CAUSES OF DEATH

Life Tables for National Populations

STUDIES IN POPULATION

Under The Editorship of: H. H. Winsborough

Department of Sociology
University of Wisconsin
Madison, Wisconsin

Samuel H. Preston, Nathan Keyfitz, and Robert Schoen. **Causes of Death:** *Life Tables for National Populations.*

In preparation

Otis Dudley Duncan, David Featherman, and Beverly Duncan. **Socioeconomic Background and Achievement.**

Tertius Chandler and Gerald Fox. **3000 Years of Urban Growth.**

CAUSES OF DEATH

Life Tables for National Populations

SAMUEL H. PRESTON   NATHAN KEYFITZ   ROBERT SCHOEN

With the collaboration of Verne E. Nelson

SEMINAR PRESS   *New York and London   1972*

SEMINAR PRESS, INC.
111 Fifth Avenue, New York, New York 10003

United Kingdom Edition published by
SEMINAR PRESS LIMITED
24/28 Oval Road, London NW1

LIBRARY OF CONGRESS CATALOG CARD NUMBER: 72-80305

CONTENTS

LIST OF TABLES

PREFACE

This book presents data on mortality from recorded causes of death in 180 populations, with detail provided on age and sex. Despite the considerable effort and expense incurred by a nation to assign a cause to each death, many of these data have remained inaccessible to potential users. This volume should reduce substantially problems of data availability by providing information on mortality experience spanning a period of 103 years, for 48 nations, and encompassing a range of life expectancies from 27 to 77. The data will assist the social scientist in documenting such matters as the sources of the vital revolution, causes of increasing sex mortality differentials, components of age curves of mortality, geographic and temporal variations in mortality structure, and economic and social costs of a disease.

Tables for all populations are presented in an identical format. One table displays death rates from each of 12 causes of death in 5-year age groups; another displays the implications of these rates for duration of life, considering all causes acting in combination; a third shows the chances of dying from a particular cause of death; and a fourth presents the survivorship function that would have applied if a particular cause of death, or combination of causes, had been eliminated.

The tables are accompanied by a text outlining the procedures used to classify causes of death and derive life-table parameters. Fundamentally, the approach to classification was to translate all international, regional, and national classifications of causes of death into constructs equivalent to those in the "Seventh Revision of the International Classification of Diseases, Injuries and Causes of Death." Recorded numbers of deaths in a population were then coded to this master list, unaltered except through grouping. In producing the published figures, the computational procedures relied on the methods of iteration, which permitted us to take rough account of the age composition of the population *within* a 5-year interval. In the text the interested reader will find simplified, but workable, computer programs, in FORTRAN, for each of the iterative cause-of-death life tables.

The text also includes a discussion of the accuracy and comparability of cause-of-death certification in our populations. Constructing comparability factors for each population is clearly impossible, but major problems are described and occasionally given quantitative dimension. The text concludes with references to the sources of data and a description of the various data adjustments performed.

ACKNOWLEDGMENTS

This book would not have been possible without the cooperation of many individuals and institutions. Missing data of one form or another were sent, upon request, by the central statistical bureaus of the following nations: Australia, Canada, Chile, Costa Rica, El Salvador, England and Wales, Guatemala, Ireland, Israel, Japan, Malta and Gozo, Mexico, the Netherlands, Poland, Puerto Rico, Scotland, Spain, South Africa, Sweden, Switzerland, and the United States. Dr. Iwao Moriyama and Dean E. Krueger of the United States Office of Health Statistics Analysis are given special thanks for undertaking the difficult task of reviewing our categorizations of causes of death under various revisions of the international classification and making a large number of suggestions that fortified our boundaries. Special thanks are also due to Dr. Jan Hoem and Mrs. Ellen Blix of the Norwegian Central Statistical Bureau for advice and guidance in interpreting the Scandanavian lists of causes of death. Dr. Sergio Chaparro Ruiz, Director, Estadistica y Censos, Chile, was exceedingly generous in providing a long series of very informative data.

Publications of the World Health Organization greatly facilitated our work. Without these initial compilations of postwar data, the task which we set would have appeared totally intractable.

Libraries at the University of California, Berkeley, and Princeton University, together with the New York Public Library, were the principal additional sources of the data processed here.

Peter Chen, translator, Mina Vasiri, statistical clerk, Elizabeth Eisenberg, programmer, and Ann Harrington and Judy Guthartz, typists, did outstanding jobs on what invariably turned out to be difficult tasks. Other individuals helping at various stages include Professors Etienne van de Walle and Eduardo Arriaga, M. Grais, Delores C. Schoen, Harriet Fishlow, Robert Gardner, and Robert Lundy.

We are grateful to Professor Judith Blake, Chairman of the Demography Department, and our former colleagues at the University of California, Berkeley, for offering abundant support at every stage of the project. The facilities of International Population and Urban Research were generously made available by its chairman, Professor Kingsley Davis. Grants to the Demography Department from the Ford Foundation and the National Institute of Child Health and Human Development (9 T01 HD 00375-08), together with National Institutes of Health research contract NIH-69-2200 and National Science Foundation grant NSF-GZ 995, provided financial support.

Chapter I INTRODUCTION

The circumstances under which men die are closely related to the conditions under which they live. The extent of violence, poverty, passivity, and ignorance in a population is reflected in the statistics of its causes and ages of death. Vigorous attempts to delay death are so nearly universal that accurate mortality statistics provide a reliable touchstone of a population's level of social organization and technological sophistication.

Not only do mortality conditions mirror those in the general society, but they also have their own important social implications. A population in which death is almost always deferred until the older ages is one that grows faster, is more willing to train individuals for the "long-run," can rely more heavily on the nuclear family for emotional gratification, and can dispense more readily with fatalistic or supernatural philosophies. Mortality declines in the last century have had a subtle but possibly decisive impact on a wide range of human activities.

Our purpose in writing this volume is to advance the study of causes and consequences of the level and structure of mortality in a population. Research along these lines has been inhibited by the inaccessibility and alleged inaccuracy and incomparability of cause-of-death data. We believe our collection of data to be extensive enough so that accessibility should no longer pose a serious impediment to research on national patterns of mortality by cause. We believe that by carefully choosing broad groupings of causes and tracing the life histories of terms in cause-of-death nosologies, we have also minimized problems of intertemporal and interspatial comparability in the lists of causes used. However, there remain important inaccuracies and inconsistencies in the way nations diagnose and code their deaths to conform to the reasonably "standard" list. Consequently, we offer an operational definition of the material in the tables.

Strictly defined, our tables provide an accurate account of the frequency with which particular causes of death were recorded in particular age and sex groups in various human populations, and suggest some statistical implications of these frequencies. These statistical expressions are the life table from all causes combined, the life table disaggregated into 12 selected cause-of-death categories, and the life table with particular causes and combinations of causes eliminated.

An understanding of the concept of cause of death is central to an appreciation of the tables. Death is one possible outcome of an encounter between a specific morbid process and a vulnerable

Table I–1a

Average Percentage of Newborns Who Would Ultimately Succumb to Particular Causes of Death at Various Ranges of Life Expectancy—Males

Expectation of life at birth	Respiratory TB	Other infectious and parasitic	Neoplasms	Cardio-vascular	Influenza, pneumonia, bronchitis	Diarrheal	Certain degener-ative	Maternal	Certain diseases of infancy	Violence	All other and unknown	Number of populations
<35	7.67	12.48	1.27	7.99	25.98	5.11	1.74	—	6.67	4.71	26.37	3
35–39	8.00	11.89	2.72	14.05	17.99	7.80	1.75	—	5.93	4.49	25.38	5
40–44	11.19	9.47	2.98	15.25	19.06	7.28	2.95	—	3.89	4.53	23.39	9
45–49	6.68	7.38	4.88	19.73	13.30	8.17	4.32	—	4.33	5.55	25.63	15
50–54	5.50	5.32	7.15	19.80	13.79	4.71	3.54	—	3.86	7.49	28.84	6
55–59	5.45	4.48	9.39	26.36	10.73	2.61	6.29	—	3.23	7.33	24.11	21
60–64	4.03	2.60	12.46	32.63	8.18	1.62	5.39	—	2.36	6.43	24.30	36
65–69	2.35	.97	16.56	45.35	6.65	.58	4.18	—	1.81	6.52	15.03	55
70–74	.87	.71	18.61	48.53	5.21	.43	3.01	—	1.33	5.96	15.34	15

human target. It is quite clearly a joint function of the potency of an agent and the vitality of the host. The importance of the agent is clear from records of dramatic annual fluctuations of death rates in populations whose members are virtually identical from year to year. The importance of the state of the host is just as clearly evident from the steeply sloping age curve of human mortality.

Despite the basic duality of the death process, "cause of death" in medicolegal terminology traditionally describes only the agent. The official international definition of the cause of death (or the underlying cause if more than one condition is involved) (World Health Organization, 1955) is "the disease or injury that initiated the train of morbid events leading to death, or the circumstances of the accident or violence which produced the fatal injury [p. 357]."[1] This definition, or one closely akin to it, forms the basis

of all published mortality statistics, and the user has little choice but to adopt the same definition. Thus death cannot be directly attributed to particular environmental deficiencies or to special characteristics or habits of the decedent. The interaction between agent and host must be studied indirectly, often by starting with comparisons of the incidence of a cause of death according to age, sex, nation, and period.

Not only has the interaction between agent and host been obscured in published mortality statistics, but the interaction among various agents has suffered a similar and somewhat less excusable fate. Death must be assigned to one underlying cause even when multiple conditions are listed on the death certificate. Most objectionable from a logical standpoint is the failure to record, in published lists, multiple causes even when, in the certifier's opinion, the death would have been averted without the intervention of secondary diseases or conditions. One consequence, for example, is that a portion of the decline in recorded rates from measles during the 20th century is due not to any factor associated

[1] For a concise history of the concept of cause of death, see Moriyama (1956, pp. 436–441).

Table I–1b

Average Percentage of Newborns Who Would Ultimately Succumb to Particular Causes of Death at Various Ranges of Life Expectancy—Females

Expectation of life at birth	Respiratory TB	Other infectious and parasitic	Neoplasms	Cardio-vascular	Influenza, pneumonia, bronchitis	Diarrheal	Certain degener-ative	Maternal	Certain diseases of infancy	Violence	All other and unknown	Number of populations
<40	7.43	12.31	2.74	11.92	21.13	7.42	1.38	1.62	5.54	1.45	27.06	6
40–44	10.08	8.98	4.20	16.95	17.22	7.88	2.56	1.73	3.80	1.78	24.80	7
45–49	7.17	8.69	5.43	19.30	15.68	7.55	2.75	1.25	3.27	1.86	27.07	9
50–54	5.08	6.20	6.80	24.86	12.63	7.88	4.25	.98	3.59	1.79	25.95	10
55–59	5.58	4.65	9.42	24.09	13.67	3.94	4.28	1.08	2.90	2.13	28.25	11
60–64	4.37	3.54	12.27	30.58	9.76	2.16	5.28	.96	2.37	2.82	25.89	20
65–69	2.59	2.04	13.24	37.71	8.70	1.54	5.61	.61	1.82	2.88	23.88	31
70–74	.96	.68	15.83	52.13	6.21	.67	3.70	.17	1.31	3.70	14.63	58
75+	.31	.45	18.31	51.49	6.05	.45	3.44	.12	.83	4.33	14.21	8

with its treatment or prevention but to the increased use of sulfa drugs in the treatment of pneumonia, a frequent complication. Such interaction among diseases cannot be adequately studied, directly or indirectly, by examination of published national mortality statistics.

However, the social scientist will not find that our tables have been rendered useless by error, inconsistency, or illogic in death assignment. Empirical regularities do emerge from the tables; frequencies of particular causes of death are highly predictable; errors have not obscured fundamental changes in the structure of mortality in the past century. An indication of the basic patterns underlying these tables is presented in Tables I-1a and b. Our populations have been grouped according to level of life expectancy, and for each level, the average proportion of newborns who would ultimately succumb to a cause is shown. It is evident from the table that, with few exceptions, the cause structure of mortality changes systematically as the level of mortality changes. In the aggregate, the life tables will surely support a detailed examination of the manifest changes in human mortality during the past century.

A. Scope of the Populations Included

In order for a population[2] to be included in this collection, two sets of data had to be available: numbers of deaths by cause, age, and sex; and numbers of persons alive by age and sex. Additional criteria are cited below. In this volume figures on numbers of deaths will always represent actual counts made by the various national statistical offices. In a majority of the included populations, statistics on numbers of persons alive represent a complete census of the population. When censuses were not available, population estimates from a variety of sources were employed.

The availability of data on causes of death by age and sex was

[2] By the term "population," we refer to the aggregation of individuals that were alive within some political boundaries during some time period.

the more important constraint on the total number of populations represented in the tables. Even so statistically advanced a country as Sweden did not collect cause-of-death data for the entire nation before 1911. Today, many countries can provide information on numbers of deaths by age and sex but have not yet undertaken the expense of assigning a cause to each death. The number of populations in our tables begins at the earliest date with 1, England and Wales in 1861, growing to 3 in 1881 with the addition of Italy and New Zealand, and ultimately to 42 in 1964. In total, 180 populations are included, representing 48 nations.

Virtually all nations providing the requisite information are represented in the tables at least once every 10 years. Tabulations in shorter intervals, or for period averages, were not performed because of the considerable effort required to process mortality information for a single population in a given calendar year. By presenting data at intervals of approximately 10 years, usually coinciding with a population census, we hope that a balance has been struck between the desire for exhaustiveness and its considerable expense.

B. Classification of Data on Cause of Death

In the course of eight revisions, the basis of the international statistical classification of causes of death has shifted gradually from anatomic to etiologic criteria. Nevertheless, there remain important elements of anatomic classifications that necessarily color any compilation, such as this, which is based predominantly on statistics of populations employing one of the international classifications. To the degree possible, the categories employed in this compilation are etiologic entities. A similarity of disease processes connotes a similarity in physical and environmental conditions affecting the incidence of the diseases. Classification according to etiology is thus a logical step in studying the determinants of a population's mortality characteristics. Three very

broad etiologic groupings suggest themselves:

(1) *External, organic.* Deaths which result from an initial invasion of the human body by other living organisms.

(2) *External, inorganic.* Deaths which result from accident or injury.

(3) *Internal.* Deaths whose origin is organ malfunction due to malformation, to cell mutation, or to deterioration which, in the present state of knowledge, seems predominantly a function of age.

Adherence to a reasonable etiologic classification was only one of several criteria employed to construct the classification of causes of death used in this study. Additional considerations include the following:

(1) The categories had to be readily constituted from available data.

(2) In order to facilitate comparisons, when two or more diseases were likely to be mistaken for one another diagnostically, or when the same disease sequence was likely to be coded in two or more different ways in different populations, the diseases in question should be grouped.

(3) Ill-defined, symptomatic, and unknown causes should be isolated from the remainder of the categories.

(4) Each category should be of major significance for some of the populations investigated.

(5) Since data from a sizable number of populations were to be processed, economy in the number of categories was desirable.

Needless to say, groupings suggested by one criterion frequently violate another. Rheumatic heart disease is infectious in origin, therefore belonging with other infectious diseases under the etiologic criterion; but it is often confused with other types of heart diseases, suggesting, alternatively, its inclusion with cardiovascular diseases under criterion (2). The categories which resulted from the numerous compromises and accommodations are presented in Table I-2. A verbal description of each category is provided, as well as the code numbers which each category comprises in the various International Lists of Diseases, Injuries, and Causes of Death.[3]

One of the principal determinants of the structure of the categories in Table I-2 was the widespread availability of data based upon the Abridged, or B, list of causes of death in the Sixth and Seventh Revisions of the International List, which covers the years 1949–1967. Data in this format, from individual countries, have been processed and published by the World Health Organization.[4] Therefore, the categories employed in this study are essentially combinations of B-list titles appearing in the Sixth and Seventh Revisions of the International Classification (the titles were identical in the Sixth and Seventh Revisions, as were, for all practical purposes, the terms comprising a title). In other cases, conformation to this B list was the goal. For only one cause of death was it deemed necessary to secure more detail than was provided by the Abridged List; our category, cardiovascular diseases, includes A85 and A86 of the Intermediate List—diseases of the arteries and other diseases of the circulatory system—which appeared in the "all other causes" category in the Abridged List.

The classification scheme employed in this volume is not particularly unusual. For the most part, the classification adheres to the simple divisions already cited, with external, organic diseases divided into respiratory tuberculosis and all other infectious and parasitic diseases; external, inorganic divided into automobile accidents and all other accidents and violence; and internal divided into neoplasms, cardiovascular diseases, and certain other degenerative diseases. The remaining categories are symptomatic (diarrhea), anatomic (influenza, pneumonia, bronchitis), or reflective of risks peculiar to particular age or sex groups (certain diseases of early infancy and complications of pregnancy).

Although "diarrhea, gastritis, and enteritis" is essentially a symptomatic category, a large majority of deaths assigned to this title are infectious or parasitic in origin.[5] Therefore, it has been carried as a separate category, permitting infectious and parasitic diseases to be studied both alone and in combination with these diarrheal diseases.

For several reasons, it was necessary to combine influenza and pneumonia, despite their distinctly different clinical courses and modes of infection. Prior to the Third Revision of the International List, the two diseases could not be satisfactorily separated. Moreover, deaths ascribed to influenza usually result directly from the complication of pneumonia, a situation making death rates from either of the two separate causes highly vulnerable to differing national coding practices (see United States Department of Health, Education, and Welfare, 1950, p. 179).

Bronchitis is also included in the category of respiratory diseases. It is an important enough cause of death to warrant extrication from the residual category, but correctly placing it elsewhere presents a problem. Deaths from acute and chronic bronchitis are often infectious in origin, but they are also frequently associated with myocardial degeneration. It has been asserted that many deaths assigned to bronchitis in England and Wales, Australia, and New Zealand would elsewhere be assigned to heart disease, and that, as a consequence, the two titles should be grouped (see United Nations, 1962, pp. 112–115). However, in other countries,

---

[3] The helpful advice of Iwao M. Moriyama and his staff at the National Center for Health Statistics, Washington, D.C., regarding the composition of categories from Revision to Revision is gratefully acknowledged.

[4] These data can be found in the *Annual Epidemiologic and Vital Statistics Report*, or *World Health Statistics Annual*. Geneva.

[5] For an international review of evidence on the etiology of diseases assigned to diarrhea and enteritis, see Verhoestraete and Puffer (1958). Certain deaths assigned to this category may be the result of malnutrition (usually accompanied by an infectious complication) or the ingestion of toxic substances.

Table I-2

Composition of Cause-of-Death Categories Employed under the Various Revisions of the International Classification of Causes of Death

Category	Titles in the 6th and 7th Revisions, Abridged List 1948, 1955	Terms in the 6th and 7th Revisions, Detailed List 1948, 1955	Terms in the 5th Revision, Detailed List 1939	Terms in the 4th Revision, Detailed List 1929	Terms in the 3rd Revision, Detailed List 1920	Terms in the 2nd Revision, Detailed List 1909	Terms in the 5th Revision, Intermediate List 1939	Terms in the 4th Revision, Abridged List 1929	Terms in the 3rd Revision, Abridged List 1920
(1) Respiratory tuberculosis	B1	001–008	13	23	31	28	6	10	13
(2) Other infectious and parasitic diseases	B2–17	010–138	1–12, 14–32, 34–43, 44a,c,d 177	1–10, 12–22, 24–44, 80, 83, 96, 177	1–10, 12–14, 16–30, 32–42, 72, 76, 91a, 115, 116, 121, 175	1–9, 11–12, 14–25, 29–35, 37, 38, 61c, 62, 67, 106, 107, 112, 164	1–5, 7–11, 13–17[a]	1–7, 9, 11–14, 21[d]	1–8, 10, 12, 14, 15[i]
(3) Malignant and benign neoplasms	B18–19	140–239	44b, 45–57, 74	45–55, 72, 139a	43–50, 65, 137, 139	39–46, 53, 129, 131	18–24[b]	15, 16[b]	16[j]
(4) Cardiovascular diseases	B22, 24–29, A85, 86	330–34, 400–68	58, 83, 90–103	56, 82, 90–95, 97–103	51, 74, 75, 83, 87–90, 91b,c, 92–96, 151	47, 64–66, 77–85, 142	25, 37, 42–48	22, 24, 25[e]	18, 19[k]
(5) Influenza, pneumonia, bronchitis	B30–32	480–502	33, 106–109	11, 106–109	11, 99–101	10, 89–92	12, 49–50	8, 26, 27	9, 20–22[l]
(6) Diarrhea, gastritis, enteritis	B36	543, 571, 572	119, 120	119, 120	15, 113, 114	13, 104, 105	54, 55	29	11, 25
(7) Certain degenerative diseases (nephritis, cirrhosis of liver, ulcers of stomach and duodenum, diabetes)	B20, 33, 37, 38	260, 540–541, 581, 590–594	61, 117, 124, 130–132	59, 117, 124, 130–132	57, 111, 122, 128, 129	50, 102, 113, 119, 120	27, 53, 58, 61	18, 33[f]	28, 29[f]
(8) Complications of pregnancy	B40	640–689	140–150	140–150	143–150	134–141	68–72	35, 36	31, 32
(9) Certain diseases of infancy	B42–44	760–776	158–161	158–161	160–162	151–152	76–79	38[g]	33[m]
(10) Motor vehicle accidents	BE47	E810–E835	170	206, 208, 210–211	188c, 188e	N.A.	83	N.A.	N.A.
(11) Other accidents and violence	BE48–50	E800–E802, E840–E999	78, 163–169, 171–176, 178–198	77, 163–176, 178–198, minus 206, 208, 210, 211	67, 163, 165–174, 176–187, 188a,b,d,f,g 189–203	58, 153, 155–163, 165–186	81, 82, 84–86[e]	40–42[h]	35, 36[n]
(12) All other and unknown causes	Residual	Residual	Residual	Residual	Residual	Residual	Residual	Residual	Residual

[a] Includes Hodgkin's disease (44b); does not include food poisoning (177).

[b] Does not include leukemia and Hodgkin's disease in both years and ovarian cysts in 1929.

[c] Does not include lead poisoning (78); includes food poisoning (177).

[d] Does not include aneurysm (96) and food poisoning (177).

[e] Does not include acute rheumatic fever (56); includes aneurysm (96).

[f] Does not include ulcers of stomach and duodenum (117 or 111) and cirrhosis of liver (124 or 122).

[g] Includes congenital malformations (157).

[h] Includes motor vehicle accidents (206, 208, 210, 211), food poisoning (177); excludes chronic poisoning by mineral substances (77).

[i] Does not include glanders (26), anthrax (27), rabies (28), tetanus (29), mycosis (30), syphilis (38), soft chancre (39), gonococcus infection (40), purulent infection (41), other infectious diseases (42), tabes dorsalis (72), general paralysis of insane (76), aneurysm (91a), ancylostomiasis (115), diseases due to other intestinal parasites (116), hydatid tumor of liver (121), and food poisoning (175).

[j] Does not include leukemia and Hodgkin's disease (65), benign and unspecified tumors (50, 137, 139).

[k] Does not include acute rheumatic fever (51), paralysis without specified cause (75), diseases of parts of the circulatory system other than the heart (91b,c; 92–96), and gangrene (151).

[l] Does not include bronchopneumonia (100).

[m] Includes congenital malformations (159); excludes "other diseases peculiar to early infancy" (162).

[n] Includes motor vehicle accidents (188c,e), food poisoning (175); excludes chronic poisoning by mineral substances (67).

bronchitis is apparently confused with pneumonia as often as with cardiovascular diseases. For example, deaths in the United States during 1950 were coded under both the Fifth and the substantially different Sixth Revisions and under the two different sets of procedures for coding multiple causes of death. Bronchitis, which grew considerably in numbers of deaths as a result of the revision, gained twice as many deaths from bronchopneumonia as from any cardiovascular disease (see United States Department of Health, Education, and Welfare, 1963, p. 150).[6]

Surprisingly, Heasman and Lipworth (1966), in a study of diagnostic accuracy in the hospitals of England and Wales, discovered that bronchitis was very frequently mistaken for bronchopneumonia prior to autopsy and concluded that "it would seem logical, therefore, to combine all categories relating to pneumonia and bronchitis [p. 33]." Moreover, Reid and Rose (1964) discovered a "remarkable similarity" in assignment of deaths involving bronchitis among a sample of certifiers in England, Norway, and the United States. In view of these considerations, bronchitis was placed with influenza and pneumonia.

It might be noted that the category "cardiovascular diseases" is nonetheless still partly an anatomic as well as an etiologic construct. Acute endocarditis, rheumatic fever, and rheumatic heart disease are prominent examples of diseases which are infectious in origin but included in this category. Their inclusion resulted from frequent diagnostic confusion among the various forms of heart disease and early publication practices making it difficult or impossible to separate the various diseases. The vast majority of deaths in the category, however, are produced either by arteriosclerosis or hypertension.[7]

Finally, the category "certain degenerative diseases" includes four rather diverse diseases: diabetes, nephritis, ulcers of the stomach and duodenum, and cirrhosis of the liver. The need for economy prevented these diseases from being individually enumerated. But because of their specificity and relative importance, it was considered desirable to extricate the group from the residual. Since all are characterized by a sharply upward-sloping age curve of mortality, this distinctive feature of the diseases is retained substantially intact by the grouping. It should be noted that this category includes acute nephritis along with the chronic forms of the disease, which are numerically more important.

Alternative classifications would have placed nephritis and/or diabetes with the cardiovascular diseases. When the method of coding multiple cases of death changed in the United States in 1950, each of these disease categories lost approximately half of its deaths, the large majority going to cardiovascular diseases (see United States Department of Health, Education, and Welfare, 1963). Nevertheless, the logic of an etiologic classification is violated by the placement of these diseases in the cardiovascular category. Diabetes is a genetically transmitted disorder resulting in malfunction of the pancreas, which, in later life, is often associated with coronary thrombosis. The etiology of nephritis is somewhat mysterious. Many deaths from this disease are the short- or long-term sequels of acute infection. Hypertension and the hypertensive or arteriosclerotic kidney, which nephritis often produces, are among its principal clinical manifestations. On the other hand, many cases of nephritis seem to be a product of hypertension rather than a cause. To cloud the picture still further, it is possible that all hypertension is a result of renal malfunction.[8] The complicated and somewhat obscure etiology of nephritis has encouraged its separation from the cardiovascular diseases, although in retrospect the alternative classification seems equally attractive.

[6] Of the 2989 bronchitis deaths in 1950 under the Sixth Revision List, 447 would formerly have been coded to bronchopneumonia, compared to 205 for "other chronic myocarditis," the only cardiovascular disease listed.

[7] For a review of difficulties in classifying cardiovascular diseases, see World Health Organization (1959).

[8] Discussion abstracted from Boyd (1962, pp. 309–317).

REFERENCES

Boyd, W. *An introduction to the study of disease.* (5th ed.) Philadelphia: Lea & Febiger, 1962.

Heasman, M. A., & Lipworth, L. *Studies on medical and population subjects no. 20. Accuracy of certification of cause of death.* London: General Register Office of England and Wales, 1966.

Moriyama, I. M. Development of the present concept of cause of death. *American Journal of Public Health,* 1956, **46,** 436–441.

Reid, D. D., & Rose, G. A. Assessing the comparability of mortality statistics. *British Medical Journal,* 1964, Vol. 2, 1437–1439.

United Nations, Department of Economic and Social Affairs. *Population Bulletin of the United Nations No. 6.* New York: United Nations, 1962.

United States Department of Health, Education, and Welfare. *Vital Statistics of the United States.* Vol. 1. Washington, D.C.: National Office of Vital Statistics, 1950.

United States Department of Health, Education, and Welfare, Public Health Service. Comparability of mortality statistics for the Fifth and Sixth Revisions: United States, 1950. *Vital statistics—Special Reports,* 1963, **51**(2), 133–178.

Verhoestraete, L. J., & Puffer, R. R. Diarrheal disease with special reference to the Americas. *Bulletin of the World Health Organization,* 1958, **19,** 23–51.

World Health Organization. *International Classification of Diseases.* (Rev. ed.), Vol. I, 1955.

World Health Organization. Classification of cardiovascular diseases. *World Health Organization Chronicle,* 1959, **13**(5), 205–207.

Chapter II METHODS OF CALCULATION

A. The Life Table for All Causes of Death Combined

Everyone dies at a certain age and from a cause that is, in principle, specifiable. The recording of age and cause of death goes back to the early concerns for public health and civic order in the 18th century when registers were set up in Sweden, England, and elsewhere. These registers consisted essentially of lists of the dead and provided, among other information, the sex, age, and cause of death of each person:

Male	73	Heart disease
Male	2	Smallpox
Female	34	Cancer
Male	28	Homicide
⋮	⋮	⋮

By the end of the 19th century, an increasing number of countries came to maintain these death records with commendable completeness, and today they are included in the statistical systems of all advanced countries. Taken along with censuses, which list living persons and which, for quite other purposes, became widespread in the 19th century, such lists can be used to calculate probabilities of dying from various causes for people of different ages; they form the basis of this book.

The present chapter describes how to proceed from a list like the one just given to life tables by cause. Our contribution is the last stage of a process that starts with the reporting of individual deaths by relatives and physicians, goes on through the classifying and counting performed by national statistical offices, and culminates in the tabulated form in which these offices issue their results. The tabulations tell us, for example, that in the United States, in the calendar year 1967, deaths of men 70–74 years of age at last birthday numbered 138,250, and that of these deaths 26,664 were due to neoplasms, a category made up in considerable part of cancer. The information comes from the National Office of Vital Statistics. The Bureau of the Census estimated the male population aged 70–74, of the United States, to be 2,236,000, in mid-1967. This is taken as the average number of persons exposed to risk through the year, that is to say, persons who, *if* they had died, would have been among the recorded deaths; the age-specific death rate is

$$_5M_{70} = \frac{138,250}{2,236,000} = .061829.$$

Such numbers bring us closer to useful analysis than lists of deaths; they provide the basis for the calculations of the chance that a man of exact age 70 will die before he reaches age 75 and also of the probability that he will die of heart cancer.

From Rates to Probabilities by Estimate of Exposure

One instructive approach to the matter is to suppose a stationary situation, in which the deaths are evenly distributed through both time and age. If the midyear population were 2,236,000 and deaths were occurring at 138,250/year, and half the deaths took place before the middle of the 5-year age interval, then the 2,236,000 men at midyear would be the survivors of $2,236,000 + \frac{5}{2}(138,250)$ men who are imagined as having started down the 70–74 age interval. This is the denominator of the required probability: With $2,236,000 + \frac{5}{2}(138,250)$ men aged 70 starting out, and $5 \times 138,250$ deaths occurring during the next 5 years of age, the probability $_5q_{70}$ of an individual person dying must be the ratio

$$_5q_{70} = \frac{5 \times 138,250}{2,236,000 + \frac{5}{2}(138,250)} = .267758.$$

(Note that we are now confusing age and time and leaning much too heavily on the assumption of stationarity. All this will be straightened out later.)

More generally, suppose $_5P_x$ persons alive at the middle of a calendar year and $_5D_x$ deaths occurring among them, so that the age-specific death rate $_5M_x$ is $_5D_x/_5P_x$. To find $_5q_x$, the probability of dying during the 5 years for someone who starts the 5-year period at exactly age x, we assume that exactly half of the $_5D_x$ deaths occurred during the first half of the time and age interval. Then, in the absence of migration, the number of individuals present $2\frac{1}{2}$ years earlier would have been $_5P_x + \frac{5}{2}\,_5D_x$, and at that time they would have been of exact age x. Out of these $5\,_5D_x$ subsequently died, so the probability of dying must be

$$_5q_x = \frac{5\,_5D_x}{_5P_x + \frac{5}{2}\,_5D_x},$$

or dividing numerator and denominator by $_5P_x$,

$$_5q_x = \frac{5\,_5M_x}{1 + \frac{5}{2}\,_5M_x}. \tag{1}$$

The problem of going from rates like $_5M_x$ to probabilities like $_5q_x$ is central to our work and deserves a diagrammatic presentation that will make the issues clearer.

Location of Death in Time and Age

Suppose each individual in a population is represented by a straight line that starts at the date of his birth. The result is a Lexis diagram (Figure 1), whose coordinates are age and time. Such a diagram can help us with the problem of translating deaths

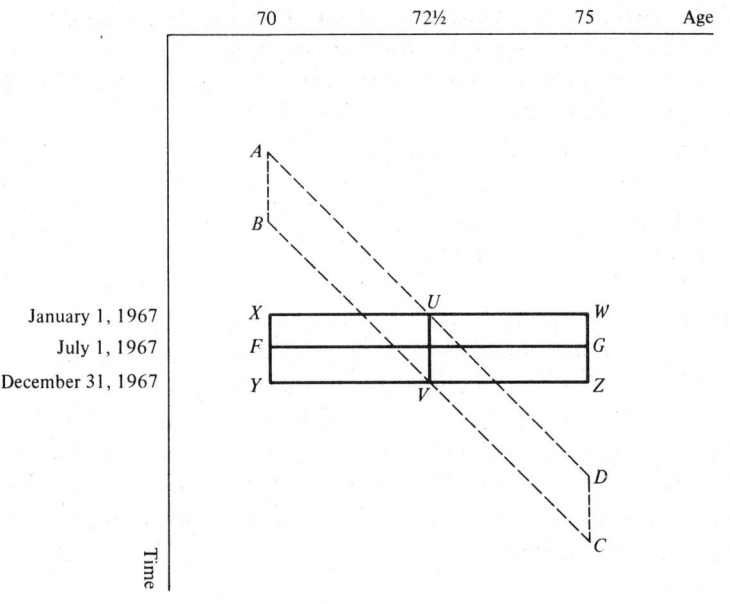

Figure 1. *Lexis diagram for locating deaths and population in time and age.*

and population into probabilities. The line continues down at 45° to either axis, ending at the age and time of the person's death. The deaths, in 1967, of men aged 70–74 at last birthday, are terminations that fall within the rectangle $XYZW$. A census taken on July 1, 1967 would count all the lines that cross FG.

Now for a probability we need the deaths among a group of individuals who start through a particular age interval. The probability is the deaths within the lozenge $ABCD$ divided by the number of life lines that cross AB. Unfortunately this is not directly available and must be approximated.

A crude means of approximating is to assume that half the deaths of area $XYZW$ have occurred in $XYVU$ and that the same number of deaths occur in $ABVU$ as in $XYVU$. Now suppose that the average density of lines crossing UV is the same as that of lines crossing FG, so that the total crossing UV is one-fifth the number observed crossing FG. With these approximations, and the additional assumption that net migration is negligible, we assume that the population that started through the age interval by crossing AB numbered one-fifth the count through FG plus half the deaths in $XYZW$. The probability of dying is thus

$$\frac{\text{deaths in } ABCD}{\text{population crossing } AB}$$

$$= \frac{\text{deaths in } XYZW}{\frac{1}{5}(\text{population crossing } FG) + \frac{1}{2}(\text{deaths in } XYZW)}.$$

If the deaths in $XYZW$ are designated $_5D_{70}$, and the population crossing FG is $_5P_{70}$, both observed, then the probability of dying $_5q_{70}$ is

$$_5q_{70} = \frac{_5D_{70}}{\frac{1}{5}\,_5P_{70} + \frac{1}{2}\,_5D_{70}} = \frac{5\,_5D_{70}}{_5P_{70} + 2\frac{1}{2}\,_5D_{70}},$$

which becomes the same as Eq. (1) for $x = 70$ if we divide numerator and denominator by $_5P_{70}$.

Assumption that Death Rate Is Fixed through the Interval

An alternative approach is possible when we suppose that the rate $_5M_x$ is the same through the whole interval. Then the probability of dying in a part, say δ, of a year, where δ is small enough so that the number of persons exposed at the beginning and the end of it is sensibly the same, is $_5M_x\,\delta$. The chance of surviving through the small interval δ is $1 - _5M_x\,\delta$ and hence that of surviving through the $5/\delta$ intervals of the 5 years is

$$(1 - _5M_x\,\delta)^{5/\delta} = 1 - _5q_x.$$

But the left-hand side, as δ tends to zero, is the exponential $\exp(-5\,_5M_x)$, so for the chance of dying we have

$$_5q_x = 1 - \exp(-5\,_5M_x). \qquad (2)$$

From Eq. (1) we have worked out the United States, 1967, male probability at $_5q_{70} = .267758$. From Eq. (2) we obtain $_5q_{70} = .265926$. The first is larger than the second and, in this instance, more nearly correct, but we will not pursue these approximations further. The purpose of including them was only to provide an intuitive sense of the problem of inferring probabilities from rates. As formulas for actual calculations they are not grossly in error, but whatever error they contain is unnecessary. With a computer we need not rely on the shortcuts necessary for hand work. Among other defects these shortcuts do not take into account that when the observed population is on the increase, it is younger than the stationary population of the life table—younger within each separate age interval as well as in total.

The Equation for Single Decrement

The method for making the single-decrement life table used here has been set down elsewhere (see Keyfitz, 1968, p. 19) and can be summarized briefly. Suppose the distribution of persons within the x to $x + 5$ age interval to be $e^{-rt}l(x + t)$, where r is the rate of increase of successive annual cohorts, and $l(x + t)$ is the probability that a child just born will live to age $x + t$. If the population is increasing, r will be positive, and in this case, as compared with the life table $l(x + t)$, the distribution within the age interval will be diminished toward the older end. In most real populations successive cohorts are an increasing series, and the population is shifted to the left within most age intervals. We write $\mu(x + t)$ for the age-specific death rate between ages $x + t$ and $x + t + dt$.

In this notation the equation involving the age-specific death rate $_5M_x$ is

$$_5M_x = \frac{\int_0^5 e^{-rt}l(x + t)\mu(x + t)\,dt}{\int_0^5 e^{-rt}l(x + t)\,dt}. \tag{3}$$

Integration by parts reduces the equation to

$$l_{x+5} = e^{5r}\left(l_x - (_5M_x + r)\int_0^5 e^{-rt}l(x + t)\,dt\right). \tag{4}$$

Equation (4) still has too many unknowns for direct solution and must be simplified. If r is set equal to zero and $l(x + t)$ is taken as a straight line between x and $x + 5$, then it reduces to the equation for $_5q_x$ given as Eq. (1). [This helps to understand the assumptions on which Eq. (1) was based.] If r is taken as zero and the $l(x + t)$ as a cubic between x and $x + 5$, then the integral of $l(x + t)$ is

$$_5L_x = \int_0^5 l(x + t)\,dt$$

$$= \tfrac{65}{24}(l_x + l_{x+5}) - \tfrac{5}{24}(l_{x-5} + l_{x+10}). \tag{5}$$

We now cannot solve for $_5q_x$ at each age x separately from the other ages but must use a set of simultaneous equations, or what is equivalent and more convenient, an iterative process.

More generally, if r is any small number, Eq. (5) is modified to provide

$$_5L_x{}' = \int_0^5 e^{-rt}l(x + t)\,dt$$

by writing $e^{-5r}l_{x+5}$ for l_{x+5}, $e^{5r}l_{x-5}$ for l_{x-5}, and $e^{-10r}l_{x+10}$ for l_{x+10}; then inserting this in Eq. (4) and simplifying gives

$$l_{x+5}^* = \frac{e^{5r}\{l_x^* - (_5M_x + r)[\tfrac{65}{24}l_x^* - \tfrac{5}{24}(e^{5r}l_{x-5}^* + e^{-10r}l_{x+10})]\}}{1 + \tfrac{65}{24}(_5M_x + r)}, \tag{6}$$

where the asterisks designate improved values obtained from a more recent iteration than the unstarred l_{x+10}.

Between each cycle of Eq. (6) we need a cycle of r from

$$r = \frac{1}{10}\ln\left(\frac{_5P_{x-5}/_5L_{x-5}'}{_5P_{x+5}/_5L_{x+5}'}\right), \tag{7}$$

where $_5P_{x-5}$ and $_5P_{x+5}$ are the observed population in the preceding and subsequent age intervals, respectively. The initial values of both l_x and r in Eqs. (6) and (7) can be arbitrary. Convergence requires less than 20 cycles, and the computing time to convergence on the CDC6400 is about $\tfrac{1}{3}$ sec/life table, a cost of about 4 cents. (The entire four tiers of tables, described below for one sex, took about $2\tfrac{1}{2}$ sec of computing time, including a variety of checks and ancillary calculations.)

Youngest Ages[1]

The difficulties of curve fitting, along with problems of defective enumeration, drive one to special methods for the youngest ages more primitive than those for the remainder of the table.

For each of the three age intervals 0, 1–4, 5–9, defining age as at last birthday, we assume a value for $_na_x$, the average years lived in the interval by those dying in the interval. For 0, this may be taken as the empirical regression:

$$a_0 = 0.07 + 1.7M_0, \tag{8}$$

[1] This material has been taken from N. Keyfitz (1970).

obtained from a number of countries in which day, month, and year of birth are available. For 1–4, $_4a_1$ would be about 1.5 years; for 5–9, $_5a_5$ about 2.5 years. Further investigation could produce improvements on these values.

If the interval be n years, then the total years lived, $_nL_x$, equals the average years lived by those dying, $_na_x$, multiplied by $_nd_x$, the number dying, plus the average years lived by those surviving, n, multiplied by the number surviving, l_{x+n}:

$$_nL_x = {_na_{xn}d_x} + nl_{x+n} = {_na_xl_x} + (n - {_na_x})l_{x+n}. \qquad (9)$$

Since usually r is not obtainable, owing to undercounts in censuses of those under 5, we are tempted to suppose for this part of the table that $r = 0$, i.e. that the stationary $_nm_x$ is the same as the observed $_nM_x$, so that the equation for l_{x+n}/l_x is

$$_nM_x = {_nm_x} = \frac{l_x - l_{x+n}}{_nL_x} = \frac{l_x - l_{x+n}}{_na_xl_x + (n - {_na_x})l_{x+n}}, \qquad (10)$$

and hence that

$$l_{x+n} = l_x \frac{1 - {_na_x}{_nM_x}}{1 + (n - {_na_x}){_nM_x}}, \qquad (11)$$

and no iteration is required [Chiang, 1968, p. 203].

Terminating the Table

For the terminal age interval inaccuracy in age statement by older people discourages attempts to estimate r and suggests assuming $r = 0$ [once again].

If $_\infty m_x = {_\infty M_x}$, then from the definition $_\infty m_x = (l_x - l_\infty)/{_\infty L_x}$ and the fact that $l_\infty = 0$, it follows that $M_x = l_x/{_\infty L_x}$, and hence

$$_\infty L_x = l_x/{_\infty M_x}, \qquad (12)$$

where x is the start of the terminal age interval. Having $l_\infty = 0$ gives $_\infty q_x = 1$, and no further assumptions are needed. For example, to find the expectation of life at this age x

we have

$$\mathring{e}_x = \frac{\int_0^\infty l(x + t)\,dt}{l_x} = \frac{1}{_\infty M_x}, \qquad (13)$$

so that among the very old the expectation of life is taken as the reciprocal of the observed death rate.

B. Multiple-Decrement Tables

The common life table discussed up to this point shows the probability of survivorship of an individual subject to the one undifferentiated hazard of death. In multiple-decrement tables the individual is subject to a number of mutually exclusive hazards, such as death from cancer, heart disease, or other cause. The person is followed in the table only to his exit, as in the ordinary life table, but there is now more than one way of exiting.

The concept of double decrement embraces all the issues of multiple decrement. Think of a table providing for three causes of death, say cancer, heart disease, and all others combined. If we could make a table providing for a consolidation into two classes, say cancer and noncancer, this would enable us to answer all questions concerning cancer including the probability of ultimately dying of cancer, the expected years of life of those who will ultimately die of cancer, etc. None of the probabilities concerning cancer are in any way affected by the distribution of noncancer deaths between heart and other diseases. A double-decrement table for cancer versus noncancer, plus another for heart versus nonheart, and another for all other versus heart and cancer, would include among them whatever information is contained in a triple-decrement table showing heart, cancer, and all others separately. This is a convenience of which advantage will be taken for computation: Nothing beyond a two-decrement table need be programmed. Wherever the theory is made simpler thereby, we will speak of methods for making a life table with two kinds of death—those due to the ith cause and those due to all other causes [designated with superscripts (i) and $(-i)$, respectively]—and will consider that this does not restrict the generality of the methods developed.

Two probabilities and hence two kinds of tables are commonly recognized in the study of cause of death. One is the probability of dying of cancer, say, during a 1- or 5-year period in the presence of other causes; the other is the probability of dying of cancer in the absence of other causes. The first gives rise to the multiple-decrement table proper, in which, for our work, 12 causes will be shown acting simultaneously. The second gives rise to an associated single-decrement table and will be applied to find the probabilities of dying, age by age, if cancer were to disappear as a cause of death. For each population our program calculates 12 associated single-decrement columns, each eliminating one cause of death, plus four columns in which combinations are eliminated.

Additive Properties of Multiple Decrement

A convenient starting point for theory on the probability of dying is the force of mortality from the ith cause at age x, written $\mu_x^{(i)}$. This is the age-specific death rate from the ith cause in an infinitesimally narrow age interval. If the survivors of the ordinary life table, representing all causes of death together, are l_x, then the life-table deaths from the ith cause during the age interval x to $x + dx$ are $l_x\mu_x^{(i)}\,dx$.

In any finite interval, say of n years, the number of deaths from the ith cause is

$$_nd_x^{(i)} = \int_0^n l_{x+t}\mu_{x+t}^{(i)}\,dt. \qquad (14)$$

These may be cumulated from the end of life backward to provide an $l_x^{(i)}$ column for those ultimately dying from this cause:

$$l_x^{(i)} = \sum_{t=0}^{\omega-x} d_{x+t}^{(i)} = \int_0^{\omega-x} l_{x+t}\mu_{x+t}^{(i)}\,dt. \qquad (15)$$

Then $l_0^{(i)}/l_0$ will be the probability of ultimately dying from the ith cause for a child just born and $l_x^{(i)}/l_x$ for a person aged x.

All the quantities mentioned above are additive, in the sense that the total of the several causes equals the corresponding function of the ordinary life table. For the force of mortality we have

$$\mu_x = \mu_x^{(1)} + \mu_x^{(2)} + \cdots + \mu_x^{(i)} + \cdots$$

or, in the case with which we shall most often deal,

$$\mu_x = \mu_x^{(i)} + \mu_x^{(-i)}.$$

Since the $_nd_x^{(i)}$ are obtained by multiplying the several $\mu_x^{(i)}$ by the same l_x and integrating over a finite age interval, the additivity of the $_nd_x^{(i)}$ follows from that of the $\mu_x^{(i)}$:

$$_nd_x = \,_nd_x^{(1)} + \,_nd_x^{(2)} + \cdots + \,_nd_x^{(i)} + \cdots;$$

similarly for the $l_x^{(i)}$:

$$l_x = l_x^{(1)} + l_x^{(2)} + \cdots + l_x^{(i)} + \cdots.$$

Additivity is related to the fact that the several causes are each acting in the presence of the others. In real life it results from the fact that the several causes of death are mutually exclusive and exhaustive. Since the effects of the several decrements will be calculated separately, and the single-decrement table for all deaths is constructed independently of these, the additivity will be available as an overall check on the computation.

The Multiple-Decrement Computation

One method of proceeding to multiple decrement, given an ordinary life table for the population in question, is to take the ratio of the observed deaths from the ith cause to all deaths in each age interval (Spiegelman, 1968, p. 137) $D_x^{(i)}/D_x$, and then suppose that this also applies to the life table $d_x^{(i)}/d_x$. With this supposition and the total decrement d_x already available, nothing stands in the way of calculating the $d_x^{(i)}$ of the multiple-decrement table and hence its $l_x^{(i)}$. This assumption is perfectly valid if the observed population is stationary, but it is unnecessarily crude otherwise. It should be clear that the proportion of deaths from cause i at ages x to $x + n$ in a population is a function not only of the relative levels of $\mu^{(i)}$ and $\mu^{(-i)}$ but also of the age composition in the interval. If $\mu^{(i)}$ increases rapidly with age, while $\mu^{(-i)}$ is decreasing (or increasing less rapidly), a growing population will have a smaller proportion of deaths from cause i than the stationary population. The magnitude of error introduced by the equal-ratio assumption is usually less than 1 part in 300, but worth avoiding nonetheless.

Let us formulate an equation for the unknown $_nd_x^{(i)}$, again in n-year age intervals, assuming not that the distribution of the observed population within an age group is the same as for the life-table population, but that it deviates from the latter by an exponential factor. The equation is

$$\frac{_nD_x^{(i)}}{_nD_x} = \frac{\int_0^n e^{-rt}l_{x+t}\mu_{x+t}^{(i)}\,dt}{\int_0^n e^{-rt}l_{x+t}\mu_{x+t}\,dt} \qquad (16)$$

with the observations on the left-hand side and the unknowns under the integrals on the right.

The numerator on the right-hand side of Eq. (16) may be written as

$$-\int_0^n e^{-rt}\,dl_{x+t}^{(i)}$$

and then integrated by parts:

$$-\int_0^n e^{-rt}\,dl_{x+t}^{(i)} = -e^{-rt}l_{x+t}^{(i)}\Big|_0^n - r\int_0^n e^{-rt}l_{x+t}^{(i)}\,dt$$

$$= l_x^{(i)} - e^{-nr}l_{x+n}^{(i)} - r_nL_x'^{(i)},$$

where $_nL_x' = \int_0^n e^{-rt}l_{x+t}^{(i)}\,dt$ is a discounted form of $L_x^{(i)}$. With this and the corresponding expression for deaths from all causes in the denominator of Eq. (16), we have

$$\frac{_nD_x^{(i)}}{_nD_x} = \frac{l_x^{(i)} - e^{-nr}l_{x+n}^{(i)} - r_nL_x'^{(i)}}{l_x - e^{-nr}l_{x+n} - r_nL_x'},$$

from which we obtain the recurrence form

$$l_x^{(i)} = e^{-nr}l_{x+n}^{(i)} + (_nD_x^{(i)}/_nD_x)(l_x - e^{-nr}l_{x+n} - r_nL_x') + r_nL_x'^{(i)}. \qquad (17)$$

The method iterating on Eq. (17) has been set forth in detail because it is a natural refinement of the approach used until the advent of the computer. Even if we did not iterate at all but simply took $_nd_x^{(i)} = _nD_x^{(i)}\,_5d_x/_nD_x$, we would not be far out. However, since we did iterate, it turned out to be convenient to produce the tables of this book by an alternative method, starting not with the observed ratio of the deaths from the given cause to the deaths from all causes, $_nD_x^{(i)}/_nD_x$, but with the age-specific death rate from the given cause $_nD_x^{(i)}/_nP_x$. The equation is

$$\frac{_nD_x^{(i)}}{_nP_x} = \frac{\int_0^n e^{-rt}l_{x+t}\mu_{x+t}^{(i)}\,dt}{\int_0^n e^{-rt}l_{x+t}\,dt},$$

and this leads to the recurrence form

$$l_x^{(i)} = e^{-nr}l_{x+n}^{(i)} + \frac{_nD_x^{(i)}\,_nL_x'}{_nP_x} + r_nL_x'^{(i)}. \qquad (17a)$$

In application, we entered expressions of form (5) for $_nL_x'$ and $_nL_x'^{(i)}$. It may be shown that Eqs. (17) and (17a) are equivalent.

Expression (17a) provided our multiple-decrement life tables. The value of r is the one to which Eq. (7) converged, in a preceding calculation of the single-decrement table for all causes, and like l_x and $_nL_x'$ is not subject to any alteration in Eq. (17a).

Each of 12 causes of death is recognized in our work, and the $l_x^{(i)}$ were added over the various causes (i). The total $\sum_i l_x^{(i)}$ agreed with the l_x of the ordinary life table for all causes together to within .005 on a radix $l_0 = 100{,}000$, an accuracy of the order of 5 parts in 100,000,000. Convergence to this accuracy for each cause required only two to four iterations once the basic life table was made.

C. The Associated Single-Decrement Table

In addition to seeking the numerical effects of the several causes, each in the presence of the other causes, we want to find what effect each would have if it were acting alone.

Two types of interdependencies among the several causes of death can be troublesome. First, the removal of the jth cause of death may alter the vitality of the survivors at any age and thereby affect $\mu_x^{(i)}$. We have no data on this aspect of interdependence of causes, and it is difficult even to specify the kind of data that would describe it. Certainly the passive analysis of vital statistics records must disregard what may be called the medical interdependence of causes. We will suppose throughout that $\mu_x^{(i)}$ is not changed by the removal of another cause of death from the population, or indeed by the removal of all other causes.

Second, even supposing $\mu_x^{(i)}$ unaffected by the removal of some other cause of death, the observed death rate in a finite age range would be changed by the altered age composition of the population within that range exposed to death from cause i. This we can deal with.

Let $\bar{l}_x^{(i)}$ be the survivorship column for an ordinary single-decrement life table in which only the ith cause is acting. Then the number of deaths in an interval of n years will be

$$_n\bar{d}_x^{(i)} = \int_0^n \bar{l}_{x+t}^{(i)} \mu_{x+t}^{(i)}\, dt.$$

The definition of $\bar{l}_x^{(i)}$ is equivalent to

$$\bar{l}_x^{(i)} = \bar{l}_0^{(i)} \left[\exp\left(-\int_0^x \mu_t^{(i)}\, dt \right) \right], \tag{18}$$

exactly as in the ordinary life table.

The additivity of the multiple-decrement table gives way here to a multiplicative property. If the several $\bar{l}_x^{(i)}$ are on radix $\bar{l}_0 = 1$, then their product is equal to the ordinary l_x:

$$l_x = \bar{l}_x^{(1)} \bar{l}_x^{(2)} \cdots \bar{l}_x^{(i)} \cdots, \tag{19}$$

a fact that follows from the expression of $\bar{l}_x^{(i)}$ as an exponential in Eq. (18) together with the additivity of the $\mu_x^{(i)}$. In words, Eq. (19) means that the probability of surviving to age x is the probability of not dying from the first cause of death, if no other cause is operative, times the probability of not dying from the second cause, if no other cause is operative, etc.

In any finite period of n years, the probability of dying from cause (i) is

$$_n q_x^{(i)} = (1/l_x) \int_0^n l_{x+t} \mu_{x+t}^{(i)}\, dt \tag{20}$$

in the multiple-decrement table and

$$_n \bar{q}_x^{(i)} = (1/\bar{l}_x^{(i)}) \int_0^n \bar{l}_{x+t}^{(i)} \mu_{x+t}^{(i)}\, dt \tag{21}$$

in the associated single-decrement table. Expressions (20) and (21) give the chances of dying in the presence and absence, respectively, of causes other than the ith; they have the same $\mu_{x+t}^{(i)}$ but different l_x and l_{x+t}.

Calculation of the Associated Single-Decrement Table

For the calculation we begin with

$$\frac{_n D_x^{(i)}}{_n P_x} \equiv {_n M_x^{(i)}} = \frac{\int_0^n e^{-rt} l_{x+t} \mu_{x+t}^{(i)}\, dt}{\int_0^n e^{-rt} l_{x+t}\, dt} \tag{22}$$

and factor the l_{x+t} on the right-hand side into

$$l_{x+t} = \bar{l}_{x+t}^{(i)}\, \bar{l}_{x+t}^{(-i)} = \bar{l}_{x+t}^{(i)}\, e^{-ht}.$$

(The mean force of mortality for the cause not of interest is here written h, and the associated single decrement $\bar{l}_x^{(i)}$ is still distinguished by a bar from the multiple decrement $l_x^{(i)}$). This converts Eq. (22) into an equation in the independent probabilities $\bar{l}_x^{(i)}$:

$$_nM_x^{(i)} = \frac{\int_0^n e^{-(r+h)t}\bar{l}_{x+t}^{(i)}\mu_{x+t}^{(i)}\,dt}{\int_0^n e^{-(r+h)t}\bar{l}_{x+t}^{(i)}\,dt}. \tag{23}$$

But Eq. (23) is exactly the same equation as for a single-decrement life table, except that r is now replaced by $r + h$.

We have shown that to calculate the life table that would apply if people were subject only to the ith cause, we can use exactly the procedure for the single-decrement table for all causes together, except that now we must add to r an allowance for the reduction of exposure due to people dying from causes other than the ith. Since the equation to be solved for $\bar{l}_x^{(i)}$ is the same as that for l_x once $r + h$ is put in place of r, we can use the same iterative procedure. However, r and h require different procedures for updating, and hence it is both more convenient and more elegant to use the previously calculated multiple-decrement table (where r is known to be 0) as the source of input data.

A number of writers suppose that all death rates are constant during each age interval. The procedure of the preceding paragraph makes the weaker assumption that the death rate from the cause of interest, the ith cause, may vary during the interval, and that only the complementary cause, designated $(-i)$, is constant. The constant $h = \mu_x^{(-i)}$, calculated in each round of iteration from the current value of $\bar{l}_{x+t}^{(i)}/\bar{l}_x$ as

$$h = \frac{1}{n}\ln\left(\frac{\bar{l}_{x+n}^{(i)}/\bar{l}_x^{(i)}}{l_{x+n}/l_x}\right),$$

turns out at convergence to be extremely close to $_nM_x^{(-i)}$, the central death rate in the population from the complementary causes.

D. Comparison with Other Methods

Our method for calculating the multiple-decrement table and the associated single-decrement table was chosen for its simplicity and because it requires a minimum of assumptions. It is very different from the standard method, as shown, for example, in Jordan's textbook (1952, Chapter 15, pp. 251–269). It does require a good deal of computation, but that is not a difficulty once the program is written and tested. This section is devoted to a consideration of the general problem of inferring probabilities and competing risks, to which our method is one solution.

Single Decrement

Result (2) is the basis of a simple way to make a life table (Neyman, 1950, p. 90). Suppose that the underlying μ_{x+t} is equal to the observed $_5M_x$ at all values $0 \le t \le 5$. Then $l_{x+t} = l_xe^{-_5M_xt}$, and in particular, $l_{x+5} = l_xe^{-_{55}M_x}$. The entire table can be constructed in 15 min on a modern desk calculator that has an exponential button.

With this method of construction, the observed death rate will be the same as that in the life table for each 5-year age interval, for the death rate in the life table is

$$_5m_x = \frac{l_x - l_{x+5}}{\int_0^5 l_{x+t}\,dt} = \frac{l_x - e^{-_{55}M_x}l_x}{l_x\int_0^5 e^{-_5M_xt}\,dt},$$

and this simplifies down to $_5M_x$ on evaluating the integral and canceling.

One difficulty of this simple method is that it implies a step function for the μ_x and, therefore, discontinuities in the derivative of l_x. This is the consequence of its agreement with the data in respect of 5-year mortality rates. The alternative that we have chosen produces, as nearly as possible, a life table whose underlying force of mortality, assumed continuous, is close to that underlying the data.

The calculation for Colombia, 1964, males will exemplify the numerical magnitude of differences between our method and that of assuming a step function for μ_x, which is to say, taking it as equal to the observed $_5M_x$ in each 5-year age interval. One kind of summary of the differences is given by the survivors l_x to age x out of 100,000 births. For age 50 this is $l_{50} = 72{,}435$ with our method and 72,327 with the step-function method. For age 85 the corresponding numbers are 13,441 and 13,427. The expectation of life at age 0 is 58.23 years with our method and 58.04 with the step-function method. The refinement has not resulted in any gross difference in results; rather its advantage is logical coherence.

Chiang (1968, p. 203) uses the mean length of time lived in each age interval by those dying in the interval. Applied to 5-year intervals, this quantity, say $_5a_x$ for those dying between ages x and $x + 5$, is very nearly $2\frac{1}{2}$ years, and in general he has

$$_5q_x = \frac{5 \, _5M_x}{1 + (5 - _na_x) _5M_x}.$$

For Colombia, males, our $_5a_{20}$ was 2.59, our $_5a_{40}$ was 2.61, and our $_5a_{60}$ was 2.61, all calculated as a by-product of our method. The resulting differences in l_x and $\overset{\circ}{e}_x$ are not numerically important as long as 2.6 years or other reasonable values of $_5a_x$ are used.

One can see the methods developed by Reed and Merrill (1939) and Greville (1943) as modifications of Eq. (2) that add to the exponent higher powers of the age-specific rate $_5M_x$. By a variant of the argument leading to Eq. (2), a more general formula, in which change of μ_{x+t} within the age group is provided for, may be derived:

$$l_{x+5} = l_x \exp\left(- \int_0^5 \mu_{x+t} \, dt\right) = l_x \exp(-5 \, _5M_x - k \, _5M_x^2), \quad (24)$$

where k is a number close to unity.

The factor $\exp(-k \, _5M_x^2)$ in Eq. (24) may be thought of as the Reed–Merrill–Greville correction to the straight exponential. As an example of why it is needed, consider the probability of surviving from age 70 to age 75 for Colombia, 1964, males. The age-specific death rate $_5M_x$ is .05609, and the first approximation exponential or step function, $\exp(-5 \, _5M_x)$, is .75545 for l_{75}/l_{70}. The value given by our method is $l_{75}/l_{70} = .75279$. Evidently the straight exponential is too high. If we put $k = 1$ in Eq. (24), the Reed–Merrill–Greville improvement is the factor $\exp(-_5M_x^2)$, which is equal to .99685. Multiplying this by the straight exponential gives .75545 × .99685 = .75307. Thus the Reed–Merrill–Greville improvement covers 90% of the distance from the step function down to the estimate given by our method.

The Chiang method, even putting $_5a_{70} = 2.5$, is better than the step function. It works out to

$$_5q_{70} = \frac{5(.05609)}{1 + 2.5(.05609)} = .24596,$$

so that $l_{75}/l_{70} = .75404$, which is slightly too high. If $_5a_{70}$ is put equal to 2.6, a better approximation for most ages, we have

$$l_{75}/l_{70} = 1 - \frac{5(.05609)}{1 + 2.4(.05609)} = .75282,$$

which is just about right.

Net Probabilities

Neyman (1950) develops the logic of finding what he calls net probabilities, which are the same as those of our associated single-decrement table. He discusses in detail the fact that persons who die of cause j are no longer exposed to cause of death i, all in terms of fixed forces of mortality for each of the two causes over the time and age interval considered. If the person is subject to the ith cause of death with force $\mu^{(i)}$, and to no other mortality risks, then the same argument that leads to Eq. (2) now gives

$$\bar{l}_{x+t}^{(i)}/\bar{l}_x^{(i)} = \exp(-5\mu^{(i)}), \qquad (25)$$

where $\bar{l}_x^{(i)}$ is the number living to age x in the presence of the ith cause of death only. Berkson and Elveback (1960) show how to make maximum likelihood estimates using this method.

If the assumption of a fixed force of mortality in the age interval is unsuitable, an application of the first part of Eq. (24) to cause (i) permits writing

$$\bar{l}_{x+5}^{(i)} = \bar{l}_x^{(i)} \exp\left(-\int_0^5 \mu_{x+t}^{(i)}\, dt\right), \qquad (26)$$

and we have the number living $\bar{l}_{x+t}^{(i)}$ in the single-decrement table that would apply if only the ith cause was operative. This is the method proposed by Cornfield (1957); it makes the minimum of assumptions but does leave aside the problem of estimating the curve of $\mu_{x+t}^{(i)}$.

Chiang (1968) shows how assuming fixed ratios of the force of mortality for the several causes in each age interval permits one to proceed from the probability of dying from all causes to a probability of dying if only the ith cause is operative. Since we have

$$\mu_x = \mu_x^{(i)} + \mu_x^{(-i)},$$

then l_{x+5}, for all causes, obtained by the first part of Eq. (24), leads easily to an $\bar{l}_{x+5}^{(i)}$ if only one can suppose that the ratio $\mu_{x+t}^{(i)}/\mu_{x+t}$ is constant through the interval (Chiang, 1968, p. 244). For, from Eq. (26), we have

$$\bar{l}_{x+5}^{(i)} = \bar{l}_x^{(i)} \exp\left(-\int_0^5 \mu_{x+t}^{(i)}\, dt\right)$$

$$= \bar{l}_x^{(i)} \exp\left[-(\mu_x^{(i)}/\mu_x)\int_0^5 \mu_{x+t}\, dt\right].$$

(Since $\mu_{x+t}^{(i)}/\mu_{x+t}$ is supposed constant, we can remove it from the integral.) Hence

$$\bar{l}_{x+5}^{(i)}/\bar{l}_x^{(i)} = (l_{x+5}/l_x)^{\mu_x^{(i)}/\mu_x}. \qquad (27)$$

Greville (1948) develops this result in more general terms. He does not require that $\mu_{x+t}^{(i)}/\mu_{x+t}$ be constant for $0 < t < 5$ but uses a suitable mean of its values through the interval.

Individuals Subject to Two Different Causes in Succession

The method proposed by Schwartz and Lazar (1963) is ingenious enough to be worth our attention here. They suppose that after a person has died of the ith cause he is still subject to risk from the $(-i)$th cause. This fiction leads to a new and apparently satisfactory formula. The method requires that among those who died of the two causes in succession, the proportion of those who died first of the ith cause be ascertained. The remainder, who died of the $(-i)$th cause and then of the ith cause, are eliminated from the total of the ith cause.

These considerations provide two equations. The first is that the observed $D_x^{(i)}/N_x$, where N_x is the estimated population at the beginning of the 1-year age interval, must be equal to the chance that the person dies of the ith and not of the $(-i)$th cause during the period, say 1 year, which is $\bar{q}_x^{(i)}(1 - \bar{q}_x^{(-i)})$, plus part of the chance that he died of both causes, which would be $\bar{q}_x^{(i)}\bar{q}_x^{(-i)}$. To eliminate the fictional cases who died of the $(-i)$th cause first, suppose that $\lambda^{(i)}$ is the chance of dying of the ith cause first among those who die of both causes. Then the first equation is

$$D_x^{(i)}/N_x = \bar{q}_x^{(i)}(1 - \bar{q}_x^{(-i)}) + \lambda^{(i)}\bar{q}_x^{(i)}\bar{q}_x^{(-i)}.$$

The second equation, by symmetry, is the same, with (i) and $(-i)$ interchanged.

Eliminating $\bar{q}_x^{(-i)}$ from the two equations gives a quadratic in $\bar{q}_x^{(i)}$. We still have to estimate $\lambda_x^{(i)}$ and $\lambda_x^{(-i)}$, but the values of these are not critical. Once estimates of the λ are made, the quadratic in $\bar{q}_x^{(i)}$ is readily solved.

Other Assumptions

In all tables, we assume that when a cause of death is eliminated, the other causes continue to operate unchanged. Krall and Hickman (1971) avoid supposition of independent action of the several causes; they assume that part of the mortality that is eliminated is retained by the increase of other causes. The device is interesting, but interdependencies can operate in both directions, and empirical investigation of their direction and amount is lacking.

Kimball (1958) works out a different probability: the chance of dying from the ith cause for those individuals who do not die of some other cause. This is not the same as the concept that we apply throughout this book: finding the probability of dying of the ith cause were the $(-i)$th cause not to exist.

Appendix to Chapter II

ITERATIVE LIFE TABLE PROGRAMS

It is our hope that the concepts of life-table construction employed here will be seen as both useful and broadly applicable. Iterative life tables, particularly when multiple decrements or associated single decrements are involved, are as hard to program as they are easy to prepare once the programs are available. To permit the reader to benefit from the advantages of the iterative technique with a minimum of difficulty, the following simplified FORTRAN programs and output are provided.

General

Program MULDEC, which computes both the basic life table and multiple-decrement columns for additional causes, is shown in Table A-1. Program ASIDEC, which calculates associated single-decrement tables (ASDTs), is given in Table A-2. The programs have been designed in a single overall pattern; the same symbolism applies throughout, and all of the three iterative sequences have been made comparable to the extent possible. Statement numbers have been keyed accordingly, with the 0–99 set pertaining to the iteration of the basic life table, the 100–199 set applying to the multiple-decrement column, and the 200–299 set dealing with the ASDTs. To simplify the illustration and allow for maximum user flexibility, the printed results have been held to a minimum (see Table A-3), and no routines for input data checks, adjustments for nonmidyear census dates, or prorations for unknown ages have been included. Such steps, as well as consistency and quality control procedures, were incorporated into the program that calculated the tables in this book, and hence the results are not strictly comparable. The only safety device included in the programs presented here is that no results will be printed if convergence is not achieved in less than 25 iterations. (Experience has indicated that convergence can be expected in less than 20 iterations.)

The basic system of computation, identical in all three sequences, can be divided into six steps as follows:

1. Read input data.
2. Initialize variables.
3. Iterate to improve function values.
4. Check for convergence to desired tolerance (here .001 on l_{80}); return to step 3 if tolerance is exceeded.
5. Print iterated results.
6. Go to next set of input data.

Comment cards have been included to mark the transition from one phase to another in most instances.

Program MULDEC

MULDEC will calculate a series of life tables and, for each life table, compute double-decrement columns for the number of causes desired. The input required for the basic life table consists of five cards. The first, or title, card identifies the population under consideration. The first column must be left blank, but the remaining 79 columns can be used for any information deemed

```
      PROGRAM MULDEC (INPUT,OUTPUT)
      DIMENSION TITLE(8),PP(20),DD(20),VMM(20),VL(20),
     2VLLP(20),VR(20),VL18(26),Q(3,19),HEADER(8),DDD(20),VMM1(20),
     3VL1(20),D1(20),VL118(26),R(3,19)

C  TO READ THE LIFE TABLE DATA

    1 READ 3, TITLE
    3 FORMAT( 8A10)
      IF(TITLE(1).EQ.10H 999999999) GO TO 199
      PRINT 3, TITLE
      READ 5, PP,DD
    5 FORMAT (10F8.0)

C  INITIALIZE LIFE TABLE VARIABLES

      DO 10 I=1,19
      VMM(I)=DD(I)/PP(I)
   10 VR(I)=0.
      SEP= .07+1.7*VMM(1)
      VL(1)=100000.
      VL(2)=VL(1)*(1.-SEP*VMM(1))/(1.+(1.-SEP)*VMM(1))
      VL(3)=VL(2)*(1.-1.5*VMM(2))/(1.+2.5*VMM(2))
      VLLP(1)=SEP*VL(1)+(1.-SEP)*VL(2)
      VLLP(2)=1.5*VL(2)+2.5*VL(3)
      DO 12 I=3,19
      VL(I+1)=VL(I)*(1.-2.5*VMM(I))/(1.+2.5*VMM(I))
   12 VLLP(I)=2.5*(VL(I)+VL(I+1))
      VL18(1)=VL(18)

C  TO ITERATE THE LIFE TABLE

      DO 21 J=1,25
      DO 15 I=4,18
      S=EXP(5.*VR(I))
      VL(I+1)=S*(VL(I)-(VMM(I)+VR(I))*((65./24.)*VL(I)-
     2(5./24.)*(S*VL(I-1)+VL(I+2)/(S**2))))/(1.+(65./24.)*
     3(VMM(I)+VR(I)))
   15 VLLP(I)=(65./24.)*(VL(I)+VL(I+1)/S)-(5./24 )*(VL(I-1)
     2*S+VL(I+2)/S**2)
      VL(20)=VL(19)*(1.-2.5*VMM(19))/(1.+2.5*VMM(19))
      VLLP(3)=5./2.*(VL(3)+VL(4)/EXP(5.*VR(3)))
      DO 18 I=4,17
   18 VR(I)=.1*ALOG((PP(I-1)/VLLP(I-1))/(PP(I+1)/VLLP(I+1)))
      VR(18)=VR(17)
      VL18(J+1)=VL(18)

C  TO CHECK FOR LIFE TABLE CONVERGENCE, ABORTING AFTER 24 ITERATIONS

      IF(J.EQ.25) GO TO 101
      IF(ABS(VL18(J+1)-VL18(J)).GE..001) GO TO 21
      IF(J.LE.1) GO TO 21
      GO TO 50
   21 CONTINUE

C  TO PRINT THE LIFE TABLE IN MATRIX Q

   50 DO 55 I=1,19
      Q(1,I)+5*I-10
   55 Q(2,I)=VL(I)
      Q(1,1)=0.
      Q(1,2)=1.

C  TO CALCULATE THE PERSON-YEARS LIVED COLUMN

      Q(3,1)=SEP*VL(1)+(1.-SEP)*VL(2)
      Q(3,2)=1.5*VL(2)+2.5*VL(3)
      Q(3,3)=2.5*(VL(3)+VL(4))
      DO 60 I=4,18
   60 Q(3,I)=(65./24.)*(VL(I)+VL(I+1))-(5./24.)*(VL(I-1)+VL(I+2))
      Q(3,19)=VL(19)/VMM(19)
      PRINT 65, Q
   65 FORMAT(1X,F3.0,2F9.0)

C  TO CONSIDER ADDITIONAL, OR SPECIFIC, CAUSES OF DECREMENT

  101 READ 3, HEADER
      IF(HEADER(1).EQ.10H 777777777) GO TO 1
      PRINT 3, HEADER
      READ 5, DDD
      IF(J.EQ.25) GO TO 101

C  TO INITIALIZE ADDITIONAL DECREMENT VARIABLES

      DO 110 I=1,19
      VMM1(I)=DDD(I)/PP(I)
  110 D1(I)=(VL(I)-VL(I+1))*VMM1(I)/VMM(I)
      VL1(19)=VL(19)*VMM1(19)/VMM(19)
      DO 112 I=2,19
  112 VL1(20-I)=VL1(21-I)+D1(20-I)
      VL118(1)=VL1(18)

C  TO ITERATE THE ADDITIONAL DECREMENT COLUMNS

      DO 121 K=1,25
      DO 115 I=4,17
      S=EXP(5.*VR(I))
      SS=(1./(S*S))
  115 VL1(I+1)=S*(VL1(I)-VR(I)*((65./24.)*VL1(I)-(5./24)
     2*(VL1(I-1)*S+VL1(I+2)*SS))-VMM1(I)*VLLP(I))/
     3(1.+(65./24.)*VR(I))
      VL118(K+1)=VL1(18)

C  TO CHECK FOR CONVERGENCE

      IF(K.EQ.25) GO TO 101
      IF(K.LE.1) GO TO 117
      IF(ABS(VL118(K+1)-VL118(K)).GE..001) GO TO 117
      GO TO 150
  117 CONTINUE
  121 CONTINUE

C  TO PRINT THE MULTIPLE DECREMENT COLUMNS IN MATRIX R

  150 DO 155 I=1,19
      R(1,I)=Q(1,I)
      R(2,I)= VL1(I)
  155 R(3,I)=VL(I)-VL1(I)
      PRINT 165, R
  165 FORMAT(1X,F3.0,2F8.0)
      GO TO 101
  199 STOP
      END
```

Table A-2

```
      PROGRAM ASIDEC(INPUT,OUTPUT)
      DIMENSION CAPTION(8),VLL(20),D1(20),DQ(20),QQ(20),VL(20),
     2VM1(20),AL(20),VH(20),AL18(26),T(2,19)

C  TO READ THE INPUT DATA

  201 READ 203,CAPTION
      IF(CAPTION(1).EQ.10H 888888888) GO TO 299
  203 FORMAT( 8A10 )
      PRINT 203, CAPTION
      READ 205,VLL,D1,VL
  205 FORMAT( 10F8.0 )

C  INITIALIZE VARIABLES

      DO 210 I=1,19
      VM1(I)= D1(I)/VLL(I)
  210 VH(I)=0.
      AL(I)=100000.
      DO 212 I=1,18
      DQ(I)=(VL(I)-VL(I+1))/VL(I)
      QQ(I)=1.-(1.-DQ(I))**(D1(I)/(VL(I)*DQ(I)))
  212 AL(I+1)=AL(I)*(1-QQ(I))
      AL18(1)=AL(18)

C  TO ITERATE THE ASSOCIATED SINGLE DECREMENT TABLE

      DO 221 J=1,25
      DO 215 I=4,17
      VH(I)=.2*ALOG((AL(I+1)*VL(I))/(AL(I)*VL(I+1)))
      S=EXP(.5*VH(I))
  215 AL(I+1)=S*(AL(I)-(VM1(I)+VH(I))*((65./24.)*AL(I)-
     2(5./24.)*(S*AL(I-1)+AL(I+2)/(S**2)))/(1.+(65./24.)*
     3(VM1(I)+VH(I)))
      AL(19)=AL(18)*(1.-QQ(18))
      AL18(J+1)=AL(18)

C  TO CHECK FOR ASDT CONVERGENCE

      IF(J.EQ.25) GO TO 201
      IF(J.LE.1) GO TO 217
      IF(ABS(AL18(J+1)-AL18(J)).GE..001) GO TO 217
      GO TO 250
  217 CONTINUE
  221 CONTINUE

C  TO PRINT THE ASDT IN MATRIX T

  250 DO 255 I=1,19
      T(1,I)=5*I-10
  255 T(2,I)=AL(I)
      T(1,1)=0.
      T(1,2)=1.
  265 FORMAT(1X,F3.0,F9.0)
      PRINT 265, T
      GO TO 201
  299 STOP
      END
```

Table A-3

Sample Output- MULDEC			Sample Output- ASIDEC	
JAPAN MALE 1960			**JAPAN 1960 MALES ASDT EXCL TB**	
0.	100000.	97103.	0.	100000.
1.	96677.	384132.	1.	96679.
5.	95467.	477018.	5.	95653.
10.	95160.	475133.	10.	95169.
15.	94881.	472987.	15.	94893.
20.	94252.	468813.	20.	94278.
25.	93237.	463545.	25.	93304.
30.	92175.	458236.	30.	92343.
35.	91095.	452268.	35.	91432.
40.	89750.	444497.	40.	90311.
45.	87392.	433295.	45.	88743.
50.	85814.	416104.	50.	86280.
55.	80939.	389339.	55.	82353.
60.	74375.	349887.	60.	76111.
65.	65068.	294841.	65.	67085.
70.	52354.	223791.	70.	54516.
75.	36874.	143273.	75.	38875.
80.	20705.	71024.	80.	22120.
85.	8468.	29949.	85.	9133.
	TUBERCULOSIS		**JAPAN 1960 MALES ASDT EXCL INF MORT**	
0.	4188.	95812.	0.	100000.
1.	4186.	92491.	1.	98351.
5.	4182.	91465.	5.	97303.
10.	4179.	90981.	10.	96808.
15.	4176.	90705.	15.	96524.
20.	4162.	90090.	20.	95884.
25.	4120.	89117.	25.	94851.
30.	4018.	88158.	30.	93771.
35.	3846.	87249.	35.	92672.
40.	3616.	86134.	40.	91304.
45.	3353.	84579.	45.	89454.
50.	3042.	82142.	50.	86659.
55.	2665.	78274.	55.	82340.
60.	2216.	72158.	60.	75662.
65.	1696.	63371.	65.	66194.
70.	1114.	51240.	70.	53260.
75.	562.	36313.	75.	37512
80.	182.	20523.	80.	21063.
85.	42.	8426.	85.	8614.

appropriate. To terminate the program, a signal title card is used, consisting of a blank in the first column and the number 9 in columns 2–10.

The second and third cards of life-table input data contain the figures on population (PP) for ages 0, 1–4, 5–9, . . . , 80–84, and 85+. The format is 10F8.0; hence the first eight columns contain the midyear population under 1 year of age, the second eight columns the number aged 1 through 4, etc. The last eight columns of the third data card are not utilized here.

The fourth and fifth cards of life-table input data contain the figures on deaths from all causes (DD). The format is identical to the PP cards.

Each additional decrement requires three cards. The first, or header, card identifies the decrement involved using the same format as the title card. After the last additional decrement set, or after the last life-table data card, if there are no additional decrements, a signal card is inserted. The card has a blank first column and the number 7 punched in columns 2–10.

The second and third additional decrement data cards contain the figures on the number of decrements (DDD), usually the number of deaths due to the cause given on the header card. The format is the same as the PP cards.

The meanings of other symbols used are as follows:

VMM   The population central death rate.
VL   Lower case l (survivorship) column of the life table.
VLLP   Capital L (person-years) column of the life table when distorted by growth.
VR   Sectionally stable rate of growth.
SEP   Proportion of deaths below age 1 occurring to persons born the previous year.

When "1" is appended to a life-table variable, the corresponding multiple-decrement variable is intended.

Program ASIDEC

ASIDEC will calculate a series of ASDTs for previously computed multiple-decrement life tables.

The input required for each ASDT consists of seven cards. The first, or caption, card identifies the population and decrement under consideration. The first column must be left blank, but the remaining 79 columns can be used. To terminate the program, a signal caption card is inserted after the last data card. The signal card has a blank first column and the figure 8 punched in columns 2–10.

The second and third input data cards contain the numbers in the life-table population (the VLL or capital L column of the life table, which reflects the number of person-years lived in the interval by the life-table cohort) for ages 0, 1–4, 5–9, . . . , 80–84, and 85+. The format is 10F8.0; hence the first eight columns of the second data card contain the person-years lived by those under 1 year of age, the second eight columns the number for ages 1–4, etc. The last eight columns of the third data card are not utilized here.

The fourth and fifth ASDT data cards contain the number of life-table deaths (D1) from the cause(s) still decrementing the life-table population after the other cause(s) has (have) been eliminated. The format is the same as for the VLL cards.

The sixth and seventh ASDT data cards contain the number of those surviving to a given age from a cohort of 100,000 births, or the number in the lower case l column of a life table. Designated VL, this is the same VL as in the preceding MULDEC program. The format is identical to that of the VLL cards.

The meaning of other symbols used are as follows:

AL   Survivors of a birth cohort under mortality conditions prevailing in the ASDT. Analogous to VL.
VH   Analogous to VR. Reflective of the deformation of the stationary age distribution of the life table produced by the decrease in mortality.
VM1   Life table central death rate for the remaining cause(s).
DQ   Life table probability of death.
QQ   ASDT probability of death.

DIFFERENCES BETWEEN THESE PROGRAMS AND THE PROGRAMS USED FOR THE TABLES

The tables given in this book were produced by a single execution of one computer program, called MBC. The program, about four times as long as the sample MULDEC and ASIDEC programs combined, can conveniently be divided into seven sections, each of which was applied to all of the 360 one-sex populations tabulated.

The first, or checking section, read the input data and checked it for card order, formating, and internal consistency. Because of the large volume of data involved, elaborate procedures were considered necessary to preserve accuracy. For example, the matrix of death figures was checked against both row and column totals with no inconsistencies permitted, and each set of figures, although previously checked, was again scrutinized by the computer at the time of the final run.

The second, or data-adjustment section, prorated the number of persons and deaths at unknown ages and calculated the estimated population as of July 1 of the year for which the data on deaths applied (almost always the same year as the census). The estimate for the rate of population growth was based on the excess of the year's births over deaths, or the population's crude rate of natural increase.

The third section calculated the basic life table and the fourth section calculated the multiple-decrement columns, in much the same way as was indicated by program MULDEC. However there were some slight refinements at the upper end of the table, and a separate iteration equation for $l_{10}[\text{VL}(4)]$ was used to make the tables agree with the data to the fullest extent possible. Section five computed the associated single-decrement table and, subject to refinements similar to those previously described, was quite similar to program ASIDEC.

The sixth section examined the results of the calculations performed and checked for deviations from consistency. If the sum of the survivors for each individual cause in the multiple-decrement table, at each age, differed significantly from the separately iterated number of survivors for the total cohort, a warning message would be printed. Otherwise, figures were then rounded separately and any discrepancy put in the residual category. In the ASDT, a similar check was done to see how closely the analogous multiplicative relationship held. The small inconsistencies were then prorated across all of the causes.

The seventh section of program MBC produced the additional calculations presented, and caused the results to be printed in the format shown. The computer then returned to the start of the program to begin the cycle once again. In all, the CDC 6400 computer took 818.6 sec of central processor time to transform 11,609 input cards into the final results.

REFERENCES

Berkson, J., & Elveback, L. Competing exponential risks, with particular reference to smoking and lung cancer. *Journal of the American Statistical Association*, 1960, **55**, 415–428.

• Chiang, C. L. *Introduction to stochastic processes in biostatistics.* New York: Wiley, 1968.

Cornfield, J. The estimation of the probability of developing a disease in the presence of competing risks. *Journal of the American Public Health Association*, 1957, **47**, 601–607.

Greville, T. N. E. Short methods of constructing abridged life tables. *Record of the American Institute of Actuaries*, 1943, **32**, 29–43.

Greville, T. N. E. Mortality tables analyzed by cause of death. *Record of the American Institute of Actuaries*, 1948, **37**, 283–294.

Jordan, C. W. *Life contingencies.* Chicago: The Society of Actuaries, 1952.

Keyfitz, N. *Introduction to the mathematics of population.* Reading, Massachusetts: Addison-Wesley, 1968.

Keyfitz, N. Finding probabilities from observed rates, or how to make a life table. *The American Statistician*, 1970, **24**, 28–33.

Kimball, A. W. Disease incidence estimation in populations subject to multiple causes of death. *Bulletin of the International Statistical Institute*, 1958, **36**, 193–204.

Krall, J. M., & Hickman, J. C. Adjusting multiple-decrement tables. *Transactions of the Society of Actuaries*, 1971, **22**, 163–179.

Neyman, J. *First course in probability and statistics.* New York: Holt, 1950.

Reed, L. J., & Merrill, M. A short method for constructing an abridged life table. *American Journal of Hygiene*, 1939, **30**, 33–62.

Schwartz, D., & Lazar, P. *Taux de mortalité par une cause donnée de décès en tenant compte des autres causes de décès ou de disparition.* Unité de Recherches Statistiques de l'Institut National d'Hygiène, Ministère de la Santé Publique, France, 1963.

Spiegelman, M. *Introduction to demography.* (Rev. ed.) Cambridge, Massachusetts: Harvard Univ. Press, 1968.

Chapter III ACCURACY AND COMPARABILITY

A. Numbers of Persons and Deaths (All Causes Combined)

The primary sources of error in the tables are unquestionably the diagnosis and coding of cause of death, which will occupy most of our attention. Errors in counts of population and deaths, whose general characteristics have been dealt with in a number of other publications, will be briefly considered (see Barclay, 1958; Spiegelman, 1968; United Nations, 1955, 1958; United Nations Statistical Office, 1955).

Accuracy of Censuses

Errors in censuses can be conveniently divided into errors of coverage and content. Errors of coverage involve the mistaken inclusion or exclusion of persons from the census count. Past experience indicates that, in the absence of fraud on a rather large scale, census counts tend to be low rather than high and, furthermore, that certain groups of people are especially likely to be undernumerated. Children below the age of 5, and infants in particular, are almost universally underreported in censuses. Transients and those at ages of high geographical mobility, frequently males in their twenties, are also very likely to be missed.

Errors of content involve the misstatement or nonstatement of a characteristic of an enumerated person. We are interested in the age and sex characteristics, but it is only the misstatement of age that presents any real problem. There is a tendency for persons who are slightly short of some landmark age, especially the age of majority, to report themselves as being that age. In the United States, for example, there is a conspicuously large number of persons at age 21 and a smaller, but still unduly large, number of females at age 18. Age 65 also seems to be favored, an occurrence that is probably connected with the receipt of retirement benefits. Moreover there seems to be an overall trend for persons at the higher and lower ages to be reported at ages in excess of their true age, while persons between 21 and 65 are reported at somewhat under their true ages. The number of persons at the youngest ages is affected by the tendency to round age upward, or to report age at the nearest rather than the last birthday, as requested. At the highest ages there is likely to be more than a little exaggeration of age, those reported as over 100 years of age being worthy of special skepticism (Myers, 1966).

Characteristic forms of age misreporting found in Asia and Latin America have been examined by Coale and Demeny (see United Nations, 1967, p. 17ff.). In brief, they found that the Latin American countries tend to have a surplus in the 5–9 age groups and a corresponding deficit in the 0–4 age groups. African or Asian

Table III-1

Indicators of Accuracy and Completeness of Systems of Census and Death Registration

Country and range of years included in study	Census year and joint score, UN Secretariat method[a]		Death registration completeness code 1946–1964[b]	Remarks
Australia, 1911–1964	1947	11.1	C*	
	1933	9.9		
Austria, 1961–1964	1939	11.7	C	
Belgium, 1960–1964	1947	10.3	C	
Bulgaria, 1964	1934	17.7	C	
Canada, 1921–1964	1941	11.7	C	Survey found birth registration 98% complete during 1940–1942.
Ceylon, 1960	1946	52.3	U	Death registration found 88.6% complete, birth registration 88.1% complete in a 1953 survey.
Chile, 1909–1964	1940	30.1	C	Recorded as incomplete for 1946–1954.
Colombia, 1960–1964	1938	51.3	U	
Costa Rica, 1960–1964	1927	32.3	C	
Czechoslovakia, 1930–1964	1947	9.9	C	Joint score completed assuming male age-ratio score same as female.
Denmark, 1921–1964	1945	7.6	C	
El Salvador, 1950			C	Infant mortality coded U.
England and Wales, 1861–1964	1931	10.2	C	See text.
Finland, 1951–1964	1940	14.1	C	
France, 1926–1964	1946	10.0	C	
Germany, West				
Excluding West Berlin, 1960–1964	1950	13.9	C	Joint score computed assuming male age-ratio score same as female.
West Berlin, 1960–1964	1946	9.7	C	
Greece, 1928–1964	1940	24.8	U	
Guatemala, 1961–1964	1940	35.8	C	
Hong Kong, 1961–1964			C*	
Hungary, 1960–1964	1941	12.4	C	
Iceland, 1964	1940	15.3	C	Adjusted for the smallness of the country, the joint score is 8.3.
Ireland, 1951–1961	1946	15.5	C	
Israel (Jewish population only), 1951–1964			C	Registration and census data considered almost complete (Bachi, 1954).
Italy, 1881–1964	1936	8.2	C	1921 census considered inflated by some 800,000 persons (Frumkin, 1954).
Japan, 1899–1964	1948	11.5	C	1950 census judged .5% low. Nation has had a fairly accurate registration system since 1875, improved after 1919 (Morita, 1954; Taueber, 1958, esp. pp. 40–42 and 300–305).
	1940	13.1		
Malta and Gozo, 1964	1948	25.2	C	
Mauritius, 1960–1964	1944	42.1	C*	

Table III-1 (Continued)

Country and range of years included in study	Census year and joint score, UN Secretariat method[a]		Death registration completeness code 1946–1964[b]	Remarks
Mexico, 1960–1964	1940	33.7	C*	
Netherlands, 1931–1964	1947	6.6	C	
	1930	5.8		
New Zealand (excluding Maoris), 1881–1964	1945	18.4	C*	
Northern Ireland, 1960–1964	1937	11.1	C*	
Norway, 1910–1964	1946	9.0	C	
	1930	12.2		
Panama, 1960–1964	1940	37.4	U	
Phillipines, 1964	1939	50.8	U	
Poland, 1960–1964	1949	16.3	C	
Portugal, 1920–1964	1940	14.6	C	
Puerto Rico, 1960–1964	1950	14.7	C	As population returns examined were based on a sample of 8700 persons, the joint score was adjusted for smallness.
Scotland, 1951–1964	1931	12.4	C*	
South Africa, 1941–1960				
Colored population			C	Colored birth registration 4.1% low for 1951–1960, while death registration deemed nearly complete; census undercounts estimated as 1.2% in 1960 and 3.8% in 1951 (see Sadie, 1970). Data on Whites held to be accurate.
White population	1946	13.2	C	
Spain, 1930–1960	1940	14.5	C	
Sweden, 1911–1964	1945	7.6	C	
Switzerland, 1930–1964	1941	10.8	C	
Taiwan, 1920–1964	1940	17.0	C*	Registration system held to be very good overall, although infant mortality underreported and child (1–4 years) mortality exaggerated (Sullivan, 1971).
Trinidad and Tobago, 1963	1946	26.6	C	
United States of America	1940	10.5	C	Death registration states only before 1940. See discussion in text.
Total Population, 1900–1964				
White population, 1920–1950				
Nonwhite population, 1920–1950				
Venezuela, 1960–1964	1941	42.4	U	
Yugoslavia, 1961–1964	1948	22.4	C	

[a] Joint Scores from *United Nations Population Bulletin No. 2.* Under 20: Census reliable. 20–40: Census fairly unreliable. Over 40: Census quite unreliable.

[b] Completeness of death registration data from *United Nations Demographic Yearbooks.* C: Completeness on the order of 90% or more. U: Completeness less than 90%. (*) Deaths tabulated by data of registration rather than date of occurrence.

populations, on the other hand, seem to be identified by a large shortage between ages 10 and 20.

In addition to all of the aforementioned forms of age misreporting, there is the problem of digit preferences. To varying degrees, respondents show a greater liking for some numbers than for others, and while preferences vary, the even numbers and multiples of 5 generally are favored. The resulting errors are considerably reduced by using data in broader age groups, but these are still affected.

A procedure for evaluating grouped census data originated in the United Nations Secretariat (United Nations, 1952, pp. 59–79). The method compares sex ratios at successive ages to arrive at a sex-ratio score and age ratios separately for each sex to arrive at two age-ratio scores. It then combines them into a joint score, first tripling the sex-ratio score. A joint score of less than 20 is indicative of a reliable census, one in the 20 through 40 range suggests a fairly unreliable census, and a joint score above 40 is held to indicate a quite unreliable census. Populations listed in the 1949–1950 and 1951 *United Nations Demographic Yearbooks* were examined, and the results for countries included in this study are shown in Table III-1. As might be expected, the United Nations Secretariat method has a number of flaws, some mentioned in the original article and others pointed out by Das Gupta (1954, pp. 63–74). The index is only a rough measure and does not differentiate between censal errors and real variations in demographic rates; large-scale migrations, heavy war casualties, and major swings in birth rates, such as occurred in the West during the 1930's, appear as census discrepancies unless special care is taken. As a result, we will present only those indexes, calculated by the United Nations Secretariat, which include adjustments for the past experience of the populations.

Table III-1 also presents comments, when available, on investigations made into the accuracy of several censuses. Two countries merit further treatment. England and Wales have a long history of decennial censuses, and the data seem to be of very high quality. Benjamin and Carrier (1954) examined population censuses back through the census of 1911 and found them to be highly accurate. Myers (1940) tested the censuses of 1911 and 1931 for age heaping and found it to be extremely small, a sign of accuracy.

Evaluations of United States censuses show them to be of substantial accuracy, but not as complete as those of England and Wales. After the 1950 census the Post-Enumeration Survey officially estimated an undercount of 1.4% of the total population, Whites being short by 1.2% and Nonwhites by 3.2%. There is evidence, however, that the 1950 Post-Enumeration Survey was affected by many of the same problems that affected the 1950 census itself (Coale, 1955). The census of 1960, believed to be a more comprehensive and accurate count than that of 1950, was officially considered a 1.7% undercount by the 1960 Post-Enumeration Survey. In other words, about 3,000,000 persons were missed by the census. In a sweeping study, Coale and Zelnik (1963) performed a wholesale reconstruction of the native White United States population by age and sex from 1880 through 1950, after first adjusting for the rather sizable amounts of age heaping present. In general they found that females were undercounted by some 2–3%, and males by about 5%, the undercounts varying greatly with age as well as by census year.

The Accuracy of Mortality Data (All Causes Combined)

In every population of this study, mortality information was derived from official death registration data. Errors of coverage in registration data are really synonymous with incomplete reporting, as overregistration of deaths is virtually unheard of. By the nature of the event, death registration is normally considered more complete than birth registration, though the latter has been the subject of more checks of registration accuracy. Direct checks of the accuracy of death registration have rarely been attempted, since they are difficult to devise and interpret. The group whose deaths are most likely to escape registration are infants, whose passing often carries less legal and emotional significance than the death of persons at other ages. Greville (1946) found that in the United States for 1939–1941, underregistration of deaths in the first year of life roughly equaled the estimated 6% underregistration of births for Whites, but exceeded, by 50%, the estimated 18% underregistration of births for Nonwhites. All in all, it is difficult to escape the conclusion that data on the first year of life, both registration and censual, are the least accurate of those for any age group.

Errors of content in death registration statistics are usually similar to those in census statistics. In comparing deaths in 1935 to the census of 1940 for the United States, Greville reported that age heaping occurred to the same order of magnitude in both for Whites and Nonwhites alike, although digital preference patterns were somewhat different. Probably the best available source on the accuracy of death registration statistics for most countries is the series of *Demographic Yearbooks* issued by the United Nations since 1948. Based on responses from the Statistical Office of the country concerned, the United Nations codes for death registration statistics are C, U, or . . . , depending on the degree of completeness. The code C suggests 90% or greater completeness ("virtually complete" in earlier volumes), U a lesser completeness, and . . . an unknown degree of completeness. These codes are shown in Table III-1 for the countries involved in this study. Should the code have changed between 1946 and 1964 (involving a date included in the study), or should the infant mortality completeness code be different, a comment is included to that effect. A remark is also made concerning surveys of birth or death registration accuracy.

England and Wales have a remarkably long record of accurate birth and death registration. Benjamin and Carrier (1954) reported that studies of the underregistration of births by Glass and Registrar General Farr indicated an underreporting of only 1–2%

between 1861 and 1880, and a trifling amount after 1880. Birth and death registration in the United States lagged well behind. The Death Registration Area, first established in 1900, was not complete until 1933, and for the 1900–1930 period our study must be confined to the Death Registration States. Since admission to the Death Registration Area was contingent upon 90% completeness of registration, which traditionally is associated with more favorable mortality, figures cannot be considered representative of the country as a whole.

Because there is no ready way to check the accuracy or completeness of death registration figures, their acceptance involves more of an act of faith than is the case with census data. It must be realized, however, that fundamentally we are interested neither in death registration data nor census data, but only in their ratio. Combining the two sets of data not only allows for additional comparative checks on the accuracy of both, but gives the user the benefit of what are nearly always partially compensating errors.

The tables prepared for this volume have been carefully scrutinized for palpable errors in death rates. In a large majority of cases, comparisons with official life tables were possible, and the two life expectancies calculated almost invariably differed by less than 2 years. On occasion, a table was discarded because of an implausible life expectancy (such as the 61.94 figure calculated for the Dominican Republic, 1951). As a further check, the tables were also examined for plausible age and sex patterns of mortality. For example, as a result of this check all tables for the South African–Asian population were discarded because of declining death rates after age 75. On the other hand, Spain, 1940, was retained because an extraordinary discrepancy between male and female life expectancies could be traced to excessive male deaths from violence, reasonable in the national context. The tables which remain are surely not free of "errors" in customary mortality parameters (excepting errors of transcription and calculation), but we believe that they reliably document a population's general level of mortality.

B. Causes of Death

In this section we are concerned with inaccuracies in recorded causes of death which can affect the total number of deaths assigned to any of the categories used in this study. Transfers of deaths between two terms within the same title, or two titles within the same category, have no effect on the number of deaths in the category as a whole and need not be considered here. The gain from aggregation is considerable. Moriyama, Dawber, and Kannel (1966; pp. 405–420) studied a representative sample of 1960 United States death certificates in which a cardiovascular–renal disease was listed as the underlying cause of death. For 15.1% of the certificates, another diagnosis was well established, or the stated diagnosis was "probably incorrect."[1] However in 95% of these cases, the preferred diagnosis of the reviewers was another cardio-vascular–renal disease. Less than 1% of the total deaths ascribed to cardiovascular–renal disease "clearly" belonged in another category altogether (Moriyama *et al.*, 1966, p. 409).

Two important factors affect the accuracy and comparability of cause-of-death statistics: the accuracy of diagnosis and the manner in which a diagnosis is translated into a notation in published statistics. Variations in both diagnostic and coding procedures are regrettably common and present a major obstacle to a meaningful interpretation of variation in population death rates by cause.

1. The Accuracy of Diagnosis

The accuracy of a cause-of-death diagnosis depends on the medical knowledge and acumen possessed by the person respon-

[1] Compiled from Moriyama *et al.* (1966, Table 2).

sible for the diagnosis and the adequacy of the data available to him. We will consider variation in diagnostic accuracy as it is likely to affect both trends and differentials in mortality rates by cause.

Influence on Trends in Mortality by Cause

Probably the most important diagnostic factor affecting trends in causes of death has been a declining proportion of deaths assigned to ill-defined and unknown causes. This decline has necessarily been reflected in an increased proportion of deaths ascribed to well-defined diseases. The amount of upward bias imparted to trends in death rates from the well-defined diseases varies with age, country, and cause of death. A review of trends in deaths from ill-defined and unknown causes by the United Nations (1962, pp. 70–73) permits an assessment of the amount of bias introduced.

At ages below 65 years, the bias is likely to be quite small. In England and Wales, for example, for ages 45–64 the number of all male deaths ascribed to ill-defined and unknown causes declined from 1.8% in 1848–1872 to 0% in 1956–1957. The corresponding decline in the United States from 1900–1904 to 1955–1957 was from 2.3% to 1.0%. Of the 12 western countries examined, the only one showing a substantial trend in the proportion of deaths in this age category from 1936–1938 to 1954–1956 was France, where 30.5% of all male deaths in the former period were assigned to this category, compared to 15.6% by the later date. Both of these figures were at least double that in any other country surveyed during the same period.

Above age 65 the picture is much less satisfactory. For ages 75 and above in 1848–1872, 49.6% of all male deaths were assigned to ill-defined or unknown causes (including senility) in England and Wales. This figure had declined to 2.9% by 1956–1957. In 8 out of the 12 Western countries surveyed, at least 10% of male deaths over age 75 were assigned to this category in 1936–1938, while 8 out of 12 were below 4% in 1954–1956.

There is no satisfactory procedure for reducing the spurious trends introduced by the increasing specificity of diagnosis. One circumstance that partially mitigates its effect on calculations relating to life expectancy at birth or a young age is that proportions surviving to older ages tended to be quite low when large proportions of deaths at these ages were assigned to ill-defined or unknown causes. Thus, experience at older ages was a much less important component of life expectancy, and customs of death assignment at these ages had substantially less impact. For example, only 16% of the male population in the period life table for England and Wales, 1861, survived to age 75, compared to about 60% today.

The causes of death most likely to have experienced an inflow of deaths from ill-defined conditions are those whose incidence is high at older ages. Neoplasms are one category that has almost surely increased as a result of increased specificity of diagnosis (Pascua, 1952). Cardiovascular diseases have grown as well, but it is not clear that in every case the net result of increased specificity of diagnosis has produced an upward trend in this disease group. According to Woolsey and Moriyama (1948),

> Heart disease was probably over-reported as a cause of death during the first two decades of the [20th] century in that many deaths were improperly returned as some ill-defined heart disease when actually they were due to an undiagnosed condition other than heart disease. On the other hand, it is probable that a large proportion of deaths certified as due to senility had, in fact, some cardiopathy [p. 1253].

In most countries and periods, however, numbers of cardiovascular deaths have probably suffered a net outflow to ill-defined conditions. The Inter-American Mortality Investigation examined original death certificates on file in 10 cities of Latin America plus San Francisco and Bristol, England. After reviewing additional clinical and pathological evidence on each decedent, a second set of certifiers transferred 414 of the 967 deaths originally assigned to ill-defined conditions to a cardiovascular disease (Puffer & Griffith, 1967, pp. 240–241). In another study, 62 deaths were originally assigned to symptoms or senility in 75 hospitals of England and Wales in 1959. After autopsy, 11 of these were assigned to cardiac diseases, 11 to malignant diseases, 9 to bronchitis and pneumonia, and 10 to abdominal diseases. Altogether, only 6 deaths remained in the ill-defined category (Heasman & Lipworth, 1966, p. 47).

Improving levels of diagnostic accuracy have not only decreased the proportion of ill-defined death assignments, but they have also effected transfers of deaths among the well-defined diseases. Many such transfers, however, have undoubtedly occurred between two diseases within one of our categories. For example, Lew (1957) contends that

> a substantial part of the increase in coronary disease and arteriosclerotic heart disease death rates reflects also more precise certification in the light of current concepts of heart disease. Thus, more and better instruction in diagnosis (including postgraduate courses in cardiology), much greater numbers of heart specialists, and greatly improved facilities for diagnosis have all served to increase the proportion of deaths ascribed to these categories of heart disease. ... [However,] a substantial part of the increase in the death rate from coronary disease undoubtedly represents deaths that formerly would have been reported as due to other diseases of the cardiovascular–renal system [pp. 194–195].[2]

One diagnostic factor that has probably produced transfers of deaths among causes, thereby affecting mortality trends, has been an increasing proportion of deaths brought to autopsy. Several studies in different nations have compared the number of deaths assigned to particular causes before and after autopsy information became available (James, Patton, & Heslin, 1955; Swartout & Webster, 1940; Pohlen & Emerson, 1942, 1943; Jablon, Augerine, Matsumoto, & Ishida, 1966, pp. 445–465; Heasman & Lipworth, 1966). One may conclude from such studies that total numbers of

---

[2] From E. A. Lew. Some implications of mortality statistics relating to coronary artery diseases. *Journal of Chronic Diseases*, 1957, 6 (3), 192–209.

Table III-2

Deaths from Senility and Ill-Defined and Unknown Conditions (B 45) as Percentages of All Deaths in Various Populations

Age	Australia 1964	Austria 1964	Belgium 1964	Bulgaria 1964	Canada 1964	Ceylon 1960	Chile 1964	Colombia 1964	Costa Rica 1963	Czecho- slovakia 1964
<1	.32	.46	9.88	.19	.31	1.70	4.48	11.01	12.14	.17
1–24	.33	.62	7.95	2.73	.60	9.16	6.90	11.60	11.64	.07
25–44	.28	.20	5.95	1.76	.60	8.75	4.07	9.22	5.87	.10
45–64	.23	.37	5.25	2.01	.51	12.05	4.80	13.63	6.24	.16
65–74	1.00	1.30	5.26	2.49	.49	31.86	8.61	19.68	10.49	.68
75+	.71	8.35	10.64	12.29	1.18	67.23	18.88	29.96	18.52	5.22
Unknown	11.11	—	—	43.33	9.09	—	13.16	19.22	44.55	—
All	.61	3.87	7.77	5.80	.75	21.02	7.24	14.16	11.99	2.10

Age	Denmark 1964	El Salvador 1950	England and Wales 1964	Finland 1960	France 1964	West Germany 1964	West Berlin 1964	Greece 1964	Guatamala 1964	Hong Kong 1964
<1	1.41	23.34	.21	.46	6.69	1.02	.13	.89	5.32	1.50
1–24	1.15	25.85	.18	.76	9.21	2.09	.73	5.03	16.00	3.03
25–44	1.42	24.28	.14	.71	8.96	2.32	.98	5.35	17.68	4.76
45–64	.49	17.98	.07	.41	7.91	2.36	1.40	6.74	21.16	6.76
65–74	.64	55.51	.14	.80	9.56	2.56	2.51	11.25	26.96	14.60
75+	1.42	48.77	2.12	6.03	20.09	10.29	7.38	29.31	37.13	30.25
Unknown	—	37.34	—	—	25.76	77.27	—	11.86	5.26	—
All	1.12	27.38	.97	2.35	13.82	5.42	4.24	18.03	16.26	10.00

Age	Hungary 1964	Iceland 1964	Ireland 1961	Israel 1964	Italy 1964	Japan 1964	Malta and Gozo 1964	Mauritius 1964	Mexico 1964	Netherlands 1964
<1	.25	1.19	.55	1.28	.53	2.58	—	8.39	1.48	2.80
1–24	.18	1.45	.74	4.64	1.92	2.78	—	19.33	19.80	3.91
25–44	.11	1.52	.74	3.90	1.32	3.25	—	17.07	16.54	5.28
45–64	.07	1.22	.65	2.60	.79	1.98	.15	19.50	19.27	3.27
65–74	.08	1.35	2.21	3.15	9.15	4.23	1.84	30.97	27.17	2.70
75+	4.09	2.56	14.07	3.40	8.54	18.98	14.03	41.36	43.00	4.07
Unknown	41.67	—	—	3.92	—	15.56	—	—	35.68	—
All	.80	1.83	7.21	3.03	3.93	8.90	5.33	20.50	17.57	3.55

Table III-2 (Continued)

Age	New Zealand 1964	Nicaragua 1964	Northern Ireland 1964	Norway 1964	Panama 1964	Philippines 1964	Poland 1964	Portugal 1964	Puerto Rico 1964	Scotland 1964
<1	.08	13.10	.11	6.12	20.15	.98	3.73	5.56	5.08	.72
1–24	.23	28.80	.63	3.53	22.01	4.11	4.03	5.37	7.23	.75
25–44	.47	24.13	.56	8.47	15.82	4.31	3.54	3.90	6.57	.54
45–64	.16	28.17	.30	6.18	15.38	4.50	3.41	3.48	5.07	.29
65–74	.18	36.75	.41	4.75	15.74	16.79	9.09	7.69	5.45	.30
75+	1.04	47.04	1.26	7.91	21.27	55.22	28.93	32.94	11.38	1.31
Unknown	—	89.61	—	—	38.75	11.90	20.83	23.08	9.09	—
All	.56	30.00	.72	6.57	19.34	11.40	11.94	14.44	7.28	.71

Age	South Africa (White) 1960	South Africa (Colored) 1960	Spain 1960	Sweden 1964	Switzerland 1964	Taiwan 1964	Trinidad and Tobago 1963	United States 1964	Venezuela 1964	Yugoslavia 1964
<1	2.93	6.60	5.24	.34	.56	1.40	.22	2.59	27.28	15.85
1–24	3.24	4.38	6.12	.82	1.26	1.50	2.30	2.42	32.13	21.38
25–44	3.07	4.81	3.75	.73	1.42	2.66	1.70	2.74	18.79	11.00
45–64	2.49	5.23	3.81	.35	1.19	2.51	1.96	1.55	23.29	16.97
65–74	3.24	7.41	9.87	.33	1.04	7.64	4.44	1.04	26.25	25.57
75+	10.84	21.44	36.07	1.79	2.39	22.51	15.06	1.05	32.46	40.99
Unknown	—	50.00	27.71	—	—	9.09	—	7.53	33.33	46.83
All	5.28	7.11	15.56	1.75	1.64	5.82	4.59	1.40	27.21	25.28

deaths assigned to infectious and parasitic diseases, cardiovascular disease, neoplasms, and accidents are affected only in a minor way by the availability of data from autopsy. Tuberculosis trends are probably biased upward to some extent, perhaps rather strongly in England and Wales; diabetes trends are biased strongly downward and cirrhosis of the liver slightly upward. The fact that the large disease groupings employed here are relatively unaffected by variation in autopsy practices does not imply that important diagnostic "errors" were not made prior to autopsy, but rather that in the samples of death certificates studied, such errors

tended to be largely compensating. It might be noted that the frequency of autopsy typically declines with the age of decedent, as does the quality of medical evidence in general (Beadenkopf *et al.*, 1965; Moriyama *et al.*, 1966).

The effects of greater availability of other types of diagnostic evidence on mortality trends are difficult to study, since apparently no systematic attempt has been made to compare death certificates filled out in the presence and absence of other types of information. One feels fairly certain that coronary heart disease is more frequently detected with the aid of an electrocardiogram, brain tumors are detected more readily with an electroencephalogram, and blood diseases such as leukemia have grown in relative importance due to the greater availability of hematological laboratories. The effect on the broader groupings employed in this study cannot be reliably estimated.

Our discussion of trends in diagnostic accuracy would not be complete without mentioning that exact diagnosis, in the sense of choosing the initiating condition in a sequence of morbid events, is very difficult for an increasing number of deaths in industrialized countries. As mortality declines, more and more deaths are concentrated at older ages. As pointed out by the World Health Organization Expert Committee on Health Statistics (1967), "at these ages, several pathological conditions are usually found, and it may be difficult, if not impossible, to order a series of conditions into a realistic chain of events [p. 5]." While diagnostic accuracy for particular causes and at particular ages has undoubtedly improved, a randomly chosen diagnosis made in 1965 is likely to be no more reliable than one made in 1900, in the sense of denoting *the* underlying cause of death, because of the changing cause and age structure of death.

Influence on Differentials in Mortality by Cause

The same diagnostic factors that have influenced mortality trends have influenced mortality differentials. Table III-2 presents the proportion of deaths coded to senility and ill-defined and unknown causes in each nation during the last year that the nation appears in the life tables. A breakdown by sex is not presented since the proportion varies little by sex. Once again it is clear that, with few exceptions, death rates by cause below ages 65 or 75 cannot be strongly affected by variations in the specificity of diagnosis. And once again, it is generally the populations where relatively few survive to older ages than have the highest proportion of ill-defined or unknown deaths at the older ages. Among western countries, the highest percentage of deaths in the ill-defined category for all ages combined occurs in Spain (15.56), followed by Portugal (14.44) and France (13.82). No other western country has a percentage greater than 8. In Eastern Europe the percentage of deaths in the ill-defined category ranges from 25.28 in Yugoslavia to .80 in Hungary. In the rest of the world, the highest percentages are recorded in Latin America, with Nicaragua (30.00), El Salvador (28.30), and Venezuela (27.41) far out in front. Israel, Malta and Gozo, Taiwan, and Trinidad and Tobago record less than 6% in the category. Populations in which more than half of the hypothetical life-table cohort would die from "other, unknown and ill-defined conditions" are excluded from the tables.

The largest variation in diagnostic specificity, and by implication diagnostic accuracy, occurs between more- and less-developed countries. Surely one major reason for this disparity is the substantially higher ratio of inhabitants to physicians in most less-developed countries. Table III-3 shows that the ratio varies from about 4000 per physician in Ceylon, El Salvador, Guatemala, and Mauritius to under 1000 in most Western countries. Some insight into the diagnostic reliability of data in less-developed countries is provided by a study of cause-of-death certification in Ceylon, a country with a large proportion of deaths in the ill-defined category and with a high ratio of inhabitants to physicians (Padley, 1959). The study reached the following conclusions

(1) In urban areas of Ceylon, cause of death is assigned by medical registrars, who, in a majority of cases, can rely on the statements of medical practitioners in attendance during the decedent's illness. When no statement from a medical practitioner is available, the registrar conducts his own examination of the corpse.

(2) In rural areas registration takes place through lay registrars, and contrary to practice in urban areas, no proof of registration is required for burial. In a large majority of cases, the registrar chooses the underlying cause of death on the basis of information provided only by the deceased's relatives and friends.

Table III-3

Population per Physician in Countries Included in Cause-of-Death Tables[a]

Country	Year	Population per physician	Country	Year	Population per physician
Australia	1966	850	Malta and Gozo	1965	680
Austria[b]	1968	560	Mauritius	1969	4590
Belgium[b]	1968	640	Mexico	1968	1850
Bulgaria	1969	550	Netherlands	1968	840
Canada	1968–1969	740	New Zealand[c]	1968	630
Ceylon	1968	3700	Nicaragua	1968	1970
Chile	1968	1810	Northern Ireland[d]	1969	760
Colombia	1967	2220	Norway	1968	740
Costa Rica	1968	1970	Panama	1968	1970
Czechoslovakia	1969	480	Philippines[c]	1967	1390
Denmark	1968	690	Poland	1969	690
El Salvador	1968	4670	Portugal[b]	1969	1190
England and Wales	1967	860	Puerto Rico	1968	1010
France[b]	1969	770	Scotland	1969	750
West Germany	1968	580	South Africa	1967	1500
Greece	1969	640	Spain	1968	770
Guatemala	1969	4030	Sweden	1968	800
Hong Kong[c]	1969	2120	Switzerland	1969	650
Hungary	1969	520	Taiwan	1969	3170
Iceland	1967	750	Trinidad	1966	2320
Ireland	1966	960	United States	1967	650
Israel	1969	410	Venezuela	1968	1120
Italy	1969	560	Yugoslavia	1969	1050
Japan	1968	910			

[a] Source: United Nations Statistical Office, Department of Economic and Social Affairs. *Statistical Yearbook*. New York: United Nations, 1970. Copyright United Nations (1970). Reproduced by permission.

[b] Includes stomatologists and odontologists.

[c] Registered persons. Not all are resident and working in the country.

[d] Persons employed in a government service or in a service of the Ministry of Health only.

(3) Attributions of underlying cause to symptomatic terms or causes which are merely terminal are frequent in both urban and rural areas.

The situation in Korea, 1940 (not included in the tables), probably represents the extreme lower boundary of diagnostic accuracy which we face. According to Park (1955), "A majority of the population consulted herb doctors, whose low level of training in scientific medicine makes it reasonable to assume that there was a high proportion of wrong diagnoses. In addition, certification of death by the police, village chiefs, and even neighbors gave no true indication of the real cause of death [p. 71]."

No population included in the tables probably approaches the low level of diagnostic accuracy which apparently characterized Korea in 1940. The Inter-American Investigation of Mortality reached some surprisingly optimistic conclusions about the quality of diagnosis in 10 major cities of Latin America during the early 1960's and the comparability of their published statistics to those of more industrialized countries (Puffer & Griffith, 1967). As previously noted, original death certificates on file in these 10 cities (plus San Francisco and Bristol, England) were compared to death certifications prepared by trained medical referees who utilized additional clinical, autopsy, and other data. Numbers of deaths in broad groupings, like those employed in this study, typically were insignificantly changed by the presumably more accurate certification. The more important "corrections" from our standpoint were rather large additions to automobile accidents at the expense of other accidents, a loss of 15% for respiratory diseases (presumably because of a tendency to report terminal rather than underlying causes), and a net gain of 26% for complications of pregnancy (presumably absorbing deaths originally assigned to infectious diseases). These transfers were generally larger in the Latin American cities than in San Francisco and Bristol, but differences were not striking. Nor were differences particularly large in the percentage of deaths which occurred in hospitals or for which many types of specific diagnostic evidence were available. However autopsies were considerably more frequent in San Francisco.

It appears that diagnostic accuracy is better in cities than in rural areas of Latin America (United States Public Health Service, 1964, p. 31),[3] as was the case in Ceylon. Even so, it is encouraging to find that a substantial portion of the Latin American population is covered by certification practices roughly comparable to those in most industrialized countries. In areas and countries where the accuracy is much lower, the exercise of computing cause-of-death life tables might be justified by noting that the "correct" data are irretrievable and that the recorded frequency of causes of death in such cases may provide some useful insights into the structure of a population's mortality that would not be possible otherwise.

In relative terms, the variation in diagnostic accuracy among industrialized countries is probably small, although information on the matter is limited. A study under the auspices of the World Health Organization (1967) found that a large proportion of death certificates in Sweden are issued by pathologists after autopsy, while in England and Wales, Denmark, and the Netherlands, this is almost never the case. One might surmise that the causes found more frequently at autopsy, identified in the foregoing, would be assigned with greater frequency in Sweden.

2. THE METHOD OF CODING A DIAGNOSIS

Once a term or set of terms has been chosen by the person certifying cause of death, diagnosis is complete. However, where that death will be recorded in published mortality statistics depends on the prevailing nomenclature and classification of causes of death on which publication is based. For a large majority of populations in the tables, the death would be assigned to a term

---

[3] In Chile 72% of deaths in 1958 were accompanied by a medical certificate, the figure being as high as 95% in Santiago Province and as low as 31% in Chiloe, a poor rural province.

and title in some particular Revision of the International List and Classification of causes of death.

There is little difficulty in translating a diagnostic term into a term in the international nomenclature for most western countries, which were well represented among the countries that cooperated in the formulation of the international nomenclature. These countries naturally attempted to establish a niche for terms in common national usage. The translation problem is occasionally more severe for countries whose terminologies are not heavily weighted in the international nomenclature. In Ceylon, for example, a term translated into English as "long" or "continued" fever almost always refers to typhoid. But since the English translation implies that it is a symptomatic term, it is placed with pyrexia of unknown origin (Padley, 1959). The one instance when an inappropriate translation is liable to have a perceptible impact on our categories occurs among Latin American countries. Verhoestraete and Puffer (1958) note that "in practically all Spanish-speaking countries toxicosis is used to signify a specific clinical entity essentially the result of severe and rapid dehydration from diarrheal disease [p. 27]." Instead of including the term under diarrheal diseases, however, the Sixth and Seventh Revisions of the International Classification assign deaths from toxicosis under age 1 to ill-defined diseases of early infancy. Thus, except in Venezuela, which violates the International Classification instructions, the category "certain diseases of early infancy" is inflated and "diarrheal diseases" deflated in Latin America relative to other regions.

If data were published for each individual term appearing in a nomenclature, all questions of coding comparability would relate to the changing meaning of the terms. But providing such detail would be expensive and for some purposes counterproductive. *Terms* are normally combined into *titles,* and data published only for the latter. However, additional questions of comparability are introduced by changes in the set of terms comprising a title. Fortunately, most transfers of terms have occurred between titles within one of our categories. Among the most important of transfers which have not so occurred and which, as a result, affect numbers of deaths in one of our categories, are the following:[4]

(a) Many terms under acute miliary tuberculosis were transferred to respiratory tuberculosis at the Third Revision of the International Classification, when miliary tuberculosis was eliminated as a separate title.

(b) Brain tumors were transferred to neoplasms in the Fourth Revision from their previous location in other diseases of the nervous system, where they had not been separately enumerated.

(c) Upon the Fifth Revision, 10 terms were transferred from somewhere in circulatory diseases to chronic nephritis. The transfer resulted in a gain of about 15% in the number of deaths assigned to chronic nephritis in the United States, and the loss of about 2% of the total deaths in the cardiovascular category. The effect of the change on numbers of deaths assigned to nephritis was more than offset when the Sixth Revision introduced a new coding procedure.

(d) Complications of pregnancy grew by about 2% when criminal abortion was transferred to that category from accidental deaths at the Fifth Revision.

(e) Aortic aneurysm was transferred to syphilis from aneurysm, a title in the circulatory diseases, upon the Fifth Revision. Since we have included the whole group of deaths under aneurysm prior to the Fifth Revision with syphilis, the effect of the change was to transfer certain terms (representing aneurysm of sites other than the aorta) from our category of infectious and parasitic diseases to that of circulatory diseases.

All of the transfers cited below occurred at the time of the Sixth Revision:

(f) Various infectious diseases were transferred from the organ system affected to infectious diseases (streptococcal sore throat

[4] Principal sources: Van Buren (1939); Dunn and Schakley (1944); World Health Organization (1952, Table III).

amoebiasis with liver abscess, acute infectious encephalitis, infectious hepatitis, and trachoma). The effect of these transfers was small, however; total numbers of deaths from infectious diseases changed by less than 3% in England and Wales as a result of these and other transfers (Campbell, 1965).

(g) Malnutrition above age 1 was moved from accidents to deficiency diseases (in our residual category).

(h) Rheumatism (unqualified) was transferred to joint diseases from acute rheumatic fever, included with our cardiovascular diseases.

(i) Pneumonia and diarrhea deaths in the first 4 weeks of life were transferred from pneumonia and diarrhea to certain diseases of early infancy, representing one of the most important changes in this list. In Canada, the gain for certain diseases of early infancy was 10% of the deaths assigned to this title under the new list; the losses for pneumonia and diarrhea were 6% and 16%, respectively, of the deaths assigned to the old titles (compiled from World Health Organization, 1952, Table V).

(j) Tachycardia, edema, cardiac failure, dropsy, and certain other vague terms were transferred from other diseases of the heart to "ill-defined conditions."

(k) Gastritis was removed from other diseases of the stomach (in our "residual") and combined with duodenitis, to form a new category (543) in our diarrheal diseases.

(l) Pulmonary edema due to heart disease was transferred from the respiratory disease category to other and unspecified diseases of the heart.

(m) Bronchiectasis was separated from chronic bronchitis, moving into our "residual."

(n) Interstitial nephritis was removed from chronic nephritis and into our "residual" (under other renal sclerosis).

(o) Jaundice and icterus of newborn were transferred from certain diseases of early infancy to "ill-defined conditions."

(p) Uremia (unqualified) was transferred from nephritis (unspecified) to "ill-defined conditions."

It is evident from the above list that the categories employed in this study do not represent closed sets of terms. The movement of terms among categories is itself sufficient to introduce spurious trends (or, more precisely, discontinuities) in series of death rates by cause. However, the major transfers are few in number—(a), (b), (d), (e), (i), and (j) in the list—and none would appear to affect the number of deaths in one of our categories by as much as 20%. The majority of the changes cited probably affect the numbers of deaths by less than 2%. The ambiguities introduced, while vexing, are typically not important enough to force serious qualification of comparisons between death rates in broad categories.

Finally, we come to one of the most serious matters affecting the comparability of cause-of-death statistics, the treatment of deaths in which more than one disease or condition is involved. Of the death certificates filed in the United States in 1917, 35% listed more than one cause of death, a percentage which has grown to about 60 in 1939, where it has remained relatively constant (Van Buren, 1939, p. 206; Kreuger, 1966, pp. 431–443). Around 1947, between 50 and 70% of the death certificates filed in Australia, Denmark, England and Wales, New Zealand, and Switzerland listed more than one cause of death, while in Argentina, France, Greece, Nicaragua, and Peru the percentage was less than 15 (United Nations Statistical Office, 1951, p. 22). A low percentage probably does not connote less complex morbid processes in a nation; more likely, the certifier or attending physician more frequently makes the underlying cause determination himself, failing to list other causes involved.

The principles for ascertaining *the* cause of death in a situation where several causes have been operative have not changed significantly. In general, the philosophy has been similar to that implied by the current definition of cause of death as heretofore cited. In the 1900 Revision of the International List, Jacques Bertillon, pioneer in cause-of-death classification, suggested several rules for determining "primary" cause of death, the most important of which was that "if one of the two diseases is an immediate and frequent complication of the other, the death should be classified under the head of the primary disease." In other instances a more commonly fatal disease, a communicable disease, and an acute disease were to be accorded priority (United States Bureau of the Census, 1902, p. 13).

A survey of national coding practices by Huber, in 1926, discovered that, in large part, Bertillon's recommendations were being followed. The main variations therefrom occurred in England, Scotland, and New Zealand where a priority system was in effect, giving highest precedence to violent causes, then to infectious causes, then to the most dangerous causes. The selection procedures were quite relaxed in all countries, and apparently little attempt was made to ensure compliance with the stated principles.

A more rigid set of selection principles was in effect in the United States at the time, and several other countries followed her lead. All diseases and conditions were assigned different "weights," and the cause with the highest weight in a particular combination was selected as *the* cause of death. *The United States Manual of Joint Causes of Death*, providing these selection rules, was first issued by the Bureau of the Census in 1914 and later revised in 1925, 1933, and 1940 in response to revisions of the International Classification.

A major consideration in the revisions of the *Manual of Joint Causes* was the maintenance of statistical continuity. According to Dunn and Shackley (1940), only two exceptions occurred: In 1937 angina pectoris was devaluated with respect to other heart diseases; in 1939, tetanus was assigned less weight than all major accidents, having previously taken precedence. However, joint-cause relationships could also be altered by the transfer of terms among titles, since a transferred term would assume the weight of the new title and lose that of the old. The one transfer of this type perceptibly affecting our categories was apparently the transfer of aortic aneurysm to syphilis at the Fifth Revision, where its joint-cause weight was higher than it had been in the circulatory cate-

gory. Clarification of previously ambiguous selection rules at the time of the 1925 revision of the *Manual of Joint Causes* also affected the statistics to some extent. In particular, terms under nephritis scored gains in relative weights, causing a 13% increase in total deaths from chronic nephritis. At this time leukemia gained 14% and duodenal ulcers about the same amount (Van Buren, 1939, p. 206).

An opportunity to assess the quantitative importance of national differences in selection rules and their applications during the period is provided by a study administered by the United States Bureau of the Census in 1935. One thousand thirty two completed death certificates containing two to five diseases or injuries were distributed to the statistical offices of 18 countries, with the instruction that underlying cause be assigned in accordance with national selection principles then in effect. The proportion of deaths assigned to each of the 18 major subdivisions of the Fourth Revision of the International List showed considerable national variation. The highest proportion assigned to a cause was typically about twice the size of the lowest, with proportions of deaths assigned to neoplasms being the most consistent from country to country and respiratory diseases the least consistent (of the causes which concern us here). Of course, this comparison overstates the amount of national disagreement in cause-of-death statistics, since the sample was composed of certificates chosen because confusion was likely.

The nations which were using the United States *Manual of Joint Causes*—Ceylon, Australia, the Philippines, and New Zealand—showed a high degree of consistency in cause-of-death assignment with the United States and with one another. England and Wales, on the other hand, generally displayed less agreement with the countries using the *Manual of Joint Causes* but closer agreement with Scotland, Switzerland, and South Africa. Relative to the United States group, the England and Wales group generally showed a higher propensity to assign death to infectious and parasitic diseases, diseases of the blood, and violence, and a lower number of assignments to nervous diseases and diseases of pregnancy. Further generalization about the frequency of agreement is difficult, except to note that Sweden and Norway showed an exceptionally strong preference for assigning infectious and parasitic diseases, and that New Zealand and Australia (both included in our tables during this period) displayed assignments that were close to the average for all countries examined.

If arbitrary selection rules were in use, they were discarded when nations adopted the Sixth Revision of the International Classification,[5] where the changes in classification were so significant that assuring intertemporal comparability would have been impossible in any case. Instead of referring to selection rules, the certifier was to accept the opinion of the attending physician about the underlying cause. The physician was assisted in the determination of underlying cause by a new form of death certificate, uniform from country to country for the first time, which asked for the *sequence* of conditions, connected by the phrase "as a consequence of," that in his opinion produced death. The physician's opinion was to stand unless the sequence of morbid conditions appeared illogical or improbable. At this point he was either queried again or an arbitrary coding rule was to be applied. It has been estimated that the physician's judgment was not reflected on only about 5% of the cause-of-death assignments in the United States in 1950 (Moriyama, 1956).

The transition from arbitrary coding rules, whether strict or loose, to physician's judgment (occasionally modified) introduces some of the most serious problems of comparability in countries where multiple-cause deaths were a high percentage of the total. The sequences previously imposed by the arbitrary selection rules evidently did not represent, in the physicians' judgment, the only reasonable path by which a set of morbid conditions could combine to produce death. But judging from studies of changes in the

[5] The selection rules had been discarded in 1940 in England and Wales.

number of deaths in different categories that occurred at the time of the coding change in the United States, Canada, and England and Wales, most of the broad categories which we are using were relatively unaffected by the change (United States Department of Health, Education, and Welfare, 1963; World Health Organization, 1952; Great Britain, 1940). Total numbers of deaths in cardiovascular diseases, neoplasms, infectious and parasitic diseases, violence, and certain diseases of early infancy changed by less than 5%. Although arteriosclerotic heart disease lost a very large number of deaths to cerebrovascular lesions, this flow was contained within one of our categories. Numbers of deaths from bronchitis, however, about doubled in England and Wales and the United States. (However, as already noted, a large proportion of the additions in the United States came from bronchopneumonia.) Numbers of deaths from nephritis about doubled in Canada and the United States. Diabetes lost about one-third to one-half its deaths. Maternal mortality, which had enjoyed a high weight under the arbitrary selection rules, lost 9% of its deaths in the United States and 8% in Canada. These are far and away the most important discontinuities introduced by the change in coding procedure and are of major significance only for the category certain degenerative diseases, and possibly respiratory diseases and maternal mortality.

All problems of international comparability in coding customs have not been solved by the standardization of procedures for selecting an underlying cause of death. In fact, the abandonment of arbitrary selection rules may have allowed divergences in national coding customs to find more ready expression in cause-of-death statistics. The importance of national differences in coding fashions was demonstrated by a study conducted by the World Health Organization, which distributed the same 1000 completed death certificates, all with multiple causes listed, to six European nations (World Health Organization, 1967). Even though the physician's preferences regarding underlying cause were already specified on the certificates distributed, substantial differences in the distribution of underlying causes assigned by the certifiers resulted. The major source of national differences was variation in the criteria for overruling the physician's certification and in the sequences of morbid conditions considered probable and improbable. For example, according to the provisions of the International Classification, death from aortic aneurysm (unqualified) is to be returned under syphilis; but since this etiology was considered highly unlikely in certain countries, their certifiers placed the death with circulatory diseases. Few data have been published from the study, however, and an estimate of resulting national biases cannot be made.

3. Summary

By way of summarizing the section on the quality of cause-of-death statistics, we shall list each of the categories employed in this study and the major problems of accuracy and comparability pertaining to each.

(1) *Respiratory Tuberculosis.* Deaths were added at the time of the Third Revision because of the transfer of terms from acute miliary tuberculosis. The trend has perhaps been biased upward by the occasional new discovery of tuberculosis at autopsy.

(2) *Other Infectious and Parasitic Diseases.* Many problems exist but all are seemingly minor.

(3) *Neoplasms.* Trends have been biased upward by the declining proportion of deaths assigned to "ill-defined" and "unknown" causes.

(4) *Cardiovascular Diseases.* Declining proportions assigned to "ill-defined" and "unknown" causes probably resulted in a growth of the number of deaths in this category. There was a loss of about 2% of deaths at the Fifth Revision when 10 terms were transferred to chronic nephritis. Frequent association with other chronic conditions—nephritis, bronchitis, diabetes—makes death rates from this cause susceptible to national coding idiosyncracies.

(5) *Certain Respiratory Diseases.* Probably this category has been artificially inflated in statistically poor populations because of a tendency to assign the underlying cause to conditions that are merely terminal (pneumonia). There may be a possible tendency in England and Wales, Australia, and New Zealand to assign to chronic bronchitis deaths that would elsewhere be assigned to cardiovascular diseases. There was a loss of about 5% of deaths in this category when deaths from pneumonia under age 5 weeks were transferred to certain diseases of early infancy at the Sixth Revision.

(6) *Diarrhea.* There was a loss of about 16% of deaths in this category when diarrhea deaths under 5 weeks of age were transferred to certain diseases of early infancy at the Sixth Revision. The understatement of diarrheal deaths under age 1 is probable in most Latin American countries due to improper coding of deaths from toxicosis.

(7) *Certain Degenerative Diseases.* Diabetes deaths were reduced substantially and nephritis deaths raised substantially when arbitrary selection rules for use in multiple-cause assignments were abandoned at the Sixth Revision. Transfer of terms to nephritis at the Fifth Revision caused a growth of about 10% in this category as a whole. Diabetes trends have been biased upward by improving levels of diagnostic accuracy and increasing recognition of the disease. As with cardiovascular diseases, a high frequency of association with other causes renders death rates in this category susceptible to variation in methods of multiple-cause disposition.

(8) *Complication of Pregnancy.* This category apparently has been understated in statistically poor populations, including England during the 19th Century (Great Britain, 1883), since some deaths from this cause have been incorrectly assigned to infectious diseases. This category lost 8 or 9% of its deaths when the method of coding multiple causes changed at the Sixth Revision.

(9) *Certain Diseases of Early Infancy*. The number of deaths increased by about 10% as a result of the transfer of deaths from pneumonia and diarrhea under 5 weeks of age at the Sixth Revision. This category has been overstated in Latin America at the expense of diarrhea. In early years many ill-defined conditions dominated this category.

(10) *Motor Vehicle Accidents*. The number of deaths in this category is considerably understated in Latin America.

(11) *Other Accidents and Violence*. No important difficulties exist.

(12) *Residual*. Improving diagnostic specificity has reduced the proportion of "ill-defined" and "unknown" causes in this category, biasing trends downward. Ill-defined conditions still dominate the category in statistically poor nations.

There is no satisfactory way of eliminating the statistical problems described in this list. The choice is between proceeding with calculations in full knowledge of the statistical deficiencies or ignoring the vast bulk of cause-of-death data altogether, despite their relevance to a wide range of social and demographic problems. We have chosen the former course, somewhat reassured by a remark of Greenwood (1942): "The scientific purist, who will wait for medical statistics until they are nosologically exact, is no wiser than Horace's rustic waiting for the river to flow away [p. 204]."

C. Precision of the Tables and of Inferences Drawn from Them

In this section we first study two additional sources of error—chance and the inference of probabilities from rates. As a necessary preliminary, we must consider what difference a hypothetical variation in the raw data makes for computed results. The subject is dealt with in statistical literature under the heading of propagation of error (Deming, 1950, p. 127).

Propagation of Error

In order to exemplify propagation of error with a result in the field of overall mortality, disregarding cause, we shall consider the probability that a person of age a will survive to age b: l_b/l_a. How is this quantity affected by an error $\Delta_5 D_x$, $a < x < x + 5 < b$, in the number of deaths at age x to $x + 4$ at last birthday?

If the exposed population $_5P_x$ at the age x to $x + 4$ is correctly given, then the error in the number of deaths will produce an error $\Delta_5 D_x/_5P_x = \Delta_5 M_x$ in the age-specific rate. This in turn will produce a proportionate error of about $-(5\Delta_5 M_x)$ in the probability l_{x+5}/l_x of living through the age interval in question, and an error $\Delta l_b = -l_b(5\Delta_5 M_x)$ in the number of survivors to any age b greater than $x + 5$. Since with $a < x$ the survivors to age a are not affected by the error, the answer to our question of the effect on l_b/l_a is

$$\Delta(l_b/l_a) = -(l_b/l_a)(5\Delta_5 M_x), \qquad a < x < x + 5 < b.$$

In application to United States males, 1964, let us suppose that 10% of the deaths at age 25–29 have been omitted, so that the true number is not 9796, as published, but 10,884. The true survivors from birth to age 60, who are 73,862 on our calculation, would then be obtained by the adjustment

$$\Delta l_{60} = -l_{60}(5\Delta_5 M_{25})$$

$$= -(73,862)(5)\frac{1088}{5,441,000} = -73.848.$$

Thus the probability of living to age 60 would be not .73862, as shown in our tables, but the smaller quantity

$$.73862 - .00073848 = .73788.$$

Sampling Variance

Sampling errors arise when the death tabulations are based on a random selection from all deaths. Random errors in the observations are propagated throughout all the calculations made from them. We can easily show, for example, that a random error having variance $E(\Delta_5 M_x)^2$ in the age group x to $x + 4$ results in a variance

$$E(\Delta \overset{\circ}{e}_a)^2 = [(_5L_x/l_a)(\overset{\circ}{e}_x - 2.5)]^2 E(\Delta_5 M_x)^2$$

for $\overset{\circ}{e}_a$, to a first approximation. If the errors of the several age groups are independent, these quantities may be added through x to obtain the total variance of the expectation of life at age $a < x$.

Insofar as sampling is not of individuals at random, all such variances are too low. Most samples are in some degree clustered, and socioeconomic similarity among the elements of each cluster is reflected in similarity in mortality. In these circumstances, the mortality at the several ages is positively correlated, and correlation terms would have to be added to the expressions for the variance cited above. In practice it will not be practicable to do this, and in order to find a more realistic estimate of the variance, we would resort to one or another of the methods comparing independent subsamples.

Error of Inference from the Age-Specific Rates

Random variation in mortality measures has received extensive treatment and need not be considered here (for a summary, see Keyfitz, 1968, Chapter 15). Instead, we concentrate on errors in the inference of life-table quantities from the observations.

From this evidence alone, the $_5M_x = {_5D_x}/{_5P_x}$ of the observations might refer to the beginning or the end of the interval $(x, x + 5)$. Whether the population is concentrated at the beginning or the end of the interval determines whether the rate $_5M_x$ refers to exact age x or to exact age $x + 5$. If we assume that the population is distributed more or less evenly through the interval, we obtain an intermediate figure, and the two numbers for the extremes provide outside limits.

In fact, such limits are so unlikely to be attained that they hardly provide a realistic statement of error. Nonetheless, it is useful to have conservative limits as well as tighter ones, and these are easily calculated: If they shift the curve of $_5q_x$ sideways by

about $2\frac{1}{2}$ years in either direction from the central estimate that is published, they shift all curves derived from $_5q_x$ in the same way.

As an example, consider the United States, 1967, male table, and note that its $\overset{\circ}{e}_{50}$ is 23.049 years. Suppose that all entries in the 45–49, 50–54, and subsequent age intervals really refer to their lower limits rather than to their midpoints. Then the figure calculated for $\overset{\circ}{e}_{50}$, 23.049 years, would really refer to age 47.5; the true $\overset{\circ}{e}_{50}$ would be roughly the mean of 23.049 and $\overset{\circ}{e}_{55} = 19.315$, or 21.182. The expectation of life at age 50 would be 1.867 years lower if all populations were really at the lower points of their intervals. The same calculation can be made for all other life-table functions, with single or double decrement.

But the likelihood that all of the population is concentrated at one end of an age interval is remote, and that this would happen by coincidence in each of the several age groups is even more remote. Fortunately, our method of making the life table, based on the parameter r, permits a more subtle means of varying the distribution within the age group. Making this parameter slightly greater than the r of expression (7) in Chapter II supposes a shift to the left in the internal distribution. Making r slightly less supposes a shift to the right. (At the extremes, if r is infinitely large and positive, we have the case of the whole population concentrated at the left, while if r is infinitely large and negative, the whole population is concentrated on the right.)

In order to ascertain the effect of a departure of .01 in r, the life table for England and Wales, 1968, was made in the way described, and then again with r incremented by .01 at each age and in every iteration. The effect of a larger r is to impute a higher death rate to the stationary population. For instance, the incrementing of r by .01 raised $_5q_{70}$ from .2952 to .2957, or about 2 parts/thousand. Summarizing the effect on all ages together, we find that incrementing r by .01 lowered $\overset{\circ}{e}_0$ from 68.646 to 68.626, or only .02 of a year. The maximum likely variation in r could hardly affect $\overset{\circ}{e}_0$ by as much as .1.

The Problem of Causal Inference

Aside from the sampling at a given time, any attempt to draw general conclusions must face what is, in effect, a sampling variation through time and space. For in comparing the death rate from cardiovascular–renal causes in England and the United States, we would usually not be interested in a particular year but would require to know which is higher in general. For such comparisons year-to-year fluctuations become analogous to sampling error, and they are likely to be large.

The importance as well as the difficulty of the inference problem may be illustrated for automobile accidents.

At the time of this writing, the automobile fatalities of the United States for 1970 have been estimated at just over 55,000, or about 1000 less than in 1969. Is the drop due to increased use of seat belts?

If the deaths are independent random events, the Poisson distribution applies to them, and year-to-year fluctuations would have a standard deviation of $(55,000)^{1/2}$ or about 235. The difference between 2 years would have a standard deviation of this times $\sqrt{2}$, or about 332. The difference of 1000 would be 3 times its standard error, and hence significant—it would be properly attributable to the increased use of seat belts, if this were the only difference between 1969 and 1970 in the underlying causal complex. The 1000 difference is on the edge of significance: Insofar as the weather during a particular year affects the accident rate, the variance among years would be larger, and the significance of the difference between 1969 and 1970 would disappear.

Beyond this, the further factor of trend enters into the picture. We note that motor vehicle fatalities were reported at 38,137 in 1960 and 53,041 in 1966, a sharply rising trend. In relation to population, the ratio went from 21.3 to 27.1 deaths per 100,000 resident population over the 6 years. Such considerations, including the tapering off of fatalities since 1966, when seat belts started to be used, strengthen the conviction that seat belts helped. In relation to the number of automobiles and trucks in use, this conviction is further strengthened, since these went from 68,000,000 in 1960 to 84,000,000 in 1966, and they are now over the 95,000,000 mark.

If we wish to establish the effect of seat belts, we must not only ask whether the 1970 figure was significantly below that of 1969, but we must take into account other elements that would help to establish an expected figure for 1970 in the absence of seat belts. Insofar as the age distribution of cars relates to safety, we would have to take into account that the mean age fell considerably during the 1960's. In some other countries where seat belts have not been widespread, a decline in fatalities has appeared in the statistics and is attributed to legal measures against drunken drivers. The error of the expected figure, in its nature not estimable as a matter of probability, is the major element in the certainty of our inference.

The example suggests also how other kinds of data are needed to supplement those of the present volume. We might distinguish drivers who use seat belts and those who do not and ascertain their respective accident rates. If those who use seat belts have fewer accidents, this would constitute evidence, but even this evidence would be far from decisive, since drivers who use seat belts are probably more careful in other regards.

One purpose of this discussion is to show that the stochastic and other errors of the year-to-year difference can only provide a lower limit to the error of attribution of a given difference to a given cause. When the year-to-year difference is barely significant, the other difficulties should make us cautious.

REFERENCES

Bachi, R. On the accuracy of demographic statistics in Palestine and Israel. In Vol. 4, *Proceedings of the world population conference*. New York: United Nations, 1954.

Barclay, G. W. *Techniques of population analysis*. New York: Wiley, 1958.

Beadenkopf, W. G. *et al*. Some demographic characteristics of an autopsied population. *Journal of Chronic Diseases*, 1965, 18, 333–351.

Benjamin, B., & Carrier, N. H. An evaluation of the quality of demographic statistics in England and Wales. In Vol. 4, *Proceedings of the world population conference*. New York: United Nations, 1954.

Campbell, H. Changes in mortality trends in England and Wales, 1931–1961. United States National Center for Health Statistics. *Vital and Health Statistics*, 1965 (Ser. 3, No. 3).

Coale, A. J. The population of the United States in 1950 classified by age, sex, and color—A revision of census figures. *Journal of the American Statistical Association*, 1955, **50**(269), 16–54.

Coale, A. J., & Zelnick, M. *New estimates of fertility and population in the United States*. Princeton, New Jersey: Princeton Univ. Press, 1963.

Das Gupta, A. Accuracy index of census age distributions. In Vol. 4, *Proceedings of the world population conference*. New York: United Nations, 1954.

Deming, W. E. *Some theory of sampling*. New York: Wiley, 1950.

Dunn, H. L., & Schakley, W. Comparison of cause-of-death assignments by the 1929 and 1938 Revisions of the International List: Deaths in the United States, 1940. United States, Bureau of the Census. *Vital Statistics—Special Reports*, 1944, **19**, 153–277.

Frumkin, G. Estimation de la qualité des statistiques démographiques. In Vol. 4, *Proceedings of the world population conference*. New York: United Nations, 1954.

Great Britain. 44th annual report of the Registrar General of births, deaths, and marriages in England. 1881. *House of Commons Sessional Papers*, 1883, **20**.

Great Britain. The Registrar General's statistical review of England and Wales for the year 1940. Tables, Part I, Medical. London.

Greenwood, M. Medical statistics from Graunt to Farr. *Biometrika*, 1942, **32**, 101–127; 203–225.

Greville, T. N. E. *United States life tables and actuarial tables 1939–1941*. United States Bureau of the Census, Washington, D.C.: United States Government Printing Office, 1946.

Heasman, M. A., & Lipworth, L. *Studies on medical and population subjects no. 20. Accuracy of certification of cause of death*. London: General Register Office of England and Wales, 1966.

Huber, M. M. Rapport sur les modes de constation des décès et de leur causes. *Bulletin de l'institut international de statistique*, 1926, **22** (2), 23–66.

Jablon, S., Augerine, D. M., Matsumoto, Y., & Ishida, M. On the significance of cause of death as recorded on death certificates in Hiroshima and Nagasaki, Japan. In W. Haenszel (Ed.), *Epidemiological approaches to the study of cancer and other chronic diseases*, 1966, National Cancer Institute Monograph No. 19.

James, G., Patton, R. E., and Heslin, S. Accuracy of cause-of-death statements on death certificates. *Public Health Reports* (United States Department of Health, Education, and Welfare), 1955, **7**(1), 39–51.

Keyfitz, N. *Introduction to the mathematics of population*. Reading, Massachusetts: Addison-Wesley, 1968.

Krueger, D. E. New numerators for old denominators—Multiple causes of death. In W. Haenszel (Ed.), *Epidemiological approaches to the study of cancer and other chronic diseases*, 1966, National Cancer Institute Monograph No. 19.

Lew, E. A. Some implications of mortality statistics relating to coronary artery diseases. *Journal of Chronic Diseases*, 1957, **6**(3), 192–209.

Morita, Y. On the accuracy of demographic statistics of Japan. In vol. 4, *Proceedings of the world population conference*. New York: United Nations, 1954.

Moriyama, I. M. Development of the present concept of cause of death. *American Journal of Public Health*, 1956, **46**, 436–441.

Moriyama, I. M., Dawber, T. R., & Kannel, W. B. Evaluation of diagnostic information supporting medical certification of deaths from cardiovascular disease. In W. Haenszel (Ed.), *Epidemiological approaches to the study of cancer and other chronic diseases*, 1966, National Cancer Institute Monograph No. 19.

Myers, R. Errors and bias in the reporting of ages in census data. *Transactions of the Actuarial Society of America*, 1940, **41**(Pt 2), 395–415.

Myers, R. Validity of centenarian data in the 1960 census. *Demography*, 1966, **3**(2), 470–476.

Padley, R. Cause of death statements in Ceylon: A study in levels of diagnostic reporting. *Bulletin of the World Health Organization*, 1959, **20**, 677–695.

Park, C. B. Statistical observations on death rates and causes of death in Korea. *Bulletin of the World Health Organization*, 1955, **13**, 69–108.

Pascua, M. Evolution of mortality in Europe during the twentieth century. *Epidemiological and Vital Statistics Report* (World Health Organization), 1952, **5**(1–2), 4–8.

Pohlen, K., & Emerson, H. Errors in clinical statements of causes of death. *American Journal of Public Health*, 1942, **32**, 251–260.

Pohlen, K., & Emerson, H. Errors in clinical statements of causes of death. (Second Rep.). *American Journal of Public Health*, 1943, **33**, 505–516.

Puffer, R. R., & Griffith, G. W. *Patterns of urban mortality*, 1967, Pan American Health Organization Scientific Publication No. 151.

Sadie, J. L. An evaluation of demographic data pertaining to the non-White population of South Africa. *South African Journal of Economics*, 1970, **38**(1), 1–34.

Spiegelman, M. *Introduction to demography*, Chicago: The Society of Actuaries, 1968.

Sullivan, J. M. *A review of Taiwanese infant and child mortality statistics 1961–1968*. (Taiwan Population Studies Working Paper No. 10) Ann Arbor, Univ. of Michigan Population Studies Center, 1971.

Swartout, H. O., & Webster, R. G. To what degree are mortality statistics dependable? *American Journal of Public Health*, 1940, **30**, 811–815.

Taeuber, I. *The population of Japan*. Princeton, New Jersey: Princeton Univ. Press, 1958.

United Nations, Department of Economic and Social Affairs. *Handbook of population census methods*. Ser. F, No. 5, Rev. 1. Vol. I. *General aspects of a population census*, 1958.

United Nations, Department of Economic and Social Affairs. *Manuals on methods of estimating population*. ST/SOA/Ser. A. Population Studies No. 23. Manual II. *Methods of appraisal of quality of basic data for population estimates*, 1955.

United Nations, Department of Economic and Social Affairs. *Manuals on methods of estimating population*. ST/SOA/Ser. A/42. Manual IV. *Methods of estimating basic demographic measures from incomplete data*. New York: United Nations, 1967.

United Nations, Department of Economic and Social Affairs. *Population Bulletin of the United Nations No. 6*. New York: United Nations, 1962.

United Nations Department of Social Affairs: Population Division. *Population Bulletin No. 2*. New York: United Nations, 1952.

United Nations Statistical Office. *Demographic yearbook*. New York: United Nations, 1951.

United Nations Statistical Office, Department of Economic and Social Affairs. *Handbook of vital statistics methods*. Ser. F, No. 7. New York: United Nations, 1955.

United Nations Statistical Office, Department of Economic and Social Affairs. *Statistical yearbook*. New York: United Nations, 1970.

United States, Bureau of the Census. *Manual of international classification of causes of death*. Washington, D.C.: United States Government Printing Office, 1902.

United States, Bureau of the Census. Classification of joint causes of death. *Vital Statistics—Special Report*, 1935, **5**, 385–469.

United States, Department of Health, Education, and Welfare. Comparability of statistics of cause of death according to the Fifth and Sixth Revisions of the international list. *Vital Statistics–Special Reports. Selected Studies*, 1963, **51**.

United States Public Health Service, National Center for Health Statistics. *Recent mortality rates in Chile*, 1964 (Ser. 3, No. 2).

Van Buren, G. H. Some things you can't prove by mortality statistics. United States, Bureau of the Census. *Vital Statistics—Special Reports*, 1939, **12**, 195–210.

Verhoestraete, L. J., & Puffer, R. R. Diarrheal disease with special reference to the Americas. *Bulletin of the World Health Organization*, 1958, **19**, 23–51.

Woolsey, T. D., & Moriyama, I. M. Statistical studies of heart diseases. II. Important factors in heart disease mortality trends. *Public Health Reports* (United States Department of Health, Education, and Welfare), 1948, **63**(39), 1247–1273.

World Health Organization. The accuracy and comparability of death statistics. *Chronicle*, 1967, **21**, 11–17.

World Health Organization. Comparability of statistics of causes of death according to the Fifth and Sixth Revisions of the International List. *Bulletin of the World Health Organization*, 1952 (Suppl. 4).

World Health Organization Expert Committee on Health Statistics. *World Health Organization technical report series*. No. 365. *Epidemiological methods in the study of chronic diseases*, 1967.

Chapter IV GUIDE TO LIFE TABLES

Mortality information for each population (one country, sex, and year) is presented in four tables, printed on two facing pages. The tables are described as follows.

Table 1. *Population, Deaths, Death Rates for All Causes Combined, and for Specified Causes.*

The first two columns in this table represent, respectively, an estimated midyear population and the number of deaths from all causes combined recorded in the population during that year. Both provide detail on ages. The remaining columns represent age-specific death rates from all causes combined or from one of the individual causes identified. The exact composition of cause-of-death categories employed, according to the various International Classifications of Cause of Death, may be found in Table I-2. The composition is subject to the variations for individual populations noted below. In all cases the numbers of people or deaths at unknown ages are first distributed to the known age categories in proportion to the total numbers at those ages. The adjusted numbers are then rounded to integer quantities in such a way as to retain the correct total population and number of deaths.

The death rate at ages x to $x + n$, from cause i, in year t, $_nM_x^i$, is calculated by dividing $_nD_x^i$, the number of deaths recorded at ages x to $x + n$, from cause i, in year t, by $_nP_x^t$, the number of persons aged x to $x + n$ at the midpoint of year t:

$$_nM_x^i = {_nD_x^i}/{_nP_x^t}.$$

Thus the number of deaths used in the computation may be inferred by multiplying the published population by the published death rate.

Four summary measures of mortality are provided. The crude death rate, for all causes combined and for each cause, is computed by the same formula as the age-specific death rate, with $x = 0$ and $n = \infty$. Two age-standardized death rates are provided in order to facilitate interpopulation comparisons that are independent of age. In one case the standard age distribution used [Standardized Rate (1)] was a Coale–Demeny (1966) "West" stable female population with a life expectancy of 45 and an annual growth rate of .02; in the other case [Standardized Rate (2)], $\mathring{e}_0 = 65$ and $r = .01$. The proportionate age distributions used for standardization may be found in Table IV-1. An age-standardized death rate for cause i in year t, ASDR_i^t, is calculated by the following formula:

$$\text{ASDR}_i^t = \sum {_nM_x^i} \cdot {_nC_x^s},$$

where $_nC_x^s$ is the proportion of the standard population aged x to

Table IV-1

Proportionate Age Distributions Used for Standardization[a]

Age interval (age last birthday)	Proportion of total population in age interval	
	Standard population (1)[b]	Standard population (2)[c]
0	.0352	.0207
1–4	.1187	.0791
5–9	.1292	.0935
10–14	.1141	.0884
15–19	.1006	.0835
20–24	.0881	.0787
25–29	.0767	.0740
30–34	.0664	.0694
35–39	.0572	.0649
40–44	.0490	.0604
45–49	.0417	.0560
50–54	.0349	.0513
55–59	.0286	.0463
60–64	.0224	.0406
65–69	.0165	.0340
70–74	.0110	.0264
75–79	.0063	.0181
80–84	.0027	.0107
85+	.0008	.0039
All	1.0000	1.0000

[a] Source: A. J. Coale & P. Demeny (1966). *Regional model life tables and stable populations.* (Copyright 1966, Princeton Univ. Press): Selections from column 1, p. 46; column 2, p. 62.

[b] Coale–Demeny "West" female stable population with $\mathring{e}_0 = 45$ and $r = .02$.

[c] Coale–Demeny "West" female stable population with $\mathring{e}_0 = 65$ and $r = .01$.

$x + n$. Note that the age-standardized death rates by cause must sum to the age-standardized death rate from all causes combined (except for rounding errors), because our list of causes is mutually exclusive and exhaustive.

The final summary measure of death rates is the geometric mean, presented only for deaths from all causes combined:[1]

$$\text{Geometric mean} = ({}_1m_0 \cdot {}_4m_1 \cdot {}_5m_5 \cdot {}_5m_{10} \cdots {}_\infty m_{85})^{1/19}.$$

Table 2. *Life Table for All Causes Combined*

The age-specific death rates from all causes combined are converted into standard life-table parameters according to the procedures outlined in Chapter II, Section A. It bears repeating that all computations refer to *hypothetical* cohorts of persons, numbering 100,000 at birth, who pass through their lives subject to the mortality conditions currently experienced in the population identified. No attempt was made to follow an actual cohort through life.

An understanding of the following notation is necessary for interpreting the columns in the second table.

x Exact age at beginning of age interval.

n Length of age interval $(1, 4, 5, 5, 5, \ldots, \infty)$.

${}_nM_x$ Population death rate (all causes combined) in the age interval x to $x + n$.

${}_nq_x$ Probability that an individual aged x will die prior to the attainment of age $x + n$.

l_x Number surviving to age x out of 100,000 starting at age 0.

${}_nd_x$ Number dying between ages x and $x + n$.

${}_nL_x$ Number of person-years lived between ages x and $x + n$ by survivors of the original 100,000.

${}_nm_x$ Life-table death rate in age interval x to $x + n$: ${}_nd_x/{}_nL_x$.

[1] For a discussion of the properties of this index, see Schoen (1970).

TABLE 4   49

$_na_x$ Average number of years lived in interval x to $x + n$ by the $_nd_x$ persons dying in the interval.

T_x Total person-years lived beyond age x by survivors of original 100,000.

$_nr_x$ Average annual growth rate of entrances into cohorts currently aged x to $x + n$ that is consistent with computed survivorship and observed age distribution.

$\overset{\circ}{e}_x$ Life expectancy at age x, or average duration of subsequent life for a survivor to age x.

Table 3.   *Number of Persons Dying (out of 100,000 at Birth) above Age x from Specified Causes*

This table presents the information of greatest interest in a multiple-decrement life table. It permits a calculation of the probability that a person surviving to some age will eventually die of a particular cause. Table IV-2 presents this table for English females in 1861. The left-hand column shows the number who will die above age x, from all causes combined, out of 100,000 at birth. It is identical to the l_x column, in the second table, showing the survivors *up to* age x, out of 100,000 at birth. The remaining columns show the number who will die from a specified disease above a particular age. Thus, out of 100,000 at birth, eventually 11,618 will die of tuberculosis. The probability of a newborn eventually dying of tuberculosis is thus

$$_\infty q_0^{TB} = l_0^{TB}/l_0 = 11{,}618/100{,}000 = .11618.$$

Similarly, the probability that a survivor to age 15 will ultimately die of tuberculosis is

$$_\infty q_{15}^{TB} = l_{15}^{TB}/l_{15} = 10{,}470/70{,}657 = .14818.$$

The probability that a newborn will die above age 15 from tuberculosis is $10{,}470/100{,}000 = .10470$. Finally, the probability that a survivor to age 15 will die from tuberculosis prior to age 35 is $(10{,}470 - 4{,}987)/70{,}657 = .07760$. That is, the number of deaths from tuberculosis between ages 15 and 35 (out of 100,000 persons at age 0) can be found by subtracting the number of people who will die from tuberculosis above age 35 from the number who will die from it above age 15.

The method of computing the multiple-decrement columns is described in Chapter II, Section B. To a close approximation, one can obtain the life-table deaths by cause, in some age interval, by apportioning life-table deaths from all causes, $_nd_x$, according to the cause distribution of deaths in the population at that age. For example,

$$_nd_x^{TB} \cong {}_nd_x \cdot {}_nM_x^{TB}/{}_nM_x.$$

The l_x^{TB} column is then obtained by summing $_nd_x^{TB}$ from the bottom of the table back to age x. Our method improves upon the one just described by recognizing that differences in age patterns of mortality from various causes can produce a distribution of deaths by cause, within an n-year interval, in the observed population, that differs from the corresponding distribution in a stationary population. For deaths at ages where r is set equal to 0 (0–10 and 85+), the results of the two methods are identical.

Summed across columns, the l_x^i columns reproduce the l_x column from all causes. This property is another way of stating that people alive at some age must eventually succumb to one of the 12 mutually exclusive and exhaustive causes of death. Additivity is not assured by the iterative technique used, but in practice the difference between l_x and $\sum_i l_x^i$ almost never exceeds 1 (out of a radix of 100,000). The difference, if any, together with rounding errors, are deposited in the residual, so that the l_x^i columns in the printed tables always sum to l_x.

Table 4.   *Number of Persons Surviving to Age x if Death from Specified Causes Were Eliminated*

This table presents estimates of what the l_x column would look like if particular disease or injury processes had been removed from the population. We denote an element in this table as $\bar{l}_x^{(-i)}$, read

Table IV-2

Number of Persons Dying (out of 100,000 at Birth) above Age x from Specified Causes: England and Wales, Females, 1861

Age (x)	All causes	Respiratory TB	Other infectious and parasitic	Neoplasms	Cardio-vascular	Influenza, pneumonia, bronchitis	Diarrheal	Certain degener-ative	Maternal	Certain diseases of infancy	Motor vehicle	Other violence	Other and unknown
0	100,000	11,618	12,199	3,173	13,251	12,495	4,603	677	1,257	3986	0	1,676	35,065
1	85,768	11,475	10,160	3,173	13,204	10,558	2,981	668	1,257	0	0	1,502	30,790
5	74,706	11,147	5,347	3,169	13,111	8,689	2,207	652	1,257	0	0	1,221	27,906
10	72,215	10,939	3,999	3,167	13,032	8,529	2,151	640	1,257	0	0	1,082	27,419
15	70,657	10,470	3,447	3,165	12,916	8,468	2,124	628	1,257	0	0	1,029	27,153
20	68,219	9,224	2,972	3,158	12,762	8,387	2,083	607	1,200	0	0	978	26,848
25	65,521	7,799	2,630	3,149	12,591	8,286	2,028	579	1,023	0	0	931	26,505
30	62,636	6,372	2,343	3,120	12,372	8,170	1,972	542	769	0	0	895	26,081
35	59,567	4,987	2,110	3,047	12,095	8,022	1,906	497	477	0	0	859	25,567
40	56,436	3,800	1,879	2,897	11,765	7,837	1,831	442	224	0	0	811	24,950
45	53,131	2,782	1,663	2,667	11,317	7,582	1,746	385	32	0	0	755	24,202
50	49,787	1,966	1,464	2,335	10,717	7,253	1,655	334	5	0	0	696	23,362
55	45,777	1,322	1,260	1,931	9,842	6,738	1,545	278	1	0	0	629	22,231
60	40,950	803	1,031	1,506	8,637	5,967	1,424	205	1	0	0	562	20,814
65	34,839	426	787	1,072	7,041	4,926	1,243	132	1	0	0	484	18,727
70	27,665	182	544	656	5,023	3,635	975	74	1	0	0	398	16,177
75	19,133	59	318	325	2,972	2,265	647	33	1	0	0	287	12,226
80	11,124	18	135	136	1,343	1,117	334	16	1	0	0	170	7,854
85+	4,321	2	32	42	377	357	110	7	0	0	0	66	3,328

"the number of persons surviving to age x if disease process i were eliminated from the population." In order to estimate accurately the effect on longevity of eliminating disease process i in a population, information is required about the interaction of disease i with diseases $(-i)$. In the absence of such information, one must make some assumption. The assumption that produced our $\bar{l}_x^{(-i)}$ columns is that *no* interaction exists between i and $-i$, i.e., that μ_x^{-i}, the force of mortality from cause $(-i)$ at age x, would be unaffected by the removal of disease process i from the population. Our

published $\bar{l}_x^{(-i)}$ would be identical to l_x in the population after the elimination of disease process i only if the assumption were accurate. It is probably quite accurate in the case of accidents. On the other hand, it probably results in an understatement of the increase in l_x that would result from eliminating pneumonia. Pneumonia typically has the effect of speeding death from some underlying condition to which the death is ascribed, and its elimination as a disease could be expected to reduce recorded death rates from these other diseases. The same is probably true of most acute conditions, if only because of coding inaccuracies. The principal effect of an antimalarial campaign in Ceylon was to reduce death rates from other causes (Newman, 1965). Similarly, death rates from other causes rose during the 1918 influenza epidemic in the United States (Collins & Lehman, 1953).

The assumption of no interaction may produce results incorrect in the opposite direction for most chronic diseases, which usually appear in multiples at the time of death. For example, "saving" people from death due to cirrhosis of the liver may increase the prevalence of and death rate from hypertension, since this condition is frequently present among decedents from cirrhosis. (On the other hand, it would also reduce the death rate in cases where hypertension was the underlying process and cirrhosis a contributory factor.)

Assuming no interaction and a radix of 1, the relation among $\bar{l}_x{}^i$ columns is multiplicative, as shown in Chapter II, Section C. That is,

$$l_x = \bar{l}_x{}^1 \cdot \bar{l}_x{}^2 \cdots \bar{l}_x^{12}.$$

We have published not the $\bar{l}_x{}^i$ but the $\bar{l}_x^{(-i)}$ columns. The $\bar{l}_x{}^i$ column may be derived from published results by the relation

$$\bar{l}_x{}^i = (l_x/\bar{l}_x^{(-i)}) \cdot 100{,}000.$$

Our initial formulas for computing the $l_x{}^i$ and $\bar{l}_x^{(-i)}$ columns do not force the $\bar{l}_x{}^i$ to multiply to l_x. However, the errors are once again quite small—rarely exceeding 15 persons (out of 100,000 at birth). They are allocated proportionally throughout the table.

Two summary measures are presented in this table: the gain in life expectancy at age 0 resulting from the "elimination" of a cause, and the gain in average person-years lived between ages 15 and 65 for a survivor to age 15, $\Delta[(T_{15} - T_{65})/l_{15}]$. The method of computing $_n\bar{L}_x^{(-i)}$ is the same as that used for computing $_nL_x$ (polynomial graduation through $\bar{l}_x^{(-i)}$).

The effect of simultaneously eliminating two cause-of-death processes from the population cannot be inferred from observing the effect of eliminating each individually. The total gain in life always exceeds the sum of the individual gains, a proposition made obvious by considering a population with only two causes of death *in toto*. Consequently, we present calculations of the gain from eliminating combinations of causes. Reading from left to right in the table, the first combination involves only "respiratory tuberculosis" and "other infectious and parasitic diseases"; the second adds to it "influenza, pneumonia, and bronchitis," "diarrheal diseases," and "maternal mortality"; the third combination includes deaths from the second combination, together with the proportion (by age) of deaths from the residual and "certain diseases of early infancy" equal to the ratio of deaths from the second combination to deaths from all causes *excepting* the residual and "certain diseases of early infancy"; the fourth combination eliminated is "automobile accidents" and "other violence."

Sources of and Adjustments to Data

The following pages provide references to the sources of the data used in the tables and the various data adjustments that were required. For convenience of presentation, the following abbreviations of frequently cited sources are used:

WHO. *AEVS* World Health Organization. *Annual epidemiological and vital statistics.* Geneva. (In 1962, the title was changed to *World health statistics annual.*)

UN. *DY* United Nations Statistical Office, Department of Economic and Social Affairs. *Demographic yearbook.* New York.

Bunle H. Bunle, *Le mouvement naturel de la population dans le monde de 1906 à 1936.* Paris: L'Institut National d'Études Démographiques, 1954.

World Population   N. Keyfitz & W. Flieger, *World population: An analysis of vital data*. Chicago: Univ. of Chicago Press, 1968.

Mitchell   B. R. Mitchell, *Abstract of British historical statistics*. London and New York: Cambridge Univ. Press, 1962.

Coale-Demeny   A. J. Coale & P. Demeny, *Regional model life tables and stable populations*. Princeton, New Jersey: Princeton Univ. Press, 1960.

The first entry following the source of death data designates the number of the International List Revision into which the deaths were classified. "N" designates a nonstandard list; the detailed allocations which were necessary in such cases were normally so extensive that they could not be presented here. When an International List Revision is indicated but national customs of presenting data prevented our strict adherence to the rules set out in Table I-2, the necessary adjustments are indicated. For example, in Canada, 1921, cause X (automobile accidents) excluded term 186e in the Third Revision, deaths from which were placed instead in cause XI (other accidents and violence).

When cause-of-death data were provided in age intervals larger than those used in the program (0, 1–4, 5–9, 10–14, . . . , 85+), the exact age at the beginning of the age interval in question is shown. Deaths in the deviant intervals for each cause were apportioned into the appropriate age intervals by one of two methods: indirect standardization (IS) or graduation (G). Returning to Canada, 1921, we can see that age intervals 30–39, 40–49, 50–59, 60–69, 70–79, and 80+ were available. Data referring to ages 30–79 were graduated, and those referring to ages 80+ were indirectly standardized.

The graduation formula was a simple second-degree polynomial fit through death rates at the midpoint of age intervals. That is, death rates in three successive age intervals were assumed to follow an age curve of the form

$$M(x) = a + b \cdot x + c \cdot x^2.$$

For example, in order to graduate the interval 40–49 in Canada, 1921, a polynomial was fitted to death rates at ages 30–39 (assumed correct for exact age 35), 40–49, and 50–59. Values of x equal to 42.5 and 47.5 were then substituted in the formula to yield death rates at ages 40–44 and 45–49. The number of deaths in a 5-year interval was inferred from death rates and population. This number of deaths was then scaled up or down by the (invariably small) factor which would be required to reproduce exactly the observed number of deaths at ages 40–49. This procedure was followed for each of the 12 causes, and the number of deaths from all causes combined was obtained as a simple sum.

When deaths were available only for very large age intervals, or for a large and open-ended age group, indirect standardization was employed. One of the striking preliminary findings of this study is the parallelism of age curves of mortality from a cause drawn from widely differing populations, when plotted on semilog paper. Exact parallelism would imply that one age curve is precisely a constant multiple of another.[2] Indirect standardization would produce, in this case, results which are perfectly accurate.

Suppose we are indirectly standardizing for the purpose of apportioning 80+ deaths into the two age-intervals 80–84 and 85+. The formulas for estimating death rates are

$$_5\bar{M}_{80} = {_5}M^s_{80} \cdot K,$$

$$\bar{M}_{85+} = M^s_{85+} \cdot K,$$

$$K = \frac{D_{80+}}{_5M^s_{80} \cdot {_5}P_{80} + M^s_{85+} \cdot P_{85+}},$$

where s denotes death rates in the standard population.

[2] If $\log x = a + \log y$, then $x = e^a \cdot y$.

Table IV-3

Comparison of Estimates of Life Expectancies at Birth for Populations Where Data from Two Sources Were Available

Population	Life expectancy based upon figures obtained by aggregation of cause-of-death data indirectly standardized or graduated to 5-year age intervals		Life expectancy based upon published data in 5-year age intervals for all causes combined	Population	Life expectancy based upon figures obtained by aggregation of cause-of-death data indirectly standardized or graduated to 5-year age intervals		Life expectancy based upon published data in 5-year age intervals for all causes combined
Canada, 1921	M	57.98	57.98	Netherlands, 1931	M	63.73	63.69
	F	60.14	60.14		F	65.06	65.02
Chile, 1920	M	28.35	28.47	Norway, 1930	M	62.55	62.56
	F	29.73	29.85		F	65.79	65.78
Chile, 1930	M	35.93	35.87	Spain, 1930	M	47.25	47.21
	F	38.26	38.24		F	50.88	50.78
Denmark, 1921	M	61.06	60.93	Sweden, 1911	M	56.62	56.59
	F	62.63	62.51		F	59.62	59.49
Denmark, 1930	M	61.41	61.44	Sweden, 1920	M	57.56	57.52
	F	63.33	63.30		F	60.25	60.21
France, 1931	M	55.18	55.18	Sweden, 1930	M	62.22	62.14
	F	59.83	59.82		F	64.24	64.18
France, 1936	M	56.63	56.64	Sweden, 1940	M	65.29	65.29
	F	62.33	62.36		F	68.00	67.99
Italy, 1891	M	38.48	38.48	Switzerland, 1930	M	59.11	59.12
	F	38.80	38.76		F	63.36	63.37
Italy, 1901	M	43.09	43.03	Switzerland, 1941	M	62.77	62.78
	F	43.70	43.65		F	66.97	66.99

An indirect standardization would be performed for each cause-of-death category and numbers of deaths from all causes combined then derived as a simple sum. The standard age curve of mortality used for each cause was that of the United States male population, 1930, which had reliable reporting and produced a life expectancy near the median found in the tables.[3] The age curve of mortality from each cause was plotted on semilog paper

[3] For maternal mortality, death rates for United States, females, 1930 are employed.

for 10 populations at widely varying life expectancies, and the United States, 1930, curves were found to parallel quite closely those of the majority of other populations. Tuberculosis is the one cause of death where the parallelism assumption of indirect standardization might lead to pronounced distortion.

It was frequently possible to compare results obtained when indirect standardization and/or graduation were employed against other results. Even for populations where cause-of-death data were available only in large age intervals, data on deaths from all causes combined were often available for 5-year intervals. To discover whether it was necessary to modify our procedures substantially by taking account of the 5-year data, we computed two life tables (by identical methods) for all populations where both sources of data were available. Results are compared in Table IV-3. Indirect standardization and/or graduation of cause-of-death data in large age groupings provided results which differed from those for which the "correct" 5-year totals were used by no more than .13 years of life expectancy. Results for Italy, 1891, are particularly interesting, since it was here that the original age

intervals were the broadest: 10–19, 20–39, 40–59, 60–79, 80+. Nonetheless, life expectancies were within .05 year of the "correct" figures. Naturally, results based on graduation may be the more accurate of the two if considerable age misstatement is present. As a result of this analysis, we did not consider it worth making the adjustments required to reproduce exactly published 5-year totals from all causes combined.

Descriptions of adjustments to population figures should be self-explanatory. Adjustments required to obtain midyear from off-center population estimates are not indicated. Population numbers were adjusted to midyear if the date to which the census or estimate referred differed from July 1 by more than 1 month. Midyear adjustment was required for about half the populations. The method of adjustment was to determine the rate of natural increase at the time (for each sex separately) and assume that the rate for the entire sex applied to each age group, with zero net migration, over the portion of the year(s) between the midpoint and the census date.

REFERENCES

Coale, A. J., & Demeny, P. *Regional model life tables and stable populations.* Princeton, New Jersey: Princeton Univ. Press, 1966.

Collins, D. S., & Lehman, J. *Excess deaths from influenza and pneumonia and from important chronic diseases during epidemic periods, 1918–1951,* 1953,

United States Public Health Service, Public Health Monograph No. 10.

Newman, P. *Malaria eradication and population growth.* (Bureau of Public Health Economics Research Ser. No. 10) Ann Arbor, Michigan, Univ. of Michigan, School of Public Health, 1965.

Schoen, R. The geometric mean of the age-specific death rates as a summary index of mortality. *Demography,* 1970, 7(3), 317–324.

AUSTRALIA—1911

Deaths: Commonwealth Bureau of Census and Statistics. *Population and Vital Statistics—1911 and Previous Years.* (Bulletin No. 29.)
* 2nd* II, −61c; XII, +61c. *

Population: Bunle.

AUSTRALIA—1921

Deaths: Commonwealth Bureau of Census and Statistics. *Population and Vital Statistics—1921 and Previous Years.* (Bulletin No. 39.)
* 2nd *

Population: Bunle.
* Population 0–4 apportioned as Australia, 1921, *World Population.* *

AUSTRALIA—1933

Deaths: Commonwealth Bureau of Census and Statistics. *Population and Vital Statistics—1933 and Previous Years.* (Bulletin No. 51.)
* 4th * Cause X uses 186e of published list. *

Population: Bunle.

AUSTRALIA—1940

Deaths: Bureau of Census and Statistics. *Demography—1940.*
* 5th *

Population: UN. *DY—60.*

AUSTRALIA—1951

Deaths: WHO. *AEVS—51.*
* 6th * Deaths 75+ from Bureau of Census and Statistics. *Demography—1951.* * A85 and A86 deaths obtained from data received in correspondence with Bureau of Census and Statistics, Canberra, Australia. *

Population: UN. *DY—60.*
* Population 75+ apportioned as population 1950 (UN. *DY—51*). *

AUSTRALIA—1960

Deaths: WHO. *AEVS—60.*
* 7th *

Population: UN: *DY—61.*

AUSTRALIA—1964

Deaths: WHO. *AEVS—64.*
* 7th *

Population: UN. *DY—65.*

AUSTRIA—1961

Deaths: WHO. *AEVS—61.*
* 7th *

Population: UN. *DY—67.*

AUSTRIA—1964

Deaths: WHO. *AEVS—64.*
* 7th *

Population: UN. *DY—65.*
* Population 0–4 from WHO. *AEVS—64.* *

BELGIUM—1960

Deaths: WHO. *AEVS—60.*
* 7th *

Population: UN. *DY—61.*

BELGIUM—1964

Deaths: WHO. *AEVS—64.*
* 7th *

Population: UN. *DY—66.*

BULGARIA—1964

Deaths: WHO. *AEVS—64.*
* 7th *

Population: UN. *DY—65.*

CANADA (REGISTRATION AREA)—1921

(Excluding Quebec, Yukon, and NW Territories)
Deaths: Dominion Bureau of Statistics. *Vital Statistics—1921.*
* 3rd * X, −186e; XI, +186e * 30, 40, 50, 60, 70 (G); 80+ (IS). *

Population: Bunle. Regional division from Dominion Bureau of Statistics. *Census of Canada. 1921.* Vol. I.

CANADA—1931

(Excluding Yukon and NW Territories)
Deaths: Dominion Bureau of Statistics. *Vital Statistics—1931.*
* 4th *

Population: Bunle. Regional division from *World Population.*

CANADA—1941

(Excluding Yukon and NW Territories)
Deaths: Dominion Bureau of Statistics. *Vital Statistics—1941.*
* 5th *

Population: UN. *DY—60.* Regional division from Bureau of Statistics. *Census of Canada. 1941.* Vol. II.

CANADA—1951

(Excluding Yukon and NW Territories)
Deaths: WHO. *AEVS—51.*
* 6th * Deaths 75–85+ from Dominion Bureau of Statistics. *Vital Statistics—1951.* * A85 and A86 deaths obtained from data received in correspondence with Dominion Bureau of Statistics, Ottawa, Canada. *

Population: UN. *DY—60.* Regional division from Dominion Bureau of Statistics. *Census of Population. 1951.* Vol. I.

CANADA—1960

Deaths: WHO. *AEVS—60.*
* 6th *

Population: WHO. *AEVS—60.*
* Population 0–4 prorated as population 1961 in UN. *DY—62.* *

CANADA—1964

Deaths: WHO. *AEVS—64.*
* 7th *

Population: UN. *DY—64.*

CEYLON—1960

Deaths: WHO. *AEVS—60.*
* 6th *

Population: WHO. *AEVS—60.*
* 0–4 apportioned as 0–1, 1–4, interpolated from 1963 and 1955 data from UN. *DY—68, 62.* *

CHILE—1909

Deaths: Oficina Central de Estadística. *Anuario Estadístico. 1909.* Tomo II.
* 2nd *

Population: Age distribution 0–19 from 1907 population as adjusted by Julio Morales Vergara, *Análisis Demográfico del Censo Chileno de 1907.* 20+ from 1907 population in Bunle, graduated by polynomial fitting to 10-year death rates to insure smooth sequence of 5-year death rates by age.

CHILE—1920

Deaths: Oficina Central de Estadística. *Anuario Estadístico. 1920.* Vol. I.
* 2nd * Deaths (by cause) 3–9 apportioned to 3–4 and 5–9 as distribution in Sweden, 1911.
* 30, 40, 50, 60, 70 (G); 80+ (IS) * II, −61c; XII, +61c. *

Population: Bunle.
* Population 45–80 graduated by polynomial fitting to 10-year death rates to insure smooth sequence of 5-year death rates by age. *

CHILE—1930

Deaths: Dirección General de Estadística. *Anuario Estadístico. 1930.*
* 3rd * 30, 40, 50 (G); 60+ (IS) *
* II, −91a; IV, +91a. *

Population: Bunle.
* Population 45–80 graduated by polynomial fitting to 10-year death rates to insure smooth sequence of 5-year death rates by age. *

CHILE—1940

Deaths: Dirección General de Estadística. *Anuario Estadístico. 1940.*
* 5th * 65+ (IS) * "2" added to male overall total to correct for sum of age groups in published figures. *

Population: UN. *DY—60.*

CHILE—1950

Deaths: WHO. *AEVS—50.*
* 6th * 75+ (IS) * Published data corrected for omission of bronchial-pneumonia (their list no. 812-0) as determined from comparison with information in Dirección General de Estadística y Censos. *Demografia y Asistencia Social, Año 1950.* * A85 and A86 deaths obtained from data received in correspondence with Dirección General de Estadística y Censos, Santiago, Chile. *

Population: UN. *DY—60.*

CHILE—1959

Deaths: WHO. *AEVS—60.*
* 6th * A85 and A86 deaths obtained from data received in correspondence with Dirección General de Estadística y Censos, Santiago, Chile. *

Population: WHO. *AEVS—60.*

CHILE—1964

Deaths: WHO. *AEVS—64.*
* 7th *

Population: WHO. *AEVS—64.*
* 65+ prorated as 1960 population from *DY—67.* *

COLOMBIA—1960

Deaths: WHO. *AEVS—60.*
* 7th * A85 and A86 deaths obtained from data received in correspondence with Ministerio de Salud, Bogota, Colombia. *

Population: WHO. *AEVS—60.*

COLOMBIA—1964

Deaths: WHO. *AEVS—64.*
* 7th * A85 and A86 deaths obtained from data received in correspondence with Ministerio de Salud, Bogota, Colombia. *

Population: UN. *DY—67.*

COSTA RICA—1960

Deaths: WHO. *AEVS—60.*
* 7th * A85 and A86 deaths obtained in correspondence with Dirección General de Estadística, San Jose, Costa Rica. *

Population: UN. *DY—61.*

COSTA RICA—1964

Deaths: WHO. *AEVS—64.*
* 7th * A85 and A86 deaths obtained in correspondence with Dirección General de Estadística, San Jose, Costa Rica. *

Population: UN. *DY—68.*

CZECHOSLOVAKIA—1934

Deaths: Statni Urad Statisticky. *Annuaire Statistique de la République Tchecoslovaque—1934.*
* N * 5, 15, 25, 40, 50 (G); 60+ (IS). *

Population: Bunle.

CZECHOSLOVAKIA—1960

Deaths: WHO. *AEVS—60.*
* 7th *

Population: WHO. *AEVS—60.*

CZECHOSLOVAKIA—1964

Deaths: WHO. *AEVS—64.*
* 7th *

Population: UN. *DY—66.*

DENMARK—1921

Deaths: *Sundhedsstyrelsen Dødsaarsagerne i Kongeriget Danmark.*
* 2nd * 35, 45, 55, 65, 75 (G) * II, −22, 37, 38b, 61c, 164, +61b, 68, part of 63; XI, +164, −58; IV, +part of 74; V, −part of 91; VI, +108; VIII, −138; XII, +22, 37, 38b, 61c, 58, part of 91, −61b, 68, part of 63, 108. *

Population: Bunle.

DENMARK—1930

Deaths: *Sundhedsstyrelsen Dødsaarsagerne i Kongeriget Danmark.*
* 3rd * 25, 35, 45, 55, 65, 75 (G) * II, −175, part of 91a, + part of 73; III, −91b, part of 151, + part of 91a, 58, 80–82, 84; VI, +117, VII, −122a; XI, +68, 175; XII, + part of 151, 91b, 122a, − part of 73, 58, 80–82, 84, 117, 68. *

Population: Statens Statistiske Bureau. *Folketaellingen i Kongeriget Danmark.*

DENMARK—1940

Deaths: *Sundhedsstyrelsen Dødsaarsagerne i Kongeriget Danmark.*
*4th * 25, 35, 45, 55, 65, 75 (G) * XI, +76, 177; II, −177; III, −139a, 72b; VI, −120b; V, −109; XII, +72b, 109, 120b, 139a. *

Population: UN. *DY—60.*
* Population 75+ prorated as population 75–85+ in 1945 census from UN. *DY—60.* *

DENMARK—1960

Deaths: WHO. *AEVS—60.*
* 7th *

Population: UN. *DY—62.*

DENMARK—1964

Deaths: WHO. *AEVS—64.*
* 7th *

Population: UN. *DY—66.*

EL SALVADOR—1950

Deaths: WHO. *AEVS—50.*
* 6th * 75+ (IS) * A85 and A86 deaths obtained from data received in correspondence with Dirección General de Estadística y Censos, San Salvador, El Salvador. *

ENGLAND AND WALES—1861

Deaths: House of Commons. *Sessional Papers.* 1863. Vol. 14. *24th Annual Report of the Registrar General in England. 1861.*
* N * 25, 35, 45, 55, 65, 75 (G). *
* Note: deaths subject to small errors because of need to hand-copy from microprint records. *

Population: Mitchell.

ENGLAND AND WALES—1871

Deaths: House of Commons. *Sessional Papers.* 1873. Vol. 20. *34th Annual Report of the Registrar General in England. 1871.*
* N * 25, 35, 45, 55, 65, 75 (G). *

Population: Mitchell.

ENGLAND AND WALES—1881

Deaths: House of Commons. *Sessional Papers.* 1883. Vol. 20. *44th Annual Report of the Registrar General in England. 1881.*
* N * 25, 35, 45, 55, 65, 75 (G). *

Population: Mitchell.

ENGLAND AND WALES—1891

Deaths: House of Commons. *Sessional Papers.* 1892. Vol. 24. *54th Annual Report of the Registrar General in England. 1891.*
* N * 25, 35, 45, 55, 65, 75 (G). *

Population: Mitchell.

ENGLAND AND WALES—1901

Deaths: Parliament. *Sessional Papers.* 1902. Vol. 18. "Births, Deaths, and Marriages (England and Wales, 1901)."
* N * 25, 35, 45, 55, 65, 75 (G). *

Population: Mitchell.

ENGLAND AND WALES—1911

Deaths: Parliament. *Sessional Papers.* 1912–1913. Vol. 13. "General Abstract of Marriages, Births, and Deaths Registered in England and Wales. 1911."
* 2nd *

Population: Bunle.

ENGLAND AND WALES—1921

Deaths: Registrar General. *Statistical Review of England and Wales—1921. Tables.* Part I.
* 3rd * 80+ (IS). *

Population: Bunle.

ENGLAND AND WALES—1931

Deaths: Registrar General. *Statistical Review of England and Wales—1931. Tables.* Part I.
* 4th * 80+ (IS). *

Population: Bunle.

ENGLAND AND WALES—1940

Deaths: Registrar General. *Statistical Review of England and Wales—1940. Tables.* Part I.
* 5th * 80+ (IS). *

Population: UN. *DY—60.*

ENGLAND AND WALES—1951

Deaths: WHO. *AEVS—51.*
* 6th * Deaths 75–85+ from Registrar General. *Statistical Review of England and Wales—1951. Tables.* Part I. * A85 and A86 deaths obtained from data received in correspondence with Office of Population Census and Surveys, London, England. *

Population: UN. *DY—60.*

ENGLAND AND WALES—1960

Deaths: WHO. *AEVS—60.*
* 7th *

Population: UN. *DY—61.*

ENGLAND AND WALES—1964

Deaths: WHO. *AEVS—64.*
* 7th *

Population: WHO. *AEVS—64.*

FINLAND—1951

Deaths: WHO. *AEVS—51.*
* 6th * Deaths 75–85+ and A85 and A86 from Suomen Virallinen Tilasto. *Voestotilastoa. Befolkningsstatistik. Dödsorsaker. 1951.* *

Population: UN. *DY—60.*

FINLAND—1960

Deaths: WHO. *AEVS—60.*
* 6th *

Population: UN. *DY—62.*

FINLAND—1964

Deaths: WHO. *AEVS—64.*
* 7th *

Population: Tilastollinen Paatoimisto. *Suomen Tilastollinen Vuosileirja. 1965.*
* Population 0–4 prorated as the average of 1963 and 1965 populations as found in *DY—65, 66.* *

FRANCE—1926

Deaths: Bureau de la Statistique Générale. Statistique Générale de la France. *Statistique Annuelle.* "Statistique du Mouvement de la Population, 1926."
* 3rd Abr. *

Population: Bureau de la Statistique Générale. *Resultats statistiques du recensement général de la population effectué le 7 mars 1926.*
* Population 70–80+ prorated as 1931 population as found in Institut National de la Statistique et des Etudes Economiques. *Annuaire Statistique de la France. 1966. Résumé Retrospectif.* *

FRANCE—1931

Deaths: Bureau de la Statistique Générale. Statistique Générale de la France. *Statistique Annuelle.* "Statistique du Mouvement de la Population, 1931."
* 4th Abr. * 70, 80+ (IS). *

Population: Bunle.

FRANCE—1936

Deaths: Bureau de la Statistique Générale. Statistique Générale de la France. *Statistique Annuelle.* "Statistique du Mouvement de la Population, 1936."
* 4th Abr. * 70, 80+ (IS). *

Population: Bureau de la Statistique Générale. *Résultats statistiques du recensement général de la population effectué le 3 mars 1936.*
* Population 70+ prorated as population of France 1936 as found in *Annuaire Statistique de la France. 1966. Résumé Rétrospectif.* *

FRANCE—1951

Deaths: Institut National de la Statistique et des Etudes Economiques. *Statistique du Mouvement de la Population. 1951.* Deuxième Partie. "Les Causes des Décès."
* 6th * Includes deaths to children whose birth was not registered (cause assumed unknown). *

Population: UN. *DY—60.*

FRANCE—1960

Deaths: WHO. *AEVS—60.*
* 7th * Includes deaths to children whose birth was not registered (cause assumed unknown). *

Population: UN. *DY—61.*

FRANCE—1964

Deaths: WHO. *AEVS—64.*
* 7th *

Population: UN. *DY—65.*

GERMANY (FEDERAL REPUBLIC)—1960

Deaths: WHO. *AEVS—60.*
* 7th *

Population: WHO. *AEVS—60.*

GERMANY (FEDERAL REPUBLIC)—1964

Deaths: WHO. *AEVS—64.*
* 7th *

Population: UN. *DY—66.*
* 80+ from *AEVS—64.* *

GERMANY (WEST BERLIN)—1960

Deaths: WHO. *AEV—60.*
* 7th *

Population: WHO. *AEVS—60.*

GERMANY (WEST BERLIN)—1964

Deaths: WHO. *AEVS—64.*
* 7th *

Population: UN. *DY—66.*
* 80+ from *AEVS—64.* *

GREECE—1928

Deaths: *Statistique des Causes de Décès. 1928.*
* 3rd Abr. *

Population: Institut International de Statistique. *Apercu de la démographie des divers pays du monde. 1929–1936.* La Haye. 1939.

GREECE—1960

Deaths: WHO. *AEVS—60.*
* 7th *

Population: UN. *DY—61.*

GREECE—1964

Deaths: WHO. *AEVS—64.*
* 7th *

Population: UN. *DY—65.*

GUATEMALA—1961

Deaths: WHO. *AEVS—61.*
* 7th * A85 and A86 deaths obtained from data received in correspondence with Dirección General de Estadística, Republic of Guatemala. *

Population: WHO. *AEVS—61.*

GUATEMALA—1964

Deaths: WHO. *AEVS—64.*
* 7th *

Population: UN. *DY—67.*
* Population includes 74,653 additional persons of unknown age and sex but not 3.7% adjustment for underenumeration. *

HONG KONG—1961

Deaths: WHO. *AEVS—61.*
* 7th * A85 and A86 deaths obtained from data received in correspondence with Medical and Health Department, Hong Kong. *

Population: WHO. *AEVS—61.*

HONG KONG—1964

Deaths: WHO. *AEVS—64.*
* 7th *

Population: UN. *DY—64.*
* Population 0–4 from *AEVS—64.* * Population 80+ prorated using 1961 population from UN. *DY—62.* *

HUNGARY—1960

Deaths: WHO. *AEVS—60.*
* 7th *

Population: UN. *DY—61.*
* Population 0–4 prorated using 1961 data (*DY—62*) * Population 80+ from *AEVS—60.* *

HUNGARY—1964

Deaths: WHO. *AEVS—64.*
* 7th *

Population: WHO. *AEVS—64.*

ICELAND—1964

Deaths: WHO. *AEVS—64.*
* 7th *

Population: WHO. *AEVS—64.*

IRELAND—1951

Deaths: WHO. *AEVS—51.*
* 6th * Deaths 75–85+ obtained from data received in correspondence with Central Statistics Office, Dublin, Ireland. * A85 and A86 deaths obtained from data received in correspondence with Central Statistics Office, Dublin, Ireland. *

Population: UN. *DY—60.*

IRELAND—1961

Deaths: WHO. *AEVS—61.*
* 7th *

Population: UN. *DY—65.*

ISRAEL (JEWISH POPULATION)—1951

Deaths: WHO. *AEVS—51.*
* 6th * Deaths 75–85+ obtained from data received in correspondence with Central Bureau of Statistics, Jerusalem, Israel. * A85 and A86 deaths obtained from data received in correspondence with Central Bureau of Statistics, Jerusalem, Israel. *

Population: UN. *DY—60.*
* Population 75+ prorated as population, 1948 (UN. *DY—60*). *

ISRAEL (JEWISH POPULATION)—1960

Deaths: WHO. *AEVS—60.*
* 7th *

Population: Central Bureau of Statistics. *Statistical Abstract of Israel.* 1961.
* Population 75+ prorated according to population in 1961 (UN. *DY—62*). *

ISRAEL (JEWISH POPULATION)—1964

Deaths: WHO. *AEVS—64.*
* 7th *

Population: Central Bureau of Statistics. *Statistical Abstract of Israel. 1964.*
* Population 75+ prorated according to average of population in 1961 and 1967 (*DY—62, 68*). *

ITALY—1881

Deaths: Direzione Generale della Statistica. *Generale Statistica delle Cause di Morte, 1881.*
* N * 5, 20, 60+ (IS) * Cause distribution available for only 25.1% of total deaths. Deaths in a particular age–sex category (from France. Statistique Générale. *Statistique Annuelle du Mouvement de la Population.* 1904) assumed to have same cause distribution as published cause figures in that category. *

Population: Direzione Generale della Statistica. *Annuario Statistico Italiano, 1905–1907.*
* Population 15–24 prorated by Coale–Demeny "West" stable population, level 7, $r = .005$. *

ITALY—1891

Deaths: Direzione Generale della Statistica. *Generale Statistica delle Cause di Morte. 1891.*
* N * 10, 20, 40, 60, 80+ (IS). *

Population: Estimate provided by Massimo Livi-Bacci in correspondence.
* 80+ prorated as Coale–Demeny "West" stable population, level 9, $r = .005$. *

ITALY—1901

Deaths: Direzione Generale della Statistica. *Statistica delle Cause di Morte nell'anno 1901.*
* N * 10 (G), 20, 30, 40, 50, 60, 70, 80+ (IS). *

Population: Direzione Generale della Statistica. *Annuario Statistico Italiano, 1905–1907.*
* Population 15–24 prorated by Coale–Demeny "West" stable population, level 9, $r = .005$. *

ITALY—1910

Deaths: Direzione Generale della Statistica e del Lavoro. *Statistica delle Cause di Morte. 1910.*
* N *

Population: Bunle.

ITALY—1921

Deaths: Direzione Generale della Statistica. *Statistica delle Cause di Morte. 1921.*
* N *

Population: Bunle.
* Population 0–4 split by projecting forward births in each of the preceding 5 years. *

ITALY—1931

Deaths: Statistica Direzione Generale. *Statistica delle Cause di Morte. 1931.*
* 4th * II, −177; III, −72, 139a; XI, +177, 76; XII, +72, 139a, −76. *

Population: Bunle.
* Population 0–4 prorated as population of Italy 1931 in *World Population*. *

ITALY—1960

Deaths: WHO. *AEVS—60.*
* 7th *

Population: UN. *DY—61.*
* Population 0–4 prorated as population in 1961 (*DY—64*). *

ITALY—1964

Deaths: WHO. *AEVS—64.*
* 7th *

Population: WHO. *AEVS—64.*
* Population figures scaled down to conform with midyear total as found in introduction to *AEVS—64*. *

JAPAN—1899

Deaths: Bureau de la Statistique Générale. *Résumé Statistique de l'Empire du Japon.* 1903.
* N *

Population: Tokei Kyoku Hensan. *Tokei Nenkan.* 1898.

JAPAN—1908

Deaths: Bureau de la Statistique Générale. *Résumé Statistique de l'Empire du Japon.* 1911.
* N *

Population: Bunle.

JAPAN—1940

Deaths: Cabinet Bureau of Statistics. *Vital Statistics. 1940.*
* 4th *

Population: *World Population.*

JAPAN—1951

Deaths: WHO. *AEVS—51.*
* 6th * 75+ prorated as deaths 75–85+, Japan, 1950, obtained from data received in correspondence with Bureau of Statistics, Tokyo. * A85 and A86 deaths obtained from data received in correspondence with Bureau of Statistics. Tokyo, Japan. *

Population: UN. *DY—60.*
* 80+ prorated to 1950 population from same source. *

JAPAN—1960

Deaths: WHO. *AEVS—60.*
* 7th *

Population: UN. *DY—61.*

JAPAN—1964

Deaths: WHO. *AEVS—64.*
* 7th *

Population: WHO. *AEVS—64.*

MALTA AND GOZO—1964

Deaths: WHO. *AEVS—64.*
* 7th * A85 and A86 graduated from 10-year age groupings, received in correspondence with Central Office of Statistics and Electoral Office, Valletta, Malta. *

Population: UN. *DY—65.*

MAURITIUS—1960

Deaths: WHO. *AEVS—60.*
* 7th * A85 and A86 indirectly standardized by age using Mauritius, 1964 (*AEVS—64*).

Population: UN. *DY—62.*
* 1962 midyear scaled down by total (1960)/total (1962) for each sex. *

MAURITIUS—1964

Deaths: WHO. *AEVS—64*
* 7th *

Population: UN. *DY—67.*
* Excluding dependents. *

MEXICO—1960

Deaths: WHO. *AEVS—61.*
* 7th * A85 and A86 deaths obtained from data received in correspondence with Dirección General de Estadística, Mexico City, Mexico. *

Population: UN. *DY—65.*

MEXICO—1964

Deaths: WHO. *AEVS—64.*
* 7th *

Population: WHO. *AEVS—64.*
* Scaled up by factor midyear total/stated total. Midyear total from introduction of same volume. *

NETHERLANDS—1931

Deaths: Centraal Bureau voor de Statistiek. *Statistiek van de Sterfte naar dem Leeftijd en de oorzaken van den dood over het jaar—1931.*
* 4th * 65, 80+ (IS) * Cause X uses 186a³. *

Population: Bunle.

NETHERLANDS—1940

Deaths: Centraal Bureau voor de Statistiek. *Statistiek van de Sterfte naar dem leeftijd en de oorzaken van den dood over het jaar—1940.*
* 4th * 80+ (IS) * Cause X uses 186d & e. *

Population: UN. *DY—60.*

NETHERLANDS—1950

Deaths: WHO. *AEVS—50.*
* 6th * Deaths 75–85+ and A85 and A86 obtained from data received in correspondence with Netherlands Centraal Bureau voor de Statistiek, The Hague, Netherlands. *

Population: UN. *DY—60.*

NETHERLANDS—1960

Deaths: WHO. *AEVS—60.*
* 7th *

Population: UN. *DY—61.*

NETHERLANDS—1964

Deaths: WHO. *AEVS—64.*
* 7th *

Population: WHO. *AEVS—64.*

NEW ZEALAND—1881

Deaths: Registrar General's Office. *Statistics of the Colony of New Zealand. 1881.*
* N * 80+ (IS). *

Population: Bureau of Census and Statistics. *Results of Census. 1901.*

NEW ZEALAND—1891

Deaths: Registrar General's Office. *Statistics of the Colony of New Zealand. 1891.*
* N * 80+ (IS). *

Population: Bureau of Census and Statistics. *Results of Census. 1901.*

NEW ZEALAND—1901

Deaths: Census and Statistics Office. *Statistics of the Colony of New Zealand. 1901.*
* N * 80+ (IS). *

Population: Bureau of Census and Statistics. *Results of Census. 1901.*

NEW ZEALAND—1911

Deaths: Government Statistician. *Statistics of the Dominion of New Zealand for the Year 1911.* Vol. I, Part III., *Population and Vital Statistics.*
* 2nd * II, −61c; XII, +61c. *

Population: Bunle.

NEW ZEALAND—1921

Deaths: Census and Statistics Office. *Report on the Vital Statistics of New Zealand, 1921.*
* 2nd * II, −61c; XII, +61c. *

Population: Bunle.

NEW ZEALAND—1926

Deaths: Census and Statistics Office. *Report on the Vital Statistics of the Dominion of New Zealand. 1926.*
* 3rd * IV, +91a; II, −91a. *

Population: Census and Statistics Office. *Population Census—1926.* Vol. 3.

NEW ZEALAND—1936

Deaths: Census and Statistics Department. *Report of the Vital Statistics of the Dominion of New Zealand. 1936.*
* 4th * III, −139a; XI uses 186c,e,g,h; XII, +139a. *

Population: United States Public Health Service. *Summary of International Vital Statistics. 1937–1944.*
* 80+ prorated according to average of 1926 and 1945 populations. *

NEW ZEALAND—1945

Deaths: Census and Statistics Department. *Report on the Vital Statistics of the Dominion of New Zealand. 1945.*
* 5th *

Population: UN. *DY—60.*

NEW ZEALAND—1951

Deaths: WHO. *AEVS—51.*
* 6th * Deaths 75–85+ from Department of Health. *Report on the Medical Statistics of New Zealand. 1951.*

Population: UN. *DY—60.*

NEW ZEALAND—1964
(Includes Maori)

Deaths: WHO. *AEVS—64.*
* 7th *

Population: UN. *DY—65.*

NORTHERN IRELAND—1960

Deaths: WHO. *AEVS—60.*
* 7th *

Population: WHO. *AEVS—60.*
* 0–4 prorated using 1961 data (UN. *DY—67*). *

NORTHERN IRELAND—1964

Deaths: WHO. *AEVS—46.*
* 7th *

Population interpolated linearly between 1963 and 1965 (UN.*DY—64* and *65*)*
* 0–4 prorated using 1963 population in UN. *DY—64.* *

NORWAY—1910

Deaths: Statistisk Sentralbyrå. *Norges Officielle Statistikk. 1910.* (Raekke V. Bund 28), Vol. 181.
* N * 20, 30, 40, 50, 60, 70 (G); 80+ (IS) * Residual deaths by age altered to achieve conformity with total deaths by age as found in Bunle. *

Population: Bunle.

NORWAY—1920

Deaths: Direktoren for det Civile Medisinalvesen. *Sundhetstilstanden og Medisinalforholdene. 1918–1921.*
 * N * 30, 40, 50, 60, 70 (G); 80+ (IS). *
 * Residual deaths by age altered to achieve conformity with total deaths by age as found in Bunle. *

Population: Bunle.

NORWAY—1930

Deaths: Direktoren for det Civile Medisinalvesen. *Sundhetstilstanden og Medisinalforholdene. 1930.*
 * N * 30, 40, 50, 60, 70 (G); 80+ (IS). *

Population: Bunle.

NORWAY—1946

Deaths: Direktoren for det Civile Medisinalvesen. *Sundhetstilstanden og Medisinalforholdene. 1946.*
 * 5th * 30, 40, 50, 60, 70 (G); 80+ (IS). *

Population: UN. *DY—60.*
 * Population 0–4 prorated as average of 1945 and 1947 (same source). *

NORWAY—1951

Deaths: WHO. *AEVS—51.*
 * 6th * Deaths 75–85+ and A85 and A86 from Statistisk Sentralbyra. *Sundhetstilstanden og Medisinalforholdene. 1951.*

Population: UN. *DY—60.*

NORWAY—1960

Deaths: WHO. *AEVS—60.*
 * 7th *

Population: UN. *DY—62.*

NORWAY—1964

Deaths: WHO. *AEVS—64.*
 * 7th *

Population: UN. *DY—66.*

PANAMA—1960

(Excluding Canal Zone and Jungle Population)
Deaths: WHO. *AEVS—60.*
 * 7th * Deaths from A85 and A86 estimated from 1964 rates, added to IV, subtracted from XII. *

Population: UN. *DY—61.*

PANAMA—1964

Deaths: WHO. *AEVS—64.*
 * 7th *

Population: UN. *DY—65, 66.*
 * Population interpolated linearly between 1962 and 1966. *

PHILIPPINES—1964

Deaths: WHO. *AEVS—64.*
 * 7th *

Population: WHO. *AEVS—64.*
 * 70+ prorated according to 1960 population (UN. *DY—68*). *

POLAND—1960

Deaths: WHO. *AEVS—60.*
 * 7th * A85 and A86 deaths obtained from data received in correspondence with Central Statistics Office, Warsaw, Poland. *

Population: UN. *DY—64.*
 * 345,653 added to male "age unknowns," 24,126 added to female "age unknowns," as result of footnote in source. *

POLAND—1964

Deaths: WHO. *AEVS—64.*
 * 7th *

Population: WHO. *AEVS—64.*

PORTUGAL—1920

Deaths: Direcção Geral da Estatística. *Anuário Demográfico. 1920.*
 * 3rd Abr. * 80+ (IS). *
Correction of errors in published table:

Sex	Cause	Age	Change
M	II	5	−3
M	II	30	+2
M	IV	50	−7
M	V	50	+9
M	XI	25	−70
M	XII	50	−2
F	V	10	+3
F	V	60	+1
F	XII	5	−100
F	XII	25	+100

Population: Bunle.

PORTUGAL—1930

Deaths: Direcção Geral da Estatística. *Anuário Demográfico. 1930.*
 * 3rd Abr. * 80+ (IS). *
Correction of errors in published table:

Sex	Cause	Age	Change
M	II	15	+60
M	II	20	−1
F	VII	80	+3
F	XII	20	+1

Population: Bunle.

PORTUGAL—1940

Deaths: Direcção Geral da Estatística. *Anuário Demográfico. 1940.*
 * 4th Abr. * 80+ (IS). *

Population: UN. *DY—60.*

PORTUGAL—1960

Deaths: WHO. *AEVS—60.*
* 7th *

Population: UN. *DY—67.*

PORTUGAL—1964

Deaths: WHO. *AEVS—64.*
* 7th *

Population: UN. *DY—65.*

PUERTO RICO—1960

Deaths: WHO. *AEVS—61.*
* 7th * A85 and A86 deaths obtained from data received in correspondence with Junta de Planificacion, Santurce, Puerto Rico. *

Population: UN. *DY—61.*

PUERTO RICO—1964

Deaths: WHO. *AEVS—64.*
* 7th *

Population: UN. *DY—65.*
* Population 75+ prorated from 1960 data (UN. *DY—62.*). *

SCOTLAND—1951

Deaths: WHO. *AEVS—51.*
* 6th * Deaths 75–85+ and A85 and A86 obtained from data received in correspondence with General Registrar's Office, Edinburgh, Scotland. *

Population: UN. *DY—60.*

SCOTLAND—1960

Deaths: WHO. *AEVS—60.*
* 7th *

Population: UN. *DY—61.*

SCOTLAND—1964

Deaths: WHO. *AEVS—64.*
* 7th *

Population: WHO. *AEVS—64.*

SOUTH AFRICA (colored)—1941

Deaths: Bureau of Census and Statistics. *Deaths. South Africa and Southwest Africa. 1958 and Previous Years.*
* 5th Abr. *

Population: Population in 1936 and 1946 estimated by Jan Sadie, *South African Journal of Economics.* March, 1970. These were projected forward and backward by appropriate life tables, and the mean of the two available estimates is presented for ages above 5. For 0–4, births in preceding 5 years were projected forward.

SOUTH AFRICA (white)—1941

Deaths: Bureau of Census and Statistics. *Deaths. South Africa and Southwest Africa. 1958 and Previous Years.*
* 5th Abr. *

Population: Bureau of Census and Statistics. *Population Census. 1941.*
* 0–4 divided by projecting forward births 1937–1941 by weighted mean of 1936 and 1946 life tables. *

SOUTH AFRICA (colored, white)—1951

Deaths: WHO. *AEVS—51.*
* 6th * Deaths 70+ from Bureau of Census and Statistics. *Deaths. South Africa and Southwest Africa. 1958 and Previous Years.* Vol. 2. *

Population: UN. *DY—60.*

SOUTH AFRICA (colored, white)—1960

Deaths: WHO. *AEVS—60.*
* 7th *

Population: Bureau of Census and Statistics. *Census of Population. 1960.*

SPAIN—1930

Deaths: Dirección General de Estadística. *Movimiento de la Población de España. 1930.*
* 3rd Abr. * 60, 70, 80+ (IS). *

Population: United States Public Health Service. *Summary of International Vital Statistics. 1937–1944. 1947.*

* Population 75+ prorated using 1940 data, UN. *DY—60.* *

SPAIN—1940

Deaths: Dirección General de Estadística. *Movimiento de la Población de España. 1940.*
* 4th Abr. * 70+ (IS). *

Population: UN. *DY—60.*

SPAIN—1960

Deaths: WHO. *AEVS—62.*
* 7th * Includes deaths of children whose birth was not registered (cause assumed "unknown"). * A85 and A86 deaths obtained from data received in correspondence with Instituto Nacional de Estadística, Madrid, Spain. *

Population: UN. *DY—66.*

SWEDEN—1911

Deaths: Statistika Centralbyrån. *Dödsorsaker år 1911.*
* N * 20, 30, 40, 50, 60 (G); 70+ (IS). *

Population: Bunle.

SWEDEN—1920

Deaths: Statistika Centralbyrån. *Dödsorsaker år 1920.*
* N * 20, 30, 40, 50 (G); 60, 70+ (IS). *

Population: Bunle.
* Population 0–4 prorated as 1920 population in *World Population.* *

SWEDEN—1930

Deaths: Statistika Centralbyrån. *Dödsorsaker år 1930.*
* * N * 60, 70+ (IS). *

Population: Bunle.

SWEDEN—1940

Deaths: Statistika Centralbyrån. *Dödsorsaker år 1940.*
* * N * 60, 70, 70+ (IS). *

Population: UN. *DY—60.*

SWEDEN—1951

Deaths: WHO. *AEVS—51.*
* * 6th * Deaths 75–85+ and A85 and A86 obtained from Central Bureau of Statistics, *Dödsorsaker. 1951.* *

Population: UN. *DY—60.*

SWEDEN—1960

Deaths: WHO. *AEVS—60.*
* * 7th *

Population: UN. *DY—61.*

SWEDEN—1964

Deaths: WHO. *AEVS—64.*
* * 7th *

Population: WHO. *AEVS—64.*

SWITZERLAND—1930

Deaths: Statistische Bureau. *Statistische Quellenwerke der Schweiz.* "Bevolkerung-bewegung in der Schweiz. 1930. "
* * N * 5–14 G, 20 (IS); 30, 40, 50, 60, 70 (G); 80+ (IS). *

Population: Bunle.

SWITZERLAND—1941

Deaths: Statistische Bureau. *Statistische Quellenwerke der Schweiz,* Heft 123. "Bevolkerung-bewegung in der Schweiz. 1941."
* * N * 20, 30, 40, 50, 60, 70 (G); 80+ (IS). *

Population: UN. *DY—60.*

SWITZERLAND—1951

Deaths: WHO. *AEVS—51.*
* * 6th * Deaths 75–85+ and A85 and A86 obtained from data received in correspondence with Federal Office of Statistics, Bern, Switzerland. *

Population: UN. *DY—60.*

SWITZERLAND—1960

Deaths: WHO. *AEVS—60.*
* * 7th *

Population: UN. *DY—61.*

SWITZERLAND—1964

Deaths: WHO. *AEVS—64.*
* * 7th *

Population: UN. *DY—65.*
* * 0–4 from *AEVS—64*; 80+ prorated from 1960 data in UN. *DY—67.* *

TAIWAN—1920

Deaths: Sotoku Kanbo Chosaka. *Jinko Dotai Tokei. 1920.*
* * N * 70+ (IS). *

Population: Sotoku Kanbo Chosaka. *Jinko Dotai Tokei. 1922.*
* * 70+ prorated according to 1930 population (see following). *

TAIWAN—1930

Deaths: Sotoku Kanbo Chosaka. *Jinko Dotai Tokei. 1930.*
* * N * 70+ (IS). *

Population: Sotoku Kanbo Chosaka. *Sotokufu Dai Yonju Tokeisho. 1936.*
* * 0–4 prorated according to population in 1926, from *Jinko Dotai Tokei. 1930.*
* * 80+ graduated by polynomial through 70–74. *

TAIWAN—1936

Deaths: Sotoku Kanbo Chosaka. *Jinko Dotai Tokei. 1936.*
* * N * 70+ (IS). *

Population: Same source as deaths.
* * 70+ prorated according to 1930 population (see preceding). *

TAIWAN—1960

Deaths: WHO. *AEVS—60.*
* * 7th * Deaths from A85 and A86 estimated from 1964 rates, added to IV and subtracted from XII. *
* * Includes deaths of infants whose births not registered (cause assumed "unknown"). *

Population: UN. *DY—61.*
* * 80+ prorated using 1956 data in UN. *DY—62.* *

TAIWAN—1964

Deaths: WHO. *AEVS—64.*
* * 7th *

Population: UN. *DY—65.*
* * 80+ prorated by projection of 1956 population to 1966 and linear interpolation between 1956 and 1966. *

TRINIDAD AND TOBAGO—1963

Deaths: WHO. *AEVS—63*.
  * 7th * "6" added to total of cause XI as result of published error. * A85 and A86 deaths obtained from data received in correspondence with Central Statistical Office, Port-of-Spain, Trinidad. *

Population: UN. *DY—65*.

UNITED STATES (REGISTRATION STATES)—1900

Deaths: Bureau of Census. *Special Reports. Mortality Statistics 1900–1904*.
  * N * The cause distribution of deaths in a particular age–sex category, available only for the Registration Area, is assumed to apply in the Registration States. *

Population: Supplied by United States Office of Health Statistics Analysis, Public Health Service.

UNITED STATES (REGISTRATION STATES)—1910
(Includes District of Columbia)

Deaths: Bureau of Census. *Mortality Statistics. 1910*.
  * 2nd * Cause X uses 175c. * The cause distribution of deaths in a particular age–sex category, available only for the Registration Area, is assumed to apply in the Registration States. *

Population: Supplied by United States Office of Health Statistics Analysis, Public Health Service. Washington, D.C. from United States Bureau of Census. *Census of Population. 1910*.

UNITED STATES (TOTAL, WHITE, NONWHITE) (REGISTRATION STATES)—1920
(Includes District of Columbia)

Deaths: Bureau of Census. *Mortality Statistics. 1920*.
  * 2nd *

Population: Supplied by United States Office of Health Statistics Analysis, Public Health Service. Washington, D.C. from United States Bureau of Census. *Census of Population. 1920*.

UNITED STATES (REGISTRATION STATES)—1930
(Includes District of Columbia)

Deaths: Bureau of Census. *Mortality Statistics. 1930*.
  * 4th *

Population: Supplied by United States Office of Health Statistics Analysis, Public Health Service. Washington, D.C. from United States Bureau of Census. *Census of Population. 1930*.

UNITED STATES—1940

Deaths: Bureau of Census. *Vital Statistics of the United States. 1940*. Part I.
  * 5th * II + 446; III − 446. *

Population: UN. *DY—60*.

UNITED STATES (TOTAL, WHITE, NONWHITE)—1950

Deaths: WHO. *AEVS—51*.
  * 6th * Deaths 75–85+ from United States Public Health Service, *Vital Statistics of the United States. 1950*. Vol. III, "Mortality Data." *

Population: Bureau of Census. *Census of Population. 1950*. Vol. II, Part I.
  * 75–85+ prorated using 20% sample in same volume. *

UNITED STATES—1960

Deaths: WHO. *AEVS—60*.
  * 7th *

Population: UN. *DY—61*.

UNITED STATES—1964

Deaths: WHO. *AEVS—64*.
  * 7th *

Population: WHO. *AEVS—64*.

VENEZUELA—1960
(Excluding Tribal Indians)

Deaths: WHO. *AEVS—60*.
  * 7th *

Population: WHO. *AEVS—60*.

VENEZUELA—1964
(Excluding Tribal Indians)

Deaths: WHO. *AEVS—64*.
  * 7th *

Population: UN. *DY—64*.
  * 0–4 from *AEVS—64*; 70+ prorated using 1961 data from UN. *DY—62*. *

YUGOSLAVIA—1961

Deaths: WHO. *AEVS—61*.
  * 7th * Deaths from A85 and A86 estimated from 1962 rates, added to IV, subtracted from XII. *

Population: UN. *DY—65*.

YUGOSLAVIA—1964

Deaths: WHO. *AEVS—64*.
  * 7th * BE 47, 49, 50 completely blank; probably in BE 48. *

Population: WHO. *AEVS—64*.

LIFE TABLES

POPULATION, DEATHS, DEATH RATES FOR ALL CAUSES COMBINED, AND SPECIFIED CAUSES

Age Start of Interval	Midyear Population	Deaths During Year	All Causes	Respiratory T. B.	Other Infec. and Paras.	Neoplasms	Cardiovascular	Infl., Pneu., Bronch.	Diarrheal	Certain Degenerative	Maternal	Cert. Dis. of Infancy	Motor Vehicle	Other Violence	Other and Unknown	Age Start of Interval
0	60553	4750	.07844	.00008	.00497	.00008	.00064	.00824	.01950	.00030	.00000	.03024	.00000	.00216	.01222	0
1	213422	1386	.00649	.00005	.00183	.00004	.00015	.00116	.00125	.00009	.00000	.00000	.00000	.00053	.00139	1
5	235222	515	.00219	.00001	.00080	.00005	.00020	.00018	.00005	.00006	.00000	.00000	.00000	.00043	.00041	5
10	221100	357	.00161	.00007	.00037	.00004	.00022	.00008	.00003	.00007	.00000	.00000	.00000	.00041	.00034	10
15	232399	556	.00239	.00024	.00036	.00006	.00031	.00015	.00001	.00010	.00000	.00000	.00000	.00066	.00049	15
20	233779	852	.00364	.00061	.00056	.00006	.00033	.00023	.00027	.00027	.00000	.00000	.00000	.00100	.00056	20
25	204829	867	.00423	.00093	.00060	.00009	.00030	.00021	.00002	.00019	.00000	.00000	.00000	.00114	.00075	25
30	175319	900	.00513	.00115	.00054	.00017	.00056	.00038	.00006	.00031	.00000	.00000	.00000	.00127	.00070	30
35	155599	986	.00634	.00111	.00060	.00021	.00088	.00061	.00005	.00044	.00000	.00000	.00000	.00150	.00094	35
40	148423	1262	.00850	.00156	.00067	.00056	.00139	.00073	.00003	.00082	.00000	.00000	.00000	.00153	.00118	40
45	136345	1471	.01079	.00153	.00086	.00098	.00203	.00085	.00004	.00115	.00000	.00000	.00000	.00164	.00171	45
50	110786	1677	.01514	.00136	.00086	.00190	.00367	.00135	.00013	.00170	.00000	.00000	.00000	.00181	.00235	50
55	73827	1575	.02133	.00171	.00095	.00289	.00626	.00140	.00019	.00228	.00000	.00000	.00000	.00232	.00336	55
60	52678	1627	.03089	.00159	.00087	.00475	.00907	.00266	.00038	.00319	.00000	.00000	.00000	.00247	.00590	60
65	41214	1958	.04751	.00150	.00080	.00764	.01606	.00355	.00066	.00425	.00000	.00000	.00000	.00247	.01017	65
70	29777	2116	.07106	.00131	.00087	.00692	.02354	.00823	.00144	.00463	.00000	.00000	.00000	.00249	.02163	70
75	19293	2158	.11185	.00073	.00109	.00788	.03416	.01374	.00223	.00658	.00000	.00000	.00000	.00342	.04204	75
80	9024	1570	.17398	.00055	.00144	.00942	.04499	.02493	.00388	.00898	.00000	.00000	.00000	.00377	.07602	80
85+	3513	1008	.28693	.00057	.00114	.01252	.05522	.03672	.00541	.00911	.00000	.00000	.00000	.00541	.16083	85+
ALL	2357102	27591														

CRUDE DEATH RATE			.01171	.00073	.00085	.00078	.00215	.00116	.00073	.00071	.00000	.00078	.00000	.00117	.00264	
STANDARDIZED RATE (1)			.01126	.00062	.00092	.00067	.00183	.00113	.00093	.00061	.00000	.00106	.00000	.00109	.00239	
STANDARDIZED RATE (2)			.01668	.00080	.00085	.00130	.00376	.00174	.00072	.00107	.00000	.00063	.00000	.00132	.00448	
GEOMETRIC MEAN			.01544													

LIFE TABLE FOR ALL CAUSES COMBINED

Age (x)	Midyear Population	Deaths During Year	$_nM_x$	$_nq_x$	l_x	$_nd_x$	$_nL_x$	$_nm_x$	$_na_x$	T_x	$_nr_x$	$\overset{\circ}{e}_x$	Age (x)
0	60553	4750	.078444	.073830	100000	7383	94118	.078444	.203354	5762663	.000000	57.627	0
1	213422	1386	.006494	.025557	92617	2367	364551	.006493	1.500000	5668545	.000000	61.204	1
5	235222	515	.002189	.010892	90250	983	448793	.002190	2.500000	5303994	.000000	58.770	5
10	221100	357	.001615	.008043	89267	718	444554	.001615	2.520021	4855202	.001372	54.390	10
15	232399	556	.002392	.011880	88549	1052	440255	.002389	2.670905	4410647	-.008281	49.810	15
20	233779	852	.003644	.018069	87497	1581	433689	.003645	2.598830	3970353	.002303	45.377	20
25	204829	867	.004233	.020974	85916	1802	425191	.004238	2.564165	3536664	.019246	41.164	25
30	175319	900	.005133	.025394	84114	2136	415389	.005142	2.574224	3111473	.023482	36.991	30
35	155599	986	.006337	.031264	81978	2563	403727	.006348	2.595429	2696085	.014506	32.888	35
40	148423	1262	.008503	.041680	79415	3310	389101	.008507	2.590886	2292358	.005676	28.866	40
45	136345	1471	.010789	.052651	76105	4007	370920	.010803	2.603049	1903257	.010727	25.008	45
50	110786	1677	.015137	.073400	72098	5292	347848	.015214	2.611056	1532336	.035841	21.254	50
55	73827	1575	.021334	.102206	66806	6828	317663	.021494	2.603007	1184489	.052655	17.730	55
60	52678	1627	.030886	.144520	59978	8668	279079	.031059	2.599119	866825	.034879	14.452	60
65	41214	1958	.047508	.213448	51310	10952	229506	.047637	2.567225	587746	.015711	11.455	65
70	29777	2116	.071062	.302344	40358	12202	171559	.071124	2.522435	358740	.004499	8.867	70
75	19293	2158	.111854	.435644	28156	12266	109545	.111972	2.453530	186281	.004535	6.616	75
80	9024	1570	.173980	.595721	15890	9466	54348	.174175	2.348163	76736	.004535	4.829	80
85+	3513	1008	.286934	1.000000	6424	6424	22388	.286934	3.485119	22388	.000000	3.485	85+

NUMBER OF PERSONS DYING (OUT OF 100,000 AT BIRTH) ABOVE AGE X FROM SPECIFIED CAUSES

Age (x)	All Causes	Respiratory T. B.	Other Infec. and Paras.	Neo-plasms	Cardio-vascular	Infl., Pneu., Bronch.	Diar-rheal	Certain Degen-erative	Maternal	Cert. Dis. of Infancy	Motor Vehicle	Other Violence	Other and Unknown	Age (x)
0	100000	5086	4763	8414	23611	10254	3619	6825	0	2846	0	8089	26493	0
1	92617	5079	4295	8407	23550	9478	1783	6797	0	0	0	7886	25342	1
5	90250	5060	3629	8391	23497	9055	1329	6763	0	0	0	7691	24835	5
10	89267	5056	3269	8370	23405	8975	1306	6736	0	0	0	7500	24650	10
15	88549	5026	3106	8354	23307	8940	1294	6706	0	0	0	7317	24499	15
20	87497	4922	2949	8328	23169	8872	1288	6661	0	0	0	7026	24282	20
25	85916	4658	2708	8300	23024	8772	1279	6542	0	0	0	6592	24041	25
30	84114	4263	2452	8262	22895	8681	1269	6463	0	0	0	6107	23722	30
35	81978	3784	2230	8193	22662	8523	1245	6332	0	0	0	5578	23431	35
40	79415	3337	1988	8107	22305	8277	1224	6153	0	0	0	4973	23051	40
45	76105	2732	1726	7889	21762	7991	1203	5833	0	0	0	4378	22591	45
50	72098	2166	1407	7526	21007	7675	1187	5405	0	0	0	3769	21956	50
55	66806	1692	1109	6859	19718	7202	1143	4811	0	0	0	3136	21136	55
60	59978	1148	808	5934	17711	6756	1082	4084	0	0	0	2398	20057	60
65	51310	704	564	4600	15162	6009	975	3190	0	0	0	1709	18397	65
70	40358	358	380	2840	11457	5096	823	2212	0	0	0	1139	16053	70
75	28156	133	230	1653	7416	3683	575	1417	0	0	0	713	12336	75
80	15890	54	111	790	3671	2177	331	695	0	0	0	338	7723	80
85+	6424	13	25	280	1236	822	121	204	0	0	0	121	3602	85+

NUMBER OF PERSONS SURVIVING TO AGE X IF SPECIFIED CAUSES WERE ELIMINATED

Age (x)	No Causes	Respiratory T. B.	Other Infec. and Paras.	Neo-plasms	Cardio-vascular	Infl., Pneu., Bronch.	Diar-rheal	Certain Degener-ative	Maternal	Cert. Dis. of Infancy	Motor Vehicle	Other Violence	Other and Unknown	(1) + (2)	(1) + (2) + (5) + (6) + (8)	(1)+(2)+ (5)+(6)+ (8)+part of(9)&(12)	(10) + (11)	Age (x)
		(1)	(2)	(3)	(4)	(5)	(6)	(7)	(8)	(9)	(10)	(11)	(12)					
0	100000	100000	100000	100000	100000	100000	100000	100000	100000	100000	100000	100000	100000	100000	100000	100000	100000	0
1	92617	92624	93068	92624	92676	93367	94400	92644	92617	95356	92617	92813	93731	93075	95635	99325	92813	1
5	90250	90275	91353	90272	90360	91402	92446	90310	90250	92958	90250	90634	91843	91379	94797	98914	90634	5
10	89267	89296	90721	89310	89467	90487	91546	89353	89267	91946	89267	89837	91031	90751	94254	98466	89837	10
15	88549	88608	90156	88608	88845	89795	90739	88664	88549	91206	88549	89298	90452	90216	93748	98008	89298	15
20	87497	87659	89244	87581	87927	88797	89667	87656	87497	90123	87497	88530	89558	89409	92988	97309	88530	20
25	85916	86337	87876	86026	86483	87293	88056	86190	85916	88494	85916	87366	88224	88307	91956	96353	87366	25
30	84114	84920	86292	84259	84798	85554	86219	84461	84114	86638	84114	86023	86698	87119	90828	95351	86023	30
35	81978	83242	84326	82188	82877	83540	84054	82446	81978	84438	81978	84374	84793	85626	89467	94081	84374	35
40	79415	81088	81935	79703	80642	81175	81447	80046	79415	81798	79415	82351	82530	83660	87703	92416	82351	40
45	76105	78315	78785	76556	77823	78078	78074	77026	76105	78389	76105	79525	79559	81072	85326	90130	79525	45
50	72098	74459	74958	72920	74481	74284	73979	73394	72098	74115	72098	75559	75559	77725	82171	87066	75559	50
55	66806	69746	69755	66221	70310	69302	68592	68591	66806	68811	66806	71028	71277	72824	77565	82466	71028	55
60	59978	63156	62923	62150	65157	62658	61641	62291	59978	61778	59978	64514	65092	66257	71137	75936	64514	60
65	51310	54460	54065	54462	58362	54330	52835	54152	51310	52850	51310	55876	57378	57384	62567	67228	55876	65
70	40358	43159	42695	44516	49791	43600	41697	43513	40358	41569	40358	44498	47522	45658	50962	55286	44498	70
75	28156	30307	29917	32148	39128	31718	29304	31072	28156	29001	28156	31433	37026	32203	37757	42064	31433	75
80	15890	17163	16977	18877	26273	19206	16727	18133	15890	16367	15890	18050	25954	18338	23333	27476	18050	80
85+	6424	6966	6920	8013	13408	8839	6900	7683	6424	6617	6424	7450	15564	7504	11090	14796	7450	85

ADDED YRS OF LIFE

	No Causes	(1)	(2)	(3)	(4)	(5)	(6)	(7)	(8)	(9)	(10)	(11)	(12)				
TOTAL		1.276	1.759	1.122	3.305	1.891	1.538	1.070	.000	1.723	.000	2.157	4.653	3.095	6.879	11.000	2.157
WORK	6.827	.927	.584	.381	.987	.453	.043	.487	.000	.000	.000	1.231	.960	1.531	2.059	2.463	1.231

POPULATION, DEATHS, DEATH RATES FOR ALL CAUSES COMBINED, AND SPECIFIED CAUSES

Age Start of Interval	Midyear Population	Deaths During Year	All Causes	Respiratory T.B.	Other Infec. and Paras.	Neoplasms	Cardiovascular	Infl., Pneu., Bronch.	Diarrheal	Certain Degenerative	Maternal	Cert. Dis. of Infancy	Motor Vehicle	Other Violence	Other and Unknown	Age Start of Interval
0	58192	3627	.06233	.00009	.00407	.00005	.00046	.00708	.01540	.00022	.00000	.02413	.00000	.00180	.00902	0
1	207370	1251	.00603	.00005	.00171	.00003	.00017	.00100	.00108	.00006	.00000	.00000	.00000	.00068	.00126	1
5	230019	458	.00199	.00003	.00083	.00003	.00018	.00013	.00009	.00005	.00000	.00000	.00000	.00024	.00040	5
10	218394	322	.00147	.00008	.00036	.00002	.00033	.00010	.00001	.00008	.00000	.00000	.00000	.00013	.00037	10
15	228008	491	.00215	.00052	.00042	.00004	.00029	.00008	.00001	.00017	.00015	.00000	.00000	.00018	.00030	15
20	224291	767	.00342	.00092	.00051	.00005	.00034	.00021	.00003	.00023	.00049	.00000	.00000	.00020	.00045	20
25	193812	807	.00416	.00118	.00035	.00011	.00042	.00024	.00005	.00026	.00075	.00000	.00000	.00019	.00062	25
30	164385	772	.00470	.00111	.00035	.00027	.00046	.00029	.00005	.00030	.00086	.00000	.00000	.00025	.00074	30
35	143528	837	.00583	.00104	.00044	.00047	.00086	.00048	.00009	.00045	.00088	.00000	.00000	.00027	.00086	35
40	128194	799	.00623	.00097	.00036	.00088	.00117	.00037	.00009	.00067	.00041	.00000	.00000	.00028	.00103	40
45	111622	893	.00800	.00082	.00029	.00167	.00194	.00051	.00018	.00088	.00005	.00000	.00000	.00024	.00142	45
50	87197	919	.01054	.00050	.00044	.00241	.00294	.00079	.00013	.00116	.00000	.00000	.00000	.00034	.00183	50
55	58541	871	.01488	.00072	.00044	.00313	.00459	.00113	.00013	.00190	.00000	.00000	.00000	.00043	.00188	55
60	45224	962	.02127	.00088	.00049	.00411	.00732	.00203	.00031	.00239	.00000	.00000	.00000	.00031	.00343	60
65	37500	1321	.03523	.00091	.00061	.00539	.01277	.00333	.00104	.00357	.00000	.00000	.00000	.00061	.00699	65
70	26746	1516	.05668	.00056	.00086	.00632	.02195	.00752	.00168	.00408	.00000	.00000	.00000	.00097	.01275	70
75	16970	1630	.09605	.00035	.00100	.00849	.03229	.01332	.00265	.00572	.00000	.00000	.00000	.00183	.03041	75
80	7908	1142	.14441	.00063	.00089	.00885	.04173	.02377	.00405	.00367	.00000	.00000	.00000	.00228	.05855	80
85+	3666	893	.24359	.00027	.00055	.01118	.05456	.03164	.00300	.00436	.00000	.00000	.00000	.00736	.13066	85+
ALL	2191567	20278														

		All Causes	Respiratory T.B.	Other Infec. and Paras.	Neoplasms	Cardiovascular	Infl., Pneu., Bronch.	Diarrheal	Certain Degenerative	Maternal	Cert. Dis. of Infancy	Motor Vehicle	Other Violence	Other and Unknown
CRUDE DEATH RATE		.00925	.00061	.00068	.00077	.00182	.00095	.00065	.00055	.00028	.00064	.00000	.00036	.00195
STANDARDIZED RATE (1)		.00912	.00054	.00075	.00070	.00163	.00094	.00080	.00050	.00025	.00085	.00000	.00037	.00179
STANDARDIZED RATE (2)		.01339	.00062	.00066	.00130	.00335	.00150	.00066	.00084	.00025	.00050	.00000	.00042	.00329
GEOMETRIC MEAN		.01280												

LIFE TABLE FOR ALL CAUSES COMBINED

Age (x)	Midyear Population	Deaths During Year	$_nM_x$	$_nq_x$	l_x	$_nd_x$	$_nL_x$	$_nm_x$	$_na_x$	T_x	$_nr_x$	$\overset{\circ}{e}_x$	Age (x)
0	58192	3627	.062328	.059280	100000	5928	95115	.062325	.175958	6143286	.000000	61.433	0
1	207370	1251	.006033	.023780	94072	2237	370696	.006035	1.500000	6048171	.000000	64.293	1
5	230019	458	.001991	.009898	91835	909	456903	.001989	2.500000	5677475	.000000	61.823	5
10	218394	322	.001474	.007347	90926	668	452972	.001475	2.517777	5220573	.000702	57.416	10
15	228008	491	.002153	.010703	90258	966	449052	.002151	2.682885	4767601	-.006221	52.822	15
20	224291	767	.003420	.016978	89292	1516	442846	.003423	2.616122	4318549	.005923	48.364	20
25	193812	807	.004164	.020632	87776	1811	434453	.004164	2.555563	3875703	.022145	44.154	25
30	164385	772	.004696	.023254	85965	1999	424954	.004704	2.563157	3441250	.025464	40.031	30
35	143528	837	.005832	.028765	83966	2417	413893	.005840	2.543701	3016296	.021050	35.923	35
40	128194	799	.006233	.030730	81549	2506	401624	.006240	2.557612	2602403	.017997	31.912	40
45	111622	893	.008000	.039546	79043	3110	387736	.008021	2.595056	2200779	.023599	27.843	45
50	87197	919	.010539	.051650	75933	3925	370290	.010600	2.611465	1813043	.046306	23.877	50
55	58541	871	.014878	.072353	72008	5210	347614	.014988	2.614923	1442753	.054321	20.036	55
60	45224	962	.021272	.101784	66798	6799	317946	.021384	2.640217	1095139	.030273	16.395	60
65	37500	1321	.035227	.163103	59999	9786	276729	.035363	2.622560	777193	.019038	12.953	65
70	26746	1516	.056681	.250055	50213	12556	220687	.056895	2.580639	500464	.018367	9.967	70
75	16970	1630	.096052	.388932	37657	14646	151577	.096624	2.493656	279776	.023782	7.430	75
80	7908	1142	.144411	.526270	23011	12110	83448	.145120	2.390001	128199	.023782	5.571	80
85+	3666	893	.243590	1.000000	10901	10901	44751	.243590	4.105263	44751	.000000	4.105	85+

NUMBER OF PERSONS DYING (OUT OF 100,000 AT BIRTH) ABOVE AGE X FROM SPECIFIED CAUSES

Age (x)	All Causes	Respiratory T. B.	Other Infec. and Paras.	Neoplasms	Cardiovascular	Infl., Pneu., Bronch.	Diarrheal	Certain Degenerative	Maternal	Cert. Dis. of Infancy	Motor Vehicle	Other Violence	Other and Unknown	Age (x)
0	100000	4055	3801	10178	27032	11428	3900	6443	1525	2295	0	2827	26516	0
1	94072	4047	3414	10173	26988	10754	2436	6422	1525	0	0	2655	25658	1
5	91835	4027	2781	10162	26925	10382	2035	6400	1525	0	0	2405	25193	5
10	90926	4015	2402	10148	26844	10321	1994	6376	1525	0	0	2294	25007	10
15	90258	3980	2240	10138	26696	10277	1987	6341	1525	0	0	2234	24840	15
20	89292	3748	2051	10120	26566	10240	1981	6266	1458	0	0	2155	24707	20
25	87776	3339	1826	10058	26414	10149	1970	6166	1238	0	0	2068	24508	25
30	85965	2827	1674	10051	26232	10043	1949	6051	913	0	0	1987	24238	30
35	83966	2355	1524	9934	26035	9919	1926	5924	548	0	0	1881	23920	35
40	81549	1925	1342	9739	25679	9720	1888	5739	185	0	0	1768	23564	40
45	79043	1537	1198	9384	25208	9569	1851	5469	24	0	0	1656	23147	45
50	75933	1222	1087	8734	24450	9370	1781	5128	4	0	0	1562	22595	50
55	72008	1036	925	7837	23354	9075	1734	4696	4	0	0	1434	21913	55
60	66758	785	771	6745	21603	8679	1638	4031	4	0	0	1285	21257	60
65	59999	504	616	5433	19262	8029	1539	3269	4	0	0	1187	20156	65
70	50213	253	446	3940	15712	7101	1249	2278	4	0	0	1016	18214	70
75	37657	130	255	2543	10852	5434	877	1377	4	0	0	801	15384	75
80	23011	76	103	1252	5934	3402	473	508	4	0	0	522	10737	80
85+	10901	12	24	500	2441	1416	134	195	0	0	0	330	5849	85+

NUMBER OF PERSONS SURVIVING TO AGE X IF SPECIFIED CAUSES WERE ELIMINATED

Age (x)	No Causes	Respiratory T. B. (1)	Other Infec. and Paras. (2)	Neoplasms (3)	Cardiovascular (4)	Infl., Pneu., Bronch. (5)	Diarrheal (6)	Certain Degenerative (7)	Maternal (8)	Cert. Dis. of Infancy (9)	Motor Vehicle (10)	Other Violence (11)	Other and Unknown (12)	(1) + (2)	(1) + (2) + (5) + (6) + (8)	(1)+(2)+ (5)+(6)+ (8)+part of(9)&(12)	(10) + (11)	Age (x)
0	100000	100000	100000	100000	100000	100000	100000	100000	100000	100000	100000	100000	100000	100000	100000	100000	100000	0
1	94072	94080	94448	94077	94115	94728	95502	94092	94072	96324	94072	94239	94908	94456	96561	99468	94239	1
5	91835	91862	92832	91851	91939	92846	93635	91877	91835	94034	91835	92246	93116	92860	95722	99002	92246	5
10	90926	90965	92295	90955	91110	91989	92749	90991	90926	93103	90926	91444	92382	92335	95287	98689	91444	10
15	90258	90332	91781	90297	90588	91357	92075	90358	90258	92415	90258	90832	91872	91856	94846	98323	90832	15
20	89292	89596	90990	89349	89748	90417	91096	89465	89359	91430	89292	89939	91024	91300	94388	97940	89939	20
25	87776	88483	89673	87854	88376	88973	89560	88046	88060	89877	87776	88499	89680	90395	93793	97481	88499	25
30	85965	87169	87676	86088	86734	87244	87734	86343	86567	88023	85965	86754	88103	89209	93045	96922	86754	30
35	83966	85617	86083	84202	84914	85339	85717	84462	84918	85976	83966	84842	86277	87775	92103	96183	84842	35
40	81549	83585	83789	81971	82826	83082	83288	82214	82836	83501	81549	82513	84252	85881	90770	95032	82513	40
45	79043	81409	81359	79805	80753	80661	80765	79956	80451	80935	79043	80089	82088	83794	88951	93331	80089	45
50	75933	78524	78270	77211	78339	77706	77658	77149	77305	77751	75933	77031	79422	80941	86242	90669	77031	50
55	72008	74652	74387	74209	75400	73984	73690	73590	73309	73732	72008	73176	76014	77118	82550	86958	73176	55
60	66758	69501	69158	69932	71723	69024	68453	68923	68005	68397	66758	68027	71184	71957	77574	81868	68027	60
65	59999	62704	62271	64126	66859	62638	61582	62656	61083	61435	59999	61197	65062	65078	70994	75196	61197	65
70	50213	52715	52275	55139	59660	53317	51812	53388	51120	51415	50213	51375	56413	54880	61214	65315	51375	70
75	37657	39642	39374	42687	50030	41546	39188	40867	38337	38559	37657	38719	45157	41450	48451	52524	38719	75
80	23011	24267	24182	27230	36036	27187	24273	25704	23427	23562	23011	23883	32307	25502	32357	36579	23883	80
85+	10901	11541	11512	13512	21177	14558	11742	12414	11101	11162	10901	11449	20692	12188	17854	22378	11449	85+

ADDED YRS OF LIFE

		(1)	(2)	(3)	(4)	(5)	(6)	(7)	(8)	(9)	(10)	(11)	(12)				
TOTAL		1.285	1.577	1.547	3.902	1.911	1.450	1.104	.592	1.467	.000	.774	4.584	2.907	7.267	11.125	.774
WORK	5.789	.939	.425	.557	.938	.341	.069	.458	.501	.000	.000	.240	.806	1.377	2.337	2.767	.240

POPULATION, DEATHS, DEATH RATES FOR ALL CAUSES COMBINED, AND SPECIFIED CAUSES

Age Start of Interval	Midyear Population	Deaths During Year	All Causes	Respiratory T.B.	Other Infec. and Paras.	Neoplasms	Cardio-vascular	Infl., Pneu., Bronch.	Diarrheal	Certain Degenerative	Maternal	Cert. Dis. of Infancy	Motor Vehicle	Other Violence	Other and Unknown	Age Start of Interval
0	68557	5119	.07467	.00004	.00474	.00007	.00034	.00786	.01677	.00023	.00000	.03294	.00000	.00059	.01068	0
1	238833	1695	.00710	.00002	.00188	.00005	.00009	.00112	.00170	.00008	.00000	.00000	.00000	.00069	.00146	1
5	303416	605	.00199	.00002	.00060	.00008	.00014	.00016	.00010	.00005	.00000	.00000	.00000	.00033	.00053	5
10	269641	465	.00172	.00001	.00029	.00004	.00018	.00008	.00004	.00011	.00000	.00000	.00000	.00048	.00049	10
15	235386	522	.00222	.00023	.00028	.00003	.00025	.00019	.00003	.00011	.00000	.00000	.00000	.00062	.00048	15
20	221174	709	.00321	.00062	.00038	.00005	.00030	.00024	.00004	.00017	.00000	.00000	.00000	.00089	.00051	20
25	225596	841	.00373	.00091	.00031	.00009	.00039	.00023	.00004	.00018	.00000	.00000	.00000	.00099	.00061	25
30	228269	1008	.00442	.00054	.00040	.00013	.00049	.00041	.00006	.00031	.00000	.00000	.00000	.00105	.00063	30
35	197556	1166	.00590	.00116	.00047	.00031	.00061	.00059	.00011	.00045	.00000	.00000	.00000	.00115	.00105	35
40	170598	1250	.00733	.00143	.00049	.00050	.00113	.00073	.00013	.00049	.00000	.00000	.00000	.00133	.00123	40
45	145065	1458	.01005	.00143	.00053	.00105	.00176	.00097	.00014	.00102	.00000	.00000	.00000	.00134	.00182	45
50	136392	1758	.01289	.00122	.00061	.00180	.00297	.00095	.00016	.00135	.00000	.00000	.00000	.00155	.00228	50
55	116584	2231	.01914	.00136	.00075	.00315	.00510	.00122	.00037	.00188	.00000	.00000	.00000	.00175	.00356	55
60	90827	2629	.02895	.00122	.00081	.00459	.00885	.00222	.00059	.00283	.00000	.00000	.00000	.00170	.00573	60
65	56221	2413	.04292	.00130	.00092	.00681	.01448	.00356	.00075	.00354	.00000	.00000	.00000	.00231	.00925	65
70	33435	2087	.06242	.00093	.00060	.00945	.02064	.00514	.00099	.00529	.00000	.00000	.00000	.00176	.01762	70
75	19645	1999	.10176	.00081	.00087	.01100	.03146	.01038	.00204	.00570	.00000	.00000	.00000	.00265	.03685	75
80	9608	1463	.15227	.00042	.00052	.00874	.04236	.01457	.00250	.00635	.00000	.00000	.00000	.00406	.07275	80
85+	4984	1234	.24759	.00040	.00140	.00903	.05377	.02909	.00682	.00762	.00000	.00000	.00000	.00381	.13563	85+
ALL	2771787	30652														

	All Causes	Respiratory T.B.	Other Infec. and Paras.	Neoplasms	Cardio-vascular	Infl., Pneu., Bronch.	Diarrheal	Certain Degenerative	Maternal	Cert. Dis. of Infancy	Motor Vehicle	Other Violence	Other and Unknown
CRUDE DEATH RATE	.01106	.00067	.00070	.00091	.00203	.00102	.00072	.00066	.00000	.00081	.00000	.00100	.00253
STANDARDIZED RATE (1)	.01042	.00055	.00078	.00071	.00161	.00100	.00092	.00053	.00000	.00116	.00000	.00092	.00224
STANDARDIZED RATE (2)	.01512	.00070	.00069	.00140	.00337	.00140	.00072	.00053	.00000	.00068	.00000	.00111	.00411
GEOMETRIC MEAN	.01413												

LIFE TABLE FOR ALL CAUSES COMBINED

Age (x)	Midyear Population	Deaths During Year	$_nM_x$	$_nq_x$	l_x	$_nd_x$	$_nL_x$	$_nm_x$	$_na_x$	T_x	$_nr_x$	$\overset{\circ}{e}_x$	Age (x)
0	68557	5119	.074668	.070440	100000	7044	94343	.074664	.196935	5904212	.000000	59.042	0
1	238833	1695	.007097	.027895	92956	2593	365342	.007097	1.500000	5809869	.000000	62.501	1
5	303416	605	.001994	.009916	90363	896	449575	.001994	2.500000	5444528	.000000	60.252	5
10	269641	465	.001725	.008595	89467	769	445430	.001726	2.523028	4994953	.018502	55.830	10
15	235386	522	.002218	.011060	88698	981	441168	.002224	2.633155	4549522	.020203	51.292	15
20	221174	709	.003206	.015915	87717	1396	435223	.003208	2.591482	4108354	.007584	46.836	20
25	225596	841	.003728	.018466	86321	1594	427715	.003737	2.559468	3673132	-.005727	42.552	25
30	228269	1008	.004416	.021847	84727	1851	419179	.004416	2.592518	3245417	-.002785	38.304	30
35	197556	1166	.005902	.029152	82876	2416	408559	.005913	2.590801	2826238	.018105	34.102	35
40	170598	1250	.007327	.036092	80460	2904	395331	.007346	2.600221	2417679	.023783	30.048	40
45	145065	1458	.010051	.049164	77556	3813	378604	.010071	2.593540	2022348	.016102	26.076	45
50	136392	1758	.012889	.062596	73743	4616	357702	.012905	2.614141	1643744	.008643	22.290	50
55	116584	2231	.019136	.091744	69127	6342	330558	.019183	2.629001	1286042	.014789	18.604	55
60	90827	2629	.028945	.136068	62785	8543	293459	.029111	2.604398	955444	.034138	15.218	60
65	56221	2413	.042920	.155845	54242	10623	245348	.043298	2.565444	661984	.053533	12.204	65
70	33435	2087	.062420	.272358	43619	11880	188871	.062900	2.540106	416636	.045354	9.552	70
75	19645	1999	.101756	.406755	31739	12910	126086	.102391	2.474100	227765	.026172	7.176	75
80	9608	1463	.152269	.545701	18829	10275	67131	.153060	2.370864	101679	.026172	5.400	80
85+	4984	1234	.247592	1.000000	8554	8554	34549	.247592	4.038858	34549	.000000	4.039	85+

NUMBER OF PERSONS DYING (OUT OF 100,000 AT BIRTH) ABOVE AGE X FROM SPECIFIED CAUSES

Age (x)	All Causes	Respiratory T.B.	Other Infec. and Paras.	Neo-plasms	Cardio-vascular	Infl., Pneu., Bronch.	Diar-rheal	Certain Degen-erative	Maternal	Cert. Dis. of Infancy	Motor Vehicle	Other Violence	Other and Unknown	Age (x)
0	100000	4607	3950	9873	23767	9179	3876	6454	0	3107	0	7024	28163	0
1	92956	4603	3502	9866	23735	8438	2294	6432	0	0	0	6930	27156	1
5	90363	4595	2816	9846	23703	8029	1671	6401	0	0	0	6680	26622	5
10	89467	4588	2548	9812	23640	7957	1628	6380	0	0	0	6530	26384	10
15	88658	4581	2419	9794	23560	7920	1612	6332	0	0	0	6315	26165	15
20	87717	4478	2295	9779	23449	7838	1599	6285	0	0	0	6040	25954	20
25	86321	4206	2132	9755	23317	7733	1581	6212	0	0	0	5652	25733	25
30	84727	3818	2001	9717	23151	7637	1566	6137	0	0	0	5230	25470	30
35	82876	3425	1834	9664	22945	7464	1542	6006	0	0	0	4789	25207	35
40	80460	2951	1642	9535	22696	7224	1497	5822	0	0	0	4319	24774	40
45	77556	2436	1447	9337	22249	6935	1443	5626	0	0	0	3793	24290	45
50	73743	1895	1246	8938	21581	6567	1391	5239	0	0	0	3286	23600	50
55	69127	1458	1028	8295	20517	6226	1333	4756	0	0	0	2732	22782	55
60	62785	1007	778	7251	18827	5822	1211	4133	0	0	0	2154	21602	60
65	54242	648	539	5779	16210	5165	1035	3299	0	0	0	1656	19911	65
70	43619	330	312	4056	12623	4283	851	2425	0	0	0	1086	17613	70
75	31739	156	200	2301	8658	3303	663	1420	0	0	0	754	14244	75
80	18829	54	90	912	4710	1984	405	699	0	0	0	418	9557	80
85+	8554	14	49	312	1858	1005	236	263	0	0	0	132	4685	85+

NUMBER OF PERSONS SURVIVING TO AGE X IF SPECIFIED CAUSES WERE ELIMINATED

Age (x)	No Causes	Respiratory T.B. (1)	Other Infec. and Paras. (2)	Neo-plasms (3)	Cardio-vascular (4)	Infl., Pneu., Bronch. (5)	Diar-rheal (6)	Certain Degen-erative (7)	Maternal (8)	Cert. Dis. of Infancy (9)	Motor Vehicle (10)	Other Violence (11)	Other and Unknown (12)	(1)+(2)	(1)+(2)+(5)+(6)+(8)	(1)+(2)+(5)+(6)+(8)+part of(9)&(12)	(10)+(11)	Age (x)
0	100000	100000	100000	100000	100000	100000	100000	100000	100000	100000	100000	100000	100000	100000	100000	100000	100000	0
1	92956	92960	93389	92963	92987	93673	94494	92977	92956	96000	92956	93047	93932	93393	95670	99614	93047	1
5	90363	90375	91466	90389	90425	91467	92484	90414	90363	93322	90363	90658	91845	91478	94765	99160	90698	5
10	89467	89485	90829	89527	89591	90633	91611	89539	89467	92396	89467	89949	91175	90848	94237	98758	89949	10
15	88658	88723	90179	88775	88900	89891	90840	88817	88658	91602	88658	89391	90614	90205	93626	98200	89391	15
20	87717	87845	89307	87808	88028	88980	89848	87881	87717	90589	87717	88679	89827	89437	92929	97567	88679	20
25	86321	86717	88050	86435	86758	87669	88437	86555	86321	89147	86321	87657	88622	88455	92038	96748	87657	25
30	84727	85503	86557	84876	85322	86147	86819	85032	84727	87501	84727	86464	87253	87350	91007	95803	86464	30
35	82876	84028	84835	83075	83663	84439	84947	83304	82876	85590	82876	85021	86014		89826	94702	85021	35
40	80460	82053	82556	80781	81473	82219	82516	81058	80460	83095	80460	83019	83561	84190	88229	93255	83019	40
45	77556	79609	79772	78061	78978	79542	79592	78327	77556	80095	77556	80557	81040	81884	86185	91338	80557	45
50	73743	76238	76052	74616	75762	76000	75731	74858	73743	76158	73743	77111	77762	78625	83216	88490	77111	50
55	69127	71903	71509	70579	72087	71583	71048	70648	69127	71390	69127	72847	73735	74381	79165	84451	72847	55
60	62785	65754	65195	65128	67176	65416	64650	64776	62785	64841	62785	66744	68180	68278	73251	78475	66744	60
65	54242	57155	56554	57701	60658	57155	56021	56766	54242	56018	54242	58155	60635	59592	64851	69898	58155	65
70	43619	46260	45689	48029	52540	46801	46473	46473	43619	45047	43619	47313	51122	48456	53898	58625	47313	70
75	31739	33815	33343	36660	42458	34961	33070	34734	31739	32778	31739	34730	40731	35524	40771	45042	34730	75
80	18829	20141	19868	22984	29579	21880	19825	21206	18829	19446	18829	20885	29257	21253	26003	29952	20885	80
85+	8554	9178	9055	10934	16728	10716	9124	9962	8554	8834	8554	9699	19322	9715	12982	16282	9699	85+

ADDED YRS OF LIFE

	No Causes	(1)	(2)	(3)	(4)	(5)	(6)	(7)	(8)	(9)	(10)	(11)	(12)	(1)+(2)	(1)+(2)+(5)+(6)+(8)	(1)+(2)+(5)+(6)+(8)+part of(9)&(12)	(10)+(11)
TOTAL		1.211	1.523	1.339	3.305	1.848	1.605	1.016	.000	1.927	.000	1.936	5.132	2.780	6.550	10.929	1.936
WORK	6.171	.879	.414	.397	.861	.459	.081	.415	.000	.000	.000	1.065	.570	1.306	1.876	2.284	1.065

POPULATION, DEATHS, DEATH RATES FOR ALL CAUSES COMBINED, AND SPECIFIED CAUSES

Age Start of Interval	Midyear Population	Deaths During Year	All Causes	Respiratory T. B.	Other Infec. and Paras.	Neoplasms	Cardiovascular	Infl., Pneu., Bronch.	Diarrheal	Certain Degenerative	Maternal	Cert. Dis. of Infancy	Motor Vehicle	Other Violence	Other and Unknown	Age Start of Interval
0	65708	3843	.05849	.00005	.00391	.00002	.00017	.00618	.01365	.00012	.00000	.02464	.00000	.00102	.00874	0
1	230763	1407	.00610	.00003	.00171	.00010	.00009	.00113	.00139	.00009	.00000	.00000	.00000	.00038	.00118	1
5	295969	567	.00192	.00001	.00071	.00016	.00018	.00016	.00006	.00007	.00000	.00000	.00000	.00017	.00053	5
10	262620	335	.00128	.00005	.00026	.00003	.00019	.00014	.00002	.00007	.00000	.00000	.00000	.00013	.00039	10
15	229857	478	.00208	.00032	.00032	.00006	.00026	.00019	.00003	.00011	.00016	.00000	.00000	.00016	.00049	15
20	233890	667	.00285	.00073	.00031	.00005	.00024	.00022	.00004	.00022	.00044	.00000	.00000	.00012	.00050	20
25	237625	894	.00376	.00092	.00025	.00011	.00036	.00031	.00002	.00021	.00071	.00000	.00000	.00019	.00066	25
30	222071	942	.00424	.00077	.00027	.00023	.00056	.00036	.00005	.00035	.00067	.00000	.00000	.00019	.00077	30
35	190428	1024	.00538	.00065	.00029	.00051	.00087	.00050	.00006	.00047	.00070	.00000	.00000	.00021	.00091	35
40	161628	911	.00564	.00062	.00023	.00100	.00108	.00050	.00007	.00042	.00003	.00000	.00000	.00019	.00102	40
45	135992	947	.00696	.00067	.00026	.00168	.00153	.00050	.00015	.00068	.00003	.00000	.00000	.00017	.00130	45
50	120218	1133	.00942	.00050	.00032	.00228	.00255	.00052	.00025	.00099	.00000	.00000	.00000	.00025	.00176	50
55	99808	1295	.01297	.00054	.00040	.00320	.00380	.00085	.00024	.00151	.00000	.00000	.00000	.00028	.00215	55
60	78904	1509	.01912	.00042	.00022	.00458	.00655	.00161	.00035	.00158	.00000	.00000	.00000	.00042	.00290	60
65	49019	1556	.03174	.00055	.00061	.00608	.01179	.00284	.00073	.00304	.00000	.00000	.00000	.00033	.00577	65
70	31906	1613	.05055	.00031	.00038	.00755	.01868	.00486	.00129	.00448	.00000	.00000	.00000	.00094	.01207	70
75	20470	1719	.08398	.00020	.00054	.01085	.03014	.00796	.00205	.00518	.00000	.00000	.00000	.00122	.02584	75
80	10392	1353	.13020	.00019	.00077	.00885	.03936	.01299	.00356	.00491	.00000	.00000	.00000	.00327	.05629	80
85+	5473	1231	.22492	.00037	.00055	.01005	.05153	.02796	.00512	.00439	.00000	.00000	.00000	.00420	.12077	85+
ALL	2682741	23424														
CRUDE DEATH RATE			.00873	.00046	.00055	.00093	.00175	.00084	.00059	.00053	.00024	.00060	.00000	.00026	.00197	
STANDARDIZED RATE (1)			.00835	.00041	.00065	.00076	.00142	.00083	.00076	.00045	.00021	.00087	.00000	.00026	.00174	
STANDARDIZED RATE (2)			.01210	.00046	.00054	.00142	.00299	.00116	.00062	.00077	.00021	.00051	.00000	.00031	.00310	
GEOMETRIC MEAN			.01161													

LIFE TABLE FOR ALL CAUSES COMBINED

Age (x)	Midyear Population	Deaths During Year	$_nM_x$	$_nq_x$	l_x	$_nd_x$	$_nL_x$	$_nm_x$	$_na_x$	T_x	$_nr_x$	$\overset{\circ}{e}_x$	Age (x)
0	65708	3843	.058486	.055780	100000	5578	95367	.058490	.169426	6305308	.000000	63.053	0
1	230763	1407	.006097	.024020	94422	2268	372018	.006096	1.500000	6209941	.000000	65.768	1
5	295969	567	.001916	.009538	92154	879	458573	.001917	2.500000	5837923	.000000	63.350	5
10	262620	335	.001276	.006354	91275	580	454938	.001275	2.521911	5379350	.019960	58.936	10
15	229857	478	.002080	.010364	90695	940	451269	.002083	2.653147	4924413	.015000	54.296	15
20	233890	667	.002852	.014161	89755	1271	445745	.002851	2.616214	4473144	-.002032	49.837	20
25	237625	894	.003762	.018636	88484	1649	438413	.003761	2.569992	4027398	-.001879	45.516	25
30	222071	942	.004242	.021017	86835	1825	429740	.004247	2.569635	3588985	.011866	41.331	30
35	190428	1024	.005377	.026573	85010	2259	419502	.005385	2.544083	3159246	.022732	37.163	35
40	161628	911	.005636	.027830	82751	2303	408102	.005643	2.545502	2739744	.027517	33.108	40
45	135992	947	.006964	.034333	80448	2762	395603	.006982	2.597076	2331642	.023927	28.983	45
50	120218	1133	.009425	.046212	77686	3590	379854	.009451	2.611247	1936038	.021422	24.921	50
55	99808	1295	.012975	.063148	74096	4679	359368	.013020	2.625071	1556184	.023618	21.002	55
60	78904	1509	.019125	.092182	69417	6399	332072	.019270	2.653800	1196816	.042592	17.241	60
65	49019	1556	.031743	.149211	63018	9403	292784	.032116	2.627756	864745	.058248	13.722	65
70	31906	1613	.050565	.226933	53615	12167	238715	.050969	2.586933	571960	.040892	10.668	70
75	20470	1719	.083977	.349353	41448	14480	171259	.084551	2.515093	333245	.029240	8.040	75
80	10392	1353	.130196	.490062	26968	13216	100846	.131052	2.427786	161987	.029240	6.007	80
85+	5473	1231	.224922	1.000000	13752	13752	61141	.224922	4.445979	61141	.000000	4.446	85+

NUMBER OF PERSONS DYING (OUT OF 100,000 AT BIRTH) ABOVE AGE X FROM SPECIFIED CAUSES

Age (x)	All Causes	Respiratory T. B.	Other Infec. and Paras.	Neoplasms	Cardiovascular	Infl., Pneu., Bronch.	Diarrheal	Certain Degenerative	Maternal	Cert. Dis. of Infancy	Motor Vehicle	Other Violence	Other and Unknown	Age (x)
0	100000	3082	3100	12102	27117	9687	3893	6360	1297	2350	0	2349	28663	0
1	94422	3077	2726	12101	27101	9098	2591	6348	1297	0	0	2251	27832	1
5	92154	3064	2090	12065	27069	8678	2075	6314	1297	0	0	2110	27392	5
10	91275	3058	1763	12053	26988	8606	2046	6283	1297	0	0	2034	27147	10
15	90655	3037	1646	12039	26903	8543	2035	6250	1297	0	0	1975	26970	15
20	89755	2893	1502	12011	26786	8459	2023	6201	1225	0	0	1904	26751	20
25	88484	2569	1365	11990	26677	8362	2006	6102	1031	0	0	1853	26529	25
30	86835	2165	1254	11942	26520	8225	1992	6008	719	0	0	1771	26239	30
35	85010	1832	1136	11841	26278	8068	1968	5859	431	0	0	1690	25907	35
40	82751	1475	1015	11624	25911	7858	1944	5662	136	0	0	1602	25524	40
45	80448	1140	922	11215	25468	7654	1914	5490	14	0	0	1526	25105	45
50	77686	876	817	10549	24860	7456	1855	5222	3	0	0	1459	24589	50
55	74096	686	654	9681	23889	7257	1760	4844	3	0	0	1364	23918	55
60	69417	492	550	8528	22518	6949	1673	4299	3	0	0	1263	23142	60
65	63018	319	478	7001	20321	6409	1554	3639	3	0	0	1124	22170	65
70	53615	158	297	5210	16825	5568	1336	2740	3	0	0	1028	20450	70
75	41448	84	208	3398	12330	4398	1027	1664	3	0	0	801	17535	75
80	26968	51	115	1534	7138	3025	673	775	3	0	0	590	13064	80
85+	13752	22	34	614	3150	1709	313	268	0	0	0	257	7385	85+

NUMBER OF PERSONS SURVIVING TO AGE X IF SPECIFIED CAUSES WERE ELIMINATED

Age (x)	No Causes	Respiratory T. B.	Other Infec. and Paras.	Neoplasms	Cardiovascular	Infl., Pneu., Bronch.	Diarrheal	Certain Degenerative	Maternal	Cert. Dis. of Infancy	Motor Vehicle	Other Violence	Other and Unknown	(1) + (2)	(1) + (2) + (5) + (6) + (8)	(1)+(2)+(5)+(6)+(8)+part of(9)&(12)	(10) + (11)	Age (x)
		(1)	(2)	(3)	(4)	(5)	(6)	(7)	(8)	(9)	(10)	(11)	(12)					
0	100000	100000	100000	100000	100000	100000	100000	100000	100000	100000	100000	100000	100000	100000	100000	100000	100000	0
1	94422	94427	94786	94423	94438	94996	95656	94434	94422	96733	94422	94517	95233	94791	96653	99696	94517	1
5	92154	92172	93142	92151	92201	93133	93515	92199	92154	94410	92154	92387	93385	93160	95948	99375	92387	5
10	91275	91298	92583	91323	91402	92317	93049	91350	91275	93509	91275	91581	92741	92607	95484	99075	91581	10
15	90655	90739	92113	90757	90906	91794	92469	90803	90655	92915	90655	91058	92232	92158	95059	98776	91058	15
20	89755	89942	91304	89844	90081	90927	91522	89911	89827	91952	89755	90185	91597	91495	94590	98398	90185	20
25	88484	88592	90150	88593	88914	89737	90243	88736	88748	90650	88484	88959	90525	90667	94059	98025	88959	25
30	86835	87736	88582	86989	87413	88202	88576	87176	87404	88960	86835	87383	89132	89501	93341	97509	87383	30
35	85010	86226	86839	85261	85818	86506	86738	85492	85855	87091	85010	85627	87597	88081	92363	96717	85627	35
40	82751	84293	84654	83211	83904	84419	84458	83416	83867	84776	82751	83439	85659	86231	90994	95517	83439	40
45	80448	82391	81302	82013	82275	82137	81265	81655	81655	82217	80448	81193	83704	84271	89315	93955	81193	45
50	77686	79724	79668	79175	79809	79649	79377	78742	78862	79587	77686	78472	81360	81758	86946	91632	78472	50
55	74096	76230	76110	76385	77101	76168	75803	75478	75218	75910	74096	74939	78289	78302	83593	88261	74939	55
60	69417	71609	71447	72721	73628	71666	71103	71251	70468	71116	69417	70306	74142	73703	79118	83706	70306	60
65	63018	65178	64931	67557	69099	65593	64665	65331	63972	64650	63018	63959	68305	67157	72813	77224	63959	65
70	53615	55605	55414	59267	62429	56619	55223	56447	54427	54927	53615	54505	55862	57471	63457	67666	54505	70
75	41448	43052	42918	47600	53073	44867	42971	44637	42076	42462	41448	42339	49235	44579	50787	54754	42339	75
80	26968	28038	28002	32716	40265	30406	28254	29810	27376	27628	26968	27721	36621	29113	34910	38586	27721	80
85+	13752	14319	14338	17464	25160	16580	14674	15599	13962	14089	13752	14378	24942	14929	19501	23087	14378	85+

ADDED YRS OF LIFE

		(1)	(2)	(3)	(4)	(5)	(6)	(7)	(8)	(9)	(10)	(11)	(12)				
TOTAL		1.016	1.384	1.870	3.875	1.854	1.454	1.068	.527	1.539	.000	.580	5.149	2.429	6.583	10.573	.580
WORK	5.238	.732	.307	.587	.840	.384	.071	.396	.436	.000	.000	.188	.882	1.045	1.973	2.434	.188

POPULATION, DEATHS, DEATH RATES FOR ALL CAUSES COMBINED, AND SPECIFIED CAUSES

Age Start of Interval	Midyear Population	Deaths During Year	All Causes	Respiratory T. B.	Other Infec. and Paras.	Neoplasms	Cardiovascular	Infl., Pneu., Bronch.	Diarrheal	Certain Degenerative	Maternal	Cert. Dis. of Infancy	Motor Vehicle	Other Violence	Other and Unknown	Age Start of Interval
0	54054	2500	.04625	.00002	.00185	.00011	.00013	.00614	.00259	.00019	.00000	.02586	.00002	.00096	.00840	0
1	237289	928	.00391	.00001	.00096	.00010	.00005	.00099	.00040	.00006	.00000	.00000	.00008	.00052	.00073	1
5	319902	467	.00146	.00001	.00034	.00006	.00012	.00016	.00003	.00004	.00000	.00000	.00014	.00023	.00034	5
10	318490	367	.00115	.00002	.00014	.00005	.00014	.00011	.00001	.00007	.00000	.00000	.00006	.00027	.00030	10
15	311433	525	.00169	.00011	.00012	.00009	.00018	.00013	.00002	.00008	.00000	.00000	.00017	.00042	.00036	15
20	297657	679	.00228	.00031	.00012	.00010	.00014	.00015	.00001	.00016	.00000	.00000	.00033	.00063	.00032	20
25	277143	689	.00249	.00039	.00014	.00013	.00018	.00018	.00001	.00020	.00000	.00000	.00021	.00065	.00039	25
30	251224	747	.00297	.00054	.00016	.00018	.00027	.00030	.00002	.00024	.00000	.00000	.00015	.00066	.00043	30
35	228394	881	.00386	.00067	.00027	.00028	.00048	.00038	.00002	.00039	.00000	.00000	.00021	.00070	.00046	35
40	229557	1219	.00531	.00076	.00031	.00053	.00093	.00054	.00003	.00036	.00000	.00000	.00013	.00074	.00098	40
45	209083	1685	.00806	.00095	.00041	.00082	.00193	.00075	.00003	.00119	.00000	.00000	.00024	.00091	.00084	45
50	171489	1992	.01162	.00112	.00048	.00161	.00311	.00105	.00004	.00147	.00000	.00000	.00016	.00108	.00149	50
55	132164	2378	.01799	.00132	.00073	.00268	.00586	.00154	.00008	.00216	.00000	.00000	.00022	.00120	.00221	55
60	114725	3031	.02642	.00108	.00072	.00489	.00980	.00191	.00013	.00271	.00000	.00000	.00021	.00126	.00371	60
65	92842	3757	.04047	.00102	.00090	.00748	.01686	.00276	.00011	.00436	.00000	.00000	.00033	.00137	.00528	65
70	65943	4243	.06434	.00097	.00074	.01130	.02777	.00510	.00035	.00623	.00000	.00000	.00032	.00135	.01022	70
75	35880	3482	.09705	.00056	.00098	.01290	.04083	.00981	.00047	.00875	.00000	.00000	.00042	.00198	.02035	75
80	13845	2185	.15782	.00022	.00072	.01423	.06414	.01758	.00116	.01264	.00000	.00000	.00036	.00274	.04363	80
85+	5997	1495	.24929	.00017	.00133	.01267	.09055	.03335	.00100	.01451	.00000	.00000	.00067	.00467	.09038	85+
ALL	3367111	33250														

			All Causes	Respiratory T. B.	Other Infec. and Paras.	Neoplasms	Cardiovascular	Infl., Pneu., Bronch.	Diarrheal	Certain Degenerative	Maternal	Cert. Dis. of Infancy	Motor Vehicle	Other Violence	Other and Unknown
CRUDE DEATH RATE			.00987	.00047	.00039	.00117	.00290	.00096	.00011	.00086	.00000	.00042	.00018	.00070	.00171
STANDARDIZED RATE (1)			.00811	.00036	.00042	.00077	.00184	.00087	.00017	.00059	.00000	.00091	.00017	.00062	.00141
STANDARDIZED RATE (2)			.01323	.00048	.00043	.00155	.00420	.00132	.00015	.00113	.00000	.00054	.00019	.00075	.00251
GEOMETRIC MEAN			.01117												

LIFE TABLE FOR ALL CAUSES COMBINED

Age (x)	Midyear Population	Deaths During Year	$_nM_x$	$_nq_x$	l_x	$_nd_x$	$_nL_x$	$_nm_x$	$_na_x$	T_x	$_nr_x$	$\overset{\circ}{e}_x$	Age (x)
0	54054	2500	.046250	.044500	100000	4450	96211	.046252	.148625	6357299	.000000	63.573	0
1	237289	928	.003911	.015489	95550	1480	378500	.003910	1.500000	6261088	.000000	65.527	1
5	319902	467	.001460	.007271	94070	684	468640	.001460	2.500000	5882588	.000000	62.534	5
10	318490	367	.001152	.005750	93386	537	465607	.001153	2.537244	5413948	.000501	57.974	10
15	311433	525	.001686	.008401	92849	780	462401	.001687	2.635417	4948341	.003377	53.294	15
20	297657	679	.002281	.011339	92069	1044	457807	.002280	2.569045	4485940	.007334	48.724	20
25	277143	689	.002486	.012370	91025	1126	452369	.002489	2.552731	4028133	.012002	44.253	25
30	251224	747	.002973	.014783	89899	1329	446291	.002978	2.589039	3575763	.017095	39.775	30
35	228394	881	.003857	.019126	88570	1694	438813	.003860	2.616834	3129473	.008807	35.333	35
40	229557	1219	.005310	.026233	86876	2279	429028	.005312	2.651656	2690660	.002009	30.971	40
45	209083	1685	.008059	.039635	84597	3353	415089	.008078	2.645206	2261632	.013993	26.734	45
50	171489	1992	.011616	.056817	81244	4616	395365	.011675	2.648352	1846542	.030663	22.728	50
55	132164	2378	.017993	.086652	76628	6640	367393	.018073	2.628514	1451177	.026524	18.938	55
60	114725	3031	.026420	.124478	69988	8712	329135	.026469	2.611915	1083784	.011665	15.485	60
65	92842	3757	.040467	.184738	61276	11320	279167	.040549	2.595995	754649	.010994	12.316	65
70	65943	4243	.064343	.278805	49956	13928	215549	.064616	2.542301	475482	.021040	9.518	70
75	35880	3482	.097046	.392655	36028	14148	144436	.097953	2.476395	259933	.048170	7.215	75
80	13845	2185	.157819	.563300	21880	12325	77169	.159715	2.384872	115497	.048170	5.279	80
85+	5997	1495	.249291	1.000000	9555	9555	38329	.249291	4.011371	38329	.000000	4.011	85+

NUMBER OF PERSONS DYING (OUT OF 100,000 AT BIRTH) ABOVE AGE X FROM SPECIFIED CAUSES

Age (x)	All Causes	Respiratory T.B.	Other Infec. and Paras.	Neoplasms	Cardiovascular	Infl., Pneu., Bronch.	Diarrheal	Certain Degenerative	Maternal	Cert. Dis. of Infancy	Motor Vehicle	Other Violence	Other and Unknown	Age (x)
0	100000	3529	2791	12279	33708	9751	872	8887	0	2488	1253	5246	19196	0
1	95550	3527	2614	12269	33696	9160	622	8869	0	0	1252	5154	18387	1
5	94070	3522	2251	12230	33678	8785	471	8845	0	0	1221	4956	18111	5
10	93386	3518	2091	12204	33624	8711	458	8828	0	0	1156	4848	17948	10
15	92849	3509	2027	12181	33560	8658	455	8797	0	0	1129	4722	17811	15
20	92069	3458	1972	12139	33475	8597	447	8759	0	0	1050	4527	17645	20
25	91025	3318	1916	12091	33409	8526	444	8685	0	0	898	4239	17499	25
30	89899	3143	1853	12032	33325	8446	438	8593	0	0	802	3944	17323	30
35	88570	2901	1781	11950	33202	8311	427	8484	0	0	736	3647	17131	35
40	86876	2607	1664	11825	32991	8144	417	8313	0	0	646	3340	16929	40
45	84557	2282	1531	11597	32590	7914	403	8158	0	0	592	3022	16508	45
50	81244	1888	1360	11255	31786	7603	391	7664	0	0	492	2644	16161	50
55	76628	1445	1171	10614	30546	7187	374	7081	0	0	428	2217	15565	55
60	69988	961	903	9623	28381	6618	346	6283	0	0	347	1775	14751	60
65	61276	605	665	8010	25148	5588	303	5350	0	0	278	1361	13528	65
70	49956	320	412	5920	20431	5217	273	4170	0	0	185	979	12049	70
75	36028	111	252	3477	14421	4112	198	2822	0	0	116	688	9831	75
80	21880	32	111	1608	8472	2676	128	1548	0	0	56	400	6849	80
85+	9555	6	51	486	3470	1278	38	556	0	0	26	179	3465	85+

NUMBER OF PERSONS SURVIVING TO AGE X IF SPECIFIED CAUSES WERE ELIMINATED

Age (x)	No Causes	Respiratory T.B. (1)	Other Infec. and Paras. (2)	Neoplasms (3)	Cardiovascular (4)	Infl., Pneu., Bronch. (5)	Diarrheal (6)	Certain Degenerative (7)	Maternal (8)	Cert. Dis. of Infancy (9)	Motor Vehicle (10)	Other Violence (11)	Other and Unknown (12)	(1)+(2)	(1)+(2)+(5)+(6)+(8)	(1)+(2)+(5)+(6)+(8)+part of(9)&(12)	(10)+(11)	Age (x)
0	100000	100000	100000	100000	100000	100000	100000	100000	100000	100000	100000	100000	100000	100000	100000	100000	100000	0
1	95550	95552	95723	95560	95562	96129	95795	95568	95550	98013	95551	95640	96344	95725	96552	99476	95641	1
5	94070	94077	94602	94118	94099	95016	94461	94111	94070	96495	94102	94355	95128	94609	95957	99077	94387	5
10	93386	93397	94075	93460	93469	94399	93787	93444	93386	95793	93482	93777	94601	94086	95515	98703	93874	10
15	92849	92869	93558	92545	92955	93910	93251	92937	92849	95242	92972	93364	94195	93618	95097	98318	93488	15
20	92069	92139	92867	92206	92299	93182	92476	92195	92069	94442	92270	92775	93572	92938	94477	97727	92978	20
25	91025	91234	91870	91209	91318	92197	91430	91223	91025	93371	91375	92012	92659	92081	93682	96951	92366	25
30	89899	90280	90797	90139	90272	91137	90305	90186	89899	92216	90340	91171	91691	91182	92855	96159	91619	30
35	88570	89187	89527	88888	89061	89926	88981	88961	88570	90853	89071	90123	90530	90150	91955	95310	90632	35
40	86876	87775	87932	87313	87568	88374	87289	87430	86876	89115	87457	88709	89003	88841	90803	94201	89302	40
45	84557	85797	85759	85249	85671	86287	85013	85291	84557	86778	85216	86703	87095	86974	89148	92656	87337	45
50	81244	82788	82529	82209	83077	83178	81655	82400	81244	83338	81937	83646	83993	84097	86536	90052	84360	50
55	76628	78524	78026	78171	79599	78667	77033	78294	76628	78603	77344	79321	79822	79956	82727	86261	80063	55
60	69988	72193	71526	72371	74885	72594	70385	72293	69988	71792	70720	72885	73720	73780	76961	80455	73648	60
65	61276	63549	62850	64942	68883	64171	61664	64162	61276	62656	61982	64215	65759	65181	68692	72037	64955	65
70	49956	52074	51472	54578	61151	53049	50299	53472	49956	51244	50616	52712	55063	53654	57368	60380	53409	70
75	36028	37737	37259	41979	50780	39268	36340	39979	36028	36957	36563	38274	41844	39027	42905	45472	38842	75
80	21880	22979	22739	27208	38022	25093	22124	25276	21880	22444	22251	23480	28256	23881	27693	29838	23879	80
85+	9555	10052	9970	12813	23240	12038	9720	11799	9555	9801	9737	10407	15491	10489	13443	15076	10605	85+

ADDED YRS OF LIFE

	No Causes	(1)	(2)	(3)	(4)	(5)	(6)	(7)	(8)	(9)	(10)	(11)	(12)	(1)+(2)	(1)+(2)+(5)+(6)+(8)	part of(9)&(12)	(10)+(11)
TOTAL		.848	.890	1.604	4.599	1.773	.326	1.240	.000	1.635	.382	1.429	3.104	1.758	3.982	6.809	1.825
WORK	4.833	.538	.232	.417	.815	.365	.023	.431	.000	.000	.223	.725	.631	.775	1.197	1.404	.953

POPULATION, DEATHS, DEATH RATES FOR ALL CAUSES COMBINED, AND SPECIFIED CAUSES

Age Start of Interval	Midyear Population	Deaths During Year	All Causes	Respiratory T.B.	Other Infec. and Paras.	Neoplasms	Cardiovascular	Infl., Pneu., Bronch.	Diarrheal	Certain Degenerative	Maternal	Cert. Dis. of Infancy	Motor Vehicle	Other Violence	Other and Unknown	Age Start of Interval
0	51637	1897	.03674	.00004	.00190	.00008	.00012	.00471	.00174	.00008	.00000	.02088	.00010	.00081	.00629	0
1	227608	798	.00351	.00004	.00104	.00010	.00006	.00082	.00036	.00006	.00000	.00000	.00005	.00032	.00067	1
5	309264	361	.00117	.00001	.00038	.00003	.00008	.00014	.00003	.00005	.00000	.00000	.00007	.00010	.00027	5
10	308514	264	.00086	.00004	.00017	.00003	.00012	.00008	.00001	.00007	.00000	.00000	.00003	.00009	.00021	10
15	303310	405	.00134	.00025	.00009	.00004	.00015	.00013	.00000	.00014	.00010	.00000	.00004	.00012	.00029	15
20	286324	573	.00200	.00053	.00010	.00010	.00017	.00017	.00002	.00014	.00035	.00000	.00003	.00012	.00027	20
25	256250	663	.00259	.00068	.00015	.00017	.00020	.00016	.00000	.00017	.00044	.00000	.00004	.00018	.00040	25
30	237426	703	.00296	.00053	.00009	.00030	.00035	.00030	.00002	.00023	.00059	.00000	.00003	.00014	.00039	30
35	237257	908	.00383	.00048	.00014	.00058	.00056	.00034	.00004	.00045	.00050	.00000	.00003	.00015	.00058	35
40	226242	980	.00433	.00037	.00013	.00108	.00075	.00038	.00003	.00052	.00027	.00000	.00001	.00018	.00061	40
45	199188	1169	.00587	.00034	.00014	.00149	.00142	.00048	.00005	.00081	.00005	.00000	.00006	.00017	.00086	45
50	162610	1367	.00841	.00028	.00017	.00232	.00252	.00055	.00058	.00098	.00000	.00000	.00007	.00022	.00123	50
55	128728	1491	.01158	.00032	.00015	.00307	.00400	.00068	.00006	.00153	.00000	.00000	.00008	.00023	.00147	55
60	113631	1991	.01752	.00034	.00021	.00399	.00708	.00100	.00009	.00246	.00000	.00000	.00008	.00015	.00212	60
65	90407	2614	.02891	.00038	.00037	.00531	.01303	.00205	.00017	.00348	.00000	.00000	.00013	.00038	.00363	65
70	64219	2987	.04651	.00037	.00044	.00656	.02191	.00416	.00020	.00526	.00000	.00000	.00009	.00055	.00657	70
75	36219	2822	.07791	.00030	.00041	.00975	.03755	.00715	.00041	.00826	.00000	.00000	.00017	.00097	.01295	75
80	15722	1950	.12403	.00045	.00045	.01018	.05629	.01336	.00070	.00700	.00000	.00000	.00013	.00318	.03231	80
85+	8172	1924	.23544	.00000	.00024	.01309	.09410	.02753	.00196	.01138	.00000	.00000	.00000	.00698	.08015	85+
ALL	3262728	25867														
CRUDE DEATH RATE			.00793	.00031	.00027	.00112	.00252	.00073	.00010	.00074	.00018	.00033	.00005	.00022	.00136	
STANDARDIZED RATE (1)			.00636	.00027	.00034	.00074	.00151	.00065	.00013	.00049	.00016	.00073	.00005	.00021	.00107	
STANDARDIZED RATE (2)			.01027	.00031	.00029	.00137	.00352	.00097	.00012	.00092	.00016	.00043	.00005	.00027	.00186	
GEOMETRIC MEAN			.00902													

LIFE TABLE FOR ALL CAUSES COMBINED

Age (x)	Midyear Population	Deaths During Year	$_nM_x$	$_nq_x$	l_x	$_nd_x$	$_nL_x$	$_nm_x$	$_na_x$	T_x	$_nr_x$	$\overset{\circ}{e}_x$	Age (x)
0	51637	1897	.036737	.035600	100000	3560	96912	.036735	.132453	6734910	.000000	67.349	0
1	227608	798	.003506	.013905	96440	1341	382408	.003507	1.500000	6637998	.000000	68.830	1
5	309264	361	.001167	.005815	95099	553	474113	.001166	2.500000	6255591	.000000	65.780	5
10	308514	264	.000856	.004273	94546	404	471735	.000856	2.538160	5781478	.000098	61.150	10
15	303310	405	.001335	.006660	94142	627	469253	.001336	2.675771	5309743	.003274	56.401	15
20	286324	573	.002001	.009977	93515	933	465340	.002005	2.626161	4840490	.011497	51.762	20
25	256250	663	.002587	.012875	92582	1192	460016	.002591	2.571833	4375130	.016927	47.257	25
30	237426	703	.002961	.014706	91390	1344	453697	.002962	2.579830	3915114	.008516	42.840	30
35	237257	908	.003827	.018957	90046	1707	446077	.003827	2.567248	3461417	.001202	38.441	35
40	226242	980	.004332	.021451	88339	1895	437125	.004335	2.588171	3015340	.008123	34.134	40
45	199188	1169	.005869	.029025	86444	2509	426277	.005886	2.631194	2578215	.020775	29.825	45
50	162610	1367	.008407	.041401	83935	3475	411414	.008446	2.622602	2151938	.033527	25.638	50
55	128728	1491	.011583	.056600	80460	4554	391526	.011631	2.634177	1740525	.027556	21.632	55
60	113631	1991	.017522	.084420	75906	6408	364525	.017579	2.659046	1348999	.017931	17.772	60
65	90407	2614	.028914	.135918	69498	9446	325175	.029049	2.637580	984470	.023141	14.165	65
70	64219	2987	.046513	.210584	60052	12646	269940	.046847	2.602387	659295	.035018	10.979	70
75	36219	2822	.077915	.330359	47406	15661	198389	.078941	2.532671	389355	.055967	8.213	75
80	15722	1950	.124030	.475728	31745	15102	120277	.125561	2.454090	190966	.055967	6.016	80
85+	8172	1924	.235438	1.000000	16643	16643	70689	.235438	4.247401	70689	.000000	4.247	85+

NUMBER OF PERSONS DYING (OUT OF 100,000 AT BIRTH) ABOVE AGE X FROM SPECIFIED CAUSES

Age (x)	All Causes	Respiratory T. B.	Other Infec. and Paras.	Neo-plasms	Cardio-vascular	Infl., Pneu., Bronch.	Diar-rheal	Certain Degenerative	Maternal	Cert. Dis. of Infancy	Motor Vehicle	Other Violence	Other and Unknown	Age (x)
0	100000	2183	1816	13056	38181	9416	891	8967	1039	2023	391	2354	19643	0
1	96440	2179	1632	13089	38170	8960	722	8960	1039	0	381	2275	19033	1
5	95099	2165	1235	13050	38146	8647	586	8936	1039	0	363	2152	18780	5
10	94546	2162	1053	13035	38106	8583	574	8910	1039	0	331	2105	18648	10
15	94142	2146	973	13023	38048	8543	569	8877	1039	C	317	2060	18547	15
20	93515	2029	933	13002	37978	8484	568	8813	991	C	300	2003	18414	20
25	92582	1782	888	12955	37900	8403	560	8748	828	C	284	1946	18288	25
30	91390	1469	818	12876	37810	8329	560	8671	625	0	266	1862	18104	30
35	90046	1231	777	12740	37651	8191	550	8568	359	0	250	1799	17930	35
40	88339	1016	715	12482	37403	8041	533	8368	137	C	239	1731	17674	40
45	86444	854	659	12010	37074	7875	520	8140	20	0	233	1654	17405	45
50	83935	709	599	11372	36465	7671	458	7794	1	0	208	1581	17037	50
55	80460	593	528	10414	35423	7445	473	7388	1	0	177	1489	16529	55
60	75906	468	471	9209	33848	7177	448	6786	1	0	147	1401	15950	60
65	69498	343	393	7753	31257	6810	416	5885	1	0	118	1347	15175	65
70	60052	220	274	6022	26998	6140	362	4748	1	0	75	1224	13988	70
75	47406	119	156	4134	21038	5007	307	3318	1	0	49	1076	12201	75
80	31745	59	74	2186	13492	3568	224	1666	1	0	16	880	9579	80
85+	16643	0	17	926	6652	1946	138	804	C	0	0	493	5667	85+

NUMBER OF PERSONS SURVIVING TO AGE X IF SPECIFIED CAUSES WERE ELIMINATED

Age (x)	No Causes	Respiratory T. B. (1)	Other Infec. and Paras. (2)	Neo-plasms (3)	Cardio-vascular (4)	Infl., Pneu., Bronch. (5)	Diar-rheal (6)	Certain Degenerative (7)	Maternal (8)	Cert. Dis. of Infancy (9)	Motor Vehicle (10)	Other Violence (11)	Other and Unknown (12)	(1)+(2)	(1)+(2)+(5)+(6)+(8)	(1)+(2)+(5)+(6)+(8)+part of(9)&(12)	(10)+(11)	Age (x)
0	100000	100000	100000	100000	100000	100000	100000	100000	100000	100000	100000	100000	100000	100000	100000	100000	100000	0
1	96440	96444	96621	96447	96451	96889	96606	96647	96440	98447	96450	96518	97041	96625	97242	99555	96527	1
5	95099	95117	95673	95145	95133	95854	95398	95130	95099	97078	95127	95298	95545	95691	96754	99264	95325	5
10	94546	94567	95300	94606	94620	95361	94855	94602	94546	96514	94605	94791	95520	95320	96457	99044	94850	10
15	94142	94179	94973	94214	94274	94994	94455	94231	94142	96101	94215	94431	95213	95010	96188	98817	94504	15
20	93515	93668	94380	93607	93716	94421	93827	93667	93563	95541	93605	93859	94713	94535	95818	98512	93949	20
25	92582	92980	93484	92720	92859	93560	92899	92798	92792	94509	92687	92979	93895	93886	95418	98190	93084	25
30	91390	92096	92351	91605	91753	92430	91703	91680	91800	93292	91511	91866	92872	93064	94868	97752	91988	30
35	90046	90980	91034	90394	90562	91209	90364	90434	90715	91920	90181	90578	91682	91977	94190	97163	90714	35
40	88339	89470	89370	88537	89093	89631	88668	88919	89217	90178	88483	88528	90203	90514	93096	96162	89073	40
45	86444	87713	87509	87501	87511	87875	86779	87239	87420	88243	86590	87098	88540	88794	91636	94746	87245	45
50	83935	85312	85029	85600	85581	85529	84282	85051	84901	85682	84102	84642	86342	86424	89447	92567	84810	50
55	80460	81896	81579	83018	83085	82213	80817	81934	81386	82135	80650	81229	83280	83035	86202	89289	81421	55
60	75906	77384	77018	79535	79979	77827	76267	77894	76780	77486	76115	76717	79151	78517	81818	84824	76928	60
65	69498	70973	70592	74293	75888	71618	69860	72208	70298	70944	69717	70293	73246	72090	75534	78398	70514	65
70	60052	61443	61109	65932	70042	62530	60415	63499	60743	61302	60281	60855	64464	62524	66251	68911	61087	70
75	47406	48594	48346	53911	61812	50420	47741	51483	47952	48393	47610	48173	52622	49558	53693	56092	48380	75
80	31745	32590	32442	37932	50206	35032	32038	35953	32110	32406	31908	32423	37705	33305	37520	39538	32589	80
85+	16643	17129	17050	20988	35264	19685	16858	19557	16835	16989	16740	17282	23367	17548	21267	23031	17383	85+

ADDED YRS OF LIFE

	No Causes	(1)	(2)	(3)	(4)	(5)	(6)	(7)	(8)	(9)	(10)	(11)	(12)	(1)+(2)	(1)+(2)+(5)+(6)+(8)	(1)+(2)+(5)+(6)+(8)+part of(9)&(12)	(10)+(11)
TOTAL		.727	.789	2.052	5.347	1.605	.288	1.329	.432	1.399	.121	.522	3.011	1.527	3.965	6.463	.645
WORK	4.056	.494	.130	.636	.707	.301	.024	.399	.338	.000	.041	.168	.556	.626	1.306	1.540	.210

POPULATION, DEATHS, DEATH RATES FOR ALL CAUSES COMBINED, AND SPECIFIED CAUSES

Age Start of Interval	Midyear Population	Deaths During Year	All Causes	Respiratory T. B.	Other Infec. and Paras.	Neoplasms	Cardiovascular	Infl., Pneu., Bronch.	Diarrheal	Certain Degenerative	Maternal	Cert. Dis. of Infancy	Motor Vehicle	Other Violence	Other and Unknown	Age Start of Interval
0	61569	2766	.04493	.00006	.00218	.00015	.00013	.00578	.00283	.00010	.00000	.02459	.00005	.00062	.00845	0
1	230911	779	.00337	.00003	.00072	.00013	.00005	.00068	.00037	.00005	.00000	.00000	.00013	.00045	.00076	1
5	268958	368	.00137	.00000	.00026	.00010	.00012	.00013	.00003	.00005	.00000	.00000	.00012	.00023	.00032	5
10	312692	337	.00108	.00001	.00012	.00007	.00013	.00005	.00002	.00004	.00000	.00000	.00013	.00025	.00026	10
15	326955	594	.00182	.00007	.00010	.00007	.00013	.00011	.00000	.00007	.00000	.00000	.00067	.00055	.00030	15
20	301593	716	.00237	.00018	.00010	.00011	.00019	.00010	.00000	.00012	.00000	.00000	.00067	.00057	.00034	20
25	306165	699	.00228	.00021	.00012	.00018	.00021	.00010	.00001	.00019	.00000	.00000	.00041	.00053	.00031	25
30	283073	703	.00248	.00031	.00012	.00019	.00031	.00015	.00002	.00021	.00000	.00000	.00028	.00053	.00035	30
35	256409	882	.00344	.00043	.00015	.00028	.00059	.00022	.00002	.00035	.00000	.00000	.00031	.00061	.00048	35
40	227293	1207	.00531	.00068	.00018	.00065	.00114	.00035	.00002	.00053	.00000	.00000	.00028	.00073	.00076	40
45	225159	1728	.00767	.00078	.00030	.00092	.00218	.00050	.00004	.00089	.00000	.00000	.00029	.00088	.00088	45
50	206140	2443	.01185	.00092	.00038	.00160	.00429	.00075	.00004	.00132	.00000	.00000	.00033	.00102	.00121	50
55	171172	3069	.01793	.00116	.00047	.00263	.00731	.00125	.00004	.00199	.00000	.00000	.00037	.00101	.00171	55
60	127541	3615	.02834	.00125	.00080	.00435	.01244	.00223	.00007	.00269	.00000	.00000	.00038	.00133	.00281	60
65	96332	4090	.04246	.00116	.00086	.00651	.02040	.00280	.00013	.00385	.00000	.00000	.00043	.00116	.00515	65
70	74950	4643	.06195	.00093	.00072	.01070	.02945	.00374	.00019	.00582	.00000	.00000	.00051	.00156	.00834	70
75	45434	4691	.10325	.00099	.00064	.01442	.05230	.00744	.00024	.00927	.00000	.00000	.00073	.00196	.01527	75
80	21651	3365	.15542	.00037	.00074	.01598	.07510	.01256	.00060	.01349	.00000	.00000	.00097	.00291	.03270	80
85+	6211	1913	.30800	.00032	.00113	.01868	.13701	.03059	.00193	.02174	.00000	.00000	.00032	.00660	.08968	85+
ALL	3550208	38608														

CRUDE DEATH RATE			.01087	.00041	.00032	.00129	.00354	.00083	.00011	.00091	.00000	.00043	.00033	.00069	.00162	
STANDARDIZED RATE (1)			.00805	.00029	.00035	.00077	.00223	.00070	.00017	.00055	.00000	.00087	.00029	.00058	.00125	
STANDARDIZED RATE (2)			.01347	.00041	.00035	.00157	.00514	.00106	.00013	.00111	.00000	.00051	.00033	.00072	.00214	
GEOMETRIC MEAN			.01101													

LIFE TABLE FOR ALL CAUSES COMBINED

Age (x)	Midyear Population	Deaths During Year	$_nM_x$	$_nq_x$	l_x	$_nd_x$	$_nL_x$	$_nm_x$	$_na_x$	T_x	$_nr_x$	$\overset{\circ}{e}_x$	Age (x)
0	61569	2766	.044925	.043270	100000	4327	96306	.044930	.146373	6377256	.000000	63.773	0
1	230911	779	.003374	.013379	95673	1280	379492	.003373	1.500000	6280950	.000000	65.650	1
5	268958	368	.001368	.006823	94393	644	470355	.001369	2.500000	5901458	.000000	62.520	5
10	312692	337	.001078	.005365	93749	503	467529	.001076	2.582422	5431103	-.019865	57.932	10
15	326955	594	.001817	.009041	93246	843	464245	.001816	2.645314	4963574	-.003878	53.231	15
20	301593	716	.002374	.011807	92403	1091	459328	.002375	2.536855	4499329	.002876	48.692	20
25	306165	699	.002283	.011346	91312	1036	453975	.002282	2.505027	4040001	.001956	44.244	25
30	283073	703	.002483	.012362	90276	1116	448692	.002487	2.591286	3586026	.011094	39.723	30
35	256409	882	.003440	.017104	89160	1525	442235	.003448	2.662158	3137334	.018217	35.188	35
40	227293	1207	.005310	.026279	87635	2303	432770	.005322	2.653152	2695099	.011594	30.754	40
45	225159	1728	.007675	.037712	85332	3218	419123	.007678	2.657901	2262329	.002189	26.512	45
50	206140	2443	.011851	.057749	82114	4742	399437	.011872	2.652230	1843206	.009882	22.447	50
55	171172	3069	.017929	.086375	77372	6683	371130	.018007	2.646204	1443769	.024246	18.660	55
60	127541	3615	.028344	.133430	70689	9432	330934	.028500	2.613333	1072639	.030721	15.174	60
65	96332	4090	.042457	.192660	61257	11814	277558	.042564	2.568422	741705	-.015186	12.108	65
70	74950	4643	.061948	.269239	49443	13312	214568	.062041	2.547545	464147	-.008624	9.388	70
75	45434	4691	.103249	.411060	36131	14852	143207	.103710	2.478608	249579	.017959	6.908	75
80	21651	3365	.155420	.553926	21279	11787	75554	.156008	2.383470	106372	.017959	4.999	80
85+	6211	1913	.308002	1.000000	9492	9492	30818	.308002	3.246733	30818	.000000	3.247	85+

NUMBER OF PERSONS DYING (OUT OF 100,000 AT BIRTH) ABOVE AGE X FROM SPECIFIED CAUSES

Age (x)	All Causes	Respiratory T. B.	Other Infec. and Paras.	Neo-plasms	Cardio-vascular	Infl., Pneu., Bronch.	Diar-rheal	Certain Degenerative	Maternal	Cert. Dis. of Infancy	Motor Vehicle	Other Violence	Other and Unknown	Age (x)
0	100000	3106	2304	12230	40219	7626	752	8614	0	2368	2172	5003	15606	0
1	95673	3100	2095	12216	40207	7069	479	8605	0	0	2167	4944	14791	1
5	94393	3088	1820	12165	40189	6811	338	8587	0	0	2118	4773	14504	5
10	93749	3086	1700	12116	40134	6752	322	8562	0	0	2062	4663	14352	10
15	93246	3082	1643	12083	40075	6728	315	8544	0	0	1999	4548	14229	15
20	92403	3048	1596	12052	40014	6675	313	8510	0	0	1809	4294	14092	20
25	91312	2966	1551	12000	39928	6629	313	8454	0	0	1503	4031	13937	25
30	90276	2869	1495	11919	39832	6583	310	8366	0	0	1316	3791	13795	30
35	89160	2731	1440	11833	39690	6517	301	8271	0	0	1190	3551	13636	35
40	87635	2541	1372	11710	39430	6420	294	8114	0	0	1052	3280	13422	40
45	85332	2247	1296	11427	38938	6267	286	7885	0	0	932	2962	13092	45
50	82114	1920	1171	11040	38025	6057	270	7510	0	0	809	2591	12721	50
55	77372	1551	1020	10399	36306	5758	254	6982	0	0	679	2184	12239	55
60	70689	1121	844	9419	33577	5291	241	6243	0	0	542	1809	11602	60
65	61257	708	578	7970	29435	4548	218	5349	0	0	418	1370	10663	65
70	49443	386	339	6158	23758	3769	180	4277	0	0	300	1047	9229	70
75	36131	186	184	3859	17429	2966	140	3027	0	0	191	711	7438	75
80	21279	44	93	1789	9906	1895	105	1695	0	0	86	430	5236	80
85+	9492	10	35	576	4223	943	60	670	0	0	10	203	2762	85+

NUMBER OF PERSONS SURVIVING TO AGE X IF SPECIFIED CAUSES WERE ELIMINATED

Age (x)	No Causes	Respiratory T. B.	Other Infec. and Paras.	Neo-plasms	Cardio-vascular	Infl., Pneu., Bronch.	Diar-rheal	Certain Degener-ative	Maternal	Cert. Dis. of Infancy	Motor Vehicle	Other Violence	Other and Unknown	(1) + (2)	(1) + (2) + (5) + (6) + (8)	(1)+(2)+ (5)+(6)+ (8)+part of(9)&(12)	(10) + (11)	Age (x)
		(1)	(2)	(3)	(4)	(5)	(6)	(7)	(8)	(9)	(10)	(11)	(12)					
0	100000	100000	100000	100000	100000	100000	100000	100000	100000	100000	100000	100000	100000	100000	100000	100000	100000	0
1	95673	95679	95878	95687	95685	96219	95940	95682	95673	98017	95678	95731	96473	95884	96701	99618	95736	1
5	94393	94411	94869	94457	94422	95190	94797	94420	94393	96706	94447	94620	95471	94887	96098	99204	94674	5
10	93749	93769	94342	93862	93833	94600	94167	93800	93749	96046	93858	94084	94973	94362	95642	98798	94194	10
15	93246	93269	93893	93391	93389	94117	93668	93315	93246	95531	93417	93695	94587	93917	95223	98396	93867	15
20	92403	92460	93091	92578	92605	93319	92824	92505	92403	94667	92763	93102	93871	93149	94500	97677	93464	20
25	91312	91450	92037	91536	91597	92263	91728	91469	91312	93549	91973	92267	92919	92176	93561	96736	92935	25
30	90276	90509	91049	90575	90654	91263	90690	90519	90276	92488	91117	91461	92009	91284	92705	95885	92313	30
35	89160	89528	89979	89545	89675	90201	89578	89494	89160	91345	90117	90573	91032	90350	91833	95030	91545	35
40	87635	88186	88508	88136	88401	88755	88053	88120	87635	89782	88714	89297	89692	89064	90633	93851	90396	40
45	85332	86161	86258	86101	86569	86576	85747	86032	85332	87423	86502	87270	87669	87095	88795	92042	88467	45
50	82114	83236	83129	83238	84219	83520	82529	83159	82114	84126	83363	84737	84352	84264	86140	89385	85634	50
55	77372	78792	78477	79064	81087	78993	77778	78878	77372	79268	78676	79887	80328	79917	82020	85210	81233	55
60	70689	72405	71869	73199	76869	72627	71073	72787	70689	72421	72014	73356	74024	73614	76043	79123	74731	60
65	61257	63137	62531	64843	70940	63650	61611	63936	61257	62758	62522	63992	65070	64450	67355	70253	65314	65
70	49443	51256	50689	54087	63471	52104	49763	52618	49443	50655	50572	51952	53907	52548	55735	58333	53138	70
75	36131	37630	37175	41722	53843	38803	36399	39600	36131	37016	37050	38265	41094	38718	41889	44035	39239	75
80	21279	22272	21963	26434	41472	23745	21464	24453	21279	21800	21902	22761	26191	22988	25875	27430	23427	80
85+	9492	9958	9836	12813	27302	11306	9604	11701	9492	9725	9821	10312	13840	10319	12436	13447	10669	85+

ADDED YRS OF LIFE

	No Causes	(1)	(2)	(3)	(4)	(5)	(6)	(7)	(8)	(9)	(10)	(11)	(12)				
TOTAL		.663	.731	1.578	5.640	1.360	.319	1.129	.000	1.559	.682	1.317	2.554	1.408	3.167	5.694	2.021
WORK	4.723	.384	.171	.436	1.000	.263	.014	.395	.000	.000	.435	.684	.549	.558	.842	.969	1.128

POPULATION, DEATHS, DEATH RATES FOR ALL CAUSES COMBINED, AND SPECIFIED CAUSES

Age Start of Interval	Midyear Population	Deaths During Year	All Causes	Respiratory T. B.	Other Infec. and Paras.	Neoplasms	Cardiovascular	Infl., Pneu., Bronch.	Diarrheal	Certain Degenerative	Maternal	Cert. Dis. of Infancy	Motor Vehicle	Other Violence	Other and Unknown	Age Start of Interval
0	58823	2089	.03551	.00003	.00201	.00009	.00014	.00418	.00218	.00007	.00000	.01974	.00003	.00078	.00627	0
1	221985	614	.00277	.00002	.00060	.00015	.00005	.00062	.00030	.00006	.00000	.00000	.00009	.00027	.00060	1
5	259567	295	.00114	.00001	.00025	.00007	.00010	.00011	.00003	.00005	.00000	.00000	.00007	.00012	.00029	5
10	300437	219	.00073	.00004	.00010	.00005	.00012	.00006	.00002	.00005	.00000	.00000	.00004	.00006	.00020	10
15	317204	332	.00105	.00016	.00008	.00005	.00011	.00007	.00001	.00005	.00010	.00000	.00007	.00009	.00022	15
20	292753	510	.00174	.00032	.00009	.00006	.00019	.00008	.00002	.00015	.00033	.00000	.00011	.00010	.00029	20
25	298114	581	.00195	.00044	.00007	.00011	.00022	.00010	.00002	.00017	.00044	.00000	.00006	.00009	.00024	25
30	266216	616	.00231	.00046	.00010	.00025	.00024	.00011	.00001	.00021	.00042	.00000	.00002	.00015	.00034	30
35	237805	651	.00274	.00035	.00012	.00042	.00047	.00014	.00002	.00032	.00037	.00000	.00004	.00013	.00037	35
40	231292	884	.00382	.00035	.00009	.00083	.00082	.00022	.00002	.00047	.00023	.00000	.00005	.00018	.00056	40
45	230721	1242	.00538	.00023	.00013	.00154	.00154	.00028	.00003	.00066	.00002	.00000	.00006	.00021	.00069	45
50	202149	1633	.00808	.00027	.00011	.00226	.00276	.00039	.00004	.00097	.00000	.00000	.00008	.00020	.00100	50
55	166706	1831	.01098	.00025	.00016	.00299	.00421	.00053	.00003	.00131	.00000	.00000	.00014	.00014	.00124	55
60	129191	2309	.01787	.00036	.00027	.00392	.00771	.00107	.00008	.00212	.00000	.00000	.00015	.00028	.00191	60
65	103173	2894	.02805	.00034	.00040	.00560	.01332	.00165	.00011	.00334	.00000	.00000	.00017	.00047	.00266	65
70	80382	3606	.04486	.00032	.00034	.00743	.02331	.00264	.00019	.00511	.00000	.00000	.00024	.00087	.00442	70
75	50075	4011	.08010	.00040	.00030	.01000	.04320	.00523	.00030	.00829	.00000	.00000	.00030	.00196	.01012	75
80	25554	3162	.12374	.00043	.00063	.01162	.06398	.01014	.00039	.00924	.00000	.00000	.00027	.00423	.02281	80
85+	8682	2297	.26457	.00023	.00069	.01474	.13085	.02396	.00035	.01555	.00000	.00000	.00046	.00910	.06865	85+
ALL	3480829	29776														

	All Causes	Respiratory T. B.	Other Infec. and Paras.	Neoplasms	Cardiovascular	Infl., Pneu., Bronch.	Diarrheal	Certain Degenerative	Maternal	Cert. Dis. of Infancy	Motor Vehicle	Other Violence	Other and Unknown
CRUDE DEATH RATE	.00855	.00025	.00021	.00127	.00327	.00060	.00009	.00080	.00015	.00033	.00008	.00026	.00124
STANDARDIZED RATE (1)	.00594	.00020	.00026	.00073	.00164	.00049	.00014	.00046	.00013	.00069	.00007	.00021	.00090
STANDARDIZED RATE (2)	.00696	.00024	.00023	.00139	.00394	.00073	.00011	.00050	.00013	.00041	.00009	.00030	.00149
GEOMETRIC MEAN	.00815												

LIFE TABLE FOR ALL CAUSES COMBINED

Age (x)	Midyear Population	Deaths During Year	$_nM_x$	$_nq_x$	l_x	$_nd_x$	$_nL_x$	$_nm_x$	$_na_x$	T_x	$_nr_x$	$\overset{\circ}{e}_x$	Age (x)
0	58823	2089	.035913	.034450	100000	3445	97004	.035514	.130373	6841059	.000000	68.411	0
1	221985	614	.002766	.010989	96555	1061	383568	.002766	1.500000	6744055	.000000	69.847	1
5	259567	295	.001137	.005665	95494	541	476118	.001136	2.500000	6360488	.000000	66.606	5
10	300437	219	.000729	.003633	94953	345	473893	.000728	2.471618	5884370	-.019895	61.971	10
15	317204	332	.001047	.005222	94608	494	471903	.001047	2.699055	5410477	-.004191	57.188	15
20	292753	510	.001742	.008681	94114	817	468613	.001743	2.604804	4938574	.002575	52.474	20
25	298114	581	.001949	.009700	93297	905	464274	.001949	2.556860	4469961	.003820	47.911	25
30	266216	616	.002314	.011516	92392	1064	459171	.002316	2.566377	4005687	.017517	43.355	30
35	237805	651	.002738	.013621	91328	1244	453664	.002742	2.607516	3546316	.015059	38.831	35
40	231292	884	.003822	.018938	90084	1706	446386	.003822	2.635185	3092653	.001904	34.331	40
45	230721	1242	.005383	.026602	88378	2351	436369	.005388	2.651708	2646267	.003857	29.943	45
50	202149	1633	.008078	.039592	86027	3418	422026	.008099	2.627572	2209898	.018131	25.688	50
55	166706	1831	.010983	.053796	82609	4444	402628	.011037	2.655875	1787872	.029710	21.643	55
60	129191	2309	.017873	.086266	78165	6743	375006	.017981	2.653956	1385244	.031775	17.722	60
65	103173	2894	.028050	.131990	71422	9427	334766	.028160	2.629769	1010238	.020786	14.145	65
70	80382	3606	.044861	.203484	61995	12615	279308	.045064	2.618939	675473	-.021573	10.896	70
75	50075	4011	.080100	.336756	49380	16629	205929	.080751	2.536144	395535	.031647	8.010	75
80	25554	3162	.123738	.473268	32751	15500	124402	.124596	2.461116	189606	.031647	5.789	80
85+	8682	2297	.264570	1.000000	17251	17251	65204	.264570	3.779713	65204	.000000	3.780	85+

NUMBER OF PERSONS DYING (OUT OF 100,000 AT BIRTH) ABOVE AGE X FROM SPECIFIED CAUSES

Age (x)	All Causes	Respiratory T.B.	Other Infec. and Paras.	Neoplasms	Cardio-vascular	Infl., Pneu., Bronch.	Diarrheal	Certain Degenerative	Maternal	Cert. Dis. of Infancy	Motor Vehicle	Other Violence	Other and Unknown	Age (x)
0	100000	1794	1546	13687	44060	7172	689	9205	875	1915	679	2866	15512	0
1	96555	1791	1351	13678	44047	6766	478	9199	875	0	675	2790	14905	1
5	95494	1784	1121	13620	44028	6528	362	9175	875	0	641	2686	14674	5
10	94953	1780	984	13587	43980	6475	348	9153	875	0	606	2631	14534	10
15	94608	1763	934	13563	43925	6448	340	9127	875	0	587	2604	14442	15
20	94114	1686	897	13541	43874	6414	335	9086	830	0	554	2561	14336	20
25	93297	1537	856	13504	43786	6377	327	9014	676	0	505	2516	14199	25
30	92392	1335	823	13454	43683	6332	318	8933	473	0	477	2476	14088	30
35	91328	1123	778	13338	43574	6280	313	8836	279	0	466	2408	13933	35
40	90084	964	725	13148	43362	6215	305	8692	113	0	447	2349	13764	40
45	88378	808	686	12777	42997	6114	295	8482	9	0	424	2270	13516	45
50	86027	710	627	12105	42323	5993	282	8194	1	0	400	2178	13214	50
55	82609	595	579	11151	41156	5830	263	7782	1	0	366	2094	12792	55
60	78165	496	516	9944	39449	5616	251	7253	1	0	310	2036	12293	60
65	71422	359	414	8470	36537	5213	222	6453	1	0	252	1931	11570	65
70	61995	245	281	6589	32057	4659	186	5329	1	0	194	1774	10680	70
75	49380	155	187	4505	25498	3917	134	3892	1	0	127	1529	9435	75
80	32751	72	125	2434	16530	2829	72	2175	1	0	65	1121	7327	80
85+	17251	15	45	961	8532	1562	23	1014	0	0	30	593	4476	85+

NUMBER OF PERSONS SURVIVING TO AGE X IF SPECIFIED CAUSES WERE ELIMINATED

Age (x)	No Causes	Respiratory T.B. (1)	Other Infec. and Paras. (2)	Neoplasms (3)	Cardiovascular (4)	Infl., Pneu., Bronch. (5)	Diarrheal (6)	Certain Degenerative (7)	Maternal (8)	Cert. Dis. of Infancy (9)	Motor Vehicle (10)	Other Violence (11)	Other and Unknown (12)	(1)+(2)	(1)+(2)+(5)+(6)+(8)	(1)+(2)+(5)+(6)+(8)+part of (9)&(12)	(10)+(11)	Age (x)
0	100000	100000	100000	100000	100000	100000	100000	100000	100000	100000	100000	100000	100000	100000	100000	100000	100000	0
1	96555	96558	96747	96564	96568	96955	96763	96561	96555	98455	96559	96630	97153	96750	97359	99591	96634	1
5	95494	95504	95913	95560	95526	96127	95815	95524	95494	97373	95532	95671	96317	95923	96884	99274	95709	5
10	94953	94967	95507	95052	95032	95636	95286	95004	94953	96822	95025	95184	95912	95521	96546	99003	95257	10
15	94608	94639	95210	94731	94742	95316	94948	94685	94608	96470	94699	94866	95657	95241	96298	98788	94957	15
20	94114	94221	94750	94258	94298	94852	94457	94232	94159	95966	94238	94413	95264	94858	95997	98535	94537	20
25	93297	93552	93969	93477	93567	94066	93645	93486	93495	95133	93468	93639	94575	94226	95559	98168	93811	25
30	92392	92846	93090	92620	92763	93199	92746	92660	92791	94210	92590	92770	93770	93548	95135	97805	92969	30
35	91328	91989	92063	91669	91803	92177	91683	91689	91916	93125	91534	91770	92847	92730	94561	97307	91977	35
40	90084	90895	90862	90610	90765	90987	90442	90584	90830	91857	90306	90579	91753	91681	93738	96535	90802	40
45	88378	89330	89181	89265	89411	89365	88739	89078	89214	90117	88619	88942	90266	90141	92386	95217	89185	45
50	86027	87051	86867	87562	87708	87106	86391	86995	86848	87700	86285	86667	88169	87901	90237	93049	86928	50
55	82609	83707	83463	85040	85398	83809	82977	83948	83358	84235	82891	83307	85091	84572	87006	89770	83591	55
60	78165	79301	79035	81682	82540	79512	78525	79956	78911	79703	78486	78882	81015	80184	82724	85404	79206	60
65	71422	72593	72316	76120	78418	73046	71779	73845	72104	72827	71771	72179	74745	73501	76270	78825	72531	65
70	61995	63118	62856	67563	72809	63934	62339	65189	62587	63215	62352	62800	65752	64035	67039	69375	63161	70
75	49380	50356	50181	56197	65282	51611	49700	53284	49851	50352	49724	50243	53565	51173	54346	56349	50593	75
80	32751	33466	33333	39210	54024	35166	33014	36862	33064	33395	33029	33663	37439	34061	37217	38771	33949	80
85+	17251	17669	17616	21951	39613	19519	17425	20371	17416	17590	17423	18123	22188	18043	20818	21984	18303	85+

ADDED YRS OF LIFE

	No Causes	(1)	(2)	(3)	(4)	(5)	(6)	(7)	(8)	(9)	(10)	(11)	(12)	(1)+(2)	(1)+(2)+(5)+(6)+(8)	combo	(10)+(11)
TOTAL		.555	.613	2.059	6.272	1.177	.292	1.254	.372	1.344	.190	.512	2.387	1.175	3.084	5.265	.705
WORK	3.490	.360	.107	.578	.734	-.170	.021	.354	.292	.000	.074	.142	.458	.468	.960	1.129	.216

POPULATION, DEATHS, DEATH RATES FOR ALL CAUSES COMBINED, AND SPECIFIED CAUSES

Age Start of Interval	Midyear Population	Deaths During Year	All Causes	Respiratory T. B.	Other Infec. and Paras.	Neoplasms	Cardiovascular	Infl., Pneu., Bronch.	Diarrheal	Certain Degenerative	Maternal	Cert. Dis. of Infancy	Motor Vehicle	Other Violence	Other and Unknown	Age Start of Interval
0	97780	2749	.02811	.00002	.00076	.00013	.00011	.00213	.00094	.00007	.00000	.01710	.00002	.00074	.00610	0
1	378081	710	.00188	.00000	.00027	.00011	.00003	.00030	.00013	.00002	.00000	.00000	.00017	.00037	.00048	1
5	379024	314	.00083	.00000	.00015	.00010	.00004	.00004	.00002	.00002	.00000	.00000	.00011	.00017	.00018	5
10	309709	237	.00077	.00000	.00012	.00005	.00004	.00004	.00000	.00003	.00000	.00000	.00008	.00027	.00012	10
15	283357	479	.00169	.00001	.00018	.00011	.00007	.00005	.00000	.00005	.00000	.00000	.00061	.00048	.00013	15
20	331423	737	.00222	.00004	.00016	.00011	.00011	.00002	.00001	.00008	.00000	.00000	.00099	.00055	.00016	20
25	361401	653	.00181	.00006	.00010	.00013	.00020	.00003	.00001	.00009	.00000	.00000	.00056	.00046	.00018	25
30	326477	626	.00192	.00009	.00009	.00023	.00031	.00006	.00001	.00012	.00000	.00000	.00039	.00040	.00022	30
35	323437	879	.00272	.00013	.00007	.00032	.00066	.00009	.00003	.00021	.00000	.00000	.00035	.00054	.00032	35
40	301415	1182	.00392	.00019	.00005	.00041	.00132	.00013	.00002	.00034	.00000	.00000	.00039	.00061	.00045	40
45	257456	1697	.00659	.00033	.00012	.00087	.00272	.00024	.00003	.00049	.00000	.00000	.00034	.00077	.00068	45
50	228408	2507	.01098	.00062	.00020	.00171	.00509	.00046	.00005	.00088	.00000	.00000	.00028	.00073	.00097	50
55	193491	3639	.01881	.00074	.00027	.00294	.00985	.00085	.00006	.00117	.00000	.00000	.00043	.00083	.00167	55
60	180907	5126	.02834	.00101	.00030	.00455	.01544	.00118	.00006	.00162	.00000	.00000	.00048	.00103	.00267	60
65	130374	5684	.04360	.00095	.00035	.00710	.02527	.00190	.00010	.00206	.00000	.00000	.00051	.00126	.00409	65
70	87022	5710	.06562	.00106	.00048	.00976	.03919	.00364	.00024	.00293	.00000	.00000	.00076	.00121	.00635	70
75	51201	5303	.10357	.00092	.00059	.01377	.06166	.00666	.00031	.00396	.00000	.00000	.00102	.00207	.01262	75
80	26399	4255	.16118	.00080	.00030	.01678	.09637	.01125	.00064	.00576	.00000	.00000	.00129	.00371	.02428	80
85+	12394	3466	.27965	.00073	.00065	.01977	.16121	.02469	.00137	.00637	.00000	.00000	.00105	.00766	.05616	85+
ALL	4259756	45953														

CRUDE DEATH RATE			.01079	.00024	.00019	.00134	.00513	.00059	.00007	.00050	.00000	.00039	.00041	.00061	.00132	
STANDARDIZED RATE (1)			.00697	.00015	.00019	.00077	.00272	.00039	.00007	.00030	.00000	.00060	.00037	.00051	.00090	
STANDARDIZED RATE (2)			.01273	.00025	.00019	.00158	.00635	.00072	.00007	.00056	.00000	.00035	.00042	.00064	.00158	
GEOMETRIC MEAN			.00929													

LIFE TABLE FOR ALL CAUSES COMBINED

Age (x)	Midyear Population	Deaths During Year	$_nM_x$	$_nq_x$	l_x	$_nd_x$	$_nL_x$	$_nm_x$	$_na_x$	T_x	$_nr_x$	$\overset{\circ}{e}_x$	Age (x)
0	97780	2749	.028114	.027430	100000	2743	97580	.028110	.117794	6602353	.000000	66.024	0
1	378081	710	.001878	.007485	97257	728	387208	.001880	1.500000	6504773	.000000	66.882	1
5	379024	314	.000828	.004113	96529	397	481653	.000824	2.500000	6117565	.000000	63.375	5
10	309709	237	.000765	.003838	96132	369	479823	.000769	2.730917	5635912	.027066	58.627	10
15	283357	479	.001690	.008417	95763	806	476942	.001690	2.676282	5156089	.004186	53.842	15
20	331423	737	.002224	.011068	94957	1051	472165	.002226	2.507533	4679147	-.023337	49.276	20
25	361401	653	.001807	.008988	93906	844	467386	.001806	2.460012	4206982	-.007864	44.800	25
30	326477	626	.001917	.009553	93062	889	463171	.001919	2.593973	3739596	.006290	40.184	30
35	323437	879	.002718	.013507	92173	1245	457936	.002719	2.647758	3276425	.003177	35.546	35
40	301415	1182	.003922	.019488	90928	1772	450556	.003933	2.695283	2818488	.014577	30.997	40
45	257456	1697	.006591	.032595	89156	2906	439112	.006618	2.705394	2367932	.019586	26.559	45
50	228408	2507	.010976	.053762	86250	4637	420585	.011025	2.700066	1928820	.019857	22.363	50
55	193491	3639	.018807	.090169	81613	7359	390756	.018833	2.647916	1508235	.007644	18.480	55
60	180907	5126	.028335	.132841	74254	9864	347732	.028367	2.613734	1117479	.006289	15.049	60
65	130374	5684	.043598	.197919	64390	12744	291087	.043781	2.578207	769747	.023632	11.954	65
70	87022	5710	.065616	.283623	51646	14648	222126	.065944	2.535244	478660	.026925	9.268	70
75	51201	5303	.103572	.411428	36998	15222	146459	.103934	2.468727	256534	.015543	6.934	75
80	26399	4255	.161180	.567735	21776	12363	76415	.161788	2.374019	110075	.015543	5.055	80
85+	12394	3466	.279651	1.000000	9413	9413	33660	.279651	3.575880	33660	.000000	3.576	85+

NUMBER OF PERSONS DYING (OUT OF 100,000 AT BIRTH) ABOVE AGE X FROM SPECIFIED CAUSES

Age (x)	All Causes	Respiratory T.B.	Other Infec. and Paras.	Neoplasms	Cardiovascular	Infl., Pneu., Bronch.	Diarrheal	Certain Degenerative	Maternal	Cert. Dis. of Infancy	Motor Vehicle	Other Violence	Other and Unknown	Age (x)
0	100000	2024	1302	12801	51875	5624	489	4550	0	1668	2897	4655	12115	0
1	97257	2022	1228	12788	51864	5417	357	4543	0	0	2895	4583	11520	1
5	96529	2021	1124	12744	51852	5301	348	4537	0	0	2830	4440	11332	5
10	96132	2019	1052	12697	51835	5280	340	4527	0	0	2778	4359	11245	10
15	95763	2018	993	12675	51815	5260	339	4511	0	0	2738	4227	11187	15
20	94957	2013	906	12623	51781	5238	339	4489	0	0	2445	3999	11124	20
25	93906	1996	832	12570	51729	5228	333	4454	0	0	1977	3738	11049	25
30	93062	1969	786	12511	51637	5214	328	4411	0	0	1716	3524	10966	30
35	92173	1929	742	12406	51492	5186	324	4354	0	0	1538	3339	10863	35
40	90928	1869	708	12257	51190	5146	311	4259	0	0	1376	3091	10721	40
45	89156	1784	687	12069	50591	5088	300	4105	0	0	1202	2816	10514	45
50	86250	1636	636	11685	49389	4980	288	3891	0	0	1053	2478	10214	50
55	81613	1376	553	10964	47238	4785	268	3518	0	0	937	2170	9804	55
60	74254	1087	448	9815	43382	4452	244	3061	0	0	770	1845	9150	60
65	64390	735	342	8229	38007	4042	225	2497	0	0	604	1487	8222	65
70	51646	458	239	6154	30618	3485	195	1895	0	0	454	1121	7027	70
75	36998	223	132	3978	21869	2670	141	1241	0	0	285	852	5607	75
80	21776	89	46	1956	12807	1691	96	659	0	0	136	548	3748	80
85+	9413	24	22	665	5426	831	46	215	0	0	35	258	1891	85+

NUMBER OF PERSONS SURVIVING TO AGE X IF SPECIFIED CAUSES WERE ELIMINATED

Age (x)	No Causes	Respiratory T.B. (1)	Other Infec. and Paras. (2)	Neoplasms (3)	Cardiovascular (4)	Infl., Pneu., Bronch. (5)	Diarrheal (6)	Certain Degenerative (7)	Maternal (8)	Cert. Dis. of Infancy (9)	Motor Vehicle (10)	Other Violence (11)	Other and Unknown (12)	(1) + (2)	(1) + (2) + (5) + (6) + (8)	(1)+(2)+ (5)+(6)+ (8)+part of(9)&(12)	(10) + (11)	Age (x)
0	100000	100000	100000	100000	100000	100000	100000	100000	100000	100000	100000	100000	100000	100000	100000	100000	100000	0
1	97257	97259	97330	97270	97268	97461	97348	97264	97257	98916	97259	97328	97846	97332	97628	99393	97330	1
5	96529	96532	96705	96586	96552	96848	96668	96542	96529	98175	96556	96742	97302	96708	97167	99021	96809	5
10	96132	96137	96379	96235	96172	96470	96278	96155	96132	97772	96250	96425	96989	96384	96871	98749	96544	10
15	95763	95769	96069	95888	95822	96120	95910	95802	95763	97396	95921	96187	96675	96075	96581	98468	96346	15
20	94957	94968	95347	95133	95050	95333	95103	95017	94957	96577	95406	95606	95925	95538	95882	97766	96059	20
25	93906	93934	94366	94133	94050	94288	94056	94000	93906	95508	94819	94810	94939	94393	94929	96802	95732	25
30	93062	93116	93563	93345	93296	93455	93216	93158	93062	94649	94230	94173	94169	93618	94168	96037	95354	30
35	92173	92267	92714	92559	92550	92590	92329	92365	92173	93745	93509	93460	93373	92808	93385	95254	94814	35
40	90928	91080	91495	91457	91601	91379	91095	91212	90928	92479	92409	92447	92255	91648	92272	94138	93953	40
45	89156	89389	89733	89862	90416	89656	89331	89588	89156	90677	90783	90923	90665	89968	90650	92507	92583	45
50	86250	86622	86859	87315	88677	86841	86431	86879	86250	87721	87973	88299	88010	87233	88015	89855	90063	50
55	81613	82219	82270	83334	86089	82363	81803	82574	81613	83005	83359	83858	83687	82881	83838	85647	85652	55
60	74254	75083	74953	76947	82305	75258	74450	75570	74254	75521	76005	76615	76783	75790	77017	78752	78421	60
65	64390	65440	65095	68272	77139	65648	64578	66067	64390	65488	66066	66781	67482	66157	67646	69262	68519	65
70	51646	52738	52305	56760	70317	53166	51824	53544	51646	52527	53127	53902	55257	53411	55172	56588	55448	70
75	36998	37981	37561	42720	61480	38803	37171	38932	36998	37629	38206	38850	40889	38559	40630	41796	40118	75
80	21776	22456	22172	26566	49612	23633	21912	23380	21776	22147	22603	23110	25687	22865	24970	25844	23987	80
85+	9413	9750	9600	12723	35384	10829	9504	10416	9413	9574	9838	10188	12594	9944	11551	12099	10648	85+

ADDED YRS OF LIFE

	No Causes	(1)	(2)	(3)	(4)	(5)	(6)	(7)	(8)	(9)	(10)	(11)	(12)	(1)+(2)	+(5)+(6)+(8)	part(9)&(12)	(10)+(11)
TOTAL		.333	.418	1.646	8.440	.749	.141	.638	.000	1.124	.916	1.195	1.857	.755	1.674	3.132	2.138
WORK	4.196	.148	.141	.446	1.208	.124	.018	.239	.000	.000	.609	.594	.368	.290	.434	.480	1.214

POPULATION, DEATHS, DEATH RATES FOR ALL CAUSES COMBINED, AND SPECIFIED CAUSES

Age Start of Interval	Midyear Population	Deaths During Year	All Causes	Respiratory T.B.	Other Infec. and Paras.	Neoplasms	Cardiovascular	Infl., Pneu., Bronch.	Diarrheal	Certain Degenerative	Maternal	Cert. Dis. of Infancy	Motor Vehicle	Other Violence	Other and Unknown	Age Start of Interval
0	93140	2129	.02286	.00003	.00064	.00010	.00004	.00191	.00104	.00009	.00000	.01351	.00004	.00060	.00485	0
1	361398	573	.00159	.00002	.00024	.00009	.00004	.00027	.00012	.00004	.00000	.00000	.00009	.00024	.00043	1
5	363924	198	.00054	.00000	.00011	.00007	.00003	.00004	.00001	.00002	.00000	.00000	.00005	.00008	.00014	5
10	297985	149	.00050	.00000	.00011	.00005	.00009	.00005	.00001	.00003	.00000	.00000	.00002	.00005	.00009	10
15	270266	171	.00063	.00001	.00010	.00007	.00005	.00003	.00001	.00006	.00003	.00000	.00008	.00006	.00013	15
20	310674	270	.00087	.00008	.00010	.00007	.00008	.00005	.00001	.00005	.00010	.00000	.00009	.00009	.00015	20
25	337584	358	.00106	.00010	.00008	.00016	.00015	.00005	.00001	.00008	.00014	.00000	.00007	.00009	.00015	25
30	316510	480	.00152	.00013	.00009	.00027	.00023	.00005	.00003	.00017	.00017	.00000	.00006	.00010	.00024	30
35	310700	616	.00198	.00015	.00005	.00044	.00047	.00005	.00001	.00017	.00015	.00000	.00007	.00015	.00027	35
40	280021	789	.00282	.00017	.00006	.00076	.00080	.00011	.00002	.00028	.00001	.00000	.00008	.00012	.00037	40
45	234988	1074	.00457	.00012	.00007	.00125	.00175	.00014	.00005	.00040	.00001	.00000	.00008	.00017	.00053	45
50	230369	1593	.00691	.00015	.00009	.00190	.00303	.00022	.00003	.00052	.00000	.00000	.00008	.00019	.00071	50
55	205913	2111	.01025	.00012	.00011	.00268	.00510	.00027	.00003	.00070	.00000	.00000	.00005	.00025	.00095	55
60	189433	2931	.01547	.00014	.00011	.00345	.00840	.00048	.00012	.00096	.00000	.00000	.00020	.00026	.00136	60
65	143206	3684	.02573	.00015	.00012	.00476	.01523	.00097	.00009	.00173	.00000	.00000	.00014	.00041	.00214	65
70	104932	4564	.04349	.00028	.00014	.00716	.02718	.00167	.00020	.00226	.00000	.00000	.00034	.00072	.00355	70
75	66974	4975	.07428	.00021	.00028	.00915	.04824	.00409	.00035	.00318	.00000	.00000	.00021	.00166	.00687	75
80	34889	4640	.13299	.00037	.00037	.01210	.08624	.00825	.00072	.00530	.00000	.00000	.00000	.00046	.00450	80
85+	18729	4530	.24187	.00005	.00037	.01468	.15148	.01810	.00117	.00555	.00000	.00000	.00000	.00046	.01468	85+
ALL	4171635	35835														

	All Causes	Respiratory T.B.	Other Infec. and Paras.	Neoplasms	Cardiovascular	Infl., Pneu., Bronch.	Diarrheal	Certain Degenerative	Maternal	Cert. Dis. of Infancy	Motor Vehicle	Other Violence	Other and Unknown
CRUDE DEATH RATE	.00859	.00010	.00012	.00127	.00442	.00044	.00008	.00043	.00005	.00030	.00009	.00028	.00101
STANDARDIZED RATE (1)	.00469	.00007	.00013	.00067	.00185	.00026	.00007	.00023	.00005	.00048	.00007	.00018	.00063
STANDARDIZED RATE (2)	.00874	.00009	.00012	.00127	.00458	.00045	.00008	.00044	.00005	.00028	.00009	.00028	.00101
GEOMETRIC MEAN	.00603												

LIFE TABLE FOR ALL CAUSES COMBINED

Age (x)	Midyear Population	Deaths During Year	$_nM_x$	$_nq_x$	l_x	$_nd_x$	$_nL_x$	$_nm_x$	$_na_x$	T_x	$_nr_x$	$\overset{\circ}{e}_x$	Age (x)
0	93140	2129	.022858	.022400	100000	2240	98004	.022856	.108859	7146148	.000000	71.461	0
1	361398	573	.001586	.006322	97760	618	389495	.001587	1.500000	7048144	.000000	72.096	1
5	363924	198	.000544	.002718	97142	264	485050	.000544	2.500000	6658649	.000000	68.546	5
10	297985	149	.000500	.002498	96878	242	483794	.000500	2.535296	6173599	.027516	63.726	10
15	270266	171	.000633	.003156	96636	305	482454	.000632	2.619536	5689805	.006819	58.879	15
20	310674	270	.000869	.004329	96331	417	480655	.000868	2.600919	5207351	-.019229	54.057	20
25	337584	358	.001060	.005286	95914	507	478366	.001060	2.624918	4726697	-.008623	49.281	25
30	316510	480	.001517	.007557	95407	721	475322	.001517	2.623671	4248331	.003235	44.529	30
35	310700	616	.001983	.009875	94686	935	471217	.001984	2.632799	3773009	.005607	39.848	35
40	280021	789	.002818	.014048	93751	1317	465705	.002828	2.683814	3301793	.021853	35.219	40
45	234988	1074	.004570	.022686	92434	2097	457294	.004566	2.674952	2836088	.018088	30.682	45
50	230369	1593	.006915	.034072	90337	3078	444464	.006925	2.654050	2378794	-.008734	26.332	50
55	205913	2111	.010252	.050115	87259	4373	426014	.010265	2.649021	1934330	.007526	22.168	55
60	189433	2931	.015472	.074874	82886	6206	399953	.015517	2.667244	1508315	.014865	18.197	60
65	143206	3684	.025725	.122001	76680	9355	361500	.025878	2.659028	1108363	.028504	14.454	65
70	104932	4564	.043495	.198247	67325	13347	304867	.043780	2.620626	746862	.029787	11.093	70
75	66974	4975	.074283	.316481	53978	17083	228252	.074843	2.562599	441995	.031028	8.188	75
80	34889	4640	.132993	.500881	36895	18480	137607	.134295	2.463869	213743	.031028	5.793	80
85+	18729	4530	.241871	1.000000	18415	18415	76136	.241871	4.134437	76136	.000000	4.134	85+

NUMBER OF PERSONS DYING (OUT OF 100,000 AT BIRTH) ABOVE AGE X FROM SPECIFIED CAUSES

Age (x)	All Causes	Respiratory T.B.	Other Infec. and Paras.	Neo-plasms	Cardio-vascular	Infl., Pneu., Bronch.	Diar-rheal	Certain Degenerative	Maternal	Cert. Dis. of Infancy	Motor Vehicle	Other Violence	Other and Unknown	Age (x)
0	100000	783	891	13706	57108	5294	663	4734	309	1325	736	3108	11343	0
1	97760	780	828	13696	57104	5107	561	4726	309	1	732	3049	10867	1
5	97142	774	733	13662	57088	5000	513	4709	309	0	696	2957	10701	5
10	96878	772	681	13628	57072	4981	509	4701	309	0	672	2920	10633	10
15	96636	772	627	13602	57030	4959	504	4688	309	0	662	2895	10588	15
20	96331	767	577	13567	57005	4944	499	4662	293	0	622	2869	10526	20
25	95914	728	531	13534	56965	4921	496	4640	245	0	578	2824	10452	25
30	95407	682	491	13458	56895	4897	493	4603	178	0	546	2781	10383	30
35	94686	618	451	13332	56784	4875	481	4524	99	0	519	2735	10268	35
40	93751	552	425	13125	56561	4850	475	4443	27	0	487	2665	10141	40
45	92434	474	398	12769	56184	4800	467	4313	5	0	451	2608	9965	45
50	90337	417	365	12197	55381	4734	445	4130	1	0	416	2528	9723	50
55	87259	350	325	11353	54033	4637	432	3898	1	0	379	2443	9408	55
60	82886	300	277	10212	51855	4523	419	3600	1	0	358	2338	9003	60
65	76680	243	233	8831	48485	4330	373	3214	1	0	280	2234	8456	65
70	67325	190	190	7105	42942	3977	340	2585	1	0	230	2087	7678	70
75	53978	105	146	4913	34597	3464	278	1894	1	0	125	1864	6591	75
80	36895	58	81	2816	23500	2521	189	1164	1	0	77	1481	5007	80
85+	18415	4	28	1118	11533	1378	89	423	0	0	12	858	2972	85+

NUMBER OF PERSONS SURVIVING TO AGE X IF SPECIFIED CAUSES WERE ELIMINATED

Age (x)	No Causes	Respiratory T.B. (1)	Other Infec. and Paras. (2)	Neo-plasms (3)	Cardio-vascular (4)	Infl., Pneu., Bronch. (5)	Diar-rheal (6)	Certain Degenerative (7)	Maternal (8)	Cert. Dis. of Infancy (9)	Motor Vehicle (10)	Other Violence (11)	Other and Unknown (12)	(1)+(2)	(1)+(2)+(5)+(6)+(8)	(1)+(2)+(5)+(6)+(8)+part of(9)&(12)	(10)+(11)	Age (x)
0	100000	100000	100000	100000	100000	100000	100000	100000	100000	100000	100000	100000	100000	100000	100000	100000	100000	0
1	97760	97763	97822	97770	97764	97945	97861	97768	97760	99078	97764	97818	98232	97825	98112	99563	97822	1
5	97142	97151	97299	97186	97162	97343	97250	97167	97142	98453	97182	97292	97777	97308	97748	99251	97332	5
10	96878	96889	97086	96956	96914	97187	97030	96911	96878	98185	96942	97064	97580	97097	97560	99127	97128	10
15	96636	96647	96858	96739	96714	96966	96792	96682	96636	97940	96710	96847	97381	96909	97397	98981	96921	15
20	96331	96347	96642	96469	96433	96675	96492	96402	96347	97631	96444	96567	97136	96658	97182	98785	96681	20
25	95914	95969	96270	96084	96056	96280	96077	96007	95578	97208	96011	96194	96790	96325	96921	98556	96352	25
30	95407	95507	95801	95653	95618	95795	95572	95537	95537	96654	95555	95729	96348	95902	96590	98249	95917	30
35	94686	94849	95117	95056	95006	95093	94862	94893	94854	95963	94899	95051	95736	95281	96080	97771	95266	35
40	93751	93979	94204	94324	94291	94179	93931	94037	94029	95016	93994	94183	94918	94432	95328	97038	94427	40
45	92434	92736	92907	93355	93344	92620	92620	92644	92730	93681	92710	92917	93762	93211	94175	95894	93194	45
50	90337	90689	90832	91810	92032	90864	90540	90921	90630	91556	90641	90888	91878	91186	92222	93930	91194	50
55	87259	87665	87777	89529	90257	87664	87468	88053	87542	88436	87589	87875	89063	88185	89298	90977	88208	55
60	82886	83320	83425	86190	87958	83572	83097	83934	83155	84004	83220	83574	85003	83862	85047	86669	83910	60
65	76680	77137	77221	81128	84887	77503	76920	78026	76929	77714	77064	77418	79179	77681	79016	80556	77806	65
70	67325	67776	67841	72958	80508	68382	67567	69108	67543	68233	67709	68112	70275	68295	69842	71247	68591	70
75	53978	54416	54431	60647	74116	55295	54227	56042	54153	54706	54380	54811	57367	54872	56654	57854	55220	75
80	36895	37232	37258	43417	64866	38601	37139	38930	37015	37393	37209	37788	40623	37599	39726	40674	38110	80
85+	18415	18621	18633	23099	50775	20112	18607	19980	18475	18663	18617	19308	21888	18842	20861	21494	19520	85+

ADDED YRS OF LIFE

	No Causes	(1)	(2)	(3)	(4)	(5)	(6)	(7)	(8)	(9)	(10)	(11)	(12)	(1)+(2)	(1)+(2)+(5)+(6)+(8)	part of(9)&(12)	(10)+(11)
TOTAL		.203	.342	2.035	5.810	.691	.174	.676	.134	.963	.206	.491	1.739	.546	1.566	2.905	.699
WORK	2.591	.113	.098	.551	.779	.085	.019	.200	.102	.000	.087	.126	.316	.211	.419	.492	.214

POPULATION, DEATHS, DEATH RATES FOR ALL CAUSES COMBINED, AND SPECIFIED CAUSES

Age Start of Interval	Midyear Popula- tion	Deaths During Year	All Causes	Respira- tory T. B.	Other Infec. and Paras.	Neo- plasms	Cardio- vascular	Infl., Pneu., Bronch.	Diar- rheal	Certain Degen- erative	Maternal	Cert. Dis. of Infancy	Motor Vehicle	Other Violence	Other and Unknown	Age Start of Interval
0	115347	2653	.02300	.00000	.00033	.00010	.00015	.00164	.00043	.00003	.00000	.01343	.00003	.00064	.00621	0
1	444609	522	.00117	.00000	.00007	.00011	.00002	.00018	.00008	.00001	.00000	.00000	.00011	.00029	.00031	1
5	522115	291	.00056	.00000	.00002	.00010	.00002	.00002	.00000	.00001	.00000	.00000	.00011	.00016	.00012	5
10	502772	252	.00050	.00000	.00002	.00008	.00004	.00001	.00000	.00001	.00000	.00000	.00011	.00015	.00009	10
15	394470	512	.00130	.00000	.00002	.00008	.00005	.00004	.00001	.00002	.00000	.00000	.00062	.00031	.00015	15
20	347068	549	.00158	.00000	.00001	.00010	.00007	.00001	.00000	.00004	.00000	.00000	.00080	.00045	.00010	20
25	342331	513	.00150	.00001	.00002	.00014	.00014	.00003	.00001	.00006	.00000	.00000	.00050	.00048	.00011	25
30	392283	667	.00170	.00002	.00002	.00021	.00027	.00004	.00001	.00008	.00000	.00000	.00041	.00049	.00016	30
35	388023	847	.00218	.00002	.00003	.00028	.00052	.00006	.00001	.00015	.00000	.00000	.00034	.00056	.00021	35
40	334779	1209	.00361	.00004	.00003	.00053	.00142	.00011	.00001	.00024	.00000	.00000	.00035	.00056	.00030	40
45	333034	1923	.00577	.00004	.00003	.00056	.00275	.00019	.00001	.00029	.00000	.00000	.00037	.00071	.00044	45
50	286647	2847	.00993	.00011	.00006	.00191	.00530	.00036	.00004	.00050	.00000	.00000	.00032	.00065	.00068	50
55	234220	3853	.01645	.00016	.00008	.00309	.00927	.00075	.00006	.00079	.00000	.00000	.00045	.00070	.00111	55
60	184498	4905	.02659	.00031	.00017	.00520	.01546	.00117	.00006	.00116	.00000	.00000	.00052	.00078	.00177	60
65	148703	6309	.04243	.00032	.00017	.00775	.02551	.00238	.00016	.00160	.00000	.00000	.00062	.00101	.00291	65
70	115952	7236	.06241	.00056	.00021	.01010	.03894	.00394	.00019	.00231	.00000	.00000	.00068	.00101	.00447	70
75	64047	6276	.09799	.00053	.00020	.01341	.06167	.00735	.00023	.00342	.00000	.00000	.00105	.00156	.00856	75
80	32116	4552	.14174	.00059	.00025	.01765	.09145	.01093	.00056	.00423	.00000	.00000	.00078	.00243	.01286	80
85+	13551	3713	.27400	.00037	.00022	.02568	.17128	.02856	.00162	.00598	.00000	.00000	.00118	.00694	.03217	85+
ALL	5196565	49629														

			All Causes	Respira- tory T. B.	Other Infec. and Paras.	Neo- plasms	Cardio- vascular	Infl., Pneu., Bronch.	Diar- rheal	Certain Degen- erative	Maternal	Cert. Dis. of Infancy	Motor Vehicle	Other Violence	Other and Unknown
CRUDE DEATH RATE			.00955	.00007	.00005	.00140	.00499	.00057	.00005	.00035	.00000	.00030	.00038	.00051	.00089
STANDARDIZED RATE (1)			.00614	.00004	.00005	.00083	.00269	.00035	.00004	.00021	.00000	.00047	.00035	.00043	.00067
STANDARDIZED RATE (2)			.01161	.00008	.00006	.00169	.00631	.00073	.00005	.00041	.00000	.00028	.00040	.00055	.00106
GEOMETRIC MEAN			.00776												

LIFE TABLE FOR ALL CAUSES COMBINED

Age (x)	Midyear Popula- tion	Deaths During Year	$_nM_x$	$_nq_x$	l_x	$_nd_x$	$_nL_x$	$_nm_x$	$_na_x$	T_x	$_nr_x$	$\overset{\circ}{e}_x$	Age (x)
0	115347	2653	.023000	.022540	100000	2254	97992	.023002	.109100	6781893	.000000	67.819	0
1	444609	522	.001174	.004666	97746	458	389839	.001175	1.500000	6683901	.000000	68.380	1
5	522115	291	.000557	.002765	97288	269	485768	.000554	2.500000	6294062	.000000	64.695	5
10	502772	252	.000501	.002515	97019	244	484560	.000504	2.808231	5808295	.018727	59.868	10
15	394470	512	.001298	.006510	96775	630	482407	.001306	2.669974	5323734	.035009	55.011	15
20	347068	549	.001582	.007864	96145	758	478847	.001583	2.522537	4841327	.022290	50.354	20
25	342331	513	.001499	.007464	95387	712	475164	.001498	2.512582	4362480	-.004051	45.735	25
30	392283	667	.001700	.008461	94675	801	471437	.001699	2.580108	3887308	-.016875	41.060	30
35	388023	847	.002183	.010866	93874	1020	467000	.002184	2.676879	3415880	-.006423	36.388	35
40	334779	1209	.003611	.017953	92854	1667	460432	.003621	2.697710	2948879	-.011374	31.758	40
45	333034	1923	.005774	.028535	91187	2602	449982	.005782	2.712337	2488447	.007229	27.289	45
50	286647	2847	.009932	.048755	88585	4319	432983	.009975	2.698107	2038465	.020200	23.011	50
55	234220	3853	.016450	.079617	84266	6709	405687	.016537	2.668337	1605482	.026365	19.053	55
60	184498	4905	.026586	.125565	77557	9740	364758	.026703	2.635844	1199795	.022800	15.470	60
65	148703	6309	.042427	.192577	67817	13060	307458	.042472	2.581371	835037	.005636	12.313	65
70	115952	7236	.062410	.271024	54757	14841	237242	.062556	2.537705	527539	-.014105	9.634	70
75	64047	6276	.097991	.394478	39916	15746	159738	.098574	2.465715	290297	-.026819	7.273	75
80	32116	4552	.141736	.519321	24170	12552	88157	.142382	2.395435	130559	-.026819	5.402	80
85+	13551	3713	.274002	1.000000	11618	11618	42401	.274002	3.649609	42401	.000000	3.650	85+

NUMBER OF PERSONS DYING (OUT OF 100,000 AT BIRTH) ABOVE AGE X FROM SPECIFIED CAUSES

Age (x)	All Causes	Respiratory T. B.	Other Infec. and Paras.	Neoplasms	Cardiovascular	Infl., Pneu., Bronch.	Diarrheal	Certain Degenerative	Maternal	Cert. Dis. of Infancy	Motor Vehicle	Other Violence	Other and Unknown	Age (x)
0	100000	679	435	14795	56575	6383	410	3606	0	1316	2904	4160	8737	0
1	97746	679	402	14785	56560	6222	367	3602	0	0	2901	4097	8131	1
5	97288	677	377	14742	56552	6154	335	3599	0	0	2859	3984	8009	5
10	97019	677	367	14693	56544	6144	335	3595	0	0	2804	3908	7952	10
15	96775	677	358	14654	56527	6138	334	3589	0	0	2752	3836	7910	15
20	96145	677	347	14613	56505	6119	332	3578	0	0	2452	3684	7838	20
25	95387	677	343	14565	56468	6112	332	3560	0	0	2070	3467	7793	25
30	94675	673	335	14498	56401	6097	329	3534	0	0	1833	3238	7737	30
35	93874	663	328	14398	56276	6080	325	3495	0	0	1642	3005	7662	35
40	92854	652	313	14266	56032	6053	320	3425	0	0	1484	2743	7566	40
45	91187	632	299	14021	55374	6001	315	3315	0	0	1322	2485	7423	45
50	88585	614	287	13589	54135	5917	312	3183	0	0	1155	2164	7229	50
55	84266	565	260	12759	51828	5762	295	2966	0	0	1015	1882	6934	55
60	77557	499	227	11500	48044	5457	273	2646	0	0	831	1598	6482	60
65	67817	386	165	9594	42379	5030	251	2221	0	0	641	1314	5836	65
70	54757	287	114	7210	34525	4297	201	1729	0	0	450	1004	4940	70
75	39916	154	64	4810	25263	3358	156	1179	0	0	289	764	3879	75
80	24170	69	32	2658	15352	2175	119	630	0	0	121	514	2500	80
85+	11618	16	9	1089	7262	1211	69	253	0	0	50	294	1365	85+

NUMBER OF PERSONS SURVIVING TO AGE X IF SPECIFIED CAUSES WERE ELIMINATED

Age (x)	No Causes	Respiratory T. B.	Other Infec. and Paras.	Neoplasms	Cardiovascular	Infl., Pneu., Bronch.	Diarrheal	Certain Degenerative	Maternal	Cert. Dis. of Infancy	Motor Vehicle	Other Violence	Other and Unknown	(1) + (2)	(1) + (2) + (5) + (6) + (8)	(1)+(2)+ (5)+(6)+ (8)+part of(9)&(12)	(10) + (11)	Age (x)
		(1)	(2)	(3)	(4)	(5)	(6)	(7)	(8)	(9)	(10)	(11)	(12)					
0	100000	100000	100000	100000	100000	100000	100000	100000	100000	100000	100000	100000	100000	100000	100000	100000	100000	0
1	97746	97746	97779	97756	97761	97905	97789	97750	97746	99056	97749	97808	98347	97779	97981	99350	97811	1
5	97288	97290	97345	97311	97315	97362	97295	97288	97288	98592	97343	97463	98009	97347	97649	99060	97508	5
10	97019	97021	97086	97121	97050	97255	97093	97030	97019	98319	97119	97269	97795	97088	97399	98812	97369	10
15	96775	96777	96851	96915	96823	97016	96850	96792	96775	98072	96926	97097	97591	96853	97170	98583	97249	15
20	96145	96147	96232	96325	96214	96404	96221	96173	96145	97433	96595	96617	97028	96234	96569	97978	97070	20
25	95387	95389	95477	95614	95493	95651	95463	95432	95387	96665	96217	96073	96309	95479	95819	97217	96909	25
30	94675	94681	94772	94967	94847	94952	94753	94746	94675	95944	95737	95586	95646	94778	95134	96525	96658	30
35	93874	93890	93977	94264	94169	94165	93956	93983	93874	95132	95120	95011	94912	93993	94367	95751	96272	35
40	92854	92881	92971	93371	93390	93169	92940	93032	92854	94098	94245	94243	93578	92998	93399	94775	95655	40
45	91187	91233	91316	91939	92372	91548	91276	91471	91187	92409	92716	92811	92434	91362	91813	93174	94367	45
50	88585	88647	88722	89747	90982	89019	88674	88991	88585	89772	90238	90485	89990	88785	89310	90643	92173	50
55	84266	84373	84423	86195	88888	84831	84368	84865	84266	85395	85977	86354	85896	84530	85200	86490	88108	55
60	77557	77719	77733	80577	85732	78372	77672	78418	77557	78596	79312	79758	79500	77895	78831	80055	81562	60
65	67817	68064	68029	72332	81053	68935	67938	68972	67817	68726	69533	70014	70137	68277	69526	70649	71785	65
70	54757	55046	54974	60724	74432	56333	54900	56140	54757	55491	56317	56817	57468	55264	57003	57989	58436	70
75	39916	40240	40116	46578	66098	41897	40058	41405	39916	40451	41194	41629	42852	40442	42600	43421	42961	75
80	24170	24431	24316	30193	54897	26347	24285	25512	24170	24494	25077	25409	27118	24578	26919	27551	26362	80
85+	11618	11780	11704	15905	42311	13397	11707	12536	11618	11774	12104	12371	13928	11867	13789	14202	12889	85+

ADDED YRS OF LIFE																		
TOTAL		.089	.110	1.534	9.903	.732	.086	.469	.000	.907	.903	1.081	1.451	.199	1.031	2.101	2.008	
WORK	3.617	.027	.027	.484	1.202	.103	.010	.154	.000	.000	.577	.551	.263	.055	.168	.182	1.137	

POPULATION, DEATHS, DEATH RATES FOR ALL CAUSES COMBINED, AND SPECIFIED CAUSES

Age Start of Interval	Midyear Population	Deaths During Year	All Causes	Respiratory T. B.	Other Infec. and Paras.	Neoplasms	Cardiovascular	Infl., Pneu., Bronch.	Diarrheal	Certain Degenerative	Maternal	Cert. Dis. of Infancy	Motor Vehicle	Other Violence	Other and Unknown	Age Start of Interval
0	109502	1992	.01819	.00000	.00029	.00005	.00014	.00143	.00045	.00002	.00000	.01052	.00009	.00037	.00482	0
1	423139	473	.00112	.00000	.00007	.00013	.00002	.00019	.00005	.00001	.00000	.00000	.00012	.00023	.00031	1
5	499764	205	.00041	.00000	.00003	.00007	.00001	.00003	.00000	.00001	.00000	.00000	.00008	.00008	.00011	5
10	478433	150	.00031	.00000	.00001	.00006	.00003	.00002	.00000	.00001	.00000	.00000	.00005	.00004	.00010	10
15	376304	198	.00053	.00001	.00002	.00006	.00004	.00001	.00001	.00002	.00001	.00000	.00022	.00004	.00009	15
20	323868	185	.00057	.00000	.00002	.00005	.00008	.00001	.00000	.00001	.00005	.00000	.00013	.00007	.00014	20
25	312937	221	.00071	.00000	.00002	.00013	.00008	.00001	.00002	.00003	.00008	.00000	.00006	.00012	.00015	25
30	355305	351	.00099	.00002	.00001	.00026	.00021	.00003	.00000	.00005	.00007	.00000	.00006	.00011	.00017	30
35	367518	562	.00153	.00003	.00002	.00051	.00035	.00003	.00001	.00011	.00008	.00000	.00006	.00013	.00020	35
40	326206	798	.00245	.00003	.00002	.00078	.00068	.00006	.00001	.00017	.00005	.00000	.00011	.00019	.00034	40
45	318744	1239	.00389	.00003	.00003	.00131	.00135	.00012	.00001	.00024	.00001	.00000	.00014	.00025	.00041	45
50	267156	1440	.00539	.00003	.00004	.00168	.00229	.00009	.00003	.00035	.00000	.00000	.00014	.00023	.00050	50
55	225927	1886	.00835	.00003	.00003	.00237	.00399	.00018	.00002	.00045	.00000	.00000	.00020	.00025	.00076	55
60	204479	2796	.01367	.00004	.00005	.00326	.00768	.00031	.00005	.00069	.00000	.00000	.00022	.00031	.00107	60
65	183205	4166	.02274	.00003	.00008	.00464	.01388	.00054	.00006	.00117	.00000	.00000	.00024	.00034	.00177	65
70	145464	5252	.03611	.00008	.00009	.00571	.02403	.00117	.00010	.00177	.00000	.00000	.00038	.00060	.00217	70
75	91061	5802	.06372	.00010	.00024	.00819	.04336	.00279	.00035	.00256	.00000	.00000	.00032	.00134	.00451	75
80	51041	5469	.10715	.00008	.00018	.01148	.07547	.00505	.00065	.00310	.00000	.00000	.00037	.00300	.00778	80
85+	24124	5650	.23421	.00008	.00054	.01675	.16241	.01724	.00079	.00415	.00000	.00000	.00037	.00929	.02259	85+
ALL	5084177	38835														

CRUDE DEATH RATE			.00764	.00002	.00005	.00122	.00429	.00033	.00004	.00030	.00002	.00023	.00013	.00026	.00074	
STANDARDIZED RATE (1)			.00384	.00001	.00004	.00063	.00162	.00018	.00003	.00015	.00002	.00037	.00012	.00017	.00050	
STANDARDIZED RATE (2)			.00736	.00002	.00004	.00119	.00412	.00031	.00004	.00029	.00002	.00022	.00013	.00025	.00072	
GEOMETRIC MEAN			.00473													

LIFE TABLE FOR ALL CAUSES COMBINED

Age (x)	Midyear Population	Deaths During Year	$_nM_x$	$_nq_x$	l_x	$_nd_x$	$_nL_x$	$_nm_x$	$_na_x$	T_x	$_nr_x$	$\overset{\circ}{e}_x$	Age (x)
0	109502	1992	.018191	.017900	100000	1790	98391	.018193	.100925	7383600	.000000	73.836	0
1	423139	473	.001118	.004460	98210	438	391745	.001118	1.500000	7285210	.000000	74.180	1
5	499764	205	.000410	.002046	97772	200	488360	.000410	2.500000	6893465	.000000	70.506	5
10	478433	150	.000314	.001568	97572	153	487489	.000314	2.577614	6405105	.018968	65.645	10
15	376304	198	.000526	.002638	97419	257	486478	.000528	2.600519	5917615	.036650	60.744	15
20	323868	185	.000571	.002851	97162	277	485135	.000571	2.563929	5431137	.026647	55.898	20
25	312937	221	.000706	.003530	96885	342	483611	.000707	2.620005	4946002	.000871	51.050	25
30	355305	351	.000988	.004910	96543	474	481611	.000984	2.671414	4462391	-.017004	46.222	30
35	367518	562	.001529	.007620	96069	732	478658	.001529	2.695811	3980780	.000471	41.437	35
40	326206	798	.002446	.012188	95337	1162	474006	.002451	2.694528	3502121	.008873	36.734	40
45	318744	1239	.003887	.019294	94175	1817	466605	.003894	2.649743	3028115	.011830	32.154	45
50	267156	1440	.005390	.026722	92358	2468	456011	.005412	2.658614	2561511	.026283	27.735	50
55	225927	1886	.008348	.041117	89890	3696	440888	.008383	2.683532	2105499	.021919	23.423	55
60	204479	2796	.013674	.066408	86194	5724	417702	.013704	2.682019	1664611	.010212	19.312	60
65	183205	4166	.022740	.108078	80470	8697	381914	.022772	2.650155	1246909	.007305	15.495	65
70	145464	5252	.036105	.167110	71773	11994	330532	.036287	2.637725	864995	.024382	12.052	70
75	91061	5802	.063716	.278124	59779	16626	258665	.064276	2.580271	534463	.036126	8.941	75
80	51041	5469	.107149	.426390	43153	18400	170110	.108165	2.518750	275799	.036126	6.391	80
85+	24124	5650	.234207	1.000000	24753	24753	105689	.234207	4.269735	105689	.000000	4.270	85+

NUMBER OF PERSONS DYING (OUT OF 100,000 AT BIRTH) ABOVE AGE X FROM SPECIFIED CAUSES

Age (x)	All Causes	Respiratory T. B.	Other Infec. and Paras.	Neoplasms	Cardiovascular	Infl., Pneu., Bronch.	Diarrheal	Certain Degenerative	Maternal	Cert. Dis. of Infancy	Motor Vehicle	Other Violence	Other and Unknown	Age (x)
0	100000	192	411	14326	62116	4629	457	3648	171	1035	1144	3153	8718	0
1	98210	192	382	14321	62103	4487	413	3646	171	0	1135	3116	8244	1
5	97772	192	354	14272	62096	4413	395	3644	171	0	1089	3025	8121	5
10	97572	192	342	14237	62091	4400	394	3640	171	0	1049	2988	8068	10
15	97419	192	335	14207	62077	4391	394	3635	171	0	1025	2971	8021	15
20	97162	189	326	14180	62059	4384	390	3623	164	0	917	2950	7980	20
25	96885	189	314	14156	62019	4378	388	3617	140	0	856	2915	7913	25
30	96543	187	304	14091	61978	4372	380	3601	103	0	827	2858	7842	30
35	96069	178	297	13964	61880	4360	380	3576	68	0	800	2807	7759	35
40	95337	162	288	13722	61711	4345	378	3525	29	0	770	2743	7664	40
45	94175	148	277	13349	61386	4318	375	3446	4	0	716	2654	7502	45
50	92358	132	264	12739	60756	4264	372	3336	0	0	650	2537	7308	50
55	89890	118	246	11968	59703	4221	360	3175	0	0	587	2433	7079	55
60	86194	104	232	10919	57935	4142	352	2960	0	0	499	2306	6745	60
65	80470	86	211	9555	54720	4013	332	2672	0	0	407	2177	6297	65
70	71773	76	180	7782	49411	3807	309	2225	0	0	315	2048	5620	70
75	59779	48	150	5888	41426	3417	274	1639	0	0	188	1846	4903	75
80	43153	23	87	3756	30108	2687	194	973	0	0	106	1495	3724	80
85+	24753	9	57	1770	17165	1823	83	438	0	0	39	981	2388	85+

NUMBER OF PERSONS SURVIVING TO AGE X IF SPECIFIED CAUSES WERE ELIMINATED

Age (x)	No Causes	Respiratory T. B. (1)	Other Infec. and Paras. (2)	Neoplasms (3)	Cardiovascular (4)	Infl., Pneu., Bronch. (5)	Diarrheal (6)	Certain Degenerative (7)	Maternal (8)	Cert. Dis. of Infancy (9)	Motor Vehicle (10)	Other Violence (11)	Other and Unknown (12)	(1)+(2)	(1)+(2)+(5)+(6)+(8)	(1)+(2)+(5)+(6)+(8)+part of (9)&(12)	(10)+(11)	Age (x)
0	100000	100000	100000	100000	100000	100000	100000	100000	100000	100000	100000	100000	100000	100000	100000	100000	100000	0
1	98210	98210	98239	98215	98223	98351	98254	98212	98210	99241	98219	98247	98681	98239	98423	99577	98256	1
5	97772	97772	97829	97826	97792	97986	97833	97776	97772	98798	97827	97899	98364	97829	98104	99302	97954	5
10	97572	97572	97640	97661	97597	97799	97634	97580	97572	98596	97667	97736	98216	97640	97930	99134	97831	10
15	97419	97419	97494	97538	97458	97664	97481	97432	97419	98442	97538	97600	98109	97494	97792	99002	97719	15
20	97162	97165	97246	97307	97219	97404	97228	97187	97169	98182	97388	97363	97892	97249	97564	98777	97590	20
25	96885	96888	96981	97054	96981	97132	96953	96916	96916	97902	97172	97121	97680	96984	97330	98555	97408	25
30	96543	96548	96649	96776	96680	96795	96619	96590	96611	97557	96858	96835	97407	96654	97050	98288	97151	30
35	96069	96083	96181	96428	96303	96332	96144	96140	96171	97078	96409	96411	97012	96195	96637	97883	96752	35
40	95337	95367	95457	95936	95738	95613	95414	95459	95478	96338	95705	95740	96369	95487	95982	97231	96109	40
45	94175	94218	94305	95140	94897	94475	94254	94374	94339	95164	94592	94662	95357	94348	94892	96140	95081	45
50	92358	92416	92498	93917	93697	92705	92438	92662	92522	93328	92833	92952	93712	92556	93151	94387	93430	50
55	89890	89961	90044	92184	92253	90271	89980	90346	90050	90834	90414	90571	91437	90115	90748	91962	91100	55
60	86194	86275	86355	89453	90256	86637	86288	86843	86347	87099	86783	86973	88011	86437	87131	88307	87567	60
65	80470	80563	80641	84889	87580	81005	80577	81356	80613	81315	81110	81323	82609	80735	81528	82645	81969	65
70	71773	71866	71955	77497	83768	72450	71890	72991	71901	72527	72431	72656	74339	72048	72976	73598	73322	70
75	59779	59882	59958	66430	78807	60704	59909	61338	59885	60407	60443	60702	62596	60061	61232	62118	61376	75
80	43153	43248	43335	49990	71026	44454	43315	44856	43230	43606	43702	44123	46244	43431	44988	45701	44684	80
85+	24753	24818	24880	30448	60232	26174	24929	26149	24797	25013	25118	25706	27618	24946	26612	27099	26085	85+

ADDED YRS OF LIFE

	No Causes	(1)	(2)	(3)	(4)	(5)	(6)	(7)	(8)	(9)	(10)	(11)	(12)	(1)+(2)	(1)+(2)+(5)+(6)+(8)	part	(10)+(11)
TOTAL		.040	.113	2.175	12.062	.536	.087	.483	.075	.774	.344	.519	1.479	.153	.858	1.854	.868
WORK	2.055	.018	.026	.544	.630	.045	.010	.113	.055	.000	.143	.143	.256	.044	.153	.182	.287

POPULATION, DEATHS, DEATH RATES FOR ALL CAUSES COMBINED, AND SPECIFIED CAUSES

Age Start of Interval	Midyear Popula- tion	Deaths During Year	All Causes	Respira- tory T. B.	Other Infec. and Paras.	Neo- plasms	Cardio- vascular	Infl., Pneu., Bronch.	Diar- rheal	Certain Degen- erative	Maternal	Cert. Dis. of Infancy	Motor Vehicle	Other Violence	Other and Unknown	Age Start of Interval
0	117737	2511	.02133	.00000	.00022	.00012	.00012	.00166	.00037	.00002	.00000	.01250	.00004	.00090	.00538	0
1	472776	509	.00108	.00000	.00005	.00008	.00002	.00019	.00005	.00001	.00000	.00000	.00011	.00026	.00030	1
5	567793	302	.00053	.00000	.00002	.00008	.00001	.00003	.00000	.00001	.00000	.00000	.00012	.00013	.00013	5
10	536587	285	.00053	.00000	.00001	.00010	.00002	.00001	.00000	.00000	.00000	.00000	.00012	.00015	.00011	10
15	502242	587	.00117	.00000	.00001	.00007	.00004	.00002	.00000	.00001	.00000	.00000	.00061	.00027	.00014	15
20	398801	683	.00171	.00000	.00001	.00011	.00011	.00003	.00001	.00003	.00000	.00000	.00080	.00050	.00012	20
25	360541	483	.00134	.00000	.00001	.00013	.00009	.00002	.00001	.00004	.00000	.00000	.00045	.00047	.00013	25
30	364549	671	.00184	.00000	.00001	.00021	.00030	.00004	.00000	.00007	.00000	.00000	.00043	.00063	.00013	30
35	398627	921	.00231	.00001	.00002	.00033	.00058	.00005	.00001	.00014	.00000	.00000	.00034	.00060	.00023	35
40	384966	1533	.00398	.00003	.00002	.00057	.00156	.00014	.00001	.00018	.00000	.00000	.00038	.00074	.00036	40
45	328073	2042	.00622	.00004	.00005	.00105	.00297	.00023	.00001	.00032	.00000	.00000	.00037	.00073	.00045	45
50	317691	3266	.01028	.00007	.00003	.00179	.00552	.00035	.00003	.00050	.00000	.00000	.00050	.00080	.00069	50
55	260358	4542	.01745	.00012	.00010	.00347	.00979	.00084	.00007	.00085	.00000	.00000	.00046	.00081	.00094	55
60	209305	5902	.02820	.00020	.00007	.00548	.01637	.00179	.00008	.00118	.00000	.00000	.00048	.00082	.00173	60
65	148487	6572	.04426	.00034	.00017	.00841	.02614	.00323	.00008	.00155	.00000	.00000	.00055	.00090	.00289	65
70	117171	7983	.06813	.00045	.00020	.01111	.04210	.00552	.00018	.00226	.00000	.00000	.00070	.00107	.00453	70
75	77291	7642	.09887	.00053	.00021	.01461	.06186	.00888	.00028	.00338	.00000	.00000	.00091	.00142	.00681	75
80	35517	5509	.15511	.00059	.00034	.01917	.09790	.01577	.00056	.00473	.00000	.00000	.00121	.00211	.01273	80
85+	16508	4303	.26066	.00103	.00061	.02138	.16677	.03162	.00103	.00575	.00000	.00000	.00091	.00624	.02532	85+
ALL	5615020	56246														

			All Causes	Respira- tory T. B.	Other Infec. and Paras.	Neo- plasms	Cardio- vascular	Infl., Pneu., Bronch.	Diar- rheal	Certain Degen- erative	Maternal	Cert. Dis. of Infancy	Motor Vehicle	Other Violence	Other and Unknown
CRUDE DEATH RATE			.01002	.00005	.00004	.00149	.00527	.00073	.00004	.00035	.00000	.00026	.00039	.00055	.00083
STANDARDIZED RATE (1)			.00631	.00003	.00004	.00087	.00280	.00043	.00004	.00020	.00000	.00044	.00036	.00046	.00063
STANDARDIZED RATE (2)			.01207	.00007	.00005	.00179	.00656	.00092	.00005	.00041	.00000	.00026	.00041	.00057	.00098
GEOMETRIC MEAN			.00791												

LIFE TABLE FOR ALL CAUSES COMBINED

Age (x)	Midyear Popula- tion	Deaths During Year	$_nM_x$	$_nq_x$	l_x	$_nd_x$	$_nL_x$	$_nm_x$	$_na_x$	T_x	$_nr_x$	$\overset{\circ}{e}_x$	Age (x)
0	117737	2511	.021327	.020930	100000	2093	98129	.021329	.106256	6745799	.000000	67.458	0
1	472776	509	.001077	.004290	97907	420	390578	.001075	1.500000	6647670	.000000	67.898	1
5	567793	302	.000532	.002657	97487	259	486788	.000532	2.500000	6257092	.000000	64.184	5
10	536587	285	.000531	.002654	97228	258	485559	.000531	2.749516	5770304	.006168	59.348	10
15	502242	587	.001169	.005857	96970	568	483548	.001175	2.707233	5284745	.021955	54.499	15
20	398801	683	.001713	.008537	96402	823	479967	.001715	2.517720	4801197	.032919	49.804	20
25	360541	483	.001340	.006675	95579	638	476310	.001339	2.515347	4321230	.016735	45.211	25
30	364549	671	.001841	.009164	94941	870	472622	.001841	2.605364	3844920	-.004783	40.498	30
35	398627	921	.002310	.011459	94071	1078	467862	.002304	2.687075	3372299	-.011544	35.848	35
40	384966	1533	.003982	.019765	92993	1838	460730	.003989	2.695638	2904437	-.009464	31.233	40
45	328073	2042	.006224	.030761	91155	2804	449308	.006241	2.693771	2443707	-.012409	26.808	45
50	317691	3266	.010280	.050322	88351	4446	431527	.010303	2.699430	1994399	-.010524	22.574	50
55	260358	4542	.017445	.084143	83905	7060	403075	.017515	2.669942	1562872	-.019672	18.627	55
60	209305	5902	.028198	.132800	76845	10205	360026	.028345	2.628715	1159798	-.027128	15.093	60
65	148487	6572	.044260	.200555	66640	13365	300895	.044417	2.582866	799772	-.019318	12.001	65
70	117171	7983	.068131	.291337	53275	15521	227902	.068104	2.521221	498877	-.002086	9.364	70
75	77291	7642	.098873	.395879	37754	14946	150799	.099112	2.459479	270975	-.012791	7.177	75
80	35517	5509	.155109	.553052	22808	12614	81067	.155600	2.386006	120175	-.012791	5.269	80
85+	16508	4303	.260661	1.000000	10194	10194	39108	.260661	3.836393	39108	.000000	3.836	85+

NUMBER OF PERSONS DYING (OUT OF 100,000 AT BIRTH) ABOVE AGE X FROM SPECIFIED CAUSES

Age (x)	All Causes	Respiratory T. B.	Other Infec. and Paras.	Neo-plasms	Cardio-vascular	Infl., Pneu., Bronch.	Diar-rheal	Certain Degen-erative	Maternal	Cert. Dis. of Infancy	Motor Vehicle	Other Violence	Other and Unknown	Age (x)
0	100000	562	370	15110	56207	7736	346	3467	0	1228	2938	4293	7743	0
1	97907	562	349	15058	56195	7573	310	3466	0	1	2934	4205	7214	1
5	97487	562	328	15066	56189	7499	289	3462	0	0	2892	4103	7097	5
10	97228	562	320	15025	56185	7485	288	3458	0	0	2832	4038	7035	10
15	96970	562	316	14976	56175	7478	286	3456	0	0	2774	3964	6983	15
20	96402	562	311	14941	56158	7467	285	3449	0	0	2480	3831	6918	20
25	95579	561	306	14890	56106	7454	282	3435	0	0	2097	3589	6859	25
30	94941	561	303	14827	56063	7445	280	3416	0	0	1881	3366	6799	30
35	94071	559	297	14726	55921	7424	278	3381	0	0	1679	3068	6738	35
40	92993	554	289	14571	55652	7400	273	3316	0	0	1520	2787	6631	40
45	91155	542	282	14309	54931	7336	267	3234	0	0	1344	2446	6464	45
50	88351	522	260	13838	53591	7234	261	3090	0	0	1177	2116	6262	50
55	83905	492	245	13063	51201	7083	250	2874	0	0	960	1772	5965	55
60	76845	444	204	11659	47238	6740	224	2530	0	0	774	1446	5586	60
65	66640	373	180	9674	41213	6092	194	2104	0	0	600	1150	4960	65
70	53215	272	129	7136	33418	5115	170	1637	0	0	434	878	4086	70
75	37754	169	83	4604	23827	3857	129	1121	0	0	274	635	3055	75
80	22808	88	51	2398	14476	2515	86	611	0	0	137	420	2026	80
85+	10194	40	24	836	6522	1237	40	225	0	0	36	244	990	85+

NUMBER OF PERSONS SURVIVING TO AGE X IF SPECIFIED CAUSES WERE ELIMINATED

Age (x)	No Causes	Respiratory T. B. (1)	Other Infec. and Paras. (2)	Neo-plasms (3)	Cardio-vascular (4)	Infl., Pneu., Bronch. (5)	Diar-rheal (6)	Certain Degener-ative (7)	Maternal (8)	Cert. Dis. of Infancy (9)	Motor Vehicle (10)	Other Violence (11)	Other and Unknown (12)	(1) + (2)	(1) + (2) + (5) + (6) + (8)	(1)+(2)+ (5)+(6)+ (8)+part of(9)&(12)	(10) + (11)	Age (x)
0	100000	100000	100000	100000	100000	100000	100000	100000	100000	100000	100000	100000	100000	100000	100000	100000	100000	0
1	97907	97907	97928	97919	97919	98068	97943	97908	97907	99129	97911	97994	98432	97928	98125	99268	97998	1
5	97487	97487	97529	97531	97505	97722	97543	97492	97487	98704	97533	97676	98127	97529	97820	99006	97722	5
10	97228	97228	97278	97313	97250	97476	97285	97237	97228	98442	97334	97481	97929	97278	97583	98773	97587	10
15	96970	96970	97023	97103	97002	97224	97029	96981	96970	98181	97133	97297	97721	97023	97337	98528	97461	15
20	96402	96402	96460	96570	96450	96666	96462	96420	96402	97606	96859	96860	97214	96460	96784	97970	97319	20
25	95579	95580	95642	95796	95679	95854	95641	95611	95579	96773	96416	96275	96443	95643	95980	97158	97118	25
30	94941	94942	95006	95220	95083	95223	95005	94991	94941	96127	95989	95857	95860	95007	95353	96525	96915	30
35	94071	94074	94142	94448	94354	94371	94136	94156	94071	95246	95313	95278	95043	94114	94510	95674	96537	35
40	92993	93001	93071	93520	93541	93314	93082	93142	92993	94154	94381	94470	94061	93079	93469	94625	95880	40
45	91155	91175	91238	91933	92413	91533	91229	91382	91155	92293	92693	92946	92370	91258	91711	92853	94514	45
50	88351	88390	88453	89574	90919	88818	88429	88713	88351	89454	90008	90418	89730	88492	89038	90159	92115	50
55	83905	83971	84017	85636	88774	84499	83990	84461	83905	84953	85654	86211	85509	84083	84761	85843	88050	55
60	76845	76951	76986	80000	85418	77719	76947	77686	76845	77805	78665	79277	78684	77093	78074	79096	81155	60
65	66640	66799	66785	71325	80464	68012	66757	67770	66640	67472	68384	69033	68834	66944	68441	69387	70839	65
70	53215	53492	53437	59492	73424	55270	53390	54603	53215	53940	54820	55438	55841	53654	55783	56630	57046	70
75	37754	37994	37907	44586	64382	40279	37870	39140	37754	38225	38987	39458	40488	38148	40824	41539	40788	75
80	22808	23015	22925	29004	53323	25463	22911	24055	22808	23093	23661	24035	25325	23133	25943	26497	24934	80
85+	10194	10318	10264	14323	39602	12348	10270	11020	10194	10321	10644	10864	12093	10389	12679	13053	11343	85+

ADDED YRS OF LIFE																	
TOTAL		.063	.081	1.967	10.107	.864	.072	.436	.000	.841	.905	1.140	1.327	.144	1.094	2.001	2.071
WORK	3.749	.016	.019	.500	1.265	.111	.010	.143	.000	.000	.579	.602	.265	.036	.158	.170	1.191

POPULATION, DEATHS, DEATH RATES FOR ALL CAUSES COMBINED, AND SPECIFIED CAUSES

Age Start of Interval	Midyear Population	Deaths During Year	All Causes	Respiratory T. B.	Other Infec. and Paras.	Neoplasms	Cardiovascular	Infl., Pneu., Bronch.	Diarrheal	Certain Degenerative	Maternal	Cert. Dis. of Infancy	Motor Vehicle	Other Violence	Other and Unknown	Age Start of Interval
0	111256	1859	.01671	.00000	.00017	.00007	.00006	.00148	.00029	.00002	.00000	.00955	.00006	.00047	.00453	0
1	450043	414	.00092	.00000	.00005	.00010	.00002	.00012	.00006	.00000	.00000	.00000	.00009	.00022	.00025	1
5	541501	210	.00039	.00000	.00001	.00006	.00001	.00003	.00000	.00001	.00000	.00000	.00010	.00006	.00011	5
10	512470	164	.00032	.00000	.00000	.00007	.00003	.00003	.00000	.00001	.00000	.00000	.00005	.00005	.00008	10
15	476150	265	.00056	.00000	.00001	.00008	.00004	.00002	.00000	.00001	.00001	.00000	.00021	.00008	.00009	15
20	377460	236	.00063	.00001	.00001	.00007	.00006	.00002	.00000	.00002	.00002	.00000	.00017	.00012	.00013	20
25	340489	236	.00069	.00001	.00000	.00015	.00009	.00003	.00001	.00003	.00004	.00000	.00007	.00014	.00012	25
30	336017	326	.00097	.00000	.00002	.00022	.00018	.00003	.00000	.00004	.00004	.00000	.00010	.00018	.00015	30
35	369365	590	.00160	.00002	.00002	.00045	.00034	.00005	.00001	.00009	.00007	.00000	.00008	.00024	.00024	35
40	368638	883	.00240	.00000	.00002	.00075	.00069	.00010	.00001	.00015	.00002	.00000	.00008	.00028	.00028	40
45	323257	1276	.00395	.00002	.00003	.00123	.00131	.00010	.00001	.00019	.00000	.00000	.00012	.00041	.00053	45
50	304285	1724	.00567	.00004	.00006	.00180	.00219	.00016	.00003	.00029	.00000	.00000	.00014	.00033	.00063	50
55	249628	2152	.00862	.00002	.00004	.00247	.00409	.00022	.00003	.00044	.00000	.00000	.00015	.00036	.00078	55
60	216891	3014	.01390	.00004	.00006	.00339	.00771	.00036	.00006	.00067	.00000	.00000	.00015	.00030	.00117	60
65	185965	4109	.02210	.00004	.00006	.00436	.01360	.00058	.00006	.00099	.00000	.00000	.00024	.00047	.00170	65
70	156685	6103	.03895	.00006	.00013	.00635	.02548	.00134	.00018	.00177	.00000	.00000	.00038	.00070	.00257	70
75	110441	7229	.06546	.00005	.00011	.00848	.04476	.00325	.00034	.00255	.00000	.00000	.00043	.00129	.00418	75
80	57759	6706	.11610	.00010	.00010	.01221	.08111	.00691	.00059	.00325	.00000	.00000	.00054	.00279	.00850	80
85+	32189	6852	.21287	.00012	.00028	.01451	.15331	.01647	.00068	.00401	.00000	.00000	.00016	.00808	.01525	85+
ALL	5520489	44348														

CRUDE DEATH RATE			.00803	.00001	.00003	.00126	.00460	.00039	.00004	.00029	.00001	.00019	.00014	.00031	.00074	
STANDARDIZED RATE (1)			.00383	.00001	.00003	.00063	.00164	.00019	.00003	.00013	.00001	.00034	.00012	.00021	.00049	
STANDARDIZED RATE (2)			.00746	.00001	.00003	.00120	.00420	.00035	.00004	.00028	.00001	.00020	.00014	.00030	.00070	
GEOMETRIC MEAN			.00473													

LIFE TABLE FOR ALL CAUSES COMBINED

Age (x)	Midyear Population	Deaths During Year	$_nM_x$	$_nq_x$	l_x	$_nd_x$	$_nL_x$	$_nm_x$	$_na_x$	T_x	$_nr_x$	$\overset{\circ}{e}_x$	Age (x)
0	111256	1859	.016709	.016460	100000	1646	98516	.016708	.098406	7383153	.000000	73.832	0
1	450043	414	.000920	.003670	98354	361	392514	.000920	1.500000	7284638	.000000	74.065	1
5	541501	210	.000388	.001939	97993	190	489490	.000388	2.500000	6892124	.000000	70.333	5
10	512470	164	.000320	.001595	97803	156	488642	.000319	2.610844	6402634	.006684	65.465	10
15	476150	265	.000557	.002796	97647	273	487583	.000560	2.612943	5913992	.023388	60.565	15
20	377460	236	.000625	.003122	97374	304	486123	.000625	2.543174	5426408	.033852	55.727	20
25	340489	236	.000693	.003461	97070	336	484544	.000693	2.601687	4940285	.019548	50.894	25
30	336017	326	.000970	.004838	96734	468	482589	.000970	2.690972	4455741	-.001233	46.062	30
35	369365	590	.001597	.007947	96266	765	479557	.001595	2.682462	3973152	-.012344	41.273	35
40	368638	883	.002395	.011916	95501	1138	474886	.002396	2.698448	3493595	.004662	36.582	40
45	323257	1276	.003947	.019555	94363	1849	467496	.003955	2.664053	3018709	.012205	31.990	45
50	304285	1724	.005666	.028039	92514	2594	456495	.005682	2.658057	2551213	.016958	27.577	50
55	249628	2152	.008621	.042449	89920	3817	440728	.008661	2.675749	2094718	.024488	23.295	55
60	216891	3014	.013896	.067524	86103	5814	416946	.013944	2.666230	1653990	.018336	19.209	60
65	185965	4109	.022096	.105320	80289	8456	381767	.022150	2.672880	1237043	.011289	15.407	65
70	156685	6103	.038951	.178623	71833	12831	328816	.039022	2.634732	855276	.008226	11.906	70
75	110441	7229	.065456	.283956	59002	16754	254433	.065848	2.578066	526460	.026103	8.923	75
80	57759	6706	.116103	.452305	42248	19109	163326	.116999	2.492586	272027	.026103	6.439	80
85+	32189	6852	.212868	1.000000	23139	23139	108701	.212868	4.697752	108701	.000000	4.698	85+

NUMBER OF PERSONS DYING (OUT OF 100,000 AT BIRTH) ABOVE AGE X FROM SPECIFIED CAUSES

Age (x)	All Causes	Respiratory T.B.	Other Infec. and Paras.	Neoplasms	Cardiovascular	Infl., Pneu., Bronch.	Diarrheal	Certain Degenerative	Maternal	Cert. Dis. of Infancy	Motor Vehicle	Other Violence	Other and Unknown	Age (x)
0	100000	153	302	14369	62428	5127	460	3462	100	942	1150	3385	8122	0
1	98354	153	285	14362	62422	4981	432	3460	100	1	1144	3339	7675	1
5	97993	153	265	14323	62413	4932	408	3459	100	0	1109	3251	7580	5
10	97803	153	262	14292	62408	4919	406	3456	100	0	1059	3222	7526	10
15	97647	153	261	14259	62396	4905	405	3451	100	0	1034	3198	7485	15
20	97374	153	255	14218	62374	4896	405	3445	94	0	931	3159	7444	20
25	97070	152	252	14184	62343	4887	404	3433	85	0	848	3100	7382	25
30	96734	149	251	14110	62299	4875	400	3417	65	0	814	3033	7321	30
35	96266	148	241	14004	62213	4859	400	3399	44	0	765	2949	7244	35
40	95501	140	233	13789	62051	4835	397	3355	10	0	728	2835	7128	40
45	94363	132	222	13431	61725	4789	395	3284	0	0	688	2701	6996	45
50	92514	122	208	12857	61108	4743	392	3196	0	0	631	2508	6749	50
55	89920	104	181	12031	60105	4671	378	3065	0	0	565	2360	6460	55
60	86103	93	163	10938	58289	4571	366	2868	0	0	498	2201	6116	60
65	80289	78	140	9522	55060	4423	341	2588	0	0	435	2076	5626	65
70	71833	64	118	7855	49854	4200	318	2210	0	0	344	1897	4973	70
75	59002	45	76	5765	41460	3758	259	1625	0	0	218	1668	4128	75
80	42248	31	48	3598	30000	2924	171	973	0	0	107	1338	3058	80
85+	23139	14	30	1577	16665	1790	74	436	0	0	17	878	1658	85+

NUMBER OF PERSONS SURVIVING TO AGE X IF SPECIFIED CAUSES WERE ELIMINATED

Age (x)	No Causes	Respiratory T.B. (1)	Other Infec. and Paras. (2)	Neoplasms (3)	Cardiovascular (4)	Infl., Pneu., Bronch. (5)	Diarrheal (6)	Certain Degenerative (7)	Maternal (8)	Cert. Dis. of Infancy (9)	Motor Vehicle (10)	Other Violence (11)	Other and Unknown (12)	(1)+(2)	(1)+(2)+(5)+(6)+(8)	(1)+(2)+(5)+(6)+(8)+part of(9)&(12)	(10)+(11)	Age (x)
0	100000	100000	100000	100000	100000	100000	100000	100000	100000	100000	100000	100000	100000	100000	100000	100000	100000	0
1	98354	98354	98371	98361	98360	98499	98382	98356	98354	99292	98360	98400	98798	98371	98544	99570	98406	1
5	97993	97993	98030	98039	98008	98186	98045	97996	97993	98928	98034	98126	98531	98030	98275	99333	98167	5
10	97803	97803	97843	97880	97823	98009	97857	97809	97803	98736	97894	97965	98394	97843	98102	99165	98056	10
15	97647	97647	97688	97757	97679	97867	97701	97658	97647	98579	97763	97833	98278	97688	97962	99029	97949	15
20	97374	97374	97421	97524	97428	97602	97428	97391	97380	98303	97592	97598	98045	97421	97709	98777	97817	20
25	97070	97071	97119	97254	97155	97306	97125	97099	97085	97996	97371	97353	97801	97120	97427	98498	97654	25
30	96734	96738	96764	96991	96882	96952	96793	96779	96769	97657	97068	97083	97524	96788	97130	98207	97418	30
35	96266	96271	96326	96628	96480	96528	96325	96328	96322	97185	96647	96697	97130	96331	96708	97790	97080	35
40	95501	95514	95568	96075	95875	95785	95562	95607	95590	96412	95916	96043	96474	95581	96017	97105	96461	40
45	94363	94384	94441	95289	95058	94690	94425	94538	94461	95264	94813	95033	95457	94441	94950	96036	95486	45
50	92514	92544	92604	93958	93813	92880	92578	92773	92610	93397	93012	93363	93835	92634	93162	94239	93866	50
55	89920	89967	90034	92193	92192	90347	89956	90301	90013	90778	90469	90892	91493	90081	90680	91745	91448	55
60	86103	86159	86230	89382	90120	86610	86188	86662	86192	86925	86695	87191	87952	86286	86970	88005	87791	60
65	80289	80356	80429	84777	87364	80906	80392	81083	80372	81055	80902	81426	82498	80496	81303	82290	82048	65
70	71833	71906	71979	77527	83710	72598	71947	72905	71908	72519	72468	73022	74445	72052	73011	73920	73668	70
75	59002	59079	59160	65746	78210	60038	59149	60421	59063	59565	59638	60189	61944	59237	60491	61281	60839	75
80	42248	42315	42385	49142	70385	43714	42428	43826	42292	42651	42797	43383	45311	42452	44157	44793	43947	80
85+	23139	23188	23227	28884	58678	24813	23309	24413	23163	23360	23506	24108	25936	23276	25169	25612	24490	85+

ADDED YRS OF LIFE	No Causes	(1)	(2)	(3)	(4)	(5)	(6)	(7)	(8)	(9)	(10)	(11)	(12)	(1)+(2)	(1)+(2)+(5)+(6)+(8)	(1)+(2)+(5)+(6)+(8)+part of(9)&(12)	(10)+(11)
TOTAL		.027	.077	2.190	13.498	.595	.081	.443	.044	.704	.350	.645	1.436	.105	.832	1.709	1.001
WORK	2.104	.011	.020	.544	.617	.061	.007	.058	.032	.000	.153	.219	.265	.030	.130	.152	.373

POPULATION, DEATHS, DEATH RATES FOR ALL CAUSES COMBINED, AND SPECIFIED CAUSES

Age Start of Interval	Midyear Population	Deaths During Year	All Causes	Respiratory T.B.	Other Infec. and Paras.	Neoplasms	Cardiovascular	Infl., Pneu., Bronch.	Diarrheal	Certain Degenerative	Maternal	Cert. Dis. of Infancy	Motor Vehicle	Other Violence	Other and Unknown	Age Start of Interval
0	63356	2506	.03953	.00002	.00028	.00017	.00024	.00382	.00235	.00008	.00000	.02333	.00000	.00069	.00855	0
1	235388	356	.00151	.00000	.00009	.00011	.00002	.00016	.00009	.00004	.00000	.00000	.00013	.00039	.00048	1
5	249113	140	.00056	.00000	.00003	.00008	.00002	.00001	.00001	.00001	.00000	.00000	.00014	.00015	.00011	5
10	263060	136	.00052	.00000	.00003	.00007	.00003	.00003	.00001	.00001	.00000	.00000	.00008	.00018	.00008	10
15	263771	345	.00131	.00001	.00000	.00010	.00007	.00002	.00000	.00002	.00000	.00000	.00046	.00052	.00011	15
20	265143	491	.00185	.00002	.00002	.00011	.00010	.00002	.00000	.00001	.00000	.00000	.00068	.00075	.00014	20
25	207769	413	.00199	.00005	.00005	.00016	.00017	.00003	.00000	.00006	.00000	.00000	.00049	.00078	.00019	25
30	229122	479	.00209	.00011	.00003	.00023	.00028	.00001	.00001	.00011	.00000	.00000	.00041	.00065	.00024	30
35	210947	583	.00217	.00017	.00005	.00032	.00057	.00004	.00000	.00023	.00000	.00000	.00033	.00071	.00034	35
40	147116	550	.00374	.00022	.00004	.00060	.00098	.00012	.00000	.00035	.00000	.00000	.00035	.00064	.00043	40
45	194880	1072	.00550	.00024	.00004	.00106	.00157	.00005	.00003	.00047	.00000	.00000	.00031	.00109	.00065	45
50	224455	2171	.00967	.00048	.00009	.00250	.00312	.00020	.00002	.00082	.00000	.00000	.00037	.00112	.00095	50
55	226068	3854	.01705	.00071	.00011	.00497	.00626	.00041	.00005	.00130	.00000	.00000	.00042	.00115	.00159	55
60	186158	5127	.02754	.00058	.00019	.00833	.01130	.00066	.00005	.00192	.00000	.00000	.00037	.00124	.00250	60
65	131863	5399	.04094	.00125	.00024	.01189	.01838	.00111	.00008	.00231	.00000	.00000	.00051	.00127	.00391	65
70	95978	6007	.06259	.00109	.00028	.01616	.02994	.00248	.00017	.00310	.00000	.00000	.00043	.00204	.00689	70
75	63060	6023	.09551	.00103	.00027	.02138	.04979	.00479	.00032	.00373	.00000	.00000	.00051	.00289	.01082	75
80	32633	4947	.15160	.00104	.00049	.02467	.08320	.00987	.00052	.00380	.00000	.00000	.00120	.00484	.02197	80
85+	13116	3195	.24360	.00122	.00030	.02455	.13487	.01975	.00130	.00343	.00000	.00000	.00122	.01029	.04666	85+
ALL	3303036	43794														

CRUDE DEATH RATE			.01326	.00030	.00008	.00285	.00542	.00057	.00009	.00064	.00000	.00045	.00037	.00088	.00162	
STANDARDIZED RATE (1)			.00687	.00015	.00006	.00119	.00203	.00033	.00011	.00029	.00000	.00082	.00032	.00063	.00094	
STANDARDIZED RATE (2)			.01205	.00026	.00008	.00246	.00488	.00054	.00009	.00055	.00000	.00048	.00036	.00083	.00152	
GEOMETRIC MEAN			.00845													

LIFE TABLE FOR ALL CAUSES COMBINED

Age (x)	Midyear Population	Deaths During Year	nM_x	nq_x	l_x	nd_x	nL_x	nm_x	na_x	T_x	nr_x	$\overset{\circ}{e}_x$	Age (x)
0	63356	2506	.039529	.038230	100000	3823	96702	.039534	.137200	6637578	.000000	66.376	0
1	235388	356	.001512	.006020	96177	579	383261	.001511	1.500000	6540876	.000000	68.009	1
5	249113	140	.000562	.002814	95598	269	477318	.000564	2.500000	6157616	.000000	64.412	5
10	263060	136	.000517	.002581	95329	246	476103	.000517	2.796409	5680298	-.004634	59.586	10
15	263771	345	.001308	.006510	95083	619	473958	.001306	2.710353	5204195	-.007098	54.733	15
20	265143	491	.001852	.009220	94464	871	470207	.001852	2.573670	4730198	.015746	50.074	20
25	207769	413	.001988	.009905	93593	927	465667	.001991	2.520676	4259991	.018418	45.516	25
30	229122	479	.002091	.010392	92666	963	460993	.002089	2.572906	3794324	-.007606	40.946	30
35	210947	583	.002764	.013784	91703	1264	455504	.002775	2.618176	3333332	.034319	36.349	35
40	147116	550	.003739	.018576	90439	1680	448230	.003748	2.639757	2877827	.021381	31.821	40
45	194880	1072	.005501	.026938	88759	2391	438312	.005455	2.706939	2429597	-.034993	27.373	45
50	224455	2171	.009672	.046950	86368	4055	422607	.009595	2.723181	1991285	-.031177	23.056	50
55	226068	3854	.017048	.081822	82313	6735	395923	.017011	2.677555	1568678	-.010885	19.057	55
60	186158	5127	.027541	.129601	75578	9795	354562	.027626	2.618385	1172754	.017259	15.517	60
65	131863	5399	.040944	.186994	65783	12301	299149	.041120	2.580227	818192	.024812	12.438	65
70	95978	6007	.062587	.271718	53482	14532	231645	.062734	2.538908	519043	.013004	9.705	70
75	63060	6023	.095512	.385494	38950	15015	156898	.095699	2.479076	287397	.009482	7.379	75
80	32633	4947	.151555	.544140	23935	13024	85708	.151958	2.391946	130499	.009482	5.452	80
85+	13116	3195	.243596	1.000000	10911	10911	44791	.243596	4.105164	44791	.000000	4.105	85+

NUMBER OF PERSONS DYING (OUT OF 100,000 AT BIRTH) ABOVE AGE X FROM SPECIFIED CAUSES

Age (x)	All Causes	Respiratory T. B.	Other Infec. and Paras.	Neoplasms	Cardiovascular	Infl., Pneu., Bronch.	Diarrheal	Certain Degenerative	Maternal	Cert. Dis. of Infancy	Motor Vehicle	Other Violence	Other and Unknown	Age (x)
0	100000	2147	560	21169	43013	4458	570	4620	0	2256	2497	6293	12417	0
1	96177	2145	533	21152	42990	4089	343	4612	0	0	2497	6226	11590	1
5	95598	2144	497	21112	42982	4027	309	4598	0	0	2449	6076	11404	5
10	95329	2144	484	21071	42974	4021	305	4592	0	0	2383	6003	11352	10
15	95083	2144	471	21037	42960	4008	301	4587	0	0	2344	5918	11313	15
20	94464	2140	469	20990	42927	3999	301	4578	0	0	2125	5671	11264	20
25	93593	2129	462	20937	42881	3991	300	4572	0	0	1804	5317	11200	25
30	92666	2105	437	20863	42802	3977	297	4543	0	0	1578	4952	11112	30
35	91703	2052	425	20758	42674	3971	291	4491	0	0	1389	4652	11000	35
40	90439	1974	403	20610	42411	3951	289	4386	0	0	1238	4330	10847	40
45	88759	1874	385	20338	41970	3899	289	4227	0	0	1079	4044	10654	45
50	86368	1769	370	19879	41291	3877	278	4022	0	0	944	3568	10370	50
55	82313	1567	338	18832	39987	3792	269	3678	0	0	787	3094	9969	55
60	75578	1285	303	16870	37514	3629	234	3162	0	0	618	2621	9342	60
65	65783	936	234	13909	33491	3396	217	2479	0	0	489	2181	8451	65
70	53482	561	164	10339	27967	3060	191	1788	0	0	337	1801	7274	70
75	38950	308	98	6589	21011	2484	153	1067	0	0	238	1327	5675	75
80	23935	146	56	3232	13182	1730	103	482	0	0	158	873	3973	80
85+	10911	55	14	1100	6041	884	58	154	0	0	55	461	2089	85+

NUMBER OF PERSONS SURVIVING TO AGE X IF SPECIFIED CAUSES WERE ELIMINATED

Age (x)	No Causes	Respiratory T. B.	Other Infec. and Paras.	Neoplasms	Cardiovascular	Infl., Pneu., Bronch.	Diarrheal	Certain Degenerative	Maternal	Cert. Dis. of Infancy	Motor Vehicle	Other Violence	Other and Unknown	(1) + (2)	(1) + (2) + (5) + (6) + (8)	(1)+(2)+ (5)+(6)+ (8)+part of(9)&(12)	(10) + (11)	Age (x)
		(1)	(2)	(3)	(4)	(5)	(6)	(7)	(8)	(9)	(10)	(11)	(12)					
0	100000	100000	100000	100000	100000	100000	100000	100000	100000	100000	100000	100000	100000	100000	100000	100000	100000	0
1	96177	96179	96203	96194	96200	96540	96400	96185	96177	98415	96177	96243	96991	96205	96792	99396	96243	1
5	95598	95601	95660	95654	95628	96020	95854	95620	95598	97822	95646	95813	96595	95663	96343	99000	95861	5
10	95329	95332	95404	95426	95367	95756	95588	95357	95329	97547	95443	95617	96375	95407	96095	98751	95731	10
15	95083	95086	95171	95214	95135	95522	95345	95116	95083	97296	95235	95455	96166	95174	95877	98533	95608	15
20	94464	94471	94553	94641	94549	94909	94724	94505	94464	96662	94834	95081	95589	94560	95268	97908	95454	20
25	93593	93611	93688	93821	93723	94042	93852	93640	93593	95771	94281	94560	94773	93706	94417	97035	95255	25
30	92666	92708	92785	92966	92873	93125	92925	92741	92666	94822	93574	93991	93923	92827	93548	96150	94912	30
35	91703	91797	91833	92105	92036	92163	91966	91829	91703	93837	92792	93317	93060	91927	92653	95240	94425	35
40	90439	90609	90589	90983	91030	90913	90700	90668	90439	92543	91664	92357	91931	90760	91498	94071	93608	40
45	88759	89025	88924	89564	89780	89276	89015	89142	88759	90824	90121	90931	90418	89191	89969	92522	92327	45
50	86368	86731	86544	87610	88042	86893	86628	86944	86368	88378	87829	88963	88268	86907	87699	90208	90468	50
55	82313	82857	82512	84541	85217	82897	82570	83201	82313	84228	83861	85263	84525	83057	83907	86345	86867	55
60	75578	76350	75794	79579	80737	76271	75847	76894	75578	77337	77164	78756	78228	76568	77546	79852	80409	60
65	65783	66784	66036	72233	74401	66606	66033	67578	65783	67314	67286	68955	68955	67040	68137	70230	70552	65
70	53482	54637	53750	62356	66388	54460	53709	55582	53482	54726	54843	56437	57184	54912	56153	57961	57873	70
75	38950	40009	39201	49271	56287	40167	39148	41118	38950	39856	40027	41529	43126	40267	41736	43188	42677	75
80	23935	24713	24122	33731	44615	25298	24096	25746	23935	24492	24660	25897	28010	24906	26501	27539	26682	80
85+	10911	11327	11024	17487	31288	12136	11014	11971	10911	11165	11312	12103	14305	11445	12850	13494	12547	85+

ADDED YRS OF LIFE																		
TOTAL		.345	.135	2.819	6.574	.650	.213	.663	.000	1.541	.791	1.552	2.046	.482	1.368	3.351	2.375	
WORK	3.872	.144	.037	.620	.822	.061	.010	.224	.000	.000	.508	.823	.360	.181	.253	.282	1.343	

POPULATION, DEATHS, DEATH RATES FOR ALL CAUSES COMBINED, AND SPECIFIED CAUSES

Age Start of Interval	Midyear Population	Deaths During Year	All Causes	Respiratory T. B.	Other Infec. and Paras.	Neoplasms	Cardiovascular	Infl., Pneu., Bronch.	Diarrheal	Certain Degenerative	Maternal	Cert. Dis. of Infancy	Motor Vehicle	Other Violence	Other and Unknown	Age Start of Interval
0	60390	1796	.02974	.00003	.C0028	.00010	.00022	.00272	.0019C	.00002	.C00C0	.01754	.00000	.00041	.00652	0
1	225572	254	.00113	.00001	.0C0C7	.00011	.00004	.00016	.00008	.00002	.00000	.00000	.00008	.00024	.00033	1
5	239297	109	.00046	.00000	.00005	.00007	.00002	.00002	.C0001	.00000	.00000	.00000	.00011	.00005	.00013	5
10	251254	76	.00030	.00000	.00003	.00004	.00001	.00002	.00000	.00001	.00000	.00000	.00003	.00007	.00009	10
15	254340	128	.00050	.00000	.00001	.00006	.00004	.00002	.00001	.00001	.00000	.00000	.00010	.00014	.00010	15
20	252177	145	.00057	.00002	.00001	.00008	.00006	.00001	.00000	.00004	.00004	.00000	.00005	.00014	.00013	20
25	202420	162	.0008C	.00001	.00003	.00023	.00006	.0000C	.00002	.00002	.00007	.00000	.00006	.00015	.00012	25
30	232597	262	.00113	.00004	.00003	.00028	.00015	.03000	.0C002	.C0005	.00011	.00000	.00006	.00018	.00020	30
35	282722	428	.00151	.00006	.00003	.00050	.00026	.C0002	.00002	.00006	.0000C8	.00000	.00004	.00020	.00024	35
40	200264	469	.00234	.0000C5	.00002	.00055	.00044	.00004	.00001	.00012	.00006	.00000	.00007	.00025	.00033	40
45	254248	862	.00339	.00006	.00004	.00162	.00076	.00005	.00001	.00013	.00000	.00000	.00006	.00029	.00037	45
50	281089	1520	.00541	.00008	.00005	.00239	.00144	.0C007	.C0002	.00027	.00000	.00000	.00007	.00037	.00063	50
55	267630	2209	.00825	.00010	.CCCC8	.00337	.00271	.00012	.00004	.00043	.00000	.C0000	.00009	.00034	.00098	55
60	241388	3264	.01352	.00014	.00010	.00479	.00535	.00025	.00005	.00073	.0C000	.00000	.00008	.00039	.00164	60
65	198949	4412	.02218	.00021	.00015	.00607	.01080	.00056	.0000C8	.00116	.00000	.00000	.00021	.00055	.00240	65
70	153304	6143	.04007	.00037	.00018	.00925	.02171	.00119	.00018	.00186	.00000	.00000	.00023	.00104	.00407	70
75	104519	7459	.07137	.00044	.00029	.01293	.04235	.00293	.00024	.00220	.00000	.00000	.00026	.00224	.00750	75
80	56452	6860	.12152	.00066	.00044	.01621	.07505	.00701	.00066	.00244	.00000	.00000	.00043	.00535	.01316	80
85+	24878	5321	.21388	.00068	.00044	.01877	.13245	.01339	.00129	.00289	.00000	.00000	.00052	.00993	.03352	85+
ALL	3783490	41879														

			All Causes	Respiratory T. B.	Other Infec. and Paras.	Neoplasms	Cardiovascular	Infl., Pneu., Bronch.	Diarrheal	Certain Degenerative	Maternal	Cert. Dis. of Infancy	Motor Vehicle	Other Violence	Other and Unknown
CRUDE DEATH RATE			.01107	.00009	.00007	.00239	.00537	.00045	.00008	.00038	.00002	.00028	.00010	.00047	.00137
STANDARDIZED RATE (1)			.00434	.00004	.00005	.00085	.00135	.00021	.00005	.00013	.00002	.00062	.00007	.00023	.00067
STANDARDIZED RATE (2)			.00787	.00007	.00006	.00166	.00356	.00033	.0000C8	.00026	.0000C2	.00036	.00009	.00036	.00102
GEOMETRIC MEAN			.00493												

LIFE TABLE FOR ALL CAUSES COMBINED

Age (x)	Midyear Population	Deaths During Year	$_nM_x$	$_nq_x$	l_x	$_nd_x$	$_nL_x$	$_nm_x$	$_na_x$	T_x	$_nr_x$	$\overset{\circ}{e}_x$	Age (x)
0	60390	1796	.029740	.028980	100000	2898	97451	.029738	.120558	7277988	.000000	72.780	0
1	225572	254	.001126	.004490	97102	436	387318	.001126	1.500000	7180537	.000000	73.948	1
5	239297	109	.000456	.002276	96666	220	482780	.000456	2.500000	6793219	.000000	70.275	5
10	251254	76	.000302	.001514	96446	146	481870	.000303	2.531393	6310439	-.004965	65.430	10
15	254340	128	.000503	.002513	96300	242	480922	.000503	2.611915	5828569	-.006054	60.525	15
20	252177	145	.000575	.002873	96058	276	479630	.000575	2.607186	5347647	-.016022	55.671	20
25	202420	162	.000800	.004009	95782	384	478004	.000803	2.639431	4868017	.018903	50.824	25
30	232597	262	.001126	.005587	95398	533	475727	.001120	2.629769	4390014	-.030285	46.018	30
35	282722	428	.001514	.007548	94865	716	472653	.001515	2.664688	3914287	-.001737	41.262	35
40	200264	469	.002342	.011673	94149	1099	468173	.002347	2.659425	3441634	-.016018	36.555	40
45	254248	862	.003390	.016733	93050	1557	461636	.003373	2.678629	2973462	-.029023	31.956	45
50	281089	1520	.005408	.026603	91493	2434	451807	.005387	2.675380	2511826	-.017813	27.454	50
55	267630	2209	.008254	.040490	89059	3606	436942	.008253	2.683722	2060019	-.000578	23.131	55
60	241388	3264	.013522	.065697	85453	5614	414240	.013553	2.679944	1623077	.010779	18.994	60
65	198949	4412	.022177	.105901	79839	8455	379623	.022272	2.685171	1208836	.019149	15.141	65
70	153304	6143	.040071	.183921	71384	13129	326045	.040267	2.648367	829213	.020754	11.616	70
75	104519	7459	.071365	.305639	58255	17805	247964	.071805	2.567479	503168	.024753	8.637	75
80	56452	6860	.121519	.467145	40450	18896	154430	.122360	2.469284	255204	.024753	6.309	80
85+	24878	5321	.213884	1.000000	21554	21554	100774	.213884	4.675437	100774	.000000	4.675	85+

NUMBER OF PERSONS DYING (OUT OF 100,000 AT BIRTH) ABOVE AGE X FROM SPECIFIED CAUSES

Age (x)	All Causes	Respiratory T. B.	Other Infec. and Paras.	Neo-plasms	Cardio-vascular	Infl., Pneu., Bronch.	Diar-rheal	Certain Degen-erative	Maternal	Cert. Dis. of Infancy	Motor Vehicle	Other Violence	Other and Unknown	Age (x)
0	100000	743	579	19381	51747	4378	686	3096	172	1709	749	4251	12509	0
1	97102	740	552	19372	51726	4113	500	3094	172	0	749	4211	11873	1
5	96666	736	526	19329	51712	4053	469	3087	172	0	720	4117	11745	5
10	96446	734	502	19294	51704	4045	465	3087	172	0	667	4090	11686	10
15	96300	734	489	19275	51700	4036	465	3081	172	0	652	4056	11640	15
20	96058	732	483	19247	51679	4026	461	3078	170	0	603	3988	11591	20
25	95782	725	477	19207	51649	4022	461	3060	153	0	578	3921	11529	25
30	95398	717	461	19095	51618	4015	452	3051	119	0	547	3850	11473	30
35	94865	697	444	18961	51547	4015	444	3029	66	0	521	3765	11376	35
40	94149	667	429	18725	51423	4007	435	3000	28	0	501	3671	11263	40
45	93050	644	420	18280	51217	3988	428	2944	0	0	468	3554	11107	45
50	91493	617	404	17536	50868	3965	423	2886	0	0	439	3418	10937	50
55	89059	581	380	16458	50218	3933	413	2763	0	0	407	3251	10655	55
60	85453	536	345	14987	49036	3879	397	2574	0	0	369	3104	10226	60
65	79839	479	302	12999	46812	3774	380	2271	0	0	336	2941	9545	65
70	71384	400	245	10689	42691	3559	351	1831	0	0	258	2730	8630	70
75	58255	281	185	7663	35573	3169	291	1223	0	0	183	2390	7297	75
80	40450	171	114	4446	25001	2436	231	676	0	0	119	1830	5426	80
85+	21554	69	45	1892	13347	1349	130	292	0	0	53	1001	3376	85+

NUMBER OF PERSONS SURVIVING TO AGE X IF SPECIFIED CAUSES WERE ELIMINATED

Age (x)	No Causes	Respiratory T. B.	Other Infec. and Paras.	Neo-plasms	Cardio-vascular	Infl., Pneu., Bronch.	Diar-rheal	Certain Degen-erative	Maternal	Cert. Dis. of Infancy	Motor Vehicle	Other Violence	Other and Unknown	(1) + (2)	(1) + (2) + (5) + (6) + (8)	(1)+(2)+ (5)+(6)+ (8)+part of(9)&(12)	(10) + (11)	Age (x)
		(1)	(2)	(3)	(4)	(5)	(6)	(7)	(8)	(9)	(10)	(11)	(12)					
0	100000	100000	100000	100000	100000	100000	100000	100000	100000	100000	100000	100000	100000	100000	100000	100000	100000	0
1	97102	97105	97129	97111	97123	97363	97285	97104	97102	98801	97102	97141	97731	97132	97577	99618	97141	1
5	96666	96673	96718	96718	96701	96966	96880	96675	96666	98357	96695	96799	97421	96725	97260	99346	96828	5
10	96446	96455	96522	96533	96488	96774	96663	96455	96446	98133	96528	96606	97258	96531	97077	99173	96688	10
15	96300	96309	96389	96405	96346	96636	96517	96315	96300	97985	96397	96494	97157	96398	96952	99056	96591	15
20	96058	96069	96153	96191	96125	96403	96278	96076	96060	97738	96203	96319	96963	96164	96733	98838	96465	20
25	95782	95800	95883	95955	95879	96130	96002	95818	95801	97458	95952	96110	96746	95901	96489	98599	96280	25
30	95398	95424	95514	95682	95526	95752	95626	95443	95451	97067	95558	95795	96415	95540	96177	98293	95997	30
35	94865	94911	94998	95282	95063	95217	95099	94931	94970	96525	95090	95345	95974	95043	95738	97867	95572	35
40	94149	94224	94296	94799	94469	94506	94351	94244	94292	95756	94393	94720	95364	94371	95116	97250	94965	40
45	93050	93147	93204	94139	93572	93422	93296	93199	93219	94678	93324	93731	94408	93301	94092	96218	94007	45
50	91493	91615	91660	93313	92355	91882	91740	91658	91659	93094	91791	92299	92999	91783	92589	94690	92599	50
55	89059	89214	89245	91922	90548	89469	89309	89380	89220	90617	89381	90010	90808	89400	90228	92289	90334	55
60	85453	85645	85666	89699	88068	85900	85759	85947	85608	86948	85799	86510	87561	85859	86723	88725	86661	60
65	79839	80074	80089	85845	84530	80359	80094	80595	79984	81236	80194	80986	82485	80316	81244	83150	81347	65
70	71384	71669	71653	79132	79822	72054	71640	72481	71513	72633	71776	72612	74648	71939	73007	74765	73011	70
75	58255	58595	58529	67663	72740	59159	58518	59707	58361	59274	58642	59571	62188	58870	60163	61680	59966	75
80	40450	40777	40699	50158	62739	41703	40683	41920	40523	41158	40772	41843	44867	41028	42620	43797	42176	80
85+	21554	21802	21737	29101	49290	23041	21751	22625	21593	21931	21773	22921	25558	21987	23762	24554	23154	85+

ADDED YRS OF LIFE		(1)	(2)	(3)	(4)	(5)	(6)	(7)	(8)	(9)	(10)	(11)	(12)					
TOTAL		.120	.145	2.934	8.610	.574	.215	.406	.074	1.271	.213	.710	1.970	.265	1.142	2.848	.928	
WORK	2.028	.040	.032	.704	.414	.029	.015	.085	.054	.000	.079	.225	.279	.072	.172	.204	.304	

POPULATION, DEATHS, DEATH RATES FOR ALL CAUSES COMBINED, AND SPECIFIED CAUSES

Age Start of Interval	Midyear Population	Deaths During Year	All Causes	Respiratory T. B.	Other Infec. and Paras.	Neoplasms	Cardiovascular	Infl., Pneu., Bronch.	Diarrheal	Certain Degenerative	Maternal	Cert. Dis. of Infancy	Motor Vehicle	Other Violence	Other and Unknown	Age Start of Interval
0	66820	2265	.03390	.00001	.00025	.00010	.00010	.00317	.00156	.00010	.00000	.02110	.00004	.00052	.00691	0
1	256309	346	.00135	.00000	.00009	.00012	.00005	.00016	.00006	.00002	.00000	.00000	.00014	.00035	.00037	1
5	279225	168	.00060	.00000	.00004	.00011	.00001	.00002	.00001	.00001	.00000	.00000	.00016	.00011	.00012	5
10	244122	128	.00052	.00001	.00002	.00008	.00001	.00002	.00000	.00001	.00000	.00000	.00009	.00019	.00010	10
15	252522	314	.00124	.00000	.00001	.00010	.00007	.00002	.00000	.00003	.00000	.00000	.00040	.00048	.00014	15
20	299726	536	.00179	.00000	.00001	.00013	.00008	.00001	.00000	.00004	.00000	.00000	.00068	.00069	.00013	20
25	216119	388	.00180	.00006	.00001	.00015	.00013	.00002	.00000	.00008	.00000	.00000	.00053	.00069	.00011	25
30	218519	439	.00201	.00007	.00002	.00023	.00023	.00003	.00001	.00009	.00000	.00000	.00044	.00068	.00022	30
35	219520	581	.00265	.00016	.00001	.00039	.00048	.00003	.00001	.00020	.00000	.00000	.00041	.00072	.00023	35
40	201018	706	.00351	.00012	.00004	.00053	.00102	.00006	.00001	.00025	.00000	.00000	.00041	.00072	.00033	40
45	133612	801	.00599	.00023	.00001	.00123	.00183	.00011	.00001	.00056	.00000	.00000	.00050	.00093	.00058	45
50	210419	2027	.00963	.00040	.00007	.00240	.00313	.00025	.00004	.00074	.00000	.00000	.00048	.00124	.00088	50
55	215819	3475	.01610	.00063	.00006	.00461	.00561	.00040	.00004	.00143	.00000	.00000	.00061	.00135	.00135	55
60	200518	5605	.02795	.00094	.00017	.00798	.01125	.00093	.00010	.00228	.00000	.00000	.00064	.00130	.00235	60
65	146113	6271	.04292	.00112	.00025	.01187	.01914	.00185	.00019	.00279	.00000	.00000	.00055	.00123	.00391	65
70	97509	6256	.06416	.00134	.00032	.01621	.03055	.00312	.00013	.00352	.00000	.00000	.00072	.00163	.00661	70
75	64206	6228	.09700	.00137	.00028	.02065	.04911	.00502	.00033	.00427	.00000	.00000	.00100	.00249	.01249	75
80	33303	5017	.15065	.00132	.00057	.02345	.07777	.00799	.00060	.00462	.00000	.00000	.00081	.00489	.02862	80
85+	14501	3487	.24047	.00097	.00041	.02372	.11710	.01296	.00097	.00393	.00000	.00000	.00110	.00862	.07068	85+
ALL	3369900	45038														

CRUDE DEATH RATE			.01336	.00029	.00008	.00281	.00535	.00059	.00008	.00071	.00000	.00042	.00044	.00085	.00175	
STANDARDIZED RATE (1)			.00667	.00014	.00005	.00117	.00199	.00032	.00008	.00032	.00000	.00074	.00036	.00060	.00089	
STANDARDIZED RATE (2)			.01198	.00025	.00007	.00241	.00475	.00054	.00008	.00061	.00000	.00044	.00042	.00079	.00162	
GEOMETRIC MEAN			.00827													

LIFE TABLE FOR ALL CAUSES COMBINED

Age (x)	Midyear Population	Deaths During Year	$_nM_x$	$_nq_x$	l_x	$_nd_x$	$_nL_x$	$_nm_x$	$_na_x$	T_x	$_nr_x$	$\overset{\circ}{e}_x$	Age (x)
0	66820	2265	.033897	.032920	100000	3292	97128	.033893	.127625	6679627	.000000	66.796	0
1	256309	346	.001350	.005387	96708	521	385530	.001351	1.500000	6582499	.000000	68.066	1
5	279225	168	.000602	.002994	96187	288	480215	.000600	2.500000	6196970	.000000	64.426	5
10	244122	128	.000524	.002628	95899	252	478928	.000526	2.749669	5716755	.014067	59.612	10
15	252522	314	.001243	.006169	95647	590	476884	.001237	2.710099	5237827	-.018718	54.762	15
20	299726	536	.001788	.008910	95057	847	473220	.001790	2.561983	4760943	.001994	50.085	20
25	216119	388	.001795	.008937	94210	842	468963	.001795	2.521526	4287723	.029156	45.512	25
30	218519	439	.002009	.010003	93368	934	464583	.002010	2.583200	3818760	.004410	40.900	30
35	219520	581	.002647	.013145	92434	1215	459271	.002645	2.614198	3354177	-.003507	36.287	35
40	201018	706	.003512	.017540	91219	1600	452395	.003537	2.687630	2894906	-.041963	31.736	40
45	133612	801	.005995	.029637	89619	2656	441966	.006010	2.692253	2442510	-.011996	27.254	45
50	210419	2027	.009633	.046583	86963	4051	425468	.009521	2.692648	2000545	-.048909	23.005	50
55	215819	3475	.016101	.077214	82912	6402	399800	.016013	2.694503	1575077	-.024371	18.997	55
60	200518	5605	.027953	.131068	76510	10028	358849	.027945	2.636493	1175277	-.001003	15.361	60
65	146113	6271	.042519	.195120	66482	12972	300987	.043098	2.577619	816428	.023218	12.280	65
70	97509	6256	.064158	.277724	53510	14861	230836	.064379	2.529482	515441	.019328	9.633	70
75	64206	6228	.097000	.390049	38649	15075	155120	.097183	2.470978	284605	.009447	7.364	75
80	33303	5017	.150647	.541317	23574	12761	84519	.150985	2.386454	129485	.009447	5.493	80
85+	14501	3487	.240466	1.000000	10813	10813	44967	.240466	4.158589	44967	.000000	4.159	85+

NUMBER OF PERSONS DYING (OUT OF 100,000 AT BIRTH) ABOVE AGE X FROM SPECIFIED CAUSES

Age (x)	All Causes	Respiratory T.B.	Other Infec. and Paras.	Neo-plasms	Cardio-vascular	Infl., Pneu., Bronch.	Diar-rheal	Certain Degenerative	Maternal	Cert. Dis. of Infancy	Motor Vehicle	Other Violence	Other and Unknown	Age (x)
0	100000	2073	518	20718	41702	4444	510	5185	0	2049	3025	6056	13720	0
1	96708	2072	494	20708	41692	4136	358	5175	0	0	3021	6005	13047	1
5	96187	2072	461	20662	41674	4072	334	5169	0	0	2967	5869	12907	5
10	95899	2072	443	20607	41667	4064	327	5164	0	0	2888	5818	12849	10
15	95647	2068	432	20568	41663	4054	327	5160	0	0	2846	5727	12802	15
20	95057	2066	428	20521	41631	4047	327	5145	0	0	2655	5502	12735	20
25	94210	2064	423	20458	41595	4040	326	5125	0	0	2331	5175	12673	25
30	93368	2038	417	20386	41532	4029	326	5085	0	0	2085	4849	12621	30
35	92434	2006	408	20280	41425	4014	322	5045	0	0	1881	4532	12521	35
40	91219	1933	402	20100	41204	4000	317	4955	0	0	1692	4202	12414	40
45	89619	1876	384	19859	40735	3970	311	4839	0	0	1508	3875	12262	45
50	86963	1774	377	19314	39926	3920	304	4590	0	0	1286	3464	12008	50
55	82912	1606	349	18307	38611	3815	288	4280	0	0	1080	2940	11636	55
60	76510	1355	323	16473	36386	3655	271	3710	0	0	838	2399	11100	60
65	66482	1018	261	13610	32351	3322	234	2891	0	0	607	1932	10256	65
70	53510	680	184	10024	26561	2760	176	2048	0	0	440	1563	9074	70
75	38649	369	111	6271	19481	2038	145	1235	0	0	274	1186	7539	75
80	23574	157	67	3064	11848	1258	94	572	0	0	119	798	5597	80
85+	10813	43	19	1067	5265	583	43	177	0	0	50	388	3178	85+

NUMBER OF PERSONS SURVIVING TO AGE X IF SPECIFIED CAUSES WERE ELIMINATED

Age (x)	No Causes	Respiratory T.B. (1)	Other Infec. and Paras. (2)	Neo-plasms (3)	Cardio-vascular (4)	Infl., Pneu., Bronch. (5)	Diar-rheal (6)	Certain Degenerative (7)	Maternal (8)	Cert. Dis. of Infancy (9)	Motor Vehicle (10)	Other Violence (11)	Other and Unknown (12)	(1)+(2)	(1)+(2)+(5)+(6)+(8)	(1)+(2)+(5)+(6)+(8)+part of (9)&(12)	(10)+(11)	Age (x)
0	100000	100000	100000	100000	100000	100000	100000	100000	100000	100000	100000	100000	100000	100000	100000	100000	100000	0
1	96708	96709	96732	96718	96718	97011	96858	96718	96708	98744	96712	96758	97372	96733	97186	99502	96762	1
5	96187	96188	96243	96243	96215	96553	96360	96203	96187	98212	96245	96373	96988	96244	96784	99136	96431	5
10	95899	95900	95973	96009	95934	96272	96078	95920	95899	97918	96036	96135	96756	95974	96527	98882	96272	10
15	95647	95652	95732	95796	95686	96029	95826	95672	95647	97661	95825	95974	96549	95737	96299	98653	96153	15
20	95057	95064	95145	95252	95127	95443	95235	95096	95057	97058	95425	95607	96021	95152	95718	98060	95977	20
25	94210	94219	94303	94466	94315	94600	94387	94269	94210	96193	94899	95083	95228	94312	94880	97203	95779	25
30	93368	93403	93466	93694	93535	93765	93543	93466	93368	95334	94298	94561	94429	93501	94075	96381	95503	30
35	92434	92500	92540	92863	92706	92842	92612	92571	92434	94380	93560	93935	93585	92606	93194	95486	95080	35
40	91219	91357	91329	91822	91708	91744	91444	91219	91219	93139	93220	93034	92643	91467	92067	94341	94361	40
45	89619	89811	89745	90452	90569	90059	89802	89955	89619	91506	91082	91733	90994	89938	90564	92812	93231	45
50	86963	87250	87092	88315	88694	87439	87148	87536	86963	88794	88605	89430	88551	87380	88045	90249	91119	50
55	82912	83351	83063	85206	85882	83469	83104	83764	82912	84658	84683	85791	84757	83502	84258	86400	87623	55
60	76510	77157	76674	80459	81497	77179	76703	77851	76510	78121	78381	79704	78778	77323	78196	80226	81653	60
65	66482	67361	66683	72773	74939	67378	66685	68426	66482	67882	68327	69710	69267	67564	68683	70536	71644	65
70	53510	54524	53741	62191	66461	54745	53725	55854	53510	54637	55148	56453	56867	54758	56247	57865	58181	70
75	38649	39648	38877	48752	56063	40172	38830	41063	38649	39463	39977	41112	42483	39882	41648	42969	42524	75
80	23574	24349	23747	33005	43940	25138	23725	25591	23574	24070	24507	25398	27633	24528	26323	27302	26403	80
85+	10813	11247	10924	17103	30130	12016	10916	12025	10813	11041	11288	11945	14693	11362	12747	13390	12470	85+

ADDED YRS OF LIFE

	No Causes	(1)	(2)	(3)	(4)	(5)	(6)	(7)	(8)	(9)	(10)	(11)	(12)	(1)+(2)	sum	sum	(10)+(11)
TOTAL		.307	.115	2.770	6.072	.643	.159	.716	.000	1.404	.900	1.489	1.996	.423	1.246	3.015	2.425
WORK	3.774	.115	.022	.620	.800	.064	.009	.229	.000	.000	.550	.801	.311	.137	.211	.232	1.364

POPULATION, DEATHS, DEATH RATES FOR ALL CAUSES COMBINED, AND SPECIFIED CAUSES

Age Start of Interval	Midyear Population	Deaths During Year	All Causes	Respiratory T. B.	Other Infec. and Paras.	Neoplasms	Cardiovascular	Infl., Pneu., Bronch.	Diarrheal	Certain Degenerative	Maternal	Cert. Dis. of Infancy	Motor Vehicle	Other Violence	Other and Unknown	Age Start of Interval
0	63905	1648	.02579	.00000	.00023	.00011	.00013	.00263	.00128	.00005	.00000	.01519	.00002	.00038	.00577	0
1	245635	290	.00118	.00000	.00008	.00014	.00001	.00016	.00007	.00001	.00000	.00000	.00000	.00013	.00021	.00037	1
5	268535	117	.00044	.00000	.00003	.00009	.00001	.00003	.00001	.00000	.00000	.00000	.00011	.00004	.00011	5
10	234530	76	.00032	.00000	.00002	.00006	.00002	.00002	.00000	.00003	.00000	.00000	.00004	.00003	.00010	10
15	242332	116	.00048	.00000	.00002	.00006	.00003	.00002	.00000	.00002	.00001	.00000	.00010	.00012	.00008	15
20	288838	175	.00061	.00001	.00000	.00010	.00006	.00001	.00001	.00002	.00006	.00000	.00012	.00012	.00010	20
25	207927	152	.00073	.00002	.00000	.00011	.00011	.00001	.00000	.00005	.00007	.00000	.00004	.00015	.00015	25
30	213128	208	.00098	.00002	.00002	.00029	.00018	.00002	.00001	.00004	.00004	.00000	.00011	.00008	.00017	30
35	246032	390	.00159	.00004	.00002	.00058	.00028	.00002	.00001	.00011	.00005	.00000	.00008	.00020	.00020	35
40	279036	595	.00213	.00006	.00003	.00096	.00036	.00004	.00002	.00011	.00003	.00000	.00005	.00021	.00026	40
45	180423	616	.00341	.00010	.00002	.00167	.00068	.00005	.00001	.00016	.00000	.00000	.00006	.00026	.00042	45
50	272735	1455	.00533	.00009	.00003	.00238	.00129	.00009	.00003	.00025	.00000	.00000	.00011	.00041	.00065	50
55	269735	2102	.00779	.00008	.00009	.00318	.00242	.00016	.00003	.00049	.00000	.00000	.00006	.00036	.00085	55
60	251533	3290	.01308	.00010	.00008	.00460	.00503	.00028	.00004	.00071	.00000	.00000	.00016	.00050	.00158	60
65	214128	4874	.02276	.00019	.00018	.00665	.01040	.00077	.00009	.00127	.00000	.00000	.00018	.00052	.00251	65
70	162021	6414	.03959	.00023	.00020	.00930	.02034	.00149	.00020	.00193	.00000	.00000	.00033	.00122	.00437	70
75	114015	7803	.06844	.00040	.00032	.01241	.03853	.00254	.00025	.00262	.00000	.00000	.00000	.00219	.00837	75
80	61208	7456	.12181	.00077	.00029	.01678	.07109	.00526	.00049	.00323	.00000	.00000	.00044	.00425	.01921	80
85+	29804	6266	.21024	.00081	.00060	.01825	.11680	.00966	.00060	.00285	.00000	.00000	.00030	.01060	.04976	85+
ALL	3845500	44043														

CRUDE DEATH RATE			.01145	.00008	.00007	.00247	.00531	.00045	.00007	.00043	.00002	.00025	.00013	.00048	.00169	
STANDARDIZED RATE (1)			.00414	.00003	.00005	.00086	.00125	.00021	.00007	.00014	.00002	.00053	.00010	.00021	.00067	
STANDARDIZED RATE (2)			.00768	.00006	.00006	.00166	.00330	.00032	.00006	.00029	.00002	.00031	.00011	.00034	.00115	
GEOMETRIC MEAN			.00480													

LIFE TABLE FOR ALL CAUSES COMBINED

Age (x)	Midyear Population	Deaths During Year	$_nM_x$	$_nq_x$	l_x	$_nd_x$	$_nL_x$	$_nm_x$	$_na_x$	T_x	$_nr_x$	$\overset{\circ}{e}_x$	Age (x)
0	63905	1648	.025788	.025210	100000	2521	97766	.025786	.113840	7325374	.000000	73.254	0
1	245635	290	.001181	.004709	97479	459	388769	.001181	1.500000	7227608	.000000	74.145	1
5	268535	117	.000436	.002175	97020	211	484573	.000435	2.500000	6838840	.000000	70.489	5
10	234530	76	.000324	.001622	96809	157	483657	.000325	2.526539	6354267	.014496	65.637	10
15	242332	116	.000479	.002390	96652	231	482710	.000479	2.620851	5870611	-.018323	60.740	15
20	288838	175	.000606	.003018	96421	291	481403	.000604	2.586627	5387900	.002510	55.879	20
25	207927	152	.000731	.003662	96130	352	479806	.000734	2.603755	4906498	.030743	51.040	25
30	213128	208	.000976	.004865	95778	466	477808	.000975	2.677486	4426691	-.001888	46.218	30
35	246032	390	.001585	.007858	95312	749	474800	.001578	2.650200	3948883	-.033206	41.431	35
40	279036	595	.002132	.010638	94563	1006	470475	.002138	2.673956	3474083	.017098	36.738	40
45	180423	616	.003414	.016984	93557	1589	464104	.003424	2.683554	3003608	.013038	32.105	45
50	272735	1455	.005335	.026161	91968	2406	454206	.005297	2.658545	2539504	-.039617	27.613	50
55	269735	2102	.007793	.038186	89562	3420	439899	.007775	2.686830	2085298	-.010867	23.283	55
60	251533	3290	.013080	.063535	86142	5473	418138	.013089	2.702890	1645399	.002656	19.101	60
65	214128	4874	.022762	.108468	80669	8750	383053	.022843	2.680881	1227261	.015894	15.214	65
70	162021	6414	.039587	.181732	71919	13070	328713	.039761	2.637210	844208	.019566	11.738	70
75	114015	7803	.068438	.294958	58849	17358	252176	.068833	2.576406	515495	.023870	8.760	75
80	61208	7456	.121814	.468439	41491	19436	158415	.122691	2.476836	263319	.023870	6.346	80
85+	29804	6266	.210240	1.000000	22055	22055	104904	.210240	4.756463	104904	.000000	4.756	85+

NUMBER OF PERSONS DYING (OUT OF 100,000 AT BIRTH) ABOVE AGE X FROM SPECIFIED CAUSES

Age (x)	All Causes	Respiratory T.B.	Other Infec. and Paras.	Neo-plasms	Cardio-vascular	Infl., Pneu., Bronch.	Diar-rheal	Certain Degen-erative	Maternal	Cert. Dis. of Infancy	Motor Vehicle	Other Violence	Other and Unknown	Age (x)
0	100000	698	553	19667	48657	4030	532	3490	127	1485	951	4203	15607	0
1	97479	698	530	19656	48645	3773	406	3486	127	0	950	4166	15042	1
5	97020	696	498	19600	48642	3711	378	3483	127	0	901	4085	14899	5
10	96809	696	482	19559	48638	3695	374	3481	127	0	847	4063	14847	10
15	96652	694	472	19530	48630	3687	372	3468	127	0	828	4047	14797	15
20	96421	694	462	19502	48616	3677	370	3456	121	0	778	3987	14758	20
25	96130	691	460	19456	48588	3674	368	3446	91	0	718	3931	14707	25
30	95778	679	458	19404	48534	3667	366	3423	57	0	700	3857	14633	30
35	95312	668	449	19268	48449	3658	361	3405	39	0	646	3816	14553	35
40	94563	649	437	18994	48216	3650	358	3351	14	0	610	3724	14460	40
45	93557	620	422	18539	48147	3633	348	3301	0	0	586	3625	14336	45
50	91568	574	412	17763	47832	3610	345	3226	0	0	560	3503	14143	50
55	89562	532	397	16688	47251	3570	333	3113	0	0	512	3315	13851	55
60	86142	498	359	15289	46189	3502	322	2899	0	0	449	3159	13476	60
65	80669	458	326	13365	44082	3384	307	2603	0	0	380	2948	12816	65
70	71919	384	258	10810	40080	3089	271	2117	0	0	312	2747	11851	70
75	58849	309	193	7747	33361	2597	204	1482	0	0	204	2345	10407	75
80	41491	207	111	4607	23583	1852	142	819	0	0	103	1788	8279	80
85+	22055	84	63	1915	12252	1014	63	299	0	0	32	1112	5221	85+

NUMBER OF PERSONS SURVIVING TO AGE X IF SPECIFIED CAUSES WERE ELIMINATED

Age (x)	No Causes	Respiratory T.B. (1)	Other Infec. and Paras. (2)	Neo-plasms (3)	Cardio-vascular (4)	Infl., Pneu., Bronch. (5)	Diar-rheal (6)	Certain Degener-ative (7)	Maternal (8)	Cert. Dis. of Infancy (9)	Motor Vehicle (10)	Other Violence (11)	Other and Unknown (12)	(1)+(2)	(1)+(2)+(5)+(6)+(8)	(1)+(2)+(5)+(6)+(8)+part of(9)&(12)	(10)+(11)	Age (x)
0	100000	100000	100000	100000	100000	100000	100000	100000	100000	100000	100000	100000	100000	100000	100000	100000	100000	0
1	97479	97479	97502	97490	97491	97733	97603	97483	97479	98956	97480	97516	98038	97502	97881	99648	97517	1
5	97020	97022	97075	97087	97035	97335	97172	97027	97020	98490	97070	97137	97720	97077	97544	99363	97187	5
10	96809	96811	96879	96917	96828	97139	96965	96818	96809	98276	96913	96948	97560	96881	97368	99156	97052	10
15	96652	96656	96732	96788	96679	96990	96809	96674	96652	98117	96775	96807	97452	96736	97232	99068	96930	15
20	96421	96425	96511	96585	96462	96768	96580	96455	96427	97882	96593	96635	97259	96515	97028	98866	96808	20
25	96130	96137	96222	96340	96158	96475	96290	96174	96166	97587	96362	96400	97017	96229	96775	98617	96632	25
30	95778	95787	95871	96039	95900	96133	95945	95845	95848	97229	96027	96121	96736	95890	96478	98330	96371	30
35	95312	95342	95414	95708	95519	95674	95478	95396	95399	96756	95614	95694	96346	95444	96061	97916	95997	35
40	94563	94611	94676	95230	94901	94930	94731	94700	94675	95996	94898	95034	95682	94725	95374	97224	95371	40
45	93557	93634	93684	94674	94060	93937	93733	93743	93681	94975	93913	94122	94789	93761	94444	96289	94480	45
50	91568	92089	92103	93848	92777	92365	92144	92225	92090	93362	92344	92646	93373	92224	92922	94749	93024	50
55	89562	89721	89708	92481	90931	89988	89745	89924	89681	90919	89975	90409	91224	89868	90600	92397	90826	55
60	86142	86329	86320	90377	88523	86619	86329	86701	86256	87447	86602	87111	88116	86507	87290	89040	87576	60
65	80669	80883	80867	86609	85023	81231	80859	81482	80776	81891	81166	81783	83173	81082	81947	83618	82287	65
70	71919	72179	72160	79841	79892	72701	72122	73108	72015	73009	72427	73104	75096	72421	73513	75070	73621	70
75	58849	59130	59105	68463	72484	59940	59076	60405	58927	59741	59363	60190	62826	59387	60802	62173	60715	75
80	41491	41775	41740	51395	62237	42899	41703	43156	41546	42120	41937	42915	46241	42025	43731	44842	43376	80
85+	22055	22295	22222	29818	47819	23433	22225	23331	22084	22389	22344	23319	27149	22464	24083	24858	23624	85+

ACCED YRS OF LIFE

	No Causes	(1)	(2)	(3)	(4)	(5)	(6)	(7)	(8)	(9)	(10)	(11)	(12)				
TOTAL		.107	.128	2.997	7.394	.578	.160	.461	.059	1.109	.280	.666	2.185	.235	1.043	2.552	.952
WORK	1.958	.037	.023	.694	.390	.034	.010	.099	.044	.000	.105	.200	.258	.060	.148	.174	.306

POPULATION, DEATHS, DEATH RATES FOR ALL CAUSES COMBINED, AND SPECIFIED CAUSES

Age Start of Interval	Midyear Population	Deaths During Year	All Causes	Respiratory T.B.	Other Infec. and Paras.	Neoplasms	Cardiovascular	Infl., Pneu., Bronch.	Diarrheal	Certain Degenerative	Maternal	Cert. Dis. of Infancy	Motor Vehicle	Other Violence	Other and Unknown	Age Start of Interval
0	78788	2820	.03579	.00003	.00052	.00011	.00015	.00267	.00090	.00004	.00000	.02017	.00001	.00075	.01045	0
1	304373	350	.00115	.00000	.00010	.00011	.00003	.00015	.00003	.00000	.00000	.00000	.00000	.00006	.00023	.00045	1
5	361327	224	.00062	.00000	.00003	.00010	.00002	.00003	.00000	.00001	.00000	.00000	.00016	.00011	.00015	5
10	351794	165	.00047	.00000	.00001	.00009	.00003	.00002	.00000	.00002	.00000	.00000	.00006	.00011	.00012	10
15	275762	261	.00095	.00000	.00003	.00009	.00007	.00001	.00000	.00001	.00000	.00000	.00026	.00032	.00016	15
20	286647	471	.00164	.00002	.00001	.00016	.00007	.00001	.00000	.00005	.00000	.00000	.00061	.00046	.00025	20
25	311141	483	.00155	.00003	.00003	.00014	.00016	.00001	.00001	.00008	.00000	.00000	.00045	.00040	.00023	25
30	328739	550	.00167	.00009	.00003	.00025	.00023	.00001	.00001	.00010	.00000	.00000	.00034	.00037	.00026	30
35	351204	728	.00207	.00014	.00003	.00031	.00037	.00005	.00001	.00014	.00000	.00000	.00027	.00040	.00035	35
40	234657	808	.00344	.00020	.00003	.00071	.00095	.00005	.00000	.00017	.00000	.00000	.00029	.00049	.00054	40
45	304650	1883	.00618	.00034	.00009	.00137	.00150	.00018	.00001	.00030	.00000	.00000	.00033	.00059	.00108	45
50	306799	3262	.01063	.00056	.00008	.00255	.00374	.00045	.00002	.00049	.00000	.00000	.00032	.00083	.00160	50
55	290553	5177	.01782	.00068	.00009	.00466	.00664	.00075	.00003	.00091	.00000	.00000	.00031	.00091	.00285	55
60	237509	6551	.02758	.00086	.00020	.00656	.01077	.00144	.00005	.00127	.00000	.00000	.00040	.00108	.00455	60
65	177150	7250	.04093	.00082	.00024	.00927	.01814	.00277	.00004	.00182	.00000	.00000	.00048	.00099	.00635	65
70	131850	8380	.06356	.00074	.00027	.01283	.02995	.00451	.00012	.00256	.00000	.00000	.00042	.00168	.01046	70
75	89933	8985	.09991	.00077	.00024	.01690	.04749	.00768	.00019	.00391	.00000	.00000	.00054	.00254	.01964	75
80	46123	7338	.15910	.00078	.00024	.02099	.07302	.01288	.00030	.00455	.00000	.00000	.00074	.00507	.04052	80
85+	18838	5371	.28512	.00021	.00048	.02532	.11397	.02431	.00048	.00504	.00000	.00000	.00058	.00807	.10665	85+
ALL	4487877	61057														

	All Causes	Respiratory T.B.	Other Infec. and Paras.	Neoplasms	Cardiovascular	Infl., Pneu., Bronch.	Diarrheal	Certain Degenerative	Maternal	Cert. Dis. of Infancy	Motor Vehicle	Other Violence	Other and Unknown
CRUDE DEATH RATE	.01360	.00026	.00008	.00247	.00529	.00087	.00004	.00051	.00000	.00035	.00031	.00065	.00278
STANDARDIZED RATE (1)	.00671	.00013	.00007	.00106	.00198	.00040	.00005	.00022	.00000	.00071	.00026	.00043	.00140
STANDARDIZED RATE (2)	.01224	.00022	.00008	.00213	.00467	.00079	.00004	.00045	.00000	.00042	.00030	.00060	.00256
GEOMETRIC MEAN	.00797												

LIFE TABLE FOR ALL CAUSES COMBINED

Age (x)	Midyear Population	Deaths During Year	$_nM_x$	$_nq_x$	l_x	$_nd_x$	$_nL_x$	$_nm_x$	$_na_x$	T_x	$_nr_x$	$\overset{\circ}{e}_x$	Age (x)
0	78788	2820	.035792	.034710	100000	3471	96983	.035790	.130847	6678228	.000000	66.782	0
1	304373	350	.001150	.004589	96529	443	385009	.001151	1.500000	6581245	.000000	68.179	1
5	361327	224	.000620	.003091	96086	297	479688	.000619	2.500000	6196237	.000000	64.486	5
10	351794	165	.000469	.002349	95789	225	478415	.000470	2.645370	5716949	.020100	59.679	10
15	275762	261	.000946	.004751	95564	454	476800	.000952	2.753763	5238134	.025588	54.813	15
20	286647	471	.001643	.008180	95110	778	473662	.001643	2.573640	4761334	-.004464	50.061	20
25	311141	483	.001552	.007728	94332	729	469838	.001552	2.500286	4287671	-.010973	45.453	25
30	328739	550	.001673	.008322	93603	779	466116	.001673	2.561778	3817834	-.021675	40.788	30
35	351204	728	.002073	.010342	92824	960	461886	.002078	2.673177	3351718	-.020590	36.108	35
40	234657	808	.003443	.017167	91864	1577	455747	.003460	2.734623	2889832	.021859	31.458	40
45	304650	1883	.006181	.030303	90287	2736	445210	.006145	2.724857	2434084	-.024675	26.959	45
50	306799	3262	.010632	.051741	87551	4530	427339	.010600	2.700699	1988874	-.012604	22.717	50
55	290553	5177	.017818	.085521	83021	7100	398463	.017818	2.656103	1561535	.000136	18.809	55
60	237509	6551	.027582	.129740	75921	9850	356071	.027663	2.610808	1163072	.016792	15.319	60
65	177150	7250	.040926	.186754	66071	12339	300536	.041057	2.583323	807000	.018862	12.214	65
70	131850	8380	.063557	.275162	53732	14785	232339	.063628	2.545203	506465	.005869	9.426	70
75	89933	8985	.099908	.399184	38947	15547	155528	.099962	2.478184	274099	.002506	7.038	75
80	46123	7338	.159096	.562265	23400	13157	82645	.159200	2.388811	118570	.002506	5.067	80
85+	18838	5371	.285115	1.000000	10243	10243	35926	.285115	3.507354	35926	.000000	3.507	85+

NUMBER OF PERSONS DYING (OUT OF 100,000 AT BIRTH) ABOVE AGE X FROM SPECIFIED CAUSES

Age (x)	All Causes	Respiratory T.B.	Other Infec. and Paras.	Neo-plasms	Cardio-vascular	Infl., Pneu., Bronch.	Diar-rheal	Certain Degen-erative	Maternal	Cert. Dis. of Infancy	Motor Vehicle	Other Violence	Other and Unknown	Age (x)
0	100000	1804	574	18001	39793	6510	268	3744	0	1956	2124	4572	20654	0
1	96529	1802	523	17990	39778	6251	181	3740	0	0	2123	4499	19642	1
5	96086	1800	496	17948	39767	6194	168	3740	0	0	2102	4411	19470	5
10	95789	1800	470	17899	39757	6180	167	3735	0	0	2026	4358	19397	10
15	95564	1799	465	17855	39745	6169	167	3724	0	0	1999	4303	19338	15
20	95110	1797	453	17812	39714	6164	167	3718	0	0	1875	4148	19262	20
25	94332	1789	446	17738	39679	6159	165	3654	0	0	1586	3932	19144	25
30	93603	1774	434	17673	39602	6153	161	3656	0	0	1374	3741	19035	30
35	92824	1734	419	17557	39498	6147	158	3611	0	0	1213	3571	18916	35
40	91864	1668	406	17414	39324	6123	155	3545	0	0	1089	3386	18754	40
45	90287	1579	392	17088	38888	6100	153	3467	0	0	954	3160	18506	45
50	87551	1429	351	16483	38049	6022	150	3335	0	0	808	2896	18028	50
55	83021	1191	316	15398	36455	5832	142	3128	0	0	673	2540	17346	55
60	75921	921	282	13543	33808	5534	128	2766	0	0	550	2179	16210	60
65	66071	614	210	11057	29958	5018	112	2313	0	0	409	1795	14585	65
70	53732	366	137	8265	24486	4183	100	1764	0	0	264	1496	12671	70
75	38947	193	75	5281	17518	3133	72	1168	0	0	166	1105	10236	75
80	23400	74	37	2651	10128	1937	42	559	0	0	81	710	7181	80
85+	10243	8	17	910	4095	873	17	181	0	0	21	290	3831	85+

NUMBER OF PERSONS SURVIVING TO AGE X IF SPECIFIED CAUSES WERE ELIMINATED

Age (x)	No Causes	Respiratory T.B. (1)	Other Infec. and Paras. (2)	Neo-plasms (3)	Cardio-vascular (4)	Infl., Pneu., Bronch. (5)	Diar-rheal (6)	Certain Degener-ative (7)	Maternal (8)	Cert. Dis. of Infancy (9)	Motor Vehicle (10)	Other Violence (11)	Other and Unknown (12)	(1)+(2)	(1)+(2)+(5)+(6)+(8)	(1)+(2)+(5)+(6)+(8)+part of(9)&(12)	(10)+(11)	Age (x)
0	100000	100000	100000	100000	100000	100000	100000	100000	100000	100000	100000	100000	100000	100000	100000	100000	100000	0
1	96529	96531	96579	96540	96544	96784	96615	96533	96529	98470	96530	96601	97528	96581	96922	99272	96602	1
5	96086	96090	96173	96139	96112	96357	96184	96090	96086	98018	96108	96245	97254	96177	96586	99000	96267	5
10	95789	95793	95892	95890	95825	96113	95888	95798	95789	97715	95887	96001	97028	95895	96319	98736	96099	10
15	95564	95569	95671	95709	95611	95898	95663	95584	95564	97486	95689	95830	96876	95676	96110	98528	95955	15
20	95110	95117	95229	95298	95188	95447	95208	95136	95110	97022	95358	95530	96476	95236	95672	98083	95779	20
25	94332	94347	94457	94592	94444	94672	94431	94381	94332	96229	94867	94965	95806	94472	94912	97307	95504	25
30	93603	93633	93739	93926	93791	93946	93706	93690	93603	95485	94346	94423	95176	93769	94215	96600	95173	30
35	92824	92893	92974	93260	93115	93317	92929	92955	92824	94690	93723	93808	94809	93043	93495	95874	94716	35
40	91864	91998	92025	92439	92326	92231	91971	92060	91864	93711	92878	93024	93691	92160	92635	95013	94051	40
45	90287	90507	90459	91178	91176	90670	90394	90557	90287	92102	91419	91654	92334	90680	91172	93538	92803	45
50	87551	87913	87758	89018	89252	88000	87657	87943	87551	89311	88794	89141	90019	88121	88681	91041	90407	50
55	83021	83597	83252	85494	86231	83633	83130	83595	83021	84690	84333	84882	86046	83829	84558	86893	86223	55
60	75921	76708	76165	80030	81530	76768	76034	76795	75921	77448	77240	77975	79822	76954	77928	80199	79330	60
65	66071	67044	66350	72131	74917	67298	66184	67260	66071	67399	67352	68226	71076	67328	68695	70877	69549	65
70	53732	54744	54025	61463	66784	55502	53835	55204	53732	54907	55762	59685	65046	55047	56969	58990	56981	70
75	38947	39832	39212	47528	56339	41161	39045	40535	38947	39730	39882	40764	45623	40102	42489	44245	41743	75
80	23400	24023	23588	31104	43118	25720	23482	24842	23400	23871	24028	24811	30317	24216	26710	28127	25477	80
85+	10243	10560	10338	15188	27567	12036	10295	11136	10243	10449	10558	11151	16378	10658	12587	13593	11493	85+

ADDED YRS OF LIFE

	No Causes	(1)	(2)	(3)	(4)	(5)	(6)	(7)	(8)	(9)	(10)	(11)	(12)	(1)+(2)	(1)+(2)+(5)+(6)+(8)	...+part of(9)&(12)	(10)+(11)
TOTAL		.306	.151	2.421	5.311	.784	.088	.480	.000	1.340	.657	1.018	3.132	.459	1.353	3.304	1.692
WORK	3.632	.138	.039	.644	.849	.087	.007	.157	.000	.000	.418	.503	.538	.177	.272	.325	.928

POPULATION, DEATHS, DEATH RATES FOR ALL CAUSES COMBINED, AND SPECIFIED CAUSES

Age Start of Interval	Midyear Popula-tion	Deaths During Year	All Causes	Respira-tory T. B.	Other Infec. and Paras.	Neo-plasms	Cardio-vascular	Infl., Pneu., Bronch.	Diar-rheal	Certain Degen-erative	Maternal	Cert. Dis. of Infancy	Motor Vehicle	Other Violence	Other and Unknown	Age Start of Interval
U	75275	2004	.02662	.COCCC	.00044	.COOC4	.00017	.00218	.0CC60	.0C005	.CCCC0	.01460	.00000	.00046	.00808	0
1	291485	291	.00100	.CCCC0	.00006	.00012	.000C3	.00012	.00004	.00001	.00000	.00000	.00005	.00018	.00038	1
5	348666	129	.00037	.CCCC0	.0CC03	.CCCC4	.000C2	.00001	.00001	.00001	.00000	.CCCC0	.00008	.00005	.00013	5
10	342365	110	.00032	.000C0	.00002	.00007	.00004	.00003	.C0001	.00000	.00000	.CCCC0	.00004	.00002	.00010	10
15	268969	110	.00041	.CCCC1	.C0001	.00007	.00003	.00001	.00000	.00004	.00001	.CCCC0	.00006	.00006	.00010	15
20	285099	185	.00065	.00001	.C0001	.0CCC9	.00007	.C0003	.00000	.00002	.00003	.CCCC0	.00009	.00014	.00014	20
25	311137	228	.00073	.000C2	.00002	.00014	.00011	.00003	.00000	.00004	.00003	.00000	.00009	.00010	.00015	25
30	323528	326	.00101	.C0CC4	.0CC02	.00025	.00017	.00003	.00000	.00005	.0CC05	.00000	.00005	.00012	.00022	30
35	338791	459	.00135	.000C6	.00004	.00047	.00022	.00003	.00000	.00007	.00006	.00000	.00004	.00015	.00023	35
40	230911	475	.00206	.00CC7	.C0003	.00079	.00040	.00006	.00000	.00010	.00002	.C0000	.00005	.00014	.00039	40
45	307751	1053	.00342	.00CC7	.00003	.00149	.00072	.00006	.C0001	.00019	.0C000	.CCCC0	.00008	.00023	.00053	45
50	317935	1593	.00501	.00006	.0CC06	.00201	.00140	.00014	.00001	.00032	.CC000	.CCCC0	.00009	.00025	.00067	50
55	312977	2609	.00834	.00CC5	.CCC10	.00296	.00289	.00026	.0CC03	.00057	.CCCC0	.CCCC0	.00006	.00030	.00113	55
60	279190	3970	.01422	.00012	.00008	.00447	.C0566	.00052	.00004	.C0C58	.CC000	.C0000	.00009	.00044	.00181	60
65	227593	5433	.02387	.CCC1C	.C0011	.00593	.01089	.00104	.C0C05	.00186	.CC000	.CC000	.00012	.00056	.00322	65
70	175786	7627	.04339	.00018	.00011	.00860	.02121	.00245	.00010	.C0287	.C0000	.C0000	.00017	.00097	.00673	70
75	124537	9513	.07639	.00028	.00018	.01188	.03837	.C0456	.00016	.00398	.C0000	.CCCC0	.00023	.00172	.01502	75
80	68924	8813	.12787	.CCC20	.00022	.01502	.06156	.00914	.C0036	.00428	.00001	.00000	.00028	.00382	.03298	80
85+	34693	7953	.22924	.00023	.00023	.01862	.C9244	.01767	.C0049	.00427	.CC000	.CC000	.00014	.00839	.08676	85+
ALL	4665612	52861														

CRUDE DEATH RATE			.01133	.0CCC6	.0CC06	.00212	.00470	.00065	.00004	.00055	.00001	.00024	.00008	.00037	.00246	
STANDARDIZED RATE (1)			.00430	.00003	.00005	.00078	.C0126	.00025	.C0004	.00019	.00001	.00051	.00007	.00018	.00094	
STANDARDIZED RATE (2)			.00813	.00005	.0CC05	.00152	.00320	.00046	.00003	.00039	.00001	.00030	.00007	.00029	.00174	
GECMETRIC MEAN			.00479													

LIFE TABLE FOR ALL CAUSES COMBINED

Age (x)	Midyear Popula-tion	Deaths During Year	$_nM_x$	$_nq_x$	l_x	$_nd_x$	$_nL_x$	$_nm_x$	$_na_x$	T_x	$_nr_x$	$\overset{\circ}{e}_x$	Age (x)
0	75275	2004	.026622	.026010	100000	2601	97699	.026623	.115258	7277460	.000000	72.775	0
1	291485	291	.000998	.003984	97399	388	388626	.000998	1.500000	7179761	.000000	73.715	1
5	348666	129	.000370	.001845	97011	179	484608	.000369	2.500000	6791135	.000000	70.004	5
10	342365	110	.000321	.001611	96832	156	483774	.000322	2.525374	6306528	.019579	65.129	10
15	268969	110	.000409	.002048	96676	198	482917	.C00410	2.664141	5822754	.024343	60.230	15
20	285099	185	.000649	.003234	96478	312	481642	.000648	2.602831	5339836	-.006501	55.348	20
25	311137	228	.000733	.003660	96166	352	479985	.000733	2.599432	4858194	-.010555	50.519	25
30	323528	326	.001008	.005010	95814	480	477931	.001004	2.627604	4378209	-.017835	45.695	30
35	338791	459	.001355	.006776	95334	646	475158	.001360	2.658991	3900278	.022885	40.912	35
40	230911	475	.002057	.010276	94688	973	471203	.002065	2.700625	3425120	.019922	36.173	40
45	307751	1053	.003422	.016892	93715	1583	464889	.C03405	2.671352	2953918	-.027119	31.520	45
50	317935	1593	.005010	.024693	92132	2275	455408	.004996	2.651484	2489029	-.013330	27.016	50
55	312977	2609	.008336	.040887	89857	3674	440865	.008334	2.708220	2033621	-.002002	22.632	55
60	279190	3970	.014220	.069004	86183	5947	417181	.014255	2.690572	1592756	.011749	18.481	60
65	227593	5433	.023872	.113590	80236	9114	380081	.023979	2.685040	1175575	.019613	14.651	65
70	175786	7627	.043388	.197435	71122	14042	322444	.043549	2.638112	795493	.015834	11.185	70
75	124537	9513	.076387	.322758	57080	18423	240314	.076662	2.552753	473049	.014765	8.287	75
80	68924	8813	.127865	.483923	38657	18707	145708	.128387	2.456712	232735	.014765	6.021	80
85+	34693	7953	.229239	1.000000	19950	19950	87027	.229239	4.362253	87027	.000000	4.362	85+

NUMBER OF PERSONS DYING (OUT OF 100,000 AT BIRTH) ABOVE AGE X FROM SPECIFIED CAUSES

Age (x)	All Causes	Respiratory T.B.	Other Infec. and Paras.	Neoplasms	Cardiovascular	Infl., Pneu., Bronch.	Diarrheal	Certain Degenerative	Maternal	Cert. Dis. of Infancy	Motor Vehicle	Other Violence	Other and Unknown	Age (x)
0	100000	451	453	17466	42466	5949	312	4665	98	1426	611	3246	22857	0
1	97399	451	410	17462	42449	5736	254	4660	98	0	611	3200	22068	1
5	97011	451	386	17415	42437	5691	237	4657	98	0	590	3130	21919	5
10	96832	451	370	17394	42428	5687	237	4654	98	0	552	3107	21854	10
15	96676	450	360	17362	42411	5674	234	4653	98	0	532	3096	21806	15
20	96478	445	354	17327	42396	5667	232	4633	94	0	503	3069	21758	20
25	96166	438	348	17284	42363	5654	230	4621	81	0	458	3001	21688	25
30	95814	430	337	17217	42310	5640	230	4599	64	0	416	2955	21616	30
35	95334	410	328	17098	42229	5626	229	4576	38	0	391	2899	21510	35
40	94688	380	311	16876	42126	5614	227	4543	12	0	373	2827	21399	40
45	93715	345	297	16502	41938	5587	225	4494	4	0	348	2762	21213	45
50	92132	314	282	15811	41605	5559	219	4406	2	0	312	2656	20966	50
55	89857	286	253	14899	40570	5494	215	4260	2	0	272	2543	20663	55
60	86183	262	210	13595	39699	5382	204	4009	2	0	247	2412	20161	60
65	80236	212	175	11727	37331	5164	186	3597	2	0	209	2228	19405	65
70	71122	175	132	9468	33169	4768	166	2888	2	0	164	2016	18174	70
75	57080	118	95	6690	26302	3974	134	1959	2	0	109	1703	15994	75
80	38657	50	52	3830	17047	2873	96	1001	2	0	53	1288	12365	80
85+	19950	20	20	1620	8045	1538	43	371	0	0	13	730	7550	85+

NUMBER OF PERSONS SURVIVING TO AGE X IF SPECIFIED CAUSES WERE ELIMINATED

Age (x)	No Causes	Respiratory T.B. (1)	Other Infec. and Paras. (2)	Neoplasms (3)	Cardiovascular (4)	Infl., Pneu., Bronch. (5)	Diarrheal (6)	Certain Degenerative (7)	Maternal (8)	Cert. Dis. of Infancy (9)	Motor Vehicle (10)	Other Violence (11)	Other and Unknown (12)	(1) + (2)	(1) + (2) + (5) + (6) + (8)	(1)+(2)+(5)+(6)+(8)+part of(9)&(12)	(10) + (11)	Age (x)
0	100000	100000	100000	100000	100000	100000	100000	100000	100000	100000	100000	100000	100000	100000	100000	100000	100000	0
1	97399	97399	97441	97403	97416	97609	97456	97404	97399	98817	97399	97444	98181	97441	97709	99510	97444	1
5	97011	97011	97077	97062	97040	97266	97085	97019	97011	98423	97032	97126	97806	97540	97077	99256	97147	5
10	96832	96832	96914	96904	96870	97090	96906	96843	96832	98241	96891	96970	97825	96914	97247	99105	97029	10
15	96676	96677	96768	96780	96731	96947	96753	96688	96676	98083	96755	96825	97715	96769	97117	98985	96904	15
20	96478	96484	96576	96616	96547	96755	96557	96510	96482	97882	96586	96653	97564	96582	96942	98815	96761	20
25	96166	96179	96269	96347	96268	96455	96246	96210	96183	97566	96318	96409	97319	96282	96670	98549	96562	25
30	95814	95835	95928	96061	95969	96116	95994	95880	95848	97208	96008	96102	97035	95949	96366	98253	96296	30
35	95334	95375	95457	95699	95569	95649	95415	95422	95394	96721	95552	95677	96656	95497	95954	97852	95895	35
40	94688	94758	94827	95273	95024	95013	94770	94808	94773	96066	94922	95100	96114	94897	95391	97297	95336	40
45	93715	93820	93866	94669	94236	94063	93798	93883	93807	95079	93972	94188	95314	93971	94497	96406	94444	45
50	92132	92265	92296	93765	92977	92502	92220	92385	92225	93473	92420	92703	93953	92429	92983	94876	92993	50
55	89857	90015	90045	92370	91316	90283	89947	90248	89947	91165	90178	90526	91939	90203	90812	92682	90849	55
60	86183	86358	86406	89916	88857	86702	86280	86805	86270	87437	86515	86954	88684	86581	87287	89115	87289	60
65	80236	80447	80477	85610	85117	80931	80343	81217	80317	81404	80582	81133	83319	80689	81578	83333	81482	65
70	71122	71344	71376	78182	79723	72116	71236	72669	71194	72157	71471	72118	75068	71599	72789	74431	72472	70
75	57080	57309	57317	65524	71251	58603	57200	59173	57137	57911	57409	58164	62346	57547	59266	60765	58500	75
80	38657	38868	38853	47121	58681	40625	38770	40888	38696	39220	38926	39739	45612	39064	41214	42534	40016	80
85+	19950	20080	20074	26295	41635	21979	20046	21576	19971	20240	20117	20917	27909	20204	22390	23522	21092	85+

ADDED YRS OF LIFE

	No Causes	(1)	(2)	(3)	(4)	(5)	(6)	(7)	(8)	(9)	(10)	(11)	(12)	(1)+(2)	(1)+(2)+(5)+(6)+(8)	+part of(9)&(12)	(10)+(11)
TOTAL		.090	.134	2.551	5.472	.686	.082	.568	.042	1.058	.190	.525	3.146	.225	1.044	2.673	.718
WORK	1.930	.042	.030	.618	.418	.053	.006	.110	.031	.000	.081	.156	.318	.072	.163	.200	.237

POPULATION, DEATHS, DEATH RATES FOR ALL CAUSES COMBINED, AND SPECIFIED CAUSES

Age Start of Interval	Midyear Population	Deaths During Year	All Causes	Respiratory T. B.	Other Infec. and Paras.	Neoplasms	Cardiovascular	Infl., Pneu., Bronch.	Diarrheal	Certain Degenerative	Maternal	Cert. Dis. of Infancy	Motor Vehicle	Other Violence	Other and Unknown	Age Start of Interval
0	80822	2351	.02909	.00000	.00042	.00007	.00025	.00145	.00063	.00005	.00000	.01664	.00005	.00082	.00871	0
1	316317	301	.00095	.00000	.00005	.00013	.00003	.00007	.00002	.00003	.00000	.00000	.00010	.00015	.00037	1
5	383884	193	.00050	.00000	.00002	.00009	.00002	.00001	.00000	.00001	.00000	.00000	.00014	.00008	.00012	5
10	361634	160	.00044	.00000	.00001	.00004	.00001	.00001	.00000	.00001	.00000	.00000	.00009	.00011	.00014	10
15	349344	375	.00107	.00001	.00000	.00012	.00005	.00001	.00000	.00002	.00000	.00000	.00037	.00030	.00018	15
20	280552	451	.00161	.00000	.00001	.00009	.00008	.00001	.00000	.00003	.00000	.00000	.00076	.00041	.00022	20
25	305220	456	.00149	.00001	.00001	.00015	.00016	.00001	.00000	.00004	.00000	.00000	.00048	.00042	.00021	25
30	330028	541	.00164	.00004	.00003	.00017	.00025	.00001	.00000	.00007	.00000	.00000	.00042	.00042	.00024	30
35	329390	746	.00226	.00004	.00002	.00036	.00049	.00004	.00000	.00010	.00000	.00000	.00035	.00052	.00036	35
40	327048	1186	.00363	.00012	.00004	.00071	.00114	.00005	.00001	.00015	.00000	.00000	.00031	.00051	.00059	40
45	218519	1342	.00614	.00022	.00005	.00145	.00212	.00008	.00002	.00028	.00000	.00000	.00044	.00057	.00092	45
50	291729	2843	.00975	.00027	.00005	.00247	.00363	.00024	.00001	.00039	.00000	.00000	.00037	.00073	.00158	50
55	281871	4766	.01691	.00051	.00010	.00470	.00641	.00055	.00001	.00070	.00000	.00000	.00033	.00085	.00275	55
60	253109	6784	.02680	.00059	.00010	.00721	.01103	.00080	.00003	.00111	.00000	.00000	.00091	.00456	60
65	193470	7954	.04111	.00062	.00017	.01052	.01874	.00169	.00006	.00165	.00000	.00000	.00046	.00110	.00611	65
70	134134	8076	.06021	.00078	.00010	.01350	.03020	.00255	.00011	.00207	.00000	.00000	.00056	.00127	.00907	70
75	90094	8120	.09013	.00055	.00023	.01654	.04904	.00428	.00013	.00312	.00000	.00000	.00053	.00181	.01389	75
80	49950	6932	.13878	.00058	.00032	.02084	.07708	.00691	.00034	.00392	.00000	.00000	.00066	.00370	.02442	80
85+	22377	5477	.24476	.00031	.00022	.02570	.13465	.01457	.00036	.00501	.00000	.00000	.00054	.00778	.05564	85+
ALL	4599492	59054														

CRUDE DEATH RATE			.01284	.00017	.00006	.00256	.00561	.00051	.00003	.00043	.00000	.00029	.00036	.00059	.00222	
STANDARDIZED RATE (1)			.00619	.00008	.00005	.00108	.00205	.00023	.00003	.00019	.00000	.00059	.00032	.00040	.00117	
STANDARDIZED RATE (2)			.01134	.00015	.00005	.00218	.00487	.00045	.00003	.00037	.00000	.00034	.00035	.00055	.00198	
GEOMETRIC MEAN			.00752													

LIFE TABLE FOR ALL CAUSES COMBINED

Age (x)	Midyear Population	Deaths During Year	$_nM_x$	$_nq_x$	l_x	$_nd_x$	$_nL_x$	$_nm_x$	$_na_x$	T_x	$_nr_x$	$\overset{\circ}{e}_x$	Age (x)
0	80822	2351	.029089	.028360	100000	2836	97503	.029086	.119451	6774926	.000000	67.749	0
1	316317	301	.000952	.003758	97164	369	387734	.000952	1.500000	6677423	.000000	68.723	1
5	383884	193	.000503	.002510	96795	243	483368	.000503	2.500000	6289690	.000000	64.979	5
10	361634	160	.000442	.002216	96552	214	482282	.000444	2.767718	5806322	.003784	60.137	10
15	349344	375	.001073	.005377	96338	518	480510	.001078	2.722812	5324040	.020389	55.264	15
20	280552	451	.001608	.008015	95820	768	477219	.001609	2.551270	4843530	.019743	50.548	20
25	305220	456	.001494	.007438	95052	707	473493	.001493	2.500589	4366310	-.010592	45.936	25
30	330028	541	.001639	.008162	94345	770	469872	.001639	2.593344	3892817	-.009218	41.262	30
35	329390	746	.002265	.011242	93575	1052	465433	.002260	2.679024	3422946	-.011084	36.580	35
40	327048	1186	.003626	.018093	92523	1674	458786	.003649	2.712689	2957512	.029581	31.965	40
45	218519	1342	.006141	.030391	90849	2761	447863	.006165	2.688413	2498726	.019556	27.504	45
50	291729	2843	.009745	.047350	88088	4171	430856	.009681	2.702290	2050863	-.028299	23.282	50
55	281871	4766	.016908	.081164	83917	6811	403714	.016871	2.669732	1620007	-.010925	19.305	55
60	253109	6784	.026803	.126060	77106	9720	362443	.026818	2.624766	1216294	.002941	15.774	60
65	193470	7954	.041112	.187472	67386	12633	306320	.041241	2.576948	853851	.018319	12.671	65
70	134134	8076	.060208	.262764	54753	14386	238261	.060309	2.532019	547531	.016801	10.000	70
75	90094	8120	.090128	.367726	40367	14844	164447	.090266	2.481263	309271	.007869	7.661	75
80	49950	6932	.138779	.511343	25523	13051	93868	.139036	2.414199	144824	.007869	5.674	80
85+	22377	5477	.244760	1.000000	12472	12472	50956	.244760	4.085631	50956	.000000	4.086	85+

NUMBER OF PERSONS DYING (OUT OF 100,000 AT BIRTH) ABOVE AGE X FROM SPECIFIED CAUSES

Age (x)	All Causes	Respiratory T. B.	Other Infec. and Paras.	Neoplasms	Cardio-vascular	Infl., Pneu., Bronch.	Diarrheal	Certain Degenerative	Maternal	Cert. Dis. of Infancy	Motor Vehicle	Other Violence	Other and Unknown	Age (x)
0	100000	1276	404	19533	45309	4120	226	3336	0	1622	2528	4368	17278	0
1	97164	1276	363	19526	45285	3978	164	3331	0	0	2524	4289	16428	1
5	96795	1276	343	19474	45273	3953	158	3319	0	0	2484	4231	16284	5
10	96552	1276	333	19429	45264	3946	157	3314	0	0	2415	4191	16227	10
15	96338	1276	329	19409	45252	3940	156	3309	0	0	2372	4136	16159	15
20	95820	1270	328	19352	45230	3933	154	3298	0	0	2192	3991	16072	20
25	95052	1268	322	19312	45192	3926	153	3282	0	0	1831	3797	15969	25
30	94345	1264	318	19242	45118	3920	151	3264	0	0	1604	3597	15867	30
35	93575	1245	305	19161	45001	3914	150	3232	0	0	1408	3402	15757	35
40	92523	1226	294	18996	44776	3897	150	3187	0	0	1247	3160	15590	40
45	90849	1172	275	18669	44249	3873	147	3118	0	0	1103	2926	15317	45
50	88088	1073	255	18016	43293	3838	137	2993	0	0	906	2671	14906	50
55	83917	959	231	16960	41740	3738	131	2827	0	0	748	2356	14227	55
60	77106	751	193	15068	39159	3516	128	2544	0	0	616	2012	13119	60
65	67386	538	156	12452	35160	3227	116	2141	0	0	450	1682	11464	65
70	54753	349	103	9222	29398	2707	99	1633	0	0	309	1345	9588	70
75	40367	163	80	5999	22177	2097	72	1138	0	0	176	1043	7422	75
80	25523	72	42	3277	14100	1391	50	625	0	0	88	745	5133	80
85+	12472	16	11	1309	6661	742	18	255	0	0	27	396	2837	85+

NUMBER OF PERSONS SURVIVING TO AGE X IF SPECIFIED CAUSES WERE ELIMINATED

Age (x)	No Causes	Respiratory T. B. (1)	Other Infec. and Paras. (2)	Neoplasms (3)	Cardiovascular (4)	Infl., Pneu., Bronch. (5)	Diarrheal (6)	Certain Degenerative (7)	Maternal (8)	Cert. Dis. of Infancy (9)	Motor Vehicle (10)	Other Violence (11)	Other and Unknown (12)	(1) + (2)	(1) + (2) + (5) + (6) + (8)	(1)+(2)+(5)+(6)+(8)+part of(9)&(12)	(10) + (11)	Age (x)
0	100000	100000	100000	100000	100000	100000	100000	100000	100000	100000	100000	100000	100000	100000	100000	100000	100000	0
1	97164	97164	97204	97171	97188	97304	97225	97169	97164	98776	97168	97242	98005	97204	97406	99064	97246	1
5	96795	96795	96855	96854	96831	96960	96862	96812	96795	98401	96839	96931	97778	96855	97087	98773	96974	5
10	96552	96552	96622	96656	96556	96723	96620	96574	96552	98154	96665	96727	97590	96622	96861	98549	96840	10
15	96338	96338	96412	96461	96394	96515	96407	96365	96338	97936	96493	96568	97443	96412	96658	98347	96724	15
20	95820	95826	95895	96000	95858	96003	95850	95858	95820	97410	96155	96194	97007	95901	96154	97838	96530	20
25	95052	95060	95132	95270	95167	95123	95105	95123	95052	95629	95745	95617	96333	95140	95399	97072	96314	25
30	94345	94357	94428	94631	94533	94538	94417	94416	94345	95910	95261	95106	95720	94440	94706	96365	96030	30
35	93575	93606	93671	93940	93879	93772	93648	93677	93575	95127	94681	94526	95050	93701	93972	95629	95643	35
40	92523	92572	92628	93049	93048	92735	92595	92669	92523	94058	93779	93707	94150	92678	92962	94611	94978	40
45	90849	90951	90971	91692	91891	91081	90922	91061	90849	92356	92247	92246	92722	91073	91380	93020	93645	45
50	88088	88284	88226	89557	90056	88348	88169	88417	88088	89549	89621	89658	90318	88423	88765	90388	91259	50
55	83917	84216	84072	86371	87356	84262	84000	84393	83917	85309	85534	85764	86724	84372	84803	86400	87416	55
60	77106	77581	77285	81249	82883	77637	77185	77816	77106	78385	78720	79140	80790	77761	78377	79944	80796	60
65	67386	68000	67577	73627	76568	68123	67466	68388	67386	68504	68955	69479	72243	68193	69022	70512	71097	65
70	54753	55423	54956	63080	68402	55828	54834	56032	54753	55661	56157	56766	60535	55629	56805	58161	58222	70
75	40367	41021	40536	49779	58785	41696	40450	41744	40367	41037	41518	42119	46726	41193	42636	43793	43320	75
80	25523	26008	25660	34212	47721	26945	25593	26814	25523	25946	26321	26877	31711	26147	27680	28569	27718	80
85+	12472	12748	12560	18624	34691	13644	12528	13372	12472	12679	12905	13388	17576	12838	14108	14693	13853	85+

ADDED YRS OF LIFE

	No Causes	(1)	(2)	(3)	(4)	(5)	(6)	(7)	(8)	(9)	(10)	(11)	(12)	(1)+(2)	(1)+(2)+(5)+(6)+(8)	part	(10)+(11)
TOTAL		.200	.104	2.665	7.098	.490	.066	.431	.000	1.122	.816	1.007	2.775	.305	.871	2.201	1.844
WORK	3.599	.077	.025	.640	.892	.059	.006	.123	.000	.000	.512	.505	.523	.102	.167	.198	1.025

POPULATION, DEATHS, DEATH RATES FOR ALL CAUSES COMBINED, AND SPECIFIED CAUSES

Age Start of Interval	Midyear Population	Deaths During Year	All Causes	Respiratory T.B.	Other Infec. and Paras.	Neoplasms	Cardio-vascular	Infl., Pneu., Bronch.	Diarrheal	Certain Degenerative	Maternal	Cert. Dis. of Infancy	Motor Vehicle	Other Violence	Other and Unknown	Age Start of Interval
0	76843	1726	.02246	.00000	.00035	.00009	.00026	.00122	.00052	.00008	.00000	.01162	.00000	.00052	.00780	0
1	300900	248	.00082	.00000	.00005	.00008	.00003	.00006	.00002	.00001	.00000	.00000	.00006	.00017	.00036	1
5	367665	149	.00041	.00000	.00002	.00009	.00001	.00000	.00000	.00001	.00000	.00000	.00012	.00006	.00010	5
10	346413	86	.00025	.00000	.00001	.00006	.00002	.00001	.00000	.00001	.00000	.00000	.00006	.00003	.00004	10
15	336438	143	.00043	.00000	.00000	.00006	.00005	.00001	.00000	.00001	.00000	.00000	.00007	.00012	.00012	15
20	268893	172	.00064	.00000	.00000	.00007	.00009	.00001	.00001	.00003	.00002	.00000	.00014	.00016	.00012	20
25	295244	206	.00070	.00001	.00001	.00016	.00009	.00001	.00000	.00003	.00003	.00000	.00007	.00011	.00017	25
30	322803	289	.00090	.00002	.00001	.00026	.00016	.00001	.00000	.00005	.00003	.00000	.00007	.00010	.00019	30
35	327101	477	.00146	.00003	.00002	.00057	.00024	.00002	.00001	.00005	.00004	.00000	.00007	.00016	.00027	35
40	329692	688	.00209	.00004	.00002	.00092	.00035	.00003	.00000	.00009	.00002	.00000	.00007	.00018	.00037	40
45	223218	778	.00349	.00004	.00004	.00151	.00084	.00004	.00000	.00022	.00000	.00000	.00007	.00021	.00052	45
50	304536	1579	.00518	.00006	.00005	.00219	.00136	.00004	.00000	.00027	.00001	.00000	.00013	.00024	.00083	50
55	305661	2354	.00770	.00003	.00004	.00292	.00252	.00009	.00002	.00048	.00000	.00000	.00016	.00032	.00118	55
60	291386	3655	.01254	.00005	.00004	.00401	.00513	.00019	.00002	.00084	.00000	.00000	.00011	.00040	.00175	60
65	246942	5551	.02249	.00009	.00012	.00568	.01073	.00045	.00003	.00167	.00000	.00000	.00014	.00061	.00296	65
70	188800	7280	.03856	.00007	.00014	.00812	.02034	.00080	.00006	.00267	.00000	.00000	.00025	.00087	.00524	70
75	130451	8943	.06855	.00010	.00019	.01118	.03887	.00166	.00019	.00377	.00000	.00000	.00028	.00185	.01046	75
80	76020	8589	.11298	.00014	.00028	.01517	.06560	.00416	.00025	.00459	.00000	.00000	.00018	.00329	.01932	80
85+	39595	8133	.20540	.00025	.00033	.01899	.11476	.01008	.00058	.00487	.00000	.00000	.00025	.00846	.04682	85+
ALL	4778621	51046														

	All Causes	Respiratory T.B.	Other Infec. and Paras.	Neoplasms	Cardio-vascular	Infl., Pneu., Bronch.	Diarrheal	Certain Degenerative	Maternal	Cert. Dis. of Infancy	Motor Vehicle	Other Violence	Other and Unknown
CRUDE DEATH RATE	.01068	.00003	.00005	.00212	.00509	.00030	.00003	.00054	.00001	.00019	.00010	.00038	.00184
STANDARDIZED RATE (1)	.00389	.00002	.00004	.00077	.00126	.00011	.00003	.00017	.00001	.00041	.00009	.00019	.00080
STANDARDIZED RATE (2)	.00737	.00003	.00004	.00150	.00327	.00020	.00003	.00037	.00001	.00024	.00010	.00029	.00130
GEOMETRIC MEAN	.00448												

LIFE TABLE FOR ALL CAUSES COMBINED

Age (x)	Midyear Population	Deaths During Year	$_nM_x$	$_nq_x$	l_x	$_nd_x$	$_nL_x$	$_nm_x$	$_na_x$	T_x	$_nr_x$	$\overset{\circ}{e}_x$	Age (x)
0	76843	1726	.022461	.022020	100000	2202	98036	.022461	.108184	7389892	.000000	73.899	0
1	300900	248	.000824	.003293	97798	322	390387	.000825	1.500000	7291855	.000000	74.560	1
5	367665	149	.000405	.002021	97476	197	486888	.000405	2.500000	6901468	.000000	70.802	5
10	346413	86	.000248	.001244	97279	121	486095	.000249	2.517218	6414581	.003427	65.940	10
15	336438	143	.000425	.002131	97158	207	485312	.000427	2.690217	5928486	.020698	61.019	15
20	268893	172	.000640	.003197	96951	310	484007	.000640	2.586694	5443174	.020408	56.144	20
25	295244	206	.000698	.003477	96641	336	482390	.000697	2.574405	4959168	-.011243	51.315	25
30	322803	289	.000895	.004465	96305	430	480525	.000895	2.673934	4476778	-.010725	46.485	30
35	327101	477	.001458	.007249	95875	695	477755	.001455	2.668765	3996253	-.013170	41.682	35
40	329692	688	.002087	.010433	95180	993	473613	.002097	2.697004	3518498	.028025	36.967	40
45	223218	778	.003485	.017348	94187	1634	467135	.003458	2.674164	3044885	.018708	32.328	45
50	304536	1579	.005185	.025568	92553	2359	457236	.005159	2.656316	2577750	-.029254	27.852	50
55	305661	2354	.007701	.037741	90194	3404	443071	.007683	2.679568	2120514	-.011356	23.511	55
60	291386	3655	.012543	.060966	86790	5293	421828	.012548	2.705790	1677443	.001353	19.328	60
65	246942	5551	.022479	.107170	81497	8734	387238	.022555	2.681856	1255615	.015059	15.407	65
70	188800	7280	.038559	.177522	72763	12917	333381	.038745	2.643916	868377	.021444	11.934	70
75	130451	8943	.068554	.295041	59846	17657	256278	.068898	2.567407	534995	.020622	8.940	75
80	76020	8589	.112983	.441584	42189	18630	164022	.113582	2.481314	278717	.020622	6.606	80
85+	39595	8133	.205405	1.000000	23559	23559	114696	.205405	4.868437	114696	.000000	4.868	85+

NUMBER OF PERSONS DYING (OUT OF 100,000 AT BIRTH) ABOVE AGE X FROM SPECIFIED CAUSES

Age (x)	All Causes	Respiratory T.B.	Other Infec. and Paras.	Neoplasms	Cardiovascular	Infl., Pneu., Bronch.	Diarrheal	Certain Degenerative	Maternal	Cert. Dis. of Infancy	Motor Vehicle	Other Violence	Other and Unknown	Age (x)
0	100000	273	403	18257	49776	3059	278	4767	74	1139	808	3564	17602	0
1	97758	273	369	18248	49751	2940	227	4760	74	0	808	3513	16835	1
5	97476	272	349	18219	49740	2917	219	4757	74	0	783	3448	16698	5
10	97279	272	340	18176	49736	2916	219	4753	74	0	724	3419	16650	10
15	97158	272	334	18145	49725	2913	219	4749	74	0	694	3402	16631	15
20	96951	270	333	18115	49702	2909	218	4743	73	0	651	3366	16571	20
25	96641	268	331	18081	49660	2905	214	4730	63	0	584	3290	16515	25
30	96305	265	325	18006	49616	2899	212	4714	50	0	548	3236	16434	30
35	95875	253	320	17881	49541	2894	212	4690	34	0	515	3190	16345	35
40	95180	240	313	17612	49425	2887	210	4666	15	0	482	3114	16216	40
45	94187	221	301	17176	49257	2874	208	4623	5	0	450	3031	16041	45
50	92553	203	280	16470	48864	2853	208	4523	3	0	419	2934	15796	50
55	90194	175	258	15471	48249	2834	207	4399	0	0	359	2827	15415	55
60	86790	161	242	14178	47138	2792	198	4185	0	0	314	2686	14896	60
65	81497	138	226	12486	44973	2711	189	3832	0	0	269	2517	14156	65
70	72763	103	180	10281	40802	2538	177	3182	0	0	215	2280	13005	70
75	59846	79	133	7566	33984	2269	157	2289	0	0	132	1988	11249	75
80	42189	53	83	4690	23970	1840	108	1319	0	0	59	1512	8555	80
85+	23559	29	38	2178	13163	1156	67	559	0	0	29	970	5370	85+

NUMBER OF PERSONS SURVIVING TO AGE X IF SPECIFIED CAUSES WERE ELIMINATED

Age (x)	No Causes	Respiratory T.B.	Other Infec. and Paras.	Neoplasms	Cardiovascular	Infl., Pneu., Bronch.	Diarrheal	Certain Degenerative	Maternal	Cert. Dis. of Infancy	Motor Vehicle	Other Violence	Other and Unknown	(1) + (2)	(1) + (2) + (5) + (6) + (8)	(1)+(2)+ (5)+(6)+ (8)+part of(9)&(12)	(10) + (11)	Age (x)
		(1)	(2)	(3)	(4)	(5)	(6)	(7)	(8)	(9)	(10)	(11)	(12)					
0	100000	100000	100000	100000	100000	100000	100000	100000	100000	100000	100000	100000	100000	100000	100000	100000	100000	0
1	97798	97798	97832	97807	97823	97916	97848	97805	97798	98931	97798	97848	98559	97832	98000	99310	97848	1
5	97476	97477	97529	97514	97512	97616	97534	97486	97476	98605	97501	97591	98373	97530	97729	99075	97616	5
10	97279	97280	97341	97360	97319	97420	97337	97293	97279	98406	97363	97423	98222	97342	97542	98888	97507	10
15	97158	97159	97226	97270	97209	97302	97216	97176	97158	98283	97272	97319	98119	97227	97430	98776	97433	15
20	96951	96954	97020	97092	97024	97099	97010	96975	96952	98074	97108	97148	97971	97023	97231	98579	97304	20
25	96641	96646	96712	96816	96756	96792	96704	96678	96652	97760	96864	96913	97714	96717	96942	98291	97137	25
30	96305	96313	96382	96554	96464	96462	96370	96358	96329	97421	96563	96630	97456	96390	96635	97989	96889	30
35	95875	95895	95956	96248	96108	96036	95939	95951	95915	96986	96165	96245	97111	95976	96242	97600	96536	35
40	95180	95213	95268	95820	95527	95347	95246	95280	95238	96283	95501	95623	96537	95300	95592	96953	95946	40
45	94187	94238	94286	95258	94699	94365	94254	94328	94255	95278	94537	94708	95707	94337	94651	96010	95060	45
50	92553	92621	92671	94316	93448	92749	92619	92791	92622	93625	92927	93162	94294	92739	93070	94418	93539	50
55	90194	90288	90331	92922	91682	90404	90259	90549	90264	91239	90618	90894	92274	90425	90771	92099	91321	55
60	86790	86894	86937	90731	89337	87033	86862	87343	86857	87795	87243	87603	89314	87042	87425	88719	88060	60
65	81497	81617	81651	86527	86078	81804	81573	82361	81560	82441	81966	82426	84608	81771	82219	83457	82900	65
70	72763	72903	72944	79659	81133	73201	72842	74157	72819	73606	73233	73818	76677	73084	73662	74810	74295	70
75	59846	59983	60037	68426	73590	60452	59929	61820	59892	60539	60308	60983	64765	60175	60916	61919	61453	75
80	42189	42307	42365	51046	63608	42982	42289	44420	42222	42678	42575	43398	48162	42484	43419	44222	43795	80
85+	23559	23643	23691	30834	49803	24521	23645	25401	23577	23832	23797	24648	29712	23775	24855	25445	24897	85+

ADDED YRS OF LIFE																		
TOTAL		.053	.101	2.773	7.808	.347	.066	.575	.032	.855	.263	.586	2.636	.155	.603	1.721	.853	
WORK	1.904	.022	.017	.650	.409	.023	.005	.093	.023	.000	.105	.166	.328	.040	.090	.111	.272	

POPULATION, DEATHS, DEATH RATES FOR ALL CAUSES COMBINED, AND SPECIFIED CAUSES

Age Start of Interval	Midyear Population	Deaths During Year	All Causes	Respiratory T. B.	Other Infec. and Paras.	Neoplasms	Cardiovascular	Infl., Pneu., Bronch.	Diarrheal	Certain Degenerative	Maternal	Cert. Dis. of Infancy	Motor Vehicle	Other Violence	Other and Unknown	Age Start of Interval
0	65808	2407	.03658	.00002	.00093	.00008	.00012	.01302	.00070	.00002	.00000	.01649	.00000	.00099	.00422	0
1	268003	475	.00177	.00000	.00019	.00015	.00003	.00069	.00004	.00000	.00000	.00000	.00004	.00032	.00031	1
5	333270	216	.00065	.00000	.00005	.00010	.00004	.00008	.00000	.00002	.00000	.00000	.00007	.00017	.00012	5
10	359765	195	.00054	.00000	.00003	.00009	.00004	.00003	.00000	.00003	.00000	.00000	.00004	.00020	.00008	10
15	343425	331	.00096	.00001	.00003	.00007	.00010	.00003	.00000	.00003	.00000	.00000	.00006	.00045	.00017	15
20	292300	385	.00132	.00001	.00002	.00016	.00011	.00003	.00000	.00006	.00000	.00000	.00017	.00059	.00015	20
25	297045	366	.00123	.00005	.00002	.00012	.00014	.00002	.00000	.00010	.00000	.00000	.00011	.00053	.00013	25
30	327595	496	.00151	.00016	.00002	.00017	.00023	.00002	.00001	.00009	.00000	.00000	.00012	.00054	.00016	30
35	335195	686	.00205	.00019	.00004	.00033	.00032	.00007	.00001	.00015	.00000	.00000	.00015	.00057	.00022	35
40	307642	952	.00309	.00020	.00009	.00068	.00069	.00011	.00001	.00021	.00000	.00000	.00012	.00055	.00041	40
45	195397	927	.00474	.00026	.00005	.00138	.00125	.00021	.00002	.00027	.00000	.00000	.00012	.00063	.00056	45
50	244146	1743	.00714	.00040	.00009	.00210	.00190	.00053	.00001	.00045	.00000	.00000	.00015	.00075	.00077	50
55	226272	2643	.01168	.00045	.00010	.00358	.00395	.00093	.00001	.00062	.00000	.00000	.00008	.00080	.00117	55
60	177187	3492	.01971	.00050	.00015	.00641	.00692	.00212	.00002	.00087	.00000	.00000	.00007	.00071	.00193	60
65	121227	3953	.03294	.00063	.00015	.00846	.01440	.00337	.00001	.00142	.00000	.00000	.00014	.00106	.00327	65
70	74104	3807	.05137	.00059	.00028	.01220	.02418	.00584	.00003	.00152	.00000	.00000	.00013	.00134	.00525	70
75	55225	4443	.08045	.00071	.00038	.01329	.04373	.00905	.00000	.00159	.00000	.00000	.00007	.00181	.00981	75
80	30251	3705	.12248	.00060	.00043	.01160	.06608	.01329	.00010	.00192	.00000	.00000	.00026	.00235	.02585	80
85+	14351	2561	.17845	.00077	.00042	.01192	.09254	.02028	.00007	.00118	.00000	.00000	.00014	.00328	.04787	85+
ALL	4068208	33823														

	All Causes	Respiratory T. B.	Other Infec. and Paras.	Neoplasms	Cardiovascular	Infl., Pneu., Bronch.	Diarrheal	Certain Degenerative	Maternal	Cert. Dis. of Infancy	Motor Vehicle	Other Violence	Other and Unknown
CRUDE DEATH RATE	.00831	.00018	.00009	.00160	.00311	.00097	.00002	.00028	.00000	.00027	.00010	.00058	.00111
STANDARDIZED RATE (1)	.00563	.00011	.00010	.00091	.00153	.00090	.00003	.00017	.00000	.00058	.00009	.00050	.00070
STANDARDIZED RATE (2)	.00562	.00018	.00010	.00176	.00374	.00118	.00002	.00029	.00000	.00034	.00010	.00059	.00131
GEOMETRIC MEAN	.00688												

LIFE TABLE FOR ALL CAUSES COMBINED

Age (x)	Midyear Population	Deaths During Year	$_nM_x$	$_nq_x$	l_x	$_nd_x$	$_nL_x$	$_nm_x$	$_na_x$	T_x	$_nr_x$	$\overset{\circ}{e}_x$	Age (x)
0	65808	2407	.036576	.035450	100000	3545	96924	.036575	.132179	6939333	.000000	69.393	0
1	268003	475	.001772	.007060	96455	681	384118	.001773	1.500000	6842409	.000000	70.939	1
5	333270	216	.000648	.003237	95774	310	478095	.000648	2.500000	6458292	.000000	67.433	5
10	359765	195	.000542	.002703	95464	258	476706	.000541	2.620317	5980197	-.007041	62.643	10
15	343425	331	.000964	.004821	95206	459	474958	.000966	2.665214	5503491	.013604	57.806	15
20	292300	385	.001317	.006565	94747	622	472205	.001317	2.540193	5028532	.017940	53.073	20
25	297045	366	.001232	.006151	94125	579	469195	.001234	2.529505	4556327	-.005087	48.407	25
30	327595	496	.001514	.007526	93546	704	466046	.001511	2.608014	4087133	-.012649	43.691	30
35	335195	686	.002047	.010168	92842	944	461999	.002043	2.658236	3621087	-.008983	39.003	35
40	307642	952	.003095	.015463	91898	1421	456186	.003115	2.674613	3159087	.040570	34.376	40
45	195397	927	.004744	.023597	90477	2135	447396	.004772	2.663056	2702902	.032278	29.874	45
50	244146	1743	.007139	.035000	88342	3092	434547	.007115	2.683336	2255506	-.016244	25.532	50
55	226272	2643	.011681	.056962	85250	4856	415054	.011700	2.694390	1820959	.008118	21.360	55
60	177187	3492	.019708	.094821	80394	7623	384229	.019839	2.674007	1405905	.031163	17.488	60
65	121227	3953	.032938	.154224	72771	11223	337155	.033287	2.620920	1021666	.052543	14.039	65
70	74104	3807	.051374	.229691	61548	14137	273376	.051713	2.569204	684512	.034707	11.122	70
75	55225	4443	.080453	.335766	47411	15919	197372	.080655	2.507185	411136	.012357	8.672	75
80	30251	3705	.122475	.466341	31492	14686	119589	.122804	2.421269	213764	.012357	6.788	80
85+	14351	2561	.178454	1.000000	16806	16806	94175	.178454	5.603670	94175	.000000	5.604	85+

NUMBER OF PERSONS DYING (OUT OF 100,000 AT BIRTH) ABOVE AGE X FROM SPECIFIED CAUSES

Age (x)	All Causes	Respiratory T.B.	Other Infec. and Paras.	Neoplasms	Cardiovascular	Infl., Pneu., Bronch.	Diarrheal	Certain Degenerative	Maternal	Cert. Dis. of Infancy	Motor Vehicle	Other Violence	Other and Unknown	Age (x)
0	100000	1619	780	17746	43359	11292	144	2790	0	1558	736	4811	15125	0
1	96455	1618	690	17739	43347	10029	76	2789	0	0	736	4715	14716	1
5	95774	1618	617	17682	43335	9766	60	2787	0	0	721	4593	14595	5
10	95464	1618	591	17633	43317	9730	60	2779	0	0	688	4511	14537	10
15	95206	1616	575	17589	43300	9715	60	2767	0	0	666	4417	14501	15
20	94747	1614	559	17554	43253	9700	60	2751	0	0	636	4202	14418	20
25	94125	1607	547	17480	43200	9685	60	2724	0	0	553	3923	14346	25
30	93546	1583	536	17422	43132	9676	60	2675	0	0	503	3676	14283	30
35	92842	1507	528	17344	43025	9665	56	2634	0	0	447	3426	14210	35
40	91898	1419	509	17190	42878	9634	55	2564	0	0	377	3163	14109	40
45	90477	1329	468	16878	42561	9582	52	2468	0	0	321	2894	13924	45
50	88342	1214	446	16257	41996	9485	45	2349	0	0	268	2610	13672	50
55	85250	1040	408	15349	41172	9256	41	2153	0	0	204	2284	13343	55
60	80394	855	366	13859	39531	8870	37	1896	0	0	173	1952	12855	60
65	72771	662	309	11382	36847	8051	29	1560	0	0	144	1679	12108	65
70	61548	449	245	8512	31925	6900	26	1078	0	0	97	1320	10996	70
75	47411	287	167	5163	25261	5291	19	661	0	0	60	954	9548	75
80	31492	148	92	2539	16606	3500	19	346	0	0	46	596	7600	80
85+	16806	72	39	1122	8715	1910	7	112	0	0	13	308	4508	85+

NUMBER OF PERSONS SURVIVING TO AGE X IF SPECIFIED CAUSES WERE ELIMINATED

Age (x)	No Causes	Respiratory T.B. (1)	Other Infec. and Paras. (2)	Neoplasms (3)	Cardiovascular (4)	Infl., Pneu., Bronch. (5)	Diarrheal (6)	Certain Degenerative (7)	Maternal (8)	Cert. Dis. of Infancy (9)	Motor Vehicle (10)	Other Violence (11)	Other and Unknown (12)	(1)+(2)	(1)+(2)+(5)+(6)+(8)	(1)+(2)+(5)+(6)+(8)+part of(9)&(12)	(10)+(11)	Age (x)
0	100000	100000	100000	100000	100000	100000	100000	100000	100000	100000	100000	100000	100000	100000	100000	100000	100000	0
1	96455	96456	96543	96462	96467	97703	96522	96456	96455	98017	96455	96549	96858	96544	97862	99728	96549	1
5	95774	95775	95935	95838	95798	97279	95856	95777	95774	97345	95789	95989	96295	95936	97527	99466	96004	5
10	95464	95465	95650	95576	95506	97001	95546	95475	95464	97030	95512	95761	96041	95651	97275	99223	95809	10
15	95206	95209	95408	95362	95264	96754	95288	95229	95206	96768	95276	95596	95818	95411	97045	98995	95666	15
20	94747	94752	94964	94937	94828	96303	94828	94786	94747	96301	94846	95351	95439	94969	96611	98559	95451	20
25	94125	94137	94352	94388	94282	95686	94206	94190	94125	95665	94307	95005	94885	94364	96011	97952	95188	25
30	93546	93582	93783	93865	93770	95106	93626	93660	93546	95080	93776	94670	94365	93819	95465	97401	94903	30
35	92842	92953	93085	93237	93171	94402	92926	92996	92842	94365	93127	94210	93728	93197	94848	96783	94498	35
40	91898	92096	92158	92443	92371	93473	91982	92120	91898	93405	92250	93517	92877	92356	94025	95960	93875	40
45	90477	90761	90773	91326	91260	92080	90563	90791	90477	91961	90879	92343	91626	91058	92760	94698	92753	45
50	88342	88734	88653	89792	89671	90005	88432	88767	88342	89791	88787	90451	89716	89046	90816	92747	90907	50
55	85250	85800	85588	87561	87359	87085	85341	85854	85250	86648	85742	87613	86505	86139	88087	90015	88119	55
60	80394	81093	80753	84073	84032	82508	80484	81215	80394	81713	80889	82954	82439	81455	83691	85594	83464	60
65	72771	73589	73151	78602	78784	75489	72860	73837	72771	73965	73246	75356	75354	73972	76829	78696	75848	65
70	61548	62437	61928	69383	71720	64953	61626	62899	61548	62558	61993	64076	64799	62822	66382	68155	64539	70
75	47411	48238	47772	56840	62495	51543	47477	48823	47411	48189	47786	49691	51270	48606	52916	54543	50085	75
80	31492	32155	31793	40353	51876	35847	31536	32691	31492	32009	31753	33310	35823	32462	37003	38418	33586	80
85+	16806	17216	17005	22880	38795	20476	16838	17621	16806	17082	16969	17997	21820	17420	21264	22518	18171	85+

ADDED YRS OF LIFE

	No Causes	(1)	(2)	(3)	(4)	(5)	(6)	(7)	(8)	(9)	(10)	(11)	(12)	(1)+(2)	(1)+(2)+(5)+(6)+(8)	part of (9)&(12)	(10)+(11)
TOTAL		.313	.244	2.718	7.220	2.156	.069	.467	.000	1.136	.248	1.352	2.182	.559	2.872	4.602	1.608
WORK	2.925	.140	.046	.595	.596	.131	.004	-.161	.000	.000	.137	.644	.321	.186	.323	.365	.784

POPULATION, DEATHS, DEATH RATES FOR ALL CAUSES COMBINED, AND SPECIFIED CAUSES

Age Start of Interval	Midyear Population	Deaths During Year	All Causes	Respiratory T. B.	Other Infec. and Paras.	Neoplasms	Cardiovascular	Infl., Pneu., Bronch.	Diarrheal	Certain Degenerative	Maternal	Cert. Dis. of Infancy	Motor Vehicle	Other Violence	Other and Unknown	Age Start of Interval
0	62321	1899	.03047	.00002	.00071	.00010	.00010	.01157	.00067	.00002	.00000	.01272	.00000	.00083	.00374	0
1	254172	423	.00166	.00001	.00017	.00011	.00003	.00071	.00004	.00002	.00000	.00000	.00004	.00024	.00030	1
5	319424	153	.00048	.00000	.00003	.00008	.00003	.00007	.00000	.00001	.00000	.00000	.00005	.00007	.00013	5
10	345955	125	.00036	.00001	.00003	.00008	.00005	.00003	.00000	.00003	.00000	.00000	.00001	.00006	.00006	10
15	332591	187	.00056	.00002	.00003	.00006	.00010	.00004	.00001	.00003	.00001	.00000	.00001	.00015	.00011	15
20	285099	183	.00064	.00001	.00003	.00011	.00008	.00003	.00000	.00005	.00004	.00000	.00003	.00011	.00014	20
25	296850	228	.00077	.00010	.00004	.00012	.00014	.00004	.00000	.00004	.00006	.00000	.00002	.00012	.00007	25
30	324565	325	.00100	.00011	.00003	.00020	.00024	.00003	.00000	.00006	.00005	.00000	.00004	.00010	.00015	30
35	331560	457	.00138	.00009	.00005	.00036	.00042	.00004	.00000	.00010	.00002	.00000	.00002	.00011	.00017	35
40	309808	640	.00207	.00005	.00003	.00075	.00056	.00008	.00001	.00014	.00001	.00000	.00004	.00013	.00027	40
45	195387	579	.00296	.00007	.00007	.00108	.00090	.00019	.00001	.00016	.00000	.00000	.00002	.00013	.00034	45
50	239880	1086	.00453	.00011	.00007	.00151	.00172	.00024	.00001	.00024	.00000	.00000	.00002	.00021	.00039	50
55	225126	1729	.00768	.00015	.00005	.00242	.00316	.00053	.00001	.00028	.00000	.00000	.00003	.00028	.00077	55
60	184629	2357	.01277	.00015	.00003	.00334	.00605	.00111	.00009	.00065	.00000	.00000	.00006	.00025	.00108	60
65	138809	3288	.02369	.00022	.00018	.00516	.01276	.00206	.00000	.00099	.00000	.00000	.00002	.00032	.00197	65
70	97132	4067	.04187	.00032	.00009	.00666	.02575	.00387	.00003	.00117	.00000	.00000	.00006	.00051	.00340	70
75	74057	5424	.07324	.00031	.00018	.00778	.04884	.00705	.00005	.00159	.00000	.00000	.00004	.00088	.00652	75
80	38251	4410	.11529	.00013	.00029	.00808	.07247	.01082	.00013	.00118	.00000	.00000	.00008	.00110	.02102	80
85+	20515	3096	.15091	.00015	.00015	.00629	.09154	.01375	.00005	.00093	.00000	.00000	.00000	.00127	.03680	85+
ALL	4076131	30656														

CRUDE DEATH RATE			.00752	.00008	.00007	.00115	.00380	.00081	.00002	.00021	.00001	.00019	.00003	.00019	.00094	
STANDARDIZED RATE (1)			.00432	.00005	.00008	.00061	.00151	.00074	.00003	.00012	.00001	.00045	.00003	.00017	.00052	
STANDARDIZED RATE (2)			.00761	.00008	.00007	.00112	.00378	.00088	.00002	.00021	.00001	.00026	.00003	.00020	.00094	
GEOMETRIC MEAN			.00488													

LIFE TABLE FOR ALL CAUSES COMBINED

Age (x)	Midyear Population	Deaths During Year	$_nM_x$	$_nq_x$	l_x	$_nd_x$	$_nL_x$	$_nm_x$	$_na_x$	T_x	$_nr_x$	$\overset{\circ}{e}_x$	Age (x)
0	62321	1899	.030471	.029680	100000	2968	97394	.030474	.121801	7318162	.000000	73.182	0
1	254172	423	.001664	.006627	97032	643	386521	.001664	1.500000	7220768	.000000	74.416	1
5	319424	153	.000479	.002397	96389	231	481368	.000480	2.500000	6834248	.000000	70.903	5
10	345955	125	.000361	.001799	96158	173	480366	.000360	2.546965	6352880	-.007702	66.067	10
15	332591	187	.000562	.002813	95985	270	479278	.000563	2.603395	5872515	.012989	61.182	15
20	285099	183	.000642	.003207	95715	307	477827	.000642	2.564468	5393237	.015690	56.347	20
25	296850	228	.000768	.003826	95408	365	476162	.000767	2.595320	4915409	-.006978	51.520	25
30	324565	325	.001001	.004987	95043	474	474824	.001000	2.624824	4439242	-.011465	46.708	30
35	331560	457	.001378	.006883	94569	649	471326	.001377	2.659540	3965158	-.009414	41.929	35
40	309808	640	.002066	.010339	93920	971	467324	.002078	2.655767	3493832	-.039728	37.200	40
45	195387	579	.002963	.014793	92949	1375	461532	.002979	2.663030	3026508	.035364	32.561	45
50	239880	1086	.004527	.022254	91574	2047	453171	.004517	2.704947	2564977	-.012394	28.010	50
55	225126	1729	.007680	.037799	89527	3384	439869	.007693	2.704947	2111805	.008523	23.588	55
60	184629	2357	.012766	.062408	86143	5376	418477	.012847	2.723524	1671937	.026878	19.409	60
65	138809	3288	.023687	.113314	80767	9152	382691	.023915	2.685690	1253460	.040122	15.519	65
70	97132	4067	.041871	.191426	71615	13709	325656	.042097	2.635176	870769	.023545	12.159	70
75	74057	5424	.073241	.311660	57906	18047	245262	.073583	2.547065	545114	.019401	9.414	75
80	38251	4410	.115291	.446223	39859	17786	153590	.115802	2.430259	299852	.019401	7.523	80
85+	20515	3096	.150914	1.000000	22073	22073	146262	.150914	6.626252	146262	.000000	6.626	85+

NUMBER OF PERSONS DYING (OUT OF 100,000 AT BIRTH) ABOVE AGE X FROM SPECIFIED CAUSES

Age (x)	All Causes	Respira- tory T. B.	Other Infec. and Paras.	Neo- plasms	Cardio- vascular	Infl., Pneu., Bronch.	Diar- rheal	Certain Degen- erative	Maternal	Cert. Dis. of Infancy	Motor Vehicle	Other Violence	Other and Unknown	Age (x)
0	100000	716	570	12796	55894	9948	156	2302	95	1239	220	1824	14240	0
1	97032	714	501	12787	55885	8822	90	2300	95	0	220	1743	13875	1
5	96389	711	437	12744	55873	8546	75	2291	95	0	205	1652	13760	5
10	96158	710	421	12708	55856	8513	75	2285	95	0	182	1619	13694	10
15	95985	705	407	12669	55830	8501	74	2271	95	0	177	1590	13666	15
20	95715	694	394	12639	55781	8481	70	2257	92	0	174	1519	13614	20
25	95408	687	380	12585	55740	8465	70	2232	71	0	160	1467	13551	25
30	95043	639	360	12526	55672	8448	70	2214	43	0	149	1409	13513	30
35	94569	588	345	12432	55558	8435	70	2185	18	0	131	1364	13443	35
40	93920	547	322	12264	55362	8416	70	2138	8	0	123	1310	13360	40
45	92949	521	307	11911	55100	8378	65	2074	2	0	106	1251	13234	45
50	91574	488	276	11410	54680	8290	63	1999	2	0	99	1192	13075	50
55	89527	437	246	10726	53905	8183	57	1891	0	0	90	1096	12896	55
60	86143	370	223	9661	52510	7948	53	1768	0	0	78	972	12560	60
65	80767	309	205	8259	49958	7480	51	1478	0	0	51	866	12106	65
70	71615	223	139	6274	45018	6683	51	1096	0	0	43	741	11347	70
75	57906	119	109	4100	36968	5415	41	713	0	0	23	573	10233	75
80	39859	43	66	2189	24545	3678	27	321	0	0	13	357	8620	80
85+	22073	21	21	920	13389	2011	7	135	0	0	0	185	5384	85+

NUMBER OF PERSONS SURVIVING TO AGE X IF SPECIFIED CAUSES WERE ELIMINATED

Age (x)	No Causes	Respira- tory T. B.	Other Infec. and Paras.	Neo- plasms	Cardio- vascular	Infl., Pneu., Bronch.	Diar- rheal	Certain Degener- ative	Maternal	Cert. Dis. of Infancy	Motor Vehicle	Other Violence	Other and Unknown	(1) + (2)	(1) + (2) + (5) + (6) + (8)	(1)+(2)+ (5)+(6)+ (8)+part of(9)&(12)	(10) + (11)	Age (x)
		(1)	(2)	(3)	(4)	(5)	(6)	(7)	(8)	(9)	(10)	(11)	(12)					
0	100000	100000	100000	100000	100000	100000	100000	100000	100000	100000	100000	100000	100000	100000	100000	100000	100000	0
1	97032	97034	97100	97041	97041	98147	97097	97034	97032	98260	97032	97112	97392	97102	98284	99777	97112	1
5	96389	96394	96520	96441	96410	97776	96469	96400	96389	97609	96404	96559	96862	96525	97955	99564	96574	5
10	96158	96164	96305	96246	96196	97575	96237	96175	96158	97375	96196	96361	96696	96311	97811	99397	96399	10
15	95985	95996	96146	96111	96049	97411	96065	96016	95985	97200	96028	96216	96550	96157	97667	99258	96259	15
20	95715	95737	95888	95871	95827	97158	95799	95760	95718	96926	95761	96017	96331	95910	97444	99044	96063	20
25	95408	95437	95595	95618	95561	96882	95492	95478	95432	96616	95468	95761	96085	95624	97191	98802	95821	25
30	95043	95120	95249	95311	95263	96609	95126	95130	95095	96246	95113	95453	95756	95326	96934	98554	95523	30
35	94569	94696	94789	94930	94902	96041	94652	94685	94646	95766	94657	95022	95349	94917	96556	98189	95110	35
40	93920	94087	94162	94446	94447	95401	94002	94082	94006	95109	94015	94424	94778	94329	95988	97626	94520	40
45	92949	93140	93203	93824	93733	94453	93040	93173	93040	94179	93060	93507	93924	93395	95088	96723	93618	45
50	91574	91795	91855	92939	92768	93145	91661	91869	91664	92733	91691	92182	92655	92077	93837	95472	92300	50
55	89527	89794	89832	91550	91474	91170	89618	89923	89617	90660	89650	90217	90802	90099	91939	93560	90341	55
60	86143	86466	86459	89164	89427	87959	86235	86645	86229	87233	86273	86930	87704	86783	88796	90399	87061	60
65	80767	81129	81077	85015	86452	82934	80855	81521	80848	81789	80915	81608	82680	81440	83800	85364	81757	65
70	71615	72017	71955	77368	81804	74311	71693	72646	71687	72521	71754	72479	74045	72359	75240	76732	72620	70
75	57906	58324	58208	64688	75401	61279	57978	59087	57964	58639	58036	58757	60914	58628	62183	63538	58889	75
80	39859	40209	40103	46303	66582	43723	39920	41000	39899	40363	39957	40626	43371	40455	44489	45634	40725	80
85+	22073	22283	22241	26746	53417	25592	22122	22846	22095	22352	22137	22626	26744	22453	26116	27137	22692	85+

ADDED YRS OF LIFE

TOTAL		.170	.210	2.133	11.825	2.037	.072	.386	.045	.525	.079	.497	2.070	.381	2.560	4.012	.576	
WORK	1.877	.078	.045	.503	.548	.097	.004	.103	.033	.000	.027	.155	.225	.124	.259	.298	.182	

POPULATION, DEATHS, DEATH RATES FOR ALL CAUSES COMBINED, AND SPECIFIED CAUSES

Age Start of Interval	Midyear Population	Deaths During Year	All Causes	Respiratory T.B.	Other Infec. and Paras.	Neoplasms	Cardiovascular	Infl., Pneu., Bronch.	Diarrheal	Certain Degenerative	Maternal	Cert. Dis. of Infancy	Motor Vehicle	Other Violence	Other and Unknown	Age Start of Interval
0	73863	8568	.11600	.00039	.00727	.00003	.00130	.01577	.01844	.00046	.00000	.04717	.00000	.00096	.02421	0
1	301179	2275	.00755	.00012	.00217	.00006	.00015	.00143	.00101	.00008	.00000	.00000	.00000	.00076	.00171	1
5	375633	1169	.00311	.00006	.00109	.00003	.00019	.00031	.00009	.00008	.00000	.00000	.00007	.00050	.00070	5
10	323982	676	.00209	.00011	.00050	.00003	.00017	.00014	.00001	.00010	.00000	.00000	.00003	.00040	.00059	10
15	283277	869	.00307	.00049	.00044	.00003	.00023	.00027	.00000	.00014	.00000	.00000	.00004	.00077	.00066	15
20	253177	950	.00375	.00103	.00041	.00004	.00035	.00035	.00019	.00000	.00000	.00000	.00004	.00081	.00058	20
25	263229	1049	.00399	.00106	.00033	.00005	.00035	.00031	.00001	.00022	.00000	.00000	.00004	.00091	.00071	25
30	266337	1057	.00397	.00082	.00039	.00009	.00039	.00039	.00002	.00021	.00000	.00000	.00003	.00095	.00068	30
35	270208	1206	.00446	.00073	.00043	.00020	.00054	.00047	.00003	.00026	.00000	.00000	.00003	.00099	.00078	35
40	225036	1230	.00547	.00070	.00052	.00043	.00077	.00064	.00001	.00036	.00000	.00000	.00000	.00101	.00099	40
45	184285	1366	.00741	.00071	.00059	.00081	.00141	.00083	.00002	.00054	.00000	.00000	.00005	.00105	.00141	45
50	151987	1493	.00982	.00081	.00060	.00126	.00227	.00099	.00002	.00075	.00000	.00000	.00007	.00106	.00200	50
55	113773	1719	.01511	.00091	.00065	.00225	.00432	.00143	.00003	.00123	.00000	.00000	.00008	.00114	.00305	55
60	96700	1976	.02043	.00102	.00070	.00362	.00645	.00178	.00005	.00184	.00000	.00000	.00006	.00119	.00371	60
65	68117	2418	.03550	.00107	.00082	.00564	.01279	.00342	.00019	.00294	.00000	.00000	.00004	.00145	.00713	65
70	44791	2380	.05314	.00094	.00092	.00781	.02175	.00580	.00040	.00424	.00000	.00000	.00007	.00163	.00958	70
75	26535	2538	.09565	.00075	.00132	.00972	.03693	.01089	.00087	.00558	.00000	.00000	.00004	.00286	.02668	75
80	13649	1834	.13437	.00051	.00190	.00952	.04887	.01495	.00132	.00549	.00000	.00000	.00000	.00440	.04740	80
85+	7211	1638	.22715	.00028	.00250	.00985	.07239	.02663	.00222	.00749	.00000	.00000	.00000	.00777	.09804	85+
ALL	3342969	36411														

	All Causes	Respiratory T.B.	Other Infec. and Paras.	Neoplasms	Cardiovascular	Infl., Pneu., Bronch.	Diarrheal	Certain Degenerative	Maternal	Cert. Dis. of Infancy	Motor Vehicle	Other Violence	Other and Unknown
CRUDE DEATH RATE	.01089	.00059	.00088	.00072	.00199	.00125	.00055	.00050	.00000	.00104	.00004	.00085	.00243
STANDARDIZED RATE (1)	.01121	.00054	.00101	.00056	.00156	.00135	.00081	.00042	.00000	.00166	.00004	.00084	.00242
STANDARDIZED RATE (2)	.01433	.00063	.00088	.00114	.00339	.00162	.00054	.00073	.00000	.00098	.00005	.00098	.00341
GEOMETRIC MEAN	.01357												

LIFE TABLE FOR ALL CAUSES COMBINED

Age (x)	Midyear Population	Deaths During Year	nM_x	nq_x	l_x	nd_x	nL_x	nm_x	na_x	T_x	nr_x	$\overset{\circ}{e}_x$	Age (x)
0	73863	8568	.115999	.106910	100000	10691	92166	.115998	.267198	5798332	.000000	57.983	0
1	301179	2275	.007554	.029650	89309	2648	350616	.007552	1.500000	5706166	.000000	63.892	1
5	375633	1169	.003112	.015451	86661	1339	429958	.003114	2.500000	5355550	.000000	61.799	5
10	323982	676	.002087	.010372	85322	885	424387	.002085	2.488230	4925592	.019753	57.729	10
15	283277	869	.003068	.015266	84437	1289	419100	.003076	2.606995	4501205	.023942	53.308	15
20	253177	950	.003752	.018605	83148	1547	411939	.003755	2.543229	4082105	.010624	49.094	20
25	263229	1049	.003985	.019730	81601	1610	403985	.003985	2.503106	3670166	-.004204	44.977	25
30	266337	1057	.003969	.019640	79991	1571	396053	.003967	2.516179	3266181	-.008645	40.832	30
35	270208	1206	.004463	.022086	78420	1732	387875	.004465	2.560503	2870128	.003657	36.599	35
40	225036	1230	.005466	.027045	76688	2074	378462	.005480	2.599948	2482253	.026352	32.368	40
45	184285	1366	.007412	.036548	74614	2727	366543	.007440	2.606497	2103791	.029225	28.196	45
50	151987	1493	.009823	.048242	71887	3468	351241	.009874	2.637327	1737248	.037008	24.166	50
55	113773	1719	.015109	.072269	68419	5013	330134	.015185	2.613912	1386006	.032604	20.258	55
60	96700	1976	.020434	.097924	63406	6209	302427	.020531	2.648172	1055873	.027470	16.653	60
65	68117	2418	.035485	.164851	57197	9429	263477	.035787	2.612949	753445	.038751	13.173	65
70	44791	2380	.053136	.237000	47768	11321	211521	.053522	2.586878	489968	.038889	10.257	70
75	26535	2538	.095647	.388225	36447	14150	146818	.056378	2.497041	278447	.027643	7.640	75
80	13649	1834	.134369	.498722	22297	11120	82424	.134912	2.386597	131629	.027643	5.903	80
85+	7211	1638	.227153	1.000000	11177	11177	49205	.227153	4.402320	49205	.000000	4.402	85+

NUMBER OF PERSONS DYING (OUT OF 100,000 AT BIRTH) ABOVE AGE X FROM SPECIFIED CAUSES

Age (x)	All Causes	Respira-tory T. B.	Other Infec. and Paras.	Neo-plasms	Cardio-vascular	Infl., Pneu., Bronch.	Diar-rheal	Certain Degen-erative	Maternal	Cert. Dis. of Infancy	Motor Vehicle	Other Violence	Other and Unknown	Age (x)
0	100000	3894	4860	8842	27161	11083	2650	5457	0	4347	267	6311	25128	0
1	89309	3857	4190	8839	27041	9629	950	5414	0	0	267	6222	22900	1
5	86661	3815	3429	8817	26987	9126	596	5386	0	0	249	5957	22299	5
10	85322	3790	2962	8802	26905	8995	558	5351	0	0	220	5743	21996	10
15	84437	3742	2752	8789	26833	8935	553	5309	0	0	206	5572	21746	15
20	83148	3535	2567	8776	26738	8820	552	5250	0	0	191	5249	21470	20
25	81601	3111	2398	8758	26614	8677	550	5171	0	0	175	4917	21230	25
30	79991	2685	2265	8738	26473	8553	547	5082	0	0	158	4548	20942	30
35	78420	2359	2110	8704	26318	8398	538	4999	0	0	147	4172	20675	35
40	76688	2075	1944	8626	26109	8214	528	4899	0	0	137	3788	20368	40
45	74614	1811	1747	8462	25814	7973	523	4762	0	0	122	3406	19994	45
50	71887	1552	1532	8162	25294	7668	517	4564	0	0	102	3020	19476	50
55	68419	1267	1321	7717	24490	7320	510	4299	0	0	77	2647	18771	55
60	63406	965	1106	6969	23052	6845	499	3890	0	0	51	2270	17759	60
65	57197	655	893	5869	21089	6305	483	3331	0	0	32	1910	16630	65
70	47768	372	676	4374	17686	5394	432	2552	0	0	20	1526	14736	70
75	36447	175	482	2714	13050	4156	346	1650	0	0	6	1180	12688	75
80	22297	64	287	1281	7589	2545	217	828	0	0	1	756	8729	80
85+	11177	14	123	484	3562	1310	109	368	0	0	0	382	4825	85+

NUMBER OF PERSONS SURVIVING TO AGE X IF SPECIFIED CAUSES WERE ELIMINATED

Age (x)	No Causes	Respira-tory T. B.	Other Infec. and Paras.	Neo-plasms	Cardio-vascular	Infl., Pneu., Bronch.	Diar-rheal	Certain Degener-ative	Maternal	Cert. Dis. of Infancy	Motor Vehicle	Other Violence	Other and Unknown	(1) + (2)	(1) + (2) + (5) + (6) + (8)	(1)+(2)+ (5)+(6)+ (8)+part of(9)&(12)	(10) + (11)	Age (x)
		(1)	(2)	(3)	(4)	(5)	(6)	(7)	(8)	(9)	(10)	(11)	(12)					
0	100000	100000	100000	100000	100000	100000	100000	100000	100000	100000	100000	100000	100000	100000	100000	100000	100000	0
1	89309	89344	89944	89312	89422	90693	90929	89350	89309	93511	89309	89393	91438	89979	93031	99302	89393	1
5	86661	86736	88035	86685	86824	88509	88589	86728	86661	90738	86679	87004	89335	88112	91992	98739	87022	5
10	85322	85421	87147	85361	85564	87274	87259	85423	85322	89336	85368	85873	88266	87248	91270	98184	85920	10
15	84437	84583	86457	84488	84749	86430	86359	84579	84437	88410	84497	85154	87608	86606	90668	97682	85214	15
20	83148	83498	85325	83212	83550	85227	85041	83346	83148	87060	83222	84178	86555	85684	89827	96936	84253	20
25	81601	82367	83910	81681	82119	83787	83461	81874	81601	85440	81689	82945	85192	84697	88949	96146	83035	25
30	79991	81169	82390	80090	80639	82260	81818	80347	79991	83754	80094	81681	83810	83603	87937	95229	81787	30
35	78420	79903	80930	78550	79210	80802	80220	78852	78420	82109	78532	80458	82441	82460	86915	94279	80573	35
40	76688	78425	79312	76893	77670	79205	78458	77210	76688	80296	76808	79071	80940	81108	85704	93132	79195	40
45	74614	76570	77368	74976	75865	77309	76341	75258	74614	78124	74745	77322	79141	79396	84169	91652	77458	45
50	71887	74033	74759	72532	73613	74794	73557	72703	71887	75269	72033	74890	76790	76991	81966	89478	75042	50
55	68419	70748	71367	69473	70871	71540	70016	69458	68419	71638	68532	71656	73824	73796	78963	86467	71827	55
60	63406	65865	66354	65119	67128	66778	64896	64770	63406	66389	63582	66786	69474	68927	74299	81673	66972	60
65	57197	59721	60067	59824	62563	60781	58557	58972	57197	59888	57374	60606	63856	62718	68233	75304	60794	65
70	47768	50144	50373	51407	55765	51654	48952	49988	47768	50015	47927	50986	55293	52878	58597	65124	51156	70
75	36447	38438	38612	40803	47533	40596	37427	38968	36447	38162	36580	39224	44315	40721	46577	52238	39368	75
80	22297	23603	23781	26218	35133	26263	23000	24522	22297	23346	22382	24352	31145	25174	30587	35276	24445	80
85+	11177	11869	12043	13810	22616	14215	11607	12648	11177	11703	11220	12494	19896	12788	16889	20524	12542	85+

ADDED YRS OF LIFE

		(1)	(2)	(3)	(4)	(5)	(6)	(7)	(8)	(9)	(10)	(11)	(12)				
TOTAL		1.198	1.979	1.168	3.812	2.578	1.355	.861	.000	2.716	.093	1.812	5.321	3.232	7.535	13.654	1.909
WORK	5.615	.855	.467	.305	.731	.458	.013	.314	.000	.000	.042	.971	.954	1.335	1.870	2.303	1.014

POPULATION, DEATHS, DEATH RATES FOR ALL CAUSES COMBINED, AND SPECIFIED CAUSES

Age Start of Interval	Midyear Population	Deaths During Year	All Causes	Respiratory T. B.	Other Infec. and Paras.	Neoplasms	Cardiovascular	Infl., Pneu., Bronch.	Diarrheal	Certain Degenerative	Maternal	Cert. Dis. of Infancy	Motor Vehicle	Other Violence	Other and Unknown	Age Start of Interval
0	71920	6345	.08822	.00026	.00672	.00004	.00065	.01192	.01356	.00018	.00000	.03605	.00000	.00072	.01812	0
1	293843	1972	.00671	.00012	.00205	.00004	.00011	.00139	.00087	.00011	.00000	.00000	.00003	.00051	.00148	1
5	366237	979	.00267	.00008	.00115	.00002	.00016	.00024	.00007	.00008	.00000	.00000	.00003	.00019	.00065	5
10	314546	611	.00194	.00022	.00052	.00003	.00022	.00018	.00002	.00008	.00000	.00000	.00000	.00013	.00054	10
15	275548	741	.00269	.00078	.00044	.00002	.00025	.00020	.00000	.00008	.00016	.00000	.00000	.00015	.00060	15
20	255722	947	.00370	.00120	.00044	.00004	.00025	.00032	.00002	.00014	.00054	.00000	.00002	.00016	.00059	20
25	249857	1034	.00414	.00115	.00052	.00014	.00028	.00027	.00002	.00016	.00076	.00000	.00001	.00014	.00068	25
30	231953	1093	.00471	.00097	.00041	.00025	.00040	.00040	.00002	.00021	.00091	.00000	.00001	.00017	.00097	30
35	221079	1176	.00532	.00084	.00037	.00052	.00058	.00045	.00003	.00028	.00086	.00000	.00000	.00018	.00119	35
40	182661	1043	.00571	.00070	.00033	.00102	.00078	.00045	.00004	.00042	.00042	.00000	.00001	.00015	.00141	40
45	149255	1094	.00733	.00062	.00033	.00163	.00139	.00057	.00005	.00060	.00015	.00000	.00000	.00018	.00179	45
50	126482	1201	.00950	.00063	.00037	.00229	.00222	.00068	.00006	.00080	.00000	.00000	.00001	.00030	.00213	50
55	98756	1422	.01440	.00067	.00045	.00328	.00413	.00123	.00008	.00120	.00000	.00000	.00001	.00037	.00298	55
60	83679	1638	.01957	.00075	.00054	.00435	.00618	.00194	.00012	.00172	.00000	.00000	.00006	.00027	.00364	60
65	59591	1992	.03343	.00086	.00067	.00571	.01212	.00399	.00029	.00257	.00000	.00000	.00007	.00049	.00668	65
70	41398	2006	.04846	.00104	.00075	.00696	.02005	.00684	.00048	.00331	.00000	.00000	.00005	.00072	.00826	70
75	26427	2312	.08749	.00095	.00098	.00806	.03432	.01177	.00110	.00439	.00000	.00000	.00004	.00219	.02369	75
80	14672	1855	.12643	.00041	.00123	.00757	.04716	.01465	.00184	.00491	.00000	.00000	.00000	.00443	.04382	80
85+	8544	1850	.21653	.00023	.00176	.00831	.07058	.02633	.00316	.00667	.00000	.00000	.00000	.00796	.09153	85+
ALL	3072170	31311														

	All Causes	Respiratory T. B.	Other Infec. and Paras.	Neoplasms	Cardiovascular	Infl., Pneu., Bronch.	Diarrheal	Certain Degenerative	Maternal	Cert. Dis. of Infancy	Motor Vehicle	Other Violence	Other and Unknown
CRUDE DEATH RATE	.01019	.00063	.00084	.00088	.00193	.00118	.00047	.00045	.00028	.00084	.00002	.00030	.00238
STANDARDIZED RATE (1)	.00992	.00059	.00056	.00072	.00146	.00118	.00063	.00037	.00026	.00127	.00002	.00028	.00218
STANDARDIZED RATE (2)	.01317	.00066	.00080	.00132	.00321	.00153	.00046	.00065	.00026	.00075	.00002	.00036	.00317
GEOMETRIC MEAN	.01299												

LIFE TABLE FOR ALL CAUSES COMBINED

Age (x)	Midyear Population	Deaths During Year	$_nM_x$	$_nq_x$	l_x	$_nd_x$	$_nL_x$	$_nm_x$	$_na_x$	T_x	$_nr_x$	$\overset{\circ}{e}_x$	Age (x)
0	71920	6345	.088223	.082540	100000	8254	93562	.088220	.219979	6014414	.000000	60.144	0
1	293843	1972	.006711	.026399	91746	2422	360929	.006710	1.500000	5920852	.000000	64.535	1
5	366237	979	.002673	.013289	89324	1187	443653	.002676	2.500000	5559923	.000000	62.244	5
10	314546	611	.001942	.009655	88137	851	438554	.001940	2.495838	5116271	.021035	58.049	10
15	275548	741	.002689	.013404	87286	1170	433657	.002698	2.629986	4677717	.020769	53.591	15
20	255722	947	.003703	.018359	86116	1581	426745	.003705	2.574188	4244060	.009729	49.283	20
25	249857	1034	.004138	.020500	84535	1733	418415	.004142	2.541835	3817315	.006514	45.157	25
30	231953	1093	.004712	.023297	82802	1929	409269	.004713	2.542228	3398900	.005946	41.049	30
35	221079	1176	.005319	.026263	80873	2124	399116	.005325	2.528641	2989631	.012880	36.967	35
40	182661	1043	.005710	.028204	78749	2221	388326	.005719	2.560033	2590515	.029410	32.896	40
45	149255	1094	.007330	.036117	76528	2764	375984	.007351	2.591881	2202190	.028889	28.776	45
50	126482	1201	.009495	.046635	73764	3440	360668	.009538	2.630269	1826206	.031461	24.757	50
55	98756	1422	.014399	.069591	70324	4915	339896	.014460	2.614742	1465537	.028057	20.840	55
60	83679	1638	.019575	.093978	65409	6147	312577	.019666	2.646311	1125641	.027285	17.209	60
65	59591	1992	.033428	.155783	59262	9232	274222	.033666	2.607506	813064	.036100	13.720	65
70	41398	2006	.048456	.218089	50030	10911	223890	.048734	2.593274	538842	.031833	10.770	70
75	26427	2312	.067486	.360873	39119	14117	160517	.087590	2.515230	314951	.020166	8.051	75
80	14672	1855	.126431	.477682	25002	11943	94122	.126888	2.413757	154434	.020166	6.177	80
85+	8544	1850	.216526	1.000000	13059	13059	60311	.216526	4.618378	60311	.000000	4.618	85+

NUMBER OF PERSONS DYING (OUT OF 100,000 AT BIRTH) ABOVE AGE X FROM SPECIFIED CAUSES

Age (x)	All Causes	Respiratory T.B.	Other Infec. and Paras.	Neoplasms	Cardiovascular	Infl., Pneu., Bronch.	Diarrheal	Certain Degenerative	Maternal	Cert. Dis. of Infancy	Motor Vehicle	Other Violence	Other and Unknown	Age (x)
0	100000	4143	4455	10468	28094	11660	2508	5148	1547	3373	111	2728	25765	0
1	91746	4118	3826	10464	28032	10545	1240	5131	1547	0	111	2660	24072	1
5	89324	4075	3087	10448	27992	10044	924	5093	1547	0	102	2477	23535	5
10	88137	4041	2578	10437	27920	9937	891	5057	1547	0	88	2392	23249	10
15	87286	3943	2353	10423	27825	9856	883	5021	1546	0	87	2335	23014	15
20	86116	3601	2165	10414	27715	9770	882	4984	1478	0	87	2269	22751	20
25	84535	3086	1976	10399	27608	9634	875	4923	1249	0	80	2202	22503	25
30	82802	2606	1758	10340	27489	9520	867	4857	932	0	75	2142	22216	30
35	80873	2211	1591	10236	27325	9356	858	4772	561	0	72	2071	21820	35
40	78749	1877	1443	10025	27094	9176	847	4658	217	0	70	1999	21343	40
45	76528	1606	1316	9627	26790	9001	832	4496	57	0	66	1942	20795	45
50	73764	1372	1192	9010	26263	8787	814	4269	3	0	61	1874	20119	50
55	70324	1143	1058	8179	25456	8540	794	3979	3	0	58	1765	19349	55
60	65409	916	906	7060	24043	8121	767	3568	3	0	54	1637	18334	60
65	59262	680	738	5696	22100	7512	729	3028	3	0	35	1551	17190	65
70	50030	445	553	4125	18748	6406	650	2320	3	0	17	1417	15346	70
75	39119	212	385	2565	14231	4866	541	1577	3	0	6	1253	13480	75
80	25002	60	226	1268	8695	2968	364	870	3	0	0	898	9650	80
85+	13059	14	106	501	4257	1588	191	402	0	0	0	480	5520	85+

NUMBER OF PERSONS SURVIVING TO AGE X IF SPECIFIED CAUSES WERE ELIMINATED

Age (x)	No Causes	Respiratory T.B. (1)	Other Infec. and Paras. (2)	Neoplasms (3)	Cardiovascular (4)	Infl., Pneu., Bronch. (5)	Diarrheal (6)	Certain Degenerative (7)	Maternal (8)	Cert. Dis. of Infancy (9)	Motor Vehicle (10)	Other Violence (11)	Other and Unknown (12)	(1)+(2)	(1)+(2)+(5)+(6)+(8)	(1)+(2)+(5)+(6)+(8)+part of(9)&(12)	(10)+(11)	Age (x)
0	100000	100000	100000	100000	100000	100000	100000	100000	100000	100000	100000	100000	100000	100000	100000	100000	100000	0
1	91746	91770	92350	91750	91805	92820	92568	91762	91746	95033	91746	91811	93382	92374	94701	99593	91811	1
5	89324	89390	90649	89344	89421	90871	90830	89377	89324	92525	89333	89568	91457	90716	93844	99189	89577	5
10	88137	88236	89959	88167	88305	89772	89657	88225	88137	91255	88160	88463	90533	90060	93312	98869	88486	10
15	87286	87481	89319	87330	87547	88987	88759	87409	87287	90414	87309	87666	89900	89519	92847	98553	87689	15
20	86116	86650	88313	86118	86483	87881	87610	86275	86185	89202	86139	86556	88964	88861	92329	98228	86580	20
25	84535	85574	86884	84601	85002	86406	86009	84751	84830	87564	84565	85034	87565	87952	91785	97878	85064	25
30	82802	84302	85325	82925	83378	84750	84253	83079	83406	85769	82836	83350	86084	86871	91133	97446	83385	30
35	80873	82736	83507	81097	81599	82541	82300	81228	81833	83771	80909	81479	84487	85431	90221	96808	81516	35
40	78749	80901	81465	79176	75686	80945	80149	79208	80028	81571	78786	79411	82761	83691	88977	95826	79449	40
45	76528	78894	79297	77339	77743	78840	77904	77135	77931	79270	76568	77228	80997	81749	87304	94321	77268	45
50	73764	76281	76559	75160	75463	76209	75108	74574	75170	76407	73808	74506	78777	79172	84875	91951	74550	50
55	70324	72955	73125	72487	72755	72905	71625	71383	71644	72644	70368	71139	75510	75861	81627	88655	71184	55
60	65409	68084	68166	66542	65055	68230	66646	66798	66656	67753	65454	66292	71668	70954	76851	83732	66338	60
65	59262	61919	61927	63473	64588	62426	60420	61047	60392	61385	59321	60145	66137	64703	70813	77453	60205	65
70	50030	52498	52457	55147	57989	53783	51081	52209	50984	51823	50096	50900	57753	55044	61569	67838	50968	70
75	39119	41263	41171	44654	50205	43540	40040	41509	39865	40521	39180	39548	47107	43428	50417	56085	40011	75
80	25002	26497	26445	29721	38229	29547	25735	27125	25479	25898	25046	25823	34031	28026	34743	39762	25869	80
85+	13059	13874	13903	16185	25418	16636	13569	14533	13310	13527	13082	13758	22251	14771	19928	23565	13822	85+

ADDED YRS OF LIFE

	No Causes	(1)	(2)	(3)	(4)	(5)	(6)	(7)	(8)	(9)	(10)	(11)	(12)				
TOTAL		1.383	1.949	1.666	3.991	2.435	1.120	.835	.614	2.147	.033	.593	5.312	3.390	8.006	13.630	.626
WORK	5.724	.972	.443	.576	.709	.413	.025	.295	.526	.000	.010	.181	1.095	1.428	2.442	3.084	.190

POPULATION, DEATHS, DEATH RATES FOR ALL CAUSES COMBINED, AND SPECIFIED CAUSES

Age Start of Interval	Midyear Population	Deaths During Year	All Causes	Respiratory T. B.	Other Infec. and Paras.	Neo-plasms	Cardio-vascular	Infl., Pneu., Bronch.	Diar-rheal	Certain Degenerative	Maternal	Cert. Dis. of Infancy	Motor Vehicle	Other Violence	Other and Unknown	Age Start of Interval
0	102855	11677	.11348	.00046	.00573	.00014	.00017	.01638	.02291	.00015	.00000	.05049	.00000	.00053	.01613	0
1	439565	2847	.00648	.00018	.00144	.00006	.00010	.00151	.00087	.00008	.00000	.00000	.00012	.00066	.00146	1
5	571588	1241	.00217	.00009	.00055	.00005	.00012	.00018	.00006	.00006	.00000	.00000	.00016	.00036	.00055	5
10	542568	822	.00152	.00013	.00026	.00004	.00014	.00010	.00002	.00003	.00000	.00000	.00006	.00034	.00040	10
15	525196	1312	.00250	.00041	.00022	.00007	.00018	.00016	.00002	.00007	.00000	.00000	.00013	.00071	.00053	15
20	463756	1508	.00325	.00080	.00027	.00009	.00018	.00021	.00001	.00008	.00000	.00000	.00022	.00090	.00048	20
25	410262	1390	.00339	.00081	.00031	.00011	.00021	.00021	.00001	.00016	.00000	.00000	.00019	.00082	.00054	25
30	368281	1301	.00353	.00076	.00022	.00016	.00030	.00024	.00001	.00023	.00000	.00000	.00017	.00077	.00069	30
35	359066	1512	.00421	.00075	.00024	.00027	.00048	.00035	.00002	.00031	.00000	.00000	.00021	.00084	.00074	35
40	347427	1888	.00543	.00079	.00031	.00050	.00082	.00048	.00002	.00049	.00000	.00000	.00020	.00088	.00095	40
45	321306	2312	.00720	.00080	.00043	.00104	.00145	.00057	.00003	.00068	.00000	.00000	.00022	.00091	.00106	45
50	267396	2855	.01068	.00088	.00052	.00164	.00258	.00073	.00002	.00122	.00000	.00000	.00024	.00116	.00169	50
55	199492	3055	.01531	.00080	.00064	.00274	.00444	.00113	.00006	.00179	.00000	.00000	.00025	.00122	.00224	55
60	157119	3581	.02279	.00074	.00068	.00421	.00784	.00150	.00010	.00274	.00000	.00000	.00030	.00137	.00331	60
65	120880	4244	.03511	.00056	.00073	.00635	.01352	.00246	.00007	.00389	.00000	.00000	.00038	.00144	.00532	65
70	88685	4867	.05488	.00090	.00088	.00889	.02269	.00449	.00027	.00593	.00000	.00000	.00035	.00170	.00878	70
75	50135	4361	.08699	.00082	.00104	.01123	.03979	.00734	.00046	.00876	.00000	.00000	.00056	.00195	.01504	75
80	23950	3203	.13374	.00046	.00138	.01324	.05879	.01420	.00079	.01311	.00000	.00000	.00050	.00334	.02793	80
85+	11244	2553	.22705	.00044	.00151	.01272	.09472	.02348	.00240	.01805	.00000	.00000	.00071	.00685	.06617	85+
ALL	5370871	56529														

CRUDE DEATH RATE	.01053	.00056	.00058	.00095	.00231	.00105	.00055	.00072	.00000	.00097	.00018	.00083	.00182
STANDARDIZED RATE (1)	.01065	.00051	.00069	.00069	.00160	.00121	.00094	.00053	.00000	.00178	.00017	.00077	.00178
STANDARDIZED RATE (2)	.01388	.00058	.00061	.00138	.00370	.00136	.00060	.00106	.00000	.00105	.00020	.00090	.00244
GEOMETRIC MEAN	.01257												

LIFE TABLE FOR ALL CAUSES COMBINED

Age (x)	Midyear Population	Deaths During Year	nM_x	nq_x	l_x	nd_x	nL_x	nm_x	na_x	T_x	nr_x	$\overset{\circ}{e}_x$	Age (x)
0	102895	11677	.113485	.104720	100000	10472	92281	.113479	.262924	5908851	.000000	59.089	0
1	439565	2847	.006477	.025500	89528	2283	352405	.006478	1.500000	5816570	.000000	64.969	1
5	571588	1241	.002171	.010797	87245	942	433870	.002171	2.500000	5464165	.000000	62.630	5
10	542568	822	.001515	.007543	86303	651	429913	.001514	2.539363	5030295	.004177	58.286	10
15	525196	1312	.002498	.012434	85652	1065	425746	.002501	2.639867	4600382	.009649	53.710	15
20	463756	1508	.003251	.016149	84587	1366	419590	.003256	2.550939	4174636	.018804	49.353	20
25	410262	1390	.003388	.016811	83221	1399	412621	.003391	2.509977	3755046	.020883	45.121	25
30	368281	1301	.003533	.017514	81822	1433	405565	.003533	2.540271	3342425	.013846	40.850	30
35	359066	1512	.004211	.020849	80389	1676	397896	.004212	2.584402	2936840	.004054	36.533	35
40	347427	1888	.005434	.026832	78713	2112	388501	.005436	2.602490	2538943	.003633	32.256	40
45	321306	2312	.007196	.035443	76601	2715	376583	.007210	2.634515	2150442	.012047	28.073	45
50	267396	2855	.010677	.052310	73886	3865	360286	.010728	2.634056	1773859	.030660	24.008	50
55	199492	3055	.015314	.074292	70021	5202	337762	.015401	2.627235	1413573	.037454	20.188	55
60	157119	3581	.022792	.108641	64819	7042	307362	.022870	2.623870	1075811	.030268	16.597	60
65	120880	4244	.035109	.162504	57777	9389	266397	.035244	2.604866	768449	.021633	13.300	65
70	88685	4867	.054880	.243201	48388	11768	213308	.055169	2.566972	502052	.027075	10.376	70
75	50135	4361	.086995	.359694	36620	13172	150161	.087719	2.499320	288744	.039062	7.885	75
80	23950	3203	.133737	.500043	23448	11725	86952	.134844	2.416809	138583	.039062	5.910	80
85+	11244	2553	.227054	1.000000	11723	11723	51631	.227054	4.404230	51631	.000000	4.404	85+

NUMBER OF PERSONS DYING (OUT OF 100,000 AT BIRTH) ABOVE AGE X FROM SPECIFIED CAUSES

Age (x)	All Causes	Respiratory T.B.	Other Infec. and Paras.	Neoplasms	Cardiovascular	Infl., Pneu., Bronch.	Diarrheal	Certain Degenerative	Maternal	Cert. Dis. of Infancy	Motor Vehicle	Other Violence	Other and Unknown	Age (x)
0	100000	3715	3545	10890	30597	9340	2905	8489	0	4659	1286	5927	18247	0
1	89528	3673	3016	10877	30980	7829	791	8476	0	0	1286	5841	16759	1
5	87245	3610	2508	10855	30946	7297	483	8448	0	0	1244	5609	16245	5
10	86303	3570	2270	10831	30895	7219	458	8420	0	0	1176	5455	16009	10
15	85652	3514	2159	10815	30836	7178	450	8406	0	0	1149	5306	15839	15
20	84587	3337	2064	10786	30759	7109	443	8377	0	0	1095	5005	15612	20
25	83221	3001	1952	10746	30683	7019	438	8342	0	0	1003	4626	15411	25
30	81822	2667	1823	10700	30596	6931	432	8277	0	0	924	4287	15185	30
35	80389	2360	1734	10636	30473	6835	429	8185	0	0	853	3976	14908	35
40	78713	2063	1638	10528	30281	6697	422	8062	0	0	768	3641	14613	40
45	76601	1756	1519	10334	29563	6511	413	7871	0	0	691	3299	14244	45
50	73886	1455	1356	9943	29416	6297	401	7613	0	0	606	2955	13844	50
55	70021	1140	1168	9349	28478	6033	393	7171	0	0	520	2535	13234	55
60	64819	871	951	8417	26565	5650	372	6563	0	0	435	2122	12473	60
65	57777	642	742	7117	24539	5188	341	5718	0	0	343	1699	11448	65
70	48388	386	548	5421	20921	4530	321	4679	0	0	242	1315	10025	70
75	36620	194	360	3519	16051	3567	263	3408	0	0	167	951	8140	75
80	23448	71	203	1825	10021	2454	193	2083	0	0	83	656	5859	80
85+	11723	23	78	657	4890	1212	124	932	0	0	37	354	3416	85+

NUMBER OF PERSONS SURVIVING TO AGE X IF SPECIFIED CAUSES WERE ELIMINATED

Age (x)	No Causes	Respiratory T.B.	Other Infec. and Paras.	Neoplasms	Cardiovascular	Infl., Pneu., Bronch.	Diarrheal	Certain Degenerative	Maternal	Cert. Dis. of Infancy	Motor Vehicle	Other Violence	Other and Unknown	(1) + (2)	(1) + (2) + (5) + (6) + (8)	(1)+(2)+ (5)+(6)+ (8)+part of(9)&(12)	(10) + (11)	Age (x)
		(1)	(2)	(3)	(4)	(5)	(6)	(7)	(8)	(9)	(10)	(11)	(12)					
0	100000	100000	100000	100000	100000	100000	100000	100000	100000	100000	100000	100000	100000	100000	100000	100000	100000	0
1	89528	89568	90030	89540	89544	90968	91550	89540	89528	94044	89528	89609	90946	90070	93585	99671	89609	1
5	87245	87346	88240	87279	87294	89184	89527	87285	87245	91646	87286	87554	89144	88342	92667	99151	87595	5
10	86303	86443	87527	86360	86402	88300	88586	86370	86303	90657	86412	86762	88422	87668	92070	98657	86872	10
15	85652	85847	86979	85725	85810	87676	87925	85733	85652	89973	85787	86257	87928	87176	91605	98246	86393	15
20	84587	84956	85993	84688	84819	86656	86839	84695	84587	88854	84774	85486	87067	86368	90836	97530	85675	20
25	83221	83919	84717	83360	83525	85348	85442	83362	83221	87419	83496	84487	85866	85428	89950	96686	84766	25
30	81822	82843	83423	82004	82208	84003	84012	82026	81822	85950	82171	83408	84654	84464	89037	95829	83764	30
35	80389	81701	82052	80632	80891	82630	82544	80681	80389	84403	80803	82262	83456	83391	88013	94865	82689	35
40	78713	80297	80439	79058	79396	81047	80830	79121	78713	82684	79203	80887	82020	82057	86763	93653	81391	40
45	76601	78451	78400	77129	77583	79062	78670	77188	76601	80465	77154	79064	80199	80294	85112	92027	79635	45
50	73886	75974	75786	74783	75379	76477	74708	73886	77613	74504	76611	77769	77927	82852	89725	77251	50
55	70021	72315	72009	71459	72375	72743	71932	71236	70021	73553	70691	73028	74329	74368	79367	86125	73727	55
60	64819	67210	66874	67072	68521	67722	66609	66542	64819	68089	65521	68018	69588	69340	74446	80968	68755	60
65	57777	60132	59812	61068	63548	60822	59402	60136	57777	60692	58491	61047	63075	62250	67373	73465	61801	65
70	48388	50603	50275	52807	56950	51576	49768	51361	48388	50829	49079	51497	54265	52577	57639	63090	52232	70
75	36620	38469	38217	41758	48410	39934	37716	40056	36620	38467	37208	39308	42944	40146	45090	49668	39939	75
80	23448	24732	24600	28329	38023	26554	24207	26821	23448	24631	23892	25420	29711	25947	30336	33766	25902	80
85+	11723	12400	12390	15176	25747	14287	12152	14354	11723	12314	11978	12938	17162	13106	16558	18860	13219	85+

ADDED YRS OF LIFE

		(1)	(2)	(3)	(4)	(5)	(6)	(7)	(8)	(9)	(10)	(11)	(12)				
TOTAL		1.139	1.357	1.492	4.358	2.301	1.603	1.136	.000	2.968	.369	1.689	3.781	2.531	6.726	12.115	2.076
WORK	5.262	.766	.314	.412	.699	.345	.019	.347	.000	.000	.203	.912	.812	1.088	1.466	1.776	1.121

POPULATION, DEATHS, DEATH RATES FOR ALL CAUSES COMBINED, AND SPECIFIED CAUSES

Age Start of Interval	Midyear Population	Deaths During Year	All Causes	Respiratory T. B.	Other Infec. and Paras.	Neoplasms	Cardiovascular	Infl., Pneu., Bronch.	Diarrheal	Certain Degenerative	Maternal	Cert. Dis. of Infancy	Motor Vehicle	Other Violence	Other and Unknown	Age Start of Interval
0	99676	8698	.08726	.00030	.00579	.00008	.00009	.01283	.01653	.00013	.00000	.03836	.00003	.00076	.01235	0
1	430755	2535	.00589	.00018	.00144	.00006	.00013	.00154	.00067	.00006	.00000	.00000	.00010	.00039	.00131	1
5	559124	963	.00172	.00010	.00052	.00004	.00011	.00020	.00005	.00006	.00000	.00000	.00007	.00012	.00045	5
10	530674	806	.00152	.00023	.00030	.00003	.00018	.00012	.00001	.00006	.00000	.00000	.00002	.00008	.00047	10
15	514198	1132	.00220	.00079	.00030	.00006	.00018	.00013	.00001	.00006	.00013	.00000	.00005	.00012	.00037	15
20	447649	1454	.00325	.00128	.00029	.00012	.00019	.00013	.00002	.00012	.00043	.00000	.00004	.00017	.00045	20
25	376810	1414	.00375	.00130	.00031	.00016	.00031	.00018	.00005	.00011	.00067	.00000	.00005	.00014	.00048	25
30	340914	1433	.00420	.00104	.00028	.00044	.00037	.00020	.00002	.00027	.00079	.00000	.00004	.00016	.00060	30
35	329360	1574	.00478	.00089	.00024	.00067	.00054	.00033	.00002	.00035	.00080	.00000	.00003	.00017	.00073	35
40	298326	1493	.00500	.00056	.00023	.00113	.00077	.00036	.00004	.00042	.00048	.00000	.00004	.00015	.00083	40
45	263789	1738	.00659	.00053	.00015	.00179	.00136	.00050	.00003	.00067	.00008	.00000	.00007	.00020	.00121	45
50	221632	1993	.00899	.00053	.00032	.00248	.00221	.00053	.00005	.00110	.00008	.00000	.00010	.00019	.00148	50
55	168273	2245	.01334	.00049	.00037	.00352	.00405	.00087	.00004	.00153	.00000	.00000	.00016	.00029	.00203	55
60	138010	2854	.02068	.00061	.00038	.00470	.00733	.00121	.00012	.00300	.00000	.00000	.00012	.00031	.00290	60
65	110692	3346	.03023	.00076	.00046	.00576	.01148	.00255	.00015	.00407	.00000	.00000	.00017	.00057	.00426	65
70	83188	4070	.04893	.00067	.00058	.00778	.02041	.00511	.00020	.00642	.00000	.00000	.00010	.00094	.00672	70
75	48766	4029	.08262	.00066	.00096	.01017	.03886	.00880	.00053	.00835	.00000	.00000	.00033	.00211	.01185	75
80	25383	3214	.12662	.00063	.00098	.01056	.05921	.01422	.00098	.01119	.00000	.00000	.00024	.00504	.02356	80
85+	14135	2997	.21203	.00050	.00085	.01153	.08971	.02731	.00241	.01415	.00000	.00000	.00014	.01075	.05469	85+
ALL	5001354	47988														

	All Causes	Respiratory T. B.	Other Infec. and Paras.	Neoplasms	Cardiovascular	Infl., Pneu., Bronch.	Diarrheal	Certain Degenerative	Maternal	Cert. Dis. of Infancy	Motor Vehicle	Other Violence	Other and Unknown
CRUDE DEATH RATE	.00960	.00064	.00054	.00108	.00225	.00101	.00044	.00071	.00024	.00076	.00006	.00028	.00159
STANDARDIZED RATE (1)	.00926	.00061	.00066	.00082	.00151	.00107	.00070	.00052	.00023	.00135	.00006	.00025	.00149
STANDARDIZED RATE (2)	.01247	.00065	.00055	.00151	.00349	.00129	.00046	.00103	.00024	.00079	.00007	.00036	.00204
GEOMETRIC MEAN	.01172												

LIFE TABLE FOR ALL CAUSES COMBINED

Age (x)	Midyear Population	Deaths During Year	$_nM_x$	$_nq_x$	l_x	$_nd_x$	$_nL_x$	$_nm_x$	$_na_x$	T_x	$_nr_x$	$\overset{\circ}{e}_x$	Age (x)
0	99676	8698	.087263	.081690	100000	8169	93615	.087262	.218347	6157957	.000000	61.580	0
1	430755	2535	.005885	.023195	91831	2130	361999	.005884	1.500000	6064343	.000000	66.038	1
5	559124	963	.001722	.008573	89701	769	446583	.001722	2.500000	5702344	.000000	63.571	5
10	530674	806	.001519	.007568	88932	673	443019	.001519	2.561602	5255761	.004216	59.099	10
15	514198	1132	.002201	.010968	88259	968	439029	.002205	2.658833	4812742	.009874	54.530	15
20	447649	1454	.003248	.016164	87291	1411	433059	.003258	2.593019	4373714	.023986	50.105	20
25	376810	1414	.003753	.018607	85880	1598	425477	.003756	2.544848	3940655	.026046	45.886	25
30	340914	1433	.004203	.020823	84282	1755	417056	.004208	2.541667	3515178	.013540	41.707	30
35	329360	1574	.004779	.023617	82527	1949	407812	.004779	2.525547	3098083	.008460	37.540	35
40	298326	1493	.005005	.024746	80578	1994	398031	.005010	2.563315	2690270	.014373	33.387	40
45	263789	1738	.006589	.032513	78584	2555	386817	.006605	2.611546	2292239	.018806	29.169	45
50	221632	1993	.008992	.044220	76029	3362	372192	.009033	2.634593	1905421	.031670	25.062	50
55	168273	2245	.013341	.065050	72667	4727	352218	.013421	2.648130	1533229	.035102	21.099	55
60	138010	2854	.020680	.098955	67940	6723	323711	.020769	2.621752	1181011	.024990	17.383	60
65	110692	3346	.030228	.141399	61217	8656	285454	.030324	2.616514	857300	.018305	14.004	65
70	83188	4070	.048925	.220011	52561	11564	235039	.049200	2.598942	571847	.026965	10.880	70
75	48766	4029	.082619	.345058	40997	14148	169891	.083277	2.519540	336808	.033403	8.215	75
80	25383	3214	.126620	.480130	26849	12891	101065	.127527	2.427647	166916	.033403	6.217	80
85+	14135	2997	.212027	1.000000	13958	13958	65831	.212027	4.716383	65831	.000000	4.716	85+

NUMBER OF PERSONS DYING (OUT OF 100,000 AT BIRTH) ABOVE AGE X FROM SPECIFIED CAUSES

Age (x)	All Causes	Respiratory T. B.	Other Infec. and Paras.	Neoplasms	Cardiovascular	Infl., Pneu., Bronch.	Diarrheal	Certain Degenerative	Maternal	Cert. Dis. of Infancy	Motor Vehicle	Other Violence	Other and Unknown	Age (x)
0	100000	4084	3145	12573	33037	10234	2410	9001	1414	3591	502	3012	16997	0
1	91831	4056	2603	12566	33028	9033	862	8989	1414	0	499	2941	15840	1
5	89701	3989	2081	12544	32583	8476	618	8966	1414	0	464	2798	15368	5
10	88932	3943	1851	12526	32933	8387	556	8941	1414	0	433	2743	15165	10
15	88259	3839	1716	12511	32854	8333	591	8915	1413	0	423	2705	14959	15
20	87291	3492	1586	12486	32776	8275	587	8888	1353	0	402	2652	14794	20
25	85880	2937	1461	12433	32692	8220	577	8835	1165	0	385	2579	14596	25
30	84282	2385	1330	12366	32558	8142	558	8787	878	0	365	2522	14391	30
35	82527	1953	1215	12182	32403	8058	550	8674	547	0	349	2453	14143	35
40	80578	1589	1117	11909	32181	7924	540	8533	219	0	336	2383	13847	40
45	78584	1365	1027	11457	31872	7781	526	8367	31	0	321	2321	13516	45
50	76029	1159	968	10761	31343	7589	514	8108	1	0	293	2245	13048	50
55	72667	961	848	9835	30514	7390	497	7656	1	0	256	2173	12496	55
60	67940	789	716	8590	29077	7083	482	7154	1	0	199	2070	11779	60
65	61217	591	592	7066	26690	6689	442	6178	1	0	162	1969	10837	65
70	52561	375	460	5418	23400	5958	398	5015	1	0	113	1805	9618	70
75	40997	217	324	3584	18570	4749	350	3500	1	0	90	1583	8029	75
80	26849	105	159	1849	11910	3242	258	2074	1	0	34	1220	5997	80
85+	13958	33	56	759	5905	1798	158	931	0	0	9	708	3601	85+

NUMBER OF PERSONS SURVIVING TO AGE X IF SPECIFIED CAUSES WERE ELIMINATED

Age (x)	No Causes	Respiratory T. B.	Other Infec. and Paras.	Neoplasms	Cardiovascular	Infl., Pneu., Bronch.	Diarrheal	Certain Degenerative	Maternal	Cert. Dis. of Infancy	Motor Vehicle	Other Violence	Other and Unknown	(1) + (2)	(1) + (2) + (5) + (6) + (8)	(1)+(2)+ (5)+(6)+ (8)+part of(9)&(12)	(10) + (11)	Age (x)
	(1)	(2)	(3)	(4)	(5)	(6)	(7)	(8)	(9)	(10)	(11)	(12)						
0	100000	100000	100000	100000	100000	100000	100000	100000	100000	100000	100000	100000	100000	100000	100000	100000	100000	0
1	91831	91858	92352	91838	91840	92589	93326	91842	91831	95336	91834	91899	92946	92379	95066	99746	91902	1
5	89701	89793	90730	89729	89754	91391	91407	89735	89701	93125	89738	89909	91264	90823	94294	99369	89547	5
10	88932	89069	90184	88978	89034	90658	90645	88991	88932	92227	89000	89193	90687	90323	93892	99098	89261	10
15	88259	88499	89638	88320	88439	90066	89965	88343	88260	91628	88336	88556	90210	89882	93496	98828	88634	15
20	87291	87875	88786	87547	87547	89137	88962	87401	87352	90623	87388	87638	89389	89381	93104	98551	87736	20
25	85880	87011	87477	86016	86216	87752	87554	86041	86127	89158	85993	86294	88145	88629	92592	98181	86407	25
30	84282	85948	85982	84482	84745	86199	85944	84488	84810	87499	84413	84745	86714	87681	92015	97751	84876	30
35	82527	84595	84308	82906	83135	84489	84162	82841	83374	85677	82671	83049	85161	86420	91153	97020	83194	35
40	80578	82986	82415	81220	81393	82629	82185	81024	81733	83654	80731	81157	83452	84858	90025	96016	81311	40
45	78584	81141	80467	79661	79687	80729	80165	79184	79898	81584	78748	79211	81726	83085	88527	94574	79376	45
50	76029	78712	77910	77768	77626	78299	77571	76867	77330	78931	76215	76711	79549	80659	86203	92224	76899	50
55	72667	75432	74585	75261	75026	75037	74157	73876	73911	75441	72881	73389	76558	77423	82984	88506	73606	55
60	67940	70697	69864	71622	71597	70463	69348	69606	69103	70533	68196	68716	72349	72700	78280	83999	68975	60
65	61217	63897	63072	66075	66945	63880	62525	63674	62265	63554	61483	62013	66149	65833	71365	76726	62282	65
70	52561	55070	54279	58399	60912	55560	53725	55801	53461	54567	52834	53399	58027	56870	62499	67412	53676	70
75	40997	43098	42461	47373	52716	44478	41949	44960	41699	42562	41230	41850	46832	44637	50400	54651	42088	75
80	26849	28318	27944	32661	42147	30472	27548	30718	27309	27874	27047	27710	32599	29474	34910	38214	27914	80
85+	13958	14776	14604	17945	29717	17046	14394	16923	14198	14491	14079	14785	19138	15459	19804	22115	14913	85+

ADDED YRS OF LIFE																		
TOTAL		1.456	1.355	2.027	4.832	2.226	1.252	1.243	.567	2.343	.140	.563	3.456	2.851	7.248	11.914	.706	
WORK	5.184	1.013	.295	.700	.658	.276	.029	.340	.475	.000	.053	.170	.733	1.317	2.134	2.522	.224	

POPULATION, DEATHS, DEATH RATES FOR ALL CAUSES COMBINED, AND SPECIFIED CAUSES

Age Start of Interval	Midyear Population	Deaths During Year	All Causes	Respiratory T. B.	Other Infec. and Paras.	Neoplasms	Cardiovascular	Infl., Pneu., Bronch.	Diarrheal	Certain Degenerative	Maternal	Cert. Dis. of Infancy	Motor Vehicle	Other Violence	Other and Unknown	Age Start of Interval
0	108944	8791	.08069	.00028	.00418	.00005	.00019	.01573	.00916	.00020	.00000	.03433	.00003	.00116	.01535	0
1	423881	1878	.00443	.00010	.00079	.00011	.00012	.00105	.00050	.00004	.00000	.00000	.00014	.00058	.00100	1
5	528134	888	.00168	.00008	.00031	.00007	.00009	.00013	.00003	.00003	.00000	.00000	.00019	.00034	.00042	5
10	555519	787	.00142	.00010	.00021	.00007	.00013	.00006	.00001	.00005	.00000	.00000	.00013	.00031	.00035	10
15	564548	1119	.00198	.00026	.00021	.00005	.00013	.00012	.00001	.00007	.00000	.00000	.00019	.00054	.00036	15
20	517145	1332	.00258	.00048	.00019	.00009	.00019	.00009	.00000	.00009	.00000	.00000	.00023	.00084	.00036	20
25	487396	1321	.00271	.00058	.00017	.00011	.00023	.00013	.00001	.00011	.00000	.00000	.00026	.00081	.00028	25
30	430664	1212	.00281	.00053	.00016	.00023	.00035	.00008	.00001	.00018	.00000	.00000	.00024	.00067	.00035	30
35	395653	1498	.00379	.00061	.00024	.00038	.00063	.00015	.00002	.00033	.00000	.00000	.00021	.00078	.00044	35
40	348039	1745	.00501	.00065	.00026	.00055	.00127	.00018	.00003	.00041	.00000	.00000	.00021	.00079	.00062	40
45	332008	2417	.00728	.00067	.00030	.00101	.00215	.00031	.00001	.00078	.00000	.00000	.00034	.00092	.00078	45
50	315404	3355	.01064	.00066	.00041	.00166	.00393	.00045	.00002	.00116	.00000	.00000	.00028	.00095	.00111	50
55	274893	4394	.01598	.00071	.00061	.00288	.00644	.00068	.00005	.00173	.00000	.00000	.00030	.00108	.00151	55
60	218202	5287	.02423	.00080	.00068	.00468	.01056	.00093	.00004	.00270	.00000	.00000	.00044	.00134	.00206	60
65	162233	6054	.03732	.00092	.00070	.00677	.01765	.00157	.00004	.00444	.00000	.00000	.00046	.00129	.00348	65
70	110944	6490	.05850	.00072	.00081	.00997	.02894	.00260	.00006	.00739	.00000	.00000	.00049	.00157	.00594	70
75	67104	6420	.09567	.00067	.00048	.01258	.05025	.00507	.00015	.01255	.00000	.00000	.00058	.00270	.01025	75
80	34038	5019	.14745	.00062	.00059	.01534	.07686	.01022	.00041	.01858	.00000	.00000	.00094	.00423	.01927	80
85+	15889	3845	.24199	.00044	.00076	.01422	.12531	.02165	.00063	.02971	.00000	.00000	.00069	.00818	.04041	85+
ALL	5890638	63852														

		All Causes	Respiratory T. B.	Other Infec. and Paras.	Neoplasms	Cardiovascular	Infl., Pneu., Bronch.	Diarrheal	Certain Degenerative	Maternal	Cert. Dis. of Infancy	Motor Vehicle	Other Violence	Other and Unknown
CRUDE DEATH RATE		.01084	.00045	.00041	.00123	.00363	.00082	.00023	.00058	.00000	.00063	.00025	.00081	.00140
STANDARDIZED RATE (1)		.00916	.00038	.00048	.00077	.00210	.00056	.00040	.00059	.00000	.00121	.00022	.00071	.00135
STANDARDIZED RATE (2)		.01336	.00046	.00044	.00154	.00485	.00100	.00026	.00128	.00000	.00071	.00026	.00086	.00171
GEOMETRIC MEAN		.01152												

LIFE TABLE FOR ALL CAUSES COMBINED

Age (x)	Midyear Population	Deaths During Year	$_nM_x$	$_nq_x$	l_x	$_nd_x$	$_nL_x$	$_nm_x$	$_na_x$	T_x	$_nr_x$	$\overset{\circ}{e}_x$	Age (x)
0	108944	8791	.080693	.075840	100000	7584	93987	.080692	.207178	6180463	.000000	61.805	0
1	423881	1878	.004430	.017529	92416	1620	365614	.004431	1.500000	6086475	.000000	65.860	1
5	528134	888	.001681	.008370	90796	760	452080	.001681	2.500000	5720861	.000000	63.008	5
10	555519	787	.001417	.007064	90036	636	448615	.001418	2.539963	5268781	-.008476	58.519	10
15	564548	1119	.001982	.009866	89400	882	444899	.001982	2.617394	4820166	.000813	53.917	15
20	517145	1332	.002576	.012800	88518	1133	439819	.002576	2.554244	4375267	.009036	49.428	20
25	487396	1321	.002710	.013469	87385	1177	433998	.002712	2.512921	3935449	-.013683	45.036	25
30	430664	1212	.002814	.013989	86208	1206	428113	.002817	2.572727	3501451	.016843	40.616	30
35	395653	1498	.003786	.018800	85002	1598	421195	.003794	2.612771	3073338	.017814	36.156	35
40	348039	1745	.005014	.024831	83404	2071	412116	.005025	2.632183	2652143	.015495	31.799	40
45	332008	2417	.007280	.035803	81333	2912	399802	.007284	2.643229	2240027	-.004916	27.541	45
50	315404	3355	.010637	.051938	78421	4073	382512	.010648	2.644652	1840225	.005276	23.466	50
55	274893	4394	.015984	.077204	74348	5740	358186	.016025	2.638611	1457713	.015659	19.607	55
60	218202	5287	.024230	.115030	68608	7892	324290	.024336	2.624229	1099527	.024701	16.026	60
65	162233	6054	.037317	.172047	60716	10446	278515	.037506	2.600557	775237	.028104	12.768	65
70	110944	6490	.058498	.257291	50270	12934	219852	.058831	2.564687	496721	.028427	9.881	70
75	67104	6420	.095672	.387347	37336	14462	150377	.096172	2.489743	276870	.022036	7.416	75
80	34038	5019	.147453	.534318	22874	12222	82475	.148190	2.390362	126493	.022036	5.530	80
85+	15889	3845	.241991	1.000000	10652	10652	44018	.241991	4.132380	44018	.000000	4.132	85+

NUMBER OF PERSONS DYING (OUT OF 100,000 AT BIRTH) ABOVE AGE X FROM SPECIFIED CAUSES

Age (x)	All Causes	Respiratory T.B.	Other Infec. and Paras.	Neo-plasms	Cardio-vascular	Infl., Pneu., Bronch.	Diar-rheal	Certain Degen-erative	Maternal	Cert. Dis. of Infancy	Motor Vehicle	Other Violence	Other and Unknown	Age (x)
0	100000	3102	2696	12300	40283	6699	1245	10491	0	3226	1708	5902	12348	0
1	92416	3076	2304	12291	40265	5220	384	10472	0	0	1705	5794	10905	1
5	90796	3039	2016	12250	40220	4838	203	10457	0	0	1652	5581	10540	5
10	90036	3005	1875	12220	40180	4780	189	10442	0	0	1568	5428	10349	10
15	89400	2960	1779	12188	40122	4751	185	10421	0	0	1510	5291	10193	15
20	88518	2843	1685	12147	40063	4700	182	10390	0	0	1424	5050	10034	20
25	87385	2630	1600	12107	39978	4658	181	10350	0	0	1322	4681	9878	25
30	86208	2380	1525	12057	39878	4601	175	10300	0	0	1208	4328	9756	30
35	85002	2153	1455	11960	39727	4566	170	10222	0	0	1105	4040	9604	35
40	83404	1897	1383	11800	39462	4503	164	10084	0	0	1015	3711	9415	40
45	81333	1628	1247	11558	38935	4428	152	9913	0	0	928	3385	9159	45
50	78421	1359	1126	11153	38075	4303	147	9601	0	0	791	3018	8848	50
55	74348	1107	969	10515	36570	4130	139	9158	0	0	683	2654	8423	55
60	68608	851	750	9480	34257	3885	121	8536	0	0	576	2268	7884	60
65	60716	591	530	7956	30814	3582	109	7655	0	0	434	1832	7213	65
70	50270	335	336	6063	25870	3142	98	6410	0	0	305	1471	6240	70
75	37336	177	157	3862	19468	2565	84	4774	0	0	198	1125	4926	75
80	22874	76	86	1904	11870	1798	62	2878	0	0	111	717	3372	80
85+	10652	19	33	626	5516	953	28	1308	0	0	30	360	1779	85+

NUMBER OF PERSONS SURVIVING TO AGE X IF SPECIFIED CAUSES WERE ELIMINATED

Age (x)	No Causes	Respiratory T.B. (1)	Other Infec. and Paras. (2)	Neo-plasms (3)	Cardio-vascular (4)	Infl., Pneu., Bronch. (5)	Diar-rheal (6)	Certain Degen-erative (7)	Maternal (8)	Cert. Dis. of Infancy (9)	Motor Vehicle (10)	Other Violence (11)	Other and Unknown (12)	(1)+(2)	(1)+(2)+(5)+(6)+(8)	(1)+(2)+(5)+(6)+(8)+part of(9)&(12)	(10)+(11)	Age (x)
0	100000	100000	100000	100000	100000	100000	100000	100000	100000	100000	100000	100000	100000	100000	100000	100000	100000	0
1	92416	92441	92794	92425	92433	93848	93247	92434	92416	95569	92419	92520	93813	92819	95105	99576	92523	1
5	90796	90857	91454	90845	90858	92569	91794	90829	90796	93894	90851	91110	92537	91516	94348	99062	91165	5
10	90036	90131	90830	90115	90137	91873	91040	90083	90036	93108	90175	90500	91956	90925	93814	98592	90639	10
15	89400	89539	90285	89510	89558	91253	90401	89468	89400	92450	89596	89998	91446	90425	93332	98148	90195	15
20	88518	88772	89489	88668	88733	90405	89512	88616	88518	91538	88797	89352	90725	89746	92687	97533	89634	20
25	87385	87848	88429	87573	87682	89290	88367	87522	87385	90366	87763	88579	89723	88898	91856	96719	88962	25
30	86208	86915	87313	86443	86601	88145	87183	86393	86208	89149	86694	87742	88639	88029	91025	95893	88237	30
35	85002	85927	86162	85330	85540	86948	85968	85262	85002	87902	85554	86806	87554	87099	90106	94978	87401	35
40	83404	84568	84645	83885	84197	85377	84358	83796	83404	86250	84065	85508	86101	85826	88861	93730	86185	40
45	81333	82738	82649	82043	82634	83333	82275	81885	81333	84108	82064	83715	84225	84077	87142	91990	84468	45
50	78421	80044	79811	79508	80538	80475	79334	79263	78421	81597	79262	81089	81526	81463	84570	89344	81959	50
55	74348	76137	75821	76012	77676	76468	75222	75583	74348	76885	75251	77244	77723	77646	80799	85437	78183	55
60	68608	70511	70182	71167	74230	70807	69432	70358	68608	70949	69546	71666	72265	72129	75335	79744	72646	60
65	60716	62651	62320	64484	69291	62957	61457	63120	60716	62788	61681	63851	64620	64306	67493	71525	64865	65
70	50270	52111	51778	55246	62736	52542	50893	53451	50270	51985	51187	53209	54453	53675	56796	60289	54180	70
75	37336	38842	38613	43154	53993	39546	37811	41221	37336	38610	38110	39834	41684	40171	43089	45850	40660	75
80	22874	23877	23711	28234	42800	24869	23183	26928	22874	23654	23417	24744	26922	24750	27272	29134	25331	80
85+	10652	11159	11078	14242	29655	12209	10819	13834	10652	11015	10960	11783	13850	11605	13510	14567	12124	85+

ADDED YRS OF LIFE

	No Causes	(1)	(2)	(3)	(4)	(5)	(6)	(7)	(8)	(9)	(10)	(11)	(12)	(1)+(2)	...	...	(10)+(11)
TOTAL		.878	.982	1.665	6.259	1.802	.711	1.257	.000	2.102	.493	1.614	2.742	1.881	4.515	8.184	2.128
WORK	4.755	.560	.250	.461	.975	.181	.014	.336	.000	.000	.258	.831	.521	.815	1.015	1.163	1.095

POPULATION, DEATHS, DEATH RATES FOR ALL CAUSES COMBINED, AND SPECIFIED CAUSES

Age Start of Interval	Midyear Population	Deaths During Year	All Causes	Respiratory T. B.	Other Infec. and Paras.	Neoplasms	Cardiovascular	Infl., Pneu., Bronch.	Diarrheal	Certain Degenerative	Maternal	Cert. Dis. of Infancy	Motor Vehicle	Other Violence	Other and Unknown	Age Start of Interval
0	105424	6449	.06117	.00018	.00355	.00004	.00014	.01222	.00659	.00015	.00000	.02383	.00002	.00120	.01286	0
1	411492	1566	.00381	.00012	.00077	.00010	.00008	.00093	.00039	.00004	.00000	.00000	.00011	.00036	.00090	1
5	515791	670	.00130	.00009	.00031	.00007	.00008	.00013	.00002	.00003	.00000	.00000	.00009	.00015	.00034	5
10	543815	536	.00099	.00016	.00016	.00003	.00012	.00007	.00000	.00004	.00000	.00000	.00003	.00009	.00028	10
15	554190	823	.00149	.00048	.00019	.00006	.00015	.00007	.00001	.00006	.00008	.00000	.00006	.00007	.00025	15
20	513846	1039	.00202	.00072	.00015	.00006	.00021	.00007	.00000	.00010	.00031	.00000	.00006	.00009	.00026	20
25	478017	1174	.00246	.00079	.00017	.00015	.00024	.00009	.00001	.00007	.00045	.00000	.00004	.00013	.00029	25
30	411703	1148	.00279	.00063	.00017	.00033	.00034	.00010	.00001	.00013	.00049	.00000	.00005	.00011	.00042	30
35	362690	1242	.00342	.00052	.00012	.00069	.00050	.00012	.00001	.00027	.00051	.00000	.00005	.00015	.00048	35
40	327566	1464	.00447	.00050	.00016	.00119	.00098	.00014	.00001	.00040	.00025	.00000	.00005	.00014	.00065	40
45	302361	1817	.00601	.00038	.00020	.00182	.00158	.00021	.00001	.00076	.00002	.00000	.00005	.00022	.00074	45
50	275611	2227	.00808	.00024	.00017	.00258	.00255	.00025	.00002	.00091	.00000	.00000	.00005	.00023	.00107	50
55	231450	2851	.01232	.00036	.00025	.00352	.00447	.00035	.00002	.00163	.00000	.00000	.00010	.00021	.00140	55
60	188415	3483	.01849	.00046	.00023	.00461	.00748	.00070	.00002	.00275	.00000	.00000	.00013	.00042	.00170	60
65	145099	4412	.03041	.00042	.00029	.00669	.01367	.00110	.00008	.00479	.00000	.00000	.00019	.00064	.00256	65
70	105878	4980	.04704	.00050	.00043	.00757	.02374	.00237	.00009	.00710	.00000	.00000	.00022	.00113	.00388	70
75	68457	5460	.07976	.00058	.00044	.01058	.04257	.00463	.00028	.01112	.00000	.00000	.00025	.00253	.00679	75
80	37410	4905	.13111	.00045	.00035	.01235	.07132	.01005	.00045	.01625	.00000	.00000	.00019	.00599	.01371	80
85+	19815	4541	.22917	.00030	.00061	.01241	.11986	.02397	.00066	.02160	.00000	.00000	.00015	.01292	.03669	85+
ALL	5599030	50787														

			All Causes	Respiratory T. B.	Other Infec. and Paras.	Neoplasms	Cardiovascular	Infl., Pneu., Bronch.	Diarrheal	Certain Degenerative	Maternal	Cert. Dis. of Infancy	Motor Vehicle	Other Violence	Other and Unknown
CRUDE DEATH RATE			.00907	.00042	.00031	.00128	.00307	.00071	.00017	.00091	.00016	.00045	.00007	.00032	.00119
STANDARDIZED RATE (1)			.00736	.00038	.00040	.00084	.00168	.00077	.00029	.00054	.00015	.00084	.00007	.00026	.00114
STANDARDIZED RATE (2)			.01101	.00041	.00033	.00156	.00401	.00084	.00019	.00117	.00015	.00049	.00008	.00039	.00139
GEOMETRIC MEAN			.00949												

LIFE TABLE FOR ALL CAUSES COMBINED

Age (x)	Midyear Population	Deaths During Year	$_nM_x$	$_nq_x$	l_x	$_nd_x$	$_nL_x$	$_nm_x$	$_na_x$	T_x	$_nr_x$	$\overset{\circ}{e}_x$	Age (x)
0	105424	6449	.061172	.058230	100000	5823	95190	.061172	.173992	6548374	.000000	65.484	0
1	411492	1566	.003806	.015078	94177	1420	373158	.003805	1.500000	6453184	.000000	68.522	1
5	515791	670	.001299	.006479	92757	601	462283	.001300	2.500000	6080026	.000000	65.548	5
10	543815	536	.000986	.004916	92156	453	459664	.000986	2.535412	5617744	-.008329	60.959	10
15	554190	823	.001485	.007393	91703	678	456517	.001484	2.642576	5158080	-.000080	56.248	15
20	513846	1039	.002022	.010074	91025	917	452921	.002025	2.596101	4701163	.008774	51.647	20
25	478017	1174	.002456	.012219	90108	1101	447854	.002458	2.559983	4248243	.016103	47.146	25
30	411703	1148	.002788	.013864	89007	1234	442032	.002792	2.566349	3800389	.023511	42.698	30
35	362690	1242	.003424	.017021	87773	1494	435271	.003432	2.594405	3358357	.021195	38.262	35
40	327566	1464	.004469	.022149	86279	1911	426828	.004477	2.609999	2923086	.016058	33.879	40
45	302361	1817	.006009	.029668	84368	2503	415862	.006019	2.611699	2496259	.011354	29.588	45
50	275611	2227	.008080	.039736	81865	3253	401655	.008099	2.642176	2080397	.015434	25.413	50
55	231450	2851	.012318	.060080	78612	4723	381945	.012366	2.646579	1678742	.022828	21.355	55
60	188415	3483	.018486	.088958	73889	6576	354019	.018575	2.654191	1296797	.026225	17.551	60
65	145099	4412	.030407	.142469	67313	9590	313772	.030564	2.623306	942778	.026628	14.006	65
70	105878	4980	.047035	.212255	57723	12252	259159	.047276	2.595784	629005	.026154	10.897	70
75	68457	5460	.079758	.334785	45471	15223	189853	.080183	2.536485	369847	.022470	8.134	75
80	37410	4905	.131115	.493190	30248	14918	113100	.131901	2.443371	179994	.022470	5.951	80
85+	19815	4541	.229170	1.000000	15330	15330	66894	.229170	4.363576	66894	.000000	4.364	85+

NUMBER OF PERSONS DYING (OUT OF 100,000 AT BIRTH) ABOVE AGE X FROM SPECIFIED CAUSES

Age (x)	All Causes	Respiratory T. B.	Other Infec. and Paras.	Neoplasms	Cardiovascular	Infl., Pneu., Bronch.	Diarrheal	Certain Degenerative	Maternal	Cert. Dis. of Infancy	Motor Vehicle	Other Violence	Other and Unknown	Age (x)
0	100000	2757	1996	14280	42004	7034	1030	11583	941	2268	558	3605	11904	0
1	94177	2780	1620	14276	41990	5871	403	11568	941	0	557	3491	10680	1
5	92757	2736	1333	14240	41962	5524	256	11552	941	0	517	3355	10341	5
10	92156	2696	1191	14209	41926	5466	247	11537	941	0	475	3286	10182	10
15	91703	2623	1117	14196	41871	5433	245	11516	941	0	459	3247	10055	15
20	91025	2405	1031	14169	41804	5400	243	11487	903	0	432	3214	9937	20
25	90108	2079	963	14140	41710	5370	242	11443	761	0	405	3175	9820	25
30	89007	1723	889	14074	41600	5329	236	11410	558	0	381	3117	9690	30
35	87773	1444	815	13928	41452	5284	231	11351	340	0	358	3066	9504	35
40	86279	1216	763	13626	41232	5231	225	11234	119	0	337	3000	9296	40
45	84368	1002	695	13118	40811	5171	220	11063	13	0	316	2940	9019	45
50	81865	845	614	12358	40152	5082	216	10746	4	0	293	2848	8707	50
55	78612	750	547	11320	39124	4980	207	10378	4	0	271	2756	8275	55
60	73889	613	450	9973	37409	4843	200	9753	2	0	233	2675	7738	60
65	67313	451	367	8337	34745	4596	195	8774	2	0	188	2526	7132	65
70	57723	319	276	6233	30428	4247	171	7263	2	0	136	2323	6325	70
75	45471	189	165	4266	24238	3628	148	5414	2	0	79	2027	5315	75
80	30248	78	82	2251	16110	2743	95	3294	2	0	32	1544	4017	80
85+	15330	20	41	830	8018	1604	44	1445	0	0	10	864	2454	85+

NUMBER OF PERSONS SURVIVING TO AGE X IF SPECIFIED CAUSES WERE ELIMINATED

Age (x)	No Causes	Respiratory T. B. (1)	Other Infec. and Paras. (2)	Neoplasms (3)	Cardiovascular (4)	Infl., Pneu., Bronch. (5)	Diarrheal (6)	Certain Degenerative (7)	Maternal (8)	Cert. Dis. of Infancy (9)	Motor Vehicle (10)	Other Violence (11)	Other and Unknown (12)	(1)+(2)	(1)+(2)+(5)+(6)+(8)	(1)+(2)+(5)+(6)+(8)+part of(9)&(12)	(10)+(11)	Age (x)
0	100000	100000	100000	100000	100000	100000	100000	100000	100000	100000	100000	100000	100000	100000	100000	100000	100000	0
1	94177	94193	94543	94181	94191	95312	94787	94192	94177	96404	94178	94288	95372	94559	96319	99620	94289	1
5	92757	92817	93403	92757	92798	94224	93505	92787	92757	94950	92758	93001	94275	93464	95708	99262	93042	5
10	92156	92255	92941	92226	92233	93673	92908	92201	92156	94335	92238	92468	93826	93041	95344	98981	92550	10
15	91703	91875	92558	91786	91834	93246	92454	91769	91703	93871	91801	92052	93494	92732	95064	98765	92150	15
20	91025	91414	91961	91134	91222	92590	91119	91063	91025	93177	91149	91405	92922	92353	94751	98526	91529	20
25	90108	90819	91103	90245	90357	91687	90849	90245	90287	92238	90258	90523	92105	91821	94386	98236	90673	25
30	89007	90066	90064	89208	89402	90608	89745	89175	89386	91111	89179	89475	91112	91136	93943	97875	89647	30
35	87773	89098	88890	88117	88311	89398	88505	87998	88365	89848	87965	88285	90038	90232	93293	97319	88478	35
40	86279	87812	87429	86918	87027	87930	87005	86616	87081	88319	86489	86848	88717	88982	92297	96380	87059	40
45	84368	86082	85560	85501	85521	86042	85083	84868	85258	86363	84594	84984	87034	87299	90733	94832	85212	45
50	81865	83686	83103	83727	83645	83579	82562	82665	82738	83800	82107	82554	84770	84951	88401	92449	82798	50
55	78612	80456	79867	81146	81357	80360	79291	79745	79450	80471	78866	79365	81841	81740	85178	89124	79621	55
60	73889	75758	75164	77917	78210	75668	74534	74534	74678	75636	74165	74676	77467	77065	80460	84242	74954	60
65	67313	69174	68555	72646	73994	69176	67905	69808	68032	68904	67607	68174	71181	70450	73817	77342	68472	65
70	57723	59444	58874	64426	68004	59654	58253	61330	58340	59088	58024	58652	61834	60629	63908	67018	58957	70
75	45471	46944	46477	52722	60441	47564	45909	50080	45957	46546	45758	46471	49676	47983	51217	53793	46764	75
80	30248	31320	30985	37001	45989	32402	30583	35252	30571	30963	30477	31318	34216	32083	35120	36991	31555	80
85+	15330	15915	15733	20006	36629	17296	15536	19436	15495	15692	15461	16372	18621	16333	18877	20021	16512	85+

ADDED YRS OF LIFE

	No Causes	(1)	(2)	(3)	(4)	(5)	(6)	(7)	(8)	(9)	(10)	(11)	(12)	(1)+(2)	(1)+(2)+(5)+(6)+(8)	+part of(9)&(12)	(10)+(11)
TOTAL		.980	.872	2.262	6.465	1.630	.559	1.428	.388	1.544	.169	.617	2.629	1.868	4.575	7.641	.789
WORK	4.033	.638	.184	.715	.769	.132	.011	.309	.313	.000	.062	.140	.505	.825	1.293	1.506	.203

POPULATION, DEATHS, DEATH RATES FOR ALL CAUSES COMBINED, AND SPECIFIED CAUSES

Age Start of Interval	Midyear Population	Deaths During Year	All Causes	Respiratory T.B.	Other Infec. and Paras.	Neoplasms	Cardiovascular	Infl., Pneu., Bronch.	Diarrheal	Certain Degenerative	Maternal	Cert. Dis. of Infancy	Motor Vehicle	Other Violence	Other and Unknown	Age Start of Interval
0	182022	8328	.04575	.00007	.00114	.00008	.00012	.00637	.00255	.00011	.00000	.02348	.00005	.00133	.01045	0
1	702674	1401	.00199	.00005	.00024	.00012	.00002	.00039	.00008	.00003	.00000	.00000	.00018	.00042	.00045	1
5	718674	699	.00097	.00002	.00012	.00007	.00003	.00006	.00002	.00003	.00000	.00000	.00024	.00024	.00013	5
10	579074	452	.00078	.00002	.00009	.00007	.00005	.00003	.00002	.00003	.00000	.00000	.00013	.00028	.00008	10
15	535782	715	.00133	.00010	.00007	.00009	.00008	.00006	.00000	.00004	.00000	.00000	.00030	.00045	.00015	15
20	540534	1005	.00186	.00019	.00008	.00013	.00010	.00004	.00000	.00006	.00000	.00000	.00045	.00066	.00015	20
25	556008	985	.00177	.00023	.00008	.00012	.00017	.00003	.00002	.00009	.00000	.00000	.00030	.00058	.00016	25
30	515655	1062	.00206	.00022	.00006	.00020	.00035	.00005	.00001	.00014	.00000	.00000	.00027	.00056	.00020	30
35	506876	1279	.00252	.00026	.00008	.00029	.00061	.00007	.00002	.00016	.00000	.00000	.00026	.00058	.00020	35
40	448729	1750	.00390	.00031	.00006	.00047	.00140	.00009	.00002	.00025	.00000	.00000	.00026	.00065	.00039	40
45	390287	2450	.00628	.00031	.00011	.00098	.00274	.00017	.00002	.00037	.00000	.00000	.00031	.00076	.00050	45
50	342841	3515	.01025	.00039	.00011	.00179	.00498	.00021	.00003	.00070	.00000	.00000	.00030	.00086	.00089	50
55	294712	4730	.01605	.00052	.00026	.00306	.00843	.00042	.00004	.00094	.00000	.00000	.00036	.00092	.00112	55
60	266229	6453	.02424	.00063	.00024	.00470	.01348	.00071	.00004	.00126	.00000	.00000	.00034	.00098	.00186	60
65	229816	7998	.03480	.00067	.00027	.00681	.01962	.00120	.00003	.00190	.00000	.00000	.00044	.00112	.00274	65
70	161611	8736	.05406	.00067	.00025	.00929	.03193	.00237	.00009	.00275	.00000	.00000	.00054	.00129	.00487	70
75	94821	8245	.08695	.00077	.00020	.01296	.05253	.00479	.00022	.00426	.00000	.00000	.00060	.00197	.00865	75
80	46310	6224	.13440	.00067	.00022	.01578	.08195	.01080	.00015	.00570	.00000	.00000	.00082	.00311	.01520	80
85+	22915	5326	.23242	.00061	.00044	.01763	.14650	.02151	.00048	.00908	.00000	.00000	.00065	.00655	.02898	85+
ALL	7135570	71353														

	All Causes	Respiratory T.B.	Other Infec. and Paras.	Neoplasms	Cardiovascular	Infl., Pneu., Bronch.	Diarrheal	Certain Degenerative	Maternal	Cert. Dis. of Infancy	Motor Vehicle	Other Violence	Other and Unknown
CRUDE DEATH RATE	.01000	.00024	.00015	.00132	.00449	.00059	.00009	.00045	.00000	.00060	.00029	.00066	.00111
STANDARDIZED RATE (1)	.00686	.00018	.00016	.00076	.00235	.00047	.00011	.00027	.00000	.00083	.00027	.00058	.00088
STANDARDIZED RATE (2)	.01133	.00025	.00015	.00154	.00544	.00065	.00008	.00052	.00000	.00049	.00030	.00069	.00121
GEOMETRIC MEAN	.00877												

LIFE TABLE FOR ALL CAUSES COMBINED

Age (x)	Midyear Population	Deaths During Year	$_nM_x$	$_nq_x$	l_x	$_nd_x$	$_nL_x$	$_nm_x$	$_na_x$	T_x	$_nr_x$	$\overset{\circ}{e}_x$	Age (x)
0	182022	8328	.045753	.044040	100000	4404	96247	.045757	.147780	6637705	.000000	66.377	0
1	702674	1401	.001994	.007929	95596	758	380489	.001992	1.500000	6541459	.000000	68.428	1
5	718674	699	.000973	.004850	94838	460	473040	.000972	2.500000	6160970	.000000	64.963	5
10	579074	452	.000781	.003899	94378	368	471005	.000781	2.594543	5687930	.025326	60.268	10
15	535782	715	.001334	.006670	94010	627	468586	.001338	2.664806	5216925	.012460	55.493	15
20	540534	1005	.001859	.009252	93383	864	464794	.001859	2.545573	4748339	.002551	50.848	20
25	556008	985	.001772	.008820	92519	816	460571	.001772	2.519404	4283545	.000862	46.299	25
30	515655	1062	.002060	.010250	91703	940	456232	.002060	2.571587	3822974	.005442	41.689	30
35	506876	1279	.002523	.012543	90763	1139	451134	.002525	2.646144	3366742	.007861	37.094	35
40	448729	1750	.003900	.019403	89624	1739	444104	.003916	2.690603	2915608	.019014	32.532	40
45	390287	2450	.006277	.031063	87885	2730	433129	.006303	2.693834	2471504	.020292	28.122	45
50	342841	3515	.010253	.050250	85155	4279	415814	.010291	2.672207	2038374	.019281	23.937	50
55	294712	4730	.016050	.077489	80876	6267	389602	.016086	2.641914	1622560	.013133	20.062	55
60	266229	6453	.024239	.114571	74609	8548	352582	.024244	2.606068	1232958	.001652	16.526	60
65	229816	7998	.034802	.160745	66061	10619	304749	.034845	2.593327	880377	.007753	13.327	65
70	161611	8736	.054056	.239981	55442	13305	244891	.054330	2.570885	575628	.026011	10.383	70
75	94821	8245	.086953	.359447	42137	15146	172869	.087615	2.503260	330737	.034142	7.849	75
80	46310	6224	.134399	.501723	26991	13542	100004	.135415	2.419064	157868	.034142	5.849	80
85+	22915	5326	.232424	1.000000	13449	13449	57864	.232424	4.302478	57864	.000000	4.302	85+

NUMBER OF PERSONS DYING (OUT OF 100,000 AT BIRTH) ABOVE AGE X FROM SPECIFIED CAUSES

Age (x)	All Causes	Respiratory T. B.	Other Infec. and Paras.	Neoplasms	Cardiovascular	Infl., Pneu., Bronch.	Diarrheal	Certain Degenerative	Maternal	Cert. Dis. of Infancy	Motor Vehicle	Other Violence	Other and Unknown	Age (x)
0	100000	1977	999	13963	52322	5642	485	4746	0	2261	2102	5218	10285	0
1	95596	1970	890	13955	52311	5029	239	4736	0	1	2097	5090	9278	1
5	94838	1950	797	13910	52303	4880	208	4723	0	0	2030	4930	9107	5
10	94378	1941	738	13878	52288	4851	198	4710	0	0	1914	4816	9044	10
15	94010	1930	658	13845	52264	4838	197	4697	0	0	1854	4683	9004	15
20	93383	1881	667	13803	52225	4812	195	4679	0	0	1715	4474	8932	20
25	92519	1793	630	13744	52180	4793	194	4649	0	0	1508	4165	8863	25
30	91703	1687	594	13691	52101	4781	187	4609	0	0	1369	3897	8787	30
35	90763	1565	565	13600	51941	4760	182	4546	0	0	1246	3639	8699	35
40	89624	1467	529	13469	51667	4730	173	4475	0	0	1127	3378	8609	40
45	87885	1330	501	13259	51042	4691	165	4363	0	0	1011	3089	8434	45
50	85155	1195	453	12831	49851	4615	159	4200	0	0	877	2758	8216	50
55	80876	1034	410	12083	47770	4529	146	3909	0	0	753	2399	7843	55
60	74609	831	309	10889	44479	4365	130	3544	0	0	614	2042	7406	60
65	66061	607	225	9232	39723	4116	115	3100	0	0	495	1698	6750	65
70	55442	405	143	7153	33736	3750	105	2520	0	0	361	1357	5912	70
75	42137	239	83	4870	25874	3165	82	1843	0	0	227	1040	4714	75
80	26991	106	48	2617	16722	2328	43	1101	0	0	123	697	3206	80
85+	13449	35	25	1020	8477	1245	28	525	0	0	38	379	1677	85+

NUMBER OF PERSONS SURVIVING TO AGE X IF SPECIFIED CAUSES WERE ELIMINATED

Age (x)	No Causes	Respiratory T. B. (1)	Other Infec. and Paras. (2)	Neoplasms (3)	Cardiovascular (4)	Infl., Pneu., Bronch. (5)	Diarrheal (6)	Certain Degenerative (7)	Maternal (8)	Cert. Dis. of Infancy (9)	Motor Vehicle (10)	Other Violence (11)	Other and Unknown (12)	(1)+(2)	(1)+(2)+(5)+(6)+(8)	(1)+(2)+(5)+(6)+(8)+part of(9)&(12)	(10)+(11)	Age (x)
0	100000	100000	100000	100000	100000	100000	100000	100000	100000	100000	100000	100000	100000	100000	100000	100000	100000	0
1	95596	95603	95703	95604	95607	96197	95837	95606	95596	97831	95601	95721	96586	95709	96554	99360	95726	1
5	94838	94865	95037	94891	94857	95584	95108	94861	94838	97057	94910	95122	95992	95063	96084	98566	95194	5
10	94378	94414	94635	94462	94412	95149	94657	94414	94378	96586	94565	94775	95590	94670	95726	98615	94963	10
15	94010	94056	94306	94127	94067	94791	94288	94058	94010	96209	94256	94539	95258	94352	95518	98306	94786	15
20	93383	93478	93708	93541	93479	94185	93662	93449	93383	95567	93767	94118	94695	93803	94891	97778	94505	20
25	92519	92701	92878	92734	92659	93333	92796	92614	92519	94683	93106	93557	93889	93060	94160	97038	94151	25
30	91703	91989	92094	91969	91920	92522	91985	91837	91703	93848	92424	93002	93137	92382	93493	96367	93734	30
35	90763	91148	91179	91138	91318	91955	91047	90955	90763	92886	91600	92310	92272	91566	92694	95561	93162	35
40	89624	90122	90071	90105	90268	90475	89913	89888	89624	91721	90570	91415	91205	90572	91727	94581	92381	40
45	87885	88510	88351	88566	89143	88759	88176	88255	87885	89941	88929	89934	89612	88979	90162	92952	91002	45
50	85155	85894	85654	86241	87571	86077	85443	85675	85155	87147	86300	87474	87047	86398	87629	90404	88650	50
55	80876	81736	81392	82649	85283	81837	81163	81656	80876	82768	82086	83438	83045	82258	83530	86205	84686	55
60	74609	75600	75183	77425	82080	75655	74889	75683	74609	76354	75860	77326	77042	76181	77539	80059	78623	60
65	66061	67151	66649	70191	77768	67225	66323	67436	66061	67606	67283	68802	68856	67749	69216	71514	70074	65
70	55442	56544	56010	60962	72048	56762	55671	57140	55442	56739	56592	58067	58593	57124	58725	60732	59271	70
75	42137	43121	42621	48558	64403	43666	42331	44637	42137	43123	43129	44420	45648	43616	45407	47039	45466	75
80	26991	27728	27329	33221	54000	28673	27146	28828	26991	27622	27710	28741	30569	28075	29996	31181	29507	80
85+	13449	13867	13633	17971	41121	15106	13537	14797	13449	13764	13868	14557	16478	14057	15891	16648	15011	85+

ADDED YRS OF LIFE

	No Causes	(1)	(2)	(3)	(4)	(5)	(6)	(7)	(8)	(9)	(10)	(11)	(12)	(1)+(2)	(1)+(2)+(5)+(6)+(8)	combined	(10)+(11)
TOTAL		.466	.353	1.904	9.696	.953	.224	.643	.000	1.549	.668	1.434	1.943	.823	2.072	4.256	2.125
WORK	3.871	.255	.091	.466	1.169	.088	.014	.199	.000	.000	.350	.679	.310	.347	.450	.494	1.036

POPULATION, DEATHS, DEATH RATES FOR ALL CAUSES COMBINED, AND SPECIFIED CAUSES

Age Start of Interval	Midyear Population	Deaths During Year	All Causes	Respiratory T. B.	Other Infec. and Paras.	Neo-plasms	Cardio-vascular	Infl., Pneu., Bronch.	Diar-rheal	Certain Degen-erative	Maternal	Cert. Dis. of Infancy	Motor Vehicle	Other Violence	Other and Unknown	Age Start of Interval
0	174181	6265	.03597	.00003	.00104	.00015	.00009	.00535	.00202	.00005	.00000	.01697	.00002	.00119	.00907	0
1	674817	1128	.00167	.00004	.00025	.00010	.00003	.00038	.00007	.00002	.00000	.00000	.00013	.00023	.00042	1
5	689034	458	.00066	.00003	.00009	.00006	.00004	.00007	.00000	.00002	.00000	.00000	.00012	.00008	.00015	5
10	559861	276	.00049	.00005	.00008	.00006	.00004	.00003	.00001	.00002	.00000	.00000	.00004	.00006	.00010	10
15	529817	449	.00085	.00017	.00010	.00006	.00006	.00005	.00001	.00004	.00003	.00000	.00012	.00006	.00014	15
20	555320	543	.00098	.00019	.00008	.00007	.00011	.00003	.00001	.00006	.00014	.00000	.00008	.00010	.00012	20
25	582699	654	.00112	.00024	.00006	.00014	.00013	.00003	.00001	.00005	.00015	.00000	.00004	.00009	.00018	25
30	534211	772	.00145	.00025	.00006	.00030	.00022	.00003	.00001	.00009	.00016	.00000	.00004	.00008	.00019	30
35	499432	1011	.00202	.00020	.00004	.00060	.00040	.00007	.00002	.00011	.00018	.00000	.00006	.00012	.00023	35
40	426185	1259	.00295	.00022	.00006	.00099	.00081	.00007	.00001	.00014	.00010	.00000	.00006	.00012	.00037	40
45	359924	1603	.00445	.00021	.00007	.00163	.00140	.00011	.00002	.00029	.00002	.00000	.00007	.00016	.00046	45
50	324877	2076	.00639	.00016	.00006	.00229	.00243	.00021	.00002	.00034	.00001	.00000	.00009	.00017	.00060	50
55	280469	2827	.01008	.00017	.00007	.00314	.00445	.00024	.00001	.00072	.00000	.00000	.00012	.00024	.00091	55
60	243914	3896	.01597	.00022	.00009	.00427	.00813	.00052	.00005	.00107	.00000	.00000	.00009	.00028	.00125	60
65	207208	5115	.02469	.00029	.00011	.00542	.01373	.00079	.00007	.00176	.00000	.00000	.00010	.00037	.00205	65
70	156038	6432	.04122	.00033	.00011	.00719	.02474	.00188	.00013	.00281	.00000	.00000	.00022	.00065	.00315	70
75	95088	6902	.07259	.00041	.00022	.01021	.04586	.00411	.00021	.00428	.00001	.00000	.00014	.00167	.00546	75
80	51268	6122	.11941	.00033	.00021	.01190	.07767	.00852	.00029	.00651	.00000	.00000	.00023	.00386	.00987	80
85+	30050	6313	.21008	.00027	.00027	.01448	.13478	.01947	.00067	.00722	.00000	.00000	.00013	.00935	.02346	85+
ALL	6974393	54101														

CRUDE DEATH RATE			.00776	.00016	.00012	.00125	.00352	.00051	.00008	.00039	.00006	.00042	.00009	.00026	.00089	
STANDARDIZED RATE (1)			.00508	.00014	.00013	.00077	.00168	.00039	.00009	.00022	.00005	.00060	.00009	.00020	.00072	
STANDARDIZED RATE (2)			.00865	.00017	.00011	.00143	.00417	.00054	.00007	.00046	.00005	.00035	.00009	.00028	.00093	
GEOMETRIC MEAN			.00627													

LIFE TABLE FOR ALL CAUSES COMBINED

Age (x)	Midyear Population	Deaths During Year	$_nM_x$	$_nq_x$	l_x	$_nd_x$	$_nL_x$	$_nm_x$	$_na_x$	T_x	$_nr_x$	$\overset{\circ}{e}_x$	Age (x)
0	174181	6265	.035968	.034880	100000	3488	96969	.035970	.131146	7079482	.000000	70.795	0
1	674817	1128	.001672	.006652	96512	642	384443	.001670	1.500000	6982513	.000000	72.349	1
5	689034	458	.000665	.003317	95870	318	478555	.000665	2.500000	6598070	.000000	68.823	5
10	559861	276	.000493	.002470	95552	236	477188	.000495	2.575035	6119515	.023688	64.044	10
15	529817	449	.000847	.004228	95316	403	475620	.000847	2.617349	5642327	.007918	59.196	15
20	555320	543	.000978	.004878	94913	463	473434	.000978	2.556246	5166707	-.008104	54.436	20
25	582699	654	.001122	.005590	94450	528	470975	.001121	2.584833	4693274	-.001678	49.691	25
30	534211	772	.001445	.007219	93922	678	468001	.001449	2.626905	4222299	.009528	44.955	30
35	499432	1011	.002024	.010092	93244	941	464010	.002028	2.650992	3754298	.016068	40.263	35
40	426185	1259	.002967	.014734	92303	1360	458338	.002967	2.664062	3290288	.027604	35.647	40
45	359924	1603	.004454	.022124	90943	2012	449987	.004471	2.650037	2831950	.024614	31.140	45
50	324877	2076	.006390	.031586	88931	2809	438100	.006412	2.666429	2381963	.019522	26.784	50
55	280469	2827	.010080	.049418	86122	4256	420701	.010116	2.671767	1943863	.019342	22.571	55
60	243914	3896	.015973	.077175	81866	6318	394490	.016016	2.651089	1523162	.014903	18.606	60
65	207208	5115	.024685	.116985	75548	8838	356954	.024760	2.648082	1128673	.015176	14.940	65
70	156038	6432	.041221	.188877	66710	12600	303710	.041487	2.631713	771719	.029375	11.568	70
75	95088	6902	.072585	.310553	54110	16804	229501	.073220	2.557216	468009	.035208	8.649	75
80	51268	6122	.119412	.461454	37306	17215	142874	.120490	2.464094	238508	.035208	6.393	80
85+	30050	6313	.210083	1.000000	20091	20091	95634	.210083	4.760019	95634	.000000	4.760	85+

NUMBER OF PERSONS DYING (OUT OF 100,000 AT BIRTH) ABOVE AGE X FROM SPECIFIED CAUSES

Age (x)	All Causes	Respira-tory T. B.	Other Infec. and Paras.	Neo-plasms	Cardio-vascular	Infl., Pneu., Bronch.	Diar-rheal	Certain Degen-erative	Maternal	Cert. Dis. of Infancy	Motor Vehicle	Other Violence	Other and Unknown	Age (x)
0	100000	1346	762	15477	54850	6197	519	5388	367	1646	660	3074	9714	0
1	96512	1342	661	15463	54841	5679	324	5383	367	1	659	2958	8834	1
5	95870	1326	566	15425	54830	5532	297	5374	367	0	607	2870	8676	5
10	95552	1314	521	15395	54813	5499	295	5363	367	0	551	2831	8603	10
15	95316	1291	483	15369	54792	5485	292	5351	366	0	531	2800	8556	15
20	94913	1212	437	15339	54761	5461	288	5331	351	0	474	2771	8488	20
25	94450	1123	401	15306	54709	5445	286	5303	287	0	434	2725	8431	25
30	93922	1010	374	15238	54648	5433	281	5278	218	0	414	2682	8346	30
35	93244	891	347	15096	54543	5417	274	5235	146	0	396	2642	8257	35
40	92303	797	330	14818	54355	5387	265	5185	63	0	367	2585	8151	40
45	90943	696	303	14363	53979	5353	261	5120	16	0	340	2528	7984	45
50	88931	601	272	13625	53344	5302	252	4989	6	0	310	2456	7774	50
55	86122	532	245	12618	52275	5208	244	4837	4	0	269	2381	7509	55
60	81866	462	213	11295	50392	5106	241	4533	4	0	217	2278	7125	60
65	75548	376	179	9607	47173	4900	222	4111	4	0	180	2168	6628	65
70	66710	272	141	7667	42255	4618	196	3480	4	0	145	2037	5895	70
75	54110	171	108	5475	34687	4040	155	2621	4	0	79	1838	4932	75
80	37306	76	57	3119	24064	3085	106	1632	1	0	47	1449	3670	80
85+	20091	25	25	1384	12889	1862	64	691	0	0	13	894	2244	85+

NUMBER OF PERSONS SURVIVING TO AGE X IF SPECIFIED CAUSES WERE ELIMINATED

Age (x)	No Causes	Respira-tory T. B.	Other Infec. and Paras.	Neo-plasms	Cardio-vascular	Infl., Pneu., Bronch.	Diar-rheal	Certain Degener-ative	Maternal	Cert. Dis. of Infancy	Motor Vehicle	Other Violence	Other and Unknown	(1) + (2)	(1) + (2) + (5) + (6) + (8)	(1)+(2)+ (5)+(6)+ (8)+part of(9)&(12)	(10) + (11)	Age (x)
		(1)	(2)	(3)	(4)	(5)	(6)	(7)	(8)	(9)	(10)	(11)	(12)					
0	100000	100000	100000	100000	100000	100000	100000	100000	100000	100000	100000	100000	100000	100000	100000	100000	100000	0
1	96512	96516	96611	96526	96521	97022	96704	96517	96512	98142	96513	96626	97380	96615	97319	99467	96627	1
5	95870	95890	96063	95922	95890	96524	96087	95884	95870	97490	95923	96071	96892	96083	96958	99195	96124	5
10	95552	95584	95790	95633	95589	96237	95771	95577	95552	97166	95661	95791	96644	95822	96730	98989	95900	10
15	95316	95371	95591	95423	95374	96014	95537	95353	95317	96926	95444	95586	96453	95646	96571	98847	95715	15
20	94913	95046	95233	95050	95001	95632	95137	94970	94929	96517	95098	95211	96114	95367	96332	98639	95396	20
25	94450	94672	94805	94619	94590	95181	94675	94534	94530	96046	94674	94792	95702	95027	96072	98402	95017	25
30	93922	94255	94302	94158	94122	94661	94151	94031	94070	95509	94165	94306	95253	94636	95765	98133	94549	30
35	93244	93694	93648	93620	93547	93994	93478	93395	93463	94819	93503	93665	94656	94100	95319	97713	93925	35
40	92303	92843	92720	92954	92791	93076	92544	92502	92603	93862	92588	92777	93807	93262	94594	97001	93063	40
45	90943	91575	91381	92040	91800	91738	91184	91204	91285	92480	91251	91466	92594	92016	93417	95826	91776	45
50	88931	89644	89390	90745	90405	89560	89176	89316	89275	90434	89262	89514	90757	90106	91549	93934	89847	50
55	86122	86881	86593	88856	88626	87018	86637	86645	86457	87577	86483	86761	88157	87356	88860	91196	87125	55
60	81866	82656	82345	85844	86158	82818	82102	82662	82185	83249	82260	82575	84184	83140	84677	86925	82972	60
65	75548	76360	76023	80935	82832	76627	75784	76693	75842	76824	75947	76309	78180	76840	78486	80599	76712	65
70	66710	67526	67165	73440	78390	67933	66943	68325	66970	67837	67095	67506	69745	67987	69745	71664	67896	70
75	54110	54863	54509	61769	72110	55635	54336	56215	54321	55024	54442	54938	57487	55268	57285	58922	55315	75
80	37306	37904	37623	44848	62902	39180	37502	39611	37454	37936	37588	38206	40756	38226	40518	41762	38496	80
85+	20091	20450	20285	25707	50625	22049	20227	22067	20171	20430	20268	20991	23104	20648	22905	23712	21175	85+

ADDED YRS OF LIFE																		
TOTAL		.412	.322	2.455	10.242	1.013	.201	.677	.157	1.194	.230	.536	1.900	.736	2.139	4.017	.769	
WORK	2.645	.235	.078	.673	.690	.076	.013	.146	.118	.000	.086	.122	.291	.314	.523	.604	.208	

POPULATION, DEATHS, DEATH RATES FOR ALL CAUSES COMBINED, AND SPECIFIED CAUSES

Age Start of Interval	Midyear Population	Deaths During Year	All Causes	Respiratory T.B.	Other Infec. and Paras.	Neoplasms	Cardiovascular	Infl., Pneu., Bronch.	Diarrheal	Certain Degenerative	Maternal	Cert. Dis. of Infancy	Motor Vehicle	Other Violence	Other and Unknown	Age Start of Interval
0	234645	7573	.03227	.00000	.00053	.00009	.00008	.00399	.00120	.00003	.00000	.01796	.00002	.00134	.00702	0
1	903755	1153	.00128	.00000	.00007	.00012	.00001	.00019	.00006	.00001	.00000	.00001	.00016	.00032	.00033	1
5	1026600	698	.00068	.00000	.00003	.00009	.00001	.00002	.00000	.00001	.00000	.00000	.00019	.00020	.00013	5
10	887300	541	.00061	.00000	.00001	.00007	.00001	.00001	.00000	.00002	.00000	.00000	.00014	.00025	.00009	10
15	701000	893	.00127	.00001	.00002	.00011	.00004	.00003	.00000	.00002	.00000	.00000	.00043	.00046	.00015	15
20	615500	923	.00150	.00000	.00002	.00011	.00006	.00002	.00001	.00005	.00000	.00000	.00056	.00058	.00009	20
25	625100	920	.00147	.00001	.00001	.00014	.00010	.00003	.00001	.00004	.00000	.00000	.00042	.00060	.00011	25
30	641900	1015	.00158	.00003	.00001	.00022	.00025	.00002	.00001	.00010	.00000	.00000	.00030	.00052	.00012	30
35	605600	1444	.00238	.00006	.00002	.00031	.00069	.00003	.00000	.00015	.00000	.00000	.00028	.00058	.00025	35
40	559100	1835	.00328	.00004	.00003	.00050	.00133	.00007	.00001	.00017	.00000	.00000	.00026	.00056	.00031	40
45	507100	3042	.00600	.00010	.00004	.00107	.00289	.00013	.00002	.00035	.00000	.00000	.00027	.00069	.00043	45
50	430300	4028	.00936	.00009	.00006	.00184	.00495	.00017	.00002	.00050	.00000	.00000	.00035	.00078	.00060	50
55	356500	5511	.01546	.00014	.00011	.00332	.00856	.00033	.00004	.00077	.00000	.00000	.00035	.00081	.00104	55
60	283200	6870	.02426	.00020	.00013	.00499	.01409	.00066	.00004	.00129	.00000	.00000	.00038	.00083	.00165	60
65	233300	8325	.03568	.00022	.00018	.00745	.02116	.00123	.00005	.00142	.00000	.00000	.00046	.00096	.00255	65
70	192400	10596	.05507	.00029	.00020	.01115	.03348	.00221	.00010	.00220	.00000	.00000	.00047	.00100	.00397	70
75	130300	10887	.08355	.00038	.00018	.01442	.05284	.00402	.00019	.00337	.00000	.00000	.00056	.00151	.00607	75
80	63900	8407	.13156	.00055	.00020	.01851	.08556	.00778	.00045	.00515	.00000	.00000	.00059	.00247	.01030	80
85+	30000	7135	.23783	.00043	.00033	.02403	.15623	.01897	.00067	.00747	.00000	.00000	.00100	.00610	.02260	85+
ALL	9027500	81796														

	All Causes	Respiratory T.B.	Other Infec. and Paras.	Neoplasms	Cardiovascular	Infl., Pneu., Bronch.	Diarrheal	Certain Degenerative	Maternal	Cert. Dis. of Infancy	Motor Vehicle	Other Violence	Other and Unknown
CRUDE DEATH RATE	.00906	.00006	.00006	.00141	.00449	.00044	.00006	.00035	.00000	.00047	.00030	.00058	.00084
STANDARDIZED RATE (1)	.00605	.00004	.00006	.00085	.00241	.00032	.00006	.00021	.00000	.00063	.00029	.00052	.00066
STANDARDIZED RATE (2)	.01071	.00007	.00006	.00173	.00563	.00050	.00005	.00042	.00000	.00037	.00032	.00062	.00093
GEOMETRIC MEAN	.00768	.00006	.00006	.00173	.00563	.00050	.00005	.00042	.00000	.00037	.00032	.00062	.00093

LIFE TABLE FOR ALL CAUSES COMBINED

Age (x)	Midyear Population	Deaths During Year	$_nM_x$	$_nq_x$	l_x	$_nd_x$	$_nL_x$	$_nm_x$	$_na_x$	T_x	$_nr_x$	$\overset{\circ}{e}_x$	Age (x)
0	234645	7573	.032274	.031390	100000	3139	97253	.032277	.124866	6808144	.000000	68.081	0
1	903755	1153	.001276	.005090	96861	493	386212	.001277	1.500000	6710891	.000000	69.284	1
5	1026600	698	.000680	.003372	96368	325	481028	.000676	2.500000	6324680	.000000	65.630	5
10	887300	541	.000610	.003061	96043	294	479540	.000613	2.702664	5843652	.028145	60.844	10
15	701000	893	.001274	.006381	95749	611	477305	.001280	2.642526	5364113	.037546	56.023	15
20	615500	923	.001500	.007484	95138	712	473927	.001502	2.523701	4886808	.019405	51.365	20
25	625100	920	.001472	.007328	94426	692	470405	.001471	2.507828	4412881	-.000689	46.734	25
30	641900	1015	.001581	.007873	93734	738	466911	.001581	2.616305	3942476	-.000791	42.060	30
35	605600	1444	.002384	.011871	92996	1104	462379	.002388	2.643984	3475565	.008308	37.373	35
40	559100	1835	.003282	.016334	91892	1501	456036	.003291	2.719159	3013186	.011874	32.791	40
45	507100	3042	.005999	.029682	90391	2683	445776	.006019	2.696919	2557150	.017356	28.290	45
50	430300	4028	.009361	.046028	87708	4037	429195	.009406	2.685214	2111374	.023229	24.073	50
55	356500	5511	.015459	.074960	83671	6272	403690	.015537	2.661764	1682178	.026135	20.105	55
60	283200	6870	.024258	.115079	77399	8907	365768	.024352	2.616785	1278489	.022357	16.518	60
65	233300	8325	.035684	.164472	68492	11265	315335	.035724	2.592099	912721	.007113	13.326	65
70	192400	10596	.055073	.242665	57227	13887	252201	.055063	2.556408	597386	-.000906	10.439	70
75	130300	10887	.083553	.346677	43340	15025	179156	.083866	2.501220	345185	.018952	7.965	75
80	63900	8407	.131565	.493555	28315	13975	105735	.132170	2.435435	166030	.018952	5.864	80
85+	30000	7135	.237833	1.000000	14340	14340	60294	.237833	4.204625	60294	.000000	4.205	85+

NUMBER OF PERSONS DYING (OUT OF 100,000 AT BIRTH) ABOVE AGE X FROM SPECIFIED CAUSES

Age (x)	All Causes	Respira-tory T.B.	Other Infec. and Paras.	Neo-plasms	Cardio-vascular	Infl., Pneu., Bronch.	Diar-rheal	Certain Degen-erative	Maternal	Cert. Dis. of Infancy	Motor Vehicle	Other Violence	Other and Unknown	Age (x)
0	100000	587	470	16402	56368	4721	377	4028	0	1748	2324	4749	8226	0
1	96861	587	418	16393	56360	4334	261	4025	0	1	2321	4619	7542	1
5	96368	586	390	16347	56356	4261	238	4019	0	0	2261	4495	7415	5
10	96043	586	378	16305	56350	4251	237	4014	0	0	2168	4401	7353	10
15	95749	586	371	16272	56343	4244	237	4005	0	0	2101	4279	7311	15
20	95138	583	362	16218	56326	4232	235	3994	0	0	1893	4058	7237	20
25	94426	581	354	16164	56295	4220	232	3970	0	0	1630	3785	7195	25
30	93734	577	348	16098	56247	4206	227	3952	0	0	1432	3500	7147	30
35	92956	563	342	15996	56132	4196	224	3905	0	0	1290	3258	7090	35
40	91892	535	331	15850	55813	4183	222	3837	0	0	1159	2988	6974	40
45	90391	514	318	15623	55206	4150	215	3759	0	0	1040	2733	6833	45
50	87708	469	300	15144	53910	4093	205	3605	0	0	918	2424	6640	50
55	83671	431	273	14349	51774	4017	197	3391	0	0	769	2090	6380	55
60	77399	373	230	13001	48300	3882	181	3080	0	0	630	1765	5957	60
65	68492	297	183	11171	43126	3637	165	2607	0	0	491	1461	5354	65
70	57227	227	125	8820	36445	3249	149	2158	0	0	345	1159	4550	70
75	43340	154	75	6007	28002	2692	123	1604	0	0	226	908	3549	75
80	28315	85	42	3418	18498	1968	88	998	0	0	126	636	2456	80
85+	14340	26	20	1449	9420	1144	40	450	0	0	60	368	1363	85+

NUMBER OF PERSONS SURVIVING TO AGE X IF SPECIFIED CAUSES WERE ELIMINATED

Age (x)	No Causes	Respira-tory T.B. (1)	Other Infec. and Paras. (2)	Neo-plasms (3)	Cardio-vascular (4)	Infl., Pneu., Bronch. (5)	Diar-rheal (6)	Certain Degener-ative (7)	Maternal (8)	Cert. Dis. of Infancy (9)	Motor Vehicle (10)	Other Violence (11)	Other and Unknown (12)	(1)+(2)	(1)+(2)+(5)+(6)+(8)	(1)+(2)+(5)+(6)+(8)+part of(9)&(12)	(10)+(11)	Age (x)
0	100000	100000	100000	100000	100000	100000	100000	100000	100000	100000	100000	100000	100000	100000	100000	100000	100000	0
1	96861	96865	96912	96870	96865	97243	96975	96864	96861	96856	96864	96989	97536	96912	97409	99313	96992	1
5	96368	96369	96447	96423	96380	96821	96505	96377	96368	98095	96431	96619	97168	96448	97038	98980	96682	5
10	96043	96044	96134	96139	96061	96504	96180	96057	96043	97764	96199	96388	96902	96135	96734	98676	96544	10
15	95749	95750	95846	95878	95774	96216	95886	95772	95749	97465	95971	96215	96648	95847	96452	98391	96438	15
20	95138	95142	95244	95320	95180	95614	95276	95172	95138	96843	95567	95823	96106	95248	95863	97793	96254	20
25	94426	94432	94539	94661	94498	94910	94566	94483	94426	96118	95115	95380	95429	94545	95171	97088	96076	25
30	93734	93744	93852	94033	93853	94229	93878	93809	93734	95414	94617	94968	94778	93862	94502	96409	95863	30
35	92956	93020	93119	93395	93229	93497	93142	93117	92956	94662	94015	94465	94089	93143	93791	95686	95500	35
40	91892	91943	92025	92442	92441	92400	92038	92079	91892	93539	93030	93616	93089	92076	92732	94612	94776	40
45	90391	90462	90534	91149	91539	90924	90541	90653	90391	92011	91630	92345	91710	90606	91291	93150	93611	45
50	87708	87822	87865	88921	90125	88281	87864	88114	87708	89280	89032	89915	89181	87979	88711	90527	91273	50
55	83671	83816	83847	85619	88147	84293	83828	84269	83671	85170	85082	86111	85335	83993	84775	86521	87563	55
60	77399	77589	77603	80538	85137	78105	77559	78254	77399	78786	78840	79978	79354	77794	78666	80305	81466	60
65	68492	68732	68717	73083	80886	69350	68649	69699	68492	65719	69900	71069	70806	68958	69982	71467	72530	65
70	57227	57491	57468	63395	75185	58305	57373	58653	57227	58252	58539	59665	59924	57734	58970	60261	61033	70
75	43340	43604	43566	50785	67429	44653	43473	44915	43340	44117	44438	45413	46301	43831	45297	46339	46564	75
80	28315	28543	28489	35688	57682	29780	28430	29852	28315	28822	29114	29899	31201	28718	30327	31084	30743	80
85+	14340	14419	14443	19892	45447	15699	14432	15527	14340	14597	14792	15341	16665	14601	16088	16555	15825	85+

ADDED YRS OF LIFE

	No Causes	(1)	(2)	(3)	(4)	(5)	(6)	(7)	(8)	(9)	(10)	(11)	(12)	(1)+(2)	(1)+(2)+(5)+(6)+(8)	(1)+(2)+(5)+(6)+(8)+part of(9)&(12)	(10)+(11)
TOTAL		.093	.130	2.211	10.844	.711	.126	.524	.000	1.218	.767	1.340	1.509	.223	1.069	2.506	2.130
WORK	3.510	.038	.028	.508	1.167	.063	.011	.155	.000	.000	.434	.647	.255	.065	.139	.151	1.090

POPULATION, DEATHS, DEATH RATES FOR ALL CAUSES COMBINED, AND SPECIFIED CAUSES

Age Start of Interval	Midyear Population	Deaths During Year	All Causes	Respiratory T. B.	Other Infec. and Paras.	Neoplasms	Cardiovascular	Infl., Pneu., Bronch.	Diarrheal	Certain Degenerative	Maternal	Cert. Dis. of Infancy	Motor Vehicle	Other Violence	Other and Unknown	Age Start of Interval
0	223760	5505	.02460	.00000	.00053	.00010	.00005	.00314	.00094	.00004	.00000	.01281	.00004	.00101	.00593	0
1	862440	914	.00106	.00000	.00008	.00011	.00001	.00015	.00004	.00001	.00000	.00000	.00011	.00022	.00033	1
5	990000	427	.00043	.00000	.00003	.00006	.00001	.00003	.00001	.00001	.00000	.00000	.00012	.00006	.00010	5
10	847100	292	.00034	.00000	.00001	.00006	.00002	.00002	.00000	.00002	.00000	.00000	.00006	.00008	.00008	10
15	674700	346	.00051	.00001	.00002	.00006	.00003	.00001	.00000	.00002	.00002	.00000	.00017	.00008	.00009	15
20	602000	336	.00056	.00001	.00001	.00006	.00005	.00002	.00000	.00003	.00005	.00000	.00011	.00008	.00012	20
25	590200	406	.00069	.00001	.00002	.00015	.00009	.00002	.00000	.00004	.00006	.00000	.00007	.00011	.00010	25
30	627600	548	.00087	.00003	.00003	.00026	.00013	.00004	.00000	.00005	.00007	.00000	.00006	.00011	.00011	30
35	612400	896	.00146	.00003	.00002	.00053	.00027	.00005	.00001	.00006	.00008	.00000	.00009	.00012	.00019	35
40	555800	1162	.00209	.00003	.00003	.00091	.00044	.00005	.00001	.00012	.00006	.00000	.00007	.00012	.00025	40
45	486500	1699	.00349	.00002	.00002	.00157	.00099	.00005	.00001	.00019	.00002	.00000	.00009	.00017	.00036	45
50	402100	2156	.00536	.00004	.00004	.00220	.00188	.00010	.00002	.00029	.00000	.00000	.00011	.00017	.00051	50
55	340300	2759	.00811	.00005	.00004	.00297	.00335	.00017	.00002	.00049	.00000	.00000	.00011	.00018	.00073	55
60	285900	3802	.01330	.00005	.00006	.00395	.00667	.00026	.00004	.00085	.00000	.00000	.00015	.00023	.00104	60
65	238200	5168	.02170	.00009	.00009	.00547	.01201	.00052	.00009	.00145	.00000	.00000	.00018	.00029	.00150	65
70	198600	7082	.03566	.00009	.00012	.00708	.02188	.00106	.00011	.00194	.00000	.00000	.00017	.00052	.00265	70
75	138100	8231	.05960	.00017	.00012	.00970	.03891	.00222	.00025	.00287	.00000	.00000	.00017	.00109	.00410	75
80	72100	7662	.10627	.00032	.00014	.01202	.07430	.00473	.00039	.00393	.00000	.00000	.00043	.00305	.00696	80
85+	38700	8506	.21979	.00023	.00021	.01705	.15341	.01488	.00121	.00646	.00000	.00000	.00021	.00819	.01793	85+
ALL	8786500	57897														

CRUDE DEATH RATE	.00659	.00003	.00005	.00122	.00328	.00031	.00005	.00029	.00002	.00033	.00011	.00023	.00067
STANDARDIZED RATE (1)	.00394	.00002	.00005	.00074	.00143	.00022	.00005	.00016	.00002	.00045	.00010	.00018	.00052
STANDARDIZED RATE (2)	.00722	.00003	.00005	.00139	.00373	.00032	.00005	.00033	.00002	.00027	.00011	.00024	.00069
GEOMETRIC MEAN	.00464												

LIFE TABLE FOR ALL CAUSES COMBINED

Age (x)	Midyear Population	Deaths During Year	$_nM_x$	$_nq_x$	l_x	$_nd_x$	$_nL_x$	$_nm_x$	$_na_x$	T_x	$_nr_x$	$\overset{\circ}{e}_x$	Age (x)
0	223760	5505	.024602	.024060	100000	2408	97861	.024606	.111824	7381653	.000000	73.817	0
1	862440	914	.001060	.004222	97592	412	389338	.001058	1.500000	7283792	.000000	74.635	1
5	990000	427	.000431	.002161	97180	210	485375	.000433	2.500000	6894454	.000000	70.945	5
10	847100	292	.000345	.001722	96970	167	484440	.000345	2.547405	6409079	.029165	66.093	10
15	674700	346	.000513	.002562	96803	248	483416	.000513	2.586526	5924638	.035643	61.203	15
20	602000	336	.000558	.002796	96555	270	482117	.000560	2.563272	5441222	.021136	56.354	20
25	590200	406	.000688	.003427	96285	330	480631	.000687	2.593434	4959105	.001770	51.504	25
30	627600	548	.000873	.004356	95955	418	478806	.000873	2.682915	4478474	-.005547	46.673	30
35	612400	896	.001463	.007296	95537	697	476062	.001464	2.670971	3999668	.005382	41.865	35
40	555800	1162	.002091	.010439	94840	990	471920	.002098	2.656970	3523606	.015846	37.153	40
45	486500	1699	.003492	.017400	93850	1633	465472	.003508	2.686773	3051686	.025383	32.517	45
50	402100	2156	.005362	.026611	92217	2454	455358	.005389	2.666140	2586213	.029876	28.045	50
55	340300	2759	.008108	.039994	89763	3590	440492	.008150	2.681639	2130856	.026897	23.739	55
60	285900	3802	.013298	.064800	86173	5584	417896	.013362	2.677441	1690364	.024136	19.616	60
65	238200	5168	.021696	.103563	80589	8346	383397	.021769	2.657835	1272468	.016492	15.790	65
70	198600	7082	.035660	.164819	72243	11907	333006	.035756	2.630928	889071	.013285	12.307	70
75	138100	8231	.059602	.262348	60336	15829	263558	.060059	2.591617	556064	.033311	9.216	75
80	72100	7662	.106269	.423933	44507	18868	175856	.107292	2.526014	292506	.033311	6.572	80
85+	38700	8506	.219793	1.000000	25639	25639	116651	.219793	4.549730	116651	.000000	4.550	85+

NUMBER OF PERSONS DYING (OUT OF 100,000 AT BIRTH) ABOVE AGE X FROM SPECIFIED CAUSES

Age (x)	All Causes	Respiratory T.B.	Other Infec. and Paras.	Neoplasms	Cardiovascular	Infl., Pneu., Bronch.	Diarrheal	Certain Degenerative	Maternal	Cert. Dis. of Infancy	Motor Vehicle	Other Violence	Other and Unknown	Age (x)
0	100000	319	382	16938	59460	4463	515	4390	172	1255	908	2959	8239	0
1	97592	319	330	16928	59455	4156	423	4386	172	1	904	2860	7658	1
5	97180	318	301	16884	59451	4098	407	4380	172	0	862	2775	7532	5
10	96970	318	288	16854	59445	4084	405	4375	172	0	802	2744	7483	10
15	96803	318	281	16827	59437	4073	403	4367	172	0	774	2707	7444	15
20	96555	314	273	16798	59421	4066	401	4355	162	0	691	2671	7403	20
25	96285	309	267	16767	59397	4056	399	4342	137	0	640	2631	7340	25
30	95955	302	258	16694	59353	4045	397	4321	110	0	604	2577	7294	30
35	95537	290	246	16570	59292	4027	396	4298	75	0	575	2527	7241	35
40	94840	275	236	16316	59163	4003	390	4269	37	0	532	2467	7152	40
45	93850	261	223	15884	58953	3978	388	4214	9	0	497	2409	7034	45
50	92217	251	215	15149	58488	3953	383	4126	0	0	453	2330	6869	50
55	89763	232	197	14144	57627	3906	374	3994	0	0	402	2252	6635	55
60	86173	211	178	12833	56140	3830	366	3776	0	0	354	2172	6313	60
65	80589	192	154	11178	53337	3719	348	3418	0	0	289	2074	5880	65
70	72243	157	120	9075	48715	3517	313	2861	0	0	220	1962	5303	70
75	60336	128	82	6712	41405	3164	276	2214	0	0	148	1789	4418	75
80	44507	84	49	4146	31062	2574	211	1453	0	0	102	1497	3329	80
85+	25639	27	24	1989	17895	1736	142	754	0	0	24	956	2092	85+

NUMBER OF PERSONS SURVIVING TO AGE X IF SPECIFIED CAUSES WERE ELIMINATED

Age (x)	No Causes	Respiratory T.B. (1)	Other Infec. and Paras. (2)	Neoplasms (3)	Cardiovascular (4)	Infl., Pneu., Bronch. (5)	Diarrheal (6)	Certain Degenerative (7)	Maternal (8)	Cert. Dis. of Infancy (9)	Motor Vehicle (10)	Other Violence (11)	Other and Unknown (12)	(1)+(2)	(1)+(2)+(5)+(6)+(8)	(1)+(2)+(5)+(6)+(8)+part of(9)&(12)	(10)+(11)	Age (x)
0	100000	100000	100000	100000	100000	100000	100000	100000	100000	100000	100000	100000	100000	100000	100000	100000	100000	0
1	97592	97592	97643	97602	97597	97896	97683	97596	97592	98839	97690	98168	97643	98039	99482	97694	1
5	97180	97181	97260	97234	97189	97541	97287	97190	97180	98422	97226	97362	97880	97261	97729	99215	97408	5
10	96970	96971	97063	97054	96985	97344	97078	96985	96970	98210	97076	97183	97718	97064	97547	99040	97289	10
15	96803	96804	96903	96913	96826	97187	96913	96826	96803	98041	96937	97053	97589	96904	97399	98896	97187	15
20	96555	96560	96663	96694	96594	96945	96667	96590	96565	97789	96771	96840	97380	96668	97181	98680	97057	20
25	96285	96295	96398	96455	96348	96684	96399	96333	96320	97516	96552	96609	97171	96408	96957	98468	96877	25
30	95955	95972	96077	96197	96061	96364	96070	96023	96017	97182	96257	96332	96884	96094	96681	98197	96635	30
35	95537	95566	95670	95902	95704	95962	95653	95628	95633	96758	95867	95963	96516	95699	96338	97861	96294	35
40	94840	94884	94982	95457	95135	95286	94961	94959	94974	96053	95210	95323	95901	95026	95729	97256	95655	40
45	93850	93907	94004	94894	94351	94316	93971	94023	94010	95050	94251	94386	95019	94061	94812	96335	94789	45
50	92217	92283	92376	93583	93114	92700	92341	92474	92383	93356	92655	92822	93531	92442	93219	94724	93263	50
55	89763	89846	89936	92497	91558	90280	89853	90144	89925	90911	90240	90429	91277	90019	90832	92307	90910	55
60	86173	86273	86357	90131	89395	86744	86306	86754	86328	87275	86678	86892	87947	86458	87322	88753	87401	60
65	80589	80701	80785	85979	86464	81231	80730	81481	80734	81619	81124	81357	82676	80897	81832	83187	81897	65
70	72243	72377	72451	79223	82352	73012	72403	73577	72373	73167	72789	73038	74677	72585	73652	74894	73590	70
75	60336	60474	60544	68585	76829	61306	60503	62053	60445	61107	60857	61160	63208	60682	61940	63020	61689	75
80	44507	44647	44688	53117	69156	45740	44686	46445	44587	45076	44931	45371	47610	44829	46339	47196	45803	80
85+	25639	25762	25762	32590	58541	27003	25754	27308	25685	25967	25942	26553	28436	25886	27478	28042	26867	85+

ADDED YRS OF LIFE

	No Causes	(1)	(2)	(3)	(4)	(5)	(6)	(7)	(8)	(9)	(10)	(11)	(12)	(1)+(2)	(1)+(2)+(5)+(6)+(8)	(1)+(2)+(5)+(6)+(8)+part of(9)&(12)	(10)+(11)
TOTAL		.057	.129	2.659	11.752	.638	.123	.544	.076	.942	.305	.532	1.493	.186	1.032	2.247	.840
WORK	1.942	.024	.025	.650	.495	.047	.008	.101	.054	.000	.122	.130	.221	.048	.158	.184	.252

POPULATION, DEATHS, DEATH RATES FOR ALL CAUSES COMBINED, AND SPECIFIED CAUSES

Age Start of Interval	Midyear Population	Deaths During Year	All Causes	Respira- tory T. B.	Other Infec. and Paras.	Neo- plasms	Cardio- vascular	Infl., Pneu., Bronch.	Diar- rheal	Certain Degen- erative	Maternal	Cert. Dis. of Infancy	Motor Vehicle	Other Violence	Other and Unknown	Age Start of Interval
0	230500	6467	.028C6	.000C0	.00024	.00010	.00012	.00262	.00055	.C0004	.00000	.01692	.00010	.00128	.00609	0
1	937400	1066	.00114	.000C0	.0C005	.00014	.00001	.00013	.0CC03	.00002	.00000	.0C000	.00017	.00029	.00030	1
5	1115600	715	.00064	.000C0	.0C002	.000C9	.00001	.00002	.C0000	.C0001	.00000	.C0000	.00021	.00020	.00010	5
10	1025200	475	.00046	.C0C0C	.00CC1	.00006	.00001	.00001	.00000	.00001	.00000	.00000	.00012	.00020	.00005	10
15	864000	1009	.00117	.C0000	.00001	.00010	.00002	.00001	.00000	.00002	.00000	.00000	.00052	.00036	.00012	15
20	657200	1180	.C0180	.000C0	.00001	.000C9	.00005	.00003	.00001	.00004	.0C0C0	.0C000	.00084	.00058	.00015	20
25	587200	869	.00148	.000C1	.C00C1	.00012	.00012	.00003	.00000	.00007	.C0000	.00000	.00048	.00054	.00010	25
30	628400	1073	.00171	.00002	.00001	.00020	.00022	.00003	.C0001	.00008	.C0000	.00000	.00040	.00057	.00017	30
35	643000	1400	.00218	.00CC2	.C00C1	.00033	.00058	.00002	.00000	.00012	.00000	.00000	.00034	.00059	.00016	35
40	598800	2191	.00366	.000C4	.00002	.0C060	.00137	.C0CC8	.0000C	.00019	.00000	.00000	.00038	.00067	.00030	40
45	530900	3044	.00573	.C00C5	.00003	.00100	.00279	.00009	.00002	.00033	.0C0C0	.C0000	.00036	.00064	.00043	45
50	476800	4534	.00951	.C0CC8	.C00C4	.00191	.00459	.00021	.00003	.00052	.00000	.00000	.00074	.00064	.00064	50
55	394400	5909	.01498	.00012	.0C007	.00334	.00797	.00C38	.00004	.00C79	.0C000	.00000	.00040	.00082	.00106	55
60	311900	7797	.02500	.CC016	.C00C7	.00584	.01389	.00066	.00005	.00108	.0C000	.00000	.00047	.00085	.00191	60
65	245800	8730	.03552	.00022	.00014	.00823	.02024	.00115	.00012	.00156	.C0000	.00000	.00050	.00075	.00262	65
70	192700	10424	.054C9	.00032	.00018	.01132	.03203	.00210	.00016	.00226	.C0000	.00000	.00054	.00058	.00420	70
75	140000	11216	.08011	.00C32	.C0019	.01427	.C4920	.00381	.00034	.00349	.00000	.00000	.00067	.00134	.00646	75
80	78100	9470	.12125	.0C038	.00019	.01786	.07810	.00694	.C0038	.03439	.00000	.00000	.00065	.00245	.00990	80
85+	41300	8210	.19879	.00048	.00024	.02036	.13063	.01574	.00077	.00632	.00000	.C0000	.00070	.00487	.01867	85+
ALL	9659200	85779														

CRUDE DEATH RATE			.00884	.000C4	.00004	.00147	.00437	.00039	.00004	.00035	.C0000	.00040	.00037	.00055	.00082	
STANDARDIZED RATE (1)			.00580	.00003	.00003	.00088	.00228	.00026	.00004	.00021	.00000	.C0060	.00036	.00050	.00062	
STANDARDIZED RATE (2)			.01028	.C00C5	.0C004	.0C177	.00527	.00044	.C0004	.00041	.00000	.00035	.00039	.00059	.00091	
GEOMETRIC MEAN			.00738													

LIFE TABLE FOR ALL CAUSES COMBINED

Age (x)	Midyear Population	Deaths During Year	$_nM_x$	$_nq_x$	l_x	$_nd_x$	$_nL_x$	$_nm_x$	$_na_x$	T_x	$_nr_x$	$\overset{\circ}{e}_x$	Age (x)
0	230500	6467	.028056	.027380	100000	2738	97584	.028058	.117696	6863887	.000000	68.639	0
1	937400	1066	.001137	.004534	97262	441	387946	.001137	1.500000	6766303	.000000	69.568	1
5	1115600	715	.00C641	.003191	96821	309	483333	.000639	2.500000	6378357	.000000	65.878	5
10	1025200	475	.0C0463	.002321	96512	224	482054	.000465	2.739025	5895025	.015843	61.081	10
15	864000	1009	.001168	.005878	96288	566	480157	.001179	2.732995	5412971	.036866	56.216	15
20	657200	1180	.0C1795	.0C8953	95722	857	476495	.001799	2.532332	4932814	.042393	51.533	20
25	587200	869	.001480	.007368	94865	699	472566	.001479	2.483011	4456319	.014907	46.975	25
30	628400	1073	.0C1708	.0C8456	94166	800	468895	.001706	2.581250	3983754	-.006622	42.306	30
35	643000	1400	.0C2177	.010828	93366	1011	464486	.002177	2.681339	3514859	-.001984	37.646	35
40	598800	2191	.0C3659	.018191	92355	1680	457900	.003669	2.693700	3050373	.011174	33.029	40
45	530900	3044	.0C5734	.028376	90675	2573	447449	.005750	2.696917	2592472	.015162	28.591	45
50	476800	4534	.0C9509	.046673	88102	4112	430567	.009541	2.679150	2145023	.017604	24.347	50
55	394400	5909	.014982	.072735	83990	6109	405743	.015056	2.674401	1714056	.024904	20.408	55
60	311900	7797	.024998	.118462	77881	9226	367412	.025111	2.616180	1308314	.024513	16.799	60
65	245800	8730	.035517	.163921	68655	11254	316075	.035605	2.583119	940902	.016140	13.705	65
70	192700	10424	.054094	.238951	57401	13716	253410	.054126	2.550686	624826	.003319	10.885	70
75	140000	11216	.C80114	.334005	43685	14591	181896	.080216	2.496473	371416	.006943	8.502	75
80	78100	9470	.121255	.462548	29094	13469	110919	.121431	2.434789	189520	.006943	6.514	80
85+	41300	8210	.198789	1.C00000	15625	15625	78601	.198789	5.030451	78601	.000000	5.030	85+

NUMBER OF PERSONS DYING (OUT OF 100,000 AT BIRTH) ABOVE AGE X FROM SPECIFIED CAUSES

Age (x)	All Causes	Respiratory T. B.	Other Infec. and Paras.	Neoplasms	Cardiovascular	Infl., Pneu., Bronch.	Diarrheal	Certain Degenerative	Maternal	Cert. Dis. of Infancy	Motor Vehicle	Other Violence	Other and Unknown	Age (x)
0	100000	497	332	17255	55344	4541	381	4044	0	1651	2839	4619	8497	0
1	97262	497	308	17245	55333	4285	327	4040	0	0	2830	4495	7902	1
5	96821	456	290	17192	55329	4234	314	4032	0	0	2764	4381	7789	5
10	96512	496	281	17151	55325	4225	312	4029	0	0	2664	4287	7742	10
15	96288	496	279	17123	55319	4220	312	4026	0	0	2606	4192	7715	15
20	95722	495	275	17075	55308	4215	311	4017	0	0	2353	4017	7656	20
25	94865	494	272	17032	55282	4201	308	3999	0	0	1951	3740	7586	25
30	94166	490	267	16976	55226	4186	306	3966	0	0	1724	3486	7539	30
35	93366	482	263	16884	55122	4172	301	3926	0	0	1534	3220	7462	35
40	92355	472	257	16733	54852	4161	301	3870	0	0	1377	2944	7388	40
45	90675	452	248	16456	54222	4126	300	3784	0	0	1201	2637	7249	45
50	88102	430	235	16007	52969	4084	292	3635	0	0	1040	2352	7058	50
55	83990	397	218	15178	50813	3995	279	3410	0	0	885	2035	6780	55
60	77881	347	191	13816	47562	3841	264	3087	0	0	724	1702	6347	60
65	68655	288	165	11658	42434	3598	244	2689	0	0	549	1389	5641	65
70	57401	220	122	9053	36020	3234	207	2194	0	0	391	1151	4809	70
75	43685	139	76	6183	27898	2701	166	1621	0	0	253	904	3744	75
80	29094	81	41	3585	18936	2006	103	985	0	0	131	659	2567	80
85+	15625	38	19	1601	10268	1237	61	497	0	0	55	383	1466	85+

NUMBER OF PERSONS SURVIVING TO AGE X IF SPECIFIED CAUSES WERE ELIMINATED

Age (x)	No Causes	Respiratory T. B.	Other Infec. and Paras.	Neoplasms	Cardiovascular	Infl., Pneu., Bronch.	Diarrheal	Certain Degenerative	Maternal	Cert. Dis. of Infancy	Motor Vehicle	Other Violence	Other and Unknown	(1) + (2)	(1) + (2) + (5) + (6) + (8)	(1)+(2)+ (5)+(6)+ (8)+part of(9)&(12)	(10) + (11)	Age (x)
		(1)	(2)	(3)	(4)	(5)	(6)	(7)	(8)	(9)	(10)	(11)	(12)					
0	100000	100000	100000	100000	100000	100000	100000	100000	100000	100000	100000	100000	100000	100000	100000	100000	100000	0
1	97262	97286	97286	97272	97273	97515	97315	97266	97262	98904	97271	97384	97851	97286	97592	99112	97393	1
5	96821	96822	96863	96884	96836	97124	96887	96833	96821	98455	96896	97057	97520	96864	97233	98777	97132	5
10	96512	96513	96562	96615	96531	96823	96580	96527	96512	98141	96686	96841	97256	96563	96942	98485	97016	10
15	96288	96289	96340	96419	96313	96603	96356	96306	96288	97913	96520	96712	97058	96341	96724	98265	96945	15
20	95722	95724	95778	95900	95758	96040	95750	95749	95722	97338	96206	96319	96547	95780	96167	97700	96806	20
25	94865	94868	94923	95085	94926	95154	94936	94909	94865	96466	95748	95734	95753	94926	95327	96848	96625	25
30	94166	94173	94229	94440	94283	94508	94238	94243	94166	95756	95271	95284	95094	94236	94650	96163	96402	30
35	93366	93381	93432	93730	93585	93719	93442	93482	93366	94942	94653	94743	94364	93447	93877	95381	96049	35
40	92355	92380	92427	92866	92842	92715	92411	92526	92355	93914	93786	93996	93416	92451	92888	94378	95453	40
45	90675	90719	90754	91453	91783	91063	90750	90928	90675	92206	92257	92596	91857	90798	91263	92733	94212	45
50	88102	88166	88192	89305	90438	88521	88183	88495	88102	89569	89801	90256	89441	88256	88758	90194	91996	50
55	83990	84084	84092	85962	88405	84477	84080	84586	83990	85408	85764	86360	85542	84186	84765	86147	88184	55
60	77881	78016	78002	81063	85337	78482	77979	78747	77881	79196	79664	80408	79746	78137	78839	80143	82270	60
65	68655	68829	68786	73599	80690	69415	68760	69797	68655	69814	70412	71186	70981	68961	69831	71014	73007	65
70	57401	57609	57550	64136	74714	58374	57523	58817	57401	58370	59017	59741	60136	57758	58863	59899	61424	70
75	43685	43914	43838	51672	66847	44901	43814	45276	43685	44422	45038	45690	46748	44068	45428	46283	47105	75
80	29094	29293	29224	36981	57163	30492	29231	30691	29094	29585	30096	30638	32172	29424	30983	31632	31693	80
85+	15625	15763	15711	21765	45802	16567	15729	16858	15625	15889	16220	16665	18179	15850	17326	17753	17300	85+

ADDED YRS OF LIFE

		(1)	(2)	(3)	(4)	(5)	(6)	(7)	(8)	(9)	(10)	(11)	(12)				
TOTAL		.073	.079	2.432	11.598	.628	.083	.541	.000	1.157	.963	1.305	1.511	.152	.872	2.028	2.298
WORK	3.555	.024	.016	.511	1.123	.062	.009	.152	.000	.000	.565	.627	.258	.040	.111	.120	1.203

POPULATION, DEATHS, DEATH RATES FOR ALL CAUSES COMBINED, AND SPECIFIED CAUSES

Age Start of Interval	Midyear Population	Deaths During Year	All Causes	Respiratory T.B.	Other Infec. and Paras.	Neoplasms	Cardiovascular	Infl., Pneu., Bronch.	Diarrheal	Certain Degenerative	Maternal	Cert. Dis. of Infancy	Motor Vehicle	Other Violence	Other and Unknown	Age Start of Interval
0	219500	4704	.02143	.00000	.00023	.00010	.00004	.00206	.00039	.00005	.00000	.01202	.00005	.00095	.00554	0
1	896200	820	.00091	.00000	.00006	.00009	.00001	.00013	.00002	.00002	.00000	.00000	.00013	.00020	.00025	1
5	1065500	420	.00039	.00000	.00001	.00007	.00001	.00002	.00000	.00000	.00000	.00000	.00012	.00007	.00009	5
10	979200	290	.00030	.00000	.00001	.00005	.00001	.00001	.00000	.00001	.00000	.00000	.00007	.00005	.00007	10
15	828800	416	.00050	.00000	.00000	.00007	.00003	.00001	.00000	.00002	.00000	.00000	.00018	.00009	.00009	15
20	653700	386	.00059	.00000	.00000	.00008	.00005	.00002	.00000	.00003	.00003	.00000	.00018	.00010	.00010	20
25	587500	373	.00063	.00001	.00001	.00013	.00010	.00002	.00001	.00003	.00004	.00000	.00010	.00010	.00009	25
30	606300	550	.00091	.00001	.00001	.00024	.00015	.00002	.00000	.00005	.00006	.00000	.00009	.00014	.00013	30
35	638400	807	.00126	.00002	.00001	.00046	.00021	.00002	.00000	.00005	.00005	.00000	.00010	.00016	.00019	35
40	609600	1231	.00202	.00002	.00001	.00087	.00044	.00006	.00001	.00010	.00003	.00000	.00011	.00015	.00022	40
45	527300	1679	.00318	.00003	.00004	.00136	.00089	.00005	.00001	.00020	.00000	.00000	.00012	.00018	.00029	45
50	463600	2366	.00510	.00003	.00003	.00218	.00169	.00009	.00002	.00024	.00000	.00000	.00013	.00021	.00047	50
55	380800	2942	.00773	.00002	.00002	.00296	.00306	.00013	.00003	.00045	.00000	.00000	.00016	.00025	.00065	55
60	310900	3988	.01283	.00005	.00006	.00426	.00575	.00028	.00005	.00089	.00000	.00000	.00019	.00024	.00106	60
65	259700	5268	.02028	.00006	.00006	.00548	.01099	.00037	.00006	.00128	.00000	.00000	.00019	.00028	.00152	65
70	213000	6985	.03279	.00006	.00006	.00692	.01995	.00070	.00015	.00190	.00000	.00000	.00025	.00045	.00231	70
75	156900	8729	.05563	.00011	.00005	.00926	.03633	.00198	.00027	.00273	.00000	.00000	.00025	.00090	.00375	75
80	88300	8545	.09677	.00019	.00009	.01216	.06672	.00428	.00044	.00365	.00000	.00000	.00027	.00246	.00651	80
85+	52600	9572	.18198	.00029	.00013	.01409	.13129	.01186	.00097	.00494	.00000	.00000	.00036	.00551	.01253	85+
ALL	9537800	60071														
CRUDE DEATH RATE			.00630	.00002	.00003	.00123	.00319	.00026	.00004	.00028	.00001	.00028	.00013	.00023	.00061	
STANDARDIZED RATE (1)			.00360	.00001	.00003	.00072	.00129	.00017	.00003	.00015	.00001	.00042	.00013	.00018	.00047	
STANDARDIZED RATE (2)			.00661	.00002	.00003	.00136	.00336	.00025	.00004	.00030	.00002	.00025	.00014	.00023	.00062	
GEOMETRIC MEAN			.00430													

LIFE TABLE FOR ALL CAUSES COMBINED

Age (x)	Midyear Population	Deaths During Year	$_nM_x$	$_nq_x$	l_x	$_nd_x$	$_nL_x$	$_nm_x$	$_na_x$	T_x	$_nr_x$	$\overset{\circ}{e}_x$	Age (x)
0	219500	4704	.021431	.021030	100000	2103	98121	.021433	.106432	7495464	.000000	74.955	0
1	896200	820	.000915	.003647	97897	357	390696	.000914	1.500000	7397343	.000000	75.563	1
5	1065500	420	.000394	.001968	97540	192	487220	.000394	2.500000	7006647	.000000	71.834	5
10	979200	290	.000296	.001479	97348	144	486391	.000296	2.576678	6519427	.016235	66.970	10
15	828800	416	.000502	.002520	97204	245	485437	.000505	2.620748	6033036	.034596	62.066	15
20	653700	386	.000590	.002950	96959	286	484093	.000591	2.545163	5547599	.038104	57.216	20
25	587500	373	.000635	.003176	96673	307	482629	.000636	2.601792	5063506	.017121	52.378	25
30	606300	550	.000907	.004524	96366	436	480802	.000907	2.641915	4580878	-.003617	47.536	30
35	638400	807	.001264	.006296	95930	604	478249	.001263	2.680740	4100076	-.005418	42.740	35
40	609600	1231	.002019	.010071	95326	960	474416	.002024	2.693793	3621826	.010592	37.994	40
45	527300	1679	.003184	.015864	94366	1497	468378	.003196	2.693860	3147410	.020567	33.353	45
50	463600	2366	.005104	.025337	92869	2353	458870	.005128	2.673360	2679033	.024805	28.847	50
55	380800	2942	.007726	.038170	90516	3455	444588	.007771	2.686746	2220162	.031043	24.528	55
60	310900	3988	.012827	.062600	87061	5450	422612	.012896	2.671063	1775575	.027783	20.395	60
65	259700	5268	.020285	.097168	81611	7930	389437	.020363	2.652191	1352962	.019545	16.578	65
70	213000	6985	.032793	.152590	73681	11243	341854	.032888	2.638475	963525	.014295	13.077	70
75	156900	8729	.055634	.246693	62438	15403	275188	.055973	2.597749	621671	.026568	9.957	75
80	88300	8545	.096772	.392666	47035	18470	189513	.097460	2.527759	346483	.026568	7.366	80
85+	52600	9572	.181977	1.000000	28565	28565	156970	.181977	5.495194	156970	.000000	5.495	85+

NUMBER OF PERSONS DYING (OUT OF 100,000 AT BIRTH) ABOVE AGE X FROM SPECIFIED CAUSES

Age (x)	All Causes	Respiratory T.B.	Other Infec. and Paras.	Neo-plasms	Cardio-vascular	Infl., Pneu., Bronch.	Diar-rheal	Certain Degen-erative	Maternal	Cert. Dis. of Infancy	Motor Vehicle	Other Violence	Other and Unknown	Age (x)
0	100000	241	249	17372	60025	4220	494	4317	106	1180	1127	2828	7841	0
1	97897	241	227	17363	60021	4018	455	4312	106	0	1122	2734	7298	1
5	97540	241	203	17328	60015	3568	447	4305	106	0	1070	2656	7201	5
10	97348	241	198	17294	60013	3956	446	4303	106	0	1012	2621	7158	10
15	97204	241	191	17271	60006	3950	446	4296	106	0	977	2596	7124	15
20	96959	240	189	17236	59992	3945	443	4285	105	0	889	2554	7081	20
25	96673	238	187	17199	59970	3937	442	4271	88	0	803	2507	7031	25
30	96366	235	180	17134	59923	3930	439	4259	70	0	753	2457	6986	30
35	95930	230	174	17020	59852	3918	439	4236	39	0	709	2388	6925	35
40	95326	221	171	16799	59754	3908	437	4211	15	0	664	2312	6834	40
45	94366	213	164	16386	59544	3878	433	4161	1	0	612	2242	6732	45
50	92869	198	145	15745	59124	3853	430	4067	0	0	556	2158	6593	50
55	90516	183	130	14741	58343	3810	420	3956	0	0	494	2063	6376	55
60	87061	174	122	13421	56973	3753	407	3755	0	0	422	1950	6084	60
65	81611	154	96	11615	54524	3633	386	3378	0	0	341	1849	5635	65
70	73681	131	72	9478	50225	3488	362	2879	0	0	266	1738	5042	70
75	62438	112	53	7110	43382	3225	312	2227	0	0	181	1585	4251	75
80	47035	82	39	4553	33318	2677	236	1474	0	0	111	1335	3210	80
85+	28565	45	21	2211	20609	1862	152	776	0	0	57	865	1967	85+

NUMBER OF PERSONS SURVIVING TO AGE X IF SPECIFIED CAUSES WERE ELIMINATED

Age (x)	No Causes	Respiratory T.B. (1)	Other Infec. and Paras. (2)	Neo-plasms (3)	Cardio-vascular (4)	Infl., Pneu., Bronch. (5)	Diar-rheal (6)	Certain Degener-ative (7)	Maternal (8)	Cert. Dis. of Infancy (9)	Motor Vehicle (10)	Other Violence (11)	Other and Unknown (12)	(1) + (2)	(1) + (2) + (5) + (6) + (8)	(1)+(2)+(5)+(6)+(8)+part of(9)&(12)	(10) + (11)	Age (x)
0	100000	100000	100000	100000	100000	100000	100000	100000	100000	100000	100000	100000	100000	100000	100000	100000	100000	0
1	97897	97897	97919	97906	97901	98097	97936	97902	97897	99071	97902	97990	98436	97919	98158	99348	97995	1
5	97540	97540	97586	97584	97550	97789	97586	97552	97540	98710	97597	97711	98174	97586	97882	99100	97768	5
10	97348	97348	97399	97426	97360	97609	97395	97362	97348	98516	97463	97553	98024	97399	97707	98928	97668	10
15	97204	97204	97261	97305	97223	97471	97251	97225	97204	98370	97354	97434	97913	97261	97576	98799	97584	15
20	96959	96960	97018	97094	96992	97230	97009	96991	96960	98122	97196	97231	97710	97019	97342	98565	97469	20
25	96673	96676	96734	96845	96728	96951	96724	96719	96691	97833	96996	96991	97472	96737	97085	98311	97315	25
30	96366	96372	96434	96602	96468	96650	96420	96424	96402	97522	96738	96733	97208	96440	96814	98044	97106	30
35	95930	95941	96004	96279	96102	95984	96010	95957	95937	97081	96364	96364	96829	96015	96431	97664	96780	35
40	95326	95346	95402	95895	95595	95629	95381	95431	95416	96470	95783	95834	96311	95422	95872	97107	96293	40
45	94366	94394	94448	95343	94842	94656	94425	94519	94469	95458	94870	94939	95444	94476	94969	96200	95446	45
50	92869	92911	92969	94475	93757	93219	92930	93113	92972	93583	93421	93516	94065	93011	93525	94744	94072	50
55	90516	90572	90628	93095	92164	90895	90505	90864	90616	91602	91115	91241	91903	90684	91238	92436	91846	55
60	87061	87123	87177	90883	90025	87486	87140	87594	87157	88105	87709	87870	88666	87239	87842	89003	88524	60
65	81611	81689	81745	87036	86879	82126	81706	82479	81701	82590	82297	82468	83578	81823	82526	83633	83161	65
70	73681	73773	73824	80769	82912	74285	73789	74945	73762	74565	74372	74561	76036	73917	74715	75734	75261	70
75	62438	62534	62577	70865	77719	63195	62576	64120	62507	63187	63102	63327	65188	62673	63643	64537	64000	75
80	47035	47133	47152	55938	70464	48090	47205	48972	47087	47599	47596	47926	50054	47250	48538	49263	48497	80
85+	28565	28653	28650	36190	60313	29856	28733	30307	28597	28908	28948	29478	31436	28738	30247	30756	29873	85+

ADDED YRS OF LIFE

	No Causes	(1)	(2)	(3)	(4)	(5)	(6)	(7)	(8)	(9)	(10)	(11)	(12)	(1)+(2)	(1)+(2)+(5)+(6)+(8)	(1)+(2)+(5)+(6)+(8)+part of(9)&(12)	(10)+(11)
TOTAL		.039	.080	2.823	14.181	.557	.082	.560	.048	.898	.387	.567	1.462	.120	.815	1.817	.959
WORK	1.853	.014	.015	.622	.453	.038	.008	.093	.034	.000	.158	.153	.207	.029	.108	.124	.312

POPULATION, DEATHS, DEATH RATES FOR ALL CAUSES COMBINED, AND SPECIFIED CAUSES

Age Start of Interval	Midyear Population	Deaths During Year	All Causes	Respiratory T.B.	Other Infec. and Paras.	Neo-plasms	Cardio-vascular	Infl., Pneu., Bronch.	Diar-rheal	Certain Degen-erative	Maternal	Cert. Dis. of Infancy	Motor Vehicle	Other Violence	Other and Unknown	Age Start of Interval
0	173000	11321	.06544	.00005	.00175	.00003	.00005	.00588	.00312	.00006	.00000	.03765	.00000	.00026	.01658	0
1	645000	5797	.00899	.00002	.00144	.00003	.00005	.00168	.00099	.00007	.00000	.00000	.00001	.00027	.00443	1
5	661000	1567	.00237	.00000	.00053	.00002	.00007	.00033	.00016	.00003	.00000	.00000	.00001	.00022	.00098	5
10	571000	703	.00123	.00000	.00023	.00001	.00011	.00012	.00006	.00002	.00000	.00000	.00002	.00027	.00038	10
15	438000	609	.00139	.00001	.00015	.00004	.00013	.00010	.00004	.00004	.00000	.00000	.00003	.00049	.00037	15
20	475000	739	.00156	.00003	.00012	.00005	.00019	.00009	.00006	.00004	.00000	.00000	.00002	.00059	.00036	20
25	446000	744	.00167	.00007	.00017	.00004	.00019	.00008	.00005	.00007	.00000	.00000	.00004	.00059	.00037	25
30	343000	806	.00235	.00016	.00015	.00013	.00037	.00014	.00009	.00010	.00000	.00000	.00003	.00059	.00059	30
35	351000	1044	.00297	.00022	.00023	.00017	.00048	.00013	.00013	.00018	.00000	.00000	.00004	.00067	.00073	35
40	253000	913	.00361	.00023	.00023	.00029	.00072	.00017	.00015	.00017	.00000	.00000	.00003	.00075	.00088	40
45	254000	1383	.00544	.00032	.00022	.00044	.00125	.00021	.00019	.00043	.00000	.00000	.00004	.00085	.00146	45
50	192000	1510	.00786	.00037	.00036	.00076	.00197	.00036	.00043	.00057	.00000	.00000	.00006	.00064	.00234	50
55	131000	1844	.01408	.00053	.00055	.00126	.00402	.00068	.00048	.00094	.00000	.00000	.00005	.00109	.00448	55
60	101000	2424	.02400	.00089	.00055	.00171	.00622	.00139	.00109	.00150	.00000	.00000	.00011	.00147	.00867	60
65	74000	2453	.03315	.00103	.00085	.00164	.00747	.00222	.00116	.00169	.00000	.00000	.00009	.00158	.01542	65
70	49000	2633	.05373	.00129	.00102	.00210	.00941	.00247	.00186	.00212	.00000	.00000	.00012	.00169	.03165	70
75	28000	2080	.07429	.00061	.00096	.00225	.01071	.00286	.00218	.00257	.00000	.00000	.00018	.00132	.05064	75
80	19000	2259	.11889	.00111	.00163	.00200	.01089	.00305	.00311	.00179	.00000	.00000	.00037	.00242	.09253	80
85+	14000	3825	.27321	.00071	.00164	.00171	.01336	.00521	.00464	.00200	.00000	.00000	.00000	.00350	.24043	85+
ALL	5218000	44654														

	All Causes	Respiratory T.B.	Other Infec. and Paras.	Neo-plasms	Cardio-vascular	Infl., Pneu., Bronch.	Diar-rheal	Certain Degen-erative	Maternal	Cert. Dis. of Infancy	Motor Vehicle	Other Violence	Other and Unknown
CRUDE DEATH RATE	.00856	.00015	.00050	.00024	.00085	.00067	.00042	.00022	.00000	.00125	.00003	.00055	.00370
STANDARDIZED RATE (1)	.00831	.00015	.00050	.00024	.00087	.00068	.00042	.00023	.00000	.00133	.00003	.00055	.00370
STANDARDIZED RATE (2)	.01189	.00024	.00049	.00042	.00164	.00071	.00048	.00040	.00000	.00078	.00004	.00069	.00333
GEOMETRIC MEAN	.01002												

LIFE TABLE FOR ALL CAUSES COMBINED

Age (x)	Midyear Population	Deaths During Year	$_nM_x$	$_nq_x$	l_x	$_nd_x$	$_nL_x$	$_nm_x$	$_na_x$	T_x	$_nr_x$	$\overset{\circ}{e}_x$	Age (x)
0	173000	11321	.065439	.062110	100000	6211	94915	.065438	.181247	6351081	.000000	63.511	0
1	645000	5797	.008988	.035164	93789	3298	366911	.008989	1.500000	6256167	.000000	66.705	1
5	661000	1567	.002371	.011835	90491	1071	449778	.002381	2.500000	5889256	.000000	65.081	5
10	571000	703	.001231	.006084	89420	544	445645	.001221	2.325751	5439478	.033186	60.831	10
15	438000	609	.001390	.006921	88876	616	442869	.001391	2.547348	4993833	.025984	56.189	15
20	475000	739	.001556	.007750	88260	684	439614	.001556	2.534418	4550964	-.003030	51.563	20
25	446000	744	.001668	.008324	87576	729	436127	.001672	2.595450	4111350	.024696	46.946	25
30	343000	806	.002350	.011722	86847	1018	431803	.002358	2.610715	3675223	.021482	42.318	30
35	351000	1044	.002974	.014757	85829	1270	426074	.002981	2.582021	3243420	.025302	37.789	35
40	253000	913	.003609	.017952	84559	1518	419202	.003621	2.632987	2817346	.030388	33.318	40
45	254000	1383	.005445	.026963	83041	2239	409947	.005462	2.651760	2398144	.017573	28.879	45
50	192000	1510	.007865	.038972	80802	3149	396786	.007936	2.706084	1988197	.049259	24.606	50
55	131000	1844	.014078	.068948	77653	5354	375945	.014241	2.698839	1591411	.052269	20.494	55
60	101000	2424	.024000	.114234	72299	8259	341791	.024164	2.614194	1215466	.037664	16.812	60
65	74000	2453	.033149	.154294	64040	9881	296477	.033328	2.599180	873675	.034732	13.643	65
70	49000	2633	.053735	.239351	54159	12963	239025	.054233	2.549195	577198	.046925	10.657	70
75	28000	2080	.074286	.314157	41196	12942	173631	.074537	2.500451	338173	.021933	8.209	75
80	19000	2259	.118895	.459793	28254	12991	108677	.119537	2.491132	164542	.021933	5.824	80
85+	14000	3825	.273214	1.000000	15263	15263	55865	.273214	3.660131	55865	.000000	3.660	85+

NUMBER OF PERSONS DYING (OUT OF 100,000 AT BIRTH) ABOVE AGE X FROM SPECIFIED CAUSES

Age (x)	All Causes	Respiratory T. B.	Other Infec. and Paras.	Neo-plasms	Cardio-vascular	Infl., Pneu., Bronch.	Diar-rheal	Certain Degen-erative	Maternal	Cert. Dis. of Infancy	Motor Vehicle	Other Violence	Other and Unknown	Age (x)
0	100000	1989	3194	3588	14281	5032	3570	3361	0	3574	322	5035	56054	0
1	93789	1984	3028	3585	14276	4473	3273	3355	0	0	322	5011	54482	1
5	90491	1978	2498	3574	14257	3855	2912	3331	0	0	320	4912	52854	5
10	89420	1976	2257	3563	14223	3707	2838	3315	0	0	317	4812	52412	10
15	88876	1974	2156	3557	14175	3653	2812	3305	0	0	308	4690	52246	15
20	88260	1971	2092	3538	14119	3609	2792	3289	0	0	293	4474	52083	20
25	87576	1957	2040	3517	14037	3569	2765	3269	0	0	283	4216	51923	25
30	86847	1927	1968	3497	13954	3532	2743	3239	0	0	268	3957	51762	30
35	85829	1859	1905	3443	13795	3473	2703	3195	0	0	255	3696	51505	35
40	84559	1765	1806	3372	13590	3420	2645	3119	0	0	237	3409	51196	40
45	83041	1669	1712	3251	13288	3346	2581	3049	0	0	225	3096	50824	45
50	80802	1538	1621	3071	12759	3261	2501	2873	0	0	209	2749	50220	50
55	77653	1390	1475	2768	11966	3114	2330	2646	0	0	184	2495	49285	55
60	72299	1191	1266	2290	10436	2855	2148	2289	0	0	167	2081	47576	60
65	64040	884	940	1703	8300	2377	1773	1772	0	0	130	1578	44583	65
70	54159	579	688	1218	6078	1717	1427	1270	0	0	102	1109	39971	70
75	41196	271	443	713	3818	1125	980	760	0	0	72	704	32310	75
80	28254	167	275	323	1557	629	601	314	0	0	41	474	23473	80
85+	15263	40	92	96	746	291	259	112	0	0	0	196	13431	85+

NUMBER OF PERSONS SURVIVING TO AGE X IF SPECIFIED CAUSES WERE ELIMINATED

Age (x)	No Causes	Respiratory T. B. (1)	Other Infec. and Paras. (2)	Neo-plasms (3)	Cardio-vascular (4)	Infl., Pneu., Bronch. (5)	Diar-rheal (6)	Certain Degener-ative (7)	Maternal (8)	Cert. Dis. of Infancy (9)	Motor Vehicle (10)	Other Violence (11)	Other and Unknown (12)	(1) + (2)	(1) + (2) + (5) + (6) + (8)	(1)+(2)+ (5)+(6)+ (8)+part of(9)&(12)	(10) + (11)	Age (x)
0	100000	100000	100000	100000	100000	100000	100000	100000	100000	100000	100000	100000	100000	100000	100000	100000	100000	0
1	93789	93794	93950	93792	93794	94332	94077	93795	93789	97314	93789	93812	95324	93955	94789	99771	93812	1
5	90491	90502	91169	90505	90514	91627	91125	90520	90491	93892	90493	90611	93611	91180	92972	99441	90613	5
10	89420	89432	90332	89444	89477	90692	90121	89465	89420	92781	89425	89638	92959	90344	92348	99132	89643	10
15	88876	88890	89884	88906	88980	90195	89599	88930	88876	92217	88890	89215	92566	89899	91974	98821	89229	15
20	88260	88277	89326	88309	88420	89614	88958	88330	88260	91577	88289	88813	92093	89343	91472	98333	88842	20
25	87576	87607	88686	87646	87816	88960	88335	87665	87576	90868	87614	88383	91546	88717	90901	97764	88422	25
30	86847	86908	88020	86936	87168	88257	87622	86966	86847	90111	86900	87908	90952	88082	90311	97180	87962	30
35	85829	85957	87052	85971	86305	87282	86635	85990	85829	89055	85894	87141	90154	87181	89490	96384	87207	35
40	84559	84778	85864	84769	85233	86044	85411	84793	84559	87737	84641	86141	89142	86086	88481	95407	86225	40
45	83041	83352	84417	83368	84005	84534	83942	83341	83041	86162	83134	84911	87932	84733	87233	94181	85006	45
50	80802	81234	82232	81298	82270	82379	81759	81268	80802	83839	80908	82972	86194	82672	85283	92236	83081	50
55	77653	78214	79173	78429	79860	79316	78742	78325	77653	80572	77779	79994	83815	79745	82595	89621	80124	55
60	72299	73015	73920	73489	75887	74103	73491	73273	72299	75017	72433	74891	79841	74652	77776	84843	75030	60
65	64040	64566	65789	65656	69357	66101	65455	65356	64040	66447	64194	66827	73505	66741	70411	77770	66987	65
70	54159	55226	55875	55982	60902	56530	55681	55777	54159	56195	54315	56965	67606	56976	61142	69123	57128	70
75	41196	42279	42720	43037	48577	43531	42754	42884	41196	42744	41340	43699	60484	43844	48088	57076	43852	75
80	28254	29082	29442	29850	35157	30291	29647	29793	28254	29316	28379	30170	53727	30305	34091	43498	30303	80
85+	15263	15805	16043	16300	20114	16628	16277	16249	15263	15837	15360	16514	46717	16613	19301	28894	16619	85+

ADDED YRS OF LIFE																		
TOTAL		.358	1.089	.586	2.183	1.423	.883	.539	.000	2.381	.073	1.339	20.730	1.457	3.882	11.017	1.414	
WORK	3.642	.157	.215	.217	.658	.172	.135	.183	.000	.000	.038	.713	.926	.373	.687	.943	.752	

POPULATION, DEATHS, DEATH RATES FOR ALL CAUSES COMBINED, AND SPECIFIED CAUSES

Age Start of Interval	Midyear Population	Deaths During Year	All Causes	Respiratory T. B.	Other Infec. and Paras.	Neoplasms	Cardiovascular	Infl., Pneu., Bronch.	Diarrheal	Certain Degenerative	Maternal	Cert. Dis. of Infancy	Motor Vehicle	Other Violence	Other and Unknown	Age Start of Interval
0	168000	9228	.05493	.00005	.00158	.00003	.00003	.00536	.00260	.00004	.00000	.03048	.00000	.00020	.01458	0
1	629000	6837	.01087	.00001	.00194	.00001	.00010	.00197	.00107	.00007	.00000	.00000	.00001	.00026	.00543	1
5	644000	1763	.00274	.00001	.00059	.00002	.00006	.00032	.00021	.00006	.00000	.00000	.00001	.00025	.00123	5
10	536000	651	.00121	.00002	.00019	.00002	.00013	.00012	.00008	.00003	.00000	.00000	.00001	.00022	.00037	10
15	408000	640	.00157	.00002	.00011	.00003	.00020	.00015	.00008	.00005	.00016	.00000	.00000	.00031	.00046	15
20	448000	1070	.00239	.00008	.00015	.00002	.00027	.00014	.00008	.00008	.00058	.00000	.00000	.00030	.00069	20
25	406000	1063	.00262	.00011	.00019	.00005	.00027	.00020	.00015	.00006	.00064	.00000	.00000	.00022	.00073	25
30	283000	965	.00341	.00014	.00017	.00012	.00050	.00018	.00018	.00010	.00079	.00000	.00001	.00020	.00102	30
35	293000	1129	.00385	.00017	.00019	.00025	.00054	.00029	.00018	.00016	.00072	.00000	.00000	.00022	.00114	35
40	194000	776	.00400	.00019	.00022	.00044	.00058	.00034	.00020	.00015	.00030	.00000	.00000	.00022	.00134	40
45	191000	981	.00514	.00024	.00031	.00071	.00076	.00042	.00029	.00032	.00008	.00000	.00001	.00022	.00177	45
50	142000	957	.00674	.00039	.00030	.00093	.00099	.00051	.00039	.00042	.00000	.00000	.00003	.00015	.00263	50
55	96000	1134	.01181	.00037	.00041	.00128	.00221	.00080	.00054	.00081	.00000	.00000	.00001	.00030	.00507	55
60	84000	1484	.01767	.00038	.00052	.00176	.00382	.00125	.00099	.00070	.00001	.00000	.00000	.00039	.00782	60
65	60000	1660	.02767	.00047	.00060	.00133	.00515	.00203	.00103	.00127	.00000	.00000	.00005	.00032	.01542	65
70	43000	2086	.04851	.00035	.00081	.00128	.00688	.00267	.00184	.00147	.00000	.00000	.00005	.00051	.03265	70
75	26000	1813	.06973	.00019	.00056	.00135	.00715	.00273	.00212	.00088	.00000	.00000	.00008	.00038	.05388	75
80	16000	2052	.12825	.00025	.00054	.00156	.01062	.00350	.00275	.00087	.00000	.00000	.00006	.00131	.10637	80
85+	13000	3975	.30577	.00046	.00292	.00054	.01231	.00454	.00392	.00154	.00000	.00000	.00000	.00131	.27823	85+
ALL	4680000	40264														

CRUDE DEATH RATE	.00860	.00010	.00056	.00022	.00061	.00077	.00045	.00016	.00023	.00109	.00001	.00026	.00415
STANDARDIZED RATE (1)	.00813	.00011	.00053	.00025	.00065	.00075	.00044	.00017	.00023	.00107	.00001	.00026	.00367
STANDARDIZED RATE (2)	.01155	.00015	.00048	.00041	.00119	.00078	.00049	.00028	.00023	.00063	.00001	.00028	.00662
GEOMETRIC MEAN	.01057												

LIFE TABLE FOR ALL CAUSES COMBINED

Age (x)	Midyear Population	Deaths During Year	$_nM_x$	$_nq_x$	l_x	$_nd_x$	$_nL_x$	$_nm_x$	$_na_x$	T_x	$_nr_x$	$\overset{\circ}{e}_x$	Age (x)
0	168000	9228	.054929	.052520	100000	5252	95606	.054934	.163379	6374200	.000000	63.742	0
1	629000	6837	.010870	.042323	94748	4010	368967	.010868	1.500000	6278594	.000000	66.266	1
5	644000	1763	.002738	.013666	90738	1240	450590	.002752	2.500000	5909627	.000000	65.128	5
10	536000	651	.001215	.005989	89498	536	446037	.001202	2.288946	5459037	.037448	60.996	10
15	408000	640	.001569	.007835	88962	697	443174	.001573	2.653037	5013000	.026464	56.350	15
20	448000	1070	.002388	.011873	88265	1048	438797	.002388	2.587468	4569826	.003782	51.774	20
25	406000	1063	.002618	.013036	87217	1137	433328	.002624	2.575308	4131029	.034816	47.365	25
30	283000	965	.003410	.016909	86080	1459	426852	.003418	2.568540	3697701	.030121	42.957	30
35	293000	1129	.003853	.019109	84621	1617	419101	.003858	2.524093	3270849	.031398	38.653	35
40	194000	776	.004000	.019830	83004	1646	410999	.004005	2.557209	2851747	.040751	34.357	40
45	191000	981	.005136	.025431	81358	2069	401358	.005149	2.601358	2440748	.022506	30.000	45
50	142000	957	.006739	.033460	79289	2653	390307	.006797	2.686503	2038921	.055563	25.715	50
55	96000	1134	.011812	.057988	76636	4444	372799	.011921	2.664079	1648614	.046507	21.512	55
60	84000	1484	.017667	.085231	72192	6153	346451	.017760	2.641970	1275814	.031225	17.673	60
65	60000	1660	.027667	.130766	66039	8637	309936	.027847	2.654350	929363	.035643	14.073	65
70	43000	2086	.048512	.218668	57402	12552	256623	.048912	2.579088	619428	.038055	10.791	70
75	26000	1813	.069731	.298818	44850	13402	191333	.070045	2.543899	362805	.025353	8.089	75
80	16000	2052	.128250	.488934	31448	15376	118909	.129309	2.507100	171472	.025353	5.453	80
85+	13000	3975	.305769	1.000000	16072	16072	52563	.305769	3.270440	52563	.000000	3.270	85+

NUMBER OF PERSONS DYING (OUT OF 100,000 AT BIRTH) ABOVE AGE X FROM SPECIFIED CAUSES

Age (x)	All Causes	Respiratory T.B.	Other Infec. and Paras.	Neoplasms	Cardiovascular	Infl., Pneu., Bronch.	Diarrheal	Certain Degenerative	Maternal	Cert. Dis. of Infancy	Motor Vehicle	Other Violence	Other and Unknown	Age (x)
0	100000	1173	3076	3380	10672	5611	3704	2310	1404	2914	92	1888	63776	0
1	94748	1169	2925	3377	10669	5099	3456	2306	1404	0	92	1869	62382	1
5	90738	1164	2210	3372	10634	4371	3061	2282	1404	0	89	1771	60380	5
10	89458	1161	1943	3362	10609	4226	2968	2257	1404	0	87	1657	59824	10
15	88962	1152	1862	3351	10550	4172	2932	2242	1402	0	80	1557	59662	15
20	88265	1141	1816	3337	10463	4103	2898	2218	1328	0	80	1421	59460	20
25	87217	1106	1749	3328	10343	4042	2861	2190	1074	0	79	1288	59157	25
30	86080	1059	1668	3305	10225	3954	2797	2162	798	0	78	1155	58839	30
35	84621	998	1595	3254	10012	3875	2720	2120	461	0	73	1109	58404	35
40	83004	927	1517	3147	9784	3753	2642	2054	162	0	73	1019	57926	40
45	81358	850	1425	2965	9544	3615	2559	1977	42	0	73	930	57378	45
50	79289	753	1301	2680	9236	3446	2443	1846	9	0	69	841	56665	50
55	76636	601	1185	2315	8844	3247	2288	1680	9	0	58	784	55625	55
60	72192	461	1033	1835	8011	2945	2085	1375	9	0	54	670	53714	60
65	66039	329	851	1224	6680	2510	1741	1131	5	0	50	534	50984	65
70	57402	184	665	812	5077	1876	1420	736	5	0	34	436	46157	70
75	44850	95	455	484	3303	1187	945	360	5	0	22	304	37690	75
80	31448	59	271	226	1933	664	539	192	5	0	8	230	27321	80
85+	16072	24	154	28	647	239	206	81	0	0	0	69	14624	85+

NUMBER OF PERSONS SURVIVING TO AGE X IF SPECIFIED CAUSES WERE ELIMINATED

Age (x)	No Causes	(1) Respiratory T.B.	(2) Other Infec. and Paras.	(3) Neoplasms	(4) Cardiovascular	(5) Infl., Pneu., Bronch.	(6) Diarrheal	(7) Certain Degenerative	(8) Maternal	(9) Cert. Dis. of Infancy	(10) Motor Vehicle	(11) Other Violence	(12) Other and Unknown	(1)+(2)	(1)+(2)+(5)+(6)+(8)	(1)+(2)+(5)+(6)+(8)+part of (9)&(12)	(10)+(11)	Age (x)
0	100000	100000	100000	100000	100000	100000	100000	100000	100000	100000	100000	100000	100000	100000	100000	100000	100000	0
1	94748	94752	94855	94751	94751	95248	94990	94752	94748	97627	94748	94766	96114	94899	95643	99834	94766	1
5	90738	90747	91582	90746	90775	91935	91358	90765	90738	93495	90741	90852	94056	91591	93434	99480	90855	5
10	89458	89509	90599	89516	89559	90825	90202	89550	89458	92217	89503	89724	93344	90610	92678	99129	89728	10
15	88962	88982	90138	88990	89082	90336	89698	89028	88964	91665	88974	89286	92954	90159	92311	98823	89298	15
20	88265	88296	89478	88307	88471	89698	89030	88355	88341	90947	88277	88723	92436	89510	91830	98415	88735	20
25	87217	87283	88483	87268	87540	88694	88010	87334	87545	89867	87230	87802	92150	88550	91210	97957	87815	25
30	86080	86192	87411	86153	86517	87627	86927	86223	86679	88696	86093	86751	90792	87525	90601	97545	86764	30
35	84621	84791	86003	84743	85263	86222	85530	84803	85547	87192	84639	85366	89710	86176	89722	96900	85385	35
40	83004	83241	84439	83230	83861	84697	83974	83248	84212	85526	83022	83825	88499	84680	88650	96097	83843	40
45	81358	81667	82857	81761	82439	83157	82392	81674	82663	83830	81375	82252	87234	83172	87472	95072	82269	45
50	79289	79687	80874	79965	81213	80413	79727	80593	81658	81658	79310	80249	85862	81280	85822	93607	80270	50
55	76636	77170	78285	77652	78346	78696	77817	77224	77897	78965	76667	77620	84104	78831	83614	91670	77652	55
60	72192	72832	73896	73622	74634	74434	73561	73044	73380	74386	72225	73231	81289	74551	79613	87992	73265	60
65	66039	66752	67776	67944	69601	68521	67627	67054	67129	68046	66073	67121	77363	68507	73993	82824	67156	65
70	57402	58157	59089	59451	62088	60174	59089	58659	58350	59146	57447	58435	72739	59867	65668	75482	58481	70
75	44850	45518	46358	46748	50224	47653	46600	46169	45590	46213	44895	45775	67157	47049	52798	64429	45822	75
80	31448	31946	32663	33001	36505	33875	33025	32513	31967	32404	31491	32155	62026	33180	38153	51671	32204	80
85+	16072	16352	16778	17012	19734	17636	17125	16697	16341	16560	16100	16552	55180	17070	20293	33212	16580	85+

ADDED YRS OF LIFE

	No Causes	(1)	(2)	(3)	(4)	(5)	(6)	(7)	(8)	(9)	(10)	(11)	(12)	(1)+(2)	(1)+(2)+(5)+(6)+(8)	part	(10)+(11)
TOTAL		.277	1.169	.833	1.647	1.624	.963	.430	.591	1.932	.020	.611	27.769	1.454	4.807	12.949	.631
WORK	4.097	.150	.207	.265	.545	.281	.192	.162	.491	.000	.005	.274	1.279	.358	1.343	1.989	.279

POPULATION, DEATHS, DEATH RATES FOR ALL CAUSES COMBINED, AND SPECIFIED CAUSES

Age Start of Interval	Midyear Population	Deaths During Year	All Causes	Respira-tory T. B.	Other Infec. and Paras.	Neo-plasms	Cardio-vascular	Infl., Pneu., Bronch.	Diar-rheal	Certain Degen-erative	Maternal	Cert. Dis. of Infancy	Motor Vehicle	Other Violence	Other and Unknown	Age Start of Interval
0	59942	21602	.36038	.00275	.04204	.00002	.03802	.05952	.02841	.00042	.00000	.03832	.00000	.00344	.14744	0
1	204055	6733	.03300	.00121	.00757	.00001	.00272	.00785	.00287	.00011	.00000	.00000	.00000	.00105	.00961	1
5	211756	1382	.00653	.00055	.00188	.00053	.00129	.00031	.00005	.00000	.00000	.00000	.00040	.00150	5	
10	194416	1104	.00568	.00080	.00116	.00001	.00045	.00132	.00015	.00004	.00000	.00000	.00000	.00069	.00106	10
15	173864	2099	.01207	.00242	.00252	.00001	.00076	.00255	.00019	.00007	.00000	.00000	.00000	.00209	.00146	15
20	128720	2358	.01832	.00357	.00371	.00001	.00127	.00388	.00030	.00017	.00000	.00000	.00000	.00319	.00222	20
25	126299	2625	.02078	.00412	.00336	.00000	.00175	.00475	.00040	.00028	.00000	.00000	.00000	.00366	.00247	25
30	98649	1883	.01909	.00390	.00295	.00012	.00202	.00427	.00027	.00031	.00000	.00000	.00000	.00302	.00222	30
35	105368	2215	.02102	.00382	.00292	.00052	.00293	.00477	.00039	.00055	.00000	.00000	.00000	.00251	.00259	35
40	71631	1648	.02301	.00369	.00299	.00071	.00364	.00572	.00056	.00068	.00000	.00000	.00000	.00207	.00295	40
45	79936	2037	.02548	.00395	.00283	.00056	.00418	.00647	.00074	.00078	.00000	.00000	.00000	.00186	.00372	45
50	59375	1586	.02671	.00391	.00271	.00135	.00497	.00665	.00098	.00093	.00000	.00000	.00000	.00141	.00381	50
55	42463	1473	.03469	.00447	.00325	.00186	.00706	.00853	.00137	.00115	.00000	.00000	.00000	.00148	.00551	55
60	34946	1273	.03643	.00403	.00352	.00200	.00830	.00787	.00143	.00089	.00000	.00000	.00000	.00183	.00655	60
65	27034	1308	.04838	.00418	.00436	.00222	.01047	.01243	.00178	.00111	.00000	.00000	.00000	.00181	.01002	65
70	15874	1144	.07207	.00611	.00653	.00277	.01575	.01713	.00290	.00214	.00000	.00000	.00000	.00170	.01663	70
75	10223	888	.08686	.00606	.00783	.00274	.01702	.01937	.00323	.00245	.00000	.00000	.00000	.00166	.02651	75
80	4703	446	.09483	.00680	.00829	.00276	.01510	.01701	.00298	.00213	.00000	.00000	.00000	.00213	.03764	80
85+	8418	857	.10181	.00285	.00713	.00178	.01426	.01936	.00321	.00190	.00000	.00000	.00000	.00226	.04906	85+
ALL	1657712	54661														

CRUDE DEATH RATE			.03297	.00262	.00476	.00036	.00388	.00674	.00181	.00035	.00000	.00139	.00000	.00185	.00920	
STANDARDIZED RATE (1)			.03239	.00265	.00471	.00036	.00383	.00664	.00177	.00035	.00000	.00135	.00000	.00187	.00887	
STANDARDIZED RATE (2)			.03166	.00309	.00425	.00061	.00439	.00681	.00146	.00051	.00000	.00079	.00000	.00194	.00780	
GEOMETRIC MEAN			.03233													

LIFE TABLE FOR ALL CAUSES COMBINED

Age (x)	Midyear Population	Deaths During Year	$_nM_x$	$_nq_x$	l_x	$_nd_x$	$_nL_x$	$_nm_x$	$_na_x$	T_x	$_nr_x$	$\overset{\circ}{e}_x$	Age (x)
0	59942	21602	.360382	.323400	100000	32340	89737	.360387	.682649	2940482	.000000	29.405	0
1	204055	6733	.032996	.121918	67660	8249	250018	.032994	1.500000	2850746	.000000	42.133	1
5	211756	1382	.006525	.032048	59411	1904	292295	.006514	2.500000	2600728	.000000	43.775	5
10	194416	1104	.005679	.028049	57507	1613	283794	.005684	2.680564	2308433	.006037	40.142	10
15	173864	2099	.012073	.059076	55894	3302	271842	.012147	2.689784	2024639	.026362	36.223	15
20	128720	2358	.018219	.087865	52592	4621	251706	.018359	2.564696	1752798	.018003	33.328	20
25	126299	2625	.020784	.098747	47971	4737	227870	.020788	2.469830	1501091	.011320	31.292	25
30	98649	1883	.019088	.091016	43234	3935	206163	.019087	2.457010	1273222	-.001155	29.450	30
35	105368	2215	.021022	.099875	39299	3925	186665	.021027	2.495435	1067058	.008537	27.152	35
40	71631	1648	.023007	.108809	35374	3849	167216	.023018	2.491773	880394	.009165	24.888	40
45	79936	2037	.025483	.119683	31525	3773	148115	.025473	2.479570	713178	-.010535	22.623	45
50	59375	1586	.026712	.125360	27752	3479	130085	.026744	2.506467	565062	.026508	20.361	50
55	42463	1473	.034685	.159890	24273	3881	111647	.034761	2.495974	434977	.024690	17.920	55
60	34946	1273	.036428	.166928	20392	3404	93409	.036442	2.487882	323331	.006702	15.856	60
65	27034	1308	.048384	.216800	16988	3683	75872	.048542	2.537766	229922	.024087	13.534	65
70	15874	1144	.072068	.306050	13305	4072	56260	.072379	2.479023	154050	.025088	11.578	70
75	10223	888	.086663	.354489	9233	3273	37604	.087039	2.384344	97791	.033602	10.591	75
80	4703	446	.094833	.378356	5960	2255	23794	.094773	2.336475	60187	.033602	10.098	80
85+	8418	857	.101806	1.000000	3705	3705	36393	.101806	9.822637	36393	.000000	9.823	85+

NUMBER OF PERSONS DYING (OUT OF 100,000 AT BIRTH) ABOVE AGE X FROM SPECIFIED CAUSES

Age (x)	All Causes	Respiratory T. B.	Other Infec. and Paras.	Neoplasms	Cardiovascular	Infl., Pneu., Bronch.	Diarrheal	Certain Degenerative	Maternal	Cert. Dis. of Infancy	Motor Vehicle	Other Violence	Other and Unknown	Age (x)
0	100000	8704	13528	1526	12916	20807	4970	1365	0	3439	0	5760	26985	0
1	67660	8457	9755	1525	9504	15466	2421	1327	0	0	0	5452	13753	1
5	59411	8155	7863	1522	8823	13504	1704	1299	0	0	0	5188	11353	5
10	57507	7994	7314	1519	8667	13128	1614	1284	0	0	0	5071	10916	10
15	55894	7765	6984	1518	8540	12753	1572	1274	0	0	0	4875	10613	15
20	52592	7104	6293	1516	8331	12056	1520	1253	0	0	0	4303	10216	20
25	47971	6203	5359	1514	8009	11078	1446	1210	0	0	0	3498	9654	25
30	43234	5264	4555	1514	7610	9995	1354	1147	0	0	0	2664	9091	30
35	39299	4460	3987	1489	7194	9115	1297	1082	0	0	0	2042	8633	35
40	35374	3746	3441	1392	6646	8224	1224	979	0	0	0	1572	8150	40
45	31525	3129	2941	1272	6036	7266	1131	864	0	0	0	1227	7659	45
50	27752	2544	2522	1130	5418	6308	1022	750	0	0	0	951	7107	50
55	24273	2036	2170	954	4770	5442	894	629	0	0	0	767	6611	55
60	20392	1536	1806	746	3979	4489	741	500	0	0	0	601	5994	60
65	16988	1159	1477	559	3203	3753	608	417	0	0	0	430	5382	65
70	13305	841	1145	390	2407	2807	473	333	0	0	0	293	4616	70
75	9233	496	754	234	1517	1839	309	211	0	0	0	197	3676	75
80	5960	268	459	131	877	1111	187	119	0	0	0	135	2673	80
85+	3705	104	259	65	519	705	117	69	0	0	0	82	1785	85+

NUMBER OF PERSONS SURVIVING TO AGE X IF SPECIFIED CAUSES WERE ELIMINATED

Age (x)	No Causes	Respiratory T. B.	Other Infec. and Paras.	Neoplasms	Cardiovascular	Infl., Pneu., Bronch.	Diarrheal	Certain Degenerative	Maternal	Cert. Dis. of Infancy	Motor Vehicle	Other Violence	Other and Unknown	(1) + (2)	(1) + (2) + (5) + (6) + (8)	(1)+(2)+ (5)+(6)+ (8)+part of(9)&(12)	(10) + (11)	Age (x)
		(1)	(2)	(3)	(4)	(5)	(6)	(7)	(8)	(9)	(10)	(11)	(12)					
0	100000	100000	100000	100000	100000	100000	100000	100000	100000	100000	100000	100000	100000	100000	100000	100000	100000	0
1	67660	67862	70815	67661	70507	72169	69776	67691	67660	70530	67660	67912	79387	71027	78130	91053	67912	1
5	59411	59873	64064	59415	62579	65361	61965	59465	59411	61931	59411	59881	72356	64562	74081	89099	59881	5
10	57507	58114	62596	57513	60735	63674	60072	57574	57507	59946	57507	58078	70602	63066	73164	88526	58078	10
15	55894	56712	61195	55901	59164	62299	58430	55969	55894	58265	55894	56645	68989	62091	72347	87886	56645	15
20	52592	54017	58318	52601	55884	59377	55031	52683	52592	54823	52592	53864	65390	59898	70762	86417	53864	20
25	47971	50162	54191	47981	51302	55225	50270	48095	47971	50006	47971	49924	60316	56666	68361	84151	49924	25
30	43234	46150	49665	43243	46643	50969	45397	43406	43234	45068	43234	45825	55035	53015	65627	81477	45825	30
35	39299	42776	45815	39331	42829	47329	41322	39518	39299	40966	39299	42287	50585	49868	63150	78992	42287	35
40	35374	39247	41847	35496	39123	43633	37268	35669	35374	36875	35374	38545	46126	46648	60334	76103	38545	40
45	31525	35628	37855	31748	35509	40017	33306	31898	31525	32862	31525	34706	41717	42781	57373	73059	34706	45
50	27752	31989	33799	28083	31919	36386	29428	28189	27752	28929	27752	30838	37416	38959	54166	69807	30838	50
55	24273	28531	29965	24730	28624	32903	25867	24770	24273	25303	24273	27163	33356	35221	50879	66355	27163	55
60	20392	24512	25588	20971	24918	28850	21881	20930	20392	21257	20392	22991	28811	30759	46693	61922	22991	60
65	16988	20836	21696	17646	21641	25002	18359	17514	16988	17709	16988	19329	24805	26612	42325	57182	19329	65
70	13305	16666	17371	13976	17868	20851	14508	13794	13305	13869	13305	15276	20442	21759	37183	51778	15276	70
75	9233	11928	12485	9834	13429	15780	10217	9678	9233	9625	9233	10691	15441	16129	30504	44682	10691	75
80	5960	7937	8383	6436	9439	11224	6703	6324	5960	6213	5960	6959	11414	11164	23645	37595	6959	80
85+	3705	5107	5436	4057	6328	7601	4229	3973	3705	3862	3705	4374	8556	7493	17547	31300	4374	85+

ADDED YRS OF LIFE																	
TOTAL		2.414	4.524	.261	3.529	6.659	1.584	.280	.000	1.219	.000	1.714	9.713	7.544	20.243	38.572	1.714
WORK	17.891	2.446	2.097	.184	1.462	3.083	.259	.230	.000	.000	.000	1.811	1.648	4.787	9.010	10.625	1.811

POPULATION, DEATHS, DEATH RATES FOR ALL CAUSES COMBINED, AND SPECIFIED CAUSES

Age Start of Interval	Midyear Population	Deaths During Year	All Causes	Respiratory T. B.	Other Infec. and Paras.	Neo-plasms	Cardio-vascular	Infl., Pneu., Bronch.	Diar-rheal	Certain Degen-erative	Maternal	Cert. Dis. of Infancy	Motor Vehicle	Other Violence	Other and Unknown	Age Start of Interval
0	59916	19504	.32552	.00302	.04046	.00008	.03366	.05548	.02515	.00018	.00000	.03168	.00000	.00254	.13327	0
1	199959	6628	.03315	.00135	.00780	.00000	.00262	.00815	.00258	.00011	.00000	.00000	.00000	.00099	.00956	1
5	209200	1343	.00642	.00067	.00170	.00000	.00043	.00146	.00024	.00003	.00000	.00000	.00000	.00025	.00163	5
10	191944	1197	.00624	.00128	.00136	.00000	.00048	.00156	.00014	.00002	.00003	.00000	.00000	.00016	.00122	10
15	172315	1826	.01060	.00309	.00191	.00002	.00077	.00233	.00020	.00007	.00058	.00000	.00000	.00033	.00129	15
20	125569	1985	.01581	.00456	.00270	.00010	.00126	.00360	.00024	.00013	.00116	.00000	.00000	.00038	.00168	20
25	133328	2452	.01839	.00445	.00252	.00017	.00176	.00455	.00036	.00032	.00156	.00000	.00000	.00034	.00197	25
30	110160	1620	.01471	.00346	.00176	.00042	.00141	.00333	.00027	.00031	.00159	.00000	.00000	.00020	.00196	30
35	98251	1916	.01950	.00405	.00222	.00091	.00264	.00424	.00056	.00036	.00184	.00000	.00026	.00242	35
40	71873	1423	.01980	.00317	.00189	.00135	.00371	.00402	.00058	.00038	.00068	.00000	.00000	.00039	.00362	40
45	78595	1705	.02169	.00332	.00235	.00156	.00425	.00519	.00074	.00047	.00034	.00000	.00000	.00031	.00316	45
50	55412	1261	.02276	.00262	.00260	.00171	.00487	.00518	.00097	.00054	.00005	.00000	.00000	.00029	.00361	50
55	45170	1209	.02677	.00306	.00288	.00193	.00607	.00615	.00124	.00069	.00004	.00000	.00000	.00029	.00443	55
60	36414	1170	.03213	.00382	.00277	.00214	.00769	.00763	.00148	.00091	.00003	.00000	.00000	.00025	.00541	60
65	27414	1183	.04315	.00434	.00361	.00248	.01021	.01032	.00182	.00106	.00000	.00000	.00000	.00040	.00890	65
70	17468	1092	.06251	.00481	.00613	.00326	.01448	.01534	.00223	.00126	.00000	.00000	.00000	.00086	.01414	70
75	11871	916	.07716	.00446	.00716	.00320	.01601	.01710	.00261	.00101	.00000	.00000	.00000	.00101	.02460	75
80	5910	513	.08680	.00525	.00745	.00288	.01506	.01387	.00288	.00034	.00000	.00000	.00000	.00068	.03841	80
85+	11258	1103	.09797	.00222	.00675	.00187	.01457	.01626	.00320	.00036	.00000	.00000	.00000	.00071	.05205	85+
ALL	1662027	50046														

CRUDE DEATH RATE	.03011	.00274	.00429	.00052	.00365	.00624	.00164	.00025	.00057	.00114	.00000	.00046	.00862
STANDARDIZED RATE (1)	.02925	.00275	.00422	.00051	.00353	.00609	.00160	.00025	.00058	.00112	.00000	.00046	.00816
STANDARDIZED RATE (2)	.02823	.00304	.00370	.00081	.00409	.00606	.00133	.00034	.00058	.00066	.00000	.00042	.00719
GEOMETRIC MEAN	.02892													

LIFE TABLE FOR ALL CAUSES COMBINED

Age (x)	Midyear Population	Deaths During Year	$_nM_x$	$_nq_x$	l_x	$_nd_x$	$_nL_x$	$_nm_x$	$_na_x$	T_x	$_nr_x$	$\overset{\circ}{e}_x$	Age (x)
0	59916	19504	.325522	.289970	100000	28997	89079	.325519	.623388	3253274	.000000	32.533	0
1	199959	6628	.033147	.122446	71003	8694	262277	.033148	1.500000	3164194	.000000	44.564	1
5	209200	1343	.006420	.031552	62309	1966	306630	.006412	2.500000	2901917	.000000	46.573	5
10	191944	1197	.006236	.030741	60343	1855	297301	.006239	2.620620	2595287	.005188	43.009	10
15	172315	1826	.010597	.051976	58488	3040	285335	.010654	2.662692	2297986	.028656	39.290	15
20	125569	1985	.015808	.076270	55448	4229	266571	.015841	2.571875	2012652	.017643	36.298	20
25	133328	2452	.018391	.087838	51219	4499	244656	.018389	2.457537	1745680	-.001476	34.083	25
30	110160	1620	.014706	.070890	46720	3312	225225	.014705	2.471442	1501024	-.007573	32.128	30
35	98251	1916	.019501	.093186	43408	4045	207011	.019540	2.520602	1275798	.024266	29.391	35
40	71873	1423	.015799	.094302	39363	3712	187456	.015802	2.478785	1068787	.007980	27.152	40
45	78595	1705	.021693	.102858	35651	3667	169032	.021694	2.484831	881331	-.000159	24.721	45
50	55412	1261	.022757	.107710	31984	3445	151291	.022771	2.495102	712299	.027549	22.270	50
55	45170	1209	.026766	.125653	28539	3586	133787	.026804	2.515918	561009	.018202	19.658	55
60	36414	1170	.032130	.145040	24953	3719	115586	.032175	2.531931	427222	.014679	17.121	60
65	27414	1183	.043153	.195724	21234	4156	95970	.043305	2.545617	311635	.027081	14.676	65
70	17468	1092	.062514	.271050	17078	4629	73787	.062734	2.493519	215666	.021713	12.628	70
75	11871	916	.077163	.322275	12449	4012	51872	.077344	2.414527	141878	.030002	11.397	75
80	5910	513	.086802	.353562	8437	2983	34339	.086870	2.365678	90006	.030002	10.668	80
85+	11258	1103	.097975	1.000000	5454	5454	55667	.097975	10.206709	55667	.000000	10.207	85+

NUMBER OF PERSONS DYING (OUT OF 100,000 AT BIRTH) ABOVE AGE X FROM SPECIFIED CAUSES

Age (x)	All Causes	Respira-tory T. B.	Other Infec. and Paras.	Neo-plasms	Cardio-vascular	Infl., Pneu., Bronch.	Diar-rheal	Certain Degen-erative	Maternal	Cert. Dis. of Infancy	Motor Vehicle	Other Violence	Other and Unknown	Age (x)
0	100000	9780	12976	2500	13882	20892	4892	1044	1907	2822	0	1440	27865	0
1	71003	9511	9372	2493	10883	15951	2651	1028	1907	0	0	1214	15993	1
5	62309	9158	7327	2493	10197	13812	1974	999	1907	0	0	955	13487	5
10	60343	8952	6806	2491	10064	13364	1901	990	1907	0	0	879	12989	10
15	58488	8572	6401	2491	9921	12900	1861	984	1900	0	0	833	12625	15
20	55448	7685	5854	2484	9702	12231	1803	964	1732	0	0	738	12255	20
25	51219	6467	5133	2457	9365	11267	1739	930	1420	0	0	636	11805	25
30	46720	5379	4516	2414	8935	10155	1651	851	941	0	0	553	11325	30
35	43408	4600	4120	2320	8618	9405	1589	782	584	0	0	508	10882	35
40	39363	3761	3660	2132	8070	8525	1473	708	203	0	0	453	10378	40
45	35651	3167	3305	1878	7373	7771	1363	637	75	0	0	380	9702	45
50	31984	2605	2907	1614	6655	6894	1239	558	17	0	0	329	9166	50
55	28539	2164	2514	1354	5916	6110	1091	476	10	0	0	285	8619	55
60	24953	1754	2129	1096	5103	5285	925	384	4	0	0	246	8027	60
65	21234	1313	1808	849	4213	4402	753	279	0	0	0	218	7399	65
70	17078	896	1460	610	3229	3407	578	177	0	0	0	179	6542	70
75	12449	540	1006	369	2158	2271	413	84	0	0	0	115	5493	75
80	8437	309	634	203	1327	1384	277	32	0	0	0	63	4208	80
85+	5454	124	376	104	811	905	178	20	0	0	0	40	2896	85+

NUMBER OF PERSONS SURVIVING TO AGE X IF SPECIFIED CAUSES WERE ELIMINATED

Age (x)	No Causes	Respira-tory T. B. (1)	Other Infec. and Paras. (2)	Neo-plasms (3)	Cardio-vascular (4)	Infl., Pneu., Bronch. (5)	Diar-rheal (6)	Certain Degener-ative (7)	Maternal (8)	Cert. Dis. of Infancy (9)	Motor Vehicle (10)	Other Violence (11)	Other and Unknown (12)	(1) + (2)	(1) + (2) + (5) + (6) + (8)	(1)+(2)+ (5)+(6)+ (8)+part of(9)&(12)	(10) + (11)	Age (x)
0	100000	100000	100000	100000	100000	100000	100000	100000	100000	100000	100000	100000	100000	100000	100000	100000	100000	0
1	71003	71229	74090	71009	73563	75269	72907	71016	71003	73409	71003	71193	81690	74326	80905	92518	71193	1
5	62309	62840	67047	62314	65224	68210	64634	62348	62309	64421	62309	62719	74438	67618	76784	90636	62719	5
10	60343	61061	65486	60350	63303	66542	62669	60390	60343	62398	60343	60815	72677	66265	75890	90201	60815	10
15	58488	59564	63906	58495	61505	65002	60784	58539	58845	60470	58488	58992	70875	65083	75180	89833	58992	15
20	55448	57355	61169	55461	58533	62352	57683	55516	55619	57327	55448	56019	67629	63273	74247	89223	56019	20
25	51219	54204	57273	51257	54412	58648	53348	51315	51679	52955	51219	51845	63000	60611	72935	88291	51845	25
30	46720	50554	52904	46796	50071	54726	48749	46883	47604	48303	46720	47371	58033	57245	71291	87016	47371	30
35	43408	47789	48587	43570	46850	51700	45356	43626	44581	44879	43408	44057	54453	54592	69773	85851	44057	35
40	39363	44223	45469	39691	43053	47890	41245	39632	40800	40697	39363	40005	49985	51083	67497	83819	40005	40
45	35651	40691	41573	36193	39726	44256	37466	35963	37077	36859	35651	36303	46096	47451	64378	80873	36303	45
50	31984	37118	37739	32725	36406	40748	33736	32339	33320	33068	31984	32618	42015	43797	61313	77814	32618	50
55	28539	33606	34115	29452	33289	37314	30250	28934	29738	29506	28539	29147	38175	40172	58012	74444	29147	55
60	24953	29837	30261	26001	30006	33650	26614	25386	26007	25799	24953	25522	34126	36184	54242	70536	25522	60
65	21234	25881	26111	22364	26540	29753	22817	21701	22135	21954	21234	21744	29844	31825	49951	66010	21744	65
70	17078	21273	21388	18213	22475	25211	18520	17547	17803	17657	17078	17524	25108	26642	44459	60324	17524	70
75	12449	15886	16082	13496	17624	19859	13653	12872	12977	12871	12449	12831	19669	20523	37427	52987	12831	75
80	8437	11009	11299	9294	12942	14661	9375	8767	8755	8723	8437	8739	15119	14743	29677	45293	8739	80
85+	5454	7312	7585	6096	9022	10165	6149	5677	5685	5639	5454	5668	11841	10168	22274	38223	5668	85+

ADDED YRS OF LIFE																	
TOTAL		3.028	4.583	.458	3.850	7.046	1.611	.238	.613	1.082	.000	.467	10.579	8.257	22.575	42.766	.467
WORK	16.038	2.831	1.660	.374	1.522	2.871	.289	.190	.818	.000	.000	.229	1.556	4.692	9.707	11.465	.229

POPULATION, DEATHS, DEATH RATES FOR ALL CAUSES COMBINED, AND SPECIFIED CAUSES

Age Start of Interval	Midyear Population	Deaths During Year	All Causes	Respiratory T. B.	Other Infec. and Paras.	Neoplasms	Cardiovascular	Infl., Pneu., Bronch.	Diarrheal	Certain Degenerative	Maternal	Cert. Dis. of Infancy	Motor Vehicle	Other Violence	Other and Unknown	Age Start of Interval
0	56071	20120	.35883	.00162	.02586	.00020	.00323	.06078	.03749	.00020	.00000	.13228	.00000	.00811	.08907	0
1	181979	8792	.04831	.00118	.00875	.00005	.00071	.01727	.00635	.00019	.00000	.00000	.00000	.00060	.01322	1
5	255745	2460	.00962	.00042	.00194	.00001	.00034	.00213	.00059	.00004	.00000	.00000	.00000	.00043	.00371	5
10	224766	1107	.00493	.00049	.00076	.00005	.00034	.00136	.00013	.00003	.00000	.00000	.00000	.00055	.00122	10
15	192928	1681	.00871	.00206	.00081	.00003	.00049	.00258	.00007	.00009	.00000	.00000	.00000	.00136	.00122	15
20	172879	2167	.01253	.00290	.00124	.00010	.00061	.00325	.00010	.00010	.00000	.00000	.00000	.00276	.00147	20
25	153953	2074	.01347	.00297	.00149	.00007	.00084	.00322	.00006	.00012	.00000	.00000	.00000	.00285	.00185	25
30	124327	1971	.01585	.00324	.00179	.00010	.00146	.00382	.00012	.00024	.00000	.00000	.00000	.00299	.00209	30
35	117872	1963	.01665	.00311	.00150	.00020	.00196	.00408	.00015	.00034	.00000	.00000	.00000	.00257	.00234	35
40	101713	2051	.02016	.00341	.00233	.00063	.00272	.00516	.00020	.00052	.00000	.00000	.00000	.00218	.00301	40
45	80448	1936	.02407	.00367	.00267	.00062	.00385	.00630	.00073	.00073	.00000	.00000	.00000	.00209	.00388	45
50	55623	1660	.02984	.00372	.00304	.00128	.00543	.00759	.00041	.00101	.00000	.00000	.00000	.00227	.00511	50
55	49570	1658	.03345	.00347	.00255	.00161	.00702	.00878	.00061	.00109	.00000	.00000	.00000	.00192	.00601	55
60	32488	1581	.04866	.00489	.00422	.00249	.01139	.01351	.00102	.00126	.00000	.00000	.00000	.00228	.00760	60
65	23897	1755	.07344	.00603	.00523	.00364	.01707	.02050	.00163	.00167	.00000	.00000	.00000	.00268	.01498	65
70	14786	1592	.10767	.00852	.00656	.00514	.02516	.03118	.00250	.00271	.00000	.00000	.00000	.00392	.02198	70
75	9270	1403	.15135	.00820	.00744	.00529	.03031	.03862	.00280	.00270	.00000	.00000	.00000	.00388	.05210	75
80	5976	1221	.20432	.00904	.00937	.00569	.03581	.04284	.00251	.00218	.00000	.00000	.00000	.00301	.09388	80
85+	4889	1432	.29290	.00491	.01023	.00470	.04336	.06198	.00368	.00245	.00000	.00000	.00000	.00389	.15770	85+
ALL	1859180	58624														

	All Causes	Respiratory T. B.	Other Infec. and Paras.	Neoplasms	Cardiovascular	Infl., Pneu., Bronch.	Diarrheal	Certain Degenerative	Maternal	Cert. Dis. of Infancy	Motor Vehicle	Other Violence	Other and Unknown
CRUDE DEATH RATE	.03153	.00229	.00326	.00039	.00232	.00759	.00203	.00031	.00000	.00399	.00000	.00190	.00746
STANDARDIZED RATE (1)	.03441	.00232	.00357	.00043	.00248	.00832	.00236	.00033	.00000	.00466	.00000	.00192	.00802
STANDARDIZED RATE (2)	.03650	.00291	.00338	.00080	.00436	.00911	.00171	.00052	.00000	.00274	.00000	.00208	.00890
GEOMETRIC MEAN	.03672												

LIFE TABLE FOR ALL CAUSES COMBINED

Age (x)	Midyear Population	Deaths During Year	$_nM_x$	$_nq_x$	l_x	$_nd_x$	$_nL_x$	$_nm_x$	$_na_x$	T_x	$_nr_x$	$\overset{\circ}{e}_x$	Age (x)
0	56071	20120	.358831	.321870	100000	32187	89701	.358827	.680012	2846616	.000000	28.466	0
1	181979	8792	.048313	.172430	67813	11693	242020	.048314	1.500000	2756916	.000000	40.655	1
5	255745	2460	.009619	.047024	56120	2639	274003	.009631	2.500000	2514896	.000000	44.813	5
10	224766	1107	.004925	.024270	53481	1298	264076	.004915	2.435317	2240894	.016572	41.901	10
15	192928	1681	.008713	.042849	52183	2236	255688	.008745	2.662306	1976818	.019089	37.882	15
20	172879	2167	.012535	.060865	49947	3040	242307	.012546	2.556469	1721130	.010886	34.459	20
25	153953	2074	.013472	.065235	46907	3060	226949	.013483	2.520833	1478823	.018144	31.527	25
30	124327	1971	.015653	.076311	43847	3346	210907	.015865	2.511145	1251874	.014782	28.551	30
35	117872	1963	.016654	.079973	40501	3239	194457	.016657	2.515180	1040967	.003755	25.702	35
40	101713	2051	.020165	.096130	37262	3582	177479	.020183	2.534606	846510	.010977	22.718	40
45	80448	1936	.024065	.113836	33680	3834	158934	.024123	2.530973	669032	.032995	19.864	45
50	55623	1660	.029844	.139114	29846	4152	138079	.029896	2.507075	510098	.022908	17.091	50
55	49570	1658	.033448	.154705	25694	3975	118655	.033500	2.530818	371218	.017581	14.448	55
60	32488	1581	.048664	.218242	21719	4740	97016	.048858	2.557270	252563	.024654	11.629	60
65	23897	1755	.073440	.310855	16979	5278	71740	.073571	2.507658	155547	.009724	9.161	65
70	14786	1592	.107669	.421673	11701	4934	45826	.107669	2.430204	83807	−.000748	7.162	70
75	9270	1403	.151348	.535688	6767	3625	24170	.149982	2.333678	37981	−.050493	5.613	75
80	5976	1221	.204217	.649268	3142	2040	10049	.203006	2.224980	13811	−.050493	4.396	80
85+	4889	1432	.292902	1.000000	1102	1102	3762	.292902	3.414106	3762	.000000	3.414	85+

NUMBER OF PERSONS DYING (OUT OF 100,000 AT BIRTH) ABOVE AGE X FROM SPECIFIED CAUSES

Age (x)	All Causes	Respiratory T. B.	Other Infec. and Paras.	Neoplasms	Cardiovascular	Infl., Pneu., Bronch.	Diarrheal	Certain Degenerative	Maternal	Cert. Dis. of Infancy	Motor Vehicle	Other Violence	Other and Unknown	Age (x)
0	100000	7593	9775	1678	9220	24180	5856	1211	0	11865	0	5931	22691	0
1	67813	7447	7455	1660	8931	18728	2493	1194	0	0	0	5204	14701	1
5	56120	7162	5338	1647	8759	14549	956	1148	0	0	0	5057	11504	5
10	53481	7048	4805	1643	8667	13963	793	1139	0	0	0	4938	10485	10
15	52183	6917	4605	1629	8578	13605	759	1132	0	0	0	4792	10166	15
20	49947	6387	4396	1621	8453	12944	741	1109	0	0	0	4441	9855	20
25	46907	5683	4096	1598	8304	12156	715	1085	0	0	0	3772	9498	25
30	43847	5007	3757	1581	8113	11425	702	1059	0	0	0	3126	9077	30
35	40501	4324	3380	1561	7804	10618	677	1007	0	0	0	2495	8635	35
40	37262	3720	3010	1521	7422	9825	647	941	0	0	0	1995	8181	40
45	33680	3114	2596	1409	6938	8908	612	849	0	0	0	1608	7646	45
50	29846	2537	2171	1310	6323	7903	566	732	0	0	0	1276	7028	50
55	25694	2020	1748	1132	5567	6848	509	592	0	0	0	961	6317	55
60	21719	1608	1399	940	4732	5805	437	462	0	0	0	734	5602	60
65	16979	1132	988	697	3622	4488	338	340	0	0	0	513	4861	65
70	11701	699	613	436	2395	3014	220	219	0	0	0	320	3785	70
75	6767	309	312	200	1242	1586	106	95	0	0	0	141	2776	75
80	3142	111	133	73	513	658	38	30	0	0	0	47	1539	80
85+	1102	18	38	18	163	233	14	9	0	0	0	15	594	85+

NUMBER OF PERSONS SURVIVING TO AGE X IF SPECIFIED CAUSES WERE ELIMINATED

Age (x)	No Causes	Respiratory T. B. (1)	Other Infec. and Paras. (2)	Neoplasms (3)	Cardiovascular (4)	Infl., Pneu., Bronch. (5)	Diarrheal (6)	Certain Degenerative (7)	Maternal (8)	Cert. Dis. of Infancy (9)	Motor Vehicle (10)	Other Violence (11)	Other and Unknown (12)	(1) + (2)	(1) + (2) + (5) + (6) + (8)	(1)+(2)+(5)+(6)+(8)+part of(9)&(12)	(10) + (11)	Age (x)
0	100000	100000	100000	100000	100000	100000	100000	100000	100000	100000	100000	100000	100000	100000	100000	100000	100000	0
1	67813	67933	69738	67828	68050	72425	70622	67827	67813	78252	67813	68411	74677	69861	77702	96744	68411	1
5	56120	56479	59725	56144	56473	64131	59917	56173	56120	64759	56120	56749	65083	60107	73334	95933	56749	5
10	53481	53935	57473	53508	53908	61772	57269	53541	53481	61714	53481	54198	63187	57961	71689	95297	54198	10
15	52183	52757	56291	52223	52688	60683	55915	52248	52183	60216	52183	53029	62026	56910	70913	94686	53029	15
20	49947	51023	54100	49993	50554	58839	53538	50032	49947	57636	49947	51108	59731	55266	69786	93599	51108	20
25	46907	48620	51123	46973	47624	56164	50307	47010	46907	54128	46907	48665	56511	52990	68046	91722	48665	25
30	43847	46130	48147	43925	44705	53353	47038	43969	43847	50597	43847	46143	53317	50653	66121	89682	46143	30
35	40501	43306	44872	40592	41598	50235	43475	40663	40501	46736	40501	43264	49767	47979	63879	87234	43264	35
40	37262	40466	41678	37385	38650	47170	40029	37475	37262	42958	37262	40318	46326	45262	61552	84692	40318	40
45	33680	37206	38114	33898	35415	43754	36216	33961	33680	38865	33680	36842	42510	42105	58818	81725	36842	45
50	29846	33575	34231	30133	31559	40021	32140	30206	29846	34440	29846	32990	38412	38508	55605	78228	32990	50
55	25694	29447	29921	26109	28310	35790	27726	26136	25694	29649	25694	28725	33928	34292	51545	73634	28725	55
60	21719	25328	25668	22250	24792	31618	23509	22214	21719	25062	21719	24514	29555	29933	47166	68561	24514	60
65	16979	20295	20498	17615	20533	26468	18473	17476	16979	19593	16979	19384	24016	24501	41556	61761	19384	65
70	11701	14418	14503	12364	15428	20239	12837	12147	11701	13502	11701	13541	17860	17870	33912	52644	13541	70
75	6767	8705	8670	7340	10139	13714	7518	7122	6767	7809	6767	7988	11564	11153	25116	41582	7988	75
80	3142	4210	4179	3499	5485	7738	3541	3351	3142	3626	3142	3781	7040	5600	15545	30077	3781	80
85+	1102	1549	1539	1262	2303	3376	1257	1188	1102	1272	1102	1348	4012	2163	7562	19405	1348	85+

ADDED YRS OF LIFE

	No Causes	(1)	(2)	(3)	(4)	(5)	(6)	(7)	(8)	(9)	(10)	(11)	(12)				
TOTAL		1.838	3.037	.220	1.521	7.356	2.045	.204	.000	4.277	.000	1.601	7.020	5.176	17.929	37.214	1.601
WORK	15.098	2.246	1.212	.183	1.208	3.072	.103	.200	.000	.000	.000	1.786	1.649	3.588	7.349	8.816	1.786

POPULATION, DEATHS, DEATH RATES FOR ALL CAUSES COMBINED, AND SPECIFIED CAUSES

Age Start of Interval	Midyear Population	Deaths During Year	All Causes	Respiratory T. B.	Other Infec. and Paras.	Neo-plasms	Cardio-vascular	Infl., Pneu., Bronch.	Diar-rheal	Certain Degen-erative	Maternal	Cert. Dis. of Infancy	Motor Vehicle	Other Violence	Other and Unknown	Age Start of Interval
0	55074	18644	.33853	.00151	.02891	.00013	.00303	.05985	.03504	.00016	.00000	.12401	.00000	.00775	.07813	0
1	179323	9030	.05036	.00101	.00921	.00007	.00083	.01781	.00704	.00011	.00000	.00000	.00000	.00078	.01350	1
5	249199	2704	.01085	.00069	.00220	.00004	.00041	.00260	.00060	.00008	.00000	.00000	.00000	.00032	.00390	5
10	215768	1128	.00523	.00057	.00074	.00004	.00036	.00172	.00012	.00004	.00002	.00000	.00000	.00013	.00109	10
15	203922	1736	.00851	.00257	.00088	.00003	.00056	.00229	.00006	.00009	.00045	.00000	.00000	.00033	.00124	15
20	179484	2025	.01128	.00357	.00087	.00008	.00075	.00291	.00007	.00012	.00104	.00000	.00000	.00032	.00154	20
25	163891	2022	.01234	.00373	.00101	.00013	.00111	.00289	.00012	.00015	.00132	.00000	.00000	.00024	.00163	25
30	126803	1887	.01488	.00386	.00121	.00031	.00147	.00345	.00013	.00026	.00188	.00000	.00000	.00026	.00207	30
35	117124	1808	.01544	.00341	.00133	.00051	.00184	.00363	.00018	.00031	.00175	.00000	.00000	.00021	.00226	35
40	99923	1740	.01741	.00309	.00186	.00079	.00257	.00447	.00025	.00037	.00102	.00000	.00000	.00022	.00276	40
45	81202	1586	.01953	.00289	.00188	.00116	.00349	.00537	.00026	.00033	.00057	.00000	.00000	.00020	.00339	45
50	55987	1324	.02365	.00226	.00246	.00175	.00454	.00641	.00039	.00052	.00013	.00000	.00000	.00030	.00418	50
55	51559	1402	.02719	.00268	.00246	.00200	.00607	.00733	.00056	.00060	.00000	.00000	.00000	.00035	.00514	55
60	35790	1513	.04227	.00351	.00335	.00251	.01065	.01140	.00123	.00098	.00000	.00000	.00000	.00047	.00777	60
65	25532	1737	.06803	.00529	.00427	.00372	.01770	.01825	.00164	.00145	.00000	.00000	.00000	.00070	.01500	65
70	16451	1668	.10139	.00784	.00547	.00632	.02796	.02900	.00170	.00231	.00000	.00000	.00000	.00109	.01969	70
75	9991	1406	.14073	.00721	.00561	.00581	.03313	.03423	.00180	.00180	.00000	.00000	.00000	.00110	.05005	75
80	8152	1548	.18989	.00932	.00785	.00491	.03974	.03668	.00258	.00098	.00000	.00000	.00000	.00098	.08685	80
85+	6833	1896	.27748	.00458	.00878	.00424	.04903	.05473	.00366	.00117	.00000	.00000	.00000	.00132	.14957	85+
ALL	1882008	56804														

	All Causes	Respiratory T. B.	Other Infec. and Paras.	Neo-plasms	Cardio-vascular	Infl., Pneu., Bronch.	Diar-rheal	Certain Degen-erative	Maternal	Cert. Dis. of Infancy	Motor Vehicle	Other Violence	Other and Unknown
CRUDE DEATH RATE	.03018	.00252	.00312	.00052	.00251	.00734	.00198	.00024	.00058	.00363	.00000	.00056	.00718
STANDARDIZED RATE (1)	.03264	.00247	.00347	.00054	.00251	.00801	.00235	.00025	.00054	.00437	.00000	.00062	.00751
STANDARDIZED RATE (2)	.03400	.00294	.00309	.00095	.00446	.00847	.00169	.00038	.00056	.00257	.00000	.00053	.00835
GEOMETRIC MEAN	.03359												

LIFE TABLE FOR ALL CAUSES COMBINED

Age (x)	Midyear Population	Deaths During Year	$_nM_x$	$_nq_x$	l_x	$_nd_x$	$_nL_x$	$_nm_x$	$_na_x$	T_x	$_nr_x$	$\overset{\circ}{e}_x$	Age (x)
0	55074	18644	.338526	.302250	100000	30225	89285	.338522	.645495	2985340	.000000	29.853	0
1	179323	9030	.050356	.178904	69775	12483	247893	.050357	1.500000	2896055	.000000	41.506	1
5	249199	2704	.010851	.052870	57292	3029	278888	.010861	2.500000	2648162	.000000	46.222	5
10	215768	1128	.005228	.025763	54263	1398	267649	.005223	2.377802	2369275	.010097	43.663	10
15	203922	1736	.008513	.041786	52865	2209	259091	.008526	2.630527	2101625	.010498	39.755	15
20	179484	2025	.011282	.054919	50656	2782	246462	.011288	2.549425	1842535	.008866	36.373	20
25	163891	2022	.012337	.059928	47874	2869	232291	.012351	2.532750	1596072	.018972	33.339	25
30	126803	1887	.014881	.071836	45005	3233	216992	.014899	2.515208	1363781	.021375	30.303	30
35	117124	1808	.015437	.074332	41772	3105	201097	.015440	2.499732	1146789	.010007	27.454	35
40	99923	1740	.017413	.083508	38667	3229	185305	.017425	2.513033	945692	.013279	24.457	40
45	81202	1586	.019532	.093318	35438	3307	168999	.019568	2.523120	760388	.034715	21.457	45
50	55987	1324	.023648	.111917	32131	3596	151735	.023699	2.519524	591389	.026765	18.406	50
55	51559	1402	.027192	.127703	28535	3644	133815	.027232	2.568720	439654	.015310	15.408	55
60	35790	1513	.042274	.192760	24891	4798	112923	.042489	2.596481	305838	.026752	12.287	60
65	25532	1737	.068032	.291942	20093	5866	85995	.068213	2.533278	192915	.013110	9.601	65
70	16451	1668	.101392	.403107	14227	5735	56476	.101548	2.443912	106920	.007570	7.515	70
75	9991	1406	.140727	.508950	8492	4322	31000	.139421	2.348353	50444	-.057039	5.940	75
80	8152	1548	.189892	.620863	4170	2589	13747	.188334	2.256421	19445	-.057039	4.663	80
85+	6833	1896	.277477	1.000000	1581	1581	5698	.277477	3.603903	5698	.000000	3.604	85+

NUMBER OF PERSONS DYING (OUT OF 100,000 AT BIRTH) ABOVE AGE X FROM SPECIFIED CAUSES

Age (x)	All Causes	Respiratory T.B.	Other Infec. and Paras.	Neo-plasms	Cardio-vascular	Infl., Pneu., Bronch.	Diar-rheal	Certain Degenerative	Maternal	Cert. Dis. of Infancy	Motor Vehicle	Other Violence	Other and Unknown	Age (x)
0	100000	8370	9639	2391	10691	24478	5912	1010	1751	11073	0	1728	22957	0
1	69775	8235	7058	2379	10421	19134	2783	995	1751	0	0	1036	15983	1
5	57292	7983	4776	2361	10216	14720	1037	968	1751	0	0	842	12638	5
10	54263	7791	4163	2350	10101	13993	869	944	1751	0	0	753	11548	10
15	52865	7531	3567	2340	10004	13532	838	933	1746	0	0	718	11256	15
20	50656	6863	3738	2331	9859	12937	823	909	1628	0	0	632	10936	20
25	47874	5982	3522	2311	9673	12218	806	880	1371	0	0	553	10558	25
30	45005	5116	3287	2279	9414	11546	779	845	1063	0	0	498	10178	30
35	41772	4280	3025	2212	9095	10798	750	788	655	0	0	442	9727	35
40	38667	3595	2756	2109	8724	10067	714	726	303	0	0	399	9274	40
45	35438	3022	2411	1962	8247	9238	668	657	115	0	0	358	8760	45
50	32131	2533	2092	1765	7655	8328	624	601	20	0	0	325	8188	50
55	28535	2084	1718	1499	6565	7353	564	522	2	0	0	278	7550	55
60	24891	1725	1388	1231	6150	6371	489	442	2	0	0	232	6861	60
65	20093	1282	1008	947	4941	5077	349	331	2	0	0	178	5978	65
70	14227	826	640	626	3414	3503	207	206	2	0	0	117	4686	70
75	8492	383	331	268	1833	1863	111	75	2	0	0	55	3571	75
80	4170	160	158	88	812	807	56	19	2	0	0	21	2047	80
85+	1581	28	50	24	279	312	21	7	0	0	0	8	852	85+

NUMBER OF PERSONS SURVIVING TO AGE X IF SPECIFIED CAUSES WERE ELIMINATED

Age (x)	No Causes	Respiratory T.B. (1)	Other Infec. and Paras. (2)	Neo-plasms (3)	Cardio-vascular (4)	Infl., Pneu., Bronch. (5)	Diar-rheal (6)	Certain Degenerative (7)	Maternal (8)	Cert. Dis. of Infancy (9)	Motor Vehicle (10)	Other Violence (11)	Other and Unknown (12)	(1)+(2)	(1)+(2) +(5)+ (6)+(8)	(1)+(2)+ (5)+(6)+ (8)+part of(9)&(12)	(10) +(11)	Age (x)
0	100000	100000	100000	100000	100000	100000	100000	100000	100000	100000	100000	100000	100000	100000	100000	100000	100000	0
1	69775	69887	71953	69785	70000	74359	72424	69787	69775	79609	69775	70352	75817	72068	79719	97120	70352	1
5	57292	57613	61248	57316	57663	65464	61129	57327	57292	65366	57292	57943	65629	61591	75089	96194	57943	5
10	54263	54755	58651	54297	54727	62816	58072	54319	54263	61911	54263	54967	63387	59182	73320	95552	54967	10
15	52865	53604	57349	52908	53414	61727	56609	52931	52870	60316	52865	53586	62091	58151	72714	95208	53586	15
20	50656	52032	55196	50706	51325	59831	54259	50742	50777	57795	50656	51433	55865	56696	71898	94641	51433	20
25	47874	50062	52394	47941	48690	57377	51297	47984	48239	54621	47874	48686	57013	54789	70895	93945	48686	25
30	45005	47947	49504	45099	46029	54724	48251	45142	45651	51348	45005	45822	54037	52741	69742	93060	45822	30
35	41772	45368	46227	41924	43038	51677	44814	41955	42772	47659	41772	42586	50680	50206	68230	91823	42586	35
40	38667	42717	43078	38908	40209	48714	41521	38896	39940	44117	38667	39462	47444	47590	66499	90285	39462	40
45	35438	39759	39850	35801	37329	45657	38101	35714	36790	40432	35438	36207	44091	44710	64293	88179	36207	45
50	32131	36574	36415	32650	34445	42528	34590	32435	33450	36659	32131	32860	40660	41519	61587	85446	32860	50
55	28535	32565	32795	29252	31296	39003	30780	28881	29724	32557	28535	29228	36878	37886	58186	81811	29228	55
60	24891	29144	28962	25774	28148	35298	26925	25268	25928	28399	24891	25539	33010	33911	54187	77359	25539	60
65	20093	23995	23778	21070	23983	30188	21871	20499	20930	22925	20093	20666	27720	28396	48372	70646	20666	65
70	14227	17450	17203	15203	18579	23449	15615	14621	14820	16232	14227	14685	21178	21100	39763	60579	14685	70
75	8492	10838	10555	9371	12784	16222	9400	8830	8846	9689	8492	8814	13985	13471	29674	47735	8814	75
80	4170	5516	5331	4736	7415	9461	4657	4375	4344	4758	4170	4352	8898	7051	18614	34424	4352	80
85+	1581	2197	2104	1839	3433	4318	1789	1666	1648	1804	1581	1658	5278	2925	9424	22332	1658	85+

ADDED YRS OF LIFE

	No Causes	(1)	(2)	(3)	(4)	(5)	(6)	(7)	(8)	(9)	(10)	(11)	(12)	(1)+(2)	(1)+(2)+(5)+(6)+(8)	big	(10)+(11)
TOTAL		2.243	3.190	.347	1.786	7.691	2.140	.184	.518	4.117	.000	.540	7.082	5.769	20.152	39.910	.540
WORK	13.895	2.674	.982	.310	1.288	2.868	.116	.171	.824	.000	.000	.215	1.656	3.769	8.357	10.117	.215

POPULATION, DEATHS, DEATH RATES FOR ALL CAUSES COMBINED, AND SPECIFIED CAUSES

Age Start of Interval	Midyear Population	Deaths During Year	All Causes	Respiratory T. B.	Other Infec. and Paras.	Neoplasms	Cardiovascular	Infl., Pneu., Bronch.	Diarrheal	Certain Degenerative	Maternal	Cert. Dis. of Infancy	Motor Vehicle	Other Violence	Other and Unknown	Age Start of Interval
0	71191	21146	.29703	.00185	.02226	.00003	.00327	.07738	.04779	.00051	.00000	.05784	.00000	.00426	.08184	0
1	223796	8204	.03666	.00102	.00569	.00001	.00029	.01415	.00663	.00034	.00000	.00000	.00000	.00083	.00769	1
5	268738	1221	.00454	.00034	.00109	.00001	.00015	.00145	.00009	.00004	.00000	.00000	.00000	.00045	.00092	5
10	236673	797	.00337	.00051	.00041	.00002	.00019	.00102	.00006	.00003	.00000	.00000	.00000	.00049	.00063	10
15	228048	1556	.00682	.00212	.00063	.00004	.00030	.00148	.00002	.00005	.00000	.00000	.00000	.00128	.00091	15
20	204704	2017	.00985	.00304	.00081	.00006	.00046	.00184	.00013	.00013	.00000	.00000	.00000	.00245	.00103	20
25	171453	1699	.00991	.00303	.00057	.00012	.00062	.00151	.00003	.00016	.00000	.00000	.00000	.00258	.00128	25
30	144740	1609	.01112	.00312	.00067	.00013	.00095	.00204	.00004	.00029	.00000	.00000	.00000	.00244	.00144	30
35	131754	1574	.01195	.00302	.00063	.00030	.00140	.00225	.00005	.00042	.00000	.00000	.00000	.00219	.00167	35
40	109519	1672	.01527	.00343	.00073	.00073	.00230	.00286	.00009	.00068	.00000	.00000	.00000	.00217	.00227	40
45	94632	1678	.01773	.00346	.00075	.00113	.00323	.00334	.00013	.00089	.00000	.00000	.00000	.00203	.00278	45
50	68218	1554	.02278	.00358	.00078	.00170	.00465	.00484	.00021	.00122	.00000	.00000	.00000	.00220	.00362	50
55	51775	1494	.02886	.00382	.00091	.00261	.00728	.00479	.00031	.00176	.00000	.00000	.00000	.00230	.00508	55
60	41524	1628	.03921	.00426	.00123	.00340	.00992	.00848	.00034	.00219	.00000	.00000	.00000	.00262	.00677	60
65	28836	1521	.05275	.00444	.00132	.00499	.01567	.01144	.00052	.00326	.00000	.00000	.00000	.00198	.00912	65
70	16934	1275	.07529	.00661	.00136	.00620	.01884	.01653	.00059	.00378	.00000	.00000	.00000	.00171	.01966	70
75	9513	944	.09923	.00557	.00137	.00673	.02660	.02365	.00105	.00515	.00000	.00000	.00000	.00200	.02712	75
80	6908	1042	.15084	.00478	.00174	.00738	.03923	.03764	.00232	.00709	.00000	.00000	.00000	.00275	.04792	80
85+	4930	1307	.26511	.00325	.00223	.00791	.06045	.06978	.00426	.00994	.00000	.00000	.00000	.00467	.10264	85+
ALL	2113866	53938														

CRUDE DEATH RATE			.02552	.00223	.00200	.00052	.00200	.00656	.00241	.00048	.00000	.00195	.00000	.00168	.00568	
STANDARDIZED RATE (1)			.02644	.00222	.00210	.00056	.00208	.00685	.00257	.00050	.00000	.00204	.00000	.00166	.00586	
STANDARDIZED RATE (2)			.02763	.00267	.00164	.00107	.00385	.00672	.00169	.00086	.00000	.00120	.00000	.00181	.00613	
GEOMETRIC MEAN			.02708													

LIFE TABLE FOR ALL CAUSES COMBINED

Age (x)	Midyear Population	Deaths During Year	$_nM_x$	$_nq_x$	l_x	$_nd_x$	$_nL_x$	$_nm_x$	$_na_x$	T_x	$_nr_x$	$\overset{\circ}{e}_x$	Age (x)
0	71191	21146	.297032	.263730	100000	26373	88790	.297026	.574954	3592746	.000000	35.927	0
1	223796	8204	.036658	.134326	73627	9890	269783	.036659	1.500000	3503956	.000000	47.591	1
5	268738	1221	.004543	.022436	63737	1430	315110	.004538	2.500000	3234173	.000000	50.742	5
10	236673	797	.003368	.016724	62307	1042	309061	.003371	2.625960	2919063	.010365	46.850	10
15	228048	1556	.006823	.033624	61265	2060	301552	.006831	2.683050	2610002	.006682	42.602	15
20	204704	2017	.009853	.048172	59205	2852	289034	.009867	2.548650	2308450	.015084	38.991	20
25	171453	1699	.009909	.048374	56353	2726	274960	.009914	2.503821	2019416	.023874	35.835	25
30	144740	1609	.011116	.054115	53627	2902	260926	.011122	2.515865	1744456	.017364	32.529	30
35	131754	1574	.011947	.058058	50725	2947	246386	.011961	2.543688	1483530	.015707	29.247	35
40	109519	1672	.015267	.073674	47778	3520	230261	.015287	2.548532	1237143	.016103	25.894	40
45	94632	1678	.017732	.085115	44258	3767	212052	.017764	2.547783	1006882	.023973	22.750	45
50	68218	1554	.022780	.108271	40491	4384	191726	.022866	2.552796	794830	.037278	19.630	50
55	51775	1494	.028856	.135098	36107	4878	168592	.028934	2.551720	603103	.024623	16.703	55
60	41524	1628	.039206	.179160	31229	5595	142391	.039293	2.541778	434511	.017809	13.914	60
65	28836	1521	.052747	.234064	25634	6000	113306	.052954	2.522639	292120	.029373	11.396	65
70	16934	1275	.075292	.318173	19634	6247	82404	.075809	2.476294	178814	.043337	9.107	70
75	9513	944	.099233	.395085	13387	5289	53323	.099187	2.426420	96410	-.003843	7.202	75
80	6908	1042	.150840	.540751	8098	4379	29058	.150697	2.389434	43086	-.003843	5.321	80
85+	4930	1307	.265112	1.000000	3719	3719	14028	.265112	3.771997	14028	.000000	3.772	85+

NUMBER OF PERSONS DYING (OUT OF 100,000 AT BIRTH) ABOVE AGE X FROM SPECIFIED CAUSES

Age (x)	All Causes	Respiratory T.B.	Other Infec. and Paras.	Neo-plasms	Cardio-vascular	Infl., Pneu., Bronch.	Diar-rheal	Certain Degenerative	Maternal	Cert. Dis. of Infancy	Motor Vehicle	Other Violence	Other and Unknown	Age (x)
0	100000	9624	6113	3618	12973	24266	6609	2924	0	5136	0	6619	22118	0
1	73627	9459	4136	3616	12682	17395	2366	2879	0	0	0	6241	14853	1
5	63737	9183	2600	3612	12605	13577	577	2787	0	0	0	6018	12778	5
10	62307	9077	2258	3607	12557	13121	549	2775	0	0	0	5875	12488	10
15	61265	8919	2132	3601	12497	12806	529	2767	0	0	0	5722	12292	15
20	59205	8279	1943	3589	12405	12360	524	2753	0	0	0	5334	12018	20
25	56353	7398	1710	3570	12272	11829	513	2715	0	0	0	4625	11721	25
30	53627	6564	1554	3537	12102	11414	503	2671	0	0	0	3914	11368	30
35	50725	5749	1379	3502	11854	10881	492	2595	0	0	0	3278	10995	35
40	47778	5005	1224	3427	11507	10325	479	2492	0	0	0	2738	10581	40
45	44258	4214	1056	3258	10976	9666	458	2336	0	0	0	2238	10056	45
50	40491	3481	857	3017	10288	8956	431	2147	0	0	0	1808	9466	50
55	36107	2795	748	2689	9391	8026	391	1913	0	0	0	1386	8768	55
60	31229	2150	594	2248	8159	7216	339	1616	0	0	0	998	7909	60
65	25634	1542	419	1763	6742	6005	291	1303	0	0	0	624	6945	65
70	19634	1038	270	1195	4959	4703	232	932	0	0	0	401	5904	70
75	13387	491	158	682	3399	3331	183	619	0	0	0	260	4264	75
80	8098	193	85	324	1981	2070	127	345	0	0	0	154	2819	80
85+	3719	46	31	111	848	979	60	139	0	0	0	65	1440	85+

NUMBER OF PERSONS SURVIVING TO AGE X IF SPECIFIED CAUSES WERE ELIMINATED

Age (x)	No Causes	Respiratory T.B. (1)	Other Infec. and Paras. (2)	Neo-plasms (3)	Cardio-vascular (4)	Infl., Pneu., Bronch. (5)	Diar-rheal (6)	Certain Degenerative (7)	Maternal (8)	Cert. Dis. of Infancy (9)	Motor Vehicle (10)	Other Violence (11)	Other and Unknown (12)	(1)+(2)	(1)+(2)+(5)+(6)+(8)	(1)+(2)+(5)+(6)+(8)+part of (9)&(12)	(10)+(11)	Age (x)
0	100000	100000	100000	100000	100000	100000	100000	100000	100000	100000	100000	100000	100000	100000	100000	100000	100000	0
1	73627	73768	75336	73629	73876	79740	77344	73665	73627	78150	73627	73951	80106	75481	85875	98443	73951	1
5	63737	64117	66694	63742	64025	72982	68725	63856	63737	67653	63737	64226	71476	67092	82836	97726	64226	5
10	62307	62783	65553	62317	62636	71863	67213	62435	62307	66135	62307	62927	70195	66054	82184	97323	62927	10
15	61265	61892	64588	61281	61648	71022	66110	61399	61265	65029	61265	62029	69240	65249	81623	96883	62029	15
20	59205	60450	62612	59232	59666	69144	63893	59348	59205	62842	59205	60331	67217	63929	80572	95948	60331	20
25	56353	58422	59837	56397	56523	66421	60826	56527	56353	59815	56353	58134	64309	62034	78921	94295	58134	25
30	53627	56446	57104	53701	54337	63686	57895	53835	53627	56922	53627	56042	61592	60105	77061	92426	56042	30
35	50725	54232	54195	50830	51642	60859	54773	50996	50725	53841	50725	53659	58678	57942	75066	90425	53659	35
40	47778	51858	51208	47950	48987	57974	51605	48134	47778	50713	47778	51098	55735	55581	72844	88177	51098	40
45	44258	48870	47608	44581	45905	54478	47825	44740	44258	46977	44258	47850	52222	52570	69924	85172	47850	45
50	40491	45490	43720	41020	42687	50684	43782	41115	40491	42979	40491	44223	48448	49118	66480	81558	44223	50
55	36107	41297	39138	36894	38569	46308	39083	36889	36107	38325	36107	39872	43958	44764	62143	76921	39872	55
60	31229	36409	34006	32331	34964	41029	33855	32188	31229	33148	31229	34885	39040	39646	56468	70639	34885	60
65	25634	30532	28086	26597	30174	35151	27837	26715	25634	27209	25634	29013	33154	33452	49814	63256	29013	65
70	19634	23913	21654	21206	25017	28527	21377	20802	19634	20840	19634	22441	26602	26374	41722	53592	22441	70
75	13387	16859	14865	14919	18764	21159	14619	14457	13387	14209	13387	15432	20070	18720	32313	43773	15432	75
80	8098	10485	9054	9334	12991	14434	8891	8976	8098	8596	8098	9429	13933	11723	22942	33017	9429	80
85+	3719	4943	4198	4452	7297	8047	4132	4276	3719	3947	3719	4399	8176	5579	13414	21571	4399	85+

ADDED YRS OF LIFE																		
TOTAL		2.598	2.371	.499	2.056	8.107	2.825	.473	.000	2.172	.000	1.943	6.716	5.192	19.049	31.819	1.943	
WORK	12.166	2.568	.576	.303	1.120	1.878	.049	.292	.000	.000	.000	1.827	1.365	3.202	5.398	6.357	1.827	

POPULATION, DEATHS, DEATH RATES FOR ALL CAUSES COMBINED, AND SPECIFIED CAUSES

Age Start of Interval	Midyear Population	Deaths During Year	All Causes	Respiratory T. B.	Other Infec. and Paras.	Neo-plasms	Cardio-vascular	Infl., Pneu., Bronch	Diar-rheal	Certain Degen-erative	Maternal	Cert. Dis. of Infancy	Motor Vehicle	Other Violence	Other and Unknown	Age Start of Interval
0	69969	18642	.26643	.CC176	.0218C	.00000	.00266	.06787	.04458	.00097	.00000	.04946	.00000	.00394	.07339	0
1	222587	7924	.03560	.00110	.0C576	.00003	.00024	.01347	.0C689	.00035	.00000	.00000	.00000	.00062	.00715	1
5	264469	1163	.00440	.00045	.CC092	.00001	.00014	.C0154	.00014	.00006	.00000	.00000	.00000	.00022	.00092	5
10	229933	906	.00394	.00106	.0C060	.00002	.00023	.00115	.0C003	.00003	.00001	.00000	.00000	.00017	.00063	10
15	239381	1849	.0C772	.00317	.0C065	.00004	.00039	.00160	.00005	.00008	.00057	.00000	.00000	.00034	.00083	15
20	210472	2153	.01023	.0C429	.0CC67	.0000S	.00055	.C0156	.00003	.00012	.00055	.C0000	.00000	.00034	.00124	20
25	188835	1905	.0100S	.00380	.00069	.00017	.00069	.00183	.00003	.00017	.00130	.00000	.00000	.00031	.00111	25
30	142673	1695	.C1188	.00350	.0C060	.00045	.00114	.00211	.00005	.00032	.0C161	.00000	.00000	.00036	.00173	30
35	136571	1510	.01106	.00264	.0CC48	.00068	.00144	.00197	.00007	.00031	.00138	.00000	.00000	.00026	.00182	35
40	107573	1402	.013C3	.0C28C	.00054	.00112	.00212	.00238	.00011	.00057	.00086	.00000	.00000	.00032	.00222	40
45	94697	1321	.01395	.00244	.0CC53	.00155	.00286	.00263	.00013	.00070	.00043	.CC000	.00000	.00024	.00244	45
50	68115	1185	.C1740	.00241	.00060	.00285	.00414	.00324	.00010	.00085	.00012	.00000	.00000	.00025	.00283	50
55	58412	1220	.02089	.0C219	.00060	.00257	.00599	.00435	.C0017	.00113	.00000	.00000	.00000	.00027	.00361	55
60	42889	1379	.03215	.00289	.00077	.00371	.00900	.00720	.00037	.00175	.00000	.C0000	.00000	.00065	.00581	60
65	30281	1390	.04590	.003C7	.00086	.00561	.01460	.00994	.00063	.00271	.00000	.00000	.00000	.00050	.00799	65
70	20876	1431	.C6855	.00546	.00115	.00647	.01878	.01346	.00043	.00273	.00000	.00000	.00000	.00057	.01950	70
75	11674	1103	.C9448	.C0480	.00128	.00737	.02758	.02004	.00086	.00385	.C0000	.00000	.00000	.00077	.C2793	75
80	9809	1355	.13814	.0C398	.00143	.00775	.03905	.03058	.C0194	.C0520	.C0000	.C0000	.00000	.00092	.04730	80
85+	7271	1669	.22954	.CC248	.00179	.00798	.05653	.05350	.00330	.C0688	.C0000	.C0000	.00000	.00151	.09559	85+
ALL	2156487	51202														

CRUDE DEATH RATE			.02374	.00243	.0C189	.00071	.00208	.00599	.00226	.00044	.00053	.00160	.00000	.00046	.00535	
STANDARDIZED RATE (1)			.02430	.00235	.00202	.00071	.00198	.00623	.00248	.00044	.00049	.00174	.00000	.00047	.00539	
STANDARDIZED RATE (2)			.02502	.00259	.00153	.00128	.00368	.00596	.00162	.00068	.00050	.00102	.00000	.00043	.00570	
GEOMETRIC MEAN			.02496													

LIFE TABLE FOR ALL CAUSES COMBINED

Age (x)	Midyear Population	Deaths During Year	$_nM_x$	$_nq_x$	l_x	$_nd_x$	$_nL_x$	$_nm_x$	$_na_x$	T_x	$_nr_x$	$\overset{\circ}{e}_x$	Age (x)
0	69969	18642	.266432	.236390	100000	23639	88723	.266437	.522935	3825712	.000000	38.257	0
1	222587	7924	.035600	.130760	76361	9985	280482	.035599	1.500000	3736989	.000000	48.938	1
5	264469	1163	.0C4397	.021710	66376	1441	328278	.CC4390	2.500000	3456508	.000000	52.075	5
10	229933	906	.0C3940	.C19543	64935	1269	321705	.003945	2.659903	3128230	.004934	48.175	10
15	239381	1849	.007724	.037932	63666	2415	312665	.007724	2.654244	2806525	.000646	44.082	15
20	210472	2153	.010229	.049909	61251	3057	298706	.010234	2.530667	2493860	.008149	40.715	20
25	188835	1905	.010088	.049232	58194	2865	283836	.010094	2.509962	2195154	.024647	37.721	25
30	142673	1695	.011880	.057727	55329	3194	268647	.011889	2.496086	1911318	.023030	34.545	30
35	136571	1510	.011057	.C53803	52135	2805	253646	.011059	2.494281	1642670	.016978	31.508	35
40	107573	1402	.013033	.063187	49330	3117	238923	.013046	2.521121	1389024	.021117	28.158	40
45	94697	1321	.013950	.067535	46213	3121	223364	.013973	2.532508	1150100	.028505	24.887	45
50	68115	1185	.017357	.083635	43092	3604	206620	.017443	2.547170	926736	.032270	21.506	50
55	58412	1220	.020886	.099701	39488	3937	187957	.020946	2.591440	720116	.023598	18.236	55
60	42889	1379	.032153	.149982	35551	5332	164909	.032333	2.590687	532159	.033225	14.969	60
65	30281	1390	.045903	.207088	30219	6258	135808	.046080	2.557160	367250	.024134	12.153	65
70	20876	1431	.068548	.294186	23961	7049	102218	.C68961	2.504995	231443	.034698	9.659	70
75	11674	1103	.C94483	.380026	16912	6427	68132	.094332	2.443857	129225	-.011405	7.641	75
80	9809	1355	.138138	.507105	10485	5317	38579	.137822	2.395853	61093	-.011405	5.827	80
85+	7271	1669	.229542	1.000000	5168	5168	22514	.229542	4.356501	22514	.000000	4.357	85+

NUMBER OF PERSONS DYING (OUT OF 100,000 AT BIRTH) ABOVE AGE X FROM SPECIFIED CAUSES

Age (x)	All Causes	Respiratory T.B.	Other Infec. and Paras.	Neo-plasms	Cardio-vascular	Infl., Pneu., Bronch.	Diar-rheal	Certain Degenerative	Maternal	Cert. Dis. of Infancy	Motor Vehicle	Other Violence	Other and Unknown	Age (x)
0	100000	10034	5551	5111	14778	23677	6513	2729	1950	4389	0	1701	23167	0
1	76361	9878	4017	5111	14542	17655	2558	2643	1950	0	0	1351	16656	1
5	66376	9569	2403	5102	14474	13877	626	2545	1950	0	0	1178	14652	5
10	64935	9422	2103	5099	14428	13372	582	2524	1950	0	0	1106	14349	10
15	63666	9080	1912	5092	14354	13002	571	2512	1945	0	0	1050	14148	15
20	61251	8090	1709	5081	14231	12501	555	2486	1766	0	0	944	13888	20
25	58194	6809	1510	5054	14068	11914	545	2451	1482	0	0	842	13519	25
30	55329	5733	1315	5005	13872	11396	537	2402	1111	0	0	755	13203	30
35	52135	4794	1153	4884	13564	10829	524	2316	678	0	0	657	12736	35
40	49330	4127	1031	4711	13197	10329	507	2237	328	0	0	590	12273	40
45	46213	3458	902	4443	12689	9760	481	2102	122	0	0	515	11741	45
50	43092	2914	784	4094	12048	9171	452	1945	27	0	0	461	11196	50
55	39488	2417	660	3504	11188	8499	431	1769	3	0	0	409	10608	55
60	35551	2005	547	3021	10058	7678	399	1556	3	0	0	357	9927	60
65	30219	1527	420	2406	8564	6483	337	1266	3	0	0	249	8964	65
70	23961	1108	303	1641	6574	5129	251	897	3	0	0	182	7873	70
75	16912	547	185	978	4645	3745	207	617	3	0	0	123	5862	75
80	10485	220	97	477	2769	2382	149	355	3	0	0	70	3963	80
85+	5168	56	40	180	1273	1205	74	155	0	0	0	34	2151	85+

NUMBER OF PERSONS SURVIVING TO AGE X IF SPECIFIED CAUSES WERE ELIMINATED

Age (x)	No Causes	Respiratory T.B. (1)	Other Infec. and Paras. (2)	Neo-plasms (3)	Cardio-vascular (4)	Infl., Pneu., Bronch. (5)	Diar-rheal (6)	Certain Degenerative (7)	Maternal (8)	Cert. Dis. of Infancy (9)	Motor Vehicle (10)	Other Violence (11)	Other and Unknown (12)	(1)+(2)	(1)+(2)+(5)+(6)+(8)	(1)+(2)+(5)+(6)+(8)+part of(9)&(12)	(10)+(11)	Age (x)
0	100000	100000	100000	100000	100000	100000	100000	100000	100000	100000	100000	100000	100000	100000	100000	100000	100000	0
1	76361	76497	78065	76361	76567	81752	79886	76436	76361	80282	76361	76667	82249	78204	87632	98587	76667	1
5	66376	66783	65412	66384	66619	74568	71348	66533	66376	69784	66376	66804	73534	69837	84786	97987	66804	5
10	64935	65479	68216	64946	65218	73907	69846	65109	64935	68269	64935	65425	72270	68788	84213	97719	65425	10
15	63666	64543	67681	63684	64017	72881	68453	63849	63671	66935	63666	64202	71080	68005	83757	97450	64202	15
20	61251	63087	64747	61279	61710	70681	65912	61452	61432	64396	61251	61872	68669	66687	83054	96586	61872	20
25	58194	61238	61721	58247	58791	67816	62632	58419	58644	61182	58194	58884	65646	64949	82091	96384	58884	25
30	55329	59337	58884	55427	56090	65065	59557	55591	56123	58170	55329	56071	62763	63149	81088	95658	56071	30
35	52135	56896	55652	52346	53156	61963	56133	52466	53311	54812	52135	52931	59656	60734	79472	94386	52931	35
40	49330	54547	52785	49699	50662	59210	53131	49721	50792	51863	49330	50149	56565	58367	77691	92867	50149	40
45	46213	51821	49583	46821	47569	56134	49801	46711	47787	48586	46213	47054	53963	55600	75258	90581	47054	45
50	43092	48913	46357	44003	45377	53038	46467	43710	44654	45305	43092	43929	50937	52618	72369	87672	43929	50
55	39488	45364	42607	40903	42459	49401	42603	40226	40943	41516	39488	40306	47347	48948	68500	83511	40306	55
60	35551	41292	38475	37302	39396	45461	38388	36422	36861	37377	35551	36338	43408	44688	63979	78602	36338	60
65	30219	35612	32831	32307	35049	40076	32693	31234	31333	31771	30219	30990	37996	38690	57556	71600	30990	65
70	23961	28679	26145	26352	29918	33410	26005	25106	24844	25191	23961	24633	31378	31292	49100	62039	24633	70
75	16912	20810	18561	19215	23224	25249	18394	17965	17535	17780	16912	17437	24476	22839	38453	50662	17437	75
80	10485	13213	11582	12361	16557	17328	11454	11357	10871	11023	10485	10853	17483	14596	27322	38125	10853	80
85+	5168	6656	5752	6338	9958	9989	5702	5749	5361	5433	5168	5375	10967	7409	16389	25314	5375	85+

ADDED YRS OF LIFE

	No Causes	(1)	(2)	(3)	(4)	(5)	(6)	(7)	(8)	(9)	(10)	(11)	(12)	(1)+(2)	(1)+(2)+(5)+(6)+(8)	(1)+(2)+(5)+(6)+(8)+part of(9)&(12)	(10)+(11)
TOTAL		3.138	2.454	.801	2.442	8.059	2.898	.488	.663	1.938	.000	.560	6.893	5.839	20.868	33.562	.560
WORK	11.686	2.977	.530	.497	1.160	1.863	.053	.260	.826	.000	.000	.273	1.377	3.563	6.741	7.958	.273

POPULATION, DEATHS, DEATH RATES FOR ALL CAUSES COMBINED, AND SPECIFIED CAUSES

Age Start of Interval	Midyear Population	Deaths During Year	All Causes	Respiratory T.B.	Other Infec. and Paras.	Neoplasms	Cardiovascular	Infl., Pneu., Bronch.	Diarrheal	Certain Degenerative	Maternal	Cert. Dis. of Infancy	Motor Vehicle	Other Violence	Other and Unknown	Age Start of Interval
0	76398	19129	.25039	.00164	.01808	.00007	.00037	.06920	.04198	.00022	.00000	.07229	.00000	.00120	.04534	0
1	236292	7353	.03112	.00124	.00401	.00006	.00027	.01204	.00652	.00037	.00000	.00000	.00001	.00080	.00580	1
5	320950	908	.00283	.00029	.00029	.00003	.00012	.00086	.00010	.00004	.00000	.00000	.00001	.00027	.00049	5
10	305852	984	.00322	.00049	.00063	.00004	.00018	.00076	.00005	.00005	.00000	.00000	.00001	.00040	.00061	10
15	255523	1630	.00638	.00215	.00088	.00008	.00032	.00105	.00003	.00007	.00000	.00000	.00003	.00094	.00083	15
20	218190	2080	.00953	.00338	.00077	.00008	.00053	.00132	.00004	.00010	.00000	.00000	.00004	.00198	.00128	20
25	203759	1907	.00936	.00303	.00074	.00010	.00058	.00122	.00003	.00016	.00000	.00000	.00003	.00195	.00151	25
30	176879	1902	.01075	.00345	.00064	.00019	.00103	.00155	.00005	.00025	.00000	.00000	.00005	.00188	.00165	30
35	154921	1756	.01133	.00323	.00069	.00037	.00115	.00165	.00010	.00047	.00000	.00000	.00005	.00182	.00181	35
40	136557	1990	.01457	.00349	.00087	.00067	.00220	.00207	.00012	.00054	.00000	.00000	.00006	.00177	.00242	40
45	108805	1970	.01811	.00367	.00095	.00127	.00365	.00278	.00012	.00114	.00000	.00000	.00006	.00145	.00302	45
50	85813	1926	.02244	.00400	.00096	.00190	.00609	.00305	.00016	.00133	.00000	.00000	.00001	.00154	.00340	50
55	67969	2140	.03148	.00400	.00109	.00344	.00827	.00496	.00038	.00263	.00000	.00000	.00001	.00156	.00513	55
60	55270	2267	.04102	.00380	.00107	.00485	.01333	.00667	.00043	.00241	.00000	.00000	.00000	.00174	.00639	60
65	32485	1644	.05061	.00388	.00123	.00539	.01545	.00967	.00028	.00286	.00000	.00000	.00003	.00132	.01050	65
70	22492	1647	.07323	.00387	.00120	.00742	.02339	.01547	.00044	.00436	.00000	.00000	.00004	.00151	.01552	70
75	11762	1273	.10823	.00357	.00136	.00893	.03707	.02423	.00077	.00663	.00000	.00000	.00000	.00196	.02372	75
80	6936	1181	.17027	.00317	.00173	.01024	.06070	.03676	.00202	.00952	.00000	.00000	.00000	.00303	.04311	80
85+	5322	1557	.29256	.00225	.00225	.01071	.10992	.05505	.00357	.01297	.00000	.00000	.00000	.00545	.09038	85+
ALL	2482175	55244														

			All Causes	Respiratory T.B.	Other Infec. and Paras.	Neoplasms	Cardiovascular	Infl., Pneu., Bronch.	Diarrheal	Certain Degenerative	Maternal	Cert. Dis. of Infancy	Motor Vehicle	Other Violence	Other and Unknown
CRUDE DEATH RATE			.02226	.00228	.00162	.00067	.00236	.00525	.00201	.00057	.00000	.00223	.00002	.00123	.00401
STANDARDIZED RATE (1)			.02389	.00226	.00178	.00070	.00235	.00582	.00235	.00058	.00000	.00254	.00002	.00121	.00428
STANDARDIZED RATE (2)			.02639	.00262	.00146	.00133	.00478	.00576	.00154	.00101	.00000	.00150	.00003	.00136	.00501
GEOMETRIC MEAN			.02602												

LIFE TABLE FOR ALL CAUSES COMBINED

Age (x)	Midyear Population	Deaths During Year	$_nM_x$	$_nq_x$	l_x	$_nd_x$	$_nL_x$	$_nm_x$	$_na_x$	T_x	$_nr_x$	$\overset{\circ}{e}_x$	Age (x)
0	76398	19129	.250386	.222310	100000	22231	88788	.250383	.495656	3911495	.000000	39.115	0
1	236292	7353	.031118	.115496	77769	8982	288621	.031120	1.500000	3822707	.000000	49.155	1
5	320950	908	.002829	.013985	68787	962	341530	.002817	2.500000	3534086	.000000	51.377	5
10	305852	984	.003217	.016012	67825	1086	336649	.003226	2.720035	3192556	.012564	47.070	10
15	255523	1630	.006379	.031601	66739	2109	328824	.006414	2.690552	2855907	.026211	42.792	15
20	218190	2080	.009533	.046650	64630	3015	315760	.009548	2.548991	2527083	.017420	39.101	20
25	203759	1907	.009359	.045736	61615	2818	301044	.009361	2.504879	2211323	.011457	35.889	25
30	176879	1902	.010753	.052401	58797	3081	286336	.010760	2.517378	1910279	.016363	32.489	30
35	154921	1756	.011335	.055191	55716	3075	271024	.011346	2.542615	1623943	.013631	29.147	35
40	136557	1990	.014573	.070477	52641	3710	254175	.014596	2.566038	1352919	.017774	25.701	40
45	108805	1970	.018106	.086877	48931	4251	234248	.018147	2.551851	1098744	.026035	22.455	45
50	85813	1926	.022444	.106714	44680	4768	211812	.022511	2.565561	864496	.026918	19.349	50
55	67969	2140	.031485	.146397	39912	5843	185284	.031535	2.556656	652685	.012472	16.353	55
60	55270	2267	.041017	.186592	34069	6357	154537	.041136	2.513273	467401	.027446	13.719	60
65	32485	1644	.050608	.225462	27712	6248	123006	.050794	2.510570	312864	.035635	11.290	65
70	22492	1647	.073226	.310939	21464	6674	90641	.073631	2.500968	189858	.032402	8.845	70
75	11762	1273	.108230	.424544	14790	6279	57906	.108435	2.444756	99217	.010171	6.708	75
80	6936	1181	.170271	.588532	8511	5009	29341	.170718	2.361915	41311	.010171	4.854	80
85+	5322	1557	.292559	1.000000	3502	3502	11970	.292559	3.418112	11970	.000000	3.418	85+

NUMBER OF PERSONS DYING (OUT OF 100,000 AT BIRTH) ABOVE AGE X FROM SPECIFIED CAUSES

Age (x)	All Causes	Respiratory T. B.	Other Infec. and Paras.	Neo-plasms	Cardio-vascular	Infl., Pneu., Bronch.	Diar-rheal	Certain Degen-erative	Maternal	Cert. Dis. of Infancy	Motor Vehicle	Other Violence	Other and Unknown	Age (x)
0	100000	10417	5745	4834	16875	21771	6186	3680	0	6419	106	5368	18599	0
1	77769	10272	4140	4828	16843	15627	2459	3660	0	0	106	5261	14573	1
5	68787	9913	2982	4811	16766	12150	578	3554	0	0	103	5031	12899	5
10	67825	9813	2774	4802	16724	11859	544	3540	0	0	99	4938	12732	10
15	66739	9647	2563	4787	16663	11603	529	3524	0	0	97	4803	12523	15
20	64630	8933	2274	4761	16555	11256	520	3500	0	0	88	4492	12251	20
25	61615	7865	2030	4737	16387	10837	507	3468	0	0	75	3865	11844	25
30	58797	6952	1807	4707	16211	10471	497	3420	0	0	64	3278	11390	30
35	55716	5964	1622	4652	15914	10025	482	3348	0	0	51	2739	10919	35
40	52641	5088	1435	4552	15602	9579	454	3220	0	0	39	2246	10426	40
45	48931	4202	1213	4380	15041	9053	422	2981	0	0	32	1796	9811	45
50	44680	3342	991	4081	14182	8399	394	2713	0	0	19	1456	9103	50
55	39912	2495	789	3676	12885	7750	359	2431	0	0	16	1130	8381	55
60	34069	1754	587	3037	11350	6830	288	1942	0	0	14	841	7426	60
65	27712	1167	422	2286	9281	5749	221	1570	0	0	8	573	6435	65
70	21464	690	270	1621	7374	4554	187	1217	0	0	4	411	5136	70
75	14790	339	161	946	5241	3142	147	819	0	0	0	273	3722	75
80	8511	132	83	428	3090	1736	102	435	0	0	0	160	2345	80
85+	3502	27	27	128	1316	659	43	155	0	0	0	65	1082	85+

NUMBER OF PERSONS SURVIVING TO AGE X IF SPECIFIED CAUSES WERE ELIMINATED

Age (x)	No Causes	Respiratory T. B. (1)	Other Infec. and Paras. (2)	Neo-plasms (3)	Cardio-vascular (4)	Infl., Pneu., Bronch. (5)	Diar-rheal (6)	Certain Degener-ative (7)	Maternal (8)	Cert. Dis. of Infancy (9)	Motor Vehicle (10)	Other Violence (11)	Other and Unknown (12)	(1) + (2)	(1) + (2) + (5) + (6) + (8)	(1)+(2)+ (5)+(6)+ (8)+part of(9)&(12)	(10) + (11)	Age (x)
0	100000	100000	100000	100000	100000	100000	100000	100000	100000	100000	100000	100000	100000	100000	100000	100000	100000	0
1	77769	77897	79194	77774	77797	83365	81117	77787	77769	83625	77769	77863	81392	79324	88692	99649	77863	1
5	68787	69239	71164	68808	68884	77325	73616	68902	68787	73966	68790	69087	73657	71631	86175	98927	69090	5
10	67825	68370	70383	67854	67963	76569	72623	67953	67825	72932	67832	68214	72805	70949	85761	98643	68220	10
15	66739	67442	69474	66783	66935	75630	71476	66880	66739	71764	66748	67256	71862	70205	85205	98228	67265	15
20	64630	65025	67574	64698	64927	73628	69227	64791	64630	69496	64647	65440	69880	69033	84237	97411	65458	20
25	61615	64019	64671	61703	62063	70660	66011	61800	61615	66254	61644	63011	67051	67195	82557	95880	63040	25
30	58797	62024	61943	58911	59358	67840	63002	59020	58797	63224	58836	60718	64469	65343	80785	94276	60758	30
35	55716	59797	58887	55877	56579	64788	59717	55998	55716	59911	55765	58080	61596	63200	78768	92397	58131	35
40	52641	57417	55829	52891	53765	61718	56450	53033	52641	56605	52699	55376	58728	60895	76562	90297	55437	40
45	48931	54310	52122	49331	50532	57966	52505	49528	48931	52615	48992	51931	55255	57851	73539	87299	51595	45
50	44680	50511	47820	45335	47000	53675	47972	45485	44680	48044	44748	47764	51224	54060	69729	83401	47837	50
55	39912	46032	42921	40888	43294	48690	42888	40904	39912	42917	39975	42997	46546	49502	64893	78186	43065	55
60	34069	40086	36838	35512	38527	42612	36680	35381	34069	36634	34125	36990	40773	43344	58368	71048	37051	60
65	27712	33232	30125	29599	33520	35902	29901	29128	27712	29799	27763	30350	34252	36125	50497	62173	30406	65
70	21464	26243	23478	23556	28067	29203	23191	22889	21464	23080	21507	23662	27582	28705	42197	53004	23709	70
75	14790	18436	16275	16653	21788	21775	16016	16126	14790	15904	14823	16430	20864	20288	32345	41811	16466	75
80	8511	10800	9429	10145	15157	14182	9253	9598	8511	9152	8530	9549	13557	11965	21678	29254	9570	80
85+	3502	4527	3919	4403	8542	7063	3848	4150	3502	3766	3510	3996	6978	5066	11226	16370	4005	85+

ADDED YRS OF LIFE

		(1)	(2)	(3)	(4)	(5)	(6)	(7)	(8)	(9)	(10)	(11)	(12)				
TOTAL		2.928	2.163	.659	2.568	7.159	2.776	.577	.000	2.908	.031	1.538	5.080	5.309	17.635	28.271	1.571
WORK	11.896	2.748	.676	.357	1.234	1.416	.060	.347	.000	.000	.030	1.412	1.485	3.496	5.197	6.236	1.444

POPULATION, DEATHS, DEATH RATES FOR ALL CAUSES COMBINED, AND SPECIFIED CAUSES

Age Start of Interval	Midyear Population	Deaths During Year	All Causes	Respiratory T. B.	Other Infec. and Paras.	Neoplasms	Cardiovascular	Infl., Pneu., Bronch.	Diarrheal	Certain Degenerative	Maternal	Cert. Dis. of Infancy	Motor Vehicle	Other Violence	Other and Unknown	Age Start of Interval
0	74000	17127	.23145	.00147	.01841	.00007	.00042	.06458	.03822	.00018	.00000	.06524	.00000	.00108	.04178	0
1	233435	7523	.03223	.00145	.00455	.00004	.00029	.01256	.00685	.00024	.00000	.00000	.00001	.00075	.00548	1
5	311990	860	.00276	.00041	.00064	.00002	.00014	.00078	.00007	.00004	.00000	.00000	.00000	.00016	.00047	5
10	301606	1056	.00350	.00106	.00068	.00003	.00022	.00079	.00005	.00005	.00003	.00000	.00000	.00016	.00044	10
15	255732	1786	.00698	.00257	.00082	.00005	.00038	.00116	.00004	.00006	.00044	.00000	.00000	.00039	.00068	15
20	237363	2231	.00940	.00412	.00073	.00009	.00058	.00131	.00003	.00011	.00114	.00000	.00000	.00031	.00098	20
25	221856	2168	.00977	.00382	.00067	.00016	.00081	.00142	.00005	.00011	.00144	.00000	.00000	.00027	.00102	25
30	174463	1682	.00964	.00284	.00059	.00038	.00104	.00141	.00007	.00025	.00151	.00000	.00000	.00030	.00124	30
35	165103	1745	.01057	.00283	.00065	.00061	.00131	.00156	.00010	.00035	.00148	.00000	.00000	.00028	.00138	35
40	131307	1477	.01125	.00238	.00067	.00110	.00208	.00169	.00009	.00050	.00081	.00000	.00000	.00024	.00168	40
45	106528	1385	.01300	.00232	.00057	.00176	.00325	.00198	.00008	.00070	.00021	.00000	.00000	.00026	.00186	45
50	87683	1436	.01638	.00224	.00065	.00251	.00473	.00247	.00022	.00092	.00003	.00000	.00000	.00030	.00230	50
55	66214	1548	.02338	.00267	.00085	.00362	.00668	.00349	.00018	.00168	.00005	.00000	.00000	.00024	.00393	55
60	62597	1942	.03102	.00227	.00062	.00438	.01113	.00522	.00038	.00156	.00000	.00000	.00002	.00029	.00474	60
65	33685	1464	.04346	.00273	.00074	.00520	.01443	.00799	.00027	.00235	.00000	.00000	.00003	.00030	.00944	65
70	28454	1805	.06344	.00214	.00074	.00713	.02182	.01276	.00039	.00355	.00000	.00000	.00000	.00035	.01395	70
75	14125	1332	.09430	.00255	.00085	.00857	.03455	.01996	.00071	.00538	.00000	.00000	.00000	.00042	.02131	75
80	11077	1646	.14860	.00226	.00099	.00984	.05651	.03024	.00172	.00767	.00000	.00000	.00000	.00072	.03864	80
85+	8992	2316	.25756	.00145	.00145	.01034	.10265	.04560	.00311	.01068	.00000	.00000	.00000	.00122	.08107	85+
ALL	2526210	52529														

	All Causes	Respiratory T. B.	Other Infec. and Paras.	Neoplasms	Cardiovascular	Infl., Pneu., Bronch.	Diarrheal	Certain Degenerative	Maternal	Cert. Dis. of Infancy	Motor Vehicle	Other Violence	Other and Unknown
CRUDE DEATH RATE	.02079	.00228	.00157	.00081	.00251	.00494	.00185	.00046	.00054	.00191	.00000	.00034	.00360
STANDARDIZED RATE (1)	.02190	.00222	.00177	.00077	.00216	.00546	.00224	.00043	.00050	.00230	.00000	.00035	.00370
STANDARDIZED RATE (2)	.02335	.00236	.00137	.00140	.00437	.00516	.00147	.00076	.00050	.00135	.00000	.00033	.00427
GEOMETRIC MEAN	.02314												

LIFE TABLE FOR ALL CAUSES COMBINED

Age (x)	Midyear Population	Deaths During Year	$_nM_x$	$_nq_x$	l_x	$_nd_x$	$_nL_x$	$_nm_x$	$_na_x$	T_x	$_nr_x$	$\overset{\circ}{e}_x$	Age (x)
0	74000	17127	.231446	.205880	100000	20588	88954	.231446	.463458	4131083	.000000	41.311	0
1	233435	7523	.032227	.119302	79412	9474	293963	.032229	1.500000	4042129	.000000	50.901	1
5	311990	860	.002756	.013626	69938	953	347308	.002744	2.500000	3748166	.000000	53.593	5
10	301606	1056	.003501	.017410	68985	1201	342211	.003510	2.740078	3400859	.011223	49.299	10
15	255732	1786	.006984	.034477	67784	2337	333454	.007008	2.660997	3058648	.018630	45.123	15
20	237363	2231	.009399	.045946	65447	3007	319851	.009401	2.544410	2725194	.005481	41.640	20
25	221856	2168	.009772	.047694	62440	2978	304712	.009773	2.485519	2405343	.017494	38.522	25
30	174463	1682	.009641	.047089	59462	2800	290298	.009645	2.495610	2100631	.020133	35.327	30
35	165103	1745	.010569	.051516	56662	2919	276042	.010574	2.510277	1810333	.015597	31.950	35
40	131307	1477	.011248	.054779	53743	2944	261415	.011262	2.520310	1534291	.029805	28.549	40
45	106528	1385	.013001	.063111	50799	3206	246151	.013025	2.553286	1272876	.026106	25.057	45
50	87683	1436	.016377	.079087	47593	3764	228899	.016444	2.591326	1026725	.034054	21.573	50
55	66214	1548	.023379	.110794	43829	4856	207356	.023414	2.580485	797827	.011322	18.203	55
60	62597	1942	.031024	.144716	38973	5640	181124	.031139	2.563608	590431	.030176	15.150	60
65	33685	1464	.043461	.197342	33333	6578	150579	.043685	2.554633	409307	.034361	12.279	65
70	28454	1805	.063436	.275276	26755	7365	115531	.063749	2.522856	258728	.029099	9.670	70
75	14125	1332	.094301	.380918	19390	7386	78292	.094339	2.473853	143197	.002441	7.385	75
80	11077	1646	.148596	.536321	12004	6438	43295	.148702	2.402079	64905	.002441	5.407	80
85+	8992	2316	.257562	1.000000	5566	5566	21610	.257562	3.882556	21610	.000000	3.883	85+

NUMBER OF PERSONS DYING (OUT OF 100,000 AT BIRTH) ABOVE AGE X FROM SPECIFIED CAUSES

Age (x)	All Causes	Respiratory T. B.	Other Infec. and Paras.	Neoplasms	Cardiovascular	Infl., Pneu., Bronch.	Diarrheal	Certain Degenerative	Maternal	Cert. Dis. of Infancy	Motor Vehicle	Other Violence	Other and Unknown	Age (x)
0	100000	9884	5588	6194	19403	21781	6021	3353	2092	5804	11	1379	18490	0
1	79412	9753	3951	6188	19366	16037	2622	3337	2092	0	11	1283	14772	1
5	69938	9327	2612	6177	19280	12343	609	3266	2092	0	7	1063	13162	5
10	68985	9184	2390	6169	19231	12073	585	3251	2092	0	7	1006	12997	10
15	67784	8819	2157	6158	19157	11803	569	3234	2080	0	7	951	12849	15
20	65447	7825	1883	6141	19032	11415	557	3214	1931	0	7	822	12620	20
25	62440	6507	1650	6111	18847	10996	549	3178	1566	0	7	724	12305	25
30	59462	5345	1445	6061	18599	10565	533	3145	1127	0	7	641	11994	30
35	56662	4523	1274	5949	18296	10155	513	3071	688	0	7	555	11631	35
40	53743	3741	1095	5782	17932	9724	484	2974	279	0	7	476	11249	40
45	50799	3119	920	5493	17386	9281	460	2842	70	0	7	413	10808	45
50	47593	2548	779	5057	16583	8793	439	2668	20	0	7	348	10351	50
55	43829	2036	630	4480	15494	8224	390	2455	13	0	7	280	9820	55
60	38973	1482	454	3727	14107	7499	352	2107	3	0	7	230	9005	60
65	33333	1071	342	2932	12080	6548	282	1751	3	0	4	178	8142	65
70	26755	659	230	2147	9897	5338	242	1396	3	0	0	133	6710	70
75	19390	342	145	1320	7362	3856	197	984	3	0	0	92	5089	75
80	12004	143	78	649	4656	2292	142	562	3	0	0	59	3420	80
85+	5566	31	31	224	2218	985	67	231	0	0	0	26	1753	85+

NUMBER OF PERSONS SURVIVING TO AGE X IF SPECIFIED CAUSES WERE ELIMINATED

Age (x)	No Causes	Respiratory T. B. (1)	Other Infec. and Paras. (2)	Neoplasms (3)	Cardiovascular (4)	Infl., Pneu., Bronch. (5)	Diarrheal (6)	Certain Degenerative (7)	Maternal (8)	Cert. Dis. of Infancy (9)	Motor Vehicle (10)	Other Violence (11)	Other and Unknown (12)	(1)+(2)	(1)+(2)+(5)+(6)+(8)	(1)+(2)+(5)+(6)+(8)+part of(9)&(12)	(10)+(11)	Age (x)
0	100000	100000	100000	100000	100000	100000	100000	100000	100000	100000	100000	100000	100000	100000	100000	100000	100000	0
1	79412	79529	80881	79417	79445	84687	82493	79426	79412	84744	79412	79497	82788	81000	89731	99678	79497	1
5	69938	70442	72522	69953	70048	78371	74639	70017	69938	74634	69942	70220	74502	73045	87354	99048	70224	5
10	68985	69625	71763	69008	69142	77605	73647	69078	68985	73617	68989	69320	73662	72429	86985	98826	69324	10
15	67784	68779	70754	67817	68012	76555	72382	67892	67756	72335	67788	68168	72536	71793	86598	98568	68172	15
20	65447	67407	68596	65496	65790	74347	69899	65571	65605	69841	65451	65945	70276	70650	85925	98092	65949	20
25	62440	65649	65683	62516	62950	71398	66696	62594	62950	66633	62443	63012	67379	69059	85037	97495	63015	25
30	59462	63721	62761	59583	60192	68475	63532	59641	60381	63455	59465	60088	64494	67256	84030	96757	60092	30
35	56662	61585	59982	56688	57658	65713	60561	56905	57975	60467	56665	57344	61842	65194	82682	95661	57347	35
40	53743	59246	57077	54121	55050	62817	57471	54069	55397	57352	53746	54467	59064	62921	81065	94260	54470	40
45	50799	56670	54131	51440	52562	59881	54348	51236	52571	54210	50802	51546	56302	60387	78813	92096	51549	45
50	47593	53713	50860	48624	50075	56661	50940	48173	49303	50789	47596	48357	53241	57400	75770	88921	48359	50
55	43829	50021	46991	45347	47228	52834	46961	44570	45410	46772	43831	44598	49604	53630	71768	84615	44601	55
60	38973	45077	41962	41064	43430	47812	41797	39967	40389	41590	38975	39705	44496	48535	66176	78595	39707	60
65	33333	38994	36001	35502	39293	41986	35817	34522	34544	35571	33338	34008	39409	42114	59071	70703	34013	65
70	26755	31731	29004	25581	33924	35093	28787	28039	27727	28551	26762	27338	33187	34398	50308	61219	27345	70
75	19390	23313	21097	22225	27470	27137	20904	20690	20094	20692	19395	19848	25817	25366	39664	49428	19853	75
80	12004	14617	13117	14366	20277	18566	12988	13164	12440	12810	12007	12313	17816	15973	27745	35835	12317	80
85+	5566	6869	6117	7008	12579	10078	6076	6350	5770	5940	5567	5732	10080	7548	15469	21308	5734	85+

ADDED YRS OF LIFE

	No Causes	(1)	(2)	(3)	(4)	(5)	(6)	(7)	(8)	(9)	(10)	(11)	(12)	(1)+(2)	(1)+(2)+(5)+(6)+(8)	(1)+(2)+(5)+(6)+(8)+part of(9)&(12)	(10)+(11)
TOTAL		3.266	2.328	.948	3.089	7.402	2.812	.513	.732	2.743	.003	.471	4.899	5.823	19.621	29.962	.474
WORK	10.915	2.893	.618	.527	1.266	1.383	.061	.263	.854	.000	.000	.268	1.137	3.572	6.223	7.168	.268

POPULATION, DEATHS, DEATH RATES FOR ALL CAUSES COMBINED, AND SPECIFIED CAUSES

Age Start of Interval	Midyear Population	Deaths During Year	All Causes	Respiratory T. B.	Other Infec. and Paras.	Neoplasms	Cardiovascular	Infl., Pneu., Bronch.	Diarrheal	Certain Degenerative	Maternal	Cert. Dis. of Infancy	Motor Vehicle	Other Violence	Other and Unknown	Age Start of Interval
0	80694	15432	.19124	.00076	.00662	.00006	.00021	.04756	.01600	.00011	.00000	.10049	.00000	.00004	.01939	0
1	300440	4221	.01405	.00054	.00158	.00004	.00017	.00512	.00180	.00017	.00000	.00225	.00001	.00036	.00202	1
5	381294	1033	.00271	.00020	.00056	.00006	.00011	.00080	.00006	.00008	.00000	.00001	.00001	.00038	.00046	5
10	318613	701	.00220	.00027	.00040	.00006	.00015	.00047	.00002	.00003	.00000	.00000	.00001	.00038	.00042	10
15	273379	1189	.00435	.00107	.00053	.00007	.00027	.00061	.00001	.00010	.00000	.00000	.00002	.00098	.00069	15
20	266856	1600	.00600	.00173	.00054	.00013	.00040	.00064	.00000	.00012	.00000	.00000	.00003	.00153	.00086	20
25	206481	1469	.00711	.00159	.00042	.00013	.00059	.00068	.00003	.00016	.00000	.00000	.00005	.00185	.00122	25
30	179987	1493	.00830	.00231	.00042	.00025	.00090	.00076	.00004	.00033	.00000	.00000	.00006	.00193	.00130	30
35	173767	1785	.01027	.00257	.00048	.00039	.00134	.00110	.00003	.00050	.00000	.00000	.00005	.00193	.00187	35
40	158814	1943	.01223	.00254	.00047	.00067	.00247	.00117	.00005	.00091	.00000	.00000	.00004	.00189	.00203	40
45	123721	1993	.01611	.00287	.00056	.00150	.00407	.00161	.00006	.00112	.00000	.00000	.00005	.00189	.00239	45
50	111229	2140	.01924	.00281	.00056	.00235	.00557	.00155	.00005	.00151	.00000	.00000	.00005	.00176	.00263	50
55	76803	2306	.03002	.00349	.00103	.00402	.00960	.00324	.00016	.00225	.00000	.00000	.00007	.00198	.00419	55
60	66861	2541	.03800	.00299	.00085	.00504	.01509	.00405	.00028	.00292	.00000	.00000	.00001	.00176	.00500	60
65	43097	2383	.05529	.00343	.00060	.00794	.02422	.00726	.00032	.00297	.00000	.00000	.00000	.00167	.00687	65
70	29898	2317	.07750	.00348	.00100	.00870	.03412	.01161	.00033	.00388	.00000	.00000	.00007	.00204	.01228	70
75	14974	1342	.08962	.00314	.00073	.00955	.03853	.01262	.00027	.00354	.00000	.00000	.00007	.00127	.01990	75
80	8644	1204	.13929	.00278	.00093	.01099	.05842	.02071	.00058	.00509	.00000	.00000	.00000	.00197	.03783	80
85+	5960	1407	.23607	.00185	.00117	.01141	.08809	.03758	.00101	.00688	.00000	.00000	.00000	.00352	.08456	85+
ALL	2821512	48499														
CRUDE DEATH RATE			.01719	.00152	.00082	.00084	.00276	.00319	.00070	.00055	.00000	.00311	.00003	.00117	.00251	
STANDARDIZED RATE (1)			.01820	.00149	.00087	.00082	.00265	.00351	.00083	.00053	.00000	.00380	.00003	.00114	.00253	
STANDARDIZED RATE (2)			.02164	.00184	.00077	.00155	.00540	.00351	.00055	.00088	.00000	.00226	.00003	.00134	.00351	
GEOMETRIC MEAN			.02109													

LIFE TABLE FOR ALL CAUSES COMBINED

Age (x)	Midyear Population	Deaths During Year	$_nM_x$	$_nq_x$	l_x	$_nd_x$	$_nL_x$	$_nm_x$	$_na_x$	T_x	$_nr_x$	$\overset{\circ}{e}_x$	Age (x)
0	80694	15432	.191241	.171410	100000	17141	89632	.191238	.395110	4663364	.000000	46.634	0
1	300440	4221	.014049	.054297	82859	4499	320189	.014051	1.500000	4573732	.000000	55.199	1
5	381294	1033	.002709	.013412	78360	1051	389173	.002701	2.500000	4253543	.000000	54.282	5
10	318613	701	.002200	.010982	77309	849	384547	.002208	2.647232	3864371	.026614	49.986	10
15	273379	1189	.004349	.021593	76460	1651	378457	.004362	2.672244	3479823	.015662	45.512	15
20	266856	1600	.005996	.029555	74809	2214	368656	.006006	2.584030	3101367	.018022	41.457	20
25	206481	1469	.007114	.035044	72595	2544	356748	.007131	2.552165	2732671	.032659	37.643	25
30	179987	1493	.008295	.040699	70051	2851	343299	.008305	2.560213	2375923	.016278	33.917	30
35	173767	1785	.010272	.050119	67200	3368	327777	.010275	2.558578	2032624	.002021	30.247	35
40	158814	1943	.012234	.055500	63832	3798	309934	.012254	2.570871	1704846	.017447	26.708	40
45	123721	1993	.016109	.077623	60034	4660	288792	.016136	2.558476	1394912	.017878	23.235	45
50	111229	2140	.019240	.092209	55374	5106	264604	.019297	2.597802	1106120	.025442	19.975	50
55	76803	2306	.030025	.140388	50268	7057	234201	.030132	2.571413	841515	.023509	16.741	55
60	66861	2541	.038004	.174546	43211	7525	197586	.038085	2.545709	607314	.018226	14.055	60
65	43097	2383	.055294	.244017	35686	8708	156917	.055494	2.529547	409727	.021932	11.481	65
70	29898	2317	.077497	.324709	26978	8760	112558	.077827	2.453675	252810	.029215	9.371	70
75	14974	1342	.089622	.364145	18218	6634	73922	.089744	2.412069	140252	.027475	7.699	75
80	8644	1204	.139287	.514503	11584	5960	42507	.140211	2.414010	66331	.027475	5.726	80
85+	5960	1407	.236074	1.000000	5624	5624	23823	.236074	4.235963	23823	.000000	4.236	85+

NUMBER OF PERSONS DYING (OUT OF 100,000 AT BIRTH) ABOVE AGE X FROM SPECIFIED CAUSES

Age (x)	All Causes	Respiratory T.B.	Other Infec. and Paras.	Neo-plasms	Cardio-vascular	Infl., Pneu., Bronch.	Diar-rheal	Certain Degen-erative	Maternal	Cert. Dis. of Infancy	Motor Vehicle	Other Violence	Other and Unknown	Age (x)
0	100000	8917	3524	7287	25170	15808	2379	4185	0	9730	152	6476	16372	0
1	82859	8849	2930	7281	25151	11545	945	4175	0	722	152	6473	14636	1
5	78360	8678	2425	7269	25097	9906	368	4120	0	3	149	6357	13988	5
10	77309	8601	2208	7244	25055	9597	347	4089	0	0	146	6211	13811	10
15	76460	8495	2054	7222	24997	9418	341	4077	0	0	144	6064	13648	15
20	74809	8089	1852	7197	24893	9188	335	4040	0	0	137	5692	13386	20
25	72595	7450	1852	7148	24743	8951	334	3998	0	0	126	5125	13068	25
30	70051	6739	1502	7102	24533	8708	323	3938	0	0	107	4466	12633	30
35	67200	5947	1357	7016	24223	8446	308	3825	0	0	88	3804	12186	35
40	63832	5104	1199	6890	23783	8084	297	3661	0	0	71	3172	11571	40
45	60034	4317	1052	6682	23015	7720	281	3380	0	0	59	2587	10941	45
50	55374	3488	891	6246	21838	7255	265	3057	0	0	45	2041	10248	50
55	50268	2745	743	5622	20359	6737	250	2656	0	0	31	1574	9551	55
60	43211	1927	501	4676	18100	5974	214	2126	0	0	16	1111	8566	60
65	35686	1336	333	3678	15108	5171	157	1549	0	0	13	762	7579	65
70	26978	797	239	2429	11292	4026	106	1083	0	0	13	500	6493	70
75	18218	405	125	1448	7436	2713	69	645	0	0	5	270	5102	75
80	11584	174	71	742	4585	1779	49	384	0	0	0	177	3623	80
85+	5624	44	28	272	2099	895	24	164	0	0	0	84	2014	85+

NUMBER OF PERSONS SURVIVING TO AGE X IF SPECIFIED CAUSES WERE ELIMINATED

Age (x)	No Causes	Respiratory T.B.	Other Infec. and Paras.	Neo-plasms	Cardio-vascular	Infl., Pneu., Bronch.	Diar-rheal	Certain Degener-ative	Maternal	Cert. Dis. of Infancy	Motor Vehicle	Other Violence	Other and Unknown	(1)+(2)	(1)+(2)+(5)+(6)+(8)	(1)+(2)+(5)+(6)+(8)+part of(9)&(12)	(10)+(11)	Age (x)
		(1)	(2)	(3)	(4)	(5)	(6)	(7)	(8)	(9)	(10)	(11)	(12)					
0	100000	100000	100000	100000	100000	100000	100000	100000	100000	100000	100000	100000	100000	100000	100000	100000	100000	0
1	82859	82921	83401	82864	82876	86826	84113	82868	82859	91465	82859	82862	84452	83463	88845	99888	82862	1
5	78360	78585	79368	78377	78429	83758	80174	78422	78360	87274	78363	78475	80511	79596	87091	99462	78478	5
10	77309	77608	78522	77350	77419	83004	79120	77401	77309	86107	77315	77568	79612	78826	86615	99082	77574	10
15	76460	76861	77816	76523	76626	82283	78258	76563	76460	85161	76468	76863	78905	78224	86161	98698	76871	15
20	74809	75607	76339	74895	75075	80752	76574	74946	74809	83322	74824	75574	77469	77153	85246	97856	75589	20
25	72595	74008	74281	72727	73001	78614	74309	72770	72595	80856	72620	73904	75502	75727	83941	96594	73930	25
30	70051	72130	71828	70224	70651	76110	71716	70279	70051	78023	70094	71976	73301	73960	82275	94984	72020	30
35	67200	69998	69051	67450	68083	73299	68812	67530	67200	74847	67260	69716	70778	71925	80336	93050	69778	35
40	63832	67350	65748	64193	65107	70012	65314	64306	63832	71096	63905	66863	67865	69372	77926	90683	66940	40
45	60034	64152	61983	60578	61999	66234	61500	60755	60034	66866	60114	63481	64479	66235	74860	87483	63566	45
50	55374	60028	57332	56300	58367	61557	56742	56354	55374	61675	55462	59110	60193	62150	70832	83145	59203	50
55	50268	55264	52191	51718	54492	56460	51525	51548	50268	55988	50361	54135	55369	57379	66058	77871	54235	55
60	43211	48343	45057	45368	49171	49334	44326	44818	43211	48128	43305	46997	48611	50454	59089	70107	47099	60
65	35686	40526	37402	38431	43826	41585	36660	37558	35686	39747	35766	39157	41165	42474	50845	60701	39245	65
70	26978	31169	28360	30240	37456	32619	27759	28819	26978	30048	27039	29850	32227	32765	40763	49075	29917	70
75	18218	21417	19249	21333	30065	23365	18776	19846	18218	20291	18266	20365	23174	22630	29912	36586	20418	75
80	11584	13832	12284	14231	23219	15833	11955	12844	11584	12902	11618	13029	16319	14668	20690	25935	13068	80
85+	5624	6822	5995	7314	15238	8556	5822	6404	5624	6264	5641	6398	9630	7272	11453	15070	6416	85+

ACCED YRS OF LIFE

	No Causes	(1)	(2)	(3)	(4)	(5)	(6)	(7)	(8)	(9)	(10)	(11)	(12)	(1)+(2)	(1)+(2)+(5)+(6)+(8)	+part	(10)+(11)
TOTAL		2.335	1.284	1.034	4.109	5.006	1.123	.703	.000	5.245	.042	1.815	3.718	3.714	10.678	20.237	1.859
WORK	9.847	1.884	.460	.453	1.384	.861	.030	.397	.000	.000	.036	1.505	1.302	2.377	3.357	4.037	1.544

POPULATION, DEATHS, DEATH RATES FOR ALL CAUSES COMBINED, AND SPECIFIED CAUSES

Age Start of Interval	Midyear Population	Deaths During Year	All Causes	Respiratory T. B.	Other Infec. and Paras.	Neoplasms	Cardiovascular	Infl., Pneu., Bronch.	Diarrheal	Certain Degenerative	Maternal	Cert. Dis. of Infancy	Motor Vehicle	Other Violence	Other and Unknown	Age Start of Interval
0	78918	13474	.17073	.00080	.00642	.00003	.00013	.04310	.01412	.00022	.00000	.08827	.00000	.00006	.01760	0
1	297331	4392	.01477	.00060	.00148	.00007	.00012	.00567	.00211	.00019	.00000	.00228	.00000	.00024	.00202	1
5	375934	932	.00248	.00021	.00055	.00005	.00007	.00073	.00007	.00009	.00000	.00001	.00000	.00024	.00046	5
10	313696	622	.00198	.00040	.00036	.00005	.00015	.00045	.00001	.00006	.00000	.00000	.00001	.00016	.00034	10
15	282522	1115	.00395	.00141	.00050	.00004	.00027	.00053	.00001	.00007	.00028	.00000	.00000	.00028	.00055	15
20	290128	1359	.00482	.00195	.00046	.00007	.00038	.00059	.00001	.00007	.00044	.00000	.00000	.00024	.00064	20
25	227513	1243	.00546	.00197	.00055	.00018	.00048	.00055	.00001	.00011	.00058	.00000	.00002	.00023	.00076	25
30	189401	1177	.00621	.00190	.00042	.00042	.00082	.00064	.00001	.00020	.00078	.00000	.00001	.00022	.00081	30
35	191446	1345	.00703	.00145	.00033	.00085	.00122	.00071	.00003	.00019	.00084	.00000	.00002	.00020	.00120	35
40	154225	1296	.00840	.00161	.00026	.00108	.00194	.00088	.00001	.00036	.00051	.00000	.00001	.00028	.00147	40
45	129276	1318	.01020	.00141	.00030	.00178	.00307	.00098	.00003	.00064	.00017	.00000	.00002	.00023	.00156	45
50	112897	1466	.01299	.00135	.00031	.00269	.00447	.00125	.00003	.00080	.00003	.00000	.00001	.00019	.00186	50
55	79233	1529	.01930	.00154	.00053	.00406	.00689	.00193	.00009	.00126	.00000	.00000	.00000	.00018	.00281	55
60	75977	1884	.02480	.00146	.00045	.00451	.01042	.00275	.00016	.00128	.00000	.00000	.00000	.00028	.00349	60
65	47104	1931	.04099	.00217	.00030	.00728	.01785	.00478	.00023	.00191	.00000	.00000	.00002	.00036	.00609	65
70	36425	2142	.05881	.00173	.00049	.00835	.02874	.00758	.00036	.00261	.00000	.00000	.00000	.00052	.00843	70
75	18913	1492	.07889	.00190	.00053	.00883	.03495	.00925	.00021	.00280	.00000	.00000	.00000	.00053	.01988	75
80	13788	1701	.12337	.00167	.00065	.01001	.05302	.01509	.00051	.00399	.00000	.00000	.00000	.00080	.03764	80
85+	10506	2223	.21159	.00114	.00095	.01057	.07986	.02741	.00086	.00552	.00000	.00000	.00000	.00152	.08376	85+
ALL	2925233	42681														

			All Causes	Respiratory T. B.	Other Infec.	Neoplasms	Cardiovascular	Infl., Pneu.	Diarrheal	Certain Degen.	Maternal	Cert. Dis. Infancy	Motor Vehicle	Other Violence	Other Unknown
CRUDE DEATH RATE			.01459	.00121	.00070	.00056	.00255	.00278	.00064	.00035	.00026	.00261	.00001	.00024	.00228
STANDARDIZED RATE (1)			.01509	.00118	.00077	.00086	.00211	.00309	.00078	.00032	.00024	.00338	.00001	.00023	.00210
STANDARDIZED RATE (2)			.01727	.00131	.00064	.00157	.00439	.00284	.00052	.00054	.00025	.00201	.00001	.00025	.00295
GEOMETRIC MEAN			.01661												

LIFE TABLE FOR ALL CAUSES COMBINED

Age (x)	Midyear Population	Deaths During Year	$_nM_x$	$_nq_x$	l_x	$_nd_x$	$_nL_x$	$_nm_x$	$_na_x$	T_x	$_nr_x$	$\overset{\circ}{e}_x$	Age (x)
0	78918	13474	.170734	.153920	100000	15392	90153	.170732	.360248	5130731	.000000	51.307	0
1	297331	4392	.014771	.056580	84608	4821	326380	.014771	1.500000	5040578	.000000	59.576	1
5	375934	932	.002479	.012295	79787	981	396483	.002474	2.500000	4714198	.000000	59.085	5
10	313696	622	.001983	.009858	78806	780	392154	.001989	2.645833	4317716	.024135	54.789	10
15	282522	1115	.003947	.019570	78026	1527	386530	.003951	2.642436	3925522	.007612	50.310	15
20	290128	1399	.004822	.023843	76499	1824	378037	.004825	2.555853	3538992	.010058	46.262	20
25	227513	1243	.005463	.026997	74675	2016	368419	.005472	2.541543	3160955	.035419	42.329	25
30	189401	1177	.006214	.030636	72659	2226	357817	.006221	2.539121	2792537	.017102	38.433	30
35	191446	1345	.007025	.034558	70433	2434	346201	.007031	2.549558	2434719	.010605	34.568	35
40	154225	1296	.008403	.041251	67999	2805	333152	.008420	2.560532	2088519	.028626	30.714	40
45	129276	1318	.010195	.049836	65194	3249	318079	.010214	2.571304	1755367	.019482	26.925	45
50	112897	1466	.012985	.063234	61945	3917	300374	.013040	2.612650	1437287	.034317	23.203	50
55	79233	1529	.019298	.092490	58028	5367	277195	.019362	2.587999	1136914	.023330	19.593	55
60	75977	1884	.024797	.117430	52661	6184	248542	.024881	2.612757	859719	.023468	16.326	60
65	47104	1931	.040994	.187491	46477	8714	211339	.041232	2.584801	611177	.029876	13.150	65
70	36425	2142	.058806	.257686	37763	9731	164598	.059120	2.511325	399838	.034962	10.588	70
75	18913	1492	.078888	.329730	28032	9243	116867	.079090	2.479917	235240	.017799	8.392	75
80	13788	1701	.123368	.470488	18789	8840	71354	.123890	2.444405	118373	.017799	6.300	80
85+	10506	2223	.211593	1.000000	9949	9949	47019	.211593	4.726046	47019	.000000	4.726	85+

NUMBER OF PERSONS DYING (OUT OF 100,000 AT BIRTH) ABOVE AGE X FROM SPECIFIED CAUSES

Age (x)	All Causes	Respiratory T. B.	Other Infec. and Paras.	Neo-plasms	Cardio-vascular	Infl., Pneu., Bronch.	Diar-rheal	Certain Degen-erative	Maternal	Cert. Dis. of Infancy	Motor Vehicle	Other Violence	Other and Unknown	Age (x)
0	100000	7030	3084	9751	28972	15240	2313	3312	1294	8704	33	1367	18860	0
1	84608	6958	2505	9788	28961	11355	1041	3293	1294	746	33	1361	17273	1
5	79787	6763	2023	9766	28921	9505	352	3230	1294	2	33	1283	16615	5
10	78806	6679	1805	9749	28894	9216	322	3196	1294	0	32	1189	16430	10
15	78026	6520	1663	9730	28836	9039	318	3173	1292	0	29	1128	16298	15
20	76499	5976	1468	9713	28730	8832	314	3146	1184	0	28	1020	16088	20
25	74675	5237	1302	9689	28587	8608	312	3121	1018	0	28	930	15843	25
30	72659	4510	1098	9620	28409	8404	307	3082	802	0	22	844	15561	30
35	70433	3832	949	9468	28114	8175	305	3010	524	0	20	767	15269	35
40	67999	3332	835	9172	27690	7931	294	2945	233	0	14	698	14855	40
45	65194	2794	748	8810	27040	7637	292	2825	63	0	12	605	14368	45
50	61945	2346	652	8242	26060	7324	282	2620	10	0	7	531	13871	50
55	58028	1942	559	7429	24709	6947	274	2380	2	0	5	473	13308	55
60	52661	1515	412	6299	22791	6410	249	2029	2	0	5	424	12525	60
65	46477	1151	301	5174	20189	5723	210	1711	2	0	5	355	11656	65
70	37763	693	238	3628	16390	4707	160	1305	2	0	0	278	10362	70
75	28032	409	156	2252	11632	3453	101	874	2	0	0	192	8961	75
80	18789	186	94	1219	7540	2369	77	546	2	0	0	130	6626	80
85+	9949	54	45	497	3755	1289	40	260	0	0	0	72	3937	85+

NUMBER OF PERSONS SURVIVING TO AGE X IF SPECIFIED CAUSES WERE ELIMINATED

Age (x)	No Causes	Respiratory T. B.	Other Infec. and Paras.	Neo-plasms	Cardio-vascular	Infl., Pneu., Bronch.	Diar-rheal	Certain Degener-ative	Maternal	Cert. Dis. of Infancy	Motor Vehicle	Other Violence	Other and Unknown	(1) + (2)	(1) + (2) + (5) + (6) + (8)	(1)+(2)+ (5)+(6)+ (8)+part of(9)&(12)	(10) + (11)	Age (x)
		(1)	(2)	(3)	(4)	(5)	(6)	(7)	(8)	(9)	(10)	(11)	(12)					
0	100000	100000	100000	100000	100000	100000	100000	100000	100000	100000	100000	100000	100000	100000	100000	100000	100000	0
1	84608	84674	85142	84611	84618	88254	85785	84625	84608	92245	84608	84614	86079	85208	90116	99889	84614	1
5	79787	80039	80763	79811	79835	85120	81578	79865	79787	89868	79787	79868	81827	81018	88373	99541	79868	5
10	78806	79139	79989	78847	78881	84380	80605	78917	78806	86703	78807	78980	81009	80327	87973	99273	78981	10
15	78026	78515	79341	78085	78158	83734	79812	78158	78028	85844	78030	78259	80343	79838	87641	99024	78263	15
20	76499	77522	77985	76574	76733	82315	78254	76656	76608	84164	76504	76834	78985	79028	87111	98640	76839	20
25	74675	76417	76293	74772	75046	80591	76390	74853	74946	82158	74680	75092	77352	78073	86506	98215	75097	25
30	72659	75091	74439	72821	73196	78633	74333	72870	73137	79940	72670	73150	75552	76931	85734	97631	73160	30
35	70433	73484	72309	70741	71247	76468	72057	70709	71172	77491	70445	70985	73537	75440	84673	96695	70997	35
40	67999	71458	69925	68589	69208	74086	69578	68330	69002	74813	68017	68600	71422	73482	83128	95257	68618	40
45	65194	69066	67128	66619	67005	71345	66710	65629	66324	71727	65213	65862	68978	71115	81014	93155	65672	45
50	61945	66087	63879	63388	64656	68124	63396	62560	63071	68152	61968	62653	66055	68151	78098	90036	62676	50
55	58028	62326	59932	60191	61948	64218	59395	58839	59091	63843	58051	58748	62462	64372	74252	85816	58771	55
60	52661	56999	54534	55751	58204	58848	53926	53737	53625	57938	52682	53361	57493	59026	68782	79773	53383	60
65	46477	50676	48237	50334	54144	52664	47631	47732	47328	51134	46496	47161	51640	52595	62194	72419	47180	65
70	37763	41624	39252	42428	48165	43839	38747	39159	38454	41547	37783	38389	43272	43265	52479	61510	38409	70
75	28032	31165	29210	32643	41364	33816	28814	29453	28545	30841	28047	28572	33539	32475	41006	48484	28586	75
80	18789	21090	19631	23011	33080	23753	19333	20022	19133	20672	18799	19202	24899	22035	29187	35228	19212	80
85+	9949	11274	10432	12834	22997	13593	10264	10822	10133	10946	9954	10210	15998	11821	16970	21336	10215	85+

ADDED YRS OF LIFE

	No Causes	(1)	(2)	(3)	(4)	(5)	(6)	(7)	(8)	(9)	(10)	(11)	(12)				
TOTAL		2.252	1.305	1.576	4.789	5.157	1.190	.566	.478	5.088	.011	.421	4.009	3.632	11.303	20.649	.432
WORK	7.523	1.694	.424	.656	1.263	.717	.016	.233	.468	.000	.007	.235	.982	2.140	3.440	4.061	.243

POPULATION, DEATHS, DEATH RATES FOR ALL CAUSES COMBINED, AND SPECIFIED CAUSES

Age Start of Interval	Midyear Population	Deaths During Year	All Causes	Respiratory T. B.	Other Infec. and Paras.	Neoplasms	Cardiovascular	Infl., Pneu., Bronch.	Diarrheal	Certain Degenerative	Maternal	Cert. Dis. of Infancy	Motor Vehicle	Other Violence	Other and Unknown	Age Start of Interval
0	104858	17127	.16334	.00021	.00645	.00014	.00243	.05115	.01368	.00026	.00000	.06964	.00001	.00085	.01853	0
1	390304	3893	.00997	.00008	.00155	.00014	.00029	.00411	.00081	.00010	.00000	.00000	.00006	.00064	.00219	1
5	495362	799	.00161	.00002	.00028	.00012	.00007	.00049	.00002	.00003	.00000	.00000	.00005	.00027	.00024	5
10	413907	591	.00143	.00005	.00016	.00010	.00010	.00028	.00001	.00004	.00000	.00000	.00005	.00038	.00026	10
15	355150	752	.00212	.00015	.00011	.00015	.00015	.00025	.00002	.00005	.00000	.00000	.00008	.00088	.00029	15
20	346713	963	.00278	.00031	.00010	.00017	.00014	.00025	.00003	.00008	.00000	.00000	.00010	.00124	.00035	20
25	268271	1151	.00429	.00060	.00011	.00032	.00031	.00033	.00001	.00021	.00000	.00000	.00013	.00172	.00054	25
30	233821	1349	.00577	.00080	.00017	.00038	.00059	.00042	.00002	.00047	.00000	.00000	.00018	.00156	.00078	30
35	225786	1382	.00612	.00085	.00016	.00051	.00063	.00063	.00002	.00062	.00000	.00000	.00016	.00163	.00091	35
40	206300	1763	.00855	.00128	.00016	.00080	.00110	.00090	.00005	.00106	.00000	.00000	.00016	.00181	.00123	40
45	160701	2027	.01261	.00152	.00027	.00159	.00228	.00125	.00008	.00134	.00000	.00000	.00021	.00205	.00202	45
50	144531	2339	.01618	.00180	.00026	.00248	.00377	.00141	.00008	.00196	.00000	.00000	.00021	.00181	.00240	50
55	99735	2624	.02631	.00221	.00043	.00455	.00654	.00306	.00014	.00251	.00000	.00000	.00016	.00216	.00416	55
60	86879	2833	.03261	.00199	.00047	.00581	.00967	.00416	.00015	.00265	.00000	.00000	.00014	.00191	.00566	60
65	55944	2948	.05270	.00231	.00072	.00919	.01593	.00711	.00039	.00325	.00000	.00000	.00021	.00198	.01160	65
70	38870	3118	.08022	.00273	.00080	.01317	.02516	.01279	.00046	.00345	.00000	.00000	.00010	.00224	.01932	70
75	15485	2442	.12553	.00236	.00056	.01704	.03899	.02356	.00082	.00436	.00000	.00000	.00008	.00308	.03495	75
80	11249	1537	.13663	.00187	.00107	.01333	.04169	.02569	.00018	.00284	.00000	.00000	.00009	.00222	.04765	80
85+	7734	1239	.16020	.00246	.00155	.02017	.05366	.03685	.00078	.00815	.00000	.00000	.00013	.00181	.03465	85+
ALL	3665600	50877														

CRUDE DEATH RATE			.01388	.00062	.00054	.00109	.00193	.00301	.00052	.00058	.00000	.00199	.00011	.00117	.00232	
STANDARDIZED RATE (1)			.01486	.00060	.00059	.00107	.00190	.00335	.00062	.00056	.00000	.00245	.00011	.00116	.00243	
STANDARDIZED RATE (2)			.01882	.00087	.00049	.00205	.00387	.00352	.00043	.00092	.00000	.00144	.00012	.00137	.00372	
GEOMETRIC MEAN			.01581													

LIFE TABLE FOR ALL CAUSES COMBINED

Age (x)	Midyear Population	Deaths During Year	$_nM_x$	$_nq_x$	l_x	$_nd_x$	$_nL_x$	$_nm_x$	$_na_x$	T_x	$_nr_x$	$\overset{\circ}{e}_x$	Age (x)
0	104858	17127	.163335	.147610	100000	14761	90371	.163338	.347670	5214029	.000000	52.140	0
1	390304	3893	.009974	.038926	85239	3318	332661	.009974	1.500000	5123658	.000000	60.109	1
5	495362	799	.001613	.008020	81921	657	407963	.001610	2.500000	4790997	.000000	58.483	5
10	413907	591	.001428	.007125	81264	579	404913	.001430	2.570164	4383035	.027371	53.936	10
15	355150	752	.002117	.010560	80685	852	401405	.002123	2.628619	3978122	.017282	49.304	15
20	346713	963	.002778	.013841	79833	1105	396575	.002786	2.656109	3576717	.020658	44.802	20
25	268271	1151	.004290	.021239	78728	1680	389667	.004311	2.635169	3180124	.035496	40.394	25
30	233821	1349	.005769	.028489	77048	2195	379873	.005778	2.554954	2790475	.019096	36.217	30
35	225786	1382	.006121	.030179	74853	2259	368796	.006125	2.578851	2410602	.005447	32.204	35
40	206300	1763	.008546	.042014	72594	3050	355164	.008573	2.637227	2041806	.021241	28.126	40
45	160701	2027	.012613	.061371	69544	4268	337479	.012647	2.600457	1686043	.021397	24.244	45
50	144531	2339	.016183	.078252	65276	5108	314277	.016253	2.630637	1348564	.028712	20.659	50
55	99735	2624	.026310	.124169	60168	7471	282762	.026422	2.580199	1034287	.027190	17.190	55
60	86879	2833	.032609	.151508	52697	7984	244154	.032701	2.578830	751525	.022618	14.261	60
65	55944	2948	.052696	.234652	44713	10492	198064	.052973	2.569497	507371	.026124	11.347	65
70	38870	3118	.080216	.335583	34221	11484	142450	.080618	2.504789	309307	.025777	9.039	70
75	19485	2442	.125327	.473062	22737	10756	85641	.125595	2.392676	166857	.009212	7.339	75
80	11249	1537	.136634	.456035	11981	5943	43526	.136539	2.243952	81216	.009212	6.779	80
85+	7734	1239	.160202	1.000000	6038	6038	37690	.160202	6.242131	37690	.000000	6.242	85+

NUMBER OF PERSONS DYING (OUT OF 100,000 AT BIRTH) ABOVE AGE X FROM SPECIFIED CAUSES

Age (x)	All Causes	Respiratory T. B.	Other Infec. and Paras.	Neoplasms	Cardiovascular	Infl., Pneu., Bronch.	Diarrheal	Certain Degenerative	Maternal	Cert. Dis. of Infancy	Motor Vehicle	Other Violence	Other and Unknown	Age (x)
0	100000	4993	2405	11583	21679	17876	1957	5380	0	6253	669	7557	19608	0
1	85239	4974	1822	11570	21459	13254	721	5356	0	0	668	7481	17934	1
5	81921	4948	1307	11522	21362	11887	451	5324	0	0	648	7268	17204	5
10	81264	4938	1193	11472	21331	11686	445	5311	0	0	626	7157	17105	10
15	80685	4917	1129	11430	21291	11574	439	5296	0	0	608	7001	17000	15
20	79833	4855	1086	11367	21232	11472	431	5278	0	0	577	6648	16887	20
25	78728	4732	1045	11300	21175	11375	419	5246	0	0	537	6155	16744	25
30	77048	4497	1003	11173	21053	11245	414	5162	0	0	485	5483	16533	30
35	74853	4191	938	11029	20828	11086	406	4984	0	0	416	4739	16236	35
40	72594	3877	879	10841	20596	10852	397	4757	0	0	356	4139	15900	40
45	69544	3421	822	10554	20202	10530	380	4378	0	0	301	3495	15461	45
50	65276	2908	729	10016	19427	10107	353	3923	0	0	231	2802	14780	50
55	60168	2341	649	9230	18235	9661	329	3306	0	0	164	2233	14020	55
60	52697	1717	526	7937	16262	8791	289	2595	0	0	119	1623	12838	60
65	44713	1231	411	6513	13893	7773	252	1948	0	0	85	1157	11450	65
70	34221	773	269	4685	10721	6355	174	1303	0	0	42	763	9136	70
75	22737	384	155	2801	7119	4521	107	811	0	0	28	443	6368	75
80	11981	182	107	1340	3824	2499	37	437	0	0	10	179	3366	80
85+	6038	93	58	760	2022	1389	29	307	0	0	5	68	1307	85+

NUMBER OF PERSONS SURVIVING TO AGE X IF SPECIFIED CAUSES WERE ELIMINATED

Age (x)	No Causes	Respiratory T. B. (1)	Other Infec. and Paras. (2)	Neoplasms (3)	Cardiovascular (4)	Infl., Pneu., Bronch. (5)	Diarrheal (6)	Certain Degenerative (7)	Maternal (8)	Cert. Dis. of Infancy (9)	Motor Vehicle (10)	Other Violence (11)	Other and Unknown (12)	(1)+(2)	(1)+(2)+(5)+(6)+(8)	(1)+(2)+(5)+(6)+(8)+part of(9)&(12)	(10)+(11)	Age (x)
0	100000	100000	100000	100000	100000	100000	100000	100000	100000	100000	100000	100000	100000	100000	100000	100000	100000	0
1	85239	85257	85758	85251	85442	89610	86387	85261	85239	91245	85240	85309	86757	85796	91410	99218	85310	1
5	81921	81963	82949	81980	82212	87542	83293	81974	81921	87653	81941	82198	84150	82992	90172	98596	82218	5
10	81264	81316	82399	81372	81583	87054	82631	81329	81264	86990	81306	81649	83577	82452	89812	98273	81692	10
15	80685	80758	81876	80834	81042	86554	82048	80765	80685	86370	80745	81224	83089	81950	89396	97872	81284	15
20	79833	79567	81055	80043	80245	85749	81190	79930	79833	85458	79923	80721	82327	81191	88689	97138	80812	20
25	78728	78982	79975	79002	79191	84665	80078	78855	78728	84275	78857	80100	81334	80233	87763	96174	80231	25
30	77048	77530	78310	77443	77623	82997	78374	77256	77048	82477	77225	79070	79815	78801	86346	94692	79252	30
35	74853	75626	76144	75379	75636	80802	76149	75231	74853	80127	75094	77573	77745	76930	84483	92752	77822	35
40	72594	73657	73906	73291	73584	78612	73860	73186	72594	77709	72887	75846	75840	74987	82621	90840	76152	40
45	69544	71016	70857	70496	70885	75651	70774	70486	69544	74444	69878	73321	73104	72357	80104	88251	73673	45
50	65276	67167	66600	66701	67305	71456	66457	66608	65276	69875	65658	69531	69315	68529	76374	84393	69938	50
55	60168	62472	61467	62258	63231	66335	61280	62003	60168	64407	60585	64673	64670	63821	71663	79434	65121	55
60	52697	55323	53952	55794	57355	59003	53709	54992	52697	56410	53104	57257	57842	56641	64637	72043	57699	60
65	44713	47410	45896	48748	51099	51125	45607	47284	44713	47864	45090	49048	50504	48655	56743	63701	49461	65
70	34221	36709	35246	39086	42402	40571	34975	36785	34221	36632	34547	37914	41007	37808	45811	52214	38275	70
75	22737	24726	23512	27764	32026	28783	23293	24868	22737	24339	22965	25477	30076	25569	33159	38842	25732	75
80	11981	13182	12424	15946	20534	17119	12325	13399	11981	12825	12114	13636	18979	13669	20092	24859	13787	80
85+	6038	6712	6297	8592	12738	9806	6217	6853	6038	6463	6109	6961	12128	6999	11704	15636	7042	85+

ADDED YRS OF LIFE

	No Causes	(1)	(2)	(3)	(4)	(5)	(6)	(7)	(8)	(9)	(10)	(11)	(12)	(1)+(2)	(1)+(2)+(5)+(6)+(8)	+part	(10)+(11)
TOTAL		1.046	.954	1.704	3.395	5.407	.932	.932	.000	3.650	.190	2.140	4.052	2.027	8.884	15.744	2.343
WORK	6.984	.729	.151	.644	.853	.588	.033	.522	.000	.000	.135	1.552	.885	.884	1.532	1.802	1.694

POPULATION, DEATHS, DEATH RATES FOR ALL CAUSES COMBINED, AND SPECIFIED CAUSES

Age Start of Interval	Midyear Population	Deaths During Year	All Causes	Respiratory T. B.	Other Infec. and Paras.	Neoplasms	Cardiovascular	Infl., Pneu., Bronch.	Diarrheal	Certain Degenerative	Maternal	Cert. Dis. of Infancy	Motor Vehicle	Other Violence	Other and Unknown	Age Start of Interval
0	102483	14357	.14009	.00023	.00650	.00026	.00192	.04433	.01144	.00013	.00000	.05842	.00001	.00071	.01614	0
1	386267	3963	.01026	.00010	.00163	.00010	.00018	.00443	.00093	.00011	.00000	.00000	.00002	.00052	.00223	1
5	488349	684	.00140	.00003	.00030	.00005	.00005	.00046	.00003	.00004	.00000	.00000	.00001	.00015	.00029	5
10	407426	401	.00098	.00009	.00013	.00004	.00011	.00029	.00000	.00002	.00000	.00000	.00001	.00010	.00017	10
15	367014	616	.00168	.00023	.00009	.00007	.00016	.00037	.00001	.00004	.00014	.00000	.00001	.00024	.00032	15
20	376841	743	.00197	.00038	.00010	.00012	.00016	.00032	.00001	.00004	.00030	.00000	.00001	.00020	.00033	20
25	295517	885	.00299	.00065	.00010	.00016	.00033	.00037	.00002	.00009	.00048	.00000	.00000	.00026	.00053	25
30	245980	989	.00402	.00069	.00017	.00039	.00041	.00052	.00002	.00023	.00061	.00000	.00001	.00019	.00079	30
35	248687	1056	.00425	.00069	.00015	.00055	.00055	.00056	.00004	.00027	.00051	.00000	.00002	.00016	.00086	35
40	200354	1127	.00563	.00062	.00012	.00118	.00091	.00064	.00001	.00057	.00033	.00000	.00001	.00019	.00103	40
45	167964	1305	.00777	.00063	.00024	.00181	.00149	.00083	.00002	.00096	.00008	.00000	.00002	.00026	.00143	45
50	146605	1513	.01032	.00074	.00016	.00262	.00235	.00103	.00012	.00105	.00001	.00000	.00003	.00028	.00193	50
55	102884	1803	.01752	.00076	.00024	.00441	.00492	.00206	.00019	.00162	.00001	.00000	.00002	.00032	.00296	55
60	98673	2131	.02160	.00077	.00021	.00472	.00644	.00287	.00012	.00154	.00004	.00000	.00001	.00035	.00452	60
65	61169	2324	.03799	.00152	.00033	.00747	.01249	.00582	.00028	.00216	.00002	.00000	.00002	.00044	.00745	65
70	47331	2726	.05759	.00091	.00049	.00936	.02013	.00923	.00040	.00256	.00000	.00000	.00006	.00065	.01380	70
75	24568	2518	.10249	.00163	.00057	.01482	.03570	.01783	.00090	.00301	.00000	.00000	.00008	.00094	.02703	75
80	17950	1973	.10992	.00100	.00067	.00964	.03699	.02279	.00072	.00201	.00000	.00000	.00017	.00084	.03510	80
85+	13638	2510	.18404	.00081	.00051	.01349	.05793	.03542	.00117	.00279	.00000	.00000	.00000	.00084	.03510	85+
ALL	3799700	43624														

CRUDE DEATH RATE			.01148	.00041	.00050	.00103	.00178	.00270	.00045	.00037	.00018	.00158	.00001	.00027	.00221	
STANDARDIZED RATE (1)			.01182	.00039	.00057	.00093	.00149	.00256	.00055	.00035	.00017	.00206	.00001	.00027	.00206	
STANDARDIZED RATE (2)			.01455	.00051	.00044	.00174	.00315	.00299	.00039	.00057	.00017	.00121	.00002	.00029	.00308	
GEOMETRIC MEAN			.01190													

LIFE TABLE FOR ALL CAUSES COMBINED

Age (x)	Midyear Population	Deaths During Year	$_nM_x$	$_nq_x$	l_x	$_nd_x$	$_nL_x$	$_nm_x$	$_na_x$	T_x	$_nr_x$	$\overset{\circ}{e}_x$	Age (x)
0	102483	14357	.140092	.127710	100000	12771	91164	.140087	.308156	5728949	.000000	57.289	0
1	386267	3963	.010260	.040021	87229	3491	340189	.010262	1.500000	5637785	.000000	64.632	1
5	488349	684	.001401	.006974	83738	584	417230	.001400	2.500000	5297596	.000000	63.264	5
10	407426	401	.000984	.004907	83154	408	414773	.000984	2.555658	4880366	.025005	58.691	10
15	367014	616	.001678	.008375	82746	693	412080	.001682	2.615649	4465594	.009319	53.967	15
20	376841	743	.001972	.009823	82053	806	408359	.001974	2.634926	4053513	.012530	49.401	20
25	295517	885	.002995	.014954	81247	1215	403362	.003012	2.635288	3645154	.037953	44.865	25
30	245980	989	.004021	.019930	80032	1595	396263	.004025	2.556818	3241792	.019472	40.506	30
35	248687	1056	.004246	.021036	78437	1650	388173	.004251	2.568687	2845529	.013143	36.278	35
40	200354	1127	.005625	.027856	76787	2139	378839	.005646	2.617364	2457356	.031289	32.002	40
45	167964	1305	.007770	.038246	74648	2855	366415	.007792	2.609457	2078517	.022128	27.844	45
50	146605	1513	.010320	.050687	71793	3639	350471	.010383	2.665911	1712102	.036844	23.848	50
55	102884	1803	.017525	.084412	68154	5753	326970	.017595	2.601215	1361631	.025633	19.979	55
60	98673	2131	.021597	.103107	62401	6434	296765	.021680	2.631398	1034661	.025962	16.581	60
65	61169	2324	.037993	.175300	55967	9811	256411	.038263	2.612459	737896	.033485	13.184	65
70	47331	2726	.057594	.254138	46156	11730	202331	.057974	2.574702	481485	.034157	10.432	70
75	24568	2518	.102491	.407163	34426	14017	136452	.102725	2.454653	279154	.008815	8.109	75
80	17950	1973	.109916	.425254	20409	8679	78967	.109906	2.340996	142702	.008815	6.992	80
85+	13638	2510	.184045	1.000000	11730	11730	63735	.184045	5.433466	63735	.000000	5.433	85+

NUMBER OF PERSONS DYING (OUT OF 100,000 AT BIRTH) ABOVE AGE X FROM SPECIFIED CAUSES

Age (x)	All Causes	Respiratory T.B.	Other Infec. and Paras.	Neoplasms	Cardiovascular	Infl., Pneu., Bronch.	Diarrheal	Certain Degenerative	Maternal	Cert. Dis. of Infancy	Motor Vehicle	Other Violence	Other and Unknown	Age (x)
0	100000	3275	2250	12988	25001	19035	1969	4095	995	5326	108	1801	23157	0
1	87229	3254	1658	12964	24826	14994	926	4083	995	0	107	1736	21686	1
5	83738	3221	1102	12929	24764	13486	610	4045	995	0	100	1560	20926	5
10	83154	3208	978	12908	24742	13295	599	4030	995	0	96	1499	20804	10
15	82746	3172	926	12891	24695	13173	597	4020	993	0	91	1456	20732	15
20	82053	3077	888	12861	24629	13023	594	4005	935	0	88	1356	20597	20
25	81247	2921	849	12811	24564	12893	590	3985	813	0	83	1274	20460	25
30	80032	2656	809	12745	24429	12744	584	3953	619	0	82	1168	20243	30
35	78437	2382	743	12590	24268	12539	577	3862	377	0	77	1093	19929	35
40	76787	2137	685	12373	24078	12322	561	3756	178	0	71	1030	19596	40
45	74648	1903	638	11924	23730	12077	558	3539	52	0	67	958	19202	45
50	71793	1673	548	11258	23180	11773	549	3186	25	0	61	864	18676	50
55	68154	1412	491	10334	22348	11410	508	2817	22	0	51	766	17995	55
60	62401	1164	411	8887	20731	10732	444	2285	19	0	45	661	17022	60
65	55967	935	348	7482	18812	9876	408	1827	7	0	42	556	15674	65
70	46156	544	264	5556	15584	8372	336	1272	3	0	37	442	13746	70
75	34426	361	165	3654	11481	6490	254	753	3	0	24	309	10932	75
80	20409	138	87	1629	6599	4051	132	342	3	0	13	181	7234	80
85+	11730	51	33	860	3692	2257	75	178	0	0	0	112	4472	85+

NUMBER OF PERSONS SURVIVING TO AGE X IF SPECIFIED CAUSES WERE ELIMINATED

Age (x)	No Causes	Respiratory T.B. (1)	Other Infec. and Paras. (2)	Neoplasms (3)	Cardiovascular (4)	Infl., Pneu., Bronch. (5)	Diarrheal (6)	Certain Degenerative (7)	Maternal (8)	Cert. Dis. of Infancy (9)	Motor Vehicle (10)	Other Violence (11)	Other and Unknown (12)	(1)+(2)	(1)+(2)+(5)+(6)+(8)	(1)+(2)+(5)+(6)+(8)+part of(9)&(12)	(10)+(11)	Age (x)
0	100000	100000	100000	100000	100000	100000	100000	100000	100000	100000	100000	100000	100000	100000	100000	100000	100000	0
1	87229	87249	87783	87251	87392	91083	88208	87240	87229	92344	87230	87290	88613	87803	92711	99368	87291	1
5	83738	83789	84820	83794	83956	88954	84951	83786	83738	88648	83746	83969	85826	84872	91549	98897	83977	5
10	83154	83218	84354	83230	83392	88576	84410	83217	83154	88030	83166	83444	85352	84418	91281	98713	83456	10
15	82746	82845	83992	82839	83030	88271	83998	82818	82748	87598	82763	83078	85007	84093	91067	98537	83095	15
20	82053	82246	83327	82175	82401	87691	83297	82140	82113	86864	82072	82482	84433	83524	90683	98219	82502	20
25	81247	81594	82548	81418	81656	86968	82483	81349	81428	86011	81271	81754	83744	82901	90289	97904	81778	25
30	80032	80639	81354	80266	80570	85826	81255	80168	80403	84725	80057	80637	82714	81971	89663	97397	80662	30
35	78437	79305	79799	78820	79125	84333	79643	78661	79042	83036	78466	79105	81388	80683	88761	96654	79135	35
40	76787	77882	78179	77379	77650	82791	77984	77111	77578	81289	76822	77504	80018	79294	87720	95750	77539	40
45	74648	75947	76048	75671	75835	80745	75814	75179	75542	79025	74686	75417	78195	77372	86017	94074	75455	45
50	71793	73272	73230	73442	73485	77980	72924	72653	72679	76003	71835	72625	75747	74738	83476	91481	72668	50
55	68154	69818	69575	70646	70596	74413	69268	69335	68998	72150	68204	69041	72611	71273	80070	87958	69091	55
60	62401	64167	63780	66133	66260	68844	63483	64001	63177	66060	62452	62314	67481	65585	74527	82143	63366	60
65	55967	57774	57264	60738	61390	62647	56972	57847	56674	59249	56016	56887	61919	59113	68209	75584	56937	65
70	46156	48012	47304	52018	53946	53216	47052	48228	46743	48862	46201	47020	53035	49206	58569	65546	47065	70
75	34426	35972	35369	40679	44582	41605	35166	36437	34864	36445	34471	35187	42450	36957	46204	52637	35232	75
80	20409	21503	21029	25994	31704	27021	20943	21930	20669	21606	20444	20959	28902	22155	30484	36094	20995	80
85+	11730	12427	12128	15651	21935	17414	12081	12737	11881	12418	11760	12099	19813	12849	19899	25004	12130	85+

ADDED YRS OF LIFE

	No Causes	(1)	(2)	(3)	(4)	(5)	(6)	(7)	(8)	(9)	(10)	(11)	(12)	(1)+(2)	(1)+(2)+(5)+(6)+(8)	+part	(10)+(11)
TOTAL		.853	1.038	2.049	3.759	5.666	.931	.730	.383	3.342	.029	.552	4.690	1.911	9.394	16.306	.581
WORK	4.950	.566	.139	.719	.732	.586	.027	.323	.348	.000	.012	.239	.850	.708	1.700	2.106	.251

POPULATION, DEATHS, DEATH RATES FOR ALL CAUSES COMBINED, AND SPECIFIED CAUSES

Age Start of Interval	Midyear Population	Deaths During Year	All Causes	Respiratory T. B.	Other Infec. and Paras.	Neoplasms	Cardiovascular	Infl., Pneu., Bronch.	Diarrheal	Certain Degenerative	Maternal	Cert. Dis. of Infancy	Motor Vehicle	Other Violence	Other and Unknown	Age Start of Interval
0	134000	17055	.12728	.00013	.00763	.00016	.00182	.03450	.01754	.00012	.00000	.04939	.00000	.00097	.01501	0
1	501000	3599	.00718	.00005	.00185	.00009	.00019	.00222	.00060	.00006	.00000	.00000	.00006	.00070	.00137	1
5	545000	734	.00135	.00002	.00027	.00006	.00006	.00027	.00003	.00003	.00000	.00000	.00005	.00031	.00023	5
10	491000	505	.00103	.00001	.00009	.00008	.00008	.00013	.00001	.00003	.00000	.00000	.00003	.00035	.00022	10
15	415000	723	.00174	.00008	.00007	.00009	.00012	.00017	.00001	.00305	.00000	.00000	.00005	.00086	.00025	15
20	350000	998	.00285	.00020	.00008	.00014	.00023	.00015	.00002	.00005	.00000	.00000	.00013	.00140	.00040	20
25	285000	1038	.00364	.00045	.00007	.00016	.00029	.00016	.00002	.00020	.00000	.00000	.00010	.00166	.00052	25
30	257000	1345	.00523	.00070	.00011	.00026	.00051	.00025	.00001	.00063	.00000	.00000	.00015	.00189	.00072	30
35	235000	1600	.00681	.00089	.00011	.00038	.00075	.00036	.00005	.00123	.00000	.00000	.00012	.00184	.00108	35
40	198000	1824	.00921	.00121	.00018	.00087	.00118	.00058	.00002	.00173	.00000	.00000	.00016	.00196	.00132	40
45	170000	1988	.01169	.00124	.00015	.00134	.00219	.00069	.00005	.00238	.00000	.00000	.00009	.00183	.00173	45
50	151000	2480	.01642	.00172	.00019	.00226	.00371	.00097	.00006	.00301	.00000	.00000	.00019	.00206	.00225	50
55	122000	2628	.02154	.00172	.00018	.00357	.00615	.00150	.00011	.00311	.00000	.00000	.00017	.00203	.00300	55
60	95000	3006	.03164	.00226	.00025	.00604	.00987	.00231	.00006	.00336	.00000	.00000	.00024	.00226	.00498	60
65	70084	3075	.04388	.00228	.00027	.00913	.01485	.00348	.00011	.00347	.00000	.00000	.00016	.00251	.00761	65
70	43973	3078	.07000	.00239	.00030	.01260	.02556	.00735	.00030	.00412	.00000	.00000	.00027	.00291	.01421	70
75	26292	2539	.09657	.00221	.00034	.01506	.03670	.01202	.00038	.00418	.00000	.00000	.00019	.00198	.02351	75
80	14009	1767	.12613	.00214	.00057	.01485	.04997	.01656	.00057	.00414	.00000	.00000	.00021	.00186	.03526	80
85+	8642	1213	.14036	.00104	.00058	.01238	.05010	.02129	.00104	.00370	.00000	.00000	.00000	.00197	.04825	85+
ALL	4112000	51195														

CRUDE DEATH RATE			.01245	.00053	.00060	.00055	.00156	.00203	.00068	.00077	.00000	.00161	.00010	.00120	.00199	
STANDARDIZED RATE (1)			.01246	.00053	.00061	.00095	.00184	.00207	.00072	.00076	.00000	.00174	.00010	.00121	.00193	
STANDARDIZED RATE (2)			.01618	.00078	.00045	.00187	.00384	.00208	.00047	.00120	.00000	.00102	.00011	.00143	.00293	
GEOMETRIC MEAN			.01393													

LIFE TABLE FOR ALL CAUSES COMBINED

Age (x)	Midyear Population	Deaths During Year	$_nM_x$	$_nq_x$	l_x	$_nd_x$	$_nL_x$	$_nm_x$	$_na_x$	T_x	$_nr_x$	$\overset{\circ}{e}_x$	Age (x)
0	134000	17055	.127276	.116680	100000	11668	91673	.127278	.286369	5582919	.000000	55.829	0
1	501000	3599	.007184	.028223	88332	2493	347056	.007182	1.500000	5491246	.000000	62.166	1
5	545000	734	.001347	.006710	85839	576	427755	.001347	2.500000	5144150	.000000	59.928	5
10	491000	505	.001029	.005137	85263	438	425254	.001030	2.578006	4716395	.019003	55.316	10
15	415000	723	.001742	.008724	84825	740	422433	.001752	2.713682	4291141	.028354	50.588	15
20	350000	998	.002851	.014236	84085	1197	417591	.002866	2.632623	3868708	.034134	46.009	20
25	285000	1038	.003642	.018121	82888	1502	410875	.003656	2.626359	3451117	.031149	41.636	25
30	257000	1345	.005233	.025901	81386	2108	401901	.005245	2.614544	3040242	.017394	37.356	30
35	235000	1600	.006809	.033565	79278	2661	390019	.006823	2.605928	2638340	.017638	33.280	35
40	198000	1824	.009212	.045173	76617	3461	374747	.009236	2.590773	2248321	.023392	29.345	40
45	170000	1988	.011694	.056988	73156	4169	355774	.011718	2.599894	1873574	.016867	25.611	45
50	151000	2480	.016424	.079145	68987	5460	331775	.016457	2.589820	1517800	.015513	22.001	50
55	122000	2628	.021541	.102681	63527	6523	301941	.021604	2.593994	1186025	.022208	18.670	55
60	95000	3006	.031642	.147411	57004	8403	264669	.031749	2.578097	884084	.022161	15.509	60
65	70084	3075	.043876	.199029	48601	9673	219502	.044068	2.570299	619416	.028507	12.745	65
70	43973	3078	.069997	.299707	38928	11667	165569	.070428	2.515964	399913	.030507	10.273	70
75	26292	2539	.096569	.387623	27261	10567	109102	.096854	2.425673	234254	.019551	8.593	75
80	14009	1767	.126133	.473044	16694	7897	62478	.126396	2.341791	125152	.019551	7.497	80
85+	8642	1213	.140361	1.000000	8797	8797	62674	.140361	7.124485	62674	.000000	7.124	85+

NUMBER OF PERSONS DYING (OUT OF 100,000 AT BIRTH) ABOVE AGE X FROM SPECIFIED CAUSES

Age (x)	All Causes	Respiratory T.B.	Other Infec. and Paras.	Neoplasms	Cardiovascular	Infl., Pneu., Bronch.	Diarrheal	Certain Degenerative	Maternal	Cert. Dis. of Infancy	Motor Vehicle	Other Violence	Other and Unknown	Age (x)
0	100000	4907	2198	12231	25823	12075	2189	7670	0	4528	675	8521	19183	0
1	88332	4894	1499	12216	25656	8912	581	7659	0	0	675	8432	17808	1
5	85839	4878	856	12185	25592	8143	371	7639	0	0	655	8189	17331	5
10	85263	4870	741	12158	25565	8027	356	7624	0	0	633	8057	17232	10
15	84825	4865	704	12126	25532	7971	353	7610	0	0	618	7905	17141	15
20	84085	4831	676	12088	25481	7900	350	7590	0	0	596	7539	17034	20
25	82888	4746	641	12029	25384	7839	341	7551	0	0	540	6950	16867	25
30	81386	4558	611	11964	25262	7771	333	7467	0	0	499	6267	16654	30
35	79278	4276	567	11859	25055	7670	329	7212	0	0	439	5507	16364	35
40	76617	3927	525	11710	24760	7531	310	6731	0	0	391	4788	15944	40
45	73156	3474	459	11381	24317	7314	303	6080	0	0	329	4054	15445	45
50	68987	3034	405	10902	23533	7069	286	5231	0	0	295	3403	14829	50
55	63527	2464	341	10151	22299	6745	266	4230	0	0	231	2719	14081	55
60	57004	1944	286	9067	20434	6290	234	3292	0	0	179	2105	13173	60
65	48601	1344	219	7461	17810	5678	217	2402	0	0	115	1506	11849	65
70	38928	843	160	5448	14532	4908	192	1641	0	0	81	954	10169	70
75	27261	447	111	3351	10269	3681	143	957	0	0	35	471	7796	75
80	16694	206	73	1706	6252	2365	101	500	0	0	15	256	5220	80
85+	8797	65	36	776	3140	1334	65	232	0	0	0	123	3026	85+

NUMBER OF PERSONS SURVIVING TO AGE X IF SPECIFIED CAUSES WERE ELIMINATED

Age (x)	No Causes	Respiratory T.B.	Other Infec. and Paras.	Neoplasms	Cardiovascular	Infl., Pneu., Bronch.	Diarrheal	Certain Degenerative	Maternal	Cert. Dis. of Infancy	Motor Vehicle	Other Violence	Other and Unknown	(1) + (2)	(1) + (2) + (5) + (6) + (8)	(1)+(2)+(5)+(6)+(8)+part of(9)&(12)	(10) + (11)	Age (x)
		(1)	(2)	(3)	(4)	(5)	(6)	(7)	(8)	(9)	(10)	(11)	(12)					
0	100000	100000	100000	100000	100000	100000	100000	100000	100000	100000	100000	100000	100000	100000	100000	100000	100000	0
1	88332	88344	88991	88346	88489	91353	89855	88342	88332	92689	88332	88416	89633	89003	93635	99395	88416	1
5	85839	85867	87120	85883	86055	89563	87530	85869	85839	90073	85859	86160	87582	87148	92720	98863	86180	5
10	85263	85298	86652	85334	85504	89082	86958	85308	85263	89469	85305	85714	87095	86688	92372	98552	85756	10
15	84825	84865	86244	84927	85098	88683	86514	84883	84825	89009	84881	85427	86740	86285	92006	98193	85483	15
20	84085	84159	85520	84224	84407	87983	85763	84163	84085	88232	84163	85049	86092	85595	91351	97520	85128	20
25	82888	83045	84338	83084	83302	86794	84551	83003	82888	86976	83020	84432	85037	84498	90256	96386	84567	25
30	81386	81727	82840	81643	81914	85292	83027	81583	81386	85400	81557	83594	83713	83188	88938	95035	83769	30
35	79278	79891	80739	79633	79998	83187	80880	79723	79278	83188	79503	82203	81839	81363	87100	93151	82436	35
40	76617	77555	78071	77107	77606	80539	78185	77524	76617	80396	76882	80179	79520	79027	84772	90781	80457	40
45	73156	74501	74610	73949	74541	77124	74660	74668	73156	76764	73470	77311	76435	75982	81750	87691	77642	45
50	68987	70692	70411	70207	71074	72980	70422	71260	68987	72390	69316	73575	72707	72151	77915	83732	73926	50
55	63527	65659	64901	65388	66682	67534	64868	66618	63527	66660	63892	68454	67713	67080	72816	78435	68847	55
60	57004	59427	58290	59742	61209	61059	58238	60714	57004	59816	57381	62053	61684	60768	66501	71838	62643	60
65	48601	51246	49761	52513	55311	52667	49669	52642	48601	50998	48981	53509	53931	52469	58108	63061	53928	65
70	38928	41518	39911	44048	47767	42935	35807	42903	38928	40848	39263	43402	44899	42566	48012	52446	43776	70
75	27261	29424	27991	32878	38107	31224	27918	30674	27261	28606	27534	30841	33814	30212	35438	39237	31150	75
80	16694	18218	17171	21719	28128	20331	17130	19182	16694	17517	16876	19070	23354	18739	23417	26576	19279	80
85+	8797	9711	9076	12342	19079	11648	9053	10330	8797	9231	8904	10158	14704	10018	13651	16107	10282	85+

ADDED YRS OF LIFE

	No Causes	(1)	(2)	(3)	(4)	(5)	(6)	(7)	(8)	(9)	(10)	(11)	(12)	(1)+(2)	(1)+(2)+(5)+(6)+(8)	part of(9)&(12)	(10)+(11)
TOTAL		1.034	1.057	1.835	4.418	3.631	1.153	1.492	.000	2.740	.188	2.480	4.055	2.116	7.257	12.233	2.684
WORK	6.714	.631	.105	.534	.897	.346	.025	.817	.000	.000	.117	1.610	.854	.739	1.123	1.318	1.734

POPULATION, DEATHS, DEATH RATES FOR ALL CAUSES COMBINED, AND SPECIFIED CAUSES

Age Start of Interval	Midyear Popula-tion	Deaths During Year	All Causes	Respira-tory T. B.	Other Infec. and Paras.	Neo-plasms	Cardio-vascular	Infl., Pneu., Bronch.	Diar-rheal	Certain Degen-erative	Maternal	Cert. Dis. of Infancy	Motor Vehicle	Other Violence	Other and Unknown	Age Start of Interval
0	129000	14403	.11165	.00011	.00744	.00009	.00160	.03184	.01567	.00011	.00000	.04146	.00001	.00079	.01253	0
1	491000	3564	.00726	.00004	.00205	.00007	.00018	.00226	.00078	.00004	.00000	.00000	.00002	.00047	.00134	1
5	544000	659	.00121	.00002	.00032	.00005	.00007	.00026	.00003	.00002	.00000	.00000	.00003	.00020	.00021	5
10	490000	417	.00085	.00006	.00011	.00002	.00007	.00015	.00001	.00003	.00000	.00000	.00001	.00017	.00022	10
15	417000	549	.00132	.00015	.00006	.00008	.00017	.00013	.00000	.00004	.00013	.00000	.00001	.00023	.00031	15
20	370000	691	.00187	.00023	.00011	.00009	.00024	.00015	.00001	.00006	.00034	.00000	.00002	.00021	.00041	20
25	310000	740	.00239	.00038	.00008	.00016	.00032	.00015	.00001	.00013	.00052	.00000	.00001	.00020	.00042	25
30	282000	975	.00346	.00044	.00011	.00037	.00050	.00021	.00001	.00024	.00062	.00000	.00001	.00024	.00070	30
35	252000	1091	.00433	.00052	.00012	.00067	.00059	.00029	.00002	.00051	.00056	.00000	.00001	.00024	.00080	35
40	215000	1011	.00470	.00044	.00007	.00108	.00084	.00027	.00000	.00062	.00025	.00000	.00002	.00021	.00090	40
45	180000	1146	.00637	.00051	.00011	.00177	.00141	.00033	.00002	.00081	.00006	.00000	.00002	.00022	.00111	45
50	163000	1566	.00961	.00054	.00007	.00252	.00260	.00053	.00004	.00128	.00001	.00000	.00003	.00033	.00167	50
55	129000	1704	.01321	.00056	.00011	.00364	.00404	.00071	.00008	.00167	.00000	.00000	.00003	.00037	.00202	55
60	106000	2228	.02102	.00075	.00015	.00570	.00704	.00142	.00009	.00169	.00000	.00000	.00005	.00045	.00368	60
65	78464	2435	.03103	.00088	.00015	.00754	.01180	.00266	.00018	.00189	.00000	.00000	.00009	.00051	.00533	65
70	53880	2636	.04892	.00121	.00011	.00957	.01997	.00455	.00022	.00243	.00000	.00000	.00004	.00074	.00969	70
75	33617	2502	.07443	.00110	.00024	.01351	.03088	.00818	.00057	.00208	.00000	.00000	.00009	.00134	.01645	75
80	21686	2187	.10085	.00101	.00028	.01273	.04431	.01323	.00074	.00189	.00000	.00000	.00009	.00148	.02509	80
85+	16353	2359	.14425	.00073	.00031	.01162	.05840	.02155	.00092	.00165	.00000	.00000	.00000	.00171	.04696	85+
ALL	4282000	42863														

		All Causes	Respira-tory T. B.	Other Infec. and Paras.	Neo-plasms	Cardio-vascular	Infl., Pneu., Bronch.	Diar-rheal	Certain Degen-erative	Maternal	Cert. Dis. of Infancy	Motor Vehicle	Other Violence	Other and Unknown
CRUDE DEATH RATE		.01001	.00029	.00057	.00106	.00187	.00176	.00060	.00038	.00017	.00125	.00002	.00030	.00174
STANDARDIZED RATE (1)		.00959	.00028	.00062	.00092	.00146	.00181	.00067	.00035	.00017	.00146	.00002	.00030	.00154
STANDARDIZED RATE (2)		.01156	.00037	.00043	.00175	.00311	.00168	.00044	.00057	.00017	.00086	.00002	.00033	.00223
GEOMETRIC MEAN		.01001												

LIFE TABLE FOR ALL CAUSES COMBINED

Age (x)	Midyear Popula-tion	Deaths During Year	$_nM_x$	$_nq_x$	l_x	$_nd_x$	$_nL_x$	$_nm_x$	$_na_x$	T_x	$_nr_x$	$\overset{\circ}{e}_x$	Age (x)
0	129000	14403	.111651	.103130	100000	10313	92366	.111653	.259807	6165902	.000000	61.659	0
1	491000	3564	.007259	.028510	89687	2557	352356	.007257	1.500000	6073536	.000000	67.719	1
5	544000	659	.001211	.006048	87130	527	434333	.001213	2.500000	5721180	.000000	65.663	5
10	490000	417	.000851	.004238	86603	367	432106	.000849	2.523274	5286848	.019410	61.047	10
15	417000	549	.001317	.006587	86236	568	429850	.001321	2.658451	4854742	.024835	56.296	15
20	370000	691	.001868	.009327	85668	799	426435	.001874	2.615509	4424892	.027336	51.652	20
25	310000	740	.002387	.011912	84869	1011	421951	.002396	2.632295	3998457	.026742	47.113	25
30	282000	975	.003457	.017184	83858	1441	415845	.003465	2.609444	3576506	.018804	42.650	30
35	252000	1091	.004329	.021452	82417	1768	407756	.004336	2.551612	3160660	.020612	38.350	35
40	215000	1011	.004702	.023298	80649	1879	398695	.004713	2.578721	2752904	.028239	34.134	40
45	180000	1146	.006367	.031459	78770	2478	388012	.006386	2.644270	2354209	.022454	29.887	45
50	163000	1566	.009607	.047122	76292	3595	372931	.009640	2.627434	1966196	.022433	25.772	50
55	129000	1704	.013209	.064336	72697	4677	352469	.013269	2.644546	1593266	.027819	21.917	55
60	106000	2228	.021019	.100559	68020	6840	323876	.021119	2.628137	1240797	.027279	18.242	60
65	78464	2435	.031033	.145211	61180	8884	284662	.031209	2.609443	916921	.032797	14.987	65
70	53880	2636	.048924	.220036	52296	11507	233536	.049273	2.571533	632258	.037397	12.090	70
75	33617	2502	.074427	.314668	40789	12835	171797	.074710	2.495293	398723	.020652	9.775	75
80	21686	2187	.100848	.401266	27954	11217	110902	.101143	2.426395	226926	.020652	8.118	80
85+	16353	2359	.144255	1.000000	16737	16737	116024	.144255	6.932175	116024	.000000	6.932	85+

NUMBER OF PERSONS DYING (OUT OF 100,000 AT BIRTH) ABOVE AGE X FROM SPECIFIED CAUSES

Age (x)	All Causes	Respiratory T.B.	Other Infec. and Paras.	Neoplasms	Cardiovascular	Infl., Pneu., Bronch.	Diarrheal	Certain Degenerative	Maternal	Cert. Dis. of Infancy	Motor Vehicle	Other Violence	Other and Unknown	Age (x)
0	100000	2724	2155	15429	31708	12718	2236	4510	1032	3829	170	2356	21133	0
1	89687	2714	1467	15422	31559	9777	788	4500	1032	0	169	2282	19977	1
5	87130	2698	745	15399	31498	8579	513	4485	1032	0	160	2118	19503	5
10	86603	2688	667	15378	31467	8866	501	4475	1032	0	147	2031	19411	10
15	86236	2664	555	15368	31436	8802	497	4462	1030	0	140	1960	19318	15
20	85668	2597	534	15335	31363	8747	496	4444	974	0	134	1860	19184	20
25	84869	2500	487	15297	31262	8682	490	4416	830	0	127	1771	19007	25
30	83859	2337	451	15229	31128	8617	487	4361	609	0	125	1685	18829	30
35	82417	2153	407	15075	30921	8529	482	4259	351	0	119	1583	18538	35
40	80649	1939	360	14801	30680	8413	472	4050	125	0	114	1486	18209	40
45	78770	1765	334	14366	30344	8303	470	3802	28	0	106	1401	17851	45
50	76292	1567	293	13676	29794	8176	461	3489	5	0	98	1317	17416	50
55	72697	1365	266	12735	28821	7976	448	3011	3	0	86	1195	16791	55
60	68020	1168	227	11447	27390	7726	420	2423	3	0	75	1064	16077	60
65	61180	926	178	9594	25096	7261	389	1876	3	0	60	917	14880	65
70	52296	675	135	7438	21714	6497	338	1337	3	0	35	771	13353	70
75	40789	392	109	5100	17013	5425	286	768	3	0	26	596	11071	75
80	27954	203	68	2774	11687	4013	188	411	3	0	11	366	8230	80
85+	16737	85	35	1348	6776	2547	106	192	0	0	0	199	5449	85+

NUMBER OF PERSONS SURVIVING TO AGE X IF SPECIFIED CAUSES WERE ELIMINATED

Age (x)	No Causes	Respiratory T.B. (1)	Other Infec. and Paras. (2)	Neoplasms (3)	Cardiovascular (4)	Infl., Pneu., Bronch. (5)	Diarrheal (6)	Certain Degenerative (7)	Maternal (8)	Cert. Dis. of Infancy (9)	Motor Vehicle (10)	Other Violence (11)	Other and Unknown (12)	(1)+(2)	(1)+(2)+(5)+(6)+(8)	(1)+(2)+(5)+(6)+(8)+part of(9)&(12)	(10)+(11)	Age (x)
0	100000	100000	100000	100000	100000	100000	100000	100000	100000	100000	100000	100000	100000	100000	100000	100000	100000	0
1	89687	89656	90341	89694	89828	92515	91068	89696	89687	93386	89688	89757	90788	90350	94634	99509	89758	1
5	87130	87155	88485	87159	87327	90692	88747	87154	87130	90723	87140	87360	88674	88510	93839	99134	87370	5
10	86603	86638	88089	86653	86830	90261	88223	86637	86603	90174	86626	86919	88231	88125	93565	98910	86941	10
15	86236	86295	87765	86296	86493	89945	87853	86283	86238	89792	86266	86621	87951	87824	93321	98708	86651	15
20	85668	85793	87212	85760	85997	89410	87215	85732	85726	89201	85703	86151	87509	87339	92927	98363	86187	20
25	84869	85090	86446	84598	85295	88643	86467	84961	85070	88369	84911	85437	86872	86671	92449	97974	85479	25
30	83858	84239	85453	84053	84413	87655	85440	84003	84277	87316	83901	84505	86019	85841	91877	97489	84545	30
35	82417	82975	84029	82762	83170	86240	83977	82661	83086	85816	82246	83155	84837	84597	90929	96653	83204	35
40	80649	81408	82274	81260	81626	84510	82186	81096	81529	83975	80702	81468	83353	83048	89650	95457	81521	40
45	78770	79685	80383	79801	80062	82655	80273	79453	79726	82018	78829	79655	81777	81317	88011	93825	79715	45
50	76292	77375	77896	77982	78095	80186	77757	77265	77241	79438	76357	77232	79650	79002	85681	91441	77298	50
55	72697	73929	74252	75252	75395	76613	74106	73603	73615	75655	72771	73714	76537	75510	82131	87763	73789	55
60	68020	69367	69513	71712	71595	71939	69366	69912	68868	70825	68100	69100	72343	70890	77411	82828	69181	60
65	61180	62625	62571	66378	67101	65174	62420	63415	61943	63703	61266	62292	66287	64049	70481	75609	62380	65
70	52296	53769	53525	58937	60891	56468	53404	54724	52948	54453	52393	53384	58212	55032	61439	66177	53483	70
75	40789	42193	41771	48342	52570	45077	41700	43207	41258	42471	40872	41795	47701	43209	49427	53649	41881	75
80	27954	29075	28662	35465	42148	32209	28662	29919	28303	29107	28023	28838	35551	29811	35658	39275	28910	80
85+	16737	17503	17187	22665	31590	20622	17225	18094	16948	17427	16787	17399	24172	17973	23078	26080	17451	85+

ADDED YRS OF LIFE	No Causes	(1)	(2)	(3)	(4)	(5)	(6)	(7)	(8)	(9)	(10)	(11)	(12)	(1)+(2)	(1)+(2)+(5)+(6)+(8)	part	(10)+(11)
TOTAL		.690	1.206	2.583	5.629	3.810	1.208	.902	.429	2.533	.050	.691	4.360	1.912	7.715	12.610	.741
WORK	4.337	.396	.099	.713	.772	.255	.016	.385	.363	.000	.017	.255	.759	.496	1.143	1.426	.271

POPULATION, DEATHS, DEATH RATES FOR ALL CAUSES COMBINED, AND SPECIFIED CAUSES

Age Start of Interval	Midyear Population	Deaths During Year	All Causes	Respiratory T. B.	Other Infec. and Paras.	Neoplasms	Cardio-vascular	Infl., Pneu., Bronch.	Diarrheal	Certain Degenerative	Maternal	Cert. Dis. of Infancy	Motor Vehicle	Other Violence	Other and Unknown	Age Start of Interval
0	256700	32673	.12728	.00048	.01028	.00009	.00053	.02112	.02118	.00019	.00000	.03677	.00002	.00046	.03617	0
1	907500	17685	.01949	.00019	.00358	.00009	.00018	.00362	.00405	.00020	.00000	.00000	.00007	.00059	.00693	1
5	972100	3678	.00378	.00007	.00080	.00006	.00009	.00039	.00033	.00009	.00000	.00000	.00010	.00039	.00146	5
10	837100	1628	.00194	.00002	.00035	.00005	.00011	.00011	.00008	.00003	.00000	.00000	.00008	.00047	.00064	10
15	667000	1678	.00252	.00000	.00025	.00008	.00014	.00010	.00003	.00004	.00000	.00000	.00011	.00109	.00067	15
20	651500	2386	.00366	.00021	.00023	.00007	.00015	.00008	.00003	.00006	.00000	.00000	.00015	.00190	.00078	20
25	500900	2182	.00436	.00032	.00021	.00009	.00021	.00010	.00003	.00008	.00000	.00000	.00019	.00207	.00096	25
30	418800	2099	.00501	.00035	.00032	.00021	.00036	.00013	.00004	.00013	.00000	.00000	.00018	.00214	.00114	30
35	388700	2161	.00556	.00043	.00033	.00027	.00048	.00015	.00006	.00020	.00000	.00000	.00022	.00156	.00146	35
40	304100	2093	.00688	.00046	.00045	.00044	.00094	.00026	.00010	.00037	.00000	.00000	.00013	.00185	.00189	40
45	237000	2370	.01000	.00062	.00062	.00089	.00162	.00036	.00014	.00053	.00000	.00000	.00018	.00212	.00292	45
50	224000	2791	.01246	.00056	.00080	.00144	.00242	.00045	.00015	.00064	.00000	.00000	.00017	.00165	.00418	50
55	135100	2849	.02109	.00088	.00115	.00274	.00485	.00092	.00019	.00108	.00000	.00000	.00024	.00217	.00688	55
60	131300	3995	.03043	.00102	.00166	.00344	.00738	.00133	.00035	.00171	.00000	.00000	.00017	.00189	.01147	60
65	75300	3099	.04116	.00116	.00198	.00530	.01061	.00212	.00052	.00268	.00000	.00000	.00029	.00197	.01453	65
70	56200	3771	.06710	.00116	.00237	.00811	.01681	.00391	.00071	.00320	.00000	.00000	.00034	.00228	.02820	70
75	29100	2828	.09718	.00003	.00320	.01000	.02632	.00694	.00082	.00443	.00000	.00000	.00038	.00320	.04186	75
80	20400	2395	.11740	.00206	.00240	.00794	.02892	.00877	.00123	.00466	.00000	.00000	.00034	.00265	.05843	80
85+	14700	2853	.19408	.00034	.00347	.01034	.04782	.01306	.00197	.00639	.00000	.00000	.00000	.00041	.00415	.10612	85+
ALL	6827500	99214		.00034	.00347	.01034	.04782	.01306	.00197	.00639	.00000	.00000		.00041	.00415	.10612	

CRUDE DEATH RATE			.01395	.00027	.00132	.00051	.00113	.00161	.00145	.00030	.00000		.00138	.00013	.00125	.00458
STANDARDIZED RATE (1)			.01404	.00030	.00127	.00061	.00130	.00153	.00135	.00034	.00000		.00129	.00014	.00131	.00460
STANDARDIZED RATE (2)			.01700	.00039	.00116	.00119	.00271	.00141	.00093	.00060	.00000		.00076	.00016	.00153	.00616
GEOMETRIC MEAN			.01596													

LIFE TABLE FOR ALL CAUSES COMBINED

Age (x)	Midyear Population	Deaths During Year	$_nM_x$	$_nq_x$	l_x	$_nd_x$	$_nL_x$	$_nm_x$	$_na_x$	T_x	$_nr_x$	$\overset{\circ}{e}_x$	Age (x)
0	256700	32673	.127281	.116680	100000	11668	91673	.127278	.286377	5294606	.000000	52.946	0
1	907500	17685	.019488	.074333	88332	6566	336913	.019489	1.500000	5202932	.000000	58.902	1
5	972100	3678	.003784	.018758	81766	1537	404988	.003795	2.500000	4866019	.000000	59.512	5
10	837100	1628	.001945	.009622	80229	772	399102	.001934	2.354005	4461032	.029136	55.604	10
15	667000	1678	.002516	.012535	79457	996	394932	.002522	2.637216	4061930	.024355	51.121	15
20	651500	2386	.003662	.018200	78461	1428	388874	.003672	2.597456	3666998	.021510	46.737	20
25	500900	2182	.004356	.021601	77033	1664	381097	.004366	2.555088	3278124	.039086	42.555	25
30	418800	2099	.005012	.024785	75369	1868	372249	.005018	2.539592	2897027	.024531	38.438	30
35	388700	2161	.005560	.027469	73501	2019	362575	.005569	2.558054	2524778	.022001	34.350	35
40	304100	2093	.006883	.034009	71482	2431	351616	.006914	2.616636	2162203	.042321	30.248	40
45	237000	2370	.010000	.048949	69051	3380	337131	.010026	2.596524	1810587	.021609	26.221	45
50	224000	2791	.012460	.060864	65671	3997	318957	.012531	2.648653	1473456	.039162	22.437	50
55	135100	2849	.021088	.101047	61674	6232	293600	.021226	2.629907	1154499	.035293	18.719	55
60	131300	3995	.030427	.142185	55442	7883	258068	.030546	2.571726	860900	.027026	15.528	60
65	75300	3099	.041155	.188103	47559	8946	216117	.041394	2.576827	602832	.039099	12.675	65
70	56200	3771	.067100	.289592	38613	11182	165471	.067577	2.532325	386715	.033978	10.015	70
75	29100	2828	.097182	.389377	27431	10681	109689	.097375	2.428534	221243	.011506	8.065	75
80	20400	2395	.117402	.448836	16750	7518	63986	.117494	2.371170	111554	.011506	6.660	80
85+	14700	2853	.194082	1.000000	9232	9232	47568	.194082	5.152471	47568	.000000	5.152	85+

NUMBER OF PERSONS DYING (OUT OF 100,000 AT BIRTH) ABOVE AGE X FROM SPECIFIED CAUSES

Age (x)	All Causes	Respiratory T. B.	Other Infec. and Paras.	Neo-plasms	Cardio-vascular	Infl., Pneu., Bronch.	Diar-rheal	Certain Degen-erative	Maternal	Cert. Dis. of Infancy	Motor Vehicle	Other Violence	Other and Unknown	Age (x)
0	100000	2307	6044	7573	17818	7604	4312	3813	0	3370	900	8618	37641	0
1	88332	2264	5102	7564	17770	5668	2370	3795	0	0	898	8576	34325	1
5	81766	2199	3896	7535	17710	4449	1007	3729	0	0	875	8376	31990	5
10	80229	2170	3569	7510	17674	4289	874	3693	0	0	833	8218	31399	10
15	79457	2163	3433	7489	17631	4247	841	3680	0	0	801	8027	31145	15
20	78461	2161	3335	7456	17577	4207	829	3664	0	0	757	7594	30881	20
25	77033	2079	3245	7430	17519	4175	818	3640	0	0	699	6854	30574	25
30	75369	1958	3127	7395	17438	4137	806	3608	0	0	625	6064	30211	30
35	73501	1829	3008	7317	17303	4087	790	3558	0	0	559	5267	29783	35
40	71482	1671	2890	7219	17129	4032	769	3486	0	0	479	4556	29251	40
45	69051	1510	2730	7064	16796	3941	735	3353	0	0	433	3906	28583	45
50	65671	1299	2522	6763	16247	3820	688	3174	0	0	374	3191	27593	50
55	61674	1121	2265	6301	15467	3676	640	2969	0	0	319	2666	26250	55
60	55442	861	1926	5492	14032	3405	585	2649	0	0	248	2028	24216	60
65	47559	597	1496	4600	12119	3059	494	2205	0	0	204	1541	21244	65
70	38613	347	1067	3447	9812	2596	382	1622	0	0	141	1116	18083	70
75	27431	156	674	2097	7009	1943	263	1090	0	0	85	738	13376	75
80	16750	153	323	999	4116	1179	173	603	0	0	43	387	8774	80
85+	9232	16	165	492	2275	621	94	304	0	0	19	197	5049	85+

NUMBER OF PERSONS SURVIVING TO AGE X IF SPECIFIED CAUSES WERE ELIMINATED

Age (x)	No Causes	Respiratory T. B. (1)	Other Infec. and Paras. (2)	Neo-plasms (3)	Cardio-vascular (4)	Infl., Pneu., Bronch. (5)	Diar-rheal (6)	Certain Degener-ative (7)	Maternal (8)	Cert. Dis. of Infancy (9)	Motor Vehicle (10)	Other Violence (11)	Other and Unknown (12)	(1) + (2)	(1) + (2) + (5) + (6) + (8)	(1)+(2)+ (5)+(6)+ (8)+part of(9)&(12)	(10) + (11)	Age (x)
0	100000	100000	100000	100000	100000	100000	100000	100000	100000	100000	100000	100000	100000	100000	100000	100000	100000	0
1	88332	88372	89221	88340	88377	90169	90175	88349	88332	91555	88334	88371	91502	89262	93020	99704	88373	1
5	81766	81866	83769	81802	81866	84672	84821	81845	81766	84749	81790	81995	87059	83872	90098	99018	82019	5
10	80229	80356	82527	80289	80362	83245	83364	80342	80229	83156	80294	80611	86048	82658	89116	98431	80676	10
15	79457	79590	81872	79537	79632	82487	82595	79582	79457	82356	79553	80027	85492	82009	88499	97881	80124	15
20	78461	78594	80946	78573	78688	81494	81573	78601	78461	81324	78600	79458	84703	81084	87558	96907	79599	20
25	77033	77245	79565	77169	77313	80044	80099	77194	77033	79843	77227	78758	83490	79784	86203	95479	78956	25
30	75369	75697	77967	75537	75724	78354	78381	75558	75369	78119	75632	77860	82077	78306	84661	93871	78132	30
35	73501	73949	76156	73742	73981	76464	76455	73735	73501	76183	73823	76747	80504	76620	82912	92047	77083	35
40	71482	72074	74185	71813	72122	74420	74377	71781	71482	74090	71874	75374	78870	74800	81027	90111	75788	40
45	69051	69783	71826	69524	70000	71982	71882	69471	69051	71570	69476	73487	76916	72587	78770	87811	73939	45
50	65671	66575	68521	66418	67119	68582	68411	66246	65671	68067	66133	70635	74234	69464	75570	84549	71131	50
55	61674	62698	64611	62830	63812	64553	64296	62415	61674	63924	62161	66884	71203	65683	71672	80589	67412	55
60	55442	56613	58419	57267	58789	58300	57853	56416	55442	57465	55948	60783	66274	59653	65456	74166	61337	60
65	47559	48813	50534	49985	52344	50349	49715	48815	47559	49294	48034	52634	60236	51866	57398	65908	53159	65
70	38613	39861	41438	41687	44844	41322	40469	40174	38613	40022	39056	43156	52646	42778	47980	55980	43651	70
75	27431	28481	29792	30859	34708	29950	28854	29005	27431	28432	27793	31013	43203	30932	35524	42716	31422	75
80	16750	17391	18487	19815	24227	18948	17692	18113	16750	17361	17003	19246	32645	19195	22935	28773	19537	80
85+	9232	9690	10318	11369	15450	10916	9812	10223	9232	9569	9390	10768	24171	10830	13610	18358	10952	85+

ADDED YRS OF LIFE																		
TOTAL		.543	2.173	1.071	2.557	2.499	2.160	.588	.000	1.921	.259	2.596	10.061	2.750	7.824	15.474	2.877	
WORK	6.466	.319	.378	.358	.672	.184	.060	.208	.000	.000	.166	1.888	1.596	.702	.954	1.322	2.065	

POPULATION, DEATHS, DEATH RATES FOR ALL CAUSES COMBINED, AND SPECIFIED CAUSES

Age Start of Interval	Midyear Population	Deaths During Year	All Causes	Respiratory T. B.	Other Infec. and Paras.	Neoplasms	Cardiovascular	Infl., Pneu., Bronch.	Diarrheal	Certain Degenerative	Maternal	Cert. Dis. of Infancy	Motor Vehicle	Other Violence	Other and Unknown	Age Start of Interval
0	245800	27213	.11071	.00038	.01049	.00008	.00041	.01954	.01894	.00019	.00000	.02907	.00001	.00045	.03114	0
1	882200	17709	.02007	.00019	.00399	.00006	.00013	.00391	.00401	.00020	.00000	.00000	.00004	.00046	.00707	1
5	941000	3215	.00342	.00006	.00075	.00004	.00008	.00043	.00033	.00006	.00000	.00000	.00004	.00020	.00142	5
10	804900	1174	.00146	.00002	.00027	.00004	.00011	.00015	.00006	.00004	.00000	.00000	.00003	.00015	.00059	10
15	740900	1288	.00174	.00011	.00018	.00009	.00014	.00009	.00003	.00004	.00018	.00000	.00002	.00023	.00062	15
20	673700	1639	.00243	.00011	.00021	.00009	.00023	.00009	.00004	.00006	.00040	.00000	.00003	.00027	.00090	20
25	547300	1748	.00319	.00021	.00029	.00015	.00032	.00015	.00005	.00008	.00059	.00000	.00002	.00021	.00112	25
30	412800	1869	.00453	.00034	.00031	.00032	.00056	.00015	.00005	.00012	.00077	.00000	.00004	.00031	.00157	30
35	409000	2139	.00523	.00039	.00033	.00063	.00067	.00020	.00007	.00016	.00080	.00000	.00004	.00031	.00162	35
40	293400	1977	.00674	.00043	.00033	.00112	.00114	.00026	.00010	.00025	.00051	.00000	.00002	.00028	.00229	40
45	240700	2043	.00849	.00041	.00043	.00163	.00179	.00033	.00013	.00040	.00012	.00000	.00007	.00032	.00285	45
50	214900	2337	.01087	.00053	.00057	.00201	.00241	.00047	.00013	.00060	.00000	.00000	.00009	.00027	.00378	50
55	129400	2220	.01716	.00061	.00065	.00352	.00433	.00084	.00023	.00095	.00000	.00000	.00008	.00043	.00552	55
60	143100	3557	.02514	.00067	.00100	.00448	.00608	.00138	.00139	.00000	.00000	.00000	.00006	.00045	.00929	60
65	77500	2889	.03728	.00066	.00102	.00597	.00996	.00228	.00057	.00214	.00000	.00000	.00010	.00053	.01404	65
70	70000	3952	.05503	.00089	.00166	.00691	.01434	.00387	.00073	.00311	.00000	.00000	.00017	.00086	.02249	70
75	33500	2901	.08660	.00072	.00212	.01048	.02537	.00543	.00096	.00487	.00000	.00000	.00015	.00104	.03546	75
80	30400	3279	.10786	.00115	.00332	.00878	.02671	.00826	.00138	.00441	.00000	.00000	.00023	.00178	.05184	80
85+	22900	4799	.20956	.00127	.00389	.01258	.04764	.01485	.00205	.00742	.00000	.00000	.00009	.00371	.11607	85+
ALL	6913400	87888														
CRUDE DEATH RATE			.01271	.00023	.00126	.00070	.00124	.00158	.00131	.00029	.00022	.00103	.00004	.00031	.00448	
STANDARDIZED RATE (1)			.01246	.00025	.00123	.00077	.00125	.00152	.00127	.00030	.00023	.00102	.00004	.00031	.00427	
STANDARDIZED RATE (2)			.01507	.00032	.00103	.00143	.00256	.00139	.00089	.00055	.00023	.00060	.00005	.00031	.00565	
GEOMETRIC MEAN			.01371													

LIFE TABLE FOR ALL CAUSES COMBINED

Age (x)	Midyear Population	Deaths During Year	$_nM_x$	$_nq_x$	l_x	$_nd_x$	$_nL_x$	$_nm_x$	$_na_x$	T_x	$_nr_x$	$\overset{\circ}{e}_x$	Age (x)
0	245800	27213	.110712	.102310	100000	10231	92411	.110712	.258210	5564495	.000000	55.645	0
1	882200	17709	.020074	.076463	89769	6864	341916	.020075	1.500000	5472084	.000000	60.957	1
5	941000	3215	.003417	.016971	82905	1407	411008	.003423	2.500000	5130168	.000000	61.880	5
10	804900	1174	.001459	.007227	81498	589	405871	.001451	2.250637	4719160	.018106	57.905	10
15	740900	1288	.001738	.008676	80909	702	402870	.001742	2.613663	4313290	.015324	53.310	15
20	673700	1639	.002433	.012119	80207	972	398722	.002438	2.620027	3910420	.020974	48.754	20
25	547300	1748	.003194	.015927	79235	1262	393182	.003210	2.628599	3511698	.043606	44.320	25
30	412800	1869	.004528	.022456	77973	1751	385636	.004541	2.584595	3118516	.029383	39.995	30
35	409000	2139	.005230	.025885	76222	1973	376328	.005243	2.576132	2732880	.024526	35.854	35
40	293400	1977	.006738	.033293	74249	2472	365277	.006767	2.585794	2356553	.046838	31.739	40
45	240700	2043	.008488	.041671	71777	2991	351657	.008505	2.583375	1991276	.022129	27.743	45
50	214900	2337	.010875	.053339	68786	3669	335258	.010944	2.636447	1639619	.048732	23.837	50
55	129400	2220	.017156	.082836	65117	5394	312816	.017243	2.632748	1304361	.029068	20.031	55
60	143100	3557	.025136	.118983	59723	7106	281609	.025234	2.606864	991545	.024801	16.602	60
65	77500	2889	.037277	.171789	52617	9039	241219	.037472	2.580969	709935	.031609	13.493	65
70	70000	3952	.055029	.243678	43578	10619	191901	.055336	2.552559	468716	.032149	10.756	70
75	33500	2901	.086597	.355533	32959	11718	135156	.086700	2.470665	276815	.005896	8.399	75
80	30400	3279	.107862	.422249	21241	8969	83099	.107931	2.423812	141659	.005896	6.669	80
85+	22900	4799	.209563	1.000000	12272	12272	58560	.209563	4.771827	58560	.000000	4.772	85+

NUMBER OF PERSONS DYING (OUT OF 100,000 AT BIRTH) ABOVE AGE X FROM SPECIFIED CAUSES

Age (x)	All Causes	Respiratory T.B.	Other Infec. and Paras.	Neoplasms	Cardiovascular	Infl., Pneu., Bronch.	Diarrheal	Certain Degenerative	Maternal	Cert. Dis. of Infancy	Motor Vehicle	Other Violence	Other and Unknown	Age (x)
0	100000	2042	5580	10260	19474	8263	4316	4015	1298	2687	309	2235	39521	0
1	89769	2006	4611	10253	19436	6457	2565	3998	1298	0	308	2193	36644	1
5	82905	1941	3248	10231	19389	5119	1192	3929	1298	0	295	2036	34227	5
10	81498	1917	2937	10214	19355	4940	1058	3904	1298	0	280	1952	33643	10
15	80909	1907	2828	10198	19312	4881	1033	3889	1296	0	269	1891	33405	15
20	80207	1864	2754	10163	15256	4843	1020	3871	1224	0	260	1798	33154	20
25	79235	1819	2669	10128	19164	4809	1002	3846	1063	0	248	1692	32795	25
30	77973	1736	2555	10068	19038	4751	984	3913	829	0	239	1608	32352	30
35	76222	1605	2438	9942	18822	4694	965	3767	531	0	224	1489	31745	35
40	74249	1458	2312	9705	18568	4617	939	3706	230	0	208	1372	31134	40
45	71777	1300	2189	9292	18148	4522	903	3615	46	0	201	1269	30292	45
50	68786	1157	2039	8717	17516	4406	856	3474	5	0	175	1155	29286	50
55	65117	980	1846	8037	16701	4246	811	3271	5	0	145	1063	28012	55
60	59723	788	1642	6930	15340	3981	738	2972	5	0	121	929	26277	60
65	52617	599	1360	5665	13621	3591	643	2579	5	0	103	803	23648	65
70	43578	440	1113	4219	11204	3036	505	2059	5	0	78	675	20244	70
75	32959	270	794	2888	8435	2289	365	1458	5	0	45	510	15900	75
80	21241	173	507	1470	5002	1554	235	800	5	0	25	368	11102	80
85+	12272	74	228	736	2790	869	120	435	0	0	5	217	6798	85+

NUMBER OF PERSONS SURVIVING TO AGE X IF SPECIFIED CAUSES WERE ELIMINATED

Age (x)	No Causes	Respiratory T.B.	Other Infec. and Paras.	Neoplasms	Cardiovascular	Infl., Pneu., Bronch.	Diarrheal	Certain Degenerative	Maternal	Cert. Dis. of Infancy	Motor Vehicle	Other Violence	Other and Unknown	(1) + (2)	(1) + (2) + (5) + (6) + (8)	(1)+(2)+ (5)+(6)+ (8)+part of(9)&(12)	(10) + (11)	Age (x)
		(1)	(2)	(3)	(4)	(5)	(6)	(7)	(8)	(9)	(10)	(11)	(12)					
0	100000	100000	100000	100000	100000	100000	100000	100000	100000	100000	100000	100000	100000	100000	100000	100000	100000	0
1	89769	89803	90691	89776	89805	91496	91443	89785	89769	92350	89770	89809	92535	90726	94195	99757	89810	1
5	82905	82999	85090	82932	82983	85820	85805	82986	82905	85289	82918	83093	87887	85187	91267	99209	83106	5
10	81498	81614	83963	81542	81609	84548	84487	81603	81498	83841	81526	81766	87012	84083	90428	98849	81794	10
15	80909	81034	83468	80968	81062	83997	83902	81028	80911	83235	80948	81236	86636	83598	90001	98551	81275	15
20	80207	80374	82820	80301	80415	83308	83187	80343	80281	82513	80254	80624	86153	82993	89487	98150	80672	20
25	79235	79445	81904	79362	79532	82333	82198	79394	79468	81513	79294	79753	85493	82121	88783	97625	79812	25
30	77973	78262	80716	78158	78391	81062	80907	78162	78436	80215	78040	78567	84607	81016	87935	97029	78634	30
35	76222	76635	79023	76528	76845	79320	79110	76453	76971	78414	76302	76921	83360	79452	86656	96029	77002	35
40	74249	74797	77107	74782	75109	77346	77088	74534	75279	76384	74343	75047	81865	77676	85176	94770	75141	40
45	71777	72463	74665	72703	73028	74868	74559	72143	72956	73841	71875	72650	80057	75380	83014	92755	72749	45
50	68786	65585	71707	70246	70617	71867	71500	69275	69956	70764	68905	69736	77828	72540	80119	89841	69857	50
55	65117	66048	68078	67178	67670	68196	67731	65779	66225	66989	65259	66107	75092	69051	76500	86175	66251	55
60	59723	60763	62643	62716	63434	62814	62194	60620	60739	61440	59876	60761	70815	63734	70993	80419	60917	60
65	52617	53713	55467	56513	57626	55726	54887	53783	53512	54130	52769	53652	65384	56623	63620	72793	53806	65
70	43578	44633	46175	48233	50154	46691	45589	45029	44319	44831	43726	44554	58139	47293	53912	62546	44705	70
75	32959	33907	35217	37774	40833	36014	34606	34599	33520	33907	33100	33843	49297	36231	42275	50289	33988	75
80	21241	21931	22941	25667	29921	23858	22411	22853	21602	21852	21348	21927	38044	23686	28548	35084	22037	80
85+	12272	12747	13483	15510	19798	14374	13040	13501	12485	12625	12349	12786	28600	14005	17731	23295	12866	85+

ADDED YRS OF LIFE

	No Causes	(1)	(2)	(3)	(4)	(5)	(6)	(7)	(8)	(9)	(10)	(11)	(12)				
TOTAL		.501	2.225	1.623	2.860	2.690	2.160	.597	.495	1.593	.080	.613	10.419	2.754	8.599	16.458	.695
WORK	5.464	.283	.318	.622	.793	.204	.070	.184	.461	.000	.038	.286	1.736	.604	1.360	2.099	.324

POPULATION, DEATHS, DEATH RATES FOR ALL CAUSES COMBINED, AND SPECIFIED CAUSES

Age Start of Interval	Midyear Population	Deaths During Year	All Causes	Respiratory T. B.	Other Infec. and Paras.	Neoplasms	Cardiovascular	Infl., Pneu., Bronch.	Diarrheal	Certain Degenerative	Maternal	Cert. Dis. of Infancy	Motor Vehicle	Other Violence	Other and Unknown	Age Start of Interval
0	318769	30864	.09682	.00027	.00743	.00009	.00024	.01725	.01700	.00026	.00000	.03443	.00003	.00042	.01940	0
1	1243488	15353	.01235	.00010	.00221	.00007	.00011	.00267	.00283	.00012	.00000	.00000	.00009	.00049	.00367	1
5	1418522	3370	.00238	.00004	.00048	.00007	.00005	.00028	.00022	.00005	.00000	.00000	.00012	.00025	.00080	5
10	1148494	1503	.00131	.00002	.00018	.00006	.00008	.00008	.00004	.00002	.00000	.00000	.00012	.00031	.00040	10
15	836284	1815	.00217	.00005	.00017	.00008	.00015	.00008	.00003	.00005	.00000	.00000	.00016	.00087	.00054	15
20	671272	2305	.00343	.00015	.00016	.00008	.00018	.00007	.00002	.00008	.00000	.00000	.00028	.00184	.00057	20
25	549667	2036	.00370	.00023	.00018	.00013	.00025	.00008	.00003	.00010	.00000	.00000	.00024	.00190	.00057	25
30	500217	2005	.00401	.00021	.00020	.00018	.00034	.00010	.00004	.00013	.00000	.00000	.00025	.00184	.00073	30
35	443163	2176	.00491	.00038	.00024	.00028	.00054	.00013	.00005	.00020	.00000	.00000	.00028	.00180	.00102	35
40	359936	1987	.00552	.00035	.00035	.00052	.00081	.00014	.00004	.00033	.00000	.00000	.00023	.00141	.00134	40
45	291251	2384	.00819	.00050	.00045	.00087	.00169	.00027	.00007	.00047	.00000	.00000	.00027	.00155	.00203	45
50	262251	3075	.01173	.00057	.00055	.00158	.00278	.00042	.00016	.00079	.00000	.00000	.00032	.00140	.00316	50
55	167127	2935	.01756	.00071	.00076	.00242	.00486	.00054	.00014	.00136	.00000	.00000	.00035	.00164	.00476	55
60	163818	4439	.02710	.00097	.00122	.00379	.00768	.00111	.00034	.00162	.00000	.00000	.00031	.00160	.00846	60
65	92211	3673	.03983	.00110	.00141	.00531	.01215	.00154	.00036	.00260	.00000	.00000	.00029	.00187	.01321	65
70	68296	3835	.05615	.00122	.00176	.00668	.01709	.00253	.00067	.00306	.00000	.00000	.00038	.00206	.02040	70
75	39384	3186	.08090	.00096	.00201	.00937	.02631	.00482	.00053	.00449	.00000	.00000	.00061	.00201	.02978	75
80	23652	2368	.10012	.00140	.00309	.00947	.03095	.00617	.00118	.00567	.00000	.00000	.00034	.00190	.03995	80
85+	16850	2818	.16724	.00119	.00404	.00961	.04807	.01068	.00172	.00760	.00000	.00000	.00024	.00303	.08107	85+
ALL	8814652	92127														

CRUDE DEATH RATE			.01069	.00021	.00090	.00050	.00112	.00127	.00113	.00029	.00000	.00127	.00018	.00099	.00284	
STANDARDIZED RATE (1)			.01100	.00024	.00085	.00061	.00133	.00119	.00102	.00034	.00000	.00121	.00020	.00110	.00291	
STANDARDIZED RATE (2)			.01397	.00035	.00080	.00117	.00281	.00106	.00071	.00062	.00000	.00071	.00023	.00127	.00424	
GEOMETRIC MEAN			.01308													

LIFE TABLE FOR ALL CAUSES COMBINED

Age (x)	Midyear Population	Deaths During Year	$_nM_x$	$_nq_x$	l_x	$_nd_x$	$_nL_x$	$_nm_x$	$_na_x$	T_x	$_nr_x$	$\overset{\circ}{e}_x$	Age (x)
0	318769	30864	.096822	.090140	100000	9014	93101	.096820	.234598	5826011	.000000	58.260	0
1	1243488	15353	.012347	.047908	90986	4359	353047	.012347	1.500000	5732910	.000000	63.009	1
5	1418522	3370	.002376	.011844	86627	1026	430570	.002383	2.500000	5379864	.000000	62.104	5
10	1148494	1503	.001309	.006484	85601	555	426597	.001301	2.462838	4949294	.038769	57.818	10
15	836284	1815	.002170	.010900	85046	927	423097	.002191	2.658670	4522697	.050403	53.179	15
20	671272	2305	.003434	.017107	84119	1439	417121	.003450	2.585563	4099600	.043299	48.736	20
25	549667	2036	.003704	.018360	82680	1518	409641	.003706	2.523880	3682480	.031521	44.539	25
30	500217	2005	.004008	.019874	81162	1613	401864	.004014	2.553601	3272838	.019253	40.325	30
35	443163	2176	.004910	.024299	79549	1933	393018	.004918	2.554751	2870974	.023927	36.091	35
40	359936	1987	.005520	.027327	77616	2121	383009	.005538	2.608931	2477956	.036433	31.926	40
45	291251	2384	.008185	.040294	75495	3042	370295	.008215	2.639574	2094948	.022282	27.749	45
50	262251	3075	.011725	.057403	72453	4159	352440	.011801	2.637553	1724653	.041088	23.804	50
55	167127	2935	.017561	.084751	68294	5788	327798	.017657	2.637857	1372213	.031862	20.093	55
60	163818	4439	.027097	.127812	62506	7989	293427	.027226	2.608900	1044416	.028495	16.709	60
65	92211	3673	.039833	.182769	54517	9964	248308	.040128	2.563541	750988	.046316	13.775	65
70	68296	3835	.056153	.247525	44553	11028	195471	.056417	2.525069	502680	.031664	11.283	70
75	39384	3186	.080896	.336793	33525	11291	138946	.081262	2.460035	307208	.027650	9.164	75
80	23652	2368	.100118	.398579	22234	8862	88305	.100356	2.419930	168262	.027650	7.568	80
85+	16850	2818	.167240	1.000000	13372	13372	79957	.167240	5.979418	79957	.000000	5.979	85+

NUMBER OF PERSONS DYING (OUT OF 100,000 AT BIRTH) ABOVE AGE X FROM SPECIFIED CAUSES

Age (x)	All Causes	Respiratory T.B.	Other Infec. and Paras.	Neoplasms	Cardiovascular	Infl., Pneu., Bronch.	Diarrheal	Certain Degenerative	Maternal	Cert. Dis. of Infancy	Motor Vehicle	Other Violence	Other and Unknown	Age (x)
0	100000	2405	4823	9013	23146	6657	3543	4819	0	3205	1424	8008	32957	0
1	90986	2380	4131	9005	23124	5051	1961	4795	0	0	1422	7969	31148	1
5	86627	2344	3350	8980	23086	4110	963	4754	0	0	1391	7796	29853	5
10	85601	2328	3141	8949	23063	3989	868	4732	0	0	1338	7688	29505	10
15	85046	2321	3064	8923	23030	3954	851	4723	0	0	1287	7555	29338	15
20	84119	2301	2992	8889	22968	3920	839	4702	0	0	1220	7181	29107	20
25	82680	2239	2924	8855	22893	3891	829	4670	0	0	1103	6407	28869	25
30	81162	2144	2852	8802	22789	3859	818	4629	0	0	1004	5629	28636	30
35	79549	2060	2773	8728	22654	3819	802	4579	0	0	903	4890	28341	35
40	77616	1911	2679	8616	22440	3769	783	4498	0	0	793	4185	27942	40
45	75495	1776	2544	8416	22129	3713	767	4370	0	0	704	3648	27428	45
50	72453	1589	2378	8091	21500	3611	741	4194	0	0	605	3073	26671	50
55	68294	1387	2185	7529	20510	3464	685	3913	0	0	492	2582	25547	55
60	62506	1153	1935	6730	18905	3284	638	3464	0	0	376	2044	23977	60
65	54517	867	1575	5613	16640	2956	539	2987	0	0	285	1574	21481	65
70	44553	594	1224	4285	13599	2571	449	2337	0	0	212	1110	18172	70
75	33525	357	880	2914	10242	2072	317	1736	0	0	137	706	14164	75
80	22234	223	600	1608	6570	1398	243	1109	0	0	52	427	10004	80
85+	13372	95	323	769	3844	854	138	607	0	0	19	242	6481	85+

NUMBER OF PERSONS SURVIVING TO AGE X IF SPECIFIED CAUSES WERE ELIMINATED

Age (x)	No Causes	Respiratory T.B. (1)	Other Infec. and Paras. (2)	Neoplasms (3)	Cardiovascular (4)	Infl., Pneu., Bronch. (5)	Diarrheal (6)	Certain Degenerative (7)	Maternal (8)	Cert. Dis. of Infancy (9)	Motor Vehicle (10)	Other Violence (11)	Other and Unknown (12)	(1)+(2)	(1)+(2)+(5)+(6)+(8)	(1)+(2)+(5)+(6)+(8)+part of(9)&(12)	(10)+(11)	Age (x)
0	100000	100000	100000	100000	100000	100000	100000	100000	100000	100000	100000	100000	100000	100000	100000	100000	100000	0
1	90986	91010	91648	90994	91007	92530	92507	91009	90986	94094	90988	91023	92727	91672	94787	99776	91025	1
5	86627	86685	88028	86659	86664	89036	89071	86689	86627	89586	86659	86831	89582	88087	93091	99285	86864	5
10	85601	85674	87197	85663	85680	88105	88113	85684	85601	88525	85685	85911	88880	87272	92461	98872	85995	10
15	85046	85126	86710	85134	85158	87570	87559	85137	85046	87951	85181	85487	88476	86791	92008	98455	85622	15
20	84119	84218	85838	84240	84291	86650	86617	84230	84119	86992	84319	84930	87751	85939	91153	97594	85132	20
25	82680	82839	84438	82832	82924	85197	85145	82821	82680	85504	82993	84255	86496	84600	89776	96158	84574	25
30	81162	81412	82961	81364	81505	83666	83593	81341	81162	83934	81568	83498	85150	83216	88354	94678	83915	30
35	79549	79878	81392	79821	80019	82044	81948	79774	79549	82266	80047	82594	83765	81728	86834	93107	83111	35
40	77616	78084	79509	77992	78288	80101	79976	77916	77616	80267	78211	81313	82146	79989	85061	91300	81937	40
45	75495	76085	77473	76059	76459	77969	77807	75914	75495	78074	76163	79647	80439	78078	83107	89330	80352	45
50	72453	73204	74518	73316	74005	74931	74698	73029	72453	74928	73192	77034	77992	75291	80279	86476	77819	50
55	68294	69200	70434	69662	70746	70777	70466	69112	68294	70627	69101	73119	74700	71368	76316	82467	73983	55
60	62506	63562	64711	64543	66361	64958	64541	63691	62506	64641	63357	67474	70032	65805	70612	76613	68392	60
65	54517	55709	56789	57380	60169	56975	56387	56005	54517	56379	55344	59324	63750	58031	62728	68629	60224	65
70	44553	45779	46740	48170	52297	46926	46165	46375	44553	46075	45256	48937	55714	48026	52415	57984	49753	70
75	33525	34657	35483	37548	42912	35770	34857	35440	33525	34670	34150	37207	46493	36681	40692	45827	37901	75
80	22234	23096	23773	26109	32529	24315	23179	24046	22234	22993	22718	24925	35877	24694	28152	32498	25468	80
85+	13372	13993	14526	16477	22876	15087	14025	14885	13372	13829	13689	15150	26411	15200	17987	21609	15510	85+

ADDED YRS OF LIFE

	No Causes	(1)	(2)	(3)	(4)	(5)	(6)	(7)	(8)	(9)	(10)	(11)	(12)				
TOTAL		.522	1.639	1.358	3.586	2.198	1.808	.737	.000	1.982	.430	2.500	7.729	2.187	6.472	11.920	2.962
WORK	5.651	.266	.266	.387	.731	.144	.048	.230	.000	.000	.257	1.682	1.151	.535	.732	.950	1.952

POPULATION, DEATHS, DEATH RATES FOR ALL CAUSES COMBINED, AND SPECIFIED CAUSES

Age Start of Interval	Midyear Population	Deaths During Year	All Causes	Respiratory T. B.	Other Infec. and Paras.	Neo-plasms	Cardio-vascular	Infl., Pneu., Bronch.	Diar-rheal	Certain Degen-erative	Maternal	Cert. Dis. of Infancy	Motor Vehicle	Other Violence	Other and Unknown	Age Start of Interval
0	311725	25414	.08153	.00023	.00706	.00006	.00020	.01555	.01469	.00020	.00000	.02693	.00002	.00032	.01625	0
1	1211765	15129	.01249	.00011	.00234	.00006	.00011	.00295	.00275	.00011	.00000	.00000	.00006	.00037	.00362	1
5	1382217	2796	.00202	.00003	.00046	.00004	.00005	.00027	.00018	.00005	.00000	.00000	.00005	.00015	.00075	5
10	1120549	1075	.00096	.00002	.00017	.00004	.00006	.00009	.00004	.00004	.00001	.00000	.00003	.00012	.00033	10
15	929756	1402	.00151	.00006	.00013	.00007	.00015	.00008	.00002	.00004	.00017	.00000	.00003	.00031	.00044	15
20	746103	1512	.00203	.00014	.00018	.00009	.00009	.00009	.00003	.00005	.00036	.00000	.00004	.00025	.00060	20
25	616153	1577	.00256	.00020	.00022	.00015	.00032	.00008	.00003	.00010	.00052	.00000	.00003	.00023	.00068	25
30	530081	1819	.00343	.00028	.00028	.00030	.00043	.00012	.00006	.00012	.00067	.00000	.00004	.00022	.00093	30
35	481253	2248	.00467	.00033	.00028	.00062	.00073	.00016	.00005	.00017	.00083	.00000	.00005	.00023	.00123	35
40	358742	1973	.00550	.00037	.00030	.00112	.00100	.00018	.00008	.00022	.00049	.00000	.00006	.00021	.00147	40
45	300973	1977	.00657	.00030	.00038	.00152	.00138	.00019	.00011	.00039	.00009	.00000	.00007	.00024	.00191	45
50	256047	2496	.00975	.00041	.00042	.00230	.00245	.00029	.00012	.00062	.00002	.00000	.00007	.00025	.00278	50
55	164475	2321	.01411	.00042	.00051	.00330	.00418	.00054	.00025	.00103	.00000	.00000	.00010	.00026	.00351	55
60	176149	3742	.02124	.00050	.00069	.00410	.00603	.00099	.00024	.00134	.00000	.00000	.00014	.00042	.00678	60
65	97338	3064	.03148	.00052	.00100	.00519	.01010	.00152	.00031	.00237	.00000	.00000	.00009	.00045	.00992	65
70	80691	3696	.04580	.00069	.00129	.00610	.01464	.00269	.00066	.00261	.00000	.00000	.00010	.00066	.01637	70
75	44313	3096	.06987	.00090	.00162	.00855	.02304	.00402	.00104	.00451	.00000	.00000	.00014	.00063	.02541	75
80	33480	3070	.09170	.00116	.00227	.00893	.02694	.00603	.00134	.00481	.00000	.00000	.00027	.00146	.03847	80
85+	28046	4815	.17168	.00096	.00285	.01230	.04767	.01269	.00193	.00610	.00000	.00000	.00025	.00367	.08326	85+
ALL	8869856	83222														

		All Causes	Respiratory T.B.	Other Infec.	Neo-plasms	Cardio-vascular	Infl. Pneu.	Diarrheal	Certain Degen.	Maternal	Cert. Dis. Infancy	Motor Vehicle	Other Violence	Other Unknown
CRUDE DEATH RATE		.00938	.00018	.00085	.00063	.00112	.00122	.00098	.00026	.00019	.00095	.00005	.00026	.00269
STANDARDIZED RATE (1)		.00936	.00019	.00081	.00072	.00119	.00115	.00093	.00029	.00021	.00095	.00005	.00026	.00259
STANDARDIZED RATE (2)		.01188	.00026	.00071	.00132	.00247	.00104	.00066	.00053	.00022	.00056	.00006	.00029	.00374
GEOMETRIC MEAN		.01081												

LIFE TABLE FOR ALL CAUSES COMBINED

Age (x)	Midyear Population	Deaths During Year	$_nM_x$	$_nq_x$	l_x	$_nd_x$	$_nL_x$	$_nm_x$	$_na_x$	T_x	$_nr_x$	$\overset{\circ}{e}_x$	Age (x)
0	311725	25414	.081527	.076590	100000	7659	93939	.081532	.208596	6160573	.000000	61.606	0
1	1211765	15129	.012485	.048429	92341	4472	358184	.012485	1.500000	6066634	.000000	65.698	1
5	1382217	2796	.002023	.010083	87869	886	437130	.002027	2.500000	5708450	.000000	64.965	5
10	1120549	1075	.000959	.004760	86983	414	433432	.000954	2.383253	5271320	.029272	60.602	10
15	929756	1402	.001508	.007555	86569	654	431305	.001516	2.645260	4837488	.036759	55.880	15
20	746103	1512	.002027	.010126	85915	870	427490	.002035	2.603209	4406183	.039393	51.285	20
25	616153	1577	.002559	.012758	85045	1085	422630	.002567	2.698103	3978694	.035631	46.783	25
30	530081	1819	.003432	.017068	83960	1433	416390	.003441	2.620086	3556064	.022658	42.354	30
35	481253	2248	.004671	.023156	82527	1911	408016	.004684	2.582963	3139674	.029653	38.044	35
40	358742	1973	.005500	.027215	80616	2194	397727	.005516	2.560012	2731658	.042529	33.885	40
45	300973	1977	.006569	.032427	78422	2543	386054	.006587	2.618626	2333932	.025033	29.761	45
50	256047	2496	.009748	.047997	75879	3642	370792	.009822	2.637916	1947877	.049736	25.671	50
55	164475	2321	.014112	.068580	72237	4954	349464	.014176	2.634109	1577085	.028240	21.832	55
60	176149	3742	.021243	.101526	67283	6831	320160	.021336	2.620407	1227621	.027029	18.246	60
65	97338	3064	.031478	.147257	60452	8902	280806	.031702	2.590031	907461	.043788	15.011	65
70	80691	3696	.045804	.207139	51550	10678	231741	.046077	2.564287	626654	.036045	12.156	70
75	44313	3096	.069867	.298419	40872	12197	173872	.070149	2.500359	394913	.022402	9.662	75
80	33480	3070	.091657	.373112	28675	10699	116336	.091967	2.472739	221041	.022402	7.708	80
85+	28046	4815	.171682	1.000000	17976	17976	104705	.171682	5.824714	104705	.000000	5.825	85+

NUMBER OF PERSONS DYING (OUT OF 100,000 AT BIRTH) ABOVE AGE X FROM SPECIFIED CAUSES

Age (x)	All Causes	Respiratory T.B.	Other Infec. and Paras.	Neoplasms	Cardiovascular	Infl., Pneu., Bronch.	Diarrheal	Certain Degenerative	Maternal	Cert. Dis. of Infancy	Motor Vehicle	Other Violence	Other and Unknown	Age (x)
0	100000	1940	4486	11646	24550	7454	3606	4834	1304	2530	431	2245	34974	0
1	92341	1918	3822	11641	24531	5993	2226	4815	1304	0	430	2214	33447	1
5	87869	1877	2983	11620	24492	4938	1241	4774	1304	0	409	2082	32149	5
10	86983	1866	2781	11604	24470	4820	1161	4752	1304	0	385	2018	31822	10
15	86569	1856	2707	11587	24443	4780	1143	4736	1301	0	370	1967	31679	15
20	85915	1830	2652	11557	24378	4744	1136	4717	1228	0	356	1831	31486	20
25	85045	1770	2576	11520	24292	4704	1125	4694	1071	0	340	1722	31231	25
30	83960	1684	2483	11456	24158	4671	1111	4653	850	0	326	1627	30941	30
35	82527	1566	2366	11332	23979	4620	1087	4603	571	0	311	1537	30555	35
40	80616	1431	2254	11076	23680	4555	1069	4534	233	0	291	1444	30049	40
45	78422	1284	2133	10630	23279	4483	1035	4445	42	0	267	1362	29462	45
50	75879	1167	1988	10041	22746	4409	993	4293	10	0	240	1271	28721	50
55	72237	1013	1831	9182	21828	4301	946	4060	5	0	213	1176	27682	55
60	67283	866	1653	8026	20359	4111	859	3698	5	0	176	1085	26445	60
65	60452	706	1432	6711	18417	3791	780	3267	5	0	131	950	24262	65
70	51550	559	1150	5248	15558	3360	693	2596	5	0	105	823	21453	70
75	40872	397	850	3830	12145	2732	539	1987	5	0	82	670	17635	75
80	28675	240	567	2339	8124	2031	358	1199	5	0	58	559	13195	80
85+	17976	101	299	1288	4991	1329	202	638	0	0	26	385	8717	85+

NUMBER OF PERSONS SURVIVING TO AGE X IF SPECIFIED CAUSES WERE ELIMINATED

Age (x)	No Causes	Respiratory T.B. (1)	Other Infec. and Paras. (2)	Neoplasms (3)	Cardiovascular (4)	Infl., Pneu., Bronch. (5)	Diarrheal (6)	Certain Degenerative (7)	Maternal (8)	Cert. Dis. of Infancy (9)	Motor Vehicle (10)	Other Violence (11)	Other and Unknown (12)	(1)+(2)	(1)+(2)+(5)+(6)+(8)	(1)+(2)+(5)+(6)+(8)+part of (9)&(12)	(10)+(11)	Age (x)
0	100000	100000	100000	100000	100000	100000	100000	100000	100000	100000	100000	100000	100000	100000	100000	100000	100000	0
1	92341	92362	92981	92346	92359	93755	93676	92359	92341	94804	92342	92371	93820	93002	95792	99834	92372	1
5	87869	87929	89306	87954	87924	90266	90120	87926	87869	90213	87890	88026	90572	89367	94156	99438	88048	5
10	86983	87053	88610	87024	87060	89476	89293	87062	86983	89303	87028	87202	89994	88682	93646	99172	87248	10
15	86569	86649	88263	86627	86672	89091	88886	86663	86572	88878	86629	86838	89714	88345	93356	98952	86898	15
20	85915	86020	87653	86002	86082	88455	88222	86028	85951	88206	85988	86218	89236	87760	92863	98523	86392	20
25	85045	85209	86842	85168	85297	87601	87340	85179	85277	87313	85134	85553	88596	87010	92293	98083	85642	25
30	83960	84208	85829	84145	84342	86517	86240	84133	84409	86199	84061	84557	87766	86082	91599	97533	84659	30
35	82527	82888	84482	82832	83081	85092	84792	82747	83247	84728	82641	83203	86669	84852	90675	96801	83319	35
40	80616	81103	82639	81169	81455	83188	82847	80899	81657	82766	80748	81365	85189	83138	89303	95618	81502	40
45	78422	79041	80513	79404	79639	80997	80627	78786	79625	80514	78574	79237	83485	81149	87492	93922	79390	45
50	75879	76594	78048	77418	77591	78446	78055	76382	77075	77903	76052	76758	81557	78784	85105	91560	76933	50
55	72237	73070	74460	74562	74789	74790	74355	72945	73380	74164	72428	73167	78739	75318	81537	87944	73361	55
60	67283	68202	69531	70609	71144	69651	69343	68296	68348	69077	67497	68238	74653	70480	76604	82860	68455	60
65	60452	61431	62688	64759	65857	63075	62379	61778	61409	62064	60687	61440	69410	63703	69672	75797	61679	65
70	51550	52522	53727	56684	59144	54204	53277	53316	52366	52925	51774	52511	62242	54740	60428	66257	52740	70
75	40872	41790	42876	46345	50504	43568	42383	42835	41519	41962	41070	41772	53624	43838	49224	54792	41975	75
80	28675	29452	30329	33949	39820	31156	29852	30748	29129	29440	28834	29401	42812	31151	35886	40836	29565	80
85+	17976	18576	19236	22281	28621	20165	18867	19753	18264	18455	18101	18572	32632	19878	23779	28160	18701	85+

ADDED YRS OF LIFE

	No Causes	(1)	(2)	(3)	(4)	(5)	(6)	(7)	(8)	(9)	(10)	(11)	(12)	(1)+(2)	(1)+(2)+(5)+(6)+(8)	part of (9)&(12)	(10)+(11)
TOTAL		.474	1.690	1.958	3.834	2.363	1.780	.739	.525	1.638	.122	.613	8.051	2.183	7.196	12.644	.737
WORK	4.602	.245	.266	.636	.763	.153	.058	.192	.438	.000	.049	.271	1.191	.514	1.178	1.639	.320

POPULATION, DEATHS, DEATH RATES FOR ALL CAUSES COMBINED, AND SPECIFIED CAUSES

Age Start of Interval	Midyear Population	Deaths During Year	All Causes	Respiratory T.B.	Other Infec. and Paras.	Neoplasms	Cardiovascular	Infl., Pneu., Bronch.	Diarrheal	Certain Degenerative	Maternal	Cert. Dis. of Infancy	Motor Vehicle	Other Violence	Other and Unknown	Age Start of Interval
0	29780	2235	.07505	.00003	.00873	.00007	.00057	.01081	.01807	.00017	.00000	.01854	.00000	.00060	.01746	0
1	93280	654	.00701	.00004	.00191	.00014	.00009	.00108	.00150	.00009	.00000	.00000	.00002	.00026	.00189	1
5	83036	142	.00171	.00004	.00053	.00010	.00000	.00012	.00012	.00002	.00000	.00000	.00005	.00020	.00053	5
10	68192	87	.00128	.00000	.00025	.00007	.00006	.00003	.00001	.00003	.00000	.00000	.00001	.00035	.00045	10
15	55985	72	.00129	.00000	.00007	.00007	.00007	.00007	.00004	.00002	.00000	.00000	.00014	.00048	.00032	15
20	48188	87	.00181	.00002	.00008	.00012	.00015	.00006	.00000	.00012	.00000	.00000	.00010	.00081	.00033	20
25	40996	67	.00163	.00000	.00012	.00017	.00010	.00005	.00000	.00007	.00000	.00000	.00007	.00061	.00044	25
30	35390	70	.00198	.00023	.00008	.00011	.00017	.00000	.00006	.00011	.00000	.00000	.00003	.00073	.00045	30
35	28499	86	.00302	.00014	.00021	.00035	.00035	.00014	.00007	.00028	.00000	.00000	.00014	.00070	.00063	35
40	23319	103	.00442	.00030	.00026	.00099	.00056	.00026	.00004	.00013	.00000	.00000	.00021	.00073	.00094	40
45	21074	136	.00645	.00066	.00028	.00095	.00133	.00005	.00000	.00057	.00000	.00000	.00009	.00114	.00138	45
50	17231	159	.00923	.00035	.00052	.00267	.00192	.00017	.00017	.00081	.00000	.00000	.00012	.00052	.00197	50
55	13098	176	.01344	.00038	.00023	.00420	.00336	.00053	.00015	.00084	.00000	.00000	.00015	.00099	.00260	55
60	9858	233	.02364	.00030	.00071	.00751	.00650	.00061	.00041	.00122	.00000	.00000	.00000	.00081	.00497	60
65	6772	246	.03633	.00059	.00089	.00916	.01196	.00118	.00044	.00310	.00000	.00000	.00015	.00103	.00783	65
70	4747	246	.05182	.00063	.00021	.00990	.02001	.00190	.00105	.00190	.00000	.00000	.00000	.00169	.01454	70
75	2878	220	.07644	.00139	.00139	.01529	.02397	.00278	.00104	.00313	.00000	.00000	.00035	.00243	.02467	75
80	1250	169	.13520	.00080	.00080	.01840	.04960	.00640	.00400	.00560	.00000	.00000	.00240	.00400	.04320	80
85+	457	154	.33698	.00000	.00000	.02845	.12035	.02845	.01094	.00875	.00000	.00000	.00240	.00400	.04320	85+
ALL	584030	5342														

CRUDE DEATH RATE			.00915	.00012	.00057	.00080	.00104	.00089	.00124	.00024	.00000	.00095	.00008	.00055	.00228	
STANDARDIZED RATE (1)			.00857	.00014	.00077	.00100	.00129	.00070	.00091	.00029	.00000	.00065	.00009	.00059	.00214	
STANDARDIZED RATE (2)			.01252	.00021	.00061	.00199	.00309	.00074	.00070	.00053	.00000	.00038	.00012	.00075	.00338	
GEOMETRIC MEAN			.01023													

LIFE TABLE FOR ALL CAUSES COMBINED

Age (x)	Midyear Population	Deaths During Year	$_nM_x$	$_nq_x$	l_x	$_nd_x$	$_nL_x$	$_nm_x$	$_na_x$	T_x	$_nr_x$	$\overset{\circ}{e}_x$	Age (x)
0	29780	2235	.075050	.070790	100000	7079	94320	.075053	.197586	6306681	.000000	63.067	0
1	93280	654	.007011	.027561	92921	2561	365282	.007011	1.500000	6212361	.000000	66.856	1
5	83036	142	.001710	.008533	90360	771	449873	.001714	2.500000	5847079	.000000	64.709	5
10	68192	87	.001276	.006340	89589	568	446484	.001272	2.427010	5397207	.029872	60.244	10
15	55985	72	.001286	.006425	89021	572	443722	.001289	2.583042	4950723	.033162	55.613	15
20	48188	87	.001805	.009000	88449	796	440284	.001808	2.536903	4507001	.030575	50.956	20
25	40996	67	.001634	.008134	87653	713	436496	.001633	2.518408	4066717	.028832	46.396	25
30	35390	70	.001978	.009880	86940	859	432674	.001985	2.641880	3630221	.031754	41.755	30
35	28499	86	.003018	.015079	86081	1298	427369	.003037	2.660985	3197547	.039158	37.146	35
40	23319	103	.004417	.021962	84783	1862	419540	.004438	2.650600	2770178	.029669	32.674	40
45	21074	136	.006453	.031886	82921	2644	408366	.006475	2.640333	2350637	.022624	28.348	45
50	17231	159	.009228	.045380	80277	3643	392775	.009275	2.636449	1942271	.034090	24.195	50
55	13098	176	.013437	.065637	76634	5030	371520	.013539	2.683855	1549497	.039340	20.219	55
60	9858	233	.023636	.112871	71604	8082	338990	.023841	2.645385	1177977	.042104	16.451	60
65	6772	246	.036326	.167973	63522	10670	291793	.036567	2.580385	838987	.039091	13.208	65
70	4747	246	.051822	.230814	52852	12199	234293	.052070	2.542609	547194	.030375	10.353	70
75	2878	220	.076442	.323838	40653	13165	170732	.077109	2.528817	312912	.047477	7.697	75
80	1250	169	.135200	.510041	27488	14020	102213	.137164	2.487384	142180	.047477	5.172	80
85+	457	154	.336980	1.000000	13468	13468	39967	.336980	2.967532	39967	.000000	2.968	85+

NUMBER OF PERSONS DYING (OUT OF 100,000 AT BIRTH) ABOVE AGE X FROM SPECIFIED CAUSES

Age (x)	All Causes	Respiratory T. B.	Other Infec. and Paras.	Neoplasms	Cardiovascular	Infl., Pneu., Bronch.	Diarrheal	Certain Degenerative	Maternal	Cert. Dis. of Infancy	Motor Vehicle	Other Violence	Other and Unknown	Age (x)
0	100000	1630	3510	17190	27933	5301	4076	4501	0	1748	904	5460	27747	0
1	92921	1627	2687	17183	27879	4281	2372	4485	0	0	904	5403	26100	1
5	90360	1612	1990	17132	27848	3885	1824	4454	0	0	896	5309	25410	5
10	89589	1595	1751	17089	27848	3831	1769	4443	0	0	874	5217	25172	10
15	89021	1595	1641	17056	27821	3818	1763	4430	0	0	868	5059	24970	15
20	88449	1595	1610	17024	27789	3786	1747	4422	0	0	804	4843	24829	20
25	87653	1586	1573	16969	27725	3759	1747	4367	0	0	758	4486	24683	25
30	86940	1586	1520	16895	27683	3738	1747	4335	0	0	727	4221	24488	30
35	86081	1487	1483	16846	27609	3738	1722	4285	0	0	714	3902	24295	35
40	84783	1427	1392	16693	27458	3677	1693	4165	0	0	654	3603	24021	40
45	82921	1300	1284	16277	27222	3569	1675	4111	0	0	564	3296	23623	45
50	80277	1029	1168	15587	26676	3550	1675	3877	0	0	525	2831	23059	50
55	76634	893	962	14829	25919	3480	1606	3557	0	0	479	2627	22282	55
60	71604	751	877	13256	24658	3280	1548	3244	0	0	422	2257	21311	60
65	63522	648	634	10653	22294	3072	1410	2826	0	0	353	1982	19610	65
70	52852	474	376	8015	18773	2725	1279	1916	0	0	311	1679	17304	70
75	40653	325	327	5688	14062	2278	1031	1473	0	0	311	1282	13876	75
80	27488	86	87	3060	9941	1798	851	934	0	0	249	863	9619	80
85+	13468	0	0	1137	4810	1137	437	350	0	0	0	437	5160	85+

NUMBER OF PERSONS SURVIVING TO AGE X IF SPECIFIED CAUSES WERE ELIMINATED

Age (x)	No Causes	Respiratory T. B.	Other Infec. and Paras.	Neoplasms	Cardiovascular	Infl., Pneu., Bronch.	Diarrheal	Certain Degenerative	Maternal	Cert. Dis. of Infancy	Motor Vehicle	Other Violence	Other and Unknown	(1) + (2)	(1) + (2) + (5) + (6) + (8)	(1)+(2)+ (5)+(6)+ (8)+part of(9)&(12)	(10) + (11)	Age (x)
		(1)	(2)	(3)	(4)	(5)	(6)	(7)	(8)	(9)	(10)	(11)	(12)					
0	100000	100000	100000	100000	100000	100000	100000	100000	100000	100000	100000	100000	100000	100000	100000	100000	100000	0
1	92921	92924	93718	92928	92973	93909	94578	92936	92921	94621	92921	92976	94522	93720	96406	99733	92976	1
5	90360	90378	91830	90417	90441	91716	92523	90406	90360	92013	90368	90506	92612	91848	95459	99414	90514	5
10	89589	89623	91289	89688	89670	90989	91789	89645	89589	91228	89619	89826	92065	91324	95029	99145	89856	10
15	89021	89055	90822	89153	89128	90425	91214	89090	89021	90650	89057	89414	91688	90857	94563	98738	89450	15
20	88449	88483	90270	88612	88587	89876	90644	88525	88449	90067	88548	89056	91244	90305	94039	98219	89156	20
25	87653	87696	89495	87869	87854	89095	89828	87783	87653	89257	87797	88613	90573	89539	93270	97434	88759	25
30	86940	86982	88821	87228	87181	88391	89097	87101	86940	88531	87114	88160	90037	88864	92590	96755	88336	30
35	86081	86221	87981	86415	86394	87518	88243	86291	86081	87656	86266	87611	89346	88125	91846	96029	87800	35
40	84783	84981	86747	85265	85241	86260	86942	85109	84783	86334	85025	86592	88282	86950	90716	94920	86840	40
45	82921	83241	84951	83807	83605	84414	85050	83293	82921	84438	83247	85001	86754	85279	89107	93345	85335	45
50	80277	80854	82359	81524	81482	81799	82338	80865	80277	81746	80631	82761	84570	82952	86696	90941	83126	50
55	76634	77319	78828	78882	78539	78157	78671	77515	76634	78036	77017	79210	81536	79533	83270	87493	79606	55
60	71604	72382	73739	75286	74645	73225	73565	72733	71604	72914	72017	74381	77189	74540	78315	82415	74810	60
65	63522	64310	65652	69371	68584	65160	65355	64926	63522	64646	63954	66254	70225	66446	70191	74068	66704	65
70	52852	53668	54865	60434	60640	54541	54534	54872	52852	53819	53249	55413	60804	55713	59323	62872	55830	70
75	40653	41413	42245	48864	51616	42358	42171	42606	40653	41397	40959	42989	50363	43036	46515	49671	43312	75
80	27488	28201	28770	35713	39435	29053	28668	29274	27488	27991	27748	29431	38653	29517	32537	35314	29710	80
85+	13468	13878	14159	19297	25086	14722	14345	14776	13468	13714	13769	14736	23762	14590	16987	18991	15065	85+

ADDED YRS OF LIFE																		
TOTAL		.323	1.551	2.374	3.287	1.346	1.695	.648	.000	1.150	.206	1.410	4.918	1.886	5.083	8.506	1.625	
WORK	3.812	.163	.175	.626	.538	.111	.045	.221	.000	.000	.125	.783	.772	.340	.499	.639	.911	

POPULATION, DEATHS, DEATH RATES FOR ALL CAUSES COMBINED, AND SPECIFIED CAUSES

Age Start of Interval	Midyear Population	Deaths During Year	All Causes	Respiratory T. B.	Other Infec. and Paras.	Neoplasms	Cardiovascular	Infl., Pneu., Bronch.	Diarrheal	Certain Degenerative	Maternal	Cert. Dis. of Infancy	Motor Vehicle	Other Violence	Other and Unknown	Age Start of Interval
0	28661	1834	.06399	.00003	.00754	.00017	.00038	.01005	.01661	.00003	.00000	.01444	.00007	.00031	.01434	0
1	90412	655	.00769	.00006	.00213	.00007	.00013	.00137	.00175	.00012	.00000	.00000	.00001	.00019	.00186	1
5	80892	136	.00168	.00000	.00040	.00004	.00010	.00012	.00015	.00006	.00000	.00000	.00002	.00014	.00066	5
10	66080	63	.00095	.00003	.00015	.00005	.00008	.00003	.00005	.00003	.00000	.00000	.00002	.00008	.00045	10
15	54702	46	.00084	.00004	.00007	.00002	.00011	.00002	.00002	.00004	.00013	.00000	.00005	.00009	.00026	15
20	48077	61	.00127	.00002	.00010	.00023	.00015	.00004	.00002	.00008	.00027	.00000	.00002	.00004	.00029	20
25	43331	76	.00175	.00021	.00018	.00014	.00025	.00007	.00000	.00000	.00032	.00000	.00002	.00005	.00046	25
30	37918	86	.00227	.00018	.00021	.00026	.00042	.00013	.00003	.00005	.00042	.00000	.00008	.00005	.00042	30
35	29771	82	.00275	.00010	.00020	.00060	.00040	.00007	.00000	.00013	.00060	.00000	.00000	.00003	.00060	35
40	23843	70	.00294	.00025	.00021	.00071	.00046	.00000	.00008	.00017	.00021	.00000	.00004	.00000	.00080	40
45	21554	100	.00464	.00032	.00014	.00167	.00111	.00009	.00000	.00028	.00005	.00000	.00000	.00009	.00088	45
50	17493	122	.00697	.00023	.00017	.00240	.00160	.00011	.00011	.00046	.00000	.00000	.00000	.00034	.00154	50
55	13065	137	.01049	.00000	.00031	.00360	.00344	.00038	.00008	.00084	.00000	.00000	.00000	.00023	.00161	55
60	9906	186	.01878	.00061	.00030	.00555	.00646	.00081	.00020	.00172	.00000	.00000	.00000	.00010	.00303	60
65	6848	197	.02877	.00029	.00058	.00716	.00978	.00131	.00044	.00219	.00000	.00000	.00000	.00015	.00686	65
70	4742	219	.04618	.00021	.00042	.00970	.01392	.00190	.00105	.00337	.00000	.00000	.00000	.00021	.01539	70
75	2819	191	.06775	.00071	.00106	.00958	.02164	.00461	.00177	.00390	.00000	.00000	.00000	.00106	.02306	75
80	1242	165	.13285	.00000	.00161	.01852	.04267	.00966	.00322	.01127	.00000	.00000	.00000	.00564	.03945	80
85+	216	255	1.18056	.00000	.01389	.11574	.41667	.09259	.01852	.03241	.00000	.00000	.00000	.00000	.44444	85+
ALL	581572	4721														

	All Causes	Respiratory T. B.	Other Infec.	Neoplasms	Cardiovascular	Infl. Pneu.	Diarrheal	Certain Degen.	Maternal	Cert. Dis. Infancy	Motor Vehicle	Other Violence	Other and Unknown
CRUDE DEATH RATE	.00812	.00010	.00088	.00074	.00103	.00089	.00117	.00024	.00013	.00071	.00003	.00015	.00205
STANDARDIZED RATE (1)	.00814	.00011	.00072	.00095	.00141	.00077	.00089	.00030	.00014	.00051	.00003	.00017	.00214
STANDARDIZED RATE (2)	.01430	.00015	.00061	.00208	.00390	.00106	.00071	.00068	.00014	.00030	.00004	.00037	.00428
GEOMETRIC MEAN	.00933												

LIFE TABLE FOR ALL CAUSES COMBINED

Age (x)	Midyear Population	Deaths During Year	$_nM_x$	$_nq_x$	l_x	$_nd_x$	$_nL_x$	$_nm_x$	$_na_x$	T_x	$_nr_x$	$\overset{\circ}{e}_x$	Age (x)
0	28661	1834	.063989	.060790	100000	6079	95008	.063984	.178782	6514221	.000000	65.142	0
1	90412	655	.007687	.030174	93921	2834	368599	.007689	1.500000	6419213	.000000	68.347	1
5	80892	136	.001661	.008399	91087	765	453523	.001687	2.500000	6050614	.000000	66.427	5
10	66080	63	.000953	.004728	90322	427	450462	.000948	2.311183	5597091	.030092	61.968	10
15	54702	46	.000841	.004205	89895	378	448559	.000843	2.577712	5146630	.032158	57.252	15
20	48077	61	.001269	.006345	89517	568	446249	.001273	2.647080	4698070	.024826	52.482	20
25	43331	76	.001754	.008758	88949	779	442887	.001759	2.614730	4251822	.020745	47.801	25
30	37918	86	.002268	.011308	88170	997	438444	.002274	2.586718	3808935	.029889	43.200	30
35	29771	82	.002754	.013697	87173	1194	432934	.002758	2.545540	3370491	.042877	38.664	35
40	23843	70	.002936	.014631	85979	1258	426908	.002947	2.625656	2937556	.033370	34.166	40
45	21554	100	.004640	.023052	84721	1953	419056	.004660	2.670678	2510648	.025050	29.634	45
50	17493	122	.006974	.034530	82768	2858	407148	.007020	2.658400	2091592	.038400	25.271	50
55	13065	137	.010486	.051633	79910	4126	390072	.010578	2.702931	1684445	.043774	21.079	55
60	9906	186	.018776	.090745	75784	6877	362815	.018955	2.658196	1294372	.045457	17.080	60
65	6848	197	.028768	.135661	68907	9348	322326	.029002	2.624247	931557	.044822	13.519	65
70	4742	219	.046183	.209070	59559	12452	267597	.046533	2.574837	609231	.039823	10.229	70
75	2819	191	.067755	.293396	47107	13821	201943	.068440	2.569475	341634	.055703	7.252	75
80	1242	165	.132850	.512558	33286	17061	125947	.135461	2.627191	139691	.055703	4.197	80
85+	216	255	1.180556	1.000000	16225	16225	13744	1.180556	.847059	13744	.000000	.847	85+

NUMBER OF PERSONS DYING (OUT OF 100,000 AT BIRTH) ABOVE AGE X FROM SPECIFIED CAUSES

Age (x)	All Causes	Respiratory T. B.	Other Infec. and Paras.	Neoplasms	Cardiovascular	Infl., Pneu., Bronch.	Diarrheal	Certain Degenerative	Maternal	Cert. Dis. of Infancy	Motor Vehicle	Other Violence	Other and Unknown	Age (x)
0	100000	1137	3460	16933	28348	6600	3982	5872	879	1372	302	2322	28793	0
1	93921	1134	2744	16917	28312	5645	2404	5868	879	0	295	2292	27431	1
5	91087	1113	1957	16892	28263	5139	1760	5824	879	0	291	2223	26746	5
10	90322	1113	1777	16875	28218	5083	1693	5795	879	0	280	2161	26448	10
15	89895	1099	1710	16855	28184	5070	1673	5782	879	0	273	2127	26243	15
20	89517	1083	1677	16846	28135	5062	1664	5765	821	0	248	2086	26130	20
25	88949	1073	1631	16744	28069	5043	1655	5728	700	0	239	2067	26000	25
30	88170	981	1549	16683	27956	5012	1655	5728	556	0	229	2026	25795	30
35	87173	900	1456	16566	27771	4954	1644	5705	371	0	194	2004	25608	35
40	85979	857	1369	16302	27597	4926	1644	5646	109	0	194	1989	25346	40
45	84721	749	1280	15955	27398	4926	1608	5574	21	0	176	1989	25005	45
50	82768	613	1221	15291	26929	4887	1608	5457	2	0	176	1950	24634	50
55	79910	520	1151	14308	26271	4839	1561	5269	2	0	176	1809	24004	55
60	75784	520	1031	12894	24911	4688	1531	4937	2	0	176	1720	23374	60
65	68907	298	921	10866	22544	4391	1456	4309	2	0	176	1684	22260	65
70	59559	205	731	8549	19369	3965	1313	3598	2	0	176	1637	20014	70
75	47107	149	618	5943	15618	3451	1028	2690	2	0	176	1579	15853	75
80	33286	4	400	4004	11200	2504	665	1894	2	0	102	1356	11155	80
85+	16225	0	191	1591	5726	1273	255	445	0	0	0	636	6108	85+

NUMBER OF PERSONS SURVIVING TO AGE X IF SPECIFIED CAUSES WERE ELIMINATED

Age (x)	No Causes	Respiratory T. B.	Other Infec. and Paras.	Neoplasms	Cardiovascular	Infl., Pneu., Bronch.	Diarrheal	Certain Degenerative	Maternal	Cert. Dis. of Infancy	Motor Vehicle	Other Violence	Other and Unknown	(1) + (2)	(1) + (2) + (5) + (6) + (8)	(1)+(2)+ (5)+(6)+ (8)+part of(9)&(12)	(10) + (11)	Age (x)
		(1)	(2)	(3)	(4)	(5)	(6)	(7)	(8)	(9)	(10)	(11)	(12)					
0	100000	100000	100000	100000	100000	100000	100000	100000	100000	100000	100000	100000	100000	100000	100000	100000	100000	0
1	93921	93924	94617	93937	93556	94851	95463	93925	93921	95260	93928	93950	95250	94620	97126	99826	93957	1
5	91087	91111	92546	91127	91169	92493	93229	91134	91087	92385	91098	91183	93063	92570	96210	99554	91194	5
10	90322	90345	91951	90378	90448	91773	92514	90358	90322	91610	90343	90479	92585	91975	95721	99260	90501	10
15	89895	89932	91585	89971	90055	91353	92097	89983	89895	91176	89923	90085	92357	91623	95389	99031	90114	15
20	89517	89570	91233	89602	89725	90977	91719	89622	89575	90793	89570	89748	92084	91287	95120	98810	89801	20
25	88949	89012	90701	89135	89222	90419	91146	89090	89127	90217	89011	89197	91634	90765	94733	98476	89259	25
30	88170	88324	89990	88415	88553	89656	90348	88310	88491	89427	88241	88457	91041	90147	94275	98137	88528	30
35	87173	87406	89067	87532	87737	88703	89338	87334	87675	88416	87278	87479	90204	89305	93665	97612	87584	35
40	85979	86251	87935	86597	86709	87516	88114	86197	86736	87205	86083	86295	89238	88214	92831	96875	86400	40
45	84721	85097	86739	85638	85640	86236	86862	85007	85555	85929	84841	85033	88285	87124	91817	95951	85153	45
50	82768	83270	84799	84370	84136	84287	84859	83164	83601	83948	82885	83111	86632	85314	89972	94089	83229	50
55	79910	80487	81942	82447	81891	81425	81976	80478	80715	81049	80023	80381	84291	82533	87141	91210	80495	55
60	75784	76331	77830	79623	79033	77371	77774	76649	76547	76864	75891	76317	80588	78392	82962	86897	76425	60
65	68907	69618	70875	74455	74253	70640	70790	70301	69601	65889	69005	69426	74416	71606	76172	79935	69525	65
70	59559	60259	61442	66717	67434	61463	61324	61441	60159	60408	59643	60052	66624	62164	66717	70310	60137	70
75	47107	47711	48699	55410	57237	49088	48765	49431	47581	47779	47174	47550	57000	49324	53743	57161	47618	75
80	33286	33835	34600	41091	45191	35525	34773	35634	33621	33761	33396	33793	45309	35172	39610	43052	33905	80
85+	16225	16496	17015	22172	27740	18238	17245	18463	16390	16456	16349	16979	27317	17299	20877	23449	17109	85+

ADDED YRS OF LIFE																		
TOTAL		.282	1.487	2.203	2.798	1.395	1.700	.636	.364	.926	.068	.305	4.172	1.777	5.410	8.600	.374	
WORK	3.111	.156	.178	.686	.596	.084	.031	.153	.301	.000	.036	.090	.641	.334	.755	.985	.126	

POPULATION, DEATHS, DEATH RATES FOR ALL CAUSES COMBINED, AND SPECIFIED CAUSES

Age Start of Interval	Midyear Population	Deaths During Year	All Causes	Respira-tory T. B.	Other Infec. and Paras.	Neo-plasms	Cardio-vascular	Infl., Pneu., Bronch.	Diar-rheal	Certain Degen-erative	Maternal	Cert. Dis. of Infancy	Motor Vehicle	Other Violence	Other and Unknown	Age Start of Interval
0	31422	2748	.08745	.00006	.00678	.00006	.00051	.01200	.02279	.00032	.00000	.02880	.00000	.00035	.01579	0
1	114286	783	.00685	.00003	.00157	.00006	.00010	.00113	.00174	.00005	.00000	.00000	.00003	.00024	.00190	1
5	118286	159	.00134	.00000	.00019	.00012	.00005	.00014	.00014	.00006	.00000	.00000	.00007	.00009	.00048	5
10	92367	76	.00082	.00000	.00009	.00011	.00001	.00001	.00002	.00002	.00000	.00000	.00004	.00009	.00028	10
15	69356	90	.00130	.00006	.00007	.00019	.00010	.00004	.00001	.00004	.00000	.00000	.00027	.00029	.00022	15
20	54004	117	.00217	.00002	.00006	.00019	.00011	.00002	.00004	.00009	.00000	.00000	.00031	.00094	.00039	20
25	45380	87	.00192	.00007	.00002	.00015	.00011	.00000	.00000	.00009	.00000	.00000	.00020	.00090	.00037	25
30	40842	118	.00289	.00010	.00015	.00029	.00017	.00000	.00002	.00015	.00000	.00000	.00012	.00115	.00073	30
35	35559	122	.00343	.00045	.00022	.00034	.00034	.00011	.00000	.00022	.00000	.00000	.00017	.00093	.00065	35
40	28969	118	.00407	.00028	.00014	.00062	.00100	.00014	.00007	.00024	.00000	.00000	.00024	.00066	.00069	40
45	24848	143	.00575	.00036	.00012	.00097	.00113	.00020	.00004	.00040	.00000	.00000	.00012	.00101	.00141	45
50	21019	180	.00856	.00024	.00033	.00205	.00152	.00038	.00005	.00109	.00000	.00000	.00010	.00109	.00171	50
55	16002	199	.01244	.00044	.00025	.00344	.00350	.00025	.00012	.00100	.00000	.00000	.00006	.00094	.00244	55
60	12383	253	.02043	.00032	.00057	.00541	.00686	.00032	.00032	.00113	.00000	.00000	.00008	.00097	.00444	60
65	9877	278	.03132	.00113	.00079	.00834	.00879	.00068	.00045	.00214	.00000	.00000	.00011	.00113	.00777	65
70	6047	350	.05788	.00066	.00017	.01323	.02051	.00182	.00083	.00265	.00000	.00000	.00033	.00132	.01637	70
75	3999	283	.07077	.00100	.00100	.01625	.02376	.00200	.00050	.00300	.00000	.00000	.00075	.00250	.02001	75
80	2258	262	.11603	.00354	.00044	.01860	.04296	.00797	.00266	.00443	.00000	.00000	.00089	.00177	.03277	80
85+	1473	235	.15954	.00000	.00272	.01901	.04820	.01697	.00407	.00611	.00000	.00000	.00000	.00000	.05771	85+
ALL	727377	6601														

CRUDE DEATH RATE			.00908	.00013	.00067	.00080	.00105	.00086	.00133	.00026	.00000	.00124	.00013	.00055	.00205	
STANDARDIZED RATE (1)			.00861	.00015	.00056	.00094	.00117	.00071	.00108	.00029	.00000	.00101	.00014	.00061	.00194	
STANDARDIZED RATE (2)			.01154	.00025	.00046	.00189	.00264	.00069	.00075	.00051	.00000	.00060	.00016	.00075	.00285	
GEOMETRIC MEAN			.00960													

LIFE TABLE FOR ALL CAUSES COMBINED

Age (x)	Midyear Population	Deaths During Year	$_nM_x$	$_nq_x$	l_x	$_nd_x$	$_nL_x$	$_nm_x$	$_na_x$	T_x	$_nr_x$	$\overset{\circ}{e}_x$	Age (x)
0	31422	2748	.087455	.081860	100000	8186	93604	.087453	.218673	6335398	.000000	63.354	0
1	114286	783	.006851	.026946	91814	2474	361071	.006852	1.500000	6241794	.000000	67.983	1
5	118286	159	.001344	.006716	89340	600	445200	.001348	2.500000	5880723	.000000	65.824	5
10	92367	76	.000823	.004091	88740	363	442787	.000820	2.486226	5435523	.039864	61.252	10
15	69356	90	.001298	.006518	88377	576	440567	.001307	2.711950	4992736	.051006	56.494	15
20	54004	117	.002167	.010809	87801	949	436685	.002173	2.555760	4552168	.045269	51.846	20
25	45380	87	.001917	.009556	86852	830	432245	.001920	2.572289	4115483	.031296	47.385	25
30	40842	118	.002889	.014380	86022	1237	427146	.002896	2.603746	3683238	.022307	42.817	30
35	35559	122	.003431	.017055	84785	1446	420404	.003440	2.564690	3256092	.028500	38.404	35
40	28969	118	.004073	.020231	83339	1686	412664	.004086	2.608862	2835689	.032159	34.026	40
45	24848	143	.005755	.028495	81653	2327	402754	.005777	2.648707	2423025	.026096	29.675	45
50	21019	180	.008564	.042193	79326	3347	388740	.008610	2.642790	2020232	.032350	25.467	50
55	16002	199	.012436	.060819	75979	4621	369104	.012520	2.664827	1631491	.038342	21.473	55
60	12383	253	.020431	.098139	71358	7003	340290	.020580	2.643837	1262387	.037983	17.691	60
65	8877	278	.031317	.146935	64355	9456	299591	.031563	2.653937	922097	.039228	14.328	65
70	6047	350	.057880	.254832	54899	13990	240114	.058264	2.542471	622507	.029280	11.339	70
75	3999	283	.070768	.300863	40909	12308	173539	.070924	2.480822	382392	.022465	9.347	75
80	2258	262	.116032	.449530	28601	12857	110169	.116703	2.446041	208853	.022465	7.302	80
85+	1473	235	.159538	1.000000	15744	15744	98685	.159538	6.268085	98685	.000000	6.268	85+

NUMBER OF PERSONS DYING (OUT OF 100,000 AT BIRTH) ABOVE AGE X FROM SPECIFIED CAUSES

Age (x)	All Causes	Respiratory T.B.	Other Infec. and Paras.	Neo-plasms	Cardio-vascular	Infl., Pneu., Bronch.	Diar-rheal	Certain Degenerative	Maternal	Cert. Dis. of Infancy	Motor Vehicle	Other Violence	Other and Unknown	Age (x)
0	100000	2006	2840	17686	26843	5714	4204	4691	0	2696	1108	5632	26580	0
1	91814	2000	2206	17680	26795	4591	2071	4661	0	0	1108	5599	25103	1
5	89340	1988	1640	17658	26760	4184	1442	4642	0	0	1098	5511	24417	5
10	88740	1988	1553	17605	26738	4120	1382	4616	0	0	1068	5469	24201	10
15	88377	1987	1515	17557	26733	4115	1373	4607	0	0	1048	5363	24079	15
20	87801	1962	1484	17474	26688	4096	1367	4587	0	0	926	5234	23983	20
25	86852	1954	1460	17393	26640	4089	1350	4547	0	0	789	4818	23812	25
30	86022	1925	1450	17327	26592	4089	1350	4508	0	0	704	4427	23650	30
35	84785	1883	1387	17201	26519	4088	1340	4445	0	0	651	3935	23336	35
40	83339	1693	1292	17058	26375	4041	1340	4350	0	0	580	3546	23064	40
45	81653	1579	1236	16800	25959	3984	1311	4250	0	0	480	3276	22778	45
50	79326	1433	1187	16408	25504	3902	1295	4087	0	0	432	2870	22208	50
55	75979	1341	1057	15606	24907	3754	1277	3659	0	0	395	2444	21539	55
60	71358	1179	964	14328	23601	3662	1230	3290	0	0	372	2099	20633	60
65	64355	1068	770	12474	21249	3551	1119	2903	0	0	345	1769	19107	65
70	54899	728	534	9960	18593	3346	983	2258	0	0	311	1431	16755	70
75	40909	570	495	6765	13633	2905	783	1620	0	0	230	1111	12797	75
80	28601	395	321	3942	9501	2556	696	1099	0	0	100	676	9315	80
85+	15744	0	268	1876	4757	1675	402	603	0	0	0	469	5694	85+

NUMBER OF PERSONS SURVIVING TO AGE X IF SPECIFIED CAUSES WERE ELIMINATED

Age (x)	No Causes	Respiratory T.B. (1)	Other Infec. and Paras. (2)	Neo-plasms (3)	Cardio-vascular (4)	Infl., Pneu., Bronch. (5)	Diar-rheal (6)	Certain Degenerative (7)	Maternal (8)	Cert. Dis. of Infancy (9)	Motor Vehicle (10)	Other Violence (11)	Other and Unknown (12)	(1)+(2)	(1)+(2)+(5)+(6)+(8)	(1)+(2)+(5)+(6)+(8)+part of(9)&(12)	(10)+(11)	Age (x)
0	100000	100000	100000	100000	100000	100000	100000	100000	100000	100000	100000	100000	100000	100000	100000	100000	100000	0
1	91814	91820	92423	91820	91860	92856	93880	91843	91814	94433	91814	91846	93240	92429	95623	99751	91846	1
5	89340	89357	90497	89367	89419	90800	91987	89387	89340	91889	89350	89458	91417	90514	94719	99486	89468	5
10	88740	88757	89977	88820	88841	90255	91431	88812	88740	91271	88780	88889	91024	89994	94306	99185	88939	10
15	88377	88395	89647	88505	88482	89891	91066	88458	88377	90898	88437	88641	90776	89666	93977	98868	88701	15
20	87801	87844	89094	88011	87951	89324	90479	87901	87801	90306	87982	88193	90283	89138	93450	98332	88374	20
25	86852	86903	88155	87140	87048	88366	89518	86991	86852	89330	87168	87656	89482	88207	92499	97346	87974	25
30	86022	86101	87323	86373	86264	87521	88663	86199	86022	89204	87212	86793	88793	87043	91657	96469	87615	30
35	84785	84905	86131	85257	85096	86264	87358	85022	84785	87204	85230	86454	87839	86253	90462	95256	86908	35
40	83339	83645	84758	83946	83788	84840	85907	83666	83339	85716	83847	85374	86621	85069	89271	94088	85894	40
45	81653	82067	83099	82505	82508	83181	84199	82073	81653	83982	82250	83921	85163	83520	87736	92529	84534	45
50	79326	79872	80780	80546	80611	80893	81585	79896	79326	81589	79954	81941	82324	81337	85547	90327	82348	50
55	75979	76593	77502	77949	77807	77628	78382	76948	75979	78146	76617	78915	80499	78128	82348	87057	79577	55
60	71358	72093	72880	74489	74384	72997	73662	72630	71358	73394	71979	74462	76539	73630	77754	82308	75111	60
65	64355	65124	65916	69041	69451	65941	66542	65877	64355	66191	64941	67481	70601	66704	70671	74972	68096	65
70	54899	55873	56452	61435	61953	56447	56854	56809	54899	56655	55431	57892	62695	57453	61221	65279	58453	70
75	40909	41771	42100	48954	51246	42455	42573	42901	40909	42076	41376	43431	50746	42987	46426	49848	43927	75
80	28601	29355	29584	37142	40401	29989	29840	30450	28601	29417	29038	30751	39258	30364	33217	35992	31220	80
85+	15744	16458	16325	22504	27720	17197	16652	17152	15744	16193	16059	17091	25567	17066	19716	22004	17433	85+

ADDED YRS OF LIFE

	No Causes	(1)	(2)	(3)	(4)	(5)	(6)	(7)	(8)	(9)	(10)	(11)	(12)	(1)+(2)	(1)+(2)+(5)+(6)+(8)	+part of(9)&(12)	(10)+(11)
TOTAL		.380	1.163	2.661	3.978	1.508	2.058	.756	.000	1.801	.352	1.574	5.464	1.554	5.310	9.419	1.941
WORK	3.940	.177	.130	.576	.554	.084	.032	.240	.000	.000	.233	.919	.746	.307	.425	.533	1.158

POPULATION, DEATHS, DEATH RATES FOR ALL CAUSES COMBINED, AND SPECIFIED CAUSES

Age Start of Interval	Midyear Population	Deaths During Year	All Causes	Respiratory T. B.	Other Infec. and Paras.	Neoplasms	Cardiovascular	Infl., Pneu., Bronch.	Diarrheal	Certain Degenerative	Maternal	Cert. Dis. of Infancy	Motor Vehicle	Other Violence	Other and Unknown	Age Start of Interval
0	30230	2180	.07211	.00007	.00615	.00003	.00036	.01078	.02127	.00017	.00000	.02051	.00000	.00056	.01221	0
1	110186	791	.00718	.00002	.00180	.00005	.00005	.00127	.00191	.00010	.00000	.00000	.00002	.00025	.00172	1
5	114374	150	.00131	.00001	.00029	.00007	.00003	.00016	.00016	.00001	.00000	.00000	.00001	.00010	.00048	5
10	90239	61	.00068	.00001	.00002	.00009	.00009	.00002	.00006	.00002	.00000	.00000	.00000	.00009	.00022	10
15	70330	64	.00091	.00001	.00006	.00003	.00007	.00004	.00001	.00006	.00006	.00000	.00003	.00020	.00034	15
20	56467	62	.00110	.00000	.00007	.00009	.00019	.00004	.00002	.00009	.00019	.00000	.00002	.00009	.00034	20
25	46905	70	.00149	.00009	.00009	.00015	.00015	.00002	.00002	.00004	.00034	.00000	.00002	.00011	.00047	25
30	41124	67	.00163	.00010	.00005	.00012	.00036	.00012	.00000	.00012	.00039	.00000	.00002	.00005	.00029	30
35	35830	114	.00318	.00022	.00011	.00073	.00022	.00017	.00003	.00025	.00070	.00000	.00000	.00011	.00064	35
40	28967	104	.00359	.00017	.00021	.00090	.00055	.00003	.00007	.00024	.00031	.00000	.00000	.00007	.00104	40
45	24485	127	.00519	.00029	.00004	.00204	.00118	.00008	.00008	.00041	.00004	.00000	.00000	.00008	.00094	45
50	20673	148	.00716	.00029	.00024	.00218	.00189	.00005	.00024	.00048	.00000	.00000	.00000	.00024	.00155	50
55	15610	151	.00967	.00026	.00006	.00320	.00224	.00051	.00000	.00115	.00000	.00000	.00006	.00006	.00211	55
60	12164	239	.01965	.00041	.00033	.00510	.00691	.00082	.00066	.00148	.00000	.00000	.00000	.00049	.00345	60
65	8944	228	.02549	.00022	.00011	.00671	.00872	.00134	.00045	.00268	.00000	.00000	.00000	.00000	.00525	65
70	6012	256	.04258	.00050	.00050	.00981	.01397	.00266	.00067	.00299	.00000	.00000	.00017	.00067	.01065	70
75	3967	238	.05999	.00050	.00025	.01185	.02193	.00529	.00050	.00302	.00000	.00000	.00000	.00101	.01563	75
80	2508	252	.10048	.00040	.00040	.01356	.03668	.00957	.00199	.00478	.00000	.00000	.00000	.00000	.03110	80
85+	2003	366	.18273	.00100	.00349	.01797	.06490	.01598	.00749	.00300	.00000	.00000	.00000	.00199	.03110	85+
ALL	721018	5668														

	All Causes	Respiratory T. B.	Other Infec. and Paras.	Neoplasms	Cardiovascular	Infl., Pneu., Bronch.	Diarrheal	Certain Degenerative	Maternal	Cert. Dis. of Infancy	Motor Vehicle	Other Violence	Other and Unknown
CRUDE DEATH RATE	.00786	.00008	.00065	.00074	.00104	.00087	.00129	.00025	.00011	.00086	.00002	.00018	.00177
STANDARDIZED RATE (1)	.00727	.00010	.00054	.00085	.00105	.00074	.00107	.00028	.00013	.00072	.00002	.00017	.00159
STANDARDIZED RATE (2)	.00982	.00014	.00041	.00165	.00238	.00081	.00076	.00052	.00014	.00042	.00002	.00020	.00237
GEOMETRIC MEAN	.00791												

LIFE TABLE FOR ALL CAUSES COMBINED

Age (x)	Midyear Population	Deaths During Year	$_nM_x$	$_nq_x$	l_x	$_nd_x$	$_nL_x$	$_nm_x$	$_na_x$	T_x	$_nr_x$	$\overset{\circ}{e}_x$	Age (x)
0	30230	2180	.072114	.068150	100000	6815	94498	.072118	.192593	6630952	.000000	66.310	0
1	110186	791	.007179	.028202	93185	2628	366170	.007177	1.500000	6536455	.000000	70.145	1
5	114374	150	.001311	.006570	90557	595	451298	.001318	2.500000	6170285	.000000	68.137	5
10	90239	61	.000676	.003346	89962	301	449019	.000670	2.370570	5718987	.036766	63.571	10
15	70330	64	.000910	.004550	89661	408	447324	.000912	2.596507	5269969	.044763	58.777	15
20	56467	62	.001098	.005490	89253	490	445093	.001101	2.607993	4822644	.041926	54.033	20
25	46905	70	.001492	.007458	88763	662	442207	.001497	2.571752	4377551	.034168	49.317	25
30	41124	67	.001629	.008150	88101	718	438861	.001636	2.710074	3935344	.025988	44.669	30
35	35830	114	.003182	.015861	87383	1386	433620	.003196	2.622805	3496483	.030061	40.013	35
40	28967	104	.003590	.017849	85997	1535	426311	.003601	2.606813	3062863	.034596	35.616	40
45	24485	127	.005187	.025728	84462	2173	417164	.005209	2.631730	2636551	.028472	31.216	45
50	20673	148	.007159	.035351	82289	2909	404509	.007191	2.615661	2219388	.034773	26.971	50
55	15610	151	.009673	.047720	79380	3788	388313	.009755	2.733138	1814879	.041209	22.863	55
60	12164	239	.019648	.094560	75592	7148	361024	.019799	2.630602	1426565	.037227	18.872	60
65	8944	228	.025492	.120814	68444	8269	322496	.025641	2.614761	1065542	.041307	15.568	65
70	6012	256	.042582	.194463	60175	11703	272545	.042940	2.575271	743045	.042601	12.348	70
75	3967	238	.059995	.262461	48472	12722	211126	.060258	2.544886	470500	.026806	9.707	75
80	2508	252	.100478	.404028	35750	14444	142773	.101167	2.509231	259374	.026806	7.255	80
85+	2003	366	.182726	1.000000	21306	21306	116601	.182726	5.472678	116601	.000000	5.473	85+

NUMBER OF PERSONS DYING (OUT OF 100,000 AT BIRTH) ABOVE AGE X FROM SPECIFIED CAUSES

Age (x)	All Causes	Respiratory T.B.	Other Infec. and Paras.	Neoplasms	Cardiovascular	Infl., Pneu., Bronch.	Diarrheal	Certain Degenerative	Maternal	Cert. Dis. of Infancy	Motor Vehicle	Other Violence	Other and Unknown	Age (x)
0	100000	1258	2584	17245	29599	7832	4835	5146	889	1538	147	1930	26597	0
1	93185	1252	2003	17242	29565	6813	2825	5130	889	0	147	1877	25442	1
5	90557	1245	1345	17222	29548	6348	2127	5094	889	0	141	1787	24811	5
10	89962	1241	1214	17190	29532	6276	2056	5090	889	0	137	1743	24594	10
15	89661	1236	1205	17151	29493	6267	2032	5080	889	0	112	1703	24493	15
20	89253	1230	1180	17138	29461	6248	2026	5054	863	0	99	1614	24340	20
25	88763	1230	1148	17098	29374	6232	2018	5015	775	0	91	1575	24207	25
30	88101	1191	1110	17032	29307	6223	2009	4996	624	0	82	1528	24000	30
35	87383	1149	1089	16978	29147	6169	2008	4942	452	0	71	1507	23871	35
40	85997	1051	1040	16661	29050	6096	1996	4832	149	0	71	1458	23593	40
45	84462	978	952	16275	28812	6082	1966	4729	19	0	71	1429	23149	45
50	82289	858	935	15419	28314	6048	1932	4558	3	0	71	1395	22756	50
55	79380	741	837	14536	27548	6027	1834	4361	3	0	71	1297	22125	55
60	75592	641	812	13284	26665	5826	1834	3909	3	0	46	1272	21300	60
65	68444	492	693	11432	24149	5527	1594	3371	3	0	46	1093	20044	65
70	60175	421	657	9258	21322	5090	1450	2501	3	0	46	1093	18334	70
75	48472	284	520	6567	17480	4355	1268	1683	3	0	0	909	15403	75
80	35750	177	467	4061	12827	3230	1161	1043	3	0	0	695	12086	80
85+	21306	116	407	2096	7568	1863	873	349	0	0	0	407	7627	85+

NUMBER OF PERSONS SURVIVING TO AGE X IF SPECIFIED CAUSES WERE ELIMINATED

Age (x)	No Causes	Respiratory T.B.	Other Infec. and Paras.	Neoplasms	Cardiovascular	Infl., Pneu., Bronch.	Diarrheal	Certain Degenerative	Maternal	Cert. Dis. of Infancy	Motor Vehicle	Other Violence	Other and Unknown	(1)+(2)	(1)+(2)+(5)+(6)+(8)	(1)+(2)+(5)+(6)+(8)+part of (9)&(12)	(10)+(11)	Age (x)
		(1)	(2)	(3)	(4)	(5)	(6)	(7)	(8)	(9)	(10)	(11)	(12)					
0	100000	100000	100000	100000	100000	100000	100000	100000	100000	100000	100000	100000	100000	100000	100000	100000	100000	0
1	93185	93191	93747	93188	93218	94174	95145	93200	93185	95074	93185	93236	94306	93753	96741	99799	93236	1
5	90557	90570	91758	90580	90606	91982	93167	90608	90557	92393	90563	90696	92278	91771	95902	99558	90701	5
10	89962	89978	91288	90016	90026	91451	92628	90016	89962	91786	89972	90144	91893	91305	95566	99384	90153	10
15	89661	89682	90992	89754	89764	91154	92343	89725	89661	91479	89696	89882	91688	91013	95296	99130	89917	15
20	89253	89280	90603	89359	89388	90758	91929	89343	89279	91063	89301	89562	91427	90631	94949	98824	89610	20
25	88763	88790	90139	88908	88884	90276	91432	88891	88877	90563	88818	89109	91061	90165	94581	98500	89165	25
30	88101	88167	89504	88311	88387	89612	90760	88247	88365	89887	88165	88492	90594	89571	94138	98163	88556	30
35	87383	87490	88796	87645	87827	88537	90021	87582	87816	89155	87457	87792	89988	88905	93679	97755	87866	35
40	85997	86200	87437	86571	86530	87600	88605	86302	86726	87741	86070	86448	88845	87643	92764	96950	86521	40
45	84462	84734	85565	85412	85224	86050	87054	84864	85308	86174	84534	84934	87715	86241	91467	95747	85006	45
50	82289	82673	83770	84073	83529	83870	84849	82851	83129	83957	82359	82782	85862	84161	89350	93585	82853	50
55	79380	79865	80907	81992	81343	80927	80117	80190	80989	79448	79953		83476	81402	86548	90755	80021	55
60	75592	76152	77071	79350	78351	77265	78039	76740	76363	77125	75681	76162	80343	77642	82766	86890	76251	60
65	68444	69094	69898	73719	73468	70251	70895	70005	69142	69832	68524	69131	74027	70562	75784	79751	69212	65
70	60175	60813	61488	67042	67497	62186	62469	62386	60789	61395	60246	60775	66843	62140	67345	71070	60851	70
75	48472	49110	49655	56750	58373	50780	50489	50117	48967	49455	48570	49127	56844	50309	55457	58957	49226	75
80	35750	36312	36668	44426	48128	38478	37333	38202	36115	36475	35822	36419	45396	37245	42289	45493	36492	80
85+	21306	21689	21900	28408	34631	24683	22480	23340	21526	21738	21349	21930	31742	22293	26862	29732	21974	85+

ADDED YRS OF LIFE

	No Causes	(1)	(2)	(3)	(4)	(5)	(6)	(7)	(8)	(9)	(10)	(11)	(12)	(1)+(2)	(1)+(2)+(5)+(6)+(8)	big	(10)+(11)
TOTAL		.272	1.171	2.739	4.298	1.745	2.182	.822	.365	1.341	.053	.435	5.055	1.450	5.989	9.672	.488
WORK	3.108	.126	.104	.673	.543	.054	.046	.217	.289	.000	.019	.133	.699	.231	.664	.885	.153

POPULATION, DEATHS, DEATH RATES FOR ALL CAUSES COMBINED, AND SPECIFIED CAUSES

Age Start of Interval	Midyear Population	Deaths During Year	All Causes	Respiratory T. B.	Other Infec. and Paras.	Neoplasms	Cardiovascular	Infl., Pneu., Bronch.	Diarrheal	Certain Degenerative	Maternal	Cert. Dis. of Infancy	Motor Vehicle	Other Violence	Other and Unknown	Age Start of Interval
0	151952	25583	.16836	.00301	.00973	.00011	.00094	.03621	.03824	.00000	.00000	.05706	.00000	.00059	.02247	0
1	577314	5473	.00948	.00096	.00220	.00002	.00014	.00292	.00103	.00000	.00000	.00000	.00000	.00066	.00154	1
5	786937	2218	.00282	.00034	.00095	.00002	.00013	.00036	.00026	.00000	.00000	.00000	.00000	.00066	.00154	5
10	487502	1054	.00216	.00048	.00052	.00001	.00016	.00023	.00007	.00000	.00000	.00000	.00000	.00029	.00047	10
15	700019	2152	.00307	.00091	.00023	.00003	.00019	.00019	.00015	.00000	.00000	.00000	.00000	.00028	.00041	15
20	754310	3444	.00457	.00207	.00025	.00004	.00023	.00025	.00021	.00000	.00000	.00000	.00000	.00104	.00034	20
25	684155	2941	.00430	.00184	.00017	.00009	.00024	.00022	.00022	.00000	.00000	.00000	.00000	.00113	.00040	25
30	587386	2836	.00483	.00198	.00021	.00014	.00037	.00027	.00026	.00000	.00000	.00000	.00000	.00098	.00050	30
35	464179	2651	.00571	.00200	.00024	.00022	.00061	.00037	.00039	.00000	.00000	.00000	.00000	.00096	.00063	35
40	400721	3023	.00754	.00230	.00023	.00061	.00088	.00059	.00055	.00000	.00000	.00000	.00000	.00103	.00085	40
45	367922	3551	.00965	.00242	.00029	.00102	.00152	.00072	.00068	.00000	.00000	.00000	.00000	.00105	.00134	45
50	336852	5086	.01510	.00289	.00035	.00225	.00249	.00181	.00086	.00000	.00000	.00000	.00000	.00115	.00185	50
55	304365	6189	.02033	.00292	.00038	.00365	.00397	.00222	.00137	.00000	.00000	.00000	.00000	.00138	.00307	55
60	256935	7221	.02810	.00288	.00041	.00552	.00649	.00298	.00172	.00000	.00000	.00000	.00000	.00149	.00433	60
65	191194	8653	.04526	.00227	.00046	.00651	.00893	.00527	.00101	.00000	.00000	.00000	.00000	.00170	.00641	65
70	135779	9124	.06720	.00228	.00045	.00899	.01431	.00798	.00161	.00000	.00000	.00000	.00000	.00128	.01952	70
75	74302	7331	.09866	.00213	.00051	.01087	.02238	.01262	.00293	.00000	.00000	.00000	.00000	.00217	.02942	75
80	30831	4657	.15105	.00188	.00062	.01245	.03393	.02066	.00730	.00000	.00000	.00000	.00000	.00273	.04448	80
85+	10769	2603	.24171	.00130	.00084	.01309	.05107	.03742	.01300	.00000	.00000	.00000	.00000	.00405	.07016	85+
ALL	7303424	105790														

CRUDE DEATH RATE			.01448	.00170	.00071	.00110	.00177	.00206	.00137	.00000	.00000	.00119	.00000	.00099	.00359	
STANDARDIZED RATE (1)			.01457	.00152	.00095	.00074	.00123	.00238	.00185	.00000	.00000	.00201	.00000	.00088	.00301	
STANDARDIZED RATE (2)			.01784	.00173	.00072	.00149	.00254	.00251	.00150	.00000	.00000	.00118	.00000	.00105	.00512	
GEOMETRIC MEAN			.01635													

LIFE TABLE FOR ALL CAUSES COMBINED

Age (x)	Midyear Population	Deaths During Year	$_nM_x$	$_nq_x$	l_x	$_nd_x$	$_nL_x$	$_nm_x$	$_na_x$	T_x	$_nr_x$	$\overset{\circ}{e}_x$	Age (x)
0	151952	25583	.168362	.151900	100000	15190	90221	.168364	.356216	5238037	.000000	52.380	0
1	577314	5473	.009480	.037036	84810	3141	331388	.009478	1.500000	5147817	.000000	60.698	1
5	786937	2218	.002819	.013996	81669	1143	405488	.002819	2.500000	4816429	.000000	58.975	5
10	487502	1054	.002162	.010754	80526	866	400479	.002162	2.515637	4410942	.018984	54.777	10
15	700019	2152	.003074	.015164	79660	1208	395468	.003055	2.655905	4010463	-.038591	50.345	15
20	754310	3444	.004566	.022562	78452	1770	387923	.004563	2.549670	3614995	-.014152	46.079	20
25	684155	2941	.004299	.021257	76682	1630	379340	.004297	2.503067	3227072	.010064	42.084	25
30	587386	2836	.004828	.023903	75052	1794	370866	.004837	2.550980	2847732	.028076	37.943	30
35	464179	2651	.005711	.028243	73258	2069	361295	.005727	2.585589	2476865	.033984	33.810	35
40	400721	3023	.007544	.037141	71189	2644	349579	.007563	2.592190	2115571	.021356	29.718	40
45	367922	3551	.009652	.047254	68545	3239	335069	.009667	2.636230	1765992	.010874	25.764	45
50	336852	5086	.015099	.072918	65306	4762	315173	.015109	2.615148	1430923	.005628	21.911	50
55	304365	6189	.020334	.096971	60544	5871	288553	.020346	2.587010	1115750	-.004394	18.429	55
60	256935	7221	.028104	.131948	54673	7214	256129	.028165	2.610751	827197	.013679	15.130	60
65	191194	8653	.045258	.204513	47459	9706	213799	.045398	2.579225	571068	.016439	12.033	65
70	135779	9124	.067197	.288851	37753	10905	161700	.067440	2.518111	357269	.020106	9.463	70
75	74302	7331	.098665	.396827	26848	10654	107170	.099413	2.459131	195569	.041349	7.284	75
80	30831	4657	.151049	.544337	16194	8815	57871	.152321	2.379585	88399	.041349	5.459	80
85+	10769	2603	.241712	1.000000	7379	7379	30528	.241712	4.137149	30528	.000000	4.137	85+

NUMBER OF PERSONS DYING (OUT OF 100,000 AT BIRTH) ABOVE AGE X FROM SPECIFIED CAUSES

Age (x)	All Causes	Respiratory T. B.	Other Infec. and Paras.	Neoplasms	Cardiovascular	Infl., Pneu., Bronch.	Diarrheal	Certain Degenerative	Maternal	Cert. Dis. of Infancy	Motor Vehicle	Other Violence	Other and Unknown	Age (x)
0	100000	9582	3407	9116	15471	13525	7546	0	0	5148	0	5868	30337	0
1	84810	9311	2529	9106	15386	10259	4096	0	0	0	0	5814	28309	1
5	81669	8992	1800	9099	15239	9292	3754	0	0	0	0	5594	27799	5
10	80526	8856	1414	9093	15285	9145	3649	0	0	0	0	5479	27605	10
15	79660	8664	1207	9088	15219	9053	3622	0	0	0	0	5367	27440	15
20	78452	8311	1116	9075	15144	8978	3563	0	0	0	0	4959	27306	20
25	76682	7511	1018	9061	15056	8883	3482	0	0	0	0	4519	27152	25
30	75052	6811	952	9026	14966	8799	3385	0	0	0	0	4149	26964	30
35	73258	6076	874	8974	14826	8698	3288	0	0	0	0	3793	26729	35
40	71189	5353	789	8892	14605	8564	3148	0	0	0	0	3419	26419	40
45	68545	4548	709	8677	14297	8356	2956	0	0	0	0	3053	25949	45
50	65306	3736	613	8335	13786	8114	2726	0	0	0	0	2666	25330	50
55	60544	2826	502	7625	13000	7541	2456	0	0	0	0	2230	24364	55
60	54673	1984	391	6570	11855	6900	2059	0	0	0	0	1802	23112	60
65	47459	1248	287	5153	10190	6135	1620	0	0	0	0	1365	21461	65
70	37753	763	189	3759	8275	5004	1403	0	0	0	0	1091	17269	70
75	26848	394	117	2302	5952	3709	1141	0	0	0	0	740	12493	75
80	16194	166	62	1132	3534	2344	823	0	0	0	0	445	7688	80
85+	7379	40	26	400	1559	1142	397	0	0	0	0	204	3611	85+

NUMBER OF PERSONS SURVIVING TO AGE X IF SPECIFIED CAUSES WERE ELIMINATED

Age (x)	No Causes	Respiratory T. B. (1)	Other Infec. and Paras. (2)	Neoplasms (3)	Cardiovascular (4)	Infl., Pneu., Bronch. (5)	Diarrheal (6)	Certain Degenerative (7)	Maternal (8)	Cert. Dis. of Infancy (9)	Motor Vehicle (10)	Other Violence (11)	Other and Unknown (12)	(1)+(2)	(1)+(2)+(5)+(6)+(8)	(1)+(2)+(5)+(6)+(8)+part of(9)&(12)	(10)+(11)	Age (x)
0	100000	100000	100000	100000	100000	100000	100000	100000	100000	100000	100000	100000	100000	100000	100000	100000	100000	0
1	84810	85060	85622	84819	84888	87868	88044	84810	84810	89680	84810	84860	86696	85874	92362	99694	84860	1
5	81669	82224	83176	81665	81791	85603	85132	81669	81669	86359	81669	81933	83598	83741	91496	99303	81933	5
10	80526	81209	82403	80547	80700	84558	84049	80526	80526	85150	80526	80901	83021	83102	91081	99046	80901	10
15	79660	80529	81728	79686	79897	83745	83173	79660	79660	84235	79660	80143	82298	82619	90686	98766	80143	15
20	78452	79663	80581	78491	78761	82553	81973	78452	78452	82957	78452	79336	81187	81825	89966	98072	79336	20
25	76682	78673	78863	76734	77071	80789	80208	76682	76682	81177	76682	77987	79513	80910	89163	97324	77987	25
30	75052	77714	77253	75137	75522	79160	78603	75052	75052	79362	75052	76703	78016	79994	88364	96609	76703	30
35	73258	76612	75486	73393	73856	77373	76825	73258	73258	77465	73258	75229	76393	78942	87435	95791	75229	35
40	71189	75197	73440	71401	71991	75327	74800	71189	71189	75277	71189	73484	74555	77575	86248	94740	73484	40
45	68545	73243	70754	68961	69623	72746	72220	68545	68545	72681	68545	71126	72271	75646	84586	93285	71126	45
50	65306	70633	67545	66040	66842	69560	69044	65306	65306	69056	65306	68158	69496	73055	82268	91171	68158	50
55	60544	66435	62731	61920	62748	65078	64285	60544	60544	64021	60544	63627	65426	68835	78561	87722	63627	55
60	54673	60875	56757	56551	57803	59425	58453	54673	54673	57813	54673	57885	60381	63195	73437	82772	57885	60
65	47459	53606	49368	50828	51177	52364	51177	47459	47459	50184	47459	50678	54151	55763	66346	75679	50678	65
70	37753	43128	39362	41778	43142	42781	40917	37753	37753	39921	37753	40573	47568	44966	55224	65218	40573	70
75	26848	31022	28054	31090	32994	31681	29338	26848	26848	28390	26848	29171	39276	32416	41800	51824	29171	75
80	16194	18911	16965	19813	22323	20391	17968	16194	16194	17124	16194	17842	29764	19812	27680	37062	17842	80
85+	7379	8715	7755	9637	12130	10342	8504	7379	7379	7803	7379	8307	19508	9159	14795	22727	8307	85+

ADDED YRS OF LIFE

	No Causes	(1)	(2)	(3)	(4)	(5)	(6)	(7)	(8)	(9)	(10)	(11)	(12)	(1)+(2)	(1)+(2)+(5)+(6)+(8)	(1)+(2)+(5)+(6)+(8)+part of(9)&(12)	(10)+(11)
TOTAL		2.896	1.581	1.213	2.120	3.816	2.886	.000	.000	2.988	.000	1.625	5.825	4.583	12.378	20.612	1.625
WORK	6.824	1.950	.239	.422	.669	.449	.361	.000	.000	.000	.000	1.095	.927	2.205	3.097	3.672	1.095

POPULATION, DEATHS, DEATH RATES FOR ALL CAUSES COMBINED, AND SPECIFIED CAUSES

Age Start of Interval	Midyear Population	Deaths During Year	All Causes	Respiratory T. B.	Other Infec. and Paras.	Neoplasms	Cardiovascular	Infl., Pneu., Bronch.	Diarrheal	Certain Degenerative	Maternal	Cert. Dis. of Infancy	Motor Vehicle	Other Violence	Other and Unknown	Age Start of Interval
0	147402	20191	.13698	.00248	.C0893	.00007	.00069	.03003	.02905	.00000	.00000	.04625	.00000	.00062	.01887	0
1	564778	5213	.00923	.00094	.00233	.00004	.00012	.00298	.00101	.00000	.00000	.00000	.00000	.00046	.00135	1
5	765478	2156	.00280	.00042	.00099	.00002	.00014	.00037	.00030	.00000	.00000	.00000	.00000	.00013	.00044	5
10	474336	1020	.00215	.C0060	.C0054	.00001	.00017	.00023	.00008	.00000	.00000	.00000	.00000	.00013	.00038	10
15	698800	1851	.00265	.001C7	.00019	.00004	.00021	.00016	.00013	.00000	.00018	.0000C	.00000	.00034	.00033	15
20	745983	3277	.00439	.00243	.00022	.00004	.00025	.00020	.00017	.00000	.00032	.00000	.00000	.00038	.00039	20
25	697748	2734	.00392	.00169	.00017	.00017	.00027	.00020	.00020	.00000	.00049	.00000	.00000	.00025	.00047	25
30	636980	2866	.00450	.00182	.00021	.00026	.00043	.00025	.00021	.00000	.00049	.00000	.00000	.00024	.00060	30
35	536594	2863	.00533	.00183	.00024	.00042	.00070	.00033	.00031	.00000	.00044	.00000	.00000	.00026	.00081	35
40	469401	2634	.00561	.00134	.00017	.00091	.00087	.00043	.00033	.00000	.00022	.0000C	.00000	.00027	.00107	40
45	425069	3148	.00741	.00141	.00022	.00153	.00151	.00052	.00041	.00000	.00004	.00000	.00000	.00030	.00148	45
50	386095	4249	.01101	.00168	.00026	.00204	.00231	.00128	.00052	.00000	.00000	.00000	.00000	.00034	.00257	50
55	343378	5279	.01537	.00169	.00029	.00332	.00368	.00156	.00082	.00000	.00000	.00000	.00000	.00037	.00363	55
60	293035	6432	.02195	.00167	.00031	.00502	.00603	.00210	.00103	.00000	.00000	.00000	.00000	.00042	.00537	60
65	222595	9092	.04085	.00175	.00037	.00540	.00887	.00404	.00068	.00000	.00000	.00000	.00000	.00047	.01927	65
70	167791	10201	.06080	.00176	.00036	.00744	.01421	.00611	.00108	.00000	.00000	.00000	.00000	.00079	.02904	70
75	96803	8696	.08983	.00163	.00042	.00901	.02221	.00968	.00197	.00000	.00000	.00000	.00000	.00099	.04391	75
80	44830	6160	.13741	.00145	.00051	.01031	.03366	.01584	.00491	.00000	.00000	.00000	.00000	.00147	.06926	80
85+	17538	3858	.21998	.00097	.00068	.01083	.05069	.02874	.00878	.00000	.00000	.00000	.00000	.00239	.11689	85+
ALL	7738834	101919														

CRUDE DEATH RATE			.01317	.00145	.00065	.00117	.00199	.00173	.00101	.00000	.00018	.00088	.00000	.00033	.00378	
STANDARDIZED RATE (1)			.01244	.00133	.00092	.00072	.00121	.00201	.00142	.00000	.00015	.00163	.00000	.00031	.00274	
STANDARDIZED RATE (2)			.01540	.00142	.00069	.00137	.00249	.00203	.00111	.00000	.00015	.C0096	.00000	.00035	.00484	
GEOMETRIC MEAN			.01429													

LIFE TABLE FOR ALL CAUSES COMBINED

Age (x)	Midyear Population	Deaths During Year	$_nM_x$	$_nq_x$	l_x	$_nd_x$	$_nL_x$	$_nm_x$	$_na_x$	T_x	$_nr_x$	$\overset{\circ}{e}_x$	Age (x)
0	147402	20191	.136979	.125040	100000	12504	91283	.136981	.302865	5590719	.000000	55.907	0
1	564778	5213	.009230	.036082	87496	3157	342092	.009229	1.500000	5499436	.000000	62.854	1
5	765478	2156	.002802	.013920	84339	1174	418760	.002804	2.500000	5157345	.000000	61.150	5
10	474336	1020	.002150	.010690	83165	889	413582	.002150	2.476565	4738585	.017438	56.978	10
15	698800	1851	.002649	.013054	82276	1074	408877	.002627	2.669732	4325003	-.040152	52.567	15
20	745983	3277	.004393	.021724	81202	1764	401697	.004391	2.555154	3916126	-.014861	48.227	20
25	697748	2734	.003918	.019399	79438	1541	393331	.003918	2.496079	3514429	.003792	44.241	25
30	636980	2866	.004499	.022273	77897	1735	385245	.004504	2.555956	3121097	.016590	40.067	30
35	536594	2863	.005334	.026352	76162	2007	375859	.005340	2.533217	2735853	.024504	35.921	35
40	469401	2634	.005611	.027712	74155	2055	365767	.005618	2.563058	2359993	.020001	31.825	40
45	425069	3148	.007406	.036443	72100	2629	354277	.007421	2.632813	1994226	.013979	27.659	45
50	386095	4249	.011005	.053706	69471	3731	338497	.011022	2.625748	1639950	.011150	23.606	50
55	343378	5278	.015371	.074247	65740	4881	317049	.015395	2.612895	1301453	.010351	19.797	55
60	293035	6432	.021950	.104767	60859	6376	289456	.022027	2.672751	984404	.017684	16.175	60
65	222595	9092	.040845	.186627	54483	10168	248113	.040981	2.609965	694948	.015492	12.755	65
70	167791	10201	.060796	.264989	44315	11743	192597	.060972	2.532342	446835	.016424	10.083	70
75	96803	8696	.089832	.368138	32572	11991	132619	.090417	2.478056	254238	.034917	7.805	75
80	44830	6160	.137408	.509208	20581	10480	75700	.138441	2.404123	121618	.034917	5.909	80
85+	17538	3858	.219979	1.000000	10101	10101	45918	.219979	4.545879	45918	.000000	4.546	85+

NUMBER OF PERSONS DYING (OUT OF 100,000 AT BIRTH) ABOVE AGE X FROM SPECIFIED CAUSES

Age (x)	All Causes	Respiratory T.B.	Other Infec. and Paras.	Neoplasms	Cardiovascular	Infl., Pneu., Bronch.	Diarrheal	Certain Degenerative	Maternal	Cert. Dis. of Infancy	Motor Vehicle	Other Violence	Other and Unknown	Age (x)
0	100000	8167	3355	9740	18326	12341	5967	0	840	4222	0	2085	34957	0
1	87496	7941	2539	9734	18263	9600	3316	0	840	0	0	2029	33234	1
5	84339	7619	1742	9721	18224	8582	2970	0	840	0	0	1872	32769	5
10	83165	7442	1326	9714	18165	8427	2846	0	840	0	0	1817	32588	10
15	82276	7192	1102	9709	18093	8332	2815	0	839	0	0	1765	32429	15
20	81202	6764	1021	9694	18007	8267	2764	0	766	0	0	1625	32294	20
25	79438	5790	934	9676	17905	8186	2695	0	640	0	0	1474	32138	25
30	77897	5125	866	9609	17799	8107	2615	0	447	0	0	1377	31952	30
35	76162	4425	786	9508	17633	8011	2536	0	259	0	0	1283	31721	35
40	74155	3738	697	9348	17370	7886	2421	0	95	0	0	1185	31415	40
45	72100	3249	635	9012	17049	7729	2301	0	16	0	0	1086	31023	45
50	69471	2749	558	8470	16513	7544	2156	0	4	0	0	979	30499	50
55	65740	2181	469	7777	15729	7111	1981	0	3	0	0	862	29627	55
60	60859	1644	377	6722	14558	6614	1720	0	3	0	0	746	28475	60
65	54483	1160	288	5267	12809	6004	1421	0	3	0	0	623	26908	65
70	44315	726	196	3926	10602	4998	1252	0	3	0	0	507	22105	70
75	32572	387	127	2490	7857	3818	1042	0	3	0	0	355	16493	75
80	20581	170	70	1291	4891	2525	778	0	3	0	0	223	10630	80
85+	10101	45	31	497	2328	1320	403	0	0	0	0	110	5367	85+

NUMBER OF PERSONS SURVIVING TO AGE X IF SPECIFIED CAUSES WERE ELIMINATED

Age (x)	No Causes	Respiratory T.B. (1)	Other Infec. and Paras. (2)	Neoplasms (3)	Cardiovascular (4)	Infl., Pneu., Bronch. (5)	Diarrheal (6)	Certain Degenerative (7)	Maternal (8)	Cert. Dis. of Infancy (9)	Motor Vehicle (10)	Other Violence (11)	Other and Unknown (12)	(1)+(2)	(1)+(2)+(5)+(6)+(8)	(1)+(2)+(5)+(6)+(8)+part of(9)&(12)	(10)+(11)	Age (x)
0	100000	100000	100000	100000	100000	100000	100000	100000	100000	100000	100000	100000	100000	100000	100000	100000	100000	0
1	87496	87707	88262	87502	87555	90096	90009	87496	87496	91533	87496	87548	89121	88475	93721	99746	87548	1
5	84339	84860	85870	84357	84434	87880	87112	84339	84339	88230	84339	84544	86372	86401	92989	99462	84544	5
10	83165	83856	85097	83190	83317	86818	86026	83165	83165	87002	83165	83422	85354	85804	92654	99292	83422	10
15	82276	83211	84415	82306	82499	85988	85139	82276	82277	86072	82276	82582	84604	85374	92332	99103	82582	15
20	81202	82556	83396	81246	81507	84933	84080	81202	81276	84948	81202	81644	83638	84786	91909	98770	81644	20
25	79438	81748	81673	79499	79838	83172	82324	79438	79635	83103	79438	80020	81980	84048	91421	98405	80020	25
30	77897	80842	80158	78023	78395	81641	80809	77897	78282	81491	77897	78565	80580	83188	90893	98021	78565	30
35	76162	79763	78454	76386	76814	79922	79090	76162	76725	79676	76162	76909	79022	82163	90197	97493	76909	35
40	74155	78374	76477	74531	75052	77945	77124	74155	74867	77576	74155	74980	77253	80828	89209	96698	74980	40
45	72100	76713	74420	72800	73294	75948	75110	72100	72870	75526	72100	73001	75516	79182	87819	95567	73001	45
50	69471	74441	71785	70685	71158	73371	72520	69471	70225	72676	69471	70445	73304	76920	85723	93494	70445	50
55	65740	71035	68019	67578	68123	69876	68803	65740	66454	68773	65740	66777	70268	73498	82651	90659	66777	55
60	60859	66321	63060	63613	64244	65198	63958	60859	61520	63667	60859	61932	66246	68719	78208	86368	61932	60
65	54483	59871	56541	58401	55284	58589	57553	54483	55035	56957	54483	55562	60952	62132	71834	80000	55562	65
70	44315	49125	46074	48807	50429	48970	46972	44315	44797	46359	44315	45299	54672	51075	60475	69471	45299	70
75	32572	36427	33926	37245	39835	37125	34716	32572	32926	34075	32572	33428	46555	37941	46592	55881	33428	75
80	20581	23205	21483	24630	28198	24650	22161	20581	20805	21531	20581	21228	36825	24222	31578	40508	21228	80
85+	10101	11486	10572	12758	16471	13130	11157	10101	10213	10567	10101	10499	25839	12021	17451	25232	10499	85+

ADDED YRS OF LIFE

	No Causes	(1)	(2)	(3)	(4)	(5)	(6)	(7)	(8)	(9)	(10)	(11)	(12)	(1)+(2)	(1)+(2)+(5)+(6)+(8)	+part	(10)+(11)
TOTAL		2.791	1.659	1.453	2.575	3.553	2.392	.000	.332	2.566	.000	.615	6.733	4.547	11.740	19.103	.615
WORK	5.880	1.787	.217	.545	.718	.368	.265	.000	.312	.000	.000	.318	.853	2.016	3.036	3.588	.318

POPULATION, DEATHS, DEATH RATES FOR ALL CAUSES COMBINED, AND SPECIFIED CAUSES

Age Start of Interval	Midyear Population	Deaths During Year	All Causes	Respiratory T. B.	Other Infec. and Paras.	Neo-plasms	Cardio-vascular	Infl., Pneu., Bronch.	Diar-rheal	Certain Degen-erative	Maternal	Cert. Dis. of Infancy	Motor Vehicle	Other Violence	Other and Unknown	Age Start of Interval
0	109400	2947	.02694	.00000	.00056	.00013	.00020	.00346	.00145	.00006	.00000	.01276	.00002	.00144	.00685	0
1	490800	678	.00138	.00001	.00014	.00013	.00008	.00018	.00007	.00002	.00000	.00000	.00008	.00036	.00032	1
5	663200	332	.00050	.00000	.00003	.00006	.00002	.00002	.00000	.00001	.00000	.00000	.00007	.00018	.00011	5
10	640100	321	.00050	.00000	.00002	.00008	.00003	.00002	.00000	.00001	.00000	.00000	.00004	.00021	.00009	10
15	523000	626	.00120	.00002	.00002	.00011	.00009	.00003	.00000	.00004	.00000	.00000	.00029	.00050	.00011	15
20	427500	767	.00179	.00003	.00002	.00010	.00013	.00001	.00000	.00005	.00000	.00000	.00046	.00089	.00009	20
25	457300	805	.00176	.00004	.00001	.00019	.00018	.00002	.00000	.00008	.00000	.00000	.00035	.00079	.00010	25
30	486500	933	.00192	.00012	.00002	.00025	.00028	.00001	.00000	.00007	.00000	.00000	.00025	.00079	.00011	30
35	501000	1228	.00245	.00020	.00004	.00041	.00047	.00004	.00000	.00010	.00000	.00000	.00021	.00079	.00019	35
40	290500	1004	.00346	.00021	.00003	.00064	.00089	.00008	.00001	.00021	.00000	.00000	.00014	.00092	.00032	40
45	443700	2427	.00547	.00032	.00005	.00125	.00160	.00013	.00001	.00034	.00000	.00000	.00019	.00115	.00044	45
50	446100	4133	.00926	.00046	.00015	.00256	.00314	.00041	.00002	.00047	.00000	.00000	.00021	.00114	.00071	50
55	392800	6369	.01621	.00087	.00018	.00519	.00568	.00081	.00003	.00073	.00000	.00000	.00020	.00120	.00132	55
60	295000	7827	.02653	.00121	.00028	.00839	.00994	.00178	.00004	.00107	.00000	.00000	.00020	.00117	.00244	60
65	201900	8066	.03995	.00153	.00038	.01134	.01695	.00266	.00006	.00181	.00000	.00000	.00014	.00139	.00368	65
70	137400	8498	.06185	.00187	.00043	.01452	.02962	.00453	.00009	.00215	.00000	.00000	.00020	.00181	.00663	70
75	89800	8114	.09036	.00182	.00039	.01503	.04777	.00772	.00026	.00218	.00000	.00000	.00020	.00238	.01261	75
80	44400	6504	.14649	.00194	.00043	.01547	.08394	.01367	.00029	.00264	.00000	.00000	.00038	.00421	.02351	80
85+	21500	4396	.20447	.00149	.00033	.01033	.11795	.01912	.00047	.00167	.00000	.00000	.00000	.00019	.00647	.04647	85+
ALL	6661900	65975															
CRUDE DEATH RATE			.00990	.00032	.00010	.00205	.00394	.00068	.00005	.00034	.00000	.00021	.00020	.00083	.00120	
STANDARDIZED RATE (1)			.00616	.00018	.00008	.00111	.00193	.00044	.00007	.00019	.00000	.00045	.00019	.00070	.00081	
STANDARDIZED RATE (2)			.01123	.00033	.00010	.00217	.00465	.00081	.00006	.00036	.00000	.00026	.00020	.00086	.00143	
GEOMETRIC MEAN			.00779													

LIFE TABLE FOR ALL CAUSES COMBINED

Age (x)	Midyear Population	Deaths During Year	$_nM_x$	$_nq_x$	l_x	$_nd_x$	$_nL_x$	$_nm_x$	$_na_x$	T_x	$_nr_x$	$\overset{\circ}{e}_x$	Age (x)
0	109400	2947	.026938	.026310	100000	2631	97674	.026937	.115794	6780273	.000000	67.803	0
1	490800	678	.001381	.005505	97369	536	388136	.001381	1.500000	6682599	.000000	68.632	1
5	663200	332	.000501	.002489	96833	241	483563	.000498	2.500000	6294463	.000000	65.003	5
10	640100	321	.000501	.002516	96592	243	482423	.000504	2.790638	5810900	.013941	60.159	10
15	523000	626	.001197	.006020	96349	580	480423	.001207	2.720546	5328477	.037237	55.304	15
20	427500	767	.001794	.008949	95769	857	476755	.001798	2.561260	4848054	.021915	50.622	20
25	457300	805	.001760	.008766	94912	832	472488	.001761	2.509766	4371299	-.003983	46.056	25
30	486500	933	.001918	.009524	94080	896	468224	.001914	2.571615	3898811	-.021185	41.441	30
35	501000	1228	.002451	.012234	93184	1140	463214	.002461	2.625914	3430587	-.036912	36.815	35
40	290500	1004	.003456	.017220	92044	1585	456524	.003472	2.668375	2967374	.027513	32.239	40
45	443700	2427	.005470	.026764	90459	2421	446742	.005419	2.706440	2510849	-.039119	27.757	45
50	446100	4133	.009265	.045253	88038	3984	431098	.009242	2.717798	2064107	-.010878	23.446	50
55	392800	6369	.016214	.078354	84054	6586	405001	.016262	2.681635	1633009	.013641	19.428	55
60	295000	7827	.026532	.125549	77468	9726	364239	.026702	2.624859	1228008	.033854	15.852	60
65	201900	8066	.039950	.183269	67742	12415	308701	.040210	2.586841	863769	.037494	12.751	65
70	137400	8498	.061849	.269326	55327	14901	239904	.062112	2.535009	555018	.022738	10.032	70
75	89800	8114	.090356	.369045	40426	14919	164555	.090662	2.481427	315114	.018669	7.795	75
80	44400	6504	.146486	.532050	25507	13571	92182	.147220	2.394935	150558	.018669	5.903	80
85+	21500	4396	.204465	1.000000	11936	11936	58377	.204465	4.890810	58377	.000000	4.891	85+

NUMBER OF PERSONS DYING (OUT OF 100,000 AT BIRTH) ABOVE AGE X FROM SPECIFIED CAUSES

Age (x)	All Causes	Respiratory T.B.	Other Infec. and Paras.	Neoplasms	Cardiovascular	Infl., Pneu., Bronch.	Diarrheal	Certain Degenerative	Maternal	Cert. Dis. of Infancy	Motor Vehicle	Other Violence	Other and Unknown	Age (x)
0	100000	2920	800	19305	43987	7310	353	3108	0	1246	1400	6612	12959	0
1	97369	2920	746	19292	43967	6971	211	3101	0	0	1398	6471	12292	1
5	96833	2915	692	19243	43938	6903	185	3092	0	0	1367	6333	12165	5
10	96592	2914	679	19215	43928	6893	185	3086	0	0	1332	6247	12113	10
15	96349	2914	671	19176	43913	6885	185	3081	0	0	1310	6144	12070	15
20	95769	2905	663	19125	43872	6870	184	3063	0	0	1167	5900	12020	20
25	94912	2890	654	19076	43809	6865	181	3040	0	0	946	5475	11976	25
30	94080	2870	651	18986	43722	6854	181	3002	0	0	782	5104	11928	30
35	93184	2814	642	18869	43590	6849	180	2968	0	0	663	4734	11875	35
40	92044	2721	622	18678	43371	6828	180	2920	0	0	567	4367	11790	40
45	90459	2624	608	18382	42961	6792	176	2825	0	0	502	3948	11641	45
50	88038	2484	584	17830	42257	6736	173	2673	0	0	417	3436	11448	50
55	84054	2286	522	16730	40906	6558	166	2471	0	0	328	2945	11142	55
60	77468	1935	448	14621	38600	6227	154	2173	0	0	246	2457	10607	60
65	67742	1492	344	11546	34951	5575	139	1780	0	0	172	2030	9713	65
70	55327	1019	227	8029	29673	4746	119	1219	0	0	128	1599	8568	70
75	40426	570	124	4538	22529	3655	97	703	0	0	80	1163	6967	75
80	25507	271	60	2063	14636	2379	54	344	0	0	47	769	4884	80
85+	11936	87	19	603	6886	1116	27	98	0	0	11	377	2712	85+

NUMBER OF PERSONS SURVIVING TO AGE X IF SPECIFIED CAUSES WERE ELIMINATED

Age (x)	No Causes	Respiratory T.B. (1)	Other Infec. and Paras. (2)	Neoplasms (3)	Cardiovascular (4)	Infl., Pneu., Bronch. (5)	Diarrheal (6)	Certain Degenerative (7)	Maternal (8)	Cert. Dis. of Infancy (9)	Motor Vehicle (10)	Other Violence (11)	Other and Unknown (12)	(1)+(2)	(1)+(2)+(5)+(6)+(8)	(1)+(2)+(5)+(6)+(8)+part of(9)&(12)	(10)+(11)	Age (x)
0	100000	100000	100000	100000	100000	100000	100000	100000	100000	100000	100000	100000	100000	100000	100000	100000	100000	0
1	97369	97369	97422	97382	97389	97704	97509	97376	97369	98606	97371	97508	98029	97422	97898	99323	97510	1
5	96833	96838	96940	96895	96882	97234	96998	96849	96833	98063	96866	97109	97617	96945	97513	98980	97142	5
10	96592	96598	96712	96681	96650	97002	96757	96614	96592	97819	96660	96954	97427	96718	97294	98765	97022	10
15	96349	96355	96476	96477	96422	96766	96514	96376	96349	97573	96439	96813	97225	96482	97066	98536	96903	15
20	95769	95784	95504	95947	95883	96199	95934	95814	95769	96986	96001	96475	96690	95918	96515	97980	96709	20
25	94912	94942	95054	95138	95088	95343	95078	94979	94912	96118	95363	96039	95869	95084	95683	97138	96495	25
30	94080	94129	94224	94354	94341	94518	94245	94184	94080	95275	94691	95572	95077	94274	94878	96323	96192	30
35	93184	93289	93336	93612	93574	93623	93348	93321	93184	94368	93908	95036	94225	93441	94046	95483	95775	35
40	92044	92240	92214	92657	92648	92499	92206	92227	92044	93214	92855	94246	93157	92410	93030	94462	95077	40
45	90459	90748	90640	91358	91463	90942	90622	90734	90459	91608	91321	93049	91703	90929	91579	93005	93937	45
50	88038	88458	88238	89465	89720	88563	88200	88456	88038	89157	88962	91080	89442	88658	89352	90762	92036	50
55	84054	84649	84305	86516	87016	84731	84215	84651	84054	85122	85024	87455	85669	84903	85751	87142	88464	55
60	77468	78357	77771	81848	82523	78413	77628	78307	77468	78452	78441	81089	79509	78663	79788	81150	82108	60
65	67742	68938	68104	74671	75692	68189	67856	68848	67742	68603	68663	71326	70390	69307	70948	72282	72295	65
70	55327	56738	55729	64576	67565	57278	55471	56746	55327	56030	56119	58663	58575	57150	59320	60580	59503	70
75	40426	41848	40807	50761	57403	42826	40550	41912	40426	40940	41046	43258	44273	42243	44889	46037	43921	75
80	25507	26645	25798	34533	46247	28111	25620	26736	25507	25831	25924	27627	29801	26949	29831	30855	28079	80
85+	11936	12598	12100	17535	33391	14118	12007	12684	11936	12088	12156	13215	15748	12770	15194	15972	13458	85+

ADDED YRS OF LIFE

	No Causes	(1)	(2)	(3)	(4)	(5)	(6)	(7)	(8)	(9)	(10)	(11)	(12)	(1)+(2)	(1)+(2)+(5)+(6)+(8)	+part of(9)&(12)	(10)+(11)
TOTAL		.445	.188	2.816	7.388	.969	.135	.462	.000	.860	.493	1.774	1.930	.636	1.785	3.014	2.288
WORK	3.661	.161	.038	.677	.798	.095	.005	.154	.000	.000	.324	.918	.255	.200	.302	.328	1.251

POPULATION, DEATHS, DEATH RATES FOR ALL CAUSES COMBINED, AND SPECIFIED CAUSES

Age Start of Interval	Midyear Population	Deaths During Year	All Causes	Respiratory T. B.	Other Infec. and Paras.	Neo-plasms	Cardio-vascular	Infl., Pneu., Bronch.	Diar-rheal	Certain Degen-erative	Maternal	Cert. Dis. of Infancy	Motor Vehicle	Other Violence	Other and Unknown	Age Start of Interval
0	103400	2162	.02091	.00003	.00060	.00005	.00020	.00310	.00119	.00007	.00000	.00896	.00001	.00101	.00570	0
1	466200	473	.00101	.00000	.00015	.00009	.00005	.00013	.00006	.00001	.00000	.00000	.00001	.00101	.00570	0
5	629500	203	.00032	.00000	.00003	.00008	.00002	.00001	.00001	.00001	.00000	.00000	.00005	.00022	.00026	1
10	615900	177	.00029	.00000	.00001	.00006	.00005	.00001	.00000	.00000	.00000	.00000	.00005	.00004	.00007	5
15	511900	230	.00045	.00001	.00002	.00007	.00005	.00002	.00000	.00002	.00001	.00000	.00004	.00015	.00006	10
20	421400	280	.00066	.00005	.00001	.00011	.00010	.00001	.00001	.00005	.00000	.00000	.00004	.00015	.00006	15
25	454400	353	.00078	.00007	.00003	.00014	.00013	.00002	.00000	.00004	.00003	.00005	.00000	.00004	.00016	20
30	496900	466	.00094	.00007	.00002	.00024	.00015	.00003	.00000	.00006	.00003	.00000	.00003	.00015	.00010	25
35	529600	736	.00139	.00007	.00003	.00047	.00027	.00003	.00000	.00006	.00004	.00000	.00002	.00020	.00019	30
40	306300	622	.00203	.00005	.00007	.00069	.00046	.00007	.00000	.00008	.00002	.00000	.00004	.00021	.00030	35
45	467300	1593	.00341	.00008	.00003	.00148	.00080	.00012	.00001	.00014	.00000	.00000	.00003	.00038	.00040	40
50	477300	2527	.00529	.00010	.00007	.00210	.00164	.00013	.00001	.00028	.00000	.00000	.00004	.00036	.00038	45
55	432700	3712	.00858	.00018	.00009	.00319	.00292	.00028	.00003	.00049	.00000	.00000	.00004	.00041	.00057	50
60	370300	5089	.01374	.00034	.00014	.00442	.00546	.00053	.00002	.00080	.00000	.00000	.00007	.00051	.00094	55
65	274700	6793	.02473	.00054	.00027	.00622	.01166	.00119	.00005	.00148	.00000	.00000	.00007	.00074	.00144	60
70	203000	8863	.04366	.00084	.00022	.00858	.02363	.00243	.00011	.00202	.00000	.00000	.00009	.00109	.00249	65
75	133600	9991	.07478	.00125	.00032	.01045	.04513	.00472	.00021	.00243	.00000	.00000	.00019	.00193	.00464	70
80	65000	8678	.13351	.00123	.00049	.01217	.08431	.00960	.00042	.00257	.00000	.00000	.00000	.00015	.00815	75
85+	32900	6549	.19906	.00094	.00049	.00970	.12410	.01441	.00052	.00164	.00000	.00000	.00000	.00015	.01832	80
ALL	6992300	59497														85+

	All Causes	Respiratory T. B.	Other Infec. and Paras.	Neo-plasms	Cardio-vascular	Infl., Pneu., Bronch.	Diar-rheal	Certain Degen-erative	Maternal	Cert. Dis. of Infancy	Motor Vehicle	Other Violence	Other and Unknown
CRUDE DEATH RATE	.00851	.00015	.00008	.00165	.00409	.00049	.00004	.00032	.00001	.00013	.00004	.00038	.00111
STANDARDIZED RATE (1)	.00409	.00007	.00008	.00076	.00145	.00028	.00006	.00014	.00002	.00032	.00004	.00026	.00062
STANDARDIZED RATE (2)	.00796	.00014	.00008	.00145	.00380	.00049	.00005	.00028	.00002	.00019	.00004	.00037	.00107
GEOMETRIC MEAN	.00469												

LIFE TABLE FOR ALL CAUSES COMBINED

Age (x)	Midyear Population	Deaths During Year	$_nM_x$	$_nq_x$	l_x	$_nd_x$	$_nL_x$	$_nm_x$	$_na_x$	T_x	$_nr_x$	$\overset{\circ}{e}_x$	Age (x)
0	103400	2162	.020909	.020530	100000	2053	98164	.020914	.105545	7320997	.000000	73.210	0
1	466200	473	.001015	.004043	97947	396	390758	.001013	1.500000	7222833	.000000	73.742	1
5	629500	203	.000322	.001609	97551	157	487363	.000322	2.500000	6832035	.000000	70.036	5
10	615900	177	.000287	.001437	97394	140	486633	.000288	2.592262	6344673	-.011699	65.144	10
15	511900	230	.000449	.002252	97254	219	485761	.000451	2.674087	5858040	-.035128	60.234	15
20	421400	280	.000664	.003329	97035	323	484400	.000667	2.600619	5372279	-.021288	55.364	20
25	454400	353	.000777	.003877	96712	375	482649	.000777	2.570000	4887879	-.005448	50.541	25
30	496900	466	.000938	.004661	96337	449	480623	.000934	2.635486	4405230	-.025905	45.727	30
35	529600	736	.001390	.006956	95888	667	477881	.001396	2.662106	3924607	-.033440	40.929	35
40	306300	622	.002031	.010166	95221	968	473875	.002043	2.696711	3446727	-.028317	36.197	40
45	467300	1593	.003409	.016774	94253	1581	467615	.003381	2.691203	2972851	-.038431	31.541	45
50	477300	2527	.005294	.026103	92672	2419	457775	.005284	2.691281	2505236	-.009588	27.033	50
55	432700	3712	.008579	.042126	90253	3802	442462	.008593	2.684662	2047461	-.008129	22.686	55
60	370300	5089	.013743	.066963	86451	5789	418970	.013817	2.705166	1604999	-.024477	18.565	60
65	274700	6793	.024729	.117813	80662	9503	381295	.024923	2.683363	1186029	-.033524	14.704	65
70	203000	8863	.043660	.158893	71159	14153	322214	.043924	2.627259	804734	-.026638	11.309	70
75	133600	9991	.074783	.318405	57006	18151	240764	.075389	2.561223	482520	-.033011	8.464	75
80	65000	8678	.133508	.501531	38855	19487	144457	.134898	2.443552	241756	-.033011	6.222	80
85+	32900	6549	.199058	1.000000	19368	19368	97298	.199058	5.023668	97298	.000000	5.024	85+

NUMBER OF PERSONS DYING (OUT OF 100,000 AT BIRTH) ABOVE AGE X FROM SPECIFIED CAUSES

Age (x)	All Causes	Respiratory T.B.	Other Infec. and Paras.	Neoplasms	Cardiovascular	Infl., Pneu., Bronch.	Diarrheal	Certain Degenerative	Maternal	Cert. Dis. of Infancy	Motor Vehicle	Other Violence	Other and Unknown	Age (x)
0	100000	1537	746	16288	52824	6109	401	3247	101	879	370	3908	13590	0
1	97947	1534	687	16284	52805	5805	284	3240	101	0	369	3809	13029	1
5	97551	1534	629	16249	52787	5753	259	3237	101	0	349	3722	12931	5
10	97394	1533	612	16211	52775	5747	257	3234	101	0	326	3701	12897	10
15	97254	1533	607	16181	52750	5741	256	3232	101	0	318	3667	12868	15
20	97035	1529	599	16147	52727	5733	255	3224	95	0	296	3592	12838	20
25	96712	1507	593	16095	52676	5727	254	3207	69	0	277	3515	12792	25
30	96337	1475	580	16028	52615	5717	254	3192	45	0	266	3421	12744	30
35	95888	1439	571	15912	52541	5703	254	3163	28	0	254	3331	12692	35
40	95221	1404	557	15684	52409	5687	252	3136	8	0	244	3236	12604	40
45	94253	1362	523	15354	52188	5656	251	3098	0	0	225	3135	12461	45
50	92672	1326	508	14666	51817	5602	248	3035	0	0	213	2972	12285	50
55	90253	1279	475	13704	51070	5541	244	2908	0	0	197	2809	12026	55
60	86451	1199	434	12292	49775	5418	230	2689	0	0	178	2627	11609	60
65	80662	1056	374	10433	47472	5193	220	2350	0	0	150	2411	11003	65
70	71159	848	270	8049	42982	4736	199	1781	0	0	122	2128	10044	70
75	57006	575	198	5275	35312	3946	162	1128	0	0	92	1776	8542	75
80	38855	273	120	2751	24348	2798	111	541	0	0	46	1306	6561	80
85+	19368	92	47	943	12075	1402	50	160	0	0	24	686	3889	85+

NUMBER OF PERSONS SURVIVING TO AGE X IF SPECIFIED CAUSES WERE ELIMINATED

Age (x)	No Causes	Respiratory T.B. (1)	Other Infec. and Paras. (2)	Neoplasms (3)	Cardiovascular (4)	Infl., Pneu., Bronch. (5)	Diarrheal (6)	Certain Degenerative (7)	Maternal (8)	Cert. Dis. of Infancy (9)	Motor Vehicle (10)	Other Violence (11)	Other and Unknown (12)	(1)+(2)	(1)+(2)+(5)+(6)+(8)	(1)+(2)+(5)+(6)+(8)+part of (9)&(12)	(10)+(11)	Age (x)
0	100000	100000	100000	100000	100000	100000	100000	100000	100000	100000	100000	100000	100000	100000	100000	100000	100000	0
1	97947	97950	98005	97951	97966	98248	98063	97954	97947	98821	97948	98045	98504	98008	98426	99561	98046	1
5	97551	97554	97667	97590	97588	97903	97691	97561	97551	98421	97572	97736	98204	97670	98164	99341	97757	5
10	97394	97398	97527	97471	97443	97752	97536	97407	97394	98263	97438	97559	98080	97531	98032	99215	97643	10
15	97254	97258	97392	97361	97328	97617	97397	97269	97254	98122	97306	97493	97968	97396	97903	99087	97545	15
20	97035	97043	97180	97175	97131	97405	97179	97058	97041	97901	97109	97349	97778	97188	97710	98896	97423	20
25	96712	96742	96863	96904	96859	97087	96856	96752	96744	97575	96804	97102	97459	96893	97446	98639	97195	25
30	96337	96399	96500	96595	96544	96721	96481	96392	96393	97169	96440	96819	97169	96562	97147	98349	96923	30
35	95888	95985	96060	96261	96169	96284	96031	95971	95960	96743	96003	96459	96768	96157	96771	97978	96574	35
40	95221	95353	95405	95820	95632	95630	95365	95331	95313	96070	95345	95883	96184	95537	96186	97399	96007	40
45	94253	94425	94469	95177	94881	94689	94356	94399	94352	95054	94394	95009	95350	94662	95324	96547	95152	45
50	92672	92877	92900	94272	93660	93154	92878	92769	93499	93499	92823	93579	93575	93105	93834	95051	93731	50
55	90253	90499	90507	92782	91564	90783	90357	90580	90348	91058	90416	91298	91135	90754	91529	92735	91463	55
60	86451	86765	86735	90305	89391	87780	86603	86979	86542	87222	86626	87633	88286	87050	87930	89120	87809	60
65	80662	81094	80985	86151	85740	81469	80813	81485	80747	81382	80852	81976	82574	81419	82474	83641	82169	65
70	71159	71736	71542	78423	80261	72306	71212	72426	71234	71794	71353	72598	74130	72122	73519	74647	72786	70
75	57006	57714	57377	65601	72524	58647	57162	58614	57066	57515	57188	58472	60801	58089	59988	61042	58659	75
80	38855	39587	39172	47134	62335	40056	39003	40443	38896	39202	39017	40252	43216	39910	42273	43192	40420	80
85+	19368	19861	19577	25062	48173	21459	19484	20436	19388	19541	19464	20514	23699	20075	22400	23110	20616	85+

ADDED YRS OF LIFE

	No Causes	(1)	(2)	(3)	(4)	(5)	(6)	(7)	(8)	(9)	(10)	(11)	(12)	(1)+(2)	(1)+(2)+(5)+(6)+(8)	(1)+(2)+(5)+(6)+(8)+part of (9)&(12)	(10)+(11)
TOTAL		.230	.199	2.527	5.269	.793	.131	.435	.047	.652	.108	.757	1.919	.430	1.425	2.473	.867
WORK	1.961	.074	.036	.622	.464	.056	.004	.091	.035	.000	.039	.245	.229	.110	.205	.235	.285

POPULATION, DEATHS, DEATH RATES FOR ALL CAUSES COMBINED, AND SPECIFIED CAUSES

Age Start of Interval	Midyear Population	Deaths During Year	All Causes	Respiratory T. B.	Other Infec. and Paras.	Neoplasms	Cardiovascular	Infl., Pneu., Bronch.	Diarrheal	Certain Degenerative	Maternal	Cert. Dis. of Infancy	Motor Vehicle	Other Violence	Other and Unknown	Age Start of Interval
0	120206	2995	.02492	.00000	.00038	.00022	.00022	.00293	.00133	.00003	.00000	.01279	.00002	.00088	.00611	0
1	440142	550	.00125	.00000	.00012	.00015	.00005	.00015	.00005	.00001	.00000	.00000	.00008	.00030	.00035	1
5	620363	370	.00060	.00000	.00002	.00009	.00001	.00001	.00000	.00001	.00000	.00000	.00013	.00018	.00014	5
10	667159	295	.00044	.00000	.00001	.00007	.00003	.00001	.00000	.00002	.00000	.00000	.00007	.00014	.00008	10
15	623831	695	.00111	.00001	.00001	.00010	.00006	.00002	.00000	.00002	.00000	.00000	.00032	.00047	.00009	15
20	511470	892	.00174	.00000	.00001	.00011	.00009	.00003	.00000	.00004	.00000	.00000	.00058	.00079	.00008	20
25	422571	694	.00164	.00001	.00001	.00014	.00016	.00001	.00001	.00008	.00000	.00000	.00037	.00075	.00010	25
30	467458	851	.00182	.00004	.00001	.00024	.00033	.00002	.00000	.00007	.00000	.00000	.00028	.00069	.00013	30
35	476347	1158	.00243	.00008	.00002	.00037	.00056	.00004	.00001	.00011	.00000	.00000	.00027	.00079	.00019	35
40	480179	1756	.00366	.00015	.00003	.00078	.00104	.00007	.00000	.00022	.00000	.00000	.00022	.00087	.00027	40
45	278616	1455	.00522	.00020	.00005	.00130	.00174	.00017	.00002	.00029	.00000	.00000	.00025	.00084	.00037	45
50	453187	3942	.00870	.00023	.00007	.00266	.00316	.00033	.00002	.00048	.00000	.00000	.00026	.00095	.00055	50
55	416965	6576	.01577	.00047	.00012	.00501	.00605	.00082	.00004	.00088	.00000	.00000	.00024	.00110	.00104	55
60	346956	9363	.02699	.00079	.00020	.00883	.01060	.00157	.00005	.00122	.00000	.00000	.00023	.00114	.00156	60
65	237214	10167	.04286	.00094	.00028	.01309	.01813	.00349	.00005	.00197	.00000	.00000	.00032	.00127	.00331	65
70	145605	9492	.06519	.00150	.00037	.01600	.03021	.00590	.00023	.00283	.00000	.00000	.00034	.00179	.00602	70
75	88885	8693	.09780	.00128	.00043	.01896	.05044	.00992	.00035	.00326	.00000	.00000	.00044	.00261	.01011	75
80	44416	6705	.15096	.00122	.00027	.01975	.08495	.01628	.00045	.00297	.00000	.00000	.00054	.00473	.01981	80
85+	18834	4591	.24376	.00112	.00053	.01673	.14097	.02846	.00069	.00234	.00000	.00000	.00069	.00865	.04359	85+
ALL	6860444	71240														

	All Causes	Respiratory T. B.	Other Infec. and Paras.	Neoplasms	Cardiovascular	Infl., Pneu., Bronch.	Diarrheal	Certain Degenerative	Maternal	Cert. Dis. of Infancy	Motor Vehicle	Other Violence	Other and Unknown
CRUDE DEATH RATE	.01038	.00020	.00008	.00234	.00421	.00081	.00005	.00040	.00000	.00022	.00026	.00077	.00105
STANDARDIZED RATE (1)	.00620	.00011	.00006	.00122	.00204	.00047	.00007	.00021	.00000	.00045	.00024	.00077	.00105
STANDARDIZED RATE (2)	.01165	.00021	.00008	.00243	.00491	.00097	.00006	.00041	.00000	.00026	.00024	.00062	.00072
GEOMETRIC MEAN	.00778										.00026	.00026	.00080	.00125

LIFE TABLE FOR ALL CAUSES COMBINED

Age (x)	Midyear Population	Deaths During Year	$_nM_x$	$_nq_x$	l_x	$_nd_x$	$_nL_x$	$_nm_x$	$_na_x$	T_x	$_nr_x$	$\overset{\circ}{e}_x$	Age (x)
0	120206	2995	.024916	.024380	100000	2438	97836	.024919	.112356	6774202	.000000	67.742	0
1	440142	550	.001250	.004981	97562	486	389033	.001249	1.500000	6676366	.000000	68.432	1
5	620363	370	.000596	.002977	97076	289	484658	.000596	2.500000	6287333	.000000	64.767	5
10	667159	295	.000442	.002211	96787	214	483452	.000443	2.742407	5802676	-.004953	59.953	10
15	623831	695	.001114	.005571	96573	538	481650	.001117	2.740861	5319224	-.015191	55.080	15
20	511470	892	.001744	.008705	96035	836	478135	.001748	2.560058	4837574	-.036760	50.373	20
25	422571	694	.001642	.008183	95199	779	474051	.001643	2.505081	4359439	-.017656	45.793	25
30	467458	851	.001820	.009055	94420	855	470035	.001819	2.585039	3885388	-.005348	41.150	30
35	476347	1158	.002431	.012056	93565	1128	465178	.002425	2.653480	3415353	-.016510	36.502	35
40	480179	1756	.003657	.018239	92437	1686	458225	.003679	2.650998	2950174	-.040571	31.916	40
45	278616	1455	.005222	.025895	90751	2350	448305	.005242	2.680940	2491950	.021125	27.459	45
50	453187	3942	.008698	.042160	88401	3727	433539	.008697	2.728401	2043645	-.043120	23.118	50
55	416965	6576	.015771	.076009	84674	6436	408579	.015752	2.701795	1610106	-.005064	19.015	55
60	346956	9363	.026986	.127317	78238	9961	367728	.027088	2.644585	1201527	-.018098	15.357	60
65	237214	10167	.042860	.195512	68277	13349	309168	.043177	2.586555	833799	.038811	12.212	65
70	145605	9492	.065190	.282315	54928	15507	236320	.065619	2.528885	524632	.035380	9.551	70
75	88885	8693	.097801	.393166	39421	15499	157833	.098199	2.466167	288311	.020932	7.314	75
80	44416	6705	.150959	.543015	23922	12990	85631	.151698	2.384206	130478	-.020932	5.454	80
85+	18834	4591	.243761	1.000000	10932	10932	44847	.243761	4.102374	44847	.000000	4.102	85+

NUMBER OF PERSONS DYING (OUT OF 100,000 AT BIRTH) ABOVE AGE X FROM SPECIFIED CAUSES

Age (x)	All Causes	Respiratory T.B.	Other Infec. and Paras.	Neoplasms	Cardiovascular	Infl., Pneu., Bronch.	Diarrheal	Certain Degenerative	Maternal	Cert. Dis. of Infancy	Motor Vehicle	Other Violence	Other and Unknown	Age (x)
0	100000	1813	615	21332	44082	8464	409	3579	0	1251	1837	6096	10522	0
1	97562	1813	578	21311	44060	8177	279	3576	0	0	1835	6010	9923	1
5	97076	1813	530	21251	44041	8121	261	3571	0	0	1805	5895	9788	5
10	96787	1813	518	21209	44035	8114	260	3566	0	0	1741	5809	9722	10
15	96573	1812	512	21173	44020	8108	260	3558	0	0	1708	5741	9681	15
20	96035	1808	507	21123	43989	8099	259	3549	0	0	1553	5511	9637	20
25	95199	1806	501	21069	43944	8085	258	3532	0	0	1273	5130	9601	25
30	94420	1800	494	21003	43870	8079	257	3495	0	0	1096	4774	9552	30
35	93565	1781	490	20893	43714	8069	255	3463	0	0	962	4448	9490	35
40	92437	1742	480	20724	43454	8053	252	3411	0	0	837	4082	9402	40
45	90751	1673	466	20361	42973	8021	250	3311	0	0	734	3684	9278	45
50	88401	1585	442	19777	42191	7943	242	3179	0	0	623	3309	9110	50
55	84674	1488	413	18640	40839	7802	233	2975	0	0	511	2857	8876	55
60	78238	1299	365	16596	38369	7468	216	2614	0	0	411	2450	8450	60
65	68277	1007	291	13338	34455	6740	198	2164	0	0	325	2031	7728	65
70	54928	715	203	9269	28801	5651	180	1551	0	0	227	1636	6695	70
75	39421	360	115	5475	21607	4246	125	879	0	0	147	1210	5257	75
80	23922	158	48	2477	13607	2672	69	363	0	0	78	796	3654	80
85+	10932	50	24	750	6322	1276	31	105	0	0	31	388	1955	85+

NUMBER OF PERSONS SURVIVING TO AGE X IF SPECIFIED CAUSES WERE ELIMINATED

Age (x)	No Causes	Respiratory T.B. (1)	Other Infec. and Paras. (2)	Neoplasms (3)	Cardiovascular (4)	Infl., Pneu., Bronch. (5)	Diarrheal (6)	Certain Degenerative (7)	Maternal (8)	Cert. Dis. of Infancy (9)	Motor Vehicle (10)	Other Violence (11)	Other and Unknown (12)	(1)+(2)	(1)+(2)+(5)+(6)+(8)	(1)+(2)+(5)+(6)+(8)+part of(9)&(12)	(10)+(11)	Age (x)
0	100000	100000	100000	100000	100000	100000	100000	100000	100000	100000	100000	100000	100000	100000	100000	100000	100000	0
1	97562	97562	97599	97583	97584	97846	97690	97565	97562	98805	97564	97647	98155	97599	98011	99439	97649	1
5	97076	97076	97160	97157	97117	97415	97222	97084	97076	98313	97108	97275	97802	97160	97646	99116	97307	5
10	96787	96787	96883	96909	96833	97132	96933	96800	96787	98021	96883	97072	97577	96883	97375	98847	97168	10
15	96573	96574	96675	96731	96634	96923	96719	96573	96573	97804	96702	96925	97403	96925	97173	98645	97054	15
20	96035	96040	96141	96242	96127	96392	96181	96065	96035	97259	96318	96616	96904	96146	96650	98116	96900	20
25	95199	95206	95310	95458	95335	95567	95345	95245	95199	96412	95759	96157	96057	95317	95832	97287	96723	25
30	94420	94433	94537	94743	94629	94791	94566	94503	94420	95623	95153	95729	95360	94550	95068	96512	96472	30
35	93565	93597	93665	93995	93928	93942	93711	93679	93565	94758	94426	95192	94559	93717	94242	95677	96008	35
40	92437	92507	92566	93031	93055	92826	92585	92601	92437	93615	93413	94415	93507	92636	93174	94598	95412	40
45	90751	90888	90891	91667	91839	91165	90858	91012	90751	91908	91812	93096	91926	91029	91592	93001	94185	45
50	88401	88622	88561	89907	90246	88881	88552	88786	88401	89528	89546	91066	89714	88782	89417	90809	92245	50
55	84674	84981	84856	87256	87802	85273	84828	85243	84674	85753	85881	87642	86164	85163	85921	87277	88892	55
60	78238	78704	78452	82674	83628	79116	78356	79114	78238	79235	79451	81425	80033	78920	79967	81270	82687	60
65	68277	68958	68533	75432	76955	69735	68432	69467	68277	69147	69416	71464	70537	69217	70855	72096	72657	65
70	54928	55740	55213	64834	67928	57107	55069	56446	54928	55628	55934	57862	57711	56029	58401	59545	58921	70
75	39421	40307	39700	50439	56881	42238	35569	41095	39421	39923	40211	41906	42716	40592	43656	44698	42746	75
80	23922	24616	24143	33678	44714	26969	24055	25350	23922	24227	24455	25772	27303	24843	28162	29039	26346	80
85+	10932	11322	11049	17079	31701	13406	11018	11766	10932	11071	11207	12071	13823	11443	14144	14793	12375	85+

ADDED YRS OF LIFE

	No Causes	(1)	(2)	(3)	(4)	(5)	(6)	(7)	(8)	(9)	(10)	(11)	(12)	(1)+(2)	(1)+(2)+(5)+(6)+(8)	(1)+(2)+(5)+(6)+(8)+part of(9)&(12)	(10)+(11)
TOTAL		.246	.140	2.953	6.851	.988	.128	.482	.000	.862	.609	1.545	1.567	.388	1.538	2.713	2.177
WORK	3.554	.081	.026	.685	.847	.095	.007	.151	.000	.000	.388	.832	.223	.108	.210	.226	1.229

POPULATION, DEATHS, DEATH RATES FOR ALL CAUSES COMBINED, AND SPECIFIED CAUSES

Age Start of Interval	Midyear Population	Deaths During Year	All Causes	Respiratory T. B.	Other Infec. and Paras.	Neo-plasms	Cardio-vascular	Infl., Pneu., Bronch.	Diar-rheal	Certain Degen-erative	Maternal	Cert. Dis. of Infancy	Motor Vehicle	Other Violence	Other and Unknown	Age Start of Interval
0	114130	2180	.01910	.00000	.00051	.00009	.00021	.00252	.00083	.00004	.00000	.00831	.00001	.00086	.00573	0
1	418955	403	.00096	.00000	.00013	.00010	.00002	.00013	.00004	.00001	.00000	.00000	.00007	.00017	.00028	1
5	593897	210	.00035	.00000	.00001	.00008	.00002	.00002	.00000	.00001	.00000	.00000	.00007	.00006	.00009	5
10	638424	151	.00024	.00000	.00000	.00006	.00002	.00001	.00000	.00001	.00000	.00000	.00003	.00004	.00007	10
15	603718	266	.00044	.00000	.00001	.00007	.00003	.00001	.00000	.00003	.00001	.00000	.00005	.00014	.00007	15
20	496435	247	.00050	.00001	.00000	.00010	.00007	.00001	.00000	.00002	.00002	.00000	.00003	.00016	.00007	20
25	418632	253	.00060	.00002	.00001	.00016	.00012	.00000	.00000	.00005	.00002	.00000	.00002	.00012	.00008	25
30	467801	450	.00096	.00005	.00001	.00030	.00018	.00002	.00001	.00005	.00005	.00000	.00005	.00012	.00012	30
35	494964	605	.00122	.00006	.00001	.00044	.00025	.00002	.00000	.00004	.00005	.00000	.00005	.00018	.00014	35
40	508965	1043	.00205	.00007	.00002	.00088	.00048	.00005	.00001	.00007	.00003	.00000	.00005	.00020	.00018	40
45	296592	965	.00325	.00006	.00004	.00143	.00088	.00009	.00000	.00018	.00000	.00000	.00006	.00023	.00027	45
50	481163	2471	.00514	.00005	.00004	.00209	.00156	.00012	.00001	.00027	.00000	.00000	.00006	.00033	.00056	50
55	452807	3686	.00814	.00011	.00006	.00315	.00289	.00025	.00002	.00050	.00000	.00000	.00000	.00037	.00073	55
60	404625	5542	.01370	.00016	.00012	.00447	.00557	.00065	.00002	.00101	.00000	.00000	.00008	.00041	.00121	60
65	324435	7676	.02365	.00031	.00018	.00630	.01107	.00122	.00007	.00177	.00000	.00000	.00011	.00067	.00197	65
70	223940	9554	.04266	.00051	.00020	.00880	.02254	.00276	.00017	.00283	.00000	.00000	.00018	.00101	.00366	70
75	146442	10827	.07393	.00057	.00029	.01119	.04324	.00564	.00026	.00280	.00000	.00000	.00026	.00270	.00700	75
80	76281	9639	.12636	.00093	.00034	.01240	.07957	.01017	.00033	.00281	.00000	.00000	.00026	.00488	.01467	80
85+	35318	7451	.21097	.00037	.00057	.01277	.13353	.01934	.00074	.00235	.00000	.00000	.00017	.01002	.03112	85+
ALL	7197524	63619														

CRUDE DEATH RATE			.00884	.00009	.00006	.00178	.00430	.00058	.00004	.00040	.00001	.00013	.00006	.00039	.00098	
STANDARDIZED RATE (1)			.00392	.00004	.00006	.00079	.00141	.00027	.00004	.00016	.00001	.00029	.00005	.00023	.00056	
STANDARDIZED RATE (2)			.00774	.00008	.00006	.00150	.00370	.00052	.00004	.00033	.00001	.00017	.00006	.00036	.00090	
GEOMETRIC MEAN			.00443													

LIFE TABLE FOR ALL CAUSES COMBINED

Age (x)	Midyear Population	Deaths During Year	$_nM_x$	$_nq_x$	l_x	$_nd_x$	$_nL_x$	$_nm_x$	$_na_x$	T_x	$_nr_x$	$\overset{\circ}{e}_x$	Age (x)
0	114130	2180	.019101	.018780	100000	1878	98314	.019102	.102472	7366188	.000000	73.662	0
1	418955	403	.000962	.003842	98122	377	391546	.000963	1.500000	7267874	.000000	74.070	1
5	593897	210	.000354	.001760	97745	172	488295	.000352	2.500000	6876329	.000000	70.350	5
10	638424	151	.000237	.001189	97573	116	487584	.000238	2.575431	6388034	-.005571	65.469	10
15	603718	266	.000441	.002196	97457	214	486776	.000440	2.622664	5900450	.014560	60.544	15
20	496435	247	.000498	.002489	97243	242	485627	.000498	2.568871	5413674	.035714	55.672	20
25	418632	253	.000604	.003031	97001	294	484316	.000607	2.656604	4928047	.016162	50.804	25
30	467801	450	.000962	.004788	96707	463	482438	.000960	2.630490	4443731	-.008305	45.950	30
35	494964	605	.001222	.006068	96244	584	479868	.001217	2.685502	3961293	-.021263	41.159	35
40	508965	1043	.002049	.010190	95660	983	476041	.002065	2.701551	3481425	.038285	36.394	40
45	296592	965	.003254	.016213	94677	1535	469831	.003267	2.684582	3005384	-.022070	31.744	45
50	481163	2471	.005135	.025155	93142	2343	460288	.005090	2.685837	2535553	-.041056	27.222	50
55	452807	3686	.008140	.039923	90799	3625	445653	.008134	2.698736	2075265	-.004332	22.856	55
60	404625	5542	.013697	.066545	87174	5801	422525	.013729	2.699606	1629612	.010929	18.694	60
65	324435	7676	.023660	.112851	81373	9183	385635	.023813	2.688074	1207087	.028303	14.834	65
70	223940	9554	.042663	.195193	72190	14091	327624	.043010	2.634941	821452	.034230	11.379	70
75	146442	10827	.073934	.315152	58099	18310	245774	.074499	2.557562	493828	.031128	8.500	75
80	76281	9639	.126362	.481289	39789	19150	150225	.127476	2.455864	248054	.031128	6.234	80
85+	35318	7451	.210969	1.000000	20639	20639	97830	.210969	4.740035	97830	.000000	4.740	85+

NUMBER OF PERSONS DYING (OUT OF 100,000 AT BIRTH) ABOVE AGE X FROM SPECIFIED CAUSES

Age (x)	All Causes	Respiratory T.B.	Other Infec. and Paras.	Neoplasms	Cardiovascular	Infl., Pneu., Bronch.	Diarrheal	Certain Degenerative	Maternal	Cert. Dis. of Infancy	Motor Vehicle	Other Violence	Other and Unknown	Age (x)
0	100000	893	570	17232	52938	7066	399	3974	88	817	532	4226	11265	0
1	98122	893	520	17224	52918	6818	317	3970	88	0	531	4142	10701	1
5	97745	892	469	17183	52908	6765	301	3967	88	0	504	4074	10594	5
10	97573	891	463	17146	52901	6755	300	3964	88	0	470	4045	10550	10
15	97457	891	462	17118	52893	6752	298	3961	88	0	455	4025	10514	15
20	97243	889	457	17081	52876	6746	298	3946	83	0	432	3955	10480	20
25	97001	884	455	17032	52843	6743	298	3935	71	0	416	3878	10446	25
30	96707	875	451	16957	52785	6742	297	3908	60	0	406	3820	10406	30
35	96244	850	446	16811	52696	6732	294	3885	37	0	382	3760	10351	35
40	95660	821	442	16602	52576	6724	293	3863	14	0	370	3672	10283	40
45	94677	789	431	16178	52345	6698	290	3827	2	0	348	3575	10194	45
50	93142	759	414	15502	51929	6657	289	3741	0	0	318	3466	10067	50
55	90799	718	394	14545	51217	6602	286	3619	0	0	289	3316	9813	55
60	87174	671	366	13141	49932	6490	279	3396	0	0	256	3153	9490	60
65	81373	604	314	11249	47573	6216	270	2970	0	0	224	2979	8974	65
70	72190	485	245	8811	43269	5741	242	2284	0	0	181	2721	8211	70
75	58099	318	179	5916	35813	4827	186	1353	0	0	121	2387	6999	75
80	39789	178	108	3157	25095	3429	122	664	0	0	57	1717	5262	80
85+	20639	36	55	1249	13063	1892	72	230	0	0	17	981	3044	85+

NUMBER OF PERSONS SURVIVING TO AGE X IF SPECIFIED CAUSES WERE ELIMINATED

Age (x)	No Causes	Respiratory T.B.	Other Infec. and Paras.	Neoplasms	Cardiovascular	Infl., Pneu., Bronch.	Diarrheal	Certain Degenerative	Maternal	Cert. Dis. of Infancy	Motor Vehicle	Other Violence	Other and Unknown	(1)+(2)	(1)+(2)+(5)+(6)+(8)	(1)+(2)+(5)+(6)+(8)+part of (9)&(12)	(10)+(11)	Age (x)
		(1)	(2)	(3)	(4)	(5)	(6)	(7)	(8)	(9)	(10)	(11)	(12)					
0	100000	100000	100000	100000	100000	100000	100000	100000	100000	100000	100000	100000	100000	100000	100000	100000	100000	0
1	98122	98122	98172	98130	98142	98368	98203	98126	98122	98935	98123	98205	98682	98172	98459	99555	98206	1
5	97745	97746	97845	97794	97775	98043	97842	97752	97745	98555	97773	97896	98411	97846	98242	99343	97924	5
10	97573	97575	97679	97659	97610	97881	97671	97583	97573	98381	97635	97753	98282	97681	98087	99193	97815	10
15	97457	97459	97564	97571	97502	97767	97557	97470	97457	98264	97534	97656	98201	97566	97977	99084	97733	15
20	97243	97247	97355	97393	97305	97559	97342	97271	97248	98048	97343	97512	98020	97359	97780	98888	97612	20
25	97001	97010	97114	97200	97095	97319	97100	97040	97018	97804	97116	97347	97810	97123	97558	98668	97462	25
30	96707	96725	96824	96981	96859	97025	96807	96773	96735	97508	96832	97110	97554	96842	97289	98400	97235	30
35	96244	96287	96366	96662	96484	96631	96332	96295	96255	97142	96392	96705	97112	96408	96889	98005	96854	35
40	95660	95731	95785	96285	96019	95992	95763	95770	95733	96452	95819	96206	96621	95856	96367	97485	96367	40
45	94677	94780	94811	95722	95263	95032	94782	94821	94762	95461	94857	95315	95718	94914	95460	96577	95496	45
50	93142	93273	93291	94850	94135	93532	93246	93370	93227	93913	93349	93878	94293	93422	94004	95111	94087	50
55	90799	90967	90964	93431	91234	90903	91142	90900	90882	91551	91029	91666	92176	91132	91758	92853	91898	55
60	87174	87381	87360	91127	90080	87702	87281	87723	87254	87896	87427	88168	88817	87568	88287	89360	88424	60
65	81373	81631	81597	86993	86476	82133	81482	82301	81447	82047	81640	82470	83416	81856	82806	83852	82741	65
70	72190	72532	72454	79662	81152	73317	72313	73668	72256	72788	72468	73410	74742	72797	74127	75125	73692	70
75	58099	58524	58370	67022	73277	59845	58346	60141	58152	58580	58376	59387	61288	58797	60775	61701	59670	75
80	39789	40195	40033	48567	62660	42188	39944	41769	39825	40119	40031	41240	43512	40442	43086	43902	41492	80
85+	20639	20951	20803	26895	49094	23067	20755	21991	20658	20810	20793	21938	24353	21118	23757	24401	22102	85+

ADDED YRS OF LIFE

	No Causes	(1)	(2)	(3)	(4)	(5)	(6)	(7)	(8)	(9)	(10)	(11)	(12)	(1)+(2)	(1)+(2)+(5)+(6)+(8)	(1)+(2)+(5)+(6)+(8)+part of (9)&(12)	(10)+(11)
TOTAL		.135	.143	2.657	9.094	.812	.102	.517	.038	.609	.150	.694	1.648	.279	1.249	2.204	.847
WORK	1.842	.044	.018	.647	.460	.043	.003	.098	.028	.000	.049	.204	.188	.062	.137	.154	.253

POPULATION, DEATHS, DEATH RATES FOR ALL CAUSES COMBINED, AND SPECIFIED CAUSES

Age Start of Interval	Midyear Population	Deaths During Year	All Causes	Respiratory T. B.	Other Infec. and Paras.	Neoplasms	Cardiovascular	Infl., Pneu., Bronch.	Diarrheal	Certain Degenerative	Maternal	Cert. Dis. of Infancy	Motor Vehicle	Other Violence	Other and Unknown	Age Start of Interval
0	39990	3495	.08740	.00013	.00558	.00008	.00040	.02231	.01235	.00020	.00000	.02343	.00000	.00103	.02191	0
1	134036	744	.00555	.00009	.00210	.00006	.00011	.00143	.00028	.00012	.00000	.00000	.00000	.00049	.00087	1
5	170897	330	.00193	.00010	.00054	.00002	.00015	.00009	.00006	.00004	.00000	.00000	.00000	.00022	.00032	5
10	171380	249	.00145	.00012	.00054	.00001	.00016	.00005	.00005	.00005	.00000	.00000	.00000	.00018	.00030	10
15	157221	378	.00240	.00058	.00050	.00004	.00017	.00016	.00009	.00013	.00000	.00000	.00000	.00042	.00032	15
20	138216	483	.00349	.00101	.00056	.00009	.00024	.00025	.00009	.00021	.00000	.00000	.00000	.00062	.00041	20
25	115617	396	.00331	.00108	.00043	.00016	.00015	.00021	.00013	.00014	.00000	.00000	.00000	.00063	.00038	25
30	109798	405	.00369	.00113	.00038	.00026	.00022	.00027	.00015	.00018	.00000	.00000	.00000	.00064	.00046	30
35	102533	395	.00385	.00082	.00039	.00031	.00037	.00042	.00015	.00028	.00000	.00000	.00000	.00050	.00060	35
40	94215	469	.00498	.00075	.00044	.00064	.00071	.00057	.00017	.00039	.00000	.00000	.00000	.00049	.00082	40
45	80671	568	.00704	.00092	.00058	.00124	.00121	.00076	.00020	.00050	.00000	.00000	.00000	.00060	.00104	45
50	68974	719	.01042	.00096	.00067	.00225	.00223	.00104	.00022	.00072	.00000	.00000	.00000	.00070	.00164	50
55	57626	819	.01421	.00085	.00064	.00368	.00352	.00120	.00021	.00115	.00000	.00000	.00000	.00083	.00213	55
60	52434	1169	.02229	.00092	.00065	.00555	.00601	.00208	.00023	.00153	.00000	.00000	.00000	.00097	.00437	60
65	40906	1368	.03344	.00130	.00061	.00819	.01007	.00364	.00032	.00196	.00000	.00000	.00000	.00108	.00628	65
70	29494	1694	.05744	.00129	.00061	.01071	.01549	.00658	.00037	.00227	.00000	.00000	.00000	.00136	.01875	70
75	18855	1578	.08369	.00074	.00064	.01236	.02111	.01024	.00048	.00223	.00000	.00000	.00000	.00133	.03458	75
80	9281	1474	.15882	.00043	.00054	.01411	.02931	.01746	.00043	.00215	.00000	.00000	.00000	.00280	.09158	80
85+	3735	1039	.27818	.00054	.00054	.01339	.03534	.02624	.00027	.00161	.00000	.00000	.00000	.00616	.19411	85+
ALL	1599879	17772														

	All Causes	Respiratory T. B.	Other Infec. and Paras.	Neoplasms	Cardiovascular	Infl., Pneu., Bronch.	Diarrheal	Certain Degenerative	Maternal	Cert. Dis. of Infancy	Motor Vehicle	Other Violence	Other and Unknown
CRUDE DEATH RATE	.01111	.00065	.00082	.00125	.00171	.00152	.00046	.00040	.00000	.00059	.00000	.00058	.00314
STANDARDIZED RATE (1)	.00959	.00059	.00093	.00084	.00112	.00151	.00058	.00031	.00000	.00082	.00000	.00053	.00234
STANDARDIZED RATE (2)	.01353	.00069	.00079	.00168	.00235	.00172	.00042	.00049	.00000	.00049	.00000	.00063	.00428
GEOMETRIC MEAN	.01223												

LIFE TABLE FOR ALL CAUSES COMBINED

Age (x)	Midyear Population	Deaths During Year	$_nM_x$	$_nq_x$	l_x	$_nd_x$	$_nL_x$	$_nm_x$	$_na_x$	T_x	$_nr_x$	$\overset{\circ}{e}_x$	Age (x)
0	39990	3495	.087397	.081810	100000	8181	93607	.087397	.218575	6093261	.000000	60.933	0
1	134036	744	.005551	.021902	91819	2011	362249	.005551	1.500000	5999654	.000000	65.342	1
5	170897	330	.001931	.009598	89808	862	446885	.001929	2.500000	5637406	.000000	62.772	5
10	171380	249	.001453	.007240	88946	644	443161	.001453	2.563729	5190521	.003022	58.356	10
15	157221	378	.002404	.011953	88302	1059	439044	.002412	2.670955	4747359	.014312	53.763	15
20	138216	483	.003495	.017342	87243	1513	432505	.003498	2.548056	4308316	.022351	49.383	20
25	115617	396	.003311	.016424	85730	1408	425136	.003312	2.504291	3875811	.021499	45.210	25
30	109798	405	.003689	.018287	84322	1542	417791	.003691	2.523373	3450675	.014422	40.923	30
35	102533	395	.003852	.019099	82780	1581	410043	.003856	2.560484	3032884	.010839	36.638	35
40	94215	469	.004978	.024643	81199	2001	401236	.004987	2.621918	2622841	.016158	32.301	40
45	80671	568	.007041	.034748	79198	2752	389506	.007065	2.643835	2221604	.021813	28.051	45
50	68974	719	.010424	.051029	76446	3901	372946	.010460	2.620055	1832098	.024702	23.966	50
55	57626	819	.014212	.068923	72545	5000	350905	.014249	2.635958	1459152	.015768	20.114	55
60	52434	1169	.022295	.106063	67545	7164	320729	.022337	2.627547	1108248	.010740	16.408	60
65	40906	1368	.033443	.155446	60381	9386	279634	.033565	2.627162	787519	.019470	13.042	65
70	29494	1694	.057435	.252829	50995	12893	223547	.057675	2.562421	507885	.019650	9.960	70
75	18855	1578	.083691	.347725	38102	13249	157641	.084046	2.519105	284338	.022472	7.463	75
80	9281	1474	.158819	.567658	24853	14108	88071	.160188	2.434523	126697	.022472	5.098	80
85+	3735	1039	.278179	1.000000	10745	10745	38626	.278179	3.594803	38626	.000000	3.595	85+

NUMBER OF PERSONS DYING (OUT OF 100,000 AT BIRTH) ABOVE AGE X FROM SPECIFIED CAUSES

Age (x)	All Causes	Respiratory T. B.	Other Infec. and Paras.	Neo-plasms	Cardio-vascular	Infl., Pneu., Bronch.	Diar-rheal	Certain Degen-erative	Maternal	Cert. Dis. of Infancy	Motor Vehicle	Other Violence	Other and Unknown	Age (x)
0	100000	4547	4466	13497	19078	11913	2238	3684	0	2193	0	4238	34146	0
1	91819	4535	3944	13490	19040	9825	1082	3665	0	0	0	4142	32096	1
5	89808	4502	3184	13468	19000	9307	982	3622	0	0	0	3964	31779	5
10	88946	4458	2766	13458	18935	9265	956	3604	0	0	0	3867	31637	10
15	88302	4404	2528	13452	18865	9244	933	3581	0	0	0	3789	31506	15
20	87243	4148	2311	13433	18792	9174	894	3525	0	0	0	3604	31362	20
25	85730	3712	2067	13392	18689	9064	853	3434	0	0	0	3335	31184	25
30	84322	3253	1886	13324	18625	8975	796	3373	0	0	0	3068	31022	30
35	82780	2782	1726	13217	18533	8861	731	3297	0	0	0	2802	30831	35
40	81199	2442	1566	13089	18381	8689	671	3181	0	0	0	2598	30582	40
45	79198	2140	1391	12832	18094	8458	603	3023	0	0	0	2402	30255	45
50	76446	1782	1164	12347	17619	8163	526	2829	0	0	0	2170	29846	50
55	72545	1425	915	11504	16782	7773	444	2558	0	0	0	1910	29234	55
60	67545	1127	690	10209	15541	7352	371	2155	0	0	0	1618	28482	60
65	60381	833	482	8426	13610	6683	298	1665	0	0	0	1305	27079	65
70	50995	470	311	6131	10784	5660	209	1117	0	0	0	1004	25309	70
75	38102	183	174	3730	7308	4183	125	609	0	0	0	701	21089	75
80	24853	66	74	1780	3971	2563	50	258	0	0	0	491	15600	80
85+	10745	21	21	517	1365	1013	10	62	0	0	0	238	7498	85+

NUMBER OF PERSONS SURVIVING TO AGE X IF SPECIFIED CAUSES WERE ELIMINATED

Age (x)	No Causes	Respiratory T. B. (1)	Other Infec. and Paras. (2)	Neo-plasms (3)	Cardio-vascular (4)	Infl., Pneu., Bronch. (5)	Diar-rheal (6)	Certain Degener-ative (7)	Maternal (8)	Cert. Dis. of Infancy (9)	Motor Vehicle (10)	Other Violence (11)	Other and Unknown (12)	(1) + (2)	(1) + (2) + (5) + (6) + (8)	(1)+(2)+ (5)+(6)+ (8)+part of(9)&(12)	(10) + (11)	Age (x)
0	100000	100000	100000	100000	100000	100000	100000	100000	100000	100000	100000	100000	100000	100000	100000	100000	100000	0
1	91819	91830	92320	91826	91855	93841	92933	91837	91819	93944	91819	91911	93804	92332	95510	99654	91911	1
5	89808	89852	91057	89836	89883	92311	90958	89868	89808	91886	89808	90074	92070	91102	94881	99286	90074	5
10	88946	89033	90606	88984	89085	91468	90151	89024	88946	91004	88946	89307	91332	90695	94530	99033	89307	10
15	88302	88443	90192	88346	88510	90827	89521	88402	88302	90346	88302	88738	90804	90335	94202	98785	88738	15
20	87243	87637	89331	87305	87521	89809	88487	87398	87243	89262	87243	87859	89863	89734	93691	98353	87859	20
25	85730	86553	88030	85832	86106	88364	86993	85972	85730	87714	85730	86604	88486	88874	92955	97705	86604	25
30	84322	85592	86768	84490	84756	87004	85622	84621	84322	86273	84322	85450	87199	88075	92278	97110	85450	30
35	82780	84502	85345	83051	83297	85530	84122	83149	82780	84696	82780	84155	85800	87120	91473	96394	84155	35
40	81199	83232	83878	81592	81858	84072	82576	81677	81199	83078	81199	82753	84418	85978	90530	95561	82753	40
45	79198	81487	81990	79837	80127	82237	80609	79821	79198	81031	79198	80911	82674	84360	89157	94290	80911	45
50	76446	79018	79372	77545	77817	79681	77885	77240	76446	78215	76446	78333	80221	82042	87124	92337	78333	50
55	72545	75345	75574	74426	74681	76012	73992	73565	72545	74224	72545	74595	76756	78491	83882	89140	74595	55
60	67545	70451	70591	70591	70778	71199	68964	68890	67545	69108	67545	69744	72238	73628	79241	84426	69744	60
65	60381	63268	63309	64889	65214	64319	61720	62057	60381	61778	60381	62652	66011	66336	72229	77320	62652	65
70	50995	53782	53631	57108	57949	55331	52209	52928	50995	52175	50995	53199	57565	56563	62833	67730	53199	70
75	38102	40443	40195	45035	46829	42746	39083	39999	38102	38984	38102	40020	47347	42664	49096	54100	40020	75
80	24853	26476	26301	31259	33994	29375	25554	26382	24853	25428	24853	26280	36926	28019	34051	39214	26280	80
85+	10745	11477	11407	14568	17159	13926	11074	11540	10745	10994	10745	11534	25840	12184	16275	21460	11534	85+

ADDED YRS OF LIFE																		
TOTAL		1.385	1.946	1.860	2.502	2.856	1.052	.685	.000	1.405	.000	1.177	6.705	3.390	7.695	12.361	1.177	
WORK	5.156	.966	.519	.533	.590	.411	.145	.299	.000	.000	.000	.611	.672	1.500	2.087	2.432	.611	

POPULATION, DEATHS, DEATH RATES FOR ALL CAUSES COMBINED, AND SPECIFIED CAUSES

Age Start of Interval	Midyear Population	Deaths During Year	All Causes	Respiratory T. B.	Other Infec. and Paras.	Neoplasms	Cardiovascular	Infl., Pneu., Bronch.	Diarrheal	Certain Degenerative	Maternal	Cert. Dis. of Infancy	Motor Vehicle	Other Violence	Other and Unknown	Age Start of Interval
0	38876	2597	.06680	.00010	.00499	.00005	.00033	.01860	.00857	.00021	.00000	.01775	.00000	.00087	.01533	0
1	131232	576	.00439	.00005	.00169	.00005	.00004	.00121	.00022	.00008	.00000	.00000	.00000	.00037	.00068	1
5	168374	303	.00180	.00012	.00093	.00001	.00014	.00014	.00007	.00007	.00000	.00000	.00000	.00006	.00027	5
10	169074	274	.00162	.00035	.00063	.00001	.00017	.00009	.00003	.00011	.00000	.00000	.00000	.00004	.00019	10
15	157095	373	.00237	.00056	.00048	.00003	.00022	.00013	.00006	.00015	.00003	.00000	.00000	.00012	.00019	15
20	148820	457	.00307	.00132	.00041	.00005	.00022	.00013	.00003	.00018	.00015	.00000	.00000	.00011	.00042	20
25	131235	442	.00337	.00123	.00034	.00010	.00025	.00023	.00006	.00023	.00023	.00000	.00000	.00007	.00063	25
30	119946	480	.00400	.00124	.00031	.00026	.00034	.00029	.00008	.00028	.00029	.00000	.00000	.00008	.00084	30
35	110343	527	.00478	.00115	.00036	.00055	.00050	.00033	.00010	.00027	.00034	.00000	.00000	.00015	.00100	35
40	99920	557	.00557	.00109	.00040	.00107	.00084	.00043	.00011	.00035	.00029	.00000	.00000	.00018	.00121	40
45	84858	614	.00724	.00101	.00047	.00173	.00125	.00053	.00013	.00051	.00004	.00000	.00000	.00020	.00137	45
50	75814	764	.01008	.00055	.00053	.00264	.00230	.00084	.00016	.00070	.00000	.00000	.00000	.00025	.00171	50
55	64773	861	.01329	.00068	.00049	.00375	.00374	.00124	.00015	.00100	.00000	.00000	.00000	.00026	.00178	55
60	60577	1268	.02093	.00086	.00056	.00528	.00667	.00239	.00021	.00127	.00000	.00000	.00000	.00036	.00332	60
65	46851	1498	.03197	.00094	.00075	.00749	.01178	.00450	.00032	.00143	.00000	.00000	.00000	.00049	.00427	65
70	35088	1938	.05523	.00088	.00077	.00975	.01841	.00778	.00046	.00174	.00000	.00000	.00000	.00083	.01462	70
75	22573	1870	.08284	.00075	.00053	.01170	.02605	.01174	.00053	.00226	.00000	.00000	.00000	.00128	.02800	75
80	12026	1829	.15209	.00050	.00042	.01397	.03426	.01821	.00075	.00233	.00000	.00000	.00000	.00258	.07908	80
85+	5818	1488	.25576	.00034	.00052	.01392	.03541	.02458	.00086	.00155	.00000	.00000	.00000	.00481	.17377	85+
ALL	1683293	18756														

CRUDE DEATH RATE			.01114	.00080	.00072	.00140	.00219	.00152	.00032	.00040	.00010	.00041	.00000	.00024	.00305	
STANDARDIZED RATE (1)			.00866	.00073	.00083	.00087	.00128	.00137	.00041	.00030	.00009	.00062	.00000	.00021	.00196	
STANDARDIZED RATE (2)			.01274	.00081	.00071	.00169	.00269	.00170	.00031	.00046	.00009	.00037	.00000	.00027	.00365	
GEOMETRIC MEAN			.01193													

LIFE TABLE FOR ALL CAUSES COMBINED

Age (x)	Midyear Population	Deaths During Year	$_nM_x$	$_nq_x$	l_x	$_nd_x$	$_nL_x$	$_nm_x$	$_na_x$	T_x	$_nr_x$	$\overset{\circ}{e}_x$	Age (x)
0	38876	2597	.06680	.063350	100000	6335	94828	.066805	.183564	6250710	.000000	62.507	0
1	131232	576	.004389	.017360	93665	1626	370595	.004388	1.500000	6155882	.000000	65.722	1
5	168374	303	.001800	.008964	92039	825	458133	.001801	2.500000	5785287	.000000	62.857	5
10	169074	274	.001621	.008069	91214	736	454281	.001620	2.569067	5327154	.003108	58.403	10
15	157095	373	.002374	.011815	90478	1069	449848	.002376	2.622389	4872874	.008049	53.857	15
20	148820	457	.003071	.015256	89409	1364	443719	.003074	2.561553	4423025	.012636	49.470	20
25	131235	442	.003368	.016719	88045	1472	436619	.003371	2.549960	3979306	.017640	45.196	25
30	119946	480	.004002	.019833	86573	1717	428684	.004005	2.564672	3542688	.014601	40.921	30
35	110343	527	.004776	.023628	84856	2005	419419	.004780	2.575540	3114004	.012455	36.698	35
40	99920	557	.005975	.029499	82851	2444	408324	.005985	2.573309	2694585	.018487	32.523	40
45	84858	614	.007236	.035631	80407	2865	395160	.007250	2.600349	2286261	.019877	28.434	45
50	75814	764	.010077	.049315	77542	3824	378544	.010102	2.603132	1891101	.019204	24.388	50
55	64773	861	.013293	.064543	73718	4758	357333	.013315	2.634160	1512557	.010726	20.518	55
60	60577	1268	.020932	.099884	68960	6888	328517	.020967	2.636046	1155223	.009228	16.752	60
65	46851	1498	.031974	.149117	62072	9256	288474	.032086	2.635430	826706	.018198	13.319	65
70	35088	1938	.055233	.244339	52816	12905	232755	.055445	2.572614	538233	.017924	10.191	70
75	22573	1870	.082842	.344617	39911	13754	165475	.083118	2.522175	305478	.016995	7.654	75
80	12026	1829	.152087	.549337	26157	14369	93913	.153004	2.433900	140003	.016995	5.352	80
85+	5818	1488	.255758	1.000000	11788	11788	46090	.255758	3.909946	46090	.000000	3.910	85+

NUMBER OF PERSONS DYING (OUT OF 100,000 AT BIRTH) ABOVE AGE X FROM SPECIFIED CAUSES

Age (x)	All Causes	Respiratory T.B.	Other Infec. and Paras.	Neo-plasms	Cardio-vascular	Infl., Pneu., Bronch.	Diar-rheal	Certain Degen-erative	Maternal	Cert. Dis. of Infancy	Motor Vehicle	Other Violence	Other and Unknown	Age (x)
0	100000	5288	4100	14040	22996	12660	1762	3483	579	1683	0	1971	31438	0
1	93665	5278	3627	14035	22964	10896	950	3464	579	0	0	1888	29984	1
5	92039	5261	3000	14018	22550	10448	868	3433	579	0	0	1750	29732	5
10	91214	5207	2575	14013	22887	10382	838	3400	579	0	0	1723	29610	10
15	90478	5045	2290	14007	22812	10339	824	3352	579	0	0	1704	29526	15
20	89409	4612	2073	13996	22712	10282	796	3286	564	0	0	1649	29439	20
25	88045	4027	1891	13957	22613	10222	781	3205	498	0	0	1599	29252	25
30	86573	3488	1745	13913	22503	10122	754	3105	398	0	0	1569	28976	30
35	84856	2956	1613	13802	22356	9997	722	2987	273	0	0	1536	28614	35
40	82851	2473	1461	13554	22147	9860	680	2873	132	0	0	1476	28195	40
45	80407	2028	1297	13115	21802	9684	635	2730	14	0	0	1402	27700	45
50	77542	1628	1111	12428	21307	9474	584	2529	1	0	0	1323	27157	50
55	73718	1269	911	11426	20434	9153	524	2264	1	0	0	1228	26508	55
60	68960	954	734	10084	19096	8711	469	1905	1	0	0	1134	25872	60
65	62072	672	550	8346	16900	7922	398	1487	1	0	0	1014	24782	65
70	52816	401	334	6180	13489	6618	305	1074	1	0	0	872	23542	70
75	39911	196	155	3907	9190	4800	199	668	1	0	0	679	20116	75
80	26157	71	67	1969	4870	2852	111	294	1	0	0	466	15456	80
85+	11788	16	24	642	1632	1133	40	71	0	0	0	222	8008	85+

NUMBER OF PERSONS SURVIVING TO AGE X IF SPECIFIED CAUSES WERE ELIMINATED

Age (x)	No Causes	Respiratory T.B. (1)	Other Infec. and Paras. (2)	Neo-plasms (3)	Cardio-vascular (4)	Infl., Pneu., Bronch. (5)	Diar-rheal (6)	Certain Degen-erative (7)	Maternal (8)	Cert. Dis. of Infancy (9)	Motor Vehicle (10)	Other Violence (11)	Other and Unknown (12)	(1)+(2)	(1)+(2)+(5)+(6)+(8)	(1)+(2)+(5)+(6)+(8)+part of(9)&(12)	(10)+(11)	Age (x)
0	100000	100000	100000	100000	100000	100000	100000	100000	100000	100000	100000	100000	100000	100000	100000	100000	100000	0
1	93665	93675	94124	93670	93696	95388	94454	93683	93665	95308	93665	93745	95083	94134	96672	99716	93745	1
5	92039	92065	93117	92061	92083	94185	92856	92088	92039	95255	92039	92255	93686	93143	96203	99462	92255	5
10	91214	91294	92711	91240	91321	93408	92054	91295	91214	92814	91214	91455	92970	92792	95941	99299	91455	10
15	90478	90719	92252	90510	90659	92658	91365	90606	90478	92065	90478	90736	92305	92497	95696	99117	90736	15
20	89409	90080	91382	89452	89687	91661	90313	89602	89424	90977	89409	89719	91303	92067	95357	98839	89719	20
25	88045	89292	90173	88126	88417	90324	88951	88315	88125	89589	88045	88400	90100	91450	94868	98492	88400	25
30	86573	88343	88813	86696	87049	88915	87491	86938	86751	88091	86573	86952	88874	90629	94262	98098	86952	30
35	84856	87130	87186	85087	85469	87279	85787	85331	85155	86344	84856	85260	87480	89522	93417	97507	85260	35
40	82851	85562	85280	83323	83658	85356	83802	83429	83283	84304	82851	83305	85841	88071	92254	96583	83305	40
45	80407	83492	82931	81301	81534	83017	81375	81110	80943	81817	80407	80921	83815	86113	90578	95108	80921	45
50	77542	80926	80165	79090	79124	80272	78526	78419	78071	78902	77542	78116	81386	83663	88307	92959	78116	50
55	73718	77300	76413	76193	76096	76639	74713	74813	74221	75011	73718	74357	78039	80126	85001	89707	74357	55
60	68960	72630	71658	72629	72534	72138	69945	70338	69431	70169	68960	69694	73656	75472	80625	85270	69694	60
65	62072	65657	64682	67132	67519	65722	63027	63717	62496	63161	62072	62807	67412	68418	74057	78622	62807	65
70	52816	56130	55244	59315	60973	57209	53715	54606	53176	53742	52816	53574	58623	58710	65117	69487	53574	70
75	39911	42602	41906	47076	50572	44970	40683	41627	40183	40611	39911	40654	47745	44731	51728	56215	40654	75
80	26157	28026	27537	32726	37818	31284	26735	27594	26336	26616	26157	26819	36165	29504	36313	40903	26819	80
85+	11788	12669	12439	15875	20397	15509	12096	12590	11869	11995	11788	12251	24635	13369	18172	22913	12251	85+

ADDED YRS OF LIFE

	No Causes	(1)	(2)	(3)	(4)	(5)	(6)	(7)	(8)	(9)	(10)	(11)	(12)	(1)+(2)	(1)+(2)+(5)+(6)+(8)	(1)+(2)+(5)+(6)+(8)+part of(9)&(12)	(10)+(11)
TOTAL		1.772	1.778	2.057	3.079	2.756	.759	.697	.219	1.093	.000	.439	6.039	3.616	7.718	11.743	.439
WORK	5.280	1.223	.434	.645	.674	.338	.084	.312	.180	.000	.000	.138	.831	1.673	2.313	2.803	.138

POPULATION, DEATHS, DEATH RATES FOR ALL CAUSES COMBINED, AND SPECIFIED CAUSES

Age Start of Interval	Midyear Population	Deaths During Year	All Causes	Respiratory T. B.	Other Infec. and Paras.	Neoplasms	Cardio-vascular	Infl., Pneu., Bronch.	Diarrheal	Certain Degenerative	Maternal	Cert. Dis. of Infancy	Motor Vehicle	Other Violence	Other and Unknown	Age Start of Interval
0	31364	2978	.09495	.00019	.00740	.00026	.00010	.02854	.01059	.00010	.00000	.03450	.00000	.00108	.01221	0
1	125714	594	.00473	.00006	.00147	.00009	.00010	.00111	.00025	.00004	.00000	.00000	.00000	.00067	.00094	1
5	168815	263	.00156	.00007	.00052	.00008	.00012	.00010	.00008	.00006	.00000	.00000	.00000	.00035	.00018	5
10	165511	185	.00112	.00010	.00025	.00006	.00014	.00005	.00008	.00004	.00000	.00000	.00000	.00021	.00019	10
15	163732	351	.00214	.00043	.00035	.00004	.00014	.00016	.00012	.00009	.00000	.00000	.00000	.00057	.00019	15
20	155789	522	.00335	.00096	.00031	.00013	.00018	.00024	.00012	.00011	.00000	.00000	.00000	.00093	.00024	20
25	140287	369	.00263	.00070	.00024	.00016	.00021	.00014	.00014	.00009	.00000	.00000	.00000	.00064	.00031	25
30	129165	376	.00291	.00067	.00022	.00024	.00029	.00018	.00014	.00015	.00000	.00000	.00000	.00061	.00040	30
35	114598	404	.00353	.00058	.00027	.00031	.00038	.00031	.00010	.00031	.00000	.00000	.00000	.00063	.00062	35
40	104437	487	.00466	.00055	.00031	.00058	.00070	.00044	.00011	.00044	.00000	.00000	.00000	.00069	.00085	40
45	95887	584	.00609	.00055	.00039	.00099	.00117	.00051	.00018	.00047	.00000	.00000	.00000	.00083	.00100	45
50	86975	805	.00926	.00059	.00044	.00182	.00217	.00079	.00022	.00068	.00000	.00000	.00000	.00094	.00161	50
55	72107	981	.01360	.00067	.00047	.00302	.00355	.00115	.00019	.00115	.00000	.00000	.00000	.00103	.00237	55
60	58519	1347	.02302	.00073	.00056	.00530	.00646	.00219	.00026	.00159	.00000	.00000	.00000	.00114	.00478	60
65	44928	1590	.03539	.00080	.00078	.00908	.01082	.00361	.00038	.00203	.00000	.00000	.00000	.00111	.00679	65
70	35770	2100	.05871	.00073	.00078	.01233	.01683	.00665	.00050	.00238	.00000	.00000	.00000	.00145	.01705	70
75	22291	1936	.08685	.00036	.00045	.01462	.02490	.01122	.00054	.00256	.00000	.00000	.00000	.00220	.03001	75
80	10764	1679	.15598	.00009	.00037	.01607	.03298	.01914	.00074	.00223	.00000	.00000	.00000	.00307	.08129	80
85+	4518	1100	.24347	.00000	.00089	.01239	.03232	.02678	.00111	.00066	.00000	.00000	.00000	.00354	.16578	85+
ALL	1731171	18651														

	All Causes	Respiratory T. B.	Other Infec. and Paras.	Neoplasms	Cardio-vascular	Infl., Pneu., Bronch.	Diarrheal	Certain Degenerative	Maternal	Cert. Dis. of Infancy	Motor Vehicle	Other Violence	Other and Unknown
CRUDE DEATH RATE	.01077	.00048	.00058	.00139	.00195	.00148	.00035	.00041	.00000	.00063	.00000	.00073	.00278
STANDARDIZED RATE (1)	.00944	.00042	.00074	.00087	.00118	.00166	.00052	.00029	.00000	.00121	.00000	.00067	.00188
STANDARDIZED RATE (2)	.01326	.00048	.00061	.00175	.00251	.00182	.00039	.00048	.00000	.00071	.00000	.00077	.00374
GEOMETRIC MEAN	.01122												

LIFE TABLE FOR ALL CAUSES COMBINED

Age (x)	Midyear Population	Deaths During Year	$_nM_x$	$_nq_x$	l_x	$_nd_x$	$_nL_x$	$_nm_x$	$_na_x$	T_x	$_nr_x$	$\overset{\circ}{e}_x$	Age (x)
0	31364	2978	.094950	.088490	100000	8849	93199	.094948	.231414	6144206	.000000	61.442	0
1	125714	594	.004725	.018683	91151	1703	360347	.004726	1.500000	6051007	.000000	66.384	1
5	168815	263	.001558	.007759	89448	694	445505	.001558	2.500000	5690660	.000000	63.620	5
10	165511	185	.001118	.005577	88754	495	442584	.001118	2.603956	5245155	.001168	59.098	10
15	163732	351	.002144	.010662	88259	941	439142	.002143	2.711876	4802571	.001808	54.415	15
20	155789	522	.003351	.016629	87318	1452	432997	.003353	2.525826	4363429	.009464	49.972	20
25	140287	369	.002630	.013055	85866	1121	426480	.002628	2.457999	3930432	.014169	45.774	25
30	129165	376	.002911	.014467	84745	1226	420731	.002914	2.557946	3503951	.016332	41.347	30
35	114598	404	.003525	.017505	83519	1462	414079	.003531	2.595332	3083220	.018017	36.916	35
40	104437	487	.004663	.023094	82057	1895	405745	.004670	2.604332	2669141	.014753	32.528	40
45	95887	584	.006091	.030077	80162	2411	395123	.006102	2.641366	2263396	.011481	28.235	45
50	86975	805	.009256	.045414	77751	3531	380449	.009281	2.647680	1868273	.016355	24.029	50
55	72107	981	.013605	.066209	74220	4914	359663	.013663	2.672594	1487824	.022788	20.046	55
60	58519	1347	.023018	.109667	69306	7602	328605	.023134	2.642040	1128160	.025672	16.278	60
65	44928	1590	.035390	.163636	61704	10097	284459	.035496	2.616970	799556	.015619	12.958	65
70	35770	2100	.058708	.257155	51607	13271	225615	.058821	2.557095	515097	.009467	9.981	70
75	22291	1936	.086851	.358253	38336	13734	157445	.087230	2.507312	289482	.022854	7.551	75
80	10764	1679	.155983	.559020	24602	13753	87477	.157219	2.416321	132036	.022854	5.367	80
85+	4518	1100	.243471	1.000000	10849	10849	44560	.243471	4.107273	44560	.000000	4.107	85+

NUMBER OF PERSONS DYING (OUT OF 100,000 AT BIRTH) ABOVE AGE X FROM SPECIFIED CAUSES

Age (x)	All Causes	Respiratory T. B.	Other Infec. and Paras.	Neo-plasms	Cardio-vascular	Infl., Pneu., Bronch.	Diar-rheal	Certain Degen-erative	Maternal	Cert. Dis. of Infancy	Motor Vehicle	Other Violence	Other and Unknown	Age (x)
0	100000	3147	3495	14316	20841	12575	2186	3698	0	3215	0	5176	31351	0
1	91151	3129	2805	14292	20832	9915	1159	3689	0	0	0	5075	30215	1
5	89448	3106	2275	14260	20794	9517	1110	3675	0	0	0	4834	29877	5
10	88754	3077	2045	14223	20739	9472	1076	3648	0	0	0	4679	29795	10
15	88259	3034	1936	14197	20677	9448	1039	3632	0	0	0	4585	29711	15
20	87318	2846	1780	14178	20616	9378	985	3592	0	0	0	4335	29608	20
25	85866	2429	1647	14122	20538	9275	932	3545	0	0	0	3932	29446	25
30	84745	2131	1547	14055	20450	9215	871	3505	0	0	0	3659	29312	30
35	83519	1848	1455	13954	20326	9139	813	3440	0	0	0	3402	29142	35
40	82057	1606	1343	13823	20166	9009	773	3309	0	0	0	3142	28886	40
45	80162	1385	1219	13586	19881	8830	730	3130	0	0	0	2862	28539	45
50	77751	1166	1066	13193	19419	8628	660	2945	0	0	0	2532	28142	50
55	74220	943	900	12499	18589	8325	577	2686	0	0	0	2173	27528	55
60	69306	704	730	11406	17305	7909	507	2270	0	0	0	1803	26672	60
65	61704	462	544	9655	15170	7186	422	1746	0	0	0	1427	25092	65
70	51607	234	322	7066	12084	6157	315	1169	0	0	0	1110	23150	70
75	38336	70	146	4281	8280	4652	201	633	0	0	0	782	19291	75
80	24602	14	76	1975	4347	2878	116	230	0	0	0	434	14532	80
85+	10849	0	39	552	1440	1193	49	30	0	0	0	158	7388	85+

NUMBER OF PERSONS SURVIVING TO AGE X IF SPECIFIED CAUSES WERE ELIMINATED

Age (x)	No Causes	Respiratory T. B. (1)	Other Infec. and Paras. (2)	Neo-plasms (3)	Cardio-vascular (4)	Infl., Pneu., Bronch. (5)	Diar-rheal (6)	Certain Degener-ative (7)	Maternal (8)	Cert. Dis. of Infancy (9)	Motor Vehicle (10)	Other Violence (11)	Other and Unknown (12)	(1) + (2)	(1) + (2) + (5) + (6) + (8)	(1)+(2)+ (5)+(6)+ (8)+part of(9)&(12)	(10) + (11)	Age (x)
0	100000	100000	100000	100000	100000	100000	100000	100000	100000	100000	100000	100000	100000	100000	100000	100000	100000	0
1	91151	91168	91812	91174	91160	93725	92058	91160	91151	94272	91151	91247	92242	91829	95404	99706	91247	1
5	89448	89488	90627	89502	89494	92381	90466	89470	89448	92510	89448	89782	90858	90667	94706	99259	89782	5
10	88754	88822	90156	88845	88855	91710	89799	88803	88754	91793	88754	89240	90236	90226	94328	98914	89240	10
15	88259	88370	89764	88375	88421	91223	89335	88324	88259	91281	88259	88837	89818	89877	94028	98647	88837	15
20	87318	87615	88965	87452	87539	90323	88437	87422	87318	90307	87318	88141	88964	89267	93523	98182	88141	20
25	85866	86574	87620	86053	86161	88926	87020	86015	85866	88806	85866	87079	87649	88342	92720	97439	87079	25
30	84745	85743	86577	84997	85124	87827	85945	84932	84745	87646	84745	86218	86641	87597	92068	96834	86218	30
35	83519	84787	85418	83868	84016	86635	84760	83768	83519	86378	83519	85230	85560	86715	91287	96106	85230	35
40	82057	83547	84036	82530	82705	85252	83317	82432	82057	84866	82057	84002	84323	85562	90258	95150	84002	40
45	80162	81840	82221	80860	81080	83467	81436	80706	80162	82906	80162	82346	82728	83942	88792	93752	82346	45
50	77751	79599	79903	78820	79103	81164	79056	78462	77751	80413	77751	80203	80645	81802	86827	91824	80203	50
55	74220	76207	76441	75931	76341	77788	75549	75155	74220	76761	74220	76923	77607	78487	83733	88742	76923	55
60	69306	71398	71549	71593	72574	73060	70615	70587	69306	71679	69306	72201	73339	73709	79170	84127	72201	60
65	61704	63801	63882	65836	66758	65770	62951	63349	61704	63816	61704	64650	66891	66053	71829	76706	64650	65
70	51607	53576	53638	57641	58967	56019	52750	53524	51607	53374	51607	54374	57909	55684	61783	66423	54374	70
75	38336	39942	40000	45560	47655	43043	35284	40237	38336	35648	38336	40688	46923	41676	47951	52494	40688	75
80	24602	25677	25726	31473	34734	29253	25279	26155	24602	25444	24602	26406	35169	26850	32804	37172	26406	80
85+	10849	11332	11370	15106	18211	14261	11192	11672	10849	11220	10849	11837	23729	11876	16105	20494	11837	85+

ADDED YRS OF LIFE																		
TOTAL		1.001	1.498	1.934	2.719	3.176	.965	.643	.000	2.096	.000	1.512	5.863	2.531	6.959	11.561	1.512	
WORK	4.645	.706	.334	.480	.603	.334	.146	.270	.000	.000	.000	.784	.649	1.047	1.545	1.810	.784	

POPULATION, DEATHS, DEATH RATES FOR ALL CAUSES COMBINED, AND SPECIFIED CAUSES

Age Start of Interval	Midyear Population	Deaths During Year	All Causes	Respiratory T. B.	Other Infec. and Paras.	Neoplasms	Cardiovascular	Infl., Pneu., Bronch.	Diarrheal	Certain Degenerative	Maternal	Cert. Dis. of Infancy	Motor Vehicle	Other Violence	Other and Unknown	Age Start of Interval
0	30857	2264	.07337	.00016	.00544	.00026	.00016	.02259	.00807	.00010	.00000	.02661	.00000	.00081	.00917	0
1	123048	435	.00354	.00011	.00112	.00007	.00011	.00100	.00022	.00002	.00000	.00000	.00000	.00038	.00050	1
5	165283	204	.00123	.00002	.00050	.00006	.00007	.00009	.00010	.00004	.00000	.00000	.00000	.00018	.00018	5
10	162147	138	.00085	.00014	.00019	.00002	.00005	.00006	.00007	.00004	.00000	.00000	.00000	.00008	.00015	10
15	163488	306	.00187	.00077	.00034	.00006	.00013	.00007	.00007	.00004	.00006	.00000	.00000	.00013	.00020	15
20	161912	441	.00272	.00117	.00039	.00006	.00020	.00009	.00007	.00004	.00019	.00000	.00000	.00022	.00028	20
25	149973	436	.00291	.00109	.00022	.00016	.00021	.00012	.00009	.00009	.00035	.00000	.00000	.00017	.00038	25
30	140834	492	.00349	.00101	.00019	.00036	.00033	.00019	.00009	.00013	.00047	.00000	.00000	.00016	.00057	30
35	124257	508	.00409	.00063	.00029	.00067	.00054	.00031	.00010	.00019	.00039	.00000	.00000	.00019	.00078	35
40	113013	590	.00522	.00046	.00034	.00118	.00089	.00043	.00012	.00027	.00031	.00000	.00000	.00020	.00101	40
45	102583	671	.00654	.00052	.00033	.00196	.00127	.00048	.00014	.00039	.00005	.00000	.00000	.00024	.00117	45
50	91755	872	.00950	.00052	.00037	.00286	.00234	.00074	.00015	.00064	.00000	.00000	.00000	.00028	.00159	50
55	75575	1000	.01323	.00061	.00050	.00367	.00394	.00102	.00017	.00112	.00000	.00000	.00000	.00028	.00192	55
60	65154	1407	.02159	.00063	.00057	.00530	.00723	.00223	.00020	.00153	.00000	.00000	.00000	.00032	.00359	60
65	51892	1546	.02979	.00060	.00054	.00738	.01172	.00391	.00025	.00179	.00000	.00000	.00000	.00035	.00326	65
70	42098	2504	.05948	.00062	.00071	.01105	.02021	.00831	.00038	.00228	.00000	.00000	.00000	.00055	.01537	70
75	26469	2409	.09101	.00053	.00094	.01326	.02475	.01232	.00038	.00200	.00000	.00000	.00000	.00083	.03600	75
80	13373	1813	.13557	.00052	.00105	.01600	.03866	.01952	.00075	.00307	.00000	.00000	.00000	.00105	.05496	80
85+	6314	1496	.23693	.00032	.00048	.01774	.03659	.02835	.00032	.00238	.00000	.00000	.00000	.00238	.14840	85+
ALL	1810025	19532														

CRUDE DEATH RATE			.01079	.00059	.00051	.00163	.00239	.00147	.00027	.00039	.00014	.00045	.00000	.00025	.00271	
STANDARDIZED RATE (1)			.00837	.00052	.00062	.00096	.00130	.00144	.00040	.00025	.00012	.00094	.00000	.00024	.00158	
STANDARDIZED RATE (2)			.01235	.00056	.00054	.00184	.00279	.00174	.00030	.00043	.00013	.00055	.00000	.00026	.00319	
GEOMETRIC MEAN			.01057													

LIFE TABLE FOR ALL CAUSES COMBINED

Age (x)	Midyear Population	Deaths During Year	$_nM_x$	$_nq_x$	l_x	$_nd_x$	$_nL_x$	$_nm_x$	$_na_x$	T_x	$_nr_x$	$\overset{\circ}{e}_x$	Age (x)
0	30857	2264	.073371	.069280	100000	6928	94421	.073373	.194730	6333851	.000000	63.339	0
1	123048	435	.003535	.014011	93072	1304	369028	.003534	1.500000	6239430	.000000	67.039	1
5	165283	204	.001234	.006157	91768	565	457428	.001235	2.500000	5870402	.000000	63.970	5
10	162147	138	.000851	.004243	91203	387	455106	.000850	2.651270	5412974	.000545	59.351	10
15	163488	306	.001872	.009316	90816	846	452138	.001871	2.704639	4957868	.002372	54.592	15
20	161912	441	.002724	.013538	89970	1218	446856	.002725	2.574405	4505730	.003309	50.080	20
25	149973	436	.002907	.014433	88752	1281	440620	.002907	2.548627	4058834	.008475	45.732	25
30	140834	492	.003493	.017343	87471	1517	433659	.003498	2.563310	3618215	.013141	41.365	30
35	124257	508	.004088	.020267	85954	1742	425552	.004094	2.578573	3184556	.017356	37.050	35
40	113013	590	.005221	.025816	84212	2174	415813	.005228	2.586630	2759004	.015020	32.763	40
45	102583	671	.006541	.032253	82038	2646	403893	.006551	2.620071	2343191	.012913	28.562	45
50	91755	872	.009504	.046552	79392	3699	388177	.009529	2.625484	1939298	.019176	24.427	50
55	75575	1000	.013232	.064392	75693	4874	367029	.013280	2.653621	1551121	.020277	20.492	55
60	65154	1407	.021595	.102981	70819	7293	336694	.021661	2.614065	1184093	.018414	16.720	60
65	51892	1546	.029793	.139561	63526	8867	296910	.029864	2.663199	847398	.012275	13.339	65
70	42098	2504	.059480	.260506	54659	14239	238977	.059583	2.589850	550489	.006873	10.071	70
75	26469	2409	.091012	.371301	40420	15008	164277	.091358	2.479789	311512	.018791	7.707	75
80	13373	1813	.135572	.503030	25412	12783	93933	.136086	2.408537	147235	.018791	5.794	80
85+	6314	1496	.236934	1.000000	12629	12629	53302	.236934	4.220588	53302	.000000	4.221	85+

NUMBER OF PERSONS DYING (OUT OF 100,000 AT BIRTH) ABOVE AGE X FROM SPECIFIED CAUSES

Age (x)	All Causes	Respiratory T. B.	Other Infec. and Paras.	Neo-plasms	Cardio-vascular	Infl., Pneu., Bronch.	Diar-rheal	Certain Degen-erative	Maternal	Cert. Dis. of Infancy	Motor Vehicle	Other Violence	Other and Unknown	Age (x)
0	100000	3705	3283	15666	24440	13239	1714	3549	804	2512	0	1816	29272	0
1	93072	3689	2769	15642	24425	11106	952	3540	804	0	0	1740	28405	1
5	91768	3650	2356	15618	24383	10737	871	3531	804	0	0	1599	28219	5
10	91203	3639	2126	15590	24350	10696	826	3514	804	0	0	1518	28140	10
15	90816	3577	2039	15579	24308	10668	795	3495	804	0	0	1482	28069	15
20	89970	3229	1884	15551	24247	10637	765	3475	776	0	0	1424	27982	20
25	88752	2705	1710	15524	24156	10596	732	3459	691	0	0	1325	27854	25
30	87471	2226	1613	15453	24064	10543	694	3417	520	0	0	1251	27690	30
35	85954	1789	1530	15298	23922	10460	657	3359	317	0	0	1180	27442	35
40	84212	1523	1407	15013	23692	10326	612	3280	149	0	0	1101	27109	40
45	82038	1332	1267	14522	23320	10145	561	3166	21	0	0	1017	26687	45
50	79392	1123	1133	13729	22806	9952	505	3008	1	0	0	918	26217	50
55	75693	920	989	12618	21893	9663	446	2757	1	0	0	808	25598	55
60	70819	696	804	11269	20438	9287	383	2343	1	0	0	706	24892	60
65	63526	484	613	9481	17994	8534	316	1825	1	0	0	598	23680	65
70	54659	307	452	7286	14508	7369	241	1293	1	0	0	494	22708	70
75	40420	159	282	4644	9671	5379	150	747	1	0	0	364	19023	75
80	25412	73	126	2461	5594	3348	88	418	1	0	0	227	13076	80
85+	12629	17	25	945	1950	1511	17	127	0	0	0	127	7910	85+

NUMBER OF PERSONS SURVIVING TO AGE X IF SPECIFIED CAUSES WERE ELIMINATED

Age (x)	No Causes	Respiratory T. B. (1)	Other Infec. and Paras. (2)	Neo-plasms (3)	Cardio-vascular (4)	Infl., Pneu., Bronch. (5)	Diar-rheal (6)	Certain Degener-ative (7)	Maternal (8)	Cert. Dis. of Infancy (9)	Motor Vehicle (10)	Other Violence (11)	Other and Unknown (12)	(1) + (2)	(1) + (2) + (5) + (6) + (8)	(1)+(2)+ (5)+(6)+ (8)+part of(9)&(12)	(10) + (11)	Age (x)
0	100000	100000	100000	100000	100000	100000	100000	100000	100000	100000	100000	100000	100000	100000	100000	100000	100000	0
1	93072	93087	93569	93095	93086	95152	93810	93081	93072	95527	93072	93145	93912	93585	96435	99749	93145	1
5	91768	91822	92671	91815	91824	94194	92577	91785	91768	94188	91768	91981	92783	92726	96016	99478	91981	5
10	91203	91268	92333	91277	91292	93656	92052	91237	91203	93608	91203	91495	92291	92398	95767	99277	91495	10
15	90816	90942	92029	90901	90946	93288	91693	90869	90816	93211	90816	91143	91971	92157	95579	99133	91143	15
20	89970	90443	91328	90082	90160	92450	90869	90043	89998	92343	89970	90352	91202	91808	95310	98929	90352	20
25	88752	89743	90267	88889	89030	91241	89671	88840	88864	91093	88752	89228	90057	91275	94926	98641	89228	25
30	87471	88930	89062	87617	87836	89978	88415	87599	87752	89778	87471	88014	88962	90547	94450	98284	88014	30
35	85954	87829	87601	86311	86455	88502	86919	86137	86432	88221	85954	86558	87669	89512	93718	97708	86558	35
40	84212	86318	85950	84846	84932	86845	85203	84470	84847	86433	84212	84882	86229	88099	92616	96756	84882	40
45	82038	84283	83872	82115	83111	84788	83054	82402	82784	82038	82038	82775	84431	86167	90978	95235	82775	45
50	79392	81776	81302	81258	80944	82249	80431	79901	80134	81486	79392	80203	82185	83743	88713	93017	80203	50
55	75693	78170	77658	78590	78088	78710	76742	76426	76400	77689	75693	76575	78963	80199	85341	89642	76575	55
60	70819	73360	72841	74896	74527	74021	71862	71910	71481	72687	70819	71744	74614	75455	80776	85013	71744	60
65	63526	66013	65525	68956	69335	67150	64526	65003	64120	65201	63526	64459	68148	68090	73790	77943	64459	65
70	54659	56968	56533	61611	63287	58931	55590	56435	55170	56101	54659	55559	59619	58921	65211	69111	55559	70
75	40420	42258	41955	48169	51830	45455	41187	42214	40798	41486	40420	41199	47708	43863	50733	54743	41199	75
80	25412	26637	26504	32380	36939	30428	25944	26807	25649	26082	25412	26011	36102	27782	34279	38802	26011	80
85+	12629	13278	13245	17483	22407	16721	12943	13536	12748	12962	12629	12998	23800	13926	19074	23310	12998	85+

ADDED YRS OF LIFE																		
TOTAL		1.280	1.323	2.338	3.277	2.919	.772	.569	.314	1.666	.000	.537	5.025	2.639	6.950	10.874	.537	
WORK	4.738	.920	.338	.731	.680	.274	.102	.203	.258	.000	.000	.203	.677	1.268	1.932	2.271	.203	

POPULATION, DEATHS, DEATH RATES FOR ALL CAUSES COMBINED, AND SPECIFIED CAUSES

Age Start of Interval	Midyear Population	Deaths During Year	All Causes	Respiratory T. B.	Other Infec. and Paras.	Neoplasms	Cardiovascular	Infl., Pneu., Bronch.	Diarrheal	Certain Degenerative	Maternal	Cert. Dis. of Infancy	Motor Vehicle	Other Violence	Other and Unknown	Age Start of Interval
0	34309	2021	.05891	.00005	.00256	.00009	.00003	.01338	.00347	.00003	.00000	.02512	.00000	.00085	.01329	0
1	127570	312	.00245	.00005	.00041	.00013	.00006	.00056	.00005	.00003	.00000	.00000	.00000	.00045	.00069	1
5	149873	114	.00076	.00001	.00015	.00007	.00005	.00007	.00001	.00002	.00000	.00000	.00000	.00020	.00018	5
10	154555	105	.00068	.00004	.00010	.00006	.00005	.00003	.00001	.00005	.00000	.00000	.00000	.00017	.00018	10
15	166372	204	.00123	.00016	.00008	.00009	.00009	.00007	.00001	.00006	.00000	.00000	.00000	.00035	.00032	15
20	160048	266	.00166	.00028	.00011	.00015	.00008	.00005	.00001	.00008	.00000	.00000	.00000	.00056	.00034	20
25	160705	260	.00162	.00037	.00008	.00016	.00007	.00005	.00001	.00008	.00000	.00000	.00000	.00047	.00034	25
30	157034	321	.00204	.00042	.00010	.00023	.00017	.00007	.00000	.00013	.00000	.00000	.00000	.00049	.00043	30
35	141556	404	.00285	.00038	.00017	.00033	.00036	.00012	.00000	.00029	.00000	.00000	.00000	.00054	.00066	35
40	128223	534	.00416	.00038	.00022	.00062	.00076	.00018	.00001	.00043	.00000	.00000	.00000	.00065	.00092	40
45	111858	646	.00578	.00040	.00024	.00109	.00126	.00022	.00000	.00056	.00000	.00000	.00000	.00082	.00117	45
50	99202	905	.00912	.00042	.00029	.00197	.00255	.00038	.00001	.00079	.00000	.00000	.00000	.00096	.00175	50
55	87931	1180	.01342	.00045	.00036	.00325	.00432	.00059	.00001	.00101	.00000	.00000	.00000	.00106	.00235	55
60	75607	1718	.02272	.00050	.00042	.00533	.00821	.00116	.00003	.00147	.00000	.00000	.00000	.00120	.00439	60
65	57442	1973	.03435	.00057	.00045	.00839	.01356	.00158	.00003	.00225	.00000	.00000	.00000	.00125	.00625	65
70	40070	2544	.06349	.00060	.00052	.01215	.02451	.00444	.00010	.00285	.00000	.00000	.00000	.00185	.01607	70
75	25107	2468	.09830	.00052	.00052	.01565	.03895	.00892	.00016	.00295	.00000	.00000	.00000	.00255	.02808	75
80	11898	2202	.18507	.00059	.00076	.01950	.06589	.01874	.00042	.00311	.00000	.00000	.00000	.00521	.07085	80
85+	5564	1610	.28936	.00072	.00108	.01833	.09112	.03001	.00090	.00270	.00000	.00000	.00000	.00935	.13515	85+
ALL	1854924	19787														

	All Causes	Respiratory T. B.	Other Infec. and Paras.	Neoplasms	Cardiovascular	Infl., Pneu., Bronch.	Diarrheal	Certain Degenerative	Maternal	Cert. Dis. of Infancy	Motor Vehicle	Other Violence	Other and Unknown
CRUDE DEATH RATE	.01044	.00030	.00026	.00157	.00300	.00090	.00008	.00046	.00000	.00045	.00000	.00069	.00274
STANDARDIZED RATE (1)	.00750	.00023	.00028	.00090	.00155	.00086	.00014	.00029	.00000	.00088	.00000	.00055	.00182
STANDARDIZED RATE (2)	.01254	.00029	.00027	.00183	.00373	.00112	.00010	.00051	.00000	.00052	.00000	.00073	.00344
GEOMETRIC MEAN	.00892												

LIFE TABLE FOR ALL CAUSES COMBINED

Age (x)	Midyear Population	Deaths During Year	$_nM_x$	$_nq_x$	l_x	$_nd_x$	$_nL_x$	$_nm_x$	$_na_x$	T_x	$_nr_x$	$\overset{\circ}{e}_x$	Age (x)
0	34309	2021	.058906	.056160	100000	5616	95340	.058905	.170140	6534371	.000000	65.344	0
1	127570	312	.002446	.009726	94384	918	375241	.002446	1.500000	6439032	.000000	68.222	1
5	149873	114	.000761	.003798	93466	355	466443	.000761	2.500000	6063791	.000000	64.877	5
10	154555	105	.000679	.003383	93111	315	464812	.000678	2.640212	5597348	-.009460	60.115	10
15	166372	204	.001226	.006110	92796	567	462656	.001226	2.664609	5132537	-.007176	55.310	15
20	160048	266	.001662	.008273	92229	763	459273	.001661	2.546418	4669881	.000454	50.634	20
25	160705	260	.001618	.008058	91466	737	455521	.001618	2.545511	4210608	-.001359	46.035	25
30	157034	321	.002044	.010184	90729	924	451447	.002047	2.621528	3755087	.006641	41.388	30
35	141556	404	.002854	.014209	89805	1276	446024	.002861	2.647923	3303639	.014511	36.787	35
40	128223	534	.004165	.020671	88529	1830	438320	.004175	2.636840	2857616	.018039	32.279	40
45	111858	646	.005775	.028582	86699	2478	427705	.005794	2.663270	2419295	.019895	27.905	45
50	99202	905	.009123	.044787	84221	3772	412252	.009150	2.652936	1991591	.016628	23.647	50
55	87931	1180	.013420	.065221	80449	5247	390036	.013453	2.673194	1579339	.012719	19.632	55
60	75607	1718	.022723	.108162	75202	8134	356812	.022796	2.639794	1189303	.016836	15.815	60
65	57442	1973	.034348	.159614	67068	10705	310127	.034518	2.644773	832490	.024665	12.413	65
70	40070	2544	.063489	.276298	56363	15573	244014	.063820	2.572628	522363	.021261	9.268	70
75	25107	2468	.098299	.395538	40790	16134	163588	.098626	2.458321	278350	-.015380	6.824	75
80	11898	2202	.185073	.626338	24656	15443	82922	.186234	2.386680	114762	-.015380	4.655	80
85+	5564	1610	.289360	1.000000	9213	9213	31839	.289360	3.455901	31839	.000000	3.456	85+

NUMBER OF PERSONS DYING (OUT OF 100,000 AT BIRTH) ABOVE AGE X FROM SPECIFIED CAUSES

Age (x)	All Causes	Respiratory T.B.	Other Infec. and Paras.	Neo-plasms	Cardio-vascular	Infl., Pneu., Bronch.	Diar-rheal	Certain Degen-erative	Maternal	Cert. Dis. of Infancy	Motor Vehicle	Other Violence	Other and Unknown	Age (x)
0	100000	2136	1827	15664	32111	8243	513	4240	0	2395	0	5395	27476	0
1	94384	2127	1582	15656	32108	6968	182	4237	0	0	0	5314	26210	1
5	93466	2110	1429	15606	32084	6756	161	4226	0	0	0	5143	25951	5
10	93111	2103	1361	15574	32059	6722	158	4216	0	0	0	5050	25868	10
15	92796	2085	1316	15544	32038	6710	155	4195	0	0	0	4969	25784	15
20	92229	2013	1277	15503	31997	6679	152	4167	0	0	0	4805	25636	20
25	91466	1884	1225	15434	31959	6656	150	4130	0	0	0	4550	25478	25
30	90729	1717	1188	15363	31925	6634	147	4093	0	0	0	4337	25325	30
35	89805	1527	1142	15259	31848	6602	147	4033	0	0	0	4116	25131	35
40	88529	1357	1066	15111	31686	6548	147	3903	0	0	0	3873	24838	40
45	86699	1190	970	14836	31353	6469	143	3715	0	0	0	3589	24434	45
50	84221	1017	867	14367	30811	6374	143	3473	0	0	0	3236	23933	50
55	80449	843	746	13554	29755	6215	139	3148	0	0	0	2841	23208	55
60	75202	665	604	12282	28064	5984	135	2753	0	0	0	2428	22287	60
65	67068	486	453	10374	25122	5567	125	2228	0	0	0	1999	20714	65
70	56363	308	313	7762	20894	5072	114	1529	0	0	0	1609	18762	70
75	40790	161	185	4786	14785	3980	90	833	0	0	0	1157	14813	75
80	24656	77	100	2221	8393	2514	64	351	0	0	0	739	10197	80
85+	9213	23	34	584	2901	956	29	86	0	0	0	298	4302	85+

NUMBER OF PERSONS SURVIVING TO AGE X IF SPECIFIED CAUSES WERE ELIMINATED

Age (x)	No Causes	Respiratory T.B. (1)	Other Infec. and Paras. (2)	Neo-plasms (3)	Cardio-vascular (4)	Infl., Pneu., Bronch. (5)	Diar-rheal (6)	Certain Degener-ative (7)	Maternal (8)	Cert. Dis. of Infancy (9)	Motor Vehicle (10)	Other Violence (11)	Other and Unknown (12)	(1)+(2)	(1)+(2)+(5)+(6)+(8)	(1)+(2)+(5)+(6)+(8)+part of(9)&(12)	(10)+(11)	Age (x)
0	100000	100000	100000	100000	100000	100000	100000	100000	100000	100000	100000	100000	100000	100000	100000	100000	100000	0
1	94384	94393	94622	94392	94387	95631	94706	94387	94384	96739	94384	94463	95622	94631	96208	99720	94463	1
5	93466	93492	93855	93523	93493	94915	93806	93480	93466	95758	93466	93714	94953	93880	95682	99342	93714	5
10	93111	93143	93566	93200	93163	94589	93453	93135	93111	95435	93111	93452	94677	93599	95433	99120	93452	10
15	92796	92846	93295	92915	92868	94281	93139	92841	92796	95112	92796	93217	94442	93346	95190	98897	93217	15
20	92229	92351	92764	92388	92342	93736	92513	92301	92229	94531	92229	92811	94015	92887	94757	98502	92811	20
25	91466	91716	92049	91693	91616	92984	91810	91575	91466	93749	91466	92300	93358	92300	94184	97964	92300	25
30	90729	91144	91344	91025	90912	92257	91073	90874	90729	92993	90729	91770	92801	91762	93660	97483	91770	30
35	89805	90405	90460	90202	90063	91350	90145	90008	89805	92046	89805	91058	92053	91065	92982	96853	91058	35
40	88529	89291	89251	89068	88944	90106	88864	88859	88529	90738	88529	90009	91044	90019	91970	95895	90009	40
45	86699	87612	87502	87501	87438	88323	87031	87209	86699	88863	86699	88435	89574	88423	90425	94390	88435	45
50	84221	85280	85103	85468	85479	85854	84544	84956	84221	86323	84221	86263	87526	86173	88222	92192	86263	50
55	80449	81633	81411	82451	82706	82206	80761	81472	80449	82457	80449	82795	84345	82609	84741	88671	82795	55
60	75202	76483	76240	78344	79012	77073	75458	76546	75202	77079	75202	77806	79783	77539	79781	83608	77806	60
65	67068	68382	68138	71772	73447	69141	67341	68772	67068	68742	67068	68909	72746	69473	71912	75554	69809	65
70	56363	57633	57392	62924	66113	58576	56603	58453	56363	57770	56363	59038	63110	58685	61248	64544	59038	70
75	40790	41835	41644	48425	54313	43369	40984	42913	40790	41808	40790	43127	49591	42710	45627	48560	43127	75
80	24656	25352	25238	31683	40058	27448	24793	26325	24656	25271	24656	26409	34650	25950	29050	31575	26409	80
85+	9213	9506	9470	13141	21243	11327	9285	10004	9213	9443	9213	10150	18853	9771	12107	14077	10150	85+

ADDED YRS OF LIFE

	No Causes	(1)	(2)	(3)	(4)	(5)	(6)	(7)	(8)	(9)	(10)	(11)	(12)	(1)+(2)	comb.	comb.	(10)+(11)
TOTAL		.571	.607	2.030	3.806	1.640	.255	.661	.000	1.626	.000	1.295	4.253	1.186	3.142	6.339	1.295
WORK	3.661	.366	.159	.537	.619	.138	.005	.264	.000	.000	.000	.623	.717	.527	.673	.859	.623

POPULATION, DEATHS, DEATH RATES FOR ALL CAUSES COMBINED, AND SPECIFIED CAUSES

Age Start of Interval	Midyear Population	Deaths During Year	All Causes	Respiratory T. B.	Other Infec. and Paras.	Neoplasms	Cardiovascular	Infl., Pneu., Bronch.	Diarrheal	Certain Degenerative	Maternal	Cert. Dis. of Infancy	Motor Vehicle	Other Violence	Other and Unknown	Age Start of Interval
0	32986	1496	.04535	.CCOCC	.00264	.00006	.00003	.01103	.00230	.00006	.00000	.01767	.00000	.00067	.01088	0
1	123460	260	.00211	.00004	.00050	.00007	.00009	.00053	.00011	.00003	.CC000	.00000	.00000	.00023	.00050	1
5	145313	91	.000€3	.CCOC3	.00017	.000C7	.C0003	.00002	.00001	.00003	.00000	.C0000	.00000	.0000€	.00018	5
10	151103	77	.00051	.00002	.00011	.00003	.00007	.0000I	.00000	.00004	.00000	.C0000	.00000	.00003	.00021	10
15	163196	169	.00104	.00023	.00013	.00009	.00012	.00009	.00000	.00006	.00002	.C0000	.00000	.00013	.00018	15
20	160235	219	.00137	.000C39	.00013	.00009	.00012	.C0CC6	.00001	.00004	.00015	.C0000	.00000	.00010	.00028	20
25	161895	294	.00182	.00050	.00011	.00023	.00014	.00006	.00000	.00004	.00025	.C0000	.00000	.00012	.00036	25
30	159931	365	.C0228	.000C53	.C0011	.00043	.00015	.C0CC8	.00000	.00007	.00029	.C0000	.00000	.00014	.00048	30
35	146448	420	.00287	.000C35	.C0010	.00078	.00034	.00014	.00001	.00012	.00022	.C0000	.00000	.00021	.00061	35
40	136584	529	.C0387	.00026	.C0010	.00125	.00062	.00019	.00001	.00020	.00015	.C0000	.00000	.00026	.00083	40
45	118978	601	.00505	.00023	.00013	.001€7	.00089	.00018	.00002	.C0034	.00002	.00000	.00000	.00028	.00111	45
50	106245	843	.00793	.00024	.CC016	.00275	.00192	.00032	.C0003	.C0056	.00000	.C0000	.00000	.00031	.00165	50
55	93858	1073	.01143	.000C33	.00018	.00380	.00321	.00043	.00002	.00085	.00000	.C0000	.00000	.00031	.00230	55
60	79802	1609	.02016	.000€0	.00025	.00545	.00714	.00117	.C0003	.00145	.00000	.CC000	.00000	.00046	.00381	60
65	61464	1950	.03173	.CC044	.00046	.00757	.C1337	.00215	.C00C5	.C0259	.00000	.C0000	.00000	.00059	.00452	65
70	46052	2682	.05824	.CC050	.00050	.01047	.02467	.00525	.00011	.00337	.00000	.C0000	.00000	.00152	.01186	70
75	29513	2739	.09281	.CC064	.00034	.01372	.03934	.01017	.C0027	.00359	.CC000	.00000	.00000	.00305	.02169	75
80	15085	2537	.16818	.00053	.00020	.01757	.C6430	.01889	.00033	.00338	.C0000	.C0000	.00000	.00656	.05641	80
85+	7493	1989	.26545	.00013	.00027	.01855	.08862	.02856	.00013	.00187	.C0000	.C0000	.00000	.01121	.11611	85+
ALL	1935681	19943														

CRUDE DEATH RATE			.01028	.CCC29	.00022	.00181	.C0319	.CCC57	.00006	.00045	.00009	.00030	.00000	.00037	.00253	
STANDARDIZED RATE (1)			.00654	.00023	.00027	.C0058	.00146	.C0C78	.00011	.00025	.00007	.00062	.00000	.00024	.00151	
STANDARDIZED RATE (2)			.01128	.CCC27	.00024	.C0189	.00356	.00112	.00008	.C0048	.00008	.C0037	.00000	.00040	.00281	
GEOMETRIC MEAN			.00800													

LIFE TABLE FOR ALL CAUSES COMBINED

Age (x)	Midyear Population	Deaths During Year	$_nM_x$	$_nq_x$	l_x	$_nd_x$	$_nL_x$	$_nm_x$	$_na_x$	T_x	$_nr_x$	$\overset{\circ}{e}_x$	Age (x)
0	32986	1496	.045353	.043660	100000	4366	96276	.045349	.147099	6728409	.000000	67.284	0
1	123460	260	.002106	.008386	95634	802	380531	.002108	1.500000	6632133	.000000	69.349	1
5	145313	91	.000626	.003132	94832	297	473418	.000627	2.500000	6251602	.000000	65.923	5
10	151103	77	.000510	.002539	94535	240	472114	.000508	2.664062	5778184	-.010034	61.122	10
15	163196	169	.001036	.005154	94295	486	470343	.001033	2.671039	5306070	-.008861	56.271	15
20	160235	219	.001367	.006812	93809	639	467522	.001367	2.616067	4835727	-.002012	51.549	20
25	161895	294	.001816	.009037	93170	842	463830	.001815	2.601198	4368205	-.003219	46.884	25
30	159931	365	.002282	.011351	92328	1048	459116	.002283	2.551444	3904375	.004370	42.288	30
35	146448	420	.002868	.014264	91280	1302	453287	.002872	2.608967	3445259	.010276	37.744	35
40	136584	529	.003873	.019216	89978	1729	445756	.003879	2.609288	2991972	.014699	33.252	40
45	118978	601	.005051	.025031	88249	2209	436062	.005066	2.653821	2546216	.019232	28.853	45
50	106245	843	.007934	.039052	86040	3360	422302	.007956	2.649306	2110153	.016711	24.525	50
55	93898	1073	.011427	.055842	82680	4617	402729	.011464	2.688840	1687852	.015252	20.414	55
60	79802	1609	.020162	.056653	78063	7545	372669	.020246	2.661227	1285122	.020474	16.463	60
65	61464	1950	.031726	.148274	70518	10456	328084	.031870	2.656250	912453	.021347	12.939	65
70	46052	2682	.058239	.256185	60062	15387	263181	.058466	2.586978	584370	.016381	9.729	70
75	29513	2739	.092807	.377840	44675	16880	181369	.093070	2.511466	321189	.012619	7.189	75
80	15085	2537	.168180	.587012	27795	16316	96576	.168944	2.401400	139820	.012619	5.030	80
85+	7493	1989	.265448	1.000000	11479	11479	43244	.265448	3.767220	43244	.000000	3.767	85+

NUMBER OF PERSONS DYING (OUT OF 100,000 AT BIRTH) ABOVE AGE X FROM SPECIFIED CAUSES

Age (x)	All Causes	Respiratory T.B.	Other Infec. and Paras.	Neoplasms	Cardio-vascular	Infl., Pneu., Bronch.	Diarrheal	Certain Degenerative	Maternal	Cert. Dis. of Infancy	Motor Vehicle	Other Violence	Other and Unknown	Age (x)
0	100000	2016	1552	17196	34086	9396	450	4367	503	1701	0	3456	25277	0
1	95634	2016	1298	17190	34083	8333	228	4362	503	0	0	3392	24229	1
5	94832	2001	1107	17162	34049	8133	185	4349	503	0	0	3305	24038	5
10	94535	1985	1028	17130	34033	8123	179	4333	503	0	0	3269	23952	10
15	94295	1975	978	17117	33999	8120	179	4314	503	0	0	3257	23853	15
20	93809	1869	915	17077	33944	8080	179	4288	495	0	0	3197	23765	20
25	93170	1685	854	17033	33889	8054	176	4271	425	0	0	3150	23633	25
30	92328	1453	802	16927	33823	8025	176	4251	310	0	0	3095	23466	30
35	91280	1209	753	16729	33754	7988	176	4219	175	0	0	3032	23245	35
40	89978	1052	710	16375	33599	7922	173	4166	76	0	0	2936	22969	40
45	88249	934	664	15816	33320	7838	169	4078	8	0	0	2822	22600	45
50	86040	836	609	15000	32930	7757	162	3931	1	0	0	2701	22113	50
55	82680	736	542	13836	32116	7621	150	3691	1	0	0	2570	21417	55
60	78063	603	469	12302	30819	7449	141	3347	1	0	0	2445	20487	60
65	70518	453	375	10264	28141	7012	132	2803	1	0	0	2272	19065	65
70	60062	309	225	7776	23731	6302	116	1952	1	0	0	2079	17571	70
75	44675	177	93	5015	17214	4912	87	1064	1	0	0	1676	14436	75
80	27795	60	32	2522	10060	3062	38	412	1	0	0	1121	10487	80
85+	11479	6	12	802	3832	1235	6	81	0	0	0	485	5020	85+

NUMBER OF PERSONS SURVIVING TO AGE X IF SPECIFIED CAUSES WERE ELIMINATED

Age (x)	No Causes	Respiratory T.B.	Other Infec. and Paras.	Neoplasms	Cardio-vascular	Infl., Pneu., Bronch.	Diarrheal	Certain Degenerative	Maternal	Cert. Dis. of Infancy	Motor Vehicle	Other Violence	Other and Unknown	(1)+(2)	(1)+(2)+(5)+(6)+(8)	(1)+(2)+(5)+(6)+(8)+part of(9)&(12)	(10)+(11)	Age (x)
		(1)	(2)	(3)	(4)	(5)	(6)	(7)	(8)	(9)	(10)	(11)	(12)					
0	100000	100000	100000	100000	100000	100000	100000	100000	100000	100000	100000	100000	100000	100000	100000	100000	100000	0
1	95634	95634	95883	95640	95637	96679	95851	95639	95634	97312	95634	95697	96664	95883	97151	99785	95697	1
5	94832	94847	95269	94866	94869	96070	95090	94850	94832	96496	94832	94981	96046	95284	96791	99562	94981	5
10	94535	94566	95050	94601	94588	95779	94759	94569	94535	96194	94535	94719	95832	95081	96601	99414	94719	10
15	94295	94336	94859	94373	94381	95539	94558	94348	94295	95949	94295	94491	95685	94900	96420	99275	94491	15
20	93809	93955	94434	93927	93950	95087	94071	93887	93817	95455	93809	94064	95285	94581	96145	99042	94064	20
25	93170	93499	93852	93331	93365	94466	93423	93265	93248	94805	93170	93470	94770	94183	95842	98824	93470	25
30	92328	92886	93056	92593	92587	93641	92588	92442	92520	93948	92328	92680	94083	93618	95415	98497	92680	30
35	91280	92076	92048	91740	91605	92616	91537	91424	91604	92881	91280	91691	93239	92851	94811	98005	91691	35
40	89978	90920	90778	90786	90453	91361	90235	90173	90356	91557	89978	90479	92189	91729	93839	97106	90479	40
45	88249	89291	89080	89602	88993	89590	88505	88528	88727	89797	88249	88854	90793	90132	92367	95676	88854	45
50	86040	87154	86905	88181	87155	87526	86296	86458	86513	87550	86040	86750	89016	88030	90311	93622	86750	50
55	82680	83850	83578	85914	84564	84244	82938	83318	83134	84131	82680	83492	86249	84760	87109	90390	83492	55
60	78063	79298	78982	82679	81143	79710	78315	79003	78492	79433	78063	78952	82380	80232	82642	85859	78952	60
65	70518	71778	71439	76764	75597	72432	70755	71892	70905	71755	70518	71487	75855	72716	75352	78454	71487	65
70	60062	61270	60986	67919	69265	62370	60278	62036	60392	61116	60062	61069	66109	62213	65193	68055	61069	70
75	44675	45688	45476	53258	58397	47654	44861	46931	44920	45459	44675	45779	52241	46508	50089	52726	45779	75
80	27795	28518	28340	35517	44406	31235	27949	29729	27948	28283	27795	28932	36348	29077	33037	35410	28932	80
85+	11479	11812	11717	16101	25703	14242	11563	12500	11543	11680	11479	12367	20188	12057	15152	17121	12367	85+

ADDED YRS OF LIFE

	No Causes	(1)	(2)	(3)	(4)	(5)	(6)	(7)	(8)	(9)	(10)	(11)	(12)	(1)+(2)	(1)+(2)+(5)+(6)+(8)	+part of(9)&(12)	(10)+(11)
TOTAL		.604	.614	2.539	4.083	1.626	.206	.599	.203	1.178	.000	.559	3.872	1.225	3.331	6.005	.559
WORK	3.406	.403	.137	.819	.527	.142	.006	.163	.162	.000	.000	.190	.664	.542	.858	1.082	.190

POPULATION, DEATHS, DEATH RATES FOR ALL CAUSES COMBINED, AND SPECIFIED CAUSES

Age Start of Interval	Midyear Population	Deaths During Year	All Causes	Respiratory T.B.	Other Infec. and Paras.	Neoplasms	Cardiovascular	Infl., Pneu., Bronch.	Diarrheal	Certain Degenerative	Maternal	Cert. Dis. of Infancy	Motor Vehicle	Other Violence	Other and Unknown	Age Start of Interval
0	38107	933	.02448	.00000	.00039	.00005	.00005	.00126	.00037	.00003	.00000	.01535	.00000	.00031	.00667	0
1	150918	170	.00113	.00000	.00003	.00013	.00001	.00011	.00002	.00001	.00000	.00001	.00017	.00025	.00038	1
5	190218	98	.00052	.00000	.00001	.00010	.00001	.00002	.00000	.00001	.00000	.00000	.00015	.00012	.00011	5
10	213036	75	.00035	.00000	.00001	.00001	.00008	.00000	.00000	.00001	.00000	.00000	.00008	.00009	.00007	10
15	194715	156	.00080	.00000	.00001	.00012	.00003	.00003	.00001	.00002	.00000	.00000	.00029	.00023	.00007	15
20	153404	154	.00100	.00000	.00000	.00013	.00006	.00002	.00000	.00004	.00000	.00000	.00031	.00033	.00012	20
25	138853	170	.00122	.00001	.00001	.00018	.00007	.00003	.00001	.00008	.00000	.00000	.00028	.00045	.00009	25
30	141925	203	.00143	.00002	.00004	.00024	.00020	.00003	.00003	.00013	.00000	.00000	.00018	.00044	.00016	30
35	153348	256	.00167	.00003	.00000	.00040	.00029	.00001	.00001	.00010	.00000	.00000	.00014	.00044	.00025	35
40	148419	358	.00241	.00003	.00001	.00067	.00060	.00002	.00002	.00011	.00000	.00000	.00013	.00057	.00023	40
45	151273	669	.00442	.00005	.00003	.00114	.00149	.00005	.00005	.00028	.00000	.00000	.00021	.00071	.00046	45
50	143807	1050	.00730	.00008	.00003	.00202	.00309	.00011	.00001	.00026	.00000	.00000	.00030	.00069	.00070	50
55	124502	1526	.01226	.00009	.00010	.00371	.00551	.00021	.00002	.00054	.00000	.00000	.00025	.00081	.00102	55
60	105755	2077	.01964	.00017	.00014	.00553	.00982	.00036	.00006	.00072	.00000	.00000	.00044	.00054	.00147	60
65	83840	2661	.03174	.00019	.00018	.00895	.01630	.00074	.00005	.00099	.00000	.00000	.00050	.00105	.00279	65
70	63361	3190	.05035	.00027	.00019	.01204	.02828	.00166	.00019	.00152	.00000	.00000	.00062	.00104	.00455	70
75	43006	3623	.08424	.00021	.00026	.01709	.04909	.00407	.00016	.00216	.00000	.00000	.00077	.00212	.00832	75
80	23298	3175	.13628	.00030	.00017	.02429	.07953	.00940	.00043	.00176	.00000	.00000	.00107	.00352	.01580	80
85+	10478	2486	.23726	.00010	.00029	.02882	.14707	.01899	.00086	.00286	.00000	.00000	.00086	.00802	.02939	85+
ALL	2272263	23030														

			All Causes	Resp. T.B.	Other Infec.	Neoplasms	Cardio.	Infl. Pneu.	Diarrheal	Cert. Degen.	Maternal	Cert. Infancy	Motor Veh.	Other Viol.	Other Unk.
CRUDE DEATH RATE			.01014	.00005	.00005	.00218	.00495	.00041	.00003	.00028	.00000	.00026	.00026	.00056	.00110
STANDARDIZED RATE (1)			.00507	.00002	.00004	.00057	.00185	.00019	.00003	.00014	.00000	.00054	.00021	.00056	.00068
STANDARDIZED RATE (2)			.00957	.00004	.00005	.00201	.00455	.00040	.00003	.00026	.00000	.00032	.00025	.00039	.00107
GEOMETRIC MEAN			.00615												

LIFE TABLE FOR ALL CAUSES COMBINED

Age (x)	Midyear Population	Deaths During Year	$_nM_x$	$_nq_x$	l_x	$_nd_x$	$_nL_x$	$_nm_x$	$_na_x$	T_x	$_nr_x$	$\overset{\circ}{e}_x$	Age (x)
0	38107	933	.024484	.023960	100000	2396	97871	.024481	.111622	7049646	.000000	70.496	0
1	150918	170	.001126	.004498	97604	439	389319	.001128	1.500000	6951774	.000000	71.224	1
5	190218	98	.000515	.002573	97165	250	485200	.000515	2.500000	6562456	.000000	67.535	5
10	213036	75	.000352	.001754	96915	170	484179	.000351	2.670343	6077256	-.008192	62.707	10
15	194715	156	.000801	.004021	96745	389	482818	.000806	2.667631	5593077	.021649	57.813	15
20	153404	154	.001004	.005013	96356	483	480614	.001005	2.584972	5110259	.034111	53.035	20
25	138853	170	.001224	.006112	95873	586	477941	.001226	2.569681	4629646	.016348	48.289	25
30	141925	203	.001430	.007126	95287	679	474779	.001430	2.561365	4151705	-.005529	43.571	30
35	153348	256	.001669	.008308	94608	786	471168	.001668	2.618215	3676926	-.007074	38.865	35
40	148419	358	.002412	.011991	93822	1125	466556	.002411	2.729815	3205758	-.002143	34.169	40
45	151273	669	.004422	.021867	92697	2027	458862	.004417	2.719536	2739202	-.003677	29.550	45
50	143807	1050	.007301	.035966	90670	3261	445864	.007314	2.704245	2280339	.007089	25.150	50
55	124502	1526	.012257	.059765	87409	5224	424918	.012294	2.678663	1834476	.015384	20.987	55
60	105755	2077	.019640	.094190	82185	7741	392781	.019708	2.656068	1409557	.018157	17.151	60
65	83840	2661	.031739	.148071	74444	11023	346024	.031856	2.623511	1016777	.019197	13.658	65
70	63361	3190	.050346	.225099	63421	14276	282696	.050499	2.589734	670753	.015057	10.576	70
75	43006	3623	.084244	.349415	49145	17172	203191	.084512	2.523075	388057	.013573	7.896	75
80	23298	3175	.136278	.505989	31973	16178	118293	.136762	2.430319	184866	.013573	5.782	80
85+	10478	2486	.237259	1.000000	15795	15795	66573	.237259	4.214803	66573	.000000	4.215	85+

NUMBER OF PERSONS DYING (OUT OF 100,000 AT BIRTH) ABOVE AGE X FROM SPECIFIED CAUSES

Age (x)	All Causes	Respiratory T.B.	Other Infec. and Paras.	Neoplasms	Cardiovascular	Infl., Pneu., Bronch.	Diarrheal	Certain Degenerative	Maternal	Cert. Dis. of Infancy	Motor Vehicle	Other Violence	Other and Unknown	Age (x)
0	100000	432	434	20961	51803	4483	313	2616	0	1505	2017	4792	10644	0
1	97604	432	395	20956	51797	4359	277	2614	0	3	2017	4762	9992	1
5	97165	432	382	20907	51792	4316	269	2611	0	0	1950	4663	9843	5
10	96915	432	377	20858	51787	4308	269	2606	0	0	1878	4607	9793	10
15	96745	432	370	20822	51785	4306	269	2601	0	0	1840	4562	9758	15
20	96356	432	365	20762	51772	4293	266	2591	0	0	1700	4450	9725	20
25	95873	432	365	20699	51744	4284	266	2572	0	0	1550	4292	9669	25
30	95287	428	358	20613	51710	4270	260	2534	0	0	1416	4075	9623	30
35	94608	418	342	20500	51616	4257	260	2471	0	0	1332	3865	9547	35
40	93822	406	342	20309	51481	4250	256	2425	0	0	1265	3659	9429	40
45	92697	390	335	19995	51202	4241	247	2371	0	0	1202	3392	9322	45
50	90670	369	320	19474	50517	4217	247	2244	0	0	1105	3064	9113	50
55	87409	332	308	18570	49138	4167	241	2126	0	0	972	2757	8798	55
60	82185	294	263	16688	46788	4078	234	1897	0	0	866	2412	8365	60
65	74444	227	207	14809	42917	3936	212	1614	0	0	691	2044	7787	65
70	63421	161	145	11704	37252	3679	195	1270	0	0	517	1681	6817	70
75	49145	85	92	8293	29229	3208	141	841	0	0	343	1386	5527	75
80	31973	43	40	4812	19223	2377	108	401	0	0	187	954	3828	80
85+	15795	6	19	1919	9791	1264	57	191	0	0	57	534	1957	85+

NUMBER OF PERSONS SURVIVING TO AGE X IF SPECIFIED CAUSES WERE ELIMINATED

Age (x)	No Causes	Respiratory T.B. (1)	Other Infec. and Paras. (2)	Neoplasms (3)	Cardiovascular (4)	Infl., Pneu., Bronch. (5)	Diarrheal (6)	Certain Degenerative (7)	Maternal (8)	Cert. Dis. of Infancy (9)	Motor Vehicle (10)	Other Violence (11)	Other and Unknown (12)	(1)+(2)	(1)+(2)+(5)+(6)+(8)	(1)+(2)+(5)+(6)+(8)+part of(9)&(12)	(10)+(11)	Age (x)
0	100000	100000	100000	100000	100000	100000	100000	100000	100000	100000	100000	100000	100000	100000	100000	100000	100000	0
1	97604	97604	97643	97609	97610	97727	97640	97606	97604	99099	97604	97634	98250	97643	97801	99570	97634	1
5	97165	97165	97216	97219	97230	97208	97208	97170	97165	98657	97232	97293	97958	97216	97425	99222	97360	5
10	96915	96915	96971	97018	96931	97008	96958	96925	96915	98403	97054	97099	97756	96971	97187	98983	97238	10
15	96745	96745	96808	96883	96763	96819	96788	96760	96745	98230	96921	96974	97620	96808	97026	98821	97151	15
20	96356	96356	96424	96554	96387	96543	96402	96381	96356	97835	96672	96656	97261	96424	96657	98447	97013	20
25	95873	95873	95941	96133	95932	96068	95919	95917	95873	97345	96337	96370	96830	95941	96181	97964	96836	25
30	95287	95291	95361	95631	95379	95494	95339	95368	95287	96750	95883	95998	96284	95365	95624	97400	96599	30
35	94608	94622	94658	95063	94793	94827	94659	94752	94608	96060	95284	95525	95615	94711	94982	96750	96208	35
40	93822	93848	93911	94465	94141	94406	93817	94010	93822	95282	94560	94939	94955	93937	94216	95974	95685	40
45	92697	92738	92792	93647	93291	92927	92760	92937	92697	94120	93489	94069	93967	92833	93127	94869	94873	45
50	90670	90731	90777	92121	91935	90919	90732	91031	90670	92062	91541	92342	92122	90839	91150	92862	93229	50
55	87409	87504	87524	89714	90013	87698	87474	87873	87409	88751	88381	89328	89124	87620	87976	89640	90321	55
60	82185	82312	82337	85541	87013	82544	82253	82845	82185	83447	83202	84331	84226	82464	82893	84477	85375	60
65	74444	74622	74635	80044	82816	74905	74527	75313	74444	75587	75534	76747	76859	74814	75361	76824	77871	65
70	63421	63634	63641	71336	76615	64054	63507	64483	63421	64395	64512	65727	66409	63855	64579	65870	66858	70
75	49145	49376	49362	58738	68527	50057	49259	50351	49145	49899	50145	51200	52661	49594	50633	51705	52242	75
80	31973	32157	32155	41673	57278	33257	32074	33117	31973	32464	32750	33673	35752	32340	33745	34551	34492	80
85+	15795	15911	15900	23354	42685	17246	15880	16510	15795	16037	16271	16942	19163	16017	17582	18128	17453	85+

ADDED YRS OF LIFE

	No Causes	(1)	(2)	(3)	(4)	(5)	(6)	(7)	(8)	(9)	(10)	(11)	(12)	(1)+(2)	sum	sum	(10)+(11)
TOTAL		.067	.101	2.838	8.611	.465	.060	.385	.000	1.080	.575	1.087	1.704	.169	.701	2.074	1.678
WORK	2.697	.023	.020	.606	.706	.042	.008	.129	.000	.000	.279	.505	.251	.043	.094	.104	.788

POPULATION, DEATHS, DEATH RATES FOR ALL CAUSES COMBINED, AND SPECIFIED CAUSES

Age Start of Interval	Midyear Population	Deaths During Year	All Causes	Respiratory T.B.	Other Infec. and Paras.	Neoplasms	Cardiovascular	Infl., Pneu., Bronch.	Diarrheal	Certain Degenerative	Maternal	Cert. Dis. of Infancy	Motor Vehicle	Other Violence	Other and Unknown	Age Start of Interval
0	36216	703	.01941	.00000	.00028	.00003	.00008	.00127	.00033	.00000	.00000	.01171	.00003	.00039	.00530	0
1	142990	107	.00075	.00000	.00005	.00012	.00001	.00010	.00000	.00000	.00000	.00000	.00011	.00006	.00030	1
5	180585	49	.00027	.00000	.00002	.00008	.00001	.00001	.00001	.00001	.00000	.00000	.00007	.00002	.00006	5
10	203636	40	.00020	.00000	.00000	.00004	.00000	.00000	.00000	.00001	.00000	.00000	.00004	.00001	.00007	10
15	186216	62	.00033	.00000	.00000	.00006	.00002	.00001	.00001	.00003	.00000	.00000	.00000	.00010	.00002	15
20	149677	52	.00035	.00000	.00000	.00007	.00001	.00001	.00001	.00003	.00002	.00000	.00004	.00007	.00009	20
25	139955	80	.00057	.00001	.00001	.00017	.00004	.00002	.00000	.00001	.00004	.00000	.00000	.00015	.00012	25
30	144963	152	.00105	.00003	.00001	.00032	.00013	.00001	.00001	.00011	.00005	.00000	.00005	.00015	.00018	30
35	158053	239	.00151	.00001	.00000	.00068	.00014	.00001	.00001	.00008	.00003	.00000	.00000	.00019	.00031	35
40	151288	333	.00220	.00004	.00003	.00096	.00030	.00003	.00001	.00010	.00003	.00000	.00000	.00025	.00038	40
45	154461	492	.00319	.00003	.00004	.00173	.00045	.00003	.00001	.00014	.00000	.00000	.00006	.00027	.00042	45
50	148747	763	.00513	.00003	.00003	.00236	.00120	.00011	.00001	.00018	.00000	.00000	.00010	.00036	.00074	50
55	133303	1070	.00803	.00005	.00006	.00363	.00233	.00019	.00002	.00029	.00000	.00000	.00008	.00033	.00106	55
60	118140	1519	.01286	.00002	.00005	.00485	.00499	.00026	.00007	.00068	.00000	.00000	.00011	.00036	.00146	60
65	95478	2015	.02110	.00009	.00018	.00639	.01010	.00048	.00006	.00081	.00000	.00000	.00016	.00060	.00228	65
70	74086	2933	.03959	.00005	.00015	.00933	.02189	.00136	.00007	.00162	.00000	.00000	.00024	.00101	.00386	70
75	50675	3626	.07155	.00018	.00022	.01377	.04227	.00312	.00041	.00172	.00000	.00000	.00020	.00276	.00691	75
80	27070	3410	.12597	.00033	.00018	.01999	.07854	.00680	.00044	.00296	.00000	.00000	.00044	.00543	.01086	80
85+	13169	3006	.22826	.00030	.00053	.02498	.14397	.01838	.00076	.00205	.00000	.00000	.00008	.01359	.02362	85+
ALL	2308708	20651														
CRUDE DEATH RATE			.00894	.00003	.00005	.00213	.00433	.00038	.00004	.00027	.00001	.00018	.00008	.00041	.00103	
STANDARDIZED RATE (1)			.00379	.00001	.00003	.00090	.00128	.00016	.00002	.00011	.00001	.00041	.00007	.00019	.00059	
STANDARDIZED RATE (2)			.00754	.00002	.00004	.00178	.00353	.00032	.00003	.00023	.00001	.00024	.00008	.00035	.00090	
GEOMETRIC MEAN			.00414													

LIFE TABLE FOR ALL CAUSES COMBINED

Age (x)	Midyear Population	Deaths During Year	$_nM_x$	$_nq_x$	l_x	$_nd_x$	$_nL_x$	$_nm_x$	$_na_x$	T_x	$_nr_x$	$\overset{\circ}{e}_x$	Age (x)
0	36216	703	.019411	.019080	100000	1908	98289	.019412	.102999	7401007	.000000	74.010	0
1	142990	107	.000748	.002987	98092	293	391636	.000748	1.500000	7302719	.000000	74.448	1
5	180585	49	.000271	.001360	97799	133	488663	.000272	2.500000	6911083	.000000	70.666	5
10	203636	40	.000196	.000973	97666	95	488099	.000195	2.565789	6422421	-.008488	65.759	10
15	186216	62	.000333	.001671	97571	163	487463	.000334	2.595859	5934322	.020873	60.821	15
20	149677	52	.000347	.001745	97408	170	486639	.000349	2.640931	5446859	.030323	55.918	20
25	139955	80	.000572	.002859	97238	278	485565	.000573	2.751799	4960220	.012135	51.011	25
30	144963	152	.001049	.005219	96960	506	483628	.001046	2.684453	4474655	-.008265	46.149	30
35	158053	239	.001512	.007527	96454	726	480568	.001511	2.655533	3991027	-.007640	41.378	35
40	151288	333	.002201	.010948	95728	1048	476180	.002201	2.653069	3510459	-.001019	36.671	40
45	154461	492	.003185	.015801	94680	1496	469934	.003183	2.683266	3034278	-.003336	32.048	45
50	148747	763	.005130	.025369	93184	2364	460446	.005134	2.684275	2564344	.005697	27.519	50
55	133303	1070	.008027	.039496	90820	3587	445778	.008047	2.680048	2103899	.011827	23.166	55
60	118140	1519	.012858	.062637	87233	5464	423481	.012903	2.678555	1658120	.017327	19.008	60
65	95478	2015	.021104	.101139	81769	8270	389819	.021215	2.699365	1234640	.022781	15.099	65
70	74086	2933	.039589	.182016	73499	13378	336166	.039796	2.658189	844821	.021119	11.494	70
75	50675	3626	.071554	.306515	60121	18428	255921	.072007	2.575203	508655	.024776	8.461	75
80	27070	3410	.125970	.480416	41693	20030	157830	.126909	2.472052	252734	.024776	6.062	80
85+	13169	3006	.228263	1.000000	21663	21663	94904	.228263	4.380905	94904	.000000	4.381	85+

NUMBER OF PERSONS DYING (OUT OF 100,000 AT BIRTH) ABOVE AGE X FROM SPECIFIED CAUSES

Age (x)	All Causes	Respiratory T.B.	Other Infec. and Paras.	Neoplasms	Cardiovascular	Infl., Pneu., Bronch.	Diarrheal	Certain Degenerative	Maternal	Cert. Dis. of Infancy	Motor Vehicle	Other Violence	Other and Unknown	Age (x)
0	100000	269	418	21526	52647	4756	392	2718	75	1151	683	4548	10817	0
1	98092	269	390	21523	52639	4631	360	2718	75	0	680	4510	10297	1
5	97799	269	371	21477	52636	4590	360	2718	75	0	637	4488	10178	5
10	97666	269	363	21439	52633	4585	357	2713	75	0	604	4480	10148	10
15	97571	269	361	21417	52631	4585	357	2705	75	0	585	4473	10113	15
20	97408	269	361	21388	52620	4580	354	2692	75	0	538	4428	10103	20
25	97238	269	361	21356	52614	4576	351	2679	65	0	518	4392	10057	25
30	96960	266	354	21272	52593	4566	351	2676	48	0	518	4319	9997	30
35	96454	252	350	21116	52530	4559	348	2622	25	0	495	4246	9911	35
40	95728	246	350	20791	52463	4556	345	2583	12	0	465	4155	9762	40
45	94680	227	338	20335	52318	4540	338	2536	0	0	433	4035	9580	45
50	93184	212	320	19523	52106	4525	335	2469	0	0	403	3910	9381	50
55	90820	197	304	18435	51554	4473	332	2385	0	0	356	3743	9041	55
60	87233	173	277	16814	50513	4389	325	2258	0	0	320	3596	8568	60
65	81769	166	256	14756	48387	4277	297	1970	0	0	273	3442	7945	65
70	73499	146	186	12258	44424	4088	272	1654	0	0	211	3208	7052	70
75	60121	127	136	9112	37020	3626	249	1108	0	0	130	2865	5748	75
80	41693	82	80	5571	26128	2821	142	667	0	0	79	2152	3971	80
85+	21663	29	50	2371	13664	1744	72	195	0	0	7	1290	2241	85+

NUMBER OF PERSONS SURVIVING TO AGE X IF SPECIFIED CAUSES WERE ELIMINATED

Age (x)	No Causes	Respiratory T.B. (1)	Other Infec. and Paras. (2)	Neoplasms (3)	Cardiovascular (4)	Infl., Pneu., Bronch. (5)	Diarrheal (6)	Certain Degenerative (7)	Maternal (8)	Cert. Dis. of Infancy (9)	Motor Vehicle (10)	Other Violence (11)	Other and Unknown (12)	(1)+(2)	(1)+(2)+(5)+(6)+(8)	(1)+(2)+(5)+(6)+(8)+part of (9)&(12)	(10)+(11)	Age (x)
0	100000	100000	100000	100000	100000	100000	100000	100000	100000	100000	100000	100000	100000	100000	100000	100000	100000	0
1	98092	98092	98120	98095	98100	98216	98124	98092	98092	99239	98095	98130	98608	98120	98275	99578	98133	1
5	97799	97799	97846	97848	97810	97964	97821	97799	97799	98942	97845	97859	98433	97846	98042	99383	97904	5
10	97666	97666	97721	97753	97680	97835	97701	97671	97666	98808	97745	97733	98330	97721	97925	99269	97812	10
15	97571	97571	97628	97680	97587	97740	97666	97584	97571	98712	97669	97645	98269	97628	97831	99176	97743	15
20	97408	97408	97464	97546	97435	97582	97445	97434	97408	98547	97553	97527	98115	97464	97676	99019	97672	20
25	97238	97238	97294	97407	97271	97416	97278	97277	97248	98375	97402	97393	97990	97294	97522	98870	97558	25
30	96960	96963	97023	97213	97014	97147	97000	97002	96987	98093	97124	97188	97770	97026	97281	98635	97352	30
35	96454	96471	96521	96662	96570	96647	96497	96549	96504	97581	96640	96753	97347	96538	96824	98182	96940	35
40	95728	95751	95794	96458	95910	95923	95774	95862	95790	96847	95943	96116	96764	95817	96120	97475	96332	40
45	94680	94721	94758	95661	95005	94888	94732	94859	94754	95787	94924	95184	95888	94799	95134	96489	95429	45
50	93184	93240	93278	95165	93715	93404	93238	93427	93256	94273	93454	93805	94573	93334	93682	95024	94076	50
55	90820	90889	90928	93854	91888	91086	90876	91140	90891	91882	91130	91591	92515	90997	91390	92714	91903	55
60	87233	87323	87363	91803	89298	87571	87294	87665	87301	88253	87566	88119	89334	87453	87921	89216	88455	60
65	81769	81860	81911	88173	85841	82195	81853	82455	81833	82725	82127	82750	84358	82002	82578	83816	83112	65
70	73499	73600	73693	81843	81210	74063	73598	74418	73556	74358	73879	74605	76703	73794	74518	75671	74991	70
75	60121	60221	60325	70172	74251	61005	60223	61371	60168	60824	60505	61342	63581	60425	61465	62473	61734	75
80	41693	41800	41880	52187	63943	42991	41853	42931	41725	42180	42001	43149	45959	41987	43494	44302	43468	80
85+	21663	21756	21782	30105	49933	23138	21756	22653	21680	21916	21875	23060	25269	21875	23526	24054	23285	85+

ADDED YRS OF LIFE

	No Causes	(1)	(2)	(3)	(4)	(5)	(6)	(7)	(8)	(9)	(10)	(11)	(12)	(1)+(2)	(1)+(2)+(5)+(6)+(8)	(1)+(2)+(5)+(6)+(8)+part of(9)&(12)	(10)+(11)
TOTAL		.043	.092	3.166	8.367	.479	.062	.361	.033	.864	.200	.612	1.724	.135	.715	1.815	.815
WORK	1.833	.018	.014	.743	.310	.032	.008	.088	.024	.000	.067	.193	.278	.031	.095	.115	.261

POPULATION, DEATHS, DEATH RATES FOR ALL CAUSES COMBINED, AND SPECIFIED CAUSES

Age Start of Interval	Midyear Population	Deaths During Year	All Causes	Respiratory T. B.	Other Infec. and Paras.	Neoplasms	Cardiovascular	Infl., Pneu., Bronch.	Diarrheal	Certain Degenerative	Maternal	Cert. Dis. of Infancy	Motor Vehicle	Other Violence	Other and Unknown	Age Start of Interval
0	42162	915	.02170	.00000	.00019	.00012	.00005	.00055	.00045	.00002	.00000	.01376	.00002	.00036	.00579	0
1	153779	145	.00094	.00001	.00001	.00017	.00003	.00004	.00002	.00001	.00000	.00001	.00014	.00025	.00027	1
5	188702	93	.00049	.00000	.00001	.00011	.00000	.00001	.00001	.00001	.00000	.00000	.00019	.00008	.00009	5
10	191161	84	.00044	.00000	.00000	.00010	.00003	.00002	.00000	.00001	.00000	.00000	.00008	.00013	.00008	10
15	218557	201	.00092	.00000	.00001	.00009	.00004	.00001	.00000	.00001	.00000	.00000	.00008	.00026	.00008	15
20	179822	173	.00096	.00000	.00002	.00013	.00004	.00002	.00001	.00003	.00000	.00000	.00042	.00029	.00008	20
25	148467	159	.00107	.00001	.00001	.00020	.00007	.00001	.00001	.00007	.00000	.00000	.00021	.00039	.00010	25
30	138175	178	.00129	.00000	.00001	.00026	.00015	.00001	.00000	.00009	.00000	.00000	.00023	.00042	.00012	30
35	143901	255	.00177	.00001	.00001	.00034	.00040	.00001	.00001	.00010	.00000	.00000	.00015	.00049	.00025	35
40	154296	379	.00246	.00003	.00002	.00058	.00078	.00005	.00001	.00008	.00000	.00000	.00017	.00049	.00025	40
45	145119	678	.00467	.00001	.00005	.00121	.00163	.00014	.00004	.00020	.00000	.00000	.00023	.00065	.00052	45
50	148600	1123	.00756	.00005	.00002	.00208	.00325	.00019	.00001	.00026	.00000	.00000	.00030	.00083	.00056	50
55	134081	1789	.01334	.00005	.00004	.00362	.00641	.00045	.00004	.00056	.00000	.00000	.00039	.00071	.00107	55
60	112638	2495	.02215	.00012	.00010	.00655	.01098	.00077	.00007	.00059	.00000	.00000	.00049	.00087	.00162	60
65	91422	3101	.03392	.00010	.00019	.00980	.01755	.00103	.00008	.00095	.00000	.00000	.00059	.00091	.00273	65
70	66804	3501	.05241	.00012	.00018	.01284	.02877	.00235	.00013	.00133	.00000	.00000	.00066	.00138	.00464	70
75	45539	3885	.08531	.00011	.00040	.01856	.04952	.00428	.00024	.00158	.00000	.00000	.00083	.00165	.00775	75
80	24597	3303	.13428	.00028	.00016	.02330	.08139	.00833	.00037	.00191	.00000	.00000	.00102	.00362	.01390	80
85+	12007	2895	.24111	.00025	.00050	.03173	.15108	.01699	.00050	.00192	.00000	.00000	.00083	.00858	.02873	85+
ALL	2339829	25352														
CRUDE DEATH RATE			.01083	.00003	.00005	.00238	.00540	.00048	.00004	.00026	.00000	.00025	.00030	.00056	.00109	
STANDARDIZED RATE (1)			.00512	.00001	.00003	.00103	.00196	.00020	.00003	.00012	.00000	.00048	.00024	.00038	.00063	
STANDARDIZED RATE (2)			.00982	.00003	.00004	.00213	.00481	.00043	.00004	.00023	.00000	.00029	.00028	.00053	.00101	
GEOMETRIC MEAN			.00623													

LIFE TABLE FOR ALL CAUSES COMBINED

Age (x)	Midyear Population	Deaths During Year	$_nM_x$	$_nq_x$	l_x	$_nd_x$	$_nL_x$	$_nm_x$	$_na_x$	T_x	$_n r_x$	$\overset{\circ}{e}_x$	Age (x)
0	42162	915	.021702	.021290	100000	2129	98099	.021703	.106893	7029091	.000000	70.291	0
1	153779	145	.000943	.003760	97871	368	390564	.000942	1.500000	6930993	.000000	70.818	1
5	188702	93	.000493	.002472	97503	241	486913	.000495	2.500000	6540429	.000000	67.079	5
10	191161	84	.000439	.002190	97262	213	485820	.000438	2.699531	6053516	-.013895	62.239	10
15	218557	201	.000920	.004585	97049	445	484185	.000919	2.617509	5567696	-.005333	57.370	15
20	179822	173	.000962	.004803	96604	464	481874	.000963	2.530981	5083511	.029053	52.622	20
25	148467	159	.001071	.005346	96140	514	479446	.001072	2.561203	4601637	.029609	47.864	25
30	138175	178	.001288	.006431	95626	615	476660	.001290	2.609417	4122190	-.011241	43.107	30
35	143901	255	.001772	.008810	95011	837	473074	.001769	2.632915	3645531	-.008682	38.370	35
40	154296	379	.002456	.012201	94174	1149	468271	.002454	2.737888	3172457	-.005385	33.687	40
45	145119	678	.004672	.023101	93025	2149	460216	.004670	2.715604	2704186	-.001564	29.069	45
50	148600	1123	.007557	.037117	90876	3373	446682	.007551	2.717783	2243970	-.002954	24.693	50
55	134081	1789	.013343	.064855	87503	5675	424424	.013371	2.693172	1797288	.009684	20.540	55
60	112638	2495	.022151	.105526	81828	8635	388769	.022211	2.640827	1372864	.013981	16.777	60
65	91422	3101	.033920	.157283	73193	11512	338381	.034021	2.603931	984096	.016785	13.445	65
70	66804	3501	.052407	.233103	61681	14378	273537	.052563	2.574941	645714	.015652	10.469	70
75	45539	3885	.085311	.352705	47303	16684	195001	.085559	2.511750	372177	.013017	7.868	75
80	24597	3303	.134285	.500310	30619	15319	113719	.134709	2.429609	177176	.013017	5.786	80
85+	12007	2895	.241109	1.000000	15300	15300	63457	.241109	4.147496	63457	.000000	4.147	85+

NUMBER OF PERSONS DYING (OUT OF 100,000 AT BIRTH) ABOVE AGE X FROM SPECIFIED CAUSES

Age (x)	All Causes	Respiratory T. B.	Other Infec. and Paras.	Neoplasms	Cardiovascular	Infl., Pneu., Bronch.	Diarrheal	Certain Degenerative	Maternal	Cert. Dis. of Infancy	Motor Vehicle	Other Violence	Other and Unknown	Age (x)
0	100000	261	392	21667	52329	4672	316	2285	0	1352	2227	4627	9872	0
1	97871	261	373	21655	52324	4579	272	2283	0	3	2224	4592	9305	1
5	97503	259	368	21589	52314	4564	264	2278	0	0	2171	4495	9201	5
10	97262	259	363	21535	52314	4562	261	2275	0	0	2080	4456	9157	10
15	97049	259	363	21486	52301	4554	261	2270	0	0	2043	4396	9116	15
20	96604	259	359	21442	52283	4547	261	2266	0	0	1839	4270	9078	20
25	96140	259	351	21380	52265	4537	259	2252	0	0	1671	4127	9039	25
30	95626	255	347	21283	52232	4530	256	2220	0	0	1571	3939	8993	30
35	95011	255	344	21159	52159	4527	256	2178	0	0	1461	3739	8933	35
40	94174	249	337	20958	51972	4523	252	2129	0	0	1392	3506	8816	40
45	93025	234	328	20728	51609	4502	249	2090	0	0	1313	3275	8697	45
50	90876	227	306	20173	50861	4439	230	1998	0	0	1205	2977	8460	50
55	87503	203	297	19245	49410	4355	227	1880	0	0	1070	2605	8211	55
60	81828	181	278	17703	46685	4161	211	1643	0	0	905	2304	7757	60
65	73193	136	240	15149	42403	3860	184	1415	0	0	715	1965	7126	65
70	61681	103	177	11825	36446	3511	158	1092	0	0	515	1658	6196	70
75	47303	70	128	8305	28550	2865	121	726	0	0	334	1280	4924	75
80	30619	49	50	4678	18664	2027	73	340	0	0	171	958	3409	80
85+	15300	16	32	2014	9587	1078	32	122	0	0	53	544	1822	85+

NUMBER OF PERSONS SURVIVING TO AGE X IF SPECIFIED CAUSES WERE ELIMINATED

Age (x)	No Causes	Respiratory T. B. (1)	Other Infec. and Paras. (2)	Neoplasms (3)	Cardiovascular (4)	Infl., Pneu., Bronch. (5)	Diarrheal (6)	Certain Degenerative (7)	Maternal (8)	Cert. Dis. of Infancy (9)	Motor Vehicle (10)	Other Violence (11)	Other and Unknown (12)	(1)+(2)	(1)+(2)+(5)+(6)+(8)	(1)+(2)+(5)+(6)+(8)+part of(9)&(12)	(10)+(11)	Age (x)
0	100000	100000	100000	100000	100000	100000	100000	100000	100000	100000	100000	100000	100000	100000	100000	100000	100000	0
1	97871	97871	97890	97883	97876	97963	97915	97873	97871	99215	97874	97906	98434	97890	98025	99426	97909	1
5	97503	97505	97527	97581	97518	97610	97554	97510	97503	98845	97559	97634	98168	97529	97687	99095	97690	5
10	97262	97264	97291	97394	97277	97370	97316	97272	97262	98600	97409	97432	97969	97293	97455	98862	97579	10
15	97049	97051	97078	97229	97077	97165	97103	97064	97049	98384	97232	97279	97796	97080	97250	98656	97463	15
20	96604	96606	96636	96827	96650	96727	96658	96623	96604	97933	96591	96959	97386	96638	96815	98216	97347	20
25	96140	96142	96180	96424	96203	96272	96196	96173	96140	97463	96693	96636	96957	96182	96370	97766	97192	25
30	95626	95632	95670	96006	95722	95764	95684	95690	95626	96942	96277	96308	96485	95676	95873	97263	96964	30
35	95011	95017	95058	95513	95179	95151	95069	95117	95011	96318	95768	95890	95925	95064	95262	96645	96654	35
40	94174	94186	94227	94833	94528	94317	94235	94328	94174	95470	94993	95280	95198	94239	94444	95818	96109	40
45	93025	93052	93087	93946	93737	93187	93089	93216	93025	94305	93914	94350	94156	93113	93340	94703	95251	45
50	90876	90909	90958	92332	92320	91097	90957	91154	90876	92126	91852	92469	92218	90991	91293	92641	93462	50
55	87503	87558	87591	89835	90352	87799	87584	87887	87503	88707	88577	89408	89043	87646	88023	89332	90505	55
60	81828	81901	81928	85553	87258	82293	81919	82417	81828	82993	82993	83907	83716	82001	82559	83808	85120	60
65	73193	73301	73319	79092	82489	73895	73300	73937	73193	74200	74417	75381	75495	73427	74240	75395	76642	65
70	61681	61802	61845	70023	75956	62558	61795	62607	61681	62530	62899	63814	64507	61966	63003	64023	65074	70
75	47303	47424	47471	57292	67400	48584	47423	48338	47303	47954	48397	49281	50647	47593	49006	49868	50421	75
80	30619	30714	30790	40741	56179	32145	30735	31603	30619	31040	31460	32167	34105	30886	32548	33206	33050	80
85+	15300	15371	15398	22968	42731	16768	15387	15948	15300	15511	15804	16378	18312	15469	17049	17489	16918	85+

ADDED YRS OF LIFE

		Respiratory T. B.	Other Infec. and Paras.	Neoplasms	Cardiovascular	Infl., Pneu., Bronch.	Diarrheal	Certain Degenerative	Maternal	Cert. Dis. of Infancy	Motor Vehicle	Other Violence	Other and Unknown	(1)+(2)	(1)+(2)+(5)+(6)+(8)	(1)+(2)+...	(10)+(11)
TOTAL		.039	.072	2.938	8.878	.485	.069	.327	.000	.966	.640	1.041	1.544	.111	.671	1.752	1.698
WORK	2.770	.013	.018	.598	.783	.057	.009	.105	.000	.000	.321	.486	.242	.031	.097	.107	.812

POPULATION, DEATHS, DEATH RATES FOR ALL CAUSES COMBINED, AND SPECIFIED CAUSES

Age Start of Interval	Midyear Population	Deaths During Year	All Causes	Respiratory T. B.	Other Infec. and Paras.	Neoplasms	Cardiovascular	Infl., Pneu., Bronch.	Diarrheal	Certain Degenerative	Maternal	Cert. Dis. of Infancy	Motor Vehicle	Other Violence	Other and Unknown	Age Start of Interval
0	40040	645	.01611	.00000	.00007	.00022	.00000	.00070	.00037	.00005	.00000	.00914	.00002	.00050	.00502	0
1	147551	99	.00067	.00000	.00003	.00014	.00001	.00006	.00001	.00000	.00000	.00000	.00012	.00012	.00018	1
5	179466	60	.00033	.00000	.00002	.00008	.00000	.00001	.00000	.00000	.00000	.00000	.00011	.00002	.00009	5
10	182464	39	.00021	.00000	.00001	.00004	.00001	.00001	.00000	.00001	.00000	.00000	.00008	.00001	.00005	10
15	207351	76	.00037	.00000	.00000	.00010	.00002	.00000	.00000	.00001	.00001	.00000	.00009	.00006	.00006	15
20	173243	70	.00040	.00000	.00000	.00010	.00002	.00000	.00000	.00002	.00002	.00000	.00010	.00010	.00005	20
25	146893	102	.00069	.00000	.00002	.00021	.00008	.00000	.00000	.00003	.00002	.00000	.00007	.00017	.00009	25
30	139662	103	.00074	.00000	.00001	.00032	.00006	.00000	.00001	.00009	.00001	.00000	.00002	.00011	.00011	30
35	146818	205	.00140	.00001	.00001	.00061	.00012	.00001	.00000	.00011	.00001	.00000	.00002	.00024	.00027	35
40	158392	312	.00197	.00001	.00000	.00102	.00024	.00005	.00001	.00004	.00001	.00000	.00006	.00021	.00031	40
45	148226	475	.00320	.00002	.00003	.00148	.00059	.00004	.00002	.00016	.00000	.00000	.00005	.00036	.00045	45
50	152583	729	.00478	.00000	.00002	.00242	.00109	.00003	.00003	.00018	.00000	.00000	.00010	.00039	.00051	50
55	141770	1016	.00717	.00001	.00002	.00329	.00212	.00009	.00003	.00027	.00000	.00000	.00013	.00037	.00082	55
60	125248	1510	.01206	.00002	.00007	.00468	.00455	.00032	.00003	.00039	.00000	.00000	.00023	.00038	.00137	60
65	106850	2253	.02109	.00005	.00010	.00670	.00997	.00055	.00004	.00086	.00000	.00000	.00017	.00056	.00209	65
70	80641	3004	.03725	.00004	.00005	.00926	.02052	.00124	.00015	.00115	.00000	.00000	.00035	.00105	.00343	70
75	56287	3694	.06563	.00004	.00018	.01343	.03893	.00297	.00030	.00156	.00000	.00000	.00032	.00268	.00522	75
80	31060	3680	.11848	.00023	.00019	.01822	.07457	.00583	.00026	.00248	.00000	.00000	.00029	.00731	.00911	80
85+	15797	3387	.21441	.00013	.00025	.02488	.13680	.01418	.00089	.00165	.00000	.00000	.00044	.01684	.01836	85+
ALL	2380342	21459														
CRUDE DEATH RATE			.00902	.00001	.00003	.00220	.00445	.00036	.00004	.00024	.00001	.00015	.00011	.00050	.00092	
STANDARDIZED RATE (1)			.00350	.00000	.00002	.00089	.00121	.00012	.00003	.00010	.00001	.00032	.00009	.00021	.00051	
STANDARDIZED RATE (2)			.00705	.00001	.00003	.00174	.00333	.00027	.00003	.00019	.00001	.00019	.00010	.00040	.00076	
GEOMETRIC MEAN			.00401													

LIFE TABLE FOR ALL CAUSES COMBINED

Age (x)	Midyear Population	Deaths During Year	$_nM_x$	$_nq_x$	l_x	$_nd_x$	$_nL_x$	$_nm_x$	$_na_x$	T_x	$_nr_x$	$\overset{\circ}{e}_x$	Age (x)
0	40040	645	.016109	.015880	100000	1588	98567	.016111	.097385	7483154	.000000	74.832	0
1	147551	99	.000671	.002672	98412	263	392991	.000669	1.500000	7384588	.000000	75.037	1
5	179466	60	.000334	.001671	98149	164	490335	.000334	2.500000	6991597	.000000	71.235	5
10	182464	39	.000214	.001072	97985	105	489666	.000214	2.529762	6501262	-.013450	66.350	10
15	207351	76	.000367	.001829	97880	179	488972	.000366	2.608240	6011596	-.005065	61.418	15
20	173243	70	.000404	.002027	97701	198	488043	.000406	2.668350	5522625	.026447	56.526	20
25	146893	102	.000694	.003477	97503	339	486701	.000697	2.598328	5034581	.025438	51.635	25
30	139662	103	.000737	.003684	97164	358	484955	.000738	2.694367	4547880	.008101	46.806	30
35	146818	205	.001396	.006952	96806	673	482469	.001395	2.680473	4062886	-.010510	41.969	35
40	158392	312	.001970	.009789	96133	941	478488	.001967	2.686194	3580417	-.005622	37.244	40
45	148226	475	.003205	.015905	95192	1514	472440	.003205	2.674895	3101929	-.000273	32.586	45
50	152583	729	.004778	.023613	93678	2212	463217	.004775	2.661618	2629489	-.002571	28.069	50
55	141770	1016	.007167	.035314	91466	3230	449875	.007180	2.692079	2166272	.008319	23.684	55
60	125248	1510	.012056	.058820	88236	5190	429279	.012050	2.706888	1716396	.012869	19.452	60
65	106850	2253	.021086	.100956	83046	8384	395866	.021179	2.690343	1287118	.019195	15.499	65
70	80641	3004	.037252	.172109	74662	12850	343106	.037452	2.649497	891252	.023365	11.937	70
75	56287	3694	.065628	.284815	61812	17605	266601	.066035	2.588244	548146	.025327	8.868	75
80	31060	3680	.118480	.459362	44207	20307	170075	.119400	2.490521	281545	.025327	6.369	80
85+	15797	3387	.214408	1.000000	23900	23900	111470	.214408	4.664009	111470	.000000	4.664	85+

NUMBER OF PERSONS DYING (OUT OF 100,000 AT BIRTH) ABOVE AGE X FROM SPECIFIED CAUSES

Age (x)	All Causes	Respiratory T.B.	Other Infec. and Paras.	Neoplasms	Cardiovascular	Infl., Pneu., Bronch.	Diarrheal	Certain Degenerative	Maternal	Cert. Dis. of Infancy	Motor Vehicle	Other Violence	Other and Unknown	Age (x)
0	100000	129	283	21951	53487	4369	395	2371	39	901	913	5664	9498	0
1	98412	129	275	21929	53487	4300	359	2366	39	0	910	5615	9003	1
5	98149	129	262	21876	53482	4276	353	2366	39	0	865	5570	8931	5
10	97985	129	254	21835	53482	4271	353	2366	39	0	813	5559	8884	10
15	97880	129	248	21816	53479	4266	353	2363	39	0	773	5553	8861	15
20	97701	129	246	21767	53470	4263	351	2356	35	0	728	5525	8831	20
25	97503	129	246	21719	53458	4263	351	2345	26	0	680	5477	8809	25
30	97164	129	236	21615	53419	4263	351	2328	16	0	647	5394	8766	30
35	96806	129	233	21462	53387	4263	347	2283	13	0	637	5338	8714	35
40	96133	126	229	21171	53232	4260	347	2230	6	0	627	5223	8582	40
45	95192	120	225	20662	53217	4236	341	2212	0	0	600	5121	8434	45
50	93678	110	217	19980	52937	4217	332	2139	0	0	578	4949	8219	50
55	91466	110	207	18858	52430	4201	317	2057	0	0	532	4770	7984	55
60	88236	104	198	17374	51472	4160	304	1936	0	0	472	4601	7615	60
65	83046	94	167	15362	49510	4022	290	1768	0	0	372	4437	7024	65
70	74662	75	126	12702	45541	3803	275	1425	0	0	306	4213	6196	70
75	61812	62	109	9513	38455	3374	224	1029	0	0	186	3849	5011	75
80	44207	53	62	5918	28006	2576	143	610	0	0	101	3126	3612	80
85+	23900	14	28	2773	15249	1581	99	183	0	0	49	1977	2047	85+

NUMBER OF PERSONS SURVIVING TO AGE X IF SPECIFIED CAUSES WERE ELIMINATED

Age (x)	No Causes	Respiratory T.B.	Other Infec. and Paras.	Neoplasms	Cardiovascular	Infl., Pneu., Bronch.	Diarrheal	Certain Degenerative	Maternal	Cert. Dis. of Infancy	Motor Vehicle	Other Violence	Other and Unknown	(1)+(2)	(1)+(2)+(5)+(6)+(8)	(1)+(2)+(5)+(6)+(8)+part of(9)&(12)	(10)+(11)	Age (x)
		(1)	(2)	(3)	(4)	(5)	(6)	(7)	(8)	(9)	(10)	(11)	(12)					
0	100000	100000	100000	100000	100000	100000	100000	100000	100000	100000	100000	100000	100000	100000	100000	100000	100000	0
1	98412	98412	98420	98434	98412	98480	98448	98417	98412	99310	98415	98461	98904	98420	98524	99344	98464	1
5	98149	98149	98170	98224	98154	98241	98191	98154	98149	99044	98197	98242	98712	98170	98304	99138	98290	5
10	97985	97985	98014	98101	97990	98082	98027	97990	97985	98879	98085	98089	98595	98014	98153	98990	98189	10
15	97880	97880	97915	98014	97888	97982	97922	97888	97880	98713	98020	97990	98512	97915	98058	98899	98130	15
20	97701	97701	97738	97884	97718	97806	97744	97716	97705	98592	97886	97839	98362	97738	97890	98731	98024	20
25	97503	97503	97540	97734	97532	97608	97546	97529	97516	98393	97735	97689	98185	97540	97701	98541	97921	25
30	97164	97164	97211	97498	97232	97268	97207	97207	97187	98050	97428	97432	97887	97211	97381	98222	97697	30
35	96806	96806	96855	97292	96905	96910	96853	96894	96832	97689	97079	97129	97578	96855	97032	97872	97404	35
40	96133	96136	96186	96908	96287	96239	96180	96273	96166	97010	96415	96569	97033	96189	96375	97213	96852	40
45	95192	95201	95244	96451	95459	95321	95244	95348	95230	96061	95498	95726	96232	95253	95473	96311	96033	45
50	93678	93697	93742	95625	94220	93824	93738	93904	93716	94533	94001	94375	94917	93760	94004	94838	94700	50
55	91466	91484	91518	94506	92500	91624	91540	91768	91503	92301	91827	92325	92911	91556	91825	92644	92689	55
60	88236	88260	88314	92686	90191	88429	88320	88647	88271	89041	88643	89232	89999	88338	88651	89450	89644	60
65	83046	83078	83150	89307	86857	83362	83139	83597	83079	83804	83527	84144	85292	83182	83625	84403	84631	65
70	74662	74709	74794	83042	82129	75155	74759	75485	74692	75343	75157	75865	77490	74841	75464	76197	76367	70
75	61812	61862	61937	72037	75468	62615	61939	62856	61837	62376	62331	63146	65278	61987	62947	63608	63676	75
80	44207	44251	44336	55145	65870	45469	44366	45312	44225	44610	44649	45792	47942	44380	45829	46381	46250	80
85+	23900	23952	23994	32793	52406	25334	24018	24816	23910	24118	24177	25711	27177	24046	25626	26007	26009	85+

ADDED YRS OF LIFE

	No Causes	(1)	(2)	(3)	(4)	(5)	(6)	(7)	(8)	(9)	(10)	(11)	(12)	(1)+(2)	...	...	(10)+(11)
TOTAL		.017	.062	3.305	8.944	.408	.069	.324	.018	.882	.266	.736	1.540	.078	.578	1.274	1.008
WORK	1.732	.004	.011	.737	.295	.018	.008	.081	.013	.000	.081	.203	.229	.016	.056	.065	.284

POPULATION, DEATHS, DEATH RATES FOR ALL CAUSES COMBINED, AND SPECIFIED CAUSES

Age Start of Interval	Midyear Population	Deaths During Year	All Causes	Respiratory T. B.	Other Infec. and Paras.	Neoplasms	Cardiovascular	Infl., Pneu., Bronch.	Diarrheal	Certain Degenerative	Maternal	Cert. Dis. of Infancy	Motor Vehicle	Other Violence	Other and Unknown	Age Start of Interval
0	35435	3981	.11235	.00014	.02122	.00008	.00037	.01851	.02088	.00000	.00000	.01750	.00003	.00031	.03330	0
1	110830	2818	.02543	.00007	.00596	.00004	.00002	.00239	.00858	.00007	.00000	.00024	.00000	.00018	.00788	1
5	126599	832	.00657	.00005	.00167	.00001	.00002	.00056	.00128	.00004	.00000	.00000	.00001	.00015	.00278	5
10	116570	277	.00238	.00004	.00046	.00001	.00003	.00013	.00034	.00002	.00000	.00000	.00001	.00029	.00104	10
15	97155	434	.00447	.00026	.00083	.00001	.00008	.00024	.00076	.00001	.00000	.00000	.00001	.00101	.00126	15
20	83904	612	.00729	.00070	.00080	.00005	.00023	.00029	.00080	.00007	.00000	.00000	.00004	.00250	.00182	20
25	66516	476	.00716	.00056	.00081	.00006	.00027	.00024	.00048	.00014	.00000	.00000	.00005	.00262	.00194	25
30	55076	439	.00797	.00049	.00085	.00007	.00044	.00038	.00062	.00020	.00000	.00000	.00004	.00252	.00236	30
35	54371	461	.00848	.00092	.00068	.00026	.00033	.00026	.00044	.00020	.00000	.00000	.00013	.00263	.00263	35
40	44403	476	.01072	.00077	.00144	.00034	.00050	.00043	.00079	.00020	.00000	.00000	.00009	.00243	.00374	40
45	34374	434	.01263	.00070	.00154	.00032	.00090	.00029	.00105	.00049	.00000	.00000	.00000	.00332	.00401	45
50	30946	505	.01632	.00055	.00197	.00052	.00107	.00068	.00129	.00058	.00000	.00000	.00000	.00372	.00595	50
55	17449	318	.01822	.00080	.00189	.00063	.00172	.00080	.00206	.00109	.00000	.00000	.00000	.00189	.00734	55
60	18733	477	.02546	.00069	.00187	.00096	.00214	.00144	.00304	.00149	.00000	.00000	.00000	.00187	.01196	60
65	10244	378	.03690	.00078	.00303	.00225	.00361	.00127	.00420	.00156	.00000	.00000	.00000	.00195	.01825	65
70	6908	394	.05704	.00072	.00608	.00188	.00391	.00246	.00594	.00188	.00000	.00000	.00014	.00246	.03156	70
75	4298	251	.05840	.00116	.00535	.00140	.00605	.00419	.00396	.00209	.00000	.00000	.00000	.00140	.03281	75
80	2649	267	.10079	.00113	.00642	.00189	.00906	.00680	.01019	.00415	.00000	.00000	.00000	.00189	.05927	80
85+	2009	380	.18915	.00050	.00896	.00199	.01344	.01244	.01792	.00597	.00000	.00000	.00000	.00189	.12444	85+
ALL	918469	14210	.01547													

	All Causes	Respiratory T. B.	Other Infec. and Paras.	Neoplasms	Cardiovascular	Infl., Pneu., Bronch.	Diarrheal	Certain Degenerative	Maternal	Cert. Dis. of Infancy	Motor Vehicle	Other Violence	Other and Unknown
CRUDE DEATH RATE	.01547	.00038	.00255	.00017	.00044	.00140	.00271	.00022	.00000	.00070	.00003	.00142	.00544
STANDARDIZED RATE (1)	.01549	.00040	.00251	.00020	.00049	.00134	.00266	.00025	.00000	.00064	.00003	.00148	.00548
STANDARDIZED RATE (2)	.01744	.00049	.00231	.00035	.00090	.00122	.00244	.00044	.00000	.00038	.00003	.00176	.00714
GEOMETRIC MEAN	.01889												

LIFE TABLE FOR ALL CAUSES COMBINED

Age (x)	Midyear Population	Deaths During Year	$_nM_x$	$_nq_x$	l_x	$_nd_x$	$_nL_x$	$_nm_x$	$_na_x$	T_x	$_nr_x$	$\overset{\circ}{e}_x$	Age (x)
0	35435	3981	.112347	.103730	100000	10373	92334	.112342	.260989	4992897	.000000	49.929	0
1	110830	2818	.025426	.095630	89627	8571	337081	.025427	1.500000	4900562	.000000	54.677	1
5	126599	832	.006572	.032385	81056	2625	398718	.006584	2.500000	4563482	.000000	56.300	5
10	116570	277	.002376	.011756	78431	922	389662	.002366	2.296186	4164764	.016357	53.101	10
15	97155	434	.004467	.022230	77509	1723	383613	.004492	2.717885	3775102	.025397	48.705	15
20	83904	612	.007294	.035943	75786	2724	372296	.007317	2.564703	3391489	.028415	44.751	20
25	66516	476	.007156	.035162	73062	2569	358894	.007158	2.502595	3019193	.036952	41.324	25
30	55076	439	.007971	.039096	70493	2756	345626	.007974	2.518596	2660299	.019101	37.738	30
35	54371	461	.008479	.041558	67737	2815	331782	.008484	2.547661	2314673	.009392	34.171	35
40	44403	476	.010720	.052371	64922	3400	316310	.010749	2.558762	1982891	.032791	30.543	40
45	34374	434	.012626	.061344	61522	3774	298414	.012647	2.563372	1666581	.019505	27.089	45
50	30946	505	.016319	.078756	57748	4548	277553	.016386	2.540265	1368167	.047779	23.692	50
55	17449	318	.018225	.087462	53200	4653	254637	.018273	2.557938	1090614	.036912	20.500	55
60	18733	477	.025463	.120337	48547	5842	228680	.025547	2.594217	835977	.022540	17.220	60
65	10244	378	.036900	.170823	42705	7295	195521	.037234	2.586846	607296	.056903	14.221	65
70	6908	394	.057035	.250861	35410	8883	154730	.057410	2.487288	411375	.040116	11.617	70
75	4298	251	.058399	.254571	26527	6753	115574	.058430	2.473592	256646	.030952	9.675	75
80	2649	267	.100793	.405937	19774	8027	78967	.101659	2.520504	141072	.030952	7.134	80
85+	2009	380	.189149	1.000000	11747	11747	62105	.189149	5.286842	62105	.000000	5.287	85+

NUMBER OF PERSONS DYING (OUT OF 100,000 AT BIRTH) ABOVE AGE X FROM SPECIFIED CAUSES

Age (x)	All Causes	Respiratory T. B.	Other Infec. and Paras.	Neoplasms	Cardio-vascular	Infl., Pneu., Bronch.	Diarrheal	Certain Degenerative	Maternal	Cert. Dis. of Infancy	Motor Vehicle	Other Violence	Other and Unknown	Age (x)
0	100000	2601	11857	2081	5768	6670	12874	2803	0	1658	149	9280	44219	0
1	89627	2588	9858	2073	5734	4961	10945	2803	0	82	146	9251	41146	1
5	81056	2564	7891	2061	5728	4155	8053	2779	0	0	146	9191	38488	5
10	78431	2545	7222	2058	5719	3931	7542	2763	0	0	143	9131	37377	10
15	77509	2528	7043	2055	5705	3882	7409	2756	0	0	140	9016	36975	15
20	75786	2428	6722	2051	5673	3790	7116	2752	0	0	136	8625	36493	20
25	73062	2165	6425	2033	5589	3684	6819	2725	0	0	123	7689	35810	25
30	70493	1966	6133	2011	5491	3597	6647	2676	0	0	106	6750	35116	30
35	67737	1796	5838	1986	5340	3466	6434	2607	0	0	94	5877	34299	35
40	64922	1491	5612	1900	5230	3380	6287	2540	0	0	51	5005	33426	40
45	61522	1249	5154	1793	5073	3244	6037	2476	0	0	23	4235	32238	45
50	57748	1041	4693	1657	4803	3157	5723	2328	0	0	23	3243	31040	50
55	53200	889	4145	1553	4505	2967	5362	2165	0	0	23	2214	29377	55
60	48547	684	3664	1392	4065	2762	4834	1886	0	0	23	1738	27499	60
65	42705	526	3236	1171	3575	2432	4136	1543	0	0	23	1310	24753	65
70	35410	372	2635	726	2861	2182	3307	1237	0	0	23	927	21140	70
75	26527	260	1686	436	2254	1797	2385	944	0	0	0	545	16220	75
80	19774	125	1070	275	1552	1311	1929	702	0	0	0	385	12425	80
85+	11747	31	556	124	835	773	1113	371	0	0	0	216	7728	85+

NUMBER OF PERSONS SURVIVING TO AGE X IF SPECIFIED CAUSES WERE ELIMINATED

Age (x)	No Causes	Respiratory T. B. (1)	Other Infec. and Paras. (2)	Neoplasms (3)	Cardio-vascular (4)	Infl., Pneu., Bronch. (5)	Diarrheal (6)	Certain Degenerative (7)	Maternal (8)	Cert. Dis. of Infancy (9)	Motor Vehicle (10)	Other Violence (11)	Other and Unknown (12)	(1)+(2)	(1)+(2)+(5)+(6)+(8)	(1)+(2)+(5)+(6)+(8)+part of (9)&(12)	(10)+(11)	Age (x)
0	100000	100000	100000	100000	100000	100000	100000	100000	100000	100000	100000	100000	100000	100000	100000	100000	100000	0
1	89627	89639	91500	89635	89659	91259	91471	89627	89627	91169	89630	89654	92582	91513	95096	99858	89657	1
5	81056	81090	84721	81074	81091	83316	85577	81079	81056	82530	81059	81138	86380	84756	91979	99682	81140	5
10	78431	78482	82668	78452	78474	80844	83338	78469	78431	79857	78436	78569	84755	82722	90603	99485	78575	10
15	77509	77577	81884	77532	77565	79944	82499	77553	77509	78919	77517	77760	84192	81955	89972	99164	77769	15
20	75786	75952	80399	75813	75872	78261	80974	75833	75786	77164	75798	76421	82839	80575	88902	98385	76433	20
25	73062	73481	77819	73106	73228	75555	78376	73134	73062	74391	73086	74607	80598	78265	86822	96500	74632	25
30	70493	71094	75389	70557	70750	72987	75801	70611	70493	71775	70533	72932	78520	76032	84649	94450	72973	30
35	67737	68483	72751	67823	68132	70267	73062	67918	67737	68969	67788	70971	76348	73552	82297	92280	71024	35
40	64922	65939	69966	65089	65409	67434	70181	65161	64922	66103	65013	68921	74145	71062	79791	89535	69017	40
45	61522	62725	66784	61784	62138	64040	66770	61812	61522	62641	61635	66112	71555	68091	76923	87506	66234	45
50	57748	59083	63174	58088	58591	60159	63005	58164	57748	58798	57854	63098	68567	64634	73512	84325	63214	50
55	53200	54579	58777	53652	54268	55649	58422	53741	53200	54167	53298	59215	65092	60300	69268	80499	59323	55
60	48547	50007	54145	49115	49953	50987	53870	49311	48547	49430	48636	54541	61637	55773	64999	76981	54641	60
65	42705	44141	48078	43416	44417	45177	48119	43704	42705	43482	42783	48429	57591	49695	59236	72397	48518	65
70	35410	36745	40487	36412	37510	37700	40756	36523	35410	36054	35475	40551	52402	42013	51485	65909	40626	70
75	26527	27627	31282	27533	28660	28601	31458	27622	26527	27009	26596	30756	46076	32579	41656	58691	30836	75
80	19774	20716	23947	20667	22029	21779	23517	20809	19774	20134	19825	23084	40516	25088	33421	51756	23143	80
85+	11747	12382	14709	12398	13710	13397	14981	12630	11747	11961	11777	13864	32644	15503	22549	41788	13900	85+

ADDED YRS OF LIFE

	No Causes	(1)	(2)	(3)	(4)	(5)	(6)	(7)	(8)	(9)	(10)	(11)	(12)	(1)+(2)	(1)+(2)+(5)+(6)+(8)	+part of (9)&(12)	(10)+(11)
TOTAL		.718	4.214	.344	.857	2.136	4.471	.444	.000	.901	.048	2.820	13.905	5.024	12.869	26.856	2.873
WORK	9.130	.550	.937	.140	.369	.308	.719	.181	.000	.000	.039	2.237	2.515	1.506	2.602	3.856	2.279

POPULATION, DEATHS, DEATH RATES FOR ALL CAUSES COMBINED, AND SPECIFIED CAUSES

Age Start of Interval	Midyear Population	Deaths During Year	All Causes	Respiratory T. B.	Other Infec. and Paras.	Neo-plasms	Cardio-vascular	Infl., Pneu., Bronch.	Diar-rheal	Certain Degen-erative	Maternal	Cert. Dis. of Infancy	Motor Vehicle	Other Violence	Other and Unknown	Age Start of Interval
0	33744	3403	.10085	.00018	.01989	.00012	.00024	.01820	.01876	.00015	.00000	.01467	.00003	.00030	.02833	0
1	109234	2690	.02463	.00005	.00657	.00000	.00006	.00250	.00715	.00003	.00000	.00000	.00000	.00014	.00813	1
5	123741	867	.00701	.00003	.00183	.00003	.00002	.00041	.00160	.00004	.00000	.00000	.00000	.00011	.00293	5
10	107746	248	.00230	.00006	.00044	.00001	.00005	.00012	.00028	.00001	.00001	.00000	.00001	.00009	.00123	10
15	101817	384	.00377	.00030	.00073	.00003	.00014	.00023	.00036	.00002	.00026	.00000	.00002	.00028	.00141	15
20	93349	456	.00488	.00058	.00071	.00010	.00022	.00024	.00035	.00007	.00037	.00000	.00001	.00025	.00198	20
25	73898	444	.00601	.00057	.00097	.00028	.00020	.00018	.00039	.00005	.00072	.00000	.00001	.00015	.00248	25
30	57426	442	.00770	.00073	.00111	.00030	.00031	.00026	.00064	.00009	.00073	.00000	.00001	.00014	.00338	30
35	57630	419	.00727	.00069	.00102	.00043	.00031	.00026	.00066	.00014	.00054	.00000	.00000	.00017	.00304	35
40	45186	456	.01009	.00058	.00133	.00089	.00035	.00042	.00089	.00018	.00049	.00000	.00002	.00022	.00474	40
45	34852	335	.00961	.00020	.00132	.00077	.00072	.00052	.00086	.00034	.00009	.00000	.00000	.00009	.00471	45
50	32343	411	.01271	.00043	.00136	.00053	.00114	.00056	.00170	.00049	.00000	.00000	.00000	.00015	.00634	50
55	18613	287	.01542	.00048	.00145	.00124	.00097	.00075	.00177	.00048	.00000	.00000	.00005	.00038	.00784	55
60	19073	552	.02894	.00068	.00283	.00189	.00173	.00173	.00288	.00105	.00000	.00000	.00000	.00016	.01599	60
65	10195	337	.03306	.00020	.00392	.00167	.00275	.00147	.00412	.00147	.00000	.00000	.00000	.00049	.01697	65
70	7581	406	.05355	.00053	.00554	.00409	.00435	.00251	.00554	.00132	.00000	.00000	.00000	.00026	.02928	70
75	4319	232	.05372	.00046	.00509	.00208	.00556	.00255	.00347	.00139	.00000	.00000	.00023	.00046	.03241	75
80	3611	334	.09250	.00055	.00609	.00249	.00831	.00443	.00858	.00166	.00000	.00000	.00000	.00083	.05926	80
85+	3090	541	.17508	.00032	.00809	.00259	.01294	.00777	.01553	.00227	.00000	.00000	.00000	.00129	.12427	85+
ALL	937448	13244														

	All Causes	Respiratory T. B.	Other Infec. and Paras.	Neo-plasms	Cardio-vascular	Infl., Pneu., Bronch.	Diar-rheal	Certain Degen-erative	Maternal	Cert. Dis. of Infancy	Motor Vehicle	Other Violence	Other and Unknown
CRUDE DEATH RATE	.01413	.00033	.00254	.00032	.00042	.00131	.00235	.00016	.00023	.00053	.00001	.00018	.00575
STANDARDIZED RATE (1)	.01413	.00033	.00256	.00035	.00043	.00130	.00237	.00017	.00022	.00052	.00001	.00018	.00568
STANDARDIZED RATE (2)	.01592	.00038	.00235	.00058	.00079	.00114	.00219	.00029	.00022	.00030	.00002	.00021	.00744
GEOMETRIC MEAN	.01692												

LIFE TABLE FOR ALL CAUSES COMBINED

Age (x)	Midyear Population	Deaths During Year	$_nM_x$	$_nq_x$	l_x	$_nd_x$	$_nL_x$	$_nm_x$	$_na_x$	T_x	$_nr_x$	$\overset{\circ}{e}_x$	Age (x)
0	33744	3403	.100848	.093680	100000	9368	92894	.100846	.241441	5229444	.000000	52.294	0
1	109234	2690	.024626	.092793	90632	8410	341503	.024626	1.500000	5136550	.000000	56.675	1
5	123741	867	.007007	.034492	82222	2836	404020	.007019	2.500000	4795047	.000000	58.318	5
10	107746	248	.002302	.011375	79386	903	394388	.002290	2.184616	4391027	.013380	55.312	10
15	101817	384	.003771	.018717	78483	1469	388942	.003777	2.636147	3996639	.009323	50.924	15
20	93349	456	.004885	.024190	77014	1863	380572	.004895	2.585436	3607697	.019409	46.845	20
25	73898	444	.006008	.029714	75151	2233	370359	.006029	2.583408	3227125	.041147	42.942	25
30	57426	442	.007697	.037810	72918	2757	357755	.007706	2.520705	2856766	.024631	39.178	30
35	57630	419	.007271	.035732	70161	2507	344659	.007274	2.548531	2499012	.012488	35.618	35
40	45186	456	.010092	.049384	67654	3341	330025	.010123	2.532051	2154353	.038864	31.844	40
45	34852	335	.009612	.046973	64313	3021	314107	.009618	2.531309	1824328	.021258	28.366	45
50	32343	411	.012708	.061917	61292	3795	297240	.012767	2.570378	1510221	.046085	24.640	50
55	18613	287	.015419	.074839	57497	4303	277443	.015509	2.666357	1212981	.038765	21.096	55
60	19073	552	.028941	.135936	53194	7231	248466	.029103	2.579317	935538	.030569	17.587	60
65	10195	337	.033055	.153515	45963	7056	212596	.033190	2.559701	687072	.052014	14.948	65
70	7581	406	.053555	.237824	38907	9253	171395	.053987	2.499144	474476	.045186	12.195	70
75	4319	232	.053716	.236663	29654	7018	130581	.053745	2.479428	303081	.018331	10.221	75
80	3611	334	.092495	.378159	22636	8560	92104	.092939	2.537797	172501	.018331	7.621	80
85+	3090	541	.175081	1.000000	14076	14076	80397	.175081	5.711645	80397	.000000	5.712	85+

NUMBER OF PERSONS DYING (OUT OF 100,000 AT BIRTH) ABOVE AGE X FROM SPECIFIED CAUSES

Age (x)	All Causes	Respira- tory T. B.	Other Infec. and Paras.	Neo- plasms	Cardio- vascular	Infl., Pneu., Bronch.	Diar- rheal	Certain Degen- erative	Maternal	Cert. Dis. of Infancy	Motor Vehicle	Other Violence	Other and Unknown	Age (x)
0	100000	2082	12719	3721	5767	6409	12441	1949	1149	1363	124	1202	51074	0
1	90632	2065	10872	3710	5745	4718	10658	1936	1149	0	121	1175	48443	1
5	82222	2050	8628	3710	5723	3865	8257	1926	1149	0	121	1128	45665	5
10	79386	2037	7885	3697	5714	3698	7609	1910	1149	0	121	1085	44481	10
15	78483	2011	7714	3693	5695	3651	7501	1906	1145	0	118	1049	44000	15
20	77014	1892	7432	3681	5642	3563	7359	1899	1045	0	110	942	43449	20
25	75151	1671	7162	3644	5556	3473	7225	1870	902	0	106	848	42694	25
30	72918	1460	6800	3538	5481	3408	7079	1850	635	0	101	793	41773	30
35	70161	1198	6401	3432	5368	3315	6848	1819	373	0	101	743	40563	35
40	67654	959	6048	3282	5260	3225	6620	1771	188	0	101	684	39516	40
45	64313	771	5609	2988	5143	3085	6327	1712	28	0	94	611	37945	45
50	61292	708	5194	2746	4916	2923	6056	1603	2	0	94	584	36466	50
55	57497	578	4789	2589	4575	2757	5547	1456	2	0	94	537	34573	55
60	53194	444	4385	2243	4306	2546	5054	1321	2	0	79	432	32382	60
65	45963	274	3677	1773	3873	2114	4333	1058	2	0	79	393	28387	65
70	38907	234	2838	1417	3284	1802	3452	745	2	0	79	288	24766	70
75	29654	143	1882	710	2532	1368	2499	519	2	0	56	243	19700	75
80	22636	82	1218	439	1805	1036	2046	337	2	0	25	183	15463	80
85+	14076	26	650	208	1041	624	1249	182	0	0	0	104	9992	85+

NUMBER OF PERSONS SURVIVING TO AGE X IF SPECIFIED CAUSES WERE ELIMINATED

Age (x)	No Causes	Respira- tory T. B. (1)	Other Infec. and Paras. (2)	Neo- plasms (3)	Cardio- vascular (4)	Infl., Pneu., Bronch. (5)	Diar- rheal (6)	Certain Degen- erative (7)	Maternal (8)	Cert. Dis. of Infancy (9)	Motor Vehicle (10)	Other Violence (11)	Other and Unknown (12)	(1) + (2)	(1) + (2) + (5) + (6) + (8)	(1)+(2)+ (5)+(6)+ (8)+part of(9)&(12)	(10) + (11)	Age (x)
0	100000	100000	100000	100000	100000	100000	100000	100000	100000	100000	100000	100000	100000	100000	100000	100000	100000	0
1	90632	90648	92407	90642	90653	92256	92306	90644	90632	91938	90635	90658	93171	92423	95817	99861	90661	1
5	82222	82251	86039	82231	82262	84526	86141	82243	82222	83407	82225	82290	87288	86069	92699	99725	82293	5
10	79386	79427	83839	79408	79433	81779	83840	79422	79386	80530	79388	79494	85522	83882	91259	99553	79496	10
15	78483	78549	83065	78509	78549	80897	83000	78522	78487	79614	78488	78626	85066	83135	90628	99375	78631	15
20	77014	77197	81806	77051	77131	79473	81595	77060	77117	78124	77027	77260	84067	82001	89772	98993	77274	20
25	75151	75549	80111	75224	75350	77642	79762	75224	75393	76234	75168	75484	82852	80535	88594	98448	75501	25
30	72918	73513	78112	73093	73186	75401	77544	73009	73417	73969	72939	73296	81396	78749	87191	97859	73317	30
35	70161	70993	75579	70434	70530	72645	74854	70279	70901	71172	70182	70574	79655	76475	85369	97130	70594	35
40	67654	68694	73252	68066	68116	70141	72418	67815	68551	68629	67674	68110	77985	74379	83637	96250	68130	40
45	64313	65488	70100	64993	64868	66818	69149	64524	65323	65240	64339	64818	75921	71380	80990	94746	64844	45
50	61292	62474	67250	62179	62045	63844	66166	61600	62280	62175	61316	61800	74079	68547	78345	92974	61825	50
55	57497	58734	63517	58484	58538	60059	62623	57929	58424	58326	57520	58020	71744	64884	75007	90836	58043	55
60	53194	54470	59194	54447	54421	55777	58454	53724	54052	53961	53230	53779	69058	60615	70969	87972	53815	60
65	45963	47227	51886	47493	47437	48617	51250	46669	46704	46622	45994	46505	64686	53312	63890	83313	46536	65
70	38907	40014	44800	40542	40718	41457	44294	39797	39534	39468	38933	39464	59645	46074	56793	77976	39490	70
75	29654	30580	35114	31548	31728	32003	34713	30533	30132	30081	29694	30118	52758	36210	46483	69585	30158	75
80	22636	23397	27494	24329	24908	24743	26961	23470	23001	22962	22654	23043	47420	28419	37596	61504	23102	80
85+	14076	14595	17645	15324	16159	15742	17524	14721	14305	14279	14132	14392	39949	18295	25885	50716	14449	85+

ADDED YRS OF LIFE																	
TOTAL		.652	4.630	.699	.890	2.189	4.247	.335	.444	.750	.023	.346	17.962	5.365	13.589	31.612	.369
WORK	7.831	.512	.984	.339	.330	.296	.614	.127	.422	.000	.011	.197	3.205	1.514	2.942	5.476	.208

POPULATION, DEATHS, DEATH RATES FOR ALL CAUSES COMBINED, AND SPECIFIED CAUSES

Age Start of Interval	Midyear Population	Deaths During Year	All Causes	Respiratory T. B.	Other Infec. and Paras.	Neoplasms	Cardiovascular	Infl., Pneu., Bronch.	Diarrheal	Certain Degenerative	Maternal	Cert. Dis. of Infancy	Motor Vehicle	Other Violence	Other and Unknown	Age Start of Interval
0	299704	59673	.19911	.00158	.02465	.00001	.00070	.02824	.02176	.00014	.00000	.05524	.00000	.00232	.06446	0
1	1059437	37804	.03568	.00096	.01456	.00002	.00026	.00601	.00247	.00007	.00000	.00000	.00000	.00123	.01011	1
5	1176672	7926	.00674	.00050	.00325	.00001	.00023	.00040	.00016	.00005	.00000	.00000	.00000	.00063	.01011	5
10	1063218	4606	.00433	.00070	.00140	.00001	.00030	.00014	.00012	.00004	.00000	.00000	.00000	.00078	.00152	10
15	960898	6191	.00644	.00249	.00130	.00002	.00042	.00024	.00013	.00006	.00000	.00000	.00000	.00086	.00086	15
20	862893	7117	.00825	.00405	.00119	.00002	.00043	.00040	.00011	.00009	.00000	.00000	.00000	.00096	.00101	20
25	736599	6208	.00843	.00363	.00087	.00004	.00070	.00049	.00014	.00014	.00000	.00000	.00000	.00096	.00126	25
30	663771	6679	.01006	.00406	.00119	.00008	.00099	.00070	.00016	.00019	.00000	.00000	.00000	.00104	.00166	30
35	592148	6675	.01127	.00355	.00093	.00014	.00138	.00098	.00019	.00024	.00000	.00000	.00000	.00117	.00230	35
40	552825	7347	.01329	.00389	.00093	.00025	.00192	.00140	.00024	.00030	.00000	.00000	.00000	.00130	.00305	40
45	454719	7060	.01553	.00374	.00104	.00042	.00251	.00194	.00029	.00034	.00000	.00000	.00000	.00146	.00379	45
50	393428	7871	.02001	.00359	.00116	.00064	.00379	.00289	.00044	.00041	.00000	.00000	.00000	.00162	.00548	50
55	299936	7667	.02556	.00349	.00128	.00093	.00552	.00409	.00069	.00049	.00000	.00000	.00000	.00178	.00729	55
60	266331	9814	.03685	.00311	.00159	.00123	.00864	.00619	.00112	.00060	.00000	.00000	.00000	.00186	.01250	60
65	176049	9198	.05225	.00230	.00223	.00158	.01378	.00945	.00161	.00076	.00000	.00000	.00000	.00173	.01881	65
70	128802	10751	.08347	.00154	.00266	.00188	.01951	.01338	.00303	.00097	.00000	.00000	.00000	.00178	.03873	70
75	72025	8488	.11785	.00093	.00265	.00201	.02476	.01676	.00408	.00067	.00000	.00000	.00000	.00189	.06410	75
80	34407	7090	.20606	.00029	.00285	.00206	.03063	.02256	.00680	.00038	.00000	.00000	.00000	.00256	.13753	80
85+	13041	4116	.31562	.00061	.00284	.00161	.02945	.02738	.00982	.00008	.00000	.00000	.00000	.00256	.13753	85+
ALL	9806903	222281														

	All Causes	Respiratory T. B.	Other Infec. and Paras.	Neoplasms	Cardiovascular	Infl., Pneu., Bronch.	Diarrheal	Certain Degenerative	Maternal	Cert. Dis. of Infancy	Motor Vehicle	Other Violence	Other and Unknown
CRUDE DEATH RATE	.02267	.00249	.00364	.00022	.00200	.00294	.00125	.00019	.00000	.00169	.00000	.00114	.00711
STANDARDIZED RATE (1)	.02283	.00241	.00390	.00020	.00178	.00297	.00134	.00017	.00000	.00194	.00000	.00112	.00698
STANDARDIZED RATE (2)	.02612	.00262	.00303	.00036	.00329	.00342	.00117	.00024	.00000	.00114	.00000	.00122	.00962
GEOMETRIC MEAN	.02683												

LIFE TABLE FOR ALL CAUSES COMBINED

Age (x)	Midyear Population	Deaths During Year	$_nM_x$	$_nq_x$	l_x	$_nd_x$	$_nL_x$	$_nm_x$	$_na_x$	T_x	$_nr_x$	$\overset{\circ}{e}_x$	Age (x)
0	299704	59673	.199106	.178130	100000	17813	89463	.199110	.408481	4047025	.000000	40.470	0
1	1059437	37804	.035683	.131043	82187	10770	301823	.035683	1.500000	3957562	.000000	48.153	1
5	1176672	7926	.006736	.033129	71417	2366	351170	.006737	2.500000	3655739	.000000	51.189	5
10	1063218	4606	.004332	.021419	69051	1479	341512	.004331	2.469151	3304569	.011613	47.857	10
15	960898	6191	.006443	.031774	67572	2147	332736	.006453	2.613336	2963057	.013151	43.850	15
20	862893	7117	.008248	.040459	65425	2647	320600	.008256	2.535103	2630321	.017457	40.204	20
25	736599	6208	.008428	.041304	62778	2593	307472	.008433	2.524987	2309721	.018181	36.792	25
30	663771	6679	.010062	.049148	60185	2958	293644	.010073	2.538455	2002246	.014484	33.268	30
35	592148	6675	.011273	.054852	57227	3139	278397	.011275	2.534844	1708605	.007641	29.857	35
40	552825	7347	.013290	.064395	54088	3483	261868	.013301	2.538939	1430208	.011214	26.442	40
45	454719	7060	.015526	.074894	50605	3790	243756	.015548	2.554474	1168340	.015460	23.087	45
50	393428	7871	.020006	.095568	46815	4474	223164	.020048	2.561187	924584	.021857	19.750	50
55	299936	7667	.025562	.120545	42341	5104	199327	.025606	2.574941	701420	.014058	16.566	55
60	266331	9814	.036849	.169455	37237	6310	170843	.036934	2.568641	502092	.014829	13.484	60
65	176049	9198	.052247	.232257	30927	7183	137073	.052403	2.555107	331249	.018692	10.711	65
70	128802	10751	.083469	.345772	23744	8210	98162	.083637	2.496041	194176	.009237	8.178	70
75	72025	8488	.117848	.452363	15534	7027	59572	.117958	2.424517	96013	.005532	6.181	75
80	34407	7090	.206063	.665805	8507	5664	27434	.206463	2.333782	36441	.005532	4.284	80
85+	13041	4116	.315620	1.000000	2843	2843	9008	.315620	3.168367	9008	.000000	3.168	85+

NUMBER OF PERSONS DYING (OUT OF 100,000 AT BIRTH) ABOVE AGE X FROM SPECIFIED CAUSES

Age (x)	All Causes	Respiratory T.B.	Other Infec. and Paras.	Neoplasms	Cardiovascular	Infl., Pneu., Bronch.	Diarrheal	Certain Degenerative	Maternal	Cert. Dis. of Infancy	Motor Vehicle	Other Violence	Other and Unknown	Age (x)
0	100000	10946	12027	1398	12434	13218	4610	982	0	4942	0	4942	34501	0
1	82187	10804	9822	1357	12372	10691	2663	969	0	0	0	4734	28735	1
5	71417	10515	5426	1392	12293	8877	1918	949	0	0	0	4364	25683	5
10	69051	10341	4284	1390	12212	8738	1861	933	0	0	0	4141	25151	10
15	67572	10102	3809	1387	12110	8692	1821	919	0	0	0	3875	24857	15
20	65425	9269	3378	1381	11970	8613	1778	897	0	0	0	3589	24550	20
25	62778	7968	2996	1373	11832	8484	1742	868	0	0	0	3290	24225	25
30	60185	6791	2728	1361	11616	8333	1701	824	0	0	0	2996	23835	30
35	57227	5599	2378	1337	11324	8127	1655	770	0	0	0	2692	23345	35
40	54088	4500	2119	1298	10940	7855	1601	703	0	0	0	2366	22706	40
45	50605	3481	1875	1233	10436	7488	1537	624	0	0	0	2024	21907	45
50	46815	2569	1621	1131	9824	7013	1466	542	0	0	0	1668	20981	50
55	42341	1769	1362	988	8576	6367	1367	451	0	0	0	1307	19754	55
60	37237	1074	1106	803	7873	5549	1230	354	0	0	0	951	18297	60
65	30927	544	833	593	6392	4488	1037	251	0	0	0	633	16156	65
70	23744	230	528	376	4498	3190	816	146	0	0	0	396	13564	70
75	15534	79	266	191	2579	1875	518	51	0	0	0	221	9754	75
80	8507	24	108	71	1104	876	275	11	0	0	0	109	5929	80
85+	2843	6	26	15	265	247	88	1	0	0	0	35	2160	85+

NUMBER OF PERSONS SURVIVING TO AGE X IF SPECIFIED CAUSES WERE ELIMINATED

Age (x)	No Causes	Respiratory T.B. (1)	Other Infec. and Paras. (2)	Neoplasms (3)	Cardiovascular (4)	Infl., Pneu., Bronch. (5)	Diarrheal (6)	Certain Degenerative (7)	Maternal (8)	Cert. Dis. of Infancy (9)	Motor Vehicle (10)	Other Violence (11)	Other and Unknown (12)	(1)+(2)	(1)+(2)+(5)+(6)+(8)	(1)+(2)+(5)+(6)+(8)+part of(9)&(12)	(10)+(11)	Age (x)
0	100000	100000	100000	100000	100000	100000	100000	100000	100000	100000	100000	100000	100000	100000	100000	100000	100000	0
1	82187	82316	84207	82188	82243	84506	83968	82199	82187	86784	82187	82375	87575	84339	88599	99219	82375	1
5	71417	71799	77490	71422	71539	75190	73677	71446	71417	75412	71417	71927	75189	77905	84617	98367	71927	5
10	69051	69592	76152	69058	69249	72843	71294	69095	69051	72913	69051	69765	77148	76748	83594	97787	69765	10
15	67572	68341	75040	67582	67867	71331	69808	67629	67572	71352	67572	68537	75821	75894	82767	97101	68537	15
20	65425	67004	73128	65441	65849	69147	67634	65501	65425	69084	65425	66646	73752	74893	81826	96331	66646	20
25	62778	65612	70588	62801	63321	66634	64934	62880	62778	66289	62778	64248	71128	73775	80812	95522	64248	25
30	60185	64117	67968	60219	60920	63854	62293	60326	60185	63551	60185	61890	68624	72409	79564	94492	61890	30
35	57227	62216	65014	57282	58215	60967	59278	57414	57227	60428	57227	59153	65799	70682	78001	93200	59153	35
40	54088	59976	61734	54178	55403	57906	56081	54330	54088	57113	54088	56237	62908	68454	75987	91498	56237	40
45	50605	57216	58029	50753	52337	54559	52534	50908	50605	53436	50605	52961	59763	65609	73431	89278	52961	45
50	46815	53930	53963	47050	49031	50968	48670	47175	46815	49434	46815	49354	56350	62165	70362	86524	49354	50
55	42341	49658	49090	42691	45158	46771	44117	42754	42341	44709	42341	45000	52389	57574	66266	82744	45000	55
60	37237	44439	43451	37720	40870	41989	38933	37692	37237	39320	37237	39931	47797	51856	61138	77819	39931	60
65	30927	37484	36379	31522	35458	35981	32520	31399	30927	32657	30927	33474	42283	44092	53940	70827	33474	65
70	23744	29107	28244	24394	29187	28974	25171	24200	23744	25072	23744	25923	35723	34624	44790	61491	25923	70
75	15534	19187	18727	16111	21077	20283	16724	15909	15534	16403	15534	17111	28492	23132	32517	48903	17111	75
80	8507	10555	10393	8913	13084	12092	9351	8741	8507	8983	8507	9460	21726	12894	20146	35215	9460	80
85+	2843	3540	3529	3011	5143	4564	3240	2927	2843	3002	2843	3207	15057	4393	8038	19990	3207	85+

ADDED YRS OF LIFE

	No Causes	(1)	(2)	(3)	(4)	(5)	(6)	(7)	(8)	(9)	(10)	(11)	(12)	(1)+(2)	(1)+(2)+(5)+(6)+(8)	...+part	(10)+(11)
TOTAL		3.386	5.186	.155	1.916	3.464	1.543	.203	.000	2.241	.000	1.437	10.115	9.110	15.810	29.807	1.437
WORK	11.052	3.312	.976	.122	1.068	.777	.163	.155	.000	.000	.000	.948	1.800	4.405	5.535	6.983	.948

POPULATION, DEATHS, DEATH RATES FOR ALL CAUSES COMBINED, AND SPECIFIED CAUSES

Age Start of Interval	Midyear Population	Deaths During Year	All Causes	Respiratory T.B.	Other Infec. and Paras.	Neoplasms	Cardiovascular	Infl., Pneu., Bronch.	Diarrheal	Certain Degenerative	Maternal	Cert. Dis. of Infancy	Motor Vehicle	Other Violence	Other and Unknown	Age Start of Interval
0	297532	46755	.15714	.00158	.02252	.00001	.00051	.02139	.01791	.00009	.00000	.04401	.00000	.00193	.04719	0
1	1052074	36897	.03507	.00104	.01526	.00001	.00030	.00593	.00245	.00005	.00000	.00000	.00000	.00089	.00914	1
5	1174412	7964	.00678	.00057	.00367	.00001	.00021	.00044	.00015	.00003	.00000	.00000	.00000	.00038	.00132	5
10	1048256	4574	.00436	.00130	.00155	.00000	.00032	.00017	.00008	.00003	.00000	.00000	.00000	.00038	.00132	10
15	977456	6857	.00702	.00359	.00137	.00002	.00045	.00023	.00012	.00006	.00015	.00000	.00000	.00015	.00088	15
20	972041	7838	.00806	.00426	.00102	.00003	.00051	.00030	.00016	.00008	.00053	.00000	.00000	.00014	.00103	20
25	837261	7534	.00900	.00445	.00089	.00009	.00068	.00036	.00018	.00011	.00079	.00000	.00000	.00011	.00132	25
30	727150	7296	.01003	.00453	.00076	.00024	.00090	.00048	.00021	.00015	.00095	.00000	.00000	.00012	.00168	30
35	636094	6865	.01079	.00410	.00080	.00052	.00114	.00064	.00026	.00019	.00087	.00000	.00000	.00017	.00213	35
40	584749	7050	.01206	.00372	.00079	.00084	.00163	.00093	.00031	.00021	.00070	.00000	.00000	.00020	.00272	40
45	478850	6212	.01297	.00317	.00077	.00129	.00232	.00127	.00035	.00020	.00011	.00000	.00000	.00023	.00325	45
50	415572	6947	.01672	.00270	.00085	.00168	.00364	.00214	.00046	.00023	.00002	.00000	.00000	.00028	.00472	50
55	315891	7004	.02217	.00239	.00105	.00156	.00553	.00354	.00056	.00034	.00000	.00000	.00000	.00031	.00650	55
60	291522	9362	.03211	.00158	.00128	.00228	.00838	.00547	.00038	.00038	.00000	.00000	.00000	.00041	.01098	60
65	201568	9199	.04564	.00156	.00155	.00265	.01284	.00822	.00171	.00037	.00000	.00000	.00000	.00055	.01619	65
70	153332	11142	.07267	.00105	.00192	.00282	.01748	.01167	.00279	.00035	.00000	.00000	.00000	.00095	.03363	70
75	89151	9469	.10621	.00055	.00242	.00251	.02162	.01523	.00415	.00024	.00000	.00000	.00000	.00155	.05795	75
80	45528	8198	.18007	.00004	.00266	.00246	.02563	.02016	.00555	.00022	.00000	.00000	.00000	.00275	.12019	80
85+	20658	5670	.27447	.00015	.00203	.00266	.02396	.02270	.00657	.00044	.00000	.00000	.00000	.00421	.21135	85+
ALL	10319097	212833														

CRUDE DEATH RATE			.02063	.00267	.00346	.00049	.00199	.00250	.00111	.00013	.00030	.00127	.00000	.00037	.00633	
STANDARDIZED RATE (1)			.02045	.00258	.00388	.00042	.00166	.00251	.00121	.00012	.00028	.00155	.00000	.00038	.00588	
STANDARDIZED RATE (2)			.02336	.00265	.00294	.00070	.00302	.00290	.00108	.00015	.00029	.00091	.00000	.00040	.00833	
GEOMETRIC MEAN			.02474													

LIFE TABLE FOR ALL CAUSES COMBINED

Age (x)	Midyear Population	Deaths During Year	$_nM_x$	$_nq_x$	l_x	$_nd_x$	$_nL_x$	$_nm_x$	$_na_x$	T_x	$_nr_x$	$\overset{\circ}{e}_x$	Age (x)
0	297532	46755	.157143	.142220	100000	14232	90566	.157145	.337143	4308885	.000000	43.089	0
1	1052074	36897	.035071	.128976	85768	11062	315417	.035071	1.500000	4218319	.000000	49.183	1
5	1174412	7964	.006781	.033344	74706	2491	367303	.006782	2.500000	3902902	.000000	52.243	5
10	1048256	4574	.004363	.021574	72215	1558	357169	.004362	2.492913	3535600	.012060	48.959	10
15	977456	6857	.007015	.034505	70657	2438	347427	.007017	2.597416	3178431	.002957	44.984	15
20	972041	7838	.008063	.039549	68219	2698	334443	.008067	2.534516	2831003	.004092	41.499	20
25	837261	7534	.008998	.044032	65521	2885	320470	.009002	2.526791	2496560	.016424	38.103	25
30	727150	7296	.010034	.048957	62636	3069	305559	.010044	2.516699	2176090	.018647	34.742	30
35	636094	6865	.010792	.052563	59567	3131	290057	.010794	2.515703	1870531	.011791	31.402	35
40	584749	7050	.012056	.058562	56436	3305	273962	.012064	2.513427	1580475	.014925	28.005	40
45	478850	6212	.012973	.062939	53131	3344	257442	.012989	2.543922	1306513	.018100	24.590	45
50	415572	6947	.016717	.080543	49787	4010	239219	.016763	2.577047	1049071	.025265	21.071	50
55	315891	7004	.022172	.105446	45777	4827	217255	.022218	2.590679	809852	.015621	17.691	55
60	291522	9362	.032114	.149231	40950	6111	189961	.032170	2.580013	592597	.012161	14.471	60
65	201568	9199	.045637	.205919	34839	7174	156764	.045763	2.570306	402635	.016505	11.557	65
70	153332	11142	.072666	.308404	27665	8532	117169	.072818	2.520389	245871	.010237	8.887	70
75	89151	9469	.106213	.418556	19133	8009	75282	.106386	2.455025	128702	.008589	6.727	75
80	45528	8198	.180065	.611561	11124	6803	37677	.180563	2.362438	53420	.008589	4.802	80
85+	20658	5670	.274470	1.000000	4321	4321	15743	.274470	3.643386	15743	.000000	3.643	85+

NUMBER OF PERSONS DYING (OUT OF 100,000 AT BIRTH) ABOVE AGE X FROM SPECIFIED CAUSES

Age (x)	All Causes	Respira- tory T.B.	Other Infec. and Paras.	Neo- plasms	Cardio- vascular	Infl., Pneu., Bronch.	Diar- rheal	Certain Degen- erative	Maternal	Cert. Dis. of Infancy	Motor Vehicle	Other Violence	Other and Unknown	Age (x)
0	100000	11618	12199	3173	13251	12495	4603	677	1257	3986	0	1676	35065	0
1	85768	11475	10160	3173	13204	10558	2981	668	1257	0	0	1502	30790	1
5	74706	11147	5347	3169	13111	8689	2207	652	1257	0	0	1221	27906	5
10	72215	10939	3999	3167	13032	8529	2151	640	1257	0	0	1082	27419	10
15	70657	10470	3447	3165	12916	8468	2124	628	1257	0	0	1029	27153	15
20	68219	9224	2972	3158	12762	8387	2083	607	1200	0	0	978	26848	20
25	65521	7799	2630	3149	12591	8286	2028	579	1023	0	0	931	26505	25
30	62636	6372	2343	3120	12372	8170	1972	542	769	0	0	895	26081	30
35	59567	4987	2110	3047	12095	8022	1906	497	477	0	0	859	25567	35
40	56436	3800	1879	2897	11765	7837	1831	442	224	0	0	811	24950	40
45	53131	2782	1663	2667	11317	7582	1746	385	32	0	0	755	24202	45
50	49787	1966	1464	2335	10717	7253	1655	334	5	0	0	696	23362	50
55	45777	1322	1260	1931	9842	6738	1545	278	1	0	0	629	22231	55
60	40950	803	1031	1506	8637	5967	1424	205	1	0	0	562	20814	60
65	34839	426	787	1072	7041	4926	1243	132	1	0	0	484	18727	65
70	27665	182	544	656	5023	3635	975	74	1	0	0	398	16177	70
75	19133	59	318	325	2972	2265	647	33	1	0	0	287	12226	75
80	11124	18	135	136	1343	1117	334	16	1	0	0	170	7854	80
85+	4321	2	32	42	377	357	110	7	0	0	0	66	3328	85+

NUMBER OF PERSONS SURVIVING TO AGE X IF SPECIFIED CAUSES WERE ELIMINATED

Age (x)	No Causes	Respira- tory T.B.	Other Infec. and Paras.	Neo- plasms	Cardio- vascular	Infl., Pneu., Bronch.	Diar- rheal	Certain Degener- ative	Maternal	Cert. Dis. of Infancy	Motor Vehicle	Other Violence	Other and Unknown	(1) + (2)	(1) + (2) + (5) + (6) + (8)	(1)+(2)+ (5)+(6)+ (8)+part of(9)&(12)	(10) + (11)	Age (x)
		(1)	(2)	(3)	(4)	(5)	(6)	(7)	(8)	(9)	(10)	(11)	(12)					
0	100000	100000	100000	100000	100000	100000	100000	100000	100000	100000	100000	100000	100000	100000	100000	100000	100000	0
1	85768	85900	87675	85768	85811	87579	87282	85776	85768	89536	85768	85929	89816	87811	91248	99410	85929	1
5	74706	75128	81096	74710	74831	78084	76763	74728	74706	77988	74706	75109	81099	81555	87589	98751	75109	5
10	72215	72828	79645	72221	72413	75645	74260	72248	72215	75388	72215	72743	78917	80523	86736	98364	72743	10
15	70657	71727	78727	70664	70966	74076	72685	70701	70657	73761	70657	71226	77502	79920	86192	98061	71226	15
20	68219	70507	76532	68233	68670	71604	70215	68283	68275	71216	68219	68819	75157	79099	85527	97686	68819	20
25	65521	69177	73882	65543	66123	68876	67497	65610	65749	68400	65521	66143	72556	78004	84766	97260	66143	25
30	62636	67620	70945	62686	63428	65563	64581	62757	63104	65388	62636	63267	69822	76591	83785	96689	63267	30
35	59567	65781	67727	59686	60594	62883	61484	59726	60299	62184	59567	60202	66963	74792	82498	95872	60202	35
40	56436	63611	64423	56655	57737	59976	58327	56640	57380	58916	56436	57085	64122	72614	80807	94678	57085	40
45	53131	61008	60890	53600	54803	56531	54997	53379	54208	55465	53131	53797	61198	69917	78565	92924	53797	45
50	49787	58081	57279	50552	51957	53313	51627	50069	50823	51974	49787	50469	58291	66820	75741	90441	50469	50
55	45777	54126	52890	46875	48657	49552	47578	46090	46733	47788	45777	46469	54881	62536	71826	86815	46469	55
60	40950	48999	47564	42345	44755	45124	42680	41300	41805	42749	40950	41633	50728	56913	66729	81934	41633	60
65	34839	42102	40727	36441	39719	39462	36486	35204	35567	36370	34839	35493	45609	49218	59603	75059	35493	65
70	27665	33692	32593	29324	33651	32662	29224	28007	28243	28880	27665	28263	39321	39694	50538	66001	28263	70
75	19133	23422	22761	20569	25419	23962	20499	19403	19533	19974	19133	19641	32289	27864	38169	53825	19641	75
80	11124	13653	13397	12109	16484	15049	12173	11293	11356	11613	11124	11510	25303	16443	24852	40249	11510	80
85+	4321	5315	5279	4166	7323	6497	4878	4392	4412	4511	4321	4536	18438	6494	11255	24728	4536	85+

ADDED YRS OF LIFE																		
TOTAL		4.026	5.556	.526	2.115	3.212	1.510	.159	.421	1.878	.000	.496	10.308	10.203	17.211	30.147	.496	
WORK	10.715	3.680	.875	.349	1.042	.588	.198	.119	.476	.000	.000	.141	1.719	4.666	6.180	7.700	.141	

POPULATION, DEATHS, DEATH RATES FOR ALL CAUSES COMBINED, AND SPECIFIED CAUSES

Age Start of Interval	Midyear Population	Deaths During Year	All Causes	Respiratory T.B.	Other Infec. and Paras.	Neo-plasms	Cardio-vascular	Infl., Pneu., Bronch.	Diar-rheal	Certain Degen-erative	Maternal	Cert. Dis. of Infancy	Motor Vehicle	Other Violence	Other and Unknown	Age Start of Interval
0	346500	69699	.20115	.00159	.02889	.00000	.00074	.03002	.02686	.00017	.00000	.05590	.00000	.00259	.05438	0
1	1194628	40824	.03417	.00063	.01562	.00001	.00028	.00585	.00242	.00014	.00000	.00000	.00000	.00106	.00816	1
5	1354956	11206	.00827	.00036	.00489	.00001	.00031	.00044	.00014	.00008	.00000	.00000	.00000	.00057	.00148	5
10	1224556	5421	.00443	.00051	.00177	.00001	.00038	.00016	.00008	.00005	.00000	.00000	.00000	.00066	.00081	10
15	1088038	6951	.00639	.00200	.00184	.00001	.00053	.00024	.00009	.00011	.00000	.00000	.00000	.00079	.00077	15
20	954829	8772	.00919	.00357	.00262	.00003	.00052	.00035	.00007	.00016	.00000	.00000	.00000	.00094	.00093	20
25	845895	8674	.01025	.00358	.00221	.00004	.00089	.00056	.00011	.00023	.00000	.00000	.00000	.00101	.00123	25
30	748556	8981	.01200	.00442	.00213	.00008	.00131	.00082	.00013	.00032	.00000	.00000	.00000	.00113	.00164	30
35	642772	8609	.01339	.00427	.00190	.00017	.00194	.00110	.00014	.00041	.00000	.00000	.00000	.00129	.00216	35
40	591916	9214	.01557	.00422	.00175	.00030	.00265	.00165	.00017	.00054	.00000	.00000	.00000	.00142	.00286	40
45	508460	9060	.01782	.00405	.00167	.00048	.00321	.00242	.00022	.00072	.00000	.00000	.00000	.00146	.00360	45
50	457203	10245	.02241	.00382	.00162	.00074	.00468	.00366	.00035	.00089	.00000	.00000	.00000	.00160	.00504	50
55	346964	9918	.02859	.00348	.00168	.00114	.00651	.00528	.00057	.00105	.00000	.00000	.00000	.00187	.00660	55
60	295607	11868	.04015	.00301	.00180	.00157	.01065	.00793	.00053	.00124	.00000	.00000	.00000	.00203	.01099	60
65	206032	11314	.05491	.00241	.00209	.00205	.01640	.01161	.00139	.00148	.00000	.00000	.00000	.00197	.01552	65
70	150361	12715	.08456	.00165	.00229	.00247	.02278	.01648	.00220	.00154	.00000	.00000	.00000	.00209	.03307	70
75	82353	9628	.11691	.00057	.00227	.00253	.02811	.02099	.00306	.00127	.00000	.00000	.00000	.00225	.05586	75
80	38719	7929	.20478	.00080	.00291	.00284	.03531	.02921	.00504	.00068	.00000	.00000	.00000	.00294	.12526	80
85+	14545	4535	.31179	.00034	.00282	.00309	.03609	.03499	.00715	.00034	.00000	.00000	.00000	.00406	.22289	85+
ALL	11092930	265563														

	All Causes	Respiratory T.B.	Other Infec. and Paras.	Neo-plasms	Cardio-vascular	Infl., Pneu., Bronch.	Diar-rheal	Certain Degen-erative	Maternal	Cert. Dis. of Infancy	Motor Vehicle	Other Violence	Other and Unknown
CRUDE DEATH RATE	.02394	.00240	.00464	.00028	.00247	.00332	.00135	.00035	.00000	.00175	.00000	.00114	.00624
STANDARDIZED RATE (1)	.02389	.00234	.00492	.00024	.00219	.00329	.00145	.00032	.00000	.00197	.00000	.00112	.00604
STANDARDIZED RATE (2)	.02741	.00260	.00389	.00045	.00399	.00400	.00116	.00046	.00000	.00116	.00000	.00125	.00847
GEOMETRIC MEAN	.02901												

LIFE TABLE FOR ALL CAUSES COMBINED

Age (x)	Midyear Population	Deaths During Year	$_nM_x$	$_nq_x$	l_x	$_nd_x$	$_nL_x$	$_nm_x$	$_na_x$	T_x	$_nr_x$	$\overset{\circ}{e}_x$	Age (x)
0	346500	69699	.201152	.179870	100000	17987	89423	.201145	.411958	3916465	.000000	39.165	0
1	1194628	40824	.034173	.125943	82013	10329	302230	.034176	1.500000	3827042	.000000	46.664	1
5	1354956	11206	.008270	.040553	71684	2907	351153	.008278	2.500000	3524813	.000000	49.172	5
10	1224556	5421	.004427	.021853	68777	1503	339964	.004421	2.391190	3173660	.011902	46.144	10
15	1088038	6951	.006389	.031543	67274	2122	331363	.006404	2.640296	2833696	.017149	42.122	15
20	954829	8772	.009187	.045002	65152	2932	318637	.009202	2.570487	2502334	.017120	38.408	20
25	845895	8674	.010254	.050048	62220	3114	303422	.010263	2.534455	2183697	.014121	35.096	25
30	748556	8981	.011997	.058319	59106	3447	287016	.012010	2.529978	1880275	.016176	31.812	30
35	642772	8609	.013394	.064859	55659	3610	269365	.013402	2.526316	1593259	.011630	28.625	35
40	591916	9214	.015566	.074987	52049	3903	250592	.015575	2.526742	1323894	.009183	25.436	40
45	508460	9060	.017819	.085386	48146	4111	230615	.017826	2.539528	1073302	.006447	22.293	45
50	457203	10245	.022408	.106347	44035	4683	208708	.022438	2.551383	842687	.013703	19.137	50
55	346964	9918	.028585	.133818	39352	5266	183919	.028632	2.561558	633979	.014305	16.110	55
60	295607	11868	.040148	.183037	34086	6239	155140	.040215	2.549354	450060	.012454	13.204	60
65	206032	11314	.054914	.242180	27847	6744	122610	.055004	2.534846	294919	.010900	10.591	65
70	150361	12715	.084563	.349097	21103	7367	86979	.084658	2.483937	172309	.007974	8.165	70
75	82353	9628	.116911	.449621	13736	6176	52751	.117079	2.420796	85330	.008780	6.212	75
80	38719	7929	.204783	.663889	7560	5019	24430	.205448	2.336040	32579	.008780	4.309	80
85+	14545	4535	.311791	1.000000	2541	2541	8150	.311791	3.207277	8150	.000000	3.207	85+

NUMBER OF PERSONS DYING (OUT OF 100,000 AT BIRTH) ABOVE AGE X FROM SPECIFIED CAUSES

Age (x)	All Causes	Respira-tory T.B.	Other Infec. and Paras.	Neo-plasms	Cardio-vascular	Infl., Pneu., Bronch.	Diar-rheal	Certain Degen-erative	Maternal	Cert. Dis. of Infancy	Motor Vehicle	Other Violence	Other and Unknown	Age (x)
0	100000	10466	15279	1595	13850	14464	4497	1744	0	4999	0	4855	28251	0
1	82013	10324	12696	1595	13783	11779	2096	1729	0	0	0	4623	23388	1
5	71684	10134	7976	1592	13698	10012	1363	1687	0	0	0	4301	20921	5
10	68777	10006	6256	1590	13591	9858	1314	1660	0	0	0	4099	20403	10
15	67274	9831	5656	1587	13463	9805	1286	1644	0	0	0	3876	20126	15
20	65152	9163	5045	1582	13288	9726	1256	1606	0	0	0	3614	19872	20
25	62220	8023	4210	1572	13123	9615	1233	1555	0	0	0	3314	19575	25
30	59106	6814	3539	1561	12853	9446	1199	1485	0	0	0	3008	19201	30
35	55659	5544	2927	1537	12474	9209	1161	1393	0	0	0	2682	18732	35
40	52049	4394	2415	1490	11951	8912	1123	1282	0	0	0	2335	18147	40
45	48146	3336	1976	1415	11287	8499	1080	1145	0	0	0	1979	17429	45
50	44035	2401	1592	1305	10547	7940	1028	979	0	0	0	1643	16600	50
55	39352	1605	1253	1149	9569	7175	955	793	0	0	0	1308	15545	55
60	34086	964	945	938	8294	6202	850	599	0	0	0	965	14329	60
65	27847	497	665	694	6638	4969	706	407	0	0	0	650	12621	65
70	21103	202	409	443	4624	3542	535	226	0	0	0	409	10713	70
75	13736	59	210	228	2640	2107	343	92	0	0	0	226	7831	75
80	7560	29	91	95	1156	999	181	25	0	0	0	108	4876	80
85+	2541	3	23	25	294	285	58	3	0	0	0	33	1817	85+

NUMBER OF PERSONS SURVIVING TO AGE X IF SPECIFIED CAUSES WERE ELIMINATED

Age (x)	No Causes	Respira-tory T.B.	Other Infec. and Paras.	Neo-plasms	Cardio-vascular	Infl., Pneu., Bronch.	Diar-rheal	Certain Degener-ative	Maternal	Cert. Dis. of Infancy	Motor Vehicle	Other Violence	Other and Unknown	(1)+(2)	(1)+(2)+(5)+(6)+(8)	(1)+(2)+(5)+(6)+(8)+part of(9)&(12)	(10)+(11)	Age (x)
		(1)	(2)	(3)	(4)	(5)	(6)	(7)	(8)	(9)	(10)	(11)	(12)					
0	100000	100000	100000	100000	100000	100000	100000	100000	100000	100000	100000	100000	100000	100000	100000	100000	100000	0
1	82013	82141	84382	82013	82074	84477	84213	82027	82013	86660	82013	82223	86530	84514	89388	99237	82223	1
5	71684	71974	78434	71687	71816	75558	74313	71735	71684	75745	71684	72170	78103	78751	86052	98472	72170	5
10	68777	69181	77120	68782	69009	72653	71349	68852	68777	69442	68777	69442	75491	77573	85009	97897	69442	10
15	67274	67844	76102	67282	67628	71120	69819	67364	67274	71086	67274	68148	74142	76747	84204	97246	68148	15
20	65152	66371	74385	65164	65668	68959	67647	65276	65152	68843	65152	66260	72079	75776	83276	96449	66260	20
25	62220	64529	71974	62241	62876	65971	64626	62389	62220	65745	62220	63577	69157	74646	82207	95566	63577	25
30	59106	62654	69132	59137	59996	62844	61426	59335	59106	62455	59106	60700	66103	73141	80820	94386	60700	30
35	55659	60205	65758	55712	56872	59425	57882	55964	55659	58812	55659	57486	62755	71172	79022	92844	57486	35
40	52049	57514	62118	52144	53703	55878	54166	52442	52049	54998	52049	54105	59330	68640	76687	90750	54105	40
45	48146	54336	57965	48306	50440	52117	50148	48643	48146	50874	48146	50405	55675	65418	73757	88053	50405	45
50	44035	50714	53458	44287	46788	48250	45918	44650	44035	46530	44035	46438	51846	61567	70344	84872	46438	50
55	39352	46193	48163	39726	42807	43919	41107	40080	39352	41582	39352	41835	47522	56535	65910	80625	41835	55
60	34086	40714	42069	34609	38393	39066	35708	34901	34086	36017	34086	36576	42553	50249	60331	75037	36576	60
65	27847	33765	34681	28499	33097	33218	29309	28690	27847	29425	27847	30187	36745	42051	52794	67390	30187	65
70	21103	25895	26558	21820	27247	26694	22368	21903	21103	22299	21103	23102	30129	32589	43694	57759	23102	70
75	13736	16992	17486	14380	19901	18886	14723	14367	13736	14514	13736	15196	23230	21631	31878	45392	15196	75
80	7560	9376	9733	8015	12627	11562	8231	7957	7560	7988	7560	8458	17072	12072	20101	32513	8458	80
85+	2541	3169	3320	2735	5118	4538	2841	2687	2541	2685	2541	2890	11152	4141	8270	18342	2890	85+

ADDED YRS OF LIFE

	No Causes	(1)	(2)	(3)	(4)	(5)	(6)	(7)	(8)	(9)	(10)	(11)	(12)	(1)+(2)	(1)+(2)+(5)+(6)+(8)	(1)+(2)+(5)+(6)+(8)+part of(9)&(12)	(10)+(11)
TOTAL		3.061	6.473	.213	2.230	3.609	1.614	.348	.000	2.196	.000	1.343	7.712	10.198	17.473	29.806	1.343
WORK	12.262	3.122	1.748	.133	1.309	.856	.117	.272	.000	.000	.000	.926	1.568	5.078	6.290	7.589	.926

POPULATION, DEATHS, DEATH RATES FOR ALL CAUSES COMBINED, AND SPECIFIED CAUSES

Age Start of Interval	Midyear Population	Deaths During Year	All Causes	Respiratory T. B.	Other Infec. and Paras.	Neoplasms	Cardiovascular	Infl., Pneu., Bronch.	Diarrheal	Certain Degenerative	Maternal	Cert. Dis. of Infancy	Motor Vehicle	Other Violence	Other and Unknown	Age Start of Interval
0	343001	56169	.16376	.00138	.02662	.00000	.00071	.02314	.02257	.00011	.00000	.04610	.00000	.00241	.04072	0
1	1196353	39921	.03337	.00065	.01604	.00001	.00031	.00570	.00238	.00008	.00000	.00000	.00000	.00076	.00745	1
5	1359622	10239	.00753	.00039	.00469	.00001	.00028	.00045	.00014	.00006	.00000	.00000	.00000	.00028	.00124	5
10	1207070	5404	.00448	.00086	.00197	.00001	.00047	.00017	.00006	.00006	.00000	.00000	.00000	.00011	.00076	10
15	1098951	7310	.00665	.00277	.00190	.00002	.00053	.00019	.00007	.00008	.00021	.00000	.00000	.00014	.00073	15
20	1055923	8676	.00822	.00367	.00179	.00002	.00058	.00027	.00009	.00011	.00066	.00000	.00000	.00013	.00088	20
25	940081	8575	.00912	.00396	.00164	.00009	.00074	.00036	.00011	.00017	.00090	.00000	.00000	.00013	.00103	25
30	816114	8495	.01041	.00418	.00149	.00026	.00102	.00053	.00013	.00023	.00108	.00000	.00000	.00014	.00135	30
35	702578	8091	.01152	.00390	.00133	.00059	.00140	.00077	.00016	.00028	.00105	.00000	.00000	.00019	.00184	35
40	641558	8384	.01307	.00358	.00121	.00095	.00207	.00116	.00021	.00035	.00087	.00000	.00000	.00022	.00244	40
45	547720	7710	.01408	.00291	.00118	.00139	.00299	.00155	.00026	.00041	.00013	.00000	.00000	.00025	.00299	45
50	490350	8821	.01799	.00244	.00117	.00185	.00447	.00264	.00038	.00051	.00002	.00000	.00000	.00031	.00420	50
55	373404	8789	.02354	.00225	.00122	.00231	.00633	.00441	.00051	.00066	.00001	.00000	.00000	.00043	.00543	55
60	328973	11226	.03412	.00186	.00132	.00274	.00961	.00713	.00085	.00077	.00000	.00000	.00000	.00050	.00934	60
65	236600	11483	.04853	.00138	.00154	.00305	.01491	.01110	.00139	.00084	.00000	.00000	.00000	.00058	.01375	65
70	174616	13347	.07644	.00089	.00171	.00329	.02050	.01613	.00223	.00084	.00000	.00000	.00000	.00092	.02994	70
75	100196	10899	.10878	.00056	.00175	.00326	.02520	.02126	.00321	.00071	.00000	.00000	.00000	.00141	.05141	75
80	51452	9356	.18184	.00012	.00183	.00297	.03024	.02768	.00490	.00049	.00000	.00000	.00000	.00247	.11115	80
85+	23269	6421	.27595	.00009	.00176	.00211	.02909	.02961	.00653	.00017	.00000	.00000	.00000	.00382	.20276	85+
ALL	11687871	249316														

	All Causes	Respiratory T.B.	Other Infec. and Paras.	Neoplasms	Cardiovascular	Infl., Pneu., Bronch.	Diarrheal	Certain Degenerative	Maternal	Cert. Dis. of Infancy	Motor Vehicle	Other Violence	Other and Unknown
CRUDE DEATH RATE	.02133	.00229	.00416	.00057	.00238	.00290	.00118	.00023	.00035	.00135	.00000	.00037	.00556
STANDARDIZED RATE (1)	.02058	.00221	.00460	.00048	.00197	.00281	.00130	.00021	.00033	.00162	.00000	.00037	.00509
STANDARDIZED RATE (2)	.02411	.00232	.00351	.00080	.00356	.00352	.00106	.00028	.00034	.00095	.00000	.00039	.00736
GEOMETRIC MEAN	.02567												

LIFE TABLE FOR ALL CAUSES COMBINED

Age (x)	Midyear Population	Deaths During Year	$_nM_x$	$_nq_x$	l_x	$_nd_x$	$_nL_x$	$_nm_x$	$_na_x$	T_x	$_nr_x$	$\overset{\circ}{e}_x$	Age (x)
0	343001	56169	.163758	.147970	100000	14797	90358	.163760	.348388	4246132	.000000	42.461	0
1	1196353	39921	.033369	.123200	85203	10497	314570	.033369	1.500000	4155774	.000000	48.775	1
5	1359622	10239	.007531	.036965	74706	2763	366623	.007536	2.500000	3841204	.000000	51.418	5
10	1207070	5404	.004477	.022101	71943	1590	355645	.004471	2.440121	3474582	.013407	48.296	10
15	1098951	7310	.006652	.032778	70353	2306	346240	.006660	2.603986	3118937	.008711	44.333	15
20	1055923	8676	.008217	.040281	68047	2741	333509	.008219	2.546288	2772697	.006345	40.747	20
25	940081	8575	.009122	.044636	65306	2915	319332	.009128	2.530589	2439188	.013517	37.350	25
30	816114	8495	.010409	.050793	62391	3169	304116	.010420	2.526428	2119856	.018677	33.977	30
35	702578	8091	.011516	.056010	59222	3317	287855	.011522	2.523302	1815740	.013882	30.660	35
40	641558	8384	.013067	.063322	55905	3540	270726	.013076	2.514536	1527845	.012758	27.329	40
45	547720	7710	.014077	.068061	52365	3564	253055	.014084	2.539359	1257119	.010791	24.007	45
50	490350	8821	.017989	.086351	48801	4214	233764	.018027	2.569758	1004063	.018613	20.575	50
55	373404	8789	.023538	.111580	44587	4975	210922	.023587	2.585385	770299	.017010	17.276	55
60	328973	11226	.034124	.157856	39612	6253	182902	.034188	2.575864	559377	.012087	14.121	60
65	236600	11483	.048563	.217393	33359	7252	149111	.048635	2.561563	376475	.012601	11.286	65
70	174616	13347	.076436	.321600	26107	8396	109605	.076602	2.507196	227364	.010648	8.709	70
75	100196	10899	.108777	.425837	17711	7542	69253	.108905	2.440776	117758	.007054	6.649	75
80	51452	9356	.181839	.614810	10169	6252	34310	.182221	2.355246	48505	.007054	4.770	80
85+	23269	6421	.275947	1.000000	3917	3917	14195	.275947	3.623890	14195	.000000	3.624	85+

NUMBER OF PERSONS DYING (OUT OF 100,000 AT BIRTH) ABOVE AGE X FROM SPECIFIED CAUSES

Age (x)	All Causes	Respiratory T.B.	Other Infec. and Paras.	Neoplasms	Cardiovascular	Infl., Pneu., Bronch.	Diarrheal	Certain Degenerative	Maternal	Cert. Dis. of Infancy	Motor Vehicle	Other Violence	Other and Unknown	Age (x)
0	100000	16072	14513	3501	14903	14606	4452	1235	1491	4165	0	1627	29435	0
1	85203	9947	12108	3501	14838	12516	2412	1225	1491	1491	0	1410	25755	1
5	74706	9742	7063	3499	14741	10723	1664	1199	1491	1491	0	1171	23413	5
10	71943	9599	5341	3497	14639	10560	1612	1178	1491	1491	0	1068	22958	10
15	70353	9290	4644	3494	14472	10499	1592	1156	1491	1491	0	1028	22687	15
20	68047	8328	3984	3488	14290	10433	1566	1128	1418	0	0	978	22434	20
25	65306	7103	3387	3481	14096	10341	1535	1092	1196	0	0	934	22141	25
30	62391	5840	2864	3453	13859	10226	1500	1037	907	0	0	894	21811	30
35	59222	4569	2413	3375	13549	10063	1459	966	577	0	0	852	21399	35
40	55905	3448	2030	3205	13144	9841	1412	884	275	C	0	799	20867	40
45	52365	2478	1701	2947	12583	9526	1355	789	40	0	0	738	20208	45
50	48801	1742	1402	2596	11825	9132	1288	684	8	0	0	674	19450	50
55	44587	1172	1129	2164	10776	8513	1200	565	3	0	0	600	18465	55
60	39612	697	873	1676	9437	7579	1091	425	1	0	0	517	17316	60
65	33359	357	632	1174	7675	6271	936	285	1	0	0	425	15603	65
70	26107	151	402	719	5448	4613	729	160	1	0	0	338	13546	70
75	17711	54	214	359	3197	2842	483	69	1	0	0	238	10254	75
80	10169	15	93	133	1451	1368	261	20	1	0	0	139	6688	80
85+	3917	1	25	30	413	420	93	2	C	0	0	54	2879	85+

NUMBER OF PERSONS SURVIVING TO AGE X IF SPECIFIED CAUSES WERE ELIMINATED

Age (x)	No Causes	Respiratory T.B. (1)	Other Infec. and Paras. (2)	Neoplasms (3)	Cardiovascular (4)	Infl., Pneu., Bronch. (5)	Diarrheal (6)	Certain Degenerative (7)	Maternal (8)	Cert. Dis. of Infancy (9)	Motor Vehicle (10)	Other Violence (11)	Other and Unknown (12)	(1)+(2)	(1)+(2)+(5)+(6)+(8)	(1)+(2)+(5)+(6)+(8)+part of (9)&(12)	(10)+(11)	Age (x)
0	100000	100000	100000	100000	100000	100000	100000	100000	100000	100000	100000	100000	100000	100000	100000	100000	100000	0
1	85203	85318	87450	85203	85263	87152	87105	85212	85203	89131	85203	85403	88665	87568	91571	99330	85403	1
5	74706	74999	81677	74708	74849	78150	77093	74738	74706	78150	74706	75106	80055	81998	88519	98748	75106	5
10	71943	72366	80527	71947	72181	75428	74294	71995	71943	75260	71943	72430	77575	81000	87698	98382	72430	10
15	70353	71075	79521	70360	70752	73824	72672	70425	70353	73597	70353	70869	76150	80338	87080	97996	70869	15
20	68047	69709	77651	68059	68613	71472	70317	68145	68119	71184	68047	68596	73923	79548	86430	97574	68596	20
25	65306	68141	75193	65325	66041	68688	67516	65435	65594	68317	65306	65876	71258	78458	85689	97114	65876	25
30	62391	66400	72427	62436	63328	65740	64537	62568	62950	65268	62391	62975	68430	77082	84767	96498	62975	30
35	59222	64359	69341	59341	60419	62569	61301	59460	60078	61952	59222	59818	65397	75267	83502	95587	59818	35
40	55905	61948	65817	56184	57439	59293	57915	56209	57011	58483	55905	56519	62308	72931	81718	94190	56519	40
45	52365	59073	62025	52878	54363	55863	54305	52743	53633	54779	52365	53000	59078	69971	79284	92125	53000	45
50	48801	55858	58146	49623	51429	52469	50676	49255	50013	51051	48801	49456	55889	66555	76152	89211	49456	50
55	44587	51660	53436	45759	48057	48580	46387	45117	45699	46643	44587	45257	52153	61913	71933	85128	45257	55
60	39612	46415	47763	41128	44077	44130	41319	40216	40602	41438	39612	40286	47618	55966	66661	79898	40286	60
65	33359	39452	40490	35115	38962	38525	34945	33998	34193	34897	33359	34013	42036	47885	59378	72694	34013	65
70	26107	31088	31933	27904	32874	31888	27540	26719	26760	27311	26107	26697	35276	38026	50221	63414	26697	70
75	17711	21182	21851	19244	24735	23472	18957	18154	18201	18528	17711	18195	27893	28133	37877	51252	18195	75
80	10169	12195	12656	11231	16130	15011	11028	10487	10423	10638	10169	10523	20875	15178	24906	38145	10523	80
85+	3917	4708	4926	4395	7279	6682	4358	4051	4016	4098	3917	4106	14379	5920	11520	23467	4106	85+

ADDED YRS OF LIFE

	No Causes	(1)	(2)	(3)	(4)	(5)	(6)	(7)	(8)	(9)	(10)	(11)	(12)	(1)+(2)	(1)+(2)+(5)+(6)+(8)	(1)+(2)+(5)+(6)+(8)+part of (9)&(12)	(10)+(11)
TOTAL		3.323	6.611	.566	2.435	3.477	1.581	.266	.489	1.942	.000	.471	7.951	10.574	18.268	29.855	.471
WORK	11.019	3.182	1.402	.378	1.225	.662	.132	.192	.561	.000	.000	.149	1.433	4.740	6.379	7.619	.149

POPULATION, DEATHS, DEATH RATES FOR ALL CAUSES COMBINED, AND SPECIFIED CAUSES

Age Start of Interval	Midyear Population	Deaths During Year	All Causes	Respiratory T. B.	Other Infec. and Paras.	Neo-plasms	Cardio-vascular	Infl., Pneu., Bronch.	Diar-rheal	Certain Degen-erative	Maternal	Cert. Dis. of Infancy	Motor Vehicle	Other Violence	Other and Unknown	Age Start of Interval
0	397649	64165	.16136	.00105	.02404	.00003	.00054	.02771	.01457	.00015	.00000	.04562	.00000	.00259	.04506	0
1	1366496	35265	.02581	.00045	.01156	.00003	.00015	.00565	.00098	.00019	.00000	.00000	.00000	.00090	.00591	1
5	1574442	9108	.00578	.00026	.00297	.00001	.00023	.00044	.00010	.00012	.00000	.00000	.00000	.00049	.00115	5
10	1407322	4557	.00324	.00043	.00059	.00002	.00034	.00015	.00005	.00012	.00000	.00000	.00000	.00046	.00074	10
15	1273023	5766	.00453	.00139	.00083	.00002	.00042	.00025	.00006	.00011	.00000	.00000	.00000	.00068	.00077	15
20	1116543	6759	.00605	.00254	.00083	.00003	.00045	.00042	.00007	.00007	.00000	.00000	.00000	.00077	.00076	20
25	984955	7231	.00734	.00300	.00086	.00005	.00066	.00061	.00007	.00027	.00000	.00000	.00000	.00090	.00093	25
30	843430	7861	.00932	.00354	.00094	.00011	.00104	.00093	.00008	.00040	.00000	.00000	.00000	.00104	.00125	30
35	747674	8712	.01165	.00366	.00114	.00019	.00171	.00132	.00009	.00054	.00000	.00000	.00000	.00117	.00184	35
40	675506	9764	.01445	.00376	.00124	.00038	.00248	.00195	.00011	.00077	.00000	.00000	.00000	.00132	.00244	40
45	549539	9301	.01693	.00353	.00117	.00069	.00311	.00275	.00015	.00115	.00000	.00000	.00000	.00146	.00292	45
50	487609	10694	.02193	.00333	.00120	.00110	.00481	.00407	.00023	.00147	.00000	.00000	.00000	.00166	.00406	50
55	383423	10911	.02846	.00310	.00125	.00169	.00737	.00583	.00034	.00171	.00000	.00000	.00000	.00190	.00527	55
60	341868	13686	.04003	.00270	.00139	.00228	.01166	.00846	.00056	.00204	.00000	.00000	.00000	.00209	.00884	60
65	232362	12832	.05522	.00207	.00166	.00256	.01851	.01194	.00087	.00255	.00000	.00000	.00000	.00213	.01254	65
70	158890	13662	.08598	.00139	.00199	.00343	.02672	.01736	.00150	.00265	.00000	.00000	.00000	.00228	.02866	70
75	90134	10709	.11881	.00089	.00236	.00323	.03375	.02289	.00207	.00200	.00000	.00000	.00000	.00236	.04926	75
80	41353	8311	.20098	.00022	.00249	.00322	.04297	.03233	.00416	.00150	.00000	.00000	.00000	.00295	.11114	80
85+	14755	4311	.29217	.00027	.00183	.00312	.04290	.03802	.00705	.00142	.00000	.00000	.00000	.00393	.19363	85+
ALL	12686973	253605														

CRUDE DEATH RATE			.01999	.00192	.00315	.00037	.00250	.00333	.00073	.00050	.00000	.00143	.00000	.00104	.00502	
STANDARDIZED RATE (1)			.01997	.00186	.00336	.00034	.00226	.00332	.00078	.00047	.00000	.00161	.00000	.00102	.00494	
STANDARDIZED RATE (2)			.02449	.00212	.00262	.00062	.00434	.00419	.00066	.00070	.00000	.00094	.00000	.00118	.00711	
GEOMETRIC MEAN			.02496													

LIFE TABLE FOR ALL CAUSES COMBINED

Age (x)	Midyear Population	Deaths During Year	$_nM_x$	$_nq_x$	l_x	$_nd_x$	$_nL_x$	$_nm_x$	$_na_x$	T_x	$_nr_x$	$\overset{\circ}{e}_x$	Age (x)
0	397649	64165	.161361	.145920	100000	14592	90432	.161358	.344314	4425869	.000000	44.259	0
1	1366496	35265	.025807	.096970	85408	8282	320927	.025806	1.500000	4335437	.000000	50.761	1
5	1574442	9108	.005785	.028551	77126	2202	380125	.005793	2.500000	4014510	.000000	52.051	5
10	1407322	4557	.003238	.016030	74924	1201	371504	.003233	2.405114	3634385	.012856	48.508	10
15	1273023	5766	.004529	.022449	73723	1655	364676	.004538	2.619965	3262881	.017167	44.259	15
20	1116543	6759	.006054	.029888	72068	2154	355136	.006065	2.584242	2898205	.018918	40.215	20
25	984955	7231	.007341	.036130	69914	2526	343447	.007355	2.576125	2543068	.020229	36.374	25
30	843430	7861	.009220	.045661	67388	3077	329481	.009239	2.575899	2199621	.020302	32.641	30
35	747674	8712	.011652	.056709	64311	3647	312680	.011664	2.566379	1870140	.011609	29.080	35
40	675506	9764	.014454	.069877	60664	4239	292919	.014472	2.546395	1557461	.015587	25.674	40
45	549539	9301	.016925	.081365	56425	4591	270890	.016948	2.552866	1264541	.015156	22.411	45
50	487609	10694	.021932	.104256	51834	5404	245992	.021968	2.561413	993651	.015603	19.170	50
55	383423	10911	.028457	.133190	46430	6184	217094	.028485	2.565357	747659	.008088	16.103	55
60	341868	13686	.040033	.182478	40246	7344	183252	.040076	2.551970	530565	.007403	13.183	60
65	232362	12832	.055224	.243633	32902	8016	144776	.055368	2.538153	347313	.017468	10.556	65
70	158890	13662	.085984	.354095	24886	8812	102253	.086178	2.483332	202538	.011388	8.139	70
75	90134	10709	.118812	.454834	16074	7311	61452	.118971	2.412404	100285	.007815	6.239	75
80	41353	8311	.200977	.654799	8763	5738	28479	.201482	2.327284	38832	.007815	4.431	80
85+	14755	4311	.292172	1.000000	3025	3025	10353	.292172	3.422640	10353	.000000	3.423	85+

NUMBER OF PERSONS DYING (OUT OF 100,000 AT BIRTH) ABOVE AGE X FROM SPECIFIED CAUSES

Age (x)	All Causes	Respiratory T.B.	Other Infec. and Paras.	Neo-plasms	Cardio-vascular	Infl., Pneu., Bronch.	Diar-rheal	Certain Degen-erative	Maternal	Cert. Dis. of Infancy	Motor Vehicle	Other Violence	Other and Unknown	Age (x)
0	100000	9812	11130	2609	17423	17088	2716	3094	0	4125	0	5219	26784	0
1	85408	9717	8956	2606	17375	14582	1399	3080	0	0	0	4985	22708	1
5	77126	9573	5245	2598	17327	12770	1085	3019	0	0	0	4697	20812	5
10	74924	9472	4113	2594	17238	12603	1048	2974	0	0	0	4508	20374	10
15	73723	9313	3747	2589	17110	12547	1028	2952	0	0	0	4338	20099	15
20	72068	8802	3443	2583	16955	12455	1006	2913	0	0	0	4091	19820	20
25	69914	7896	3147	2571	16780	12306	983	2861	0	0	0	3819	19551	25
30	67389	6865	2852	2555	16551	12097	959	2769	0	0	0	3511	19229	30
35	64311	5699	2542	2519	16206	11791	933	2637	0	0	0	3169	18815	35
40	60664	4555	2184	2459	15669	11377	906	2469	0	0	0	2804	18241	40
45	56425	3455	1822	2348	14941	10804	873	2242	0	0	0	2416	17524	45
50	51834	2500	1504	2161	14097	10057	834	1931	0	0	0	2019	16731	50
55	46430	1680	1210	1889	12910	9053	777	1568	0	0	0	1612	15731	55
60	40246	1009	938	1522	11307	7786	703	1196	0	0	0	1198	14587	60
65	32902	514	684	1103	9167	6234	599	821	0	0	0	815	12965	65
70	24886	214	443	673	6480	4501	473	452	0	0	0	507	11143	70
75	16074	72	240	322	3742	2722	319	181	0	0	0	274	8202	75
80	8763	18	94	124	1667	1314	191	58	0	0	0	128	5169	80
85+	3025	3	19	32	444	394	73	15	0	0	0	41	2004	85+

NUMBER OF PERSONS SURVIVING TO AGE X IF SPECIFIED CAUSES WERE ELIMINATED

Age (x)	No Causes	Respiratory T.B. (1)	Other Infec. and Paras. (2)	Neo-plasms (3)	Cardio-vascular (4)	Infl., Pneu., Bronch. (5)	Diar-rheal (6)	Certain Degener-ative (7)	Maternal (8)	Cert. Dis. of Infancy (9)	Motor Vehicle (10)	Other Violence (11)	Other and Unknown (12)	(1)+(2)	(1)+(2)+(5)+(6)+(8)	(1)+(2)+(5)+(6)+(8)+part of(9)&(12)	(10)+(11)	Age (x)
0	100000	100000	100000	100000	100000	100000	100000	100000	100000	100000	100000	100000	100000	100000	100000	100000	100000	0
1	85408	85496	87439	85411	85452	87753	86633	85421	85408	89302	85408	85624	89255	87529	91221	99265	85624	1
5	77126	77342	82652	77136	77212	81032	78535	77196	77126	80643	77126	77596	82504	82884	88673	98625	77596	5
10	74924	75234	81498	74938	75095	78892	76330	75036	74924	78340	74924	75568	80612	81835	87785	98097	75568	10
15	73723	74187	80587	73741	74019	77686	75127	73855	73723	77085	73723	74527	79614	81093	87079	97542	74527	15
20	72068	73032	79107	72092	72511	76038	73462	72236	72068	75354	72068	73101	78125	80165	86216	96825	73101	20
25	69914	71759	77063	69949	70517	73920	71290	70128	69914	73102	69914	71189	76077	79097	85274	96032	71189	25
30	67388	70213	74598	67438	68197	71467	68738	67685	67388	70461	67388	68925	73674	77726	84081	95003	68925	30
35	64311	68204	71528	64394	65425	68521	65625	64724	64311	67243	64311	66120	70753	75857	82475	93588	66120	35
40	60664	65524	67859	60800	62248	65066	61930	61218	60664	63430	60664	62736	67357	73296	80255	91599	62736	40
45	56425	62100	63509	56660	58624	61115	57635	57162	56425	58998	56425	58740	63423	69897	77331	88898	58740	45
50	51834	58062	58685	52230	54702	56924	52984	52814	51834	54198	51834	54358	59123	65735	73793	85508	54358	50
55	46430	52882	52882	47045	50200	52044	47515	47659	46430	48547	46430	49056	54050	60230	69091	80869	49056	55
60	40246	46552	46127	41127	45159	46454	41258	41667	40246	42081	40246	42965	48108	53354	63132	74784	42965	60
65	32902	38573	37972	34010	39155	39630	33826	34415	32902	34402	32902	35494	41121	44517	55125	66533	35494	65
70	24886	29477	28962	26111	32523	31838	25657	26366	24886	26021	24886	27134	33152	34305	45319	56066	27134	70
75	16074	19170	18895	17158	24053	22457	16725	17257	16074	16807	16074	17727	24809	22534	32757	42905	17727	75
80	8763	10495	10425	9506	15558	13753	9216	9501	8763	9163	8763	9780	17454	12486	20608	29946	9780	80
85+	3025	3633	3649	3338	6737	5630	3252	3306	3025	3163	3025	3431	10833	4383	8768	16479	3431	85+

ADDED YRS OF LIFE

	No Causes	(1)	(2)	(3)	(4)	(5)	(6)	(7)	(8)	(9)	(10)	(11)	(12)	(1)+(2)			(10)+(11)
TOTAL		2.799	4.821	.354	2.651	4.202	.954	.581	.000	2.002	.000	1.402	6.907	8.005	14.618	24.421	1.402
WORK	10.452	2.598	.859	.194	1.293	1.045	.082	.392	.000	.000	.000	.894	1.374	3.544	4.862	5.862	.894

POPULATION, DEATHS, DEATH RATES FOR ALL CAUSES COMBINED, AND SPECIFIED CAUSES

Age Start of Interval	Midyear Population	Deaths During Year	All Causes	Respiratory T.B.	Other Infec. and Paras.	Neoplasms	Cardiovascular	Infl., Pneu., Bronch.	Diarrheal	Certain Degenerative	Maternal	Cert. Dis. of Infancy	Motor Vehicle	Other Violence	Other and Unknown	Age Start of Interval
0	393385	50811	.12916	.00089	.02128	.00002	.00041	.02093	.01174	.00012	.00000	.03727	.00000	.00250	.03400	0
1	1375884	33941	.02467	.00044	.01151	.00002	.00016	.00542	.00098	.00016	.00000	.00000	.00000	.00064	.00535	1
5	1584224	8976	.00567	.00035	.00304	.00001	.00025	.00047	.00012	.00008	.00000	.00000	.00000	.00023	.00112	5
10	1402992	4545	.00324	.00077	.00105	.00001	.00042	.00015	.00005	.00006	.00000	.00000	.00000	.00011	.00062	10
15	1283475	6040	.00471	.00202	.00087	.00002	.00047	.00019	.00006	.00009	.00013	.00000	.00000	.00013	.00074	15
20	1220154	7344	.00602	.00268	.00074	.00004	.00052	.00027	.00008	.00017	.00065	.00000	.00000	.00011	.00077	20
25	1070432	7700	.00719	.00299	.00073	.00009	.00070	.00041	.00008	.00022	.00087	.00000	.00000	.00013	.00098	25
30	908367	7889	.00868	.00321	.00070	.00027	.00102	.00063	.00010	.00031	.00105	.00000	.00000	.00015	.00125	30
35	799287	8078	.01011	.00302	.00069	.00064	.00151	.00091	.00012	.00043	.00096	.00000	.00000	.00019	.00163	35
40	728942	8668	.01189	.00280	.00068	.00107	.00222	.00129	.00015	.00056	.00078	.00000	.00000	.00024	.00210	40
45	606013	7865	.01298	.00230	.00069	.00164	.00300	.00159	.00016	.00065	.00008	.00000	.00000	.00027	.00256	45
50	538176	9207	.01711	.00192	.00072	.00223	.00467	.00260	.00023	.00089	.00001	.00000	.00000	.00034	.00350	50
55	425985	9808	.02302	.00166	.00078	.00284	.00709	.00428	.00035	.00116	.00000	.00000	.00000	.00045	.00441	55
60	388454	12932	.03329	.00135	.00091	.00343	.01093	.00680	.00057	.00137	.00000	.00000	.00000	.00059	.00734	60
65	271848	12853	.04728	.00111	.00118	.00399	.01709	.01038	.00088	.00151	.00000	.00000	.00000	.00068	.01047	65
70	192270	14260	.07417	.00076	.00143	.00436	.02390	.01574	.00142	.00152	.00000	.00000	.00000	.00113	.02390	70
75	112894	11617	.10290	.00043	.00158	.00410	.02965	.02175	.00206	.00120	.00000	.00000	.00000	.00182	.04029	75
80	54791	9577	.17479	.00011	.00184	.00387	.03568	.02999	.00318	.00102	.00000	.00000	.00000	.00325	.09565	80
85+	23582	6219	.26372	.00021	.00199	.00343	.03380	.03337	.00411	.00114	.00000	.00000	.00000	.00488	.18077	85+
ALL	13381155	238330														
CRUDE DEATH RATE			.01781	.00173	.00280	.00069	.00255	.00280	.00063	.00037	.00032	.00110	.00000	.00037	.00448	
STANDARDIZED RATE (1)			.01734	.00168	.00311	.00058	.00212	.00271	.00068	.00033	.00030	.00131	.00000	.00037	.00415	
STANDARDIZED RATE (2)			.02117	.00177	.00233	.00100	.00396	.00348	.00059	.00047	.00031	.00077	.00000	.00042	.00607	
GEOMETRIC MEAN			.02214													

LIFE TABLE FOR ALL CAUSES COMBINED

Age (x)	Midyear Population	Deaths During Year	$_nM_x$	$_nq_x$	l_x	$_nd_x$	$_nL_x$	$_nm_x$	$_na_x$	T_x	$_nr_x$	$\overset{\circ}{e}_x$	Age (x)
0	393385	50811	.129164	.118310	100000	11831	91595	.129166	.289578	4748832	.000000	47.488	0
1	1375884	33941	.024669	.092935	88169	8194	332191	.024667	1.500000	4657237	.000000	52.822	1
5	1584224	8976	.005666	.027971	79975	2237	394283	.005674	2.500000	4325046	.000000	54.080	5
10	1402992	4545	.003240	.016028	77738	1246	385490	.003232	2.424090	3930763	.014300	50.564	10
15	1283475	6040	.004706	.023310	76492	1783	378205	.004714	2.613573	3545283	.010447	46.348	15
20	1220154	7344	.006019	.029689	74709	2218	368163	.006025	2.573546	3167078	.009988	42.392	20
25	1070432	7700	.007193	.035397	72491	2566	356198	.007204	2.561623	2798915	.019301	38.611	25
30	908367	7889	.008685	.042514	69925	2977	342336	.008696	2.551646	2442717	.021991	34.933	30
35	799287	8078	.010107	.049352	66948	3304	326626	.010116	2.544265	2100380	.013421	31.373	35
40	728942	8668	.011891	.057806	63644	3679	309121	.011901	2.526728	1773754	.015398	27.870	40
45	606013	7865	.012978	.062970	59965	3776	290582	.012995	2.552194	1464633	.015851	24.425	45
50	538176	9207	.017108	.082311	56189	4625	269769	.017144	2.583604	1174051	.019054	20.895	50
55	425985	9808	.023024	.109223	51564	5632	244252	.023058	2.590961	904282	.011164	17.537	55
60	388454	12932	.033291	.154228	45932	7084	212497	.033337	2.577228	660030	.009225	14.370	60
65	271848	12853	.047280	.212572	38848	8258	174119	.047427	2.563398	447533	.019192	11.520	65
70	192270	14260	.074167	.313730	30590	9597	129023	.074382	2.506795	273414	.015088	8.938	70
75	112894	11617	.102902	.408279	20993	8571	83093	.103150	2.448105	144391	.014895	6.878	75
80	54791	9577	.174791	.600708	12422	7462	42491	.175615	2.370762	61299	.014895	4.935	80
85+	23582	6219	.263718	1.000000	4960	4960	18808	.263718	3.791928	18808	.000000	3.792	85+

NUMBER OF PERSONS DYING (OUT OF 100,000 AT BIRTH) ABOVE AGE X FROM SPECIFIED CAUSES

Age (x)	All Causes	Respiratory T.B.	Other Infec. and Paras.	Neoplasms	Cardiovascular	Infl., Pneu., Bronch.	Diarrheal	Certain Degenerative	Maternal	Cert. Dis. of Infancy	Motor Vehicle	Other Violence	Other and Unknown	Age (x)
0	100000	8658	10337	5036	19412	16416	2700	2356	1538	3414	0	1947	28186	0
1	88169	8576	8388	5035	19375	14499	1624	2345	1538	0	0	1718	25071	1
5	79975	8430	4565	5029	19320	12700	1300	2292	1538	0	0	1507	23294	5
10	77738	8291	3363	5027	19220	12515	1253	2260	1538	0	0	1417	22854	10
15	76492	7992	2960	5022	19059	12458	1235	2237	1538	0	0	1374	22617	15
20	74709	7226	2633	5016	18882	12387	1213	2202	1488	0	0	1324	22338	20
25	72491	6237	2360	5002	18651	12288	1184	2141	1250	0	0	1285	22053	25
30	69925	5170	2099	4971	18441	12142	1154	2063	940	0	0	1241	21704	30
35	66948	4071	1860	4876	18090	11927	1120	1958	581	0	0	1190	21275	35
40	63644	3086	1634	4665	17595	11629	1080	1817	266	0	0	1127	20745	40
45	59965	2221	1422	4333	16907	11230	1035	1643	27	0	0	1054	20093	45
50	56189	1553	1222	3857	16033	10765	989	1441	5	0	0	975	19349	50
55	51564	1037	1027	3254	14770	10061	928	1202	2	0	0	883	18400	55
60	45932	633	836	2561	13035	9013	843	917	2	0	0	772	17320	60
65	38848	346	642	1831	10708	7564	722	626	2	0	0	648	15759	65
70	30590	154	436	1135	7723	5752	568	363	2	0	0	529	13928	70
75	20993	56	251	572	4632	3715	385	167	2	0	0	383	10830	75
80	12422	20	120	232	2166	1904	213	67	2	0	0	230	7468	80
85+	4960	4	37	65	636	628	77	22	0	0	0	92	3399	85+

NUMBER OF PERSONS SURVIVING TO AGE X IF SPECIFIED CAUSES WERE ELIMINATED

Age (x)	No Causes	Respiratory T.B.	Other Infec. and Paras.	Neoplasms	Cardiovascular	Infl., Pneu., Bronch.	Diarrheal	Certain Degenerative	Maternal	Cert. Dis. of Infancy	Motor Vehicle	Other Violence	Other and Unknown	(1)+(2)	(1)+(2)+(5)+(6)+(8)	(1)+(2)+(5)+(6)+(8)+part of(9)&(12)	(10)+(11)	Age (x)
		(1)	(2)	(3)	(4)	(5)	(6)	(7)	(8)	(9)	(10)	(11)	(12)					
0	100000	100000	100000	100000	100000	100000	100000	100000	100000	100000	100000	100000	100000	100000	100000	100000	100000	0
1	88169	88246	90017	88170	88204	89986	89184	88179	88169	91431	88169	88384	91141	90096	93012	99342	88384	1
5	79975	80184	85453	79982	80059	83390	81209	80035	79975	82934	79975	80372	84438	85676	90713	98852	80372	5
10	77738	78078	84339	77746	77918	81248	78984	77828	77738	80615	77738	78213	82536	84708	89953	98504	78213	10
15	76492	77126	83422	76505	76830	80005	77736	76603	76492	79322	76492	77002	81463	84113	89407	98138	77002	15
20	74709	76095	81830	74728	75215	78214	75947	74852	74759	77473	74709	75257	75858	83349	88763	97727	75257	20
25	72491	74835	79695	72523	73171	75994	73721	72690	72774	75173	72491	73061	77788	82273	88054	97263	73061	25
30	69925	73276	77157	69987	70830	73454	71141	70194	70505	72512	69925	70519	75403	80854	87128	96628	70519	30
35	66948	71291	74130	67100	68163	70545	66146	67309	67858	69425	66948	67567	72647	78939	85824	95638	67567	35
40	63644	68802	70716	63996	65293	67374	64823	64126	64821	65999	63644	64294	69625	76447	83950	94062	64294	40
45	59965	65738	66857	60622	62208	63891	61120	60585	61310	62184	59965	60649	66296	73293	81381	91744	60649	45
50	56189	62310	62863	57272	59176	60350	57317	56972	57470	58268	56189	56908	62923	69711	78117	88586	56908	50
55	51564	57730	57897	53150	55595	56112	52659	52515	52742	53472	51564	52313	58771	64821	73682	84151	52313	55
60	45932	51851	51776	48023	51321	51072	46989	47053	46982	47632	45932	46705	53526	58448	68004	78323	46705	60
65	38848	44150	43992	41321	45863	44702	39856	40070	39736	40285	38848	39618	46574	49996	60372	70494	39618	65
70	30590	34956	34847	33196	39371	37095	31524	31792	31289	31722	30590	31304	39011	39821	50900	60610	31304	70
75	20993	24080	24087	23285	30489	27573	21790	21984	21473	21770	20993	21606	30258	27628	38526	48094	21606	75
80	12422	14278	14366	14062	20957	18222	13030	13086	12706	12882	12422	12906	22046	16513	25990	35363	12906	80
85+	4960	5712	5795	5731	10101	8513	5291	5254	5075	5144	4960	5241	14522	6674	12501	21263	5241	85+

ADDED YRS OF LIFE

	No Causes	(1)	(2)	(3)	(4)	(5)	(6)	(7)	(8)	(9)	(10)	(11)	(12)	(1)+(2)	(1)+(2)+(5)+(6)+(8)	+part of(9)&(12)	(10)+(11)
TOTAL		2.872	4.852	.809	3.101	3.864	.926	.485	.518	1.747	.000	.521	7.146	8.073	14.815	23.853	.521
WORK	9.502	2.496	.692	.467	1.329	.738	.100	.307	.543	.000	.000	.157	1.334	3.248	4.826	5.822	.157

POPULATION, DEATHS, DEATH RATES FOR ALL CAUSES COMBINED, AND SPECIFIED CAUSES

Age Start of Interval	Midyear Population	Deaths During Year	All Causes	Respiratory T. B.	Other Infec. and Paras.	Neo-plasms	Cardio-vascular	Infl., Pneu., Bronch.	Diar-rheal	Certain Degen-erative	Maternal	Cert. Dis. of Infancy	Motor Vehicle	Other Violence	Other and Unknown	Age Start of Interval
0	384524	76257	.19832	.00087	.02616	.00003	.00087	.04320	.01714	.00029	.00000	.05561	.00000	.00344	.05071	0
1	1395410	38016	.02724	.00040	.01113	.00003	.00018	.00782	.00107	.00016	.00000	.00000	.00000	.00081	.00563	1
5	1698012	7959	.00469	.00024	.00205	.00001	.00025	.00057	.00007	.00009	.00000	.00000	.00000	.00044	.00094	5
10	1615287	4243	.00263	.00029	.00073	.00001	.00031	.00021	.00004	.00007	.00000	.00000	.00000	.00037	.00058	10
15	1469190	6157	.00419	.00117	.00064	.00004	.00045	.00049	.00005	.00011	.00000	.00000	.00000	.00056	.00067	15
20	1250697	7077	.00566	.00217	.00062	.00005	.00049	.00080	.00006	.00013	.00000	.00000	.00000	.00065	.00069	20
25	1114126	7664	.00688	.00253	.00059	.00008	.00064	.00111	.00006	.00025	.00000	.00000	.00000	.00078	.00084	25
30	980563	8829	.00900	.00307	.00064	.00015	.00095	.00167	.00007	.00040	.00000	.00000	.00000	.00093	.00112	30
35	867857	10206	.01176	.00346	.00085	.00026	.00143	.00241	.00008	.00059	.00000	.00000	.00000	.00107	.00161	35
40	747530	11555	.01545	.00372	.00096	.00051	.00230	.00355	.00011	.00088	.00000	.00000	.00000	.00125	.00218	40
45	643949	12395	.01925	.00359	.00096	.00090	.00334	.00490	.00015	.00127	.00000	.00000	.00000	.00142	.00271	45
50	551097	14367	.02607	.00343	.00101	.00148	.00557	.00717	.00021	.00177	.00000	.00000	.00000	.00161	.00381	50
55	414426	14257	.03440	.00304	.00103	.00231	.00862	.01016	.00026	.00240	.00000	.00000	.00000	.00176	.00481	55
60	357872	17467	.04881	.00260	.00111	.00319	.01391	.01444	.00044	.00296	.00000	.00000	.00000	.00198	.00818	60
65	260407	17389	.06678	.00205	.00123	.00416	.02195	.01966	.00070	.00339	.00000	.00000	.00000	.00222	.01142	65
70	185704	18830	.10140	.00138	.00142	.00495	.03191	.02758	.00127	.00370	.00000	.00000	.00000	.00248	.02671	70
75	101977	14210	.13935	.00059	.00173	.00510	.04154	.03556	.00203	.00352	.00000	.00000	.00000	.00255	.04674	75
80	43819	10296	.23497	.00052	.00156	.00493	.05393	.05073	.00347	.00319	.00000	.00000	.00000	.00317	.11306	80
85+	16244	5320	.32751	.00006	.00179	.00357	.05307	.06015	.00449	.00259	.00000	.00000	.00000	.00400	.19780	85+
ALL	14098691	302494														

			All Causes	Respiratory T. B.	Other Infec. and Paras.	Neo-plasms	Cardio-vascular	Infl., Pneu., Bronch.	Diar-rheal	Certain Degen-erative	Maternal	Cert. Dis. of Infancy	Motor Vehicle	Other Violence	Other and Unknown
CRUDE DEATH RATE			.02146	.00178	.00267	.00052	.00286	.00509	.00071	.00062	.00000	.00152	.00000	.00058	.00471
STANDARDIZED RATE (1)			.02238	.00170	.00308	.00047	.00257	.00528	.00085	.00057	.00000	.00196	.00000	.00098	.00492
STANDARDIZED RATE (2)			.02781	.00196	.00232	.00087	.00507	.00678	.00068	.00091	.00000	.00115	.00000	.00114	.00694
GEOMETRIC MEAN			.02650												

LIFE TABLE FOR ALL CAUSES COMBINED

Age (x)	Midyear Population	Deaths During Year	nM_x	nq_x	l_x	nd_x	nL_x	nm_x	na_x	T_x	nr_x	$\overset{\circ}{e}_x$	Age (x)
0	384524	76257	.198315	.177450	100000	17745	89480	.198313	.407136	4189425	.000000	41.894	0
1	1395410	38016	.027244	.102024	82255	8392	308040	.027243	1.500000	4099945	.000000	49.844	1
5	1698012	7959	.004687	.023178	73863	1712	365035	.004690	2.500000	3791905	.000000	51.337	5
10	1615287	4243	.002627	.013042	72151	941	358354	.002626	2.448858	3426870	.006623	47.496	10
15	1469190	6157	.004191	.020758	71210	1481	352558	.004201	2.642077	3068516	.017728	43.091	15
20	1250697	7077	.005658	.027980	69729	1951	343937	.005673	2.587135	2715958	.021858	38.950	20
25	1114126	7664	.006879	.033890	67778	2297	333343	.006891	2.585256	2372020	.018542	34.997	25
30	980563	8829	.009004	.044150	65481	2891	320446	.009022	2.592745	2038677	.016658	31.134	30
35	867857	10206	.011760	.057262	62590	3584	304305	.011778	2.587832	1718231	.015436	27.452	35
40	747530	11555	.015458	.074603	59006	4402	284325	.015462	2.568245	1413927	.015705	23.962	40
45	643949	12395	.019248	.092045	54604	5026	260806	.019271	2.569928	1129601	.010183	20.687	45
50	551097	14367	.026070	.122817	49578	6089	233060	.026126	2.564661	868795	.017470	17.524	50
55	414426	14257	.034402	.158891	43489	6910	200561	.034453	2.556651	635735	.011631	14.618	55
60	357872	17467	.048808	.217830	36579	7968	163241	.048811	2.533363	435173	.000710	11.897	60
65	260407	17389	.066776	.286114	28611	8186	122642	.066747	2.506388	271932	-.002582	9.504	65
70	185704	18830	.101358	.402399	20425	8219	81168	.101259	2.450141	149290	-.006703	7.309	70
75	101977	14210	.139345	.509504	12206	6219	44662	.139245	2.368113	68122	-.005278	5.581	75
80	43819	10296	.234567	.715216	5987	4282	18254	.234577	2.272108	23460	-.005278	3.919	80
85+	16244	5320	.327506	1.000000	1705	1705	5206	.327506	3.053383	5206	.000000	3.053	85+

NUMBER OF PERSONS DYING (OUT OF 100,000 AT BIRTH) ABOVE AGE X FROM SPECIFIED CAUSES

Age (x)	All Causes	Respiratory T. B.	Other Infec. and Paras.	Neo-plasms	Cardio-vascular	Infl., Pneu., Bronch.	Diar-rheal	Certain Degenerative	Maternal	Cert. Dis. of Infancy	Motor Vehicle	Other Violence	Other and Unknown	Age (x)
0	100000	8674	9424	3165	16840	24490	2612	3518	0	4976	0	4606	21695	0
1	82255	8596	7083	3162	16762	20624	1079	3492	0	0	0	4299	17158	1
5	73863	8472	3654	3152	16705	18215	751	3442	0	0	0	4049	15423	5
10	72151	8363	2904	3147	16613	18005	725	3407	0	0	0	3888	15079	10
15	71210	8277	2642	3144	16500	17929	711	3381	0	0	0	3754	14872	15
20	69729	7863	2416	3130	16341	17754	693	3344	0	0	0	3555	14633	20
25	67778	7114	2203	3113	16173	17479	673	3298	0	0	0	3332	14393	25
30	65481	6271	2005	3088	15960	17106	653	3215	0	0	0	3070	14113	30
35	62590	5286	1798	3039	15655	16568	630	3087	0	0	0	2773	13754	35
40	59006	4233	1540	2959	15219	15832	606	2908	0	0	0	2445	13264	40
45	54604	3177	1266	2812	14564	14820	576	2655	0	0	0	2090	12644	45
50	49578	2240	1015	2577	13690	13541	538	2323	0	0	0	1720	11934	50
55	43489	1440	779	2231	12388	11865	490	1909	0	0	0	1345	11042	55
60	36579	830	572	1766	10656	9823	437	1428	0	0	0	991	10076	60
65	28611	406	391	1245	8384	7465	366	944	0	0	0	668	8742	65
70	20425	155	240	735	5694	5055	280	528	0	0	0	396	7342	70
75	12206	42	125	334	3107	2819	177	228	0	0	0	194	5180	75
80	5987	16	48	106	1253	1232	87	70	0	0	0	81	3094	80
85+	1705	0	9	19	276	313	23	13	0	0	0	21	1031	85+

NUMBER OF PERSONS SURVIVING TO AGE X IF SPECIFIED CAUSES WERE ELIMINATED

Age (x)	No Causes	Respiratory T. B.	Other Infec. and Paras.	Neo-plasms	Cardio-vascular	Infl., Pneu., Bronch.	Diar-rheal	Certain Degenerative	Maternal	Cert. Dis. of Infancy	Motor Vehicle	Other Violence	Other and Unknown	(1) + (2)	(1) + (2) + (5) + (6) + (8)	(1)+(2)+ (5)+(6)+ (8)+part of(9)&(12)	(10) + (11)	Age (x)
		(1)	(2)	(3)	(4)	(5)	(6)	(7)	(8)	(9)	(10)	(11)	(12)					
0	100000	100000	100000	100000	100000	100000	100000	100000	100000	100000	100000	100000	100000	100000	100000	100000	100000	0
1	82255	82326	84402	82258	82326	85831	83655	82279	82255	86886	82255	82533	86468	84475	89648	99022	82533	1
5	73863	74044	79198	73875	73981	79492	75437	73932	73863	78022	73863	74351	79393	79392	87264	98437	74351	5
10	72151	72416	78162	72168	72357	77874	73714	72253	72151	76214	72151	72788	77919	78449	86506	97944	72788	10
15	71210	71577	77425	71229	71526	76540	73061	71336	71210	75220	71210	71973	77125	77824	85925	97461	71973	15
20	69729	70502	76058	69762	70196	75527	71272	69889	69729	73655	69729	70676	75777	76901	85138	96789	70676	20
25	67778	69280	74159	67827	68399	73708	69598	67979	67778	71594	67778	68921	73915	75803	84283	96063	68921	25
30	65481	67785	71859	65553	66293	71610	67570	65757	65481	69168	65481	66848	71710	74387	83199	95110	66848	30
35	62590	65796	68908	62707	63669	69026	64036	62980	62590	66114	62590	64193	68930	72438	81732	93798	64193	35
40	59006	63111	65239	59194	60456	65867	60393	59549	59006	62328	59006	60845	65509	69778	79722	91986	60845	40
45	54604	59498	60664	54920	56595	62050	55917	55353	54604	57679	54604	56659	61288	66101	76921	89363	56659	45
50	49578	55000	55346	50091	52258	57741	50807	50809	49578	52370	49578	51810	56411	61399	73281	85811	51810	50
55	43489	49080	48795	44268	47144	52511	44613	44765	43489	45938	43489	45814	50442	55068	68211	80692	45814	55
60	36579	41913	41254	37671	41415	46486	37575	39108	36579	38639	36579	38877	43467	47270	61707	73868	38877	60
65	28611	33210	32447	29942	34750	39101	29454	30254	28611	30222	28611	30711	35428	37663	52989	64638	30711	65
70	20425	23950	23307	21827	27717	30822	21102	21568	20425	21575	20425	22170	26802	27330	42608	53276	22170	70
75	12206	14410	14028	13372	19471	21179	12693	13374	12206	12893	12206	13415	18371	16562	29882	39601	13415	75
80	5987	7087	6941	6729	11798	12449	6291	6676	5987	6324	5987	6664	11496	8216	17952	26430	6664	80
85+	1705	2028	1999	1966	4475	4642	1825	1933	1705	1801	1705	1932	5996	2378	6932	13545	1932	85+

ADDED YRS OF LIFE

TOTAL		2.291	4.091	.409	2.431	6.238	.990	.588	.000	2.336	.000	1.193	5.654	6.656	15.728	25.887	1.193	
WORK	10.728	2.293	.630	.258	1.275	1.870	.071	.422	.000	.000	.000	.784	1.203	2.980	5.208	6.148	.784	

POPULATION, DEATHS, DEATH RATES FOR ALL CAUSES COMBINED, AND SPECIFIED CAUSES

Age Start of Interval	Midyear Population	Deaths During Year	All Causes	Respiratory T. B.	Other Infec. and Paras.	Neoplasms	Cardiovascular	Infl., Pneu., Bronch.	Diarrheal	Certain Degenerative	Maternal	Cert. Dis. of Infancy	Motor Vehicle	Other Violence	Other and Unknown	Age Start of Interval
0	385050	59544	.15464	.00074	.02340	.00004	.00076	.03183	.01360	.00036	.00000	.04362	.00000	.00341	.03688	0
1	1397781	36461	.02608	.00038	.01116	.00002	.00018	.00749	.00107	.00010	.00000	.00000	.00000	.00058	.00511	1
5	1706136	8041	.00471	.00030	.00227	.00001	.00026	.00058	.00011	.00007	.00000	.00000	.00000	.00022	.00088	5
10	1616809	4629	.00286	.00063	.00082	.00001	.00041	.00021	.00005	.00008	.00000	.00000	.00000	.00010	.00056	10
15	1489485	6339	.00426	.00160	.00062	.00003	.00053	.00038	.00005	.00010	.00012	.00000	.00000	.00012	.00070	15
20	1402665	7256	.00517	.00192	.00049	.00004	.00053	.00051	.00004	.00014	.00063	.00000	.00000	.00011	.00077	20
25	1242257	7864	.00633	.00223	.00048	.00005	.00065	.00070	.00006	.00020	.00089	.00000	.00000	.00014	.00089	25
30	1052274	8376	.00796	.00246	.00046	.00029	.00098	.00101	.00007	.00032	.00107	.00000	.00000	.00017	.00113	30
35	918634	9090	.00990	.00254	.00051	.00066	.00155	.00139	.00009	.00048	.00093	.00000	.00000	.00019	.00156	35
40	803542	10010	.01246	.00247	.00053	.00119	.00245	.00208	.00012	.00068	.00072	.00000	.00000	.00024	.00198	40
45	696370	10161	.01459	.00202	.00052	.00199	.00351	.00289	.00016	.00091	.00008	.00000	.00000	.00031	.00221	45
50	612055	12290	.02008	.00173	.00054	.00278	.00559	.00461	.00023	.00120	.00001	.00000	.00000	.00040	.00299	50
55	472100	12928	.02738	.00159	.00057	.00353	.00849	.00711	.00029	.00151	.00000	.00000	.00000	.00049	.00381	55
60	417060	16785	.04025	.00133	.00065	.00434	.01320	.01114	.00048	.00186	.00000	.00000	.00000	.00062	.00663	60
65	313096	18004	.05750	.00101	.00079	.00512	.02039	.01691	.00085	.00224	.00000	.00000	.00000	.00070	.00950	65
70	233293	20577	.08820	.00070	.00102	.00572	.02866	.02492	.00132	.00245	.00000	.00000	.00000	.00107	.02236	70
75	131935	16087	.12193	.00052	.00132	.00565	.03678	.03315	.00174	.00228	.00000	.00000	.00000	.00151	.03898	75
80	62058	12698	.20462	.00026	.00174	.00567	.04547	.04799	.00274	.00200	.00000	.00000	.00000	.00301	.09573	80
85+	27570	8291	.30073	.00025	.00192	.00522	.04313	.05923	.00377	.00145	.00000	.00000	.00000	.00522	.18052	85+
ALL	14980170	285431														

	All Causes	Respiratory T. B.	Other Infec. and Paras.	Neoplasms	Cardiovascular	Infl., Pneu., Bronch.	Diarrheal	Certain Degenerative	Maternal	Cert. Dis. of Infancy	Motor Vehicle	Other Violence	Other and Unknown
CRUDE DEATH RATE	.01905	.00143	.00237	.00086	.00305	.00422	.00061	.00047	.00032	.00112	.00000	.00038	.00423
STANDARDIZED RATE (1)	.01902	.00136	.00287	.00072	.00247	.00417	.00074	.00041	.00030	.00154	.00000	.00040	.00406
STANDARDIZED RATE (2)	.02374	.00146	.00209	.00125	.00472	.00549	.00060	.00062	.00031	.00090	.00000	.00043	.00585
GEOMETRIC MEAN	.02327												

LIFE TABLE FOR ALL CAUSES COMBINED

Age (x)	Midyear Population	Deaths During Year	nM_x	nq_x	l_x	nd_x	nL_x	nm_x	na_x	T_x	nr_x	$\overset{\circ}{e}_x$	Age (x)
0	385050	59544	.154640	.140180	100000	14018	90648	.154641	.332887	4570568	.000000	45.706	0
1	1397781	36461	.026085	.097951	85982	8422	322873	.026085	1.500000	4479919	.000000	52.103	1
5	1706136	8041	.004713	.023258	77560	1807	383283	.004715	2.500000	4157046	.000000	53.598	5
10	1616809	4629	.002863	.014204	75753	1076	376027	.002861	2.455081	3773764	.007612	49.817	10
15	1489485	6339	.004256	.021091	74677	1575	369613	.004261	2.604854	3397737	.009424	45.499	15
20	1402665	7256	.005173	.025567	73102	1869	360973	.005178	2.572343	3028124	.010474	41.423	20
25	1242257	7864	.006330	.031221	71233	2224	350778	.006340	2.577844	2667152	.019386	37.443	25
30	1052274	8376	.007960	.039125	69009	2700	338500	.007976	2.576003	2316374	.022450	33.566	30
35	918634	9090	.009895	.048395	66309	3209	323756	.009912	2.572647	1977873	.018272	29.828	35
40	803542	10010	.012457	.060523	63100	3819	306155	.012474	2.553079	1654118	.017012	26.214	40
45	696370	10161	.014591	.070545	59281	4182	286256	.014609	2.573181	1347962	.011678	22.739	45
50	612055	12290	.020080	.095973	55099	5288	262739	.020126	2.587738	1061706	.018142	19.269	50
55	472100	12928	.027384	.128666	49811	6409	233589	.027437	2.586825	798967	.013441	16.040	55
60	417060	16785	.040246	.183379	43402	7959	197637	.040271	2.565858	565379	.003617	13.027	60
65	313096	18004	.057503	.251813	35443	8925	155237	.057493	2.537442	367742	.000594	10.376	65
70	233293	20577	.088202	.360623	26518	9563	108459	.088171	2.476668	212505	.001962	8.014	70
75	131935	16087	.121921	.463226	16955	7854	64401	.121955	2.405887	104046	.001153	6.137	75
80	62058	12698	.204615	.660916	9101	6015	29383	.204709	2.319722	39645	.001153	4.356	80
85+	27570	8291	.300725	1.000000	3086	3086	10262	.300725	3.325292	10262	.000000	3.325	85+

NUMBER OF PERSONS DYING (OUT OF 100,000 AT BIRTH) ABOVE AGE X FROM SPECIFIED CAUSES

Age (x)	All Causes	Respiratory T. B.	Other Infec. and Paras.	Neoplasms	Cardiovascular	Infl., Pneu., Bronch.	Diarrheal	Certain Degenerative	Maternal	Cert. Dis. of Infancy	Motor Vehicle	Other Violence	Other and Unknown	Age (x)
0	100000	6567	8904	5739	20076	22998	2560	2881	1495	3954	0	1841	22585	0
1	85982	6900	6783	5735	20007	20112	1327	2848	1495	0	0	1532	19243	1
5	77560	6778	3179	5728	19950	17695	982	2815	1495	0	0	1344	17594	5
10	75753	6661	2307	5723	19849	17472	940	2790	1495	0	0	1259	17257	10
15	74677	6425	2001	5721	19695	17391	922	2760	1495	0	0	1220	17047	15
20	73102	5832	1770	5710	19499	17251	903	2725	1449	0	0	1178	16785	20
25	71233	5139	1594	5696	19309	17066	888	2675	1223	0	0	1139	16504	25
30	69009	4358	1424	5663	19082	16819	867	2603	909	0	0	1090	16194	30
35	66309	3525	1268	5563	18749	16476	842	2495	547	0	0	1032	15812	35
40	63100	2704	1103	5349	18245	16025	812	2339	247	0	0	970	15306	40
45	59281	1949	943	4983	17493	15387	774	2130	27	0	0	896	14699	45
50	55099	1371	754	4413	16487	14559	729	1869	5	0	0	806	14066	50
55	49811	917	652	3680	15014	13343	669	1554	2	0	0	701	13279	55
60	43402	547	519	2855	13026	11679	602	1200	2	0	0	586	12386	60
65	35443	284	391	1997	10414	9475	506	833	2	0	0	464	11077	65
70	26518	127	268	1202	7250	6850	374	486	2	0	0	355	9604	70
75	16955	52	158	582	4142	4148	231	220	2	0	0	240	7180	75
80	9101	18	73	218	1773	2014	119	73	2	0	0	142	4669	80
85+	3086	3	20	54	443	608	39	15	0	0	0	54	1850	85+

NUMBER OF PERSONS SURVIVING TO AGE X IF SPECIFIED CAUSES WERE ELIMINATED

Age (x)	No Causes	Respiratory T. B.	Other Infec. and Paras.	Neoplasms	Cardiovascular	Infl., Pneu., Bronch.	Diarrheal	Certain Degenerative	Maternal	Cert. Dis. of Infancy	Motor Vehicle	Other Violence	Other and Unknown	(1)+(2)	(1)+(2)+(5)+(6)+(8)	(1)+(2)+(5)+(6)+(8)+part of(9)&(12)	(10)+(11)	Age (x)
		(1)	(2)	(3)	(4)	(5)	(6)	(7)	(8)	(9)	(10)	(11)	(12)					
0	100000	100000	100000	100000	100000	100000	100000	100000	100000	100000	100000	100000	100000	100000	100000	100000	100000	0
1	85982	86044	87969	85986	86046	88698	87132	86013	85982	89724	85982	86269	89134	88033	92028	99072	86269	1
5	77560	77732	82932	77570	77672	82412	78930	77619	77560	80936	77560	77998	82043	83116	89875	98643	77998	5
10	75753	76037	81927	75768	75962	80726	77133	75835	75753	79056	75753	76265	80485	82233	89229	98302	76265	10
15	74677	75192	81092	74693	75037	79666	76056	74788	74677	77927	74677	75221	79563	81652	88714	97937	75221	15
20	73102	74200	79630	73129	73649	78133	74471	73245	73148	76284	73102	73676	78162	80826	88061	97487	73676	20
25	71233	73000	77783	71273	71955	76331	72582	71422	71501	74333	71233	71831	76461	79713	87364	97022	71831	25
30	69009	71513	75538	69081	69935	74209	70337	69263	69580	72012	69009	69637	74401	78279	86507	96411	69637	30
35	66309	69566	72750	66476	67531	71668	67610	66660	67216	69195	66309	66970	71895	76323	85260	95421	66970	35
40	63100	67044	69406	63469	64766	68677	64368	63587	64260	65846	63100	63790	68953	73744	83380	93794	63790	40
45	59281	63768	65996	59686	61599	65198	60510	59943	60587	61861	59281	60002	65426	70323	80685	91272	60002	45
50	55099	59870	60922	56214	58271	61483	56285	55969	56334	57497	55099	55857	61488	66197	77149	87714	55857	50
55	49811	54593	55224	51626	54182	56889	50942	50903	50930	51579	49811	50598	56427	60526	72284	82698	50598	55
60	43402	47946	48256	45787	49273	51375	44451	44691	44377	45291	43402	44196	50120	53309	66080	76191	44196	60
65	35443	39415	39535	38213	43006	44377	36389	36838	36240	36986	35443	36203	42317	43965	57787	67534	36203	65
70	26518	29638	29698	29335	35661	36159	27343	27872	27114	27672	26518	27183	33223	33192	47716	56871	27183	70
75	16955	19014	19085	19302	26356	26228	17600	18041	17336	17693	16955	17474	23820	21404	35141	43974	17474	75
80	9101	10233	10313	10657	17047	16662	9531	9795	9306	9497	9101	9453	15647	11596	22734	31120	9453	80
85+	3086	3479	3531	3722	7342	7275	3279	3356	3156	3220	3086	3256	8808	3980	10197	17865	3256	85+

ADDED YRS OF LIFE																		
TOTAL		2.148	4.230	.859	3.085	5.571	.948	.524	.483	1.975	.000	.519	5.559	6.608	15.252	24.201	.519	
WORK	9.425	1.949	.482	.538	1.448	1.257	.078	.347	.536	.000	.000	.163	1.209	2.464	4.555	5.451	.163	

POPULATION, DEATHS, DEATH RATES FOR ALL CAUSES COMBINED, AND SPECIFIED CAUSES

Age Start of Interval	Midyear Population	Deaths During Year	All Causes	Respiratory T. B.	Other Infec. and Paras.	Neoplasms	Cardiovascular	Infl., Pneu., Bronch.	Diarrheal	Certain Degenerative	Maternal	Cert. Dis. of Infancy	Motor Vehicle	Other Violence	Other and Unknown	Age Start of Interval
0	400629	78493	.19592	.00049	.02035	.00004	.00051	.03003	.04006	.00039	.00000	.05586	.00000	.00298	.04521	0
1	1460175	31088	.02129	.00028	.00872	.00004	.00013	.00500	.00205	.00016	.00000	.00000	.00000	.00088	.00405	1
5	1744058	7014	.00402	.00015	.00193	.00003	.00025	.00039	.00008	.00009	.00000	.00000	.00000	.00037	.00073	5
10	1675957	3834	.00229	.00019	.00064	.00003	.00037	.00015	.00003	.00007	.00000	.00000	.00000	.00032	.00048	10
15	1612269	5557	.00345	.00080	.00063	.00003	.00046	.00032	.00003	.00013	.00000	.00000	.00000	.00055	.00055	15
20	1476568	6918	.00468	.00166	.00064	.00005	.00043	.00046	.00003	.00018	.00000	.00000	.00000	.00065	.00058	20
25	1332240	7305	.00548	.00194	.00068	.00007	.00055	.00058	.00004	.00024	.00000	.00000	.00000	.00072	.00067	25
30	1161134	8245	.00710	.00240	.00078	.00016	.00079	.00083	.00005	.00038	.00000	.00000	.00000	.00084	.00086	30
35	1037569	9568	.00922	.00275	.00101	.00029	.00117	.00119	.00008	.00059	.00000	.00000	.00000	.00097	.00117	35
40	900162	10977	.01219	.00305	.00114	.00061	.00188	.00174	.00011	.00092	.00000	.00000	.00000	.00114	.00161	40
45	762255	11778	.01545	.00316	.00112	.00111	.00273	.00240	.00014	.00137	.00000	.00000	.00000	.00134	.00208	45
50	638188	13517	.02118	.00311	.00117	.00193	.00468	.00356	.00021	.00199	.00000	.00000	.00000	.00154	.00300	50
55	498976	13926	.02791	.00271	.00123	.00313	.00745	.00499	.00029	.00276	.00000	.00000	.00000	.00172	.00363	55
60	411617	16634	.04041	.00230	.00126	.00442	.01211	.00742	.00050	.00353	.00000	.00000	.00000	.00193	.00694	60
65	283238	15756	.05563	.00183	.00120	.00575	.01877	.01047	.00082	.00418	.00000	.00000	.00000	.00181	.01080	65
70	196080	16847	.08592	.00125	.00122	.00688	.02697	.01556	.00135	.00469	.00000	.00000	.00000	.00276	.02523	70
75	113436	13125	.11570	.00082	.00134	.00689	.03404	.02082	.00185	.00452	.00000	.00000	.00000	.00237	.04305	75
80	52255	10036	.19206	.00025	.00145	.00706	.04329	.03093	.00318	.00442	.00000	.00000	.00000	.00344	.09804	80
85+	18053	5000	.27696	.00028	.00144	.00626	.04337	.03894	.00465	.00399	.00000	.00000	.00000	.00543	.17260	85+
ALL	15775259	285618														

CRUDE DEATH RATE			.01811	.00149	.00220	.00070	.00245	.00294	.00134	.00072	.00000	.00142	.00000	.00093	.00391	
STANDARDIZED RATE (1)			.01940	.00135	.00261	.00062	.00218	.00317	.00177	.00065	.00000	.00157	.00000	.00091	.00416	
STANDARDIZED RATE (2)			.02348	.00160	.00204	.00117	.00426	.00389	.00123	.00106	.00000	.00116	.00000	.00108	.00600	
GEOMETRIC MEAN			.02193													

LIFE TABLE FOR ALL CAUSES COMBINED

Age (x)	Midyear Population	Deaths During Year	$_nM_x$	$_nq_x$	l_x	$_nd_x$	$_nL_x$	$_nm_x$	$_na_x$	T_x	$_nr_x$	$\overset{\circ}{e}_x$	Age (x)
0	400629	78493	.195924	.175410	100000	17541	89529	.195925	.403071	4531941	.000000	45.319	0
1	1460175	31088	.021291	.080852	82459	6667	313169	.021289	1.500000	4442412	.000000	53.874	1
5	1744058	7014	.004022	.019923	75792	1510	375185	.004025	2.500000	4129243	.000000	54.481	5
10	1675957	3834	.002288	.011362	74282	844	369247	.002286	2.437549	3754058	.003145	50.538	10
15	1612269	5557	.003447	.017116	73438	1257	364220	.003451	2.637397	3384811	.007023	46.091	15
20	1476568	6918	.004684	.023178	72181	1673	356859	.004688	2.581441	3020591	.012058	41.847	20
25	1332240	7305	.005483	.027103	70508	1911	347914	.005493	2.579147	2663732	.016532	37.779	25
30	1161134	8245	.007101	.034972	68597	2399	337212	.007114	2.593789	2315818	.018048	33.760	30
35	1037569	9568	.009222	.045183	66198	2991	323794	.009237	2.594171	1978606	.016030	29.889	35
40	900162	10977	.012194	.059345	63207	3751	306699	.012220	2.580256	1654811	.018240	26.181	40
45	762255	11778	.015452	.074610	59456	4436	286566	.015480	2.584817	1347853	.017670	22.670	45
50	638188	13517	.021180	.101000	55020	5557	261633	.021240	2.576518	1061287	.021480	19.289	50
55	498976	13926	.027909	.130946	49463	6477	231615	.027964	2.576070	799654	.016206	16.167	55
60	411617	16634	.040411	.184293	42986	7922	195566	.040508	2.555726	568039	.015747	13.215	60
65	283238	15756	.055628	.245152	35064	8596	154129	.055771	2.534827	372472	.017267	10.623	65
70	196080	16847	.085919	.353597	26468	9359	108740	.086068	2.478319	218343	.008628	8.249	70
75	113436	13125	.115704	.445457	17109	7622	65798	.115840	2.409172	109603	.008170	6.406	75
80	52255	10036	.192058	.636239	9487	6036	31345	.192564	2.334396	43806	.008170	4.617	80
85+	18053	5000	.276962	1.000000	3451	3451	12460	.276962	3.610600	12460	.000000	3.611	85+

NUMBER OF PERSONS DYING (OUT OF 100,000 AT BIRTH) ABOVE AGE X FROM SPECIFIED CAUSES

Age (x)	All Causes	Respiratory T.B.	Other Infec. and Paras.	Neoplasms	Cardiovascular	Infl., Pneu., Bronch.	Diarrheal	Certain Degenerative	Maternal	Cert. Dis. of Infancy	Motor Vehicle	Other Violence	Other and Unknown	Age (x)
0	100000	7744	8784	5233	18149	16520	5191	4831	0	5001	0	4894	23653	0
1	82459	7700	6962	5229	18103	13832	1605	4756	0	0	0	4627	19605	1
5	75792	7614	4232	5216	18062	12267	964	4747	0	0	0	4352	18338	5
10	74282	7556	3508	5206	17970	12120	935	4712	0	0	0	4212	18063	10
15	73438	7488	3270	5156	17832	12063	925	4686	0	0	0	4094	17884	15
20	72181	7197	3040	5184	17664	11944	914	4640	0	0	0	3915	17683	20
25	70508	6602	2813	5166	17511	11781	902	4577	0	0	0	3682	17474	25
30	68597	5928	2575	5143	17319	11579	889	4492	0	0	0	3431	17241	30
35	66198	5116	2311	5090	17052	11298	871	4362	0	0	0	3147	16951	35
40	63207	4224	1983	4996	16672	10913	847	4172	0	0	0	2832	16568	40
45	59456	3287	1632	4808	16093	10378	813	3890	0	0	0	2482	16073	45
50	55020	2382	1310	4488	15308	9688	774	3496	0	0	0	2096	15478	50
55	49463	1568	1005	3981	14079	8752	720	2974	0	0	0	1693	14691	55
60	42986	942	720	3255	12349	7594	652	2334	0	0	0	1294	13846	60
65	35064	493	474	2390	9974	6139	554	1642	0	0	0	916	12482	65
70	26468	213	289	1501	7073	4521	427	997	0	0	0	637	10810	70
75	17109	77	157	753	4135	2826	279	487	0	0	0	336	8059	75
80	9487	23	68	299	1894	1455	157	190	0	0	0	180	5221	80
85+	3451	3	18	78	540	485	58	50	0	0	0	68	2151	85+

NUMBER OF PERSONS SURVIVING TO AGE X IF SPECIFIED CAUSES WERE ELIMINATED

Age (x)	No Causes	Respiratory T.B. (1)	Other Infec. and Paras. (2)	Neoplasms (3)	Cardiovascular (4)	Infl., Pneu., Bronch. (5)	Diarrheal (6)	Certain Degenerative (7)	Maternal (8)	Cert. Dis. of Infancy (9)	Motor Vehicle (10)	Other Violence (11)	Other and Unknown (12)	(1)+(2)	(1)+(2)+(5)+(6)+(8)	(1)+(2)+(5)+(6)+(8)+part of(9)&(12)	(10)+(11)	Age (x)
0	100000	100000	100000	100000	100000	100000	100000	100000	100000	100000	100000	100000	100000	100000	100000	100000	100000	0
1	82459	82499	84128	82463	82501	84532	85775	82491	82459	87120	82459	82701	86212	84168	90180	99204	82701	1
5	75792	75911	80042	75808	75870	79626	79482	75868	75792	80076	75792	76280	80521	80168	88323	98620	76280	5
10	74282	74456	79208	74307	74449	78152	77928	74391	74282	78481	74282	74900	79207	79394	87676	98116	74900	10
15	73438	73678	78560	73473	73741	77364	77053	73572	73438	77569	73438	74167	78497	78817	87118	97684	74167	15
20	72181	72707	77460	72227	72646	76164	75746	72358	72181	76261	72181	73077	77367	78025	86396	97040	73077	20
25	70508	71617	75906	70571	71115	74569	74003	70744	70508	74494	70508	71617	75795	77100	85582	96317	71617	25
30	68597	70354	74101	68681	69379	72159	72010	68911	68597	72475	68597	69927	73988	76000	84622	95452	69927	30
35	66198	68717	71791	66331	67218	70508	69511	66629	66198	69940	66198	67767	71709	74522	83346	94276	67767	35
40	63207	66522	68895	63427	64560	67724	66395	63806	63207	66780	63207	65021	68875	72509	81609	92653	65021	40
45	59456	63537	65178	59846	61305	64264	62489	60296	59456	62817	59456	61512	65313	69653	79125	90248	61512	45
50	55020	59733	60655	55692	57516	60191	57866	56183	55020	58130	55020	57308	61072	65851	75766	86875	57308	50
55	49463	54541	54848	50557	52941	55051	52076	51017	49463	52259	49463	51918	55738	60479	70919	81860	51918	55
60	42986	48043	47960	44634	47769	49094	45323	44955	42986	45416	42986	45511	49336	53602	64548	75026	45511	60
65	35064	39640	39368	37226	41424	41574	31064	37327	35064	37046	35064	37484	41684	44506	55779	65618	37484	65
70	26468	30194	25896	28927	34383	33087	28095	28774	26468	27964	26468	28553	33246	34104	44252	54178	28553	70
75	17109	19638	19443	19356	25479	23144	18286	19042	17109	18076	17109	18716	24462	22316	32265	40263	18716	75
80	9487	10933	10855	11110	16787	14267	10236	10800	9487	10023	9487	10501	16647	12509	20296	27339	10501	80
85+	3451	3990	3982	4194	7661	6105	3786	4022	3451	3646	3451	3892	10310	4604	8935	14664	3892	85+

ADDED YRS OF LIFE

	No Causes	(1)	(2)	(3)	(4)	(5)	(6)	(7)	(8)	(9)	(10)	(11)	(12)	(1)+(2)	(1)+(2)+(5)+(6)+(8)	+part	(10)+(11)
TOTAL		2.085	3.818	.658	2.692	4.178	2.309	.811	.000	2.535	.000	1.288	5.856	6.131	14.053	23.101	1.288
WORK	8.981	1.945	.760	.349	1.191	1.017	.063	.501	.000	.000	.000	.786	1.013	2.763	3.984	4.650	.786

POPULATION, DEATHS, DEATH RATES FOR ALL CAUSES COMBINED, AND SPECIFIED CAUSES

Age Start of Interval	Midyear Population	Deaths During Year	All Causes	Respiratory T. B.	Other Infec. and Paras.	Neoplasms	Cardiovascular	Infl., Pneu., Bronch.	Diarrheal	Certain Degenerative	Maternal	Cert. Dis. of Infancy	Motor Vehicle	Other Violence	Other and Unknown	Age Start of Interval
0	397548	62155	.15635	.00051	.01771	.00004	.00036	.02306	.03337	.00021	.00000	.04326	.00000	.00282	.03501	0
1	1469067	30011	.02043	.00025	.00876	.00003	.00014	.00480	.00190	.00012	.00000	.00000	.00000	.00071	.00372	1
5	1753158	7148	.00408	.00020	.00205	.00001	.00030	.00038	.00009	.00008	.00000	.00000	.00000	.00026	.00071	5
10	1675481	3955	.00238	.00040	.00071	.00002	.00046	.00014	.00003	.00005	.00000	.00000	.00000	.00009	.00045	10
15	1643191	5293	.00322	.00100	.00052	.00003	.00050	.00022	.00003	.00020	.00009	.00000	.00000	.00012	.00052	15
20	1652918	6325	.00383	.00129	.00045	.00005	.00042	.00024	.00004	.00027	.00045	.00000	.00000	.00011	.00051	20
25	1500392	7074	.00471	.00154	.00043	.00011	.00050	.00033	.00005	.00031	.00067	.00000	.00000	.00013	.00062	25
30	1277268	7693	.00602	.00175	.00044	.00033	.00075	.00048	.00007	.00042	.00082	.00000	.00000	.00016	.00081	30
35	1114012	8596	.00772	.00186	.00052	.00070	.00120	.00070	.00008	.00060	.00074	.00000	.00000	.00021	.00111	35
40	955770	9477	.00992	.00186	.00054	.00129	.00193	.00103	.00011	.00082	.00059	.00000	.00000	.00026	.00148	40
45	815478	9623	.01180	.00159	.00049	.00217	.00277	.00136	.00012	.00108	.00007	.00000	.00000	.00031	.00184	45
50	694641	11320	.01630	.00139	.00048	.00312	.00461	.00221	.00019	.00143	.00001	.00000	.00000	.00038	.00247	50
55	556655	12105	.02175	.00121	.00053	.00404	.00732	.00335	.00030	.00187	.00000	.00000	.00000	.00042	.00271	55
60	481545	15470	.03213	.00102	.00057	.00513	.01133	.00565	.00050	.00228	.00000	.00000	.00000	.00056	.00508	60
65	348273	15943	.04578	.00092	.00057	.00626	.01693	.00916	.00079	.00264	.00000	.00000	.00000	.00077	.00773	65
70	251603	18060	.07178	.00070	.00064	.00729	.02374	.01440	.00126	.00291	.00000	.00000	.00000	.00120	.01963	70
75	151824	15279	.10064	.00045	.00079	.00761	.03008	.01996	.00175	.00284	.00000	.00000	.00000	.00160	.03555	75
80	76815	12793	.16654	.00014	.00092	.00803	.03747	.02959	.00279	.00266	.00000	.00000	.00000	.00311	.08183	80
85+	30585	7607	.24872	.00003	.00095	.00749	.03773	.03796	.00396	.00206	.00000	.00000	.00000	.00559	.15295	85+
ALL	16846264	265967														

	All Causes	Respiratory T. B.	Other Infec. and Paras.	Neoplasms	Cardiovascular	Infl., Pneu., Bronch.	Diarrheal	Certain Degenerative	Maternal	Cert. Dis. of Infancy	Motor Vehicle	Other Violence	Other and Unknown
CRUDE DEATH RATE	.01579	.00105	.00181	.00104	.00258	.00245	.00110	.00060	.00026	.00102	.00000	.00037	.00349
STANDARDIZED RATE (1)	.01631	.00096	.00231	.00084	.00206	.00254	.00152	.00051	.00023	.00152	.00000	.00039	.00342
STANDARDIZED RATE (2)	.01971	.00106	.00169	.00150	.00393	.00320	.00107	.00077	.00024	.00090	.00000	.00044	.00493
GEOMETRIC MEAN	.01877												

LIFE TABLE FOR ALL CAUSES COMBINED

Age (x)	Midyear Population	Deaths During Year	$_nM_x$	$_nq_x$	l_x	$_nd_x$	$_nL_x$	$_nm_x$	$_na_x$	T_x	$_nr_x$	$\overset{\circ}{e}_x$	Age (x)
0	397548	62155	.156346	.141640	100000	14164	90592	.156349	.335788	4943286	.000000	49.433	0
1	1469067	30011	.020429	.077741	85836	6673	326662	.020428	1.500000	4852694	.000000	56.534	1
5	1753158	7148	.004077	.020186	79163	1598	391820	.004078	2.500000	4526032	.000000	57.174	5
10	1675481	3955	.002384	.011848	77565	919	385450	.002384	2.415443	4134212	.003759	53.300	10
15	1643191	5293	.003221	.015983	76646	1225	380274	.003221	2.586735	3748762	-.001078	48.910	15
20	1652918	6325	.003827	.018947	75421	1429	373637	.003825	2.573332	3368489	.001044	44.662	20
25	1500392	7074	.004715	.023354	73992	1728	365790	.004724	2.586926	2994851	.015742	40.475	25
30	1277268	7693	.006023	.029752	72264	2150	356139	.006037	2.590407	2629061	.022330	36.381	30
35	1114012	8596	.007716	.037952	70114	2661	344151	.007732	2.587843	2272922	-.021295	32.418	35
40	955770	9477	.009916	.048508	67453	3272	329299	.009936	2.565391	1928771	-.021862	28.594	40
45	815478	9623	.011800	.057462	64181	3688	311994	.011821	2.583830	1599472	.019389	24.921	45
50	694641	11320	.016296	.078621	60493	4756	291009	.016343	2.591288	1287477	.022647	21.283	50
55	556655	12105	.021746	.103558	55737	5772	264819	.021796	2.597706	996468	.016009	17.878	55
60	481545	15470	.032126	.149365	49965	7463	231793	.032197	2.583830	731649	.014124	14.643	60
65	348273	15943	.045777	.206461	42502	8775	191162	.045904	2.567165	499856	.017122	11.761	65
70	251603	18060	.071780	.305156	33727	10292	143035	.071954	2.512651	308694	.012671	9.153	70
75	151824	15279	.100636	.401109	23435	9400	93229	.100827	2.452571	165659	.011588	7.069	75
80	76815	12793	.166543	.560834	14035	8152	48776	.167130	2.375056	72430	.011588	5.161	80
85+	30585	7607	.248717	1.000000	5883	5883	23653	.248717	4.020639	23653	.000000	4.021	85+

NUMBER OF PERSONS DYING (OUT OF 100,000 AT BIRTH) ABOVE AGE X FROM SPECIFIED CAUSES

Age (x)	All Causes	Respiratory T. B.	Other Infec. and Paras.	Neoplasms	Cardiovascular	Infl., Pneu., Bronch.	Diarrheal	Certain Degenerative	Maternal	Cert. Dis. of Infancy	Motor Vehicle	Other Violence	Other and Unknown	Age (x)
0	100000	5455	7491	8263	21189	16212	4840	4188	1215	3919	0	2174	25054	0
1	85836	5409	5887	8259	21157	14123	1817	4169	1215	0	0	1919	21881	1
5	79163	5327	3024	8249	21113	12555	1197	4130	1215	0	0	1687	20666	5
10	77565	5247	2220	8244	20996	12408	1162	4100	1215	0	0	1587	20386	10
15	76646	5092	1946	8236	20818	12354	1151	4066	1215	0	0	1553	20215	15
20	75421	4713	1748	8224	20629	12269	1140	3991	1182	0	0	1508	20017	20
25	73992	4231	1580	8205	20473	12180	1124	3991	1014	0	0	1465	19829	25
30	72264	3667	1422	8163	20288	12058	1105	3777	767	0	0	1418	19599	30
35	70114	3042	1266	8046	20021	11885	1080	3626	475	0	0	1362	19311	35
40	67453	2402	1087	7803	19607	11643	1052	3420	220	0	0	1290	18929	40
45	64181	1790	909	7376	18969	11302	1017	3149	28	0	0	1204	18437	45
50	60493	1295	757	6657	18102	10875	978	2811	7	0	0	1107	17864	50
55	55737	892	617	5787	16754	10229	922	2393	5	0	0	997	17141	55
60	49965	573	475	4714	14811	9340	843	1858	4	0	0	886	16421	60
65	42502	336	344	3523	12178	8027	726	1368	4	0	0	755	15241	65
70	33727	160	236	2326	8533	6270	575	863	4	0	0	607	13753	70
75	23435	60	144	1282	5530	4206	393	446	4	0	0	434	10936	75
80	14035	18	70	572	2723	2342	230	181	4	0	0	285	7610	80
85+	5883	1	22	177	892	898	94	49	0	0	0	132	3618	85+

NUMBER OF PERSONS SURVIVING TO AGE X IF SPECIFIED CAUSES WERE ELIMINATED

Age (x)	No Causes	Respiratory T. B.	Other Infec. and Paras.	Neoplasms	Cardiovascular	Infl., Pneu., Bronch.	Diarrheal	Certain Degenerative	Maternal	Cert. Dis. of Infancy	Motor Vehicle	Other Violence	Other and Unknown	(1) + (2)	(1) + (2) + (5) + (6) + (8)	(1)+(2)+ (5)+(6)+ (8)+part of(9)&(12)	(10) + (11)	Age (x)
		(1)	(2)	(3)	(4)	(5)	(6)	(7)	(8)	(9)	(10)	(11)	(12)					
0	100000	100000	100000	100000	100000	100000	100000	100000	100000	100000	100000	100000	100000	100000	100000	100000	100000	0
1	85836	85879	87334	85840	85866	87791	88680	85854	85836	89541	85836	86072	88824	87377	92329	99333	86072	1
5	79163	79281	83390	79176	79233	82521	82403	79217	79163	82580	79163	79605	83134	83514	90620	98855	79605	5
10	77565	77760	82549	77583	77749	81007	80776	77647	77565	80913	77565	78097	81748	82757	90007	98471	78097	10
15	76646	76993	81862	76671	77006	80103	79830	76761	76646	79954	76646	77206	80959	82233	89512	98073	77206	15
20	75421	76142	80763	75458	75963	78911	78566	75609	75454	78677	75421	76017	79872	81535	88903	97580	76017	20
25	73992	75182	79411	74047	74680	77508	77094	74276	74191	77186	73992	74620	78556	80689	88303	97103	74620	25
30	72264	73995	77724	72359	73121	75825	75313	72654	72704	75383	72264	72924	76964	79586	87560	96510	72924	30
35	70114	72426	75577	70322	71212	73748	73058	70642	70830	73140	70114	70810	74977	78070	86485	95589	70810	35
40	67453	70329	72898	67893	68923	71199	70352	68165	68395	70365	67453	68194	72533	76006	84844	94083	68194	40
45	64181	67542	69550	65021	66219	68057	66975	65126	65267	66951	64181	64971	69532	73192	82410	91718	64971	45
50	60493	64167	65713	61957	63289	64626	63166	61718	61537	63104	60493	61333	66142	69704	79099	88328	61333	50
55	55737	59533	60693	57587	59684	60212	58256	57276	56700	58143	55737	56618	61705	64826	74461	83468	56618	55
60	49965	53690	54554	53048	55511	54854	52302	51828	50830	52122	49965	50861	56075	58620	68581	77175	50861	60
65	42502	45904	46537	46302	49994	48045	44603	44595	43237	44337	42502	43387	48937	50261	60656	68760	43387	65
70	33727	36594	37033	37915	43211	39934	35535	35859	34311	35183	33727	34564	40397	40181	50994	58498	34564	70
75	23435	25515	25816	27328	33853	29848	24851	25283	23841	24447	23435	24164	31038	28107	38619	45781	24164	75
80	14035	15315	15523	17003	23604	19784	15016	15358	14278	14641	14035	14589	22333	16938	25986	32875	14589	80
85+	5883	6431	6540	7434	12028	9674	6386	6529	5987	6137	5883	6216	14330	7149	12987	19451	6216	85+

ADDED YRS OF LIFE																	
TOTAL		1.724	3.726	1.286	3.337	3.851	2.173	.814	.420	2.119	.000	.597	5.966	5.602	13.258	21.165	.597
WORK	7.612	1.453	.473	.660	1.280	.658	.073	.508	.435	.000	.000	.175	.960	1.949	3.215	3.787	.175

POPULATION, DEATHS, DEATH RATES FOR ALL CAUSES COMBINED, AND SPECIFIED CAUSES

Age Start of Interval	Midyear Population	Deaths During Year	All Causes	Respiratory T.B.	Other Infec. and Paras.	Neoplasms	Cardiovascular	Infl., Pneu., Bronch.	Diarrheal	Certain Degenerative	Maternal	Cert. Dis. of Infancy	Motor Vehicle	Other Violence	Other and Unknown	Age Start of Interval
0	396215	63874	.16121	.00035	.01692	.00004	.00035	.02321	.04435	.00020	.00000	.04906	.00000	.00244	.02427	0
1	1545314	27983	.01811	.00022	.00768	.00006	.00013	.00419	.00281	.00011	.00000	.00000	.00000	.00073	.00218	1
5	1852463	6411	.00346	.00011	.00162	.00005	.00019	.00038	.00007	.00007	.00000	.00000	.00000	.00038	.00057	5
10	1752520	3574	.00204	.00015	.00058	.00004	.00029	.00013	.00003	.00008	.00000	.00000	.00000	.00032	.00042	10
15	1659524	5038	.00304	.00068	.00056	.00005	.00037	.00026	.00003	.00012	.00000	.00000	.00000	.00050	.00047	15
20	1506855	5802	.00385	.00129	.00052	.00008	.00030	.00041	.00004	.00016	.00000	.00000	.00000	.00059	.00046	20
25	1459855	6504	.00446	.00149	.00056	.00011	.00038	.00049	.00005	.00023	.00000	.00000	.00000	.00066	.00049	25
30	1379721	7623	.00553	.00177	.00064	.00015	.00055	.00072	.00007	.00032	.00000	.00000	.00000	.00070	.00061	30
35	1264961	8994	.00711	.00193	.00079	.00030	.00096	.00089	.00005	.00048	.00000	.00000	.00000	.00087	.00080	35
40	1078083	9989	.00927	.00208	.00099	.00061	.00145	.00128	.00012	.00073	.00000	.00000	.00000	.00094	.00111	40
45	928693	11596	.01249	.00210	.00099	.00130	.00235	.00175	.00020	.00112	.00000	.00000	.00000	.00115	.00152	45
50	770380	13407	.01740	.00229	.00102	.00229	.00391	.00242	.00026	.00174	.00000	.00000	.00000	.00122	.00224	50
55	609706	14971	.02455	.00214	.00099	.00354	.00644	.00381	.00041	.00241	.00000	.00000	.00000	.00150	.00332	55
60	478486	17255	.03606	.00202	.00099	.00527	.01124	.00582	.00058	.00330	.00000	.00000	.00000	.00153	.00532	60
65	366920	19106	.05207	.00158	.00093	.00700	.01743	.00871	.00101	.00435	.00000	.00000	.00000	.00164	.00942	65
70	237531	19209	.08087	.00110	.00082	.00873	.02656	.01384	.00174	.00501	.00000	.00000	.00000	.00184	.02124	70
75	127823	15287	.11960	.00055	.00092	.00952	.03574	.01948	.00267	.00512	.00000	.00000	.00000	.00265	.04296	75
80	56561	9724	.17192	.00048	.00094	.00850	.04015	.02574	.00401	.00403	.00000	.00000	.00000	.00331	.08476	80
85+	22801	6165	.27038	.00022	.00053	.00737	.04658	.03838	.00539	.00421	.00000	.00000	.00000	.00439	.16333	85+
ALL	17494412	272512														

		All Causes	Respiratory T.B.	Other Infec.	Neoplasms	Cardiovascular	Infl., Pneu.	Diarrheal	Certain Degen.	Maternal	Cert. Dis. Infancy	Motor Vehicle	Other Violence	Other and Unknown
CRUDE DEATH RATE		.01558	.00116	.00180	.00092	.00237	.00239	.00143	.00070	.00000	.00111	.00000	.00083	.00287
STANDARDIZED RATE (1)		.01654	.00101	.00222	.00075	.00196	.00256	.00204	.00059	.00000	.00173	.00000	.00080	.00288
STANDARDIZED RATE (2)		.02072	.00121	.00172	.00143	.00397	.00321	.00144	.00099	.00000	.00102	.00000	.00054	.00481
GEOMETRIC MEAN		.01892												

LIFE TABLE FOR ALL CAUSES COMBINED

Age (x)	Midyear Population	Deaths During Year	$_nM_x$	$_nq_x$	l_x	$_nd_x$	$_nL_x$	$_nm_x$	$_na_x$	T_x	$_nr_x$	$\overset{\circ}{e}_x$	Age (x)
0	396215	63874	.161210	.145790	100000	14579	90437	.161206	.344058	4938242	.000000	49.382	0
1	1545314	27983	.018108	.069304	85421	5920	326884	.018110	1.500000	4847805	.000000	56.752	1
5	1852463	6411	.003461	.017157	79501	1364	394095	.003461	2.500000	4520921	.000000	56.866	5
10	1752520	3574	.002039	.010136	78137	792	388664	.002038	2.448180	4126826	.005665	52.815	10
15	1659524	5038	.003036	.015088	77345	1167	383946	.003039	2.618359	3738162	.010973	48.331	15
20	1506855	5802	.003850	.019100	76178	1455	377352	.003856	2.568729	3354217	.010436	44.031	20
25	1459855	6504	.004455	.022041	74723	1647	369610	.004456	2.568053	2976864	.005237	39.839	25
30	1379721	7623	.005525	.027273	73076	1993	360573	.005527	2.588016	2607255	.006519	35.679	30
35	1264961	8994	.007110	.035015	71083	2489	349426	.007123	2.593913	2246682	.014153	31.606	35
40	1078083	9989	.009266	.045412	68594	3115	335493	.009285	2.599719	1897256	.020021	27.659	40
45	928693	11596	.012486	.060783	65479	3980	317870	.012521	2.606679	1561762	.020019	23.851	45
50	770380	13407	.017403	.083790	61499	5153	295149	.017459	2.604106	1243893	.023362	20.226	50
55	609706	14971	.024554	.116335	56346	6555	265993	.024643	2.599256	948744	.023976	16.838	55
60	478486	17255	.036062	.166215	49791	8276	228901	.036155	2.576854	682751	.016351	13.712	60
65	366920	19106	.052071	.231434	41515	9608	184075	.052196	2.554122	453850	.014464	10.932	65
70	237531	19209	.080869	.337606	31907	10772	132621	.081224	2.501470	269775	.021549	8.455	70
75	127823	15287	.119595	.458197	21135	9684	80627	.120108	2.413517	137154	.021748	6.489	75
80	56561	9724	.171921	.589643	11451	6752	39147	.172477	2.318171	56526	.021748	4.936	80
85+	22801	6165	.270383	1.000000	4699	4699	17379	.270383	3.698459	17379	.000000	3.658	85+

NUMBER OF PERSONS DYING (OUT OF 100,000 AT BIRTH) ABOVE AGE X FROM SPECIFIED CAUSES

Age (x)	All Causes	Respiratory T.B.	Other Infec. and Paras.	Neoplasms	Cardio-vascular	Infl., Pneu., Bronch.	Diarrheal	Certain Degenerative	Maternal	Cert. Dis. of Infancy	Motor Vehicle	Other Violence	Other and Unknown	Age (x)
0	100000	6410	7855	7445	19917	15447	6377	5223	0	4437	0	4718	22171	0
1	85421	6378	6324	7442	19885	13348	2366	5205	0	0	0	4497	19976	1
5	79501	6305	3813	7424	19842	11979	1449	5169	0	0	0	4258	19262	5
10	78137	6260	3172	7405	19765	11828	1419	5141	0	0	0	4108	19039	10
15	77345	6201	2948	7390	19653	11776	1409	5110	0	0	0	3984	18874	15
20	76178	5938	2734	7372	19513	11675	1398	5064	0	0	0	3790	18694	20
25	74723	5449	2528	7342	19400	11519	1383	5004	0	0	0	3567	18521	25
30	73076	4899	2331	7303	19261	11337	1365	4917	0	0	0	3324	18339	30
35	71083	4261	2102	7247	19061	11078	1341	4803	0	0	0	3070	18120	35
40	68594	3586	1826	7143	18726	10765	1310	4635	0	0	0	2766	17837	40
45	65479	2888	1511	6936	18237	10334	1269	4388	0	0	0	2450	17466	45
50	61499	2219	1196	6519	17488	9777	1205	4029	0	0	0	2083	16983	50
55	56346	1542	894	5839	16329	9059	1128	3513	0	0	0	1722	16320	55
60	49791	974	631	4895	14607	8040	1019	2871	0	0	0	1323	15431	60
65	41515	513	405	3685	12025	6704	886	2115	0	0	0	972	14210	65
70	31907	223	234	2394	8809	5097	699	1313	0	0	0	670	12468	70
75	21135	78	125	1233	5272	3253	467	648	0	0	0	426	9633	75
80	11451	34	52	465	2382	1677	251	235	0	0	0	211	6144	80
85+	4699	4	9	128	809	667	94	73	0	0	0	76	2839	85+

NUMBER OF PERSONS SURVIVING TO AGE X IF SPECIFIED CAUSES WERE ELIMINATED

Age (x)	No Causes	Respiratory T.B. (1)	Other Infec. and Paras. (2)	Neoplasms (3)	Cardio-vascular (4)	Infl., Pneu., Bronch. (5)	Diarrheal (6)	Certain Degenerative (7)	Maternal (8)	Cert. Dis. of Infancy (9)	Motor Vehicle (10)	Other Violence (11)	Other and Unknown (12)	(1)+(2)	(1)+(2)+(5)+(6)+(8)	(1)+(2)+(5)+(6)+(8)+part of(9)&(12)	(10)+(11)	Age (x)
0	100000	100000	100000	100000	100000	100000	100000	100000	100000	100000	100000	100000	100000	100000	100000	100000	100000	0
1	85421	85451	86846	85424	85451	87381	89206	85438	85421	89617	85421	85625	87472	86876	92807	99458	85625	1
5	79501	79599	83328	79521	79570	82667	83952	79551	79501	83407	79501	79923	82118	83430	91633	98998	79923	5
10	78137	78278	82567	78175	78281	81424	82543	78214	78137	81976	78137	78701	80938	82716	91057	98588	78701	10
15	77345	77543	81966	77398	77600	80653	81717	77452	77345	81145	77345	78028	80288	82176	90535	98137	78028	15
20	76178	76636	80954	76248	76568	79541	80496	76329	76178	79920	76178	77045	79262	81441	89856	97537	77045	20
25	74723	75661	79615	74821	75218	78183	78974	74931	74723	78394	74723	75797	77926	80614	89145	96914	75797	25
30	73076	74546	78078	73211	73699	76648	77252	73366	73076	76666	73076	74370	76397	79649	88317	96168	74370	30
35	71083	73157	76190	71270	71888	74826	75170	71478	71083	74575	71083	72597	74539	78414	87289	95237	72597	35
40	68594	71281	73814	68877	69705	72531	72570	69141	68594	71964	68594	70361	72221	76705	85809	93845	70361	40
45	65479	68756	70793	65553	67027	69684	69317	66245	65479	68696	65479	67483	69324	74336	83746	91864	67483	45
50	61499	65260	66821	62353	63701	66025	65170	62572	61499	64520	61499	63748	65608	70907	80669	88797	63748	50
55	56346	60481	61536	57793	59525	61235	59787	57834	56346	59114	56346	58765	60792	66052	76168	84216	58765	55
60	49791	54019	54646	51587	54340	55162	52941	51728	49791	52237	49791	52320	54629	59286	69837	77665	52320	60
65	41515	45495	45789	44513	47556	47364	44270	43851	41515	43554	41515	43960	46789	50179	61048	68450	43960	65
70	31907	35241	35355	35439	40253	38041	34200	34448	31907	33474	31907	34065	37730	39049	49902	56729	34065	70
75	21135	23469	23515	24531	30516	27037	22856	23400	21135	22173	21135	22774	27883	26112	36125	42409	22774	75
80	11451	12749	12799	13942	19830	16181	12554	13007	11451	12014	11451	12508	18904	14249	22074	27775	12508	80
85+	4699	5252	5282	5981	10014	7586	5259	5453	4699	4930	4699	5225	11997	5904	10668	15703	5225	85+

ADDED YRS OF LIFE

	No Causes	(1)	(2)	(3)	(4)	(5)	(6)	(7)	(8)	(9)	(10)	(11)	(12)	(1)+(2)	(1)+(2)+(5)+(6)+(8)	(1)+(2)+(5)+(6)+(8)+part of(9)&(12)	(10)+(11)
TOTAL		1.759	3.572	1.005	2.821	3.751	2.923	.843	.000	2.405	.000	1.277	4.571	5.492	13.404	20.215	1.277
WORK	7.537	1.514	.668	.437	1.027	.838	.084	.461	.000	.000	.000	.738	.811	2.220	3.232	3.715	.738

POPULATION, DEATHS, DEATH RATES FOR ALL CAUSES COMBINED, AND SPECIFIED CAUSES

Age Start of Interval	Midyear Population	Deaths During Year	All Causes	Respiratory T. B.	Other Infec. and Paras.	Neo-plasms	Cardio-vascular	Infl., Pneu., Bronch.	Diar-rheal	Certain Degen-erative	Maternal	Cert. Dis. of Infancy	Motor Vehicle	Other Violence	Other and Unknown	Age Start of Interval
0	397604	50726	.13087	.00034	.01549	.00004	.00028	.01810	.03704	.00019	.00000	.03877	.00000	.00232	.01828	0
1	1535559	26487	.01725	.00023	.00761	.00004	.00013	.00382	.00276	.00012	.00000	.00000	.00000	.00058	.00196	1
5	1854219	6257	.00337	.00015	.00171	.00003	.00023	.00037	.00010	.00008	.00000	.00000	.00000	.00022	.00050	5
10	1756526	3636	.00207	.00036	.00063	.00002	.00038	.00014	.00003	.00008	.00000	.00000	.00000	.00008	.00035	10
15	1686016	4594	.00272	.00069	.00053	.00004	.00041	.00017	.00002	.00013	.00006	.00000	.00000	.00008	.00036	15
20	1677334	5382	.00321	.00111	.00043	.00005	.00040	.00021	.00003	.00019	.00030	.00000	.00000	.00012	.00037	20
25	1627418	6078	.00373	.00123	.00043	.00010	.00042	.00025	.00004	.00023	.00048	.00000	.00000	.00011	.00045	25
30	1505133	6868	.00456	.00127	.00043	.00029	.00058	.00037	.00006	.00029	.00056	.00000	.00000	.00013	.00060	30
35	1355286	8001	.00590	.00132	.00046	.00062	.00088	.00056	.00007	.00046	.00057	.00000	.00000	.00018	.00080	35
40	1160488	8603	.00741	.00125	.00042	.00124	.00145	.00069	.00009	.00068	.00032	.00000	.00000	.00020	.00107	40
45	1002037	9878	.00986	.00113	.00048	.00204	.00236	.00097	.00014	.00101	.00004	.00000	.00000	.00027	.00141	45
50	836578	11072	.01323	.00086	.00045	.00275	.00386	.00147	.00021	.00137	.00000	.00000	.00000	.00034	.00183	50
55	672136	12832	.01909	.00092	.00056	.00400	.00584	.00259	.00034	.00181	.00000	.00000	.00000	.00040	.00264	55
60	544188	15091	.02773	.00092	.00065	.00524	.00953	.00432	.00049	.00230	.00000	.00000	.00000	.00047	.00396	60
65	442043	17444	.03946	.00081	.00054	.00639	.01423	.00661	.00078	.00283	.00000	.00000	.00000	.00061	.00667	65
70	317493	21179	.06671	.00054	.00055	.00826	.02283	.01232	.00154	.00331	.00000	.00000	.00000	.00102	.01634	70
75	192928	18203	.09951	.00037	.00046	.00910	.03025	.01761	.00225	.00347	.00000	.00000	.00000	.00158	.03442	75
80	87985	13334	.15155	.00024	.00077	.00894	.03696	.02483	.00355	.00310	.00000	.00000	.00000	.00298	.07017	80
85+	41424	9633	.23255	.00007	.00070	.00826	.04060	.03288	.00473	.00212	.00000	.00000	.00000	.00505	.13813	85+
ALL	18672355	255298														

	All Causes	Respiratory T. B.	Other Infec. and Paras.	Neo-plasms	Cardio-vascular	Infl., Pneu., Bronch.	Diar-rheal	Certain Degen-erative	Maternal	Cert. Dis. of Infancy	Motor Vehicle	Other Violence	Other and Unknown
CRUDE DEATH RATE	.01367	.00084	.00151	.00114	.00246	.00197	.00117	.00060	.00018	.00080	.00000	.00032	.00268
STANDARDIZED RATE (1)	.01382	.00075	.00202	.00084	.00179	.00201	.00176	.00047	.00016	.00080	.00000	.00032	.00268
STANDARDIZED RATE (2)	.01715	.00082	.00148	.00154	.00353	.00256	.00124	.00075	.00016	.00136	.00000	.00033	.00232
GEOMETRIC MEAN	.01591												

LIFE TABLE FOR ALL CAUSES COMBINED

Age (x)	Midyear Population	Deaths During Year	$_nM_x$	$_nq_x$	l_x	$_nd_x$	$_nL_x$	$_nm_x$	$_na_x$	T_x	$_nr_x$	$\overset{\circ}{e}_x$	Age (x)
0	397604	50726	.130871	.119780	100000	11978	91525	.130871	.292430	5339814	.000000	53.398	0
1	1535559	26487	.017249	.066143	88022	5822	337533	.017249	1.500000	5248288	.000000	59.625	1
5	1854219	6257	.003374	.016740	82200	1376	407560	.003376	2.500000	4910755	.000000	59.742	5
10	1756526	3636	.002070	.010294	80824	832	401979	.002070	2.426633	4503195	.006106	55.716	10
15	1686016	4594	.002725	.013539	79992	1083	397341	.002726	2.581564	4101216	.003470	51.270	15
20	1677334	5382	.003209	.015517	78909	1256	391479	.003208	2.558718	3703875	.000074	46.939	20
25	1627418	6078	.003735	.018505	77653	1437	384770	.003735	2.567560	3312397	.004470	42.656	25
30	1505133	6868	.004563	.022594	76216	1722	376928	.004569	2.588923	2927627	.010455	38.412	30
35	1355286	8001	.005904	.029157	74494	2172	367231	.005915	2.587957	2550699	.017357	34.240	35
40	1160488	8603	.007413	.036490	72322	2639	355261	.007428	2.594101	2183468	.021527	30.191	40
45	1002037	9878	.009858	.048276	69683	3364	340345	.009884	2.600946	1828207	.021804	26.236	45
50	836578	11072	.013235	.064371	66319	4269	321406	.013282	2.613317	1487863	.025373	22.435	50
55	672136	12832	.019091	.091636	62050	5686	296675	.019166	2.612630	1166456	.025415	18.799	55
60	544188	15091	.027731	.130278	56364	7343	264122	.027802	2.585796	869781	.017211	15.431	60
65	442043	17444	.039462	.180555	49021	8851	223855	.039539	2.599094	605659	.011253	12.355	65
70	317493	21179	.066707	.287603	40170	11553	172500	.066974	2.546110	381804	.018135	9.505	70
75	192928	18203	.099509	.398644	28617	11408	114109	.099975	2.460024	209304	.024167	7.314	75
80	87985	13334	.151549	.544134	17209	9364	61460	.152359	2.374519	95195	.024167	5.532	80
85+	41424	9633	.232546	1.000000	7845	7845	33735	.232546	4.300218	33735	.000000	4.300	85+

NUMBER OF PERSONS DYING (OUT OF 100,000 AT BIRTH) ABOVE AGE X FROM SPECIFIED CAUSES

Age (x)	All Causes	Respiratory T.B.	Other Infec. and Paras.	Neoplasms	Cardiovascular	Infl., Pneu., Bronch.	Diarrheal	Certain Degenerative	Maternal	Cert. Dis. of Infancy	Motor Vehicle	Other Violence	Other and Unknown	Age (x)
0	100000	4536	6910	9786	22431	14981	5913	4663	876	3549	0	2142	24213	0
1	88022	4505	5492	9782	22405	13325	2523	4645	876	0	0	1929	22540	1
5	82200	4429	2923	9769	22361	12034	1592	4606	876	0	0	1733	21877	5
10	80824	4368	2226	9758	22268	11885	1551	4575	876	0	0	1643	21674	10
15	79992	4223	1976	9750	22114	11829	1538	4542	875	0	0	1612	21533	15
20	78909	3868	1764	9735	21952	11760	1528	4491	851	0	0	1571	21389	20
25	77653	3432	1594	9714	21794	11678	1517	4417	735	0	0	1526	21246	25
30	76216	2959	1430	9675	21634	11583	1501	4327	550	0	0	1482	21075	30
35	74494	2481	1269	9566	21416	11444	1481	4219	339	0	0	1434	20845	35
40	72322	1995	1101	9337	21094	11240	1455	4048	131	0	0	1369	20552	40
45	69683	1551	951	8855	20577	10995	1422	3805	18	0	0	1297	20172	45
50	66319	1166	786	8199	19771	10664	1376	3459	4	0	0	1204	19690	50
55	62050	857	641	7314	18525	10190	1308	3017	2	0	0	1095	19101	55
60	56364	585	476	6122	16785	9418	1208	2480	2	0	0	975	18313	60
65	49021	342	344	4736	14259	8274	1077	1871	2	0	0	851	17265	65
70	40170	162	223	3304	11067	6791	902	1237	2	0	0	713	15769	70
75	28617	68	128	1877	7117	4658	636	664	2	0	0	536	12931	75
80	17209	26	75	838	3653	2640	378	268	0	0	0	355	8974	80
85+	7845	2	24	279	1370	1109	160	72				170	4659	85+

NUMBER OF PERSONS SURVIVING TO AGE X IF SPECIFIED CAUSES WERE ELIMINATED

Age (x)	No Causes	Respiratory T.B. (1)	Other Infec. and Paras. (2)	Neoplasms (3)	Cardiovascular (4)	Infl., Pneu., Bronch. (5)	Diarrheal (6)	Certain Degenerative (7)	Maternal (8)	Cert. Dis. of Infancy (9)	Motor Vehicle (10)	Other Violence (11)	Other and Unknown (12)	(1)+(2)	(1)+(2)+(5)+(6)+(8)	(1)+(2)+(5)+(6)+(8)+part of(9)&(12)	(10)+(11)	Age (x)
0	100000	100000	100000	100000	100000	100000	100000	100000	100000	100000	100000	100000	100000	100000	100000	100000	100000	0
1	88022	88051	89362	88026	88046	89588	91258	88039	88022	91413	88022	88222	89605	89391	94327	99508	88222	1
5	82200	82301	86009	82216	82265	84942	86160	82253	82200	85367	82200	82577	84333	86115	93274	99124	82577	5
10	80824	80993	85296	80851	80980	83673	84760	80907	80824	83938	80824	81284	83128	85464	92786	98803	81284	10
15	79992	80295	84681	80026	80301	82869	83901	80107	79993	83074	79992	80478	82416	85001	92363	98469	80478	15
20	78909	79562	83757	78958	79375	81818	82776	79074	78934	81949	78909	79430	81448	84451	91884	98086	79430	20
25	77653	78733	82603	77722	78265	80600	81470	77889	77793	80645	77653	78210	80298	83752	91368	97665	78210	25
30	76216	77753	81248	76322	76981	79207	79979	76537	76537	79152	76216	76807	78988	82886	90771	97186	76807	30
35	74494	76479	79582	74706	75460	77560	78193	74915	75017	77364	74494	75120	77439	81703	89916	96470	75120	35
40	72322	74742	77438	72755	73582	75508	75940	72900	73037	75108	72322	72994	75482	80030	88602	95281	72994	40
45	69683	72466	74770	70538	71415	73005	73203	70481	70483	72368	69683	70402	73118	77757	86561	93303	70402	45
50	66319	68359	71333	67824	68779	69819	69716	67421	67094	68874	66319	67095	70083	74603	83529	90243	67095	50
55	62050	65207	66892	64339	65614	65810	65257	63517	62777	64441	62050	62882	66176	70296	79377	85971	62882	55
60	56364	59504	60932	59633	61382	60566	59414	58222	57025	58535	56364	57236	60918	64326	73716	80124	57236	60
65	49021	51990	53126	53246	56013	53834	51803	51226	49556	50910	49021	49897	54050	56344	66154	72282	49897	65
70	40170	42774	43652	45055	49316	45613	42617	42577	40641	41718	40170	41015	45615	46482	56652	62461	41015	70
75	28617	30554	31183	33460	39440	34594	30599	30841	28952	29719	28617	29371	35498	33294	43539	49219	29371	75
80	17209	18407	18796	21062	27652	22756	18613	18872	17411	17872	17209	17806	25519	20105	29091	34815	17806	80
85+	7845	8408	8605	10062	15266	11795	8642	8746	7938	8147	7845	8244	16707	9223	15457	21086	8244	85+

ADDED YRS OF LIFE

	No Causes	(1)	(2)	(3)	(4)	(5)	(6)	(7)	(8)	(9)	(10)	(11)	(12)	(1)+(2)	(1)+(2)+(5)+(6)+(8)	(1)+(2)+(5)+(6)+(8)+part of(9)&(12)	(10)+(11)
TOTAL		1.495	3.550	1.509	3.406	3.406	2.756	.853	.220	2.046	.000	.569	4.842	5.162	12.693	18.690	.569
WORK	6.301	1.173	.474	.659	1.099	.515	.070	.442	.311	.000	.000	.161	.755	1.664	2.621	3.037	.161

POPULATION, DEATHS, DEATH RATES FOR ALL CAUSES COMBINED, AND SPECIFIED CAUSES

Age Start of Interval	Midyear Population	Deaths During Year	All Causes	Respiratory T.B.	Other Infec. and Paras.	Neoplasms	Cardiovascular	Infl., Pneu., Bronch.	Diarrheal	Certain Degenerative	Maternal	Cert. Dis. of Infancy	Motor Vehicle	Other Violence	Other and Unknown	Age Start of Interval
0	404510	40381	.09983	.00015	.00785	.00006	.00016	.01844	.01709	.00012	.00000	.03709	.00000	.00143	.01744	0
1	1276929	13913	.01090	.00016	.00345	.00005	.00009	.00370	.00104	.00008	.00000	.00000	.00000	.00060	.00173	1
5	1766560	4967	.00281	.00007	.00109	.00004	.00017	.00039	.00008	.00006	.00000	.00000	.00000	.00034	.00058	5
10	1837125	3234	.00176	.00013	.00045	.00003	.00024	.00017	.00002	.00006	.00000	.00000	.00000	.00022	.00044	10
15	1727823	4914	.00284	.00071	.00040	.00006	.00030	.00033	.00002	.00010	.00000	.00000	.00000	.00041	.00051	15
20	1448385	5171	.00357	.00136	.00030	.00008	.00036	.00042	.00001	.00014	.00000	.00000	.00000	.00043	.00046	20
25	1339960	5190	.00387	.00135	.00026	.00011	.00051	.00052	.00002	.00022	.00000	.00000	.00000	.00042	.00045	25
30	1281320	5834	.00455	.00143	.00036	.00016	.00064	.00070	.00002	.00028	.00000	.00000	.00000	.00046	.00051	30
35	1273321	7405	.00582	.00162	.00050	.00031	.00074	.00098	.00003	.00043	.00000	.00000	.00000	.00056	.00065	35
40	1223054	8901	.00728	.00177	.00057	.00057	.00105	.00125	.00004	.00056	.00000	.00000	.00000	.00067	.00080	40
45	1162158	11124	.00957	.00175	.00067	.00121	.00154	.00159	.00006	.00079	.00000	.00000	.00000	.00083	.00115	45
50	971021	13231	.01363	.00164	.00071	.00225	.00292	.00210	.00007	.00127	.00000	.00000	.00000	.00096	.00167	50
55	781608	15767	.02017	.00153	.00084	.00393	.00518	.00318	.00010	.00173	.00000	.00000	.00000	.00118	.00252	55
60	601235	17979	.02990	.00142	.00080	.00587	.00900	.00489	.00018	.00248	.00000	.00000	.00000	.00138	.00389	60
65	449363	20483	.04558	.00101	.00080	.00819	.01616	.00792	.00027	.00306	.00000	.00000	.00000	.00148	.00670	65
70	280491	20243	.07217	.00071	.00076	.01026	.02716	.01271	.00057	.00383	.00000	.00000	.00000	.00165	.01453	70
75	158540	17663	.11141	.00039	.00065	.01157	.04210	.01963	.00091	.00459	.00000	.00000	.00000	.00204	.02953	75
80	66997	10852	.16158	.00027	.00040	.01069	.05405	.02669	.00170	.00423	.00000	.00000	.00000	.00291	.06094	80
85+	24839	7039	.28338	.00016	.00056	.01119	.08140	.04839	.00306	.00596	.00000	.00000	.00000	.00479	.12786	85+
ALL	18075239	234291														

	All Causes	Respiratory T.B.	Other Infec. and Paras.	Neoplasms	Cardiovascular	Infl., Pneu., Bronch.	Diarrheal	Certain Degenerative	Maternal	Cert. Dis. of Infancy	Motor Vehicle	Other Violence	Other and Unknown
CRUDE DEATH RATE	.01296	.00100	.00093	.00119	.00260	.00228	.00053	.00062	.00000	.00083	.00000	.00065	.00232
STANDARDIZED RATE (1)	.01229	.00085	.00117	.00083	.00186	.00228	.00078	.00046	.00000	.00131	.00000	.00060	.00217
STANDARDIZED RATE (2)	.01658	.00099	.00095	.00162	.00406	.00299	.00054	.00079	.00000	.00077	.00000	.00072	.00355
GEOMETRIC MEAN	.01575												

LIFE TABLE FOR ALL CAUSES COMBINED

Age (x)	Midyear Population	Deaths During Year	$_nM_x$	$_nq_x$	l_x	$_nd_x$	$_nL_x$	$_nm_x$	$_na_x$	T_x	$_nr_x$	$\overset{\circ}{e}_x$	Age (x)
0	404510	40381	.099827	.092780	100000	9278	92946	.099821	.239706	5593577	.000000	55.936	0
1	1276929	13913	.010896	.042437	90722	3850	353263	.010898	1.500000	5500631	.000000	60.632	1
5	1766560	4967	.002812	.013952	86872	1212	431330	.002810	2.500000	5147368	.000000	59.252	5
10	1837125	3234	.001760	.008767	85660	751	426420	.001761	2.497226	4716038	-.003661	55.055	10
15	1727823	4914	.002844	.014156	84909	1202	421652	.002850	2.626872	4289618	-.014604	50.520	15
20	1448385	5171	.003570	.017717	83707	1483	414906	.003574	2.552821	3867925	-.022355	46.208	20
25	1339960	5190	.003873	.019191	82224	1578	407245	.003875	2.544096	3453020	-.012906	41.995	25
30	1281320	5834	.004553	.022531	80646	1817	399830	.004556	2.578197	3045775	-.003683	37.767	30
35	1273321	7405	.005816	.028670	78829	2260	388687	.005814	2.584900	2646945	-.000186	33.578	35
40	1223054	8901	.007278	.035759	76569	2738	376250	.007277	2.591231	2258259	-.000291	29.493	40
45	1162158	11124	.009572	.046850	73831	3459	360508	.009584	2.615701	1882009	.007943	25.491	45
50	971021	13231	.013626	.066205	70372	4659	343815	.013670	2.629275	1521101	.021095	21.615	50
55	781608	15767	.020173	.096632	65713	6350	313451	.020258	2.619915	1180286	.026499	17.961	55
60	601235	17979	.029900	.140054	59363	8314	276900	.030025	2.604668	866835	.024207	14.602	60
65	449363	20483	.045582	.206214	51049	10527	229794	.045811	2.582308	589935	.027561	11.556	65
70	280491	20243	.072170	.307808	40522	12473	171780	.072610	2.528278	360141	.029480	8.888	70
75	158540	17663	.111410	.435666	28049	12220	108971	.112140	2.440756	188360	.030112	6.715	75
80	66997	10852	.161977	.568450	15829	8998	55284	.162758	2.348230	79389	.030112	5.015	80
85+	24839	7039	.283385	1.000000	6831	6831	24105	.283385	3.528768	24105	.000000	3.529	85+

NUMBER OF PERSONS DYING (OUT OF 100,000 AT BIRTH) ABOVE AGE X FROM SPECIFIED CAUSES

Age (x)	All Causes	Respiratory T. B.	Other Infec. and Paras.	Neoplasms	Cardiovascular	Infl., Pneu., Bronch.	Diarrheal	Certain Degenerative	Maternal	Cert. Dis. of Infancy	Motor Vehicle	Other Violence	Other and Unknown	Age (x)
0	100000	5528	4949	10442	25340	17395	2601	4983	0	3447	0	4279	20636	0
1	90722	5914	4220	10436	25325	15680	1013	4972	0	0	0	4146	19016	1
5	86872	5858	3002	10417	25295	14374	645	4943	0	0	0	3934	18404	5
10	85660	5826	2534	10402	25221	14206	612	4916	0	0	0	3788	18155	10
15	84909	5772	2341	10390	25118	14135	602	4891	0	0	0	3692	17968	15
20	83707	5471	2173	10364	24990	13994	596	4847	0	0	0	3517	17755	20
25	82224	4903	2049	10331	24839	13820	593	4788	0	0	0	3337	17564	25
30	80646	4352	1941	10286	24630	13609	586	4698	0	0	0	3165	17379	30
35	78829	3781	1799	10221	24376	13329	580	4586	0	0	0	2982	17175	35
40	76569	3149	1606	10100	24089	12950	566	4419	0	0	0	2765	16925	40
45	73831	2484	1390	9885	23695	12479	553	4210	0	0	0	2514	16621	45
50	70372	1854	1150	9447	23139	11906	533	3924	0	0	0	2213	16206	50
55	65713	1296	909	8664	22139	11188	508	3488	0	0	0	1885	15636	55
60	59363	816	647	7427	20505	10188	478	2945	0	0	0	1515	14842	60
65	51049	423	426	5795	17998	8827	428	2257	0	0	0	1132	13763	65
70	40522	193	242	3907	14252	6997	366	1551	0	0	0	790	12214	70
75	28049	71	113	2139	9567	4800	268	891	0	0	0	507	9693	75
80	15829	29	42	875	4951	2648	168	390	0	0	0	283	6443	80
85+	6831	4	14	270	1962	1166	74	144	0	0	0	115	3082	85+

NUMBER OF PERSONS SURVIVING TO AGE X IF SPECIFIED CAUSES WERE ELIMINATED

Age (x)	No Causes	Respiratory T. B. (1)	Other Infec. and Paras. (2)	Neoplasms (3)	Cardiovascular (4)	Infl., Pneu., Bronch. (5)	Diarrheal (6)	Certain Degenerative (7)	Maternal (8)	Cert. Dis. of Infancy (9)	Motor Vehicle (10)	Other Violence (11)	Other and Unknown (12)	(1) + (2)	(1) + (2) + (5) + (6) + (8)	(1)+(2)+ (5)+(6)+ (8)+part of(9)&(12)	(10) + (11)	Age (x)
0	100000	100000	100000	100000	100000	100000	100000	100000	100000	100000	100000	100000	100000	100000	100000	100000	100000	0
1	90722	90735	91419	90728	90732	92370	92247	90732	90722	94064	90722	90849	92278	91432	94657	99619	90849	1
5	86872	86940	88748	86896	86915	89760	88699	86910	86872	90072	86872	87201	88973	88817	93700	99233	87201	5
10	85660	85758	87986	85699	85776	88681	87495	85725	85660	88816	85660	86130	87985	88087	93147	98855	86130	10
15	84909	85060	87412	84959	85127	87976	86738	84958	84909	98037	84909	85471	87405	87568	92686	98491	85471	15
20	83707	84156	86347	83782	84049	86876	85516	83839	83707	86791	83707	84437	86386	86810	92044	97963	84437	20
25	82224	83233	84944	82331	82711	85516	84004	82412	82224	85253	82224	83121	85051	85987	91366	97391	83121	25
30	80646	82190	83424	80795	81332	84093	82399	80520	80646	83617	80646	81698	83608	85022	90582	96694	81698	30
35	78829	80916	81690	79039	79753	82487	80549	79208	78829	81733	78829	80041	81934	83852	89658	95895	80041	35
40	76569	79238	79545	76893	77753	80514	78253	77102	76569	79290	76569	77963	79841	82318	88463	94767	77963	40
45	73831	77082	76921	74356	75367	78123	75468	74552	73831	76551	73831	75427	77298	80309	86862	93262	75427	45
50	70372	74115	73562	71305	72393	75057	71952	71342	70372	72964	70372	72194	74102	77475	84488	90965	72194	50
55	65713	69777	68935	67356	68602	70832	67213	67047	65713	68134	65713	67740	69779	73198	80702	87163	67740	55
60	59363	63518	62535	62065	63617	65019	60748	61097	59363	61550	59363	61856	63842	66912	74997	81331	61556	60
65	51049	55011	53992	54975	57259	57312	52287	53199	51049	52930	51049	53303	55988	58182	66904	72552	53303	65
70	40522	43884	43030	45478	49340	47358	41561	42885	40522	42015	40522	42628	45985	46600	55858	61444	42628	70
75	28049	30483	29897	33151	39227	34974	28852	30264	28049	29082	28049	29752	34306	32491	41672	46727	29752	75
80	15829	17235	16926	15831	27469	21826	16359	17479	15829	16412	15829	16966	22583	18429	26262	30671	16966	80
85+	6831	7455	7324	9056	15672	10817	7122	7718	6831	7083	6831	7437	13340	7993	13196	16874	7437	85+

ADDED YRS OF LIFE																		
TOTAL		1.764	2.137	1.394	3.409	3.582	1.253	.805	.000	2.052	.000	1.121	3.877	3.989	9.864	15.123	1.121
WORK	6.428	1.396	.435	.478	.908	.861	.026	.387	.000	.000	.000	.552	.717	1.852	2.805	3.229	.552

POPULATION, DEATHS, DEATH RATES FOR ALL CAUSES COMBINED, AND SPECIFIED CAUSES

Age Start of Interval	Midyear Population	Deaths During Year	All Causes	Respiratory T.B.	Other Infec. and Paras.	Neoplasms	Cardiovascular	Infl., Pneu., Bronch.	Diarrheal	Certain Degenerative	Maternal	Cert. Dis. of Infancy	Motor Vehicle	Other Violence	Other and Unknown	Age Start of Interval
0	390964	29869	.07640	.00017	.00718	.00004	.00009	.01411	.01227	.00010	.00000	.02855	.00000	.00126	.01264	0
1	1249300	12478	.00959	.00013	.00352	.00004	.00009	.00328	.00094	.00006	.00000	.00000	.00000	.00042	.00150	1
5	1752366	4740	.00270	.00012	.00115	.00002	.00020	.00036	.00007	.00006	.00000	.00000	.00000	.00017	.00054	5
10	1822701	3324	.00182	.00033	.00046	.00002	.00030	.00016	.00002	.00007	.00000	.00000	.00000	.00007	.00039	10
15	1775231	4778	.00269	.00114	.00036	.00003	.00033	.00022	.00001	.00009	.00004	.00000	.00000	.00009	.00037	15
20	1703067	5518	.00324	.00141	.00027	.00005	.00032	.00026	.00001	.00014	.00030	.00000	.00000	.00010	.00038	20
25	1620290	5761	.00356	.00129	.00025	.00014	.00038	.00035	.00003	.00015	.00047	.00000	.00000	.00010	.00042	25
30	1519649	5852	.00385	.00113	.00023	.00026	.00043	.00043	.00003	.00019	.00051	.00000	.00000	.00011	.00053	30
35	1471913	6918	.00470	.00103	.00024	.00059	.00064	.00054	.00004	.00028	.00051	.00000	.00000	.00014	.00068	35
40	1378121	7902	.00573	.00096	.00027	.00111	.00097	.00058	.00004	.00045	.00029	.00000	.00000	.00016	.00089	40
45	1243968	9228	.00742	.00085	.00029	.00188	.00163	.00079	.00005	.00057	.00004	.00000	.00000	.00022	.00111	45
50	1043130	10796	.01035	.00069	.00030	.00283	.00274	.00112	.00008	.00085	.00000	.00000	.00000	.00025	.00148	50
55	849117	12606	.01485	.00063	.00033	.00388	.00438	.00189	.00009	.00114	.00000	.00000	.00000	.00033	.00216	55
60	680768	15175	.02229	.00055	.00034	.00532	.00773	.00322	.00018	.00165	.00000	.00000	.00000	.00036	.00290	60
65	536699	18550	.03456	.00050	.00042	.00700	.01323	.00559	.00031	.00222	.00000	.00000	.00000	.00048	.00481	65
70	376320	21219	.05639	.00041	.00043	.00844	.02245	.01029	.00054	.00270	.00000	.00000	.00000	.00075	.01038	70
75	234038	21381	.09136	.00032	.00044	.01029	.03481	.01701	.00090	.00307	.00000	.00000	.00000	.00138	.02314	75
80	112857	15818	.14016	.00025	.00048	.01078	.04677	.02501	.00134	.00258	.00000	.00000	.00000	.00260	.05036	80
85+	50961	12425	.24381	.00016	.00065	.01132	.07045	.04533	.00239	.00357	.00000	.00000	.00000	.00428	.10567	85+
ALL	19811460	224338														

	All Causes	Respiratory T.B.	Other Infec. and Paras.	Neoplasms	Cardiovascular	Infl., Pneu., Bronch.	Diarrheal	Certain Degenerative	Maternal	Cert. Dis. of Infancy	Motor Vehicle	Other Violence	Other and Unknown
CRUDE DEATH RATE	.01132	.00078	.00073	.00135	.00263	.00182	.00038	.00047	.00017	.00056	.00000	.00025	.00218
STANDARDIZED RATE (1)	.01000	.00070	.00105	.00085	.00161	.00173	.00060	.00033	.00015	.00101	.00000	.00024	.00174
STANDARDIZED RATE (2)	.01315	.00073	.00080	.00160	.00346	.00230	.00043	.00055	.00015	.00059	.00000	.00029	.00286
GEOMETRIC MEAN	.01320												

LIFE TABLE FOR ALL CAUSES COMBINED

Age (x)	Midyear Population	Deaths During Year	$_nM_x$	$_nq_x$	l_x	$_nd_x$	$_nL_x$	$_nm_x$	$_na_x$	T_x	$_nr_x$	$\overset{\circ}{e}_x$	Age (x)
0	390964	29869	.076358	.072000	100000	7200	94239	.076401	.199877	5991973	.000000	59.920	0
1	1249300	12478	.009988	.038976	92800	3617	362158	.009987	1.500000	5897734	.000000	63.553	1
5	1752366	4740	.002705	.013433	89183	1198	442920	.002705	2.500000	5535577	.000000	62.070	5
10	1822701	3324	.001824	.009081	87985	799	437921	.001825	2.491656	5092657	-.004038	57.881	10
15	1775231	4778	.002691	.013374	87186	1166	433137	.002692	2.604345	4654736	.002041	53.389	15
20	1703067	5518	.003240	.016078	86020	1383	426710	.003241	2.549108	4221599	.004599	49.077	20
25	1620290	5761	.003556	.017628	84637	1492	419497	.003557	2.528346	3794889	.007418	44.837	25
30	1519649	5852	.003851	.019075	83145	1586	411844	.003851	2.553069	3375392	.006335	40.596	30
35	1471913	6918	.004702	.023247	81559	1896	403154	.004702	2.573400	2963547	.004615	36.336	35
40	1378121	7902	.005734	.028294	79663	2254	392874	.005737	2.586051	2560353	.008143	32.140	40
45	1243968	9228	.007418	.036520	77409	2827	380295	.007434	2.612457	2167479	.016131	28.000	45
50	1043130	10796	.010350	.050682	74582	3780	363933	.010387	2.625165	1787184	.024807	23.963	50
55	849117	12606	.014846	.072004	70802	5098	341932	.014909	2.630893	1423251	.027554	20.102	55
60	680768	15175	.022291	.106280	65704	6983	311962	.022384	2.628765	1081318	.023864	16.457	60
65	536699	18550	.034563	.160317	58721	9414	271174	.034716	2.617268	769357	.023106	13.102	65
70	376320	21219	.056386	.249092	49307	12282	216750	.056664	2.574923	498183	.023689	10.104	70
75	234038	21381	.091357	.373558	37025	13831	150483	.091911	2.495346	281433	.026550	7.601	75
80	112857	15818	.140160	.516211	23194	11973	84927	.140980	2.407222	130949	.026550	5.646	80
85+	50961	12425	.243814	1.000000	11221	11221	46023	.243814	4.101489	46023	.000000	4.101	85+

NUMBER OF PERSONS DYING (OUT OF 100,000 AT BIRTH) ABOVE AGE X FROM SPECIFIED CAUSES

Age (x)	All Causes	Respira- tory T. B.	Other Infec. and Paras.	Neo- plasms	Cardio- vascular	Infl., Pneu., Bronch.	Diar- rheal	Certain Degen- erative	Maternal	Cert. Dis. of Infancy	Motor Vehicle	Other Violence	Other and Unknown	Age (x)
0	100000	4442	4124	12407	28061	16656	2302	4092	888	2691	0	1953	22344	0
1	92800	4426	3447	12403	28053	15326	1146	4083	888	0	0	1875	21153	1
5	89183	4380	2172	12388	28021	14137	807	4061	888	0	0	1721	20608	5
10	87985	4325	1661	12379	27932	13976	775	4033	888	0	0	1646	20370	10
15	87186	4179	1458	12371	27801	13905	767	4002	888	0	0	1616	20199	15
20	86020	3684	1302	12355	27657	13811	761	3965	869	0	0	1577	20039	20
25	84637	3082	1188	12333	27522	13699	757	3906	741	0	0	1535	19874	25
30	83145	2542	1083	12275	27364	13554	746	3843	544	0	0	1494	19700	30
35	81559	2075	989	12166	27189	13377	732	3767	335	0	0	1447	19482	35
40	79663	1659	893	11927	26929	13160	717	3653	130	0	0	1391	19204	40
45	77409	1281	787	11490	26546	12930	700	3477	15	0	0	1327	18856	45
50	74582	959	677	10774	25923	12630	679	3261	1	0	0	1244	18434	50
55	70802	709	567	9742	24923	12220	650	2950	1	0	0	1152	17888	55
60	65704	492	452	8411	23417	11569	618	2557	1	0	0	1037	17150	60
65	58721	307	347	6746	20993	10559	563	2042	1	0	0	924	16239	65
70	49307	171	232	4844	17387	9035	479	1439	1	0	0	792	14927	70
75	37025	83	139	3011	12497	6792	361	853	1	0	0	628	12660	75
80	23194	36	73	1458	7231	4216	224	390	1	0	0	419	9146	80
85+	11221	7	30	521	3242	2086	110	164	0	0	0	197	4864	85+

NUMBER OF PERSONS SURVIVING TO AGE X IF SPECIFIED CAUSES WERE ELIMINATED

Age (x)	No Causes	Respira- tory T. B.	Other Infec. and Paras.	Neo- plasms	Cardio- vascular	Infl., Pneu., Bronch.	Diar- rheal	Certain Degen- erative	Maternal	Cert. Dis. of Infancy	Motor Vehicle	Other Violence	Other and Unknown	(1) + (2)	(1) + (2) + (5) + (6) + (8)	(1)+(2)+ (5)+(6)+ (8)+part of(9)&(12)	(10) + (11)	Age (x)
		(1)	(2)	(3)	(4)	(5)	(6)	(7)	(8)	(9)	(10)	(11)	(12)					
0	100000	100000	100000	100000	100000	100000	100000	100000	100000	100000	100000	100000	100000	100000	100000	100000	100000	0
1	92800	92815	93454	92804	92808	94090	93920	92809	92800	95428	92800	92914	93954	93470	95913	99687	92914	1
5	89183	89243	91079	89201	89222	91612	90566	89213	89183	91709	89183	89444	90835	91141	95107	99400	89444	5
10	87985	88099	90376	88012	88112	90546	89412	88042	87985	90477	87985	88317	89856	90493	94636	99119	88317	10
15	87186	87444	89763	87221	87442	89796	88608	87274	87186	89655	87186	87545	89214	90029	94236	98832	87545	15
20	86020	86770	88722	86070	86416	88692	87429	86143	86039	88456	86020	86413	88183	89495	93807	98182	86413	20
25	84637	85979	87412	84708	85162	87380	86027	84817	84783	87034	84637	85065	86933	88798	93343	98182	85065	25
30	83145	85009	85979	83273	83818	85988	84522	83384	83484	85500	83145	83607	85578	87906	92794	97759	83607	30
35	81559	83861	84435	81793	82394	84530	82924	81869	82100	83869	81559	82059	84168	86818	92093	97200	82059	35
40	79663	82335	82570	80129	80739	82787	81011	80079	80395	81919	79663	80207	82464	85340	91016	96259	80207	40
45	77409	80391	80342	78296	78838	80681	78736	77988	78235	79601	77409	78001	80518	83438	89398	94734	78001	45
50	74582	77784	77520	76151	76585	78042	75881	75354	75391	76694	74582	75234	78009	80848	87007	92362	75234	50
55	70802	74095	73703	73326	73711	74506	72064	71842	71570	72807	70802	71512	74614	77131	83509	88814	71512	55
60	65704	68979	68511	69386	69932	69805	66907	67054	66417	67565	65704	66415	69994	71926	78658	83865	66475	60
65	58721	61831	61333	63693	64588	63409	59849	60425	59358	60384	58721	59517	63479	64581	71847	76855	59517	65
70	49307	52048	51610	55397	58350	54773	50333	51307	49842	50703	49307	50058	54620	54479	62447	67176	50098	70
75	37025	39162	38837	43402	49106	43340	37899	39053	37427	38074	37025	37763	43256	41079	49756	54253	37763	75
80	23194	24571	24383	28638	36737	29618	23852	24845	23446	23851	23194	23825	30552	25830	34289	38641	23825	80
85+	11221	11908	11827	14665	22637	16305	11619	12186	11343	11539	11221	11682	19164	12551	19091	23265	11682	85+

ADDED YRS OF LIFE																		
TOTAL		1.623	2.083	1.897	3.933	3.502	1.055	.703	.345	1.692	.000	.491	3.980	3.773	9.203	13.800	.491	
WORK	5.436	1.207	.297	.671	.850	.513	.033	.292	.299	.000	.000	.139	.687	1.515	2.408	2.800	.139	

POPULATION, DEATHS, DEATH RATES FOR ALL CAUSES COMBINED, AND SPECIFIED CAUSES

Age Start of Interval	Midyear Population	Deaths During Year	All Causes	Respiratory T. B.	Other Infec. and Paras.	Neo-plasms	Cardio-vascular	Infl., Pneu., Bronch.	Diar-rheal	Certain Degen-erative	Maternal	Cert. Dis. of Infancy	Motor Vehicle	Other Violence	Other and Unknown	Age Start of Interval
0	305184	24332	.07973	.00015	.00612	.00013	.00007	.01925	.00652	.00007	.00000	.03212	.00000	.00128	.01402	0
1	1206068	9705	.00805	.00010	.00286	.00009	.00006	.00292	.00028	.00005	.00000	.00000	.00000	.00056	.00113	1
5	1678998	3820	.00228	.00005	.00080	.00007	.00013	.00030	.00002	.00005	.00000	.00000	.00000	.00038	.00048	5
10	1621545	2387	.00147	.00008	.00033	.00005	.00019	.00016	.00001	.00006	.00000	.00000	.00000	.00021	.00038	10
15	1710687	4415	.00258	.00060	.00036	.00008	.00024	.00030	.00001	.00010	.00000	.00000	.00000	.00047	.00042	15
20	1700309	5650	.00332	.00108	.00029	.00010	.00023	.00032	.00001	.00013	.00000	.00000	.00000	.00075	.00040	20
25	1630113	5409	.00332	.00111	.00024	.00014	.00026	.00037	.00001	.00018	.00000	.00000	.00000	.00075	.00040	25
30	1434274	5268	.00367	.00111	.00026	.00024	.00033	.00051	.00001	.00023	.00000	.00000	.00000	.00062	.00040	30
35	1283892	6247	.00487	.00128	.00033	.00038	.00055	.00077	.00001	.00034	.00000	.00000	.00000	.00055	.00043	35
40	1230191	8238	.00670	.00141	.00047	.00065	.00095	.00119	.00002	.00058	.00000	.00000	.00000	.00060	.00060	40
45	1187369	11416	.00961	.00160	.00057	.00131	.00168	.00161	.00002	.00092	.00000	.00000	.00000	.00067	.00075	45
50	1117086	15023	.01345	.00145	.00067	.00227	.00311	.00209	.00003	.00130	.00000	.00000	.00000	.00088	.00102	50
55	988124	19295	.01953	.00137	.00086	.00380	.00565	.00263	.00004	.00181	.00000	.00000	.00000	.00100	.00148	55
60	778599	22979	.02951	.00116	.00091	.00613	.01064	.00356	.00005	.00244	.00000	.00000	.00000	.00124	.00212	60
65	578367	27626	.04777	.00091	.00090	.00940	.01973	.00555	.00009	.00376	.00000	.00000	.00000	.00133	.00329	65
70	376739	28481	.07560	.00057	.00083	.01213	.03516	.00925	.00012	.00499	.00000	.00000	.00000	.00155	.00587	70
75	204319	24709	.12093	.00034	.00077	.01378	.05934	.01610	.00029	.00622	.00000	.00000	.00000	.00179	.01076	75
80	83697	15429	.18434	.00023	.00070	.01447	.08948	.02657	.00043	.00665	.00000	.00000	.00000	.00259	.02150	80
85+	30599	9288	.30354	.00013	.00098	.01520	.13478	.04889	.00078	.00918	.00000	.00000	.00000	.00380	.04161	85+
ALL	19146160	249717														
CRUDE DEATH RATE			.01304	.00087	.00074	.00155	.00376	.00200	.00015	.00077	.00000	.00051	.00000	.00076	.00193	
STANDARDIZED RATE (1)			.01109	.00070	.00096	.00093	.00222	.00201	.00028	.00049	.00000	.00113	.00000	.00066	.00170	
STANDARDIZED RATE (2)			.01662	.00082	.00082	.00185	.00531	.00257	.00019	.00090	.00000	.00066	.00000	.00081	.00269	
GEOMETRIC MEAN			.01463													

LIFE TABLE FOR ALL CAUSES COMBINED

Age (x)	Midyear Population	Deaths During Year	$_nM_x$	$_nq_x$	l_x	$_nd_x$	$_nL_x$	$_nm_x$	$_na_x$	T_x	$_nr_x$	$\overset{\circ}{e}_x$	Age (x)
0	305184	24332	.079729	.074980	100000	7498	94043	.079729	.205539	5820369	.000000	58.204	0
1	1206068	9705	.008047	.031556	92502	2919	362711	.008048	1.500000	5726326	.000000	61.905	1
5	1678998	3820	.002275	.011308	89583	1013	445383	.002274	2.500000	5363615	.000000	59.873	5
10	1621545	2387	.001472	.007328	88570	649	441251	.001471	2.536595	4918233	-.001990	55.529	10
15	1710687	4415	.002581	.012818	87921	1127	436950	.002579	2.644373	4476982	-.007168	50.921	15
20	1700309	5650	.003323	.016459	86794	1430	430453	.003322	2.540501	4040031	-.002238	46.547	20
25	1630113	5409	.003318	.016459	85364	1405	423329	.003319	2.514976	3609578	-.008442	42.285	25
30	1434274	5268	.003673	.018235	83959	1531	416088	.003680	2.578924	3186250	.018693	37.950	30
35	1283892	6247	.004866	.024082	82428	1985	407411	.004872	2.617758	2770162	.013958	33.607	35
40	1230191	8238	.006697	.032980	80443	2653	395931	.006701	2.631298	2362750	.004250	29.372	40
45	1187369	11416	.009615	.047011	77790	3657	380261	.009617	2.624077	1966820	.000500	25.284	45
50	1117086	15023	.013448	.065167	74133	4831	359175	.013450	2.621654	1586558	-.001833	21.402	50
55	988124	19295	.019527	.093475	69302	6478	331120	.019564	2.624202	1227383	-.011507	17.711	55
60	778599	22979	.029513	.138371	62824	8693	293462	.029622	2.623663	896263	-.019992	14.266	60
65	578367	27626	.047766	.214997	54131	11638	242580	.047576	2.587680	602801	-.022260	11.136	65
70	376739	28481	.075599	.319841	42493	13591	178856	.075988	2.527132	360221	-.024607	8.477	70
75	204319	24709	.120933	.463913	28902	13408	110157	.121718	2.437848	181364	-.026533	6.275	75
80	83697	15429	.184344	.619014	15494	9591	51760	.185296	2.319405	71208	-.026533	4.596	80
85+	30599	9288	.303539	1.000000	5903	5903	19447	.303539	3.294466	19447	.000000	3.294	85+

NUMBER OF PERSONS DYING (OUT OF 100,000 AT BIRTH) ABOVE AGE X FROM SPECIFIED CAUSES

Age (x)	All Causes	Respira-tory T. B.	Other Infec. and Paras.	Neo-plasms	Cardio-vascular	Infl., Pneu., Bronch.	Diar-rheal	Certain Degen-erative	Maternal	Cert. Dis. of Infancy	Motor Vehicle	Other Violence	Other and Unknown	Age (x)
0	100000	5172	4445	12183	32962	14937	920	5874	0	3021	0	4926	15560	0
1	92502	5158	3869	12171	32956	13126	308	5868	0	0	0	4805	14241	1
5	85583	5121	2833	12139	32935	12066	207	5850	0	0	0	4601	13831	5
10	86570	5098	2478	12109	32877	11933	197	5830	0	0	0	4433	13615	10
15	87921	5063	2331	12085	32795	11862	194	5803	0	0	0	4340	13448	15
20	86794	4800	2174	12048	32692	11731	191	5761	0	0	0	4134	13263	20
25	85364	4335	2049	12003	32595	11591	187	5705	0	0	0	3809	13090	25
30	83959	3864	1948	11944	32484	11436	183	5630	0	0	0	3548	12922	30
35	82428	3400	1841	11843	32349	11225	178	5533	0	0	0	3319	12740	35
40	80443	2877	1706	11687	32124	10911	171	5394	0	0	0	3074	12499	40
45	77790	2318	1518	11429	31746	10439	165	5164	0	0	0	2809	12202	45
50	74133	1709	1303	10929	31107	9827	156	4814	0	0	0	2474	11814	50
55	69302	1174	1062	10113	29989	9075	145	4347	0	0	0	2113	11284	55
60	62824	722	778	8851	28114	8202	131	3746	0	0	0	1701	10579	60
65	54131	381	512	7045	24976	7153	115	3029	0	0	0	1310	9610	65
70	42493	161	293	4757	20163	5801	92	2113	0	0	0	933	8180	70
75	28902	60	144	2583	13837	4138	70	1218	0	0	0	611	6241	75
80	15494	22	59	1061	7256	2352	38	530	0	0	0	325	3851	80
85+	5903	3	19	296	2621	951	15	179	0	0	0	122	1697	85+

NUMBER OF PERSONS SURVIVING TO AGE X IF SPECIFIED CAUSES WERE ELIMINATED

Age (x)	No Causes	Respira-tory T. B.	Other Infec. and Paras.	Neo-plasms	Cardio-vascular	Infl., Pneu., Bronch.	Diar-rheal	Certain Degener-ative	Maternal	Cert. Dis. of Infancy	Motor Vehicle	Other Violence	Other and Unknown	(1) + (2)	(1) + (2) + (5) + (6) + (8)	(1)+(2)+ (5)+(6)+ (8)+part of(9)&(12)	(10) + (11)	Age (x)
		(1)	(2)	(3)	(4)	(5)	(6)	(7)	(8)	(9)	(10)	(11)	(12)					
0	100000	100000	100000	100000	100000	100000	100000	100000	100000	100000	100000	100000	100000	100000	100000	100000	100000	0
1	92502	92515	93058	92514	92508	94260	93052	92502	92502	95453	92502	92618	93779	93071	95445	99643	92618	1
5	89583	89632	91152	89626	89606	92354	90255	89606	89583	92441	89583	89897	91230	91203	94729	99293	89897	5
10	88570	88642	90482	88642	88654	91447	89244	88613	88570	91395	88570	89048	90417	90555	94208	98903	89048	10
15	87921	88027	89968	88016	88086	90850	88593	87991	87921	90726	87921	88489	89925	90077	93789	98562	88489	15
20	86794	87161	88975	86925	87059	89820	87461	86904	86794	89561	86794	87561	88966	89351	93175	98040	87561	20
25	85364	86189	87636	85538	85721	88484	86024	85528	85364	88087	85364	86444	87670	88483	92426	97365	86444	25
30	83959	85244	86256	84188	84421	87187	84612	84195	83959	86637	83959	85284	86399	87617	91693	96706	85284	30
35	82428	84157	84832	82754	83016	85814	83074	82756	82428	85058	82428	83959	85009	86611	90876	95967	83959	35
40	80443	82660	82926	80916	81242	84071	81080	80501	80443	83009	80443	82184	83208	85511	89760	94947	82184	40
45	77790	80500	80382	78503	78939	81785	78412	78461	77790	80272	77790	79740	80766	83182	88154	93430	79740	45
50	74133	77332	76820	75307	75864	78571	74735	75118	74133	76458	74133	76327	77363	80136	85622	90951	76327	50
55	69302	72833	72056	71206	72037	74225	69875	70682	69302	71513	69302	71713	72858	75727	81777	87097	71713	55
60	62824	66477	65601	65797	67188	67181	63357	64660	62824	64828	62824	65416	66757	69416	75975	81159	65416	60
65	54131	57611	56781	58474	61095	59811	54605	56401	54131	55858	54131	56742	58484	60432	67358	72214	56742	65
70	42493	45429	44775	48133	53021	48251	42886	45124	42493	43849	42493	44891	47258	47869	54903	59172	44891	70
75	28902	30985	30581	34803	43165	34423	29187	31475	28902	29824	28902	30811	33997	32785	39445	42904	30811	75
80	15494	16639	16457	20001	31443	20062	15671	17415	15494	15988	15494	16737	20388	17672	23144	25678	16737	80
85+	5903	6351	6295	8230	19097	8800	5984	6873	5903	6091	5903	6508	9647	6773	10236	11859	6508	85+

ADDED YRS OF LIFE

	No Causes	(1)	(2)	(3)	(4)	(5)	(6)	(7)	(8)	(9)	(10)	(11)	(12)	(1)+(2)	(1)+(2)+(5)+(6)+(8)	(1)+(2)+(5)+(6)+(8)+part	(10)+(11)
TOTAL		1.498	1.819	1.594	4.323	2.537	.466	.853	.000	1.850	.000	1.301	2.916	3.380	7.749	11.765	1.301
WORK	5.936	1.160	.379	.532	.812	.748	.014	.381	.000	.000	.000	.689	.637	1.554	2.363	2.704	.689

POPULATION, DEATHS, DEATH RATES FOR ALL CAUSES COMBINED, AND SPECIFIED CAUSES

Age Start of Interval	Midyear Population	Deaths During Year	All Causes	Respiratory T. B.	Other Infec. and Paras.	Neoplasms	Cardiovascular	Infl., Pneu., Bronch.	Diarrheal	Certain Degenerative	Maternal	Cert. Dis. of Infancy	Motor Vehicle	Other Violence	Other and Unknown	Age Start of Interval
0	296902	1767	.05930	.00014	.00555	.00010	.00006	.01430	.00436	.00003	.00000	.02357	.00000	.00123	.00998	0
1	1184019	8333	.00704	.00008	.00276	.00008	.00004	.00251	.00027	.00004	.00000	.00000	.00000	.00038	.00088	1
5	1645742	3253	.00198	.00005	.00077	.00004	.00014	.00030	.00003	.00003	.00000	.00000	.00000	.00021	.00041	5
10	1587712	2353	.00148	.00018	.00036	.00005	.00025	.00017	.00001	.00008	.00000	.00000	.00000	.00008	.00032	10
15	1725965	4103	.00238	.00097	.00027	.00006	.00030	.00021	.00001	.00010	.00004	.00000	.00000	.00013	.00030	15
20	1796362	5180	.00288	.00122	.00021	.00010	.00030	.00023	.00001	.00011	.00024	.00000	.00000	.00016	.00031	20
25	1729085	5464	.00316	.00117	.00020	.00015	.00033	.00025	.00002	.00013	.00038	.00000	.00000	.00016	.00037	25
30	1622915	5488	.00338	.00088	.00019	.00032	.00044	.00036	.00002	.00015	.00042	.00000	.00000	.00014	.00044	30
35	1520889	6090	.00400	.00079	.00019	.00062	.00061	.00048	.00002	.00023	.00033	.00000	.00000	.00017	.00057	35
40	1435019	7254	.00505	.00072	.00020	.00115	.00088	.00060	.00003	.00034	.00017	.00000	.00000	.00019	.00077	40
45	1368159	9392	.00686	.00057	.00024	.00190	.00157	.00069	.00003	.00057	.00002	.00000	.00000	.00024	.00103	45
50	1266034	12326	.00974	.00054	.00028	.00281	.00249	.00103	.00003	.00080	.00000	.00000	.00000	.00034	.00142	50
55	1081644	15404	.01424	.00048	.00034	.00374	.00455	.00145	.00004	.00124	.00000	.00000	.00000	.00040	.00200	55
60	879384	19363	.02202	.00044	.00035	.00505	.00838	.00247	.00007	.00189	.00000	.00000	.00000	.00051	.00287	60
65	693092	24115	.03479	.00040	.00036	.00690	.01530	.00415	.00008	.00289	.00000	.00000	.00000	.00071	.00400	65
70	494551	28509	.05765	.00032	.00041	.00909	.02761	.00800	.00014	.00364	.00000	.00000	.00000	.00114	.00730	70
75	295851	28690	.09697	.00030	.00044	.01157	.04826	.01458	.00026	.00485	.00000	.00000	.00000	.00196	.01477	75
80	142268	22208	.15610	.00013	.00045	.01320	.07667	.02403	.00048	.00446	.00000	.00000	.00000	.00363	.03305	80
85+	65556	16781	.25598	.00008	.00061	.01385	.11550	.04357	.00085	.00616	.00000	.00000	.00000	.00601	.06935	85+
ALL	20831149	241913														

	All Causes	Respiratory T.B.	Other Infec. and Paras.	Neoplasms	Cardiovascular	Infl., Pneu., Bronch.	Diarrheal	Certain Degenerative	Maternal	Cert. Dis. of Infancy	Motor Vehicle	Other Violence	Other and Unknown
CRUDE DEATH RATE	.01161	.00062	.00052	.00163	.00383	.00167	.00011	.00062	.00012	.00034	.00000	.00034	.00180
STANDARDIZED RATE (1)	.00876	.00055	.00081	.00085	.00187	.00151	.00021	.00035	.00011	.00083	.00000	.00029	.00133
STANDARDIZED RATE (2)	.01313	.00058	.00062	.00168	.00440	.00199	.00015	.00065	.00011	.00049	.00000	.00037	.00209
GEOMETRIC MEAN	.01197												

LIFE TABLE FOR ALL CAUSES COMBINED

Age (x)	Midyear Population	Deaths During Year	$_nM_x$	$_nq_x$	l_x	$_nd_x$	$_nL_x$	$_nm_x$	$_na_x$	T_x	$_nr_x$	$\overset{\circ}{e}_x$	Age (x)
0	296902	1767	.059302	.056520	100000	5652	95313	.059299	.170814	6236157	.000000	62.362	0
1	1184019	8333	.007038	.027664	94348	2610	370867	.007038	1.500000	6140844	.000000	65.087	1
5	1645742	3253	.001977	.009843	91738	903	456433	.001978	2.500000	5769977	.000000	62.896	5
10	1587712	2353	.001482	.007376	90835	670	452534	.001481	2.550062	5313544	-.003149	58.497	10
15	1725965	4103	.002377	.011801	90165	1064	448291	.002373	2.618460	4861011	-.013595	53.912	15
20	1796362	5180	.002884	.014310	89101	1275	442383	.002882	2.551144	4412720	-.007233	49.525	20
25	1729085	5464	.003160	.015679	87826	1377	435724	.003160	2.526628	3970337	.003206	45.207	25
30	1622915	5488	.003382	.016784	86449	1451	428682	.003385	2.544366	3534613	.008024	40.887	30
35	1520889	6090	.004004	.019836	84998	1686	420906	.004006	2.577971	3105931	.008637	36.541	35
40	1435019	7254	.005055	.024990	83312	2082	411576	.005059	2.605968	2685025	.006398	32.229	40
45	1368159	9392	.006865	.033793	81230	2745	399633	.006869	2.625835	2273449	.004603	27.988	45
50	1266034	12326	.009736	.047652	78485	3740	383579	.009750	2.634860	1873816	.009996	23.875	50
55	1081644	15404	.014241	.069115	74745	5166	361553	.014288	2.643890	1490237	.018880	19.938	55
60	879384	19363	.022019	.105032	69579	7308	330647	.022103	2.639031	1128683	.021294	16.222	60
65	693092	24115	.034793	.161279	62271	10043	287490	.034933	2.623718	798042	.020451	12.816	65
70	494551	28509	.057646	.254117	52228	13272	229050	.057944	2.562159	510552	.023789	9.775	70
75	295851	28690	.096974	.352160	38956	15277	156570	.097573	2.498854	281502	.024606	7.226	75
80	142268	22208	.156100	.556949	23679	13188	83948	.157097	2.388014	124932	.024606	5.276	80
85+	65556	16781	.255980	1.000000	10491	10491	40984	.255980	3.906561	40984	.000000	3.907	85+

NUMBER OF PERSONS DYING (OUT OF 100,000 AT BIRTH) ABOVE AGE X FROM SPECIFIED CAUSES

Age (x)	All Causes	Respira-tory T. B.	Other Infec. and Paras.	Neo-plasms	Cardio-vascular	Infl., Pneu., Bronch.	Diar-rheal	Certain Degen-erative	Maternal	Cert. Dis. of Infancy	Motor Vehicle	Other Violence	Other and Unknown	Age (x)
0	100000	3636	3384	13546	37019	14587	818	5194	684	2246	0	2672	16214	0
1	94348	3623	2855	13536	37014	13224	402	5191	684	0	0	2555	15264	1
5	91738	3593	1821	13508	36998	12295	303	5175	684	0	0	2413	14938	5
10	90835	3570	1480	13491	36932	12158	291	5159	684	0	0	2318	14752	10
15	90165	3490	1318	13470	36819	12082	286	5125	684	0	0	2283	14608	15
20	89101	3057	1197	13444	36687	11990	281	5081	665	0	0	2226	14473	20
25	87826	2518	1104	13402	36555	11886	276	5034	560	0	0	2154	14337	25
30	86449	2008	1018	13335	36410	11776	267	4977	397	0	0	2086	14175	30
35	84998	1632	937	13195	36221	11620	256	4911	218	0	0	2024	13984	35
40	83312	1300	857	12933	35963	11417	246	4816	81	0	0	1953	13746	40
45	81230	1003	773	12458	35601	11170	233	4677	10	0	0	1873	13432	45
50	78485	775	677	11658	34974	10893	220	4450	2	0	0	1778	13018	50
55	74745	568	571	10619	34017	10499	208	4143	1	0	0	1646	12473	55
60	69579	395	448	9264	32264	9973	194	3692	1	0	0	1501	11747	60
65	62271	251	331	7591	29579	9153	171	3065	1	0	0	1332	10797	65
70	52228	138	228	5603	25159	7953	147	2231	1	0	0	1126	9642	70
75	38956	66	133	3516	18797	6108	116	1396	1	0	0	863	7960	75
80	23679	19	65	1658	11194	3811	75	635	1	0	0	554	5627	80
85+	10491	3	25	568	4734	1785	35	253	0	0	0	246	2842	85+

NUMBER OF PERSONS SURVIVING TO AGE X IF SPECIFIED CAUSES WERE ELIMINATED

Age (x)	No Causes	Respira-tory T. B.	Other Infec. and Paras.	Neo-plasms	Cardio-vascular	Infl., Pneu., Bronch.	Diar-rheal	Certain Degener-ative	Maternal	Cert. Dis. of Infancy	Motor Vehicle	Other Violence	Other and Unknown	(1) + (2)	(1) + (2) + (5) + (6) + (8)	(1)+(2)+ (5)+(6)+ (8)+part of(9)&(12)	(10) + (11)	Age (x)
		(1)	(2)	(3)	(4)	(5)	(6)	(7)	(8)	(9)	(10)	(11)	(12)					
0	100000	100000	100000	100000	100000	100000	100000	100000	100000	100000	100000	100000	100000	100000	100000	100000	100000	0
1	94348	94361	94863	94358	94353	95681	94753	94351	94348	96555	94348	94462	95275	94876	96629	99681	94462	1
5	91738	91780	93260	91775	91759	93968	92230	91757	91738	93884	91738	91989	92965	93302	96082	99434	91989	5
10	90835	90899	92698	90889	90921	93183	91334	90869	90835	92960	90835	91178	92237	92763	95683	99168	91178	10
15	90165	90309	92179	90239	90363	92573	90665	90233	90165	92274	90165	90541	91703	92326	95317	98885	90541	15
20	89101	89675	91214	89200	89428	91575	89600	89212	89120	91155	89101	89529	90757	91802	94899	98558	89529	20
25	87826	88932	90003	87966	88280	90370	88323	87982	87949	89880	87826	88320	89596	91137	94440	98194	88320	25
30	86449	88052	88679	86653	87041	89066	86947	86659	86732	88471	86449	87003	88356	90323	93901	97764	87003	30
35	84998	86954	87273	85338	85769	87730	85459	85270	85455	86986	84998	85605	87066	89282	93193	97165	85605	35
40	83312	85566	85624	83906	84326	86261	83813	83856	83896	85397	83312	83977	85581	87940	92175	96247	83977	40
45	81230	83729	83569	82283	82581	84296	81731	81720	81870	83130	81230	81958	83761	86140	90652	94802	81958	45
50	78485	81131	80842	80263	80420	81731	78982	79184	79111	80321	78485	79283	81352	83567	88273	92442	79283	50
55	74745	77473	77096	77523	77551	78238	75230	75713	75342	76493	74745	75635	78028	79911	84860	89010	75635	55
60	69579	72291	71890	73532	73867	73863	70044	70922	70135	71206	69579	70549	73370	74693	79915	83982	70549	60
65	62271	64839	64453	67500	68968	66481	62709	64080	62769	63727	62271	63301	66617	67112	72730	76623	63301	65
70	52228	54489	54155	58613	62507	56945	52618	54534	52645	53450	52228	53284	57014	56500	62558	66123	53284	70
75	38956	40706	40478	45768	53665	44244	39274	41429	39267	39967	38956	39975	44140	42296	48816	51938	39975	75
80	23679	24780	24658	29498	41792	28984	23904	25807	23868	24233	23679	24544	28965	25804	32140	34697	24544	80
85+	10491	10990	10952	14013	27589	14552	10617	11706	10575	10736	10491	11083	15240	11472	16234	18151	11083	85+

ADDED YRS OF LIFE																		
TOTAL		1.335	1.669	2.037	5.204	3.087	.385	.766	.271	1.455	.000	.607	2.855	3.047	7.079	10.339	.607	
WORK	4.939	1.007	.241	.710	.828	.455	.023	.272	.230	.000	.000	.191	.610	1.255	1.993	2.299	.191	

POPULATION, DEATHS, DEATH RATES FOR ALL CAUSES COMBINED, AND SPECIFIED CAUSES

Age Start of Interval	Midyear Population	Deaths During Year	All Causes	Respiratory T.B.	Other Infec. and Paras.	Neoplasms	Cardiovascular	Infl., Pneu., 'Bronch.	Diarrheal	Certain Degenerative	Maternal	Cert. Dis. of Infancy	Motor Vehicle	Other Violence	Other and Unknown	Age Start of Interval
0	297000	19693	.06631	.00008	.00307	.00016	.00006	.01559	.00525	.00010	.00000	.02753	.00001	.00184	.01260	0
1	1172000	6051	.00516	.00004	.00149	.00010	.00003	.00162	.00018	.00004	.00000	.00000	.00018	.00075	.00073	1
5	1417000	3003	.00212	.00002	.00069	.00009	.00008	.00016	.00001	.00004	.00000	.00000	.00020	.00047	.00036	5
10	1506000	2228	.00148	.00004	.00027	.00006	.00013	.00009	.00000	.00004	.00000	.00000	.00012	.00045	.00027	10
15	1737000	4388	.00253	.00036	.00029	.00008	.00008	.00017	.00001	.00007	.00000	.00000	.00018	.00084	.00036	15
20	1608000	3663	.00228	.00067	.00017	.00009	.00017	.00017	.00001	.00010	.00000	.00000	.00015	.00051	.00024	20
25	1735000	5169	.00298	.00078	.00019	.00013	.00021	.00025	.00001	.00014	.00000	.00000	.00016	.00080	.00031	25
30	1737000	6188	.00356	.00078	.00019	.00021	.00029	.00032	.00002	.00019	.00000	.00000	.00018	.00100	.00038	30
35	1636000	7621	.00466	.00085	.00022	.00038	.00050	.00056	.00002	.00032	.00000	.00000	.00015	.00116	.00050	35
40	1365000	8639	.00633	.00102	.00026	.00077	.00089	.00091	.00002	.00048	.00000	.00000	.00019	.00116	.00065	40
45	1240000	11733	.00946	.00106	.00036	.00182	.00163	.00163	.00003	.00069	.00000	.00000	.00019	.00138	.00098	45
50	1168000	17524	.01500	.00130	.00048	.00229	.00366	.00290	.00003	.00111	.00000	.00000	.00024	.00158	.00142	50
55	1056000	24388	.02309	.00135	.00053	.00377	.00679	.00459	.00006	.00166	.00000	.00000	.00033	.00186	.00215	55
60	922000	31546	.03421	.00121	.00070	.00606	.01234	.00616	.00004	.00217	.00000	.00000	.00041	.00203	.00309	60
65	724000	36404	.05028	.00087	.00065	.00879	.02148	.00783	.00010	.00301	.00000	.00000	.00049	.00204	.00501	65
70	487000	37799	.07762	.00051	.00063	.01166	.03697	.01174	.00012	.00409	.00000	.00000	.00064	.00236	.00890	70
75	259000	33802	.13051	.00032	.00057	.01510	.06615	.01911	.00022	.00602	.00000	.00000	.00093	.00342	.01866	75
80	110000	21584	.19622	.00017	.00041	.01455	.10347	.02804	.00034	.00652	.00000	.00000	.00097	.00445	.03690	80
85+	40000	12773	.31932	.00010	.00057	.01527	.15587	.05082	.00060	.00955	.00000	.00000	.00100	.00810	.07742	85+
ALL	20216000	294196														

	All Causes	Respiratory T.B.	Other Infec. and Paras.	Neoplasms	Cardiovascular	Infl., Pneu., 'Bronch.	Diarrheal	Certain Degenerative	Maternal	Cert. Dis. of Infancy	Motor Vehicle	Other Violence	Other and Unknown
CRUDE DEATH RATE	.01455	.00068	.00046	.00173	.00481	.00237	.00012	.00074	.00000	.00040	.00023	.00116	.00185
STANDARDIZED RATE (1)	.01052	.00050	.00059	.00093	.00242	.00185	.00022	.00042	.00000	.00057	.00019	.00096	.00146
STANDARDIZED RATE (2)	.01688	.00061	.00052	.00184	.00589	.00276	.00015	.00079	.00000	.00057	.00024	.00116	.00234
GEOMETRIC MEAN	.01412												

LIFE TABLE FOR ALL CAUSES COMBINED

Age (x)	Midyear Population	Deaths During Year	$_nM_x$	$_nq_x$	l_x	$_nd_x$	$_nL_x$	$_nm_x$	$_na_x$	T_x	$_nr_x$	$\overset{\circ}{e}_x$	Age (x)
0	297000	19693	.066306	.062590	100000	6290	94859	.066309	.182721	5938733	.000000	59.387	0
1	1172000	6051	.005163	.020382	93710	1910	370065	.005161	1.500000	5843874	.000000	62.361	1
5	1417000	3003	.002119	.010556	91800	969	456578	.002122	2.500000	5473809	.000000	59.628	5
10	1506000	2228	.001479	.007354	90831	668	452519	.001476	2.550524	5017231	-.019038	55.237	10
15	1737000	4388	.002526	.012544	90163	1131	448059	.002524	2.562813	4564712	-.012806	50.627	15
20	1608000	3663	.002278	.011333	89032	1009	442673	.002279	2.534894	4116654	-.002975	46.238	20
25	1735000	5169	.002979	.014769	88023	1300	436914	.002975	2.583654	3673981	-.010470	41.739	25
30	1737000	6188	.003562	.017654	86723	1531	429526	.003561	2.590627	3237007	-.003643	37.326	30
35	1636000	7621	.004658	.023077	85192	1966	421268	.004667	2.613598	2807081	.013066	32.950	35
40	1365000	8639	.006329	.031276	83226	2603	409592	.006349	2.641904	2385813	.021807	28.667	40
45	1240000	11733	.009462	.046376	80623	3739	394386	.009481	2.665541	1975821	-.010309	24.507	45
50	1168000	17524	.015003	.072499	76884	5574	371332	.015011	2.652008	1581435	-.003036	20.569	50
55	1056000	24388	.023095	.109466	71310	7806	337965	.023097	2.619112	1210102	.000553	16.970	55
60	922000	31546	.034215	.158053	63504	10037	293299	.034221	2.586783	872137	-.001059	13.734	60
65	724000	36404	.050282	.224194	53467	11987	238099	.050345	2.561021	578839	-.007537	10.826	65
70	487000	37799	.077616	.326615	41480	13548	173887	.077913	2.526372	340740	-.018515	8.215	70
75	259000	33802	.130510	.490548	27932	13702	104465	.131138	2.432872	166853	.017320	5.974	75
80	110000	21584	.196218	.641813	14230	9133	46406	.196808	2.290663	62367	.017320	4.383	80
85+	40000	12773	.319325	1.000000	5097	5097	15962	.319325	3.131606	15962	.000000	3.132	85+

NUMBER OF PERSONS DYING (OUT OF 100,000 AT BIRTH) ABOVE AGE X FROM SPECIFIED CAUSES

Age (x)	All Causes	Respiratory T. B.	Other Infec. and Paras.	Neo-plasms	Cardio-vascular	Infl., Pneu., Bronch.	Diar-rheal	Certain Degenerative	Maternal	Cert. Dis. of Infancy	Motor Vehicle	Other Violence	Other and Unknown	Age (x)
0	100000	4019	2908	11883	34866	16322	755	5037	0	2612	1432	7163	13003	0
1	93710	4012	2616	11868	34860	14842	257	5028	0	0	1431	6989	11807	1
5	91800	3996	2063	11831	34849	14242	191	5014	0	0	1364	6713	11537	5
10	90831	3986	1748	11790	34814	14171	185	4994	0	0	1274	6498	11371	10
15	90163	3967	1626	11762	34756	14131	183	4976	0	0	1221	6293	11248	15
20	89032	3805	1497	11728	34681	14053	181	4943	0	0	1140	5917	11087	20
25	88023	3507	1423	11690	34607	13980	177	4898	0	0	1071	5691	10979	25
30	86723	3168	1338	11634	34516	13871	172	4837	0	0	1003	5341	10843	30
35	85192	2834	1255	11544	34392	13732	163	4755	0	0	925	4910	10682	35
40	83226	2475	1161	11384	34183	13493	155	4619	0	0	861	4423	10472	40
45	80623	2057	1055	11068	33817	13119	147	4423	0	0	784	3948	10205	45
50	76884	1638	913	10543	33097	12475	136	4151	0	0	708	3404	9819	50
55	71310	1154	726	9691	31737	11398	125	3738	0	0	617	2819	9295	55
60	63504	697	558	8415	29441	9845	105	3177	0	0	507	2190	8569	60
65	53467	343	353	6636	25821	8038	92	2539	0	0	388	1596	7661	65
70	41480	135	199	4540	20697	6171	69	1822	0	0	271	1111	6465	70
75	27932	48	89	2509	14241	4123	48	1108	0	0	159	700	4907	75
80	14230	14	29	927	7293	2116	25	476	0	0	62	340	2948	80
85+	5097	2	9	244	2488	811	10	152	0	0	16	129	1236	85+

NUMBER OF PERSONS SURVIVING TO AGE X IF SPECIFIED CAUSES WERE ELIMINATED

Age (x)	No Causes	Respiratory T. B. (1)	Other Infec. and Paras. (2)	Neo-plasms (3)	Cardio-vascular (4)	Infl., Pneu., Bronch. (5)	Diar-rheal (6)	Certain Degenerative (7)	Maternal (8)	Cert. Dis. of Infancy (9)	Motor Vehicle (10)	Other Violence (11)	Other and Unknown (12)	(1)+(2)	(1)+(2)+(5)+(6)+(8)	(1)+(2)+(5)+(6)+(8)+part of(9)&(12)	(10)+(11)	Age (x)
0	100000	100000	100000	100000	100000	100000	100000	100000	100000	100000	100000	100000	100000	100000	100000	100000	100000	0
1	93710	93717	93993	93725	93716	95153	94193	93719	93710	96272	93711	93879	94875	94000	95940	99465	93880	1
5	91800	91822	92628	91851	91819	93819	92339	91822	91800	94310	91867	92239	93212	92651	95244	98960	92307	5
10	90831	90863	91967	90922	90882	92901	91370	90873	90831	93315	90987	91481	92356	91999	94655	98437	91638	10
15	90163	90214	91414	90281	90272	92258	90700	90223	90163	92628	90371	91014	91841	91465	94149	97956	91224	15
20	89032	89244	90397	89183	89214	91180	89565	89124	89032	91467	89318	90250	90852	90612	93354	97195	90540	20
25	88023	88530	89447	88210	88277	90222	88554	88159	88023	90430	88375	89455	89932	89962	92765	96641	89813	25
30	86723	87561	88212	86963	87064	89000	87251	86917	86723	89094	87137	88488	88742	89065	91959	95671	88911	30
35	85192	86350	86738	85517	85650	87570	85719	85464	85192	87522	85677	87363	87339	87918	90932	94873	87860	35
40	83226	84718	84831	83703	83882	85793	83749	83627	83226	85502	83763	85841	85536	86352	89575	93550	86395	40
45	80623	82488	82284	81398	81622	83490	81138	81206	80623	82828	81220	83640	83132	84188	87738	91748	84259	45
50	76884	79081	78610	78143	78553	80272	77386	77707	76884	78586	77528	80213	75666	80857	84971	89012	80986	50
55	71310	73828	73085	73317	74210	75544	71786	72477	71310	73260	71995	75080	74414	75666	80693	84738	75802	55
60	63504	66192	65257	66541	68383	68843	63547	65083	63504	65241	64219	67487	66987	68019	74252	78236	68247	60
65	53467	56067	55135	57759	61270	59782	53852	55398	53467	54929	54179	57400	57284	57816	65110	68882	58164	65
70	41480	43686	42913	46839	52996	48246	41799	43634	41480	42614	42136	44987	45584	45195	52970	56336	45699	70
75	27932	29490	28988	33454	43105	34485	28164	29958	27932	28696	28466	30656	32130	30605	38099	40869	31243	75
80	14230	15047	14810	18401	30950	19388	14364	15761	14230	14619	14571	15895	18041	15661	21539	23515	16276	80
85+	5097	5397	5317	7117	19027	8042	5154	5855	5097	5236	5246	5830	7834	5630	8981	10155	6001	85+

ADDED YRS OF LIFE																		
TOTAL		1.057	1.136	1.537	4.575	3.177	.378	.704	.000	1.619	.379	1.913	2.402	2.221	6.021	9.146	2.313	
WORK	5.793	.797	.261	.527	.834	.706	.016	.315	.000	.000	.185	1.006	.543	1.065	1.821	2.045	1.197	

POPULATION, DEATHS, DEATH RATES FOR ALL CAUSES COMBINED, AND SPECIFIED CAUSES

Age Start of Interval	Midyear Population	Deaths During Year	All Causes	Respiratory T. B.	Other Infec. and Paras.	Neoplasms	Cardiovascular	Infl., Pneu., Bronch.	Diarrheal	Certain Degenerative	Maternal	Cert. Dis. of Infancy	Motor Vehicle	Other Violence	Other and Unknown	Age Start of Interval
0	284000	14199	.05000	.00008	.00254	.00008	.00006	.01155	.00386	.00005	.00000	.02055	.00001	.00151	.00970	0
1	1128000	5053	.00448	.00005	.00140	.00010	.00004	.00134	.00015	.00004	.00000	.00000	.00010	.00060	.00067	1
5	1380000	2488	.00180	.00002	.00067	.00005	.00010	.00015	.00002	.00003	.00000	.00000	.00010	.00037	.00029	5
10	1488000	1949	.00131	.00010	.00028	.00005	.00014	.00008	.00001	.00005	.00000	.00000	.00004	.00035	.00021	10
15	1712000	3977	.00232	.00073	.00025	.00007	.00021	.00011	.00001	.00008	.00003	.00000	.00006	.00053	.00025	15
20	1566000	4486	.00286	.00106	.00020	.00009	.00024	.00016	.00002	.00008	.00016	.00000	.00005	.00053	.00027	20
25	1762000	5065	.00287	.00086	.00015	.00015	.00029	.00018	.00002	.00010	.00024	.00000	.00003	.00054	.00031	25
30	1773000	5328	.00301	.00066	.00014	.00028	.00036	.00022	.00013	.00013	.00024	.00000	.00003	.00054	.00037	30
35	1684000	6131	.00364	.00056	.00013	.00057	.00056	.00031	.00003	.00019	.00019	.00000	.00003	.00057	.00050	35
40	1558000	7276	.00467	.00047	.00017	.00103	.00091	.00042	.00003	.00029	.00010	.00000	.00003	.00064	.00059	40
45	1455000	9632	.00662	.00038	.00018	.00180	.00153	.00064	.00003	.00040	.00001	.00000	.00004	.00074	.00086	45
50	1356000	12979	.00957	.00033	.00023	.00255	.00272	.00101	.00004	.00062	.00000	.00000	.00006	.00083	.00118	50
55	1244000	17250	.01387	.00033	.00025	.00347	.00463	.00165	.00004	.00095	.00000	.00000	.00007	.00093	.00156	55
60	1085000	23886	.02201	.00031	.00028	.00472	.00870	.00291	.00006	.00154	.00000	.00000	.00009	.00112	.00228	60
65	869000	30663	.03529	.00029	.00027	.00646	.01612	.00499	.00009	.00222	.00000	.00000	.00013	.00137	.00336	65
70	631000	36834	.05837	.00023	.00026	.00837	.02972	.00851	.00013	.00309	.00000	.00000	.00018	.00159	.00589	70
75	390000	38147	.09781	.00016	.00033	.01023	.05257	.01485	.00022	.00395	.00000	.00000	.00023	.00313	.01213	75
80	194000	30753	.15852	.00011	.00034	.01183	.08686	.02330	.00026	.00427	.00000	.00000	.00025	.00511	.02619	80
85+	87000	22352	.25692	.00007	.00046	.01241	.13085	.04224	.00047	.00590	.00000	.00000	.00025	.00930	.05497	85+
ALL	21646000	278448														

		All Causes	Respiratory T.B.	Other Infec.	Neoplasms	Cardiovascular	Infl., Pneu.	Diarrheal	Certain Degen.	Maternal	Cert. Dis. Infancy	Motor Vehicle	Other Violence	Other Unknown
CRUDE DEATH RATE		.01286	.00045	.00033	.00174	.00495	.00179	.00010	.00059	.00008	.00027	.00006	.00082	.00169
STANDARDIZED RATE (1)		.00799	.00041	.00049	.00083	.00195	.00123	.00018	.00029	.00007	.00072	.00006	.00065	.00112
STANDARDIZED RATE (2)		.01264	.00042	.00040	.00155	.00472	.00182	.00013	.00053	.00007	.00043	.00007	.00080	.00172
GEOMETRIC MEAN		.01118												

LIFE TABLE FOR ALL CAUSES COMBINED

Age (x)	Midyear Population	Deaths During Year	$_nM_x$	$_nq_x$	l_x	$_nd_x$	$_nL_x$	$_nm_x$	$_na_x$	T_x	$_nr_x$	$\overset{\circ}{e}_x$	Age (x)
0	284000	14199	.049996	.047970	100000	4797	95947	.049997	.154994	6390099	.000000	63.901	0
1	1128000	5053	.004480	.017720	95203	1687	376555	.004480	1.500000	6294152	.000000	66.113	1
5	1380000	2488	.001803	.008993	93516	841	465478	.001807	2.500000	5917558	.000000	63.279	5
10	1488000	1949	.001310	.006507	92675	603	461914	.001305	2.576354	5452080	-.020379	58.830	10
15	1712000	3977	.002323	.011534	92072	1062	457849	.002320	2.635554	4990167	-.011302	54.199	15
20	1566000	4486	.002865	.014218	91010	1294	451860	.002864	2.535058	4532318	-.004586	49.800	20
25	1762000	5065	.002875	.014267	89716	1280	445385	.002874	2.504069	4080457	-.015476	45.482	25
30	1773000	5328	.003005	.014915	88436	1319	438944	.003005	2.546279	3635072	-.003934	41.104	30
35	1684000	6131	.003641	.018056	87117	1573	431790	.003643	2.587280	3196129	.005939	36.688	35
40	1558000	7276	.004670	.023123	85544	1978	423015	.004676	2.621440	2764339	.009303	32.315	40
45	1455000	9632	.006620	.032621	83566	2726	411392	.006626	2.638252	2341324	.007865	28.018	45
50	1356000	12979	.009572	.046846	80840	3787	395244	.009581	2.635001	1929932	.006219	23.873	50
55	1244000	17250	.013867	.067226	77053	5180	373096	.013884	2.650780	1534688	.006597	19.917	55
60	1085000	23886	.022015	.104852	71873	7536	341634	.022059	2.647155	1161592	.010891	16.162	60
65	869000	30663	.035285	.163250	64337	10503	296736	.035395	2.624548	819958	.015401	12.745	65
70	631000	36834	.058374	.256622	53834	13815	235731	.058605	2.575548	523222	.018566	9.719	70
75	390000	38147	.097813	.394263	40019	15778	160611	.098237	2.497544	287491	.017330	7.184	75
80	194000	30753	.158521	.562229	24241	13629	85575	.159264	2.385706	126880	.017330	5.234	80
85+	87000	22352	.256920	1.000000	10612	10612	41305	.256920	3.892269	41305	.000000	3.892	85+

NUMBER OF PERSONS DYING (OUT OF 100,000 AT BIRTH) ABOVE AGE X FROM SPECIFIED CAUSES

Age (x)	All Causes	Respiratory T.B.	Other Infec. and Paras.	Neoplasms	Cardiovascular	Infl., Pneu., Bronch.	Diarrheal	Certain Degenerative	Maternal	Cert. Dis. of Infancy	Motor Vehicle	Other Violence	Other and Unknown	Age (x)
0	100000	2697	2272	12781	40842	14250	693	4379	427	1972	450	5763	13474	0
1	95203	2689	2029	12773	40836	13141	322	4374	427	0	448	5618	12546	1
5	93516	2671	1503	12735	40821	12636	267	4361	427	0	411	5392	12292	5
10	92675	2660	1192	12712	40775	12566	260	4346	427	0	364	5218	12155	10
15	92072	2615	1064	12689	40708	12527	257	4322	427	0	347	5056	12060	15
20	91010	2284	948	12659	40614	12475	252	4284	413	0	322	4812	11947	20
25	89716	1805	857	12619	40508	12404	241	4246	339	0	301	4571	11825	25
30	88436	1421	791	12554	40380	12324	231	4199	232	0	286	4330	11688	30
35	87117	1133	729	12432	40221	12226	219	4141	128	0	273	4092	11523	35
40	85544	889	673	12184	39981	12094	206	4058	48	0	260	3845	11306	40
45	83566	692	600	11748	39597	11916	194	3934	7	0	248	3572	11058	45
50	80840	537	525	11007	38967	11653	182	3768	2	0	232	3267	10700	50
55	77053	408	433	9996	37890	11254	167	3523	2	0	208	2938	10234	55
60	71873	286	337	8699	36161	10638	155	3167	1	0	182	2592	9655	60
65	64337	180	242	7084	33180	9642	135	2641	1	0	150	2207	8875	65
70	53834	95	163	5165	28379	8156	110	1981	1	0	112	1801	7871	70
75	40019	41	101	3188	21341	6142	78	1250	1	0	69	1330	6478	75
80	24241	15	48	1541	12859	3746	42	614	1	0	32	825	4518	80
85+	10612	3	19	513	5405	1745	19	244	0	0	10	384	2270	85+

NUMBER OF PERSONS SURVIVING TO AGE X IF SPECIFIED CAUSES WERE ELIMINATED

Age (x)	No Causes	Respiratory T.B. (1)	Other Infec. and Paras. (2)	Neoplasms (3)	Cardiovascular (4)	Infl., Pneu., Bronch. (5)	Diarrheal (6)	Certain Degenerative (7)	Maternal (8)	Cert. Dis. of Infancy (9)	Motor Vehicle (10)	Other Violence (11)	Other and Unknown (12)	(1)+(2)	(1)+(2)+(5)+(6)+(8)	(1)+(2)+(5)+(6)+(8)+part of(9)&(12)	(10)+(11)	Age (x)
0	100000	100000	100000	100000	100000	100000	100000	100000	100000	100000	100000	100000	100000	100000	100000	100000	100000	0
1	95203	95211	95440	95211	95209	96251	95566	95208	95203	97146	95205	95345	96113	95448	96907	99571	95347	1
5	93516	93542	94273	93561	93537	95092	93927	93534	93516	95425	93555	93880	94664	94299	96310	99163	93918	5
10	92675	92711	93738	92743	92741	94408	93089	92707	92675	94567	92760	93209	93951	93775	95854	98776	93295	10
15	92072	92153	93257	92162	92205	93734	92487	92128	92072	93952	92173	92765	93436	93339	95452	98404	92868	15
20	91010	91420	92258	91129	91235	92706	91425	91103	91024	92868	91135	91940	92472	92714	94887	97887	92067	20
25	89716	90599	91078	89873	90043	91459	90136	89846	89803	91547	89860	90875	91280	91974	94292	97355	91021	25
30	88436	89692	89845	88656	88886	90235	88860	88611	88628	90241	88593	89821	90117	91121	93624	96750	89981	30
35	87117	88645	88567	87455	87719	88989	87546	87347	87410	88655	87725	88722	88540	90121	92822	96009	88893	35
40	85544	87290	87025	86123	86375	87516	85979	85852	85911	87290	85722	87369	87553	88801	91702	94943	87551	40
45	83566	85471	85086	84567	84762	85672	84003	83990	83965	85272	83751	85625	85780	87025	90114	93378	85815	45
50	80840	82838	82385	82549	82629	83143	81274	81415	81231	82490	81035	83140	83344	84422	87716	90979	83340	50
55	77053	79087	78617	79656	79841	79650	77462	77842	77426	78626	77262	79575	79910	80692	84282	87516	79792	55
60	71873	73891	73427	75644	76225	74914	72284	72957	72222	73340	72093	74571	75120	75488	79516	82685	74800	60
65	64337	66246	65819	69337	71293	68048	64724	65814	64649	65650	64565	67130	68018	67772	72463	75506	67368	65
70	53834	55510	55148	59932	64727	58394	54181	55689	54095	54933	54059	56558	57892	56865	62381	65196	56795	70
75	40019	41312	41050	46470	55975	45327	40305	42049	40213	40836	40223	42470	44345	42376	48573	51031	42687	75
80	24241	25044	24907	29642	44406	29625	24442	25984	24359	24736	24393	26141	28599	25732	31862	33858	26305	80
85+	10612	10972	10923	13810	30542	14641	10715	11633	10664	10829	10693	11754	14347	11293	15809	17220	11843	85+

ADDED YRS OF LIFE

	No Causes	(1)	(2)	(3)	(4)	(5)	(6)	(7)	(8)	(9)	(10)	(11)	(12)	(1)+(2)	(1)+(2)+(5)+(6)+(8)	(1)+(2)+(5)+(6)+(8)+part of(9)&(12)	(10)+(11)
TOTAL		1.005	1.062	1.928	5.890	2.556	.331	.631	.171	1.301	.137	1.495	2.401	2.088	5.315	7.909	1.637
WORK	4.707	.763	.203	.660	.794	.357	.026	.219	.143	.000	.045	.645	.509	.971	1.515	1.715	.691

POPULATION, DEATHS, DEATH RATES FOR ALL CAUSES COMBINED, AND SPECIFIED CAUSES

Age Start of Interval	Midyear Population	Deaths During Year	All Causes	Respiratory T.B.	Other Infec. and Paras.	Neoplasms	Cardiovascular	Infl., Pneu., Bronch.	Diarrheal	Certain Degenerative	Maternal	Cert. Dis. of Infancy	Motor Vehicle	Other Violence	Other and Unknown	Age Start of Interval
0	338255	11773	.03481	.00004	.00101	.00014	.00006	.00524	.00134	.00006	.00000	.01904	.00000	.00134	.00652	0
1	1566686	2257	.00144	.00003	.00031	.00013	.00001	.00025	.00004	.00002	.00000	.00000	.00013	.00018	.00034	1
5	1617569	1072	.00066	.00001	.00005	.00005	.00002	.00004	.00001	.00002	.00000	.00000	.00012	.00014	.00013	5
10	1429640	812	.00057	.00001	.00005	.00008	.00004	.00002	.00001	.00002	.00000	.00000	.00009	.00010	.00015	10
15	1336270	1181	.00088	.00005	.00008	.00009	.00007	.00005	.00001	.00003	.00000	.00000	.00018	.00018	.00016	15
20	1428266	1931	.00135	.00017	.00006	.00012	.00011	.00005	.00000	.00007	.00000	.00000	.00031	.00030	.00017	20
25	1626982	2396	.00147	.00028	.00005	.00015	.00016	.00006	.00001	.00009	.00000	.00000	.00020	.00031	.00017	25
30	1515023	2662	.00176	.00031	.00008	.00024	.00026	.00009	.00001	.00012	.00000	.00000	.00015	.00021	.00021	30
35	1633733	3757	.00230	.00032	.00008	.00045	.00046	.00016	.00002	.00017	.00000	.00000	.00011	.00029	.00025	35
40	1659072	5956	.00359	.00040	.00008	.00079	.00094	.00032	.00002	.00024	.00000	.00000	.00012	.00034	.00035	40
45	1557540	9890	.00635	.00052	.00011	.00151	.00193	.00074	.00002	.00039	.00000	.00000	.00012	.00042	.00057	45
50	1318880	14909	.01130	.00077	.00015	.00286	.00385	.00151	.00004	.00058	.00000	.00000	.00011	.00053	.00088	50
55	1090086	20260	.01859	.00089	.00026	.00454	.00654	.00293	.00005	.00083	.00000	.00000	.00012	.00057	.00146	55
60	939496	29107	.03098	.00109	.00036	.00674	.01299	.00531	.00007	.00117	.00000	.00000	.00020	.00075	.00229	60
65	781208	37358	.04782	.00110	.00040	.00943	.02273	.00784	.00011	.00173	.00000	.00000	.00020	.00083	.00345	65
70	591637	43312	.07321	.00076	.00044	.01238	.03876	.01158	.00017	.00229	.00000	.00000	.00027	.00100	.00557	70
75	374772	43816	.11691	.00056	.00043	.01598	.06675	.01794	.00025	.00292	.00000	.00000	.00044	.00167	.00998	75
80	164933	30499	.18492	.00035	.00046	.01789	.11140	.02721	.00050	.00382	.00000	.00000	.00056	.00271	.02003	80
85+	60872	18776	.30845	.00021	.00071	.01738	.19083	.04537	.00062	.00465	.00000	.00000	.00079	.00460	.04329	85+
ALL	21030920	281724														

		All Causes	Respiratory T.B.	Other Infec. and Paras.	Neoplasms	Cardiovascular	Infl., Pneu., Bronch.	Diarrheal	Certain Degenerative	Maternal	Cert. Dis. of Infancy	Motor Vehicle	Other Violence	Other and Unknown
CRUDE DEATH RATE		.01340	.00038	.00017	.00216	.00603	.00198	.00006	.00044	.00000	.00031	.00016	.00043	.00127
STANDARDIZED RATE (1)		.00725	.00024	.00016	.00105	.00251	.00103	.00007	.00023	.00000	.00067	.00015	.00033	.00081
STANDARDIZED RATE (2)		.01363	.00033	.00017	.00206	.00623	.00202	.00006	.00042	.00000	.00039	.00016	.00043	.00134
GEOMETRIC MEAN		.00851												

LIFE TABLE FOR ALL CAUSES COMBINED

Age (x)	Midyear Population	Deaths During Year	$_nM_x$	$_nq_x$	l_x	$_nd_x$	$_nL_x$	$_nm_x$	$_na_x$	T_x	$_nr_x$	$\overset{\circ}{e}_x$	Age (x)
0	338255	11773	.034805	.033780	100000	3378	97058	.034804	.129169	6584597	.000000	65.846	0
1	1566686	2257	.001441	.005744	96622	555	385101	.001441	1.500000	6487538	.000000	67.143	1
5	1617569	1072	.000663	.003300	96067	317	479543	.000661	2.500000	6102438	.000000	63.523	5
10	1429640	812	.000568	.002841	95750	272	478092	.000569	2.580423	5622895	.016602	58.725	10
15	1336270	1181	.000884	.004420	95478	422	476411	.000884	2.681181	5144803	.007414	53.885	15
20	1428266	1931	.001352	.006722	95056	639	473739	.001349	2.588354	4668392	-.016359	49.112	20
25	1626982	2396	.001473	.007340	94417	693	470390	.001473	2.554113	4194653	-.010966	44.427	25
30	1515023	2662	.001757	.008738	93724	819	466649	.001755	2.593610	3724263	-.002196	39.736	30
35	1633733	3757	.002300	.011420	92905	1061	462042	.002296	2.660030	3257614	-.010988	35.064	35
40	1659072	5956	.003590	.017791	91844	1634	455504	.003587	2.725546	2795572	-.004235	30.438	40
45	1557540	9890	.006350	.031371	90210	2830	444642	.006365	2.735718	2340068	.009747	25.940	45
50	1318880	14909	.011304	.055344	87380	4836	425757	.011359	2.695926	1895426	.021942	21.692	50
55	1090086	20260	.018586	.089383	82544	7378	395529	.018653	2.670016	1469668	.018212	17.805	55
60	939496	29107	.030982	.144440	75166	10857	350020	.031018	2.622770	1074139	.006201	14.290	60
65	781208	37358	.047821	.214216	64309	13776	288104	.047816	2.572484	724119	-.000510	11.260	65
70	591637	43312	.073207	.309699	50533	15650	213946	.073149	2.525932	436015	-.004133	8.628	70
75	374772	43816	.116914	.450764	34883	15724	134319	.117064	2.450023	222069	.005230	6.366	75
80	164933	30499	.184918	.619970	19159	11878	64145	.185174	2.335410	87750	.005230	4.580	80
85+	60872	18776	.308451	1.000000	7281	7281	23605	.308451	3.242011	23605	.000000	3.242	85+

NUMBER OF PERSONS DYING (OUT OF 100,000 AT BIRTH) ABOVE AGE X FROM SPECIFIED CAUSES

Age (x)	All Causes	Respiratory T.B.	Other Infec. and Paras.	Neoplasms	Cardiovascular	Infl., Pneu., Bronch.	Diarrheal	Certain Degenerative	Maternal	Cert. Dis. of Infancy	Motor Vehicle	Other Violence	Other and Unknown	Age (x)
0	100000	2607	1136	16121	46247	14939	397	3266	0	1850	1095	2983	9359	0
1	96622	2603	1038	16107	46241	14430	267	3260	0	2	1095	2853	8726	1
5	96067	2593	917	16058	46236	14336	251	3251	0	1	1046	2784	8594	5
10	95750	2589	876	16016	46226	14317	248	3241	0	0	988	2717	8532	10
15	95478	2586	850	15978	46205	14305	248	3232	0	0	946	2668	8460	15
20	95056	2564	814	15937	46174	14281	245	3216	0	0	861	2580	8384	20
25	94417	2484	787	15881	46123	14255	243	3183	0	0	717	2439	8305	25
30	93724	2355	765	15810	46048	14227	240	3142	0	0	622	2294	8221	30
35	92905	2210	728	15697	45925	14184	236	3086	0	0	554	2158	8127	35
40	91844	2060	692	15491	45713	14111	229	3009	0	0	505	2025	8009	40
45	90210	1877	654	15133	45287	13968	222	2900	0	0	451	1868	7850	45
50	87380	1644	607	14459	44425	13636	211	2725	0	0	398	1680	7595	50
55	82544	1316	542	13236	42775	12987	194	2477	0	0	349	1452	7216	55
60	75166	965	439	11435	40019	11822	173	2147	0	0	301	1226	6639	60
65	64309	584	313	9072	35465	9962	148	1737	0	0	229	963	5836	65
70	50533	268	198	6356	28917	7704	116	1238	0	0	172	722	4842	70
75	34883	105	105	3709	20634	5229	80	749	0	0	113	509	3650	75
80	19159	29	46	1561	11655	2817	47	356	0	0	54	284	2310	80
85+	7281	5	17	410	4504	1071	15	110	0	0	19	109	1021	85+

NUMBER OF PERSONS SURVIVING TO AGE X IF SPECIFIED CAUSES WERE ELIMINATED

Age (x)	No Causes	Respiratory T.B.	Other Infec. and Paras.	Neoplasms	Cardiovascular	Infl., Pneu., Bronch.	Diarrheal	Certain Degenerative	Maternal	Cert. Dis. of Infancy	Motor Vehicle	Other Violence	Other and Unknown	(1)+(2)	(1)+(2)+(5)+(6)+(8)	(1)+(2)+(5)+(6)+(8)+part of(9)&(12)	(10)+(11)	Age (x)
		(1)	(2)	(3)	(4)	(5)	(6)	(7)	(8)	(9)	(10)	(11)	(12)					
0	100000	100000	100000	100000	100000	100000	100000	100000	100000	100000	100000	100000	100000	100000	100000	100000	100000	0
1	96622	96626	96718	96636	96628	97124	96750	96628	96622	98456	96622	96750	97246	96722	97353	99404	96750	1
5	96067	96081	96284	96130	96078	96660	96210	96082	96067	97891	96116	96263	96820	96298	97036	99159	96312	5
10	95750	95768	96007	95854	95771	96360	95896	95775	95750	97569	95857	96012	96563	96025	96784	98918	96119	10
15	95478	95499	95760	95620	95520	96098	95623	95512	95478	97292	95626	95789	96361	95781	96550	98694	95938	15
20	95056	95099	95373	95238	95128	95698	95204	95106	95056	96862	95289	95454	96012	95416	96209	98365	95687	20
25	94417	94539	94759	94654	94540	95081	94566	94499	94417	96211	94792	94953	95446	94882	95699	97863	95330	25
30	93724	93974	94085	94030	93921	94411	93874	93846	93724	95505	94191	94280	94830	94336	95180	97359	94872	30
35	92905	93298	93300	93322	93223	93629	93058	93082	92905	94670	93436	93713	94096	93695	94580	96776	94249	35
40	91844	92382	92271	92462	92370	92633	92002	92096	91844	93589	92418	92776	93141	92811	93770	95981	93356	40
45	90210	90921	90667	91175	91153	91128	90373	90566	90210	91924	90828	91283	91643	91382	92478	94700	91908	45
50	87380	88300	87869	88588	89155	88600	87548	87898	87380	89040	88031	88606	89024	88794	90207	92439	89267	50
55	82544	83735	83070	85282	85873	84335	82719	83276	82544	84112	83207	83927	84473	84268	86284	88513	84601	55
60	75166	76590	75743	79453	80983	77945	75346	76150	75166	76594	75816	76644	77487	77179	80224	82441	77307	60
65	64309	65886	64920	70321	73978	68493	64486	65535	64309	65531	64932	65821	67064	66512	71034	73198	66459	65
70	50533	52056	51115	57940	65204	55987	50700	51947	50533	51493	51073	51939	53622	52656	58533	60539	52494	70
75	34883	36070	35362	42568	54791	40977	35028	36275	34883	35546	35305	36034	38077	36565	43132	44852	36470	75
80	19159	19866	19465	25350	42424	24667	19263	20221	19159	19523	19434	19962	22014	20183	26127	27419	20248	80
85+	7281	7564	7415	10581	28867	10807	7340	7840	7281	7419	7407	7695	9292	7703	11526	12318	7828	85+

ADDED YRS OF LIFE

	(1)	(2)	(3)	(4)	(5)	(6)	(7)	(8)	(9)	(10)	(11)	(12)				
TOTAL	.550	.343	2.171	6.842	1.951	.131	.460	.000	1.248	.355	.740	1.548	.898	3.063	4.848	1.101
WORK	3.699 .324	.090	.679	.900	.352	.014	.187	.000	.000	.198	.342	.338	.416	.789	.879	.542

POPULATION, DEATHS, DEATH RATES FOR ALL CAUSES COMBINED, AND SPECIFIED CAUSES

Age Start of Interval	Midyear Population	Deaths During Year	All Causes	Respiratory T.B.	Other Infec. and Paras.	Neo-plasms	Cardio-vascular	Infl., Pneu., Bronch.	Diar-rheal	Certain Degen-erative	Maternal	Cert. Dis. of Infancy	Motor Vehicle	Other Violence	Other and Unknown	Age Start of Interval
0	321194	8450	.02631	.00005	.00097	.00012	.00004	.00425	.00095	.00007	.00000	.01332	.00000	.00098	.00558	0
1	1494010	1876	.00126	.00002	.00031	.00012	.00001	.00025	.00003	.00002	.00000	.00000	.00008	.00014	.00028	1
5	1546494	699	.00045	.00001	.00008	.00007	.00003	.00004	.00000	.00002	.00000	.00000	.00005	.00005	.00012	5
10	1384185	516	.00037	.00001	.00006	.00005	.00005	.00003	.00000	.00002	.00000	.00000	.00002	.00002	.00005	10
15	1370018	880	.00064	.00011	.00008	.00006	.00008	.00004	.00001	.00004	.00001	.00000	.00002	.00002	.00005	15
20	1501155	1332	.00089	.00028	.00005	.00009	.00011	.00004	.00001	.00005	.00006	.00000	.00004	.00005	.00012	20
25	1655103	1904	.00115	.00035	.00005	.00014	.00015	.00007	.00002	.00004	.00008	.00000	.00002	.00005	.00012	25
30	1565546	2294	.00147	.00035	.00004	.00027	.00025	.00009	.00001	.00007	.00008	.00000	.00002	.00006	.00017	30
35	1691714	3237	.00191	.00026	.00005	.00055	.00037	.00013	.00001	.00009	.00008	.00000	.00002	.00007	.00024	35
40	1708391	4601	.00269	.00021	.00005	.00094	.00063	.00017	.00002	.00013	.00003	.00000	.00003	.00011	.00038	40
45	1616760	6916	.00428	.00020	.00008	.00153	.00122	.00029	.00002	.00018	.00001	.00000	.00003	.00018	.00053	45
50	1507818	9729	.00645	.00019	.00010	.00227	.00215	.00049	.00003	.00028	.00001	.00000	.00003	.00018	.00070	50
55	1334532	13548	.01015	.00018	.00011	.00321	.00394	.00099	.00005	.00039	.00000	.00000	.00005	.00025	.00099	55
60	1204768	19732	.01638	.00013	.00013	.00425	.00754	.00180	.00008	.00069	.00000	.00000	.00006	.00030	.00134	60
65	1049430	29335	.02795	.00020	.00016	.00594	.01465	.00340	.00012	.00109	.00000	.00000	.00009	.00042	.00207	65
70	837145	40336	.04818	.00020	.00018	.00761	.02816	.00635	.00020	.00155	.00000	.00000	.00011	.00070	.00312	70
75	549528	46839	.08523	.00018	.00019	.01022	.05288	.01185	.00028	.00216	.00000	.00000	.00019	.00139	.00591	75
80	281413	40563	.14414	.00011	.00021	.01231	.09299	.02012	.00045	.00258	.00000	.00000	.00023	.00306	.01207	80
85+	137054	34869	.25442	.00004	.00050	.01361	.16259	.03731	.00074	.00277	.00001	.00000	.00015	.00674	.02996	85+
ALL	22756258	267656														

	All Causes	Respiratory T.B.	Other Infec. and Paras.	Neo-plasms	Cardio-vascular	Infl., Pneu., Bronch.	Diar-rheal	Certain Degen-erative	Maternal	Cert. Dis. of Infancy	Motor Vehicle	Other Violence	Other and Unknown
CRUDE DEATH RATE	.01176	.00018	.00011	.00186	.00610	.00148	.00006	.00033	.00002	.00019	.00005	.00027	.00110
STANDARDIZED RATE (1)	.00493	.00015	.00013	.00077	.00178	.00060	.00006	.00014	.00002	.00047	.00005	.00015	.00061
STANDARDIZED RATE (2)	.00932	.00017	.00012	.00145	.00461	.00117	.00006	.00026	.00002	.00028	.00005	.00015	.00061
GEOMETRIC MEAN	.00596	.00017	.00012	.00145	.00461	.00117	.00006	.00026	.00002	.00028	.00005	.00023	.00091

LIFE TABLE FOR ALL CAUSES COMBINED

Age (x)	Midyear Population	Deaths During Year	$_nM_x$	$_nq_x$	l_x	$_nd_x$	$_nL_x$	$_nm_x$	$_na_x$	T_x	$_nr_x$	$\overset{\circ}{e}_x$	Age (x)
0	321194	8450	.026308	.025710	100000	2571	97724	.026309	.114724	7094734	.000000	70.947	0
1	1494010	1876	.001256	.005009	97429	488	388456	.001256	1.500000	6997010	.000000	71.816	1
5	1546494	699	.000452	.002249	96941	218	484160	.000450	2.500000	6608514	.000000	68.170	5
10	1384185	516	.000373	.001871	96723	181	483181	.000375	2.604742	6124354	.011985	63.318	10
15	1370018	880	.000642	.003201	96542	309	481988	.000641	2.664509	5641172	-.001270	58.432	15
20	1501155	1332	.000887	.004416	96233	425	480152	.000885	2.617647	5159184	-.017843	53.611	20
25	1655103	1904	.001150	.005730	95808	549	477724	.001149	2.602838	4679031	-.009048	48.838	25
30	1565546	2294	.001465	.007306	95259	696	474628	.001466	2.604765	4201308	-.003200	44.104	30
35	1691714	3237	.001913	.009507	94563	899	470684	.001910	2.625079	3726680	-.010924	39.409	35
40	1708391	4601	.002693	.013378	93664	1253	465408	.002692	2.676244	3255996	-.002276	34.763	40
45	1616760	6916	.004278	.021199	92411	1959	457496	.004282	2.673026	2790588	-.004933	30.198	45
50	1507818	9729	.006452	.031840	90452	2880	445559	.006464	2.673177	2333091	.010609	25.794	50
55	1334532	13548	.010152	.049708	87572	4353	427747	.010177	2.676890	1887533	.012467	21.554	55
60	1204768	19732	.016378	.079020	83219	6576	400846	.016405	2.681088	1459785	-.008214	17.541	60
65	1049430	29335	.027953	.131375	76643	10069	359677	.027995	2.662297	1058939	-.006412	13.817	65
70	837145	40336	.048183	.216601	66574	14420	298565	.048298	2.621012	699263	.010718	10.504	70
75	549528	46839	.085235	.353664	52154	18445	215361	.085651	2.538131	400698	.018738	7.683	75
80	281413	40563	.144140	.527930	33709	17796	122790	.144930	2.428917	185337	.018738	5.498	80
85+	137054	34869	.254418	1.000000	15913	15913	62547	.254418	3.930540	62547	.000000	3.931	85+

NUMBER OF PERSONS DYING (OUT OF 100,000 AT BIRTH) ABOVE AGE X FROM SPECIFIED CAUSES

Age (x)	All Causes	Respiratory T.B.	Other Infec. and Paras.	Neoplasms	Cardiovascular	Infl., Pneu., Bronch.	Diarrheal	Certain Degenerative	Maternal	Cert. Dis. of Infancy	Motor Vehicle	Other Violence	Other and Unknown	Age (x)
0	100000	1268	824	14801	53831	12803	486	2708	167	1303	369	2250	9190	0
1	97429	1263	729	14790	53826	12398	394	2702	167	1	369	2154	8646	1
5	96941	1255	610	14743	53821	12289	382	2695	167	0	339	2101	8539	5
10	96723	1251	573	14712	53808	12271	380	2687	167	0	313	2079	8482	10
15	96542	1245	544	14688	53782	12259	380	2673	167	0	303	2068	8433	15
20	96233	1193	503	14658	53744	12242	377	2652	161	0	280	2048	8375	20
25	95808	1061	481	14613	53694	12222	372	2629	134	0	262	2024	8316	25
30	95259	895	455	14546	53621	12191	365	2609	95	0	252	1995	8235	30
35	94563	730	434	14416	53502	12146	360	2575	62	0	244	1961	8133	35
40	93664	608	412	14159	53327	12084	353	2532	22	0	235	1915	8017	40
45	92411	508	389	13722	53032	12006	342	2472	8	0	223	1866	7843	45
50	90452	416	351	13022	52475	11871	331	2389	3	0	208	1784	7602	50
55	87572	334	306	12010	51513	11652	320	2265	2	0	192	1690	7288	55
60	83219	257	260	10636	49823	11228	297	2096	2	0	171	1584	6865	60
65	76643	184	210	8930	46795	10506	264	1818	2	0	147	1462	6325	65
70	66574	113	152	6864	41515	9282	222	1424	1	0	114	1310	5577	70
75	52154	54	98	4589	33085	7380	163	961	1	0	80	1099	4644	75
80	33709	16	57	2383	21638	4816	102	494	1	0	39	799	3364	80
85+	15913	2	31	851	10169	2334	47	173	0	0	10	422	1874	85+

NUMBER OF PERSONS SURVIVING TO AGE X IF SPECIFIED CAUSES WERE ELIMINATED

Age (x)	No Causes	Respiratory T.B.	Other Infec. and Paras.	Neoplasms	Cardiovascular	Infl., Pneu., Bronch.	Diarrheal	Certain Degenerative	Maternal	Cert. Dis. of Infancy	Motor Vehicle	Other Violence	Other and Unknown	(1)+(2)	(1)+(2)+(5)+(6)+(8)	(1)+(2)+(5)+(6)+(8)+part of(9)&(12)	(10)+(11)	Age (x)
		(1)	(2)	(3)	(4)	(5)	(6)	(7)	(8)	(9)	(10)	(11)	(12)					
0	100000	100000	100000	100000	100000	100000	100000	100000	100000	100000	100000	100000	100000	100000	100000	100000	100000	0
1	97429	97434	97523	97440	97434	97839	97520	97435	97429	98723	97429	97524	97967	97528	98030	99577	97524	1
5	96941	96954	97153	96999	96951	97449	97043	96954	96941	98229	96971	97088	97584	97166	97778	99390	97118	5
10	96723	96740	96972	96812	96746	97248	96827	96744	96723	98008	96779	96892	97422	96989	97620	99251	96948	10
15	96542	96565	96819	96654	96591	97078	96646	96577	96542	97825	96608	96722	97289	96842	97484	99132	96787	15
20	96233	96308	96551	96320	96320	96784	96340	96289	96239	97512	96432	97036	96626	97292	97965	98965	96521	20
25	95808	96014	96146	95994	95944	96377	95919	95886	95841	97081	95914	96030	96667	96353	97071	98773	96137	25
30	95259	95630	95621	95511	95467	95855	95376	95357	95331	96525	95374	95509	96194	95994	96787	98532	95625	30
35	94563	95097	94944	94943	94889	95200	94685	94694	94667	95820	94686	94845	95554	95479	96352	98138	94968	35
40	93664	94315	94063	94298	94162	94357	93791	93807	93807	94909	93794	93989	94802	94716	95693	97505	94120	40
45	92411	93153	92828	93475	93197	93173	92548	92641	92566	93639	92552	92781	93709	93573	94642	96472	92922	45
50	90452	91270	90898	92196	91779	91333	90597	90760	90609	91654	90604	90895	91965	91719	92921	94759	91049	50
55	87572	88445	88048	90281	89823	88643	87723	87992	87725	88789	87735	88094	89351	88926	90325	92157	88259	55
60	83219	84124	83716	87184	87066	84656	83285	83784	83364	84325	83395	83819	85331	84627	86410	88226	83996	60
65	76643	77548	77149	82025	83287	78675	76827	77432	76776	77661	76828	77313	79121	78060	80462	82233	77500	65
70	66574	67426	67068	73332	77898	69520	66773	67631	66691	67459	66765	67299	69448	67926	71269	72953	67493	70
75	52154	52874	52588	59691	70398	56245	52362	53397	52246	52847	52334	52911	55270	53314	57827	59337	53093	75
80	33709	34204	34022	40626	59674	38625	33892	34892	33768	34157	33858	34443	36824	34522	39842	41078	34595	80
85+	15913	16156	16078	20459	45697	20246	16037	16696	15942	16124	16003	16520	18511	16324	20968	21835	16613	85+

ADDED YRS OF LIFE																		
TOTAL		.427	.321	2.249	8.740	1.574	.126	.380	.070	.941	.109	.391	1.542	.750	2.566	4.049	.501	
WORK	2.536	.281	.072	.654	.623	.172	.018	.110	.054	.000	.036	.100	.306	.354	.600	.696	.136	

POPULATION, DEATHS, DEATH RATES FOR ALL CAUSES COMBINED, AND SPECIFIED CAUSES

Age Start of Interval	Midyear Population	Deaths During Year	All Causes	Respiratory T. B.	Other Infec. and Paras.	Neo-plasms	Cardio-vascular	Infl., Pneu., Bronch.	Diar-rheal	Certain Degen-erative	Maternal	Cert. Dis. of Infancy	Motor Vehicle	Other Violence	Other and Unknown	Age Start of Interval
0	381000	9911	.02601	.00000	.00023	.00011	.00010	.00308	.00047	.00004	.00000	.01495	.00002	.00070	.00632	0
1	1439000	1362	.00095	.00000	.00005	.00011	.00001	.00020	.00004	.00001	.00000	.00000	.00008	.00016	.00029	1
5	1664000	881	.00053	.00000	.00002	.00011	.00002	.00004	.00000	.00002	.00000	.00000	.00010	.00011	.00011	5
10	1879000	722	.00038	.00000	.00001	.00006	.00002	.00002	.00000	.00001	.00000	.00000	.00006	.00010	.00009	10
15	1560000	1405	.00090	.00000	.00001	.00008	.00004	.00004	.00001	.00003	.00000	.00000	.00041	.00016	.00012	15
20	1482000	1669	.00113	.00000	.00002	.00013	.00007	.00002	.00001	.00004	.00000	.00000	.00046	.00028	.00010	20
25	1446000	1460	.00101	.00001	.00001	.00017	.00011	.00004	.00001	.00006	.00000	.00000	.00023	.00025	.00012	25
30	1494000	1809	.00121	.00002	.00002	.00023	.00024	.00006	.00000	.00007	.00000	.00000	.00017	.00026	.00013	30
35	1646000	3137	.00191	.00005	.00003	.00040	.00059	.00008	.00001	.00011	.00000	.00000	.00015	.00029	.00018	35
40	1451000	4307	.00297	.00006	.00003	.00072	.00113	.00017	.00001	.00013	.00000	.00000	.00015	.00032	.00024	40
45	1615000	8331	.00516	.00010	.00005	.00144	.00217	.00030	.00002	.00019	.00000	.00000	.00016	.00039	.00033	45
50	1565000	14452	.00923	.00014	.00007	.00267	.00410	.00073	.00003	.00031	.00000	.00000	.00018	.00045	.00056	50
55	1387000	23225	.01674	.00026	.00010	.00491	.00747	.00170	.00005	.00052	.00000	.00000	.00021	.00057	.00097	55
60	1064000	29251	.02749	.00035	.00013	.00766	.01286	.00332	.00005	.00073	.00000	.00000	.00024	.00064	.00150	60
65	813000	34626	.04259	.00046	.00024	.01045	.02137	.00534	.00010	.00115	.00000	.00000	.00028	.00068	.00252	65
70	600000	39501	.06583	.00053	.00025	.01351	.03552	.00846	.00023	.00172	.00000	.00000	.00033	.00089	.00438	70
75	395000	39865	.10092	.00050	.00030	.01670	.05803	.01306	.00029	.00243	.00000	.00000	.00054	.00150	.00756	75
80	201000	31445	.15644	.00040	.00030	.01939	.09358	.02061	.00041	.00336	.00000	.00000	.00083	.00300	.01456	80
85+	94000	21813	.23205	.00026	.00035	.01874	.14317	.03112	.00052	.00406	.00000	.00000	.00094	.00471	.02818	85+
ALL	22176000	269172														

	All Causes	Respiratory T. B.	Other Infec. and Paras.	Neo-plasms	Cardio-vascular	Infl., Pneu., Bronch.	Diar-rheal	Certain Degen-erative	Maternal	Cert. Dis. of Infancy	Motor Vehicle	Other Violence	Other and Unknown
CRUDE DEATH RATE	.01214	.00011	.00006	.00241	.00592	.00141	.00005	.00032	.00000	.00026	.00021	.00039	.00100
STANDARDIZED RATE (1)	.00605	.00005	.00005	.00110	.00234	.00067	.00004	.00015	.00000	.00053	.00020	.00028	.00064
STANDARDIZED RATE (2)	.01157	.00009	.00006	.00219	.00562	.00136	.00005	.00030	.00000	.00031	.00022	.00038	.00099
GEOMETRIC MEAN	.00687												

LIFE TABLE FOR ALL CAUSES COMBINED

Age (x)	Midyear Population	Deaths During Year	$_nM_x$	$_nq_x$	l_x	$_nd_x$	$_nL_x$	$_nm_x$	$_na_x$	T_x	$_nr_x$	$\overset{\circ}{e}_x$	Age (x)
0	381000	9911	.026013	.025430	100000	2543	97747	.026016	.114222	6824174	.000000	68.242	0
1	1439000	1362	.000946	.003776	97457	368	388908	.000946	1.500000	6726427	.000000	69.019	1
5	1664000	881	.000529	.002637	97089	256	484805	.000528	2.500000	6337519	.000000	65.275	5
10	1879000	722	.000384	.001921	96833	186	483737	.000385	2.701613	5852714	.000850	60.441	10
15	1560000	1405	.000901	.004511	96647	436	482219	.000904	2.669629	5368976	.020472	55.552	15
20	1482000	1669	.001126	.005623	96211	541	479712	.001128	2.517329	4886757	.010620	50.792	20
25	1446000	1460	.001010	.005028	95670	481	477154	.001008	2.514293	4407045	.003937	46.065	25
30	1494000	1809	.001211	.006030	95189	574	474597	.001209	2.650987	3929891	-.012644	41.285	30
35	1646000	3137	.001906	.009481	94615	897	471001	.001904	2.687663	3455294	-.002509	36.520	35
40	1451000	4307	.002968	.014746	93718	1382	465437	.002969	2.718584	2984294	.001216	31.843	40
45	1615000	8331	.005159	.025418	92336	2347	456372	.005143	2.738425	2518856	-.012364	27.279	45
50	1565000	14452	.009235	.045206	89989	4068	440734	.009230	2.735630	2062484	-.001403	22.919	50
55	1387000	23225	.016745	.080865	85921	6948	413520	.016802	2.684945	1621751	.014964	18.875	55
60	1064000	29251	.027492	.129614	78973	10236	370601	.027620	2.629506	1208231	.024609	15.299	60
65	813000	34626	.042590	.193651	68737	13311	311549	.042725	2.585769	837630	.017413	12.186	65
70	600000	39501	.065835	.283549	55426	15716	238395	.065924	2.535288	526081	.007235	9.492	70
75	395000	39865	.100924	.402241	39710	15973	158087	.101040	2.466767	287686	.005616	7.245	75
80	201000	31445	.156443	.554746	23737	13168	84054	.156661	2.370076	129600	.005616	5.460	80
85+	94000	21813	.232053	1.000000	10569	10569	45546	.232053	4.309357	45546	.000000	4.309	85+

NUMBER OF PERSONS DYING (OUT OF 100,000 AT BIRTH) ABOVE AGE X FROM SPECIFIED CAUSES

Age (x)	All Causes	Respiratory T. B.	Other Infec. and Paras.	Neoplasms	Cardiovascular	Infl., Pneu., Bronch.	Diarrheal	Certain Degenerative	Maternal	Cert. Dis. of Infancy	Motor Vehicle	Other Violence	Other and Unknown	Age (x)
0	100000	813	482	19280	50476	11915	348	2570	0	1462	1552	2951	8151	0
1	97457	813	459	19270	50466	11614	301	2566	0	1	1551	2883	7533	1
5	97089	812	440	19227	50461	11537	286	2562	0	1	1521	2822	7420	5
10	96833	812	431	19175	50452	11517	284	2555	0	0	1471	2771	7365	10
15	96647	812	426	19146	50443	11505	283	2548	0	0	1440	2724	7320	15
20	96211	811	422	19107	50424	11485	280	2535	0	0	1242	2644	7261	20
25	95670	811	414	19046	50391	11474	276	2514	0	0	1023	2510	7211	25
30	95189	804	407	18966	50339	11457	272	2485	0	0	913	2390	7156	30
35	94615	792	398	18857	50223	11430	270	2452	0	0	834	2265	7094	35
40	93718	769	384	18670	49945	11391	264	2398	0	0	762	2126	7009	40
45	92336	740	369	18336	49419	11310	258	2337	0	0	694	1978	6895	45
50	89989	694	345	17683	48434	11172	247	2248	0	0	619	1801	6746	50
55	85921	632	316	16508	46630	10850	232	2112	0	0	538	1602	6501	55
60	78973	526	275	14471	43531	10145	210	1895	0	0	453	1368	6099	60
65	68737	396	225	11623	38739	8908	191	1621	0	0	364	1129	5541	65
70	55426	251	150	8362	32056	7238	159	1263	0	0	276	918	4753	70
75	39710	125	90	5138	23574	5217	103	853	0	0	198	707	3705	75
80	23737	46	42	2495	14389	3150	58	468	0	0	113	469	2507	80
85+	10569	12	16	854	6521	1417	24	185	0	0	43	215	1282	85+

NUMBER OF PERSONS SURVIVING TO AGE X IF SPECIFIED CAUSES WERE ELIMINATED

Age (x)	No Causes	Respiratory T. B.	Other Infec. and Paras.	Neoplasms	Cardiovascular	Infl., Pneu., Bronch.	Diarrheal	Certain Degenerative	Maternal	Cert. Dis. of Infancy	Motor Vehicle	Other Violence	Other and Unknown	(1) + (2)	(1) + (2) + (5) + (6) + (8)	(1)+(2)+ (5)+(6)+ (8)+part of(9)&(12)	(10) + (11)	Age (x)
		(1)	(2)	(3)	(4)	(5)	(6)	(7)	(8)	(9)	(10)	(11)	(12)					
0	100000	100000	100000	100000	100000	100000	100000	100000	100000	100000	100000	100000	100000	100000	100000	100000	100000	0
1	97457	97457	97480	97467	97467	97755	97503	97461	97457	98910	97458	97524	98069	97480	97824	99485	97525	1
5	97089	97090	97131	97142	97104	97463	97150	97097	97089	98537	97120	97217	97812	97132	97567	99274	97248	5
10	96833	96834	96883	96938	96857	97226	96896	96848	96833	98278	96914	97012	97610	96884	97341	99053	97092	10
15	96647	96648	96702	96780	96680	97051	96711	96669	96647	98089	96759	96872	97468	96703	97172	98887	96984	15
20	96211	96213	96270	96363	96263	96633	96278	96246	96211	97646	96520	96515	97087	96272	96762	98474	96825	20
25	95670	95672	95737	95902	95754	96101	95740	95725	95670	97097	96157	96107	96592	95739	96240	97946	96636	25
30	95189	95198	95262	95500	95325	95635	95263	95273	95189	96609	95823	95744	96161	95271	95792	97494	96382	30
35	94615	94636	94657	95033	94646	95065	94732	94615	94615	96027	95325	95292	95644	94718	95264	96963	96007	35
40	93718	93762	93813	94319	94244	94223	93759	93887	93718	95116	94493	94528	94823	93857	94443	96137	95310	40
45	92336	92408	92445	93263	93381	92914	92421	92563	92336	93714	93168	93282	93539	92516	93182	94864	94123	45
50	89989	90104	90119	91545	91996	90690	90083	90299	89989	91332	90874	91088	91310	90234	91032	92691	91984	50
55	85921	86092	86073	88582	89658	86908	86026	86350	85921	87203	86846	87167	87426	86244	87341	88960	88105	55
60	78973	79232	79152	83457	85567	80567	79090	79577	78973	80151	79906	80345	80749	79411	81135	82693	81294	60
65	68737	69084	68940	75497	79480	71312	68857	69520	68737	69763	69632	70157	70817	69287	72008	73473	71071	65
70	55426	55836	55657	64164	71411	59077	55551	56383	55426	56253	56228	56764	57836	56098	59896	61235	57585	70
75	39710	40110	39926	49207	61267	44179	39847	40748	39710	40302	40351	40851	42371	40327	45021	46186	41510	75
80	23737	24036	23902	32001	49267	28226	23853	24660	23737	24091	24186	24608	26329	24203	28921	29844	25073	80
85+	10569	10724	10660	15760	35573	13980	10643	11173	10569	10727	10815	11129	12639	10816	14407	15039	11388	85+

ADDED YRS OF LIFE																	
TOTAL		.119	.103	2.677	8.645	1.467	.080	.341	.000	1.016	.457	.689	1.376	.223	1.798	3.157	1.194
WORK	3.114	.044	.029	.691	.989	.193	.013	.115	.000	.000	.310	.318	.228	.073	.281	.303	.631

POPULATION, DEATHS, DEATH RATES FOR ALL CAUSES COMBINED, AND SPECIFIED CAUSES

Age Start of Interval	Midyear Population	Deaths During Year	All Causes	Respiratory T. B.	Other Infec. and Paras.	Neoplasms	Cardio-vascular	Infl., Pneu., Bronch.	Diarrheal	Certain Degen-erative	Maternal	Cert. Dis. of Infancy	Motor Vehicle	Other Violence	Other and Unknown	Age Start of Interval
0	360000	7207	.02002	.00001	.00021	.00011	.00008	.00248	.00034	.00004	.00000	.01061	.00001	.00053	.00560	0
1	1366000	1069	.00078	.00000	.00005	.00010	.00002	.00016	.00003	.00001	.00000	.00000	.00005	.00009	.00027	1
5	1586000	545	.00034	.00000	.00002	.00007	.00001	.00003	.00000	.00001	.00000	.00000	.00005	.00005	.00011	5
10	1797000	467	.00026	.00000	.00001	.00006	.00002	.00001	.00000	.00001	.00000	.00000	.00003	.00003	.00008	10
15	1509000	543	.00036	.00000	.00001	.00006	.00003	.00002	.00001	.00002	.00001	.00000	.00008	.00004	.00009	15
20	1451000	644	.00044	.00000	.00001	.00007	.00005	.00002	.00000	.00003	.00003	.00000	.00006	.00007	.00009	20
25	1414000	858	.00061	.00001	.00001	.00014	.00010	.00002	.00001	.00003	.00005	.00000	.00004	.00008	.00011	25
30	1497000	1280	.00086	.00004	.00001	.00026	.00017	.00003	.00001	.00004	.00005	.00000	.00003	.00009	.00012	30
35	1680000	2263	.00135	.00004	.00002	.00049	.00032	.00005	.00001	.00006	.00004	.00000	.00003	.00012	.00017	35
40	1499000	3241	.00216	.00004	.00003	.00096	.00055	.00009	.00001	.00006	.00002	.00000	.00004	.00015	.00023	40
45	1665000	5721	.00344	.00005	.00003	.00157	.00093	.00014	.00002	.00010	.00000	.00000	.00006	.00020	.00034	45
50	1636000	8627	.00527	.00003	.00004	.00228	.00173	.00023	.00003	.00015	.00000	.00000	.00007	.00024	.00048	50
55	1525000	12250	.00803	.00004	.00005	.00259	.00317	.00043	.00004	.00027	.00000	.00000	.00008	.00031	.00065	55
60	1346000	18053	.01341	.00005	.00008	.00409	.00634	.00082	.00007	.00046	.00000	.00000	.00013	.00035	.00103	60
65	1149000	25736	.02240	.00007	.00011	.00555	.01218	.00149	.00015	.00069	.00000	.00000	.00014	.00047	.00155	65
70	933000	35611	.03817	.00009	.00011	.00717	.02324	.00278	.00021	.00108	.00000	.00000	.00021	.00077	.00251	70
75	676000	45715	.06763	.00010	.00016	.00941	.04392	.00564	.00037	.00165	.00000	.00000	.00028	.00148	.00461	75
80	394000	44545	.11306	.00009	.00019	.01177	.07583	.01038	.00053	.00222	.00000	.00000	.00037	.00306	.00863	80
85+	203000	42721	.21045	.00006	.00030	.01410	.14090	.02188	.00079	.00263	.00000	.00000	.00028	.00655	.02297	85+
ALL	23686000	257096														

	All Causes	Respiratory T. B.	Other Infec. and Paras.	Neoplasms	Cardio-vascular	Infl., Pneu., Bronch.	Diarrheal	Certain Degen-erative	Maternal	Cert. Dis. of Infancy	Motor Vehicle	Other Violence	Other and Unknown
CRUDE DEATH RATE	.01085	.00003	.00005	.00197	.00606	.00087	.00006	.00026	.00001	.00016	.00008	.00033	.00097
STANDARDIZED RATE (1)	.00378	.00002	.00003	.00074	.00146	.00031	.00003	.00009	.00001	.00037	.00006	.00015	.00050
STANDARDIZED RATE (2)	.00732	.00003	.00004	.00139	.00381	.00058	.00005	.00018	.00001	.00022	.00007	.00024	.00071
GEOMETRIC MEAN	.00426												

LIFE TABLE FOR ALL CAUSES COMBINED

Age (x)	Midyear Population	Deaths During Year	$_nM_x$	$_nq_x$	l_x	$_nd_x$	$_nL_x$	$_nm_x$	$_na_x$	T_x	$_nr_x$	$\overset{\circ}{e}_x$	Age (x)
0	360000	7207	.020019	.019670	100000	1967	98238	.020023	.104033	7412655	.000000	74.127	0
1	1366000	1069	.000783	.003121	98033	306	391367	.000782	1.500000	7314418	.000000	74.612	1
5	1586000	545	.000344	.001719	97727	168	488215	.000344	2.500000	6923051	.000000	70.841	5
10	1797000	467	.000260	.001292	97559	126	487482	.000258	2.513228	6434836	.000067	65.558	10
15	1509000	543	.000360	.001806	97433	176	486744	.000362	2.606534	5947354	.018579	61.040	15
20	1451000	644	.000444	.002221	97257	216	485770	.000445	2.613812	5460610	.009961	56.146	20
25	1414000	858	.000607	.003030	97041	294	484511	.000607	2.638180	4974841	.002775	51.265	25
30	1497000	1280	.000855	.004248	96747	411	482781	.000851	2.678427	4490330	-.016033	46.413	30
35	1680000	2263	.001347	.006706	96336	646	480194	.001345	2.699626	4007549	-.005619	41.600	35
40	1499000	3241	.002162	.010764	95690	1030	476076	.002164	2.694984	3527355	.000222	36.862	40
45	1665000	5721	.003436	.017008	94660	1610	469565	.003429	2.680254	3051280	-.011855	32.234	45
50	1636000	8627	.005273	.026040	93050	2423	459603	.005272	2.669298	2581714	-.001446	27.745	50
55	1525000	12250	.008033	.039452	90627	3575	444865	.008045	2.689357	2122112	.007474	23.416	55
60	1346000	18053	.013412	.065205	87048	5676	422114	.013447	2.687160	1677246	.012875	19.268	60
65	1149000	25736	.022399	.106732	81372	8685	386623	.022464	2.665881	1255133	.013332	15.425	65
70	933000	35611	.038168	.175520	72687	12758	333368	.038270	2.643309	868510	.011970	11.949	70
75	676000	45715	.067626	.291361	59929	17461	257242	.067878	2.571552	535141	.015467	8.930	75
80	394000	44545	.113058	.441627	42468	18755	165221	.113515	2.487659	277900	.015467	6.544	80
85+	203000	42721	.210448	1.000000	23713	23713	112679	.210448	4.751761	112679	.000000	4.752	85+

NUMBER OF PERSONS DYING (OUT OF 100,000 AT BIRTH) ABOVE AGE X FROM SPECIFIED CAUSES

Age (x)	All Causes	Respiratory T. B.	Other Infec. and Paras.	Neoplasms	Cardiovascular	Infl., Pneu., Bronch.	Diarrheal	Certain Degenerative	Maternal	Cert. Dis. of Infancy	Motor Vehicle	Other Violence	Other and Unknown	Age (x)
0	100000	250	374	16429	58215	8300	546	2284	95	1043	637	2943	8880	0
1	98033	249	353	16418	58207	8057	513	2280	99	0	636	2891	8330	1
5	97727	248	334	16377	58201	7995	503	2274	99	0	616	2857	8223	5
10	97559	248	324	16343	58197	7981	501	2270	99	0	591	2835	8170	10
15	97433	247	321	16313	58188	7974	499	2264	99	0	575	2819	8134	15
20	97257	246	315	16281	58175	7966	497	2254	95	0	537	2800	8091	20
25	97041	245	309	16248	58149	7956	495	2238	78	0	507	2767	8049	25
30	96747	239	302	16180	58103	7944	490	2224	53	0	487	2727	7998	30
35	96336	220	296	16054	58023	7928	485	2206	28	0	472	2683	7941	35
40	95690	199	288	15818	57871	7902	481	2180	8	0	456	2626	7861	40
45	94660	182	276	15362	57611	7860	475	2151	1	0	435	2556	7751	45
50	93050	158	262	14627	57174	7794	466	2103	0	0	409	2462	7595	50
55	90627	142	244	13580	56381	7690	451	2033	0	0	379	2351	7376	55
60	87048	125	221	12249	54969	7497	432	1912	0	0	343	2213	7087	60
65	81372	104	187	10521	52284	7150	401	1717	0	0	290	2066	6652	65
70	72687	78	145	8371	47559	6573	342	1451	0	0	234	1884	6050	70
75	59929	48	107	5980	39787	5643	272	1090	0	0	165	1628	5209	75
80	42468	22	65	3555	28444	4184	176	664	0	0	93	1246	4019	80
85+	23713	7	33	1589	15877	2465	89	296	0	0	31	738	2588	85+

NUMBER OF PERSONS SURVIVING TO AGE X IF SPECIFIED CAUSES WERE ELIMINATED

Age (x)	No Causes	Respiratory T. B. (1)	Other Infec. and Paras. (2)	Neoplasms (3)	Cardiovascular (4)	Infl., Pneu., Bronch. (5)	Diarrheal (6)	Certain Degenerative (7)	Maternal (8)	Cert. Dis. of Infancy (9)	Motor Vehicle (10)	Other Violence (11)	Other and Unknown (12)	(1)+(2)	(1)+(2)+(5)+(6)+(8)	(1)+(2)+(5)+(6)+(8)+part of(9)&(12)	(10)+(11)	Age (x)
0	100000	100000	100000	100000	100000	100000	100000	100000	100000	100000	100000	100000	100000	100000	100000	100000	100000	0
1	98033	98034	98054	98044	98041	98274	98066	98037	98033	99071	98034	98084	98579	98055	98328	99597	98085	1
5	97727	97729	97767	97779	97741	98029	97770	97737	97727	98762	97748	97812	98379	97769	98114	99430	97833	5
10	97559	97561	97609	97645	97577	97875	97603	97573	97559	98592	97605	97666	98263	97611	97971	99298	97712	10
15	97433	97436	97486	97549	97449	97755	97479	97453	97433	98465	97495	97556	98172	97489	97858	99188	97618	15
20	97257	97261	97315	97404	97297	97587	97305	97287	97261	98287	97357	97399	98038	97319	97702	99037	97499	20
25	97041	97046	97105	97221	97107	97380	97091	97087	97062	98069	97171	97216	97863	97110	97521	98862	97345	25
30	96747	96758	96818	96995	96858	97097	96802	96807	96793	97772	96896	96961	97618	96829	97281	98631	97110	30
35	96336	96366	96413	96709	96527	96701	96396	96413	96407	97356	96499	96593	97260	96443	96939	98295	96757	35
40	95690	95741	95774	96297	96032	96078	95753	95793	95780	96703	95868	96002	96685	95825	96368	97728	96181	40
45	94660	94727	94755	95718	95258	95086	94729	94791	94756	95662	94857	95039	95759	94822	95415	96772	95237	45
50	93050	93140	93158	94829	94075	93534	93126	93226	93145	94035	93270	93516	94287	93247	93906	95254	93737	50
55	90627	90730	90750	93419	92420	91202	90716	90868	90720	91587	90871	91191	92051	90853	91613	92943	91436	55
60	87048	87164	87188	91083	90194	87791	87152	87398	87137	87970	87317	87726	88703	87304	88245	89549	87997	60
65	81372	81500	81536	86908	87048	82406	81500	81889	81455	82234	81675	82149	83349	81665	82917	84178	82455	65
70	72687	72826	72873	79826	82687	74165	72857	73402	72762	73011	73554	75037	73013	74748	75936	73882	70	70
75	59929	60071	60117	68228	76690	62015	60133	60849	59990	60564	60259	60879	62658	60259	62633	63701	61214	75
80	42468	42590	42636	50658	67985	45231	42653	43482	42512	42918	42762	43469	45457	42759	45829	46720	43769	80
85+	23713	23792	23831	30092	56094	26641	23903	24558	23737	23964	23923	24658	26536	23910	27106	27765	24876	85+

ADDED YRS OF LIFE

	No Causes	(1)	(2)	(3)	(4)	(5)	(6)	(7)	(8)	(9)	(10)	(11)	(12)				
TOTAL		.057	.094	2.618	11.079	.987	.093	.300	.045	.784	.169	.465	1.478	.152	1.292	2.421	.636
WORK	1.842	.026	.022	.656	.493	.079	.013	.065	.033	.000	.063	.125	.205	.048	.173	.200	.189

POPULATION, DEATHS, DEATH RATES FOR ALL CAUSES COMBINED, AND SPECIFIED CAUSES

Age Start of Interval	Midyear Population	Deaths During Year	All Causes	Respiratory T.B.	Other Infec. and Paras.	Neoplasms	Cardiovascular	Infl., Pneu., Bronch.	Diarrheal	Certain Degenerative	Maternal	Cert. Dis. of Infancy	Motor Vehicle	Other Violence	Other and Unknown	Age Start of Interval
0	433000	10011	.02312	.00000	.00022	.00009	.00008	.00254	.00048	.00004	.00000	.01244	.00002	.00087	.00594	0
1	1624000	1414	.00087	.00000	.00004	.00011	.00001	.00013	.00004	.00001	.00000	.00000	.00009	.00016	.00026	1
5	1764000	808	.00046	.00000	.00001	.00010	.00001	.00003	.00000	.00001	.00000	.00000	.00010	.00005	.00011	5
10	1695000	687	.00041	.00000	.00000	.00007	.00002	.00002	.00002	.00001	.00000	.00000	.00010	.00005	.00011	10
15	1895000	1859	.00098	.00000	.00001	.00009	.00004	.00004	.00000	.00002	.00000	.00000	.00008	.00011	.00010	15
20	1543000	1691	.00110	.00000	.00001	.00011	.00007	.00003	.00001	.00003	.00000	.00000	.00043	.00028	.00012	20
25	1516000	1509	.00100	.00000	.00001	.00016	.00013	.00009	.00000	.00004	.00000	.00000	.00023	.00027	.00012	25
30	1512000	1800	.00119	.00003	.00001	.00023	.00024	.00004	.00001	.00005	.00000	.00000	.00017	.00027	.00015	30
35	1542000	2859	.00185	.00003	.00001	.00039	.00061	.00008	.00001	.00008	.00000	.00000	.00015	.00033	.00017	35
40	1707000	5168	.00303	.00004	.00003	.00074	.00122	.00014	.00002	.00013	.00000	.00000	.00016	.00032	.00023	40
45	1416000	7452	.00526	.00007	.00004	.00133	.00239	.00032	.00002	.00017	.00000	.00000	.00016	.00040	.00037	45
50	1553000	14311	.00922	.00010	.00005	.00266	.00429	.00070	.00002	.00023	.00000	.00000	.00020	.00042	.00055	50
55	1456000	23656	.01625	.00014	.00008	.00477	.00765	.00157	.00004	.00042	.00000	.00000	.00020	.00053	.00086	55
60	1231000	33677	.02736	.00023	.00011	.00766	.01302	.00334	.00008	.00064	.00000	.00000	.00025	.00063	.00141	60
65	853000	36448	.04273	.00032	.00016	.01115	.02059	.00579	.00012	.00094	.00000	.00000	.00024	.00065	.00237	65
70	614000	39808	.06483	.00042	.00023	.01429	.03384	.00920	.00017	.00146	.00000	.00000	.00039	.00085	.00398	70
75	390000	38597	.09897	.00045	.00027	.01743	.05407	.01536	.00024	.00228	.00000	.00000	.00061	.00143	.00682	75
80	204000	30203	.14805	.00035	.00036	.02036	.08488	.02325	.00042	.00278	.00000	.00000	.00087	.00253	.01224	80
85+	98000	22815	.23281	.00039	.00031	.02069	.13893	.03757	.00076	.00383	.00000	.00000	.00096	.00500	.02438	85+
ALL	23046000	274773														

	All Causes	Respiratory T.B.	Other Infec. and Paras.	Neoplasms	Cardiovascular	Infl., Pneu., Bronch.	Diarrheal	Certain Degenerative	Maternal	Cert. Dis. of Infancy	Motor Vehicle	Other Violence	Other and Unknown
CRUDE DEATH RATE	.01192	.00007	.00005	.00247	.00572	.00152	.00005	.00027	.00000	.00023	.00023	.00039	.00092
STANDARDIZED RATE (1)	.00587	.00004	.00004	.00112	.00230	.00069	.00004	.00012	.00000	.00000	.00023	.00039	.00092
STANDARDIZED RATE (2)	.01133	.00007	.00005	.00225	.00543	.00148	.00004	.00025	.00000	.00044	.00021	.00029	.00060
GEOMETRIC MEAN	.00674	.00004	.00005	.00225	.00543	.00148	.00004	.00025	.00000	.00026	.00026	.00023	.00091

LIFE TABLE FOR ALL CAUSES COMBINED

Age (x)	Midyear Population	Deaths During Year	$_nM_x$	$_nq_x$	l_x	$_nd_x$	$_nL_x$	$_nm_x$	$_na_x$	T_x	$_nr_x$	$\overset{\circ}{e}_x$	Age (x)
0	433000	10011	.023120	.022650	100000	2265	97983	.023116	.109304	6856617	.000000	68.566	0
1	1624000	1414	.000871	.003479	97735	340	390090	.000872	1.500000	6758634	.000000	69.153	1
5	1764000	808	.000458	.002290	97395	223	486418	.000458	2.500000	6368544	.000000	65.389	5
10	1695000	687	.000405	.002027	97172	197	485420	.000406	2.765440	5882127	-.008083	60.533	10
15	1895000	1859	.000981	.004888	96975	474	483759	.000980	2.645482	5396707	.001478	55.650	15
20	1543000	1691	.001096	.005471	96501	528	481185	.001097	2.500789	4912948	.020256	50.911	20
25	1516000	1509	.000995	.004960	95973	476	478683	.000994	2.517069	4431763	.005535	46.177	25
30	1512000	1800	.001190	.005937	95497	567	476150	.001191	2.646238	3953080	.001838	41.395	30
35	1542000	2859	.001854	.009207	94930	874	472641	.001849	2.701897	3476929	-.013656	36.626	35
40	1707000	5168	.003028	.015034	94056	1414	467066	.003027	2.726750	3004288	.000246	31.941	40
45	1416000	7452	.005263	.026047	92642	2413	457729	.005272	2.728536	2537222	.006631	27.387	45
50	1553000	14311	.009215	.045008	90229	4061	441895	.009190	2.722287	2079493	-.010650	23.047	50
55	1456000	23656	.016247	.078289	86168	6746	415262	.016245	2.690823	1637598	-.000946	19.005	55
60	1231000	33677	.027357	.128932	79422	10240	372908	.027460	2.636515	1222336	.018785	15.390	60
65	853000	36448	.042729	.194501	69182	13456	313389	.042937	2.583157	849428	.026531	12.278	65
70	614000	39808	.064834	.280139	55726	15611	240111	.065016	2.532549	536039	.015212	9.619	70
75	390000	38597	.098967	.396236	40115	15895	160280	.099170	2.464939	295928	.010223	7.377	75
80	204000	30203	.148054	.534104	24220	12936	87178	.148385	2.377731	135648	.010223	5.601	80
85+	98000	22815	.232806	1.000000	11284	11284	48470	.232806	4.295420	48470	.000000	4.295	85+

NUMBER OF PERSONS DYING (OUT OF 100,000 AT BIRTH) ABOVE AGE X FROM SPECIFIED CAUSES

Age (x)	All Causes	Respiratory T.B.	Other Infec. and Paras.	Neoplasms	Cardiovascular	Infl., Pneu., Bronch.	Diarrheal	Certain Degenerative	Maternal	Cert. Dis. of Infancy	Motor Vehicle	Other Violence	Other and Unknown	Age (x)
0	100000	589	393	20110	49740	13247	346	2217	0	1221	1627	2949	7561	0
1	97735	589	371	20101	49732	12960	298	2213	0	2	1625	2864	6980	1
5	97395	588	355	20058	49728	12907	282	2208	0	0	1590	2801	6878	5
10	97172	588	348	20010	49725	12892	280	2203	0	0	1541	2760	6825	10
15	96975	588	345	19978	49717	12882	280	2198	0	0	1503	2708	6776	15
20	96501	587	342	19936	49698	12863	278	2188	0	0	1266	2625	6718	20
25	95973	585	337	19881	49664	12847	276	2172	0	0	1062	2490	6659	25
30	95497	584	333	19802	49602	12832	274	2153	0	0	950	2360	6607	30
35	94930	577	327	19694	49486	12812	269	2129	0	0	869	2230	6537	35
40	94056	563	321	19511	49197	12777	265	2094	0	0	798	2075	6455	40
45	92642	546	308	19164	48625	12713	256	2035	0	0	725	1925	6345	45
50	90229	515	291	18552	47530	12565	246	1958	0	0	651	1742	6179	50
55	86168	469	269	17380	45641	12258	237	1857	0	0	565	1556	5936	55
60	79422	410	236	15399	42466	11608	220	1685	0	0	483	1337	5578	60
65	69182	324	196	12535	37592	10357	190	1445	0	0	391	1103	5049	65
70	55726	223	145	9028	30579	8533	153	1147	0	0	315	899	4304	70
75	40115	122	89	5590	22828	6317	113	795	0	0	222	695	3344	75
80	24220	50	46	2794	14142	3849	73	429	0	0	123	464	2250	80
85+	11284	19	15	1003	6734	1821	37	185	0	0	46	242	1182	85+

NUMBER OF PERSONS SURVIVING TO AGE X IF SPECIFIED CAUSES WERE ELIMINATED

Age (x)	No Causes	Respiratory T.B. (1)	Other Infec. and Paras. (2)	Neoplasms (3)	Cardiovascular (4)	Infl., Pneu., Bronch. (5)	Diarrheal (6)	Certain Degenerative (7)	Maternal (8)	Cert. Dis. of Infancy (9)	Motor Vehicle (10)	Other Violence (11)	Other and Unknown (12)	(1)+(2)	(1)+(2)+(5)+(6)+(8)	(1)+(2)+(5)+(6)+(8)+part of(9)&(12)	(10)+(11)	Age (x)
0	100000	100000	100000	100000	100000	100000	100000	100000	100000	100000	100000	100000	100000	100000	100000	100000	100000	0
1	97735	97735	97757	97144	97743	98019	97782	97739	97735	98548	97737	97819	98311	97757	98089	99469	97821	1
5	97395	97396	97433	97447	97407	97731	97458	97404	97395	98605	97432	97542	98072	97434	97834	99249	97579	5
10	97172	97173	97217	97272	97187	97522	97237	97186	97172	98380	97258	97359	97900	97218	97634	99054	97445	10
15	96975	96976	97022	97106	96958	97335	97040	96994	96975	98180	97099	97214	97751	97023	97449	98871	97338	15
20	96501	96503	96551	96674	96543	96878	96568	96530	96501	97700	96861	96822	97332	96553	96997	98417	97183	20
25	95973	95977	96028	96200	96048	96364	96041	96018	95973	97166	96535	96427	96859	96032	96492	97907	96993	25
30	95497	95502	95556	95802	95634	95901	95567	95560	95497	96684	96169	96080	96430	95561	96035	97446	96756	30
35	94930	94942	94994	95241	95182	95352	95005	95017	94930	96110	95679	95640	95928	95006	95503	96912	96395	35
40	94056	94082	94126	94646	94555	94509	94134	94177	94056	95225	94870	94915	95128	94151	94683	96086	95736	40
45	92642	92684	92724	93571	93745	93152	92728	92820	92642	93793	93517	93638	93808	92766	93363	94755	94522	45
50	90229	90301	90325	91146	92404	90873	90322	90478	90229	91350	91154	91381	91531	90397	91136	92510	92319	50
55	86168	86281	86281	88789	90156	87086	86266	86505	86168	87239	87137	87453	87652	86395	87414	88757	88436	55
60	79422	79583	79558	83820	86348	80902	79529	79898	79422	80409	80394	80819	81140	79720	81314	82605	81808	60
65	69182	69403	69338	75884	80324	71671	69303	69822	69182	70042	70115	70620	71184	69559	72188	73410	71573	65
70	55726	55954	55857	64661	71962	55450	55856	56512	55726	56419	56547	57071	58031	56167	60061	61194	57911	70
75	40115	40394	40286	50023	61514	44842	40243	40983	40115	40614	40786	41259	42629	40565	45490	46504	41949	75
80	24220	24443	24356	32578	48557	29284	24328	25033	24220	24521	24702	25095	26651	24580	29852	30707	25595	80
85+	11284	11409	11368	17078	35323	15379	11358	11832	11284	11424	11561	11846	13225	11494	15768	16404	12137	85+

ADDED YRS OF LIFE

	No Causes	(1)	(2)	(3)	(4)	(5)	(6)	(7)	(8)	(9)	(10)	(11)	(12)	(1)+(2)	(1)+(2)+(5)+(6)+(8)	part of(9)&(12)	(10)+(11)
TOTAL		.081	.082	2.772	8.375	1.556	.079	.284	.000	.851	.525	.710	1.309	.163	1.825	2.976	1.244
WORK	3.109	.028	.020	.678	1.042	.183	.011	.085	.000	.000	.324	.327	.229	.047	.242	.261	.654

POPULATION, DEATHS, DEATH RATES FOR ALL CAUSES COMBINED, AND SPECIFIED CAUSES

Age Start of Interval	Midyear Population	Deaths During Year	All Causes	Respiratory T.B.	Other Infec. and Paras.	Neoplasms	Cardiovascular	Infl., Pneu., Bronch.	Diarrheal	Certain Degenerative	Maternal	Cert. Dis. of Infancy	Motor Vehicle	Other Violence	Other and Unknown	Age Start of Interval
0	411000	7434	.01809	.00000	.00018	.00010	.00008	.00220	.00038	.00003	.00000	.00913	.00002	.00068	.00527	0
1	1541000	1138	.00074	.00000	.00005	.00009	.00001	.00014	.00003	.00001	.00000	.00000	.00006	.00011	.00024	1
5	1676000	537	.00032	.00000	.00001	.00007	.00001	.00003	.00000	.00001	.00000	.00000	.00005	.00004	.00009	5
10	1617000	402	.00025	.00000	.00000	.00005	.00002	.00002	.00000	.00001	.00000	.00000	.00004	.00002	.00008	10
15	1813000	723	.00040	.00000	.00001	.00006	.00003	.00003	.00000	.00002	.00001	.00000	.00010	.00005	.00008	15
20	1537000	705	.00046	.00000	.00001	.00004	.00004	.00002	.00000	.00002	.00003	.00000	.00007	.00008	.00010	20
25	1462000	866	.00059	.00000	.00001	.00013	.00009	.00003	.00001	.00002	.00003	.00000	.00004	.00010	.00013	25
30	1433000	1174	.00082	.00001	.00002	.00024	.00015	.00002	.00001	.00003	.00004	.00000	.00004	.00011	.00015	30
35	1507000	1897	.00126	.00002	.00001	.00050	.00025	.00005	.00001	.00003	.00003	.00000	.00004	.00013	.00019	35
40	1706000	3816	.00224	.00003	.00001	.00100	.00053	.00010	.00001	.00006	.00001	.00000	.00004	.00018	.00027	40
45	1459000	5032	.00345	.00002	.00003	.00158	.00094	.00015	.00002	.00010	.00000	.00000	.00000	.00019	.00036	45
50	1642000	8557	.00521	.00003	.00003	.00238	.00161	.00024	.00003	.00013	.00000	.00000	.00007	.00024	.00045	50
55	1574000	12408	.00788	.00003	.00005	.00312	.00291	.00043	.00004	.00023	.00000	.00000	.00007	.00032	.00069	55
60	1419000	18378	.01295	.00003	.00006	.00426	.00585	.00085	.00007	.00036	.00000	.00000	.00010	.00040	.00097	60
65	1207000	25735	.02132	.00004	.00007	.00555	.01117	.00157	.00014	.00063	.00000	.00000	.00015	.00048	.00150	65
70	975000	35782	.03670	.00005	.00009	.00707	.02156	.00318	.00022	.00110	.00000	.00000	.00021	.00076	.00247	70
75	714000	44039	.06168	.00006	.00016	.00912	.03867	.00597	.00035	.00153	.00000	.00000	.00032	.00134	.00416	75
80	421000	45433	.10792	.00010	.00025	.01194	.07003	.01194	.00062	.00207	.00000	.00000	.00034	.00305	.00758	80
85+	241000	45908	.19049	.00006	.00025	.01381	.12490	.02413	.00091	.00240	.00000	.00000	.00027	.00575	.01796	85+
ALL	24355000	259964														

	All Causes	Respiratory T.B.	Other Infec. and Paras.	Neoplasms	Cardiovascular	Infl., Pneu., Bronch.	Diarrheal	Certain Degenerative	Maternal	Cert. Dis. of Infancy	Motor Vehicle	Other Violence	Other and Unknown
CRUDE DEATH RATE	.01067	.00002	.00004	.00202	.00577	.00099	.00007	.00024	.00001	.00015	.00008	.00034	.00093
STANDARDIZED RATE (1)	.00359	.00001	.00003	.00075	.00133	.00031	.00003	.00008	.00001	.00032	.00006	.00016	.00048
STANDARDIZED RATE (2)	.00693	.00002	.00003	.00140	.00347	.00062	.00005	.00016	.00001	.00019	.00007	.00024	.00067
GEOMETRIC MEAN	.00412												

LIFE TABLE FOR ALL CAUSES COMBINED

Age (x)	Midyear Population	Deaths During Year	$_nM_x$	$_nq_x$	l_x	$_nd_x$	$_nL_x$	$_nm_x$	$_na_x$	T_x	$_nr_x$	$\overset{\circ}{e}_x$	Age (x)
0	411000	7434	.018088	.017800	100000	1780	98399	.018090	.100749	7475586	.000000	74.756	0
1	1541000	1138	.000738	.002942	98220	289	392158	.000737	1.500000	7377187	.000000	75.109	1
5	1676000	537	.000320	.001603	97931	157	489263	.000321	2.500000	6985029	.000000	71.326	5
10	1617000	402	.000249	.001248	97774	122	488573	.000250	2.563183	6495767	-.007725	66.437	10
15	1813000	723	.000399	.001987	97652	194	487796	.000398	2.609536	6007194	-.001723	61.516	15
20	1537000	705	.000459	.002298	97458	224	486150	.000460	2.587426	5519398	-.018087	56.634	20
25	1462000	866	.000592	.002962	97234	288	485486	.000593	2.624421	5032648	.010151	51.758	25
30	1433000	1174	.000819	.004085	96946	396	483806	.000819	2.666246	4547162	.002942	46.904	30
35	1507000	1897	.001259	.006256	96550	604	481380	.001255	2.731059	4063356	-.017081	42.086	35
40	1706000	3816	.002237	.011110	95946	1066	477277	.002234	2.699343	3581977	-.003929	37.333	40
45	1459000	5032	.003449	.017116	94880	1624	470617	.003451	2.670618	3104699	.002433	32.722	45
50	1642000	8557	.005211	.025693	93256	2396	460684	.005201	2.664597	2634082	-.012504	28.246	50
55	1574000	12408	.007883	.038708	90860	3517	446155	.007883	2.683987	2173398	.000746	23.920	55
60	1419000	18378	.012951	.062993	87343	5502	423964	.012978	2.682472	1727243	.009790	19.775	60
65	1207000	25735	.021321	.101856	81841	8336	389811	.021385	2.673494	1303279	.014082	15.925	65
70	975000	35782	.036699	.169255	73505	12444	338105	.036805	2.635775	913468	.013411	12.427	70
75	714000	44039	.061679	.269337	61061	16446	265563	.061929	2.583468	575364	.017721	9.423	75
80	421000	45433	.107917	.426605	44615	19033	175505	.108447	2.500646	309801	.017721	6.944	80
85+	241000	45908	.190490	1.000000	25582	25582	134296	.190490	5.249630	134296	.000000	5.250	85+

NUMBER OF PERSONS DYING (OUT OF 100,000 AT BIRTH) ABOVE AGE X FROM SPECIFIED CAUSES

Age (x)	All Causes	Respiratory T.B.	Other Infec. and Paras.	Neo-plasms	Cardio-vascular	Infl., Pneu., Bronch.	Diar-rheal	Certain Degen-erative	Maternal	Cert. Dis. of Infancy	Motor Vehicle	Other Violence	Other and Unknown	Age (x)
0	100000	165	333	17068	56632	9778	591	2180	73	899	666	3088	8527	0
1	98220	165	316	17058	56625	9562	553	2177	73	1	664	3021	8005	1
5	97931	164	297	17023	56621	9507	542	2174	73	0	642	2976	7912	5
10	97774	164	290	16990	56617	9491	541	2171	73	0	616	2956	7865	10
15	97652	163	288	16964	56608	9482	540	2167	73	0	596	2945	7826	15
20	97458	163	283	16933	56594	9468	539	2157	70	0	545	2920	7786	20
25	97234	163	280	16894	56572	9458	538	2148	55	0	512	2880	7734	25
30	96946	160	276	16829	56529	9446	535	2138	38	0	494	2829	7672	30
35	96550	154	269	16712	56457	9437	531	2122	18	0	473	2778	7599	35
40	95946	144	263	16474	56338	9413	527	2106	5	0	456	2714	7506	40
45	94880	131	256	15997	56088	9367	520	2078	1	0	435	2629	7378	45
50	93256	119	243	15252	55643	9295	511	2033	0	0	415	2538	7207	50
55	90860	107	229	14157	54901	9184	498	1973	0	0	385	2426	7000	55
60	87343	93	208	12765	53602	8992	482	1871	0	0	352	2285	6693	60
65	81841	79	182	10958	51113	8631	453	1716	0	0	312	2117	6280	65
70	73505	62	153	8792	46742	8016	398	1468	0	0	252	1928	5694	70
75	61061	44	121	6400	39428	6937	325	1094	0	0	182	1672	4858	75
80	44615	27	78	3973	29114	5344	231	687	0	0	96	1315	3750	80
85+	25582	8	34	1855	16774	3241	122	322	0	0	36	777	2413	85+

NUMBER OF PERSONS SURVIVING TO AGE X IF SPECIFIED CAUSES WERE ELIMINATED

Age (x)	No Causes	Respiratory T.B. (1)	Other Infec. and Paras. (2)	Neo-plasms (3)	Cardio-vascular (4)	Infl., Pneu., Bronch. (5)	Diar-rheal (6)	Certain Degener-ative (7)	Maternal (8)	Cert. Dis. of Infancy (9)	Motor Vehicle (10)	Other Violence (11)	Other and Unknown (12)	(1)+(2)	(1)+(2)+(5)+(6)+(8)	(1)+(2)+(5)+(6)+(8)+part of(9)&(12)	(10)+(11)	Age (x)
0	100000	100000	100000	100000	100000	100000	100000	100000	100000	100000	100000	100000	100000	100000	100000	100000	100000	0
1	98220	98220	98237	98230	98227	98434	98258	98223	98220	99114	98222	98286	98739	98237	98489	99557	98288	1
5	97931	97932	97967	97976	97942	98200	97980	97937	97931	98823	97955	98042	98542	97968	98285	99393	98066	5
10	97774	97775	97817	97852	97789	98058	97823	97783	97774	98665	97824	97905	98431	97818	98152	99269	97955	10
15	97652	97654	97697	97756	97665	97942	97702	97665	97542	98542	97722	97794	98347	97699	98042	99164	97864	15
20	97458	97460	97508	97592	97456	97764	97509	97481	97461	98346	97579	97625	98192	97510	97871	98996	97746	20
25	97234	97236	97286	97407	97294	97550	97286	97266	97252	98120	97387	97440	98019	97288	97675	98807	97594	25
30	96946	96951	97002	97184	97049	97273	97001	96988	96981	97829	97117	97203	97791	97007	97425	98565	97374	30
35	96550	96561	96613	96904	96724	96885	96609	96608	96605	97430	96741	96857	97465	96624	97073	98220	97049	35
40	95946	95967	96015	96536	96238	96302	96008	96019	96013	96820	96153	96315	96949	96036	96523	97674	96523	40
45	94880	94914	94955	95942	95418	95278	94949	94980	94951	95745	95106	95330	96000	94988	95527	96677	95556	45
50	93256	93301	93342	95050	94230	93719	93332	93399	93326	94106	93498	93785	94529	93387	93999	95143	94032	50
55	90860	90916	90958	93716	92552	91422	90947	91059	90929	91688	91125	91490	92307	91014	91733	92864	91757	55
60	87343	87410	87458	91506	90277	88073	87443	87634	87409	88139	87630	88088	89041	87525	88424	89537	88378	60
65	81841	81917	81974	87591	87120	82978	81963	82265	81903	82587	82149	82703	83840	82050	83276	84359	83014	65
70	73505	73590	73652	80891	82785	75029	73666	74122	73560	74175	73839	74460	75871	73737	75488	76523	74798	70
75	61061	61148	61212	69624	76700	63339	61262	61917	61107	61617	61402	62091	63816	61299	63843	64802	62437	75
80	44615	44693	44762	53266	68242	47710	44842	45591	44649	45022	44937	45678	47624	44840	48231	49074	46008	80
85+	25582	25641	25699	32492	56119	29091	25794	26422	25601	25815	25812	26607	28395	25758	29556	30224	26846	85+

ADDED YRS OF LIFE

	No Causes	(1)	(2)	(3)	(4)	(5)	(6)	(7)	(8)	(9)	(10)	(11)	(12)	(1)+(2)	(1)+(2)+(5)+(6)+(8)	+part of(9)&(12)	(10)+(11)
TOTAL		.034	.080	2.786	11.073	1.136	.058	.278	.034	.680	.186	.525	1.489	.114	1.399	2.388	.714
WORK	1.830	.013	.016	.673	.459	.082	.011	.053	.025	.000	.071	.143	.226	.030	.147	.173	.214

POPULATION, DEATHS, DEATH RATES FOR ALL CAUSES COMBINED, AND SPECIFIED CAUSES

Age Start of Interval	Midyear Population	Deaths During Year	All Causes	Respiratory T. B.	Other Infec. and Paras.	Neoplasms	Cardiovascular	Infl., Pneu., Bronch.	Diarrheal	Certain Degenerative	Maternal	Cert. Dis. of Infancy	Motor Vehicle	Other Violence	Other and Unknown	Age Start of Interval
0	47600	1839	.03863	.00019	.00235	.00008	.00004	.00647	.00202	.00006	.00000	.02065	.00000	.00055	.00622	0
1	205400	458	.00223	.00007	.00042	.00010	.00003	.00033	.00012	.00003	.00000	.00000	.00000	.00077	.00035	1
5	197000	216	.00110	.00005	.00012	.00007	.00006	.00005	.00002	.00004	.00000	.00000	.00000	.00053	.00018	5
10	172000	136	.00079	.00006	.00010	.00005	.00002	.00002	.00001	.00006	.00000	.00000	.00000	.00034	.00013	10
15	157100	213	.00136	.00032	.00015	.00004	.00006	.00004	.00001	.00004	.00000	.00000	.00000	.00052	.00017	15
20	164500	469	.00285	.00089	.00017	.00007	.00017	.00002	.00001	.00008	.00000	.00000	.00000	.00120	.00024	20
25	148600	460	.00310	.00103	.00012	.00016	.00031	.00004	.00001	.00009	.00000	.00000	.00000	.00113	.00020	25
30	125300	446	.00356	.00097	.00006	.00019	.00063	.00005	.00002	.00019	.00000	.00000	.00000	.00122	.00022	30
35	132500	553	.00417	.00110	.00017	.00038	.00082	.00005	.00000	.00020	.00000	.00000	.00000	.00117	.00029	35
40	137600	902	.00656	.00126	.00025	.00078	.00198	.00017	.00001	.00030	.00000	.00000	.00000	.00134	.00047	40
45	116800	1158	.00991	.00170	.00023	.00166	.00348	.00026	.00004	.00046	.00000	.00000	.00000	.00140	.00068	45
50	95800	1498	.01564	.00258	.00030	.00304	.00603	.00034	.00003	.00061	.00000	.00000	.00000	.00165	.00105	50
55	74300	1780	.02396	.00287	.00052	.00538	.01063	.00055	.00005	.00085	.00000	.00000	.00000	.00170	.00136	55
60	59500	2083	.03501	.00257	.00057	.00824	.01704	.00113	.00005	.00116	.00000	.00000	.00000	.00139	.00245	60
65	43900	2318	.05280	.00310	.00039	.01146	.02800	.00255	.00007	.00134	.00000	.00000	.00000	.00130	.00460	65
70	29500	2307	.07820	.00258	.00044	.01539	.04108	.00325	.00003	.00122	.00000	.00000	.00000	.00132	.01247	70
75	17300	1943	.11231	.00208	.00040	.01705	.05312	.00561	.00017	.00139	.00000	.00000	.00000	.00156	.03092	75
80	7300	1225	.16781	.00164	.00041	.01425	.07000	.00890	.00027	.00123	.00000	.00000	.00000	.00260	.06849	80
85+	2700	757	.28037	.00111	.00111	.01333	.08000	.02148	.00074	.00074	.00000	.00000	.00000	.00333	.15852	85+
ALL	1934700	20761														

CRUDE DEATH RATE			.01073	.00100	.00028	.00157	.00385	.00054	.00008	.00027	.00000	.00051	.00000	.00102	.00161	
STANDARDIZED RATE (1)			.00882	.00082	.00029	.00115	.00279	.00052	.00010	.00021	.00000	.00073	.00000	.00093	.00129	
STANDARDIZED RATE (2)			.01530	.00113	.00028	.00227	.00602	.00075	.00008	.00034	.00000	.00043	.00000	.00106	.00295	
GEOMETRIC MEAN			.01186													

LIFE TABLE FOR ALL CAUSES COMBINED

Age (x)	Midyear Population	Deaths During Year	$_nM_x$	$_nq_x$	l_x	$_nd_x$	$_nL_x$	$_nm_x$	$_na_x$	T_x	$_nr_x$	$\overset{\circ}{e}_x$	Age (x)
0	47600	1839	.038634	.037390	100000	3739	96768	.038639	.135679	6225679	.000000	62.257	0
1	205400	458	.002230	.008861	96261	853	382912	.002228	1.500000	6128910	.000000	63.670	1
5	197000	216	.001096	.005471	95408	522	475735	.001097	2.500000	5745999	.000000	60.226	5
10	172000	136	.000791	.003942	94886	374	473520	.000790	2.566288	5270264	.019717	55.543	10
15	157100	213	.001356	.006782	94512	641	471156	.001360	2.810387	4796744	.007802	50.753	15
20	164500	469	.002851	.014158	93871	1329	466195	.002851	2.622586	4325588	-.000058	46.080	20
25	148600	460	.003096	.015377	92542	1423	459211	.003099	2.540993	3859392	-.020240	41.704	25
30	125300	446	.003559	.017658	91119	1609	451661	.003562	2.554900	3400181	.015372	37.316	30
35	132500	553	.004174	.020635	89510	1847	443187	.004168	2.637611	2948521	-.009794	32.941	35
40	137600	902	.006555	.032271	87663	2829	431717	.006553	2.667683	2505334	-.001164	28.579	40
45	116800	1158	.009914	.048613	84834	4124	414545	.009948	2.666050	2073617	-.018825	24.443	45
50	95800	1498	.015637	.075177	80710	6116	389169	.015716	2.648586	1659072	.027551	20.556	50
55	74300	1780	.023957	.113763	74594	8486	352710	.024059	2.612514	1269904	.025483	17.024	55
60	59500	2083	.035008	.161841	66108	10699	304731	.035110	2.587683	917194	.018324	13.874	60
65	43900	2318	.052802	.234420	55409	12989	245238	.052965	2.551229	612463	.017461	11.053	65
70	29500	2307	.078203	.327511	42420	13893	177258	.078377	2.492112	367225	.012696	8.657	70
75	17300	1943	.112312	.436884	28527	12463	110531	.112755	2.424092	189967	.021810	6.659	75
80	7300	1225	.167808	.582171	16064	9352	55456	.168517	2.345599	79436	.021810	4.945	80
85+	2700	757	.280370	1.000000	6712	6712	23940	.280370	3.566711	23940	.000000	3.567	85+

NUMBER OF PERSONS DYING (OUT OF 100,000 AT BIRTH) ABOVE AGE X FROM SPECIFIED CAUSES

Age (x)	All Causes	Respiratory T. B.	Other Infec. and Paras.	Neoplasms	Cardiovascular	Infl., Pneu., Bronch.	Diarrheal	Certain Degenerative	Maternal	Cert. Dis. of Infancy	Motor Vehicle	Other Violence	Other and Unknown	Age (x)
0	100000	7886	1754	15677	40487	4569	416	2351	0	2000	0	6941	17919	0
1	96261	7867	1526	15669	40483	3942	221	2345	0	2	0	6888	17318	1
5	95408	7839	1364	15630	40472	3818	174	2334	0	0	0	6594	17183	5
10	94886	7815	1306	15598	40445	3796	167	2317	0	0	0	6342	17100	10
15	94512	7787	1259	15576	40434	3788	162	2289	0	0	0	6180	17037	15
20	93871	7637	1187	15555	40404	3767	159	2268	0	0	0	5936	16958	20
25	92542	7223	1108	15524	40325	3755	153	2231	0	0	0	5378	16845	25
30	91119	6750	1052	15450	40182	3737	150	2188	0	0	0	4859	16751	30
35	89510	6310	1024	15363	39896	3715	143	2101	0	0	0	4307	16651	35
40	87663	5822	950	15196	39536	3692	143	2014	0	0	0	3789	16521	40
45	84834	5279	844	14861	38680	3620	140	1886	0	0	0	3209	16315	45
50	80710	4574	748	14169	37229	3513	122	1694	0	0	0	2626	16035	50
55	74594	3568	629	12979	34866	3378	110	1457	0	0	0	1984	15623	55
60	66108	2556	444	11070	31056	3182	91	1143	0	0	0	1386	15140	60
65	55409	1649	269	8553	25883	2837	75	789	0	0	0	961	14393	65
70	42420	889	175	5737	18995	2209	58	459	0	0	0	643	13255	70
75	28527	361	97	3005	11698	1631	52	243	0	0	0	408	11032	75
80	16064	131	52	1118	5810	1008	33	89	0	0	0	235	7588	80
85+	6712	27	27	319	1915	514	18	18	0	0	0	80	3794	85+

NUMBER OF PERSONS SURVIVING TO AGE X IF SPECIFIED CAUSES WERE ELIMINATED

Age (x)	No Causes	Respiratory T. B. (1)	Other Infec. and Paras. (2)	Neoplasms (3)	Cardiovascular (4)	Infl., Pneu., Bronch. (5)	Diarrheal (6)	Certain Degenerative (7)	Maternal (8)	Cert. Dis. of Infancy (9)	Motor Vehicle (10)	Other Violence (11)	Other and Unknown (12)	(1) + (2)	(1) + (2) + (5) + (6) + (8)	(1)+(2)+ (5)+(6)+ (8)+part of(9)&(12)	(10) + (11)	Age (x)
0	100000	100000	100000	100000	100000	100000	100000	100000	100000	100000	100000	100000	100000	100000	100000	100000	100000	0
1	96261	96280	96485	96269	96265	96878	96452	96267	96261	98241	96261	96313	96852	96504	97315	99763	96313	1
5	95408	95454	95792	95455	95423	96144	95645	95425	95408	97373	95408	95753	96130	95838	96817	99324	95753	5
10	94886	94956	95326	94964	94928	95640	95128	94920	94886	96840	94886	95482	95687	95396	96400	98917	95482	10
15	94512	94610	94997	94612	94565	95271	94758	94573	94512	96458	94512	95268	95373	95095	96109	98638	95268	15
20	93871	94118	94425	93991	93953	94646	94119	93953	93871	95804	93871	94867	94806	94673	95707	98261	94867	20
25	92542	93199	93167	92691	92702	93318	92792	92660	92542	94448	92542	94086	93577	93828	94871	97452	94086	25
30	91119	92239	91790	91340	91418	91901	91368	91278	91119	92995	91119	93164	92232	92919	93973	96571	93164	30
35	89510	91053	90197	89813	90089	90300	89762	89752	89510	91353	89510	92080	90704	91752	92823	95424	92080	35
40	87663	89667	88410	88126	88590	88460	87910	87987	87663	89468	87663	90708	88963	90431	91510	94121	90708	40
45	84834	87321	85662	85614	86587	85677	85076	85274	84834	86561	84834	88373	86298	88173	89303	91911	88373	45
50	80710	83786	81592	82137	83835	81617	80958	81317	80710	82372	80710	84670	82381	84702	85917	88499	84670	50
55	74594	78446	75525	77087	79880	75564	74834	75384	74594	76130	74594	78903	76543	79425	80717	83241	78903	55
60	66108	70527	67110	70200	74698	67155	66339	67107	66108	67469	66108	70522	68304	71596	72984	75357	70522	60
65	55409	60000	56410	61333	68240	56610	55575	56575	55409	55550	55409	59521	57962	61084	62642	64794	59521	65
70	42420	46652	43269	49748	60198	43903	42594	43606	42420	43294	42420	45864	45436	47585	49452	51303	45864	70
75	28527	31842	29162	36156	49846	30015	28649	29503	28527	29114	28527	31049	32592	32551	34396	35919	31049	75
80	16064	18114	16455	22181	36768	17397	16147	16731	16064	16395	16064	17623	21580	18555	20199	21444	17623	80
85+	6712	7643	6891	9985	22096	7612	6756	7037	6712	6850	6712	7471	12847	7847	8958	9904	7471	85+

ADDED YRS OF LIFE

	No Causes	(1)	(2)	(3)	(4)	(5)	(6)	(7)	(8)	(9)	(10)	(11)	(12)				
TOTAL		1.753	.574	2.053	5.969	.867	.184	.415	.000	1.279	.000	2.042	2.515	2.354	3.483	5.527	2.042
WORK	5.728	1.104	.178	.636	1.396	.101	.013	.202	.000	.000	.000	1.166	.362	1.290	1.412	1.528	1.166

POPULATION, DEATHS, DEATH RATES FOR ALL CAUSES COMBINED, AND SPECIFIED CAUSES

Age Start of Interval	Midyear Population	Deaths During Year	All Causes	Respiratory T. B.	Other Infec. and Paras.	Neo-plasms	Cardio-vascular	Infl., Pneu., Bronch.	Diar-rheal	Certain Degen-erative	Maternal	Cert. Dis. of Infancy	Motor Vehicle	Other Violence	Other and Unknown	Age Start of Interval
0	45600	1455	.03191	.00009	.00246	.00007	.00007	.00507	.00169	.00009	.00000	.01654	.00000	.00050	.00535	0
1	197000	327	.00166	.00002	.00042	.00009	.00003	.00027	.00010	.00003	.00000	.00001	.00000	.00039	.00031	1
5	188200	121	.00064	.00005	.00012	.00007	.00004	.00005	.00000	.00002	.00000	.00000	.00000	.00018	.00011	5
10	166700	106	.00064	.00010	.00007	.00010	.00005	.00005	.00000	.00005	.00000	.00000	.00000	.00008	.00013	10
15	152900	157	.00103	.00039	.00009	.00005	.00004	.00003	.00000	.00007	.00003	.00000	.00000	.00018	.00015	15
20	160900	241	.00150	.00072	.00013	.00009	.00006	.00005	.00001	.00006	.00007	.00000	.00000	.00017	.00016	20
25	159600	300	.00188	.00081	.00012	.00007	.00018	.00007	.00002	.00008	.00014	.00000	.00000	.00018	.00021	25
30	145400	302	.00208	.00059	.00008	.00028	.00037	.00001	.00002	.00009	.00020	.00000	.00000	.00018	.00026	30
35	150400	385	.00256	.00065	.00011	.00044	.00041	.00005	.00000	.00020	.00015	.00000	.00000	.00026	.00025	35
40	153000	446	.00292	.00056	.00015	.00062	.00071	.00008	.00003	.00019	.00011	.00000	.00000	.00018	.00028	40
45	132600	591	.00446	.00055	.00020	.00127	.00133	.00014	.00002	.00020	.00005	.00000	.00000	.00027	.00042	45
50	115500	828	.00717	.00055	.00022	.00204	.00294	.00027	.00003	.00022	.00000	.00000	.00000	.00029	.00061	50
55	93800	984	.01049	.00063	.00022	.00257	.00456	.00032	.00003	.00052	.00000	.00000	.00000	.00036	.00086	55
60	82400	1520	.01845	.00072	.00023	.00461	.00962	.00083	.00004	.00070	.00000	.00000	.00000	.00032	.00138	60
65	67100	2156	.03213	.00082	.00030	.00681	.01873	.00124	.00007	.00097	.00000	.00000	.00000	.00045	.00274	65
70	49000	2721	.05553	.00110	.00041	.00959	.03184	.00300	.00012	.00137	.00000	.00000	.00000	.00057	.00753	70
75	31700	3040	.09590	.00091	.00041	.01047	.05079	.00688	.00016	.00123	.00000	.00000	.00000	.00104	.02401	75
80	14300	2132	.14909	.00077	.00063	.01203	.06517	.01063	.00014	.00091	.00000	.00000	.00000	.00280	.05601	80
85+	6600	1813	.27470	.00030	.00045	.01273	.08909	.01470	.00030	.00091	.00000	.00000	.00000	.00379	.15242	85+
ALL	2112700	19625														

CRUDE DEATH RATE			.00929	.00048	.00023	.00136	.00378	.00056	.00007	.00023	.00005	.00036	.00000	.00029	.00189	
STANDARDIZED RATE (1)			.00580	.00040	.00025	.00077	.00185	.00042	.00008	.00015	.00005	.00058	.00000	.00025	.00099	
STANDARDIZED RATE (2)			.01055	.00048	.00023	.00148	.00440	.00064	.00007	.00024	.00005	.00034	.00000	.00030	.00232	
GEOMETRIC MEAN			.00751													

LIFE TABLE FOR ALL CAUSES COMBINED

Age (x)	Midyear Population	Deaths During Year	$_nM_x$	$_nq_x$	l_x	$_nd_x$	$_nL_x$	$_nm_x$	$_na_x$	T_x	$_nr_x$	$\overset{\circ}{e}_x$	Age (x)
0	45600	1455	.031908	.031040	100000	3104	97282	.031907	.124243	6882019	.000000	68.820	0
1	197000	327	.001660	.006615	96896	641	385982	.001661	1.500000	6784737	.000000	70.021	1
5	188200	121	.000643	.003200	96255	308	480505	.000641	2.500000	6398756	.000000	66.477	5
10	166700	106	.000636	.003179	95947	305	479011	.000637	2.625000	5918251	.018004	61.683	10
15	152900	157	.001027	.005134	95642	491	477067	.001029	2.671419	5439240	.008233	56.871	15
20	160900	241	.001498	.007451	95151	709	474064	.001496	2.615480	4962174	-.005048	52.151	20
25	159600	300	.001880	.009360	94442	884	470054	.001881	2.560803	4488109	.005334	47.522	25
30	145400	302	.002077	.010336	93558	967	465434	.02078	2.563340	4018055	.006806	42.947	30
35	150400	385	.002560	.012723	92591	1178	460084	.002560	2.562960	3552622	-.006734	38.369	35
40	153000	446	.002915	.014473	91413	1323	453927	.002915	2.628496	3092538	.003329	33.830	40
45	132600	591	.004457	.022133	90090	1994	445839	.004472	2.687751	2638610	.017942	29.289	45
50	115500	828	.007169	.035416	88096	3120	433175	.007203	2.658787	2192771	.025732	24.891	50
55	93800	984	.010490	.051450	84976	4372	414791	.010540	2.692222	1759595	.024848	20.707	55
60	82400	1520	.018447	.088780	80604	7156	386514	.018514	2.693369	1344804	.015719	16.684	60
65	67100	2156	.032131	.149556	73448	11014	341411	.032260	2.654860	958291	.018289	13.047	65
70	49000	2721	.055531	.245748	62434	15343	275332	.055725	2.599027	616880	.015332	9.881	70
75	31700	3040	.095899	.388758	47091	18307	189725	.096492	2.502048	341548	.023855	7.253	75
80	14300	2132	.149091	.539293	28784	15523	103548	.149911	2.399222	151823	.023855	5.275	80
85+	6600	1813	.274697	1.000000	13261	13261	48275	.274697	3.640375	48275	.000000	3.640	85+

NUMBER OF PERSONS DYING (OUT OF 100,000 AT BIRTH) ABOVE AGE X FROM SPECIFIED CAUSES

Age (x)	All Causes	Respiratory T.B.	Other Infec. and Paras.	Neoplasms	Cardiovascular	Infl., Pneu., Bronch.	Diarrheal	Certain Degenerative	Maternal	Cert. Dis. of Infancy	Motor Vehicle	Other Violence	Other and Unknown	Age (x)
0	100000	3716	1554	14190	44388	5797	408	2132	347	1610	0	2357	23501	0
1	96896	3707	1315	14183	44382	5304	244	2123	347	2	0	2308	22981	1
5	96255	3699	1152	14150	44370	5200	205	2111	347	0	0	2159	22862	5
10	95947	3674	1094	14117	44350	5177	205	2101	347	0	0	2072	22810	10
15	95642	3624	1059	14071	44327	5151	205	2078	347	0	0	2032	22748	15
20	95151	3437	1016	14046	44308	5139	205	2044	334	0	0	1948	22674	20
25	94442	3095	954	14005	44282	5115	202	2017	302	0	0	1868	22602	25
30	93558	2712	898	13972	44196	5083	193	1979	234	0	0	1786	22505	30
35	92591	2437	863	13844	44023	5076	183	1937	141	0	0	1703	22384	35
40	91413	2137	814	13621	43833	5055	183	1845	71	0	0	1583	22271	40
45	90090	1882	745	13339	43510	5016	171	1759	20	0	0	1503	22145	45
50	88096	1637	658	12768	42915	4952	161	1669	0	0	0	1382	21954	50
55	84976	1357	564	11879	41632	4835	146	1574	0	0	0	1258	21691	55
60	80604	1135	471	10640	39727	4702	133	1356	0	0	0	1108	21332	60
65	73448	859	382	8853	35590	4382	119	1084	0	0	0	986	20793	65
70	62434	578	280	6522	29567	3957	93	752	0	0	0	833	19852	70
75	47091	275	168	3876	20774	3127	59	375	0	0	0	675	17762	75
80	28784	101	89	1885	11088	1812	29	142	0	0	0	476	13162	80
85+	13261	15	22	614	4301	709	15	44	0	0	0	183	7358	85+

NUMBER OF PERSONS SURVIVING TO AGE X IF SPECIFIED CAUSES WERE ELIMINATED

Age (x)	No Causes	Respiratory T.B. (1)	Other Infec. and Paras. (2)	Neoplasms (3)	Cardiovascular (4)	Infl., Pneu., Bronch. (5)	Diarrheal (6)	Certain Degenerative (7)	Maternal (8)	Cert. Dis. of Infancy (9)	Motor Vehicle (10)	Other Violence (11)	Other and Unknown (12)	(1)+(2)	(1)+(2)+(5)+(6)+(8)	(1)+(2)+(5)+(6)+(8)+part of(9)&(12)	(10)+(11)
0	100000	100000	100000	100000	100000	100000	100000	100000	100000	100000	100000	100000	100000	100000	100000	100000	100000
1	96896	96905	97132	96903	96902	97382	97058	96905	96896	98492	96896	96944	97409	97140	97791	99771	96944
5	96255	96272	96652	96295	96273	96842	96454	96276	96255	97842	96255	96452	96884	96669	97460	99509	96452
10	95947	95989	96401	96020	95985	96556	96146	95978	95947	97529	95947	96230	96626	96443	97256	99322	96230
15	95642	95734	96130	95760	95703	96275	95840	95666	95642	97219	95642	95994	96382	96222	97059	99151	95994
20	95151	95429	95679	95294	95230	95793	95348	95238	95164	96720	95151	95556	95961	95959	96819	98953	95556
25	94442	95060	95028	94625	94547	95103	94641	94555	94487	95999	94442	94924	95318	95650	96568	98751	94924
30	93558	94555	94195	93772	93747	94245	93764	93708	93670	95101	93558	94117	94524	95199	96224	98469	94117
35	92591	93854	93256	92930	92951	93278	92805	92782	92795	94118	92591	93228	93668	94529	95660	97955	93228
40	91413	92963	92119	91971	92112	91958	91624	91693	91684	92920	91413	92162	92590	93681	94895	97222	92162
45	90090	91875	90855	90922	90551	90818	90310	90451	90408	91576	90090	90908	91377	92655	93962	96313	90908
50	88096	90089	88921	89461	89534	89872	88321	88539	88426	89545	88096	89017	89546	90942	92322	94680	89017
55	84976	87139	85874	87203	87654	85840	85497	86295	86377	85933	84976	85987	86638	88060	89533	91865	85987
60	80604	82918	81547	83964	85081	81555	80836	81312	80906	81933	80604	81711	82538	83888	85442	87714	81711
65	73448	75827	74393	78304	81389	74624	73673	74355	73723	74659	73448	74574	75739	76803	78565	80715	74574
70	62434	64723	63332	68884	76061	63923	62649	63514	62668	63464	62434	63534	65286	65654	67610	69540	63534
75	47091	49087	47866	54527	67416	48891	47283	48236	47868	48059	47091	48059	51195	49895	52208	53902	48059
80	28784	30141	29319	35132	53405	30963	28924	29665	28892	29259	28784	29535	35477	30702	33311	34900	29535
85+	13261	13946	13553	17246	34527	15072	13335	13734	13311	13480	13261	13807	21838	14253	16351	17792	13807

ADDED YRS OF LIFE

	No Causes	(1)	(2)	(3)	(4)	(5)	(6)	(7)	(8)	(9)	(10)	(11)	(12)	(1)+(2)	(1)+(2)+(5)+(6)+(8)	+part	(10)+(11)
TOTAL		1.102	.578	2.017	5.830	.913	.174	.381	.139	1.133	.000	.615	3.008	1.694	2.976	4.878	.615
WORK	3.149	.697	.141	.548	.720	.086	.015	.147	.107	.000	.000	.229	.301	.842	1.056	1.187	.229

POPULATION, DEATHS, DEATH RATES FOR ALL CAUSES COMBINED, AND SPECIFIED CAUSES

Age Start of Interval	Midyear Population	Deaths During Year	All Causes	Respiratory T.B.	Other Infec. and Paras.	Neoplasms	Cardiovascular	Infl., Pneu., Bronch.	Diarrheal	Certain Degenerative	Maternal	Cert. Dis. of Infancy	Motor Vehicle	Other Violence	Other and Unknown	Age Start of Interval
0	40190	998	.02483	.00000	.00037	.00007	.00005	.00254	.00075	.00005	.00000	.01416	.00002	.00075	.00607	0
1	167335	219	.00131	.00000	.00010	.00013	.00002	.00022	.00009	.00002	.00000	.00000	.00020	.00033	.00022	1
5	222849	140	.00063	.00000	.00001	.00006	.00002	.00003	.00000	.00002	.00000	.00000	.00016	.00021	.00011	5
10	249764	139	.00056	.00002	.00002	.00008	.00000	.00002	.00000	.00003	.00000	.00000	.00011	.00020	.00008	10
15	188543	217	.00115	.00001	.00004	.00009	.00005	.00005	.00000	.00004	.00000	.00000	.00038	.00036	.00014	15
20	158268	243	.00154	.00003	.00002	.00006	.00011	.00003	.00001	.00006	.00000	.00000	.00036	.00071	.00016	20
25	147208	294	.00200	.00014	.00001	.00018	.00021	.00001	.00004	.00000	.00000	.00000	.00029	.00095	.00015	25
30	154566	409	.00265	.00019	.00005	.00023	.00033	.00003	.00001	.00019	.00000	.00000	.00032	.00108	.00015	30
35	139352	509	.00365	.00042	.00006	.00039	.00084	.00006	.00000	.00020	.00000	.00000	.00027	.00108	.00033	35
40	116756	601	.00515	.00039	.00005	.00074	.00193	.00003	.00001	.00018	.00000	.00000	.00028	.00120	.00034	40
45	125910	1072	.00851	.00056	.00013	.00156	.00338	.00014	.00002	.00043	.00000	.00000	.00033	.00131	.00064	45
50	124258	1666	.01341	.00081	.00010	.00277	.00610	.00026	.00002	.00068	.00000	.00000	.00032	.00151	.00083	50
55	99882	2020	.02022	.00121	.00022	.00519	.00929	.00039	.00003	.00080	.00000	.00000	.00034	.00132	.00143	55
60	75143	2393	.03185	.00158	.00040	.00857	.01484	.00071	.00004	.00146	.00000	.00000	.00036	.00152	.00237	60
65	52782	2487	.04712	.00146	.00038	.01188	.02469	.00146	.00008	.00148	.00000	.00000	.00049	.00119	.00402	65
70	35396	2611	.07377	.00234	.00025	.01608	.04068	.00333	.00011	.00189	.00000	.00000	.00037	.00164	.00706	70
75	20397	2168	.10629	.00181	.00034	.01829	.06182	.00677	.00025	.00221	.00000	.00000	.00064	.00191	.01226	75
80	9360	1470	.15705	.00182	.00043	.01688	.09177	.01229	.00075	.00374	.00000	.00000	.00043	.00417	.02479	80
85+	3711	972	.26192	.00054	.00000	.01752	.15036	.02668	.00135	.00458	.00000	.00000	.00054	.00862	.05174	85+
ALL	2131670	20628														
CRUDE DEATH RATE			.00968	.00037	.00009	.00178	.00427	.00041	.00004	.00032	.00000	.00027	.00028	.00084	.00101	
STANDARDIZED RATE (1)			.00722	.00026	.00008	.00119	.00277	.00034	.00005	.00023	.00000	.00000	.00028	.00084	.00101	
STANDARDIZED RATE (2)			.01339	.00044	.00010	.00236	.00636	.00065	.00005	.00041	.00000	.00050	.00026	.00073	.00083	
GEOMETRIC MEAN			.00926										.00029	.00053	.00150	

LIFE TABLE FOR ALL CAUSES COMBINED

Age (x)	Midyear Population	Deaths During Year	$_nM_x$	$_nq_x$	l_x	$_nd_x$	$_nL_x$	$_nm_x$	$_na_x$	T_x	$_nr_x$	$\overset{\circ}{e}_x$	Age (x)
0	40190	998	.024832	.024300	100000	2430	97843	.024836	.112214	6542260	.000000	65.423	0
1	167335	219	.001309	.005217	97570	509	389008	.001308	1.500000	6444417	.000000	66.049	1
5	222849	140	.000628	.003132	97061	304	484545	.000627	2.500000	6055410	.000000	62.388	5
10	249764	139	.000557	.002780	96757	269	483165	.000557	2.696716	5570865	.006529	57.576	10
15	188543	217	.001151	.005783	96488	558	481142	.001160	2.674358	5087699	.038589	52.729	15
20	158268	243	.001535	.007672	95930	736	477891	.001540	2.610111	4606557	.030682	48.020	20
25	147208	294	.001997	.009948	95194	947	473707	.001999	2.610656	4128666	.008010	43.371	25
30	154566	409	.002646	.013146	94247	1239	468292	.002646	2.624765	3654958	-.000432	38.781	30
35	139352	509	.003653	.018160	93008	1689	461044	.003663	2.634325	3186666	.021041	34.262	35
40	116756	601	.005147	.025493	91319	2328	451195	.005160	2.680502	2725622	.012848	29.847	40
45	125910	1072	.008514	.041645	88991	3706	436360	.008493	2.680788	2274427	-.012050	25.558	45
50	124258	1666	.013408	.065006	85285	5544	413402	.013411	2.651027	1838067	.001047	21.552	50
55	99882	2020	.020224	.096876	79741	7725	380468	.020304	2.639239	1424665	.022147	17.866	55
60	75143	2393	.031846	.148675	72016	10707	334415	.032017	2.602951	1044196	.030052	14.500	60
65	52782	2487	.047118	.212302	61309	13016	274921	.047344	2.570394	709782	.027989	11.577	65
70	35396	2611	.073765	.312778	48293	15105	203887	.074085	2.512248	434860	.021805	9.005	70
75	20397	2168	.106290	.418947	33188	13904	130271	.106722	2.434596	230973	.023973	6.960	75
80	9360	1470	.157051	.556938	19284	10740	68082	.157751	2.361460	100702	.023334	5.222	80
85+	3711	972	.261924	1.000000	8544	8544	32620	.261924	3.817901	32620	.000000	3.818	85+

NUMBER OF PERSONS DYING (OUT OF 100,000 AT BIRTH) ABOVE AGE X FROM SPECIFIED CAUSES

Age (x)	All Causes	Respiratory T.B.	Other Infec. and Paras.	Neoplasms	Cardio-vascular	Infl., Pneu., Bronch.	Diarrheal	Certain Degenerative	Maternal	Cert. Dis. of Infancy	Motor Vehicle	Other Violence	Other and Unknown	Age (x)
0	100000	3392	741	18289	48564	4696	336	3120	0	1385	1971	6637	10869	0
1	97570	3392	705	18281	48559	4447	263	3115	0	0	1968	6564	10276	1
5	97061	3392	668	18233	48552	4364	229	3108	0	0	1892	6436	10187	5
10	96757	3390	663	18202	48542	4351	226	3097	0	0	1816	6334	10136	10
15	96488	3382	656	18162	48540	4341	226	3084	0	0	1763	6237	10097	15
20	95930	3377	638	18118	48516	4315	226	3066	0	0	1581	6061	10032	20
25	95194	3364	629	18088	48465	4303	223	3038	0	0	1409	5718	9957	25
30	94247	3297	622	18001	48365	4297	223	3019	0	0	1271	5267	9885	30
35	93008	3209	601	17892	48210	4282	220	2928	0	0	1122	4731	9813	35
40	91319	3013	571	17712	47820	4252	220	2836	0	0	1000	4235	9660	40
45	88991	2839	548	17379	46948	4236	216	2754	0	0	872	3694	9505	45
50	85285	2593	493	16698	45476	4174	206	2568	0	0	727	3122	9228	50
55	79741	2257	449	15553	42954	4068	196	2288	0	0	594	2497	8885	55
60	72016	1795	365	13570	39404	3919	185	1982	0	0	464	1994	8338	60
65	61309	1264	231	10689	34411	3681	171	1491	0	0	344	1486	7541	65
70	48293	863	127	7411	27585	3276	150	1084	0	0	208	1159	6430	70
75	33188	383	75	4125	19251	2591	127	697	0	0	133	824	4982	75
80	19284	148	30	1739	11161	1704	95	409	0	0	50	573	3375	80
85+	8544	18	0	571	4905	870	44	149	0	0	18	281	1688	85+

NUMBER OF PERSONS SURVIVING TO AGE X IF SPECIFIED CAUSES WERE ELIMINATED

Age (x)	No Causes	Respiratory T.B. (1)	Other Infec. and Paras. (2)	Neoplasms (3)	Cardio-vascular (4)	Infl., Pneu., Bronch. (5)	Diarrheal (6)	Certain Degenerative (7)	Maternal (8)	Cert. Dis. of Infancy (9)	Motor Vehicle (10)	Other Violence (11)	Other and Unknown (12)	(1)+(2)	(1)+(2)+(5)+(6)+(8)	(1)+(2)+(5)+(6)+(8)+part of(9)&(12)	(10)+(11)	Age (x)
0	100000	100000	100000	100000	100000	100000	100000	100000	100000	100000	100000	100000	100000	100000	100000	100000	100000	0
1	97570	97570	97606	97578	97575	97816	97642	97575	97570	98948	97573	97642	98157	97606	97924	99490	97645	1
5	97061	97061	97133	97117	97073	97389	97167	97073	97061	98431	97140	97261	97735	97133	97568	99161	97340	5
10	96757	96759	96834	96844	96779	97097	96865	96780	96757	98123	96912	97058	97480	96836	97285	98878	97213	10
15	96488	96498	96572	96614	96512	96837	96596	96524	96488	97850	96695	96885	97248	96582	97040	98633	97093	15
20	95930	95945	96031	96099	95978	96303	96037	95984	95930	97285	96318	96502	96751	96046	96528	98115	96892	20
25	95194	95224	95304	95392	95292	95576	95304	95275	95194	96538	95751	96106	96084	95331	95824	97409	96668	25
30	94247	94341	94362	94530	94444	94631	94356	94346	94247	95578	94937	95604	95201	94457	94951	96528	96303	30
35	93008	93189	93143	93396	93357	93402	93118	93196	93008	94321	93838	94888	94021	93324	93830	95396	95735	35
40	91319	91691	91481	91879	92050	91736	91427	91555	91319	92608	92256	93668	92467	91854	92382	93950	94628	40
45	88991	89526	89172	89869	90576	89413	89100	89342	88991	90248	90031	91829	90265	89708	90244	91791	92902	45
50	85285	86040	85512	86802	88284	85751	85400	85804	85285	86489	86426	88584	86781	86269	86857	88377	89768	50
55	79741	80775	79996	82295	85108	80280	79858	80499	79741	80867	80938	83454	81478	81034	81701	83163	84706	55
60	72016	73596	72327	76294	80548	72645	72132	72994	72016	73033	73222	75869	74118	73712	74476	75663	77139	60
65	61309	62982	61697	67825	73923	62067	61421	62601	61309	62175	62448	65081	63860	63381	64282	65551	66290	65
70	48293	49975	48691	56727	66004	49257	48400	49678	48293	48975	49312	51570	51340	50387	51506	52607	52658	70
75	33188	34754	33504	42280	55803	34436	33280	34468	33188	33657	33950	35735	36578	35084	36505	37408	36556	75
80	19284	20374	19501	26934	44501	20722	19362	20253	19284	19556	19791	20968	22643	20604	22230	22922	21519	80
85+	8544	9116	8660	13038	31679	9780	8612	9152	8544	8665	8790	9498	11401	9240	10661	11157	9771	85+

ADDED YRS OF LIFE

	No Causes	(1)	(2)	(3)	(4)	(5)	(6)	(7)	(8)	(9)	(10)	(11)	(12)	(1)+(2)	(1)+(2)+(5)+(6)+(8)	part of(9)&(12)	(10)+(11)
TOTAL		.560	.166	2.475	8.053	.601	.093	.462	.000	.922	.610	1.726	1.607	.730	1.454	2.668	2.363
WORK	4.627	.266	.055	.664	1.328	.071	.007	.188	.000	.000	.351	.995	.317	.322	.401	.435	1.358

POPULATION, DEATHS, DEATH RATES FOR ALL CAUSES COMBINED, AND SPECIFIED CAUSES

Age Start of Interval	Midyear Population	Deaths During Year	All Causes	Respiratory T. B.	Other Infec. and Paras.	Neoplasms	Cardiovascular	Infl., Pneu., Bronch.	Diarrheal	Certain Degenerative	Maternal	Cert. Dis. of Infancy	Motor Vehicle	Other Violence	Other and Unknown	Age Start of Interval
0	38653	729	.01886	.00000	.00039	.00010	.00008	.00186	.00083	.00008	.00000	.01035	.00000	.00054	.00463	0
1	160469	139	.00087	.00000	.00007	.00012	.00001	.00017	.00005	.00000	.00000	.00000	.00006	.00022	.00016	1
5	214487	89	.00041	.00000	.00000	.00007	.00002	.00003	.00000	.00001	.00000	.00000	.00012	.00007	.00010	5
10	240079	77	.00032	.00000	.00002	.00007	.00004	.00003	.00000	.00001	.00000	.00000	.00005	.00003	.00006	10
15	182127	78	.00043	.00002	.00001	.00008	.00003	.00002	.00000	.00002	.00000	.00000	.00005	.00003	.00006	15
20	152900	107	.00070	.00003	.00001	.00013	.00008	.00005	.00001	.00004	.00005	.00000	.00010	.00008	.00009	20
25	140767	111	.00079	.00010	.00001	.00013	.00003	.00002	.00002	.00006	.00007	.00000	.00006	.00012	.00016	25
30	152501	173	.00113	.00016	.00001	.00020	.00020	.00003	.00001	.00007	.00007	.00000	.00007	.00022	.00010	30
35	153689	255	.00166	.00019	.00004	.00049	.00030	.00002	.00001	.00007	.00010	.00000	.00005	.00021	.00017	35
40	138115	330	.00239	.00017	.00004	.00078	.00057	.00003	.00000	.00016	.00009	.00000	.00005	.00022	.00028	40
45	146019	551	.00377	.00014	.00003	.00128	.00127	.00010	.00003	.00020	.00001	.00000	.00006	.00028	.00035	45
50	144991	783	.00540	.00016	.00005	.00185	.00201	.00010	.00001	.00027	.00000	.00000	.00008	.00030	.00059	50
55	121882	1040	.00853	.00012	.00007	.00249	.00389	.00021	.00000	.00050	.00000	.00000	.00009	.00032	.00079	55
60	102204	1544	.01511	.00026	.00014	.00381	.00804	.00034	.00001	.00073	.00000	.00000	.00014	.00032	.00131	60
65	78024	2021	.02590	.00035	.00010	.00563	.01459	.00077	.00005	.00146	.00000	.00000	.00012	.00045	.00236	65
70	60102	2974	.04948	.00043	.00018	.00854	.03045	.00203	.00018	.00241	.00000	.00000	.00020	.00101	.00404	70
75	38539	3345	.08680	.00091	.00031	.01175	.05548	.00571	.00029	.00322	.00000	.00000	.00021	.00192	.00701	75
80	19293	2713	.14062	.00078	.00026	.01394	.08703	.01114	.00067	.00311	.00000	.00000	.00005	.00617	.01747	80
85+	8662	2110	.24359	.00069	.00035	.01408	.14477	.02424	.00092	.00312	.00000	.00000	.00012	.01051	.04479	85+
ALL	2293503	19169														

	All Causes	Respiratory T.B.	Other Infec.	Neoplasms	Cardiovascular	Infl. Pneu.	Diarrheal	Certain Degen.	Maternal	Cert. Dis. Infancy	Motor Vehicle	Other Violence	Other Unknown
CRUDE DEATH RATE	.00836	.00013	.00005	.00142	.00436	.00046	.00005	.00033	.00003	.00017	.00008	.00033	.00095
STANDARDIZED RATE (1)	.00433	.00008	.00005	.00073	.00177	.00025	.00005	.00016	.00003	.00036	.00007	.00021	.00056
STANDARDIZED RATE (2)	.00872	.00013	.00005	.00141	.00457	.00050	.00005	.00033	.00003	.00021	.00008	.00035	.00100
GEOMETRIC MEAN	.00506												

LIFE TABLE FOR ALL CAUSES COMBINED

Age (x)	Midyear Population	Deaths During Year	$_nM_x$	$_nq_x$	l_x	$_nd_x$	$_nL_x$	$_nm_x$	$_na_x$	T_x	$_nr_x$	$\overset{\circ}{e}_x$	Age (x)
0	38653	729	.018860	.018550	100000	1855	98334	.018864	.102062	7241464	.000000	72.415	0
1	160469	139	.000866	.003454	98145	339	391733	.000865	1.500000	7143130	.000000	72.781	1
5	214487	89	.000415	.002076	97806	203	488523	.000416	2.500000	6751397	.000000	69.028	5
10	240079	77	.000321	.001598	97603	156	487626	.000320	2.508013	6262875	.006555	64.167	10
15	182127	78	.000428	.002145	97447	209	486751	.000429	2.684410	5775249	.038359	59.266	15
20	152900	107	.000700	.003507	97238	341	485374	.000703	2.605654	5288498	.032169	54.387	20
25	140767	111	.000789	.003942	96897	382	483572	.000790	2.611257	4803124	.009533	49.569	25
30	152501	173	.001134	.005647	96515	545	481298	.001132	2.657492	4319552	-.008712	44.755	30
35	153689	255	.001659	.008273	95970	794	477987	.001661	2.654020	3838253	.004578	39.994	35
40	138115	330	.002389	.011894	95176	1132	473250	.002392	2.677047	3360266	.005865	35.306	40
45	146019	551	.003773	.018672	94044	1756	466107	.003767	2.657911	2887015	-.008485	30.699	45
50	144991	783	.005400	.026688	92288	2463	455703	.005405	2.670862	2420908	.005262	26.232	50
55	121882	1040	.008533	.042037	89825	3776	440488	.008572	2.712747	1965205	.020412	21.878	55
60	102204	1544	.015107	.073435	86049	6319	415703	.015201	2.698706	1524717	.027356	17.719	60
65	78024	2021	.025902	.122952	79730	9803	376066	.026067	2.696241	1109013	.026673	13.910	65
70	60102	2974	.049483	.222418	69927	15553	312778	.049725	2.630213	732947	.019674	10.482	70
75	38539	3345	.086795	.359069	54374	19524	223583	.087323	2.526783	420169	.023616	7.727	75
80	19293	2713	.140621	.518307	34850	18063	127672	.141479	2.421375	196587	.023616	5.641	80
85+	8662	2110	.243593	1.000000	16787	16787	68914	.243593	4.105213	68914	.000000	4.105	85+

NUMBER OF PERSONS DYING (OUT OF 100,000 AT BIRTH) ABOVE AGE X FROM SPECIFIED CAUSES

Age (x)	All Causes	Respira-tory T. B.	Other Infec. and Paras.	Neo-plasms	Cardio-vascular	Infl., Pneu., Bronch.	Diar-rheal	Certain Degen-erative	Maternal	Cert. Dis. of Infancy	Motor Vehicle	Other Violence	Other and Unknown	Age (x)
0	100000	1251	479	15342	55941	6003	481	3619	192	1018	603	3625	11446	0
1	98145	1251	441	15331	55933	5819	400	3611	192	0	603	3571	10993	1
5	97806	1251	412	15285	55928	5751	381	3611	192	0	581	3486	10928	5
10	97603	1251	410	15253	55919	5737	381	3604	192	0	522	3454	10880	10
15	97447	1249	400	15217	55901	5721	381	3598	192	0	499	3440	10849	15
20	97238	1238	397	15176	55885	5713	381	3587	192	0	462	3402	10805	20
25	96897	1222	394	15113	55847	5691	374	3568	166	0	436	3351	10735	25
30	96515	1174	387	15051	55833	5681	364	3537	132	0	409	3292	10655	30
35	95970	1095	384	14956	55736	5668	361	3502	97	0	377	3185	10609	35
40	95176	1005	365	14720	55592	5659	354	3468	47	0	352	3086	10528	40
45	94044	923	348	14349	55321	5645	354	3393	6	0	328	2979	10398	45
50	92288	856	332	13753	54729	5597	338	3300	0	0	300	2849	10234	50
55	89825	784	310	12910	53810	5553	335	3178	0	0	265	2713	9967	55
60	86049	729	281	11812	52086	5459	310	2956	0	0	225	2572	9619	60
65	79730	619	224	10223	48719	5315	306	2649	0	0	168	2438	9069	65
70	69927	488	185	8098	43194	5023	272	2096	0	0	125	2268	8178	70
75	54374	353	128	5420	33619	4383	214	1339	0	0	62	1949	6907	75
80	34850	148	58	2782	21140	3095	150	618	0	0	16	1515	5328	80
85+	16787	48	24	971	9977	1671	64	215	0	0	8	724	3085	85+

NUMBER OF PERSONS SURVIVING TO AGE X IF SPECIFIED CAUSES WERE ELIMINATED

Age (x)	No Causes	Respira-tory T. B. (1)	Other Infec. and Paras. (2)	Neo-plasms (3)	Cardio-vascular (4)	Infl., Pneu., Bronch. (5)	Diar-rheal (6)	Certain Degener-ative (7)	Maternal (8)	Cert. Dis. of Infancy (9)	Motor Vehicle (10)	Other Violence (11)	Other and Unknown (12)	(1)+(2)	(1)+(2)+(5)+(6)+(8)	(1)+(2)+(5)+(6)+(8)+part of(9)&(12)	(10)+(11)	Age (x)
0	100000	100000	100000	100000	100000	100000	100000	100000	100000	100000	100000	100000	100000	100000	100000	100000	100000	0
1	98145	98145	98183	98156	98153	98327	98225	98153	98145	99159	98145	98199	98595	98183	98446	99606	98199	1
5	97806	97806	97872	97863	97819	98056	97905	97814	97806	98816	97828	97944	98319	97872	98222	99407	97966	5
10	97603	97603	97671	97692	97625	97866	97702	97618	97603	98611	97684	97773	98184	97671	98034	99222	97854	10
15	97447	97449	97525	97572	97487	97726	97546	97468	97447	98453	97551	97631	98038	97527	97905	99099	97735	15
20	97238	97251	97319	97403	97294	97524	97336	97270	97238	98242	97379	97459	97872	97332	97718	98915	97600	20
25	96897	96926	96981	97125	96990	97204	97002	96948	96923	97858	97063	97169	97599	97010	97449	98663	97335	25
30	96515	96592	96605	96804	96622	96831	96630	96596	96575	97512	96707	96845	97295	96682	97174	98414	97038	30
35	95970	96125	96063	96352	96173	96297	96087	96086	96064	96961	96193	96405	96791	96218	96759	98006	96629	35
40	95176	95420	95287	95791	95522	95510	95299	95325	95319	96159	95422	95706	96072	95531	96135	97393	95954	40
45	94044	94366	94171	95024	94656	94388	94166	94266	94227	95015	94311	94675	95560	94494	95146	96612	94944	45
50	92288	92671	92428	93848	93481	92673	92423	92598	92473	93241	92578	93037	93449	92812	93523	94783	93329	50
55	89825	90269	89983	92193	91910	90243	89959	90248	90005	90753	90142	90689	91222	90428	91168	92414	91009	55
60	86049	86529	86229	89427	89791	86542	86202	86672	86222	86938	86392	87016	87734	86709	87537	88755	87363	60
65	79730	80281	79952	84462	86650	80327	79876	80606	79890	80553	80103	80756	81833	80504	81418	82580	81134	65
70	69927	70533	70158	76209	81833	70727	70087	71220	70067	70649	70294	70988	72631	70766	71883	72558	71361	70
75	54374	54965	54604	61869	74299	55573	54549	56058	54483	54936	54715	55485	57648	55197	56709	57631	55833	75
80	34850	35393	35053	42087	63280	36686	35014	36518	34920	35210	35104	35919	38308	35599	37726	38466	36182	80
85+	16787	17118	16908	21814	47873	18719	16925	17879	16821	16960	16915	17865	20205	17241	19422	19990	18001	85+

ADDED YRS OF LIFE

	No Causes	(1)	(2)	(3)	(4)	(5)	(6)	(7)	(8)	(9)	(10)	(11)	(12)	(1)+(2)	(1)+(2)+(5)+(6)+(8)	part of(9)&(12)	(10)+(11)
TOTAL		.247	.118	2.202	8.782	.643	.116	.464	.079	.747	.196	.596	1.547	.366	1.223	2.249	.795
WORK	2.115	.123	.024	.568	.574	.049	.014	.114	.058	.000	.073	.197	.242	.147	.269	.311	.271

POPULATION, DEATHS, DEATH RATES FOR ALL CAUSES COMBINED, AND SPECIFIED CAUSES

Age Start of Interval	Midyear Popula- tion	Deaths During Year	All Causes	Respira- tory T.B.	Other Infec. and Paras.	Neo- plasms	Cardio- vascular	Infl., Pneu., Bronch.	Diar- rheal	Certain Degen- erative	Maternal	Cert. Dis. of Infancy	Motor Vehicle	Other Violence	Other and Unknown	Age Start of Interval
0	40298	815	.02022	.00002	.00010	.00010	.00010	.00062	.00035	.00005	.00000	.01397	.00005	.00074	.00412	0
1	161885	185	.00114	.00000	.00003	.00014	.00002	.00012	.00006	.00001	.00000	.00000	.00016	.00035	.00027	1
5	210085	142	.00068	.00000	.00002	.00010	.00001	.00002	.00000	.00000	.00000	.00000	.00020	.00025	.00008	5
10	226428	112	.00049	.00000	.00000	.00006	.00003	.00001	.00000	.00002	.00000	.00000	.00012	.00020	.00005	10
15	247287	260	.00105	.00000	.00000	.00009	.00004	.00002	.00000	.00005	.00000	.00000	.00039	.00033	.00012	15
20	170422	267	.00157	.00002	.00001	.00008	.00006	.00001	.00001	.00002	.00000	.00000	.00050	.00075	.00010	20
25	158122	297	.00188	.00007	.00000	.00014	.00022	.00000	.00001	.00007	.00000	.00000	.00042	.00083	.00012	25
30	146927	314	.00214	.00010	.00001	.00024	.00036	.00001	.00001	.00009	.00000	.00000	.00033	.00084	.00016	30
35	150551	503	.00334	.00014	.00001	.00041	.00109	.00001	.00000	.00014	.00000	.00000	.00030	.00095	.00029	35
40	133941	741	.00553	.00028	.00004	.00081	.00229	.00007	.00001	.00026	.00000	.00000	.00032	.00115	.00028	40
45	110188	965	.00876	.00031	.00005	.00159	.00421	.00012	.00001	.00033	.00000	.00000	.00043	.00122	.00028	45
50	122591	1696	.01383	.00035	.00009	.00271	.00736	.00022	.00004	.00048	.00000	.00000	.00046	.00144	.00068	50
55	111397	2384	.02140	.00059	.00015	.00507	.01091	.00045	.00004	.00064	.00000	.00000	.00044	.00159	.00152	55
60	85648	2798	.03267	.00075	.00012	.00808	.01749	.00081	.00006	.00100	.00000	.00000	.00054	.00147	.00236	60
65	59820	2824	.04721	.00094	.00022	.01143	.02589	.00115	.00013	.00132	.00000	.00000	.00057	.00160	.00395	65
70	37756	2693	.07133	.00127	.00037	.01563	.04153	.00238	.00016	.00201	.00000	.00000	.00066	.00127	.00604	70
75	22321	2485	.11133	.00143	.00022	.01891	.06675	.00618	.00018	.00246	.00000	.00000	.00094	.00193	.01232	75
80	10140	1680	.16568	.00168	.00030	.02051	.10375	.00917	.00039	.00394	.00000	.00000	.00099	.00503	.01992	80
85+	4066	1067	.26242	.00123	.00049	.02017	.15568	.02041	.00049	.00369	.00000	.00000	.00049	.00959	.05017	85+
ALL	2209873	22228														

			All Causes	Respira- tory T.B.	Other Infec. and Paras.	Neo- plasms	Cardio- vascular	Infl., Pneu., Bronch.	Diar- rheal	Certain Degen- erative	Maternal	Cert. Dis. of Infancy	Motor Vehicle	Other Violence	Other and Unknown
CRUDE DEATH RATE			.01006	.00021	.00005	.00184	.00496	.00032	.00003	.00028	.00000	.00025	.00035	.00083	.00093
STANDARDIZED RATE (1)			.00710	.00014	.00004	.00118	.00308	.00022	.00003	.00019	.00000	.00049	.00032	.00070	.00071
STANDARDIZED RATE (2)			.01348	.00025	.00006	.00238	.00700	.00050	.00004	.00036	.00000	.00029	.00036	.00091	.00135
GEOMETRIC MEAN			.00900												

LIFE TABLE FOR ALL CAUSES COMBINED

Age (x)	Midyear Popula- tion	Deaths During Year	$_nM_x$	$_nq_x$	l_x	$_nd_x$	$_nL_x$	$_nm_x$	$_na_x$	T_x	$_nr_x$	$\overset{\circ}{e}_x$	Age (x)
0	40298	815	.020224	.019860	100000	1986	98221	.020220	.104381	6569632	.000000	65.696	0
1	161885	185	.001143	.004561	98014	447	390939	.001143	1.500000	6471411	.000000	66.025	1
5	210085	142	.000676	.003382	97567	330	487010	.000678	2.500000	6080472	.000000	62.321	5
10	226428	112	.000495	.002468	97237	240	485622	.000494	2.656250	5593462	-.020011	57.524	10
15	247287	260	.001051	.005258	96997	510	483817	.001054	2.710784	5107840	.012274	52.660	15
20	170422	267	.001567	.007835	96487	756	480625	.001573	2.606371	4624022	.040993	47.924	20
25	158122	297	.001878	.009360	95731	896	476468	.001881	2.558826	4143397	.021198	43.282	25
30	146927	314	.002137	.010640	94835	1009	471790	.002139	2.636274	3666929	.007397	38.666	30
35	150551	503	.003341	.016584	93826	1556	465557	.003342	2.703915	3195139	-.001744	34.054	35
40	133941	741	.005532	.027441	92270	2532	455500	.005559	2.689409	2729582	.023672	29.583	40
45	110188	965	.008758	.042992	89738	3858	439713	.008774	2.673179	2274082	.009155	25.341	45
50	122591	1696	.013835	.066826	85880	5739	415950	.013797	2.656459	1834369	-.014239	21.360	50
55	111397	2384	.021401	.101920	80141	8168	381368	.021418	2.632580	1418419	-.004806	17.699	55
60	85648	2798	.032669	.151960	71973	10937	333525	.032792	2.591642	1037051	.022567	14.409	60
65	59820	2824	.047208	.212645	61036	12979	273501	.047455	2.559246	703526	.031874	11.526	65
70	37756	2693	.071326	.304389	48057	14628	204040	.071692	2.522232	430024	.027357	8.948	70
75	22321	2485	.111330	.434952	33429	14540	130017	.111831	2.446458	225984	.019920	6.760	75
80	10140	1680	.165680	.576738	18889	10894	65501	.166219	2.343090	95967	.019920	5.081	80
85+	4066	1067	.262420	1.000000	7995	7995	30466	.262420	3.810684	30466	.000000	3.811	85+

NUMBER OF PERSONS DYING (OUT OF 100,000 AT BIRTH) ABOVE AGE X FROM SPECIFIED CAUSES

Age (x)	All Causes	Respiratory T.B.	Other Infec. and Paras.	Neoplasms	Cardiovascular	Infl., Pneu., Bronch.	Diarrheal	Certain Degenerative	Maternal	Cert. Dis. of Infancy	Motor Vehicle	Other Violence	Other and Unknown	Age (x)
0	100000	1900	429	18203	52762	3605	265	2705	0	1372	2523	6518	9718	0
1	98014	1897	419	18193	52752	3544	231	2700	0	0	2518	6445	9315	1
5	97567	1897	407	18140	52745	3498	209	2698	0	0	2456	6310	9207	5
10	97237	1897	398	18091	52741	3486	209	2695	0	0	2360	6189	9171	10
15	96997	1897	396	18061	52728	3482	209	2687	0	0	2301	6092	9144	15
20	96487	1895	394	18018	52708	3472	207	2663	0	0	2112	5931	9087	20
25	95731	1887	388	17981	52677	3466	204	2652	0	0	1870	5568	9038	25
30	94835	1853	388	17915	52571	3466	201	2619	0	0	1668	5173	8981	30
35	93826	1805	385	17802	52400	3463	198	2577	0	0	1511	4778	8907	35
40	92270	1740	379	17613	51892	3457	198	2512	0	0	1372	4336	8771	40
45	89738	1611	358	17244	50842	3423	191	2393	0	0	1225	3811	8640	45
50	85880	1475	334	16544	48986	3371	187	2249	0	0	1037	3276	8421	50
55	80141	1329	297	15422	45934	3280	170	2049	0	0	844	2676	8140	55
60	71973	1103	239	13485	41770	3108	153	1806	0	0	676	2070	7563	60
65	61036	853	200	10780	35913	2838	134	1470	0	0	497	1580	6771	65
70	48057	596	140	7639	28790	2521	97	1107	0	0	341	1141	5685	70
75	33429	336	64	4439	20269	2029	64	694	0	0	206	881	4447	75
80	18889	149	35	1976	11549	1220	41	373	0	0	83	629	2834	80
85+	7995	37	15	614	4743	622	15	112	0	0	15	292	1530	85+

NUMBER OF PERSONS SURVIVING TO AGE X IF SPECIFIED CAUSES WERE ELIMINATED

Age (x)	No Causes	Respiratory T.B. (1)	Other Infec. and Paras. (2)	Neoplasms (3)	Cardiovascular (4)	Infl., Pneu., Bronch. (5)	Diarrheal (6)	Certain Degenerative (7)	Maternal (8)	Cert. Dis. of Infancy (9)	Motor Vehicle (10)	Other Violence (11)	Other and Unknown (12)	(1)+(2)	(1)+(2)+(5)+(6)+(8)	(1)+(2)+(5)+(6)+(8)+part of(9)&(12)	(10)+(11)	Age (x)
0	100000	100000	100000	100000	100000	100000	100000	100000	100000	100000	100000	100000	100000	100000	100000	100000	100000	0
1	98014	98017	98024	98024	98024	98074	98014	98019	98014	99382	98019	98086	98414	98027	98121	99026	98091	1
5	97567	97570	97589	97630	97584	97673	97622	97574	97567	98929	97634	97774	98073	97592	97753	98680	97841	5
10	97237	97240	97268	97349	97258	97355	97292	97247	97237	98594	97400	97564	97778	97271	97444	98370	97727	10
15	96997	97000	97030	97138	97031	97118	97052	97015	96997	98351	97218	97421	97563	97033	97209	98134	97643	15
20	96487	96492	96521	96670	96540	96618	96544	96529	96487	97833	96896	97070	97108	96526	96714	97637	97482	20
25	95731	95744	95771	95950	95815	95867	95790	95783	95731	97067	96379	96674	96396	95784	95979	96896	97328	25
30	94835	94882	94875	95118	95024	94999	94897	94920	94835	96158	95680	96167	95551	94921	95118	96029	97023	30
35	93826	93920	93868	94219	94184	93962	93890	93952	93826	95135	94819	95543	94663	93962	94163	95070	96554	35
40	92270	92427	92318	92845	93129	92410	92333	92458	92270	93558	93386	94406	93175	92475	92678	93578	95548	40
45	89738	90018	89805	90664	91625	89907	89806	90039	89738	90990	90970	92346	90749	90085	90324	91212	93614	45
50	85880	86281	85968	87461	89560	86093	85949	86309	85880	87078	87246	88915	87065	86369	86654	87518	90329	50
55	80141	80657	80259	82728	86706	80428	80222	80736	80141	81259	81605	83574	81522	80776	81147	81971	85101	55
60	71973	72652	72134	76216	82256	72395	72062	72739	71973	72977	73449	75655	73772	72814	73332	74112	77207	60
65	61036	61844	61208	67324	76196	61644	61129	61999	61036	61888	62455	64632	63314	62018	62732	63442	66135	65
70	48057	48924	48246	56160	68411	48821	48163	49142	48057	48728	49315	51298	50859	49116	50007	50630	52641	70
75	33429	34251	33623	42278	58806	34382	33530	34535	33429	33895	34419	35911	36485	34450	35539	36054	36974	75
80	18889	19494	19019	26283	46825	20061	18963	19759	18889	19153	19542	20495	21973	19629	20928	21342	21203	80
85+	7995	8324	8063	12387	33913	8901	8043	8537	7995	8107	8316	8908	10309	8395	9403	9667	9266	85+

ADDED YRS OF LIFE

	No Causes	(1)	(2)	(3)	(4)	(5)	(6)	(7)	(8)	(9)	(10)	(11)	(12)				
TOTAL		.289	.076	2.429	9.224	.371	.062	.373	.000	.915	.739	1.644	1.351	.366	.811	1.508	2.415
WORK	4.593	.132	.023	.657	1.589	.052	.010	.149	.000	.000	.431	.906	.272	.155	.218	.233	1.350

POPULATION, DEATHS, DEATH RATES FOR ALL CAUSES COMBINED, AND SPECIFIED CAUSES

Age Start of Interval	Midyear Population	Deaths During Year	All Causes	Respiratory T.B.	Other Infec. and Paras.	Neoplasms	Cardiovascular	Infl., Pneu., Bronch.	Diarrheal	Certain Degenerative	Maternal	Cert. Dis. of Infancy	Motor Vehicle	Other Violence	Other and Unknown	Age Start of Interval
0	38560	554	.01437	.00000	.00016	.00008	.00010	.00052	.00023	.00013	.00000	.00884	.00000	.00034	.00397	0
1	155545	129	.00083	.00001	.00005	.00012	.00000	.00012	.00005	.00001	.00000	.00000	.00012	.00016	.00020	1
5	201563	68	.00034	.00000	.00000	.00007	.00001	.00002	.00000	.00000	.00000	.00000	.00012	.00005	.00006	5
10	218257	59	.00027	.00001	.00000	.00007	.00002	.00000	.00000	.00003	.00000	.00000	.00004	.00005	.00006	10
15	237951	137	.00058	.00000	.00001	.00008	.00004	.00001	.00000	.00004	.00000	.00000	.00004	.00004	.00007	15
20	165668	98	.00059	.00002	.00001	.00012	.00005	.00001	.00000	.00003	.00003	.00000	.00007	.00015	.00011	20
25	151909	99	.00065	.00002	.00001	.00011	.00006	.00002	.00000	.00006	.00005	.00000	.00006	.00013	.00013	25
30	141689	156	.00110	.00005	.00001	.00037	.00018	.00000	.00000	.00008	.00006	.00000	.00006	.00013	.00013	30
35	151465	222	.00147	.00007	.00001	.00037	.00029	.00003	.00000	.00013	.00008	.00000	.00007	.00013	.00017	35
40	153431	307	.00200	.00011	.00001	.00057	.00051	.00007	.00001	.00010	.00000	.00000	.00005	.00027	.00031	40
45	132409	474	.00358	.00017	.00004	.00137	.00126	.00005	.00001	.00013	.00000	.00000	.00007	.00026	.00034	45
50	145349	775	.00533	.00012	.00003	.00168	.00222	.00008	.00001	.00023	.00000	.00000	.00011	.00030	.00056	50
55	136845	1137	.00831	.00009	.00012	.00243	.00378	.00012	.00001	.00045	.00000	.00000	.00011	.00032	.00086	55
60	112526	1671	.01485	.00015	.00012	.00382	.00753	.00030	.00004	.00084	.00000	.00000	.00017	.00032	.00164	60
65	90180	2294	.02544	.00027	.00017	.00516	.01476	.00033	.00006	.00150	.00000	.00000	.00021	.00055	.00244	65
70	62502	3054	.04886	.00040	.00019	.00838	.03042	.00128	.00018	.00266	.00000	.00000	.00021	.00086	.00429	70
75	42558	3675	.08635	.00045	.00019	.01116	.05799	.00268	.00035	.00324	.00000	.00000	.00028	.00209	.00792	75
80	21328	3045	.14277	.00019	.00028	.01393	.09837	.00661	.00061	.00417	.00000	.00000	.00014	.00352	.01496	80
85+	9163	2330	.25428	.00022	.00065	.01561	.16807	.01790	.00120	.00437	.00000	.00000	.00011	.01091	.03525	85+
ALL	2368898	20284														

	All Causes	Respiratory T.B.	Other Infec. and Paras.	Neoplasms	Cardiovascular	Infl., Pneu., Bronch.	Diarrheal	Certain Degenerative	Maternal	Cert. Dis. of Infancy	Motor Vehicle	Other Violence	Other and Unknown
CRUDE DEATH RATE	.00856	.00007	.00005	.00143	.00480	.00028	.00003	.00036	.00001	.00014	.00010	.00031	.00096
STANDARDIZED RATE (1)	.00409	.00004	.00003	.00070	.00182	.00013	.00002	.00017	.00002	.00014	.00010	.00031	.00096
STANDARDIZED RATE (2)	.00855	.00007	.00005	.00137	.00481	.00029	.00002	.00017	.00002	.00031	.00009	.00020	.00055
GEOMETRIC MEAN	.00476	.00007	.00005	.00137	.00481	.00029	.00004	.00035	.00002	.00018	.00010	.00032	.00097

LIFE TABLE FOR ALL CAUSES COMBINED

Age (x)	Midyear Population	Deaths During Year	$_nM_x$	$_nq_x$	l_x	$_nd_x$	$_nL_x$	$_nm_x$	$_na_x$	T_x	$_nr_x$	$\overset{\circ}{e}_x$	Age (x)
0	38560	554	.014367	.014180	100000	1418	98716	.014364	.094424	7298494	.000000	72.985	0
1	155545	129	.000829	.003317	98592	327	393511	.000831	1.500000	7199779	.000000	73.033	1
5	201563	68	.000337	.001689	98255	166	490860	.000338	2.500000	6806268	.000000	69.271	5
10	218257	59	.000270	.001346	98089	132	490139	.000269	2.683081	6315408	-.019900	64.384	10
15	237951	137	.000576	.002877	97957	282	489112	.000577	2.615248	5825269	.011860	59.468	15
20	165668	98	.000592	.002949	97675	288	487662	.000591	2.526042	5336156	.041471	54.632	20
25	151909	99	.000652	.003265	97387	318	486191	.000654	2.660508	4848494	.023258	49.786	25
30	141689	156	.001101	.005491	97069	533	484093	.001101	2.650876	4362303	.007345	44.940	30
35	151465	222	.001466	.007293	96536	704	481008	.001464	2.625178	3878210	-.009447	40.174	35
40	153431	307	.002001	.009976	95832	956	476975	.002004	2.714217	3397202	.007358	35.450	40
45	132409	474	.003580	.017781	94876	1687	470474	.003586	2.684376	2920227	-.006058	30.779	45
50	145349	775	.005332	.026280	93189	2449	460243	.005321	2.671839	2449753	-.009542	26.288	50
55	136845	1137	.008309	.040853	90740	3707	445230	.008326	2.715190	1989510	.009035	21.925	55
60	112526	1671	.014850	.072134	87033	6278	420733	.014922	2.701165	1544280	.021232	17.744	60
65	90180	2294	.025438	.120971	80755	9769	381302	.025620	2.699611	1123547	-.029768	13.913	65
70	62502	3054	.048862	.220297	70986	15638	317921	.049188	2.633396	742245	.026332	10.456	70
75	42558	3675	.086353	.357411	55348	19782	227910	.086757	2.531615	424323	.019927	7.666	75
80	21328	3045	.142770	.524096	35566	18640	129850	.143551	2.425943	196413	.019927	5.522	80
85+	9163	2330	.254284	1.000000	16926	16926	66563	.254284	3.932618	66563	.000000	3.933	85+

NUMBER OF PERSONS DYING (OUT OF 100,000 AT BIRTH) ABOVE AGE X FROM SPECIFIED CAUSES

Age (x)	All Causes	Respiratory T. B.	Other Infec. and Paras.	Neoplasms	Cardiovascular	Infl., Pneu., Bronch.	Diarrheal	Certain Degenerative	Maternal	Cert. Dis. of Infancy	Motor Vehicle	Other Violence	Other and Unknown	Age (x)
0	100000	704	449	15093	59763	3621	389	3974	108	873	781	3304	10941	0
1	98582	704	434	15086	59753	3569	366	3962	108	0	781	3270	10549	1
5	98255	701	416	15040	59753	3521	348	3957	108	0	732	3207	10472	5
10	98089	701	416	15006	59748	3511	348	3954	108	0	674	3183	10440	10
15	97957	697	416	14972	59739	3511	348	3939	108	0	656	3165	10406	15
20	97675	697	412	14933	59720	3507	346	3918	106	0	592	3091	10353	20
25	97387	685	409	14874	59697	3501	346	3903	91	0	557	3005	10319	25
30	97069	675	403	14819	59668	3492	346	3874	65	0	528	2945	10254	30
35	96536	651	399	14641	59582	3492	346	3833	38	0	498	2883	10173	35
40	95832	616	393	14464	59443	3479	346	3770	0	0	466	2794	10061	40
45	94876	563	387	14193	59200	3445	343	3723	0	0	441	2667	9914	45
50	93189	531	369	13549	58605	3424	339	3663	0	0	409	2546	9754	50
55	90740	478	353	12777	57585	3389	336	3558	0	0	358	2407	9499	55
60	87033	435	298	11692	55899	3333	333	3356	0	0	310	2264	9113	60
65	80755	371	249	10079	52713	3206	318	3003	0	0	238	2155	8423	65
70	70986	269	185	8104	47038	3077	296	2428	0	0	158	1942	7489	70
75	55348	142	124	5427	37296	2666	240	1580	0	0	92	1665	6116	75
80	35566	40	81	2875	24007	2051	159	839	0	0	27	1186	4301	80
85+	16926	15	44	1039	11187	1191	80	291	0	0	7	726	2346	85+

NUMBER OF PERSONS SURVIVING TO AGE X IF SPECIFIED CAUSES WERE ELIMINATED

Age (x)	No Causes	Respiratory T. B. (1)	Other Infec. and Paras. (2)	Neoplasms (3)	Cardiovascular (4)	Infl., Pneu., Bronch. (5)	Diarrheal (6)	Certain Degenerative (7)	Maternal (8)	Cert. Dis. of Infancy (9)	Motor Vehicle (10)	Other Violence (11)	Other and Unknown (12)	(1)+(2)	(1)+(2)+(5)+(6)+(8)	(1)+(2)+(5)+(6)+(8)+part of(9)&(12)	(10)+(11)	Age (x)
0	100000	100000	100000	100000	100000	100000	100000	100000	100000	100000	100000	100000	100000	100000	100000	100000	100000	0
1	98582	98582	98597	98589	98592	98634	98605	98594	98582	99453	98582	98616	98972	98597	98671	99414	98616	1
5	98255	98258	98288	98308	98265	98354	98296	98272	98255	99123	98304	98352	98721	98291	98431	99199	98401	5
10	98089	98092	98122	98176	98104	98198	98130	98109	98089	98955	98196	98209	98556	98125	98275	99043	98316	10
15	97957	97964	97990	98078	97981	98066	97998	97992	97957	98822	98082	98095	98488	97997	98147	98916	98220	15
20	97675	97682	97712	97834	97718	97788	97717	97731	97677	98538	97863	97887	98257	97719	97876	98646	98076	20
25	97387	97406	97427	97605	97453	97505	97429	97458	97404	98247	97610	97684	98002	97445	97623	98396	97908	25
30	97069	97098	97114	97341	97163	97196	97118	97112	97069	97926	97320	97426	97747	97143	97356	98139	97678	30
35	96536	96589	96585	96985	96716	96662	96578	96676	96606	97389	96816	96953	97292	96638	96876	97666	97234	35
40	95832	95919	95887	96455	96149	95970	95874	96034	95939	96678	96142	96335	96695	95974	96262	97064	96646	40
45	94876	95015	94936	95765	95433	95047	94920	95122	94982	95714	95208	95501	95878	95075	95397	96210	95834	45
50	93189	93357	93266	94708	94331	93378	93216	93491	93293	94012	93546	93923	94333	93434	93776	94583	94284	50
55	90740	90956	90831	92956	92877	90958	90789	91138	90841	91541	91139	91593	92109	91047	91418	92217	91596	55
60	87033	87283	87174	90292	90790	87298	87083	87613	87130	87802	87462	87993	88731	87424	87838	88624	88427	60
65	80755	81048	80933	85404	87506	81123	80816	81637	80845	81468	81223	81751	82010	81227	81750	82512	82225	65
70	70986	71340	71202	77051	82905	71432	71060	72307	71065	71613	71472	72064	73872	71557	72162	72867	72558	70
75	55348	55736	55570	62679	75497	56063	55455	57140	55410	55837	55785	56437	58870	55959	56855	57468	56883	75
80	35566	35895	35742	42618	65324	36527	35700	37324	35606	35880	35898	36657	39357	36073	37229	37702	37000	80
85+	16926	17100	17035	21821	51807	17989	17043	18155	16945	17075	17098	17768	20268	17210	18438	18760	17948	85+

ADDED YRS OF LIFE	No Causes	(1)	(2)	(3)	(4)	(5)	(6)	(7)	(8)	(9)	(10)	(11)	(12)	(1)+(2)	...	...	(10)+(11)
TOTAL		.130	.084	2.137	10.129	.339	.057	.492	.047	.644	.251	.567	1.497	.214	.664	1.315	.822
WORK	2.002	.053	.020	.548	.567	.033	.003	.112	.035	.000	.095	.214	.252	.073	.145	.169	.310

POPULATION, DEATHS, DEATH RATES FOR ALL CAUSES COMBINED, AND SPECIFIED CAUSES

Age Start of Interval	Midyear Population	Deaths During Year	All Causes	Respiratory T.B.	Other Infec. and Paras.	Neo-plasms	Cardio-vascular	Infl., Pneu., Bronch.	Diarrheal	Certain Degenerative	Maternal	Cert. Dis. of Infancy	Motor Vehicle	Other Violence	Other and Unknown	Age Start of Interval
0	376504	42021	.11161	.00059	.00456	.00002	.00080	.00586	.02669	.00018	.00000	.02090	.00000	.00065	.05134	0
1	1469189	13523	.00920	.00019	.00150	.00001	.00008	.00069	.00072	.00003	.00000	.00000	.00000	.00052	.00546	1
5	1156050	3877	.00335	.00014	.00081	.00001	.00007	.00016	.00000	.00004	.00000	.00000	.00000	.00032	.00179	5
10	1558904	2624	.00168	.00015	.00028	.00001	.00008	.00006	.00000	.00002	.00000	.00000	.00000	.00023	.00085	10
15	1729225	6444	.00373	.00100	.00041	.00002	.00013	.00015	.00000	.00003	.00000	.00000	.00000	.00059	.00139	15
20	1660505	10354	.00624	.00209	.00054	.00002	.00018	.00028	.00000	.00009	.00000	.00000	.00000	.00096	.00208	20
25	1629354	9861	.00605	.00223	.00033	.00003	.00021	.00023	.00000	.00010	.00000	.00000	.00000	.00096	.00208	25
30	1271159	8921	.00702	.00238	.00030	.00007	.00034	.00031	.00000	.00016	.00000	.00000	.00000	.00106	.00186	30
35	1275872	10451	.00819	.00257	.00032	.00013	.00051	.00040	.00000	.00028	.00000	.00000	.00000	.00119	.00226	35
40	1248715	13173	.01055	.00276	.00032	.00032	.00094	.00056	.00000	.00050	.00000	.00000	.00000	.00113	.00284	40
45	1264600	16458	.01301	.00274	.00030	.00065	.00142	.00072	.00000	.00073	.00000	.00000	.00000	.00125	.00389	45
50	1185549	21494	.01813	.00269	.00032	.00128	.00264	.00104	.00000	.00104	.00000	.00000	.00000	.00136	.00509	50
55	1025113	24036	.02345	.00215	.00026	.00196	.00430	.00141	.00000	.00147	.00000	.00000	.00000	.00160	.00750	55
60	880156	31083	.03532	.00170	.00028	.00316	.00721	.00205	.00000	.00198	.00000	.00000	.00000	.00159	.01031	60
65	682897	35474	.05195	.00142	.00030	.00408	.01108	.00307	.00001	.00270	.00000	.00000	.00000	.00197	.01696	65
70	469075	38009	.08103	.00094	.00028	.00480	.01662	.00454	.00001	.00346	.00000	.00000	.00000	.00237	.04802	70
75	269765	36553	.13550	.00077	.00027	.00488	.02474	.00712	.00001	.00442	.00000	.00000	.00000	.00286	.09042	75
80	120907	27064	.22384	.00054	.00022	.00409	.02972	.01040	.00002	.00480	.00000	.00000	.00000	.00331	.17074	80
85+	43451	15436	.35525	.00069	.00028	.00357	.03089	.01339	.00000	.00658	.00000	.00000	.00000	.00444	.29541	85+
ALL	19316990	366856														

	All Causes	Respiratory T.B.	Other Infec. and Paras.	Neo-plasms	Cardio-vascular	Infl., Pneu., Bronch.	Diarrheal	Certain Degenerative	Maternal	Cert. Dis. of Infancy	Motor Vehicle	Other Violence	Other and Unknown
CRUDE DEATH RATE	.01899	.00163	.00054	.00077	.00240	.00102	.00058	.00066	.00000	.00041	.00000	.00111	.00988
STANDARDIZED RATE (1)	.01461	.00132	.00069	.00040	.00126	.00078	.00103	.00037	.00000	.00074	.00000	.00088	.00715
STANDARDIZED RATE (2)	.02072	.00152	.00056	.00077	.00260	.00109	.00061	.00067	.00000	.00043	.00000	.00105	.01137
GEOMETRIC MEAN	.01981												

LIFE TABLE FOR ALL CAUSES COMBINED

Age (x)	Midyear Population	Deaths During Year	$_nM_x$	$_nq_x$	l_x	$_nd_x$	$_nL_x$	$_nm_x$	$_na_x$	T_x	$_nr_x$	$\overset{\circ}{e}_x$	Age (x)
0	376504	42021	.111608	.103090	100000	10309	92369	.111607	.259734	5232979	.000000	52.330	0
1	1469189	13523	.009204	.035990	89691	3228	350694	.009205	1.500000	5140610	.000000	57.315	1
5	1156050	3877	.003354	.016678	86463	1442	428710	.003364	2.500000	4789916	.000000	55.398	5
10	1558904	2624	.001683	.008327	85021	708	423358	.001672	2.532074	4361206	-.038267	51.296	10
15	1729225	6444	.003727	.018396	84313	1551	418069	.003710	2.746078	3937848	-.017953	46.705	15
20	1660505	10354	.006235	.030690	82762	2540	407635	.006231	2.569062	3519779	-.007516	42.529	20
25	1629354	9861	.006052	.029830	80222	2393	395158	.006056	2.512885	3112144	.013394	38.794	25
30	1271159	8921	.007018	.034537	77829	2688	382555	.007026	2.548363	2716986	.020700	34.910	30
35	1275872	10451	.008191	.040151	75141	3017	368375	.008190	2.570365	2334431	.000207	31.067	35
40	1248715	13173	.010549	.051358	72124	3707	351622	.010543	2.572779	1966056	-.007062	27.259	40
45	1264600	16458	.013014	.063025	68417	4312	331692	.013000	2.589865	1614433	-.009997	23.597	45
50	1185549	21494	.018130	.086842	64105	5567	307063	.018130	2.581844	1282741	-.000473	20.010	50
55	1025113	24036	.023447	.111022	58538	6499	277048	.023458	2.593155	975678	-.003998	16.667	55
60	880156	31083	.035315	.162820	52039	8473	239753	.035341	2.587385	698630	.003829	13.425	60
65	682897	35474	.051946	.230753	43566	10053	193292	.052009	2.559103	458877	.007453	10.533	65
70	469075	38009	.081030	.337929	33513	11325	139480	.081194	2.520125	265585	.009711	7.925	70
75	269765	36553	.135499	.502389	22188	11147	82314	.135421	2.431914	126105	-.001969	5.683	75
80	120907	27064	.223841	.695770	11041	7682	34336	.223730	2.283395	43791	-.001969	3.966	80
85+	43451	15436	.355251	1.000000	3359	3359	9455	.355251	2.814913	9455	.000000	2.815	85+

NUMBER OF PERSONS DYING (OUT OF 100,000 AT BIRTH) ABOVE AGE X FROM SPECIFIED CAUSES

Age (x)	All Causes	Respiratory T.B.	Other Infec. and Paras.	Neo-plasms	Cardio-vascular	Infl., Pneu., Bronch.	Diar-rheal	Certain Degenerative	Maternal	Cert. Dis. of Infancy	Motor Vehicle	Other Violence	Other and Unknown	Age (x)
0	100000	8447	2750	4180	13043	5354	2728	3524	0	1930	0	5838	52206	0
1	89691	8392	2328	4178	12969	4812	263	3507	0	0	0	5777	47465	1
5	86463	8328	1803	4173	12941	4570	11	3495	0	0	0	5595	45547	5
10	85021	8269	1455	4167	12910	4499	10	3478	0	0	0	5456	44777	10
15	84313	8209	1337	4163	12876	4472	10	3469	0	0	0	5361	44416	15
20	82762	7793	1165	4157	12822	4408	9	3455	0	0	0	5115	43838	20
25	80222	6942	945	4149	12748	4294	9	3420	0	0	0	4723	42992	25
30	77829	6061	815	4137	12667	4202	9	3381	0	0	0	4303	42254	30
35	75141	5149	701	4109	12535	4084	9	3318	0	0	0	3849	41387	35
40	72124	4204	583	4060	12346	3937	9	3215	0	0	0	3431	40339	40
45	68417	3233	469	3948	12017	3739	8	3038	0	0	0	2990	38975	45
50	64105	2324	368	3732	11547	3502	7	2798	0	0	0	2540	37287	50
55	58538	1497	270	3338	10735	3182	7	2477	0	0	0	2047	34985	55
60	52039	903	197	2794	9544	2790	5	2070	0	0	0	1607	32129	60
65	43566	456	130	2036	7814	2298	4	1596	0	0	0	1134	28058	65
70	33513	221	71	1247	5670	1704	3	1074	0	0	0	723	22800	70
75	22188	91	32	577	3348	1070	2	591	0	0	0	392	16085	75
80	11041	27	10	176	1312	484	1	227	0	0	0	157	8647	80
85+	3359	7	3	34	292	127	0	62	0	0	0	42	2792	85+

NUMBER OF PERSONS SURVIVING TO AGE X IF SPECIFIED CAUSES WERE ELIMINATED

Age (x)	No Causes	Respiratory T.B. (1)	Other Infec. and Paras. (2)	Neo-plasms (3)	Cardio-vascular (4)	Infl., Pneu., Bronch. (5)	Diar-rheal (6)	Certain Degenerative (7)	Maternal (8)	Cert. Dis. of Infancy (9)	Motor Vehicle (10)	Other Violence (11)	Other and Unknown (12)	(1)+(2)	(1)+(2)+(5)+(6)+(8)	(1)+(2)+(5)+(6)+(8)+part of(9)&(12)	(10)+(11)	Age (x)
0	100000	100000	100000	100000	100000	100000	100000	100000	100000	100000	100000	100000	100000	100000	100000	100000	100000	0
1	89691	89743	90091	89693	89761	90206	92055	89707	89691	91537	89691	89749	94293	90144	93050	99540	89749	1
5	86463	86576	87368	86470	86558	87198	88996	86490	86463	88242	86463	86658	92901	87483	90811	98910	86698	5
10	85021	85191	86261	85034	85145	85815	87513	85065	85021	86771	85021	85390	92176	86433	89797	98434	85390	10
15	84313	84541	85662	84329	84470	85128	86784	84365	84313	86048	84313	84774	91798	85893	89265	98097	84774	15
20	82762	83401	84259	82784	82970	83626	85189	82827	82762	84465	82762	83460	90735	84909	88311	97500	83460	20
25	80222	81690	81894	80251	80497	81173	82574	80320	80222	81873	80222	81289	88868	83392	86855	96591	81289	25
30	77829	80142	79581	77869	78176	78843	80111	77962	77829	79431	77829	79284	87026	81946	85448	95620	79284	30
35	75141	78302	76947	75207	75606	76238	77344	75332	75141	76687	75141	77002	84979	80184	83740	94379	77002	35
40	72124	76128	73976	72236	72757	73323	74239	72409	72124	73608	72124	74330	82736	78084	81709	92899	74330	40
45	68417	73220	70288	68633	69342	69751	70424	68860	68417	69925	68417	70954	80023	75222	78938	90708	70954	45
50	64105	69552	65958	64518	65435	65589	65987	64755	64105	65424	64105	66935	76916	71562	75368	87661	66935	50
55	58538	64372	60327	59296	60551	60207	60256	59442	58538	59743	58538	61615	72926	66339	70233	82865	61615	55
60	52039	57841	53700	53235	55004	53904	53568	53233	52039	53110	52039	55211	68273	59686	63642	76226	55211	60
65	43566	48834	45019	45281	45595	44847	45010	44661	43566	44661	43566	46681	62258	50463	54367	66348	46681	65
70	33513	37833	34684	35553	38845	35621	34500	35058	33513	34203	33513	36294	54951	39154	42842	53691	36294	70
75	22188	25163	22995	24113	27980	24133	22842	23646	22188	22645	22188	24317	46504	26079	29200	38192	24317	75
80	11041	12570	11458	12295	15798	12455	11367	12033	11041	11268	11041	12276	37021	13044	15150	21576	12276	80
85+	3359	3836	3490	3824	5629	4005	3459	3756	3359	3428	3359	3802	27896	3985	4892	8435	3802	85+

ADDED YRS OF LIFE

	No Causes	(1)	(2)	(3)	(4)	(5)	(6)	(7)	(8)	(9)	(10)	(11)	(12)	(1)+(2)	(1)+(2)+(5)+(6)+(8)	+part of(9)&(12)	(10)+(11)
TOTAL		2.434	1.173	.520	1.628	1.119	1.522	.504	.000	1.071	.000	1.491	15.971	3.679	6.592	15.212	1.491
WORK	8.737	2.035	.354	.210	.588	.362	.001	.253	.000	.000	.000	.998	2.856	2.413	2.812	4.486	.998

POPULATION, DEATHS, DEATH RATES FOR ALL CAUSES COMBINED, AND SPECIFIED CAUSES

Age Start of Interval	Midyear Population	Deaths During Year	All Causes	Respiratory T. B.	Other Infec. and Paras.	Neoplasms	Cardiovascular	Infl., Pneu., Bronch.	Diarrheal	Certain Degenerative	Maternal	Cert. Dis. of Infancy	Motor Vehicle	Other Violence	Other and Unknown	Age Start of Interval
0	367281	32403	.08822	.00048	.00424	.00002	.00064	.00456	.02040	.00014	.00000	.01647	.00000	.00053	.04075	0
1	1448720	12598	.00870	.00019	.00148	.00001	.00008	.00073	.00062	.00002	.00000	.00518	.00000	.00038	.00518	1
5	1128541	3710	.00329	.00018	.00084	.00001	.00007	.00018	.00000	.00005	.00000	.00000	.00000	.00016	.00179	5
10	1538168	2957	.00192	.00041	.00034	.00001	.00009	.00008	.00000	.00002	.00000	.00000	.00000	.00006	.00092	10
15	1702019	7444	.00437	.00187	.00048	.00001	.00012	.00017	.00000	.00004	.00005	.00000	.00000	.00016	.00147	15
20	1707468	9898	.00580	.00250	.00044	.00002	.00018	.00024	.00000	.00007	.00020	.00000	.00000	.00021	.00194	20
25	1655855	9357	.00565	.00221	.00036	.00005	.00022	.00024	.00000	.00011	.00029	.00000	.00000	.00019	.00199	25
30	1542409	8904	.00577	.00189	.00030	.00015	.00033	.00026	.00000	.00016	.00028	.00000	.00000	.00020	.00220	30
35	1511720	9127	.00604	.00158	.00026	.00031	.00044	.00031	.00000	.00024	.00022	.00000	.00000	.00021	.00246	35
40	1451624	10564	.00728	.00140	.00023	.00063	.00077	.00034	.00000	.00040	.00011	.00000	.00000	.00025	.00314	40
45	1394497	12269	.00880	.00113	.00020	.00108	.00122	.00038	.00000	.00056	.00002	.00000	.00000	.00031	.00389	45
50	1259748	15461	.01227	.00101	.00021	.00158	.00215	.00057	.00000	.00074	.00001	.00000	.00000	.00038	.00562	50
55	1128469	17461	.01547	.00083	.00021	.00203	.00313	.00079	.00000	.00086	.00000	.00000	.00000	.00042	.00721	55
60	995556	23353	.02396	.00077	.00022	.00283	.00542	.00140	.00000	.00112	.00000	.00000	.00000	.00050	.01170	60
65	823851	30313	.03679	.00063	.00022	.00357	.00860	.00222	.00001	.00137	.00000	.00000	.00000	.00061	.01958	65
70	611539	36849	.06026	.00055	.00026	.00421	.01341	.00354	.00001	.00170	.00000	.00000	.00000	.00081	.03577	70
75	384184	42144	.10970	.00060	.00025	.00482	.02071	.00629	.00001	.00218	.00000	.00000	.00000	.00126	.07356	75
80	193186	34962	.18098	.00042	.00025	.00472	.02520	.00912	.00002	.00243	.00000	.00000	.00000	.00169	.13713	80
85+	82282	25621	.31138	.00064	.00032	.00464	.03126	.01277	.00001	.00311	.00000	.00000	.00000	.00238	.25624	85+
ALL	20927117	345895														

	All Causes	Respiratory T. B.	Other Infec. and Paras.	Neoplasms	Cardiovascular	Infl., Pneu., Bronch.	Diarrheal	Certain Degenerative	Maternal	Cert. Dis. of Infancy	Motor Vehicle	Other Violence	Other and Unknown
CRUDE DEATH RATE	.01653	.00122	.00048	.00091	.00228	.00087	.00040	.00044	.00009	.00029	.00000	.00033	.00921
STANDARDIZED RATE (1)	.01172	.00112	.00067	.00044	.00103	.00063	.00079	.00024	.00008	.00058	.00000	.00026	.00588
STANDARDIZED RATE (2)	.01625	.00115	.00053	.00082	.00213	.00086	.00047	.00040	.00008	.00034	.00000	.00032	.00915
GEOMETRIC MEAN	.01621												

LIFE TABLE FOR ALL CAUSES COMBINED

Age (x)	Midyear Population	Deaths During Year	$_nM_x$	$_nq_x$	l_x	$_nd_x$	$_nL_x$	$_nm_x$	$_na_x$	T_x	$_nr_x$	$\overset{\circ}{e}_x$	Age (x)
0	367281	32403	.088224	.082540	100000	8254	93562	.088220	.219981	5666081	.000000	56.661	0
1	1448720	12598	.008696	.034051	91746	3124	359174	.008698	1.500000	5572520	.000000	60.739	1
5	1128541	3710	.003287	.016373	88622	1451	439483	.003302	2.500000	5213346	.000000	58.827	5
10	1538168	2957	.001922	.009487	87171	827	433873	.001906	2.603537	4773863	-.038294	54.764	10
15	1702019	7444	.004374	.021565	86344	1862	427995	.004357	2.677453	4339990	-.022098	50.264	15
20	1707468	9898	.005797	.028562	84482	2413	416466	.005794	2.536694	3912595	-.008656	46.313	20
25	1655855	9357	.005651	.027867	82069	2287	404598	.005653	2.486973	3496128	.001379	42.600	25
30	1542409	8904	.005773	.028453	79782	2270	393239	.005773	2.501744	3091531	.003514	38.750	30
35	1511720	9127	.006037	.029750	77512	2306	381882	.006039	2.537854	2698292	.000676	34.811	35
40	1451624	10564	.007277	.035755	75206	2689	369478	.007278	2.563453	2316410	.000214	30.801	40
45	1394497	12269	.008798	.043093	72517	3125	355075	.008801	2.596667	1946931	.003044	26.848	45
50	1259748	15461	.012273	.059647	69392	4139	336977	.012283	2.588035	1591857	.008014	22.940	50
55	1128469	17461	.015473	.074694	65253	4874	314645	.015490	2.615921	1254880	.007383	19.231	55
60	995556	23353	.023959	.113467	60379	6851	285641	.023985	2.627475	940235	.006549	15.572	60
65	823851	30313	.036794	.169369	53528	9066	245990	.036855	2.612003	654594	.008758	12.229	65
70	611539	36849	.060256	.263708	44462	11725	194046	.060424	2.589463	408604	.012332	9.190	70
75	384184	42144	.109697	.430736	32737	14101	128369	.109848	2.495479	214557	.004695	6.554	75
80	193186	34962	.180976	.612739	18636	11419	63011	.181222	2.358003	86188	.004695	4.625	80
85+	82282	25621	.311380	1.000000	7217	7217	23177	.311380	3.211506	23177	.000000	3.212	85+

NUMBER OF PERSONS DYING (OUT OF 100,000 AT BIRTH) ABOVE AGE X FROM SPECIFIED CAUSES

Age (x)	All Causes	Respiratory T.B.	Other Infec. and Paras.	Neoplasms	Cardiovascular	Infl., Pneu., Bronch.	Diarrheal	Certain Degenerative	Maternal	Cert. Dis. of Infancy	Motor Vehicle	Other Violence	Other and Unknown	Age (x)
0	100000	6564	2710	5552	14355	5300	2142	2657	470	1541	0	1912	56797	0
1	91746	6520	2313	5550	14295	4873	234	2644	470	0	0	1863	52984	1
5	88622	6452	1781	5546	14266	4612	12	2635	470	0	0	1725	51123	5
10	87171	6372	1410	5543	14234	4534	11	2613	470	0	0	1654	50330	10
15	86344	6199	1263	5539	14197	4501	11	2603	469	0	0	1628	49934	15
20	84482	5404	1059	5534	14146	4430	11	2585	447	0	0	1560	49306	20
25	82069	4364	876	5525	14071	4332	11	2558	362	0	0	1471	48499	25
30	79782	3471	722	5503	13982	4235	11	2515	245	0	0	1395	47693	30
35	77512	2728	615	5443	13852	4132	11	2452	135	0	0	1318	46826	35
40	75206	2125	516	5323	13683	4014	10	2359	52	0	0	1236	45888	40
45	72517	1607	433	5090	13358	3888	10	2211	11	0	0	1144	44725	45
50	69392	1206	361	4706	12964	3752	9	2012	3	0	0	1035	43344	50
55	65253	865	289	4173	12238	3560	8	1764	1	0	0	908	41447	55
60	60379	605	224	3532	11253	3312	7	1493	1	0	0	774	39178	60
65	53528	385	162	2724	9702	2913	6	1173	1	0	0	631	35831	65
70	44462	229	107	1845	7585	2367	5	837	1	0	0	482	31004	70
75	32737	122	57	1028	4977	1680	3	506	1	0	0	324	24039	75
80	18636	45	23	408	2316	871	2	227	1	0	0	162	14581	80
85+	7217	15	7	108	724	296	0	72	0	0	0	55	5940	85+

NUMBER OF PERSONS SURVIVING TO AGE X IF SPECIFIED CAUSES WERE ELIMINATED

Age (x)	No Causes	Respiratory T.B.	Other Infec. and Paras.	Neoplasms	Cardiovascular	Infl., Pneu., Bronch.	Diarrheal	Certain Degenerative	Maternal	Cert. Dis. of Infancy	Motor Vehicle	Other Violence	Other and Unknown	(1)+(2)	(1)+(2)+(5)+(6)+(8)	(1)+(2)+(5)+(6)+(8)+part of(9)&(12)	(10)+(11)	Age (x)
		(1)	(2)	(3)	(4)	(5)	(6)	(7)	(8)	(9)	(10)	(11)	(12)					
0	100000	100000	100000	100000	100000	100000	100000	100000	100000	100000	100000	100000	100000	100000	100000	100000	100000	0
1	91746	91788	92127	91803	92156	93591	91758	91746	91746	93234	91746	91793	95471	92169	94443	99632	91793	1
5	88622	88730	89517	88628	88706	89276	90627	88643	88622	90059	88622	88803	94143	89625	92329	99142	88803	5
10	87171	87356	88423	87180	87285	87892	89144	87213	87171	88584	87171	87420	93441	88611	91367	98824	87420	10
15	86344	86700	87733	86357	86494	87091	88299	86396	86345	87744	86344	86616	92978	88095	90870	98656	86616	15
20	84482	85624	86046	84499	84680	85284	86395	84551	84505	85852	84482	84816	91644	87209	90055	98408	84816	20
25	82069	84224	83772	82095	82335	82946	83927	82162	82175	83400	82069	82482	89893	85972	88972	98054	82482	25
30	79782	82785	81583	79829	80129	80731	81588	79915	80001	81076	79782	80258	88263	84654	87840	97624	80258	30
35	77512	81193	79380	77617	77978	78537	79267	77704	77833	78769	77512	78051	86703	83149	86513	96963	78051	35
40	75206	79401	77118	75426	75826	76318	76910	75484	75600	76425	75206	75811	85163	81420	84938	95974	75811	40
45	72517	77101	74444	72959	73398	73715	74160	72931	72937	73693	72517	73191	83422	79149	82756	94252	73191	45
50	69392	74196	71309	70194	70666	70674	70965	69984	69802	70517	69392	70145	81356	76244	79882	91607	70145	50
55	65253	70124	67127	66533	67172	66648	66733	66053	65640	66311	65253	66085	78730	72137	75798	87590	66085	55
60	60379	65154	62177	62194	63139	61914	61750	61383	60737	61358	60379	61280	75531	67094	70780	82444	61280	60
65	53528	57984	55182	55925	57522	55276	54744	54725	53846	54356	53528	54463	71021	59775	63504	74821	54463	65
70	44462	48316	45887	47293	49855	46430	45473	45768	44726	45183	44462	45376	65128	49864	53571	64244	45376	70
75	32737	35673	33830	35565	39317	34803	33483	33989	32931	33268	32737	33547	57544	36863	40321	49948	33547	75
80	18636	20368	19284	20743	24868	20460	19061	19562	18747	18938	18636	19220	47895	21076	23808	31803	19220	80
85+	7217	7908	7478	8236	10992	8311	7383	7674	7260	7334	7217	7510	38024	8193	9710	15241	7510	85+

ADDED YRS OF LIFE	No Causes	(1)	(2)	(3)	(4)	(5)	(6)	(7)	(8)	(9)	(10)	(11)	(12)	(1)+(2)	(1)+(2)+(5)+(6)+(8)	(1)+(2)+(5)+(6)+(8)+part of(9)&(12)	(10)+(11)
TOTAL		2.337	1.262	.814	1.835	1.083	1.274	.449	.179	.915	.000	.495	17.830	3.715	6.491	14.945	.495
WORK	7.317	1.883	.345	.336	.544	.289	.001	.217	.162	.000	.000	.220	2.656	2.247	2.733	4.471	.220

POPULATION, DEATHS, DEATH RATES FOR ALL CAUSES COMBINED, AND SPECIFIED CAUSES

Age Start of Interval	Midyear Population	Deaths During Year	All Causes	Respiratory T. B.	Other Infec. and Paras.	Neoplasms	Cardiovascular	Infl., Pneu., Bronch.	Diarrheal	Certain Degenerative	Maternal	Cert. Dis. of Infancy	Motor Vehicle	Other Violence	Other and Unknown	Age Start of Interval
0	371177	31697	.08540	.00043	.00455	.00005	.00113	.01650	.01131	.00015	.00000	.02087	.00000	.00054	.02987	0
1	1447223	10055	.00695	.00016	.00113	.00002	.00010	.00194	.00038	.00004	.00000	.00271	.00000	.00046	.00271	1
5	1789515	4011	.00224	.00008	.00059	.00002	.00007	.00023	.00002	.00005	.00000	.00000	.00000	.00023	.00095	5
10	1185355	2242	.00189	.00016	.00045	.00002	.00010	.00010	.00001	.00004	.00000	.00000	.00000	.00022	.00079	10
15	1539049	4847	.00315	.00095	.00041	.00003	.00015	.00014	.00001	.00006	.00000	.00000	.00000	.00057	.00083	15
20	1719274	8874	.00516	.00181	.00047	.00004	.00020	.00031	.00001	.00009	.00000	.00000	.00000	.00092	.00132	20
25	1796910	9695	.00540	.00205	.00037	.00007	.00024	.00024	.00001	.00011	.00000	.00000	.00000	.00106	.00125	25
30	1622637	10314	.00636	.00236	.00039	.00009	.00038	.00033	.00002	.00016	.00000	.00000	.00000	.00112	.00154	30
35	1257558	9865	.00784	.00258	.00042	.00018	.00070	.00048	.00002	.00021	.00000	.00000	.00000	.00120	.00206	35
40	1224817	11626	.00949	.00261	.00047	.00036	.00108	.00066	.00002	.00034	.00000	.00000	.00000	.00123	.00273	40
45	1180908	14605	.01237	.00277	.00051	.00074	.00192	.00080	.00003	.00054	.00000	.00000	.00000	.00138	.00367	45
50	1170803	19334	.01651	.00264	.00047	.00140	.00323	.00109	.00004	.00072	.00000	.00000	.00000	.00151	.00542	50
55	1072560	26105	.02434	.00248	.00055	.00253	.00591	.00167	.00007	.00116	.00000	.00000	.00000	.00181	.00816	55
60	888025	29174	.03285	.00180	.00050	.00361	.00933	.00220	.00008	.00173	.00000	.00000	.00000	.00185	.01176	60
65	712473	36261	.05089	.00147	.00066	.00532	.01551	.00375	.00011	.00281	.00000	.00000	.00000	.00209	.01917	65
70	495194	41837	.08449	.00095	.00065	.00610	.02289	.00595	.00017	.00413	.00000	.00000	.00000	.00220	.04140	70
75	281208	35647	.12676	.00088	.00081	.00738	.03580	.00942	.00031	.00620	.00000	.00000	.00000	.00277	.06318	75
80	121118	26154	.21594	.00072	.00088	.00534	.03952	.01441	.00023	.00728	.00000	.00000	.00000	.00326	.14429	80
85+	41861	17231	.41162	.00048	.00122	.00561	.05955	.02611	.00043	.01006	.00000	.00000	.00000	.00326	.14429	85+
ALL	19917665	349574														

CRUDE DEATH RATE			.01755	.00159	.00061	.00097	.00327	.00149	.00027	.00065	.00000	.00039	.00000	.00109	.00722	
STANDARDIZED RATE (1)			.01286	.00127	.00070	.00051	.00170	.00141	.00047	.00036	.00000	.00073	.00000	.00084	.00487	
STANDARDIZED RATE (2)			.01946	.00148	.00063	.00099	.00359	.00165	.00030	.00070	.00000	.00043	.00000	.00107	.00861	
GEOMETRIC MEAN			.01815													

LIFE TABLE FOR ALL CAUSES COMBINED

Age (x)	Midyear Population	Deaths During Year	$_nM_x$	$_nq_x$	l_x	$_nd_x$	$_nL_x$	$_nm_x$	$_na_x$	T_x	$_nr_x$	$\overset{\circ}{e}_x$	Age (x)
0	371177	31697	.085396	.080030	100000	8003	93719	.085394	.215173	5517475	.000000	55.175	0
1	1447223	10055	.006948	.027316	91997	2513	361706	.006948	1.500000	5423756	.000000	58.956	1
5	1789515	4011	.002241	.011130	89484	996	444930	.002239	2.500000	5062050	.000000	56.569	5
10	1185355	2242	.001891	.009425	88488	834	440431	.001894	2.591427	4617120	-.020238	52.178	10
15	1539049	4847	.003149	.015538	87654	1362	435149	.003130	2.708180	4176689	-.029218	47.650	15
20	1719274	8874	.005161	.025437	86292	2195	426155	.005151	2.583144	3741541	-.024844	43.359	20
25	1796910	9695	.005395	.026612	84097	2238	414967	.005393	2.534536	3315386	-.011082	39.423	25
30	1622637	10314	.006356	.031347	81859	2566	403051	.006366	2.566495	2900418	.020463	35.432	30
35	1257558	9865	.007845	.038553	79293	3057	389025	.007858	2.566310	2497368	.024381	31.495	35
40	1224817	11626	.009492	.046422	76236	3539	372604	.009498	2.576823	2108343	.003775	27.655	40
45	1180908	14605	.012368	.060002	72697	4362	352972	.012358	2.589934	1735738	-.004902	23.876	45
50	1170803	19334	.016513	.079344	68335	5422	328718	.016494	2.610276	1382766	-.008802	20.235	50
55	1072560	26105	.024339	.114952	62913	7232	297122	.024340	2.588092	1054048	-.000058	16.754	55
60	888025	29174	.032853	.152296	55681	8480	257928	.032877	2.585274	756926	.005220	13.594	60
65	712473	36261	.050895	.226754	47201	10703	210138	.050933	2.583232	498998	.004327	10.572	65
70	495194	41837	.084486	.349499	36498	12756	150735	.084625	2.510616	288859	.007148	7.914	70
75	281208	35647	.126764	.478182	23742	11353	89437	.126938	2.421588	138124	.006477	5.818	75
80	121118	26154	.215938	.684720	12389	8483	39197	.216417	2.318460	48687	.006477	3.930	80
85+	41861	17231	.411624	1.000000	3906	3906	9489	.411624	2.429400	9489	.000000	2.429	85+

NUMBER OF PERSONS DYING (OUT OF 100,000 AT BIRTH) ABOVE AGE X FROM SPECIFIED CAUSES

Age (x)	All Causes	Respiratory T.B.	Other Infec. and Paras.	Neoplasms	Cardiovascular	Infl., Pneu., Bronch.	Diarrheal	Certain Degenerative	Maternal	Cert. Dis. of Infancy	Motor Vehicle	Other Violence	Other and Unknown	Age (x)
0	100000	8770	3311	5654	19241	8296	1408	3815	0	1956	0	6069	41440	0
1	91997	8729	2885	5690	19135	6750	348	3802	0	0	0	6018	38640	1
5	89484	8672	2475	5681	19058	6048	210	3786	0	0	0	5851	37663	5
10	88488	8635	2211	5673	19066	5947	201	3765	0	0	0	5747	37243	10
15	87654	8565	2015	5663	19020	5903	195	3747	0	0	0	5652	36894	15
20	86292	8156	1835	5652	18955	5841	191	3722	0	0	0	5406	36534	20
25	84097	7387	1637	5637	18870	5708	185	3685	0	0	0	5015	35973	25
30	81859	6536	1483	5609	18769	5610	181	3641	0	0	0	4575	35455	30
35	79293	5592	1326	5572	18617	5478	173	3576	0	0	0	4125	34834	35
40	76236	4586	1163	5503	18344	5292	165	3493	0	0	0	3659	34031	40
45	72697	3615	988	5368	17941	5048	156	3367	0	0	0	3201	33013	45
50	68335	2638	809	5106	17265	4765	146	3177	0	0	0	2713	31716	50
55	62913	1769	655	4647	16206	4407	132	2941	0	0	0	2217	29939	55
60	55681	1032	491	3895	14449	3912	111	2597	0	0	0	1680	27514	60
65	47201	568	361	2964	12040	3344	90	2151	0	0	0	1202	24481	65
70	36498	259	222	1846	8780	2556	67	1560	0	0	0	762	20446	70
75	23742	116	117	926	5324	1657	41	937	0	0	0	430	14194	75
80	12389	37	45	265	2118	813	13	382	0	0	0	182	8534	80
85+	3906	5	12	53	565	248	4	95	0	0	0	51	2873	85+

NUMBER OF PERSONS SURVIVING TO AGE X IF SPECIFIED CAUSES WERE ELIMINATED

Age (x)	No Causes	Respiratory T.B. (1)	Other Infec. and Paras. (2)	Neoplasms (3)	Cardiovascular (4)	Infl., Pneu., Bronch. (5)	Diarrheal (6)	Certain Degenerative (7)	Maternal (8)	Cert. Dis. of Infancy (9)	Motor Vehicle (10)	Other Violence (11)	Other and Unknown (12)	(1) + (2)	(1) + (2) + (5) + (6) + (8)	(1)+(2)+ (5)+(6)+ (8)+part of(9)&(12)	(10) + (11)	Age (x)
0	100000	100000	100000	100000	100000	100000	100000	100000	100000	100000	100000	100000	100000	100000	100000	100000	100000	0
1	91997	92036	92406	92001	92099	93491	93019	92009	91997	93892	91997	92046	94721	92446	94991	99554	92046	1
5	89484	89579	90289	89497	89619	91644	90616	89512	89484	91327	89484	89667	93121	90385	93737	99144	89667	5
10	88488	88618	89550	88508	88654	90727	89536	88536	88488	90311	88488	88802	92531	89681	93123	98826	88802	10
15	87654	87853	88903	87684	87864	89917	88778	87720	87654	89459	87654	88060	92022	89105	92577	98501	88060	15
20	86292	86896	87703	86333	86564	88583	87402	86382	86292	88069	86292	86937	90968	88317	91827	97568	86937	20
25	84097	85453	85671	84151	84446	86464	85185	84221	84097	85829	84097	85116	89240	87053	90661	97156	85116	25
30	81859	84037	83546	81940	82299	84422	82922	82023	81859	83545	81859	83291	87409	85769	89433	96226	83291	30
35	79293	82362	81085	79408	79870	81755	80331	79516	79293	80926	79293	81132	85324	84223	87975	95123	81132	35
40	76236	80217	78122	76414	77061	78792	77242	76532	76236	77806	76236	78473	82887	82202	86078	93656	78473	40
45	72697	77497	74671	72999	73883	75381	73665	73103	72697	74194	72697	75291	80127	79601	83638	91694	75291	45
50	68335	73862	70369	68875	70120	71142	69255	68902	68335	69742	68335	71265	76719	76060	80251	88748	71265	50
55	62913	68506	64937	63856	65609	65856	63773	63664	62913	64205	62913	66108	72572	71123	75468	84328	66108	55
60	55681	61745	57631	57239	59818	58775	56462	56674	55681	56828	55681	59040	66915	63908	68406	77363	59040	60
65	47201	52812	48978	49410	53148	50379	47883	48463	47201	48173	47201	50515	60180	54800	59335	67968	50515	65
70	36498	41137	37998	39241	44442	39700	37046	38009	36498	37250	36498	39472	51289	42827	47283	55165	39472	70
75	23742	26885	24804	26322	32472	26618	24119	25248	23742	24231	23742	25962	41228	28087	31991	38773	25962	75
80	12389	14091	12996	14257	20350	14578	12606	13598	12389	12644	12389	13739	29816	14781	17697	22747	13739	80
85+	3906	4462	4116	4626	7926	4563	3979	4458	3906	3986	3906	4410	20309	4702	6086	9314	4410	85+

ADDED YRS OF LIFE

		(1)	(2)	(3)	(4)	(5)	(6)	(7)	(8)	(9)	(10)	(11)	(12)				
TOTAL		2.487	1.242	.705	2.418	2.185	.730	.495	.000	1.132	.000	1.533	9.256	3.809	7.030	13.069	1.533
WORK	8.043	1.985	.416	.264	.764	.408	.018	.211	.000	.000	.000	1.007	1.992	2.431	2.899	4.052	1.007

POPULATION, DEATHS, DEATH RATES FOR ALL CAUSES COMBINED, AND SPECIFIED CAUSES

Age Start of Interval	Midyear Population	Deaths During Year	All Causes	Respiratory T. B.	Other Infec. and Paras.	Neoplasms	Cardiovascular	Infl., Pneu., Bronch.	Diarrheal	Certain Degenerative	Maternal	Cert. Dis. of Infancy	Motor Vehicle	Other Violence	Other and Unknown	Age Start of Interval
0	363995	23961	.06583	.00038	.00402	.00002	.00096	.01266	.00842	.00005	.00000	.01599	.00000	.00043	.02284	0
1	1413167	9130	.00646	.00014	.00114	.00003	.00009	.00181	.00036	.00003	.00000	.00000	.00000	.00038	.00248	1
5	1746297	3806	.00218	.00009	.00063	.00002	.00009	.00022	.00003	.00004	.00000	.00000	.00000	.00038	.00248	5
10	1147180	2349	.00205	.00034	.00049	.00002	.00014	.00014	.00001	.00005	.00000	.00000	.00000	.00015	.00092	10
15	1517165	5016	.00331	.00153	.00042	.00002	.00012	.00015	.00001	.00005	.00004	.00000	.00000	.00010	.00077	15
20	1665454	8114	.00487	.00230	.00046	.00004	.00023	.00022	.00001	.00008	.00021	.00000	.00000	.00016	.00081	20
25	1697578	8262	.00487	.00203	.00039	.00008	.00031	.00023	.00001	.00011	.00028	.00000	.00000	.00021	.00111	25
30	1646490	8087	.00491	.00168	.00035	.00019	.00041	.00026	.00001	.00014	.00025	.00000	.00000	.00021	.00122	30
35	1532986	8320	.00543	.00144	.00031	.00040	.00064	.00029	.00002	.00020	.00022	.00000	.00000	.00021	.00142	35
40	1458344	9394	.00644	.00127	.00031	.00079	.00094	.00037	.00002	.00026	.00011	.00000	.00000	.00025	.00165	40
45	1401762	11514	.00821	.00112	.00030	.00129	.00156	.00048	.00002	.00040	.00002	.00000	.00000	.00031	.00204	45
50	1320830	14001	.01060	.00089	.00028	.00183	.00245	.00062	.00003	.00055	.00001	.00000	.00000	.00035	.00267	50
55	1182915	18511	.01565	.00082	.00033	.00266	.00421	.00099	.00006	.00083	.00000	.00000	.00000	.00038	.00357	55
60	1025274	21968	.02143	.00071	.00031	.00322	.00639	.00148	.00007	.00115	.00000	.00000	.00000	.00043	.00531	60
65	863007	31415	.03640	.00075	.00040	.00461	.01165	.00281	.00011	.00178	.00000	.00000	.00000	.00050	.00759	65
70	647499	41501	.06409	.00060	.00046	.00535	.01821	.00453	.00013	.00219	.00000	.00000	.00000	.00065	.01365	70
75	402059	38730	.09633	.00055	.00054	.00647	.02847	.00781	.00024	.00329	.00000	.00000	.00000	.00086	.03137	75
80	206581	36729	.17779	.00060	.00073	.00590	.03424	.01254	.00026	.00345	.00000	.00000	.00000	.00108	.04788	80
85+	84967	28732	.33815	.00039	.00100	.00618	.05158	.02347	.00046	.00475	.00000	.00000	.00000	.00173	.11795	85+
ALL	21323550	329540														

		All Causes	Respiratory T. B.	Other Infec. and Paras.	Neoplasms	Cardiovascular	Infl., Pneu., Bronch.	Diarrheal	Certain Degenerative	Maternal	Cert. Dis. of Infancy	Motor Vehicle	Other Violence	Other and Unknown
CRUDE DEATH RATE		.01545	.00105	.00051	.00117	.00312	.00130	.00020	.00049	.00009	.00027	.00000	.00035	.00687
STANDARDIZED RATE (1)		.00999	.00099	.00064	.00056	.00136	.00111	.00036	.00024	.00008	.00056	.00000	.00027	.00381
STANDARDIZED RATE (2)		.01485	.00104	.00054	.00103	.00285	.00131	.00024	.00044	.00008	.00033	.00000	.00033	.00667
GEOMETRIC MEAN		.01440												

LIFE TABLE FOR ALL CAUSES COMBINED

Age (x)	Midyear Population	Deaths During Year	$_nM_x$	$_nq_x$	l_x	$_nd_x$	$_nL_x$	$_nm_x$	$_na_x$	T_x	$_nr_x$	$\overset{\circ}{e}_x$	Age (x)
0	363995	23961	.065828	.062460	100000	6246	94890	.065823	.181907	5981776	.000000	59.818	0
1	1413167	9130	.006461	.025439	93754	2385	369054	.006462	1.500000	5886886	.000000	62.791	1
5	1746297	3806	.002179	.010813	91369	988	454375	.002174	2.500000	5517832	.000000	60.351	5
10	1147180	2349	.002048	.010212	90381	923	449696	.002052	2.606311	5063457	.000000	56.023	10
15	1517165	5016	.003306	.016309	89458	1459	443891	.003287	2.670351	4613762	-.019439	51.575	15
20	1665454	8114	.004872	.024046	87999	2116	434831	.004866	2.559566	4169871	-.030522	47.385	20
25	1697578	8262	.004867	.024033	85883	2064	424238	.004865	2.491723	3735040	-.021125	43.490	25
30	1646490	8087	.004912	.024267	83819	2034	414036	.004913	2.513008	3310802	-.009390	39.499	30
35	1532986	8320	.005427	.026790	81785	2191	403550	.005429	2.546687	2896765	.001339	35.419	35
40	1458344	9394	.006442	.031723	79594	2525	391848	.006444	2.575330	2493215	-.006087	31.324	40
45	1401762	11514	.008214	.040276	77069	3104	377856	.008215	2.587320	2101368	-.003513	27.266	45
50	1320830	14001	.010600	.051727	73965	3826	360717	.010607	2.619359	1723512	.001483	23.302	50
55	1182915	18511	.015649	.075507	70139	5296	338037	.015667	2.609989	1362795	-.004102	19.430	55
60	1025274	21968	.021426	.102124	64843	6622	308593	.021459	2.640881	1024758	-.008569	15.804	60
65	863007	31415	.036402	.167878	58221	9774	268094	.036457	2.645646	716165	-.008837	12.301	65
70	647499	41501	.064094	.277726	48447	13455	209394	.064257	2.559210	448071	-.006687	9.249	70
75	402059	38730	.096329	.388603	34992	13598	140880	.096522	2.493749	238677	-.011439	6.821	75
80	206581	36729	.177795	.609844	21394	13047	73113	.178450	2.404991	97797	-.009720	4.571	80
85+	84967	28732	.338155	1.000000	8347	8347	24684	.338155	2.957225	24684	.000000	2.957	85+

NUMBER OF PERSONS DYING (OUT OF 100,000 AT BIRTH) ABOVE AGE X FROM SPECIFIED CAUSES

Age (x)	All Causes	Respiratory T. B.	Other Infec. and Paras.	Neo-plasms	Cardio-vascular	Infl., Pneu., Bronch.	Diar-rheal	Certain Degen-erative	Maternal	Cert. Dis. of Infancy	Motor Vehicle	Other Violence	Other and Unknown	Age (x)
0	100000	6295	3027	7542	20544	8276	1162	3165	475	1517	0	2129	45468	0
1	93754	6258	2645	7540	20852	7075	363	3157	475	0	0	2088	43301	1
5	91369	6205	2223	7528	20820	6409	231	3145	475	0	0	1948	42385	5
10	90381	6165	1936	7520	20779	6308	219	3127	475	0	0	1882	41970	10
15	89458	6011	1716	7512	20715	6248	215	3104	474	0	0	1838	41625	15
20	87999	5338	1531	7502	20662	6183	212	3081	457	0	0	1766	41267	20
25	85883	4340	1332	7486	20562	6087	207	3047	365	0	0	1673	40784	25
30	83819	3478	1168	7452	20432	5989	202	2999	246	0	0	1584	40269	30
35	81785	2782	1025	7373	20261	5883	197	2942	143	0	0	1497	39682	35
40	79594	2200	899	7212	20001	5765	190	2861	56	0	0	1396	39014	40
45	77069	1701	776	6902	19631	5619	181	2759	11	0	0	1276	38213	45
50	73965	1277	663	6415	19041	5437	173	2609	3	0	0	1143	37204	50
55	70139	958	563	5754	18154	5214	163	2410	1	0	0	1007	35915	55
60	64843	680	452	4853	16730	4879	143	2128	1	0	0	861	34116	60
65	58221	460	357	3860	14754	4420	121	1772	1	0	0	705	31771	65
70	48447	259	250	2623	11625	3666	92	1295	1	0	0	531	28105	70
75	34992	135	153	1501	7803	2630	65	836	1	0	0	351	21517	75
80	21394	57	77	590	3787	1528	31	372	1	0	0	198	14753	80
85+	8347	10	25	153	1273	579	11	117	0	0	0	71	6108	85+

NUMBER OF PERSONS SURVIVING TO AGE X IF SPECIFIED CAUSES WERE ELIMINATED

Age (x)	No Causes	Respiratory T. B.	Other Infec. and Paras.	Neo-plasms	Cardio-vascular	Infl., Pneu., Bronch.	Diar-rheal	Certain Degen-erative	Maternal	Cert. Dis. of Infancy	Motor Vehicle	Other Violence	Other and Unknown	(1) + (2)	(1) + (2) + (5) + (6) + (8)	(1)+(2)+ (5)+(6)+ (8)+part of(9)&(12)	(10) + (11)	Age (x)
		(1)	(2)	(3)	(4)	(5)	(6)	(7)	(8)	(9)	(10)	(11)	(12)					
0	100000	100000	100000	100000	100000	100000	100000	100000	100000	100000	100000	100000	100000	100000	100000	100000	100000	0
1	93754	93790	94125	93756	93843	94924	94531	93762	93754	95234	93754	93794	95876	94161	96125	99641	93794	1
5	91369	91456	92149	91383	91487	93177	92257	91388	91369	92812	91369	91546	94366	92237	94977	99299	91546	5
10	90381	90507	91441	90403	90539	92272	91272	90418	90381	91808	90381	90622	93773	91569	94406	99048	90622	10
15	89458	89736	90729	89487	89678	91391	90344	89518	89459	90870	89458	89740	93172	91011	93900	98804	89740	15
20	87999	88945	89436	88038	88268	89966	88873	88080	88017	89388	87999	88348	92023	90397	93355	98571	88348	20
25	85883	87809	87485	85937	86245	87900	86741	85996	85991	87239	85883	86316	90310	89446	92579	98215	86316	25
30	83819	86573	85548	83905	84301	85887	84662	83977	84043	85142	83819	84330	88677	88358	91692	97751	84330	30
35	81785	85185	83616	81947	82426	83910	82612	81996	82105	83076	81785	82370	87141	87092	90612	97099	82370	35
40	79594	83503	81503	79911	80477	81781	80406	79879	79992	80851	79594	80264	85511	85505	89195	96060	80264	40
45	77069	81370	79041	77683	78293	79335	77864	77446	77499	78286	77069	77837	83650	83452	87276	94452	77837	45
50	73965	78532	75971	75037	75730	76323	74736	74475	74385	75133	73965	74834	81361	80662	84579	91964	74834	50
55	70139	74799	72142	71812	72703	72600	70880	70818	70539	71246	70139	71097	78545	76935	80935	88407	71097	55
60	64843	69436	66804	67282	68648	67452	65868	65745	65213	65867	64843	65871	74577	71536	75653	83107	65871	60
65	58221	62568	60074	61393	63653	61018	58875	59373	58553	59140	58221	59294	69566	64559	68811	76130	59294	65
70	48447	52259	50089	52283	56173	51500	49018	49849	48724	49212	48447	49501	62031	54031	58443	65463	49501	70
75	34992	37857	36262	38792	44494	38140	35427	36404	35192	35544	34992	35908	52562	39231	43540	50248	35908	75
80	21394	23210	22231	24502	31437	24265	21687	22632	21516	21732	21394	22075	41098	24118	27887	33719	22075	80
85+	8347	9086	8706	9866	14704	10138	8473	8994	8395	8479	8347	8692	29917	9477	11753	16534	8692	85+

ADDED YRS OF LIFE

		(1)	(2)	(3)	(4)	(5)	(6)	(7)	(8)	(9)	(10)	(11)	(12)				
TOTAL		2.265	1.290	1.117	2.708	2.032	.618	.474	.184	.942	.000	.553	10.134	3.619	6.708	12.251	.553
WORK	6.431	1.728	.384	.433	.711	.304	.016	.189	.159	.000	.000	.245	1.703	2.131	2.646	3.687	.245

POPULATION, DEATHS, DEATH RATES FOR ALL CAUSES COMBINED, AND SPECIFIED CAUSES

Age Start of Interval	Midyear Population	Deaths During Year	All Causes	Respiratory T. B.	Other Infec. and Paras.	Neo-plasms	Cardio-vascular	Infl., Pneu., Bronch.	Diar-rheal	Certain Degen-erative	Maternal	Cert. Dis. of Infancy	Motor Vehicle	Other Violence	Other and Unknown	Age Start of Interval
0	318736	24143	.07575	.00034	.0C417	.0000 7	.0059	.01380	.00686	.00013	.00000	.02179	.00000	.00048	.02752	0
1	1343014	7556	.00563	.00010	.00085	.00004	.00009	.00138	.00026	.00004	.00000	.00000	.00000	.00040	.00246	1
5	1696922	3183	.00188	.00006	.00045	.00002	.00008	.00016	.00002	.00003	.00000	.00000	.00000	.00022	.00084	5
10	1767954	2370	.00134	.00009	.00024	.00002	.00008	.00007	.00001	.00002	.00000	.00000	.00000	.00020	.00062	10
15	1146465	3365	.00294	.00062	.00036	.00003	.00014	.00012	.00001	.00005	.00000	.00000	.00000	.00064	.00098	15
20	1483684	6044	.00407	.00128	.00035	.00004	.00016	.00021	.00001	.00007	.00000	.00000	.00000	.00080	.00115	20
25	1673184	7800	.00466	.00164	.00025	.00006	.00022	.00016	.00001	.00009	.00000	.00000	.00000	.00096	.00126	25
30	1713033	10130	.00591	.00194	.00030	.00012	.00035	.00026	.00001	.00014	.00000	.00000	.00000	.00108	.00171	30
35	1553763	12048	.00775	.00233	.00034	.00022	.00061	.00041	.00001	.00020	.00000	.00000	.00000	.00123	.00241	35
40	1179771	12063	.01022	.00256	.00039	.00043	.00110	.00055	.00001	.00029	.00000	.00000	.00000	.00131	.00359	40
45	1140868	14245	.01249	.00246	.00042	.00080	.00182	.00064	.00003	.00041	.00000	.00000	.00000	.00138	.00453	45
50	1085670	18597	.01713	.00240	.00044	.00148	.00317	.00083	.00003	.00071	.00000	.00000	.00000	.00153	.00653	50
55	1053471	24019	.02280	.00202	.00047	.00234	.00521	.00108	.00003	.00058	.00000	.00000	.00000	.00161	.00906	55
60	926692	32513	.03509	.00191	.00047	.00380	.00942	.00174	.00006	.00163	.00000	.00000	.00000	.00190	.01417	60
65	719340	34962	.04860	.00128	.00053	.00491	.01410	.00244	.00009	.00252	.00000	.00000	.00000	.00199	.02075	65
70	519666	38048	.07322	.00102	.00055	.00619	.02221	.00358	.00013	.00410	.00000	.00000	.00000	.00224	.03316	70
75	304937	41193	.13509	.00063	.00070	.00658	.03292	.00628	.00018	.00630	.00000	.00000	.00000	.00271	.07839	75
80	130657	26358	.20173	.00067	.00076	.00589	.03883	.00910	.00018	.00757	.00000	.00000	.00000	.00296	.13537	80
85+	45154	17290	.38291	.00044	.00104	.00618	.05851	.01650	.00033	.01058	.00000	.00000	.00000	.00489	.28403	85+
ALL	19802981	335927														

	All Causes	Respiratory T. B.	Other Infec. and Paras.	Neo-plasms	Cardio-vascular	Infl., Pneu., Bronch.	Diar-rheal	Certain Degen-erative	Maternal	Cert. Dis. of Infancy	Motor Vehicle	Other Violence	Other and Unknown
CRUDE DEATH RATE	.01696	.00136	.00048	.00100	.00320	.00106	.00015	.00063	.00000	.00035	.00000	.00106	.00767
STANDARDIZED RATE (1)	.01194	.00105	.00056	.00052	.00159	.00107	.00029	.00033	.00000	.00077	.00000	.00082	.00495
STANDARDIZED RATE (2)	.01849	.00126	.00051	.00099	.00340	.00118	.00019	.00067	.00000	.00045	.00000	.00103	.00879
GEOMETRIC MEAN	.01674												

LIFE TABLE FOR ALL CAUSES COMBINED

Age (x)	Midyear Population	Deaths During Year	$_nM_x$	$_nq_x$	l_x	$_nd_x$	$_nL_x$	$_nm_x$	$_na_x$	T_x	$_nr_x$	$\overset{\circ}{e}_x$	Age (x)
0	318736	24143	.075746	.071410	100000	7141	94278	.075744	.198768	5664406	.000000	56.644	0
1	1343014	7556	.005626	.022195	92859	2061	366284	.005627	1.500000	5570128	.000000	59.985	1
5	1696922	3183	.001876	.009317	90798	846	451875	.001872	2.500000	5203844	.000000	57.312	5
10	1767954	2370	.001341	.006692	89952	602	448352	.001343	2.660922	4751969	.030168	52.828	10
15	1146465	3365	.002935	.014673	89350	1311	443716	.002955	2.685768	4303617	.029361	48.166	15
20	1483684	6044	.004074	.020116	88039	1771	435908	.004063	2.579169	3859974	-.028504	43.843	20
25	1673184	7800	.004662	.022958	86268	1984	426522	.004652	2.571825	3423994	-.023922	39.690	25
30	1713033	10130	.005913	.029128	84284	2455	415520	.005908	2.596572	2997471	-.009756	35.564	30
35	1553763	12048	.007754	.038153	81829	3122	401649	.007773	2.598828	2581952	.020803	31.553	35
40	1179771	12063	.010225	.050008	78707	3936	383549	.010250	2.574685	2180303	.025131	27.702	40
45	1140868	14245	.012486	.060625	74771	4533	362905	.012491	2.584381	1796314	.003005	24.024	45
50	1085670	18597	.017130	.082178	70238	5772	337266	.017114	2.587600	1433409	-.006075	20.408	50
55	1053471	24019	.022800	.107964	64466	6960	305664	.022770	2.605514	1096143	-.009627	17.003	55
60	926692	32513	.035085	.161670	57506	9297	265020	.035080	2.578789	790479	-.000615	13.746	60
65	719340	34962	.048603	.217304	48209	10476	215360	.048644	2.548225	525459	.005724	10.900	65
70	519666	38049	.073216	.310656	37733	11722	159902	.073307	2.546245	310099	.006174	8.218	70
75	304937	41193	.135087	.502787	26011	13078	96675	.135278	2.447622	150197	.004359	5.774	75
80	130657	26358	.201734	.652130	12933	8434	41772	.201904	2.285664	53522	.004359	4.138	80
85+	45154	17290	.382912	1.000000	4499	4499	11749	.382912	2.611567	11749	.000000	2.612	85+

NUMBER OF PERSONS DYING (OUT OF 100,000 AT BIRTH) ABOVE AGE X FROM SPECIFIED CAUSES

Age (x)	All Causes	Respiratory T.B.	Other Infec. and Paras.	Neoplasms	Cardiovascular	Infl., Pneu., Bronch.	Diarrheal	Certain Degenerative	Maternal	Cert. Dis. of Infancy	Motor Vehicle	Other Violence	Other and Unknown	Age (x)
0	100000	7753	2736	5952	19108	6194	887	3782	0	2054	0	6111	45423	0
1	92859	7721	2343	5946	19052	4892	240	3770	0	0	0	6066	42829	1
5	90798	7685	2033	5932	19018	4386	144	3755	0	0	0	5919	41926	5
10	89952	7660	1831	5921	18984	4312	137	3740	0	0	0	5820	41547	10
15	89350	7620	1722	5914	18950	4282	134	3730	0	0	0	5730	41268	15
20	88039	7342	1563	5901	18888	4229	132	3707	0	0	0	5445	40832	20
25	86268	6785	1410	5885	18817	4136	128	3675	0	0	0	5098	40334	25
30	84284	6085	1301	5858	18722	4069	125	3637	0	0	0	4688	39799	30
35	81829	5278	1177	5810	18577	3961	121	3580	0	0	0	4238	39087	35
40	78707	4342	1039	5721	18330	3795	118	3501	0	0	0	3746	38115	40
45	74771	3360	888	5555	17905	3583	113	3390	0	0	0	3244	36733	45
50	70238	2468	735	5264	17246	3350	103	3241	0	0	0	2741	35090	50
55	64466	1658	588	4766	16177	3069	95	3001	0	0	0	2225	32887	55
60	57506	1039	445	4051	14589	2740	85	2702	0	0	0	1734	30121	60
65	48209	533	322	3044	12093	2281	69	2271	0	0	0	1231	26365	65
70	37733	258	207	1985	9055	1755	50	1728	0	0	0	802	21893	70
75	26011	96	112	995	5499	1182	29	1072	0	0	0	444	16582	75
80	12933	35	44	320	2313	574	12	462	0	0	0	183	8990	80
85+	4499	5	12	73	687	194	4	129	0	0	0	58	3337	85+

NUMBER OF PERSONS SURVIVING TO AGE X IF SPECIFIED CAUSES WERE ELIMINATED

Age (x)	No Causes	Respiratory T.B. (1)	Other Infec. and Paras. (2)	Neoplasms (3)	Cardiovascular (4)	Infl., Pneu., Bronch. (5)	Diarrheal (6)	Certain Degenerative (7)	Maternal (8)	Cert. Dis. of Infancy (9)	Motor Vehicle (10)	Other Violence (11)	Other and Unknown (12)	(1)+(2)	(1)+(2)+(5)+(6)+(8)	(1)+(2)+(5)+(6)+(8)+part of(9)&(12)	(10)+(11)	Age (x)
0	100000	100000	100000	100000	100000	100000	100000	100000	100000	100000	100000	100000	100000	100000	100000	100000	100000	0
1	92859	92890	93238	92865	92913	94122	93484	92871	92859	94859	92859	92902	95392	93269	95175	99647	92902	1
5	90798	90864	91477	90817	90864	92541	91505	90824	90798	92754	90798	90986	94197	91544	94028	99242	90986	5
10	89952	90042	90828	89982	90071	91754	90660	89993	89952	91889	89952	90237	93711	90919	93470	98926	90237	10
15	89350	89479	90330	89387	89503	91171	90056	89401	89350	91275	89350	89723	93374	90460	93033	98637	89723	15
20	88039	88443	89164	88088	88251	89887	88737	88112	88039	89935	88039	88691	92457	89573	92178	98001	88691	20
25	86268	87220	87524	86332	86546	86546	86955	86371	86268	88126	86268	87254	91117	88490	91164	97275	87254	25
30	84284	85917	85620	84374	84650	86212	84959	84422	84284	86099	84284	85658	89581	87279	89990	96388	85658	30
35	81829	84228	83250	81963	82328	83810	82488	82019	81829	83552	81829	83615	87721	85691	88473	95251	83615	35
40	78707	81965	80212	78924	79431	80760	79344	78968	78707	80402	78707	80915	85403	83532	86425	93700	80919	40
45	74771	78868	76351	75140	75879	76952	75381	75127	74771	76381	74771	77376	82607	80534	83560	91460	77376	45
50	70238	75003	71873	70669	71931	72520	70821	70718	70238	71751	70238	73191	79378	76749	79899	88340	73191	50
55	64466	69670	66111	65529	67078	66839	65008	65139	64466	65855	64466	67693	75280	71448	74701	83540	67693	55
60	57506	62780	59111	59145	61419	59945	57599	58392	57506	58745	57506	60872	70272	64533	67847	76783	60872	60
65	48209	53134	49670	50539	53989	50693	48637	49354	48209	49247	48209	51518	63263	54744	58077	66663	51518	65
70	37733	41852	38881	40546	45372	40168	38085	39124	37733	38546	37733	40727	54981	43236	46456	54197	40727	70
75	26011	28996	26951	28834	35002	28197	26271	27536	26011	26571	26011	28392	44854	30044	32895	39245	28392	75
80	12933	14461	13448	14849	20591	14481	13074	14140	12933	13212	12933	14311	33647	15037	17020	21482	14311	80
85+	4499	5050	4697	5328	8780	5283	4553	5128	4499	4596	4499	5057	23754	5272	6264	8865	5057	85+

ADDED YRS OF LIFE

	No Causes	(1)	(2)	(3)	(4)	(5)	(6)	(7)	(8)	(9)	(10)	(11)	(12)				
TOTAL		2.124	1.011	.760	2.369	1.730	.462	.466	.000	1.216	.000	1.538	10.408	3.191	5.567	11.353	1.538
WORK	7.715	1.647	.336	.284	.722	.316	.010	.185	.000	.000	.000	.996	2.306	2.003	2.357	3.554	.996

POPULATION, DEATHS, DEATH RATES FOR ALL CAUSES COMBINED, AND SPECIFIED CAUSES

Age Start of Interval	Midyear Population	Deaths During Year	All Causes	Respiratory T. B.	Other Infec. and Paras.	Neo-plasms	Cardio-vascular	Infl., Pneu., Bronch.	Diar-rheal	Certain Degen-erative	Maternal	Cert. Dis. of Infancy	Motor Vehicle	Other Violence	Other and Unknown	Age Start of Interval
0	315002	18102	.05747	.00023	.00381	.00004	.00038	.01087	.00493	.00005	.00000	.01646	.00000	.00046	.02023	0
1	1326816	6755	.00509	.00011	.00086	.00002	.00008	.00129	.00023	.00002	.00000	.00000	.00000	.00028	.00220	1
5	1678194	2867	.00171	.00006	.00040	.00002	.00008	.00016	.00001	.00003	.00000	.00000	.00000	.00013	.00081	5
10	1735204	2373	.00137	.00015	.00027	.00002	.00009	.00007	.00001	.00003	.00000	.00000	.00000	.00005	.00064	10
15	1122779	3250	.00289	.00104	.00037	.00003	.00014	.00011	.00001	.00004	.00003	.00000	.00000	.00018	.00094	15
20	1473846	5144	.00349	.00144	.00030	.00003	.00018	.00012	.00000	.00006	.00015	.00000	.00000	.00020	.00100	20
25	1642217	6278	.00382	.00141	.00029	.00006	.00026	.00013	.00001	.00008	.00022	.00000	.00000	.00020	.00116	25
30	1658153	6752	.00407	.00125	.00027	.00017	.00035	.00016	.00001	.00011	.00018	.00000	.00000	.00021	.00136	30
35	1605673	7466	.00465	.00112	.00028	.00035	.00052	.00020	.00001	.00015	.00014	.00000	.00000	.00002	.00168	35
40	1466096	8797	.00600	.00097	.00026	.00074	.00086	.00025	.00002	.00026	.00008	.00000	.00000	.00026	.00229	40
45	1396022	10488	.00751	.00079	.00025	.00115	.00133	.00032	.00002	.00033	.00001	.00000	.00000	.00032	.00299	45
50	1323440	13892	.01050	.00065	.00028	.00180	.00228	.00045	.00002	.00050	.00000	.00000	.00000	.00038	.00409	50
55	1236601	17094	.01382	.00060	.00027	.00223	.00346	.00060	.00004	.00072	.00000	.00000	.00000	.00044	.00547	55
60	1075201	23859	.02219	.00067	.00030	.00339	.00626	.00099	.00005	.00119	.00000	.00000	.00000	.00051	.00885	60
65	885877	28453	.03212	.00062	.00035	.00404	.00983	.00164	.00006	.00166	.00000	.00000	.00000	.00058	.01334	65
70	687956	35671	.05185	.00053	.00044	.00518	.01656	.00290	.00010	.00240	.00000	.00000	.00000	.00070	.02263	70
75	445842	44778	.10043	.00047	.00054	.00609	.02590	.00526	.00014	.00322	.00000	.00000	.00000	.00111	.05771	75
80	219664	34449	.15683	.00052	.00056	.00613	.03189	.00754	.00015	.00354	.00000	.00000	.00000	.00170	.10480	80
85+	100720	29923	.29709	.00034	.00076	.00643	.04803	.01367	.00027	.00487	.00000	.00000	.00000	.00281	.21990	85+
ALL	21395303	306391														

CRUDE DEATH RATE			.01432	.00076	.00040	.00114	.00298	.00087	.00011	.00048	.00006	.00024	.00000	.00032	.00695	
STANDARDIZED RATE (1)			.00869	.00069	.00050	.00052	.00120	.00082	.00021	.00022	.00006	.00058	.00000	.00024	.00363	
STANDARDIZED RATE (2)			.01323	.00074	.00043	.00097	.00257	.00089	.00014	.00042	.00006	.00034	.00000	.00030	.00637	
GEOMETRIC MEAN			.01238													

LIFE TABLE FOR ALL CAUSES COMBINED

Age (x)	Midyear Population	Deaths During Year	$_nM_x$	$_nq_x$	l_x	$_nd_x$	$_nL_x$	$_nm_x$	$_na_x$	T_x	$_nr_x$	$\overset{\circ}{e}_x$	Age (x)
0	315002	18102	.057466	.054840	100000	5484	95436	.057463	.167693	6235495	.000000	62.355	0
1	1326816	6755	.005091	.020113	94516	1901	373312	.005092	1.500000	6140059	.000000	64.963	1
5	1678194	2867	.001708	.008476	92615	785	461113	.001702	2.500000	5766747	.000000	62.266	5
10	1735204	2373	.001368	.006839	91830	628	457591	.001372	2.676818	5305635	.031319	57.777	10
15	1122779	3250	.002895	.014451	91202	1318	452908	.002910	2.646213	4847944	.028734	53.156	15
20	1473846	5144	.003490	.017278	89884	1553	445611	.003485	2.547355	4395036	-.029140	48.897	20
25	1642217	6278	.003823	.018917	88331	1671	437518	.003819	2.524062	3949425	-.020928	44.712	25
30	1658153	6752	.004072	.020148	86660	1746	428994	.004070	2.533648	3511907	-.008021	40.525	30
35	1605673	7466	.004650	.023000	84914	1953	419835	.004652	2.575632	3082914	.003543	36.306	35
40	1466096	8797	.006000	.029592	82961	2455	408880	.006004	2.586558	2663078	.007895	32.100	40
45	1396022	10488	.007513	.036929	80506	2973	395413	.007519	2.606164	2254198	.003969	28.000	45
50	1323440	13892	.010497	.051204	77533	3970	378147	.010499	2.602540	1858785	.001671	23.974	50
55	1236601	17094	.013823	.066977	73563	4927	356180	.013833	2.638438	1480638	.004012	20.127	55
60	1075201	23859	.022190	.105542	68636	7244	325954	.022224	2.622084	1124459	.009507	16.383	60
65	885877	28453	.032118	.149401	61392	9172	285037	.032178	2.609777	798504	.010537	13.007	65
70	687956	35671	.051851	.231272	52220	12077	232369	.051573	2.620994	513467	.010870	9.833	70
75	445842	44778	.100435	.403209	40143	16186	160517	.100837	2.516475	281099	.013242	7.002	75
80	219664	34449	.156826	.557541	23957	13357	84903	.157321	2.388464	120582	.013242	5.033	80
85+	100720	29923	.297091	1.000000	10600	10600	35679	.297091	3.365973	35679	.000000	3.366	85+

NUMBER OF PERSONS DYING (OUT OF 100,000 AT BIRTH) ABOVE AGE X FROM SPECIFIED CAUSES

Age (x)	All Causes	Respiratory T.B.	Other Infec. and Paras.	Neo-plasms	Cardio-vascular	Infl., Pneu., Bronch.	Diar-rheal	Certain Degen-erative	Maternal	Cert. Dis. of Infancy	Motor Vehicle	Other Violence	Other and Unknown	Age (x)
0	100000	4750	2519	7735	21151	5995	722	3332	360	1571	0	2122	49743	0
1	94516	4728	2156	7732	21114	4958	252	3327	360	0	0	2078	47811	1
5	92615	4688	1835	7723	21085	4475	167	3318	360	0	0	1972	46992	5
10	91830	4659	1652	7716	21050	4401	162	3302	360	0	0	1911	46617	10
15	91202	4571	1525	7709	21007	4367	158	3287	360	0	0	1889	46325	15
20	89884	4097	1361	7693	20541	4318	154	3269	344	0	0	1808	45899	20
25	88331	3455	1228	7679	20861	4265	153	3243	277	0	0	1716	45454	25
30	86660	2837	1101	7651	20749	4208	148	3209	181	0	0	1630	44946	30
35	84914	2301	986	7580	20599	4139	144	3161	102	0	0	1539	44363	35
40	82961	1832	870	7434	20379	4056	139	3096	42	0	0	1454	43659	40
45	80506	1437	764	7131	20026	3952	130	2992	7	0	0	1346	42721	45
50	77533	1126	664	6676	19498	3827	123	2860	2	0	0	1221	41536	50
55	73563	865	555	5995	18636	3657	114	2670	0	0	0	1077	39990	55
60	68636	650	463	5200	17403	3444	101	2415	0	0	0	919	38041	60
65	61392	433	366	4094	15360	3122	85	2027	0	0	0	754	35151	65
70	52220	256	265	2942	12552	2654	69	1552	0	0	0	588	31342	70
75	40143	131	162	1736	8603	1978	46	994	0	0	0	424	26069	75
80	23957	56	75	758	4434	1130	22	477	0	0	0	245	16760	80
85+	10600	12	27	230	1714	488	10	174	0	0	0	100	7845	85+

NUMBER OF PERSONS SURVIVING TO AGE X IF SPECIFIED CAUSES WERE ELIMINATED

Age (x)	No Causes	Respiratory T.B. (1)	Other Infec. and Paras. (2)	Neo-plasms (3)	Cardio-vascular (4)	Infl., Pneu., Bronch. (5)	Diar-rheal (6)	Certain Degener-ative (7)	Maternal (8)	Cert. Dis. of Infancy (9)	Motor Vehicle (10)	Other Violence (11)	Other and Unknown (12)	(1)+(2)	(1)+(2)+(5)+(6)+(8)	(1)+(2)+(5)+(6)+(8)+part of(9)&(12)	(10)+(11)	Age (x)
0	100000	100000	100000	100000	100000	100000	100000	100000	100000	100000	100000	100000	100000	100000	100000	100000	100000	0
1	94516	94537	94870	94519	94552	95529	94974	94521	94516	96056	94516	94559	96413	94891	96373	99747	94559	1
5	92615	92676	93281	92627	92679	94093	93148	92629	92615	94124	92615	92762	95304	93342	95377	99461	92762	5
10	91830	91919	92674	91849	91928	93370	92364	91859	91830	92037	91830	91987	94882	92764	94868	99215	92037	10
15	91202	91378	92164	91227	91343	92766	91736	91246	91202	92688	91202	91429	94534	92342	94476	99039	91429	15
20	89884	90530	91001	89925	90088	91475	90414	89945	89900	91348	89884	90189	93607	91655	93844	98747	90189	20
25	88331	89610	89562	88385	88611	89948	88853	88417	88413	89770	88331	88722	92450	90858	93155	98418	88722	25
30	86660	88537	87995	86741	87046	88304	87177	86778	86836	88072	86660	87129	91229	89902	92341	97999	87129	30
35	84914	87297	86338	85064	85442	86594	85425	85078	85165	86297	84914	85464	90001	88761	91331	97383	85464	35
40	82961	85767	84469	83252	83696	84686	83465	83185	83265	84312	82961	83583	88672	87326	90013	96451	83583	40
45	80506	83632	82076	81089	81571	82285	81004	80826	80836	81817	80506	81217	87041	85262	88045	94806	81217	45
50	77533	80861	79145	78546	79086	79372	78020	77972	77856	78796	77533	78341	85094	82541	85383	92363	78341	50
55	73563	76985	75196	75199	75898	75477	74034	74166	73871	74761	73563	74472	82406	78695	81599	88678	74472	55
60	68636	72046	70255	70951	72055	70633	69088	69447	68923	69754	68636	69638	79025	73745	76710	83778	69638	60
65	61392	64657	62934	64551	66511	63493	61811	62490	61649	62392	61392	62447	73901	66306	69306	76197	62447	65
70	52220	55168	53626	56031	59450	54455	52591	53600	52439	53071	52220	53272	67232	56654	59748	66319	53272	70
75	40143	42523	41316	44210	49793	42481	40449	41705	40311	40797	40143	41098	58000	43766	46863	52841	41098	75
80	23957	25437	24724	27205	33900	26044	24158	25297	24057	24347	23957	24666	46674	26251	28898	34083	24666	80
85+	10600	11285	10972	12431	17709	11984	10657	11402	10644	10773	10600	11011	35588	11681	13382	17294	11011	85+

ADDED YRS OF LIFE

	No Causes	(1)	(2)	(3)	(4)	(5)	(6)	(7)	(8)	(9)	(10)	(11)	(12)	(1)+(2)	(1)+(2)+(5)+(6)+(8)	+part of(9)&(12)	(10)+(11)
TOTAL		1.678	1.054	1.149	2.692	1.585	.387	.471	.144	1.013	.000	.536	11.657	2.769	5.023	10.151	.536
WORK	5.599	1.230	.313	.409	.642	.201	.012	.163	.121	.000	.000	.240	1.836	1.555	1.906	2.901	.240

POPULATION, DEATHS, DEATH RATES FOR ALL CAUSES COMBINED, AND SPECIFIED CAUSES

Age Start of Interval	Midyear Population	Deaths During Year	All Causes	Respiratory T. B.	Other Infec. and Paras.	Neo-plasms	Cardio-vascular	Infl., Pneu., Bronch.	Diar-rheal	Certain Degen-erative	Maternal	Cert. Dis. of Infancy	Motor Vehicle	Other Violence	Other and Unknown	Age Start of Interval
0	414400	24150	.05828	.00020	.00235	.00012	.00046	.00777	.00246	.00007	.00000	.02440	.00001	.00053	.01990	0
1	1649200	4328	.00262	.00003	.00047	.00014	.00006	.00041	.00013	.00003	.00000	.00000	.00004	.00029	.00102	1
5	1335900	945	.00071	.00001	.00013	.00008	.00005	.00004	.00000	.00002	.00000	.00000	.00007	.00012	.00019	5
10	1333900	824	.00062	.00001	.00007	.00008	.00007	.00004	.00000	.00002	.00000	.00000	.00014	.00016	10
15	1531000	1711	.00112	.00007	.00011	.00008	.00009	.00003	.00000	.00003	.00000	.00000	.00011	.00036	.00022	15
20	1668700	2788	.00167	.00029	.00012	.00010	.00012	.00003	.00000	.00005	.00000	.00000	.00017	.00051	.00028	20
25	1686200	3639	.00216	.00052	.00013	.00013	.00017	.00003	.00000	.00007	.00000	.00000	.00015	.00061	.00035	25
30	1279400	3251	.00254	.00064	.00013	.00016	.00023	.00005	.00000	.00009	.00000	.00000	.00014	.00062	.00035	30
35	1261000	4502	.00357	.00082	.00016	.00027	.00043	.00006	.00000	.00019	.00000	.00000	.00020	.00071	.00074	35
40	1520100	8137	.00535	.00106	.00019	.00059	.00081	.00012	.00000	.00035	.00000	.00000	.00018	.00092	.00114	40
45	1521800	12614	.00829	.00130	.00023	.00132	.00156	.00022	.00000	.00062	.00000	.00000	.00017	.00113	.00172	45
50	1357900	17171	.01265	.00147	.00030	.00258	.00297	.00037	.00001	.00097	.00000	.00000	.00015	.00133	.00248	50
55	978700	18118	.01851	.00158	.00037	.00406	.00517	.00070	.00001	.00138	.00000	.00000	.00019	.00129	.00378	55
60	853000	22830	.02676	.00147	.00045	.00574	.00902	.00119	.00001	.00173	.00000	.00000	.00021	.00142	.00553	60
65	729400	29904	.04100	.00134	.00058	.00818	.01529	.00237	.00001	.00230	.00000	.00000	.00021	.00171	.00901	65
70	579800	37455	.06460	.00132	.00056	.01076	.02593	.00457	.00002	.00267	.00000	.00000	.00022	.00193	.01661	70
75	400600	42530	.10617	.00110	.00065	.01391	.04283	.00945	.00006	.00319	.00000	.00000	.00018	.00268	.03211	75
80	175800	30260	.17213	.00070	.00071	.01471	.06371	.01866	.00011	.00346	.00000	.00000	.00015	.00358	.06634	80
85+	71700	21220	.29596	.00075	.00063	.01409	.09043	.03562	.00015	.00480	.00000	.00000	.00022	.00580	.14346	85+
ALL	20348500	286377														

CRUDE DEATH RATE	.01407	.00070	.00029	.00188	.00409	.00103	.00007	.00058	.00000	.00050	.00014	.00084	.00395
STANDARDIZED RATE (1)	.00826	.00046	.00029	.00090	.00172	.00065	.00010	.00030	.00000	.00086	.00014	.00084	.00395
STANDARDIZED RATE (2)	.01372	.00063	.00028	.00177	.00401	.00104	.00007	.00054	.00000	.00051	.00012	.00058	.00228
GEOMETRIC MEAN	.00999													

LIFE TABLE FOR ALL CAUSES COMBINED

Age (x)	Midyear Population	Deaths During Year	$_nM_x$	$_nq_x$	l_x	$_nd_x$	$_nL_x$	$_nm_x$	$_na_x$	T_x	$_nr_x$	$\overset{\circ}{e}_x$	Age (x)
0	414400	24150	.058277	.055590	100000	5559	95381	.058282	.169071	6360837	.000000	63.608	0
1	1649200	4328	.002624	.010419	94441	984	375304	.002622	1.500000	6265456	.000000	66.343	1
5	1335900	945	.000707	.003542	93457	331	466458	.000710	2.500000	5890152	.000000	63.025	5
10	1333900	824	.000618	.003082	93126	287	464951	.000617	2.633566	5423695	-.009113	58.240	10
15	1531000	1711	.001118	.005547	92839	515	463007	.001112	2.693770	4958744	-.020883	53.412	15
20	1668700	2788	.001671	.008297	92324	766	459803	.001666	2.627557	4495737	-.019514	48.695	20
25	1686200	3639	.002158	.010747	91558	984	455409	.002161	2.580666	4035934	.011858	44.081	25
30	1279400	3251	.002541	.012664	90574	1147	450127	.002548	2.608617	3580525	.031138	39.531	30
35	1261000	4502	.003570	.017690	89427	1582	443422	.003568	2.653287	3130397	-.007217	35.005	35
40	1520100	8137	.005353	.026308	87845	2311	433841	.005327	2.670471	2686975	-.023997	30.588	40
45	1521800	12614	.008289	.040604	85534	3473	419559	.008278	2.664603	2253133	-.008582	26.342	45
50	1357900	17171	.012645	.061601	82061	5055	398373	.012689	2.639507	1833574	.021622	22.344	50
55	978700	18118	.018512	.089058	77006	6858	368672	.018602	2.614799	1435202	.030676	18.638	55
60	853000	22830	.026764	.125934	70148	8834	329610	.026801	2.608058	1066529	.008903	15.204	60
65	729400	29904	.040998	.186581	61314	11440	279024	.041000	2.592093	736920	.000363	12.019	65
70	579800	37455	.064600	.278522	49874	13891	215402	.064489	2.554682	457896	-.008985	9.181	70
75	400600	42530	.106166	.419254	35983	15086	141888	.106324	2.479299	242494	.006157	6.739	75
80	175800	30260	.172127	.593004	20897	12392	71869	.172425	2.367976	100606	.006157	4.814	80
85+	71700	21220	.295955	1.000000	8505	8505	28737	.295955	3.378868	28737	.000000	3.379	85+

NUMBER OF PERSONS DYING (OUT OF 100,000 AT BIRTH) ABOVE AGE X FROM SPECIFIED CAUSES

Age (x)	All Causes	Respiratory T. B.	Other Infec. and Paras.	Neo-plasms	Cardio-vascular	Infl., Pneu., Bronch.	Diar-rheal	Certain Degen-erative	Maternal	Cert. Dis. of Infancy	Motor Vehicle	Other Violence	Other and Unknown	Age (x)
0	100000	4641	1814	13754	30780	7316	330	4165	0	2328	912	5609	28351	0
1	94441	4622	1590	13742	30736	6575	95	4159	0	0	912	5558	26452	1
5	93457	4611	1416	13688	30714	6421	48	4146	0	0	895	5448	26070	5
10	93126	4607	1353	13651	30692	6405	47	4136	0	0	862	5391	25982	10
15	92839	4601	1318	13615	30662	6388	47	4128	0	0	845	5326	25909	15
20	92324	4568	1268	13577	30618	6373	47	4114	0	0	793	5158	25808	20
25	91558	4434	1211	13530	30565	6358	46	4093	0	0	717	4926	25678	25
30	90574	4198	1153	13469	30487	6343	46	4063	0	0	649	4647	25519	30
35	89427	3911	1094	13395	30384	6322	45	4022	0	0	585	4366	25303	35
40	87845	3546	1025	13276	30194	6297	44	3937	0	0	498	4052	24976	40
45	85534	3086	944	13023	29847	6247	43	3787	0	0	420	3652	24485	45
50	82061	2539	846	12472	29192	6154	41	3526	0	0	350	3178	23763	50
55	77006	1954	726	11438	28003	6004	37	3137	0	0	289	2646	22772	55
60	70148	1372	591	9933	26084	5746	33	2629	0	0	219	2169	21372	60
65	61314	889	443	8038	23106	5353	29	2058	0	0	150	1700	19548	65
70	49874	516	282	5756	18840	4691	26	1416	0	0	91	1224	17032	70
75	35983	232	161	3440	13266	3709	21	841	0	0	43	808	13462	75
80	20897	76	69	1464	7180	2366	12	388	0	0	17	427	8898	80
85+	8505	22	18	405	2599	1024	4	138	0	0	6	167	4122	85+

NUMBER OF PERSONS SURVIVING TO AGE X IF SPECIFIED CAUSES WERE ELIMINATED

Age (x)	No Causes	Respiratory T. B.	Other Infec. and Paras.	Neo-plasms	Cardio-vascular	Infl., Pneu., Bronch.	Diar-rheal	Certain Degener-ative	Maternal	Cert. Dis. of Infancy	Motor Vehicle	Other Violence	Other and Unknown	(1) + (2)	(1) + (2) + (5) + (6) + (8)	(1)+(2)+ (5)+(6)+ (8)+part of(9)&(12)	(10) + (11)	Age (x)
		(1)	(2)	(3)	(4)	(5)	(6)	(7)	(8)	(9)	(10)	(11)	(12)					
0	100000	100000	100000	100000	100000	100000	100000	100000	100000	100000	100000	100000	100000	100000	100000	100000	100000	0
1	94441	94459	94659	94453	94484	95164	94670	94447	94441	96730	94441	94491	96304	94677	95633	99516	94491	1
5	93457	93486	93846	93522	93521	94327	93730	93476	93457	95723	93474	93616	95689	93876	95026	99143	93633	5
10	93126	93159	93577	93228	93212	94009	93399	93155	93126	95383	93176	93341	95440	93610	94775	98913	93391	10
15	92839	92878	93324	92977	92955	93736	93111	92876	92839	95090	92906	93118	95221	93363	94542	98690	93185	15
20	92324	92396	92856	92499	92483	93231	92595	92374	92324	94562	92442	92770	94796	92928	94117	98272	92889	20
25	91558	91763	92143	91778	91769	92473	91828	91629	91558	93777	91751	92233	94143	92349	93546	97722	92427	25
30	90574	91012	91211	90853	90860	91494	90841	90674	90574	92770	90833	91522	93294	91652	92856	97063	91783	30
35	89427	90147	90115	89776	89812	90357	89691	89566	89427	91595	89746	90645	92333	90840	92055	96318	90969	35
40	87845	88917	88589	88306	88413	88783	88106	88066	87845	89974	88245	89357	91035	89671	90897	95235	89764	40
45	85534	87039	86339	86235	86432	86497	85789	85898	85534	87607	86001	87409	89144	87858	89112	93537	87886	45
50	82061	84051	82931	83280	83574	83077	82307	82668	82061	84050	82578	84335	86264	84942	86252	90745	84866	50
55	77006	79455	77939	79173	79609	78107	77241	77956	77006	78873	77550	79670	81966	80418	81817	86306	80233	55
60	70148	72952	71129	73614	74439	71402	70366	71505	70148	71848	70711	73046	76102	73972	75528	79944	73632	60
65	61314	64234	62311	66227	68090	62786	61508	63045	61314	62800	61871	64304	68393	65278	67057	71267	64888	65
70	49874	52599	50832	56130	59824	51687	50035	51878	49874	51083	50380	52755	58222	53609	55737	59599	53291	70
75	35983	38200	36777	42749	49206	38165	36103	37934	35983	36855	36389	38433	45695	39043	41549	44937	38866	75
80	20897	22305	21428	26635	35568	23270	20974	22387	20897	21404	21152	22626	31313	22872	25563	28356	22902	80
85+	8505	9114	8753	11706	20182	10439	8541	9278	8505	8711	8616	9384	18021	9380	11562	13703	9506	85+

ADDED YRS OF LIFE

	No Causes	(1)	(2)	(3)	(4)	(5)	(6)	(7)	(8)	(9)	(10)	(11)	(12)				
TOTAL		1.071	.591	1.871	3.809	1.156	.191	.610	.000	1.538	.269	1.324	4.953	1.679	3.097	6.694	1.603
WORK	4.525	.667	.167	.548	.703	.104	.002	.236	.000	.000	.166	.731	.818	.838	.948	1.183	.901

POPULATION, DEATHS, DEATH RATES FOR ALL CAUSES COMBINED, AND SPECIFIED CAUSES

Age Start of Interval	Midyear Population	Deaths During Year	All Causes	Respiratory T. B.	Other Infec. and Paras.	Neoplasms	Cardio-vascular	Infl., Pneu., Bronch.	Diarrheal	Certain Degenerative	Maternal	Cert. Dis. of Infancy	Motor Vehicle	Other Violence	Other and Unknown	Age Start of Interval
0	398400	18004	.04519	.00014	.00210	.00010	.00041	.00627	.00180	.00005	.00000	.01855	.00001	.00044	.01534	0
1	1588600	3561	.00224	.00002	.00046	.00013	.00006	.00036	.00008	.00002	.00000	.00000	.00003	.00020	.00087	1
5	1294000	728	.00056	.00001	.00012	.00006	.00005	.00004	.00000	.00001	.00000	.00000	.00004	.00005	.00017	5
10	1311400	646	.00049	.00003	.00010	.00005	.00007	.00002	.00000	.00002	.00000	.00000	.00002	.00005	.00014	10
15	1497900	1162	.00078	.00011	.00013	.00007	.00008	.00003	.00000	.00002	.00001	.00000	.00002	.00011	.00018	15
20	1608900	1930	.00120	.00032	.00015	.00007	.00011	.00004	.00000	.00004	.00007	.00000	.00003	.00012	.00025	20
25	1621700	2574	.00159	.00046	.00015	.00013	.00017	.00004	.00000	.00005	.00010	.00000	.00003	.00013	.00032	25
30	1243600	2414	.00194	.00051	.00012	.00026	.00025	.00004	.00000	.00008	.00010	.00000	.00002	.00014	.00041	30
35	1266900	3155	.00249	.00045	.00010	.00050	.00037	.00007	.00000	.00015	.00012	.00000	.00002	.00017	.00054	35
40	1525800	4903	.00321	.00038	.00011	.00080	.00057	.00009	.00000	.00024	.00005	.00000	.00004	.00025	.00067	40
45	1534000	7294	.00475	.00035	.00013	.00133	.00109	.00012	.00001	.00042	.00001	.00000	.00003	.00034	.00093	45
50	1451800	10118	.00697	.00034	.00013	.00201	.00186	.00019	.00000	.00064	.00000	.00000	.00004	.00037	.00139	50
55	1326800	13508	.01018	.00035	.00018	.00287	.00310	.00034	.00000	.00080	.00000	.00000	.00003	.00043	.00204	55
60	1186100	18407	.01552	.00045	.00022	.00394	.00557	.00064	.00000	.00096	.00000	.00000	.00003	.00047	.00323	60
65	1058600	26366	.02491	.00052	.00030	.00533	.01000	.00138	.00001	.00132	.00000	.00000	.00006	.00058	.00541	65
70	859000	36879	.04293	.00064	.00037	.00726	.01804	.00329	.00002	.00170	.00000	.00000	.00000	.00078	.01077	70
75	626700	47535	.07585	.00071	.00042	.00980	.03219	.00703	.00004	.00209	.00000	.00000	.00007	.00136	.02213	75
80	318000	40742	.12812	.00053	.00042	.01139	.04835	.01411	.00008	.00232	.00000	.00000	.00000	.00210	.04847	80
85+	171700	39685	.23113	.00047	.00048	.01203	.07068	.02924	.00010	.00263	.00000	.00000	.00008	.00523	.11019	85+
ALL	21889900	279611														

			All Causes	Respiratory T. B.	Other Infec. and Paras.	Neoplasms	Cardio-vascular	Infl., Pneu., Bronch.	Diarrheal	Certain Degenerative	Maternal	Cert. Dis. of Infancy	Motor Vehicle	Other Violence	Other and Unknown
CRUDE DEATH RATE			.01277	.00033	.00023	.00183	.00418	.00107	.00004	.00046	.00003	.00034	.00004	.00036	.00386
STANDARDIZED RATE (1)			.00569	.00023	.00025	.00071	.00121	.00049	.00008	.00019	.00003	.00065	.00003	.00020	.00162
STANDARDIZED RATE (2)			.00933	.00029	.00022	.00133	.00285	.00077	.00005	.00034	.00003	.00038	.00003	.00029	.00274
GEOMETRIC MEAN			.00688												

LIFE TABLE FOR ALL CAUSES COMBINED

Age (x)	Midyear Population	Deaths During Year	$_nM_x$	$_nq_x$	l_x	$_nd_x$	$_nL_x$	$_nm_x$	$_na_x$	T_x	$_nr_x$	$\overset{\circ}{e}_x$	Age (x)
0	398400	18004	.045191	.043510	100000	4351	96288	.045187	.146824	6937934	.000000	69.379	0
1	1588600	3561	.002242	.008918	95649	853	380464	.002242	1.500000	6841647	.000000	71.529	1
5	1294000	728	.000563	.002817	94796	267	473313	.000564	2.500000	6461183	.000000	68.159	5
10	1311400	646	.000493	.002454	94529	232	472085	.000491	2.587105	5987871	-.010289	63.344	10
15	1497900	1162	.000776	.003860	94297	364	470643	.000773	2.667729	5515785	-.019492	58.494	15
20	1608900	1930	.001200	.005962	93933	560	468343	.001196	2.639509	5045142	-.017224	53.710	20
25	1621700	2574	.001587	.007914	93373	739	465088	.001589	2.595005	4576799	.012834	49.016	25
30	1243600	2414	.001941	.009683	92634	897	461010	.001946	2.591973	4111711	.028416	44.387	30
35	1266900	3155	.002490	.012372	91737	1135	455960	.002489	2.599486	3650701	-.010063	39.795	35
40	1525800	4903	.003213	.015883	90602	1439	449642	.003201	2.638841	3194741	-.023352	35.261	40
45	1534000	7294	.004755	.023485	89163	2094	440902	.004749	2.654011	2745129	-.006644	30.788	45
50	1451800	10118	.006969	.034306	87069	2987	428313	.006974	2.645910	2304226	-.003542	26.464	50
55	1326800	13508	.010181	.049785	84082	4186	410571	.010196	2.649457	1875913	.008830	22.311	55
60	1186100	18407	.015519	.074972	79896	5990	385447	.015540	2.657276	1465342	.006974	18.341	60
65	1058600	26366	.024906	.117825	73906	8708	349161	.024940	2.660915	1079895	.006499	14.612	65
70	859000	36879	.042932	.195037	65198	12716	295897	.042974	2.633444	730734	-.004347	11.208	70
75	626700	47535	.075850	.321120	52482	16853	221229	.076179	2.556444	434837	.017562	8.285	75
80	318000	40742	.128119	.485054	35629	17282	134229	.128751	2.458832	213608	.017562	5.995	80
85+	171700	39685	.231130	1.000000	18347	18347	79380	.231130	4.326572	79380	.000000	4.327	85+

NUMBER OF PERSONS DYING (OUT OF 100,000 AT BIRTH) ABOVE AGE X FROM SPECIFIED CAUSES

Age (x)	All Causes	Respiratory T. B.	Other Infec. and Paras.	Neo-plasms	Cardio-vascular	Infl., Pneu., Bronch.	Diar-rheal	Certain Degen-erative	Maternal	Cert. Dis. of Infancy	Motor Vehicle	Other Violence	Other and Unknown	Age (x)
0	100000	2334	1510	13774	33650	8672	254	3406	215	1786	249	2725	31425	0
1	95649	2321	1308	13764	33610	8069	81	3401	215	0	249	2683	29948	1
5	94796	2312	1131	13714	33588	7932	51	3392	215	0	239	2606	29616	5
10	94529	2308	1073	13684	33565	7912	50	3386	215	0	220	2581	29535	10
15	94297	2296	1025	13661	33533	7903	50	3377	215	0	211	2559	29467	15
20	93933	2246	964	13629	33495	7889	49	3365	208	0	200	2505	29383	20
25	93373	2099	894	13598	33444	7872	48	3346	174	0	186	2447	29265	25
30	92634	1883	824	13535	33364	7853	48	3324	127	0	174	2387	29115	30
35	91737	1647	767	13416	33248	7834	46	3285	81	0	165	2325	28923	35
40	90602	1441	719	13190	33080	7804	45	3219	27	0	150	2247	28680	40
45	89163	1269	670	12833	32825	7764	45	3110	3	0	134	2133	28377	45
50	87069	1116	614	12246	32344	7712	41	2923	0	0	119	1985	27969	50
55	84082	972	560	11384	31548	7632	40	2649	0	0	102	1824	27371	55
60	79896	811	488	10203	30274	7493	39	2321	0	0	87	1650	26530	60
65	73906	637	401	8683	28123	7244	37	1951	0	0	74	1469	25287	65
70	65198	456	296	6822	24627	6760	34	1490	0	0	53	1268	23392	70
75	52482	267	187	4672	19282	5784	29	987	0	0	37	1036	20201	75
80	35629	110	94	2499	12132	4221	19	524	0	0	20	733	15277	80
85+	18347	37	38	955	5611	2321	8	209	0	0	6	415	8747	85+

NUMBER OF PERSONS SURVIVING TO AGE X IF SPECIFIED CAUSES WERE ELIMINATED

Age (x)	No Causes	Respiratory T. B. (1)	Other Infec. and Paras. (2)	Neo-plasms (3)	Cardio-vascular (4)	Infl., Pneu., Bronch. (5)	Diar-rheal (6)	Certain Degener-ative (7)	Maternal (8)	Cert. Dis. of Infancy (9)	Motor Vehicle (10)	Other Violence (11)	Other and Unknown (12)	(1) + (2)	(1) + (2) + (5) + (6) + (8)	(1)+(2)+ (5)+(6)+ (8)+part of(9)&(12)	(10) + (11)	Age (x)
0	100000	100000	100000	100000	100000	100000	100000	100000	100000	100000	100000	100000	100000	100000	100000	100000	100000	0
1	95649	95662	95847	95659	95688	96241	95818	95654	95649	97412	95649	95690	97104	95859	96623	99604	95690	1
5	94796	94818	95169	94855	94857	95520	94994	94810	94796	96543	94806	94913	96575	95190	96117	99317	94923	5
10	94529	94554	94959	94618	94613	95271	94727	94549	94529	96271	94558	94671	96385	94984	95930	99162	94700	10
15	94297	94334	94774	94405	94412	95046	94495	94326	94297	96035	94335	94461	96218	94812	95765	99021	94499	15
20	93933	94020	94469	94077	94086	94693	94131	93974	93940	95664	93982	94150	95932	94557	95530	98820	94199	20
25	93373	93607	93976	93547	93576	94146	93571	93432	93414	95094	93435	93647	95480	94211	95234	98589	93709	25
30	92634	93082	93303	92869	92915	93420	92830	92715	92721	94341	92708	92966	94877	93754	94838	98274	93040	30
35	91737	92417	92456	92089	92131	92534	91933	91856	91869	93428	91819	92127	94155	93141	94287	97807	92210	35
40	90602	91480	91361	91175	91159	91419	90797	90785	90786	92272	90658	91065	93238	92245	93468	97055	91162	40
45	89163	90199	89959	90084	89966	90007	89355	89452	89368	90806	89273	89733	92067	91004	92275	95898	89844	45
50	87069	88234	87902	88557	88335	87945	87260	87256	87272	88674	87192	87773	90322	89077	90382	94000	87896	50
55	84082	85350	84940	86385	86102	85008	84268	84804	84278	85631	84217	84921	87835	86221	87566	91146	85057	55
60	79896	81260	80782	83275	83098	80913	80073	80905	80083	81368	80039	80864	84323	82161	83586	87103	81009	60
65	73906	75338	74810	78568	79051	75090	74072	75200	74079	75268	74051	74978	79273	76259	77837	81252	75125	65
70	65198	66634	66095	71189	73339	66707	65347	66780	65350	66399	65345	66335	71866	67551	69434	72707	66485	70
75	52482	53810	53302	59435	64672	54602	52607	54216	52605	53449	52615	53608	61096	54651	57126	60260	53744	75
80	35629	36660	36262	42396	51727	38428	35722	37196	35712	36286	35733	36648	46471	37312	40442	43412	36755	80
85+	18347	18931	18713	23165	34217	21286	18403	19387	18390	18685	18410	19103	30751	19309	22523	25355	19169	85+

ADDED YRS OF LIFE																		
TOTAL		.668	.593	2.109	4.309	1.226	.151	.545	.092	1.276	.079	.551	5.260	1.268	2.791	5.982	.631	
WORK	2.958	.400	.151	.572	.541	.079	.003	.177	.071	.000	.032	.203	.583	.553	.708	.898	.235	

POPULATION, DEATHS, DEATH RATES FOR ALL CAUSES COMBINED, AND SPECIFIED CAUSES

Age Start of Interval	Midyear Population	Deaths During Year	All Causes	Respiratory T. B.	Other Infec. and Paras.	Neo-plasms	Cardio-vascular	Infl., Pneu., Bronch.	Diar-rheal	Certain Degen-erative	Maternal	Cert. Dis. of Infancy	Motor Vehicle	Other Violence	Other and Unknown	Age Start of Interval
0	412447	13017	.03156	.00002	.00065	.00008	.00022	.00196	.00030	.00003	.00000	.01428	.00000	.00053	.01349	0
1	1620129	2128	.00131	.00000	.00010	.00013	.00004	.00013	.00002	.00001	.00000	.00000	.00000	.00031	.00056	1
5	1800653	839	.00047	.00000	.00003	.00011	.00001	.00002	.00000	.00001	.00000	.00000	.00000	.00017	.00012	5
10	2095330	855	.00041	.00000	.00001	.00008	.00002	.00001	.00000	.00001	.00000	.00000	.00000	.00017	.00011	10
15	1434425	1260	.00088	.00000	.00002	.00010	.00004	.00001	.00000	.00001	.00000	.00000	.00000	.00054	.00014	15
20	1492972	1848	.00124	.00001	.00002	.00012	.00006	.00002	.00000	.00003	.00000	.00000	.00000	.00076	.00021	20
25	1668208	2607	.00156	.00001	.00003	.00015	.00011	.00001	.00000	.00006	.00000	.00000	.00000	.00089	.00027	25
30	1674958	3502	.00209	.00015	.00003	.00022	.00020	.00003	.00000	.00011	.00000	.00000	.00000	.00093	.00042	30
35	1634486	4462	.00273	.00021	.00005	.00032	.00037	.00005	.00000	.00019	.00000	.00000	.00000	.00094	.00061	35
40	1047620	4121	.00393	.00031	.00006	.00057	.00065	.00005	.00000	.00036	.00000	.00000	.00000	.00108	.00085	40
45	1337391	8791	.00657	.00044	.00009	.00131	.00133	.00012	.00000	.00065	.00000	.00000	.00000	.00125	.00137	45
50	1433338	15737	.01098	.00063	.00011	.00266	.00247	.00025	.00000	.00112	.00000	.00000	.00000	.00149	.00225	50
55	1355467	22958	.01694	.00078	.00015	.00454	.00453	.00040	.00000	.00165	.00000	.00000	.00000	.00167	.00322	55
60	1091899	27996	.02564	.00092	.00023	.00698	.00779	.00082	.00000	.00220	.00000	.00000	.00000	.00173	.00496	60
65	730164	27299	.03739	.00098	.00031	.00921	.01340	.00150	.00002	.00264	.00000	.00000	.00000	.00177	.00758	65
70	575659	33334	.05791	.00104	.00042	.01254	.02269	.00303	.00005	.00306	.00000	.00000	.00000	.00220	.01288	70
75	394706	36559	.09262	.00109	.00055	.01632	.03881	.00636	.00004	.00318	.00000	.00000	.00000	.00300	.02326	75
80	219169	32740	.14938	.00106	.00054	.01978	.06206	.01288	.00007	.00295	.00000	.00000	.00000	.00470	.04534	80
85+	99624	25758	.25855	.00083	.00054	.02096	.09575	.02759	.00014	.00296	.00000	.00000	.00000	.00883	.10094	85+
ALL	22118645	265811														

	All Causes	Respiratory T.B.	Other Infec. and Paras.	Neo-plasms	Cardio-vascular	Infl., Pneu., Bronch.	Diar-rheal	Certain Degen-erative	Maternal	Cert. Dis. of Infancy	Motor Vehicle	Other Violence	Other and Unknown
CRUDE DEATH RATE	.01202	.00030	.00011	.00221	.00377	.00064	.00001	.00064	.00000	.00027	.00000	.00102	.00305
STANDARDIZED RATE (1)	.00634	.00016	.00009	.00103	.00151	.00030	.00001	.00032	.00000	.00050	.00000	.00074	.00168
STANDARDIZED RATE (2)	.01152	.00027	.00011	.00206	.00363	.00063	.00001	.00058	.00000	.00030	.00000	.00074	.00295
GEOMETRIC MEAN	.00772												

LIFE TABLE FOR ALL CAUSES COMBINED

Age (x)	Midyear Population	Deaths During Year	$_nM_x$	$_nq_x$	l_x	$_nd_x$	$_nL_x$	$_nm_x$	$_na_x$	T_x	$_nr_x$	$\overset{\circ}{e}_x$	Age (x)
0	412447	13017	.031560	.030710	100000	3071	97309	.031559	.123653	6740609	.000000	67.406	0
1	1620129	2128	.001313	.005241	96929	508	386446	.001315	1.500000	6643300	.000000	68.538	1
5	1800653	839	.000466	.002323	96421	224	481545	.000465	2.500000	6256854	.000000	64.891	5
10	2095330	855	.000408	.002037	96197	196	480537	.000408	2.712585	5775309	.013025	60.036	10
15	1434425	1260	.000878	.004417	96001	424	479027	.000885	2.693101	5294773	.037355	55.153	15
20	1492972	1848	.001238	.006163	95577	589	476478	.001236	2.611418	4815746	-.004289	50.386	20
25	1668208	2607	.001563	.007780	94988	739	473174	.001562	2.609946	4339268	-.011363	45.682	25
30	1674958	3502	.002091	.010387	94249	979	468908	.002088	2.612958	3866094	-.011203	41.020	30
35	1634486	4462	.002730	.013616	93270	1270	463347	.002741	2.635171	3397186	-.033729	36.423	35
40	1047620	4121	.003934	.019598	92000	1803	455833	.003955	2.688806	2933839	-.030702	31.890	40
45	1337391	8791	.006573	.032196	90197	2904	444319	.006536	2.704675	2478006	-.025989	27.473	45
50	1433338	15737	.010979	.053338	87293	4656	425621	.010939	2.671061	2033687	-.019648	23.297	50
55	1355467	22958	.016931	.081404	82637	6727	397316	.016931	2.641036	1608065	-.001678	19.459	55
60	1091899	27996	.025640	.121328	75910	9210	357517	.025761	2.607718	1210749	-.028123	15.950	60
65	730164	27299	.037387	.172249	66700	11489	305780	.037573	2.587294	853232	.029865	12.792	65
70	575659	33334	.057906	.254007	55211	14024	241829	.057991	2.559452	547452	.007815	9.916	70
75	394706	36559	.092623	.376114	41187	15491	167169	.092607	2.497512	305623	.001990	7.420	75
80	219169	32740	.149382	.538566	25696	13839	92595	.149458	2.406951	138454	.001990	5.388	80
85+	99624	25758	.258552	1.000000	11857	11857	45859	.258552	3.867692	45859	.000000	3.868	85+

NUMBER OF PERSONS DYING (OUT OF 100,000 AT BIRTH) ABOVE AGE X FROM SPECIFIED CAUSES

Age (x)	All Causes	Respiratory T. B.	Other Infec. and Paras.	Neo-plasms	Cardio-vascular	Infl., Pneu., Bronch.	Diar-rheal	Certain Degen-erative	Maternal	Cert. Dis. of Infancy	Motor Vehicle	Other Violence	Other and Unknown	Age (x)
0	100000	2312	811	18244	33198	5666	79	5078	0	1389	0	7630	25593	0
1	96929	2309	748	18236	33177	5475	50	5075	0	0	0	7578	24281	1
5	96421	2308	708	18185	33162	5424	43	5069	0	0	0	7459	24063	5
10	96197	2307	696	18132	33155	5416	43	5064	0	0	0	7377	24007	10
15	96001	2307	691	18095	33145	5409	43	5059	0	0	0	7296	23956	15
20	95577	2306	682	18046	33124	5403	43	5053	0	0	0	7035	23885	20
25	94988	2300	671	17950	33093	5395	43	5037	0	0	0	6674	23785	25
30	94249	2279	658	17920	33041	5388	43	5009	0	0	0	6252	23659	30
35	93270	2210	643	17819	32947	5372	42	4956	0	0	0	5818	23463	35
40	92000	2115	621	17668	32776	5350	42	4868	0	0	0	5383	23177	40
45	90197	1972	595	17406	32477	5327	41	4701	0	0	0	4889	22789	45
50	87293	1779	556	16828	31888	5274	40	4414	0	0	0	4333	22181	50
55	82637	1510	508	15703	30843	5170	39	3938	0	0	0	3699	21227	55
60	75910	1202	447	13901	29044	5011	37	3281	0	0	0	3037	19950	60
65	66700	872	363	11394	26241	4716	36	2493	0	0	0	2420	18165	65
70	55211	573	269	8567	22118	4254	31	1686	0	0	0	1878	15835	70
75	41187	321	168	5532	16621	3520	19	945	0	0	0	1346	12715	75
80	25656	139	75	2803	10130	2456	13	413	0	0	0	844	8823	80
85+	11857	38	25	961	4391	1265	6	136	0	0	0	405	4630	85+

NUMBER OF PERSONS SURVIVING TO AGE X IF SPECIFIED CAUSES WERE ELIMINATED

Age (x)	No Causes	Respiratory T. B.	Other Infec. and Paras.	Neo-plasms	Cardio-vascular	Infl., Pneu., Bronch.	Diar-rheal	Certain Degener-ative	Maternal	Cert. Dis. of Infancy	Motor Vehicle	Other Violence	Other and Unknown	(1) + (2)	(1) + (2) + (5) + (6) + (8)	(1)+(2)+ (5)+(6)+ (8)+part of(9)&(12)	(10) + (11)	Age (x)
		(1)	(2)	(3)	(4)	(5)	(6)	(7)	(8)	(9)	(10)	(11)	(12)					
0	100000	100000	100000	100000	100000	100000	100000	100000	100000	100000	100000	100000	100000	100000	100000	100000	100000	0
1	96929	96932	96991	96937	96950	97117	96958	96932	96929	98306	96929	96980	98229	96994	97211	99294	96980	1
5	96421	96425	96523	96480	96457	96659	96456	96430	96421	97791	96421	96591	97935	96527	96801	98951	96591	5
10	96197	96202	96310	96309	96239	96443	96232	96211	96197	97564	96197	96648	97764	96315	96597	98750	96448	10
15	96001	96006	96119	96149	96053	96253	96036	96020	96001	97365	96001	96333	97617	96124	96412	98566	96333	15
20	95577	95583	95704	95774	95650	95834	95612	95602	95577	96935	95577	96169	97258	95710	96002	98150	96169	20
25	94988	95000	95125	95239	95092	95251	95023	95029	94988	96338	94988	95939	96760	95137	95436	97576	95939	25
30	94249	94292	94398	94568	94404	94517	94284	94317	94249	95588	94249	95619	96135	94430	94734	96867	95619	30
35	93270	93371	93432	93687	93552	93552	93305	93390	93270	94595	93270	95064	95336	93533	93851	95990	95064	35
40	92000	92194	92182	92562	92414	92300	92035	92206	92000	93307	92000	94211	94328	92376	92712	94867	94211	40
45	90197	90529	90401	91010	90901	90514	90232	90565	90197	91478	90197	92867	92874	90734	91088	93259	92867	45
50	87293	87805	87529	88655	88253	87762	87328	87933	87293	88533	87293	90441	90502	88043	88440	90625	90441	50
55	82637	83385	82907	85046	84875	83078	82671	83711	82637	83811	82637	86258	86642	83658	84139	86329	86258	55
60	75910	76895	76217	79921	79758	76469	75943	77536	75910	76989	75910	79899	80882	77206	77809	79958	79899	60
65	66700	67879	67049	72739	72900	67471	66730	68886	66700	67648	66700	70814	72874	68233	69053	71131	70814	65
70	55211	56462	55585	63071	64586	56277	55241	57779	55211	55139	55211	62681	59934	56845	57973	59934	59139	70
75	41187	42341	41553	50118	54054	42634	41219	43770	41187	41772	41187	44608	49916	42718	44253	46053	44608	75
80	25656	26560	25997	33953	41100	27481	25721	27746	25656	26061	25656	28257	35078	26872	28766	30354	28257	80
85+	11857	12325	12030	17366	26136	13553	11873	13003	11857	12025	11857	13362	20460	12505	14313	15606	13362	85+

ADDED YRS OF LIFE

	No Causes	(1)	(2)	(3)	(4)	(5)	(6)	(7)	(8)	(9)	(10)	(11)	(12)	(1)+(2)	(1)+(2)+...	(1)+(2)+...	(10)+(11)
TOTAL		.403	.189	2.515	4.190	.622	.029	.763	.000	.956	.000	1.877	4.160	.594	1.267	3.134	1.877
WORK	3.734	.180	.047	.619	.597	.063	.001	.263	.000	.000	.000	1.013	.688	.228	.292	.367	1.013

POPULATION, DEATHS, DEATH RATES FOR ALL CAUSES COMBINED, AND SPECIFIED CAUSES

Age Start of Interval	Midyear Population	Deaths During Year	All Causes	Respiratory T. B.	Other Infec. and Paras.	Neoplasms	Cardiovascular	Infl., Pneu., Bronch.	Diarrheal	Certain Degenerative	Maternal	Cert. Dis. of Infancy	Motor Vehicle	Other Violence	Other and Unknown	Age Start of Interval
0	395867	9476	.02394	.00003	.00055	.00008	.00018	.00152	.00018	.00004	.00000	.01056	.00000	.00045	.01036	0
1	1562379	1668	.00107	.00000	.00010	.00011	.00002	.00013	.00002	.00001	.00000	.00000	.00000	.00020	.00048	1
5	1738355	603	.00035	.00000	.00003	.00008	.00002	.00001	.00000	.00001	.00000	.00000	.00000	.00005	.00012	5
10	2022690	531	.00026	.00000	.00001	.00006	.00003	.00001	.00000	.00001	.00000	.00000	.00000	.00005	.00008	10
15	1381544	602	.00044	.00001	.00001	.00007	.00003	.00001	.00000	.00002	.00001	.00000	.00000	.00017	.00012	15
20	1410642	956	.00068	.00002	.00003	.00010	.00006	.00002	.00000	.00003	.00004	.00000	.00000	.00023	.00015	20
25	1549824	1278	.00082	.00005	.00003	.00013	.00008	.00002	.00000	.00005	.00007	.00000	.00000	.00020	.00019	25
30	1590938	1751	.00110	.00005	.00003	.00023	.00012	.00002	.00000	.00008	.00006	.00000	.00000	.00019	.00027	30
35	1619666	2633	.00163	.00011	.00004	.00047	.00019	.00003	.00000	.00015	.00006	.00000	.00000	.00022	.00036	35
40	1059029	2468	.00233	.00010	.00004	.00079	.00034	.00005	.00000	.00027	.00004	.00000	.00000	.00031	.00047	40
45	1373653	4961	.00361	.00011	.00005	.00137	.00067	.00006	.00000	.00036	.00001	.00000	.00000	.00031	.00067	45
50	1492683	7949	.00533	.00012	.00006	.00195	.00122	.00010	.00000	.00054	.00000	.00000	.00000	.00035	.00097	50
55	1448120	11114	.00767	.00013	.00008	.00265	.00205	.00016	.00000	.00074	.00000	.00000	.00000	.00045	.00142	55
60	1316956	15843	.01203	.00015	.00011	.00371	.00387	.00036	.00001	.00097	.00000	.00000	.00000	.00055	.00231	60
65	1140332	22624	.01984	.00023	.00015	.00509	.00759	.00079	.00001	.00132	.00000	.00000	.00000	.00072	.00394	65
70	944727	32105	.03398	.00031	.00022	.00688	.01452	.00178	.00001	.00160	.00000	.00000	.00000	.00114	.00752	70
75	714630	43501	.06087	.00039	.00028	.00968	.02736	.00408	.00004	.00193	.00000	.00000	.00000	.00211	.01499	75
80	424274	46224	.10895	.00056	.00037	.01306	.04746	.00874	.00008	.00209	.00000	.00000	.00000	.00426	.03233	80
85+	236794	48862	.20635	.00042	.00054	.01530	.07756	.02151	.00014	.00184	.00000	.00000	.00000	.00934	.07971	85+
ALL	23423103	255149														
CRUDE DEATH RATE			.01089	.00010	.00009	.00191	.00395	.00070	.00001	.00044	.00002	.00018	.00000	.00052	.00298	
STANDARDIZED RATE (1)			.00386	.00005	.00007	.00069	.00093	.00020	.00001	.00017	.00002	.00037	.00000	.00025	.00109	
STANDARDIZED RATE (2)			.00707	.00008	.00007	.00132	.00236	.00041	.00001	.00031	.00002	.00022	.00000	.00038	.00188	
GEOMETRIC MEAN			.00460													

LIFE TABLE FOR ALL CAUSES COMBINED

Age (x)	Midyear Population	Deaths During Year	$_nM_x$	$_nq_x$	l_x	$_nd_x$	$_nL_x$	$_nm_x$	$_na_x$	T_x	$_nr_x$	$\overset{\circ}{e}_x$	Age (x)
0	395867	9476	.023937	.023440	100000	2344	97915	.023939	.110693	7409302	.000000	74.093	0
1	1562379	1668	.001068	.004260	97656	416	389584	.001068	1.500000	7311387	.000000	74.869	1
5	1738355	603	.000347	.001728	97240	168	485780	.000346	2.500000	6921803	.000000	71.183	5
10	2022690	531	.000263	.001319	97072	128	485049	.000264	2.571615	6436023	.013084	66.302	10
15	1381544	602	.000436	.002187	96944	212	484231	.000438	2.695558	5950973	.038915	61.386	15
20	1410642	956	.000678	.003380	96732	327	482881	.000677	2.617227	5466742	-.000265	56.514	20
25	1549824	1278	.000825	.004108	96405	396	481076	.000823	2.604693	4983861	-.009201	51.697	25
30	1590938	1751	.001101	.005479	96009	526	478809	.001099	2.650903	4502785	-.014885	46.900	30
35	1619666	2633	.001626	.008138	95483	777	475592	.001634	2.654440	4023975	-.028435	42.143	35
40	1059029	2468	.002330	.011636	94706	1102	470961	.002340	2.668444	3548383	.027823	37.467	40
45	1373653	4961	.003612	.017820	93604	1668	464123	.003594	2.663619	3077422	-.026853	32.877	45
50	1492683	7949	.005325	.026236	91936	2412	454005	.005313	2.647267	2613299	-.017017	28.425	50
55	1448120	11114	.007675	.037677	89524	3373	439737	.007670	2.662874	2159294	-.001721	24.120	55
60	1316956	15843	.012030	.056606	86151	5049	419036	.012049	2.678913	1719557	.007942	19.960	60
65	1140332	22624	.019840	.095053	81102	7709	387597	.019889	2.676363	1300521	.011841	16.036	65
70	944727	32105	.033983	.157713	73393	11575	339652	.034059	2.657649	912924	.009882	12.439	70
75	714630	43501	.060872	.266395	61818	16468	269571	.061090	2.600270	573072	-.014658	9.270	75
80	424274	46224	.108948	.430011	45350	19501	178232	.109414	2.512019	303501	-.014658	6.692	80
85+	236794	48862	.206348	1.000000	25849	25849	125269	.206348	4.846179	125269	.000000	4.846	85+

NUMBER OF PERSONS DYING (OUT OF 100,000 AT BIRTH) ABOVE AGE X FROM SPECIFIED CAUSES

Age (x)	All Causes	Respiratory T.B.	Other Infec. and Paras.	Neo-plasms	Cardio-vascular	Infl., Pneu., Bronch.	Diar-rheal	Certain Degen-erative	Maternal	Cert. Dis. of Infancy	Motor Vehicle	Other Violence	Other and Unknown	Age (x)
0	100000	862	683	16407	37339	6849	82	3619	137	1034	0	4681	28307	0
1	97656	859	630	16399	37322	6701	64	3615	137	0	0	4637	27292	1
5	97240	859	592	16356	37312	6652	58	3613	137	0	0	4557	27104	5
10	97072	858	579	16319	37305	6645	57	3611	137	0	0	4516	27045	10
15	96944	857	572	16288	37292	6639	57	3605	137	0	0	4489	27008	15
20	96732	854	565	16256	37277	6633	57	3596	133	0	0	4408	26953	20
25	96405	846	550	16206	37246	6625	57	3584	113	0	0	4298	26880	25
30	96009	821	535	16145	37206	6613	57	3562	81	0	0	4202	26787	30
35	95483	776	521	16036	37147	6605	56	3524	50	0	0	4111	26657	35
40	94706	723	503	15809	37058	6591	56	3452	21	0	0	4006	26487	40
45	93604	676	484	15434	36895	6568	55	3325	4	0	0	3899	26264	45
50	91936	625	459	14800	36586	6540	54	3161	0	0	0	3757	25954	50
55	89524	572	430	13916	36033	6496	54	2914	0	0	0	3597	25512	55
60	86151	514	393	12753	35133	6425	52	2591	0	0	0	3400	24890	60
65	81102	453	346	11196	33508	6275	48	2186	0	0	0	3169	23921	65
70	73393	365	287	9219	30556	5967	45	1674	0	0	0	2891	22389	70
75	61818	260	211	6877	25610	5361	42	1128	0	0	0	2502	19827	75
80	45350	154	135	4262	18208	4256	30	607	0	0	0	1931	15767	80
85+	25849	53	68	1917	9715	2694	17	231	0	0	0	1170	9984	85+

NUMBER OF PERSONS SURVIVING TO AGE X IF SPECIFIED CAUSES WERE ELIMINATED

Age (x)	No Causes	Respiratory T.B. (1)	Other Infec. and Paras. (2)	Neo-plasms (3)	Cardio-vascular (4)	Infl., Pneu., Bronch. (5)	Diar-rheal (6)	Certain Degener-ative (7)	Maternal (8)	Cert. Dis. of Infancy (9)	Motor Vehicle (10)	Other Violence (11)	Other and Unknown (12)	(1)+(2)	(1)+(2)+(5)+(6)+(8)	(1)+(2)+(5)+(6)+(8)+part of(9)&(12)	(10)+(11)	Age (x)
0	100000	100000	100000	100000	100000	100000	100000	100000	100000	100000	100000	100000	100000	100000	100000	100000	100000	0
1	97656	97659	97708	97664	97673	97802	97674	97660	97656	98683	97656	97699	98684	97711	97876	99415	97699	1
5	97240	97243	97330	97291	97267	97435	97264	97246	97240	98263	97240	97363	98434	97333	97552	99164	97363	5
10	97072	97076	97175	97160	97106	97273	97097	97080	97072	98093	97072	97236	98323	97179	97405	99027	97236	10
15	96944	96949	97054	97063	96991	97151	96969	96958	96944	97964	96944	97135	98231	97059	97291	98917	97135	15
20	96732	96740	96849	96882	96794	96945	96757	96755	96736	97749	96732	97004	98072	96857	97098	98728	97004	20
25	96405	96421	96536	96605	96497	96625	96440	96429	96429	97419	96405	96786	97814	96552	96821	98461	96786	25
30	96009	96050	96155	96269	96141	96240	96033	96066	96065	97019	96009	96484	97507	96195	96508	98168	96484	30
35	95483	95568	95642	95851	95673	95721	95508	95577	95569	96487	95483	96047	97104	95727	96078	97765	96047	35
40	94706	94844	94881	95298	94983	94956	94731	94871	94821	95702	94706	95371	96486	95019	95411	97118	95371	40
45	93604	93787	93796	94565	94041	93874	93630	93894	93734	94589	93604	94368	95590	93980	94408	96125	94368	45
50	91936	92166	92150	93517	92673	92229	91962	92384	92068	92903	91936	92828	94201	92380	92834	94548	92828	50
55	89524	89801	89761	91555	90794	89853	89550	90205	89652	90466	89524	90553	92177	90038	90524	92224	90553	55
60	86151	86474	86415	89669	88274	86537	86176	87126	86275	87057	86151	87336	89335	86739	87280	88958	87336	60
65	81102	81466	81396	86000	84733	81612	81131	82418	81218	81955	81102	82445	85080	81761	82423	84070	82445	65
70	73393	73806	73716	79841	79672	74151	73422	75079	73498	74165	73393	74877	78537	74131	75033	76645	74877	70
75	61818	62262	62160	69616	72217	63022	61845	63750	61907	62468	61818	63433	68715	62606	63945	65538	63433	75
80	45350	45766	45665	53629	60889	47207	45360	47223	45415	45827	45350	47037	54421	46085	48073	49668	47037	80
85+	25849	26162	26079	32705	44333	28147	25876	27210	25886	26121	25849	27405	36646	26395	28813	30406	27405	85+

ADDED YRS OF LIFE

	No Causes	(1)	(2)	(3)	(4)	(5)	(6)	(7)	(8)	(9)	(10)	(11)	(12)	(1)+(2)	(1)+(2)+(5)+(6)+(8)	...+part of(9)&(12)	(10)+(11)
TOTAL		.174	.183	2.537	4.755	.705	.024	.596	.062	.778	.000	.824	4.289	.358	1.163	2.792	.824
WORK	2.030	.074	.040	.583	.337	.040	.001	.169	.044	.000	.000	.265	.404	.114	.200	.256	.265

POPULATION, DEATHS, DEATH RATES FOR ALL CAUSES COMBINED, AND SPECIFIED CAUSES

Age Start of Interval	Midyear Population	Deaths During Year	All Causes	Respiratory T. B.	Other Infec. and Paras.	Neoplasms	Cardiovascular	Infl., Pneu., Bronch.	Diarrheal	Certain Degenerative	Maternal	Cert. Dis. of Infancy	Motor Vehicle	Other Violence	Other and Unknown	Age Start of Interval
0	437438	5776	.02235	.00001	.00047	.00007	.00017	.00094	.00020	.00003	.00000	.01213	.00003	.00070	.00760	0
1	1689363	1782	.00105	.00000	.00007	.00012	.00002	.00005	.00001	.00001	.00000	.00000	.00009	.00021	.00046	1
5	1882280	853	.00045	.00000	.00002	.00009	.00002	.00001	.00000	.00001	.00000	.00000	.00011	.00009	.00012	5
10	2105522	913	.00043	.00000	.00001	.00008	.00002	.00001	.00000	.00001	.00000	.00000	.00010	.00011	.00010	10
15	2067148	1966	.00095	.00000	.00001	.00009	.00003	.00001	.00000	.00001	.00000	.00000	.00036	.00028	.00016	15
20	1511896	2239	.00148	.00000	.00001	.00012	.00006	.00001	.00000	.00002	.00000	.00000	.00054	.00052	.00020	20
25	1606275	2657	.00165	.00003	.00002	.00016	.00010	.00001	.00000	.00006	.00000	.00000	.00042	.00059	.00027	25
30	1722664	3313	.00192	.00006	.00003	.00021	.00020	.00001	.00000	.00010	.00000	.00000	.00034	.00059	.00038	30
35	1697527	4810	.00283	.00014	.00005	.00034	.00040	.00002	.00000	.00024	.00000	.00000	.00038	.00067	.00059	35
40	1684431	6828	.00405	.00020	.00005	.00068	.00072	.00004	.00000	.00042	.00000	.00000	.00039	.00071	.00085	40
45	916746	5769	.00629	.00029	.00005	.00136	.00125	.00006	.00000	.00067	.00000	.00000	.00047	.00087	.00126	45
50	1429008	14452	.01011	.00038	.00008	.00270	.00228	.00009	.00000	.00112	.00000	.00000	.00046	.00105	.00196	50
55	1371983	22221	.01620	.00055	.00013	.00474	.00416	.00016	.00001	.00166	.00000	.00000	.00050	.00122	.00306	55
60	1236520	30815	.02492	.00067	.00020	.00742	.00744	.00034	.00002	.00230	.00000	.00000	.00049	.00135	.00468	60
65	901135	32958	.03657	.00071	.00026	.01027	.01256	.00065	.00001	.00300	.00000	.00000	.00045	.00136	.00729	65
70	592171	32559	.05498	.00086	.00035	.01315	.02161	.00134	.00003	.00342	.00000	.00000	.00051	.00162	.01209	70
75	416839	35343	.08479	.00089	.00050	.01677	.03563	.00275	.00004	.00366	.00000	.00000	.00047	.00259	.02150	75
80	227730	31012	.13618	.00078	.00047	.02084	.05799	.00638	.00009	.00382	.00000	.00000	.00049	.00457	.04075	80
85+	118782	26172	.22034	.00072	.00053	.02191	.08650	.01384	.00012	.00321	.00000	.00000	.00055	.00861	.08435	85+
ALL	23615458	266437														

	All Causes	Respiratory T.B.	Other Infec. and Paras.	Neoplasms	Cardiovascular	Infl., Pneu., Bronch.	Diarrheal	Certain Degenerative	Maternal	Cert. Dis. of Infancy	Motor Vehicle	Other Violence	Other and Unknown
CRUDE DEATH RATE	.01128	.00021	.00009	.00235	.00358	.00030	.00001	.00069	.00000	.00022	.00035	.00075	.00274
STANDARDIZED RATE (1)	.00578	.00011	.00006	.00108	.00141	.00014	.00001	.00034	.00000	.00043	.00030	.00052	.00138
STANDARDIZED RATE (2)	.01069	.00019	.00008	.00218	.00335	.00029	.00001	.00063	.00000	.00025	.00034	.00071	.00260
GEOMETRIC MEAN	.00739												

LIFE TABLE FOR ALL CAUSES COMBINED

Age (x)	Midyear Population	Deaths During Year	$_nM_x$	$_nq_x$	l_x	$_nd_x$	$_nL_x$	$_nm_x$	$_na_x$	T_x	$_nr_x$	$\overset{\circ}{e}_x$	Age (x)
0	437438	5776	.022348	.021910	100000	2191	98046	.022347	.107992	6852039	.000000	68.520	0
1	1689363	1782	.001055	.004212	97809	412	390206	.001056	1.500000	6753993	.000000	69.053	1
5	1882280	853	.000453	.002269	97397	221	486433	.000454	2.500000	6363787	.000000	65.339	5
10	2105522	913	.000434	.002161	97176	210	485405	.000433	2.739087	5877355	-.015086	60.482	10
15	2067148	1966	.000951	.004765	96966	462	483780	.000955	2.727273	5391949	.020867	55.607	15
20	1511896	2238	.001480	.007399	96504	714	480803	.001485	2.595413	4908169	.030443	50.860	20
25	1606275	2657	.001654	.008237	95790	789	477018	.001654	2.551489	4427366	-.005792	46.220	25
30	1722664	3313	.001923	.009568	95001	909	472843	.001922	2.621929	3950348	-.005669	41.582	30
35	1697527	4810	.002834	.014039	94092	1321	467359	.002827	2.652504	3477505	-.013379	36.959	35
40	1684431	6828	.004054	.020222	92771	1876	459480	.004083	2.668133	3010146	.046325	32.447	40
45	916746	5769	.006293	.031150	90895	2835	447856	.006330	2.679233	2550665	-.031244	28.062	45
50	1429008	14452	.010113	.049001	88060	4315	430280	.010028	2.677771	2102770	-.039724	23.879	50
55	1371983	22221	.016198	.077820	83745	6517	403428	.016154	2.652710	1672490	-.013579	19.971	55
60	1236520	30815	.024921	.117729	77228	9092	364449	.024947	2.614249	1269062	.005786	16.433	60
65	901135	32958	.036574	.168824	68136	11503	312899	.036763	2.584851	904614	-.031241	13.277	65
70	592171	32559	.054982	.243268	56633	13777	249455	.055228	2.553199	591715	-.025025	10.448	70
75	416839	35343	.084788	.350499	42856	15021	176786	.084967	2.503883	342260	.010640	7.986	75
80	227730	31012	.136179	.505012	27835	14057	102942	.136552	2.422444	165474	.010640	5.945	80
85+	118782	26172	.220336	1.000000	13778	13778	62532	.220336	4.538514	62532	.000000	4.539	85+

NUMBER OF PERSONS DYING (OUT OF 100,000 AT BIRTH) ABOVE AGE X FROM SPECIFIED CAUSES

Age (x)	All Causes	Respiratory T.B.	Other Infec. and Paras.	Neo-plasms	Cardio-vascular	Infl., Pneu., Bronch.	Diar-rheal	Certain Degen-erative	Maternal	Cert. Dis. of Infancy	Motor Vehicle	Other Violence	Other and Unknown	Age (x)
0	100000	1684	653	20282	33746	2970	76	5742	0	1189	2526	5950	25142	0
1	97809	1683	647	20275	33730	2877	56	5739	0	0	2523	5881	24398	1
5	97397	1682	621	20227	33721	2856	51	5735	0	0	2487	5799	24218	5
10	97176	1682	613	20184	33712	2852	51	5733	0	0	2433	5758	24158	10
15	96966	1682	609	20146	33701	2849	51	5728	0	0	2384	5707	24109	15
20	96504	1681	603	20101	33686	2844	51	5723	0	0	2209	5572	24034	20
25	95790	1679	597	20043	33658	2841	51	5712	0	0	1949	5323	23937	25
30	95001	1665	587	19568	33612	2836	50	5685	0	0	1747	5043	23808	30
35	94092	1635	573	19871	33518	2832	50	5638	0	0	1584	4763	23628	35
40	92771	1572	550	19710	33332	2823	49	5528	0	0	1405	4452	23350	40
45	90895	1481	528	19396	32999	2806	47	5333	0	0	1226	4124	22955	45
50	88060	1350	504	18780	32433	2778	46	5030	0	0	1016	3735	22388	50
55	83745	1190	469	17633	31462	2741	45	4550	0	0	820	3284	21551	55
60	77228	969	415	15725	29789	2678	40	3881	0	0	617	2793	20321	60
65	68136	724	341	13018	27075	2553	34	3042	0	0	437	2302	18610	65
70	56633	501	259	9791	23116	2347	30	2101	0	0	296	1876	16316	70
75	42856	285	171	6502	17697	2009	23	1247	0	0	168	1469	13285	75
80	27835	128	82	3534	11383	1521	16	600	0	0	86	1011	9474	80
85+	13778	45	33	1370	5409	865	7	201	0	0	34	539	5275	85+

NUMBER OF PERSONS SURVIVING TO AGE X IF SPECIFIED CAUSES WERE ELIMINATED

Age (x)	No Causes	Respiratory T.B. (1)	Other Infec. and Paras. (2)	Neo-plasms (3)	Cardio-vascular (4)	Infl., Pneu., Bronch. (5)	Diar-rheal (6)	Certain Degener-ative (7)	Maternal (8)	Cert. Dis. of Infancy (9)	Motor Vehicle (10)	Other Violence (11)	Other and Unknown (12)	(1)+(2)	(1)+(2)+(5)+(6)+(8)	(1)+(2)+(5)+(6)+(8)+part of(9)&(12)	(10)+(11)	Age (x)
0	100000	100000	100000	100000	100000	100000	100000	100000	100000	100000	100000	100000	100000	100000	100000	100000	100000	0
1	97809	97810	97855	97816	97825	97901	97829	97812	97809	98992	97812	97877	98548	97855	97967	99162	97880	1
5	97397	97399	97468	97452	97422	97510	97422	97404	97397	98575	97436	97547	98314	97470	97608	98840	97586	5
10	97176	97178	97255	97274	97210	97292	97201	97185	97176	98351	97269	97367	98151	97257	97398	98632	97460	10
15	96966	96968	97049	97101	97011	97085	96991	96980	96966	98139	97108	97207	97988	97051	97195	98428	97349	15
20	96504	96507	96593	96684	96563	96628	96528	96523	96504	97671	96820	96879	97597	96595	96744	97974	97196	20
25	95790	95795	95884	96026	95877	95916	95814	95820	95790	96949	96364	96412	96973	95889	96039	97262	96989	25
30	95001	95020	95104	95310	95133	95131	95026	95057	95001	96150	95773	95899	96304	95123	95278	96497	96678	30
35	94092	94141	94208	94495	94317	94224	94117	94195	94092	95230	95020	95263	95565	94257	94414	95634	96202	35
40	92771	92881	92908	93329	93178	92910	92756	92982	92771	93893	93865	94238	94504	93019	93184	94414	95350	40
45	90895	91093	91051	91755	91625	91048	90922	91295	90895	91994	92147	92663	92992	91250	91431	92674	93939	45
50	88060	88382	88235	89508	89331	88236	88087	88748	88060	89125	89482	90164	90664	88557	88762	90014	91620	50
55	83745	84207	83946	86267	85920	83949	83772	84872	83745	84758	85292	86196	87066	84409	84642	85892	87788	55
60	77228	77868	77465	81464	80901	77477	77257	78920	77228	78162	78852	79974	81527	78107	78388	79625	81656	60
65	68136	68932	68415	74603	74099	68474	68168	70438	68136	68960	69741	71036	73645	69214	69589	70789	72710	65
70	56633	57500	56940	65304	65645	57193	56663	59436	56633	57318	58098	59447	62514	57811	58322	59450	60985	70
75	42856	43701	43165	52803	55443	43510	42885	45755	42856	43374	44078	45357	51110	44016	44717	45752	46649	75
80	27835	28510	28107	37325	43180	28662	27859	30268	27835	28172	28655	29850	37053	28789	29670	30579	30772	80
85+	13778	14171	13947	20588	28818	14661	13796	15284	13778	13945	14241	15128	22628	14344	15284	16022	15636	85+

ADDED YRS OF LIFE

	No Causes	Respiratory T.B. (1)	Other Infec. and Paras. (2)	Neo-plasms (3)	Cardio-vascular (4)	Infl., Pneu., Bronch. (5)	Diar-rheal (6)	Certain Degener-ative (7)	Maternal (8)	Cert. Dis. of Infancy (9)	Motor Vehicle (10)	Other Violence (11)	Other and Unknown (12)	(1)+(2)	(1)+(2)+(5)+(6)+(8)	(1)+(2)+(5)+(6)+(8)+part of(9)&(12)	(10)+(11)
TOTAL		.281	.150	2.884	4.528	.315	.023	.861	.000	.828	.784	1.350	3.894	.433	.780	1.857	2.162
WORK	3.723	.112	.037	.650	.574	.028	.002	.274	.000	.000	.469	.666	.653	.150	.180	.224	1.145

POPULATION, DEATHS, DEATH RATES FOR ALL CAUSES COMBINED, AND SPECIFIED CAUSES

Age Start of Interval	Midyear Population	Deaths During Year	All Causes	Respiratory T. B.	Other Infec. and Paras.	Neoplasms	Cardiovascular	Infl., Pneu., Bronch.	Diarrheal	Certain Degenerative	Maternal	Cert. Dis. of Infancy	Motor Vehicle	Other Violence	Other and Unknown	Age Start of Interval
0	420274	7146	.01700	.00001	.00046	.00005	.00006	.00081	.00024	.00001	.00000	.00903	.00004	.00053	.00576	0
1	1625016	1516	.00093	.00000	.00006	.00012	.00003	.00006	.00001	.00001	.00000	.00000	.00007	.00015	.00042	1
5	1812938	587	.00032	.00000	.00001	.00006	.00001	.00001	.00000	.00000	.00000	.00000	.00008	.00003	.00011	5
10	2034801	500	.00025	.00000	.00001	.00006	.00002	.00001	.00000	.00001	.00000	.00000	.00005	.00003	.00006	10
15	1973297	876	.00044	.00000	.00001	.00008	.00003	.00001	.00000	.00001	.00000	.00000	.00012	.00008	.00010	15
20	1394902	889	.00064	.00001	.00002	.00009	.00006	.00001	.00000	.00002	.00002	.00000	.00014	.00012	.00014	20
25	1472105	1007	.00068	.00002	.00002	.00011	.00008	.00000	.00000	.00004	.00004	.00000	.00010	.00011	.00016	25
30	1633125	1602	.00098	.00004	.00003	.00019	.00011	.00001	.00000	.00009	.00005	.00000	.00009	.00013	.00025	30
35	1652877	2442	.00148	.00004	.00004	.00041	.00020	.00001	.00000	.00016	.00004	.00000	.00009	.00015	.00032	35
40	1688355	3677	.00218	.00006	.00003	.00074	.00032	.00002	.00000	.00026	.00002	.00000	.00010	.00017	.00045	40
45	939779	3115	.00331	.00007	.00004	.00121	.00058	.00002	.00000	.00040	.00000	.00000	.00014	.00020	.00065	45
50	1505564	7472	.00496	.00008	.00005	.00189	.00102	.00004	.00000	.00053	.00000	.00000	.00014	.00029	.00094	50
55	1479458	10502	.00710	.00008	.00007	.00260	.00182	.00006	.00000	.00071	.00000	.00000	.00015	.00032	.00130	55
60	1405527	15560	.01107	.00011	.00010	.00371	.00342	.00012	.00000	.00095	.00000	.00000	.00016	.00042	.00209	60
65	1229773	22015	.01790	.00016	.00014	.00504	.00645	.00028	.00001	.00136	.00000	.00000	.00013	.00056	.00377	65
70	1003163	30854	.03076	.00026	.00023	.00706	.01269	.00069	.00002	.00177	.00000	.00000	.00018	.00097	.00690	70
75	763247	41765	.05472	.00034	.00030	.00957	.02451	.00170	.00004	.00223	.00000	.00000	.00015	.00155	.01389	75
80	475854	45869	.09638	.00047	.00041	.01300	.04366	.00394	.00006	.00250	.00000	.00000	.00019	.00403	.02813	80
85+	285262	52647	.18456	.00059	.00054	.01548	.07497	.01056	.00009	.00229	.00000	.00000	.00016	.00981	.07007	85+
ALL	24795357	250041														

CRUDE DEATH RATE			.01008	.00008	.00008	.00191	.00373	.00033	.00001	.00047	.00001	.00015	.00011	.00046	.00275	
STANDARDIZED RATE (1)			.00334	.00003	.00005	.00067	.00082	.00009	.00001	.00018	.00001	.00032	.00010	.00018	.00087	
STANDARDIZED RATE (2)			.00629	.00005	.00006	.00129	.00212	.00018	.00001	.00033	.00001	.00019	.00011	.00030	.00163	
GEOMETRIC MEAN			.00415													

LIFE TABLE FOR ALL CAUSES COMBINED

Age (x)	Midyear Population	Deaths During Year	$_nM_x$	$_nq_x$	l_x	$_nd_x$	$_nL_x$	$_nm_x$	$_na_x$	T_x	$_nr_x$	$\overset{\circ}{e}_x$	Age (x)
0	420274	7146	.017003	.016750	100000	1675	98491	.017007	.098905	7567804	.000000	75.678	0
1	1625016	1516	.000933	.003722	98325	366	392385	.000933	1.500000	7469313	.000000	75.966	1
5	1812938	587	.000324	.001613	97959	158	489400	.000323	2.500000	7076928	.000000	72.244	5
10	2034801	500	.000246	.001227	97801	120	488717	.000246	2.604167	6587528	-.014893	67.356	10
15	1973297	876	.000444	.002232	97681	218	487900	.000447	2.682531	6098811	.024687	62.436	15
20	1394902	889	.000637	.003191	97463	311	486561	.000639	2.575697	5610911	.036126	57.570	20
25	1472105	1007	.000684	.003407	97152	331	484966	.000683	2.601964	5124350	-.005236	52.746	25
30	1633125	1602	.000981	.004885	96821	473	483001	.000979	2.665610	4639384	-.009473	47.917	30
35	1652877	2442	.001477	.007338	96348	707	480091	.001473	2.667963	4156383	-.017678	43.139	35
40	1688355	3677	.002178	.010905	95641	1043	475776	.002192	2.670981	3676292	-.042667	38.438	40
45	939779	3115	.003315	.016523	94598	1563	469037	.003330	2.663148	3200516	-.028786	33.833	45
50	1505564	7472	.004963	.024367	93035	2267	459841	.004930	2.647037	2731178	-.040506	29.356	50
55	1479458	10502	.007099	.034847	90768	3163	446445	.007085	2.662161	2271338	-.011114	25.024	55
60	1405527	15560	.011071	.053981	87605	4729	427031	.011074	2.675160	1824892	.001298	20.831	60
65	1229773	22015	.017902	.086141	82876	7139	397818	.017905	2.680026	1397861	.011705	16.867	65
70	1003163	30854	.030757	.143893	75737	10898	353232	.030852	2.664461	1000044	-.013894	13.204	70
75	763247	41765	.054720	.242786	64839	15742	286567	.054933	2.609685	646811	.016441	9.976	75
80	475854	45869	.096385	.390777	49097	19186	198175	.096813	2.534150	360245	.016441	7.337	80
85+	285262	52647	.184557	1.000000	29911	29911	162069	.184557	5.418390	162069	.000000	5.418	85+

NUMBER OF PERSONS DYING (OUT OF 100,000 AT BIRTH) ABOVE AGE X FROM SPECIFIED CAUSES

Age (x)	All Causes	Respiratory T. B.	Other Infec. and Paras.	Neo-plasms	Cardio-vascular	Infl., Pneu., Bronch.	Diar-rheal	Certain Degen-erative	Maternal	Cert. Dis. of Infancy	Motor Vehicle	Other Violence	Other and Unknown	Age (x)
0	100000	685	658	17430	38382	3579	82	4126	87	890	895	4574	28612	0
1	98325	684	613	17426	38376	3499	59	4124	87	0	891	4522	28044	1
5	97959	682	587	17377	38364	3475	55	4121	87	0	865	4465	27881	5
10	97801	682	581	17346	38357	3469	55	4120	87	0	827	4451	27826	10
15	97681	681	577	17317	38348	3464	55	4116	87	0	801	4438	27797	15
20	97463	680	570	17279	38335	3462	55	4110	85	0	741	4400	27746	20
25	97152	675	562	17234	38305	3459	55	4098	75	0	673	4341	27675	25
30	96821	665	552	17179	38266	3457	55	4080	57	0	624	4288	27598	30
35	96348	646	537	17087	38215	3454	54	4038	33	0	580	4228	27476	35
40	95641	623	521	16892	38119	3448	54	3960	13	0	536	4156	27319	40
45	94558	593	505	16536	37568	3439	54	3836	1	0	488	4074	27104	45
50	93035	559	488	15967	37654	3429	53	3646	0	0	424	3978	26797	50
55	90768	524	466	15103	37231	3413	52	3403	0	0	362	3845	26369	55
60	87605	487	435	13945	36422	3388	52	3086	0	0	297	3703	25790	60
65	82876	441	392	12360	34662	3339	49	2682	0	0	229	3523	24899	65
70	75737	379	337	10352	32387	3228	45	2138	0	0	178	3299	23394	70
75	64839	288	256	7852	27889	2983	39	1513	0	0	115	2955	20949	75
80	49097	189	170	5105	20837	2493	26	872	0	0	65	2392	16948	80
85+	29911	96	88	2508	12150	1711	15	370	0	0	27	1590	11356	85+

NUMBER OF PERSONS SURVIVING TO AGE X IF SPECIFIED CAUSES WERE ELIMINATED

Age (x)	No Causes	Respiratory T. B.	Other Infec. and Paras.	Neo-plasms	Cardio-vascular	Infl., Pneu., Bronch.	Diar-rheal	Certain Degener-ative	Maternal	Cert. Dis. of Infancy	Motor Vehicle	Other Violence	Other and Unknown	(1) + (2)	(1) + (2) + (5) + (6) + (8)	(1)+(2)+ (5)+(6)+ (8)+part of(9)&(12)	(10) + (11)	Age (x)
		(1)	(2)	(3)	(4)	(5)	(6)	(7)	(8)	(9)	(10)	(11)	(12)					
0	100000	100000	100000	100000	100000	100000	100000	100000	100000	100000	100000	100000	100000	100000	100000	100000	100000	0
1	98325	98326	98370	98329	98331	98404	98348	98327	98325	99211	98329	98377	98890	98371	98473	99472	98381	1
5	97959	97962	98029	98012	97977	98062	97986	97964	97959	98842	97989	98067	98665	98032	98162	99204	98097	5
10	97801	97804	97877	97885	97826	97910	97828	97807	97801	98683	97869	97923	98582	97880	98016	99062	97991	10
15	97681	97685	97761	97794	97715	97795	97708	97691	97681	98562	97775	97816	98490	97765	97906	98954	97910	15
20	97463	97468	97550	97613	97510	97578	97490	97479	97465	98342	97617	97636	98322	97555	97699	98749	97790	20
25	97152	97162	97247	97347	97229	97270	97178	97180	97164	98028	97373	97383	98079	97257	97414	98468	97575	25
30	96821	96841	96925	97070	96936	96941	96847	96867	96851	97694	97090	97104	97823	96945	97122	98185	97375	30
35	96348	96337	96467	96688	96514	96470	96375	96435	96402	97217	96660	96690	97468	96506	96709	97790	97003	35
40	95641	95702	95775	96174	95901	95768	95668	95806	95714	96503	95995	96053	96911	95836	96065	97157	96408	40
45	94558	94689	94746	95482	95006	94733	94625	94884	94682	95491	94996	95087	96071	94837	95084	96183	95487	45
50	93035	93158	93198	94476	93710	93177	93062	93506	93119	93874	93490	93612	94793	93321	93576	94673	94069	50
55	90768	90922	90949	93044	91888	90923	90796	91469	90850	91586	91273	91463	92915	91103	91369	92458	91972	55
60	87605	87790	87810	90975	89495	87779	87632	88596	87684	88395	88157	88416	90262	87996	88277	89350	88973	60
65	82876	83096	83112	87679	86128	83085	82904	84211	82951	83623	83465	83820	86287	83333	83650	84699	84415	65
70	75737	75998	76005	82179	81311	76038	75767	77486	75805	76420	76324	76816	80367	76267	76669	77691	77412	70
75	64839	65146	65144	72898	74226	65325	64870	66928	64898	65424	65400	66087	71246	65452	66034	67032	66658	75
80	49097	49416	49402	57927	63665	49897	49132	51251	49141	49540	49565	50543	57908	49723	50615	51594	51025	80
85+	29911	30177	30161	37739	48543	31019	29941	31631	29938	30181	30226	31436	40761	30429	31616	32561	31767	85+

ADDED YRS OF LIFE																		
TOTAL		.117	.155	2.719	5.155	.361	.026	.669	.040	.682	.308	.677	4.191	.273	.707	1.739	.991	
WORK	1.874	.039	.032	.546	.303	.014	.001	.171	.028	.000	.136	.166	.379	.071	.113	.145	.303	

POPULATION, DEATHS, DEATH RATES FOR ALL CAUSES COMBINED, AND SPECIFIED CAUSES

Age Start of Interval	Midyear Population	Deaths During Year	All Causes	Respiratory T. B.	Other Infec. and Paras.	Neoplasms	Cardiovascular	Infl., Pneu., Bronch.	Diarrheal	Certain Degenerative	Maternal	Cert. Dis. of Infancy	Motor Vehicle	Other Violence	Other and Unknown	Age Start of Interval
0	468000	18341	.03919	.00001	.00050	.00009	.00007	.00286	.00096	.00001	.00000	.02576	.00001	.00071	.00820	0
1	1724000	2501	.00145	.00000	.00011	.00013	.00002	.00019	.00004	.00002	.00000	.00000	.00016	.00030	.00048	1
5	1563000	1267	.00065	.00000	.00003	.00009	.00002	.00002	.00000	.00001	.00000	.00000	.00020	.00012	.00015	5
10	1780000	847	.00048	.00000	.00003	.00008	.00001	.00002	.00000	.00001	.00000	.00000	.00011	.00012	.00010	10
15	1993000	2531	.00127	.00001	.00003	.00011	.00004	.00003	.00000	.00002	.00000	.00000	.00052	.00037	.00015	15
20	2361000	4244	.00180	.00002	.00002	.00012	.00006	.00002	.00000	.00004	.00000	.00000	.00082	.00050	.00018	20
25	1850000	3284	.00178	.00005	.00002	.00016	.00011	.00003	.00000	.00007	.00000	.00000	.00056	.00056	.00020	25
30	1814000	3261	.00180	.00011	.00002	.00022	.00021	.00003	.00000	.00010	.00000	.00000	.00039	.00046	.00026	30
35	1573000	3863	.00246	.00015	.00004	.00037	.00042	.00006	.00001	.00016	.00000	.00000	.00036	.00051	.00039	35
40	1075000	3685	.00343	.00019	.00003	.00060	.00077	.00010	.00001	.00029	.00000	.00000	.00032	.00059	.00054	40
45	1603000	8809	.00550	.00024	.00005	.00117	.00154	.00016	.00001	.00045	.00000	.00000	.00040	.00068	.00079	45
50	1743000	16612	.00953	.00040	.00006	.00228	.00299	.00035	.00002	.00077	.00000	.00000	.00042	.00087	.00138	50
55	1676000	27374	.01633	.00061	.00011	.00426	.00569	.00079	.00003	.00105	.00000	.00000	.00046	.00050	.00242	55
60	1252000	33693	.02691	.00085	.00013	.00707	.01036	.00152	.00004	.00156	.00000	.00000	.00048	.00093	.00396	60
65	876000	36204	.04133	.00088	.00016	.01017	.01769	.00266	.00007	.00215	.00000	.00000	.00051	.00103	.00600	65
70	664000	42228	.06360	.00092	.00020	.01356	.02929	.00483	.00011	.00277	.00000	.00000	.00067	.00145	.00980	70
75	441000	44629	.10120	.00090	.00018	.01754	.04916	.00887	.00023	.00334	.00000	.00000	.00085	.00216	.01797	75
80	234000	38086	.16276	.00093	.00029	.02102	.07778	.01538	.00041	.00368	.00000	.00000	.00111	.00375	.03839	80
85+	87000	24052	.27646	.00064	.00029	.02216	.11823	.03009	.00072	.00322	.00000	.00000	.00152	.00843	.09116	85+
ALL	25177000	315511														

CRUDE DEATH RATE	.01253	.00024	.00007	.00228	.00468	.00087	.00004	.00052	.00000	.00048	.00043	.00064	.00227	
STANDARDIZED RATE (1)	.00685	.00013	.00007	.00105	.00189	.00044	.00005	.00026	.00000	.00091	.00037	.00047	.00123	
STANDARDIZED RATE (2)	.01228	.00021	.00007	.00213	.00459	.00088	.00005	.00048	.00000	.00053	.00041	.00062	.00229	
GEOMETRIC MEAN	.00831													

LIFE TABLE FOR ALL CAUSES COMBINED

Age (x)	Midyear Population	Deaths During Year	$_nM_x$	$_nq_x$	l_x	$_nd_x$	$_nL_x$	$_nm_x$	$_na_x$	T_x	$_nr_x$	$\overset{\circ}{e}_x$	Age (x)
0	468000	18341	.039190	.037910	100000	3791	96727	.039193	.136623	6651539	.000000	66.515	0
1	1724000	2501	.001451	.005779	96209	556	383446	.001450	1.500000	6554812	.000000	68.131	1
5	1563000	1267	.000645	.003220	95653	308	477495	.000645	2.500000	6171366	.000000	64.518	5
10	1780000	847	.000476	.002381	95345	227	476219	.000477	2.767070	5693871	.004551	59.719	10
15	1993000	2531	.001270	.006297	95118	599	474221	.001263	2.714942	5217653	-.026757	54.855	15
20	2361000	4244	.001798	.008940	94519	845	470530	.001796	2.556460	4743432	-.006201	50.185	20
25	1850000	3284	.001775	.008839	93674	828	466297	.001776	2.496477	4272902	.021061	45.615	25
30	1814000	3261	.001798	.008950	92846	831	462215	.001798	2.575712	3806605	.007869	40.999	30
35	1573000	3863	.002456	.012281	92015	1130	457400	.002470	2.632375	3344389	.047532	36.346	35
40	1075000	3685	.003428	.017044	90885	1549	450817	.003436	2.670675	2886990	.017137	31.765	40
45	1603000	8809	.005495	.026854	89336	2399	441199	.005437	2.715368	2436173	-.043361	27.270	45
50	1743000	16612	.009531	.046344	86937	4029	425472	.009469	2.713452	1994974	-.025893	22.947	50
55	1676000	27374	.016333	.078726	82908	6527	399407	.016342	2.681522	1569501	.001981	18.931	55
60	1252000	33693	.026911	.127204	76381	9716	358876	.027073	2.629790	1170094	.031480	15.319	60
65	876000	36204	.041329	.188705	66665	12580	302954	.041524	2.585784	811218	.026220	12.169	65
70	664000	42228	.063596	.275418	54085	14896	233856	.063697	2.545076	508264	.008315	9.397	70
75	441000	44629	.101200	.403251	39189	15803	156115	.101227	2.479579	274407	.001177	7.002	75
80	234000	38086	.162761	.570726	23386	13347	81980	.162808	2.381418	118292	.001177	5.058	80
85+	87000	24052	.276460	1.000000	10039	10039	36313	.276460	3.617163	36313	.000000	3.617	85+

NUMBER OF PERSONS DYING (OUT OF 100,000 AT BIRTH) ABOVE AGE X FROM SPECIFIED CAUSES

Age (x)	All Causes	Respiratory T.B.	Other Infec. and Paras.	Neo-plasms	Cardio-vascular	Infl., Pneu., Bronch.	Diar-rheal	Certain Degen-erative	Maternal	Cert. Dis. of Infancy	Motor Vehicle	Other Violence	Other and Unknown	Age (x)
0	100000	1792	489	18134	39317	7251	302	4083	0	2492	2890	4639	18611	0
1	96209	1791	441	18126	39310	6975	209	4082	0	0	2889	4570	17816	1
5	95653	1790	398	18077	39301	6902	193	4077	0	0	2827	4455	17633	5
10	95345	1790	382	18034	39293	6894	192	4072	0	0	2732	4397	17559	10
15	95118	1789	369	17997	39286	6885	191	4067	0	0	2681	4342	17511	15
20	94519	1786	357	17945	39267	6873	190	4056	0	0	2437	4168	17440	20
25	93674	1778	347	17888	39237	6864	190	4036	0	0	2050	3932	17352	25
30	92846	1753	335	17810	39184	6849	188	4004	0	0	1792	3673	17258	30
35	92015	1703	326	17709	39088	6834	187	3957	0	0	1611	3460	17140	35
40	90885	1632	308	17538	38894	6808	184	3884	0	0	1449	3227	16961	40
45	89336	1548	294	17268	38547	6764	182	3751	0	0	1305	2962	16715	45
50	86937	1442	271	16760	37876	6692	178	3553	0	0	1130	2664	16371	50
55	82908	1274	247	15758	36612	6546	169	3226	0	0	952	2296	15788	55
60	76381	1029	204	14094	34339	6230	159	2805	0	0	768	1935	14818	60
65	66665	725	156	11542	30592	5678	143	2244	0	0	594	1602	13389	65
70	54085	456	109	8449	25202	4868	121	1591	0	0	438	1291	11560	70
75	39189	242	63	5275	18340	3737	96	941	0	0	280	952	9263	75
80	23386	102	35	2536	10662	2352	60	420	0	0	148	614	6457	80
85+	10039	23	10	805	4293	1093	26	117	0	0	55	306	3311	85+

NUMBER OF PERSONS SURVIVING TO AGE X IF SPECIFIED CAUSES WERE ELIMINATED

Age (x)	No Causes	Respiratory T.B. (1)	Other Infec. and Paras. (2)	Neo-plasms (3)	Cardio-vascular (4)	Infl., Pneu., Bronch. (5)	Diar-rheal (6)	Certain Degener-ative (7)	Maternal (8)	Cert. Dis. of Infancy (9)	Motor Vehicle (10)	Other Violence (11)	Other and Unknown (12)	(1) + (2)	(1) + (2) + (5) + (6) + (8)	(1)+(2)+ (5)+(6)+ (8)+part of(9)&(12)	(10) + (11)	Age (x)
0	100000	100000	100000	100000	100000	100000	100000	100000	100000	100000	100000	100000	100000	100000	100000	100000	100000	0
1	96209	96210	96256	96217	96216	96480	96300	96210	96209	98684	96210	96277	96992	96257	96620	99343	96278	1
5	95653	95655	95743	95710	95669	95996	95760	95569	95653	98114	95716	95835	96616	95745	96195	98973	95898	5
10	95345	95347	95450	95444	95369	95694	95452	95356	95345	97798	95503	95585	96379	95452	95910	98688	95743	10
15	95118	95121	95236	95254	95149	95476	95226	95134	95118	97565	95326	95412	96198	95239	95706	98485	95621	15
20	94519	94525	94648	94706	94568	94886	94627	94546	94519	96951	94970	94985	95664	94654	95131	97897	95439	20
25	93674	93688	93812	93916	93753	94047	93781	93720	93674	96084	94509	94373	94897	93826	94308	97053	95214	25
30	92846	92885	92995	93164	92977	93231	92954	92924	92846	95235	93933	93799	94153	93034	93528	96258	94897	30
35	92015	92103	92172	92431	92241	92411	92124	92139	92015	94383	93275	93173	93430	92260	92767	95487	94449	35
40	90885	91043	91058	91467	91301	91302	90995	91080	90885	93223	92292	92264	92443	91216	91746	95459	93693	40
45	89336	89574	89520	90178	90092	89790	89446	89660	89336	91635	90864	90958	91136	89758	90326	93026	92515	45
50	86937	87274	87138	88264	88343	87450	87048	87449	86937	89174	88600	88815	89035	87476	88105	90774	90514	50
55	82908	83394	83124	85133	85513	83541	83023	83718	82908	85041	84671	85067	85494	83611	84366	86982	86875	55
60	76381	77065	76621	80128	81064	77271	76496	77535	76381	78346	78185	78725	79729	77307	78326	80863	80584	60
65	66665	67548	66919	72478	74568	67966	66781	68206	66665	68380	68405	69030	70993	67806	69249	71651	70832	65
70	54085	55046	54333	61898	66175	55889	54199	55937	54085	55477	55640	56293	59375	55299	57264	59443	57912	70
75	39189	40068	39408	48021	55630	41502	39293	41102	39189	40197	40453	41088	45217	40292	42783	44661	42414	75
80	23386	24018	23538	31312	42670	25916	23476	24943	23386	23988	24244	24791	29591	24174	26892	28391	25700	80
85+	10039	10362	10120	15000	27423	12049	10099	10915	10039	10297	10469	10852	15504	10446	12612	13684	11316	85+

ACCEC YRS OF LIFE																		
TOTAL		.293	.145	2.396	5.153	.860	.054	.570	.000	1.708	.913	1.130	2.715	.439	1.417	3.618	2.068	
WORK	3.674	.129	.036	.600	.721	.100	.006	.204	.000	.000	.570	.591	.474	.165	.271	.317	1.171	

POPULATION, DEATHS, DEATH RATES FOR ALL CAUSES COMBINED, AND SPECIFIED CAUSES

Age Start of Interval	Midyear Population	Deaths During Year	All Causes	Respiratory T. B.	Other Infec. and Paras.	Neoplasms	Cardio-vascular	Infl., Pneu., Bronch.	Diarrheal	Certain Degenerative	Maternal	Cert. Dis. of Infancy	Motor Vehicle	Other Violence	Other and Unknown	Age Start of Interval
0	444000	13633	.03070	.00000	.00045	.00010	.00008	.00245	.00063	.00001	.00000	.01962	.00001	.00058	.00677	0
1	1634000	1921	.00118	.00000	.00011	.00011	.00002	.00016	.00005	.00001	.00000	.00000	.00011	.00021	.00040	1
5	1867000	761	.00041	.00000	.00003	.00006	.00001	.00002	.00000	.00001	.00000	.00000	.00010	.00005	.00040	5
10	1701000	471	.00028	.00000	.00001	.00006	.00002	.00001	.00000	.00001	.00000	.00000	.00010	.00005	.00012	10
15	1911000	1002	.00052	.00000	.00002	.00008	.00003	.00002	.00000	.00002	.00002	.00000	.00004	.00003	.00009	15
20	2251000	1373	.00061	.00002	.00002	.00010	.00005	.00002	.00000	.00003	.00006	.00000	.00010	.00011	.00013	20
25	1768000	1565	.00089	.00004	.00002	.00016	.00008	.00003	.00001	.00006	.00012	.00000	.00006	.00011	.00013	25
30	1875000	2136	.00114	.00005	.00002	.00028	.00014	.00003	.00000	.00005	.00014	.00000	.00006	.00011	.00020	30
35	2113000	3671	.00174	.00007	.00002	.00061	.00023	.00004	.00001	.00007	.00014	.00000	.00005	.00015	.00022	35
40	1464000	3360	.00230	.00006	.00002	.00099	.00038	.00006	.00000	.00011	.00016	.00000	.00006	.00017	.00032	40
45	2115000	7845	.00371	.00007	.00003	.00166	.00075	.00010	.00001	.00017	.00000	.00000	.00008	.00026	.00059	45
50	2153000	11331	.00526	.00007	.00004	.00200	.00132	.00015	.00001	.00027	.00000	.00000	.00009	.00029	.00080	50
55	1921000	15961	.00831	.00008	.00006	.00313	.00257	.00029	.00002	.00049	.00000	.00000	.00010	.00034	.00123	55
60	1646000	23017	.01398	.00013	.00008	.00446	.00544	.00057	.00003	.00087	.00000	.00000	.00010	.00039	.00192	60
65	1307000	32355	.02476	.00018	.00011	.00641	.01150	.00124	.00007	.00144	.00000	.00000	.00017	.00051	.00313	65
70	969000	43289	.04467	.00025	.00015	.00904	.02297	.00254	.00011	.00215	.00000	.00000	.00023	.00092	.00590	70
75	619000	50486	.08156	.00032	.00017	.01324	.04347	.00608	.00022	.00300	.00000	.00000	.00038	.00214	.01255	75
80	322000	45308	.14071	.00041	.00025	.01660	.07309	.01135	.00039	.00296	.00000	.00000	.00045	.00498	.03023	80
85+	125000	31857	.25486	.00032	.00040	.01852	.11486	.02360	.00066	.00293	.00000	.00000	.00032	.01202	.08123	85+
ALL	28205000	291342														

	All Causes	Respiratory T. B.	Other Infec. and Paras.	Neoplasms	Cardio-vascular	Infl., Pneu., Bronch.	Diarrheal	Certain Degenerative	Maternal	Cert. Dis. of Infancy	Motor Vehicle	Other Violence	Other and Unknown
CRUDE DEATH RATE	.01033	.00007	.00006	.00209	.00433	.00066	.00004	.00039	.00004	.00031	.00010	.00038	.00186
STANDARDIZED RATE (1)	.00465	.00004	.00005	.00085	.00134	.00029	.00004	.00015	.00004	.00069	.00008	.00021	.00087
STANDARDIZED RATE (2)	.00871	.00006	.00006	.00165	.00353	.00057	.00004	.00031	.00004	.00065	.00009	.00021	.00087
GEOMETRIC MEAN	.00520	.00006	.00006	.00165	.00353	.00057	.00004	.00031	.00004	.00041	.00009	.00033	.00162

LIFE TABLE FOR ALL CAUSES COMBINED

Age (x)	Midyear Population	Deaths During Year	$_nM_x$	$_nq_x$	l_x	$_nd_x$	$_nL_x$	$_nm_x$	$_na_x$	T_x	$_nr_x$	$\overset{\circ}{e}_x$	Age (x)
0	444000	13633	.030705	.029900	100000	2990	97375	.030706	.122198	7184471	.000000	71.845	0
1	1634000	1921	.001176	.004690	97010	455	386903	.001176	1.500000	7087096	.000000	73.055	1
5	1867000	761	.000408	.002030	96555	196	482285	.000406	2.500000	6700194	.000000	69.393	5
10	1701000	471	.000277	.001391	96359	134	481471	.000278	2.585510	6217909	.003958	64.529	10
15	1911000	1002	.000524	.002608	96225	251	480530	.000522	2.631142	5736437	-.026342	59.615	15
20	2251000	1373	.000610	.003042	95974	292	479176	.000609	2.623430	5255907	-.004672	54.764	20
25	1768000	1565	.000885	.004431	95682	424	477401	.000888	2.621364	4776731	.020727	49.923	25
30	1875000	2136	.001139	.005658	95258	539	475025	.001135	2.653448	4299329	-.017822	45.134	30
35	2113000	3671	.001737	.008668	94719	821	471654	.001741	2.635759	3824304	.015864	40.375	35
40	1464000	3360	.002295	.011438	93898	1074	466987	.002300	2.669732	3352650	.010868	35.705	40
45	2115000	7845	.003709	.018271	92824	1696	460149	.003686	2.658707	2885663	-.037523	31.087	45
50	2153000	11331	.005263	.025963	91128	2366	450127	.005256	2.669942	2425514	-.008145	26.617	50
55	1921000	15961	.008309	.040851	88762	3626	435459	.008327	2.656900	1975386	.011086	22.255	55
60	1646000	23017	.013984	.068044	85136	5793	412388	.014047	2.705528	1539927	.020263	18.088	60
65	1307000	32355	.024755	.117729	79343	9341	375120	.024901	2.688171	1127539	.025063	14.211	65
70	969000	43289	.044674	.203280	70002	14230	316462	.044966	2.642422	752419	.027024	10.749	70
75	619000	50486	.081561	.341910	55772	19069	232201	.082123	2.553140	435957	.025685	7.817	75
80	322000	45308	.140708	.520230	36703	19094	134663	.141791	2.441485	203757	.025685	5.551	80
85+	125000	31857	.254856	1.000000	17609	17609	69094	.254856	3.923784	69094	.000000	3.924	85+

NUMBER OF PERSONS DYING (OUT OF 100,000 AT BIRTH) ABOVE AGE X FROM SPECIFIED CAUSES

Age (x)	All Causes	Respiratory T.B.	Other Infec. and Paras.	Neoplasms	Cardiovascular	Infl., Pneu., Bronch.	Diarrheal	Certain Degenerative	Maternal	Cert. Dis. of Infancy	Motor Vehicle	Other Violence	Other and Unknown	Age (x)
0	100000	574	444	18047	44449	6883	337	3483	248	1911	772	3617	19235	0
1	97010	574	399	18037	44441	6644	276	3481	248	0	770	3561	18579	1
5	96555	573	355	17995	44434	6584	256	3477	248	0	729	3479	18425	5
10	96359	572	340	17964	44430	6573	255	3472	248	0	682	3456	18367	10
15	96225	571	335	17935	44422	6568	254	3466	248	0	662	3441	18323	15
20	95974	569	325	17897	44409	6560	252	3455	241	0	612	3389	18265	20
25	95682	560	318	17851	44383	6551	251	3442	214	0	571	3340	18201	25
30	95258	540	307	17774	44343	6537	248	3415	159	0	545	3287	18103	30
35	94719	514	298	17641	44275	6521	245	3390	93	0	521	3218	18003	35
40	93898	479	289	17351	44166	6501	242	3355	29	0	495	3138	17853	40
45	92824	449	280	16889	43989	6475	240	3305	3	0	468	3057	17669	45
50	91128	419	265	16129	43649	6430	237	3230	1	0	433	2938	17397	50
55	88762	387	246	15137	43054	6361	233	3106	0	0	394	2805	17039	55
60	85136	352	220	13773	41930	6233	225	2892	0	0	351	2657	16503	60
65	79343	300	187	11929	39672	5997	213	2533	0	0	309	2495	15708	65
70	70002	233	147	9514	35325	5528	186	1992	0	0	246	2301	14530	70
75	55772	152	101	6642	28002	4589	150	1309	0	0	173	2006	12648	75
80	36703	78	61	3555	17839	3166	99	609	0	0	84	1505	9707	80
85+	17609	22	28	1280	7936	1631	46	202	0	0	22	830	5612	85+

NUMBER OF PERSONS SURVIVING TO AGE X IF SPECIFIED CAUSES WERE ELIMINATED

Age (x)	No Causes	Respiratory T.B.	Other Infec. and Paras.	Neoplasms	Cardiovascular	Infl., Pneu., Bronch.	Diarrheal	Certain Degenerative	Maternal	Cert. Dis. of Infancy	Motor Vehicle	Other Violence	Other and Unknown	(1)+(2)	(1)+(2)+(5)+(6)+(8)	(1)+(2)+(5)+(6)+(8)+part of(9)&(12)	(10)+(11)	Age (x)
		(1)	(2)	(3)	(4)	(5)	(6)	(7)	(8)	(9)	(10)	(11)	(12)					
0	100000	100000	100000	100000	100000	100000	100000	100000	100000	100000	100000	100000	100000	100000	100000	100000	100000	0
1	97010	97010	97054	97020	97018	97246	97070	97012	97010	98911	97012	97065	97658	97054	97350	99442	97067	1
5	96555	96556	96643	96607	96570	96850	96635	96561	96555	98447	96559	96692	97355	96644	97019	99169	96735	5
10	96359	96361	96442	96442	96378	96664	96440	96370	96359	98247	96449	96519	97216	96464	96850	99008	96608	10
15	96225	96228	96333	96336	96252	96535	96307	96242	96225	98110	96335	96399	97125	96336	96728	98889	96509	15
20	95974	95979	96091	96123	96014	96291	96057	96002	95981	97854	96133	96200	96930	96096	96504	98670	96360	20
25	95682	95696	95806	95877	95748	96007	95766	95723	95716	97557	95882	95956	96700	95820	96264	98439	96157	25
30	95258	95292	95393	95529	95363	95595	95345	95326	95347	97124	95483	95584	96370	95426	95941	98141	95810	30
35	94719	94779	94862	95122	94892	95071	94808	94811	94873	96575	94967	95112	95926	94921	95519	97737	95361	35
40	93898	93992	94048	94587	94178	94266	93989	94024	94115	95738	94170	94386	95246	94113	94822	97054	94641	40
45	92824	92947	92982	93970	93277	93214	92916	92999	93064	94643	93119	93369	94342	93105	93831	96060	93667	45
50	91128	91278	91258	93018	91912	91556	91222	91374	91366	92913	91453	91782	92893	91448	92212	94421	92109	50
55	88762	88940	88946	91608	90121	89247	88857	89124	88994	90501	89117	89531	90842	89124	89943	92120	89889	55
60	85136	85341	85338	89254	87565	85728	85235	85694	85359	86804	85519	86020	87669	85544	86464	88592	86407	60
65	79343	79584	79563	85065	83882	80124	79447	80213	79551	80897	79740	80325	82497	79805	80908	82953	80727	65
70	70002	70278	70234	77514	78454	71139	70119	71284	70185	71373	70412	71053	73944	70511	71963	73868	71468	70
75	55772	56064	55998	64642	70266	57536	55897	57413	55918	56865	56164	56877	60713	56291	58354	60060	57276	75
80	36703	36954	36883	45496	57786	39065	36827	38361	36799	37422	37033	37846	42632	37136	39763	41189	38186	80
85+	17609	17768	17718	23824	40578	19882	17704	18695	17655	17954	17810	18635	23943	17878	20348	21452	18847	85+

ADDED YRS OF LIFE

	No Causes	(1)	(2)	(3)	(4)	(5)	(6)	(7)	(8)	(9)	(10)	(11)	(12)				
TOTAL		.108	.137	2.634	5.545	.764	.086	.441	.106	1.405	.226	.571	2.580	.245	1.215	3.058	.801
WORK	2.103	.050	.027	.656	.388	.060	.007	.101	.080	.000	.086	.179	.355	.076	.223	.276	.266

POPULATION, DEATHS, DEATH RATES FOR ALL CAUSES COMBINED, AND SPECIFIED CAUSES

Age Start of Interval	Midyear Population	Deaths During Year	All Causes	Respiratory T. B.	Other Infec. and Paras.	Neo-plasms	Cardio-vascular	Infl., Pneu., Bronch.	Diar-rheal	Certain Degen-erative	Maternal	Cert. Dis. of Infancy	Motor Vehicle	Other Violence	Other and Unknown	Age Start of Interval
0	518354	15430	.02977	.00000	.00025	.00005	.00008	.00140	.00049	.00002	.00000	.02006	.00003	.00081	.00654	0
1	1945248	2411	.00124	.00000	.00006	.00014	.00002	.00010	.00006	.00001	.00000	.00000	.00016	.00027	.00042	1
5	2120204	1323	.00062	.00000	.00002	.00008	.00001	.00001	.00001	.00001	.00000	.00000	.00022	.00013	.00012	5
10	1955668	1047	.00054	.00000	.00001	.00007	.00002	.00001	.00000	.00001	.00000	.00000	.00015	.00015	.00012	10
15	1758674	2231	.00127	.00001	.00001	.00011	.00003	.00002	.00000	.00002	.00000	.00000	.00057	.00036	.00011	15
20	2253014	4206	.00187	.00001	.00001	.00014	.00006	.00001	.00000	.00005	.00000	.00000	.00087	.00057	.00016	20
25	2367255	3927	.00166	.00003	.00001	.00018	.00010	.00002	.00001	.00007	.00000	.00000	.00055	.00052	.00018	25
30	1926110	3576	.00186	.00006	.00001	.00022	.00022	.00002	.00001	.00011	.00000	.00000	.00040	.00055	.00027	30
35	1838158	4503	.00245	.00011	.00003	.00037	.00043	.00002	.00000	.00019	.00000	.00000	.00036	.00057	.00037	35
40	1589764	5778	.00363	.00017	.00003	.00064	.00096	.00006	.00001	.00029	.00000	.00000	.00034	.00059	.00055	40
45	1066509	6065	.00569	.00018	.00004	.00116	.00174	.00010	.00001	.00051	.00000	.00000	.00039	.00075	.00080	45
50	1640181	15664	.00955	.00030	.00006	.00229	.00331	.00021	.00001	.00079	.00000	.00000	.00045	.00084	.00129	50
55	1675498	28055	.01674	.00047	.00007	.00441	.00626	.00054	.00003	.00125	.00000	.00000	.00053	.00095	.00224	55
60	1490817	41845	.02807	.00066	.00012	.00769	.01129	.00102	.00005	.00179	.00000	.00000	.00061	.00107	.00378	60
65	1018397	43985	.04319	.00065	.00016	.01155	.01896	.00187	.00007	.00233	.00000	.00000	.00061	.00105	.00573	65
70	685125	44479	.06492	.00087	.00017	.01529	.03130	.00317	.00012	.00305	.00000	.00000	.00072	.00135	.00888	70
75	457452	45536	.09954	.00091	.00018	.01980	.05014	.00534	.00020	.00383	.00000	.00000	.00098	.00230	.01586	75
80	241920	36810	.15216	.00085	.00024	.02365	.07747	.00947	.00031	.00416	.00000	.00000	.00130	.00418	.03053	80
85+	108152	27008	.24972	.00068	.00028	.02544	.11759	.01734	.00062	.00350	.00000	.00000	.00156	.00976	.07294	85+
ALL	26656500	333979														

	All Causes	Respiratory T. B.	Other Infec. and Paras.	Neo-plasms	Cardio-vascular	Infl., Pneu., Bronch.	Diar-rheal	Certain Degen-erative	Maternal	Cert. Dis. of Infancy	Motor Vehicle	Other Violence	Other and Unknown
CRUDE DEATH RATE	.01253	.00020	.00005	.00252	.00499	.00056	.00004	.00058	.00000	.00039	.00046	.00068	.00205
STANDARDIZED RATE (1)	.00654	.00010	.00004	.00114	.00201	.00026	.00003	.00028	.00000	.00071	.00046	.00068	.00108
STANDARDIZED RATE (2)	.01201	.00018	.00005	.00234	.00480	.00055	.00004	.00054	.00000	.00042	.00045	.00066	.00200
GEOMETRIC MEAN	.00818												

LIFE TABLE FOR ALL CAUSES COMBINED

Age (x)	Midyear Popula-tion	Deaths During Year	$_nM_x$	$_nq_x$	l_x	$_nd_x$	$_nL_x$	$_nm_x$	$_na_x$	T_x	$_nr_x$	$\overset{\circ}{e}_x$	Age (x)
0	518354	15430	.029767	.029010	100000	2901	97449	.029769	.120604	6704447	.000000	67.044	0
1	1945248	2411	.001239	.004943	97099	480	387196	.001240	1.500000	6606998	.000000	68.044	1
5	2120204	1323	.000624	.003105	96619	300	482345	.000622	2.500000	6219802	.000000	64.375	5
10	1955668	1047	.000535	.002679	96319	258	481014	.000536	2.747901	5737457	.018638	59.567	10
15	1758674	2231	.001269	.006319	96061	607	478919	.001267	2.715884	5256443	-.002622	54.720	15
20	2253014	4206	.001867	.009292	95454	887	475089	.001867	2.540868	4777524	-.032198	50.051	20
25	2367255	3927	.001659	.008259	94567	781	470879	.001659	2.494932	4302435	.000565	45.496	25
30	1926110	3576	.001857	.009255	93786	868	466833	.001859	2.584485	3831557	.021079	40.854	30
35	1838158	4503	.002450	.012194	92918	1133	461924	.002453	2.646918	3364724	.009766	36.212	35
40	1589764	5778	.003635	.018162	91785	1667	455050	.003663	2.675465	2902800	-.049438	31.626	40
45	1066509	6065	.005687	.028152	90118	2537	444743	.005704	2.695277	2447750	-.014703	27.162	45
50	1640181	15664	.009550	.046186	87581	4045	428660	.009436	2.714514	2003007	-.046199	22.870	50
55	1675498	28055	.016744	.080229	83536	6702	402192	.016664	2.689029	1574346	-.021598	18.846	55
60	1490817	41845	.028069	.131791	76834	10126	360189	.028113	2.631777	1172155	.008357	15.256	60
65	1018397	43985	.043190	.196483	66708	13107	301796	.043430	2.578107	811965	.030890	12.172	65
70	685125	44479	.064921	.280592	53601	15040	230870	.065145	2.530945	510169	.018894	9.518	70
75	457452	45536	.099543	.357837	38561	15341	153953	.099647	2.467448	279299	.005102	7.243	75
80	241920	36810	.152158	.544488	23220	12643	82990	.152343	2.381192	125345	.005102	5.398	80
85+	108152	27008	.249723	1.000000	10577	10577	42355	.249723	4.004443	42355	.000000	4.004	85+

NUMBER OF PERSONS DYING (OUT OF 100,000 AT BIRTH) ABOVE AGE X FROM SPECIFIED CAUSES

Age (x)	All Causes	Respiratory T. B.	Other Infec. and Paras.	Neo-plasms	Cardio-vascular	Infl., Pneu., Bronch.	Diar-rheal	Certain Degen-erative	Maternal	Cert. Dis. of Infancy	Motor Vehicle	Other Violence	Other and Unknown	Age (x)
0	100000	1501	370	20073	41767	4622	257	4554	0	1955	3175	5005	16721	0
1	97099	1501	346	20065	41759	4485	210	4552	0	0	3172	4926	16083	1
5	96619	1500	323	20011	41750	4447	187	4548	0	0	3111	4821	15921	5
10	96319	1499	313	19971	41744	4440	185	4544	0	0	3004	4758	15861	10
15	96061	1499	309	19935	41733	4436	185	4538	0	0	2933	4685	15808	15
20	95454	1497	303	19884	41721	4426	183	4529	0	0	2662	4512	15737	20
25	94567	1493	298	19818	41654	4422	181	4507	0	0	2250	4242	15662	25
30	93786	1481	293	19735	41647	4413	179	4475	0	0	1989	3997	15577	30
35	92918	1454	288	19631	41546	4402	175	4425	0	0	1802	3742	15453	35
40	91785	1404	275	19460	41346	4391	173	4339	0	0	1636	3478	15283	40
45	90118	1328	263	19167	40904	4364	170	4205	0	0	1479	3209	15029	45
50	87561	1250	243	18650	40125	4320	166	3979	0	0	1303	2874	14671	50
55	83536	1123	218	17683	38728	4232	160	3643	0	0	1109	2513	14127	55
60	76834	937	190	15918	36224	4016	148	3143	0	0	898	2132	13228	60
65	66708	698	148	13144	32149	3649	131	2498	0	0	678	1745	11868	65
70	53601	442	98	9641	26390	3079	109	1792	0	0	492	1428	10130	70
75	38561	241	60	6103	19136	2343	82	1086	0	0	326	1115	8069	75
80	23220	101	32	3052	11408	1520	52	495	0	0	175	761	5624	80
85+	10577	29	12	1077	4981	734	26	148	0	0	66	414	3090	85+

NUMBER OF PERSONS SURVIVING TO AGE X IF SPECIFIED CAUSES WERE ELIMINATED

Age (x)	No Causes	Respiratory T. B.	Other Infec. and Paras.	Neo-plasms	Cardio-vascular	Infl., Pneu., Bronch.	Diar-rheal	Certain Degen-erative	Maternal	Cert. Dis. of Infancy	Motor Vehicle	Other Violence	Other and Unknown	(1) + (2)	(1) + (2) + (5) + (6) + (8)	(1)+(2)+ (5)+(6)+ (8)+part of(9)&(12)	(10) + (11)	Age (x)
		(1)	(2)	(3)	(4)	(5)	(6)	(7)	(8)	(9)	(10)	(11)	(12)					
0	100000	100000	100000	100000	100000	100000	100000	100000	100000	100000	100000	100000	100000	100000	100000	100000	100000	0
1	97099	97099	97123	97107	97107	97234	97145	97101	97099	99045	97102	97177	97730	97304	97304	99049	97180	1
5	96619	96620	96665	96681	96636	96751	96688	96625	96619	98555	96683	96801	97409	96666	96908	98650	96865	5
10	96319	96321	96375	96421	96342	96498	96390	96329	96319	98249	96490	96564	97167	96377	96627	98409	96735	10
15	96061	96063	96121	96198	96095	96243	96132	96077	96061	97986	96302	96378	96960	96123	96376	98155	96620	15
20	95454	95458	95520	95641	95499	95645	95526	95479	95454	97367	95965	95942	95559	95619	95524	97558	96456	20
25	94567	94575	94637	94818	94639	94760	94641	94613	94567	96462	95486	95321	95559	94645	94912	96668	96248	25
30	93786	93806	93861	94118	93904	93987	93861	93864	93786	95665	94960	94780	94895	93880	94157	95902	95967	30
35	92918	92965	92997	93351	93136	93128	92956	93045	92918	94780	94270	94160	94142	93043	93332	95070	95530	35
40	91785	91881	91876	92384	92200	92003	91864	91996	91785	93624	93288	93278	93165	91972	92270	94002	94806	40
45	90118	90287	90219	90966	90966	90359	90159	90459	90118	91924	91752	91855	91729	90389	90712	92436	93521	45
50	87561	87823	87699	88953	89184	87859	87663	88136	87581	89336	89346	89606	89506	87941	88303	90006	91412	50
55	83536	83891	83673	85810	86466	83887	83620	84396	83536	85210	85412	85829	85917	84028	84467	86135	87756	55
60	76834	77339	76987	80684	82055	77366	76923	78110	76834	78374	78766	79318	79915	77443	78120	79731	81312	60
65	66708	67371	66880	72815	75413	67515	66801	68428	66708	68045	68595	69236	70712	67544	68457	69969	71194	65
70	53601	54364	53784	62025	66718	54769	53696	55633	53601	54675	55288	55925	58491	54550	55837	57201	57685	70
75	38561	39281	38724	48200	56274	40043	38652	40643	38561	39334	39918	40509	44025	39447	41060	42210	41935	75
80	23220	23761	23340	32080	43764	24779	23298	24952	23220	23685	24157	24681	28756	23884	25573	26460	25677	80
85+	10577	10872	10645	16523	29731	11853	10630	11614	10577	10789	11079	11488	15334	10942	12323	12931	12033	85+

ADDED YRS OF LIFE																		
TOTAL		.228	.090	2.657	5.932	.524	.070	.634	.000	1.341	.988	1.209	2.448	.319	.926	2.316	2.228	
WORK	3.733	.091	.023	.616	.791	.062	.007	.219	.000	.000	.598	.623	.452	.114	.184	.214	1.233	

POPULATION, DEATHS, DEATH RATES FOR ALL CAUSES COMBINED, AND SPECIFIED CAUSES

Age Start of Interval	Midyear Population	Deaths During Year	All Causes	Respiratory T. B.	Other Infec. and Paras.	Neoplasms	Cardio-vascular	Infl., Pneu., Bronch.	Diarrheal	Certain Degenerative	Maternal	Cert. Dis. of Infancy	Motor Vehicle	Other Violence	Other and Unknown	Age Start of Interval
0	492162	11519	.02340	.00000	.00026	.00011	.00005	.00112	.00033	.00001	.00000	.01531	.00002	.00053	.00566	0
1	1850790	1734	.00094	.00000	.00006	.00010	.00001	.00009	.00003	.00001	.00000	.00000	.00009	.00017	.00035	1
5	2011746	843	.00042	.00000	.00001	.00007	.00001	.00001	.00000	.00001	.00000	.00000	.00013	.00005	.00012	5
10	1859540	572	.00031	.00000	.00001	.00006	.00001	.00001	.00000	.00001	.00000	.00000	.00008	.00005	.00012	10
15	1667312	795	.00048	.00000	.00001	.00007	.00002	.00001	.00000	.00001	.00000	.00000	.00008	.00004	.00010	15
20	2104502	1306	.00062	.00000	.00001	.00009	.00004	.00001	.00001	.00002	.00006	.00000	.00015	.00008	.00011	20
25	2176151	1606	.00074	.00001	.00001	.00015	.00006	.00001	.00001	.00003	.00008	.00000	.00009	.00013	.00013	25
30	1776857	1877	.00106	.00004	.00001	.00028	.00012	.00001	.00000	.00005	.00009	.00000	.00007	.00015	.00017	30
35	1957780	3086	.00158	.00005	.00002	.00057	.00022	.00002	.00000	.00007	.00009	.00000	.00007	.00015	.00023	35
40	2142784	5149	.00240	.00005	.00002	.00107	.00038	.00003	.00001	.00012	.00003	.00000	.00007	.00018	.00040	40
45	1448479	5250	.00362	.00004	.00002	.00168	.00068	.00005	.00001	.00019	.00000	.00000	.00010	.00027	.00057	45
50	2161556	11644	.00539	.00006	.00003	.00244	.00126	.00008	.00001	.00028	.00000	.00000	.00009	.00032	.00081	50
55	2077656	17385	.00837	.00006	.00006	.00334	.00249	.00018	.00002	.00051	.00000	.00000	.00013	.00037	.00121	55
60	1818510	25247	.01388	.00009	.00007	.00477	.00521	.00030	.00003	.00090	.00000	.00000	.00017	.00044	.00190	60
65	1500565	35625	.02374	.00013	.00010	.00684	.01067	.00061	.00006	.00142	.00000	.00000	.00022	.00059	.00309	65
70	1109260	46847	.04223	.00021	.00012	.00979	.02197	.00139	.00009	.00223	.00000	.00000	.00031	.00107	.00504	70
75	720210	54063	.07507	.00030	.00017	.01331	.04170	.00319	.00020	.00315	.00000	.00000	.00036	.00236	.01022	75
80	370207	47502	.12831	.00033	.00018	.01773	.07151	.00621	.00038	.00345	.00000	.00000	.00054	.00236	.01022	80
85+	170722	38199	.22375	.00033	.00036	.02005	.11352	.01221	.00071	.00306	.00000	.00000	.00046	.01343	.05962	85+
ALL	29416789	310249														

		All Causes	Respiratory T. B.	Other Infec.	Neoplasms	Cardio-vascular	Infl. Pneu.	Diarrheal	Certain Degen.	Maternal	Cert. Dis. Infancy	Motor Vehicle	Other Violence	Other Unknown
CRUDE DEATH RATE		.01055	.00006	.00005	.00235	.00464	.00038	.00003	.00044	.00003	.00026	.00013	.00045	.00174
STANDARDIZED RATE (1)		.00421	.00002	.00004	.00089	.00128	.00015	.00002	.00015	.00003	.00054	.00011	.00021	.00076
STANDARDIZED RATE (2)		.00805	.00004	.00004	.00174	.00339	.00030	.00003	.00032	.00003	.00032	.00012	.00036	.00136
GEOMETRIC MEAN		.00489												

LIFE TABLE FOR ALL CAUSES COMBINED

Age (x)	Midyear Population	Deaths During Year	$_nM_x$	$_nq_x$	l_x	$_nd_x$	$_nL_x$	$_nm_x$	$_na_x$	T_x	$_nr_x$	$\overset{\circ}{e}_x$	Age (x)
0	492162	11519	.023405	.022930	100000	2293	97959	.023408	.109788	7291287	.000000	72.913	0
1	1850790	1734	.000937	.003736	97707	365	389916	.000936	1.500000	7193328	.000000	73.621	1
5	2011746	843	.000419	.002096	97342	204	486200	.000420	2.500000	6803412	.000000	69.892	5
10	1859540	572	.000308	.001534	97138	149	485323	.000307	2.537752	6317212	.018648	65.033	10
15	1667312	795	.000477	.002382	96989	231	484399	.000477	2.635281	5831889	-.000956	60.129	15
20	2104502	1306	.000621	.003090	96758	299	483096	.000619	2.587096	5347490	-.028704	55.267	20
25	2176151	1606	.000738	.003691	96459	356	481448	.000739	2.621723	4864422	-.004901	50.430	25
30	1776857	1877	.001056	.005276	96103	507	479329	.001058	2.661078	4382974	-.016064	45.607	30
35	1957780	3086	.001576	.007825	95596	748	476241	.001571	2.675468	3903644	-.021276	40.835	35
40	2142784	5149	.002403	.011988	94848	1137	471593	.002411	2.672054	3427403	.019817	36.136	40
45	1448479	5250	.003624	.018002	93711	1687	464607	.003631	2.659677	2955810	-.009989	31.542	45
50	2161556	11644	.005387	.026406	92024	2430	454459	.005347	2.670353	2491203	-.038133	27.071	50
55	2077656	17385	.008368	.041007	89594	3674	439486	.008360	2.690755	2036744	-.004075	22.733	55
60	1818510	25247	.013883	.067435	85920	5794	416236	.013920	2.693483	1597258	-.011854	18.590	60
65	1500565	35625	.023741	.113010	80126	9055	379645	.023851	2.682473	1181022	.020688	14.740	65
70	1109260	46847	.042233	.193117	71071	13725	322971	.042496	2.640498	801377	.026433	11.276	70
75	720210	54063	.075066	.319307	57346	18311	242053	.075649	2.560085	478407	.030618	8.342	75
80	370207	47502	.128312	.486896	39035	19006	146839	.129434	2.456750	236354	.030618	6.055	80
85+	170722	38199	.223750	1.000000	20029	20029	89515	.223750	4.469279	89515	.000000	4.469	85+

NUMBER OF PERSONS DYING (OUT OF 100,000 AT BIRTH) ABOVE AGE X FROM SPECIFIED CAUSES

Age (x)	All Causes	Respiratory T. B.	Other Infec. and Paras.	Neo-plasms	Cardio-vascular	Infl., Pneu., Bronch.	Diar-rheal	Certain Degen-erative	Maternal	Cert. Dis. of Infancy	Motor Vehicle	Other Violence	Other and Unknown	Age (x)
0	100000	458	362	19576	46708	3937	310	3753	178	1500	1053	4366	17359	0
1	97707	458	337	19965	46703	3827	278	3752	178	0	1051	4314	16804	1
5	97342	457	312	19924	46698	3790	265	3789	178	0	1015	4247	16667	5
10	97138	457	305	19889	46694	3783	263	3786	178	0	952	4223	16608	10
15	96989	457	299	19862	46689	3779	263	3780	178	0	916	4205	16561	15
20	96758	456	296	19828	46680	3775	262	3773	171	0	843	4167	16507	20
25	96459	454	290	19783	46662	3772	259	3764	144	0	779	4107	16445	25
30	96103	447	284	19713	46632	3767	257	3748	104	0	737	4050	16364	30
35	95556	429	279	19577	46576	3761	255	3724	60	0	704	3977	16254	35
40	94848	406	271	19307	46472	3753	254	3689	16	0	668	3894	16118	40
45	93711	384	261	18798	46290	3738	251	3635	1	0	634	3788	15931	45
50	92024	364	252	18017	45972	3713	248	3545	0	0	585	3662	15666	50
55	89594	337	237	16913	45408	3677	243	3418	0	0	545	3517	15299	55
60	85920	309	212	15447	44314	3600	235	3194	0	0	487	3355	14767	60
65	80126	271	181	13458	42138	3476	222	2819	0	0	418	3170	13973	65
70	71071	222	141	10852	38062	3244	198	2278	0	0	334	2944	12796	70
75	57346	153	101	7679	30915	2791	168	1555	0	0	233	2596	11155	75
80	39035	80	59	4442	20739	2010	120	790	0	0	121	2017	8657	80
85+	20029	30	32	1795	10162	1093	63	274	0	0	41	1202	5337	85+

NUMBER OF PERSONS SURVIVING TO AGE X IF SPECIFIED CAUSES WERE ELIMINATED

Age (x)	No Causes	Respiratory T. B.	Other Infec. and Paras.	Neo-plasms	Cardio-vascular	Infl., Pneu., Bronch.	Diar-rheal	Certain Degener-ative	Maternal	Cert. Dis. of Infancy	Motor Vehicle	Other Violence	Other and Unknown	(1) + (2)	(1) + (2) + (5) + (6) + (8)	(1)+(2)+ (5)+(6)+ (8)+part of(9)&(12)	(10) + (11)	Age (x)
	(1)	(2)	(3)	(4)	(5)	(6)	(7)	(8)	(9)	(10)	(11)	(12)						
0	100000	100000	100000	100000	100000	100000	100000	100000	100000	100000	100000	100000	100000	100000	100000	100000	100000	0
1	97707	97707	97732	97718	97712	97816	97739	97708	97707	99201	97709	97758	98257	97732	97872	99310	97760	1
5	97342	97343	97392	97394	97352	97487	97386	97346	97342	98830	97380	97460	98028	97393	97585	99063	97498	5
10	97138	97139	97194	97225	97152	97290	97184	97145	97138	98623	97239	97280	97882	97195	97394	98878	97381	10
15	96989	96990	97051	97103	97008	97145	97035	97002	96989	98472	97126	97149	97779	97052	97255	98741	97286	15
20	96758	96760	96823	96905	96786	96917	96805	96778	96765	98237	96967	96955	97600	96825	97039	98527	97165	20
25	96459	96463	96530	96651	96505	96621	96509	96488	96493	97934	96732	96716	97361	96534	96780	98275	96989	25
30	96103	96114	96180	96364	96179	96269	96155	96148	96177	97572	96417	96416	97083	96191	96483	97992	96731	30
35	95556	95625	95677	95952	95727	95767	95650	95664	95713	97058	95941	95980	96682	95706	96049	97572	96327	35
40	94848	94900	94937	95511	95082	95026	94902	94951	95008	96298	95226	95312	96063	94988	95382	96913	95663	40
45	93711	93784	93809	94877	94124	93902	93768	93866	93884	95144	94119	94276	95100	93881	94303	95831	94686	45
50	92024	92115	92129	93956	92746	92236	92082	92266	92195	93431	92473	92704	93655	92220	92664	94175	93157	50
55	89594	89710	89711	92594	90860	89836	89656	89955	89761	90964	90071	90400	91551	89827	90299	91787	90882	55
60	85920	86058	86057	90292	88228	86228	85987	86487	86080	87234	86435	86853	88330	86195	86733	88185	87373	60
65	80126	80292	80283	86243	84467	80534	80201	81020	80275	81351	80673	81177	83165	80449	81085	82475	81731	65
70	71071	71264	71248	79177	79084	71653	71160	72380	71203	72158	71635	72219	74925	71442	72251	73540	72792	70
75	57346	57564	57525	67121	71365	58228	57445	59064	57453	58223	57892	58591	62027	57743	58841	59967	59149	75
80	39035	39243	39191	48877	60160	40293	39142	40850	39108	39632	39499	40373	44505	39399	40856	41769	40853	80
85+	20029	20171	20128	27521	44749	21351	20124	21343	20066	20335	20324	21317	25659	20271	21751	22412	21631	85+

ADDED YRS OF LIFE		(1)	(2)	(3)	(4)	(5)	(6)	(7)	(8)	(9)	(10)	(11)	(12)				
TOTAL		.077	.093	2.576	6.471	.422	.061	.476	.079	1.113	.312	.645	2.421	.170	.738	1.983	.963
WORK	2.047	.030	.018	.721	.360	.029	.006	.097	.059	.000	.124	.189	.342	.048	.142	.176	.313

POPULATION, DEATHS, DEATH RATES FOR ALL CAUSES COMBINED, AND SPECIFIED CAUSES

Age Start of Interval	Midyear Population	Deaths During Year	All Causes	Respiratory T.B.	Other Infec. and Paras.	Neoplasms	Cardiovascular	Infl., Pneu., Bronch.	Diarrheal	Certain Degenerative	Maternal	Cert. Dis. of Infancy	Motor Vehicle	Other Violence	Other and Unknown	Age Start of Interval
0	11000	420	.03818	.00009	.00027	.00018	.00000	.00300	.00027	.00009	.00000	.02655	.00000	.00027	.00745	0
1	36000	51	.00142	.00000	.00003	.00025	.00000	.00028	.00000	.00000	.00000	.00000	.00000	.00027	.00745	1
5	46000	27	.00059	.00000	.00002	.00009	.00000	.00000	.00000	.00000	.00000	.00000	.00003	.00039	.00044	5
10	50000	26	.00052	.00000	.00002	.00014	.00002	.00004	.00000	.00002	.00000	.00000	.00004	.00022	.00022	10
15	83000	72	.00087	.00001	.00001	.00006	.00008	.00001	.00000	.00001	.00000	.00000	.00012	.00004	.00012	15
20	85000	89	.00105	.00001	.00001	.00007	.00006	.00001	.00000	.00005	.00000	.00000	.00014	.00040	.00013	20
25	56000	94	.00168	.00009	.00004	.00021	.00012	.00002	.00000	.00012	.00000	.00000	.00016	.00049	.00012	25
30	51000	102	.00200	.00018	.00002	.00027	.00031	.00004	.00000	.00012	.00000	.00000	.00016	.00079	.00012	30
35	44000	128	.00291	.00032	.00005	.00041	.00048	.00002	.00000	.00016	.00000	.00000	.00018	.00059	.00025	35
40	39000	162	.00415	.00015	.00000	.00059	.00113	.00010	.00000	.00027	.00000	.00000	.00011	.00080	.00041	40
45	67000	435	.00649	.00037	.00009	.00121	.00201	.00024	.00000	.00061	.00000	.00000	.00010	.00072	.00079	45
50	84000	913	.01087	.00062	.00005	.00248	.00412	.00030	.00002	.00101	.00000	.00000	.00024	.00087	.00085	50
55	83000	1619	.01951	.00089	.00016	.00495	.00804	.00084	.00007	.00155	.00000	.00000	.00024	.00093	.00111	55
60	66000	2053	.03111	.00068	.00024	.00792	.01389	.00185	.00002	.00189	.00000	.00000	.00013	.00105	.00182	60
65	51000	2290	.04490	.00102	.00029	.01125	.02114	.00337	.00000	.00265	.00000	.00000	.00026	.00114	.00321	65
70	40000	2823	.07057	.00110	.00015	.01525	.03322	.00677	.00002	.00420	.00000	.00000	.00041	.00076	.00400	70
75	26000	2669	.10265	.00158	.00038	.01988	.05085	.01142	.00012	.00423	.00000	.00000	.00035	.00117	.00832	75
80	12000	2005	.16708	.00142	.00042	.02433	.07917	.02575	.00008	.00575	.00000	.00000	.00046	.00185	.01188	80
85+	4000	1014	.25350	.00150	.00025	.02850	.11775	.04125	.00075	.00675	.00000	.00000	.00133	.00467	.02417	85+
ALL	934000	16992														

	All Causes	Respiratory T.B.	Other Infec. and Paras.	Neoplasms	Cardiovascular	Infl., Pneu., Bronch.	Diarrheal	Certain Degenerative	Maternal	Cert. Dis. of Infancy	Motor Vehicle	Other Violence	Other and Unknown
CRUDE DEATH RATE	.01819	.00042	.00010	.00367	.00783	.00161	.00002	.00101	.00000	.00031	.00022	.00083	.00217
STANDARDIZED RATE (1)	.00718	.00017	.00005	.00119	.00224	.00055	.00002	.00036	.00000	.00093	.00014	.00054	.00100
STANDARDIZED RATE (2)	.01297	.00029	.00007	.00241	.00523	.00118	.00002	.00068	.00000	.00055	.00018	.00071	.00166
GEOMETRIC MEAN	.00839												

LIFE TABLE FOR ALL CAUSES COMBINED

Age (x)	Midyear Population	Deaths During Year	$_nM_x$	$_nq_x$	l_x	$_nd_x$	$_nL_x$	$_nm_x$	$_na_x$	T_x	$_nr_x$	$\overset{\circ}{e}_x$	Age (x)
0	11000	420	.038182	.036960	100000	3696	96803	.038181	.134909	6583067	.000000	65.831	0
1	36000	51	.001417	.005649	96304	544	383856	.001417	1.500000	6486265	.000000	67.352	1
5	46000	27	.000587	.002945	95760	282	478095	.000590	2.500000	6102409	.000000	63.726	5
10	50000	26	.000520	.002577	95478	246	476803	.000516	2.612636	5624314	-.042424	58.907	10
15	83000	72	.000867	.004358	95232	415	475175	.000873	2.625502	5147511	-.067096	54.052	15
20	85000	89	.001047	.005231	94817	496	472924	.001049	2.658350	4672336	.009768	49.277	20
25	56000	94	.001679	.008357	94321	792	469716	.001686	2.615215	4199413	.045816	44.523	25
30	51000	102	.002000	.009986	93529	934	465425	.002007	2.623126	3729697	-.024695	39.877	30
35	44000	128	.002909	.014515	92595	1344	459810	.002923	2.645244	3264272	.034607	35.253	35
40	39000	162	.004154	.020504	91251	1871	451883	.004140	2.663126	2804461	-.018460	30.733	40
45	67000	435	.006493	.031428	89380	2809	440432	.006378	2.697283	2352579	-.075514	26.321	45
50	84000	913	.010869	.052339	86571	4531	422533	.010723	2.721943	1912147	-.049507	22.088	50
55	83000	1619	.019506	.093077	82040	7636	392414	.019459	2.670792	1489614	-.011487	18.157	55
60	66000	2053	.031106	.145093	74404	10791	346137	.031175	2.601454	1097200	.012826	14.747	60
65	51000	2290	.044902	.202647	63613	12891	286761	.044954	2.571626	751063	.006949	11.807	65
70	40000	2823	.070575	.300126	50722	15223	215881	.070516	2.521582	464302	-.004217	9.154	70
75	26000	2669	.102654	.407561	35499	14468	140701	.102828	2.456873	248421	.009086	6.998	75
80	12000	2005	.167083	.581427	21031	12228	72994	.167521	2.369868	107720	.009086	5.122	80
85+	4000	1014	.253500	1.000000	8803	8803	34726	.253500	3.944773	34726	.000000	3.945	85+

NUMBER OF PERSONS DYING (OUT OF 100,000 AT BIRTH) ABOVE AGE X FROM SPECIFIED CAUSES

Age (x)	All Causes	Respiratory T. B.	Other Infec. and Paras.	Neo-plasms	Cardio-vascular	Infl., Pneu., Bronch.	Diar-rheal	Certain Degenerative	Maternal	Cert. Dis. of Infancy	Motor Vehicle	Other Violence	Other and Unknown	Age (x)
0	100000	2274	530	19305	41850	9066	145	5428	0	2570	1281	5125	12426	0
1	96304	2265	503	19288	41850	8776	118	5419	0	0	1281	5058	11706	1
5	95760	2265	493	19192	41850	8669	118	5419	0	0	1271	4949	11534	5
10	95478	2265	482	19150	41850	8669	118	5419	0	0	1250	4844	11431	10
15	95232	2265	473	19083	41841	8650	118	5410	0	0	1193	4827	11372	15
20	94817	2259	467	19053	41798	8644	118	5404	0	0	1125	4640	11309	20
25	94321	2254	461	19019	41770	8638	118	5382	0	0	1019	4406	11254	25
30	93529	2211	444	18917	41711	8630	118	5322	0	0	944	4036	11196	30
35	92555	2128	435	18789	41564	8611	118	5249	0	0	862	3763	11076	35
40	91251	1982	414	18600	41343	8601	97	5123	0	0	810	3396	10885	40
45	89380	1913	414	18335	40835	8555	97	4868	0	0	764	3072	10527	45
50	86571	1752	375	17818	39971	8450	97	4603	0	0	660	2692	10153	50
55	82040	1493	355	16790	38259	8327	88	4180	0	0	558	2300	9690	55
60	74404	1143	294	14851	35115	7998	59	3571	0	0	506	1889	8978	60
65	63613	907	210	12102	30293	7356	54	2914	0	0	417	1496	7864	65
70	50722	614	125	8872	24225	6387	54	2154	0	0	299	1277	6715	70
75	35499	377	93	5582	17058	4926	49	1248	0	0	223	1023	4920	75
80	21031	155	39	2781	9892	3314	32	652	0	0	158	763	3245	80
85+	8803	52	9	990	4089	1432	26	234	0	0	61	425	1485	85+

NUMBER OF PERSONS SURVIVING TO AGE X IF SPECIFIED CAUSES WERE ELIMINATED

Age (x)	No Causes	Respiratory T. B. (1)	Other Infec. and Paras. (2)	Neo-plasms (3)	Cardio-vascular (4)	Infl., Pneu., Bronch. (5)	Diar-rheal (6)	Certain Degenerative (7)	Maternal (8)	Cert. Dis. of Infancy (9)	Motor Vehicle (10)	Other Violence (11)	Other and Unknown (12)	(1)+(2)	(1)+(2)+(5)+(6)+(8)	(1)+(2)+(5)+(6)+(8)+part of(9)&(12)	(10)+(11)	Age (x)
0	100000	100000	100000	100000	100000	100000	100000	100000	100000	100000	100000	100000	100000	100000	100000	100000	100000	0
1	96304	96313	96330	96321	96304	96589	96330	96313	96304	98859	96304	96330	97013	96339	96651	99519	96330	1
5	95760	95769	95796	95872	95760	96150	95769	95760	95760	98301	95770	95935	96638	95805	96222	99124	95945	5
10	95478	95487	95525	95632	95478	95867	95504	95487	95478	98011	95509	95758	96457	95534	95950	98850	95789	10
15	95232	95241	95288	95453	95241	95639	95258	95250	95232	97759	95320	95528	96268	95297	95731	98633	95616	15
20	94817	94832	94879	95067	94869	95229	94843	94841	94817	97333	94972	95299	95912	94894	95332	98225	95455	20
25	94321	94341	94388	94603	94411	94736	94347	94366	94321	96824	94581	95035	95466	94408	94850	97731	95298	25
30	93529	93591	93613	93911	93667	93949	93555	93634	93529	96011	93862	94609	94723	93675	94122	96987	94946	30
35	92595	92739	92687	93101	92878	93030	92620	92772	92595	95052	93007	93940	93898	92832	93293	96150	94357	35
40	91251	91538	91363	91939	91750	91689	91297	91550	91251	93672	91709	92946	92728	91650	92137	95191	93404	40
45	89380	89730	89489	90318	90376	89855	89425	89927	89380	91752	89874	91368	91187	89840	90363	93191	91862	45
50	86571	87069	86715	87996	88400	87135	86615	87363	86571	88868	87152	88879	88697	87214	87827	90624	89476	50
55	82040	82766	82196	84414	85494	82695	82090	83207	82040	84217	82691	84619	84518	82924	83637	86348	85290	55
60	74404	75398	74604	78481	80721	75316	74477	76052	74404	76378	75044	77253	77353	75601	76602	79165	77893	60
65	63613	64683	63862	69830	74022	64997	63680	65644	63613	65301	64243	66332	67212	64936	66419	68752	66989	65
70	50722	51841	50996	58924	65663	52719	50775	53044	50722	52068	51330	53092	54686	52120	54230	56266	53729	70
75	35499	36483	35717	44532	54366	38188	35541	37918	35499	36441	35988	37380	39922	36706	39533	41242	37895	75
80	21031	21787	21202	29176	41752	23993	21069	22946	21031	21589	21371	22356	25132	21964	25103	26428	22718	80
85+	8803	9187	8893	13874	26421	11484	8823	9895	8803	9037	9007	9586	11924	9281	12134	13087	9808	85+

ADDED YRS OF LIFE

	No Causes	(1)	(2)	(3)	(4)	(5)	(6)	(7)	(8)	(9)	(10)	(11)	(12)	(1)+(2)	(1)+(2)+(5)+(6)+(8)	(1)+(2)+(5)+(6)+(8)+part of(9)&(12)	(10)+(11)
TOTAL		.381	.111	2.565	6.014	1.022	.035	.762	.000	1.743	.326	1.272	2.051	.494	1.587	3.823	1.610
WORK	3.834	.186	.035	.625	.967	.095	.009	.296	.000	.000	.186	.719	.430	.221	.326	.372	.908

POPULATION, DEATHS, DEATH RATES FOR ALL CAUSES COMBINED, AND SPECIFIED CAUSES

Age Start of Interval	Midyear Population	Deaths During Year	All Causes	Respiratory T. B.	Other Infec. and Paras.	Neoplasms	Cardio-vascular	Infl., Pneu., Bronch.	Diarrheal	Certain Degenerative	Maternal	Cert. Dis. of Infancy	Motor Vehicle	Other Violence	Other and Unknown	Age Start of Interval
0	10000	330	.03300	.00000	.00010	.00000	.00000	.00360	.00030	.00010	.00000	.02300	.00000	.00050	.00540	0
1	34000	45	.00132	.00000	.00018	.00012	.00000	.00021	.00000	.00000	.00000	.00000	.00009	.00024	.00050	1
5	43000	13	.00030	.00000	.00000	.00002	.00000	.00000	.00000	.00000	.00000	.00000	.00007	.00002	.00019	5
10	48000	11	.00023	.00000	.00002	.00004	.00000	.00002	.00000	.00002	.00000	.00000	.00000	.00004	.00008	10
15	81000	45	.00056	.00000	.00002	.00011	.00004	.00004	.00000	.00002	.00001	.00000	.00004	.00020	.00007	15
20	84000	71	.00085	.00010	.00001	.00012	.00006	.00002	.00000	.00001	.00011	.00000	.00002	.00029	.00011	20
25	58000	67	.00116	.00012	.00002	.00017	.00010	.00002	.00000	.00003	.00009	.00000	.00000	.00050	.00010	25
30	63000	101	.00160	.00016	.00000	.00032	.00025	.00005	.00000	.00006	.00013	.00000	.00003	.00035	.00025	30
35	75000	152	.00203	.00021	.00003	.00067	.00032	.00005	.00000	.00009	.00008	.00000	.00001	.00035	.00021	35
40	66000	197	.00298	.00018	.00005	.00115	.00055	.00006	.00000	.00012	.00000	.00000	.00002	.00042	.00044	40
45	107000	438	.00409	.00014	.00004	.00181	.00065	.00012	.00001	.00025	.00000	.00000	.00005	.00047	.00055	45
50	125000	675	.00540	.00007	.00003	.00234	.00133	.00013	.00002	.00035	.00000	.00000	.00002	.00043	.00067	50
55	116000	1066	.00919	.00007	.00009	.00340	.00272	.00035	.00000	.00068	.00000	.00000	.00005	.00052	.00131	55
60	109000	1595	.01463	.00009	.00008	.00468	.00589	.00061	.00000	.00088	.00000	.00000	.00007	.00051	.00181	60
65	96000	2263	.02357	.00009	.00009	.00622	.01101	.00126	.00006	.00109	.00000	.00000	.00015	.00066	.00294	65
70	75000	3240	.04320	.00017	.00020	.00913	.02237	.00324	.00005	.00191	.00000	.00000	.00013	.00105	.00493	70
75	47000	3506	.07460	.00026	.00026	.01189	.04266	.00594	.00015	.00215	.00000	.00000	.00026	.00232	.00872	75
80	24000	3112	.12967	.00033	.00017	.01633	.07217	.01308	.00033	.00342	.00000	.00000	.00046	.00612	.01725	80
85+	10000	2190	.21900	.00030	.00030	.01700	.11870	.02670	.00070	.00340	.00000	.00000	.00000	.00030	.01725	85+
ALL	1271000	19117														

	All Causes	Respiratory T.B.	Other Infec. and Paras.	Neoplasms	Cardio-vascular	Infl., Pneu., Bronch.	Diarrheal	Certain Degenerative	Maternal	Cert. Dis. of Infancy	Motor Vehicle	Other Violence	Other and Unknown
CRUDE DEATH RATE	.01504	.00011	.00007	.00313	.00704	.00112	.00003	.00058	.00002	.00018	.00007	.00070	.00200
STANDARDIZED RATE (1)	.00478	.00007	.00005	.00087	.00135	.00035	.00002	.00015	.00003	.00081	.00004	.00032	.00072
STANDARDIZED RATE (2)	.00852	.00005	.00005	.00166	.00353	.00064	.00002	.00030	.00003	.00048	.00005	.00048	.00119
GEOMETRIC MEAN	.00547												

LIFE TABLE FOR ALL CAUSES COMBINED

Age (x)	Midyear Population	Deaths During Year	$_nM_x$	$_nq_x$	l_x	$_nd_x$	$_nL_x$	$_nm_x$	$_na_x$	T_x	$_nr_x$	$\overset{\circ}{e}_x$	Age (x)
0	10000	330	.033000	.032070	100000	3207	97197	.032995	.126100	7154601	.000000	71.546	0
1	34000	45	.001324	.005279	96793	511	385895	.001324	1.500000	7057404	.000000	72.912	1
5	43000	13	.000302	.001527	96282	147	481043	.000306	2.500000	6671509	.000000	69.291	5
10	48000	11	.000229	.001134	96135	109	480428	.000227	2.733180	6190467	-.045743	64.393	10
15	81000	45	.000556	.002801	96026	269	479519	.000561	2.728470	5710039	-.069755	59.463	15
20	84000	71	.000845	.004219	95757	404	477834	.000845	2.645936	5230520	.006353	54.623	20
25	58000	67	.001155	.005789	95353	552	475458	.001161	2.632473	4752686	.033621	49.843	25
30	63000	101	.001603	.007964	94801	755	472200	.001599	2.609272	4277228	-.017620	45.118	30
35	75000	152	.002027	.010080	94046	948	467989	.002026	2.636252	3805028	-.005423	40.459	35
40	66000	197	.002985	.014769	93098	1375	462240	.002975	2.636061	3337039	-.022959	35.844	40
45	107000	438	.004093	.020126	91723	1846	454210	.004064	2.613647	2874799	-.066152	31.342	45
50	125000	675	.005400	.026503	89877	2382	443865	.005366	2.682620	2420589	-.029983	26.932	50
55	116000	1066	.009190	.044963	87495	3934	428376	.009184	2.686992	1976724	-.003553	22.592	55
60	109000	1595	.014633	.070763	83561	5913	404014	.014636	2.667604	1548349	.001119	18.530	60
65	96000	2263	.023573	.111928	77648	8691	368169	.023610	2.683643	1144335	-.007188	14.737	65
70	75000	3240	.043200	.156847	68957	13574	312705	.043408	2.636643	776226	-.020384	11.257	70
75	47000	3506	.074596	.317679	55383	17594	233568	.075198	2.558981	463522	.032671	8.369	75
80	24000	3112	.129667	.491016	37789	18555	141727	.130920	2.455268	229554	.032671	6.075	80
85+	10000	2190	.219000	1.000000	19234	19234	87826	.219000	4.566210	87826	.000000	4.566	85+

NUMBER OF PERSONS DYING (OUT OF 100,000 AT BIRTH) ABOVE AGE X FROM SPECIFIED CAUSES

Age (x)	All Causes	Respiratory T. B.	Other Infec. and Paras.	Neo-plasms	Cardio-vascular	Infl., Pneu., Bronch.	Diar-rheal	Certain Degen-erative	Maternal	Cert. Dis. of Infancy	Motor Vehicle	Other Violence	Other and Unknown	Age (x)
0	100000	746	456	18252	46946	8163	228	3396	196	2235	457	4965	13960	0
1	96793	746	446	18252	46946	7813	199	3387	196	0	457	4916	13435	1
5	96282	746	378	18207	46946	7734	199	3387	196	0	423	4825	13241	5
10	96135	746	378	18195	46946	7734	199	3387	196	0	389	4814	13151	10
15	96026	746	368	18176	46946	7724	199	3377	196	0	389	4795	13110	15
20	95757	746	356	18121	46925	7705	199	3365	191	0	371	4701	13077	20
25	95353	702	351	18065	46897	7694	199	3359	140	0	360	4565	13021	25
30	94801	644	343	17982	46847	7686	199	3342	99	0	360	4327	12972	30
35	94046	569	343	17833	46727	7663	199	3312	39	0	345	4161	12855	35
40	93098	470	330	17521	46578	7638	199	3269	1	0	338	3999	12755	40
45	91723	385	309	16992	46326	7611	199	3213	1	0	332	3803	12552	45
50	89877	321	292	16176	46034	7555	195	3100	1	0	310	3591	12302	50
55	87495	289	278	15143	45450	7499	184	2945	1	0	300	3399	12007	55
60	83561	259	241	13689	44285	7348	184	2653	1	0	277	3178	11446	60
65	77648	222	208	11798	41904	7099	184	2297	1	0	248	2970	10717	65
70	68957	188	173	9507	37843	6634	161	1894	1	0	194	2728	9634	70
75	55383	133	110	6643	30808	5615	144	1296	1	0	152	2397	8084	75
80	37789	73	50	3847	20741	4212	109	792	1	0	92	1848	6024	80
85+	19234	26	26	1493	10425	2345	61	299	0	0	26	975	3558	85+

NUMBER OF PERSONS SURVIVING TO AGE X IF SPECIFIED CAUSES WERE ELIMINATED

Age (x)	No Causes	Respiratory T. B.	Other Infec. and Paras.	Neo-plasms	Cardio-vascular	Infl., Pneu., Bronch.	Diar-rheal	Certain Degener-ative	Maternal	Cert. Dis. of Infancy	Motor Vehicle	Other Violence	Other and Unknown	(1) + (2)	(1) + (2) + (5) + (6) + (8)	(1)+(2)+ (5)+(6)+ (8)+part of(9)&(12)	(10) + (11)	Age (x)
	(1)	(2)	(3)	(4)	(5)	(6)	(7)	(8)	(9)	(10)	(11)	(12)						
0	100000	100000	100000	100000	100000	100000	100000	100000	100000	100000	100000	100000	100000	100000	100000	100000	100000	0
1	96793	96793	96803	96793	96793	97138	96822	96802	96793	99017	96793	96841	97311	96803	97176	99578	96841	1
5	96282	96282	96360	96327	96282	96704	96310	96291	96282	98494	96316	96421	96992	96360	96811	99296	96455	5
10	96135	96135	96213	96192	96135	96557	96163	96144	96135	98344	96203	96285	96934	96213	96663	99144	96353	10
15	96026	96026	96113	96102	96026	96457	96054	96045	96026	98232	96094	96194	96866	96113	96573	99065	96262	15
20	95757	95757	95856	95888	95778	96206	95785	95788	95762	97957	95843	96019	96628	95856	96339	98829	96105	20
25	95353	95397	95457	95539	95402	95811	95381	95390	95409	97544	95449	95750	96276	95501	96044	98545	95847	25
30	94801	94903	94912	95069	94899	95264	94829	94854	94857	96979	94857	95434	95768	95014	95604	98105	95531	30
35	94046	94222	94156	94461	94263	94529	94074	94129	94202	96207	94156	94841	95124	94332	95001	97517	94952	35
40	93098	93370	93220	93821	93462	93601	93125	93223	93290	95237	93214	94048	94425	93493	94219	96736	94164	40
45	91723	92076	91864	92966	92333	92245	91750	91902	91912	93830	91843	92855	93077	92218	92962	95468	92977	45
50	89877	90287	90032	91917	90766	90445	89907	90164	90062	91942	90016	91199	91456	90442	91232	93715	91340	50
55	87495	87925	87660	90529	88945	88103	87536	87928	87675	89505	87641	88974	89328	88001	88927	91364	89122	55
60	83561	84001	83755	87941	86112	84291	83600	84262	83733	85481	83722	85193	85873	84196	85146	87515	85358	60
65	77648	78093	77860	83656	82422	78569	77684	78645	77808	79432	77826	79365	80522	78306	79435	81691	79551	65
70	68957	69384	69178	76649	77376	70221	69011	70228	69099	70541	69166	70718	72574	69607	71084	73182	70933	70
75	55383	55776	55617	64461	69833	57336	55441	56948	55497	56655	55588	57102	59764	56011	58167	60028	57314	75
80	37789	38106	37997	46715	59134	40335	37858	39281	37867	38657	37979	39433	42646	38316	41057	42562	39631	80
85+	19234	19429	19357	25904	43813	21973	19303	20355	19274	19676	19377	20719	23744	19553	22465	23548	20873	85+

ADDED YRS OF LIFE

	No Causes	(1)	(2)	(3)	(4)	(5)	(6)	(7)	(8)	(9)	(10)	(11)	(12)	(1)+(2)	col	col	col
TOTAL		.206	.127	2.805	6.507	.585	.037	.462	.089	1.641	.113	.956	2.098	.333	1.463	3.524	1.072
WORK	2.453	.128	.027	.760	.437	.069	.002	.116	.068	.000	.028	.413	.305	.155	.295	.339	.442

POPULATION, DEATHS, DEATH RATES FOR ALL CAUSES COMBINED, AND SPECIFIED CAUSES

Age Start of Interval	Midyear Population	Deaths During Year	All Causes	Respiratory T. B.	Other Infec. and Paras.	Neoplasms	Cardiovascular	Infl., Pneu., Bronch.	Diarrheal	Certain Degenerative	Maternal	Cert. Dis. of Infancy	Motor Vehicle	Other Violence	Other and Unknown	Age Start of Interval
0	13426	432	.03218	.00000	.00015	.00022	.00000	.00201	.00037	.00000	.00000	.02182	.00000	.00089	.00670	0
1	46052	64	.00139	.00000	.00002	.00020	.00000	.00013	.00004	.00000	.00000	.00000	.00000	.00065	.00670	0
5	44496	19	.00043	.00000	.00000	.00004	.00002	.00000	.00002	.00000	.00000	.00000	.00004	.00030	.00065	1
10	49032	15	.00031	.00000	.00000	.00010	.00000	.00000	.00000	.00000	.00000	.00000	.00002	.00020	.00011	5
15	54626	36	.00066	.00002	.00002	.00011	.00004	.00000	.00000	.00000	.00000	.00000	.00004	.00014	.00002	10
20	103486	154	.00149	.00001	.00001	.00021	.00007	.00000	.00001	.00003	.00000	.00000	.00009	.00029	.00004	15
25	81145	119	.00147	.00002	.00002	.00016	.00007	.00002	.00000	.00007	.00000	.00000	.00022	.00078	.00014	20
30	52990	115	.00217	.00002	.00000	.00030	.00025	.00004	.00000	.00017	.00000	.00000	.00013	.00085	.00014	25
35	49142	162	.00330	.00010	.00002	.00041	.00057	.00006	.00000	.00035	.00000	.00000	.00026	.00092	.00042	30
40	44636	213	.00477	.00036	.00002	.00108	.00110	.00004	.00000	.00045	.00000	.00000	.00026	.00092	.00061	35
45	37991	234	.00616	.00029	.00003	.00118	.00205	.00021	.00000	.00053	.00000	.00000	.00008	.00103	.00067	40
50	68419	701	.01025	.00035	.00006	.00224	.00395	.00022	.00006	.00108	.00000	.00000	.00018	.00114	.00076	45
55	81402	1508	.01853	.00055	.00010	.00463	.00736	.00065	.00001	.00150	.00000	.00000	.00027	.00135	.00098	50
60	73583	2324	.03158	.00071	.00008	.00821	.01408	.00113	.00004	.00223	.00000	.00000	.00035	.00125	.00210	55
65	52903	2495	.04716	.00087	.00030	.01265	.02125	.00257	.00008	.00257	.00000	.00000	.00040	.00113	.00351	60
70	39275	2650	.06747	.00102	.00041	.01507	.03231	.00400	.00013	.00377	.00000	.00000	.00048	.00168	.00535	65
75	26948	2787	.10342	.00141	.00026	.02074	.05065	.00731	.00015	.00367	.00000	.00000	.00085	.00249	.00861	70
80	13600	2064	.15176	.00162	.00044	.02449	.07346	.01478	.00015	.00456	.00000	.00000	.00085	.00249	.01588	75
85+	5828	1288	.22100	.00086	.00051	.02316	.09935	.02557	.00017	.00309	.00000	.00000	.00125	.00485	.02618	80
ALL	938980	17380														85+

	All Causes	Respiratory T.B.	Other Infec. and Paras.	Neoplasms	Cardiovascular	Infl., Pneu., Bronch.	Diarrheal	Certain Degenerative	Maternal	Cert. Dis. of Infancy	Motor Vehicle	Other Violence	Other and Unknown
CRUDE DEATH RATE	.01851	.00033	.00008	.00385	.00791	.00111	.00004	.00096	.00000	.00031	.00024	.00103	.00266
STANDARDIZED RATE (1)	.00687	.00012	.00004	.00122	.00217	.00035	.00003	.00034	.00000	.00077	.00014	.00064	.00106
STANDARDIZED RATE (2)	.01253	.00022	.00006	.00247	.00503	.00075	.00003	.00063	.00000	.00045	.00019	.00084	.00186
GEOMETRIC MEAN	.00790												

LIFE TABLE FOR ALL CAUSES COMBINED

Age (x)	Midyear Population	Deaths During Year	$_nM_x$	$_nq_x$	l_x	$_nd_x$	$_nL_x$	$_nm_x$	$_na_x$	T_x	$_nr_x$	$\overset{\circ}{e}_x$	Age (x)
0	13426	432	.032176	.031290	100000	3129	97261	.032171	.124700	6638751	.000000	66.388	0
1	46052	64	.001390	.005543	96871	537	386142	.001391	1.500000	6541490	.000000	67.528	1
5	44496	19	.000427	.002138	96334	206	481155	.000428	2.500000	6155349	.000000	63.896	5
10	49032	15	.000306	.001529	96128	147	480294	.000306	2.647392	5674194	-.005561	59.027	10
15	54626	36	.000659	.003230	95981	310	479247	.000647	2.878360	5193899	-.060169	54.114	15
20	103486	154	.001488	.007421	95671	710	476660	.001490	2.613263	4714652	-.065028	49.280	20
25	81145	119	.001467	.007329	94961	696	473131	.001471	2.594289	4237992	.036006	44.629	25
30	52990	115	.002170	.010874	94265	1025	468936	.002186	2.669309	3764861	.052134	39.939	30
35	49142	162	.003297	.016359	93240	1529	462616	.003305	2.656284	3295925	.018870	35.349	35
40	44636	213	.004772	.023683	91711	2172	453371	.004791	2.613087	2833309	.030868	30.894	40
45	37991	234	.006159	.030244	89539	2708	441357	.006136	2.659558	2379938	-.021048	26.580	45
50	68419	701	.010246	.048900	86831	4246	424488	.010003	2.723200	1938581	-.080616	22.326	50
55	81402	1508	.018525	.087873	82585	7257	396201	.018216	2.695530	1514093	-.046240	18.334	55
60	73583	2324	.031583	.146785	75328	11057	350322	.031562	2.619815	1117892	-.003705	14.840	60
65	52903	2495	.047162	.211853	64271	13616	288061	.047268	2.554776	767569	.013893	11.943	65
70	39275	2650	.067473	.288955	50655	14637	216918	.067477	2.516112	479509	.000212	9.466	70
75	26948	2787	.103421	.409462	36018	14748	142571	.103443	2.456011	262590	-.000912	7.291	75
80	13600	2064	.151765	.541749	21270	11523	75915	.151787	2.358797	120019	-.000912	5.643	80
85+	5828	1288	.221002	1.000000	9747	9747	44104	.221002	4.524845	44104	.000000	4.525	85+

NUMBER OF PERSONS DYING (OUT OF 100,000 AT BIRTH) ABOVE AGE X FROM SPECIFIED CAUSES

Age (x)	All Causes	Respiratory T. B.	Other Infec. and Paras.	Neoplasms	Cardiovascular	Infl., Pneu., Bronch.	Diarrheal	Certain Degenerative	Maternal	Cert. Dis. of Infancy	Motor Vehicle	Other Violence	Other and Unknown	Age (x)
0	100000	1815	439	20113	41650	6059	201	5132	0	2122	1397	6230	14842	0
1	96871	1815	425	20091	41650	5864	165	5132	0	0	1397	6143	14189	1
5	96334	1815	416	20016	41650	5813	148	5132	0	0	1380	6026	13938	5
10	96128	1815	416	19994	41639	5813	137	5132	0	0	1369	5928	13885	10
15	95981	1815	416	19945	41639	5813	137	5132	0	0	1350	5860	13874	15
20	95671	1806	408	19893	41621	5813	137	5106	0	0	1307	5724	13856	20
25	94961	1801	403	19790	41586	5813	133	5092	0	0	1202	5353	13788	25
30	94265	1789	391	19714	41551	5801	133	5057	0	0	1097	5009	13723	30
35	93240	1780	391	19572	41434	5783	133	4976	0	0	1036	4610	13525	35
40	91711	1733	382	19382	41169	5755	133	4815	0	0	913	4186	13243	40
45	89539	1569	372	18892	40668	5734	133	4612	0	0	822	3800	12937	45
50	86831	1442	360	18371	39767	5642	133	4380	0	0	787	3347	12602	50
55	82585	1295	336	17453	38134	5553	108	3928	0	0	714	2866	12198	55
60	75328	1077	297	15641	35259	5298	103	3339	0	0	608	2330	11376	60
65	64271	830	269	12767	30331	4904	89	2558	0	0	484	1892	10147	65
70	50655	579	181	9118	24195	4161	67	1816	0	0	370	1565	8603	70
75	36018	358	93	5848	17186	3294	39	999	0	0	265	1201	6735	75
80	21270	157	56	2890	9963	2251	18	475	0	0	143	846	4471	80
85+	9747	38	23	1022	4392	1128	8	136	0	0	45	484	2481	85+

NUMBER OF PERSONS SURVIVING TO AGE X IF SPECIFIED CAUSES WERE ELIMINATED

Age (x)	No Causes	Respiratory T. B. (1)	Other Infec. and Paras. (2)	Neoplasms (3)	Cardiovascular (4)	Infl., Pneu., Bronch. (5)	Diarrheal (6)	Certain Degenerative (7)	Maternal (8)	Cert. Dis. of Infancy (9)	Motor Vehicle (10)	Other Violence (11)	Other and Unknown (12)	(1)+(2)	(1)+(2)+(5)+(6)+(8)	(1)+(2)+(5)+(6)+(8)+part of(9)&(12)	(10)+(11)	Age (x)
0	100000	100000	100000	100000	100000	100000	100000	100000	100000	100000	100000	100000	100000	100000	100000	100000	100000	0
1	96871	96871	96883	96893	96871	97063	96906	96871	96871	98982	96871	96957	97516	96885	97112	99026	96957	1
5	96334	96334	96357	96430	96334	96576	96386	96334	96334	98433	96351	96536	97228	96357	96651	98624	96553	5
10	96128	96128	96151	96246	96139	96369	96191	96128	96128	98223	96156	96428	97073	96151	96455	98429	96456	10
15	95981	95981	96004	96148	95992	96222	96044	95981	95981	98073	96028	96348	96936	96004	96308	98278	96396	15
20	95671	95680	95702	95889	95700	95911	95697	95671	95671	97756	95761	96174	96641	95710	96014	97979	96264	20
25	94961	94975	94996	95281	95025	95200	95027	95001	94961	97030	95155	95832	95992	95010	95315	97268	96028	25
30	94265	94291	94312	94658	94363	94514	94331	94339	94265	96319	94562	95476	95354	94338	94653	96596	95777	30
35	93240	93274	93286	93771	93454	93504	93305	93394	93240	95272	93595	94841	94517	93321	93651	95579	95202	35
40	91711	91792	91766	92423	92185	91959	91775	92023	91711	93710	92183	93714	93251	91846	92199	94117	94196	40
45	89539	89780	89602	90724	90501	89841	89602	90045	89539	91490	90090	91885	91350	89843	90209	92118	92450	45
50	86831	87190	86904	88501	88666	87214	86892	87552	86831	88723	87400	89565	88924	87264	87710	89600	90151	50
55	82585	83070	82678	85091	85972	83037	82667	83716	82585	84385	83197	85665	84580	83164	83702	85536	86305	55
60	75328	75980	75450	79418	81330	75986	75408	76931	75328	76970	75988	78672	78325	76103	76849	78598	79362	60
65	64271	65057	64401	70616	74482	65201	64352	66377	64271	65672	64950	67544	68017	65189	66215	67806	68258	65
70	50655	51499	50836	59317	65355	52063	50738	52996	50655	51759	51292	53539	55076	51683	53207	54620	54211	70
75	36018	36806	36220	45500	54722	37776	36101	38403	36018	36803	36560	38392	40910	37013	38909	40108	38970	75
80	21270	21891	21417	29845	41831	23162	21335	23100	21270	21734	21685	22962	26204	22042	24075	25030	23409	80
85+	9747	10113	9836	15521	27973	11453	9783	10831	9747	9959	10003	10782	13741	10205	12036	12742	11067	85+

ADDED YRS OF LIFE

	No Causes	(1)	(2)	(3)	(4)	(5)	(6)	(7)	(8)	(9)	(10)	(11)	(12)	(1)+(2)	(1)+(2)+(5)+(6)+(8)	part	(10)+(11)
TOTAL		.276	.073	2.761	6.223	.686	.059	.748	.000	1.444	.329	1.544	2.319	.350	1.116	2.659	1.889
WORK	3.883	.119	.022	.684	.923	.073	.005	.291	.000	.000	.194	.838	.448	.142	.221	.252	1.038

GERMANY (WEST BERLIN) 1964 FEMALES

POPULATION, DEATHS, DEATH RATES FOR ALL CAUSES COMBINED, AND SPECIFIED CAUSES

Age Start of Interval	Midyear Population	Deaths During Year	All Causes	Respiratory T.B.	Other Infec. and Paras.	Neoplasms	Cardiovascular	Infl., Pneu., Bronch.	Diarrheal	Certain Degenerative	Maternal	Cert. Dis. of Infancy	Motor Vehicle	Other Violence	Other and Unknown	Age Start of Interval
0	12538	323	.02576	.00000	.00000	.00000	.00000	.00128	.00016	.00008	.00000	.01755	.00000	.00048	.00622	0
1	43810	32	.00073	.00000	.00000	.00014	.00002	.00002	.00000	.00002	.00000	.00000	.00000	.00005	.00014	.00034	1
5	41954	16	.00038	.00000	.00002	.00012	.00000	.00002	.00000	.00000	.00000	.00000	.00000	.00005	.00012	.00005	5
10	46560	6	.00013	.00000	.00000	.00004	.00000	.00000	.00000	.00000	.00000	.00000	.00000	.00005	.00012	.00005	10
15	51288	20	.00039	.00000	.00000	.00004	.00000	.00002	.00000	.00000	.00000	.00000	.00000	.00000	.00004	.00004	15
20	89498	49	.00055	.00001	.00000	.00004	.00006	.00001	.00000	.00001	.00007	.00000	.00000	.00002	.00018	.00012	20
25	75949	53	.00070	.00001	.00000	.00007	.00009	.00001	.00001	.00000	.00003	.00000	.00000	.00003	.00008	.00017	25
30	54343	76	.00140	.00007	.00000	.00040	.00013	.00000	.00000	.00004	.00011	.00000	.00000	.00006	.00024	.00017	30
35	63620	148	.00233	.00020	.00000	.00075	.00033	.00003	.00000	.00011	.00005	.00000	.00005	.00044	.00036	35
40	76816	236	.00307	.00012	.00001	.00131	.00052	.00001	.00003	.00017	.00001	.00000	.00003	.00044	.00042	40
45	64821	285	.00440	.00005	.00002	.00184	.00082	.00008	.00000	.00045	.00000	.00000	.00005	.00046	.00065	45
50	112044	701	.00626	.00010	.00006	.00256	.00150	.00013	.00001	.00042	.00000	.00000	.00008	.00043	.00096	50
55	121944	1055	.00865	.00007	.00007	.00336	.00253	.00020	.00003	.00055	.00000	.00000	.00007	.00065	.00112	55
60	110890	1536	.01385	.00010	.00009	.00462	.00487	.00053	.00005	.00084	.00000	.00000	.00009	.00061	.00205	60
65	102635	2378	.02317	.00011	.00012	.00645	.01023	.00083	.00006	.00126	.00000	.00000	.00019	.00071	.00323	65
70	85140	3275	.03847	.00021	.00013	.00856	.01934	.00149	.00009	.00170	.00000	.00000	.00028	.00127	.00498	70
75	58290	3939	.06758	.00022	.00026	.01122	.03745	.00393	.00014	.00194	.00000	.00000	.00039	.00249	.00954	75
80	29187	3338	.11437	.00041	.00014	.01370	.06568	.00764	.00021	.00243	.00000	.00000	.00041	.00249	.00954	80
85+	13084	2760	.21094	.00046	.00054	.01842	.10624	.01697	.00061	.00268	.00000	.00000	.00054	.01796	.04655	85+
ALL	1254411	20226														

	All Causes	Respiratory T.B.	Other Infec. and Paras.	Neoplasms	Cardiovascular	Infl., Pneu., Bronch.	Diarrheal	Certain Degenerative	Maternal	Cert. Dis. of Infancy	Motor Vehicle	Other Violence	Other and Unknown
CRUDE DEATH RATE	.01612	.00010	.00006	.00338	.00744	.00081	.00004	.00060	.00002	.00018	.00011	.00087	.00252
STANDARDIZED RATE (1)	.00424	.00004	.00002	.00088	.00122	.00017	.00001	.00015	.00002	.00062	.00005	.00031	.00076
STANDARDIZED RATE (2)	.00780	.00006	.00003	.00165	.00317	.00037	.00002	.00029	.00002	.00036	.00007	.00049	.00128
GEOMETRIC MEAN	.00473												

LIFE TABLE FOR ALL CAUSES COMBINED

Age (x)	Midyear Population	Deaths During Year	$_nM_x$	$_nq_x$	l_x	$_nd_x$	$_nL_x$	$_nm_x$	$_na_x$	T_x	$_nr_x$	$\overset{\circ}{e}_x$	Age (x)
0	12538	323	.025762	.025190	100000	2519	97768	.025765	.113795	7286509	.000000	72.865	0
1	43810	32	.000730	.002913	97481	284	389214	.000730	1.500000	7188742	.000000	73.745	1
5	41954	16	.000381	.001903	97197	185	485523	.000381	2.500000	6799528	.000000	69.956	5
10	46560	6	.000129	.000649	97012	63	484903	.000130	2.509921	6314005	.000000	65.085	10
15	51288	20	.000390	.001939	96949	188	484317	.000388	2.724956	5829102	-.007014	60.125	15
20	89498	49	.000547	.002749	96761	266	483171	.000551	2.617481	5344785	-.052198	55.237	20
25	75949	53	.000698	.003503	96495	338	481715	.000702	2.752056	4861614	-.059657	50.382	25
30	54343	76	.001399	.007020	96157	675	479256	.001408	2.735185	4379898	-.026435	45.549	30
35	63620	148	.002326	.011520	95482	1100	474819	.002317	2.644508	3900642	.029898	40.852	35
40	76816	236	.003072	.015236	94382	1438	468506	.003069	2.632563	3425823	-.028093	36.297	40
45	64821	285	.004397	.021680	92944	2015	459961	.004381	2.638234	2957317	-.005644	31.818	45
50	112044	701	.006256	.030518	90929	2775	448063	.006193	2.628078	2497356	-.025791	27.465	50
55	121944	1055	.008652	.042210	88154	3721	432069	.008612	2.661639	2049294	-.069652	23.247	55
60	110890	1536	.013852	.067059	84433	5662	409038	.013842	2.681547	1617225	-.025048	19.154	60
65	102635	2378	.023169	.109875	78771	8655	373617	.023165	2.661756	1208187	-.003461	15.338	65
70	85140	3275	.038466	.176593	70116	12382	321336	.038533	2.638221	834569	-.000526	11.903	70
75	58290	3939	.067576	.292202	57734	16870	247721	.068101	2.572676	513233	-.008118	8.890	75
80	29187	3338	.114366	.447019	40864	18267	158389	.115330	2.485561	265512	.031388	6.497	80
85+	13084	2760	.210945	1.000000	22597	22597	107123	.210945	4.740580	107123	.000000	4.741	85+

NUMBER OF PERSONS DYING (OUT OF 100,000 AT BIRTH) ABOVE AGE X FROM SPECIFIED CAUSES

Age (x)	All Causes	Respiratory T. B.	Other Infec. and Paras.	Neo-plasms	Cardio-vascular	Infl., Pneu., Bronch.	Diar-rheal	Certain Degenerative	Maternal	Cert. Dis. of Infancy	Motor Vehicle	Other Violence	Other and Unknown	Age (x)
0	100000	611	346	18940	45932	5392	259	3318	136	1716	664	6074	16612	0
1	97481	611	346	18940	45932	5268	243	3310	136	0	664	6027	16004	1
5	97197	611	346	18887	45923	5259	243	3301	136	0	646	5974	15871	5
10	97012	611	335	18829	45923	5247	243	3301	136	0	623	5916	15848	10
15	96949	611	335	18808	45923	5247	243	3301	136	0	623	5895	15827	15
20	96761	611	335	18789	45922	5238	243	3301	127	0	614	5811	15770	20
25	96495	606	335	18767	45894	5232	243	3296	95	0	581	5714	15732	25
30	96157	599	335	18734	45850	5226	237	3296	82	0	568	5581	15649	30
35	95482	563	335	18538	45788	5226	237	3278	29	0	542	5466	15480	35
40	94382	466	335	18183	45632	5211	237	3226	6	0	519	5257	15310	40
45	92944	411	329	17567	45388	5205	225	3147	0	0	507	5050	15115	45
50	90929	390	322	16726	45015	5170	225	2942	0	0	486	4837	14816	50
55	88154	346	294	15589	44353	5110	221	2755	0	0	450	4647	14389	55
60	84433	318	266	14141	43266	5026	207	2518	0	0	418	4367	13906	60
65	78771	277	229	12253	41277	4809	185	2176	0	0	381	4116	13068	65
70	70116	237	185	9844	37455	4499	163	1706	0	0	312	3851	11864	70
75	57734	169	143	6961	31226	4018	133	1158	0	0	222	3442	10262	75
80	40864	113	79	4172	21869	3035	99	677	0	0	123	2820	7877	80
85+	22597	49	57	1973	11380	1818	65	287	0	0	57	1924	4987	85+

NUMBER OF PERSONS SURVIVING TO AGE X IF SPECIFIED CAUSES WERE ELIMINATED

Age (x)	No Causes	Respiratory T. B. (1)	Other Infec. and Paras. (2)	Neo-plasms (3)	Cardio-vascular (4)	Infl., Pneu., Bronch. (5)	Diar-rheal (6)	Certain Degenerative (7)	Maternal (8)	Cert. Dis. of Infancy (9)	Motor Vehicle (10)	Other Violence (11)	Other and Unknown (12)	(1)+(2)	(1)+(2)+(5)+(6)+(8)	(1)+(2)+(5)+(6)+(8)+part of(9)&(12)	(10)+(11)	Age (x)
0	100000	100000	100000	100000	100000	100000	100000	100000	100000	100000	100000	100000	100000	100000	100000	100000	100000	0
1	97481	97481	97481	97481	97481	97604	97497	97489	97481	99190	97481	97527	98083	97481	97619	99283	97527	1
5	97197	97197	97197	97250	97206	97328	97213	97214	97197	98901	97215	97296	97931	97197	97344	99011	97314	5
10	97012	97012	97023	97123	97021	97155	97028	97029	97012	98713	97053	97169	97768	97023	97182	98849	97210	10
15	96949	96949	96960	97081	96958	97092	96965	96966	96949	98649	96990	97127	97726	96960	97119	98785	97168	15
20	96761	96761	96772	96912	96771	96913	96777	96778	96770	98457	96811	97023	97593	96772	96948	98620	97073	20
25	96495	96500	96506	96667	96533	96652	96511	96517	96536	98187	96578	96853	97363	96511	96725	98400	96936	25
30	96157	96169	96168	96362	96239	96320	96179	96179	96211	97843	96252	96647	97106	96180	96418	98098	96743	30
35	95482	95530	95493	95881	95625	95643	95503	95521	95588	97156	95603	96084	96595	95541	95830	97530	96205	35
40	94382	94526	94393	95132	94679	94557	94403	94473	94510	96037	94524	95186	95653	94536	94861	96569	95330	40
45	92944	93140	92960	94300	93480	93122	92977	93112	93076	94573	93096	93944	94392	93157	93500	95198	94097	45
50	90929	91142	90952	93104	91825	91138	90961	91297	91058	92523	91098	92120	92646	91165	91536	93209	92291	50
55	88154	88404	88204	91416	89684	88416	88189	88695	88279	89699	88834	89498	90248	88454	88877	90526	89701	55
60	84433	84700	84508	89038	86988	84766	84480	85185	84553	85913	84656	85999	86924	84775	85278	86883	86226	60
65	78771	79059	78877	85011	83161	79293	78836	79806	78883	80152	79015	80478	81932	79166	79869	81428	80727	65
70	70116	70410	70252	78157	77934	70875	70195	71487	70215	71345	70398	71891	74115	70547	71492	72953	72180	70
75	57734	58038	57884	67320	70771	58803	57826	59369	57816	58746	58048	59577	62584	58189	59445	60748	59901	75
80	40864	41126	41023	50425	60689	42471	40958	42433	40922	41580	41169	42711	46518	41286	43069	44184	43030	80
85+	22597	22789	22701	29945	47158	24431	22674	23763	22629	22993	22814	24315	28251	22894	24872	25724	24549	85+

ADDED YRS OF LIFE																	
TOTAL		.131	.050	3.029	6.654	.550	.040	.487	.062	1.276	.143	.999	2.454	.181	.843	2.264	1.148
WORK	2.337	.066	.009	.765	.412	.038	.007	.122	.046	.000	.051	.353	.373	.075	.166	.204	.404

POPULATION, DEATHS, DEATH RATES FOR ALL CAUSES COMBINED, AND SPECIFIED CAUSES

Age Start of Interval	Midyear Population	Deaths During Year	All Causes	Respiratory T. B.	Other Infec. and Paras.	Neoplasms	Cardiovascular	Infl., Pneu., Bronch.	Diarrheal	Certain Degenerative	Maternal	Cert. Dis. of Infancy	Motor Vehicle	Other Violence	Other and Unknown	Age Start of Interval
0	87573	9287	.10605	.00021	.01276	.00002	.00040	.01061	.03141	.00024	.00000	.02022	.00000	.00070	.02948	0
1	304861	9336	.03062	.00031	.00928	.00003	.00009	.00421	.00324	.00024	.00000	.00000	.00000	.00056	.01267	1
5	321864	1965	.00611	.00014	.00256	.00001	.00005	.00076	.00000	.00009	.00000	.00000	.00000	.00034	.00215	5
10	314950	952	.00302	.00020	.00090	.00001	.00007	.00040	.00000	.00006	.00000	.00000	.00000	.00030	.00109	10
15	344419	1628	.00473	.00117	.00106	.00001	.00010	.00050	.00000	.00012	.00000	.00000	.00000	.00045	.00131	15
20	261201	1796	.00688	.00268	.00087	.00001	.00009	.00070	.00000	.00014	.00000	.00000	.00000	.00066	.00174	20
25	254575	1846	.00725	.00284	.00078	.00005	.00013	.00079	.00000	.00022	.00000	.00000	.00000	.00076	.00168	25
30	185285	1274	.00688	.00241	.00075	.00005	.00026	.00081	.00000	.00023	.00000	.00000	.00000	.00069	.00168	30
35	175321	1627	.00928	.00248	.00103	.00021	.00031	.00145	.00000	.00038	.00000	.00000	.00000	.00084	.00258	35
40	152918	1434	.00938	.00201	.00111	.00026	.00039	.00156	.00000	.00054	.00000	.00000	.00000	.00058	.00294	40
45	161178	2013	.01249	.00203	.00143	.00046	.00061	.00248	.00000	.00068	.00000	.00000	.00000	.00068	.00412	45
50	139927	2132	.01524	.00220	.00164	.00071	.00114	.00287	.00000	.00074	.00000	.00000	.00000	.00089	.00505	50
55	108493	2455	.02263	.00251	.00225	.00132	.00211	.00445	.00000	.00141	.00000	.00000	.00000	.00100	.00759	55
60	92555	2805	.03031	.00228	.00269	.00173	.00340	.00586	.00000	.00199	.00000	.00000	.00000	.00099	.01137	60
65	71016	3265	.04598	.00221	.00376	.00232	.00586	.00862	.00000	.00330	.00000	.00000	.00000	.00106	.01876	65
70	49052	3023	.06163	.00169	.00495	.00224	.00785	.00966	.00000	.00369	.00000	.00000	.00000	.00137	.03017	70
75	30007	2750	.09165	.00153	.00716	.00223	.01143	.01160	.00000	.00440	.00000	.00000	.00000	.00157	.05172	75
80	15216	2102	.13814	.00085	.00973	.00158	.01400	.01314	.00007	.00434	.00000	.00000	.00000	.00171	.09273	80
85+	11009	2412	.21909	.00036	.01154	.00227	.01317	.01680	.00000	.00454	.00000	.00000	.00000	.00164	.16877	85+
ALL	3081420	54102														

CRUDE DEATH RATE			.01756	.00151	.00269	.00032	.00086	.00241	.00121	.00054	.00000	.00057	.00000	.00064	.00678	
STANDARDIZED RATE (1)			.01653	.00141	.00283	.00024	.00063	.00224	.00149	.00044	.00000	.00071	.00000	.00061	.00593	
STANDARDIZED RATE (2)			.01951	.00162	.00263	.00044	.00126	.00275	.00091	.00072	.00000	.00042	.00000	.00070	.00807	
GEOMETRIC MEAN			.02056													

LIFE TABLE FOR ALL CAUSES COMBINED

Age (x)	Midyear Population	Deaths During Year	$_nM_x$	$_nq_x$	l_x	$_nd_x$	$_nL_x$	$_nm_x$	$_na_x$	T_x	$_nr_x$	$\overset{\circ}{e}_x$	Age (x)
0	87573	9287	.106049	.098240	100000	9824	92635	.106051	.250283	4840598	.000000	48.406	0
1	304861	9336	.030624	.113778	90176	10260	335054	.030622	1.500000	4747963	.000000	52.652	1
5	321864	1965	.006105	.030057	79916	2402	393575	.006103	2.500000	4412909	.000000	55.219	5
10	314950	952	.003023	.015017	77514	1164	384532	.003027	2.389748	4019334	-.012436	51.853	10
15	344419	1628	.004727	.023392	76350	1786	377569	.004730	2.659875	3634803	.006089	47.607	15
20	261201	1796	.006876	.033877	74564	2526	366667	.006889	2.564248	3257234	.019257	43.684	20
25	254575	1846	.007251	.035606	72038	2565	353741	.007251	2.485786	2890567	.024252	40.126	25
30	185285	1274	.006876	.033840	69473	2351	341588	.006883	2.542890	2536826	-.031504	36.515	30
35	175321	1627	.009280	.045425	67122	3049	328110	.009293	2.540040	2195237	.017214	32.705	35
40	152918	1434	.009378	.045839	64073	2937	313159	.009379	2.546391	1867128	-.004187	29.141	40
45	161178	2013	.012489	.060570	61136	3703	296692	.012481	2.572745	1553969	-.006484	25.418	45
50	139927	2132	.015237	.073651	57433	4230	277011	.015270	2.599537	1257277	-.016842	21.891	50
55	108493	2455	.022628	.107588	53203	5724	252222	.022694	2.590409	980266	.020164	18.425	55
60	92555	2805	.030306	.141410	47479	6714	224308	.030356	2.584308	728044	-.011500	15.334	60
65	71016	3265	.045976	.207065	40765	8441	183127	.046094	2.547931	506868	-.015840	12.434	65
70	49052	3023	.061628	.267789	32324	8656	140062	.061801	2.509531	323741	-.020247	10.015	70
75	30007	2750	.091645	.373373	23668	8837	96020	.092033	2.474209	183678	-.022507	7.761	75
80	15216	2102	.138144	.509878	14831	7562	54481	.138801	2.358285	87658	-.022507	5.910	80
85+	11009	2412	.219093	1.000000	7269	7269	33178	.219093	4.564262	33178	.000000	4.564	85+

NUMBER OF PERSONS DYING (OUT OF 100,000 AT BIRTH) ABOVE AGE X FROM SPECIFIED CAUSES

Age (x)	All Causes	Respiratory T. B.	Other Infec. and Paras.	Neo-plasms	Cardio-vascular	Infl., Pneu., Bronch.	Diar-rheal	Certain Degen-erative	Maternal	Cert. Dis. of Infancy	Motor Vehicle	Other Violence	Other and Unknown	Age (x)
0	100000	8167	12624	2379	6812	14104	3558	3844	0	1873	0	3479	42720	0
1	90176	8148	11443	2377	6775	13121	1088	3822	0	0	0	3415	39987	1
5	79916	8045	8332	2367	6746	11710	4	3743	0	0	0	3227	35742	5
10	77514	7991	7325	2363	6725	11411	4	3706	0	0	0	3092	34897	10
15	76350	7916	6979	2361	6700	11256	4	3684	0	0	0	2975	34475	15
20	74564	7474	6578	2358	6660	11066	4	3640	0	0	0	2805	33979	20
25	72038	6489	6260	2355	6628	10810	4	3588	0	0	0	2563	33341	25
30	69473	5484	5984	2335	6583	10532	4	3510	0	0	0	2295	32746	30
35	67122	4663	5727	2316	6494	10252	4	3432	0	0	0	2061	32173	35
40	64073	3851	5388	2249	6393	9776	4	3307	0	0	0	1784	31321	40
45	61136	3222	5040	2169	6270	9286	4	3139	0	0	0	1604	30402	45
50	57433	2620	4615	2033	6088	8552	4	2936	0	0	0	1403	29182	50
55	53203	2010	4159	1834	5770	7757	4	2732	0	0	0	1157	27780	55
60	47479	1378	3590	1500	5235	6631	4	2375	0	0	0	906	25860	60
65	40765	874	2995	1118	4481	5333	4	1934	0	0	0	686	23340	65
70	32324	451	2304	692	3405	3752	4	1329	0	0	0	493	19894	70
75	23668	214	1609	378	2303	2397	4	812	0	0	0	301	15650	75
80	14831	67	918	163	1201	1291	4	389	0	0	0	150	10658	80
85+	7269	12	383	75	437	558	0	151	0	0	0	54	5599	85+

NUMBER OF PERSONS SURVIVING TO AGE X IF SPECIFIED CAUSES WERE ELIMINATED

Age (x)	No Causes	Respiratory T. B.	Other Infec. and Paras.	Neo-plasms	Cardio-vascular	Infl., Pneu., Bronch.	Diar-rheal	Certain Degener-ative	Maternal	Cert. Dis. of Infancy	Motor Vehicle	Other Violence	Other and Unknown	(1) + (2)	(1) + (2) + (5) + (6) + (8)	(1)+(2)+ (5)+(6)+ (8)+part of(9)&(12)	(10) + (11)	Age (x)
		(1)	(2)	(3)	(4)	(5)	(6)	(7)	(8)	(9)	(10)	(11)	(12)					
0	100000	100000	100000	100000	100000	100000	100000	100000	100000	100000	100000	100000	100000	100000	100000	100000	100000	0
1	90176	90194	91304	90178	90211	91114	92581	90197	90176	91971	90176	90237	92808	91322	95142	99753	90237	1
5	79916	80029	83934	79927	79974	82100	83460	80009	79916	81507	79916	80147	86463	84053	90179	99142	80147	5
10	77514	77677	82460	77529	77591	79935	80952	77641	77514	79057	77514	77871	84770	82633	88993	98760	77871	10
15	76350	76585	81587	76366	76451	78894	79736	76497	76350	77870	76350	76819	83956	81839	88315	98426	76819	15
20	74564	75234	80103	74583	74702	77242	77871	74751	74564	76049	74564	75191	82533	80822	87438	97963	75191	20
25	72038	73669	77726	72059	72203	74887	75233	72270	72038	73412	72038	72884	80434	79485	86293	97376	72884	25
30	69473	72062	75251	69513	69677	72505	72554	69773	69473	70856	69473	70556	78225	78055	85074	96642	70556	30
35	67122	70465	72979	67180	67407	70339	70099	67489	67122	68458	67122	68402	76215	76613	83846	95859	68402	35
40	64073	68101	70025	64194	64444	67633	66914	64547	64073	65349	64073	65571	73704	74427	82047	94710	65571	40
45	61136	65635	67187	61330	61611	65041	63647	61753	61136	62353	61136	62745	71366	72132	80142	93504	62745	45
50	57433	62288	63572	57747	58057	61863	59980	58212	57433	58577	57433	59145	68438	68946	77558	91819	59145	50
55	53203	58340	59377	53687	54092	58136	55562	54124	53203	54262	53203	55033	65026	65111	74303	89446	55033	55
60	47479	52720	53591	48231	48790	53056	49585	48646	47479	48424	47479	49357	60290	59507	69447	85575	49357	60
65	40765	45783	46638	41771	42615	46516	42573	42187	40765	41577	40765	42589	54617	52379	62956	80157	42589	65
70	32324	36724	37689	33510	34806	38850	33757	34012	32324	32968	32324	33949	47795	42820	53748	72027	33949	70
75	23668	27117	28295	24813	26516	29861	24718	25270	23668	24139	23668	25030	40000	32418	42715	61977	25030	75
80	14831	17122	18389	15723	17610	19839	15489	16253	14831	15126	14831	15809	33343	21229	29658	49248	15809	80
85+	7269	8435	9479	7770	9276	10410	7554	8147	7269	7414	7269	7819	26332	11000	16458	35127	7819	85+

ADDED YRS OF LIFE		(1)	(2)	(3)	(4)	(5)	(6)	(7)	(8)	(9)	(10)	(11)	(12)					
TOTAL		2.472	4.562	.355	.909	3.554	2.109	.656	.000	.959	.000	1.006	14.294	7.364	14.450	28.932	1.006	
WORK	9.032	2.138	.980	.155	.298	1.119	.000	.301	.000	.000	.000	.631	2.271	3.193	4.458	6.413	.631	

POPULATION, DEATHS, DEATH RATES FOR ALL CAUSES COMBINED, AND SPECIFIED CAUSES

Age Start of Interval	Midyear Population	Deaths During Year	All Causes	Respiratory T. B.	Other Infec. and Paras.	Neoplasms	Cardiovascular	Infl., Pneu., Bronch.	Diarrheal	Certain Degenerative	Maternal	Cert. Dis. of Infancy	Motor Vehicle	Other Violence	Other and Unknown	Age Start of Interval
0	82333	8605	.10451	.00030	.01383	.00002	.00018	.00887	.03270	.00011	.00000	.02057	.00000	.00084	.02709	0
1	293329	9071	.03052	.00027	.00921	.00003	.00006	.00403	.00339	.00029	.00000	.00000	.00000	.00050	.01305	1
5	306793	1918	.00625	.00019	.00270	.00001	.00003	.00085	.00000	.00012	.00000	.00000	.00000	.00020	.00216	5
10	287719	908	.00316	.00047	.00107	.00001	.00005	.00040	.00000	.00008	.00001	.00000	.00000	.00011	.00096	10
15	352579	1716	.00487	.00185	.00059	.00001	.00007	.00045	.00000	.00012	.00010	.00000	.00000	.00014	.00113	15
20	289339	1983	.00685	.00256	.00101	.00002	.00013	.00049	.00000	.00022	.00076	.00000	.00000	.00016	.00150	20
25	266093	2118	.00796	.00220	.00109	.00005	.00018	.00070	.00000	.00035	.00123	.00000	.00000	.00016	.00200	25
30	199316	1530	.00768	.00171	.00097	.00011	.00017	.00094	.00000	.00033	.00132	.00000	.00000	.00013	.00200	30
35	201689	1841	.00913	.00179	.00112	.00024	.00023	.00130	.00000	.00042	.00126	.00000	.00000	.00016	.00260	35
40	175304	1386	.00791	.00123	.00114	.00044	.00041	.00125	.00000	.00043	.00058	.00000	.00000	.00015	.00228	40
45	153241	1397	.00912	.00119	.00123	.00065	.00057	.00162	.00000	.00047	.00027	.00000	.00000	.00018	.00294	45
50	136826	1514	.01107	.00088	.00156	.00075	.00107	.00176	.00000	.00072	.00006	.00000	.00000	.00028	.00398	50
55	101445	1590	.01567	.00090	.00220	.00121	.00179	.00311	.00000	.00071	.00004	.00000	.00000	.00024	.00548	55
60	99440	2123	.02135	.00100	.00271	.00141	.00275	.00383	.00000	.00149	.00000	.00000	.00000	.00038	.00779	60
65	70940	2484	.03502	.00104	.00433	.00168	.00540	.00593	.00000	.00209	.00000	.00000	.00000	.00047	.01408	65
70	54761	2883	.05265	.00089	.00486	.00199	.00645	.00659	.00000	.00250	.00000	.00000	.00000	.00057	.02880	70
75	29527	2769	.09378	.00061	.00809	.00244	.01382	.00972	.00000	.00379	.00000	.00000	.00000	.00064	.05466	75
80	18737	2472	.13193	.00053	.00859	.00171	.01537	.01014	.00000	.00352	.00000	.00000	.00000	.00096	.09110	80
85+	13972	3255	.23297	.00057	.01167	.00172	.01768	.01188	.00000	.00480	.00000	.00000	.00000	.00115	.18351	85+
ALL	3133383	51563														

CRUDE DEATH RATE	.01646	.00123	.00274	.00032	.00086	.00193	.00118	.00048	.00040	.00054	.00000	.00025	.00653
STANDARDIZED RATE (1)	.01562	.00114	.00256	.00025	.00058	.00186	.00155	.00038	.00037	.00072	.00000	.00025	.00556
STANDARDIZED RATE (2)	.01788	.00119	.00274	.00043	.00121	.00216	.00055	.00059	.00039	.00043	.00000	.00026	.00754
GEOMETRIC MEAN	.01887												

LIFE TABLE FOR ALL CAUSES COMBINED

Age (x)	Midyear Population	Deaths During Year	$_nM_x$	$_nq_x$	l_x	$_nd_x$	$_nL_x$	$_nm_x$	$_na_x$	T_x	$_nr_x$	$\overset{\circ}{e}_x$	Age (x)
0	82333	8605	.104515	.096900	100000	9690	92710	.104520	.247675	4976709	.000000	49.767	0
1	293329	9071	.030924	.114816	90310	10369	335318	.030923	1.500000	4883999	.000000	54.080	1
5	306793	1918	.006252	.030773	79941	2460	393555	.006251	2.500000	4548682	.000000	56.900	5
10	287719	908	.003156	.015655	77481	1213	384242	.003157	2.392141	4155127	-.015158	53.628	10
15	352579	1716	.004867	.024021	76268	1832	377031	.004859	2.647721	3770885	-.012157	49.443	15
20	289339	1983	.006854	.033747	74436	2512	366104	.006861	2.581028	3393854	.011900	45.594	20
25	266093	2118	.007960	.039055	71924	2809	352617	.007966	2.506823	3027751	.026503	42.097	25
30	199316	1530	.007676	.037676	69115	2604	339098	.007679	2.512721	2675134	.024581	38.706	30
35	201689	1841	.009128	.044624	66511	2968	325105	.009129	2.490033	2336036	.006127	35.123	35
40	175304	1386	.007906	.038745	63543	2462	311510	.007903	2.479522	2010931	.017309	31.647	40
45	153241	1397	.009116	.044629	61081	2726	298734	.009125	2.552886	1699421	.013020	27.822	45
50	136826	1514	.011065	.054048	58355	3154	284193	.011098	2.596042	1400687	.027987	24.003	50
55	101445	1590	.015674	.075723	55201	4180	265980	.015715	2.601724	1116494	.019887	20.226	55
60	99440	2123	.021350	.101821	51021	5195	242794	.021397	2.630294	850514	.012842	16.670	60
65	70940	2484	.035016	.162113	45826	7429	211353	.035150	2.607125	607719	.020008	13.261	65
70	54761	2883	.052647	.234784	38397	9015	170234	.052957	2.587216	396366	.030870	10.323	70
75	29527	2769	.093779	.381288	29382	11203	118888	.094231	2.498717	226132	.018172	7.696	75
80	18737	2472	.131931	.492106	18179	8946	67612	.132314	2.397370	107244	.018172	5.899	80
85+	13972	3255	.232966	1.000000	9233	9233	39632	.232966	4.292473	39632	.000000	4.292	85+

NUMBER OF PERSONS DYING (OUT OF 100,000 AT BIRTH) ABOVE AGE X FROM SPECIFIED CAUSES

Age (x)	All Causes	Respiratory T.B.	Other Infec. and Paras.	Neoplasms	Cardiovascular	Infl., Pneu., Bronch.	Diarrheal	Certain Degenerative	Maternal	Cert. Dis. of Infancy	Motor Vehicle	Other Violence	Other and Unknown	Age (x)
0	100000	5923	13880	2554	7727	11842	4170	3463	1899	1908	0	1346	45288	0
1	90310	5894	12598	2552	7710	11020	1139	3453	1899	0	0	1268	42777	1
5	79941	5803	9475	2541	7691	9670	3	3357	1899	0	0	1101	38401	5
10	77481	5730	8413	2537	7678	9337	1	3311	1899	0	0	1024	37551	10
15	76268	5550	7998	2533	7661	9183	0	3280	1896	0	0	983	37184	15
20	74436	4853	7624	2528	7635	9012	0	3236	1861	0	0	929	36758	20
25	71924	3916	7253	2519	7588	8831	0	3154	1582	0	0	872	36209	25
30	69115	3141	6667	2501	7523	8585	0	3030	1148	0	0	817	35503	30
35	66511	2564	6539	2463	7465	8265	0	2920	699	0	0	772	34824	35
40	63543	1982	6175	2386	7389	7843	0	2784	288	0	0	719	33977	40
45	61081	1601	5821	2246	7263	7452	0	2651	108	0	0	673	33266	45
50	58355	1246	5452	2051	7093	6968	0	2510	28	0	0	618	32389	50
55	55201	996	5006	1837	6787	6465	0	2304	12	0	0	539	31255	55
60	51021	757	4420	1513	6308	5637	0	2115	2	0	0	476	29793	60
65	45826	515	3762	1171	5640	4705	0	1752	2	0	0	383	27896	65
70	38397	295	2845	816	4495	3448	0	1311	2	0	0	285	24900	70
75	29382	143	2016	477	3391	2323	0	883	2	0	0	188	19959	75
80	18179	70	1050	186	1741	1163	0	431	2	0	0	112	13424	80
85+	9233	23	462	68	701	471	0	190	0	0	0	45	7273	85+

NUMBER OF PERSONS SURVIVING TO AGE X IF SPECIFIED CAUSES WERE ELIMINATED

Age (x)	No Causes	Respiratory T.B. (1)	Other Infec. and Paras. (2)	Neoplasms (3)	Cardiovascular (4)	Infl., Pneu., Bronch. (5)	Diarrheal (6)	Certain Degenerative (7)	Maternal (8)	Cert. Dis. of Infancy (9)	Motor Vehicle (10)	Other Violence (11)	Other and Unknown (12)	(1)+(2)	(1)+(2)+(5)+(6)+(8)	(1)+(2)+(5)+(6)+(8)+part of(9)&(12)	(10)+(11)	Age (x)
0	100000	100000	100000	100000	100000	100000	100000	100000	100000	100000	100000	100000	100000	100000	100000	100000	100000	0
1	90310	90338	91536	90312	90326	91094	93236	90319	90310	92141	90310	90384	92727	91564	95351	99793	90384	1
5	79941	80051	84058	79953	79973	81926	83641	80040	79941	81562	79941	80164	86416	84174	90256	99200	80164	5
10	77481	77659	82578	77497	77525	79741	81069	77622	77481	79052	77481	77773	84666	82768	89127	98931	77773	10
15	76268	76623	81725	76287	76328	78650	79801	76438	76271	77814	76268	76596	83739	82106	88596	98759	76596	15
20	74436	75478	80159	74460	74520	76935	77884	74645	74474	75545	74436	74810	82191	81281	87946	98539	74810	20
25	71924	73870	77847	71956	72052	74523	75256	72207	72236	73382	71924	72342	80016	79953	87056	98204	72342	25
30	69115	71769	75217	69163	69302	71863	72317	69505	69843	70516	69115	69571	77665	78106	85869	97717	69571	30
35	66511	69655	72734	66595	66748	69483	69592	66999	67658	67859	66511	66994	75491	76172	84699	97229	66994	35
40	63543	67145	69879	63699	63844	66815	66486	64143	65049	64831	63543	64057	73068	73839	83163	96515	64057	40
45	61081	64939	67554	61369	61495	64631	63910	61790	62709	62319	61081	61620	71043	71821	81633	95550	61620	45
50	58355	62410	64935	58822	58918	62245	61058	59172	59990	59538	58355	58924	68877	69452	79690	94234	58924	50
55	55201	59297	61914	55853	56035	59409	57758	56177	56764	56320	55201	55817	66470	66508	77013	92169	55817	55
60	51021	55054	57861	51939	52262	55773	53384	52109	52475	52055	51021	51652	63152	62434	73446	89393	51652	60
65	45826	49695	52680	46981	47594	51068	47949	47155	47132	46755	45826	46482	58992	57128	68511	85223	46482	65
70	38397	41856	45112	39698	40980	44086	40176	39927	39491	39175	38397	39037	53056	49176	60761	78560	39037	70
75	29382	32172	35376	30682	32402	34873	30743	30941	30219	29978	29382	29957	47071	38735	49475	69015	29957	75
80	18179	19965	22808	19218	21516	22668	19021	19515	18697	18548	18179	18595	38572	25049	33613	53510	18595	80
85+	9233	10176	12112	9848	11823	12132	9661	10094	9458	9420	9233	9492	31214	13349	18879	37507	9492	85+

ADDED YRS OF LIFE

	No Causes	(1)	(2)	(3)	(4)	(5)	(6)	(7)	(8)	(9)	(10)	(11)	(12)	(1)+(2)	(1)+(2)+(5)+(6)+(8)	(1)+(2)+(5)+(6)+(8)+part of(9)&(12)	(10)+(11)
TOTAL		2.119	5.052	.423	.567	3.155	2.266	.657	.708	1.004	.000	.409	15.261	7.460	15.109	29.054	.409
WORK	8.526	1.805	1.091	.202	.285	.923	.000	.320	.699	.000	.000	.155	2.093	2.961	4.778	6.722	.155

POPULATION, DEATHS, DEATH RATES FOR ALL CAUSES COMBINED, AND SPECIFIED CAUSES

Age Start of Interval	Midyear Population	Deaths During Year	All Causes	Respiratory T. B.	Other Infec. and Paras.	Neoplasms	Cardiovascular	Infl., Pneu., Bronch.	Diarrheal	Certain Degenerative	Maternal	Cert. Dis. of Infancy	Motor Vehicle	Other Violence	Other and Unknown	Age Start of Interval
0	81936	3349	.04087	.00004	.00443	.00016	.00033	.00820	.00206	.00005	.00000	.01734	.00000	.00033	.00793	0
1	307013	666	.00217	.00001	.00036	.00019	.00007	.00031	.00010	.00002	.00000	.00000	.00005	.00028	.00078	1
5	366521	272	.00074	.00000	.00009	.00012	.00005	.00005	.00001	.00001	.00000	.00000	.00005	.00018	.00020	5
10	368214	194	.00053	.00000	.00004	.00011	.00007	.00002	.00000	.00002	.00000	.00000	.00002	.00015	.00009	10
15	324905	297	.00091	.00000	.00003	.00009	.00008	.00003	.00000	.00005	.00000	.00000	.00007	.00038	.00020	15
20	372932	343	.00092	.00003	.00004	.00009	.00008	.00002	.00000	.00005	.00000	.00000	.00035	.00035	.00016	20
25	356428	403	.00113	.00010	.00004	.00013	.00011	.00000	.00000	.00006	.00000	.00000	.00009	.00042	.00018	25
30	316008	459	.00145	.00017	.00005	.00020	.00016	.00002	.00001	.00011	.00000	.00000	.00010	.00034	.00028	30
35	259930	427	.00164	.00022	.00004	.00035	.00023	.00002	.00001	.00015	.00000	.00000	.00008	.00028	.00026	35
40	227304	532	.00234	.00028	.00003	.00050	.00037	.00004	.00001	.00022	.00000	.00000	.00011	.00027	.00051	40
45	233767	1009	.00432	.00031	.00012	.00104	.00085	.00007	.00000	.00054	.00000	.00000	.00009	.00047	.00084	45
50	224404	1489	.00664	.00055	.00014	.00187	.00154	.00009	.00001	.00057	.00000	.00000	.00006	.00055	.00127	50
55	190079	2059	.01083	.00058	.00015	.00336	.00281	.00013	.00002	.00115	.00000	.00000	.00008	.00049	.00207	55
60	143363	2410	.01681	.00069	.00017	.00481	.00488	.00031	.00007	.00147	.00000	.00000	.00010	.00060	.00371	60
65	106795	2778	.02601	.00097	.00025	.00681	.00787	.00069	.00007	.00198	.00000	.00000	.00010	.00068	.00657	65
70	80729	3356	.04157	.00085	.00037	.00891	.01401	.00136	.00015	.00317	.00000	.00000	.00012	.00090	.01172	70
75	57278	3773	.06587	.00070	.00035	.00983	.02299	.00236	.00038	.00347	.00000	.00000	.00007	.00129	.02442	75
80	32635	3544	.10860	.00070	.00064	.01134	.03484	.00463	.00070	.00460	.00000	.00000	.00009	.00239	.04866	80
85+	14348	3414	.23794	.00091	.00091	.01087	.05834	.01143	.00153	.00774	.00000	.00000	.00000	.00000	.14190	85+
ALL	4064589	30774														

	All Causes	Respiratory T. B.	Other Infec. and Paras.	Neoplasms	Cardiovascular	Infl., Pneu., Bronch.	Diarrheal	Certain Degenerative	Maternal	Cert. Dis. of Infancy	Motor Vehicle	Other Violence	Other and Unknown
CRUDE DEATH RATE	.00757	.00022	.00020	.00124	.00183	.00039	.00008	.00045	.00000	.00035	.00007	.00041	.00235
STANDARDIZED RATE (1)	.00530	.00015	.00026	.00076	.00095	.00042	.00010	.00027	.00000	.00061	.00007	.00034	.00137
STANDARDIZED RATE (2)	.00875	.00023	.00021	.00144	.00220	.00043	.00008	.00051	.00000	.00036	.00007	.00042	.00277
GEOMETRIC MEAN	.00636												

LIFE TABLE FOR ALL CAUSES COMBINED

Age (x)	Midyear Population	Deaths During Year	$_nM_x$	$_nq_x$	l_x	$_nd_x$	$_nL_x$	$_nm_x$	$_na_x$	T_x	$_nr_x$	$\overset{\circ}{e}_x$	Age (x)
0	81936	3349	.040873	.039480	100000	3948	96603	.040868	.139485	7033212	.000000	70.332	0
1	307013	666	.002169	.008631	96052	829	382136	.002169	1.500000	6936609	.000000	72.217	1
5	366521	272	.000742	.003707	95223	353	475233	.000743	2.500000	6554474	.000000	68.833	5
10	368214	194	.000527	.002635	94870	250	473741	.000528	2.565000	6079241	.010555	64.080	10
15	324905	297	.000914	.004555	94620	431	472060	.000913	2.587974	5605500	.003317	59.242	15
20	372932	343	.000920	.004587	94189	432	469885	.000919	2.547261	5133439	-.011086	54.501	20
25	356428	403	.001131	.005642	93757	529	467513	.001132	2.556093	4663554	.006768	49.741	25
30	316008	459	.001452	.007251	93228	676	464458	.001453	2.571191	4196041	.023709	45.008	30
35	259930	427	.001643	.008212	92552	760	460942	.001649	2.608553	3731543	.033027	40.318	35
40	227304	532	.002340	.011679	91792	1072	456525	.002348	2.728933	3270600	.016336	35.631	40
45	233767	1009	.004316	.021362	90720	1938	449137	.004315	2.697046	2814075	-.000755	31.019	45
50	224404	1489	.006635	.032721	88782	2905	437194	.006645	2.687966	2364938	.007101	26.638	50
55	190079	2059	.010832	.053088	85877	4559	418761	.010887	2.669674	1927744	.026099	22.448	55
60	143363	2410	.016810	.081384	81318	6618	391013	.016925	2.646287	1508983	.039364	18.557	60
65	106795	2778	.026012	.123240	74700	9206	351695	.026176	2.631436	1117970	.034141	14.966	65
70	80729	3356	.041571	.189727	65494	12426	297635	.041749	2.599003	766275	.022241	11.700	70
75	57278	3773	.065872	.284748	53068	15111	228370	.066169	2.553410	468640	.021944	8.831	75
80	32635	3544	.108595	.429433	37957	16300	149252	.109211	2.513344	240270	.021944	6.330	80
85+	14348	3414	.237943	1.000000	21657	21657	91018	.237943	4.202695	91018	.000000	4.203	85+

NUMBER OF PERSONS DYING (OUT OF 100,000 AT BIRTH) ABOVE AGE X FROM SPECIFIED CAUSES

Age (x)	All Causes	Respiratory T.B.	Other Infec. and Paras.	Neo-plasms	Cardio-vascular	Infl., Pneu., Bronch.	Diar-rheal	Certain Degen-erative	Maternal	Cert. Dis. of Infancy	Motor Vehicle	Other Violence	Other and Unknown	Age (x)
0	100000	2224	1439	15428	27535	4183	697	5721	0	1675	549	3696	36853	0
1	96052	2221	1011	15412	27503	3391	497	5717	0	0	549	3664	36087	1
5	95223	2216	871	15340	27478	3274	457	5708	0	0	531	3558	35790	5
10	94870	2214	830	15284	27455	3252	455	5704	0	0	507	3474	35695	10
15	94620	2213	812	15234	27424	3240	455	5694	0	0	495	3402	35651	15
20	94189	2212	797	15193	27388	3227	455	5670	0	0	463	3224	35560	20
25	93757	2199	779	15149	27349	3216	455	5645	0	0	419	3060	35486	25
30	93228	2152	759	15089	27298	3214	455	5618	0	0	377	2866	35400	30
35	92552	2071	734	14996	27222	3205	452	5566	0	0	329	2709	35268	35
40	91792	1969	716	14834	27115	3196	448	5455	0	0	291	2578	35150	40
45	90720	1843	702	14604	26948	3178	444	5394	0	0	239	2456	34912	45
50	88782	1704	650	14139	26568	3146	442	5150	0	0	201	2246	34536	50
55	85877	1464	588	13321	25894	3105	439	4902	0	0	175	2007	33982	55
60	81318	1222	526	11909	24708	3051	432	4417	0	0	142	1799	33112	60
65	74700	951	460	10019	22784	2927	404	3839	0	0	104	1564	31648	65
70	65454	607	371	7614	19994	2681	378	3141	0	0	68	1323	29317	70
75	53068	353	260	4959	15803	2273	333	2194	0	0	31	1053	25809	75
80	37957	194	180	2711	10530	1732	245	1399	0	0	15	757	20194	80
85+	21657	82	82	990	5310	1040	140	704	0	0	0	393	12916	85+

NUMBER OF PERSONS SURVIVING TO AGE X IF SPECIFIED CAUSES WERE ELIMINATED

Age (x)	No Causes	Respiratory T.B.	Other Infec. and Paras.	Neo-plasms	Cardio-vascular	Infl., Pneu., Bronch.	Diar-rheal	Certain Degener-ative	Maternal	Cert. Dis. of Infancy	Motor Vehicle	Other Violence	Other and Unknown	(1)+(2)	(1)+(2)+(5)+(6)+(8)	(1)+(2)+(5)+(6)+(8)+part of(9)&(12)	(10)+(11)	Age (x)
		(1)	(2)	(3)	(4)	(5)	(6)	(7)	(8)	(9)	(10)	(11)	(12)					
0	100000	100000	100000	100000	100000	100000	100000	100000	100000	100000	100000	100000	100000	100000	100000	100000	100000	0
1	96052	96055	96472	96068	96083	96831	96248	96056	96052	97708	96052	96083	98806	96475	97457	99776	96083	1
5	95223	95231	95780	95310	95279	96113	95457	95236	95223	96864	95241	95360	98269	95788	96921	99403	95378	5
10	94870	94880	95466	95013	94949	95779	95106	94887	94870	96505	94912	95090	96008	95476	96630	99130	95132	10
15	94620	94631	95232	94813	94730	95539	94855	94647	94620	96251	94674	94912	95799	95243	96407	98908	94966	15
20	94189	94201	94814	94422	94334	95117	94423	94240	94189	95812	94274	94658	95455	94826	95997	98499	94744	20
25	93757	93782	94397	94033	93940	94691	93990	93832	93757	95373	93886	94388	95092	94422	95600	98097	94518	25
30	93228	93299	93884	93562	93461	94159	93459	93330	93228	94835	93398	94051	94662	93956	95130	97629	94222	30
35	92552	92704	93229	92977	92860	93485	92785	92705	92552	94147	92769	93526	94090	93382	94561	97074	93746	35
40	91792	92044	92481	92375	92204	92727	92027	92015	91792	93374	92045	92890	93437	92735	93920	96442	93146	40
45	90720	91095	91415	91527	91294	91662	90956	91041	90720	92284	91022	91928	92586	91793	92988	95533	92234	45
50	88782	89287	89514	90037	89723	89736	89015	89338	88782	90312	89115	90175	90989	90024	91230	93784	90514	50
55	85877	86603	86647	87911	87460	86840	86105	86661	85877	87357	86225	87463	88572	87379	88595	91160	87818	55
60	81318	82243	82108	84662	84001	82283	81541	82538	81318	82720	81680	83026	84748	83042	84258	86787	83395	60
65	74700	75813	75489	79679	79094	75708	74932	76384	74700	75988	75069	76499	79328	76613	77888	80369	76876	65
70	65454	66796	66270	72297	72168	66612	65722	67641	65494	66623	65851	67302	71910	67587	68980	71420	67669	70
75	53068	54354	53797	61261	62780	54348	53293	55691	53068	53983	53390	54782	61845	55101	56670	58996	55115	75
80	37957	39012	38546	46035	50467	39343	38193	40535	37957	38611	38201	39441	50132	39617	41319	43512	39694	80
85+	21657	22345	22068	27869	34463	22989	21871	23688	21657	22030	21807	22787	36748	22768	24407	26431	22946	85+

ADDED YRS OF LIFE

		(1)	(2)	(3)	(4)	(5)	(6)	(7)	(8)	(9)	(10)	(11)	(12)				
TOTAL		.443	.589	2.379	3.388	.960	.211	.804	.000	1.210	.191	.965	5.982	1.037	2.241	4.553	1.160
WORK	2.573	.184	.061	.523	.428	.038	.005	.214	.000	.000	.100	.431	.469	.246	.289	.358	.532

POPULATION, DEATHS, DEATH RATES FOR ALL CAUSES COMBINED, AND SPECIFIED CAUSES

Age Start of Interval	Midyear Population	Deaths During Year	All Causes	Respiratory T. B.	Other Infec. and Paras.	Neoplasms	Cardiovascular	Infl., Pneu., Bronch.	Diarrheal	Certain Degenerative	Maternal	Cert. Dis. of Infancy	Motor Vehicle	Other Violence	Other and Unknown	Age Start of Interval
0	76613	2984	.03895	.00005	.00435	.00012	.00020	.00799	.00281	.00007	.00000	.01637	.00000	.00025	.00676	0
1	285341	545	.00191	.00001	.00035	.00014	.00007	.00029	.00011	.00004	.00000	.00000	.00002	.00025	.00065	1
5	339292	175	.00052	.00000	.00008	.00009	.00005	.00005	.00005	.00001	.00000	.00000	.00002	.00004	.00016	5
10	349162	118	.00034	.00000	.00004	.00006	.00005	.00003	.00000	.00002	.00000	.00000	.00001	.00005	.00008	10
15	308097	151	.00049	.00002	.00003	.00005	.00006	.00000	.00000	.00004	.00000	.00000	.00001	.00014	.00014	15
20	368559	213	.00058	.00005	.00002	.00009	.00008	.00001	.00000	.00002	.00004	.00000	.00000	.00012	.00012	20
25	377785	277	.00073	.00010	.00002	.00008	.00012	.00001	.00001	.00006	.00007	.00000	.00001	.00009	.00017	25
30	354161	388	.00110	.00014	.00003	.00021	.00017	.00001	.00001	.00006	.00006	.00000	.00001	.00009	.00030	30
35	294072	352	.00120	.00010	.00002	.00033	.00020	.00001	.00001	.00008	.00010	.00000	.00001	.00010	.00023	35
40	255401	452	.00177	.00010	.00005	.00068	.00030	.00003	.00000	.00013	.00002	.00000	.00002	.00010	.00034	40
45	257597	677	.00263	.00011	.00004	.00116	.00051	.00003	.00001	.00015	.00001	.00000	.00003	.00010	.00047	45
50	239795	965	.00402	.00009	.00006	.00146	.00103	.00007	.00003	.00028	.00000	.00000	.00004	.00015	.00082	50
55	205958	1263	.00613	.00010	.00007	.00192	.00185	.00017	.00003	.00054	.00000	.00000	.00003	.00018	.00125	55
60	166461	1762	.01059	.00015	.00010	.00292	.00363	.00025	.00005	.00085	.00000	.00000	.00002	.00023	.00238	60
65	136561	2301	.01685	.00025	.00019	.00347	.00627	.00059	.00009	.00133	.00000	.00000	.00002	.00030	.00434	65
70	108581	3477	.03202	.00026	.00025	.00434	.01321	.00129	.00034	.00187	.00000	.00000	.00006	.00058	.00983	70
75	78205	4119	.05267	.00042	.00031	.00563	.02174	.00198	.00043	.00261	.00000	.00000	.00008	.00075	.01872	75
80	44094	4144	.09398	.00027	.00052	.00642	.03372	.00501	.00068	.00320	.00000	.00000	.00005	.00154	.04257	80
85+	17081	5426	.31766	.00029	.00111	.01147	.09121	.01405	.00205	.00720	.00000	.00000	.00000	.00006	.00509	.18512	85+
ALL	4262816	29789														ALL

	All Causes	Respiratory T. B.	Other Infec. and Paras.	Neoplasms	Cardiovascular	Infl., Pneu., Bronch.	Diarrheal	Certain Degenerative	Maternal	Cert. Dis. of Infancy	Motor Vehicle	Other Violence	Other and Unknown
CRUDE DEATH RATE	.00699	.00009	.00017	.00092	.00205	.00039	.00010	.00032	.00002	.00029	.00002	.00018	.00242
STANDARDIZED RATE (1)	.00422	.00006	.00024	.00051	.00083	.00041	.00013	.00016	.00002	.00058	.00002	.00014	.00113
STANDARDIZED RATE (2)	.00712	.00009	.00018	.00092	.00207	.00042	.00011	.00032	.00002	.00034	.00002	.00015	.00245
GEOMETRIC MEAN	.00459												

LIFE TABLE FOR ALL CAUSES COMBINED

Age (x)	Midyear Population	Deaths During Year	$_nM_x$	$_nq_x$	l_x	$_nd_x$	$_nL_x$	$_nm_x$	$_na_x$	T_x	$_nr_x$	$\overset{\circ}{e}_x$	Age (x)
0	76613	2984	.038949	.037680	100000	3768	96745	.038948	.136213	7352521	.000000	73.525	0
1	285341	545	.001910	.007607	96232	732	383058	.001911	1.500000	7255775	.000000	75.399	1
5	339292	175	.000516	.002576	95500	246	476885	.000516	2.500000	6872677	.000000	71.965	5
10	349162	118	.000338	.001690	95254	161	475865	.000338	2.481884	6395792	.008925	67.145	10
15	308097	151	.000490	.002440	95093	232	474909	.000489	2.601473	5919928	.001214	62.254	15
20	368559	213	.000578	.002888	94861	274	473644	.000578	2.586679	5445019	-.019322	57.400	20
25	377785	277	.000733	.003658	94587	346	472120	.000733	2.645111	4971375	-.005407	52.559	25
30	354161	388	.001096	.005465	94241	515	469962	.001096	2.586574	4499255	.015091	47.742	30
35	294072	352	.001197	.005986	93726	561	467292	.001201	2.614379	4029293	.030721	42.990	35
40	255401	452	.001770	.008834	93165	823	463902	.001774	2.663781	3562001	.017823	38.233	40
45	257597	677	.002628	.013082	92342	1208	458898	.002632	2.671944	3098099	.004754	33.550	45
50	239795	965	.004024	.019971	91134	1820	451434	.004032	2.672505	2639201	.013086	28.960	50
55	205958	1263	.006132	.030398	89314	2715	440341	.006166	2.705724	2187767	.025750	24.495	55
60	166461	1762	.010585	.051575	86599	4501	422572	.010651	2.684357	1747426	.030201	20.178	60
65	136561	2301	.016850	.081585	82098	6698	395158	.016950	2.710915	1324854	.026196	16.137	65
70	108581	3477	.032022	.149629	75400	11282	350543	.032184	2.654948	929696	.021761	12.330	70
75	78205	4119	.052669	.235332	64118	15089	284471	.053042	2.606300	579153	.031953	9.033	75
80	44094	4144	.093981	.387138	49029	18981	200091	.094862	2.626354	294682	.031953	6.010	80
85+	17081	5426	.317663	1.000000	30048	30048	94591	.317663	3.147991	94591	.000000	3.148	85+

NUMBER OF PERSONS DYING (OUT OF 100,000 AT BIRTH) ABOVE AGE X FROM SPECIFIED CAUSES

Age (x)	All Causes	Respira- tory T. B.	Other Infec. and Paras.	Neo- plasms	Cardio- vascular	Infl., Pneu., Bronch.	Diar- rheal	Certain Degen- erative	Maternal	Cert. Dis. of Infancy	Motor Vehicle	Other Violence	Other and Unknown	Age (x)
0	100000	841	1285	10992	32399	4780	991	4274	141	1583	184	2091	40439	0
1	96232	836	865	10980	32380	4007	719	4268	141	0	184	2067	39785	1
5	95500	833	730	10928	32355	3894	678	4255	141	0	178	1973	39535	5
10	95254	832	691	10884	32332	3872	676	4248	141	0	166	1952	39460	10
15	95093	830	673	10857	32308	3859	675	4239	141	0	162	1927	39422	15
20	94861	823	659	10832	32277	3858	675	4221	141	0	158	1862	39355	20
25	94587	799	648	10790	32241	3854	674	4211	124	0	149	1803	39294	25
30	94241	752	638	10753	32186	3850	671	4185	90	0	144	1759	39213	30
35	93726	686	622	10655	32106	3843	668	4154	59	0	140	1717	39076	35
40	93165	642	611	10502	32011	3837	665	4116	15	0	133	1669	38964	40
45	92342	594	585	10186	31872	3824	663	4054	6	0	126	1624	38808	45
50	91134	545	566	9653	31637	3812	658	3986	2	0	110	1576	38589	50
55	89314	503	537	8991	31170	3782	647	3861	1	0	91	1510	38221	55
60	86599	458	505	8144	30352	3706	634	3623	1	0	78	1430	37668	60
65	82098	394	462	6905	28807	3599	611	3263	1	0	68	1334	36654	65
70	75400	296	386	5531	26312	3362	576	2734	1	0	60	1214	34928	70
75	64118	205	299	4007	21658	2908	455	2077	1	0	37	1010	31461	75
80	49029	85	211	2402	15436	2339	331	1332	1	0	15	794	26083	80
85+	30048	28	105	1085	8628	1329	194	681	0	0	6	482	17510	85+

NUMBER OF PERSONS SURVIVING TO AGE X IF SPECIFIED CAUSES WERE ELIMINATED

Age (x)	No Causes	Respira- tory T. B. (1)	Other Infec. and Paras. (2)	Neo- plasms (3)	Cardio- vascular (4)	Infl., Pneu., Bronch. (5)	Diar- rheal (6)	Certain Degener- ative (7)	Maternal (8)	Cert. Dis. of Infancy (9)	Motor Vehicle (10)	Other Violence (11)	Other and Unknown (12)	(1) + (2)	(1) + (2) + (5) + (6) + (8)	(1)+(2)+ (5)+(6)+ (8)+part of(9)&(12)	(10) + (11)	Age (x)
0	100000	100000	100000	100000	100000	100000	100000	100000	100000	100000	100000	100000	100000	100000	100000	100000	100000	0
1	96232	96237	96645	96244	96251	96993	96459	96238	96232	97797	96232	96256	96876	96650	97685	99847	96256	1
5	95500	95508	96045	95564	95543	96369	95806	95519	95500	97053	95506	95617	96390	96053	97237	99541	95623	5
10	95254	95263	95837	95361	95320	96143	95561	95280	95254	96803	95272	95392	96217	95846	97052	99386	95410	10
15	95093	95104	95693	95227	95183	95994	95401	95128	95093	96640	95115	95256	96093	95704	96923	99265	95278	15
20	94861	94879	95473	95020	94982	95760	95168	94914	94861	96404	94887	95088	95926	95491	96709	99055	95114	20
25	94587	94629	95209	94787	94744	95488	94894	94649	94604	96126	94622	94873	95711	95251	96487	98845	94908	25
30	94241	94330	94870	94478	94452	95143	94550	94329	94292	95774	94281	94570	95442	94960	96234	98617	94609	30
35	93726	93880	94368	94059	94016	94630	94036	93845	93808	95251	93769	94095	95059	94523	95834	98253	94138	35
40	93165	93362	93814	93650	93548	94069	93477	93321	93290	94680	93215	93580	94604	94013	95370	97806	93630	40
45	92342	92585	93012	92139	92861	93251	92653	92558	92475	93844	92299	92758	93926	93256	94628	97069	92855	45
50	91134	91423	91814	92456	91881	92043	91446	91415	91269	92616	91206	91632	92919	92105	93480	95913	91704	50
55	89314	89639	90009	91277	90514	90235	89630	89714	89447	90767	89403	89868	91435	90336	91728	94145	89958	55
60	86599	86958	87305	89358	88583	87568	86919	87222	86728	88008	86698	87215	89215	87667	89108	91500	87315	60
65	82098	82501	82809	85967	85532	83122	82423	83043	82221	83433	82202	82776	85602	83216	84714	87059	82881	65
70	75400	75864	76127	80339	81086	76571	75733	76781	75513	76627	75503	76139	80363	76596	78245	80570	76243	70
75	64118	64597	64817	69824	73722	65540	64513	65910	64214	65161	64227	64936	71835	65301	67260	69592	65046	75
80	49029	49500	49640	54927	62954	50627	49439	51067	49102	49827	49131	49845	60465	50117	52262	54560	49949	80
85+	30048	30381	30506	34926	45989	31847	30407	31827	30094	30537	30118	30795	46228	30844	33131	35565	30866	85+

ADDED YRS OF LIFE																		
TOTAL		.199	.559	1.773	3.438	.974	.293	.540	.063	1.194	.053	.421	5.227	.760	2.117	4.316	.475	
WORK	1.678	.095	.040	.466	.334	.024	.008	.112	.046	.000	.019	.136	.352	.135	.213	.276	.155	

POPULATION, DEATHS, DEATH RATES FOR ALL CAUSES COMBINED, AND SPECIFIED CAUSES

Age Start of Interval	Midyear Population	Deaths During Year	All Causes	Respiratory T. B.	Other Infec. and Paras.	Neoplasms	Cardiovascular	Infl., Pneu., Bronch.	Diarrheal	Certain Degenerative	Maternal	Cert. Dis. of Infancy	Motor Vehicle	Other Violence	Other and Unknown	Age Start of Interval
0	78028	3007	.03854	.00004	.001C4	.00018	.00008	.C0611	.00138	.00004	.00000	.02258	.00003	.00068	.00638	0
1	305074	476	.00156	.00001	.00020	.00015	.00004	.00029	.00005	.00001	.00000	.00000	.00006	.00024	.00051	1
5	375769	241	.00064	.CCCC0	.00004	.00013	.00004	.C0004	.00001	.00001	.00000	.C0000	.00008	.00014	.00016	5
10	361288	159	.00044	.00000	.00002	.00007	.00003	.00002	.00000	.00001	.00000	.C00C0	.00005	.00011	.00011	10
15	372809	337	.CC090	.00002	.00003	.0C0C9	.C0008	.00003	.00000	.00002	.00000	.CC000	.00020	.00030	.00014	15
20	295213	356	.00121	.00001	.000C2	.00015	.00008	.C0004	.CCC00	.00004	.00000	.CC000	.00033	.00037	.00016	20
25	325754	364	.00112	.000C4	.0CC01	.00015	.00013	.00002	.00000	.00006	.00000	.00000	.00026	.00029	.00017	25
30	324275	439	.00135	.CCC12	.0CC02	.00021	.C0012	.00002	.CCC0C	.00005	.00000	.CC000	.00026	.00031	.00021	30
35	306823	594	.00194	.00015	.000C4	.00033	.00029	.00002	.00001	.00017	.00000	.CC000	.00019	.00031	.00039	35
40	230447	587	.00255	.00014	.0CC05	.00052	.00049	.00003	.00001	.00029	.00000	.C0000	.00020	.00034	.00047	40
45	213143	935	.00439	.00032	.0C0C9	.00114	.00101	.C0007	.CCC00	.00045	.00000	.CC000	.00014	.00036	.00080	45
50	236386	1649	.00698	.00035	.00CC8	.00204	.00180	.00017	.C0001	.00070	.00000	.C0000	.00017	.00045	.00120	50
55	213772	2357	.01103	.00039	.C00C9	.00335	.003C1	.00034	.00003	.001C9	.C0000	.00000	.00020	.00045	.00201	55
60	173120	3277	.01893	.CCC79	.00013	.00533	.00550	.00084	.0C002	.00184	.CC000	.00000	.00018	.00056	.00373	60
65	126176	3603	.02856	.0CC91	.0CC17	.00774	.00902	.00159	.CC006	.00220	.C0000	.00000	.00020	.00074	.00593	65
70	84828	3975	.04666	.00100	.00019	.00975	.01578	.00336	.00012	.00373	.00000	.C0000	.00022	.00091	.01180	70
75	61932	4565	.C7371	.00111	.00021	.01164	.02522	.00691	.00034	.00438	.00000	.C0000	.00026	.00113	.02251	75
80	38120	4354	.11422	.0CC81	.0CC47	.01207	.03712	.C1123	.00050	.00548	.CC000	.CC000	.00018	.00247	.04389	80
85+	16861	4404	.26119	.00C71	.00059	.01352	.07224	.02888	.00142	.00724	.CC000	.CC000	.00047	.00522	.13089	85+
ALL	4139818	35679														

CRUDE DEATH RATE			.00862	.00C20	.CCCC9	.00148	.C0224	.00C66	.CC006	.00053	.C0000	.00043	.00018	.00039	.00236	
STANDARDIZED RATE (1)			.00542	.00012	.0001C	.C0083	.00104	.00047	.CCC07	.C0029	.00000	.00079	.00016	.00032	.00123	
STANDARDIZED RATE (2)			.0C931	.00021	.0C010	.00159	.C0246	.00073	.CC006	.00057	.CC000	.00047	.00017	.00040	.00255	
GECMETRIC MEAN			.00649													

LIFE TABLE FOR ALL CAUSES COMBINED

Age (x)	Midyear Population	Deaths During Year	$_nM_x$	$_nq_x$	l_x	$_nd_x$	$_nL_x$	$_nm_x$	$_na_x$	T_x	$_nr_x$	$\overset{\circ}{e}_x$	Age (x)
C	78028	3007	.038537	.037290	1C0000	3729	96776	.C38532	.135514	6987903	.000000	69.879	0
1	305074	476	.0C1560	.006222	96271	599	383587	.001562	1.500000	6891127	.000000	71.581	1
5	375769	241	.000641	.003198	95672	306	477595	.000641	2.500000	6507541	.000000	68.019	5
10	361288	159	.000440	.002202	95366	210	476331	.000441	2.623016	6C29946	-.003329	63.230	10
15	372809	337	.0C0904	.004519	95156	430	474780	.000906	2.674419	5553615	.014204	58.363	15
20	295213	356	.001206	.006017	94726	570	472225	.C01207	2.534722	5C78835	.017323	53.616	20
25	325754	364	.0C1117	.005576	94156	525	469480	.001118	2.524206	4606610	-.005685	48.925	25
30	324275	439	.0C1354	.006739	93631	631	466655	.001352	2.623481	4137130	-.002372	44.185	30
35	306823	594	.0C1936	.009667	93000	899	462865	.001942	2.625603	3670474	.022303	39.467	35
40	230447	587	.002547	.012736	92101	1173	457797	.002562	2.691461	3207609	.038013	34.827	40
45	213143	935	.0C4387	.021742	90928	1977	450C88	.004392	2.697585	2749812	.004549	30.242	45
50	236386	1649	.CC6976	.034266	88951	3048	437687	.006964	2.681158	2299724	-.008985	25.854	50
55	213772	2357	.011026	.053815	85903	4628	418852	.011049	2.695954	1862036	.010662	21.676	55
60	173120	2277	.018929	.091061	81275	7401	388980	.019027	2.649958	1443185	.026520	17.757	60
65	126176	3603	.028555	.134635	73874	9946	345782	.C28764	2.628423	1C54204	.040243	14.270	65
70	84828	3975	.046860	.211676	63928	13532	287016	.C47147	2.58C094	708422	.030228	11.082	70
75	61932	4565	.C7371C	.312187	50396	15733	213040	.073850	2.524921	421406	.009349	8.362	75
80	38120	4354	.114218	.444682	34663	15414	134671	.114457	2.492904	208367	.009349	6.011	80
85+	16861	4404	.261194	1.C00000	19249	19249	73696	.261194	3.828565	73696	.000000	3.829	85+

NUMBER OF PERSONS DYING (OUT OF 100,000 AT BIRTH) ABOVE AGE X FROM SPECIFIED CAUSES

Age (x)	All Causes	Respiratory T.B.	Other Infec. and Paras.	Neo-plasms	Cardio-vascular	Infl., Pneu., Bronch.	Diar-rheal	Certain Degen-erative	Maternal	Cert. Dis. of Infancy	Motor Vehicle	Other Violence	Other and Unknown	Age (x)
0	100000	2025	718	16375	28683	8023	499	6066	0	2185	1297	3438	30691	0
1	96271	2021	617	16358	28675	7432	365	6062	0	0	1295	3372	30074	1
5	95672	2019	540	16300	28659	7321	345	6057	0	0	1273	3281	29877	5
10	95366	2019	521	16240	28641	7301	342	6052	0	0	1235	3214	29801	10
15	95156	2019	509	16205	28625	7290	341	6048	0	0	1212	3160	29747	15
20	94726	2011	494	16163	28588	7277	341	6037	0	0	1117	3020	29678	20
25	94156	2004	485	16090	28550	7260	341	6017	0	0	960	2845	29604	25
30	93631	1986	480	16020	28499	7253	341	5989	0	0	839	2711	29523	30
35	93000	1930	472	15924	28432	7245	340	5945	0	0	720	2567	29425	35
40	92101	1841	455	15772	28298	7236	335	5865	0	0	631	2422	29246	40
45	90928	1775	431	15533	28072	7220	329	5731	0	0	541	2265	29031	45
50	88951	1629	389	15017	27617	7189	329	5530	0	0	478	2103	28670	50
55	85903	1477	352	14127	26830	7113	324	5225	0	0	404	1905	28146	55
60	81275	1314	314	12703	25567	6971	310	4768	0	0	322	1701	27305	60
65	73874	1007	265	10620	23413	6643	301	4048	0	0	250	1482	25845	65
70	63928	692	207	7932	20267	6086	279	3285	0	0	181	1224	23775	70
75	50396	403	153	5125	15707	5112	244	2211	0	0	117	962	20362	75
80	34663	166	108	2643	10324	3637	172	1278	0	0	62	721	15552	80
85+	19249	52	44	997	5324	2129	105	533	0	0	35	385	9645	85+

NUMBER OF PERSONS SURVIVING TO AGE X IF SPECIFIED CAUSES WERE ELIMINATED

Age (x)	No Causes	Respiratory T.B. (1)	Other Infec. and Paras. (2)	Neo-plasms (3)	Cardio-vascular (4)	Infl., Pneu., Bronch. (5)	Diar-rheal (6)	Certain Degenerative (7)	Maternal (8)	Cert. Dis. of Infancy (9)	Motor Vehicle (10)	Other Violence (11)	Other and Unknown (12)	(1)+(2)	(1)+(2)+(5)+(6)+(8)	(1)+(2)+(5)+(6)+(8)+part of(9)&(12)	(10)+(11)	Age (x)
0	100000	100000	100000	100000	100000	100000	100000	100000	100000	100000	100000	100000	100000	100000	100000	100000	100000	0
1	96271	96275	96370	96288	96279	96853	96403	96275	96271	98439	96273	96336	96878	96374	97089	99603	96338	1
5	95672	95678	95847	95746	95656	96361	95823	95681	95672	97826	95696	95827	96473	95853	96656	99207	95851	5
10	95366	95372	95560	95500	95408	96073	95519	95380	95366	97513	95428	95588	96241	95566	96429	99047	95650	10
15	95156	95162	95361	95325	95214	95873	95310	95174	95156	97299	95241	95431	96084	95367	96241	98862	95516	15
20	94726	94740	94945	94936	94820	95453	94879	94755	94726	96859	94905	95140	95719	94959	95842	98460	95320	20
25	94156	94177	94383	94438	94288	94895	94308	94204	94156	96276	94491	94743	95218	94404	95299	97907	95080	25
30	93631	93670	93862	93981	93823	94373	93782	93707	93631	95739	94085	94349	94769	93901	94798	97398	94807	30
35	93000	93094	93237	93444	93247	93745	93151	93120	93000	95094	93570	93858	94229	93332	94233	96881	94434	35
40	92101	92283	92353	92693	92480	92848	92256	92299	92101	94175	92755	93097	93499	92535	93443	96050	93758	40
45	90928	91173	91201	91752	91528	91682	91087	91257	90928	92975	91664	92069	92525	91447	92366	94569	92814	45
50	88951	89336	89259	90273	89992	89719	89106	89473	88951	90954	89734	90229	90877	89646	90578	93182	91023	50
55	85903	86425	86237	88072	87655	86720	86058	86709	85903	87837	86732	87335	88291	86761	87745	90325	88178	55
60	81275	81928	81628	84759	84234	82188	81435	82487	81275	83105	82140	82831	84379	82284	83373	85906	83713	60
65	73874	74763	74242	79138	78722	75021	74028	75675	73874	75537	74729	75501	78155	75135	76462	78958	76375	65
70	63928	64993	64301	71207	71314	65450	64082	66216	63928	65368	64733	65581	69702	65372	67090	69534	66406	70
75	50396	51495	50737	58958	60911	52491	50549	53192	50396	51531	51087	51936	58356	51844	54162	56590	52649	75
80	34663	35616	34935	42995	47613	37357	34828	37400	34663	35444	35184	35928	45030	35896	38912	41449	36468	80
85+	19249	19865	19448	25424	31999	21997	19390	21368	19249	19682	19558	20209	31329	20070	23103	25655	20534	85+

ADDED YRS OF LIFE

	No Causes	(1)	(2)	(3)	(4)	(5)	(6)	(7)	(8)	(9)	(10)	(11)	(12)	(1)+(2)	(1)+(2)+(5)+(6)+(8)	(1)+(2)+(5)+(6)+(8)+part of(9)&(12)	(10)+(11)
TOTAL		.352	.235	2.437	3.468	1.127	.140	.814	.000	1.571	.445	.867	4.301	.590	1.892	4.368	1.321
WORK	2.715	.133	.041	.558	.481	.056	.005	.212	.000	.000	.267	.384	.445	.174	.236	.286	.654

POPULATION, DEATHS, DEATH RATES FOR ALL CAUSES COMBINED, AND SPECIFIED CAUSES

Age Start of Interval	Midyear Population	Deaths During Year	All Causes	Respiratory T. B.	Other Infec. and Paras.	Neo-plasms	Cardio-vascular	Infl., Pneu., Bronch.	Diar-rheal	Certain Degen-erative	Maternal	Cert. Dis. of Infancy	Motor Vehicle	Other Violence	Other and Unknown	Age Start of Interval
0	73213	2484	.03393	.00003	.00058	.00007	.00005	.00579	.00163	.00005	.00000	.01919	.00001	.00044	.00568	0
1	288286	398	.00138	.00001	.00015	.00015	.00004	.00032	.00005	.00002	.00000	.00000	.00003	.00020	.00042	1
5	355183	152	.00043	.00000	.00003	.00008	.00003	.00006	.00000	.00001	.00000	.00000	.00004	.00007	.00012	5
10	342533	99	.00029	.00000	.00001	.00005	.00003	.00002	.00000	.00001	.00000	.00000	.00002	.00006	.00008	10
15	361797	154	.00043	.00000	.00001	.00006	.00005	.00001	.00000	.00003	.00001	.00000	.00000	.00009	.00014	15
20	297988	157	.00053	.00001	.00001	.00010	.00009	.00002	.00000	.00003	.00003	.00000	.00004	.00009	.00011	20
25	364190	265	.00073	.00006	.00002	.00014	.00011	.00003	.00000	.00003	.00004	.00000	.00003	.00008	.00019	25
30	363221	333	.00092	.00009	.00002	.00020	.00016	.00002	.00000	.00004	.00009	.00000	.00006	.00006	.00023	30
35	337740	447	.00132	.00007	.00003	.00044	.00023	.00002	.00000	.00011	.00005	.00000	.00002	.00010	.00025	35
40	254789	451	.00177	.00007	.00001	.00072	.00034	.00004	.00001	.00011	.00002	.00000	.00002	.00012	.00031	40
45	235567	633	.00269	.00005	.00003	.00109	.00060	.00006	.00001	.00022	.00000	.00000	.00005	.00011	.00048	45
50	254547	980	.00385	.00002	.00004	.00152	.00097	.00012	.00000	.00033	.00000	.00000	.00000	.00009	.00064	50
55	221949	1462	.00659	.00009	.00007	.00219	.00187	.00030	.00002	.00067	.00000	.00000	.00009	.00021	.00106	55
60	192046	2268	.01181	.00014	.00005	.00256	.00428	.00059	.00002	.00115	.00000	.00000	.00006	.00032	.00223	60
65	155674	2988	.01919	.00015	.00017	.00382	.00743	.00115	.00007	.00159	.00000	.00000	.00010	.00034	.00437	65
70	112526	4173	.03708	.00022	.00022	.00536	.01477	.00307	.00012	.00287	.00000	.00000	.00012	.00084	.00948	70
75	82563	5199	.06297	.00023	.00030	.00541	.02544	.00604	.00039	.00352	.00000	.00000	.00012	.00149	.02002	75
80	49628	5203	.10484	.00032	.00032	.00679	.04084	.01072	.00071	.00437	.00000	.00000	.00010	.00262	.03804	80
85+	27171	5904	.21729	.00026	.00074	.00729	.06971	.02274	.00132	.00526	.00000	.00000	.00007	.00534	.10456	85+
ALL	4370611	33750														

	All Causes	Respiratory T. B.	Other Infec. and Paras.	Neo-plasms	Cardio-vascular	Infl., Pneu., Bronch.	Diar-rheal	Certain Degen-erative	Maternal	Cert. Dis. of Infancy	Motor Vehicle	Other Violence	Other and Unknown
CRUDE DEATH RATE	.00772	.00006	.00007	.00102	.00247	.00068	.00006	.00043	.00002	.00032	.00004	.00023	.00230
STANDARDIZED RATE (1)	.00409	.00004	.00008	.00054	.00090	.00043	.00007	.00019	.00002	.00068	.00003	.00015	.00097
STANDARDIZED RATE (2)	.00714	.00006	.00008	.00096	.00223	.00064	.00007	.00040	.00002	.00040	.00004	.00022	.00203
GEOMETRIC MEAN	.00441												

LIFE TABLE FOR ALL CAUSES COMBINED

Age (x)	Midyear Population	Deaths During Year	$_nM_x$	$_nq_x$	l_x	$_nd_x$	$_nL_x$	$_nm_x$	$_na_x$	T_x	$_nr_x$	$\overset{\circ}{e}_x$	Age (x)
0	73213	2484	.033928	.032950	100000	3295	97126	.033925	.127678	7376488	.000000	73.765	0
1	288286	398	.001381	.005512	96705	533	385488	.001383	1.500000	7279362	.000000	75.274	1
5	355183	152	.000428	.002132	96172	205	480348	.000427	2.500000	6893875	.000000	71.683	5
10	342533	99	.000289	.001448	95967	139	479487	.000290	2.498501	6413527	-.004883	66.831	10
15	361797	154	.000426	.002129	95828	204	478653	.000426	2.614379	5934040	.010805	61.924	15
20	297988	157	.000527	.002625	95624	251	477522	.000526	2.617862	5455387	.006027	57.050	20
25	364190	265	.000728	.003628	95373	346	476038	.000727	2.610790	4977865	-.018055	52.194	25
30	363221	333	.000917	.004578	95027	435	474106	.000918	2.634100	4501826	-.003850	47.374	30
35	337740	447	.001324	.006618	94592	626	471478	.001323	2.632122	4027720	.023758	42.580	35
40	254789	451	.001770	.008854	93966	832	467879	.001778	2.654958	3556243	.038319	37.846	40
45	235567	633	.002687	.013368	93134	1245	462749	.002690	2.654116	3088364	.006925	33.160	45
50	254547	980	.003850	.019077	91889	1753	455415	.003849	2.700965	2625614	-.000436	28.574	50
55	221949	1462	.006587	.032573	90136	2936	444024	.006612	2.732814	2170200	.016104	24.077	55
60	192046	2268	.011810	.057729	87200	5034	424388	.011862	2.693228	1726176	.019965	19.796	60
65	155674	2988	.019194	.092557	82166	7605	393435	.019330	2.712689	1301788	.030324	15.843	65
70	112526	4173	.037085	.171645	74561	12798	342752	.037339	2.651782	908353	.027961	12.183	70
75	82563	5199	.062970	.274096	61763	16929	267726	.063233	2.572841	565601	.018647	9.158	75
80	49628	5203	.104840	.417473	44834	18717	177681	.105340	2.516229	297875	.018647	6.644	80
85+	27171	5904	.217290	1.000000	26117	26117	120194	.217290	4.602134	120194	.000000	4.602	85+

NUMBER OF PERSONS DYING (OUT OF 100,000 AT BIRTH) ABOVE AGE X FROM SPECIFIED CAUSES

Age (x)	All Causes	Respiratory T. B.	Other Infec. and Paras.	Neoplasms	Cardiovascular	Infl., Pneu., Bronch.	Diarrheal	Certain Degenerative	Maternal	Cert. Dis. of Infancy	Motor Vehicle	Other Violence	Other and Unknown	Age (x)
0	100000	591	674	11247	34441	9041	674	5219	120	1864	365	2689	33075	0
1	96705	588	578	11241	34436	8479	516	5213	120	0	364	2647	32523	1
5	96172	586	519	11184	34421	8357	496	5204	120	0	352	2571	32362	5
10	95967	586	507	11145	34406	8330	495	5198	120	0	334	2538	32308	10
15	95828	584	501	11121	34391	8322	494	5191	120	0	324	2512	32268	15
20	95624	583	497	11052	34368	8316	494	5177	114	0	313	2468	32202	20
25	95373	577	491	11046	34323	8308	494	5162	101	0	295	2426	32150	25
30	95027	547	481	10981	34272	8295	492	5148	82	0	280	2388	32061	30
35	94592	506	473	10887	34198	8287	491	5129	40	0	270	2360	31951	35
40	93966	473	459	10680	34087	8276	491	5078	15	0	260	2313	31834	40
45	93134	438	455	10340	33926	8260	487	5025	4	0	253	2258	31688	45
50	91889	414	443	9837	33647	8232	483	4924	2	0	231	2209	31467	50
55	90136	384	427	9143	33207	8177	476	4772	1	0	210	2168	31171	55
60	87200	344	395	8168	32370	8042	466	4473	1	0	170	2074	30697	60
65	82166	286	373	6908	30544	7789	457	3983	1	0	143	1936	29746	65
70	74561	228	304	5402	27600	7331	429	3353	1	0	103	1802	28008	70
75	61763	152	228	3560	22502	6268	389	2364	1	0	60	1510	24729	75
80	44834	90	147	2109	15664	4642	285	1419	1	0	27	1109	19341	80
85+	26117	31	88	876	8378	2734	159	633	0	0	9	641	12568	85+

NUMBER OF PERSONS SURVIVING TO AGE X IF SPECIFIED CAUSES WERE ELIMINATED

Age (x)	No Causes	Respiratory T. B.	Other Infec. and Paras.	Neoplasms	Cardiovascular	Infl., Pneu., Bronch.	Diarrheal	Certain Degenerative	Maternal	Cert. Dis. of Infancy	Motor Vehicle	Other Violence	Other and Unknown	(1) + (2)	(1) + (2) + (5) + (6) + (8)	(1)+(2)+ (5)+(6)+ (8)+part of(9)&(12)	(10) + (11)	Age (x)
		(1)	(2)	(3)	(4)	(5)	(6)	(7)	(8)	(9)	(10)	(11)	(12)					
0	100000	100000	100000	100000	100000	100000	100000	100000	100000	100000	100000	100000	100000	100000	100000	100000	100000	0
1	96705	96708	96799	96711	96710	97259	96860	96711	96705	98555	96706	96746	97249	96802	97514	99772	96747	1
5	96172	96177	96325	96235	96192	96684	96347	96187	96172	98012	96185	96289	96875	96330	97181	99521	96302	5
10	95967	95972	96132	96069	96002	96666	96142	95988	95967	97803	95958	96117	96723	96136	97014	99365	96148	10
15	95828	95835	95998	95953	95878	96534	96004	95856	95828	97662	95869	96004	96623	96005	96891	99246	96044	15
20	95624	95632	95798	95778	95697	96335	95800	95666	95630	97454	95676	95843	96484	95806	96701	99061	95895	20
25	95373	95387	95552	95573	95490	96090	95548	95392	95198	97198	95443	95634	96283	95566	96481	98844	95703	25
30	95027	95071	95216	95291	95155	95755	95204	95097	95065	96845	95111	95325	96023	95260	96206	98588	95409	30
35	94592	94677	94788	94949	94833	95324	94769	94681	94672	96402	94686	94916	95695	94873	95866	98276	95011	35
40	93966	94083	94175	94528	94317	94704	94142	94105	94070	95764	94069	94335	95179	94292	95316	97731	94439	40
45	93134	93285	93345	94032	93643	93882	93312	93325	93248	94916	93210	93555	94484	93496	94542	96554	93665	45
50	91889	92062	92109	93281	92670	92655	92069	92178	92004	93647	92019	92353	93444	92282	93349	95746	92484	50
55	90136	90335	90368	92202	91343	90942	90319	90571	90249	91861	90284	90632	91960	90567	91678	94055	90781	55
60	87200	87432	87456	90184	89206	88114	87387	87916	87310	88869	87263	87773	89442	87688	88909	91257	87957	60
65	82166	82441	82428	86250	85890	83276	82351	83322	82269	83738	82364	82841	85231	82704	84116	86418	83041	65
70	74561	74866	74865	79783	80927	76013	74756	76220	74655	75988	74779	75302	79080	75171	76931	79221	75522	70
75	61763	62084	62084	67894	72258	63961	61961	64060	61841	62945	61983	62646	68753	62407	64916	67277	62868	75
80	44834	45120	45135	50641	59691	47882	45067	47333	44890	45692	45021	45821	55282	45423	48824	51450	46012	80
85+	26117	26328	26337	30569	42912	29472	26348	28206	26151	26617	26240	27055	39159	26551	30265	33037	27182	85+

ADDED YRS OF LIFE																		
TOTAL		.128	.200	1.858	4.212	1.255	.175	.671	.054	1.409	.104	.459	4.607	.329	1.840	4.255	.564	
WORK	1.661	.057	.023	.504	.348	.048	.004	.121	.039	.000	.036	.112	.321	.080	.171	.218	.148	

POPULATION, DEATHS, DEATH RATES FOR ALL CAUSES COMBINED, AND SPECIFIED CAUSES

Age Start of Interval	Midyear Population	Deaths During Year	All Causes	Respiratory T.B.	Other Infec. and Paras.	Neoplasms	Cardiovascular	Infl., Pneu., Bronch.	Diarrheal	Certain Degenerative	Maternal	Cert. Dis. of Infancy	Motor Vehicle	Other Violence	Other and Unknown	Age Start of Interval
0	73600	9011	.12243	.00014	.01906	.00001	.00004	.02102	.01546	.00005	.00000	.05702	.00001	.00022	.00939	0
1	260500	7997	.03070	.00010	.01157	.00004	.00006	.00544	.00664	.00006	.00000	.00000	.00004	.00015	.00660	1
5	272600	2005	.00736	.00006	.00282	.00003	.00003	.00097	.00104	.00004	.00000	.00000	.00006	.00011	.00220	5
10	240800	910	.00378	.00005	.00120	.00001	.00004	.00058	.00042	.00002	.00000	.00000	.00004	.00022	.00121	10
15	209700	762	.00363	.00009	.00059	.00004	.00010	.00048	.00028	.00005	.00000	.00000	.00009	.00037	.00114	15
20	188300	853	.00453	.00028	.00054	.00005	.00012	.00049	.00034	.00005	.00000	.00000	.00022	.00085	.00116	20
25	152900	787	.00515	.00031	.00053	.00008	.00014	.00047	.00046	.00010	.00000	.00000	.00018	.00105	.00141	25
30	118200	921	.00779	.00058	.00144	.00010	.00021	.00088	.00056	.00016	.00000	.00000	.00030	.00118	.00237	30
35	109400	890	.00814	.00068	.00149	.00011	.00038	.00079	.00056	.00025	.00000	.00000	.00027	.00117	.00244	35
40	79600	831	.01044	.00070	.00200	.00028	.00062	.00119	.00083	.00036	.00000	.00000	.00030	.00102	.00314	40
45	74300	841	.01132	.00069	.00219	.00051	.00082	.00121	.00081	.00044	.00000	.00000	.00019	.00077	.00369	45
50	58300	800	.01372	.00063	.00226	.00062	.00106	.00163	.00111	.00062	.00000	.00000	.00019	.00105	.00455	50
55	43200	839	.01942	.00086	.00333	.00093	.00164	.00229	.00169	.00065	.00000	.00000	.00032	.00097	.00674	55
60	38800	1273	.03281	.00116	.00508	.00183	.00289	.00459	.00278	.00137	.00000	.00000	.00046	.00116	.01149	60
65	20400	962	.04716	.00157	.00603	.00216	.00456	.00716	.00510	.00206	.00000	.00000	.00025	.00058	.01730	65
70	11400	769	.06746	.00167	.00842	.00360	.00649	.01000	.00640	.00228	.00000	.00000	.00026	.00114	.02719	70
75	7300	644	.08822	.00164	.01014	.00452	.01096	.01370	.00863	.00233	.00000	.00000	.00014	.00137	.03479	75
80	4900	529	.10796	.00184	.01510	.00551	.01306	.01531	.00694	.00143	.00000	.00000	.00000	.00082	.04796	80
85+	3900	576	.14769	.00256	.01308	.00308	.01590	.02282	.00846	.00282	.00000	.00000	.00051	.00231	.07615	85+
ALL	1968100	32200														

	All Causes	Respiratory T.B.	Other Infec. and Paras.	Neoplasms	Cardiovascular	Infl., Pneu., Bronch.	Diarrheal	Certain Degenerative	Maternal	Cert. Dis. of Infancy	Motor Vehicle	Other Violence	Other and Unknown
CRUDE DEATH RATE	.01636	.00032	.00383	.00022	.00045	.00249	.00216	.00020	.00000	.00213	.00014	.00059	.00381
STANDARDIZED RATE (1)	.01672	.00036	.00376	.00028	.00056	.00252	.00213	.00025	.00000	.00201	.00015	.00062	.00407
STANDARDIZED RATE (2)	.01901	.00051	.00364	.00055	.00114	.00276	.00209	.00042	.00000	.00118	.00018	.00074	.00580
GEOMETRIC MEAN	.01932												

LIFE TABLE FOR ALL CAUSES COMBINED

Age (x)	Midyear Population	Deaths During Year	$_nM_x$	$_nq_x$	l_x	$_nd_x$	$_nL_x$	$_nm_x$	$_na_x$	T_x	$_nr_x$	$\overset{\circ}{e}_x$	Age (x)
0	73600	9011	.122432	.112490	100000	11249	91880	.122432	.278135	4838468	.000000	48.385	0
1	260500	7997	.030699	.114038	88751	10121	329702	.030697	1.500000	4746588	.000000	53.482	1
5	272600	2005	.007355	.036208	78630	2847	386033	.007375	2.500000	4416887	.000000	56.173	5
10	240800	910	.003779	.018619	75783	1411	375074	.003762	2.277640	4030854	.016784	53.189	10
15	209700	762	.003634	.018031	74372	1341	368555	.003639	2.535266	3655781	.019472	49.155	15
20	188300	853	.004530	.022429	73031	1638	361160	.004535	2.561304	3287226	.022316	45.011	20
25	152900	787	.005147	.025535	71393	1823	352622	.005170	2.617595	2926066	.039449	40.985	25
30	118200	921	.007792	.038335	69570	2667	341359	.007813	2.566320	2573444	.028496	36.991	30
35	109400	890	.008135	.039938	66903	2672	327962	.008147	2.547561	2232084	.030149	33.363	35
40	79600	831	.010440	.051019	64231	3277	313106	.010466	2.543676	1904122	.031639	29.645	40
45	74300	841	.011319	.055107	60954	3359	296490	.011329	2.534919	1591017	.017748	26.102	45
50	58300	800	.013722	.066672	57595	3840	278719	.013777	2.589572	1294527	.038990	22.476	50
55	43200	839	.019421	.093201	53755	5010	257003	.019494	2.650366	1015808	.021748	18.897	55
60	38800	1273	.032809	.152959	48745	7456	225875	.033009	2.605983	758804	.031133	15.567	60
65	20400	962	.047157	.213204	41289	8803	184849	.047623	2.546717	532929	.069753	12.907	65
70	11400	769	.067456	.290279	32486	9430	138748	.067965	2.488644	348081	.049812	10.715	70
75	7300	644	.088219	.359516	23056	8289	93887	.088287	2.419170	209333	.006386	9.079	75
80	4900	529	.107959	.420803	14767	6214	57534	.108005	2.376757	115445	.006386	7.818	80
85+	3900	576	.147692	1.000000	8553	8553	57911	.147692	6.770833	57911	.000000	6.771	85+

NUMBER OF PERSONS DYING (OUT OF 100,000 AT BIRTH) ABOVE AGE X FROM SPECIFIED CAUSES

Age (x)	All Causes	Respiratory T.B.	Other Infec. and Paras.	Neoplasms	Cardio-vascular	Infl., Pneu., Bronch.	Diarrheal	Certain Degenerative	Maternal	Cert. Dis. of Infancy	Motor Vehicle	Other Violence	Other and Unknown	Age (x)
0	100000	2773	17927	3054	6652	14445	10358	2323	0	5239	941	3820	32468	0
1	88751	2760	16176	3053	6648	12514	8938	2318	0	0	940	3800	31604	1
5	78630	2728	12360	3039	6629	10720	6749	2297	0	0	926	3752	29430	5
10	75783	2704	11269	3028	6618	10345	6348	2282	0	0	904	3708	28577	10
15	74372	2687	10824	3023	6602	10128	6193	2274	0	0	889	3627	28125	15
20	73031	2653	10458	3007	6567	9951	6089	2255	0	0	855	3491	27705	20
25	71393	2551	10119	2990	6524	9774	5966	2237	0	0	776	3167	27289	25
30	69570	2442	9791	2962	6473	9607	5802	2200	0	0	712	2795	26786	30
35	66903	2242	9298	2927	6401	9306	5611	2145	0	0	607	2390	25976	35
40	64231	2020	8809	2891	6274	9048	5428	2063	0	0	518	2007	25173	40
45	60954	1800	8182	2804	6080	8673	5168	1949	0	0	423	1689	24186	45
50	57595	1596	7531	2652	5836	8314	4928	1817	0	0	368	1462	23091	50
55	53755	1419	6898	2479	5538	7857	4615	1644	0	0	315	1169	21821	55
60	48745	1199	6039	2240	5114	7265	4179	1477	0	0	231	919	20082	60
65	41289	936	4887	1824	4458	6221	3546	1166	0	0	126	657	17468	65
70	32486	644	3766	1423	3605	4884	2591	782	0	0	82	477	14232	70
75	23056	412	2590	919	2696	3486	1697	465	0	0	46	318	10427	75
80	14767	258	1638	494	1666	2199	887	247	0	0	33	190	7155	80
85+	8553	148	757	178	921	1322	490	163	0	0	30	134	4410	85+

NUMBER OF PERSONS SURVIVING TO AGE X IF SPECIFIED CAUSES WERE ELIMINATED

Age (x)	No Causes	Respiratory T.B.	Other Infec. and Paras.	Neoplasms	Cardio-vascular	Infl., Pneu., Bronch.	Diarrheal	Certain Degenerative	Maternal	Cert. Dis. of Infancy	Motor Vehicle	Other Violence	Other and Unknown	(1)+(2)	(1)+(2)+(5)+(6)+(8)	(1)+(2)+(5)+(6)+(8)+part of(9)&(12)	(10)+(11)	Age (x)
		(1)	(2)	(3)	(4)	(5)	(6)	(7)	(8)	(9)	(10)	(11)	(12)					
0	100000	100000	100000	100000	100000	100000	100000	100000	100000	100000	100000	100000	100000	100000	100000	100000	100000	0
1	88751	88763	90415	88752	88755	90588	90098	88756	88751	93823	88752	88770	89568	90427	93700	99928	88771	1
5	78630	78671	83846	78644	78651	81958	81941	78654	78630	83124	78644	78692	81445	83890	91168	99752	78706	5
10	75783	75846	81960	75807	75814	79414	79386	75821	75783	80114	75818	75886	79368	82029	90046	99562	75921	10
15	74372	74451	80912	74401	74419	78161	78069	74417	74372	78622	74421	74553	78361	80998	89356	99318	74603	15
20	73031	73142	79849	73075	73111	76937	76765	73094	73031	77205	73113	73344	77388	79970	88559	98848	73427	20
25	71393	71603	78425	71453	71514	75115	75175	71472	71393	76022	71222	72022	76089	78656	87466	97969	72182	25
30	69570	69882	76779	69656	69739	73645	73427	69684	69570	73546	69788	70554	74677	77124	86166	96915	70775	30
35	66903	67401	74371	67020	67136	71134	70810	67067	66903	70727	67216	68253	72672	74925	84315	95554	68572	35
40	64231	64928	71936	64379	64580	68563	68172	64469	64231	67902	64619	65911	70630	72717	82383	94072	66309	40
45	60954	61833	68953	61180	61415	65456	64963	61291	60954	64415	62866		68092	69947	80053	92350	63342	45
50	57595	58627	65873	57957	58328	62225	61632	58043	57595	60887	58085	59630	65540	67052	77520	90495	60137	50
55	53755	54892	62184	54261	54731	58555	57848	54342	53755	56827	54264	55948	62582	63499	74435	88122	56477	55
60	48745	49990	57341	49434	50043	53716	52905	49438	48745	51531	49287	50581	58710	58806	70333	85107	51548	60
65	41289	42592	49830	42262	43013	46571	46167		41289	43649	41845	43434	52711	51402	63820	80153	44019	65
70	32486	33778	40419	33617	34638	38001	36702	33525	32486	34343	32962	34340	45299	42026	55542	73978	34844	70
75	23056	24174	29937	24300	25412	28376	26907	24067	23056	24374	23424	24513	36925	31389	45087	65780	24904	75
80	14767	15611	20182	15923	17207	19477	17998	15594	14767	15611	15013	15808	28202	21335	34298	55590	16071	80
85+	8553	9130	12630	9482	10641	12185	10795	9099	8553	9042	8698	9201	20791	13482	24241	46323	9357	85+

ADDED YRS OF LIFE

	No Causes	(1)	(2)	(3)	(4)	(5)	(6)	(7)	(8)	(9)	(10)	(11)	(12)	(1)+(2)	(1)+(2)+(5)+(6)+(8)	+part	(10)+(11)
TOTAL		.610	6.325	.443	.949	4.053	3.370	.394	.000	2.750	.261	1.082	8.752	7.080	17.076	35.195	1.354
WORK	8.010	.413	1.372	.167	.332	.777	.539	.188	.000	.000	.205	.872	2.190	1.808	3.244	4.810	1.083

POPULATION, DEATHS, DEATH RATES FOR ALL CAUSES COMBINED, AND SPECIFIED CAUSES

Age Start of Interval	Midyear Population	Deaths During Year	All Causes	Respiratory T. B.	Other Infec. and Paras.	Neo-plasms	Cardio-vascular	Infl., Pneu., Bronch.	Diar-rheal	Certain Degen-erative	Maternal	Cert. Dis. of Infancy	Motor Vehicle	Other Violence	Other and Unknown	Age Start of Interval
0	69900	7431	.10631	.00007	.01801	.00003	.00007	.01853	.01567	.00003	.00000	.04574	.00000	.00016	.00801	0
1	250100	8187	.03273	.00010	.01305	.00002	.00003	.00578	.00686	.00006	.00000	.00000	.00003	.00013	.00666	1
5	257700	2078	.00806	.00005	.00308	.00001	.00001	.00117	.00122	.00006	.00000	.00000	.00004	.00007	.00235	5
10	217300	752	.00346	.00004	.00114	.00003	.00003	.00057	.00039	.00004	.00000	.00000	.00001	.00008	.00112	10
15	217200	793	.00365	.00014	.00092	.00002	.00010	.00056	.00029	.00001	.00030	.00000	.00000	.00010	.00121	15
20	196900	955	.00485	.00028	.00107	.00000	.00011	.00069	.00032	.00006	.00048	.00000	.00002	.00012	.00165	20
25	152600	920	.00603	.00037	.00140	.00009	.00022	.00085	.00052	.00005	.00047	.00000	.00003	.00018	.00186	25
30	109000	944	.00866	.00057	.00174	.00029	.00036	.00121	.00069	.00017	.00088	.00000	.00007	.00014	.00253	30
35	108000	898	.00831	.00045	.00173	.00039	.00039	.00112	.00066	.00016	.00069	.00000	.00005	.00017	.00252	35
40	84600	775	.00916	.00046	.00162	.00067	.00048	.00129	.00087	.00018	.00046	.00000	.00004	.00020	.00288	40
45	71400	724	.01014	.00043	.00160	.00095	.00074	.00125	.00095	.00020	.00017	.00000	.00006	.00008	.00371	45
50	60000	840	.01400	.00060	.00240	.00103	.00095	.00203	.00135	.00032	.00000	.00000	.00003	.00013	.00515	50
55	38300	764	.01995	.00078	.00303	.00138	.00149	.00253	.00198	.00081	.00000	.00000	.00000	.00018	.00762	55
60	36700	1252	.03411	.00063	.00510	.00199	.00309	.00526	.00354	.00112	.00000	.00000	.00003	.00038	.01300	60
65	17500	936	.05349	.00120	.00703	.00440	.00531	.00640	.00554	.00183	.00006	.00000	.00011	.00040	.02120	65
70	12400	819	.06605	.00089	.00645	.00476	.00694	.01056	.00556	.00185	.00000	.00000	.00024	.00048	.02831	70
75	7200	615	.08542	.00056	.00847	.00361	.01250	.01222	.00833	.00222	.00000	.00000	.00014	.00111	.03625	75
80	6500	668	.10277	.00092	.01092	.00415	.01138	.01554	.00800	.00138	.00000	.00000	.00000	.00154	.04892	80
85+	4300	736	.17116	.00140	.01047	.00465	.02326	.02372	.01116	.00186	.00000	.00000	.00023	.00047	.09395	85+
ALL	1917600	31087														

CRUDE DEATH RATE			.01621	.00027	.00399	.00034	.00049	.00258	.00225	.00016	.00024	.00167	.00003	.00014	.00406	
STANDARDIZED RATE (1)			.01663	.00029	.00393	.00042	.00059	.00262	.00225	.00020	.00024	.00161	.00004	.00015	.00431	
STANDARDIZED RATE (2)			.01915	.00038	.00367	.00076	.00121	.00268	.00222	.00034	.00024	.00095	.00005	.00015	.00626	
GEOMETRIC MEAN			.01962													

LIFE TABLE FOR ALL CAUSES COMBINED

Age (x)	Midyear Population	Deaths During Year	$_nM_x$	$_nq_x$	l_x	$_nd_x$	$_nL_x$	$_nm_x$	$_na_x$	T_x	$_nr_x$	$\overset{\circ}{e}_x$	Age (x)
0	69900	7431	.106309	.098470	100000	9847	92622	.106314	.250725	4834681	.000000	48.347	0
1	250100	8187	.022735	.121028	90153	10911	333335	.032733	1.500000	4742059	.000000	52.600	1
5	257700	2078	.008064	.039600	79242	3138	388365	.008080	2.500000	4408724	.000000	55.636	5
10	217300	752	.003461	.017082	76104	1300	376898	.003449	2.214103	4020359	.011425	52.827	10
15	217200	793	.003651	.018101	74804	1354	370732	.003652	2.571393	3643461	.004123	48.707	15
20	196900	955	.004850	.024016	73450	1764	363004	.004859	2.592947	3272729	.019525	44.557	20
25	152600	920	.006029	.029866	71686	2141	353326	.006060	2.616087	2909725	.049173	40.590	25
30	109000	944	.008661	.042519	69545	2957	340451	.008686	2.540229	2556399	.034277	36.759	30
35	108000	898	.008315	.040728	66588	2712	326141	.008315	2.492856	2215948	.017348	33.278	35
40	84600	775	.009161	.044837	63876	2864	312285	.009171	2.522696	1889807	.031558	29.586	40
45	71400	724	.010140	.049564	61012	3024	297727	.010157	2.574956	1577522	.020265	25.856	45
50	60000	840	.014000	.068152	57988	3952	280568	.014089	2.613339	1279795	.045732	22.070	50
55	38300	764	.019948	.095751	54036	5174	258039	.020051	2.653532	999288	.029723	18.493	55
60	36700	1252	.034114	.158917	48862	7765	225859	.034380	2.623873	741248	.037139	15.170	60
65	17500	936	.053486	.238241	41097	9791	181238	.054023	2.523576	515389	.056684	12.541	65
70	12400	819	.066048	.283428	31306	8873	133942	.066245	2.454309	334150	.036166	10.674	70
75	7200	615	.085417	.349708	22433	7845	91936	.085331	2.421447	200208	-.009222	8.925	75
80	6500	668	.102769	.405470	14588	5915	57601	.102689	2.406770	108272	-.009222	7.422	80
85+	4300	736	.171163	1.000000	8673	8673	50671	.171163	5.842391	50671	.000000	5.842	85+

NUMBER OF PERSONS DYING (OUT OF 100,000 AT BIRTH) ABOVE AGE X FROM SPECIFIED CAUSES

Age (x)	All Causes	Respiratory T. B.	Other Infec. and Paras.	Neo-plasms	Cardio-vascular	Infl., Pneu., Bronch.	Diar-rheal	Certain Degen-erative	Maternal	Cert. Dis. of Infancy	Motor Vehicle	Other Violence	Other and Unknown	Age (x)
0	100000	2008	17729	4163	7051	14859	11030	1842	1181	4236	247	975	34679	0
1	90153	2002	16061	4160	7044	13143	9579	1840	1181	0	247	960	33936	1
5	79242	1967	11710	4152	7033	11216	7292	1821	1181	0	236	916	31718	5
10	76104	1948	10511	4148	7030	10760	6817	1798	1181	0	220	888	30803	10
15	74804	1932	10083	4137	7018	10547	6671	1784	1179	0	214	856	30383	15
20	73450	1879	9741	4129	6981	10341	6565	1779	1068	0	214	819	29934	20
25	71686	1777	9352	4106	6940	10091	6449	1759	894	0	207	776	29335	25
30	69545	1644	8856	4076	6863	9791	6262	1740	729	0	195	714	28675	30
35	66588	1450	8261	3975	6740	9378	6027	1680	428	0	170	667	27812	35
40	63876	1302	7697	3848	6613	9012	5813	1629	205	0	155	612	26990	40
45	61012	1158	7192	3636	6461	8610	5539	1574	62	0	144	550	26086	45
50	57988	1029	6716	3352	6240	8238	5255	1515	13	0	127	525	24978	50
55	54036	860	6038	3061	5972	7664	4874	1425	13	0	118	487	23524	55
60	48862	657	5253	2703	5585	7006	4359	1215	13	0	84	440	21547	60
65	41097	516	4095	2249	4883	5810	3552	961	13	0	78	353	18587	65
70	31306	296	2813	1441	3908	4640	2539	626	3	0	57	280	14703	70
75	22433	178	1949	804	2574	3218	1793	378	3	0	24	215	10897	75
80	14588	127	1171	472	1826	2095	1027	174	3	0	12	113	7568	80
85+	8673	71	530	236	1178	1202	566	94	0	0	12	24	4760	85+

NUMBER OF PERSONS SURVIVING TO AGE X IF SPECIFIED CAUSES WERE ELIMINATED

Age (x)	No Causes	Respiratory T. B.	Other Infec. and Paras.	Neo-plasms	Cardio-vascular	Infl., Pneu., Bronch.	Diar-rheal	Certain Degen-erative	Maternal	Cert. Dis. of Infancy	Motor Vehicle	Other Violence	Other and Unknown	(1)+(2)	(1)+(2) +(5)+ (6)+(8)	(1)+(2)+ (5)+(6)+ (8)+part of(9)&(12)	(10) +(11)	Age (x)
		(1)	(2)	(3)	(4)	(5)	(6)	(7)	(8)	(9)	(10)	(11)	(12)					
0	100000	100000	100000	100000	100000	100000	100000	100000	100000	100000	100000	100000	100000	100000	100000	100000	100000	0
1	90153	90159	91750	90156	90160	91796	91541	90155	90153	94264	90153	90167	90861	91756	94867	99943	90167	1
5	79242	79280	84903	79252	79258	82546	82667	79261	79242	82856	79252	79296	81986	84943	92310	99805	79306	5
10	76104	76159	82810	76118	76122	79744	79881	76145	76104	79575	76130	76183	79673	82869	91142	99671	76209	10
15	74804	74874	81859	74828	74834	78603	78668	74858	74806	78215	74835	74914	78749	81934	90546	99524	74945	15
20	73450	73571	80748	73482	73516	77395	77355	73508	73562	76800	73481	73594	77793	80881	89893	99350	73625	20
25	71686	71905	79232	71740	71791	75797	75618	71763	71968	74955	71723	71865	76554	80127	89073	99072	71906	25
30	69545	69889	77407	69627	69723	73847	73554	69638	69982	72716	69592	69784	74965	77791	87912	98667	69832	30
35	66588	67105	74767	66765	66879	71137	70670	66736	67303	69625	66658	66863	72694	75352	86351	97940	66933	35
40	63876	64522	72345	64171	64281	68624	68015	64068	64783	66789	63958	64194	70618	73076	84781	97135	64276	40
45	61012	61771	69662	61503	61548	65970	65251	61250	62020	63794	61101	61377	68435	70528	82905	96022	61466	45
50	57988	58837	66741	58734	58715	63094	62313	58272	58994	60632	58089	58359	66267	67718	80550	94490	58461	50
55	54036	54993	62950	55016	54976	59400	58463	54388	54973	56500	54139	54419	63375	64064	77515	92650	54522	55
60	48862	49923	57798	50096	50089	54404	53398	49382	49710	51090	48987	49253	59554	59053	73101	89676	49379	60
65	41097	42121	49892	42564	42794	46993	45727	41769	41810	42971	41208	41506	53506	51125	66175	84942	41618	65
70	31306	32282	39371	33161	33495	36981	35826	32115	31858	32734	31409	31682	45410	40599	55850	76698	31786	70
75	22433	23234	29137	24334	24863	27958	26399	23227	22828	23456	22535	22758	37547	30177	45040	67607	22861	75
80	14588	15150	19775	16110	17224	19333	17905	15273	14845	15253	14663	14883	29315	20537	33997	56971	14960	80
85+	8673	9052	12438	9779	10840	12433	11085	9145	8828	9069	8718	8918	22308	12982	24212	47766	8964	85+

ADDED YRS OF LIFE																	
TOTAL		.488	6.550	.656	.962	4.240	3.541	.299	.422	2.194	.062	.239	9.267	7.143	18.004	35.045	.301
WORK	8.183	.364	1.441	.308	.337	.999	.606	.124	.442	.000	.033	.135	2.431	1.825	4.073	6.300	.168

POPULATION, DEATHS, DEATH RATES FOR ALL CAUSES COMBINED, AND SPECIFIED CAUSES

Age Start of Interval	Midyear Population	Deaths During Year	All Causes	Respiratory T.B.	Other Infec. and Paras.	Neoplasms	Cardiovascular	Infl., Pneu., Bronch.	Diarrheal	Certain Degenerative	Maternal	Cert. Dis. of Infancy	Motor Vehicle	Other Violence	Other and Unknown	Age Start of Interval
0	80504	9443	.11730	.00005	.01553	.00005	.00011	.02256	.01635	.00005	.00000	.05248	.00001	.00015	.00996	0
1	303994	7911	.02602	.00008	.00862	.00003	.00009	.00513	.00604	.00004	.00000	.00000	.00003	.00018	.00579	1
5	344091	2247	.00653	.00005	.00206	.00002	.00005	.00105	.00123	.00003	.00000	.00000	.00003	.00011	.00188	5
10	282019	942	.00334	.00005	.00089	.00004	.00008	.00046	.00043	.00002	.00000	.00000	.00004	.00020	.00113	10
15	208724	980	.00470	.00017	.00108	.00002	.00010	.00067	.00039	.00003	.00000	.00000	.00014	.00072	.00138	15
20	166332	901	.00542	.00031	.00099	.00009	.00010	.00063	.00033	.00010	.00000	.00000	.00017	.00120	.00149	20
25	142576	952	.00668	.00038	.00118	.00011	.00024	.00084	.00053	.00012	.00000	.00000	.00019	.00135	.00175	25
30	133176	1037	.00779	.00047	.00143	.00008	.00026	.00058	.00058	.00016	.00000	.00000	.00023	.00116	.00243	30
35	119067	1063	.00893	.00049	.00153	.00018	.00040	.00102	.00073	.00031	.00000	.00000	.00024	.00123	.00280	35
40	93938	1003	.01068	.00053	.00188	.00031	.00046	.00134	.00100	.00036	.00000	.00000	.00015	.00110	.00354	40
45	75466	1067	.01414	.00082	.00239	.00044	.00097	.00167	.00118	.00042	.00000	.00000	.00019	.00115	.00488	45
50	59123	1043	.01764	.00074	.00310	.00079	.00096	.00225	.00178	.00076	.00000	.00000	.00025	.00113	.00587	50
55	43498	950	.02184	.00087	.00280	.00120	.00237	.00276	.00207	.00099	.00000	.00000	.00011	.00122	.00745	55
60	43109	1541	.03575	.00125	.00538	.00169	.00332	.00464	.00353	.00057	.00000	.00000	.00028	.00102	.01366	60
65	25210	1161	.04605	.00131	.00567	.00198	.00464	.00686	.00452	.00190	.00000	.00000	.00016	.00099	.01761	65
70	16527	1089	.06589	.00103	.00720	.00303	.00702	.01083	.00563	.00224	.00000	.00000	.00073	.00145	.02674	70
75	9727	773	.07947	.00123	.00843	.00288	.01038	.01234	.00874	.00195	.00000	.00000	.00031	.00247	.03074	75
80	5141	614	.11943	.00097	.01089	.00428	.01478	.01692	.00817	.00078	.00000	.00000	.00019	.00175	.06069	80
85+	4014	640	.15944	.00075	.01071	.00523	.01146	.02143	.01196	.00448	.00000	.00000	.00025	.00149	.09168	85+
ALL	2156236	35357														

	All Causes	Respiratory T.B.	Other Infec. and Paras.	Neoplasms	Cardiovascular	Infl., Pneu., Bronch.	Diarrheal	Certain Degenerative	Maternal	Cert. Dis. of Infancy	Motor Vehicle	Other Violence	Other and Unknown
CRUDE DEATH RATE	.01640	.00030	.00329	.00023	.00051	.00270	.00232	.00021	.00000	.00196	.00012	.00067	.00408
STANDARDIZED RATE (1)	.01652	.00034	.00317	.00028	.00061	.00267	.00222	.00025	.00000	.00185	.00013	.00075	.00425
STANDARDIZED RATE (2)	.01927	.00046	.00318	.00052	.00121	.00293	.00222	.00041	.00000	.00109	.00016	.00089	.00621
GEOMETRIC MEAN	.02042												

LIFE TABLE FOR ALL CAUSES COMBINED

Age (x)	Midyear Population	Deaths During Year	$_nM_x$	$_nq_x$	l_x	$_nd_x$	$_nL_x$	$_nm_x$	$_na_x$	T_x	$_nr_x$	$\overset{\circ}{e}_x$	Age (x)
0	80504	9443	.117299	.108040	100000	10804	92107	.117299	.269407	4850686	.000000	48.507	0
1	303994	7911	.026024	.097740	89196	8718	334989	.026025	1.500000	4758579	.000000	53.350	1
5	344091	2247	.006530	.032245	80478	2595	395903	.006555	2.500000	4423590	.000000	54.966	5
10	282019	942	.003340	.016425	77883	1280	386047	.003316	2.368490	4027688	.034009	51.715	10
15	208724	980	.004695	.023329	76603	1787	378698	.004719	2.584406	3641641	.047272	47.539	15
20	166332	901	.005417	.026786	74816	2004	369197	.005428	2.563311	3262943	.038573	43.613	20
25	142576	952	.006677	.032907	72812	2396	358213	.006689	2.559822	2893746	.022400	39.743	25
30	133176	1037	.007787	.038230	70416	2692	345648	.007792	2.543803	2535532	.010673	36.008	30
35	119067	1063	.008928	.043736	67724	2962	331358	.008939	2.548391	2190064	.020609	32.338	35
40	93938	1003	.010677	.052191	64762	3380	315620	.010709	2.576800	1858706	.032287	28.701	40
45	75466	1067	.014139	.068554	61382	4208	296697	.014183	2.572877	1543086	.030081	25.139	45
50	59123	1043	.017641	.084864	57174	4852	273597	.017708	2.552899	1246390	.041208	21.800	50
55	43498	950	.021840	.103972	52322	5440	248609	.021882	2.610064	972793	.014453	18.585	55
60	43109	1541	.035747	.164757	46882	7726	215655	.035826	2.572536	723784	.013214	15.438	60
65	25210	1161	.046053	.207631	39156	8130	175690	.046277	2.527650	508129	.042939	12.977	65
70	16527	1089	.065892	.283794	31026	8805	132956	.066225	2.481639	332449	.033532	10.715	70
75	9727	773	.079470	.330948	22221	7354	92306	.079670	2.443738	199493	.032262	8.978	75
80	5141	614	.119432	.458667	14867	6819	56711	.120241	2.415463	107187	.032262	7.210	80
85+	4014	640	.159442	1.000000	8048	8048	50476	.159442	6.271875	50476	.000000	6.272	85+

NUMBER OF PERSONS DYING (OUT OF 100,000 AT BIRTH) ABOVE AGE X FROM SPECIFIED CAUSES

Age (x)	All Causes	Respiratory T.B.	Other Infec. and Paras.	Neoplasms	Cardiovascular	Infl., Pneu., Bronch.	Diarrheal	Certain Degenerative	Maternal	Cert. Dis. of Infancy	Motor Vehicle	Other Violence	Other and Unknown	Age (x)
0	100000	2395	15601	2847	6621	14929	11015	2280	0	4835	824	4522	34131	0
1	89196	2391	14171	2842	6611	12851	9509	2276	0	1	822	4508	33214	1
5	80478	2364	11285	2831	6580	11134	7487	2264	0	0	813	4446	31274	5
10	77883	2343	10466	2823	6559	10717	6997	2251	0	0	799	4401	30527	10
15	76603	2323	10127	2810	6529	10542	6836	2243	0	0	782	4322	30089	15
20	74816	2258	9718	2800	6491	10289	6690	2232	0	0	729	4046	29563	20
25	72812	2142	9354	2767	6453	10058	6567	2194	0	0	664	3599	29014	25
30	70416	2006	8931	2729	6367	9756	6376	2151	0	0	596	3117	28387	30
35	67724	1843	8435	2701	6279	9416	6176	2096	0	0	516	2718	27544	35
40	64762	1681	7928	2639	6145	9079	5933	1993	0	0	438	2309	26617	40
45	61382	1512	7332	2541	5999	8654	5617	1879	0	0	391	1963	25494	45
50	57174	1268	6622	2410	5711	8157	5265	1752	0	0	336	1609	24044	50
55	52322	1064	5772	2191	5445	7538	4776	1542	0	0	267	1298	22429	55
60	46882	847	5073	1893	4855	6851	4261	1296	0	0	238	996	20572	60
65	39156	576	3910	1527	4138	5848	3499	1086	0	0	178	776	17618	65
70	31026	347	2912	1177	3317	4633	2631	749	0	0	150	601	14509	70
75	22221	210	1951	773	2378	3185	1879	450	0	0	53	407	10935	75
80	14867	96	1172	508	1416	2045	1070	271	0	0	25	178	8086	80
85+	8048	38	541	264	578	1081	604	226	0	0	13	75	4628	85+

NUMBER OF PERSONS SURVIVING TO AGE X IF SPECIFIED CAUSES WERE ELIMINATED

Age (x)	No Causes	Respiratory T.B. (1)	Other Infec. and Paras. (2)	Neoplasms (3)	Cardiovascular (4)	Infl., Pneu., Bronch. (5)	Diarrheal (6)	Certain Degenerative (7)	Maternal (8)	Cert. Dis. of Infancy (9)	Motor Vehicle (10)	Other Violence (11)	Other and Unknown (12)	(1)+(2)	(1)+(2)+(5)+(6)+(8)	(1)+(2)+(5)+(6)+(8)+part of(9)&(12)	(10)+(11)	Age (x)
0	100000	100000	100000	100000	100000	100000	100000	100000	100000	100000	100000	100000	100000	100000	100000	100000	100000	0
1	89196	89200	90556	89201	89205	91179	90629	89200	89196	93878	89198	89209	90066	90560	94061	99921	89211	1
5	80478	80507	84535	80493	80516	83551	83745	80493	80478	84703	80488	80549	83144	84565	91796	99731	80559	5
10	77883	77932	82660	77905	77940	81673	81548	77910	77883	81972	77907	77996	81226	82712	90818	99553	78019	10
15	76603	76671	81659	76638	76685	80513	80375	76638	76603	80625	76643	76793	80345	81731	90133	99265	76833	15
20	74816	74947	80186	74860	74938	78898	78651	74861	74816	78744	74908	75275	79018	80326	89051	98546	75368	20
25	72812	73054	78424	72887	72568	77025	76612	72893	72812	76635	72965	73704	77475	78684	87650	97411	73859	25
30	70416	70784	76292	70526	70652	74805	74347	70537	70416	74113	70631	71760	75585	76691	86020	96099	71979	30
35	67724	68239	73905	67657	68038	72301	71712	67894	67724	71279	68010	69416	73589	74467	84181	94791	69709	35
40	64762	65414	71215	64950	65194	69491	68828	65026	64762	68162	65112	66791	71362	71933	82031	93168	67152	40
45	61382	62167	68139	61656	61935	66310	65564	61744	61382	64605	61760	63653	68853	69010	79629	91522	64045	45
50	57174	58144	64233	57557	57970	62284	61433	57634	57174	60176	57579	59644	65722	65323	76462	89298	60067	50
55	52322	53408	59702	52884	53310	57647	56724	52946	52322	55069	52759	54893	61946	60941	72793	86705	55352	55
60	46882	48065	54254	47671	48340	52375	51358	47677	46882	49343	47301	49485	57627	55623	68072	82900	49928	60
65	39156	40398	46557	40156	41054	44779	43663	40015	39156	41212	39561	41541	51562	48034	61255	78127	41971	65
70	31026	32219	37956	32138	33304	36740	35467	32015	31026	32655	31372	33081	44661	39415	53356	72164	33450	70
75	22221	23194	28191	23372	24719	27799	26135	23189	22221	23388	22552	23868	36629	29425	43297	63781	24224	75
80	14867	15615	19679	15664	17434	19751	18277	15664	14867	15648	15110	16170	28648	20669	33827	54989	16435	80
85+	8048	8497	11276	8778	10177	11685	10318	8514	8048	8471	8189	8835	21170	11904	22159	43831	8990	85+

ADDED YRS OF LIFE

	No Causes	(1)	(2)	(3)	(4)	(5)	(6)	(7)	(8)	(9)	(10)	(11)	(12)	(1)+(2)	(1)+(2)+(5)+(6)+(8)	(1)+(2)+(5)+(6)+(8)+part of(9)&(12)	(10)+(11)
TOTAL		.555	5.230	.430	.966	4.282	3.491	.389	.000	2.533	.221	1.282	9.346	5.893	15.929	33.234	1.514
WORK	9.094	.393	1.406	.181	.346	.971	.640	.201	.000	.000	.172	1.049	2.505	1.823	3.591	5.412	1.227

POPULATION, DEATHS, DEATH RATES FOR ALL CAUSES COMBINED, AND SPECIFIED CAUSES

Age Start of Interval	Midyear Population	Deaths During Year	All Causes	Respiratory T. B.	Other Infec. and Paras.	Neo-plasms	Cardio-vascular	Infl., Pneu., Bronch.	Diar-rheal	Certain Degen-erative	Maternal	Cert. Dis. of Infancy	Motor Vehicle	Other Violence	Other and Unknown	Age Start of Interval
0	80021	7824	.09777	.00004	.01531	.00004	.00010	.01941	.01395	.00000	.00000	.04044	.00001	.00019	.00830	0
1	295493	8210	.02778	.00006	.01010	.00002	.00009	.00532	.00641	.00005	.00000	.00000	.00002	.00011	.00560	1
5	331634	2254	.00680	.00005	.00228	.00001	.00005	.00096	.00137	.00003	.00000	.00000	.00004	.00010	.00190	5
10	267338	810	.00303	.00006	.00080	.00002	.00004	.00058	.00042	.00001	.00000	.00000	.00002	.00005	.00102	10
15	224461	842	.00375	.00011	.00084	.00004	.00012	.00065	.00034	.00003	.00022	.00000	.00002	.00016	.00122	15
20	178819	993	.00555	.00029	.00120	.00008	.00018	.00093	.00048	.00004	.00044	.00000	.00002	.00013	.00175	20
25	152793	969	.00634	.00041	.00132	.00016	.00024	.00096	.00054	.00006	.00045	.00000	.00004	.00018	.00197	25
30	132399	948	.00716	.00044	.00153	.00023	.00026	.00108	.00061	.00008	.00062	.00000	.00003	.00008	.00220	30
35	122510	962	.00785	.00052	.00130	.00037	.00046	.00117	.00061	.00014	.00065	.00000	.00002	.00017	.00244	35
40	92266	819	.00888	.00037	.00134	.00054	.00042	.00150	.00083	.00017	.00040	.00000	.00005	.00013	.00311	40
45	70151	720	.01026	.00033	.00171	.00081	.00077	.00128	.00121	.00021	.00009	.00000	.00000	.00016	.00369	45
50	62310	864	.01387	.00058	.00205	.00100	.00106	.00197	.00172	.00032	.00000	.00000	.00003	.00014	.00499	50
55	42960	839	.01953	.00047	.00265	.00193	.00154	.00275	.00216	.00063	.00000	.00000	.00005	.00012	.00724	55
60	42100	1372	.03259	.00055	.00430	.00235	.00266	.00513	.00311	.00069	.00000	.00000	.00002	.00033	.01304	60
65	23650	1043	.04410	.00055	.00520	.00393	.00457	.00643	.00524	.00097	.00000	.00000	.00017	.00025	.01679	65
70	16708	1060	.06344	.00096	.00628	.00473	.00700	.00934	.00736	.00150	.00000	.00000	.00006	.00042	.02580	70
75	8456	725	.08574	.00166	.00674	.00485	.01265	.01183	.00946	.00189	.00000	.00000	.00000	.00071	.03595	75
80	5918	817	.13805	.00118	.01065	.00575	.01707	.02129	.01081	.00253	.00000	.00000	.00000	.00051	.06827	80
85+	4156	850	.20452	.00048	.01035	.00722	.02093	.02671	.01853	.00217	.00000	.00000	.00000	.00000	.11598	85+
ALL	2154143	32921														

CRUDE DEATH RATE			.01528	.00024	.00334	.00036	.00051	.00263	.00229	.00013	.00019	.00150	.00003	.00014	.00392	
STANDARDIZED RATE (1)			.01538	.00027	.00321	.00044	.00060	.00262	.00223	.00015	.00020	.00142	.00003	.00014	.00392	
STANDARDIZED RATE (2)			.01840	.00036	.00305	.00082	.00124	.00292	.00231	.00027	.00020	.00084	.00003	.00014	.00408	
GEOMETRIC MEAN			.01918												.00618	

LIFE TABLE FOR ALL CAUSES COMBINED

Age (x)	Midyear Population	Deaths During Year	$_nM_x$	$_nq_x$	l_x	$_nd_x$	$_nL_x$	$_nm_x$	$_na_x$	T_x	$_nr_x$	$\overset{\circ}{e}_x$	Age (x)
0	80021	7824	.097774	.090980	100000	9098	93051	.097774	.236216	5020107	.000000	50.201	0
1	295493	8210	.027784	.103914	90902	9446	339993	.027783	1.500000	4927056	.000000	54.202	1
5	331634	2254	.006797	.033552	81456	2733	400448	.006825	2.500000	4587063	.000000	56.313	5
10	267338	810	.003030	.014900	78723	1173	390415	.003004	2.271775	4186615	.026477	53.182	10
15	224461	842	.003751	.018672	77550	1448	384322	.003752	2.632366	3796200	.034361	48.952	15
20	178819	993	.005553	.027503	76102	2093	375458	.005575	2.586200	3411879	.034671	44.833	20
25	152793	969	.006342	.031266	74009	2314	364350	.006351	2.538804	3036421	.028075	41.028	25
30	132399	948	.007160	.035205	71695	2524	352238	.007166	2.529054	2672071	.016588	37.270	30
35	122510	962	.007852	.038542	69171	2666	339267	.007858	2.528992	2319833	.021402	33.538	35
40	92266	819	.008877	.043531	66505	2895	325357	.008897	2.537925	1980565	.044653	29.781	40
45	70151	720	.010264	.050197	63610	3193	310313	.010290	2.576861	1655168	.030406	26.021	45
50	62310	864	.013866	.067415	60417	4073	292337	.013933	2.606659	1344855	.037033	22.260	50
55	42960	839	.019530	.093692	56344	5279	269287	.019604	2.644914	1052518	.021586	18.680	55
60	42100	1372	.032589	.151669	51065	7745	236667	.032725	2.591000	783231	.022994	15.338	60
65	23650	1043	.044101	.199954	43320	8662	195321	.044348	2.543365	546563	.041670	12.617	65
70	16708	1060	.063443	.275492	34658	9548	149042	.063882	2.504429	351243	.044574	10.135	70
75	8456	725	.085738	.353047	25110	8865	103126	.085963	2.470483	201780	.018476	8.036	75
80	5918	817	.138053	.510434	16245	8292	59769	.138734	2.412466	98655	.018476	6.073	80
85+	4156	850	.204524	1.000000	7953	7953	38885	.204524	4.889412	38885	.000000	4.889	85+

NUMBER OF PERSONS DYING (OUT OF 100,000 AT BIRTH) ABOVE AGE X FROM SPECIFIED CAUSES

Age (x)	All Causes	Respiratory T. B.	Other Infec. and Paras.	Neoplasms	Cardiovascular	Infl., Pneu., Bronch.	Diarrheal	Certain Degenerative	Maternal	Cert. Dis. of Infancy	Motor Vehicle	Other Violence	Other and Unknown	Age (x)
0	100000	1955	15342	4751	7361	15592	12089	1560	1013	3763	170	921	35483	0
1	90902	1952	13918	4747	7352	13786	10791	1560	1013	0	169	903	34711	1
5	81456	1931	10484	4740	7319	11976	8611	1543	1013	0	164	867	32808	5
10	78723	1913	9566	4737	7299	11590	8059	1530	1013	0	147	828	32041	10
15	77550	1889	9257	4728	7283	11366	7900	1524	1013	0	138	809	31643	15
20	76102	1846	8934	4712	7238	11117	7768	1512	928	0	129	745	31173	20
25	74009	1738	8481	4681	7168	10765	7587	1497	761	0	121	697	30513	25
30	71695	1587	8001	4621	7080	10414	7388	1476	596	0	107	630	29795	30
35	69171	1433	7461	4538	6989	10033	7173	1446	378	0	96	604	29020	35
40	66505	1256	7021	4413	6834	9637	6965	1399	157	0	88	545	28190	40
45	63610	1137	6583	4235	6696	9149	6692	1342	28	0	70	503	27175	45
50	60417	1035	6050	3982	6455	8751	6314	1276	2	0	70	454	26028	50
55	56344	865	5448	3689	6144	8170	5810	1181	2	0	61	412	24562	55
60	51065	740	4731	3167	5729	7427	5225	1011	2	0	48	381	22604	60
65	43320	514	3710	2609	5096	6208	4485	848	2	0	42	302	19504	65
70	34658	408	2691	1836	4196	4947	3454	657	2	0	9	252	16206	70
75	25110	263	1748	1127	3139	3542	2346	431	2	0	0	189	12323	75
80	16245	92	1052	627	1830	2319	1369	236	2	0	0	116	8602	80
85+	7953	19	402	281	814	1039	720	84	0	0	0	84	4510	85+

NUMBER OF PERSONS SURVIVING TO AGE X IF SPECIFIED CAUSES WERE ELIMINATED

Age (x)	No Causes	Respiratory T. B. (1)	Other Infec. and Paras. (2)	Neoplasms (3)	Cardiovascular (4)	Infl., Pneu., Bronch. (5)	Diarrheal (6)	Certain Degenerative (7)	Maternal (8)	Cert. Dis. of Infancy (9)	Motor Vehicle (10)	Other Violence (11)	Other and Unknown (12)	(1) + (2)	(1) + (2) + (5) + (6) + (8)	(1)+(2)+ (5)+(6)+ (8)+part of(9)&(12)	(10) + (11)	Age (x)
0	100000	100000	100000	100000	100000	100000	100000	100000	100000	100000	100000	100000	100000	100000	100000	100000	100000	0
1	90902	90905	92269	90906	90911	92640	92148	90902	90902	94560	90903	90919	91641	92272	95325	99933	90920	1
5	81456	81478	86046	81466	81495	84777	84690	81472	81456	84734	81462	81505	83953	86070	93135	99791	81511	5
10	78723	78762	84118	78736	78780	82328	82414	78751	78723	81891	78745	78809	81917	84160	92141	99632	78831	10
15	77550	77613	83193	77571	77622	81334	81352	77584	77550	80671	77581	77654	81109	83260	91604	99518	77685	15
20	76102	76206	81983	76139	76218	80075	79970	76147	76186	79164	76141	76267	80083	82095	90872	99238	76306	20
25	74009	74217	80211	74075	74191	78239	77958	74068	74256	76987	74055	74217	78568	80437	89870	98906	74263	25
30	71695	72046	78217	71819	71958	76158	75727	71773	72097	74580	71753	71963	76866	78600	88684	98415	72021	30
35	69171	69662	76044	69372	69514	73876	73285	69275	69775	71955	69238	69455	74980	76583	87413	97930	69522	35
40	66505	67152	73589	66821	66988	71444	70677	66652	67304	69181	66577	66836	72978	74304	85850	97107	66909	40
45	63610	64346	70861	64088	64208	68849	67885	63806	64502	66170	63697	63968	70899	71681	83959	96116	64055	45
50	60417	61217	67885	61120	61223	65814	64872	60668	61290	62848	60499	60805	68558	68783	81614	94653	60888	50
55	56344	57256	63964	57287	57401	61991	61023	56670	57158	58611	56430	56747	65601	65000	78572	92771	56833	55
60	51065	52012	58751	52427	52427	56967	55911	51523	51803	53120	51155	51460	61665	59841	74148	89661	51550	60
65	43320	44335	50931	45005	45078	49594	48183	43860	43946	45063	43402	43728	55872	52125	67332	85203	43811	65
70	34658	35566	41828	36730	36912	40986	39587	35263	35159	36053	34753	35029	48663	42924	58819	78566	35125	70
75	25110	25855	31280	27252	27719	31136	29773	25744	25473	26120	25186	25433	40200	32258	48112	69852	25510	75
80	16245	16894	20936	18064	19127	21390	20203	16815	16480	16899	16294	16513	31240	21772	36169	58577	16563	80
85+	7953	8323	10840	9111	10221	11692	10460	8340	8069	8273	7977	8107	21757	11344	22255	45035	8131	85+

ADDED YRS OF LIFE

	No Causes	(1)	(2)	(3)	(4)	(5)	(6)	(7)	(8)	(9)	(10)	(11)	(12)	(1)+(2)	+(5)+(6)+(8)	part	(10)+(11)
TOTAL		.464	5.477	.706	.975	4.363	3.651	.239	.368	2.011	.051	.237	8.827	6.022	16.732	32.342	.289
WORK	8.096	.336	1.320	.314	.353	1.095	.668	.107	.373	.000	.027	.141	2.431	1.673	4.003	6.208	.169

POPULATION, DEATHS, DEATH RATES FOR ALL CAUSES COMBINED, AND SPECIFIED CAUSES

Age Start of Interval	Midyear Population	Deaths During Year	All Causes	Respiratory T.B.	Other Infec. and Paras.	Neo-plasms	Cardio-vascular	Infl., Pneu., Bronch.	Diar-rheal	Certain Degen-erative	Maternal	Cert. Dis. of Infancy	Motor Vehicle	Other Violence	Other and Unknown	Age Start of Interval
0	55600	2289	.04117	.00004	.00273	.00004	.00004	.00854	.00523	.00002	.00000	.01937	.00000	.00023	.00453	0
1	211500	921	.00435	.00003	.00153	.00005	.00004	.00147	.00052	.00003	.00000	.00000	.00001	.00026	.00040	1
5	226400	219	.00097	.00002	.00013	.00007	.00003	.00015	.00005	.00005	.00000	.00000	.00010	.00023	.00016	5
10	183200	122	.00067	.00002	.00007	.00005	.00007	.00007	.00001	.00002	.00000	.00000	.00010	.00023	.00016	10
15	96700	73	.00075	.00003	.00007	.00014	.00006	.00005	.00000	.00003	.00000	.00000	.00007	.00020	.00011	15
20	111400	145	.00130	.00022	.00004	.00013	.00014	.00006	.00001	.00011	.00000	.00000	.00004	.00004	.00020	20
25	141100	220	.00156	.00035	.00011	.00019	.00007	.00006	.00001	.00012	.00000	.00000	.00002	.00044	.00019	25
30	141100	311	.00220	.00055	.00012	.00040	.00021	.00008	.00000	.00011	.00000	.00000	.00006	.00043	.00019	30
35	125900	384	.00305	.00075	.00021	.00052	.00034	.00011	.00002	.00024	.00000	.00000	.00006	.00043	.00025	35
40	107000	519	.00485	.00106	.00017	.00107	.00072	.00024	.00004	.00038	.00000	.00000	.00011	.00041	.00065	40
45	87400	649	.00743	.00135	.00016	.00170	.00149	.00056	.00006	.00066	.00000	.00000	.00006	.00041	.00065	45
50	60800	861	.01416	.00262	.00039	.00312	.00332	.00110	.00012	.00087	.00000	.00000	.00006	.00037	.00102	50
55	38300	760	.01984	.00347	.00034	.00423	.00603	.00136	.00005	.00089	.00000	.00000	.00016	.00051	.00194	55
60	23500	898	.03821	.00553	.00058	.00668	.01200	.00238	.00026	.00200	.00000	.00000	.00021	.00119	.00269	60
65	13400	639	.04769	.00470	.00045	.00769	.01799	.00388	.00022	.00254	.00000	.00000	.00000	.00045	.00698	65
70	7500	580	.07733	.00813	.00053	.00747	.02907	.00747	.00053	.00427	.00000	.00000	.00040	.00080	.00978	70
75	3600	365	.10139	.00750	.00056	.00944	.04139	.00972	.00111	.00472	.00000	.00000	.00000	.00111	.01867	75
80	1400	231	.16500	.01071	.00000	.01357	.05071	.01857	.00000	.00643	.00000	.00000	.00214	.00083	.02500	80
85+	500	108	.21600	.00400	.00000	.00800	.06800	.03400	.00600	.00800	.00000	.00000	.00000	.00143	.06143	85+
ALL	1636300	10294														

	All Causes	Respiratory T.B.	Other Infec. and Paras.	Neo-plasms	Cardio-vascular	Infl., Pneu., Bronch.	Diar-rheal	Certain Degen-erative	Maternal	Cert. Dis. of Infancy	Motor Vehicle	Other Violence	Other and Unknown
CRUDE DEATH RATE	.00629	.00066	.00042	.00073	.00108	.00081	.00028	.00026	.00000	.00066	.00007	.00035	.00096
STANDARDIZED RATE (1)	.00816	.00081	.00042	.00093	.00180	.00099	.00029	.00035	.00000	.00066	.00007	.00035	.00096
STANDARDIZED RATE (2)	.01399	.00144	.00037	.00171	.00407	.00145	.00025	.00066	.00000	.00068	.00008	.00035	.00145
GEOMETRIC MEAN	.00978									.00040	.00012	.00041	.00311

LIFE TABLE FOR ALL CAUSES COMBINED

Age (x)	Midyear Population	Deaths During Year	$_nM_x$	$_nq_x$	l_x	$_nd_x$	$_nL_x$	$_nm_x$	$_na_x$	T_x	$_nr_x$	$\overset{\circ}{e}_x$	Age (x)
0	55600	2289	.041169	.039760	100000	3976	96581	.041168	.139987	6368818	.000000	63.688	0
1	211500	921	.004355	.017235	96024	1655	379959	.004356	1.500000	6272238	.000000	65.319	1
5	226400	219	.000967	.004927	94369	465	470683	.000988	2.500000	5892279	.000000	62.439	5
10	183200	122	.000666	.003216	93904	302	468741	.000644	2.419978	5421597	.067529	57.736	10
15	96700	73	.000755	.003729	93602	349	467200	.000747	2.680277	4952856	.069103	52.914	15
20	111400	145	.001302	.006477	93253	604	464832	.001299	2.626932	4485655	-.015018	48.102	20
25	141100	220	.001559	.007739	92649	717	461536	.001554	2.617097	4020824	-.028463	43.398	25
30	141100	311	.002204	.010954	91932	1007	457281	.002202	2.637372	3559287	-.002323	38.717	30
35	125900	384	.003050	.015188	90925	1381	451412	.003059	2.673636	3102006	.017409	34.116	35
40	107000	519	.004850	.024100	89544	2158	442709	.004875	2.677441	2650594	.026128	29.601	40
45	87400	649	.007426	.036837	87386	3219	429649	.007492	2.738104	2207886	.039801	25.266	45
50	60800	861	.014161	.069350	84167	5837	407137	.014337	2.653261	1778237	.061521	21.127	50
55	38300	760	.019843	.095915	78330	7513	374269	.020074	2.686566	1371100	.070544	17.504	55
60	23500	898	.038213	.177429	70817	12565	323710	.038816	2.582587	996831	.070395	14.076	60
65	13400	639	.047687	.214482	58252	12494	260528	.047956	2.540253	673121	.065055	11.555	65
70	7500	580	.077333	.327353	45758	14979	191327	.078290	2.498985	412593	.057554	9.017	70
75	3600	365	.101389	.403554	30779	12421	121942	.101859	2.427542	221266	.058643	7.189	75
80	1400	231	.165000	.580619	18358	10659	63680	.167385	2.362753	99323	.058643	5.410	80
85+	500	108	.216000	1.000000	7699	7699	35644	.216000	4.629630	35644	.000000	4.630	85+

NUMBER OF PERSONS DYING (OUT OF 100,000 AT BIRTH) ABOVE AGE X FROM SPECIFIED CAUSES

Age (x)	All Causes	Respiratory T.B.	Other Infec. and Paras.	Neoplasms	Cardio-vascular	Infl., Pneu., Bronch.	Diarrheal	Certain Degenerative	Maternal	Cert. Dis. of Infancy	Motor Vehicle	Other Violence	Other and Unknown	Age (x)
0	100000	10731	2241	12790	30120	9853	1453	4904	0	1873	821	2818	22396	0
1	96024	10728	1977	12786	30117	8990	948	4903	0	2	821	2795	21957	1
5	94369	10715	1895	12768	30100	8433	748	4890	0	0	816	2696	21808	5
10	93904	10707	1333	12736	30088	8363	725	4865	0	0	769	2588	21730	10
15	93602	10700	1301	12714	30056	8334	723	4858	0	0	739	2496	21681	15
20	93253	10685	1267	12646	30029	8310	723	4843	0	0	705	2380	21665	20
25	92649	10581	1247	12584	29962	8281	719	4793	0	0	684	2225	21573	25
30	91932	10422	1194	12496	29930	8255	715	4737	0	0	675	2023	21485	30
35	90925	10169	1139	12312	29833	8219	715	4689	0	0	649	1828	21372	35
40	89544	9828	1046	12078	29678	8169	705	4581	0	0	623	1646	21190	40
45	87386	9359	972	11603	29357	8060	688	4410	0	0	574	1464	20899	45
50	84167	8774	902	10864	28709	7817	663	4123	0	0	549	1306	20460	50
55	78330	7697	740	9577	27334	7363	616	3767	0	0	481	1097	19658	55
60	70817	6386	612	7980	25039	6851	597	3432	0	0	423	860	18637	60
65	58252	4578	290	5792	21085	6067	512	2773	0	0	354	471	16330	65
70	45758	3358	178	3790	16356	5043	454	2108	0	0	354	360	13757	70
75	30779	1784	75	2358	10723	3593	350	1282	0	0	276	205	10133	75
80	18358	874	8	1203	5652	2401	213	706	0	0	138	103	7060	80
85+	7699	143	0	285	2424	1212	213	285	0	0	0	0	3137	85+

NUMBER OF PERSONS SURVIVING TO AGE X IF SPECIFIED CAUSES WERE ELIMINATED

Age (x)	No Causes	Respiratory T.B. (1)	Other Infec. and Paras. (2)	Neoplasms (3)	Cardio-vascular (4)	Infl., Pneu., Bronch. (5)	Diarrheal (6)	Certain Degenerative (7)	Maternal (8)	Cert. Dis. of Infancy (9)	Motor Vehicle (10)	Other Violence (11)	Other and Unknown (12)	(1)+(2)	(1)+(2)+(5)+(6)+(8)	(1)+(2)+(5)+(6)+(8)+part of (9)&(12)	(10)+(11)	Age (x)
0	100000	100000	100000	100000	100000	100000	100000	100000	100000	100000	100000	100000	100000	100000	100000	100000	100000	0
1	96024	96027	96283	96028	96027	96873	96520	96025	96024	97875	96024	96047	96455	96286	97639	99925	96047	1
5	94369	94385	95204	94391	94389	95762	95056	94383	94369	96190	94374	94489	94941	95220	97329	99749	94494	5
10	93904	93928	94797	93958	93936	95361	94611	93943	93904	95716	93956	94132	94552	94821	97017	99464	94184	10
15	93602	93633	94525	93677	93665	95084	94309	93648	93602	95408	93684	93921	94297	94555	96778	99233	94003	15
20	93253	93298	94206	93356	93343	94754	93957	93313	93253	95052	93368	93687	93961	94252	96492	98944	93803	20
25	92649	92798	93616	92853	92805	94170	93352	92759	92649	94437	92785	93236	93445	93767	96029	98499	93372	25
30	91932	92239	92945	92222	92119	93467	92634	92097	91932	93700	92075	92717	92811	93255	95536	98029	92861	30
35	90925	91481	91982	91356	91207	92480	91619	91136	90925	92680	91093	91897	91907	92545	94846	97367	92067	35
40	89544	90433	90679	90242	89976	91126	90238	89855	89544	91272	89735	90684	90684	91579	93918	96495	90877	40
45	87386	88722	88567	88541	88127	89039	88080	87863	87386	89072	87621	88680	88800	89922	92350	94996	88919	45
50	84167	86039	85375	86017	85525	86003	84860	84910	84167	85791	84418	85571	85968	87273	89911	92644	85826	50
55	78330	81141	79612	81330	80955	80487	79021	79368	78330	79842	78629	79842	80800	82469	85487	88387	80147	55
60	70817	74658	72100	75120	75491	73268	71460	72079	70817	72184	71143	72413	74060	76011	79356	82390	72746	60
65	58252	63156	59604	63925	66031	61008	58858	59901	58252	59376	58582	59924	63149	64622	68384	71747	60264	65
70	45758	50788	46919	52184	56839	48885	46286	47662	45758	46641	46017	47170	52140	52076	56277	59766	47437	70
75	30779	35612	31646	36442	44384	34171	31221	32767	30779	31373	31019	31859	38611	36614	41234	45006	32108	75
80	18358	22048	18927	22804	32686	21419	18728	20014	18358	18712	18610	19083	26194	22730	27055	30481	19344	80
85+	7699	9814	7943	10307	17835	9897	7854	8686	7699	7848	7893	8070	15125	10125	13278	16393	8274	85+

ADDED YRS OF LIFE

	No Causes	(1)	(2)	(3)	(4)	(5)	(6)	(7)	(8)	(9)	(10)	(11)	(12)	(1)+(2)	(1)+(2)+(5)+(6)+(8)	...part	(10)+(11)
TOTAL		1.684	.859	1.938	4.006	1.893	.547	.673	.000	1.226	.169	.793	3.155	2.582	5.311	8.095	.966
WORK	4.277	.745	.148	.759	.727	.228	.022	.256	.000	.000	.071	.416	.517	.897	1.160	1.347	.488

POPULATION, DEATHS, DEATH RATES FOR ALL CAUSES COMBINED, AND SPECIFIED CAUSES

Age Start of Interval	Midyear Population	Deaths During Year	All Causes	Respiratory T.B.	Other Infec. and Paras.	Neoplasms	Cardiovascular	Infl., Pneu., Bronch.	Diarrheal	Certain Degenerative	Maternal	Cert. Dis. of Infancy	Motor Vehicle	Other Violence	Other and Unknown	Age Start of Interval
0	52700	1811	.03436	.00004	.00241	.00002	.00002	.00860	.00391	.00008	.00000	.01548	.00006	.00034	.00342	0
1	199300	889	.00446	.00007	.00155	.00004	.00002	.00151	.00046	.00005	.00000	.00001	.00005	.00023	.00049	1
5	210300	173	.00082	.00000	.00025	.00004	.00004	.00011	.00003	.00002	.00000	.00000	.00008	.00010	.00013	5
10	163100	75	.00046	.00001	.00006	.00005	.00006	.00009	.00000	.00002	.00000	.00000	.00003	.00009	.00004	10
15	80500	54	.00067	.00001	.00005	.00006	.00017	.00005	.00001	.00001	.00000	.00000	.00001	.00017	.00011	15
20	90900	74	.00081	.00009	.00007	.00009	.00006	.00001	.00004	.00004	.00000	.00000	.00000	.00017	.00017	20
25	119200	151	.00127	.00018	.00004	.00023	.00014	.00005	.00000	.00006	.00009	.00000	.00001	.00023	.00023	25
30	122800	195	.00159	.00034	.00006	.00029	.00022	.00004	.00000	.00006	.00009	.00000	.00001	.00021	.00027	30
35	113400	246	.00217	.00026	.00010	.00056	.00033	.00007	.00004	.00004	.00011	.00000	.00004	.00026	.00034	35
40	96400	298	.00309	.00045	.00008	.00092	.00054	.00013	.00003	.00015	.00010	.00000	.00004	.00027	.00037	40
45	81500	343	.00421	.00060	.00004	.00142	.00083	.00021	.00000	.00033	.00001	.00000	.00001	.00027	.00048	45
50	64800	453	.00699	.00074	.00009	.00250	.00159	.00045	.00005	.00020	.00000	.00000	.00005	.00039	.00094	50
55	51000	466	.00914	.00114	.00010	.00253	.00269	.00053	.00012	.00045	.00000	.00000	.00000	.00022	.00137	55
60	39600	614	.01551	.00152	.00033	.00389	.00576	.00109	.00010	.00066	.00000	.00000	.00013	.00028	.00177	60
65	28300	572	.02021	.00145	.00011	.00392	.00724	.00177	.00011	.00059	.00000	.00000	.00000	.00071	.00389	65
70	18400	699	.03799	.00228	.00022	.00495	.01413	.00489	.00033	.00141	.00000	.00000	.00033	.00038	.00908	70
75	10100	623	.06168	.00317	.00010	.00574	.02386	.00713	.00059	.00218	.00000	.00000	.00010	.00119	.01762	75
80	4100	392	.09561	.00146	.00049	.00655	.03073	.01439	.00122	.00146	.00000	.00000	.00000	.00122	.03805	80
85+	1600	315	.19687	.00312	.00062	.00500	.06000	.03875	.00187	.00437	.00000	.00000	.00000	.00122	.07875	85+
ALL	1548000	8443														

	All Causes	Respiratory T.B.	Other Infec. and Paras.	Neoplasms	Cardiovascular	Infl., Pneu., Bronch.	Diarrheal	Certain Degenerative	Maternal	Cert. Dis. of Infancy	Motor Vehicle	Other Violence	Other and Unknown
CRUDE DEATH RATE	.00545	.00033	.00037	.00072	.00106	.00083	.00023	.00015	.00003	.00053	.00004	.00023	.00094
STANDARDIZED RATE (1)	.00510	.00029	.00036	.00063	.00096	.00080	.00022	.00014	.00003	.00055	.00004	.00022	.00087
STANDARDIZED RATE (2)	.00808	.00048	.00027	.00109	.00221	.00107	.00018	.00025	.00003	.00032	.00005	.00027	.00184
GEOMETRIC MEAN	.00631												

LIFE TABLE FOR ALL CAUSES COMBINED

Age (x)	Midyear Population	Deaths During Year	$_nM_x$	$_nq_x$	l_x	$_nd_x$	$_nL_x$	$_nm_x$	$_na_x$	T_x	$_nr_x$	$\overset{\circ}{e}_x$	Age (x)
0	52700	1811	.034364	.033370	100000	3337	97092	.034370	.128419	7095353	.000000	70.954	0
1	199300	889	.004461	.017639	96663	1705	382390	.004459	1.500000	6998261	.000000	72.399	1
5	210300	173	.000823	.004286	94958	407	473773	.000859	2.500000	6615872	.000000	69.672	5
10	163100	75	.000460	.002115	94551	200	472234	.000424	2.393750	6142099	.076201	64.961	10
15	80500	54	.000671	.003233	94351	305	471030	.000648	2.623634	5669865	.079509	60.093	15
20	90900	74	.000814	.004051	94046	381	469337	.000812	2.655293	5198835	-.012680	55.280	20
25	119200	151	.001267	.006288	93665	589	466926	.001261	2.625566	4729498	-.032425	50.494	25
30	122800	195	.001588	.007908	93076	736	463625	.001587	2.615772	4262572	-.008236	45.797	30
35	113400	246	.002169	.010808	92340	998	459345	.002173	2.640072	3798947	.013631	41.141	35
40	96400	298	.003091	.015404	91342	1407	453377	.003103	2.631189	3339602	.025441	36.562	40
45	81500	343	.004209	.020948	89935	1884	443306	.004231	2.681241	2886225	.031991	32.092	45
50	64800	453	.006991	.034594	88051	3046	433044	.007034	2.632756	2440918	.038534	27.722	50
55	51000	466	.009137	.044997	85005	3825	416101	.009192	2.666939	2007874	.038554	23.621	55
60	39600	614	.015505	.075277	81180	6111	391347	.015615	2.618502	1591773	.041266	19.608	60
65	28300	572	.020212	.057257	75069	7301	358211	.020376	2.666958	1200426	.050045	15.991	65
70	18400	699	.037989	.176514	67768	11962	310572	.038516	2.636840	842115	.057294	12.426	70
75	10100	623	.061683	.271620	55806	15158	241951	.062649	2.553849	531543	.081396	9.525	75
80	4100	392	.095610	.390671	40648	15880	163786	.096956	2.515494	289592	.081396	7.124	80
85+	1600	315	.196875	1.000000	24768	24768	125806	.196875	5.079365	125806	.000000	5.079	85+

NUMBER OF PERSONS DYING (OUT OF 100,000 AT BIRTH) ABOVE AGE X FROM SPECIFIED CAUSES

Age (x)	All Causes	Respiratory T.B.	Other Infec. and Paras.	Neo-plasms	Cardio-vascular	Infl., Pneu., Bronch.	Diar-rheal	Certain Degen-erative	Maternal	Cert. Dis. of Infancy	Motor Vehicle	Other Violence	Other and Unknown	Age (x)
0	100000	4974	1673	11477	30783	13827	1448	3027	210	1506	499	2570	28006	0
1	96663	4970	1439	11475	30781	12993	1068	3020	210	2	494	2537	27674	1
5	94958	4946	848	11460	30773	12415	892	3001	210	0	476	2451	27486	5
10	94551	4943	726	11438	30752	12359	875	2989	210	0	439	2399	27421	10
15	94351	4938	700	11417	30726	12318	875	2981	210	0	425	2356	27405	15
20	94046	4932	677	11389	30648	12297	870	2975	210	0	419	2273	27356	20
25	93665	4891	646	11348	30607	12271	865	2955	190	0	419	2196	27277	25
30	93076	4806	626	11243	30540	12247	865	2927	147	0	416	2090	27169	30
35	92340	4648	600	11107	30439	12228	865	2901	105	0	412	1992	27043	35
40	91342	4526	555	10847	30288	12196	848	2880	53	0	392	1870	26887	40
45	89935	4323	517	10426	30043	12135	834	2814	6	0	373	1748	26716	45
50	88051	4054	501	9788	29668	12041	834	2666	1	0	367	1628	26503	50
55	85005	3732	461	8700	28974	11846	814	2579	1	0	347	1460	26091	55
60	81180	3256	419	7645	27844	11624	765	2390	1	0	347	1371	25518	60
65	75069	2661	290	6116	25572	11195	725	2131	1	0	297	1261	24820	65
70	67768	2141	253	4710	22956	10551	687	1774	1	0	285	1007	23403	70
75	55806	1425	185	3166	18503	9007	584	1331	1	0	182	889	20533	75
80	40648	655	162	1771	12643	7256	437	799	1	0	160	594	16170	80
85+	24768	393	79	629	7548	4875	236	550	0	0	157	393	9908	85+

NUMBER OF PERSONS SURVIVING TO AGE X IF SPECIFIED CAUSES WERE ELIMINATED

Age (x)	No Causes	Respiratory T.B. (1)	Other Infec. and Paras. (2)	Neo-plasms (3)	Cardio-vascular (4)	Infl., Pneu., Bronch. (5)	Diar-rheal (6)	Certain Degenerative (7)	Maternal (8)	Cert. Dis. of Infancy (9)	Motor Vehicle (10)	Other Violence (11)	Other and Unknown (12)	(1)+(2)	(1)+(2)+(5)+(6)+(8)	(1)+(2)+(5)+(6)+(8)+part of (9)&(12)	(10)+(11)	Age (x)
0	100000	100000	100000	100000	100000	100000	100000	100000	100000	100000	100000	100000	100000	100000	100000	100000	100000	0
1	96663	96667	96893	96665	96665	97486	97037	96670	96663	98153	96668	96695	96990	96897	98101	99889	96700	1
5	94958	94986	95773	94975	94968	96346	95501	94984	94958	96424	94981	95075	95466	95801	97758	99718	95098	5
10	94551	94582	95486	94590	94582	95990	95109	94588	94551	96010	94611	94720	95122	95516	97542	99538	94779	10
15	94351	94386	95310	94411	94408	95829	94908	94396	94351	95807	94424	94562	94937	95346	97410	99410	94636	15
20	94046	94087	95025	94133	94180	95540	94606	94097	94046	95498	94125	94340	94680	95067	97152	99157	94419	20
25	93665	93747	94671	93793	93840	95180	94228	93736	93665	95111	93744	94035	94375	94754	96885	98919	94114	25
30	93076	93242	94096	93308	93317	94605	93635	93174	93139	94513	93157	93549	93891	94264	96454	98519	93631	30
35	92340	92663	93378	92706	92680	93876	92855	92464	92444	93765	92425	92908	93275	93705	95944	98052	92993	35
40	91342	91783	92414	91564	91829	92894	91908	91485	91497	92752	91446	92026	92423	92861	95184	97328	92130	40
45	89935	90572	91029	90069	90069	91125	90506	90142	90134	91323	90056	90730	91172	91674	94404	96267	90852	45
50	88051	88943	89138	89705	89135	89702	88610	88400	88251	89410	88175	88949	89476	90041	92521	94710	89075	50
55	85005	86186	86094	87697	86745	86795	85564	85428	85198	86317	85145	86039	86793	87291	89918	92141	86180	55
60	81180	82781	82262	84820	83977	83111	81762	81770	81364	82433	81313	82255	83461	83884	86692	88984	82391	60
65	75069	77134	76195	79584	79949	77229	75546	75866	75239	76228	75241	76171	77872	78291	81399	83716	76345	65
70	67768	70140	68820	73637	74869	70397	68326	68830	67922	68814	67934	69007	71713	71229	74770	77223	69177	70
75	55806	58433	56734	62170	66277	59443	56360	57089	55933	56667	56036	56935	61879	59405	64050	66982	57170	75
80	40648	43245	41344	46613	54554	44914	41178	42044	40740	41275	40833	41727	49402	43986	49347	52803	41917	80
85+	24768	26567	25257	29433	38568	29477	25249	25818	24825	25150	24883	25586	36596	27092	32945	37412	25705	85+

ADDED YRS OF LIFE																		
TOTAL		.920	.847	2.090	4.187	2.338	.506	.448	.088	1.093	.110	.648	3.876	1.782	4.930	7.795	.761	
WORK	2.630	.320	.075	.651	.502	.126	.019	.107	.064	.000	.020	.256	.368	.396	.609	.719	.276	

POPULATION, DEATHS, DEATH RATES FOR ALL CAUSES COMBINED, AND SPECIFIED CAUSES

Age Start of Interval	Midyear Population	Deaths During Year	All Causes	Respiratory T.B.	Other Infec. and Paras.	Neoplasms	Cardiovascular	Infl., Pneu., Bronch.	Diarrheal	Certain Degenerative	Maternal	Cert. Dis. of Infancy	Motor Vehicle	Other Violence	Other and Unknown	Age Start of Interval
0	54115	1630	.03012	.00002	.00115	.00006	.00011	.00477	.00144	.00004	.00000	.01850	.00002	.00048	.00355	0
1	228485	435	.00190	.00001	.00037	.00008	.00002	.00068	.00013	.00003	.00000	.00000	.00004	.00030	.00025	1
5	262000	173	.00066	.00000	.00010	.00006	.00003	.00005	.00000	.00002	.00000	.00000	.00010	.00019	.00010	5
10	224100	149	.00066	.00000	.00005	.00007	.00007	.00002	.00000	.00003	.00000	.00000	.00005	.00028	.00010	10
15	163100	136	.00083	.00002	.00006	.00012	.00007	.00004	.00001	.00006	.00000	.00000	.00006	.00028	.00012	15
20	111700	143	.00128	.00013	.00009	.00012	.00013	.00004	.00000	.00009	.00000	.00000	.00008	.00047	.00014	20
25	141100	200	.00142	.00018	.00004	.00022	.00009	.00002	.00000	.00015	.00000	.00000	.00007	.00045	.00019	25
30	154400	262	.00170	.00025	.00008	.00028	.00021	.00000	.00000	.00014	.00000	.00000	.00006	.00036	.00028	30
35	139400	417	.00299	.00035	.00012	.00068	.00039	.00012	.00002	.00022	.00000	.00000	.00008	.00049	.00047	35
40	122800	545	.00444	.00053	.00011	.00120	.00067	.00020	.00002	.00038	.00000	.00000	.00008	.00036	.00049	40
45	99800	704	.00705	.00118	.00016	.00185	.00156	.00035	.00001	.00043	.00000	.00000	.00010	.00058	.00082	45
50	78600	956	.01216	.00178	.00023	.00307	.00352	.00084	.00001	.00056	.00000	.00000	.00020	.00059	.00136	50
55	48600	935	.01924	.00350	.00027	.00486	.00576	.00088	.00006	.00084	.00000	.00000	.00014	.00062	.00230	55
60	31000	1036	.03342	.00403	.00039	.00677	.01145	.00277	.00006	.00171	.00000	.00000	.00052	.00084	.00487	60
65	17000	816	.04800	.00435	.00024	.00965	.01824	.00388	.00006	.00282	.00000	.00000	.00018	.00094	.00765	65
70	9600	727	.07573	.00385	.00010	.01219	.03083	.00521	.00000	.00427	.00000	.00000	.00021	.00115	.01792	70
75	4500	499	.11089	.00556	.00022	.01111	.04511	.01200	.00022	.00400	.00000	.00000	.00067	.00133	.03067	75
80	1851	276	.14911	.00486	.00162	.01026	.05348	.01351	.00000	.00554	.00000	.00000	.00054	.00270	.05619	80
85+	749	158	.21095	.00267	.00134	.01202	.06008	.03338	.00134	.01068	.00000	.00000	.00000	.00401	.08545	85+
ALL	1892900	10197														

CRUDE DEATH RATE			.00539	.00051	.00017	.00086	.00119	.00050	.00006	.00025	.00000	.00053	.00009	.00039	.00084	
STANDARDIZED RATE (1)			.00717	.00058	.00018	.00106	.00184	.00068	.00008	.00032	.00000	.00065	.00009	.00041	.00128	
STANDARDIZED RATE (2)			.01307	.00102	.00019	.00156	.00417	.00117	.00006	.00062	.00000	.00038	.00012	.00051	.00287	
GEOMETRIC MEAN			.00866													

LIFE TABLE FOR ALL CAUSES COMBINED

Age (x)	Midyear Population	Deaths During Year	$_nM_x$	$_nq_x$	l_x	$_nd_x$	$_nL_x$	$_nm_x$	$_na_x$	T_x	$_nr_x$	$\overset{\circ}{e}_x$	Age (x)
0	54115	1630	.030121	.029340	100000	2934	97422	.030117	.121206	6569260	.000000	65.693	0
1	228485	435	.001904	.007582	97066	736	386424	.001905	1.500000	6471839	.000000	66.675	1
5	262000	173	.000660	.003291	96330	317	480858	.000659	2.500000	6085415	.000000	63.173	5
10	224100	149	.000665	.003322	96013	319	479284	.000666	2.550940	5604557	.030295	58.373	10
15	163100	136	.000834	.004128	95694	395	477543	.000827	2.654008	5125273	.067491	53.559	15
20	111700	143	.001280	.006411	95299	611	475024	.001286	2.592744	4647730	.035426	48.770	20
25	141100	200	.001417	.007044	94688	667	471811	.001414	2.557159	4172706	-.022753	44.068	25
30	154400	262	.001697	.008445	94021	794	468270	.001696	2.688917	3700895	-.009310	39.362	30
35	139400	417	.002991	.014878	93227	1387	462924	.002996	2.685052	3232625	.011631	34.675	35
40	122800	545	.004438	.022060	91840	2026	454500	.004458	2.680055	2769701	.024113	30.158	40
45	99800	704	.007054	.034939	89814	3138	441881	.007101	2.709156	2315201	.030701	25.778	45
50	78600	956	.012163	.059728	86676	5177	421366	.012286	2.679399	1873320	.050764	21.613	50
55	48600	935	.019239	.093204	81499	7596	389840	.019485	2.675750	1451954	.067617	17.816	55
60	31000	1036	.033419	.156760	73903	11585	341785	.033896	2.606388	1062014	.071472	14.372	60
65	17000	816	.048000	.216823	62318	13512	278669	.048488	2.563539	720329	.069361	11.559	65
70	9600	727	.075729	.321805	48806	15706	204943	.076636	2.511315	441660	.059674	9.049	70
75	4500	499	.110889	.433988	33100	14365	128400	.111877	2.417305	236717	.054256	7.152	75
80	1851	276	.149109	.533574	18735	10004	66928	.145473	2.326403	108318	.054256	5.782	80
85+	749	158	.210948	1.000000	8731	8731	41389	.210948	4.740506	41389	.000000	4.741	85+

NUMBER OF PERSONS DYING (OUT OF 100,000 AT BIRTH) ABOVE AGE X FROM SPECIFIED CAUSES

Age (x)	All Causes	Respiratory T.B.	Other Infec. and Paras.	Neo-plasms	Cardio-vascular	Infl., Pneu., Bronch.	Diar-rheal	Certain Degen-erative	Maternal	Cert. Dis. of Infancy	Motor Vehicle	Other Violence	Other and Unknown	Age (x)
0	100000	8132	1255	15573	32674	8814	367	4908	0	1802	874	3588	22013	0
1	97066	8130	1143	15568	32663	8349	227	4905	0	0	872	3541	21668	1
5	96330	8125	1001	15537	32655	8087	178	4894	0	0	857	3426	21570	5
10	96013	8123	952	15506	32642	8063	178	4885	0	0	808	3333	21523	10
15	95694	8121	926	15474	32610	8055	178	4872	0	0	784	3198	21476	15
20	95299	8109	900	15419	32576	8035	175	4846	0	0	755	3066	21418	20
25	94688	8049	857	15363	32517	8018	175	4803	0	0	717	2839	21350	25
30	94021	7966	837	15260	32474	8008	175	4733	0	0	683	2625	21260	30
35	93227	7851	798	15127	32377	7990	175	4669	0	0	656	2455	21129	35
40	91840	7667	741	14810	32194	7933	165	4569	0	0	619	2226	20916	40
45	89814	7243	689	14264	31888	7840	157	4395	0	0	582	2063	20693	45
50	86676	6719	618	13440	31190	7683	153	4204	0	0	538	1806	20325	50
55	81499	5959	521	12135	29686	7326	147	3967	0	0	451	1559	19748	55
60	73903	4580	416	10222	27406	6976	123	3633	0	0	395	1318	18834	60
65	62318	3197	283	7883	23423	6008	101	3038	0	0	216	1029	17140	65
70	48806	1985	219	5173	18276	4917	85	2241	0	0	170	766	14974	70
75	33100	1156	199	2663	11875	3836	85	1359	0	0	126	530	11231	75
80	18735	478	169	1242	6035	2272	56	846	0	0	39	358	7240	80
85+	8731	111	55	497	2487	1381	55	442	0	0	0	166	3537	85+

NUMBER OF PERSONS SURVIVING TO AGE X IF SPECIFIED CAUSES WERE ELIMINATED

Age (x)	No Causes	Respiratory T.B.	Other Infec. and Paras.	Neo-plasms	Cardio-vascular	Infl., Pneu., Bronch.	Diar-rheal	Certain Degen-erative	Maternal	Cert. Dis. of Infancy	Motor Vehicle	Other Violence	Other and Unknown	(1) + (2)	(1) + (2) + (5) + (6) + (8)	(1)+(2)+ (5)+(6)+ (8)+part of(9)&(12)	(10) + (11)	Age (x)
		(1)	(2)	(3)	(4)	(5)	(6)	(7)	(8)	(9)	(10)	(11)	(12)					
0	100000	100000	100000	100000	100000	100000	100000	100000	100000	100000	100000	100000	100000	100000	100000	100000	100000	0
1	97066	97068	97176	97071	97077	97525	97204	97069	97066	98858	97068	97112	97406	97178	97777	99743	97114	1
5	96330	96337	96581	96366	96349	97048	96516	96344	96330	98108	96347	96491	96766	96588	97496	99529	96508	5
10	96013	96022	96313	96080	96045	96753	96158	96036	96013	97785	96079	96266	96495	96321	97251	99252	96332	10
15	95694	95705	96019	95792	95758	96440	95879	95730	95694	97460	95784	96082	96221	96029	96965	99006	96171	15
20	95299	95322	95648	95452	95356	96062	95486	95361	95299	97058	95417	95817	95882	95671	96626	98671	95936	20
25	94688	94771	95078	94856	94843	95463	94874	94792	94688	96436	94843	95431	95336	95161	96128	98178	95587	25
30	94021	94186	94428	94330	94218	94800	94205	94194	94021	95756	94209	94974	94755	94594	95565	97622	95164	30
35	93227	93505	93670	93667	93519	94018	93410	93463	93227	94948	93441	94343	94086	93949	94932	97010	94559	35
40	91840	92297	92333	92590	92311	92676	92030	92172	91840	93535	92087	93169	92900	92753	93832	95944	93420	40
45	89814	90684	90348	91093	90579	90725	90008	90311	89814	91472	90092	91277	91074	91223	92347	94499	91560	45
50	86676	88036	87261	88735	88109	87711	86867	87344	86676	88276	86988	88345	88255	88631	89887	92087	88663	50
55	81499	83530	82144	84741	84343	82823	81864	82359	81499	83003	81877	83312	83559	84191	85754	88013	83699	55
60	73903	77100	74589	78757	78763	75444	74054	75005	73903	75267	74299	75781	76669	77815	79643	82010	76188	60
65	62318	66345	63019	68734	70431	64452	62499	63805	62318	63468	62817	64173	66285	67091	69676	72201	64687	65
70	48806	53102	49411	56528	60550	51545	48962	50696	48806	49707	49236	50498	53999	53760	56958	59510	50943	70
75	33100	36714	33526	40769	48111	35907	33206	35135	33100	33711	33429	34446	40198	37186	40469	42911	34788	75
80	18735	21378	19000	24382	34311	21636	18817	20289	18735	19081	18987	19630	26687	21681	25148	27651	19894	80
85+	8731	10246	8932	12027	20963	10793	8770	9751	8731	8892	8875	9283	16499	10482	13015	15219	9436	85+

ADDED YRS OF LIFE

	No Causes	(1)	(2)	(3)	(4)	(5)	(6)	(7)	(8)	(9)	(10)	(11)	(12)	(1)+(2)	(1)+(2)+(5)+(6)+(8)	(1)+(2)+(5)+(6)+(8)+part of(9)&(12)	(10)+(11)
TOTAL		1.275	.391	2.333	4.400	1.344	.147	.656	.000	1.210	.210	.956	2.983	1.682	3.316	5.484	1.171
WORK	3.968	.540	.107	.811	.749	.172	.009	.232	.000	.000	.092	.471	.460	.650	.839	.563	.564

POPULATION, DEATHS, DEATH RATES FOR ALL CAUSES COMBINED, AND SPECIFIED CAUSES

Age Start of Interval	Midyear Population	Deaths During Year	All Causes	Respiratory T.B.	Other Infec. and Paras.	Neo-plasms	Cardio-vascular	Infl., Pneu., Bronch.	Diar-rheal	Certain Degen-erative	Maternal	Cert. Dis. of Infancy	Motor Vehicle	Other Violence	Other and Unknown	Age Start of Interval
0	51116	1237	.02420	.00000	.00084	.00010	.00016	.00505	.00133	.00004	.00000	.01348	.00002	.00045	.00274	0
1	213484	355	.00166	.00000	.00033	.00006	.00002	.00059	.00011	.00001	.00000	.00000	.00003	.00029	.00023	1
5	243800	160	.00066	.00000	.00010	.00006	.00004	.00010	.00001	.00002	.00000	.00000	.00006	.00014	.00013	5
10	204100	87	.00043	.00000	.00006	.00004	.00007	.00003	.00000	.00002	.00000	.00000	.00003	.00008	.00009	10
15	139700	77	.00055	.00002	.00006	.00007	.00010	.00001	.00000	.00001	.00000	.00000	.00001	.00016	.00009	15
20	87100	66	.00076	.00008	.00006	.00011	.00007	.00000	.00001	.00000	.00007	.00000	.00000	.00022	.00011	20
25	116600	119	.00102	.00012	.00006	.00015	.00009	.00002	.00001	.00006	.00006	.00000	.00002	.00027	.00017	25
30	134600	160	.00119	.00011	.00007	.00025	.00021	.00004	.00000	.00008	.00007	.00000	.00002	.00013	.00022	30
35	127700	235	.00184	.00026	.00005	.00057	.00030	.00006	.00000	.00009	.00004	.00000	.00003	.00016	.00024	35
40	114800	269	.00234	.00017	.00008	.00078	.00048	.00006	.00002	.00011	.00012	.00000	.00005	.00015	.00032	40
45	94400	338	.00358	.00023	.00005	.00135	.00100	.00011	.00002	.00014	.00001	.00000	.00004	.00020	.00043	45
50	80800	492	.00609	.00053	.00007	.00207	.00173	.00024	.00005	.00025	.00000	.00000	.00009	.00033	.00073	50
55	61400	499	.00813	.00062	.00013	.00244	.00275	.00029	.00003	.00041	.00000	.00000	.00007	.00018	.00121	55
60	49700	665	.01338	.00062	.00020	.00330	.00559	.00070	.00000	.00056	.00000	.00000	.00018	.00044	.00177	60
65	35200	669	.01901	.00099	.00009	.00429	.00781	.00125	.00000	.00080	.00000	.00000	.00011	.00037	.00330	65
70	23500	816	.03472	.00106	.00017	.00638	.01464	.00255	.00009	.00162	.00000	.00000	.00013	.00064	.00745	70
75	13100	707	.05397	.00092	.00023	.00568	.02328	.00664	.00038	.00229	.00000	.00000	.00031	.00115	.01290	75
80	5936	545	.09181	.00168	.00034	.00825	.02746	.01257	.00034	.00219	.00000	.00000	.00051	.00202	.03605	80
85+	2264	417	.18419	.00044	.00044	.01104	.05830	.02606	.00088	.00486	.00000	.00000	.00000	.00177	.08039	85+
ALL	1799300	7913														

CRUDE DEATH RATE			.00440	.00017	.00013	.00074	.00116	.00047	.00006	.00015	.00002	.00038	.00005	.00022	.00083	
STANDARDIZED RATE (1)			.00401	.00015	.00014	.00062	.00096	.00046	.00007	.00012	.00002	.00047	.00004	.00022	.00072	
STANDARDIZED RATE (2)			.00693	.00024	.00013	.00112	.00219	.00071	.00006	.00025	.00003	.00028	.00006	.00026	.00161	
GEOMETRIC MEAN			.00517													

LIFE TABLE FOR ALL CAUSES COMBINED

Age (x)	Midyear Population	Deaths During Year	$_nM_x$	$_nq_x$	l_x	$_nd_x$	$_nL_x$	$_nm_x$	$_na_x$	T_x	$_nr_x$	$\overset{\circ}{e}_x$	Age (x)
0	51116	1237	.024200	.023690	100000	2369	97894	.024200	.111140	7381764	.000000	73.818	0
1	213484	355	.001663	.006627	97631	647	388907	.001664	1.500000	7283870	.000000	74.606	1
5	243800	160	.000656	.003289	96984	319	484123	.000659	2.500000	6894963	.000000	71.094	5
10	204100	87	.000426	.002110	96665	204	482801	.000423	2.429534	6410841	.035261	66.320	10
15	139700	77	.000551	.002592	96461	250	481714	.000519	2.634167	5928040	.082376	61.455	15
20	87100	66	.000758	.003794	96211	365	480192	.000760	2.635274	5446327	.044539	56.608	20
25	116600	119	.001021	.005081	95846	487	478054	.001019	2.585130	4966135	-.028884	51.814	25
30	134600	160	.001189	.005914	95359	564	475465	.001186	2.641105	4488081	-.018691	47.065	30
35	127700	235	.001840	.009167	94795	869	471914	.001841	2.628021	4012616	-.004030	42.329	35
40	114800	269	.002343	.011690	93926	1098	467049	.002351	2.649514	3540702	.021791	37.697	40
45	54400	338	.003581	.017850	92828	1657	460342	.003599	2.707956	3073653	.028178	33.111	45
50	80800	492	.006089	.030185	91171	2752	449369	.006124	2.643078	2613311	.034587	28.664	50
55	61400	499	.008127	.040116	88419	3547	433809	.008176	2.663871	2163942	.038560	24.474	55
60	49700	665	.013380	.065298	84872	5542	411283	.013475	2.640405	1730134	.039748	20.385	60
65	35200	669	.019006	.091764	79330	7282	379727	.019177	2.676119	1318851	.049662	16.625	65
70	23500	816	.034723	.162364	72048	11698	332515	.035180	2.629955	939123	.057804	13.035	70
75	13100	707	.053969	.241574	60350	14579	266489	.054708	2.581410	606608	.076210	10.051	75
80	5936	545	.091813	.380044	45771	17395	186058	.093492	2.539691	340119	.076210	7.431	80
85+	2264	417	.184187	1.000000	28376	28376	154061	.184197	5.429257	154061	.000000	5.429	85+

NUMBER OF PERSONS DYING (OUT OF 100,000 AT BIRTH) ABOVE AGE X FROM SPECIFIED CAUSES

Age (x)	All Causes	Respiratory T.B.	Other Infec. and Paras.	Neoplasms	Cardiovascular	Infl., Pneu., Bronch.	Diarrheal	Certain Degenerative	Maternal	Cert. Dis. of Infancy	Motor Vehicle	Other Violence	Other and Unknown	Age (x)
0	100000	2613	965	13629	33826	11055	572	3415	174	1320	559	2601	29271	0
1	97631	2613	883	13620	33811	10561	442	3411	174	0	557	2557	29002	1
5	96984	2613	755	13596	33802	10332	400	3408	174	0	546	2446	28912	5
10	96665	2613	707	13566	33782	10284	396	3398	174	0	517	2378	28850	10
15	96461	2613	677	13547	33748	10268	396	3386	174	0	503	2340	28809	15
20	96211	2603	646	13514	33706	10267	396	3380	174	0	496	2260	28769	20
25	95846	2564	618	13459	33674	10267	390	3380	140	0	485	2155	28714	25
30	95359	2506	590	13390	33629	10259	386	3351	112	0	477	2027	28632	30
35	94795	2454	558	13271	33530	10241	386	3313	80	0	466	1967	28529	35
40	93926	2332	517	13001	33390	10211	386	3272	61	0	451	1890	28415	40
45	92828	2250	481	12637	33165	10183	378	3219	4	0	427	1820	28264	45
50	91171	2142	456	12014	32703	10134	368	3155	0	0	407	1727	28065	50
55	88419	1902	423	11081	31919	10027	346	3043	0	0	368	1577	27733	55
60	84872	1633	366	10018	30713	9899	332	2865	0	0	340	1499	27207	60
65	79330	1375	283	8654	28394	9606	332	2632	0	0	265	1316	26473	65
70	72048	996	251	7016	25400	9125	332	2327	0	0	222	1176	25203	70
75	60350	642	194	4880	20466	8259	302	1782	0	0	179	961	22685	75
80	45771	398	132	3319	14193	6446	198	1168	0	0	96	650	19171	80
85+	28376	68	68	1701	8982	4015	136	749	0	0	0	272	12385	85+

NUMBER OF PERSONS SURVIVING TO AGE X IF SPECIFIED CAUSES WERE ELIMINATED

Age (x)	No Causes	Respiratory T.B. (1)	Other Infec. and Paras. (2)	Neoplasms (3)	Cardiovascular (4)	Infl., Pneu., Bronch. (5)	Diarrheal (6)	Certain Degenerative (7)	Maternal (8)	Cert. Dis. of Infancy (9)	Motor Vehicle (10)	Other Violence (11)	Other and Unknown (12)	(1)+(2)	(1)+(2)+(5)+(6)+(8)	(1)+(2)+(5)+(6)+(8)+part of(9)&(12)	(10)+(11)	Age (x)
0	100000	100000	100000	100000	100000	100000	100000	100000	100000	100000	100000	100000	100000	100000	100000	100000	100000	0
1	97631	97631	97712	97640	97646	98120	97760	97635	97631	98544	97633	97674	97857	97712	98331	99773	97676	1
5	96984	96984	97192	97017	97008	97700	97154	96991	96984	98288	96957	97139	97338	97192	98081	99585	97151	5
10	96665	96665	96921	96728	96709	97427	96838	96682	96665	97765	96707	96886	97080	96921	97859	99385	96928	10
15	96461	96461	96746	96542	96538	97237	96634	96490	96461	97758	96517	96720	96917	96746	97699	99234	96776	15
20	96211	96221	96526	96325	96330	96986	96383	96246	96211	97505	96274	96550	96706	96536	97488	99028	96612	20
25	95846	95895	96188	96015	95997	96618	96024	95881	95880	97135	95919	96288	96394	96237	97227	98782	96362	25
30	95359	95466	95728	95596	95554	96135	95540	95422	95421	96641	95440	95928	95986	95835	96860	98436	96009	30
35	94795	94953	95193	95150	95088	95585	94975	94896	94888	96070	94886	95420	95522	95252	96423	98023	95512	35
40	93926	94204	94362	94547	94356	94735	94104	94067	94037	95189	94032	94623	94761	94641	95754	97375	94729	40
45	92828	93185	93295	93807	93478	93659	93012	93020	92995	94076	92956	93587	93805	93653	94849	96490	93716	45
50	91171	91629	91654	92759	92272	92036	91362	91423	91339	92357	91317	92009	92330	92114	93355	94997	92156	50
55	88419	89101	88920	90898	90272	89365	88625	88774	88582	89608	88599	89381	89875	89606	90943	92600	89563	55
60	84872	85792	85409	88328	87866	85507	85084	85388	85028	86013	85072	85873	86795	86335	87767	89450	86075	60
65	79330	80442	79913	83943	84483	80585	79528	80039	79476	80397	79590	80444	81856	81033	82672	84357	80708	65
70	72048	73424	72608	77504	79826	73655	72228	72986	72181	73017	72325	73195	75604	73995	75974	77716	73476	70
75	60350	61831	60871	67391	72054	62515	60529	61642	60461	61162	60621	61511	65795	62365	64914	66766	61787	75
80	45771	47110	46221	52632	61525	49080	45997	47295	45855	46387	46049	46928	53367	47573	51359	53548	47213	80
85+	28376	29472	29705	34114	44016	32530	28565	29661	28428	28758	28624	29397	35869	29814	34470	37810	29654	85+

ADDED YRS OF LIFE

	No Causes	(1)	(2)	(3)	(4)	(5)	(6)	(7)	(8)	(9)	(10)	(11)	(12)	(1)+(2)	...	...	(10)+(11)
TOTAL		.510	.369	2.316	4.803	1.552	.175	.460	.076	.992	.134	.672	4.074	.883	2.758	4.810	.808
WORK	2.217	.184	.081	.554	.490	.061	.011	.092	.053	.000	.036	.230	.300	.265	.392	.459	.266

POPULATION, DEATHS, DEATH RATES FOR ALL CAUSES COMBINED, AND SPECIFIED CAUSES

Age Start of Interval	Midyear Population	Deaths During Year	All Causes	Respiratory T.B.	Other Infec. and Paras.	Neoplasms	Cardiovascular	Infl., Pneu., Bronch.	Diarrheal	Certain Degenerative	Maternal	Cert. Dis. of Infancy	Motor Vehicle	Other Violence	Other and Unknown	Age Start of Interval
0	77330	3989	.05158	.00009	.00106	.00010	.00000	.01072	.00295	.00001	.00000	.02558	.00000	.00057	.01050	0
1	340910	567	.00166	.00003	.00019	.00013	.00003	.00043	.00015	.00002	.00000	.00000	.00001	.00028	.00040	1
5	468164	265	.00057	.00000	.00004	.00009	.00003	.00005	.00000	.00001	.00000	.00000	.00004	.00015	.00015	5
10	421348	241	.00057	.00000	.00002	.00007	.00005	.00003	.00001	.00001	.00000	.00000	.00002	.00021	.00015	10
15	381950	453	.00119	.00002	.00003	.00013	.00013	.00003	.00001	.00004	.00000	.00000	.00007	.00059	.00013	15
20	335234	503	.00150	.00007	.00003	.00013	.00013	.00003	.00000	.00005	.00000	.00000	.00020	.00077	.00010	20
25	361198	587	.00163	.00014	.00003	.00017	.00019	.00003	.00001	.00005	.00000	.00000	.00022	.00067	.00012	25
30	367113	695	.00189	.00025	.00003	.00019	.00028	.00005	.00000	.00007	.00000	.00000	.00014	.00067	.00020	30
35	352276	911	.00259	.00034	.00004	.00036	.00049	.00007	.00000	.00016	.00000	.00000	.00013	.00075	.00024	35
40	210022	705	.00336	.00041	.00005	.00049	.00075	.00009	.00001	.00021	.00000	.00000	.00017	.00079	.00038	40
45	340346	1754	.00515	.00050	.00009	.00113	.00138	.00018	.00001	.00032	.00000	.00000	.00014	.00087	.00054	45
50	309670	2773	.00895	.00076	.00016	.00219	.00294	.00042	.00001	.00052	.00000	.00000	.00009	.00098	.00089	50
55	272879	4292	.01573	.00105	.00017	.00410	.00588	.00071	.00004	.00083	.00000	.00000	.00015	.00116	.00165	55
60	219847	5380	.02447	.00148	.00019	.00618	.01029	.00126	.00002	.00115	.00000	.00000	.00013	.00115	.00262	60
65	145562	5837	.04010	.00161	.00021	.00969	.01843	.00254	.00002	.00166	.00000	.00000	.00010	.00131	.00453	65
70	109673	6850	.06246	.00177	.00025	.01232	.03189	.00426	.00012	.00186	.00000	.00000	.00013	.00160	.00827	70
75	70576	7151	.10132	.00154	.00028	.01539	.05547	.00764	.00016	.00237	.00000	.00000	.00011	.00227	.01610	75
80	34020	5312	.15614	.00135	.00029	.01464	.08933	.01170	.00038	.00232	.00000	.00000	.00015	.00332	.03266	80
85+	11694	3402	.29092	.00086	.00077	.01616	.16068	.02411	.00077	.00291	.00000	.00000	.00000	.00034	.07628	85+
ALL	4829812	51667														

	All Causes	Respiratory T.B.	Other Infec. and Paras.	Neoplasms	Cardiovascular	Infl., Pneu., Bronch.	Diarrheal	Certain Degenerative	Maternal	Cert. Dis. of Infancy	Motor Vehicle	Other Violence	Other and Unknown
CRUDE DEATH RATE	.01070	.00042	.00011	.00179	.00433	.00079	.00008	.00035	.00000	.00041	.00011	.00074	.00158
STANDARDIZED RATE (1)	.00713	.00025	.00011	.00096	.00207	.00072	.00013	.00020	.00000	.00090	.00009	.00060	.00110
STANDARDIZED RATE (2)	.01226	.00041	.00011	.00190	.00511	.00096	.00009	.00036	.00000	.00053	.00011	.00076	.00192
GEOMETRIC MEAN	.00828												

LIFE TABLE FOR ALL CAUSES COMBINED

Age (x)	Midyear Population	Deaths During Year	nM_x	nq_x	l_x	nd_x	nL_x	nm_x	na_x	T_x	nr_x	$\overset{\circ}{e}_x$	Age (x)
0	77330	3989	.051584	.049440	100000	4944	95836	.051588	.157693	6605357	.000000	66.054	0
1	340910	567	.001663	.006617	95056	629	378652	.001661	1.500000	6509521	.000000	68.481	1
5	468164	265	.000566	.002817	94427	266	471470	.000564	2.500000	6130870	.000000	64.927	5
10	421348	241	.000572	.002867	94161	270	470191	.000574	2.725309	5659400	.014075	60.103	10
15	381950	453	.001186	.005943	93891	558	468149	.001192	2.659797	5189209	.022519	55.268	15
20	335234	503	.001500	.007479	93333	698	464960	.001501	2.557008	4721060	.010956	50.583	20
25	361198	587	.001625	.008085	92635	749	461337	.001624	2.546451	4256100	-.005049	45.945	25
30	367113	695	.001893	.009414	91886	865	457356	.001891	2.602601	3794763	-.011791	41.299	30
35	352276	911	.002586	.012909	91021	1175	452300	.002598	2.612766	3337407	.045137	36.666	35
40	210022	705	.003357	.016706	89846	1501	445697	.003368	2.646153	2885107	.020889	32.112	40
45	340346	1754	.005154	.025219	88345	2228	436630	.005103	2.713009	2439410	-.039153	27.612	45
50	309670	2773	.008955	.043882	86117	3779	421977	.008955	2.722226	2002780	.000079	23.257	50
55	272879	4292	.015729	.076016	82338	6259	397099	.015762	2.668857	1580803	.010607	19.199	55
60	219847	5380	.024472	.116353	76079	8852	359538	.024620	2.643823	1183703	-.031671	15.559	60
65	145562	5837	.040100	.184003	67227	12370	306468	.040363	2.601691	824165	-.033136	12.259	65
70	109673	6850	.062458	.271433	54857	14890	237851	.062602	2.553140	517697	.011697	9.437	70
75	70576	7151	.101323	.404534	39967	16168	159068	.101642	2.478520	279846	-.013361	7.002	75
80	34020	5312	.156143	.555612	23799	13223	84425	.156625	2.385584	120778	-.013361	5.075	80
85+	11694	3402	.290918	1.000000	10576	10576	36354	.290918	3.437390	36354	.000000	3.437	85+

NUMBER OF PERSONS DYING (OUT OF 100,000 AT BIRTH) ABOVE AGE X FROM SPECIFIED CAUSES

Age (x)	All Causes	Respiratory T.B.	Other Infec. and Paras.	Neoplasms	Cardiovascular	Infl., Pneu., Bronch.	Diarrheal	Certain Degenerative	Maternal	Cert. Dis. of Infancy	Motor Vehicle	Other Violence	Other and Unknown	Age (x)
0	100000	3384	765	16297	44387	7239	513	3028	0	2452	762	5656	15517	0
1	95056	3375	664	16287	44387	6212	231	3027	0	0	762	5601	14510	1
5	94427	3363	592	16236	44377	6050	175	3020	0	0	758	5496	14360	5
10	94161	3363	571	16193	44363	6025	173	3014	0	0	740	5428	14291	10
15	93891	3362	559	16160	44339	6009	170	3008	0	0	731	5330	14223	15
20	93333	3353	544	16101	44277	5996	166	2987	0	0	697	5050	14162	20
25	92635	3321	531	16039	44217	5983	165	2962	0	0	605	4694	14118	25
30	91886	3257	518	15959	44130	5971	162	2938	0	0	505	4385	14061	30
35	91021	3144	503	15871	44001	5947	161	2906	0	0	443	4078	13967	35
40	89846	2988	487	15707	43779	5913	160	2833	0	0	383	3739	13857	40
45	88345	2803	463	15487	43442	5875	153	2738	0	0	308	3386	13690	45
50	86117	2585	422	15001	42850	5797	150	2600	0	0	249	3006	13457	50
55	82338	2265	357	14077	41610	5621	144	2379	0	0	210	2594	13081	55
60	76079	1848	290	12445	39269	5339	128	2049	0	0	150	2134	12427	60
65	67227	1313	223	10212	35541	4883	120	1635	0	0	103	1722	11475	65
70	54857	818	158	7226	29850	4099	113	1125	0	0	73	1319	10076	70
75	39967	397	99	4292	22244	3084	85	682	0	0	43	939	8102	75
80	23799	151	54	1841	13390	1865	60	305	0	0	25	577	5531	80
85+	10576	31	28	588	5841	877	28	106	0	0	12	292	2773	85+

NUMBER OF PERSONS SURVIVING TO AGE X IF SPECIFIED CAUSES WERE ELIMINATED

Age (x)	No Causes	Respiratory T.B. (1)	Other Infec. and Paras. (2)	Neoplasms (3)	Cardiovascular (4)	Infl., Pneu., Bronch. (5)	Diarrheal (6)	Certain Degenerative (7)	Maternal (8)	Cert. Dis. of Infancy (9)	Motor Vehicle (10)	Other Violence (11)	Other and Unknown (12)	(1)+(2)	(1)+(2)+(5)+(6)+(8)	(1)+(2)+(5)+(6)+(8)+part of(9)&(12)	(10)+(11)	Age (x)
0	100000	100000	100000	100000	100000	100000	100000	100000	100000	100000	100000	100000	100000	100000	100000	100000	100000	0
1	95056	95065	95155	95066	95056	96062	95331	95057	95056	97477	95056	95110	96043	95163	96449	99775	95110	1
5	94427	94448	94597	94488	94437	95590	94756	94435	94427	96832	94431	94585	95558	94617	96117	99530	94589	5
10	94161	94182	94351	94264	94185	95346	94492	94175	94161	96559	94183	94387	95359	94372	95895	99318	94409	10
15	93891	93913	94093	94027	93939	95089	94224	93911	93891	96282	93922	94214	95154	94114	95653	99079	94245	15
20	93333	93363	93549	93527	93442	94537	93668	93374	93333	95710	93398	93935	94650	93579	95126	98538	94000	20
25	92635	92697	92862	92890	92803	93843	92968	92700	92635	94994	92791	93590	93987	92924	94474	97868	93747	25
30	91886	92011	92124	92218	92140	93056	92219	91975	91886	94226	92140	93145	93285	92250	93804	97181	93403	30
35	91021	91258	91272	91438	91401	92244	91352	91141	91021	93339	91335	92578	92502	91509	93077	96447	92897	35
40	89846	90309	90109	90422	90443	91088	90174	90037	89846	92134	90216	91726	91419	90500	92086	95443	92103	40
45	88345	88912	88628	89131	89269	89604	88675	88627	88345	90595	88783	90551	90060	89197	90806	94150	91001	45
50	86117	86887	86433	87369	87611	87423	86441	86529	86117	88310	86603	88653	88024	87206	88861	92176	89153	50
55	82338	83390	82704	84457	85010	83761	82654	82949	82338	84435	82841	85178	84538	83761	85536	88792	85698	55
60	76079	77458	76482	79662	80907	77670	76386	76963	76079	78016	76601	79160	78759	77868	79818	82952	79704	60
65	67227	68957	67646	72623	75320	69073	67506	68403	67227	68939	67733	70352	70528	69387	71589	74533	70881	65
70	54857	56726	55258	62235	67457	57095	55051	56284	54857	56254	55297	57786	58891	57140	59725	62359	58250	70
75	39967	41696	40309	48243	57828	42507	40162	41392	39967	40985	40313	42441	44752	42053	44943	47158	42808	75
80	23799	25020	24037	31046	45767	26321	23934	24944	23799	24405	24018	25566	28954	25270	28107	29769	25802	80
85+	10576	11201	10699	14898	32316	12427	10657	11221	10576	10845	10682	11561	15238	11331	13416	14480	11677	85+

ADDED YRS OF LIFE

	No Causes	(1)	(2)	(3)	(4)	(5)	(6)	(7)	(8)	(9)	(10)	(11)	(12)	(1)+(2)	(1)+(2)+(5)+(6)+(8)	+part of(9)&(12)	(10)+(11)
TOTAL		.602	.237	2.208	6.312	1.396	.251	.440	.000	1.678	.241	1.471	2.323	.844	2.541	5.194	1.721
WORK	3.509	.280	.053	.578	.784	.106	.008	.164	.000	.000	.165	.831	.321	.334	.451	.501	1.000

POPULATION, DEATHS, DEATH RATES FOR ALL CAUSES COMBINED, AND SPECIFIED CAUSES

Age Start of Interval	Midyear Population	Deaths During Year	All Causes	Respiratory T. B.	Other Infec. and Paras.	Neoplasms	Cardiovascular	Infl., Pneu., Bronch.	Diarrheal	Certain Degenerative	Maternal	Cert. Dis. of Infancy	Motor Vehicle	Other Violence	Other and Unknown	Age Start of Interval
0	74436	2989	.04016	.00005	.00107	.00007	.00001	.00667	.00254	.00003	.00000	.01904	.00001	.00054	.00813	0
1	331077	477	.00144	.00001	.00024	.00008	.00004	.00040	.00012	.00001	.00000	.00000	.00002	.00015	.00037	1
5	440683	171	.00039	.00000	.00004	.00005	.00002	.00006	.00000	.00001	.00000	.00000	.00003	.00005	.00013	5
10	387377	114	.00029	.00001	.00002	.00004	.00005	.00001	.00000	.00002	.00000	.00000	.00001	.00005	.00013	10
15	386775	217	.00056	.00002	.00001	.00006	.00009	.00003	.00001	.00003	.00002	.00000	.00001	.00018	.00010	15
20	357517	271	.00076	.00004	.00003	.00009	.00011	.00002	.00000	.00003	.00004	.00000	.00003	.00024	.00012	20
25	363930	332	.00091	.00001	.00001	.00012	.00017	.00004	.00000	.00004	.00007	.00000	.00002	.00017	.00016	25
30	381465	505	.00132	.00021	.00004	.00034	.00024	.00003	.00000	.00007	.00006	.00000	.00001	.00016	.00017	30
35	396094	720	.00182	.00018	.00005	.00062	.00040	.00007	.00000	.00006	.00006	.00000	.00002	.00017	.00018	35
40	241885	636	.00263	.00021	.00005	.00095	.00059	.00006	.00002	.00012	.00005	.00000	.00002	.00021	.00034	40
45	376855	1453	.00386	.00020	.00006	.00154	.00113	.00011	.00001	.00013	.00000	.00000	.00002	.00029	.00037	45
50	348899	2013	.00577	.00018	.00009	.00215	.00201	.00017	.00002	.00028	.00000	.00000	.00001	.00028	.00058	50
55	304811	2741	.00899	.00025	.00009	.00302	.00368	.00028	.00001	.00047	.00000	.00000	.00002	.00033	.00085	55
60	257917	4185	.01623	.00033	.00016	.00466	.00760	.00054	.00003	.00086	.00000	.00000	.00002	.00047	.00154	60
65	203408	5615	.02760	.00052	.00024	.00638	.01460	.00136	.00005	.00130	.00000	.00000	.00004	.00065	.00246	65
70	156414	7502	.04796	.00052	.00022	.00824	.02808	.00266	.00016	.00160	.00000	.00000	.00005	.00098	.00544	70
75	96293	8702	.09037	.00080	.00036	.01152	.05618	.00567	.00017	.00188	.00000	.00000	.00009	.00187	.01183	75
80	44745	6725	.15030	.00060	.00029	.01276	.09313	.00568	.00034	.00174	.00000	.00000	.00013	.00443	.02720	80
85+	18482	4490	.24294	.00027	.00043	.01266	.14246	.01742	.00032	.00124	.00000	.00000	.00027	.00752	.06033	85+
ALL	5169063	49858														
CRUDE DEATH RATE			.00965	.00017	.00010	.00169	.00471	.00062	.00006	.00028	.00002	.00027	.00002	.00034	.00135	
STANDARDIZED RATE (1)			.00532	.00010	.00011	.00079	.00177	.00054	.00011	.00013	.00002	.00027	.00002	.00034	.00135	
STANDARDIZED RATE (2)			.00953	.00015	.00010	.00151	.00457	.00068	.00008	.00025	.00002	.00067	.00002	.00023	.00082	
GEOMETRIC MEAN			.00571													

LIFE TABLE FOR ALL CAUSES COMBINED

Age (x)	Midyear Population	Deaths During Year	$_nM_x$	$_nq_x$	l_x	$_nd_x$	$_nL_x$	$_nm_x$	$_na_x$	T_x	$_nr_x$	$\overset{\circ}{e}_x$	Age (x)
0	74436	2989	.040155	.038810	100000	3881	96656	.040153	.138264	7030314	.000000	70.303	0
1	331077	477	.001441	.005743	96119	552	383096	.001441	1.500000	6933658	.000000	72.136	1
5	440683	171	.000388	.001936	95567	185	477373	.000388	2.500000	6550562	.000000	68.544	5
10	387377	114	.000294	.001478	95382	141	476575	.000296	2.621158	6073190	.010624	63.672	10
15	386775	217	.000561	.002803	95241	267	475583	.000561	2.670100	5596615	.008227	58.763	15
20	357517	271	.000758	.003780	94974	359	474007	.000757	2.595172	5121032	.007619	53.920	20
25	363930	332	.000912	.004555	94615	431	472052	.000913	2.626160	4647026	-.000912	49.115	25
30	381465	505	.001324	.006583	94184	620	469457	.001321	2.641129	4174974	-.018425	44.328	30
35	396094	720	.001818	.009055	93564	851	465816	.001827	2.645662	3705516	.034127	39.604	35
40	241885	636	.002629	.013105	92713	1215	460712	.002637	2.651749	3239700	-.019853	34.943	40
45	376855	1453	.003856	.018973	91498	1736	453430	.003829	2.661050	2778988	-.036232	30.372	45
50	348899	2013	.005770	.028486	89762	2557	442859	.005774	2.672647	2325558	.002245	25.908	50
55	304811	2741	.008992	.044206	87205	3855	427219	.009023	2.715791	1882699	.015580	21.589	55
60	257917	4185	.016226	.078584	83350	6550	401656	.016308	2.695515	1455480	.022206	17.462	60
65	203408	5615	.027605	.130234	76800	10002	360641	.027734	2.664592	1053824	-.021251	13.722	65
70	156414	7502	.047962	.216354	66798	14452	299836	.048200	2.636703	693183	-.020833	10.377	70
75	96293	8702	.090370	.372235	52346	19485	213730	.091166	2.536577	393348	.030385	7.514	75
80	44745	6725	.150296	.543897	32861	17873	117923	.151565	2.404908	179617	.030385	5.466	80
85+	18482	4490	.242939	1.000000	14988	14988	61694	.242939	4.116258	61694	.000000	4.116	85+

NUMBER OF PERSONS DYING (OUT OF 100,000 AT BIRTH) ABOVE AGE X FROM SPECIFIED CAUSES

Age (x)	All Causes	Respiratory T.B.	Other Infec. and Paras.	Neoplasms	Cardiovascular	Infl., Pneu., Bronch.	Diarrheal	Certain Degenerative	Maternal	Cert. Dis. of Infancy	Motor Vehicle	Other Violence	Other and Unknown	Age (x)
0	100000	1390	770	15499	52571	6354	499	2563	140	1840	190	3205	14979	0
1	96119	1385	666	15493	52569	5516	253	2561	140	0	189	3153	14194	1
5	95567	1382	574	15463	52555	5363	207	2556	140	0	181	3094	14052	5
10	95382	1380	557	15439	52548	5335	205	2553	140	0	167	3069	13989	10
15	95241	1378	547	15422	52523	5329	205	2542	140	0	164	3044	13947	15
20	94974	1371	542	15392	52480	5314	201	2529	129	0	160	2957	13899	20
25	94615	1351	529	15350	52430	5304	201	2513	107	0	145	2841	13844	25
30	94184	1299	523	15293	52348	5284	200	2496	76	0	136	2762	13767	30
35	93564	1199	504	15135	52235	5268	199	2466	49	0	132	2687	13690	35
40	92713	1116	483	14842	52046	5235	197	2436	21	0	124	2606	13607	40
45	91498	1019	460	14401	51772	5207	190	2379	0	0	114	2509	13447	45
50	89762	926	433	13707	51266	5155	186	2319	0	0	108	2379	13283	50
55	87205	846	393	12755	50376	5080	179	2195	0	0	102	2254	13025	55
60	83350	739	357	11461	48796	4962	176	1992	0	0	94	2114	12659	60
65	76800	608	293	9581	45725	4742	162	1644	0	0	84	1925	12036	65
70	66798	419	206	7274	40429	4248	144	1174	0	0	68	1650	11146	70
75	52346	262	140	4797	31963	3446	96	692	0	0	53	1394	9503	75
80	32861	90	62	2323	19845	2222	60	289	0	0	33	990	6947	80
85+	14988	17	27	781	8789	1075	20	77	0	0	17	464	3721	85+

NUMBER OF PERSONS SURVIVING TO AGE X IF SPECIFIED CAUSES WERE ELIMINATED

Age (x)	No Causes	Respiratory T.B. (1)	Other Infec. and Paras. (2)	Neoplasms (3)	Cardiovascular (4)	Infl., Pneu., Bronch. (5)	Diarrheal (6)	Certain Degenerative (7)	Maternal (8)	Cert. Dis. of Infancy (9)	Motor Vehicle (10)	Other Violence (11)	Other and Unknown (12)	(1)+(2)	(1)+(2)+(5)+(6)+(8)	(1)+(2)+(5)+(6)+(8)+part of (9)&(12)	(10)+(11)	Age (x)
0	100000	100000	100000	100000	100000	100000	100000	100000	100000	100000	100000	100000	100000	100000	100000	100000	100000	0
1	96119	96124	96221	96125	96121	96944	96360	96121	96119	97940	96120	96170	96892	96226	97296	99802	96171	1
5	95567	95575	95760	95603	95583	96541	95853	95574	95567	97377	95576	95677	96478	95768	97034	99639	95686	5
10	95382	95392	95592	95442	95405	96383	95670	95392	95382	97189	95405	95516	96355	95602	96896	99524	95539	10
15	95241	95253	95461	95318	95289	96246	95528	95262	95241	97045	95267	95400	96255	95473	96771	99403	95426	15
20	94974	94993	95198	95080	95065	95992	95264	95008	94985	96773	95004	95220	96033	95217	96542	99178	95250	20
25	94615	94654	94851	94763	94755	95639	94904	94665	94648	96407	94660	94976	95726	94890	96243	98883	95021	25
30	94184	94274	94425	94388	94406	95406	94413	94250	94248	95968	94237	94623	95368	94516	95917	98572	94676	30
35	93564	93754	93823	93925	93897	94613	93852	93660	93654	95336	93621	94075	94818	94013	95451	98118	94132	35
40	92713	92984	92990	93364	93232	93785	93000	92838	92830	94469	92778	93300	94039	93262	94752	97419	93365	40
45	91498	91862	91794	92583	92285	92584	91789	91678	91635	93231	91572	92175	92568	92159	93689	96354	92249	45
50	89762	90211	90080	91524	91041	90051	89998	89896	89762	91462	89840	90555	91369	90531	92090	94729	90634	50
55	87205	87721	87553	89879	89342	88366	87493	87557	87335	88857	87287	88100	89026	88071	89672	92264	88183	55
60	83350	83948	83718	87218	86991	84577	83628	83886	83474	84929	83436	84344	85456	84319	85973	88487	84431	60
65	76800	77478	77201	82272	83293	78145	77070	77631	76915	78255	76889	77899	79356	77882	79643	82019	77989	65
70	66798	67565	67228	73890	78007	68439	67049	67963	66898	68063	66890	67976	69885	67999	70037	72203	68070	70
75	52346	53086	52741	60359	70526	54363	52585	53690	52424	53338	52431	53535	56308	53487	55885	57749	53623	75
80	32861	33461	33170	40172	59151	35140	33039	34026	32910	33484	32930	33935	37585	33776	36369	37788	34006	80
85+	14988	15311	15152	19606	43845	16856	15096	15664	15010	15272	15030	15839	19752	15479	17559	18474	15884	85+

ADDED YRS OF LIFE

	No Causes	(1)	(2)	(3)	(4)	(5)	(6)	(7)	(8)	(9)	(10)	(11)	(12)	(1)+(2)	(1)+(2)+(5)+(6)+(8)	+part of(9)&(12)	(10)+(11)
TOTAL		.291	.251	2.312	6.058	1.205	.233	.362	.061	1.329	.052	.603	2.122	.544	2.071	4.188	.656
WORK	2.302	.145	.041	.670	.611	.071	.007	.098	.047	.000	.020	.242	.260	.186	.312	.358	.262

POPULATION, DEATHS, DEATH RATES FOR ALL CAUSES COMBINED, AND SPECIFIED CAUSES

Age Start of Interval	Midyear Population	Deaths During Year	All Causes	Respiratory T. B.	Other Infec. and Paras.	Neo-plasms	Cardio-vascular	Infl., Pneu., Bronch.	Diar-rheal	Certain Degen-erative	Maternal	Cert. Dis. of Infancy	Motor Vehicle	Other Violence	Other and Unknown	Age Start of Interval
0	66000	3030	.04591	.00000	.00074	.00009	.00000	.00524	.00255	.00002	.00000	.02645	.00000	.00056	.01026	0
1	273000	342	.00125	.00000	.00016	.00010	.00004	.00022	.00010	.00001	.00000	.00000	.00003	.00019	.00040	1
5	438000	199	.00045	.00000	.00002	.00007	.00003	.00003	.00000	.00000	.00000	.00000	.00006	.00011	.00014	5
10	457000	193	.00042	.00000	.00001	.00006	.00004	.00000	.00000	.00001	.00000	.00000	.00004	.00016	.00009	10
15	396000	425	.00107	.00000	.00001	.00010	.00011	.00002	.00000	.00002	.00000	.00000	.00013	.00056	.00012	15
20	369000	591	.00160	.00003	.00002	.00012	.00010	.00001	.00001	.00005	.00000	.00000	.00032	.00085	.00011	20
25	327000	548	.00168	.00004	.00002	.00014	.00021	.00002	.00001	.00008	.00000	.00000	.00032	.00073	.00011	25
30	354000	669	.00189	.00014	.00002	.00022	.00031	.00002	.00000	.00007	.00000	.00000	.00019	.00079	.00013	30
35	362000	918	.00254	.00020	.00004	.00033	.00059	.00005	.00000	.00011	.00000	.00000	.00023	.00078	.00023	35
40	349000	1168	.00335	.00024	.00007	.00058	.00092	.00009	.00001	.00017	.00000	.00000	.00017	.00080	.00030	40
45	211000	1103	.00523	.00031	.00011	.00117	.00165	.00004	.00000	.00035	.00000	.00000	.00013	.00089	.00056	45
50	327000	2725	.00833	.00055	.00009	.00217	.00289	.00017	.00001	.00041	.00000	.00000	.00014	.00105	.00085	50
55	288000	4092	.01421	.00084	.00016	.00396	.00548	.00031	.00003	.00074	.00000	.00000	.00017	.00111	.00141	55
60	250000	6044	.02418	.00123	.00021	.00673	.01050	.00038	.00005	.00122	.00000	.00000	.00015	.00117	.00253	60
65	182000	7018	.03856	.00176	.00026	.01001	.01892	.00075	.00007	.00138	.00000	.00000	.00015	.00134	.00393	65
70	115000	6863	.05968	.00199	.00024	.01323	.03327	.00103	.00010	.00197	.00000	.00000	.00019	.00188	.00577	70
75	74000	6912	.09341	.00218	.00031	.01636	.05678	.00212	.00011	.00207	.00000	.00000	.00028	.00281	.01038	75
80	37000	5490	.14838	.00165	.00027	.01668	.10154	.00354	.00024	.00254	.00000	.00000	.00019	.00489	.01684	80
85+	14000	3572	.25514	.00121	.00036	.01800	.17921	.00714	.00050	.00214	.00000	.00000	.00029	.00807	.03821	85+
ALL	4889000	51902														

CRUDE DEATH RATE			.01062	.00037	.00009	.00201	.00492	.00028	.00006	.00034	.00000	.00036	.00016	.00080	.00122	
STANDARDIZED RATE (1)			.00663	.00019	.00009	.00059	.00216	.00031	.00011	.00018	.00000	.00093	.00014	.00061	.00092	
STANDARDIZED RATE (2)			.01149	.00035	.00009	.00199	.00541	.00034	.00008	.00033	.00000	.00055	.00016	.00080	.00138	
GEOMETRIC MEAN			.00767													

LIFE TABLE FOR ALL CAUSES COMBINED

Age (x)	Midyear Population	Deaths During Year	$_nM_x$	$_nq_x$	l_x	$_nd_x$	$_nL_x$	$_nm_x$	$_na_x$	T_x	$_nr_x$	$\overset{\circ}{e}_x$	Age (x)
0	66000	3030	.045909	.044180	100000	4418	96236	.045908	.148045	6704914	.000000	67.049	0
1	273000	342	.001253	.005001	95582	478	381133	.001254	1.500000	6608678	.000000	69.141	1
5	438000	199	.000454	.002261	95104	215	474983	.000453	2.500000	6227545	.000000	65.481	5
10	457000	193	.000422	.002118	94889	201	474004	.000424	2.803690	5752563	.005336	60.624	10
15	396000	425	.001073	.005365	94688	508	472285	.001076	2.726378	5278559	.016824	55.747	15
20	369000	591	.001602	.007995	94180	753	469074	.001605	2.575255	4806274	.019587	51.033	20
25	327000	548	.001676	.008349	93427	780	465210	.001677	2.531517	4337200	.008955	46.423	25
30	354000	669	.001890	.009401	92647	871	461136	.001889	2.589696	3871990	-.006628	41.793	30
35	362000	918	.002536	.012585	91776	1155	456126	.002532	2.615801	3410855	-.031112	37.165	35
40	349000	1168	.003347	.016656	90621	1513	449563	.003365	2.659038	2954728	.042132	32.605	40
45	211000	1103	.005227	.025924	89108	2310	440183	.005248	2.681006	2505165	.020243	28.114	45
50	327000	2725	.008333	.040554	86798	3520	425902	.008265	2.702356	2064982	-.034880	23.791	50
55	288000	4092	.014208	.068754	83278	5729	403187	.014209	2.695351	1639080	-.000023	19.682	55
60	250000	6044	.024176	.114663	77549	8892	366861	.024238	2.651330	1235893	-.012914	15.937	60
65	182000	7018	.038560	.177520	68657	12188	314041	.038810	2.600611	869033	.033562	12.658	65
70	115000	6863	.059678	.261701	56469	14778	246158	.060035	2.551273	554991	.031443	9.828	70
75	74000	6912	.093405	.379578	41691	15825	168710	.093800	2.488441	308834	.019480	7.408	75
80	37000	5490	.148378	.537385	25866	13900	93225	.149102	2.402503	140124	.019480	5.417	80
85+	14000	3572	.255143	1.000000	11966	11966	46899	.255143	3.919373	46899	.000000	3.919	85+

NUMBER OF PERSONS DYING (OUT OF 100,000 AT BIRTH) ABOVE AGE X FROM SPECIFIED CAUSES

Age (x)	All Causes	Respiratory T.B.	Other Infec. and Paras.	Neoplasms	Cardiovascular	Infl., Pneu., Bronch.	Diarrheal	Certain Degenerative	Maternal	Cert. Dis. of Infancy	Motor Vehicle	Other Violence	Other and Unknown	Age (x)
0	100000	3084	685	17918	50858	2574	444	2921	0	2546	1113	6244	11613	0
1	95582	3084	613	17909	50858	2070	199	2920	0	0	1113	6190	10626	1
5	95104	3084	552	17870	50842	1587	160	2914	0	0	1102	6118	10475	5
10	94889	3084	543	17835	50829	1574	160	2914	0	0	1074	6068	10408	10
15	94688	3084	540	17805	50811	1567	158	2911	0	0	1053	5994	10365	15
20	94180	3084	534	17757	50758	1558	158	2904	0	0	990	5729	10308	20
25	93427	3072	530	17703	50709	1553	156	2881	0	0	839	5329	10255	25
30	92647	3053	523	17637	50610	1944	153	2845	0	0	688	4988	10206	30
35	91776	2989	513	17536	50467	1934	151	2813	0	0	601	4626	10146	35
40	90621	2899	497	17386	50199	1912	151	2764	0	0	497	4272	10044	40
45	89108	2791	467	17123	49782	1874	146	2686	0	0	419	3912	9908	45
50	86798	2655	417	16605	49051	1855	144	2531	0	0	361	3522	9657	50
55	83278	2424	379	15691	47831	1783	142	2356	0	0	300	3075	9297	55
60	77549	2084	315	14095	45622	1657	130	2058	0	0	230	2629	8729	60
65	68657	1631	237	11621	41756	1517	111	1611	0	0	174	2200	7799	65
70	56469	1075	155	8461	35765	1281	91	1177	0	0	127	1780	6557	70
75	41691	584	95	5191	27515	1026	65	691	0	0	80	1315	5129	75
80	25866	216	43	2425	17888	666	46	342	0	0	32	839	3369	80
85+	11966	57	17	844	8405	335	23	100	0	0	13	379	1793	85+

NUMBER OF PERSONS SURVIVING TO AGE X IF SPECIFIED CAUSES WERE ELIMINATED

Age (x)	No Causes	Respiratory T.B. (1)	Other Infec. and Paras. (2)	Neoplasms (3)	Cardiovascular (4)	Infl., Pneu., Bronch. (5)	Diarrheal (6)	Certain Degenerative (7)	Maternal (8)	Cert. Dis. of Infancy (9)	Motor Vehicle (10)	Other Violence (11)	Other and Unknown (12)	(1)+(2)	(1)+(2)+(5)+(6)+(8)	(1)+(2)+(5)+(6)+(8)+part of(9)&(12)	(10)+(11)	Age (x)
0	100000	100000	100000	100000	100000	100000	100000	100000	100000	100000	100000	100000	100000	100000	100000	100000	100000	0
1	95582	95582	95652	95591	95582	96076	95822	95583	95582	98104	95582	95635	96552	95652	96388	99674	95635	1
5	95104	95104	95235	95152	95120	95679	95382	95111	95104	97613	95115	95228	96221	95235	96090	99454	95239	5
10	94889	94889	95029	94972	94918	95476	95166	94896	94889	97392	94928	95063	96071	95029	95895	99263	95102	10
15	94688	94688	94830	94800	94735	95280	94966	94698	94688	97186	94748	94936	95911	94830	95704	99068	94996	15
20	94180	94180	94328	94340	94279	94778	94457	94197	94180	96665	94302	94692	95454	94328	95206	98554	94815	20
25	93427	93439	93577	93639	93575	94025	93704	93467	93427	95892	93699	94336	94745	93589	94468	97792	94611	25
30	92647	92678	92803	92923	92892	93249	92924	92722	92647	95051	93068	93892	94003	92834	93717	97018	94319	30
35	91776	91870	91941	92151	92162	92383	92053	91882	91776	94197	92280	93375	93180	92035	92923	96202	93888	35
40	90621	90804	90800	91141	91270	91242	90894	90775	90621	93012	91222	92559	92110	90983	91882	95138	93173	40
45	89108	89395	89313	89882	90163	89757	89382	89337	89108	91459	89777	91378	90710	89601	90530	93757	92065	45
50	86798	87212	87047	88069	88559	87449	87067	87174	86798	89088	87507	89405	88611	87463	88391	91568	90136	50
55	83278	83903	83555	85411	86196	83974	83538	83811	83278	85475	84019	86231	85378	84182	85150	88250	86998	55
60	77549	78462	77869	81131	82505	78319	77802	78335	77549	79595	78307	80744	80069	78785	79828	82796	81533	60
65	68657	69897	69013	74302	77021	69472	68899	69778	68657	70468	69381	71905	71756	70260	71345	74079	72663	65
70	56469	58002	56836	64282	69748	57356	56686	57791	56469	57959	57107	59539	60237	58379	59525	61906	60212	70
75	41691	43253	42013	50738	61023	42568	41874	43092	41691	42791	42203	44378	45797	43588	44700	46573	44923	75
80	25866	27130	26107	34187	50671	26700	25994	27014	25866	26548	26221	27931	29966	27382	28405	29684	28314	80
85+	11966	12662	12095	17265	39662	12581	12041	12666	11966	12282	12143	13255	15129	12798	13539	14203	13451	85+

ADDED YRS OF LIFE

	No Causes	(1)	(2)	(3)	(4)	(5)	(6)	(7)	(8)	(9)	(10)	(11)	(12)	(1)+(2)	(1)+(2)+(5)+(6)+(8)	+part of(9)&(12)	(10)+(11)
TOTAL		.458	.189	2.428	5.407	.615	.214	.418	.000	1.765	.370	1.548	2.016	.649	1.496	3.990	1.932
WORK	3.431	.167	.041	.578	.826	.051	.006	.146	.000	.000	.245	.879	.293	.207	.265	.292	1.130

POPULATION, DEATHS, DEATH RATES FOR ALL CAUSES COMBINED, AND SPECIFIED CAUSES

Age Start of Interval	Midyear Population	Deaths During Year	All Causes	Respiratory T.B.	Other Infec. and Paras.	Neoplasms	Cardiovascular	Infl., Pneu., Bronch.	Diarrheal	Certain Degenerative	Maternal	Cert. Dis. of Infancy	Motor Vehicle	Other Violence	Other and Unknown	Age Start of Interval
0	62012	2256	.03638	.00005	.00063	.00013	.00000	.00450	.00184	.00003	.00000	.01913	.00002	.00060	.00947	0
1	258049	319	.00124	.00000	.00021	.00012	.00010	.00021	.00007	.00001	.00000	.00000	.00002	.00013	.00037	1
5	417080	152	.00036	.00000	.00002	.00011	.00003	.00004	.00000	.00001	.00000	.00000	.00002	.00003	.00011	5
10	439084	102	.00023	.00000	.00001	.00005	.00003	.00001	.00000	.00002	.00000	.00000	.00001	.00004	.00006	10
15	384073	161	.00042	.00001	.00001	.00007	.00007	.00001	.00001	.00003	.00001	.00000	.00003	.00014	.00005	15
20	369071	222	.00060	.00001	.00002	.00009	.00010	.00002	.00000	.00002	.00002	.00000	.00002	.00021	.00011	20
25	349067	249	.00071	.00005	.00001	.00012	.00013	.00001	.00000	.00005	.00004	.00000	.00002	.00016	.00011	25
30	368070	369	.00100	.00008	.00003	.00024	.00023	.00001	.00000	.00007	.00005	.00000	.00004	.00015	.00011	30
35	383073	588	.00153	.00010	.00001	.00058	.00032	.00002	.00001	.00006	.00005	.00000	.00002	.00018	.00019	35
40	390075	860	.00220	.00009	.00003	.00052	.00054	.00001	.00001	.00007	.00002	.00000	.00003	.00025	.00023	40
45	240046	859	.00358	.00013	.00005	.00151	.00102	.00004	.00000	.00015	.00000	.00000	.00002	.00031	.00035	45
50	368070	1938	.00527	.00012	.00004	.00204	.00187	.00004	.00001	.00024	.00000	.00000	.00004	.00033	.00054	50
55	324062	2700	.00833	.00018	.00009	.00257	.00332	.00008	.00001	.00038	.00000	.00000	.00004	.00044	.00084	55
60	286055	3952	.01382	.00024	.00012	.00415	.00665	.00021	.00003	.00077	.00000	.00000	.00002	.00044	.00118	60
65	238045	5811	.02441	.00041	.00017	.00605	.01342	.00032	.00004	.00113	.00000	.00000	.00004	.00074	.00209	65
70	166032	7343	.04423	.00066	.00027	.00865	.02755	.00067	.00010	.00140	.00000	.00000	.00017	.00129	.00347	70
75	112021	8458	.07586	.00074	.00031	.01115	.05162	.00146	.00020	.00171	.00000	.00000	.00020	.00221	.00627	75
80	57011	7408	.12994	.00075	.00030	.01351	.09398	.00314	.00039	.00172	.00000	.00000	.00011	.00446	.01159	80
85+	22004	5141	.23364	.00068	.00064	.01427	.17270	.00523	.00032	.00186	.00000	.00000	.00014	.01068	.02713	85+
ALL	5233000	48928														
CRUDE DEATH RATE			.00935	.00013	.00007	.00179	.00520	.00022	.00004	.00027	.00001	.00023	.00003	.00040	.00095	
STANDARDIZED RATE (1)			.00470	.00006	.00008	.00078	.00170	.00024	.00008	.00012	.00001	.00067	.00003	.00023	.00070	
STANDARDIZED RATE (2)			.00843	.00011	.00008	.00149	.00448	.00025	.00006	.00023	.00001	.00040	.00003	.00037	.00070	
GEOMETRIC MEAN			.00490													

LIFE TABLE FOR ALL CAUSES COMBINED

Age (x)	Midyear Population	Deaths During Year	$_nM_x$	$_nq_x$	l_x	$_nd_x$	$_nL_x$	$_nm_x$	$_na_x$	T_x	$_nr_x$	$\overset{\circ}{e}_x$	Age (x)
0	62012	2256	.036380	.035270	100000	3527	96938	.036384	.131846	7189366	.000000	71.894	0
1	258049	319	.001236	.004924	96473	475	384705	.001235	1.500000	7092428	.000000	73.517	1
5	417080	152	.000364	.001823	95998	175	479553	.000365	2.500000	6707723	.000000	69.874	5
10	439084	102	.000232	.001159	95823	111	478841	.000232	2.548799	6228171	.004195	64.997	10
15	384073	161	.000419	.002100	95712	201	478094	.000420	2.682421	5749328	.015071	60.069	15
20	369071	222	.000602	.003005	95511	287	476866	.000602	2.600900	5271234	.011791	55.190	20
25	349067	249	.000713	.003571	95224	340	475309	.000715	2.614583	4794367	.003726	50.348	25
30	368070	369	.001003	.004996	94884	474	473314	.001001	2.667018	4319058	-.005060	45.519	30
35	383073	588	.001535	.007626	94410	720	470366	.001531	2.661748	3845744	-.017314	40.735	35
40	390075	860	.002205	.011026	93690	1033	466061	.002216	2.687561	3375378	-.035328	36.027	40
45	240046	859	.003578	.017808	92657	1650	459435	.003591	2.666540	2909317	.019019	31.399	45
50	368070	1938	.005265	.025844	91007	2352	449560	.005232	2.675205	2449882	-.032158	26.920	50
55	324062	2700	.008332	.040923	88655	3628	434904	.008342	2.692657	2000315	.005518	22.563	55
60	286055	3952	.013816	.067120	85027	5707	412031	.013851	2.703916	1565411	.011579	18.411	60
65	238045	5811	.024411	.116162	79320	9214	375317	.024550	2.690154	1153379	.024304	14.541	65
70	166032	7343	.044226	.201367	70106	14117	317071	.044523	2.629852	778062	.028483	11.098	70
75	112021	8458	.075861	.321724	55989	18013	235859	.076372	2.552520	460992	.027676	8.234	75
80	57011	7408	.129940	.491310	37976	18658	142450	.130979	2.457938	225133	.027676	5.928	80
85+	22004	5141	.233639	1.000000	19318	19318	82683	.233639	4.280101	82683	.000000	4.280	85+

NUMBER OF PERSONS DYING (OUT OF 100,000 AT BIRTH) ABOVE AGE X FROM SPECIFIED CAUSES

Age (x)	All Causes	Respiratory T.B.	Other Infec. and Paras.	Neo-plasms	Cardio-vascular	Infl., Pneu., Bronch.	Diar-rheal	Certain Degen-erative	Maternal	Cert. Dis. of Infancy	Motor Vehicle	Other Violence	Other and Unknown	Age (x)
0	100000	1162	655	16507	60112	2302	411	2499	89	1854	290	4060	10059	0
1	96473	1157	594	16494	60112	1866	232	2496	89	0	289	4002	9142	1
5	95998	1157	515	16449	60074	1786	206	2492	89	0	281	3951	8998	5
10	95823	1156	506	16398	60060	1768	206	2487	89	0	272	3935	8946	10
15	95712	1156	500	16376	60045	1762	206	2479	89	0	268	3914	8917	15
20	95511	1153	497	16345	60010	1757	203	2466	85	0	255	3848	8892	20
25	95224	1148	489	16301	59962	1749	203	2457	78	0	246	3750	8841	25
30	94884	1122	482	16242	59902	1744	203	2433	58	0	235	3672	8791	30
35	94410	1084	468	16128	59794	1740	203	2401	34	0	217	3602	8739	35
40	93690	1037	465	15855	59645	1729	201	2372	11	0	206	3517	8652	40
45	92657	995	450	15424	59392	1723	196	2337	0	0	194	3402	8544	45
50	91007	936	427	14730	58918	1706	194	2268	0	0	185	3260	8383	50
55	88655	882	407	13818	58085	1686	189	2162	0	0	169	3110	8147	55
60	85027	806	368	12525	56638	1653	186	1997	0	0	153	2921	7780	60
65	79320	706	319	10814	53887	1566	173	1681	0	0	143	2738	7293	65
70	70106	552	254	8534	48814	1444	159	1257	0	0	127	2460	6505	70
75	55989	341	170	5781	40011	1228	128	811	0	0	73	2049	5397	75
80	37976	166	96	3142	27746	882	82	405	0	0	27	1523	3907	80
85+	19318	56	53	1180	14279	432	26	154	0	0	11	883	2244	85+

NUMBER OF PERSONS SURVIVING TO AGE X IF SPECIFIED CAUSES WERE ELIMINATED

Age (x)	No Causes	Respiratory T.B. (1)	Other Infec. and Paras. (2)	Neo-plasms (3)	Cardio-vascular (4)	Infl., Pneu., Bronch. (5)	Diar-rheal (6)	Certain Degen-erative (7)	Maternal (8)	Cert. Dis. of Infancy (9)	Motor Vehicle (10)	Other Violence (11)	Other and Unknown (12)	(1)+(2)	(1)+(2)+(5)+(6)+(8)	(1)+(2)+(5)+(6)+(8)+part of(9)&(12)	(10)+(11)	Age (x)
0	100000	100000	100000	100000	100000	100000	100000	100000	100000	100000	100000	100000	100000	100000	100000	100000	100000	0
1	96473	96478	96533	96486	96473	96902	96649	96476	96473	98311	96474	96530	97378	96538	97144	99644	96531	1
5	95998	96003	96137	96056	96036	96505	96159	96005	95998	97827	96007	96106	97043	96141	96852	99428	96115	5
10	95823	95829	95970	95932	95875	96347	96024	95835	95823	97649	95841	95946	96919	95976	96704	99288	95964	10
15	95712	95718	95865	95842	95779	96242	95912	95732	95712	97536	95734	95856	96836	95871	96604	99189	95878	15
20	95511	95520	95667	95672	95613	96045	95714	95544	95515	97331	95546	95721	96658	95676	96419	99002	95756	20
25	95224	95238	95387	95429	95373	95764	95426	95266	95235	97038	95268	95532	96419	95401	96157	98740	95575	25
30	94884	94924	95054	95147	95093	95427	95086	94950	94915	96692	94939	95269	96125	95094	95873	98458	95323	30
35	94410	94487	94593	94786	94726	94955	94611	94507	94465	96209	94482	94863	95698	94670	95474	98059	94935	35
40	93690	93814	93874	94336	94152	94241	93891	93815	93767	95475	93773	94224	95056	93998	94833	97413	94308	40
45	92657	92821	92854	93729	93368	93208	92861	92816	92744	94422	92751	93301	94117	93019	93867	96430	93395	45
50	91007	91227	91224	92758	92180	91565	91209	91232	91093	92741	91108	91781	92603	91444	92297	94828	91883	50
55	88655	88923	88886	91283	90634	89219	88857	88979	88739	90344	88769	89558	90447	89154	90010	92491	89674	55
60	85027	85358	85287	88660	88387	85600	85224	85500	85107	86647	85152	86080	87113	85619	86477	88877	86207	60
65	79320	79726	79610	84638	85265	79940	79516	80068	79395	80831	79446	80481	81749	80017	80918	83187	80610	65
70	70106	70610	70423	77122	80670	70769	70293	71169	70172	71442	70233	71398	73019	70930	71859	73907	71527	70
75	55989	56581	56317	64339	74139	56714	56166	57241	56042	57056	56139	57395	59353	56912	57886	59579	57548	75
80	37976	38520	38259	46169	65534	39757	38134	39162	38012	38700	38115	39374	41572	38807	39807	41023	39517	80
85+	19318	19673	19492	25216	54300	20039	19438	20103	19336	19686	19400	20499	22460	19851	20739	21422	20585	85+

ADDED YRS OF LIFE																	
TOTAL		.193	.187	2.494	12.565	.546	.170	.354	.038	1.368	.072	.672	1.807	.381	1.146	3.152	.745
WORK	1.981	.073	.027	.640	.550	.023	.005	.089	.029	.000	.031	.236	.213	.099	.156	.177	.267

POPULATION, DEATHS, DEATH RATES FOR ALL CAUSES COMBINED, AND SPECIFIED CAUSES

Age Start of Interval	Midyear Population	Deaths During Year	All Causes	Respiratory T. B.	Other Infec. and Paras.	Neoplasms	Cardiovascular	Infl., Pneu., Bronch.	Diarrheal	Certain Degenerative	Maternal	Cert. Dis. of Infancy	Motor Vehicle	Other Violence	Other and Unknown	Age Start of Interval
0	2400	49	.02042	.CCCCC	.CC000	.CCCC0	.00000	.00208	.CC000	.CC000	.00000	.01042	.00000	.00083	.00708	0
1	9600	10	.00104	.C0000	.00010	.00000	.00000	.00000	.0001C	.00000	.00000	.00000	.00031	.00042	.00010	1
5	11500	6	.00052	.CCCCC	.C0000	.00017	.00000	.00000	.CC000	.00000	.00000	.C0000	.00009	.00009	.00017	5
10	10300	7	.00068	.C0000	.00000	.00039	.C0000	.C0C00	.00000	.C00C0	.00000	.00000	.00000	.00010	.00019	10
15	8800	9	.00102	.00CCC	.00000	.00023	.00000	.00000	.00000	.00011	.00000	.00000	.00000	.00068	.00000	15
20	6700	13	.00194	.C0CCC	.C0C00	.C0030	.00015	.00015	.00000	.C0000	.CC000	.C0000	.00030	.0C0S0	.00015	20
25	5800	9	.00155	.00000	.00000	.00017	.00017	.00000	.CC900	.00000	.00000	.00000	.00017	.00069	.00034	25
30	6100	7	.00115	.0CCCC	.00000	.0000C	.00000	.C0033	.00000	.00000	.00000	.00000	.00000	.0004S	.0C033	30
35	5800	10	.00172	.00000	.00C00	.00034	.00034	.00017	.00000	.00017	.CC000	.00000	.00000	.00069	.00000	35
40	5400	20	.00370	.C0CCC	.00000	.00056	.00093	.00019	.00000	.00000	.00000	.C0000	.00000	.00148	.00056	40
45	4700	23	.00489	.CCCC0	.00000	.0004C	.CC213	.00021	.00000	.CC064	.00000	.C0000	.00021	.00106	.00021	45
50	4200	32	.00762	.00CC0	.CC000	.00333	.00286	.00024	.00000	.CCCC0	.00024	.00000	.00024	.00048	.00024	50
55	3800	51	.01342	.CCCCC	.00C00	.00368	.00632	.00026	.00000	.00000	.00000	.0C000	.00000	.00211	.00105	55
60	3200	49	.01531	.00CC0	.00000	.0046S	.CC781	.C0000	.00000	.00062	.C0000	.00000	.00000	.00062	.00156	60
65	2900	91	.03250	.00CCC	.00000	.01036	.01286	.00107	.00000	.00107	.00000	.C0000	.00107	.00250	.00357	65
70	2200	85	.03864	.CCCCC	.00045	.00727	.02045	.00273	.C0000	.00045	.00000	.00000	.00000	.00182	.00545	70
75	1300	80	.06154	.C0000	.00077	.01385	.03462	.00462	.C0CCC	.00077	.C0000	.00000	.00077	.00077	.00538	75
80	600	72	.12000	.CCC00	.00167	.C1167	.08500	.00833	.00167	.00000	.00000	.00000	.00000	.00167	.C1000	80
85+	400	98	.24500	.C0000	.CC000	.02000	.14250	.04250	.CC500	.00000	.CC000	.00000	.00000	.00250	.00500	.02750	85+
ALL	95600	721														

	All Causes	Respiratory T. B.	Other Infec. and Paras.	Neoplasms	Cardiovascular	Infl., Pneu., Bronch.	Diarrheal	Certain Degenerative	Maternal	Cert. Dis. of Infancy	Motor Vehicle	Other Violence	Other and Unknown
CRUDE DEATH RATE	.00754	.00000	.00004	.00145	.00331	.C0050	.00004	.00014	.CC0C0	.00026	.00015	.00074	.00091
STANDARDIZED RATE (1)	.00480	.C0000	.00003	.00091	.00166	.C0026	.00002	.00010	.00000	.00037	.00013	.00066	.00068
STANDARDIZED RATE (2)	.00877	.00000	.00005	.00172	.00407	.C0056	.000C5	.C0016	.00000	.00022	.00015	.00080	.00100
GEOMETRIC MEAN	.00654												

LIFE TABLE FOR ALL CAUSES COMBINED

Age (x)	Midyear Population	Deaths During Year	$_nM_x$	$_nq_x$	l_x	$_nd_x$	$_nL_x$	$_nm_x$	$_na_x$	T_x	$_nr_x$	$\overset{\circ}{e}_x$	Age (x)
0	2400	49	.020417	.020050	100000	2005	98205	.020416	.104708	7098095	.000000	70.981	0
1	9600	10	.001042	.004153	97995	407	390963	.001041	1.500000	6999890	.000000	71.431	1
5	11500	6	.000522	.002603	97588	254	487305	.000521	2.500000	6608928	.000000	67.723	5
10	10300	7	.000680	.003401	97334	331	485893	.000681	2.653575	6121623	.017362	62.893	10
15	8800	9	.001023	.005134	97003	498	483856	.001029	2.753096	5635730	.035318	58.099	15
20	6700	13	.001940	.009659	96505	936	480235	.001949	2.553196	5151834	.044194	53.384	20
25	5800	9	.001552	.007712	95569	737	475920	.001549	2.388625	4671599	.018281	48.882	25
30	6100	7	.001148	.005715	94832	542	472821	.001146	2.528828	4195678	.001465	44.243	30
35	5800	10	.001724	.008612	94290	812	469666	.001729	2.802494	3722858	.006987	39.483	35
40	5400	20	.003704	.018411	93478	1721	463382	.003714	2.671170	3253192	.014346	34.802	40
45	4700	23	.004894	.024260	91757	2226	453562	.004908	2.653583	2789810	.019980	30.404	45
50	4200	32	.007619	.037551	89531	3362	439956	.007642	2.709944	2336248	.014216	26.094	50
55	3800	51	.013421	.065151	86169	5614	417354	.013451	2.596893	1896292	.014935	22.007	55
60	3200	49	.015312	.074148	80555	5973	389017	.015354	2.696684	1478938	.014030	18.359	60
65	2800	91	.032500	.150881	74582	11253	345667	.032536	2.596826	1089921	.005735	14.614	65
70	2200	85	.038636	.176902	63329	11203	289235	.038733	2.553297	744054	.023075	11.749	70
75	1300	80	.061538	.270863	52126	14119	226712	.062277	2.597656	454819	.055159	8.725	75
80	600	72	.120000	.468966	38007	17824	145728	.122310	2.514190	228108	.055159	6.002	80
85+	400	98	.245000	1.000000	20183	20183	82380	.245000	4.081633	82380	.000000	4.082	85+

NUMBER OF PERSONS DYING (OUT OF 100,000 AT BIRTH) ABOVE AGE X FROM SPECIFIED CAUSES

Age (x)	All Causes	Respiratory T. B.	Other Infec. and Paras.	Neo-plasms	Cardio-vascular	Infl., Pneu., Bronch.	Diar-rheal	Certain Degen-erative	Maternal	Cert. Dis. of Infancy	Motor Vehicle	Other Violence	Other and Unknown	Age (x)
0	100000	0	597	18317	51508	7715	700	1455	0	1023	1345	6719	10621	0
1	97995	0	597	18317	51508	7511	700	1455	0	0	1345	6637	9925	1
5	97588	0	556	18317	51508	7511	659	1455	0	0	1223	6475	9884	5
10	97334	0	556	18232	51508	7511	659	1455	0	0	1181	6432	9800	10
15	97003	0	556	18043	51508	7511	659	1455	0	0	1181	6384	9706	15
20	96505	0	556	17934	51508	7510	659	1400	0	0	1180	6051	9707	20
25	95569	0	556	17791	51436	7438	659	1400	0	0	1036	5620	9633	25
30	94832	0	556	17709	51354	7438	659	1400	0	0	954	5293	9469	30
35	94290	0	556	17709	51198	7438	659	1400	0	0	954	5060	9316	35
40	93478	0	556	17547	51036	7358	659	1320	0	0	954	4736	9312	40
45	91757	0	556	17289	50605	7272	659	1319	0	0	954	4049	9054	45
50	89531	0	556	17092	49636	7175	659	1029	0	0	857	3568	8959	50
55	86169	0	556	15621	48374	7070	659	925	0	0	752	3358	8854	55
60	80555	0	556	14081	45731	6961	659	925	0	0	752	2478	8412	60
65	74582	0	556	12252	42666	6960	659	680	0	0	752	2235	7802	65
70	63329	0	556	8667	38233	6588	659	310	0	0	381	1370	6565	70
75	52126	0	423	6565	32292	5795	659	179	0	0	381	846	4986	75
80	38007	0	246	3358	24324	4736	658	4	0	0	205	676	3760	80
85+	20183	0	0	1648	11739	3501	412	0	0	0	205	412	2266	85+

NUMBER OF PERSONS SURVIVING TO AGE X IF SPECIFIED CAUSES WERE ELIMINATED

Age (x)	No Causes	Respiratory T. B. (1)	Other Infec. and Paras. (2)	Neo-plasms (3)	Cardio-vascular (4)	Infl., Pneu., Bronch. (5)	Diar-rheal (6)	Certain Degener-ative (7)	Maternal (8)	Cert. Dis. of Infancy (9)	Motor Vehicle (10)	Other Violence (11)	Other and Unknown (12)	(1) + (2)	(1) + (2) + (5) + (6) + (8)	(1)+(2)+ (5)+(6)+ (8)+part of(9)&(12)	(10) + (11)	Age (x)
0	100000	100000	100000	100000	100000	100000	100000	100000	100000	100000	100000	100000	100000	100000	100000	100000	100000	0
1	97995	97995	97995	97995	97995	98197	97995	97995	97995	99013	97995	98076	98686	97995	98197	99421	98076	1
5	97588	97588	97629	97588	97588	97789	97629	97588	97588	98602	97710	97831	98318	97629	97871	99100	97953	5
10	97334	97334	97375	97419	97334	97535	97375	97334	97334	98345	97498	97619	98146	97375	97617	98842	97783	10
15	97003	97003	97044	97277	97003	97203	97044	97003	97003	98011	97166	97335	97907	97044	97285	98506	97499	15
20	96505	96505	96545	96886	96505	96705	96545	96560	96505	97507	96668	97169	97404	96545	96786	98002	97334	20
25	95569	95569	95609	96090	95641	95839	95609	95623	95569	96562	95874	96660	96533	95609	95919	97130	96969	25
30	94832	94832	94872	95431	94985	95100	94872	94886	94832	95817	95217	96244	95954	94872	95180	96381	96635	30
35	94290	94290	94330	94885	94598	94556	94330	94344	94290	95269	94673	95530	95560	94330	94636	95830	96320	35
40	93478	93478	93517	94231	93945	93822	93517	93611	93478	94449	93857	95433	94741	93517	93901	95086	95820	40
45	91757	91757	91795	92754	92646	92180	91795	91889	91757	92710	92129	94373	93256	91795	92257	93438	94756	45
50	89531	89531	89569	90701	91370	90040	89569	89947	89531	90461	89991	92573	91089	89569	90116	91273	93048	50
55	86169	86169	86205	88770	89213	86763	86205	86671	86169	87064	86715	89310	87774	86205	86835	87954	89876	55
60	80555	80555	80589	84533	86089	81216	80569	81025	80555	81392	81065	84377	82493	80589	81284	82340	84911	60
65	74582	74582	74613	80134	82895	75195	74613	75255	74582	75357	75055	78365	76980	74613	75258	76236	78862	65
70	63329	63329	63356	71673	75099	64200	63356	64243	63329	63987	64074	67382	66553	63356	64254	65134	68175	70
75	52126	52126	52270	61179	68556	53579	52148	52997	52126	52667	52738	55963	56301	52270	53750	54630	56620	75
80	38007	38007	38263	47863	59783	40002	38026	38792	38007	38402	38604	40956	42182	38263	40292	41058	41599	80
85+	20183	20183	20497	27046	49634	22195	20370	20603	20183	20393	20500	21954	23621	20497	22749	23313	22299	85+

ADDED YRS OF LIFE		(1)	(2)	(3)	(4)	(5)	(6)	(7)	(8)	(9)	(10)	(11)	(12)				
TOTAL		.000	.068	2.810	8.336	.787	.058	.285	.000	.736	.350	1.887	1.802	.068	.933	1.929	2.253
WORK	3.137	.000	.000	.605	.835	.106	.000	.113	.000	.000	.118	.942	.268	.000	.106	.113	1.062

POPULATION, DEATHS, DEATH RATES FOR ALL CAUSES COMBINED, AND SPECIFIED CAUSES

Age Start of Interval	Midyear Population	Deaths During Year	All Causes	Respiratory T. B.	Other Infec. and Paras.	Neo-plasms	Cardio-vascular	Infl., Pneu., Bronch.	Diar-rheal	Certain Degen-erative	Maternal	Cert. Dis. of Infancy	Motor Vehicle	Other Violence	Other and Unknown	Age Start of Interval
0	2300	35	.01522	.00000	.00174	.00000	.00000	.00087	.00000	.00000	.00000	.01000	.00000	.00000	.00261	0
1	9100	10	.00110	.00000	.00011	.00011	.00011	.00011	.00000	.00000	.00000	.00000	.00022	.00022	.00022	1
5	10900	4	.00037	.00000	.00000	.00009	.00000	.00009	.00000	.00000	.00000	.00000	.00009	.00009	.00000	5
10	9600	2	.00021	.00000	.00000	.00000	.00000	.00010	.00000	.00000	.00000	.00000	.00000	.00000	.00010	10
15	8300	1	.00012	.00000	.00000	.00000	.00000	.00000	.00000	.00012	.00000	.00000	.00000	.00000	.00000	15
20	6600	7	.00106	.00000	.00000	.00000	.00000	.00000	.00000	.00015	.00015	.00000	.00015	.00045	.00015	20
25	5600	2	.00036	.00000	.00000	.00000	.00000	.00000	.00000	.00000	.00018	.00000	.00000	.00000	.00018	25
30	5900	6	.00102	.00017	.00000	.00068	.00000	.00000	.00000	.00000	.00000	.00000	.00000	.00000	.00017	30
35	5500	4	.00073	.00000	.00000	.00036	.00000	.00000	.00000	.00000	.00018	.00000	.00000	.00018	.00000	35
40	5200	8	.00154	.00000	.00000	.00077	.00058	.00000	.00000	.00000	.00000	.00000	.00000	.00000	.00019	40
45	4600	16	.00348	.00000	.00000	.00174	.00087	.00000	.00000	.00022	.00000	.00000	.00000	.00000	.00065	45
50	4200	12	.00286	.00000	.00000	.00143	.00071	.00000	.00000	.00000	.00000	.00000	.00024	.00000	.00048	50
55	3800	31	.00816	.00026	.00000	.00395	.00211	.00053	.00000	.00000	.00000	.00000	.00000	.00026	.00105	55
60	3300	32	.00970	.00000	.00000	.00485	.00273	.00000	.00000	.00030	.00000	.00000	.00030	.00030	.00121	60
65	3000	51	.01700	.00000	.00000	.00533	.00900	.00067	.00033	.00067	.00000	.00000	.00000	.00033	.00067	65
70	2400	69	.02875	.00000	.00000	.00875	.01083	.00250	.00083	.00083	.00000	.00000	.00042	.00083	.00375	70
75	1600	82	.05125	.00000	.00062	.00812	.02437	.00687	.00062	.00062	.00000	.00000	.00187	.00187	.00625	75
80	900	85	.09444	.00000	.00000	.00667	.05889	.01333	.00000	.00111	.00000	.00000	.00000	.00444	.01000	80
85+	700	130	.18571	.00000	.00000	.02143	.11429	.02143	.00143	.00286	.00000	.00000	.00000	.00000	.00571	.01857	85+
ALL	93500	587														

CRUDE DEATH RATE			.00628	.00002	.00006	.00137	.00272	.00056	.00005	.00013	.00003	.00025	.00011	.00025	.00074	
STANDARDIZED RATE (1)			.00307	.00002	.00008	.00074	.00091	.00021	.00002	.00007	.00004	.00035	.00008	.00015	.00041	
STANDARDIZED RATE (2)			.00590	.00002	.00006	.00140	.00246	.00050	.00005	.00013	.00004	.00021	.00011	.00024	.00070	
GEOMETRIC MEAN			.00352													

LIFE TABLE FOR ALL CAUSES COMBINED

Age (x)	Midyear Population	Deaths During Year	$_nM_x$	$_nq_x$	l_x	$_nd_x$	$_nL_x$	$_nm_x$	$_na_x$	T_x	$_nr_x$	$\overset{\circ}{e}_x$	Age (x)
0	2300	35	.015217	.015010	100000	1501	98643	.015217	.095870	7652852	.000000	76.529	0
1	9100	10	.001099	.004386	98499	432	392916	.001099	1.500000	7554209	.000000	76.693	1
5	10900	4	.000367	.001835	98067	180	489885	.000367	2.500000	7161293	.000000	73.024	5
10	9600	2	.000208	.001042	97887	102	489155	.000209	2.254902	6671408	.019225	68.154	10
15	8300	1	.000120	.000614	97785	60	488862	.000123	3.951389	6182253	.031667	63.223	15
20	6600	7	.001061	.005321	97725	520	487349	.001067	2.545272	5693391	.041580	58.259	20
25	5600	2	.000357	.001780	97205	173	485587	.000356	2.466281	5206043	.019799	53.557	25
30	5900	6	.001017	.005070	97032	492	483567	.001017	2.575373	4720456	.003668	48.648	30
35	5500	4	.000727	.003636	96540	351	481874	.000728	2.647792	4236489	.009151	43.883	35
40	5200	8	.001538	.007704	96189	741	479363	.001546	2.864935	3754615	.013841	39.034	40
45	4600	16	.003478	.017276	95448	1649	473242	.003484	2.575424	3275252	.018220	34.315	45
50	4200	12	.002857	.014265	93799	1338	466080	.002871	2.821375	2802010	.015136	29.872	50
55	3800	31	.008158	.040157	92461	3713	453622	.008185	2.661538	2335930	.017227	25.264	55
60	3300	32	.009697	.047517	88748	4217	433868	.009720	2.658930	1882307	.014120	21.210	60
65	3000	51	.017000	.081982	84531	6930	406641	.017042	2.689214	1448440	.011488	17.135	65
70	2400	69	.028750	.135449	77601	10511	363505	.028916	2.669128	1041798	.025466	13.425	70
75	1600	82	.051250	.230481	67090	15463	298766	.051756	2.627616	678293	.040035	10.110	75
80	900	85	.094444	.387065	51627	19983	209137	.095550	2.547999	379527	.040035	7.351	80
85+	700	130	.185714	1.000000	31644	31644	170391	.185714	5.384615	170391	.000000	5.385	85+

NUMBER OF PERSONS DYING (OUT OF 100,000 AT BIRTH) ABOVE AGE X FROM SPECIFIED CAUSES

Age (x)	All Causes	Respiratory T.B.	Other Infec. and Paras.	Neoplasms	Cardiovascular	Infl., Pneu., Bronch.	Diarrheal	Certain Degenerative	Maternal	Cert. Dis. of Infancy	Motor Vehicle	Other Violence	Other and Unknown	Age (x)
0	100000	202	403	19247	50180	10146	873	1856	249	986	1167	3614	11077	0
1	98499	202	232	19247	50180	10060	873	1856	249	0	1167	3614	10819	1
5	98067	202	189	19204	50137	10017	873	1856	249	0	1080	3527	10733	5
10	97887	202	189	19159	50137	9972	873	1856	249	0	1035	3482	10733	10
15	97785	202	189	19159	50086	9972	873	1856	249	0	1035	3482	10682	15
20	97725	202	189	19159	50086	9972	873	1797	248	0	1035	3481	10683	20
25	97205	202	189	19159	50086	9972	873	1723	173	0	961	3259	10608	25
30	97032	201	189	19158	50086	9972	873	1723	87	0	961	3259	10523	30
35	96540	119	189	18830	50086	9972	873	1723	87	0	961	3259	10441	35
40	96189	119	189	18654	50086	9972	873	1723	0	0	961	3172	10440	40
45	95448	119	189	18284	49808	9972	873	1723	0	0	961	3172	10347	45
50	93799	119	189	17459	49397	9972	873	1620	0	0	961	3172	10037	50
55	92461	119	189	16791	49062	9971	873	1620	0	0	850	3172	9814	55
60	88748	0	189	14994	48103	9732	873	1620	0	0	850	3052	9335	60
65	84531	0	189	12889	46913	9732	872	1488	0	0	718	2920	8810	65
70	77601	0	189	10717	43244	9459	736	1216	0	0	718	2784	8538	70
75	67090	0	188	7528	39284	8540	432	913	0	0	564	2479	7162	75
80	51627	0	0	5105	31900	6459	247	727	0	0	0	1911	5278	80
85+	31644	0	0	3651	19473	3651	243	487	0	0	0	974	3165	85+

NUMBER OF PERSONS SURVIVING TO AGE X IF SPECIFIED CAUSES WERE ELIMINATED

Age (x)	No Causes	Respiratory T.B. (1)	Other Infec. and Paras. (2)	Neoplasms (3)	Cardiovascular (4)	Infl., Pneu., Bronch. (5)	Diarrheal (6)	Certain Degenerative (7)	Maternal (8)	Cert. Dis. of Infancy (9)	Motor Vehicle (10)	Other Violence (11)	Other and Unknown (12)	(1)+(2)	(1)+(2) +(5)+ (6)+(8)	(1)+(2)+ (5)+(6)+ (8)+part of(9)&(12)	(10) +(11)	Age (x)
0	100000	100000	100000	100000	100000	100000	100000	100000	100000	100000	100000	100000	100000	100000	100000	100000	100000	0
1	98499	98499	98669	98499	98499	98584	98499	98499	98499	99482	98499	98499	98755	98669	98754	100000	98499	1
5	98067	98067	98279	98110	98110	98195	98067	98067	98067	99046	98154	98154	98408	98279	98407	99670	98241	5
10	97887	97887	98099	97975	97930	98060	97887	97887	97887	98864	98019	98019	98228	98099	98272	99533	98151	10
15	97785	97785	97996	97873	97879	97958	97785	97785	97785	98761	97917	97917	98177	97996	98169	99429	98048	15
20	97725	97725	97936	97813	97819	97897	97725	97784	97726	98701	97856	97857	98115	97936	98110	99369	97989	20
25	97205	97205	97415	97292	97298	97377	97205	97338	97281	98176	97410	97559	97668	97415	97663	98925	97764	25
30	97032	97033	97242	97120	97125	97203	97032	97164	97194	98001	97236	97385	97580	97243	97577	98927	97590	30
35	96540	96623	96749	96956	96633	96710	96540	96672	96701	97504	96743	96891	97167	96832	97164	98526	97095	35
40	96189	96272	96397	96780	96281	96359	96189	96320	96436	97149	96392	96626	96815	96480	96899	98257	96830	40
45	95448	95530	95654	96406	95817	95616	95448	95578	95693	96401	95649	95882	96163	95736	96152	97500	96084	45
50	93799	93879	94002	95570	94532	93965	93799	94029	94040	94736	93997	94225	94811	94083	94491	95815	94424	50
55	92461	92540	92661	94885	93559	92625	92461	92688	92699	93384	92766	92881	93683	92741	93144	94450	93188	55
60	88748	88941	98940	92899	90757	89140	88748	88966	88976	89634	89041	89270	90397	89133	89757	91069	89564	60
65	84531	84714	84714	90659	87644	84905	84532	84868	84718	85375	84939	85157	86624	84898	85493	86743	85569	65
70	77601	77769	77769	85484	84185	78209	77733	78172	77801	78376	77976	78308	79792	77938	78885	80054	78686	70
75	67090	67236	67237	77228	76886	68487	67487	67866	67262	67760	67560	67988	70314	67383	69371	70580	68465	75
80	51627	51739	51904	61883	67092	54558	52092	52387	51760	52142	52484	52826	55858	52017	55648	56946	53703	80
85+	31644	31713	31814	39305	55756	35848	31932	32299	31725	31960	32170	33131	36056	31883	36541	37699	33681	85+

ADDED YRS OF LIFE																		
TOTAL		.066	.181	3.164	8.744	.973	.087	.273	.123	.763	.264	.538	1.584	.247	1.453	2.653	.806	
WORK	1.590	.035	.000	.648	.267	.017	.000	.079	.087	.000	.048	.129	.239	.035	.140	.186	.177	

POPULATION, DEATHS, DEATH RATES FOR ALL CAUSES COMBINED, AND SPECIFIED CAUSES

Age Start of Interval	Midyear Population	Deaths During Year	All Causes	Respiratory T. B.	Other Infec. and Paras.	Neo-plasms	Cardio-vascular	Infl., Pneu., Bronch.	Diar-rheal	Certain Degen-erative	Maternal	Cert. Dis. of Infancy	Motor Vehicle	Other Violence	Other and Unknown	Age Start of Interval
0	32679	1679	.05138	.00009	.00226	.00006	.00034	.00759	.00282	.00003	.00000	.02604	.00000	.00107	.01108	0
1	127791	351	.00275	.00003	.00070	.00016	.00006	.00056	.00010	.00002	.00000	.00000	.00008	.00023	.00081	1
5	143704	133	.00093	.00000	.00017	.00006	.00005	.00011	.00001	.00003	.00000	.00000	.00007	.00010	.00031	5
10	132924	79	.00059	.00002	.00016	.00008	.00005	.00005	.00000	.00002	.00000	.00000	.00002	.00005	.00014	10
15	125930	167	.00133	.00030	.00020	.00007	.00011	.00010	.00001	.00009	.00000	.00000	.00005	.00014	.00026	15
20	105537	209	.00198	.00069	.00025	.00012	.00014	.00010	.00000	.00009	.00000	.00000	.00008	.00022	.00029	20
25	99744	252	.00253	.00081	.00017	.00026	.00028	.00015	.00000	.00011	.00000	.00000	.00012	.00032	.00030	25
30	96585	268	.00277	.00090	.00024	.00025	.00040	.00008	.00001	.00023	.00000	.00000	.00009	.00022	.00035	30
35	102431	370	.00361	.00102	.00021	.00036	.00064	.00021	.00001	.00027	.00000	.00000	.00011	.00034	.00045	35
40	94146	441	.00468	.00057	.00025	.00075	.00108	.00017	.00003	.00036	.00000	.00000	.00011	.00020	.00075	40
45	82497	614	.00744	.00125	.00018	.00125	.00221	.00062	.00000	.00055	.00000	.00000	.00013	.00030	.00096	45
50	83046	973	.01172	.00170	.00029	.00250	.00384	.00126	.00008	.00069	.00000	.00000	.00007	.00037	.00144	50
55	65125	1152	.01769	.00129	.00026	.00326	.00719	.00192	.00008	.00086	.00000	.00000	.00006	.00034	.00244	55
60	61437	1715	.02791	.00142	.00024	.00526	.01175	.00365	.00003	.00112	.00000	.00000	.00016	.00057	.00371	60
65	54226	2335	.04306	.00077	.00035	.00706	.02073	.00546	.00007	.00127	.00000	.00000	.00015	.00081	.00638	65
70	49194	3500	.07115	.00061	.00016	.00978	.03502	.00915	.00022	.00270	.00000	.00000	.00012	.00083	.01254	70
75	31689	3752	.11840	.00044	.00009	.01067	.05522	.01616	.00016	.00278	.00000	.00000	.00022	.00079	.03187	75
80	14671	2872	.19576	.00020	.00027	.01111	.07573	.02202	.00048	.00389	.00000	.00000	.00027	.00164	.08016	80
85+	5489	1614	.29404	.00000	.00055	.00929	.09164	.02733	.00055	.00474	.00000	.00000	.00000	.00273	.15722	85+
ALL	1508845	22476														

	All Causes	Respiratory T. B.	Other Infec. and Paras.	Neo-plasms	Cardio-vascular	Infl., Pneu., Bronch.	Diar-rheal	Certain Degen-erative	Maternal	Cert. Dis. of Infancy	Motor Vehicle	Other Violence	Other and Unknown
CRUDE DEATH RATE	.01490	.00062	.00030	.00165	.00543	.00176	.00010	.00048	.00000	.00056	.00009	.00033	.00356
STANDARDIZED RATE (1)	.00830	.00051	.00034	.00083	.00224	.00099	.00013	.00026	.00000	.00092	.00008	.00027	.00173
STANDARDIZED RATE (2)	.01428	.00063	.00030	.00156	.00512	.00167	.00010	.00046	.00000	.00054	.00009	.00032	.00349
GEOMETRIC MEAN	.01042												

LIFE TABLE FOR ALL CAUSES COMBINED

Age (x)	Midyear Population	Deaths During Year	$_nM_x$	$_nq_x$	l_x	$_nd_x$	$_nL_x$	$_nm_x$	$_na_x$	T_x	$_nr_x$	$\overset{\circ}{e}_x$	Age (x)
0	32679	1679	.051379	.049250	100000	4925	95850	.051382	.157344	6364469	.000000	63.645	0
1	127791	351	.002747	.010907	95075	1037	377708	.002746	1.500000	6268619	.000000	65.933	1
5	143704	133	.000926	.004615	94038	434	469105	.000925	2.500000	5890912	.000000	62.644	5
10	132924	79	.000594	.002970	93604	278	467364	.000595	2.638639	5421807	.007880	57.923	10
15	125930	167	.001326	.006623	93326	619	465216	.001331	2.715065	4954443	.018112	53.087	15
20	105537	209	.001980	.009891	92707	917	461354	.001988	2.621320	4489227	.022764	48.424	20
25	99744	252	.002526	.012561	91790	1153	456137	.002528	2.559988	4027874	.012356	43.881	25
30	96585	268	.002775	.013780	90637	1249	450156	.002775	2.574560	3571737	-.001280	39.407	30
35	102431	370	.003612	.017899	89388	1600	443104	.003611	2.602734	3121581	-.004834	34.922	35
40	94146	441	.004684	.023215	87788	2038	434166	.004694	2.657426	2678477	.013953	30.511	40
45	82497	614	.007443	.036618	85750	3140	421458	.007450	2.677813	2244311	.005940	26.173	45
50	83046	973	.011716	.057112	82610	4718	401982	.011737	2.654108	1822853	.009554	22.066	50
55	65125	1152	.017689	.085118	77892	6630	373844	.017735	2.644702	1420871	.014582	18.242	55
60	61437	1715	.027915	.130827	71262	9323	334132	.027902	2.621116	1047026	-.002353	14.693	60
65	54226	2335	.043061	.194546	61939	12050	280764	.042919	2.559049	712895	-.018042	11.510	65
70	49194	3500	.071147	.301710	49889	15052	212605	.070798	2.552457	432131	-.023342	8.662	70
75	31689	3752	.118401	.454689	34837	15840	133990	.118218	2.462411	219527	-.005916	6.302	75
80	14671	2872	.195760	.641891	18997	12194	62401	.195414	2.327852	85537	-.005916	4.503	80
85+	5489	1614	.294043	1.000000	6803	6803	23136	.294043	3.400867	23136	.000000	3.401	85+

NUMBER OF PERSONS DYING (OUT OF 100,000 AT BIRTH) ABOVE AGE X FROM SPECIFIED CAUSES

Age (x)	All Causes	Respiratory T. B.	Other Infec. and Paras.	Neo-plasms	Cardio-vascular	Infl., Pneu., Bronch.	Diar-rheal	Certain Degen-erative	Maternal	Cert. Dis. of Infancy	Motor Vehicle	Other Violence	Other and Unknown	Age (x)
0	100000	4502	1776	11829	37819	11715	546	3399	0	2496	597	2182	23139	0
1	95075	4493	1559	11823	37787	10988	276	3396	0	0	597	2079	22077	1
5	94038	4481	1256	11764	37763	10775	238	3390	0	0	567	1994	21770	5
10	93604	4481	1215	11735	37741	10723	232	3377	0	0	535	1945	21620	10
15	93326	4474	1141	11700	37716	10698	232	3366	0	0	524	1920	21555	15
20	92707	4332	1048	11666	37664	10654	228	3326	0	0	502	1853	21434	20
25	91790	4012	934	11609	37598	10606	228	3286	0	0	467	1752	21298	25
30	90637	3641	857	11490	37470	10537	228	3236	0	0	412	1606	21160	30
35	89388	3236	750	11378	37288	10500	223	3133	0	0	370	1508	21002	35
40	87788	2786	659	11218	37003	10409	219	3012	0	0	323	1357	20802	40
45	85750	2366	548	10890	36531	10335	205	2855	0	0	276	1269	20475	45
50	82610	1840	471	10363	35599	10074	205	2625	0	0	220	1141	20072	50
55	77892	1375	355	9354	34052	9565	171	2349	0	0	191	991	19489	55
60	71262	892	258	8135	31356	8845	142	2027	0	0	168	865	18574	60
65	61939	419	176	6379	27432	7627	132	1652	0	0	114	675	17333	65
70	49889	201	78	4400	21634	6099	111	1296	0	0	72	447	15551	70
75	34837	71	43	2325	14222	4165	64	723	0	0	46	270	12908	75
80	18997	12	30	897	6832	2003	43	351	0	0	17	164	8648	80
85+	6803	0	13	215	2120	632	13	110	0	0	0	63	3637	85+

NUMBER OF PERSONS SURVIVING TO AGE X IF SPECIFIED CAUSES WERE ELIMINATED

Age (x)	No Causes	Respiratory T. B.	Other Infec. and Paras.	Neo-plasms	Cardio-vascular	Infl., Pneu., Bronch.	Diar-rheal	Certain Degener-ative	Maternal	Cert. Dis. of Infancy	Motor Vehicle	Other Violence	Other and Unknown	(1) + (2)	(1) + (2) + (5) + (6) + (8)	(1)+(2)+ (5)+(6)+ (8)+part of(9)&(12)	(10) + (11)	Age (x)
		(1)	(2)	(3)	(4)	(5)	(6)	(7)	(8)	(9)	(10)	(11)	(12)					
0	100000	100000	100000	100000	100000	100000	100000	100000	100000	100000	100000	100000	100000	100000	100000	100000	100000	0
1	95075	95084	95287	95081	95106	95786	95339	95078	95075	97540	95075	95175	96116	95296	96275	99469	95175	1
5	94038	94059	94510	94102	94093	94955	94337	94047	94038	96476	94068	94222	95377	94531	95756	99165	94252	5
10	93604	93625	94155	93697	93680	94570	93907	93626	93604	96031	93666	93836	95089	94176	95455	98931	93898	10
15	93326	93353	93950	93454	93427	94314	93628	93359	93326	95746	93398	93583	94872	93977	95280	98783	93655	15
20	92707	92876	93420	92868	92859	93733	93011	92779	92707	95111	92801	93029	94366	93590	94936	98500	93123	20
25	91790	92277	92610	92006	92007	92854	92091	91902	91790	94170	91918	92210	93570	93102	94490	98126	92338	25
30	90637	91489	91524	90969	90979	91757	90935	90797	90637	92987	90818	91197	92534	92385	93833	97519	91379	30
35	89388	90035	90370	89827	89907	90530	89686	89648	89388	91705	89608	90038	91420	91631	93111	96855	90260	35
40	87788	88466	88844	88582	89001	88085	88164	87788	89064	88051	88577	89986	90542	92103	95905	88843		40
45	85750	87813	86892	86654	86998	87009	86054	86273	85750	87973	86054	86609	88229	88983	90609	94478	86915	45
50	82610	85127	83787	84006	84746	84083	82903	83341	82610	84752	82957	83564	85406	86340	88191	92096	83916	50
55	77892	80731	79116	80210	81463	79786	78201	78852	77892	79911	78248	78939	81116	82000	84327	88234	79300	55
60	71262	74338	72476	74593	77270	72726	71573	72452	71262	73110	71610	72342	75128	75604	78536	82410	72695	60
65	61939	65071	63071	66567	71254	65246	62218	63329	61939	63545	62292	63057	66530	66261	70114	73875	63417	65
70	49889	52614	50890	55550	63695	54014	50133	51335	49889	51182	50211	50997	55333	53669	58391	61882	51326	70
75	34837	36851	35564	40743	53072	39498	35047	36339	34837	35740	35083	35759	41174	37621	42911	45980	36012	75
80	18997	20139	19403	23439	38356	23393	19126	20094	18997	19490	19152	19578	26502	20569	25501	28223	19738	80
85+	6803	7219	6958	8890	20426	9403	6867	7343	6803	6979	6868	7071	14473	7384	10301	12400	7139	85+

ADDED YRS OF LIFE																		
TOTAL		1.228	.722	1.673	4.557	1.812	.235	.533	.000	1.646	.178	.576	3.569	1.970	4.141	7.290	.757	
WORK	4.551	.872	.236	.578	.988	.304	.014	.257	.000	.000	.096	.269	.574	1.115	1.447	1.689	.366	

POPULATION, DEATHS, DEATH RATES FOR ALL CAUSES COMBINED, AND SPECIFIED CAUSES

Age Start of Interval	Midyear Population	Deaths During Year	All Causes	Respiratory T. B.	Other Infec. and Paras.	Neoplasms	Cardiovascular	Infl., Pneu., Bronch.	Diarrheal	Certain Degenerative	Maternal	Cert. Dis. of Infancy	Motor Vehicle	Other Violence	Other and Unknown	Age Start of Interval
0	30979	1197	.03864	.00010	.00229	.00000	.00013	.00571	.00194	.00006	.00000	.01846	.00000	.00074	.00920	0
1	121978	293	.00240	.00003	.00070	.00007	.00005	.00065	.00013	.00001	.00000	.00000	.00002	.00012	.00062	1
5	137784	95	.00069	.00001	.00013	.00002	.00008	.00007	.00002	.00001	.00000	.00000	.00005	.00012	.00062	5
10	128424	91	.00071	.00008	.00018	.00006	.00013	.00004	.00001	.00001	.00000	.00000	.00001	.00007	.00022	10
15	115634	144	.00125	.00045	.00022	.00006	.00010	.00006	.00002	.00002	.00002	.00000	.00004	.00009	.00017	15
20	96954	204	.00210	.00098	.00031	.00010	.00018	.00007	.00000	.00007	.00007	.00000	.00004	.00000	.00028	20
25	98992	240	.00242	.00115	.00021	.00017	.00036	.00011	.00000	.00004	.00011	.00000	.00002	.00005	.00019	25
30	95285	246	.00258	.00094	.00009	.00020	.00046	.00015	.00000	.00007	.00021	.00000	.00001	.00007	.00037	30
35	98804	376	.00381	.00100	.00015	.00048	.00079	.00026	.00002	.00022	.00036	.00000	.00001	.00011	.00039	35
40	86465	364	.00421	.00069	.00017	.00091	.00093	.00038	.00002	.00021	.00028	.00000	.00001	.00002	.00059	40
45	78673	423	.00538	.00064	.00020	.00145	.00154	.00033	.00005	.00022	.00000	.00000	.00001	.00009	.00081	45
50	80198	764	.00953	.00070	.00010	.00226	.00379	.00061	.00006	.00057	.00000	.00000	.00002	.00004	.00137	50
55	63927	874	.01367	.00053	.00014	.00344	.00541	.00138	.00002	.00056	.00000	.00000	.00000	.00013	.00206	55
60	60816	1354	.02226	.00054	.00008	.00439	.01085	.00276	.00007	.00077	.00000	.00000	.00003	.00033	.00243	60
65	53493	1927	.03602	.00071	.00019	.00581	.01735	.00520	.00007	.00151	.00000	.00000	.00004	.00036	.00479	65
70	51081	3076	.06022	.00037	.00020	.00650	.03032	.00932	.00025	.00178	.00000	.00000	.00004	.00084	.01059	70
75	32968	3442	.10440	.00027	.00006	.00761	.04984	.01686	.00024	.00237	.00000	.00000	.00006	.00136	.02572	75
80	16265	2788	.17141	.00012	.00018	.00861	.06837	.02275	.00043	.00203	.00000	.00000	.00000	.00000	.06542	80
85+	7817	2008	.25688	.00000	.00013	.00588	.08789	.02942	.00013	.00230	.00000	.00000	.00000	.00350	.06542	85+
ALL	1456437	19906														

			All Causes	Respiratory T. B.	Other Infec.	Neoplasms	Cardiovascular	Infl. Pneu. Bronch.	Diarrheal	Certain Degen.	Maternal	Cert. Dis. Infancy	Motor Vehicle	Other Violence	Other Unknown
CRUDE DEATH RATE			.01367	.00053	.00026	.00142	.00526	.00179	.00009	.00035	.00007	.00039	.00002	.00023	.00326
STANDARDIZED RATE (1)			.00694	.00049	.00031	.00071	.00199	.00087	.00010	.00017	.00007	.00065	.00003	.00013	.00140
STANDARDIZED RATE (2)			.01211	.00054	.00026	.00130	.00455	.00156	.00008	.00032	.00007	.00038	.00002	.00020	.00282
GEOMETRIC MEAN			.00916												

LIFE TABLE FOR ALL CAUSES COMBINED

Age (x)	Midyear Population	Deaths During Year	$_nM_x$	$_nq_x$	l_x	$_nd_x$	$_nL_x$	$_nm_x$	$_na_x$	T_x	$_nr_x$	$\overset{\circ}{e}_x$	Age (x)
0	30979	1197	.038639	.037390	100000	3739	96768	.038639	.135686	6623001	.000000	66.230	0
1	121978	293	.002404	.009557	96261	920	382744	.002404	1.500000	6526232	.000000	67.797	1
5	137784	95	.000689	.003440	95341	328	475685	.000689	2.500000	6143488	.000000	64.437	5
10	128424	91	.000709	.003536	95013	336	474280	.000708	2.663070	5667603	.010578	59.651	10
15	115634	144	.001245	.006242	94677	591	472043	.001252	2.729836	5193324	.024825	54.853	15
20	96954	204	.002104	.010501	94086	988	468071	.002111	2.611969	4721280	.018583	50.180	20
25	98992	240	.002424	.012052	93098	1122	462725	.002425	2.535465	4253210	.004415	45.685	25
30	95285	246	.002582	.012819	91976	1179	457055	.002580	2.604255	3790485	-.001845	41.212	30
35	98804	376	.003806	.018855	90797	1712	449847	.003806	2.582749	3333430	-.001247	36.713	35
40	86465	364	.004210	.020868	89085	1859	440904	.004216	2.567913	2883583	.017816	32.369	40
45	78673	423	.005377	.026575	87226	2318	430773	.005381	2.689010	2442679	.003801	28.004	45
50	80198	764	.009526	.046662	84908	3962	415272	.009541	2.660746	2011906	-.008671	23.695	50
55	63927	874	.013672	.066402	80946	5375	392133	.013707	2.656434	1596634	-.014756	19.725	55
60	60816	1354	.022264	.105834	75571	7998	359070	.022274	2.651236	1204501	-.002076	15.939	60
65	53493	1927	.036023	.165465	67573	11181	311324	.035914	2.626200	845431	-.015147	12.511	65
70	51081	3076	.060218	.261934	56392	14771	246293	.059973	2.585316	534108	-.019235	9.471	70
75	32968	3442	.104404	.413974	41621	17230	164954	.104454	2.495562	287815	-.001864	6.915	75
80	16265	2788	.171411	.590546	24391	14404	83983	.171511	2.363768	122861	-.001864	5.037	80
85+	7817	2008	.256876	1.000000	9987	9987	38879	.256876	3.892928	38879	.000000	3.893	85+

NUMBER OF PERSONS DYING (OUT OF 100,000 AT BIRTH) ABOVE AGE X FROM SPECIFIED CAUSES

Age (x)	All Causes	Respiratory T. B.	Other Infec. and Paras.	Neo-plasms	Cardio-vascular	Infl., Pneu., Bronch.	Diar-rheal	Certain Degen-erative	Maternal	Cert. Dis. of Infancy	Motor Vehicle	Other Violence	Other and Unknown	Age (x)
0	100000	3797	1521	11034	39882	12990	519	2695	492	1787	160	1581	23542	0
1	96261	3787	1299	11034	39869	12437	331	2688	492	0	160	1509	22655	1
5	95341	3775	1032	11006	39851	12189	281	2685	492	0	150	1462	22418	5
10	95013	3768	970	10996	39813	12154	271	2678	492	0	126	1431	22314	10
15	94677	3731	885	10966	39750	12136	267	2675	492	0	123	1405	22247	15
20	94086	3516	782	10937	39701	12107	259	2666	484	0	102	1364	22168	20
25	93058	3056	637	10889	39618	12073	259	2632	450	0	83	1364	22037	25
30	91976	2523	539	10809	39450	12022	259	2614	399	0	73	1341	21947	30
35	90797	2091	496	10718	39239	11955	259	2580	303	0	69	1307	21780	35
40	89085	1641	428	10504	38864	11836	250	2480	139	0	64	1257	21602	40
45	87226	1335	351	10100	38475	11668	245	2388	17	0	59	1247	21341	45
50	84908	1062	264	9475	37811	11525	223	2255	1	0	54	1209	20989	50
55	80946	772	222	8536	36234	11271	197	2057	1	0	43	1193	20420	55
60	75571	563	167	7184	34104	10729	191	1836	1	0	43	1144	19609	60
65	67573	369	138	5608	30206	9736	167	1558	1	0	31	1026	18733	65
70	56392	147	80	3799	24822	8124	144	1087	1	0	20	916	17252	70
75	41621	55	31	2200	17383	5839	81	649	1	0	10	709	14663	75
80	24391	10	21	944	9158	3056	41	259	1	0	0	484	10417	80
85+	9987	0	5	229	3417	1144	5	90	0	0	0	189	4908	85+

NUMBER OF PERSONS SURVIVING TO AGE X IF SPECIFIED CAUSES WERE ELIMINATED

Age (x)	No Causes	Respiratory T. B.	Other Infec. and Paras.	Neo-plasms	Cardio-vascular	Infl., Pneu., Bronch.	Diar-rheal	Certain Degener-ative	Maternal	Cert. Dis. of Infancy	Motor Vehicle	Other Violence	Other and Unknown	(1) + (2)	(1) + (2) + (5) + (6) + (8)	(1)+(2)+ (5)+(6)+ (8)+part of(9)&(12)	(10) + (11)	Age (x)
		(1)	(2)	(3)	(4)	(5)	(6)	(7)	(8)	(9)	(10)	(11)	(12)					
0	100000	100000	100000	100000	100000	100000	100000	100000	100000	100000	100000	100000	100000	100000	100000	100000	100000	0
1	96261	96271	96479	96261	96274	96805	96446	96268	96261	98030	96261	96332	97135	96489	97220	99671	96332	1
5	95341	95363	95824	95369	95372	96128	95574	95351	95341	97093	95351	95458	96445	95845	96873	99523	95468	5
10	95013	95042	95556	95051	95081	95833	95255	95030	95013	96759	95047	95160	96218	95585	96655	99355	95194	10
15	94677	94742	95304	94745	94808	95512	94922	94697	94677	96417	94714	94850	95946	95370	96460	99191	94887	15
20	94086	94366	94812	94182	94265	94945	94338	94115	94094	95815	94143	94299	95427	95094	96227	99011	94356	20
25	93058	93835	93962	93241	93358	93982	93347	93160	93140	94809	93174	93308	94557	94706	95904	98786	93384	25
30	91976	93240	92928	92197	92401	92901	92055	92068	92061	93666	92061	92207	93508	94204	95501	98440	92292	30
35	90797	92480	91780	91106	91427	91777	91040	90909	90983	92466	90885	91059	92478	93481	94938	97972	91147	35
40	89085	91191	90117	89601	90058	90166	89332	89294	89431	90722	89176	89392	90915	92248	93990	97095	89483	40
45	87226	89599	88314	88135	88589	88453	87473	87522	87686	88829	87320	87536	89281	90716	92739	95923	87630	45
50	84908	87494	86054	86418	86645	86245	85170	85288	85371	86469	85004	85247	87265	88675	90843	94068	85344	50
55	80946	83703	82080	83324	84440	82474	81221	81542	81388	82434	81049	81285	83766	84876	87245	90454	81388	55
60	75571	78354	76683	79146	81011	77533	75834	76343	75983	76960	75667	75935	79018	79507	82302	85486	76032	60
65	67573	70251	68595	72343	76458	70299	67831	68529	67942	68815	67670	68011	71526	71314	74880	77943	68109	65
70	56392	58836	57299	62158	69651	60218	56628	57626	56700	57428	56483	56859	61143	59782	64456	67413	56950	70
75	41621	43505	42332	47395	59897	46584	41850	42914	41848	42386	41697	42145	47612	44248	50068	52942	42221	75
80	24391	25529	24815	28860	45252	29753	24555	25450	24524	24839	24443	24871	31882	25973	32069	34928	24924	80
85+	9987	10459	10171	12352	26449	13715	10077	10530	10042	10171	10008	10372	18365	10652	14841	17437	10394	85+

ADDED YRS OF LIFE																	
TOTAL		1.274	.706	1.700	5.449	1.837	.205	.397	.178	1.215	.061	.281	3.480	1.998	4.348	7.072	.342
WORK	4.077	.916	.216	.600	.937	.252	.015	.149	.139	.000	.027	.068	.491	1.138	1.562	1.789	.095

POPULATION, DEATHS, DEATH RATES FOR ALL CAUSES COMBINED, AND SPECIFIED CAUSES

Age Start of Interval	Midyear Population	Deaths During Year	All Causes	Respiratory T. B.	Other Infec. and Paras.	Neoplasms	Cardiovascular	Infl., Pneu., Bronch.	Diarrheal	Certain Degenerative	Maternal	Cert. Dis. of Infancy	Motor Vehicle	Other Violence	Other and Unknown	Age Start of Interval
0	32198	1029	.03156	.00000	.00071	.00012	.00000	.00398	.00096	.00006	.00000	.01736	.00000	.00040	.00835	0
1	121524	166	.00137	.00000	.00012	.00015	.00002	.00035	.00007	.00002	.00000	.00000	.00009	.00010	.00046	1
5	147271	77	.00052	.00000	.00006	.00006	.00001	.00003	.00001	.00001	.00000	.00000	.00009	.00008	.00018	5
10	148601	61	.00041	.00000	.00003	.00008	.00003	.00001	.00001	.00001	.00000	.00000	.00007	.00009	.00010	10
15	120576	76	.00063	.00001	.00002	.00010	.00008	.00000	.00000	.00007	.00000	.00000	.00012	.00012	.00011	15
20	80573	84	.00104	.00001	.00001	.00006	.00012	.00006	.00001	.00001	.00000	.00000	.00030	.00024	.00021	20
25	72427	85	.00117	.00006	.00004	.00019	.00015	.00008	.00000	.00007	.00000	.00000	.00018	.00022	.00018	25
30	75384	119	.00158	.00008	.00001	.00021	.00033	.00008	.00000	.00016	.00000	.00000	.00027	.00017	.00027	30
35	81781	185	.00226	.00017	.00004	.00033	.00068	.00017	.00001	.00022	.00000	.00000	.00012	.00027	.00024	35
40	84957	286	.00337	.00014	.00005	.00073	.00121	.00022	.00001	.00011	.00000	.00000	.00026	.00026	.00038	40
45	89206	477	.00535	.00015	.00004	.00121	.00222	.00040	.00002	.00029	.00000	.00000	.00016	.00030	.00055	45
50	81844	784	.00958	.00033	.00010	.00219	.00456	.00079	.00002	.00028	.00000	.00000	.00012	.00037	.00082	50
55	68750	1033	.01503	.00054	.00009	.00361	.00666	.00161	.00006	.00071	.00000	.00000	.00013	.00045	.00116	55
60	64558	1604	.02485	.00068	.00011	.00520	.01204	.00301	.00006	.00101	.00000	.00000	.00019	.00048	.00208	60
65	51238	2047	.03995	.00082	.00008	.00751	.02077	.00521	.00006	.00139	.00000	.00000	.00027	.00059	.00326	65
70	44194	2714	.06141	.00061	.00007	.01016	.03367	.00695	.00014	.00208	.00000	.00000	.00027	.00104	.00643	70
75	29751	2888	.09707	.00024	.00013	.01277	.05469	.01146	.00017	.00269	.00000	.00000	.00044	.00097	.01351	75
80	16706	2794	.16725	.00048	.00018	.01538	.09488	.01868	.00054	.00353	.00000	.00000	.00018	.00120	.03220	80
85+	7709	2241	.29070	.00013	.00013	.01492	.15203	.03009	.00052	.00441	.00000	.00000	.00013	.00258	.08535	85+
ALL	1419248	18750														
CRUDE DEATH RATE			.01321	.00017	.00007	.00186	.00632	.00147	.00006	.00039	.00000	.00039	.00016	.00030	.00202	
STANDARDIZED RATE (1)			.00622	.00010	.00007	.00085	.00230	.00069	.00006	.00019	.00000	.00061	.00015	.00022	.00097	
STANDARDIZED RATE (2)			.01169	.00016	.00007	.00167	.00552	.00130	.00005	.00036	.00000	.00036	.00017	.00029	.00174	
GEOMETRIC MEAN			.00720													

LIFE TABLE FOR ALL CAUSES COMBINED

Age (x)	Midyear Population	Deaths During Year	$_nM_x$	$_nq_x$	l_x	$_nd_x$	$_nL_x$	$_nm_x$	$_na_x$	T_x	$_nr_x$	$\overset{\circ}{e}_x$	Age (x)
0	32198	1029	.031959	.031090	100000	3109	97278	.031960	.124329	6791225	.000000	67.912	0
1	121524	166	.001366	.005439	96891	527	386247	.001364	1.500000	6693948	.000000	69.087	1
5	147271	77	.000523	.002615	96364	252	481190	.000524	2.500000	6307701	.000000	65.457	5
10	148601	61	.000410	.002050	96112	197	480078	.000410	2.554992	5826511	.007620	60.622	10
15	120576	76	.000630	.003169	95915	304	478878	.000635	2.706277	5346433	.048584	55.741	15
20	80573	84	.001043	.005209	95611	498	476863	.001044	2.605840	4867555	.056772	50.910	20
25	72427	85	.001174	.005856	95113	557	474224	.001175	2.591637	4390692	.020663	46.163	25
30	75384	119	.001579	.007858	94556	743	471026	.001577	2.639356	3916469	-.005551	41.420	30
35	81781	185	.002262	.011235	93813	1054	466597	.002259	2.658523	3445443	-.012352	36.727	35
40	84957	286	.003366	.016656	92759	1545	460214	.003357	2.682174	2978846	-.013200	32.114	40
45	89206	477	.005347	.026367	91214	2405	450605	.005337	2.727477	2518632	-.008296	27.612	45
50	81844	784	.009579	.046566	88809	4171	434399	.009602	2.687305	2068027	.011938	23.286	50
55	68750	1033	.015025	.072721	84638	6155	408855	.015054	2.670931	1633628	.009382	19.301	55
60	64558	1604	.024846	.117490	78483	9221	370710	.024874	2.646156	1224774	.005872	15.606	60
65	51238	2047	.039951	.182264	69262	12624	315974	.039953	2.596971	854064	.000280	12.331	65
70	44194	2714	.061411	.266552	56638	15097	246193	.061322	2.549375	538089	-.007919	9.501	70
75	29751	2888	.097072	.390024	41541	16202	167126	.096945	2.495448	291897	-.005889	7.027	75
80	16706	2794	.167245	.581830	25339	14743	88320	.166927	2.397084	124770	-.005889	4.924	80
85+	7709	2241	.290699	1.000000	10596	10596	36450	.290699	3.439982	36450	.000000	3.440	85+

NUMBER OF PERSONS DYING (OUT OF 100,000 AT BIRTH) ABOVE AGE X FROM SPECIFIED CAUSES

Age (x)	All Causes	Respiratory T. B.	Other Infec. and Paras.	Neo-plasms	Cardio-vascular	Infl., Pneu., Bronch.	Diar-rheal	Certain Degen-erative	Maternal	Cert. Dis. of Infancy	Motor Vehicle	Other Violence	Other and Unknown	Age (x)
0	100000	1396	458	14705	49276	11143	360	3109	0	1689	1187	2238	14439	0
1	96891	1396	388	14693	49276	10756	266	3103	0	0	1187	2199	13627	1
5	96364	1396	344	14636	49269	10620	241	3097	0	0	1152	2161	13448	5
10	96112	1396	314	14607	49266	10607	234	3094	0	0	1109	2121	13364	10
15	95915	1396	302	14568	49253	10603	231	3090	0	0	1077	2079	13316	15
20	95611	1392	294	14520	49213	10603	231	3054	0	0	1021	2019	13264	20
25	95113	1386	288	14451	49155	10574	225	3049	0	0	878	1906	13161	25
30	94556	1360	268	14399	49083	10534	225	3016	0	0	793	1801	13077	30
35	93813	1322	262	14299	48927	10497	225	2941	0	0	668	1720	12952	35
40	92759	1243	245	14146	48608	10417	219	2838	0	0	611	1595	12837	40
45	91214	1178	223	13811	48052	10314	214	2790	0	0	491	1476	12665	45
50	88809	1112	203	13267	47055	10133	204	2658	0	0	421	1339	12417	50
55	84638	968	160	12214	45070	9787	193	2536	0	0	367	1180	12063	55
60	78483	748	125	10837	42341	9125	169	2244	0	0	314	995	11585	60
65	69262	495	85	8906	37873	8009	146	1870	0	0	245	817	10816	65
70	56638	236	60	6531	31312	6363	128	1433	0	0	159	632	9784	70
75	41541	86	43	4032	23035	4655	94	921	0	0	92	376	8207	75
80	25339	46	21	1899	13908	2742	66	472	0	0	19	213	5953	80
85+	10596	5	5	544	5542	1097	19	161	0	0	5	109	3109	85+

NUMBER OF PERSONS SURVIVING TO AGE X IF SPECIFIED CAUSES WERE ELIMINATED

Age (x)	No Causes	Respiratory T. B.	Other Infec. and Paras.	Neo-plasms	Cardio-vascular	Infl., Pneu., Bronch.	Diar-rheal	Certain Degener-ative	Maternal	Cert. Dis. of Infancy	Motor Vehicle	Other Violence	Other and Unknown	(1) + (2)	(1) + (2) + (5) + (6) + (8)	(1)+(2)+ (5)+(6)+ (8)+part of(9)&(12)	(10) + (11)	Age (x)
		(1)	(2)	(3)	(4)	(5)	(6)	(7)	(8)	(9)	(10)	(11)	(12)					
0	100000	100000	100000	100000	100000	100000	100000	100000	100000	100000	100000	100000	100000	100000	100000	100000	100000	0
1	96891	96891	96960	96903	96891	97273	96984	96897	96891	98568	96891	96929	97654	96960	97435	99704	96929	1
5	96364	96364	96476	96433	96371	96880	96481	96376	96364	98032	96359	96440	97342	96476	97111	99481	96475	5
10	96112	96112	96254	96209	96122	96640	96236	96127	96112	97775	96190	96228	97173	96254	96907	99298	96306	10
15	95915	95915	96069	96051	95938	96445	96041	95934	95915	97575	96025	96073	97022	96069	96728	99112	96182	15
20	95611	95615	95772	95795	95674	96140	95737	95666	95611	97266	95776	95828	96767	95776	96433	98822	95994	20
25	95113	95123	95280	95225	95233	95668	95244	95172	95113	96759	95420	95442	96367	95290	95978	98368	95751	25
30	94556	94592	94742	94859	94748	95148	94687	94648	94556	96192	94947	94988	95887	94777	95503	97896	95381	30
35	93813	93886	94003	94213	94159	94427	93943	93979	93813	95437	94264	94323	95260	94077	94834	97228	94838	35
40	92759	92910	92964	93308	93420	93457	92893	93026	92759	94364	93323	93388	94306	93115	93951	96346	93956	40
45	91214	91427	91437	92088	92421	92003	91351	91524	91214	92793	91888	91952	92909	91651	92583	94967	92631	45
50	88809	89082	89046	90204	90987	89757	88952	89242	88809	90346	89535	89663	90709	89320	90419	92781	90396	50
55	84638	85039	84906	86518	88722	85884	85170	84638	86103	85383	85609	86802	85309	86715	89032	86362	55
60	78483	79068	78765	82070	85071	80289	78643	79260	78483	79841	79225	79563	80963	79352	81343	83598	80316	60
65	69262	70017	69549	74345	79767	71936	69424	70302	69262	70461	69982	70384	72199	70307	73193	75355	71116	65
70	56638	57491	56855	63135	72425	60387	56787	57890	56638	57618	57305	57726	60021	57752	61736	63736	58405	70
75	41541	42294	41744	48733	62568	45868	41679	42907	41541	42260	42088	42561	45480	42500	47084	48833	43121	75
80	25339	25828	25480	31703	50748	29658	25445	26530	25339	25778	25729	26088	29735	25971	30525	31976	26490	80
85+	10596	10827	10665	14363	34805	13669	10670	11300	10596	10779	10768	10977	14712	10897	14156	15200	11155	85+

ADDED YRS OF LIFE

	No Causes	(1)	(2)	(3)	(4)	(5)	(6)	(7)	(8)	(9)	(10)	(11)	(12)	(1)+(2)	(1)+(2)+(5)+(6)+(8)	(1)+(2)+(5)+(6)+(8)+part	(10)+(11)
TOTAL		.245	.167	2.025	7.236	1.477	.116	.430	.000	1.173	.380	.534	2.123	.413	2.037	3.981	.919
WORK	3.163	.110	.036	.573	1.048	.225	.010	.158	.000	.000	.220	.256	.340	.147	.384	.433	.478

POPULATION, DEATHS, DEATH RATES FOR ALL CAUSES COMBINED, AND SPECIFIED CAUSES

Age Start of Interval	Midyear Population	Deaths During Year	All Causes	Respiratory T. B.	Other Infec. and Paras.	Neoplasms	Cardiovascular	Infl., Pneu., Bronch.	Diarrheal	Certain Degenerative	Maternal	Cert. Dis. of Infancy	Motor Vehicle	Other Violence	Other and Unknown	Age Start of Interval
0	30700	798	.02599	.00000	.00036	.00007	.00003	.00336	.00094	.00003	.00000	.01290	.00000	.00059	.00772	0
1	116972	148	.00127	.00000	.00016	.00005	.00001	.00027	.00007	.00003	.00000	.00000	.00003	.00014	.00051	1
5	140975	56	.00040	.00001	.00008	.00006	.00003	.00002	.00001	.00000	.00000	.00000	.00004	.00003	.00013	5
10	140779	53	.00038	.00000	.00004	.00005	.00003	.00006	.00000	.00001	.00000	.00000	.00001	.00003	.00014	10
15	113725	36	.00032	.00001	.00001	.00005	.00003	.00003	.00003	.00002	.00000	.00000	.00003	.00004	.00011	15
20	77751	50	.00064	.00004	.00000	.00010	.00013	.00008	.00004	.00006	.00001	.00000	.00000	.00005	.00009	20
25	73243	68	.00093	.00004	.00008	.00023	.00018	.00010	.00003	.00001	.00001	.00000	.00004	.00004	.00016	25
30	77710	106	.00136	.00012	.00001	.00031	.00026	.00005	.00000	.00008	.00012	.00000	.00003	.00010	.00030	30
35	85347	169	.00198	.00018	.00002	.00057	.00045	.00013	.00002	.00007	.00014	.00000	.00004	.00005	.00032	35
40	85679	204	.00238	.00019	.00004	.00079	.00077	.00014	.00002	.00007	.00005	.00000	.00005	.00004	.00023	40
45	85770	348	.00406	.00017	.00008	.00140	.00125	.00029	.00007	.00023	.00000	.00000	.00001	.00007	.00048	45
50	75594	514	.00680	.00020	.00001	.00231	.00279	.00046	.00004	.00019	.00000	.00000	.00007	.00007	.00066	50
55	67647	638	.00943	.00021	.00003	.00268	.00418	.00075	.00001	.00030	.00000	.00000	.00010	.00010	.00106	55
60	66766	1067	.01598	.00018	.00007	.00424	.00804	.00117	.00006	.00064	.00000	.00000	.00006	.00013	.00138	60
65	52458	1409	.02686	.00025	.00006	.00536	.01485	.00248	.00013	.00086	.00000	.00000	.00004	.00031	.00254	65
70	48783	2247	.04606	.00016	.00006	.00685	.02712	.00457	.00023	.00166	.00000	.00000	.00010	.00066	.00465	70
75	33587	2626	.07819	.00030	.00015	.00741	.04725	.00819	.00027	.00226	.00000	.00000	.00012	.00143	.01081	75
80	20409	2811	.13773	.00005	.00015	.01049	.08124	.01578	.00024	.00240	.00000	.00000	.00015	.00220	.02504	80
85+	10864	2665	.24531	.00009	.00055	.01197	.13669	.02522	.00055	.00322	.00000	.00000	.00009	.00479	.06213	85+
ALL	1404759	16013														

			All Causes	Respiratory T. B.	Other Infec. and Paras.	Neoplasms	Cardiovascular	Infl., Pneu., Bronch.	Diarrheal	Certain Degenerative	Maternal	Cert. Dis. of Infancy	Motor Vehicle	Other Violence	Other and Unknown
CRUDE DEATH RATE			.01140	.00010	.00007	.00154	.00579	.00114	.00007	.00030	.00002	.00028	.00004	.00021	.00185
STANDARDIZED RATE (1)			.00468	.00007	.00007	.00070	.00174	.00048	.00006	.00012	.00002	.00045	.00004	.00011	.00083
STANDARDIZED RATE (2)			.00886	.00009	.00006	.00130	.00434	.00088	.00006	.00024	.00002	.00027	.00004	.00016	.00139
GEOMETRIC MEAN			.00540												

LIFE TABLE FOR ALL CAUSES COMBINED

Age (x)	Midyear Population	Deaths During Year	$_nM_x$	$_nq_x$	l_x	$_nd_x$	$_nL_x$	$_nm_x$	$_na_x$	T_x	$_nr_x$	$\overset{\circ}{e}_x$	Age (x)
0	30700	798	.025993	.025410	100000	2541	97749	.025995	.114189	7160573	.000000	71.606	0
1	116972	148	.001265	.005048	97459	492	388606	.001266	1.500000	7062823	.000000	72.470	1
5	140975	56	.000397	.001980	96967	192	484355	.000396	2.500000	6674217	.000000	68.830	5
10	140779	53	.000376	.001881	96775	182	483412	.000376	2.454212	6189862	.009210	63.961	10
15	113725	36	.000317	.001574	96593	152	482612	.000315	2.676809	5706451	.048607	59.077	15
20	77751	50	.000643	.003225	96441	311	481489	.000646	2.697615	5223839	.051742	54.166	20
25	73243	68	.000928	.004650	96130	447	479603	.000932	2.657532	4742350	.014263	49.333	25
30	77710	106	.001364	.006783	95683	649	476894	.001361	2.656651	4262747	-.010028	44.551	30
35	85347	169	.001980	.009839	95034	935	472929	.001977	2.603387	3785853	-.012462	39.837	35
40	85679	204	.002381	.011828	94099	1113	469007	.002379	2.675015	3312924	-.006858	35.207	40
45	85770	348	.004057	.020111	92986	1870	460660	.004059	2.716578	2845016	.002451	30.596	45
50	75594	514	.006799	.033551	91116	3057	448395	.006818	2.649725	2384356	.016598	26.168	50
55	67647	638	.009431	.046185	88059	4067	430841	.009440	2.675498	1935961	.004261	21.985	55
60	66766	1067	.015981	.077186	83992	6483	404948	.016009	2.684393	1505120	.008376	17.920	60
65	52458	1409	.026860	.126501	77509	9805	364607	.026892	2.660611	1100172	.005808	14.194	65
70	48783	2247	.046061	.207403	67704	14042	305043	.046033	2.615917	735565	-.002899	10.864	70
75	33587	2626	.078185	.328314	53662	17618	225170	.078243	2.551392	430522	-.003061	8.023	75
80	20409	2811	.137733	.510154	36044	18388	133376	.137866	2.452471	205352	.003061	5.697	80
85+	10864	2665	.245306	1.000000	17656	17656	71976	.245306	4.076548	71976	.000000	4.077	85+

NUMBER OF PERSONS DYING (OUT OF 100,000 AT BIRTH) ABOVE AGE X FROM SPECIFIED CAUSES

Age (x)	All Causes	Respiratory T. B.	Other Infec. and Paras.	Neoplasms	Cardiovascular	Infl., Pneu., Bronch.	Diarrheal	Certain Degenerative	Maternal	Cert. Dis. of Infancy	Motor Vehicle	Other Violence	Other and Unknown	Age (x)
0	100000	824	449	13587	52804	9925	511	2630	156	1261	341	1720	15792	0
1	97459	824	414	13581	52801	9597	418	2627	156	0	341	1663	15037	1
5	96967	824	351	13561	52797	9494	392	2617	156	0	328	1610	14837	5
10	96775	821	314	13533	52783	9484	385	2617	156	0	311	1596	14775	10
15	96593	821	296	13509	52770	9453	385	2610	156	0	304	1582	14707	15
20	96441	816	292	13484	52757	9441	385	2601	156	0	291	1565	14653	20
25	96130	797	292	13434	52655	9403	366	2570	150	0	272	1541	14610	25
30	95683	778	253	13322	52610	9357	353	2564	143	0	253	1521	14529	30
35	95034	723	247	13175	52488	9333	353	2527	88	0	241	1472	14387	35
40	94099	640	236	12904	52278	9272	342	2494	21	0	224	1450	14238	40
45	92986	552	219	12533	51918	9207	331	2461	0	0	202	1433	14130	45
50	91116	472	182	11888	51343	9072	299	2354	0	0	197	1401	13908	50
55	88059	383	176	10848	50086	8864	281	2270	0	0	167	1371	13613	55
60	83992	293	163	9655	48282	8539	275	2143	0	0	122	1327	13153	60
65	77509	221	133	7576	45018	8065	250	1882	0	0	98	1272	12594	65
70	67704	130	112	6022	39556	7160	202	1569	0	0	84	1161	11668	70
75	53662	80	93	3934	31329	5766	133	1062	0	0	53	961	10251	75
80	36044	13	60	2264	20682	3921	72	553	0	0	26	639	7814	80
85+	17656	7	40	861	9838	1815	40	232	0	0	7	345	4471	85+

NUMBER OF PERSONS SURVIVING TO AGE X IF SPECIFIED CAUSES WERE ELIMINATED

Age (x)	No Causes	Respiratory T. B.	Other Infec. and Paras.	Neoplasms	Cardiovascular	Infl., Pneu., Bronch.	Diarrheal	Certain Degenerative	Maternal	Cert. Dis. of Infancy	Motor Vehicle	Other Violence	Other and Unknown	(1) + (2)	(1) + (2) + (5) + (6) + (8)	(1)+(2)+ (5)+(6)+ (8)+part of(9)&(12)	(10) + (11)	Age (x)
		(1)	(2)	(3)	(4)	(5)	(6)	(7)	(8)	(9)	(10)	(11)	(12)					
0	100000	100000	100000	100000	100000	100000	100000	100000	100000	100000	100000	100000	100000	100000	100000	100000	100000	0
1	97459	97459	97494	97465	97462	97783	97551	97462	97459	98712	97459	97515	98207	97494	97910	99662	97515	1
5	96967	96967	97064	96993	96974	97393	97084	96980	96967	98214	96980	97076	97913	97064	97609	99450	97089	5
10	96775	96778	96909	96829	96796	97210	96899	96788	96775	97835	96805	96898	97781	96912	97473	99379	96928	10
15	96593	96596	96745	96671	96627	97058	96717	96613	96593	97835	96630	96729	97666	96748	97339	99272	96766	15
20	96441	96449	96597	96544	96488	96918	96565	96470	96441	97681	96491	96594	97567	96605	97207	99150	96644	20
25	96130	96157	96285	96282	96239	96643	96272	96190	96136	97366	96199	96307	97296	96312	96976	98928	96376	25
30	95683	95729	95876	95946	95876	96240	95838	95748	95696	96913	95770	95879	96925	95922	96650	98623	95966	30
35	95034	95134	95232	95443	95348	95611	95188	95136	95102	96256	95133	95278	96411	95333	96135	98139	95376	35
40	94099	94281	94306	94775	94620	94732	94262	94233	94233	95309	94214	94362	95613	94489	95424	97458	94477	40
45	92986	93254	93208	94026	93861	93676	93158	93151	93139	94181	93121	93263	94591	93476	94499	96536	93398	45
50	91116	91458	91370	92783	92550	91927	91316	91253	91253	89191	91253	91419	92913	91712	92885	94926	91557	50
55	88059	88477	88310	90717	90709	89049	88270	88401	88204	89191	88221	88382	90092	88729	90091	92106	88544	55
60	83992	84479	84244	87694	88355	85258	84199	84443	84130	85072	84191	84343	86392	84733	86364	88353	84542	60
65	77509	78028	77771	82665	84902	79141	77725	78177	77637	78505	77715	77886	80277	78291	80294	82201	78093	65
70	67704	68242	67952	74174	79926	69999	67937	68583	67815	68574	67897	68138	71024	68492	71175	72977	68332	70
75	53662	54133	53876	60844	72644	56777	53908	54816	53750	54352	53843	54185	57634	54348	57862	59497	54368	75
80	36044	36415	36214	42415	62054	39760	36259	37241	36103	36507	36187	36661	40918	36587	40666	42123	36807	80
85+	17656	17842	17753	21942	46303	21135	17783	18471	17685	17883	17739	18164	22820	17940	21665	22864	18250	85+

ADDED YRS OF LIFE

	No Causes	(1)	(2)	(3)	(4)	(5)	(6)	(7)	(8)	(9)	(10)	(11)	(12)				
TOTAL		.202	.168	2.142	8.077	1.274	.153	.344	.062	.919	.099	.281	2.257	.371	1.884	3.585	.381
WORK	2.312	.109	.033	.643	.702	.159	.027	.091	.045	.000	.043	.064	.303	.143	.375	.442	.107

POPULATION, DEATHS, DEATH RATES FOR ALL CAUSES COMBINED, AND SPECIFIED CAUSES

Age Start of Interval	Midyear Population	Deaths During Year	All Causes	Respiratory T. B.	Other Infec. and Paras.	Neoplasms	Cardiovascular	Infl., Pneu., Bronch.	Diarrheal	Certain Degenerative	Maternal	Cert. Dis. of Infancy	Motor Vehicle	Other Violence	Other and Unknown	Age Start of Interval
0	20652	941	.04556	.00010	.00368	.00010	.00034	.00581	.00765	.00000	.00000	.01859	.00000	.00077	.00852	0
1	71656	221	.00308	.00001	.00134	.00008	.00006	.00040	.00028	.00006	.00000	.00000	.00003	.00031	.00052	1
5	62302	58	.00093	.00003	.00018	.00005	.00006	.00005	.00002	.00003	.00000	.00000	.00006	.00029	.00016	5
10	53031	33	.00062	.00000	.00002	.00006	.00008	.00002	.00000	.00004	.00000	.00000	.00004	.00023	.00015	10
15	58139	95	.00163	.00003	.00009	.00007	.00012	.00002	.00000	.00010	.00000	.00000	.00012	.00083	.00026	15
20	55966	152	.00272	.00016	.00013	.00009	.00023	.00002	.00002	.00007	.00000	.00000	.00034	.00139	.00027	20
25	58829	113	.00192	.00019	.00007	.00020	.00008	.00005	.00000	.00010	.00000	.00000	.00020	.00076	.00025	25
30	48534	86	.00177	.00016	.00004	.00023	.00014	.00004	.00000	.00000	.00000	.00000	.00008	.00070	.00029	30
35	52601	113	.00215	.00011	.00008	.00034	.00042	.00000	.00000	.00013	.00000	.00000	.00015	.00059	.00032	35
40	55334	131	.00237	.00013	.00011	.00040	.00085	.00004	.00000	.00014	.00000	.00000	.00004	.00036	.00031	40
45	42910	190	.00443	.00051	.00009	.00079	.00168	.00005	.00000	.00023	.00000	.00000	.00009	.00037	.00061	45
50	33878	279	.00824	.00027	.00032	.00159	.00410	.00012	.00000	.00044	.00000	.00000	.00006	.00059	.00074	50
55	21874	267	.01221	.00055	.00027	.00315	.00576	.00023	.00000	.00046	.00000	.00000	.00009	.00037	.00133	55
60	16313	368	.02256	.00092	.00043	.00435	.01195	.00049	.00012	.00061	.00000	.00000	.00000	.00031	.00337	60
65	10721	372	.03470	.00121	.00056	.00756	.01651	.00103	.00028	.00131	.00000	.00000	.00019	.00075	.00532	65
70	7510	419	.05579	.00067	.00200	.00799	.02663	.00186	.00040	.00186	.00000	.00000	.00053	.00120	.01265	70
75	3794	332	.08751	.00105	.00211	.00896	.04560	.00527	.00053	.00290	.00000	.00000	.00026	.00211	.01871	75
80	1768	249	.14084	.00170	.00396	.01697	.05373	.00622	.00057	.00226	.00000	.00000	.00057	.00566	.04921	80
85+	911	162	.17783	.00000	.00329	.01647	.06586	.01317	.00439	.00329	.00000	.00000	.00000	.00549	.06586	85+
ALL	676723	4581														

			All Causes	Respiratory T. B.	Other Infec. and Paras.	Neoplasms	Cardiovascular	Infl., Pneu., Bronch.	Diarrheal	Certain Degenerative	Maternal	Cert. Dis. of Infancy	Motor Vehicle	Other Violence	Other and Unknown
CRUDE DEATH RATE			.00677	.00019	.00041	.00079	.00201	.00037	.00029	.00020	.00000	.00057	.00011	.00061	.00123
STANDARDIZED RATE (1)			.00666	.00017	.00044	.00071	.00185	.00039	.00033	.00018	.00000	.00065	.00011	.00060	.00122
STANDARDIZED RATE (2)			.01082	.00026	.00045	.00143	.00413	.00051	.00024	.00032	.00000	.00038	.00012	.00069	.00227
GEOMETRIC MEAN			.00830												

LIFE TABLE FOR ALL CAUSES COMBINED

Age (x)	Midyear Population	Deaths During Year	$_nM_x$	$_nq_x$	l_x	$_nd_x$	$_nL_x$	$_nm_x$	$_na_x$	T_x	$_nr_x$	$\overset{\circ}{e}_x$	Age (x)
0	20652	941	.045565	.043860	100000	4386	96261	.045564	.147460	6701192	.000000	67.012	0
1	71656	221	.003084	.012247	95614	1171	379529	.003085	1.500000	6604931	.000000	69.079	1
5	62302	58	.000931	.004638	94443	438	471120	.000930	2.500000	6225403	.000000	65.917	5
10	53031	33	.000622	.003106	94005	292	469362	.000622	2.731164	5754283	.006949	61.213	10
15	58139	95	.001634	.008131	93713	762	466860	.001632	2.763014	5284920	-.003766	56.395	15
20	55966	152	.002716	.013491	92951	1254	461644	.002716	2.518939	4818060	-.006185	51.834	20
25	58829	113	.001921	.009553	91697	876	456201	.001920	2.392266	4356416	-.007050	47.509	25
30	48534	86	.001772	.008820	90821	801	452120	.001772	2.522108	3900215	-.014376	42.944	30
35	52601	113	.002148	.010675	90020	961	447749	.002146	2.553980	3448095	-.013161	38.304	35
40	55334	131	.002367	.011790	89059	1050	442875	.002371	2.695437	3000346	.006221	33.689	40
45	42910	190	.004428	.022111	88009	1946	435693	.004466	2.763682	2557471	.032994	29.059	45
50	33878	279	.008235	.040819	86063	3513	422159	.008322	2.678385	2121777	.052851	24.654	50
55	21874	267	.012206	.060012	82550	4954	401384	.012342	2.705642	1699618	.059663	20.589	55
60	16313	368	.022559	.108292	77596	8403	368267	.022818	2.654012	1298235	.052588	16.731	60
65	10721	372	.034698	.161375	69193	11166	319292	.034971	2.611275	929968	.043123	13.440	65
70	7510	419	.055792	.247592	58027	14367	255186	.056300	2.567400	610675	.044512	10.524	70
75	3794	332	.087507	.362208	43660	15814	178786	.088452	2.501344	355490	.051826	8.142	75
80	1768	249	.140837	.515608	27846	14469	101478	.142582	2.390859	176703	.051826	6.346	80
85+	911	162	.177827	1.000000	13377	13377	75225	.177827	5.623457	75225	.000000	5.623	85+

NUMBER OF PERSONS DYING (OUT OF 100,000 AT BIRTH) ABOVE AGE X FROM SPECIFIED CAUSES

Age (x)	All Causes	Respiratory T. B.	Other Infec. and Paras.	Neoplasms	Cardiovascular	Infl., Pneu., Bronch.	Diarrheal	Certain Degenerative	Maternal	Cert. Dis. of Infancy	Motor Vehicle	Other Violence	Other and Unknown	Age (x)
0	100000	2217	3365	13708	41115	4558	1580	2952	0	1790	892	5154	22669	0
1	95614	2208	3011	13699	41082	3999	844	2952	0	0	892	5079	21848	1
5	94443	2203	2502	13667	41061	3845	738	2931	0	0	881	4963	21652	5
10	94005	2188	2419	13644	41031	3822	730	2916	0	0	851	4827	21577	10
15	93713	2188	2410	13618	40995	3813	730	2898	0	0	833	4720	21508	15
20	92951	2172	2370	13566	40939	3805	730	2850	0	0	777	4335	21387	20
25	91697	2097	2312	13545	40832	3797	722	2817	0	0	621	3692	21262	25
30	90821	2012	2281	13451	40793	3774	722	2770	0	0	528	3343	21147	30
35	90020	1938	2263	13349	40727	3755	722	2733	0	0	491	3027	21015	35
40	89059	1887	2229	13196	40541	3755	722	2674	0	0	422	2762	20871	40
45	88009	1830	2181	13019	40164	3739	722	2610	0	0	406	2602	20736	45
50	86063	1606	2140	12671	39424	3719	722	2507	0	0	366	2439	20469	50
55	82550	1495	2001	11988	37671	3668	722	2319	0	0	341	2189	20156	55
60	77556	1271	1891	10707	35331	3575	722	2135	0	0	304	2045	19615	60
65	69193	930	1732	9089	30878	3391	676	1907	0	0	304	1931	18355	65
70	58027	542	1550	6662	25571	3060	585	1486	0	0	243	1690	16638	70
75	43660	374	1034	4620	18708	2577	483	1006	0	0	106	1382	13370	75
80	27846	183	656	3008	10472	1620	388	484	0	0	60	998	9977	80
85+	13377	0	248	1239	4954	991	330	248	0	0	0	413	4954	85+

NUMBER OF PERSONS SURVIVING TO AGE X IF SPECIFIED CAUSES WERE ELIMINATED

Age (x)	No Causes	Respiratory T. B. (1)	Other Infec. and Paras. (2)	Neoplasms (3)	Cardiovascular (4)	Infl., Pneu., Bronch. (5)	Diarrheal (6)	Certain Degenerative (7)	Maternal (8)	Cert. Dis. of Infancy (9)	Motor Vehicle (10)	Other Violence (11)	Other and Unknown (12)	(1) + (2)	(1) + (2) + (5) + (6) + (8)	(1)+(2)+ (5)+(6)+ (8)+part of(9)&(12)	(10) + (11)	Age (x)
0	100000	100000	100000	100000	100000	100000	100000	100000	100000	100000	100000	100000	100000	100000	100000	100000	100000	0
1	95614	95623	95961	95623	95646	96162	96336	95614	95614	97380	95614	95687	96420	95970	97249	99705	95687	1
5	94443	94457	95295	94484	94496	95138	95263	94464	94443	96188	94454	94631	95436	95308	96843	99452	94642	5
10	94005	94034	94936	94068	94087	94720	94825	94041	94005	95742	94046	94328	95069	94965	96526	99154	94369	10
15	93713	93741	94650	93802	93831	94435	94534	93767	93713	95444	93772	94142	94843	94679	96245	98871	94201	15
20	92951	92995	93921	93071	93124	93675	93766	93052	92951	94668	93065	93763	94194	93966	95528	98147	93878	20
25	91697	91815	92712	91856	91974	92420	92509	91829	91697	93391	91965	93144	93049	92832	94391	96997	93416	25
30	90821	91023	91858	91073	91135	91560	91625	90599	90821	92499	91179	92608	92277	92062	93632	96239	92973	30
35	90020	90294	91066	90371	90397	90771	90817	90233	90020	91683	90412	92112	91596	91343	92920	95530	92513	35
40	89059	89381	90128	89560	89618	89802	89847	89329	89059	90704	89516	91399	90764	90453	92016	94616	91868	40
45	88009	88384	89113	88681	88639	88760	88788	88340	88009	89635	88476	90485	89831	89493	91055	93647	90965	45
50	86063	86652	87184	87067	87716	86817	86825	86489	86063	87653	86560	88650	88115	87781	89334	91925	89161	50
55	82550	83225	83763	84193	85904	83324	83281	83143	82550	84075	83051	85283	84832	84448	85994	88518	85801	55
60	77596	78449	78844	80417	83144	78414	78283	78333	77596	79029	78103	80309	80283	79711	81265	83706	80834	60
65	69193	70280	70459	73308	78782	70099	69850	70068	69193	70471	69645	71724	72831	71565	73190	75521	72192	65
70	58027	59299	59260	63869	71828	59099	58662	59152	58027	59099	58463	60379	62760	60557	62346	64516	60832	70
75	43660	44762	45046	50021	61916	44855	44227	44931	43660	44467	44107	45707	50385	46182	48105	50150	46175	75
80	27846	28704	29038	33390	49889	29427	28283	29082	27846	28360	28166	29475	35411	29932	32128	33922	29814	80
85+	13377	13918	14241	17544	31698	14594	13627	14139	13377	13624	13572	14585	21941	14816	16467	17995	14798	85+

ADDED YRS OF LIFE																		
TOTAL		.438	.977	1.931	6.444	.867	.645	.460	.000	1.235	.283	1.555	3.562	1.427	3.016	5.281	1.848	
WORK	3.529	.199	.117	.462	.885	.046	.004	.156	.000	.000	.175	.877	.421	.317	.368	.422	1.056	

POPULATION, DEATHS, DEATH RATES FOR ALL CAUSES COMBINED, AND SPECIFIED CAUSES

Age Start of Interval	Midyear Population	Deaths During Year	All Causes	Respiratory T. B.	Other Infec. and Paras.	Neoplasms	Cardiovascular	Infl., Pneu., Bronch.	Diarrheal	Certain Degenerative	Maternal	Cert. Dis. of Infancy	Motor Vehicle	Other Violence	Other and Unknown	Age Start of Interval
0	15678	777	.03949	.00020	.00381	.00005	.00010	.00457	.00778	.00000	.00000	.01530	.00005	.00086	.00676	0
1	67288	230	.00342	.00001	.00131	.00007	.00007	.00028	.00062	.00001	.00000	.00010	.00009	.00012	.00082	1
5	58995	42	.00071	.00002	.00012	.00007	.00002	.00007	.00002	.00002	.00000	.00000	.00007	.00019	.00014	5
10	50034	36	.00072	.00000	.00014	.00008	.00012	.00002	.00002	.00006	.00000	.00000	.00000	.00007	.00014	10
15	53552	42	.00078	.00007	.00004	.00006	.00007	.00004	.00000	.00006	.00000	.00000	.00000	.00004	.00008	15
20	55231	58	.00105	.00013	.00011	.00011	.00018	.00002	.00000	.00004	.00002	.00009	.00000	.00004	.00028	20
25	58054	62	.00107	.00005	.00012	.00022	.00012	.00003	.00002	.00005	.00005	.00007	.00000	.00003	.00020	25
30	46814	69	.00147	.00009	.00002	.00028	.00038	.00000	.00002	.00006	.00023	.00007	.00000	.00012	.00022	30
35	55281	110	.00199	.00013	.00007	.00060	.00040	.00004	.00004	.00011	.00011	.00023	.00000	.00019	.00019	35
40	50122	129	.00257	.00010	.00006	.00106	.00058	.00002	.00000	.00012	.00011	.00010	.00000	.00016	.00033	40
45	36068	149	.00413	.00014	.00017	.00139	.00128	.00017	.00003	.00017	.00000	.00000	.00008	.00025	.00044	45
50	30964	187	.00604	.00019	.00006	.00165	.00216	.00010	.00006	.00042	.00000	.00000	.00008	.00025	.00047	50
55	19195	179	.00933	.00021	.00026	.00313	.00396	.00000	.00000	.00042	.00005	.00006	.00000	.00019	.00113	55
60	17777	303	.01704	.00039	.00023	.00394	.00793	.00028	.00023	.00062	.00005	.00006	.00000	.00056	.00094	60
65	12128	343	.02828	.00025	.00074	.00627	.01418	.00058	.00025	.00099	.00000	.00000	.00000	.00000	.00281	65
70	8588	417	.04856	.00058	.00082	.01095	.02271	.00175	.00058	.00116	.00000	.00000	.00000	.00107	.00396	70
75	4115	333	.08092	.00073	.00097	.01312	.04107	.00535	.00000	.00122	.00000	.00000	.00000	.00116	.00885	75
80	2220	244	.10991	.00090	.00225	.01351	.05315	.00541	.00225	.00270	.00000	.00000	.00000	.00194	.01652	80
85+	1155	196	.16970	.00000	.00260	.00952	.07446	.01299	.00260	.00346	.00000	.00000	.00000	.00405	.02568	85+
ALL	647259	3906												.01039	.05368	

			All Causes	Resp. T.B.	Other Infec.	Neoplasms	Cardiovascular	Infl.	Diarrheal	Certain Degen.	Maternal	Cert. Dis. Infancy	Motor Vehicle	Other Violence	Other Unknown
CRUDE DEATH RATE			.00603	.00011	.00038	.00097	.00181	.00032	.00034	.00016	.00005	.00047	.00004	.00027	.00111
STANDARDIZED RATE (1)			.00554	.00010	.00041	.00081	.00150	.00032	.00038	.00013	.00004	.00054	.00004	.00026	.00101
STANDARDIZED RATE (2)			.00904	.00014	.00037	.00156	.00351	.00043	.00029	.00024	.00005	.00032	.00003	.00038	.00173
GEOMETRIC MEAN			.00663												

LIFE TABLE FOR ALL CAUSES COMBINED

Age (x)	Midyear Population	Deaths During Year	nM_x	nq_x	l_x	nd_x	nL_x	nm_x	na_x	T_x	nr_x	$\overset{\circ}{e}_x$	Age (x)
0	15678	777	.039486	.038180	100000	3818	96706	.039481	.137126	6987798	.000000	69.878	0
1	67288	230	.003418	.013558	96182	1304	381468	.003418	1.500000	6891093	.000000	71.646	1
5	58995	42	.000712	.003552	94878	337	473548	.000712	2.500000	6509625	.000000	68.610	5
10	50034	36	.000720	.003596	94541	340	471862	.000721	2.519608	6036077	.010198	63.846	10
15	53552	42	.000784	.003917	94201	369	470114	.000785	2.585253	5564216	-.004971	59.067	15
20	55231	58	.001050	.005233	93832	491	467559	.001049	2.554311	5094102	-.012766	54.290	20
25	58054	62	.001068	.005325	93341	497	465502	.001068	2.580483	4626143	-.009788	49.562	25
30	46814	69	.001474	.007356	92844	683	462599	.001476	2.626281	4160640	.009200	44.813	30
35	55281	110	.001990	.009885	92161	911	458629	.001986	2.611828	3698041	-.013270	40.126	35
40	50122	129	.002574	.012844	91250	1172	453517	.002584	2.667804	3239412	.027357	35.500	40
45	36068	149	.004131	.020593	90078	1855	446060	.004159	2.665768	2785895	.037659	30.928	45
50	30964	187	.006039	.030015	88223	2648	434931	.006088	2.664590	2339835	.053696	26.522	50
55	19195	179	.009325	.046123	85575	3947	418860	.009423	2.715881	1904905	.050653	22.260	55
60	17777	303	.017044	.082545	81628	6738	392557	.017164	2.687370	1486045	.031493	18.205	60
65	12128	343	.028282	.133623	74890	10007	351000	.028510	2.656661	1093487	.037732	14.601	65
70	8588	417	.048556	.219826	64883	14263	290259	.049139	2.605269	742487	.053497	11.443	70
75	4115	333	.080923	.340063	50620	17214	210085	.081938	2.501174	452228	.055046	8.934	75
80	2220	244	.109910	.429863	33406	14360	129908	.110540	2.414882	242143	.055046	7.248	80
85+	1155	196	.169697	1.000000	19046	19046	112235	.169697	5.892857	112235	.000000	5.893	85+

NUMBER OF PERSONS DYING (OUT OF 100,000 AT BIRTH) ABOVE AGE X FROM SPECIFIED CAUSES

Age (x)	All Causes	Respira-tory T. B.	Other Infec. and Paras.	Neo-plasms	Cardio-vascular	Infl., Pneu., Bronch.	Diar-rheal	Certain Degen-erative	Maternal	Cert. Dis. of Infancy	Motor Vehicle	Other Violence	Other and Unknown	Age (x)
0	100000	1217	2781	16451	42561	4906	2006	2598	323	1479	206	4126	20946	0
1	96182	1198	2413	16446	42951	4464	1255	2598	323	0	202	4042	20290	1
5	94878	1192	1914	16417	42923	4356	1017	2593	323	C	168	3997	19978	5
10	94541	1184	1857	16385	42915	4324	1009	2585	323	0	135	3909	19915	10
15	94201	1184	1792	16348	42858	4314	1009	2556	323	0	117	3824	19876	15
20	93832	1149	1774	16321	42823	4297	1009	2539	323	C	99	3754	19744	20
25	93341	1089	1723	16271	42738	4288	1009	2530	280	0	99	3660	19654	25
30	92844	1065	1667	16166	42682	4272	1001	2506	248	C	83	3604	19550	30
35	92161	1026	1657	16037	42504	4272	991	2476	139	C	83	3515	19461	35
40	91250	968	1624	15765	42322	4256	974	2427	90	0	75	3440	19309	40
45	90078	923	1597	15283	42057	4247	974	2372	45	0	66	3404	19110	45
50	88223	860	1522	14663	41483	4172	961	2297	45	0	28	3292	18900	50
55	85575	776	1495	13940	40531	4131	933	2113	45	0	1	3208	18402	55
60	81628	688	1384	12620	38850	4131	933	1938	23	0	1	3054	18006	60
65	74890	533	1295	11067	35712	4019	944	1694	1	C	1	2831	16893	65
70	64883	446	1032	8850	30694	3813	757	1345	1	0	1	2453	15491	70
75	50620	275	755	5642	24025	3293	586	1005	1	0	1	2113	12884	75
80	33406	121	589	2870	15281	2151	586	748	1	C	1	1698	9360	80
85+	19046	0	292	1069	8357	1458	292	389	0	0	0	1166	6023	85+

NUMBER OF PERSONS SURVIVING TO AGE X IF SPECIFIED CAUSES WERE ELIMINATED

Age (x)	No Causes	Respira-tory T. B. (1)	Other Infec. and Paras. (2)	Neo-plasms (3)	Cardio-vascular (4)	Infl., Pneu., Bronch. (5)	Diar-rheal (6)	Certain Degener-ative (7)	Maternal (8)	Cert. Dis. of Infancy (9)	Motor Vehicle (10)	Other Violence (11)	Other and Unknown (12)	(1) + (2)	(1) + (2) + (5) + (6) + (8)	(1)+(2)+ (5)+(6)+ (8)+part of(9)&(12)	(10) + (11)	Age (x)
0	100000	100000	100000	100000	100000	100000	100000	100000	100000	100000	100000	100000	100000	100000	100000	100000	100000	0
1	96182	96201	96544	96187	96192	96616	96921	96182	96182	97643	96186	96264	96827	96562	97744	99762	96268	1
5	94878	94902	95733	94912	94915	95414	95846	94883	94878	96320	94916	95004	95827	95758	97282	99569	95042	5
10	94541	94573	95451	94606	94586	95108	95513	94554	94541	95977	94611	94755	95550	95483	97044	99350	94825	10
15	94201	94233	95173	94303	94303	94776	95170	94243	94201	95632	94289	94499	95006	95206	96771	99082	94587	15
20	93832	93899	94818	93961	93969	94421	94757	93891	93832	95258	93938	94199	95006	94886	96464	98808	94305	20
25	93341	93468	94374	93519	93562	93936	94301	93408	93364	94759	93446	93800	94600	94502	96127	98501	93906	25
30	92844	92994	93928	93126	93120	93452	93807	92935	92919	94255	92965	93357	94202	94079	95755	98158	93478	30
35	92161	92349	93247	92570	92613	92765	93127	92281	92344	93561	92281	92759	93599	93437	95223	97639	92880	35
40	91250	91494	92358	91927	91879	91864	92224	91418	91480	92636	91377	91917	92827	92605	94460	96893	92045	40
45	90078	90363	91199	91230	90965	90693	91039	90298	90350	91447	90212	90773	91836	91488	93376	95809	90908	45
50	88223	88565	89396	89975	89667	88900	89177	88513	88489	89563	88392	89015	90157	89743	91685	94105	89186	50
55	85575	85990	86740	88004	87935	86272	86528	86039	85833	86875	85756	86427	87953	87160	89118	91513	86619	55
60	81628	82110	82849	85280	85584	82293	82538	82242	81856	82868	81810	82593	84296	83338	85232	87549	82776	60
65	74890	75481	76097	79808	81735	75609	75811	75689	75157	76028	75057	75991	78446	76698	78665	80899	76160	65
70	64883	65476	66178	71375	76092	65701	65763	65903	65114	65869	65027	66194	69345	66783	68785	70845	66341	70
75	50620	51235	51842	58871	66672	51729	51458	51719	50800	51389	50733	51948	56619	52472	54703	56584	52063	75
80	33406	33937	34383	41514	54348	35096	33959	34343	33525	33914	33480	34629	40692	34929	37437	39090	34706	80
85+	19046	19441	19832	25397	40628	20559	19586	19857	19115	19335	19089	20159	26436	20243	22551	23942	20204	85+

ACCED YRS OF LIFE																		
TOTAL		.271	.966	2.572	7.014	.826	.817	.395	.126	1.060	.101	.752	3.369	1.242	3.090	5.175	.855
WORK	2.541	.122	.097	.641	.666	.045	.019	.111	.092	.000	.029	.200	.412	.219	.376	.462	.229

POPULATION, DEATHS, DEATH RATES FOR ALL CAUSES COMBINED, AND SPECIFIED CAUSES

Age Start of Interval	Midyear Population	Deaths During Year	All Causes	Respiratory T. B.	Other Infec. and Paras.	Neoplasms	Cardiovascular	Infl., Pneu., Bronch.	Diarrheal	Certain Degenerative	Maternal	Cert. Dis. of Infancy	Motor Vehicle	Other Violence	Other and Unknown	Age Start of Interval
0	22700	685	.03018	.00000	.00066	.00009	.00022	.00295	.00203	.00004	.00000	.01586	.00000	.00044	.00789	0
1	90300	140	.00155	.00000	.00010	.00021	.00002	.00017	.00010	.00001	.00000	.00001	.00012	.00028	.00053	1
5	120200	73	.00061	.00000	.00001	.00022	.00001	.00001	.00001	.00001	.00000	.00000	.00010	.00011	.00013	5
10	104500	50	.00048	.00000	.00001	.00020	.00002	.00001	.00001	.00000	.00000	.00000	.00010	.00011	.00013	10
15	70400	70	.00099	.00000	.00000	.00013	.00006	.00000	.00000	.00007	.00000	.00000	.00003	.00012	.00007	15
20	68800	72	.00105	.00001	.00000	.00013	.00001	.00001	.00000	.00004	.00000	.00000	.00000	.00045	.00016	20
25	66800	67	.00100	.00003	.00003	.00012	.00018	.00000	.00000	.00006	.00000	.00000	.00016	.00058	.00009	25
30	60600	62	.00102	.00007	.00002	.00020	.00015	.00000	.00000	.00007	.00000	.00000	.00009	.00039	.00010	30
35	64400	102	.00158	.00003	.00002	.00028	.00034	.00002	.00000	.00007	.00000	.00000	.00003	.00036	.00013	35
40	50100	114	.00228	.00008	.00008	.00048	.00084	.00000	.00000	.00018	.00000	.00000	.00050	.00023	40
45	61000	209	.00343	.00003	.00003	.00097	.00146	.00002	.00000	.00023	.00000	.00000	.00006	.00034	.00022	45
50	56700	389	.00686	.00009	.00007	.00180	.00374	.00002	.00000	.00026	.00000	.00000	.00003	.00026	.00039	50
55	42500	508	.01195	.00021	.00005	.00289	.00659	.00009	.00000	.00047	.00000	.00000	.00005	.00037	.00046	55
60	31600	628	.01987	.00025	.00016	.00484	.01066	.00016	.00000	.00063	.00000	.00000	.00006	.00028	.00132	60
65	19100	627	.03283	.00016	.00031	.00723	.01885	.00037	.00021	.00110	.00000	.00000	.00021	.00073	.00237	65
70	12500	615	.04920	.00032	.00032	.00840	.02904	.00112	.00008	.00216	.00000	.00000	.00048	.00026	.00414	70
75	6500	516	.07938	.00123	.00046	.01292	.04769	.00246	.00031	.00154	.00000	.00000	.00062	.00112	.00616	75
80	3600	386	.10722	.00028	.00056	.01444	.06528	.00306	.00167	.00194	.00000	.00000	.00056	.00108	.01108	80
85+	2000	301	.15050	.00050	.00000	.01650	.08400	.01100	.00250	.00150	.00000	.00000	.00100	.00500	.02850	85+
ALL	954300	5614														

CRUDE DEATH RATE			.00588	.00006	.00006	.00105	.00257	.00018	.00008	.00018	.00000	.00038	.00009	.00036	.00088	
STANDARDIZED RATE (1)			.00509	.00004	.00007	.00081	.00190	.00019	.00010	.00018	.00000	.00038	.00009	.00036	.00088	
STANDARDIZED RATE (2)			.00889	.00008	.00008	.00155	.00442	.00025	.00009	.00014	.00000	.00056	.00009	.00035	.00083	
GEOMETRIC MEAN			.00602	.00008	.00008	.00155	.00442	.00025	.00009	.00026	.00000	.00033	.00011	.00042	.00129	

LIFE TABLE FOR ALL CAUSES COMBINED

Age (x)	Midyear Population	Deaths During Year	$_nM_x$	$_nq_x$	l_x	$_nd_x$	$_nL_x$	$_nm_x$	$_na_x$	T_x	$_nr_x$	$\overset{\circ}{e}_x$	Age (x)
0	22700	685	.030176	.029400	100000	2940	97417	.030180	.121300	7085695	.000000	70.857	0
1	90300	140	.001550	.006171	97060	599	386743	.001549	1.500000	6988278	.000000	72.000	1
5	120200	73	.000607	.003027	96461	292	481515	.000606	2.500000	6601535	.000000	68.437	5
10	104500	50	.000478	.002402	96169	231	480306	.000481	2.667749	6119960	.041132	63.638	10
15	70400	70	.000994	.004982	95938	478	478551	.000999	2.616370	5639654	.047932	58.784	15
20	68800	72	.001047	.005217	95460	498	476054	.001046	2.498745	5161104	.012421	54.066	20
25	66800	67	.001003	.005002	94962	475	473619	.001003	2.492982	4685049	.014202	49.336	25
30	60600	62	.001023	.005101	94487	482	471286	.001023	2.616269	4211430	.002280	44.572	30
35	64400	102	.001584	.007914	94005	744	468285	.001589	2.661010	3740144	.015212	39.787	35
40	50100	114	.002275	.011334	93261	1057	463832	.002279	2.660833	3271859	.011230	35.083	40
45	61000	209	.003426	.016919	92204	1560	457540	.003410	2.769364	2808027	-.017316	30.454	45
50	56700	389	.006861	.033913	90644	3074	446279	.006888	2.742152	2350486	.015673	25.931	50
55	42500	508	.011953	.058616	87570	5133	426025	.012049	2.696320	1904207	.036804	21.745	55
60	31600	628	.019873	.095964	82437	7911	393726	.020093	2.666646	1478182	.054086	17.931	60
65	19100	627	.032827	.153785	74526	11461	345243	.033197	2.610392	1084456	.058518	14.551	65
70	12500	615	.049200	.221739	63065	13984	281392	.049696	2.573462	739213	.058317	11.721	70
75	6500	516	.079385	.333979	49081	16392	204381	.080203	2.497318	457821	.048324	9.328	75
80	3600	386	.107222	.421334	32689	13773	127752	.107810	2.408502	253440	.048324	7.753	80
85+	2000	301	.150500	1.000000	18916	18916	125688	.150500	6.644518	125688	.000000	6.645	85+

NUMBER OF PERSONS DYING (OUT OF 100,000 AT BIRTH) ABOVE AGE X FROM SPECIFIED CAUSES

Age (x)	All Causes	Respiratory T. B.	Other Infec. and Paras.	Neoplasms	Cardiovascular	Infl., Pneu., Bronch.	Diarrheal	Certain Degenerative	Maternal	Cert. Dis. of Infancy	Motor Vehicle	Other Violence	Other and Unknown	Age (x)
0	100000	848	675	16846	53822	3228	932	2685	0	1549	986	3711	14718	0
1	97060	848	610	16837	53800	2940	735	2681	0	4	986	3668	13951	1
5	96461	848	572	16756	53792	2876	696	2677	0	0	939	3561	13744	5
10	96169	848	568	16648	53788	2872	692	2673	0	0	891	3509	13680	10
15	95938	848	563	16552	53778	2863	688	2672	0	0	878	3448	13648	15
20	95460	848	563	16491	53752	2863	688	2638	0	0	816	3228	13573	20
25	94962	841	563	16429	53745	2856	688	2617	0	0	740	2951	13532	25
30	94487	827	549	16372	53659	2856	688	2589	0	0	697	2767	13483	30
35	94005	796	541	16279	53589	2856	688	2558	0	0	682	2596	13420	35
40	93261	782	534	16148	53428	2849	688	2514	0	0	645	2364	13309	40
45	92204	745	497	15925	53038	2849	688	2431	0	0	618	2206	13207	45
50	90644	730	482	15484	52376	2841	688	2326	0	0	603	2087	13027	50
55	87570	690	450	14679	50700	2833	688	2207	0	0	579	1921	12823	55
60	82437	599	430	13437	47871	2793	688	2006	0	0	559	1800	12254	60
65	74526	499	367	11511	43624	2729	687	1754	0	0	533	1512	11310	65
70	63065	446	257	8997	37036	2600	614	1369	0	0	459	1423	9864	70
75	49081	353	167	6621	28777	2278	592	756	0	0	323	1103	8111	75
80	32689	98	72	3957	18926	1768	527	443	0	0	196	882	5820	80
85+	18916	63	0	2074	10558	1383	314	189	0	0	126	628	3581	85+

NUMBER OF PERSONS SURVIVING TO AGE X IF SPECIFIED CAUSES WERE ELIMINATED

Age (x)	No Causes	Respiratory T. B. (1)	Other Infec. and Paras. (2)	Neoplasms (3)	Cardiovascular (4)	Infl., Pneu., Bronch. (5)	Diarrheal (6)	Certain Degenerative (7)	Maternal (8)	Cert. Dis. of Infancy (9)	Motor Vehicle (10)	Other Violence (11)	Other and Unknown (12)	(1)+(2)	(1)+(2)+(5)+(6)+(8)	(1)+(2)+(5)+(6)+(8)+part of(9)&(12)	(10)+(11)	Age (x)
0	100000	100000	100000	100000	100000	100000	100000	100000	100000	100000	100000	100000	100000	100000	100000	100000	100000	0
1	97060	97060	97124	97069	97082	97344	97254	97064	97060	98554	97060	97102	97819	97124	97603	99630	97102	1
5	96461	96461	96563	96551	96491	96807	96693	96469	96461	97590	96508	96610	97423	96563	97142	99238	96657	5
10	96169	96169	96274	96366	96202	96518	96404	96181	96169	97693	96264	96369	97193	96274	96860	98954	96464	10
15	95938	95938	96048	96231	95981	96296	96177	95951	95938	97458	96045	96199	96992	96048	96646	98737	96307	15
20	95460	95460	95569	95813	95529	95816	95658	95507	95460	96973	95629	95940	96584	95569	96164	98245	96110	20
25	94962	94969	95071	95375	95038	95323	95158	95029	94962	96467	95206	95718	96121	95078	95677	97749	95964	25
30	94487	94508	94609	94955	94648	94846	94722	94582	94487	95584	94773	95424	95690	94630	95226	97292	95713	30
35	94005	94057	94135	94564	94235	94362	94239	94131	94005	95495	94304	95110	95266	94187	94780	96841	95412	35
40	93261	93326	93397	93547	93651	93622	93493	93429	93261	94739	93595	94591	94624	93462	94058	96109	94930	40
45	92204	92305	92375	93106	92579	92561	92433	92453	92204	93665	92561	93678	93364	92477	93066	95103	94041	45
50	90644	90759	90827	91573	92071	91003	90870	90993	90644	92080	91010	92213	92251	90942	91529	93538	92585	50
55	87570	87720	87778	89660	90638	87925	87788	88025	87570	88958	87947	89252	89327	87929	88505	90453	89636	55
60	82437	82667	82652	85647	88213	82810	82642	83061	82437	83743	82811	84140	84657	82883	83465	85321	84522	60
65	74526	74829	74781	79352	84187	74925	74713	75332	74526	75707	74889	76344	77460	75085	75675	77389	76717	65
70	63065	63370	63382	65648	78421	63523	63290	64106	63065	64064	63441	64687	66943	63688	64380	65888	65073	70
75	49081	49402	49407	56554	70774	49726	49275	50441	49081	49859	49494	50634	53764	49730	50583	51838	51060	75
80	32689	33111	32983	40230	60184	33541	32874	33851	32689	33207	33067	33907	37907	33409	34474	35462	34299	80
85+	18916	19187	19141	25088	48557	19708	19184	19787	18916	19216	19188	19820	23975	19415	20515	21219	20105	85+

ADDED YRS OF LIFE

	No Causes	(1)	(2)	(3)	(4)	(5)	(6)	(7)	(8)	(9)	(10)	(11)	(12)	(1)+(2)	+(5)+(6)+(8)	+part	(10)+(11)
TOTAL		.135	.167	2.639	11.168	.518	.229	.425	.000	1.121	.264	1.025	2.512	.303	1.068	2.722	1.296
WORK	2.519	.046	.027	.501	.834	.011	.000	.128	.000	.000	.105	.500	.261	.073	.085	.095	.606

POPULATION, DEATHS, DEATH RATES FOR ALL CAUSES COMBINED, AND SPECIFIED CAUSES

Age Start of Interval	Midyear Population	Deaths During Year	All Causes	Respiratory T. B.	Other Infec. and Paras.	Neoplasms	Cardiovascular	Infl., Pneu., Bronch.	Diarrheal	Certain Degenerative	Maternal	Cert. Dis. of Infancy	Motor Vehicle	Other Violence	Other and Unknown	Age Start of Interval
0	21500	551	.02563	.00000	.00065	.00005	.00005	.00242	.00251	.00005	.00000	.01153	.00000	.00037	.00800	0
1	85200	122	.00143	.00000	.00018	.00009	.00006	.00016	.00008	.00001	.00000	.00000	.00006	.00028	.00050	1
5	113400	51	.00045	.00000	.00003	.00012	.00003	.00001	.00001	.00003	.00000	.00000	.00001	.00005	.00017	5
10	98600	28	.00028	.00000	.00000	.00009	.00005	.00001	.00001	.00000	.00000	.00000	.00002	.00005	.00005	10
15	66200	32	.00048	.00000	.00005	.00006	.00009	.00000	.00000	.00005	.00002	.00000	.00003	.00005	.00005	15
20	64700	35	.00054	.00002	.00005	.00014	.00008	.00000	.00000	.00003	.00003	.00000	.00003	.00014	.00006	20
25	64400	56	.00087	.00002	.00005	.00017	.00009	.00003	.00000	.00006	.00011	.00000	.00000	.00022	.00012	25
30	64100	58	.00090	.00002	.00002	.00028	.00016	.00002	.00000	.00002	.00014	.00000	.00003	.00012	.00011	30
35	64000	88	.00137	.00002	.00003	.00053	.00014	.00000	.00000	.00005	.00012	.00000	.00003	.00027	.00019	35
40	52200	99	.00190	.00002	.00002	.00080	.00040	.00000	.00000	.00006	.00004	.00000	.00004	.00031	.00021	40
45	63500	208	.00328	.00003	.00000	.00153	.00093	.00002	.00000	.00006	.00004	.00000	.00003	.00011	.00057	45
50	52500	282	.00537	.00002	.00011	.00244	.00171	.00002	.00000	.00019	.00000	.00000	.00002	.00017	.00069	50
55	38900	342	.00879	.00000	.00003	.00316	.00370	.00010	.00013	.00033	.00000	.00000	.00005	.00031	.00098	55
60	30300	424	.01399	.00007	.00003	.00422	.00726	.00017	.00007	.00026	.00000	.00000	.00030	.00033	.00129	60
65	18700	509	.02722	.00011	.00000	.00663	.01599	.00048	.00000	.00080	.00000	.00000	.00005	.00053	.00262	65
70	15300	604	.03948	.00013	.00033	.00810	.02471	.00072	.00000	.00105	.00000	.00000	.00013	.00111	.00320	70
75	7500	520	.06933	.00013	.00027	.01253	.04467	.00213	.00040	.00093	.00000	.00000	.00040	.00160	.00627	75
80	4600	439	.09543	.00043	.00109	.01174	.06391	.00304	.00065	.00130	.00000	.00000	.00022	.00326	.00627	80
85+	2700	342	.12667	.00000	.00037	.01148	.09000	.00667	.00111	.00222	.00000	.00000	.00037	.00481	.00963	85+
ALL	928300	4790														

CRUDE DEATH RATE			.00516	.00002	.00007	.00113	.00230	.00016	.00009	.00011	.00003	.00027	.00004	.00023	.00070	
STANDARDIZED RATE (1)			.00413	.00001	.00008	.00081	.00151	.00016	.00011	.00009	.00003	.00041	.00004	.00021	.00068	
STANDARDIZED RATE (2)			.00730	.00003	.00008	.00152	.00372	.00021	.00005	.00016	.00003	.00024	.00005	.00029	.00087	
GEOMETRIC MEAN			.00467													

LIFE TABLE FOR ALL CAUSES COMBINED

Age (x)	Midyear Population	Deaths During Year	$_nM_x$	$_nq_x$	l_x	$_nd_x$	$_nL_x$	$_nm_x$	$_na_x$	T_x	$_nr_x$	$\overset{\circ}{e}_x$	Age (x)
0	21500	551	.025628	.025060	100000	2506	97779	.025629	.113567	7384724	.000000	73.847	0
1	85200	122	.001432	.005703	97494	556	388586	.001431	1.500000	7286945	.000000	74.742	1
5	113400	51	.000450	.002259	96938	219	484143	.000452	2.500000	6898359	.000000	71.163	5
10	98600	28	.000284	.001406	96719	136	483258	.000281	2.522978	6414216	.041536	66.318	10
15	66200	32	.000483	.002423	96583	234	482356	.000485	2.610399	5930958	.048664	61.408	15
20	64700	35	.000541	.002699	96349	260	481133	.000540	2.647436	5448603	.013009	56.551	20
25	64400	56	.000870	.004350	96089	418	479436	.000872	2.585227	4967469	.004252	51.697	25
30	64100	58	.000905	.004505	95671	431	477327	.000903	2.614559	4488034	-.003515	46.911	30
35	64000	88	.001375	.006877	95240	655	474659	.001380	2.647265	4010707	-.016928	42.112	35
40	52200	99	.001897	.009452	94585	894	470870	.001899	2.701342	3536048	.005484	37.385	40
45	63500	208	.003276	.016213	93691	1519	464584	.003267	2.714917	3065178	-.010232	32.716	45
50	52500	282	.005371	.026700	92172	2461	455202	.005406	2.701053	2600194	-.031090	28.210	50
55	38900	342	.008792	.043406	89711	3894	439534	.008859	2.683455	2144991	-.039826	23.910	55
60	30300	424	.013993	.068634	85817	5890	415697	.014169	2.727080	1705457	-.056641	19.873	60
65	18700	509	.027219	.129043	79927	10314	375258	.027465	2.636546	1289760	-.044081	16.137	65
70	15300	604	.039477	.181719	69613	12650	317841	.039800	2.610771	914501	-.046733	13.137	70
75	7500	520	.069333	.299142	56963	17040	242783	.070186	2.533328	596660	-.051191	10.475	75
80	4600	439	.095435	.385141	39923	15376	160085	.096049	2.429110	353877	-.051191	8.864	80
85+	2700	342	.126667	1.000000	24547	24547	193792	.126667	7.894737	193792	.000000	7.895	85+

NUMBER OF PERSONS DYING (OUT OF 100,000 AT BIRTH) ABOVE AGE X FROM SPECIFIED CAUSES

Age (x)	All Causes	Respiratory T. B.	Other Infec. and Paras.	Neoplasms	Cardiovascular	Infl., Pneu., Bronch.	Diarrheal	Certain Degenerative	Maternal	Cert. Dis. of Infancy	Motor Vehicle	Other Violence	Other and Unknown	Age (x)
0	100000	275	738	18400	59125	3182	790	2030	219	1128	560	3550	10003	0
1	97494	275	674	18395	59121	2946	544	2026	219	0	560	3513	9221	1
5	96938	275	606	18359	59098	2882	513	2021	219	0	537	3404	9024	5
10	96719	275	593	18298	59098	2878	508	2008	219	0	533	3378	8944	10
15	96583	275	592	18255	59061	2873	503	2008	219	0	523	3353	8920	15
20	96349	275	571	18226	59017	2873	503	1986	211	0	508	3288	8891	20
25	96089	268	548	18159	58580	2873	503	1971	196	0	486	3250	8855	25
30	95671	260	526	18077	58935	2858	503	1942	144	0	486	3146	8794	30
35	95240	253	519	17943	58861	2850	503	1934	77	0	471	3087	8742	35
40	94585	245	504	17690	58794	2850	503	1912	18	0	456	2960	8653	40
45	93691	236	495	17310	58604	2850	503	1885	0	0	438	2816	8554	45
50	92172	222	495	16602	58173	2843	503	1856	0	0	424	2764	8290	50
55	89711	213	443	15487	57386	2834	503	1768	0	0	415	2686	7976	55
60	85817	213	432	14091	55740	2789	446	1621	0	0	392	2550	7543	60
65	79927	185	418	12321	52672	2719	420	1510	0	0	267	2412	7003	65
70	69613	145	417	9816	46604	2536	420	1206	0	0	248	2209	6012	70
75	56963	103	312	7227	38680	2304	419	872	0	0	206	1852	4988	75
80	39923	70	247	4158	27696	1777	320	646	0	0	107	1459	3443	80
85+	24547	0	72	2225	17441	1292	215	431	0	0	72	933	1866	85+

NUMBER OF PERSONS SURVIVING TO AGE X IF SPECIFIED CAUSES WERE ELIMINATED

Age (x)	No Causes	Respiratory T. B.	Other Infec. and Paras.	Neoplasms	Cardiovascular	Infl., Pneu., Bronch.	Diarrheal	Certain Degenerative	Maternal	Cert. Dis. of Infancy	Motor Vehicle	Other Violence	Other and Unknown	(1) + (2)	(1) + (2) + (5) + (6) + (8)	(1)+(2)+ (5)+(6)+ (8)+part of(9)&(12)	(10) + (11)	Age (x)
		(1)	(2)	(3)	(4)	(5)	(6)	(7)	(8)	(9)	(10)	(11)	(12)					
0	100000	100000	100000	100000	100000	100000	100000	100000	100000	100000	100000	100000	100000	100000	100000	100000	100000	0
1	97494	97499	97557	97499	97498	97727	97737	97498	97494	98614	97494	97531	98265	97557	98035	99787	97531	1
5	96938	96938	97069	96979	96965	97234	97211	96947	96938	98052	96961	97083	97907	97069	97639	99476	97106	5
10	96719	96719	96862	96821	96759	97018	96996	96741	96719	97830	96746	96890	97767	96862	97441	99287	96917	10
15	96583	96583	96726	96728	96647	96887	96865	96605	96583	97693	96620	96779	97653	96726	97314	99160	96816	15
20	96349	96349	96514	96522	96457	96652	96630	96393	96357	97456	96401	96609	97446	96514	97108	98955	96661	20
25	96089	96096	96276	96329	96233	96391	96369	96148	96112	97193	96163	96387	97219	96283	96891	98741	96460	25
30	95671	95686	95880	95992	95860	95987	95950	95758	95746	96770	95744	96071	96858	95895	96568	98428	96145	30
35	95240	95262	95455	95694	95502	95563	95518	95335	95381	96334	95328	95658	96474	95477	96222	98089	95786	35
40	94585	94615	94813	95289	94912	94905	94861	94701	94784	95672	94687	95167	95901	94843	95643	97512	95270	40
45	93691	93729	93926	94770	94205	94008	93964	93833	93906	94767	93810	94412	95094	93964	94775	96631	94532	45
50	92172	92224	92403	93947	93109	92491	92441	92341	92384	93231	92303	92933	93819	92455	93260	95091	93065	50
55	89711	89770	89987	92566	91411	90031	89973	89962	89917	90742	89848	90529	91629	90047	90840	92634	90667	55
60	85817	85874	86092	89567	89100	86167	86123	86201	86014	86803	85970	86734	88085	86149	87008	88741	86889	60
65	79927	80007	80197	85599	86119	80321	80237	80393	80111	80845	80190	80915	82576	80277	81172	82802	81182	65
70	69613	69720	69849	77092	81363	70128	69883	70304	69773	70413	69860	70666	72880	69956	70910	72357	70916	70
75	56963	57088	57252	65719	75495	57557	57186	57832	57094	57617	57203	58153	60612	57378	58377	59600	58398	75
80	39923	40038	40180	49087	66545	40816	40163	40722	40015	40382	40174	41093	43875	40296	41540	42475	41351	80
85+	24547	24673	24842	32085	56593	25484	24777	25209	24603	24829	24729	25690	28356	24969	26225	26896	25880	85+
ADDED YRS OF LIFE TOTAL		.049	.213	3.213	17.906	.528	.267	.318	.058	.847	.126	.710	2.099	.262	1.171	2.664	.839	
WORK	1.946	.016	.044	.679	.498	.015	.005	.071	.071	.000	.037	.203	.242	.061	.152	.175	.240	

POPULATION, DEATHS, DEATH RATES FOR ALL CAUSES COMBINED, AND SPECIFIED CAUSES

Age Start of Interval	Midyear Population	Deaths During Year	All Causes	Respiratory T.B.	Other Infec. and Paras.	Neoplasms	Cardiovascular	Infl., Pneu., Bronch.	Diarrheal	Certain Degenerative	Maternal	Cert. Dis. of Infancy	Motor Vehicle	Other Violence	Other and Unknown	Age Start of Interval
0	25068	695	.02772	.00000	.00064	.00012	.00012	.00243	.00140	.00004	.00000	.01472	.00008	.00040	.00778	0
1	96453	99	.00103	.00000	.00009	.00009	.00000	.00013	.00004	.00000	.00000	.00000	.00010	.00009	.00047	1
5	123560	69	.00056	.00000	.00002	.00008	.00001	.00004	.00001	.00001	.00000	.00000	.00010	.00011	.00018	5
10	132465	51	.00039	.00000	.00002	.00008	.00002	.00001	.00000	.00002	.00000	.00000	.00003	.00009	.00011	10
15	118352	102	.00086	.00001	.00001	.00014	.00005	.00001	.00000	.00002	.00000	.00000	.00014	.00032	.00017	15
20	75250	93	.00124	.00000	.00001	.00019	.00009	.00000	.00000	.00003	.00000	.00000	.00027	.00054	.00011	20
25	69208	69	.00100	.00001	.00000	.00017	.00013	.00000	.00000	.00001	.00000	.00000	.00017	.00033	.00016	25
30	65626	70	.00107	.00003	.00002	.00021	.00020	.00000	.00000	.00008	.00000	.00000	.00012	.00032	.00009	30
35	62368	110	.00176	.00002	.00002	.00027	.00051	.00003	.00002	.00010	.00000	.00000	.00019	.00032	.00024	35
40	69661	167	.00240	.00003	.00006	.00055	.00095	.00003	.00000	.00014	.00000	.00000	.00011	.00037	.00029	40
45	52940	220	.00416	.00009	.00006	.00081	.00155	.00009	.00000	.00009	.00000	.00000	.00011	.00024	.00029	45
50	67581	470	.00695	.00007	.00009	.00132	.00380	.00007	.00001	.00025	.00000	.00000	.00030	.00030	.00045	50
55	57658	643	.01115	.00007	.00007	.00272	.00609	.00024	.00000	.00043	.00000	.00000	.00018	.00034	.00081	55
60	43236	842	.01947	.00012	.00014	.00421	.01152	.00028	.00000	.00090	.00000	.00000	.00017	.00028	.00108	60
65	28089	946	.03368	.00043	.00011	.00719	.01937	.00085	.00000	.00114	.00000	.00000	.00021	.00039	.00171	65
70	17724	926	.05225	.00017	.00062	.00954	.03205	.00141	.00011	.00164	.00000	.00000	.00050	.00032	.00374	70
75	9571	796	.08317	.00063	.00052	.01212	.05067	.00355	.00031	.00240	.00000	.00000	.00028	.00062	.00581	75
80	4684	577	.12319	.00064	.00043	.01516	.07899	.00598	.00043	.00278	.00000	.00000	.00063	.00219	.01013	80
85+	2715	453	.16685	.00184	.00074	.01179	.10350	.01400	.00184	.00295	.00000	.00000	.00000	.00256	.02578	85+
ALL	1122209	7398	.00659	.00005	.00007	.00107	.00321	.00024	.00005	.00020	.00000	.00033	.00016	.00031	.00091	

	All Causes	Resp. T.B.	Other Infec.	Neoplasms	Cardiovascular	Infl., Pneu.	Diarrheal	Certain Degen.	Maternal	Cert. Dis. Infancy	Motor Vehicle	Other Violence	Other and Unknown
CRUDE DEATH RATE	.00659	.00005	.00007	.00107	.00321	.00024	.00005	.00020	.00000	.00033	.00016	.00031	.00091
STANDARDIZED RATE (1)	.00507	.00003	.00007	.00074	.00205	.00021	.00006	.00013	.00000	.00033	.00016	.00031	.00091
STANDARDIZED RATE (2)	.00921	.00007	.00009	.00146	.00485	.00035	.00006	.00027	.00000	.00052	.00015	.00029	.00080
GEOMETRIC MEAN	.00599									.00030	.00019	.00036	.00121

LIFE TABLE FOR ALL CAUSES COMBINED

Age (x)	Midyear Population	Deaths During Year	$_nM_x$	$_nq_x$	l_x	$_nd_x$	$_nL_x$	$_nm_x$	$_na_x$	T_x	$_nr_x$	$\overset{\circ}{e}_x$	Age (x)
0	25068	695	.027725	.027060	100000	2706	97611	.027722	.117132	7070001	.000000	70.700	0
1	96453	99	.001026	.004101	97294	399	388179	.001028	1.500000	6972390	.000000	71.663	1
5	123560	69	.000558	.002787	96895	270	483800	.000558	2.500000	6584211	.000000	67.952	5
10	132465	51	.000385	.001925	96625	186	482691	.000385	2.665771	6100411	-.006103	63.135	10
15	118352	102	.000862	.004334	96439	418	481234	.000869	2.701356	5617720	-.040313	58.252	15
20	75250	93	.001236	.006144	96021	590	478642	.001233	2.519774	5136486	-.056894	53.493	20
25	69208	69	.000997	.004967	95431	474	475953	.000996	2.463520	4657844	-.022430	48.809	25
30	65626	70	.001067	.005319	94957	507	473591	.001071	2.645464	4181892	-.016339	44.040	30
35	62368	110	.001764	.008767	94450	828	470307	.001761	2.653986	3708301	-.006303	39.262	35
40	69661	167	.002397	.011952	93622	1119	465537	.002404	2.700700	3237993	.010667	34.566	40
45	52940	220	.004156	.020605	92503	1906	458160	.004160	2.715329	2772456	.005996	29.972	45
50	67581	470	.006955	.034006	90597	3089	445860	.006928	2.693563	2314296	-.018526	25.545	50
55	57658	643	.011152	.054578	87508	4776	426577	.011196	2.704626	1868435	.017684	21.352	55
60	43236	842	.019475	.094039	82732	7780	395674	.019663	2.688223	1441858	.043128	17.428	60
65	28089	946	.033679	.157501	74952	11805	346704	.034049	2.623341	1046183	.052408	13.958	65
70	17724	926	.052246	.233883	63147	14769	279853	.052774	2.570474	699480	.053842	11.077	70
75	9571	796	.083168	.347286	48378	16801	199900	.084047	2.500769	419627	.049599	8.674	75
80	4684	577	.123185	.465677	31577	14831	119361	.124253	2.402471	219726	.049599	6.958	80
85+	2715	453	.166851	1.000000	16746	16746	100365	.166851	5.993377	100365	.060000	5.993	85+

NUMBER OF PERSONS DYING (OUT OF 100,000 AT BIRTH) ABOVE AGE X FROM SPECIFIED CAUSES

Age (x)	All Causes	Respiratory T.B.	Other Infec. and Paras.	Neoplasms	Cardiovascular	Infl., Pneu., Bronch.	Diarrheal	Certain Degenerative	Maternal	Cert. Dis. of Infancy	Motor Vehicle	Other Violence	Other and Unknown	Age (x)
0	100000	785	768	15326	56707	4177	514	2870	0	1437	1575	3161	12680	0
1	97294	785	705	15314	56695	3940	378	2866	0	0	1567	3122	11922	1
5	96895	785	685	15278	56695	3887	362	2866	0	0	1527	3086	11740	5
10	96625	785	657	15239	56692	3868	358	2862	0	0	1480	3031	11653	10
15	96439	785	646	15199	56681	3864	358	2854	0	0	1465	2988	11599	15
20	96021	781	642	15133	56656	3860	358	2846	0	0	1395	2831	11519	20
25	95431	781	636	15044	56613	3860	358	2834	0	0	1267	2570	11468	25
30	94957	774	636	14962	56551	3860	358	2827	0	0	1185	2412	11392	30
35	94450	759	629	14860	56456	3860	358	2790	0	0	1127	2260	11351	35
40	93622	752	621	14732	56216	3845	350	2745	0	0	1037	2087	11237	40
45	92503	738	594	14478	55773	3832	350	2678	0	0	983	1973	11104	45
50	90557	695	565	14105	54880	3788	350	2635	0	0	845	1835	10895	50
55	87508	662	529	13522	53192	3756	344	2523	0	0	765	1683	10532	55
60	82732	632	499	12356	50584	3652	344	2338	0	0	691	1565	10071	60
65	74952	586	444	10676	45981	3540	344	1978	0	0	608	1409	9386	65
70	63147	436	406	8159	39190	3239	331	1580	0	0	434	1297	8075	70
75	48378	389	230	5474	30123	2838	299	1118	0	0	356	1120	6431	75
80	31577	262	126	3036	19885	2117	235	634	0	0	228	674	4380	80
85+	16746	185	74	1183	10388	1405	185	296	0	0	74	370	2586	85+

NUMBER OF PERSONS SURVIVING TO AGE X IF SPECIFIED CAUSES WERE ELIMINATED

Age (x)	No Causes	(1) Respiratory T.B.	(2) Other Infec. and Paras.	(3) Neoplasms	(4) Cardiovascular	(5) Infl., Pneu., Bronch.	(6) Diarrheal	(7) Certain Degenerative	(8) Maternal	(9) Cert. Dis. of Infancy	(10) Motor Vehicle	(11) Other Violence	(12) Other and Unknown	(1)+(2)	(1)+(2)+(5)+(6)+(8)	(1)+(2)+(5)+(6)+(8)+part of (9)&(12)	(10)+(11)	Age (x)
0	100000	100000	100000	100000	100000	100000	100000	100000	100000	100000	100000	100000	100000	100000	100000	100000	100000	0
1	97294	97294	97356	97306	97306	97528	97428	97298	97294	98722	97302	97332	98045	97356	97725	99598	97340	1
5	96895	96895	96993	96943	96907	97181	97045	96899	96895	98317	96943	96969	97826	96993	97430	99387	97017	5
10	96625	96625	96735	96712	96640	96778	96633	96625	96625	98043	96720	96754	97641	96735	97193	99163	96849	10
15	96439	96439	96559	96565	96465	96747	96552	96455	96439	97854	96548	96611	97507	96559	97021	98994	96720	15
20	96021	96025	96145	96213	96072	96331	96173	96045	96021	97430	96200	96349	97165	96149	96613	98580	96529	20
25	95431	95435	95560	95711	95524	95740	95582	95467	95431	96831	95737	96019	96620	95564	96025	97581	96326	25
30	94957	94968	95085	95317	95112	95108	94999	94957	94957	96350	95343	95700	96217	95096	95555	97503	96090	30
35	94450	94476	94585	94911	94699	94755	94600	94529	94450	95836	94892	95342	95745	94611	95067	97007	95789	35
40	93622	93655	93764	94207	94109	93940	93778	93745	93622	94956	94151	94680	95020	93796	94272	96201	95215	40
45	92503	92549	92670	93335	93428	92830	92658	92691	92503	93079	93663	94019		92716	93199	95114	94247	45
50	90557	90685	90785	91785	92040	90561	90748	90824	90557	91926	91299	91872	92292	90873	91390	93283	92583	50
55	87508	87625	87729	89238	90957	87891	87660	87838	87508	88792	88265	88891	89509	87846	88384	90229	89659	55
60	82732	82872	82970	85532	88670	83196	82876	83225	82732	83946	83520	84156	85083	83110	83722	85487	84957	60
65	74952	75123	75220	79158	85165	75480	75082	75743	74952	76052	76054	76392	77756	74976		77678	77201	65
70	63147	63428	63408	69169	79188	63871	63269	64183	63147	64074	63976	64465	66769	63691	64545	65984	65312	70
75	48378	48634	48733	55610	71453	49290	48500	49582	48378	49088	49082	49548	52654	48991	50040	51231	50268	75
80	31577	31847	31891	38599	60490	32771	31708	32761	31577	32040	32141	32711	36234	32164	33519	34441	33296	80
85+	16746	16945	16950	22158	48152	17916	16852	17627	16746	16992	17158	17574	20748	17152	18466	19074	18007	85+

ADDED YRS OF LIFE

	No Causes	(1)	(2)	(3)	(4)	(5)	(6)	(7)	(8)	(9)	(10)	(11)	(12)	(1)+(2)	(1)+(2)+(5)+(6)+(8)	(1)+(2)+(5)+(6)+(8)+part of (9)&(12)	(10)+(11)
TOTAL		.101	.174	2.235	12.024	.574	.140	.386	.000	1.036	.432	.812	2.210	.276	1.009	2.554	1.253
WORK	2.557	.028	.027	.480	.913	.030	.003	.092	.000	.000	.211	.416	.288	.056	.088	.100	.630

POPULATION, DEATHS, DEATH RATES FOR ALL CAUSES COMBINED, AND SPECIFIED CAUSES

Age Start of Interval	Midyear Population	Deaths During Year	All Causes	Respira- tory T. B.	Other Infec. and Paras.	Neo- plasms	Cardio- vascular	Infl., Pneu., Bronch.	Diar- rheal	Certain Degen- erative	Maternal	Cert. Dis. of Infancy	Motor Vehicle	Other Violence	Other and Unknown	Age Start of Interval
0	23624	486	.02057	.00000	.00034	.00013	.00000	.00229	.00080	.00000	.00000	.01054	.00000	.00051	.00597	0
1	91619	85	.00093	.00000	.00013	.00005	.00000	.00015	.00007	.00000	.00000	.00000	.00008	.00007	.00038	1
5	116757	47	.00040	.00000	.00003	.00006	.00002	.00002	.00002	.00003	.00000	.00000	.00006	.00003	.00014	5
10	125117	39	.00031	.00000	.00001	.00008	.00004	.00001	.00000	.00005	.00000	.00000	.00002	.00005	.00006	10
15	109702	57	.00052	.00000	.00001	.00011	.00011	.00000	.00000	.00001	.00000	.00000	.00005	.00011	.00012	15
20	71766	50	.00070	.00000	.00000	.00013	.00010	.00000	.00000	.00004	.00003	.00000	.00007	.00018	.00015	20
25	69393	41	.00059	.00000	.00004	.00006	.00013	.00003	.00000	.00004	.00003	.00000	.00004	.00012	.00010	25
30	69682	76	.00109	.00001	.00001	.00036	.00017	.00001	.00000	.00006	.00003	.00000	.00004	.00020	.00019	30
35	70412	106	.00151	.00001	.00001	.00055	.00028	.00004	.00003	.00001	.00001	.00000	.00003	.00018	.00033	35
40	70736	155	.00219	.00003	.00001	.00058	.00044	.00001	.00000	.00008	.00001	.00000	.00006	.00018	.00038	40
45	55408	194	.00350	.00002	.00005	.00137	.00097	.00005	.00000	.00009	.00000	.00000	.00004	.00036	.00054	45
50	67974	374	.00550	.00003	.00003	.00235	.00206	.00006	.00003	.00022	.00000	.00000	.00009	.00018	.00046	50
55	50483	445	.00881	.00002	.00006	.00317	.00359	.00022	.00000	.00042	.00000	.00000	.00010	.00030	.00095	55
60	40917	664	.01623	.00002	.00010	.00406	.00863	.00027	.00005	.00071	.00000	.00000	.00012	.00034	.00193	60
65	27429	745	.02716	.00004	.00011	.00623	.01560	.00062	.00000	.00095	.00000	.00000	.00033	.00040	.00288	65
70	17972	759	.04223	.00011	.00022	.00718	.02693	.00055	.00006	.00134	.00000	.00000	.00022	.00117	.00406	70
75	10957	809	.07383	.00027	.00018	.01159	.04737	.00237	.00018	.00173	.00000	.00000	.00027	.00228	.00758	75
80	5692	625	.10980	.00000	.00070	.01177	.07502	.00439	.00035	.00334	.00000	.00000	.00053	.00369	.01001	80
85+	3679	553	.15031	.00082	.00027	.01142	.10709	.01033	.00136	.00136	.00000	.00000	.00000	.00544	.01223	85+
ALL	1099319	6310														

CRUDE DEATH RATE			.00574	.00002	.00005	.00117	.00280	.00021	.00004	.00017	.00001	.00023	.00007	.00024	.00075	
STANDARDIZED RATE (1)			.00409	.00001	.00005	.00077	.00163	.00018	.00005	.00012	.00001	.00037	.00006	.00019	.00065	
STANDARDIZED RATE (2)			.00769	.00002	.00006	.00145	.00408	.00027	.00004	.00023	.00001	.00022	.00008	.00019	.00093	
GEOMETRIC MEAN			.00476													

LIFE TABLE FOR ALL CAUSES COMBINED

Age (x)	Midyear Population	Deaths During Year	$_nM_x$	$_nq_x$	l_x	$_nd_x$	$_nL_x$	$_nm_x$	$_na_x$	T_x	$_nr_x$	$\overset{\circ}{e}_x$	Age (x)
0	23624	486	.020572	.020200	100000	2020	98192	.020572	.104973	7340458	.000000	73.405	0
1	91619	85	.000928	.003705	97980	363	391013	.000928	1.500000	7242266	.000000	73.916	1
5	116757	47	.000403	.002008	97617	196	487595	.000402	2.500000	6851253	.000000	70.185	5
10	125117	39	.000312	.001560	97421	152	486737	.000312	2.578125	6363658	-.004298	65.321	10
15	109702	57	.000520	.002601	97269	253	485751	.000521	2.652339	5876921	.041328	60.419	15
20	71766	50	.000697	.003474	97016	337	484244	.000696	2.520401	5391170	.051796	55.570	20
25	69393	41	.000591	.002958	96679	286	482719	.000592	2.636218	4906926	-.014201	50.755	25
30	69682	76	.001091	.005436	96393	524	480745	.001090	2.671756	4424207	.002758	45.898	30
35	70412	106	.001505	.007489	95869	718	477658	.001503	2.650012	3943462	-.006953	41.134	35
40	70736	155	.002191	.010941	95151	1041	473344	.002199	2.683718	3465804	-.018521	36.424	40
45	55408	194	.003501	.017384	94110	1636	466766	.003505	2.687194	2992461	.005607	31.797	45
50	67974	374	.005502	.027154	92474	2511	456567	.005500	2.689002	2525694	-.002590	27.312	50
55	50483	445	.008815	.043507	89963	3914	440921	.008877	2.727655	2069127	-.030967	23.000	55
60	40917	664	.016228	.078885	86049	6788	414587	.016373	2.693325	1628206	.039171	18.922	60
65	27429	745	.027161	.128853	79261	10213	372142	.027444	2.634082	1213619	-.052260	15.312	65
70	17972	759	.042232	.193503	69048	13361	313335	.042621	2.614341	841477	.048732	12.187	70
75	10957	809	.073834	.315083	55687	17546	235209	.074597	2.536416	528112	.042421	9.484	75
80	5692	625	.109803	.430718	38141	16428	148451	.110663	2.427905	292903	-.042421	7.679	80
85+	3679	553	.150313	1.000000	21713	21713	144452	.150313	6.652803	144452	.000000	6.653	85+

NUMBER OF PERSONS DYING (OUT OF 100,000 AT BIRTH) ABOVE AGE X FROM SPECIFIED CAUSES

Age (x)	All Causes	Respiratory T.B.	Other Infec. and Paras.	Neo-plasms	Cardio-vascular	Infl., Pneu., Bronch.	Diar-rheal	Certain Degen-erative	Maternal	Cert. Dis. of Infancy	Motor Vehicle	Other Violence	Other and Unknown	Age (x)
0	100000	—300	556	16743	59551	3851	470	2667	55	1035	699	3508	10565	0
1	97980	300	523	16730	59551	3627	391	2667	55	0	699	3458	9979	1
5	97617	300	472	16709	59551	3567	366	2667	55	0	669	3433	9828	5
10	97421	300	455	16680	59542	3558	357	2654	55	0	640	3416	9764	10
15	97269	300	451	16641	59523	3555	357	2631	55	0	632	3393	9731	15
20	97016	300	447	16588	59470	3555	357	2627	55	0	605	3339	9673	20
25	96679	300	447	16527	59424	3555	357	2606	41	0	572	3251	9599	25
30	96393	300	426	16499	59361	3541	357	2585	27	0	551	3196	9550	30
35	95869	293	419	16327	59278	3534	357	2558	13	0	530	3099	9461	35
40	95151	286	412	16062	59143	3513	344	2551	6	0	517	3011	9306	40
45	94110	273	405	15599	58534	3507	344	2511	0	0	490	2923	9124	45
50	92474	264	380	14958	58478	3481	344	2469	0	0	473	2755	8872	50
55	89963	251	367	13884	57539	3455	330	2368	0	0	433	2674	8662	55
60	86049	242	340	12482	55941	3358	330	2183	0	0	389	2543	8241	60
65	79261	232	299	10791	52325	3245	310	1887	0	0	338	2401	7433	65
70	69048	218	258	8455	46447	3012	310	1532	0	0	215	2249	6352	70
75	55687	183	188	6194	37917	2711	292	1111	0	0	145	1877	5069	75
80	38141	118	145	3447	26656	2145	249	700	0	0	80	1334	3267	80
85+	21713	118	39	1649	15470	1492	196	196	0	0	0	785	1768	85+

NUMBER OF PERSONS SURVIVING TO AGE X IF SPECIFIED CAUSES WERE ELIMINATED

Age (x)	No Causes	Respiratory T.B.	Other Infec. and Paras.	Neo-plasms	Cardio-vascular	Infl., Pneu., Bronch.	Diar-rheal	Certain Degener-ative	Maternal	Cert. Dis. of Infancy	Motor Vehicle	Other Violence	Other and Unknown	(1) + (2)	(1) + (2) + (5) + (6) + (8)	(1)+(2)+ (5)+(6)+ (8)+part of(9)&(12)	(10) + (11)	Age (x)
		(1)	(2)	(3)	(4)	(5)	(6)	(7)	(8)	(9)	(10)	(11)	(12)					
0	100000	100000	100000	100000	100000	100000	100000	100000	100000	100000	100000	100000	100000	100000	100000	100000	100000	0
1	97980	97980	98013	97993	97980	98202	98058	97980	97980	99010	97980	98030	98562	98013	98313	99678	98030	1
5	97617	97617	97700	97651	97617	97898	97720	97617	97617	98643	97647	97691	98348	97700	98085	99546	97721	5
10	97421	97421	97521	97484	97430	97711	97533	97434	97421	98445	97480	97512	98215	97521	97923	99399	97571	10
15	97269	97269	97373	97371	97297	97561	97381	97305	97269	98291	97336	97383	98095	97373	97778	99253	97450	15
20	97016	97016	97124	97170	97097	97307	97127	97056	97016	98036	97110	97184	97899	97124	97527	99000	97277	20
25	96679	96679	96787	96894	96806	96995	96790	96740	96693	97695	96805	96934	97633	96787	97203	98674	97061	25
30	96393	96393	96521	96582	96582	96697	96504	96474	96421	97406	96540	96702	97394	96521	96964	98443	96850	30
35	95869	95876	96003	96282	96140	96178	95979	95977	95911	96877	96036	96274	96954	96010	96472	97951	96442	35
40	95151	95165	95291	95826	95555	95479	95273	95265	95199	96151	95330	95641	96384	95305	95805	97288	95821	40
45	94110	94137	94256	95243	94719	94440	94231	94263	94164	95059	94314	94683	95513	94283	94789	96263	94888	45
50	92474	92509	92642	94233	93528	92824	92593	92666	92527	93446	92691	93204	94106	92677	93201	94662	93423	50
55	89963	90010	90139	92759	91931	90329	90092	90250	90014	90909	90214	90754	91762	90187	90736	92164	91007	55
60	86049	86103	86244	90147	89544	86495	86173	86505	86098	86953	86332	86935	88191	86298	86919	88304	87220	60
65	79261	79320	79480	84751	86174	79781	79354	79966	79306	80094	79571	80214	82032	79539	80241	81544	80528	65
70	69048	69113	69277	76191	81280	69720	69164	69997	69087	69774	69433	70023	72512	69342	70175	71347	70413	70
75	55687	55771	55935	63717	75206	56503	55797	56835	55719	56272	56060	56813	59700	56019	56984	57978	57194	75
80	38141	38252	38346	46290	65681	39178	38252	39273	38163	38542	38450	39371	42508	38457	39640	40404	39690	80
85+	21713	21776	21909	28028	54674	22808	21816	22747	21725	21941	21949	22839	25476	21973	23204	23717	23088	85+

ADDED YRS OF LIFE																		
TOTAL		.039	.147	2.775	15.875	.567	.118	.385	.025	.771	.182	.623	1.974	.186	.908	2.095	.809	
WORK	2.058	.011	.024	.677	.567	.031	.006	.077	.019	.000	.062	.208	.304	.035	.090	.109	.270	

POPULATION, DEATHS, DEATH RATES FOR ALL CAUSES COMBINED, AND SPECIFIED CAUSES

Age Start of Interval	Midyear Population	Deaths During Year	All Causes	Respiratory T. B.	Other Infec. and Paras.	Neoplasms	Cardiovascular	Infl., Pneu., Bronch.	Diarrheal	Certain Degenerative	Maternal	Cert. Dis. of Infancy	Motor Vehicle	Other Violence	Other and Unknown	Age Start of Interval
0	404149	112210	.27765	.00119	.04327	.00008	.00368	.03567	.04292	.00000	.00000	.08156	.00000	.00560	.06368	0
1	1344428	83140	.06184	.00142	.02792	.00005	.00068	.00754	.00931	.00001	.00000	.00000	.00000	.00088	.01402	1
5	1528092	17781	.01164	.00055	.00596	.00004	.00042	.00091	.00092	.00001	.00000	.00000	.00000	.00088	.01402	5
10	1381296	6991	.00506	.00050	.00210	.00003	.00033	.00037	.00015	.00001	.00000	.00000	.00000	.00053	.00228	10
15	1300985	7954	.00611	.00191	.00174	.00002	.00030	.00049	.00007	.00001	.00000	.00000	.00000	.00033	.00124	15
20	1209712	11184	.00925	.00255	.00172	.00007	.00032	.00155	.00038	.00001	.00000	.00000	.00000	.00047	.00111	20
25	1047924	8835	.00843	.00247	.00126	.00008	.00035	.00141	.00033	.00001	.00000	.00000	.00000	.00069	.00196	25
30	1013064	8310	.00820	.00223	.00127	.00011	.00047	.00146	.00028	.00001	.00000	.00000	.00000	.00063	.00175	30
35	884637	8885	.01004	.00227	.00147	.00017	.00078	.00200	.00043	.00002	.00000	.00000	.00000	.00069	.00175	35
40	891865	10229	.01147	.00222	.00164	.00029	.00127	.00235	.00051	.00003	.00000	.00000	.00000	.00069	.00222	40
45	690599	11105	.01608	.00258	.00229	.00053	.00242	.00315	.00071	.00005	.00000	.00000	.00000	.00069	.00247	45
50	722154	13108	.01815	.00230	.00232	.00082	.00363	.00344	.00083	.00007	.00000	.00000	.00000	.00084	.00350	50
55	538114	15601	.02899	.00287	.00314	.00164	.00714	.00521	.00164	.00014	.00000	.00000	.00000	.00081	.00394	55
60	540657	17858	.03303	.00081	.00363	.00109	.00779	.00761	.00177	.00008	.00000	.00000	.00000	.00107	.00614	60
65	300696	18158	.06039	.00114	.00531	.00216	.01648	.01371	.00373	.00016	.00000	.00000	.00000	.00095	.00928	65
70	247554	19937	.08054	.00102	.00467	.00269	.02389	.01878	.00537	.00023	.00000	.00000	.00000	.00097	.01673	70
75	116499	15395	.13215	.00101	.00566	.00352	.04015	.03197	.01054	.00033	.00000	.00000	.00000	.00149	.02239	75
80	60372	9355	.15496	.00065	.00489	.00283	.04257	.03662	.01825	.00038	.00000	.00000	.00000	.00201	.03675	80
85+	18829	4629	.24584	.00048	.00590	.00250	.05731	.05927	.02926	.00048	.00000	.00000	.00000	.00209	.04668	85+
ALL	14241626	400665														

CRUDE DEATH RATE	.02813	.00172	.00614	.00037	.00270	.00444	.00293	.00004	.00000	.00231	.00000	.00085	.00662
STANDARDIZED RATE (1)	.02915	.00166	.00706	.00028	.00208	.00428	.00329	.00003	.00000	.00287	.00000	.00085	.00662
STANDARDIZED RATE (2)	.02965	.00173	.00553	.00050	.00400	.00516	.00286	.00005	.00000	.00287	.00000	.00086	.00674
GEOMETRIC MEAN	.02801									.00169	.00000	.00086	.00727

LIFE TABLE FOR ALL CAUSES COMBINED

Age (x)	Midyear Population	Deaths During Year	$_nM_x$	$_nq_x$	l_x	$_nd_x$	$_nL_x$	$_nm_x$	$_na_x$	T_x	$_nr_x$	$\overset{\circ}{e}_x$	Age (x)
0	404149	112210	.277645	.246320	100000	24632	88718	.277642	.541997	3325602	.000000	33.256	0
1	1344428	83140	.061840	.214242	75368	16147	261105	.061841	1.500000	3236883	.000000	42.948	1
5	1528092	17781	.011636	.056618	59221	3353	287723	.011654	2.500000	2975779	.000000	50.249	5
10	1381296	6991	.005061	.024898	55868	1391	275506	.005049	2.243889	2688056	.007749	48.114	10
15	1300985	7954	.006114	.030160	54477	1643	268486	.006120	2.626674	2412550	.005717	44.286	15
20	1209712	11184	.009245	.045236	52834	2390	258286	.009253	2.538180	2144064	.012289	40.581	20
25	1047924	8835	.008431	.041254	50444	2081	246925	.008428	2.455450	1885778	.009668	37.384	25
30	1013064	8310	.008203	.040217	48363	1945	236993	.008207	2.520780	1638853	.010072	33.887	30
35	884637	8885	.010044	.049011	46418	2275	226511	.010044	2.547711	1401860	.002544	30.201	35
40	891865	10229	.011469	.055864	44143	2466	214748	.011483	2.580343	1175349	.011481	26.626	40
45	690599	11105	.016080	.077405	41677	3226	200504	.016089	2.556895	960601	.006986	23.049	45
50	722154	13108	.018191	.087046	38451	3347	184205	.018170	2.594986	760098	.006551	19.768	50
55	538114	15601	.028992	.135369	35104	4752	163912	.028991	2.557169	575892	-.000145	16.405	55
60	540657	17858	.033030	.153235	30352	4651	140557	.033090	2.591244	411981	.015012	13.573	60
65	300696	18158	.060387	.264153	25701	6789	111884	.060679	2.551769	271424	.021432	10.561	65
70	247554	19937	.080536	.335131	18912	6338	78593	.080643	2.480771	159540	.009487	8.436	70
75	116499	15395	.132147	.493359	12574	6204	46761	.132675	2.403456	80947	.014359	6.438	75
80	60372	9355	.154956	.543642	6370	3463	22361	.154868	2.259902	34186	.014359	5.367	80
85+	18829	4629	.245844	1.000000	2907	2907	11825	.245844	4.067617	11825	.000000	4.068	85+

NUMBER OF PERSONS DYING (OUT OF 100,000 AT BIRTH) ABOVE AGE X FROM SPECIFIED CAUSES

Age (x)	All Causes	Respiratory T.B.	Other Infec. and Paras.	Neoplasms	Cardio-vascular	Infl., Pneu., Bronch.	Diarrheal	Certain Degenerative	Maternal	Cert. Dis. of Infancy	Motor Vehicle	Other Violence	Other and Unknown	Age (x)
0	100000	5877	18963	1603	12197	16914	9926	154	0	7236	0	2948	24182	0
1	75368	5771	15125	1596	11870	13749	6118	154	0	0	0	2451	18534	1
5	59221	5359	7834	1582	11694	11782	3687	151	0	0	0	2222	14870	5
10	55868	5241	6116	1570	11572	11518	3421	147	0	0	0	2069	14214	10
15	54477	5102	5539	1562	11481	11416	3379	146	0	0	0	1978	13874	15
20	52834	4588	5073	1556	11401	11284	3361	144	0	0	0	1851	13576	20
25	50444	3929	4629	1538	11317	10883	3263	142	0	0	0	1673	13070	25
30	48363	3320	4318	1519	11229	10535	3180	139	0	0	0	1485	12638	30
35	46418	2792	4018	1493	11118	10189	3114	136	0	0	0	1336	12222	35
40	44143	2277	3685	1454	10942	9737	3017	132	0	0	0	1180	11719	40
45	41677	1801	3333	1393	10668	9231	2906	125	0	0	0	1031	11189	45
50	38451	1284	2974	1297	10182	8599	2764	114	0	0	0	862	10485	50
55	35104	861	2446	1136	9513	7966	2610	100	0	0	0	714	9758	55
60	30352	391	1932	867	8342	7111	2341	77	0	0	0	538	8753	60
65	25701	279	1420	713	7244	6038	2091	66	0	0	0	404	7446	65
70	18912	151	825	470	5391	4496	1671	48	0	0	0	296	5564	70
75	12574	71	458	258	3510	3018	1248	30	0	0	0	179	3802	75
80	6370	23	183	93	1625	1518	752	14	0	0	0	85	2077	80
85+	2907	6	70	30	678	701	346	6	0	0	0	37	1033	85+

NUMBER OF PERSONS SURVIVING TO AGE X IF SPECIFIED CAUSES WERE ELIMINATED

Age (x)	No Causes	Respiratory T.B. (1)	Other Infec. and Paras. (2)	Neoplasms (3)	Cardio-vascular (4)	Infl., Pneu., Bronch. (5)	Diarrheal (6)	Certain Degenerative (7)	Maternal (8)	Cert. Dis. of Infancy (9)	Motor Vehicle (10)	Other Violence (11)	Other and Unknown (12)	(1)+(2)	(1)+(2)+(5)+(6)+(8)	(1)+(2)+(5)+(6)+(8)+part of(9)&(12)	(10)+(11)	Age (x)
0	100000	100000	100000	100000	100000	100000	100000	100000	100000	100000	100000	100000	100000	100000	100000	100000	100000	0
1	75368	75460	78763	75374	75651	78157	78736	75368	75368	81896	75368	75799	80417	78859	85432	98020	75799	1
5	59221	59623	69007	59238	59600	63243	64154	59224	59221	64351	59221	59764	66742	69476	80375	97224	59764	5
10	55868	56402	67074	55896	56345	59937	60803	55874	55868	60707	55868	56530	63665	67715	79063	96615	56530	10
15	54477	55137	66091	54512	55033	58552	59334	54484	54477	59156	54477	55214	62483	66891	78305	96173	55214	15
20	52834	53989	64656	52874	53453	56927	57564	52843	52834	57411	52834	53675	60936	66069	77560	95703	53675	20
25	50444	52209	62264	50500	51118	54776	55064	50455	50444	54814	50444	51424	58753	64442	76385	95042	51424	25
30	48363	50676	60072	48435	49096	52887	52882	48376	48363	52552	48363	49491	56824	62945	75265	94321	49491	30
35	46418	49183	58023	46513	47233	51132	50826	46433	46418	50439	46418	47650	55020	61478	74153	93592	47650	35
40	44143	47307	55586	44271	45093	49114	48438	44162	44143	47967	44143	45471	52908	59570	72728	92601	45471	40
45	41677	45162	52913	41858	42847	46921	45851	41701	41677	45287	41677	43080	50573	57338	71017	91260	43080	45
50	38451	42207	49380	38720	40014	43978	42452	38484	38451	41782	38451	39914	47486	54204	68445	89034	39914	50
55	35104	38978	45609	35496	37204	40847	38920	35148	35104	38145	35104	36586	44218	50643	65333	86041	36586	55
60	30352	34187	40059	30944	33342	36255	33930	30411	30352	32981	30352	31804	39429	45122	60250	80735	31804	60
65	25701	29062	34547	26346	29364	31902	28988	25761	25701	27927	25701	27059	34987	39065	54692	75312	27059	65
70	18912	21508	26109	19601	23498	25168	21740	18972	18912	20550	18912	20008	28029	29694	45427	65525	20008	70
75	12574	14373	17769	13210	17638	18405	14855	12628	12574	13663	12574	13403	20874	20311	35125	53702	13403	75
80	6370	7319	9273	6813	10987	10993	7950	6409	6370	6922	6370	6860	12779	10654	22953	38723	6860	80
85+	2907	3353	4342	3154	6214	6036	3978	2930	2907	3159	2907	3165	7387	5008	14232	27405	3165	85+

ADDED YRS OF LIFE

	No Causes	(1)	(2)	(3)	(4)	(5)	(6)	(7)	(8)	(9)	(10)	(11)	(12)	(1)+(2)	(1)+(2)+(5)+(6)+(8)	(1)+(2)+(5)+(6)+(8)+part of(9)&(12)	(10)+(11)
TOTAL		1.854	8.051	.235	1.858	4.355	3.304	.025	.000	2.834	.000	.880	7.314	10.461	22.154	39.830	.880
WORK	10.697	2.087	1.501	.173	.844	1.549	.342	.019	.000	.000	.000	.597	1.927	3.704	5.916	7.730	.597

POPULATION, DEATHS, DEATH RATES FOR ALL CAUSES COMBINED, AND SPECIFIED CAUSES

Age Start of Interval	Midyear Population	Deaths During Year	All Causes	Respiratory T. B.	Other Infec. and Paras.	Neoplasms	Cardiovascular	Infl., Pneu., Bronch.	Diarrheal	Certain Degenerative	Maternal	Cert. Dis. of Infancy	Motor Vehicle	Other Violence	Other and Unknown	Age Start of Interval
0	386335	95619	.24750	.00099	.04101	.00008	.00335	.03083	.04146	.00001	.00000	.06829	.00000	.00383	.05765	0
1	1299410	80866	.06223	.00151	.02766	.00004	.00061	.00783	.00967	.00000	.00000	.00000	.00000	.00076	.01414	1
5	1476156	18149	.01229	.00095	.00659	.00003	.00041	.00090	.00115	.00000	.00000	.00000	.00000	.00014	.00214	5
10	1324525	7791	.00588	.00095	.00256	.00002	.00036	.00040	.00021	.00000	.00001	.00000	.00000	.00014	.00214	10
15	1329105	9170	.00690	.00303	.00178	.00002	.00027	.00044	.00007	.00000	.00001	.00000	.00000	.00009	.00128	15
20	1234169	10423	.00845	.00268	.00113	.00014	.00029	.00092	.00036	.00000	.00122	.00000	.00000	.00012	.00158	20
25	1076409	10555	.00981	.00329	.00105	.00020	.00041	.00107	.00041	.00000	.00142	.00000	.00000	.00017	.00179	25
30	1040030	10288	.00989	.00313	.00111	.00028	.00057	.00116	.00036	.00001	.00125	.00000	.00000	.00015	.00188	30
35	889130	10307	.01159	.00316	.00127	.00045	.00094	.00157	.00054	.00001	.00113	.00000	.00000	.00016	.00237	35
40	900852	9574	.01063	.00260	.00120	.00063	.00129	.00156	.00055	.00001	.00043	.00000	.00000	.00013	.00221	40
45	688081	9594	.01394	.00289	.00160	.00111	.00235	.00200	.00073	.00002	.00007	.00000	.00000	.00016	.00300	45
50	737033	11205	.01520	.00244	.00153	.00164	.00334	.00206	.00081	.00003	.00001	.00000	.00000	.00015	.00320	50
55	530640	14055	.02649	.00323	.00220	.00350	.00699	.00332	.00169	.00006	.00000	.00000	.00000	.00020	.00529	55
60	547465	17325	.03165	.00066	.00288	.00150	.00872	.00721	.00181	.00002	.00000	.00000	.00000	.00062	.00823	60
65	283184	18451	.06516	.00100	.00463	.00329	.02041	.01439	.00425	.00005	.00000	.00000	.00000	.00070	.01643	65
70	243140	20548	.08451	.00087	.00393	.00356	.02855	.01900	.00590	.00005	.00000	.00000	.00000	.00101	.02124	70
75	103069	15119	.14669	.00090	.00518	.00541	.05062	.03412	.01216	.00010	.00000	.00000	.00000	.00147	.03672	75
80	62201	9507	.15284	.00050	.00387	.00392	.04786	.03482	.01881	.00010	.00000	.00000	.00000	.00132	.04164	80
85+	19673	4970	.25263	.00030	.00498	.00381	.06781	.05957	.03177	.00015	.00000	.00000	.00000	.00203	.08219	85+
ALL	14170607	383516														

CRUDE DEATH RATE			.02706	.00217	.00573	.00065	.00295	.00388	.00293	.00001	.00043	.00186	.00000	.00036	.00609	
STANDARDIZED RATE (1)			.02851	.00210	.00685	.00050	.00229	.00384	.00337	.00001	.00041	.00240	.00000	.00038	.00636	
STANDARDIZED RATE (2)			.02956	.00214	.00523	.00086	.00456	.00472	.00299	.00002	.00041	.00141	.00000	.00037	.00684	
GEOMETRIC MEAN			.02849													

LIFE TABLE FOR ALL CAUSES COMBINED

Age (x)	Midyear Population	Deaths During Year	$_nM_x$	$_nq_x$	l_x	$_nd_x$	$_nL_x$	$_nm_x$	$_na_x$	T_x	$_nr_x$	$\overset{\circ}{e}_x$	Age (x)
0	386335	95619	.247503	.219800	100000	21980	88807	.247504	.490755	3398967	.000000	33.990	0
1	1299410	80866	.062233	.215419	78020	16807	270063	.062234	1.500000	3310160	.000000	42.427	1
5	1476156	18149	.012295	.059693	61213	3654	296930	.012306	2.500000	3040098	.000000	49.664	5
10	1324525	7791	.005882	.028927	57559	1665	283266	.005878	2.280030	2743168	.003154	47.658	10
15	1329105	9170	.006899	.033921	55894	1896	274849	.006898	2.562742	2459902	-.001559	44.010	15
20	1234169	10423	.008445	.041409	53998	2236	264521	.008453	2.554226	2185053	.010380	40.465	20
25	1076409	10555	.009806	.047873	51762	2478	252645	.009808	2.512107	1920531	.007684	37.103	25
30	1040030	10288	.009892	.048292	49284	2380	240504	.009896	2.514356	1667886	.010024	33.842	30
35	889130	10307	.011592	.056328	46904	2642	227897	.011593	2.493061	1427382	.002750	30.432	35
40	900852	9574	.010628	.051783	44262	2292	215619	.010630	2.517179	1199485	.012830	27.100	40
45	688081	9594	.013943	.067453	41970	2831	202894	.013953	2.542903	983866	.007576	23.442	45
50	737033	11205	.015203	.073456	39139	2875	188858	.015223	2.622029	780972	.009777	19.954	50
55	530640	14055	.026487	.124504	36264	4515	170410	.026495	2.583702	592114	.002560	16.328	55
60	547465	17325	.031646	.147690	31749	4689	147674	.031752	2.638978	421703	.020442	13.282	60
65	283184	18451	.065156	.282446	27060	7643	116626	.065534	2.556670	274029	.022086	10.127	65
70	243140	20548	.084511	.348561	19417	6768	79971	.084630	2.471373	157404	.011737	8.106	70
75	103069	15119	.146688	.530714	12649	6713	45714	.146848	2.388494	77432	.003500	6.122	75
80	62201	9507	.152843	.534872	5936	3175	20789	.152722	2.199803	31718	.003500	5.343	80
85+	19673	4970	.252631	1.000000	2761	2761	10929	.252631	3.958350	10929	.000000	3.958	85+

NUMBER OF PERSONS DYING (OUT OF 100,000 AT BIRTH) ABOVE AGE X FROM SPECIFIED CAUSES

Age (x)	All Causes	Respiratory T.B.	Other Infec. and Paras.	Neoplasms	Cardiovascular	Infl., Pneu., Bronch.	Diarrheal	Certain Degenerative	Maternal	Cert. Dis. of Infancy	Motor Vehicle	Other Violence	Other and Unknown	Age (x)
0	100000	7393	18306	2857	13896	15417	10365	54	1406	6064	0	1290	22952	0
1	78020	7305	14664	2850	13598	12679	6683	53	1406	0	0	950	17832	1
5	61213	6896	7194	2840	13434	10563	4072	52	1406	0	0	744	14012	5
10	57559	6615	5237	2832	13312	10297	3731	51	1406	0	0	702	13376	10
15	55894	6345	4513	2826	13212	10184	3672	50	1403	0	0	676	13013	15
20	53998	5513	4025	2822	13137	10062	3651	49	1346	0	0	644	12749	20
25	51762	4804	3726	2786	13059	9818	3555	49	1023	0	0	612	12330	25
30	49284	3972	3462	2735	12955	9549	3452	48	664	0	0	568	11879	30
35	46904	3219	3195	2668	12818	9270	3365	46	364	0	0	532	11427	35
40	44262	2499	2905	2565	12604	8913	3242	43	108	0	0	495	10888	40
45	41970	1939	2647	2428	12324	8576	3123	40	16	0	0	467	10410	45
50	39139	1352	2322	2202	11846	8170	2974	36	2	0	0	434	9801	50
55	36264	892	2033	1891	11214	7780	2822	31	1	0	0	406	9194	55
60	31749	342	1657	1295	10023	7213	2533	21	1	0	0	371	8293	60
65	27060	247	1221	1075	8729	6143	2265	19	1	0	0	280	7070	65
70	19417	130	689	689	6333	4455	1766	12	1	0	0	198	5144	70
75	12649	61	375	372	4046	2933	1293	8	1	0	0	117	3443	75
80	5936	19	138	124	1729	1372	737	4	1	0	0	50	1762	80
85+	2761	3	54	42	741	651	347	2	0	0	0	22	899	85+

NUMBER OF PERSONS SURVIVING TO AGE X IF SPECIFIED CAUSES WERE ELIMINATED

Age (x)	No Causes	Respiratory T.B. (1)	Other Infec. and Paras. (2)	Neoplasms (3)	Cardiovascular (4)	Infl., Pneu., Bronch. (5)	Diarrheal (6)	Certain Degenerative (7)	Maternal (8)	Cert. Dis. of Infancy (9)	Motor Vehicle (10)	Other Violence (11)	Other and Unknown (12)	(1)+(2)	(1)+(2)+(5)+(6)+(8)	(1)+(2)+(5)+(6)+(8)+part of(9)&(12)	(10)+(11)	Age (x)
0	100000	100000	100000	100000	100000	100000	100000	100000	100000	100000	100000	100000	100000	100000	100000	100000	100000	0
1	78020	78098	81296	78026	78283	80470	81332	78021	78020	83550	78020	78320	82664	81376	87495	98526	78320	1
5	61213	61637	71045	61227	61565	65093	66263	61215	61213	65552	61213	61631	68533	71537	82347	97827	61631	5
10	57559	58231	69044	57580	58009	61483	62667	57561	57559	61639	57559	57993	65136	69851	81233	97483	57993	10
15	55894	56818	67907	55920	56430	59823	60917	55897	55897	59856	55894	56342	63658	69029	80525	97191	56342	15
20	53998	55728	66188	54027	54591	57922	58873	54002	54057	57825	53998	54462	61755	68309	79976	96961	54462	20
25	51762	54141	63806	51825	52407	55781	56538	51766	52137	55431	51762	52239	59708	66739	79126	96632	52239	25
30	49284	52406	61070	49394	50001	53394	53941	49289	49995	52777	49284	49781	57359	64938	78112	96165	49781	30
35	46904	50662	58444	47074	47723	51112	51429	46911	47878	50228	46904	47413	55105	63127	76992	95568	47413	35
40	44262	48569	55504	44523	45247	48612	48663	44271	45435	47399	44262	44778	52620	60905	75492	94631	44778	40
45	41970	46656	52946	42353	43184	46457	46271	41982	43174	44945	41970	42487	50451	58857	73886	93394	42487	45
50	39139	44143	49772	39717	40750	43759	43309	39154	40275	41913	39139	39654	47760	56135	71464	91241	39654	50
55	36264	41401	46471	37105	38396	40566	40290	36282	37318	38834	36264	36768	44970	53054	68522	88290	36768	55
60	31749	36835	41138	33059	34816	36472	35575	31774	32672	33999	31749	32224	40432	47728	63221	82534	32224	60
65	27060	31493	35574	28386	31014	32243	30599	27083	27846	28978	27060	27550	35928	41402	57405	76637	27550	65
70	19417	22712	26130	20712	24658	24894	22438	19440	19981	20793	19417	19838	28027	30564	46600	64852	19838	70
75	12649	14859	17358	13765	18601	17858	15063	12667	13017	13546	12649	12990	20333	20392	35282	51644	12990	75
80	5936	7005	8363	6640	11336	9995	7531	5947	6109	6357	5936	6142	11534	9870	21704	34790	6142	80
85+	2761	3271	3970	3150	6691	5531	3848	2768	2842	2957	2761	2876	6606	4703	13521	24171	2876	85+

ADDED YRS OF LIFE

	No Causes	(1)	(2)	(3)	(4)	(5)	(6)	(7)	(8)	(9)	(10)	(11)	(12)	(1)+(2)	(1)+(2)+(5)+(6)+(8)	+part of(9)&(12)	(10)+(11)
TOTAL		2.450	7.942	.441	2.054	3.845	3.427	.010	.481	2.374	.000	.376	6.895	11.080	23.098	39.155	.376
WORK	10.893	2.709	1.211	.377	.664	1.081	.376	.008	.715	.000	.000	.128	1.765	4.038	6.617	8.379	.128

POPULATION, DEATHS, DEATH RATES FOR ALL CAUSES COMBINED, AND SPECIFIED CAUSES

Age Start of Interval	Midyear Population	Deaths During Year	All Causes	Respiratory T. B.	Other Infec. and Paras.	Neo-plasms	Cardio-vascular	Infl., Pneu., Bronch.	Diar-rheal	Certain Degen-erative	Maternal	Cert. Dis. of Infancy	Motor Vehicle	Other Violence	Other and Unknown	Age Start of Interval
0	497909	112361	.22567	.00035	.02104	.00008	.00206	.00910	.04881	.00001	.00000	.06582	.00000	.00036	.07804	0
1	1620091	83432	.05150	.00034	.01593	.00004	.00044	.00368	.01252	.00001	.00000	.00000	.00000	.00036	.01778	1
5	1813000	15049	.00830	.00017	.00373	.00002	.00024	.00055	.00063	.00000	.00000	.00000	.00000	.00076	.01778	5
10	1550000	7015	.00453	.00035	.00186	.00002	.00024	.00026	.00023	.00001	.00000	.00000	.00000	.00025	.00271	10
15	1474000	5823	.00395	.00066	.00107	.00003	.00031	.00049	.00014	.00001	.00000	.00000	.00000	.00021	.00134	15
20	1302000	7504	.00576	.00125	.00147	.00004	.00026	.00093	.00017	.00002	.00000	.00000	.00000	.00044	.00081	20
25	1179000	7912	.00671	.00155	.00148	.00006	.00035	.00104	.00019	.00002	.00000	.00000	.00000	.00046	.00117	25
30	1088000	8395	.00772	.00171	.00150	.00010	.00055	.00128	.00019	.00003	.00000	.00000	.00000	.00062	.00139	30
35	904000	8362	.00925	.00173	.00153	.00016	.00050	.00173	.00028	.00005	.00000	.00000	.00000	.00061	.00174	35
40	854000	8042	.00942	.00128	.00146	.00029	.00108	.00244	.00044	.00005	.00000	.00000	.00000	.00066	.00221	40
45	777000	9427	.01213	.00109	.00156	.00049	.00186	.00297	.00055	.00007	.00000	.00000	.00000	.00068	.00170	45
50	721000	12205	.01693	.00085	.00174	.00086	.00317	.00368	.00074	.00011	.00000	.00000	.00000	.00075	.00280	50
55	577000	13807	.02393	.00085	.00202	.00140	.00506	.00451	.00118	.00018	.00000	.00000	.00000	.00081	.00486	55
60	519000	20217	.03895	.00084	.00257	.00146	.01018	.00671	.00240	.00015	.00000	.00000	.00000	.00087	.00787	60
65	381000	21022	.05518	.00080	.00308	.00217	.01620	.00911	.00381	.00023	.00000	.00000	.00000	.00116	.01349	65
70	299000	24859	.08314	.00074	.00371	.00299	.02597	.01378	.00605	.00035	.00000	.00000	.00000	.00089	.01889	70
75	123000	15582	.12668	.00066	.00445	.00362	.04061	.02181	.01102	.00054	.00000	.00000	.00000	.00149	.02806	75
80	63239	13576	.21468	.00057	.00492	.00244	.05384	.02130	.01385	.00036	.00000	.00000	.00000	.00189	.04209	80
85+	19761	7906	.40008	.00040	.00683	.00258	.08112	.03856	.02475	.00051	.00000	.00000	.00000	.00217	.11523	85+
ALL	15762000	402496														

	All Causes	Respiratory T. B.	Other Infec. and Paras.	Neo-plasms	Cardio-vascular	Infl., Pneu., Bronch.	Diar-rheal	Certain Degen-erative	Maternal	Cert. Dis. of Infancy	Motor Vehicle	Other Violence	Other and Unknown
CRUDE DEATH RATE	.02554	.00087	.00404	.00037	.00266	.00276	.00358	.00005	.00000	.00208	.00000	.00060	.00853
STANDARDIZED RATE (1)	.02474	.00084	.00431	.00028	.00199	.00243	.00380	.00004	.00000	.00232	.00000	.00056	.00818
STANDARDIZED RATE (2)	.02736	.00091	.00355	.00050	.00413	.00338	.00313	.00007	.00000	.00136	.00000	.00067	.00966
GEOMETRIC MEAN	.02525												

LIFE TABLE FOR ALL CAUSES COMBINED

Age (x)	Midyear Population	Deaths During Year	$_nM_x$	$_nq_x$	l_x	$_nd_x$	$_nL_x$	$_nm_x$	$_na_x$	T_x	$_nr_x$	$\overset{\circ}{e}_x$	Age (x)
0	497909	112361	.225666	.200900	100000	20090	89023	.225671	.453632	3847807	.000000	38.478	0
1	1620091	83432	.051498	.182493	79910	14583	283183	.051497	1.500000	3758783	.000000	47.038	1
5	1813000	15049	.008301	.040749	65327	2662	319980	.008319	2.500000	3475601	.000000	53.203	5
10	1550000	7015	.004526	.022293	62665	1397	309528	.004513	2.281824	3155621	.012420	50.357	10
15	1474000	5823	.003950	.019570	61268	1199	303408	.003952	2.554386	2846093	.011931	46.453	15
20	1302000	7504	.005763	.028467	60069	1710	296222	.005773	2.588816	2542685	.016591	42.329	20
25	1179000	7912	.006711	.033037	58359	1928	287064	.006716	2.546356	2246463	.011174	38.494	25
30	1088000	8395	.007716	.037905	56431	2139	276918	.007724	2.551523	1959399	.017178	34.722	30
35	904000	8362	.009250	.045255	54292	2457	265369	.009259	2.520944	1682481	.017427	30.989	35
40	854000	8042	.009417	.046031	51835	2386	253306	.009419	2.540078	1417112	.008546	27.339	40
45	777000	9427	.012133	.058970	49449	2916	240248	.012137	2.600380	1163807	.003781	23.535	45
50	721000	12205	.016928	.081469	46533	3791	223590	.016955	2.606063	923559	.011346	19.847	50
55	577000	13807	.023929	.113378	42742	4846	202212	.023965	2.627339	699969	.008632	16.377	55
60	519000	20217	.038954	.178198	37896	6753	173162	.038998	2.583667	497757	.006111	13.135	60
65	381000	21022	.055176	.242687	31143	7558	137110	.055124	2.538315	324595	-.005639	10.423	65
70	299000	24859	.083140	.345262	23585	8143	97535	.083488	2.496009	187485	.021232	7.949	70
75	123000	15582	.126683	.479342	15442	7402	58154	.127283	2.425555	89950	.021538	5.825	75
80	63239	13576	.214678	.683831	8040	5498	25442	.216055	2.315842	31796	.021538	3.955	80
85+	19761	7906	.400081	1.000000	2542	2542	6354	.400081	2.499494	6354	.000000	2.499	85+

NUMBER OF PERSONS DYING (OUT OF 100,000 AT BIRTH) ABOVE AGE X FROM SPECIFIED CAUSES

Age (x)	All Causes	Respiratory T. B.	Other Infec. and Paras.	Neo-plasms	Cardio-vascular	Infl., Pneu., Bronch.	Diar-rheal	Certain Degen-erative	Maternal	Cert. Dis. of Infancy	Motor Vehicle	Other Violence	Other and Unknown	Age (x)
0	100000	3597	13363	1937	14373	12542	11775	266	0	5860	0	2552	33735	0
1	79910	3565	11490	1930	14190	11733	7430	265	0	0	0	2520	26787	1
5	65327	3469	6978	1919	14065	10691	3884	264	0	0	0	2305	21752	5
10	62665	3413	5783	1914	13989	10514	3681	264	0	0	0	2225	20882	10
15	61268	3303	5210	1908	13914	10434	3610	262	0	0	0	2159	20468	15
20	60069	3101	4886	1900	13819	10286	3568	260	0	0	0	2027	20222	20
25	58359	2729	4451	1887	13743	10010	3516	255	0	0	0	1891	19877	25
30	56431	2284	4027	1868	13642	9710	3462	249	0	0	0	1712	19477	30
35	54292	1810	3611	1841	13489	9355	3409	240	0	0	0	1542	18995	35
40	51835	1351	3205	1799	13250	8895	3334	227	0	0	0	1366	18408	40
45	49449	1028	2834	1725	12977	8275	3222	215	0	0	0	1195	17978	45
50	46533	766	2460	1608	12529	7562	3089	198	0	0	0	1016	17305	50
55	42742	555	2070	1415	11818	6739	2924	173	0	0	0	834	16214	55
60	37896	384	1662	1132	10793	5825	2665	137	0	0	0	657	14621	60
65	31143	238	1218	880	9027	4662	2270	111	0	0	0	457	12280	65
70	23585	129	795	583	6808	3414	1748	79	0	0	0	335	9694	70
75	15442	58	433	290	4264	2064	1155	44	0	0	0	189	6945	75
80	8040	19	174	80	1892	791	511	13	0	0	0	79	4481	80
85+	2542	3	43	16	515	245	157	3	0	0	0	23	1537	85+

NUMBER OF PERSONS SURVIVING TO AGE X IF SPECIFIED CAUSES WERE ELIMINATED

Age (x)	No Causes	Respiratory T. B. (1)	Other Infec. and Paras. (2)	Neo-plasms (3)	Cardio-vascular (4)	Infl., Pneu., Bronch. (5)	Diar-rheal (6)	Certain Degen-erative (7)	Maternal (8)	Cert. Dis. of Infancy (9)	Motor Vehicle (10)	Other Violence (11)	Other and Unknown (12)	(1) + (2)	(1) + (2) + (5) + (6) + (8)	(1)+(2)+ (5)+(6)+ (8)+part of(9)&(12)	(10) + (11)	Age (x)
0	100000	100000	100000	100000	100000	100000	100000	100000	100000	100000	100000	100000	100000	100000	100000	100000	100000	0
1	79910	79939	81598	79916	80073	80635	83882	79911	79910	85212	79910	79939	86355	81628	86462	99316	79939	1
5	65327	65437	70998	65342	65574	66876	72017	65329	65327	69743	65327	65545	75682	71118	80260	98581	65545	5
10	62665	62825	69389	62684	62976	64328	69302	62667	62665	66901	62665	62952	73592	69567	78977	98213	62952	10
15	61268	61534	68473	61293	61647	62975	67835	61272	61268	65410	61268	61615	72433	68770	78263	97878	61615	15
20	60069	60531	67492	60101	60535	61894	66553	60074	60069	64130	60069	60541	71304	68011	77642	97398	60541	20
25	58359	59179	66054	58403	58888	60413	64716	58369	58359	62304	58359	58952	69679	66982	76892	96925	58952	25
30	56431	57669	64345	56492	57043	58723	62636	56447	56431	60246	56431	57183	67849	65757	75953	96277	57183	30
35	54292	55960	62373	54378	55032	56861	60320	54316	54292	57562	54292	55184	65848	64290	74807	95474	55184	35
40	51835	53892	60007	51958	52779	54761	57672	51871	51835	55339	51835	52862	63567	62388	73332	94369	52862	40
45	49449	51739	57666	49639	50622	52884	55139	49495	49449	52792	49449	50599	61158	60337	71954	93171	50599	45
50	46533	48954	54690	46826	48085	50510	52031	46593	46533	49679	46533	47793	58366	57536	69833	91267	47793	50
55	42742	45179	50675	43198	44878	47258	47970	42821	42742	45632	42742	44079	54940	53563	66467	88127	44079	55
60	37896	40226	45386	38570	40817	42861	42785	38000	37896	40458	37896	39253	50678	48176	61517	83300	39253	60
65	31143	33197	37781	31929	35314	36433	35588	31252	31143	33248	31143	32445	44579	40273	53838	75379	32445	65
70	23585	25241	29059	24446	29022	28886	27414	23695	23585	25179	23585	24681	37127	31099	44365	64914	24681	70
75	15442	16586	19384	16250	21692	20288	18553	15542	15442	16486	15442	16282	28041	20821	32867	51208	16282	75
80	8040	8665	10322	8616	13916	11812	10225	8114	8040	8584	8040	8559	18175	11124	20788	35729	8559	80
85+	2542	2749	3354	2761	5870	4187	3482	2571	2542	2714	2542	2738	10646	3627	8184	18111	2738	85+

ADDED YRS OF LIFE																		
TOTAL		1.100	5.535	.265	1.907	2.751	4.425	.041	.000	2.571	.000	.685	10.364	6.838	16.125	33.261	.685	
WORK	8.845	1.197	1.374	.176	.822	1.429	.273	.033	.000	.000	.000	.554	1.806	2.629	4.531	6.030	.554	

POPULATION, DEATHS, DEATH RATES FOR ALL CAUSES COMBINED, AND SPECIFIED CAUSES

Age Start of Interval	Midyear Population	Deaths During Year	All Causes	Respiratory T. B.	Other Infec. and Paras.	Neoplasms	Cardiovascular	Infl., Pneu., Bronch.	Diarrheal	Certain Degenerative	Maternal	Cert. Dis. of Infancy	Motor Vehicle	Other Violence	Other and Unknown	Age Start of Interval
0	480229	95942	.19978	.00029	.01919	.00008	.00175	.00694	.04485	.00001	.00000	.05858	.00000	.00037	.06772	0
1	1566771	82335	.05255	.00034	.01580	.00004	.00041	.00349	.01352	.00000	.00000	.00000	.00000	.00073	.01822	1
5	1732000	16096	.00929	.00030	.00433	.00003	.00024	.00059	.00078	.00000	.00000	.00000	.00000	.00023	.00280	5
10	1471000	8348	.00568	.00088	.00242	.00002	.00028	.00025	.00027	.00000	.00000	.00000	.00000	.00006	.00149	10
15	1415000	7334	.00518	.00134	.00150	.00003	.00038	.00050	.00018	.00001	.00008	.00000	.00000	.00014	.00103	15
20	1251000	8814	.00705	.00172	.00170	.00009	.00036	.00060	.00021	.00001	.00069	.00000	.00000	.00009	.00158	20
25	1251000	9710	.00776	.00191	.00158	.00013	.00048	.00067	.00023	.00002	.00078	.00000	.00000	.00012	.00185	25
30	1118000	9527	.00852	.00196	.00147	.00020	.00076	.00083	.00023	.00003	.00077	.00000	.00000	.00012	.00215	30
35	1000000	9646	.00965	.00187	.00139	.00032	.00124	.00111	.00035	.00004	.00070	.00000	.00000	.00013	.00249	35
40	907000	7319	.00807	.00130	.00120	.00048	.00113	.00137	.00043	.00002	.00054	.00000	.00000	.00014	.00145	40
45	833000	8174	.00981	.00103	.00121	.00008	.00195	.00166	.00054	.00004	.00054	.00000	.00000	.00016	.00233	45
50	767000	10879	.01418	.00083	.00133	.00142	.00332	.00207	.00072	.00006	.00001	.00000	.00000	.00017	.00425	50
55	627000	13179	.02102	.00067	.00156	.00231	.00530	.00253	.00116	.00009	.00000	.00000	.00000	.00019	.00722	55
60	576000	22504	.03907	.00064	.00178	.00176	.01161	.00605	.00248	.00007	.00000	.00000	.00000	.00053	.01416	60
65	380000	21540	.05668	.00059	.00252	.00262	.01848	.00822	.00394	.00010	.00000	.00000	.00000	.00040	.01982	65
70	284000	24567	.08650	.00055	.00376	.00361	.02962	.01243	.00626	.00015	.00000	.00000	.00000	.00068	.02945	70
75	107000	14238	.13307	.00051	.00551	.00436	.04632	.01968	.01141	.00022	.00000	.00000	.00000	.00086	.04418	75
80	44095	13915	.31557	.00057	.00730	.00465	.07785	.02969	.02365	.00014	.00000	.00000	.00000	.00279	.16893	80
85+	14905	8764	.58799	.00040	.01006	.00490	.11721	.05381	.04227	.00020	.00000	.00000	.00000	.00463	.35451	85+
ALL	15825000	392831														

	All Causes	Respiratory T. B.	Other Infec. and Paras.	Neoplasms	Cardiovascular	Infl., Pneu., Bronch.	Diarrheal	Certain Degenerative	Maternal	Cert. Dis. of Infancy	Motor Vehicle	Other Violence	Other and Unknown
CRUDE DEATH RATE	.02482	.00107	.00355	.00053	.00296	.00219	.00351	.00003	.00026	.00178	.00000	.00025	.00830
STANDARDIZED RATE (1)	.02480	.00105	.00437	.00040	.00229	.00197	.00387	.00002	.00025	.00206	.00000	.00025	.00826
STANDARDIZED RATE (2)	.02906	.00107	.00359	.00072	.00495	.00290	.00335	.00003	.00026	.00121	.00000	.00029	.01068
GEOMETRIC MEAN	.02694												

LIFE TABLE FOR ALL CAUSES COMBINED

Age (x)	Midyear Population	Deaths During Year	$_nM_x$	$_nq_x$	l_x	$_nd_x$	$_nL_x$	$_nm_x$	$_na_x$	T_x	$_nr_x$	$\overset{\circ}{e}_x$	Age (x)
0	480229	95942	.199784	.178710	100000	17871	89450	.199789	.409633	3875889	.000000	38.759	0
1	1566771	82335	.052551	.185793	82129	15259	290369	.052550	1.500000	3786440	.000000	46.104	1
5	1732000	16096	.009293	.045491	66870	3042	326745	.009310	2.500000	3496071	.000000	52.282	5
10	1471000	8348	.005675	.027887	63828	1780	314387	.005662	2.329939	3169326	.010942	49.654	10
15	1415000	7334	.005183	.025609	62048	1589	306333	.005187	2.541300	2854939	.011372	46.012	15
20	1251000	8814	.007046	.034652	60459	2095	297190	.007049	2.563047	2548606	.007751	42.154	20
25	1251000	9710	.007762	.038089	58364	2223	286314	.007764	2.523242	2251416	.002546	38.575	25
30	1118000	9527	.008521	.041734	56141	2343	274912	.008523	2.527564	1965102	.011420	35.003	30
35	1000000	9646	.009646	.047084	53798	2533	262592	.009646	2.474010	1690190	.011998	31.417	35
40	907000	7319	.008069	.039540	51265	2027	251222	.008069	2.482425	1427598	.011010	27.847	40
45	833000	8174	.009813	.047971	49238	2362	240534	.009820	2.605490	1176377	.005826	23.892	45
50	767000	10879	.014184	.068756	46876	3223	226743	.014214	2.630443	935842	.013892	19.964	50
55	627000	13179	.021019	.100337	43653	4380	208109	.021047	2.681174	709100	.006011	16.244	55
60	576000	22504	.039069	.179054	39273	7032	179545	.039166	2.608077	500991	.011306	12.757	60
65	380000	21540	.056684	.249000	32241	8028	141473	.056746	2.542066	321446	.006989	9.970	65
70	284000	24567	.086504	.357370	24213	8653	99378	.087071	2.493740	179973	.032122	7.433	70
75	107000	14238	.133065	.499229	15560	7768	57978	.133982	2.448238	80595	.032165	5.180	75
80	44095	13915	.315569	.862808	7792	6723	20799	.323237	2.258670	22617	.032165	2.903	80
85+	14905	8764	.587991	1.000000	1069	1069	1818	.587991	1.700707	1818	.000000	1.701	85+

NUMBER OF PERSONS DYING (OUT OF 100,000 AT BIRTH) ABOVE AGE X FROM SPECIFIED CAUSES

Age (x)	All Causes	Respiratory T. B.	Other Infec. and Paras.	Neo-plasms	Cardio-vascular	Infl., Pneu., Bronch.	Diar-rheal	Certain Degen-erative	Maternal	Cert. Dis. of Infancy	Motor Vehicle	Other Violence	Other and Unknown	Age (x)
0	100000	4199	13439	2772	16195	10067	12140	135	1006	5240	0	997	33810	0
1	82129	4173	11722	2765	16038	9447	8128	134	1006	0	0	964	27752	1
5	66870	4073	7135	2754	15920	8434	4202	133	1006	0	0	751	22462	5
10	63828	3976	5718	2745	15841	8241	3947	133	1006	0	0	676	21545	10
15	62048	3700	4960	2739	15753	8162	3861	131	1005	0	0	657	21080	15
20	60459	3287	4501	2730	15637	8009	3807	129	980	0	0	615	20764	20
25	58364	2777	3995	2704	15532	7830	3744	125	775	0	0	589	20293	25
30	56141	2229	3543	2667	15394	7638	3678	121	553	0	0	556	19762	30
35	53798	1689	3139	2612	15183	7411	3614	113	341	0	0	524	19172	35
40	51265	1197	2774	2529	14857	7119	3522	103	158	0	0	490	18517	40
45	49238	872	2473	2407	14573	6773	3413	97	22	0	0	454	18154	45
50	46876	624	2181	2214	14104	6373	3282	88	1	0	0	416	17593	50
55	43653	437	1878	1891	13348	5903	3118	75	0	0	0	377	16626	55
60	39273	297	1553	1411	12244	5375	2877	57	0	0	0	338	15121	60
65	32241	183	1233	1095	10153	4285	2430	45	0	0	0	243	12574	65
70	24213	100	875	724	7535	3122	1873	31	0	0	0	186	9767	70
75	15560	46	499	364	4571	1879	1246	16	0	0	0	118	6821	75
80	7792	16	178	110	1870	731	579	3	0	0	0	68	4237	80
85+	1069	1	18	9	213	98	77	0	0	0	0	8	645	85+

NUMBER OF PERSONS SURVIVING TO AGE X IF SPECIFIED CAUSES WERE ELIMINATED

Age (x)	No Causes	Respiratory T. B.	Other Infec. and Paras.	Neo-plasms	Cardio-vascular	Infl., Pneu., Bronch.	Diar-rheal	Certain Degener-ative	Maternal	Cert. Dis. of Infancy	Motor Vehicle	Other Violence	Other and Unknown	(1) + (2)	(1) + (2) + (5) + (6) + (8)	(1)+(2)+ (5)+(6)+ (8)+part of(9)&(12)	(10) + (11)	Age (x)
		(1)	(2)	(3)	(4)	(5)	(6)	(7)	(8)	(9)	(10)	(11)	(12)					
0	100000	100000	100000	100000	100000	100000	100000	100000	100000	100000	100000	100000	100000	100000	100000	100000	100000	0
1	82129	82153	83697	82135	82271	82692	85840	82130	82129	87010	82129	82159	87797	83721	88104	99409	82159	1
5	66870	66979	72490	66885	67092	68253	73687	66872	66870	70844	66870	67087	76765	72609	81667	98708	67087	5
10	63828	64027	70710	63851	64118	65341	70611	63830	63828	67621	63828	64108	74309	70930	80328	98356	64108	10
15	62048	62515	69571	62076	62417	63599	68735	62051	62049	65735	62048	62339	72772	70095	79591	98113	62339	15
20	60459	61327	68299	60496	60934	62125	67034	60464	60485	64052	60459	60784	71275	69279	78963	97776	60784	20
25	58364	59712	66496	58425	58926	60153	64780	58373	58591	61832	58364	58704	69353	68031	78127	97435	58704	25
30	56141	57990	64470	56236	56819	58057	62384	56154	56578	59477	56141	56500	67333	66593	77120	96961	56500	30
35	53798	56118	62235	53943	54657	55864	59850	53818	54426	56695	53798	54174	65219	64919	75872	96242	54174	35
40	51265	53979	59718	51485	52408	53532	57133	51294	52045	54311	51265	51657	62928	62879	74288	95128	51657	40
45	49238	52181	57701	49569	50622	51770	54993	49272	50122	52164	49238	49650	60878	61150	73098	94099	49650	45
50	46876	49934	55268	47382	48667	49698	52498	46917	47738	49662	46876	47305	58693	58873	71189	92293	47305	50
55	43653	46693	51813	44440	46084	46764	49066	43704	44457	46247	43653	44091	55788	55421	67961	89052	44091	55
60	39273	42149	46980	40446	42582	42612	44400	39335	39996	41607	39273	39704	52049	50421	62989	83835	39704	60
65	32241	34712	38915	33497	37013	36069	36911	32303	32835	34154	32241	32682	45854	41967	54649	75054	32682	65
70	24213	26145	29600	25491	30570	28233	28277	24272	24659	25652	24213	24594	38092	31962	44327	63448	24594	70
75	15560	16847	19390	16684	22860	19333	18764	15610	15847	16485	15560	15860	28450	20994	32037	48723	15860	75
80	7792	8458	9988	8542	14539	10715	9972	7826	7936	8255	7792	7977	17953	10843	19437	32565	7977	80
85+	1069	1166	1437	1207	3254	1772	1587	1075	1089	1133	1069	1114	7118	1566	3927	10257	1114	85+

ADDED YRS OF LIFE																	
TOTAL		1.414	5.658	.399	2.060	2.076	4.479	.024	.343	2.279	.000	.283	9.883	7.330	16.291	32.263	.283
WORK 9.169		1.499	1.417	.303	.569	.905	.304	.022	.457	.000	.000	.120	1.991	2.985	4.868	6.575	.120

POPULATION, DEATHS, DEATH RATES FOR ALL CAUSES COMBINED, AND SPECIFIED CAUSES

Age Start of Interval	Midyear Population	Deaths During Year	All Causes	Respiratory T. B.	Other Infec. and Paras.	Neoplasms	Cardiovascular	Infl., Pneu., Bronch.	Diarrheal	Certain Degenerative	Maternal	Cert. Dis. of Infancy	Motor Vehicle	Other Violence	Other and Unknown	Age Start of Interval
0	482653	94657	.19612	.00049	.01130	.00010	.00085	.03846	.05109	.00001	.00000	.05565	.00000	.00036	.03781	0
1	1622297	58384	.03599	.00043	.00666	.00009	.00026	.00866	.01047	.00000	.00000	.00000	.00000	.00079	.00863	1
5	1817815	10397	.00572	.00022	.00189	.00003	.00019	.00081	.00065	.00000	.00000	.00000	.00000	.00026	.00167	5
10	1718585	5833	.00339	.00028	.00106	.00002	.00020	.00039	.00026	.00001	.00000	.00000	.00000	.00026	.00093	10
15	1449651	6562	.00453	.00109	.00091	.00003	.00030	.00062	.00014	.00001	.00000	.00000	.00000	.00046	.00095	15
20	1358754	7489	.00551	.00169	.00088	.00005	.00025	.00058	.00017	.00001	.00000	.00000	.00000	.00045	.00103	20
25	1074928	6731	.00626	.00201	.00079	.00008	.00034	.00110	.00018	.00001	.00000	.00000	.00000	.00061	.00113	25
30	997946	7255	.00727	.00216	.00095	.00012	.00054	.00135	.00018	.00002	.00000	.00000	.00000	.00060	.00135	30
35	955289	8401	.00879	.00218	.00109	.00019	.00088	.00182	.00027	.00003	.00000	.00000	.00000	.00065	.00169	35
40	897358	8416	.00938	.00124	.00071	.00033	.00101	.00265	.00040	.00004	.00000	.00000	.00000	.00062	.00237	40
45	813142	9773	.01202	.00131	.00090	.00054	.00175	.00322	.00051	.00005	.00000	.00000	.00000	.00069	.00305	45
50	763773	12017	.01573	.00132	.00104	.00097	.00298	.00400	.00068	.00009	.00000	.00000	.00000	.00075	.00392	50
55	667841	13778	.02063	.00134	.00114	.00157	.00475	.00490	.00108	.00013	.00000	.00000	.00000	.00080	.00493	55
60	563728	21274	.03774	.00086	.00138	.00183	.01043	.00803	.00200	.00012	.00000	.00000	.00000	.00106	.01203	60
65	418431	22236	.05314	.00091	.00152	.00272	.01660	.01090	.00317	.00018	.00000	.00000	.00000	.00082	.01632	65
70	301306	24127	.08007	.00092	.00147	.00374	.02660	.01649	.00504	.00028	.00000	.00000	.00000	.00138	.02415	70
75	176530	21712	.12299	.00085	.00172	.00453	.04160	.02611	.00918	.00042	.00000	.00000	.00000	.00173	.03686	75
80	75464	15434	.20452	.00029	.00186	.00294	.05358	.03155	.01075	.00017	.00000	.00000	.00000	.00219	.10120	80
85+	23582	8941	.37915	.00021	.00254	.00310	.08070	.05720	.01921	.00025	.00000	.00000	.00000	.00356	.21237	85+
ALL	16179073	363417														

			All Causes	Respiratory T.B.	Other Infec. and Paras.	Neoplasms	Cardiovascular	Infl., Pneu., Bronch.	Diarrheal	Certain Degenerative	Maternal	Cert. Dis. of Infancy	Motor Vehicle	Other Violence	Other and Unknown
CRUDE DEATH RATE			.02246	.00108	.00159	.00047	.00284	.00463	.00329	.00004	.00000	.00166	.00000	.00060	.00586
STANDARDIZED RATE (1)			.02104	.00106	.00214	.00034	.00191	.00434	.00358	.00003	.00000	.00196	.00000	.00056	.00514
STANDARDIZED RATE (2)			.02444	.00114	.00178	.00061	.00410	.00455	.00285	.00005	.00000	.00115	.00000	.00065	.00715
GEOMETRIC MEAN			.02305												

LIFE TABLE FOR ALL CAUSES COMBINED

Age (x)	Midyear Population	Deaths During Year	$_nM_x$	$_nq_x$	l_x	$_nd_x$	$_nL_x$	$_nm_x$	$_na_x$	T_x	$_nr_x$	$\overset{\circ}{e}_x$	Age (x)
0	482653	94657	.196118	.175580	100000	17558	89525	.196124	.403401	4302729	.000000	43.027	0
1	1622297	58384	.035988	.132069	82442	10888	302548	.035988	1.500000	4213204	.000000	51.105	1
5	1817815	10397	.005720	.028216	71554	2019	352723	.005724	2.500000	3910656	.000000	54.653	5
10	1718585	5833	.003394	.016797	69535	1168	344654	.003389	2.413492	3557934	.014164	51.168	10
15	1449651	6562	.004527	.022438	68367	1534	338136	.004537	2.588548	3213280	.017170	47.000	15
20	1358754	7489	.005512	.027232	66833	1820	329714	.005520	2.554144	2875144	.021945	43.020	20
25	1074928	6731	.006262	.030871	65013	2007	320137	.006269	2.544843	2545431	.027390	39.153	25
30	997946	7255	.007270	.035743	63006	2252	309527	.007276	2.556246	2225293	.010357	35.319	30
35	955289	8401	.008794	.043042	60754	2615	297319	.008795	2.532983	1915766	.003161	31.533	35
40	897358	8416	.009379	.045656	58139	2666	284160	.009382	2.548918	1618448	.005963	27.838	40
45	813142	9773	.012019	.058425	55473	3241	269532	.012025	2.583179	1334287	.004530	24.053	45
50	763773	12017	.015734	.075816	52232	3960	251575	.015741	2.579651	1064755	.003595	20.385	50
55	667841	13778	.020631	.098504	48272	4755	230219	.020654	2.656940	813180	.005862	16.846	55
60	563728	21274	.037738	.173312	43517	7542	199503	.037804	2.602454	582961	.009191	13.396	60
65	418431	22236	.053141	.235214	35975	8464	159057	.053214	2.540441	383458	.008534	10.659	65
70	301306	24127	.080075	.353866	27511	9185	114616	.080137	2.502586	224401	.003852	8.157	70
75	176530	21712	.122993	.468078	18326	8578	69616	.123218	2.433697	109785	.008419	5.991	75
80	75464	15434	.204521	.662187	9748	6455	31483	.205030	2.326588	40168	.008419	4.121	80
85+	23582	8941	.379145	1.000000	3293	3293	8685	.379145	2.637513	8685	.000000	2.638	85+

NUMBER OF PERSONS DYING (OUT OF 100,000 AT BIRTH) ABOVE AGE X FROM SPECIFIED CAUSES

Age (x)	All Causes	Respiratory T.B.	Other Infec. and Paras.	Neoplasms	Cardio-vascular	Infl., Pneu., Bronch.	Diarrheal	Certain Degenerative	Maternal	Cert. Dis. of Infancy	Motor Vehicle	Other Violence	Other and Unknown	Age (x)
0	100000	5081	7384	2703	16686	20627	11659	234	0	4983	0	2791	27852	0
1	82442	5037	6372	2694	16611	17184	7085	233	0	0	0	2759	24467	1
5	71554	4905	4358	2667	16533	14566	3917	232	0	0	0	2520	21856	5
10	69535	4827	3691	2657	16467	14281	3688	231	0	0	0	2427	21266	10
15	68367	4728	3328	2652	16398	14149	3600	229	0	0	0	2335	20948	15
20	66833	4356	3020	2640	16296	13940	3551	225	0	0	0	2180	20625	20
25	65013	3799	2729	2623	16213	13616	3496	221	0	0	0	2031	20285	25
30	63006	3154	2475	2599	16104	13263	3437	217	0	0	0	1835	19922	30
35	60754	2484	2181	2563	15936	12844	3381	210	0	0	0	1649	19506	35
40	58139	1837	1858	2507	15676	12303	3300	200	0	0	0	1456	19002	40
45	55473	1486	1655	2414	15388	11548	3185	190	0	0	0	1279	18328	45
50	52232	1134	1413	2267	14917	10604	3048	175	0	0	0	1094	17504	50
55	48272	801	1151	2024	14166	9674	2878	154	0	0	0	906	16518	55
60	43517	494	889	1663	13072	8546	2630	123	0	0	0	721	15379	60
65	35975	321	614	1298	10986	6941	2230	98	0	0	0	509	12978	65
70	27511	176	372	865	8341	5205	1725	69	0	0	0	379	10379	70
75	18326	71	203	436	5289	3313	1146	37	0	0	0	221	7610	75
80	9748	12	84	120	2389	1493	506	8	0	0	0	101	5035	80
85+	3293	2	22	27	701	497	167	2	0	0	0	31	1844	85+

NUMBER OF PERSONS SURVIVING TO AGE X IF SPECIFIED CAUSES WERE ELIMINATED

Age (x)	No Causes	Respiratory T.B. (1)	Other Infec. and Paras. (2)	Neoplasms (3)	Cardio-vascular (4)	Infl., Pneu., Bronch. (5)	Diarrheal (6)	Certain Degenerative (7)	Maternal (8)	Cert. Dis. of Infancy (9)	Motor Vehicle (10)	Other Violence (11)	Other and Unknown (12)	(1)+(2)+(6)+(8)	(1)+(2)+(5)+(6)+(8)	(1)+(2)+(5)+(6)+(8)+part of(9)&(12)	(10)+(11)	Age (x)
0	100000	100000	100000	100000	100000	100000	100000	100000	100000	100000	100000	100000	100000	100000	100000	100000	100000	0
1	82442	82482	83365	82450	82510	85623	86655	82443	82442	87085	82442	82471	85569	83405	91092	99754	82471	1
5	71554	71712	74275	71586	71686	76890	78411	71556	71554	75584	71554	71802	76834	74439	87655	99167	71802	5
10	69535	69765	72866	69576	69728	75023	76446	69538	69535	73452	69535	69868	75293	73107	86716	98830	69868	10
15	68367	68692	72020	68412	68626	73904	75258	68372	68367	72218	68367	68786	74370	72362	86107	98500	68786	15
20	66833	67522	70725	66889	67187	72469	73623	66841	66833	70597	66833	67397	73050	71454	85351	97997	67397	20
25	65013	66240	69103	65085	65440	70843	71678	65025	65013	68675	65013	65710	71428	70408	84587	97536	65710	25
30	63006	64846	67236	63099	63528	69036	69529	63022	63006	66555	63006	63877	69616	69199	83672	96918	63877	30
35	60754	63208	65142	60879	61424	67021	67105	60776	60754	64176	60754	61779	67581	67773	82579	96158	61779	35
40	58139	61119	62677	58314	59038	64723	64304	58170	58139	61414	58139	59312	65223	65922	81170	95123	59312	40
45	55473	58706	60017	55731	56617	62582	61480	55512	55473	58597	55473	56769	62976	63515	79413	93858	56769	45
50	52232	55638	56765	52619	53779	59883	58035	52284	52232	55174	52232	53636	60211	60467	77026	91963	53636	50
55	48272	51761	52736	48866	50451	56462	53817	48340	48272	50991	48272	49755	56749	56548	73740	89073	49755	55
60	43517	46974	47812	44400	46562	52167	48779	43608	43517	45968	43517	45035	52448	51611	69351	84900	45035	60
65	35975	39001	39800	37043	40594	44906	40735	36073	35975	38001	35975	37429	46069	43148	60986	76849	37429	65
70	27511	29962	30669	28719	33762	36282	31654	27611	27511	29061	27511	28740	38252	33401	50683	66262	28740	70
75	18326	20050	20581	19495	25743	26278	21634	18419	18326	19358	18326	19279	28798	22517	38116	52511	19279	75
80	9748	10710	11042	10610	16942	15974	12063	9818	9748	10297	9748	10345	18544	12132	24605	36870	10345	80
85+	3293	3624	3769	3641	7601	6380	4314	3320	3293	3478	3293	3536	10712	4148	10530	19885	3536	85+

ADDED YRS OF LIFE

	No Causes	(1)	(2)	(3)	(4)	(5)	(6)	(7)	(8)	(9)	(10)	(11)	(12)	C14	C15	C16	C17
TOTAL		1.604	3.010	.374	2.136	5.778	4.667	.037	.000	2.401	.000	.779	6.986	4.760	17.536	29.664	.779
WORK	8.608	1.591	.871	.205	.800	1.580	.261	.026	.000	.000	.000	.547	1.636	2.509	4.549	5.915	.547

POPULATION, DEATHS, DEATH RATES FOR ALL CAUSES COMBINED, AND SPECIFIED CAUSES

Age Start of Interval	Midyear Population	Deaths During Year	All Causes	Respiratory T. B.	Other Infec. and Paras.	Neoplasms	Cardio-vascular	Infl., Pneu., Bronch.	Diarrheal	Certain Degenerative	Maternal	Cert. Dis. of Infancy	Motor Vehicle	Other Violence	Other and Unknown	Age Start of Interval
0	462984	81367	.17574	.00047	.01072	.00005	.00064	.03155	.04777	.00000	.00000	.05096	.00000	.00030	.03324	0
1	1559010	57939	.03716	.00045	.00640	.00008	.00021	.00891	.01135	.00000	.00000	.00000	.00000	.00075	.00901	1
5	1755958	11100	.00632	.00035	.00204	.00002	.00021	.00095	.00074	.00000	.00000	.00000	.00000	.00026	.00175	5
10	1678700	7592	.00452	.00102	.00130	.00001	.00024	.00054	.00025	.00001	.00000	.00000	.00000	.00014	.00102	10
15	1481164	6501	.00439	.00157	.00092	.00003	.00029	.00044	.00019	.00001	.00005	.00000	.00000	.00008	.00082	15
20	1388385	8488	.00611	.00197	.00091	.00005	.00034	.00074	.00023	.00001	.00046	.00000	.00000	.00010	.00127	20
25	1137880	7848	.00690	.00234	.00082	.00013	.00046	.00083	.00025	.00001	.00052	.00000	.00000	.00014	.00139	25
30	1058015	8489	.00802	.00252	.00098	.00020	.00073	.00102	.00025	.00002	.00052	.00000	.00000	.00013	.00165	30
35	986588	9501	.00963	.00254	.00113	.00032	.00119	.00137	.00038	.00002	.00047	.00000	.00000	.00014	.00207	35
40	929713	7259	.00781	.00113	.00059	.00052	.00112	.00163	.00039	.00002	.00041	.00000	.00000	.00015	.00184	40
45	829954	8171	.00985	.00119	.00075	.00087	.00194	.00158	.00049	.00003	.00007	.00000	.00000	.00017	.00237	45
50	800383	10637	.01329	.00121	.00086	.00153	.00330	.00246	.00066	.00025	.00000	.00000	.00000	.00018	.00303	50
55	677241	12240	.01807	.00122	.00095	.00249	.00526	.00301	.00105	.00008	.00000	.00000	.00000	.00020	.00382	55
60	591355	21681	.03666	.00066	.00112	.00192	.01134	.00795	.00191	.00006	.00000	.00000	.00000	.00055	.01115	60
65	426649	22312	.05230	.00069	.00123	.00226	.01804	.01080	.00303	.00009	.00000	.00000	.00000	.00042	.01513	65
70	307747	24354	.07914	.00069	.00120	.00395	.02890	.01633	.00481	.00014	.00000	.00000	.00000	.00072	.02239	70
75	172894	21084	.12195	.00064	.00139	.00478	.04521	.02587	.00877	.00021	.00000	.00000	.00000	.00090	.03417	75
80	78118	15395	.19707	.00050	.00192	.00356	.04951	.02994	.01013	.00008	.00000	.00000	.00000	.00175	.09968	80
85+	26406	9661	.36586	.00034	.00265	.00371	.07457	.05431	.01814	.00011	.00000	.00000	.00000	.00292	.20912	85+
ALL	16349184	351619														

CRUDE DEATH RATE			.02151	.00128	.00189	.00061	.00309	.00403	.00317	.00002	.00017	.00144	.00000	.00027	.00553
STANDARDIZED RATE (1)			.02044	.00128	.00211	.00043	.00206	.00383	.00358	.00002	.00017	.00179	.00000	.00026	.00491
STANDARDIZED RATE (2)			.02375	.00131	.00172	.00076	.00435	.00441	.00285	.00003	.00017	.00105	.00000	.00029	.00681
GEOMETRIC MEAN			.02287												

LIFE TABLE FOR ALL CAUSES COMBINED

Age (x)	Midyear Population	Deaths During Year	$_nM_x$	$_nq_x$	l_x	$_nd_x$	$_nL_x$	$_nm_x$	$_na_x$	T_x	$_nr_x$	$\overset{\circ}{e}_x$	Age (x)
0	462984	81367	.175745	.158200	100000	15820	90014	.175751	.368766	4365202	.000000	43.652	0
1	1559010	57939	.037164	.136018	84180	11450	308095	.037164	1.500000	4275188	.000000	50.786	1
5	1755958	11100	.006321	.031143	72730	2265	357588	.006327	2.500000	3967093	.000000	54.545	5
10	1678700	7592	.004523	.022223	70465	1573	348232	.004517	2.398284	3609505	.009117	51.218	10
15	1481164	6501	.004389	.021730	68892	1497	340814	.004392	2.564156	3260873	.012041	47.333	15
20	1388385	8488	.006114	.030180	67395	2034	332040	.006126	2.573951	2920059	.018038	43.328	20
25	1137880	7848	.006897	.033950	65361	2219	321352	.006905	2.542437	2588019	.022067	39.596	25
30	1058015	8489	.008024	.039372	63142	2486	309627	.008029	2.552963	2266667	.010386	35.898	30
35	986588	9501	.009630	.047003	60656	2851	296096	.009629	2.480051	1957040	.004580	32.265	35
40	929713	7259	.007808	.038284	57805	2213	283456	.007807	2.483431	1660945	.008399	28.734	40
45	829954	8171	.009845	.048118	55592	2675	271522	.009852	2.593224	1377489	.005479	24.779	45
50	800383	10637	.013290	.064441	52917	3410	256399	.013300	2.599462	1105967	.006290	20.900	50
55	677241	12240	.018073	.086917	49507	4303	237658	.018106	2.704702	849568	.008422	17.161	55
60	591355	21681	.036663	.168567	45204	7638	207845	.036749	2.620450	611910	.010031	13.537	60
65	426649	22312	.052296	.232098	37566	8719	166430	.052388	2.545590	404065	.011070	10.756	65
70	307747	24354	.079136	.330918	28847	9546	120424	.079270	2.505652	237635	.008972	8.238	70
75	172894	21084	.121948	.465157	19301	8978	73462	.122213	2.433402	117211	.010010	6.073	75
80	78118	15395	.197074	.646711	10323	6676	33780	.197629	2.328553	43749	.010010	4.238	80
85+	26406	9661	.365864	1.000000	3647	3647	9968	.365864	2.733257	9968	.000000	2.733	85+

NUMBER OF PERSONS DYING (OUT OF 100,000 AT BIRTH) ABOVE AGE X FROM SPECIFIED CAUSES

Age (x)	All Causes	Respiratory T.B.	Other Infec. and Paras.	Neoplasms	Cardiovascular	Infl., Pneu., Bronch.	Diarrheal	Certain Degenerative	Maternal	Cert. Dis. of Infancy	Motor Vehicle	Other Violence	Other and Unknown	Age (x)
0	100000	5780	7232	3519	18768	18733	11877	133	775	4587	0	1202	27394	0
1	84180	5737	6267	3511	18710	15893	7577	133	775	0	0	1175	24402	1
5	72730	5599	4296	3485	18644	13147	4080	133	775	0	0	943	21628	5
10	70465	5475	3565	3477	18570	12805	3816	132	775	0	0	848	21002	10
15	68892	5120	3114	3413	18486	12617	3730	130	775	0	0	772	20646	15
20	67395	4585	2801	3463	18387	12468	3666	127	758	0	0	739	20368	20
25	65361	3931	2498	3433	18273	12223	3589	125	604	0	0	739	19946	25
30	63142	3177	2234	3392	18125	11956	3508	122	435	0	0	695	19468	30
35	60656	2396	1929	3330	17900	11641	3429	117	274	0	0	654	18980	35
40	57805	1645	1595	3235	17548	11235	3317	110	135	0	0	611	18314	40
45	55592	1326	1428	3087	17231	10772	3205	105	18	0	0	568	17852	45
50	52917	1004	1225	2851	16704	10235	3070	96	1	0	0	522	17209	50
55	49507	694	1004	2457	15856	9605	2902	84	0	0	0	474	16431	55
60	45204	405	779	1865	14603	8887	2651	65	0	0	0	427	15522	60
65	37566	269	546	1465	12240	7230	2254	52	0	0	0	312	13198	65
70	28847	154	341	987	9231	5430	1750	37	0	0	0	241	10676	70
75	19301	71	197	511	5744	3459	1169	20	0	0	0	155	7975	75
80	10323	24	95	159	2417	1555	523	4	0	0	0	89	5457	80
85+	3647	3	26	37	743	541	181	1	0	0	0	29	2086	85+

NUMBER OF PERSONS SURVIVING TO AGE X IF SPECIFIED CAUSES WERE ELIMINATED

Age (x)	No Causes	Respiratory T.B.	Other Infec. and Paras.	Neoplasms	Cardiovascular	Infl., Pneu., Bronch.	Diarrheal	Certain Degenerative	Maternal	Cert. Dis. of Infancy	Motor Vehicle	Other Violence	Other and Unknown	(1)+(2)	(1)+(2)+(5)+(6)+(8)	(1)+(2)+(5)+(6)+(8)+part of(9)&(12)	(10)+(11)	Age (x)
		(1)	(2)	(3)	(4)	(5)	(6)	(7)	(8)	(9)	(10)	(11)	(12)					
0	100000	100000	100000	100000	100000	100000	100000	100000	100000	100000	100000	100000	100000	100000	100000	100000	100000	0
1	84180	84219	85069	84187	84233	86823	88214	84180	84180	88490	84180	84205	86967	85109	91988	99806	84205	1
5	72730	72892	75371	72760	72837	77690	79696	72730	72730	78454	72730	72967	77847	75540	88420	99262	72967	5
10	70465	70744	73774	70502	70642	75632	77499	70466	70465	74073	70465	70789	76085	74066	87432	98922	70789	10
15	68892	69519	72595	68933	69148	74143	75896	68895	68892	72419	68892	69255	74768	73255	86816	98671	69255	15
20	67395	68544	71344	67445	67744	72691	74284	67401	67412	70846	67395	67779	73442	72561	86284	98420	67779	20
25	65361	67134	69507	65439	65812	70758	72126	65369	65529	68708	65361	65766	71680	71393	85506	98086	65766	25
30	63142	65620	67424	63257	63725	68640	69765	63152	63471	66375	63142	63577	69731	70070	84600	97635	63577	30
35	60656	63837	65089	60828	61439	67104	60671	61131	63762	65158	60656	61114	67542	68503	83453	96975	61114	35
40	57805	61612	62381	58062	58901	63594	64071	57826	58395	60765	57805	58284	65036	66489	81903	95944	58284	40
45	55592	59587	60169	55595	56964	61661	61740	55617	56275	58438	55592	56095	63125	64493	80421	94813	56095	45
50	52917	57057	57489	53524	54753	59278	58915	52950	53584	55626	52917	53441	60804	61986	78282	92947	53441	50
55	49507	53704	54017	50462	52081	56144	55300	49549	50132	52622	49507	50044	57756	58596	75164	89932	50044	55
60	45204	49335	49556	46654	48831	52049	50762	45261	45774	47518	45204	45740	53762	54084	70813	85442	45740	60
65	37566	41132	41414	39146	42974	45027	42593	37625	38040	39489	37566	38117	47268	45346	62403	77254	38117	65
70	28847	31695	31999	30498	36154	36512	33211	28905	29211	30324	28847	29333	39175	35158	51879	66332	29333	70
75	19301	21280	21538	20817	28017	24772	19354	19544	20289	19301	19697	29365	23746	39015	52239	19697		75
80	10323	11418	11601	11406	18880	16204	12741	10363	10453	10852	10323	10583	18753	12831	25174	36306	10583	80
85+	3647	4047	4143	4107	8658	6705	4748	3663	3693	3834	3647	3774	11204	4597	11142	20221	3774	85+

ADDED YRS OF LIFE																		
TOTAL		1.995	3.029	.528	2.502	5.118	4.792	.022	.269	2.216	.000	.353	6.905	5.200	17.766	29.448	.353	
WORK	8.532	1.858	.864	.330	.957	1.058	.311	.016	.317	.000	.000	.124	1.625	2.775	4.709	6.111	.124	

POPULATION, DEATHS DEATH RATES FOR ALL CAUSES COMBINED, AND SPECIFIED CAUSES

Age Start of Interval	Midyear Population	Deaths During Year	All Causes	Respiratory T. B.	Other Infec. and Paras.	Neo-plasms	Cardio-vascular	Infl., Pneu., Bronch.	Diar-rheal	Certain Degen-erative	Maternal	Cert. Dis. of Infancy	Motor Vehicle	Other Violence	Other and Unknown	Age Start of Interval
0	490723	85989	.17523	.00067	.00777	.00022	.00083	.03446	.05279	.00000	.00000	.04378	.00000	.00033	.03437	0
1	1713496	54584	.03186	.00041	.00584	.00015	.00021	.00853	.00912	.00000	.00000	.00000	.00000	.00079	.00680	1
5	1917534	9306	.00485	.00017	.00145	.00005	.00018	.00073	.00062	.00000	.00000	.00000	.00000	.00025	.00141	5
10	1868016	4832	.00259	.00020	.00067	.00004	.00018	.00025	.00022	.00000	.00000	.00000	.00000	.00028	.00076	10
15	1565027	6547	.00418	.00106	.00077	.00004	.00032	.00049	.00022	.00001	.00000	.00000	.00000	.00044	.00084	15
20	1397673	8685	.00621	.00230	.00091	.00010	.00036	.00074	.00022	.00002	.00000	.00000	.00000	.00061	.00094	20
25	1134372	6842	.00603	.00227	.00070	.00011	.00037	.00077	.00024	.00002	.00000	.00000	.00000	.00057	.00095	25
30	1026185	6468	.00630	.00199	.00058	.00017	.00058	.00088	.00026	.00003	.00000	.00000	.00000	.00061	.00120	30
35	934489	6578	.00704	.00171	.00055	.00026	.00077	.00116	.00033	.00004	.00000	.00000	.00000	.00062	.00160	35
40	886665	7402	.00835	.00151	.00057	.00046	.00128	.00144	.00036	.00004	.00000	.00000	.00000	.00067	.00202	40
45	848557	9078	.01070	.00154	.00056	.00077	.00191	.00190	.00046	.00006	.00000	.00000	.00000	.00075	.00276	45
50	807584	11129	.01378	.00134	.00063	.00117	.00308	.00255	.00070	.00010	.00000	.00000	.00000	.00082	.00341	50
55	692426	13795	.01992	.00127	.00069	.00187	.00543	.00388	.00091	.00022	.00000	.00000	.00000	.00096	.00471	55
60	626088	18280	.02920	.00107	.00069	.00263	.00968	.00525	.00143	.00025	.00000	.00000	.00000	.00107	.00713	60
65	478164	21776	.04554	.00090	.00081	.00349	.01760	.00813	.00225	.00034	.00000	.00000	.00000	.00114	.01089	65
70	335171	25262	.07537	.00074	.00087	.00418	.03088	.01225	.00378	.00037	.00000	.00000	.00000	.00129	.02101	70
75	184257	23212	.12598	.00055	.00078	.00482	.04962	.01917	.00587	.00037	.00000	.00000	.00000	.00166	.04314	75
80	84542	16829	.19906	.00047	.00095	.00371	.06275	.02583	.00764	.00021	.00000	.00000	.00000	.00233	.09516	80
85+	30721	9647	.31402	.00029	.00094	.00374	.07041	.03392	.00567	.00013	.00000	.00000	.00000	.00221	.19270	85+
ALL	17021690	346241														

	All Causes	Respiratory T. B.	Other Infec.	Neo-plasms	Cardio-vascular	Infl., Pneu.	Diar-rheal	Certain Degen.	Maternal	Cert. Dis. Infancy	Motor Vehicle	Other Violence	Other Unknown
CRUDE DEATH RATE	.02034	.00111	.00150	.00062	.00321	.00374	.00304	.00006	.00000	.00126	.00000	.00063	.00516
STANDARDIZED RATE (1)	.01885	.00110	.00165	.00044	.00206	.00360	.00340	.00004	.00000	.00154	.00000	.00058	.00442
STANDARDIZED RATE (2)	.02210	.00118	.00132	.00077	.00448	.00384	.00257	.00007	.00000	.00091	.00000	.00068	.00628
GEOMETRIC MEAN	.02065												

LIFE TABLE FOR ALL CAUSES COMBINED

Age (x)	Midyear Population	Deaths During Year	$_nM_x$	$_nq_x$	l_x	$_nd_x$	$_nL_x$	$_nm_x$	$_na_x$	T_x	$_nr_x$	$\overset{\circ}{e}_x$	Age (x)
0	490723	85989	.175229	.157760	100000	15776	90028	.175235	.367890	4589380	.000000	45.894	0
1	1713496	54584	.031855	.118019	84224	9940	312046	.031854	1.500000	4499352	.000000	53.421	1
5	1917534	9306	.004853	.023989	74284	1782	366565	.004856	2.500000	4187306	.000000	56.369	5
10	1868016	4832	.002587	.012841	72502	931	360121	.002585	2.434211	3820341	.011531	52.693	10
15	1565027	6547	.004183	.020791	71571	1488	354389	.004199	2.670531	3460220	.021447	48.347	15
20	1397673	8685	.006214	.030664	70083	2149	345153	.006226	2.551380	3105831	.025155	44.316	20
25	1134372	6842	.006032	.029705	67934	2018	334604	.006031	2.489367	2760678	.026724	40.638	25
30	1026185	6468	.006303	.031040	65916	2046	324505	.006305	2.519652	2426075	.016945	36.806	30
35	934489	6578	.007039	.034617	63870	2211	313922	.007043	2.545040	2101570	.010649	32.904	35
40	886665	7402	.008348	.040935	61659	2524	302167	.008353	2.571976	1787648	.004113	28.992	40
45	848557	9078	.010698	.052135	59135	3083	288221	.010697	2.582239	1485481	.001498	25.120	45
50	807584	11129	.013781	.066742	56052	3741	271302	.013789	2.605531	1197260	.004398	21.360	50
55	692426	13795	.019923	.095162	52311	4978	249677	.019938	2.613960	925958	.004923	17.701	55
60	626088	18280	.029197	.136564	47333	6464	221219	.029220	2.610451	676280	.004968	14.288	60
65	478164	21776	.045541	.205657	40869	8405	184143	.045644	2.596470	455061	.011785	11.135	65
70	335171	25262	.075370	.319000	32464	10356	136878	.075659	2.543252	270918	.016940	8.345	70
75	184257	23212	.125976	.477429	22108	10555	83557	.126321	2.443569	134040	.010244	6.063	75
80	84542	16829	.199061	.648922	11553	7497	37567	.199564	2.305839	50483	.010244	4.370	80
85+	30721	9647	.314020	1.000000	4056	4056	12916	.314020	3.184513	12916	.000000	3.185	85+

NUMBER OF PERSONS DYING (OUT OF 100,000 AT BIRTH) ABOVE AGE X FROM SPECIFIED CAUSES

Age (x)	All Causes	Respiratory T. B.	Other Infec. and Paras.	Neo-plasms	Cardio-vascular	Infl., Pneu., Bronch.	Diar-rheal	Certain Degen-erative	Maternal	Cert. Dis. of Infancy	Motor Vehicle	Other Violence	Other and Unknown	Age (x)
0	100000	5594	5692	3860	21255	17466	11140	362	0	3942	0	3179	27510	0
1	84224	5534	4992	3840	21180	14363	6388	362	0	0	0	3150	24415	1
5	74284	5405	3169	3794	21113	11702	3541	362	0	0	0	2903	22295	5
10	72502	5341	2638	3775	21048	11434	3315	362	0	0	0	2813	21776	10
15	71571	5269	2396	3760	20985	11345	3236	361	0	0	0	2714	21505	15
20	70083	4890	2122	3748	20872	11169	3160	358	0	0	0	2558	21206	20
25	67934	4093	1807	3714	20748	10913	3083	351	0	0	0	2346	20879	25
30	65916	3333	1572	3676	20623	10653	3001	344	0	0	0	2153	20561	30
35	63870	2689	1384	3621	20434	10368	2917	333	0	0	0	1954	20170	35
40	61659	2153	1211	3538	20193	10003	2813	321	0	0	0	1759	19668	40
45	59135	1696	1040	3358	19807	9567	2705	309	0	0	0	1557	19056	45
50	56052	1252	879	3176	19256	9021	2573	290	0	0	0	1341	18264	50
55	52311	890	709	2859	18420	8329	2382	264	0	0	0	1120	17338	55
60	47333	573	536	2391	17063	7361	2156	211	0	0	0	880	16162	60
65	40869	336	384	1810	14919	6199	1839	154	0	0	0	644	14584	65
70	32464	170	235	1167	11669	4699	1424	92	0	0	0	434	12574	70
75	22108	69	116	594	7425	3017	905	41	0	0	0	257	9684	75
80	11553	23	51	190	3270	1412	413	10	0	0	0	118	6066	80
85+	4056	4	12	48	909	438	125	2	0	0	0	29	2489	85+

NUMBER OF PERSONS SURVIVING TO AGE X IF SPECIFIED CAUSES WERE ELIMINATED

Age (x)	No Causes	Respiratory T. B. (1)	Other Infec. and Paras. (2)	Neo-plasms (3)	Cardio-vascular (4)	Infl., Pneu., Bronch. (5)	Diar-rheal (6)	Certain Degener-ative (7)	Maternal (8)	Cert. Dis. of Infancy (9)	Motor Vehicle (10)	Other Violence (11)	Other and Unknown (12)	(1) + (2)	(1) + (2) + (5) + (6) + (8)	(1)+(2)+ (5)+(6)+ (8)+part of(9)&(12)	(10) + (11)	Age (x)
0	100000	100000	100000	100000	100000	100000	100000	100000	100000	100000	100000	100000	100000	100000	100000	100000	100000	0
1	84224	84279	84868	84242	84293	87117	86654	84224	84224	87916	84224	84251	87109	84924	92503	99757	84251	1
5	74284	74454	76556	74343	74408	79463	81092	74284	74284	77540	74284	74540	78914	76771	89649	99182	74540	5
10	72502	72731	75302	72579	72687	77840	79391	72502	72502	75680	72502	72841	77568	75539	88807	98851	72841	10
15	71571	71869	74565	71662	71816	76935	78457	71572	71571	74708	71571	72004	76860	74895	88255	98506	72004	15
20	70083	70753	73317	70184	70436	75523	76908	70087	70083	73155	70083	70663	75581	74018	87532	98013	70663	20
25	67934	69380	71394	68065	68399	73480	74613	67945	67934	70912	67934	68707	73611	72914	86643	97384	68707	25
30	65916	68086	69517	66081	66491	71575	72505	65933	65916	68805	65916	66858	71765	71807	85766	96759	66858	30
35	63870	66632	67554	64084	64615	69658	70346	63898	63870	66670	63870	64982	69958	70476	84656	95925	64982	35
40	61659	64877	65396	61948	62619	67639	68023	61697	61659	64362	61659	62928	68079	68808	83273	94880	62928	40
45	59135	62693	62896	59550	60441	65341	65355	59184	59135	61727	59135	60554	65997	66681	81429	93357	60554	45
50	56052	59884	59784	56663	57841	62524	62090	56117	56052	58509	56052	57613	63384	63871	78922	91182	57613	50
55	52311	56261	55669	53192	54821	59102	58151	52397	52311	54604	52311	53987	60174	60196	75603	88100	53987	55
60	47333	51231	50819	48585	50978	54527	52857	47461	47333	49408	47333	49085	55749	55004	70759	83322	49085	60
65	40869	44472	44030	42507	46217	48339	45968	41032	40869	42609	40869	42609	49892	47912	63740	76091	42609	65
70	32464	35485	35117	34362	40136	40006	36932	32649	32464	33887	32464	34040	41877	38385	53813	65486	34040	70
75	22108	24254	24019	23898	31991	28992	25639	22275	22108	23077	22108	23332	31761	26351	40075	50499	23332	75
80	11553	12709	12600	12796	21560	16713	13807	11662	11553	12059	11553	12296	20785	13861	23965	32441	12296	80
85+	4056	4474	4448	4582	10525	6722	5046	4099	4056	4234	4056	4371	12024	4906	10116	16202	4371	85+

ADDED YRS OF LIFE

		(1)	(2)	(3)	(4)	(5)	(6)	(7)	(8)	(9)	(10)	(11)	(12)				
TOTAL		1.834	2.503	.577	2.778	5.151	4.767	.055	.000	1.996	.000	.891	6.757	4.463	16.265	25.889	.891
WORK	8.012	1.740	.683	.289	.900	1.068	.305	.035	.000	.000	.000	.594	1.475	2.461	3.971	5.061	.594

POPULATION, DEATHS, DEATH RATES FOR ALL CAUSES COMBINED, AND SPECIFIED CAUSES

Age Start of Interval	Midyear Population	Deaths During Year	All Causes	Respiratory T. B.	Other Infec. and Paras.	Neoplasms	Cardiovascular	Infl., Pneu., Bronch.	Diarrheal	Certain Degenerative	Maternal	Cert. Dis. of Infancy	Motor Vehicle	Other Violence	Other and Unknown	Age Start of Interval
0	471062	74418	.15758	.00068	.00708	.00019	.00046	.02946	.04939	.00000	.00000	.04001	.00000	.00032	.03039	0
1	1652147	53037	.03210	.00035	.00538	.00014	.00026	.00839	.00956	.00000	.00000	.00000	.00000	.00070	.00689	1
5	1846546	9843	.00533	.00028	.00156	.00003	.00017	.00091	.00076	.00000	.00000	.00000	.00000	.00022	.00140	5
10	1814569	5812	.00320	.00061	.00087	.00004	.00023	.00035	.00026	.00000	.00000	.00000	.00000	.00010	.00073	10
15	1675286	8155	.00486	.00188	.00051	.00006	.00030	.00048	.00025	.00001	.00005	.00000	.00000	.00015	.00077	15
20	1526336	9243	.00606	.00237	.00082	.00009	.00036	.00060	.00028	.00001	.00036	.00000	.00000	.00016	.00100	20
25	1313156	8755	.00667	.00248	.00073	.00014	.00047	.00070	.00031	.00001	.00048	.00000	.00000	.00014	.00119	25
30	1150544	7995	.00695	.00208	.00066	.00030	.00068	.00081	.00039	.00002	.00052	.00000	.00000	.00012	.00137	30
35	1021542	7491	.00733	.00167	.00061	.00051	.00095	.00092	.00042	.00002	.00053	.00000	.00000	.00014	.00157	35
40	950032	7465	.00786	.00142	.00053	.00084	.00133	.00100	.00047	.00002	.00034	.00000	.00000	.00016	.00174	40
45	884250	7511	.00849	.00109	.00044	.00131	.00190	.00115	.00050	.00004	.00006	.00000	.00000	.00015	.00186	45
50	841293	9497	.01129	.00087	.00045	.00187	.00325	.00169	.00063	.00006	.00000	.00000	.00000	.00020	.00225	50
55	705079	11186	.01586	.00084	.00052	.00236	.00523	.00260	.00092	.00011	.00000	.00000	.00000	.00020	.00309	55
60	654330	16900	.02583	.00075	.00053	.00287	.00999	.00471	.00140	.00016	.00000	.00000	.00000	.00025	.00516	60
65	480574	21212	.04414	.00072	.00062	.00379	.01913	.00790	.00231	.00018	.00000	.00000	.00000	.00035	.00915	65
70	348393	26323	.07556	.00054	.00070	.00447	.03255	.01260	.00386	.00022	.00000	.00000	.00000	.00060	.02000	70
75	185957	23106	.12425	.00055	.00074	.00474	.04939	.01993	.00587	.00019	.00000	.00000	.00000	.00104	.04179	75
80	89879	17637	.19623	.00024	.00107	.00466	.05975	.02602	.00822	.00008	.00000	.00000	.00000	.00135	.09484	80
85+	34712	10632	.30629	.00043	.00115	.00386	.06419	.03080	.00928	.00012	.00000	.00000	.00000	.00190	.19457	85+
ALL	17649667	336218														

	All Causes	Respiratory T. B.	Other Infec. and Paras.	Neoplasms	Cardiovascular	Infl., Pneu., Bronch.	Diarrheal	Certain Degenerative	Maternal	Cert. Dis. of Infancy	Motor Vehicle	Other Violence	Other and Unknown
CRUDE DEATH RATE	.01905	.00122	.00139	.00077	.00329	.00330	.00291	.00003	.00016	.00107	.00000	.00025	.00466
STANDARDIZED RATE (1)	.01812	.00121	.00160	.00056	.00212	.00328	.00344	.00003	.00016	.00141	.00000	.00025	.00408
STANDARDIZED RATE (2)	.02128	.00122	.00127	.00054	.00456	.00353	.00262	.00004	.00016	.00083	.00000	.00026	.00584
GEOMETRIC MEAN	.02027												

LIFE TABLE FOR ALL CAUSES COMBINED

Age (x)	Midyear Population	Deaths During Year	$_nM_x$	$_nq_x$	l_x	$_nd_x$	$_nL_x$	$_nm_x$	$_na_x$	T_x	$_nr_x$	$\overset{\circ}{e}_x$	Age (x)
0	471062	74418	.157979	.143030	100000	14303	90539	.157975	.338565	4679160	.000000	46.792	0
1	1652147	53037	.032102	.118872	85697	10187	317221	.032103	1.500000	4588621	.000000	53.545	1
5	1846546	9843	.005330	.026301	75510	1986	372585	.005330	2.500000	4271300	.000000	56.566	5
10	1814569	5812	.003203	.015886	73524	1168	364649	.003203	2.455943	3898715	.003057	53.026	10
15	1675286	8155	.004856	.024034	72356	1739	357629	.004863	2.612732	3534066	.009442	48.843	15
20	1526336	9243	.006056	.029865	70617	2109	347919	.006062	2.550281	3176438	.015872	44.981	20
25	1313156	8755	.006667	.032814	68508	2248	336952	.006672	2.514365	2828519	.020713	41.287	25
30	1150544	7995	.006949	.034168	66260	2264	325652	.006952	2.505245	2491567	.019700	37.603	30
35	1021542	7491	.007333	.036018	63996	2305	314241	.007335	2.510304	2165915	.014333	33.845	35
40	950032	7465	.007858	.038547	61691	2378	302544	.007860	2.514280	1851674	.009358	30.015	40
45	884250	7511	.008494	.041610	59313	2468	290551	.008494	2.563310	1549130	.003133	26.118	45
50	841293	9497	.011289	.055027	56845	3128	276748	.011303	2.609628	1258579	.009825	22.141	50
55	705079	11186	.015865	.076587	53717	4114	258909	.015890	2.648072	981831	.008381	18.278	55
60	654330	16900	.025828	.122009	49603	6052	233845	.025880	2.658660	722922	.009559	14.574	60
65	480574	21212	.044139	.200294	43551	8723	197007	.044278	2.621494	489076	.014713	11.230	65
70	348393	26323	.075555	.319829	34828	11139	146806	.075876	2.546122	292069	.017808	8.386	70
75	185957	23106	.124255	.472329	23689	11189	89827	.124562	2.442258	145263	.009720	6.132	75
80	89879	17637	.196230	.643200	12500	8040	40875	.196698	2.310297	55436	.009720	4.435	80
85+	34712	10632	.306292	1.000000	4460	4460	14561	.306292	3.264861	14561	.000000	3.265	85+

NUMBER OF PERSONS DYING (OUT OF 100,000 AT BIRTH) ABOVE AGE X FROM SPECIFIED CAUSES

Age (x)	All Causes	Respiratory T. B.	Other Infec. and Paras.	Neoplasms	Cardio-vascular	Infl., Pneu., Bronch.	Diarrheal	Certain Degenerative	Maternal	Cert. Dis. of Infancy	Motor Vehicle	Other Violence	Other and Unknown	Age (x)
0	100000	5719	5534	4566	23147	16579	11619	220	762	3622	0	1200	26632	0
1	85697	5657	4892	4949	23105	13912	7147	220	762	0	0	1171	23882	1
5	75510	5534	3186	4905	23024	11250	3987	219	762	0	0	950	21693	5
10	73524	5430	2607	4893	22960	10912	3703	218	762	0	0	867	21172	10
15	72356	5208	2289	4877	22876	10783	3607	216	762	0	0	832	20906	15
20	70617	4536	1964	4856	22768	10612	3519	214	742	0	0	777	20629	20
25	68508	3710	1681	4824	22641	10403	3420	210	615	0	0	722	20282	25
30	66260	2874	1433	4776	22483	10165	3314	206	453	0	0	674	19882	30
35	63996	2197	1218	4680	22262	9901	3187	199	284	0	0	635	19433	35
40	61691	1675	1028	4518	21961	9612	3056	191	119	0	0	591	18940	40
45	59313	1247	867	4264	21557	9309	2915	184	17	0	0	542	18411	45
50	56845	929	740	3882	21005	8974	2770	173	0	0	0	499	17873	50
55	53717	687	614	3365	20104	8505	2594	157	0	0	0	443	17248	55
60	49603	469	480	2753	18747	7830	2355	129	0	0	0	393	16447	60
65	43551	293	356	2081	16405	6727	2026	91	0	0	0	335	15237	65
70	34828	151	233	1334	12623	5167	1570	55	0	0	0	266	13429	70
75	23689	71	130	676	7825	3310	1001	22	0	0	0	177	10477	75
80	12500	22	64	251	3380	1515	472	5	0	0	0	83	6708	80
85+	4460	6	17	56	935	448	135	2	0	0	0	28	2833	85+

NUMBER OF PERSONS SURVIVING TO AGE X IF SPECIFIED CAUSES WERE ELIMINATED

Age (x)	No Causes	Respiratory T. B. (1)	Other Infec. and Paras. (2)	Neoplasms (3)	Cardio-vascular (4)	Infl., Pneu., Bronch. (5)	Diarrheal (6)	Certain Degenerative (7)	Maternal (8)	Cert. Dis. of Infancy (9)	Motor Vehicle (10)	Other Violence (11)	Other and Unknown (12)	(1)+(2)	(1)+(2)+(5)+(6)+(8)	(1)+(2)+(5)+(6)+(8)+part of (9)&(12)	(10)+(11)	Age (x)
0	100000	100000	100000	100000	100000	100000	100000	100000	100000	100000	100000	100000	100000	100000	100000	100000	100000	0
1	85697	85754	86293	85713	85736	88199	89934	85697	85697	89113	85697	85724	88278	86351	93266	99829	85724	1
5	75510	75676	77664	75565	75620	80328	82416	75511	75510	78520	75510	75741	79929	77834	90374	99282	75741	5
10	73524	73788	76211	73590	73695	78571	80555	73526	73524	76455	73524	73831	78373	76485	89551	98994	73831	10
15	72356	72838	75328	72436	72608	77459	79380	72360	72356	75240	72356	72693	77409	75829	89058	98753	72693	15
20	70617	71759	73852	70716	70970	75775	77567	70623	70637	73432	70617	71001	75842	75046	88483	98448	71001	20
25	68508	70447	71939	68636	68947	73737	75358	68518	68653	71239	68508	68935	73945	73975	87767	98079	68935	25
30	66260	68586	69834	66431	66869	71570	73000	66273	66560	68901	66260	66720	71545	72708	86914	97623	66720	30
35	63996	67325	67671	64256	64804	69405	70643	64016	64453	66547	63996	64479	69967	71191	85836	96946	64479	35
40	61691	65441	65431	62102	62770	67214	68241	61718	62294	64150	61691	62200	67979	69408	84469	95940	62200	40
45	59313	63365	63077	59960	60755	64947	65944	59346	59994	61677	59313	59851	65932	67385	82751	94493	59851	45
50	56845	61061	60584	57844	58784	62605	63185	56887	57514	59111	56845	57403	63777	65078	80603	92458	57403	50
55	53717	57554	57381	55175	56463	59665	59858	53772	54349	55858	53717	54300	60953	61907	77576	89393	54300	55
60	49603	53741	53124	51556	53529	55821	55567	49681	50187	51580	49603	50189	57165	57555	73412	85098	50189	60
65	43551	47362	46766	45922	49428	50186	49134	43655	44064	45287	43551	44121	51513	50858	66898	78271	44121	65
70	34828	38012	37516	37430	43552	41769	39754	34943	35238	36216	34828	35346	43154	40946	56711	67377	35346	70
75	23689	25925	25609	26038	34961	30290	27576	23794	23968	24633	23689	24115	32528	28024	42204	51810	24115	75
80	12500	13717	13562	14069	23745	17701	14955	12567	12647	12998	12500	12793	21348	14883	25581	33742	12793	80
85+	4460	4904	4868	5147	11591	7241	5586	4486	4513	4638	4460	4597	12517	5353	11016	17308	4597	85+

ADDED YRS OF LIFE

	No Causes	(1)	(2)	(3)	(4)	(5)	(6)	(7)	(8)	(9)	(10)	(11)	(12)	(1)+(2)	(1)+(2)+(5)+(6)+(8)	(1)+(2)+(5)+(6)+(8)+part of(9)&(12)	(10)+(11)
TOTAL		2.075	2.493	.806	3.087	4.779	4.994	.036	.275	1.852	.000	.371	6.515	4.704	16.713	25.942	.371
WORK	7.917	1.901	.696	.459	.973	.844	.372	.021	.301	.000	.000	.148	1.351	2.637	4.316	5.394	.148

POPULATION, DEATHS, DEATH RATES FOR ALL CAUSES COMBINED, AND SPECIFIED CAUSES

Age Start of Interval	Midyear Population	Deaths During Year	All Causes	Respiratory T. B.	Other Infec. and Paras.	Neoplasms	Cardiovascular	Infl., Pneu., Bronch.	Diarrheal	Certain Degenerative	Maternal	Cert. Dis. of Infancy	Motor Vehicle	Other Violence	Other and Unknown	Age Start of Interval
0	513655	78961	.15372	.00047	.00599	.00020	.00080	.02752	.05556	.00001	.00000	.03306	.00000	.00025	.02987	0
1	1332705	37674	.02827	.00029	.00420	.00013	.00029	.00724	.00961	.00000	.00000	.00000	.00000	.00065	.00587	1
5	2099891	8707	.00415	.00014	.00120	.00003	.00017	.00061	.00055	.00001	.00000	.00000	.00000	.00026	.00117	5
10	2169448	5486	.00253	.00015	.00068	.00003	.00019	.00028	.00026	.00001	.00000	.00000	.00000	.00027	.00067	10
15	1913204	7864	.00411	.00085	.00087	.00004	.00031	.00051	.00020	.00001	.00000	.00000	.00000	.00056	.00076	15
20	1656486	10051	.00607	.00232	.00087	.00006	.00030	.00061	.00012	.00001	.00000	.00000	.00000	.00087	.00091	20
25	1330742	7341	.00552	.00215	.00050	.00008	.00036	.00056	.00013	.00002	.00000	.00000	.00000	.00082	.00090	25
30	1227912	6759	.00550	.00171	.00052	.00013	.00052	.00064	.00013	.00002	.00000	.00000	.00000	.00075	.00107	30
35	1113234	6552	.00589	.00140	.00049	.00024	.00064	.00087	.00017	.00004	.00000	.00000	.00000	.00071	.00134	35
40	1041651	7302	.00701	.00118	.00053	.00042	.00101	.00113	.00021	.00003	.00000	.00000	.00000	.00075	.00175	40
45	963912	8525	.00884	.00108	.00055	.00071	.00154	.00164	.00029	.00005	.00000	.00000	.00000	.00078	.00221	45
50	856831	10320	.01204	.00105	.00058	.00125	.00263	.00211	.00039	.00009	.00000	.00000	.00000	.00090	.00304	50
55	789044	13422	.01701	.00102	.00058	.00203	.00465	.00297	.00060	.00018	.00000	.00000	.00000	.00091	.00408	55
60	695784	18120	.02589	.00095	.00068	.00288	.00863	.00453	.00109	.00022	.00000	.00000	.00000	.00103	.00589	60
65	527240	21462	.04071	.00083	.00073	.00371	.01569	.00703	.00164	.00032	.00000	.00000	.00000	.00119	.00956	65
70	392294	26686	.06803	.00065	.00085	.00464	.02797	.01057	.00285	.00030	.00000	.00000	.00000	.00126	.01853	70
75	223565	25709	.11500	.00051	.00081	.00477	.04698	.01636	.00434	.00035	.00000	.00000	.00000	.00147	.03940	75
80	97035	17788	.18332	.00040	.00073	.00407	.05922	.02062	.00537	.00025	.00000	.00000	.00000	.00189	.09077	80
85+	34190	9591	.28052	.00029	.00070	.00269	.06511	.02557	.00626	.00018	.00000	.00000	.00000	.00173	.17760	85+
ALL	18982823	328320														

			All Causes	Respiratory T.B.	Other Infec.	Neoplasms	Cardiovascular	Infl. Pneu.	Diarrheal	Certain Degen.	Maternal	Cert. Dis. Infancy	Motor Vehicle	Other Violence	Other Unknown
CRUDE DEATH RATE			.01730	.00099	.00111	.00065	.00299	.00289	.00263	.00005	.00000	.00089	.00000	.00068	.00442
STANDARDIZED RATE (1)			.01673	.00095	.00134	.00044	.00187	.00298	.00344	.00004	.00000	.00116	.00000	.00064	.00388
STANDARDIZED RATE (2)			.01571	.00101	.00109	.00079	.00408	.00319	.00245	.00006	.00000	.00068	.00000	.00073	.00562
GEOMETRIC MEAN			.01844												

LIFE TABLE FOR ALL CAUSES COMBINED

Age (x)	Midyear Population	Deaths During Year	$_nM_x$	$_nq_x$	l_x	$_nd_x$	$_nL_x$	$_nm_x$	$_na_x$	T_x	$_nr_x$	$\overset{\circ}{e}_x$	Age (x)
0	513655	78961	.153724	.139400	100000	13940	90679	.153730	.331330	4885061	.000000	48.851	0
1	1332705	37674	.028269	.105612	86060	9089	321518	.028269	1.500000	4794382	.000000	55.710	1
5	2099891	8707	.004146	.020514	76971	1579	380908	.004145	2.500000	4472865	.000000	58.111	5
10	2169448	5486	.002529	.012561	75392	947	374580	.002528	2.487020	4091957	.001988	54.276	10
15	1913204	7864	.004110	.020418	74445	1520	368683	.004123	2.669545	3717377	.016391	49.935	15
20	1656486	10051	.006068	.029949	72925	2184	359249	.006079	2.538442	3348695	.028125	45.920	20
25	1330742	7341	.005516	.027184	70741	1923	348832	.005513	2.465874	2989446	.027232	42.259	25
30	1227912	6759	.005504	.027159	68818	1869	339422	.005506	2.502229	2640614	.015917	38.371	30
35	1113234	6552	.005888	.029022	66949	1943	329965	.005888	2.539994	2301192	.012413	34.372	35
40	1041651	7302	.007010	.034489	65006	2242	319587	.007015	2.572201	1971227	.007876	30.324	40
45	963912	8525	.008844	.043337	62764	2720	307206	.008852	2.597866	1651640	.010027	26.315	45
50	856831	10320	.012044	.058624	60044	3520	291816	.012062	2.612571	1344354	.009596	22.389	50
55	789044	13422	.017010	.081771	56524	4622	271653	.017014	2.627200	1052537	.002336	18.621	55
60	695784	18120	.025894	.122192	51902	6342	244457	.025943	2.626505	780885	.010538	15.045	60
65	527240	21462	.040706	.185975	45560	8473	207556	.040823	2.610793	536427	.014340	11.774	65
70	392294	26686	.068026	.292501	37087	10848	158994	.068229	2.562588	328871	.013266	8.868	70
75	223565	25709	.114996	.447121	26239	11732	101472	.115618	2.466509	169877	.020174	6.474	75
80	97035	17788	.183315	.617771	14507	8962	48638	.184259	2.333533	68405	.020174	4.715	80
85+	34190	9591	.280521	1.000000	5545	5545	19767	.280521	3.564800	19767	.000000	3.565	85+

NUMBER OF PERSONS DYING (OUT OF 100,000 AT BIRTH) ABOVE AGE X FROM SPECIFIED CAUSES

Age (x)	All Causes	Respira-tory T.B.	Other Infec. and Paras.	Neo-plasms	Cardio-vascular	Infl., Pneu., Bronch.	Diar-rheal	Certain Degen-erative	Maternal	Cert. Dis. of Infancy	Motor Vehicle	Other Violence	Other and Unknown	Age (x)
0	100000	5065	5004	4496	22675	16073	11019	361	0	2998	0	3698	28611	0
1	86060	5022	4461	4478	22603	13577	5980	361	0	0	0	3676	25902	1
5	76971	4929	3110	4437	22511	11251	2890	360	0	0	0	3467	24016	5
10	75392	4874	2654	4424	22446	11017	2682	357	0	0	0	3369	23569	10
15	74445	4818	2400	4411	22376	10911	2586	355	0	0	0	3269	23319	15
20	72925	4503	2079	4397	22261	10722	2514	351	0	0	0	3060	23038	20
25	70741	3665	1766	4376	22155	10503	2469	346	0	0	0	2747	22714	25
30	68818	2917	1591	4347	22030	10309	2424	341	0	0	0	2461	22398	30
35	66949	2337	1414	4302	21854	10090	2379	334	0	0	0	2206	22033	35
40	65006	1876	1253	4223	21643	9804	2323	322	0	0	0	1971	21591	40
45	62764	1498	1083	4089	21319	9444	2257	312	0	0	0	1732	21030	45
50	60044	1166	916	3871	20845	8938	2168	297	0	0	0	1491	20352	50
55	56524	860	747	3506	20076	8320	2053	269	0	0	0	1228	19465	55
60	51902	585	589	2956	18813	7513	1891	221	0	0	0	980	18354	60
65	45560	353	424	2250	16698	6403	1624	167	0	0	0	727	16914	65
70	37087	182	272	1479	13430	4940	1283	99	0	0	0	480	14922	70
75	26239	79	137	741	8568	3192	829	51	0	0	0	279	11963	75
80	14507	28	54	256	4179	1524	387	16	0	0	0	129	7934	80
85+	5545	6	14	53	1287	513	124	3	0	0	0	34	3511	85+

NUMBER OF PERSONS SURVIVING TO AGE X IF SPECIFIED CAUSES WERE ELIMINATED

Age (x)	No Causes	Respira-tory T.B. (1)	Other Infec. and Paras. (2)	Neo-plasms (3)	Cardio-vascular (4)	Infl., Pneu., Bronch. (5)	Diar-rheal (6)	Certain Degener-ative (7)	Maternal (8)	Cert. Dis. of Infancy (9)	Motor Vehicle (10)	Other Violence (11)	Other and Unknown (12)	(1) + (2)	(1) + (2) + (5) + (6) + (8)	(1)+(2)+ (5)+(6)+ (8)+part of(9)&(12)	(10) + (11)	Age (x)
0	100000	100000	100000	100000	100000	100000	100000	100000	100000	100000	100000	100000	100000	100000	100000	100000	100000	0
1	86060	86100	86565	86077	86127	88405	90859	86060	86060	88884	86060	86080	86608	86605	93926	99796	86080	1
5	76971	77095	78718	77025	77118	81359	84406	76972	76971	79497	76971	77187	81107	78844	91389	99267	77187	5
10	75392	75568	77566	75457	75600	79935	82901	75396	75392	77866	75392	75701	79910	77746	90642	98942	75701	10
15	74445	74674	76852	74523	74720	79043	81964	74451	74445	76888	74445	74850	79170	77088	90117	98611	74850	15
20	72925	73463	75611	73015	73309	77628	80369	72935	72925	75318	72925	73530	77850	76169	89358	98051	73530	20
25	70741	72100	73667	70849	71219	75533	78011	70755	70741	73062	70741	71639	75860	75082	88407	97340	71639	25
30	68818	70896	71844	68952	69407	73684	75940	68837	68818	71076	68818	69978	74133	74013	87447	96600	69978	30
35	66949	69562	70075	67124	67697	71915	73926	66974	66949	69146	66949	68334	72508	72810	86361	95749	68334	35
40	65006	68016	68208	65254	65943	70131	71842	65042	65006	67139	65006	66587	70877	71366	85089	94745	66587	40
45	62764	66060	66031	63136	63953	68355	69436	62804	62764	64824	62764	64532	69038	69498	83416	93356	64532	45
50	60044	63539	63341	60615	61655	65683	66523	60102	60044	62014	60044	61978	66778	67028	81235	91455	61978	50
55	56524	60129	59801	57420	58850	62492	62747	56606	56524	58375	56524	58608	63828	63614	78074	88511	58608	55
60	51902	55492	55071	53263	55315	58243	57789	52023	51902	53605	51902	54062	59822	58880	73567	84087	54062	60
65	45560	48943	48505	47437	50716	52306	51006	45717	45560	47055	45560	47703	54089	52107	66973	77373	47703	65
70	37087	40005	39629	39341	44699	44116	41866	37276	37087	38304	37087	39063	48216	42747	57401	67377	39063	70
75	26239	28394	28157	28490	36461	32996	30051	26412	26239	27100	26239	27813	35949	30470	43884	53040	27813	75
80	14507	15738	15631	16133	25654	19834	16987	14628	14507	14983	14507	15492	24417	16957	27147	34835	15492	80
85+	5545	6030	6000	6302	13374	8450	6679	5599	5545	5727	5545	5982	15002	6525	11976	17672	5982	85+

ADDED YRS OF LIFE																		
TOTAL		1.723	2.184	.660	2.970	4.625	5.178	.057	.000	1.592	.000	1.090	6.859	4.006	15.379	23.554	1.090	
WORK	7.271	1.572	.659	.284	.800	.891	.154	.029	.000	.000	.000	.762	1.341	2.263	3.440	4.353	.762	

POPULATION, DEATHS, DEATH RATES FOR ALL CAUSES COMBINED, AND SPECIFIED CAUSES

Age Start of Interval	Midyear Population	Deaths During Year	All Causes	Respiratory T. B.	Other Infec. and Paras.	Neoplasms	Cardiovascular	Infl., Pneu., Bronch.	Diarrheal	Certain Degenerative	Maternal	Cert. Dis. of Infancy	Motor Vehicle	Other Violence	Other and Unknown	Age Start of Interval
0	491242	66895	.13618	.00042	.00551	.00022	.00086	.02256	.05093	.00001	.00000	.02990	.00000	.00022	.02556	0
1	1280154	34978	.02732	.00028	.00379	.00012	.00022	.00700	.00991	.00000	.00000	.00000	.00000	.00051	.00549	1
5	2029393	8466	.00417	.00020	.00126	.00003	.00018	.00069	.00059	.00000	.00000	.00000	.00000	.00016	.00106	5
10	2099936	5868	.00279	.00044	.00081	.00002	.00023	.00035	.00026	.00000	.00000	.00000	.00000	.00007	.00060	10
15	1899752	8225	.00433	.00158	.00095	.00005	.00027	.00048	.00020	.00001	.00005	.00000	.00000	.00013	.00061	15
20	1737462	9446	.00544	.00208	.00086	.00007	.00028	.00053	.00020	.00001	.00031	.00000	.00000	.00019	.00091	20
25	1529943	8645	.00565	.00196	.00077	.00010	.00038	.00059	.00019	.00001	.00043	.00000	.00000	.00015	.00108	25
30	1401386	7848	.00560	.00171	.00066	.00021	.00047	.00064	.00018	.00002	.00046	.00000	.00000	.00013	.00111	30
35	1238738	7469	.00603	.00142	.00057	.00039	.00073	.00077	.00021	.00002	.00047	.00000	.00000	.00013	.00132	35
40	1101133	7182	.00652	.00115	.00054	.00071	.00103	.00082	.00030	.00003	.00028	.00000	.00000	.00014	.00152	40
45	985742	7426	.00753	.00104	.00052	.00116	.00155	.00100	.00032	.00004	.00005	.00000	.00000	.00016	.00168	45
50	877887	9047	.01031	.00080	.00050	.00166	.00290	.00155	.00044	.00008	.00001	.00000	.00000	.00020	.00216	50
55	797141	11198	.01405	.00071	.00053	.00221	.00475	.00223	.00056	.00012	.00000	.00000	.00000	.00023	.00271	55
60	727404	16637	.02287	.00069	.00056	.00291	.00882	.00379	.00101	.00019	.00000	.00000	.00000	.00026	.00464	60
65	537458	20457	.03806	.00060	.00065	.00380	.01633	.00665	.00174	.00024	.00000	.00000	.00000	.00038	.00766	65
70	409007	27611	.06751	.00058	.00083	.00448	.02965	.01128	.00292	.00020	.00000	.00000	.00000	.00048	.01708	70
75	224818	25857	.11501	.00048	.00089	.00522	.04723	.01661	.00448	.00025	.00000	.00000	.00000	.00088	.03897	75
80	109102	19539	.17909	.00027	.00053	.00428	.05709	.02125	.00554	.00018	.00000	.00000	.00000	.00124	.08871	80
85+	42193	11120	.26355	.00021	.00083	.00358	.06025	.02472	.00581	.00009	.00000	.00000	.00000	.00140	.16666	85+
ALL	19519891	313914														

CRUDE DEATH RATE			.01608	.00105	.00109	.00074	.00309	.00255	.00242	.00004	.00015	.00075	.00000	.00021	.00399	
STANDARDIZED RATE (1)			.01566	.00099	.00133	.00051	.00190	.00268	.00334	.00003	.00014	.00105	.00000	.00021	.00347	
STANDARDIZED RATE (2)			.01863	.00102	.00110	.00089	.00414	.00293	.00241	.00005	.00014	.00062	.00000	.00023	.00511	
GEOMETRIC MEAN			.01758													

LIFE TABLE FOR ALL CAUSES COMBINED

Age (x)	Midyear Population	Deaths During Year	$_nM_x$	$_nq_x$	l_x	$_nd_x$	$_nL_x$	$_nm_x$	$_na_x$	T_x	$_nr_x$	$\overset{\circ}{e}_x$	Age (x)
0	491242	66895	.136175	.124350	100000	12435	91314	.136178	.301498	5042002	.000000	50.420	0
1	1280154	34978	.027323	.102301	87565	8958	327865	.027322	1.500000	4950688	.000000	56.537	1
5	2029393	8466	.004172	.020647	78607	1623	388978	.004172	2.500000	4622823	.000000	58.809	5
10	2099936	5868	.002794	.013873	76984	1068	382251	.002794	2.501170	4233845	.000380	54.996	10
15	1899752	8225	.004330	.021458	75916	1629	375700	.004336	2.618426	3851594	.011088	50.735	15
20	1737462	9446	.005437	.026842	74287	1994	366530	.005440	2.540329	3475894	.015189	46.790	20
25	1529943	8645	.005651	.027873	72293	2015	356416	.005653	2.494520	3109363	.015935	43.011	25
30	1401386	7848	.005600	.027619	70278	1941	346541	.005601	2.501610	2752947	.014986	39.172	30
35	1238738	7469	.006030	.029706	68337	2030	336649	.006030	2.519397	2406406	.017655	35.214	35
40	1101133	7182	.006522	.032123	66307	2130	326282	.006528	2.534038	2069757	.016767	31.215	40
45	985742	7426	.007533	.037054	64177	2378	315145	.007546	2.586119	1743474	.015547	27.167	45
50	877887	9047	.010305	.050373	61799	3113	301549	.010323	2.608082	1428329	.013675	23.112	50
55	797141	11198	.014048	.068040	58686	3993	284039	.014058	2.648072	1126780	.004080	19.200	55
60	727404	16637	.022872	.108807	54693	5951	259535	.022930	2.659147	842742	.012643	15.409	60
65	537458	20457	.038062	.175188	48742	8539	223561	.038195	2.640312	583207	.015961	11.965	65
70	409007	27611	.067507	.291073	40203	11702	172633	.067785	2.574631	359646	.016937	8.946	70
75	224818	25857	.115013	.446686	28501	12731	110235	.115490	2.465226	187013	.015328	6.562	75
80	109102	19539	.179089	.607292	15770	9577	53280	.179748	2.330062	76778	.015328	4.869	80
85+	42193	11120	.263551	1.000000	6193	6193	23498	.263551	3.794335	23498	.000000	3.794	85+

NUMBER OF PERSONS DYING (OUT OF 100,000 AT BIRTH) ABOVE AGE X FROM SPECIFIED CAUSES

Age (x)	All Causes	Respiratory T.B.	Other Infec. and Paras.	Neo-plasms	Cardio-vascular	Infl., Pneu., Bronch.	Diar-rheal	Certain Degen-erative	Maternal	Cert. Dis. of Infancy	Motor Vehicle	Other Violence	Other and Unknown	Age (x)
0	100000	5133	5146	5372	24899	15497	11158	286	714	2730	0	1192	27873	0
1	87565	5095	4642	5352	24821	13438	6507	285	714	0	0	1173	25538	1
5	78607	5004	3400	5313	24747	11142	3259	284	714	0	0	1006	23738	5
10	76984	4926	2909	5301	24679	10874	3030	283	714	0	0	944	23324	10
15	75916	4759	2599	5291	24592	10740	2930	281	714	0	0	917	23093	15
20	74287	4165	2241	5274	24492	10558	2855	279	695	0	0	867	22861	20
25	72293	3402	1924	5249	24391	10364	2782	277	580	0	0	797	22527	25
30	70278	2705	1649	5213	24257	10155	2713	274	426	0	0	744	22142	30
35	68337	2114	1420	5139	24093	9932	2650	267	267	0	0	698	21757	35
40	66307	1636	1229	5007	23845	9672	2581	260	109	0	0	655	21313	40
45	64177	1262	1051	4776	23507	9406	2481	250	18	0	0	611	20815	45
50	61799	933	886	4408	23017	9091	2379	236	2	0	0	562	20285	50
55	58686	692	734	3905	22141	8622	2246	212	0	0	0	501	19633	55
60	54693	491	585	3276	20791	7989	2088	177	0	0	0	434	18862	60
65	48742	313	439	2520	18495	7003	1824	128	0	0	0	366	17654	65
70	40203	178	294	1669	14829	5511	1434	75	0	0	0	280	15933	70
75	28501	79	149	893	9691	3556	929	40	0	0	0	197	12967	75
80	15770	26	52	317	4466	1719	433	12	0	0	0	100	8645	80
85+	6193	5	19	84	1416	581	136	2	0	0	0	33	3917	85+

NUMBER OF PERSONS SURVIVING TO AGE X IF SPECIFIED CAUSES WERE ELIMINATED

Age (x)	No Causes	Respiratory T.B. (1)	Other Infec. and Paras. (2)	Neo-plasms (3)	Cardio-vascular (4)	Infl., Pneu., Bronch. (5)	Diar-rheal (6)	Certain Degen-erative (7)	Maternal (8)	Cert. Dis. of Infancy (9)	Motor Vehicle (10)	Other Violence (11)	Other and Unknown (12)	(1)+(2)	(1)+(2)+(5)+(6)+(8)	(1)+(2)+(5)+(6)+(8)+part of(9)&(12)	(10)+(11)	Age (x)
0	100000	100000	100000	100000	100000	100000	100000	100000	100000	100000	100000	100000	100000	100000	100000	100000	100000	0
1	87565	87601	88038	87584	87638	89512	92024	87566	87565	90155	87565	87583	89776	88073	94616	99788	87583	1
5	78607	78725	80223	78661	78743	82608	85906	78609	78607	80932	78607	78781	82358	80343	92273	99366	78781	5
10	76984	77177	79064	77049	77184	81182	84381	76987	76984	79261	76984	77216	81088	79262	91615	99121	77216	10
15	75916	76273	78284	75990	76200	80196	83319	75921	75916	78162	75916	76172	80205	78652	91188	98913	76172	15
20	74287	75229	76970	74376	74664	78666	81612	74294	74306	76485	74287	74587	78727	77946	90702	98653	74587	20
25	72293	73976	75228	72404	72761	76757	79501	72301	72425	74432	72293	72654	76964	76980	90046	98334	72654	25
30	70278	72620	73414	70422	70866	74837	77360	70289	70559	72357	70278	70682	75861	75224	89277	97949	70682	30
35	68337	71219	71623	68550	69072	73004	75292	68355	68768	70359	68337	68775	73554	74643	88410	97437	68775	35
40	66307	69596	69692	66644	67268	71110	73130	66331	66881	68268	66307	66775	71841	73149	87269	96643	66775	40
45	64177	67747	67638	64733	65545	69107	70890	64823	66075	66177	64177	64673	70067	71400	85782	95445	64673	45
50	61799	65578	65302	62699	63513	66880	68373	61845	62437	63627	61799	62326	66040	69296	83827	93664	62326	50
55	58686	62524	62169	60040	61198	64008	65073	58753	59294	60422	58686	59246	65316	66235	80932	90827	59246	55
60	54693	58476	58092	56579	58411	60323	60815	54789	55259	56311	54693	55280	61706	62110	76959	86784	55280	60
65	48742	52292	51917	51165	54423	54795	54475	48874	50184	49330	48742	49330	55698	56293	70706	80353	49330	65
70	40203	43262	42961	43015	48761	46742	45329	40360	40619	41392	40203	40767	48273	46229	61229	70447	40767	70
75	28501	30757	30585	31190	40196	35090	32614	28641	28796	29344	28501	28971	37359	33006	46983	55542	28971	75
80	15770	17059	16998	17717	28319	21133	18464	15868	15933	16237	15770	16102	25336	18387	29147	36589	16102	80
85+	6193	6713	6657	7118	14977	9274	7464	6237	6257	6376	6193	6365	15784	7259	13237	19146	6365	85+

ADDED YRS OF LIFE

	No Causes	(1)	(2)	(3)	(4)	(5)	(6)	(7)	(8)	(9)	(10)	(11)	(12)	(1)+(2)	(1)+(2)+(5)+(6)+(8)	...+part	(10)+(11)
TOTAL		1.883	2.276	.849	3.322	4.328	5.238	.045	.268	1.483	.000	.351	6.544	4.268	15.736	23.508	.351
WORK	6.947	1.642	.748	.406	.832	.755	.243	.022	.274	.000	.000	.155	1.218	2.426	3.816	4.769	.155

POPULATION, DEATHS, DEATH RATES FOR ALL CAUSES COMBINED, AND SPECIFIED CAUSES

Age Start of Interval	Midyear Population	Deaths During Year	All Causes	Respiratory T. B.	Other Infec. and Paras.	Neoplasms	Cardiovascular	Infl., Pneu., Bronch.	Diarrheal	Certain Degenerative	Maternal	Cert. Dis. of Infancy	Motor Vehicle	Other Violence	Other and Unknown	Age Start of Interval
0	513934	62596	.12180	.00031	.00678	.00004	.00032	.02683	.04342	.00066	.00000	.03084	.00000	.00031	.01229	0
1	1818949	29974	.01648	.00016	.00329	.00005	.00009	.00515	.00466	.00043	.00000	.00000	.00000	.00068	.00197	1
5	2731961	5987	.00219	.00005	.00074	.00003	.00012	.00038	.00013	.00011	.00000	.00000	.00000	.00022	.00043	5
10	1556944	3167	.00203	.00010	.00060	.00003	.00018	.00025	.00006	.00007	.00000	.00000	.00000	.00030	.00046	10
15	2071239	6356	.00307	.00060	.00067	.00004	.00021	.00048	.00004	.00009	.00000	.00000	.00000	.00047	.00048	15
20	1832941	8087	.00441	.00132	.00071	.00007	.00024	.00063	.00005	.00014	.00000	.00000	.00000	.00068	.00057	20
25	1522939	6895	.00453	.00144	.00064	.00009	.00026	.00058	.00005	.00022	.00000	.00000	.00000	.00068	.00057	25
30	1292806	6589	.00510	.00148	.00056	.00014	.00040	.00072	.00006	.00032	.00000	.00000	.00000	.00072	.00070	30
35	1126911	6558	.00585	.00140	.00060	.00026	.00060	.00058	.00006	.00045	.00000	.00000	.00000	.00069	.00082	35
40	1060206	7448	.00703	.00121	.00069	.00049	.00092	.00118	.00008	.00061	.00000	.00000	.00000	.00083	.00101	40
45	964782	8938	.00926	.00121	.00082	.00082	.00154	.00158	.00012	.00087	.00000	.00000	.00000	.00097	.00134	45
50	922318	11197	.01214	.00116	.00076	.00131	.00264	.00203	.00017	.00129	.00000	.00000	.00000	.00110	.00168	50
55	766965	14016	.01827	.00113	.00103	.00217	.00482	.00310	.00030	.00187	.00000	.00000	.00000	.00126	.00259	55
60	685451	18288	.02668	.00098	.00104	.00321	.00893	.00455	.00051	.00250	.00000	.00000	.00000	.00129	.00367	60
65	558613	24665	.04415	.00081	.00136	.00475	.01747	.00764	.00055	.00343	.00000	.00000	.00000	.00147	.00628	65
70	402190	29607	.07361	.00054	.00153	.00591	.03212	.01263	.00174	.00433	.00000	.00000	.00000	.00169	.01313	70
75	225182	29274	.13000	.00040	.00184	.00605	.05732	.02218	.00334	.00540	.00000	.00000	.00000	.00213	.03134	75
80	91070	21069	.23135	.00024	.00253	.00582	.08688	.03724	.00535	.00609	.00000	.00000	.00000	.00257	.08464	80
85+	26791	11706	.43694	.00045	.00358	.00605	.12754	.06364	.00806	.00780	.00000	.00000	.00000	.00332	.21649	85+
ALL	20172192	312457														

	All Causes	Respiratory T.B.	Other Infec.	Neoplasms	Cardiovascular	Infl. Pneu.	Diarrheal	Certain Degen.	Maternal	Cert. Dis. Infancy	Motor Vehicle	Other Violence	Other Unknown
CRUDE DEATH RATE	.01549	.00079	.00116	.00072	.00322	.00294	.00175	.00073	.00000	.00079	.00000	.00071	.00269
STANDARDIZED RATE (1)	.01408	.00074	.00125	.00050	.00206	.00283	.00224	.00056	.00000	.00109	.00000	.00065	.00218
STANDARDIZED RATE (2)	.01935	.00083	.00114	.00054	.00493	.00350	.00159	.00091	.00000	.00064	.00000	.00079	.00409
GEOMETRIC MEAN	.01712												

LIFE TABLE FOR ALL CAUSES COMBINED

Age (x)	Midyear Population	Deaths During Year	$_nM_x$	$_nq_x$	l_x	$_nd_x$	$_nL_x$	$_nm_x$	$_na_x$	T_x	$_nr_x$	$\overset{\circ}{e}_x$	Age (x)
0	513934	62596	.121798	.111940	100000	11194	91907	.121797	.277056	5342786	.000000	53.428	0
1	1818949	29974	.016479	.063307	88806	5622	341169	.016479	1.500000	5250878	.000000	59.128	1
5	2731961	5987	.002191	.010879	83184	905	413658	.002188	2.500000	4909709	.000000	59.022	5
10	1556944	3167	.002034	.010136	82279	834	409379	.002037	2.583183	4496052	.025446	54.644	10
15	2071239	6356	.003069	.015200	81445	1238	404321	.003062	2.654483	4086672	-.016092	50.177	15
20	1832941	8087	.004412	.021843	80207	1752	396763	.004416	2.561834	3682351	.015810	45.911	20
25	1522939	6895	.004527	.022408	78455	1758	387918	.004532	2.521450	3285588	.027438	41.879	25
30	1292806	6589	.005097	.025203	76697	1933	378736	.005104	2.543326	2897670	.027346	37.781	30
35	1126911	6558	.005855	.028891	74764	2160	368540	.005861	2.555748	2518934	.017825	33.692	35
40	1060206	7448	.007025	.034585	72604	2511	356654	.007035	2.584379	2150393	.011385	29.618	40
45	964782	8938	.009264	.045325	70093	3177	342823	.009267	2.594560	1793439	.005322	25.587	45
50	922318	11197	.012140	.055074	66916	3953	325116	.012156	2.623693	1450616	.008533	21.678	50
55	766965	14016	.018275	.087734	62963	5524	301684	.018311	2.622948	1125430	.012034	17.874	55
60	685451	18288	.026680	.125577	57439	7213	270104	.026705	2.630465	823745	.004890	14.341	60
65	558613	24665	.044154	.199916	50226	10041	227142	.044206	2.611045	553642	.005734	11.023	65
70	402190	29607	.073614	.312679	40185	12565	170240	.073807	2.557932	326499	.011289	8.125	70
75	225182	29274	.130002	.490043	27620	13535	103742	.130468	2.461520	156259	.011964	5.657	75
80	91070	21069	.231350	.714590	14085	10065	43317	.232357	2.306694	52517	.011964	3.729	80
85+	26791	11706	.436938	1.000000	4020	4020	9200	.436938	2.288655	9200	.000000	2.289	85+

NUMBER OF PERSONS DYING (OUT OF 100,000 AT BIRTH) ABOVE AGE X FROM SPECIFIED CAUSES

Age (x)	All Causes	Respiratory T. B.	Other Infec. and Paras.	Neoplasms	Cardiovascular	Infl., Pneu., Bronch.	Diarrheal	Certain Degenerative	Maternal	Cert. Dis. of Infancy	Motor Vehicle	Other Violence	Other and Unknown	Age (x)
0	100000	4712	5758	5707	26802	17581	7274	5339	0	2834	0	4429	19124	0
1	88806	4684	5174	5704	26772	15516	3283	5278	0	0	0	4400	17995	1
5	83184	4629	4053	5687	26740	13758	1692	5132	0	0	0	4169	17324	5
10	82279	4610	3748	5675	26692	13603	1640	5086	0	0	0	4079	17146	10
15	81445	4570	3505	5664	26617	13502	1617	5057	0	0	0	3957	16956	15
20	80207	4330	3236	5647	26531	13310	1601	5020	0	0	0	3768	16764	20
25	78455	3805	2952	5619	26435	13059	1582	4966	0	0	0	3499	16538	25
30	76657	3245	2706	5585	26335	12834	1563	4881	0	0	0	3235	16313	30
35	74764	2684	2494	5531	26183	12560	1540	4760	0	0	0	2962	16050	35
40	72604	2168	2273	5435	25962	12199	1520	4594	0	0	0	2706	15747	40
45	70093	1734	2026	5260	25632	11779	1491	4377	0	0	0	2408	15386	45
50	66916	1319	1747	4978	25104	11237	1450	4080	0	0	0	2075	14926	50
55	62963	942	1498	4550	24243	10576	1395	3658	0	0	0	1718	14383	55
60	57439	602	1188	3893	22785	9638	1306	3093	0	0	0	1337	13597	60
65	50226	339	906	3026	20370	8407	1166	2418	0	0	0	989	12605	65
70	40185	155	597	1946	16397	6670	951	1637	0	0	0	654	11178	70
75	27620	62	337	939	10913	4514	655	900	0	0	0	367	8933	75
80	14085	20	146	311	4947	2205	306	339	0	0	0	145	5666	80
85+	4020	4	33	56	1173	586	74	72	0	0	0	31	1991	85+

NUMBER OF PERSONS SURVIVING TO AGE X IF SPECIFIED CAUSES WERE ELIMINATED

Age (x)	No Causes	Respiratory T. B.	Other Infec. and Paras.	Neoplasms	Cardiovascular	Infl., Pneu., Bronch.	Diarrheal	Certain Degenerative	Maternal	Cert. Dis. of Infancy	Motor Vehicle	Other Violence	Other and Unknown	(1) + (2)	(1) + (2) + (5) + (6) + (8)	(1)+(2)+ (5)+(6)+ (8)+part of(9)&(12)	(10) + (11)	Age (x)
		(1)	(2)	(3)	(4)	(5)	(6)	(7)	(8)	(9)	(10)	(11)	(12)					
0	100000	100000	100000	100000	100000	100000	100000	100000	100000	100000	100000	100000	100000	100000	100000	100000	100000	0
1	88806	88832	89396	88809	88834	91158	92645	88863	88806	91516	88806	88833	89876	89422	95759	99798	88833	1
5	83184	83252	84835	83203	83241	87151	88401	83379	83184	85722	83184	83433	84846	84915	94545	99238	83433	5
10	82279	82375	84222	82310	82384	86365	87495	82518	82279	84789	82279	82616	84103	84321	94119	98946	82616	10
15	81445	81580	83617	81486	81623	85595	86632	81711	81445	83930	81445	81900	83444	83755	93629	98576	81900	15
20	80207	80579	82620	80265	80468	84494	85332	80505	80207	82654	80207	80844	82371	83003	93027	98102	80844	20
25	78455	79342	81105	78539	78806	82911	83488	78801	78455	80849	78455	79347	80802	82022	92242	97469	79347	25
30	76657	78126	79519	76813	77139	81288	81637	77119	76657	79037	76657	77833	79221	81022	91403	96776	77833	30
35	74764	76724	77752	74931	75346	79527	79604	75296	74764	77045	74764	76145	77493	79790	90367	95892	76145	35
40	72604	75030	75732	72861	73389	77609	77325	73286	72604	74819	72604	74203	75564	78263	89098	94779	74203	40
45	70093	72877	73367	70514	71180	75367	74681	70567	70093	72232	70093	71936	73321	76281	87389	93209	71936	45
50	66916	69996	70327	67596	68480	72523	71339	68045	66916	68958	66916	69010	70469	73564	84998	90945	69010	50
55	62963	66244	66426	64023	65296	68937	67182	64442	62963	64884	62963	65291	66663	69888	81646	87646	65291	55
60	57439	60773	60911	59048	61031	63877	61378	59343	57439	59192	57439	59541	61199	64447	76586	82595	59541	60
65	50226	53401	53541	52472	55825	57149	53811	52546	50226	51758	50226	52752	55045	56925	69395	75266	52752	65
70	40185	42898	43131	42997	48793	47522	43260	42773	40185	41411	40185	42519	45462	46042	58615	64149	42519	70
75	27620	29564	29873	30444	39504	34830	29997	30046	27620	28463	27620	29473	33426	31975	43793	48815	29473	75
80	14085	15106	15376	16003	27088	19916	15565	15747	14085	14515	14085	15194	20058	16491	25770	30094	15194	80
85+	4020	4320	4451	4715	12371	6955	4573	4646	4020	4143	4020	4398	9067	4783	9413	12667	4398	85+

ADDED YRS OF LIFE																		
TOTAL		1.453	2.199	.756	3.066	4.527	3.515	.505	.000	1.622	.000	1.186	3.240	3.735	12.857	17.512	1.186	
WORK	6.621	1.230	.693	.318	.744	.929	.072	.406	.000	.000	.000	.731	.827	1.951	3.026	3.542	.731	

POPULATION, DEATHS, DEATH RATES FOR ALL CAUSES COMBINED, AND SPECIFIED CAUSES

Age Start of Interval	Midyear Population	Deaths During Year	All Causes	Respiratory T. B.	Other Infec. and Paras.	Neoplasms	Cardio-vascular	Infl., Pneu., Bronch.	Diarrheal	Certain Degenerative	Maternal	Cert. Dis. of Infancy	Motor Vehicle	Other Violence	Other and Unknown	Age Start of Interval
0	495183	53279	.10759	.00023	.00624	.00003	.00028	.02188	.04068	.00059	.00000	.02657	.00000	.00033	.01075	0
1	1755454	29024	.01653	.00014	.00320	.00003	.00011	.00503	.00518	.00043	.00000	.00000	.00000	.00055	.00188	1
5	2643572	5691	.00215	.00007	.00078	.00002	.00010	.00040	.00015	.00012	.00000	.00000	.00000	.00055	.00188	5
10	1510889	3082	.00204	.00026	.00067	.00002	.00021	.00028	.00007	.00008	.00000	.00000	.00000	.00011	.00041	10
15	2049010	6393	.00312	.00116	.00069	.00003	.00022	.00037	.00005	.00010	.00007	.00000	.00000	.00007	.00038	15
20	1860898	7920	.00426	.00175	.00072	.00005	.00028	.00044	.00005	.00014	.00026	.00000	.00000	.00011	.00033	20
25	1619060	7377	.00456	.00169	.00066	.00010	.00035	.00050	.00005	.00018	.00038	.00000	.00000	.00014	.00043	25
30	1492067	6929	.00464	.00135	.00060	.00021	.00043	.00059	.00005	.00023	.00043	.00000	.00000	.00014	.00061	30
35	1347290	6855	.00509	.00107	.00056	.00044	.00064	.00068	.00008	.00032	.00044	.00000	.00000	.00012	.00073	35
40	1254884	7442	.00593	.00093	.00056	.00085	.00098	.00085	.00008	.00043	.00027	.00000	.00000	.00018	.00079	40
45	1092666	7950	.00728	.00087	.00055	.00127	.00166	.00098	.00013	.00064	.00003	.00000	.00000	.00019	.00096	45
50	986389	9340	.00947	.00066	.00058	.00168	.00272	.00139	.00019	.00088	.00001	.00000	.00000	.00021	.00114	50
55	816584	11907	.01458	.00064	.00070	.00237	.00499	.00235	.00028	.00127	.00000	.00000	.00000	.00027	.00173	55
60	729623	16090	.02205	.00058	.00069	.00300	.00879	.00386	.00047	.00182	.00000	.00000	.00000	.00030	.00255	60
65	597550	22900	.03832	.00061	.00101	.00411	.01724	.00705	.00092	.00255	.00000	.00000	.00000	.00043	.00440	65
70	434052	28487	.06563	.00044	.00117	.00505	.03081	.01223	.00157	.00335	.00000	.00000	.00000	.00064	.01039	70
75	250782	29545	.11781	.00025	.00152	.00573	.05346	.02110	.00257	.00416	.00000	.00000	.00000	.00104	.02755	75
80	108178	22858	.21130	.00030	.00263	.00634	.08030	.03547	.00487	.00502	.00000	.00000	.00000	.00174	.07463	80
85+	36113	13879	.38432	.00019	.00396	.00609	.11184	.05610	.00761	.00601	.00000	.00000	.00000	.00277	.18974	85+
ALL	21080244	296948														

		All Causes	Respiratory T. B.	Other Infec. and Paras.	Neoplasms	Cardio-vascular	Infl., Pneu., Bronch.	Diarrheal	Certain Degenerative	Maternal	Cert. Dis. of Infancy	Motor Vehicle	Other Violence	Other and Unknown
CRUDE DEATH RATE		.01409	.00081	.00105	.00079	.00332	.00257	.00161	.00058	.00014	.00062	.00000	.00023	.00237
STANDARDIZED RATE (1)		.01271	.00077	.00119	.00053	.00202	.00245	.00220	.00044	.00013	.00094	.00000	.00022	.00183
STANDARDIZED RATE (2)		.01725	.00080	.00105	.00097	.00472	.00309	.00156	.00070	.00013	.00055	.00000	.00025	.00344
GEOMETRIC MEAN		.01539												

LIFE TABLE FOR ALL CAUSES COMBINED

Age (x)	Midyear Population	Deaths During Year	$_nM_x$	$_nq_x$	l_x	$_nd_x$	$_nL_x$	$_nm_x$	$_na_x$	T_x	$_nr_x$	$\overset{\circ}{e}_x$	Age (x)
0	495183	53279	.107595	.099590	100000	9959	92560	.107595	.252911	5551617	.000000	55.516	0
1	1755454	29024	.016534	.063504	90041	5718	345869	.016532	1.500000	5459057	.000000	60.629	1
5	2643572	5691	.002153	.010685	84323	901	419363	.002148	2.500000	5113188	.000000	60.638	5
10	1510889	3082	.002040	.010177	83422	849	415065	.002045	2.591775	4693826	.000000	56.266	10
15	2049010	6393	.003120	.015441	82573	1275	409857	.003111	2.641176	4278760	-.019606	51.818	15
20	1860898	7920	.004256	.021071	81298	1713	402316	.004258	2.563120	3868903	-.010452	47.589	20
25	1619060	7377	.004556	.022542	79585	1794	393455	.004560	2.508477	3466587	.016517	43.558	25
30	1492067	6929	.004644	.022959	77791	1786	384514	.004645	2.513648	3073132	.014696	39.505	30
35	1347290	6855	.005088	.025143	76005	1911	375327	.005092	2.541645	2688618	.012299	35.374	35
40	1254884	7442	.005930	.029260	74094	2168	365188	.005937	2.563807	2313291	.014130	31.221	40
45	1092666	7950	.007276	.035801	71926	2575	353412	.007286	2.585113	1948102	.015581	27.085	45
50	986389	9340	.009469	.046430	69351	3220	339142	.009495	2.635870	1594691	.018624	22.994	50
55	816584	11907	.014581	.070693	66131	4675	319641	.014626	2.644162	1255548	.017553	18.986	55
60	729623	16090	.022052	.105034	61456	6455	292186	.022092	2.661696	935907	.009323	15.229	60
65	597550	22900	.038322	.176088	55001	9685	252130	.038413	2.638100	643720	.010320	11.704	65
70	434052	28487	.065630	.284116	45316	12875	195457	.065871	2.582718	391590	.015835	8.641	70
75	250782	29545	.117811	.456120	32441	14797	125025	.118352	2.487329	196133	.015277	6.046	75
80	108178	22858	.211300	.678701	17644	11975	56357	.212484	2.339231	71108	.015277	4.030	80
85+	36113	13879	.384321	1.000000	5669	5669	14751	.384321	2.601989	14751	.000000	2.602	85+

NUMBER OF PERSONS DYING (OUT OF 100,000 AT BIRTH) ABOVE AGE X FROM SPECIFIED CAUSES

Age (x)	All Causes	Respiratory T. B.	Other Infec. and Paras.	Neo-plasms	Cardio-vascular	Infl., Pneu., Bronch.	Diar-rheal	Certain Degen-erative	Maternal	Cert. Dis. of Infancy	Motor Vehicle	Other Violence	Other and Unknown	Age (x)
0	100000	4515	5470	6513	30291	17733	7430	4477	726	2460	0	1441	18944	0
1	90041	4493	4892	6509	30265	15707	3665	4422	726	0	0	1411	17951	1
5	84323	4446	3786	6498	30228	13967	1874	4275	726	0	0	1221	17302	5
10	83422	4417	3459	6491	30186	13799	1811	4226	726	0	0	1175	17132	10
15	82573	4306	3183	6482	30098	13685	1781	4192	726	0	0	1146	16974	15
20	81298	3832	2898	6469	30010	13535	1762	4153	699	0	0	1100	16840	20
25	79585	3128	2609	6450	29898	13357	1742	4056	595	0	0	1042	16668	25
30	77791	2465	2351	6412	29761	13161	1720	4026	445	0	0	984	16466	30
35	76005	1948	2120	6329	29596	12934	1700	3939	279	0	0	931	16229	35
40	74094	1545	1908	6165	29355	12679	1668	3819	115	0	0	884	15956	40
45	71926	1208	1703	5853	28996	12369	1639	3661	15	0	0	819	15663	45
50	69351	900	1508	5405	28408	12022	1593	3435	4	0	0	750	15326	50
55	66131	676	1310	4833	27481	11549	1529	3135	1	0	0	678	14939	55
60	61456	470	1086	4075	25881	10797	1439	2728	1	0	0	593	14386	60
65	55001	302	884	3198	23307	9668	1302	2156	1	0	0	505	13638	65
70	45316	149	629	2160	18550	7886	1069	1552	1	0	0	397	12523	70
75	32441	64	401	1172	12906	5486	761	897	1	0	0	271	10482	75
80	17644	27	210	454	6195	2837	388	376	1	0	0	140	7016	80
85+	5669	3	58	90	1650	828	112	89	0	0	0	41	2798	85+

NUMBER OF PERSONS SURVIVING TO AGE X IF SPECIFIED CAUSES WERE ELIMINATED

Age (x)	No Causes	Respiratory T. B.	Other Infec. and Paras.	Neo-plasms	Cardio-vascular	Infl., Pneu., Bronch.	Diar-rheal	Certain Degener-ative	Maternal	Cert. Dis. of Infancy	Motor Vehicle	Other Violence	Other and Unknown	(1) + (2)	(1) + (2) + (5) + (6) + (8)	(1)+(2)+ (5)+(6)+ (8)+part of(9)&(12)	(10) + (11)	Age (x)
		(1)	(2)	(3)	(4)	(5)	(6)	(7)	(8)	(9)	(10)	(11)	(12)					
0	100000	100000	100000	100000	100000	100000	100000	100000	100000	100000	100000	100000	100000	100000	100000	100000	100000	0
1	90041	90062	90591	90045	90090	91983	93684	90093	90041	92405	90041	90069	90588	90612	96311	99815	90069	1
5	84323	84388	85921	84337	84382	87879	89556	84514	84323	86537	84323	84534	85847	85988	95175	99319	84534	5
10	83422	83515	85336	83443	83522	87114	88666	83660	83422	85612	83422	83676	85102	85431	94820	99109	83676	10
15	82573	82776	84748	82603	82760	86346	87795	82843	82573	84741	82573	82854	84396	84957	94457	98874	82854	15
20	81298	81971	83730	81340	81569	85169	86459	81602	81325	83432	81298	81620	83225	84423	94089	98624	81620	20
25	79585	80949	82261	79645	79962	83555	84659	79940	79714	81674	79585	79958	81650	83671	93601	98289	79958	25
30	77791	79794	80671	77887	78296	81879	82774	78207	78066	79833	77791	78213	80014	82747	93002	97863	78213	30
35	76005	78487	79056	76182	76663	80236	80894	76498	76439	78000	76005	76470	78419	81638	92249	97295	76470	35
40	74094	76926	77286	74429	74976	78485	78954	74694	74680	76039	74094	74594	76725	80239	91216	96433	74594	40
45	71926	75020	75235	72561	73141	76512	76616	72666	72594	73814	71926	72476	74780	78472	89744	95076	72476	45
50	69351	72650	72742	70408	71112	74137	73921	70289	70006	71172	69351	69950	72448	76203	87649	93036	69950	50
55	66131	69506	69568	67708	68746	71190	70556	67323	66758	67867	66131	66773	69480	73118	84774	90160	66773	55
60	61456	64801	64877	63674	65511	66460	66093	62093	62039	63069	61456	62135	65130	68408	80368	85702	62135	60
65	55001	58161	58264	57850	61286	61186	58903	56868	55523	56445	55001	55693	59043	61612	73977	79178	55693	65
70	45316	48065	48249	48658	55096	52156	48757	47459	45746	46506	45316	45985	49747	51176	63973	68906	45985	70
75	32441	34483	34743	35729	46137	39734	35184	34553	32749	33293	32441	33027	37567	36931	49524	54143	33027	75
80	17644	18782	19043	20002	33036	24088	19431	19192	17811	18107	17644	18059	23610	20272	30769	35069	18059	80
85+	5669	6048	6207	6652	16332	9363	6409	6337	5723	5818	5669	5857	11316	6623	12485	16156	5857	85+

ADDED YRS OF LIFE

		(1)	(2)	(3)	(4)	(5)	(6)	(7)	(8)	(9)	(10)	(11)	(12)				
TOTAL		1.618	2.214	.963	3.643	4.195	3.645	.787	.274	1.451	.000	.395	3.051	3.917	13.139	17.455	.395
WORK	5.978	1.354	.672	.444	.828	.702	.080	.315	.257	.000	.000	.155	.657	2.053	3.172	3.623	.155

POPULATION, DEATHS, DEATH RATES FOR ALL CAUSES COMBINED, AND SPECIFIED CAUSES

Age Start of Interval	Midyear Population	Deaths During Year	All Causes	Respiratory T.B.	Other Infec. and Paras.	Neoplasms	Cardiovascular	Infl., Pneu., Bronch.	Diarrheal	Certain Degenerative	Maternal	Cert. Dis. of Infancy	Motor Vehicle	Other Violence	Other and Unknown	Age Start of Interval
0	451072	22267	.04936	.00005	.00123	.00010	.00012	.00829	.00463	.00006	.00000	.02763	.00000	.00006	.00719	0
1	1709436	3630	.00212	.00001	.00031	.00015	.00004	.00043	.00023	.00002	.00000	.00000	.00008	.00026	.00060	1
5	2057937	1370	.00067	.00000	.00009	.00010	.00003	.00005	.00001	.00002	.00000	.00000	.00009	.00011	.00016	5
10	2200017	1347	.00061	.00000	.00005	.00008	.00006	.00003	.00001	.00002	.00000	.00000	.00009	.00014	.00014	10
15	1939941	2131	.00110	.00002	.00004	.00010	.00010	.00003	.00000	.00003	.00000	.00000	.00032	.00029	.00016	15
20	2087876	2687	.00129	.00005	.00003	.00012	.00010	.00002	.00001	.00006	.00000	.00000	.00043	.00033	.00014	20
25	2015937	2808	.00139	.00011	.00003	.00015	.00015	.00004	.00000	.00009	.00000	.00000	.00036	.00030	.00016	25
30	1992479	3266	.00164	.00018	.00003	.00022	.00024	.00004	.00001	.00014	.00000	.00000	.00030	.00028	.00020	30
35	1882540	4125	.00219	.00022	.00005	.00037	.00043	.00006	.00001	.00021	.00000	.00000	.00029	.00030	.00027	35
40	1238429	4306	.00348	.00033	.00006	.00071	.00082	.00012	.00001	.00031	.00000	.00000	.00033	.00038	.00040	40
45	1689533	9218	.00546	.00041	.00009	.00129	.00148	.00021	.00001	.00056	.00000	.00000	.00037	.00047	.00057	45
50	1517553	13848	.00913	.00055	.00013	.00237	.00288	.00047	.00002	.00089	.00000	.00000	.00036	.00057	.00088	50
55	1232138	18528	.01504	.00068	.00019	.00407	.00534	.00092	.00003	.00129	.00000	.00000	.00041	.00069	.00141	55
60	963881	22775	.02363	.00076	.00026	.00622	.00957	.00162	.00006	.00195	.00000	.00000	.00041	.00070	.00208	60
65	741750	26536	.03577	.00071	.00032	.00810	.01686	.00259	.00010	.00258	.00000	.00000	.00045	.00086	.00320	65
70	578850	31374	.05420	.00066	.00034	.00993	.02909	.00406	.00015	.00318	.00000	.00000	.00050	.00104	.00525	70
75	384691	34280	.08911	.00056	.00037	.01264	.05159	.00755	.00030	.00352	.00000	.00000	.00056	.00159	.01043	75
80	193642	29927	.15455	.00039	.00035	.01437	.09054	.01457	.00080	.00340	.00000	.00000	.00063	.00254	.02696	80
85+	74520	20868	.28003	.00050	.00032	.01460	.14858	.03141	.00181	.00356	.00000	.00000	.00067	.00464	.07394	85+
ALL	24952222	255291														

	All Causes	Respiratory T.B.	Other Infec. and Paras.	Neoplasms	Cardiovascular	Infl., Pneu., Bronch.	Diarrheal	Certain Degenerative	Maternal	Cert. Dis. of Infancy	Motor Vehicle	Other Violence	Other and Unknown
CRUDE DEATH RATE	.01023	.00024	.00013	.00163	.00416	.00085	.00013	.00054	.00000	.00050	.00030	.00041	.00134
STANDARDIZED RATE (1)	.00678	.00015	.00015	.00091	.00195	.00066	.00021	.00031	.00000	.00097	.00025	.00032	.00090
STANDARDIZED RATE (2)	.01150	.00023	.00014	.00175	.00483	.00099	.00015	.00056	.00000	.00057	.00029	.00043	.00155
GEOMETRIC MEAN	.00800												

LIFE TABLE FOR ALL CAUSES COMBINED

Age (x)	Midyear Population	Deaths During Year	$_nM_x$	$_nq_x$	l_x	$_nd_x$	$_nL_x$	$_nm_x$	$_na_x$	T_x	$_nr_x$	$\overset{\circ}{e}_x$	Age (x)
0	451072	22267	.049365	.047390	100000	4739	95990	.049370	.153920	6675770	.000000	66.758	0
1	1709436	3630	.002124	.008440	95261	804	379034	.002121	1.500000	6579779	.000000	69.071	1
5	2057937	1370	.000666	.003324	94457	314	471500	.000666	2.500000	6200745	.000000	65.646	5
10	2200017	1347	.000612	.003059	94143	288	470037	.000613	2.645399	5729245	.003628	60.857	10
15	1939941	2131	.001098	.005487	93855	515	468052	.001100	2.625405	5259208	.006194	56.035	15
20	2087876	2687	.001287	.006407	93340	598	465232	.001293	2.544941	4791156	-.004340	51.330	20
25	2015937	2808	.001393	.006944	92742	644	462132	.001394	2.549819	4325924	-.003074	46.645	25
30	1992479	3266	.001639	.008165	92098	752	458684	.001639	2.598903	3863792	-.003593	41.953	30
35	1882540	4125	.002191	.010958	91346	1001	454397	.002203	2.669206	3405108	.038753	37.277	35
40	1238429	4306	.003477	.017322	90345	1565	448100	.003493	2.683573	2950711	.022540	32.660	40
45	1689533	9218	.005456	.026808	88780	2380	438430	.005428	2.701593	2502611	-.022983	28.189	45
50	1517553	13848	.009125	.044769	86400	3868	423089	.009142	2.696269	2064181	.010034	23.891	50
55	1232138	18528	.015037	.072950	82532	6024	398586	.015113	2.663616	1641092	.025491	19.884	55
60	963881	22775	.023628	.112393	76508	8599	362124	.023746	2.625814	1242507	.028178	16.240	60
65	741750	26536	.035775	.165177	67909	11217	312544	.035889	2.592828	880382	-.018639	12.964	65
70	578850	31374	.054201	.239840	56692	13597	250416	.054298	2.565761	567838	.009628	10.016	70
75	384691	34280	.089110	.365936	43095	15770	176373	.089413	2.520477	317422	.014487	7.366	75
80	193642	29927	.154548	.554328	27325	15147	97562	.155256	2.421051	141050	.014487	5.162	80
85+	74520	20868	.280032	1.000000	12178	12178	43488	.280032	3.571018	43488	.000000	3.571	85+

NUMBER OF PERSONS DYING (OUT OF 100,000 AT BIRTH) ABOVE AGE X FROM SPECIFIED CAUSES

Age (x)	All Causes	Respiratory T. B.	Other Infec. and Paras.	Neoplasms	Cardiovascular	Infl., Pneu., Bronch.	Diarrheal	Certain Degenerative	Maternal	Cert. Dis. of Infancy	Motor Vehicle	Other Violence	Other and Unknown	Age (x)
0	100000	1928	984	15684	45448	8344	883	4982	0	2652	2135	3331	13629	0
1	95261	1923	865	15674	45437	7548	438	4976	0	0	2135	3326	12939	1
5	94457	1920	748	15619	45422	7386	351	4968	0	0	2104	3227	12712	5
10	94143	1920	708	15570	45406	7364	346	4957	0	0	2063	3173	12636	10
15	93855	1917	684	15532	45377	7350	344	4949	0	0	2022	3108	12572	15
20	93340	1910	665	15484	45330	7338	342	4934	0	0	1870	2971	12496	20
25	92742	1888	652	15430	45283	7326	339	4907	0	0	1668	2818	12431	25
30	92098	1839	637	15363	45213	7309	338	4865	0	0	1502	2677	12355	30
35	91346	1754	621	15260	45104	7292	335	4801	0	0	1365	2548	12266	35
40	90345	1655	598	15091	44909	7265	331	4707	0	0	1234	2410	12145	40
45	88780	1508	570	14772	44539	7210	327	4566	0	0	1085	2240	11963	45
50	86400	1330	529	14212	43895	7116	323	4321	0	0	924	2034	11716	50
55	82532	1095	473	13205	42673	6918	313	3946	0	0	771	1793	11345	55
60	76508	824	397	11574	40529	6551	299	3428	0	0	607	1518	10781	60
65	67909	548	301	9313	37041	5960	278	2719	0	0	457	1266	10026	65
70	56692	328	200	6776	31749	5149	247	1910	0	0	317	996	9020	70
75	43095	163	114	4287	24447	4129	210	1114	0	0	193	735	7703	75
80	27325	64	49	2054	15315	2792	157	492	0	0	94	454	5854	80
85+	12178	22	14	635	6461	1366	79	155	0	0	29	202	3215	85+

NUMBER OF PERSONS SURVIVING TO AGE X IF SPECIFIED CAUSES WERE ELIMINATED

Age (x)	No Causes	Respiratory T. B. (1)	Other Infec. and Paras. (2)	Neoplasms (3)	Cardiovascular (4)	Infl., Pneu., Bronch. (5)	Diarrheal (6)	Certain Degenerative (7)	Maternal (8)	Cert. Dis. of Infancy (9)	Motor Vehicle (10)	Other Violence (11)	Other and Unknown (12)	(1) + (2)	(1) + (2) + (5) + (6) + (8)	(1)+(2)+ (5)+(6)+ (8)+part of(9)&(12)	(10) + (11)	Age (x)
0	100000	100000	100000	100000	100000	100000	100000	100000	100000	100000	100000	100000	100000	100000	100000	100000	100000	0
1	95261	95266	95377	95271	95272	96041	95696	95267	95261	97885	95261	95266	95937	95382	96602	99889	95266	1
5	94457	94465	94689	94521	94483	95353	94976	94471	94457	97058	94488	94560	95355	94697	96161	99584	94591	5
10	94143	94151	94414	94256	94184	95058	94665	94168	94143	96736	94215	94300	95115	94422	95909	99346	94372	10
15	93855	93866	94149	94006	93925	94821	94377	93888	93855	96440	93967	94077	94888	94160	95659	99101	94189	15
20	93340	93358	93652	93538	93457	94313	93862	93387	93340	95911	93604	93697	94444	93670	95175	98606	93962	20
25	92742	92782	93065	92993	92905	93721	93263	92816	92742	95296	93206	93250	93905	93104	94616	98034	93717	25
30	92098	92186	92434	92414	92330	93087	92617	92213	92098	94635	92725	92744	93329	92522	94043	97451	93376	30
35	91346	91518	91695	91762	91685	92344	91863	91524	91346	93862	92106	92116	92657	91868	93398	96800	92883	35
40	90345	90614	90713	90926	90875	91360	90861	90615	90345	92833	91228	91245	91764	90983	92530	95923	92137	40
45	88780	89191	89169	89670	89671	89852	89251	89186	88780	91225	89797	89835	90358	89582	91165	94540	90864	45
50	86400	86976	86820	87826	87911	87518	86901	87038	86400	88780	87550	87633	88184	87398	89043	92378	88799	50
55	82532	83314	82988	84500	85200	83796	83020	83511	82532	84805	83782	83948	84607	83774	85560	88821	85220	55
60	76508	77496	77004	80335	81142	78040	76974	77922	76508	78615	77827	78090	78990	77998	80045	83174	79436	60
65	67909	69048	68440	73574	75556	68839	68343	69846	67909	69775	69223	69555	70849	69589	72023	74937	70901	65
70	56692	57846	57228	63974	68732	59069	57083	59072	56692	58253	57918	58318	60113	58393	61261	63857	59580	70
75	43095	44117	43577	51120	60554	45837	43424	45626	43095	44282	44137	44564	46928	44611	47812	49979	45641	75
80	27325	28051	27682	34549	50002	30210	27576	29446	27325	28078	28065	28486	31401	28418	31707	33345	29257	80
85+	12178	12530	12360	16609	35741	14528	12341	13361	12178	12513	12551	12867	16111	12717	15375	16459	13261	85+

ADDED YRS OF LIFE																		
TOTAL		.394	.323	2.257	6.477	1.369	.400	.741	.000	1.834	.639	.795	2.037	.720	2.538	5.214	1.448	
WORK	3.345	.203	.059	.619	.745	.122	.009	.254	.000	.000	.394	.390	.340	.263	.396	.444	.789	

POPULATION, DEATHS, DEATH RATES FOR ALL CAUSES COMBINED, AND SPECIFIED CAUSES

Age Start of Interval	Midyear Population	Deaths During Year	All Causes	Respiratory T. B.	Other Infec. and Paras.	Neo-plasms	Cardio-vascular	Infl., Pneu., Bronch.	Diar-rheal	Certain Degen-erative	Maternal	Cert. Dis. of Infancy	Motor Vehicle	Other Violence	Other and Unknown	Age Start of Interval
0	432570	17683	.04088	.00003	.00115	.00013	.00010	.00741	.00432	.00006	.00000	.02158	.00000	.00004	.00605	0
1	1635715	3283	.00201	.00001	.00032	.00012	.00004	.00046	.00026	.00002	.00000	.00000	.00005	.00018	.00055	1
5	1971060	1019	.00052	.00000	.00008	.00007	.00004	.00005	.00001	.00002	.00000	.00000	.00003	.00005	.00016	5
10	2101121	792	.00038	.00001	.00004	.00006	.00006	.00003	.00001	.00002	.00000	.00000	.00003	.00003	.00010	10
15	1870560	901	.00048	.00002	.00003	.00007	.00007	.00002	.00000	.00003	.00001	.00000	.00003	.00003	.00010	15
20	2047990	1291	.00063	.00004	.00003	.00009	.00011	.00002	.00001	.00004	.00006	.00000	.00004	.00007	.00011	20
25	1598976	1725	.00086	.00008	.00004	.00014	.00014	.00002	.00001	.00005	.00014	.00000	.00003	.00007	.00014	25
30	1993595	2223	.00112	.00008	.00005	.00027	.00021	.00004	.00001	.00006	.00013	.00000	.00003	.00008	.00018	30
35	1988038	3058	.00154	.00008	.00005	.00049	.00032	.00004	.00001	.00009	.00013	.00000	.00003	.00006	.00023	35
40	1332021	2875	.00216	.00008	.00005	.00082	.00052	.00007	.00001	.00015	.00007	.00000	.00004	.00007	.00028	40
45	1779683	5829	.00328	.00008	.00006	.00134	.00096	.00010	.00001	.00020	.00001	.00000	.00004	.00011	.00036	45
50	1606778	8001	.00498	.00008	.00007	.00191	.00168	.00015	.00002	.00035	.00000	.00000	.00005	.00013	.00054	50
55	1357128	10559	.00778	.00011	.00010	.00267	.00298	.00030	.00002	.00055	.00000	.00000	.00007	.00017	.00080	55
60	1199417	15327	.01278	.00013	.00014	.00372	.00573	.00060	.00003	.00096	.00000	.00000	.00008	.00020	.00118	60
65	990067	22255	.02248	.00018	.00018	.00493	.01207	.00131	.00007	.00151	.00000	.00000	.00011	.00032	.00180	65
70	785774	30948	.03939	.00021	.00018	.00682	.02315	.00262	.00015	.00211	.00000	.00000	.00015	.00060	.00339	70
75	511551	36862	.07206	.00027	.00025	.00908	.04513	.00575	.00030	.00258	.00000	.00000	.00023	.00116	.00731	75
80	260645	33415	.12820	.00023	.00027	.01057	.07936	.01154	.00068	.00278	.00000	.00000	.00023	.00275	.01978	80
85+	114997	27595	.23996	.00018	.00026	.01117	.13344	.02535	.00137	.00247	.00000	.00000	.00012	.00517	.06043	85+
ALL	25977686	225641														

	All Causes	Respiratory T. B.	Other Infec. and Paras.	Neo-plasms	Cardio-vascular	Infl., Pneu., Bronch.	Diar-rheal	Certain Degen-erative	Maternal	Cert. Dis. of Infancy	Motor Vehicle	Other Violence	Other and Unknown
CRUDE DEATH RATE	.00869	.00007	.00011	.00139	.00413	.00070	.00012	.00035	.00004	.00036	.00005	.00019	.00116
STANDARDIZED RATE (1)	.00464	.00005	.00013	.00068	.00148	.00051	.00020	.00017	.00004	.00076	.00004	.00011	.00068
STANDARDIZED RATE (2)	.00828	.00007	.00011	.00126	.00383	.00070	.00014	.00032	.00004	.00045	.00005	.00018	.00113
GEOMETRIC MEAN	.00527												

LIFE TABLE FOR ALL CAUSES COMBINED

Age (x)	Midyear Population	Deaths During Year	nM_x	nq_x	l_x	nd_x	nL_x	nm_x	na_x	T_x	nr_x	$\overset{\circ}{e}_x$	Age (x)
0	432570	17683	.040879	.039490	100000	3949	96602	.040879	.135494	7169085	.000000	71.691	0
1	1635715	3283	.002007	.007985	96051	767	382287	.002006	1.500000	7072483	.000000	73.633	1
5	1971060	1019	.000517	.002582	95284	246	475805	.000517	2.500000	6690197	.000000	70.213	5
10	2101121	792	.000377	.001883	95038	179	474739	.000377	2.479050	6214392	.003640	65.388	10
15	1870560	901	.000477	.002404	94859	228	473750	.000481	2.608735	5739653	.004652	60.507	15
20	2047990	1291	.000630	.003149	94631	298	472447	.000631	2.624441	5265903	-.006656	55.647	20
25	1598976	1725	.000863	.004304	94333	406	470697	.000863	2.614943	4793456	.002124	50.814	25
30	1993595	2223	.001115	.005558	93927	522	468395	.001114	2.624920	4322759	-.007821	46.023	30
35	1988038	3058	.001538	.007668	93405	719	465327	.001545	2.637923	3854364	.031462	41.265	35
40	1332021	2875	.002158	.010768	92686	998	461055	.002164	2.659903	3389037	-.021554	36.565	40
45	1779683	5829	.003275	.016196	91688	1485	454983	.003264	2.672138	2927943	-.019793	31.934	45
50	1606778	8001	.004980	.024667	90203	2225	445846	.004991	2.676966	2472960	.012137	27.415	50
55	1357128	10559	.007780	.038362	87978	3375	432087	.007811	2.688086	2027113	.019586	23.041	55
60	1199417	15327	.012779	.062315	84603	5272	410904	.012830	2.702840	1595026	.018308	18.853	60
65	990067	22255	.022478	.107247	79331	8508	376958	.022570	2.684924	1184122	.018085	14.926	65
70	785774	30948	.039385	.181071	70823	12824	324016	.039578	2.652903	807163	.020653	11.397	70
75	511551	36862	.072059	.308971	57999	17920	246596	.072669	2.578183	483148	.032065	8.330	75
80	260645	33415	.128201	.487762	40079	19549	150997	.129466	2.473102	236552	.032065	5.902	80
85+	114997	27595	.239963	1.000000	20530	20530	85555	.239963	4.167313	85555	.000000	4.167	85+

NUMBER OF PERSONS DYING (OUT OF 100,000 AT BIRTH) ABOVE AGE X FROM SPECIFIED CAUSES

Age (x)	All Causes	Respiratory T. B.	Other Infec. and Paras.	Neo-plasms	Cardio-vascular	Infl., Pneu., Bronch.	Diar-rheal	Certain Degen-erative	Maternal	Cert. Dis. of Infancy	Motor Vehicle	Other Violence	Other and Unknown	Age (x)
0	100000	618	809	14068	52414	8221	955	3645	256	2085	446	2052	14431	0
1	96051	615	698	14055	52405	7504	538	3639	256	0	446	2048	13847	1
5	95284	610	576	14009	52390	7330	439	3630	256	0	427	1977	13640	5
10	95038	608	536	13976	52372	7309	433	3622	256	0	413	1952	13561	10
15	94859	603	518	13949	52342	7297	430	3613	256	0	398	1936	13517	15
20	94631	593	506	13916	52308	7286	428	3599	250	0	379	1902	13464	20
25	94333	573	492	13872	52257	7275	425	3582	221	0	360	1866	13410	25
30	93927	537	472	13804	52189	7264	422	3560	156	0	345	1834	13344	30
35	93405	502	450	13678	52089	7247	419	3532	97	0	330	1798	13263	35
40	92686	464	429	13446	51937	7229	416	3491	35	0	315	1768	13156	40
45	91688	426	403	13067	51697	7198	410	3421	5	0	299	1734	13028	45
50	90203	389	377	12460	51260	7152	404	3331	2	0	281	1684	12863	50
55	87978	353	347	11608	50507	7083	396	3175	1	0	260	1625	12623	55
60	84603	306	305	10449	49213	6654	386	2935	1	0	229	1551	12274	60
65	79331	254	247	8917	46845	6705	372	2539	1	0	196	1467	11788	65
70	70823	187	185	7054	42270	6208	345	1967	1	0	153	1345	11108	70
75	57999	118	127	4838	34727	5355	296	1281	1	0	103	1150	10003	75
80	40079	52	65	2590	23500	3923	221	641	1	0	47	861	8178	80
85+	20530	16	22	956	11416	2169	118	211	0	0	10	442	5170	85+

NUMBER OF PERSONS SURVIVING TO AGE X IF SPECIFIED CAUSES WERE ELIMINATED

Age (x)	No Causes	Respiratory T. B.	Other Infec. and Paras.	Neo-plasms	Cardio-vascular	Infl., Pneu., Bronch.	Diar-rheal	Certain Degen-erative	Maternal	Cert. Dis. of Infancy	Motor Vehicle	Other Violence	Other and Unknown	(1) + (2)	(1) + (2) + (5) + (6) + (8)	(1)+(2)+ (5)+(6)+ (8)+part of(9)&(12)	(10) + (11)	Age (x)
		(1)	(2)	(3)	(4)	(5)	(6)	(7)	(8)	(9)	(10)	(11)	(12)					
0	100000	100000	100000	100000	100000	100000	100000	100000	100000	100000	100000	100000	100000	100000	100000	100000	100000	0
1	96051	96054	96160	96064	96060	96756	96461	96057	96051	98116	96051	96055	96625	96163	97282	99899	96055	1
5	95284	95292	95514	95342	95308	96158	95789	95299	95284	97333	95303	95359	96061	95522	96909	99671	95378	5
10	95038	95048	95307	95129	95080	95931	95548	95061	95038	97081	95071	95137	95893	95317	96729	99520	95170	10
15	94859	94874	95146	94977	94931	95763	95371	94891	94859	96899	94907	94974	95756	95161	96586	99385	95022	15
20	94631	94656	94929	94782	94736	95544	95144	94677	94637	96666	94698	94780	95580	94954	96395	99202	94847	20
25	94333	94378	94644	94527	94489	95254	94847	94395	94368	96361	94418	94518	95333	94689	96170	98988	94603	25
30	93927	94007	94257	94189	94150	94855	94442	94011	94027	95946	94027	94143	94989	94338	95894	98731	94243	30
35	93405	93520	93755	93791	93727	94345	93920	93517	93563	95413	93519	93655	94543	93870	95499	98351	93770	35
40	92686	92838	93054	93302	93158	93637	93200	92838	92905	94679	92815	92965	93923	93207	94909	97765	93093	40
45	91688	91876	92078	92677	92395	92660	92203	91908	91934	93659	91831	91997	93041	92267	94020	96874	92141	45
50	90203	90425	90613	91787	91336	91205	90715	90509	90448	92142	90362	90557	91700	90836	92618	95444	90716	50
55	87978	88230	88407	90383	89840	89024	88486	88431	88218	89870	88154	88382	89680	88661	90479	93259	88558	55
60	84603	84892	85057	88090	87700	85737	85101	85276	84834	86422	84802	85064	86589	85347	87238	89546	85265	60
65	79331	79652	79813	84158	84648	80640	79812	80349	79548	81037	79550	79845	81676	80136	82176	84765	80065	65
70	70823	71173	71312	77017	80329	72471	71278	72280	71016	72346	71059	71398	73580	71665	74004	76394	71636	70
75	57999	58348	58452	65276	73994	60144	58416	59825	58157	59246	58237	58648	61305	58804	61584	63670	58889	75
80	40079	40374	40443	47226	64455	42809	40430	41883	40188	40941	40290	40770	43999	40741	44017	45684	40985	80
85+	20530	20707	20747	25582	49925	23285	20783	21772	20587	20971	20664	21186	24982	20926	24093	25308	21324	85+

ACCED YRS OF LIFE																		
TOTAL		.149	.315	2.194	7.793	1.287	.424	.510	.112	1.539	.119	.331	2.011	.465	2.323	4.650	.451	
WORK	1.976	.073	.051	.595	.517	.063	.010	.121	.084	.000	.045	.095	.256	.124	.282	.333	.140	

POPULATION, DEATHS, DEATH RATES FOR ALL CAUSES COMBINED, AND SPECIFIED CAUSES

Age Start of Interval	Midyear Population	Deaths During Year	All Causes	Respiratory T.B.	Other Infec. and Paras.	Neoplasms	Cardiovascular	Infl., Pneu., Bronch.	Diarrheal	Certain Degenerative	Maternal	Cert. Dis. of Infancy	Motor Vehicle	Other Violence	Other and Unknown	Age Start of Interval
0	479000	20474	.04274	.00001	.00092	.00010	.00010	.00611	.00338	.00003	.00000	.02536	.00002	.00014	.00658	0
1	1774000	2809	.00158	.00001	.00016	.00015	.00002	.00029	.00015	.00002	.00000	.00000	.00011	.00022	.00046	1
5	2059000	1288	.00063	.00000	.00004	.00011	.00003	.00004	.00001	.00002	.00000	.00000	.00011	.00011	.00016	5
10	2015000	1076	.00053	.00000	.00004	.00008	.00005	.00002	.00000	.00002	.00000	.00000	.00009	.00013	.00011	10
15	2051000	2334	.00114	.00001	.00003	.00010	.00008	.00002	.00000	.00003	.00000	.00000	.00041	.00030	.00015	15
20	1972000	2592	.00131	.00003	.00002	.00012	.00008	.00002	.00000	.00006	.00000	.00000	.00053	.00032	.00014	20
25	1931000	2598	.00135	.00006	.00002	.00016	.00014	.00003	.00001	.00008	.00000	.00000	.00043	.00028	.00015	25
30	1891000	3202	.00169	.00009	.00003	.00025	.00028	.00004	.00001	.00012	.00000	.00000	.00036	.00029	.00022	30
35	1855000	4367	.00235	.00015	.00004	.00042	.00053	.00006	.00001	.00024	.00000	.00000	.00036	.00028	.00026	35
40	1665000	6198	.00372	.00026	.00005	.00075	.00103	.00009	.00001	.00042	.00000	.00000	.00038	.00033	.00041	40
45	1259000	6723	.00534	.00029	.00007	.00130	.00167	.00015	.00002	.00056	.00000	.00000	.00040	.00037	.00051	45
50	1601000	14183	.00886	.00038	.00009	.00236	.00295	.00034	.00002	.00056	.00000	.00000	.00048	.00049	.00077	50
55	1344000	20608	.01523	.00059	.00014	.00441	.00550	.00075	.00004	.00146	.00000	.00000	.00056	.00057	.00132	55
60	1064000	26243	.02466	.00072	.00019	.00681	.01005	.00140	.00005	.00218	.00000	.00000	.00057	.00068	.00202	60
65	780000	28867	.03701	.00072	.00027	.00940	.01666	.00249	.00007	.00291	.00000	.00000	.00059	.00077	.00312	65
70	592000	32639	.05513	.00062	.00025	.01174	.02857	.00373	.00013	.00351	.00000	.00000	.00069	.00110	.00478	70
75	402000	34476	.08576	.00052	.00038	.01369	.04946	.00640	.00023	.00404	.00000	.00000	.00076	.00151	.00876	75
80	213000	29043	.13635	.00044	.00026	.01547	.08196	.01113	.00050	.00410	.00000	.00000	.00093	.00231	.01924	80
85+	102000	22562	.22120	.00033	.00025	.01426	.12581	.02136	.00097	.00343	.00000	.00000	.00068	.00435	.04974	85+
ALL	25049000	262282														

	All Causes	Respiratory T.B.	Other Infec. and Paras.	Neoplasms	Cardiovascular	Infl., Pneu., Bronch.	Diarrheal	Certain Degenerative	Maternal	Cert. Dis. of Infancy	Motor Vehicle	Other Violence	Other and Unknown
CRUDE DEATH RATE	.01047	.00020	.00010	.00188	.00435	.00074	.00010	.00062	.00000	.00048	.00037	.00039	.00123
STANDARDIZED RATE (1)	.00642	.00012	.00010	.00099	.00192	.00051	.00015	.00034	.00000	.00089	.00031	.00030	.00079
STANDARDIZED RATE (2)	.01056	.00019	.00010	.00192	.00464	.00079	.00011	.00063	.00000	.00052	.00037	.00040	.00129
GEOMETRIC MEAN	.00767												

LIFE TABLE FOR ALL CAUSES COMBINED

Age (x)	Midyear Population	Deaths During Year	$_nM_x$	$_nq_x$	l_x	$_nd_x$	$_nL_x$	$_nm_x$	$_na_x$	T_x	$_nr_x$	$\overset{\circ}{e}_x$	Age (x)
0	479000	20474	.042743	.041230	100000	4123	96465	.042741	.142663	6743224	.000000	67.432	0
1	1774000	2809	.001583	.006310	95877	605	381996	.001584	1.500000	6646759	.000000	65.326	1
5	2059000	1288	.000626	.003128	95272	298	475615	.000627	2.500000	6264763	.000000	65.757	5
10	2015000	1076	.000534	.002664	94974	253	474287	.000533	2.696805	5789148	-.000316	60.955	10
15	2051000	2334	.001138	.005669	94721	537	472338	.001137	2.641217	5314861	.000052	56.111	15
20	1972000	2592	.001314	.006551	94184	617	469356	.001314	2.530727	4842522	.003963	51.416	20
25	1931000	2598	.001345	.006712	93567	628	466300	.001347	2.555401	4373126	.003177	46.738	25
30	1891000	3202	.001693	.008436	92939	784	462829	.001694	2.619845	3906826	.002398	42.036	30
35	1855000	4367	.002354	.011709	92155	1079	458266	.002355	2.674930	3443997	.002701	37.372	35
40	1665000	6198	.003723	.018556	91076	1690	451422	.003744	2.658161	2985731	.033069	32.783	40
45	1259000	6723	.005340	.026425	89386	2362	441457	.005350	2.682843	2534309	-.010575	28.352	45
50	1601000	14183	.008859	.043241	87024	3763	426508	.008823	2.711489	2092852	-.016796	24.049	50
55	1344000	20608	.015333	.074248	83261	6182	401945	.015380	2.677195	1666344	.014304	20.013	55
60	1064000	26243	.024664	.117036	77079	9021	363972	.024785	2.625217	1264398	.026866	16.404	60
65	780000	28867	.037009	.170502	68058	11604	312262	.037161	2.584669	900426	.024260	13.230	65
70	592000	32639	.055133	.243331	56454	13737	248660	.055244	2.553323	588164	.011678	10.418	70
75	402000	34476	.085761	.353957	42717	15120	175830	.085992	2.502949	339504	.013040	7.948	75
80	213000	29043	.136352	.505526	27597	13951	101982	.136799	2.419331	163674	.013040	5.931	80
85+	102000	22562	.221196	1.000000	13646	13646	61692	.221196	4.520876	61692	.000000	4.521	85+

NUMBER OF PERSONS DYING (OUT OF 100,000 AT BIRTH) ABOVE AGE X FROM SPECIFIED CAUSES

Age (x)	All Causes	Respiratory T.B.	Other Infec. and Paras.	Neoplasms	Cardiovascular	Infl., Pneu., Bronch.	Diarrheal	Certain Degenerative	Maternal	Cert. Dis. of Infancy	Motor Vehicle	Other Violence	Other and Unknown	Age (x)
0	100000	1611	726	17587	46133	7162	667	5630	0	2446	2728	3184	12126	0
1	95877	1610	638	17577	46124	6572	341	5628	0	0	2726	3171	11490	1
5	95272	1608	575	17518	46114	6462	285	5620	0	0	2684	3088	11318	5
10	94974	1607	557	17467	46100	6444	281	5612	0	0	2630	3036	11240	10
15	94721	1607	540	17431	46077	6434	281	5603	0	0	2586	2974	11188	15
20	94184	1602	526	17382	46039	6423	279	5590	0	0	2394	2833	11116	20
25	93567	1590	516	17224	46001	6413	278	5563	0	0	2148	2683	11051	25
30	92939	1562	507	17250	45537	6401	275	5526	0	0	1947	2554	10980	30
35	92155	1520	493	17135	45806	6384	272	5469	0	0	1780	2419	10877	35
40	91076	1450	474	16941	45565	6357	267	5361	0	0	1613	2289	10759	40
45	89386	1334	452	16601	45095	6315	261	5172	0	0	1443	2138	10575	45
50	87024	1205	419	16024	44357	6250	254	4926	0	0	1266	1976	10347	50
55	83261	1042	381	15021	43103	6107	244	4517	0	0	1062	1767	10017	55
60	77079	803	326	13242	40685	5804	227	3929	0	0	838	1537	9488	60
65	68058	540	257	10753	37204	5293	208	3132	0	0	631	1289	8751	65
70	56454	315	173	7808	31954	4511	185	2220	0	0	447	1048	7773	70
75	42717	160	110	4884	24851	3582	152	1346	0	0	275	774	6583	75
80	27597	68	43	2474	16127	2454	111	636	0	0	141	507	5036	80
85+	13646	21	16	880	7762	1318	60	212	0	0	42	269	3066	85+

NUMBER OF PERSONS SURVIVING TO AGE X IF SPECIFIED CAUSES WERE ELIMINATED

Age (x)	No Causes	Respiratory T.B. (1)	Other Infec. and Paras. (2)	Neoplasms (3)	Cardiovascular (4)	Infl., Pneu., Bronch. (5)	Diarrheal (6)	Certain Degenerative (7)	Maternal (8)	Cert. Dis. of Infancy (9)	Motor Vehicle (10)	Other Violence (11)	Other and Unknown (12)	(1)+(2)	(1)+(2)+(5)+(6)+(8)	(1)+(2)+(5)+(6)+(8)+part of(9)&(12)	(10)+(11)	Age (x)
0	100000	100000	100000	100000	100000	100000	100000	100000	100000	100000	100000	100000	100000	100000	100000	100000	100000	0
1	95877	95878	95963	95887	95886	96456	96197	95879	95877	98302	95879	95890	96502	95964	96866	99855	95892	1
5	95272	95275	95421	95341	95291	95958	95646	95282	95272	97682	95316	95367	96066	95424	96488	99560	95411	5
10	94974	94978	95140	95053	95007	95676	95351	94992	94974	97376	95072	95121	95844	95144	96227	99307	95219	10
15	94721	94725	94904	94876	94777	95431	95097	94748	94721	97117	94862	94930	95641	94908	95958	99078	95071	15
20	94184	94193	94380	94387	94277	94901	94559	94224	94184	96566	94517	94533	95171	94389	95486	98554	94866	20
25	93567	93588	93771	93827	93697	94290	93941	93633	93567	95934	94144	94063	94613	93792	94894	97947	94643	25
30	92939	92988	93151	93271	93133	93669	93313	93042	92939	95290	93714	93561	94050	93200	94310	97351	94341	30
35	92155	92245	92379	92599	92478	92896	92529	92314	92155	94486	93091	92908	93360	92469	93591	96621	93851	35
40	91076	91235	91316	91709	91636	91835	91451	91341	91076	93380	92169	91950	92386	91476	92618	95632	93053	40
45	89386	89657	89644	90347	90405	90173	89760	89834	89386	91647	90629	90395	90857	89915	91087	94074	91652	45
50	87024	87415	87308	88537	88756	87855	87395	87704	87024	89225	88411	88168	88665	87700	88915	91858	89573	50
55	83261	83796	83570	85713	86179	84198	83626	84316	83261	85367	84791	84563	85179	84106	85425	88287	86116	55
60	77079	77805	77418	81130	82021	78242	77433	78630	77079	79029	78714	78505	79377	78147	79691	82420	80174	60
65	68058	68948	68422	74136	76199	69574	68389	70194	68058	69779	69700	69557	70803	69317	71206	73722	71235	65
70	56454	57399	56833	64477	68773	58444	56749	59085	56454	57882	57987	57921	59664	57784	60133	62361	59494	70
75	42717	43567	43058	51755	60155	45065	42969	45504	42717	43797	44029	44071	46252	43915	46602	48439	45425	75
80	27597	28219	27871	35821	50035	30080	27793	29999	27597	28295	28554	28692	31255	28499	31284	32661	29686	80
85+	13646	13987	13800	19197	37741	15752	13778	15155	13646	13991	14190	14359	17071	14145	16486	17393	14931	85+

ADDED YRS OF LIFE																		
TOTAL		.305	.220	2.595	7.612	1.135	.297	.841	.000	1.702	.804	.758	1.925	.527	1.992	4.360	1.579	
WORK	3.395	.140	.044	.651	.801	.097	.010	.272	.000	.000	.479	.363	.326	.184	.292	.326	.848	

POPULATION, DEATHS, DEATH RATES FOR ALL CAUSES COMBINED, AND SPECIFIED CAUSES

Age Start of Interval	Midyear Population	Deaths During Year	All Causes	Respiratory T. B.	Other Infec. and Paras.	Neoplasms	Cardiovascular	Infl., Pneu., Bronch.	Diarrheal	Certain Degenerative	Maternal	Cert. Dis. of Infancy	Motor Vehicle	Other Violence	Other and Unknown	Age Start of Interval
0	457000	16197	.03544	.00001	.00090	.00014	.00008	.00556	.00299	.00003	.00000	.02021	.00002	.00011	.00540	0
1	1693000	2446	.00144	.00001	.00018	.00013	.00003	.00029	.00015	.00002	.00000	.00000	.00006	.00041	.00041	1
5	1978000	797	.00040	.00000	.00004	.00008	.00002	.00003	.00001	.00001	.00000	.00000	.00005	.00004	.00012	5
10	1935000	678	.00035	.00000	.00003	.00007	.00005	.00002	.00000	.00002	.00000	.00000	.00003	.00003	.00010	10
15	1983000	886	.00045	.00001	.00002	.00008	.00006	.00002	.00000	.00002	.00001	.00000	.00006	.00006	.00010	15
20	1932000	1110	.00057	.00003	.00003	.00010	.00008	.00002	.00001	.00003	.00005	.00000	.00007	.00006	.00010	20
25	1910000	1415	.00074	.00004	.00003	.00014	.00012	.00002	.00001	.00005	.00010	.00000	.00005	.00006	.00013	25
30	1901000	1850	.00097	.00005	.00002	.00023	.00018	.00002	.00000	.00007	.00011	.00000	.00005	.00006	.00016	30
35	1899000	2683	.00141	.00006	.00003	.00046	.00030	.00003	.00001	.00009	.00010	.00000	.00006	.00007	.00021	35
40	1787000	3884	.00217	.00006	.00003	.00087	.00054	.00005	.00002	.00016	.00006	.00000	.00006	.00008	.00026	40
45	1348000	4216	.00313	.00004	.00006	.00137	.00086	.00008	.00001	.00021	.00000	.00000	.00007	.00010	.00033	45
50	1682000	8226	.00489	.00007	.00006	.00202	.00157	.00010	.00001	.00038	.00000	.00000	.00009	.00013	.00045	50
55	1453000	11069	.00762	.00007	.00008	.00272	.00285	.00023	.00002	.00069	.00000	.00000	.00011	.00014	.00071	55
60	1229000	15201	.01237	.00011	.00010	.00378	.00544	.00046	.00003	.00108	.00000	.00000	.00000	.00021	.00103	60
65	1043000	22077	.02117	.00012	.00015	.00508	.01082	.00095	.00005	.00180	.00000	.00000	.00019	.00032	.00169	65
70	818000	30807	.03766	.00017	.00016	.00692	.02195	.00158	.00010	.00252	.00000	.00000	.00023	.00060	.00303	70
75	567000	38357	.06765	.00021	.00021	.00910	.04282	.00432	.00023	.00320	.00000	.00000	.00024	.00124	.00608	75
80	299000	34950	.11689	.00019	.00024	.01085	.07584	.00879	.00058	.00326	.00000	.00000	.00025	.00242	.01446	80
85+	155000	30919	.19948	.00014	.00027	.01070	.12028	.01778	.00103	.00272	.00000	.00000	.00023	.00516	.04117	85+
ALL	26069000	227768														

CRUDE DEATH RATE			.00874	.00005	.00008	.00149	.00430	.00058	.00009	.00043	.00003	.00035	.00008	.00020	.00105
STANDARDIZED RATE (1)			.00438	.00003	.00009	.00069	.00138	.00037	.00014	.00019	.00003	.00071	.00006	.00011	.00057
STANDARDIZED RATE (2)			.00759	.00005	.00008	.00129	.00358	.00052	.00010	.00037	.00003	.00042	.00008	.00017	.00091
GEOMETRIC MEAN			.00477												

LIFE TABLE FOR ALL CAUSES COMBINED

Age (x)	Midyear Population	Deaths During Year	$_nM_x$	$_nq_x$	l_x	$_nd_x$	$_nL_x$	$_nm_x$	$_na_x$	T_x	$_nr_x$	$\overset{\circ}{e}_x$	Age (x)
0	457000	16197	.035442	.034380	100000	3438	97010	.035440	.130251	7294584	.000000	72.946	0
1	1693000	2446	.001445	.005758	96562	556	384858	.001445	1.500000	7197574	.000000	74.538	1
5	1978000	797	.000403	.002010	96006	193	479548	.000402	2.500000	6812716	.000000	70.961	5
10	1935000	678	.000350	.001753	95813	168	478649	.000351	2.526042	6333169	-.000378	66.099	10
15	1983000	886	.000447	.002237	95645	214	477712	.000448	2.602220	5854519	-.001029	61.211	15
20	1932000	1110	.000575	.002861	95431	273	476501	.000573	2.605311	5376807	.002564	56.342	20
25	1910000	1415	.000741	.003699	95158	352	474949	.000741	2.611269	4900306	.001394	51.497	25
30	1901000	1850	.000973	.004863	94806	461	472942	.000975	2.640998	4425357	.000457	46.678	30
35	1899000	2683	.001413	.007038	94345	664	470181	.001412	2.674448	3952414	-.002154	41.893	35
40	1787000	3884	.002173	.010856	93681	1017	466025	.002182	2.659374	3482234	.028299	37.171	40
45	1348000	4216	.003128	.015562	92664	1442	459961	.003135	2.670914	3016209	.013039	32.550	45
50	1682000	8226	.004891	.024117	91222	2200	451006	.004878	2.679924	2556248	-.013098	28.022	50
55	1453000	11069	.007618	.037541	89022	3342	437374	.007641	2.685268	2105242	.015371	23.649	55
60	1229000	15201	.012369	.060364	85680	5172	416473	.012419	2.693913	1667868	.019369	19.466	60
65	1043000	22077	.021167	.101307	80508	8156	383691	.021257	2.688946	1251395	.018378	15.544	65
70	818000	30807	.037661	.173720	72352	12569	332280	.037827	2.654547	867704	.018767	11.993	70
75	567000	38357	.067649	.292391	59783	17480	256558	.068122	2.579138	535424	.027883	8.956	75
80	299000	34950	.116890	.454081	42303	19209	163053	.117809	2.477105	278825	.027883	6.591	80
85+	155000	30919	.199477	1.000000	23094	23094	115773	.199477	5.013099	115773	.000000	5.013	85+

NUMBER OF PERSONS DYING (OUT OF 100,000 AT BIRTH) ABOVE AGE X FROM SPECIFIED CAUSES

Age (x)	All Causes	Respiratory T.B.	Other Infec. and Paras.	Neoplasms	Cardiovascular	Infl., Pneu., Bronch.	Diarrheal	Certain Degenerative	Maternal	Cert. Dis. of Infancy	Motor Vehicle	Other Violence	Other and Unknown	Age (x)
0	100000	460	635	14971	54236	6769	734	4447	205	1960	675	2193	12715	0
1	96562	459	548	14958	54229	6230	443	4444	205	0	674	2182	12190	1
5	96006	457	478	14909	54216	6119	386	4436	205	0	651	2116	12033	5
10	95813	456	459	14872	54205	6106	381	4431	205	0	625	2095	11978	10
15	95645	455	447	14840	54183	6095	379	4422	205	0	611	2079	11929	15
20	95431	449	436	14800	54153	6087	378	4414	202	0	583	2051	11878	20
25	95158	436	421	14754	54113	6079	375	4400	179	0	550	2020	11831	25
30	94806	417	408	14685	54054	6071	372	4378	133	0	525	1992	11771	30
35	94345	392	398	14576	53968	6060	370	4344	79	0	503	1962	11693	35
40	93681	365	384	14359	53829	6045	368	4302	31	0	477	1929	11592	40
45	92664	335	368	13953	53575	6024	361	4230	2	0	450	1893	11473	45
50	91222	315	342	13319	53179	5988	355	4135	1	0	418	1848	11322	50
55	89022	282	313	12411	52472	5941	349	3966	0	0	379	1790	11119	55
60	85680	250	278	11220	51222	5840	341	3662	0	0	333	1727	10807	60
65	80508	205	238	9644	48942	5646	327	3211	0	0	280	1640	10375	65
70	72352	158	181	7651	44769	5280	307	2519	0	0	208	1517	9722	70
75	59783	102	127	5386	37437	4617	273	1681	0	0	130	1317	8713	75
80	42303	49	72	3042	26367	3498	214	857	0	0	70	996	7138	80
85+	23094	16	31	1239	13925	2059	119	314	0	0	27	598	4766	85+

NUMBER OF PERSONS SURVIVING TO AGE X IF SPECIFIED CAUSES WERE ELIMINATED

Age (x)	No Causes	Respiratory T.B.	Other Infec. and Paras.	Neoplasms	Cardiovascular	Infl., Pneu., Bronch.	Diarrheal	Certain Degenerative	Maternal	Cert. Dis. of Infancy	Motor Vehicle	Other Violence	Other and Unknown	(1) + (2)	(1) + (2) + (5) + (6) + (8)	(1)+(2)+(5)+(6)+(8)+part of(9)&(12)	(10) + (11)	Age (x)
		(1)	(2)	(3)	(4)	(5)	(6)	(7)	(8)	(9)	(10)	(11)	(12)					
0	100000	100000	100000	100000	100000	100000	100000	100000	100000	100000	100000	100000	100000	100000	100000	100000	100000	0
1	96562	96563	96648	96575	96569	97093	96848	96565	96562	98507	96563	96573	97079	96649	97468	99872	96574	1
5	96006	96009	96068	96026	96026	96645	96348	96017	96006	97940	96030	96083	96678	96164	97149	99642	96107	5
10	95813	95817	95987	95911	95844	96464	96159	95829	95813	97743	95863	95910	96539	95991	96992	99497	95960	10
15	95645	95650	95830	95775	95658	96306	95992	95670	95645	97572	95709	95758	96419	95835	96848	99360	95822	15
20	95431	95442	95627	95601	95514	96099	95779	95464	95434	97353	95523	95572	96254	95638	96661	99178	95664	20
25	95158	95182	95368	95374	95280	95832	95508	95205	95184	97075	95282	95330	96026	95392	96447	98972	95454	25
30	94806	94849	95029	95090	94987	95485	95157	94874	94878	96716	94955	95005	95732	95071	96180	98717	95154	30
35	94345	94413	94577	94737	94611	95032	94697	94447	94470	96246	94515	94573	95345	94644	95816	98365	94744	35
40	93681	93775	93925	94287	94084	94378	94032	93824	93853	95568	93876	93940	94776	94019	95249	97802	94136	40
45	92664	92787	92921	93671	93317	93375	93018	92877	92863	94531	92884	92956	93866	93044	94319	96862	93177	45
50	91222	91363	91501	92851	92261	91958	91577	91527	91419	93060	91470	91555	92558	91642	92941	95457	91804	50
55	89022	89192	89323	91529	90746	89787	89374	89487	89215	90815	89303	89404	90529	89494	90817	93287	89686	55
60	85680	85875	86004	89302	88559	86516	86027	86428	85686	87406	85955	86110	87442	86200	87584	89985	86427	60
65	80508	80735	80851	85517	85569	81484	80848	81653	80683	82130	80856	80997	82592	81079	82588	84879	81347	65
70	72352	72600	72715	78840	81226	73581	72676	74048	72509	73810	72733	72908	74862	72965	74699	76815	73292	70
75	59783	60035	60132	67452	75029	61415	60082	61964	59913	60987	60169	60426	62813	60389	62484	64323	60816	75
80	42303	42528	42596	49975	66104	44434	42565	44559	42395	43155	42626	43031	45860	42822	45356	46809	43359	80
85+	23094	23241	23284	28877	53410	25382	23306	24746	23144	23559	23302	23788	26979	23432	26047	27075	24002	85+

ACCED YRS OF LIFE																		
TOTAL		.104	.225	2.412	9.427	1.034	.300	.619	.090	1.467	.186	.343	1.860	.330	1.776	3.853	.531	
WORK	1.873	.049	.039	.607	.480	.046	.008	.127	.066	.000	.072	.086	.232	.088	.209	.246	.158	

POPULATION, DEATHS, DEATH RATES FOR ALL CAUSES COMBINED, AND SPECIFIED CAUSES

Age Start of Interval	Midyear Population	Deaths During Year	All Causes	Respiratory T. B.	Other Infec. and Paras.	Neoplasms	Cardiovascular	Infl., Pneu., Bronch.	Diarrheal	Certain Degenerative	Maternal	Cert. Dis. of Infancy	Motor Vehicle	Other Violence	Other and Unknown	Age Start of Interval
0	614296	115085	.18735	.C0049	.0C940	.00001	.00597	.C2938	.01666	.C0074	.C0000	.03083	.00000	.00158	.09228	0
1	2127991	59350	.02789	.0003C	.00421	.00001	.00091	.00419	.00328	.C0037	.C0000	.00000	.00000	.00118	.01344	1
5	2342420	14246	.006C8	.C0016	.0C118	.C0000	.00033	.00051	.C0049	.00015	.C0000	.0C000	.00000	.00048	.00278	5
10	2228848	8271	.00371	.C0028	.00074	.00000	.00032	.00023	.C0017	.C0005	.CC000	.00000	.00000	.00029	.00159	10
15	2205895	14124	.C0640	.00137	.0CC98	.00001	.00049	.00035	.C0021	.C0010	.C0000	.00000	.00000	.00052	.00238	15
20	2045221	17577	.C0859	.00217	.C0121	.C0000	.00061	.00052	.C0025	.00011	.00000	.0C000	.00000	.00081	.00292	20
25	1602013	13134	.C0820	.00193	.C0112	.00001	.00067	.C0C48	.C0027	.00011	.00000	.0C00C	.00000	.00079	.00283	25
30	1594440	131C7	.C0822	.C017C	.C01C6	.00001	.00091	.00049	.C0030	.00014	.C0000	.0C015	.00000	.00066	.00295	30
35	1251235	12236	.CC978	.00168	.00103	.C00C8	.CC126	.00065	.C0039	.C0019	.C0000	.0C015	.00000	.00077	.00373	35
40	1368905	15800	.01154	.C0163	.001C3	.00039	.00177	.00076	.C0051	.C0025	.00000	.0C000	.00000	.00078	.00442	40
45	1243523	19334	.01555	.C0187	.C01C8	.00081	.00272	.00103	.C0073	.00038	.C0000	.00000	.00000	.00087	.00606	45
50	1C75924	22668	.021C7	.C02C1	.00120	.00138	.00404	.00148	.CCC99	.00053	.C0000	.0C000	.00000	.00100	.00842	50
55	843166	24716	.02931	.CC2CC	.0C118	.00216	.00630	.00231	.C0158	.00079	.C0000	.0C000	.00000	.00100	.01201	55
60	58C706	24901	.04288	.C0196	.C0134	.00286	.01054	.00356	.C0244	.00111	.C0000	.0C000	.00000	.00105	.01803	60
65	498345	30660	.06152	.C0184	.00147	.00309	.01544	.00501	.C0362	.00158	.C0000	.0C000	.00000	.00129	.02820	65
70	329826	26018	.C7888	.C0134	.C0159	.00232	.01893	.00536	.C0342	.00165	.C0000	.00000	.00000	.00133	.04294	70
75	174922	2C978	.11993	.C0125	.00186	.00281	.02960	.00848	.C0623	.00248	.C0000	.00000	.00000	.00167	.06555	75
80	66464	13678	.2C580	.C0111	.C0223	.00322	.04485	.01389	.01544	.C0357	.C0000	.00000	.00000	.00247	.11903	80
85+	26842	10366	.38619	.C0C75	.00305	.00335	.06754	.02518	.C27E1	.C0492	.C0000	.0C000	.00000	.004C6	.24972	85+
ALL	22220972	476249														

	All Causes														
CRUDE DEATH RATE	.02143	.CC128	.CC163	.00044	.CC266	.00217	.CC145	.C0035	.CCCC0	.00085	.00000	.00079	.00981		
STANDARDIZED RATE (1)	.02150	.00118	.00175	.00034	.00227	.00234	.CC155	.00032	.00000	.00109	.00000	.00078	.00989		
STANDARDIZED RATE (2)	.02580	.00134	.00156	.C0063	.00403	.00233	.00166	.00046	.00000	.00064	.00000	.00084	.01231		
GEOMETRIC MEAN	.02632														

LIFE TABLE FOR ALL CAUSES COMBINED

Age (x)	Midyear Population	Deaths During Year	$_nM_x$	$_nq_x$	l_x	$_nd_x$	$_nL_x$	$_nm_x$	$_na_x$	T_x	$_nr_x$	$\overset{\circ}{e}_x$	Age (x)
0	614286	115085	.187348	.168090	1C0000	16809	89721	.187347	.388491	4238074	.000000	42.381	0
1	2127991	59350	.027890	.1C4290	83191	8676	311074	.027890	1.500000	4148353	.000000	49.865	1
5	2342420	14246	.CC6082	.029954	74515	2232	366995	.C06082	2.500000	3837279	.000000	51.497	5
10	2228848	8271	.0C3711	.018386	72283	1329	358094	.003711	2.500784	3470284	.001612	48.010	10
15	2205895	14124	.006403	.031527	70954	2237	349504	.CC6401	2.645843	3112190	-.001966	43.862	15
20	2045221	17577	.0C8594	.042129	68717	2895	336432	.C08605	2.529145	2762686	-.019238	40.204	20
25	1602013	13134	.0C8198	.04013S	65822	2642	322432	.008194	2.472559	2426255	-.017016	36.861	25
30	1594440	13107	.008220	.040313	63180	2547	309586	.008227	2.520858	2103822	-.017396	33.299	30
35	1251235	12236	.CC9779	.047779	60633	2897	296067	.CC9785	2.549764	1794236	-.012085	29.592	35
40	1368905	15800	.011542	.05610C	57736	3239	280830	.011534	2.576412	1498170	-.009200	25.949	40
45	1243523	19334	.015548	.C74958	54497	4085	262652	.015553	2.592921	1217340	-.003356	22.338	45
50	1C75924	22668	.02106E	.1CC393	50412	5061	239855	.021100	2.588421	954688	-.010903	18.938	50
55	843166	24716	.029313	.137439	45351	6233	211704	.029442	2.585198	714833	-.029949	15.762	55
60	580706	24901	.042881	.194540	39118	7610	177016	.042991	2.559242	503129	-.016779	12.862	60
65	498345	30660	.061524	.2665C4	31508	8397	136547	.061495	2.499926	326113	-.003531	10.350	65
70	329826	26018	.C78884	.329151	23111	7607	96277	.C75011	2.465821	189566	-.013761	8.202	70
75	174922	2C978	.119928	.461107	15504	7149	59226	.12C7C7	2.441076	93289	-.029873	6.017	75
80	66464	13678	.2C579E	.668462	8355	5585	26890	.207658	2.334825	34063	-.029873	4.077	80
85+	26842	10366	.386186	1.C00000	2770	2770	7173	.386186	2.589427	7173	.000000	2.589	85+

NUMBER OF PERSONS DYING (OUT OF 100,000 AT BIRTH) ABOVE AGE X FROM SPECIFIED CAUSES

Age (x)	All Causes	Respiratory T.B.	Other Infec. and Paras.	Neoplasms	Cardiovascular	Infl., Pneu., Bronch.	Diarrheal	Certain Degenerative	Maternal	Cert. Dis. of Infancy	Motor Vehicle	Other Violence	Other and Unknown	Age (x)
0	100000	5849	6495	2580	15053	9228	6360	1794	0	2766	0	3514	46321	0
1	83191	5805	5652	2579	14557	6592	4866	1727	0	0	0	3372	38041	1
5	74515	5711	4341	2577	14274	5289	3847	1613	0	0	0	3004	33859	5
10	72283	5653	3908	2576	14152	5103	3667	1556	0	0	0	2829	32839	10
15	70954	5551	3643	2575	14036	5022	3607	1525	0	0	0	2725	32270	15
20	68717	5071	3300	2574	13865	4900	3533	1492	0	0	0	2543	31439	20
25	65822	4341	2893	2572	13661	4725	3449	1454	0	0	0	2271	30456	25
30	63180	3721	2530	2570	13446	4569	3362	1419	0	0	0	2018	29545	30
35	60633	3195	2201	2567	13162	4418	3269	1376	0	0	0	1814	28631	35
40	57736	2698	1897	2542	12788	4225	3154	1318	0	0	0	1587	27527	40
45	54497	2240	1609	2434	12291	4012	3010	1247	0	0	0	1368	26286	45
50	50412	1748	1326	2221	11577	3743	2818	1146	0	0	0	1138	24695	50
55	45351	1266	1037	1890	10606	3386	2580	1018	0	0	0	898	22670	55
60	39118	843	787	1431	9265	2894	2244	851	0	0	0	687	20116	60
65	31508	496	550	924	7393	2263	1811	654	0	0	0	501	16916	65
70	23111	244	350	502	5286	1579	1317	439	0	0	0	326	13068	70
75	15504	115	196	279	3462	1063	987	280	0	0	0	197	8925	75
80	8355	41	85	113	1698	557	615	132	0	0	0	98	5016	80
85+	2770	5	22	24	484	181	198	35	0	0	0	29	1792	85+

NUMBER OF PERSONS SURVIVING TO AGE X IF SPECIFIED CAUSES WERE ELIMINATED

Age (x)	No Causes	Respiratory T.B. (1)	Other Infec. and Paras. (2)	Neoplasms (3)	Cardiovascular (4)	Infl., Pneu., Bronch. (5)	Diarrheal (6)	Certain Degenerative (7)	Maternal (8)	Cert. Dis. of Infancy (9)	Motor Vehicle (10)	Other Violence (11)	Other and Unknown (12)	(1)+(2)	(1)+(2)+(5)+(6)+(8)	(1)+(2)+(5)+(6)+(8)+part of(9)&(12)	(10)+(11)	Age (x)
0	100000	100000	100000	100000	100000	100000	100000	100000	100000	100000	100000	100000	100000	100000	100000	100000	100000	0
1	83231	83231	83962	83192	83681	85627	84563	83252	83191	85749	83191	83320	91085	84003	87888	97646	83320	1
5	74515	74640	76468	74518	75223	77976	76730	74678	74515	76806	74515	74980	86034	76596	82537	95828	74980	5
10	72283	72461	74617	72287	73091	75832	74615	72497	72283	74505	72283	72908	84625	74800	81005	94978	72908	10
15	70954	71231	73516	70959	71864	74522	73304	71195	70954	73136	70954	71672	83732	73803	80081	94395	71672	15
20	68717	69461	71549	68722	69769	72299	71068	68983	68717	70830	68717	69593	82062	72323	78697	93567	69593	20
25	65822	67261	68950	65829	67033	69434	68159	66114	65822	67846	65822	66931	79762	70458	76962	92486	66931	25
30	63180	65184	66556	63189	64557	66808	65512	63495	63180	65123	63180	64497	77650	68668	75291	91387	64497	30
35	60633	63090	64213	60644	62240	64271	62965	60977	60633	62497	60633	62102	75628	66816	73549	90165	62102	35
40	57736	60582	61460	57771	59642	61400	60074	58121	57736	59511	57736	59362	73371	64490	71360	88495	59362	40
45	54497	57652	58310	54636	56797	58176	56849	54930	54497	56173	54497	56250	70804	61686	68693	86234	56250	45
50	50412	53833	54231	50747	53261	54092	52781	50910	50412	51962	50412	52262	67515	57911	65058	82909	52262	50
55	45351	48917	49082	45969	48897	49027	47719	45922	45351	46745	45351	47252	63364	52941	60221	78218	47252	55
60	39118	42618	42587	40085	43542	42785	41490	39768	39118	40321	39118	40961	58070	46397	53824	71658	40961	60
65	31508	34665	34533	32754	36990	35086	33833	32211	31508	32477	31508	33167	51231	37993	45428	62571	33167	65
70	23111	25661	25516	24399	29326	26392	25272	23815	23111	23822	23111	24485	43331	28332	35379	51277	24485	70
75	15504	17329	17256	16557	21647	18189	17248	16109	15504	15981	15504	16536	36157	19287	25173	39168	16536	75
80	8355	9397	9387	9050	13585	10240	9602	8793	8355	8612	8355	8987	27333	10558	14871	25863	8987	80
85+	2770	3138	3151	3054	5726	3657	3457	2971	2770	2855	2770	3020	17139	3570	5881	13012	3020	85+

ADDED YRS OF LIFE

	No Causes	(1)	(2)	(3)	(4)	(5)	(6)	(7)	(8)	(9)	(10)	(11)	(12)	(1)+(2)	(1)+(2)+(5)+(6)+(8)	(1)+(2)+(5)+(6)+(8)+part of(9)&(12)	(10)+(11)
TOTAL		1.637	2.367	.338	2.492	2.849	1.850	.355	.000	1.291	.000	1.031	14.702	4.133	9.621	22.982	1.031
WORK	10.734	1.596	.967	.191	1.131	.563	.344	.164	.000	.000	.000	.651	3.503	2.619	3.633	5.990	.651

POPULATION, DEATHS, DEATH RATES FOR ALL CAUSES COMBINED, AND SPECIFIED CAUSES

Age Start of Interval	Midyear Population	Deaths During Year	All Causes	Respiratory T. B.	Other Infec. and Paras.	Neo-plasms	Cardio-vascular	Infl., Pneu., Bronch.	Diar-rheal	Certain Degen-erative	Maternal	Cert. Dis. of Infancy	Motor Vehicle	Other Violence	Other and Unknown	Age Start of Interval
0	603300	98283	.16291	.00038	.00871	.00001	.00532	.02413	.01457	.00056	.00000	.02767	.00000	.00167	.07988	0
1	2073778	57492	.02772	.00028	.00395	.00000	.00085	.00430	.00324	.00036	.00000	.00000	.00000	.00101	.01373	1
5	2291096	13808	.00603	.00026	.00113	.00000	.00031	.00060	.00049	.00019	.00000	.00000	.00000	.00023	.00282	5
10	2182057	9872	.00452	.00086	.00077	.00000	.00035	.00037	.00021	.00010	.00000	.00000	.00000	.00018	.00167	10
15	2165089	16972	.00784	.00208	.00105	.00001	.00057	.00059	.00027	.00012	.00026	.00000	.00000	.00044	.00246	15
20	1999208	19680	.00984	.00235	.00110	.00000	.00079	.00071	.00035	.00017	.00061	.00000	.00000	.00041	.00335	20
25	1559555	15705	.01007	.00220	.00103	.00001	.00091	.00066	.00043	.00018	.00073	.00000	.00000	.00032	.00362	25
30	1527750	15323	.01003	.00176	.00090	.00010	.00101	.00061	.00043	.00022	.00081	.00000	.00000	.00028	.00389	30
35	1196379	13607	.01137	.00151	.00088	.00042	.00132	.00064	.00053	.00026	.00096	.00000	.00000	.00026	.00458	35
40	1279049	14744	.01153	.00125	.00088	.00066	.00157	.00065	.00059	.00029	.00060	.00000	.00000	.00030	.00474	40
45	1170904	14342	.01225	.00124	.00093	.00108	.00198	.00067	.00066	.00029	.00012	.00000	.00000	.00032	.00496	45
50	1020103	16598	.01627	.00122	.00113	.00136	.00302	.00103	.00096	.00043	.00000	.00000	.00000	.00033	.00678	50
55	827272	18558	.02243	.00117	.00117	.00172	.00468	.00157	.00153	.00057	.00000	.00000	.00000	.00041	.00961	55
60	613494	19773	.03223	.00103	.00131	.00210	.00738	.00214	.00229	.00083	.00000	.00000	.00000	.00060	.01455	60
65	550353	26816	.04873	.00088	.00155	.00213	.01166	.00316	.00337	.00104	.00000	.00000	.00000	.00072	.02422	65
70	398529	26827	.06732	.00083	.00156	.00170	.01444	.00363	.00319	.00120	.00001	.00000	.00000	.00081	.03993	70
75	229942	23590	.10259	.00078	.00182	.00207	.02258	.00574	.00581	.00181	.00000	.00000	.00000	.00102	.06096	75
80	99228	17665	.17802	.00070	.00218	.00236	.03421	.00940	.01438	.00260	.00000	.00000	.00000	.00151	.11068	80
85+	47765	16173	.33860	.00046	.00301	.00247	.05154	.01704	.02573	.00360	.00000	.00000	.00000	.00249	.23224	85+
ALL	21834851	455828														

CRUDE DEATH RATE			.02088	.00126	.00154	.00044	.00242	.00195	.00150	.00033	.00029	.00076	.00000	.00046	.00993	
STANDARDIZED RATE (1)			.02001	.00121	.00165	.00033	.00190	.00208	.00151	.00030	.00028	.00097	.00000	.00046	.00932	
STANDARDIZED RATE (2)			.02322	.00125	.00147	.00056	.00320	.00193	.00161	.00039	.00029	.00057	.00000	.00047	.01147	
GEOMETRIC MEAN			.02505													

LIFE TABLE FOR ALL CAUSES COMBINED

Age (x)	Midyear Population	Deaths During Year	$_nM_x$	$_nq_x$	l_x	$_nd_x$	$_nL_x$	$_nm_x$	$_na_x$	T_x	$_nr_x$	$\overset{\circ}{e}_x$	Age (x)
0	603300	98283	.162909	.147240	100000	14724	90384	.162904	.346945	4367628	.000000	43.676	0
1	2073778	57492	.027723	.103710	85276	8844	318994	.027725	1.500000	4277244	.000000	50.158	1
5	2291096	13808	.006027	.029673	76432	2268	376490	.006024	2.500000	3958250	.000000	51.788	5
10	2182057	9872	.004524	.022383	74164	1660	366779	.004526	2.565387	3581760	.000792	48.295	10
15	2165089	16972	.007839	.038467	72504	2789	355900	.007836	2.626464	3214981	-.003047	44.342	15
20	1999208	19680	.009844	.048096	69715	3353	340290	.009853	2.529203	2859081	.018323	41.011	20
25	1559555	15705	.010070	.049109	66362	3259	323607	.010071	2.483060	2518790	.017119	37.955	25
30	1527750	15323	.010030	.048936	63103	3088	307808	.010032	2.504115	2195183	.017226	34.787	30
35	1196379	13607	.011373	.055320	60015	3320	291793	.011378	2.505522	1887375	.012787	31.448	35
40	1279049	14744	.011527	.056019	56695	3176	275506	.011528	2.491013	1595582	-.007488	28.143	40
45	1170904	14342	.012249	.059474	53519	3183	259798	.012252	2.550463	1320076	.004755	24.666	45
50	1020103	16598	.016271	.078413	50336	3947	242182	.016298	2.593531	1060278	.012689	21.064	50
55	827272	18558	.022433	.106814	46389	4955	220029	.022520	2.595106	818096	.027255	17.636	55
60	613494	19773	.032230	.149853	41434	6209	192211	.032303	2.590756	598067	.014876	14.434	60
65	550353	26816	.048725	.217488	35225	7661	157336	.048692	2.547508	405856	-.004371	11.522	65
70	398529	26827	.067315	.288637	27564	7956	118006	.067420	2.509532	248519	.009895	9.016	70
75	229942	23590	.102591	.409272	19608	8025	77794	.103157	2.477181	130514	.026317	6.656	75
80	99228	17665	.178024	.610982	11583	7077	39411	.175568	2.385368	52719	.026317	4.551	80
85+	47765	16173	.338595	1.000000	4506	4506	13308	.338595	2.953379	13308	.000000	2.953	85+

NUMBER OF PERSONS DYING (OUT OF 100,000 AT BIRTH) ABOVE AGE X FROM SPECIFIED CAUSES

Age (x)	All Causes	Respiratory T. B.	Other Infec. and Paras.	Neoplasms	Cardiovascular	Infl., Pneu., Bronch.	Diarrheal	Certain Degenerative	Maternal	Cert. Dis. of Infancy	Motor Vehicle	Other Violence	Other and Unknown	Age (x)
0	100000	5526	6340	2566	13945	8287	6879	1721	1268	2501	0	2020	48947	0
1	85276	5492	5552	2565	13465	6105	5561	1670	1268	0	0	1870	41728	1
5	76432	5403	4292	2563	13193	4734	4527	1555	1268	0	0	1547	37350	5
10	74164	5303	3866	2563	13076	4510	4344	1484	1268	0	0	1461	36289	10
15	72504	4987	3582	2562	12948	4374	4267	1448	1267	0	0	1395	35674	15
20	69715	4245	3209	2560	12744	4166	4170	1406	1174	0	0	1240	34801	20
25	66362	3444	2836	2559	12474	3925	4051	1349	967	0	0	1099	33658	25
30	63103	2733	2503	2557	12180	3713	3911	1291	731	0	0	997	32487	30
35	60015	2192	2225	2525	11870	3524	3777	1223	480	0	0	911	31288	35
40	56695	1752	1967	2401	11484	3337	3622	1147	199	0	0	834	29952	40
45	53519	1409	1724	2219	11053	3158	3459	1066	33	0	0	752	28646	45
50	50336	1088	1482	1938	10538	2983	3287	990	3	0	0	670	27357	50
55	46389	792	1209	1609	9805	2734	3053	885	2	0	0	589	25711	55
60	41434	533	952	1231	8771	2387	2716	758	1	0	0	498	23587	60
65	35225	336	699	826	7349	1975	2274	599	1	0	0	383	20783	65
70	27564	198	456	490	5516	1479	1744	435	1	0	0	270	16975	70
75	19608	100	272	289	3810	1050	1368	293	0	0	0	174	12252	75
80	11583	39	130	128	2044	601	912	151	0	0	0	94	7484	80
85+	4506	6	40	33	686	227	342	48	0	0	0	33	3091	85+

NUMBER OF PERSONS SURVIVING TO AGE X IF SPECIFIED CAUSES WERE ELIMINATED

Age (x)	No Causes	Respiratory T. B.	Other Infec. and Paras.	Neoplasms	Cardiovascular	Infl., Pneu., Bronch.	Diarrheal	Certain Degenerative	Maternal	Cert. Dis. of Infancy	Motor Vehicle	Other Violence	Other and Unknown	(1) + (2)	(1) + (2) + (5) + (6) + (8)	(1)+(2)+ (5)+(6)+ (8)+part of(9)&(12)	(10) + (11)	Age (x)
		(1)	(2)	(3)	(4)	(5)	(6)	(7)	(8)	(9)	(10)	(11)	(12)					
0	100000	100000	100000	100000	100000	100000	100000	100000	100000	100000	100000	100000	100000	100000	100000	100000	100000	0
1	85276	85307	86006	85277	85720	87313	86501	85323	85276	87615	85276	85414	92202	86038	89358	97853	85414	1
5	76432	76544	78298	76435	77089	79597	78528	76583	76432	78528	76432	76863	87243	78413	83900	96159	76863	5
10	74164	74371	76406	74167	74918	77465	76384	74381	74164	76198	74164	74667	85856	76620	82426	95504	74667	10
15	72504	73021	74986	72508	73369	75872	74752	72752	72505	74492	72504	73062	84640	75520	81480	95027	73062	15
20	69715	70949	72480	69720	70749	73167	71975	69994	69807	71627	69715	70405	82390	73763	80031	94247	70405	20
25	66362	68336	68373	66368	67615	69895	68633	66684	66653	68182	66362	67157	79757	71437	78157	93266	67157	25
30	63103	65658	66307	63111	64587	66681	65404	63466	63611	64834	63103	63960	77225	69033	76216	92245	63960	30
35	60015	63034	63347	60054	61737	63613	62339	60427	60746	61661	60015	60915	74891	66533	74145	91037	60915	35
40	56695	59597	60108	56853	58709	60287	59047	57159	57662	58250	56695	57621	72367	63609	71646	89230	57621	40
45	53519	56989	56992	53846	55856	57095	55905	54036	54596	54987	53519	54474	69971	60687	68988	87207	54474	45
50	50336	53932	53852	50919	53058	53880	52754	50897	51378	51716	50336	51315	67465	57700	66070	84553	51315	50
55	46389	50008	49910	47246	49645	49912	48854	47008	47350	47661	46389	47371	64329	53804	62229	80888	47371	55
60	41434	44930	44841	42564	45401	44935	43972	42108	42293	42570	41434	42395	60309	48624	57123	75751	42395	60
65	35225	38393	38373	36570	40061	38615	37817	35947	35955	36191	35225	36154	55176	41824	50244	68562	36154	65
70	27564	30175	30261	28923	33241	30699	30097	28277	28136	28320	27564	28393	48789	33127	41121	58670	28393	70
75	19608	21554	21695	20750	25434	22242	21756	20237	20015	20146	19608	20280	42505	23848	30638	46796	20280	75
80	11583	12783	12934	12386	16866	13531	13245	12066	11824	11901	11583	12043	34334	14274	19463	33076	12043	80
85+	4506	4995	5092	4880	7664	5533	5560	4759	4600	4630	4506	4723	24001	5645	8730	18728	4723	85+

ADDED YRS OF LIFE																		
TOTAL		1.834	2.329	.412	2.430	2.755	1.942	.386	.430	1.188	.000	.639	15.942	4.296	10.340	24.407	.639	
WORK	11.256	1.658	.885	.259	1.082	.606	.422	.191	.476	.000	.000	.307	3.727	2.595	4.274	7.085	.307	

POPULATION, DEATHS, DEATH RATES FOR ALL CAUSES COMBINED, AND SPECIFIED CAUSES

Age Start of Interval	Midyear Population	Deaths During Year	All Causes	Respiratory T. B.	Other Infec. and Paras.	Neoplasms	Cardiovascular	Infl., Pneu., Bronch.	Diarrheal	Certain Degenerative	Maternal	Cert. Dis. of Infancy	Motor Vehicle	Other Violence	Other and Unknown	Age Start of Interval
0	739905	140669	.19012	.00063	.01066	.00001	.00451	.03972	.00573	.00106	.00000	.03912	.00000	.00154	.08293	0
1	2414636	63595	.02634	.00040	.00328	.00001	.00068	.00556	.00401	.00058	.00000	.00000	.00000	.00120	.01061	1
5	2872335	15991	.00557	.00022	.00092	.00000	.00031	.00054	.00043	.00026	.00000	.00000	.00000	.00050	.00239	5
10	2548211	8854	.00347	.00037	.00060	.00001	.00032	.00023	.00015	.00014	.00000	.00000	.00000	.00026	.00140	10
15	2244428	15966	.00711	.00203	.00100	.00001	.00047	.00035	.00020	.00014	.00000	.00000	.00000	.00057	.00235	15
20	2082481	18720	.00899	.00300	.00120	.00001	.00054	.00039	.00022	.00017	.00000	.00000	.00000	.00086	.00261	20
25	1996964	16010	.00802	.00243	.00054	.00001	.00061	.00040	.00023	.00016	.00000	.00000	.00000	.00078	.00246	25
30	1869001	14074	.00753	.00184	.00089	.00008	.00081	.00044	.00026	.00019	.00000	.00000	.00000	.00068	.00235	30
35	1468948	12671	.00863	.00175	.00093	.00021	.00113	.00050	.00033	.00023	.00000	.00000	.00000	.00082	.00282	35
40	1440242	15257	.01059	.00184	.00089	.00049	.00166	.00061	.00048	.00038	.00000	.00000	.00000	.00074	.00351	40
45	1110767	15720	.01415	.00185	.00099	.00109	.00256	.00085	.00065	.00057	.00000	.00000	.00000	.00084	.00476	45
50	1172785	22360	.01907	.00203	.00103	.00185	.00392	.00131	.00095	.00083	.00000	.00000	.00000	.00089	.00626	50
55	1004676	27037	.02691	.00223	.00102	.00278	.00623	.00212	.00151	.00117	.00000	.00000	.00000	.00100	.00896	55
60	798983	30843	.03860	.00199	.00104	.00390	.00976	.00338	.00230	.00173	.00000	.00000	.00000	.00108	.01341	60
65	548818	30629	.05581	.00163	.00106	.00439	.01508	.00527	.00352	.00242	.00000	.00000	.00000	.00124	.02119	65
70	310196	20010	.06451	.00113	.00089	.00322	.01615	.00505	.00276	.00253	.00000	.00000	.00000	.00118	.03159	70
75	198254	19386	.09778	.00105	.00103	.00389	.02526	.00800	.00502	.00381	.00000	.00000	.00000	.00149	.04823	75
80	89769	14873	.16568	.00094	.00125	.00446	.03828	.01310	.01243	.00547	.00000	.00000	.00000	.00221	.08756	80
85+	49374	15090	.30563	.00063	.00170	.00468	.05766	.02376	.02224	.00755	.00000	.00000	.00000	.00365	.18376	85+
ALL	24960773	517755														

	All Causes	Respiratory T. B.	Other Infec. and Paras.	Neoplasms	Cardiovascular	Infl., Pneu., Bronch.	Diarrheal	Certain Degenerative	Maternal	Cert. Dis. of Infancy	Motor Vehicle	Other Violence	Other and Unknown
CRUDE DEATH RATE	.02074	.00148	.00146	.00062	.00247	.00262	.00131	.00054	.00000	.00116	.00000	.00079	.00829
STANDARDIZED RATE (1)	.02040	.00141	.00156	.00047	.00203	.00281	.00133	.00048	.00000	.00138	.00000	.00078	.00815
STANDARDIZED RATE (2)	.02338	.00154	.00134	.00087	.00362	.00256	.00144	.00070	.00000	.00081	.00000	.00083	.00967
GEOMETRIC MEAN	.02406												

LIFE TABLE FOR ALL CAUSES COMBINED

Age (x)	Midyear Population	Deaths During Year	$_nM_x$	$_nq_x$	l_x	$_nd_x$	$_nL_x$	$_nm_x$	$_na_x$	T_x	$_nr_x$	$\overset{\circ}{e}_x$	Age (x)
0	739905	140669	.190118	.170450	100000	17045	89657	.190113	.393200	4342134	.000000	43.421	0
1	2414636	63595	.026337	.098849	82955	8200	311320	.026339	1.500000	4252476	.000000	51.262	1
5	2872335	15991	.005567	.027436	74755	2051	368648	.005564	2.500000	3941156	.000000	52.721	5
10	2548211	8854	.003475	.017234	72704	1253	360482	.003476	2.575819	3572509	.015992	49.138	10
15	2244428	15966	.007114	.035087	71451	2507	351358	.007135	2.647753	3212026	.015702	44.954	15
20	2082481	18720	.008989	.043963	68944	3031	337160	.008990	2.505636	2860669	.007159	41.493	20
25	1996964	16010	.008017	.039279	65913	2589	322949	.008017	2.444477	2523509	-.000144	38.285	25
30	1869001	14074	.007530	.036969	63324	2341	310765	.007533	2.499110	2200560	-.018550	34.751	30
35	1468948	12671	.008628	.042290	60983	2579	298609	.008637	2.554931	1889795	-.017393	30.989	35
40	1440242	15257	.010593	.051726	58404	3021	284721	.010610	2.583926	1591186	-.018238	27.244	40
45	1110767	15720	.014152	.068541	55383	3796	267774	.014176	2.591983	1306465	-.012600	23.590	45
50	1172785	22360	.019066	.091050	51587	4697	246637	.019044	2.594653	1038690	-.007806	20.135	50
55	1004676	27037	.026911	.126466	46890	5930	220155	.026936	2.589376	792053	.005588	16.892	55
60	798983	30843	.038603	.176782	40960	7241	187190	.038683	2.567987	571898	.013675	13.962	60
65	548818	30629	.055805	.245944	33719	8293	147825	.056100	2.495528	384709	.035055	11.409	65
70	310196	20010	.064508	.277787	25426	7063	109252	.064649	2.468763	236883	.035055	9.317	70
75	198254	19386	.097784	.393944	18363	7234	73607	.098278	2.483037	127631	.023778	6.950	75
80	89769	14873	.165681	.581723	11129	6474	38793	.166886	2.396960	54024	.023778	4.854	80
85+	49374	15090	.305626	1.000000	4655	4655	15231	.305626	3.271968	15231	.000000	3.272	85+

NUMBER OF PERSONS DYING (OUT OF 100,000 AT BIRTH) ABOVE AGE X FROM SPECIFIED CAUSES

Age (x)	All Causes	Respiratory T.B.	Other Infec. and Paras.	Neoplasms	Cardiovascular	Infl., Pneu., Bronch.	Diarrheal	Certain Degenerative	Maternal	Cert. Dis. of Infancy	Motor Vehicle	Other Violence	Other and Unknown	Age (x)
0	100000	6855	5764	3870	15557	10868	6063	3021	0	3507	0	3591	40904	0
1	82955	6798	4791	3869	15153	7306	5191	2926	0	0	0	3453	33468	1
5	74755	6674	3769	3867	14940	5576	3941	2746	0	0	0	3078	30164	5
10	72704	6594	3429	3865	14828	5377	3783	2651	0	0	0	2893	29284	10
15	71451	6457	3212	3864	14713	5295	3728	2600	0	0	0	2800	28782	15
20	68944	5742	2859	3862	14548	5172	3657	2552	0	0	0	2599	27953	20
25	65913	4731	2455	3859	14366	5040	3583	2494	0	0	0	2310	27075	25
30	63324	3946	2153	3856	14169	4912	3510	2441	0	0	0	2057	26280	30
35	60983	3376	1878	3830	13918	4776	3428	2382	0	0	0	1846	25549	35
40	58404	2855	1599	3768	13579	4627	3329	2295	0	0	0	1646	24706	40
45	55383	2330	1345	3629	13106	4453	3194	2187	0	0	0	1435	23794	45
50	51587	1835	1080	3337	12419	4225	3019	2035	0	0	0	1209	22428	50
55	46890	1335	827	2881	11455	3903	2784	1830	0	0	0	990	20885	55
60	40960	866	602	2268	10081	3437	2452	1573	0	0	0	769	18912	60
65	33719	493	407	1537	8249	2803	2021	1248	0	0	0	567	16394	65
70	25426	253	251	887	6008	2019	1458	888	0	0	0	382	13240	70
75	18363	130	154	537	4241	1467	1197	611	0	0	0	254	9772	75
80	11129	53	78	251	2373	875	825	329	0	0	0	144	6201	80
85+	4655	10	26	71	878	362	339	115	0	0	0	56	2798	85+

NUMBER OF PERSONS SURVIVING TO AGE X IF SPECIFIED CAUSES WERE ELIMINATED

Age (x)	No Causes	Respiratory T.B.	Other Infec. and Paras.	Neoplasms	Cardiovascular	Infl., Pneu., Bronch.	Diarrheal	Certain Degenerative	Maternal	Cert. Dis. of Infancy	Motor Vehicle	Other Violence	Other and Unknown	(1) + (2)	(1) + (2) + (5) + (6) + (8)	(1)+(2)+(5)+(6)+(8)+part of(9)&(12)	(10) + (11)	Age (x)
		(1)	(2)	(3)	(4)	(5)	(6)	(7)	(8)	(9)	(10)	(11)	(12)					
0	100000	100000	100000	100000	100000	100000	100000	100000	100000	100000	100000	100000	100000	100000	100000	100000	100000	0
1	82955	83007	83845	82956	83323	86259	83752	83041	82955	86207	82955	83081	90001	83897	88076	98065	83081	1
5	74755	74920	76543	74758	75290	79458	76680	75004	74755	77685	74755	75225	84578	76712	83637	96473	75225	5
10	72704	72943	74787	72709	73336	77487	74736	73040	72704	75554	72704	73345	83246	75033	82204	95574	73345	10
15	71451	71822	73720	71457	72187	76238	73504	71832	71451	74252	71451	72174	82383	74103	81340	95001	72174	15
20	68944	70012	71492	68951	69818	73692	70997	69359	68944	71646	68944	69842	80436	72600	79910	94163	69842	20
25	65913	67546	68760	65923	66929	70590	67950	66367	65913	68497	65913	67058	77508	70880	78256	93123	67058	25
30	63324	66075	66368	63337	64497	67992	65355	63813	63324	65806	63324	64677	75774	69251	76696	92076	64677	30
35	60983	64218	64198	61021	62364	65583	62022	61512	60983	63373	60983	62498	73837	67603	75134	90504	62498	35
40	58404	62041	61771	58501	60067	62567	60457	58997	58404	60693	58404	60055	71720	65618	73231	89360	60055	40
45	55383	59377	58838	55611	57436	59893	57466	56051	55383	57554	55383	57161	69219	63081	70783	87196	57161	45
50	51587	55821	55077	52084	54192	56026	53703	52358	51587	53609	51587	53468	66032	59597	67381	83923	53468	50
55	46890	51255	50320	47783	50233	51260	49047	47790	46890	48728	46890	48816	61932	55004	62897	79365	48816	55
60	40960	45253	44181	42227	45278	45256	43170	41991	40960	42566	40960	42857	56590	48812	56841	72950	42857	60
65	33719	37625	36561	35534	39156	37896	35953	34871	33719	35041	33719	35472	49849	40796	48889	64227	35472	65
70	25426	28601	27714	27390	31666	29348	27596	26618	25426	26423	25426	26916	41865	31176	39056	53173	26916	70
75	18363	20772	20105	20099	24964	21740	20207	19471	18363	19083	18363	19553	35499	22742	29627	42311	19553	75
80	11129	12655	12248	12422	17215	13726	12569	12032	11129	11565	11129	11940	27551	13927	19400	29883	11940	80
85+	4655	5324	5159	5323	8806	6152	5613	5180	4655	4837	4655	5054	18221	5900	9402	17050	5054	85+

ACCED YRS OF LIFE

	No Causes	(1)	(2)	(3)	(4)	(5)	(6)	(7)	(8)	(9)	(10)	(11)	(12)	(1)+(2)	(1)+(2)+(5)+(6)+(8)	part of(9)&(12)	(10)+(11)
TOTAL		2.114	2.190	.543	2.572	3.638	1.714	.597	.000	1.687	.000	1.086	12.791	4.451	10.727	23.433	1.086
WORK	10.430	2.011	.900	.279	1.081	.488	.318	.250	.000	.000	.000	.664	2.918	2.974	3.883	5.874	.664

POPULATION, DEATHS, DEATH RATES FOR ALL CAUSES COMBINED, AND SPECIFIED CAUSES

Age Start of Interval	Midyear Population	Deaths During Year	All Causes	Respiratory T. B.	Other Infec. and Paras.	Neoplasms	Cardiovascular	Infl., Pneu., Bronch.	Diarrheal	Certain Degenerative	Maternal	Cert. Dis. of Infancy	Motor Vehicle	Other Violence	Other and Unknown	Age Start of Interval
0	718128	122147	.17009	.00047	.01051	.00001	.00363	.03466	.00854	.00093	.00000	.03576	.00000	.00156	.07401	0
1	2349507	63168	.02689	.00040	.00321	.00000	.00064	.00584	.00414	.00058	.00000	.00000	.00000	.00099	.01107	1
5	2783257	16940	.00609	.00043	.00104	.00000	.00031	.00073	.00050	.00032	.00000	.00000	.00000	.00025	.00250	5
10	2488606	12901	.00518	.00120	.00095	.00000	.00037	.00038	.00025	.00018	.00000	.00000	.00000	.00015	.00169	10
15	2173815	20914	.00962	.00330	.00137	.00000	.00061	.00059	.00033	.00017	.00024	.00000	.00000	.00040	.00262	15
20	2035975	22184	.01090	.00339	.00129	.00001	.00074	.00063	.00041	.00026	.00067	.00000	.00000	.00040	.00308	20
25	1978600	20326	.01027	.00280	.00106	.00009	.00089	.00058	.00045	.00028	.00071	.00000	.00000	.00029	.00313	25
30	1807369	18359	.01016	.00213	.00099	.00026	.00105	.00053	.00048	.00032	.00084	.00000	.00000	.00026	.00331	30
35	1402617	15319	.01092	.00182	.00087	.00055	.00131	.00054	.00053	.00042	.00055	.00000	.00000	.00025	.00369	35
40	1358835	14984	.01103	.00150	.00080	.00056	.00161	.00058	.00058	.00042	.00061	.00000	.00000	.00024	.00373	40
45	1058256	12755	.01205	.00136	.00077	.00140	.00211	.00066	.00073	.00049	.00012	.00000	.00000	.00032	.00410	45
50	1118140	16854	.01507	.00141	.00077	.00186	.00309	.00089	.00104	.00060	.00000	.00000	.00000	.00030	.00510	50
55	984970	20408	.02072	.00128	.00087	.00245	.00453	.00150	.00164	.00093	.00000	.00000	.00000	.00038	.00715	55
60	810153	23929	.02954	.00110	.00085	.00283	.00724	.00229	.00239	.00132	.00000	.00000	.00000	.00049	.01100	60
65	591260	26134	.04420	.00074	.00088	.00312	.01139	.00325	.00358	.00187	.00000	.00000	.00000	.00065	.01871	65
70	367592	22274	.06059	.00060	.00081	.00237	.01322	.00304	.00216	.00000	.00000	.00000	.00000	.00087	.03375	70
75	254613	23528	.09241	.00056	.00095	.00286	.02067	.00597	.00555	.00324	.00000	.00000	.00000	.00110	.05151	75
80	122131	19487	.15956	.00050	.00113	.00328	.03133	.00977	.01375	.00466	.00000	.00000	.00000	.00162	.09353	80
85+	63547	19076	.30019	.00031	.00157	.00343	.04719	.01772	.02458	.00644	.00000	.00000	.00000	.00268	.19626	85+
ALL	24467371	511687														

CRUDE DEATH RATE			.02091	.00162	.00150	.00062	.00229	.00245	.00148	.00055	.00029	.00105	.00000	.00044	.00863	
STANDARDIZED RATE (1)			.02004	.00161	.00162	.00047	.00178	.00263	.00143	.00048	.00028	.00126	.00000	.00044	.00804	
STANDARDIZED RATE (2)			.02244	.00160	.00137	.00079	.00303	.00227	.00158	.00065	.00029	.00074	.00000	.00045	.00967	
GEOMETRIC MEAN			.02454													

LIFE TABLE FOR ALL CAUSES COMBINED

Age (x)	Midyear Population	Deaths During Year	$_nM_x$	$_nq_x$	l_x	$_nd_x$	$_nL_x$	$_nm_x$	$_na_x$	T_x	$_nr_x$	$\overset{\circ}{e}_x$	Age (x)
0	718128	122147	.170091	.153370	100000	15337	90171	.170087	.359154	4344726	.000000	43.447	0
1	2349507	63168	.026886	.100776	84663	8532	317322	.026888	1.500000	4254555	.000000	50.253	1
5	2783257	16940	.006086	.029922	76131	2278	374560	.006075	2.500000	3937233	.000000	51.717	5
10	2488606	12901	.005184	.025632	73853	1893	364164	.005190	2.622491	3562273	.014827	48.235	10
15	2173815	20914	.009621	.047123	71960	3391	351686	.009642	2.607085	3197508	.014131	44.435	15
20	2035975	22184	.010896	.053027	68569	3636	333726	.010895	2.491978	2845823	.002916	41.503	20
25	1978600	20326	.010273	.050067	64933	3251	316416	.010274	2.462768	2512097	-.002456	38.688	25
30	1807369	18359	.010158	.049528	61682	3055	300745	.010158	2.490930	2195681	.019042	35.597	30
35	1402617	15319	.010922	.053184	58627	3118	285324	.010928	2.494922	1894936	.018007	32.322	35
40	1358835	14984	.011027	.053607	55509	2979	270089	.011030	2.497133	1609612	.018146	28.997	40
45	1058256	12755	.012053	.058576	52530	3077	255085	.012063	2.541572	1339523	.013163	25.500	45
50	1118140	16854	.015073	.072655	49453	3593	238585	.015060	2.584249	1084437	-.006562	21.929	50
55	984970	20408	.020719	.098779	45860	4530	218416	.020740	2.597360	845852	.005916	18.444	55
60	810153	23929	.029536	.138156	41330	5710	192918	.029558	2.595155	627436	.014155	15.181	60
65	591260	26134	.044201	.200393	35620	7138	160633	.044437	2.553003	434518	.032199	12.199	65
70	367592	22274	.060594	.264237	28482	7526	123750	.060816	2.520623	273884	.024966	9.616	70
75	254613	23528	.092407	.376169	20956	7883	85048	.092689	2.496881	150134	.014522	7.164	75
80	122131	19487	.159558	.566664	13073	7408	46215	.160296	2.414901	65086	.014522	4.979	80
85+	63547	19076	.300187	1.000000	5665	5665	18872	.300187	3.331254	18872	.000000	3.331	85+

NUMBER OF PERSONS DYING (OUT OF 100,000 AT BIRTH) ABOVE AGE X FROM SPECIFIED CAUSES

Age (x)	All Causes	Respiratory T. B.	Other Infec. and Paras.	Neo-plasms	Cardio-vascular	Infl., Pneu., Bronch.	Diar-rheal	Certain Degen-erative	Maternal	Cert. Dis. of Infancy	Motor Vehicle	Other Violence	Other and Unknown	Age (x)
0	100000	6961	5863	3670	13908	9903	6958	2930	1251	3224	0	1949	43343	0
1	84663	6918	4915	3669	13580	6778	6228	2846	1251	0	0	1808	36670	1
5	76131	6791	3896	3667	13377	4925	4914	2661	1251	0	0	1493	33156	5
10	73853	6629	3506	3667	13259	4654	4726	2541	1251	0	0	1399	32221	10
15	71960	6189	3159	3665	13122	4514	4634	2477	1251	0	0	1344	31605	15
20	68569	5027	2678	3665	12907	4308	4519	2418	1165	0	0	1203	30679	20
25	64933	3894	2246	3662	12660	4098	4381	2329	943	0	0	1068	29652	25
30	61682	3008	1909	3635	12378	3914	4239	2242	720	0	0	975	28662	30
35	58627	2370	1613	3556	12063	3755	4095	2145	467	0	0	898	27665	35
40	55509	1851	1366	3398	11690	3600	3945	2025	195	0	0	827	26612	40
45	52530	1447	1150	3139	11255	3444	3788	1911	30	0	0	762	25604	45
50	49453	1101	954	2781	10715	3275	3601	1785	1	0	0	681	24559	50
55	45860	766	770	2338	9978	3061	3352	1642	1	0	0	608	23344	55
60	41330	486	580	1803	8588	2734	2993	1439	1	0	0	526	21780	60
65	35620	275	409	1258	7588	2291	2531	1185	1	0	0	432	19650	65
70	28482	156	267	756	5749	1766	1954	883	1	0	0	328	16622	70
75	20956	82	166	464	4108	1298	1577	615	1	0	0	220	12425	75
80	13073	35	85	220	2346	789	1103	338	1	0	0	126	8030	80
85+	5665	6	30	65	891	334	464	121	0	0	0	50	3704	85+

NUMBER OF PERSONS SURVIVING TO AGE X IF SPECIFIED CAUSES WERE ELIMINATED

Age (x)	No Causes	Respiratory T. B. (1)	Other Infec. and Paras. (2)	Neo-plasms (3)	Cardio-vascular (4)	Infl., Pneu., Bronch. (5)	Diar-rheal (6)	Certain Degener-ative (7)	Maternal (8)	Cert. Dis. of Infancy (9)	Motor Vehicle (10)	Other Violence (11)	Other and Unknown (12)	(1) + (2)	(1) + (2) + (5) + (6) + (8)	(1)+(2)+ (5)+(6)+ (8)+part of(9)&(12)	(10) + (11)	Age (x)
0	100000	100000	100000	100000	100000	100000	100000	100000	100000	100000	100000	100000	100000	100000	100000	100000	100000	0
1	84663	84703	85539	84664	84965	87584	85374	84740	84663	87679	84663	84793	91024	85579	89275	98319	84793	1
5	76131	76287	77901	76134	76596	80596	78036	76376	76131	78843	76131	76547	85511	78060	84707	96862	76547	5
10	73853	74164	75964	73856	74421	78468	75891	74210	73853	76483	73853	74350	83993	76283	83287	96137	74350	10
15	71960	72701	74370	71965	72650	76603	74039	72371	71960	74523	71960	72499	82535	75135	82295	95635	72499	15
20	68569	70431	71352	68573	69439	73208	70666	69018	68653	71011	68569	69221	79689	73289	80739	94861	69221	20
25	64933	67837	68007	64940	66000	69544	67057	65446	65230	67246	64933	65683	76634	71048	78943	93926	65683	25
30	61682	65349	64946	61715	62976	66255	63843	62255	62183	63879	61682	62486	73945	68807	77119	92887	62486	30
35	58627	62774	62034	58736	60172	63140	60827	59267	59352	60715	58627	59468	71457	66422	75137	91593	59468	35
40	55509	59978	58990	55767	57345	59944	57743	56233	56464	57486	55509	56375	68917	63739	72834	89857	56375	40
45	52530	57185	56047	53028	54707	56891	54804	53328	53597	54401	52530	53414	66448	61014	70340	87686	53414	45
50	49453	54201	52967	50274	52052	53737	51783	50328	50486	51214	49453	50365	63851	58053	67434	84853	50365	50
55	45860	50617	49309	47057	49023	50057	48273	46812	46817	47493	45860	46777	60742	54424	63836	81176	46777	55
60	41330	45941	44632	42932	45197	45453	43865	42385	42193	42802	41330	42236	56744	49579	59076	76182	42236	60
65	35620	39784	38637	37528	40400	39628	38262	36772	36364	36889	35620	36490	51657	43154	52646	69258	36490	65
70	28482	31929	31031	30480	34218	32211	31151	29682	29077	29496	28482	29273	45467	34786	43925	59636	29273	70
75	20956	23562	22925	22691	26914	24155	23272	22078	21394	21702	20956	21633	39719	25776	33683	48199	21633	75
80	13073	14739	14370	14361	18653	15534	14939	14002	13346	13539	13073	13571	32236	16202	22460	34959	13571	80
85+	5665	6408	6266	6333	9526	7086	6958	6218	5784	5867	5665	5931	22764	7088	11118	20860	5931	85+

ADDED YRS OF LIFE																		
TOTAL		2.493	2.305	.618	2.413	3.509	1.910	.640	.434	1.535	.000	.612	13.660	4.973	11.999	25.502	.612	
WORK	11.604	2.246	.945	.378	1.087	.550	.456	.290	.477	.000	.000	.283	3.152	3.263	4.951	7.409	.283	

POPULATION, DEATHS, DEATH RATES FOR ALL CAUSES COMBINED, AND SPECIFIED CAUSES

Age Start of Interval	Midyear Population	Deaths During Year	All Causes	Respiratory T.B.	Other Infec. and Paras.	Neoplasms	Cardiovascular	Infl., Pneu., Bronch.	Diarrheal	Certain Degenerative	Maternal	Cert. Dis. of Infancy	Motor Vehicle	Other Violence	Other and Unknown	Age Start of Interval
0	1002158	103900	.10367	.00027	.00719	.00007	.00045	.02396	.01616	.00060	.00000	.03749	.00000	.00062	.01686	0
1	3560861	68980	.01937	.00020	.00410	.00006	.00015	.00368	.00533	.00062	.00000	.00000	.00000	.00084	.00439	1
5	4409497	17580	.00399	.00011	.00111	.00003	.00012	.00043	.00044	.00025	.00000	.00000	.00000	.00041	.00108	5
10	4190675	11306	.00270	.00031	.00066	.00003	.00015	.00023	.00012	.00014	.00000	.00000	.00000	.00022	.00083	10
15	3682703	30164	.00819	.00314	.00145	.00005	.00021	.00051	.00022	.00020	.00000	.00000	.00000	.00064	.00178	15
20	3030013	28039	.00925	.00435	.00147	.00005	.00018	.00050	.00022	.00023	.00000	.00000	.00000	.00066	.00159	20
25	2813826	23849	.00848	.00358	.00116	.00009	.00023	.00059	.00021	.00029	.00000	.00000	.00000	.00081	.00151	25
30	2485963	19020	.00765	.00264	.00100	.00016	.00039	.00067	.00019	.00039	.00000	.00000	.00000	.00074	.00147	30
35	2240113	18183	.00812	.00199	.00099	.00031	.00078	.00083	.00021	.00058	.00000	.00000	.00000	.00079	.00163	35
40	1957943	19141	.00978	.00162	.00105	.00063	.00155	.00097	.00026	.00095	.00000	.00000	.00000	.00085	.00189	40
45	1631437	22224	.01362	.00164	.00115	.00122	.00313	.00125	.00036	.00145	.00000	.00000	.00000	.00085	.00257	45
50	1441031	29192	.02026	.00168	.00121	.00241	.00583	.00173	.00060	.00232	.00000	.00000	.00000	.00098	.00351	50
55	1226108	35757	.02916	.00160	.00126	.00367	.00949	.00281	.00116	.00339	.00000	.00000	.00000	.00107	.00473	55
60	1036577	45097	.04351	.00158	.00142	.00521	.01571	.00419	.00157	.00493	.00000	.00000	.00000	.00118	.00771	60
65	693141	43959	.06342	.00132	.00148	.00627	.02386	.00617	.00250	.00705	.00000	.00000	.00000	.00149	.01328	65
70	415195	40483	.09750	.00093	.00142	.00688	.03418	.00895	.00430	.01047	.00000	.00000	.00000	.00182	.02856	70
75	213252	30068	.14100	.00075	.00175	.00625	.04152	.01158	.00661	.01289	.00000	.00000	.00000	.00250	.05713	75
80	89562	18867	.21066	.00035	.00147	.00439	.04618	.01362	.01010	.01550	.00000	.00000	.00000	.00274	.11631	80
85+	30726	9502	.30925	.00029	.00182	.00329	.04648	.01549	.01308	.01865	.00000	.00000	.00000	.00378	.20637	85+
ALL	36150821	615311														

	All Causes	Resp. T.B.	Other Infec.	Neoplasms	Cardio.	Infl.	Diarrheal	Certain Degen.	Maternal	Cert. Dis. Infancy	Motor Vehicle	Other Violence	Other and Unknown
CRUDE DEATH RATE	.01702	.00171	.00161	.00077	.00267	.00207	.00143	.00110	.00000	.00104	.00000	.00073	.00389
STANDARDIZED RATE (1)	.01742	.00167	.00171	.00068	.00242	.00225	.00164	.00103	.00000	.00132	.00000	.00072	.00398
STANDARDIZED RATE (2)	.02364	.00174	.00154	.00124	.00496	.00245	.00155	.00182	.00000	.00078	.00000	.00084	.00672
GEOMETRIC MEAN	.02403												

LIFE TABLE FOR ALL CAUSES COMBINED

Age (x)	Midyear Population	Deaths During Year	$_nM_x$	$_nq_x$	l_x	$_nd_x$	$_nL_x$	$_nm_x$	$_na_x$	T_x	$_nr_x$	$\overset{\circ}{e}_x$	Age (x)
0	1002158	103900	.103672	.056160	100000	5616	92752	.103674	.246243	4795131	.000000	47.951	0
1	3560861	68980	.019372	.073907	90384	6680	344836	.019372	1.500000	4702379	.000000	52.027	1
5	4409497	17580	.003987	.019700	83704	1649	414398	.003979	2.500000	4357543	.000000	52.059	5
10	4190675	11306	.002698	.013430	82055	1102	407857	.002702	2.806072	3943146	.008273	48.055	10
15	3682703	30164	.008191	.040369	80953	3268	397097	.008230	2.653700	3535288	.022326	43.671	15
20	3030013	28039	.009254	.045221	77685	3513	379602	.009254	2.488554	3138191	.020279	40.396	20
25	2813826	23849	.008476	.041458	74172	3075	362996	.008471	2.442751	2758589	.012717	37.192	25
30	2485963	19020	.007651	.037526	71097	2668	348742	.007650	2.472670	2395592	.014559	33.695	30
35	2240113	18183	.008117	.039822	68429	2725	335432	.008124	2.536391	2046850	.014115	29.912	35
40	1957943	19141	.009776	.047851	65704	3144	320955	.009796	2.593697	1711419	.020411	26.047	40
45	1631437	22224	.013622	.066160	62560	4139	302975	.013661	2.626339	1390464	.018692	22.226	45
50	1441031	29192	.020258	.096780	58421	5654	278606	.020294	2.612568	1087489	.011690	18.615	50
55	1226108	35757	.029163	.136335	52767	7194	246542	.029180	2.596174	808882	.003657	15.329	55
60	1036577	45097	.043506	.196937	45573	8975	206026	.043562	2.566690	562340	.008272	12.339	60
65	693141	43959	.063420	.275070	36598	10067	158121	.063666	2.529655	356314	.022357	9.736	65
70	415195	40483	.097504	.392256	26531	10408	106268	.097941	2.464711	198193	.021856	7.470	70
75	213252	30068	.140998	.515041	16123	8304	58776	.141283	2.370017	91926	.010475	5.702	75
80	89562	18867	.210659	.665500	7819	5227	24768	.211036	2.259103	33150	.010475	4.240	80
85+	30726	9502	.309249	1.000000	2592	2592	8382	.309249	3.233635	8382	.000000	3.234	85+

NUMBER OF PERSONS DYING (OUT OF 100,000 AT BIRTH) ABOVE AGE X FROM SPECIFIED CAUSES

Age (x)	All Causes	Respiratory T. B.	Other Infec. and Paras.	Neo-plasms	Cardio-vascular	Infl., Pneu., Bronch.	Diar-rheal	Certain Degenerative	Maternal	Cert. Dis. of Infancy	Motor Vehicle	Other Violence	Other and Unknown	Age (x)
0	100000	8634	7212	5746	20919	10701	6525	7821	0	3477	0	3916	25049	0
1	90384	8610	6546	5739	20877	8478	5027	7765	0	0	0	3858	23484	1
5	83704	8540	5133	5719	20824	7210	3189	7551	0	0	0	3569	21969	5
10	82055	8493	4673	5707	20774	7032	3006	7446	0	0	0	3400	21524	10
15	80953	8366	4406	5693	20712	6938	2956	7390	0	0	0	3309	21183	15
20	77685	7111	3827	5674	20628	6735	2869	7312	0	0	0	3054	20475	20
25	74172	5457	3269	5654	20558	6547	2786	7223	0	0	0	2810	19873	25
30	71097	4159	2849	5621	20474	6331	2711	7117	0	0	0	2510	19325	30
35	68429	3241	2501	5565	20336	6096	2644	6980	0	0	0	2253	18813	35
40	65704	2575	2169	5462	20073	5817	2573	6784	0	0	0	1987	18264	40
45	62560	2055	1831	5257	19571	5505	2490	6478	0	0	0	1715	17658	45
50	58421	1557	1483	4886	18618	5126	2381	6037	0	0	0	1458	16875	50
55	52767	1088	1147	4212	16991	4642	2215	5350	0	0	0	1185	15897	55
60	45573	695	837	3307	14650	3950	1930	4552	0	0	0	922	14730	60
65	36598	370	545	2231	11408	3084	1606	3535	0	0	0	679	13140	65
70	26531	161	312	1239	7622	2106	1208	2416	0	0	0	443	11024	70
75	16123	63	161	506	3976	1150	749	1299	0	0	0	249	7970	75
80	7819	18	57	139	1533	469	359	541	0	0	0	102	4601	80
85+	2592	2	15	28	390	130	110	156	0	0	0	32	1729	85+

NUMBER OF PERSONS SURVIVING TO AGE X IF SPECIFIED CAUSES WERE ELIMINATED

Age (x)	No Causes	Respiratory T. B. (1)	Other Infec. and Paras. (2)	Neo-plasms (3)	Cardio-vascular (4)	Infl., Pneu., Bronch. (5)	Diar-rheal (6)	Certain Degener-ative (7)	Maternal (8)	Cert. Dis. of Infancy (9)	Motor Vehicle (10)	Other Violence (11)	Other and Unknown (12)	(1)+(2)	(1)+(2)+(5)+(6)+(8)	(1)+(2)+(5)+(6)+(8)+part of(9)&(12)	(10)+(11)	Age (x)
0	100000	100000	100000	100000	100000	100000	100000	100000	100000	100000	100000	100000	100000	100000	100000	100000	100000	0
1	90384	90407	91019	90391	90424	92521	91819	90437	90384	93749	90384	90439	91884	91042	94674	99640	90439	1
5	83704	83793	85672	83729	83792	86541	86848	83960	83704	86821	83704	84034	86587	85763	92426	98791	84034	5
10	82055	82188	84452	82092	82191	85412	85326	82410	82055	85110	82055	82546	85339	84589	91559	98244	82546	10
15	80953	81211	83591	81003	81149	84362	84231	81359	80953	83967	80953	81529	84546	83858	90928	97855	81529	15
20	77685	79177	80804	77752	77955	81164	80920	78151	77685	80578	77685	78489	81860	82356	89626	97171	78489	20
25	74172	77262	77719	74255	74499	77686	77345	74705	74172	76934	74172	75186	78780	80957	88419	96512	75186	25
30	71097	75393	74929	71209	71493	74687	74215	71713	71097	73744	71097	72363	76086	79457	87130	95677	72363	30
35	68429	73525	72478	68592	68947	72127	71499	69157	68429	70977	68429	69904	73770	77875	85765	94683	69904	35
40	65704	71300	69937	65962	66462	69544	68724	66598	65704	68150	65704	67387	71415	75894	84021	93229	67387	40
45	62560	68441	66942	63007	63780	66535	65520	63715	62560	64889	62560	64435	68643	73234	81578	90941	64435	45
50	58421	64440	62873	59202	60508	62527	61296	59935	58421	60556	58421	60428	64937	69351	77878	87263	60428	50
55	52767	58695	57132	54125	56278	56970	55530	54769	52767	54732	52767	54848	59693	63551	72205	81351	54848	55
60	45573	51099	49654	47616	50983	49902	48238	48116	45573	47270	45573	47624	52796	55675	64529	73185	47624	60
65	36598	41360	40160	39255	44322	40931	40531	39046	36598	39612	36598	38472	44082	45385	54155	62006	38472	65
70	26531	30181	29328	29368	36259	30613	28669	29760	26531	27519	26531	28100	34206	33363	41598	48375	28100	70
75	16123	18424	17950	18475	26216	19472	17810	19075	16123	16723	16123	17234	24106	20512	27365	32907	17234	75
80	7819	8969	8783	9241	15693	10016	8937	9876	7819	8110	7819	8465	15778	10075	14751	19109	8465	80
85+	2592	2983	2939	3136	6623	3567	3123	3551	2592	2689	2592	2848	9594	3381	5605	8575	2848	85+

ACCED YRS OF LIFE

	No Causes	(1)	(2)	(3)	(4)	(5)	(6)	(7)	(8)	(9)	(10)	(11)	(12)	(1)+(2)	(1)+(2)+(5)+(6)+(8)	(1)+(2)+(5)+(6)+(8)+part of(9)&(12)	(10)+(11)
TOTAL		2.789	2.649	.770	2.803	3.050	2.268	1.204	.000	1.776	.000	1.062	5.697	5.652	11.994	18.552	1.062
WORK	10.731	2.681	1.108	.385	1.032	.702	.238	.550	.000	.000	.000	.674	1.710	3.887	4.973	6.254	.674

POPULATION, DEATHS, DEATH RATES FOR ALL CAUSES COMBINED, AND SPECIFIED CAUSES

Age Start of Interval	Midyear Population	Deaths During Year	All Causes	Respiratory T. B.	Other Infec. and Paras.	Neo-plasms	Cardio-vascular	Infl., Pneu., Bronch.	Diar-rheal	Certain Degen-erative	Maternal	Cert. Dis. of Infancy	Motor Vehicle	Other Violence	Other and Unknown	Age Start of Interval
0	974112	86609	.08891	.00023	.00691	.00007	.00036	.02021	.01446	.00053	.00000	.03165	.00000	.00062	.01385	0
1	3479800	65818	.01891	.00018	.00427	.00005	.00014	.00365	.00531	.00050	.00000	.00000	.00000	.00066	.00414	1
5	4317457	17315	.00401	.00016	.00120	.00004	.00013	.00045	.00050	.00025	.00000	.00000	.00000	.00016	.00113	5
10	4115533	14300	.00347	.00078	.00080	.00003	.00018	.00030	.00018	.00016	.00000	.00000	.00000	.00008	.00096	10
15	3657933	30846	.00843	.00340	.00171	.00004	.00026	.00054	.00026	.00023	.00004	.00000	.00000	.00017	.00178	15
20	3017475	27948	.00926	.00349	.00159	.00006	.00031	.00065	.00029	.00032	.00028	.00000	.00000	.00030	.00197	20
25	2789069	23718	.00850	.00286	.00129	.00015	.00045	.00071	.00028	.00040	.00034	.00000	.00000	.00027	.00177	25
30	2414559	19108	.00791	.00193	.00102	.00034	.00063	.00069	.00029	.00051	.00048	.00000	.00000	.00025	.00176	30
35	2137615	17932	.00839	.00135	.00090	.00068	.00107	.00066	.00033	.00072	.00059	.00000	.00000	.00023	.00185	35
40	1835454	16510	.00900	.00105	.00084	.00111	.00157	.00067	.00040	.00085	.00035	.00000	.00000	.00026	.00191	40
45	1536975	15806	.01028	.00056	.00084	.00158	.00240	.00069	.00045	.00108	.00004	.00000	.00000	.00029	.00196	45
50	1412063	20086	.01422	.00091	.00090	.00222	.00407	.00094	.00078	.00151	.00001	.00000	.00000	.00037	.00253	50
55	1301886	24305	.01867	.00079	.00083	.00273	.00607	.00145	.00135	.00198	.00000	.00000	.00000	.00041	.00306	55
60	1162776	32117	.02762	.00072	.00101	.00356	.00950	.00208	.00184	.00304	.00000	.00000	.00000	.00051	.00538	60
65	840020	35354	.04209	.00055	.00106	.00429	.01516	.00302	.00287	.00462	.00000	.00000	.00000	.00069	.00982	65
70	564219	40151	.07116	.00045	.00119	.00457	.02361	.00471	.00455	.00727	.00000	.00000	.00000	.00109	.02327	70
75	325063	35913	.11048	.00037	.00129	.00416	.02998	.00630	.00771	.00988	.00000	.00000	.00000	.00150	.04929	75
80	160776	28380	.17652	.00017	.00126	.00344	.03365	.00847	.01144	.01259	.00000	.00000	.00000	.00208	.10342	80
85+	70990	19068	.26860	.00020	.00180	.00220	.03362	.01024	.01490	.01447	.00000	.00000	.00000	.00249	.18867	85+
ALL	36113775	571284														

CRUDE DEATH RATE			.01582	.00140	.00160	.00075	.00232	.00171	.00156	.00058	.00014	.00085	.00000	.00033	.00416	
STANDARDIZED RATE (1)			.01499	.00139	.00172	.00061	.00178	.00184	.00167	.00081	.00014	.00111	.00000	.00033	.00358	
STANDARDIZED RATE (2)			.01926	.00136	.00149	.00103	.00352	.00177	.00166	.00137	.00015	.00066	.00000	.00038	.00588	
GEOMETRIC MEAN			.02082													

LIFE TABLE FOR ALL CAUSES COMBINED

Age (x)	Midyear Population	Deaths During Year	$_nM_x$	$_nq_x$	l_x	$_nd_x$	$_nL_x$	$_nm_x$	$_na_x$	T_x	$_nr_x$	$\overset{\circ}{e}_x$	Age (x)
0	974112	86609	.088911	.083150	100000	8315	93524	.088908	.221148	5072563	.000000	50.726	0
1	3479800	65818	.018914	.072247	91685	6624	350180	.018916	1.500000	4979039	.000000	54.306	1
5	4317457	17315	.004010	.019809	85061	1685	421093	.004001	2.500000	4628859	.000000	54.418	5
10	4115533	14300	.003475	.017259	83376	1439	413640	.003479	2.748147	4207767	.006833	50.467	10
15	3657933	30846	.008433	.041483	81937	3399	401628	.008463	2.629655	3794127	.020420	46.305	15
20	3017475	27948	.009262	.045265	78538	3555	383744	.009264	2.483591	3392499	.019597	43.196	20
25	2789069	23718	.008504	.041556	74983	3119	366957	.008500	2.448702	3008755	.014206	40.126	25
30	2414559	19108	.007914	.038782	71864	2787	352294	.007911	2.479144	2641797	.017636	36.761	30
35	2137615	17932	.008389	.041114	69077	2840	338312	.008395	2.509536	2289503	.017620	33.144	35
40	1835454	16510	.008995	.044039	66237	2917	323964	.009004	2.524426	1951191	.023467	29.458	40
45	1536975	15806	.010284	.050253	63320	3182	308900	.010301	2.580007	1627227	.019366	25.698	45
50	1412063	20086	.014225	.068825	60138	4139	290722	.014237	2.591659	1318327	.007314	21.922	50
55	1301886	24305	.018669	.089341	55999	5003	268004	.018668	2.603188	1027605	-.000590	18.350	55
60	1162776	32117	.027621	.129755	50996	6617	239170	.027667	2.610668	759602	.009439	14.895	60
65	840020	35354	.042087	.191938	44379	8518	201495	.042274	2.605056	520432	.023881	11.727	65
70	564219	40151	.071162	.304342	35861	10914	152491	.071571	2.543178	318937	.024880	8.894	70
75	325063	35913	.110480	.432116	24947	10780	97290	.110803	2.454043	166445	.013312	6.672	75
80	160776	28380	.176519	.602527	14167	8536	48192	.177126	2.347313	69156	.013312	4.881	80
85+	70990	19068	.268601	1.000000	5631	5631	20964	.268601	3.722991	20964	.000000	3.723	85+

NUMBER OF PERSONS DYING (OUT OF 100,000 AT BIRTH) ABOVE AGE X FROM SPECIFIED CAUSES

Age (x)	All Causes	Respiratory T. B.	Other Infec. and Paras.	Neoplasms	Cardiovascular	Infl., Pneu., Bronch.	Diarrheal	Certain Degenerative	Maternal	Cert. Dis. of Infancy	Motor Vehicle	Other Violence	Other and Unknown	Age (x)
0	100000	6886	7289	5762	19470	8846	8289	7417	745	2960	0	1958	30378	0
1	91685	6864	6642	5755	19436	6956	6936	7367	745	0	0	1900	29084	1
5	85061	6802	5145	5738	19387	5677	5076	7191	745	0	0	1667	27633	5
10	83376	6735	4642	5723	19332	5488	4867	7086	745	0	0	1601	27157	10
15	81937	6410	4311	5711	19259	5362	4794	7018	744	0	0	1567	26761	15
20	78538	5039	3623	5655	19155	5143	4689	6927	727	0	0	1497	26043	20
25	74983	3699	3014	5671	19035	4891	4580	6804	619	0	0	1381	25289	25
30	71864	2652	2543	5617	18869	4631	4476	6658	495	0	0	1283	24640	30
35	69077	1973	2186	5495	18646	4387	4373	6477	326	0	0	1194	24020	35
40	66237	1516	1880	5265	18284	4163	4262	6232	127	0	0	1117	23391	40
45	63320	1177	1609	4904	17773	3946	4133	5956	15	0	0	1033	22774	45
50	60138	882	1351	4415	17029	3732	3993	5621	4	0	0	943	22168	50
55	55999	619	1091	3770	15843	3458	3766	5183	1	0	0	835	21433	55
60	50996	407	867	3038	14218	3070	3405	4653	0	0	0	726	20612	60
65	44379	236	626	2185	11941	2573	2964	3925	0	0	0	605	19324	65
70	35861	126	412	1320	8873	1962	2382	2991	0	0	0	466	17329	70
75	24947	57	230	622	5256	1240	1617	1876	0	0	0	299	13750	75
80	14167	21	105	217	2335	626	865	913	0	0	0	153	8932	80
85+	5631	4	38	46	705	215	312	303	0	0	0	52	3956	85+

NUMBER OF PERSONS SURVIVING TO AGE X IF SPECIFIED CAUSES WERE ELIMINATED

Age (x)	No Causes	Respiratory T. B.	Other Infec. and Paras.	Neoplasms	Cardiovascular	Infl., Pneu., Bronch.	Diarrheal	Certain Degenerative	Maternal	Cert. Dis. of Infancy	Motor Vehicle	Other Violence	Other and Unknown	(1)+(2)	(1)+(2)+(5)+(6)+(8)	(1)+(2)+(5)+(6)+(8)+part of(9)&(12)	(10)+(11)	Age (x)
		(1)	(2)	(3)	(4)	(5)	(6)	(7)	(8)	(9)	(10)	(11)	(12)					
0	100000	100000	100000	100000	100000	100000	100000	100000	100000	100000	100000	100000	100000	100000	100000	100000	100000	0
1	91685	91706	92306	91692	91718	93512	92989	91733	91685	94563	91685	91741	92932	92328	95507	99682	91741	1
5	85061	85140	87101	85084	85138	88021	88107	85275	85061	87731	85061	85337	87646	87182	93447	98998	85337	5
10	83376	83519	85887	83413	83506	86472	86576	83690	83376	85993	83376	83712	86397	86035	92655	98604	83712	10
15	81937	82402	84744	81985	82138	85109	85157	82313	81938	84509	81937	82301	85313	85225	92004	98297	82301	15
20	78538	80345	81928	78600	78832	81801	81731	78988	78556	81003	78538	78956	82509	83813	90865	97861	78956	20
25	74983	78059	78842	75066	75382	78056	78143	75534	75106	77324	74983	75496	79552	82076	89529	97243	75496	25
30	71864	75886	76048	71996	72410	75363	74999	72536	72104	74120	71864	72453	76920	80305	88181	96468	72453	30
35	69077	73649	73470	69324	69823	72691	72195	69903	69474	71245	69077	69731	74591	78333	86648	95390	69731	35
40	66237	71099	70769	66701	67312	69934	69341	67272	66814	68316	66237	66940	72192	75963	84692	93747	66940	40
45	63320	68324	67936	64120	64858	67078	66415	64584	63981	65307	63320	64075	69673	73304	82308	91511	64075	45
50	60138	65201	64792	61383	62347	63929	63225	61673	60777	62025	60138	60944	66825	70247	79342	88522	60944	50
55	55999	60989	60603	57757	59255	59811	59105	57863	56597	57757	55999	56855	63018	66003	75199	84221	56855	55
60	50996	55760	55420	53358	55628	54864	54189	53219	51541	52597	50996	51881	58277	60597	70016	78758	51881	60
65	44379	48658	48473	47272	50782	48246	47596	47027	44854	45772	44379	45264	52108	53190	62680	70992	45264	65
70	35861	39458	39378	39030	44307	39585	39025	38898	36244	36987	35861	36703	44273	43328	52604	60278	36703	70
75	24947	27511	27558	27780	34744	28204	27847	28078	25214	25730	24947	25675	34724	30391	38763	45700	25675	75
80	14167	15652	15751	16106	22962	16537	16449	16766	14318	14612	14167	14692	25475	17402	23838	30014	14692	80
85+	5631	6233	6306	6521	10885	6872	6941	7118	5691	5808	5631	5904	17338	6980	10611	15653	5904	85+

ADDED YRS OF LIFE

	No Causes	(1)	(2)	(3)	(4)	(5)	(6)	(7)	(8)	(9)	(10)	(11)	(12)	(1)+(2)	(1)+(2)+(5)+(6)+(8)	part of (9)&(12)	(10)+(11)
TOTAL		2.583	2.954	.568	2.832	2.851	2.553	1.252	.258	1.585	.000	.528	7.239	5.735	12.560	19.431	.528
WORK	10.046	2.242	1.165	.503	.989	.638	.334	.540	.246	.000	.000	.237	1.815	3.489	4.869	6.289	.237

POPULATION, DEATHS, DEATH RATES FOR ALL CAUSES COMBINED, AND SPECIFIED CAUSES

Age Start of Interval	Midyear Population	Deaths During Year	All Causes	Respiratory T. B.	Other Infec. and Paras.	Neoplasms	Cardiovascular	Infl., Pneu., Bronch.	Diarrheal	Certain Degenerative	Maternal	Cert. Dis. of Infancy	Motor Vehicle	Other Violence	Other and Unknown	Age Start of Interval
0	1093635	66869	.06114	.00014	.00373	.00007	.00009	.01133	.00558	.00013	.00000	.02890	.00000	.00106	.00972	0
1	4852629	40937	.00844	.00018	.00251	.00008	.00008	.00121	.00183	.00023	.00000	.00000	.00009	.00084	.00138	1
5	4593663	8818	.00192	.00008	.00052	.00004	.00008	.00013	.00016	.00010	.00000	.00000	.00006	.00041	.00034	5
10	4463184	4510	.00101	.00008	.00018	.00004	.00011	.00006	.00004	.00006	.00000	.00000	.00003	.00016	.00026	10
15	4364577	8673	.00199	.00049	.00020	.00005	.00014	.00007	.00003	.00009	.00000	.00000	.00004	.00051	.00036	15
20	3897442	14302	.00367	.00134	.00027	.00007	.00018	.00007	.00005	.00015	.00000	.00000	.00006	.00102	.00047	20
25	3028909	12957	.00428	.00186	.00032	.00011	.00023	.00009	.00005	.00019	.00000	.00000	.00006	.00085	.00051	25
30	2333684	10184	.00436	.00180	.00032	.00018	.00033	.00009	.00005	.00026	.00000	.00000	.00007	.00070	.00057	30
35	2376514	11674	.00491	.00172	.00035	.00034	.00054	.00011	.00006	.00038	.00000	.00000	.00006	.00069	.00066	35
40	2251015	14156	.00629	.00171	.00046	.00066	.00096	.00014	.00009	.00062	.00000	.00000	.00007	.00073	.00085	40
45	1994040	17612	.00883	.00175	.00054	.00131	.00178	.00022	.00012	.00102	.00000	.00000	.00007	.00084	.00118	45
50	1767943	22267	.01259	.00193	.00057	.00220	.00322	.00035	.00020	.00145	.00000	.00000	.00008	.00095	.00166	50
55	1423319	27610	.01940	.00205	.00066	.00372	.00602	.00066	.00042	.00226	.00000	.00000	.00009	.00107	.00246	55
60	1131484	34679	.03065	.00241	.00076	.00551	.01070	.00136	.00082	.00330	.00000	.00000	.00009	.00113	.00457	60
65	788851	39611	.05021	.00228	.00087	.00770	.01884	.00310	.00182	.00495	.00000	.00000	.00008	.00142	.00915	65
70	541837	41561	.07670	.00183	.00104	.00868	.02873	.00544	.00356	.00661	.00000	.00000	.00007	.00178	.01895	70
75	290839	30849	.10607	.00108	.00118	.00738	.03825	.00452	.00492	.00682	.00000	.00000	.00007	.00212	.03611	75
80	102600	17127	.16693	.00075	.00124	.00564	.04309	.01274	.01220	.00936	.00000	.00000	.00011	.00267	.07913	80
85+	30866	8144	.26385	.00052	.00091	.00473	.05313	.01814	.02180	.01137	.00000	.00000	.00013	.00267	.14952	85+
ALL	41327031	432540														

	All Causes	Respiratory T.B.	Other Infec.	Neoplasms	Cardiovascular	Infl. Pneu.	Diarrheal	Certain Degen.	Maternal	Cert. Dis. Infancy	Motor Vehicle	Other Violence	Other Unknown
CRUDE DEATH RATE	.01047	.00103	.00074	.00087	.00206	.00082	.00063	.00070	.00000	.00076	.00006	.00074	.00204
STANDARDIZED RATE (1)	.01030	.00098	.00076	.00076	.00181	.00089	.00067	.00062	.00000	.00102	.00006	.00073	.00201
STANDARDIZED RATE (2)	.01573	.00120	.00069	.00139	.00392	.00111	.00084	.00113	.00000	.00060	.00006	.00083	.00395
GEOMETRIC MEAN	.01390												

LIFE TABLE FOR ALL CAUSES COMBINED

Age (x)	Midyear Population	Deaths During Year	$_nM_x$	$_nq_x$	l_x	$_nd_x$	$_nL_x$	$_nm_x$	$_na_x$	T_x	$_nr_x$	$\overset{\circ}{e}_x$	Age (x)
0	1093635	66869	.061144	.058200	100000	5820	95192	.061139	.173944	5937623	.000000	59.376	0
1	4852629	40937	.008436	.033054	94180	3113	368938	.008438	1.500000	5842431	.000000	62.035	1
5	4593663	8818	.001920	.009553	91067	870	453160	.001920	2.500000	5473493	.000000	60.104	5
10	4463184	4510	.001010	.005033	90197	454	449854	.001009	2.508719	5020333	.002142	55.660	10
15	4364577	8673	.001987	.009906	89743	889	446736	.001990	2.773716	4570479	.006168	50.929	15
20	3897442	14302	.003670	.018255	88854	1622	440415	.003683	2.623305	4123743	.023500	46.410	20
25	3028909	12957	.004278	.021196	87232	1849	431584	.004284	2.525014	3683328	.045522	42.225	25
30	2333684	10184	.004364	.021597	85383	1844	422342	.004366	2.520223	3251745	.029997	38.084	30
35	2376514	11674	.004912	.024276	83539	2028	412767	.004913	2.570266	2829402	.003746	33.869	35
40	2251015	14156	.006289	.031014	81511	2528	401526	.006296	2.614962	2416635	.008805	29.648	40
45	1994040	17612	.008832	.043338	78983	3423	386796	.008850	2.628177	2015109	.012834	25.513	45
50	1767943	22267	.012595	.061329	75560	4634	366878	.012631	2.643055	1628313	.018231	21.550	50
55	1423319	27610	.019398	.093125	70926	6605	339076	.019479	2.645061	1261435	.022529	17.785	55
60	1131484	34679	.030649	.143546	64321	9233	299726	.030805	2.630397	922359	.026434	14.340	60
65	788851	39611	.050214	.224690	55088	12384	245427	.050459	2.576443	622633	.024404	11.303	65
70	541837	41561	.076704	.322616	42704	13777	179022	.076957	2.496008	377206	.017676	8.833	70
75	290839	30849	.106069	.418986	28927	12120	113508	.106776	2.431776	198184	.047969	6.851	75
80	102600	17127	.166930	.583566	16807	9808	58149	.168670	2.360743	84676	.047969	5.038	80
85+	30866	8144	.263850	1.000000	6999	6999	26526	.263850	3.790029	26526	.000000	3.790	85+

NUMBER OF PERSONS DYING (OUT OF 100,000 AT BIRTH) ABOVE AGE X FROM SPECIFIED CAUSES

Age (x)	All Causes	Respiratory T. B.	Other Infec. and Paras.	Neo-plasms	Cardio-vascular	Infl., Pneu., Bronch.	Diar-rheal	Certain Degen-erative	Maternal	Cert. Dis. of Infancy	Motor Vehicle	Other Violence	Other and Unknown	Age (x)
0	100000	7815	3915	9659	26381	6594	4940	7601	0	2751	391	5132	24821	0
1	94180	7802	3560	9653	26373	5516	4371	7589	0	0	391	5032	23893	1
5	91067	7735	2634	9623	26344	5067	3695	7505	0	0	357	4720	23387	5
10	90197	7697	2397	9603	26307	5010	3621	7462	0	0	332	4534	23234	10
15	89743	7661	2317	9584	26258	4984	3601	7433	0	0	319	4464	23122	15
20	88854	7441	2229	9559	26195	4953	3586	7395	0	0	300	4235	22961	20
25	87232	6849	2109	9530	26116	4921	3566	7330	0	0	271	3785	22755	25
30	85383	6042	1972	9482	26015	4883	3544	7246	0	0	245	3418	22536	30
35	83539	5282	1839	9406	25875	4846	3521	7135	0	0	217	3124	22294	35
40	81511	4570	1695	9264	25652	4803	3494	6978	0	0	192	2839	22024	40
45	78983	3885	1509	8958	25265	4746	3458	6729	0	0	164	2545	21684	45
50	75560	3209	1301	8492	24574	4661	3410	6333	0	0	135	2219	21226	50
55	70926	2501	1090	7683	23387	4532	3337	5801	0	0	106	1872	20617	55
60	64321	1805	865	6416	21335	4309	3193	5031	0	0	77	1511	19779	60
65	55088	1081	636	4757	18109	3898	2946	4039	0	0	51	1171	18400	65
70	42704	521	422	2862	13461	3132	2495	2820	0	0	32	822	16137	70
75	28927	193	235	1307	8300	2155	1855	1633	0	0	19	503	12727	75
80	16807	73	101	475	3940	1224	1291	859	0	0	10	261	8573	80
85+	6999	14	24	125	1409	481	578	302	0	0	3	95	3968	85+

NUMBER OF PERSONS SURVIVING TO AGE X IF SPECIFIED CAUSES WERE ELIMINATED

Age (x)	No Causes	Respiratory T. B. (1)	Other Infec. and Paras. (2)	Neo-plasms (3)	Cardio-vascular (4)	Infl., Pneu., Bronch. (5)	Diar-rheal (6)	Certain Degener-ative (7)	Maternal (8)	Cert. Dis. of Infancy (9)	Motor Vehicle (10)	Other Violence (11)	Other and Unknown (12)	(1) + (2)	(1) + (2) + (5) + (6) + (8)	(1)+(2)+(5)+(6)+(8)+part of(9)&(12)	(10) + (11)	Age (x)
0	100000	100000	100000	100000	100000	100000	100000	100000	100000	100000	100000	100000	100000	100000	100000	100000	100000	0
1	94180	94193	94525	94186	94188	95232	94734	94192	94180	96888	94277	95085	94538	94538	96156	99648	94277	1
5	91067	91145	92319	91102	91103	92532	92273	91161	91067	93685	91100	91468	92446	92398	95128	99021	91502	5
10	90197	90312	91677	90252	90270	91705	91467	90333	90197	92790	90255	90781	91717	91794	94642	98610	90839	10
15	89743	89894	91296	89816	89864	91270	91026	89907	89743	92323	89814	90394	91369	91449	94336	98348	90465	15
20	88854	89223	90481	88952	89037	90357	90140	89054	88854	91408	88943	89729	90627	90922	93772	97847	89818	20
25	87232	88185	88950	87357	87490	88779	88515	87493	87232	89740	87348	88542	89181	89922	92863	97020	88660	25
30	85383	87127	87203	85553	85736	86636	86660	85722	85383	87838	85522	87034	87513	88984	91958	96226	87176	30
35	83539	86016	85454	83780	84023	85056	84812	83981	83539	85941	83703	85451	85868	87989	90993	95378	85619	35
40	81511	84655	83526	81887	82206	83073	82780	82099	81511	83854	81696	83665	84058	86747	89786	94275	83855	40
45	78983	82732	81123	79611	80041	80554	80249	79800	78983	81254	79190	81368	81797	84973	88052	92627	81581	45
50	75560	79841	77816	76662	77261	77148	76819	76734	75560	77732	75786	78170	78718	82225	85351	89968	78404	50
55	70926	75671	73254	72761	73710	72544	72179	72553	70926	72965	71166	73724	74507	78155	81351	85551	73974	55
60	64321	69333	66653	67233	68909	66006	66006	66550	64321	66170	64567	67216	68412	71847	75193	79665	67473	60
65	55088	60103	57305	59205	62304	56924	56416	57953	55088	56672	55322	57895	59967	62521	66162	70431	58142	65
70	42704	47125	44617	47711	53143	44830	44142	46062	42704	43932	42902	45202	48711	49236	53428	57401	45412	70
75	28927	32213	30382	33755	41648	31220	30449	32260	28927	29759	29072	30895	36366	33833	38436	42129	31050	75
80	16807	18812	17757	20338	29390	18913	18147	19397	16807	17290	16898	18145	25519	19876	24150	27599	18243	80
85+	6999	7875	7446	8738	15343	8416	8054	8489	6999	7200	7041	7669	16034	8378	11593	15026	7715	85+

ADDED YRS OF LIFE

	No Causes	(1)	(2)	(3)	(4)	(5)	(6)	(7)	(8)	(9)	(10)	(11)	(12)	(1)+(2)	(1)+(2)+(5)+(6)+(8)	part	(10)+(11)
TOTAL		2.138	1.488	1.380	2.463	1.496	1.151	1.125	.000	1.702	.125	1.494	4.202	3.702	6.671	10.563	1.624
WORK	6.009	1.544	.350	.493	.805	.134	.080	.428	.000	.000	.064	.809	.725	1.914	2.145	2.489	.874

POPULATION, DEATHS, DEATH RATES FOR ALL CAUSES COMBINED, AND SPECIFIED CAUSES

Age Start of Interval	Midyear Population	Deaths During Year	All Causes	Respiratory T.B.	Other Infec. and Paras.	Neoplasms	Cardiovascular	Infl., Pneu., Bronch.	Diarrheal	Certain Degenerative	Maternal	Cert. Dis. of Infancy	Motor Vehicle	Other Violence	Other and Unknown	Age Start of Interval
0	1046111	56005	.05354	.00015	.00386	.00006	.00011	.01007	.00530	.00010	.00000	.02511	.00000	.00103	.00774	0
1	4666651	38699	.00829	.00021	.00267	.00006	.00007	.00131	.00187	.00017	.00000	.00000	.00006	.00061	.00127	1
5	4463407	7765	.00174	.00011	.00059	.00003	.00007	.00015	.00020	.00010	.00000	.00000	.00002	.00016	.00032	5
10	4367761	4435	.00102	.00016	.00018	.00004	.00012	.00007	.00005	.00008	.00000	.00000	.00002	.00009	.00023	10
15	4282080	8043	.00188	.00072	.00021	.00005	.00016	.00006	.00004	.00009	.00002	.00000	.00001	.00021	.00031	15
20	3946329	12936	.00328	.00138	.00032	.00007	.00024	.00010	.00005	.00013	.00016	.00000	.00001	.00039	.00044	20
25	3467110	13700	.00395	.00164	.00038	.00014	.00035	.00012	.00007	.00019	.00026	.00000	.00001	.00054	.00044	25
30	2877303	11833	.00411	.00145	.00036	.00030	.00044	.00012	.00007	.00024	.00030	.00000	.00001	.00024	.00059	30
35	2700959	12184	.00451	.00118	.00036	.00063	.00065	.00011	.00009	.00032	.00029	.00000	.00001	.00022	.00066	35
40	2395096	12559	.00524	.00101	.00038	.00103	.00098	.00014	.00011	.00041	.00016	.00000	.00001	.00023	.00077	40
45	1958718	13696	.00659	.00093	.00036	.00168	.00179	.00018	.00016	.00057	.00002	.00000	.00001	.00030	.00077	45
50	1723592	15999	.00928	.00091	.00039	.00224	.00294	.00025	.00023	.00079	.00000	.00000	.00002	.00025	.00098	50
55	1410755	19336	.01371	.00103	.00047	.00297	.00487	.00044	.00044	.00121	.00000	.00000	.00003	.00039	.00184	55
60	1206515	25196	.02088	.00104	.00054	.00392	.00813	.00089	.00080	.00186	.00000	.00000	.00002	.00051	.00318	60
65	958437	33178	.03462	.00055	.00066	.00497	.01410	.00181	.00175	.00292	.00000	.00000	.00003	.00074	.00669	65
70	740248	41114	.05554	.00066	.00084	.00552	.02217	.00323	.00334	.00418	.00000	.00000	.00003	.00097	.01461	70
75	452318	37229	.08231	.00052	.00094	.00528	.03072	.00470	.00475	.00533	.00000	.00000	.00004	.00133	.02871	75
80	186184	26315	.14134	.00025	.00108	.00464	.03307	.00859	.01177	.00579	.00000	.00000	.00003	.00189	.07422	80
85+	68867	16236	.23576	.00023	.00112	.00376	.05181	.01378	.02106	.00746	.00000	.00000	.00001	.00240	.13413	85+
ALL	42918441	406458														

CRUDE DEATH RATE			.00947	.00079	.00072	.00082	.00206	.00072	.00067	.00051	.00009	.00061	.00002	.00035	.00211	
STANDARDIZED RATE (1)			.00852	.00075	.00077	.00066	.00151	.00076	.00066	.00041	.00008	.00088	.00002	.00034	.00168	
STANDARDIZED RATE (2)			.01253	.00082	.00067	.00114	.00320	.00083	.00082	.00073	.00008	.00052	.00002	.00038	.00332	
GEOMETRIC MEAN			.01168													

LIFE TABLE FOR ALL CAUSES COMBINED

Age (x)	Midyear Population	Deaths During Year	$_nM_x$	$_nq_x$	l_x	$_nd_x$	$_nL_x$	$_nm_x$	$_na_x$	T_x	$_nr_x$	$\overset{\circ}{e}_x$	Age (x)
0	1046111	56005	.053536	.051240	100000	5124	95701	.053542	.161012	6267214	.000000	62.672	0
1	4666651	38699	.008293	.032495	94876	3083	371797	.008292	1.500000	6171513	.000000	65.048	1
5	4463407	7765	.001740	.008661	91793	795	456978	.001740	2.500000	5799716	.000000	63.183	5
10	4367761	4435	.001015	.005066	90998	461	453848	.001016	2.523500	5342739	.001462	58.713	10
15	4282080	8043	.001878	.009355	90537	847	450776	.001879	2.746212	4888891	.005292	53.999	15
20	3946329	12936	.003278	.016301	89690	1462	444979	.003286	2.625541	4438115	.013099	49.483	20
25	3467110	13700	.003951	.015586	88228	1728	436882	.003955	2.536169	3993136	.025157	45.259	25
30	2877303	11833	.004113	.020370	86500	1762	428129	.004116	2.519273	3556253	.023597	41.113	30
35	2700959	12184	.004511	.022316	84738	1891	419043	.004513	2.542746	3128125	.013752	36.915	35
40	2395096	12559	.005244	.025951	82847	2150	409046	.005256	2.586434	2709081	.023739	32.700	40
45	1958718	13696	.006992	.034487	80697	2783	356819	.007013	2.604803	2300035	.025823	28.502	45
50	1723592	15999	.009282	.045563	77914	3550	381147	.009314	2.627465	1903216	.023877	24.427	50
55	1410755	19336	.013706	.066632	74364	4955	360137	.013759	2.642196	1522069	.022822	20.468	55
60	1206515	25196	.020883	.099872	69409	6932	330770	.020957	2.652163	1161932	.018590	16.740	60
65	958437	33178	.034617	.160347	62477	10018	288574	.034716	2.623174	831162	.014538	13.303	65
70	740248	41114	.055541	.245049	52459	12855	230907	.055672	2.558343	542588	.012345	10.343	70
75	452318	37229	.082307	.343854	39604	13618	164130	.082971	2.511382	311680	.043050	7.870	75
80	186184	26315	.141339	.523320	25986	13599	95009	.143133	2.432118	147550	.043050	5.678	80
85+	68867	16236	.235759	1.000000	12387	12387	52541	.235759	4.241624	52541	.000000	4.242	85+

NUMBER OF PERSONS DYING (OUT OF 100,000 AT BIRTH) ABOVE AGE X FROM SPECIFIED CAUSES

Age (x)	All Causes	Respira-tory T. B.	Other Infec. and Paras.	Neo-plasms	Cardio-vascular	Infl., Pneu., Bronch.	Diar-rheal	Certain Degen-erative	Maternal	Cert. Dis. of Infancy	Motor Vehicle	Other Violence	Other and Unknown	Age (x)
0	100000	5388	3921	9117	27812	6046	6375	5967	519	2403	119	2619	29714	0
1	94876	5374	3552	9112	27801	5082	5867	5958	519	0	119	2520	28972	1
5	91793	5296	2558	9088	27774	4596	5174	5896	519	0	97	2294	28501	5
10	90998	5248	2290	9075	27741	4528	5082	5849	519	0	86	2221	28359	10
15	90537	5174	2208	9059	27687	4498	5061	5814	519	0	81	2182	28254	15
20	89690	4850	2115	9038	27613	4472	5044	5773	509	0	75	2085	28116	20
25	88228	4234	1972	9008	27508	4428	5021	5714	439	0	71	1913	27920	25
30	86500	3519	1806	8946	27356	4374	4991	5632	325	0	66	1798	27687	30
35	84738	2900	1651	8816	27167	4325	4960	5529	198	0	63	1697	27432	35
40	82847	2404	1502	8553	26896	4278	4923	5396	75	0	61	1603	27156	40
45	80697	1992	1347	8128	26491	4221	4878	5228	8	0	55	1508	26841	45
50	77914	1622	1202	7460	25777	4150	4815	4999	2	0	50	1387	26450	50
55	74364	1275	1055	6603	24652	4056	4727	4656	1	0	42	1278	25995	55
60	69409	903	884	5530	22889	3896	4567	4258	1	0	32	1138	25311	60
65	62477	559	705	4232	20190	3598	4302	3642	1	0	25	970	24253	65
70	52459	285	514	2797	16109	3074	3795	2798	1	0	16	754	22316	70
75	39604	132	320	1522	10978	2328	3023	1831	1	0	10	530	18929	75
80	25986	48	166	657	5912	1549	2235	953	1	0	4	310	14151	80
85+	12387	12	59	198	2722	724	1106	392	0	0	1	126	7047	85+

NUMBER OF PERSONS SURVIVING TO AGE X IF SPECIFIED CAUSES WERE ELIMINATED

Age (x)	No Causes	Respira-tory T. B.	Other Infec. and Paras.	Neo-plasms	Cardio-vascular	Infl., Pneu., Bronch.	Diar-rheal	Certain Degen-erative	Maternal	Cert. Dis. of Infancy	Motor Vehicle	Other Violence	Other and Unknown	(1) + (2)	(1) + (2) + (5) + (6) + (8)	(1)+(2)+ (5)+(6)+ (8)+part of(9)&(12)	(10) + (11)	Age (x)
		(1)	(2)	(3)	(4)	(5)	(6)	(7)	(8)	(9)	(10)	(11)	(12)					
0	100000	100000	100000	100000	100000	100000	100000	100000	100000	100000	100000	100000	100000	100000	100000	100000	100000	0
1	94876	94890	95236	94881	94887	95820	95372	94885	94876	97245	94876	94972	95601	95250	96700	99671	94972	1
5	91793	91883	93128	91821	91830	93150	92961	91862	91793	94085	91815	92109	92963	93219	95842	99217	92131	5
10	90998	91135	92593	91039	91067	92452	92248	91114	90998	93271	91030	91384	92301	92732	95508	98983	91417	10
15	90537	90747	92207	90594	90660	92014	91802	90687	90537	92758	90574	90960	91940	92421	95241	98773	90998	15
20	89690	90222	91438	89767	89866	91179	90961	89880	89700	91930	89733	90207	91219	91981	94843	98461	90250	20
25	88228	89368	90093	88334	88525	89737	89501	88473	88307	90431	88274	88908	89930	91257	94242	97989	88954	25
30	86500	88338	88456	86665	86942	88034	87778	86822	86691	88660	86550	87281	88404	90376	93544	97451	87332	30
35	84738	87166	86850	85029	85360	86290	86021	85156	85051	86854	84790	85604	86862	89339	92694	96753	85657	35
40	82847	85727	85063	83393	83725	84412	84139	83388	83275	84916	82900	83788	85204	88020	91552	95726	83841	40
45	80697	83923	83013	81652	81958	82279	82000	81391	81180	82712	80754	81708	83313	86332	89982	94230	81766	45
50	77914	81408	80297	79504	79847	79512	79235	78811	78387	79860	77974	79011	80837	83897	87598	91858	79072	50
55	74364	78053	76786	76740	77345	75583	75713	75520	74816	76221	74429	75519	77633	80595	84353	88576	75585	55
60	69409	73230	71840	72703	73985	71079	70826	70919	69831	71142	69480	70624	73137	75795	79683	83829	70696	60
65	62477	66260	64841	66742	69382	64271	64010	64436	62857	64037	62547	63733	66900	68767	72917	76938	63805	65
70	52459	55899	54625	57454	62555	54461	54225	54905	52778	53769	52526	53715	58111	58207	62842	66726	53784	70
75	39604	42340	41413	44591	52826	41792	41634	42334	39845	40593	39660	40751	47265	44275	49414	53245	40808	75
80	25986	27852	27302	30038	40501	28090	27995	28535	26144	26635	26027	26920	36013	29262	34284	38099	26963	80
85+	12387	13302	13090	14681	22970	14006	14191	14024	12463	12696	12409	12962	25280	14058	18321	23072	12984	85+

ADDED YRS OF LIFE

TOTAL		1.832	1.649	1.565	3.928	1.500	1.339	.935	.203	1.561	.043	.748	5.016	3.544	6.918	10.833	.792
WORK	5.182	1.278	.356	.606	.848	.136	.100	.311	.168	.000	.012	.292	.675	1.648	2.076	2.432	.304

POPULATION, DEATHS, DEATH RATES FOR ALL CAUSES COMBINED, AND SPECIFIED CAUSES

Age Start of Interval	Midyear Population	Deaths During Year	All Causes	Respiratory T. B.	Other Infec. and Paras.	Neoplasms	Cardiovascular	Infl., Pneu., Bronch.	Diarrheal	Certain Degenerative	Maternal	Cert. Dis. of Infancy	Motor Vehicle	Other Violence	Other and Unknown	Age Start of Interval
0	809800	27714	.03422	.00002	.00088	.00010	.00023	.00664	.00228	.00003	.00000	.01738	.00003	.00056	.00567	0
1	3175658	8514	.00268	.00001	.00040	.00011	.00003	.00041	.00028	.00006	.00000	.00000	.00018	.00069	.00050	1
5	4690417	4788	.00102	.00001	.00014	.00006	.00004	.00007	.00005	.00005	.00000	.00000	.00011	.00032	.00018	5
10	5558673	3263	.00059	.00001	.00005	.00007	.00006	.00003	.00001	.00004	.00000	.00000	.00005	.00016	.00012	10
15	4662985	6169	.00132	.00003	.00005	.00008	.00010	.00004	.00001	.00007	.00000	.00000	.00021	.00054	.00020	15
20	4084912	8828	.00216	.00009	.00005	.00008	.00013	.00004	.00001	.00010	.00000	.00000	.00034	.00106	.00026	20
25	4084414	9357	.00229	.00022	.00005	.00012	.00017	.00005	.00002	.00013	.00000	.00000	.00032	.00092	.00030	25
30	3747246	8821	.00235	.00037	.00006	.00022	.00024	.00006	.00002	.00015	.00000	.00000	.00025	.00064	.00034	30
35	2752303	8150	.00296	.00051	.00009	.00037	.00041	.00008	.00002	.00021	.00000	.00000	.00025	.00061	.00041	35
40	2281765	9299	.00408	.00059	.00012	.00069	.00086	.00009	.00003	.00032	.00000	.00000	.00028	.00059	.00051	40
45	2237874	14166	.00633	.00072	.00015	.00132	.00174	.00015	.00004	.00054	.00000	.00000	.00029	.00070	.00069	45
50	2047743	20849	.01018	.00091	.00022	.00239	.00343	.00024	.00005	.00086	.00000	.00000	.00031	.00079	.00099	50
55	1793571	30158	.01681	.00115	.00028	.00403	.00667	.00049	.00013	.00127	.00000	.00000	.00031	.00092	.00156	55
60	1443036	38200	.02647	.00148	.00035	.00608	.01145	.00107	.00023	.00191	.00000	.00000	.00035	.00108	.00247	60
65	1027562	44072	.04289	.00197	.00040	.00882	.01958	.00205	.00051	.00300	.00000	.00000	.00040	.00132	.00484	65
70	704161	48425	.06877	.00246	.00048	.01123	.03203	.00424	.00122	.00452	.00000	.00000	.00043	.00166	.01049	70
75	381358	42751	.11210	.00265	.00068	.01197	.05041	.00887	.00310	.00643	.00000	.00000	.00046	.00211	.02540	75
80	171377	29365	.17135	.00186	.00068	.01026	.06773	.01552	.00656	.00809	.00000	.00000	.00041	.00298	.05724	80
85+	51772	14637	.28272	.00139	.00097	.00854	.08690	.02662	.01192	.01004	.00000	.00000	.00054	.00417	.13163	85+
ALL	45706627	377526														

CRUDE DEATH RATE	.00826	.00040 .00016 .00117 .00271 .00053 .00018 .00049 .00000 .00031 .00023 .00070 .00138
STANDARDIZED RATE (1)	.00730	.00032 .00018 .00090 .00202 .00057 .00021 .00038 .00000 .00061 .00022 .00067 .00121
STANDARDIZED RATE (2)	.01309	.00053 .00019 .00171 .00468 .00090 .00032 .00075 .00000 .00036 .00025 .00078 .00261
GEOMETRIC MEAN	.00964	

LIFE TABLE FOR ALL CAUSES COMBINED

Age (x)	Midyear Population	Deaths During Year	$_nM_x$	$_nq_x$	l_x	$_nd_x$	$_nL_x$	$_nm_x$	$_na_x$	T_x	$_nr_x$	$\overset{\circ}{e}_x$	Age (x)
0	809800	27714	.034223	.023230	100000	3323	97103	.034221	.128180	6545220	.000000	65.452	0
1	3175658	8514	.002681	.010654	96677	1030	384133	.002681	1.500000	6448117	.000000	66.698	1
5	4690417	4788	.001021	.005092	95647	487	477018	.001021	2.500000	6063984	.000000	63.400	5
10	5558673	3263	.000587	.002932	95160	279	475132	.000587	2.606033	5586967	-.006173	58.711	10
15	4662985	6169	.001323	.006629	94881	629	472986	.001330	2.743773	5111835	.023907	53.876	15
20	4084912	8828	.002161	.010769	94252	1015	468813	.002165	2.588875	4638849	.016192	49.218	20
25	4084414	9357	.002291	.011390	93237	1062	463544	.002291	2.512751	4170036	.003810	44.725	25
30	3747246	8821	.002354	.011717	92175	1080	458234	.002357	2.554591	3706943	.026525	40.211	30
35	2752303	8150	.002961	.014765	91095	1345	452266	.002974	2.614467	3248259	.046742	35.658	35
40	2281765	9299	.004075	.020267	89750	1819	444455	.004092	2.660574	2795992	.025827	31.153	40
45	2237874	14166	.006330	.031240	87931	2747	433293	.006340	2.684064	2351498	.008119	26.743	45
50	2047743	20849	.010181	.049845	85184	4246	416100	.010204	2.687284	1918205	.009995	22.518	50
55	1793571	30158	.016815	.081059	80938	6564	389334	.016860	2.660598	1502104	.014090	18.559	55
60	1443036	38200	.026472	.125124	74374	9306	349886	.026597	2.637680	1112770	.024989	14.962	60
65	1027562	44072	.042890	.195396	65068	12714	294841	.043122	2.601152	762884	.026779	11.724	65
70	704161	48425	.068770	.295660	52354	15479	223792	.069167	2.546501	468004	.027365	8.940	70
75	381358	42751	.112102	.438481	36875	16169	143277	.112851	2.458253	244251	.027145	6.624	75
80	171377	29365	.171347	.591085	20706	12239	71025	.172320	2.344129	100973	.027145	4.877	80
85+	51772	14637	.282720	1.000000	8467	8467	29948	.282720	3.537064	29948	.000000	3.537	85+

NUMBER OF PERSONS DYING (OUT OF 100,000 AT BIRTH) ABOVE AGE X FROM SPECIFIED CAUSES

Age (x)	All Causes	Respiratory T. B.	Other Infec. and Paras.	Neo-plasms	Cardio-vascular	Infl., Pneu., Bronch.	Diar-rheal	Certain Degen-erative	Maternal	Cert. Dis. of Infancy	Motor Vehicle	Other Violence	Other and Unknown	Age (x)
0	100000	4188	1317	13559	37486	6496	2274	5983	0	1688	1738	5382	19489	0
1	96677	4186	1232	13948	37464	5851	2053	5981	0	0	1735	5289	18938	1
5	95647	4182	1077	13904	37452	5694	1946	5957	0	0	1666	5022	18747	5
10	95160	4179	1009	13874	37434	5661	1924	5934	0	0	1613	4870	18662	10
15	94881	4176	985	13841	37407	5647	1918	5916	0	0	1590	4794	18607	15
20	94252	4162	963	13804	37362	5628	1911	5885	0	0	1489	4535	18513	20
25	93237	4120	941	13765	37300	5608	1906	5837	0	0	1330	4038	18392	25
30	92175	4017	917	13707	37223	5587	1899	5778	0	0	1181	3614	18252	30
35	91095	3846	889	13607	37112	5557	1892	5708	0	0	1065	3321	18098	35
40	89750	3616	848	13438	36923	5522	1883	5613	0	0	951	3046	17910	40
45	87931	3353	793	13131	36538	5483	1870	5470	0	0	827	2783	17683	45
50	85184	3042	727	12559	35781	5416	1854	5237	0	0	704	2481	17383	50
55	80938	2665	637	11561	34351	5315	1833	4880	0	0	573	2154	16969	55
60	74374	2216	529	9990	31747	5123	1781	4383	0	0	451	1794	16360	60
65	65068	1696	405	7854	27717	4746	1701	3713	0	0	329	1415	15492	65
70	52354	1114	286	5246	21911	4137	1547	2825	0	0	212	1024	14052	70
75	36875	562	177	2726	14701	3180	1271	1809	0	0	115	651	11683	75
80	20706	182	79	1009	7434	1898	822	882	0	0	49	347	8004	80
85+	8467	42	29	256	2603	797	357	301	0	0	16	125	3941	85+

NUMBER OF PERSONS SURVIVING TO AGE X IF SPECIFIED CAUSES WERE ELIMINATED

Age (x)	No Causes	Respiratory T. B. (1)	Other Infec. and Paras. (2)	Neo-plasms (3)	Cardio-vascular (4)	Infl., Pneu., Bronch. (5)	Diar-rheal (6)	Certain Degener-ative (7)	Maternal (8)	Cert. Dis. of Infancy (9)	Motor Vehicle (10)	Other Violence (11)	Other and Unknown (12)	(1) + (2)	(1) + (2) + (5) + (6) + (8)	(1)+(2)+ (5)+(6)+ (8)+part of(9)&(12)	(10) + (11)	Age (x)
0	100000	100000	100000	100000	100000	100000	100000	100000	100000	100000	100000	100000	100000	100000	100000	100000	100000	0
1	96677	96679	96761	96688	96659	97313	96855	96679	96677	98351	96680	96768	97220	96763	97619	99592	96771	1
5	95647	95653	95884	95701	95680	96434	95969	95673	95647	97303	95719	96004	96376	95890	97004	99065	96076	5
10	95160	95169	95464	95244	95211	95976	95502	95209	95160	96808	95284	95667	95970	95473	96638	98718	95792	10
15	94881	94893	95208	94998	94959	95709	95228	94947	94881	96524	95028	95463	95744	95220	96402	98490	95611	15
20	94252	94278	94599	94405	94374	95093	94604	94349	94252	95884	94499	95090	95204	94625	95826	97912	95339	20
25	93237	93304	93602	93427	93420	94089	93590	93381	93237	94851	93640	94566	94301	93670	94884	96962	94975	25
30	92175	92344	92560	92421	92432	93039	92531	92376	92175	93771	92722	93918	93368	92730	93960	96043	94475	30
35	91095	91433	91503	91438	91460	91979	91454	91363	91095	92672	91752	93114	92429	91843	93099	95203	93785	35
40	89750	90193	90193	90256	90298	90656	90113	90109	89750	91304	90511	92019	91254	90758	92044	94178	92799	40
45	87931	88744	88420	88733	88853	88857	88299	88425	87931	89454	88800	90421	89633	89237	90555	92709	91315	45
50	85184	86281	85723	86531	86834	86148	85557	85893	85184	86659	86148	87902	87134	86827	88193	90350	88897	50
55	80938	82353	81538	83213	83940	81954	81313	81564	80938	82339	81983	83850	83204	82964	84393	86523	84932	55
60	74374	76112	75030	78027	79766	75454	74768	75800	74374	75662	75453	77407	77059	76784	78353	80415	78530	60
65	65068	67087	65758	70389	73947	66408	65488	66956	65068	66195	66127	68090	68264	67799	69642	71591	69198	65
70	52354	54516	53017	59210	65710	53993	52832	54697	52354	53261	53312	55151	56301	55206	57454	59253	56160	70
75	36875	38877	37433	44131	54484	38867	37447	39419	36875	37513	37631	39172	41859	39465	42243	43909	39976	75
80	20706	22122	21093	26314	39624	22853	21371	22873	20706	21065	21180	22234	26854	22535	25671	27324	22742	80
85+	8467	9139	8657	11369	23062	10128	9041	9759	8467	8614	8682	9240	14776	9344	11934	13539	9475	85+

	ADDED YRS OF LIFE																
TOTAL		.738	.385	1.940	4.852	1.053	.377	.786	.000	1.131	.523	1.579	2.630	1.132	2.651	4.519	2.122
WORK	4.164	.375	.092	.581	.836	.097	.026	.266	.000	.000	.307	.830	.455	.468	.593	.676	1.145

POPULATION, DEATHS, DEATH RATES FOR ALL CAUSES COMBINED, AND SPECIFIED CAUSES

Age Start of Interval	Midyear Population	Deaths During Year	All Causes	Respiratory T. B.	Other Infec. and Paras.	Neoplasms	Cardiovascular	Infl., Pneu., Bronch.	Diarrheal	Certain Degenerative	Maternal	Cert. Dis. of Infancy	Motor Vehicle	Other Violence	Other and Unknown	Age Start of Interval
0	774835	21579	.02785	.00003	.00082	.00012	.00017	.00565	.00180	.00003	.00000	.01402	.00001	.00086	.00433	0
1	3063027	6886	.00225	.00001	.00040	.00008	.00003	.00041	.00026	.00004	.00000	.00000	.00014	.00044	.00044	1
5	4506851	3422	.00076	.00001	.00016	.00005	.00004	.00007	.00006	.00004	.00000	.00000	.00006	.00011	.00016	5
10	5375660	2282	.00042	.00001	.00005	.00005	.00006	.00003	.00001	.00003	.00000	.00000	.00002	.00005	.00011	10
15	4571995	3661	.00080	.00004	.00003	.00006	.00009	.00004	.00001	.00005	.00001	.00000	.00003	.00028	.00015	15
20	4181335	5711	.00137	.00012	.00004	.00009	.00013	.00006	.00001	.00007	.00009	.00000	.00003	.00052	.00021	20
25	4116292	6379	.00155	.00023	.00005	.00015	.00018	.00007	.00002	.00010	.00017	.00000	.00002	.00032	.00025	25
30	3730221	6755	.00181	.00033	.00006	.00029	.00026	.00007	.00002	.00011	.00014	.00000	.00002	.00023	.00028	30
35	3267136	7369	.00226	.00036	.00008	.00053	.00038	.00008	.00003	.00014	.00010	.00000	.00003	.00020	.00032	35
40	2739107	8129	.00297	.00036	.00008	.00090	.00065	.00008	.00003	.00020	.00004	.00000	.00004	.00020	.00039	40
45	2556446	11511	.00450	.00036	.00010	.00146	.00129	.00011	.00005	.00031	.00000	.00000	.00006	.00024	.00051	45
50	2141745	14327	.00669	.00038	.00012	.00199	.00244	.00018	.00008	.00043	.00000	.00000	.00008	.00030	.00070	50
55	1859424	18466	.00993	.00044	.00014	.00279	.00404	.00031	.00011	.00064	.00000	.00000	.00010	.00033	.00103	55
60	1493804	23697	.01586	.00054	.00021	.00382	.00712	.00057	.00023	.00104	.00000	.00000	.00012	.00046	.00175	60
65	1128783	30218	.02677	.00067	.00028	.00515	.01313	.00121	.00046	.00168	.00000	.00000	.00015	.00068	.00337	65
70	876590	40877	.04663	.00076	.00030	.00656	.02334	.00251	.00132	.00280	.00000	.00000	.00020	.00095	.00788	70
75	577310	47575	.08241	.00082	.00047	.00749	.03819	.00541	.00312	.00402	.00000	.00000	.00022	.00148	.02118	75
80	313944	41414	.13192	.00058	.00053	.00710	.05208	.00960	.00652	.00526	.00000	.00000	.00025	.00207	.04792	80
85+	139065	28815	.20721	.00038	.00065	.00575	.06147	.01586	.01097	.00593	.00000	.00000	.00012	.00264	.10343	85+
ALL	47413570	329073														

	All Causes	Respiratory T. B.	Other Infec. and Paras.	Neoplasms	Cardiovascular	Infl., Pneu., Bronch.	Diarrheal	Certain Degenerative	Maternal	Cert. Dis. of Infancy	Motor Vehicle	Other Violence	Other and Unknown
CRUDE DEATH RATE	.00694	.00023	.00013	.00095	.00243	.00046	.00023	.00035	.00004	.00023	.00006	.00033	.00151
STANDARDIZED RATE (1)	.00516	.00018	.00016	.00067	.00145	.00044	.00019	.00023	.00004	.00049	.00006	.00032	.00095
STANDARDIZED RATE (2)	.00915	.00025	.00015	.00120	.00335	.00061	.00031	.00045	.00004	.00029	.00007	.00037	.00206
GEOMETRIC MEAN	.00676												

LIFE TABLE FOR ALL CAUSES COMBINED

Age (x)	Midyear Population	Deaths During Year	$_nM_x$	$_nq_x$	l_x	$_nd_x$	$_nL_x$	$_nm_x$	$_na_x$	T_x	$_nr_x$	$\overset{\circ}{e}_x$	Age (x)
0	774835	21579	.027850	.027180	100000	2718	97601	.027848	.117345	7037810	.000000	70.378	0
1	3063027	6886	.002248	.008943	97282	870	386953	.002248	1.500000	6940209	.000000	71.341	1
5	4506851	3422	.000759	.003786	96412	365	481148	.000759	2.500000	6553256	.000000	67.971	5
10	5375660	2282	.000425	.002124	96047	204	479729	.000425	2.520425	6072109	-.006877	63.220	10
15	4571995	3661	.000801	.004017	95843	385	478346	.000805	2.741883	5592380	-.019605	58.349	15
20	4181335	5711	.001366	.006820	95458	651	475735	.001368	2.631047	5114034	-.011923	53.574	20
25	4116292	6379	.001550	.007721	94807	732	472246	.001550	2.556352	4638299	-.008655	48.924	25
30	3730221	6755	.001811	.009025	94075	849	468319	.001813	2.577788	4166053	-.016746	44.284	30
35	3267136	7369	.002255	.011252	93226	1049	463614	.002263	2.601883	3697734	-.027012	39.664	35
40	2739107	8129	.002968	.014776	92177	1362	457684	.002976	2.650055	3234120	-.023176	35.086	40
45	2556446	11511	.004503	.022353	90815	2030	449328	.004518	2.661433	2776436	-.019794	30.572	45
50	2141745	14327	.006689	.033057	88785	2935	437036	.006716	2.652896	2327108	-.024037	26.211	50
55	1859424	18466	.009931	.048736	85850	4184	419488	.009974	2.666906	1890072	-.023674	22.016	55
60	1493804	23697	.015864	.076964	81666	6287	393730	.015968	2.677814	1470583	-.032168	18.007	60
65	1128783	30218	.026770	.126693	75379	9550	354601	.026932	2.665532	1076853	-.027953	14.286	65
70	876590	40877	.046632	.210713	65829	13875	296189	.046845	2.624805	722252	-.019857	10.972	70
75	577310	47575	.082408	.343804	51954	17862	215733	.082797	2.534617	426063	-.018738	8.201	75
80	313944	41414	.131915	.494046	34092	16843	127084	.132535	2.424672	210330	-.018738	6.169	80
85+	139065	28815	.207205	1.000000	17249	17249	83246	.207205	4.826132	83246	.000000	4.826	85+

NUMBER OF PERSONS DYING (OUT OF 100,000 AT BIRTH) ABOVE AGE X FROM SPECIFIED CAUSES

Age (x)	All Causes	Respiratory T. B.	Other Infec. and Paras.	Neoplasms	Cardiovascular	Infl., Pneu., Bronch.	Diarrheal	Certain Degenerative	Maternal	Cert. Dis. of Infancy	Motor Vehicle	Other Violence	Other and Unknown	Age (x)
0	100000	2171	1154	12045	38717	6331	3540	4834	261	1368	534	3047	25998	0
1	97282	2168	1074	12033	38700	5779	3364	4831	261	0	532	2963	25577	1
5	96412	2164	918	12001	38687	5621	3263	4818	261	0	480	2794	25405	5
10	96047	2161	839	11978	38667	5585	3234	4800	261	0	451	2742	25329	10
15	95843	2155	817	11952	38638	5570	3229	4784	261	0	442	2716	25279	15
20	95458	2137	801	11921	38594	5549	3225	4762	258	0	426	2580	25205	20
25	94807	2079	781	11880	38532	5521	3219	4729	213	0	410	2335	25108	25
30	94075	1970	758	11810	38448	5489	3211	4683	131	0	398	2185	24992	30
35	93226	1814	731	11673	38324	5458	3201	4632	67	0	387	2078	24861	35
40	92177	1645	693	11425	38149	5422	3190	4566	19	0	371	1986	24711	40
45	90815	1479	656	11013	37849	5383	3176	4477	2	0	354	1895	24531	45
50	88785	1315	611	10356	37266	5333	3155	4336	1	0	326	1785	24301	50
55	85850	1148	558	9483	36195	5252	3120	4149	1	0	293	1655	23996	55
60	81666	963	497	8310	34490	5122	3073	3881	1	0	251	1517	23561	60
65	75379	750	413	6801	31663	4895	2980	3470	1	0	204	1335	22867	65
70	65829	513	314	4970	26978	4463	2813	2872	1	0	151	1092	21662	70
75	51954	288	224	3025	20035	3715	2420	2039	1	0	91	809	19307	75
80	34092	111	123	1406	11763	2542	1741	1168	1	0	42	488	14707	80
85+	17249	32	54	479	5118	1320	913	494	0	0	10	220	8609	85+

NUMBER OF PERSONS SURVIVING TO AGE X IF SPECIFIED CAUSES WERE ELIMINATED

Age (x)	No Causes	Respiratory T. B.	Other Infec. and Paras.	Neoplasms	Cardiovascular	Infl., Pneu., Bronch.	Diarrheal	Certain Degenerative	Maternal	Cert. Dis. of Infancy	Motor Vehicle	Other Violence	Other and Unknown	(1) + (2)	(1) + (2) + (5) + (6) + (8)	(1)+(2)+ (5)+(6)+ (8)+part of(9)&(12)	(10) + (11)	Age (x)
		(1)	(2)	(3)	(4)	(5)	(6)	(7)	(8)	(9)	(10)	(11)	(12)					
0	100000	100000	100000	100000	100000	100000	100000	100000	100000	100000	100000	100000	100000	100000	100000	100000	100000	0
1	97282	97285	97361	97294	97299	97828	97456	97285	97282	98641	97284	97365	97698	97364	98085	99651	97367	1
5	96412	96419	96646	96456	96442	97111	96685	96428	96412	97758	96466	96663	96997	96653	97629	99293	96717	5
10	96047	96057	96359	96113	96056	96780	96348	96081	96047	97388	96130	96349	96706	96369	97409	99109	96432	10
15	95843	95859	96176	95935	95921	96589	96148	95893	95843	97182	95934	96170	96551	96192	97250	98964	96262	15
20	95458	95492	95806	95581	95580	96223	95766	95529	95461	96791	95565	95920	96237	95840	96922	98645	96028	20
25	94807	94898	95173	94970	94990	95595	95119	94911	94855	96131	94929	95512	95678	95294	96420	98163	95635	25
30	94075	94275	94461	94307	94340	94889	94393	94224	94204	95389	94208	94925	95056	94661	95934	97717	95059	30
35	93226	93579	93635	93592	93613	94063	93551	93425	93418	94528	93369	94176	94330	93990	95361	97187	94320	35
40	92177	92695	92620	92787	92735	93041	92509	92439	92415	93464	92334	93208	93420	93140	94595	96460	93367	40
45	90815	91491	91288	91829	91664	91705	91156	91162	91066	92083	90587	91922	92221	91968	93476	95382	92096	45
50	88785	89610	89292	90435	90200	89710	89139	89264	89031	90025	88981	89978	90390	90122	91673	93559	90176	50
55	85850	86813	86393	88324	88295	86821	86227	86498	86088	87049	86072	87133	87708	87362	88984	90856	87358	55
60	81666	82765	82242	85204	85720	82718	82071	82547	81893	82807	81918	83023	83868	83349	85076	86916	83279	60
65	75379	76600	75992	80170	82025	76571	75843	76592	75588	76432	75657	76809	77223	77223	79146	80937	77092	65
70	65829	67120	66457	71849	76557	67282	66392	67457	66012	66748	66121	67309	69384	67760	70042	71765	67608	70
75	51954	53175	52530	58605	68009	53784	52753	53999	52098	52680	52238	53378	57021	53764	56671	58364	53670	75
80	34092	35037	34552	39931	54201	36286	35178	36164	34187	34568	34317	35292	41748	35509	39106	40994	35525	80
85+	17249	17784	17530	20975	35880	19289	18405	18803	17298	17490	17385	18051	27032	18074	21627	23845	18193	85+

ADDED YRS OF LIFE

	No Causes	(1)	(2)	(3)	(4)	(5)	(6)	(7)	(8)	(9)	(10)	(11)	(12)				
TOTAL		.516	.387	1.998	5.340	1.083	.484	.655	.114	.981	.152	.842	3.658	.908	2.678	4.574	.997
WORK	2.886	.272	.072	.607	.658	.094	.030	.171	.088	.000	.043	.350	.365	.345	.559	.653	.394

POPULATION, DEATHS, DEATH RATES FOR ALL CAUSES COMBINED, AND SPECIFIED CAUSES

Age Start of Interval	Midyear Population	Deaths During Year	All Causes	Respiratory T.B.	Other Infec. and Paras.	Neoplasms	Cardiovascular	Infl., Pneu., Bronch.	Diarrheal	Certain Degenerative	Maternal	Cert. Dis. of Infancy	Motor Vehicle	Other Violence	Other and Unknown	Age Start of Interval
0	853650	19925	.02334	.00001	.00047	.00010	.00023	.00325	.00134	.00004	.00000	.01279	.00002	.00082	.00428	0
1	3213155	5244	.00163	.00001	.00014	.00011	.00003	.00019	.00010	.00003	.00000	.00000	.00016	.00055	.00032	1
5	4043868	3090	.00076	.00000	.00005	.00007	.00002	.00004	.00002	.00003	.00000	.00000	.00011	.00029	.00014	5
10	4938406	2485	.00050	.00000	.00002	.00007	.00003	.00003	.00001	.00003	.00000	.00000	.00005	.00015	.00012	10
15	5257527	5160	.00098	.00001	.00003	.00009	.00006	.00003	.00001	.00005	.00000	.00000	.00025	.00030	.00016	15
20	4690089	7288	.00155	.00003	.00002	.00010	.00010	.00002	.00001	.00009	.00000	.00000	.00038	.00062	.00018	20
25	4049852	7343	.00181	.00008	.00003	.00015	.00015	.00003	.00001	.00012	.00000	.00000	.00037	.00064	.00024	25
30	3993008	8189	.00205	.00018	.00004	.00023	.00026	.00003	.00001	.00015	.00000	.00000	.00034	.00053	.00029	30
35	3585131	9660	.00269	.00029	.00005	.00041	.00046	.00004	.00002	.00022	.00000	.00000	.00031	.00054	.00036	35
40	2552972	9527	.00373	.00039	.00007	.00070	.00080	.00005	.00002	.00032	.00000	.00000	.00033	.00057	.00048	40
45	2171024	12343	.00569	.00048	.00010	.00130	.00161	.00009	.00003	.00049	.00000	.00000	.00035	.00064	.00061	45
50	2158059	19450	.00901	.00060	.00015	.00233	.00308	.00015	.00005	.00074	.00000	.00000	.00038	.00072	.00083	50
55	1865864	27973	.01499	.00082	.00022	.00358	.00593	.00027	.00007	.00111	.00000	.00000	.00043	.00084	.00132	55
60	1610566	39083	.02427	.00112	.00029	.00627	.01079	.00053	.00017	.00162	.00000	.00000	.00042	.00100	.00206	60
65	1178755	46126	.03913	.00155	.00036	.00905	.01869	.00126	.00036	.00237	.00000	.00000	.00048	.00117	.00384	65
70	759908	48956	.06442	.00223	.00043	.01185	.03280	.00252	.00090	.00371	.00000	.00000	.00051	.00151	.00796	70
75	433806	44526	.10264	.00257	.00047	.01328	.05254	.00529	.00225	.00526	.00000	.00000	.00047	.00204	.01846	75
80	185489	30082	.16218	.00233	.00055	.01241	.07605	.01092	.00490	.00664	.00000	.00000	.00058	.00280	.04501	80
85+	70805	17081	.24124	.00188	.00064	.00955	.09275	.01816	.00932	.00727	.00000	.00000	.00038	.00387	.09742	85+
ALL	47611934	363531														

	All Causes	Respiratory T.B.	Other Infec. and Paras.	Neoplasms	Cardiovascular	Infl., Pneu., Bronch.	Diarrheal	Certain Degenerative	Maternal	Cert. Dis. of Infancy	Motor Vehicle	Other Violence	Other and Unknown
CRUDE DEATH RATE	.00764	.00030	.00010	.00127	.00285	.00032	.00013	.00044	.00000	.00023	.00028	.00057	.00115
STANDARDIZED RATE (1)	.00618	.00022	.00010	.00093	.00159	.00031	.00013	.00032	.00000	.00045	.00025	.00053	.00094
STANDARDIZED RATE (2)	.01163	.00040	.00012	.00179	.00472	.00054	.00022	.00063	.00000	.00026	.00029	.00064	.00201
GEOMETRIC MEAN	.00806												

LIFE TABLE FOR ALL CAUSES COMBINED

Age (x)	Midyear Population	Deaths During Year	$_nM_x$	$_nq_x$	l_x	$_nd_x$	$_nL_x$	$_nm_x$	$_na_x$	T_x	$_nr_x$	$\overset{\circ}{e}_x$	Age (x)
0	853650	19925	.023341	.022870	100000	2287	97964	.023345	.109680	6777206	.000000	67.772	0
1	3213155	5244	.001632	.006459	97713	635	389265	.001631	1.500000	6679242	.000000	68.356	1
5	4043868	3090	.000764	.003822	97078	371	484463	.000766	2.500000	6289977	.000000	64.793	5
10	4938406	2485	.000503	.002502	96707	242	482951	.000501	2.586949	5805515	-.025204	60.032	10
15	5257527	5160	.000981	.004893	96465	472	481250	.000981	2.721575	5322564	-.006813	55.176	15
20	4690089	7288	.001554	.007751	95993	744	478186	.001556	2.608927	4841314	-.018623	50.434	20
25	4049852	7343	.001813	.009039	95249	861	474138	.001816	2.553233	4363128	-.017265	45.808	25
30	3993008	8189	.002051	.010213	94388	964	469612	.002053	2.585149	3888990	.006544	41.202	30
35	3585131	9660	.002694	.013433	93424	1255	464139	.002704	2.624834	3419378	-.031651	36.601	35
40	2552972	9527	.003732	.018618	92169	1716	456824	.003756	2.656978	2955238	-.048895	32.063	40
45	2171024	12343	.005685	.028169	90453	2548	446347	.005709	2.677427	2498414	-.020866	27.621	45
50	2158059	19450	.009013	.044207	87905	3886	430150	.009026	2.690427	2052067	-.007922	23.344	50
55	1865864	27973	.014992	.072603	84019	6100	405904	.015028	2.673634	1621517	-.011698	19.299	55
60	1610566	39083	.024267	.115120	77919	8970	368484	.024343	2.646507	1215613	-.016268	15.601	60
65	1178755	46126	.039131	.179959	68949	12408	315155	.039371	2.615215	847129	-.030317	12.286	65
70	759908	48956	.064424	.280009	56541	15832	244018	.064880	2.556399	531974	-.032583	9.409	70
75	433806	44526	.102640	.410081	40709	16694	161370	.103452	2.473643	287956	-.034562	7.074	75
80	185489	30082	.162177	.571310	24015	13720	83911	.163507	2.364128	126586	-.034562	5.271	80
85+	70805	17081	.241240	1.000000	10295	10295	42675	.241240	4.145249	42675	.000000	4.145	85+

NUMBER OF PERSONS DYING (OUT OF 100,000 AT BIRTH) ABOVE AGE X FROM SPECIFIED CAUSES

Age (x)	All Causes	Respiratory T.B.	Other Infec. and Paras.	Neoplasms	Cardiovascular	Infl., Pneu., Bronch.	Diarrheal	Certain Degenerative	Maternal	Cert. Dis. of Infancy	Motor Vehicle	Other Violence	Other and Unknown	Age (x)
0	100000	3411	929	15814	42288	4513	1859	5470	0	1253	2139	4785	17539	0
1	97713	3411	883	15805	42266	4195	1728	5466	0	0	2137	4705	17117	1
5	97078	3409	830	15762	42255	4119	1690	5456	0	0	2073	4490	16994	5
10	96707	3408	804	15729	42247	4099	1680	5442	0	0	2021	4351	16926	10
15	96465	3407	793	15698	42230	4085	1675	5427	0	0	1999	4280	16871	15
20	95993	3403	777	15655	42201	4073	1671	5402	0	0	1880	4137	16794	20
25	95249	3389	766	15609	42153	4062	1668	5359	0	0	1696	3840	16707	25
30	94388	3351	751	15540	42080	4047	1663	5301	0	0	1521	3539	16595	30
35	93424	3267	733	15433	41959	4034	1658	5229	0	0	1363	3290	16458	35
40	92169	3133	708	15243	41746	4013	1650	5125	0	0	1219	3041	16291	40
45	90453	2954	676	14920	41374	3989	1640	4979	0	0	1069	2782	16070	45
50	87905	2741	630	14336	40652	3949	1629	4761	0	0	912	2498	15797	50
55	84019	2484	567	13332	39322	3884	1609	4442	0	0	750	2189	15440	55
60	77919	2149	477	11714	36907	3773	1579	3991	0	0	576	1849	14904	60
65	68949	1737	371	9396	32916	3578	1515	3351	0	0	423	1482	14140	65
70	56541	1245	256	6533	26985	3178	1398	2640	0	0	273	1113	12920	70
75	40709	699	151	3630	18920	2556	1176	1729	0	0	147	742	10959	75
80	24015	283	75	1482	10378	1692	808	876	0	0	71	410	7940	80
85+	10295	80	27	407	3958	775	398	310	0	0	16	165	4159	85+

NUMBER OF PERSONS SURVIVING TO AGE X IF SPECIFIED CAUSES WERE ELIMINATED

Age (x)	No Causes	Respiratory T.B. (1)	Other Infec. and Paras. (2)	Neoplasms (3)	Cardiovascular (4)	Infl., Pneu., Bronch. (5)	Diarrheal (6)	Certain Degenerative (7)	Maternal (8)	Cert. Dis. of Infancy (9)	Motor Vehicle (10)	Other Violence (11)	Other and Unknown (12)	(1) + (2)	(1) + (2) + (5) + (6) + (8)	(1)+(2)+(5)+(6)+(8)+part of(9)&(12)	(10) + (11)	Age (x)
0	100000	100000	100000	100000	100000	100000	100000	100000	100000	100000	100000	100000	100000	100000	100000	100000	100000	0
1	97713	97713	97758	97722	97735	98028	97843	97717	97713	98959	97715	97792	98131	97758	98204	99559	97794	1
5	97078	97080	97176	97130	97111	97467	97245	97092	97078	98316	97144	97371	97617	97118	97735	99125	97437	5
10	96707	96710	96831	96791	96747	97114	96883	96735	96707	97941	96824	97138	97312	96834	97419	98817	97256	10
15	96465	96469	96599	96580	96522	96885	96646	96508	96465	97696	96604	96967	97124	96603	97206	98611	97107	15
20	95993	96001	96143	96151	96079	96423	96177	96060	95993	97218	96250	96636	96726	96151	96767	98172	96895	20
25	95249	95271	95408	95451	95382	95687	95434	95359	95249	96644	95588	96063	96430	95430	96056	97456	96629	25
30	94388	94448	94561	94657	94593	94837	94577	94555	94388	95592	94999	95619	95307	94621	95261	96661	96237	30
35	93424	93567	93613	93797	93747	93881	93616	93661	93424	94616	94187	94893	94472	93756	94408	95816	95668	35
40	92169	92443	92381	92727	92701	92641	92366	92506	92169	93345	93066	93870	93371	92655	93329	94750	94783	40
45	90453	90900	90692	91323	91346	90540	90656	90929	90453	91607	91483	92384	91854	91140	91838	93273	93436	45
50	87905	88551	88183	89334	89495	88418	88113	88584	87905	89026	89063	90068	89540	88831	89561	90999	91254	50
55	84019	84889	84347	86389	86874	84574	84238	84983	84019	85091	85286	86396	85938	85220	86006	87428	87698	55
60	77919	79052	78310	81734	83009	78541	78151	79253	77919	78913	79264	80460	80228	79449	80321	81705	81848	60
65	68949	70345	69395	74645	77564	69565	69215	70705	68949	69829	70285	71553	71736	70800	71832	73141	72939	65
70	56541	58140	57011	64071	69939	57513	56866	58680	56541	57262	57774	59022	59989	58623	59973	61187	60309	70
75	40709	42335	41136	48973	59533	41949	41134	43053	40709	41228	41704	42822	44998	42779	44542	45645	43869	75
80	24015	25300	24324	30886	45992	25437	24553	26087	24015	24321	24660	25526	29241	25625	27751	28790	26212	80
85+	10295	10982	10459	14149	29306	11540	10795	11581	10295	10426	10607	11110	15831	11157	13114	14118	11447	85+

ADDED YRS OF LIFE

	No Causes	(1)	(2)	(3)	(4)	(5)	(6)	(7)	(8)	(9)	(10)	(11)	(12)				
TOTAL		.528	.220	2.228	5.803	.633	.250	.743	.000	.863	.638	1.313	2.313	.752	1.686	2.943	1.972
WORK	3.606	.220	.060	.607	.786	.056	.018	.251	.000	.000	.374	.614	.389	.281	.356	.404	.994

POPULATION, DEATHS, DEATH RATES FOR ALL CAUSES COMBINED, AND SPECIFIED CAUSES

Age Start of Interval	Midyear Population	Deaths During Year	All Causes	Respiratory T.B.	Other Infec. and Paras.	Neo-plasms	Cardio-vascular	Infl., Pneu., Bronch.	Diar-rheal	Certain Degen-erative	Maternal	Cert. Dis. of Infancy	Motor Vehicle	Other Violence	Other and Unknown	Age Start of Interval
0	809827	15045	.01858	.00000	.00040	.00008	.00018	.00273	.00104	.00003	.00000	.00994	.00003	.00068	.00347	0
1	3054804	3990	.00131	.00000	.00013	.00009	.00003	.00019	.00010	.00001	.00000	.00000	.00013	.00034	.00029	1
5	3869617	1893	.00049	.00000	.00005	.00005	.00002	.00005	.00002	.00002	.00000	.00000	.00006	.00010	.00012	5
10	4738287	1544	.00033	.00000	.00002	.00002	.00005	.00004	.00002	.00001	.00002	.00000	.00002	.00004	.00010	10
15	5074385	2328	.00046	.00001	.00002	.00007	.00006	.00002	.00001	.00004	.00000	.00000	.00003	.00010	.00011	15
20	4681439	3992	.00085	.00003	.00002	.00009	.00008	.00003	.00001	.00006	.00006	.00000	.00004	.00027	.00015	20
25	4131914	4595	.00111	.00010	.00003	.00016	.00013	.00003	.00001	.00007	.00013	.00000	.00003	.00022	.00020	25
30	4012235	5340	.00133	.00016	.00003	.00030	.00018	.00004	.00001	.00008	.00012	.00000	.00004	.00016	.00022	30
35	3670153	6528	.00178	.00022	.00004	.00051	.00030	.00004	.00001	.00012	.00007	.00000	.00004	.00016	.00026	35
40	3157528	7812	.00247	.00023	.00005	.00083	.00055	.00004	.00002	.00017	.00003	.00000	.00005	.00018	.00033	40
45	2587059	9956	.00385	.00024	.00008	.00134	.00109	.00006	.00003	.00025	.00000	.00000	.00007	.00022	.00046	45
50	2451423	13890	.00567	.00024	.00009	.00193	.00202	.00009	.00004	.00037	.00000	.00000	.00010	.00024	.00056	50
55	1998637	17016	.00851	.00028	.00012	.00267	.00341	.00017	.00007	.00055	.00000	.00000	.00010	.00027	.00087	55
60	1703430	23156	.01359	.00035	.00017	.00375	.00619	.00031	.00014	.00084	.00000	.00000	.00013	.00035	.00136	60
65	1304500	30483	.02337	.00050	.00024	.00509	.01191	.00068	.00035	.00137	.00000	.00000	.00018	.00055	.00249	65
70	930503	38987	.04190	.00067	.00029	.00672	.02251	.00150	.00083	.00215	.00000	.00000	.00025	.00094	.00603	70
75	626320	46016	.07347	.00081	.00040	.00783	.03862	.00326	.00210	.00322	.00000	.00000	.00029	.00143	.01551	75
80	340088	42459	.12485	.00072	.00048	.00742	.05838	.00671	.00498	.00405	.00000	.00000	.00031	.00223	.03956	80
85+	169545	34506	.20352	.00052	.00047	.00600	.07511	.01252	.00930	.00489	.00000	.00000	.00032	.00297	.09142	85+
ALL	49311694	305536														

	All Causes	Respiratory T.B.	Other Infec. and Paras.	Neo-plasms	Cardio-vascular	Infl., Pneu., Bronch.	Diar-rheal	Certain Degen-erative	Maternal	Cert. Dis. of Infancy	Motor Vehicle	Other Violence	Other and Unknown
CRUDE DEATH RATE	.00628	.00015	.00008	.00100	.00251	.00028	.00016	.00029	.00003	.00016	.00007	.00026	.00129
STANDARDIZED RATE (1)	.00414	.00010	.00008	.00066	.00135	.00024	.00011	.00018	.00003	.00035	.00006	.00023	.00075
STANDARDIZED RATE (2)	.00792	.00016	.00009	.00119	.00329	.00036	.00021	.00036	.00003	.00021	.00008	.00029	.00166
GEOMETRIC MEAN	.00525												

LIFE TABLE FOR ALL CAUSES COMBINED

Age (x)	Midyear Population	Deaths During Year	$_nM_x$	$_nq_x$	l_x	$_nd_x$	$_nL_x$	$_nm_x$	$_na_x$	T_x	$_nr_x$	$\overset{\circ}{e}_x$	Age (x)
0	809827	15045	.018578	.018270	100000	1827	98359	.018575	.101583	7298088	.000000	72.981	0
1	3054804	3990	.001306	.005215	98173	512	391412	.001308	1.500000	7199729	.000000	73.337	1
5	3869617	1893	.000489	.002437	97661	238	487710	.000488	2.500000	6808317	.000000	69.714	5
10	4738287	1544	.000326	.001632	97423	159	486714	.000327	2.479036	6320607	-.025219	64.878	10
15	5074385	2328	.000459	.002282	97264	222	485818	.000457	2.739302	5833893	-.009068	59.980	15
20	4681439	3992	.000853	.004266	97042	414	484241	.000855	2.658514	5348075	-.013671	55.111	20
25	4131914	4595	.001112	.005557	96628	537	481844	.001114	2.586903	4863834	.015226	50.336	25
30	4012235	5340	.001331	.006640	96091	638	478925	.001332	2.601228	4381990	.010020	45.603	30
35	3670153	6528	.001779	.008873	95453	847	475258	.001782	2.630608	3903065	.017081	40.890	35
40	3157528	7812	.002474	.012357	94606	1169	470304	.002486	2.667879	3427807	.030642	36.232	40
45	2587059	9956	.003848	.019147	93437	1789	463005	.003864	2.663266	2957503	.024116	31.652	45
50	2451423	13890	.005666	.028053	91648	2571	452218	.005685	2.657688	2494499	.019543	27.218	50
55	1998637	17016	.008514	.041930	89077	3735	436690	.008553	2.671966	2042281	.025888	22.927	55
60	1703430	23156	.013594	.066251	85342	5654	413651	.013669	2.690278	1605591	.026246	18.814	60
65	1304500	30483	.023368	.111673	79688	8899	377845	.023552	2.685672	1191940	.034346	14.958	65
70	930503	38987	.041896	.191908	70789	13585	321861	.042208	2.638250	814096	.031401	11.500	70
75	626320	46016	.073470	.313160	57204	17914	242303	.073932	2.559637	492235	-.025472	8.605	75
80	340088	42459	.124847	.476279	39290	18713	148827	.125737	2.455067	249932	-.025472	6.361	80
85+	169545	34506	.203521	1.000000	20577	20577	101105	.203521	4.913493	101105	.000000	4.913	85+

NUMBER OF PERSONS DYING (OUT OF 100,000 AT BIRTH) ABOVE AGE X FROM SPECIFIED CAUSES

Age (x)	All Causes	Respiratory T. B.	Other Infec. and Paras.	Neoplasms	Cardiovascular	Infl., Pneu., Bronch.	Diarrheal	Certain Degenerative	Maternal	Cert. Dis. of Infancy	Motor Vehicle	Other Violence	Other and Unknown	Age (x)
0	100000	1615	825	13001	43763	4559	2905	4264	202	978	680	2767	24441	0
1	98173	1615	786	12994	43745	4290	2803	4260	202	0	678	2700	24100	1
5	97661	1614	734	12558	43735	4215	2764	4255	202	0	628	2568	23988	5
10	97423	1613	708	12933	43725	4192	2755	4246	202	0	598	2520	23931	10
15	97264	1612	698	12906	43708	4181	2751	4236	202	0	588	2500	23882	15
20	97042	1607	691	12873	43681	4171	2748	4217	201	0	575	2451	23827	20
25	96628	1590	681	12828	43641	4156	2745	4188	170	0	556	2320	23753	25
30	96091	1540	668	12748	43576	4139	2742	4155	106	0	542	2217	23658	30
35	95453	1462	653	12606	43492	4122	2736	4118	47	0	525	2140	23552	35
40	94606	1358	634	12364	43347	4103	2729	4059	14	0	505	2062	23431	40
45	93437	1249	611	11973	43088	4082	2720	3981	2	0	479	1979	23273	45
50	91648	1140	574	11350	42579	4052	2708	3862	1	0	446	1875	23061	50
55	89077	1032	531	10474	41662	4013	2691	3656	1	0	400	1768	22809	55
60	85342	912	479	9304	40162	3937	2661	3453	1	0	358	1649	22426	60
65	79688	768	407	7747	37584	3809	2601	3106	1	0	304	1502	21859	65
70	70789	577	314	5816	33043	3551	2468	2587	1	0	234	1291	20907	70
75	57204	361	220	3647	25745	3065	2197	1890	1	0	152	986	18940	75
80	39290	165	121	1747	16335	2267	1683	1106	1	0	81	638	15146	80
85+	20577	53	48	606	7594	1266	940	494	0	0	32	300	9244	85+

NUMBER OF PERSONS SURVIVING TO AGE X IF SPECIFIED CAUSES WERE ELIMINATED

Age (x)	No Causes	Respiratory T. B.	Other Infec. and Paras.	Neoplasms	Cardiovascular	Infl., Pneu., Bronch.	Diarrheal	Certain Degenerative	Maternal	Cert. Dis. of Infancy	Motor Vehicle	Other Violence	Other and Unknown	(1) + (2)	(1) + (2) + (5) + (6) + (8)	(1)+(2)+(5)+(6)+(8)+part of(9)&(12)	(10) + (11)	Age (x)
		(1)	(2)	(3)	(4)	(5)	(6)	(7)	(8)	(9)	(10)	(11)	(12)					
0	100000	100000	100000	100000	100000	100000	100000	100000	100000	100000	100000	100000	100000	100000	100000	100000	100000	0
1	98173	98173	98212	98180	98191	98440	98274	98177	98173	99147	98175	98239	98511	98212	98580	99645	98241	1
5	97661	97662	97751	97704	97689	98002	97801	97670	97661	98630	97713	97859	98110	97752	98233	99342	97911	5
10	97423	97425	97539	97491	97441	97786	97571	97441	97423	98389	97505	97668	97928	97541	98053	99179	97750	10
15	97264	97267	97390	97359	97319	97637	97416	97292	97264	98229	97356	97529	97817	97393	97919	99055	97621	15
20	97042	97050	97175	97169	97123	97424	97197	97089	97043	98005	97146	97356	97649	97183	97722	98864	97460	20
25	96628	96653	96770	96800	96749	97024	96785	96704	96660	97586	96751	97071	97307	96795	97382	98536	97195	25
30	96091	96166	96245	96342	96276	96502	96250	96199	96187	97044	96227	96635	96882	96320	96988	98171	96772	30
35	95453	95605	95621	95844	95721	95878	95617	95597	95607	96400	95605	96071	96325	95774	96520	97733	96224	35
40	94606	94860	94792	95236	95017	95046	94776	94808	94791	95544	94777	95296	95592	95047	95847	97082	95469	40
45	93437	93797	93643	94451	94101	93893	93613	93714	93632	94364	93632	94202	94570	94004	94838	96088	94398	45
50	91648	92109	91887	92809		92125	91833	92038	91840	92557	91872	92502	92972	92350	93213	94467	92728	50
55	89077	89632	89352	91535	91126	89579	89274	89621	89264	89961	89340	90014	90616	89909	90805	92050	90279	55
60	85342	85992	85656	88881	88821	85898	85560	86102	85521	86189	85635	86357	87199	86309	87276	88504	86654	60
65	79688	80435	80051	84572	85571	80332	79950	80737	79855	80478	80014	80780	81983	80802	81894	83092	81110	65
70	70789	71634	71200	77078	80753	71607	71148	72217	70938	71491	71145	71960	73759	72050	73405	74559	72322	70
75	57204	58082	57620	64428	73168	58309	57740	58998	57324	57771	57565	58429	61482	58505	60320	61444	58797	75
80	39290	40056	39657	46027	61185	40727	40091	41189	39372	39680	39596	40424	45759	40430	42853	44055	40739	80
85+	20577	21059	20822	25075	43349	22081	21543	22033	20621	20781	20772	21420	29388	21310	23991	25434	21623	85+

ADDED YRS OF LIFE

	No Causes	(1)	(2)	(3)	(4)	(5)	(6)	(7)	(8)	(9)	(10)	(11)	(12)	(1)+(2)	(1)+(2)+(5)+(6)+(8)	+part	(10)+(11)
TOTAL		.329	.208	2.163	6.098	.849	.326	.578	.090	.723	.179	.658	3.223	.539	1.652	2.907	.839
WORK	2.275	.148	.044	.600	.545	.050	.017	.144	.067	.000	.051	.222	.300	.192	.328	.386	.273

POPULATION, DEATHS, DEATH RATES FOR ALL CAUSES COMBINED, AND SPECIFIED CAUSES

Age Start of Interval	Midyear Popula-tion	Deaths During Year	All Causes	Respira-tory T. B.	Other Infec. and Paras.	Neo-plasms	Cardio-vascular	Infl., Pneu., Bronch.	Diar-rheal	Certain Degen-erative	Maternal	Cert. Dis. of Infancy	Motor Vehicle	Other Violence	Other and Unknown	Age Start of Interval
0	3293	119	.03614	.00000	.00000	.00000	.00061	.00364	.00182	.00030	.00000	.02429	.00000	.00091	.00456	0
1	14825	14	.00094	.00000	.00000	.00020	.00000	.00007	.00000	.00000	.00000	.00000	.00013	.00000	.00054	1
5	18969	7	.00037	.00000	.00016	.00005	.00005	.00000	.00000	.00000	.00000	.00000	.00000	.00000	.00011	5
10	19109	4	.00021	.00000	.00000	.00005	.00010	.00000	.00000	.00000	.00000	.00000	.00000	.00005	.00000	10
15	19075	9	.00047	.00000	.00000	.00021	.00005	.00000	.00000	.00000	.00000	.00000	.00005	.00010	.00005	15
20	9320	6	.00064	.00000	.00000	.00000	.00000	.00000	.00000	.00000	.00000	.00000	.00011	.00021	.00032	20
25	8250	5	.00061	.00000	.00000	.00024	.00000	.00000	.00000	.00012	.00000	.00000	.00011	.00000	.00012	25
30	7644	8	.00105	.00000	.00000	.00026	.00000	.00013	.00000	.00013	.00000	.00000	.00013	.00026	.00013	30
35	8270	17	.00206	.00012	.00012	.00048	.00121	.00000	.00012	.00000	.00000	.00000	.00000	.00000	.00000	35
40	8073	23	.00285	.00000	.00000	.00062	.00149	.00012	.00000	.00012	.00000	.00000	.00025	.00012	.00012	40
45	6657	35	.00510	.00015	.00000	.00088	.00190	.00044	.00000	.00044	.00000	.00000	.00000	.00015	.00044	.00073	45
50	6988	63	.00902	.00000	.00000	.00172	.00515	.00029	.00000	.00057	.00000	.00000	.00029	.00014	.00086	50
55	7113	110	.01546	.00014	.00000	.00351	.00844	.00014	.00000	.00127	.00000	.00000	.00000	.00028	.00169	55
60	5478	168	.03067	.00000	.00000	.00730	.01752	.00091	.00018	.00237	.00000	.00000	.00000	.00000	.00237	60
65	4407	190	.04311	.00068	.00023	.00726	.02519	.00113	.00000	.00340	.00000	.00000	.00000	.00045	.00477	65
70	3555	211	.05935	.00028	.00000	.00900	.03882	.00197	.00028	.00309	.00000	.00000	.00000	.00000	.00591	70
75	1736	205	.11809	.00058	.00000	.01152	.07604	.00806	.00000	.00346	.00000	.00000	.00000	.00058	.01786	75
80	977	137	.14023	.00000	.00000	.00819	.09519	.00512	.00000	.00512	.00000	.00000	.00000	.00102	.02559	80
85+	432	97	.22454	.00231	.00000	.01852	.11111	.01389	.00000	.00926	.00000	.00000	.00000	.00000	.06713	85+
ALL	154371	1428														

			All Causes	Respira-tory T. B.	Other Infec. and Paras.	Neo-plasms	Cardio-vascular	Infl., Pneu., Bronch.	Diar-rheal	Certain Degen-erative	Maternal	Cert. Dis. of Infancy	Motor Vehicle	Other Violence	Other and Unknown
CRUDE DEATH RATE			.00925	.00006	.00003	.00133	.00489	.00041	.00006	.00048	.00000	.00052	.00007	.00014	.00126
STANDARDIZED RATE (1)			.00626	.00004	.00003	.00084	.00275	.00032	.00008	.00030	.00000	.00086	.00008	.00014	.00084
STANDARDIZED RATE (2)			.01164	.00007	.00003	.00160	.00638	.00053	.00006	.00059	.00000	.00050	.00008	.00017	.00164
GEOMETRIC MEAN			.00599												

LIFE TABLE FOR ALL CAUSES COMBINED

Age (x)	Midyear Popula-tion	Deaths During Year	$_nM_x$	$_nq_x$	l_x	$_nd_x$	$_nL_x$	$_nm_x$	$_na_x$	T_x	$_nr_x$	$\overset{\circ}{e}_x$	Age (x)
0	3293	119	.036137	.035040	100000	3504	96957	.036140	.131433	6797849	.000000	67.978	0
1	14825	14	.000944	.003762	96496	363	385077	.000943	1.500000	6700892	.000000	69.442	1
5	18969	7	.000369	.001852	96133	178	480220	.000371	2.500000	6315816	.000000	65.699	5
10	19109	4	.000209	.001042	95955	100	479535	.000209	2.602083	5835596	-.012508	60.816	10
15	19075	9	.000472	.002368	95855	227	478746	.000474	2.671623	5356060	.047521	55.877	15
20	9320	6	.000644	.003001	95628	287	477436	.000601	2.545732	4877314	.085682	51.003	20
25	8250	5	.000606	.003042	95341	290	476024	.000609	2.650862	4399878	.037418	46.149	25
30	7644	8	.001047	.005229	95051	497	474153	.001048	2.783367	3923854	-.009697	41.282	30
35	8270	17	.002056	.010216	94554	966	470528	.002053	2.679218	3449701	-.007562	36.484	35
40	8073	23	.002849	.014190	93588	1328	464905	.002856	2.714765	2979173	.010243	31.833	40
45	6657	35	.005104	.025309	92260	2335	456011	.005120	2.735100	2514268	.014001	27.252	45
50	6988	63	.009015	.044070	89925	3963	440569	.008995	2.714905	2058256	-.009614	22.889	50
55	7113	110	.015465	.074719	85962	6423	415304	.015466	2.741547	1617687	-.000263	18.819	55
60	5478	168	.030668	.143452	79539	11410	370598	.030788	2.625183	1202383	.018271	15.117	60
65	4407	190	.043113	.194910	68129	13279	308045	.043107	2.544964	831785	-.000868	12.209	65
70	3555	211	.059353	.260273	54850	14278	239655	.059569	2.576688	523740	.020655	9.549	70
75	1736	205	.118088	.456795	40574	18534	155856	.118887	2.465503	284086	.019768	7.002	75
80	977	137	.140225	.508485	22040	11207	79944	.140186	2.300255	128190	.019768	5.816	80
85+	432	97	.224537	1.000000	10833	10833	48246	.224537	4.453608	48246	.000000	4.454	85+

NUMBER OF PERSONS DYING (OUT OF 100,000 AT BIRTH) ABOVE AGE X FROM SPECIFIED CAUSES

Age (x)	All Causes	Respiratory T. B.	Other Infec. and Paras.	Neoplasms	Cardiovascular	Infl., Pneu., Bronch.	Diarrheal	Certain Degenerative	Maternal	Cert. Dis. of Infancy	Motor Vehicle	Other Violence	Other and Unknown	Age (x)
0	100000	661	203	14074	56573	4391	369	5258	0	2356	553	1245	14317	0
1	96496	661	203	14074	56514	4038	192	5229	0	0	553	1157	13875	1
5	96133	661	203	13997	56514	4012	192	5229	0	0	501	1157	13667	5
10	95955	661	127	13971	56489	4012	192	5229	0	0	501	1157	13616	10
15	95855	661	127	13946	56439	4012	192	5229	0	0	501	1132	13616	15
20	95628	661	127	13846	56415	4012	192	5229	0	0	476	1081	13589	20
25	95341	661	127	13846	56415	4012	192	5229	0	0	424	978	13457	25
30	95051	661	127	13735	56415	4012	192	5171	0	0	366	978	13394	30
35	94554	661	127	13610	56415	3950	192	5109	0	0	304	854	13332	35
40	93588	604	70	13383	55860	3950	135	5109	0	0	304	854	13319	40
45	92260	604	70	13095	55168	3892	135	5051	0	0	189	796	13260	45
50	89925	538	70	12694	54299	3692	135	4851	0	0	122	596	12928	50
55	85962	538	70	11940	52035	3566	135	4600	0	0	0	533	12545	55
60	79539	480	70	10480	48532	3508	135	4074	0	0	0	417	11843	60
65	68129	479	70	7766	42010	3168	68	3191	0	0	0	417	10960	65
70	54850	269	0	5530	34253	2818	68	2143	0	0	0	277	9492	70
75	40574	203	0	3370	24912	2342	0	1402	0	0	0	277	8068	75
80	22040	112	0	1567	12977	1075	0	861	0	0	0	186	5262	80
85+	10833	112	0	893	5361	670	0	447	0	0	0	112	3238	85+

NUMBER OF PERSONS SURVIVING TO AGE X IF SPECIFIED CAUSES WERE ELIMINATED

Age (x)	No Causes	Respiratory T. B. (1)	Other Infec. and Paras. (2)	Neoplasms (3)	Cardiovascular (4)	Infl., Pneu., Bronch. (5)	Diarrheal (6)	Certain Degenerative (7)	Maternal (8)	Cert. Dis. of Infancy (9)	Motor Vehicle (10)	Other Violence (11)	Other and Unknown (12)	(1) + (2)	(1) + (2) + (5) + (6) + (8)	(1)+(2)+(5)+(6)+(8)+part of(9)&(12)	(10) + (11)	Age (x)
0	100000	100000	100000	100000	100000	100000	100000	100000	100000	100000	100000	100000	100000	100000	100000	100000	100000	0
1	96496	96496	96496	96496	96554	96843	96670	96524	96496	98838	96496	96582	96931	96496	97018	99115	96582	1
5	96133	96133	96133	96210	96191	96505	96306	96161	96133	98466	96185	96215	96775	96133	96679	98804	96271	5
10	95955	95955	96031	96058	96038	96326	96128	95983	95955	98284	96007	96041	96647	96031	96577	98731	96093	10
15	95855	95855	95931	95958	95588	96226	96028	95883	95855	98182	95907	95966	96547	95931	96476	98628	96018	15
20	95628	95628	95704	95855	95784	95998	95800	95656	95628	97949	95705	95790	96345	95704	96247	98394	95866	20
25	95341	95341	95416	95568	95457	95710	95513	95369	95341	97655	95469	95605	96189	95416	95959	98099	95734	25
30	95051	95051	95126	95388	95206	95419	95222	95137	95051	97358	95237	95314	95560	95126	95667	97801	95501	30
35	94554	94554	94629	95015	94705	94982	94725	94701	94554	96849	94801	94940	95520	94629	95229	97362	95188	35
40	93588	93645	93719	94271	94296	94012	93814	93734	93588	95860	93832	93970	94558	93776	94427	96545	94216	40
45	92260	92316	92389	93222	93652	92736	92482	92462	92260	94499	92616	92695	93275	92445	93145	95237	93052	45
50	89925	90045	90051	91263	92158	90587	90142	90320	89925	92108	90338	90547	91247	90171	91053	93143	90963	50
55	85962	86076	86082	87593	90395	86719	86169	86586	85962	88049	86479	86618	87606	86197	87165	89179	87140	55
60	79539	79700	79650	82869	87259	80296	79731	80628	79539	81470	80017	80258	81750	79812	80766	82646	80741	60
65	68129	68269	68225	73639	81661	69056	68355	69894	68129	69783	68539	68745	70868	68365	69565	71218	69158	65
70	54850	55152	54990	61480	74632	55947	55032	57239	54850	56181	55180	55473	58441	55292	56586	58005	55806	70
75	40574	40852	40677	47586	67257	41810	40767	43000	40574	41559	40818	41034	44556	40956	42404	43531	41280	75
80	22040	22257	22096	27400	54133	23683	22143	23771	22040	22575	22172	22358	26566	22313	24090	24929	22493	80
85+	10833	10940	10860	14055	43115	11943	10884	11994	10833	11096	10898	11041	14845	10967	12148	12643	11107	85+

ADDED YRS OF LIFE

	No Causes	(1)	(2)	(3)	(4)	(5)	(6)	(7)	(8)	(9)	(10)	(11)	(12)	(1)+(2)	(1)+(2)+(5)+(6)+(8)	(1)+(2)+(5)+(6)+(8)+part of(9)&(12)	(10)+(11)
TOTAL		.085	.075	2.013	9.671	.658	.157	.665	.000	1.647	.201	.332	1.956	.161	.983	2.603	.534
WORK	2.801	.030	.015	.577	1.156	.092	.017	.173	.000	.000	.125	.167	.297	.045	.153	.168	.293

POPULATION, DEATHS, DEATH RATES FOR ALL CAUSES COMBINED, AND SPECIFIED CAUSES

Age Start of Interval	Midyear Population	Deaths During Year	All Causes	Respiratory T.B.	Other Infec. and Paras.	Neoplasms	Cardiovascular	Infl., Pneu., Bronch.	Diarrheal	Certain Degenerative	Maternal	Cert. Dis. of Infancy	Motor Vehicle	Other Violence	Other and Unknown	Age Start of Interval
0	3033	100	.03297	.00000	.00000	.00000	.00033	.00264	.00231	.00000	.00000	.02143	.00000	.00000	.00626	0
1	13756	8	.00058	.00000	.00007	.00000	.00000	.00014	.00007	.00000	.00000	.00000	.00000	.00014	.00014	1
5	17697	3	.00017	.00000	.00000	.00000	.00000	.00006	.00000	.00000	.00000	.00000	.00000	.00000	.00011	5
10	18002	6	.00033	.00000	.00011	.00000	.00000	.00000	.00000	.00000	.00000	.00000	.00006	.00000	.00017	10
15	19105	5	.00026	.00000	.00000	.00000	.00005	.00000	.00000	.00000	.00000	.00000	.00000	.00005	.00016	15
20	11333	5	.00044	.00000	.00000	.00018	.00000	.00000	.00000	.00000	.00018	.00000	.00000	.00000	.00009	20
25	11753	8	.00068	.00000	.00000	.00009	.00034	.00000	.00000	.00000	.00000	.00000	.00000	.00000	.00026	25
30	11500	6	.00052	.00000	.00009	.00017	.00000	.00000	.00000	.00000	.00017	.00000	.00009	.00000	.00000	30
35	10390	18	.00173	.00000	.00000	.00077	.00029	.00000	.00000	.00000	.00029	.00000	.00000	.00000	.00038	35
40	9446	22	.00233	.00000	.00000	.00064	.00064	.00011	.00011	.00000	.00032	.00000	.00000	.00011	.00042	40
45	7757	25	.00322	.00000	.00000	.00103	.00116	.00026	.00026	.00000	.00000	.00000	.00013	.00000	.00039	45
50	7532	43	.00571	.00000	.00027	.00119	.00279	.00027	.00000	.00080	.00000	.00000	.00000	.00000	.00040	50
55	7775	85	.01093	.00000	.00013	.00219	.00553	.00026	.00000	.00180	.00000	.00000	.00000	.00000	.00103	55
60	6124	133	.02172	.00000	.00000	.00523	.01192	.00016	.00000	.00261	.00000	.00000	.00000	.00000	.00180	60
65	5458	172	.03151	.00000	.00037	.00476	.01924	.00018	.00000	.00366	.00000	.00000	.00000	.00018	.00311	65
70	4482	188	.04195	.00000	.00000	.00424	.02834	.00156	.00067	.00312	.00000	.00000	.00000	.00022	.00379	70
75	2252	193	.08570	.00000	.00000	.00622	.05906	.00178	.00089	.00666	.00000	.00000	.00000	.00044	.01066	75
80	1235	171	.13846	.00000	.00000	.00648	.10040	.00243	.00081	.00891	.00000	.00000	.00000	.00162	.01781	80
85+	550	137	.24909	.00000	.00000	.00909	.16545	.01091	.00000	.00545	.00000	.00000	.00000	.00364	.05455	85+
ALL	169220	1328														

			All Causes	Resp. T.B.	Other Infec.	Neoplasms	Cardiovascular	Infl., Pneu.	Diarrheal	Certain Degen.	Maternal	Cert. Dis. Infancy	Motor Vehicle	Other Violence	Other and Unknown
CRUDE DEATH RATE			.00785	.00000	.00005	.00093	.00438	.00023	.00009	.00060	.00006	.00038	.00002	.00007	.00104
STANDARDIZED RATE (1)			.00488	.00000	.00005	.00056	.00207	.00019	.00011	.00032	.00006	.00075	.00002	.00004	.00071
STANDARDIZED RATE (2)			.00921	.00000	.00005	.00104	.00523	.00027	.00010	.00070	.00006	.00044	.00002	.00004	.00071
GEOMETRIC MEAN			.00455												

LIFE TABLE FOR ALL CAUSES COMBINED

Age (x)	Midyear Population	Deaths During Year	$_nM_x$	$_nq_x$	l_x	$_nd_x$	$_nL_x$	$_nm_x$	$_na_x$	T_x	$_nr_x$	$\overset{\circ}{e}_x$	Age (x)
0	3033	100	.032971	.032050	100000	3205	97199	.032974	.126050	7121328	.000000	71.213	0
1	13756	8	.000580	.002314	96795	224	386620	.000579	1.500000	7024129	.000000	72.567	1
5	17697	3	.000170	.000849	96571	82	482650	.000170	2.500000	6637509	.000000	68.732	5
10	18002	6	.000333	.001658	96489	160	482054	.000332	2.557292	6154859	-.015125	63.788	10
15	19105	5	.000262	.001308	96329	126	481341	.000262	2.587632	5672805	.029145	58.890	15
20	11333	5	.000441	.002214	96203	213	480524	.000443	2.695618	5191464	.053211	53.964	20
25	11753	8	.000681	.003356	95990	326	479143	.000680	2.523645	4710939	-.008492	49.077	25
30	11500	6	.000522	.002613	95664	250	477799	.000523	2.916667	4231797	.009986	44.236	30
35	10390	18	.001732	.008657	95414	826	475182	.001738	2.714134	3753998	.014612	39.344	35
40	9446	22	.002329	.011619	94588	1099	470334	.002337	2.628336	3278816	.024193	34.664	40
45	7757	25	.003223	.016077	93489	1503	463999	.003239	2.706947	2808482	.025417	30.041	45
50	7532	43	.005709	.028178	91986	2592	454132	.005708	2.763069	2344484	-.001212	25.487	50
55	7775	85	.010932	.053426	89394	4776	436317	.010946	2.769490	1890352	.004453	21.146	55
60	6124	133	.021718	.103642	84618	8770	402482	.021790	2.650133	1454035	-.015906	17.184	60
65	5458	172	.031513	.146293	75848	11096	352258	.031500	2.568343	1051553	-.003367	13.864	65
70	4482	188	.041946	.191654	64752	12410	294327	.042164	2.628307	699295	.029734	10.800	70
75	2252	193	.065702	.358011	52342	18739	215676	.086805	2.554076	404967	.040531	7.737	75
80	1235	171	.138462	.514061	33603	17274	123537	.139828	2.425152	189091	.040531	5.627	80
85+	550	137	.249091	1.000000	16329	16329	65554	.249091	4.014959	65554	.000000	4.015	85+

NUMBER OF PERSONS DYING (OUT OF 100,000 AT BIRTH) ABOVE AGE X FROM SPECIFIED CAUSES

Age (x)	All Causes	Respiratory T.B.	Other Infec. and Paras.	Neo-plasms	Cardio-vascular	Infl., Pneu., Bronch.	Diarrheal	Certain Degenerative	Maternal	Cert. Dis. of Infancy	Motor Vehicle	Other Violence	Other and Unknown	Age (x)
0	100000	0	425	10660	61137	2715	773	7513	456	2083	129	799	13306	0
1	96755	0	429	10660	61105	2458	549	7513	456	0	129	799	12697	1
5	96571	0	401	10660	61105	2402	521	7513	456	0	129	743	12641	5
10	96489	0	401	10660	61105	2402	493	7513	456	0	129	743	12587	10
15	96329	0	347	10660	61105	2402	493	7513	456	0	102	743	12508	15
20	96203	0	347	10659	61080	2402	493	7513	456	0	102	718	12433	20
25	95950	0	347	10574	61080	2402	493	7513	370	0	102	718	12391	25
30	95664	0	347	10533	60917	2402	493	7513	370	0	102	718	12269	30
35	95414	0	306	10449	60917	2402	493	7513	287	0	60	718	12269	35
40	94588	0	306	10083	60779	2402	493	7513	149	0	60	718	12085	40
45	93489	0	306	9783	60479	2352	493	7463	0	0	60	668	11885	45
50	91986	0	306	9303	59935	2232	493	7342	0	0	0	668	11707	50
55	89394	0	185	8761	58670	2111	493	6980	0	0	0	668	11526	55
60	84618	0	129	7805	56253	1999	493	6194	0	0	0	668	11077	60
65	75848	0	129	5697	51437	1933	493	5139	0	0	0	668	10352	65
70	64752	0	0	4019	44664	1869	493	3849	0	0	0	604	9254	70
75	52342	0	0	2772	36274	1406	295	2928	0	0	0	538	8129	75
80	33603	0	0	1419	23354	1020	102	1473	0	0	0	440	5795	80
85+	16329	0	0	596	10846	715	0	358	0	0	0	238	3576	85+

NUMBER OF PERSONS SURVIVING TO AGE X IF SPECIFIED CAUSES WERE ELIMINATED

Age (x)	No Causes	Respiratory T.B. (1)	Other Infec. and Paras. (2)	Neo-plasms (3)	Cardio-vascular (4)	Infl., Pneu., Bronch. (5)	Diarrheal (6)	Certain Degenerative (7)	Maternal (8)	Cert. Dis. of Infancy (9)	Motor Vehicle (10)	Other Violence (11)	Other and Unknown (12)	(1)+(2)	(1)+(2)+(5)+(6)+(8)	(1)+(2)+(5)+(6)+(8)+part of(9)&(12)	(10)+(11)	Age (x)
0	100000	100000	100000	100000	100000	100000	100000	100000	100000	100000	100000	100000	100000	100000	100000	100000	100000	0
1	96795	96795	96795	96795	96826	97048	97016	96795	96795	98866	96795	96795	97396	96795	97269	99797	96795	1
5	96571	96571	96599	96571	96602	96880	96819	96571	96571	98637	96571	96627	97227	96599	97157	99720	96627	5
10	96489	96489	96517	96489	96520	96797	96765	96489	96489	98554	96489	96545	97159	96517	97102	99720	96545	10
15	96329	96329	96517	96329	96360	96637	96605	96329	96329	98350	96356	96385	97117	96411	96996	99665	96412	15
20	96203	96203	96285	96204	96259	96511	96478	96203	96203	98261	96230	96284	97066	96285	96869	99534	96311	20
25	95990	95990	96072	96076	96046	96297	96265	95990	96076	98044	96017	96071	96893	96072	96741	99425	96097	25
30	95664	95664	95745	95791	95883	95970	95938	95664	95750	97711	95691	95744	96687	95745	96412	99087	95771	30
35	95414	95414	95536	95624	95632	95719	95667	95414	95582	97456	95483	95494	96434	95536	96285	98557	95563	35
40	94588	94588	94709	95162	94942	94890	94859	94568	94893	95612	94656	94667	95785	94709	95590	98283	94736	40
45	93489	93489	93609	94357	94139	93838	93756	93539	93939	95489	93556	93617	94873	93609	94680	97393	93685	45
50	91986	91986	92104	93322	93171	92449	92249	92155	92428	93954	92112	92112	93527	92104	93278	95968	92238	50
55	89394	89394	89628	91236	91818	89963	89650	89917	89824	91307	89516	89517	91074	89628	90892	93531	89639	55
60	84618	84618	84894	87316	89362	85266	84860	85885	85025	86429	84734	84734	86654	84894	86201	88722	84850	60
65	75848	75848	76095	80249	85065	76492	76065	78002	76213	77471	75952	75952	78379	76095	77331	79598	76056	65
70	64752	64752	65083	70246	79951	65363	64928	67824	65063	66137	64840	64900	67969	65083	66203	68165	64989	70
75	52342	52342	52608	58000	74673	53258	52672	55693	52594	53462	52414	52521	56015	52608	54125	55792	52593	75
80	33603	33603	33774	38432	65085	34500	33967	37002	33765	34322	33649	33797	38006	33774	35220	36375	33843	80
85+	16329	16329	16412	19329	53334	16980	16576	18838	16408	16678	16351	16563	20263	16412	17408	18024	16585	85+

ACCED YRS OF LIFE

	No Causes	(1)	(2)	(3)	(4)	(5)	(6)	(7)	(8)	(9)	(10)	(11)	(12)	(1)+(2)			(10)+(11)
TOTAL		.000	.125	1.646	11.131	.459	.237	.887	.179	1.521	.051	.110	1.891	.125	1.008	3.064	.161
WORK	2.026	.000	.032	.513	.716	.056	.000	.156	.133	.000	.024	.023	.294	.032	.221	.257	.046

POPULATION, DEATHS, DEATH RATES FOR ALL CAUSES COMBINED, AND SPECIFIED CAUSES

Age Start of Interval	Midyear Population	Deaths During Year	All Causes	Respiratory T.B.	Other Infec. and Paras.	Neoplasms	Cardiovascular	Infl., Pneu., Bronch.	Diarrheal	Certain Degenerative	Maternal	Cert. Dis. of Infancy	Motor Vehicle	Other Violence	Other and Unknown	Age Start of Interval
0	11123	980	.08811	.00000	.00557	.00000	.00009	.01025	.02158	.00000	.00000	.03884	.00000	.00045	.01133	0
1	42343	439	.01037	.00005	.00085	.00005	.00012	.00203	.00319	.00002	.00000	.00000	.00005	.00026	.00376	1
5	49746	83	.00167	.00000	.00022	.00004	.00012	.00014	.00012	.00004	.00000	.00000	.00008	.00016	.00074	5
10	43568	43	.00099	.00000	.00009	.00005	.00009	.00009	.00005	.00000	.00000	.00000	.00007	.00009	.00046	10
15	29356	41	.00140	.00000	.00000	.00003	.00017	.00000	.00000	.00007	.00000	.00000	.00020	.00041	.00051	15
20	22248	43	.00193	.00022	.00004	.00004	.00018	.00004	.00004	.00005	.00000	.00000	.00018	.00040	.00072	20
25	20775	42	.00202	.00000	.00014	.00000	.00024	.00005	.00010	.00014	.00000	.00000	.00024	.00034	.00077	25
30	18758	75	.00400	.00011	.00016	.00011	.00091	.00027	.00005	.00037	.00000	.00000	.00005	.00021	.00176	30
35	20532	92	.00448	.00024	.00005	.00024	.00146	.00010	.00024	.00019	.00000	.00000	.00024	.00034	.00136	35
40	15658	117	.00747	.00051	.00026	.00026	.00204	.00038	.00013	.00057	.00000	.00000	.00038	.00038	.00255	40
45	14225	191	.01343	.00035	.00014	.00063	.00506	.00049	.00042	.00070	.00000	.00000	.00007	.00028	.00527	45
50	11335	270	.02382	.00053	.00053	.00150	.00856	.00168	.00053	.00115	.00000	.00000	.00053	.00079	.00803	50
55	8800	278	.03159	.00057	.00136	.00182	.00841	.00239	.00080	.00136	.00000	.00000	.00023	.00034	.01432	55
60	6642	315	.04743	.00030	.00075	.00256	.01536	.00256	.00120	.00181	.00000	.00000	.00060	.00105	.02123	60
65	3880	249	.06418	.00103	.00129	.00232	.01778	.00593	.00155	.00464	.00000	.00000	.00000	.00077	.02887	65
70	2326	199	.08555	.00129	.00129	.00473	.02193	.00860	.00172	.00301	.00000	.00000	.00043	.00000	.04256	70
75	1009	140	.13875	.00000	.00099	.00297	.03568	.01685	.00297	.00496	.00000	.00000	.00000	.00000	.07433	75
80	403	79	.19603	.00248	.00496	.00744	.04218	.00744	.00248	.00248	.00000	.00000	.00000	.00000	.12655	80
85+	173	30	.17341	.00578	.00000	.00578	.05780	.00000	.00578	.00578	.00000	.00000	.00000	.00000	.09249	85+
ALL	322900	3706														

CRUDE DEATH RATE	.01148	.00015	.00050	.00032	.00197	.00109	.00135	.00034	.00000	.00134	.00015	.00031	.00395	
STANDARDIZED RATE (1)	.01291	.00017	.00051	.00037	.00235	.00120	.00135	.00040	.00000	.00137	.00016	.00032	.00470	
STANDARDIZED RATE (2)	.01941	.00028	.00053	.00071	.00460	.00159	.00109	.00071	.00000	.00080	.00019	.00035	.00856	
GEOMETRIC MEAN	.01466													

LIFE TABLE FOR ALL CAUSES COMBINED

Age (x)	Midyear Population	Deaths During Year	$_nM_x$	$_nq_x$	l_x	$_nd_x$	$_nL_x$	$_nm_x$	$_na_x$	T_x	$_nr_x$	$\overset{\circ}{e}_x$	Age (x)
0	11123	980	.088106	.082440	100000	8244	93568	.088107	.219780	5554520	.000000	55.545	0
1	42343	439	.010368	.040422	91756	3709	357752	.010368	1.500000	5460952	.000000	59.516	1
5	49746	83	.001668	.008336	88047	734	438400	.001674	2.500000	5103201	.000000	57.960	5
10	43568	43	.000987	.004890	87313	427	435471	.000981	2.437549	4664801	.035873	53.426	10
15	29356	41	.001397	.006975	86886	606	432959	.001400	2.639233	4229330	.064252	48.677	15
20	22248	43	.001933	.009643	86280	832	429374	.001938	2.564353	3796330	.042337	44.000	20
25	20775	42	.002022	.010100	85448	863	425258	.002029	2.703747	3366957	.024519	39.404	25
30	18758	75	.003998	.019814	84585	1676	418939	.004001	2.621445	2941699	.001864	34.778	30
35	20532	92	.004481	.022193	82909	1840	410220	.004485	2.649457	2522760	.007144	30.428	35
40	15658	117	.007472	.036956	81069	2996	398536	.007518	2.727178	2112540	.025981	26.059	40
45	14225	191	.013427	.065413	78073	5107	378694	.013486	2.714616	1714004	.018311	21.954	45
50	11335	270	.023820	.113162	72966	8257	345106	.023926	2.611269	1335311	.024825	18.300	50
55	8800	278	.031591	.147074	64709	9517	300485	.031672	2.577011	990205	.018868	15.302	55
60	6642	315	.047425	.213346	55192	11775	247050	.047662	2.544781	689719	.030329	12.497	60
65	3880	249	.064175	.277455	43417	12048	186820	.064490	2.487982	442669	.037050	10.196	65
70	2326	199	.085555	.353215	31369	11080	128806	.086021	2.469446	255849	.043208	8.156	70
75	1009	140	.138751	.513727	20289	10423	74386	.140121	2.403898	127043	.037715	6.262	75
80	403	79	.196030	.635719	9866	6272	31931	.196421	2.225958	52657	.037715	5.337	80
85+	173	30	.173410	1.000000	3594	3594	20725	.173410	5.766667	20725	.000000	5.767	85+

NUMBER OF PERSONS DYING (OUT OF 100,000 AT BIRTH) ABOVE AGE X FROM SPECIFIED CAUSES

Age (x)	All Causes	Respiratory T.B.	Other Infec. and Paras.	Neoplasms	Cardio-vascular	Infl., Pneu., Bronch.	Diar-rheal	Certain Degenerative	Maternal	Cert. Dis. of Infancy	Motor Vehicle	Other Violence	Other and Unknown	Age (x)
0	100000	1586	2710	3889	24841	7985	5284	3979	0	3634	1111	2016	42965	0
1	91756	1586	2188	3889	24832	7026	3265	3979	0	0	1111	1974	41906	1
5	88047	1569	1884	3873	24790	6300	2125	3971	0	0	1094	1881	40560	5
10	87313	1569	1787	3855	24737	6238	2072	3953	0	0	1059	1811	40232	10
15	86886	1569	1747	3835	24697	6198	2052	3953	0	0	1029	1770	40036	15
20	86280	1568	1747	3821	24624	6198	2052	3923	0	0	939	1590	39818	20
25	85448	1471	1728	3821	24547	6180	2033	3884	0	0	862	1417	39505	25
30	84585	1471	1667	3821	24443	6159	1992	3822	0	0	760	1274	39176	30
35	82909	1427	1600	3776	24063	6047	1970	3666	0	0	737	1185	38438	35
40	81069	1327	1580	3676	23463	6007	1870	3586	0	0	637	1045	37878	40
45	78073	1123	1477	3573	22642	5853	1818	3356	0	0	485	892	36854	45
50	72966	990	1424	3332	20716	5666	1658	3089	0	0	458	785	34848	50
55	64709	807	1239	2812	17754	5083	1475	2692	0	0	275	510	32062	55
60	55192	636	829	2265	15222	4365	1235	2281	0	0	207	408	27744	60
65	43417	562	644	1631	11407	3729	936	1831	0	0	57	146	22474	65
70	31369	367	402	1196	8076	2611	646	958	0	0	57	3	17053	70
75	20289	201	236	583	5239	1495	424	574	0	0	3	3	11531	75
80	9866	201	162	363	2560	230	201	203	0	0	3	3	5940	80
85+	3594	120	0	120	1198	0	120	120	0	0	0	0	1916	85+

NUMBER OF PERSONS SURVIVING TO AGE X IF SPECIFIED CAUSES WERE ELIMINATED

Age (x)	No Causes	Respiratory T.B. (1)	Other Infec. and Paras. (2)	Neoplasms (3)	Cardio-vascular (4)	Infl., Pneu., Bronch. (5)	Diar-rheal (6)	Certain Degenerative (7)	Maternal (8)	Cert. Dis. of Infancy (9)	Motor Vehicle (10)	Other Violence (11)	Other and Unknown (12)	(1)+(2)	(1)+(2)+(5)+(6)+(8)	(1)+(2)+(5)+(6)+(8)+part of(9)&(12)	(10)+(11)	Age (x)
0	100000	100000	100000	100000	100000	100000	100000	100000	100000	100000	100000	100000	100000	100000	100000	100000	100000	0
1	91756	91756	92257	91756	91765	92679	93710	91756	91756	95303	91756	91796	92776	92257	95170	99877	91796	1
5	88047	88064	88828	88063	88096	89654	91070	88055	88047	91450	88064	88177	90369	88845	93572	99570	88193	5
10	87313	87330	88185	87346	87415	88969	90365	87339	87313	90688	87364	87512	89951	88202	93016	99173	87563	10
15	86886	86902	87794	86939	87027	88575	89944	86912	86886	90244	86967	87125	89713	87811	92668	98897	87206	15
20	86280	86297	87182	86347	86493	87957	89316	86335	86280	89615	86450	86697	89312	87159	92022	98209	86868	20
25	85448	85562	86360	85514	85736	87127	88475	85542	85448	88751	85693	86034	88774	86475	91298	97540	86281	25
30	84585	84698	85549	84651	84974	86205	87623	84739	84585	87855	84930	85308	88218	85663	90506	96781	85656	30
35	82909	83063	83921	83018	83669	84672	85910	83215	82909	86114	83270	83707	87235	84077	88973	95361	84071	35
40	81069	81319	82079	81275	82413	82834	84106	81448	81069	84203	81521	81989	85883	82332	87275	93671	82446	40
45	78073	78514	79148	78372	80192	79927	81050	78665	78073	81091	78658	79111	83781	79595	84593	91096	79704	45
50	72966	73507	74022	73480	76883	74885	75909	73779	72966	75786	73539	74041	80409	74572	79620	86133	74622	50
55	64709	65363	65824	65660	71179	66977	67458	65809	64709	67210	65391	65925	74262	66489	71786	78317	66619	55
60	55192	55908	56528	56517	63334	57815	57803	56516	55192	57325	55837	56324	68088	57262	62820	70016	56982	60
65	43417	44047	44634	45035	53850	46075	45749	44871	43417	45095	44058	44545	59633	45281	50634	57556	45203	65
70	31369	31993	32460	32922	42552	34316	33312	33193	31369	32582	31831	32305	45879	33105	38459	45548	32781	70
75	20289	20826	21130	21813	30763	23195	21734	21797	20289	21073	20632	20892	40116	21689	26561	33590	21245	75
80	9866	10124	10327	10760	18000	12309	10733	10868	9866	10247	10031	10159	28803	10597	14382	20625	10330	80
85+	3594	3736	3861	4076	8165	4653	3961	4012	3594	3733	3656	3703	20056	4014	5728	9636	3767	85+

ADDED YRS OF LIFE																		
TOTAL		.275	.812	.515	3.840	1.771	2.194	.578	.000	2.139	.297	.582	9.547	1.095	5.276	10.985	.884	
WORK	6.418	.183	.145	.228	1.584	.264	.141	.306	.000	.000	.214	.375	2.196	.329	.744	1.229	.591	

POPULATION, DEATHS, DEATH RATES FOR ALL CAUSES COMBINED, AND SPECIFIED CAUSES

Age Start of Interval	Midyear Population	Deaths During Year	All Causes	Respiratory T. B.	Other Infec. and Paras.	Neoplasms	Cardiovascular	Infl., Pneu., Bronch.	Diarrheal	Certain Degenerative	Maternal	Cert. Dis. of Infancy	Motor Vehicle	Other Violence	Other and Unknown	Age Start of Interval
0	10869	780	.07176	.00000	.00432	.00000	.00028	.01113	.01536	.00000	.00000	.03027	.00000	.00018	.01021	0
1	40735	510	.01252	.00005	.00130	.00005	.00007	.00196	.00378	.00007	.00000	.00000	.00005	.00044	.00474	1
5	48341	108	.00223	.00000	.00019	.00002	.00019	.00021	.00025	.00002	.00000	.00000	.00017	.00029	.00091	5
10	42654	32	.00075	.00000	.00009	.00002	.00007	.00007	.00005	.00000	.00000	.00000	.00002	.00002	.00040	10
15	28906	57	.00197	.00000	.00003	.00003	.00017	.00010	.00007	.00003	.00017	.00000	.00000	.00028	.00107	15
20	22090	104	.00471	.00005	.00009	.00009	.00032	.00023	.00014	.00018	.00032	.00000	.00005	.00027	.00294	20
25	20647	107	.00518	.00024	.00005	.00010	.00048	.00039	.00015	.00010	.00044	.00000	.00010	.00044	.00271	25
30	18003	96	.00533	.00017	.00022	.00011	.00078	.00039	.00011	.00011	.00056	.00000	.00000	.00017	.00272	30
35	18726	118	.00630	.00016	.00016	.00053	.00085	.00032	.00032	.00032	.00064	.00000	.00000	.00005	.00288	35
40	13955	85	.00609	.00029	.00021	.00064	.00115	.00050	.00029	.00029	.00014	.00000	.00000	.00029	.00229	40
45	12476	70	.00561	.00008	.00000	.00088	.00096	.00000	.00008	.00048	.00000	.00000	.00000	.00024	.00289	45
50	9864	105	.01064	.00010	.00051	.00203	.00203	.00112	.00010	.00051	.00000	.00000	.00020	.00010	.00395	50
55	8589	140	.01630	.00000	.00023	.00116	.00489	.00151	.00023	.00105	.00000	.00000	.00012	.00000	.00710	55
60	7184	204	.02840	.00000	.00000	.00390	.00821	.00195	.00125	.00125	.00000	.00000	.00000	.00056	.01128	60
65	5188	256	.04934	.00000	.00096	.00289	.01311	.00270	.00270	.00308	.00000	.00000	.00000	.00077	.02313	65
70	3717	231	.06215	.00027	.00108	.00323	.01641	.00377	.00242	.00350	.00000	.00000	.00000	.00027	.03121	70
75	2078	234	.11261	.00000	.00096	.00385	.02406	.00626	.00577	.00385	.00000	.00000	.00000	.00096	.06689	75
80	1105	173	.15656	.00000	.00090	.00543	.02896	.01357	.00362	.00362	.00000	.00000	.00090	.00181	.09774	80
85+	673	132	.19614	.00000	.00000	.00892	.04755	.00594	.00149	.00000	.00000	.00000	.00149	.00149	.12927	85+
ALL	315800	3542														

CRUDE DEATH RATE			.01122	.00007	.00046	.00046	.00146	.00110	.00129	.00029	.00014	.00104	.00006	.00027	.00456	
STANDARDIZED RATE (1)			.01090	.00008	.00045	.00046	.00139	.00108	.00126	.00030	.00016	.00107	.00006	.00027	.00435	
STANDARDIZED RATE (2)			.01538	.00008	.00040	.00082	.00282	.00122	.00109	.00054	.00016	.00063	.00007	.00029	.00726	
GEOMETRIC MEAN			.01380													

LIFE TABLE FOR ALL CAUSES COMBINED

Age (x)	Midyear Population	Deaths During Year	nM_x	nq_x	l_x	nd_x	nL_x	nm_x	na_x	T_x	nr_x	$\overset{\circ}{e}_x$	Age (x)
0	10869	780	.071764	.067830	100000	6783	94519	.071763	.191958	5819825	.000000	58.198	0
1	40735	510	.012520	.048564	93217	4527	361551	.012521	1.500000	5725306	.000000	61.419	1
5	48341	108	.002234	.011140	88690	988	440580	.002240	2.500000	5363755	.000000	60.478	5
10	42654	32	.000750	.003706	87702	325	437674	.000743	2.426923	4922775	.034839	56.131	10
15	28906	57	.001972	.010003	87377	874	435055	.002009	2.905940	4485101	.062569	51.330	15
20	22090	104	.004708	.023444	86503	2028	427713	.004741	2.632314	4050047	.038925	46.820	20
25	20647	107	.005182	.025593	84475	2162	416999	.005185	2.513394	3622333	.023180	42.881	25
30	18003	96	.005332	.026326	82313	2167	406215	.005335	2.531245	3205334	.006621	38.941	30
35	18726	118	.006301	.031031	80146	2487	394546	.006303	2.513487	2799119	.013459	34.925	35
40	13955	85	.006091	.029977	77659	2328	382393	.006088	2.464651	2404573	.031005	30.963	40
45	12476	70	.005611	.027771	75331	2092	371737	.005628	2.649379	2022180	.028277	26.844	45
50	9864	105	.010645	.052267	73239	3828	357328	.010713	2.683734	1650443	.029650	22.535	50
55	8589	140	.016300	.078777	69411	5468	334369	.016353	2.679910	1293114	.016557	18.630	55
60	7184	204	.028396	.133713	63943	8550	299749	.028524	2.664815	958746	.019935	14.994	60
65	5188	256	.049345	.220822	55393	12232	247032	.049516	2.552884	658997	.018161	11.897	65
70	3717	231	.062147	.270035	43161	11655	187005	.062325	2.528940	411965	.022683	9.545	70
75	2078	234	.112608	.439631	31506	13851	122504	.113066	2.471242	224960	.013547	7.140	75
80	1105	173	.156561	.551855	17655	9743	62116	.156851	2.315145	102456	.013547	5.803	80
85+	673	132	.196137	1.000000	7912	7912	40339	.196137	5.098485	40339	.000000	5.098	85+

NUMBER OF PERSONS DYING (OUT OF 100,000 AT BIRTH) ABOVE AGE X FROM SPECIFIED CAUSES

Age (x)	All Causes	Respiratory T.B.	Other Infec. and Paras.	Neo-plasms	Cardio-vascular	Infl., Pneu., Bronch.	Diar-rheal	Certain Degenerative	Maternal	Cert. Dis. of Infancy	Motor Vehicle	Other Violence	Other and Unknown	Age (x)
0	100000	515	2188	5750	19880	7390	6020	3660	929	2861	410	1761	48636	0
1	93217	515	1779	5750	19854	6338	4568	3660	929	0	410	1744	47670	1
5	88690	497	1309	5732	19827	5628	3201	3634	929	0	392	1584	45957	5
10	87702	497	1227	5723	19745	5536	3091	3624	929	0	319	1456	45555	10
15	87377	497	1186	5712	19714	5506	3071	3624	928	0	309	1446	45384	15
20	86503	497	1171	5697	19639	5461	3041	3609	851	0	309	1324	44904	20
25	84475	457	1133	5658	19502	5363	2982	3531	715	0	290	1207	43637	25
30	82313	356	1112	5618	19259	5201	2922	3491	532	0	249	1025	42508	30
35	80146	289	1022	5573	18983	5043	2877	3445	307	0	249	958	41400	35
40	77659	225	959	5361	18646	4916	2750	3319	54	0	228	937	40264	40
45	75331	116	877	5114	18207	4725	2641	3209	1	0	228	826	39387	45
50	73239	86	876	4784	17848	4724	2612	3030	1	0	228	737	38313	50
55	69411	50	694	4057	17115	4322	2575	2847	1	0	155	702	36893	55
60	63943	50	617	3667	15474	3815	2496	2496	1	0	116	701	34510	60
65	55393	50	617	2455	13002	3230	2118	2119	1	0	116	533	31112	65
70	43161	50	377	1781	9754	2561	1449	1354	1	0	116	343	25375	70
75	31506	0	176	1177	6679	1854	995	699	1	0	116	293	19516	75
80	17655	0	58	704	3722	1084	285	227	1	0	116	174	11284	80
85+	7912	0	0	360	1918	240	60	0	0	0	60	60	5214	85+

NUMBER OF PERSONS SURVIVING TO AGE X IF SPECIFIED CAUSES WERE ELIMINATED

Age (x)	No Causes	Respiratory T.B.	Other Infec. and Paras.	Neo-plasms	Cardio-vascular	Infl., Pneu., Bronch.	Diar-rheal	Certain Degener-ative	Maternal	Cert. Dis. of Infancy	Motor Vehicle	Other Violence	Other and Unknown	(1) + (2)	(1)+(2)+(5)+(6)+(8)	(1)+(2)+(5)+(6)+(8)+part of (9)&(12)	(10) + (11)	Age (x)
		(1)	(2)	(3)	(4)	(5)	(6)	(7)	(8)	(9)	(10)	(11)	(12)					
0	100000	100000	100000	100000	100000	100000	100000	100000	100000	100000	100000	100000	100000	100000	100000	100000	100000	0
1	93217	93217	93613	93217	93242	94238	94629	93217	93217	96020	93217	93233	94154	93613	96072	99898	93233	1
5	88690	88708	89528	88708	88740	89364	90364	88715	88690	91357	88708	88862	91285	89546	94021	99459	88879	5
10	87702	87719	88613	87728	87833	89451	90492	87737	87702	90339	87792	88000	90681	88631	93274	98886	88090	10
15	87377	87394	88326	87414	87539	89150	90177	87412	87378	90004	87477	87683	90521	88343	93026	98739	87783	15
20	86503	86520	87458	86555	86738	88304	89306	86552	86581	89104	86602	86928	90112	87475	92272	98168	87027	20
25	84475	84531	85445	84564	84840	86333	87272	84600	84665	87015	84590	85007	89313	85502	90501	96982	85122	25
30	82313	82468	83279	82439	82871	84287	85100	82475	82699	84788	82466	83012	88213	83436	88744	95758	83166	30
35	80146	80363	81177	80314	81004	82227	82906	80349	80746	82556	80255	80893	87071	81396	87032	94622	81043	35
40	77659	77932	78721	78031	78826	79804	80463	77980	78491	79994	77824	78404	85592	78998	85012	93051	78570	40
45	75331	75704	76443	75937	76903	77605	78162	75752	76191	77596	75491	76164	83984	76821	83051	91296	76326	45
50	73239	73631	74321	74157	75130	75452	76021	73826	74075	75441	73394	74137	82840	74719	80811	88911	74295	50
55	69411	69818	70616	71000	71940	71912	72085	70147	70203	71498	69630	70257	80089	71030	77297	85507	70518	55
60	63943	64318	65128	65791	67926	66752	66486	64962	64673	65866	64182	64760	76466	65509	71918	80171	65002	60
65	55393	55718	56420	58123	61334	58396	57964	56633	56025	57059	55599	56260	70134	56751	63318	71342	56469	65
70	43161	43414	44178	45945	51061	46125	45784	44822	43653	44459	43322	44005	61443	44438	50950	59068	44169	70
75	31506	31734	32423	34086	40489	34319	33832	33298	31866	32453	31623	32164	52568	32657	38634	46560	32284	75
80	17655	17782	18256	19477	25648	19862	19528	19024	17856	18186	17721	18115	41634	18387	23141	30780	18183	80
85+	7912	7969	8220	8979	13336	9542	8915	8686	8003	8150	7978	8195	30764	8279	11380	17650	8264	85+
ADDED YRS OF LIFE TOTAL		.167	.825	.895	2.864	1.560	2.240	.551	.358	1.744	.119	.536	12.716	.996	5.790	12.276	.656	
WORK	6.212	.131	.128	.388	.836	.365	.163	.225	.323	.000	.042	.256	2.664	.259	1.126	2.311	.298	

POPULATION, DEATHS, DEATH RATES FOR ALL CAUSES COMBINED, AND SPECIFIED CAUSES

Age Start of Interval	Midyear Population	Deaths During Year	All Causes	Respiratory T. B.	Other Infec. and Paras.	Neo-plasms	Cardio-vascular	Infl., Pneu., Bronch.	Diar-rheal	Certain Degen-erative	Maternal	Cert. Dis. of Infancy	Motor Vehicle	Other Violence	Other and Unknown	Age Start of Interval
0	13250	880	.06642	.00015	.00136	.00000	.00053	.00823	.01555	.00030	.00000	.03049	.00000	.00008	.00974	0
1	48100	273	.00568	.00000	.00023	.00008	.00008	.00091	.00183	.00008	.00000	.00000	.00010	.00023	.00212	1
5	53550	82	.00153	.00000	.00015	.00009	.00009	.00015	.00015	.00006	.00000	.00000	.00011	.00009	.00063	5
10	50100	45	.00090	.00000	.00014	.00006	.00008	.00012	.00002	.00000	.00000	.00000	.00006	.00018	.00024	10
15	36300	46	.00127	.00003	.00008	.00003	.00014	.00011	.00003	.00003	.00000	.00000	.00014	.00030	.00039	15
20	24850	31	.00125	.00000	.00004	.00004	.00028	.00012	.00000	.00000	.00000	.00000	.00020	.00020	.00032	20
25	22600	36	.00159	.00000	.00009	.00004	.00022	.00004	.00000	.00004	.00000	.00000	.00022	.00044	.00049	25
30	19600	51	.00260	.00010	.00000	.00010	.00061	.00015	.00000	.00010	.00000	.00000	.00005	.00041	.00107	30
35	21800	91	.00417	.00009	.00023	.00018	.00115	.00032	.00000	.00014	.00000	.00000	.00037	.00046	.00124	35
40	18150	142	.00782	.00028	.00022	.00061	.00215	.00066	.00017	.00039	.00000	.00000	.00055	.00066	.00215	40
45	15000	146	.00973	.00033	.00013	.00060	.00267	.00087	.00040	.00060	.00000	.00000	.00007	.00080	.00327	45
50	13200	207	.01568	.00068	.00030	.00091	.00576	.00189	.00015	.00061	.00000	.00000	.00023	.00068	.00447	50
55	9600	242	.02521	.00052	.00031	.00219	.00948	.00125	.00062	.00156	.00000	.00000	.00052	.00031	.00844	55
60	7450	279	.03745	.00054	.00027	.00349	.01315	.00242	.00054	.00107	.00000	.00000	.00040	.00067	.01450	60
65	4750	221	.04653	.00126	.00021	.00421	.01495	.00274	.00084	.00168	.00000	.00000	.00063	.00063	.01937	65
70	2600	227	.08731	.00115	.00038	.00423	.03077	.00731	.00231	.00346	.00000	.00000	.00077	.00115	.03577	70
75	1350	145	.10741	.00074	.00000	.00444	.03852	.00889	.00222	.00296	.00000	.00000	.00000	.00074	.04889	75
80	450	71	.15778	.00000	.00222	.00444	.03778	.01778	.00000	.00222	.00000	.00000	.00000	.00000	.09111	80
85+	100	34	.34000	.00000	.00000	.00000	.07000	.02000	.00000	.00000	.00000	.00000	.00000	.01000	.24000	85+
ALL	362800	3249														

CRUDE DEATH RATE			.00896	.00013	.00020	.00038	.00178	.00088	.00093	.00024	.00000	.00111	.00018	.00033	.00278	
STANDARDIZED RATE (1)			.01008	.00015	.00020	.00044	.00218	.00095	.00090	.00028	.00000	.00107	.00019	.00035	.00337	
STANDARDIZED RATE (2)			.01617	.00024	.00021	.00079	.00444	.00138	.00071	.00047	.00000	.00063	.00023	.00047	.00662	
GEOMETRIC MEAN			.01213													

LIFE TABLE FOR ALL CAUSES COMBINED

Age (x)	Midyear Population	Deaths During Year	$_nM_x$	$_nq_x$	l_x	$_nd_x$	$_nL_x$	$_nm_x$	$_na_x$	T_x	$_nr_x$	$\overset{\circ}{e}_x$	Age (x)
0	13250	880	.066415	.063000	100000	6300	94852	.066419	.182906	6015277	.000000	60.153	0
1	48100	273	.005676	.022380	93700	2097	369558	.005674	1.500000	5920424	.000000	63.185	1
5	53550	82	.001531	.007642	91603	700	456265	.001534	2.500000	5550867	.000000	60.597	5
10	50100	45	.000898	.004466	90903	406	453473	.000895	2.433805	5094602	.022733	56.044	10
15	36300	46	.001267	.006310	90497	571	451089	.001266	2.555458	4641129	.061630	51.285	15
20	24850	31	.001247	.006205	89926	558	448265	.001245	2.553017	4190040	.053017	46.594	20
25	22600	36	.001593	.007978	89368	713	445180	.001602	2.672394	3741775	.032694	41.869	25
30	19600	51	.002602	.012949	88655	1148	440633	.002605	2.658897	3296595	.009173	37.185	30
35	21800	91	.004174	.020673	87507	1809	433462	.004173	2.748411	2855961	-.000727	32.637	35
40	18150	142	.007824	.038566	85698	3305	420670	.007857	2.633825	2422499	.024680	28.268	40
45	15000	146	.009733	.047723	82393	3932	402689	.009764	2.640832	2001830	.020957	24.296	45
50	13200	207	.015682	.076000	78461	5963	378384	.015759	2.665355	1599141	.026014	20.381	50
55	9600	242	.025208	.119534	72498	8666	341872	.025349	2.620851	1220757	.030685	16.838	55
60	7450	279	.037450	.172171	63832	10990	292193	.037612	2.546254	878885	.029494	13.769	60
65	4750	221	.046526	.210174	52842	11106	237302	.046801	2.577135	586691	.049452	11.103	65
70	2600	227	.087308	.361846	41736	15102	170938	.088348	2.500869	349390	.041800	8.371	70
75	1350	145	.107407	.419351	26634	11169	103910	.107487	2.380249	178452	.057940	6.700	75
80	450	71	.157778	.561357	15465	8682	54592	.159035	2.381556	74542	.057940	4.820	80
85+	100	34	.340000	1.000000	6783	6783	19950	.340000	2.941176	19950	.000000	2.941	85+

NUMBER OF PERSONS DYING (OUT OF 100,000 AT BIRTH) ABOVE AGE X FROM SPECIFIED CAUSES

Age (x)	All Causes	Respiratory T. B.	Other Infec. and Paras.	Neo-plasms	Cardio-vascular	Infl., Pneu., Bronch.	Diar-rheal	Certain Degenerative	Maternal	Cert. Dis. of Infancy	Motor Vehicle	Other Violence	Other and Unknown	Age (x)
0	100000	1655	1227	5339	28878	8278	3733	3159	0	2892	1477	2935	40427	0
1	93700	1640	1098	5339	28828	7498	2258	3130	0	0	1477	2928	39504	1
5	91603	1640	1013	5308	28797	7160	1582	3100	0	0	1438	2843	38722	5
10	90903	1640	945	5266	28755	7092	1514	3074	0	0	1387	2801	38429	10
15	90497	1640	882	5239	28718	7037	1505	3074	0	0	1360	2719	38323	15
20	89926	1628	845	5227	28657	6988	1493	3061	0	0	1297	2561	38149	20
25	89368	1628	827	5209	28530	6934	1493	3043	0	0	1206	2491	38007	25
30	88655	1628	788	5189	28431	6915	1493	3024	0	0	1108	2294	37785	30
35	87507	1583	788	5144	28160	6847	1493	2979	0	0	1085	2114	37314	35
40	85658	1543	688	5064	27663	6708	1493	2919	0	0	926	1915	36779	40
45	82393	1427	596	4808	26756	6428	1423	2756	0	0	695	1636	35868	45
50	78461	1292	542	4566	25677	6078	1261	2514	0	0	669	1314	34548	50
55	72498	1033	427	4219	23484	5359	1204	2283	0	0	582	1057	32850	55
60	63832	855	320	3466	20227	4932	989	1746	0	0	403	950	29944	60
65	52842	579	242	2441	16370	4222	832	1433	0	0	286	753	25684	65
70	41736	278	192	1441	12803	3567	629	1029	0	0	135	603	21059	70
75	26634	81	126	715	7476	2300	230	431	0	0	3	404	14868	75
80	15465	6	126	256	3477	1374	2	127	0	0	3	328	9766	80
85+	6783	0	0	0	1396	399	0	0	0	0	0	199	4789	85+

NUMBER OF PERSONS SURVIVING TO AGE X IF SPECIFIED CAUSES WERE ELIMINATED

Age (x)	No Causes	Respiratory T. B. (1)	Other Infec. and Paras. (2)	Neo-plasms (3)	Cardio-vascular (4)	Infl., Pneu., Bronch. (5)	Diar-rheal (6)	Certain Degenerative (7)	Maternal (8)	Cert. Dis. of Infancy (9)	Motor Vehicle (10)	Other Violence (11)	Other and Unknown (12)	(1) + (2)	(1) + (2) + (5) + (6) + (8)	(1)+(2)+ (5)+(6)+ (8)+part of(9)&(12)	(10) + (11)	Age (x)
0	100000	100000	100000	100000	100000	100000	100000	100000	100000	100000	100000	100000	100000	100000	100000	100000	100000	0
1	93700	93715	93825	93700	93748	95458	95138	93728	93700	96541	93700	93707	94598	93839	96051	99775	93707	1
5	91603	91617	91809	91634	91681	92681	93690	91660	91603	94381	91642	91694	93264	91824	95022	99405	91732	5
10	90903	90917	91176	90975	91022	92042	93044	90986	90903	93659	90992	91035	92849	91190	94507	99025	91124	10
15	90497	90511	90832	90596	90653	91686	92637	90579	90497	93241	90613	90710	92543	90846	94216	98770	90826	15
20	89926	89952	90295	90036	90142	91157	92065	90021	89926	92653	90104	90276	92136	90321	93736	98319	90454	20
25	89368	89394	89753	89496	89709	90646	91494	89480	89368	92078	89636	89806	91710	89779	93229	97814	90075	25
30	88655	88681	89076	88801	89053	89942	90764	88785	88655	91343	89018	89287	91205	89102	92546	97126	89653	30
35	87507	87577	87923	87696	87946	88846	89569	87680	87507	90160	87889	88311	90507	87993	91465	96077	88696	35
40	85658	85806	86205	85963	86884	87149	87737	85927	85658	88297	86230	86684	89185	86313	89863	94522	87222	40
45	82393	82611	82971	82900	84440	84068	84423	82774	82393	84891	83132	83618	86680	83190	86973	91714	84368	45
50	78461	78801	79064	79181	81497	80406	80556	79061	78461	80840	79190	79947	83910	79407	83548	88491	80690	50
55	72498	73062	73167	73502	77526	75005	74490	73277	72498	74696	73257	74121	79298	73736	78382	83524	74897	55
60	63832	64496	64522	65437	71603	66453	65754	65028	63832	65767	64669	65363	72869	65193	69956	75059	66221	60
65	52842	53646	53484	55134	63334	55688	54613	54121	52842	54444	53643	54293	64914	54298	59140	64305	55116	65
70	41736	42642	42288	44475	53960	44602	43322	43115	41736	43002	42504	43019	56565	43205	47927	53079	43810	70
75	26634	27368	27038	28992	40352	29560	27977	28006	26634	27442	27229	27614	43400	27784	32390	37334	28231	75
80	15465	15947	15700	17211	28449	17958	16422	16499	15465	15934	15808	16092	32372	16189	19962	24212	16449	80
85+	6783	6998	6969	7734	15203	8640	7204	7324	6783	6989	6935	7145	22773	7190	9727	13590	7305	85+
ADDED YRS OF LIFE																		
TOTAL		.264	.378	.756	4.129	1.634	1.588	.481	.000	1.818	.386	.720	7.806	.645	3.985	8.168	1.115	
WORK	5.198	.128	.118	.273	1.352	.365	.074	.200	.000	.000	.233	.442	1.494	.246	.692	1.015	.678	

POPULATION, DEATHS, DEATH RATES FOR ALL CAUSES COMBINED, AND SPECIFIED CAUSES

Age Start of Interval	Midyear Population	Deaths During Year	All Causes	Respiratory T. B.	Other Infec. and Paras.	Neoplasms	Cardiovascular	Infl., Pneu., Bronch.	Diarrheal	Certain Degenerative	Maternal	Cert. Dis. of Infancy	Motor Vehicle	Other Violence	Other and Unknown	Age Start of Interval
0	13050	681	.05218	.00000	.00092	.00008	.00077	.00659	.01333	.00008	.00000	.02314	.00000	.00000	.00728	0
1	46800	318	.00679	.00002	.00036	.00004	.00000	.00130	.00224	.00006	.00000	.00000	.00000	.00021	.00254	1
5	52450	72	.00137	.00000	.00013	.00004	.00010	.00017	.00011	.00002	.00000	.00000	.00008	.00008	.00065	5
10	49700	43	.00087	.00000	.00008	.00004	.00014	.00010	.00004	.00006	.00000	.00000	.00000	.00014	.00026	10
15	36300	35	.00096	.00003	.00014	.00003	.00006	.00003	.00003	.00006	.00000	.00000	.00003	.00017	.00039	15
20	24800	70	.00282	.00008	.00020	.00000	.00028	.00020	.00000	.00004	.00048	.00000	.00000	.00040	.00113	20
25	23000	74	.00322	.00009	.00017	.00009	.00022	.00004	.00009	.00000	.00039	.00000	.00000	.00022	.00191	25
30	19200	73	.00380	.00010	.00021	.00010	.00052	.00010	.00005	.00010	.00026	.00000	.00000	.00036	.00198	30
35	20650	90	.00436	.00005	.00019	.00058	.00044	.00019	.00005	.00039	.00058	.00000	.00000	.00010	.00179	35
40	16450	105	.00638	.00018	.00036	.00091	.00128	.00043	.00006	.00036	.00006	.00000	.00012	.00024	.00237	40
45	13400	82	.00612	.00007	.00015	.00112	.00194	.00037	.00037	.00030	.00000	.00000	.00007	.00000	.00172	45
50	11650	108	.00927	.00000	.00000	.00146	.00283	.00043	.00009	.00026	.00000	.00000	.00009	.00009	.00403	50
55	9300	127	.01366	.00000	.00022	.00151	.00484	.00075	.00043	.00086	.00000	.00000	.00011	.00011	.00484	55
60	7950	178	.02239	.00013	.00000	.00226	.00755	.00126	.00050	.00075	.00000	.00000	.00000	.00025	.00969	60
65	6200	205	.03306	.00000	.00032	.00242	.01065	.00242	.00048	.00161	.00000	.00000	.00016	.00000	.01500	65
70	4300	235	.05465	.00000	.00047	.00209	.01744	.00419	.00116	.00302	.00000	.00000	.00023	.00047	.02558	70
75	2600	190	.07308	.00115	.00115	.00346	.02192	.00500	.00462	.00154	.00000	.00000	.00038	.00000	.03385	75
80	1200	138	.11500	.00000	.00083	.00250	.03667	.00833	.00333	.00167	.00000	.00000	.00000	.00000	.06167	80
85+	300	111	.37000	.00000	.00000	.00667	.08667	.02000	.00667	.00667	.00000	.00000	.00000	.00000	.24333	85+
ALL	355300	2935														

CRUDE DEATH RATE			.00817	.00005	.00022	.00039	.00141	.00075	.00093	.00022	.00011	.00084	.00004	.00017	.00304	
STANDARDIZED RATE (1)			.00801	.00005	.00022	.00040	.00139	.00072	.00088	.00022	.00013	.00081	.00004	.00018	.00298	
STANDARDIZED RATE (2)			.01222	.00007	.00023	.00067	.00296	.00091	.00074	.00038	.00013	.00048	.00005	.00018	.00542	
GEOMETRIC MEAN			.01076													

LIFE TABLE FOR ALL CAUSES COMBINED

Age (x)	Midyear Population	Deaths During Year	$_nM_x$	$_nq_x$	l_x	$_nd_x$	$_nL_x$	$_nm_x$	$_na_x$	T_x	$_nr_x$	$\overset{\circ}{e}_x$	Age (x)
0	13050	681	.052184	.049990	100000	4999	95794	.052185	.158713	6374342	.000000	63.743	0
1	46800	318	.006795	.026726	95001	2539	373657	.006795	1.500000	6278547	.000000	66.089	1
5	52450	72	.001373	.006846	92462	633	460728	.001374	2.500000	5904891	.000000	63.863	5
10	49700	43	.000865	.004312	91829	396	458115	.000864	2.400042	5444163	.020934	59.286	10
15	36300	35	.000964	.004845	91433	443	456244	.000971	2.519959	4986048	.061065	54.532	15
20	24800	70	.002823	.014166	90990	1289	451934	.002852	2.660169	4529804	.050324	49.784	20
25	23000	74	.003217	.015986	89701	1434	444998	.003222	2.554480	4077870	.031307	45.461	25
30	19200	73	.003802	.018852	88267	1664	437266	.003805	2.554462	3632872	.013178	41.158	30
35	20650	90	.004358	.021581	86603	1869	428552	.004361	2.612025	3195607	.006189	36.899	35
40	16450	105	.006383	.031499	84734	2669	417125	.006399	2.547615	2767055	.031917	32.656	40
45	13400	82	.006119	.030208	82065	2479	404327	.006131	2.580510	2349930	.028626	28.635	45
50	11650	108	.009270	.045573	79586	3627	389398	.009314	2.647620	1945603	.027802	24.447	50
55	9300	127	.013656	.066470	75959	5049	367992	.013720	2.662367	1556205	.025965	20.487	55
60	7950	178	.022390	.106642	70910	7562	336624	.022464	2.629402	1188213	.018519	16.757	60
65	6200	205	.033065	.153849	63348	9746	293503	.033206	2.615774	851589	.023926	13.443	65
70	4300	235	.054651	.242118	53602	12978	236162	.054954	2.545975	558086	.028240	10.412	70
75	2600	190	.073077	.310408	40624	12610	171527	.073516	2.494647	321924	.046375	7.924	75
80	1200	138	.115000	.451703	28014	12654	108883	.116216	2.535430	150397	.046375	5.369	80
85+	300	111	.370000	1.000000	15360	15360	41514	.370000	2.702703	41514	.000000	2.703	85+

NUMBER OF PERSONS DYING (OUT OF 100,000 AT BIRTH) ABOVE AGE X FROM SPECIFIED CAUSES

Age (x)	All Causes	Respiratory T. B.	Other Infec. and Paras.	Neo-plasms	Cardio-vascular	Infl., Pneu., Bronch.	Diar-rheal	Certain Degen-erative	Maternal	Cert. Dis. of Infancy	Motor Vehicle	Other Violence	Other and Unknown	Age (x)
0	100000	511	1518	5492	26309	7013	4679	3177	809	2217	371	1108	46796	0
1	95001	511	1430	5484	26236	6382	3402	3169	809	0	371	1108	46099	1
5	92462	503	1294	5468	26236	5895	2564	3145	809	0	371	1028	45149	5
10	91829	503	1233	5451	26192	5816	2511	3137	809	0	336	993	44848	10
15	91433	503	1196	5432	26127	5770	2493	3109	809	0	336	929	44729	15
20	90990	490	1132	5420	26103	5758	2481	3057	782	0	324	852	44551	20
25	89701	453	1041	5420	25974	5666	2481	3079	561	0	324	669	44033	25
30	88267	414	964	5381	25877	5647	2442	3079	387	0	324	572	43180	30
35	86603	369	873	5335	25649	5601	2419	3033	273	0	324	413	42314	35
40	84734	348	789	5086	25462	5518	2398	2866	24	0	324	372	41547	40
45	82065	271	637	4704	24925	5340	2372	2714	1	0	273	270	40558	45
50	79586	242	578	4250	24137	5189	2221	2594	1	0	243	270	39861	50
55	75959	242	578	3681	23028	5021	2188	2493	1	0	209	237	38281	55
60	70910	242	498	3126	21239	4743	2028	2175	1	0	170	197	36491	60
65	63348	199	498	2362	18690	4317	1859	1920	1	0	170	113	33219	65
70	53602	199	403	1652	15553	3603	1716	1444	1	0	122	113	28796	70
75	40624	199	292	1157	11413	2610	1437	727	1	0	67	2	22719	75
80	28014	0	93	560	7632	1748	636	469	1	0	1	2	16872	80
85+	15360	0	0	277	3598	830	277	277	0	0	0	0	10101	85+

NUMBER OF PERSONS SURVIVING TO AGE X IF SPECIFIED CAUSES WERE ELIMINATED

Age (x)	No Causes	Respiratory T. B.	Other Infec. and Paras.	Neo-plasms	Cardio-vascular	Infl., Pneu., Bronch.	Diar-rheal	Certain Degener-ative	Maternal	Cert. Dis. of Infancy	Motor Vehicle	Other Violence	Other and Unknown	(1) + (2)	(1) + (2) + (5) + (6) + (8)	(1)+(2)+ (5)+(6)+ (8)+part of(9)&(12)	(10) + (11)	Age (x)
		(1)	(2)	(3)	(4)	(5)	(6)	(7)	(8)	(9)	(10)	(11)	(12)					
0	100000	100000	100000	100000	100000	100000	100000	100000	100000	100000	100000	100000	100000	100000	100000	100000	100000	0
1	95001	95001	95087	95009	95072	95618	96254	95009	95001	97186	95001	95001	95683	95087	96966	99781	95001	1
5	92462	92470	92680	92485	92531	93547	94523	92493	92462	94589	92462	92541	94074	92688	95866	99577	92541	5
10	91829	91837	92106	91869	91942	92987	93930	91868	91829	93941	91864	91942	93736	92114	95409	99291	91977	10
15	91433	91441	91746	91492	91610	92632	93543	91500	91433	93536	91468	91610	93453	91754	95102	99019	91645	15
20	90990	91011	91366	91061	91190	92195	93102	91068	91017	93083	91037	91243	93182	91387	94774	98771	91290	20
25	89701	89758	90162	89771	90027	90982	91783	89796	89947	91764	89747	90133	92390	90220	93889	98170	90179	25
30	88267	88362	88798	88374	88684	89546	90355	88361	88683	90297	88312	88788	91789	88893	92750	97537	88834	30
35	86603	86741	87214	86754	87240	87905	88675	86741	87124	88595	86647	87273	90955	87353	91334	96429	87318	35
40	84734	84890	85416	85129	85544	86091	86783	85034	85492	86683	84777	85430	89792	85573	89842	95207	85474	40
45	82065	82292	82876	82826	83385	83557	84076	82506	82822	83953	82157	82841	88001	83105	87489	93012	82934	45
50	79586	79834	80431	80777	81659	81185	81688	80132	80320	81417	79705	80338	86082	80682	85256	90809	80458	50
55	75959	76196	76766	77661	79057	77653	77999	76580	76659	77706	76106	76709	83845	77005	81581	87068	76858	55
60	70910	71131	71741	73049	75623	72766	72913	71800	71564	72541	71085	71650	80205	71965	76698	82175	71826	60
65	63348	63586	64090	66005	70175	65421	65355	64387	63932	64805	63504	64089	75238	64332	69174	74654	64247	65
70	53602	53803	54319	56530	62657	56039	55436	54929	54096	54835	53778	54229	68679	54523	59496	65088	54407	70
75	40624	40778	41266	43295	51873	43380	42270	42269	40999	41559	40806	41197	59265	41423	46450	52164	41381	75
80	28014	28288	28624	30384	39985	30683	29849	29363	28272	28658	28194	28407	48568	28904	34043	40303	28589	80
85+	15360	15510	15764	16885	26553	17573	16648	16247	15502	15713	15459	15577	36730	15918	19921	25420	15678	85+

ADDED YRS OF LIFE																	
TOTAL		.123	.498	.560	3.482	1.485	1.719	.492	.334	1.463	.082	.427	9.035	.623	4.290	8.802	.510
WORK	4.782	.079	.199	.403	.836	.207	.086	.171	.280	.000	.030	.243	1.920	.279	.860	1.576	.273

POPULATION, DEATHS, DEATH RATES FOR ALL CAUSES COMBINED, AND SPECIFIED CAUSES

Age Start of Interval	Midyear Population	Deaths During Year	All Causes	Respiratory T. B.	Other Infec. and Paras.	Neoplasms	Cardiovascular	Infl., Pneu., Bronch.	Diarrheal	Certain Degenerative	Maternal	Cert. Dis. of Infancy	Motor Vehicle	Other Violence	Other and Unknown	Age Start of Interval
0	588206	65746	.11177	.00008	.00754	.00003	.00002	.02192	.02389	.00005	.00000	.04533	.00001	.00058	.01231	0
1	2359125	33361	.01414	.00007	.00261	.00004	.00008	.00230	.00446	.00005	.00000	.00000	.00002	.00036	.00415	1
5	2715955	7230	.00266	.00003	.00059	.00004	.00008	.00027	.00046	.00002	.00000	.00000	.00003	.00027	.00087	5
10	2242824	3578	.00160	.00003	.00029	.00004	.00016	.00010	.00016	.00002	.00000	.00000	.00002	.00034	.00045	10
15	1745311	4275	.00245	.00005	.00024	.00005	.00030	.00009	.00011	.00004	.00000	.00000	.00005	.00096	.00053	15
20	1410105	5462	.00387	.00026	.00029	.00007	.00041	.00010	.00012	.00010	.00000	.00000	.00005	.00178	.00070	20
25	1200445	5863	.00488	.00031	.00032	.00008	.00062	.00014	.00016	.00020	.00000	.00000	.00009	.00204	.00092	25
30	1012866	5724	.00565	.00038	.00039	.00011	.00070	.00018	.00016	.00035	.00000	.00000	.00008	.00216	.00114	30
35	962715	6969	.00724	.00051	.00042	.00017	.00118	.00025	.00020	.00063	.00000	.00000	.00008	.00236	.00144	35
40	676820	5658	.00842	.00056	.00049	.00029	.00172	.00032	.00031	.00091	.00000	.00000	.00006	.00194	.00181	40
45	612757	6788	.01108	.00068	.00070	.00054	.00256	.00044	.00039	.00129	.00000	.00000	.00005	.00212	.00230	45
50	529293	7059	.01334	.00074	.00084	.00083	.00405	.00052	.00051	.00180	.00000	.00000	.00006	.00175	.00222	50
55	406712	7782	.01913	.00059	.00118	.00132	.00651	.00090	.00083	.00252	.00000	.00000	.00006	.00180	.00302	55
60	373375	8991	.02408	.00100	.00137	.00169	.00902	.00133	.00112	.00265	.00000	.00000	.00009	.00168	.00413	60
65	204212	7621	.03732	.00111	.00168	.00303	.01520	.00220	.00168	.00358	.00000	.00000	.00011	.00190	.00642	65
70	161889	8653	.05345	.00148	.00227	.00393	.02037	.00317	.00265	.00466	.00000	.00000	.00014	.00185	.01294	70
75	91493	7011	.07663	.00154	.00280	.00521	.02955	.00543	.00392	.00624	.00000	.00000	.00015	.00227	.01950	75
80	58063	6014	.10358	.00134	.00403	.00543	.03307	.00766	.00543	.00599	.00000	.00000	.00012	.00239	.03811	80
85+	63114	8701	.13786	.00103	.00390	.00412	.03638	.01122	.00602	.00551	.00000	.00000	.00011	.00192	.06766	85+
ALL	17415320	212526														

		All Causes	Respiratory T. B.	Other Infec. and Paras.	Neoplasms	Cardiovascular	Infl., Pneu., Bronch.	Diarrheal	Certain Degenerative	Maternal	Cert. Dis. of Infancy	Motor Vehicle	Other Violence	Other and Unknown
CRUDE DEATH RATE		.01220	.00028	.00106	.00030	.00165	.00140	.00174	.00051	.00000	.00153	.00005	.00114	.00254
STANDARDIZED RATE (1)		.01239	.00031	.00104	.00033	.00177	.00139	.00170	.00057	.00000	.00160	.00005	.00123	.00240
STANDARDIZED RATE (2)		.01494	.00044	.00101	.00064	.00347	.00127	.00139	.00100	.00000	.00094	.00006	.00144	.00329
GEOMETRIC MEAN		.01478												

LIFE TABLE FOR ALL CAUSES COMBINED

Age (x)	Midyear Population	Deaths During Year	$_nM_x$	$_nq_x$	l_x	$_nd_x$	$_nL_x$	$_nm_x$	$_na_x$	T_x	$_nr_x$	$\overset{\circ}{e}_x$	Age (x)
0	588206	65746	.111774	.103240	100000	10324	92360	.111780	.260015	5568836	.000000	55.688	0
1	2359125	33361	.014141	.054630	89676	4899	346457	.014140	1.500000	5476475	.000000	61.070	1
5	2715955	7230	.002662	.013247	84777	1123	421078	.002667	2.500000	5130019	.000000	60.512	5
10	2242824	3578	.001595	.007914	83654	662	416593	.001589	2.467271	4708941	.031691	56.291	10
15	1745311	4275	.002449	.012278	82992	1019	412604	.002470	2.686684	4292348	.042829	51.720	15
20	1410105	5462	.003873	.019275	81973	1580	406108	.003891	2.622059	3879744	.036073	47.330	20
25	1200445	5863	.004884	.024194	80393	1945	397230	.004896	2.565338	3473636	.032792	43.208	25
30	1012866	5724	.005651	.027917	78448	2190	386926	.005660	2.573630	3076407	.017422	39.216	30
35	962715	6969	.007239	.035655	76258	2719	374670	.007257	2.565358	2689480	.027915	35.268	35
40	676820	5658	.008419	.041379	73539	3043	360314	.008445	2.574556	2314810	.039209	31.477	40
45	612757	6788	.011078	.054017	70496	3808	343226	.011095	2.569919	1954496	.016528	27.725	45
50	529293	7059	.013337	.064594	66688	4321	323034	.013376	2.591800	1611270	.027431	24.161	50
55	406712	7782	.019134	.091587	62367	5712	298004	.019168	2.578563	1288235	.014269	20.656	55
60	373375	8991	.024080	.114288	56655	6475	267700	.024188	2.594627	990232	.035312	17.478	60
65	204212	7621	.037319	.172439	50180	8653	225970	.037627	2.581162	722531	.047128	14.399	65
70	161889	8653	.053450	.237099	41527	9846	183344	.053702	2.532924	492562	.030371	11.861	70
75	91493	7011	.076629	.322244	31681	10209	132664	.076954	2.478552	309217	.026395	9.760	75
80	58063	6014	.103577	.409603	21472	8795	84599	.103961	2.412055	176554	.026395	8.223	80
85+	63114	8701	.137862	1.000000	12677	12677	91955	.137862	7.253649	91955	.000000	7.254	85+

NUMBER OF PERSONS DYING (OUT OF 100,000 AT BIRTH) ABOVE AGE X FROM SPECIFIED CAUSES

Age (x)	All Causes	Respiratory T. B.	Other Infec. and Paras.	Neoplasms	Cardiovascular	Infl., Pneu., Bronch.	Diarrheal	Certain Degenerative	Maternal	Cert. Dis. of Infancy	Motor Vehicle	Other Violence	Other and Unknown	Age (x)
0	100000	2851	5919	4602	25938	7832	7684	6990	0	4187	357	8553	25087	0
1	89676	2843	5222	4599	25936	5808	5477	6986	0	0	355	8500	23950	1
5	84777	2818	4317	4584	25909	5011	3933	6970	0	0	350	8374	22511	5
10	83654	2805	4069	4569	25873	4897	3739	6961	0	0	339	8259	22143	10
15	82992	2793	3951	4554	25805	4856	3675	6954	0	0	330	8117	21957	15
20	81973	2755	3853	4532	25680	4820	3632	6939	0	0	311	7716	21735	20
25	80393	2650	3733	4505	25512	4780	3584	6898	0	0	289	6990	21452	25
30	78448	2526	3606	4471	25267	4725	3519	6818	0	0	253	6177	21086	30
35	76258	2378	3454	4429	24995	4654	3457	6684	0	0	220	5341	20646	35
40	73539	2185	3297	4364	24552	4562	3382	6448	0	0	189	4456	20104	40
45	70496	1981	3118	4261	23927	4446	3269	6118	0	0	168	3757	19451	45
50	66688	1746	2877	4076	23045	4296	3133	5674	0	0	150	3029	18662	50
55	62367	1507	2603	3806	21729	4126	2967	5090	0	0	131	2464	17944	55
60	56655	1211	2251	3411	19784	3858	2718	4339	0	0	114	1926	17043	60
65	50180	944	1884	2957	17354	3500	2416	3628	0	0	91	1477	15929	65
70	41527	688	1496	2255	13829	2588	2025	2706	0	0	66	1038	14436	70
75	31681	417	1077	1532	10079	2404	1536	1849	0	0	41	699	12047	75
80	21472	212	705	838	6143	1679	1014	1019	0	0	21	357	9444	80
85+	12677	95	358	379	3345	1032	554	507	0	0	10	176	6221	85+

NUMBER OF PERSONS SURVIVING TO AGE X IF SPECIFIED CAUSES WERE ELIMINATED

Age (x)	No Causes	Respiratory T. B.	Other Infec. and Paras.	Neoplasms	Cardiovascular	Infl., Pneu., Bronch.	Diarrheal	Certain Degenerative	Maternal	Cert. Dis. of Infancy	Motor Vehicle	Other Violence	Other and Unknown	(1) + (2)	(1) + (2) + (5) + (6) + (8)	(1)+(2)+ (5)+(6)+ (8)+part of(9)&(12)	(10) + (11)	Age (x)
		(1)	(2)	(3)	(4)	(5)	(6)	(7)	(8)	(9)	(10)	(11)	(12)					
0	100000	100000	100000	100000	100000	100000	100000	100000	100000	100000	100000	100000	100000	100000	100000	100000	100000	0
1	89676	89684	90338	89679	89678	91612	91789	89680	89676	93728	89678	89726	90759	90346	94472	99861	89728	1
5	84777	84808	86294	84794	84805	87403	88325	84796	84777	88608	84784	84947	87228	86326	92724	99555	84954	5
10	83654	83698	85402	83686	83717	86362	87356	83682	83654	87434	83671	83936	86450	85447	92117	99228	83954	10
15	82992	83048	84846	83039	83123	85721	86731	83027	82992	86742	83018	83414	85957	84903	91646	98830	83441	15
20	81973	82066	83904	82041	82227	84705	85711	82022	81973	85677	82018	82792	85130	83999	90757	97942	82837	20
25	80393	80588	82408	80486	80809	83113	84109	80482	80393	84025	80459	81925	83781	82608	89351	96506	81992	25
30	78448	78761	80543	78573	79057	81159	82141	78614	78448	81993	78548	80766	82132	80865	87598	94715	80868	30
35	76258	76709	78449	76421	77160	78965	79912	76552	76258	79704	76388	79364	80295	78913	85630	92718	79499	35
40	73539	74165	75810	73760	74851	76244	77140	74056	73539	76882	73654	77443	77994	76456	83149	90187	77607	40
45	70496	71298	72854	70809	72380	73206	74064	71317	70496	73681	70666	74962	75448	73683	80389	87396	75142	45
50	66688	67678	69162	67166	69357	69404	70203	67904	66688	69701	66866	71669	72158	70188	76896	83841	71860	50
55	62367	63528	64956	63077	66201	65078	65823	64081	62367	65185	62552	67613	68275	66164	72867	79656	67814	55
60	56655	57997	59357	57682	62139	59385	60046	58952	56655	59215	56839	61978	62965	60763	67503	74064	62179	60
65	50180	51625	52935	51527	57605	52953	53485	52914	50180	52447	50365	55357	56550	54460	61254	67548	55561	65
70	41527	42962	44180	43301	51492	44315	44642	44680	41527	43403	41703	46251	48699	45707	52435	58233	46447	70
75	31681	33020	34094	33696	43544	34356	34519	34896	31681	33112	31837	35613	39683	35535	41988	47364	35788	75
80	21472	22553	23437	23447	34278	23939	23866	24407	21472	22442	21594	24415	29716	24617	30505	35246	24553	80
85+	12677	13409	14128	14229	23931	14692	14484	14859	12677	13250	12757	14607	21281	14943	19788	24142	14699	85+

ADDED YRS OF LIFE																	
TOTAL		.652	1.968	.708	4.735	2.501	3.026	1.229	.000	2.505	.104	2.678	6.366	2.661	8.784	15.186	2.791
WORK	6.986	.376	.412	.209	1.196	.217	.213	.495	.000	.000	.066	1.853	1.207	.794	1.241	1.549	1.923

POPULATION, DEATHS, DEATH RATES FOR ALL CAUSES COMBINED, AND SPECIFIED CAUSES

Age Start of Interval	Midyear Population	Deaths During Year	All Causes	Respiratory T. B.	Other Infec. and Paras.	Neo-plasms	Cardio-vascular	Infl., Pneu., Bronch.	Diar-rheal	Certain Degen-erative	Maternal	Cert. Dis. of Infancy	Motor Vehicle	Other Violence	Other and Unknown	Age Start of Interval
0	559728	53629	.09581	.00008	.00683	.00004	.00001	.01945	.02200	.00001	.00000	.03647	.00001	.00050	.01040	0
1	2288584	33874	.01480	.00007	.00286	.00003	.00009	.00245	.00469	.00005	.00000	.00009	.00001	.00029	.00425	1
5	2618444	6746	.00258	.00003	.00057	.00002	.00008	.00029	.00048	.00002	.00000	.00000	.00001	.00017	.00091	5
10	2129766	2853	.00134	.00003	.00026	.00004	.00016	.00011	.00017	.00002	.00000	.00000	.00001	.00012	.00043	10
15	1801463	3438	.00191	.00011	.00025	.00005	.00038	.00010	.00012	.00003	.00021	.00000	.00001	.00017	.00049	15
20	1546521	4667	.00302	.00025	.00035	.00008	.00058	.00013	.00018	.00007	.00040	.00000	.00001	.00021	.00074	20
25	1312568	4722	.00360	.00028	.00034	.00010	.00076	.00017	.00020	.00010	.00049	.00000	.00001	.00019	.00094	25
30	1045449	4405	.00421	.00030	.00039	.00029	.00093	.00019	.00020	.00019	.00055	.00000	.00001	.00020	.00096	30
35	964232	5242	.00544	.00031	.00038	.00047	.00143	.00022	.00027	.00029	.00063	.00000	.00002	.00024	.00116	35
40	688940	4258	.00618	.00028	.00050	.00076	.00172	.00029	.00035	.00047	.00028	.00000	.00001	.00025	.00126	40
45	624871	4959	.00794	.00032	.00057	.00123	.00235	.00037	.00041	.00070	.00011	.00000	.00002	.00034	.00153	45
50	537532	5386	.01002	.00038	.00067	.00158	.00349	.00047	.00050	.00098	.00003	.00000	.00002	.00029	.00161	50
55	395802	5976	.01510	.00050	.00087	.00223	.00588	.00078	.00079	.00175	.00000	.00000	.00003	.00038	.00189	55
60	373764	7874	.02107	.00051	.00134	.00250	.00852	.00108	.00105	.00207	.00000	.00000	.00003	.00044	.00351	60
65	211300	6897	.03264	.00059	.00147	.00365	.01409	.00190	.00155	.00304	.00000	.00000	.00003	.00058	.00534	65
70	172565	8491	.04920	.00069	.00213	.00437	.02159	.00332	.00285	.00384	.00000	.00000	.00002	.00075	.00964	70
75	96891	7063	.07290	.00111	.00262	.00564	.03262	.00493	.00431	.00537	.00000	.00000	.00000	.00100	.01526	75
80	70688	7210	.10200	.00079	.00351	.00583	.03824	.00754	.00550	.00545	.00000	.00000	.00000	.00127	.03384	80
85+	68701	12329	.17946	.00074	.00418	.00603	.05432	.01486	.00929	.00635	.00000	.00000	.00000	.00191	.08169	85+
ALL	17507809	190019														

CRUDE DEATH RATE			.01085	.00019	.00103	.00047	.00183	.00131	.00170	.00037	.00018	.00117	.00001	.00025	.00236	
STANDARDIZED RATE (1)			.01078	.00021	.00102	.00051	.00182	.00131	.00170	.00039	.00019	.00128	.00001	.00025	.00212	
STANDARDIZED RATE (2)			.01323	.00027	.00097	.00091	.00361	.00122	.00142	.00072	.00019	.00076	.00002	.00030	.00285	
GEOMETRIC MEAN			.01261													

LIFE TABLE FOR ALL CAUSES COMBINED

Age (x)	Midyear Population	Deaths During Year	$_nM_x$	$_nq_x$	l_x	$_nd_x$	$_nL_x$	$_nm_x$	$_na_x$	T_x	$_nr_x$	$\overset{\circ}{e}_x$	Age (x)
0	559728	53629	.095813	.089250	100000	8925	93153	.095810	.232881	5870645	.000000	58.706	0
1	2288584	33874	.014801	.057096	91075	5200	351300	.014802	1.500000	5777491	.000000	63.437	1
5	2618444	6746	.002576	.012833	85875	1102	426620	.002583	2.500000	5426191	.000000	63.187	5
10	2129766	2853	.001340	.006641	84773	563	422395	.001333	2.389728	4999571	.028194	58.976	10
15	1801463	3438	.001908	.009548	84210	804	419184	.001918	2.679053	4577176	.030204	54.354	15
20	1546521	4667	.003018	.015035	83406	1254	414033	.003029	2.610314	4157992	.027453	49.852	20
25	1312568	4722	.003590	.017869	82152	1468	407180	.003605	2.561308	3743959	.035630	45.574	25
30	1045449	4405	.004214	.020896	80684	1686	399342	.004222	2.581183	3336779	.027101	41.356	30
35	964232	5242	.005436	.026899	78998	2125	389815	.005451	2.564804	2937437	.033137	37.184	35
40	688940	4258	.006181	.030531	76873	2347	378660	.006198	2.569415	2547622	.040569	33.141	40
45	624871	4959	.007938	.039007	74526	2907	365607	.007951	2.584064	2168961	.018383	29.103	45
50	537532	5386	.010020	.049149	71619	3520	349726	.010065	2.622573	1803354	.034386	25.180	50
55	395802	5976	.015098	.073099	68099	4978	328642	.015147	2.619024	1453628	.021061	21.346	55
60	373764	7874	.021067	.100822	63121	6364	300461	.021181	2.620306	1124985	.035099	17.823	60
65	211300	6897	.032641	.152457	56757	8653	263039	.032856	2.602469	824525	.044261	14.527	65
70	172565	8491	.049205	.220772	48104	10620	214581	.049492	2.557556	561486	.033397	11.672	70
75	96891	7063	.072896	.309119	37484	11587	158431	.073136	2.498130	346904	.019142	9.255	75
80	70688	7210	.101998	.406070	25897	10516	102766	.102330	2.459189	188474	.019142	7.278	80
85+	68701	12329	.179459	1.000000	15381	15381	85708	.179459	5.572309	85708	.000000	5.572	85+

NUMBER OF PERSONS DYING (OUT OF 100,000 AT BIRTH) ABOVE AGE X FROM SPECIFIED CAUSES

Age (x)	All Causes	Respiratory T.B.	Other Infec. and Paras.	Neoplasms	Cardiovascular	Infl., Pneu., Bronch.	Diarrheal	Certain Degenerative	Maternal	Cert. Dis. of Infancy	Motor Vehicle	Other Violence	Other and Unknown	Age (x)
0	100000	1872	5995	7145	31209	8227	8585	5888	1077	3358	105	2031	24468	0
1	91075	1865	5359	7141	31207	6415	6535	5887	1077	0	104	1985	23500	1
5	85875	1839	4355	7132	31174	5554	4889	5870	1077	0	99	1881	22005	5
10	84773	1825	4112	7122	31141	5431	4682	5862	1077	0	94	1809	21618	10
15	84210	1812	4003	7106	31073	5386	4612	5853	1075	0	90	1759	21441	15
20	83406	1765	3900	7086	30914	5343	4563	5840	986	0	87	1689	21233	20
25	82152	1659	3753	7054	30673	5287	4486	5809	819	0	81	1603	20928	25
30	80684	1544	3616	7011	30362	5216	4403	5767	620	0	76	1526	20543	30
35	78998	1425	3462	6895	29988	5139	4322	5691	401	0	72	1446	20157	35
40	76873	1304	3312	6708	29430	5052	4216	5576	155	0	65	1351	19704	40
45	74526	1197	3122	6417	28777	4941	4083	5397	51	0	59	1255	19227	45
50	71619	1081	2914	5967	27917	4807	3934	5141	12	0	50	1131	18665	50
55	68099	948	2680	5411	26690	4641	3758	4794	4	0	44	1028	18101	55
60	63121	785	2393	4676	24748	4383	3499	4217	4	0	36	904	17476	60
65	56757	630	1988	3923	22171	4056	3181	3592	4	0	28	771	16413	65
70	48104	474	1599	2958	18432	3550	2664	2788	4	0	20	619	14998	70
75	37484	325	1141	2017	13771	2833	2048	1960	4	0	15	456	12914	75
80	25897	148	725	1123	8587	2049	1363	1108	4	0	12	297	10481	80
85+	15381	64	358	516	4656	1274	796	544	0	0	9	163	7001	85+

NUMBER OF PERSONS SURVIVING TO AGE X IF SPECIFIED CAUSES WERE ELIMINATED

Age (x)	No Causes	Respiratory T.B.	Other Infec. and Paras.	Neoplasms	Cardiovascular	Infl., Pneu., Bronch.	Diarrheal	Certain Degenerative	Maternal	Cert. Dis. of Infancy	Motor Vehicle	Other Violence	Other and Unknown	(1)+(2)	(1)+(2)+(5)+(6)+(8)	(1)+(2)+(5)+(6)+(8)+part of(9)&(12)	(10)+(11)	Age (x)
		(1)	(2)	(3)	(4)	(5)	(6)	(7)	(8)	(9)	(10)	(11)	(12)					
0	100000	100000	100000	100000	100000	100000	100000	100000	100000	100000	100000	100000	100000	100000	100000	100000	100000	0
1	91075	91082	91684	91079	91077	92820	93052	91076	91075	94375	91076	91119	92003	91690	95476	99889	91120	1
5	85875	85907	87436	85887	85909	88377	89387	85892	85875	88987	85881	86017	88229	87468	93697	99623	86023	5
10	84773	84818	86560	84795	84839	87368	88454	84798	84773	87845	84784	84985	87493	86606	93134	99393	84996	10
15	84210	84268	86096	84248	84344	86834	87940	84244	84212	87261	84225	84471	87094	86155	92777	99141	84485	15
20	83406	83510	85379	83463	83657	86049	87151	83453	83457	86423	83423	83734	86477	85485	92255	98719	83752	20
25	82152	82360	84245	82240	82679	84813	85921	82229	82407	85129	82175	82561	85491	84458	91477	98097	82584	25
30	80684	81002	82879	80814	81512	83370	84471	80801	81133	83608	80712	81162	84361	83206	90512	97320	81190	30
35	78998	79428	81303	79240	80184	81707	82790	79188	79656	81860	79029	79546	82999	81746	89345	96297	79577	35
40	76873	77412	79269	77294	78588	79558	80613	77172	77758	79658	76910	77501	81237	79824	87737	94798	77538	40
45	74526	75154	77042	75223	76849	77281	78347	74993	75487	77226	74568	75230	79254	77691	85786	92891	75272	45
50	71619	72337	74248	72735	74726	74403	75445	72321	72581	74214	71668	72418	76751	74993	83172	90251	72468	50
55	68099	68913	70835	69713	72313	70914	71918	69109	69022	70567	68152	68960	73570	71682	79900	86870	69014	55
60	63121	64034	65945	65345	69043	65950	66924	64623	63976	65408	63177	64040	68845	66900	75159	81889	64098	60
65	56757	57727	59698	59499	64813	59662	60458	58717	57526	58814	56815	57711	63014	60719	68954	75433	57771	65
70	48104	49072	50974	51365	59003	51058	51784	50534	48756	49847	48161	49055	54875	51999	60219	66266	49113	70
75	37484	38372	40149	40916	51297	40462	40939	40149	37992	38842	37533	38371	44908	41100	49111	54648	38421	75
80	25897	26660	28107	29082	41804	28663	28909	28499	26248	26835	25933	26644	38935	28935	36235	41038	26681	80
85+	15381	15900	17000	17800	30167	17650	17659	17406	15593	15938	15405	15930	23675	17574	23525	27842	15955	85+
ADDED YRS OF LIFE																		
TOTAL		.467	2.052	1.201	5.412	2.521	3.238	.912	.434	2.119	.031	.548	5.594	2.545	9.380	15.405	.580
WORK	5.437	.277	.423	.451	1.353	.231	.265	.301	.381	.000	.014	.234	1.053	.704	1.612	2.090	.249

POPULATION, DEATHS, DEATH RATES FOR ALL CAUSES COMBINED, AND SPECIFIED CAUSES

Age Start of Interval	Midyear Population	Deaths During Year	All Causes	Respiratory T. B.	Other Infec. and Paras.	Neoplasms	Cardiovascular	Infl., Pneu., Bronch.	Diarrheal	Certain Degenerative	Maternal	Cert. Dis. of Infancy	Motor Vehicle	Other Violence	Other and Unknown	Age Start of Interval
0	694566	65845	.09480	.00013	.00566	.00007	.00013	.02320	.01760	.00012	.00000	.04054	.00002	.00079	.00655	0
1	2786294	33209	.01192	.00006	.00228	.00005	.00006	.00265	.00255	.00004	.00000	.00000	.00004	.00043	.00376	1
5	3208856	7246	.00226	.00003	.00045	.00004	.00004	.00031	.00020	.00001	.00000	.00000	.00005	.00025	.00087	5
10	2649789	3581	.00135	.00002	.00016	.00005	.00006	.00013	.00006	.00001	.00000	.00000	.00005	.00032	.00049	10
15	2061616	4263	.00207	.00008	.00014	.00005	.00011	.00013	.00005	.00002	.00000	.00000	.00009	.00082	.00057	15
20	1666155	5542	.00333	.00020	.00014	.00008	.00018	.00016	.00005	.00007	.00000	.00000	.00013	.00155	.00078	20
25	1418239	5801	.00409	.00024	.00014	.00008	.00024	.00020	.00005	.00016	.00000	.00000	.00014	.00182	.00101	25
30	1196420	5880	.00491	.00031	.00021	.00012	.00031	.00026	.00007	.00033	.00000	.00000	.00016	.00186	.00127	30
35	1137201	6718	.00591	.00038	.00021	.00017	.00041	.00039	.00011	.00058	.00000	.00000	.00018	.00184	.00164	35
40	798952	6314	.00790	.00050	.00030	.00028	.00079	.00056	.00017	.00103	.00000	.00000	.00020	.00181	.00227	40
45	723673	6120	.00846	.00049	.00028	.00041	.00093	.00064	.00016	.00112	.00000	.00000	.00017	.00154	.00272	45
50	625310	7551	.01208	.00073	.00042	.00084	.00176	.00088	.00025	.00161	.00000	.00000	.00018	.00154	.00387	50
55	480776	7514	.01563	.00082	.00055	.00124	.00253	.00129	.00039	.00205	.00000	.00000	.00020	.00146	.00510	55
60	440628	10606	.02407	.00095	.00082	.00208	.00413	.00194	.00065	.00293	.00000	.00000	.00021	.00156	.00880	60
65	240890	8016	.03328	.00113	.00097	.00256	.00648	.00306	.00091	.00344	.00000	.00000	.00025	.00169	.01239	65
70	190705	8710	.04567	.00110	.00109	.00357	.00885	.00415	.00166	.00392	.00000	.00000	.00031	.00157	.01906	70
75	108400	7381	.06809	.00110	.00156	.00554	.01283	.00709	.00213	.00565	.00000	.00000	.00032	.00186	.03001	75
80	69256	6546	.09452	.00136	.00188	.00565	.01562	.01034	.00295	.00611	.00000	.00000	.00027	.00211	.04824	80
85+	74274	9200	.12387	.00094	.00171	.00394	.01608	.01358	.00381	.00576	.00000	.00000	.00000	.00219	.07515	85+
ALL	20572000	216043														

CRUDE DEATH RATE			.01050	.00024	.00076	.00031	.00071	.00163	.00111	.00047	.00000	.00137	.00011	.00101	.00281	
STANDARDIZED RATE (1)			.01066	.00026	.00073	.00034	.00076	.00161	.00109	.00052	.00000	.00143	.00011	.00108	.00272	
STANDARDIZED RATE (2)			.01303	.00038	.00065	.00066	.00150	.00157	.00085	.00092	.00000	.00084	.00014	.00124	.00429	
GEOMETRIC MEAN			.01281													

LIFE TABLE FOR ALL CAUSES COMBINED

Age (x)	Midyear Population	Deaths During Year	$_nM_x$	$_nq_x$	l_x	$_nd_x$	$_nL_x$	$_nm_x$	$_na_x$	T_x	$_nr_x$	$\overset{\circ}{e}_x$	Age (x)
0	694566	65845	.094800	.088360	100000	8836	93207	.094800	.231160	5909957	.000000	59.100	0
1	2786294	33209	.011919	.046290	91164	4220	354106	.011917	1.500000	5816750	.000000	63.805	1
5	3208856	7246	.002258	.011260	86944	979	432273	.002265	2.500000	5462644	.000000	62.829	5
10	2649789	3581	.001351	.006712	85965	577	428363	.001347	2.466060	5030372	.031944	58.517	10
15	2061616	4263	.002068	.010364	85388	885	424899	.002083	2.693974	4602009	.043141	53.895	15
20	1666155	5542	.003326	.016579	84503	1401	419180	.003342	2.619260	4177109	.036541	49.431	20
25	1418239	5801	.004090	.020300	83102	1687	411413	.004101	2.571503	3757930	.033455	45.221	25
30	1196420	5880	.004915	.024320	81415	1980	402257	.004922	2.566498	3346517	.018259	41.104	30
35	1137201	6718	.005907	.029194	79435	2319	391590	.005922	2.591544	2944260	.028896	37.065	35
40	798952	6314	.007903	.038889	77116	2999	378240	.007929	2.552587	2552670	.040315	33.102	40
45	723673	6120	.008457	.041502	74117	3076	363142	.008471	2.580258	2174430	.018024	29.338	45
50	625310	7551	.012076	.058896	71041	4184	345156	.012122	2.598192	1811288	.029339	25.496	50
55	480776	7514	.015629	.075504	66857	5048	322267	.015664	2.619230	1466132	.016552	21.929	55
60	440628	10606	.024070	.114433	61809	7073	292076	.024216	2.600941	1143865	.037060	18.506	60
65	240890	8016	.033277	.154834	54736	8475	253007	.033497	2.560767	851789	.050103	15.562	65
70	190705	8710	.045673	.206329	46261	9545	207914	.045908	2.549437	598782	.036211	12.944	70
75	108400	7381	.068090	.292516	36716	10740	156808	.068491	2.507255	390867	.033457	10.646	75
80	69256	6546	.094519	.381852	25976	9919	104427	.094985	2.433502	234059	.033457	9.011	80
85+	74274	9200	.123866	1.000000	16057	16057	129632	.123866	8.073261	129632	.000000	8.073	85+

NUMBER OF PERSONS DYING (OUT OF 100,000 AT BIRTH) ABOVE AGE X FROM SPECIFIED CAUSES

Age (x)	All Causes	Respiratory T. B.	Other Infec. and Paras.	Neoplasms	Cardio-vascular	Infl., Pneu., Bronch.	Diarrheal	Certain Degenerative	Maternal	Cert. Dis. of Infancy	Motor Vehicle	Other Violence	Other and Unknown	Age (x)
0	100000	2667	3861	5385	13104	11159	5039	7351	0	3778	918	7967	38771	0
1	91164	2655	3334	5378	13092	8997	3398	7339	0	0	916	7893	38162	1
5	86944	2632	2526	5361	13072	8057	2497	7324	0	0	903	7741	36831	5
10	85965	2620	2332	5343	13056	7922	2410	7318	0	0	879	7632	36453	10
15	85388	2610	2263	5323	13031	7865	2383	7313	0	0	860	7493	36247	15
20	84503	2576	2203	5300	12983	7809	2363	7302	0	0	823	7141	36003	20
25	83102	2493	2146	5267	12909	7743	2341	7272	0	0	769	6487	35675	25
30	81415	2392	2087	5234	12810	7659	2318	7207	0	0	710	5737	35261	30
35	79435	2267	2002	5185	12684	7554	2288	7074	0	0	645	4990	34746	35
40	77116	2118	1919	5120	12522	7400	2244	6848	0	0	574	4271	34100	40
45	74117	1930	1804	5012	12221	7188	2179	6456	0	0	500	3588	33239	45
50	71041	1752	1703	4861	11883	6957	2120	6051	0	0	437	3027	32250	50
55	66857	1499	1557	4570	11272	6651	2034	5494	0	0	375	2496	30909	55
60	61809	1235	1379	4171	10455	6234	1908	4832	0	0	310	2024	29261	60
65	54736	956	1139	3559	9241	5663	1717	3972	0	0	248	1569	26672	65
70	46261	670	894	2605	7589	4881	1485	3099	0	0	184	1141	23513	70
75	36716	441	667	1975	5740	4013	1138	2282	0	0	120	815	19525	75
80	25976	269	422	1103	3717	2892	802	1392	0	0	69	522	14788	80
85+	16057	122	222	511	2084	1812	494	747	0	0	38	284	9743	85+

NUMBER OF PERSONS SURVIVING TO AGE X IF SPECIFIED CAUSES WERE ELIMINATED

Age (x)	No Causes	Respiratory T. B. (1)	Other Infec. and Paras. (2)	Neoplasms (3)	Cardio-vascular (4)	Infl., Pneu., Bronch. (5)	Diarrheal (6)	Certain Degenerative (7)	Maternal (8)	Cert. Dis. of Infancy (9)	Motor Vehicle (10)	Other Violence (11)	Other and Unknown (12)	(1)+(2)	(1)+(2)+(5)+(6)+(8)	(1)+(2)+(5)+(6)+(8)+part of(9)&(12)	(10)+(11)	Age (x)
0	100000	100000	100000	100000	100000	100000	100000	100000	100000	100000	100000	100000	100000	100000	100000	100000	100000	0
1	91164	91175	91668	91171	91175	93251	92744	91175	91164	94842	91166	91235	91747	91680	95404	99778	91237	1
5	86944	86977	88222	86967	86974	89878	89350	86970	86944	90452	86959	87160	88818	88256	93760	99423	87175	5
10	85965	86010	87425	86006	86011	89005	88433	85956	85965	89433	86003	86287	88203	87470	93164	99100	86326	10
15	85388	85443	86908	85448	85459	88647	87867	85424	85388	88833	85445	85847	87822	86963	92715	98726	85905	15
20	84503	84591	86068	84546	84586	87607	86977	84550	84503	87912	84596	85310	87161	86157	91938	97973	85405	20
25	83102	83271	84698	83216	83291	86223	85557	83178	83102	86455	83247	84553	86052	84871	90660	96692	84701	25
30	81415	81681	83039	81559	81699	84559	83844	81554	81415	84700	81616	83596	84731	83310	89108	95137	83802	30
35	79435	79818	81105	79624	79837	82610	81836	79702	79435	82640	79665	82323	83201	81496	87315	93363	82593	35
40	77116	77636	78820	77364	77667	80356	79491	77599	77116	80227	77439	80657	81442	79352	85233	91331	80995	40
45	74117	74802	75870	74462	74944	77448	76465	74969	74117	77107	74500	78223	79171	76572	82549	88729	78628	45
50	71041	71874	72823	71520	72170	74471	73352	72260	71041	73907	71470	75558	76927	73677	79746	86035	76015	50
55	66857	67889	68675	67553	68524	70357	69118	68556	66857	69554	67321	71657	73819	69740	75915	82347	72155	55
60	61809	63021	63670	62879	64161	65505	64025	64035	61809	64303	62301	66734	70018	64919	71267	77881	67265	60
65	54736	56077	56617	56272	58018	58581	56884	57551	54736	56944	55231	59559	64827	58004	64515	71405	60098	65
70	46261	47663	48083	48276	50670	50286	48299	49488	46261	48127	46738	50765	58339	49541	56224	63374	51289	70
75	36716	38038	38372	39092	42055	40759	38657	40060	36716	38197	37152	40608	51002	39753	46464	53919	41090	75
80	25976	27060	27362	28442	31753	29899	27646	29164	25976	27024	26327	29001	42048	28504	34918	42507	29393	80
85+	16057	16846	17079	18093	21246	19476	17347	18600	16057	16705	16299	18135	33196	17918	23479	31183	18408	85+

ADDED YRS OF LIFE

	No Causes	(1)	(2)	(3)	(4)	(5)	(6)	(7)	(8)	(9)	(10)	(11)	(12)	(1)+(2)	(1)+(2)+(5)+(6)+(8)	+part of(9)&(12)	(10)+(11)
TOTAL		.620	1.461	.866	2.143	3.353	2.042	1.334	.000	2.376	.263	2.578	11.116	2.107	7.984	15.487	2.861
WORK	6.080	.316	.215	.213	.497	.350	.103	.473	.000	.000	.150	1.623	1.587	.534	.999	1.413	1.781

POPULATION, DEATHS, DEATH RATES FOR ALL CAUSES COMBINED, AND SPECIFIED CAUSES

Age Start of Interval	Midyear Popula- tion	Deaths During Year	All Causes	Respira- tory T. B.	Other Infec. and Paras.	Neo- plasms	Cardio- vascular	Infl., Pneu., Bronch.	Diar- rheal	Certain Degen- erative	Maternal	Cert. Dis. of Infancy	Motor Vehicle	Other Violence	Other and Unknown	Age Start of Interval
0	661856	53412	.08070	.00011	.00531	.00007	.00009	.02068	.01574	.00012	.00000	.03274	.00001	.00067	.00516	0
1	2703582	33425	.01236	.00007	.00262	.00004	.00006	.00289	.00258	.00005	.00000	.00000	.00003	.00036	.00367	1
5	3092674	6795	.00220	.00002	.00047	.00003	.00004	.00034	.00021	.00002	.00000	.00000	.00002	.00017	.00088	5
10	2516056	2722	.00108	.00004	.00017	.00003	.00006	.00012	.00007	.00001	.00000	.00000	.00001	.00011	.00045	10
15	2127968	3212	.00151	.00007	.00011	.00005	.00012	.00013	.00005	.00003	.00017	.00000	.00001	.00015	.00061	15
20	1827124	4413	.00242	.00017	.00015	.00006	.00020	.00019	.00007	.00006	.00037	.00000	.00002	.00017	.00096	20
25	1550348	4413	.00285	.00022	.00019	.00009	.00027	.00023	.00008	.00008	.00039	.00000	.00001	.00016	.00113	25
30	1234462	4544	.00368	.00024	.00020	.00026	.00036	.00027	.00010	.00016	.00051	.00000	.00002	.00015	.00136	30
35	1139195	5431	.00477	.00028	.00023	.00050	.00053	.00036	.00011	.00027	.00057	.00000	.00003	.00022	.00167	35
40	814284	4520	.00555	.00029	.00022	.00074	.00072	.00039	.00015	.00043	.00032	.00000	.00004	.00021	.00205	40
45	738070	4563	.00618	.00030	.00021	.00107	.00082	.00049	.00017	.00060	.00008	.00000	.00003	.00021	.00221	45
50	635783	5462	.00859	.00028	.00031	.00143	.00139	.00058	.00025	.00101	.00001	.00000	.00003	.00026	.00305	50
55	467311	5790	.01239	.00042	.00043	.00208	.00216	.00088	.00034	.00142	.00000	.00000	.00009	.00032	.00424	55
60	441237	8835	.02002	.00058	.00061	.00275	.00350	.00160	.00063	.00220	.00000	.00000	.00008	.00040	.00768	60
65	248657	7109	.02858	.00055	.00073	.00360	.00560	.00253	.00107	.00287	.00000	.00000	.00011	.00044	.01108	65
70	203571	8789	.04317	.00064	.00097	.00438	.00865	.00414	.00165	.00350	.00000	.00000	.00015	.00057	.01852	70
75	114321	7502	.06562	.00068	.00146	.00617	.01349	.00586	.00276	.00523	.00000	.00000	.00015	.00108	.02874	75
80	83233	8030	.09648	.00074	.00171	.00620	.01931	.00982	.00342	.00572	.00000	.00000	.00005	.00117	.04835	80
85+	81228	13265	.16331	.00069	.00183	.00569	.02573	.01918	.00582	.00581	.00000	.00000	.00010	.00214	.09631	85+
ALL	20681000	192232														

CRUDE DEATH RATE			.00930	.00016	.00075	.00046	.00075	.00151	.00103	.00035	.00016	.00105	.00003	.00024	.00280	
STANDARDIZED RATE (1)			.00920	.00018	.00074	.00050	.00073	.00150	.00104	.00036	.00017	.00115	.00003	.00024	.00257	
STANDARDIZED RATE (2)			.01152	.00023	.00063	.00090	.00149	.00145	.00085	.00069	.00017	.00068	.00004	.00027	.00412	
GEOMETRIC MEAN			.01079													

LIFE TABLE FOR ALL CAUSES COMBINED

Age (x)	Midyear Popula- tion	Deaths During Year	$_nM_x$	$_nq_x$	l_x	$_nd_x$	$_nL_x$	$_nm_x$	$_na_x$	T_x	$_nr_x$	$\overset{\circ}{e}_x$	Age (x)
0	661856	53412	.080700	.075850	100000	7585	93987	.080703	.207191	6200367	.000000	62.004	0
1	2703582	33425	.012363	.047968	92415	4433	358578	.012363	1.500000	6106381	.000000	66.076	1
5	3092674	6795	.002197	.010957	87982	964	437500	.002203	2.500000	5747803	.000000	65.329	5
10	2516056	2722	.001082	.005367	87018	467	433858	.001076	2.361706	5310303	.028418	61.025	10
15	2127968	3212	.001509	.007556	86551	654	431238	.001517	2.680938	4876445	.030533	56.342	15
20	1827124	4413	.002415	.012049	85897	1035	427012	.002424	2.610507	4445207	.027965	51.750	20
25	1550348	4413	.002846	.014176	84862	1203	421406	.002855	2.585723	4018195	.036324	47.350	25
30	1234462	4544	.003681	.018289	83659	1530	414624	.003690	2.600490	3596789	.027745	42.993	30
35	1139195	5431	.004767	.023634	82129	1941	405932	.004782	2.571913	3182166	.033620	38.746	35
40	814284	4520	.005551	.027436	80188	2200	395531	.005562	2.541572	2776233	.041342	34.622	40
45	738070	4563	.006182	.030518	77988	2380	384158	.006195	2.587447	2380702	.019499	30.527	45
50	635783	5462	.008591	.042310	75608	3199	370458	.008635	2.629989	1996504	.036034	26.406	50
55	467311	5790	.012390	.060434	72409	4376	351802	.012439	2.659202	1626046	.023129	22.456	55
60	441237	8835	.020023	.096174	68033	6543	324621	.020156	2.624274	1274244	.037250	18.730	60
65	248657	7109	.028585	.134640	61490	8279	287569	.028790	2.598618	949623	.047378	15.444	65
70	203571	8789	.043174	.196613	53211	10462	240659	.043465	2.576407	662054	.038330	12.442	70
75	114321	7502	.065622	.283422	42749	12116	183761	.065933	2.525259	421355	.025627	9.856	75
80	83233	8030	.096476	.389482	30633	11931	123072	.096943	2.477789	237594	.025627	7.756	80
85+	81228	13265	.163306	1.000000	18702	18702	114521	.163306	6.123483	114521	.000000	6.123	85+

NUMBER OF PERSONS DYING (OUT OF 100,000 AT BIRTH) ABOVE AGE X FROM SPECIFIED CAUSES

Age (x)	All Causes	Respiratory T. B.	Other Infec. and Paras.	Neoplasms	Cardiovascular	Infl., Pneu., Bronch.	Diarrheal	Certain Degenerative	Maternal	Cert. Dis. of Infancy	Motor Vehicle	Other Violence	Other and Unknown	Age (x)
0	100000	1759	3854	7981	15256	11292	5546	6307	1005	3077	279	2045	41599	0
1	92415	1749	3354	7974	15247	9348	4066	6296	1005	0	278	1982	41116	1
5	87982	1725	2414	7958	15225	8311	3142	6279	1005	0	268	1855	39800	5
10	87018	1714	2209	7945	15208	8163	3050	6271	1005	0	258	1780	39415	10
15	86551	1697	2138	7932	15181	8110	3021	6265	1003	0	253	1731	39220	15
20	85897	1664	2089	7911	15128	8052	3001	6251	928	0	247	1668	38958	20
25	84862	1590	2026	7884	15042	7972	2973	6223	771	0	239	1597	38545	25
30	83659	1498	1947	7844	14930	7876	2940	6188	604	0	234	1531	38067	30
35	82129	1397	1866	7734	14780	7765	2897	6121	392	0	224	1450	37503	35
40	80188	1284	1771	7532	14563	7619	2852	6011	161	0	212	1362	36821	40
45	77988	1170	1685	7237	14279	7465	2792	5841	36	0	196	1279	36008	45
50	75608	1056	1605	6825	13962	7277	2724	5611	6	0	185	1199	35158	50
55	72409	951	1491	6291	13444	7063	2632	5236	3	0	173	1102	34023	55
60	68033	802	1339	5556	12681	6752	2512	4735	3	0	141	988	32524	60
65	61490	614	1140	4660	11537	6228	2307	4016	3	0	114	858	30013	65
70	53211	456	929	3621	9913	5493	1998	3187	3	0	82	730	26799	70
75	42749	301	693	2562	7818	4490	1558	2341	3	0	45	592	22306	75
80	30633	175	424	1425	5327	3408	1089	1376	3	0	18	392	16996	80
85+	18702	79	210	651	2947	2197	667	665	0	0	11	245	11030	85+

NUMBER OF PERSONS SURVIVING TO AGE X IF SPECIFIED CAUSES WERE ELIMINATED

Age (x)	No Causes	Respiratory T. B.	Other Infec. and Paras.	Neoplasms	Cardiovascular	Infl., Pneu., Bronch.	Diarrheal	Certain Degenerative	Maternal	Cert. Dis. of Infancy	Motor Vehicle	Other Violence	Other and Unknown	(1) + (2)	(1) + (2) + (5) + (6) + (8)	(1)+(2)+ (5)+(6)+ (8)+part of(9)&(12)	(10) + (11)	Age (x)
		(1)	(2)	(3)	(4)	(5)	(6)	(7)	(8)	(9)	(10)	(11)	(12)					
0	100000	100000	100000	100000	100000	100000	100000	100000	100000	100000	100000	100000	100000	100000	100000	100000	100000	0
1	92415	92425	92897	92422	92424	94302	93848	92426	92415	95420	92416	92476	92880	92906	96274	99822	92477	1
5	87982	88015	89367	88004	88012	90817	90267	88009	87982	90843	87993	88164	89725	89400	94678	99520	88174	5
10	87018	87061	88596	87053	87064	89974	89372	87052	87018	89848	87039	87273	89133	88639	94130	99287	87293	10
15	86551	86611	88192	86558	86624	89546	88922	86591	86553	89365	86576	86853	88854	88253	93810	99091	86879	15
20	85897	85989	87576	85965	86022	88929	88270	85951	85974	88690	85928	86260	88451	87670	93356	98791	86291	20
25	84862	85027	86584	84956	85071	87940	87235	84943	85094	87621	84901	85291	87809	86752	92666	98368	85330	25
30	83659	83913	85437	83792	83977	86752	86032	83774	84054	86379	83702	84148	87057	85696	91860	97869	84192	30
35	82129	82479	83956	82368	82591	85319	84503	82308	82728	84800	82181	82690	86048	84314	90778	97091	82743	35
40	80188	80642	82068	80622	80655	83453	82551	80472	81003	82795	80251	80823	84723	82533	89323	95937	80887	40
45	77988	78542	79903	78704	78919	81321	80348	78433	78905	78905	78065	78688	83251	80471	87466	94318	78766	45
50	75608	76259	77546	76712	76827	79033	77965	76267	76527	78067	75693	76366	81608	78213	85328	92333	76453	50
55	72409	73136	74379	73599	74094	75908	74759	73412	73292	74764	72503	73231	79363	75126	82303	89409	73326	55
60	68033	68862	70035	70258	70377	71637	70361	69469	69863	70245	68152	68917	76177	70889	78140	85349	69038	60
65	61490	62420	63495	64385	64744	65275	63796	63489	62240	63489	61623	62414	71576	64455	71853	79331	62549	65
70	53211	54164	55148	56735	57640	57217	55506	55741	53860	54941	53356	54131	65518	56136	63733	71477	54279	70
75	42749	43655	44524	46598	48382	46942	44568	45579	43270	44139	42899	43614	57830	45468	53159	61330	43767	75
80	30633	31390	32141	34447	37127	34653	32677	33537	31007	31629	30763	31425	47968	32936	40229	48438	31558	80
85+	18702	19241	19797	21715	25012	22243	20301	21086	18932	19310	18787	19303	37481	20367	26619	34738	19390	85+

ADDED YRS OF LIFE																		
TOTAL		.441	1.550	1.356	2.243	3.258	2.078	.991	.419	2.010	.069	.565	10.211	2.007	8.246	15.459	.636	
WORK	4.630	.232	.207	.438	.512	.322	.117	.281	.349	.000	.026	.202	1.624	.441	1.246	2.022	.229	

POPULATION, DEATHS, DEATH RATES FOR ALL CAUSES COMBINED, AND SPECIFIED CAUSES

Age Start of Interval	Midyear Population	Deaths During Year	All Causes	Respiratory T. B.	Other Infec. and Paras.	Neoplasms	Cardiovascular	Infl., Pneu., Bronch.	Diarrheal	Certain Degenerative	Maternal	Cert. Dis. of Infancy	Motor Vehicle	Other Violence	Other and Unknown	Age Start of Interval
0	90314	5142	.05693	.00028	.00333	.00007	.00008	.01119	.00401	.00006	.00000	.02050	.00000	.00079	.01664	0
1	340618	1824	.00535	.00014	.00141	.00009	.00004	.00172	.00016	.00001	.00000	.00000	.00009	.00058	.00110	1
5	431060	687	.00159	.00005	.00045	.00009	.00004	.00019	.00002	.00003	.00000	.00000	.00013	.00027	.00033	5
10	388165	446	.00115	.00004	.00025	.00007	.00006	.00010	.00001	.00003	.00000	.00000	.00007	.00013	.00038	10
15	377822	702	.00186	.00041	.00033	.00010	.00007	.00017	.00001	.00006	.00000	.00000	.00007	.00032	.00033	15
20	354004	883	.00249	.00080	.00033	.00010	.00011	.00023	.00001	.00008	.00000	.00000	.00013	.00034	.00036	20
25	323421	761	.00235	.00082	.00022	.00019	.00011	.00016	.00001	.00015	.00000	.00000	.00030	.00030	.00030	25
30	285656	787	.00275	.00067	.00028	.00021	.00021	.00027	.00002	.00022	.00000	.00000	.00009	.00037	.00042	30
35	254983	773	.00303	.00052	.00032	.00036	.00026	.00038	.00002	.00028	.00000	.00000	.00006	.00030	.00054	35
40	226185	913	.00404	.00059	.00021	.00055	.00041	.00049	.00002	.00036	.00000	.00000	.00010	.00039	.00078	40
45	204613	1184	.00579	.00056	.00054	.00104	.00083	.00065	.00001	.00065	.00000	.00000	.00011	.00049	.00091	45
50	185416	1631	.00880	.00057	.00058	.00194	.00170	.00099	.00003	.00090	.00000	.00000	.00009	.00065	.00135	50
55	156217	2130	.01363	.00072	.00063	.00333	.00328	.00134	.00002	.00131	.00000	.00000	.00010	.00077	.00213	55
60	126770	2931	.02312	.00058	.00074	.00547	.00658	.00254	.00007	.00206	.00000	.00000	.00018	.00088	.00361	60
65	100748	4227	.04196	.00101	.00079	.00908	.01346	.00558	.00011	.00260	.00000	.00000	.00016	.00058	.00778	65
70	66372	4106	.06186	.00101	.00078	.01252	.02156	.00904	.00017	.00358	.00000	.00000	.00018	.00111	.01151	70
75	41292	3740	.09057	.00094	.00092	.01514	.03371	.01431	.00031	.00596	.00000	.00000	.00022	.00148	.01758	75
80	19671	3255	.16547	.00056	.00071	.01637	.05338	.03365	.00051	.00554	.00000	.00000	.00031	.00264	.05180	80
85+	8535	2409	.28225	.00035	.00094	.01711	.08049	.06104	.00082	.00773	.00000	.00000	.00035	.00480	.10861	85+
ALL	3981902	38531														

CRUDE DEATH RATE			.00968	.00049	.00056	.00129	.00204	.00151	.00013	.00052	.00000	.00046	.00010	.00046	.00211	
STANDARDIZED RATE (1)			.00819	.00044	.00061	.00090	.00131	.00133	.00018	.00037	.00000	.00072	.00010	.00043	.00181	
STANDARDIZED RATE (2)			.01293	.00052	.00057	.00182	.00317	.00206	.00013	.00070	.00000	.00042	.00011	.00051	.00292	
GEOMETRIC MEAN			.01072													

LIFE TABLE FOR ALL CAUSES COMBINED

Age (x)	Midyear Population	Deaths During Year	$_nM_x$	$_na_x$	l_x	$_nd_x$	$_nL_x$	$_nm_x$	$_na_x$	T_x	$_nr_x$	$\overset{\circ}{e}_x$	Age (x)
0	90314	5142	.056935	.054360	100000	5436	95471	.056939	.166789	6368777	.000000	63.688	0
1	340618	1824	.005355	.021129	94564	1998	373261	.005353	1.500000	6273306	.000000	66.339	1
5	431060	687	.001594	.007940	92566	735	460993	.001594	2.500000	5900045	.000000	63.739	5
10	388165	446	.001149	.005728	91831	526	457863	.001149	2.543964	5439052	.009984	59.229	10
15	377822	702	.001858	.009266	91305	846	454534	.001861	2.646769	4981189	.007162	54.555	15
20	354004	883	.002494	.012403	90459	1122	449531	.002496	2.536950	4526655	.010881	50.041	20
25	323421	761	.002353	.011697	89337	1045	444091	.002353	2.517344	4077124	.016673	45.638	25
30	285656	787	.002755	.013693	88292	1209	438493	.002757	2.546009	3633033	.020155	41.148	30
35	254983	773	.003032	.015066	87083	1312	432241	.003035	2.581142	3194540	.020398	36.684	35
40	226185	913	.004037	.020053	85771	1720	424783	.004049	2.632389	2762298	.019253	32.206	40
45	204613	1184	.005787	.028614	84051	2405	414619	.005801	2.656618	2337516	.014690	27.811	45
50	185416	1631	.008796	.043211	81646	2528	399589	.008820	2.664163	1922897	.015941	23.552	50
55	156217	2130	.013635	.066374	78118	5185	378567	.013696	2.681172	1522907	.022775	19.495	55
60	126770	2931	.023121	.110157	72933	8037	346080	.023223	2.687570	1144341	.019299	15.690	60
65	100748	4227	.041956	.191399	64896	12421	294697	.042148	2.602213	798261	.021490	12.301	65
70	66372	4106	.061863	.269250	52475	14131	227420	.062136	2.526360	503563	.025435	9.596	70
75	41292	3740	.090574	.370566	38344	14209	156184	.090976	2.499047	276143	.023499	7.202	75
80	19671	3255	.165472	.582805	24135	14066	84285	.166885	2.412940	119960	.023499	4.970	80
85+	8535	2409	.282250	1.000000	10069	10069	35674	.282250	3.542964	35674	.000000	3.543	85+

NUMBER OF PERSONS DYING (OUT OF 100,000 AT BIRTH) ABOVE AGE X FROM SPECIFIED CAUSES

Age (x)	All Causes	Respiratory T. B.	Other Infec. and Paras.	Neoplasms	Cardiovascular	Infl., Pneu., Bronch.	Diarrheal	Certain Degenerative	Maternal	Cert. Dis. of Infancy	Motor Vehicle	Other Violence	Other and Unknown	Age (x)
0	100000	3619	3564	15090	26747	15767	728	5738	0	1957	708	3604	22478	0
1	94564	3592	3246	15083	26740	14698	345	5732	0	0	708	3529	20891	1
5	92566	3539	2720	15049	26727	14055	286	5727	0	0	673	3311	20479	5
10	91831	3516	2511	15009	26707	13968	279	5714	0	0	613	3188	20326	10
15	91305	3496	2397	14977	26679	13922	273	5700	0	0	581	3126	20154	15
20	90459	3308	2245	14933	26648	13845	270	5675	0	0	551	2982	20002	20
25	89337	2946	2098	14886	26597	13740	266	5639	0	0	494	2831	19840	25
30	88292	2581	1999	14801	26549	13668	261	5571	0	0	459	2697	19706	30
35	87083	2287	1878	14707	26456	13551	253	5476	0	0	417	2535	19523	35
40	85771	2064	1740	14551	26344	13386	246	5355	0	0	390	2406	19289	40
45	84051	1814	1609	14300	26168	13178	239	5201	0	0	347	2240	18955	45
50	81646	1583	1383	13868	25824	12907	235	4931	0	0	300	2035	18580	50
55	78118	1354	1152	13091	25140	12512	224	4572	0	0	263	1774	18036	55
60	72933	1082	912	11825	23888	12000	217	4075	0	0	225	1483	17226	60
65	64896	743	655	9923	21599	11116	192	3361	0	0	162	1177	15968	65
70	52475	444	421	7236	17611	9345	160	2592	0	0	115	887	13664	70
75	38344	215	243	4379	12683	7279	122	1683	0	0	74	632	11034	75
80	24135	68	99	2012	7396	5031	72	751	0	0	40	401	8265	80
85+	10069	13	33	610	2871	2178	29	276	0	0	13	171	3875	85+

NUMBER OF PERSONS SURVIVING TO AGE X IF SPECIFIED CAUSES WERE ELIMINATED

Age (x)	No Causes	Respiratory T. B.	Other Infec. and Paras.	Neoplasms	Cardiovascular	Infl., Pneu., Bronch	Diarrheal	Certain Degenerative	Maternal	Cert. Dis. of Infancy	Motor Vehicle	Other Violence	Other and Unknown	(1) + (2)	(1) + (2) + (5) + (6) + (8)	(1)+(2)+ (5)+(6)+ (8)+part of(9)&(12)	(10) + (11)	Age (x)
	(1)	(2)	(3)	(4)	(5)	(6)	(7)	(8)	(9)	(10)	(11)	(12)						
0	100000	100000	100000	100000	100000	100000	100000	100000	100000	100000	100000	100000	100000	100000	100000	100000	100000	0
1	94564	94590	94874	94571	94571	95609	94937	94570	94564	96486	94637	94637	96120	94900	96327	99720	94637	1
5	92566	92644	93393	92606	92586	94234	92990	92577	92566	94447	92601	92854	94504	93472	95592	99311	92888	5
10	91831	91931	92861	91911	91870	93574	92259	91855	91831	93698	91925	92239	93909	92963	95169	98963	92334	10
15	91305	91425	92445	91416	91372	93085	91736	91342	91305	93161	91431	91773	93547	92556	94816	98694	91899	15
20	90459	90756	91741	90613	90556	92301	90889	90521	90459	92298	90613	91067	92835	92052	94373	98332	91222	20
25	89337	90001	90752	89536	89484	91263	89766	89434	89337	91153	89546	90088	91849	91426	93845	97896	90299	25
30	88292	89315	89790	88573	88485	90268	88721	88456	88292	90087	88534	89169	90912	90830	93314	97429	89413	30
35	87083	88388	88683	87454	87366	89151	87514	87339	87083	88853	87363	88111	89654	90011	92605	96795	88394	35
40	85771	87281	87466	86292	86161	87796	86202	86144	85771	87514	86074	86913	88741	89026	91774	96054	87220	40
45	84051	85783	85664	84812	84609	86423	84481	84569	84051	85759	84390	85337	87304	87633	90567	94952	85681	45
50	81646	83560	83635	82817	82530	84225	82067	82418	81646	83306	82022	83100	85190	85596	88756	93205	83483	50
55	78118	80179	80253	80013	79644	80985	78532	79212	78118	79764	78514	79976	82066	82370	85846	90327	80174	55
60	72933	75127	75164	75966	75602	76124	73326	74442	72933	74415	73340	74762	77446	77425	81249	85707	75179	60
65	64896	67177	67130	69466	65548	68613	65270	66928	64896	66215	65318	66818	70184	69490	73893	78264	67252	65
70	52475	54596	54498	58825	60212	57189	52806	54832	52475	53542	52858	54296	59033	56700	62184	66465	54693	70
75	38344	40095	39978	45790	49092	43752	38619	40884	38344	39123	38659	39899	45731	41804	48041	52007	40227	75
80	24135	25356	25280	31106	36701	29640	24347	26521	24135	24626	24360	25303	31524	26559	32904	36369	25538	80
85+	10069	10614	10590	14159	20284	14765	10185	11396	10069	10274	10180	10708	17277	11164	16559	19927	10826	85+

ADDED YRS OF LIFE

TOTAL	4.187	1.056	1.329	1.993	3.060	2.743	.331	.808	.000	1.291	.223	.963	3.942	2.416	5.707	9.524	1.191	
WORK		.701	.376	.524	.453	.398	.014	.301	.000	.000	.100	.411	.623	1.085	1.513	1.807	.512	

POPULATION, DEATHS, DEATH RATES FOR ALL CAUSES COMBINED, AND SPECIFIED CAUSES

Age Start of Interval	Midyear Population	Deaths During Year	All Causes	Respiratory T. B.	Other Infec. and Paras.	Neoplasms	Cardiovascular	Infl., Pneu., Bronch.	Diarrheal	Certain Degenerative	Maternal	Cert. Dis. of Infancy	Motor Vehicle	Other Violence	Other and Unknown	Age Start of Interval
0	85591	3655	.04270	.00027	.00338	.00007	.00005	.00876	.00291	.00006	.00000	.01363	.00000	.00056	.01302	0
1	327409	1524	.00465	.00009	.00148	.00009	.00003	.00141	.00012	.00003	.00000	.00000	.00005	.00033	.00103	1
5	416125	537	.00129	.00003	.00049	.00004	.00006	.00014	.00002	.00004	.00000	.00000	.00005	.00006	.00036	5
10	375415	400	.00107	.00015	.00031	.00005	.00009	.00011	.00000	.00007	.00000	.00000	.00002	.00003	.00022	10
15	373313	686	.00184	.00081	.00030	.00006	.00012	.00011	.00001	.00008	.00002	.00000	.00002	.00007	.00025	15
20	361994	758	.00209	.00097	.00025	.00006	.00008	.00015	.00001	.00007	.00015	.00000	.00002	.00009	.00023	20
25	334339	842	.00252	.00090	.00021	.00016	.00016	.00019	.00002	.00012	.00032	.00000	.00001	.00012	.00032	25
30	297221	882	.00297	.00079	.00021	.00027	.00018	.00030	.00001	.00014	.00048	.00000	.00002	.00010	.00046	30
35	265676	944	.00355	.00061	.00023	.00056	.00030	.00035	.00001	.00018	.00056	.00000	.00001	.00011	.00063	35
40	233718	1040	.00445	.00062	.00018	.00094	.00046	.00050	.00003	.00039	.00042	.00000	.00001	.00018	.00073	40
45	210926	1273	.00604	.00061	.00027	.00181	.00089	.00056	.00003	.00061	.00004	.00000	.00001	.00015	.00105	45
50	191606	1755	.00916	.00046	.00035	.00281	.00194	.00081	.00003	.00102	.00000	.00000	.00001	.00024	.00149	50
55	162570	2159	.01328	.00057	.00041	.00394	.00339	.00119	.00005	.00165	.00000	.00000	.00000	.00023	.00185	55
60	132848	2906	.02187	.00063	.00045	.00595	.00644	.00224	.00005	.00270	.00000	.00000	.00001	.00032	.00309	60
65	107216	4228	.03943	.00079	.00053	.00768	.01410	.00581	.00015	.00362	.00000	.00000	.00003	.00053	.00619	65
70	71509	4209	.05886	.00080	.00053	.01060	.02260	.00878	.00024	.00552	.00000	.00000	.00003	.00060	.00916	70
75	46622	4054	.08695	.00075	.00062	.01283	.03533	.01390	.00043	.00830	.00000	.00000	.00002	.00079	.01398	75
80+	23242	3639	.15657	.00056	.00060	.01407	.05404	.03167	.00060	.00558	.00000	.00000	.00009	.00185	.04711	80
85+	11354	3026	.26651	.00035	.00079	.01480	.08147	.05734	.00114	.00828	.00000	.00000	.00009	.00335	.09891	85+
ALL	4028694	38517														

CRUDE DEATH RATE			.00956	.00055	.00048	.00140	.00232	.00144	.00011	.00067	.00014	.00029	.00002	.00019	.00195	
STANDARDIZED RATE (1)			.00745	.00050	.00056	.00094	.00137	.00116	.00014	.00045	.00013	.00048	.00002	.00017	.00154	
STANDARDIZED RATE (2)			.01217	.00055	.00048	.00180	.00328	.00189	.00011	.00067	.00013	.00028	.00002	.00022	.00253	
GEOMETRIC MEAN			.01030													

LIFE TABLE FOR ALL CAUSES COMBINED

Age (x)	Midyear Population	Deaths During Year	$_nM_x$	$_nq_x$	l_x	$_nd_x$	$_nL_x$	$_nm_x$	$_na_x$	T_x	$_nr_x$	$\overset{\circ}{e}_x$	Age (x)
0	85591	3655	.042703	.041190	100000	4119	96468	.042698	.142555	6501483	.000000	65.015	0
1	327409	1524	.004655	.018408	95881	1765	379112	.004656	1.500000	6405014	.000000	66.802	1
5	416125	537	.001290	.006428	94116	605	469068	.001290	2.500000	6025903	.000000	64.026	5
10	375415	400	.001065	.005315	93511	497	466364	.001066	2.603119	5556835	.008903	59.424	10
15	373313	686	.001838	.009149	93014	851	463039	.001838	2.613592	5090471	.002647	54.728	15
20	361994	758	.002094	.010427	92163	961	458473	.002096	2.563059	4627432	.006045	50.209	20
25	334339	842	.002518	.012522	91202	1142	453232	.002520	2.567134	4168959	.014116	45.711	25
30	297221	882	.002967	.014757	90060	1329	447066	.002973	2.566309	3715727	.018524	41.258	30
35	265676	944	.003553	.017638	88731	1565	439846	.003558	2.579207	3268662	.020110	36.838	35
40	233718	1040	.004450	.022073	87166	1924	431223	.004462	2.605683	2828795	.019840	32.453	40
45	210926	1273	.006035	.029809	85242	2541	420231	.006047	2.647006	2397572	.014721	28.127	45
50	191606	1755	.009159	.044945	82701	3717	404747	.009184	2.643765	1977341	.015055	23.910	50
55	162570	2159	.013280	.064646	78984	5106	382989	.013332	2.663329	1572594	.021791	19.910	55
60	132848	2906	.021875	.104497	73878	7720	351520	.021962	2.685233	1189605	.018209	16.102	60
65	107216	4228	.039434	.180930	66158	11970	302169	.039614	2.608918	838085	.021249	12.668	65
70	71509	4209	.058860	.257954	54188	13978	236504	.059103	2.536382	535916	.023500	9.890	70
75	46622	4054	.086955	.358393	40210	14411	165122	.087275	2.506939	299413	.019211	7.446	75
80	23242	3639	.156570	.560409	25799	14458	91737	.157602	2.423039	134290	.019211	5.205	80
85+	11354	3026	.266514	1.000000	11341	11341	42553	.266514	3.752148	42553	.000000	3.752	85+

NUMBER OF PERSONS DYING (OUT OF 100,000 AT BIRTH) ABOVE AGE X FROM SPECIFIED CAUSES

Age (x)	All Causes	Respiratory T. B.	Other Infec. and Paras.	Neo-plasms	Cardio-vascular	Infl., Pneu., Bronch.	Diar-rheal	Certain Degen-erative	Maternal	Cert. Dis. of Infancy	Motor Vehicle	Other Violence	Other and Unknown	Age (x)
0	100000	3770	2939	15405	29357	15539	710	7452	885	1315	139	1625	20864	0
1	95881	3744	2613	15398	29353	14694	430	7447	885	0	139	1571	19607	1
5	94116	3710	2053	15364	29341	14158	386	7436	885	0	119	1445	19219	5
10	93511	3695	1822	15344	29313	14094	377	7416	885	0	95	1418	19052	10
15	93014	3622	1677	15322	29272	14041	375	7384	885	0	85	1402	18949	15
20	92163	3249	1539	15294	29215	13990	370	7346	877	0	78	1370	18835	20
25	91202	2804	1424	15265	29178	13922	365	7312	807	0	70	1328	18727	25
30	90060	2395	1328	15190	29107	13837	357	7257	663	0	68	1275	18583	30
35	88731	2041	1234	15069	29026	13703	351	7195	446	0	59	1231	18376	35
40	87166	1774	1132	14822	28895	13547	348	7117	197	0	54	1183	18097	40
45	85242	1507	1052	14414	28696	13333	337	6948	19	0	48	1108	17780	45
50	82701	1252	941	13650	28320	13095	325	6690	2	0	42	1046	17338	50
55	78984	1066	799	12511	27533	12765	312	6277	2	0	38	948	16733	55
60	73878	849	641	10998	26228	12308	293	5643	2	0	33	861	16022	60
65	66158	627	482	8903	23950	11514	277	4690	2	0	30	750	14933	65
70	54188	387	321	6577	19666	9749	232	3593	2	0	22	589	13050	70
75	40210	198	195	4063	14296	7662	175	2281	2	0	15	446	10877	75
80	25799	74	93	1942	8443	5356	104	908	2	0	12	314	8551	80
85+	11341	15	34	630	3467	2440	49	352	0	0	4	142	4208	85+

NUMBER OF PERSONS SURVIVING TO AGE X IF SPECIFIED CAUSES WERE ELIMINATED

Age (x)	No Causes	Respiratory T. B.	Other Infec. and Paras.	Neo-plasms	Cardio-vascular	Infl., Pneu., Bronch.	Diar-rheal	Certain Degener-ative	Maternal	Cert. Dis. of Infancy	Motor Vehicle	Other Violence	Other and Unknown	(1) + (2)	(1) + (2) + (5) + (6) + (8)	(1)+(2)+ (5)+(6)+ (8)+part of(9)&(12)	(10) + (11)	Age (x)
		(1)	(2)	(3)	(4)	(5)	(6)	(7)	(8)	(9)	(10)	(11)	(12)					
0	100000	100000	100000	100000	100000	100000	100000	100000	100000	100000	100000	100000	100000	100000	100000	100000	100000	0
1	95881	95906	96201	95888	95885	96712	96156	95886	95881	97177	95881	95934	97120	96226	97338	99810	95934	1
5	94116	94175	94988	94156	94132	95469	94429	94132	94116	95388	94136	94293	95722	95047	96734	99537	94313	5
10	93511	93584	94610	93571	93555	94920	93831	93547	93511	94775	93555	93714	95276	94684	96440	99363	93757	10
15	93014	93160	94254	93096	93098	94469	93335	93081	93014	94271	93067	93232	94875	94402	96209	99200	93285	15
20	92163	92680	93531	92272	92303	93656	92466	92268	92171	93409	92223	92411	94122	94056	95922	99000	92471	20
25	91202	92160	92672	91339	91378	92748	91526	91339	91280	92435	91269	91489	93251	93645	95663	98818	91556	25
30	90060	91417	91608	90270	90304	91673	90388	90250	90280	91278	90128	90396	92229	92989	95231	98499	90465	30
35	88731	90426	90351	89058	89052	90456	89060	88980	89164	89931	88807	89106	91079	92077	94675	98086	89183	35
40	87166	89101	88861	87734	87612	89018	87452	87488	87840	88344	87246	87582	89757	90833	93830	97397	87662	40
45	85242	87404	86980	86204	85676	87270	85572	85725	86078	86394	85326	85724	88099	89186	92560	96244	85808	45
50	82701	85056	84499	84399	83691	84908	83033	83426	83529	83819	82788	83230	85924	86905	90480	94230	83318	50
55	78984	81420	80843	81750	80712	81424	79314	80085	79775	80052	79071	79585	82679	83336	87133	90891	79673	55
60	73878	76373	75773	77994	76796	76617	74205	75532	74617	74877	73965	74525	78056	78332	82413	86122	74612	60
65	66158	68609	68009	71962	71052	69397	66466	68565	66820	67052	66238	66843	70557	70528	75069	78668	66924	65
70	54188	56420	55853	61265	62512	58541	54481	57194	54730	54921	54261	54896	60007	58153	63797	67317	54970	70
75	40210	42033	41556	47959	52027	45420	40477	43646	40612	40754	40270	40859	46642	43440	49889	53153	40920	75
80	25799	27070	26745	32825	39961	31294	26027	29203	26057	26148	25840	26322	32173	28063	34685	37543	26364	80
85+	11341	11940	11797	15547	23310	16237	11477	13249	11456	11494	11364	11685	18104	12419	18176	21215	11709	85+

ADDED YRS OF LIFE																		
TOTAL		1.240	1.240	2.249	3.512	2.513	.267	1.010	.331	.877	.055	.384	3.557	2.511	5.859	9.025	.439	
WORK	4.282	.854	.277	.696	.488	.351	.018	.297	.266	.000	.015	.128	.598	1.137	1.798	2.114	.143	

POPULATION, DEATHS, DEATH RATES FOR ALL CAUSES COMBINED, AND SPECIFIED CAUSES

Age Start of Interval	Midyear Popula-tion	Deaths During Year	All Causes	Respira-tory T. B.	Other Infec. and Paras.	Neo-plasms	Cardio-vascular	Infl., Pneu., Bronch.	Diar-rheal	Certain Degen-erative	Maternal	Cert. Dis. of Infancy	Motor Vehicle	Other Violence	Other and Unknown	Age Start of Interval
0	90778	4168	.04591	.00012	.00240	.00014	.00003	.00809	.00207	.00006	.00000	.01818	.00000	.00077	.01406	0
1	340188	1261	.00371	.00005	.00071	.00014	.00003	.00095	.00014	.00005	.00000	.00000	.00009	.00065	.00090	1
5	420360	599	.00142	.00002	.00024	.00006	.00006	.00011	.00003	.00004	.00000	.00000	.00014	.00036	.00036	5
10	416152	423	.00102	.00002	.00015	.00007	.00005	.00006	.00001	.00004	.00000	.00000	.00006	.00033	.00023	10
15	424180	850	.00200	.00025	.00021	.00012	.00008	.00012	.00001	.00005	.00000	.00000	.00005	.00083	.00029	15
20	369510	1647	.00446	.00050	.00017	.00015	.00007	.00010	.00001	.00006	.00000	.00000	.00008	.00298	.00034	20
25	361549	1399	.00387	.00040	.00019	.00016	.00012	.00012	.00000	.00012	.00000	.00000	.00013	.00224	.00038	25
30	338556	1315	.00388	.00040	.00016	.00022	.00017	.00018	.00002	.00021	.00000	.00000	.00008	.00198	.00047	30
35	307576	1121	.00364	.00035	.00017	.00032	.00025	.00020	.00001	.00029	.00000	.00000	.00010	.00146	.00049	35
40	272313	1249	.00459	.00036	.00029	.00060	.00054	.00027	.00001	.00041	.00000	.00000	.00010	.00126	.00076	40
45	239426	1526	.00637	.00043	.00036	.00107	.00081	.00046	.00004	.00064	.00000	.00000	.00010	.00146	.00101	45
50	210801	1991	.00944	.00039	.00043	.00198	.00187	.00067	.00002	.00095	.00000	.00000	.00014	.00150	.00148	50
55	183956	2647	.01439	.00041	.00049	.00344	.00363	.00092	.00003	.00142	.00000	.00000	.00021	.00152	.00232	55
60	159077	3689	.02319	.00068	.00064	.00562	.00739	.00157	.00004	.00189	.00000	.00000	.00015	.00155	.00368	60
65	122100	4586	.03756	.00057	.00076	.00872	.01337	.00340	.00011	.00253	.00000	.00000	.00016	.00176	.00618	65
70	86232	5359	.06215	.00068	.00066	.01281	.02481	.00626	.00016	.00356	.00000	.00000	.00023	.00182	.01114	70
75	53714	5515	.10267	.00047	.00056	.01709	.04366	.01115	.00028	.00519	.00000	.00000	.00028	.00277	.02122	75
80	24090	4148	.17219	.00025	.00058	.01864	.06737	.02113	.00058	.00527	.00000	.00000	.00021	.00357	.05459	80
85+	10231	2965	.28981	.00020	.00088	.01955	.10146	.03831	.00098	.00733	.00000	.00000	.00000	.00645	.11446	85+
ALL	4430789	46458														

	All Causes	Respira-tory T. B.	Other Infec. and Paras.	Neo-plasms	Cardio-vascular	Infl., Pneu., Bronch.	Diar-rheal	Certain Degen-erative	Maternal	Cert. Dis. of Infancy	Motor Vehicle	Other Violence	Other and Unknown
CRUDE DEATH RATE	.01049	.00031	.00036	.00148	.00263	.00103	.00008	.00055	.00000	.00037	.00011	.00139	.00217
STANDARDIZED RATE (1)	.00811	.00026	.00038	.00093	.00149	.00087	.00011	.00036	.00000	.00064	.00010	.00126	.00170
STANDARDIZED RATE (2)	.01325	.00031	.00038	.00190	.00372	.00135	.00009	.00067	.00000	.00038	.00011	.00126	.00291
GEOMETRIC MEAN	.01148												

LIFE TABLE FOR ALL CAUSES COMBINED

Age (x)	Midyear Popula-tion	Deaths During Year	$_nM_x$	$_nq_x$	l_x	$_nd_x$	$_nL_x$	$_nm_x$	$_na_x$	T_x	$_nr_x$	$\overset{\circ}{e}_x$	Age (x)
0	90778	4168	.045914	.044190	100000	4419	96235	.045919	.148054	6357986	.000000	63.580	0
1	340188	1261	.003707	.014689	95581	1404	378814	.003706	1.500000	6261751	.000000	65.513	1
5	420360	599	.001425	.007104	94177	669	469213	.001426	2.500000	5882937	.000000	62.467	5
10	416152	423	.001016	.005058	93508	473	466412	.001014	2.614958	5413724	-.003598	57.896	10
15	424180	850	.002004	.009996	93035	930	463175	.002008	2.849686	4947312	.005606	53.177	15
20	369510	1647	.004457	.022083	92105	2034	455606	.004464	2.581428	4484137	.012276	48.685	20
25	361549	1399	.003869	.019152	90071	1725	445973	.003868	2.459541	4028531	.005277	44.726	25
30	338556	1315	.003884	.019231	88346	1699	437449	.003884	2.480503	3582559	.009836	40.551	30
35	307576	1121	.003645	.018073	86647	1566	429369	.003647	2.531263	3145109	.015539	36.298	35
40	272313	1249	.004587	.022731	85081	1934	420789	.004596	2.613323	2715740	.019397	31.919	40
45	239426	1526	.006374	.031486	83147	2618	409565	.006392	2.643080	2294951	.019363	27.601	45
50	210801	1991	.009445	.046344	80529	3732	393886	.009475	2.652956	1885387	.017973	23.413	50
55	183956	2647	.014389	.069768	76797	5358	371454	.014424	2.661169	1491501	.013801	19.421	55
60	159077	3689	.023190	.110262	71439	7877	338678	.023258	2.649248	1120047	.015083	15.678	60
65	122100	4586	.037559	.173015	63562	11001	291632	.037722	2.620425	781369	.021276	12.293	65
70	86232	5359	.062146	.270847	52561	14236	228195	.062385	2.568825	489737	.017754	9.317	70
75	53714	5515	.102673	.409959	38325	15704	152205	.103176	2.489838	261542	.019911	6.824	75
80	24090	4148	.172188	.595464	22621	13470	77760	.173225	2.376036	109337	.019911	4.833	80
85+	10231	2965	.289805	1.000000	9151	9151	31576	.289805	3.450550	31576	.000000	3.451	85+

NUMBER OF PERSONS DYING (OUT OF 100,000 AT BIRTH) ABOVE AGE X FROM SPECIFIED CAUSES

Age (x)	All Causes	Respira-tory T.B.	Other Infec. and Paras.	Neo-plasms	Cardio-vascular	Infl., Pneu., Bronch.	Diar-rheal	Certain Degen-erative	Maternal	Cert. Dis. of Infancy	Motor Vehicle	Other Violence	Other and Unknown	Age (x)
0	100000	2192	2452	15407	30272	9978	533	5361	0	1749	747	9542	21767	0
1	95581	2180	2221	15393	30269	9199	334	5355	0	0	747	9468	20415	1
5	94177	2160	1953	15341	30259	8839	282	5335	0	0	713	9221	20074	5
10	93508	2150	1841	15313	30231	8788	266	5317	0	0	646	9050	19906	10
15	93035	2140	1772	15281	30209	8759	259	5300	0	0	618	8896	19801	15
20	92105	2026	1677	15223	30174	8702	256	5279	0	0	594	8508	19666	20
25	90071	1798	1599	15154	30144	8657	251	5249	0	0	558	7149	19512	25
30	88346	1619	1515	15081	30088	8605	250	5195	0	0	499	6152	19342	30
35	86647	1442	1447	14983	30016	8527	242	5104	0	0	464	5287	19135	35
40	85081	1290	1373	14844	29906	8442	238	4979	0	0	422	4661	18926	40
45	83147	1137	1252	14589	29680	8329	233	4804	0	0	388	4130	18605	45
50	80529	962	1106	14149	29344	8140	218	4540	0	0	349	3531	18190	50
55	76797	807	936	13365	28604	7874	210	4163	0	0	295	2938	17605	55
60	71439	654	752	12085	27252	7530	200	3635	0	0	218	2373	16740	60
65	63562	423	534	10176	24740	6997	187	2996	0	0	167	1849	15493	65
70	52561	256	312	7623	20822	6000	156	2255	0	0	119	1335	13683	70
75	38325	100	161	4691	15136	4565	119	1441	0	0	66	919	11127	75
80	22621	30	76	2083	8459	2858	76	648	0	0	23	495	7873	80
85+	9151	6	28	617	3204	1210	31	231	0	0	6	204	3614	85+

NUMBER OF PERSONS SURVIVING TO AGE X IF SPECIFIED CAUSES WERE ELIMINATED

Age (x)	No Causes	Respira-tory T.B. (1)	Other Infec. and Paras. (2)	Neo-plasms (3)	Cardio-vascular (4)	Infl., Pneu., Bronch. (5)	Diar-rheal (6)	Certain Degener-ative (7)	Maternal (8)	Cert. Dis. of Infancy (9)	Motor Vehicle (10)	Other Violence (11)	Other and Unknown (12)	(1)+(2)	(1)+(2)+(5)+(6)+(8)	(1)+(2)+(5)+(6)+(8)+part of(9)&(12)	(10)+(11)	Age (x)
0	100000	100000	100000	100000	100000	100000	100000	100000	100000	100000	100000	100000	100000	100000	100000	100000	100000	0
1	95581	95593	95807	95595	95584	96346	95776	95587	95581	97306	95581	95653	96512	95819	96782	99668	95653	1
5	94177	94208	94667	94242	94190	95251	94421	94203	94177	95877	94211	94494	95832	94698	96067	99166	94528	5
10	93508	93549	94107	93601	93549	94666	93766	93551	93508	95196	93608	93994	95322	94148	95576	98726	94095	10
15	93035	93086	93700	93159	93097	94216	93299	93095	93035	94714	93163	93673	94947	93751	95210	98383	93802	15
20	92105	92269	92858	92286	92202	93332	92369	92185	92105	93767	92255	93126	94135	93024	94533	97731	93278	20
25	90071	90457	90885	90316	90195	91316	90179	90345	90071	91854	90254	92439	92211	91275	92807	95977	92626	25
30	88346	88903	89229	88659	88523	89619	88605	88506	88346	89941	88584	91687	90618	89792	91353	94510	91934	30
35	86647	87370	87581	87051	86893	87974	86909	86894	86647	88211	86915	90817	89086	88312	89936	93093	91098	35
40	85081	85943	86072	85617	85432	86470	85342	85448	85081	86617	85386	89828	87689	86944	88635	91798	90150	40
45	83147	84142	84237	83925	83714	84618	83407	83479	83147	84648	83479	88342	86024	85245	87025	90214	88694	45
50	80529	81667	81730	81721	81412	82143	80796	81307	80529	81982	80889	86188	83739	82885	84827	88042	86573	50
55	76797	78036	78111	78715	78374	78602	77059	77911	76797	78183	77193	82815	80454	79371	81514	84723	83242	55
60	71439	72741	72842	74499	74251	73458	71693	72994	71439	72728	71882	77625	75720	74170	76537	79693	78107	60
65	63562	64942	65019	68188	68575	65878	63800	65562	63562	64709	64004	69603	68628	66431	69110	72160	70087	65
70	52561	53856	53971	58925	60684	55425	52786	54912	52561	53510	52970	58067	58554	55301	58564	61444	58519	70
75	38325	39404	39483	45840	50207	41722	38521	40766	38325	39017	38669	42729	45192	40595	44419	47009	43112	75
80	22621	23310	23369	29503	37078	26081	22769	24705	22621	23029	22856	25580	29781	24082	27947	30082	25846	80
85+	9151	9445	9484	13170	21350	11786	9239	10278	9151	9316	9257	10552	16039	9789	12729	14473	10674	85+

ADDED YRS OF LIFE

	No Causes	(1)	(2)	(3)	(4)	(5)	(6)	(7)	(8)	(9)	(10)	(11)	(12)	(1)+(2)	(1)+(2)+(5)+(6)+(8)	part	(10)+(11)
TOTAL		.616	.824	2.002	3.475	1.687	.207	.778	.000	1.145	.226	3.053	3.618	1.452	3.430	6.119	3.296
WORK	5.222	.410	.240	.524	.462	.239	.013	.290	.000	.000	.098	1.942	.622	.653	.912	1.052	2.046

POPULATION, DEATHS, DEATH RATES FOR ALL CAUSES COMBINED, AND SPECIFIED CAUSES

Age Start of Interval	Midyear Population	Deaths During Year	All Causes	Respiratory T. B.	Other Infec. and Paras.	Neoplasms	Cardiovascular	Infl., Pneu., Bronch.	Diarrheal	Certain Degenerative	Maternal	Cert. Dis. of Infancy	Motor Vehicle	Other Violence	Other and Unknown	Age Start of Interval
0	86994	3068	.03527	.00010	.00238	.00003	.00006	.00640	.00162	.00001	.00000	.01309	.00001	.00062	.01093	0
1	324509	992	.00306	.00002	.00077	.00011	.00001	.00076	.00009	.00003	.00000	.00000	.00005	.00039	.00083	1
5	401221	436	.00109	.00002	.00024	.00006	.00002	.00009	.00001	.00003	.00000	.00000	.00005	.00039	.00083	5
10	401272	352	.00088	.00004	.00017	.00008	.00006	.00007	.00001	.00004	.00000	.00000	.00003	.00025	.00029	10
15	410749	526	.00128	.00033	.00022	.00005	.00008	.00006	.00000	.00006	.00002	.00000	.00003	.00025	.00019	15
20	360554	594	.00165	.00034	.00017	.00009	.00011	.00011	.00001	.00007	.00010	.00000	.00002	.00028	.00025	20
25	363838	626	.00172	.00041	.00011	.00013	.00011	.00007	.00001	.00006	.00026	.00000	.00002	.00028	.00025	25
30	350102	746	.00213	.00036	.00013	.00029	.00018	.00008	.00001	.00012	.00033	.00000	.00001	.00031	.00032	30
35	319434	898	.00281	.00031	.00017	.00055	.00027	.00017	.00002	.00022	.00036	.00000	.00002	.00029	.00043	35
40	283369	1025	.00362	.00039	.00019	.00100	.00040	.00018	.00002	.00027	.00022	.00000	.00000	.00037	.00057	40
45	249647	1296	.00519	.00037	.00015	.00176	.00076	.00023	.00004	.00054	.00022	.00000	.00001	.00037	.00094	45
50	217774	1774	.00815	.00029	.00025	.00265	.00173	.00040	.00003	.00096	.00000	.00000	.00000	.00002	.00049	.00132	50
55	190385	2335	.01226	.00042	.00028	.00383	.00344	.00071	.00002	.00130	.00000	.00000	.00002	.00049	.00132	55
60	165386	3305	.01998	.00058	.00046	.00522	.00704	.00125	.00007	.00201	.00000	.00000	.00002	.00075	.00168	60
65	129216	4278	.03311	.00073	.00044	.00802	.01338	.00238	.00015	.00311	.00000	.00000	.00003	.00088	.00399	65
70	93265	5404	.05794	.00080	.00053	.01072	.02568	.00545	.00027	.00495	.00000	.00000	.00005	.00132	.00817	70
75	59252	5674	.09576	.00068	.00064	.01489	.04385	.00582	.00049	.00657	.00000	.00000	.00005	.00209	.01669	75
80	27582	4392	.15923	.00047	.00054	.01615	.06229	.02009	.00051	.00591	.00000	.00000	.00000	.00417	.04847	80
85+	13272	3543	.26695	.00030	.00075	.01756	.09381	.03624	.00090	.00814	.00000	.00000	.00004	.00417	.04847	85+
ALL	4447821	41264												.00008	.00753	.10164	

	All Causes	Respiratory T. B.	Other Infec. and Paras.	Neoplasms	Cardiovascular	Infl., Pneu., Bronch.	Diarrheal	Certain Degenerative	Maternal	Cert. Dis. of Infancy	Motor Vehicle	Other Violence	Other and Unknown
CRUDE DEATH RATE	.00928	.00031	.00031	.00157	.00281	.00090	.00008	.00062	.00010	.00026	.00003	.00044	.00187
STANDARDIZED RATE (1)	.00646	.00025	.00035	.00095	.00146	.00070	.00009	.00037	.00008	.00046	.00003	.00037	.00134
STANDARDIZED RATE (2)	.01128	.00031	.00032	.00186	.00362	.00113	.00009	.00073	.00009	.00027	.00003	.00037	.00235
GEOMETRIC MEAN	.00868												

LIFE TABLE FOR ALL CAUSES COMBINED

Age (x)	Midyear Population	Deaths During Year	$_nM_x$	$_nq_x$	l_x	$_nd_x$	$_nL_x$	$_nm_x$	$_na_x$	T_x	$_nr_x$	$\overset{\circ}{e}_x$	Age (x)
0	86994	3068	.035267	.034220	100000	3422	97023	.035270	.129954	6728511	.000000	67.285	0
1	324509	992	.003057	.012135	96578	1172	383382	.003057	1.500000	6631488	.000000	68.665	1
5	401221	436	.001087	.005419	95406	517	475738	.001087	2.500000	6248106	.000000	65.490	5
10	401272	352	.000877	.004374	94889	415	473425	.000877	2.543173	5772369	.000000	60.833	10
15	410749	526	.001281	.006383	94474	603	470937	.001280	2.622996	5298943	-.004714	56.089	15
20	360554	594	.001647	.008213	93871	771	467468	.001649	2.552691	4828007	-.005426	51.432	20
25	363838	626	.001721	.008571	93100	798	463548	.001722	2.554302	4360538	.011375	46.837	25
30	350102	746	.002131	.010606	92302	979	459162	.002132	2.601932	3896990	.002096	42.220	30
35	319434	898	.002811	.013983	91323	1277	453556	.002816	2.604411	3437828	-.007552	37.645	35
40	283369	1025	.003617	.017980	90046	1619	446391	.003627	2.628552	2984272	-.015365	33.142	40
45	249647	1296	.005191	.025739	88427	2276	436827	.005210	2.668058	2537881	-.019574	28.700	45
50	217774	1774	.008146	.040104	86151	3455	422673	.008174	2.660878	2101054	-.020764	24.388	50
55	190385	2335	.012265	.059785	82696	4944	401951	.012300	2.668175	1678381	-.020087	20.296	55
60	165386	3305	.019984	.095766	77752	7446	371374	.020050	2.665077	1276429	-.015512	16.417	60
65	129216	4278	.033107	.154240	70306	10844	326029	.033261	2.648373	905055	-.016420	12.873	65
70	93265	5404	.057942	.255104	59462	15169	260709	.058184	2.587088	579026	-.021654	9.738	70
75	59252	5674	.095760	.387985	44293	17185	178534	.096256	2.501831	318317	-.018178	7.187	75
80	27582	4392	.159234	.565147	27108	15320	95626	.160208	2.394637	139783	-.021330	5.157	80
85+	13272	3543	.266953	1.000000	11788	11788	44158	.266953	3.745978	44158	.000000	3.746	85+

NUMBER OF PERSONS DYING (OUT OF 100,000 AT BIRTH) ABOVE AGE X FROM SPECIFIED CAUSES

Age (x)	All Causes	Respiratory T.B.	Other Infec. and Paras.	Neoplasms	Cardiovascular	Infl., Pneu., Bronch.	Diarrheal	Certain Degenerative	Maternal	Cert. Dis. of Infancy	Motor Vehicle	Other Violence	Other and Unknown	Age (x)
0	100000	2377	2118	16946	34758	9816	599	6748	598	1270	177	3864	20729	0
1	96578	2367	1887	16943	34753	9195	442	6747	598	0	176	3804	19666	1
5	95406	2359	1591	16899	34749	8904	408	6734	598	0	157	3657	19350	5
10	94889	2350	1476	16871	34737	8859	401	6721	598	0	130	3536	19210	10
15	94474	2331	1396	16832	34707	8827	397	6703	598	0	114	3451	19118	15
20	93871	2176	1291	16806	34669	8801	395	6675	590	0	100	3335	19033	20
25	93100	1972	1212	16765	34617	8752	389	6642	542	0	92	3203	18914	25
30	92302	1781	1161	16702	34567	8720	383	6614	420	0	84	3073	18797	30
35	91323	1617	1104	16571	34495	8683	376	6557	270	0	79	2930	18651	35
40	90046	1476	1025	16321	34361	8605	366	6459	107	0	72	2797	18457	40
45	88427	1303	939	15872	34182	8523	358	6339	10	0	71	2630	18200	45
50	86151	1140	874	15101	33849	8421	342	6099	2	0	65	2467	17791	50
55	82696	1016	767	13977	33113	8249	331	5694	2	0	56	2259	17232	55
60	77752	847	655	12435	31725	7963	322	5172	2	0	49	2025	16557	60
65	70306	631	484	10492	29100	7499	297	4422	2	0	40	1746	15593	65
70	59462	393	340	7870	24713	6719	247	3404	2	0	30	1458	14286	70
75	44293	184	203	5068	17987	5292	177	2108	2	0	16	1113	12143	75
80	27108	63	88	2401	10122	3527	89	933	2	0	7	737	9139	80
85+	11789	13	33	775	4142	1600	40	359	0	0	3	333	4490	85+

NUMBER OF PERSONS SURVIVING TO AGE X IF SPECIFIED CAUSES WERE ELIMINATED

Age (x)	No Causes	Respiratory T.B. (1)	Other Infec. and Paras. (2)	Neoplasms (3)	Cardiovascular (4)	Infl., Pneu., Bronch. (5)	Diarrheal (6)	Certain Degenerative (7)	Maternal (8)	Cert. Dis. of Infancy (9)	Motor Vehicle (10)	Other Violence (11)	Other and Unknown (12)	(1)+(2)	(1)+(2)+(5)+(6)+(8)	(1)+(2)+(5)+(6)+(8)+part of(9)&(12)	(10)+(11)	Age (x)
0	100000	100000	100000	100000	100000	100000	100000	100000	100000	100000	100000	100000	100000	100000	100000	100000	100000	0
1	96578	96588	96805	96581	96583	97190	96732	96579	96578	97834	96579	96637	97628	96815	97585	99776	96638	1
5	95406	95424	95926	95453	95415	96302	95592	95420	95406	96647	95426	95611	96762	95944	97034	99454	95630	5
10	94889	94916	95521	94963	94910	95826	95081	94916	94889	96123	94936	95213	96379	95548	96687	99166	95260	10
15	94474	94519	95184	94587	94525	95439	94670	94519	94474	95703	94536	94882	96051	95230	96401	98914	94945	15
20	93871	94071	94682	94009	93959	94856	94067	93943	93879	95092	93947	94393	95524	94884	96088	98642	94469	20
25	93100	93502	93984	93278	93239	94126	93301	93205	93156	94311	93183	93750	94860	94390	95693	98311	93834	25
30	92302	92892	93229	92541	92490	93352	92507	92434	92479	93503	92393	93077	94166	93825	95285	97965	93168	30
35	91323	92071	92298	91691	91591	92399	91533	91510	91648	92511	91418	92233	93315	93054	94701	97442	92329	35
40	90046	90924	91087	90658	90434	91185	90263	90328	90529	91217	90146	91077	92207	91975	93863	96670	91178	40
45	88427	89463	89535	89477	88966	89628	88648	88823	88997	89577	88526	89607	90811	90584	92637	95497	89707	45
50	86151	87323	87255	87948	87027	87423	86382	86775	86715	87272	86254	87463	88889	88483	90619	93500	87568	50
55	82696	83944	83901	85552	84270	84088	82928	83696	83237	83772	82804	84163	85891	85167	87412	90276	84272	55
60	77752	79092	78995	81998	80617	79344	77979	79206	78261	78763	77860	79362	81438	80356	82779	85588	79472	60
65	70306	71726	71595	76117	75533	72157	70535	72350	70766	71220	70412	72032	74604	73041	75743	78451	72141	65
70	59462	60885	60686	67030	68369	61804	59702	62159	59851	60235	59561	61193	64385	62139	65271	67779	61294	70
75	44293	45536	45324	52706	58037	47334	44532	47477	44583	44869	44379	45888	50005	46596	50391	52638	45976	75
80	27108	27962	27829	34787	44450	30472	27323	30037	27285	27461	27167	28387	33382	28706	32737	34640	28445	80
85+	11788	12193	12138	16525	26754	14714	11913	13475	11866	11941	11816	12618	18690	12554	15942	17722	12649	85+

ADDED YRS OF LIFE

		(1)	(2)	(3)	(4)	(5)	(6)	(7)	(8)	(9)	(10)	(11)	(12)				
TOTAL		.660	.804	2.415	4.128	1.500	.185	.887	.233	.873	.069	.906	3.255	1.475	3.483	5.830	.977
WORK	3.491	.419	.196	.701	.469	.165	.018	.256	.183	.000	.019	.355	.503	.618	.993	1.174	.374

POPULATION, DEATHS, DEATH RATES FOR ALL CAUSES COMBINED, AND SPECIFIED CAUSES

Age Start of Interval	Midyear Population	Deaths During Year	All Causes	Respiratory T. B.	Other Infec. and Paras.	Neoplasms	Cardiovascular	Infl., Pneu., Bronch.	Diarrheal	Certain Degenerative	Maternal	Cert. Dis. of Infancy	Motor Vehicle	Other Violence	Other and Unknown	Age Start of Interval
0	117226	3331	.02842	.00004	.00052	.00018	.00009	.00176	.00044	.00005	.00000	.01545	.00002	.00068	.00879	0
1	502883	908	.00181	.00002	.00039	.00010	.00003	.00013	.00006	.00001	.00000	.00000	.00011	.00051	1
5	477640	384	.00080	.00001	.00011	.00009	.00003	.00002	.00001	.00001	.00000	.00000	.00013	.00023	.00016	5
10	420698	217	.00052	.00001	.00003	.00005	.00003	.00002	.00000	.00002	.00000	.00000	.00007	.00014	.00015	10
15	413561	368	.00089	.00003	.00007	.00010	.00006	.00002	.00001	.00004	.00000	.00000	.00010	.00022	.00023	15
20	404416	478	.00118	.00006	.00006	.00013	.00007	.00002	.00001	.00005	.00000	.00000	.00008	.00029	.00041	20
25	394778	498	.00126	.00017	.00005	.00016	.00013	.00003	.00001	.00005	.00000	.00000	.00013	.00024	.00030	25
30	341059	441	.00129	.00018	.00005	.00026	.00013	.00002	.00005	.00008	.00000	.00000	.00008	.00023	.00026	30
35	335570	580	.00173	.00017	.00007	.00035	.00023	.00003	.00016	.00000	.00000	.00010	.00024	.00042	35
40	317245	826	.00260	.00023	.00011	.00064	.00042	.00010	.00001	.00020	.00000	.00000	.00012	.00024	.00053	40
45	288762	1195	.00414	.00021	.00014	.00111	.00091	.00015	.00001	.00027	.00000	.00000	.00015	.00036	.00082	45
50	252148	1814	.00719	.00026	.00020	.00224	.00197	.00029	.00004	.00043	.00000	.00000	.00009	.00038	.00130	50
55	217781	2326	.01068	.00034	.00027	.00339	.00333	.00035	.00003	.00060	.00000	.00000	.00015	.00057	.00166	55
60	183262	3137	.01712	.00037	.00021	.00516	.00631	.00059	.00004	.00085	.00000	.00000	.00019	.00066	.00264	60
65	147711	4210	.02850	.00051	.00043	.00763	.01211	.00128	.00008	.00132	.00000	.00000	.00018	.00062	.00433	65
70	111479	5258	.04717	.00077	.00051	.01132	.02147	.00251	.00006	.00187	.00000	.00000	.00043	.00096	.00726	70
75	68528	5414	.07900	.00069	.00042	.01626	.03928	.00458	.00019	.00261	.00000	.00000	.00038	.00134	.01286	75
80	32704	4398	.13448	.00055	.00052	.02030	.06910	.01046	.00040	.00352	.00000	.00000	.00040	.00211	.02712	80
85+	13554	3134	.23122	.00037	.00059	.02213	.11325	.02140	.00037	.00332	.00000	.00000	.00037	.00211	.02712	85+
ALL	5041005	38917														

	All Causes	Respiratory T. B.	Other Infec. and Paras.	Neoplasms	Cardiovascular	Infl., Pneu., Bronch.	Diarrheal	Certain Degenerative	Maternal	Cert. Dis. of Infancy	Motor Vehicle	Other Violence	Other and Unknown
CRUDE DEATH RATE	.00772	.00016	.00018	.00153	.00272	.00042	.00003	.00029	.00000	.00036	.00012	.00038	.00153
STANDARDIZED RATE (1)	.00513	.00012	.00017	.00090	.00138	.00026	.00003	.00018	.00000	.00054	.00011	.00033	.00110
STANDARDIZED RATE (2)	.00925	.00018	.00018	.00183	.00351	.00052	.00004	.00034	.00000	.00032	.00013	.00040	.00181
GEOMETRIC MEAN	.00654												

LIFE TABLE FOR ALL CAUSES COMBINED

Age (x)	Midyear Population	Deaths During Year	$_nM_x$	$_nq_x$	l_x	$_nd_x$	$_nL_x$	$_nm_x$	$_na_x$	T_x	$_nr_x$	$\overset{\circ}{e}_x$	Age (x)
0	117226	3331	.028415	.027720	100000	2772	97556	.028414	.118306	7045676	.000000	70.457	0
1	502883	908	.001806	.007189	97228	699	387165	.001805	1.500000	6948120	.000000	71.462	1
5	477640	384	.000804	.004009	96529	387	481678	.000803	2.500000	6560956	.000000	67.969	5
10	420698	217	.000516	.002580	96142	248	480098	.000517	2.532762	6079278	.012322	63.232	10
15	413561	368	.000890	.004442	95894	426	478471	.000890	2.654049	5599180	.005679	58.389	15
20	404416	478	.001182	.005857	95468	563	475968	.001183	2.563277	5120709	.001881	53.638	20
25	394778	498	.001261	.006291	94905	597	473042	.001262	2.515704	4644741	.012244	48.941	25
30	341059	441	.001293	.006447	94308	608	470064	.001293	2.571957	4171699	.016189	44.235	30
35	335570	580	.001728	.008613	93700	807	466607	.001730	2.654120	3701636	.006554	39.505	35
40	317245	826	.002604	.012972	92893	1205	461677	.002610	2.686549	3235029	.010059	34.825	40
45	288762	1195	.004138	.020570	91688	1886	454138	.004153	2.719159	2773351	.016101	30.248	45
50	252148	1814	.007194	.035511	89802	3189	441588	.007222	2.672664	2319213	.019953	25.826	50
55	217781	2326	.010680	.052290	86613	4529	422491	.010720	2.665323	1877625	.020423	21.678	55
60	183262	3137	.017118	.082635	82084	6783	394622	.017189	2.670954	1455134	.021092	17.727	60
65	147711	4210	.028502	.134062	75301	10095	352746	.028618	2.646421	1060512	.019462	14.084	65
70	111479	5258	.047166	.212833	65206	13878	292795	.047398	2.605187	707766	.023434	10.854	70
75	68528	5414	.079004	.333190	51328	17102	214590	.079696	2.541199	414971	.036813	8.085	75
80	32704	4398	.134479	.504295	34226	17260	127007	.135898	2.443608	200382	.036813	5.855	80
85+	13554	3134	.231223	1.000000	16966	16966	73375	.231223	4.324825	73375	.000000	4.325	85+

NUMBER OF PERSONS DYING (OUT OF 100,000 AT BIRTH) ABOVE AGE X FROM SPECIFIED CAUSES

Age (x)	All Causes	Respiratory T. B.	Other Infec. and Paras.	Neoplasms	Cardiovascular	Infl., Pneu., Bronch.	Diarrheal	Certain Degenerative	Maternal	Cert. Dis. of Infancy	Motor Vehicle	Other Violence	Other and Unknown	Age (x)
0	100000	1573	1393	19649	42004	6105	304	3479	0	1507	1030	3437	19519	0
1	97228	1569	1303	19632	41996	5934	261	3474	0	0	1028	3371	18660	1
5	96529	1561	1151	19594	41986	5883	239	3470	0	0	987	3194	18464	5
10	96142	1557	1100	19551	41971	5875	234	3463	0	0	923	3083	18385	10
15	95894	1551	1086	19528	41957	5864	233	3455	C	C	889	3016	18315	15
20	95468	1536	1054	19480	41928	5852	230	3436	0	C	840	2909	18203	20
25	94905	1505	1026	19416	41896	5843	229	3412	0	0	801	2771	18006	25
30	94308	1424	1001	19341	41835	5831	226	3389	0	0	740	2659	17862	30
35	93700	1341	978	19218	41773	5821	226	3350	0	0	703	2550	17742	35
40	92893	1263	946	19053	41685	5807	222	3275	0	0	658	2436	17548	40
45	91688	1155	894	18759	41491	5759	219	3184	0	0	602	2325	17300	45
50	89802	1059	829	18253	41076	5690	213	3060	0	0	533	2161	16928	50
55	86613	945	740	17261	40202	5563	195	2870	0	0	492	1991	16354	55
60	82084	803	627	15824	38786	5415	182	2617	C	C	428	1750	15652	60
65	75301	657	506	13782	36281	5181	166	2280	0	0	353	1489	14606	65
70	65206	475	353	11083	31988	4727	138	1813	0	0	288	1269	13072	70
75	51328	248	203	7756	25667	3987	119	1262	C	0	161	987	10938	75
80	34226	101	113	4247	17156	2907	78	658	0	0	80	697	8149	80
85+	16966	27	43	1624	8310	1570	27	244	0	0	27	422	4672	85+

NUMBER OF PERSONS SURVIVING TO AGE X IF SPECIFIED CAUSES WERE ELIMINATED

Age (x)	No Causes	Respiratory T. B.	Other Infec. and Paras.	Neoplasms	Cardiovascular	Infl., Pneu., Bronch.	Diarrheal	Certain Degenerative	Maternal	Cert. Dis. of Infancy	Motor Vehicle	Other Violence	Other and Unknown	(1) + (2)	(1) + (2) + (5) + (6) + (8)	(1)+(2)+ (5)+(6)+ (8)+part of(9)&(12)	(10) + (11)	Age (x)
		(1)	(2)	(3)	(4)	(5)	(6)	(7)	(8)	(9)	(10)	(11)	(12)					
0	100000	100000	100000	100000	100000	100000	100000	100000	100000	100000	100000	100000	100000	100000	100000	100000	100000	0
1	97228	97232	97317	97245	97236	97397	97270	97233	97228	98725	97230	97293	98079	97321	97532	99324	97295	1
5	96529	96541	96769	96584	96547	96747	96593	96538	96529	98016	96572	96770	97571	96781	97064	98940	96813	5
10	96142	96158	96432	96239	96175	96368	96211	96158	96142	97623	96249	96493	97259	96448	96743	98631	96600	10
15	95894	95916	96197	96014	95941	96130	95964	95918	95894	97371	96034	96312	97079	96219	96526	98422	96453	15
20	95468	95505	95802	95635	95543	95715	95540	95511	95468	96938	95657	95991	96761	95839	96159	98071	96181	20
25	94905	94972	95265	95135	95012	95160	94978	94971	94905	96367	95131	95563	96390	95333	95662	97601	95792	25
30	94308	94456	94691	94612	94475	94573	94383	94397	94308	95760	94594	95075	95929	94839	95182	97151	95363	30
35	93700	93930	94103	94127	93928	93973	93775	93827	93700	95143	94021	94571	95433	94334	94685	96673	94896	35
40	92893	93199	93325	93480	93207	93178	92971	93094	92893	94324	93256	93872	94808	93632	93998	96014	94239	40
45	91688	92097	92166	92561	92191	92017	91768	91977	91688	93100	92103	92765	93830	92578	92991	95041	93185	45
50	89802	90298	90335	91165	90709	90193	89887	90208	89802	91185	90277	91021	92277	90834	91315	93388	91502	50
55	86613	87204	87215	88922	88360	87115	86712	87192	86613	87947	87111	87958	89581	87810	88421	90508	88464	55
60	82084	82783	82765	85720	85158	82705	82191	82881	82084	82619	82619	83597	85606	83470	84211	86275	84142	60
65	75301	76083	76043	80704	80653	76097	75414	76359	75301	76461	75864	76943	79583	76833	77762	79763	77518	65
70	65206	66054	65992	72622	74253	66324	65330	66563	65206	66210	65754	66837	70438	66850	68126	70026	67399	70
75	51328	52199	52080	60531	65189	52880	51442	52894	51328	52118	51873	52867	57525	52963	54686	56412	53428	75
80	34226	34925	34800	43837	53195	36178	34336	35742	34226	34753	34654	35494	40986	35511	37657	39091	35938	80
85+	16966	17365	17300	24176	37783	18936	17056	18047	16966	17227	17215	17793	23402	17706	19867	20950	18054	85+

ADDED YRS OF LIFE																		
TOTAL		.342	.423	2.714	5.756	.650	.079	.496	.000	1.083	.303	.883	3.110	.768	1.562	3.271	1.193	
WORK	2.670	.165	.096	.592	.476	.074	.009	.151	.000	.000	.122	.313	.546	.262	.347	.447	.436	

POPULATION, DEATHS, DEATH RATES FOR ALL CAUSES COMBINED, AND SPECIFIED CAUSES

Age Start of Interval	Midyear Population	Deaths During Year	All Causes	Respiratory T. B.	Other Infec. and Paras.	Neoplasms	Cardiovascular	Infl., Pneu., Bronch.	Diarrheal	Certain Degenerative	Maternal	Cert. Dis. of Infancy	Motor Vehicle	Other Violence	Other and Unknown	Age Start of Interval
0	108962	2446	.02245	.00002	.00093	.00012	.00009	.00150	.00032	.00003	.00000	.01083	.00000	.00039	.00822	0
1	473375	707	.00149	.00003	.00036	.00011	.00003	.00017	.00004	.00001	.00000	.00000	.00008	.00025	.00043	1
5	481907	220	.00046	.00001	.00010	.00006	.00004	.00004	.00000	.00001	.00000	.00000	.00007	.00006	.00007	5
10	410367	127	.00031	.00001	.00004	.00005	.00003	.00001	.00000	.00001	.00000	.00000	.00001	.00003	.00011	10
15	394585	199	.00050	.00004	.00005	.00009	.00003	.00001	.00001	.00004	.00002	.00000	.00003	.00005	.00014	15
20	397920	290	.00073	.00011	.00010	.00009	.00007	.00002	.00001	.00004	.00006	.00000	.00004	.00005	.00016	20
25	397727	357	.00090	.00013	.00007	.00019	.00008	.00003	.00001	.00005	.00010	.00000	.00002	.00006	.00017	25
30	360297	381	.00106	.00011	.00008	.00022	.00012	.00003	.00001	.00006	.00014	.00000	.00001	.00006	.00020	30
35	349108	543	.00156	.00013	.00008	.00046	.00017	.00004	.00001	.00009	.00023	.00000	.00001	.00006	.00025	35
40	334369	711	.00213	.00011	.00011	.00084	.00027	.00007	.00001	.00013	.00010	.00000	.00002	.00007	.00039	40
45	310768	1064	.00342	.00010	.00007	.00145	.00062	.00008	.00001	.00021	.00002	.00000	.00003	.00012	.00072	45
50	273722	1389	.00507	.00010	.00009	.00213	.00123	.00011	.00002	.00028	.00000	.00000	.00002	.00018	.00091	50
55	237757	1908	.00803	.00018	.00015	.00327	.00231	.00022	.00004	.00048	.00000	.00000	.00003	.00021	.00114	55
60	197527	2723	.01379	.00023	.00024	.00446	.00506	.00048	.00004	.00089	.00000	.00000	.00008	.00017	.00215	60
65	161359	3929	.02435	.00035	.00028	.00649	.01111	.00094	.00011	.00149	.00000	.00000	.00004	.00042	.00312	65
70	122734	5200	.04237	.00042	.00037	.00913	.02231	.00205	.00011	.00238	.00000	.00000	.00009	.00050	.00501	70
75	79340	5804	.07315	.00049	.00053	.01262	.04053	.00427	.00020	.00337	.00000	.00000	.00011	.00110	.00993	75
80	39548	4805	.12150	.00061	.00043	.01578	.06605	.00920	.00051	.00351	.00000	.00000	.00003	.00200	.02339	80
85+	18174	3860	.21239	.00044	.00083	.01772	.10823	.01959	.00094	.00550	.00000	.00000	.00006	.00550	.05359	85+
ALL	5149546	36663														

			All Causes	Respiratory T. B.	Other Infec. and Paras.	Neoplasms	Cardiovascular	Infl., Pneu., Bronch.	Diarrheal	Certain Degenerative	Maternal	Cert. Dis. of Infancy	Motor Vehicle	Other Violence	Other and Unknown
CRUDE DEATH RATE			.00712	.00011	.00016	.00147	.00286	.00039	.00004	.00032	.00005	.00023	.00004	.00018	.00129
STANDARDIZED RATE (1)			.00419	.00008	.00016	.00082	.00126	.00022	.00003	.00017	.00004	.00038	.00004	.00013	.00087
STANDARDIZED RATE (2)			.00790	.00012	.00016	.00160	.00330	.00044	.00004	.00035	.00005	.00022	.00004	.00019	.00142
GEOMETRIC MEAN			.00503												

LIFE TABLE FOR ALL CAUSES COMBINED

Age (x)	Midyear Population	Deaths During Year	$_nM_x$	$_nq_x$	l_x	$_nd_x$	$_nL_x$	$_nm_x$	$_na_x$	T_x	$_nr_x$	$\overset{\circ}{e}_x$	Age (x)
0	108962	2446	.022448	.022010	100000	2201	98037	.022451	.108162	7297575	.000000	72.976	0
1	473375	707	.001494	.005951	97799	582	389741	.001493	1.500000	7199538	.000000	73.616	1
5	481907	220	.000457	.002284	97217	222	485530	.000457	2.500000	6809797	.000000	70.047	5
10	410367	127	.000309	.001536	96995	149	484607	.000307	2.532159	6324267	.017792	65.202	10
15	394585	199	.000504	.002530	96846	245	483660	.000507	2.671769	5839660	.007279	60.298	15
20	397920	290	.000729	.003634	96601	351	482166	.000728	2.610399	5356000	-.001156	55.445	20
25	397727	357	.000898	.004478	96250	431	480205	.000898	2.574923	4873834	.005856	50.637	25
30	360297	381	.001057	.005281	95819	506	477894	.001059	2.627223	4393629	.011651	45.853	30
35	349108	543	.001555	.007764	95313	740	474818	.001558	2.639640	3915735	.006903	41.083	35
40	334369	711	.002126	.010595	94573	1002	470538	.002129	2.677354	3440917	.007682	36.384	40
45	310768	1064	.003424	.017025	93571	1593	464146	.003432	2.671584	2970379	.013706	31.745	45
50	273722	1389	.005074	.025158	91978	2314	454512	.005091	2.676102	2506233	.019240	27.248	50
55	237757	1908	.008025	.039581	89664	3549	440171	.008063	2.703755	2051721	.022880	22.882	55
60	197527	2723	.013785	.067178	86115	5785	417311	.013863	2.707145	1611550	.024324	18.714	60
65	161359	3929	.024349	.115785	80330	9301	380055	.024473	2.678184	1194239	.022187	14.867	65
70	122734	5200	.042368	.193442	71029	13740	322587	.042593	2.630413	814184	.023543	11.463	70
75	79340	5804	.073154	.312466	57289	17902	242664	.073773	2.554417	491598	.034842	8.581	75
80	39548	4805	.121498	.467565	39387	18416	150196	.122613	2.462035	248933	.034842	6.320	80
85+	18174	3860	.212391	1.000000	20971	20971	98738	.212391	4.708290	98738	.000000	4.708	85+

NUMBER OF PERSONS DYING (OUT OF 100,000 AT BIRTH) ABOVE AGE X FROM SPECIFIED CAUSES

Age (x)	All Causes	Respiratory T.B.	Other Infec. and Paras.	Neo-plasms	Cardio-vascular	Infl., Pneu., Bronch.	Diar-rheal	Certain Degen-erative	Maternal	Cert. Dis. of Infancy	Motor Vehicle	Other Violence	Other and Unknown	Age (x)
0	100000	1112	1272	18635	46485	6114	422	4265	320	1062	289	2092	17932	0
1	97799	1110	1181	18623	46476	5568	390	4262	320	0	289	2053	17127	1
5	97217	1101	1041	18581	46465	5903	375	4259	320	0	258	1955	16959	5
10	96955	1098	993	18551	46447	5884	373	4256	320	0	226	1924	16923	10
15	96846	1094	974	18528	46431	5877	371	4252	320	0	219	1909	16871	15
20	96601	1073	951	18486	46419	5875	369	4232	310	0	203	1883	16800	20
25	96250	1019	905	18443	46388	5865	366	4211	283	0	185	1861	16724	25
30	95819	958	872	18352	46350	5853	360	4188	234	0	176	1831	16645	30
35	95313	904	832	18244	46293	5837	355	4159	167	0	170	1803	16549	35
40	94573	843	793	18027	46214	5820	351	4117	57	0	158	1768	16425	40
45	93571	792	742	17632	46088	5789	344	4055	8	0	148	1733	16240	45
50	91978	746	710	16956	45800	5753	338	3956	1	0	136	1677	15905	50
55	89664	699	670	15983	45238	5701	329	3830	1	0	126	1596	15491	55
60	86115	619	604	14538	44214	5602	313	3615	1	0	115	1505	14989	60
65	80330	524	505	12672	42087	5400	296	3242	1	0	83	1435	14085	65
70	71029	392	399	10198	37836	5039	255	2671	1	0	66	1277	12895	70
75	57289	257	277	7245	30595	4372	219	1901	1	0	37	1115	11270	75
80	39387	138	148	4167	20673	3324	169	1080	1	0	10	846	8831	80
85+	20971	43	81	1749	10687	1934	92	543	0	0	5	543	5294	85+

NUMBER OF PERSONS SURVIVING TO AGE X IF SPECIFIED CAUSES WERE ELIMINATED

Age (x)	No Causes	Respiratory T.B. (1)	Other Infec. and Paras. (2)	Neo-plasms (3)	Cardio-vascular (4)	Infl., Pneu., Bronch. (5)	Diar-rheal (6)	Certain Degener-ative (7)	Maternal (8)	Cert. Dis. of Infancy (9)	Motor Vehicle (10)	Other Violence (11)	Other and Unknown (12)	(1)+(2)	(1)+(2)+(5)+(6)+(8)	(1)+(2)+(5)+(6)+(8)+part of(9)&(12)	(10)+(11)	Age (x)
0	100000	100000	100000	100000	100000	100000	100000	100000	100000	100000	100000	100000	100000	100000	100000	100000	100000	0
1	97799	97801	97889	97811	97808	97943	97831	97802	97799	98855	97799	97838	98558	97891	98067	99581	97838	1
5	97217	97228	97446	97271	97237	97426	97263	97223	97217	98267	97248	97353	98181	97457	97713	99316	97384	5
10	96955	97009	97272	97079	97033	97222	97043	97004	96955	98042	97058	97162	97993	97286	97562	99177	97225	10
15	96846	96864	97141	96952	96900	97080	96896	96859	96846	97892	96916	97028	97855	97159	97444	99075	97097	15
20	96601	96640	96919	96749	96667	96883	96653	96634	96611	97644	96687	96808	97719	96958	97256	98907	96894	20
25	96250	96343	96613	96441	96346	96494	96305	96304	96287	97289	96353	96478	97440	96706	97044	98731	96582	25
30	95819	95972	96213	96100	95953	96074	95880	95895	95905	96854	95931	96076	97084	96367	96771	98491	96188	30
35	95313	95519	95745	95700	95503	95583	95378	95418	95465	96342	95430	95597	96668	95952	96444	98201	95715	35
40	94573	94839	95041	95175	94840	94858	94642	94719	94834	95554	94701	94890	96043	95308	95928	97724	95018	40
45	93571	93885	94085	94563	93961	93884	93646	93777	93878	94581	93708	93919	95213	94400	95102	96927	94057	45
50	91978	92332	92515	93633	92649	92321	92058	92279	92286	92971	92124	92376	93930	92871	93611	95442	92523	50
55	89664	90056	90227	92260	90879	90050	89751	90083	89965	90632	89817	90132	91985	90621	91405	93226	90286	55
60	86115	86570	86721	90076	88306	86583	86214	86729	86404	87045	86272	86654	88851	87179	88048	89846	86813	60
65	80330	80847	80991	85929	84510	80563	80439	81266	80599	81197	80508	80901	83787	81512	82542	84305	81080	65
70	71029	71610	71714	78502	79056	71932	71164	72401	71267	71796	71202	71684	75259	72301	73605	75271	71858	70
75	57289	57879	57952	66298	71421	58628	57430	59101	57481	57908	57455	57964	62225	58549	60266	61754	58131	75
80	39387	39891	39949	48591	60435	41205	39525	41331	39519	39812	39523	40076	45063	40460	42619	43868	40215	80
85+	20971	21309	21319	28104	45288	23008	21100	22414	21042	21197	21047	21560	27080	21662	23994	25027	21639	85+

ADDED YRS OF LIFE																	
TOTAL		.253	.411	2.772	6.656	.674	.080	.539	.135	.787	.104	.378	2.725	.666	1.581	3.098	.483
WORK	2.033	.122	.095	.645	.340	.050	.012	.117	.057	.000	.031	.087	.367	.217	.378	.470	.117

NETHERLANDS 1960 MALES

POPULATION, DEATHS, DEATH RATES FOR ALL CAUSES COMBINED, AND SPECIFIED CAUSES

Age Start of Interval	Midyear Population	Deaths During Year	All Causes	Respiratory T. B.	Other Infec. and Paras.	Neoplasms	Cardiovascular	Infl., Pneu., Bronch.	Diarrheal	Certain Degenerative	Maternal	Cert. Dis. of Infancy	Motor Vehicle	Other Violence	Other and Unknown	Age Start of Interval
0	121172	2266	.01870	.00000	.00012	.00008	.00006	.00061	.00017	.00001	.00000	.01067	.00001	.00045	.00654	0
1	470322	629	.00134	.00000	.00007	.00014	.00001	.00010	.00003	.00001	.00000	.00000	.00018	.00035	.00044	1
5	567864	348	.00061	.00000	.00003	.00010	.00002	.00001	.00000	.00001	.00000	.00000	.00018	.00013	.00013	5
10	606832	221	.00036	.00000	.00001	.00007	.00001	.00000	.00000	.00001	.00000	.00000	.00008	.00008	.00009	10
15	467582	333	.00071	.00000	.00001	.00012	.00004	.00001	.00000	.00003	.00000	.00000	.00008	.00016	.00009	15
20	410286	411	.00100	.00000	.00001	.00017	.00004	.00001	.00000	.00003	.00000	.00000	.00020	.00016	.00014	20
25	389973	407	.00104	.00001	.00001	.00021	.00007	.00002	.00001	.00005	.00000	.00000	.00027	.00020	.00015	25
30	376260	398	.00106	.00000	.00002	.00026	.00014	.00003	.00001	.00006	.00000	.00000	.00018	.00018	.00019	30
35	376625	548	.00146	.00002	.00001	.00039	.00026	.00003	.00001	.00010	.00000	.00000	.00016	.00020	.00017	35
40	329400	801	.00243	.00002	.00003	.00067	.00062	.00009	.00001	.00012	.00000	.00000	.00025	.00029	.00035	40
45	323105	1280	.00396	.00003	.00005	.00127	.00115	.00010	.00001	.00019	.00000	.00000	.00025	.00027	.00066	45
50	303178	2172	.00716	.00005	.00009	.00247	.00241	.00025	.00001	.00029	.00000	.00000	.00029	.00034	.00097	50
55	269552	3264	.01211	.00009	.00007	.00402	.00441	.00047	.00004	.00059	.00000	.00000	.00038	.00041	.00163	55
60	225142	4250	.01888	.00011	.00014	.00603	.00752	.00080	.00005	.00069	.00000	.00000	.00043	.00056	.00255	60
65	182068	5449	.02993	.00020	.00020	.00897	.01297	.00159	.00010	.00113	.00000	.00000	.00047	.00064	.00375	65
70	137808	6277	.04555	.00011	.00028	.01199	.02218	.00216	.00012	.00181	.00000	.00000	.00060	.00076	.00554	70
75	91373	6883	.07533	.00020	.00031	.01558	.03869	.00543	.00014	.00270	.00000	.00000	.00095	.00161	.00932	75
80	49664	6344	.12774	.00028	.00022	.02138	.06892	.01023	.00022	.00421	.00000	.00000	.00083	.00266	.01879	80
85+	21985	5020	.22834	.00032	.00032	.02652	.12704	.02124	.00086	.00546	.00000	.00000	.00077	.00600	.03980	85+
ALL	5720191	47301														

	All Causes	Respiratory T. B.	Other Infec. and Paras.	Neoplasms	Cardiovascular	Infl., Pneu., Bronch.	Diarrheal	Certain Degenerative	Maternal	Cert. Dis. of Infancy	Motor Vehicle	Other Violence	Other and Unknown
CRUDE DEATH RATE	.00827	.00003	.00006	.00190	.00343	.00047	.00003	.00029	.00000	.00023	.00026	.00033	.00126
STANDARDIZED RATE (1)	.00463	.00002	.00004	.00101	.00149	.00022	.00002	.00015	.00000	.00038	.00026	.00023	.00082
STANDARDIZED RATE (2)	.00887	.00003	.00006	.00202	.00374	.00051	.00003	.00031	.00000	.00022	.00027	.00034	.00134
GEOMETRIC MEAN	.00579												

LIFE TABLE FOR ALL CAUSES COMBINED

Age (x)	Midyear Population	Deaths During Year	$_nM_x$	$_nq_x$	l_x	$_nd_x$	$_nL_x$	$_nm_x$	$_na_x$	T_x	$_nr_x$	$\overset{\circ}{e}_x$	Age (x)
0	121172	2266	.018701	.018390	100000	1839	98348	.018699	.101791	7152945	.000000	71.529	0
1	470322	629	.001337	.005338	98161	524	391334	.001339	1.500000	7054597	.000000	71.868	1
5	567864	348	.000613	.003052	97637	298	487440	.000611	2.500000	6663263	.000000	68.245	5
10	606832	221	.000364	.001818	97339	177	486263	.000364	2.558851	6175823	.010227	63.447	10
15	467582	333	.000712	.003562	97162	348	485004	.000718	2.683788	5689560	.035350	58.557	15
20	410286	411	.001002	.004999	96814	484	482892	.001002	2.566288	5204556	.022800	53.758	20
25	389973	407	.001044	.005211	96330	502	480400	.001045	2.509130	4721664	.012468	49.016	25
30	376260	398	.001058	.005280	95828	506	477915	.001059	2.578228	4241264	.003184	44.259	30
35	376625	548	.001455	.007260	95322	692	475014	.001457	2.692979	3763350	.009123	39.480	35
40	329400	801	.002432	.012121	94630	1147	470521	.002438	2.708152	3288350	.013754	34.749	40
45	323105	1280	.003962	.019661	93483	1838	463255	.003968	2.736784	2817815	.005369	30.143	45
50	303178	2172	.007164	.035310	91645	3236	450840	.007178	2.717797	2354560	.008336	25.692	50
55	269552	3264	.012109	.059055	88409	5221	429890	.012145	2.671862	1903720	.014828	21.533	55
60	225142	4250	.018877	.090674	83188	7543	398203	.018943	2.648510	1473830	.018758	17.717	60
65	182068	5449	.029928	.140102	75645	10598	352949	.030027	2.615018	1075627	.018242	14.219	65
70	137808	6277	.045549	.205913	65047	13394	292978	.045717	2.591661	722679	.019879	11.110	70
75	91373	6883	.075329	.319265	51653	16491	217796	.075717	2.546023	429701	.022582	8.319	75
80	49664	6344	.127738	.484529	35162	17037	132526	.128556	2.459427	211904	.022582	6.027	80
85+	21985	5020	.228338	1.000000	18125	18125	79378	.228338	4.379482	79378	.000000	4.379	85+

NUMBER OF PERSONS DYING (OUT OF 100,000 AT BIRTH) ABOVE AGE X FROM SPECIFIED CAUSES

Age (x)	All Causes	Respiratory T. B.	Other Infec. and Paras.	Neo-plasms	Cardio-vascular	Infl., Pneu., Bronch.	Diar-rheal	Certain Degenerative	Maternal	Cert. Dis. of Infancy	Motor Vehicle	Other Violence	Other and Unknown	Age (x)
0	100000	318	523	22020	45967	6318	294	3468	0	1051	2205	3184	14652	0
1	98161	318	511	22012	45561	6258	278	3468	0	2	2204	3140	14009	1
5	97637	318	483	21958	45955	6217	266	3464	0	1	2133	3003	13839	5
10	97339	318	470	21909	45948	6211	266	3458	0	0	2045	2939	13775	10
15	97162	318	465	21873	45541	6208	265	3454	0	0	2008	2901	13729	15
20	96814	318	461	21816	45924	6201	263	3442	0	0	1910	2820	13659	20
25	96330	316	457	21733	45906	6194	262	3426	0	0	1722	2729	13585	25
30	95828	312	455	21630	45870	6185	258	3401	0	0	1590	2631	13496	30
35	95322	311	444	21506	45803	6171	255	3371	0	0	1502	2545	13414	35
40	94630	301	438	21319	45677	6159	249	3326	0	0	1425	2449	13287	40
45	93483	292	424	21002	45385	6119	245	3271	0	0	1308	2313	13124	45
50	91645	279	401	20415	44853	6073	242	3181	0	0	1192	2190	12819	50
55	88409	258	361	19300	43765	5961	237	3050	0	0	1060	2035	12382	55
60	83188	221	330	17567	41864	5758	220	2796	0	0	895	1858	11679	60
65	75645	179	275	15159	38857	5436	198	2521	0	0	723	1635	10662	65
70	65047	138	205	11985	34242	4872	163	2120	0	0	557	1409	9336	70
75	51653	106	122	8463	27734	4237	129	1587	0	0	382	1185	7708	75
80	35162	63	55	4972	19261	3046	98	995	0	0	174	833	5665	80
85+	18125	25	25	2105	10084	1686	69	433	0	0	61	477	3160	85+

NUMBER OF PERSONS SURVIVING TO AGE X IF SPECIFIED CAUSES WERE ELIMINATED

Age (x)	No Causes	Respiratory T. B. (1)	Other Infec. and Paras. (2)	Neo-plasms (3)	Cardio-vascular (4)	Infl., Pneu., Bronch. (5)	Diar-rheal (6)	Certain Degenerative (7)	Maternal (8)	Cert. Dis. of Infancy (9)	Motor Vehicle (10)	Other Violence (11)	Other and Unknown (12)	(1)+(2)	(1)+(2)+(5)+(6)+(8)	(1)+(2)+(5)+(6)+(8)+part of(9)&(12)	(10)+(11)	Age (x)
0	100000	100000	100000	100000	100000	100000	100000	100000	100000	100000	100000	100000	100000	100000	100000	100000	100000	0
1	98161	98161	98173	98169	98167	98220	98177	98161	98161	99206	98162	98205	98800	98173	98248	99258	98206	1
5	97637	97637	97677	97669	97649	97737	97665	97641	97637	98677	97709	97817	98444	97677	97805	98849	97889	5
10	97339	97339	97392	97450	97358	97445	97367	97349	97339	98377	97499	97583	98207	97392	97525	98572	97743	10
15	97162	97162	97220	97308	97188	97271	97191	97176	97162	98198	97358	97443	98075	97220	97357	98405	97640	15
20	96814	96814	96875	97017	96857	96929	96844	96840	96814	97846	97108	97175	97795	96875	97021	98069	97470	20
25	96330	96332	96395	96615	96390	96452	96361	96372	96330	97357	96811	96781	97380	96397	96550	97996	97263	25
30	95828	95834	95895	96214	95924	95958	95863	95894	95828	96850	96438	96375	96963	95901	96066	97110	96988	30
35	95322	95329	95399	95831	95484	95465	95360	95418	95322	96339	96018	95952	96533	95406	95588	96633	96652	35
40	94630	94647	94713	95322	94917	94784	94674	94770	94630	95639	95398	95392	95961	94730	94928	95973	96125	40
45	93483	93509	93579	94485	94058	93530	93450	93676	93483	94480	94359	94332	94962	93604	93844	94889	95216	45
50	91645	91683	91762	93217	92741	91879	91694	91524	91645	92622	92619	92600	93402	91800	92083	93125	93585	50
55	88409	88466	88561	91046	90554	88745	88461	88807	88409	89352	89480	89485	90543	88618	89008	90043	90569	55
60	83188	83278	83361	87417	87117	83702	83254	83810	83188	84075	84358	84357	85897	83451	84033	85055	85560	60
65	75645	75767	75855	81939	82279	76423	75726	76475	75645	76452	76875	76939	79115	75977	76840	77841	78189	65
70	65047	65189	65292	73713	75543	66246	65149	66138	65047	65741	66260	66372	69327	65435	66746	67713	67610	70
75	51653	51795	51922	62180	67131	53185	51764	53003	51653	52204	52775	52909	56615	52064	53723	54604	54058	75
80	35162	35294	35399	45892	55652	37230	35263	36580	35162	35537	36099	36314	40423	35532	37729	38518	37282	80
85+	18125	18220	18269	26446	41022	20233	18158	19273	18125	18318	18690	18980	22970	18364	20582	21219	19572	85+

ADDED YRS OF LIFE

	No Causes	(1)	(2)	(3)	(4)	(5)	(6)	(7)	(8)	(9)	(10)	(11)	(12)	(1)+(2)	+(5)+(6)+(8)	+part(9)&(12)	(10)+(11)
TOTAL		.047	.112	3.151	6.956	.634	.052	.432	.000	.762	.637	.711	2.291	.159	.855	1.760	1.359
WORK	2.513	.015	.024	.676	.577	.068	.009	.110	.000	.000	.297	.251	.369	.040	.117	.138	.551

POPULATION, DEATHS, DEATH RATES FOR ALL CAUSES COMBINED, AND SPECIFIED CAUSES

Age Start of Interval	Midyear Population	Deaths During Year	All Causes	Respiratory T. B.	Other Infec. and Paras.	Neoplasms	Cardiovascular	Infl., Pneu., Bronch.	Diarrheal	Certain Degenerative	Maternal	Cert. Dis. of Infancy	Motor Vehicle	Other Violence	Other and Unknown	Age Start of Interval
0	115601	1681	.01454	.00000	.00011	.00015	.00009	.00053	.00012	.00003	.00000	.00753	.00000	.00028	.00571	0
1	447784	449	.00100	.00000	.00007	.00013	.00003	.00011	.00002	.00001	.00000	.00000	.00000	.00016	.00036	1
5	538398	208	.00039	.00000	.00003	.00008	.00001	.00002	.00000	.00001	.00000	.00000	.00010	.00016	.00036	1
10	576576	132	.00023	.00000	.00000	.00006	.00001	.00001	.00000	.00000	.00000	.00000	.00007	.00005	.00012	5
15	446769	125	.00028	.00000	.00001	.00004	.00002	.00002	.00000	.00001	.00000	.00000	.00000	.00002	.00009	10
20	396388	180	.00045	.00000	.00001	.00011	.00003	.00001	.00000	.00001	.00000	.00000	.00005	.00004	.00009	15
25	381235	218	.00057	.00001	.00001	.00013	.00007	.00003	.00000	.00003	.00003	.00000	.00007	.00004	.00013	20
30	380039	262	.00069	.00001	.00000	.00027	.00007	.00004	.00001	.00003	.00005	.00000	.00005	.00004	.00017	25
35	389956	402	.00103	.00001	.00002	.00045	.00013	.00004	.00001	.00003	.00004	.00000	.00004	.00008	.00011	30
40	340117	602	.00177	.00001	.00004	.00092	.00025	.00003	.00001	.00008	.00005	.00000	.00004	.00006	.00018	35
45	338950	923	.00272	.00001	.00002	.00148	.00046	.00007	.00002	.00011	.00001	.00000	.00005	.00009	.00023	40
50	322524	1365	.00423	.00001	.00003	.00212	.00094	.00009	.00001	.00017	.00000	.00000	.00000	.00011	.00039	45
55	291678	2021	.00693	.00003	.00007	.00301	.00209	.00023	.00004	.00033	.00000	.00000	.00010	.00020	.00058	50
60	250392	2704	.01080	.00002	.00013	.00403	.00394	.00027	.00005	.00063	.00000	.00000	.00008	.00020	.00085	55
65	204648	3372	.01892	.00004	.00013	.00561	.00853	.00067	.00007	.00121	.00000	.00000	.00014	.00020	.00139	60
70	154997	5654	.03648	.00008	.00018	.00801	.01932	.00173	.00012	.00227	.00000	.00000	.00014	.00039	.00213	65
75	104560	6867	.06568	.00013	.00023	.01183	.03698	.00357	.00021	.00364	.00000	.00000	.00015	.00074	.00386	70
80	57864	6638	.11472	.00026	.00028	.01649	.06842	.00758	.00041	.00572	.00000	.00000	.00022	.00168	.00677	75
85+	27964	5882	.21034	.00011	.00029	.02267	.12223	.01917	.00086	.00608	.00000	.00000	.00010	.00315	.01191	80
ALL	5766440	40185														85+

	All Causes	Respiratory T.B.	Other Infec. and Paras.	Neoplasms	Cardiovascular	Infl., Pneu., Bronch.	Diarrheal	Certain Degen.	Maternal	Cert. Dis. of Infancy	Motor Vehicle	Other Violence	Other and Unknown
CRUDE DEATH RATE	.00697	.00002	.00005	.00159	.00317	.00038	.00003	.00033	.00002	.00015	.00007	.00021	.00096
STANDARDIZED RATE (1)	.00332	.00001	.00003	.00078	.00111	.00016	.00002	.00014	.00002	.00027	.00006	.00012	.00060
STANDARDIZED RATE (2)	.00673	.00002	.00004	.00153	.00305	.00036	.00003	.00033	.00002	.00016	.00007	.00021	.00096
GEOMETRIC MEAN	.00382												

LIFE TABLE FOR ALL CAUSES COMBINED

Age (x)	Midyear Population	Deaths During Year	$_nM_x$	$_nq_x$	l_x	$_nd_x$	$_nL_x$	$_nm_x$	$_na_x$	T_x	$_nr_x$	$\overset{\circ}{e}_x$	Age (x)
0	115601	1681	.014541	.014350	100000	1435	98701	.014539	.094720	7543366	.000000	75.434	0
1	447784	449	.001003	.004008	98565	395	393273	.001004	1.500000	7444665	.000000	75.531	1
5	538398	208	.000386	.001925	98170	189	490378	.000385	2.500000	7051392	.000000	71.828	5
10	576576	132	.000229	.001143	97981	112	489614	.000229	2.403274	6561015	.000000	66.962	10
15	446769	125	.000280	.001400	97869	137	489026	.000280	2.668796	6071401	.009924	62.036	15
20	396388	180	.000454	.002282	97732	223	488132	.000457	2.631726	5582375	.034312	57.119	20
25	381235	218	.000572	.002851	97509	278	486873	.000571	2.583933	5094243	.021509	52.244	25
30	380039	262	.000689	.003445	97231	335	485364	.000690	2.637438	4607370	.009515	47.386	30
35	389956	402	.001031	.005150	96896	499	483340	.001032	2.715848	4122006	-.002181	42.541	35
40	340117	602	.001770	.008838	96397	852	480020	.001775	2.694151	3638666	-.006257	37.747	40
45	338950	923	.002723	.013533	95545	1293	474727	.002724	2.681587	3158646	.012846	33.059	45
50	322524	1365	.004232	.020997	94252	1979	466700	.004240	2.696017	2683918	.003746	28.476	50
55	291678	2021	.006929	.034192	92273	3155	454048	.006949	2.680732	2217218	.007811	24.029	55
60	250392	2704	.010799	.052919	89118	4716	434747	.010848	2.700868	1763170	.014930	19.785	60
65	204648	3372	.018520	.091254	84402	7702	404476	.019042	2.723427	1328423	.021280	15.739	65
70	154997	5654	.036478	.169179	76700	12976	353242	.036734	2.668163	923947	.025751	12.046	70
75	104560	6867	.065675	.285230	63724	18176	274731	.066159	2.585323	570705	.027954	8.956	75
80	57864	6638	.114717	.448318	45548	20420	176512	.115686	2.491267	295974	.029407	6.498	80
85+	27964	5882	.210342	1.000000	25128	25128	119463	.210342	4.754165	119463	.000000	4.754	85+

NUMBER OF PERSONS DYING (OUT OF 100,000 AT BIRTH) ABOVE AGE X FROM SPECIFIED CAUSES

Age (x)	All Causes	Respiratory T.B.	Other Infec. and Paras.	Neoplasms	Cardiovascular	Infl., Pneu., Bronch.	Diarrheal	Certain Degenerative	Maternal	Cert. Dis. of Infancy	Motor Vehicle	Other Violence	Other and Unknown	Age (x)
0	100000	194	466	19937	50595	6183	394	4732	121	744	624	2927	12683	0
1	98565	194	455	19923	50587	6131	382	4729	121	2	624	2899	12118	1
5	98170	194	427	19871	50575	6088	373	4723	121	1	584	2837	11976	5
10	97981	194	412	19832	50572	6078	371	4721	121	0	551	2813	11916	10
15	97869	194	411	19802	50567	6072	371	4719	121	0	532	2805	11875	15
20	97732	194	407	19782	50556	6063	371	4712	120	0	507	2788	11832	20
25	97509	193	402	19729	50542	6059	371	4697	106	0	475	2768	11767	25
30	97231	190	398	19665	50510	6045	371	4682	82	0	450	2750	11688	30
35	96896	184	398	19535	50875	6027	369	4667	63	0	431	2713	11634	35
40	96397	180	390	19315	50813	6010	366	4651	27	0	413	2685	11547	40
45	95545	173	373	18872	50693	5994	362	4611	3	0	386	2641	11437	45
50	94252	169	361	18170	50475	5961	352	4559	0	0	363	2588	11254	50
55	92273	165	348	17181	50037	5920	348	4479	0	0	318	2496	10981	55
60	89118	151	319	15813	49082	5816	329	4329	0	0	281	2408	10590	60
65	84402	142	263	14056	47357	5697	308	4053	0	0	220	2319	9987	65
70	76700	126	212	11779	43877	5423	278	3560	0	0	163	2162	9120	70
75	63724	96	147	8937	36996	4806	235	2753	0	0	110	1897	7747	75
80	45548	59	84	5670	26754	3706	176	1746	0	0	50	1431	5872	80
85+	25128	13	34	2708	14602	2290	103	726	0	0	30	871	3751	85+

NUMBER OF PERSONS SURVIVING TO AGE X IF SPECIFIED CAUSES WERE ELIMINATED

Age (x)	No Causes	Respiratory T.B. (1)	Other Infec. and Paras. (2)	Neoplasms (3)	Cardiovascular (4)	Infl., Pneu., Bronch. (5)	Diarrheal (6)	Certain Degenerative (7)	Maternal (8)	Cert. Dis. of Infancy (9)	Motor Vehicle (10)	Other Violence (11)	Other and Unknown (12)	(1)+(2)	(1)+(2)+(5)+(6)+(8)	(1)+(2)+(5)+(6)+(8)+part of(9)&(12)	(10)+(11)	Age (x)
0	100000	100000	100000	100000	100000	100000	100000	100000	100000	100000	100000	100000	100000	100000	100000	100000	100000	0
1	98565	98565	98576	98579	98573	98617	98577	98568	98565	99304	98565	98593	99128	98576	98639	99403	98593	1
5	98170	98170	98209	98236	98190	98264	98191	98179	98170	98260	98054	98094	98873	98209	98324	99131	98300	5
10	97981	97981	98035	98086	98004	98065	98004	97992	97981	98718	98054	98094	98743	98035	98162	98981	98167	10
15	97869	97869	97924	98004	97897	97979	97892	97882	97869	98605	97961	97990	98671	97924	98057	98879	98082	15
20	97732	97732	97791	97886	97771	97851	97755	97752	97733	98467	97849	97870	98577	97791	97933	98761	97987	20
25	97509	97510	97572	97716	97562	97632	97532	97544	97524	98242	97657	97667	98417	97573	97734	98570	97815	25
30	97231	97235	97298	97502	97316	97367	97254	97281	97270	97962	97404	97406	98216	97302	97500	98352	97580	30
35	96896	96906	96963	97296	97015	97050	96921	96961	96954	97625	97087	97108	97932	96973	97210	98067	97300	35
40	96397	96411	96472	97015	96578	96567	96424	96477	96490	97122	96605	96636	97716	96486	96777	97646	96845	40
45	95545	95566	95636	96603	95844	95729	95576	95664	95661	96421	95778	95826	96765	95657	95990	96861	96060	45
50	94252	94276	94354	96003	94764	94467	94293	94421	94370	94961	94505	94582	95639	94378	94752	95623	94836	50
55	92273	92301	92385	94989	93211	92524	92317	92518	92388	92967	92566	92687	93906	92413	92825	93688	92981	55
60	89118	89159	89255	93135	90978	89463	89179	89503	89229	89788	89437	89605	91087	89296	89815	91658	89314	60
65	84402	84449	84586	90009	87856	84845	84480	85037	84508	85037	84764	84950	86668	84634	85263	86108	85314	65
70	76700	76758	76916	84137	83410	77366	76800	77752	76796	77277	77083	77349	79795	76975	77841	78659	77735	70
75	63724	63800	63963	72787	76464	64848	63846	65345	63804	64203	64090	64507	67607	64039	65375	66146	64878	75
80	45548	45633	45771	55244	66050	47306	45685	47581	45605	45891	45860	46507	50024	45857	47830	48523	46826	80
85+	25128	25209	25288	33223	51914	27197	25257	27041	25159	25317	25315	26079	29356	25369	27633	28185	26273	85+

ADDED YRS OF LIFE

	No Causes	(1)	(2)	(3)	(4)	(5)	(6)	(7)	(8)	(9)	(10)	(11)	(12)	(1)+(2)	(1)+(2)+(5)+(6)+(8)	(1)+(2)+(5)+(6)+(8)+part of(9)&(12)	(10)+(11)
TOTAL		.027	.103	2.965	7.799	.586	.055	.509	.053	.567	.194	.402	1.942	.130	.833	1.589	.598
WORK	1.537	.008	.018	.644	.275	.046	.006	.068	.037	.000	.065	.081	.249	.027	.116	.144	.146

POPULATION, DEATHS, DEATH RATES FOR ALL CAUSES COMBINED, AND SPECIFIED CAUSES

Age Start of Interval	Midyear Population	Deaths During Year	All Causes	Respiratory T. B.	Other Infec. and Paras.	Neo-plasms	Cardio-vascular	Infl., Pneu., Bronch.	Diar-rheal	Certain Degen-erative	Maternal	Cert. Dis. of Infancy	Motor Vehicle	Other Violence	Other and Unknown	Age Start of Interval
0	127000	2154	.01656	.00000	.00013	.00007	.00009	.00031	.00014	.00004	.00000	.01033	.00002	.00031	.00551	0
1	492000	555	.00113	.00000	.00004	.00013	.00001	.00004	.00004	.00001	.00000	.00000	.00016	.00033	.00036	1
5	583000	345	.00059	.00000	.00002	.00009	.00001	.00001	.00000	.00000	.00000	.00000	.00016	.00015	.00015	5
10	568000	277	.00049	.00000	.00000	.00007	.00001	.00000	.00000	.00002	.00000	.00000	.00012	.00011	.00015	10
15	590000	501	.00085	.00000	.00001	.00009	.00003	.00001	.00000	.00002	.00000	.00000	.00034	.00017	.00017	15
20	455000	465	.00102	.00000	.00000	.00011	.00005	.00000	.00000	.00003	.00000	.00000	.00047	.00020	.00016	20
25	405000	414	.00102	.00000	.00001	.00015	.00006	.00000	.00001	.00003	.00000	.00000	.00036	.00021	.00018	25
30	392000	439	.00112	.00000	.00001	.00023	.00015	.00002	.00000	.00005	.00000	.00000	.00027	.00020	.00019	30
35	373000	599	.00161	.00001	.00001	.00039	.00038	.00002	.00001	.00008	.00000	.00000	.00025	.00017	.00030	35
40	372000	923	.00248	.00001	.00003	.00062	.00077	.00004	.00000	.00014	.00000	.00000	.00024	.00019	.00044	40
45	321000	1457	.00454	.00001	.00002	.00132	.00169	.00006	.00002	.00021	.00000	.00000	.00025	.00030	.00065	45
50	314000	2233	.00711	.00002	.00004	.00259	.00257	.00014	.00001	.00029	.00000	.00000	.00026	.00032	.00087	50
55	287000	3692	.01286	.00003	.00005	.00437	.00512	.00033	.00003	.00046	.00000	.00000	.00039	.00045	.00164	55
60	243000	5044	.02076	.00006	.00012	.00698	.00865	.00071	.00007	.00079	.00000	.00000	.00042	.00045	.00252	60
65	196000	6432	.03282	.00011	.00013	.01054	.01494	.00113	.00010	.00116	.00000	.00000	.00053	.00059	.00359	65
70	148000	7021	.04744	.00014	.00022	.01307	.02303	.00167	.00013	.00170	.00000	.00000	.00072	.00097	.00582	70
75	101000	7630	.07554	.00020	.00028	.01829	.03949	.00290	.00018	.00255	.00000	.00000	.00100	.00169	.00897	75
80	54000	6317	.11698	.00028	.00026	.02237	.06626	.00458	.00044	.00304	.00000	.00000	.00100	.00315	.01520	80
85+	27000	5492	.20341	.00015	.00022	.02926	.11607	.01181	.00100	.00430	.00000	.00000	.00063	.00656	.03341	85+
ALL	6048000	51990														

	All Causes	Respiratory T.B.	Other Infec.	Neo-plasms	Cardio-vascular	Infl. Pneu.	Diar-rheal	Certain Degen.	Maternal	Cert. Dis. Infancy	Motor Vehicle	Other Violence	Other Unknown
CRUDE DEATH RATE	.00860	.00002	.00004	.00212	.00373	.00029	.00003	.00027	.00000	.00022	.00031	.00034	.00122
STANDARDIZED RATE (1)	.00469	.00001	.00003	.00108	.00161	.00013	.00002	.00014	.00000	.00036	.00027	.00026	.00078
STANDARDIZED RATE (2)	.00894	.00002	.00004	.00221	.00390	.00031	.00003	.00029	.00000	.00021	.00031	.00035	.00126
GEOMETRIC MEAN	.00556												

LIFE TABLE FOR ALL CAUSES COMBINED

Age (x)	Midyear Population	Deaths During Year	$_nM_x$	$_nq_x$	l_x	$_nd_x$	$_nL_x$	$_nm_x$	$_na_x$	T_x	$_nr_x$	$\overset{\circ}{e}_x$	Age (x)
0	127000	2154	.016961	.016710	100000	1671	98494	.016965	.098833	7134027	.000000	71.340	0
1	492000	555	.001128	.004495	98329	442	392211	.001127	1.500000	7035533	.000000	71.551	1
5	583000	345	.000592	.002952	97887	289	488713	.000591	2.500000	6643322	.000000	67.867	5
10	568000	277	.000488	.002439	97598	238	487421	.000488	2.608543	6154609	-.004688	63.061	10
15	590000	501	.000849	.004242	97360	413	485821	.000850	2.629641	5667189	.011671	58.209	15
20	455000	465	.001022	.005106	96947	495	483514	.001024	2.533249	5181367	.034661	53.445	20
25	405000	414	.001022	.005101	96452	492	481039	.001023	2.517361	4697854	.019674	48.707	25
30	392000	439	.001120	.005586	95960	536	478517	.001120	2.605721	4216815	.010953	43.943	30
35	373000	599	.001606	.008006	95424	764	475342	.001607	2.672884	3738298	.003853	39.176	35
40	372000	923	.002481	.012360	94660	1170	470655	.002486	2.738690	3262956	.009858	34.470	40
45	321000	1457	.004539	.022526	93490	2106	462608	.004552	2.700914	2792302	.013731	29.867	45
50	314000	2233	.007111	.035028	91384	3201	449629	.007119	2.722196	2329694	.004427	25.493	50
55	287000	3692	.012864	.062597	88183	5520	428157	.012892	2.688745	1880065	.009869	21.320	55
60	243000	5044	.020757	.099222	82663	8202	394025	.020816	2.648185	1451908	.015006	17.564	60
65	196000	6432	.032816	.152483	74461	11354	345014	.032909	2.596332	1057882	.016489	14.207	65
70	148000	7021	.047439	.213162	63107	13452	282844	.047560	2.569816	712869	.015118	11.296	70
75	101000	7630	.075545	.319444	49655	15862	209002	.075894	2.524101	430025	.021886	8.660	75
80	54000	6317	.116981	.452372	33793	15287	130042	.117554	2.453869	221022	.021886	6.540	80
85+	27000	5492	.203407	1.000000	18506	18506	90980	.203407	4.916242	90980	.000000	4.916	85+

NUMBER OF PERSONS DYING (OUT OF 100,000 AT BIRTH) ABOVE AGE X FROM SPECIFIED CAUSES

Age (x)	All Causes	Respiratory T. B.	Other Infec. and Paras.	Neo-plasms	Cardio-vascular	Infl., Pneu., Bronch.	Diar-rheal	Certain Degen-erative	Maternal	Cert. Dis. of Infancy	Motor Vehicle	Other Violence	Other and Unknown	Age (x)
0	100000	227	382	24075	47476	3806	358	3130	0	1018	2484	3331	13713	0
1	98329	227	370	24068	47467	3775	344	3126	0	0	2482	3300	13170	1
5	97887	227	352	24018	47462	3757	328	3123	0	0	2418	3171	13031	5
10	97598	227	342	23973	47457	3755	327	3121	0	0	2340	3100	12956	10
15	97360	227	341	23939	47453	3753	326	3109	0	0	2284	3045	12883	15
20	96947	227	337	23895	47437	3749	325	3100	0	0	2116	2961	12800	20
25	96452	227	337	23840	47412	3749	324	3087	0	0	1886	2866	12724	25
30	95960	227	333	23768	47382	3747	319	3071	0	0	1712	2763	12638	30
35	95424	227	331	23660	47310	3736	319	3046	0	0	1583	2668	12544	35
40	94660	224	324	23475	47129	3727	317	3010	0	0	1466	2586	12402	40
45	93490	220	311	23181	46763	3708	315	2946	0	0	1352	2498	12196	45
50	91384	214	301	22568	45978	3682	305	2849	0	0	1237	2358	11892	50
55	88183	204	283	21404	44821	3618	302	2717	0	0	1118	2213	11503	55
60	82663	190	263	19531	42625	3478	287	2520	0	0	952	2022	10795	60
65	74461	167	218	16775	39206	3198	258	2208	0	0	786	1843	9802	65
70	63107	130	174	13132	34033	2808	223	1805	0	0	603	1639	8560	70
75	49655	91	112	9430	27501	2334	187	1324	0	0	400	1364	6912	75
80	33793	50	54	5596	19205	1725	149	789	0	0	190	1008	5027	80
85+	18506	13	20	2662	10560	1075	91	391	0	0	57	596	3041	85+

NUMBER OF PERSONS SURVIVING TO AGE X IF SPECIFIED CAUSES WERE ELIMINATED

Age (x)	No Causes	Respiratory T. B.	Other Infec. and Paras.	Neo-plasms	Cardio-vascular	Infl., Pneu., Bronch.	Diar-rheal	Certain Degen-erative	Maternal	Cert. Dis. of Infancy	Motor Vehicle	Other Violence	Other and Unknown	(1) + (2)	(1) + (2) + (5) + (6) + (8)	(1)+(2)+(5)+(6)+(8)+part of(9)&(12)	(10) + (11)	Age (x)
		(1)	(2)	(3)	(4)	(5)	(6)	(7)	(8)	(9)	(10)	(11)	(12)					
0	100000	100000	100000	100000	100000	100000	100000	100000	100000	100000	100000	100000	100000	100000	100000	100000	100000	0
1	98329	98329	98341	98336	98338	98360	98343	98333	98329	99344	98331	98360	98869	98341	98386	99191	98362	1
5	97887	97887	97917	97944	97901	97936	97917	97894	97887	98897	97953	98046	98564	97917	97995	98822	98112	5
10	97598	97598	97638	97700	97617	97648	97629	97607	97598	98605	97742	97828	98348	97638	97719	98548	97972	10
15	97360	97360	97401	97495	97383	97412	97352	97381	97360	98365	97559	97645	98182	97401	97485	98313	97844	15
20	96947	96947	96991	97126	96986	97003	96979	96977	96947	97947	97314	97314	97849	96991	97080	97908	97682	20
25	96452	96452	96496	96685	96515	96508	96485	96495	96452	97447	97047	96913	97426	96496	96585	97409	97511	25
30	95960	95960	96008	96264	96053	96018	95958	96018	95960	96950	96727	96522	97016	96008	96104	96925	97293	30
35	95424	95424	95474	95834	95588	95452	95462	95507	95424	96409	96316	96078	96569	95474	95580	96400	96976	35
40	94660	94663	94716	95252	95004	94737	94700	94778	94660	95637	95663	95391	95535	94719	94836	95654	96402	40
45	93490	93496	93559	94356	94156	93555	93510	93670	93490	94455	94595	94300	94961	93565	93701	94518	95415	45
50	91384	91397	91461	92857	92859	91502	91434	91656	91384	92327	92579	92315	93127	91474	91642	92450	93523	50
55	88183	88205	88275	90774	90769	88360	88234	88576	88183	89093	89455	89226	90255	88297	88526	89319	90512	55
60	82663	82697	82768	86979	87304	82965	82726	83223	82663	83516	84018	83827	85210	82803	83168	83941	85201	60
65	74461	74514	74599	81147	82145	75000	74545	75264	74461	75229	75841	75682	77823	74652	75277	76027	77085	65
70	63107	63186	63264	72518	75075	63926	63210	64163	63107	63758	64448	64332	67161	63343	64271	64970	65700	70
75	49655	49751	49834	60939	66374	50727	49768	50920	49655	50167	50894	50868	54420	49930	51124	51759	52137	75
80	33793	33892	33962	45493	55263	35037	33901	35105	33793	34142	34812	34920	38769	34062	35429	35956	35972	80
85+	18506	18587	18623	27965	42542	19685	18608	19528	18506	18697	19164	19436	22958	18705	20006	20397	20127	85+

ADDED YRS OF LIFE																		
TOTAL		.027	.077	3.477	8.015	.393	.057	.410	.000	.735	.751	.714	2.213	.105	.560	1.245	1.478	
WORK	2.657	.005	.015	.661	.690	.040	.007	.099	.000	.000	.383	.245	.384	.020	.068	.080	.630	

POPULATION, DEATHS, DEATH RATES FOR ALL CAUSES COMBINED, AND SPECIFIED CAUSES

Age Start of Interval	Midyear Population	Deaths During Year	All Causes	Respiratory T. B.	Other Infec. and Paras.	Neoplasms	Cardiovascular	Infl., Pneu., Bronch.	Diarrheal	Certain Degenerative	Maternal	Cert. Dis. of Infancy	Motor Vehicle	Other Violence	Other and Unknown	Age Start of Interval
0	120000	1565	.01304	.00000	.00011	.00012	.00008	.00032	.00012	.00000	.00000	.00723	.00001	.00028	.00477	0
1	469000	404	.00086	.00000	.00004	.00013	.00001	.00004	.00004	.00001	.00000	.00000	.00010	.00016	.00033	1
5	556000	217	.00039	.00000	.00000	.00009	.00001	.00002	.00001	.00001	.00000	.00000	.00010	.00004	.00012	5
10	540000	155	.00029	.00000	.00001	.00006	.00001	.00001	.00000	.00001	.00000	.00000	.00006	.00003	.00009	10
15	564000	176	.00031	.00000	.00000	.00007	.00002	.00000	.00000	.00001	.00000	.00000	.00007	.00003	.00010	15
20	432000	157	.00036	.00000	.00000	.00008	.00003	.00000	.00000	.00003	.00003	.00000	.00006	.00005	.00008	20
25	384000	184	.00048	.00000	.00000	.00012	.00005	.00001	.00000	.00003	.00003	.00000	.00007	.00006	.00011	25
30	381000	264	.00069	.00000	.00001	.00025	.00009	.00000	.00001	.00004	.00005	.00000	.00005	.00006	.00012	30
35	378000	393	.00104	.00001	.00003	.00046	.00015	.00002	.00001	.00004	.00007	.00000	.00004	.00007	.00017	35
40	385000	626	.00163	.00000	.00002	.00085	.00026	.00002	.00001	.00003	.00003	.00000	.00006	.00008	.00026	40
45	233000	892	.00268	.00001	.00002	.00152	.00043	.00002	.00001	.00010	.00001	.00000	.00008	.00014	.00035	45
50	332000	1383	.00417	.00001	.00002	.00226	.00081	.00006	.00002	.00019	.00000	.00000	.00010	.00017	.00056	50
55	312000	1928	.00618	.00002	.00004	.00276	.00174	.00010	.00002	.00033	.00000	.00000	.00010	.00021	.00087	55
60	273000	2880	.01055	.00001	.00005	.00418	.00368	.00018	.00005	.00064	.00000	.00000	.00014	.00023	.00138	60
65	228000	4092	.01755	.00003	.00009	.00559	.00795	.00029	.00008	.00116	.00000	.00000	.00017	.00040	.00219	65
70	174000	5796	.03331	.00002	.00010	.00857	.01720	.00072	.00012	.00206	.00000	.00000	.00018	.00068	.00366	70
75	119000	6985	.05870	.00012	.00014	.01197	.03331	.00166	.00026	.00258	.00000	.00000	.00018	.00182	.00626	75
80	66000	6755	.10235	.00009	.00009	.01594	.06353	.00332	.00045	.00361	.00000	.00000	.00023	.00415	.01094	80
85+	35000	6595	.18843	.00011	.00040	.02223	.11354	.00834	.00086	.00571	.00000	.00000	.00009	.00911	.02803	85+
ALL	6081000	41447														
CRUDE DEATH RATE			.00682	.00001	.00003	.00167	.00315	.00018	.00003	.00031	.00001	.00014	.00009	.00025	.00094	
STANDARDIZED RATE (1)			.00306	.00000	.00002	.00078	.00101	.00007	.00002	.00013	.00001	.00025	.00008	.00013	.00055	
STANDARDIZED RATE (2)			.00616	.00001	.00003	.00153	.00279	.00016	.00003	.00028	.00001	.00015	.00008	.00023	.00086	
GEOMETRIC MEAN			.00362													

LIFE TABLE FOR ALL CAUSES COMBINED

Age (x)	Midyear Population	Deaths During Year	$_nM_x$	$_nq_x$	l_x	$_nd_x$	$_nL_x$	$_nm_x$	$_na_x$	T_x	$_nr_x$	$\overset{\circ}{e}_x$	Age (x)
0	120000	1565	.013042	.012890	100000	1289	98830	.013043	.092171	7636225	.000000	76.362	0
1	469000	404	.000861	.003434	98711	339	393997	.000860	1.500000	7537395	.000000	76.358	1
5	556000	217	.000390	.001952	98372	192	491380	.000391	2.500000	7143399	.000000	72.616	5
10	540000	155	.000287	.001436	98180	141	490539	.000287	2.442376	6652019	-.004707	67.753	10
15	564000	176	.000312	.001561	98039	153	489820	.000312	2.550381	6161479	-.011906	62.847	15
20	432000	157	.000363	.001818	97886	178	489002	.000364	2.594803	5671659	-.036213	57.941	20
25	384000	184	.000479	.002395	97708	234	487988	.000480	2.642450	5182657	-.019422	53.042	25
30	381000	264	.000693	.003468	97474	338	486581	.000695	2.665804	4694669	-.006260	48.163	30
35	378000	393	.001040	.005178	97136	503	484515	.001038	2.684725	4208088	-.002340	43.322	35
40	385000	626	.001626	.008113	96633	784	481367	.001629	2.706207	3723573	-.007140	38.533	40
45	333000	892	.002679	.013344	95849	1279	476291	.002685	2.690253	3242206	-.013049	33.826	45
50	332000	1383	.004166	.020641	94570	1952	468292	.004168	2.665215	2765915	-.003160	29.247	50
55	312000	1928	.006179	.030523	92618	2827	456583	.006192	2.698164	2297623	-.009537	24.808	55
60	273000	2880	.010549	.051687	89791	4641	438301	.010589	2.704293	1841040	-.017041	20.504	60
65	228000	4092	.017947	.086647	85150	7378	408857	.018045	2.710423	1402739	-.023117	16.474	65
70	174000	5796	.033310	.155493	77772	12093	360635	.033533	2.666005	993882	-.027578	12.779	70
75	119000	6985	.058697	.259048	65679	17014	287507	.059178	2.596808	633247	-.033851	9.642	75
80	66000	6755	.102348	.410952	48665	19999	193608	.103297	2.514011	345740	-.033851	7.104	80
85+	35000	6595	.188429	1.000000	28666	28666	152132	.188429	5.307051	152132	.000000	5.307	85+

NUMBER OF PERSONS DYING (OUT OF 100,000 AT BIRTH) ABOVE AGE X FROM SPECIFIED CAUSES

Age (x)	All Causes	Respira-tory T. B.	Other Infec. and Paras.	Neo-plasms	Cardio-vascular	Infl., Pneu., Bronch.	Diar-rheal	Certain Degen-erative	Maternal	Cert. Dis. of Infancy	Motor Vehicle	Other Violence	Other and Unknown	Age (x)
									104	715	714	3776	12984	0
0	100000	120	319	21278	52171	3032	452	4335	104	0	713	3748	12512	1
1	98711	120	308	21267	52163	3001	440	4335	104	0	673	3685	12383	5
5	98372	120	292	21217	52158	2983	426	4331	104	0	622	3665	12327	10
10	98180	120	291	21173	52154	2974	423	4327	104	0	590	3652	12280	15
15	98039	120	286	21142	52148	2972	422	4323	104	0	557	3636	12232	20
20	97886	120	284	21107	52138	2971	421	4316	104	0	530	3610	12195	25
25	97708	118	283	21068	52121	2968	421	4303	91	0	498	3581	12140	30
30	97474	118	283	21010	52096	2963	420	4288	77	0	472	3550	12081	35
35	97136	117	277	20890	52052	2962	417	4267	51	0	453	3517	11998	40
40	96633	115	264	20670	51982	2953	417	4246	18	0	424	3479	11876	45
45	95849	113	254	20260	51855	2942	414	4229	3	0	384	3415	11710	50
50	94570	108	247	19534	51649	2933	409	4181	0	0	349	3334	11450	55
55	92618	103	235	18476	51270	2906	402	4093	0	0	305	3237	11052	60
60	89791	95	216	17216	50474	2861	392	3943	0	0	242	3134	10444	65
65	85150	88	196	15380	48850	2784	371	3661	0	0	174	2971	9544	70
70	77772	76	158	13086	45577	2662	339	3185	0	0	110	2724	8218	75
75	65679	69	120	9980	39325	2399	295	2439	0	0	59	2195	6405	80
80	48665	35	79	6523	29658	1915	219	1577	0	0	13	1387	4265	85+
85+	28666	17	61	3382	17273	1269	130	869						

NUMBER OF PERSONS SURVIVING TO AGE X IF SPECIFIED CAUSES WERE ELIMINATED

Age (x)	No Causes	Respira-tory T. B.	Other Infec. and Paras.	Neo-plasms	Cardio-vascular	Infl., Pneu., Bronch.	Diar-rheal	Certain Degener-ative	Maternal	Cert. Dis. of Infancy	Motor Vehicle	Other Violence	Other and Unknown	(1) + (2)	(1) + (2) + (5) + (6) + (8)	(1)+(2)+ (5)+(6)+ (8)+part of(9)&(12)	(10) + (11)	Age (x)
		(1)	(2)	(3)	(4)	(5)	(6)	(7)	(8)	(9)	(10)	(11)	(12)					
0	100000	100000	100000	100000	100000	100000	100000	100000	100000	100000	100000	100000	100000	100000	100000	100000	100000	0
1	98711	98711	98722	98722	98719	98742	98723	98711	98711	99424	98712	98735	99181	98722	98765	99391	98740	1
5	98372	98372	98399	98433	98385	98421	98398	98376	98372	99082	98413	98463	98970	98399	98473	99128	98504	5
10	98180	98180	98208	98285	98197	98238	98209	98188	98180	98889	98272	98290	98833	98208	98294	98953	98382	10
15	98039	98039	98072	98175	98062	98058	98069	98051	98039	98747	98163	98162	98738	98072	98161	98823	98286	15
20	97886	97886	97921	98056	97919	97946	97917	97905	97886	98593	98043	98025	98633	97921	98012	98675	98182	20
25	97708	97710	97744	97917	97758	97771	97739	97740	97721	98414	97891	97873	98491	97744	97853	98519	98056	25
30	97474	97476	97510	97741	97549	97542	97506	97521	97501	98178	97689	97668	98310	97512	97638	98310	97883	30
35	97136	97139	97177	97522	97254	97205	97170	97204	97189	97838	97376	97360	98029	97180	97337	98014	97601	35
40	96633	96638	96687	97238	96821	96711	96667	96721	96718	97331	96891	96889	97605	96692	96890	97575	97147	40
45	95849	95856	95913	96860	96162	95937	95886	95953	95949	96541	96134	96141	96935	95920	96145	96832	96426	45
50	94570	94582	94640	96299	95084	94666	94611	94721	94671	95253	94891	94921	95809	94652	94890	95574	95243	50
55	92618	92634	92698	95384	93500	92738	92666	92853	92717	93287	92967	93043	94092	92715	92983	93660	93393	55
60	89791	89815	89888	93758	91441	89952	89847	90167	89887	90440	90173	90299	91619	89911	90226	90896	90683	60
65	85150	85179	85261	90797	88342	85378	85224	85783	85241	85765	85574	85732	87490	85291	85684	86340	86159	65
70	77772	77810	77910	85295	84003	78097	77870	78809	77855	78334	78224	78461	80797	77948	78457	79084	78917	70
75	65679	65718	65830	75218	77427	66197	65802	67251	65749	66153	66119	66491	69508	65869	66585	67158	66936	75
80	48665	48723	48812	59212	68044	49470	48822	50588	48717	49016	49035	49730	53172	48870	49892	50389	50108	80
85+	28666	28714	28766	37902	55626	29643	28826	30362	28697	28873	28919	29927	33146	28814	29994	30367	30191	85+
ADDED YRS OF LIFE																		
TOTAL		.017	.069	3.248	8.855	.295	.064	.503	.046	.551	.238	.484	1.957	.086	.495	1.078	.726	
WORK	1.461	.004	.013	.639	.256	.018	.005	.066	.032	.000	.074	.087	.230	.018	.073	.089	.161	

POPULATION, DEATHS, DEATH RATES FOR ALL CAUSES COMBINED, AND SPECIFIED CAUSES

Age Start of Interval	Midyear Population	Deaths During Year	All Causes	Respiratory T. B.	Other Infec. and Paras.	Neo-plasms	Cardio-vascular	Infl., Pneu., Bronch.	Diar-rheal	Certain Degen-erative	Maternal	Cert. Dis. of Infancy	Motor Vehicle	Other Violence	Other and Unknown	Age Start of Interval
0	9292	990	.10654	.00043	.01378	.00011	.00075	.01421	.02012	.00000	.00000	.02873	.00000	.00226	.02615	0
1	32720	365	.01116	.00009	.00391	.00000	.00012	.00153	.00119	.00000	.00000	.00000	.00000	.00226	.00290	1
5	34614	132	.00381	.00003	.00179	.00000	.00026	.00020	.00012	.00003	.00000	.00000	.00000	.00141	.00290	5
10	29136	83	.00285	.00014	.00062	.00000	.00027	.00014	.00014	.00007	.00000	.00000	.00000	.00075	.00064	10
15	21250	77	.00362	.00071	.00108	.00000	.00014	.00014	.00014	.00000	.00000	.00000	.00000	.00072	.00076	15
20	22277	119	.00534	.00166	.00072	.00000	.00040	.00027	.00009	.00000	.00000	.00000	.00000	.00080	.00061	20
25	24132	131	.00543	.00170	.00054	.00012	.00041	.00029	.00008	.00025	.00000	.00000	.00000	.00121	.00099	25
30	20384	133	.00652	.00186	.00049	.00005	.00078	.00034	.00010	.00010	.00000	.00000	.00000	.00112	.00091	30
35	20502	168	.00819	.00185	.00068	.00015	.00122	.00054	.00005	.00015	.00000	.00000	.00000	.00142	.00137	35
40	20281	219	.01080	.00178	.00084	.00035	.00197	.00104	.00039	.00000	.00000	.00000	.00000	.00200	.00156	40
45	14099	194	.01376	.00099	.00099	.00085	.00319	.00099	.00050	.00064	.00000	.00000	.00000	.00212	.00232	45
50	9640	148	.01535	.00156	.00104	.00104	.00394	.00145	.00021	.00041	.00000	.00000	.00000	.00248	.00312	50
55	4899	132	.02694	.00286	.00122	.00122	.00674	.00306	.00102	.00286	.00000	.00000	.00000	.00166	.00405	55
60	3844	117	.03044	.00156	.00104	.00182	.00832	.00364	.00130	.00104	.00000	.00000	.00000	.00286	.00735	60
65	1896	81	.04272	.00158	.00211	.00316	.01424	.00527	.00000	.00053	.00000	.00000	.00000	.00264	.01319	65
70	1185	67	.05654	.00000	.00169	.00253	.02025	.01013	.00169	.00169	.00000	.00000	.00000	.00286	.01319	70
75	586	45	.07679	.00171	.00341	.00171	.01536	.01195	.00000	.00000	.00000	.00000	.00000	.00169	.01688	75
80	262	32	.12214	.00000	.00000	.00382	.01527	.01527	.00000	.00382	.00000	.00000	.00000	.00171	.04096	80
85+	62	14	.22581	.00000	.00000	.00000	.01613	.03226	.00000	.00000	.00000	.00000	.00000	.00382	.08015	85+
ALL	271061	3247													.17742	

CRUDE DEATH RATE			.01198	.00100	.00174	.00023	.00127	.00125	.00101	.00014	.00000	.00099	.00000	.00139	.00297	
STANDARDIZED RATE (1)			.01346	.00096	.00179	.00029	.00166	.00149	.00104	.00017	.00000	.00101	.00000	.00137	.00367	
STANDARDIZED RATE (2)			.01702	.00112	.00152	.00052	.00295	.00159	.00078	.00027	.00000	.00059	.00000	.00152	.00575	
GEOMETRIC MEAN			.01804													

LIFE TABLE FOR ALL CAUSES COMBINED

Age (x)	Midyear Population	Deaths During Year	$_nM_x$	$_nq_x$	l_x	$_nd_x$	$_nL_x$	$_nm_x$	$_na_x$	T_x	$_nr_x$	$\overset{\circ}{e}_x$	Age (x)
0	9292	990	.106543	.098670	100000	9867	92611	.106543	.251124	5333940	.000000	53.339	0
1	32720	365	.011155	.043414	90133	3913	350750	.011156	1.500000	5241329	.000000	58.151	1
5	34614	132	.003813	.018917	86220	1631	427023	.003819	2.500000	4890580	.000000	56.722	5
10	29136	83	.002849	.014115	84589	1194	419934	.002843	2.477841	4463557	.037111	52.768	10
15	21250	77	.003624	.018035	83395	1504	413416	.003638	2.633533	4043624	.034340	48.488	15
20	22277	119	.005342	.026352	81891	2158	404191	.005339	2.560917	3630208	-.008799	44.330	20
25	24132	131	.005428	.026777	79733	2135	393358	.005427	2.532884	3226016	-.001789	40.460	25
30	20384	133	.006525	.032153	77598	2495	381936	.006533	2.573480	2832619	.011347	36.504	30
35	20502	168	.008194	.040145	75103	3015	368249	.008187	2.590036	2450683	-.008406	32.631	35
40	20281	219	.010798	.052686	72088	3798	351267	.010812	2.584749	2082434	.013617	28.887	40
45	14099	194	.013760	.066774	68290	4560	330246	.013808	2.542900	1731167	.044726	25.350	45
50	9640	148	.015353	.074329	63730	4737	307430	.015408	2.631412	1400921	.081914	21.982	50
55	4899	132	.026944	.127947	58993	7548	276629	.027286	2.570769	1093491	.071796	18.536	55
60	3844	117	.030437	.141919	51445	7301	239192	.030524	2.530133	816862	.061638	15.878	60
65	1896	81	.042722	.194908	44144	8604	199534	.043121	2.537604	577670	.075132	13.086	65
70	1185	67	.056540	.249128	35540	8854	155574	.056912	2.501035	378136	.061325	10.640	70
75	586	45	.076792	.324065	26686	8648	111736	.077397	2.491424	222562	.068380	8.340	75
80	262	32	.122137	.471117	18038	8498	68577	.123918	2.456755	110826	.068380	6.144	80
85+	62	14	.225806	1.000000	9540	9540	42249	.225806	4.428571	42249	.000000	4.429	85+

NUMBER OF PERSONS DYING (OUT OF 100,000 AT BIRTH) ABOVE AGE X FROM SPECIFIED CAUSES

Age (x)	All Causes	Respiratory T. B.	Other Infec. and Paras.	Neoplasms	Cardiovascular	Infl., Pneu., Bronch.	Diarrheal	Certain Degenerative	Maternal	Cert. Dis. of Infancy	Motor Vehicle	Other Violence	Other and Unknown	Age (x)
0	100000	6290	7670	3126	17837	11897	3801	1627	0	2661	0	8377	36714	0
1	90133	6250	6394	3116	17767	10581	1938	1627	0	0	0	8167	34293	1
5	86220	6218	5022	3116	17724	10045	1520	1627	0	0	0	7674	33274	5
10	84589	6206	4256	3116	17613	9959	1470	1615	0	0	0	7353	33001	10
15	83395	6146	4000	3116	17498	9901	1412	1586	0	0	0	7050	32686	15
20	81891	5650	3552	3116	17440	9843	1354	1586	0	0	0	6718	32432	20
25	79733	5180	3261	3116	17277	9734	1318	1586	0	0	0	6229	32032	25
30	77598	4511	3049	3068	17114	9620	1285	1489	0	0	0	5788	31674	30
35	75103	3799	2862	3049	16813	9488	1248	1451	0	0	0	5244	31149	35
40	72088	3116	2611	2995	16365	9291	1230	1397	0	0	0	4508	30575	40
45	68290	2494	2316	2873	15670	8927	1091	1397	0	0	0	3763	29759	45
50	63730	2168	1987	2590	14609	8598	927	1184	0	0	0	2944	28723	50
55	58993	1683	1669	2270	13389	8146	865	1059	0	0	0	2441	27471	55
60	51445	885	1329	1929	11502	7286	575	887	0	0	0	1644	25408	60
65	44144	520	1080	1488	9497	6411	266	637	0	0	0	1277	22968	65
70	35540	207	654	851	6614	5344	266	534	0	0	0	746	20324	70
75	26686	207	392	461	3450	3750	4	269	0	0	0	488	17665	75
80	18038	16	7	273	1759	2412	4	269	0	0	0	296	13002	80
85+	9540	0	0	0	681	1363	0	0	0	0	0	0	7496	85+

NUMBER OF PERSONS SURVIVING TO AGE X IF SPECIFIED CAUSES WERE ELIMINATED

Age (x)	No Causes	Respiratory T. B.	Other Infec. and Paras.	Neoplasms	Cardiovascular	Infl., Pneu., Bronch.	Diarrheal	Certain Degenerative	Maternal	Cert. Dis. of Infancy	Motor Vehicle	Other Violence	Other and Unknown	(1) + (2)	(1) + (2) + (5) + (6) + (8)	(1)+(2)+ (5)+(6)+ (8)+part of(9)&(12)	(10) + (11)	Age (x)
		(1)	(2)	(3)	(4)	(5)	(6)	(7)	(8)	(9)	(10)	(11)	(12)					
0	100000	100000	100000	100000	100000	100000	100000	100000	100000	100000	100000	100000	100000	100000	100000	100000	100000	0
1	90133	90171	91352	90142	90199	91391	91918	90133	90133	92694	90133	90333	92460	91391	94501	99372	90333	1
5	86220	86288	88757	86229	86326	87596	88346	86220	86220	88672	86220	86895	89474	88826	92849	98555	86895	5
10	84589	84667	87862	84598	84803	86379	86725	84601	84589	86992	84589	85573	88063	87944	92073	97945	85573	10
15	83395	83532	86886	83404	83720	85219	85560	83436	83395	85764	83395	84670	87146	87029	91241	97240	84670	15
20	81891	82320	85783	81900	82268	83741	84076	81931	81891	84218	81891	83477	85838	86232	90533	96669	83477	20
25	79733	80818	83823	79741	80262	81644	81857	79772	79733	81598	79733	81771	83990	84964	89362	95736	81771	25
30	77598	79326	81799	77654	78275	79573	79737	77732	77598	79803	77598	80029	82114	83620	88113	94647	80029	30
35	75103	77494	79363	75176	76058	77148	77211	75270	75103	77237	75103	78010	80022	81890	86481	93241	78010	35
40	72088	75076	76437	72211	73451	74249	74130	72301	72088	74136	72088	75630	77412	79606	84315	91240	75630	40
45	68290	71753	72715	68526	70274	70703	70364	68492	68290	70230	68290	72410	74191	76402	81504	88688	72410	45
50	63730	67292	68199	64225	66646	66312	65828	64125	63730	65541	63730	68418	70333	72011	77395	84649	68418	50
55	58993	62786	63457	59762	62931	61838	60997	59480	58993	60669	58993	63853	66449	67537	73199	80680	63853	55
60	51445	55549	55679	52439	56791	54774	53474	52032	51445	52907	51445	56491	60159	60120	66536	74491	56491	60
65	44144	48028	48027	45416	50828	47871	46181	44882	44144	45398	44144	48846	54333	52253	59280	67634	48846	65
70	35540	38970	39083	37155	44011	39595	37179	36228	35540	36550	35540	39854	46753	42855	49947	58146	39854	70
75	26686	29259	29596	28248	36555	31309	28155	27436	26686	27444	26686	30172	38287	32449	40167	48180	30172	75
80	18038	19950	20355	19255	26663	22476	19027	18543	18038	18551	18038	20572	32045	22513	29590	39325	20572	80
85+	9540	10564	10771	10394	15288	12860	10066	10007	9540	9811	9540	11124	25607	11927	16964	26153	11124	85+

ADDED YRS OF LIFE																		
TOTAL		1.857	3.136	.485	3.092	2.529	1.649	.283	.000	1.509	.000	2.580	10.815	5.144	10.020	18.708	2.580	
WORK	8.439	1.464	.754	.198	1.121	.510	.173	.139	.000	.000	.000	1.398	1.569	2.256	3.009	3.849	1.398	

POPULATION, DEATHS, DEATH RATES FOR ALL CAUSES COMBINED, AND SPECIFIED CAUSES

Age Start of Interval	Midyear Popula-tion	Deaths During Year	All Causes	Respira-tory T. B.	Other Infec. and Paras.	Neo-plasms	Cardio-vascular	Infl., Pneu., Bronch.	Diar-rheal	Certain Degen-erative	Maternal	Cert. Dis. of Infancy	Motor Vehicle	Other Violence	Other and Unknown	Age Start of Interval
0	8823	744	.08433	.00091	.01235	.00011	.00045	.00861	.01621	.00000	.00000	.02595	.00000	.00170	.01802	0
1	32192	347	.01078	.00006	.00457	.00006	.00016	.00149	.00099	.00003	.00000	.00000	.00000	.00084	.00258	1
5	33908	98	.00289	.00015	.00124	.00000	.00021	.00029	.00009	.00000	.00000	.00000	.00000	.00024	.00068	5
10	29003	78	.00269	.00024	.00076	.00000	.00024	.00014	.00003	.00014	.00003	.00000	.00000	.00017	.00093	10
15	21741	82	.00377	.00124	.00115	.00000	.00018	.00014	.00005	.00005	.00023	.00000	.00000	.00064	.00093	15
20	19458	80	.00411	.00128	.00057	.00000	.00026	.00021	.00015	.00015	.00077	.00000	.00000	.00010	.00062	20
25	16819	104	.00618	.00208	.00030	.00012	.00071	.00018	.00012	.00012	.00131	.00000	.00000	.00018	.00107	25
30	14521	102	.00702	.00172	.00069	.00041	.00076	.00062	.00007	.00021	.00110	.00000	.00000	.00014	.00131	30
35	13362	109	.00816	.00187	.00067	.00037	.00090	.00022	.00037	.00015	.00172	.00000	.00000	.00037	.00150	35
40	11099	93	.00838	.00126	.00072	.00081	.00153	.00036	.00027	.00009	.00059	.00000	.00000	.00036	.00198	40
45	7434	76	.01022	.00148	.00108	.00121	.00215	.00054	.00040	.00013	.00040	.00000	.00000	.00054	.00229	45
50	5054	72	.01425	.00139	.00020	.00277	.00356	.00059	.00059	.00040	.00000	.00000	.00000	.00020	.00416	50
55	2991	40	.01337	.00167	.00201	.00134	.00334	.00167	.00100	.00000	.00000	.00000	.00000	.00067	.00167	55
60	2552	50	.01959	.00000	.00196	.00353	.00627	.00196	.00078	.00118	.00000	.00000	.00000	.00000	.00392	60
65	1365	48	.03516	.00073	.00000	.00586	.01026	.00293	.00220	.00000	.00000	.00000	.00000	.00073	.01245	65
70	921	40	.04343	.00000	.00217	.00109	.00977	.00651	.00109	.00326	.00000	.00000	.00000	.00000	.01954	70
75	415	42	.10120	.00000	.00723	.00723	.01687	.01687	.00000	.00000	.00000	.00000	.00000	.00000	.05301	75
80	196	24	.12245	.00510	.00510	.00000	.02041	.00510	.00000	.00000	.00000	.00000	.00000	.00000	.08673	80
85+	67	15	.22388	.00000	.00000	.00000	.02985	.00000	.00000	.00000	.00000	.00000	.00000	.00000	.19403	85+
ALL	221921	2244														

CRUDE DEATH RATE			.01011	.00089	.00187	.00033	.00082	.00090	.00054	.00012	.00043	.00103	.00000	.00036	.00242	
STANDARDIZED RATE (1)			.01144	.00095	.00177	.00053	.00129	.00103	.00050	.00016	.00043	.00091	.00000	.00035	.00312	
STANDARDIZED RATE (2)			.01480	.00105	.00158	.00089	.00233	.00131	.00073	.00023	.00045	.00054	.00000	.00032	.00537	
GEOMETRIC MEAN			.01576													

LIFE TABLE FOR ALL CAUSES COMBINED

Age (x)	Midyear Popula-tion	Deaths During Year	$_nM_x$	$_nq_x$	l_x	$_nd_x$	$_nL_x$	$_nm_x$	$_na_x$	T_x	$_nr_x$	$\overset{\circ}{e}_x$	Age (x)
0	8823	744	.084325	.079080	100000	7908	93779	.084326	.213353	5680331	.000000	56.803	0
1	32192	347	.010779	.041980	92092	3866	358703	.010778	1.500000	5586552	.000000	60.663	1
5	33908	98	.002890	.014338	88226	1265	437968	.002888	2.500000	5227849	.000000	59.255	5
10	29003	78	.002689	.013374	86961	1163	431969	.002692	2.561443	4789882	.032088	55.081	10
15	21741	82	.003772	.018742	85798	1608	425086	.003783	2.572036	4357913	.038228	50.793	15
20	19458	80	.004111	.020418	84190	1719	416842	.004124	2.610048	3932827	.024411	46.714	20
25	16819	104	.006183	.030544	82471	2519	406275	.006200	2.586344	3515985	.024823	42.633	25
30	14521	102	.007024	.034558	79952	2763	392971	.007031	2.542828	3109710	.018533	38.895	30
35	13362	109	.008157	.039993	77189	3087	378286	.008160	2.519099	2716739	.013947	35.196	35
40	11099	93	.008379	.041106	74102	3046	362594	.008391	2.532488	2338452	.039111	31.557	40
45	7434	76	.010223	.050129	71056	3562	346712	.010274	2.594692	1975458	.058838	27.801	45
50	5054	72	.014246	.069117	67494	4665	325913	.014314	2.522597	1628746	.077966	24.132	50
55	2991	40	.013373	.064747	62829	4068	304161	.013374	2.545835	1302833	.058705	20.736	55
60	2552	50	.019592	.094621	58761	5560	280875	.019795	2.674498	998672	.055497	16.995	60
65	1365	48	.035165	.164001	53201	8725	244872	.035631	2.577913	717796	.066228	13.492	65
70	921	40	.043431	.198377	44476	8823	201568	.043772	2.641156	472924	.066580	10.633	70
75	415	42	.101205	.412392	35653	14703	141681	.103775	2.511817	271356	.062781	7.611	75
80	196	24	.122449	.460955	20950	9657	79233	.121881	2.357659	129675	.062781	6.190	80
85+	67	15	.223881	1.000000	11293	11293	50442	.223881	4.466667	50442	.000000	4.467	85+

NUMBER OF PERSONS DYING (OUT OF 100,000 AT BIRTH) ABOVE AGE X FROM SPECIFIED CAUSES

Age (x)	All Causes	Respiratory T. B.	Other Infec. and Paras.	Neo-plasms	Cardio-vascular	Infl., Pneu., Bronch.	Diar-rheal	Certain Degen-erative	Maternal	Cert. Dis. of Infancy	Motor Vehicle	Other Violence	Other and Unknown	Age (x)
0	100000	6099	8800	6142	16902	8558	3958	1546	2554	2434	0	1757	41250	0
1	92092	6014	7642	6131	16859	7750	2438	1546	2554	0	0	1597	39561	1
5	88226	5991	6004	6109	16803	7215	2081	1535	2554	0	0	1296	38638	5
10	86961	5927	5462	6109	16713	7086	2043	1535	2554	0	0	1193	38339	10
15	85798	5820	5135	6109	16609	7027	2028	1475	2539	0	0	1119	37937	15
20	84190	5287	4646	6109	16531	6568	2008	1456	2439	0	0	1080	37666	20
25	82471	4750	4412	6109	16423	6882	1943	1391	2115	0	0	1037	37409	25
30	79952	3903	4292	6060	16131	6809	1895	1343	1583	0	0	965	36971	30
35	77189	3227	4020	5897	15834	6565	1868	1261	1149	0	0	910	36458	35
40	74102	2520	3766	5755	15493	6481	1726	1205	498	0	0	769	35889	40
45	71056	2064	3503	5458	14933	6349	1628	1172	143	0	0	637	35169	45
50	67494	1550	3130	5032	14179	6162	1487	1125	8	0	0	451	34370	50
55	62829	1100	3070	4119	12877	5966	1291	995	8	0	0	389	33014	55
60	58761	594	2450	3717	11859	5451	984	995	8	0	0	184	32519	60
65	53201	594	1904	2712	10077	4898	763	661	8	0	0	184	31400	65
70	44476	419	1904	1270	7540	4168	218	661	8	0	0	3	28285	70
75	35653	419	1459	1071	5576	2829	8	0	0	0	0	3	24280	75
80	20950	419	407	18	3136	385	8	0	0	8	0	3	16566	80
85+	11293	0	0	0	1506	0	0	0	0	0	0	0	9787	85+

NUMBER OF PERSONS SURVIVING TO AGE X IF SPECIFIED CAUSES WERE ELIMINATED

Age (x)	No Causes	Respiratory T. B. (1)	Other Infec. and Paras. (2)	Neo-plasms (3)	Cardio-vascular (4)	Infl., Pneu., Bronch. (5)	Diar-rheal (6)	Certain Degen-erative (7)	Maternal (8)	Cert. Dis. of Infancy (9)	Motor Vehicle (10)	Other Violence (11)	Other and Unknown (12)	(1) + (2)	(1) + (2) + (5) + (6) + (8)	(1)+(2)+(5)+(6)+(8)+part of(9)&(12)	(10) + (11)	Age (x)
0	100000	100000	100000	100000	100000	100000	100000	100000	100000	100000	100000	100000	100000	100000	100000	100000	100000	0
1	92092	92174	93210	92103	92133	92870	93562	92092	92092	94457	92092	92246	93727	93292	95582	99535	92246	1
5	88226	88327	90934	88258	88320	89501	89990	88237	88226	90492	88226	88669	90716	91038	94200	98971	88669	5
10	86961	87124	90187	86992	87144	88348	88738	86972	86961	89194	86961	87500	89721	90355	93673	98686	87500	10
15	85758	86065	89318	85829	86082	87226	87566	85868	85813	88001	85798	86404	88934	89596	92981	98271	86404	15
20	84190	84984	88150	84220	84546	85651	85946	84278	84304	86352	84190	84824	87546	88981	92537	98083	84824	20
25	82471	83787	86592	82501	82927	83989	84256	82621	82905	84589	82471	83135	86023	87974	92013	97784	83135	25
30	79952	82079	84071	80029	80684	81497	81731	80145	80900	82005	79952	80667	83847	86308	91000	97114	80667	30
35	77189	79927	81448	77424	78191	78925	78934	77456	78537	79171	77189	77934	81480	84337	89723	96212	77934	35
40	74102	77450	78453	74468	75403	75852	75920	74413	76048	76005	74102	74957	78812	81998	88252	95156	74957	40
45	71056	74734	75502	71700	72864	72867	72897	71387	73279	72881	71056	72006	76326	79410	86158	93415	72006	45
50	67494	71516	72103	68527	69970	69401	69384	67855	69740	69227	67494	68580	73342	76400	83447	90987	68580	50
55	62829	67035	67182	64690	66450	64800	64784	63291	64915	64442	62829	63901	65708	71679	78764	86369	63901	55
60	58761	63217	63478	60903	63198	61121	60856	59193	60716	60270	58761	59965	65726	68292	76064	83779	59965	60
65	53201	57234	58031	56141	59070	55886	55352	53912	54971	54567	53201	54291	60717	62430	70503	78119	54291	65
70	44476	48019	48513	48335	52017	47430	46794	45073	45556	45618	44476	45556	54125	52377	60722	68412	45556	70
75	35653	38492	39331	38933	43786	39324	37703	36737	36839	36569	35653	36517	47987	42463	51176	60129	36517	75
80	20950	22624	24005	23763	28085	25223	22151	21574	21647	21488	20950	21458	37326	25922	34098	46102	21458	80
85+	11293	12527	13281	12824	16803	13935	11946	11630	11675	11583	11293	11569	31048	14732	19881	32342	11569	85+

ADDED YRS OF LIFE																		
TOTAL		2.057	3.372	1.083	2.788	1.898	1.568	.310	.951	1.453	.000	.677	15.419	5.592	10.808	17.407	.677	
WORK	7.573	1.547	.745	.441	.972	.343	.208	.139	.821	.000	.000	.211	1.315	2.330	3.835	4.775	.211	

POPULATION, DEATHS, DEATH RATES FOR ALL CAUSES COMBINED, AND SPECIFIED CAUSES

Age Start of Interval	Midyear Population	Deaths During Year	All Causes	Respiratory T.B.	Other Infec. and Paras.	Neoplasms	Cardiovascular	Infl., Pneu., Bronch.	Diarrheal	Certain Degenerative	Maternal	Cert. Dis. of Infancy	Motor Vehicle	Other Violence	Other and Unknown	Age Start of Interval
0	8437	945	.11201	.00012	.01482	.00012	.00012	.01825	.02323	.00012	.00000	.03105	.00000	.00190	.02228	0
1	34077	293	.00860	.00006	.00340	.00006	.00003	.00141	.00070	.00000	.00000	.03105	.00000	.00190	.00200	1
5	43757	133	.00304	.00002	.00096	.00000	.00018	.00032	.00007	.00007	.00000	.00000	.00000	.00094	.00200	5
10	41001	84	.00205	.00017	.00054	.00000	.00022	.00007	.00002	.00002	.00000	.00000	.00000	.00048	.00094	10
15	32776	99	.00302	.00043	.00079	.00006	.00018	.00021	.00000	.00012	.00000	.00000	.00000	.00046	.00054	15
20	28509	152	.00533	.00147	.00053	.00007	.00025	.00028	.00011	.00011	.00000	.00000	.00000	.00067	.00055	20
25	23847	108	.00453	.00092	.00063	.00000	.00050	.00029	.00017	.00017	.00000	.00000	.00000	.00182	.00070	25
30	22154	114	.00515	.00126	.00059	.00009	.00032	.00041	.00018	.00018	.00000	.00000	.00000	.00109	.00075	30
35	20637	139	.00674	.00150	.00048	.00024	.00097	.00048	.00010	.00024	.00000	.00000	.00000	.00144	.00068	35
40	17862	139	.00778	.00134	.00056	.00050	.00129	.00101	.00011	.00056	.00000	.00000	.00000	.00141	.00131	40
45	17131	183	.01068	.00123	.00082	.00053	.00216	.00146	.00000	.00111	.00000	.00000	.00000	.00146	.00095	45
50	16871	272	.01612	.00154	.00089	.00148	.00379	.00243	.00000	.00095	.00000	.00000	.00000	.00210	.00128	50
55	11011	252	.02289	.00163	.00154	.00218	.00599	.00327	.00036	.00191	.00000	.00000	.00000	.00190	.00314	55
60	7731	227	.02936	.00103	.00103	.00285	.00854	.00375	.00026	.00233	.00000	.00000	.00000	.00227	.00372	60
65	3946	217	.05499	.00177	.00152	.00634	.01926	.00710	.00025	.00329	.00000	.00000	.00000	.00285	.00673	65
70	2519	184	.07304	.00079	.00159	.00675	.01866	.01032	.00198	.00357	.00000	.00000	.00000	.00152	.01394	70
75	1199	134	.11176	.00083	.00083	.00584	.02252	.01835	.00167	.00667	.00000	.00000	.00000	.00516	.02422	75
80	485	60	.12371	.00000	.00000	.00412	.02268	.02062	.00000	.00825	.00000	.00000	.00000	.00250	.05254	80
85+	237	52	.21941	.00000	.00000	.00422	.03376	.03376	.00000	.00844	.00000	.00000	.00000	.00412	.06392	85+
ALL	334187	3787														

	All Causes	Respiratory T.B.	Other Infec. and Paras.	Neoplasms	Cardiovascular	Infl., Pneu., Bronch.	Diarrheal	Certain Degenerative	Maternal	Cert. Dis. of Infancy	Motor Vehicle	Other Violence	Other and Unknown
CRUDE DEATH RATE	.01133	.00076	.00137	.00046	.00148	.00151	.00076	.00043	.00000	.00078	.00000	.00124	.00253
STANDARDIZED RATE (1)	.01306	.00073	.00156	.00050	.00161	.00178	.00101	.00045	.00000	.00109	.00000	.00125	.00307
STANDARDIZED RATE (2)	.01741	.00087	.00129	.00055	.00314	.00242	.00071	.00085	.00000	.00064	.00000	.00149	.00505
GEOMETRIC MEAN	.01672												

LIFE TABLE FOR ALL CAUSES COMBINED

Age (x)	Midyear Population	Deaths During Year	$_nM_x$	$_nq_x$	l_x	$_nd_x$	$_nL_x$	$_nm_x$	$_na_x$	T_x	$_nr_x$	$\overset{\circ}{e}_x$	Age (x)
0	8437	945	.112007	.103440	100000	10344	92350	.112009	.260411	5450328	.000000	54.503	0
1	34077	293	.008598	.033662	89656	3018	351079	.008596	1.500000	5357979	.000000	59.762	1
5	43757	133	.003040	.015097	86638	1308	429920	.003042	2.500000	5006900	.000000	57.791	5
10	41001	84	.002049	.010184	85330	869	424471	.002047	2.492089	4576980	.018867	53.639	10
15	32776	99	.003021	.015056	84461	1275	419394	.003040	2.716503	4152509	.030645	49.165	15
20	28509	152	.005332	.026373	83186	2194	410557	.005344	2.550991	3733115	.028675	44.877	20
25	23847	108	.004529	.022313	80992	1812	400392	.004526	2.479305	3322558	.024485	41.023	25
30	22154	114	.005146	.025436	79180	2014	391021	.005151	2.577375	2922166	.011693	36.905	30
35	20637	139	.006735	.033175	77166	2560	379605	.006744	2.568359	2531145	.014069	32.801	35
40	17862	139	.007782	.038254	74606	2854	366140	.007795	2.585771	2151540	.015335	28.839	40
45	17131	183	.010682	.052054	71752	3735	349931	.010674	2.636044	1785400	.005551	24.883	45
50	16871	272	.016122	.077819	68017	5293	327499	.016162	2.622055	1435470	.015899	21.105	50
55	11011	252	.022886	.109001	62724	6837	297036	.023017	2.574381	1107971	.043820	17.664	55
60	7731	227	.029362	.138386	55887	7734	261142	.029616	2.634687	810935	.064685	14.510	60
65	3946	217	.054992	.245821	48153	11837	211906	.055860	2.561935	549793	.064254	11.418	65
70	2519	184	.073045	.309863	36316	11253	153264	.073422	2.483671	337888	.043506	9.304	70
75	1199	134	.111760	.437059	25063	10955	96941	.113007	2.409935	184624	.055756	7.366	75
80	485	60	.123711	.461936	14108	6517	53086	.122764	2.321716	87683	.055756	6.215	80
85+	237	52	.219409	1.000000	7591	7591	34597	.219409	4.557692	34597	.000000	4.558	85+

NUMBER OF PERSONS DYING (OUT OF 100,000 AT BIRTH) ABOVE AGE X FROM SPECIFIED CAUSES

Age (x)	All Causes	Respiratory T.B.	Other Infec. and Paras.	Neoplasms	Cardiovascular	Infl., Pneu., Bronch.	Diarrheal	Certain Degenerative	Maternal	Cert. Dis. of Infancy	Motor Vehicle	Other Violence	Other and Unknown	Age (x)
0	100000	5110	6591	5808	19167	13827	3392	5103	0	2868	0	8528	29606	0
1	89656	5099	5222	5797	19156	12142	1246	5092	0	0	0	8353	27549	1
5	86638	5078	4028	5777	19146	11647	999	5092	0	0	0	8023	26848	5
10	85330	5069	3615	5777	19067	11509	970	5063	0	0	0	7816	26444	10
15	84461	4995	3387	5777	18974	11479	959	5052	0	0	0	7620	26218	15
20	83186	4813	3054	5751	18897	11389	959	5001	0	0	0	7335	25987	20
25	80992	4206	2839	5722	18796	11273	916	4957	0	0	0	6584	25699	25
30	79180	3838	2587	5722	18594	11155	848	4890	0	0	0	6149	25397	30
35	77166	3343	2358	5687	18470	10996	778	4819	0	0	0	5583	25132	35
40	74606	2772	2174	5594	18101	10812	741	4727	0	0	0	5050	24635	40
45	71752	2281	1968	5409	17628	10442	700	4521	0	0	0	4516	24287	45
50	68017	1852	1683	5226	16873	9932	700	4133	0	0	0	3781	23837	50
55	62724	1347	1391	4739	15627	9134	700	3822	0	0	0	3160	22804	55
60	55887	862	930	4087	13833	8158	591	3251	0	0	0	2483	21692	60
65	48153	595	663	3336	11574	7172	524	2640	0	0	0	1741	19908	65
70	36316	216	338	1971	7427	5644	468	1935	0	0	0	1421	16896	70
75	25063	97	95	938	4571	4050	160	1385	0	0	0	623	13144	75
80	14108	16	16	374	2375	2247	0	729	0	0	0	386	7965	80
85+	7591	0	0	146	1168	1168	0	292	0	0	0	146	4671	85+

NUMBER OF PERSONS SURVIVING TO AGE X IF SPECIFIED CAUSES WERE ELIMINATED

Age (x)	No Causes	Respiratory T.B. (1)	Other Infec. and Paras. (2)	Neoplasms (3)	Cardiovascular (4)	Infl., Pneu., Bronch. (5)	Diarrheal (6)	Certain Degenerative (7)	Maternal (8)	Cert. Dis. of Infancy (9)	Motor Vehicle (10)	Other Violence (11)	Other and Unknown (12)	(1)+(2)	(1)+(2)+(5)+(6)+(8)	(1)+(2)+(5)+(6)+(8)+part of(9)&(12)	(10)+(11)	Age (x)
0	100000	100000	100000	100000	100000	100000	100000	100000	100000	100000	100000	100000	100000	100000	100000	100000	100000	0
1	89656	89666	90961	89666	89666	91265	91710	89666	89656	92412	89656	89822	91624	91036	94726	99582	89822	1
5	86638	86669	89098	86668	86658	86869	86648	86638	86638	89301	86638	87124	89130	89247	93592	99053	87124	5
10	85330	85369	88175	85359	85428	87491	87560	85369	85330	87953	85330	86015	88313	88216	92813	98530	86015	10
15	84461	84573	87512	84490	84651	86630	86679	84510	84461	87057	84461	85336	87647	87629	92240	98060	85336	15
20	83186	83478	86534	83240	83449	85414	85371	83285	83186	85743	83186	84334	86562	86838	91505	97435	84334	20
25	80992	81880	84472	81074	81349	83279	83161	81132	80992	83481	80992	82865	84575	85398	90163	96179	82865	25
30	79180	80416	82843	79260	79730	81536	81371	79383	79180	81614	79180	81452	82995	84136	89038	95170	81452	30
35	77166	78869	80972	77278	77825	79624	79372	77434	77166	79538	77166	79957	81159	82759	87837	94060	79957	35
40	74606	76828	78476	74806	75610	77170	76777	74957	74606	76899	74606	77849	78982	80813	86022	92403	77849	40
45	71752	74386	75687	72127	73190	74554	73881	72293	71752	73957	71752	75419	76323	78465	83993	90413	75419	45
50	68017	70948	72040	68552	70134	71229	70035	68911	68017	70108	68017	72248	72818	75144	81027	87430	72248	50
55	62724	65933	66732	63691	65923	66494	64585	63851	62724	64652	62724	67261	68222	70146	76568	83109	67261	55
60	55887	59228	59921	57377	60545	60229	57651	57443	55887	57605	55887	60618	61935	63503	70597	77140	60618	60
65	48153	51292	51893	50158	54491	52888	49737	50078	48153	49633	48153	52976	55237	55277	62709	69152	52976	65
70	36316	39032	39440	39077	45358	41367	37562	38405	36316	37432	36316	40257	44770	42389	49943	56115	40257	70
75	25063	27039	27435	27893	34361	30094	26190	26988	25063	25833	25063	28526	35007	29598	37138	43339	28526	75
80	14108	15284	15503	16160	21682	18628	14862	15727	14108	14542	14108	16246	25935	16795	23361	30167	16246	80
85+	7591	8236	8354	8886	13085	11106	7997	8821	7591	7824	7591	8943	19089	9064	13971	20098	8943	85+

ADDED YRS OF LIFE

	No Causes	(1)	(2)	(3)	(4)	(5)	(6)	(7)	(8)	(9)	(10)	(11)	(12)	(1)+(2)	(1)+(2)+(5)+(6)+(8)	big	(10)+(11)
TOTAL		1.431	2.745	.785	2.854	2.975	1.581	.749	.000	1.667	.000	2.358	6.584	4.273	9.450	15.462	2.358
WORK	7.345	1.133	.662	.273	.928	.634	.098	.339	.000	.000	.000	1.402	1.023	1.821	2.609	3.121	1.402

POPULATION, DEATHS, DEATH RATES FOR ALL CAUSES COMBINED, AND SPECIFIED CAUSES

Age Start of Interval	Midyear Population	Deaths During Year	All Causes	Respiratory T.B.	Other Infec. and Paras.	Neoplasms	Cardiovascular	Infl., Pneu., Bronch.	Diarrheal	Certain Degenerative	Maternal	Cert. Dis. of Infancy	Motor Vehicle	Other Violence	Other and Unknown	Age Start of Interval
0	8104	725	.08946	.00037	.01505	.00012	.00025	.01370	.01839	.00000	.00000	.02419	.00000	.00197	.01542	0
1	33081	233	.00704	.00015	.00287	.00003	.00006	.00109	.00060	.00003	.00000	.00000	.00000	.00045	.00175	1
5	42836	107	.00250	.00002	.00119	.00000	.00009	.00030	.00007	.00005	.00000	.00000	.00000	.00014	.00063	5
10	40565	76	.00187	.00025	.00067	.00000	.00017	.00007	.00000	.00005	.00000	.00000	.00000	.00025	.00042	10
15	32849	124	.00377	.00125	.00073	.00000	.00033	.00024	.00009	.00006	.00003	.00000	.00000	.00018	.00085	15
20	29980	147	.00490	.00170	.00100	.00003	.00030	.00037	.00000	.00010	.00030	.00000	.00000	.00020	.00090	20
25	22507	107	.00475	.00147	.00053	.00013	.00018	.00049	.00009	.00013	.00071	.00000	.00000	.00009	.00093	25
30	17995	104	.00578	.00117	.00078	.00011	.00061	.00078	.00011	.00028	.00056	.00000	.00000	.00022	.00117	30
35	15194	137	.00902	.00191	.00072	.00066	.00112	.00086	.00033	.00053	.00138	.00000	.00000	.00020	.00132	35
40	13514	104	.00770	.00111	.00067	.00104	.00133	.00081	.00000	.00030	.00067	.00000	.00000	.00015	.00163	40
45	11901	113	.00950	.00084	.00042	.00151	.00227	.00101	.00000	.00059	.00017	.00000	.00000	.00034	.00235	45
50	9980	124	.01242	.00070	.00080	.00281	.00271	.00120	.00060	.00090	.00000	.00000	.00000	.00000	.00271	50
55	6186	110	.01778	.00113	.00016	.00291	.00533	.00307	.00000	.00178	.00000	.00000	.00000	.00065	.00275	55
60	4494	119	.02648	.00045	.00089	.00401	.00846	.00401	.00000	.00134	.00000	.00000	.00000	.00067	.00668	60
65	2579	93	.03606	.00039	.00116	.00659	.01163	.00620	.00155	.00078	.00000	.00000	.00000	.00000	.00775	65
70	1385	116	.08375	.00144	.00217	.00650	.03321	.01661	.00289	.00144	.00000	.00000	.00000	.00217	.01733	70
75	942	87	.09236	.00212	.00106	.00531	.01911	.02442	.00000	.00106	.00000	.00000	.00000	.00531	.03397	75
80	442	28	.06335	.00000	.00000	.00000	.01357	.01584	.00226	.00000	.00000	.00000	.00000	.00226	.02941	80
85+	653	77	.11111	.00000	.00000	.00000	.01876	.02742	.00144	.00144	.00000	.00000	.00000	.00226	.02941	85+
ALL	295227	2731												.00144	.06061	

	All Causes	Respiratory T.B.	Other Infec. and Paras.	Neoplasms	Cardiovascular	Infl., Pneu., Bronch.	Diarrheal	Certain Degenerative	Maternal	Cert. Dis. of Infancy	Motor Vehicle	Other Violence	Other and Unknown
CRUDE DEATH RATE	.00925	.00081	.00142	.00049	.00109	.00129	.00068	.00023	.00023	.00066	.00000	.00031	.00203
STANDARDIZED RATE (1)	.01126	.00083	.00155	.00066	.00155	.00166	.00086	.00028	.00024	.00085	.00000	.00036	.00243
STANDARDIZED RATE (2)	.01460	.00091	.00125	.00115	.00299	.00244	.00067	.00041	.00026	.00050	.00000	.00045	.00359
GEOMETRIC MEAN	.01452												

LIFE TABLE FOR ALL CAUSES COMBINED

Age (x)	Midyear Population	Deaths During Year	$_nM_x$	$_nq_x$	l_x	$_nd_x$	$_nL_x$	$_nm_x$	$_na_x$	T_x	$_nr_x$	$\overset{\circ}{e}_x$	Age (x)
0	8104	725	.089462	.083640	100000	8364	93494	.089461	.222085	5772582	.000000	57.726	0
1	33081	233	.007043	.027666	91636	2537	360202	.007043	1.500000	5679089	.000000	61.974	1
5	42836	107	.002498	.012391	89099	1104	442735	.002494	2.500000	5318887	.000000	59.696	5
10	40565	76	.001874	.009341	87995	822	438031	.001877	2.635341	4876152	.018143	55.414	10
15	32849	124	.003775	.018790	87173	1638	432031	.003791	2.659493	4438121	.024160	50.912	15
20	29980	147	.004903	.024271	85535	2076	422552	.004913	2.532414	4006090	.028396	46.836	20
25	22507	107	.004754	.023497	83459	1961	412446	.004755	2.527409	3583537	.043832	42.938	25
30	17995	104	.005779	.028639	81498	2334	401975	.005806	2.637193	3171091	.037508	38.910	30
35	15194	137	.009017	.044187	79164	3498	387184	.009034	2.531089	2769116	.025295	34.979	35
40	13514	104	.007696	.037745	75666	2856	371166	.007695	2.491684	2381932	.018499	31.480	40
45	11901	113	.009495	.046477	72810	3384	355872	.009509	2.583358	2010766	.014973	27.617	45
50	9980	124	.012425	.060640	69426	4210	337069	.012490	2.610105	1654894	.042240	23.837	50
55	6186	110	.017782	.086007	65216	5609	312738	.017935	2.621345	1317825	.058046	20.207	55
60	4494	119	.026480	.125438	59607	7477	280001	.026703	2.588104	1005087	.056477	16.862	60
65	2579	93	.036060	.168252	52130	8771	240330	.036496	2.683251	725086	.078424	13.909	65
70	1385	116	.083755	.350377	43359	15192	179154	.084799	2.522312	484756	.036925	11.180	70
75	942	87	.092357	.369155	28167	10398	112669	.092288	2.291166	305602	.029203	10.850	75
80	442	28	.063348	.268389	17769	4769	75934	.062805	2.292671	192934	.029203	10.858	80
85+	693	77	.111111	1.000000	13000	13000	117000	.111111	9.000000	117000	.000000	9.000	85+

NUMBER OF PERSONS DYING (OUT OF 100,000 AT BIRTH) ABOVE AGE X FROM SPECIFIED CAUSES

Age (x)	All Causes	Respiratory T. B.	Other Infec. and Paras.	Neo-plasms	Cardio-vascular	Infl., Pneu., Bronch.	Diar-rheal	Certain Degen-erative	Maternal	Cert. Dis. of Infancy	Motor Vehicle	Other Violence	Other and Unknown	Age (x)
0	100000	5315	6581	7654	21700	17786	3660	2795	1501	2261	0	2782	27925	0
1	91636	5280	5173	7683	21677	16506	1942	2795	1501	0	0	2597	26482	1
5	89099	5225	4139	7672	21656	16114	1724	2784	1501	0	0	2434	25850	5
10	87995	5215	3612	7672	21614	15980	1693	2764	1501	0	0	2372	25572	10
15	87173	5105	3322	7672	21538	15948	1693	2742	1501	0	0	2264	25388	15
20	85535	4563	3006	7672	21393	15842	1653	2716	1487	0	0	2185	25018	20
25	83459	3843	2583	7657	21267	15686	1653	2673	1359	0	0	2101	24637	25
30	81498	3240	2365	7602	21193	15483	1616	2618	1064	0	0	2064	24253	30
35	79164	2771	2051	7556	20945	15169	1571	2505	840	0	0	1974	23782	35
40	75666	2031	1771	7299	20510	14838	1444	2301	303	0	0	1898	23271	40
45	72810	1621	1524	6914	20014	14535	1444	2191	58	0	0	1843	22666	45
50	69426	1322	1375	6374	19205	14176	1443	1981	0	0	0	1724	21826	50
55	65216	1086	1104	5422	18286	13766	1240	1674	0	0	0	1724	20914	55
60	59607	731	1056	4510	16596	12793	1240	1114	0	0	0	1517	20050	60
65	52130	610	802	3378	14206	11663	1240	744	0	0	0	1332	18155	65
70	43359	516	521	1782	11365	10146	855	562	0	0	0	1332	16280	70
75	28167	254	129	614	5346	7127	334	301	0	0	0	937	13125	75
80	17769	14	12	19	3216	4371	334	182	0	0	0	336	9285	80
85+	13000	0	0	0	2195	3208	169	169	0	0	0	169	7090	85+

NUMBER OF PERSONS SURVIVING TO AGE X IF SPECIFIED CAUSES WERE ELIMINATED

Age (x)	No Causes	Respiratory T. B. (1)	Other Infec. and Paras. (2)	Neo-plasms (3)	Cardio-vascular (4)	Infl., Pneu., Bronch. (5)	Diar-rheal (6)	Certain Degener-ative (7)	Maternal (8)	Cert. Dis. of Infancy (9)	Motor Vehicle (10)	Other Violence (11)	Other and Unknown (12)	(1) + (2)	(1) + (2) + (5) + (6) + (8)	(1)+(2)+ (5)+(6)+ (8)+part of(9)&(12)	(10) + (11)	Age (x)
0	100000	100000	100000	100000	100000	100000	100000	100000	100000	100000	100000	100000	100000	100000	100000	100000	100000	0
1	91636	91669	92593	91647	91658	92669	93295	91636	91636	93825	91636	91813	93027	93027	95986	99590	91813	1
5	89099	89164	91459	89120	89141	90651	90931	89109	91228	90099	89099	89432	91087	91549	95100	99288	89432	5
10	87995	88091	90865	88016	88078	89703	89836	88026	87995	90097	87995	88386	90241	90964	94669	99103	88386	10
15	87173	87377	90315	87194	87231	88897	86957	87225	87173	89256	87173	87669	85586	90527	94249	98803	87669	15
20	85535	86276	88943	85555	85834	87334	87365	85612	85549	87579	85535	86100	88280	89713	93574	98434	86100	20
25	83459	84902	87220	83494	83876	85372	85244	83577	83599	85453	83459	84094	86527	88728	92859	98053	84094	25
30	81498	83515	85395	81586	81979	83571	83279	81667	81928	83445	81498	82155	84888	87509	92180	97726	82155	30
35	79164	81598	83275	79295	79677	81496	80939	79440	79804	81055	79164	79891	82942	85835	91075	96971	79891	35
40	75666	78742	79883	76044	76779	78228	77490	76130	76808	77474	75666	76436	79802	83130	89346	95554	76436	40
45	72810	76188	77124	73555	74377	75584	74565	73366	74153	74550	72810	73606	77419	80703	87378	93859	73606	45
50	69426	72953	73694	70672	71731	72436	71101	70163	70764	71085	69426	70302	74658	77437	84337	90957	70302	50
55	65216	68770	65504	67231	68309	68460	66950	66210	66472	66774	65216	66039	71124	73291	80552	87275	66039	55
60	59607	63213	63574	62446	64151	63556	61228	61060	60755	61031	59607	60560	65915	67420	75265	81874	60560	60
65	52130	55402	55854	55733	56560	56721	53550	53754	53134	53376	52130	53138	55641	59360	67625	74242	53138	65
70	43359	46171	46731	47527	51709	48708	44903	44879	44194	44395	43359	44198	51594	49762	59007	65628	44198	70
75	28167	30219	30694	32163	39829	34484	29598	29369	28710	28840	28167	29043	36679	32930	43182	49573	29043	75
80	17769	19268	19458	20822	27533	24607	18664	18623	18111	18194	17769	18825	27517	21100	31282	39013	18825	80
85+	13000	14110	14247	15253	21537	19428	13903	13637	13250	13311	13000	13924	23246	15463	25010	33642	13924	85+

ADDED YRS OF LIFE																	
TOTAL		1.822	2.975	1.410	3.950	3.547	1.479	.598	.538	1.374	.000	.720	7.743	4.918	11.985	21.062	.720
WORK	7.406	1.364	.717	.525	.935	.679	.107	.300	.457	.000	.000	.191	1.315	2.111	3.462	4.362	.191

POPULATION, DEATHS, DEATH RATES FOR ALL CAUSES COMBINED, AND SPECIFIED CAUSES

Age Start of Interval	Midyear Population	Deaths During Year	All Causes	Respiratory T.B.	Other Infec. and Paras.	Neoplasms	Cardiovascular	Infl., Pneu., Bronch.	Diarrheal	Certain Degenerative	Maternal	Cert. Dis. of Infancy	Motor Vehicle	Other Violence	Other and Unknown	Age Start of Interval
0	9658	823	.08521	.00021	.0C466	.00010	.00114	.01315	.01118	.00021	.00000	.03375	.00000	.00362	.01719	0
1	34879	233	.00668	.00011	.00129	.00000	.00017	.00143	.00034	.00006	.00000	.00000	.00000	.00112	.00215	1
5	43524	89	.00204	.00002	.0C064	.00005	.00016	.00018	.00007	.00005	.00000	.00000	.00000	.00034	.00053	5
10	43307	76	.00175	.00005	.00032	.00000	.00018	.00012	.00005	.00007	.00000	.00000	.00000	.00039	.00058	10
15	42660	133	.00312	.00052	.00059	.00005	.00030	.00014	.00005	.00021	.00000	.00000	.00000	.00063	.00063	15
20	41394	164	.00396	.00128	.00058	.00005	.00022	.00022	.00002	.00012	.00000	.00000	.00000	.00092	.00056	20
25	35477	132	.00372	.00110	.00045	.00003	.00034	.00025	.00003	.00025	.00000	.00000	.00000	.00079	.00048	25
30	29837	128	.00429	.00101	.00054	.00003	.00030	.00037	.00007	.00023	.00000	.00000	.00000	.00137	.00037	30
35	24418	154	.00631	.00139	.00049	.00033	.00078	.00061	.00004	.00029	.00000	.00000	.00000	.00152	.00086	35
40	21693	131	.00604	.00074	.00069	.00028	.00124	.00069	.00005	.00028	.00000	.00000	.00000	.00101	.00106	40
45	19225	191	.00993	.00114	.00078	.00120	.00156	.00114	.00005	.00088	.00000	.00000	.00000	.00198	.00120	45
50	15487	225	.01453	.00116	.00103	.00149	.00342	.00194	.00013	.00090	.00000	.00000	.00000	.00174	.00271	50
55	13777	263	.01909	.00167	.00054	.00225	.00414	.00156	.00000	.00152	.00000	.00000	.00000	.00312	.00348	55
60	12865	355	.02759	.00140	.00070	.00326	.01003	.00303	.00016	.00202	.00000	.00000	.00000	.00187	.00513	60
65	10209	408	.03996	.00137	.00078	.00509	.01342	.00549	.00078	.00255	.00000	.00000	.00000	.00176	.00872	65
70	5374	383	.07127	.00056	.00112	.00819	.02698	.00800	.00074	.00354	.00000	.00000	.00000	.00112	.02103	70
75	2296	254	.11063	.00087	.00044	.01002	.03702	.02003	.00218	.00610	.00000	.00000	.00000	.00131	.03267	75
80	1055	168	.15924	.00095	.00095	.00379	.04645	.02180	.00000	.00569	.00000	.00000	.00000	.00284	.07678	80
85+	376	108	.28723	.00000	.00000	.00532	.07181	.03989	.00000	.00798	.00000	.00000	.00000	.00266	.15957	85+
ALL	407511	4418														
CRUDE DEATH RATE			.01084	.00075	.00076	.00066	.00204	.00136	.00038	.00049	.00000	.00080	.00000	.00113	.00247	
STANDARDIZED RATE (1)			.01103	.00066	.00082	.00055	.00177	.00145	.00051	.00042	.00000	.00119	.00000	.00112	.00254	
STANDARDIZED RATE (2)			.01593	.00079	.00077	.00107	.00376	.00209	.00039	.00075	.00000	.00070	.00000	.00124	.00437	
GEOMETRIC MEAN			.01483													

LIFE TABLE FOR ALL CAUSES COMBINED

Age (x)	Midyear Population	Deaths During Year	$_nM_x$	$_nq_x$	l_x	$_nd_x$	$_nL_x$	$_nm_x$	$_na_x$	T_x	$_nr_x$	$\overset{\circ}{e}_x$	Age (x)
0	9658	823	.085214	.079870	100000	7987	93729	.085214	.214864	5804524	.000000	58.045	0
1	34879	233	.006680	.026279	92013	2418	362007	.006679	1.500000	5710795	.000000	62.065	1
5	43524	89	.002045	.010179	89595	912	445695	.002046	2.500000	5348788	.000000	59.700	5
10	43307	76	.001755	.008728	88683	774	441574	.001753	2.620855	4903093	-.000044	55.288	10
15	42660	133	.003118	.015482	87909	1361	436335	.003119	2.641440	4461520	-.000646	50.752	15
20	41394	164	.003962	.019619	86548	1698	428537	.003962	2.524907	4025185	.008786	46.508	20
25	35477	132	.003721	.018433	84850	1564	420356	.003721	2.510257	3596647	.023326	42.388	25
30	29837	128	.004290	.021312	83286	1775	412195	.004306	2.614202	3176291	.031312	38.137	30
35	24418	154	.006307	.031125	81511	2537	401333	.006321	2.547546	2764096	.029254	33.911	35
40	21693	131	.006039	.029807	78974	2354	389234	.006048	2.605937	2362763	.018569	29.918	40
45	19225	191	.009935	.048734	76620	3734	374344	.009975	2.654995	1973529	.022613	25.757	45
50	15487	225	.014528	.070411	72886	5132	352111	.014575	2.599579	1599185	.023135	21.941	50
55	13777	263	.019090	.091316	67754	6187	323892	.019102	2.595294	1247074	.005130	18.406	55
60	12865	355	.027594	.129323	61567	7962	288688	.027580	2.595192	923182	-.003213	14.995	60
65	10209	408	.039965	.183285	53605	9825	244613	.040165	2.617091	634494	.026586	11.836	65
70	5374	383	.071269	.307995	43780	13484	185886	.072539	2.551651	385881	.070616	8.905	70
75	2296	254	.110627	.434645	30296	13168	117757	.111824	2.439009	203995	.054092	6.733	75
80	1055	168	.159242	.562179	17128	9629	60130	.160136	2.350711	86238	.054092	5.035	80
85+	376	108	.287234	1.000000	7499	7499	26108	.287234	3.481481	26108	.000000	3.481	85+

NUMBER OF PERSONS DYING (OUT OF 100,000 AT BIRTH) ABOVE AGE X FROM SPECIFIED CAUSES

Age (x)	All Causes	Respiratory T. B.	Other Infec. and Paras.	Neoplasms	Cardiovascular	Infl., Pneu., Bronch.	Diarrheal	Certain Degenerative	Maternal	Cert. Dis. of Infancy	Motor Vehicle	Other Violence	Other and Unknown	Age (x)
0	100000	4980	4395	7344	25137	13046	2031	4964	0	3164	0	7597	27342	0
1	92013	4961	3959	7334	25030	11813	983	4944	0	0	0	7257	25732	1
5	89595	4919	3492	7334	24968	11295	859	4924	0	0	0	6852	24952	5
10	88683	4909	3205	7314	24896	11213	828	4903	0	0	0	6698	24717	10
15	87909	4889	3062	7314	24815	11162	808	4873	0	0	0	6525	24461	15
20	86548	4664	2806	7293	24682	11100	787	4780	0	0	0	6249	24187	20
25	84850	4115	2558	7273	24589	11007	777	4729	0	0	0	5855	23947	25
30	83286	3653	2368	7261	24446	10900	765	4622	0	0	0	5523	23748	30
35	81511	3238	2147	7246	24321	10747	737	4525	0	0	0	4954	23596	35
40	78974	2679	1950	7114	24006	10500	721	4410	0	0	0	4347	23247	40
45	76620	2393	1680	7005	23521	10230	703	4301	0	0	0	3952	22835	45
50	72886	1964	1388	6555	22923	9799	683	3969	0	0	0	3210	22385	50
55	67754	1554	1023	6031	21723	9116	638	3650	0	0	0	2595	21424	55
60	61567	1013	718	5301	20381	8481	638	3156	0	0	0	1584	20295	60
65	53605	609	516	4359	17488	7606	593	2573	0	0	0	1045	18816	65
70	43780	274	324	3107	14188	6258	400	1948	0	0	0	614	16667	70
75	30296	175	115	1564	9078	4742	261	1282	0	0	0	411	12668	75
80	17128	72	65	382	4684	2345	1	556	0	0	0	255	8768	80
85+	7499	0	0	139	1875	1042	0	208	0	0	0	69	4166	85+

NUMBER OF PERSONS SURVIVING TO AGE X IF SPECIFIED CAUSES WERE ELIMINATED

Age (x)	No Causes	Respiratory T. B. (1)	Other Infec. and Paras. (2)	Neoplasms (3)	Cardiovascular (4)	Infl., Pneu., Bronch. (5)	Diarrheal (6)	Certain Degenerative (7)	Maternal (8)	Cert. Dis. of Infancy (9)	Motor Vehicle (10)	Other Violence (11)	Other and Unknown (12)	(1) + (2)	(1) + (2) + (5) + (6) + (8)	(1)+(2)+ (5)+(6)+ (8)+part of(9)&(12)	(10) + (11)	Age (x)
0	100000	100000	100000	100000	100000	100000	100000	100000	100000	100000	100000	100000	100000	100000	100000	100000	100000	0
1	92013	92031	92432	92023	92116	93203	93023	92032	92013	95098	92013	92340	93570	92450	94674	98772	92340	1
5	89595	89654	90467	89604	89756	91273	90703	89633	89595	92599	89595	90315	91897	90527	93363	97993	90315	5
10	88683	88751	89835	88712	88914	90427	89811	88742	88683	91656	88683	89550	91202	89904	92838	97598	89550	10
15	87909	87997	89195	87938	88219	89690	89047	87997	87909	90856	87909	88943	90668	89285	92272	97130	88943	15
20	86548	86859	88072	86597	86986	88364	87689	86727	86548	89450	86548	87843	89545	88388	91433	96404	87843	20
25	84850	85702	86595	84918	85372	86724	85979	85076	84850	87695	84850	86517	88035	87464	90586	95676	86517	25
30	83286	84586	85191	83365	83941	85234	84406	83615	83286	86078	83286	85258	86617	86520	89735	94904	85258	30
35	81511	83201	83599	81603	82277	83573	82636	81929	81511	84244	81511	84019	84927	85332	88698	93894	84019	35
40	78974	81174	81156	79193	80030	81221	80079	79493	78974	81622	78974	82022	82643	83459	87035	92321	82022	40
45	76620	79045	79050	76941	78130	79074	77711	77232	76620	79189	76620	79982	80605	81551	85362	90754	79982	45
50	72886	75625	75492	73634	74910	75656	73943	73795	72886	75329	72886	76843	77140	78328	82484	87884	76843	50
55	67754	70711	70541	68961	70845	71015	68781	68911	67754	70025	67754	72060	72697	73620	78332	83873	72060	55
60	61567	64793	64402	63376	65731	65167	62500	63099	61567	63631	61567	66510	67223	67776	72827	78377	66510	60
65	53605	56810	56269	56092	60188	57611	54461	55498	53605	55402	53605	58449	60056	59633	65113	70501	58449	65
70	43780	46715	46137	47007	52617	48377	44656	45911	43780	45248	43780	48158	51280	49230	55488	60802	48158	70
75	30296	32411	32108	33922	41859	34897	31020	32352	30296	31312	30296	33506	39591	34349	40510	45410	33506	75
80	17128	18406	18188	20168	28554	21906	17736	18874	17128	17702	17128	19071	26536	19545	25885	30567	19071	80
85+	7499	8108	8008	9016	15930	10725	7766	8514	7499	7750	7499	8484	17241	8658	12824	16958	8484	85+

ADDED YRS OF LIFE																		
TOTAL		1.412	1.610	.555	3.385	2.552	.849	.768	.000	1.939	.000	2.277	5.174	3.081	6.820	11.474	2.277	
WORK	6.466	1.057	.614	.315	.838	.523	.046	.346	.000	.000	.000	1.183	.880	1.693	2.300	2.723	1.183	

POPULATION, DEATHS, DEATH RATES FOR ALL CAUSES COMBINED, AND SPECIFIED CAUSES

Age Start of Interval	Midyear Population	Deaths During Year	All Causes	Respiratory T. B.	Other Infec. and Paras.	Neoplasms	Cardiovascular	Infl., Pneu., Bronch.	Diarrheal	Certain Degenerative	Maternal	Cert. Dis. of Infancy	Motor Vehicle	Other Violence	Other and Unknown	Age Start of Interval
0	8815	640	.07260	.00023	.00366	.00000	.00034	.01248	.01168	.00011	.00000	.02711	.00000	.00250	.01429	0
1	33889	180	.00531	.00006	.00115	.00000	.00012	.00148	.00032	.00000	.00000	.00000	.00000	.00077	.00142	1
5	42643	78	.00183	.00009	.00066	.00000	.00014	.00012	.00000	.00005	.00000	.00000	.00000	.00023	.00054	5
10	42345	62	.00146	.00014	.00028	.00000	.00024	.00009	.00005	.00005	.00000	.00000	.00000	.00019	.00043	10
15	42579	128	.00301	.00087	.00033	.00005	.00038	.00021	.00002	.00012	.00005	.00000	.00000	.00019	.00090	15
20	42179	176	.00417	.00135	.00066	.00007	.00026	.00038	.00005	.00017	.00036	.00000	.00000	.00012	.00076	20
25	33407	155	.00464	.00141	.00012	.00051	.00036	.00036	.00003	.00027	.00036	.00000	.00000	.00015	.00108	25
30	27415	133	.00485	.00139	.00044	.00026	.00055	.00022	.00004	.00018	.00055	.00000	.00000	.00018	.00106	30
35	21328	120	.00563	.00136	.00028	.00056	.00070	.00042	.00014	.00028	.00070	.00000	.00000	.00028	.00089	35
40	17438	140	.00803	.00120	.00034	.00143	.00092	.00103	.00006	.00034	.00063	.00000	.00000	.00034	.00172	40
45	14070	126	.00896	.00100	.00036	.00220	.00178	.00078	.00007	.00092	.00000	.00000	.00000	.00021	.00163	45
50	12054	152	.01261	.00108	.00025	.00307	.00315	.00166	.00017	.00100	.00000	.00000	.00000	.00008	.00216	50
55	10015	161	.01608	.00080	.00040	.00339	.00509	.00210	.00030	.00130	.00000	.00000	.00000	.00000	.00270	55
60	8059	191	.02370	.00050	.00037	.00472	.00807	.00347	.00025	.00236	.00000	.00000	.00000	.00012	.00385	60
65	6059	224	.03697	.00066	.00066	.00380	.01601	.00759	.00017	.00248	.00000	.00000	.00000	.00050	.00512	65
70	3253	180	.05533	.00031	.00031	.00584	.01906	.01045	.00184	.00277	.00000	.00000	.00000	.00123	.01353	70
75	1688	151	.08945	.00237	.00000	.00652	.03258	.01126	.00118	.00178	.00000	.00000	.00000	.00118	.03258	75
80	856	126	.14720	.00117	.00117	.00467	.02804	.01752	.00350	.00234	.00000	.00000	.00000	.00350	.08528	80
85+	342	93	.27193	.00000	.00000	.00292	.04386	.03216	.00585	.00292	.00000	.00000	.00000	.00585	.17836	85+
ALL	368434	3216														

CRUDE DEATH RATE			.00873	.00079	.00059	.00068	.00147	.00121	.00040	.00035	.00019	.00065	.00000	.00033	.00208	
STANDARDIZED RATE (1)			.00965	.00073	.00064	.00072	.00158	.00142	.00054	.00036	.00017	.00095	.00000	.00037	.00234	
STANDARDIZED RATE (2)			.01416	.00082	.00055	.00125	.00320	.00199	.00047	.00059	.00018	.00056	.00000	.00039	.00415	
GEOMETRIC MEAN			.01378													

LIFE TABLE FOR ALL CAUSES COMBINED

Age (x)	Midyear Population	Deaths During Year	$_nM_x$	$_nq_x$	l_x	$_nd_x$	$_nL_x$	$_nm_x$	$_na_x$	T_x	$_nr_x$	$\overset{\circ}{e}_x$	Age (x)
0	8815	640	.072604	.068590	100000	6859	94468	.072607	.193426	5993232	.000000	59.932	0
1	33889	180	.005311	.020968	93141	1953	367682	.005312	1.500000	5898764	.000000	63.332	1
5	42643	78	.001829	.009102	91188	830	453865	.001829	2.500000	5531082	.000000	60.656	5
10	42345	62	.001464	.007293	90358	659	450248	.001464	2.660281	5077217	-.000399	56.190	10
15	42579	128	.003006	.014905	89699	1337	445396	.003002	2.682000	4626969	-.005345	51.583	15
20	42179	176	.004173	.020676	88362	1827	437378	.004177	2.574120	4181573	-.011044	47.323	20
25	33407	155	.004640	.022962	86535	1987	427750	.004645	2.521179	3744195	-.031902	43.268	25
30	27415	133	.004851	.023998	84548	2029	417732	.004857	2.532035	3316446	-.038031	39.226	30
35	21328	120	.005626	.027860	82519	2299	407085	.005647	2.603356	2898713	-.039727	35.128	35
40	17438	140	.008028	.039516	80220	3170	393401	.008058	2.571372	2491628	-.036184	31.060	40
45	14070	126	.008955	.043933	77050	3385	377069	.008977	2.583087	2098227	-.030504	27.232	45
50	12054	152	.012610	.061359	73665	4520	357438	.012646	2.591399	1721158	-.023176	23.365	50
55	10015	161	.016078	.077634	69145	5368	332859	.016127	2.603156	1363720	-.023848	19.723	55
60	8059	191	.023700	.112564	63777	7179	301835	.023785	2.624988	1030861	-.021305	16.164	60
65	6059	224	.036970	.170942	56598	9675	259714	.037252	2.594229	729026	-.041982	12.881	65
70	3253	180	.055334	.246255	46923	11555	206429	.055976	2.560742	469312	-.068752	10.002	70
75	1688	151	.089455	.368808	35368	13044	144324	.090380	2.507235	262883	-.045715	7.433	75
80	856	126	.147196	.537896	22324	12008	80622	.148942	2.418561	118558	-.045715	5.311	80
85+	342	93	.271930	1.000000	10316	10316	37936	.271930	3.677419	37936	.000000	3.677	85+

NUMBER OF PERSONS DYING (OUT OF 100,000 AT BIRTH) ABOVE AGE X FROM SPECIFIED CAUSES

Age (x)	All Causes	Respiratory T.B.	Other Infec. and Paras.	Neoplasms	Cardiovascular	Infl., Pneu., Bronch.	Diarrheal	Certain Degenerative	Maternal	Cert. Dis. of Infancy	Motor Vehicle	Other Violence	Other and Unknown	Age (x)
0	100000	5199	3104	9157	24376	14006	2754	4261	1096	2561	0	2451	31035	0
1	93141	5177	2739	9157	24344	12827	1650	4250	1096	0	0	2215	29686	1
5	91188	5155	2316	9157	24301	12284	1531	4250	1096	0	0	1933	29165	5
10	90358	5113	2018	9157	24237	12231	1531	4229	1096	0	0	1827	28919	10
15	89659	5049	1891	9157	24131	12189	1510	4207	1096	0	0	1741	28728	15
20	88362	4663	1744	9136	23963	12095	1499	4155	1075	0	0	1658	28374	20
25	86535	4071	1454	9104	23849	11929	1479	4082	919	0	0	1606	28042	25
30	84548	3469	1237	9053	23695	11775	1466	3967	765	0	0	1542	27579	30
35	82519	2890	1055	8945	23465	11684	1450	3891	535	0	0	1465	27139	35
40	80220	2337	941	8712	23178	11510	1393	3776	249	0	0	1350	26775	40
45	77050	1865	805	8143	22814	11102	1371	3639	2	0	0	1215	26094	45
50	73665	1490	671	7309	22139	10807	1344	3289	2	0	0	1135	25479	50
55	69145	1105	582	6209	21007	10211	1284	2932	2	0	0	1106	24707	55
60	63777	840	449	5077	19304	9510	1184	2498	2	0	0	1106	23807	60
65	56598	690	337	3652	16857	8455	1109	1785	2	0	0	1068	22643	65
70	46923	519	165	2667	12666	6465	1064	1141	2	0	0	937	21297	70
75	35368	455	104	1450	8704	4293	675	570	2	0	0	679	18436	75
80	22324	108	104	508	3963	2662	504	316	2	0	0	507	13650	80
85+	10316	0	0	111	1664	1220	222	111	0	0	0	222	6766	85+

NUMBER OF PERSONS SURVIVING TO AGE X IF SPECIFIED CAUSES WERE ELIMINATED

Age (x)	No Causes	Respiratory T.B. (1)	Other Infec. and Paras. (2)	Neoplasms (3)	Cardiovascular (4)	Infl., Pneu., Bronch. (5)	Diarrheal (6)	Certain Degenerative (7)	Maternal (8)	Cert. Dis. of Infancy (9)	Motor Vehicle (10)	Other Violence (11)	Other and Unknown (12)	(1) + (2)	(1) + (2) + (5) + (6) + (8)	(1)+(2)+ (5)+(6)+ (8)+part of(9)&(12)	(10) + (11)	Age (x)
0	100000	100000	100000	100000	100000	100000	100000	100000	100000	100000	100000	100000	100000	100000	100000	100000	100000	0
1	93141	93162	93494	93141	93172	94286	94212	93152	93141	95645	93141	93369	94452	93515	95753	99330	93369	1
5	91188	91231	91955	91188	91261	92854	92356	91198	91188	93640	91188	91691	92996	91997	94878	98853	91691	5
10	90358	90442	91417	90358	90494	92063	91515	90389	90358	92787	90358	90963	92359	91502	94423	98558	90963	10
15	89659	89846	90879	89659	89940	91434	90869	89752	89659	92111	89659	90386	91520	91028	93999	98229	90386	15
20	88362	88892	89672	88383	88766	90166	89526	88466	88383	90738	88362	89122	90911	90210	93286	97744	89122	20
25	86535	87645	88110	86587	87044	88470	87655	86709	86710	88862	86535	87331	89370	89240	92645	97375	87331	25
30	84548	86237	86305	84649	85199	86594	85694	84832	84872	86821	84548	85389	87791	88029	91732	96806	85389	30
35	82519	84753	84417	82725	83384	84608	83654	82872	83064	84738	82519	83417	86137	86703	90715	96082	83417	35
40	80220	82953	82180	80651	81347	82247	81380	80677	81035	82377	80220	81208	84113	84981	89481	95035	81208	40
45	77050	80154	79070	78028	78496	79582	78186	77624	77624	79122	77050	78133	81492	82255	87358	93196	78133	45
50	73665	77015	75730	75430	75723	76384	74778	74560	74645	75646	73665	74779	78550	79174	84446	90309	74779	50
55	69145	72680	71172	71901	72215	72299	70249	70335	70065	71004	69145	70219	74532	74810	80529	86401	70219	55
60	63777	67304	65778	67458	68340	67354	64853	65301	64626	65492	63777	64768	69683	69416	75629	81439	64768	60
65	56598	59876	58483	61296	63172	60870	57660	58641	57351	58120	56598	57514	63047	61870	68689	74298	57514	65
70	46923	49805	48646	51791	56801	52450	47847	49224	47547	48185	46923	47805	53658	51634	59634	64990	47805	70
75	35368	37600	36720	40213	47159	41680	36410	37618	35839	36319	35368	36261	43407	39037	47989	53451	36261	75
80	22324	24027	23177	26225	35153	27848	23117	23951	22621	22924	22324	23026	32515	24945	17091	38035	23026	80
85+	10316	11180	10782	12432	18832	14118	10878	11215	10455	10593	10316	10837	23389	11685	17091	23536	10837	85+

ADDED YRS OF LIFE																		
TOTAL		1.667	1.311	1.559	3.498	2.785	.947	.757	.399	1.606	.000	.735	6.214	3.027	7.595	12.714	.735
WORK	6.544	1.241	.436	.685	.878	.544	.065	.341	.337	.000	.000	.187	1.184	1.693	2.703	3.440	.187

POPULATION, DEATHS, DEATH RATES FOR ALL CAUSES COMBINED, AND SPECIFIED CAUSES

Age Start of Interval	Midyear Population	Deaths During Year	All Causes	Respiratory T. B.	Other Infec. and Paras.	Neoplasms	Cardiovascular	Infl., Pneu., Bronch.	Diarrheal	Certain Degenerative	Maternal	Cert. Dis. of Infancy	Motor Vehicle	Other Violence	Other and Unknown	Age Start of Interval
0	12680	859	.06774	.00CC8	.CC3CC	.00016	.0026C	.C0789	.01073	.00008	.CCCCC	.03021	.00000	.00071	.01230	0
1	47627	251	.00527	.0CC02	.0C124	.00004	.00015	.000C4	.00C78	.C0006	.00000	.C0000	.00000	.00080	.00134	1
5	54142	111	.002C5	.0CC02	.00057	.000C4	.00022	.00018	.00004	.00004	.CC000	.C0000	.00000	.0C035	.00059	5
10	46678	82	.00176	.CCCCS	.00034	.00000	.00009	.00006	.00006	.00004	.00004	.C0000	.00000	.00047	.00060	10
15	45045	93	.002C6	.0CC13	.0CC33	.000C7	.00022	.00007	.00007	.00013	.00000	.C0000	.00000	.0CC58	.00047	15
20	49967	137	.00274	.0CC64	.CC028	.00002	.00020	.C0016	.0000C	.00006	.C0000	.00000	.00000	.00086	.00052	20
25	54996	181	.00329	.0CC6C	.00051	.00011	.00025	.00015	.00002	.0CC20	.00000	.C0000	.00000	.00084	.00062	25
30	49684	225	.00453	.0CC89	.CC054	.00014	.00028	.00020	.00006	.00020	.C0000	.C0000	.00000	.00141	.00081	30
35	39676	223	.00562	.00113	.00C48	.00030	.00048	.00038	.00003	.00048	.C0000	.C0000	.00000	.00146	.00088	35
40	31371	223	.00711	.00102	.00C73	.00067	.00112	.00073	.00000	.00029	.C0000	.C0000	.00000	.00134	.00121	40
45	24347	216	.00887	.00123	.00C74	.00082	.00103	.000C4	.C0000	.0CC86	.00000	.C0000	.00000	.00144	.00181	45
50	20402	278	.01363	.00074	.00103	.00240	.00250	.00074	.00000	.00147	.00000	.C0000	.00000	.00167	.00309	50
55	16779	283	.01687	.001C1	.00C66	.00304	.0C477	.C0113	.CCOC6	.0C167	.CC000	.C0000	.00000	.00167	.00286	55
60	12886	336	.026C7	.00085	.00C93	.00457	.00745	.00186	.00031	.00178	.00000	.00000	.00000	.00225	.00567	60
65	10995	504	.04584	.001C9	.00C82	.CC728	.01610	.00409	.CC045	.00364	.C0000	.00000	.00000	.00218	.C1C19	65
70	8739	548	.06271	.0CC69	.00034	.00847	.02449	.00561	.00126	.00366	.C0000	.CC000	.00000	.00229	.01591	70
75	5241	519	.0S9C3	.00019	.0CC76	.00840	.03931	.01030	.00114	.00553	.C0000	.C0000	.00000	.00343	.02996	75
80	2049	330	.16105	.0CC0C	.00C49	.01269	.04539	.01367	.00342	.00634	.CC000	.C0000	.00000	.00390	.07516	80
85+	701	196	.27960	.C0000	.00000	.01269	.06562	.02568	.00428	.00285	.C0000	.C0000	.00000	.00390	.16833	85+
ALL	534005	5595				.00856										

CRUDE DEATH RATE .01048 .00054 .00065 .00088 .00215 .00093 .00042 .00053 .00000 .00072 .00000 .00107 .00259
STANDARDIZED RATE (1) .00979 .00046 .00069 .00072 .00170 .00090 .00055 .00044 .00000 .00106 .00000 .00097 .00230
STANDARDIZED RATE (2) .01476 .00056 .00066 .00140 .00362 .00130 .00044 .00078 .CCCC0 .00063 .00000 .00115 .00417
GEOMETRIC MEAN .01352

LIFE TABLE FOR ALL CAUSES COMBINED

Age (x)	Midyear Population	Deaths During Year	$_nM_x$	$_nq_x$	l_x	$_nd_x$	$_nL_x$	$_nm_x$	$_na_x$	T_x	$_nr_x$	$\overset{\circ}{e}_x$	Age (x)
0	12680	859	.067744	.0642C0	1CCOCO	6420	94769	.067744	.185166	6026457	.000000	60.265	0
1	47627	251	.005270	.0208C6	93580	1947	369453	.005270	1.500000	5931689	.000000	63.386	1
5	54142	111	.0C205C	.010204	91633	935	455828	.002051	2.50000C	5562236	.000000	60.701	5
10	46678	82	.0C1757	.0C8743	90698	793	451505	.001756	2.496847	5106409	.016486	56.301	10
15	45045	93	.002065	.010266	89905	923	447304	.002063	2.594122	4654904	.000086	51.776	15
20	49967	137	.0C2742	.013598	88982	1210	441991	.002738	2.587466	4207599	-.019634	47.286	20
25	54996	181	.003291	.016304	87772	1431	435434	.003286	2.605986	3765608	-.011947	42.902	25
30	49684	225	.004529	.022446	86341	1938	427051	.004538	2.598469	3330174	.016742	38.570	30
35	39676	223	.005621	.0278C7	84403	2347	416343	.005637	2.583440	2903123	.034373	34.396	35
40	31371	223	.0C71C8	.035074	82056	2878	403316	.007136	2.580279	2486780	.041049	30.306	40
45	24347	216	.0C8872	.043648	79178	3456	387695	.008914	2.628641	2083464	.037145	26.314	45
50	20402	278	.013626	.0661E5	75722	5012	366558	.013673	2.595438	1695770	.026032	22.395	50
55	16779	283	.016866	.081346	70710	5752	339795	.016928	2.608694	1329211	.029072	18.798	55
60	12886	336	.026075	.123357	64958	8013	306006	.026186	2.655815	989416	.021301	15.232	60
65	10995	504	.045839	.206252	56945	11745	256249	.045834	2.575440	683410	-.000654	12.001	65
70	9739	548	.0627C7	.271372	45200	12266	195625	.062702	2.523626	427161	-.000328	9.450	70
75	5241	519	.099027	.39885E	32934	13136	131627	.099797	2.484537	231537	.034267	7.030	75
80	2049	330	.161054	.570310	19798	11291	69484	.162497	2.386783	99910	.034267	5.046	80
85+	701	196	.279601	1.CC0OCO	8507	8507	30426	.279601	3.576531	30426	.000000	3.577	85+

NUMBER OF PERSONS DYING (OUT OF 100,000 AT BIRTH) ABOVE AGE X FROM SPECIFIED CAUSES

Age (x)	All Causes	Respiratory T. B.	Other Infec. and Paras.	Neoplasms	Cardiovascular	Infl., Pneu., Bronch.	Diarrheal	Certain Degenerative	Maternal	Cert. Dis. of Infancy	Motor Vehicle	Other Violence	Other and Unknown	Age (x)
0	100000	3729	3969	10142	26053	8724	2423	5551	0	2862	0	7792	28755	0
1	93580	3721	3685	10127	25807	7976	1407	5543	0	0	0	7725	27589	1
5	91633	3713	3227	10111	25752	7666	1120	5520	0	0	0	7430	27094	5
10	90698	3705	2966	10094	25651	7582	1103	5503	0	0	0	7270	26824	10
15	89905	3666	2812	10094	25613	7553	1074	5484	0	0	0	7057	26552	15
20	88982	3607	2663	10064	25513	7523	1044	5424	0	0	0	6799	26345	20
25	87772	3324	2540	10056	25425	7453	1044	5398	0	0	0	6419	26113	25
30	86341	3063	2318	10008	25314	7389	1036	5311	0	0	0	6055	25847	30
35	84403	2684	2086	9948	25194	7303	1011	5225	0	0	0	5453	25499	35
40	82056	2211	1886	9821	24992	7144	1000	5025	0	0	0	4844	25133	40
45	79178	1800	1589	9548	24539	6846	1000	4908	0	0	0	4305	24643	45
50	75722	1323	1302	9226	24139	6480	1000	4570	0	0	0	3747	23935	50
55	70710	1054	925	8341	23215	6210	1000	4029	0	0	0	3135	22801	55
60	64958	709	703	7303	21585	5823	980	3462	0	0	0	2567	21826	60
65	56945	448	417	5778	19293	5250	884	2914	0	0	0	1878	20083	65
70	45200	169	208	3914	15168	4201	767	1982	0	0	0	1318	17473	70
75	32934	34	140	2257	10378	3105	521	1265	0	0	0	871	14363	75
80	19798	10	39	1150	5170	1737	370	533	0	0	0	416	10373	80
85+	8507	0	0	260	1997	781	130	87	0	0	0	130	5122	85+

NUMBER OF PERSONS SURVIVING TO AGE X IF SPECIFIED CAUSES WERE ELIMINATED

Age (x)	No Causes	Respiratory T. B. (1)	Other Infec. and Paras. (2)	Neoplasms (3)	Cardiovascular (4)	Infl., Pneu., Bronch. (5)	Diarrheal (6)	Certain Degenerative (7)	Maternal (8)	Cert. Dis. of Infancy (9)	Motor Vehicle (10)	Other Violence (11)	Other and Unknown (12)	(1) + (2)	(1) + (2) + (5) + (6) + (8)	(1)+(2)+ (5)+(6)+ (8)+part of(9)&(12)	(10) + (11)	Age (x)
0	100000	100000	100000	100000	100000	100000	100000	100000	100000	100000	100000	100000	100000	100000	100000	100000	100000	0
1	93580	93588	93855	93595	93818	94306	94568	93588	93580	96389	93580	93645	94715	93863	95590	99072	93645	1
5	91633	91648	92358	91663	91921	92654	92888	91663	91633	94384	91633	91989	93241	92374	94682	98516	91989	5
10	90698	90721	91678	90745	91084	91793	91957	90745	90698	93421	90698	91210	92563	91701	94097	98069	91210	10
15	89905	89967	91031	89951	90325	91020	91182	89970	89905	92604	89905	90626	92031	91094	93534	97623	90626	15
20	88982	89102	90247	89058	89498	90115	90276	89107	88982	91653	88982	89955	91297	90369	92851	96995	89955	20
25	87772	88172	89144	87855	88596	88960	89049	87921	87772	90407	87772	89114	90292	89550	92083	96316	89114	25
30	86341	86995	87914	86470	87039	87574	87605	86574	86341	88933	86341	88029	89092	88580	91161	95490	88029	30
35	84403	85421	86175	84588	85205	85695	85664	84716	84403	86937	84403	86662	87448	87214	89872	94314	86662	35
40	82056	83519	83980	82362	83038	83293	82558	82056	82056	84519	82056	84870	85391	85477	88262	92758	84870	40
45	79178	81001	81334	79743	80577	80842	80371	79779	79178	81555	79178	82443	82899	83207	86236	90901	82443	45
50	75722	77944	78072	76581	77459	77680	76863	76630	75722	77995	75722	79414	80009	80363	83683	88541	79414	50
55	70710	73052	73280	72383	73253	72806	71776	72089	70710	72833	70710	74779	75879	75707	79126	84026	74779	55
60	64958	67451	67539	66521	67267	66780	64958	66908	64958	66908	64958	69274	70716	70131	73741	78537	69274	60
65	56945	59383	59486	60692	62753	59528	57912	59071	56945	58655	56945	61417	63756	62033	65947	70628	61417	65
70	45200	47393	47409	49967	54029	48236	46074	47754	45200	46557	45200	49285	53308	49708	54073	58452	49285	70
75	32934	34649	34602	37987	44555	36156	33785	35441	32934	33923	32934	36325	42101	36404	40998	44925	36325	75
80	19798	20846	20882	23820	32745	22917	20428	21914	19798	20392	19798	22223	29587	21988	26262	29599	22223	80
85+	8507	8964	8999	10940	17840	10577	8937	9736	8507	8762	8507	9755	18831	9483	12386	15137	9755	85+

ADDED YRS OF LIFE																	
TOTAL		1.032	1.434	1.377	3.474	1.662	.948	.857	.000	1.804	.000	2.108	5.317	2.505	5.319	9.177	2.108
WORK	5.826	.737	.520	.436	.689	.344	.032	.362	.000	.000	.000	1.140	1.007	1.271	1.666	2.066	1.140

POPULATION, DEATHS, DEATH RATES FOR ALL CAUSES COMBINED, AND SPECIFIED CAUSES

Age Start of Interval	Midyear Population	Deaths During Year	All Causes	Respiratory T. B.	Other Infec. and Paras.	Neoplasms	Cardiovascular	Infl., Pneu., Bronch.	Diarrheal	Certain Degenerative	Maternal	Cert. Dis. of Infancy	Motor Vehicle	Other Violence	Other and Unknown	Age Start of Interval
0	11800	625	.05297	.00000	.00178	.00000	.00153	.00542	.00915	.00000	.00000	.02424	.00000	.00085	.01000	0
1	46481	245	.00527	.00006	.00120	.00004	.00011	.00114	.00060	.00006	.00000	.00000	.00000	.00060	.00144	1
5	52477	91	.00173	.00002	.00042	.00004	.00023	.00017	.00002	.00013	.00000	.00000	.00000	.00023	.00048	5
10	45262	54	.00119	.00009	.00029	.00004	.00015	.00009	.00000	.00011	.00000	.00000	.00000	.00011	.00031	10
15	43922	102	.00232	.00066	.00022	.00005	.00023	.00016	.00000	.00009	.00000	.00000	.00000	.00014	.00059	15
20	46401	148	.00319	.00099	.00045	.00000	.00032	.00022	.00000	.00015	.00028	.00000	.00000	.00013	.00065	20
25	47806	211	.00441	.00123	.00042	.00015	.00040	.00027	.00008	.00019	.00054	.00000	.00000	.00025	.00088	25
30	42970	184	.00428	.00077	.00019	.00023	.00051	.00037	.00005	.00030	.00088	.00000	.00000	.00021	.00077	30
35	33638	156	.00464	.00054	.00033	.00068	.00065	.00030	.00006	.00024	.00065	.00000	.00000	.00021	.00098	35
40	27423	145	.00529	.00058	.00044	.00073	.00098	.00026	.00000	.00040	.00036	.00000	.00000	.00018	.00135	40
45	20820	152	.00730	.00058	.00034	.00168	.00159	.00019	.00005	.00062	.00005	.00000	.00000	.00043	.00178	45
50	16672	163	.00978	.00024	.00024	.00234	.00300	.00054	.00000	.00078	.00000	.00000	.00000	.00030	.00234	50
55	12685	190	.01498	.00055	.00071	.00323	.00449	.00118	.00032	.00189	.00000	.00000	.00000	.00016	.00244	55
60	10286	222	.02158	.00029	.00019	.00515	.00681	.00204	.00058	.00224	.00000	.00000	.00000	.00039	.00389	60
65	8760	281	.03208	.00046	.00046	.00651	.01393	.00183	.00057	.00194	.00000	.00000	.00000	.00068	.00571	65
70	6067	320	.05274	.00066	.00049	.00742	.02209	.00527	.00099	.00264	.00000	.00000	.00000	.00099	.01220	70
75	3280	300	.09146	.00061	.00152	.00976	.03262	.01220	.00244	.00366	.00000	.00000	.00000	.00091	.02774	75
80	1454	198	.13618	.00000	.00000	.01376	.03851	.01100	.00413	.00344	.00000	.00000	.00000	.00344	.06190	80
85+	689	152	.22061	.00000	.00000	.01161	.04354	.02758	.00000	.00145	.00000	.00000	.00000	.00290	.13353	85+
ALL	478893	3939														

CRUDE DEATH RATE			.00823	.00051	.00048	.00083	.00170	.00076	.00038	.00040	.00024	.00060	.00000	.00030	.00202	
STANDARDIZED RATE (1)			.00830	.00045	.00052	.00078	.00158	.00079	.00048	.00038	.00019	.00085	.00000	.00030	.00197	
STANDARDIZED RATE (2)			.01241	.00049	.00048	.00149	.00324	.00116	.00043	.00062	.00020	.00050	.00000	.00035	.00345	
GEOMETRIC MEAN			.01178													

LIFE TABLE FOR ALL CAUSES COMBINED

Age (x)	Midyear Population	Deaths During Year	$_nM_x$	$_nq_x$	l_x	$_nd_x$	$_nL_x$	$_nm_x$	$_na_x$	T_x	$_nr_x$	$\overset{\circ}{e}_x$	Age (x)
0	11800	625	.052966	.050710	100000	5071	95741	.052966	.160042	6306240	.000000	63.062	0
1	46481	245	.005271	.020805	94929	1975	374779	.005270	1.500000	6210500	.000000	65.423	1
5	52477	91	.001734	.008628	92954	802	462765	.001733	2.500000	5835721	.000000	62.781	5
10	45262	54	.001193	.005958	92152	549	459441	.001195	2.597146	5372956	.015781	58.305	10
15	43922	102	.002322	.011550	91603	1058	455554	.002322	2.673677	4913515	.001783	53.639	15
20	46401	148	.003190	.015804	90545	1431	449332	.003185	2.629135	4457962	-.010279	49.235	20
25	47806	211	.004414	.021826	89114	1945	440794	.004412	2.544559	4008629	-.004191	44.983	25
30	42970	184	.004282	.021189	87169	1847	431230	.004283	2.501579	3567835	-.020994	40.930	30
35	33638	156	.004638	.022960	85322	1959	421782	.004645	2.535733	3136605	-.035458	36.762	35
40	27423	145	.005288	.026187	83363	2183	411559	.005304	2.592476	2714822	-.040717	32.566	40
45	20820	152	.007301	.036068	81180	2928	398909	.007340	2.612207	2303263	-.042359	28.372	45
50	16672	163	.009777	.048050	78252	3760	382379	.009833	2.638076	1904354	-.040335	24.336	50
55	12685	190	.014978	.072759	74492	5420	359608	.015072	2.628728	1521975	-.037995	20.431	55
60	10286	222	.021583	.102922	69072	7109	328387	.021648	2.612445	1162368	-.020211	16.828	60
65	8760	281	.032078	.149396	61963	9257	287779	.032167	2.619549	833981	-.015510	13.459	65
70	6067	320	.052744	.235666	52706	12421	233705	.053148	2.558858	546202	-.034876	10.363	70
75	3280	300	.091463	.376095	40285	15151	163608	.092606	2.503988	312496	-.048009	7.757	75
80	1454	198	.136176	.505729	25134	12711	92576	.137303	2.396432	148888	-.048009	5.924	80
85+	689	152	.226610	1.000000	12423	12423	56312	.220610	4.532895	56312	.000000	4.533	85+

NUMBER OF PERSONS DYING (OUT OF 100,000 AT BIRTH) ABOVE AGE X FROM SPECIFIED CAUSES

Age (x)	All Causes	Respiratory T.B.	Other Infec. and Paras.	Neoplasms	Cardiovascular	Infl., Pneu., Bronch.	Diarrheal	Certain Degenerative	Maternal	Cert. Dis. of Infancy	Motor Vehicle	Other Violence	Other and Unknown	Age (x)
0	100000	3169	2928	12449	28018	9501	2705	4887	1235	2320	0	2488	30300	0
1	94929	3169	2757	12449	27872	8982	1829	4887	1235	0	0	2407	29342	1
5	92954	3145	2306	12432	27832	8555	1603	4862	1235	0	0	2181	28803	5
10	92152	3136	2112	12415	27726	8476	1594	4801	1235	0	0	2075	28582	10
15	91603	3095	1980	12395	27655	8435	1594	4750	1234	0	0	2025	28440	15
20	90545	2794	1835	12374	27552	8362	1594	4708	1193	0	0	1963	28170	20
25	89114	2349	1632	12374	27406	8266	1594	4641	1067	0	0	1905	27880	25
30	87169	1805	1447	12309	27231	8146	1558	4558	828	0	0	1794	27493	30
35	85322	1475	1367	12208	27010	7985	1538	4427	446	0	0	1704	27162	35
40	83363	1250	1229	11918	26733	7860	1513	4327	172	0	0	1616	26745	40
45	81180	1010	1048	11615	26325	7756	1513	4160	24	0	0	1540	26189	45
50	78252	781	915	10938	25686	7679	1494	3910	7	0	0	1367	25475	50
55	74492	690	823	10039	24530	7469	1493	3609	7	0	0	1253	24579	55
60	69072	491	567	8870	22904	7040	1378	2923	7	0	0	1197	23695	60
65	61963	395	503	7173	20658	6368	1186	2189	7	0	0	1068	22416	65
70	52706	264	372	5298	16636	5840	1021	1630	7	0	0	871	20767	70
75	40285	109	255	3560	11442	4592	788	1011	7	0	0	639	17882	75
80	25134	10	3	1950	6055	2570	382	408	7	0	0	488	13261	80
85+	12423	0	0	654	2452	1553	0	82	0	0	0	163	7519	85+

NUMBER OF PERSONS SURVIVING TO AGE X IF SPECIFIED CAUSES WERE ELIMINATED

Age (x)	No Causes	Respiratory T.B. (1)	Other Infec. and Paras. (2)	Neoplasms (3)	Cardiovascular (4)	Infl., Pneu., Bronch. (5)	Diarrheal (6)	Certain Degenerative (7)	Maternal (8)	Cert. Dis. of Infancy (9)	Motor Vehicle (10)	Other Violence (11)	Other and Unknown (12)	(1)+(2)	(1)+(2)+(5)+(6)+(8)	(1)+(2)+(5)+(6)+(8)+part of(9)&(12)	(10)+(11)	Age (x)
0	100000	100000	100000	100000	100000	100000	100000	100000	100000	100000	100000	100000	100000	100000	100000	100000	100000	0
1	94929	94929	95096	94929	95071	95436	95786	94929	94929	97216	94929	95008	95867	95096	96467	99343	95008	1
5	92954	92978	93565	92971	93133	93878	94019	92979	92954	95194	92954	93255	94413	93589	95601	98896	93255	5
10	92152	92184	92953	92186	92435	93146	93217	92237	92152	94372	92152	92557	93822	92986	95075	98469	92557	10
15	91603	91676	92532	91656	91956	92632	92662	91739	91604	93810	91603	92055	93407	92606	94730	98192	92055	15
20	90545	90917	91609	90619	90996	91636	91592	90721	90587	92727	90545	91054	92602	91986	94213	97863	91054	20
25	89114	89925	90365	89186	89704	90284	90144	89354	89280	91261	89114	89673	91433	91187	93627	97493	89673	25
30	87169	88507	88578	87304	87920	88434	88213	87486	87569	89269	87169	87826	89831	89937	92758	96896	87826	30
35	85322	86963	86782	85555	86278	86722	86364	85762	86094	87378	85322	86055	88266	88451	91823	96155	86055	35
40	83363	85193	84928	83879	84575	84856	84406	83893	84391	85372	83363	84167	86667	86793	90555	95067	84167	40
45	81180	82886	82705	81984	82738	82195	81862	82329	82256	83136	81180	82039	84970	84953	88907	93598	82039	45
50	78252	80434	80030	79701	80427	79831	79250	79157	79376	80137	78252	79252	82642	82261	86212	90935	79252	50
55	74492	76660	76276	76770	77731	76205	75443	75652	75562	76287	74492	75556	79599	78497	82495	87154	75556	55
60	69072	71280	70979	72354	73728	71085	70060	70821	70064	70736	69072	70113	74722	73247	77565	82169	70113	60
65	61963	64037	63735	66611	68454	64426	63039	64247	62853	63456	61963	63021	68354	65868	70676	75128	63021	65
70	52706	54595	54338	58540	62473	55310	53776	55182	53463	53576	52706	53791	59847	56285	61130	65217	53791	70
75	40285	41868	41638	46446	53413	43440	41311	42743	40864	41256	40285	41320	48705	43273	48539	52391	41320	75
80	25134	26200	26182	30456	39367	28862	26104	27168	25495	25740	25134	25901	35140	27292	33017	37031	25901	80
85+	12423	12957	12943	16175	23760	15093	13179	13673	12606	12722	12423	13035	23879	13499	17655	21127	13035	85+

ADDED YRS OF LIFE

	No Causes	(1)	(2)	(3)	(4)	(5)	(6)	(7)	(8)	(9)	(10)	(11)	(12)	(1)+(2)	...	...	(10)+(11)
TOTAL		1.106	1.147	1.862	4.100	1.715	.900	.881	.480	1.516	.000	.671	5.969	2.280	5.618	9.555	.671
WORK	5.465	.819	.380	.579	.853	.315	.043	.336	.392	.000	.000	.215	1.082	1.208	1.993	2.550	.215

POPULATION, DEATHS, DEATH RATES FOR ALL CAUSES COMBINED, AND SPECIFIED CAUSES

Age Start of Interval	Midyear Population	Deaths During Year	All Causes	Respiratory T.B.	Other Infec. and Paras.	Neoplasms	Cardiovascular	Infl., Pneu., Bronch.	Diarrheal	Certain Degenerative	Maternal	Cert. Dis. of Infancy	Motor Vehicle	Other Violence	Other and Unknown	Age Start of Interval
0	14100	774	.05489	.00000	.00156	.00000	.00028	.00617	.00461	.00028	.00000	.02965	.00000	.00078	.01156	0
1	51939	246	.00474	.00004	.00141	.00006	.00012	.00094	.00040	.00008	.00000	.00000	.00000	.00064	.00106	1
5	67418	138	.00205	.00000	.00064	.00004	.00019	.00025	.00003	.00009	.00000	.00000	.00000	.00030	.00050	5
10	61887	101	.00163	.00002	.00015	.00000	.00024	.00016	.00000	.00008	.00000	.00000	.00000	.00040	.00053	10
15	54667	98	.00179	.00018	.00024	.00011	.00020	.00020	.00002	.00002	.00000	.00000	.00000	.00044	.00038	15
20	48164	153	.00318	.00054	.00025	.00008	.00027	.00027	.00002	.00017	.00000	.00000	.00000	.00102	.00056	20
25	44464	137	.00308	.00090	.00038	.00002	.00018	.00022	.00000	.00009	.00000	.00000	.00000	.00072	.00056	25
30	47519	191	.00402	.00093	.00021	.00011	.00023	.00048	.00002	.00032	.00000	.00000	.00000	.00107	.00065	30
35	50294	260	.00517	.00082	.00054	.00032	.00052	.00062	.00002	.00040	.00000	.00000	.00000	.00109	.00085	35
40	45968	275	.00598	.00087	.00033	.00052	.00102	.00078	.00007	.00044	.00000	.00000	.00000	.00104	.00091	40
45	37632	337	.00896	.00109	.00050	.00077	.00154	.00133	.00008	.00058	.00000	.00000	.00000	.00175	.00130	45
50	30178	315	.01044	.00093	.00043	.00149	.00305	.00086	.00007	.00070	.00000	.00000	.00000	.00166	.00126	50
55	21366	343	.01605	.00080	.00051	.00300	.00529	.00136	.00019	.00122	.00000	.00000	.00000	.00140	.00229	55
60	16933	422	.02492	.00112	.00018	.00490	.00921	.00177	.00035	.00189	.00000	.00000	.00000	.00219	.00331	60
65	13495	523	.03876	.00044	.00015	.00689	.01438	.00311	.00022	.00282	.00000	.00000	.00000	.00267	.00808	65
70	8559	496	.05795	.00047	.00023	.00841	.02325	.00561	.00012	.00386	.00000	.00000	.00000	.00175	.01425	70
75	5748	509	.08855	.00052	.00000	.01148	.03793	.00870	.00070	.00452	.00000	.00000	.00000	.00104	.02366	75
80	3201	412	.12871	.00000	.00031	.00937	.04561	.01250	.00094	.00531	.00000	.00000	.00000	.00312	.05155	80
85+	1431	369	.25786	.00000	.00140	.00839	.08805	.02725	.00070	.00629	.00000	.00000	.00000	.00419	.12159	85+
ALL	624963	6099														

	All Causes	Respiratory T.B.	Other Infec. and Paras.	Neoplasms	Cardiovascular	Infl., Pneu., Bronch.	Diarrheal	Certain Degenerative	Maternal	Cert. Dis. of Infancy	Motor Vehicle	Other Violence	Other and Unknown
CRUDE DEATH RATE	.00976	.00052	.00048	.00089	.00233	.00103	.00020	.00050	.00000	.00067	.00000	.00097	.00220
STANDARDIZED RATE (1)	.00864	.00043	.00052	.00067	.00168	.00093	.00025	.00039	.00000	.00104	.00000	.00086	.00184
STANDARDIZED RATE (2)	.01308	.00053	.00046	.00134	.00370	.00132	.00021	.00068	.00000	.00061	.00000	.00105	.00317
GEOMETRIC MEAN	.01227												

LIFE TABLE FOR ALL CAUSES COMBINED

Age (x)	Midyear Population	Deaths During Year	$_nM_x$	$_nq_x$	l_x	$_nd_x$	$_nL_x$	$_nm_x$	$_na_x$	T_x	$_nr_x$	$\overset{\circ}{e}_x$	Age (x)
0	14100	774	.054894	.052480	100000	5248	95609	.054890	.163319	6234295	.000000	62.343	0
1	51939	246	.004736	.018723	94752	1774	374573	.004736	1.500000	6138686	.000000	64.787	1
5	67418	138	.002047	.010196	92978	948	462520	.002050	2.500000	5764113	.000000	61.994	5
10	61887	101	.001632	.008117	92030	747	458255	.001630	2.463744	5301593	.013977	57.607	10
15	54667	98	.001793	.008961	91283	818	454512	.001800	2.673696	4843338	.021171	53.058	15
20	48164	153	.003177	.015759	90465	1429	448866	.003184	2.579164	4388826	.021454	48.514	20
25	44464	137	.003081	.015286	89036	1361	441843	.003080	2.548065	3939960	.006492	44.251	25
30	47519	191	.004019	.019880	87675	1743	434191	.004014	2.599326	3498117	-.012667	39.899	30
35	50294	260	.005170	.025505	85932	2192	424332	.005166	2.569476	3063927	-.008329	35.655	35
40	45968	275	.005982	.029544	83740	2474	412803	.005993	2.616293	2639594	.013837	31.521	40
45	37632	337	.008555	.043967	81266	3573	397710	.008984	2.587403	2226792	.026969	27.401	45
50	30178	315	.010438	.051137	77693	3973	378985	.010483	2.613946	1829082	.040931	23.542	50
55	21366	343	.016054	.077944	73720	5746	355080	.016182	2.647095	1450097	.045208	19.670	55
60	16933	422	.024922	.118133	67974	8030	320821	.025030	2.627776	1095016	.024382	16.109	60
65	13495	523	.038755	.178016	59944	10671	273985	.038947	2.588323	774195	.027603	12.915	65
70	8559	496	.057951	.254785	49273	12554	215532	.058247	2.543960	500210	.028854	10.152	70
75	5748	509	.088553	.362773	36719	13320	150041	.088776	2.480934	284679	.012568	7.753	75
80	3201	412	.128710	.484422	23399	11335	87853	.129023	2.428999	134637	.012568	5.754	80
85+	1431	369	.257862	1.000000	12064	12064	46785	.257862	3.878049	46785	.000000	3.878	85+

NUMBER OF PERSONS DYING (OUT OF 100,000 AT BIRTH) ABOVE AGE X FROM SPECIFIED CAUSES

Age (x)	All Causes	Respiratory T.B.	Other Infec. and Paras.	Neoplasms	Cardiovascular	Infl., Pneu., Bronch.	Diarrheal	Certain Degenerative	Maternal	Cert. Dis. of Infancy	Motor Vehicle	Other Violence	Other and Unknown	Age (x)
0	100000	3589	2694	10727	30779	9912	1213	5338	0	2834	0	7252	25662	0
1	94752	3589	2544	10727	30752	9322	772	5311	0	0	0	7177	24558	1
5	92978	3515	2018	10706	30708	8969	621	5282	0	0	0	6939	24160	5
10	92030	3575	1723	10685	30619	8852	607	5241	0	0	0	6802	23926	10
15	91283	3567	1634	10685	30508	8778	607	5204	0	0	0	6616	23684	15
20	90465	3483	1526	10635	30416	8687	599	5195	0	0	0	6416	23508	20
25	89036	3239	1414	10598	30295	8565	589	5121	0	0	0	5958	23257	25
30	87675	2841	1245	10588	30216	8466	589	5081	0	0	0	5640	23009	30
35	85932	2439	1154	10543	30116	8256	580	4944	0	0	0	5175	22725	35
40	83740	2093	926	10408	29897	7995	572	4775	0	0	0	4710	22364	40
45	81266	1734	792	10192	29474	7671	545	4596	0	0	0	4279	21983	45
50	77693	1300	591	9883	28857	7142	513	4362	0	0	0	3579	21466	50
55	73720	950	427	9312	27690	6816	488	4097	0	0	0	2953	20987	55
60	67974	667	245	8237	25793	6331	420	3661	0	0	0	2454	20166	60
65	59944	307	189	6658	22823	5760	306	3052	0	0	0	1751	19098	65
70	49273	187	148	4763	18863	4902	246	2278	0	0	0	1019	16867	70
75	36719	86	98	2945	13822	3685	220	1444	0	0	0	644	13775	75
80	23399	8	98	1220	8118	2377	116	764	0	0	0	487	10211	80
85+	12064	0	65	392	4119	1275	33	294	0	0	0	196	5690	85+

NUMBER OF PERSONS SURVIVING TO AGE X IF SPECIFIED CAUSES WERE ELIMINATED

Age (x)	No Causes	Respiratory T.B. (1)	Other Infec. and Paras. (2)	Neoplasms (3)	Cardiovascular (4)	Infl., Pneu., Bronch. (5)	Diarrheal (6)	Certain Degenerative (7)	Maternal (8)	Cert. Dis. of Infancy (9)	Motor Vehicle (10)	Other Violence (11)	Other and Unknown (12)	(1)+(2)	(1)+(2)+(5)+(6)+(8)	(1)+(2)+(5)+(6)+(8)+part of(9)&(12)	(10)+(11)	Age (x)
0	100000	100000	100000	100000	100000	100000	100000	100000	100000	100000	100000	100000	100000	100000	100000	100000	100000	0
1	94752	94752	94898	94752	94778	95328	95182	94778	94752	97551	94752	94825	95383	94898	95908	99471	94825	1
5	92978	92992	93645	92999	93047	93896	93551	93033	92978	95724	92978	93286	94438	93659	95165	99018	93286	5
10	92030	92044	92986	92071	92187	93056	92611	92125	92030	94748	92030	92472	93712	93000	94630	98610	92472	10
15	91283	91305	92321	91324	91550	92375	91859	91414	91283	93979	91283	91907	93197	92343	94037	98079	91907	15
20	90465	90570	91602	90556	90821	91639	91044	90604	90465	93137	90465	91284	92541	91709	93493	97558	91284	20
25	89036	89382	90268	89162	89507	90314	89616	89246	89036	91666	89036	90302	91334	90619	92518	96692	90302	25
30	87675	88413	89058	87809	88218	89033	88246	87922	87675	90265	87675	89242	90191	89808	91793	96096	89242	30
35	85932	87058	87379	86108	86564	87475	86500	86310	85932	88470	85932	87938	88687	88524	90709	95113	87938	35
40	83740	85184	85379	84045	84574	85506	84302	84276	83740	86214	83740	86166	86794	86851	89278	93796	86166	40
45	81266	83027	82992	81776	82498	83307	81838	81964	81266	83666	81266	84058	84619	84790	87531	92132	84058	45
50	77693	79811	79544	78486	79486	80175	78271	78591	77693	79988	77693	81073	81427	81712	84951	89643	81073	50
55	73720	76080	75639	75037	76595	76403	74293	74834	73720	75898	73720	77565	77753	78061	81532	86170	77565	55
60	67974	70431	69923	70248	72544	70932	68569	69427	67974	69982	67974	72024	72529	72449	76264	80795	72024	60
65	59944	62460	61716	63499	67020	63114	60576	61812	59944	61715	59944	64217	65043	64305	68420	72678	64217	65
70	49273	51452	50767	54039	59249	52705	49847	51535	49273	50728	49273	53495	55709	53012	57364	61255	53495	70
75	36719	38433	37876	42015	49695	40414	37169	39159	36719	37804	36719	40210	44642	39644	44169	47673	40210	75
80	23399	24555	24136	28370	38400	26518	23771	25530	23399	24090	23399	25758	32121	25328	29600	32548	25758	80
85+	12064	12666	12468	15352	25011	14802	12315	13529	12064	12420	12064	13508	21569	13090	16395	18905	13508	85+

ADDED YRS OF LIFE	No Causes	(1)	(2)	(3)	(4)	(5)	(6)	(7)	(8)	(9)	(10)	(11)	(12)	(1)+(2)	(1)+(2)+(5)+(6)+(8)	(1)+(2)+(5)+(6)+(8)+part	(10)+(11)
TOTAL		1.044	1.139	1.461	4.304	1.971	.475	.845	.000	1.837	.000	2.002	4.480	2.211	4.816	8.508	2.002
WORK	5.423	.742	.350	.386	.785	.523	.035	.299	.000	.000	.000	1.036	.792	1.101	1.683	2.027	1.036

POPULATION, DEATHS, DEATH RATES FOR ALL CAUSES COMBINED, AND SPECIFIED CAUSES

Age Start of Interval	Midyear Population	Deaths During Year	All Causes	Respiratory T. B.	Other Infec. and Paras.	Neoplasms	Cardiovascular	Infl., Pneu., Bronch.	Diarrheal	Certain Degenerative	Maternal	Cert. Dis. of Infancy	Motor Vehicle	Other Violence	Other and Unknown	Age Start of Interval
0	13271	592	.04461	.00000	.00249	.00008	.00023	.00414	.00339	.00008	.00000	.02464	.00000	.00030	.00927	0
1	50388	223	.00443	.00002	.00153	.00010	.00004	.00083	.00046	.00004	.00000	.00000	.00000	.00034	.00107	1
5	64980	96	.00148	.00000	.00057	.00000	.00012	.00018	.00003	.00006	.00000	.00000	.00000	.00009	.00042	5
10	60021	68	.00113	.00013	.00017	.00003	.00012	.00012	.00002	.00007	.00000	.00000	.00000	.00015	.00033	10
15	53102	96	.00181	.00064	.00019	.00002	.00019	.00008	.00002	.00015	.00011	.00000	.00000	.00008	.00034	15
20	49423	144	.00291	.00097	.00038	.00008	.00020	.00016	.00002	.00012	.00051	.00000	.00000	.00014	.00034	20
25	49075	173	.00353	.00096	.00037	.00006	.00022	.00020	.00000	.00031	.00077	.00000	.00000	.00018	.00045	25
30	48216	156	.00324	.00071	.00010	.00023	.00031	.00027	.00004	.00021	.00064	.00000	.00000	.00015	.00058	30
35	47458	210	.00442	.00078	.00021	.00036	.00061	.00042	.00004	.00042	.00067	.00000	.00000	.00017	.00074	35
40	42369	191	.00451	.00061	.00019	.00101	.00080	.00033	.00000	.00038	.00026	.00000	.00000	.00012	.00080	40
45	32581	211	.00648	.00049	.00006	.00129	.00190	.00031	.00000	.00046	.00006	.00000	.00000	.00034	.00157	45
50	25937	257	.00991	.00035	.00031	.00285	.00243	.00062	.00015	.00096	.00000	.00000	.00000	.00012	.00212	50
55	18630	249	.01337	.00064	.00016	.00344	.00424	.00059	.00011	.00177	.00000	.00000	.00000	.00032	.00209	55
60	14841	250	.01685	.00034	.00013	.00330	.00701	.00108	.00034	.00182	.00000	.00000	.00000	.00074	.00209	60
65	11065	317	.02865	.00045	.00000	.00606	.01166	.00226	.00018	.00271	.00000	.00000	.00000	.00027	.00506	65
70	7510	368	.04900	.00053	.00080	.00919	.02104	.00386	.00040	.00280	.00000	.00000	.00000	.00067	.00972	70
75	4928	412	.08360	.00020	.00041	.00994	.03511	.00994	.00020	.00690	.00000	.00000	.00000	.00122	.01968	75
80	2588	299	.11553	.00000	.00039	.01236	.04096	.00734	.00155	.00580	.00000	.00000	.00000	.00232	.04482	80
85+	1176	271	.23044	.00000	.00000	.01020	.07228	.01105	.00085	.00510	.00000	.00000	.00000	.00000	.04482	85+
ALL	597559	4583														

CRUDE DEATH RATE			.00767	.00048	.00042	.00091	.00182	.00062	.00017	.00049	.00024	.00055	.00000	.00022	.00175	
STANDARDIZED RATE (1)			.00722	.00044	.00050	.00075	.00145	.00062	.00022	.00041	.00021	.00087	.00000	.00021	.00155	
STANDARDIZED RATE (2)			.01103	.00047	.00041	.00144	.00321	.00088	.00019	.00073	.00021	.00051	.00000	.00027	.00271	
GEOMETRIC MEAN			.01034													

LIFE TABLE FOR ALL CAUSES COMBINED

Age (x)	Midyear Population	Deaths During Year	$_nM_x$	$_nq_x$	l_x	$_nd_x$	$_nL_x$	$_nm_x$	$_na_x$	T_x	$_nr_x$	$\overset{\circ}{e}_x$	Age (x)
0	13271	592	.044609	.042970	100000	4297	96330	.044607	.145835	6538334	.000000	65.383	0
1	50388	223	.004426	.017513	95703	1676	378622	.004427	1.500000	6442005	.000000	67.312	1
5	64980	96	.001477	.007349	94027	691	468408	.001475	2.500000	6063383	.000000	64.486	5
10	60021	68	.001133	.005657	93336	528	465391	.001135	2.558396	5594975	.014189	59.944	10
15	53102	96	.001808	.009040	92808	839	462110	.001816	2.699642	5129584	.018751	55.271	15
20	49423	144	.002914	.014483	91969	1332	456670	.002917	2.616366	4667474	.009312	50.751	20
25	49075	173	.003525	.017465	90637	1583	449248	.003524	2.512897	4210804	.001592	46.458	25
30	48216	156	.003235	.016058	89054	1430	441765	.003237	2.548805	3761556	-.000511	42.239	30
35	47458	210	.004425	.021889	87624	1918	433426	.004425	2.552572	3319792	-.002702	37.887	35
40	42369	191	.004508	.022332	85706	1914	423906	.004515	2.583921	2886366	.024191	33.678	40
45	32581	211	.006476	.032091	83792	2689	412662	.006516	2.657819	2462460	.037495	29.388	45
50	25937	257	.009909	.048716	81103	3951	396123	.009974	2.622806	2049798	.044285	25.274	50
55	18630	249	.013366	.065040	77152	5018	373615	.013431	2.579755	1653676	.044755	21.434	55
60	14841	250	.016845	.081404	72134	5872	346812	.016931	2.640036	1280060	.035082	17.746	60
65	11065	317	.028649	.135296	66262	8965	310309	.028891	2.657441	933248	.038766	14.084	65
70	7510	368	.049001	.220727	57297	12647	256234	.049357	2.608013	622939	.032384	10.872	70
75	4928	412	.083604	.347637	44650	15522	184524	.084119	2.505060	366706	.025840	8.213	75
80	2588	299	.115533	.447130	29128	13024	112299	.115976	2.440031	182182	.025840	6.255	80
85+	1176	271	.230442	1.000000	16104	16104	69883	.230442	4.335483	69883	.000000	4.339	85+

NUMBER OF PERSONS DYING (OUT OF 100,000 AT BIRTH) ABOVE AGE X FROM SPECIFIED CAUSES

Age (x)	All Causes	Respiratory T. B.	Other Infec. and Paras.	Neo-plasms	Cardio-vascular	Infl., Pneu., Bronch.	Diar-rheal	Certain Degen-erative	Maternal	Cert. Dis. of Infancy	Motor Vehicle	Other Violence	Other and Unknown	Age (x)
0	100000	3170	2388	13153	32230	7619	1226	6515	1344	2374	0	2187	27794	0
1	95703	3170	2148	13146	32208	7219	900	6508	1344	0	0	2157	26903	1
5	94027	3162	1569	13108	32193	6904	727	6493	1344	0	0	2030	26497	5
10	93336	3162	1303	13108	32136	6817	713	6464	1344	0	0	1987	26302	10
15	92808	3099	1226	13093	32081	6763	705	6433	1344	0	0	1917	26147	15
20	91969	2802	1139	13084	31994	6728	696	6363	1290	0	0	1882	25991	20
25	90637	2358	963	13047	31902	6654	687	6308	1059	0	0	1817	25842	25
30	89054	1928	798	13020	31801	6563	687	6170	711	0	0	1735	25641	30
35	87624	1616	753	12919	31664	6444	669	6079	427	0	0	1671	25382	35
40	85706	1279	661	12763	31399	6261	650	5896	135	0	0	1598	25064	40
45	83792	1019	581	12331	31056	6121	650	5736	26	0	0	1547	24725	45
50	81103	817	556	11794	30265	5994	650	5544	2	0	0	1408	24073	50
55	77152	680	433	10655	29296	5748	588	5158	2	0	0	1362	23230	55
60	72134	438	374	9369	27656	5527	548	4492	2	0	0	1240	22448	60
65	66262	323	327	8220	25249	5149	431	3860	2	0	0	983	21718	65
70	57297	182	327	6326	21600	4441	375	3015	2	0	0	900	20129	70
75	44650	45	120	3962	16169	3441	272	2294	2	0	0	727	17618	75
80	29128	9	46	2122	9656	1595	234	1013	2	0	0	501	13950	80
85+	16104	0	0	713	5051	773	59	357	0	0	0	238	8913	85+

NUMBER OF PERSONS SURVIVING TO AGE X IF SPECIFIED CAUSES WERE ELIMINATED

Age (x)	No Causes	Respira-tory T. B.	Other Infec. and Paras.	Neo-plasms	Cardio-vascular	Infl., Pneu., Bronch.	Diar-rheal	Certain Degener-ative	Maternal	Cert. Dis. of Infancy	Motor Vehicle	Other Violence	Other and Unknown	(1) + (2)	(1) + (2) + (5) + (6) + (8)	(1)+(2)+ (5)+(6)+ (8)+part of(9)&(12)	(10) + (11)	Age (x)
		(1)	(2)	(3)	(4)	(5)	(6)	(7)	(8)	(9)	(10)	(11)	(12)					
0	100000	100000	100000	100000	100000	100000	100000	100000	100000	100000	100000	100000	100000	100000	100000	100000	100000	0
1	95703	95703	95938	95710	95725	96095	96022	95710	95703	98054	95703	95732	96579	95938	96653	99720	95732	1
5	94027	94035	94835	94071	94063	94513	94513	94049	94027	96336	94027	94182	95294	94843	96042	99449	94182	5
10	93336	93344	94406	93380	93429	94117	93832	93386	93336	95629	93336	93533	94791	94414	95711	99259	93533	10
15	92808	92879	93949	92867	92955	93639	93310	92889	92808	95088	92808	93073	94412	94021	95376	99001	93073	15
20	91969	92335	93188	92036	92201	92828	92475	92119	92023	94228	91969	92267	93716	93559	95008	98737	92267	20
25	90637	91442	92015	90740	90958	91558	91145	90840	90920	92863	90637	90995	92510	92832	94595	98434	90995	25
30	89054	90276	90574	89182	89470	90050	89553	89390	89679	91241	89054	89488	91058	91817	94019	97998	89488	30
35	87624	89140	89165	87850	88170	88723	88133	88046	88523	89776	87624	88115	89858	90708	93327	97467	88115	35
40	85706	87528	87306	86083	86504	86965	86223	86300	86877	87811	85706	86259	88254	89163	92261	96558	86259	40
45	83792	85856	85437	84590	84915	85163	84257	84532	86046	85850	83792	84383	86629	87522	90829	95201	84383	45
50	81103	83285	82720	82411	82983	82557	81592	82011	82340	83095	81103	81813	84515	84946	88318	92705	81813	50
55	77152	79365	78813	79534	79914	78780	77678	78397	78329	79047	77152	77872	81258	81074	84620	88997	77872	55
60	72134	74444	73745	75652	76338	73875	72665	73956	73235	73906	72134	72927	76772	76106	79714	83954	72927	60
65	66262	68497	67787	70657	72651	68234	66862	68558	67273	67890	66262	67239	71272	70074	73924	77960	67239	65
70	57297	59365	58617	63001	66651	59683	57868	60097	58171	58704	57297	58219	63241	60732	64868	68627	58219	70
75	44650	46385	45865	51425	57809	47440	45186	47502	45331	45747	44650	45524	51790	47648	52015	55422	45524	75
80	29128	30288	29979	35270	45054	32560	29509	32100	29572	29843	29128	29884	37410	31173	35840	38847	29884	80
85+	16104	16752	16609	20791	30743	18688	16445	18285	16351	16500	16104	16721	26011	17278	20789	23224	16721	85+

ADDED YRS OF LIFE

		(1)	(2)	(3)	(4)	(5)	(6)	(7)	(8)	(9)	(10)	(11)	(12)				
TOTAL		1.135	1.129	1.979	4.519	1.446	.442	1.049	.558	1.603	.000	.510	4.929	2.289	4.897	8.333	.510
WORK	4.785	.809	.257	.566	.754	.277	.032	.368	.448	.000	.000	.170	.754	1.071	1.858	2.216	.170

POPULATION, DEATHS, DEATH RATES FOR ALL CAUSES COMBINED, AND SPECIFIED CAUSES

Age Start of Interval	Midyear Population	Deaths During Year	All Causes	Respira- tory T. B.	Other Infec. and Paras.	Neo- plasms	Cardio- vascular	Infl., Pneu., Bronch.	Diar- rheal	Certain Degen- erative	Maternal	Cert. Dis. of Infancy	Motor Vehicle	Other Violence	Other and Unknown	Age Start of Interval
0	14025	638	.04549	.00000	.00342	.00014	.00050	.00570	.00114	.00000	.00000	.02374	.00000	.00086	.00998	0
1	54963	199	.00362	.00002	.00091	.00009	.00018	.00084	.00016	.00007	.00000	.00000	.00000	.00086	.00086	1
5	68008	103	.00151	.00001	.00041	.00004	.00012	.00012	.00000	.00007	.00000	.00000	.00000	.00049	.00050	5
10	68595	73	.00106	.00001	.00012	.00004	.00010	.00009	.00000	.00004	.00000	.00000	.00000	.00026	.00039	10
15	63790	122	.00191	.00020	.00013	.00005	.00020	.00013	.00000	.00008	.00000	.00000	.00000	.00072	.00041	15
20	58184	164	.00282	.00050	.00017	.00014	.00014	.00014	.00002	.00009	.00000	.00000	.00000	.00115	.00048	20
25	52136	152	.00292	.00082	.00019	.00004	.00013	.00013	.00002	.00013	.00000	.00000	.00000	.00098	.00046	25
30	45511	174	.00382	.00101	.00033	.00020	.00029	.00024	.00002	.00020	.00000	.00000	.00000	.00092	.00062	30
35	49281	239	.00485	.00081	.00024	.00045	.00057	.00059	.00000	.00028	.00000	.00000	.00000	.00122	.00069	35
40	49140	251	.00511	.00065	.00045	.00037	.00051	.00053	.00000	.00037	.00000	.00000	.00000	.00130	.00094	40
45	46142	367	.00795	.00100	.00043	.00095	.00141	.00074	.00011	.00069	.00000	.00000	.00000	.00156	.00106	45
50	35390	398	.01125	.00079	.00051	.00175	.00297	.00119	.00000	.00093	.00000	.00000	.00000	.00161	.00150	50
55	27264	437	.01603	.00077	.00055	.00297	.00528	.00114	.00022	.00176	.00000	.00000	.00000	.00143	.00191	55
60	19380	491	.02534	.00072	.00083	.00542	.00857	.00144	.00005	.00217	.00000	.00000	.00000	.00212	.00402	60
65	14519	620	.04270	.00055	.00048	.00868	.01729	.00317	.00000	.00337	.00000	.00000	.00000	.00255	.00661	65
70	10557	627	.05939	.00057	.00019	.00966	.02425	.00493	.00000	.00417	.00000	.00000	.00000	.00284	.01279	70
75	6100	644	.10557	.00016	.00049	.01361	.04672	.01000	.00016	.00639	.00000	.00000	.00000	.00279	.02525	75
80	3123	501	.16042	.00032	.00096	.01281	.06084	.02337	.00096	.00833	.00000	.00000	.00000	.00256	.05027	80
85+	1757	473	.26921	.00000	.00057	.02220	.07911	.03130	.00000	.01024	.00000	.00000	.00000	.00455	.12123	85+
ALL	687865	6673														

CRUDE DEATH RATE			.00970	.00048	.00043	.00110	.00251	.00095	.00006	.00058	.00000	.00048	.00000	.00104	.00207	
STANDARDIZED RATE (1)			.00822	.00040	.00048	.00080	.00176	.00083	.00008	.00043	.00000	.00084	.00000	.00090	.00169	
STANDARDIZED RATE (2)			.01344	.00049	.00045	.00162	.00403	.00133	.00007	.00082	.00000	.00049	.00000	.00113	.00302	
GEOMETRIC MEAN			.01162													

LIFE TABLE FOR ALL CAUSES COMBINED

Age (x)	Midyear Population	Deaths During Year	$_nM_x$	$_nq_x$	l_x	$_nd_x$	$_nL_x$	$_nm_x$	$_na_x$	T_x	$_nr_x$	$\overset{\circ}{e}_x$	Age (x)
0	14025	638	.045490	.043790	100000	4379	96266	.045488	.147333	6330816	.000000	63.308	0
1	54963	199	.003621	.014359	95621	1373	379052	.003622	1.500000	6234550	.000000	65.201	1
5	68008	103	.001515	.007533	94248	710	469465	.001512	2.500000	5855498	.000000	62.129	5
10	68595	73	.001064	.005313	93538	497	466485	.001065	2.574614	5386033	.002207	57.581	10
15	63790	122	.001913	.009544	93041	888	463150	.001917	2.686280	4919548	.011440	52.875	15
20	58184	164	.002819	.014009	92153	1291	457627	.002821	2.569229	4456398	.014760	48.359	20
25	52136	152	.002915	.014495	90862	1317	451102	.002920	2.564382	3998771	.022743	44.009	25
30	45511	174	.003823	.018963	89545	1698	443644	.003827	2.596560	3547669	.009573	39.619	30
35	49281	239	.004850	.023951	87847	2104	434072	.004847	2.545944	3104025	-.008687	35.334	35
40	49140	251	.005108	.025215	85743	2162	423553	.005104	2.612454	2669953	-.004981	31.139	40
45	46142	367	.007954	.039136	83581	3271	410198	.007974	2.643814	2246400	.015138	26.877	45
50	35390	398	.011246	.055037	80310	4420	391047	.011303	2.623869	1836202	.034645	22.864	50
55	27264	437	.016028	.077731	75890	5899	365538	.016138	2.641655	1445155	.041953	19.043	55
60	19380	491	.025335	.120458	69991	8431	330140	.025538	2.649745	1079617	.040680	15.425	60
65	14519	620	.042703	.194266	61560	11959	278834	.042989	2.577922	749477	.022921	12.175	65
70	10557	627	.059392	.260156	49601	12904	216456	.059615	2.555070	470642	-.022869	9.489	70
75	6100	644	.105574	.418835	36697	15370	144883	.106086	2.488465	254187	.017323	6.927	75
80	3123	501	.160423	.565152	21327	12053	74855	.161018	2.363295	109304	.017323	5.125	80
85+	1757	473	.269209	1.000000	9274	9274	34449	.269209	3.714588	34449	.000000	3.715	85+

NUMBER OF PERSONS DYING (OUT OF 100,000 AT BIRTH) ABOVE AGE X FROM SPECIFIED CAUSES

Age (x)	All Causes	Respiratory T. B.	Other Infec. and Paras.	Neoplasms	Cardiovascular	Infl., Pneu., Bronch.	Diarrheal	Certain Degenerative	Maternal	Cert. Dis. of Infancy	Motor Vehicle	Other Violence	Other and Unknown	Age (x)
0	100000	3363	2782	12843	31775	9648	437	6366	0	2286	0	7886	22614	0
1	95621	3363	2452	12829	31727	9098	327	6366	0	0	0	7804	21655	1
5	94248	3356	2107	12794	31658	8781	265	6338	0	0	0	7618	21331	5
10	93538	3350	1914	12774	31603	8726	265	6304	0	0	0	7507	21095	10
15	93041	3343	1860	12753	31555	8685	265	6283	0	0	0	7385	20912	15
20	92153	3248	1802	12731	31461	8627	265	6247	0	0	0	7050	20722	20
25	90862	3019	1723	12668	31398	8564	257	6208	0	0	0	6522	20503	25
30	89545	2646	1636	12651	31237	8503	248	6147	0	0	0	6082	20295	30
35	87847	2197	1490	12563	31210	8396	239	6059	0	0	0	5672	20021	35
40	85743	1845	1384	12369	30963	8140	239	5936	0	0	0	5144	19723	40
45	83581	1569	1195	12214	30748	7916	239	5781	0	0	0	4592	19327	45
50	80310	1160	1017	11822	30167	7613	194	5495	0	0	0	3952	18890	50
55	75890	851	818	11131	28996	7148	194	5128	0	0	0	3322	18302	55
60	69991	570	616	10034	27049	6732	113	4480	0	0	0	2799	17598	60
65	61560	332	343	8230	24193	6251	97	3761	0	0	0	2097	16256	65
70	49601	178	209	5802	19348	5362	97	2817	0	0	0	1385	14403	70
75	36697	56	169	3708	14077	4291	97	1912	0	0	0	770	11617	75
80	21327	32	97	1731	7275	2832	73	982	0	0	0	366	7939	80
85+	9274	0	20	765	2725	1078	0	353	0	0	0	157	4176	85+

NUMBER OF PERSONS SURVIVING TO AGE X IF SPECIFIED CAUSES WERE ELIMINATED

Age (x)	No Causes	Respiratory T. B. (1)	Other Infec. and Paras. (2)	Neoplasms (3)	Cardiovascular (4)	Infl., Pneu., Bronch. (5)	Diarrheal (6)	Certain Degenerative (7)	Maternal (8)	Cert. Dis. of Infancy (9)	Motor Vehicle (10)	Other Violence (11)	Other and Unknown (12)	(1) + (2)	(1) + (2) + (5) + (6) + (8)	(1)+(2)+ (5)+(6)+ (8)+part of(9)&(12)	(10) + (11)	Age (x)
0	100000	100000	100000	100000	100000	100000	100000	100000	100000	100000	100000	100000	100000	100000	100000	100000	100000	0
1	95621	95621	95944	95635	95668	96160	95729	95621	95621	97883	95621	95701	96563	95944	96594	99433	95701	1
5	94248	94255	94911	94296	94363	95097	94416	94276	94248	96477	94248	94512	95502	94918	95943	98998	94512	5
10	93538	93551	94390	93606	93707	94435	93704	93599	93538	95750	93538	93911	95021	94403	95478	98651	93911	10
15	93041	93061	93943	93129	93257	93975	93207	93123	93041	95242	93041	93534	94702	93963	95075	98297	93534	15
20	92153	92267	93104	92263	92461	93136	92317	92270	92153	94333	92153	92977	93991	93220	94382	97641	92977	20
25	90862	91203	91879	91033	91228	91895	91032	91016	90862	93011	90862	92205	92896	93220	93446	96755	92205	25
30	89545	90253	90635	89730	89567	90624	89721	89758	89545	91663	89545	91313	91761	91352	92635	96021	91313	30
35	87847	88991	89063	88116	88387	89013	88029	88143	87847	89925	87847	89996	90299	90223	91609	95104	89996	35
40	85743	87212	87036	86198	86516	87138	85920	86154	85743	87771	85743	88377	88440	88527	90154	93720	88377	40
45	83581	85291	85031	84179	84549	85166	83754	84136	83581	85558	83581	86712	86614	86770	88598	92272	86712	45
50	80310	82363	81881	81273	81819	82136	80520	81126	80310	82209	80310	83971	83669	83973	86107	89835	83971	50
55	75890	78138	77571	77483	78486	78079	76089	77022	75890	77685	75890	79991	79662	79869	82387	86118	79991	55
60	69991	72341	71740	72545	74346	72421	70252	71669	69991	71646	69991	74304	74183	74149	77009	80643	74304	60
65	61560	63857	63360	65583	68300	64166	61804	63729	61560	63016	61560	66054	66595	65724	68777	72232	66054	65
70	49601	51593	51172	55206	60070	52539	49798	52230	49601	50774	49601	53907	55489	53228	56605	59681	53907	70
75	36697	38278	37894	42877	50267	39857	36843	39464	36697	37565	36697	40455	43826	39527	43102	45808	40455	75
80	21327	22263	22079	26698	37139	24397	21431	23695	21327	21831	21327	23841	29020	23048	26495	28666	23841	80
85+	9274	9702	9652	12411	22115	11976	9366	10762	9274	9493	9274	10518	16366	10098	13170	15141	10518	85+

ADDED YRS OF LIFE																		
TOTAL		.978	1.022	1.662	4.122	1.653	.154	.887	.000	1.494	.000	2.098	3.766	2.023	3.936	6.851	2.098	
WORK	5.180	.706	.282	.431	.704	.376	.023	.307	.000	.000	.000	1.177	.739	.995	1.410	1.683	1.177	

POPULATION, DEATHS, DEATH RATES FOR ALL CAUSES COMBINED, AND SPECIFIED CAUSES

Age Start of Interval	Midyear Population	Deaths During Year	All Causes	Respiratory T. B.	Other Infec. and Paras.	Neoplasms	Cardiovascular	Infl., Pneu., Bronch.	Diarrheal	Certain Degenerative	Maternal	Cert. Dis. of Infancy	Motor Vehicle	Other Violence	Other and Unknown	Age Start of Interval
0	13388	494	.03690	.00000	.00373	.00007	.00007	.00478	.00164	.00007	.00000	.01905	.00000	.00075	.00672	0
1	52705	211	.00400	.00000	.00120	.00013	.00013	.00093	.00017	.00015	.00000	.00000	.00000	.00046	.00083	1
5	65431	88	.00134	.00005	.00032	.00008	.00011	.00017	.00005	.00006	.00000	.00000	.00000	.00046	.00083	5
10	66002	81	.00123	.00009	.00018	.00006	.00020	.00009	.00000	.00011	.00002	.00000	.00000	.00018	.00034	5
15	61126	89	.00146	.00046	.00011	.00007	.00016	.00015	.00000	.00005	.00008	.00000	.00000	.00021	.00027	10
20	55174	137	.00248	.00085	.00020	.00005	.00016	.00022	.00005	.00009	.00029	.00000	.00000	.00008	.00029	15
25	52016	157	.00302	.00090	.00013	.00012	.00023	.00013	.00002	.00009	.00029	.00000	.00000	.00018	.00038	20
30	49827	166	.00333	.00066	.00014	.00024	.00040	.00032	.00010	.00013	.00054	.00000	.00000	.00023	.00058	25
35	49847	185	.00371	.00060	.00018	.00046	.00038	.00042	.00004	.00014	.00050	.00000	.00000	.00010	.00072	30
40	46880	203	.00433	.00041	.00017	.00090	.00087	.00034	.00004	.00032	.00052	.00000	.00000	.00012	.00066	35
45	41746	262	.00628	.00038	.00010	.00156	.00146	.00041	.00002	.00045	.00041	.00000	.00000	.00019	.00055	40
50	31218	284	.00910	.00026	.00016	.00240	.00256	.00051	.00000	.00057	.00002	.00000	.00000	.00031	.00144	45
55	24144	297	.01230	.00033	.00025	.00335	.00431	.00041	.00004	.00122	.00000	.00000	.00000	.00038	.00160	50
60	18171	343	.01888	.00055	.00028	.00440	.00726	.00143	.00000	.00145	.00000	.00000	.00000	.00021	.00195	55
65	13269	400	.03015	.00023	.00015	.00603	.01379	.00234	.00023	.00193	.00000	.00000	.00000	.00017	.00286	60
70	8892	480	.05398	.00011	.00000	.00855	.02800	.00371	.00034	.00249	.00000	.00000	.00000	.00030	.00460	65
75	5438	494	.09084	.00037	.00055	.00919	.04101	.00993	.00000	.00349	.00000	.00000	.00000	.00034	.00945	70
80	2929	406	.13861	.00000	.00000	.01263	.05394	.01946	.00137	.00478	.00000	.00000	.00000	.00110	.02391	75
85+	1544	369	.23899	.00000	.00000	.01263	.05394	.01946	.00137	.00580	.00000	.00000	.00000	.00239	.04302	80
ALL	659747	5146		.00000	.00000	.00842	.07254	.03174	.00065	.00777	.00000	.00000	.00000	.00259	.11528	85+

CRUDE DEATH RATE			.00780	.00040	.00033	.00101	.00218	.00076	.00009	.00050	.00018	.00039	.00000	.00025	.00171	
STANDARDIZED RATE (1)			.00691	.00036	.00043	.00078	.00163	.00072	.00012	.00040	.00016	.00067	.00000	.00025	.00141	
STANDARDIZED RATE (2)			.01125	.00038	.00034	.00145	.00371	.00112	.00011	.00070	.00017	.00039	.00000	.00028	.00260	
GEOMETRIC MEAN			.00999													

LIFE TABLE FOR ALL CAUSES COMBINED

Age (x)	Midyear Population	Deaths During Year	$_nM_x$	$_nq_x$	l_x	$_nd_x$	$_nL_x$	$_nm_x$	$_na_x$	T_x	$_nr_x$	$\overset{\circ}{e}_x$	Age (x)
0	13388	494	.036899	.035750	100000	3575	96900	.036894	.132728	6604160	.000000	66.042	0
1	52705	211	.004003	.015857	96425	1529	381878	.004004	1.500000	6507261	.000000	67.485	1
5	65431	88	.001345	.006702	94896	636	472890	.001345	2.500000	6125383	.000000	64.548	5
10	66002	81	.001227	.006121	94260	577	469867	.001228	2.516248	5652493	.002229	59.967	10
15	61126	89	.001456	.007269	93683	681	466832	.001459	2.675294	5182626	.013239	55.321	15
20	55174	137	.002483	.012365	93002	1150	462280	.002488	2.626087	4715794	.014559	50.706	20
25	52016	157	.003018	.014992	91852	1377	455889	.003020	2.552197	4253514	.010053	46.308	25
30	49827	166	.003332	.016524	90475	1495	448692	.003332	2.536232	3797625	.003071	41.974	30
35	49847	185	.003711	.018397	88980	1637	440886	.003713	2.548106	3348933	.001354	37.637	35
40	46880	203	.004330	.021444	87343	1873	432244	.004333	2.613009	2908047	.007137	33.295	40
45	41746	262	.006276	.031040	85470	2653	421100	.006300	2.644098	2475803	.025783	28.967	45
50	31218	284	.009097	.044773	82817	3708	405253	.009150	2.618157	2054703	.041856	24.810	50
55	24144	297	.012301	.060120	79109	4756	384292	.012376	2.633997	1649450	.041481	20.850	55
60	18171	343	.018876	.091012	74353	6767	355854	.019016	2.648792	1265158	.040652	17.016	60
65	13269	400	.030145	.141878	67586	9589	315458	.030397	2.656451	909303	.039869	13.454	65
70	8892	480	.053981	.240840	57997	13968	256478	.054461	2.601169	593846	.037235	10.239	70
75	5438	494	.090842	.371846	44029	16372	179253	.091335	2.502329	337367	.022301	7.662	75
80	2929	406	.138614	.511661	27657	14151	101601	.139279	2.407707	158114	.022301	5.717	80
85+	1544	369	.238990	1.000000	13506	13506	56513	.238990	4.184282	56513	.000000	4.184	85+

NUMBER OF PERSONS DYING (OUT OF 100,000 AT BIRTH) ABOVE AGE X FROM SPECIFIED CAUSES

Age (x)	All Causes	Respiratory T.B.	Other Infec. and Paras.	Neo-plasms	Cardio-vascular	Infl., Pneu., Bronch.	Diar-rheal	Certain Degen-erative	Maternal	Cert. Dis. of Infancy	Motor Vehicle	Other Violence	Other and Unknown	Age (x)
0	100000	2583	1927	12995	35747	9976	723	6245	1066	1845	0	2041	24852	0
1	96425	2583	1565	12988	35739	9513	563	6238	1066	0	0	1969	24201	1
5	94896	2583	1109	12937	35689	9158	498	6180	1066	0	0	1795	23881	5
10	94260	2561	957	12901	35638	9079	477	6151	1066	0	0	1708	23722	10
15	93683	2518	872	12872	35546	9036	477	6101	1059	0	0	1609	23593	15
20	93002	2303	818	12842	35469	8967	476	6079	1020	0	0	1570	23458	20
25	91852	1909	726	12817	35394	8867	451	6037	886	0	0	1486	23279	25
30	90475	1497	665	12764	35288	8805	442	5975	640	0	0	1381	23018	30
35	88980	1200	602	12656	35108	8661	397	5912	415	0	0	1336	22693	35
40	87343	935	522	12452	34940	8475	380	5771	185	0	0	1283	22400	40
45	85470	760	448	12064	34561	8328	361	5577	10	0	0	1200	22161	45
50	82817	599	408	11405	33942	8156	351	5333	1	0	0	1069	21553	50
55	79109	495	343	10425	32894	7948	351	4836	1	0	0	913	20903	55
60	74353	367	247	9129	31225	7787	335	4277	1	0	0	834	20151	60
65	67586	171	149	7555	28614	7272	335	3589	1	0	0	775	19125	65
70	57997	101	102	5644	24216	6529	263	2801	1	0	0	680	17660	70
75	44029	72	102	3441	16971	5566	176	1901	1	0	0	592	15207	75
80	27657	6	2	1789	9589	3771	176	1041	1	0	0	393	10889	80
85+	13506	0	0	476	4099	1793	37	439	0	0	0	146	6516	85+

NUMBER OF PERSONS SURVIVING TO AGE X IF SPECIFIED CAUSES WERE ELIMINATED

Age (x)	No Causes	Respiratory T.B. (1)	Other Infec. and Paras. (2)	Neo-plasms (3)	Cardio-vascular (4)	Infl., Pneu., Bronch. (5)	Diar-rheal (6)	Certain Degener-ative (7)	Maternal (8)	Cert. Dis. of Infancy (9)	Motor Vehicle (10)	Other Violence (11)	Other and Unknown (12)	(1)+(2)	(1)+(2)+(5)+(6)+(8)	(1)+(2)+(5)+(6)+(8)+part of(9)&(12)	(10)+(11)	Age (x)
0	100000	100000	100000	100000	100000	100000	100000	100000	100000	100000	100000	100000	100000	100000	100000	100000	100000	0
1	96425	96425	96781	96432	96433	96881	96582	96432	96425	98254	96425	96496	97066	96781	97397	99683	96496	1
5	94896	94896	95702	94953	94953	95665	95115	94560	94896	96656	94896	95138	95847	95702	96734	99245	95138	5
10	94260	94282	95213	94353	94368	95137	94499	94353	94260	96048	94260	94588	95365	95235	96365	98962	94588	10
15	93683	93748	94716	93804	93882	94598	93920	93825	93690	95460	93683	94108	94912	94781	95957	98596	94108	15
20	93002	93281	94082	93152	93276	93980	93239	93165	93048	94766	93002	93463	94358	94364	95646	98375	93463	20
25	91852	92521	93011	92025	92158	92518	92111	92055	92031	93594	91852	92391	93372	93688	95227	98091	92391	25
30	90475	91547	91678	90699	90921	91587	90739	90737	90896	92191	90475	91111	92236	92764	94616	97659	91111	30
35	88980	90332	90226	89307	89559	90219	89284	89300	89618	90668	88980	89650	91041	91598	93859	97110	89650	35
40	87343	88937	88647	87868	88118	88746	87658	87797	88199	89000	87343	88054	89663	90265	92948	96353	88054	40
45	85470	87206	86820	86371	86608	86991	85758	86108	86483	87091	85470	86248	87984	88584	91578	95027	86248	45
50	82817	84661	84165	84348	84539	84463	83144	83678	83807	84388	82817	83702	85871	86039	89149	92634	83702	50
55	79109	80974	80461	81553	81807	80889	79422	80423	80055	80609	79109	80108	82667	82359	85554	88987	80108	55
60	74353	76233	75719	77955	78582	76186	74662	76141	75242	75763	74353	75369	78481	77633	80833	84154	75369	60
65	67586	69486	68922	72449	74112	69758	67867	69885	68394	68868	67586	68566	72378	70860	74319	77535	68566	65
70	57997	59693	59187	64089	68229	60574	58306	60726	58690	59097	57997	58927	63580	60918	64727	67709	58927	70
75	44029	45342	44933	50800	59747	46871	44338	46922	44555	44864	44029	44813	50675	46273	50199	52754	44813	75
80	27657	28535	28306	33423	46232	30956	27851	30197	27988	28182	27657	28311	36020	29204	33355	35772	28311	80
85+	13506	13939	13824	17444	29815	16732	13697	15203	13668	13762	13506	14000	21951	14267	18140	20415	14000	85+

ADDED YRS OF LIFE

	No Causes	(1)	(2)	(3)	(4)	(5)	(6)	(7)	(8)	(9)	(10)	(11)	(12)	(1)+(2)	(1)+(2)+(5)+(6)+(8)	(1)+(2)+(5)+(6)+(8)+part of(9)&(12)	(10)+(11)
TOTAL		.939	.945	1.984	4.858	1.647	.241	.979	.429	1.250	.000	.595	4.005	1.901	4.343	7.135	.595
WORK	4.385	.677	.168	.595	.722	.304	.040	.314	.338	.000	.000	.188	.740	.849	1.552	1.908	.188

POPULATION, DEATHS, DEATH RATES FOR ALL CAUSES COMBINED, AND SPECIFIED CAUSES

Age Start of Interval	Midyear Population	Deaths During Year	All Causes	Respiratory T.B.	Other Infec. and Paras.	Neoplasms	Cardiovascular	Infl., Pneu., Bronch.	Diarrheal	Certain Degenerative	Maternal	Cert. Dis. of Infancy	Motor Vehicle	Other Violence	Other and Unknown	Age Start of Interval
0	11804	415	.03516	.00000	.00144	.00008	.00017	.00322	.00059	.00025	.00000	.02067	.00000	.00051	.00822	0
1	48219	135	.00280	.00002	.00062	.00008	.00012	.00062	.00004	.00002	.00000	.00000	.00000	.00048	.00068	1
5	65793	96	.00146	.00002	.00024	.00003	.00011	.00024	.00003	.00002	.00000	.00000	.00010	.00048	.00049	5
10	69286	70	.00101	.00001	.00012	.00009	.00013	.00006	.00000	.00008	.00000	.00000	.00006	.00017	.00033	10
15	67595	100	.00148	.00010	.00019	.00001	.00013	.00000	.00000	.00003	.00000	.00000	.00009	.00016	.00022	15
20	67900	175	.00258	.00019	.00022	.00015	.00015	.00013	.00001	.00016	.00000	.00000	.00024	.00041	.00022	20
25	63941	133	.00208	.00044	.00016	.00003	.00019	.00025	.00001	.00016	.00000	.00000	.00046	.00072	.00023	25
30	56229	138	.00245	.00043	.00027	.00016	.00032	.00028	.00000	.00013	.00000	.00000	.00027	.00045	.00025	30
35	50886	189	.00371	.00067	.00018	.00033	.00041	.00057	.00000	.00007	.00000	.00000	.00014	.00050	.00037	35
40	43624	225	.00516	.00062	.00023	.00060	.00096	.00066	.00000	.00035	.00000	.00000	.00018	.00065	.00071	40
45	46392	335	.00722	.00067	.00043	.00103	.00168	.00080	.00009	.00053	.00000	.00000	.00030	.00055	.00084	45
50	45956	456	.00992	.00067	.00054	.00154	.00333	.00098	.00002	.00073	.00000	.00000	.00028	.00067	.00081	50
55	41096	631	.01535	.00092	.00058	.00265	.00586	.00134	.00005	.00087	.00000	.00000	.00020	.00096	.00081	55
60	25989	717	.02391	.00093	.00090	.00420	.00994	.00157	.00007	.00129	.00000	.00000	.00032	.00092	.00141	60
65	21763	786	.03612	.00078	.00074	.00666	.01774	.00161	.00005	.00217	.00000	.00000	.00037	.00123	.00253	65
70	13332	741	.05558	.00075	.00068	.01005	.02468	.00338	.00000	.00317	.00000	.00000	.00032	.00115	.00391	70
75	8053	768	.09537	.00050	.00050	.01478	.04917	.00608	.00000	.00525	.00000	.00000	.00075	.00195	.00803	75
80	3952	592	.14980	.00000	.00051	.01594	.08730	.00987	.00025	.00782	.00000	.00000	.00037	.00186	.01416	80
85+	2018	448	.22200	.00000	.00099	.01338	.13280	.01586	.00050	.01037	.00000	.00000	.00025	.00278	.02252	85+
ALL	757828	7150														
CRUDE DEATH RATE			.00943	.00039	.00036	.00121	.00347	.00077	.00004	.00070	.00000	.00032	.00023	.00063	.00131	
STANDARDIZED RATE (1)			.00705	.00029	.00036	.00074	.00198	.00064	.00004	.00044	.00000	.00073	.00020	.00053	.00131	
STANDARDIZED RATE (2)			.01186	.00038	.00038	.00152	.00472	.00093	.00004	.00087	.00000	.00073	.00020	.00053	.00110	
GEOMETRIC MEAN			.00957		.00043								.00023	.00066	.00171	

LIFE TABLE FOR ALL CAUSES COMBINED

Age (x)	Midyear Population	Deaths During Year	$_nM_x$	$_nq_x$	l_x	$_nd_x$	$_nL_x$	$_nm_x$	$_na_x$	T_x	$_nr_x$	$\overset{\circ}{e}_x$	Age (x)
0	11804	415	.035158	.034110	100000	3411	97032	.035153	.129768	6571945	.000000	65.719	0
1	48219	135	.002800	.011130	96589	1075	383669	.002802	1.500000	6474914	.000000	67.036	1
5	65793	96	.001459	.007266	95514	694	475835	.001458	2.500000	6091245	.000000	63.773	5
10	69286	70	.001010	.005041	94820	478	472905	.001011	2.500436	5615410	-.003765	59.222	10
15	67595	100	.001479	.007367	94342	695	470123	.001479	2.716127	5142505	-.000583	54.509	15
20	67900	175	.002577	.012803	93647	1199	465292	.002577	2.545350	4672382	.000152	49.894	20
25	63941	133	.002080	.010341	92448	956	459833	.002079	2.482566	4207090	.012269	45.508	25
30	56229	138	.002454	.012231	91492	1119	454811	.002460	2.632931	3747257	.017565	40.957	30
35	50886	189	.003714	.018479	90373	1670	447928	.003728	2.642715	3292446	.023086	36.432	35
40	43624	225	.005158	.025512	88703	2263	438148	.005165	2.628425	2844517	.011763	32.068	40
45	46392	335	.007221	.035458	86440	3065	424907	.007213	2.620718	2406369	-.008409	27.839	45
50	45956	456	.009923	.048444	83375	4039	407367	.009915	2.646076	1981462	-.004697	23.766	50
55	41096	631	.015354	.074329	79336	5897	382836	.015403	2.652443	1574094	.017523	19.841	55
60	25989	717	.023909	.113754	73439	8354	347349	.024051	2.624416	1191258	.033371	16.221	60
65	21763	786	.036116	.167258	65085	10886	299256	.036377	2.596052	843909	.041442	12.966	65
70	13332	741	.055581	.246739	54199	13373	238589	.056050	2.576756	544653	.043293	10.049	70
75	8053	768	.095368	.387327	40826	15813	164629	.096053	2.501963	306064	.027930	7.497	75
80	3952	592	.149758	.540599	25013	13522	89675	.150790	2.382753	141435	.027930	5.654	80
85+	2018	448	.222002	1.000000	11491	11491	51761	.222002	4.504464	51761	.000000	4.504	85+

NUMBER OF PERSONS DYING (OUT OF 100,000 AT BIRTH) ABOVE AGE X FROM SPECIFIED CAUSES

Age (x)	All Causes	Respiratory T.B.	Other Infec. and Paras.	Neoplasms	Cardiovascular	Infl., Pneu., Bronch.	Diarrheal	Certain Degenerative	Maternal	Cert. Dis. of Infancy	Motor Vehicle	Other Violence	Other and Unknown	Age (x)
0	100000	2865	2622	13233	43153	7453	299	7484	0	2006	1641	4952	14292	0
1	96589	2865	2483	13225	43136	7141	242	7460	0	0	1641	4902	13494	1
5	95514	2857	2244	13193	43088	6902	226	7452	0	0	1601	4719	13232	5
10	94820	2850	2128	13179	43038	6786	212	7416	0	0	1572	4640	12999	10
15	94342	2843	2073	13138	42976	6759	211	7402	0	0	1531	4565	12844	15
20	93647	2795	1983	13131	42914	6696	211	7388	0	0	1420	4370	12739	20
25	92448	2706	1880	13062	42825	6580	205	7313	0	0	1208	4034	12635	25
30	91492	2504	1808	13048	42738	6494	205	7255	0	0	1086	3826	12528	30
35	90373	2310	1687	12974	42592	6364	188	7223	0	0	1021	3599	12415	35
40	88703	2010	1608	12824	42406	6107	188	7063	0	0	942	3309	12246	40
45	86440	1739	1507	12562	41983	5816	188	6832	0	0	811	3068	11934	45
50	83375	1455	1324	12123	41271	5477	152	6520	0	0	692	2784	11577	50
55	79336	1180	1103	11494	39916	5079	143	6166	0	0	612	2394	11249	55
60	73439	826	879	10475	37662	4565	124	5671	0	0	491	2040	10706	60
65	65085	501	565	9007	34184	4020	101	4913	0	0	363	1610	9821	65
70	54199	268	346	6958	28834	3536	87	3957	0	0	266	1266	8641	70
75	40826	90	185	4583	22896	2721	69	2694	0	0	86	798	6704	75
80	25013	9	104	2138	14731	1712	49	1399	0	0	26	490	4355	80
85+	11491	0	51	693	6874	821	26	462	0	0	0	231	2333	85+

NUMBER OF PERSONS SURVIVING TO AGE X IF SPECIFIED CAUSES WERE ELIMINATED

Age (x)	No Causes	Respiratory T.B. (1)	Other Infec. and Paras. (2)	Neoplasms (3)	Cardiovascular (4)	Infl., Pneu., Bronch. (5)	Diarrheal (6)	Certain Degenerative (7)	Maternal (8)	Cert. Dis. of Infancy (9)	Motor Vehicle (10)	Other Violence (11)	Other and Unknown (12)	(1) + (2)	(1)+(2)+(5)+(6)+(8)	(1)+(2)+(5)+(6)+(8)+part of(9)&(12)	(10)+(11)	Age (x)
0	100000	100000	100000	100000	100000	100000	100000	100000	100000	100000	100000	100000	100000	100000	100000	100000	100000	0
1	96589	96589	96726	96597	96606	96896	96645	96613	96589	98581	96589	96638	97376	96726	97090	99436	96638	1
5	95514	95522	95887	95554	95578	96056	95585	95545	95514	97483	95554	95745	96556	95895	96512	99011	95785	5
10	94820	94835	95307	94873	94934	95475	94905	94887	94820	96775	94888	95128	96089	95322	96066	98686	95197	10
15	94342	94364	94882	94436	94517	95021	94427	94423	94342	96287	94451	94724	95761	94903	95673	98326	94833	15
20	93647	93716	94273	93747	93883	94384	93732	93741	93647	95578	93866	94221	95162	94343	95171	97848	94441	20
25	92448	92605	93169	92616	92769	93292	92538	92615	92448	94354	92876	93351	94049	93327	94270	96953	93783	25
30	91492	91849	92278	91672	91897	92413	91561	91715	91492	93379	92037	92595	93185	92638	93661	96374	93147	30
35	90373	90920	91270	90624	90919	91414	90477	90626	90373	92236	90976	91691	92159	91822	92987	95735	92303	35
40	88703	89539	89663	89099	89424	89982	88806	89110	88703	90532	89374	90289	90627	90508	91919	94712	90972	40
45	86440	87525	87476	87086	87565	87978	86540	87066	86440	88222	87224	88227	88631	88574	90255	93109	89028	45
50	83375	84704	84557	84434	85172	85158	83507	84288	83375	85054	84249	85848	86590	85904	87922	90821	86280	50
55	79336	80873	80679	80568	82409	81468	79470	80555	79336	80972	80247	81638	82019	82242	84596	87471	82575	55
60	73439	75209	74901	75557	78571	75922	73562	75052	73439	74953	74400	75920	76465	76707	79454	82275	76913	60
65	65085	66966	66682	68760	73228	67816	65233	67247	65085	66427	66058	67702	68640	68609	71650	74348	68715	65
70	54199	55983	55732	59227	66720	56934	54335	56907	54199	55311	55099	56704	58308	57566	60623	63028	57646	70
75	40826	42327	42122	46949	56999	43635	40944	44027	40826	41668	41662	43137	45765	43671	46810	48873	44020	75
80	25013	25995	25870	31008	45024	27583	25101	28071	25013	25529	25570	26678	30154	26886	29752	31262	27272	80
85+	11491	11948	11921	15480	32503	13338	11547	13610	11491	11728	11764	12440	15561	12395	14457	15342	12736	85+

ADDED YRS OF LIFE

	No Causes	(1)	(2)	(3)	(4)	(5)	(6)	(7)	(8)	(9)	(10)	(11)	(12)	(1)+(2)	(1)+(2)+(5)+(6)+(8)	part	(10)+(11)
TOTAL		.728	.823	1.735	7.226	1.465	.092	1.023	.000	1.353	.494	1.287	2.513	1.567	3.199	5.416	1.798
WORK	4.436	.447	.272	.417	.826	.437	.017	.310	.000	.000	.294	.638	.439	.724	1.192	1.341	.938

POPULATION, DEATHS, DEATH RATES FOR ALL CAUSES COMBINED, AND SPECIFIED CAUSES

Age Start of Interval	Midyear Population	Deaths During Year	All Causes	Respiratory T. B.	Other Infec. and Paras.	Neoplasms	Cardiovascular	Infl., Pneu., Bronch.	Diarrheal	Certain Degenerative	Maternal	Cert. Dis. of Infancy	Motor Vehicle	Other Violence	Other and Unknown	Age Start of Interval
0	11310	354	.03130	.00000	.00221	.00009	.00027	.00389	.00071	.00009	.00000	.01671	.00000	.00080	.00654	0
1	45794	109	.00238	.00000	.00055	.00015	.00011	.00063	.00013	.00002	.00000	.00000	.00000	.00020	.00059	1
5	63022	75	.00119	.00000	.00021	.00011	.00010	.00014	.00002	.00002	.00000	.00000	.00005	.00008	.00048	5
10	66480	46	.00069	.00000	.00008	.00002	.00005	.00008	.00002	.00006	.00000	.00000	.00005	.00006	.00048	10
15	65091	69	.00106	.00018	.00008	.00011	.00012	.00011	.00000	.00008	.00003	.00000	.00008	.00006	.00026	15
20	66085	126	.00191	.00071	.00026	.00005	.00015	.00011	.00002	.00008	.00015	.00000	.00005	.00009	.00026	20
25	61463	150	.00244	.00063	.00011	.00005	.00021	.00020	.00004	.00010	.00059	.00000	.00002	.00013	.00041	25
30	53646	132	.00246	.00062	.00021	.00026	.00026	.00019	.00004	.00017	.00034	.00000	.00004	.00007	.00028	30
35	51257	165	.00322	.00055	.00016	.00037	.00045	.00037	.00004	.00018	.00043	.00000	.00004	.00012	.00053	35
40	47728	189	.00396	.00048	.00023	.00092	.00084	.00021	.00004	.00031	.00008	.00000	.00004	.00008	.00071	40
45	46872	253	.00540	.00028	.00021	.00152	.00113	.00036	.00002	.00053	.00000	.00000	.00004	.00017	.00073	45
50	43666	361	.00827	.00021	.00016	.00268	.00273	.00030	.00002	.00071	.00000	.00000	.00005	.00037	.00105	50
55	37705	465	.01233	.00053	.00034	.00347	.00408	.00064	.00000	.00119	.00000	.00000	.00011	.00034	.00162	55
60	28016	498	.01778	.00036	.00036	.00432	.00750	.00100	.00000	.00157	.00000	.00000	.00007	.00050	.00225	60
65	21215	662	.03120	.00024	.00042	.00655	.01513	.00156	.00009	.00339	.00000	.00000	.00019	.00038	.00325	65
70	13592	652	.04797	.00052	.00044	.00858	.02553	.00221	.00015	.00515	.00000	.00000	.00015	.00052	.00434	70
75	8005	630	.07870	.00025	.00050	.01099	.04497	.00387	.00012	.00687	.00000	.00000	.00050	.00150	.00912	75
80	4012	521	.12986	.00025	.00050	.01072	.07602	.00897	.00025	.01221	.00000	.00000	.00000	.00399	.01695	80
85+	2046	449	.21945	.00000	.00098	.01271	.12268	.01760	.00049	.00880	.00000	.00000	.00000	.00880	.04741	85+
ALL	737005	5906														

	All Causes	Respiratory T. B.	Other Infec. and Paras.	Neoplasms	Cardiovascular	Infl., Pneu., Bronch.	Diarrheal	Certain Degenerative	Maternal	Cert. Dis. of Infancy	Motor Vehicle	Other Violence	Other and Unknown
CRUDE DEATH RATE	.00801	.00033	.00026	.00133	.00305	.00054	.00004	.00063	.00012	.00026	.00006	.00023	.00116
STANDARDIZED RATE (1)	.00595	.00028	.00030	.00082	.00172	.00050	.00006	.00039	.00011	.00059	.00006	.00023	.00116
STANDARDIZED RATE (2)	.01006	.00031	.00028	.00154	.00416	.00068	.00005	.00080	.00011	.00059	.00005	.00019	.00096
GEOMETRIC MEAN	.00835									.00035	.00006	.00028	.00143

LIFE TABLE FOR ALL CAUSES COMBINED

Age (x)	Midyear Population	Deaths During Year	$_nM_x$	$_nq_x$	l_x	$_nd_x$	$_nL_x$	$_nm_x$	$_na_x$	T_x	$_nr_x$	$\overset{\circ}{e}_x$	Age (x)
0	11310	354	.031300	.030460	100000	3046	97329	.031296	.123210	6827661	.000000	68.277	0
1	45794	109	.002380	.009468	96954	918	385521	.002381	1.500000	6730331	.000000	69.418	1
5	63022	75	.001190	.005935	96036	570	478755	.001191	2.500000	6344810	.000000	66.067	5
10	66480	46	.000692	.003446	95466	329	476454	.000690	2.457573	5866055	-.003745	61.447	10
15	65091	69	.001060	.005287	95137	503	474546	.001060	2.735669	5389562	-.001476	56.651	15
20	66085	126	.001907	.009489	94634	898	471057	.001906	2.647318	4915016	-.000056	51.937	20
25	61463	150	.002440	.012140	93736	1138	465884	.002443	2.543204	4443959	-.014445	47.409	25
30	53646	132	.002461	.012246	92598	1134	460222	.002464	2.559524	3978074	.016413	42.961	30
35	51257	165	.003219	.015984	91464	1462	453797	.003222	2.590202	3517852	.010874	38.462	35
40	47728	189	.003960	.019633	90002	1767	445778	.003964	2.604933	3064055	.006818	34.044	40
45	46872	253	.005398	.026656	88235	2352	435654	.005399	2.652441	2618277	.002985	29.674	45
50	43666	361	.008267	.040613	85883	3488	421237	.008280	2.655474	2182624	.007842	25.414	50
55	37705	465	.012333	.060137	82395	4955	400246	.012380	2.632989	1761386	.025273	21.377	55
60	28016	498	.017776	.085886	77440	6651	371699	.017894	2.669335	1361140	.035082	17.577	60
65	21215	662	.031204	.146365	70789	10361	329364	.031456	2.629472	989441	.038225	13.977	65
70	13592	652	.047969	.216621	60428	13090	270532	.048386	2.585307	660057	.046252	10.923	70
75	8005	630	.078701	.332101	47338	15721	197857	.079440	2.532401	389525	.041326	8.229	75
80	4012	521	.129860	.491350	31617	15535	118346	.131267	2.441986	191629	.041326	6.061	80
85+	2046	449	.219453	1.000000	16082	16082	73282	.219453	4.556793	73282	.000000	4.557	85+

NUMBER OF PERSONS DYING (OUT OF 100,000 AT BIRTH) ABOVE AGE X FROM SPECIFIED CAUSES

Age (x)	All Causes	Respiratory T.B.	Other Infec. and Paras.	Neo-plasms	Cardio-vascular	Infl., Pneu., Bronch.	Diar-rheal	Certain Degen-erative	Maternal	Cert. Dis. of Infancy	Motor Vehicle	Other Violence	Other and Unknown	Age (x)
0	100000	2264	1964	14936	46229	6435	376	8078	746	1626	473	2704	14169	0
1	96954	2264	1749	14928	46204	6057	307	8069	746	0	473	2627	13530	1
5	96036	2264	1539	14869	46162	5813	257	8061	746	0	473	2551	13301	5
10	95466	2264	1440	14816	46116	5744	249	8053	746	0	450	2513	13075	10
15	95137	2264	1404	14808	46073	5708	242	8024	746	0	429	2484	12955	15
20	94634	2177	1368	14757	46015	5657	242	7988	731	0	392	2470	12837	20
25	93736	1842	1246	14736	45943	5607	235	7952	660	0	371	2427	12717	25
30	92598	1547	1193	14713	45845	5516	235	7907	387	0	363	2366	12526	30
35	91464	1264	1099	14592	45724	5430	217	7829	233	0	346	2332	12398	35
40	90002	1016	1028	14424	45520	5262	200	7750	38	0	329	2279	12156	40
45	88235	801	925	14012	45146	5169	181	7609	1	0	310	2242	11839	45
50	85883	681	832	13175	44653	5011	172	7377	1	0	291	2167	11523	50
55	82395	594	765	12045	43503	4885	162	7077	1	0	272	2013	11078	55
60	77440	381	626	10651	41859	4629	162	6558	1	0	229	1875	10429	60
65	70789	303	494	9039	39047	4255	162	6009	1	0	203	1689	9587	65
70	60428	224	354	6867	34014	3739	130	4881	1	0	140	1565	8513	70
75	47338	84	234	4426	27637	3137	90	3478	1	0	100	1423	7328	75
80	31617	35	135	2243	18046	2361	66	2108	1	0	0	1121	5501	80
85+	16082	0	72	931	8590	1289	36	645	0	0	0	645	3474	85+

NUMBER OF PERSONS SURVIVING TO AGE X IF SPECIFIED CAUSES WERE ELIMINATED

Age (x)	No Causes	Respiratory T.B. (1)	Other Infec. and Paras. (2)	Neo-plasms (3)	Cardio-vascular (4)	Infl., Pneu., Bronch. (5)	Diar-rheal (6)	Certain Degen-erative (7)	Maternal (8)	Cert. Dis. of Infancy (9)	Motor Vehicle (10)	Other Violence (11)	Other and Unknown (12)	(1)+(2)	(1)+(2)+(5)+(6)+(8)	(1)+(2)+(5)+(6)+(8)+part of(9)&(12)	(10)+(11)	Age (x)
0	100000	100000	100000	100000	100000	100000	100000	100000	100000	100000	100000	100000	100000	100000	100000	100000	100000	0
1	96954	96954	97166	96962	96979	97327	97022	96963	96954	98568	96954	97030	97585	97166	97608	99753	97030	1
5	96036	96036	96456	96103	96102	96649	96153	96035	96036	97635	96036	96187	96891	96456	97190	99530	96187	5
10	95466	95466	95982	95585	95578	96145	95590	95491	95466	97055	95489	95654	96543	95982	96791	99276	95677	10
15	95137	95137	95688	95264	95291	95850	95268	95190	95137	96721	95181	95353	96332	95688	96537	98988	95397	15
20	94634	94721	95218	94811	94845	95394	94764	94723	94649	96210	94715	94863	95942	95305	96219	98775	94944	20
25	93736	94156	94437	93932	94017	94539	93872	93860	93822	95297	93837	94006	95153	94860	95899	98277	94107	25
30	92598	93308	93343	92815	92974	93483	92732	92732	92765	94140	92705	92925	94190	94059	95462	97979	93033	30
35	91464	92449	92294	91799	91956	92424	91615	91707	91570	92987	91587	91821	93166	93288	94946	97535	91945	35
40	90002	91220	90890	90499	90690	91116	90167	90320	90094	91501	90140	90406	91922	92120	94150	96865	90545	40
45	88235	89645	89209	89134	89283	89420	88416	88687	88951	89704	88389	88668	90438	90634	92786	95571	89823	45
50	85883	87376	86923	87596	87397	87194	86068	86553	86579	87313	86052	86379	88348	88434	90707	93493	86549	50
55	82395	83914	83460	85174	85002	83778	82582	83335	83063	83767	82576	83023	85209	84998	87324	90052	83205	55
60	77440	79078	78577	81460	81553	78993	77616	78794	78068	78729	77651	78165	80738	80239	82659	85380	78378	60
65	70789	72362	71956	76100	77438	72574	70950	72602	71363	71968	71007	71631	74647	73555	76194	78753	71851	65
70	60428	61845	61555	67149	71392	62441	60595	63053	60918	61434	60672	61262	64773	62999	65807	68110	61509	70
75	47338	48574	48328	55043	63711	49467	47504	50701	47722	48126	47565	48119	51877	49590	52424	54349	48350	75
80	31617	32482	32359	38858	53614	33707	31747	35071	31873	32143	31850	32392	36319	33244	35877	37314	32631	80
85+	16082	16547	16505	20926	40442	17964	16169	19011	16213	16350	16200	16821	20177	16982	19228	20156	16945	85+

ADDED YRS OF LIFE

	No Causes	(1)	(2)	(3)	(4)	(5)	(6)	(7)	(8)	(9)	(10)	(11)	(12)	(1)+(2)	(1)+(2)+(5)+(6)+(8)	part	(10)+(11)
TOTAL		.763	.714	2.323	7.490	1.217	.132	1.036	.313	1.135	.122	.471	2.534	1.488	3.222	5.278	.594
WORK	3.750	.540	.195	.644	.683	.240	.020	.249	.245	.000	.052	.126	.527	.738	1.256	1.491	.178

POPULATION, DEATHS, DEATH RATES FOR ALL CAUSES COMBINED, AND SPECIFIED CAUSES

Age Start of Interval	Midyear Population	Deaths During Year	All Causes	Respiratory T.B.	Other Infec. and Paras.	Neo-plasms	Cardio-vascular	Infl., Pneu., Bronch.	Diar-rheal	Certain Degen-erative	Maternal	Cert. Dis. of Infancy	Motor Vehicle	Other Violence	Other and Unknown	Age Start of Interval
0	17919	607	.03387	.00006	.00112	.00011	.00017	.00307	.00084	.00011	.00000	.01914	.00000	.00134	.00792	0
1	64715	121	.00187	.00005	.00039	.00005	.00003	.00029	.00006	.00002	.00000	.00000	.00000	.00003	.00045	.00051	1
5	66939	63	.00094	.00000	.00022	.00010	.00012	.00007	.00004	.00001	.00000	.00000	.00003	.00045	.00051	5
10	60782	57	.00094	.00002	.00012	.00010	.00008	.00008	.00002	.00003	.00000	.00000	.00006	.00015	.00015	10
15	64622	93	.00144	.00011	.00011	.00014	.00011	.00008	.00002	.00003	.00000	.00000	.00000	.00033	.00016	15
20	46514	109	.00234	.00032	.00009	.00009	.00013	.00009	.00002	.00005	.00000	.00000	.00008	.00050	.00026	20
25	51571	124	.00240	.00058	.00012	.00021	.00027	.00006	.00002	.00015	.00000	.00000	.00026	.00082	.00039	25
30	58034	104	.00179	.00034	.00012	.00014	.00031	.00003	.00000	.00008	.00000	.00000	.00019	.00060	.00027	30
35	58495	155	.00265	.00036	.00019	.00021	.00062	.00012	.00000	.00009	.00000	.00000	.00012	.00040	.00034	35
40	53299	193	.00362	.00043	.00006	.00053	.00101	.00009	.00000	.00017	.00000	.00000	.00019	.00046	.00034	40
45	47380	304	.00642	.00061	.00034	.00114	.00213	.00023	.00006	.00038	.00000	.00000	.00015	.00056	.00036	45
50	40525	370	.00913	.00062	.00015	.00153	.00415	.00044	.00002	.00057	.00000	.00000	.00011	.00059	.00068	50
55	41583	604	.01453	.00079	.00026	.00279	.00695	.00046	.00005	.00084	.00000	.00000	.00007	.00064	.00067	55
60	38954	1025	.02631	.00123	.00067	.00436	.01384	.00116	.00021	.00125	.00000	.00000	.00014	.00070	.00113	60
65	31815	1199	.03769	.00091	.00057	.00654	.02156	.00176	.00009	.00164	.00000	.00000	.00021	.00095	.00205	65
70	19873	1270	.06391	.00106	.00065	.01142	.03698	.00292	.00015	.00245	.00000	.00000	.00025	.00072	.00283	70
75	11515	1099	.09544	.00052	.00052	.01381	.05706	.00399	.00069	.00357	.00000	.00000	.00035	.00116	.00564	75
80	4895	738	.15077	.00041	.00020	.01716	.08907	.00776	.00102	.00556	.00000	.00000	.00017	.00191	.01120	80
85+	2265	587	.25916	.00000	.00000	.01413	.15850	.01810	.00088	.00715	.00000	.00000	.00000	.00286	.02513	85+
ALL	781655	8822														
CRUDE DEATH RATE			.01129	.00040	.00026	.00154	.00527	.00057	.00008	.00064	.00000	.00044	.00013	.00061	.00136	
STANDARDIZED RATE (1)			.00676	.00029	.00024	.00078	.00241	.00038	.00007	.00034	.00000	.00067	.00011	.00054	.00136	
STANDARDIZED RATE (2)			.01191	.00038	.00025	.00157	.00572	.00060	.00008	.00065	.00000	.00040	.00012	.00054	.00093	
GEOMETRIC MEAN			.00909									.00040	.00012	.00063	.00150	

LIFE TABLE FOR ALL CAUSES COMBINED

Age (x)	Midyear Population	Deaths During Year	$_nM_x$	$_nq_x$	l_x	$_nd_x$	$_nL_x$	$_nm_x$	$_na_x$	T_x	$_nr_x$	$\overset{\circ}{e}_x$	Age (x)
0	17919	607	.033875	.032900	100000	3290	97130	.033872	.127587	6649813	.000000	66.498	0
1	64715	121	.001870	.007445	96710	720	385040	.001870	1.500000	6552683	.000000	67.756	1
5	66939	63	.000941	.004698	95990	451	478823	.000942	2.500000	6167643	.000000	64.253	5
10	60782	57	.000938	.004679	95539	447	476626	.000938	2.608594	5688821	-.001931	59.544	10
15	64622	93	.001439	.007193	95092	684	473887	.001443	2.699805	5212195	.017817	54.812	15
20	46514	109	.002343	.011683	94408	1103	469372	.002350	2.581596	4738308	.028063	50.190	20
25	51571	124	.002404	.011961	93305	1116	463676	.002407	2.447543	4268936	-.013026	45.752	25
30	58034	104	.001792	.008916	92189	822	458908	.001791	2.521796	3805259	-.017625	41.277	30
35	58495	155	.002650	.013156	91367	1202	453997	.002648	2.638831	3346351	-.001380	36.625	35
40	53299	193	.003621	.018000	90165	1623	447102	.003630	2.706280	2892354	-.011473	32.078	40
45	47380	304	.006416	.031725	88542	2809	436149	.006440	2.664353	2445252	-.021278	27.617	45
50	40525	370	.009130	.044779	85733	3839	419679	.009147	2.659384	2009103	-.010665	23.434	50
55	41583	604	.014525	.070164	81894	5746	396268	.014500	2.702387	1589423	-.007892	19.408	55
60	38954	1025	.026313	.123720	76148	9421	358400	.026286	2.628702	1193156	-.005315	15.669	60
65	31815	1199	.037687	.173333	66727	11566	305952	.037803	2.606562	834756	.017695	12.510	65
70	19873	1270	.063906	.278041	55161	15337	238262	.064370	2.552107	528803	.032407	9.587	70
75	11515	1099	.095441	.386752	39824	15402	160192	.096147	2.472528	290541	.039064	7.296	75
80	4895	738	.150766	.544837	24422	13306	87457	.152143	2.395708	130350	-.039064	5.337	80
85+	2265	587	.259161	1.000000	11116	11116	42892	.259161	3.858603	42892	.000000	3.859	85+

NUMBER OF PERSONS DYING (OUT OF 100,000 AT BIRTH) ABOVE AGE X FROM SPECIFIED CAUSES

Age (x)	All Causes	Respiratory T. B.	Other Infec. and Paras.	Neo-plasms	Cardio-vascular	Infl., Pneu., Bronch.	Diar-rheal	Certain Degen-erative	Maternal	Cert. Dis. of Infancy	Motor Vehicle	Other Violence	Other and Unknown	Age (x)
0	100000	2955	1718	13628	50979	4932	604	5618	0	1859	894	4505	12308	0
1	96710	2949	1609	13617	50562	4634	522	5607	0	0	894	4375	11541	1
5	95990	2931	1461	13599	50550	4521	499	5601	0	0	882	4203	11343	5
10	95539	2931	1353	13549	50893	4485	477	5594	0	0	854	4131	11272	10
15	95092	2924	1298	13502	50854	4446	469	5578	0	0	854	3974	11193	15
20	94408	2872	1247	13436	50803	4409	462	5556	0	0	817	3739	11067	20
25	93305	2719	1207	13396	50742	4369	452	5485	0	0	695	3355	10885	25
30	92189	2449	1153	13297	50616	4342	443	5449	0	0	605	3076	10759	30
35	91367	2291	1098	13234	50474	4326	443	5410	0	0	550	2894	10647	35
40	90165	2128	1012	13141	50155	4272	443	5332	0	0	464	2684	10494	40
45	88542	1935	987	12905	49740	4230	417	5164	0	0	397	2432	10335	45
50	85733	1667	839	12406	48805	4128	408	4914	0	0	351	2174	10041	50
55	81894	1408	777	11762	47061	3941	398	4562	0	0	320	1905	9760	55
60	76148	1094	673	10658	44213	3761	379	4067	0	0	263	1629	9311	60
65	66727	653	434	9096	39359	3347	305	3478	0	0	190	1288	8577	65
70	55161	374	261	7089	32740	2807	277	2726	0	0	113	1067	7707	70
75	39824	122	104	4350	23862	2107	240	1870	0	0	28	789	6352	75
80	24422	40	22	2130	14651	1462	127	973	0	0	1	481	4535	80
85+	11116	0	0	606	6798	776	38	341	0	0	0	227	2330	85+

NUMBER OF PERSONS SURVIVING TO AGE X IF SPECIFIED CAUSES WERE ELIMINATED

Age (x)	No Causes	Respiratory T. B. (1)	Other Infec. and Paras. (2)	Neo-plasms (3)	Cardio-vascular (4)	Infl., Pneu., Bronch. (5)	Diar-rheal (6)	Certain Degener-ative (7)	Maternal (8)	Cert. Dis. of Infancy (9)	Motor Vehicle (10)	Other Violence (11)	Other and Unknown (12)	(1) + (2)	(1) + (2) + (5) + (6) + (8)	(1)+(2)+ (5)+(6)+ (8)+part of(9)&(12)	(10) + (11)	Age (x)
0	100000	100000	100000	100000	100000	100000	100000	100000	100000	100000	100000	100000	100000	100000	100000	100000	100000	0
1	96710	96716	96817	96721	96727	97003	96791	96721	96710	98555	96710	96838	97467	96823	97198	99152	96838	1
5	95990	96014	96244	96019	96019	96394	96093	96007	95990	97822	96002	96289	96941	96268	96777	98840	96301	5
10	95539	95563	95900	95617	95624	95977	95663	95563	95539	97362	95579	95908	96557	95924	96490	98579	95948	10
15	95092	95123	95506	95217	95216	95568	95224	95131	95092	96907	95132	95617	96185	95537	96148	98254	95657	15
20	94408	94490	94871	94598	94582	94917	94546	94469	94408	96210	94484	95115	95620	94953	95605	97733	95242	20
25	93305	93539	93802	93533	93538	93848	93451	93436	93305	95085	93502	94439	94686	94037	94733	96891	94638	25
30	92189	92689	92734	92513	92545	92753	92342	92354	92189	93948	92473	93590	93681	93237	93964	96152	93879	30
35	91367	92021	91962	91751	91861	91942	91519	91570	91367	93111	91704	92940	92959	92621	93359	95570	93282	35
40	90165	90974	90839	90647	90932	90796	90315	90443	90165	91886	90583	91929	91891	91653	92438	94674	92356	40
45	88542	89529	89228	89241	89751	89194	88715	88982	88542	90232	89019	90530	90357	90223	91065	93300	91017	45
50	85733	86956	86544	86906	87842	86465	85910	86407	85733	87369	86240	87917	87825	87779	88711	90953	88437	50
55	81894	83319	82730	83655	85674	82778	82072	82885	81894	83457	82409	84250	84174	84170	85263	87461	84780	55
60	76148	77781	77027	78880	82485	77146	76332	77553	76148	77601	76682	78612	78714	78675	79903	82016	79164	60
65	66727	68579	67723	70650	77482	67995	66958	68521	66727	68000	67264	69215	69689	69603	71171	73155	69772	65
70	55161	56951	56143	60366	71428	56711	55377	57348	55161	56214	55675	57425	58441	57964	59827	61577	57960	70
75	39824	41334	40667	46186	62274	41555	40012	42161	39824	40584	40267	41704	43430	42209	44251	45654	42168	75
80	24422	25410	25002	30372	51172	26011	24627	26601	24422	24888	24714	25826	28231	26014	27938	28938	26135	80
85+	11116	11593	11395	15129	37063	12329	11268	12569	11116	11328	11249	11933	14640	11884	13362	13977	12076	85+

ADDED YRS OF LIFE																		
TOTAL		.721	.543	1.784	8.557	.800	.146	.759	.000	1.267	.270	1.311	2.047	1.273	2.260	3.967	1.589	
WORK	3.966	.431	.151	.459	1.016	.133	.022	.256	.000	.000	.172	.644	.423	.584	.743	.848	.819	

POPULATION, DEATHS, DEATH RATES FOR ALL CAUSES COMBINED, AND SPECIFIED CAUSES

Age Start of Interval	Midyear Population	Deaths During Year	All Causes	Respiratory T. B.	Other Infec. and Paras.	Neoplasms	Cardiovascular	Infl., Pneu., Bronch.	Diarrheal	Certain Degenerative	Maternal	Cert. Dis. of Infancy	Motor Vehicle	Other Violence	Other and Unknown	Age Start of Interval
0	17170	429	.02499	.00000	.00116	.00000	.00012	.00233	.00047	.00012	.00000	.01409	.00000	.00070	.00600	0
1	62270	101	.00162	.00002	.00040	.00006	.00006	.00031	.00006	.00005	.00000	.00000	.00003	.00026	.00037	1
5	65266	52	.00080	.00000	.00026	.00006	.00009	.00003	.00000	.00003	.00000	.00000	.00006	.00009	.00017	5
10	57910	42	.00073	.00003	.00016	.00007	.00005	.00012	.00002	.00007	.00000	.00000	.00000	.00005	.00016	10
15	63222	41	.00065	.00009	.00008	.00005	.00008	.00003	.00003	.00006	.00000	.00000	.00002	.00005	.00016	15
20	66384	87	.00131	.00050	.00012	.00005	.00014	.00003	.00000	.00002	.00020	.00000	.00000	.00008	.00005	.00015	20
25	64696	103	.00159	.00045	.00012	.00014	.00015	.00003	.00005	.00003	.00026	.00000	.00000	.00011	.00025	25
30	64317	105	.00163	.00033	.00008	.00025	.00019	.00005	.00002	.00005	.00036	.00000	.00002	.00005	.00026	30
35	59890	146	.00244	.00040	.00017	.00048	.00042	.00007	.00002	.00012	.00035	.00000	.00005	.00010	.00027	35
40	52026	154	.00296	.00021	.00008	.00094	.00067	.00006	.00002	.00025	.00013	.00000	.00000	.00019	.00040	40
45	48555	273	.00562	.00025	.00006	.00189	.00183	.00019	.00002	.00039	.00004	.00000	.00002	.00025	.00068	45
50	44034	346	.00786	.00016	.00011	.00232	.00307	.00027	.00014	.00082	.00000	.00000	.00000	.00011	.00086	50
55	41900	477	.01138	.00029	.00021	.00329	.00480	.00017	.00007	.00091	.00000	.00000	.00005	.00029	.00131	55
60	38428	661	.01720	.00016	.00034	.00390	.00859	.00060	.00005	.00148	.00000	.00000	.00003	.00042	.00164	60
65	32311	866	.02680	.00022	.00015	.00535	.01547	.00062	.00019	.00214	.00000	.00000	.00003	.00043	.00220	65
70	20295	983	.04844	.00039	.00005	.00788	.02892	.00187	.00030	.00340	.00000	.00000	.00000	.00074	.00488	70
75	12640	927	.07334	.00016	.00055	.00886	.04834	.00253	.00055	.00364	.00000	.00000	.00016	.00127	.00728	75
80	5798	779	.13436	.00034	.00017	.01138	.08693	.00655	.00103	.00638	.00000	.00000	.00000	.00190	.01566	80
85+	2862	657	.22956	.00000	.00140	.01188	.14885	.01188	.00175	.00734	.00000	.00000	.00000	.00629	.04018	85+
ALL	819974	7229															

	All Causes	Respiratory T. B.	Other Infec. and Paras.	Neoplasms	Cardiovascular	Infl., Pneu., Bronch.	Diarrheal	Certain Degenerative	Maternal	Cert. Dis. of Infancy	Motor Vehicle	Other Violence	Other and Unknown
CRUDE DEATH RATE	.00882	.00022	.00019	.00140	.00426	.00036	.00008	.00053	.00010	.00030	.00003	.00023	.00112
STANDARDIZED RATE (1)	.00516	.00019	.00022	.00075	.00188	.00026	.00006	.00028	.00009	.00050	.00003	.00017	.00075
STANDARDIZED RATE (2)	.00930	.00021	.00020	.00139	.00464	.00039	.00008	.00054	.00009	.00029	.00003	.00024	.00120
GEOMETRIC MEAN	.00695												

LIFE TABLE FOR ALL CAUSES COMBINED

Age (x)	Midyear Population	Deaths During Year	$_nM_x$	$_nq_x$	l_x	$_nd_x$	$_nL_x$	$_nm_x$	$_na_x$	T_x	$_nr_x$	$\overset{\circ}{e}_x$	Age (x)
0	17170	429	.024985	.024440	100000	2444	97831	.024982	.112475	7021071	.000000	70.211	0
1	62270	101	.001622	.006468	97556	631	388647	.001624	1.500000	6923240	.000000	70.967	1
5	65266	52	.000797	.003972	96925	385	483663	.000796	2.500000	6534594	.000000	67.419	5
10	57910	42	.000725	.003625	96540	350	481809	.000726	2.455357	6050931	.005370	62.678	10
15	63222	41	.000649	.003223	96190	310	480232	.000646	2.685484	5569122	-.011548	57.897	15
20	66384	87	.001311	.006529	95880	626	477928	.001310	2.648096	5088889	-.006307	53.076	20
25	64696	103	.001592	.007926	95254	755	474412	.001591	2.539459	4610961	-.000469	48.407	25
30	64317	105	.001633	.008138	94499	769	470652	.001634	2.603760	4136549	.002091	43.773	30
35	59890	146	.002438	.012141	93730	1138	465929	.002442	2.609293	3665897	.014958	39.111	35
40	52026	154	.002960	.014753	92592	1366	459836	.002957	2.713366	3199967	.017943	34.560	40
45	48555	273	.005622	.027810	91226	2537	450217	.005635	2.669163	2740131	.013393	30.037	45
50	44034	346	.007858	.038629	88689	3426	435337	.007870	2.633294	2289914	.009107	25.820	50
55	41900	477	.011384	.055464	85263	4729	415166	.011391	2.642428	1854578	.003403	21.751	55
60	38428	661	.017201	.082686	80534	6659	386988	.017207	2.645042	1439412	.002830	17.873	60
65	32311	866	.026802	.126768	73875	9365	347515	.026948	2.665777	1052423	.025631	14.246	65
70	20295	983	.048436	.218741	64510	14111	288608	.048893	2.594651	704908	.040965	10.927	70
75	12640	927	.073339	.313022	50399	15776	213268	.073973	2.545203	416300	.044620	8.260	75
80	5798	779	.134357	.506426	34623	17534	128590	.136356	2.460624	203032	.044620	5.864	80
85+	2862	657	.229560	1.000000	17089	17089	74442	.229560	4.356164	74442	.000000	4.356	85+

NUMBER OF PERSONS DYING (OUT OF 100,000 AT BIRTH) ABOVE AGE X FROM SPECIFIED CAUSES

Age (x)	All Causes	Respiratory T.B.	Other Infec. and Paras.	Neo-plasms	Cardio-vascular	Infl., Pneu., Bronch.	Diar-rheal	Certain Degen-erative	Maternal	Cert. Dis. of Infancy	Motor Vehicle	Other Violence	Other and Unknown	Age (x)
0	100000	1587	1387	14164	55012	4093	794	5705	631	1379	200	2287	12761	0
1	97556	1587	1272	14164	55001	3865	748	5693	631	0	200	2218	12176	1
5	96925	1580	1116	14139	54976	3747	723	5675	631	0	188	2118	12032	5
10	96540	1580	991	14109	54931	3732	723	5660	631	0	158	2074	11951	10
15	96190	1564	916	14076	54906	3674	715	5626	631	0	158	2049	11875	15
20	95880	1519	878	14053	54869	3658	700	5596	631	0	151	2026	11799	20
25	95254	1281	820	14032	54804	3644	700	5589	538	0	115	2005	11726	25
30	94499	1069	781	13966	54731	3629	678	5574	413	0	115	1953	11610	30
35	93730	915	725	13848	54643	3607	670	5552	245	0	107	1931	11487	35
40	92592	728	647	13622	54447	3576	663	5497	82	0	84	1884	11362	40
45	91226	631	612	13186	54136	3549	654	5382	20	0	84	1796	11176	45
50	88689	520	584	12332	53308	3466	644	5205	2	0	75	1685	10868	50
55	85263	451	535	11322	51971	3347	585	4849	2	0	75	1635	10491	55
60	80534	332	445	9954	49977	3278	555	4472	2	0	55	1516	9948	60
65	73875	272	314	8443	46652	3046	535	3898	2	0	45	1355	9313	65
70	64510	196	261	6576	41241	2829	470	3153	2	0	34	1204	8544	70
75	50399	82	247	4287	32806	2282	384	2165	2	0	34	989	7121	75
80	34623	49	127	2393	22398	1737	265	1386	2	0	0	716	5550	80
85+	17089	0	104	884	11081	884	130	546	0	0	0	468	2992	85+

NUMBER OF PERSONS SURVIVING TO AGE X IF SPECIFIED CAUSES WERE ELIMINATED

Age (x)	No Causes	Respiratory T.B. (1)	Other Infec. and Paras. (2)	Neo-plasms (3)	Cardio-vascular (4)	Infl., Pneu., Bronch. (5)	Diar-rheal (6)	Certain Degener-ative (7)	Maternal (8)	Cert. Dis. of Infancy (9)	Motor Vehicle (10)	Other Violence (11)	Other and Unknown (12)	(1)+(2)	(1)+(2)+(5)+(6)+(8)	(1)+(2)+(5)+(6)+(8)+part of (9)&(12)	(10)+(11)	Age (x)
0	100000	100000	100000	100000	100000	100000	100000	100000	100000	100000	100000	100000	100000	100000	100000	100000	100000	0
1	97556	97556	97669	97556	97567	97781	97601	97568	97556	98928	97556	97624	98136	97669	97940	99527	97624	1
5	96925	96932	97194	96950	96961	97267	96955	96955	96925	98288	96937	97094	97654	96940	97367	99075	96793	5
10	96540	96547	96933	96855	96621	96896	96610	96585	96540	97897	96582	96751	97339	96680	97172	98922	96467	10
15	96190	96213	96657	96278	96295	96602	96268	96268	96190	97542	96232	96425	97062	96426	96974	98758	96186	15
20	95880	95948	96383	95990	96022	96307	95972	95988	95880	97228	95929	96137	96826	96119	96748	98583	95615	20
25	95254	95559	95812	95384	95460	95962	95346	95368	95347	96593	95338	95531	96268	95630	96421	98330	94909	25
30	94499	95014	95112	94694	94776	95449	94612	94627	94716	95828	94582	94825	95621	95043	96031	98010	94167	30
35	93730	94395	94374	94042	94093	94198	93850	93879	94113	95048	93821	94076	94967	94537	95340	97365	93094	35
40	92592	93436	93306	93126	93146	93086	92717	92794	93133	93894	92705	92580	93940	92901	94169	96207	91808	40
45	91226	92155	91965	92188	92083	91939	91359	91540	91821	92509	91337	91697	92742	90457	91805	93828	89374	45
50	88689	89702	89435	90479	90351	89270	88828	89169	89285	89936	88806	89256	90472	87080	88559	90548	85971	50
55	85263	86306	86029	88000	88207	85939	85454	86077	85836	86462	85375	85858	87355	82458	83959	85886	81339	55
60	80534	81636	81345	84501	85345	81240	80744	81673	81075	81666	80659	81212	83052	75827	77459	79285	74778	60
65	73875	74944	74746	79045	81740	74747	74087	75479	74371	74914	74000	74653	76814	66337	68043	69684	65452	65
70	64510	65515	65320	70911	77197	65478	64756	66624	64943	65417	64629	65331	67827	51942	53872	55254	51328	70
75	50399	51286	51044	57653	69912	51648	50667	52954	50738	51108	50492	51233	54327	35812	37735	38787	35519	75
80	34623	35259	35167	41413	61542	35945	34906	37053	34856	35110	34715	35425	38750	17727	19439	20127	17707	80
85+	17089	17437	17374	21721	47912	18361	17323	18918	17205	17329	17134	17660	21201	17727	19439	20127	17707	85+

ADDED YRS OF LIFE

	No Causes	(1)	(2)	(3)	(4)	(5)	(6)	(7)	(8)	(9)	(10)	(11)	(12)	(1)+(2)	(1)+(2)+(5)+(6)+(8)	(1)+(2)+(5)+(6)+(8)+part of (9)&(12)	(10)+(11)
TOTAL		.531	.533	2.210	9.977	.653	.146	.774	.260	.586	.074	.452	2.016	1.069	2.164	3.695	.527
WORK	3.044	.354	.123	.646	.752	.078	.033	.183	.197	.000	.030	.114	.374	.479	.793	.924	.144

POPULATION, DEATHS, DEATH RATES FOR ALL CAUSES COMBINED, AND SPECIFIED CAUSES

Age Start of Interval	Midyear Population	Deaths During Year	All Causes	Respiratory T.B.	Other Infec. and Paras.	Neoplasms	Cardiovascular	Infl., Pneu., Bronch.	Diarrheal	Certain Degenerative	Maternal	Cert. Dis. of Infancy	Motor Vehicle	Other Violence	Other and Unknown	Age Start of Interval
0	21645	611	.02823	.00000	.00046	.00000	.00005	.00222	.00074	.00000	.00000	.01811	.00000	.00106	.00559	0
1	87293	123	.00141	.00002	.00016	.00007	.00007	.00013	.00007	.00001	.00000	.00000	.00009	.00053	.00026	1
5	84629	60	.00071	.00000	.00009	.00006	.00004	.00002	.00000	.00004	.00000	.00000	.00007	.00019	.00020	5
10	70686	40	.00057	.00000	.00004	.00007	.00003	.00001	.00001	.00007	.00000	.00000	.00003	.00013	.00017	10
15	60927	78	.00128	.00000	.00008	.00013	.00003	.00002	.00000	.00003	.00000	.00000	.00003	.00013	.00017	15
20	66760	118	.00177	.00006	.00004	.00009	.00001	.00001	.00001	.00006	.00000	.00000	.00064	.00048	.00008	20
25	70256	123	.00175	.00016	.00006	.00019	.00019	.00000	.00000	.00009	.00000	.00000	.00064	.00061	.00021	25
30	64327	119	.00185	.00022	.00006	.00022	.00023	.00006	.00000	.00009	.00000	.00000	.00034	.00054	.00017	30
35	66430	159	.00239	.00029	.00008	.00026	.00059	.00008	.00002	.00015	.00000	.00000	.00026	.00054	.00014	35
40	62833	221	.00352	.00030	.00006	.00043	.00121	.00013	.00002	.00022	.00000	.00000	.00011	.00057	.00027	40
45	55653	325	.00584	.00034	.00009	.00110	.00252	.00013	.00002	.00020	.00000	.00000	.00011	.00056	.00048	45
50	46957	417	.00888	.00026	.00028	.00164	.00413	.00019	.00002	.00055	.00000	.00000	.00011	.00081	.00050	50
55	38322	598	.01560	.00060	.00029	.00347	.00791	.00034	.00010	.00050	.00000	.00000	.00013	.00072	.00096	55
60	37302	921	.02469	.00064	.00035	.00472	.01405	.00083	.00008	.00121	.00000	.00000	.00029	.00094	.00117	60
65	33661	1281	.03806	.00068	.00059	.00778	.02151	.00154	.00003	.00119	.00000	.00000	.00027	.00043	.00212	65
70	25655	1491	.05812	.00074	.00019	.01134	.03383	.00253	.00023	.00226	.00000	.00000	.00030	.00086	.00356	70
75	14462	1292	.08934	.00021	.00083	.01507	.05338	.00449	.00048	.00339	.00000	.00000	.00047	.00090	.00561	75
80	6817	985	.14449	.00029	.00088	.01599	.09330	.00763	.00044	.00308	.00000	.00000	.00076	.00104	.00968	80
85+	2780	677	.24353	.00000	.00072	.01906	.15827	.02338	.00072	.00432	.00000	.00000	.00103	.00352	.01834	85+
ALL	917395	9639		.00000	.00072	.01906	.15827	.02338	.00072	.00432	.00000	.00000	.00108	.00288	.03309	

	All Causes	Resp. T.B.	Other Infec.	Neoplasms	Cardiovascular	Infl., Pneu.	Diarrheal	Cert. Degen.	Maternal	Cert. Dis. Infancy	Motor Vehicle	Other Violence	Other/Unknown
CRUDE DEATH RATE	.01051	.00021	.00016	.00162	.00519	.00048	.00006	.00036	.00000	.00043	.00024	.00059	.00118
STANDARDIZED RATE (1)	.00614	.00014	.00013	.00083	.00238	.00028	.00006	.00020	.00000	.00043	.00024	.00059	.00118
STANDARDIZED RATE (2)	.01113	.00021	.00016	.00169	.00565	.00052	.00006	.00038	.00000	.00064	.00022	.00052	.00075
GEOMETRIC MEAN	.00759		.00016	.00169	.00565	.00052	.00006	.00038	.00000	.00037	.00025	.00059	.00125

LIFE TABLE FOR ALL CAUSES COMBINED

Age (x)	Midyear Population	Deaths During Year	$_nM_x$	$_nq_x$	l_x	$_nd_x$	$_nL_x$	$_nm_x$	$_na_x$	T_x	$_nr_x$	$\overset{\circ}{e}_x$	Age (x)
0	21645	611	.028228	.027540	100000	2754	97571	.028226	.117988	6784315	.000000	67.843	0
1	87293	123	.001409	.005615	97246	546	387619	.001409	1.500000	6686744	.000000	68.761	1
5	84629	60	.000709	.003537	96700	342	482645	.000709	2.500000	6299125	.000000	65.141	5
10	70686	40	.000566	.002833	96358	273	481164	.000567	2.708333	5816480	.028505	60.363	10
15	60927	78	.001280	.006401	96085	615	479005	.001284	2.691734	5335315	.014496	55.527	15
20	66760	118	.001768	.008788	95470	839	475296	.001765	2.552145	4856310	-.011836	50.867	20
25	70256	123	.001751	.008718	94631	825	471098	.001751	2.506313	4381014	-.001920	46.296	25
30	64327	119	.001850	.009210	93806	864	466929	.001850	2.567757	3909916	-.003564	41.681	30
35	66430	159	.002393	.011900	92942	1106	462099	.002393	2.639580	3442987	-.001482	37.044	35
40	62833	221	.003517	.017477	91836	1605	455480	.003524	2.694964	2980888	.009022	32.459	40
45	55653	325	.005840	.028904	90231	2608	445100	.005859	2.678138	2525408	.018475	27.988	45
50	46957	417	.008880	.043767	87623	3835	429302	.008933	2.702086	2080308	.028382	23.742	50
55	38322	598	.015605	.075524	83788	6328	404201	.015656	2.670802	1651005	.015707	19.705	55
60	37302	921	.024690	.116486	77460	9023	365907	.024659	2.629045	1246805	-.006907	16.096	60
65	33661	1281	.038056	.174131	68437	11917	313515	.038011	2.594211	880898	-.006925	12.872	65
70	25655	1491	.058117	.254989	56520	14412	247308	.058275	2.551230	567383	-.014808	10.039	70
75	14462	1292	.089338	.367175	42108	15461	171823	.089982	2.495823	320074	.034755	7.601	75
80	6817	985	.144492	.529215	26647	14102	96737	.145777	2.411862	148251	.034755	5.564	80
85+	2780	677	.243525	1.000000	12545	12545	51514	.243525	4.106352	51514	.000000	4.106	85+

NUMBER OF PERSONS DYING (OUT OF 100,000 AT BIRTH) ABOVE AGE X FROM SPECIFIED CAUSES

Age (x)	All Causes	Respiratory T.B.	Other Infec. and Paras.	Neoplasms	Cardiovascular	Infl., Pneu., Bronch.	Diarrheal	Certain Degenerative	Maternal	Cert. Dis. of Infancy	Motor Vehicle	Other Violence	Other and Unknown	Age (x)
0	100000	1686	1241	15459	53974	4839	470	3366	0	1767	1793	4384	11021	0
1	97246	1686	1196	15459	53969	4623	398	3366	0	0	1793	4280	10476	1
5	96700	1678	1134	15433	53943	4574	371	3362	0	0	1757	4076	10372	5
10	96358	1678	1105	15387	53926	4563	371	3345	0	0	1723	3984	10276	10
15	96085	1678	1085	15353	53912	4556	365	3311	0	0	1709	3923	10193	15
20	95470	1677	1046	15290	53896	4548	365	3295	0	0	1503	3694	10156	20
25	94631	1649	1024	15248	53890	4541	358	3267	0	0	1197	3402	10055	25
30	93806	1575	997	15147	53802	4541	358	3226	0	0	1036	3147	9977	30
35	92942	1474	968	15045	53693	4512	350	3183	0	0	913	2893	9911	35
40	91836	1342	933	14927	53422	4477	343	3113	0	0	864	2629	9786	40
45	90231	1204	904	14731	52870	4419	336	3012	0	0	813	2375	9567	45
50	87623	1052	864	14241	51745	4363	312	2923	0	0	765	2015	9343	50
55	83788	942	745	13532	49959	4280	303	2685	0	0	710	1704	8928	55
60	77460	699	629	12125	46751	4142	261	2483	0	0	594	1324	8452	60
65	68437	463	501	10400	41618	3839	231	2042	0	0	496	1167	7680	65
70	56520	249	315	7963	34883	3355	222	1670	0	0	403	897	6563	70
75	42108	66	267	5152	26491	2727	164	1109	0	0	287	675	5170	75
80	26647	32	123	2551	17247	1948	80	524	0	0	155	495	3492	80
85+	12545	0	37	982	8153	1204	37	222	0	0	56	148	1706	85+

NUMBER OF PERSONS SURVIVING TO AGE X IF SPECIFIED CAUSES WERE ELIMINATED

Age (x)	No Causes	Respiratory T.B. (1)	Other Infec. and Paras. (2)	Neoplasms (3)	Cardiovascular (4)	Infl., Pneu., Bronch. (5)	Diarrheal (6)	Certain Degenerative (7)	Maternal (8)	Cert. Dis. of Infancy (9)	Motor Vehicle (10)	Other Violence (11)	Other and Unknown (12)	(1)+(2)	(1)+(2)+(5)+(6)+(8)	(1)+(2)+(5)+(6)+(8)+part of(9)&(12)	(10)+(11)	Age (x)
0	100000	100000	100000	100000	100000	100000	100000	100000	100000	100000	100000	100000	100000	100000	100000	100000	100000	0
1	97246	97246	97290	97251	97459	97317	97246	97246	97246	97246	97349	97785	97290	97575	99314	97349		1
5	96700	96708	96806	96726	96731	96981	96798	96704	96700	98448	96736	97006	97340	96814	97173	98940	97042	5
10	96358	96366	96493	96430	96406	96629	96455	96379	96358	98100	96428	96755	97092	96501	96870	98647	96825	10
15	96085	96093	96239	96191	96147	96362	96188	96140	96085	97822	96169	96542	96901	96247	96628	98416	96626	15
20	95470	95479	95662	95638	95547	95754	95572	95540	95470	97196	95759	96154	96318	95671	96058	97838	96445	20
25	94631	94668	94843	94839	94713	94919	94739	94729	94631	96342	95223	95602	95573	94880	95278	97053	96200	25
30	93806	93916	94044	94113	93975	94092	93913	93944	93806	95502	94554	95025	94818	94154	94549	96320	95783	30
35	92942	93152	93206	93348	93219	93254	93056	93121	92942	94622	93807	94407	94011	93417	93846	95618	95285	35
40	91836	92175	92132	92355	92380	92179	91956	92083	91836	93496	92740	93550	93018	92472	92939	94722	94471	40
45	90231	90701	90551	90537	91318	90626	90356	90574	90231	91862	91170	92172	91613	91023	91547	93341	93131	45
50	87623	88230	87973	88197	89808	88062	87768	88044	87623	89207	88563	89870	89189	88583	89174	90947	90855	50
55	83788	84477	84240	85616	87687	84289	83935	84425	83788	85303	84760	86249	85699	84932	85591	87332	87250	55
60	77460	78333	77989	80544	84359	78057	77617	78245	77460	78860	78471	80111	79696	78868	79657	81322	81157	60
65	68437	69432	69026	72866	79974	69253	68621	69550	68437	69674	69423	70930	71164	70029	71054	72605	71953	65
70	56520	57538	57176	62578	73591	57641	56680	57782	56520	57542	57420	58833	59836	58205	59528	60916	59770	70
75	42108	43024	42637	49369	65082	43498	42278	43545	42108	42869	42880	44029	45666	43565	45185	46333	44836	75
80	26647	27252	27098	33720	54168	28170	26821	28034	26647	27129	27242	28012	30508	27713	29489	30351	28637	80
85+	12545	12852	12816	17263	41453	13800	12656	13413	12545	12772	12893	13434	15801	13129	14570	15102	13807	85+

ADDED YRS OF LIFE

	No Causes	(1)	(2)	(3)	(4)	(5)	(6)	(7)	(8)	(9)	(10)	(11)	(12)	(1)+(2)	(1)+(2)+(5)+(6)+(8)	+part of(9)&(12)	(10)+(11)
TOTAL		.367	.295	2.059	9.854	.607	.118	.480	.000	1.225	.563	1.301	1.739	.665	1.412	2.813	1.881
WORK	3.641	.196	.093	.497	1.041	.073	.017	.155	.000	.000	.367	.653	.326	.290	.381	.423	1.027

POPULATION, DEATHS, DEATH RATES FOR ALL CAUSES COMBINED, AND SPECIFIED CAUSES

Age Start of Interval	Midyear Population	Deaths During Year	All Causes	Respiratory T. B.	Other Infec. and Paras.	Neoplasms	Cardiovascular	Infl., Pneu., Bronch.	Diarrheal	Certain Degenerative	Maternal	Cert. Dis. of Infancy	Motor Vehicle	Other Violence	Other and Unknown	Age Start of Interval
0	20971	406	.01936	.00000	.00014	.00014	.00024	.00229	.00048	.00000	.00000	.01159	.00000	.00048	.00401	0
1	83937	100	.00119	.00001	.00021	.00013	.00001	.00008	.00004	.00002	.00000	.00000	.00008	.00021	.00038	1
5	81137	35	.00043	.00000	.00014	.00005	.00002	.00002	.00000	.00004	.00000	.00000	.00006	.00005	.00005	5
10	68643	20	.00029	.00003	.00004	.00007	.00003	.00000	.00000	.00003	.00000	.00000	.00000	.00003	.00005	10
15	57866	37	.00064	.00009	.00002	.00005	.00003	.00000	.00000	.00003	.00007	.00000	.00000	.00009	.00010	.00016	15
20	64026	52	.00081	.00017	.00005	.00012	.00008	.00002	.00002	.00006	.00009	.00000	.00008	.00006	.00006	20
25	68342	73	.00107	.00025	.00006	.00013	.00023	.00000	.00001	.00004	.00010	.00000	.00000	.00007	.00016	25
30	66284	84	.00127	.00030	.00000	.00029	.00018	.00005	.00002	.00008	.00008	.00000	.00000	.00007	.00018	30
35	66357	109	.00164	.00012	.00011	.00039	.00035	.00006	.00000	.00006	.00011	.00000	.00005	.00009	.00032	35
40	60433	151	.00250	.00022	.00005	.00074	.00065	.00008	.00005	.00013	.00010	.00000	.00003	.00012	.00033	40
45	52547	217	.00413	.00013	.00008	.00158	.00129	.00008	.00006	.00019	.00000	.00000	.00000	.00010	.00063	45
50	47644	316	.00663	.00023	.00010	.00250	.00256	.00008	.00008	.00025	.00000	.00000	.00000	.00015	.00061	50
55	42201	444	.01052	.00012	.00009	.00374	.00438	.00005	.00005	.00059	.00000	.00000	.00005	.00028	.00116	55
60	39752	647	.01628	.00018	.00018	.00385	.00898	.00033	.00008	.00091	.00000	.00000	.00005	.00018	.00156	60
65	35837	872	.02433	.00017	.00017	.00525	.01418	.00050	.00020	.00120	.00000	.00000	.00011	.00028	.00234	65
70	27689	1182	.04269	.00033	.00022	.00748	.02604	.00108	.00018	.00249	.00000	.00000	.00018	.00079	.00390	70
75	16147	1203	.07450	.00025	.00019	.01071	.04880	.00248	.00062	.00266	.00000	.00000	.00031	.00124	.00725	75
80	8223	997	.12125	.00012	.00049	.01326	.08209	.00693	.00000	.00389	.00000	.00000	.00036	.00328	.01082	80
85+	3919	928	.23680	.00000	.00026	.01608	.16407	.01429	.00077	.00510	.00000	.00000	.00026	.00689	.02909	85+
ALL	911955	7873														ALL

CRUDE DEATH RATE			.00863	.00014	.00010	.00152	.00458	.00032	.00006	.00036	.00003	.00027	.00006	.00022	.00097	
STANDARDIZED RATE (1)			.00436	.00011	.00009	.00077	.00176	.00019	.00005	.00017	.00003	.00041	.00005	.00015	.00057	
STANDARDIZED RATE (2)			.00835	.00013	.00010	.00146	.00445	.00031	.00006	.00034	.00003	.00024	.00006	.00022	.00093	
GEOMETRIC MEAN			.00543													

LIFE TABLE FOR ALL CAUSES COMBINED

Age (x)	Midyear Population	Deaths During Year	$_nM_x$	$_nq_x$	l_x	$_nd_x$	$_nL_x$	$_nm_x$	$_na_x$	T_x	$_nr_x$	$\overset{\circ}{e}_x$	Age (x)
0	20971	406	.019360	.019030	100000	1903	98293	.019361	.102912	7229073	.000000	72.291	0
1	83937	100	.001191	.004750	98097	466	391223	.001191	1.500000	7130780	.000000	72.691	1
5	81137	35	.000431	.002151	97631	210	487630	.000431	2.500000	6739557	.000000	69.031	5
10	68643	20	.000291	.001458	97421	142	486771	.000292	2.649648	6251927	.029299	64.174	10
15	57866	37	.000639	.003207	97279	312	485667	.000642	2.666934	5765156	.016512	59.264	15
20	64026	52	.000812	.004043	96967	392	483857	.000810	2.607355	5279489	-.011576	54.446	20
25	68342	73	.001068	.005322	96575	514	481635	.001067	2.587143	4795592	-.007188	49.657	25
30	66284	84	.001267	.006319	96061	607	478843	.001268	2.591639	4313957	-.000932	44.909	30
35	66357	109	.001643	.008182	95454	781	475437	.001643	2.652849	3835114	-.003150	40.178	35
40	60433	151	.002499	.012464	94673	1180	470652	.002507	2.701095	3359677	-.016681	35.487	40
45	52547	217	.004130	.020536	93493	1920	463044	.004146	2.697591	2889025	-.019404	30.901	45
50	47644	316	.006633	.032772	91573	3001	450912	.006655	2.682995	2425980	-.017094	26.492	50
55	42201	444	.010521	.051438	88572	4556	432217	.010541	2.663932	1975069	-.011096	22.299	55
60	39752	647	.016278	.078390	84016	6586	404524	.016282	2.638014	1542852	-.001535	18.364	60
65	35837	872	.024332	.115188	77430	8919	366262	.024351	2.658089	1138328	-.004045	14.701	65
70	27689	1182	.042688	.194918	68511	13354	310963	.042944	2.634292	772065	-.026023	11.269	70
75	16147	1203	.074503	.317766	55157	17527	232850	.075272	2.550363	461102	-.041322	8.360	75
80	8223	997	.121245	.467473	37630	17591	143626	.122478	2.468924	228252	-.041322	6.066	80
85+	3919	928	.236795	1.000000	20039	20039	84626	.236795	4.223060	84626	.000000	4.223	85+

NUMBER OF PERSONS DYING (OUT OF 100,000 AT BIRTH) ABOVE AGE X FROM SPECIFIED CAUSES

Age (x)	All Causes	Respiratory T.B.	Other Infec. and Paras.	Neoplasms	Cardiovascular	Infl., Pneu., Bronch.	Diarrheal	Certain Degenerative	Maternal	Cert. Dis. of Infancy	Motor Vehicle	Other Violence	Other and Unknown	Age (x)
0	100000	1075	778	16058	58687	3913	577	3922	228	1139	501	2433	10689	0
1	98097	1075	764	16044	58664	3688	530	3922	228	0	501	2386	10295	1
5	97631	1070	680	15993	58659	3656	516	3912	228	0	468	2302	10147	5
10	97421	1070	614	15969	58647	3644	516	3894	228	0	438	2278	10123	10
15	97279	1056	593	15933	58633	3644	516	3880	228	0	438	2264	10094	15
20	96967	1013	585	15908	58616	3644	499	3846	228	0	396	2213	10019	20
25	96575	931	562	15847	58578	3636	492	3816	182	0	358	2183	9990	25
30	96061	811	534	15784	58466	3636	485	3795	133	0	358	2148	9911	30
35	95454	666	534	15647	58379	3615	478	3759	97	0	351	2104	9824	35
40	94673	609	484	15460	58214	3586	478	3730	47	0	330	2061	9674	40
45	93493	508	460	15108	57909	3547	454	3668	0	0	314	2007	9518	45
50	91573	446	425	14374	57306	3512	428	3579	0	0	314	1963	9226	50
55	88572	342	378	13244	56147	3474	390	3465	0	0	286	1896	8950	55
60	84016	291	337	11624	54246	3453	369	3209	0	0	265	1773	8449	60
65	77430	220	265	10067	50612	3321	339	2842	0	0	245	1702	7817	65
70	68511	179	204	8145	45415	3137	267	2402	0	0	204	1600	6958	70
75	55157	77	137	5811	37264	2797	211	1624	0	0	147	1351	5738	75
80	37630	20	93	3299	25775	2210	65	1001	0	0	75	1059	4033	80
85+	20039	0	22	1360	13885	1209	65	432	0	0	22	583	2461	85+

NUMBER OF PERSONS SURVIVING TO AGE X IF SPECIFIED CAUSES WERE ELIMINATED

Age (x)	No Causes	Respiratory T.B. (1)	Other Infec. and Paras. (2)	Neoplasms (3)	Cardiovascular (4)	Infl., Pneu., Bronch. (5)	Diarrheal (6)	Certain Degenerative (7)	Maternal (8)	Cert. Dis. of Infancy (9)	Motor Vehicle (10)	Other Violence (11)	Other and Unknown (12)	(1)+(2)	(1)+(2)+(5)+(6)+(8)	(1)+(2)+(5)+(6)+(8)+part of (9)&(12)	(10)+(11)	Age (x)
0	100000	100000	100000	100000	100000	100000	100000	100000	100000	100000	100000	100000	100000	100000	100000	100000	100000	0
1	98097	98097	98111	98111	98120	98320	98144	98097	98097	99232	98097	98144	98488	98111	98381	99565	98144	1
5	97631	97636	97729	97696	97659	97885	97691	97641	97631	98760	97664	97761	98168	97734	98048	99292	97794	5
10	97421	97426	97584	97510	97461	97687	97481	97449	97421	98548	97484	97575	97981	97589	97916	99168	97638	10
15	97279	97298	97463	97403	97333	97544	97339	97321	97279	98404	97342	97447	97868	97482	97808	99068	97510	15
20	96967	97029	97159	97116	97037	97231	97044	97043	96967	98089	97072	97185	97629	97221	97563	98842	97290	20
25	96575	96719	96789	96784	96683	96846	96659	96680	96621	97692	96717	96822	97264	96933	97335	98625	96965	25
30	96061	96324	96302	96332	96280	96331	96151	96187	96156	97172	96202	96342	96825	96565	97023	98346	96484	30
35	95454	95860	95693	95861	95759	95743	95551	95615	95584	95601	95777	96301	96460	96100	96620	97973	95925	35
40	94673	95133	94960	95264	95140	94989	94769	94862	94852	95768	94840	95037	95664	95421	96017	97407	95204	40
45	93493	94048	93801	94429	94260	93844	93611	93741	93716	94574	93674	93906	94628	94357	95057	96470	94088	45
50	91573	92178	91909	93226	92928	91951	91715	91904	91792	92632	91750	92021	92978	92516	93264	94680	92199	50
55	88572	89260	88943	91047	91210	88575	88746	89005	88783	89556	88771	89072	90207	89634	90435	91831	89272	55
60	84016	84719	84408	88253	88290	84419	84202	84678	84217	84988	84225	84610	86065	85114	85917	87259	84821	60
65	77430	78146	77861	82917	85121	77929	77630	78395	77615	78326	77642	78046	79942	78581	79482	80756	78260	65
70	68511	69184	68950	75323	80886	69127	68756	69786	68675	69303	68737	69153	71572	69627	70672	71843	69382	70
75	55157	55790	55570	62574	74342	55562	55405	56895	55289	55795	55590	55900	58773	56208	57422	58427	56136	75
80	37630	38108	37948	45366	65186	38676	37919	39341	37720	38065	37848	38382	41615	38430	39897	40676	38604	80
85+	20039	20308	20260	25896	53145	21348	20193	21382	20087	20271	20194	20791	23445	20532	22094	22612	20951	85+

ADDED YRS OF LIFE

	No Causes	(1)	(2)	(3)	(4)	(5)	(6)	(7)	(8)	(9)	(10)	(11)	(12)	(1)+(2)	...	...	(10)+(11)
TOTAL		.340	.248	2.457	11.203	.489	.126	.519	.097	.835	.138	.410	1.639	.590	1.317	2.403	.549
WORK	2.438	.209	.058	.652	.671	.041	.032	.124	.072	.000	.052	.112	.311	.268	.414	.484	.164

POPULATION, DEATHS, DEATH RATES FOR ALL CAUSES COMBINED, AND SPECIFIED CAUSES

Age Start of Interval	Midyear Population	Deaths During Year	All Causes	Respiratory T.B.	Other Infec. and Paras.	Neoplasms	Cardiovascular	Infl., Pneu., Bronch.	Diarrheal	Certain Degenerative	Maternal	Cert. Dis. of Infancy	Motor Vehicle	Other Violence	Other and Unknown	Age Start of Interval
0	32052	703	.02193	.00003	.00031	.00000	.00019	.00256	.00069	.00000	.00000	.01170	.00000	.00084	.00521	0
1	127090	169	.00133	.00001	.00007	.00019	.00004	.00018	.00006	.00002	.00000	.00001	.00012	.00031	.00033	1
5	146010	65	.00045	.00000	.00003	.00005	.00000	.00001	.00000	.00001	.00000	.00000	.00008	.00010	.00016	5
10	131290	61	.00046	.00000	.00000	.00005	.00002	.00002	.00001	.00002	.00000	.00000	.00007	.00010	.00016	10
15	117290	121	.00103	.00000	.00002	.00007	.00006	.00003	.00000	.00003	.00000	.00000	.00047	.00017	.00012	15
20	92630	129	.00139	.00000	.00001	.00017	.00002	.00001	.00001	.00004	.00000	.00000	.00056	.00049	.00008	20
25	78500	115	.00146	.00000	.00000	.00023	.00011	.00003	.00001	.00001	.00000	.00000	.00046	.00050	.00011	25
30	79710	112	.00141	.00000	.00004	.00035	.00015	.00000	.00003	.00006	.00000	.00000	.00018	.00048	.00013	30
35	83920	170	.00203	.00004	.00002	.00036	.00062	.00005	.00000	.00007	.00000	.00000	.00015	.00046	.00025	35
40	79630	259	.00325	.00003	.00001	.00050	.00129	.00009	.00001	.00018	.00000	.00000	.00019	.00060	.00035	40
45	69690	409	.00587	.00001	.00006	.00121	.00265	.00017	.00003	.00026	.00000	.00000	.00022	.00076	.00050	45
50	68760	641	.00932	.00007	.00004	.00209	.00508	.00038	.00001	.00028	.00000	.00000	.00023	.00076	.00050	50
55	58650	916	.01562	.00005	.00007	.00324	.00868	.00099	.00002	.00048	.00000	.00000	.00027	.00068	.00114	55
60	47400	1203	.02538	.00025	.00004	.00586	.01395	.00186	.00002	.00072	.00000	.00000	.00015	.00080	.00173	60
65	33700	1318	.03911	.00018	.00021	.00774	.02279	.00377	.00009	.00125	.00000	.00000	.00047	.00045	.00217	65
70	25085	1501	.05984	.00048	.00008	.01025	.03544	.00658	.00020	.00167	.00000	.00000	.00052	.00056	.00407	70
75	18420	1817	.09864	.00049	.00022	.01488	.05695	.01314	.00016	.00315	.00000	.00000	.00071	.00147	.00749	75
80	10625	1617	.15219	.00038	.00019	.01807	.08725	.02438	.00038	.00424	.00000	.00000	.00094	.00292	.01346	80
85+	4882	1309	.26813	.00020	.00041	.02315	.15260	.05285	.00061	.00696	.00000	.00000	.00020	.00655	.02458	85+
ALL	1305334	12635														

	All Causes	Respiratory T.B.	Other Infec. and Paras.	Neoplasms	Cardiovascular	Infl., Pneu., Bronch.	Diarrheal	Certain Degenerative	Maternal	Cert. Dis. of Infancy	Motor Vehicle	Other Violence	Other and Unknown
CRUDE DEATH RATE	.00968	.00005	.00005	.00151	.00481	.00105	.00004	.00028	.00000	.00029	.00025	.00047	.00088
STANDARDIZED RATE (1)	.00588	.00003	.00004	.00089	.00247	.00056	.00004	.00016	.00000	.00029	.00025	.00047	.00088
STANDARDIZED RATE (2)	.01130	.00005	.00005	.00179	.00580	.00125	.00005	.00033	.00000	.00041	.00024	.00041	.00063
GEOMETRIC MEAN	.00729									.00024	.00027	.00050	.00097

LIFE TABLE FOR ALL CAUSES COMBINED

Age (x)	Midyear Population	Deaths During Year	$_nM_x$	$_nq_x$	l_x	$_nd_x$	$_nL_x$	$_nm_x$	$_na_x$	T_x	$_nr_x$	$\overset{\circ}{e}_x$	Age (x)
0	32052	703	.021933	.021510	100000	2151	98080	.021931	.107286	6844927	.000000	68.449	0
1	127090	169	.001330	.005304	97849	519	390099	.001330	1.500000	6746847	.000000	68.952	1
5	146010	65	.000445	.002219	97330	216	486110	.000444	2.500000	6356748	.000000	65.311	5
10	131290	61	.000465	.002327	97114	226	485064	.000466	2.762721	5870638	.014478	60.451	10
15	117290	121	.001032	.005171	96888	501	483280	.001037	2.684631	5385574	.027712	55.586	15
20	92630	129	.001393	.006951	96387	670	480301	.001395	2.561567	4902294	.039807	50.861	20
25	78500	115	.001465	.007303	95717	699	476836	.001466	2.498510	4421993	.023640	46.199	25
30	79710	112	.001405	.006999	95018	665	473480	.001404	2.578947	3945156	-.001095	41.520	30
35	83920	170	.002026	.010079	94353	951	469564	.002025	2.685331	3471676	-.005090	36.795	35
40	79630	259	.003253	.016177	93402	1511	463590	.003259	2.736598	3002112	-.011300	32.142	40
45	69690	409	.005869	.029024	91891	2667	453322	.005883	2.700366	2538522	.010038	27.625	45
50	68760	641	.009322	.045669	89224	4076	436715	.009333	2.692642	2085201	.005955	23.370	50
55	58650	916	.015618	.075586	85148	6436	410773	.015668	2.674507	1648485	.016004	19.360	55
60	47400	1203	.025380	.120274	78712	9467	371142	.025508	2.631950	1237712	.026477	15.725	60
65	33700	1318	.039110	.179536	69245	12432	316265	.039309	2.590124	866571	.028139	12.515	65
70	25085	1501	.059843	.261296	56813	14845	247812	.059904	2.557876	550305	.006370	9.686	70
75	18420	1817	.098643	.394491	41968	16556	168236	.098410	2.487052	302493	-.010491	7.208	75
80	10625	1617	.152188	.543680	25412	13816	91010	.151808	2.390691	134258	-.010491	5.283	80
85+	4882	1309	.268128	1.000000	11596	11596	43248	.268128	3.729565	43248	.000000	3.730	85+

NUMBER OF PERSONS DYING (OUT OF 100,000 AT BIRTH) ABOVE AGE X FROM SPECIFIED CAUSES

Age (x)	All Causes	Respiratory T.B.	Other Infec. and Paras.	Neo-plasms	Cardio-vascular	Infl., Pneu., Bronch.	Diar-rheal	Certain Degenerative	Maternal	Cert. Dis. of Infancy	Motor Vehicle	Other Violence	Other and Unknown	Age (x)
0	100000	489	366	16043	53420	11349	322	2932	0	1150	1939	3842	8148	0
1	97849	486	335	16043	53402	11059	254	2932	0	3	1939	3760	7636	1
5	97330	483	308	15970	53387	10988	233	2923	0	0	1893	3640	7505	5
10	97114	483	294	15943	53387	10974	233	2920	0	0	1853	3594	7426	10
15	96888	483	294	15921	53376	10974	229	2912	0	0	1819	3512	7368	15
20	96387	483	286	15888	53247	10958	229	2900	0	0	1591	3404	7301	20
25	95717	483	281	15804	53337	10953	224	2879	0	0	1321	3169	7266	25
30	95018	483	281	15654	53282	10940	218	2873	0	0	1103	2933	7211	30
35	94353	483	263	15528	53210	10940	206	2843	0	0	1020	2707	7153	35
40	93402	466	252	15360	52920	10918	206	2810	0	0	948	2489	7033	40
45	91891	454	246	15127	52318	10877	200	2728	0	0	860	2209	6872	45
50	89224	448	220	14579	51111	10799	187	2611	0	0	763	1864	6642	50
55	85148	416	201	13663	48892	10633	181	2490	0	0	661	1655	6356	55
60	78712	395	173	12327	45315	10225	174	2294	0	0	549	1374	5886	60
65	69245	300	157	10141	40112	9531	166	2026	0	0	494	1077	5241	65
70	56813	244	91	7683	32865	8330	137	1630	0	0	343	937	4553	70
75	41568	125	71	5142	24072	6698	88	1214	0	0	214	798	3546	75
80	25412	43	35	2644	14514	4494	60	686	0	0	96	553	2287	80
85+	11596	9	18	1001	6600	2286	27	301	0	0	9	283	1062	85+

NUMBER OF PERSONS SURVIVING TO AGE X IF SPECIFIED CAUSES WERE ELIMINATED

Age (x)	No Causes	Respiratory T.B. (1)	Other Infec. and Paras. (2)	Neo-plasms (3)	Cardio-vascular (4)	Infl., Pneu., Bronch. (5)	Diar-rheal (6)	Certain Degenerative (7)	Maternal (8)	Cert. Dis. of Infancy (9)	Motor Vehicle (10)	Other Violence (11)	Other and Unknown (12)	(1)+(2)	(1)+(2)+(5)+(6)+(8)	(1)+(2)+(5)+(6)+(8)+part of(9)&(12)	(10)+(11)	Age (x)
0	100000	100000	100000	100000	100000	100000	100000	100000	100000	100000	100000	100000	100000	100000	100000	100000	100000	0
1	97849	97852	97880	97849	97867	98136	97916	97849	97849	98990	97849	97930	98357	97883	98238	99559	97930	1
5	97330	97336	97387	97403	97363	97687	97418	97339	97330	98468	97376	97531	97966	97393	97839	99198	97577	5
10	97114	97120	97185	97214	97147	97477	97202	97126	97114	98250	97200	97360	97829	97191	97643	99012	97446	10
15	96888	96894	96959	97009	96932	97257	96979	96908	96888	98021	97008	97216	97659	96965	97426	98796	97336	15
20	96387	96393	96466	96541	96459	96770	96478	96419	96387	97514	96734	96821	97222	96472	96947	98314	97170	20
25	95717	95723	95800	95954	95799	96103	95812	95769	95717	96836	96332	96384	96581	95806	96288	97646	97003	25
30	95018	95024	95101	95363	95154	95414	95119	95076	95018	96129	95847	95917	95931	95106	95604	96954	96754	30
35	94353	94359	94453	94862	94560	94746	94465	94441	94353	95456	95260	95473	95318	94459	94965	96309	96391	35
40	93402	93425	93512	94074	93897	93813	93513	93522	93402	94494	94372	94721	94478	93535	94058	95396	95714	40
45	91891	91925	92005	92785	92980	92336	92006	92090	91891	92966	92933	93480	93111	92039	92601	93927	94541	45
50	89224	89263	89360	90639	91493	89724	89348	89533	89224	90267	90333	91113	90639	89400	90036	91336	92245	50
55	85148	85217	85257	87412	89566	85758	85213	86144	85148	86307	87159	86782	85365	86143	87404	88345		55
60	78712	78796	78876	82134	86492	79710	78834	79284	78712	79632	79892	80847	80684	78960	80085	81294	82059	60
65	69245	69408	69405	74424	81643	70786	69360	70001	69245	70055	70335	71408	71601	69568	71234	72368	72533	65
70	56813	56997	57004	63492	75179	59201	56934	57797	56813	57477	57847	58717	59393	57189	59719	60746	59785	70
75	41568	42206	42126	45388	66443	45217	42099	43058	41568	42459	42843	43498	44787	42365	45788	46702	44405	75
80	25412	25619	25535	32240	53733	29280	25513	26492	25412	25709	26034	26537	28177	25743	29779	30554	27187	80
85+	11596	11713	11664	16151	38431	15146	11664	12356	11596	11732	11939	12296	13784	11781	15478	16083	12660	85+

ADDED YRS OF LIFE

	No Causes	(1)	(2)	(3)	(4)	(5)	(6)	(7)	(8)	(9)	(10)	(11)	(12)	(1)+(2)	(1)+(2)+(5)+(6)+(8)	part	(10)+(11)
TOTAL		.062	.098	2.171	8.638	1.211	.094	.352	.000	.799	.625	1.038	1.384	.161	1.484	2.570	1.678
WORK	3.358	.015	.024	.582	1.131	.104	.013	.105	.000	.000	.395	.529	.268	.040	.157	.172	.930

POPULATION, DEATHS, DEATH RATES FOR ALL CAUSES COMBINED, AND SPECIFIED CAUSES

Age Start of Interval	Midyear Population	Deaths During Year	All Causes	Respiratory T. B.	Other Infec. and Paras.	Neoplasms	Cardiovascular	Infl., Pneu., Bronch.	Diarrheal	Certain Degenerative	Maternal	Cert. Dis. of Infancy	Motor Vehicle	Other Violence	Other and Unknown	Age Start of Interval
0	30434	490	.01610	.00000	.00030	.00013	.00020	.00168	.00030	.00000	.00000	.00861	.00007	.00046	.00437	0
1	122020	126	.00103	.00001	.00011	.00011	.00002	.00018	.00000	.00002	.00000	.00000	.00007	.00018	.00034	1
5	139680	46	.00033	.00000	.00000	.00006	.00001	.00004	.00000	.00001	.00000	.00000	.00009	.00003	.00009	5
10	125020	36	.00029	.00000	.00001	.00006	.00002	.00004	.00000	.00000	.00000	.00000	.00004	.00005	.00006	10
15	112620	50	.00044	.00000	.00003	.00004	.00005	.00001	.00002	.00001	.00001	.00000	.00008	.00005	.00014	15
20	88040	69	.00078	.00000	.00005	.00009	.00006	.00005	.00000	.00003	.00008	.00000	.00014	.00014	.00016	20
25	75790	41	.00054	.00000	.00000	.00013	.00008	.00000	.00000	.00001	.00003	.00000	.00005	.00013	.00011	25
30	75030	70	.00093	.00000	.00000	.00035	.00019	.00007	.00000	.00005	.00003	.00000	.00001	.00008	.00016	30
35	77890	122	.00157	.00001	.00003	.00065	.00032	.00009	.00000	.00006	.00006	.00000	.00003	.00010	.00021	35
40	78260	172	.00220	.00005	.00001	.00056	.00051	.00006	.00003	.00008	.00003	.00000	.00006	.00009	.00032	40
45	71200	254	.00357	.00004	.00003	.00147	.00096	.00017	.00000	.00014	.00001	.00000	.00013	.00017	.00045	45
50	67690	369	.00545	.00000	.00009	.00192	.00216	.00021	.00007	.00021	.00000	.00000	.00009	.00027	.00044	50
55	57650	518	.00899	.00000	.00007	.00305	.00373	.00040	.00003	.00026	.00000	.00000	.00009	.00038	.00095	55
60	48480	613	.01264	.00002	.00008	.00394	.00598	.00062	.00006	.00052	.00000	.00000	.00002	.00033	.00107	60
65	40920	932	.02278	.00000	.00012	.00557	.01281	.00103	.00002	.00103	.00000	.00000	.00017	.00037	.00166	65
70	33595	1203	.03581	.00006	.00009	.00637	.02206	.00211	.00006	.00155	.00000	.00000	.00018	.00077	.00256	70
75	25415	1654	.06508	.00012	.00012	.00873	.04057	.00539	.00031	.00275	.00000	.00000	.00024	.00185	.00500	75
80	15155	1677	.11066	.00013	.00020	.00904	.07239	.01254	.00066	.00257	.00000	.00000	.00053	.00376	.00884	80
85+	8018	1784	.22250	.00025	.00025	.01522	.13657	.03081	.00087	.00362	.00000	.00000	.00087	.01098	.02307	85+
ALL	1292907	10226														

CRUDE DEATH RATE			.00791	.00002	.00005	.00134	.00411	.00067	.00004	.00025	.00002	.00020	.00009	.00031	.00082	
STANDARDIZED RATE (1)			.00371	.00001	.00005	.00072	.00146	.00028	.00002	.00011	.00002	.00030	.00008	.00017	.00050	
STANDARDIZED RATE (2)			.00727	.00001	.00005	.00132	.00373	.00058	.00004	.00024	.00002	.00018	.00009	.00028	.00074	
GEOMETRIC MEAN			.00452													

LIFE TABLE FOR ALL CAUSES COMBINED

Age (x)	Midyear Population	Deaths During Year	$_nM_x$	$_nq_x$	l_x	$_nd_x$	$_nL_x$	$_nm_x$	$_na_x$	T_x	$_nr_x$	$\overset{\circ}{e}_x$	Age (x)
0	30434	490	.016100	.015870	100000	1587	98568	.016101	.097371	7417079	.000000	74.171	0
1	122020	126	.001033	.004115	98413	405	392640	.001031	1.500000	7318512	.000000	74.365	1
5	139680	46	.000329	.001653	98008	162	489635	.000331	2.500000	6925872	.000000	70.666	5
10	125020	36	.000288	.001431	97846	140	488892	.000286	2.583333	6436237	.014217	65.779	10
15	112620	50	.000444	.002231	97706	218	488035	.000447	2.731269	5947345	.028294	60.870	15
20	88040	69	.000784	.003918	97488	382	486494	.000785	2.524542	5459310	.039958	56.000	20
25	75790	41	.000541	.002708	97106	263	484887	.000542	2.554658	4972816	.024204	51.210	25
30	75030	70	.000933	.004657	96843	451	483189	.000933	2.725425	4487929	.003690	46.342	30
35	77890	122	.001566	.007791	96392	751	480207	.001564	2.665335	4004740	-.005609	41.546	35
40	78260	172	.002198	.010947	95641	1047	475780	.002201	2.684058	3524533	.003081	36.852	40
45	71200	254	.003567	.017718	94594	1676	469084	.003573	2.681484	3048753	.008665	32.230	45
50	67690	369	.005451	.026981	92918	2507	458805	.005464	2.692461	2579668	.012027	27.763	50
55	57650	518	.008985	.044156	90411	3992	442663	.009018	2.647326	2120863	.022135	23.458	55
60	48480	613	.012644	.061676	86419	5330	419771	.012697	2.687774	1678200	.021493	19.419	60
65	40920	932	.022776	.108473	81089	8796	384836	.022856	2.657008	1258430	.016538	15.519	65
70	33595	1203	.035809	.165424	72293	11959	333278	.035883	2.643058	873593	.009901	12.084	70
75	25415	1654	.065080	.281897	60334	17008	260582	.065269	2.584201	540315	.011842	8.955	75
80	15155	1677	.110657	.434681	43326	18833	169652	.111010	2.505542	279733	.011842	6.456	80
85+	8018	1784	.222499	1.000000	24493	24493	110081	.222499	4.494395	110081	.000000	4.494	85+

NUMBER OF PERSONS DYING (OUT OF 100,000 AT BIRTH) ABOVE AGE X FROM SPECIFIED CAUSES

Age (x)	All Causes	Respiratory T.B.	Other Infec. and Paras.	Neo-plasms	Cardio-vascular	Infl., Pneu., Bronch.	Diar-rheal	Certain Degen-erative	Maternal	Cert. Dis. of Infancy	Motor Vehicle	Other Violence	Other and Unknown	Age (x)
0	100000	171	417	15551	56510	9053	446	3100	118	849	802	3683	9300	0
1	98413	171	388	15538	56491	8888	416	3100	118	0	795	3637	8871	1
5	98008	167	346	15496	56484	8818	416	3091	118	0	767	3567	8738	5
10	97846	167	346	15468	56477	8800	416	3084	118	0	721	3553	8696	10
15	97706	167	342	15437	56465	8780	416	3084	118	0	701	3529	8667	15
20	97488	167	329	15415	56439	8776	408	3079	114	0	662	3503	8596	20
25	97106	167	307	15371	56412	8754	408	3063	75	0	596	3436	8517	25
30	96843	167	307	15306	56373	8754	408	3056	62	0	570	3372	8468	30
35	96392	167	307	15139	56283	8722	408	3031	49	0	564	3334	8388	35
40	95641	161	295	14824	56129	8679	408	3000	19	0	552	3284	8290	40
45	94594	137	289	14368	55886	8648	396	2963	6	0	521	3242	8138	45
50	92918	117	276	13676	55436	8569	396	2897	0	0	462	3162	7927	50
55	90411	117	235	12793	55444	8474	362	2802	0	0	421	3040	7723	55
60	86419	109	204	11437	52785	8296	346	2686	0	0	383	2871	7302	60
65	81089	101	169	9779	50259	8036	320	2469	0	0	374	2733	6849	65
70	72293	101	122	7631	45310	7639	311	2072	0	0	308	2591	6208	70
75	60334	81	93	5507	37943	6932	291	1555	0	0	249	2332	5351	75
80	43326	50	62	3227	27340	5521	209	836	0	0	187	1849	4045	80
85+	24493	27	27	1675	15034	3391	96	358	0	0	96	1208	2541	85+

NUMBER OF PERSONS SURVIVING TO AGE X IF SPECIFIED CAUSES WERE ELIMINATED

Age (x)	No Causes	Respiratory T.B. (1)	Other Infec. and Paras. (2)	Neo-plasms (3)	Cardio-vascular (4)	Infl., Pneu., Bronch. (5)	Diar-rheal (6)	Certain Degen-erative (7)	Maternal (8)	Cert. Dis. of Infancy (9)	Motor Vehicle (10)	Other Violence (11)	Other and Unknown (12)	(1)+(2)	(1)+(2)+(5)+(6)+(8)	(1)+(2)+(5)+(6)+(8)+part of(9)&(12)	(10)+(11)	Age (x)
0	100000	100000	100000	100000	100000	100000	100000	100000	100000	100000	100000	100000	100000	100000	100000	100000	100000	0
1	98413	98413	98442	98426	98432	98577	98443	98413	98413	99259	98420	98459	98839	98442	98635	99561	98466	1
5	98008	98012	98079	98063	98034	98241	98017	98008	98008	98850	98043	98123	98566	98083	98346	99326	98159	5
10	97846	97850	97916	97929	97879	98097	97876	97862	97846	98687	97927	97975	98445	97920	98201	99186	98056	10
15	97706	97710	97780	97820	97751	97976	97736	97722	97706	98546	97807	97859	98334	97784	98085	99075	97960	15
20	97488	97492	97575	97623	97559	97762	97525	97509	97492	98326	97627	97667	98186	97579	97895	98897	97806	20
25	97106	97110	97215	97285	97203	97401	97143	97143	97149	97941	97311	97351	97880	97219	97595	98616	97556	25
30	96843	96847	96952	97086	96979	97137	96880	96887	96899	97675	97073	97151	97665	96955	97343	98365	97383	30
35	96392	96396	96500	96801	96617	96717	96429	96460	96461	97220	96627	96737	97290	96504	96935	97962	96973	35
40	95641	95651	95760	96363	96018	96006	95678	95740	95739	96463	95886	96033	96631	95770	96271	97305	96280	40
45	94594	94628	94718	95766	95210	94596	94462	94729	94704	95407	94868	95024	95726	94752	95303	96342	95299	45
50	92918	92971	93053	94766	93974	93382	92965	93116	93032	93717	93245	93420	94242	93105	93733	94771	93749	50
55	90411	90462	90582	93102	92433	90657	90451	90697	90522	91188	90770	91021	91503	90634	91373	92400	91382	55
60	86419	86476	86613	90366	90027	87116	86511	86807	86525	87162	86799	87168	88265	86670	87569	88581	87552	60
65	81089	81150	81305	86486	87064	81997	81200	81664	81188	81786	81455	81926	83270	81366	82491	83475	82296	65
70	72293	72348	72530	79292	82805	73483	72401	73184	72381	72914	72682	73175	74860	72585	73980	74897	73568	70
75	60334	60398	60558	68324	77255	61989	60442	61557	60408	60853	60712	61311	63292	60622	62474	63306	61695	75
80	43326	43398	43513	51271	68202	45762	43474	44823	43379	43698	43650	44445	46620	43585	46250	46985	44777	80
85+	24493	24551	24625	30379	55969	27594	24661	25678	24523	24704	24744	25618	27584	24683	28033	28651	25881	85+

ADDED YRS OF LIFE

	No Causes	(1)	(2)	(3)	(4)	(5)	(6)	(7)	(8)	(9)	(10)	(11)	(12)	(1)+(2)	(1)+(2)+(5)+(6)+(8)	(1)+(2)+(5)+(6)+(8)+part of(9)&(12)	(10)+(11)
TOTAL		.030	.123	2.526	9.591	.957	.068	.380	.053	.637	.226	.541	1.516	.153	1.246	2.130	.772
WORK	2.010	.011	.030	.659	.537	.083	.012	.071	.039	.000	.085	.142	.271	.041	.175	.210	.228

POPULATION, DEATHS, DEATH RATES FOR ALL CAUSES COMBINED, AND SPECIFIED CAUSES

Age Start of Interval	Midyear Population	Deaths During Year	All Causes	Respiratory T. B.	Other Infec. and Paras.	Neo-plasms	Cardio-vascular	Infl., Pneu., Bronch.	Diar-rheal	Certain Degen-erative	Maternal	Cert. Dis. of Infancy	Motor Vehicle	Other Violence	Other and Unknown	Age Start of Interval
0	15700	498	.03172	.00000	.00045	.00015	.00006	.00344	.00076	.00013	.00000	.01879	.00000	.00032	.00758	0
1	58800	71	.00121	.00000	.00007	.00019	.00003	.00014	.00009	.00002	.00000	.00000	.00014	.00024	.00031	1
5	68000	43	.00063	.00000	.00003	.00009	.00000	.00000	.00001	.00000	.00000	.00000	.00018	.00019	.00013	5
10	67600	30	.00044	.00000	.00000	.00007	.00007	.00001	.00000	.00003	.00000	.00000	.00007	.00012	.00006	10
15	63600	57	.00090	.00000	.00000	.00013	.00009	.00005	.00000	.00005	.00000	.00000	.00000	.00027	.00009	15
20	53300	56	.00105	.00000	.00000	.00011	.00008	.00000	.00000	.00000	.00000	.00000	.00043	.00028	.00009	20
25	41800	45	.00108	.00010	.00002	.00012	.00014	.00002	.00000	.00005	.00000	.00000	.00019	.00033	.00010	25
30	39600	60	.00152	.00000	.00005	.00038	.00035	.00003	.00000	.00013	.00000	.00000	.00018	.00025	.00015	30
35	42400	78	.00184	.00007	.00005	.00028	.00064	.00014	.00000	.00012	.00000	.00000	.00017	.00024	.00014	35
40	38500	127	.00330	.00005	.00005	.00060	.00135	.00023	.00000	.00016	.00000	.00000	.00013	.00042	.00031	40
45	42600	239	.00561	.00007	.00000	.00157	.00251	.00031	.00002	.00019	.00000	.00000	.00021	.00023	.00049	45
50	38400	383	.00997	.00029	.00010	.00229	.00518	.00073	.00003	.00023	.00000	.00000	.00013	.00029	.00070	50
55	34900	570	.01633	.00032	.00023	.00436	.00808	.00123	.00006	.00052	.00000	.00000	.00032	.00045	.00174	55
60	28200	809	.02869	.00032	.00032	.00589	.01603	.00294	.00014	.00067	.00000	.00000	.00018	.00050	.00170	60
65	21900	859	.03922	.00018	.00046	.00731	.02292	.00370	.00018	.00123	.00000	.00000	.00032	.00037	.00256	65
70	16000	1075	.06719	.00044	.00050	.01244	.04075	.00556	.00000	.00169	.00000	.00000	.00031	.00087	.00462	70
75	11100	1138	.10252	.00054	.00027	.01477	.06631	.00847	.00009	.00270	.00000	.00000	.00018	.00108	.00811	75
80	7100	965	.13592	.00000	.00028	.01620	.08873	.00972	.00042	.00296	.00000	.00000	.00070	.00282	.01408	80
85+	2400	789	.32875	.00042	.00042	.03083	.20458	.03458	.00000	.00583	.00000	.00000	.00042	.01000	.04167	85+
ALL	691900	7892														

CRUDE DEATH RATE			.01141	.00009	.00009	.00185	.00602	.00096	.00005	.00029	.00000	.00043	.00020	.00036	.00106	
STANDARDIZED RATE (1)			.00638	.00005	.00007	.00097	.00269	.00054	.00005	.00016	.00000	.00066	.00019	.00029	.00071	
STANDARDIZED RATE (2)			.01156	.00009	.00010	.00193	.00642	.00101	.00005	.00031	.00000	.00039	.00020	.00038	.00110	
GEOMETRIC MEAN			.00739													

LIFE TABLE FOR ALL CAUSES COMBINED

Age (x)	Midyear Population	Deaths During Year	$_nM_x$	$_nq_x$	l_x	$_nd_x$	$_nL_x$	$_nm_x$	$_na_x$	T_x	$_nr_x$	$\overset{\circ}{e}_x$	Age (x)
0	15700	498	.031720	.030860	100000	3086	97256	.031718	.123924	6752752	.000000	67.528	0
1	58800	71	.001207	.004819	96914	467	386489	.001208	1.500000	6655456	.000000	68.674	1
5	68000	43	.000632	.003152	96447	304	481475	.000631	2.500000	6268967	.000000	64.999	5
10	67600	30	.000444	.002215	96143	213	480209	.000444	2.623239	5787492	.002435	60.197	10
15	63600	57	.000896	.004462	95930	430	478635	.000898	2.639535	5307283	.014754	55.325	15
20	53300	56	.001051	.005246	95500	501	476264	.001052	2.533683	4828648	.035750	50.562	20
25	41800	45	.001077	.005379	94999	511	473762	.001079	2.586840	4352384	.036003	45.815	25
30	39600	60	.001515	.007557	94488	714	470727	.001517	2.601541	3878622	.005365	41.049	30
35	42400	78	.001840	.009160	93774	859	466891	.001840	2.695722	3407895	.002447	36.342	35
40	38500	127	.003299	.016370	92915	1521	461120	.003298	2.728468	2941004	-.001426	31.653	40
45	42600	239	.005610	.027650	91394	2527	451239	.005600	2.732159	2479884	-.007381	27.134	45
50	38400	383	.009974	.048803	88867	4337	434355	.009985	2.658870	2028645	.005275	22.828	50
55	34900	570	.016332	.078871	84530	6667	407263	.016370	2.692022	1594290	.010421	18.861	55
60	28200	809	.028688	.134621	77863	10482	364243	.028777	2.608082	1187027	.017227	15.245	60
65	21900	859	.039224	.179650	67381	12105	307785	.039329	2.594382	822784	.016301	12.211	65
70	16000	1075	.067187	.288841	55276	15966	237262	.067293	2.549924	514999	.007146	9.317	70
75	11100	1138	.102523	.405266	39310	15931	155839	.102227	2.444553	277737	-.014693	7.065	75
80	7100	965	.135915	.501561	23379	11726	86451	.135637	2.403757	121898	-.014693	5.214	80
85+	2400	789	.328750	1.000000	11653	11653	35446	.328750	3.041825	35446	.000000	3.042	85+

NUMBER OF PERSONS DYING (OUT OF 100,000 AT BIRTH) ABOVE AGE X FROM SPECIFIED CAUSES

Age (x)	All Causes	Respiratory T. B.	Other Infec. and Paras.	Neo-plasms	Cardio-vascular	Infl., Pneu., Bronch.	Diar-rheal	Certain Degen-erative	Maternal	Cert. Dis. of Infancy	Motor Vehicle	Other Violence	Other and Unknown	Age (x)
0	100000	763	761	16556	55799	8490	318	2598	0	1828	1417	2811	8659	0
1	96914	763	718	16537	55792	8156	244	2586	0	0	1417	2780	7921	1
5	96447	763	692	16465	55779	8103	211	2579	0	0	1365	2688	7802	5
10	96143	763	677	16422	55779	8103	204	2579	0	0	1280	2596	7740	10
15	95930	763	677	16387	55744	8096	204	2565	0	0	1244	2539	7711	15
20	95500	763	677	16327	55698	8074	204	2543	0	0	1138	2411	7665	20
25	94999	763	677	16273	55663	8074	204	2516	0	0	932	2276	7621	25
30	94488	717	666	16216	55594	8062	204	2493	0	0	843	2118	7575	30
35	93774	717	642	16037	55427	8050	204	2433	0	0	760	1999	7505	35
40	92915	684	620	15905	55130	7984	204	2378	0	0	683	1889	7438	40
45	91394	660	596	15630	54507	7876	204	2307	0	0	623	1697	7294	45
50	88867	629	596	14921	53377	7739	193	2222	0	0	527	1591	7072	50
55	84530	504	551	13925	51123	7422	182	2120	0	0	471	1467	6765	55
60	77863	376	457	12148	47824	6918	159	1909	0	0	342	1268	6462	60
65	67381	260	341	9999	41964	5843	107	1663	0	0	278	1087	5839	65
70	55276	203	200	7746	34888	4702	51	1283	0	0	179	975	5049	70
75	39310	99	81	4791	25203	3380	51	882	0	0	105	767	3951	75
80	23379	15	39	2492	14902	2064	37	462	0	0	77	599	2692	80
85+	11653	15	15	1093	7252	1226	0	207	0	0	15	354	1476	85+

NUMBER OF PERSONS SURVIVING TO AGE X IF SPECIFIED CAUSES WERE ELIMINATED

Age (x)	No Causes	Respiratory T. B.	Other Infec. and Paras.	Neo-plasms	Cardio-vascular	Infl., Pneu., Bronch.	Diar-rheal	Certain Degener-ative	Maternal	Cert. Dis. of Infancy	Motor Vehicle	Other Violence	Other and Unknown	(1) + (2)	(1) + (2) + (5) + (6) + (8)	(1)+(2)+ (5)+(6)+ (8)+part of(9)&(12)	(10) + (11)	Age (x)
		(1)	(2)	(3)	(4)	(5)	(6)	(7)	(8)	(9)	(10)	(11)	(12)					
0	100000	100000	100000	100000	100000	100000	100000	100000	100000	100000	100000	100000	100000	100000	100000	100000	100000	0
1	96914	96914	96956	96933	96921	97243	96987	96926	96914	98730	96914	96945	97643	96956	97359	99585	96945	1
5	96447	96447	96515	96537	96467	96828	96552	96466	96447	98255	96499	96569	97292	96515	97002	99259	96621	5
10	96143	96143	96226	96276	96163	96523	96255	96162	96143	97545	96280	96357	97048	96226	96718	98975	96494	10
15	95930	95930	96013	96058	95985	96316	96042	95963	95930	97728	96102	96200	96862	96013	96511	98764	96373	15
20	95500	95500	95582	95727	95600	95906	95611	95554	95500	97290	95778	95897	96475	95582	96101	98346	96176	20
25	94999	94999	95081	95279	95134	95403	95110	95080	94999	96779	95481	95530	96013	95081	95597	97831	96015	25
30	94488	94534	94580	94823	94651	94902	94558	94592	94488	96259	95057	95174	95543	94626	95152	97382	95748	30
35	93774	93820	93890	94286	94142	94197	93883	93937	93774	95531	94422	94575	94891	93935	94469	96687	95228	35
40	92915	92993	93052	93555	93577	93400	93023	93131	92915	94656	93634	93819	94090	93130	93725	95936	94545	40
45	91394	91495	91552	92298	92670	91979	91501	91677	91394	93107	92161	92475	92694	91653	92347	94543	93252	45
50	88867	88995	89021	90455	91245	89572	88682	89226	88867	90232	89709	90024	90353	89149	89972	92129	90877	50
55	84530	84774	84720	87035	89079	85512	84650	84972	84530	86114	85386	85753	86248	84965	86074	88176	86621	55
60	77863	78211	78129	81944	85459	79260	77995	78474	77863	79322	78776	79183	79743	78478	80021	82012	80111	60
65	67381	67790	67719	73042	80185	69615	67544	68140	67381	68644	68231	68694	69604	68130	70559	72399	69560	65
70	55276	55653	55681	62167	73657	58182	55460	56247	55276	56312	56064	56456	57843	56071	59215	60857	57260	70
75	39310	39673	39697	47080	64603	42558	39440	40344	39310	40047	39932	40328	42113	40064	43518	44834	40966	75
80	23379	23659	23640	30158	53808	26419	23468	24324	23379	23817	23770	24117	26103	23923	27136	28070	24520	80
85+	11653	11792	11800	16334	42241	13640	11723	12309	11653	11871	11892	12197	13985	11941	14267	14850	12447	85+

ADDED YRS OF LIFE																		
TOTAL		.130	.155	2.254	9.101	1.104	.102	.350	.000	1.263	.469	.692	1.450	.286	1.512	3.215	1.169	
WORK	3.252	.062	.037	.640	1.184	.179	.006	.125	.000	.000	.259	.331	.235	.099	.285	.308	.593	

POPULATION, DEATHS, DEATH RATES FOR ALL CAUSES COMBINED, AND SPECIFIED CAUSES

Age Start of Interval	Midyear Population	Deaths During Year	All Causes	Respiratory T. B.	Other Infec. and Paras.	Neoplasms	Cardio-vascular	Infl., Pneu., Bronch.	Diarrheal	Certain Degenerative	Maternal	Cert. Dis. of Infancy	Motor Vehicle	Other Violence	Other and Unknown	Age Start of Interval
0	14600	372	.02548	.00000	.00034	.00000	.00014	.00199	.00075	.00000	.00000	.01260	.00000	.00034	.00932	0
1	55400	63	.00114	.00000	.00009	.00011	.00000	.00023	.00002	.00002	.00000	.00000	.00000	.00014	.00038	1
5	64100	24	.00037	.00000	.00000	.00009	.00002	.00002	.00002	.00000	.00000	.00000	.00008	.00006	.00011	5
10	64800	13	.00020	.00000	.00002	.00002	.00003	.00002	.00000	.00000	.00000	.00000	.00002	.00003	.00008	10
15	58600	17	.00029	.00002	.00002	.00007	.00010	.00000	.00000	.00000	.00000	.00000	.00002	.00003	.00003	15
20	50500	21	.00042	.00004	.00002	.00008	.00008	.00000	.00002	.00002	.00002	.00000	.00004	.00002	.00012	20
25	45800	34	.00074	.00004	.00002	.00017	.00013	.00004	.00000	.00009	.00000	.00000	.00002	.00002	.00011	25
30	45600	43	.00094	.00009	.00002	.00024	.00022	.00000	.00000	.00009	.00009	.00000	.00000	.00000	.00011	30
35	47200	74	.00157	.00004	.00002	.00047	.00038	.00000	.00000	.00006	.00008	.00000	.00000	.00004	.00008	.00038	35
40	41000	106	.00259	.00002	.00005	.00080	.00102	.00010	.00000	.00012	.00002	.00000	.00000	.00005	.00010	.00029	40
45	46200	207	.00448	.00013	.00006	.00169	.00152	.00011	.00004	.00013	.00000	.00000	.00000	.00004	.00015	.00061	45
50	41900	273	.00652	.00007	.00005	.00270	.00251	.00026	.00005	.00017	.00000	.00000	.00000	.00002	.00010	.00060	50
55	39200	366	.00934	.00010	.00008	.00276	.00439	.00054	.00000	.00028	.00000	.00000	.00000	.00008	.00018	.00094	55
60	33600	567	.01687	.00018	.00006	.00420	.00935	.00101	.00000	.00042	.00000	.00000	.00000	.00000	.00021	.00149	60
65	27700	716	.02585	.00018	.00007	.00523	.01513	.00162	.00022	.00083	.00000	.00000	.00000	.00011	.00029	.00217	65
70	22100	1073	.04855	.00014	.00014	.00765	.03172	.00258	.00009	.00077	.00000	.00000	.00000	.00005	.00086	.00457	70
75	15500	1237	.07981	.00019	.00019	.00974	.05497	.00503	.00032	.00206	.00000	.00000	.00000	.00026	.00135	.00568	75
80	10100	1134	.11228	.00000	.00010	.01010	.07535	.00911	.00069	.00208	.00000	.00000	.00000	.00010	.00287	.01188	80
85+	4000	1064	.26600	.00000	.00075	.01850	.18375	.02150	.00050	.00325	.00000	.00000	.00000	.00000	.00625	.03150	85+
ALL	727900	7404															

	All Causes	Respiratory T. B.	Other Infec. and Paras.	Neoplasms	Cardio-vascular	Infl., Pneu., Bronch.	Diarrheal	Certain Degenerative	Maternal	Cert. Dis. of Infancy	Motor Vehicle	Other Violence	Other and Unknown
CRUDE DEATH RATE	.01017	.00005	.00005	.00162	.00580	.00066	.00005	.00022	.00002	.00025	.00005	.00022	.00117
STANDARDIZED RATE (1)	.00454	.00003	.00005	.00075	.00190	.00029	.00004	.00010	.00002	.00044	.00005	.00012	.00075
STANDARDIZED RATE (2)	.00865	.00005	.00005	.00141	.00480	.00055	.00005	.00019	.00002	.00026	.00005	.00019	.00102
GEOMETRIC MEAN	.00484												

LIFE TABLE FOR ALL CAUSES COMBINED

Age (x)	Midyear Population	Deaths During Year	$_nM_x$	$_nq_x$	l_x	$_nd_x$	$_nL_x$	$_nm_x$	$_na_x$	T_x	$_nr_x$	$\overset{\circ}{e}_x$	Age (x)
0	14600	372	.025479	.024920	100000	2492	97790	.025483	.113315	7194531	.000000	71.945	0
1	55400	63	.001137	.004533	97508	442	388927	.001136	1.500000	7096740	.000000	72.781	1
5	64100	24	.000374	.001875	97066	182	484875	.000375	2.500000	6707813	.000000	69.106	5
10	64800	13	.000201	.001001	96884	97	484169	.000200	2.409794	6222938	.003891	64.231	10
15	58600	17	.000290	.001446	96787	140	483607	.000289	2.656250	5738770	.019434	59.293	15
20	50500	21	.000416	.002090	96647	202	482775	.000418	2.724835	5255163	.024989	54.375	20
25	45800	34	.000742	.003712	96445	358	481382	.000744	2.845484	4772387	.016170	49.483	25
30	45600	43	.000943	.004704	96087	452	479386	.000943	2.679757	4291005	-.001953	44.658	30
35	47200	74	.001568	.007821	95635	748	476465	.001570	2.714182	3811619	.007739	39.856	35
40	41000	106	.002565	.012868	94887	1221	471659	.002589	2.726249	3335154	.003132	35.149	40
45	46200	207	.004481	.022143	93666	2074	463503	.004475	2.672774	2863495	-.007289	30.571	45
50	41900	273	.006516	.032110	91592	2941	451021	.006521	2.640613	2399992	.005748	26.203	50
55	39200	366	.009337	.045786	88651	4059	433930	.009354	2.702636	1948971	.009160	21.985	55
60	33600	567	.016875	.081438	84592	6889	406871	.016932	2.664574	1515041	.016518	17.910	60
65	27700	716	.025848	.122273	77703	9501	366426	.025929	2.675113	1108170	.014606	14.262	65
70	22100	1073	.048552	.218102	68202	14875	305542	.048664	2.615588	741743	.011330	10.876	70
75	15500	1237	.079806	.332927	53327	17754	222394	.079831	2.508085	436201	.001572	8.180	75
80	10100	1134	.112277	.437523	35573	15564	138586	.112306	2.476294	213808	.001572	6.010	80
85+	4000	1064	.266000	1.000000	20009	20009	75222	.266000	3.759398	75222	.000000	3.759	85+

NUMBER OF PERSONS DYING (OUT OF 100,000 AT BIRTH) ABOVE AGE X FROM SPECIFIED CAUSES

Age (x)	All Causes	Respiratory T. B.	Other Infec. and Paras.	Neo-plasms	Cardio-vascular	Infl., Pneu., Bronch.	Diar-rheal	Certain Degen-erative	Maternal	Cert. Dis. of Infancy	Motor Vehicle	Other Violence	Other and Unknown	Age (x)
0	100000	439	439	15104	60286	6569	445	2149	146	1233	384	2126	10680	0
1	97508	439	405	15104	60272	6375	371	2149	146	0	384	2092	9771	1
5	97066	439	370	15062	60272	6284	364	2142	146	0	328	2036	9623	5
10	96884	439	370	15017	60265	6276	364	2142	146	0	290	2006	9569	10
15	96787	439	363	15009	60250	6268	364	2142	146	0	282	1991	9533	15
20	96647	431	354	14976	60200	6268	364	2142	146	0	274	1974	9518	20
25	96445	431	345	14938	60162	6268	354	2132	136	0	255	1965	9459	25
30	96087	410	334	14853	60099	6247	354	2090	94	0	244	1954	9408	30
35	95635	368	324	14738	59994	6247	354	2048	52	0	244	1902	9364	35
40	94887	348	314	14515	59811	6247	354	2018	11	0	224	1861	9184	40
45	93666	336	291	14135	59328	6201	354	1960	0	0	201	1815	9045	45
50	91592	276	260	13354	58627	6151	334	1900	0	0	181	1745	8764	50
55	88651	244	239	12137	57495	6033	313	1825	0	0	170	1702	8493	55
60	84592	200	206	10940	55586	5800	313	1703	0	0	137	1624	8083	60
65	77703	151	181	9229	51768	5386	313	1533	0	0	125	1539	7478	65
70	68202	85	155	7308	46205	4790	233	1228	0	0	85	1433	6680	70
75	53327	43	113	4968	36484	3999	205	992	0	0	71	1169	5283	75
80	35573	0	70	2801	24256	2880	134	533	0	0	14	868	4017	80
85+	20009	0	56	1392	13822	1617	38	244	0	0	0	470	2370	85+

NUMBER OF PERSONS SURVIVING TO AGE X IF SPECIFIED CAUSES WERE ELIMINATED

Age (x)	No Causes	Respiratory T. B.	Other Infec. and Paras.	Neo-plasms	Cardio-vascular	Infl., Pneu., Bronch.	Diar-rheal	Certain Degener-ative	Maternal	Cert. Dis. of Infancy	Motor Vehicle	Other Violence	Other and Unknown	(1) + (2)	(1) + (2) + (5) + (6) + (8)	(1)+(2)+ (5)+(6)+ (8)+part of(9)&(12)	(10) + (11)	Age (x)
		(1)	(2)	(3)	(4)	(5)	(6)	(7)	(8)	(9)	(10)	(11)	(12)					
0	100000	100000	100000	100000	100000	100000	100000	100000	100000	100000	100000	100000	100000	100000	100000	100000	100000	0
1	97508	97508	97542	97508	97522	97700	97581	97508	97508	98733	97508	97542	98410	97542	97807	99655	97542	1
5	97066	97066	97134	97108	97348	97680	97146	97073	97066	98286	97122	97155	98113	97134	97497	99407	97211	5
10	96884	96884	96952	96971	96905	97173	96964	96891	96884	98101	96978	97003	97583	96952	97322	99232	97097	10
15	96787	96787	96862	96882	96823	97084	96867	96794	96787	98003	96889	96921	97922	96862	97239	99157	97023	15
20	96647	96655	96731	96775	96733	96944	96726	96655	96647	97861	96757	96758	97795	96739	97116	99033	96908	20
25	96445	96453	96538	96610	96568	96741	96534	96462	96455	97657	96573	96605	97650	96546	96942	98868	96733	25
30	96087	96116	96191	96337	96273	96403	96176	96146	96139	97294	96226	96257	97340	96219	96677	98615	96396	30
35	95635	95706	95748	95599	95925	95950	95723	95735	95729	96837	95773	95856	96926	95819	96317	98257	95995	35
40	94887	94977	95009	95471	95358	95159	94975	95017	95021	96079	95044	95147	96350	95099	95635	97585	95305	40
45	93666	93767	93809	94623	94614	94020	93753	93852	93809	94843	93844	93969	95250	93910	94496	96435	94147	45
50	91592	91750	91763	93312	93222	91988	91657	91833	91732	92743	91786	91958	93424	91921	92565	94489	92152	50
55	88651	88835	88837	91543	91370	89151	88773	88958	88786	89765	88849	89047	90697	89022	89784	91670	89247	55
60	84592	84811	84802	88566	89131	85258	84708	85005	84721	85655	84814	85021	85980	85021	85980	87822	85269	60
65	77703	77951	77920	83086	85822	78753	77810	78246	77822	78679	77918	78202	80471	78169	79455	81204	78419	65
70	68202	68482	68417	74869	81212	69651	68371	68966	68306	69059	68428	68741	71410	68697	70478	72099	68969	70
75	53327	53582	53532	60839	74682	55208	53483	54135	53408	53997	53516	53984	57137	53788	55935	57310	54175	75
80	35573	35778	35744	42623	65850	37785	35736	36493	35627	36020	35746	36260	39230	35950	38419	39452	36436	80
85+	20009	20124	20116	25256	54474	22269	20172	20747	20040	20260	20117	20698	23452	20232	22735	23487	20809	85+

ADDED YRS OF LIFE

		(1)	(2)	(3)	(4)	(5)	(6)	(7)	(8)	(9)	(10)	(11)	(12)				
TOTAL		.100	.122	2.308	10.998	.774	.059	.284	.062	.903	.133	.325	1.910	.223	1.170	2.717	.459
WORK	2.157	.051	.034	.658	.742	.066	.010	.085	.046	.000	.034	.078	.268	.085	.208	.242	.112

POPULATION, DEATHS, DEATH RATES FOR ALL CAUSES COMBINED, AND SPECIFIED CAUSES

Age Start of Interval	Midyear Population	Deaths During Year	All Causes	Respiratory T. B.	Other Infec. and Paras.	Neoplasms	Cardiovascular	Infl., Pneu., Bronch.	Diarrheal	Certain Degenerative	Maternal	Cert. Dis. of Infancy	Motor Vehicle	Other Violence	Other and Unknown	Age Start of Interval
0	16800	538	.03202	.00000	.00024	.00030	.00006	.00268	.00065	.00012	.00000	.01845	.00000	.00024	.00929	0
1	62600	48	.00077	.00000	.00000	.00008	.00003	.00011	.00003	.00000	.00000	.00000	.00011	.00010	.00030	1
5	70900	29	.00041	.00000	.00003	.00011	.00000	.00001	.00000	.00000	.00000	.00000	.00011	.00008	.00006	5
10	66300	26	.00039	.00000	.00000	.00009	.00002	.00003	.00000	.00002	.00000	.00000	.00008	.00009	.00008	10
15	66300	54	.00081	.00000	.00002	.00011	.00011	.00000	.00000	.00000	.00000	.00000	.00008	.00015	.00015	15
20	51300	45	.00088	.00000	.00004	.00006	.00008	.00000	.00000	.00002	.00000	.00000	.00029	.00018	.00021	20
25	42000	41	.00098	.00000	.00000	.00014	.00021	.00002	.00000	.00010	.00000	.00000	.00019	.00012	.00019	25
30	40100	56	.00140	.00000	.00000	.00012	.00040	.00002	.00002	.00015	.00000	.00000	.00022	.00022	.00022	30
35	41200	72	.00175	.00005	.00005	.00032	.00085	.00007	.00002	.00005	.00000	.00000	.00017	.00012	.00007	35
40	43900	150	.00342	.00007	.00002	.00080	.00155	.00023	.00000	.00009	.00000	.00000	.00014	.00027	.00025	40
45	39400	235	.00596	.00005	.00003	.00114	.00338	.00028	.00000	.00010	.00000	.00000	.00025	.00030	.00043	45
50	41000	409	.00998	.00010	.00007	.00224	.00571	.00054	.00005	.00037	.00000	.00000	.00010	.00029	.00051	50
55	35700	589	.01650	.00025	.00006	.00381	.00874	.00157	.00003	.00034	.00000	.00000	.00025	.00050	.00095	55
60	30700	808	.02632	.00039	.00007	.00625	.01436	.00274	.00000	.00068	.00000	.00000	.00029	.00036	.00117	60
65	24000	1024	.04267	.00021	.00029	.00892	.02404	.00475	.00004	.00092	.00000	.00000	.00050	.00062	.00237	65
70	17400	1132	.06506	.00029	.00017	.01144	.03925	.00753	.00000	.00138	.00000	.00000	.00046	.00057	.00397	70
75	11500	1087	.09452	.00052	.00017	.01304	.05861	.01243	.00009	.00235	.00000	.00000	.00052	.00148	.00530	75
80	6300	923	.14651	.00016	.00032	.01841	.08905	.02190	.00032	.00365	.00000	.00000	.00095	.00222	.00952	80
85+	3200	771	.24094	.00000	.00062	.01812	.15719	.03219	.00062	.00437	.00000	.00000	.00031	.00781	.01969	85+
ALL	710600	8037														

	All Causes	Respiratory T. B.	Other Infec. and Paras.	Neoplasms	Cardiovascular	Infl., Pneu., Bronch.	Diarrheal	Certain Degenerative	Maternal	Cert. Dis. of Infancy	Motor Vehicle	Other Violence	Other and Unknown
CRUDE DEATH RATE	.01131	.00007	.00005	.00182	.00600	.00123	.00003	.00026	.00000	.00044	.00021	.00029	.00092
STANDARDIZED RATE (1)	.00617	.00004	.00004	.00093	.00267	.00059	.00003	.00013	.00000	.00065	.00018	.00020	.00071
STANDARDIZED RATE (2)	.01149	.00007	.00005	.00185	.00616	.00126	.00003	.00027	.00000	.00038	.00021	.00029	.00091
GEOMETRIC MEAN	.00674												

LIFE TABLE FOR ALL CAUSES COMBINED

Age (x)	Midyear Population	Deaths During Year	$_nM_x$	$_nq_x$	l_x	$_nd_x$	$_nL_x$	$_nm_x$	$_na_x$	T_x	$_nr_x$	$\overset{\circ}{e}_x$	Age (x)
0	16800	538	.032024	.031150	100000	3115	97273	.032023	.124440	6796454	.000000	67.965	0
1	62600	48	.000767	.003065	96885	297	386798	.000768	1.500000	6699181	.000000	69.146	1
5	70900	29	.000409	.002040	96588	197	482448	.000408	2.500000	6312383	.000000	65.354	5
10	66300	26	.000392	.001961	96391	189	481523	.000393	2.714947	5829936	.002373	60.482	10
15	66300	54	.000814	.004075	96202	392	480078	.000817	2.622236	5348413	.015455	55.596	15
20	51300	45	.000877	.004373	95810	419	478018	.000877	2.536794	4868335	.040943	50.812	20
25	42000	41	.000976	.004885	95391	466	475840	.000979	2.608190	4390317	.031092	46.024	25
30	40100	56	.001397	.006963	94925	661	473046	.001397	2.611258	3914477	.010291	41.238	30
35	41200	72	.001748	.008688	94264	819	469465	.001745	2.734788	3441430	-.008166	36.508	35
40	43900	150	.003417	.016951	93445	1584	463657	.003416	2.747790	2971966	-.001350	31.804	40
45	39400	235	.005964	.029425	91861	2703	453123	.005965	2.712804	2508308	.000898	27.305	45
50	41000	409	.009976	.048734	89158	4345	435770	.009971	2.693949	2055185	-.002442	23.051	50
55	35700	589	.016499	.079563	84813	6748	408309	.016527	2.665049	1619415	.008587	19.094	55
60	30700	808	.026319	.124140	78065	9691	367454	.026373	2.639949	1211107	.011028	15.514	60
65	24000	1024	.042667	.193904	68374	13258	309928	.042778	2.590731	843653	.013497	12.339	65
70	17400	1132	.065057	.280590	55116	15465	237307	.065169	2.525205	533725	.009605	9.684	70
75	11500	1087	.094522	.381554	39651	15129	159922	.094603	2.466235	296418	.004493	7.476	75
80	6300	923	.146508	.530666	24522	13013	88728	.146661	2.396322	136496	.004493	5.566	80
85+	3200	771	.240937	1.000000	11509	11509	47768	.240937	4.150454	47768	.000000	4.150	85+

NUMBER OF PERSONS DYING (OUT OF 100,000 AT BIRTH) ABOVE AGE X FROM SPECIFIED CAUSES

Age (x)	All Causes	Respiratory T. B.	Other Infec. and Paras.	Neoplasms	Cardiovascular	Infl., Pneu., Bronch.	Diarrheal	Certain Degenerative	Maternal	Cert. Dis. of Infancy	Motor Vehicle	Other Violence	Other and Unknown	Age (x)
0	100000	598	404	16315	56000	11236	205	2326	0	1795	1568	2389	7164	0
1	96885	598	381	16287	55995	10976	142	2314	0	0	1568	2366	6258	1
5	96588	598	381	16256	55982	10933	129	2314	0	0	1525	2329	6141	5
10	96391	598	367	16201	55982	10926	129	2314	0	0	1470	2288	6116	10
15	96202	598	367	16158	55975	10911	129	2307	0	0	1434	2245	6078	15
20	95810	598	360	16107	55924	10911	129	2307	0	0	1296	2172	6006	20
25	95391	598	341	16079	55887	10911	129	2297	0	0	1157	2088	5904	25
30	94925	598	341	16011	55784	10900	129	2252	0	0	1066	2032	5812	30
35	94264	598	341	15952	55595	10888	118	2181	0	0	960	1925	5706	35
40	93445	575	318	15804	55197	10854	118	2158	0	0	880	1869	5672	40
45	91861	543	308	15435	54479	10748	118	2116	0	0	817	1742	5555	45
50	89158	520	296	14917	52949	10622	118	2070	0	0	702	1604	5360	50
55	84813	479	264	13940	50463	10388	96	1910	0	0	659	1476	5139	55
60	78065	375	242	12381	46889	9746	85	1773	0	0	556	1476	5139	60
65	68374	231	217	10079	41598	8738	85	1521	0	0	448	1139	4318	65
70	55116	166	127	7311	34126	7262	72	1236	0	0	293	945	3578	70
75	39651	98	86	4594	24793	5472	72	909	0	0	184	808	2635	75
80	24522	15	58	2507	15413	3481	58	533	0	0	101	571	1785	80
85+	11509	0	30	866	7508	1538	30	209	0	0	15	373	940	85+

NUMBER OF PERSONS SURVIVING TO AGE X IF SPECIFIED CAUSES WERE ELIMINATED

Age (x)	No Causes	Respiratory T. B.	Other Infec. and Paras.	Neoplasms	Cardiovascular	Infl., Pneu., Bronch.	Diarrheal	Certain Degenerative	Maternal	Cert. Dis. of Infancy	Motor Vehicle	Other Violence	Other and Unknown	(1) + (2)	(1) + (2) + (5) + (6) + (8)	(1)+(2)+ (5)+(6)+ (8)+part of(9)&(12)	(10) + (11)	Age (x)
		(1)	(2)	(3)	(4)	(5)	(6)	(7)	(8)	(9)	(10)	(11)	(12)					
0	100000	100000	100000	100000	100000	100000	100000	100000	100000	100000	100000	100000	100000	100000	100000	100000	100000	0
1	96885	96885	96908	96913	96890	97141	96947	96897	96885	98668	96885	96908	97781	96908	97226	99482	96908	1
5	96588	96588	96611	96646	96606	96887	96663	96600	96588	98365	96631	96648	97559	96611	96984	99271	96691	5
10	96391	96391	96428	96504	96409	96696	96466	96403	96391	98165	96489	96491	97425	96428	96807	99094	96589	10
15	96202	96202	96238	96358	96227	96521	96277	96221	96202	97972	96336	96345	97273	96238	96633	98919	96479	15
20	95810	95810	95853	96016	95886	96128	95884	95829	95810	97573	96081	96026	96949	95853	96246	98524	96297	20
25	95391	95391	95453	95625	95503	95708	95465	95420	95391	97146	95690	95628	96619	95453	95844	98119	96100	25
30	94925	94925	94987	95225	95140	95251	94999	94998	94925	96672	95423	95278	96249	94987	95387	97654	95778	30
35	94264	94264	94325	94621	94666	94600	94348	94408	94264	95999	94865	94722	95686	94325	94746	97002	95326	35
40	93445	93468	93529	93947	94243	93812	93528	93610	93445	95165	94121	93955	94889	93552	94003	96245	94635	40
45	91861	91915	91953	92723	93366	92327	91943	92065	91861	93551	93551	92489	93358	92007	92557	94777	93221	45
50	89158	89233	89259	90512	92164	89735	89237	89402	89158	90799	89978	89904	90845	89335	89993	92164	90731	50
55	84813	84926	84941	87074	90214	85593	84910	85201	84813	86374	85635	85649	86638	85053	85934	88025	86479	55
60	78065	78268	78204	81696	86764	79408	78165	78554	78065	79502	78922	79034	80129	78407	79857	81848	79901	60
65	68374	68686	68519	73841	81658	70516	68461	69040	68374	69632	69226	69346	70595	68832	71079	72906	70210	65
70	55116	55425	55314	62255	74369	58224	55158	55911	55116	56130	55943	56075	57597	55624	58848	60456	56917	70
75	39651	39931	39827	47440	65280	43517	39710	40504	39651	40381	40339	40459	42276	40109	44085	45408	41161	75
80	24522	24760	24653	31333	54393	28677	24570	25351	24522	24973	25013	25213	26860	24892	29166	30163	25717	80
85+	11509	11631	11589	16177	40420	15068	11550	12125	11509	11721	11798	11970	13241	11712	15389	16045	12271	85+

ADDED YRS OF LIFE																		
TOTAL		.089	.083	2.243	10.555	1.300	.068	.299	.000	1.249	.462	.487	1.514	.173	1.559	3.295	.955	
WORK	3.174	.032	.027	.566	1.362	.155	.007	.099	.000	.000	.256	.220	.272	.059	.222	.240	.477	

POPULATION, DEATHS, DEATH RATES FOR ALL CAUSES COMBINED, AND SPECIFIED CAUSES

Age Start of Interval	Midyear Population	Deaths During Year	All Causes	Respiratory T.B.	Other Infec. and Paras.	Neoplasms	Cardiovascular	Infl., Pneu., Bronch.	Diarrheal	Certain Degenerative	Maternal	Cert. Dis. of Infancy	Motor Vehicle	Other Violence	Other and Unknown	Age Start of Interval
0	15700	366	.02331	.00000	.00025	.00000	.00025	.00157	.00057	.00000	.00000	.01153	.00000	.00013	.00860	0
1	59400	36	.00061	.00000	.00007	.00002	.00003	.00007	.00002	.00000	.00000	.00000	.00008	.00007	.00025	1
5	67400	26	.00039	.00000	.00001	.00003	.00003	.00000	.00000	.00001	.00000	.00000	.00015	.00004	.00010	5
10	62600	15	.00024	.00000	.00002	.00005	.00005	.00000	.00000	.00003	.00000	.00000	.00002	.00005	.00003	10
15	63500	19	.00030	.00000	.00000	.00005	.00005	.00000	.00000	.00000	.00000	.00000	.00005	.00005	.00008	15
20	53100	19	.00036	.00000	.00000	.00006	.00004	.00000	.00000	.00002	.00000	.00000	.00011	.00006	.00008	20
25	43800	24	.00055	.00000	.00000	.00016	.00009	.00002	.00000	.00005	.00005	.00000	.00002	.00007	.00009	25
30	42900	33	.00077	.00007	.00000	.00023	.00012	.00002	.00000	.00002	.00009	.00000	.00000	.00009	.00016	30
35	44300	68	.00153	.00002	.00007	.00059	.00043	.00000	.00000	.00002	.00000	.00000	.00005	.00009	.00027	35
40	46500	91	.00196	.00002	.00000	.00067	.00077	.00011	.00000	.00006	.00000	.00000	.00002	.00009	.00022	40
45	41400	187	.00452	.00002	.00014	.00159	.00150	.00019	.00002	.00007	.00000	.00000	.00012	.00024	.00060	45
50	44000	246	.00559	.00002	.00016	.00216	.00220	.00014	.00000	.00011	.00000	.00000	.00007	.00016	.00073	50
55	39500	369	.00934	.00000	.00000	.00334	.00397	.00061	.00003	.00025	.00000	.00000	.00015	.00010	.00089	55
60	36100	544	.01507	.00017	.00014	.00402	.00795	.00094	.00008	.00044	.00000	.00000	.00011	.00019	.00102	60
65	31400	743	.02366	.00006	.00010	.00439	.01452	.00150	.00010	.00073	.00000	.00000	.00016	.00041	.00169	65
70	23800	1027	.04315	.00004	.00008	.00676	.02714	.00366	.00017	.00134	.00000	.00000	.00050	.00063	.00282	70
75	16700	1194	.07150	.00018	.00000	.01024	.04677	.00587	.00030	.00158	.00000	.00000	.00048	.00120	.00449	75
80	9500	1117	.11758	.00011	.00011	.00979	.08411	.01105	.00053	.00168	.00000	.00000	.00053	.00284	.00684	80
85+	5200	1193	.22942	.00019	.00000	.01269	.15712	.02942	.00038	.00423	.00000	.00000	.00038	.00635	.01865	85+
ALL	746800	7317														

			All Causes	Respiratory T.B.	Other Infec. and Paras.	Neoplasms	Cardiovascular	Infl., Pneu., Bronch.	Diarrheal	Certain Degenerative	Maternal	Cert. Dis. of Infancy	Motor Vehicle	Other Violence	Other and Unknown
CRUDE DEATH RATE			.00980	.00003	.00004	.00154	.00560	.00081	.00005	.00023	.00001	.00024	.00011	.00022	.00092
STANDARDIZED RATE (1)			.00411	.00002	.00004	.00069	.00172	.00030	.00003	.00009	.00001	.00041	.00008	.00011	.00063
STANDARDIZED RATE (2)			.00793	.00003	.00004	.00131	.00438	.00063	.00004	.00019	.00001	.00024	.00010	.00019	.00078
GEOMETRIC MEAN			.00434												

LIFE TABLE FOR ALL CAUSES COMBINED

Age (x)	Midyear Population	Deaths During Year	$_nM_x$	$_nq_x$	l_x	$_nd_x$	$_nL_x$	$_nm_x$	$_na_x$	T_x	$_nr_x$	$\overset{\circ}{e}_x$	Age (x)
0	15700	366	.023312	.022840	100000	2284	97966	.023314	.109631	7313774	.000000	73.138	0
1	59400	36	.000606	.002415	97716	236	390274	.000605	1.500000	7215807	.000000	73.845	1
5	67400	26	.000386	.001929	97480	188	486930	.000386	2.500000	6825533	.000000	70.020	5
10	62600	15	.000240	.001203	97292	117	486159	.000241	2.423433	6338603	.003433	65.150	10
15	63500	19	.000299	.001492	97175	145	485524	.000299	2.581897	5852445	.009073	60.226	15
20	53100	19	.000358	.001793	97030	174	484740	.000359	2.644875	5366920	.032323	55.312	20
25	43800	24	.000548	.002746	96856	266	483656	.000550	2.655075	4882180	.027066	50.407	25
30	42900	33	.000769	.003851	96590	372	482117	.000772	2.762097	4398524	.006706	45.538	30
35	44300	68	.001535	.007629	96218	734	479371	.001531	2.658663	3916407	-.008208	40.703	35
40	46500	91	.001957	.009750	95484	931	475380	.001958	2.808808	3437035	-.001648	35.996	40
45	41400	187	.004517	.022358	94553	2114	467817	.004519	2.659551	2961655	.002521	31.323	45
50	44000	246	.005591	.027586	92439	2550	456237	.005589	2.663562	2493838	-.002783	26.978	50
55	39500	369	.009342	.045790	89889	4116	439926	.009356	2.687277	2037601	.007912	22.668	55
60	36100	544	.015069	.072867	85773	6250	414245	.015088	2.660867	1597675	-.006211	18.627	60
65	31400	743	.023662	.112445	79523	8942	376846	.023729	2.677393	1183429	.013171	14.882	65
70	23800	1027	.043151	.196427	70581	13864	319988	.043327	2.625745	806583	.017647	11.428	70
75	16700	1194	.071497	.305159	56717	17310	241158	.071779	2.549008	486595	.017615	8.579	75
80	9500	1117	.117579	.455148	39407	17936	151850	.118117	2.480742	245437	.017615	6.228	80
85+	5200	1193	.229423	1.000000	21471	21471	93587	.229423	4.358759	93587	.000000	4.359	85+

NUMBER OF PERSONS DYING (OUT OF 100,000 AT BIRTH) ABOVE AGE X FROM SPECIFIED CAUSES

Age (x)	All Causes	Respiratory T.B.	Other Infec. and Paras.	Neoplasms	Cardiovascular	Infl., Pneu., Bronch.	Diarrheal	Certain Degenerative	Maternal	Cert. Dis. of Infancy	Motor Vehicle	Other Violence	Other and Unknown	Age (x)
0	100000	261	303	14746	60611	8720	399	2328	67	1130	888	2261	8286	0
1	97716	261	278	14746	60586	8526	342	2328	67	0	888	2248	7446	1
5	97480	261	252	14740	60573	8500	336	2328	67	0	856	2222	7345	5
10	97292	261	245	14725	60558	8500	336	2321	67	0	783	2201	7295	10
15	97175	261	237	14702	60535	8500	336	2305	67	0	776	2177	7279	15
20	97030	261	237	14679	60512	8485	326	2305	67	0	753	2154	7241	20
25	96856	261	237	14652	60494	8485	336	2296	67	0	698	2127	7203	25
30	96590	260	237	14574	60450	8474	336	2274	45	0	687	2094	7159	30
35	96218	227	237	14461	60393	8463	336	2263	0	0	687	2071	7080	35
40	95484	216	204	14180	60188	8463	336	2252	0	0	666	2028	6951	40
45	94553	206	204	13863	59820	8412	336	2221	0	0	655	1987	6849	45
50	92439	194	137	13117	59119	8321	324	2187	0	0	599	1874	6567	50
55	89889	184	136	12132	58114	8259	324	2135	0	0	568	1801	6236	55
60	85773	184	136	10661	56361	7991	313	2024	0	0	501	1757	5845	60
65	79523	115	79	8996	53063	7601	279	1840	0	0	455	1676	5419	65
70	70581	91	43	7338	47572	7034	243	1563	0	0	395	1520	4782	70
75	56717	78	16	5166	38850	5859	189	1131	0	0	233	1317	3878	75
80	39407	34	16	2692	27522	4438	116	654	0	0	117	1027	2791	80
85+	21471	18	0	1188	14704	2754	36	396	0	0	36	594	1745	85+

NUMBER OF PERSONS SURVIVING TO AGE X IF SPECIFIED CAUSES WERE ELIMINATED

Age (x)	No Causes	Respiratory T.B. (1)	Other Infec. and Paras. (2)	Neoplasms (3)	Cardiovascular (4)	Infl., Pneu., Bronch. (5)	Diarrheal (6)	Certain Degenerative (7)	Maternal (8)	Cert. Dis. of Infancy (9)	Motor Vehicle (10)	Other Violence (11)	Other and Unknown (12)	(1)+(2)	(1)+(2)+(5)+(6)+(8)	(1)+(2)+(5)+(6)+(8)+part of(9)&(12)	(10)+(11)	Age (x)
0	100000	100000	100000	100000	100000	100000	100000	100000	100000	100000	100000	100000	100000	100000	100000	100000	100000	0
1	97716	97716	97741	97716	97741	97908	97772	97716	97716	98839	97716	97729	98550	97741	97989	99721	97729	1
5	97480	97480	97531	97486	97518	97698	97542	97480	97480	98601	97512	97519	98414	97531	97811	99583	97551	5
10	97292	97292	97350	97313	97345	97509	97354	97299	97292	98411	97397	97352	98274	97350	97629	99401	97457	10
15	97175	97175	97240	97219	97251	97392	97237	97198	97175	98292	97287	97259	98172	97240	97520	99291	97371	15
20	97030	97030	97105	97097	97128	97262	97053	97030	97030	98146	97165	97137	98064	97105	97389	99164	97271	20
25	96856	96856	96921	96950	96972	97087	96918	96888	96856	97970	97045	96989	97927	96921	97215	98986	97179	25
30	96590	96591	96655	96761	96750	96831	96652	96644	96612	97700	96790	96756	97702	96656	96982	98755	96956	30
35	96218	96252	96283	96502	96434	96470	96279	96283	96285	97324	96417	96406	97406	96317	96697	98400	96606	35
40	95484	95525	95581	96047	95904	95734	95545	95559	95550	96582	95703	95714	96793	95626	96004	97794	95933	40
45	94553	94607	94649	95428	95337	94851	94613	94658	94619	95640	94780	94821	95952	94703	95129	96910	95050	45
50	92439	92504	92599	94042	93907	92821	92510	92575	92503	93502	92717	92814	94090	92664	93183	94956	93092	50
55	89889	89962	90046	92441	92329	90322	89958	90073	89951	90922	90190	90325	91827	90119	90685	92242	90628	55
60	85773	85843	85923	89697	89879	86450	85850	86057	85833	86759	86126	86233	88013	85993	86808	88500	86587	60
65	79523	79654	79717	84851	86728	80529	79627	79965	79578	80437	79894	80028	82021	79848	81020	82640	80401	65
70	70581	70720	70787	76989	82830	72018	70707	71236	70630	71392	70968	71177	73419	70926	72549	74050	71567	70
75	56717	56840	56906	64017	76381	58955	56867	57634	56756	57369	57173	57379	59844	57030	59478	60793	57841	75
80	39407	39529	39538	46838	67375	42205	39572	40445	39434	39860	39820	40112	42539	39661	42684	43722	40532	80
85+	21471	21549	21554	26853	56656	24345	21619	22230	21486	21718	21755	22178	24013	21633	24715	25411	22472	85+

ADDED YRS OF LIFE	No Causes	(1)	(2)	(3)	(4)	(5)	(6)	(7)	(8)	(9)	(10)	(11)	(12)	(1)+(2)	(1)+(2)+(5)+(6)+(8)	+part of(9)&(12)	(10)+(11)
TOTAL		.049	.097	2.288	11.699	.922	.079	.275	.030	.840	.221	.329	1.667	.147	1.188	2.635	.552
WORK	1.953	.021	.022	.632	.637	.077	.004	.049	.022	.000	.065	.095	.259	.042	.145	.171	.160

POPULATION, DEATHS, DEATH RATES FOR ALL CAUSES COMBINED, AND SPECIFIED CAUSES

Age Start of Interval	Midyear Population	Deaths During Year	All Causes	Respiratory T. B.	Other Infec. and Paras.	Neoplasms	Cardio-vascular	Infl., Pneu., Bronch.	Diar-rheal	Certain Degen-erative	Maternal	Cert. Dis. of Infancy	Motor Vehicle	Other Violence	Other and Unknown	Age Start of Interval
0	29329	2331	.07948	.00034	.00754	.00007	.00031	.01142	.00927	.00010	.00000	.01770	.00000	.00058	.03215	0
1	114699	904	.00788	.00022	.00261	.00009	.00007	.00181	.00059	.00004	.00000	.00000	.00000	.00062	.00183	1
5	142227	492	.00346	.00018	.00145	.00006	.00023	.00025	.00013	.00010	.00000	.00000	.00000	.00035	.00071	5
10	136063	371	.00273	.00040	.00093	.00001	.00021	.00013	.00004	.00011	.00000	.00000	.00000	.00042	.00047	10
15	113455	613	.00540	.00199	.00079	.00005	.00035	.00028	.00002	.00012	.00000	.00000	.00000	.00077	.00102	15
20	81194	655	.00807	.00360	.00086	.00000	.00036	.00034	.00001	.00017	.00000	.00000	.00000	.00111	.00161	20
25	67388	512	.00760	.00426	.00089	.00006	.00043	.00045	.00003	.00022	.00000	.00000	.00000	.00125	.00012	25
30	66045	440	.00666	.00280	.00056	.00017	.00045	.00047	.00006	.00024	.00000	.00000	.00000	.00100	.00091	30
35	58751	436	.00742	.00221	.00051	.00036	.00061	.00060	.00007	.00036	.00000	.00000	.00000	.00094	.00177	35
40	52139	433	.00830	.00194	.00067	.00052	.00081	.00084	.00008	.00067	.00000	.00000	.00000	.00100	.00178	40
45	49002	434	.00886	.00176	.00071	.00104	.00127	.00112	.00012	.00090	.00000	.00000	.00000	.00100	.00094	45
50	46461	569	.01225	.00207	.00069	.00213	.00185	.00140	.00017	.00103	.00000	.00000	.00000	.00097	.00194	50
55	41776	665	.01592	.00215	.00072	.00328	.00321	.00199	.00022	.00122	.00000	.00000	.00000	.00093	.00220	55
60	35424	765	.02160	.00226	.00073	.00466	.00517	.00265	.00028	.00133	.00000	.00000	.00000	.00082	.00370	60
65	28953	1001	.03457	.00204	.00079	.00608	.00888	.00439	.00045	.00159	.00000	.00000	.00000	.00083	.00953	65
70	21282	1104	.05187	.00122	.00103	.00747	.01499	.00766	.00070	.00221	.00000	.00000	.00000	.00094	.01565	70
75	16566	1389	.08385	.00072	.00109	.00791	.02046	.01056	.00078	.00229	.00000	.00000	.00000	.00109	.03894	75
80	9919	1420	.14316	.00081	.00071	.00585	.02157	.01018	.00050	.00121	.00000	.00000	.00000	.00101	.10132	80
85+	5320	1234	.23195	.00056	.00094	.00602	.03252	.01861	.00094	.00169	.00000	.00000	.00000	.00150	.16917	85+
ALL	1115953	15768														

CRUDE DEATH RATE			.01413	.00161	.00122	.00098	.00184	.00158	.00042	.00044	.00000	.00047	.00000	.00078	.00479	
STANDARDIZED RATE (1)			.01158	.00167	.00131	.00066	.00113	.00134	.00048	.00036	.00000	.00062	.00000	.00078	.00323	
STANDARDIZED RATE (2)			.01516	.00182	.00111	.00123	.00221	.00168	.00037	.00053	.00000	.00037	.00000	.00084	.00502	
GEOMETRIC MEAN			.01660													

LIFE TABLE FOR ALL CAUSES COMBINED

Age (x)	Midyear Population	Deaths During Year	$_nM_x$	$_nq_x$	l_x	$_nd_x$	$_nL_x$	$_nm_x$	$_na_x$	T_x	$_nr_x$	$\overset{\circ}{e}_x$	Age (x)
0	29329	2331	.079478	.074750	100000	7475	94058	.079472	.205112	5641230	.000000	56.412	0
1	114699	904	.007881	.030921	92525	2861	362948	.007883	1.500000	5547172	.000000	59.953	1
5	142227	492	.003459	.017131	89664	1536	444480	.003456	2.500000	5184225	.000000	57.818	5
10	136063	371	.002727	.013560	88128	1195	437819	.002729	2.639644	4739745	.010053	53.783	10
15	113455	613	.005403	.026883	86933	2337	429274	.005444	2.693000	4301925	.037018	49.486	15
20	81194	655	.008067	.039718	84596	3360	414723	.008102	2.542659	3872652	.048128	45.778	20
25	67388	512	.007598	.037237	81236	3025	398451	.007592	2.445041	3457928	.022687	42.566	25
30	66045	440	.006662	.032758	78211	2562	384594	.006662	2.478288	3059477	.008518	39.118	30
35	58751	436	.007421	.036458	75649	2758	371434	.007425	2.530593	2674883	.015224	35.359	35
40	52139	433	.008305	.040705	72891	2967	357095	.008309	2.519239	2303448	.012600	31.601	40
45	49002	434	.008857	.043361	69924	3032	342251	.008859	2.569605	1946354	.004515	27.835	45
50	46461	569	.012247	.059499	66892	3980	324884	.012251	2.593959	1604103	.002723	23.980	50
55	41776	665	.015918	.076726	62912	4827	302908	.015936	2.586147	1279219	.008705	20.333	55
60	35424	765	.021596	.102884	58085	5976	276217	.021635	2.622539	976310	.011691	16.808	60
65	28953	1001	.034573	.160088	52109	8342	240548	.034679	2.602818	700093	.016892	13.435	65
70	21282	1104	.051875	.230608	43767	10093	194296	.051946	2.568756	459545	.007318	10.500	70
75	16566	1389	.083846	.346647	33674	11673	139479	.083690	2.524933	265249	-.008308	7.877	75
80	9919	1420	.143160	.522249	22001	11490	80456	.142812	2.428253	125770	-.008308	5.717	80
85+	5320	1234	.231955	1.000000	10511	10511	45315	.231955	4.311183	45315	.000000	4.311	85+

NUMBER OF PERSONS DYING (OUT OF 100,000 AT BIRTH) ABOVE AGE X FROM SPECIFIED CAUSES

Age (x)	All Causes	Respiratory T. B.	Other Infec. and Paras.	Neoplasms	Cardiovascular	Infl., Pneu., Bronch.	Diarrheal	Certain Degenerative	Maternal	Cert. Dis. of Infancy	Motor Vehicle	Other Violence	Other and Unknown	Age (x)
0	100000	10489	5896	8590	15963	10901	1946	3484	0	1664	0	4847	36220	0
1	92525	10457	5187	8584	15934	9827	1073	3474	0	0	0	4793	33196	1
5	89664	10378	4241	8552	15908	9169	858	3458	0	0	0	4568	32532	5
10	88128	10296	3598	8527	15805	9060	799	3415	0	0	0	4412	32216	10
15	86933	10118	3193	8524	15712	9002	780	3366	0	0	0	4228	32010	15
20	84596	9252	2853	8501	15560	8880	772	3313	0	0	0	3897	31568	20
25	81236	7749	2495	8501	15412	8736	767	3241	0	0	0	3434	30901	25
30	78211	6052	2182	8477	15240	8559	755	3152	0	0	0	2938	30856	30
35	75649	4977	1967	8413	15065	8378	732	3059	0	0	0	2554	30504	35
40	72891	4156	1777	8280	14837	8156	707	2926	0	0	0	2206	29846	40
45	69924	3465	1537	8094	14549	7854	679	2686	0	0	0	1850	29210	45
50	66892	2864	1293	7738	14116	7470	637	2378	0	0	0	1508	28888	50
55	62912	2193	1069	7045	13514	7015	581	2043	0	0	0	1193	28259	55
60	58085	1540	852	6050	12541	6413	516	1673	0	0	0	910	27590	60
65	52109	916	649	4762	11110	5679	438	1306	0	0	0	684	26565	65
70	43767	427	457	3297	8967	4619	329	923	0	0	0	485	24263	70
75	33674	190	256	1845	6051	3129	192	454	0	0	0	302	21215	75
80	22001	89	105	742	3199	1657	83	174	0	0	0	151	15801	80
85+	10511	26	43	273	1474	843	43	77	0	0	0	68	7664	85+

NUMBER OF PERSONS SURVIVING TO AGE X IF SPECIFIED CAUSES WERE ELIMINATED

Age (x)	No Causes	Respiratory T. B. (1)	Other Infec. and Paras. (2)	Neoplasms (3)	Cardiovascular (4)	Infl., Pneu., Bronch. (5)	Diarrheal (6)	Certain Degenerative (7)	Maternal (8)	Cert. Dis. of Infancy (9)	Motor Vehicle (10)	Other Violence (11)	Other and Unknown (12)	(1) + (2)	(1) + (2) + (5) + (6) + (8)	(1)+(2)+ (5)+(6)+ (8)+part of(9)&(12)	(10) + (11)	Age (x)
0	100000	100000	100000	100000	100000	100000	100000	100000	100000	100000	100000	100000	100000	100000	100000	100000	100000	0
1	92525	92556	93209	92531	92553	93564	93368	92535	92525	94139	92525	92577	100000	95479	93240	95146	99724	92577	1
5	89664	89772	91270	89701	89717	91328	90695	89689	89664	91228	89664	89936	93204	91380	94146	99299	89936	5
10	88128	88315	90358	88189	88282	89873	89201	88195	88128	89665	88128	88551	91933	90550	93467	98840	88551	10
15	86933	87295	88546	86696	87177	88714	88010	87048	86933	88450	86933	87534	90901	89919	92898	98392	87534	15
20	84596	85811	87485	84680	84984	86452	85652	84760	84596	86072	84596	85510	88914	88741	91820	97605	85510	20
25	81236	83911	84373	81317	81755	83162	82255	81465	81236	82653	81236	82574	86071	87152	90338	96607	82574	25
30	78211	82525	81551	78313	78880	80244	79204	78519	78211	79575	78211	79995	82913	86049	89406	95650	79995	30
35	75649	80944	79100	75811	76470	77758	76623	76039	75649	76969	75649	77762	80565	84636	88172	94623	77762	35
40	72891	78859	76411	73178	73909	75186	73864	73398	72891	74163	72891	75279	78319	82668	86409	93224	75279	40
45	69924	76384	73548	70383	71188	72432	70885	70648	69924	71144	69924	72515	75803	80343	84368	91462	72515	45
50	66892	73717	70610	67683	68534	69681	67853	67889	66892	68059	66892	69776	72858	77814	82223	89333	69776	50
55	62912	70051	66638	64340	65057	65996	63871	64180	62912	64010	62912	65943	69191	74200	79024	86207	65943	55
60	58085	65377	61746	60390	61042	61543	59034	59619	58085	59098	58085	61169	64593	69498	74837	81974	61169	60
65	52109	59317	55598	55458	56205	55552	53035	53842	52109	53018	52109	55100	59041	63288	69163	76229	55100	65
70	43767	50328	46884	48025	49374	48050	44647	45586	43767	44531	43767	46471	52042	53913	60378	67536	46471	70
75	33674	38956	36260	38361	40974	38427	34473	35464	33674	34261	33674	35924	43362	41948	49004	56109	35924	75
80	22001	25543	23819	26074	29676	26477	22611	23437	22001	22385	22001	23599	34609	27654	34202	41520	23599	80
85+	10511	12253	11425	12838	15841	13329	10830	11267	10511	10694	10511	11335	27898	13318	17402	24611	11335	85+

ADDED YRS OF LIFE																		
TOTAL		3.650	2.512	1.293	2.320	2.508	.807	.714	.000	.981	.000	1.616	9.404	6.380	10.293	16.604	1.616	
WORK	8.568	2.752	.699	.391	.658	.571	.053	.349	.000	.000	.000	.973	1.174	3.513	4.218	5.042	.973	

POPULATION, DEATHS, DEATH RATES FOR ALL CAUSES COMBINED, AND SPECIFIED CAUSES

Age Start of Interval	Midyear Population	Deaths During Year	All Causes	Respiratory T. B.	Other Infec. and Paras.	Neoplasms	Cardiovascular	Infl., Pneu., Bronch.	Diarrheal	Certain Degenerative	Maternal	Cert. Dis. of Infancy	Motor Vehicle	Other Violence	Other and Unknown	Age Start of Interval
0	28137	1817	.06458	.00032	.0C636	.00004	.00021	.01070	.00793	.00004	.00000	.01450	.00000	.00028	.02420	0
1	109756	801	.00730	.00018	.00282	.00002	.00011	.00167	.00058	.00003	.00000	.00000	.00000	.00031	.00159	1
5	137014	473	.00345	.00039	.00147	.00002	.00021	.00037	.00015	.00013	.00000	.00000	.00000	.00012	.00058	5
10	131811	432	.00328	.00085	.00099	.00003	.00030	.00014	.00005	.00016	.00000	.00000	.00000	.00008	.00068	10
15	116810	512	.00438	.00227	.00075	.00003	.00032	.00016	.00002	.00013	.00008	.00000	.00000	.00006	.00057	15
20	98322	565	.00575	.00315	.00054	.00003	.00026	.00023	.00004	.00017	.00028	.00000	.00000	.00006	.00097	20
25	86056	521	.00605	.00374	.00040	.00010	.00031	.00031	.00005	.00022	.00040	.00000	.00000	.00006	.00046	25
30	80036	502	.00627	.00327	.00044	.00024	.00047	.00045	.00004	.00029	.00042	.00000	.00000	.00010	.00055	30
35	70037	505	.00721	.00297	.00040	.00044	.00063	.00056	.00004	.00034	.00043	.00000	.00000	.00011	.00129	35
40	63031	450	.00714	.00230	.00023	.00071	.00067	.00054	.00008	.00038	.00030	.00000	.00000	.00011	.00171	40
45	60247	477	.00792	.00158	.00035	.00118	.00106	.00070	.00008	.00050	.00018	.00000	.00000	.00012	.00178	45
50	55606	590	.01061	.00214	.00047	.00191	.00183	.00103	.00005	.00068	.00000	.00000	.00000	.00009	.00241	50
55	49612	663	.01336	.00206	.00050	.00278	.00314	.00163	.00008	.00095	.00000	.00000	.00000	.00010	.00212	55
60	41158	812	.01971	.00184	.00044	.00386	.00502	.00238	.00017	.00143	.00000	.00000	.00000	.00017	.00439	60
65	34529	963	.02789	.00168	.00046	.00495	.00808	.00440	.00038	.00162	.00000	.00000	.00000	.00026	.00605	65
70	25720	1214	.04720	.00159	.00051	.00579	.01291	.00836	.00082	.00128	.00000	.00000	.00000	.00035	.01559	70
75	19975	1583	.07925	.00125	.00055	.00626	.01722	.01161	.00100	.00115	.00000	.00000	.00000	.00045	.03975	75
80	12693	1560	.12290	.00039	.00039	.00536	.01765	.01079	.00047	.00102	.00000	.00000	.00000	.00039	.08643	80
85+	7563	1599	.21142	.00026	.00066	.00569	.02671	.01944	.00093	.00145	.00000	.00000	.00000	.00066	.15563	85+
ALL	1228153	16039														

CRUDE DEATH RATE			.01306	.00183	.00059	.00054	.00180	.00154	.00034	.00039	.00013	.00033	.00000	.00014	.00462	
STANDARDIZED RATE (1)			.01005	.00178	.00116	.00058	.00103	.00123	.00043	.00030	.00014	.00051	.00000	.00013	.00276	
STANDARDIZED RATE (2)			.01330	.00192	.00092	.00107	.00197	.00159	.00033	.00043	.00014	.00030	.00000	.00014	.00449	
GEOMETRIC MEAN			.01474													

LIFE TABLE FOR ALL CAUSES COMBINED

Age (x)	Midyear Population	Deaths During Year	$_nM_x$	$_nq_x$	l_x	$_nd_x$	$_nL_x$	$_nm_x$	$_na_x$	T_x	$_nr_x$	$\overset{o}{e}_x$	Age (x)
0	28137	1817	.064577	.061330	100000	6133	94970	.064579	.179781	5932437	.000000	59.324	0
1	109756	801	.007298	.028668	93867	2691	368741	.007298	1.500000	5833468	.000000	62.189	1
5	137014	473	.003452	.017099	91176	1559	451983	.003449	2.500000	5468727	.000000	59.980	5
10	131811	432	.003277	.016269	89617	1458	444514	.003280	2.551012	5016745	.007371	55.980	10
15	116810	512	.004383	.021733	88159	1916	436211	.004392	2.607646	4572230	.020371	51.863	15
20	98322	565	.005746	.028385	86243	2448	425217	.005757	2.549700	4136019	.025763	47.958	20
25	86056	521	.006054	.029835	83795	2500	412738	.006057	2.505333	3710802	.017383	44.284	25
30	80036	502	.006272	.030900	81295	2512	400256	.006276	2.524134	3298064	.014075	40.569	30
35	70037	505	.007210	.035426	78783	2791	386970	.007212	2.511495	2897808	.017716	36.782	35
40	63031	450	.007139	.035083	75992	2666	373307	.007142	2.504532	2510839	.010821	33.041	40
45	60247	477	.007917	.038854	73326	2849	359712	.007920	2.571809	2137532	.005235	29.151	45
50	55606	590	.010610	.051762	70477	3648	343515	.010618	2.584864	1777820	.006796	25.226	50
55	49612	663	.013364	.064867	66829	4335	323776	.013389	2.607987	1434245	.013816	21.461	55
60	41158	812	.019710	.094329	62494	5895	298376	.019757	2.609167	1110469	.015351	17.769	60
65	34529	963	.027890	.131168	56599	7424	265384	.027975	2.627823	812093	.018129	14.348	65
70	25720	1214	.047201	.212506	49175	10450	220873	.047312	2.607496	546709	.011129	11.118	70
75	19975	1583	.079249	.330949	38725	12816	161929	.079146	2.526871	325836	-.006030	8.414	75
80	12693	1560	.122902	.467135	25909	12103	98607	.122740	2.443747	163907	-.006030	6.326	80
85+	7563	1599	.211424	1.000000	13806	13806	65300	.211424	4.729831	65300	.000000	4.730	85+

NUMBER OF PERSONS DYING (OUT OF 100,000 AT BIRTH) ABOVE AGE X FROM SPECIFIED CAUSES

Age (x)	All Causes	Respiratory T.B.	Other Infec. and Paras.	Neoplasms	Cardiovascular	Infl., Pneu., Bronch.	Diarrheal	Certain Degenerative	Maternal	Cert. Dis. of Infancy	Motor Vehicle	Other Violence	Other and Unknown	Age (x)
0	100000	11575	4912	8282	16165	11834	1838	3002	832	1377	0	891	39292	0
1	93867	11544	4308	8278	16145	10818	1085	2999	832	0	0	864	36994	1
5	91176	11477	3270	8272	16105	10203	870	2989	832	0	0	750	36408	5
10	89617	11302	2604	8262	16009	10035	801	2929	832	0	0	693	36150	10
15	88159	10923	2163	8248	15874	9975	781	2858	832	0	0	660	35845	15
20	86243	9929	1835	8237	15736	9904	773	2802	798	0	0	634	35595	20
25	83795	8585	1607	8224	15624	9804	756	2729	676	0	0	608	35182	25
30	81295	7040	1444	8180	15494	9674	737	2637	513	0	0	584	34992	30
35	78783	5731	1269	8085	15304	9494	722	2522	343	0	0	544	34769	35
40	75992	4583	1114	7913	15060	9278	705	2390	177	0	0	499	34273	40
45	73326	3725	990	7646	14811	9077	675	2247	65	0	0	458	33632	45
50	70477	3015	865	7222	14428	8826	645	2068	0	0	0	416	32992	50
55	66829	2279	704	6566	13797	8473	627	1833	0	0	0	385	32165	55
60	62494	1614	541	5664	12776	7943	601	1526	0	0	0	353	31476	60
65	56599	1064	410	4510	11273	7231	550	1098	0	0	0	302	30161	65
70	49175	618	287	3194	9121	6057	449	667	0	0	0	232	28550	70
75	38725	266	176	1913	6265	4207	268	384	0	0	0	155	25091	75
80	25909	64	87	900	3478	2328	106	198	0	0	0	82	18666	80
85+	13806	17	43	371	1744	1269	60	95	0	0	0	43	10164	85+

NUMBER OF PERSONS SURVIVING TO AGE X IF SPECIFIED CAUSES WERE ELIMINATED

Age (x)	No Causes	Respiratory T.B. (1)	Other Infec. and Paras. (2)	Neoplasms (3)	Cardiovascular (4)	Infl., Pneu., Bronch. (5)	Diarrheal (6)	Certain Degenerative (7)	Maternal (8)	Cert. Dis. of Infancy (9)	Motor Vehicle (10)	Other Violence (11)	Other and Unknown (12)	(1)+(2)	(1)+(2)+(5)+(6)+(8)	(1)+(2)+(5)+(6)+(8)+part of(9)&(12)	(10)+(11)	Age (x)
0	100000	100000	100000	100000	100000	100000	100000	100000	100000	100000	100000	100000	100000	100000	100000	100000	100000	0
1	93867	93897	94454	93871	93886	94856	94599	93870	93867	95210	93867	93893	96120	94484	96225	99861	93893	1
5	91176	91271	92781	91186	91234	92752	92101	91189	91176	92461	91176	91314	93557	92878	95442	99627	91314	5
10	89617	89884	91870	89636	89770	91335	90555	89689	89617	90900	89617	89809	92615	92143	94935	99333	89809	10
15	88159	88800	90824	88192	88443	89910	89142	88300	88159	89421	88159	88381	91421	91484	94341	98976	88381	15
20	86243	87866	89515	86286	86658	88027	87212	86437	86277	87477	86243	86486	89691	90863	93822	98675	86486	20
25	83795	86733	86886	83850	84309	84754	84055	83948	83795	84994	83795	84057	87569	89932	93122	98363	84057	25
30	81295	85735	84460	81392	81923	83206	82244	81639	81605	82458	81295	81572	85152	89073	92582	97989	81572	30
35	78783	84455	82029	78970	79580	80816	79718	79230	79251	79911	78783	79091	82752	87935	91818	97399	79091	35
40	75992	82680	79282	76343	77004	78171	76910	76553	76608	77080	75992	76334	80334	86259	90533	96495	76334	40
45	73326	80701	77628	73929	74551	75632	74242	74031	74031	74365	73326	73696	78184	84335	88921	95310	73696	45
50	70477	78335	73778	71477	72037	72948	71387	71311	71219	71486	70477	70874	75818	82004	86880	93567	70874	50
55	66829	75080	70124	68428	68940	69529	67710	67852	67532	67785	66829	67236	72765	78781	83918	90867	67236	55
60	62494	70934	65740	64889	65496	65555	63343	63753	63152	63388	62494	62906	68774	74619	80171	87161	62906	60
65	56599	64837	59670	59918	60836	60087	57417	58156	57195	57409	56599	57021	63680	68355	74391	81443	57021	65
70	49175	56808	51963	53369	55055	53381	49982	50939	49692	49879	49175	49607	57048	60029	66930	73990	49607	70
75	38725	45093	41024	43267	46272	43850	39523	40371	39133	39279	38725	39134	48652	47770	55789	63454	39134	75
80	25909	30356	27523	29868	33759	31103	26576	27165	26182	26280	25909	26242	39903	32247	40125	49149	26242	80
85+	13806	16215	14700	16360	19687	17512	14195	14553	13951	14004	13806	14012	33088	17265	22753	32280	14012	85+

ADDED YRS OF LIFE		(1)	(2)	(3)	(4)	(5)	(6)	(7)	(8)	(9)	(10)	(11)	(12)				
TOTAL		4.235	2.345	1.335	2.442	2.554	.763	.665	.320	.847	.000	.277	10.337	6.790	11.113	17.633	.277
WORK	7.348	2.948	.499	.434	.621	.440	.045	.296	.266	.000	.000	.082	1.045	3.491	4.339	5.166	.082

POPULATION, DEATHS, DEATH RATES FOR ALL CAUSES COMBINED, AND SPECIFIED CAUSES

Age Start of Interval	Midyear Population	Deaths During Year	All Causes	Respiratory T. B.	Other Infec. and Paras.	Neoplasms	Cardiovascular	Infl., Pneu., Bronch.	Diarrheal	Certain Degenerative	Maternal	Cert. Dis. of Infancy	Motor Vehicle	Other Violence	Other and Unknown	Age Start of Interval
0	33685	2302	.06834	.00030	.00591	.00003	.00056	.01285	.00401	.00006	.00000	.02060	.00000	.00050	.02351	0
1	115382	777	.00673	.00017	.00254	.00007	.00011	.00192	.00025	.00006	.00000	.00000	.00000	.00076	.00085	1
5	142742	508	.00356	.00012	.00142	.00004	.00021	.00032	.00006	.00008	.00000	.00000	.00000	.00041	.00091	5
10	139714	347	.00248	.00038	.00085	.00000	.00019	.00021	.00003	.00009	.00000	.00000	.00000	.00038	.00036	10
15	134385	688	.00512	.00201	.00099	.00005	.00022	.00051	.00004	.00018	.00000	.00000	.00000	.00065	.00048	15
20	117806	1013	.00860	.00401	.00100	.00010	.00025	.00088	.00001	.00018	.00000	.00000	.00000	.00101	.00116	20
25	99240	754	.00760	.00303	.00082	.00014	.00034	.00077	.00002	.00020	.00000	.00000	.00000	.00083	.00145	25
30	81246	570	.00702	.00238	.00055	.00020	.00048	.00073	.00001	.00030	.00000	.00000	.00000	.00084	.00154	30
35	69531	442	.00636	.00180	.00043	.00035	.00068	.00073	.00001	.00039	.00000	.00000	.00000	.00081	.00116	35
40	66902	475	.00710	.00176	.00057	.00048	.00087	.00087	.00003	.00051	.00000	.00000	.00000	.00084	.00118	40
45	57995	502	.00866	.00155	.00059	.00058	.00143	.00098	.00002	.00072	.00000	.00000	.00000	.00083	.00155	45
50	49793	491	.00986	.00139	.00046	.00185	.00219	.00056	.00000	.00106	.00000	.00000	.00000	.00070	.00125	50
55	45271	632	.01396	.00135	.00046	.00318	.00389	.00135	.00004	.00133	.00000	.00000	.00000	.00068	.00168	55
60	40066	895	.02234	.00160	.00062	.00537	.00659	.00212	.00012	.00140	.00000	.00000	.00000	.00075	.00377	60
65	33906	1088	.03209	.00156	.00071	.00743	.01097	.00339	.00021	.00159	.00000	.00000	.00000	.00080	.00543	65
70	25019	1290	.05156	.00128	.00072	.00935	.01767	.00536	.00040	.00192	.00000	.00000	.00000	.00092	.01395	70
75	16874	1413	.08374	.00095	.00071	.01043	.02501	.00800	.00047	.00219	.00000	.00000	.00000	.00107	.03491	75
80	8724	1191	.13652	.00046	.00057	.00848	.02694	.00883	.00011	.00195	.00000	.00000	.00000	.00092	.08826	80
85+	5367	1409	.26253	.00037	.00093	.00894	.04043	.01602	.00019	.00261	.00000	.00000	.00000	.00149	.19154	85+
ALL	1283648	16787														

CRUDE DEATH RATE	.01308	.00153	.00111	.00110	.00206	.00151	.00017	.00044	.00000	.00054	.00000	.00071	.00389
STANDARDIZED RATE (1)	.01079	.00146	.00122	.00073	.00130	.00143	.00021	.00035	.00000	.00073	.00000	.00069	.00267
STANDARDIZED RATE (2)	.01449	.00156	.00102	.00143	.00263	.00160	.00016	.00053	.00000	.00043	.00000	.00073	.00442
GEOMETRIC MEAN	.01578													

LIFE TABLE FOR ALL CAUSES COMBINED

Age (x)	Midyear Population	Deaths During Year	$_nM_x$	$_nq_x$	l_x	$_nd_x$	$_nL_x$	$_nm_x$	$_na_x$	T_x	$_nr_x$	$\overset{\circ}{e}_x$	Age (x)
0	33685	2302	.068339	.064740	100000	6474	94731	.068341	.186176	5780765	.000000	57.808	0
1	115382	777	.006734	.026485	93526	2477	367912	.006733	1.500000	5686033	.000000	60.796	1
5	142742	508	.003559	.017639	91049	1606	451230	.003559	2.500000	5318122	.000000	58.409	5
10	139714	347	.002484	.012343	89443	1104	444587	.002483	2.619641	4866892	.000875	54.413	10
15	134385	688	.005120	.025357	88339	2240	436621	.005130	2.735026	4422305	.007525	50.061	15
20	117806	1013	.008599	.042172	86099	3631	421590	.008663	2.547565	3985683	.018078	46.292	20
25	99240	754	.007598	.037214	82468	3069	404480	.007588	2.438973	3564093	.026277	43.218	25
30	81246	570	.007016	.034408	79399	2732	390025	.007005	2.448908	3159613	.030701	39.794	30
35	69531	442	.006357	.031291	76667	2399	377309	.006358	2.487929	2769588	.017733	36.125	35
40	66902	475	.007100	.034914	74268	2593	364991	.007104	2.551581	2392279	.010482	32.211	40
45	57995	502	.008656	.042428	71675	3041	350922	.008666	2.549189	2027288	.019469	28.284	45
50	49793	491	.009861	.048241	68634	3311	335180	.009878	2.586895	1676366	.016784	24.425	50
55	45271	632	.013960	.067694	65323	4422	316217	.013984	2.648594	1341185	.009584	20.532	55
60	40066	895	.022338	.106156	60901	6465	289104	.022361	2.619328	1024968	.006156	16.830	60
65	33906	1088	.032089	.149258	54436	8125	252738	.032148	2.607154	735854	.011156	13.518	65
70	25019	1290	.051561	.229837	46311	10644	205837	.051711	2.583791	483116	.014615	10.432	70
75	16874	1413	.083738	.347829	35667	12406	147562	.084073	2.519547	277279	.017800	7.774	75
80	8724	1191	.136520	.507631	23261	11808	86091	.137156	2.441265	129717	.017800	5.577	80
85+	5367	1409	.262530	1.000000	11453	11453	43625	.262530	3.809084	43625	.000000	3.809	85+

NUMBER OF PERSONS DYING (OUT OF 100,000 AT BIRTH) ABOVE AGE X FROM SPECIFIED CAUSES

Age (x)	All Causes	Respiratory T.B.	Other Infec. and Paras.	Neoplasms	Cardiovascular	Infl., Pneu., Bronch.	Diarrheal	Certain Degenerative	Maternal	Cert. Dis. of Infancy	Motor Vehicle	Other Violence	Other and Unknown	Age (x)
0	100000	9114	5494	10557	19971	10262	842	3626	0	1952	0	4317	33865	0
1	93526	9086	4935	10554	19918	9044	462	3620	0	0	0	4269	31638	1
5	91049	9022	4001	10528	19876	8339	370	3598	0	0	0	3989	31326	5
10	89443	8568	3362	10512	19781	8194	341	3563	0	0	0	3805	30917	10
15	88339	8800	2984	10512	19656	8102	328	3525	0	0	0	3637	30755	15
20	86099	7920	2551	10490	19601	7880	312	3447	0	0	0	3350	30548	20
25	82468	6228	2129	10447	19497	7509	309	3371	0	0	0	2924	30055	25
30	79399	5005	1800	10389	19358	7198	300	3290	0	0	0	2590	29469	30
35	76667	4082	1585	10312	19170	6915	296	3174	0	0	0	2264	28869	35
40	74268	3405	1422	10181	18915	6638	290	3027	0	0	0	1960	28430	40
45	71675	2761	1215	10006	18598	6322	279	2841	0	0	0	1654	27999	45
50	68634	2217	1009	9660	18094	5976	273	2587	0	0	0	1364	27454	50
55	65323	1753	855	9038	17357	5653	273	2229	0	0	0	1129	27036	55
60	60901	1327	708	8030	16125	5226	259	1810	0	0	0	912	26504	60
65	54436	865	527	6477	14218	4612	223	1406	0	0	0	696	25412	65
70	46311	470	348	4596	11439	3753	171	1003	0	0	0	494	24037	70
75	35667	207	200	2669	7793	2648	88	607	0	0	0	305	21150	75
80	23261	67	95	1128	4094	1464	18	284	0	0	0	147	15964	80
85+	11453	16	41	390	1764	699	8	114	0	0	0	65	8356	85+

NUMBER OF PERSONS SURVIVING TO AGE X IF SPECIFIED CAUSES WERE ELIMINATED

Age (x)	No Causes	Respiratory T.B. (1)	Other Infec. and Paras. (2)	Neoplasms (3)	Cardiovascular (4)	Infl., Pneu., Bronch. (5)	Diarrheal (6)	Certain Degenerative (7)	Maternal (8)	Cert. Dis. of Infancy (9)	Motor Vehicle (10)	Other Violence (11)	Other and Unknown (12)	(1)+(2)	(1)+(2)+(5)+(6)+(8)	(1)+(2)+(5)+(6)+(8)+part of (9)&(12)	(10)+(11)	Age (x)
0	100000	100000	100000	100000	100000	100000	100000	100000	100000	100000	100000	100000	100000	100000	100000	100000	100000	0
1	93526	93553	94068	93529	93577	94711	93894	93532	93526	95433	93526	93572	95704	94095	95663	99680	93572	1
5	91049	91139	92508	91077	91140	92910	91459	91076	91049	92505	91049	91371	93485	92599	94958	99224	91371	5
10	89443	89584	91523	89487	89627	91418	89514	89505	89443	91266	89443	89443	92253	91667	94184	98738	89943	10
15	88339	88646	90778	88382	88605	90383	88817	88438	88339	90140	88339	89000	91281	91094	93705	98360	89000	15
20	86099	87275	88916	86163	86453	88316	86580	86272	86099	87854	86099	87029	89178	90131	92968	97763	87029	20
25	82468	85290	85593	82571	82909	84965	82932	82708	82468	84149	82468	83782	85519	88522	91716	96895	83782	25
30	79399	83366	82744	79556	79561	82117	79855	79710	79399	81018	79399	80997	83323	86877	90367	95993	80997	30
35	76667	81455	80117	76894	77396	79580	77111	77082	76667	78230	76667	78538	81077	85120	88866	94884	78538	35
40	74268	79616	77778	74618	75228	77373	74704	74816	74268	75782	74268	76387	78998	83379	87375	93604	76387	40
45	71675	77517	75275	72186	72918	74996	72107	72388	71675	73136	71675	74030	76651	81411	85697	92110	74030	45
50	68634	74806	72293	69465	70329	72169	69053	69569	68634	70033	68634	71183	74010	78794	83359	89897	71183	50
55	65323	71692	68964	66732	67677	69020	65722	66567	65323	66655	65323	67987	70880	75687	80459	86946	67987	55
60	60901	67290	64445	63217	64341	64784	61287	62474	60901	62142	60901	63602	66643	71206	76227	82553	63602	60
65	54436	60630	57785	58050	59449	58528	54815	56234	54436	55546	54436	57063	60709	64360	69680	75808	57063	65
70	46311	51985	49335	51265	53452	50651	46682	48224	46311	47255	46311	48741	53087	55379	61053	66825	48741	70
75	35667	40292	38133	41381	45012	40079	36026	37501	35667	36394	35667	37712	43915	43077	48893	54310	37712	75
80	23261	26401	24958	28437	33213	27220	23551	24727	23261	23735	23261	24727	34327	28326	33560	38703	24727	80
85+	11453	13039	12328	14635	18864	14032	11603	12300	11453	11686	11453	12235	26680	14035	17420	22106	12235	85+

ADDED YRS OF LIFE

	No Causes	(1)	(2)	(3)	(4)	(5)	(6)	(7)	(8)	(9)	(10)	(11)	(12)	(1)+(2)	(1)+(2)+(5)+(6)+(8)	+part of (9)&(12)	(10)+(11)
TOTAL		3.261	2.435	1.509	2.815	2.762	.355	.729	.000	1.175	.000	1.464	7.873	5.876	9.454	14.561	1.464
WORK	8.269	2.461	.732	.415	.680	.768	.020	.354	.000	.000	.000	.801	1.167	3.248	4.121	4.952	.801

POPULATION, DEATHS, DEATH RATES FOR ALL CAUSES COMBINED, AND SPECIFIED CAUSES

Age Start of Interval	Midyear Population	Deaths During Year	All Causes	Respiratory T. B.	Other Infec. and Paras.	Neoplasms	Cardiovascular	Infl., Pneu., Bronch.	Diarrheal	Certain Degenerative	Maternal	Cert. Dis. of Infancy	Motor Vehicle	Other Violence	Other and Unknown	Age Start of Interval
0	32189	1691	.05253	.00031	.00590	.00009	.00034	.00858	.00320	.00003	.00000	.01578	.00000	.00025	.01765	0
1	110748	674	.00609	.00014	.00258	.00005	.00007	.00176	.00026	.00005	.00000	.00000	.00000	.00040	.00077	1
5	137158	413	.00301	.00016	.00137	.00003	.00023	.00031	.00002	.00007	.00000	.00000	.00000	.00008	.00074	5
10	134360	369	.00275	.00060	.00100	.00001	.00019	.00020	.00000	.00019	.00000	.00000	.00000	.00008	.00045	10
15	131743	724	.00550	.00306	.00104	.00005	.00027	.00040	.00005	.00014	.00008	.00000	.00000	.00014	.00028	15
20	122226	817	.00668	.00375	.00072	.00006	.00025	.00065	.00004	.00026	.00029	.00000	.00000	.00005	.00062	20
25	104541	680	.00650	.00328	.00061	.00010	.00033	.00071	.00006	.00017	.00030	.00000	.00000	.00013	.00081	25
30	89428	549	.00614	.00283	.00040	.00028	.00042	.00066	.00003	.00022	.00045	.00000	.00000	.00012	.00072	30
35	79287	533	.00672	.00238	.00029	.00043	.00058	.00064	.00003	.00028	.00045	.00000	.00000	.00011	.00153	35
40	74443	524	.00704	.00201	.00103	.00103	.00070	.00059	.00009	.00040	.00023	.00000	.00000	.00008	.00163	40
45	64482	462	.00716	.00164	.00037	.00167	.00115	.00065	.00005	.00060	.00011	.00000	.00000	.00008	.00084	45
50	57906	538	.00929	.00149	.00047	.00252	.00178	.00081	.00003	.00092	.00000	.00000	.00000	.00014	.00114	50
55	54315	694	.01278	.00133	.00052	.00337	.00309	.00122	.00007	.00120	.00000	.00000	.00000	.00018	.00180	55
60	47683	824	.01728	.00141	.00042	.00419	.00491	.00187	.00013	.00138	.00000	.00000	.00000	.00017	.00281	60
65	41124	1086	.02641	.00134	.00044	.00540	.00875	.00309	.00024	.00163	.00000	.00000	.00000	.00022	.00530	65
70	30759	1334	.04337	.00120	.00062	.00676	.01616	.00491	.00039	.00185	.00000	.00000	.00000	.00036	.01112	70
75	21174	1629	.07693	.00094	.00066	.00756	.02220	.00756	.00052	.00158	.00000	.00000	.00000	.00052	.03500	75
80	11852	1435	.12108	.00042	.00042	.00633	.02084	.00877	.00042	.00160	.00000	.00000	.00000	.00051	.08176	80
85+	7796	1871	.23999	.00026	.00064	.00667	.03130	.01591	.00077	.00218	.00000	.00000	.00000	.00090	.18138	85+
ALL	1353254	16847														
CRUDE DEATH RATE			.01245	.00175	.00098	.00113	.00200	.00135	.00016	.00045	.00013	.00038	.00000	.00016	.00396	
STANDARDIZED RATE (1)			.00934	.00166	.00116	.00071	.00109	.00117	.00019	.00033	.00013	.00056	.00000	.00015	.00221	
STANDARDIZED RATE (2)			.01268	.00174	.00094	.00128	.00220	.00137	.00015	.00049	.00013	.00033	.00000	.00016	.00391	
GEOMETRIC MEAN			.01412													

LIFE TABLE FOR ALL CAUSES COMBINED

Age (x)	Midyear Population	Deaths During Year	$_nM_x$	$_nq_x$	l_x	$_nd_x$	$_nL_x$	$_nm_x$	$_na_x$	T_x	$_nr_x$	$\overset{\circ}{e}_x$	Age (x)
0	32189	1691	.052533	.050310	100000	5031	95770	.052532	.159307	6056449	.000000	60.564	0
1	110748	674	.006086	.023976	94969	2277	374184	.006085	1.500000	5960679	.000000	62.764	1
5	137158	413	.003010	.014931	92692	1384	460000	.003009	2.500000	5586495	.000000	60.269	5
10	134360	369	.002746	.013646	91308	1246	453646	.002747	2.677234	5126495	.000263	56.145	10
15	131743	724	.005496	.027137	90062	2444	444541	.005498	2.639457	4672849	.001515	51.885	15
20	122226	817	.006684	.032893	87618	2882	430940	.006688	2.519229	4228309	.011662	48.258	20
25	104541	680	.006505	.031982	84736	2710	416821	.006502	2.469019	3797368	.021934	44.814	25
30	89428	549	.006139	.030222	82026	2479	403916	.006137	2.493361	3380547	.023187	41.213	30
35	79287	533	.006722	.033075	79547	2631	391195	.006726	2.514412	2976631	.014254	37.420	35
40	74443	524	.007039	.034596	76916	2661	377925	.007041	2.458904	2585436	.012742	33.614	40
45	64482	462	.007165	.035243	74255	2617	364657	.007173	2.547605	2207511	.018141	29.729	45
50	57906	538	.009291	.045493	71638	3259	350381	.009301	2.603879	1842654	.010368	25.722	50
55	54315	694	.012777	.062037	68379	4242	331721	.012788	2.601662	1492273	.007090	21.824	55
60	47683	824	.017281	.083088	64137	5329	308005	.017302	2.620606	1160552	.008155	18.095	60
65	41124	1086	.026408	.124592	58808	7327	276729	.026477	2.637306	852547	.013511	14.497	65
70	30759	1334	.043369	.197316	51481	10158	233279	.043544	2.624943	575818	.019021	11.185	70
75	21174	1629	.076934	.324734	41323	13419	173652	.077275	2.543595	342539	.017721	8.289	75
80	11852	1435	.121077	.464665	27904	12966	106643	.121583	2.464394	168886	.017721	6.052	80
85+	7796	1871	.239995	1.000000	14938	14938	62243	.239995	4.166756	62243	.000000	4.167	85+

NUMBER OF PERSONS DYING (OUT OF 100,000 AT BIRTH) ABOVE AGE X FROM SPECIFIED CAUSES

Age (x)	All Causes	Respiratory T. B.	Other Infec. and Paras.	Neo-plasms	Cardio-vascular	Infl., Pneu., Bronch.	Diar-rheal	Certain Degen-erative	Maternal	Cert. Dis. of Infancy	Motor Vehicle	Other Violence	Other and Unknown	Age (x)
0	100000	10481	5115	10210	19129	10001	945	3647	765	1511	0	1044	37152	0
1	94969	10452	4550	10201	19097	9141	638	3644	765	0	0	1020	35461	1
5	92692	10401	3583	10181	19070	8482	540	3623	765	0	0	871	35176	5
10	91308	10327	2953	10167	18966	8341	530	3590	765	0	0	834	34835	10
15	90062	10054	2458	10161	18878	8250	530	3502	765	0	0	797	34627	15
20	87618	8693	2035	10137	18760	8071	510	3441	731	0	0	736	34504	20
25	84736	7078	1725	10112	18650	7792	492	3329	608	0	0	715	34235	25
30	82026	5712	1471	10072	18511	7497	468	3257	484	0	0	659	33895	30
35	79547	4571	1309	9958	18338	7231	455	3166	303	0	0	610	33606	35
40	76916	3640	1196	9790	18111	6979	445	3058	125	0	0	565	33007	40
45	74255	2879	1069	9398	17847	6756	435	2905	39	0	0	535	32392	45
50	71638	2280	933	8785	17427	6518	418	2684	0	0	0	506	32087	50
55	68379	1760	769	7900	16802	6233	406	2363	0	0	0	458	31688	55
60	64137	1320	598	6781	15774	5830	381	1965	0	0	0	397	31091	60
65	58808	888	469	5489	14260	5254	343	1539	0	0	0	345	30221	65
70	51481	518	348	3993	11830	4397	275	1088	0	0	0	285	28747	70
75	41323	237	203	2413	8047	3248	184	655	0	0	0	201	26135	75
80	27904	74	89	1100	4184	1932	93	310	0	0	0	110	20012	80
85+	14938	16	40	415	1948	990	48	136	0	0	0	56	11289	85+

NUMBER OF PERSONS SURVIVING TO AGE X IF SPECIFIED CAUSES WERE ELIMINATED

Age (x)	No Causes	Respiratory T. B. (1)	Other Infec. and Paras. (2)	Neo-plasms (3)	Cardio-vascular (4)	Infl., Pneu., Bronch. (5)	Diar-rheal (6)	Certain Degener-ative (7)	Maternal (8)	Cert. Dis. of Infancy (9)	Motor Vehicle (10)	Other Violence (11)	Other and Unknown (12)	(1) + (2)	(1) + (2) + (5) + (6) + (8)	(1)+(2)+ (5)+(6)+ (8)+part of(9)&(12)	(10) + (11)	Age (x)
0	100000	100000	100000	100000	100000	100000	100000	100000	100000	100000	100000	100000	100000	100000	100000	100000	100000	0
1	94969	94997	95521	94978	95000	95811	95269	94972	94969	96453	94969	94992	96631	95550	96701	99808	94992	1
5	92692	92770	94157	92720	92749	94173	93082	92716	92692	94140	92692	92862	94601	94276	96185	99545	92862	5
10	91308	91458	93428	91350	91468	92909	91702	91364	91308	92735	91308	91512	93535	93581	95633	99275	91512	10
15	90062	90482	92616	90109	90307	91723	90450	90205	90062	91469	90062	90300	92470	93049	95184	98988	90300	15
20	87618	89386	90573	87688	87973	89424	88016	87817	87652	88987	87618	87910	90085	92402	94770	98679	87910	20
25	84736	88082	87910	84828	85188	86763	85138	85039	84890	86060	84736	85039	87395	91380	94181	98341	85039	25
30	82026	86673	85358	82155	82601	84286	82439	82390	82297	83308	82026	82375	84546	90193	93453	97927	82375	30
35	79547	85248	82944	79784	80277	82008	79961	79991	79989	80790	79547	79934	82674	88889	92627	97342	79934	35
40	76916	83415	80316	77312	77847	79551	77326	77452	77520	78118	76916	77335	80555	87103	91278	96462	77335	40
45	74255	81344	77668	75026	75417	77026	74660	74924	74923	75415	74255	74689	78403	85083	89538	95078	74689	45
50	71638	79123	75071	72993	73180	74554	72046	72503	72321	72757	71638	72085	75956	82915	87609	93203	72085	50
55	68379	76086	71824	70559	70478	71453	68780	69523	69031	69447	68379	68853	72915	79919	84802	90394	68853	55
60	64137	71841	67542	67309	67141	67430	64538	65603	64748	65139	64137	64641	69011	75654	80798	86347	64641	60
65	58808	66335	62060	63027	63100	62410	59212	60570	59368	59727	58808	59320	64181	70003	75514	81002	59320	65
70	51481	58460	54447	56690	57734	55491	51899	53458	51972	52285	51481	51986	57713	61827	67824	73227	51986	70
75	41323	47207	43840	47076	50287	45661	41740	43310	41717	41969	41323	41804	49046	50083	56431	61698	41804	75
80	27904	32026	29701	33016	37979	32036	28260	29538	28170	28340	27904	28303	35706	34088	40013	45619	28303	80
85+	14938	17193	15938	18268	22645	17946	15161	15946	15080	15171	14938	15191	22363	18343	22580	28691	15191	85+

ADDED YRS OF LIFE

	No Causes	(1)	(2)	(3)	(4)	(5)	(6)	(7)	(8)	(9)	(10)	(11)	(12)	(1)+(2)			
TOTAL		4.016	2.420	1.695	2.723	2.487	.346	.756	.301	.944	.000	.327	8.922	6.640	10.304	15.100	.327
WORK	7.581	2.898	.607	.558	.604	.637	.042	.317	.244	.000	.000	.109	.871	3.557	4.591	5.279	.109

POPULATION, DEATHS, DEATH RATES FOR ALL CAUSES COMBINED, AND SPECIFIED CAUSES

Age Start of Interval	Midyear Population	Deaths During Year	All Causes	Respiratory T. B.	Other Infec. and Paras.	Neoplasms	Cardiovascular	Infl., Pneu., Bronch.	Diarrheal	Certain Degenerative	Maternal	Cert. Dis. of Infancy	Motor Vehicle	Other Violence	Other and Unknown	Age Start of Interval
0	23627	1241	.05252	.00025	.00326	.00000	.00055	.00851	.00262	.00008	.00000	.02362	.00000	.00034	.01329	0
1	97361	409	.00420	.00008	.00113	.00009	.00012	.00086	.00013	.00014	.00000	.00000	.00000	.00080	.00083	1
5	141698	266	.00188	.00009	.00058	.00002	.00010	.00011	.00004	.00011	.00000	.00000	.00000	.00049	.00034	5
10	144781	239	.00165	.00010	.00052	.00003	.00011	.00006	.00000	.00010	.00000	.00000	.00000	.00041	.00031	10
15	136834	425	.00311	.00088	.00063	.00011	.00016	.00015	.00001	.00013	.00000	.00000	.00000	.00064	.00041	15
20	121643	651	.00535	.00245	.00064	.00012	.00011	.00024	.00002	.00013	.00000	.00000	.00000	.00106	.00058	20
25	109950	607	.00552	.00268	.00057	.00009	.00026	.00022	.00001	.00015	.00000	.00000	.00000	.00103	.00050	25
30	103261	551	.00534	.00205	.00059	.00020	.00031	.00027	.00001	.00025	.00000	.00000	.00000	.00107	.00058	30
35	90832	506	.00557	.00171	.00056	.00035	.00048	.00034	.00001	.00033	.00000	.00000	.00000	.00109	.00069	35
40	75606	453	.00599	.00139	.00048	.00052	.00071	.00045	.00005	.00040	.00000	.00000	.00000	.00111	.00089	40
45	64206	468	.00729	.00115	.00048	.00097	.00120	.00061	.00006	.00055	.00000	.00000	.00000	.00109	.00118	45
50	61440	550	.00895	.00109	.00062	.00160	.00164	.00083	.00003	.00070	.00000	.00000	.00000	.00098	.00146	50
55	51574	695	.01348	.00107	.00068	.00291	.00330	.00116	.00006	.00109	.00000	.00000	.00000	.00095	.00227	55
60	42717	867	.02030	.00119	.00075	.00520	.00592	.00143	.00012	.00176	.00000	.00000	.00000	.00108	.00286	60
65	36361	1161	.03193	.00124	.00074	.00743	.01040	.00242	.00014	.00234	.00000	.00000	.00000	.00110	.00613	65
70	28724	1239	.04313	.00118	.00059	.00968	.01654	.00414	.00007	.00285	.00000	.00000	.00000	.00091	.00717	70
75	20276	1620	.07990	.00123	.00044	.01169	.02653	.00710	.00010	.00316	.00000	.00000	.00000	.00099	.02865	75
80	10838	1414	.13047	.00148	.00018	.01218	.03700	.00978	.00018	.00231	.00000	.00000	.00000	.00111	.06625	80
85+	5658	1324	.23236	.00088	.00035	.01281	.05581	.01790	.00035	.00333	.00000	.00000	.00000	.00193	.13900	85+
ALL	1367427	14686														
CRUDE DEATH RATE			.01074	.00117	.00067	.00122	.00216	.00091	.00009	.00049	.00000	.00041	.00000	.00086	.00277	
STANDARDIZED RATE (1)			.00845	.00104	.00074	.00075	.00119	.00083	.00013	.00035	.00000	.00083	.00000	.00081	.00178	
STANDARDIZED RATE (2)			.01221	.00116	.00068	.00149	.00261	.00106	.00010	.00057	.00000	.00049	.00000	.00087	.00319	
GEOMETRIC MEAN			.01249													

LIFE TABLE FOR ALL CAUSES COMBINED

Age (x)	Midyear Population	Deaths During Year	$_nM_x$	$_nq_x$	l_x	$_nd_x$	$_nL_x$	$_nm_x$	$_na_x$	T_x	$_nr_x$	$\overset{\circ}{e}_x$	Age (x)
0	23627	1241	.052525	.050300	100000	5030	95771	.052521	.159292	6256158	.000000	62.562	0
1	97361	409	.004201	.016637	94970	1580	375930	.004203	1.500000	6160387	.000000	64.867	1
5	141698	266	.001877	.009337	93390	872	464770	.001876	2.500000	5784457	.000000	61.939	5
10	144781	239	.001651	.008225	92518	761	460801	.001651	2.649474	5319687	-.000949	57.499	10
15	136834	425	.003106	.015454	91757	1418	455580	.003113	2.739480	4858886	.009844	52.954	15
20	121643	651	.005352	.026467	90339	2391	445921	.005362	2.585041	4403306	.016405	48.742	20
25	109950	607	.005521	.027221	87948	2394	433726	.005520	2.487991	3957385	.012111	44.997	25
30	103261	551	.005336	.026334	85554	2253	422116	.005337	2.490291	3523659	.011442	41.186	30
35	90832	506	.005571	.027479	83301	2289	410812	.005572	2.512924	3101544	.021203	37.233	35
40	75606	453	.005992	.029564	81012	2395	399183	.006000	2.546190	2690731	.029359	33.214	40
45	64206	468	.007289	.035870	78617	2820	386229	.007301	2.568853	2291548	-.017806	29.148	45
50	61440	550	.008952	.043894	75797	3327	371069	.008966	2.620792	1905319	.011552	25.137	50
55	51574	695	.013476	.065531	72470	4749	351154	.013524	2.642530	1534250	.021331	21.171	55
60	42717	867	.020296	.097104	67721	6576	323066	.020355	2.637083	1183095	.016452	17.470	60
65	36361	1161	.031930	.148434	61145	9076	283788	.031982	2.582980	860029	-.010056	14.065	65
70	28724	1239	.043135	.155721	52069	10191	235901	.043200	2.601438	576241	.009119	11.067	70
75	20276	1620	.079897	.335212	41878	14038	175018	.080209	2.551482	340340	.014830	8.127	75
80	10838	1414	.130467	.490661	27840	13660	104296	.130973	2.444836	165322	-.014830	5.938	80
85+	5658	1324	.232362	1.000000	14180	14180	61025	.232362	4.303625	61025	.000000	4.304	85+

NUMBER OF PERSONS DYING (OUT OF 100,000 AT BIRTH) ABOVE AGE X FROM SPECIFIED CAUSES

Age (x)	All Causes	Respiratory T. B.	Other Infec. and Paras.	Neoplasms	Cardio-vascular	Infl., Pneu., Bronch.	Diarrheal	Certain Degenerative	Maternal	Cert. Dis. of Infancy	Motor Vehicle	Other Violence	Other and Unknown	Age (x)
0	100000	7597	4108	12822	24006	8367	574	4507	0	2262	0	5704	30053	0
1	94970	7573	3756	12822	23953	7552	323	4499	0	0	0	5672	28780	1
5	93390	7542	3371	12787	23907	7227	272	4445	0	0	0	5371	28468	5
10	92518	7499	3102	12777	23861	7178	253	4392	0	0	0	5144	28312	10
15	91757	7452	2861	12765	23810	7150	253	4348	0	0	0	4954	28164	15
20	90339	7050	2574	12715	23737	7083	249	4288	0	0	0	4663	27980	20
25	87948	5954	2288	12660	23689	6976	242	4229	0	0	0	4190	27720	25
30	85554	4791	2040	12620	23574	6882	238	4162	0	0	0	3744	27503	30
35	83301	3925	1790	12534	23443	6767	234	4055	0	0	0	3294	27259	35
40	81012	3226	1560	12389	23244	6627	229	3919	0	0	0	2846	26972	40
45	78617	2673	1370	12181	22957	6446	208	3760	0	0	0	2403	26619	45
50	75797	2228	1183	11807	22492	6211	184	3549	0	0	0	1982	26161	50
55	72470	1823	954	11213	21881	5903	172	3289	0	0	0	1620	25615	55
60	67721	1449	715	10187	20717	5493	151	2906	0	0	0	1286	24817	60
65	61145	1063	473	8503	18796	5031	113	2338	0	0	0	938	23890	65
70	52069	712	263	6393	15839	4342	74	1674	0	0	0	626	22146	70
75	41878	433	123	4108	11933	3363	58	1000	0	0	0	412	20448	75
80	27840	216	45	2059	7274	2116	41	447	0	0	0	240	15402	80
85+	14180	54	21	782	3406	1092	21	203	0	0	0	118	8483	85+

NUMBER OF PERSONS SURVIVING TO AGE X IF SPECIFIED CAUSES WERE ELIMINATED

Age (x)	No Causes	Respiratory T. B. (1)	Other Infec. and Paras. (2)	Neoplasms (3)	Cardio-vascular (4)	Infl., Pneu., Bronch. (5)	Diarrheal (6)	Certain Degenerative (7)	Maternal (8)	Cert. Dis. of Infancy (9)	Motor Vehicle (10)	Other Violence (11)	Other and Unknown (12)	(1)+(2)	(1)+(2)+(5)+(6)+(8)	(1)+(2)+(5)+(6)+(8)+part of(9)&(12)	(10)+(11)	Age (x)
0	100000	100000	100000	100000	100000	100000	100000	100000	100000	100000	100000	100000	100000	100000	100000	100000	100000	0
1	94970	94993	95275	94570	95022	95767	95215	94978	94970	97200	94970	95001	96219	95298	96346	99679	95001	1
5	93390	93444	94113	93425	93486	94500	93682	93451	93390	95583	93390	93720	94932	94167	95584	99106	93720	5
10	92518	92614	93505	92562	92659	93667	92826	92631	92518	94650	92518	93072	94203	93602	95079	98671	93072	10
15	91757	91899	92978	91813	91948	92925	92062	91913	91757	93911	91757	92497	93579	93122	94621	98277	92497	15
20	90339	90880	91830	90444	90600	91556	90644	90553	90339	92460	90339	91359	92319	92380	93940	97691	91359	20
25	87948	89569	89687	88104	88249	89240	88251	88214	87948	90013	87948	89414	90138	91340	93002	96513	89414	25
30	85554	88307	87495	85746	85961	86905	85853	85879	85554	87563	85554	87428	87904	90311	92057	96096	87428	30
35	83301	86868	85444	83573	83827	84731	83556	83724	83301	85257	83301	85581	85837	89102	90954	95112	85581	35
40	81012	85202	83329	81420	81722	82544	81304	81558	81012	82914	81012	83684	83770	87639	89618	93891	83684	40
45	78617	83258	81058	79219	79592	80285	78921	79305	78617	80463	78617	81662	81654	85843	88004	92389	81662	45
50	75797	80735	78340	76749	77201	77642	76114	76670	75797	77577	75797	79163	79194	83443	85832	90310	79163	50
55	72470	77613	75133	73971	74424	74543	72785	73562	72470	74172	72470	76058	76278	80465	83126	87685	76058	55
60	67721	72915	70449	70145	70713	70066	68036	69118	67721	69311	67721	71413	72095	75852	78843	83417	71413	60
65	61145	66229	63847	65012	65783	63718	61465	62959	61145	62581	61145	64827	66040	69156	72443	76867	64827	65
70	52069	56748	54571	57467	59034	54927	52378	54247	52069	53292	52069	55509	58001	59475	63112	67330	55509	70
75	41878	45912	44020	48522	51611	45112	42140	44259	41878	42861	41878	44847	48393	48261	52313	56151	44847	75
80	27840	30712	29329	34211	35262	31092	28028	29892	27840	28494	27840	29961	37324	32354	36378	40066	29961	80
85+	14180	15769	14956	18559	24207	16658	14290	15410	14180	14513	14180	15353	26755	16631	19689	23080	15353	85+

ADDED YRS OF LIFE

	No Causes	(1)	(2)	(3)	(4)	(5)	(6)	(7)	(8)	(9)	(10)	(11)	(12)				
TOTAL		2.595	1.654	1.810	3.175	1.759	.251	.827	.000	1.465	.000	1.933	5.540	4.347	6.582	10.337	1.933
WORK	6.419	1.850	.611	.434	.550	.346	.022	.295	.000	.000	.000	1.016	.740	2.495	2.895	3.312	1.016

POPULATION, DEATHS, DEATH RATES FOR ALL CAUSES COMBINED, AND SPECIFIED CAUSES

Age Start of Interval	Midyear Population	Deaths During Year	All Causes	Respiratory T.B.	Other Infec. and Paras.	Neoplasms	Cardiovascular	Infl., Pneu., Bronch.	Diarrheal	Certain Degenerative	Maternal	Cert. Dis. of Infancy	Motor Vehicle	Other Violence	Other and Unknown	Age Start of Interval
0	22471	944	.04201	.00004	.00312	.00018	.00053	.00743	.00240	.C0000	.C0000	.01749	.00000	.00040	.01041	0
1	93572	320	.00342	.00004	.00115	.00009	.00006	.00069	.00025	.00004	.00000	.C0000	.00000	.00035	.00074	1
5	136709	154	.00113	.00004	.0C039	.00007	.00007	.00007	.00003	.00004	.00000	.C0000	.00000	.00015	.00026	5
10	139510	189	.00135	.00022	.00043	.00001	.00014	.00009	.00001	.00011	.00000	.00000	.00000	.00006	.00028	10
15	132645	388	.00293	.C0158	.00051	.00004	.00016	.00011	.00000	.00007	.00003	.C0000	.00000	.00008	.00035	15
20	123759	501	.00405	.00251	.0C044	.00006	.00019	.00013	.00001	.00014	.00013	.C0000	.00000	.00011	.00032	20
25	117524	544	.00463	.00284	.00049	.00009	.00022	.00009	.00002	.00018	.00028	.C0000	.00000	.00006	.00037	25
30	110233	492	.00446	.CC216	.0C042	.00024	.00031	.00016	.00003	.00020	.00035	.C0000	.00000	.00012	.00048	30
35	95697	455	.00475	.00175	.0CC38	.00053	.00047	.00022	.00003	.00027	.00037	.00000	.00000	.00014	.00061	35
40	83492	415	.00497	.C0119	.0C032	.00109	.00067	.00029	.00001	.00041	.00017	.00000	.00000	.00012	.00071	40
45	73724	449	.00609	.00090	.00021	.0017C	.00110	.00041	.00003	.00054	.00005	.00000	.00000	.00012	.00094	45
50	69128	542	.00784	.00110	.00042	.00227	.00155	.00046	.00004	.00068	.00000	.00000	.00000	.00013	.00119	50
55	58481	673	.01151	.00113	.0CC48	.00318	.00298	.00082	.0CC07	.00096	.00000	.C0000	.00000	.00014	.00176	55
60	50763	790	.01556	.00112	.00043	.00412	.00492	.00136	.00010	.00132	.C0000	.C0000	.00000	.00018	.00201	60
65	45160	1169	.02589	.00111	.0CC47	.00574	.00923	.00259	.00013	.00179	.00000	.00000	.00000	.00024	.00458	65
70	36091	1532	.04245	.00127	.0CC69	.00920	.01765	.00488	.00019	.00277	.00000	.00000	.00000	.00030	.00549	70
75	26158	1833	.07007	.CCC84	.00065	.00940	.02508	.00723	.00031	.00241	.C0000	.00000	.00000	.00050	.02366	75
80	14645	1726	.11786	.CCC82	.00082	.01004	.03476	.00963	.00048	.00137	.C0000	.C0000	.00000	.00102	.05893	80
85+	8621	1814	.21042	.00058	.00104	.01056	.05243	.01752	.00081	.00186	.CC000	.C0000	.00000	.00174	.12388	85+
ALL	1438383	14930														

			All Causes	Resp. T.B.	Other Infec.	Neoplasms	Cardiovascular	Infl. Pneu. Bronch.	Diarrheal	Certain Degen.	Maternal	Cert. Dis. Infancy	Motor Vehicle	Other Violence	Other and Unknown	
CRUDE DEATH RATE			.01038	.00125	.0CC53	.00137	.00246	.00091	.0CC10	.00045	.00010	.00027	.00000	.00017	.00277	
STANDARDIZED RATE (1)			.00703	.00111	.00061	.00077	.00112	.00070	.00014	.00029	.0C009	.00062	.00000	.00016	.00143	
STANDARDIZED RATE (2)			.01045	.00120	.00055	.00143	.00246	.00095	.00011	.00047	.CCCC9	.00036	.00000	.00017	.00264	
GEOMETRIC MEAN			.01040													

LIFE TABLE FOR ALL CAUSES COMBINED

Age (x)	Midyear Population	Deaths During Year	$_nM_x$	$_nq_x$	l_x	$_nd_x$	$_nL_x$	$_nm_x$	$_na_x$	T_x	$_nr_x$	$\overset{\circ}{e}_x$	Age (x)
0	22471	944	.042010	.040550	100000	4055	96518	.042013	.141416	6577902	.000000	65.779	0
1	93572	320	.003420	.013560	95945	1301	380528	.003419	1.500000	6481384	.000000	67.553	1
5	136709	154	.001126	.005610	94644	531	471893	.001125	2.500000	6100857	.000000	64.461	5
10	139510	189	.001355	.006758	94113	636	469148	.001356	2.771554	5628964	-.000357	59.811	10
15	132645	388	.002925	.014549	93477	1360	464237	.002930	2.685662	5159816	-.006997	55.199	15
20	123759	501	.004048	.020061	92117	1848	456112	.004052	2.579478	4695579	-.008365	50.974	20
25	117524	544	.004629	.022876	90269	2065	446203	.004628	2.509988	4239467	-.006102	46.965	25
30	110233	492	.004463	.022074	88204	1947	436145	.004464	2.496041	3793264	-.012392	43.006	30
35	95697	455	.004755	.023511	86257	2028	426241	.004758	2.512636	3357119	-.020625	38.920	35
40	83492	415	.004971	.024576	84229	2070	416062	.004975	2.544384	2930878	-.022357	34.797	40
45	73724	449	.006090	.030051	82159	2469	404831	.006099	2.584548	2514817	.014831	30.609	45
50	69128	542	.007841	.038549	79690	3072	391152	.007854	2.624376	2109985	.013719	26.477	50
55	58481	673	.011508	.056162	76618	4303	372826	.011542	2.614600	1718833	.019862	22.434	55
60	50763	790	.015563	.075213	72315	5439	348784	.015594	2.648197	1346008	.011959	18.613	60
65	45160	1169	.025886	.122196	66876	8172	315177	.025928	2.650183	997224	.008068	14.912	65
70	36091	1532	.042448	.193002	58704	11330	266453	.042522	2.611062	682047	.008593	11.618	70
75	26158	1833	.070074	.299996	47374	14212	202127	.070312	2.555396	415593	.015317	8.773	75
80	14645	1726	.117856	.455612	33162	15109	127670	.118345	2.475649	213466	.015317	6.437	80
85+	8621	1814	.210416	1.000000	18053	18053	85797	.210416	4.752481	85797	.000000	4.752	85+

NUMBER OF PERSONS DYING (OUT OF 100,000 AT BIRTH) ABOVE AGE X FROM SPECIFIED CAUSES

Age (x)	All Causes	Respiratory T. B.	Other Infec. and Paras.	Neo-plasms	Cardio-vascular	Infl., Pneu., Bronch.	Diar-rheal	Certain Degener-ative	Maternal	Cert. Dis. of Infancy	Motor Vehicle	Other Violence	Other and Unknown	Age (x)
0	100000	8100	3542	13528	26594	8941	762	4068	600	1688	0	1301	30876	0
1	95945	8095	3242	13511	26543	8223	530	4068	600	0	0	1263	29870	1
5	94644	8079	2803	13478	26518	7959	437	4052	600	0	0	1128	29590	5
10	94113	8058	2620	13444	26487	7925	423	4031	600	0	0	1056	29469	10
15	93477	7954	2418	13440	26423	7881	416	3981	600	0	0	1026	29338	15
20	92117	7218	2180	13423	26350	7832	416	3949	586	0	0	991	29172	20
25	90269	6071	1977	13393	26265	7773	412	3886	527	0	0	939	29026	25
30	88204	4803	1757	13355	26166	7735	405	3807	402	0	0	913	28861	30
35	86257	3862	1575	13252	26032	7664	393	3720	247	0	0	861	28651	35
40	84229	3120	1415	13023	25830	7570	380	3603	92	0	0	803	28393	40
45	82159	2629	1281	12567	25550	7450	375	3433	23	0	0	753	28098	45
50	79690	2266	1154	11879	25104	7285	364	3213	1	0	0	704	27720	50
55	76618	1836	990	10989	24497	7103	347	2947	1	0	0	653	27255	55
60	72315	1415	811	9801	23383	6796	321	2589	1	0	0	602	26596	60
65	66876	1024	660	8363	21660	6321	287	2128	1	0	0	540	25892	65
70	58704	675	514	6553	18743	5502	245	1562	1	0	0	463	24446	70
75	47374	335	329	4099	14033	4201	193	823	1	0	0	382	22978	75
80	33162	165	198	2198	8952	2737	131	337	1	0	0	281	18162	80
85+	18053	50	90	906	4498	1503	70	159	0	0	0	149	10628	85+

NUMBER OF PERSONS SURVIVING TO AGE X IF SPECIFIED CAUSES WERE ELIMINATED

Age (x)	No Causes	Respiratory T. B. (1)	Other Infec. and Paras. (2)	Neo-plasms (3)	Cardio-vascular (4)	Infl., Pneu., Bronch. (5)	Diar-rheal (6)	Certain Degener-ative (7)	Maternal (8)	Cert. Dis. of Infancy (9)	Motor Vehicle (10)	Other Violence (11)	Other and Unknown (12)	(1) + (2)	(1) + (2) + (5) + (6) + (8)	(1)+(2)+ (5)+(6)+ (8)+part of(9)&(12)	(10) + (11)	Age (x)
0	100000	100000	100000	100000	100000	100000	100000	100000	100000	100000	100000	100000	100000	100000	100000	100000	100000	0
1	95945	95950	96239	95962	95555	96651	96173	95945	95945	97613	95945	95982	96935	96244	97182	99678	95982	1
5	94644	94665	95373	94693	94718	95605	94961	94660	94644	96289	94644	94815	95502	95394	96685	99400	94815	5
10	94113	94154	95022	94196	94218	95103	94442	94150	94113	95749	94113	94355	95487	95063	96399	99185	94355	10
15	93477	93622	94583	93563	93645	94504	93811	93563	93477	95102	93477	93747	94974	94730	96113	98988	93747	15
20	92117	92595	93446	92219	92355	93178	92446	92234	92131	93718	92117	92418	93760	94337	95779	98797	92418	20
25	90269	92283	91775	90399	90587	91368	90556	90446	90341	91838	90269	90616	92026	93823	95385	98527	90616	25
30	88204	91462	89897	88368	88613	89316	88530	88455	88358	89737	88204	88569	90087	93218	94951	98237	88569	30
35	86257	90413	88097	86520	86790	87416	86588	86589	86601	87756	86257	86665	88211	92341	94315	97763	86665	35
40	84229	89058	86187	84713	84951	85455	84565	84670	84719	85693	84229	84685	86496	91128	93363	96969	84685	40
45	82159	87383	84204	83086	83142	83475	82492	82758	82705	83587	82159	82654	84670	89559	91969	95677	82654	45
50	79690	85138	81802	81278	81090	81132	80023	80489	80241	81075	79690	80218	82510	87395	89966	93738	80218	50
55	76618	82307	78814	79039	78572	78186	76955	77650	77148	77950	76618	77176	79803	84666	87380	91208	77176	55
60	72315	78125	74566	75800	75279	74100	72659	73643	72815	73572	72315	72892	75991	80557	83512	87368	72892	60
65	66876	72655	69107	71562	71365	68997	67227	68556	67339	68038	66876	67470	70991	75079	78405	82210	67470	65
70	58704	64131	60804	64655	65632	61363	59051	60724	59110	59724	58704	59298	63768	66425	70328	74084	59298	70
75	47374	52085	49240	54646	57899	50754	47701	49690	47702	48197	47374	47926	52930	54136	58802	62276	47926	75
80	33162	36612	34580	40056	46012	36851	33443	35202	33391	33738	33162	33634	41883	38177	43079	46723	33634	80
85+	18053	20023	18907	22993	29566	21083	18251	19301	18179	18367	18053	18407	30877	20970	24930	28734	18407	85+

ADDED YRS OF LIFE																		
TOTAL		2.997	1.442	2.163	3.601	1.666	.288	.767	.243	1.141	.000	.382	5.548	4.529	6.986	10.352	.382	
WORK	5.469	2.084	.464	.592	.544	.220	.019	.276	.186	.000	.000	.110	.591	2.576	3.038	3.426	.110	

POPULATION, DEATHS, DEATH RATES FOR ALL CAUSES COMBINED, AND SPECIFIED CAUSES

Age Start of Interval	Midyear Population	Deaths During Year	All Causes	Respiratory T. B.	Other Infec. and Paras.	Neoplasms	Cardiovascular	Infl., Pneu., Bronch.	Diarrheal	Certain Degenerative	Maternal	Cert. Dis. of Infancy	Motor Vehicle	Other Violence	Other and Unknown	Age Start of Interval
0	34317	1420	.04138	.00009	.00256	.00023	.00020	.00898	.00189	.00000	.00000	.01553	.00003	.00035	.01151	0
1	116395	348	.00299	.00003	.00087	.00011	.00002	.00038	.00008	.00002	.00000	.00000	.00009	.00066	.00073	1
5	110331	142	.00129	.00005	.00029	.00014	.00006	.00002	.00002	.00003	.00000	.00000	.00010	.00042	.00017	5
10	102926	95	.00092	.00003	.00018	.00005	.00009	.00003	.00002	.00002	.00000	.00000	.00003	.00022	.00027	10
15	115784	193	.00167	.00023	.00038	.00004	.00010	.00005	.00001	.00006	.00000	.00000	.00003	.00042	.00035	15
20	133161	341	.00256	.00071	.00036	.00010	.00010	.00006	.00000	.00004	.00000	.00000	.00005	.00072	.00044	20
25	136310	383	.00281	.00089	.00029	.00014	.00015	.00007	.00000	.00007	.00000	.00000	.00006	.00072	.00043	25
30	127821	381	.00298	.00092	.00028	.00022	.00013	.00005	.00000	.00013	.00000	.00000	.00005	.00075	.00044	30
35	119388	409	.00343	.00095	.00026	.00036	.00024	.00008	.00001	.00020	.00000	.00000	.00004	.00079	.00050	35
40	108084	429	.00397	.00072	.00027	.00055	.00047	.00012	.00003	.00027	.00000	.00000	.00003	.00086	.00066	40
45	100196	553	.00552	.00058	.00030	.00097	.00085	.00019	.00003	.00036	.00000	.00000	.00004	.00094	.00088	45
50	87157	658	.00755	.00092	.00041	.00171	.00123	.00031	.00005	.00048	.00000	.00000	.00006	.00123	.00116	50
55	69875	693	.00992	.00064	.00036	.00259	.00253	.00043	.00004	.00059	.00000	.00000	.00006	.00094	.00173	55
60	56999	917	.01609	.00082	.00042	.00428	.00496	.00054	.00004	.00093	.00000	.00000	.00005	.00107	.00296	60
65	47332	1260	.02662	.00005	.00044	.00623	.00951	.00120	.00004	.00139	.00000	.00000	.00006	.00112	.00575	65
70	37406	1380	.03689	.00091	.00037	.00845	.01508	.00171	.00016	.00201	.00000	.00000	.00005	.00104	.00711	70
75	23252	1730	.07440	.00055	.00039	.01122	.02877	.00555	.00034	.00305	.00000	.00000	.00004	.00163	.02245	75
80	14171	1758	.12406	.00113	.00042	.01334	.04608	.01164	.00042	.00395	.00000	.00000	.00000	.00268	.04425	80
85+	7594	1595	.21003	.00066	.00053	.01409	.06940	.02107	.00079	.00553	.00000	.00000	.00013	.00487	.09297	85+
ALL	1548499	14685														

	All Causes	Respiratory T. B.	Other Infec. and Paras.	Neoplasms	Cardiovascular	Infl., Pneu., Bronch.	Diarrheal	Certain Degenerative	Maternal	Cert. Dis. of Infancy	Motor Vehicle	Other Violence	Other and Unknown
CRUDE DEATH RATE	.00948	.00062	.00041	.00132	.00238	.00070	.00008	.00038	.00000	.00034	.00005	.00079	.00242
STANDARDIZED RATE (1)	.00623	.00046	.00045	.00071	.00105	.00056	.00009	.00021	.00000	.00055	.00005	.00065	.00144
STANDARDIZED RATE (2)	.00969	.00057	.00041	.00140	.00253	.00071	.00008	.00039	.00000	.00032	.00005	.00076	.00247
GEOMETRIC MEAN	.00883												

LIFE TABLE FOR ALL CAUSES COMBINED

Age (x)	Midyear Population	Deaths During Year	$_nM_x$	$_nq_x$	l_x	$_nd_x$	$_nL_x$	$_nm_x$	$_na_x$	T_x	$_n r_x$	$\overset{\circ}{e}_x$	Age (x)
0	34317	1420	.041379	.039960	100000	3996	96565	.041382	.140344	6784822	.000000	67.848	0
1	116395	348	.002990	.011864	96004	1139	381169	.002988	1.500000	6688257	.000000	69.666	1
5	110331	142	.001287	.006420	94865	609	472803	.001288	2.500000	6307089	.000000	66.485	5
10	102926	95	.000923	.004604	94256	434	470230	.000923	2.579685	5834286	-.000490	61.898	10
15	115784	193	.001667	.008260	93822	775	467328	.001658	2.701075	5364057	-.021828	57.173	15
20	133161	341	.002561	.012703	93047	1182	462386	.002556	2.589361	4896728	-.022765	52.626	20
25	136310	383	.002810	.013955	91865	1282	456153	.002810	2.525676	4434343	-.005898	48.270	25
30	127821	381	.002981	.014793	90583	1340	449614	.002980	2.536536	3978190	.005865	43.918	30
35	119388	409	.003426	.016999	89243	1517	442503	.003428	2.553148	3528576	.011595	39.539	35
40	108084	429	.003969	.019686	87726	1727	434485	.003975	2.600005	3086073	.012959	35.179	40
45	100196	553	.005519	.027279	85999	2346	424418	.005528	2.622904	2651587	.013216	30.833	45
50	87157	658	.007550	.037189	83653	3111	410816	.007573	2.605539	2227169	.024056	26.624	50
55	69875	693	.009918	.048665	80542	3922	393501	.009967	2.651868	1816353	.031389	22.552	55
60	56999	917	.016088	.077917	76620	5970	369205	.016170	2.672460	1422853	.025863	18.570	60
65	47332	1260	.026620	.125464	70650	8864	332041	.026695	2.607316	1053648	.015693	14.914	65
70	37406	1380	.036892	.170524	61786	10536	284127	.037082	2.645908	721607	.027131	11.679	70
75	23252	1730	.074402	.316937	51250	16243	216902	.074686	2.577521	437480	.022663	8.536	75
80	14171	1758	.124056	.473620	35007	16580	132845	.124807	2.455343	220578	.022663	6.301	80
85+	7594	1595	.210034	1.000000	18427	18427	87733	.210034	4.761129	87733	.000000	4.761	85+

NUMBER OF PERSONS DYING (OUT OF 100,000 AT BIRTH) ABOVE AGE X FROM SPECIFIED CAUSES

Age (x)	All Causes	Respiratory T.B.	Other Infec. and Paras.	Neo-plasms	Cardio-vascular	Infl., Pneu., Bronch.	Diar-rheal	Certain Degen-erative	Maternal	Cert. Dis. of Infancy	Motor Vehicle	Other Violence	Other and Unknown	Age (x)
0	100000	4355	2671	14462	30340	7311	570	4018	0	1500	366	5995	28412	0
1	96004	4346	2424	14440	30320	6444	387	4018	0	0	363	5961	27301	1
5	94865	4333	2093	14397	30314	6300	358	4012	0	0	327	5709	27022	5
10	94256	4312	1956	14333	30284	6291	349	3999	0	0	280	5512	26940	10
15	93822	4298	1869	14310	30243	6278	349	3990	0	0	266	5407	26812	15
20	93047	4191	1692	14290	30198	6253	345	3962	0	0	254	5210	26652	20
25	91865	3866	1525	14245	30153	6226	345	3944	0	0	233	4877	26451	25
30	90583	3461	1394	14182	30083	6196	345	3911	0	0	206	4549	26256	30
35	89243	3046	1268	14083	30023	6171	345	3851	0	0	185	4212	26059	35
40	87726	2627	1153	13923	29915	6137	342	3762	0	0	167	3863	25837	40
45	85999	2314	1036	13685	29710	6085	329	3645	0	0	155	3489	25551	45
50	83653	1898	909	13273	29349	6004	317	3492	0	0	142	3091	25178	50
55	80542	1522	739	12568	28841	5877	298	3294	0	0	118	2586	24699	55
60	76620	1269	598	11542	27836	5707	281	3062	0	0	96	2215	24014	60
65	70650	964	443	9955	25990	5505	268	2717	0	0	76	1820	22912	65
70	61786	683	295	7880	22822	5104	247	2253	0	0	55	1448	20999	70
75	51250	425	189	5474	18514	4613	201	1681	0	0	40	1151	18962	75
80	35007	220	105	3031	12235	3399	126	1016	0	0	31	795	14049	80
85+	18427	58	46	1236	6088	1848	69	485	0	0	12	427	8158	85+

NUMBER OF PERSONS SURVIVING TO AGE X IF SPECIFIED CAUSES WERE ELIMINATED

Age (x)	No Causes	Respiratory T.B. (1)	Other Infec. and Paras. (2)	Neo-plasms (3)	Cardio-vascular (4)	Infl., Pneu., Bronch. (5)	Diar-rheal (6)	Certain Degenerative (7)	Maternal (8)	Cert. Dis. of Infancy (9)	Motor Vehicle (10)	Other Violence (11)	Other and Unknown (12)	(1)+(2)	(1)+(2)+(5)+(6)+(8)	(1)+(2)+(5)+(6)+(8)+part of(9)&(12)	(10)+(11)	Age (x)
0	100000	100000	100000	100000	100000	100000	100000	100000	100000	100000	100000	100000	100000	100000	100000	100000	100000	0
1	96004	96013	96246	96026	96024	96857	96183	96004	96004	97485	96007	96037	97099	96255	97292	99768	96040	1
5	94865	94887	95435	94929	94890	95853	95071	94871	94865	96328	94904	95149	96228	95457	96660	99294	95188	5
10	94256	94298	94960	94384	94311	95246	94470	94275	94256	95710	94341	94735	95693	95002	96218	98869	94821	10
15	93822	93878	94610	93972	93918	94821	94035	93850	93822	95269	93921	94404	95382	94667	95892	98583	94504	15
20	93047	93210	94006	93216	93187	94063	93262	93102	93047	94482	93157	93822	94756	94170	95419	98182	93933	20
25	91865	92350	92980	92076	92048	92977	92077	91538	91865	93282	91955	92965	93756	93470	94737	97593	93096	25
30	90583	91466	91814	90854	90833	91629	90792	90687	90583	91980	90738	91997	92645	92709	93996	96938	92154	30
35	89243	90530	90583	89609	89549	90298	89449	89406	89243	90620	89416	90977	91475	91889	93190	96211	91153	35
40	87726	89413	89159	88245	88134	88758	87932	87974	87726	89079	87914	89784	90146	90873	92199	95293	89976	40
45	85999	87969	87521	86745	86604	87102	86214	86359	85999	87326	86195	88396	88663	89526	90901	94057	88598	45
50	83653	85990	85261	84790	84601	84807	83874	84154	83653	84943	83857	86389	86624	87643	89086	92310	86599	50
55	80542	83172	82260	82341	81961	81779	80773	81220	80542	81784	80762	83689	83891	84946	86499	89767	83917	55
60	76620	79376	78395	79362	78975	77955	76856	77494	76620	77802	76851	79990	80505	81215	82896	86163	80230	60
65	70650	73495	72439	74772	74673	72088	70881	71791	70650	71740	70882	74153	75353	75356	77141	80347	74396	65
70	61786	64546	63492	67474	68514	63428	62007	63226	61786	62739	62008	65214	67833	66328	68335	71427	65448	70
75	51250	53784	52763	58399	61345	53075	51476	52978	51250	52041	51448	54377	58347	55371	57596	60435	54587	75
80	35007	36912	36110	42218	48538	37307	35223	36752	35007	35547	35150	37453	44752	38076	40827	43541	37606	80
85+	18427	19552	19051	23822	32412	20853	18582	19747	18427	18711	18516	19997	29589	20214	23067	25579	20094	85+

ADDED YRS OF LIFE

	No Causes	(1)	(2)	(3)	(4)	(5)	(6)	(7)	(8)	(9)	(10)	(11)	(12)				
TOTAL		1.307	1.100	2.113	3.868	1.325	.193	.583	.000	1.045	.139	1.772	4.738	2.437	4.051	6.832	1.916
WORK	4.058	.806	.357	.457	.405	.110	.012	.179	.000	.000	.046	.817	.624	1.172	1.299	1.559	.864

POPULATION, DEATHS, DEATH RATES FOR ALL CAUSES COMBINED, AND SPECIFIED CAUSES

Age Start of Interval	Midyear Population	Deaths During Year	All Causes	Respiratory T. B.	Other Infec. and Paras.	Neoplasms	Cardiovascular	Infl., Pneu., Bronch.	Diarrheal	Certain Degenerative	Maternal	Cert. Dis. of Infancy	Motor Vehicle	Other Violence	Other and Unknown	Age Start of Interval
0	32486	1030	.03171	.00006	.00252	.00012	.00015	.00757	.00083	.00000	.00000	.01185	.00000	.00022	.00837	0
1	110534	247	.00223	.00004	.00070	.00011	.00003	.00029	.00002	.00003	.00000	.00000	.00005	.00033	.00064	1
5	106163	112	.00105	.00003	.00030	.00006	.00006	.00010	.00003	.00000	.00000	.00000	.00005	.00016	.00027	5
10	98843	65	.00066	.00009	.00027	.00001	.00007	.00002	.00000	.00002	.00000	.00000	.00000	.00003	.00014	10
15	112269	137	.00122	.00037	.00029	.00004	.00008	.00003	.00000	.00004	.00004	.00000	.00002	.00008	.00023	15
20	129169	205	.00159	.00065	.00026	.00007	.00007	.00003	.00001	.00004	.00008	.00000	.00004	.00008	.00026	20
25	135020	262	.00194	.00079	.00027	.00013	.00009	.00005	.00001	.00007	.00016	.00000	.00004	.00007	.00025	25
30	126473	245	.00194	.00072	.00019	.00021	.00011	.00005	.00002	.00013	.00017	.00000	.00002	.00007	.00025	30
35	120215	272	.00226	.00067	.00017	.00042	.00021	.00007	.00001	.00016	.00017	.00000	.00000	.00007	.00032	35
40	113453	326	.00287	.00052	.00020	.00078	.00038	.00012	.00001	.00020	.00010	.00000	.00001	.00011	.00055	40
45	106542	410	.00385	.00043	.00022	.00127	.00072	.00017	.00000	.00013	.00006	.00000	.00001	.00012	.00072	45
50	92671	457	.00493	.00039	.00024	.00195	.00110	.00019	.00000	.00018	.00006	.00000	.00000	.00010	.00078	50
55	77767	628	.00808	.00037	.00024	.00287	.00235	.00037	.00003	.00045	.00000	.00000	.00001	.00013	.00125	55
60	66757	816	.01222	.00046	.00022	.00383	.00401	.00055	.00006	.00099	.00000	.00000	.00003	.00019	.00186	60
65	55822	1203	.02155	.00050	.00027	.00539	.00824	.00143	.00011	.00152	.00000	.00000	.00004	.00047	.00358	65
70	45221	1400	.03096	.00051	.00038	.00736	.01413	.00234	.00009	.00210	.00000	.00000	.00007	.00080	.00318	70
75	30414	2011	.06612	.00049	.00049	.01016	.02729	.00687	.00030	.00260	.00000	.00000	.00007	.00210	.01575	75
80	20016	2373	.11856	.00060	.00050	.01369	.04506	.01409	.00065	.00230	.00000	.00000	.00000	.00410	.03757	80
85+	11700	2336	.19966	.00034	.00068	.01436	.06786	.02556	.00111	.00325	.00000	.00000	.00000	.00752	.07897	85+
ALL	1591535	14535														

	All Causes	Respiratory T. B.	Other Infec. and Paras.	Neoplasms	Cardiovascular	Infl., Pneu., Bronch.	Diarrheal	Certain Degenerative	Maternal	Cert. Dis. of Infancy	Motor Vehicle	Other Violence	Other and Unknown
CRUDE DEATH RATE	.00913	.00044	.00033	.00151	.00276	.00089	.00006	.00034	.00006	.00024	.00002	.00029	.00219
STANDARDIZED RATE (1)	.00483	.00036	.00039	.00069	.00095	.00053	.00005	.00016	.00005	.00042	.00003	.00017	.00104
STANDARDIZED RATE (2)	.00795	.00041	.00034	.00135	.00234	.00076	.00005	.00031	.00005	.00025	.00002	.00026	.00181
GEOMETRIC MEAN	.00668												

LIFE TABLE FOR ALL CAUSES COMBINED

Age (x)	Midyear Population	Deaths During Year	$_nM_x$	$_nq_x$	l_x	$_nd_x$	$_nL_x$	$_nm_x$	$_na_x$	T_x	$_nr_x$	$\overset{\circ}{e}_x$	Age (x)
0	32486	1030	.031706	.030850	100000	3085	97297	.031707	.123900	7156587	.000000	71.566	0
1	110534	247	.002235	.008884	96915	861	385508	.002233	1.500000	7059290	.000000	72.840	1
5	106163	112	.001055	.005268	96054	506	479005	.001056	2.500000	6673783	.000000	69.479	5
10	98843	65	.000658	.003276	95548	313	476972	.000656	2.547923	6194778	-.000893	64.834	10
15	112269	137	.001220	.006069	95235	578	474820	.001217	2.656070	5717805	-.022132	60.039	15
20	129169	205	.001587	.007881	94657	746	471489	.001582	2.591879	5242985	-.023819	55.389	20
25	135020	262	.001940	.009658	93911	907	467319	.001941	2.534684	4771496	-.007202	50.809	25
30	126473	245	.001937	.009645	93004	897	462805	.001938	2.530193	4304177	.005809	46.279	30
35	120215	272	.002263	.011259	92107	1037	458026	.002264	2.580963	3841373	.008017	41.706	35
40	113453	326	.002873	.014275	91070	1300	452241	.002875	2.608494	3383346	.007982	37.151	40
45	106542	410	.003848	.019093	89770	1714	444743	.003854	2.603924	2931105	.012679	32.651	45
50	92671	457	.004931	.024473	88056	2155	435248	.004951	2.664830	2486362	.023130	28.236	50
55	77767	628	.008075	.039802	85901	3419	421535	.008111	2.668787	2051115	-.024967	23.878	55
60	66757	816	.012223	.059710	82482	4925	401047	.012280	2.692766	1629580	-.021810	19.757	60
65	55822	1203	.021551	.102840	77557	7976	368924	.021620	2.635223	1228533	-.017060	15.840	65
70	45221	1400	.030959	.145183	69581	10102	324540	.031127	2.687133	859610	.025031	12.354	70
75	30414	2011	.066121	.286656	59479	17050	256715	.066416	2.614052	535069	.015469	8.996	75
80	20016	2373	.118555	.458083	42429	19436	163153	.119098	2.481360	278355	.015469	6.560	80
85+	11700	2336	.199658	1.000000	22993	22993	115162	.199658	5.008562	115162	.000000	5.009	85+

NUMBER OF PERSONS DYING (OUT OF 100,000 AT BIRTH) ABOVE AGE X FROM SPECIFIED CAUSES

Age (x)	All Causes	Respiratory T.B.	Other Infec. and Paras.	Neo-plasms	Cardio-vascular	Infl., Pneu., Bronch.	Diar-rheal	Certain Degen-erative	Maternal	Cert. Dis. of Infancy	Motor Vehicle	Other Violence	Other and Unknown	Age (x)
0	100000	3123	2336	15943	33834	9929	538	3670	355	1153	172	3208	25739	0
1	96915	3117	2090	15931	33819	9192	457	3670	355	0	172	3187	24925	1
5	96054	3103	1822	15889	33809	9080	450	3659	355	0	151	3058	24678	5
10	95548	3089	1678	15862	33782	9031	437	3659	355	0	129	2981	24545	10
15	95235	3046	1547	15858	33748	9021	437	3650	355	0	129	2966	24478	15
20	94657	2874	1408	15836	33710	9008	437	3629	338	0	120	2928	24369	20
25	93911	2568	1283	15804	33677	8994	433	3610	302	0	102	2892	24246	25
30	93004	2198	1159	15742	33635	8970	430	3576	226	0	85	2857	24126	30
35	92107	1865	1071	15643	33584	8948	422	3514	146	0	78	2824	24012	35
40	91070	1560	995	15448	33489	8917	418	3441	70	0	78	2790	23864	40
45	89770	1325	903	15093	33317	8861	414	3397	26	0	74	2742	23618	45
50	88056	1133	807	14528	32995	8786	414	3339	1	0	69	2688	23296	50
55	85901	965	704	13674	32512	8701	414	3258	1	0	69	2646	22957	55
60	82482	807	601	12461	31514	8543	403	3067	1	0	64	2591	22430	60
65	77557	621	511	10919	29895	8319	379	2669	1	0	52	2513	21678	65
70	69581	436	411	8925	26841	7788	340	2105	1	0	39	2340	20355	70
75	59479	271	289	6529	22230	7021	311	1422	1	0	17	2080	19308	75
80	42429	144	162	3915	15196	5247	234	754	1	0	0	1537	15239	80
85+	22993	39	79	1654	7815	2943	128	374	0	0	0	866	9095	85+

NUMBER OF PERSONS SURVIVING TO AGE X IF SPECIFIED CAUSES WERE ELIMINATED

Age (x)	No Causes	Respiratory T.B. (1)	Other Infec. and Paras. (2)	Neo-plasms (3)	Cardio-vascular (4)	Infl., Pneu., Bronch. (5)	Diar-rheal (6)	Certain Degener-ative (7)	Maternal (8)	Cert. Dis. of Infancy (9)	Motor Vehicle (10)	Other Violence (11)	Other and Unknown (12)	(1) + (2)	(1) + (2) + (5) + (6) + (8)	(1)+(2)+(5)+(6)+(8)+part of(9)&(12)	(10) + (11)	Age (x)
0	100000	100000	100000	100000	100000	100000	100000	100000	100000	100000	100000	100000	100000	100000	100000	100000	100000	0
1	96915	96921	97157	96927	96930	97643	96955	96915	96915	98057	96915	96936	97720	97163	97974	99866	96936	1
5	96054	96074	96562	96108	96079	96888	96065	96054	96054	97186	96015	96203	97100	96582	97508	99557	96224	5
10	95548	95582	96198	95628	95559	96427	95647	95555	95548	96674	95591	95773	96722	96232	97217	99341	95816	10
15	95235	95312	96015	95319	95320	96121	95333	95255	95235	96357	95278	95474	96473	96092	97086	99259	95517	15
20	94657	94905	95572	94762	94780	95551	94755	94698	94674	95772	94708	94933	95998	95822	96844	99095	94984	20
25	93911	94463	94944	94047	94066	94812	94012	93970	93964	95017	93980	94221	95366	95502	96576	98921	94290	25
30	93004	93922	94152	93201	93199	93920	93107	93097	93132	94100	93089	93346	94566	95081	96256	98689	93431	30
35	92107	93351	93333	92401	92351	93037	92217	92260	92313	93192	92198	92478	93769	94593	95876	98382	92570	35
40	91070	92608	92358	91555	91406	92020	91183	91294	91350	92143	91160	91471	92864	93918	95308	97886	91562	40
45	89770	91523	91133	90604	90273	90763	89885	90035	89872	90828	89863	90213	91787	92913	94396	97057	90307	45
50	88056	89970	89489	89440	88871	89105	88169	88374	88394	89093	88152	88545	90361	91434	92998	95717	88641	50
55	85901	87938	87403	88112	87179	87010	86011	86291	86231	86913	85995	86419	88494	89475	91094	93828	86514	55
60	82482	84556	84026	85833	84708	83703	82598	83045	82799	83454	82577	83034	85506	86180	87916	90639	83129	60
65	77557	79729	79098	82277	81280	78927	77690	78476	77855	78471	77658	78152	81160	81314	83210	85888	78254	65
70	69581	71710	71060	75843	76019	71324	69737	70947	69848	70401	69684	70281	74133	73234	75526	78137	70384	70
75	59479	61455	60858	67279	69804	61702	59639	61291	59708	60180	59587	60321	64418	62879	65657	68061	60430	75
80	42429	43947	43521	50520	57215	45593	42609	44296	42592	42929	42520	43495	49842	45078	48831	51294	43589	80
85+	22993	23895	23646	29400	39128	26569	23168	24294	23082	23264	23042	24075	32782	24574	28722	31335	24126	85+

ADDED YRS OF LIFE

	No Causes	(1)	(2)	(3)	(4)	(5)	(6)	(7)	(8)	(9)	(10)	(11)	(12)	(1)+(2)	(1)+(2)+(5)+(6)+(8)	part	(10)+(11)
TOTAL		1.085	1.006	2.418	4.323	1.493	.116	.528	.154	.842	.068	.508	3.937	2.112	3.976	6.433	.576
WORK	2.861	.668	.275	.550	.357	.089	.009	.124	.112	.000	.023	.097	.438	.948	1.164	1.385	.120

POPULATION, DEATHS, DEATH RATES FOR ALL CAUSES COMBINED, AND SPECIFIED CAUSES

Age Start of Interval	Midyear Population	Deaths During Year	All Causes	Respiratory T. B.	Other Infec. and Paras.	Neoplasms	Cardio-vascular	Infl., Pneu., Bronch.	Diarrheal	Certain Degenerative	Maternal	Cert. Dis. of Infancy	Motor Vehicle	Other Violence	Other and Unknown	Age Start of Interval
0	31039	907	.02922	.00000	.00113	.00019	.00006	.00359	.00093	.00000	.00000	.01472	.00006	.00029	.00783	0
1	131408	217	.00165	.00002	.00021	.00019	.00002	.00015	.00003	.00001	.00000	.00000	.00012	.00044	.00046	1
5	143988	130	.00090	.00000	.00016	.00009	.00000	.00001	.00001	.00001	.00000	.00000	.00013	.00031	.00018	5
10	109430	75	.00069	.00001	.00009	.00008	.00002	.00001	.00000	.00000	.00000	.00000	.00006	.00029	.00012	10
15	103122	108	.00105	.00004	.00014	.00013	.00007	.00003	.00000	.00005	.00000	.00000	.00009	.00037	.00015	15
20	115832	201	.00174	.00010	.00014	.00014	.00011	.00003	.00001	.00004	.00000	.00000	.00014	.00085	.00018	20
25	131441	201	.00153	.00025	.00012	.00018	.00006	.00001	.00000	.00010	.00000	.00000	.00009	.00050	.00021	25
30	133089	275	.00207	.00039	.00023	.00026	.00014	.00002	.00000	.00008	.00000	.00000	.00008	.00064	.00023	30
35	126013	286	.00227	.00034	.00019	.00034	.00019	.00006	.00001	.00015	.00000	.00000	.00002	.00071	.00026	35
40	117148	302	.00258	.00018	.00019	.00049	.00043	.00005	.00000	.00019	.00000	.00000	.00002	.00068	.00036	40
45	105626	447	.00423	.00035	.00012	.00113	.00099	.00007	.00001	.00029	.00000	.00000	.00008	.00057	.00059	45
50	97057	676	.00696	.00038	.00019	.00173	.00225	.00010	.00004	.00041	.00000	.00000	.00006	.00084	.00096	50
55	82187	836	.01017	.00038	.00030	.00285	.00365	.00017	.00001	.00055	.00000	.00000	.00007	.00085	.00096	55
60	64881	954	.01470	.00040	.00018	.00424	.00595	.00039	.00005	.00071	.00000	.00000	.00009	.00072	.00197	60
65	50660	1235	.02438	.00047	.00030	.00626	.01161	.00077	.00004	.00089	.00000	.00000	.00006	.00095	.00304	65
70	40716	1612	.03959	.00076	.00047	.00978	.01881	.00150	.00010	.00098	.00000	.00000	.00007	.00113	.00599	70
75	27748	1911	.06887	.00079	.00058	.01452	.03481	.00350	.00014	.00191	.00000	.00000	.00004	.00173	.01085	75
80	14605	1676	.11476	.00048	.00021	.01897	.05587	.00911	.00027	.00336	.00000	.00000	.00007	.00315	.02328	80
85+	8616	1936	.22470	.00104	.00046	.01985	.09981	.02008	.00058	.00209	.00000	.00000	.00000	.00812	.07266	85+
ALL	1634606	13985														

	All Causes	Respiratory T. B.	Other Infec. and Paras.	Neoplasms	Cardio-vascular	Infl., Pneu., Bronch.	Diarrheal	Certain Degenerative	Maternal	Cert. Dis. of Infancy	Motor Vehicle	Other Violence	Other and Unknown
CRUDE DEATH RATE	.00856	.00024	.00021	.00159	.00314	.00045	.00004	.00027	.00000	.00028	.00008	.00068	.00157
STANDARDIZED RATE (1)	.00499	.00016	.00021	.00080	.00127	.00029	.00005	.00015	.00000	.00052	.00009	.00055	.00091
STANDARDIZED RATE (2)	.00855	.00023	.00021	.00161	.00316	.00045	.00004	.00027	.00000	.00030	.00008	.00067	.00154
GEOMETRIC MEAN	.00687												

LIFE TABLE FOR ALL CAUSES COMBINED

Age (x)	Midyear Population	Deaths During Year	$_nM_x$	$_nq_x$	l_x	$_nd_x$	$_nL_x$	$_nm_x$	$_na_x$	T_x	$_nr_x$	$\overset{\circ}{e}_x$	Age (x)
0	31039	907	.029221	.028490	100000	2849	97492	.029223	.119676	7084638	.000000	70.846	0
1	131408	217	.001651	.006577	97151	639	387007	.001651	1.500000	6987146	.000000	71.920	1
5	143988	130	.000903	.004507	96512	435	481473	.000903	2.500000	6600140	.000000	68.387	5
10	109430	75	.000685	.003414	96077	328	479579	.000684	2.541921	6118667	.031135	63.685	10
15	103122	108	.001047	.005232	95749	501	477595	.001049	2.705422	5639088	.005769	58.894	15
20	115832	201	.001735	.008632	95248	822	474230	.001733	2.555251	5161493	-.019458	54.190	20
25	131441	201	.001529	.007614	94426	719	470362	.001529	2.540855	4687262	-.019439	49.640	25
30	133089	275	.002066	.010277	93707	963	466196	.002066	2.570959	4216901	-.004205	45.001	30
35	126013	286	.002270	.011289	92744	1047	461147	.002270	2.542582	3750705	-.006224	40.441	35
40	117148	302	.002578	.012836	91697	1177	455721	.002583	2.651338	3289558	.012927	35.874	40
45	105626	447	.004232	.021012	90520	1902	448234	.004243	2.704609	2833837	.013840	31.306	45
50	97057	676	.006965	.034361	88618	3045	435970	.006984	2.661741	2385603	.015199	26.920	50
55	82187	836	.010172	.049852	85573	4266	417776	.010211	2.635129	1949633	.025624	22.783	55
60	64881	954	.014704	.071482	81307	5812	392938	.014791	2.660551	1531856	.032845	18.840	60
65	50660	1235	.024378	.115835	75495	8745	356926	.024501	2.650253	1138918	.025113	15.086	65
70	40716	1612	.039591	.181558	66750	12119	305007	.039734	2.628259	781992	-.017329	11.715	70
75	27748	1911	.068870	.296645	54631	16206	233702	.069345	2.565511	476985	.028658	8.731	75
80	14605	1676	.114755	.448016	38425	17215	148890	.115622	2.488527	243283	.028658	6.331	80
85+	8616	1936	.224698	1.000000	21210	21210	94393	.224698	4.450413	94393	.000000	4.450	85+

NUMBER OF PERSONS DYING (OUT OF 100,000 AT BIRTH) ABOVE AGE X FROM SPECIFIED CAUSES

Age (x)	All Causes	Respiratory T.B.	Other Infec. and Paras.	Neo-plasms	Cardio-vascular	Infl., Pneu., Bronch.	Diar-rheal	Certain Degen-erative	Maternal	Cert. Dis. of Infancy	Motor Vehicle	Other Violence	Other and Unknown	Age (x)
0	100000	2035	1579	18391	41714	5666	334	2885	0	1435	535	5842	19584	0
1	97151	2035	1469	18372	41707	5277	243	2885	0	0	529	5814	18820	1
5	96512	2029	1387	18299	41701	5218	231	2882	0	0	482	5643	18640	5
10	96077	2029	1310	18255	41701	5211	227	2875	0	0	422	5493	18554	10
15	95749	2025	1266	18216	41692	5207	227	2875	0	0	391	5352	18498	15
20	95248	2006	1201	18156	41660	5193	227	2852	0	0	349	5176	18428	20
25	94426	1958	1136	18090	41607	5180	223	2832	0	0	284	4775	18341	25
30	93707	1840	1079	18004	41578	5177	223	2785	0	0	241	4538	18242	30
35	92744	1658	970	17885	41512	5166	223	2747	0	0	206	4241	18136	35
40	91697	1501	882	17728	41424	5141	220	2677	0	0	198	3911	18015	40
45	90520	1419	797	17505	41228	5117	220	2591	0	0	191	3600	17852	45
50	88618	1245	742	16999	40780	5088	215	2460	0	0	157	3346	17586	50
55	85573	1078	661	16242	39798	5043	197	2280	0	0	130	2977	17167	55
60	81307	921	533	15047	38265	4971	192	2050	0	0	99	2621	16608	60
65	75495	763	461	13373	35908	4818	174	1771	0	0	63	2337	15827	65
70	66750	594	355	11130	31742	4541	160	1453	0	0	42	1998	14735	70
75	54631	361	212	8140	25981	4082	130	1153	0	0	19	1652	12901	75
80	38425	176	77	4729	17788	3256	96	703	0	0	11	1245	10344	80
85+	21210	99	44	1873	9422	1895	55	197	0	0	0	767	6858	85+

NUMBER OF PERSONS SURVIVING TO AGE X IF SPECIFIED CAUSES WERE ELIMINATED

Age (x)	No Causes	Respiratory T.B. (1)	Other Infec. and Paras. (2)	Neo-plasms (3)	Cardio-vascular (4)	Infl., Pneu., Bronch. (5)	Diar-rheal (6)	Certain Degen-erative (7)	Maternal (8)	Cert. Dis. of Infancy (9)	Motor Vehicle (10)	Other Violence (11)	Other and Unknown (12)	(1)+(2)	(1)+(2)+(5)+(6)+(8)	(1)+(2)+(5)+(6)+(8)+part of(9)&(12)	(10)+(11)	Age (x)
0	100000	100000	100000	100000	100000	100000	100000	100000	100000	100000	100000	100000	100000	100000	100000	100000	100000	0
1	97151	97151	97259	97170	97158	97535	97241	97151	97151	98576	97157	97179	97907	97259	97734	99734	97185	1
5	96512	96518	96702	96603	96525	96953	96613	96515	96512	97927	96565	96710	97444	96708	97251	99304	96763	5
10	96077	96083	96343	96212	96090	96523	96182	96087	96077	97486	96189	96424	97091	96349	96901	98969	96537	10
15	95749	95759	96058	95922	95771	96197	95853	95759	95749	97153	95892	96236	96816	96068	96623	98696	96380	15
20	95248	95277	95620	95481	95302	95708	95352	95281	95248	96645	95432	95909	96380	95649	96216	98297	96095	20
25	94426	94502	94860	94722	94532	94895	94533	94478	94426	95811	94673	95485	95636	94937	95516	97598	95735	25
30	93707	93901	94195	94087	93841	94175	93813	93806	93707	95081	93996	94997	95008	94390	94969	97068	95289	30
35	92744	93117	93336	93239	92942	93219	92849	92880	92744	94104	93065	94320	94139	93712	94298	96420	94646	35
40	91697	92223	92370	92344	91981	92191	91804	91901	91697	93042	92022	93590	93198	92900	93509	95652	93921	40
45	90520	91121	91270	91382	90996	91032	90625	90807	90520	91847	90848	92704	92167	91876	92503	94654	93040	45
50	88618	89380	89407	89969	89531	89148	88726	89029	88618	89918	88573	91014	90498	90175	90825	92982	91378	50
55	85573	86474	86415	87636	87435	86129	85695	86148	85573	86828	85942	88260	87810	87325	88018	90159	88640	55
60	81307	82318	82233	84469	84618	81906	81428	82079	81307	82499	81688	84218	83994	83255	83994	86093	84612	60
65	75495	76587	76425	80123	80971	76200	75625	76483	75495	76602	75883	78481	78771	77531	78389	80412	78884	65
70	66750	67877	67673	73113	75918	67637	66878	67926	66750	67729	67113	69721	70726	68815	69864	71748	70100	70
75	54631	55767	55517	62864	68345	55780	54763	55869	54631	55432	54949	57389	59669	56671	58003	59720	57722	75
80	38425	39379	39161	47596	57428	39949	38546	39682	38425	38988	38655	40722	44372	40134	41857	43305	40966	80
85+	21210	21795	21641	28994	42312	23112	21307	22290	21210	21521	21345	22852	27624	22237	24342	25520	22998	85+

ADDED YRS OF LIFE

		(1)	(2)	(3)	(4)	(5)	(6)	(7)	(8)	(9)	(10)	(11)	(12)				
TOTAL		.487	.542	2.601	5.754	.755	.102	.450	.000	1.037	.230	1.594	2.880	1.035	1.922	3.747	1.832
WORK	3.000	.257	.187	.528	.503	.048	.006	.154	.000	.000	.090	.718	.366	.445	.500	.573	.810

POPULATION, DEATHS, DEATH RATES FOR ALL CAUSES COMBINED, AND SPECIFIED CAUSES

Age Start of Interval	Midyear Population	Deaths During Year	All Causes	Respiratory T.B.	Other Infec. and Paras.	Neoplasms	Cardiovascular	Infl., Pneu., Bronch.	Diarrheal	Certain Degenerative	Maternal	Cert. Dis. of Infancy	Motor Vehicle	Other Violence	Other and Unknown	Age Start of Interval
0	29150	648	.02223	.00003	.00062	.00024	.00000	.00336	.00069	.00003	.00000	.01081	.00000	.00031	.00614	0
1	123728	162	.00131	.00000	.00018	.00013	.00000	.00019	.00006	.00001	.00000	.00000	.00009	.00031	.00035	1
5	136782	80	.00058	.00000	.00014	.00006	.00000	.00003	.00002	.00001	.00000	.00000	.00006	.00010	.00017	5
10	105445	38	.00036	.00001	.00010	.00007	.00001	.00001	.00002	.00001	.00000	.00000	.00000	.00005	.00010	10
15	99510	44	.00044	.00003	.00015	.00003	.00004	.00000	.00000	.00004	.00000	.00000	.00003	.00001	.00011	15
20	110912	77	.00069	.00013	.00014	.00007	.00003	.00002	.00000	.00003	.00005	.00000	.00002	.00005	.00016	20
25	127308	123	.00097	.00020	.00012	.00018	.00008	.00001	.00001	.00004	.00006	.00000	.00002	.00005	.00020	25
30	132702	130	.00098	.00023	.00010	.00018	.00008	.00002	.00001	.00004	.00014	.00000	.00000	.00004	.00014	30
35	124641	190	.00152	.00025	.00010	.00040	.00020	.00002	.00001	.00013	.00014	.00000	.00000	.00006	.00021	35
40	118056	250	.00212	.00025	.00005	.00091	.00023	.00006	.00001	.00011	.00004	.00000	.00000	.00012	.00032	40
45	111231	326	.00293	.00019	.00005	.00143	.00052	.00006	.00003	.00013	.00003	.00000	.00000	.00004	.00045	45
50	103683	470	.00453	.00016	.00017	.00209	.00111	.00008	.00003	.00021	.00000	.00000	.00001	.00012	.00055	50
55	88332	622	.00704	.00017	.00016	.00286	.00224	.00017	.00003	.00040	.00000	.00000	.00007	.00015	.00079	55
60	73347	837	.01141	.00019	.00011	.00395	.00472	.00019	.00003	.00060	.00000	.00000	.00001	.00022	.00139	60
65	60432	1130	.01870	.00035	.00017	.00515	.00917	.00056	.00003	.00098	.00000	.00000	.00002	.00033	.00195	65
70	48812	1668	.03417	.00035	.00014	.00828	.01743	.00139	.00012	.00129	.00000	.00000	.00002	.00090	.00424	70
75	34311	2053	.05984	.00020	.00020	.01119	.03350	.00376	.00012	.00157	.00000	.00000	.00000	.00143	.00737	75
80	19842	2135	.10760	.00040	.00030	.01381	.05892	.01003	.00060	.00212	.00000	.00000	.00000	.00358	.01784	80
85+	12689	2768	.21814	.00055	.00047	.01860	.09733	.02419	.00071	.00221	.00000	.00000	.00000	.00000	.06368	85+
ALL	1660953	13751														

	All Causes	Respiratory T.B.	Other Infec.	Neoplasms	Cardiovascular	Infl., Pneu., Bronch.	Diarrheal	Certain Degenerative	Maternal	Cert. Dis. of Infancy	Motor Vehicle	Other Violence	Other and Unknown
CRUDE DEATH RATE	.00828	.00016	.00014	.00167	.00347	.00056	.00005	.00025	.00003	.00019	.00002	.00028	.00145
STANDARDIZED RATE (1)	.00375	.00011	.00015	.00074	.00107	.00026	.00005	.00011	.00003	.00038	.00003	.00014	.00068
STANDARDIZED RATE (2)	.00692	.00014	.00014	.00144	.00282	.00045	.00004	.00022	.00003	.00022	.00002	.00023	.00116
GEOMETRIC MEAN	.00469												

LIFE TABLE FOR ALL CAUSES COMBINED

Age (x)	Midyear Population	Deaths During Year	$_nM_x$	$_nq_x$	l_x	$_nd_x$	$_nL_x$	$_nm_x$	$_na_x$	T_x	$_nr_x$	$\overset{\circ}{e}_x$	Age (x)
0	29150	648	.022230	.021800	100000	2180	98055	.022232	.107791	7438219	.000000	74.382	0
1	123728	162	.001309	.005214	97820	510	390005	.001308	1.500000	7340164	.000000	75.037	1
5	136782	80	.000585	.002929	97310	285	485838	.000587	2.500000	6950159	.000000	71.423	5
10	105445	38	.000360	.001793	97025	174	484675	.000359	2.414990	6464322	.029784	66.625	10
15	99510	44	.000442	.002210	96851	214	483753	.000442	2.655763	5979646	.006415	61.741	15
20	110912	77	.000694	.003456	96637	334	482402	.000692	2.655938	5495893	-.018218	56.872	20
25	127308	123	.000966	.004818	96303	464	480383	.000966	2.560165	5013491	-.021895	52.060	25
30	132702	130	.000980	.004883	95839	468	478079	.000979	2.616186	4533108	-.006100	47.299	30
35	124641	190	.001524	.007602	95371	725	475153	.001526	2.652299	4055029	.006444	42.518	35
40	118056	250	.002117	.010545	94646	998	470868	.002119	2.633601	3579876	.008722	37.824	40
45	111231	326	.002931	.014576	93648	1365	465052	.002935	2.664377	3109007	.008515	33.199	45
50	103683	470	.004533	.022485	92283	2075	456597	.004544	2.678213	2643956	.014504	28.651	50
55	88332	622	.007042	.034808	90208	3140	443771	.007076	2.685111	2187358	.024290	24.248	55
60	73347	837	.011412	.055876	87068	4865	424066	.011472	2.682554	1743587	.026628	20.026	60
65	60432	1130	.018695	.090058	82203	7403	393970	.018750	2.697583	1319521	.022125	16.052	65
70	48812	1668	.034172	.158904	74800	11886	346190	.034334	2.660255	925551	.020080	12.374	70
75	34311	2053	.059835	.262994	62914	16546	274856	.060199	2.559758	579361	.025360	9.209	75
80	19842	2135	.107600	.427277	46368	19812	182768	.108400	2.523103	304505	.025360	6.567	80
85+	12689	2768	.218142	1.000000	26556	26556	121737	.218142	4.584176	121737	.000000	4.584	85+

NUMBER OF PERSONS DYING (OUT OF 100,000 AT BIRTH) ABOVE AGE X FROM SPECIFIED CAUSES

Age (x)	All Causes	Respiratory T.B.	Other Infec. and Paras.	Neo-plasms	Cardio-vascular	Infl., Pneu., Bronch.	Diar-rheal	Certain Degenerative	Maternal	Cert. Dis. of Infancy	Motor Vehicle	Other Violence	Other and Unknown	Age (x)
0	100000	1328	1070	18383	45842	7244	457	2714	222	1060	156	3377	18147	0
1	97820	1325	1010	18360	45842	6914	389	2711	222	0	156	3347	17544	1
5	97310	1325	941	18309	45842	6842	364	2708	222	0	121	3227	17409	5
10	97025	1325	873	18281	45842	6828	353	2704	222	0	93	3177	17327	10
15	96851	1320	822	18249	45837	6823	353	2700	222	0	93	3155	17277	15
20	96637	1305	749	18234	45818	6823	353	2680	222	0	78	3150	17225	20
25	96303	1245	680	18200	45805	6815	353	2667	196	0	70	3128	17144	25
30	95839	1147	623	18113	45767	6811	350	2648	166	0	62	3102	17050	30
35	95371	1035	576	18027	45728	6800	346	2630	101	0	62	3084	16982	35
40	94646	917	530	17836	45632	6789	342	2569	33	0	62	3053	16883	40
45	93648	801	507	17404	45524	6761	338	2517	13	0	54	2997	16732	45
50	92283	714	481	16739	45281	6731	326	2459	1	0	54	2976	16521	50
55	90208	639	402	15781	44772	6656	313	2361	1	0	50	2923	16270	55
60	87068	563	332	14506	43770	6620	298	2185	1	0	19	2858	15916	60
65	82203	482	286	12824	41754	6539	286	1929	1	0	14	2765	15323	65
70	74800	345	220	10790	38122	6315	273	1543	1	0	7	2634	14550	70
75	62914	224	171	7916	32054	5829	230	1096	1	0	0	2320	13073	75
80	46368	144	114	4830	22678	4785	198	662	1	0	0	1924	11032	80
85+	26556	67	58	2264	11849	2945	86	269	0	0	0	1266	7752	85+

NUMBER OF PERSONS SURVIVING TO AGE X IF SPECIFIED CAUSES WERE ELIMINATED

Age (x)	No Causes	Respiratory T.B.	Other Infec. and Paras.	Neo-plasms	Cardio-vascular	Infl., Pneu., Bronch.	Diar-rheal	Certain Degener-ative	Maternal	Cert. Dis. of Infancy	Motor Vehicle	Other Violence	Other and Unknown	(1) + (2)	(1) + (2) + (5) + (6) + (8)	(1)+(2)+ (5)+(6)+ (8)+part of(9)&(12)	(10) + (11)	Age (x)
		(1)	(2)	(3)	(4)	(5)	(6)	(7)	(8)	(9)	(10)	(11)	(12)					
0	100000	100000	100000	100000	100000	100000	100000	100000	100000	100000	100000	100000	100000	100000	100000	100000	100000	0
1	97820	97823	97879	97843	97820	98147	97887	97823	97820	98874	97820	97850	98418	97882	98277	99762	97850	1
5	97310	97313	97438	97384	97310	97707	97402	97316	97310	98359	97345	97459	98041	97441	97931	99471	97494	5
10	97025	97028	97221	97126	97025	97435	97128	97035	97025	98070	97088	97224	97838	97224	97738	99313	97287	10
15	96851	96859	97097	96984	96856	97265	96953	96865	96851	97895	96914	97072	97711	97105	97624	99223	97134	15
20	96637	96660	96956	96785	96661	97051	96739	96671	96637	97678	96715	96862	97547	96979	97497	99123	96940	20
25	96303	96386	96690	96484	96340	96723	96405	96350	96329	97341	96388	96549	97292	96773	97324	99001	96635	25
30	95839	96019	96281	96106	95914	96261	95943	95904	95895	96872	95932	96110	96918	96442	97049	98771	96203	30
35	95371	95662	95858	95723	95484	95802	95479	95454	95491	96399	95463	95659	96513	96151	96817	98576	95751	35
40	94646	95053	95175	95187	94854	95085	94757	94789	94833	95666	94738	94963	95880	95585	96331	98122	95055	40
45	93648	94167	94195	94616	93962	94110	93762	93842	93853	94657	93747	94017	95021	94717	95509	97320	94116	45
50	92283	92881	92848	93907	92835	92768	92407	92531	92497	93277	92380	92668	93849	93450	94286	96105	92765	50
55	90208	90867	90839	92764	91255	90717	90342	90548	90417	91180	90307	90637	91991	91502	92370	94181	90736	55
60	87068	87779	87746	90831	89081	87635	87212	87570	87270	88006	87194	87546	89144	88463	89393	91177	87673	60
65	82203	82954	82888	87476	86134	82817	82351	82927	82394	83089	82327	82745	84755	83645	84618	86337	82870	65
70	74800	75615	75487	81686	82093	75575	74947	75831	74974	75606	74919	75419	77886	76309	77431	79056	75540	70
75	62914	63711	63536	71633	75432	64020	63077	64195	63060	63592	63021	63726	66934	64341	65794	67272	63834	75
80	46368	47023	46876	55862	66090	48107	46516	47689	46476	46868	46447	47311	51229	47538	49594	50870	47391	80
85+	26556	26990	26889	34388	51331	29016	26725	27616	26618	26842	26601	27602	32176	27328	30120	31257	27649	85+

ADDED YRS OF LIFE

TOTAL		.361	.412	2.778	6.092	.834	.115	.393	.097	.800	.076	.466	2.489	.775	1.850	3.403	.542	
WORK	1.884	.195	.138	.603	.314	.034	.009	.097	.068	.000	.018	.065	.284	.334	.447	.544	.083	

POPULATION, DEATHS, DEATH RATES FOR ALL CAUSES COMBINED, AND SPECIFIED CAUSES

Age Start of Interval	Midyear Population	Deaths During Year	All Causes	Respiratory T.B.	Other Infec. and Paras.	Neoplasms	Cardiovascular	Infl., Pneu., Bronch.	Diarrheal	Certain Degenerative	Maternal	Cert. Dis. of Infancy	Motor Vehicle	Other Violence	Other and Unknown	Age Start of Interval
0	31561	671	.02126	.00000	.00057	.00010	.00010	.00165	.00057	.00000	.00000	.01137	.00000	.00048	.00643	0
1	126864	164	.00129	.00000	.00005	.00019	.00000	.00016	.00003	.00001	.00000	.00000	.00008	.00034	.00044	1
5	155015	107	.00069	.00000	.00004	.00013	.00001	.00003	.00000	.00000	.00000	.00000	.00005	.00028	.00014	5
10	162730	70	.00043	.00000	.00001	.00008	.00001	.00001	.00000	.00001	.00000	.00000	.00006	.00017	.00009	10
15	131556	121	.00092	.00001	.00002	.00008	.00004	.00002	.00000	.00003	.00000	.00000	.00021	.00040	.00012	15
20	106565	128	.00120	.00001	.00002	.00014	.00006	.00002	.00003	.00003	.00000	.00000	.00023	.00055	.00009	20
25	104206	133	.00128	.00001	.00000	.00022	.00014	.00000	.00002	.00007	.00000	.00000	.00011	.00053	.00018	25
30	116555	165	.00142	.00001	.00001	.00025	.00013	.00002	.00001	.00012	.00000	.00000	.00011	.00059	.00017	30
35	132824	254	.00191	.00000	.00005	.00042	.00027	.00001	.00002	.00012	.00000	.00000	.00009	.00054	.00037	35
40	127304	328	.00258	.00007	.00004	.00046	.00065	.00007	.00002	.00015	.00000	.00000	.00011	.00060	.00042	40
45	122356	475	.00388	.00011	.00003	.00077	.00141	.00007	.00001	.00020	.00000	.00000	.00015	.00051	.00063	45
50	110068	716	.00651	.00015	.00010	.00152	.00266	.00013	.00002	.00032	.00000	.00000	.00009	.00063	.00090	50
55	97730	1065	.01090	.00012	.00023	.00256	.00500	.00031	.00000	.00046	.00000	.00000	.00019	.00074	.00129	55
60	85431	1611	.01886	.00025	.00014	.00502	.00912	.00052	.00004	.00057	.00000	.00000	.00016	.00075	.00229	60
65	66423	1898	.02857	.00039	.00027	.00652	.01513	.00084	.00012	.00083	.00000	.00000	.00023	.00068	.00357	65
70	47590	2183	.04587	.00025	.00027	.01009	.02593	.00158	.00008	.00095	.00000	.00000	.00023	.00086	.00563	70
75	31285	2322	.07422	.00038	.00054	.01365	.04306	.00438	.00032	.00137	.00000	.00000	.00019	.00160	.00873	75
80	19446	2389	.12285	.00031	.00021	.01707	.07127	.00941	.00103	.00226	.00000	.00000	.00041	.00252	.01836	80
85+	10574	2322	.21960	.00057	.00047	.02043	.11538	.02620	.00066	.00246	.00000	.00000	.00019	.00681	.04643	85+
ALL	1786083	17122														

	All Causes	Respiratory T.B.	Other Infec. and Paras.	Neoplasms	Cardiovascular	Infl., Pneu., Bronch.	Diarrheal	Certain Degenerative	Maternal	Cert. Dis. of Infancy	Motor Vehicle	Other Violence	Other and Unknown
CRUDE DEATH RATE	.00959	.00008	.00009	.00172	.00453	.00051	.00005	.00024	.00000	.00020	.00013	.00058	.00145
STANDARDIZED RATE (1)	.00474	.00004	.00007	.00079	.00167	.00022	.00004	.00012	.00000	.00040	.00012	.00047	.00080
STANDARDIZED RATE (2)	.00881	.00007	.00008	.00158	.00410	.00046	.00005	.00022	.00000	.00024	.00013	.00056	.00132
GEOMETRIC MEAN	.00620												

LIFE TABLE FOR ALL CAUSES COMBINED

Age (x)	Midyear Population	Deaths During Year	$_nM_x$	$_nq_x$	l_x	$_nd_x$	$_nL_x$	$_nm_x$	$_na_x$	T_x	$_nr_x$	$\overset{\circ}{e}_x$	Age (x)
0	31561	671	.021260	.020860	100000	2086	58135	.021256	.106143	7130773	.000000	71.308	0
1	126864	164	.001293	.005158	97914	505	390394	.001294	1.500000	7032637	.000000	71.825	1
5	155015	107	.000690	.003449	97409	336	486205	.000691	2.500000	6642244	.000000	68.189	5
10	162730	70	.000430	.002143	97073	208	484868	.000429	2.612179	6156039	.007012	63.417	10
15	131556	121	.000920	.004625	96865	448	483282	.000927	2.672061	5671170	.035741	58.547	15
20	106565	128	.001201	.005995	96417	578	480674	.001202	2.558391	5187888	.030303	53.807	20
25	104206	133	.001276	.006365	95839	610	477689	.001277	2.531421	4707215	.002537	49.116	25
30	116555	165	.001416	.007036	95229	670	474530	.001412	2.589552	4229525	-.021093	44.414	30
35	132824	254	.001912	.009497	94559	898	470660	.001908	2.622958	3754995	-.016007	39.711	35
40	127304	328	.002577	.012812	93661	1200	465489	.002578	2.653299	3284335	-.000205	35.066	40
45	122356	475	.003682	.019262	92461	1781	458210	.003687	2.700613	2818846	.006883	30.487	45
50	110068	716	.006505	.032146	90680	2915	446716	.006525	2.707047	2360636	.014137	26.033	50
55	97730	1065	.010897	.053301	87765	4678	428090	.010928	2.705305	1913920	.013166	21.807	55
60	85431	1611	.018857	.090568	83087	7525	397763	.018918	2.651578	1485830	.016640	17.883	60
65	66423	1898	.028574	.134366	75562	10153	353690	.028706	2.624327	1088067	.025385	14.400	65
70	47590	2183	.045871	.207678	65409	13584	294367	.046146	2.594413	734377	.029920	11.227	70
75	31285	2322	.074221	.314694	51825	16309	218998	.074471	2.539600	440009	.015438	8.490	75
80	19446	2389	.122853	.469760	35516	16684	135253	.123354	2.463038	221011	.015438	6.223	80
85+	10574	2322	.219595	1.000000	18832	18832	85758	.219595	4.553833	85758	.000000	4.554	85+

NUMBER OF PERSONS DYING (OUT OF 100,000 AT BIRTH) ABOVE AGE X FROM SPECIFIED CAUSES

Age (x)	All Causes	Respiratory T. B.	Other Infec. and Paras.	Neo-plasms	Cardio-vascular	Infl., Pneu., Bronch.	Diar-rheal	Certain Degen-erative	Maternal	Cert. Dis. of Infancy	Motor Vehicle	Other Violence	Other and Unknown	Age (x)
0	100000	706	740	17434	50346	5983	473	2303	0	1116	1008	4849	15042	0
1	97914	706	684	17424	50336	5822	417	2303	0	0	1008	4802	14412	1
5	97409	706	666	17350	50336	5760	405	2300	0	0	977	4670	14239	5
10	97073	706	647	17288	50330	5744	405	2300	0	0	952	4532	14169	10
15	96865	706	641	17249	50324	5738	405	2297	0	0	925	4451	14129	15
20	96417	702	634	17208	50306	5731	405	2282	0	0	825	4255	14069	20
25	95839	702	625	17140	50278	5722	391	2268	0	0	717	3970	14026	25
30	95229	697	625	17035	50210	5722	382	2236	0	0	667	3718	13937	30
35	94559	693	621	16917	50149	5714	378	2179	0	0	614	3437	13857	35
40	93661	686	596	16719	50022	5710	367	2123	0	0	571	3182	13685	40
45	92461	653	578	16507	49719	5678	360	2053	0	0	520	2904	13489	45
50	90680	605	563	16154	49069	5648	356	1963	0	0	453	2668	13201	50
55	87765	540	518	15474	47876	5590	348	1821	0	0	412	2388	12798	55
60	83087	487	421	14375	45727	5459	348	1623	0	0	329	2072	12246	60
65	75562	389	366	12372	42086	5253	334	1395	0	0	264	1774	11329	65
70	65409	250	269	10058	36706	4953	291	1101	0	0	184	1535	10062	70
75	51825	176	189	7075	29023	4484	266	822	0	0	116	1280	8394	75
80	35516	92	69	4080	19562	3520	156	520	0	0	73	929	6475	80
85+	18832	49	41	1752	9895	2247	57	211	0	0	16	584	3980	85+

NUMBER OF PERSONS SURVIVING TO AGE X IF SPECIFIED CAUSES WERE ELIMINATED

Age (x)	No Causes	Respiratory T. B.	Other Infec. and Paras.	Neo-plasms	Cardio-vascular	Infl., Pneu., Bronch.	Diar-rheal	Certain Degen-erative	Maternal	Cert. Dis. of Infancy	Motor Vehicle	Other Violence	Other and Unknown	(1) + (2)	(1) + (2) + (5) + (6) + (8)	(1)+(2)+ (5)+(6)+ (8)+part of(9)&(12)	(10) + (11)	Age (x)
		(1)	(2)	(3)	(4)	(5)	(6)	(7)	(8)	(9)	(10)	(11)	(12)					
0	100000	100000	100000	100000	100000	100000	100000	100000	100000	100000	100000	100000	100000	100000	100000	100000	100000	0
1	97914	97914	97969	97924	97924	98073	97969	97914	97914	99025	97914	97961	98539	97969	98185	99585	97961	1
5	97409	97409	97482	97453	97419	97630	97416	97412	97409	98514	97440	97587	98205	97482	97770	99214	97618	5
10	97073	97073	97165	97218	97089	97309	97140	97076	97073	98174	97129	97389	97937	97165	97468	98917	97445	10
15	96865	96865	96963	97049	96887	97106	96932	96871	96865	97964	96948	97261	97767	96963	97271	98720	97344	15
20	96417	96421	96521	96641	96457	96664	96483	96438	96417	97511	96599	97008	97375	96525	96839	98284	97191	20
25	95839	95843	95952	96130	95906	96054	95919	95874	95839	96926	96128	96713	96835	95956	96291	97730	97004	25
30	95229	95238	95341	95623	95364	95482	95317	95295	95229	96309	95566	96351	96308	95350	95692	97125	96692	30
35	94559	94572	94674	95068	94754	94818	94651	94682	94559	95631	94947	95957	95711	94687	95039	96465	96350	35
40	93661	93681	93800	94364	93981	93922	93763	93838	93661	94723	94088	95303	94976	93820	94183	95608	95738	40
45	92461	92513	92616	93367	93079	92750	92569	92706	92461	93510	92934	94364	93957	92668	93067	94492	94846	45
50	90680	90779	90847	91923	91937	90994	90789	91010	90680	91708	91210	92785	92437	90946	91371	92789	93327	50
55	87765	87925	87971	89649	90180	88126	87879	88224	87765	88760	88319	90084	89870	88131	88608	90012	90652	55
60	83087	83290	83376	85970	87549	83557	83195	83715	83087	84029	83692	85598	85632	83580	84161	85532	86221	60
65	75562	75840	75878	80184	83365	76187	75673	76353	75562	76415	76175	78137	78783	76157	76900	78204	78771	65
70	65409	65779	65773	71727	77902	66232	65545	66369	65409	66151	66014	67867	69436	66145	67117	68335	68495	70
75	51825	52183	52184	59805	70415	52904	51955	52837	51825	52413	52365	54008	56609	52545	53774	54836	54571	75
80	35516	35831	35861	43909	60084	37081	35664	36463	35516	35919	35921	37314	40561	36179	37931	38830	37740	80
85+	18832	19030	19035	25438	46012	20637	19011	19563	18832	19046	19088	20047	23648	19235	21279	22001	20320	85+

ADDED YRS OF LIFE																	
TOTAL		.111	.171	2.442	7.945	.638	.097	.354	.000	.808	.326	1.339	2.309	.283	1.033	2.252	1.674
WORK	2.686	.036	.035	.492	.665	.043	.017	.125	.000	.000	.173	.628	.351	.071	.131	.153	.804

POPULATION, DEATHS, DEATH RATES FOR ALL CAUSES COMBINED, AND SPECIFIED CAUSES

Age Start of Interval	Midyear Population	Deaths During Year	All Causes	Respiratory T. B.	Other Infec. and Paras.	Neoplasms	Cardiovascular	Infl., Pneu., Bronch.	Diarrheal	Certain Degenerative	Maternal	Cert. Dis. of Infancy	Motor Vehicle	Other Violence	Other and Unknown	Age Start of Interval
0	29885	496	.01660	.00003	.00030	.00013	.00007	.00161	.00033	.00000	.00000	.00783	.00000	.00037	.00592	0
1	120819	108	.00089	.00000	.00004	.00013	.00000	.00009	.00002	.00001	.00000	.00000	.00013	.00012	.00035	1
5	147090	51	.00035	.00000	.00001	.00007	.00000	.00001	.00000	.00001	.00000	.00000	.00007	.00004	.00013	5
10	153874	37	.00024	.00000	.00001	.00007	.00001	.00001	.00000	.00003	.00000	.00000	.00001	.00001	.00008	10
15	125137	40	.00032	.00001	.00002	.00007	.00002	.00002	.00001	.00003	.00001	.00000	.00004	.00000	.00010	15
20	102301	45	.00044	.00001	.00002	.00012	.00005	.00003	.00000	.00004	.00003	.00000	.00002	.00003	.00010	20
25	99898	54	.00054	.00000	.00000	.00015	.00008	.00002	.00000	.00007	.00004	.00000	.00004	.00004	.00010	25
30	111538	82	.00074	.00001	.00001	.00026	.00008	.00001	.00002	.00012	.00003	.00000	.00000	.00005	.00015	30
35	130240	137	.00105	.00002	.00002	.00047	.00011	.00001	.00002	.00008	.00008	.00000	.00003	.00002	.00019	35
40	126610	181	.00143	.00001	.00001	.00086	.00021	.00002	.00001	.00006	.00002	.00000	.00001	.00002	.00018	40
45	121800	292	.00240	.00005	.00007	.00107	.00052	.00009	.00000	.00013	.00001	.00000	.00002	.00013	.00032	45
50	113381	380	.00335	.00004	.00003	.00161	.00093	.00010	.00000	.00011	.00000	.00000	.00004	.00008	.00041	50
55	105600	695	.00658	.00004	.00004	.00288	.00228	.00015	.00002	.00028	.00000	.00000	.00003	.00015	.00071	55
60	94934	978	.01030	.00005	.00006	.00370	.00434	.00033	.00002	.00032	.00000	.00000	.00005	.00013	.00126	60
65	76274	1474	.01933	.00005	.00014	.00497	.00994	.00090	.00004	.00073	.00000	.00000	.00005	.00029	.00220	65
70	58868	1961	.03331	.00007	.00014	.00679	.01962	.00149	.00008	.00105	.00000	.00000	.00003	.00066	.00336	70
75	41541	2592	.06240	.00017	.00010	.00946	.03755	.00472	.00022	.00125	.00000	.00000	.00007	.00169	.00717	75
80	25291	2675	.10577	.00004	.00024	.01238	.06394	.01004	.00036	.00214	.00000	.00000	.00000	.00387	.01277	80
85+	14059	3143	.22356	.00021	.00057	.01472	.11985	.03016	.00092	.00285	.00000	.00000	.00014	.00974	.04438	85+
ALL	1799140	15421														

	All Causes	Respiratory T. B.	Other Infec. and Paras.	Neoplasms	Cardiovascular	Infl., Pneu., Bronch.	Diarrheal	Certain Degenerative	Maternal	Cert. Dis. of Infancy	Motor Vehicle	Other Violence	Other and Unknown
CRUDE DEATH RATE	.00857	.00003	.00005	.00163	.00426	.00065	.00003	.00023	.00001	.00013	.00004	.00026	.00125
STANDARDIZED RATE (1)	.00323	.00001	.00004	.00068	.00114	.00021	.00002	.00010	.00001	.00028	.00004	.00010	.00060
STANDARDIZED RATE (2)	.00647	.00002	.00004	.00129	.00308	.00046	.00003	.00018	.00002	.00016	.00004	.00019	.00095
GEOMETRIC MEAN	.00368												

LIFE TABLE FOR ALL CAUSES COMBINED

Age (x)	Midyear Population	Deaths During Year	$_nM_x$	$_nq_x$	l_x	$_nd_x$	$_nL_x$	$_nm_x$	$_na_x$	T_x	$_nr_x$	$\overset{\circ}{e}_x$	Age (x)
0	29885	496	.016597	.016350	100000	1635	98526	.016595	.098215	7579360	.000000	75.794	0
1	120819	108	.000894	.003568	98365	351	392583	.000894	1.500000	7480834	.000000	76.052	1
5	147090	51	.000347	.001734	98014	170	489645	.000347	2.500000	7088252	.000000	72.319	5
10	153874	37	.000240	.001199	97844	117	488925	.000239	2.476852	6598607	.007271	67.440	10
15	125137	40	.000320	.001607	97727	157	488263	.000322	2.630042	6109682	.034950	62.518	15
20	102301	45	.000440	.002204	97570	215	487335	.000441	2.602713	5621419	.029799	57.614	20
25	99898	54	.000541	.002701	97355	263	486147	.000541	2.610900	5134084	.003603	52.736	25
30	111538	82	.000735	.003656	97092	355	484623	.000733	2.642606	4647938	-.021620	47.871	30
35	130240	137	.001052	.005231	96737	506	482489	.001049	2.636281	4163315	-.018895	43.037	35
40	126610	181	.001430	.007129	96231	686	479572	.001430	2.692541	3680826	-.001108	38.250	40
45	121800	292	.002397	.011932	95545	1140	475060	.002400	2.662058	3201254	.006024	33.505	45
50	113381	380	.003352	.016662	94405	1573	468483	.003358	2.748464	2726194	.009632	28.878	50
55	105600	695	.006581	.032489	92832	3016	457238	.006596	2.704810	2257711	.009349	24.320	55
60	94934	978	.010302	.050526	89816	4538	438760	.010343	2.725825	1800473	.017228	20.046	60
65	76274	1474	.019325	.093049	85278	7935	408111	.019443	2.696466	1361713	.025701	15.968	65
70	58868	1961	.033312	.155425	77343	12021	358718	.033511	2.671003	953602	.025725	12.330	70
75	41541	2592	.062396	.272527	65322	17802	283767	.062735	2.593353	594883	.021307	9.107	75
80	25291	2675	.105769	.420833	47520	19998	188007	.106368	2.520127	311117	.021307	6.547	80
85+	14059	3143	.223558	1.000000	27522	27522	123109	.223558	4.473115	123109	.000000	4.473	85+

NUMBER OF PERSONS DYING (OUT OF 100,000 AT BIRTH) ABOVE AGE X FROM SPECIFIED CAUSES

Age (x)	All Causes	Respiratory T. B.	Other Infec. and Paras.	Neo-plasms	Cardio-vascular	Infl., Pneu., Bronch.	Diar-rheal	Certain Degenerative	Maternal	Cert. Dis. of Infancy	Motor Vehicle	Other Violence	Other and Unknown	Age (x)
0	100000	258	436	16620	52637	8425	375	2393	107	771	299	3185	14494	0
1	98365	255	406	16607	52631	8267	342	2393	107	0	299	3149	13909	1
5	98014	255	390	16555	52631	8231	335	2390	107	0	247	3100	13773	5
10	97844	255	383	16522	52631	8228	335	2383	107	0	210	3080	13710	10
15	97727	255	380	16487	52624	8222	335	2371	107	0	204	3074	13668	15
20	97570	251	372	16451	52617	8214	331	2355	103	0	184	3074	13618	20
25	97355	246	363	16394	52593	8200	331	2336	88	0	175	3060	13569	25
30	97092	246	363	16321	52554	8190	331	2302	69	0	155	3040	13521	30
35	96737	242	358	16196	52515	8186	323	2245	56	0	155	3014	13447	35
40	96231	231	351	15971	52463	8182	311	2204	15	0	141	3006	13356	40
45	95545	227	340	15558	52361	8171	308	2178	4	0	137	2995	13266	45
50	94405	204	308	15051	52115	8128	308	2115	0	0	129	2933	13114	50
55	92832	187	296	14293	51675	8082	308	2062	0	0	108	2895	12926	55
60	89816	170	279	12975	50629	8013	299	1932	0	0	95	2826	12598	60
65	85278	128	251	11350	48713	7868	290	1792	0	0	72	2770	12044	65
70	77343	107	192	9315	44626	7496	274	1491	0	0	51	2652	11139	70
75	65322	82	143	6870	37541	6955	243	1112	0	0	39	2412	9925	75
80	47520	34	116	4177	26826	5605	181	756	0	0	18	1930	7877	80
85+	27522	26	70	1813	14755	3713	114	350	0	0	18	1200	5463	85+

NUMBER OF PERSONS SURVIVING TO AGE X IF SPECIFIED CAUSES WERE ELIMINATED

Age (x)	No Causes	Respiratory T. B. (1)	Other Infec. and Paras. (2)	Neo-plasms (3)	Cardio-vascular (4)	Infl., Pneu., Bronch. (5)	Diar-rheal (6)	Certain Degenerative (7)	Maternal (8)	Cert. Dis. of Infancy (9)	Motor Vehicle (10)	Other Violence (11)	Other and Unknown (12)	(1) + (2)	(1) + (2) + (5) + (6) + (8)	(1)+(2)+ (5)+(6)+ (8)+part of(9)&(12)	(10) + (11)	Age (x)
0	100000	100000	100000	100000	100000	100000	100000	100000	100000	100000	100000	100000	100000	100000	100000	100000	100000	0
1	98365	98368	98395	98378	98371	98522	98398	98365	98365	99133	98365	98401	98947	98398	98587	99676	98401	1
5	98014	98017	98060	98079	98020	98206	98054	98017	98014	98779	98066	98099	98730	98063	98295	99417	98150	5
10	97844	97847	97897	97942	97850	98039	97884	97854	97844	98608	97933	97948	98623	97900	98134	99261	98037	10
15	97727	97730	97782	97860	97740	97928	97766	97749	97727	98490	97822	97837	98547	97785	98026	99157	97932	15
20	97570	97577	97633	97738	97590	97778	97613	97608	97574	98331	97685	97680	98439	97640	97896	99039	97795	20
25	97355	97367	97427	97580	97399	97577	97398	97412	97374	98115	97478	97479	98272	97439	97724	98877	97602	25
30	97092	97104	97164	97390	97175	97323	97135	97183	97130	97850	97235	97236	98055	97176	97489	98646	97379	30
35	96737	96753	96814	97159	96858	96972	96788	96884	96788	97492	96879	96906	97771	96830	97167	98329	97049	35
40	96231	96258	96314	96876	96404	96468	96294	96418	96322	96982	96387	96407	97351	96341	96733	97907	96563	40
45	95545	95575	95639	96601	95818	95752	95610	95757	95647	96291	95704	95731	96748	95569	96084	97256	95890	45
50	94405	94458	94529	95959	94921	94692	94470	94677	94509	95142	94570	94650	95747	94583	95040	96215	94815	50
55	92832	92901	92966	95127	93779	93159	92855	93153	92935	93556	93015	93111	94340	93035	93531	94698	93294	55
60	89816	89900	89963	93374	91778	90201	89886	90254	89915	90517	90006	90154	91604	90046	90603	91747	90344	60
65	85278	85398	85445	90215	89072	85786	85353	85831	85372	85944	85480	85654	87528	85565	86246	87366	85857	65
70	77343	77472	77550	83984	84957	78161	77427	78134	77429	77947	77547	77797	80272	77679	78673	79754	78002	70
75	65322	65454	65542	73400	79269	66519	65421	66341	65394	65832	65505	65928	68962	65674	67053	68044	66113	75
80	47520	47656	47703	56011	69835	49579	47645	48567	47573	47891	47671	48378	52040	47840	50100	51017	48532	80
85+	27522	27607	27662	34603	56241	30237	27645	28442	27552	27737	27609	28583	32194	27748	30656	31454	28674	85+

ADDED YRS OF LIFE

	No Causes	(1)	(2)	(3)	(4)	(5)	(6)	(7)	(8)	(9)	(10)	(11)	(12)	(1)+(2)	(1)+(2)+(5)+(6)+(8)	part	(10)+(11)
TOTAL		.049	.104	2.560	7.557	.788	.065	.343	.048	.591	.125	.354	2.029	.153	1.068	2.125	.480
WORK	1.416	.017	.022	.582	.291	.039	.009	.093	.034	.000	.031	.048	.216	.040	.122	.150	.079

POPULATION, DEATHS, DEATH RATES FOR ALL CAUSES COMBINED, AND SPECIFIED CAUSES

Age Start of Interval	Midyear Population	Deaths During Year	All Causes	Respiratory T. B.	Other Infec. and Paras.	Neoplasms	Cardiovascular	Infl., Pneu., Bronch.	Diarrheal	Certain Degenerative	Maternal	Cert. Dis. of Infancy	Motor Vehicle	Other Violence	Other and Unknown	Age Start of Interval
0	32639	612	.01875	.00000	.00025	.00012	.00003	.00113	.00021	.00000	.00000	.01152	.00003	.00028	.00518	0
1	125459	147	.00117	.00001	.00002	.00014	.00001	.00006	.00008	.00000	.00000	.00000	.00014	.00039	.00032	1
5	157775	107	.00068	.00000	.00003	.00010	.00000	.00003	.00001	.00001	.00000	.00000	.00017	.00022	.00013	5
10	154577	56	.00036	.00000	.00002	.00005	.00002	.00001	.00000	.00002	.00000	.00000	.00005	.00012	.00008	10
15	162782	152	.00093	.00000	.00003	.00009	.00003	.00001	.00000	.00001	.00000	.00000	.00029	.00034	.00014	15
20	123350	141	.00114	.00000	.00000	.00010	.00004	.00002	.00000	.00002	.00000	.00000	.00024	.00052	.00020	20
25	101493	120	.00118	.00002	.00000	.00019	.00010	.00000	.00001	.00005	.00000	.00000	.00011	.00047	.00024	25
30	104202	138	.00132	.00001	.00002	.00020	.00023	.00005	.00000	.00005	.00000	.00000	.00012	.00044	.00020	30
35	116240	223	.00192	.00002	.00000	.00040	.00039	.00003	.00002	.00012	.00000	.00000	.00011	.00049	.00034	35
40	132212	354	.00268	.00003	.00002	.00067	.00070	.00004	.00001	.00019	.00000	.00000	.00009	.00040	.00052	40
45	123284	535	.00434	.00007	.00002	.00101	.00134	.00006	.00000	.00020	.00000	.00000	.00015	.00075	.00071	45
50	118262	830	.00702	.00005	.00004	.00151	.00300	.00012	.00001	.00041	.00000	.00000	.00012	.00073	.00104	50
55	102951	1200	.01166	.00009	.00010	.00285	.00539	.00020	.00001	.00039	.00000	.00000	.00024	.00069	.00170	55
60	90427	1746	.01931	.00012	.00013	.00495	.00969	.00043	.00002	.00069	.00000	.00000	.00022	.00066	.00239	60
65	74874	2297	.03068	.00017	.00016	.00653	.01758	.00080	.00008	.00065	.00000	.00000	.00028	.00085	.00357	65
70	54157	2498	.04613	.00024	.00017	.00971	.02640	.00140	.00011	.00105	.00000	.00000	.00018	.00098	.00587	70
75	35323	2654	.07514	.00040	.00034	.01336	.04365	.00419	.00023	.00125	.00000	.00000	.00051	.00159	.00963	75
80	19265	2377	.12338	.00005	.00026	.01827	.07288	.01023	.00031	.00187	.00000	.00000	.00062	.00275	.01614	80
85+	11553	2477	.21440	.00017	.00026	.01774	.12006	.02294	.00078	.00251	.00000	.00000	.00052	.00701	.04241	85+
ALL	1840825	18664														

	All Causes	Respiratory T. B.	Other Infec. and Paras.	Neoplasms	Cardiovascular	Infl., Pneu., Bronch.	Diarrheal	Certain Degenerative	Maternal	Cert. Dis. of Infancy	Motor Vehicle	Other Violence	Other and Unknown
CRUDE DEATH RATE	.01014	.00005	.00005	.00181	.00501	.00049	.00003	.00024	.00000	.00020	.00018	.00057	.00150
STANDARDIZED RATE (1)	.00473	.00002	.00004	.00079	.00177	.00018	.00003	.00012	.00000	.00041	.00016	.00043	.00078
STANDARDIZED RATE (2)	.00891	.00004	.00005	.00159	.00430	.00042	.00003	.00021	.00000	.00024	.00017	.00054	.00132
GEOMETRIC MEAN	.00613												

LIFE TABLE FOR ALL CAUSES COMBINED

Age (x)	Midyear Population	Deaths During Year	$_nM_x$	$_nq_x$	l_x	$_nd_x$	$_nL_x$	$_nm_x$	$_na_x$	T_x	$_nr_x$	$\overset{\circ}{e}_x$	Age (x)
0	32639	612	.018751	.018440	100000	1844	98344	.018751	.101876	7127143	.000000	71.271	0
1	125459	147	.001172	.004676	98156	459	391477	.001172	1.500000	7028799	.000000	71.608	1
5	157775	107	.000678	.003388	97697	331	487658	.000679	2.500000	6637323	.000000	67.938	5
10	154577	56	.000362	.001808	97366	176	486415	.000362	2.644413	6149665	-.006146	63.160	10
15	162782	152	.000934	.004661	97190	453	484896	.000934	2.672921	5663250	.009873	58.270	15
20	123350	141	.001143	.005706	96737	552	482329	.001144	2.543403	5178354	.041997	53.530	20
25	101493	120	.001182	.005905	96185	568	479521	.001185	2.528609	4696025	.026644	48.823	25
30	104202	138	.001324	.006589	95617	630	476580	.001322	2.611111	4216504	-.002676	44.098	30
35	116240	223	.001918	.009517	94987	904	472804	.001912	2.642653	3739924	-.022699	39.373	35
40	132212	354	.002678	.013276	94083	1249	467520	.002672	2.681979	3267120	-.014710	34.726	40
45	123284	535	.004340	.021490	92834	1995	459577	.004341	2.697577	2799600	.001090	30.157	45
50	118262	830	.007018	.034578	90839	3141	446967	.007027	2.658716	2340023	.007541	25.760	50
55	102951	1200	.011656	.056911	87698	4991	426953	.011690	2.688422	1893057	.013759	21.586	55
60	90427	1746	.019308	.092556	82707	7655	395599	.019350	2.656924	1466104	.011179	17.726	60
65	74874	2297	.030678	.143327	75052	10757	349564	.030773	2.611187	1070505	.016799	14.264	65
70	54157	2498	.046125	.208352	64295	13396	289121	.046333	2.584836	720941	.024604	11.213	70
75	35323	2654	.075135	.318513	50899	16212	214584	.075551	2.538205	431820	.025168	8.484	75
80	19265	2377	.123384	.471906	34687	16369	131758	.124197	2.456371	217235	.025168	6.263	80
85+	11553	2477	.214403	1.000000	18318	18318	85437	.214403	4.664110	85437	.000000	4.664	85+

NUMBER OF PERSONS DYING (OUT OF 100,000 AT BIRTH) ABOVE AGE X FROM SPECIFIED CAUSES

Age (x)	All Causes	Respiratory T. B.	Other Infec. and Paras.	Neoplasms	Cardiovascular	Infl., Pneu., Bronch.	Diarrheal	Certain Degenerative	Maternal	Cert. Dis. of Infancy	Motor Vehicle	Other Violence	Other and Unknown	Age (x)
0	100000	419	442	17178	52002	5473	306	2158	0	1123	1332	4747	14770	0
1	98156	419	418	17166	51999	5361	284	2198	0	0	1329	4720	14262	1
5	97697	416	411	17110	51996	5336	253	2198	0	0	1273	4567	14137	5
10	97366	416	399	17060	51996	5324	250	2195	0	0	1190	4462	14074	10
15	97190	416	390	17035	51986	5318	250	2186	0	0	1168	4405	14036	15
20	96737	416	375	16990	51971	5315	250	2183	0	0	1024	4241	13972	20
25	96185	416	375	16943	51952	5307	250	2171	0	0	908	3990	13873	25
30	95617	406	375	16853	51904	5307	245	2147	0	0	856	3763	13761	30
35	94987	402	366	16757	51794	5284	245	2124	0	0	797	3553	13665	35
40	94083	394	366	16567	51613	5268	237	2067	0	0	744	3321	13506	40
45	92834	380	355	16253	51285	5250	234	1979	0	0	702	3134	13262	45
50	90839	346	348	15791	50670	5220	234	1886	0	0	634	2772	12938	50
55	87698	323	329	15117	49325	5167	230	1704	0	0	581	2447	12475	55
60	82707	286	287	13858	47016	5080	226	1538	0	0	478	2153	11745	60
65	75052	238	235	11934	43173	4909	217	1267	0	0	390	1891	10798	65
70	64295	177	179	9646	37000	4627	189	1038	0	0	292	1591	9548	70
75	50899	107	130	6827	29339	4218	157	732	0	0	239	1308	7842	75
80	34687	22	57	3949	19518	3310	108	464	0	0	128	965	5766	80
85+	18318	15	22	1516	10257	1960	67	214	0	0	44	599	3624	85+

NUMBER OF PERSONS SURVIVING TO AGE X IF SPECIFIED CAUSES WERE ELIMINATED

Age (x)	No Causes	Respiratory T. B. (1)	Other Infec. and Paras. (2)	Neoplasms (3)	Cardiovascular (4)	Infl., Pneu., Bronch. (5)	Diarrheal (6)	Certain Degenerative (7)	Maternal (8)	Cert. Dis. of Infancy (9)	Motor Vehicle (10)	Other Violence (11)	Other and Unknown (12)	(1) + (2)	(1) + (2) + (5) + (6) + (8)	(1)+(2)+(5)+(6)+(8)+part of(9)&(12)	(10) + (11)	Age (x)
0	100000	100000	100000	100000	100000	100000	100000	100000	100000	100000	100000	100000	100000	100000	100000	100000	100000	0
1	98156	98156	98180	98168	98159	98267	98178	98156	98156	99285	98159	98183	98661	98180	98313	99588	98186	1
5	97697	97700	97728	97765	97700	97822	97750	97697	97697	98821	97756	97876	98225	97731	97919	99214	97935	5
10	97366	97369	97409	97483	97372	97513	97421	97369	97366	98486	97508	97650	98055	97412	97614	98912	97792	10
15	97190	97193	97241	97332	97206	97343	97245	97202	97190	98308	97353	97531	97916	97244	97453	98753	97694	15
20	96737	96740	96803	96924	96768	96892	96792	96752	96737	97850	97044	97240	97524	96806	97017	98314	97548	20
25	96185	96188	96251	96417	96235	96347	96240	96212	96185	97291	96606	96937	97067	96254	96471	97763	97362	25
30	95617	95630	95682	95938	95714	95778	95676	95668	95617	96717	96088	96593	96606	95695	95916	97204	97069	30
35	94987	95004	95061	95402	95153	95170	95046	95060	94987	96079	95514	96168	96067	95078	95320	96607	96701	35
40	94083	94108	94156	94684	94468	94280	94149	94212	94083	95165	94658	95487	95313	94181	94445	95727	96070	40
45	92834	92872	92917	93742	93542	93047	92903	93049	92834	93902	93443	94408	94293	92955	93237	94514	95027	45
50	90839	90910	90927	92190	92147	91077	90906	91142	90839	91884	91502	92744	92593	90998	91304	92568	93421	50
55	87698	87789	87802	89677	90312	87980	87767	88170	87698	88707	88391	89863	89856	87893	88245	89483	90573	55
60	82707	82829	82846	85793	87514	83058	82776	83314	82707	83658	83461	85041	85411	82968	83389	84588	85817	60
65	75052	75208	75228	79815	83386	75534	75123	75863	75052	75915	75821	77426	78497	75384	75940	77071	78219	65
70	64295	64485	64497	70659	78060	64971	64382	65203	64295	65034	65045	66615	68466	64688	65457	66485	67392	70
75	50899	51112	51103	58750	70640	51806	50996	51893	50899	51484	51540	52996	55839	51316	52331	53229	53663	75
80	34687	34901	34886	42842	60158	36080	34794	35588	34687	35086	35216	36410	39967	35101	36623	37398	36966	80
85+	18318	18436	18448	24877	46309	20084	18404	18978	18318	18529	18659	19504	22946	18567	20452	21061	19867	85+

ADDED YRS OF LIFE

	No Causes	(1)	(2)	(3)	(4)	(5)	(6)	(7)	(8)	(9)	(10)	(11)	(12)				
TOTAL		.068	.095	2.420	8.690	.537	.065	.336	.000	.819	.431	1.226	2.270	.163	.774	1.847	1.670
WORK	2.745	.022	.020	.516	.713	.041	.006	.112	.000	.000	.203	.561	.422	.042	.089	.106	.767

POPULATION, DEATHS, DEATH RATES FOR ALL CAUSES COMBINED, AND SPECIFIED CAUSES

Age Start of Interval	Midyear Popula- tion	Deaths During Year	All Causes	Respira- tory T. B.	Other Infec. and Paras.	Neo- plasms	Cardio- vascular	Infl., Pneu., Bronch.	Diar- rheal	Certain Degen- erative	Maternal	Cert. Dis. of Infancy	Motor Vehicle	Other Violence	Other and Unknown	Age Start of Interval
0	30868	466	.01510	.00000	.00010	.00006	.00003	.00084	.00016	.00003	.00000	.00810	.00000	.00049	.00528	0
1	119172	121	.00102	.00000	.00005	.00013	.00000	.00008	.00003	.00002	.00000	.00000	.00000	.00016	.00031	1
5	150530	43	.00029	.00000	.00002	.00005	.00000	.00002	.00001	.00001	.00000	.00000	.00007	.00005	.00007	5
10	146722	26	.00018	.00000	.00001	.00003	.00001	.00000	.00000	.00000	.00000	.00000	.00002	.00005	.00005	10
15	154332	47	.00030	.00000	.00000	.00006	.00001	.00002	.00000	.00001	.00001	.00000	.00006	.00006	.00006	15
20	117163	39	.00033	.00000	.00000	.00009	.00003	.00001	.00001	.00003	.00002	.00000	.00002	.00005	.00006	20
25	98140	42	.00043	.00000	.00000	.00013	.00005	.00000	.00000	.00004	.00003	.00000	.00000	.00005	.00012	25
30	100765	69	.00068	.00000	.00002	.00027	.00007	.00003	.00000	.00006	.00003	.00000	.00001	.00009	.00011	30
35	112751	108	.00096	.00003	.00000	.00046	.00011	.00000	.00000	.00005	.00004	.00000	.00001	.00007	.00020	35
40	130755	209	.00160	.00001	.00002	.00079	.00028	.00004	.00001	.00007	.00001	.00000	.00003	.00008	.00027	40
45	123869	278	.00224	.00005	.00001	.00119	.00040	.00003	.00000	.00008	.00001	.00000	.00002	.00010	.00035	45
50	118931	436	.00367	.00006	.00003	.00171	.00114	.00004	.00002	.00012	.00000	.00000	.00007	.00012	.00038	50
55	109181	642	.00588	.00004	.00007	.00242	.00202	.00013	.00003	.00025	.00000	.00000	.00005	.00013	.00074	55
60	100380	1045	.01041	.00007	.00007	.00365	.00443	.00028	.00004	.00030	.00000	.00000	.00003	.00020	.00134	60
65	86422	1636	.01893	.00006	.00012	.00485	.01017	.00059	.00006	.00046	.00000	.00000	.00013	.00027	.00223	65
70	65257	2194	.03362	.00005	.00009	.00683	.01961	.00152	.00015	.00093	.00000	.00000	.00011	.00069	.00363	70
75	45559	2848	.06251	.00007	.00007	.00944	.03769	.00465	.00040	.00158	.00000	.00000	.00015	.00178	.00669	75
80	26445	2935	.11099	.00008	.00019	.01078	.07045	.00987	.00042	.00223	.00000	.00000	.00015	.00424	.01259	80
85+	16272	3323	.20422	.00031	.00061	.01389	.11523	.02643	.00080	.00283	.00000	.00000	.00012	.00873	.03528	85+
ALL	1853514	16507														

CRUDE DEATH RATE			.00891	.00002	.00004	.00164	.00460	.00062	.00004	.00021	.00001	.00013	.00005	.00031	.00122	
STANDARDIZED RATE (1)			.00314	.00001	.00002	.00065	.00115	.00016	.00002	.00008	.00001	.00029	.00005	.00014	.00055	
STANDARDIZED RATE (2)			.00638	.00002	.00003	.00124	.00314	.00041	.00003	.00016	.00001	.00017	.00005	.00023	.00089	
GEOMETRIC MEAN			.00345													

LIFE TABLE FOR ALL CAUSES COMBINED

Age (x)	Midyear Popula- tion	Deaths During Year	$_nM_x$	$_nq_x$	l_x	$_nd_x$	$_nL_x$	$_nm_x$	$_na_x$	T_x	$_nr_x$	$\overset{\circ}{e}_x$	Age (x)
0	30868	466	.015097	.014890	100000	1489	98653	.015093	.095664	7608745	.000000	76.087	0
1	119172	121	.001015	.004050	98511	399	393047	.001015	1.500000	7510092	.000000	76.236	1
5	150530	43	.000286	.001427	98112	140	490210	.000286	2.500000	7117045	.000000	72.540	5
10	146722	26	.000177	.000888	97972	87	489644	.000178	2.521552	6626835	-.005391	67.640	10
15	154332	47	.000305	.001522	97885	149	489068	.000305	2.606264	6137191	-.010717	62.698	15
20	117163	39	.000333	.001668	97736	163	488285	.000334	2.576687	5648123	.041315	57.790	20
25	98140	42	.000428	.002142	97573	209	487378	.000429	2.669458	5159838	.025362	52.882	25
30	100765	69	.000685	.003420	97364	333	486040	.000685	2.657658	4672460	-.002387	47.990	30
35	112751	108	.000958	.004751	97031	461	484093	.000952	2.696132	4186420	-.023366	43.145	35
40	130755	209	.001598	.007942	96570	767	481059	.001594	2.665417	3702327	-.017149	38.338	40
45	123869	278	.002244	.011169	95803	1070	476539	.002245	2.686332	3221267	.001114	33.624	45
50	118931	436	.003666	.018199	94733	1724	469695	.003670	2.697457	2744728	.006679	28.973	50
55	109181	642	.005880	.029072	93009	2704	458885	.005893	2.721816	2275033	.009856	24.460	55
60	100380	1045	.010410	.050972	90305	4603	441081	.010436	2.731009	1816148	.010018	20.111	60
65	86422	1636	.018930	.091106	85702	7808	410576	.019017	2.703130	1375067	.019153	16.045	65
70	65257	2194	.033621	.156829	77894	12216	361043	.033835	2.672980	964491	.026463	12.382	70
75	45559	2848	.062512	.273318	65678	17951	285312	.062917	2.600250	603448	.025134	9.188	75
80	26445	2935	.110985	.436943	47727	20854	186545	.111791	2.502138	318136	.025134	6.666	80
85+	16272	3323	.204216	1.000000	26873	26873	131591	.204216	4.896780	131591	.000000	4.897	85+

NUMBER OF PERSONS DYING (OUT OF 100,000 AT BIRTH) ABOVE AGE X FROM SPECIFIED CAUSES

Age (x)	All Causes	Respira-tory T. B.	Other Infec. and Paras.	Neo-plasms	Cardio-vascular	Infl., Pneu., Bronch.	Diar-rheal	Certain Degen-erative	Maternal	Cert. Dis. of Infancy	Motor Vehicle	Other Violence	Other and Unknown	Age (x)
0	100000	229	359	16117	54433	7845	455	2256	66	799	431	3453	13557	0
1	98511	229	350	16110	54430	7762	439	2253	66	0	431	3405	13036	1
5	98112	229	330	16058	54430	7732	426	2246	66	0	368	3313	12914	5
10	97972	229	320	16032	54430	7723	422	2243	66	0	336	3290	12881	10
15	97885	229	314	16015	54426	7723	422	2243	66	0	326	3263	12858	15
20	97736	229	314	15983	54420	7713	422	2239	62	0	294	3232	12828	20
25	97573	229	314	15937	54408	7713	418	2223	54	0	286	3207	12784	25
30	97364	229	314	15872	54383	7713	418	2203	39	0	286	3182	12725	30
35	97031	229	304	15742	54349	7699	418	2174	24	0	281	3138	12673	35
40	96570	216	304	15520	54298	7699	418	2148	7	0	277	3104	12579	40
45	95803	213	297	15142	54162	7680	414	2115	4	0	262	3064	12450	45
50	94733	189	293	14573	53970	7665	414	2077	0	0	251	3017	12284	50
55	93009	162	281	13771	53436	7645	407	2021	0	0	219	2962	12105	55
60	90305	145	247	12659	52504	7586	394	1907	0	0	194	2903	11766	60
65	85702	114	216	11049	50542	7463	376	1775	0	0	181	2815	11171	65
70	77894	91	169	9053	46342	7219	352	1585	0	0	128	2705	10250	70
75	65678	74	136	6577	39211	6664	297	1245	0	0	90	2454	8930	75
80	47727	55	117	3876	28385	5324	183	792	0	0	46	1942	7007	80
85+	26873	40	81	1828	15163	3477	105	372	0	0	16	1148	4643	85+

NUMBER OF PERSONS SURVIVING TO AGE X IF SPECIFIED CAUSES WERE ELIMINATED

Age (x)	No Causes	Respira-tory T. B.	Other Infec. and Paras.	Neo-plasms	Cardio-vascular	Infl., Pneu., Bronch.	Diar-rheal	Certain Degener-ative	Maternal	Cert. Dis. of Infancy	Motor Vehicle	Other Violence	Other and Unknown	(1) + (2)	(1) + (2) + (5) + (6) + (8)	(1)+(2)+ (5)+(6)+ (8)+part of(9)&(12)	(10) + (11)	Age (x)
		(1)	(2)	(3)	(4)	(5)	(6)	(7)	(8)	(9)	(10)	(11)	(12)					
0	100000	100000	100000	100000	100000	100000	100000	100000	100000	100000	100000	100000	100000	100000	100000	100000	100000	0
1	98511	98511	98520	98518	98514	98593	98527	98514	98511	99307	98511	98559	99029	98520	98618	99460	98559	1
5	98112	98112	98141	98171	98115	98224	98141	98122	98112	98905	98175	98251	98751	98141	98282	99149	98314	5
10	97972	97972	98011	98057	97975	98093	98005	97985	97972	98764	98067	98134	98643	98011	98165	99038	98229	10
15	97885	97885	97930	97987	97892	98006	97918	97898	97885	98676	97990	98074	98579	97930	98083	98958	98179	15
20	97736	97736	97781	97870	97749	97867	97769	97753	97740	98526	97873	97956	98459	97781	97948	98825	98093	20
25	97573	97573	97618	97752	97598	97703	97610	97606	97585	98362	97717	97817	98339	97618	97797	98677	97962	25
30	97364	97364	97409	97608	97414	97494	97401	97417	97391	98151	97508	97633	98188	97409	97602	98486	97777	30
35	97031	97031	97085	97404	97115	97175	97067	97113	97073	97815	97180	97343	97904	97085	97308	98196	97492	35
40	96570	96583	96624	97164	96704	96713	96606	96677	96629	97351	96722	96915	97534	96637	96875	97768	97067	40
45	95803	95819	95864	96772	96072	95964	95843	95942	95864	96577	95969	96185	96889	95880	96142	97035	96351	45
50	94733	94773	94797	96264	95191	94907	94772	94908	94797	95499	94908	95158	95974	94837	95115	96007	95333	50
55	93009	93075	93084	95323	93992	93200	93055	93237	93072	93761	93212	93481	94407	93149	93450	94334	93685	55
60	90305	90385	90411	93681	92192	90548	90362	90639	90366	91035	90527	90821	92002	90492	90855	91732	91045	60
65	85702	85808	85833	90546	89468	86053	85774	86148	85760	86395	85925	86278	87905	85939	86423	87287	86503	65
70	77894	78013	78058	84327	85609	78448	77982	78482	77947	78524	78148	78523	80801	78176	78875	79708	78779	70
75	65678	65793	65846	73593	79145	66663	65803	66488	65723	66209	65927	66442	69395	65962	67124	67909	66694	75
80	47727	47827	47865	56087	70261	49617	47915	48705	47759	48113	47945	48726	52182	47965	50095	50843	48949	80
85+	26873	26940	26977	33413	56941	29395	27037	27743	26891	27090	27018	28042	31358	27045	29784	30440	28194	85+

ADDED YRS OF LIFE

		(1)	(2)	(3)	(4)	(5)	(6)	(7)	(8)	(9)	(10)	(11)	(12)				
TOTAL		.040	.075	2.498	8.492	.688	.065	.287	.031	.614	.147	.484	1.920	.115	.911	1.737	.633
WORK	1.350	.014	.010	.565	.280	.025	.005	.064	.022	.000	.032	.088	.214	.024	.075	.092	.121

POPULATION, DEATHS, DEATH RATES FOR ALL CAUSES COMBINED, AND SPECIFIED CAUSES

Age Start of Interval	Midyear Population	Deaths During Year	All Causes	Respiratory T. B.	Other Infec. and Paras.	Neoplasms	Cardiovascular	Infl., Pneu., Bronch.	Diarrheal	Certain Degenerative	Maternal	Cert. Dis. of Infancy	Motor Vehicle	Other Violence	Other and Unknown	Age Start of Interval
0	18900	1299	.06873	.00016	.00942	.00005	.00026	.00937	.01323	.00000	.00000	.01751	.00000	.00063	.01810	0
1	69490	650	.00935	.00013	.00245	.00004	.00009	.00178	.00161	.00010	.00000	.00000	.00001	.00024	.00289	1
5	72820	154	.00211	.00003	.00052	.00000	.00003	.00021	.00004	.00001	.00000	.00000	.00008	.00027	.00092	5
10	59190	84	.00142	.00003	.00017	.00002	.00002	.00010	.00000	.00005	.00000	.00000	.00005	.00037	.00061	10
15	50890	80	.00157	.00006	.00004	.00004	.00006	.00008	.00002	.00002	.00000	.00000	.00012	.00059	.00055	15
20	40840	121	.00296	.00017	.00020	.00002	.00012	.00010	.00002	.00002	.00000	.00000	.00022	.00125	.00083	20
25	34030	96	.00282	.00018	.00006	.00009	.00009	.00009	.00006	.00006	.00000	.00000	.00012	.00088	.00126	25
30	29590	90	.00304	.00030	.00020	.00014	.00003	.00020	.00003	.00010	.00000	.00000	.00010	.00095	.00098	30
35	27810	90	.00324	.00036	.00022	.00032	.00029	.00029	.00004	.00011	.00000	.00000	.00004	.00076	.00083	35
40	24460	123	.00503	.00065	.00025	.00049	.00049	.00020	.00012	.00033	.00000	.00000	.00016	.00086	.00147	40
45	20910	139	.00665	.00067	.00038	.00053	.00100	.00057	.00014	.00053	.00000	.00000	.00033	.00081	.00167	45
50	16770	138	.00823	.00089	.00024	.00072	.00197	.00054	.00036	.00036	.00000	.00000	.00036	.00101	.00179	50
55	12430	173	.01392	.00072	.00032	.00161	.00386	.00048	.00016	.00032	.00000	.00000	.00008	.00088	.00547	55
60	9370	205	.02188	.00107	.00021	.00256	.00832	.00117	.00043	.00085	.00000	.00000	.00032	.00107	.00587	60
65	7400	217	.02932	.00149	.00081	.00419	.01014	.00108	.00000	.00189	.00000	.00000	.00027	.00122	.00824	65
70	4730	298	.06300	.00148	.00042	.00930	.03002	.00317	.00063	.00254	.00000	.00000	.00000	.00127	.01416	70
75	2560	233	.09102	.00273	.00039	.01172	.04297	.00391	.00000	.00469	.00000	.00000	.00078	.00156	.02227	75
80	1080	174	.16111	.00093	.00370	.01204	.06481	.00833	.00093	.00278	.00000	.00000	.00093	.00648	.06019	80
85+	590	172	.29153	.00339	.00339	.01695	.08644	.01695	.00339	.00508	.00000	.00000	.00169	.00339	.15085	85+
ALL	503860	4536														

	All Causes	Respiratory T. B.	Other Infec. and Paras.	Neoplasms	Cardiovascular	Infl., Pneu., Bronch.	Diarrheal	Certain Degenerative	Maternal	Cert. Dis. of Infancy	Motor Vehicle	Other Violence	Other and Unknown
CRUDE DEATH RATE	.00900	.00028	.00091	.00046	.00134	.00088	.00078	.00020	.00000	.00066	.00012	.00066	.00271
STANDARDIZED RATE (1)	.00910	.00030	.00084	.00051	.00151	.00084	.00072	.00022	.00000	.00062	.00012	.00070	.00271
STANDARDIZED RATE (2)	.01328	.00046	.00067	.00112	.00371	.00091	.00051	.00042	.00000	.00036	.00016	.00084	.00413
GEOMETRIC MEAN	.01164												

LIFE TABLE FOR ALL CAUSES COMBINED

Age (x)	Midyear Population	Deaths During Year	$_nM_x$	$_nq_x$	l_x	$_nd_x$	$_nL_x$	$_nm_x$	$_na_x$	T_x	$_nr_x$	$\overset{\circ}{e}_x$	Age (x)
0	18900	1299	.068730	.065090	100000	6509	94707	.068728	.186841	6183566	.000000	61.836	0
1	69490	650	.009354	.036560	93491	3418	365419	.009354	1.500000	6088859	.000000	65.128	1
5	72820	154	.002115	.010547	90073	950	447990	.002121	2.500000	5723440	.000000	63.542	5
10	59190	84	.001419	.007046	89123	628	443992	.001414	2.416070	5275450	.026210	59.193	10
15	50890	80	.001572	.007876	88495	697	443872	.001581	2.699964	4831458	.032544	54.596	15
20	40840	121	.002963	.014773	87798	1297	435855	.002976	2.582562	4390586	.037480	50.008	20
25	34030	96	.002821	.014000	86501	1211	429476	.002820	2.498452	3954731	.033174	45.719	25
30	29590	90	.003042	.015101	85290	1288	423259	.003043	2.522645	3525256	.021475	41.333	30
35	27810	90	.003236	.016083	84002	1351	416793	.003241	2.619048	3101996	.015631	36.928	35
40	24460	123	.005029	.024924	82651	2060	408374	.005044	2.630663	2685203	.020822	32.488	40
45	20910	139	.006648	.032795	80591	2643	396578	.006665	2.567101	2276829	.026852	28.252	45
50	16770	138	.008229	.040404	77948	3165	382336	.008278	2.660677	1880251	.038566	24.122	50
55	12430	173	.013918	.067583	74783	5084	362062	.014042	2.668666	1497915	.045127	20.030	55
60	9370	205	.021878	.104463	69699	7281	331029	.021995	2.601177	1135853	.033599	16.297	60
65	7400	217	.029324	.138101	62418	8620	292120	.029508	2.683246	804824	.031860	12.894	65
70	4730	298	.063002	.276274	53798	14863	233060	.063773	2.562602	512704	.041782	9.530	70
75	2560	233	.091016	.372749	38935	14513	158221	.091726	2.488186	279644	.047125	7.182	75
80	1080	174	.161111	.574891	24422	14040	85810	.163617	2.414530	121423	.047521	4.972	80
85+	590	172	.291525	1.000000	10382	10382	35613	.291525	3.430233	35613	.000000	3.430	85+

NUMBER OF PERSONS DYING (OUT OF 100,000 AT BIRTH) ABOVE AGE X FROM SPECIFIED CAUSES

Age (x)	All Causes	Respiratory T. B.	Other Infec. and Paras.	Neoplasms	Cardio-vascular	Infl., Pneu., Bronch.	Diarrheal	Certain Degenerative	Maternal	Cert. Dis. of Infancy	Motor Vehicle	Other Violence	Other and Unknown	Age (x)
0	100000	3467	3775	9359	31506	6102	2706	3406	0	1659	1141	5676	31203	0
1	93491	3452	2883	9354	31481	5215	1453	3406	0	0	1141	5616	29490	1
5	90073	3405	1989	9339	31450	4563	864	3369	0	0	1135	5526	28433	5
10	89123	3392	1755	9339	31437	4470	845	3363	0	0	1098	5403	28021	10
15	88495	3377	1681	9331	31430	4425	845	3340	0	0	1076	5237	27753	15
20	87798	3351	1664	9314	31404	4391	837	3332	0	0	1023	4975	27507	20
25	86501	3276	1578	9303	31350	4348	826	3321	0	0	927	4429	27143	25
30	85290	3200	1553	9265	31313	4310	826	3296	0	0	877	4051	26599	30
35	84002	3070	1467	9207	31298	4224	812	3253	0	0	834	3651	26186	35
40	82651	2920	1377	9072	31178	4104	797	3207	0	0	819	3336	25841	40
45	80591	2652	1277	8871	30976	4020	746	3073	0	0	752	2986	25238	45
50	77948	2386	1125	8662	30575	3792	689	2864	0	0	619	2663	24573	50
55	74783	2044	1034	8386	29814	3587	552	2728	0	0	482	2275	23881	55
60	69699	1782	917	7797	28397	3411	494	2611	0	0	454	1955	21881	60
65	62418	1427	846	6943	25624	3020	352	2325	0	0	348	1601	19932	65
70	53798	992	608	5710	22636	2702	352	1769	0	0	269	1245	17515	70
75	38935	645	511	3516	15541	1953	203	1172	0	0	269	949	14176	75
80	24422	210	447	1657	8697	1331	203	425	0	0	143	698	10611	80
85+	10382	121	121	604	3078	604	121	181	0	0	60	121	5371	85+

NUMBER OF PERSONS SURVIVING TO AGE X IF SPECIFIED CAUSES WERE ELIMINATED

Age (x)	No Causes	Respiratory T. B. (1)	Other Infec. and Paras. (2)	Neoplasms (3)	Cardio-vascular (4)	Infl., Pneu., Bronch. (5)	Diarrheal (6)	Certain Degenerative (7)	Maternal (8)	Cert. Dis. of Infancy (9)	Motor Vehicle (10)	Other Violence (11)	Other and Unknown (12)	(1) + (2)	(1) + (2) + (5) + (6) + (8)	(1)+(2)+ (5)+(6)+ (8)+part of(9)&(12)	(10) + (11)	Age (x)
0	100000	100000	100000	100000	100000	100000	100000	100000	100000	100000	100000	100000	100000	100000	100000	100000	100000	0
1	93491	93506	94357	93496	93515	94352	94710	93491	93491	95109	93491	93549	95162	94372	96484	99807	93549	1
5	90073	90133	91758	90092	90127	91551	91835	90109	90073	91631	90079	90217	92745	91859	95193	99526	90223	5
10	89123	89195	91067	89142	89189	90680	90886	89165	89123	90665	89166	89388	92190	91141	94567	99175	89431	10
15	88495	88582	90501	88522	88568	90086	90245	88560	88495	90026	88559	88925	91617	90589	94042	98736	88989	15
20	87798	87910	89805	87842	87896	89411	89543	87870	87798	89317	87915	88487	91348	89920	93392	98104	88604	20
25	86501	86686	88566	86555	86651	88134	88231	86583	86501	87998	86711	87728	90375	88755	92239	96987	87941	25
30	85290	85548	87351	85381	85475	86938	86956	85396	85290	86766	85547	86881	89676	87616	91095	95911	87143	30
35	84002	84386	86120	84149	84199	85713	85696	84149	84002	85455	84298	85974	88754	86513	90055	94983	86277	35
40	82651	83178	84826	82930	82964	84456	84333	82841	82651	84081	82957	84912	87689	85367	89007	94022	85226	40
45	80591	81372	82813	81063	81097	82435	82283	80909	80591	81985	80956	83151	86137	83616	87325	92481	83528	45
50	77948	78968	80251	78611	78836	79962	79642	78462	77948	79297	78433	80752	84014	81301	85213	90514	81254	50
55	74783	76101	77084	75693	76393	76921	76545	75410	74783	76077	75383	77867	81338	78443	82566	87973	78492	55
60	69699	71185	71960	71125	72613	71867	71398	70398	69699	70905	70285	72895	77936	73494	77627	83146	73508	60
65	62418	64092	64512	64525	67820	64741	64077	63319	62418	63498	63044	65631	71884	66243	70535	75951	66289	65
70	53798	55655	55831	56810	61553	56107	55228	55099	53798	54729	54411	56913	64588	57796	61838	67029	57561	70
75	38935	40582	40499	43121	51997	41273	40099	40396	38935	39609	39379	41453	50259	42201	46073	50362	41925	75
80	24422	25811	25451	28696	40612	26410	25150	25952	24422	24845	24802	26214	35385	26899	29956	33135	26623	80
85+	10382	11032	11037	13007	24313	11735	10745	11197	10382	10562	10597	11543	20700	11728	13720	15866	11782	85+

ADDED YRS OF LIFE

		(1)	(2)	(3)	(4)	(5)	(6)	(7)	(8)	(9)	(10)	(11)	(12)				
TOTAL		.689	1.661	1.079	3.686	1.638	1.339	.463	.000	1.067	.286	1.622	6.418	2.375	5.539	9.697	1.921
WORK	4.499	.347	.184	.274	.493	.225	.066	.148	.000	.000	.168	.974	1.312	.533	.831	1.194	1.147

POPULATION, DEATHS, DEATH RATES FOR ALL CAUSES COMBINED, AND SPECIFIED CAUSES

Age Start of Interval	Midyear Population	Deaths During Year	All Causes	Respiratory T.B.	Other Infec. and Paras.	Neoplasms	Cardiovascular	Infl., Pneu., Bronch.	Diarrheal	Certain Degenerative	Maternal	Cert. Dis. of Infancy	Motor Vehicle	Other Violence	Other and Unknown	Age Start of Interval
0	18500	1066	.05762	.00038	.00762	.00011	.00011	.00935	.01022	.00000	.00000	.01249	.00005	.00043	.01686	0
1	67610	620	.00917	.00007	.00291	.00004	.00001	.00175	.00127	.00004	.00000	.00000	.00001	.00031	.00274	1
5	71220	140	.00197	.00001	.00053	.00003	.00004	.00020	.00004	.00001	.00000	.00000	.00006	.00014	.00090	5
10	58780	64	.00109	.00002	.00015	.00002	.00007	.00007	.00007	.00002	.00003	.00000	.00002	.00019	.00044	10
15	50020	78	.00156	.00004	.00012	.00008	.00008	.00010	.00002	.00002	.00024	.00000	.00002	.00008	.00076	15
20	40340	108	.00268	.00025	.00007	.00012	.00020	.00005	.00000	.00000	.00045	.00000	.00000	.00032	.00121	20
25	33640	108	.00321	.00056	.00021	.00015	.00009	.00012	.00003	.00006	.00048	.00000	.00000	.00021	.00131	25
30	30190	89	.00295	.00043	.00013	.00036	.00023	.00013	.00003	.00003	.00040	.00000	.00000	.00023	.00096	30
35	26930	100	.00371	.00059	.00011	.00048	.00041	.00015	.00004	.00007	.00067	.00000	.00007	.00004	.00108	35
40	22990	100	.00435	.00035	.00100	.00061	.00026	.00000	.00009	.00017	.00000	.00000	.00017	.00013	.00144	40
45	18840	124	.00658	.00037	.00016	.00133	.00101	.00037	.00016	.00021	.00016	.00000	.00016	.00027	.00239	45
50	15190	112	.00737	.00039	.00020	.00151	.00132	.00020	.00007	.00026	.00000	.00000	.00000	.00007	.00296	50
55	11830	133	.01124	.00034	.00059	.00211	.00287	.00051	.00000	.00034	.00000	.00000	.00008	.00008	.00431	55
60	9070	148	.01632	.00044	.00055	.00265	.00496	.00077	.00033	.00121	.00000	.00000	.00011	.00022	.00507	60
65	6800	155	.02279	.00074	.00103	.00456	.00838	.00176	.00000	.00118	.00000	.00000	.00000	.00015	.00500	65
70	4440	186	.04189	.00090	.00068	.00541	.02117	.00248	.00000	.00203	.00000	.00000	.00000	.00045	.00878	70
75	2470	148	.05992	.00081	.00081	.00729	.02591	.00364	.00040	.00283	.00000	.00000	.00000	.00081	.01741	75
80	1190	152	.12773	.00336	.00000	.01261	.05462	.00588	.00084	.00168	.00000	.00000	.00000	.00336	.04538	80
85+	690	220	.31884	.00000	.00725	.02754	.11304	.01739	.00000	.01014	.00000	.00000	.00000	.00435	.13913	85+
ALL	490740	3851														
CRUDE DEATH RATE			.00785	.00024	.00091	.00057	.00109	.00083	.00060	.00014	.00017	.00047	.00004	.00022	.00257	
STANDARDIZED RATE (1)			.00779	.00026	.00083	.00062	.00117	.00079	.00055	.00015	.00018	.00044	.00004	.00021	.00253	
STANDARDIZED RATE (2)			.01099	.00034	.00067	.00120	.00292	.00082	.00037	.00032	.00018	.00026	.00004	.00025	.00360	
GEOMETRIC MEAN			.01026													

LIFE TABLE FOR ALL CAUSES COMBINED

Age (x)	Midyear Population	Deaths During Year	$_nM_x$	$_nq_x$	l_x	$_nd_x$	$_nL_x$	$_nm_x$	$_na_x$	T_x	$_nr_x$	$\overset{\circ}{e}_x$	Age (x)
0	18500	1066	.057622	.054990	100000	5499	95425	.057627	.167957	6447790	.000000	64.478	0
1	67610	620	.009170	.035851	94501	3388	369534	.009168	1.500000	6352365	.000000	67.220	1
5	71220	140	.001966	.009801	91113	893	453333	.001970	2.500000	5982831	.000000	65.664	5
10	58780	64	.001089	.005409	90220	488	449840	.001085	2.418460	5529499	.025799	61.289	10
15	50020	78	.001559	.007823	89732	702	447051	.001570	2.708333	5079658	.033050	56.609	15
20	40340	108	.002677	.013366	89030	1190	442320	.002690	2.622199	4632607	.037853	52.034	20
25	33640	108	.003210	.015938	87840	1400	435716	.003213	2.511310	4190287	.030023	47.704	25
30	30190	89	.002948	.014646	86440	1266	429070	.002952	2.527975	3754571	.021058	43.436	30
35	26930	100	.003713	.018433	85174	1570	422057	.003720	2.571523	3325501	.021849	39.044	35
40	22990	100	.004350	.021590	83604	1805	413735	.004363	2.625808	2903443	.028272	34.729	40
45	18840	124	.006582	.032519	81799	2660	402568	.006608	2.583960	2489709	.033155	30.437	45
50	15190	112	.007373	.036354	79139	2877	388824	.007399	2.611734	2087140	.036894	26.373	50
55	11830	133	.011243	.055113	76262	4203	371388	.011317	2.639385	1698316	.039827	22.269	55
60	9070	148	.016318	.078949	72059	5689	346704	.016409	2.610996	1326928	.038406	18.414	60
65	6800	155	.022194	.108995	66370	7234	314951	.022969	2.664011	980224	.042085	14.769	65
70	4440	186	.041892	.192505	59136	11384	268342	.042423	2.598585	665273	.055810	11.250	70
75	2470	148	.059919	.264303	47752	12621	208459	.060544	2.599140	396930	.061470	8.312	75
80	1190	152	.127731	.495004	35131	17390	132829	.130920	2.537342	188472	.061470	5.365	80
85+	690	220	.318841	1.000000	17741	17741	55642	.318841	3.136364	55642	.000000	3.136	85+

NUMBER OF PERSONS DYING (OUT OF 100,000 AT BIRTH) ABOVE AGE X FROM SPECIFIED CAUSES

Age (x)	All Causes	Respiratory T. B.	Other Infec. and Paras.	Neo-plasms	Cardio-vascular	Infl., Pneu., Bronch.	Diar-rheal	Certain Degen-erative	Maternal	Cert. Dis. of Infancy	Motor Vehicle	Other Violence	Other and Unknown	Age (x)
0	100000	2723	4089	11672	32077	6459	1952	3199	1119	1192	291	2024	33203	0
1	94501	2687	3361	11661	32067	5567	977	3199	1119	0	286	1983	31594	1
5	91113	2660	2285	11645	32061	4922	507	3183	1119	0	280	1868	30583	5
10	90220	2654	2043	11632	32042	4832	488	3177	1119	0	255	1804	30174	10
15	89732	2646	1975	11624	32011	4802	457	3169	1104	0	247	1720	29977	15
20	89030	2627	1921	11568	31975	4757	448	3160	995	0	238	1684	29637	20
25	87840	2516	1888	11533	31887	4736	448	3160	797	0	238	1541	29096	25
30	86440	2269	1797	11468	31849	4684	435	3134	589	0	238	1450	28527	30
35	85174	2084	1741	11311	31749	4627	421	3120	419	0	238	1351	28113	35
40	83604	1834	1694	11106	31575	4564	405	3088	137	0	206	1336	27659	40
45	81799	1690	1640	10690	31322	4455	405	3052	66	0	134	1281	27064	45
50	79139	1541	1575	10153	30914	4306	341	2966	3	0	70	1174	26096	50
55	76262	1387	1498	9409	30398	4229	316	2863	3	0	70	1150	24939	55
60	72059	1262	1276	8622	29319	4039	315	2735	3	0	39	1118	23331	60
65	66370	1108	1084	7699	27584	3768	200	2312	3	0	1	1041	21570	65
70	59136	875	759	6255	24910	3207	200	1940	3	0	1	954	19992	70
75	47752	632	579	4795	19146	2536	200	1390	3	0	1	871	17599	75
80	35131	462	411	3265	13707	1770	114	798	3	0	1	698	13902	80
85+	17741	0	403	1532	6290	568	0	564	0	0	0	242	7742	85+

NUMBER OF PERSONS SURVIVING TO AGE X IF SPECIFIED CAUSES WERE ELIMINATED

Age (x)	No Causes	Respiratory T. B. (1)	Other Infec. and Paras. (2)	Neo-plasms (3)	Cardio-vascular (4)	Infl., Pneu., Bronch. (5)	Diar-rheal (6)	Certain Degener-ative (7)	Maternal (8)	Cert. Dis. of Infancy (9)	Motor Vehicle (10)	Other Violence (11)	Other and Unknown (12)	(1) + (2)	(1) + (2) + (5) + (6) + (8)	(1)+(2)+ (5)+(6)+ (8)+part of(9)&(12)	(10) + (11)	Age (x)
0	100000	100000	100000	100000	100000	100000	100000	100000	100000	100000	100000	100000	100000	100000	100000	100000	100000	0
1	94501	94536	95211	94512	94511	95372	95453	94501	94501	95667	94506	94541	96078	95247	97093	99860	94546	1
5	91113	91173	92868	91139	91128	92594	92499	91129	91113	92237	91124	91264	93648	92930	95877	99616	91275	5
10	90220	90286	92204	90259	90254	91778	91611	90242	90220	91333	90255	90434	93150	92271	95312	99359	90469	10
15	89732	89805	91775	89778	89757	91312	91147	89761	89747	90839	89775	90029	92849	91850	94956	99102	90072	15
20	89030	89122	91112	89112	89130	90643	90443	89068	89154	90128	89082	89360	92473	91205	94463	98831	89412	20
25	87840	88041	89927	87976	88026	89453	89234	87878	88159	88924	87891	88309	91757	90133	93583	98247	88360	25
30	86440	86884	88587	86638	86661	88075	87825	86503	86961	87506	86490	86992	90526	89041	92740	97830	87042	30
35	85174	85756	87346	85526	85492	86847	86553	85250	85858	86225	85224	85817	90027	87984	91896	97205	85867	35
40	83604	84464	85784	84153	84089	85310	84974	83710	84557	84635	83684	84250	88845	86667	90908	96465	84331	40
45	81799	82785	83987	82752	82526	83578	83139	81939	82802	82808	81949	82486	87554	84998	89353	95028	82637	45
50	79139	80241	81321	80557	80248	81010	80500	79355	80172	80115	79347	79909	85733	82453	86975	92822	80120	50
55	76262	77477	78443	78414	77847	78143	77598	76575	77258	77203	76462	77028	83856	79692	84173	90090	77231	55
60	72059	73330	74342	74883	74636	74026	73322	72481	73000	72948	72279	72814	80970	75653	80113	86131	73036	60
65	66370	67692	68663	69898	70492	68450	67646	67168	67236	67189	66609	67140	76497	70030	74574	80557	67382	65
70	59136	60538	61456	63728	65555	61537	60272	60202	59908	59865	59349	59867	69893	62953	67640	73430	60082	70
75	47752	49106	49823	52884	58989	50320	48670	49117	48375	48341	47924	48455	59041	51236	55748	60852	48629	75
80	35131	36277	36803	40375	49513	37713	35882	36654	35590	35564	35257	35800	47545	38004	42213	46636	35929	80
85+	17741	18655	18591	21826	33462	19655	18202	18681	17975	17960	17805	18406	30584	19549	22513	25628	18473	85+

ADDED YRS OF LIFE																		
TOTAL		.666	1.766	1.672	3.673	1.669	1.076	.387	.480	.793	.099	.506	6.732	2.455	5.891	10.294	.606	
WORK	4.315	.380	.164	.557	.482	.171	.036	.085	.384	.000	.045	.191	1.558	.545	1.150	1.891	.237	

POPULATION, DEATHS, DEATH RATES FOR ALL CAUSES COMBINED, AND SPECIFIED CAUSES

Age Start of Interval	Midyear Population	Deaths During Year	All Causes	Respiratory T. B.	Other Infec. and Paras.	Neoplasms	Cardiovascular	Infl., Pneu., Bronch.	Diarrheal	Certain Degenerative	Maternal	Cert. Dis. of Infancy	Motor Vehicle	Other Violence	Other and Unknown	Age Start of Interval
0	22288	1066	.04783	.00013	.00628	.00027	.00022	.00462	.00754	.00009	.00000	.01422	.00000	.00036	.01409	0
1	78027	603	.00773	.00006	.00147	.00009	.00009	.00149	.00127	.00010	.00000	.00000	.00000	.00035	.00281	1
5	82239	141	.00171	.00004	.00035	.00004	.00006	.00013	.00006	.00006	.00000	.00000	.00005	.00021	.00073	5
10	70783	65	.00092	.00003	.00014	.00004	.00003	.00006	.00000	.00003	.00000	.00000	.00004	.00016	.00040	10
15	57203	101	.00177	.00007	.00014	.00007	.00007	.00005	.00000	.00007	.00000	.00000	.00023	.00058	.00049	15
20	48446	99	.00204	.00012	.00014	.00006	.00010	.00004	.00002	.00010	.00000	.00000	.00029	.00062	.00054	20
25	40456	124	.00307	.00030	.00007	.00012	.00022	.00005	.00002	.00005	.00000	.00000	.00037	.00133	.00052	25
30	35810	90	.00251	.00017	.00014	.00017	.00014	.00017	.00006	.00006	.00000	.00000	.00017	.00073	.00073	30
35	32290	116	.00359	.00059	.00012	.00025	.00028	.00009	.00006	.00022	.00000	.00000	.00031	.00077	.00090	35
40	28714	107	.00373	.00056	.00010	.00028	.00045	.00007	.00000	.00000	.00000	.00000	.00017	.00087	.00122	40
45	24858	140	.00563	.00052	.00008	.00084	.00072	.00032	.00004	.00032	.00000	.00000	.00040	.00056	.00181	45
50	18366	172	.00937	.00049	.00022	.00114	.00212	.00044	.00000	.00065	.00000	.00000	.00022	.00152	.00256	50
55	13492	182	.01349	.00056	.00022	.00259	.00430	.00052	.00007	.00059	.00000	.00000	.00022	.00052	.00348	55
60	11841	244	.02061	.00076	.00068	.00329	.00676	.00110	.00025	.00110	.00000	.00000	.00017	.00127	.00524	60
65	7823	254	.03247	.00115	.00089	.00447	.01240	.00089	.00026	.00243	.00000	.00000	.00026	.00077	.00895	65
70	6368	292	.04585	.00204	.00141	.00550	.01837	.00236	.00047	.00110	.00000	.00000	.00031	.00173	.01256	70
75	3649	294	.08057	.00164	.00082	.01178	.03152	.00411	.00027	.00301	.00000	.00000	.00000	.00082	.02658	75
80	1700	225	.13235	.00353	.00059	.01412	.05941	.00353	.00059	.00294	.00000	.00000	.00059	.00412	.04294	80
85+	1132	209	.18463	.00177	.00265	.01148	.07155	.01413	.00000	.00618	.00000	.00000	.00088	.00265	.07332	85+
ALL	585485	4524														

	All Causes	Respiratory T. B.	Other Infec. and Paras.	Neoplasms	Cardiovascular	Infl., Pneu., Bronch.	Diarrheal	Certain Degenerative	Maternal	Cert. Dis. of Infancy	Motor Vehicle	Other Violence	Other and Unknown
CRUDE DEATH RATE	.00773	.00027	.00062	.00054	.00132	.00059	.00050	.00022	.00000	.00054	.00016	.00060	.00237
STANDARDIZED RATE (1)	.00754	.00028	.00058	.00057	.00131	.00055	.00046	.00022	.00000	.00050	.00017	.00062	.00227
STANDARDIZED RATE (2)	.01118	.00043	.00050	.00115	.00312	.00063	.00032	.00040	.00000	.00029	.00020	.00074	.00339
GEOMETRIC MEAN	.01000												

LIFE TABLE FOR ALL CAUSES COMBINED

Age (x)	Midyear Population	Deaths During Year	$_nM_x$	$_nq_x$	l_x	$_nd_x$	$_nL_x$	$_nm_x$	$_na_x$	T_x	$_nr_x$	$\overset{\circ}{e}_x$	Age (x)
0	22288	1066	.047828	.045960	100000	4596	96099	.047825	.151308	6494885	.000000	64.949	0
1	78027	603	.007728	.030334	95404	2894	374381	.007730	1.500000	6398786	.000000	67.070	1
5	82239	141	.001715	.008540	92510	790	460575	.001715	2.500000	6024405	.000000	65.122	5
10	70783	65	.000918	.004568	91720	419	457556	.000916	2.508453	5563830	.026479	60.661	10
15	57203	101	.001766	.008839	91301	807	454593	.001775	2.630370	5106274	.034624	55.928	15
20	48446	99	.002044	.010211	90494	924	450276	.002052	2.625586	4651681	.033462	51.403	20
25	40456	124	.003065	.015228	89570	1364	444477	.003069	2.527187	4201405	.030260	46.906	25
30	35810	90	.002513	.012493	88206	1102	438315	.002520	2.535920	3756928	.022262	42.593	30
35	32290	116	.003592	.017841	87104	1554	431735	.003599	2.564484	3318614	.019499	38.099	35
40	28714	107	.003726	.018504	85550	1583	423958	.003734	2.604496	2886878	.019248	33.745	40
45	24858	140	.005632	.027963	83967	2348	414421	.005666	2.694226	2462920	.031062	29.332	45
50	18366	172	.009365	.046215	81619	3772	399241	.009448	2.652826	2048949	.051021	25.098	50
55	13492	182	.013489	.065706	77847	5115	377159	.013562	2.639093	1649258	.034036	21.186	55
60	11841	244	.020606	.098815	72732	7187	346694	.020730	2.639285	1272099	.033536	17.490	60
65	7823	254	.032468	.151346	65545	9920	303829	.032650	2.591146	925405	.031968	14.119	65
70	6368	292	.045654	.207122	55625	11527	250359	.046042	2.591253	621576	.023581	11.174	70
75	3649	294	.080570	.339449	44098	14969	183684	.081493	2.541210	371217	.044377	8.418	75
80	1700	225	.132353	.497374	29129	14488	108233	.133859	2.417719	187532	.044377	6.438	80
85+	1132	209	.184629	1.000000	14641	14641	79300	.184629	5.416268	79300	.000000	5.416	85+

NUMBER OF PERSONS DYING (OUT OF 100,000 AT BIRTH) ABOVE AGE X FROM SPECIFIED CAUSES

Age (x)	All Causes	Respiratory T.B.	Other Infec. and Paras.	Neoplasms	Cardio-vascular	Infl., Pneu., Bronch.	Diarrheal	Certain Degenerative	Maternal	Cert. Dis. of Infancy	Motor Vehicle	Other Violence	Other and Unknown	Age (x)
0	100000	3594	3201	10849	32231	5322	1744	3697	0	1367	1413	5462	31120	0
1	95404	3581	2597	10823	32210	4878	1020	3688	0	0	1413	5427	29767	1
5	92510	3557	2045	10789	32176	4321	545	3650	0	0	1413	5297	28717	5
10	91720	3540	1883	10773	32148	4259	517	3628	0	0	1391	5202	28379	10
15	91301	3527	1819	10753	32135	4234	517	3615	0	0	1371	5130	28200	15
20	90494	3495	1755	10721	32103	4210	517	3583	0	0	1267	4866	27977	20
25	89570	3439	1690	10693	32057	4191	507	3536	0	0	1136	4586	27735	25
30	88206	3306	1657	10638	31957	4169	496	3514	0	0	972	3991	27506	30
35	87104	3233	1596	10564	31896	4095	472	3490	0	0	898	3674	27186	35
40	85550	2978	1543	10457	31775	4055	445	3396	0	0	765	3340	26796	40
45	83967	2742	1498	10338	31583	4026	445	3396	0	0	691	2971	26277	45
50	81619	2525	1465	9986	31279	3891	428	3261	0	0	524	2737	25523	50
55	77847	2329	1377	9523	30417	3716	428	2998	0	0	438	2125	24496	55
60	72732	1964	1292	8539	28783	3519	400	2774	0	0	354	1931	23176	60
65	65545	1700	1056	7392	26423	3137	311	2389	0	0	296	1490	21351	65
70	55625	1348	783	6028	22631	2864	233	1649	0	0	218	1258	18613	70
75	44098	836	429	4646	18012	2270	115	1375	0	0	139	824	15452	75
80	29129	534	280	2456	12152	1509	65	814	0	0	139	673	10507	80
85+	14641	140	210	911	5674	1121	0	490	0	0	70	210	5815	85+

NUMBER OF PERSONS SURVIVING TO AGE X IF SPECIFIED CAUSES WERE ELIMINATED

Age (x)	No Causes	Respiratory T.B.	Other Infec. and Paras.	Neo-plasms	Cardio-vascular	Infl., Pneu., Bronch.	Diar-rheal	Certain Degener-ative	Maternal	Cert. Dis. of Infancy	Motor Vehicle	Other Violence	Other and Unknown	(1)+(2)	(1)+(2)+(5)+(6)+(8)	(1)+(2)+(5)+(6)+(8)+part of(9)&(12)	(10)+(11)	Age (x)
		(1)	(2)	(3)	(4)	(5)	(6)	(7)	(8)	(9)	(10)	(11)	(12)					
0	100000	100000	100000	100000	100000	100000	100000	100000	100000	100000	100000	100000	100000	100000	100000	100000	100000	0
1	95404	95417	95596	95429	95425	95839	96114	95413	95404	96748	95404	95438	96735	96009	97163	99772	95438	1
5	92510	92546	93632	92568	92563	93484	93671	92556	92510	93814	92510	92671	94854	93669	95842	99379	92671	5
10	91720	91773	92996	91794	91801	92748	92899	91787	91720	93013	91742	91975	94390	93049	95302	99035	91997	10
15	91301	91366	92636	91394	91394	92350	92475	91381	91301	92508	91343	91627	94143	92702	94972	98775	91669	15
20	90494	90591	91882	90618	90619	91558	91657	90605	90494	91769	90639	91081	93540	91980	94257	98080	91227	20
25	89570	89721	91009	89721	89739	90642	90721	89727	89570	90832	89844	90432	92834	91163	93450	97298	90709	25
30	88206	88497	89657	88409	88472	89284	89361	88382	88206	89449	88639	89653	91656	89943	92234	96075	90093	30
35	87104	87455	88598	87379	87428	88243	88268	87302	87104	88332	87606	88853	90842	88955	91323	95229	89365	35
40	85550	86149	87071	85926	85988	86708	86721	85838	85550	86756	86176	87606	85626	87680	90084	94074	88247	40
45	83967	84790	85505	84455	84589	85133	85116	84250	83967	85150	84655	86360	85508	86344	88741	92837	87068	45
50	81619	82635	83147	82443	82526	82888	82753	82028	81619	82769	82454	84183	86819	84183	86679	90888	85044	50
55	77847	79091	79392	79091	79569	79231	78929	78495	77847	78944	78728	80910	83880	80579	83150	87376	81826	55
60	72732	74177	74260	74867	75974	74219	73770	73556	72732	73757	73637	75788	79755	75736	78387	82628	76731	60
65	65545	67103	67151	68597	70849	67255	66566	66659	65545	66469	66416	68736	73799	68747	71640	75877	69649	65
70	55625	57280	57246	59541	64022	57335	56565	57265	55625	56409	56437	58556	65533	58949	61787	65847	59411	70
75	44098	45879	45706	48536	55704	46003	44949	45646	44098	44719	44812	46827	55375	47551	50562	54534	47586	75
80	29129	30556	30311	34062	43285	31030	29731	30623	29129	29539	29600	31060	41956	31796	34571	37931	31562	80
85+	14641	15648	15286	18424	29591	15886	14990	15631	14641	14847	14927	15958	26351	16337	18150	20333	16270	85+

ADDED YRS OF LIFE

	No Causes	(1)	(2)	(3)	(4)	(5)	(6)	(7)	(8)	(9)	(10)	(11)	(12)	(1)+(2)	+(5)+(6)+(8)	+part of(9)&(12)	(10)+(11)
TOTAL		.716	1.239	1.497	4.607	1.240	.903	.566	.000	.913	.439	1.587	6.455	1.977	4.240	7.737	2.044
WORK	4.208	.336	.145	.354	.517	.140	.031	.160	.000	.000	.294	.904	1.051	.482	.656	.904	1.206

POPULATION, DEATHS, DEATH RATES FOR ALL CAUSES COMBINED, AND SPECIFIED CAUSES

Age Start of Interval	Midyear Population	Deaths During Year	All Causes	Respiratory T. B.	Other Infec. and Paras.	Neo-plasms	Cardio-vascular	Infl., Pneu., Bronch.	Diar-rheal	Certain Degen-erative	Maternal	Cert. Dis. of Infancy	Motor Vehicle	Other Violence	Other and Unknown	Age Start of Interval
0	21495	922	.04289	.00000	.00642	.00005	.00005	.00470	.00609	.00005	.00000	.01228	.00000	.00047	.01279	0
1	75843	605	.00798	.00005	.00186	.00007	.00004	.00160	.00121	.00005	.00000	.00000	.00003	.00025	.00282	1
5	79667	157	.00197	.00004	.00046	.00008	.00004	.00093	.00008	.00006	.00000	.00000	.00006	.00013	.00090	5
10	68103	54	.00079	.00004	.00007	.00004	.00001	.00006	.00001	.00003	.00001	.00000	.00001	.00012	.00037	10
15	57712	97	.00168	.00003	.00014	.00005	.00005	.00014	.00002	.00003	.00023	.00000	.00009	.00029	.00061	15
20	47718	92	.00193	.00013	.00013	.00004	.00015	.00006	.00002	.00010	.00021	.00000	.00004	.00025	.00080	20
25	39432	110	.00279	.00043	.00010	.00020	.00013	.00008	.00000	.00013	.00033	.00000	.00000	.00038	.00101	25
30	34085	79	.00232	.00018	.00003	.00018	.00029	.00012	.00003	.00006	.00044	.00000	.00003	.00015	.00082	30
35	30293	103	.00340	.00033	.00007	.00050	.00046	.00013	.00000	.00020	.00050	.00000	.00007	.00026	.00089	35
40	25910	105	.00405	.00046	.00004	.00073	.00066	.00027	.00000	.00015	.00019	.00000	.00000	.00019	.00135	40
45	21963	112	.00510	.00036	.00000	.00114	.00105	.00018	.00005	.00009	.00009	.00000	.00000	.00014	.00200	45
50	16272	123	.00756	.00031	.00018	.00160	.00135	.00043	.00018	.00061	.00000	.00000	.00012	.00037	.00240	50
55	13057	96	.00735	.00046	.00000	.00138	.00260	.00023	.00000	.00046	.00000	.00000	.00000	.00015	.00207	55
60	10821	198	.01830	.00046	.00028	.00351	.00647	.00028	.00018	.00074	.00000	.00000	.00046	.00046	.00545	60
65	7545	176	.02333	.00040	.00040	.00358	.00941	.00053	.00027	.00119	.00000	.00000	.00013	.00013	.00729	65
70	5641	206	.03652	.00035	.00106	.00550	.01578	.00124	.00000	.00230	.00000	.00000	.00018	.00071	.00940	70
75	3796	201	.05295	.00132	.00079	.00474	.02266	.00132	.00026	.00448	.00000	.00000	.00026	.00184	.01528	75
80	2027	188	.09275	.00197	.00049	.00789	.04440	.00296	.00099	.00395	.00000	.00000	.00049	.00099	.02861	80
85+	1547	306	.19780	.00194	.00129	.01293	.09050	.01228	.00194	.00452	.00000	.00000	.00000	.00194	.07046	85+
ALL	562927	3930														

	All Causes	Respiratory T. B.	Other Infec. and Paras.	Neo-plasms	Cardio-vascular	Infl., Pneu., Bronch.	Diar-rheal	Certain Degen-erative	Maternal	Cert. Dis. of Infancy	Motor Vehicle	Other Violence	Other and Unknown
CRUDE DEATH RATE	.00698	.00018	.00065	.00051	.00122	.00057	.00044	.00021	.00013	.00047	.00005	.00025	.00229
STANDARDIZED RATE (1)	.00653	.00019	.00059	.00053	.00109	.00052	.00040	.00021	.00014	.00043	.00005	.00025	.00213
STANDARDIZED RATE (2)	.00513	.00027	.00045	.00097	.00261	.00050	.00029	.00039	.00014	.00025	.00007	.00029	.00290
GEOMETRIC MEAN	.00870												

LIFE TABLE FOR ALL CAUSES COMBINED

Age (x)	Midyear Population	Deaths During Year	$_nM_x$	$_nq_x$	l_x	$_nd_x$	$_nL_x$	$_nm_x$	$_na_x$	T_x	$_nr_x$	$\overset{\circ}{e}_x$	Age (x)
0	21495	922	.042894	.041370	100000	4137	96454	.042891	.142919	6751980	.000000	67.520	0
1	75843	605	.007977	.031284	95863	2999	375955	.007977	1.500000	6655526	.000000	69.427	1
5	79667	157	.001971	.009821	92864	912	462040	.001974	2.500000	6279571	.000000	67.621	5
10	68103	54	.000793	.003948	91952	363	458823	.000791	2.418503	5817531	.023284	63.267	10
15	57712	97	.001681	.008407	91589	770	456126	.001688	2.638258	5358708	.031129	58.508	15
20	47718	92	.001928	.009624	90819	874	452010	.001934	2.614178	4902582	.035423	53.982	20
25	39432	110	.002790	.013886	89945	1249	446633	.002796	2.524686	4450572	.033487	49.481	25
30	34085	79	.002318	.011523	88696	1022	440974	.002318	2.547701	4003939	.025909	45.142	30
35	30293	103	.003400	.016915	87674	1483	434811	.003403	2.599882	3562965	.024341	40.639	35
40	25910	105	.004052	.020107	86191	1733	426759	.004061	2.578621	3128154	.025172	36.293	40
45	21963	112	.005099	.025303	84458	2137	417225	.005122	2.630050	2701396	.036109	31.985	45
50	16272	123	.007559	.037257	82321	3067	404093	.007590	2.550810	2284170	.045863	27.747	50
55	13057	96	.007352	.036402	79254	2885	389825	.007401	2.766176	1880077	.033292	23.722	55
60	10821	198	.018298	.088426	76369	6753	365571	.018452	2.649378	1490252	.036321	19.514	60
65	7545	176	.023327	.110995	69616	7727	329530	.023449	2.599381	1124280	.041085	16.150	65
70	5641	206	.036518	.168673	61889	10439	284270	.036722	2.588351	794750	.031660	12.842	70
75	3796	201	.052550	.236229	51450	12154	227814	.053351	2.578095	510480	.042715	9.922	75
80	2027	188	.092748	.381591	39296	14995	159811	.093830	2.554574	282666	.042715	7.193	80
85+	1547	306	.197802	1.000000	24301	24301	122855	.197802	5.055556	122855	.000000	5.056	85+

NUMBER OF PERSONS DYING (OUT OF 100,000 AT BIRTH) ABOVE AGE X FROM SPECIFIED CAUSES

Age (x)	All Causes	Respiratory T.B.	Other Infec. and Paras.	Neoplasms	Cardiovascular	Infl., Pneu., Bronch.	Diarrheal	Certain Degenerative	Maternal	Cert. Dis. of Infancy	Motor Vehicle	Other Violence	Other and Unknown	Age (x)
0	100000	2464	2823	10497	36323	4752	1824	4382	884	1185	601	2438	31827	0
1	95863	2464	2204	10492	36318	4299	1236	4377	884	0	601	2393	30595	1
5	92864	2444	1505	10467	36303	3699	780	4357	884	0	591	2299	29535	5
10	91952	2427	1290	10432	36286	3641	745	4328	884	0	562	2241	29116	10
15	91589	2406	1257	10412	36279	3614	739	4315	877	0	556	2187	28947	15
20	90819	2390	1194	10389	36255	3551	731	4299	773	0	516	2052	28669	20
25	89945	2332	1137	10369	36189	3523	721	4251	678	0	497	1938	28310	25
30	88696	2139	1092	10278	36132	3489	721	4195	530	0	497	1768	27855	30
35	87674	2062	1079	10200	36002	3437	708	4169	336	0	484	1704	27493	35
40	86191	1918	1050	9983	35800	3379	708	4082	121	0	456	1589	27105	40
45	84458	1720	1034	9669	35519	3264	708	4017	39	0	456	1507	26525	45
50	82321	1569	1034	9191	35079	3188	689	3978	2	0	456	1450	25685	50
55	79254	1444	959	8544	34528	3013	614	3727	2	0	405	1300	24718	55
60	76369	1265	959	8003	33502	2924	614	3548	2	0	405	1240	23907	60
65	69616	1096	856	6709	31112	2822	546	3275	2	0	235	1071	21892	65
70	61889	965	723	5527	27989	2645	459	2878	2	0	192	1027	19482	70
75	51450	863	419	3960	23478	2290	459	2218	2	0	142	823	16796	75
80	39296	559	241	2880	18273	1988	397	1191	2	0	81	400	13284	80
85+	24301	238	159	1588	11118	1509	238	556	0	0	0	238	8657	85+

NUMBER OF PERSONS SURVIVING TO AGE X IF SPECIFIED CAUSES WERE ELIMINATED

Age (x)	No Causes	Respiratory T.B. (1)	Other Infec. and Paras. (2)	Neoplasms (3)	Cardiovascular (4)	Infl., Pneu., Bronch. (5)	Diarrheal (6)	Certain Degenerative (7)	Maternal (8)	Cert. Dis. of Infancy (9)	Motor Vehicle (10)	Other Violence (11)	Other and Unknown (12)	(1)+(2)	(1)+(2)+(5)+(6)+(8)	(1)+(2)+(5)+(6)+(8)+part of(9)&(12)	(10)+(11)	Age (x)
0	100000	100000	100000	100000	100000	100000	100000	100000	100000	100000	100000	100000	100000	100000	100000	100000	100000	0
1	95863	95863	96471	95868	95868	96308	96440	95868	95863	97030	95863	95907	97077	96471	97502	99853	95907	1
5	92864	92884	94148	92893	92884	93890	93876	92888	92864	93995	92874	92999	95102	94168	96245	99585	93009	5
10	91952	91988	93440	92016	91988	93026	92989	92005	91952	93072	91991	92144	94596	93477	95636	99250	92182	10
15	91589	91646	93105	91673	91632	92686	92628	91655	91596	92704	91613	91834	94396	93163	95356	99048	91879	15
20	90819	90892	92386	90925	90886	91970	91857	90900	90930	91925	90503	91197	93889	92460	94818	98644	91281	20
25	89945	90075	91555	90070	90077	91113	90984	90073	90149	91040	90047	90433	93355	91687	94164	98151	90536	25
30	88696	89016	90329	88910	88883	89882	89720	88878	89045	89776	88797	89347	92529	90655	93294	97507	89449	30
35	87674	88067	89301	87963	87588	88899	88659	87880	88213	88741	87786	88382	91839	89702	92584	96976	88495	35
40	86191	86721	87820	86691	86701	87454	87199	86480	86935	87240	86329	87002	90689	88360	91486	96000	87141	40
45	84458	85175	86070	85262	85238	85811	85446	84806	85269	85486	84593	85334	89472	86801	90080	94753	85471	45
50	82321	83170	83892	83582	83521	83716	83303	82699	83148	83323	82453	83232	88091	84758	88099	92873	83366	50
55	79254	80195	80842	81115	80560	80772	80274	79866	80050	80219	79431	80280	85830	81802	85290	90143	80460	55
60	76369	77454	77899	78708	79050	77920	77352	77135	77136	77299	76540	77417	83572	79006	82468	87278	77591	60
65	69616	70768	71111	73031	74461	71130	70578	70578	70315	70464	69934	70735	78317	72288	75633	80250	71058	65
70	61889	63038	63347	66102	69423	63406	62827	63126	62511	62643	62212	62926	72224	64523	67781	72181	63254	70
75	51450	52501	52946	56492	62510	53043	52229	53097	51967	52076	51764	52503	62963	54027	57112	61104	52824	75
80	39296	40371	40596	44184	53589	40785	39947	41485	39691	39774	39590	40477	51990	41706	44445	47916	40779	80
85+	24301	25224	25171	28479	41682	25612	24830	26182	24547	24597	24546	25162	37290	26127	28420	31100	25415	85+

ADDED YRS OF LIFE

	No Causes	(1)	(2)	(3)	(4)	(5)	(6)	(7)	(8)	(9)	(10)	(11)	(12)	(1)+(2)	(1)+(2)+(5)+(6)+(8)	part	(10)+(11)
TOTAL		.564	1.312	1.690	5.399	1.256	.844	.637	.389	.821	.144	.674	6.811	1.890	4.507	8.243	.821
WORK	3.767	.279	.100	.458	.514	.161	.027	.157	.297	.000	.050	.290	1.230	.380	.872	1.349	.340

POPULATION, DEATHS, DEATH RATES FOR ALL CAUSES COMBINED, AND SPECIFIED CAUSES

Age Start of Interval	Midyear Population	Deaths During Year	All Causes	Respiratory T.B.	Other Infec. and Paras.	Neoplasms	Cardio-vascular	Infl., Pneu., Bronch.	Diarrheal	Certain Degenerative	Maternal	Cert. Dis. of Infancy	Motor Vehicle	Other Violence	Other and Unknown	Age Start of Interval
0	671000	31041	.04626	.00014	.00355	.00005	.00011	.01248	.00357	.00013	.00000	.01743	.00000	.00016	.00863	0
1	2329000	20533	.00882	.00017	.00116	.00004	.00006	.00395	.00162	.00013	.00000	.00000	.00002	.00018	.00152	1
5	2385000	6257	.00262	.00006	.00048	.00003	.00006	.00078	.00046	.00013	.00000	.00000	.00003	.00017	.00049	5
10	2035000	2503	.00123	.00006	.00021	.00004	.00008	.00024	.00012	.00004	.00000	.00000	.00001	.00016	.00026	10
15	1667000	2316	.00139	.00016	.00015	.00005	.00012	.00020	.00005	.00005	.00000	.00000	.00003	.00034	.00025	15
20	1352000	3357	.00248	.00043	.00019	.00007	.00017	.00020	.00005	.00011	.00000	.00000	.00006	.00084	.00036	20
25	1103000	3255	.00295	.00063	.00019	.00009	.00021	.00021	.00007	.00014	.00000	.00000	.00007	.00088	.00046	25
30	908000	3069	.00338	.00082	.00024	.00017	.00030	.00020	.00009	.00021	.00000	.00000	.00006	.00084	.00046	30
35	752000	3570	.00475	.00125	.00027	.00027	.00050	.00026	.00013	.00036	.00000	.00000	.00004	.00100	.00066	35
40	636000	3227	.00507	.00140	.00029	.00035	.00064	.00028	.00017	.00042	.00000	.00000	.00004	.00075	.00075	40
45	539000	3782	.00702	.00203	.00037	.00055	.00102	.00042	.00025	.00062	.00000	.00000	.00004	.00071	.00101	45
50	438000	4176	.00953	.00291	.00046	.00082	.00164	.00049	.00032	.00085	.00000	.00000	.00006	.00065	.00133	50
55	330000	3775	.01144	.00314	.00050	.00114	.00229	.00054	.00025	.00118	.00000	.00000	.00006	.00056	.00179	55
60	237000	5162	.02178	.00576	.00076	.00189	.00449	.00116	.00064	.00216	.00000	.00000	.00006	.00083	.00403	60
65	164000	3064	.01868	.00452	.00059	.00161	.00455	.00092	.00045	.00187	.00000	.00000	.00005	.00049	.00363	65
70	94228	3870	.04107	.00783	.00086	.00267	.00869	.00173	.00089	.00354	.00000	.00000	.00006	.00073	.01405	70
75	49171	3359	.06831	.01082	.00102	.00405	.01448	.00254	.00092	.00521	.00000	.00000	.00008	.00094	.02827	75
80	42777	4069	.09512	.01092	.00105	.00339	.01583	.00341	.00122	.00491	.00000	.00000	.00002	.00070	.05367	80
85+	39824	7190	.18054	.00979	.00103	.00279	.02230	.00552	.00151	.00465	.00000	.00000	.00005	.00083	.13208	85+
ALL	15772000	117575														

	All Causes	Respiratory T.B.	Other Infec. and Paras.	Neoplasms	Cardio-vascular	Infl., Pneu., Bronch.	Diarrheal	Certain Degenerative	Maternal	Cert. Dis. of Infancy	Motor Vehicle	Other Violence	Other and Unknown
CRUDE DEATH RATE	.00745	.00079	.00057	.00023	.00058	.00146	.00056	.00029	.00000	.00074	.00004	.00046	.00173
STANDARDIZED RATE (1)	.00752	.00101	.00053	.00030	.00074	.00127	.00050	.00037	.00000	.00061	.00004	.00050	.00165
STANDARDIZED RATE (2)	.01036	.00170	.00050	.00052	.00148	.00106	.00044	.00065	.00000	.00036	.00004	.00057	.00304
GEOMETRIC MEAN	.01030												

LIFE TABLE FOR ALL CAUSES COMBINED

Age (x)	Midyear Population	Deaths During Year	$_nM_x$	$_nq_x$	l_x	$_nd_x$	$_nL_x$	$_nm_x$	$_na_x$	T_x	$_nr_x$	$\overset{\circ}{e}_x$	Age (x)
0	671000	31041	.046261	.044510	100000	4451	96211	.046263	.148643	6501644	.000000	65.016	0
1	2329000	20533	.008816	.034506	95549	3297	373954	.008817	1.500000	6405433	.000000	67.038	1
5	2385000	6257	.002623	.013073	92252	1206	458245	.002632	2.500000	6031480	.000000	65.380	5
10	2035000	2503	.001230	.006065	91046	554	453721	.001221	2.283394	5573235	.025336	61.213	10
15	1667000	2316	.001389	.006962	90492	630	451002	.001397	2.685516	5119510	.036112	56.574	15
20	1352000	3357	.002483	.012408	89862	1115	446663	.002496	2.625747	4668508	.038628	51.952	20
25	1103000	3255	.002951	.014682	88747	1303	440552	.002958	2.556920	4221845	.037530	47.572	25
30	908000	3069	.003380	.016822	87444	1471	433692	.003392	2.601971	3781294	.035859	43.242	30
35	752000	3570	.004747	.023531	85973	2023	424940	.004761	2.565600	3347601	.032809	38.938	35
40	636000	3227	.005074	.025110	83950	2108	414649	.005084	2.580250	2922661	.028907	34.814	40
45	539000	3782	.007017	.034640	81842	2835	402453	.007044	2.616549	2508012	.028543	30.645	45
50	438000	4176	.009534	.046755	79007	3694	386090	.009568	2.578393	2105559	.035770	26.650	50
55	330000	3775	.011439	.056099	75313	4225	366775	.011519	2.682791	1719469	.045164	22.831	55
60	237000	5162	.021781	.104110	71088	7401	337245	.021945	2.541605	1352694	.048088	19.028	60
65	164000	3064	.018682	.089547	63687	5703	304949	.018701	2.635345	1015449	.059053	15.944	65
70	94228	3870	.041071	.191536	57984	11106	263833	.042095	2.651082	710500	.087039	12.253	70
75	49171	3359	.068213	.293464	46878	13757	200340	.068668	2.524912	446667	.025179	9.528	75
80	42777	4069	.095121	.384982	33121	12751	133501	.095512	2.482240	246326	.025179	7.437	80
85+	39824	7190	.180544	1.000000	20370	20370	112825	.180544	5.538804	112825	.000000	5.539	85+

NUMBER OF PERSONS DYING (OUT OF 100,000 AT BIRTH) ABOVE AGE X FROM SPECIFIED CAUSES

Age (x)	All Causes	Respiratory T.B.	Other Infec. and Paras.	Neoplasms	Cardiovascular	Infl., Pneu., Bronch.	Diarrheal	Certain Degenerative	Maternal	Cert. Dis. of Infancy	Motor Vehicle	Other Violence	Other and Unknown	Age (x)
0	100000	15453	3306	4876	15638	7029	2883	6166	0	1677	299	4009	38664	0
1	95549	15440	2965	4871	15627	5828	2540	6153	0	0	299	3993	37833	1
5	92252	15378	2532	4858	15607	4353	1934	6105	0	0	293	3927	37265	5
10	91046	15350	2313	4845	15581	3992	1721	6076	0	0	280	3848	37040	10
15	90492	15321	2218	4827	15545	3884	1666	6060	0	0	274	3776	36921	15
20	89862	15248	2152	4806	15490	3795	1646	6037	0	0	258	3620	36810	20
25	88747	15052	2069	4775	15414	3707	1621	5989	0	0	229	3241	36650	25
30	87444	14774	1983	4735	15322	3613	1593	5925	0	0	198	2854	36447	30
35	85973	14418	1879	4660	15192	3525	1555	5835	0	0	174	2488	36247	35
40	83950	13883	1765	4546	14978	3413	1499	5680	0	0	158	2064	35964	40
45	81842	13301	1644	4399	14714	3296	1430	5507	0	0	143	1754	35654	45
50	79007	12481	1496	4178	14300	3127	1328	5257	0	0	125	1467	35248	50
55	75313	11354	1320	3858	13662	2937	1207	4925	0	0	101	1217	34732	55
60	71088	10158	1137	3437	12814	2739	1113	4491	0	0	80	1013	34066	60
65	63687	8244	878	2797	11285	2343	895	3757	0	0	60	733	32695	65
70	57984	6872	699	2308	9894	2063	760	3188	0	0	43	584	31573	70
75	46878	4768	469	1589	7550	1598	520	2233	0	0	26	389	27736	75
80	33121	2593	265	776	4636	1086	336	1187	0	0	10	201	22031	80
85+	20370	1105	116	314	2516	623	170	524	0	0	6	93	14903	85+

NUMBER OF PERSONS SURVIVING TO AGE X IF SPECIFIED CAUSES WERE ELIMINATED

Age (x)	No Causes	Respiratory T.B. (1)	Other Infec. and Paras. (2)	Neoplasms (3)	Cardiovascular (4)	Infl., Pneu., Bronch. (5)	Diarrheal (6)	Certain Degenerative (7)	Maternal (8)	Cert. Dis. of Infancy (9)	Motor Vehicle (10)	Other Violence (11)	Other and Unknown (12)	(1)+(2)	(1)+(2)+(5)+(6)+(8)	(1)+(2)+(5)+(6)+(8)+part of(9)&(12)	(10)+(11)	Age (x)
0	100000	100000	100000	100000	100000	100000	100000	100000	100000	100000	100000	100000	100000	100000	100000	100000	100000	0
1	95562	95554	95883	95554	95560	96560	95885	95562	95549	97202	95549	95565	96365	95896	97422	99895	95565	1
5	92252	92325	93002	92269	92282	94871	93176	92311	92252	93848	92258	92332	93604	93076	96677	99698	92338	5
10	91046	91146	92006	91076	91101	94000	92172	91134	91046	92621	91065	91203	92607	92107	96272	99484	91222	10
15	90492	90620	91542	90540	90583	93540	91666	90595	90492	91417	90517	90720	92165	91672	95989	99278	90745	15
20	89862	90062	90971	89931	90007	92980	91048	89987	89862	91417	89902	90245	91636	91174	95583	98916	90285	20
25	88747	89140	89926	88846	88966	91917	89944	88918	88747	90283	88816	89504	90661	90325	94812	98191	89574	25
30	87444	88109	88692	87581	87752	90664	88651	87677	87444	88957	87543	88578	89536	89367	93937	97384	88678	30
35	85973	86984	87305	86182	86405	89229	87158	86291	85973	87461	86094	87457	88233	88331	92983	96497	87579	35
40	83950	85473	85365	84267	84585	87245	85203	84415	83950	85403	84084	85826	86444	86914	91673	95286	85962	40
45	81842	83914	83343	82297	82724	85174	83132	82467	81842	83258	81587	83984	84590	85453	90335	94069	84133	45
50	79007	81838	80604	79665	80271	82397	80354	79858	79007	80374	79165	81364	82073	83492	88559	92458	81527	50
55	75313	79159	77011	76256	77153	78738	76718	76453	75313	77616	75487	77811	78761	80944	86203	90305	77991	55
60	71088	75908	72872	72393	73674	74522	72507	72593	71088	72318	71273	73651	75022	77813	83200	87524	73842	60
65	63687	70007	65537	65476	67521	67157	65169	65748	63687	64789	63871	66258	68595	72041	77734	82558	66449	65
70	57984	65190	59844	60093	62897	61425	59465	60423	57984	58987	58168	60472	63623	67281	73094	78250	60664	70
75	46878	54862	48594	49254	53181	50103	48256	49749	46878	47689	47042	49071	55372	56870	62621	69135	49243	75
80	33121	40937	34509	35518	40435	35859	34280	36085	33121	33694	33250	34834	45223	42653	47796	55769	34970	80
85+	20370	26647	21345	22232	26962	22447	21217	22761	20370	20722	20453	21512	36498	27922	32048	41721	21599	85+

ADDED YRS OF LIFE

	No Causes	(1)	(2)	(3)	(4)	(5)	(6)	(7)	(8)	(9)	(10)	(11)	(12)	(1)+(2)	(1)+(2)+(5)+(6)+(8)	+part	(10)+(11)
TOTAL		2.956	1.218	.822	2.301	2.798	1.104	1.033	.000	1.123	.099	1.333	9.837	4.277	8.651	14.028	1.435
WORK	4.647	1.066	.262	.256	.516	.281	.120	.306	.000	.000	.056	.801	.639	1.339	1.764	2.085	.858

POPULATION, DEATHS, DEATH RATES FOR ALL CAUSES COMBINED, AND SPECIFIED CAUSES

Age Start of Interval	Midyear Population	Deaths During Year	All Causes	Respiratory T. B.	Other Infec. and Paras.	Neoplasms	Cardiovascular	Infl., Pneu., Bronch.	Diarrheal	Certain Degenerative	Maternal	Cert. Dis. of Infancy	Motor Vehicle	Other Violence	Other and Unknown	Age Start of Interval
0	656000	23304	.03552	.00011	.00264	.00004	.00008	.01035	.00274	.00007	.00000	.01287	.00000	.00010	.00651	0
1	2255000	18175	.00806	.00015	.00103	.00003	.00005	.00382	.00138	.00010	.00000	.00000	.00000	.00013	.00137	1
5	2290000	5100	.00223	.00006	.00040	.00003	.00005	.00073	.00034	.00004	.00000	.00000	.00002	.00011	.00044	5
10	1963000	1841	.00094	.00005	.00013	.00003	.00009	.00023	.00008	.00003	.00000	.00000	.00001	.00008	.00021	10
15	1618000	1580	.00098	.00014	.00009	.00004	.00011	.00013	.00003	.00003	.00005	.00000	.00001	.00008	.00025	15
20	1323000	2079	.00157	.00032	.00014	.00006	.00016	.00014	.00006	.00007	.00021	.00000	.00001	.00009	.00032	20
25	1091000	2458	.00225	.00057	.00017	.00012	.00022	.00015	.00009	.00010	.00032	.00000	.00001	.00010	.00040	25
30	902000	2563	.00284	.00082	.00015	.00015	.00027	.00016	.00012	.00012	.00050	.00000	.00001	.00009	.00045	30
35	750000	2977	.00397	.00110	.00020	.00030	.00043	.00028	.00016	.00020	.00057	.00000	.00001	.00009	.00059	35
40	637000	2844	.00446	.00150	.00021	.00049	.00052	.00023	.00018	.00020	.00034	.00000	.00002	.00011	.00066	40
45	543000	2955	.00544	.00205	.00021	.00062	.00073	.00033	.00016	.00033	.00008	.00000	.00002	.00012	.00080	45
50	448000	3093	.00690	.00253	.00032	.00082	.00101	.00045	.00023	.00045	.00000	.00000	.00003	.00013	.00102	50
55	343000	2813	.00820	.00284	.00028	.00108	.00136	.00042	.00024	.00058	.00000	.00000	.00002	.00011	.00128	55
60	250000	3745	.01498	.00451	.00046	.00162	.00277	.00084	.00042	.00120	.00000	.00000	.00003	.00015	.00297	60
65	176000	2507	.01424	.00414	.00032	.00142	.00278	.00068	.00027	.00130	.00000	.00000	.00006	.00019	.00307	65
70	100680	3539	.03515	.00681	.00055	.00254	.00662	.00151	.00066	.00292	.00000	.00000	.00005	.00042	.01308	70
75	53505	2945	.05504	.00906	.00078	.00288	.01110	.00191	.00064	.00342	.00000	.00000	.00002	.00021	.02503	75
80	50135	4278	.08533	.00708	.00076	.00217	.01396	.00299	.00090	.00317	.00000	.00000	.00008	.00066	.05356	80
85+	48680	8565	.17594	.00746	.00105	.00191	.02153	.00485	.00103	.00435	.00000	.00000	.00002	.00053	.13322	85+
ALL	15498000	97361														

	All Causes	Respiratory T. B.	Other Infec. and Paras.	Neoplasms	Cardiovascular	Infl., Pneu., Bronch.	Diarrheal	Certain Degenerative	Maternal	Cert. Dis. of Infancy	Motor Vehicle	Other Violence	Other and Unknown
CRUDE DEATH RATE	.00628	.00074	.00044	.00023	.00048	.00129	.00045	.00020	.00012	.00054	.00001	.00011	.00166
STANDARDIZED RATE (1)	.00602	.00089	.00041	.00028	.00054	.00112	.00040	.00023	.00013	.00045	.00001	.00011	.00143
STANDARDIZED RATE (2)	.00842	.00147	.00036	.00048	.00111	.00092	.00035	.00042	.00014	.00027	.00002	.00013	.00276
GEOMETRIC MEAN	.00817												

LIFE TABLE FOR ALL CAUSES COMBINED

Age (x)	Midyear Population	Deaths During Year	nM_x	nq_x	l_x	nd_x	nL_x	nm_x	na_x	T_x	nr_x	$\overset{\circ}{e}_x$	Age (x)
0	656000	23304	.035524	.034460	100000	3446	97003	.035525	.130391	6884864	.000000	68.849	0
1	2255000	18175	.008060	.031559	96554	3051	378589	.008059	1.500000	6787860	.000000	70.301	1
5	2290000	5100	.002227	.011123	93503	1040	464915	.002237	2.500000	6409272	.000000	68.546	5
10	1963000	1841	.000938	.004629	92463	428	461122	.000928	2.212812	5944357	.024787	64.289	10
15	1618000	1580	.000977	.004889	92035	450	459111	.000980	2.635648	5483235	.035303	59.578	15
20	1323000	2079	.001571	.007872	91585	721	456242	.001580	2.665569	5024124	.037525	54.857	20
25	1091000	2458	.002253	.011259	90864	1023	451877	.002264	2.612414	4567882	.036575	50.272	25
30	902000	2563	.002841	.014169	89841	1273	446173	.002853	2.618323	4116004	.035478	45.814	30
35	750000	2977	.003969	.019714	88568	1746	438610	.003981	2.577200	3669831	.032590	41.435	35
40	637000	2844	.004465	.022114	86822	1920	429422	.004471	2.558594	3231221	.028796	37.217	40
45	543000	2955	.005442	.026925	84902	2286	418981	.005456	2.581383	2801799	.028170	33.000	45
50	448000	3093	.006904	.034049	82616	2813	406245	.006924	2.570136	2382818	.034995	28.842	50
55	343000	2813	.008201	.040512	79803	3233	391507	.008258	2.677725	1976573	.045413	24.768	55
60	250000	3745	.014980	.072757	76570	5571	369275	.015086	2.563349	1585066	.049269	20.701	60
65	176000	2507	.014244	.069355	70999	4927	343809	.014331	2.729687	1215790	.062175	17.124	65
70	100680	3539	.035151	.166530	66072	11003	304622	.036120	2.660808	871981	.092841	13.197	70
75	53505	2945	.055042	.243694	55069	13420	242578	.055322	2.558355	567359	.027671	10.303	75
80	50135	4278	.085330	.354438	41649	14762	171966	.085842	2.542437	324781	.027671	7.798	80
85+	48680	8565	.175945	1.000000	26887	26887	152815	.175945	5.683556	152815	.000000	5.684	85+

NUMBER OF PERSONS DYING (OUT OF 100,000 AT BIRTH) ABOVE AGE X FROM SPECIFIED CAUSES

Age (x)	All Causes	Respiratory T.B.	Other Infec. and Paras.	Neoplasms	Cardiovascular	Infl., Pneu., Bronch.	Diarrheal	Certain Degenerative	Maternal	Cert. Dis. of Infancy	Motor Vehicle	Other Violence	Other and Unknown	Age (x)
0	100000	14914	2584	4828	14577	6577	2445	4814	911	1248	143	1075	45884	0
1	96554	14903	2328	4824	14569	5573	2179	4807	911	0	143	1065	45252	1
5	93503	14846	1936	4813	14552	4126	1658	4768	911	0	142	1017	44734	5
10	92463	14817	1749	4799	14529	3783	1498	4747	911	0	133	966	44531	10
15	92035	14793	1688	4787	14488	3681	1463	4734	911	0	129	927	44434	15
20	91585	14727	1649	4767	14439	3623	1450	4719	888	0	125	881	44317	20
25	90864	14582	1586	4740	14367	3557	1422	4688	791	0	119	839	44173	25
30	89841	14321	1508	4688	14268	3490	1380	4641	648	0	114	793	43990	30
35	88568	13953	1442	4621	14145	3418	1327	4589	426	0	108	752	43787	35
40	86822	13467	1354	4487	13556	3294	1256	4501	178	0	102	697	43530	40
45	84902	12820	1262	4276	13732	3197	1180	4413	34	0	95	649	43244	45
50	82616	11960	1175	4017	13423	3057	1114	4274	2	0	88	597	42909	50
55	79803	10931	1045	3684	13009	2911	1020	4089	2	0	75	542	42495	55
60	76570	9815	937	3259	12472	2747	925	3859	2	0	67	499	41988	60
65	70999	8141	768	2657	11441	2433	768	3410	2	0	57	443	40879	65
70	66072	6718	657	2169	10478	2199	674	2959	2	0	37	377	39802	70
75	55069	4605	488	1380	8406	1728	470	2049	2	0	22	248	35671	75
80	41649	2403	297	681	5701	1264	316	1218	2	0	18	198	29551	80
85+	26887	1140	160	292	3290	741	157	666	0	0	3	82	20356	85+

NUMBER OF PERSONS SURVIVING TO AGE X IF SPECIFIED CAUSES WERE ELIMINATED

Age (x)	No Causes	Respiratory T.B. (1)	Other Infec. and Paras. (2)	Neoplasms (3)	Cardiovascular (4)	Infl., Pneu., Bronch. (5)	Diarrheal (6)	Certain Degenerative (7)	Maternal (8)	Cert. Dis. of Infancy (9)	Motor Vehicle (10)	Other Violence (11)	Other and Unknown (12)	(1)+(2)	(1)+(2)+(5)+(6)+(8)	(1)+(2)+(5)+(6)+(8)+part of (9)&(12)	(10)+(11)	Age (x)
0	100000	100000	100000	100000	100000	100000	100000	100000	100000	100000	100000	100000	100000	100000	100000	100000	100000	0
1	96554	96565	96806	96558	96562	97546	96816	96561	96554	97788	96554	96564	97177	96817	98076	99935	96564	1
5	93503	93570	94134	93518	93527	95913	94272	93548	93503	94698	93504	93560	94621	94201	97424	99788	93561	5
10	92463	92558	93275	92491	92510	95156	93384	92528	92463	93645	92473	92570	93773	93024	97088	99631	92580	10
15	92035	92153	92904	92075	92123	94861	92987	92113	92035	93211	92049	92180	93437	93024	96872	99479	92194	15
20	91585	91769	92490	91645	91721	94456	92545	91678	91608	92756	91603	91776	93099	92675	96607	99283	91793	20
25	90864	91191	91825	90950	91071	93781	91845	90987	90983	92025	90888	91095	92512	92155	96267	99041	91119	25
30	89841	90425	90869	89978	90144	92754	90853	90009	90102	90899	89869	90115	91655	91460	95808	98709	90144	30
35	88568	89512	89648	88770	88990	91553	89619	88786	89046	89700	88602	88879	90563	90604	95281	98330	88913	35
40	86822	88236	87969	87153	87424	89875	87924	87123	87538	87932	86861	87182	89038	89401	94492	97711	87221	40
45	84902	86937	86116	85436	85714	87987	86055	85284	85746	85987	84947	85301	87359	88180	93545	96941	85347	45
50	82616	85470	83884	83393	83714	85761	83804	83125	83469	83672	82667	83056	85348	86782	92324	95907	83107	50
55	79803	83612	81158	80884	81277	82990	81045	80478	80626	80823	79865	80283	82863	85032	90730	94532	80345	55
60	76570	81378	77978	78030	78522	79795	77856	77445	77360	77549	76637	77072	80024	82874	88720	92766	77140	60
65	70999	77189	72470	72946	73835	74305	72345	72249	71732	71906	71071	71519	75327	78788	84886	89452	71592	65
70	66072	73336	67550	68368	69683	69385	67417	67680	66754	66916	66158	66620	71215	74976	81167	86187	66707	70
75	55069	63292	56458	57729	60106	58282	56379	57263	55637	55773	55154	55644	63571	64888	71033	77685	55730	75
80	41649	50097	42869	44294	48086	44505	42776	44057	42079	42181	41717	42127	54650	51564	57175	65914	42196	80
85+	26887	33574	27787	28926	33343	29180	27745	28911	27166	27231	26943	27289	46336	34698	39262	50126	27346	85+

ACCED YRS OF LIFE

	No Causes	(1)	(2)	(3)	(4)	(5)	(6)	(7)	(8)	(9)	(10)	(11)	(12)	(1)+(2)	(1)+(2)+(5)+(6)+(8)	...part	(10)+(11)
TOTAL		3.019	1.004	.906	2.063	2.665	.976	.763	.390	.879	.040	.320	12.644	4.099	8.586	13.887	.361
WORK	3.632	1.026	.187	.285	.412	.226	.123	.177	.287	.000	.015	.118	.572	1.221	1.889	2.283	.133

POPULATION, DEATHS, DEATH RATES FOR ALL CAUSES COMBINED, AND SPECIFIED CAUSES

Age Start of Interval	Midyear Population	Deaths During Year	All Causes	Respiratory T. B.	Other Infec. and Paras.	Neoplasms	Cardio-vascular	Infl., Pneu., Bronch.	Diarrheal	Certain Degenerative	Maternal	Cert. Dis. of Infancy	Motor Vehicle	Other Violence	Other and Unknown	Age Start of Interval
0	307288	21582	.07023	.00011	.00407	.00011	.00137	.01527	.00614	.00009	.00000	.02520	.00001	.00058	.01729	0
1	1453564	2558	.00176	.00002	.00021	.00007	.00013	.00031	.00005	.00002	.00000	.00000	.00004	.00042	.00048	1
5	1825760	1181	.00065	.00000	.00006	.00006	.00006	.00004	.00000	.00001	.00000	.00000	.00004	.00020	.00015	5
10	1575613	880	.00056	.00001	.00003	.00007	.00007	.00002	.00000	.00001	.00000	.00000	.00002	.00021	.00011	10
15	986080	1153	.00117	.00003	.00003	.00007	.00017	.00004	.00000	.00003	.00000	.00000	.00000	.00057	.00015	15
20	878759	2029	.00231	.00017	.00004	.00013	.00023	.00003	.00000	.00003	.00000	.00000	.00023	.00114	.00029	20
25	1154472	2350	.00204	.00036	.00003	.00011	.00026	.00003	.00000	.00007	.00000	.00000	.00014	.00080	.00023	25
30	1143518	2707	.00237	.00048	.00003	.00019	.00039	.00004	.00000	.00007	.00000	.00000	.00011	.00074	.00032	30
35	966649	2737	.00283	.00053	.00004	.00031	.00061	.00005	.00001	.00012	.00000	.00000	.00010	.00071	.00037	35
40	636068	2466	.00388	.00068	.00006	.00058	.00096	.00007	.00000	.00016	.00000	.00000	.00008	.00075	.00052	40
45	757363	4659	.00615	.00099	.00009	.00113	.00179	.00013	.00001	.00025	.00000	.00000	.00007	.00086	.00083	45
50	811398	7637	.00941	.00132	.00011	.00204	.00310	.00025	.00001	.00039	.00000	.00000	.00007	.00079	.00133	50
55	659991	10025	.01519	.00171	.00016	.00352	.00543	.00035	.00003	.00068	.00000	.00000	.00007	.00082	.00242	55
60	475069	11526	.02426	.00218	.00019	.00513	.00918	.00068	.00003	.00078	.00000	.00000	.00006	.00074	.00529	60
65	300951	11464	.03809	.00226	.00025	.00691	.01544	.00116	.00006	.00109	.00000	.00000	.00004	.00071	.01016	65
70	197554	11427	.05784	.00203	.00023	.00801	.02282	.00172	.00007	.00130	.00000	.00000	.00003	.00084	.02079	70
75	106969	9597	.08972	.00151	.00026	.00857	.03270	.00299	.00009	.00135	.00000	.00000	.00005	.00090	.04130	75
80	48577	6907	.14219	.00146	.00025	.00855	.04321	.00391	.00008	.00111	.00000	.00000	.00012	.00136	.08173	80
85+	21476	4404	.20507	.00098	.00028	.00573	.05369	.00540	.00028	.00107	.00000	.00000	.00019	.00140	.13606	85+
ALL	14307119	117289														

	All Causes	Respiratory T.B.	Other Infec. and Paras.	Neoplasms	Cardio-vascular	Infl., Pneu., Bronch.	Diarrheal	Certain Degenerative	Maternal	Cert. Dis. of Infancy	Motor Vehicle	Other Violence	Other and Unknown
CRUDE DEATH RATE	.00820	.00052	.00017	.00098	.00216	.00053	.00015	.00019	.00000	.00054	.00008	.00061	.00227
STANDARDIZED RATE (1)	.00776	.00041	.00022	.00073	.00166	.00071	.00023	.00015	.00000	.00089	.00008	.00060	.00208
STANDARDIZED RATE (2)	.01200	.00062	.00018	.00137	.00350	.00063	.00014	.00025	.00000	.00052	.00008	.00066	.00404
GEOMETRIC MEAN	.00878												

LIFE TABLE FOR ALL CAUSES COMBINED

Age (x)	Midyear Population	Deaths During Year	$_nM_x$	$_nq_x$	l_x	$_nd_x$	$_nL_x$	$_nm_x$	$_na_x$	T_x	$_nr_x$	$\overset{\circ}{e}_x$	Age (x)
0	307288	21582	.070234	.066450	100000	6645	94614	.070233	.189397	6475563	.000000	64.756	0
1	1453564	2558	.001760	.007006	93355	654	371785	.001759	1.500000	6380949	.000000	68.351	1
5	1825760	1181	.000647	.003225	92701	299	462758	.000646	2.500000	6009164	.000000	64.823	5
10	1575613	880	.000559	.002792	92402	258	461416	.000559	2.696221	5546407	.044669	60.025	10
15	986080	1153	.001169	.005882	92144	542	459530	.001179	2.805197	5084991	.066760	55.185	15
20	878759	2029	.002309	.011484	91602	1052	455458	.002310	2.574263	4625461	.005182	50.495	20
25	1154472	2350	.002036	.010127	90550	917	450458	.002036	2.500454	4170003	-.026580	46.052	25
30	1143518	2707	.002367	.011759	89633	1054	445600	.002365	2.566018	3719545	-.002605	41.497	30
35	966649	2737	.002831	.014123	88579	1251	439899	.002844	2.605416	3273945	.046089	36.961	35
40	636068	2466	.003877	.019318	87328	1687	432701	.003899	2.664587	2834046	.036556	32.453	40
45	757363	4659	.006152	.030207	85641	2587	422182	.006128	2.671772	2401345	-.019878	28.040	45
50	811398	7637	.009412	.045994	83054	3820	406397	.009400	2.677356	1979163	-.007081	23.830	50
55	659991	10025	.015190	.073693	79234	5839	382546	.015264	2.666695	1572765	-.024536	19.850	55
60	475069	11526	.024262	.115703	73395	8492	346907	.024479	2.636869	1190220	.047526	16.217	60
65	300951	11464	.038093	.175920	64903	11418	297004	.038439	2.594022	843312	.049484	12.993	65
70	197554	11427	.057842	.255118	53485	13645	233997	.058313	2.550171	546269	.044227	10.213	70
75	106969	9597	.089718	.369076	39840	14704	162335	.090578	2.492887	312272	.046694	7.838	75
80	48577	6907	.142187	.522876	25136	13143	91453	.143714	2.395778	149936	.046694	5.965	80
85+	21476	4404	.205066	1.000000	11993	11993	58484	.205066	4.876476	58484	.000000	4.876	85+

NUMBER OF PERSONS DYING (OUT OF 100,000 AT BIRTH) ABOVE AGE X FROM SPECIFIED CAUSES

Age (x)	All Causes	Respiratory T. B.	Other Infec. and Paras.	Neo-plasms	Cardio-vascular	Infl., Pneu., Bronch.	Diar-rheal	Certain Degen-erative	Maternal	Cert. Dis. of Infancy	Motor Vehicle	Other Violence	Other and Unknown	Age (x)
0	100000	4989	1036	11694	31218	4149	719	2068	0	2384	525	4542	36676	0
1	93355	4979	650	11684	31088	2704	138	2060	0	0	524	4488	35040	1
5	92701	4972	573	11656	31042	2589	118	2050	0	0	508	4332	34861	5
10	92402	4970	543	11627	31014	2569	117	2044	0	0	490	4239	34789	10
15	92144	4966	529	11596	30980	2559	115	2039	0	0	483	4139	34738	15
20	91602	4952	513	11565	30902	2540	113	2027	0	0	447	3871	34672	20
25	90550	4876	493	11507	30796	2529	111	2003	0	0	344	3352	34539	25
30	89633	4712	479	11457	30679	2516	110	1973	0	0	280	2990	34437	30
35	88579	4458	466	11371	30506	2500	108	1942	0	0	233	2659	34296	35
40	87328	4267	448	11234	30238	2479	106	1888	0	0	190	2347	34131	40
45	85641	3970	421	10981	29818	2447	104	1819	0	0	154	2021	33906	45
50	83054	3555	384	10504	29065	2393	102	1712	0	0	124	1656	33559	50
55	79234	3017	340	9678	27806	2294	96	1555	0	0	95	1335	33018	55
60	73395	2360	280	8327	25715	2158	85	1295	0	0	70	1023	32082	60
65	64903	1601	213	6535	22500	1921	74	1022	0	0	48	767	30222	65
70	53485	931	138	4470	17870	1572	55	695	0	0	37	556	27161	70
75	39840	456	83	2591	12492	1167	39	390	0	0	30	359	22233	75
80	25136	213	41	1196	7143	676	24	172	0	0	22	212	15437	80
85+	11993	57	16	335	3140	316	16	63	0	0	11	82	7957	85+

NUMBER OF PERSONS SURVIVING TO AGE X IF SPECIFIED CAUSES WERE ELIMINATED

Age (x)	No Causes	Respiratory T. B.	Other Infec. and Paras.	Neo-plasms	Cardio-vascular	Infl., Pneu., Bronch.	Diar-rheal	Certain Degener-ative	Maternal	Cert. Dis. of Infancy	Motor Vehicle	Other Violence	Other and Unknown	(1) + (2)	(1) + (2) + (5) + (6) + (8)	(1)+(2)+ (5)+(6)+ (8)+part of(9)&(12)	(10) + (11)	Age (x)
		(1)	(2)	(3)	(4)	(5)	(6)	(7)	(8)	(9)	(10)	(11)	(12)					
0	100000	100000	100000	100000	100000	100000	100000	100000	100000	100000	100000	100000	100000	100000	100000	100000	100000	0
1	93355	93365	93729	93365	93481	94761	93918	93363	93355	95687	93356	93407	94949	93738	95724	99470	93408	1
5	92701	92718	93149	92739	92872	94214	93280	92719	92701	95016	92718	92508	94465	93166	95278	99093	92925	5
10	92402	92421	92879	92468	92600	93930	92980	92426	92402	94710	92437	92702	94234	92897	95025	98848	92737	10
15	92144	92166	92633	92241	92376	93678	92723	92173	92144	94445	92186	92543	94023	92656	94790	98612	92585	15
20	91602	91638	92105	91730	91910	93146	92179	91642	91602	93890	91679	92268	93537	92141	94285	98094	92346	20
25	90550	90662	91067	90734	90961	92088	91123	90614	90550	92812	90729	91729	92558	91179	93314	97101	91911	25
30	89633	89907	90159	89865	90156	91168	90201	89726	89633	91872	89874	91166	91764	90434	92566	96348	91411	30
35	88579	89063	89111	88854	89269	90113	89142	88702	88579	90791	88864	90429	90828	89599	91729	95518	90720	35
40	87328	88036	87871	87775	88277	88861	87885	87503	87328	89509	87652	89469	89714	88584	90714	94505	89800	40
45	85641	86633	86200	86232	86694	87177	86189	85881	85641	87760	85994	88071	88210	87199	89331	93123	88435	45
50	83054	84430	83633	84199	85123	84598	83588	83392	83054	85128	83426	85781	85858	85019	87155	90940	86166	50
55	79234	81082	79830	81149	82478	80805	79749	79711	79234	81213	79618	82159	82496	81692	83853	87617	82557	55
60	73395	75756	74005	76511	78524	74984	73883	74089	73395	75228	73714	76416	77362	76385	78558	82262	76811	60
65	64903	67729	65506	69435	72750	66536	65345	65775	64903	66524	65259	67824	70282	68358	70555	74205	68196	65
70	53485	56446	54050	59250	64844	55156	53866	54504	53485	54821	53788	56091	61014	57043	59244	62741	56409	70
75	39840	42473	40308	45948	54237	41446	40138	40865	39840	40835	40072	41958	50581	42972	45038	48255	42202	75
80	25136	26997	25464	30266	40431	26554	25336	25957	25136	25764	25289	26593	39548	27349	29122	31876	26755	80
85+	11993	12994	12167	15158	24167	12929	12094	12461	11993	12293	12073	12781	28751	13183	14331	16340	12867	85+
ADDED YRS OF LIFE																		
TOTAL		1.008	.440	1.761	4.562	1.363	.421	.342	.000	1.613	.194	1.491	7.419	1.458	3.307	6.541	1.691	
WORK	3.967	.509	.054	.514	.884	.074	.006	.131	.000	.000	.131	.891	.509	.565	.646	.751	1.025	

POPULATION, DEATHS, DEATH RATES FOR ALL CAUSES COMBINED, AND SPECIFIED CAUSES

Age Start of Interval	Midyear Population	Deaths During Year	All Causes	Respiratory T. B.	Other Infec. and Paras.	Neoplasms	Cardiovascular	Infl., Pneu., Bronch.	Diarrheal	Certain Degenerative	Maternal	Cert. Dis. of Infancy	Motor Vehicle	Other Violence	Other and Unknown	Age Start of Interval
0	287222	15980	.05564	.00010	.00350	.00007	.00128	.01213	.00482	.00006	.00000	.01905	.00000	.00045	.01418	0
1	1358999	2214	.00163	.00002	.00017	.00008	.00011	.00040	.00007	.00001	.00000	.00000	.00003	.00027	.00048	1
5	1715855	750	.00044	.00001	.00005	.00006	.00006	.00003	.00001	.00001	.00000	.00000	.00002	.00008	.00012	5
10	1487608	499	.00034	.00001	.00003	.00005	.00007	.00002	.00000	.00002	.00000	.00000	.00000	.00006	.00009	10
15	953066	535	.00056	.00004	.00002	.00005	.00013	.00001	.00000	.00002	.00001	.00000	.00001	.00014	.00013	15
20	1083971	912	.00084	.00015	.00003	.00008	.00017	.00003	.00000	.00004	.00003	.00000	.00001	.00014	.00017	20
25	1144509	1281	.00112	.00029	.00003	.00014	.00021	.00004	.00000	.00003	.00005	.00000	.00001	.00011	.00021	25
30	1183446	1600	.00135	.00029	.00004	.00026	.00028	.00002	.00001	.00005	.00006	.00000	.00001	.00011	.00022	30
35	1101075	1949	.00177	.00029	.00004	.00049	.00042	.00004	.00000	.00005	.00005	.00000	.00000	.00015	.00024	35
40	722538	1762	.00244	.00031	.00003	.00083	.00063	.00000	.00000	.00007	.00004	.00000	.00000	.00010	.00038	40
45	874488	3501	.00400	.00028	.00006	.00141	.00119	.00008	.00001	.00015	.00000	.00000	.00002	.00015	.00063	45
50	896700	4871	.00543	.00030	.00006	.00188	.00183	.00009	.00001	.00020	.00000	.00000	.00002	.00020	.00085	50
55	762957	6462	.00847	.00042	.00011	.00262	.00320	.00023	.00002	.00029	.00000	.00000	.00001	.00023	.00134	55
60	625151	8678	.01388	.00053	.00013	.00347	.00560	.00040	.00003	.00046	.00000	.00000	.00003	.00025	.00298	60
65	433750	10343	.02385	.00065	.00019	.00453	.01022	.00065	.00003	.00068	.00000	.00000	.00003	.00026	.00661	65
70	318467	13158	.04132	.00071	.00022	.00523	.01696	.00112	.00005	.00055	.00000	.00000	.00004	.00035	.01569	70
75	186488	12868	.06900	.00075	.00020	.00557	.02610	.00196	.00005	.00102	.00000	.00000	.00007	.00063	.03224	75
80	93617	10835	.11574	.00053	.00022	.00668	.03814	.00299	.00010	.00100	.00000	.00000	.00003	.00080	.06523	80
85+	50066	8680	.17337	.00034	.00024	.00505	.04724	.00360	.00012	.00060	.00000	.00000	.00014	.00098	.11507	85+
ALL	15279973	106878														

	All Causes	Resp. T.B.	Other Infec.	Neoplasms	Cardiovascular	Infl. Pneu.	Diarrheal	Cert. Degen.	Maternal	Cert. Dis. Infancy	Motor Vehicle	Other Violence	Other and Unknown
CRUDE DEATH RATE	.00699	.00022	.00014	.00056	.00208	.00041	.00010	.00014	.00002	.00036	.00002	.00017	.00238
STANDARDIZED RATE (1)	.00542	.00017	.00018	.00060	.00118	.00056	.00018	.00009	.00002	.00067	.00002	.00017	.00238
STANDARDIZED RATE (2)	.00843	.00023	.00014	.00107	.00257	.00047	.00011	.00015	.00002	.00039	.00001	.00016	.00159
GEOMETRIC MEAN	.00558												

LIFE TABLE FOR ALL CAUSES COMBINED

Age (x)	Midyear Population	Deaths During Year	$_nM_x$	$_nq_x$	l_x	$_nd_x$	$_nL_x$	$_nm_x$	$_na_x$	T_x	$_nr_x$	$\overset{\circ}{e}_x$	Age (x)
0	287222	15980	.055636	.053170	100000	5317	95558	.055642	.164582	7060654	.000000	70.607	0
1	1358999	2214	.001629	.006485	94683	614	377197	.001628	1.500000	6965096	.000000	73.562	1
5	1715855	750	.000437	.002190	94069	206	469830	.000438	2.500000	6587899	.000000	70.033	5
10	1487608	499	.000335	.001673	93863	157	468935	.000335	2.576964	6118069	.047537	65.181	10
15	953066	535	.000561	.002817	93706	264	467919	.000564	2.685448	5649135	.044241	60.286	15
20	1083971	912	.000841	.004195	93442	392	466283	.000841	2.635523	5181216	-.005997	55.448	20
25	1144509	1281	.001119	.005578	93050	519	464001	.001119	2.592726	4714932	-.009154	50.671	25
30	1183446	1600	.001352	.006733	92531	623	461159	.001351	2.598315	4250932	-.008906	45.941	30
35	1101075	1949	.001770	.008846	91908	813	457609	.001777	2.625051	3789773	.036991	41.234	35
40	722538	1762	.002439	.012196	91095	1111	452899	.002453	2.681143	3332164	.033770	36.579	40
45	874488	3501	.004003	.019770	89984	1779	445734	.003991	2.646969	2879265	-.017000	31.998	45
50	896700	4871	.005432	.026824	88205	2366	435485	.005433	2.658407	2433531	-.000828	27.589	50
55	762957	6462	.008470	.041683	85839	3578	420918	.008500	2.686731	1998046	.018160	23.277	55
60	625151	8678	.013881	.067748	82261	5573	398447	.013987	2.652894	1577128	.036198	19.172	60
65	433750	10343	.023846	.113942	76688	8738	363119	.024064	2.674358	1178681	.041443	15.370	65
70	318467	13158	.041317	.189639	67950	12886	309134	.041684	2.624069	815562	.039907	12.002	70
75	186488	12868	.069002	.298053	55064	16412	235241	.069767	2.557923	506429	.048348	9.197	75
80	93617	10835	.115738	.451438	38652	17449	148890	.117194	2.457137	271188	.048348	7.016	80
85+	50066	8680	.173371	1.000000	21203	21203	122298	.173371	5.767972	122298	.000000	5.768	85+

NUMBER OF PERSONS DYING (OUT OF 100,000 AT BIRTH) ABOVE AGE X FROM SPECIFIED CAUSES

Age (x)	All Causes	Respiratory T.B.	Other Infec. and Paras.	Neo-plasms	Cardio-vascular	Infl., Pneu., Bronch.	Diar-rheal	Certain Degenerative	Maternal	Cert. Dis. of Infancy	Motor Vehicle	Other Violence	Other and Unknown	Age (x)
0	100000	2058	928	11211	32765	3688	588	1622	109	1821	139	1520	43551	0
1	94683	2048	594	11204	32643	2529	128	1616	109	0	139	1476	42197	1
5	94069	2041	528	11176	32601	2380	101	1613	109	0	128	1373	42019	5
10	93863	2038	505	11146	32573	2367	99	1607	109	0	118	1337	41964	10
15	93706	2033	494	11124	32541	2359	98	1599	109	0	116	1310	41923	15
20	93442	2014	486	11099	32481	2355	98	1588	106	0	110	1244	41861	20
25	93050	1945	471	11063	32404	2341	98	1571	91	0	106	1181	41779	25
30	92531	1811	456	10999	32305	2325	98	1555	69	0	100	1131	41682	30
35	91908	1678	436	10880	32175	2314	95	1530	41	0	95	1081	41583	35
40	91095	1546	419	10656	31980	2294	94	1507	19	0	94	1013	41473	40
45	89984	1405	404	10277	31695	2273	92	1474	2	0	93	968	41301	45
50	88205	1281	379	9652	31167	2239	89	1409	0	0	85	883	41021	50
55	85839	1152	352	8835	30368	2199	86	1320	0	0	78	797	40652	55
60	82261	973	305	7729	29015	2102	79	1198	0	0	74	700	40086	60
65	76688	760	252	6342	26766	1943	69	1012	0	0	63	598	38883	65
70	67950	524	181	4689	23020	1705	59	765	0	0	52	503	36452	70
75	55064	304	113	3070	17737	1356	42	471	0	0	39	393	31539	75
80	38652	129	65	1660	11541	891	29	229	0	0	22	242	23844	80
85+	21203	42	29	618	5777	440	15	73	0	0	17	120	14072	85+

NUMBER OF PERSONS SURVIVING TO AGE X IF SPECIFIED CAUSES WERE ELIMINATED

Age (x)	No Causes	Respiratory T.B. (1)	Other Infec. and Paras. (2)	Neo-plasms (3)	Cardio-vascular (4)	Infl., Pneu., Bronch. (5)	Diar-rheal (6)	Certain Degenerative (7)	Maternal (8)	Cert. Dis. of Infancy (9)	Motor Vehicle (10)	Other Violence (11)	Other and Unknown (12)	(1)+(2)	(1)+(2)+(5)+(6)+(8)	(1)+(2)+(5)+(6)+(8)+part of (9)&(12)	(10)+(11)	Age (x)
0	100000	100000	100000	100000	100000	100000	100000	100000	100000	100000	100000	100000	100000	100000	100000	100000	100000	0
1	94683	94693	95009	94690	94802	95817	95132	94689	94683	96471	94683	94726	96010	95018	96612	99544	94726	1
5	94069	94086	94458	94104	94229	95346	94542	94078	94069	95846	94080	94214	95567	94475	96239	99267	94225	5
10	93863	93883	94275	93928	94051	95151	94337	93878	93863	95636	93884	94044	95414	94294	96070	99109	94065	10
15	93706	93731	94128	93792	93925	95000	94180	93729	93706	95476	93729	93914	95296	94153	95935	98979	93937	15
20	93442	93485	93871	93553	93721	94736	93915	93476	93445	95207	93471	93715	95090	93915	95700	98747	93744	20
25	93050	93162	93492	93197	93405	94353	93521	93100	93068	94808	93083	93385	94775	93605	95414	98483	93418	25
30	92531	92776	92986	92741	92983	93843	92999	92597	92511	94279	92569	92914	94344	93232	95073	98177	92953	30
35	91908	92285	92380	92235	92487	93222	92376	91999	91975	93644	91951	92339	93810	92758	94633	97761	92382	35
40	91095	91601	91579	91644	91865	92418	91560	91208	91184	92816	91139	91590	93092	92088	93993	97132	91634	40
45	89984	90624	90478	90506	91030	91312	90445	90128	90089	91684	90028	90518	92131	91121	93048	96193	90562	45
50	88205	88956	88714	89736	89761	89541	88660	88411	88309	89571	88256	88813	90594	89469	91401	94528	88865	50
55	85839	86699	86361	88152	88159	87179	86285	86127	85941	87460	85896	86516	88539	87226	89152	92242	86573	55
60	82261	83262	82807	85596	85656	83642	82695	82657	82358	83815	82319	83006	85422	83815	85772	88810	83065	60
65	76688	77829	77249	81201	82339	78131	77102	77238	76779	78136	76753	77481	80852	78398	80400	83373	77547	65
70	67950	69186	68514	73608	76640	69457	68327	68671	68030	69233	68018	68743	74100	69760	71787	74663	68812	70
75	55064	56265	55582	61235	67866	56607	55384	55915	55129	56104	55131	55806	65080	56795	58796	61556	55874	75
80	38652	39642	39056	44297	54423	40135	38888	39452	38698	39382	38713	39301	53968	40056	41896	44454	39362	80
85+	21203	21812	21451	25187	36404	22361	21343	21758	21228	21603	21240	21649	41439	22067	23452	25533	21687	85+

ADDED YRS OF LIFE																	
TOTAL		.513	.412	1.966	4.815	1.241	.369	.270	.048	1.331	.040	.446	9.453	.929	2.623	5.361	.487
WORK	2.293	.260	.043	.577	.616	.050	.003	.077	.036	.000	.012	.160	.371	.304	.394	.476	.172

POPULATION, DEATHS, DEATH RATES FOR ALL CAUSES COMBINED, AND SPECIFIED CAUSES

Age Start of Interval	Midyear Population	Deaths During Year	All Causes	Respiratory T. B.	Other Infec. and Paras.	Neoplasms	Cardiovascular	Infl., Pneu., Bronch.	Diarrheal	Certain Degenerative	Maternal	Cert. Dis. of Infancy	Motor Vehicle	Other Violence	Other and Unknown	Age Start of Interval
0	290000	15492	.05342	.00003	.00212	.00011	.00073	.01153	.00504	.00004	.00000	.02123	.00001	.00050	.01207	0
1	1223000	1736	.00142	.00001	.00015	.00012	.00007	.00026	.00007	.00001	.00000	.00000	.00005	.00030	.00038	1
5	1812000	968	.00053	.00000	.00003	.00008	.00003	.00002	.00001	.00001	.00000	.00000	.00005	.00018	.00012	5
10	1748000	873	.00050	.00000	.00002	.00007	.00005	.00001	.00000	.00001	.00000	.00000	.00003	.00020	.00010	10
15	1342000	1255	.00094	.00001	.00002	.00008	.00009	.00002	.00000	.00002	.00000	.00000	.00009	.00046	.00014	15
20	1014000	1678	.00165	.00006	.00002	.00010	.00014	.00001	.00000	.00006	.00000	.00000	.00025	.00083	.00018	20
25	1131000	2133	.00189	.00023	.00002	.00015	.00019	.00002	.00001	.00006	.00000	.00000	.00025	.00079	.00017	25
30	1182000	2696	.00228	.00046	.00003	.00021	.00030	.00003	.00000	.00010	.00000	.00000	.00016	.00077	.00023	30
35	1073000	3070	.00286	.00056	.00004	.00037	.00049	.00004	.00000	.00013	.00000	.00000	.00015	.00077	.00030	35
40	882000	3470	.00393	.00063	.00006	.00072	.00086	.00007	.00000	.00021	.00000	.00000	.00015	.00079	.00044	40
45	572000	3209	.00561	.00088	.00006	.00130	.00139	.00013	.00001	.00032	.00000	.00000	.00011	.00077	.00064	45
50	785000	7231	.00921	.00128	.00007	.00232	.00267	.00021	.00001	.00056	.00000	.00000	.00012	.00082	.00114	50
55	725000	10832	.01494	.00185	.00013	.00355	.00480	.00041	.00002	.00081	.00000	.00000	.00010	.00091	.00195	55
60	561000	14335	.02555	.00255	.00018	.00653	.00908	.00081	.00004	.00124	.00000	.00000	.00013	.00097	.00401	60
65	364000	14933	.04102	.00340	.00030	.00938	.01581	.00157	.00007	.00162	.00000	.00000	.00015	.00098	.00774	65
70	212000	13390	.06316	.00302	.00025	.01142	.02688	.00275	.00012	.00245	.00000	.00000	.00017	.00118	.01492	70
75	124000	11914	.09608	.00293	.00033	.01284	.04133	.00431	.00017	.00266	.00000	.00000	.00014	.00146	.02991	75
80	53000	7987	.15070	.00192	.00038	.01217	.06460	.00708	.00026	.00221	.00000	.00000	.00021	.00202	.05985	80
85+	22000	5451	.24777	.00159	.00036	.01050	.09886	.01177	.00041	.00277	.00000	.00000	.00023	.00327	.11800	85+
ALL	15115000	122653														

CRUDE DEATH RATE			.00811	.00058	.00011	.00129	.00239	.00048	.00011	.00028	.00000	.00041	.00012	.00061	.00174	
STANDARDIZED RATE (1)			.00720	.00043	.00013	.00093	.00173	.00061	.00020	.00021	.00000	.00075	.00011	.00057	.00154	
STANDARDIZED RATE (2)			.01214	.00071	.00012	.00180	.00404	.00067	.00013	.00038	.00000	.00044	.00013	.00068	.00305	
GEOMETRIC MEAN			.00831													

LIFE TABLE FOR ALL CAUSES COMBINED

Age (x)	Midyear Population	Deaths During Year	$_nM_x$	$_nq_x$	l_x	$_nd_x$	$_nL_x$	$_nm_x$	$_na_x$	T_x	$_nr_x$	$\overset{\circ}{e}_x$	Age (x)
0	290000	15492	.053421	.051130	100000	5113	95709	.053422	.160815	6580632	.000000	65.806	0
1	1223000	1736	.001419	.005659	94887	537	378206	.001420	1.500000	6484922	.000000	68.344	1
5	1812000	968	.000534	.002660	94350	251	471123	.000533	2.500000	6106717	.000000	64.724	5
10	1748000	873	.000499	.002497	94099	235	469947	.000500	2.669326	5635594	.017127	59.890	10
15	1342000	1255	.000935	.004709	93864	442	468327	.000944	2.753582	5165647	.050268	55.033	15
20	1014000	1678	.001655	.008274	93422	773	465266	.001661	2.615082	4697320	.030171	50.281	20
25	1131000	2133	.001886	.009379	92649	869	461128	.001885	2.564250	4232054	-.009221	45.678	25
30	1182000	2696	.002281	.011342	91780	1041	456385	.002281	2.584454	3770925	-.002382	41.087	30
35	1073000	3070	.002861	.014228	90739	1291	450616	.002865	2.615059	3314540	.012210	36.528	35
40	882000	3470	.003934	.019609	89448	1754	443094	.003959	2.636474	2863924	.055463	32.018	40
45	572000	3209	.005610	.027824	87694	2440	432801	.005638	2.676571	2420829	.026131	27.605	45
50	785000	7231	.009211	.044831	85254	3822	417432	.009156	2.687729	1988029	-.027589	23.319	50
55	725000	10832	.014941	.072257	81432	5884	393562	.014951	2.689072	1570596	.003327	19.287	55
60	561000	14335	.025553	.121274	75548	9162	356215	.025720	2.650599	1177034	.030996	15.580	60
65	364000	14933	.041025	.188398	66386	12507	301844	.041435	2.594480	820819	.051794	12.364	65
70	212000	13390	.063160	.275321	53879	14834	232869	.063701	2.537709	518975	-.045413	9.632	70
75	124000	11914	.096081	.389090	39045	15192	156859	.096851	2.474617	286105	.040223	7.328	75
80	53000	7987	.150658	.544292	23853	12983	85375	.152070	2.389663	129246	.040223	5.418	80
85+	22000	5451	.247773	1.000000	10870	10870	43871	.247773	4.035957	43871	.000000	4.036	85+

NUMBER OF PERSONS DYING (OUT OF 100,000 AT BIRTH) ABOVE AGE X FROM SPECIFIED CAUSES

Age (x)	All Causes	Respiratory T.B.	Other Infec. and Paras.	Neoplasms	Cardiovascular	Infl., Pneu., Bronch.	Diarrheal	Certain Degenerative	Maternal	Cert. Dis. of Infancy	Motor Vehicle	Other Violence	Other and Unknown	Age (x)
0	100000	5895	790	15371	35500	4832	672	3221	0	2032	866	4873	25948	0
1	94887	5892	587	15360	35430	3728	190	3217	0	0	865	4824	24794	1
5	94350	5888	532	15316	35403	3629	162	3212	0	0	846	4709	24653	5
10	94099	5887	520	15279	35390	3620	159	3205	0	0	820	4623	24596	10
15	93864	5886	510	15248	35366	3614	159	3198	0	0	807	4527	24549	15
20	93422	5882	499	15212	35326	3605	157	3187	0	0	761	4307	24486	20
25	92649	5853	492	15164	35259	3599	156	3161	0	0	645	3917	24403	25
30	91780	5749	482	15093	35172	3592	153	3132	0	0	530	3554	24323	30
35	90739	5540	470	14999	35033	3577	153	3087	0	0	459	3205	24216	35
40	89448	5286	450	14831	34813	3559	151	3028	0	0	391	2857	24082	40
45	87694	5005	423	14509	34429	3529	149	2935	0	0	323	2507	23885	45
50	85254	4624	395	13943	33824	3474	146	2796	0	0	276	2173	23603	50
55	81432	4090	364	12979	32718	3387	142	2561	0	0	224	1833	23134	55
60	75548	3361	314	11424	30827	3224	133	2244	0	0	182	1474	22365	60
65	66386	2448	249	9083	27568	2932	119	1800	0	0	135	1128	20924	65
70	53879	1417	159	6231	22738	2453	96	1309	0	0	89	833	18554	70
75	39045	715	102	3561	16418	1805	67	735	0	0	50	556	15036	75
80	23853	256	50	1543	9883	1123	41	317	0	0	29	326	10285	80
85+	10870	70	16	461	4337	516	18	122	0	0	10	144	5176	85+

NUMBER OF PERSONS SURVIVING TO AGE X IF SPECIFIED CAUSES WERE ELIMINATED

Age (x)	No Causes	Respiratory T.B.	Other Infec. and Paras.	Neoplasms	Cardiovascular	Infl., Pneu., Bronch.	Diarrheal	Certain Degenerative	Maternal	Cert. Dis. of Infancy	Motor Vehicle	Other Violence	Other and Unknown	(1) + (2)	(1) + (2) + (5) + (6) + (8)	(1)+(2)+ (5)+(6)+ (8)+part of(9)&(12)	(10) + (11)	Age (x)
		(1)	(2)	(3)	(4)	(5)	(6)	(7)	(8)	(9)	(10)	(11)	(12)					
0	100000	100000	100000	100000	100000	100000	100000	100000	100000	100000	100000	100000	100000	100000	100000	100000	100000	0
1	94887	94890	95085	94898	94955	95968	95358	94891	94887	96887	94888	94935	96018	95088	96649	99633	94936	1
5	94350	94357	94602	94405	94445	95525	94846	94359	94350	96339	94370	94512	95617	94609	96291	99334	94532	5
10	94099	94107	94362	94190	94207	95280	94557	94115	94099	96082	94145	94347	95420	94370	96060	99103	94393	10
15	93864	93873	94136	93986	93995	95048	94360	93887	93864	95842	93923	94207	95229	94145	95837	98878	94266	15
20	93422	93435	93704	93580	93593	94610	93918	93456	93422	95391	93526	93984	94845	93717	95413	98444	94089	20
25	92649	92691	92936	92853	92885	93833	93142	92708	92649	94602	92868	93598	94144	92978	94667	97680	93820	25
30	91780	91925	92074	92053	92100	92560	92271	91868	91780	93714	92112	93086	93342	92220	93905	96908	93423	30
35	90739	91091	91042	91103	91155	91921	91225	90870	90739	92652	91138	92383	92391	91395	93081	96085	92789	35
40	89448	90048	89766	89974	90117	90631	89929	89636	89448	91333	89909	91421	91212	90369	92056	95064	91892	40
45	87694	88563	88033	88531	88734	88884	88167	87971	87694	89542	88214	89983	89623	88905	90598	93603	90516	45
50	85254	86479	85611	86634	86871	86446	85717	85661	85254	87051	85806	87817	87414	86841	88554	91556	88386	50
55	81432	83133	81804	83713	84086	82676	81878	82052	81432	83148	82010	84223	83966	83512	85253	88240	84821	55
60	75548	77845	75941	79218	79915	76862	75971	76431	75548	77140	76125	78494	78667	78250	80056	83013	79094	60
65	66386	69289	66793	71947	73530	67820	66771	67583	66386	67785	66937	69311	70550	69714	71632	74529	69887	65
70	53879	57206	54290	61230	64694	55485	54212	55301	53879	55015	54368	56529	59576	57643	59728	62539	57042	70
75	39045	42084	39391	47002	53784	40779	39311	40576	39045	39868	39432	41211	46621	42457	44645	47202	41620	75
80	23853	26087	24105	30629	40614	25470	24036	25121	23853	24356	24106	25363	33272	26363	28365	30537	25632	80
85+	10870	12023	11007	14903	25892	12041	10969	11584	10870	11099	10998	11686	20657	12175	13609	15148	11824	85+

ADDED YRS OF LIFE																		
TOTAL		1.022	.272	2.185	4.780	1.170	.364	.462	.000	1.384	.287	1.416	3.869	1.301	2.898	5.444	1.713	
WORK	3.711	.457	.040	.599	.728	.064	.005	.163	.000	.000	.187	.823	.402	.498	.569	.644	1.014	

POPULATION, DEATHS, DEATH RATES FOR ALL CAUSES COMBINED, AND SPECIFIED CAUSES

Age Start of Interval	Midyear Population	Deaths During Year	All Causes	Respiratory T. B.	Other Infec. and Paras.	Neo-plasms	Cardio-vascular	Infl., Pneu., Bronch.	Diar-rheal	Certain Degen-erative	Maternal	Cert. Dis. of Infancy	Motor Vehicle	Other Violence	Other and Unknown	Age Start of Interval
0	275000	11385	.04140	.00006	.00181	.00011	.00077	.00933	.00400	.00004	.00000	.01498	.00001	.00055	.00973	0
1	1159000	1494	.00129	.00001	.00015	.00010	.00006	.00031	.00005	.00001	.00000	.00000	.00004	.00020	.00035	1
5	1735000	709	.00041	.00000	.00003	.00008	.00004	.00003	.00000	.00001	.00000	.00000	.00003	.00008	.00010	5
10	1685000	500	.00030	.00000	.00002	.00005	.00004	.00001	.00000	.00001	.00000	.00000	.00001	.00006	.00009	10
15	1307000	600	.00046	.00001	.00001	.00007	.00008	.00002	.00000	.00003	.00000	.00000	.00002	.00013	.00009	15
20	992000	657	.00066	.00005	.00002	.00008	.00011	.00002	.00001	.00003	.00004	.00000	.00003	.00015	.00013	20
25	1115000	917	.00082	.00013	.00003	.00013	.00016	.00002	.00000	.00004	.00004	.00000	.00003	.00011	.00013	25
30	1183000	1322	.00112	.00019	.00003	.00026	.00022	.00002	.00000	.00005	.00005	.00000	.00002	.00011	.00018	30
35	1174000	1903	.00162	.00022	.00002	.00049	.00033	.00002	.00000	.00008	.00004	.00000	.00002	.00013	.00026	35
40	1014000	2368	.00234	.00023	.00004	.00086	.00053	.00003	.00001	.00012	.00003	.00000	.00001	.00016	.00032	40
45	680000	2419	.00356	.00022	.00005	.00148	.00090	.00005	.00001	.00017	.00001	.00000	.00002	.00019	.00046	45
50	913000	4744	.00520	.00027	.00007	.00206	.00151	.00010	.00002	.00026	.00000	.00000	.00003	.00025	.00063	50
55	841000	6861	.00816	.00036	.00010	.00294	.00278	.00019	.00002	.00045	.00000	.00000	.00004	.00024	.00104	55
60	712000	9542	.01340	.00059	.00013	.00404	.00531	.00037	.00002	.00066	.00000	.00000	.00005	.00031	.00192	60
65	528000	12675	.02401	.00087	.00017	.00568	.01056	.00087	.00005	.00117	.00000	.00000	.00006	.00037	.00420	65
70	345000	14795	.04288	.00111	.00019	.00748	.02057	.00167	.00007	.00152	.00000	.00000	.00008	.00062	.00959	70
75	228000	16401	.07193	.00096	.00028	.00869	.03439	.00307	.00012	.00174	.00000	.00000	.00011	.00107	.02152	75
80	108000	12831	.11881	.00073	.00029	.00883	.05582	.00480	.00014	.00187	.00000	.00000	.00012	.00174	.04446	80
85+	54000	11143	.20635	.00067	.00039	.00746	.08869	.00748	.00030	.00165	.00000	-.00000	.00020	.00298	.09654	85+
ALL	16048000	113266														

CRUDE DEATH RATE			.00706	.00020	.00009	.00122	.00258	.00039	.00008	.00022	.00001	.00026	.00003	.00020	.00176	
STANDARDIZED RATE (1)			.00482	.00013	.00012	.00071	.00126	.00047	.00015	.00012	.00001	.00053	.00003	.00017	.00110	
STANDARDIZED RATE (2)			.00821	.00021	.00010	.00131	.00306	.00047	.00010	.00023	.00001	.00031	.00003	.00022	.00215	
GEOMETRIC MEAN			.00509													

LIFE TABLE FOR ALL CAUSES COMBINED

Age (x)	Midyear Population	Deaths During Year	$_nM_x$	$_nq_x$	l_x	$_nd_x$	$_nL_x$	$_nm_x$	$_na_x$	T_x	$_nr_x$	$\overset{\circ}{e}_x$	Age (x)
0	275000	11385	.041400	.039980	100000	3998	96563	.041403	.140380	7175093	.000000	71.751	0
1	1159000	1494	.001289	.005135	96002	493	382776	.001288	1.500000	7078530	.000000	73.733	1
5	1735000	709	.000409	.002042	95509	195	477058	.000409	2.500000	6695755	.000000	70.106	5
10	1685000	500	.000297	.001479	95314	141	476222	.000296	2.535461	6218697	.015922	65.244	10
15	1307000	600	.000459	.002301	95173	219	475354	.000461	2.665525	5742475	.049178	60.337	15
20	992000	657	.000662	.003317	94954	315	474018	.000665	2.611772	5267121	.029545	55.470	20
25	1115000	917	.000822	.004100	94639	388	472269	.000822	2.612758	4793103	-.008996	50.646	25
30	1183000	1322	.001117	.005570	94251	525	470019	.001117	2.646032	4320834	-.008630	45.844	30
35	1174000	1903	.001621	.008066	93726	756	466857	.001619	2.654872	3850815	.000241	41.086	35
40	1014000	2368	.002335	.011692	92970	1087	462314	.002351	2.666935	3383958	.046357	36.398	40
45	680000	2419	.003557	.017707	91883	1627	455602	.003571	2.656218	2921644	.023783	31.797	45
50	913000	4744	.005196	.025561	90256	2307	445908	.005174	2.671399	2466043	-.022063	27.323	50
55	841000	6861	.008158	.040080	87949	3525	431601	.008167	2.689657	2020135	.005144	22.969	55
60	712000	9542	.013402	.065337	84424	5516	409483	.013471	2.709051	1588534	.023048	18.816	60
65	528000	12675	.024006	.114817	78908	9060	373596	.024251	2.688351	1179050	.042978	14.942	65
70	345000	14795	.042684	.196240	69848	13707	316690	.043282	2.625316	805454	.039950	11.532	70
75	228000	16401	.071934	.308242	56141	17305	238310	.072615	2.550154	488764	.041126	8.706	75
80	108000	12831	.118806	.460217	38836	17873	148865	.120062	2.464600	250453	.041126	6.449	80
85+	54000	11143	.206352	1.000000	20963	20963	101589	.206352	4.846092	101589	.000000	4.846	85+

NUMBER OF PERSONS DYING (OUT OF 100,000 AT BIRTH) ABOVE AGE X FROM SPECIFIED CAUSES

Age (x)	All Causes	Respiratory T. B.	Other Infec. and Paras.	Neo-plasms	Cardio-vascular	Infl., Pneu., Bronch.	Diar-rheal	Certain Degen-erative	Maternal	Cert. Dis. of Infancy	Motor Vehicle	Other Violence	Other and Unknown	Age (x)
0	100000	2115	750	14238	41518	4477	570	2630	100	1446	261	2152	29743	0
1	96002	2109	574	14227	41443	3575	185	2626	100	0	260	2099	28804	1
5	95509	2106	517	14187	41418	3457	164	2621	100	0	246	2023	28670	5
10	95314	2105	503	14148	41399	3444	162	2616	100	0	230	1986	28621	10
15	95173	2105	496	14125	41378	3437	162	2610	100	0	225	1957	28578	15
20	94954	2101	490	14090	41342	3428	162	2598	97	0	218	1895	28533	20
25	94639	2076	479	14051	41289	3419	159	2585	80	0	206	1824	28471	25
30	94251	2013	467	13991	41212	3412	157	2566	59	0	194	1774	28406	30
35	93726	1922	453	13869	41111	3404	156	2543	37	0	185	1722	28324	35
40	92970	1821	443	13639	40956	3394	155	2508	17	0	176	1660	28201	40
45	91883	1714	425	13237	40707	3381	151	2453	5	0	171	1587	28052	45
50	90256	1613	404	12558	40296	3358	147	2376	1	0	161	1500	27842	50
55	87949	1493	372	11644	39625	3312	139	2262	0	0	147	1391	27564	55
60	84424	1337	330	10372	38425	3232	129	2068	0	0	132	1288	27111	60
65	78908	1093	277	8715	36235	3079	120	1795	0	0	113	1162	26319	65
70	69848	766	212	6580	32244	2752	103	1354	0	0	88	1021	24728	70
75	56141	413	150	4202	25667	2217	81	871	0	0	64	823	21653	75
80	38836	185	84	2124	17396	1479	51	456	0	0	39	566	16456	80
85+	20963	68	40	758	9009	760	30	167	0	0	21	303	9807	85+

NUMBER OF PERSONS SURVIVING TO AGE X IF SPECIFIED CAUSES WERE ELIMINATED

Age (x)	No Causes	Respiratory T. B. (1)	Other Infec. and Paras. (2)	Neo-plasms (3)	Cardio-vascular (4)	Infl., Pneu., Bronch. (5)	Diar-rheal (6)	Certain Degener-ative (7)	Maternal (8)	Cert. Dis. of Infancy (9)	Motor Vehicle (10)	Other Violence (11)	Other and Unknown (12)	(1) + (2)	(1) + (2) + (5) + (6) + (8)	(1)+(2)+ (5)+(6)+ (8)+part of(9)&(12)	(10) + (11)	Age (x)
0	100000	100000	100000	100000	100000	100000	100000	100000	100000	100000	100000	100000	100000	100000	100000	100000	100000	0
1	96002	96008	96175	96013	96076	96890	96380	96006	96002	97429	96003	96054	96926	96180	97452	99636	96055	1
5	95509	95518	95738	95560	95607	96511	95906	95518	95509	96929	95524	95637	96564	95747	97153	99408	95652	5
10	95314	95324	95556	95404	95431	96337	95712	95328	95314	96731	95345	95478	96416	95566	96985	99247	95509	10
15	95173	95183	95422	95285	95311	96192	95571	95193	95173	96588	95209	95366	96317	95432	96856	99121	95402	15
20	94954	94968	95208	95101	95127	95979	95351	94986	94957	96366	94997	95209	96141	95222	96656	98922	95252	20
25	94639	94678	94903	94825	94865	95670	95037	94684	94659	96046	94694	94964	95884	94942	96401	98678	95019	25
30	94251	94352	94526	94496	94553	95285	94650	94314	94292	95662	94317	94625	95557	94628	96113	98404	94691	30
35	93726	93918	94014	94092	94127	94762	94124	93812	93789	95119	93801	94150	95108	94206	95716	98024	94225	35
40	92970	93261	93266	93563	93523	94008	93365	93090	93052	94352	93053	93452	94465	93558	95088	97410	93536	40
45	91883	92277	92193	92872	92679	92922	92278	92057	91976	93249	91970	92433	93511	92589	94133	96457	92521	45
50	90256	90744	90581	91910	91450	91300	90648	90503	90351	91558	90352	90883	92067	91071	92622	94932	90979	50
55	87949	88544	88298	90484	89786	89012	88339	88303	88043	89256	88056	88668	89994	88895	90464	92750	88776	55
60	84424	85149	84800	88149	87397	85524	84808	84954	84514	85679	84542	85216	86843	85528	87129	89375	85334	60
65	78908	79823	79311	84076	83909	80086	79276	79670	78992	80081	79036	79771	81561	80231	81895	84086	79900	65
70	69848	70969	70266	76586	78378	71204	70189	70941	69923	70886	69985	70746	74125	71394	73213	75331	70884	70
75	56141	57361	56532	63921	69961	57721	56435	57458	56201	56976	56272	57042	62584	57761	59762	61767	57176	75
80	38836	39870	39161	46196	57708	40561	39064	40096	38877	39413	38948	39676	48391	40204	42281	44128	39790	80
85+	20963	21608	21171	26139	41602	22444	21102	21860	20985	21275	21036	21611	32855	21822	23543	25028	21687	85+

ADDED YRS OF LIFE

	No Causes	(1)	(2)	(3)	(4)	(5)	(6)	(7)	(8)	(9)	(10)	(11)	(12)	(1)+(2)	(1)+(2)+(5)+(6)+(8)	part	(10)+(11)
TOTAL		.411	.272	2.331	5.834	1.089	.320	.383	.044	1.065	.073	.493	4.379	.685	2.167	4.166	.567
WORK	2.051	.168	.035	.623	.497	.038	.006	.096	.033	.000	.025	.169	.289	.203	.281	.332	.194

POPULATION, DEATHS, DEATH RATES FOR ALL CAUSES COMBINED, AND SPECIFIED CAUSES

Age Start of Interval	Midyear Population	Deaths During Year	All Causes	Respira-tory T. B.	Other Infec. and Paras.	Neo-plasms	Cardio-vascular	Infl., Pneu., Bronch.	Diar-rheal	Certain Degen-erative	Maternal	Cert. Dis. of Infancy	Motor Vehicle	Other Violence	Other and Unknown	Age Start of Interval
0	62183	18165	.29212	.00037	.01168	.00002	.00068	.01743	.07333	.00055	.00000	.04730	.00000	.00109	.13968	0
1	243707	11589	.04755	.00043	.00559	.00002	.00018	.00423	.01137	.00048	.00000	.00000	.00000	.00069	.02457	1
5	346882	2925	.00843	.00025	.00128	.00001	.00010	.00053	.00132	.00021	.00000	.00000	.00000	.00027	.00446	5
10	348049	1591	.00457	.00021	.00063	.00001	.00011	.00031	.00041	.00010	.00000	.00000	.00000	.00033	.00246	10
15	306992	1836	.00598	.00108	.00075	.00001	.00017	.00046	.00021	.00009	.00000	.00000	.00000	.00054	.00268	15
20	239862	2356	.00982	.00273	.00101	.00003	.00023	.00102	.00016	.00015	.00000	.00000	.00000	.00075	.00374	20
25	204391	1972	.00965	.00258	.00078	.00006	.00023	.00067	.00015	.00021	.00000	.00000	.00000	.00078	.00376	25
30	175487	1676	.00955	.00244	.00063	.00010	.00041	.00103	.00022	.00025	.00000	.00000	.00000	.00066	.00382	30
35	162547	1750	.01077	.00257	.00062	.00014	.00066	.00112	.00019	.00038	.00000	.00000	.00000	.00064	.00446	35
40	153205	1958	.01278	.00228	.00081	.00020	.00110	.00110	.00029	.00035	.00000	.00000	.00000	.00058	.00607	40
45	139449	2124	.01523	.00226	.00066	.00047	.00166	.00154	.00039	.00067	.00000	.00000	.00000	.00057	.00701	45
50	124236	2377	.01913	.00192	.00064	.00067	.00274	.00162	.00051	.00093	.00000	.00000	.00000	.00060	.00951	50
55	96045	2478	.02580	.00158	.00076	.00107	.00454	.00218	.00075	.00104	.00000	.00000	.00000	.00067	.01282	55
60	91337	3290	.03602	.00127	.00072	.00125	.00744	.00291	.00100	.00127	.00000	.00000	.00000	.00072	.01943	60
65	60768	3389	.05577	.00128	.00076	.00165	.01321	.00448	.00155	.00155	.00000	.00000	.00000	.00084	.03046	65
70	45326	4233	.09339	.00068	.00099	.00170	.02303	.00655	.00267	.00212	.00000	.00000	.00000	.00124	.05441	70
75	23932	3701	.15465	.00104	.00092	.00180	.03765	.00978	.00481	.00276	.00000	.00000	.00000	.00163	.09427	75
80	13554	2505	.18482	.00052	.00118	.00140	.03468	.00789	.00325	.00229	.00000	.00000	.00000	.00074	.13288	80
85+	6369	2285	.35877	.00031	.00173	.00157	.05228	.01413	.00581	.00314	.00000	.00000	.00000	.00110	.27869	85+
ALL	2844321	72200														

	All Causes	Respira-tory T.B.	Other Infec. and Paras.	Neo-plasms	Cardio-vascular	Infl., Pneu., Bronch.	Diar-rheal	Certain Degen-erative	Maternal	Cert. Dis. of Infancy	Motor Vehicle	Other Violence	Other and Unknown
CRUDE DEATH RATE	.02538	.00143	.00147	.00025	.00208	.00188	.00312	.00044	.00000	.00103	.00000	.00060	.01308
STANDARDIZED RATE (1)	.02818	.00140	.00177	.00020	.00155	.00208	.00441	.00040	.00000	.00166	.00000	.00060	.01409
STANDARDIZED RATE (2)	.03015	.00154	.00141	.00035	.00330	.00218	.00306	.00056	.00000	.00098	.00000	.00064	.01614
GEOMETRIC MEAN	.02853												

LIFE TABLE FOR ALL CAUSES COMBINED

Age (x)	Midyear Popula-tion	Deaths During Year	$_nM_x$	$_nq_x$	l_x	$_nd_x$	$_nL_x$	$_nm_x$	$_na_x$	T_x	$_nr_x$	$\overset{\circ}{e}_x$	Age (x)
0	62183	18165	.292122	.259290	100000	25929	88763	.292116	.56667	3447837	.000000	34.478	0
1	243707	11589	.041553	.170013	74071	12593	264802	.041556	1.500000	3359074	.000000	45.349	1
5	346882	2925	.008432	.041299	61478	2539	301043	.008434	2.500000	3094272	.000000	50.331	5
10	348049	1591	.004571	.022583	58939	1331	291154	.004571	2.369459	2793230	.000671	47.392	10
15	306992	1836	.005981	.029597	57608	1705	284061	.006002	2.666178	2502036	.023270	43.432	15
20	239862	2356	.009822	.048137	55903	2691	272954	.009859	2.561935	2217975	.031370	39.675	20
25	204391	1972	.009648	.047076	53212	2505	259730	.009645	2.472971	1945021	.024814	36.552	25
30	175487	1676	.009551	.046660	50707	2366	247626	.009555	2.502730	1685291	.017665	33.236	30
35	162547	1750	.010766	.052461	48341	2536	235463	.010770	2.538775	1437665	.006179	29.740	35
40	153205	1958	.012780	.061958	45805	2838	222059	.012780	2.545513	1202202	.003463	26.246	40
45	139449	2124	.015231	.073452	42967	3156	207113	.015238	2.553272	980142	.002282	22.812	45
50	124236	2377	.019133	.091558	39811	3645	190201	.019164	2.570816	773029	.016555	19.417	50
55	96045	2478	.025800	.121523	36166	4395	170181	.025825	2.576981	582829	.006788	16.115	55
60	91337	3290	.036020	.165843	31771	5269	146126	.036058	2.584100	412648	.006854	12.988	60
65	60768	3389	.055769	.246095	26502	6522	116685	.055894	2.573597	266522	.011985	10.057	65
70	45326	4233	.093390	.379029	19980	7573	81024	.093466	2.507455	149837	.003381	7.499	70
75	23932	3701	.154646	.547514	12407	6793	44188	.153728	2.372786	68813	-.021245	5.546	75
80	13554	2505	.184816	.610082	5614	3425	18524	.184900	2.212713	24625	-.021245	4.386	80
85+	6369	2285	.358769	1.000000	2189	2189	6101	.358769	2.787309	6101	.000000	2.787	85+

NUMBER OF PERSONS DYING (OUT OF 100,000 AT BIRTH) ABOVE AGE X FROM SPECIFIED CAUSES

Age (x)	All Causes	Respiratory T. B.	Other Infec. and Paras.	Neo-plasms	Cardio-vascular	Infl., Pneu., Bronch.	Diar-rheal	Certain Degen-erative	Maternal	Cert. Dis. of Infancy	Motor Vehicle	Other Violence	Other and Unknown	Age (x)
0	100000	5445	4995	1174	9602	7401	11509	1834	0	4198	0	2201	51641	0
1	74071	5412	3959	1173	9542	5853	5000	1786	0	0	0	2104	39242	1
5	61478	5299	2479	1167	9493	4734	1989	1658	0	0	0	1923	32736	5
10	58939	5224	2094	1166	9462	4574	1591	1593	0	0	0	1840	31395	10
15	57608	5163	1909	1163	9430	4484	1472	1563	0	0	0	1745	30679	15
20	55903	4851	1695	1160	9382	4354	1414	1538	0	0	0	1591	29918	20
25	53212	4103	1419	1151	9318	4075	1370	1458	0	0	0	1386	28892	25
30	50707	3329	1218	1136	9257	3902	1320	1445	0	0	0	1184	27916	30
35	48341	2726	1063	1110	9155	3648	1267	1382	0	0	0	1022	26968	35
40	45805	2122	918	1078	9000	3384	1222	1292	0	0	0	871	25918	40
45	42967	1616	738	1034	8756	3141	1157	1214	0	0	0	742	24569	45
50	39811	1148	601	937	8411	2821	1075	1076	0	0	0	624	23118	50
55	36166	784	479	809	7889	2513	978	898	0	0	0	510	21306	55
60	31771	448	350	627	7115	2143	850	721	0	0	0	397	19120	60
65	26502	262	244	444	6026	1717	705	535	0	0	0	291	16278	65
70	19980	112	156	252	4480	1193	524	354	0	0	0	193	12716	70
75	12407	57	75	114	2612	662	307	183	0	0	0	93	8304	75
80	5614	11	35	35	957	232	96	61	0	0	0	21	4166	80
85+	2189	2	11	10	319	86	35	19	0	0	0	7	1700	85+

NUMBER OF PERSONS SURVIVING TO AGE X IF SPECIFIED CAUSES WERE ELIMINATED

Age (x)	No Causes	Respiratory T. B.	Other Infec. and Paras.	Neo-plasms	Cardio-vascular	Infl., Pneu., Bronch.	Diar-rheal	Certain Degener-ative	Maternal	Cert. Dis. of Infancy	Motor Vehicle	Other Violence	Other and Unknown	(1) + (2)	(1) + (2) + (5) + (6) + (8)	(1)+(2)+ (5)+(6)+ (8)+part of(9)&(12)	(10) + (11)	Age (x)
		(1)	(2)	(3)	(4)	(5)	(6)	(7)	(8)	(9)	(10)	(11)	(12)					
0	100000	100000	100000	100000	100000	100000	100000	100000	100000	100000	100000	100000	100000	100000	100000	100000	100000	0
1	74071	74099	74565	74072	74122	75410	79868	74112	74071	77759	74071	74154	85503	74993	82324	99340	74154	1
5	61478	61604	63557	61484	61565	63625	69309	61629	61478	64539	61478	61712	78138	63728	74366	98239	61712	5
10	58939	59134	61362	58946	59053	61169	66888	59147	58939	61874	58939	59245	76599	61565	72511	97619	59245	10
15	57608	57859	60167	57618	57751	59880	65511	57841	57608	60477	57608	58002	75794	60429	71429	97040	58002	15
20	55903	56457	58607	55915	56089	58241	63637	56154	55903	58687	55903	56438	74544	59187	70193	96332	56438	20
25	53212	54481	56068	53233	53452	55722	60622	53490	53212	55862	53212	53923	72302	57406	68485	95429	53923	25
30	50707	52696	53636	50741	50996	53276	57824	51024	50707	53232	50707	51585	70205	55740	66783	94438	51585	30
35	48341	50852	51293	48399	48717	51051	55185	48706	48341	50748	48341	49339	68224	53958	65051	93320	49339	35
40	45805	48806	48752	45891	46314	48645	52340	46239	45805	48086	45805	46901	66104	51947	63039	91882	46901	40
45	42967	46307	45918	43091	43684	45882	49169	43450	42967	45107	42967	44123	63923	49487	60472	89947	44123	45
50	39811	43393	42686	40020	40815	42842	45648	40394	39811	41793	39811	40999	61342	46526	57409	87177	40999	50
55	36166	39799	38902	36478	37592	39236	41575	36868	36166	37967	36166	37357	58451	42810	53389	82975	37357	55
60	31771	35309	34305	32218	33788	34846	36661	32556	31771	33353	31771	32926	54768	38124	48249	77120	32926	60
65	26502	29640	28719	27044	29263	29496	30734	27331	26502	27822	26502	27566	50382	32120	41456	68603	27566	65
70	19980	22489	21734	20558	23591	22746	23353	20766	19980	20975	19980	20870	44324	24463	32552	56575	20870	70
75	12407	14012	13564	12875	16475	14602	14701	13034	12407	13025	12407	13041	36348	15318	21361	40117	13041	75
80	5614	6374	6165	5878	9040	6545	6818	5981	5614	5894	5614	5550	26771	7000	10515	22552	5950	80
85+	2189	2491	2420	2308	4201	2819	2703	2359	2189	2298	2189	2329	20566	2754	4380	11131	2329	85+

ADDED YRS OF LIFE																		
TOTAL		1.618	1.945	.166	1.183	2.115	4.781	.381	.000	1.689	.000	.649	19.783	3.682	11.798	33.227	.649	
WORK	11.194	2.007	.669	.130	.610	.841	.211	.252	.000	.000	.000	.569	4.291	2.725	3.899	7.167	.569	

POPULATION, DEATHS, DEATH RATES FOR ALL CAUSES COMBINED, AND SPECIFIED CAUSES

Age Start of Interval	Midyear Population	Deaths During Year	All Causes	Respiratory T. B.	Other Infec. and Paras.	Neoplasms	Cardiovascular	Infl., Pneu., Bronch.	Diarrheal	Certain Degenerative	Maternal	Cert. Dis. of Infancy	Motor Vehicle	Other Violence	Other and Unknown	Age Start of Interval
0	61710	15235	.24688	.00039	.01074	.00006	.00058	.01531	.06493	.00037	.00000	.03656	.00000	.00050	.11742	0
1	237114	10988	.04634	.00038	.00556	.00001	.00008	.00387	.01136	.00049	.00000	.00000	.00000	.00061	.02399	1
5	334972	2718	.00811	.00026	.00137	.00001	.00007	.00057	.00118	.00016	.00000	.00000	.00000	.00018	.00431	5
10	335185	1463	.00436	.00041	.00075	.00000	.00010	.00028	.00033	.00010	.00001	.00000	.00000	.00009	.00231	10
15	320634	1853	.00578	.00135	.00081	.00000	.00018	.00043	.00016	.00008	.00015	.00000	.00000	.00015	.00245	15
20	276361	2043	.00739	.00204	.00070	.00001	.00023	.00048	.00019	.00013	.00050	.00000	.00000	.00014	.00297	20
25	242475	1956	.00807	.00192	.00061	.00005	.00020	.00057	.00020	.00017	.00067	.00000	.00000	.00015	.00352	25
30	217765	1760	.00808	.00174	.00054	.00014	.00037	.00064	.00022	.00019	.00062	.00000	.00000	.00011	.00351	30
35	196294	1695	.00864	.00159	.00061	.00017	.00043	.00057	.00022	.00031	.00069	.00000	.00000	.00010	.00396	35
40	186885	1787	.00956	.00138	.00056	.00039	.00073	.00068	.00027	.00035	.00034	.00000	.00000	.00010	.00475	40
45	161451	1675	.01037	.00123	.00053	.00055	.00116	.00087	.00035	.00031	.00011	.00000	.00000	.00014	.00514	45
50	154000	2015	.01308	.00086	.00063	.00070	.00197	.00103	.00051	.00052	.00002	.00000	.00000	.00014	.00671	50
55	118198	2067	.01749	.00087	.00056	.00096	.00340	.00118	.00080	.00051	.00000	.00000	.00000	.00019	.00893	55
60	117645	3467	.02947	.00066	.00074	.00116	.00621	.00207	.00113	.00059	.00000	.00000	.00000	.00021	.01669	60
65	78202	3560	.04552	.00081	.00087	.00139	.01165	.00309	.00164	.00110	.00000	.00000	.00000	.00029	.02468	65
70	62832	4872	.07754	.00054	.00057	.00154	.01951	.00520	.00269	.00110	.00000	.00000	.00000	.00038	.04600	70
75	33375	4272	.12800	.00063	.00053	.00152	.03215	.00761	.00357	.00159	.00000	.00000	.00000	.00072	.07889	75
80	20900	3575	.17105	.00038	.00144	.00158	.03129	.00689	.00344	.00110	.00000	.00000	.00000	.00077	.12416	80
85+	11004	3661	.33270	.00027	.00191	.00164	.04707	.01254	.00609	.00154	.00000	.00000	.00000	.00118	.26045	85+
ALL	3167002	70662														

		All Causes	Respiratory T. B.	Other Infec. and Paras.	Neoplasms	Cardiovascular	Infl., Pneu., Bronch.	Diarrheal	Certain Degenerative	Maternal	Cert. Dis. of Infancy	Motor Vehicle	Other Violence	Other and Unknown
CRUDE DEATH RATE		.02231	.00107	.00132	.00029	.00208	.00149	.00266	.00032	.00022	.00071	.00000	.00020	.01195
STANDARDIZED RATE (1)		.02428	.00102	.00170	.00021	.00127	.00168	.00409	.00029	.00021	.00129	.00000	.00022	.01230
STANDARDIZED RATE (2)		.02558	.00106	.00134	.00036	.00277	.00168	.00285	.00036	.00022	.00076	.00000	.00022	.01397
GEOMETRIC MEAN		.02402												

LIFE TABLE FOR ALL CAUSES COMBINED

Age (x)	Midyear Population	Deaths During Year	$_nM_x$	$_nq_x$	l_x	$_nd_x$	$_nL_x$	$_nm_x$	$_na_x$	T_x	$_nr_x$	$\overset{\circ}{e}_x$	Age (x)
0	61710	15235	.246881	.219260	100000	21926	88811	.246884	.489697	3869865	.000000	38.699	0
1	237114	10988	.046341	.166112	78074	12969	279874	.046339	1.500000	3781053	.000000	48.429	1
5	334972	2718	.008114	.039767	65105	2589	319053	.008115	2.500000	3501180	.000000	53.777	5
10	335185	1463	.004365	.021594	62516	1350	309029	.004369	2.369599	3182127	-.003261	50.901	10
15	320634	1853	.005779	.028513	61166	1744	301639	.005782	2.596880	2873099	.008162	46.972	15
20	276361	2043	.007393	.036367	59422	2161	291816	.007405	2.550131	2571460	.018626	43.275	20
25	242475	1956	.008067	.039538	57261	2264	280649	.008067	2.501656	2279644	.016740	39.811	25
30	217765	1760	.008082	.039620	54997	2179	269531	.008084	2.497036	1998899	.015124	36.347	30
35	196294	1695	.008635	.042277	52818	2233	258546	.008637	2.517260	1729464	.007786	32.744	35
40	186885	1787	.009562	.046733	50585	2364	247058	.009569	2.518242	1470918	.010262	29.078	40
45	161451	1675	.010375	.050600	48221	2440	235118	.010378	2.546648	1223860	.006906	25.380	45
50	154000	2015	.013084	.063520	45781	2908	221878	.013106	2.583606	988741	-.017229	21.597	50
55	118198	2067	.017488	.084132	42873	3607	205870	.017521	2.644973	766863	-.009666	17.887	55
60	117645	3467	.029470	.137982	39266	5418	183484	.029528	2.629045	560993	.010291	14.287	60
65	78202	3560	.045523	.205714	33848	6963	152531	.045650	2.600352	377509	.014253	11.153	65
70	62832	4872	.077540	.326279	26885	8772	112856	.077727	2.541206	224977	.010266	8.368	70
75	33375	4272	.128000	.480208	18113	8698	68140	.127649	2.421797	112121	-.010551	6.190	75
80	20900	3575	.171053	.584918	9415	5507	32235	.170840	2.305210	43981	-.010551	4.671	80
85+	11004	3661	.332697	1.000000	3908	3908	11746	.332697	3.005736	11746	.000000	3.006	85+

NUMBER OF PERSONS DYING (OUT OF 100,000 AT BIRTH) ABOVE AGE X FROM SPECIFIED CAUSES

Age (x)	All Causes	Respiratory T. B.	Other Infec. and Paras.	Neo-plasms	Cardio-vascular	Infl., Pneu., Bronch.	Diar-rheal	Certain Degen-erative	Maternal	Cert. Dis. of Infancy	Motor Vehicle	Other Violence	Other and Unknown	Age (x)
0	100000	4135	5107	1493	10985	6637	11315	1436	841	3247	0	826	53978	0
1	78074	4100	4153	1487	10933	5277	5548	1403	841	0	0	781	43551	1
5	65105	3995	2556	1484	10910	4193	2370	1266	841	0	0	612	36838	5
10	62516	3911	2158	1482	10887	4011	1993	1216	841	0	0	554	35463	10
15	61166	3786	1927	1481	10858	3925	1890	1184	840	0	0	528	34747	15
20	59422	3377	1683	1481	10803	3794	1841	1159	793	0	0	483	34008	20
25	57261	2781	1478	1477	10737	3652	1785	1120	648	0	0	441	33142	25
30	54997	2244	1306	1462	10680	3493	1730	1072	459	0	0	398	32153	30
35	52818	1776	1160	1425	10581	3320	1671	1021	291	0	0	367	31206	35
40	50585	1365	1002	1381	10469	3174	1615	942	113	0	0	342	30182	40
45	48221	1026	863	1285	10287	3006	1547	855	29	0	0	317	29006	45
50	45781	737	737	1157	10013	2802	1466	782	4	0	0	285	27798	50
55	42873	546	558	1001	9575	2574	1353	666	0	0	0	255	26305	55
60	39266	367	467	802	8873	2330	1187	562	0	0	0	215	24463	60
65	33848	245	331	588	7731	1948	979	454	0	0	0	176	21396	65
70	26885	122	199	375	5949	1475	729	286	0	0	0	131	17619	70
75	18113	61	134	201	3742	887	425	162	0	0	0	88	12413	75
80	9415	19	71	70	1556	369	182	54	0	0	0	39	7055	80
85+	3908	3	22	19	553	147	72	18	0	0	0	14	3060	85+

NUMBER OF PERSONS SURVIVING TO AGE X IF SPECIFIED CAUSES WERE ELIMINATED

Age (x)	No Causes	Respiratory T. B.	Other Infec. and Paras.	Neo-plasms	Cardio-vascular	Infl., Pneu., Bronch.	Diar-rheal	Certain Degener-ative	Maternal	Cert. Dis. of Infancy	Motor Vehicle	Other Violence	Other and Unknown	(1) + (2)	(1) + (2) + (5) + (6) + (8)	(1)+(2)+ (5)+(6)+ (8)+part of(9)&(12)	(10) + (11)	Age (x)
		(1)	(2)	(3)	(4)	(5)	(6)	(7)	(8)	(9)	(10)	(11)	(12)					
0	100000	100000	100000	100000	100000	100000	100000	100000	100000	100000	100000	100000	100000	100000	100000	100000	100000	0
1	78074	78105	78919	78079	78120	79282	83326	78103	78074	80989	78074	78114	87826	78951	85565	99593	78114	1
5	65105	65227	67261	65112	65164	67124	72647	65254	65105	67536	65105	65292	80458	67387	77525	98637	65292	5
10	62516	62715	65031	62525	62595	64639	70172	62709	62516	64850	62516	62753	78942	65238	75714	98200	62753	10
15	61166	61485	63865	61176	61272	63331	68771	61386	61166	63450	61166	61424	78136	64198	74736	97903	61424	15
20	59422	60139	62295	59431	59580	61659	66864	59661	59469	61640	59422	59717	76844	63047	73673	97551	59717	20
25	57261	58547	60241	57274	57478	59561	64495	57529	57450	59399	57261	57587	75157	61594	72399	97131	57587	25
30	54997	56773	58037	55024	55262	57369	62005	55302	55364	57050	54997	55352	73469	59910	70928	96631	55352	30
35	52818	54598	55888	52880	53170	55273	59614	53161	53337	54790	52818	53190	71809	58196	69411	95941	53190	35
40	50585	53093	53689	50688	51032	53086	57155	50992	51258	52474	50585	50966	70150	56352	67708	95053	50966	40
45	48221	50960	51324	48413	48827	50777	54559	48694	48945	50021	48221	48608	68483	54240	65594	93570	48608	45
50	45781	48680	48858	46089	46628	48418	51888	46302	46493	47409	45781	46180	66711	51952	63242	91589	46180	50
55	42873	45784	45898	43314	44101	45576	48716	43544	43475	44474	42873	43276	64614	49015	60133	88496	43276	55
60	39266	42115	42171	39862	41088	41990	44799	39918	39880	40732	39266	39674	61896	45230	56047	84006	39674	60
65	33848	36424	36487	34563	36547	36577	38838	34512	34377	35112	33848	34236	58034	39265	49447	76391	34236	65
70	26885	29048	29107	27646	30792	29511	31104	27565	27306	27889	26885	27234	52232	31449	40562	65110	27234	70
75	18113	19623	19666	18770	22910	20414	21243	18673	18356	18789	18113	18382	44501	21305	28601	49083	18383	75
80	9415	10231	10271	9852	14029	11029	11243	9785	9562	9766	9415	9591	34686	11162	15858	30212	9591	80
85+	3908	4258	4297	4123	6835	4743	4750	4085	3969	4054	3908	3997	27246	4681	7013	15797	3997	85+

ADDED YRS OF LIFE																	
TOTAL		1.401	2.133	.231	1.316	1.983	4.951	.344	.299	1.427	.000	.266	20.885	3.630	12.017	32.691	.266
WORK	9.200	1.526	.616	.166	.522	.574	.230	.200	.391	.000	.000	.126	3.835	2.172	3.475	6.587	.126

POPULATION, DEATHS, DEATH RATES FOR ALL CAUSES COMBINED, AND SPECIFIED CAUSES

Age Start of Interval	Midyear Population	Deaths During Year	All Causes	Respiratory T. B.	Other Infec. and Paras.	Neoplasms	Cardiovascular	Infl., Pneu., Bronch.	Diarrheal	Certain Degenerative	Maternal	Cert. Dis. of Infancy	Motor Vehicle	Other Violence	Other and Unknown	Age Start of Interval
0	72807	15980	.21948	.00088	.01433	.00001	.00102	.00994	.08315	.00085	.00000	.04464	.00000	.00243	.06223	0
1	314566	7519	.02390	.00041	.00410	.00003	.00018	.00123	.00855	.00055	.00000	.00000	.00000	.00100	.00787	1
5	386244	1073	.00278	.00017	.00058	.00001	.00006	.00009	.00032	.00009	.00000	.00000	.00000	.00032	.00115	5
10	328607	793	.00241	.00023	.00045	.00001	.00016	.00011	.00010	.00010	.00000	.00000	.00000	.00033	.00092	10
15	336964	1274	.00378	.00129	.00056	.00002	.00014	.00017	.00005	.00007	.00000	.00000	.00000	.00045	.00103	15
20	302271	1850	.00612	.00303	.00068	.00004	.00022	.00022	.00006	.00011	.00000	.00000	.00000	.00052	.00124	20
25	246283	1751	.00711	.00348	.00050	.00005	.00043	.00025	.00008	.00015	.00000	.00000	.00000	.00064	.00156	25
30	201893	1614	.00799	.00346	.00053	.00013	.00062	.00033	.00006	.00026	.00000	.00000	.00000	.00060	.00200	30
35	189234	1669	.00882	.00340	.00037	.00019	.00083	.00050	.00008	.00035	.00000	.00000	.00000	.00066	.00245	35
40	171725	1617	.00942	.00298	.00044	.00035	.00101	.00049	.00010	.00052	.00000	.00000	.00000	.00061	.00292	40
45	150255	1798	.01197	.00316	.00044	.00062	.00179	.00064	.00015	.00069	.00000	.00000	.00000	.00084	.00363	45
50	143432	2040	.01422	.00252	.00058	.00086	.00250	.00103	.00020	.00099	.00000	.00000	.00000	.00086	.00468	50
55	116753	2389	.02046	.00261	.00050	.00140	.00478	.00142	.00037	.00128	.00000	.00000	.00000	.00107	.00703	55
60	101540	3032	.02986	.00215	.00061	.00206	.00877	.00221	.00071	.00194	.00000	.00000	.00000	.00110	.01032	60
65	71596	3255	.04546	.00200	.00075	.00296	.01596	.00351	.00084	.00257	.00000	.00000	.00000	.00128	.01559	65
70	51236	3851	.07516	.00176	.00082	.00357	.02867	.00552	.00150	.00308	.00000	.00000	.00000	.00144	.02879	70
75	29662	3412	.11503	.00125	.00088	.00374	.04187	.00829	.00212	.00364	.00000	.00000	.00000	.00175	.05148	75
80	14480	2347	.16209	.00048	.00083	.00345	.05311	.00829	.00207	.00331	.00000	.00000	.00000	.00180	.08874	80
85+	7548	2244	.29730	.00026	.00119	.00358	.07989	.01497	.00371	.00450	.00000	.00000	.00000	.00291	.18627	85+
ALL	3237096	59508														

	All Causes	Respiratory T. B.	Other Infec. and Paras.	Neoplasms	Cardiovascular	Infl., Pneu., Bronch.	Diarrheal	Certain Degenerative	Maternal	Cert. Dis. of Infancy	Motor Vehicle	Other Violence	Other and Unknown
CRUDE DEATH RATE	.01838	.00186	.00120	.00041	.00253	.00101	.00291	.00053	.00000	.00100	.00000	.00071	.00622
STANDARDIZED RATE (1)	.01939	.00177	.00145	.00032	.00183	.00101	.00412	.00046	.00000	.00157	.00000	.00070	.00616
STANDARDIZED RATE (2)	.02199	.00199	.00112	.00060	.00402	.00126	.00267	.00069	.00000	.00092	.00000	.00076	.00796
GEOMETRIC MEAN	.02042												

LIFE TABLE FOR ALL CAUSES COMBINED

Age (x)	Midyear Population	Deaths During Year	$_nM_x$	$_nq_x$	l_x	$_nd_x$	$_nL_x$	$_nm_x$	$_na_x$	T_x	$_nr_x$	$\overset{\circ}{e}_x$	Age (x)
0	72807	15980	.219484	.195580	100000	19558	89109	.219485	.443123	4509090	.000000	45.091	0
1	314566	7519	.023903	.090214	80442	7257	303626	.023901	1.500000	4419982	.000000	54.946	1
5	386244	1073	.002778	.013787	73185	1009	363403	.002777	2.500000	4116356	.000000	56.246	5
10	328607	793	.002413	.012012	72176	867	358781	.002417	2.578816	3752954	.010271	51.997	10
15	336964	1274	.003781	.018749	71309	1337	353462	.003783	2.694465	3394173	.002414	47.598	15
20	302271	1850	.006120	.030226	69972	2115	344789	.006134	2.602246	3040710	.018298	43.456	20
25	246283	1751	.007110	.035000	67857	2375	333442	.007123	2.539825	2695921	.031906	39.729	25
30	201893	1614	.007994	.039232	65482	2569	321059	.008002	2.527653	2362479	.023744	36.078	30
35	189234	1669	.008820	.043171	62913	2716	307817	.008823	2.515571	2041421	.009864	32.448	35
40	171725	1617	.009416	.046049	60197	2772	294185	.009423	2.546973	1733604	.013842	28.799	40
45	150255	1798	.011966	.058180	57425	3341	278570	.011976	2.559239	1439418	.007377	25.066	45
50	143432	2040	.014223	.068819	54084	3722	261444	.014236	2.588438	1160448	.009094	21.456	50
55	116753	2389	.020462	.097713	50362	4921	240054	.020500	2.611089	899004	.011966	17.851	55
60	101540	3032	.029860	.139654	45441	6346	211989	.029935	2.602328	658950	.015885	14.501	60
65	71596	3255	.045463	.205602	39095	8038	176114	.045641	2.591311	446960	.020859	11.433	65
70	51236	3851	.075162	.317771	31057	9869	130901	.075393	2.529216	270846	.013823	8.721	70
75	29662	3412	.115029	.444686	21188	9422	81719	.115298	2.429310	139945	.011238	6.605	75
80	14480	2347	.162086	.567058	11766	6672	41092	.162367	2.341439	58226	.011238	4.949	80
85+	7548	2244	.297297	1.000000	5094	5094	17134	.297297	3.363636	17134	.000000	3.364	85+

NUMBER OF PERSONS DYING (OUT OF 100,000 AT BIRTH) ABOVE AGE X FROM SPECIFIED CAUSES

Age (x)	All Causes	Respiratory T.B.	Other Infec. and Paras.	Neoplasms	Cardiovascular	Infl., Pneu., Bronch.	Diarrheal	Certain Degenerative	Maternal	Cert. Dis. of Infancy	Motor Vehicle	Other Violence	Other and Unknown	Age (x)
0	100000	9388	4756	2929	18980	5841	11254	3308	0	3578	0	3513	35973	0
1	80442	9310	3519	2928	18890	4955	3885	3232	0	0	0	3296	30427	1
5	73185	9186	2275	2920	18835	4581	1290	3065	0	0	0	2994	28039	5
10	72176	9126	2065	2917	18812	4547	1176	3034	0	0	0	2879	27620	10
15	71309	9042	1904	2914	18754	4506	1141	2997	0	0	0	2762	27289	15
20	69972	8585	1706	2907	18706	4445	1123	2974	0	0	0	2603	26923	20
25	67857	7538	1470	2893	18630	4368	1101	2937	0	0	0	2424	26496	25
30	65482	6376	1305	2879	18487	4285	1076	2887	0	0	0	2211	25976	30
35	62913	5265	1135	2838	18288	4180	1055	2804	0	0	0	2017	25331	35
40	60197	4217	1021	2779	18032	4027	1031	2696	0	0	0	1815	24579	40
45	57425	3341	892	2676	17735	3881	1001	2542	0	0	0	1637	23720	45
50	54084	2459	770	2503	17235	3702	959	2349	0	0	0	1403	22704	50
55	50362	1799	619	2277	16581	3432	908	2090	0	0	0	1177	21479	55
60	45441	1172	499	1939	15430	3090	819	1783	0	0	0	920	19789	60
65	39095	718	370	1501	13565	2621	668	1370	0	0	0	686	17596	65
70	31057	366	237	979	10739	2002	520	917	0	0	0	459	14838	70
75	21188	136	129	511	6975	1276	323	513	0	0	0	270	11055	75
80	11766	35	58	205	3546	597	149	215	0	0	0	126	6835	80
85+	5054	5	20	61	1369	257	64	77	0	0	0	50	3191	85+

NUMBER OF PERSONS SURVIVING TO AGE X IF SPECIFIED CAUSES WERE ELIMINATED

Age (x)	No Causes	Respiratory T.B. (1)	Other Infec. and Paras. (2)	Neoplasms (3)	Cardiovascular (4)	Infl., Pneu., Bronch. (5)	Diarrheal (6)	Certain Degenerative (7)	Maternal (8)	Cert. Dis. of Infancy (9)	Motor Vehicle (10)	Other Violence (11)	Other and Unknown (12)	(1)+(2)	(1)+(2)+(5)+(6)+(8)	(1)+(2)+(5)+(6)+(8)+part of(9)&(12)	(10)+(11)	Age (x)
0	100000	100000	100000	100000	100000	100000	100000	100000	100000	100000	100000	100000	100000	100000	100000	100000	100000	0
1	80442	80512	81593	80443	81239	87355		80510	80442	84083	80442	80636	85563	81664	89561	99171	80636	1
5	73185	73367	75445	73193	73311	74271	82207	73406	73185	76497	73185	73651	80304	75633	86218	98151	73651	5
10	72176	72415	74620	72187	72323	73281	81201	72425	72176	75443	72176	72751	79655	74868	85519	97755	72751	10
15	71309	71629	73890	71323	71512	72443	80265	71592	71309	74536	71309	71994	79062	74221	84871	97282	71994	15
20	69972	70743	72708	69993	70219	71146	78780	70273	69972	73139	69972	70803	77982	73509	84150	96834	70803	20
25	67857	69655	70752	67891	68172	69072	76423	68185	67857	70928	67857	68842	76095	72627	83260	96297	68842	25
30	65482	68399	68444	65529	65927	66738	73776	65848	65482	68446	65482	66645	74007	71493	82093	95523	66645	30
35	62913	66862	65934	62998	63537	64225	70905	63347	62913	65760	62913	64224	71822	70072	80620	94500	64224	35
40	60197	65074	63204	60336	61048	61605	67870	60715	60197	62922	60197	61653	69566	68324	78836	93182	61653	40
45	57425	63208	60426	57659	58532	58914	64778	58075	57425	60024	57425	58993	67340	66301	76730	91514	58993	45
50	54084	60288	57035	54473	55624	55665	61055	54886	54084	56532	54084	55794	64589	63577	73870	88953	55794	50
55	50362	56851	53264	50945	52450	52103	56909	51363	50362	52641	50362	52180	61572	60127	70293	85550	52180	55
60	45441	51570	48179	46293	48479	47349	51444	46642	45441	47498	45441	47334	57553	55102	65001	80133	47334	60
65	39095	45193	41578	40243	43599	41193	44418	40523	39095	40864	39095	40949	52157	48063	57537	72004	40949	65
70	31057	36261	33154	32449	37560	33308	35435	32610	31057	32463	31057	32741	44841	38710	47369	60397	32741	70
75	21188	24955	22713	22539	29648	23371	24360	22595	21188	22147	21188	22499	35439	33925	44590		22499	75
80	11766	13942	12668	12753	20382	13538	13674	12780	11766	12299	11766	12606	25667	15011	20072	27792	12606	80
85+	5054	6059	5511	5622	11596	6116	5984	5630	5094	5325	5094	5510	17554	6554	9244	13789	5510	85+

ADDED YRS OF LIFE	No Causes	(1)	(2)	(3)	(4)	(5)	(6)	(7)	(8)	(9)	(10)	(11)	(12)	(1)+(2)	(1)+(2)+(5)+(6)+(8)	+part of(9)&(12)	(10)+(11)
TOTAL		2.918	2.077	.400	2.485	1.327	5.700	.626	.000	2.021	.000	1.040	10.064	5.164	13.315	24.381	1.040
WORK	8.670	2.775	.504	.198	.754	.367	.086	.287	.000	.000	.000	.581	2.091	3.327	3.840	5.334	.581

POPULATION, DEATHS, DEATH RATES FOR ALL CAUSES COMBINED, AND SPECIFIED CAUSES

Age Start of Interval	Midyear Population	Deaths During Year	All Causes	Respiratory T.B.	Other Infec. and Paras.	Neoplasms	Cardiovascular	Infl., Pneu., Bronch.	Diarrheal	Certain Degenerative	Maternal	Cert. Dis. of Infancy	Motor Vehicle	Other Violence	Other and Unknown	Age Start of Interval
0	71281	13138	.18431	.00067	.01399	.00003	.00090	.00898	.07100	.00066	.00000	.03483	.00000	.00201	.05125	0
1	308257	7128	.02312	.00047	.00406	.00003	.00010	.00114	.00836	.00050	.00000	.00000	.00000	.00095	.00752	1
5	373275	989	.00265	.00019	.00063	.00001	.00013	.00012	.00032	.00009	.00000	.00000	.00000	.00015	.00101	5
10	315377	789	.00250	.00044	.00051	.00001	.00017	.00014	.00013	.00005	.00000	.00000	.00000	.00015	.00088	10
15	343412	1312	.00382	.00176	.00057	.00002	.00018	.00013	.00006	.00006	.00011	.00000	.00000	.00016	.00078	15
20	321167	1717	.00535	.00253	.00052	.00003	.00023	.00016	.00008	.00010	.00046	.00000	.00000	.00015	.00109	20
25	286979	1566	.00546	.00239	.00042	.00008	.00027	.00017	.00006	.00013	.00059	.00000	.00000	.00013	.00120	25
30	238344	1469	.00616	.00208	.00047	.00018	.00048	.00019	.00010	.00029	.00066	.00000	.00000	.00019	.00151	30
35	219390	1459	.00665	.00205	.00037	.00033	.00062	.00026	.00011	.00028	.00071	.00000	.00000	.00017	.00175	35
40	204323	1358	.00665	.00171	.00036	.00006	.00081	.00024	.00012	.00030	.00029	.00000	.00000	.00016	.00202	40
45	180460	1396	.00774	.00142	.00034	.00056	.00147	.00035	.00016	.00054	.00007	.00000	.00000	.00016	.00227	45
50	173289	1543	.00890	.00122	.00042	.00117	.00205	.00043	.00018	.00048	.00001	.00000	.00000	.00017	.00278	50
55	141209	1789	.01267	.00123	.00045	.00142	.00356	.00085	.00032	.00079	.00001	.00000	.00000	.00028	.00375	55
60	127778	2571	.02012	.00108	.00045	.00187	.00745	.00146	.00064	.00102	.00000	.00000	.00000	.00033	.00583	60
65	94011	3109	.03307	.00121	.00067	.00263	.01295	.00218	.00106	.00149	.00000	.00000	.00000	.00054	.01034	65
70	72275	4088	.05656	.00101	.00062	.00295	.02333	.00383	.00133	.00156	.00000	.00000	.00000	.00073	.02120	70
75	42903	3930	.09160	.00086	.00068	.00331	.03813	.00548	.00219	.00186	.00000	.00000	.00000	.00126	.03783	75
80	24041	3556	.14791	.00079	.00062	.00362	.04671	.00578	.00266	.00200	.00000	.00000	.00000	.00137	.08436	80
85+	14414	3937	.27314	.00056	.00090	.00382	.07042	.01055	.00479	.00278	.00000	.00000	.00000	.00229	.17705	85+
ALL	3552185	56844														

	All Causes	Respiratory T.B.	Other Infec. and Paras.	Neoplasms	Cardiovascular	Infl., Pneu., Bronch.	Diarrheal	Certain Degenerative	Maternal	Cert. Dis. of Infancy	Motor Vehicle	Other Violence	Other and Unknown
CRUDE DEATH RATE	.01600	.00136	.00107	.00052	.00270	.00080	.00240	.00039	.00021	.00070	.00000	.00033	.00552
STANDARDIZED RATE (1)	.01606	.00128	.00140	.00035	.00154	.00078	.00368	.00032	.00020	.00123	.00000	.00033	.00552
STANDARDIZED RATE (2)	.01773	.00135	.00105	.00062	.00341	.00090	.00243	.00044	.00020	.00072	.00000	.00035	.00493
GEOMETRIC MEAN	.01630												

LIFE TABLE FOR ALL CAUSES COMBINED

Age (x)	Midyear Population	Deaths During Year	$_nM_x$	$_nq_x$	l_x	$_nd_x$	$_nL_x$	$_nm_x$	$_na_x$	T_x	$_nr_x$	$\overset{\circ}{e}_x$	Age (x)
0	71281	13138	.184313	.165500	100000	16550	89794	.184310	.383332	4997002	.000000	49.970	0
1	308257	7128	.023124	.087442	83450	7297	315558	.023124	1.500000	4907208	.000000	58.804	1
5	373275	989	.002650	.013145	76153	1001	378263	.002646	2.500000	4591650	.000000	60.295	5
10	315377	789	.002502	.012441	75152	935	373506	.002503	2.589795	4213388	.006923	56.065	10
15	343412	1312	.003820	.018917	74217	1404	367781	.003817	2.646457	3839881	-.005577	51.739	15
20	321167	1717	.005346	.026396	72813	1922	359365	.005348	2.554847	3472101	.006541	47.685	20
25	286979	1566	.005457	.026943	70891	1910	349716	.005462	2.518979	3112735	.020175	43.909	25
30	238344	1469	.006163	.030385	68981	2096	339723	.006170	2.527632	2763019	.022938	40.055	30
35	219390	1459	.006650	.032713	66885	2188	328959	.006651	2.501904	2423296	.011237	36.231	35
40	204323	1358	.006646	.032706	64697	2116	318234	.006649	2.518510	2094337	.013260	32.371	40
45	180460	1396	.007736	.037967	62581	2376	307072	.007738	2.544893	1776103	.008766	28.381	45
50	173289	1543	.008904	.043651	60205	2628	294700	.008918	2.593148	1469031	.013377	24.400	50
55	141209	1789	.012669	.061674	57577	3551	279545	.012703	2.651424	1174331	.015964	20.396	55
60	127778	2571	.020121	.096417	54026	5209	257934	.020195	2.658700	894786	.018358	16.562	60
65	94011	3109	.033071	.154024	48817	7519	226352	.033218	2.641530	636852	.021353	13.046	65
70	72275	4088	.056562	.249818	41298	10317	181544	.056829	2.582045	410500	.021284	9.940	70
75	42903	3930	.091602	.373842	30981	11582	125969	.091943	2.501673	228956	.016371	7.390	75
80	24041	3556	.147914	.536626	19399	10410	70077	.148551	2.414205	102987	.016371	5.309	80
85+	14414	3937	.273137	1.000000	8989	8989	32910	.273137	3.661163	32910	.000000	3.661	85+

NUMBER OF PERSONS DYING (OUT OF 100,000 AT BIRTH) ABOVE AGE X FROM SPECIFIED CAUSES

Age (x)	All Causes	Respiratory T. B.	Other Infec. and Paras.	Neoplasms	Cardiovascular	Infl., Pneu., Bronch.	Diarrheal	Certain Degenerative	Maternal	Cert. Dis. of Infancy	Motor Vehicle	Other Violence	Other and Unknown	Age (x)
0	100000	6834	4802	3891	22704	5144	10824	2548	987	3128	0	1782	37356	0
1	83450	6774	3546	3889	22623	4338	4448	2489	987	0	0	1601	32755	1
5	76153	6624	2264	3881	22591	3979	1811	2330	987	0	0	1303	30383	5
10	75152	6552	2026	3878	22542	3933	1692	2295	987	0	0	1247	30000	10
15	74217	6387	1836	3874	22478	3881	1643	2275	987	0	0	1186	29670	15
20	72813	5741	1626	3868	22413	3835	1623	2252	947	0	0	1125	29383	20
25	70891	4830	1438	3858	22331	3779	1595	2216	782	0	0	1071	28991	25
30	68981	3994	1291	3828	22236	3719	1573	2170	574	0	0	1025	28571	30
35	66885	3288	1130	3765	22071	3653	1540	2070	350	0	0	960	28058	35
40	64697	2614	1008	3655	21867	3569	1504	1978	118	0	0	903	27481	40
45	62581	2069	895	3454	21608	3493	1465	1883	27	0	0	851	26836	45
50	60205	1632	791	3159	21156	3384	1416	1718	7	0	0	802	26140	50
55	57577	1273	668	2813	20549	3256	1361	1576	5	0	0	753	25323	55
60	54026	929	541	2417	19549	3018	1272	1354	1	0	0	673	24272	60
65	48817	650	426	1933	17618	2641	1106	1091	1	0	0	588	22763	65
70	41298	376	274	1337	14674	2145	864	753	1	0	0	465	20409	70
75	30981	193	161	802	10418	1446	622	469	1	0	0	332	16537	75
80	19399	84	76	384	5599	755	345	234	1	0	0	172	11749	80
85+	8989	18	30	126	2317	347	158	91	0	0	0	75	5827	85+

NUMBER OF PERSONS SURVIVING TO AGE X IF SPECIFIED CAUSES WERE ELIMINATED

Age (x)	No Causes	Respiratory T. B.	Other Infec. and Paras.	Neoplasms	Cardiovascular	Infl., Pneu., Bronch.	Diarrheal	Certain Degenerative	Maternal	Cert. Dis. of Infancy	Motor Vehicle	Other Violence	Other and Unknown	(1) + (2)	(1) + (2) + (5) + (6) + (8)	(1)+(2)+ (5)+(6)+ (8)+part of(9)&(12)	(10) + (11)	Age (x)
		(1)	(2)	(3)	(4)	(5)	(6)	(7)	(8)	(9)	(10)	(11)	(12)					
0	100000	100000	100000	100000	100000	100000	100000	100000	100000	100000	100000	100000	100000	100000	100000	100000	100000	0
1	83450	83505	84604	83452	83524	84189	89474	83504	83450	86353	83450	83615	87755	84659	91574	99340	83615	1
5	76153	76346	78457	76162	76251	77174	84395	76354	76153	78802	76153	76590	82499	78656	88338	98427	76590	5
10	75152	75414	77670	75164	75298	76206	83417	75385	75152	77766	75152	75639	81828	77941	87726	98126	75639	10
15	74217	74641	76899	74233	74424	75310	82433	74467	74217	76799	74217	74759	81168	77338	87165	97824	74759	15
20	72813	73876	75660	72835	73081	73931	80896	73082	72853	75346	72813	73405	79944	76764	86643	97565	73405	20
25	70891	72843	73855	70922	71233	72036	78791	71188	71093	73357	70891	71521	78259	75889	85953	97255	71521	25
30	68981	71733	72017	69041	69408	70155	76653	69316	69384	71381	68981	69640	76605	74890	85173	96868	69640	30
35	66885	70280	69994	67005	67463	68090	74398	67309	67498	69212	66885	67589	74845	73547	84045	96129	67589	35
40	64697	68680	67830	64922	65459	65947	72004	65198	65520	66948	64697	65434	73034	72006	82726	95213	65434	40
45	62581	67005	65728	62997	63577	63866	69692	63160	63467	64758	62581	63346	71366	70375	81113	93915	63346	45
50	60205	64921	63340	60898	61615	61550	67099	60925	61078	62299	60205	60990	69435	68302	78952	91857	60990	50
55	57577	62467	60702	58583	59537	58992	64230	58407	58413	59580	57577	58376	67336	65857	76365	89302	58376	55
60	54026	58976	57087	55361	56877	55590	60365	55023	54815	55905	54026	54854	64384	62318	72692	85522	54854	60
65	48817	53578	51699	50496	53363	50600	54722	49973	49530	50515	48817	49647	59911	56741	66890	79283	49647	65
70	41298	45601	43883	43286	48201	43281	46543	42593	41901	42735	41298	42115	54453	48456	58068	69642	42115	70
75	30981	34381	33023	32956	40712	33106	35151	32204	31433	32059	30981	31711	44646	36647	45080	55197	31711	75
80	19399	21621	20748	20982	30953	21312	22257	20355	19682	20074	19399	19984	33968	23124	29573	37429	19984	80
85+	8989	10068	9647	9910	18279	10178	10457	9532	9121	9302	8989	9327	24381	10804	14439	19581	9327	85+

ADDED YRS OF LIFE																		
TOTAL		2.458	2.266	.624	2.971	1.232	5.651	.554	.384	1.725	.000	.575	10.117	4.857	13.157	22.926	.575	
WORK	6.842	2.084	.470	.309	.673	.232	.103	.234	.353	.000	.000	.168	1.573	2.584	3.378	4.521	.168	

POPULATION, DEATHS, DEATH RATES FOR ALL CAUSES COMBINED, AND SPECIFIED CAUSES

Age Start of Interval	Midyear Population	Deaths During Year	All Causes	Respiratory T. B.	Other Infec. and Paras.	Neoplasms	Cardiovascular	Infl., Pneu., Bronch.	Diarrheal	Certain Degenerative	Maternal	Cert. Dis. of Infancy	Motor Vehicle	Other Violence	Other and Unknown	Age Start of Interval
0	82085	12877	.15687	.00068	.01230	.00002	.00074	.01944	.05750	.00073	.00000	.04310	.00000	.00108	.02126	0
1	342641	7638	.02229	.00048	.00398	.00002	.00019	.00386	.00860	.00063	.00000	.00000	.00000	.00097	.00356	1
5	426427	1463	.00343	.00018	.00106	.00002	.00011	.00034	.00043	.00014	.00000	.00000	.00000	.00036	.00080	5
10	408025	918	.00225	.00019	.00058	.00001	.00016	.00020	.00010	.00005	.00000	.00000	.00000	.00036	.00060	10
15	372756	1271	.00341	.00110	.00069	.00003	.00019	.00020	.00011	.00004	.00000	.00000	.00000	.00047	.00058	15
20	314583	1506	.00479	.00192	.00071	.00004	.00025	.00024	.00004	.00010	.00000	.00000	.00000	.00071	.00079	20
25	297224	1584	.00533	.00256	.00056	.00003	.00028	.00026	.00004	.00013	.00000	.00000	.00000	.00061	.00086	25
30	266808	1683	.00631	.00273	.00063	.00006	.00051	.00037	.00006	.00012	.00000	.00000	.00000	.00073	.00109	30
35	229984	1658	.00721	.00250	.00066	.00020	.00079	.00053	.00005	.00023	.00000	.00000	.00000	.00077	.00147	35
40	194343	1726	.00888	.00249	.00063	.00034	.00137	.00070	.00006	.00022	.00000	.00000	.00000	.00090	.00217	40
45	170708	2008	.01176	.00274	.00078	.00053	.00199	.00108	.00014	.00043	.00000	.00000	.00000	.00090	.00305	45
50	153891	2287	.01486	.00250	.00080	.00084	.00324	.00170	.00017	.00063	.00000	.00000	.00000	.00101	.00398	50
55	125440	2711	.02161	.00234	.00124	.00184	.00568	.00218	.00033	.00091	.00000	.00000	.00000	.00128	.00580	55
60	113974	3479	.03052	.00218	.00104	.00228	.01002	.00360	.00054	.00153	.00000	.00000	.00000	.00127	.00806	60
65	81962	3844	.04690	.00176	.00168	.00278	.01823	.00556	.00078	.00204	.00000	.00000	.00000	.00143	.01264	65
70	57103	4621	.08092	.00144	.00189	.00429	.03306	.00944	.00144	.00271	.00000	.00000	.00000	.00205	.02460	70
75	33821	4194	.12401	.00121	.00189	.00189	.04988	.01458	.00207	.00343	.00000	.00000	.00000	.00216	.04403	75
80	16846	2686	.15944	.00042	.00125	.00321	.05164	.01585	.00184	.00303	.00000	.00000	.00000	.00208	.08014	80
85+	9537	2776	.29108	.00031	.00178	.00336	.07780	.02884	.00325	.00409	.00000	.00000	.00000	.00346	.16819	85+
ALL	3698198	60930														

	All Causes	Respiratory T. B.	Other Infec. and Paras.	Neoplasms	Cardiovascular	Infl., Pneu., Bronch.	Diarrheal	Certain Degenerative	Maternal	Cert. Dis. of Infancy	Motor Vehicle	Other Violence	Other and Unknown
CRUDE DEATH RATE	.01648	.00152	.00136	.00044	.00282	.00186	.00228	.00042	.00000	.00096	.00000	.00077	.00405
STANDARDIZED RATE (1)	.01673	.00142	.00158	.00034	.00205	.00196	.00322	.00038	.00000	.00152	.00000	.00075	.00352
STANDARDIZED RATE (2)	.02051	.00162	.00134	.00064	.00448	.00229	.00213	.00055	.00000	.00089	.00000	.00086	.00569
GEOMETRIC MEAN	.01921												

LIFE TABLE FOR ALL CAUSES COMBINED

Age (x)	Midyear Population	Deaths During Year	$_nM_x$	$_nq_x$	l_x	$_nd_x$	$_nL_x$	$_nm_x$	$_na_x$	T_x	$_nr_x$	$\overset{\circ}{e}_x$	Age (x)
0	82085	12877	.156874	.142090	100000	14209	90575	.156816	.336686	4894265	.000000	48.943	0
1	342641	7638	.022292	.084461	85791	7246	325049	.022292	1.500000	4803690	.000000	55.993	1
5	426427	1463	.003431	.017005	78545	1336	389385	.003431	2.500000	4478641	.000000	57.020	5
10	408025	918	.002250	.011177	77209	863	383879	.002248	2.490102	4089256	.005918	52.963	10
15	372756	1271	.003409	.016962	76346	1295	378683	.003420	2.647362	3705377	.019154	48.534	15
20	314583	1506	.004787	.023704	75051	1779	370940	.004796	2.574246	3326694	.019857	44.326	20
25	297224	1584	.005329	.026327	73272	1929	361629	.005334	2.547412	2955754	.011804	40.339	25
30	266808	1683	.006308	.031089	71343	2218	351279	.006314	2.549125	2594125	.016685	36.361	30
35	229984	1658	.007209	.035472	69125	2452	339638	.007219	2.558371	2242846	.022793	32.446	35
40	194343	1726	.008881	.043571	66673	2905	326352	.008901	2.586059	1903208	.023013	28.545	40
45	170708	2008	.011763	.057270	63768	3652	310005	.011780	2.580835	1576856	.013319	24.728	45
50	153891	2287	.014861	.071894	60116	4322	290210	.014893	2.600648	1266850	.016046	21.073	50
55	125440	2711	.021612	.102878	55794	5740	265204	.021644	2.601771	976640	.009958	17.504	55
60	113974	3479	.030525	.142366	50054	7126	233150	.030564	2.597559	711436	.008704	14.213	60
65	81962	3844	.046900	.211447	42928	9077	192845	.047069	2.598922	478286	.018553	11.142	65
70	57103	4621	.080924	.337833	33851	11436	140965	.081126	2.526251	285441	.010324	8.432	70
75	33821	4194	.124006	.469239	22415	10518	84780	.124062	2.404945	144475	.002002	6.445	75
80	16846	2686	.159444	.557872	11897	6637	41624	.159450	2.308931	59695	.002002	5.018	80
85+	9537	2776	.291077	1.000000	5260	5260	18071	.291077	3.435519	18071	.000000	3.436	85+

NUMBER OF PERSONS DYING (OUT OF 100,000 AT BIRTH) ABOVE AGE X FROM SPECIFIED CAUSES

Age (x)	All Causes	Respiratory T.B.	Other Infec. and Paras.	Neoplasms	Cardiovascular	Infl., Pneu., Bronch.	Diarrheal	Certain Degenerative	Maternal	Cert. Dis. of Infancy	Motor Vehicle	Other Violence	Other and Unknown	Age (x)
0	100000	8417	6302	3436	22793	11104	9313	2819	0	3904	0	4314	27598	0
1	85791	8355	5188	3434	22726	9343	4105	2753	0	0	0	4216	25671	1
5	78545	8199	3893	3427	22665	8088	1310	2549	0	0	0	3899	24515	5
10	77209	8131	3482	3420	22621	7957	1143	2494	0	0	0	3757	24204	10
15	76346	8056	3260	3414	22559	7881	1106	2474	0	0	0	3620	23976	15
20	75051	7637	2999	3402	22489	7804	1063	2460	0	0	0	3441	23756	20
25	73272	6924	2737	3387	22395	7714	1048	2424	0	0	0	3179	23464	25
30	71343	5957	2535	3376	22294	7619	1034	2377	0	0	0	2959	23152	30
35	69125	5039	2314	3356	22113	7487	1012	2335	0	0	0	2704	22765	35
40	66673	4191	2091	3286	21843	7306	994	2255	0	0	0	2440	22267	40
45	63768	3380	1884	3173	21393	7077	974	2182	0	0	0	2148	21557	45
50	60116	2532	1642	3007	20776	6740	930	2049	0	0	0	1830	20610	50
55	55794	1806	1410	2763	19831	6247	881	1866	0	0	0	1537	19453	55
60	50054	1185	1082	2273	18320	5667	792	1625	0	0	0	1197	17913	60
65	42928	676	841	1741	15979	4827	665	1268	0	0	0	900	16031	65
70	33851	338	515	1204	12449	3750	514	874	0	0	0	625	13582	70
75	22415	135	249	598	7776	2416	311	491	0	0	0	335	10104	75
80	11897	33	88	194	3546	1180	135	200	0	0	0	152	6369	80
85+	5260	6	32	61	1406	521	59	74	0	0	0	63	3038	85+

NUMBER OF PERSONS SURVIVING TO AGE X IF SPECIFIED CAUSES WERE ELIMINATED

Age (x)	No Causes	Respiratory T.B. (1)	Other Infec. and Paras. (2)	Neoplasms (3)	Cardiovascular (4)	Infl., Pneu., Bronch. (5)	Diarrheal (6)	Certain Degenerative (7)	Maternal (8)	Cert. Dis. of Infancy (9)	Motor Vehicle (10)	Other Violence (11)	Other and Unknown (12)	(1)+(2)	(1)+(2)+(5)+(6)+(8)	(1)+(2)+(5)+(6)+(8)+part of(9)&(12)	(10)+(11)	Age (x)
0	100000	100000	100000	100000	100000	100000	100000	100000	100000	100000	100000	100000	100000	100000	100000	100000	100000	0
1	85791	85848	86828	85793	85853	87436	90748	85852	85791	89481	85791	85882	87593	86886	93669	99575	85882	1
5	78545	78747	80758	78553	78660	81284	85960	78796	78545	81923	78545	78932	81332	80966	91699	98728	78932	5
10	77209	77475	79805	77224	77366	80036	84679	77511	77209	80530	77209	77731	80268	80080	91043	98320	77731	10
15	76346	76684	79141	76367	76563	79220	83773	76664	76346	79629	76346	77000	79607	79491	90508	97929	77000	15
20	75051	75802	78067	75084	75334	77955	82399	75378	75051	78279	75051	75873	78484	78848	89918	97501	75873	20
25	73272	74720	76486	73319	73641	76200	80462	73627	73272	76423	73272	74336	76926	77998	89074	96863	74336	25
30	71343	73692	74681	71399	71803	74291	78359	71735	71343	74411	71343	72600	75225	77140	88227	96259	72600	30
35	69125	72381	72587	69199	69750	72117	75947	69564	69125	72098	69125	70599	73289	76007	87122	95435	70599	35
40	66673	70691	70243	66814	67545	69745	73272	67159	66673	69540	66673	68360	71210	74475	85617	94236	68360	40
45	63768	68456	67396	64013	65049	66941	70101	64305	63768	66510	63768	65674	68853	72350	83493	92477	65674	45
50	60116	65424	63784	60509	61939	63452	66133	60752	60116	62701	60116	62232	65911	69417	80602	90020	62232	50
55	55794	61485	58397	56397	59393	61431	62565	56522	55794	58194	55794	58050	62406	65498	76767	86552	58050	55
60	50054	55808	53653	51066	53944	53871	55204	50976	50054	52207	50054	52413	57640	59821	71006	80958	52413	60
65	42928	48388	46253	44300	48664	47046	47474	44056	42928	44774	42928	45239	51481	52136	63188	73006	45239	65
70	33851	38491	36784	35425	42094	38158	37584	35099	33851	35307	33851	35929	43285	41826	52348	61596	35929	70
75	22415	25670	24589	23972	32586	26510	25070	23562	22415	23379	22415	24039	32504	28160	37249	45238	24039	75
80	11897	13706	13175	13031	22575	15156	13447	12725	11897	12409	11897	12898	21658	15178	21855	28075	12898	80
85+	5260	6080	5865	5856	12586	7267	6001	5714	5260	5486	5260	5765	14423	6780	10685	15190	5765	85+

ADDED YRS OF LIFE

	No Causes	(1)	(2)	(3)	(4)	(5)	(6)	(7)	(8)	(9)	(10)	(11)	(12)	(1)+(2)	(1)+(2)+(5)+(6)+(8)	+part	(10)+(11)
TOTAL		2.516	2.486	.454	3.044	2.839	4.802	.536	.000	2.090	.000	1.213	5.867	5.174	14.131	21.366	1.213
WORK	7.731	2.176	.671	.203	.863	.502	.081	.187	.000	.000	.000	.709	1.446	2.897	3.550	4.527	.709

POPULATION, DEATHS, DEATH RATES FOR ALL CAUSES COMBINED, AND SPECIFIED CAUSES

Age Start of Interval	Midyear Population	Deaths During Year	All Causes	Respiratory T.B.	Other Infec. and Paras.	Neoplasms	Cardiovascular	Infl., Pneu., Bronch.	Diarrheal	Certain Degenerative	Maternal	Cert. Dis. of Infancy	Motor Vehicle	Other Violence	Other and Unknown	Age Start of Interval
0	75262	10834	.14395	.00054	.01311	.00004	.00050	.01803	.05466	.00041	.00000	.03626	.00000	.00078	.01920	0
1	329590	6993	.02122	.00048	.00396	.00003	.00015	.00364	.00845	.00056	.00000	.00000	.00000	.00072	.00323	1
5	409739	1199	.00293	.00018	.00085	.00001	.00011	.00042	.00035	.00011	.00000	.00000	.00000	.00022	.00068	5
10	395764	813	.00205	.00031	.00070	.00001	.00013	.00016	.00010	.00006	.00000	.00000	.00000	.00010	.00048	10
15	376109	1225	.00326	.00136	.00063	.00003	.00017	.00018	.00007	.00007	.00009	.00000	.00000	.00014	.00044	15
20	316455	1318	.00416	.00188	.00065	.00003	.00021	.00022	.00006	.00007	.00043	.00000	.00000	.00014	.00051	20
25	312022	1480	.00474	.00202	.00052	.00006	.00036	.00026	.00007	.00009	.00054	.00000	.00000	.00012	.00045	25
30	290170	1369	.00472	.00158	.00052	.00012	.00043	.00031	.00005	.00015	.00058	.00000	.00000	.00013	.00083	30
35	266242	1340	.00503	.00144	.00046	.00025	.00060	.00040	.00009	.00023	.00056	.00000	.00000	.00014	.00086	35
40	228327	1320	.00578	.00121	.00047	.00055	.00098	.00037	.00010	.00027	.00035	.00000	.00000	.00018	.00127	40
45	204728	1400	.00684	.00116	.00057	.00089	.00146	.00046	.00014	.00035	.00007	.00000	.00000	.00018	.00153	45
50	192521	1670	.00867	.00089	.00061	.00127	.00231	.00081	.00016	.00036	.00001	.00000	.00000	.00020	.00204	50
55	160189	2086	.01302	.00099	.00061	.00174	.00393	.00123	.00030	.00084	.00001	.00000	.00000	.00022	.00315	55
60	148548	3044	.02049	.00108	.00066	.00211	.00800	.00217	.00053	.00110	.00000	.00000	.00000	.00038	.00446	60
65	112457	3626	.03224	.00092	.00092	.00253	.01432	.00340	.00076	.00156	.00000	.00000	.00000	.00049	.00736	65
70	83154	4839	.05819	.00087	.00096	.00332	.02580	.00648	.00125	.00192	.00000	.00000	.00000	.00079	.01680	70
75	53227	5207	.09783	.00071	.00132	.00378	.04274	.00962	.00158	.00297	.00000	.00000	.00000	.00105	.03406	75
80	30633	5514	.18000	.00059	.00157	.00330	.05886	.01358	.00193	.00232	.00000	.00000	.00000	.00193	.09594	80
85+	12948	4279	.33048	.00039	.00216	.00348	.08866	.02464	.00348	.00317	.00000	.00000	.00000	.00193	.20134	85+
ALL	3998085	59556														

	All Causes	Respiratory T.B.	Other Infec. and Paras.	Neoplasms	Cardiovascular	Infl., Pneu., Bronch.	Diarrheal	Certain Degenerative	Maternal	Cert. Dis. of Infancy	Motor Vehicle	Other Violence	Other and Unknown
CRUDE DEATH RATE	.01490	.00106	.00117	.00056	.00312	.00156	.00194	.00039	.00019	.00068	.00000	.00028	.00394
STANDARDIZED RATE (1)	.01410	.00102	.00148	.00036	.00169	.00164	.00309	.00031	.00018	.00128	.00000	.00028	.00394
STANDARDIZED RATE (2)	.01695	.00106	.00119	.00065	.00385	.00175	.00204	.00044	.00018	.00075	.00000	.00028	.00278
GEOMETRIC MEAN	.01520												

LIFE TABLE FOR ALL CAUSES COMBINED

Age (x)	Midyear Population	Deaths During Year	$_nM_x$	$_nq_x$	l_x	$_nd_x$	$_nL_x$	$_nm_x$	$_na_x$	T_x	$_nr_x$	$\overset{\circ}{e}_x$	Age (x)
0	75262	10834	.143950	.131030	100000	13103	91021	.143956	.314716	5318207	.000000	53.182	0
1	329590	6993	.021217	.080590	86897	7003	330081	.021216	1.500000	5227187	.000000	60.154	1
5	409739	1199	.002926	.014519	79894	1160	396570	.002925	2.500000	4897106	.000000	61.295	5
10	395764	813	.002054	.010224	78734	805	391679	.002055	2.526398	4500536	.002177	57.161	10
15	376109	1225	.003257	.016194	77929	1262	386652	.003264	2.628434	4108857	.015563	52.726	15
20	316455	1318	.004165	.020648	76667	1583	379481	.004171	2.565540	3722205	.016906	48.550	20
25	312022	1480	.004743	.023440	75084	1760	371046	.004743	2.515033	3342724	.006077	44.520	25
30	290170	1369	.004718	.023321	73324	1710	362349	.004719	2.502558	2971678	.008692	40.528	30
35	266242	1340	.005033	.024869	71614	1781	353676	.005036	2.533104	2609328	.015723	36.436	35
40	228327	1320	.005781	.028540	69833	1993	344287	.005789	2.552580	2255652	.021446	32.301	40
45	204728	1400	.006838	.033667	67840	2284	333656	.006845	2.572789	1911364	.011672	28.175	45
50	192521	1670	.008674	.042574	65556	2791	321155	.008691	2.626224	1577708	.015061	24.067	50
55	160189	2086	.013022	.063331	62765	3975	304506	.013054	2.655556	1256553	.013074	20.020	55
60	148548	3044	.020492	.097959	58790	5759	280387	.020539	2.644882	952048	.012267	16.194	60
65	112457	3626	.032243	.150478	53031	7980	246411	.032385	2.651081	671661	.021358	12.665	65
70	83154	4839	.058193	.256287	45051	11546	197474	.058469	2.593864	425250	.019682	9.439	70
75	53227	5207	.097826	.393434	33505	13182	134760	.097819	2.514382	227776	-.000313	6.798	75
80	30633	5514	.180002	.612902	20323	12456	69212	.179970	2.398576	93017	-.000313	4.577	80
85+	12948	4279	.330476	1.000000	7867	7867	23805	.330476	3.025941	23805	.000000	3.026	85+

NUMBER OF PERSONS DYING (OUT OF 100,000 AT BIRTH) ABOVE AGE X FROM SPECIFIED CAUSES

Age (x)	All Causes	Respiratory T. B.	Other Infec. and Paras.	Neo-plasms	Cardio-vascular	Infl., Pneu., Bronch.	Diarrheal	Certain Degenerative	Maternal	Cert. Dis. of Infancy	Motor Vehicle	Other Violence	Other and Unknown	Age (x)
0	100000	5753	5828	4340	26463	10058	9300	2803	955	3301	0	1684	29515	0
1	86897	5667	4634	4337	26417	8417	4324	2766	955	0	0	1612	27768	1
5	79894	5510	3326	4326	26367	7216	1536	2581	955	0	0	1375	26702	5
10	78734	5440	2988	4322	26324	7048	1397	2537	955	0	0	1289	26434	10
15	77929	5319	2713	4320	26271	6584	1359	2514	955	0	0	1248	26246	15
20	76667	4789	2469	4306	26206	6913	1333	2488	918	0	0	1194	26051	20
25	75084	4076	2224	4293	26125	6829	1312	2461	754	0	0	1148	25862	25
30	73324	3326	2032	4272	25990	6732	1286	2428	555	0	0	1097	25606	30
35	71614	2753	1844	4227	25833	6619	1267	2374	345	0	0	1048	25304	35
40	69833	2244	1682	4138	25618	6478	1234	2293	147	0	0	959	25000	40
45	67840	1828	1519	3934	25281	6351	1200	2201	29	0	0	937	24560	45
50	65556	1442	1328	3635	24792	6196	1153	2083	6	0	0	872	24049	50
55	62765	1155	1131	3225	24049	5935	1103	1968	5	0	0	802	23392	55
60	58790	853	945	2694	22847	5560	1011	1713	1	0	0	735	22431	60
65	53031	549	759	2103	20598	4949	864	1403	1	0	0	629	21176	65
70	45051	324	531	1480	17053	4108	677	1018	1	0	0	508	19351	70
75	33505	153	341	823	11935	2822	429	637	1	0	0	351	16013	75
80	20323	56	164	314	6176	1526	216	237	1	0	0	209	11424	80
85+	7867	9	51	83	2111	586	83	75	0	0	0	75	4794	85+

NUMBER OF PERSONS SURVIVING TO AGE X IF SPECIFIED CAUSES WERE ELIMINATED

Age (x)	No Causes	Respiratory T. B.	Other Infec. and Paras.	Neo-plasms	Cardio-vascular	Infl., Pneu., Bronch.	Diarrheal	Certain Degenerative	Maternal	Cert. Dis. of Infancy	Motor Vehicle	Other Violence	Other and Unknown	(1)+(2)	(1)+(2)+(5)+(6)+(8)	(1)+(2)+(5)+(6)+(8)+part of(9)&(12)	(10)+(11)	Age (x)
		(1)	(2)	(3)	(4)	(5)	(6)	(7)	(8)	(9)	(10)	(11)	(12)					
0	100000	100000	100000	100000	100000	100000	100000	100000	100000	100000	100000	100000	100000	100000	100000	100000	100000	0
1	86897	86977	88016	86900	86940	88439	91658	86931	86897	90027	86897	86964	88540	88097	94573	99725	86964	1
5	79894	80118	82203	79907	79981	82492	87138	80103	79894	82771	79894	80183	82452	82434	92831	99046	80183	5
10	78734	79025	81356	78751	78863	81467	86023	78984	78734	81570	78734	79105	81530	81656	92312	98758	79105	10
15	77929	78338	80807	77948	78109	80700	85185	78199	77929	80736	77929	78337	80890	81231	91951	98563	78337	15
20	76667	77600	79749	76699	76909	79466	83833	76959	76704	79428	76667	77122	79781	80720	91531	98324	77122	20
25	75084	76715	78355	75129	75402	77911	82125	75397	75283	77788	75084	75576	78329	80057	91102	98078	75576	25
30	73324	75678	76717	73388	73768	76184	80228	73662	73715	75965	73324	73855	76757	79179	90495	97707	73855	30
35	71614	74499	75122	71721	72204	74524	78378	71998	72205	74193	71614	72181	75280	78149	89740	97209	72181	35
40	69833	73171	73422	70026	70623	72815	76464	70288	70607	72348	69833	70435	73724	76932	88808	96491	70435	40
45	67840	71513	71496	68230	68945	70868	74319	68373	68709	70283	67840	68486	72080	75367	87355	95248	68486	45
50	65556	69506	69287	66229	67114	68641	71867	66188	66345	67917	65556	66245	70189	73462	85434	93478	66245	50
55	62765	66845	66541	63816	65006	65987	68861	63484	63592	65026	62765	63494	67892	70866	82818	90961	63494	55
60	58790	62923	62517	60298	62107	62191	64598	59714	59568	60907	58790	59538	64606	66912	78806	86991	59538	60
65	53031	57068	56581	54969	58328	56716	58423	54164	53733	54941	53031	53808	59601	60888	72690	80741	53808	65
70	45051	48702	48290	47293	53275	49017	45822	46375	45648	45674	45051	45824	52561	52203	63645	71332	45824	70
75	33505	36377	36088	35765	45174	37674	37288	34826	33949	34712	33505	34217	42598	39181	49681	56795	34217	75
80	20323	22144	22035	22109	34053	23994	22799	21444	20592	21055	20323	20866	30806	24010	32222	38199	20866	80
85+	7867	8603	8604	8710	17968	9978	8915	8404	7972	8150	7867	8160	19763	9408	13703	18079	8160	85+

ADDED YRS OF LIFE

	No Causes	(1)	(2)	(3)	(4)	(5)	(6)	(7)	(8)	(9)	(10)	(11)	(12)	(1)+(2)	sum	big	(10)+(11)
TOTAL		2.061	2.603	.670	3.284	2.718	5.041	.546	.373	1.904	.000	.488	5.607	4.788	14.134	20.455	.488
WORK	5.893	1.637	.594	.311	.739	.364	.091	.185	.365	.000	.000	.157	.974	2.260	3.147	3.821	.157

POPULATION, DEATHS, DEATH RATES FOR ALL CAUSES COMBINED, AND SPECIFIED CAUSES

Age Start of Interval	Midyear Population	Deaths During Year	All Causes	Respiratory T. B.	Other Infec. and Paras.	Neoplasms	Cardiovascular	Infl., Pneu., Bronch.	Diarrheal	Certain Degenerative	Maternal	Cert. Dis. of Infancy	Motor Vehicle	Other Violence	Other and Unknown	Age Start of Interval
0	96338	9219	.05569	.00020	.00298	.00006	.00001	.01629	.02512	.00033	.00000	.03828	.00000	.00023	.01220	0
1	362543	2611	.00720	.00007	.00067	.00013	.00002	.00177	.00225	.00023	.00000	.00000	.00012	.00058	.00136	1
5	431006	509	.00118	.00001	.00016	.00007	.00005	.00022	.00005	.00005	.00000	.00000	.00011	.00020	.00136	5
10	420790	337	.00080	.00001	.00010	.00008	.00007	.00009	.00001	.00005	.00000	.00000	.00004	.00021	.00014	10
15	363662	425	.00117	.00009	.00009	.00009	.00010	.00005	.00001	.00005	.00000	.00000	.00011	.00035	.00021	15
20	334427	570	.00170	.00029	.00008	.00009	.00010	.00008	.00001	.00008	.00000	.00000	.00025	.00053	.00019	20
25	322201	639	.00198	.00056	.00006	.00015	.00016	.00006	.00000	.00017	.00000	.00000	.00015	.00044	.00025	25
30	303391	775	.00255	.00077	.00009	.00021	.00024	.00013	.00001	.00025	.00000	.00000	.00018	.00040	.00027	30
35	282762	960	.00340	.00085	.00011	.00029	.00046	.00019	.00001	.00036	.00000	.00000	.00016	.00059	.00037	35
40	238099	1110	.00466	.00107	.00014	.00057	.00070	.00024	.00001	.00062	.00000	.00000	.00024	.00054	.00053	40
45	241927	1661	.00687	.00120	.00021	.00095	.00132	.00041	.00002	.00096	.00000	.00000	.00021	.00068	.00091	45
50	222732	2149	.00965	.00134	.00018	.00167	.00249	.00077	.00004	.00110	.00000	.00000	.00019	.00084	.00102	50
55	183165	2825	.01542	.00151	.00029	.00300	.00475	.00127	.00007	.00193	.00000	.00000	.00017	.00084	.00159	55
60	144393	3442	.02384	.00177	.00026	.00423	.00905	.00215	.00012	.00256	.00000	.00000	.00020	.00101	.00247	60
65	110927	4179	.03767	.00156	.00041	.00641	.01616	.00349	.00023	.00371	.00000	.00000	.00018	.00111	.00441	65
70	83102	5179	.06232	.00154	.00036	.00723	.03056	.00562	.00032	.00454	.00000	.00000	.00020	.00138	.01055	70
75	49443	5047	.10208	.00103	.00047	.00963	.04721	.00969	.00057	.00534	.00000	.00000	.00030	.00160	.02625	75
80	23949	4000	.16702	.00079	.00033	.00814	.06681	.01432	.00058	.00505	.00000	.00000	.00025	.00238	.06835	80
85+	11193	2573	.22988	.00054	.00036	.00724	.06781	.01939	.00080	.00554	.00000	.00000	.00018	.00286	.12517	85+
ALL	4226050	48210														ALL

CRUDE DEATH RATE			.01141	.00061	.00026	.00103	.00299	.00125	.00081	.00072	.00000	.00087	.00015	.00055	.00217	
STANDARDIZED RATE (1)			.00966	.00048	.00030	.00067	.00174	.00123	.00118	.00050	.00000	.00135	.00014	.00049	.00158	
STANDARDIZED RATE (2)			.01381	.00066	.00026	.00127	.00411	.00144	.00076	.00086	.00000	.00079	.00016	.00055	.00292	
GEOMETRIC MEAN			.01048													

LIFE TABLE FOR ALL CAUSES COMBINED

Age (x)	Midyear Population	Deaths During Year	$_nM_x$	$_nq_x$	l_x	$_nd_x$	$_nL_x$	$_nm_x$	$_na_x$	T_x	$_nr_x$	$\overset{\circ}{e}_x$	Age (x)
0	96338	9219	.055694	.089150	100000	8915	93159	.055696	.232680	6118342	.000000	61.183	0
1	362543	2611	.007202	.028292	91085	2577	357898	.007200	1.500000	6025183	.000000	66.149	1
5	431006	509	.001181	.005858	88508	522	441235	.001183	2.500000	5667285	.000000	64.031	5
10	420790	337	.000801	.003989	87986	351	439050	.000799	2.494065	5226050	.010790	59.396	10
15	363662	425	.001169	.005842	87635	512	436976	.001172	2.658691	4787000	.021124	54.624	15
20	334427	570	.001704	.008505	87123	741	433834	.001708	2.595873	4350024	.013443	49.930	20
25	322201	639	.001983	.009815	86382	853	429850	.001984	2.584506	3916190	.009038	45.336	25
30	303391	775	.002554	.012709	85529	1087	425047	.002557	2.609629	3486341	.008013	40.762	30
35	282762	960	.003395	.016815	84442	1425	418821	.003402	2.621491	3061294	.018972	36.253	35
40	238099	1110	.004662	.023104	83017	1918	410564	.004672	2.642835	2642473	.015295	31.831	40
45	241927	1661	.006866	.033766	81099	2740	399017	.006867	2.635797	2231909	.000603	27.521	45
50	222732	2149	.009648	.047270	78359	3704	383127	.009668	2.659737	1832892	.011894	23.391	50
55	183165	2825	.015423	.074744	74655	5580	360185	.015492	2.654047	1449766	.023912	19.420	55
60	144393	3442	.023838	.113355	69075	7830	326850	.023956	2.634100	1089581	.026757	15.774	60
65	110927	4179	.037673	.173402	61245	10620	280906	.037806	2.615917	762731	.018225	12.454	65
70	83102	5179	.062321	.271388	50625	13739	219697	.062536	2.566917	481825	.016163	9.518	70
75	49443	5047	.102077	.407553	36886	15033	146634	.102521	2.485755	262128	.017976	7.106	75
80	23949	4000	.167022	.581797	21853	12714	75738	.167868	2.362979	115494	.017976	5.285	80
85+	11193	2573	.229876	1.000000	9139	9139	39756	.229876	4.350175	39756	.000000	4.350	85+

NUMBER OF PERSONS DYING (OUT OF 100,000 AT BIRTH) ABOVE AGE X FROM SPECIFIED CAUSES

Age (x)	All Causes	Respira- tory T.B.	Other Infec. and Paras.	Neo- plasms	Cardio- vascular	Infl., Pneu., Bronch.	Diar- rheal	Certain Degen- erative	Maternal	Cert. Dis. of Infancy	Motor Vehicle	Other Violence	Other and Unknown	Age (x)
0	100000	4717	1524	9926	33000	9739	3589	6590	0	3566	1021	4004	22324	0
1	91085	4698	1246	9921	32999	8222	1249	6559	0	0	1021	3983	21187	1
5	88508	4673	1005	9873	32992	7590	443	6477	0	0	979	3774	20702	5
10	87986	4667	937	9841	32971	7495	420	6455	0	0	929	3686	20585	10
15	87635	4662	892	9808	32941	7457	416	6431	0	0	910	3592	20526	15
20	87123	4622	846	9767	32899	7436	411	6409	0	0	863	3437	20433	20
25	86382	4496	811	9730	32853	7399	406	6373	0	0	753	3208	20353	25
30	85529	4256	784	9667	32787	7374	405	6301	0	0	690	3017	20248	30
35	84442	3927	748	9577	32686	7318	399	6196	0	0	614	2846	20131	35
40	83017	3573	702	9456	32491	7236	393	6043	0	0	549	2600	19974	40
45	81099	3132	645	9223	32203	7136	388	5787	0	0	452	2378	19755	45
50	78359	2654	562	8843	31676	6973	381	5403	0	0	367	2107	19393	50
55	74655	2141	494	8202	30718	6678	364	4979	0	0	294	1784	19001	55
60	69075	1598	389	7115	28996	6217	339	4280	0	0	233	1483	18425	60
65	61245	1018	303	5727	26018	5509	298	3439	0	0	168	1152	17613	65
70	50625	580	189	3922	21457	4526	231	2394	0	0	117	840	16369	70
75	36886	242	110	2331	14717	3287	160	1396	0	0	72	535	14036	75
80	21853	91	41	917	7769	1860	77	611	0	0	28	300	10159	80
85+	9139	21	14	288	2696	771	32	220	0	0	7	114	4976	85+

NUMBER OF PERSONS SURVIVING TO AGE X IF SPECIFIED CAUSES WERE ELIMINATED

Age (x)	No Causes	Respira- tory T.B. (1)	Other Infec. and Paras. (2)	Neo- plasms (3)	Cardio- vascular (4)	Infl., Pneu., Bronch. (5)	Diar- rheal (6)	Certain Degen- erative (7)	Maternal (8)	Cert. Dis. of Infancy (9)	Motor Vehicle (10)	Other Violence (11)	Other and Unknown (12)	(1) + (2) (5) + (6) + (8)	(1) + (2) (5)+(6)+ (8)+part of(9)&(12)	(10) + (11)	Age (x)
0	100000	100000	100000	100000	100000	100000	100000	100000	100000	100000	100000	100000	100000	100000	100000	100000	0
1	91085	91103	91351	91090	91086	92544	93345	91115	91085	94551	91085	91105	92176	91369	95136	95872	91105	1
5	88508	88550	89005	88560	88516	90561	91522	88618	88508	91876	88549	88734	90053	89047	94215	99341	88775	5
10	87986	88034	88548	88070	88015	90124	91006	88117	87986	91334	88077	88298	89641	88596	93863	99033	88390	10
15	87635	87688	88240	87751	87694	89803	90647	87789	87635	90970	87745	88040	89344	88293	93587	98762	88151	15
20	87123	87215	87771	87279	87223	89300	90123	87298	87123	90439	87279	87681	88916	87864	93160	98339	87838	20
25	86382	86599	87059	86574	86527	88558	89361	86592	86382	89669	86646	87165	88241	87278	92584	97759	87432	25
30	85529	85984	86227	85782	85739	87729	88480	85809	85529	88784	85854	86497	87477	86685	91982	97170	86825	30
35	84442	85220	85167	84782	84750	86671	87361	84823	84442	87656	84838	85569	86484	85952	91271	96477	85971	35
40	83017	84137	83776	83471	83514	85292	85893	83544	83017	86176	83471	84373	85184	84906	90255	95472	84835	40
45	81099	82636	81897	81775	81871	83423	83914	81869	81099	84185	81639	82647	83438	83449	88820	94043	83197	45
50	78359	80324	79212	79390	79630	80769	81086	79485	78359	81341	78965	80126	80986	81199	86609	91831	80746	50
55	74655	77041	75535	76274	76823	77249	77270	76148	74655	77496	75304	76661	77554	77950	83484	88639	77328	55
60	69075	71823	69991	71649	72808	71936	71520	71145	69075	71704	69735	71228	72335	72776	78472	83469	71909	60
65	61245	64249	62139	64895	67582	64475	63453	63900	61245	63576	61891	63475	64941	65187	71103	75822	64145	65
70	50625	53523	51469	55401	60633	54246	52513	53816	50625	52552	51206	52761	54897	54415	60482	64742	53367	70
75	36886	39298	37568	41861	51604	40668	38324	40116	36886	38290	37348	38712	42228	40025	45849	49483	39196	75
80	21853	23400	22310	26036	38904	25319	22770	24415	21853	22685	22160	23121	26693	23889	28841	31795	23446	80
85+	9139	9833	9347	11368	23038	11410	9552	10488	9139	9487	9281	9793	17120	10057	13123	15333	9945	85+

ADDED YRS OF LIFE

	No Causes	(1)	(2)	(3)	(4)	(5)	(6)	(7)	(8)	(9)	(10)	(11)	(12)				
TOTAL		1.117	.597	1.434	4.279	2.329	2.124	1.063	.000	2.320	.325	1.087	3.779	1.730	6.446	10.702	1.422
WORK	4.079	.704	.122	.457	.662	.224	.016	.397	.000	.000	.195	.561	.443	.829	1.078	1.225	.759

POPULATION, DEATHS, DEATH RATES FOR ALL CAUSES COMBINED, AND SPECIFIED CAUSES

Age Start of Interval	Midyear Population	Deaths During Year	All Causes	Respiratory T.B.	Other Infec. and Paras.	Neoplasms	Cardiovascular	Infl., Pneu., Bronch.	Diarrheal	Certain Degenerative	Maternal	Cert. Dis. of Infancy	Motor Vehicle	Other Violence	Other and Unknown	Age Start of Interval
0	90249	7366	.08162	.00027	.00273	.00003	.00001	.01365	.02186	.00017	.00000	.03229	.00000	.00034	.01027	0
1	346754	2319	.00669	.00010	.00071	.00007	.00004	.00169	.00202	.00024	.00000	.00000	.00005	.00056	.00121	1
5	414924	393	.00095	.00000	.00018	.00005	.00003	.00016	.00005	.00004	.00000	.00000	.00007	.00016	.00022	5
10	413472	239	.00058	.00005	.00008	.00006	.00008	.00007	.00001	.00003	.00000	.00000	.00001	.00005	.00013	10
15	379001	250	.00066	.00009	.00006	.00006	.00009	.00004	.00001	.00004	.00002	.00000	.00001	.00012	.00013	15
20	366481	347	.00095	.00022	.00006	.00010	.00013	.00004	.00000	.00005	.00011	.00000	.00001	.00008	.00015	20
25	346888	453	.00131	.00037	.00006	.00011	.00016	.00003	.00002	.00012	.00014	.00000	.00002	.00009	.00019	25
30	330177	521	.00158	.00035	.00006	.00022	.00025	.00008	.00001	.00013	.00019	.00000	.00002	.00009	.00019	30
35	304818	603	.00198	.00030	.00012	.00042	.00027	.00011	.00002	.00014	.00018	.00000	.00002	.00011	.00030	35
40	258268	647	.00251	.00031	.00008	.00073	.00048	.00009	.00002	.00019	.00010	.00000	.00002	.00014	.00036	40
45	265686	959	.00361	.00033	.00008	.00114	.00088	.00020	.00003	.00033	.00003	.00000	.00003	.00016	.00041	45
50	255770	1430	.00559	.00029	.00009	.00177	.00170	.00022	.00004	.00063	.00000	.00000	.00006	.00022	.00057	50
55	223382	1761	.00788	.00029	.00010	.00214	.00297	.00043	.00006	.00084	.00000	.00000	.00008	.00015	.00081	55
60	187607	2432	.01296	.00041	.00018	.00299	.00577	.00082	.00012	.00104	.00000	.00000	.00005	.00024	.00135	60
65	151629	3630	.02394	.00052	.00020	.00358	.01242	.00172	.00018	.00173	.00000	.00000	.00008	.00040	.00271	65
70	121955	5204	.04267	.00051	.00020	.00502	.02288	.00334	.00034	.00230	.00000	.00000	.00016	.00066	.00719	70
75	80280	6269	.07809	.00044	.00032	.00562	.04127	.00569	.00065	.00315	.00000	.00000	.00011	.00120	.01964	75
80	44841	6138	.13688	.00040	.00040	.00658	.05745	.01048	.00071	.00312	.00000	.00000	.00007	.00143	.05624	80
85+	26956	5836	.21618	.00015	.00041	.00545	.07097	.01526	.00081	.00274	.00000	.00000	.00004	.00289	.11746	85+
ALL	4609178	46797														

	All Causes	Respiratory T.B.	Other Infec. and Paras.	Neoplasms	Cardiovascular	Infl., Pneu., Bronch.	Diarrheal	Certain Degenerative	Maternal	Cert. Dis. of Infancy	Motor Vehicle	Other Violence	Other and Unknown
CRUDE DEATH RATE	.01015	.00024	.00021	.00097	.00334	.00096	.00064	.00043	.00005	.00063	.00004	.00023	.00242
STANDARDIZED RATE (1)	.00721	.00020	.00026	.00054	.00135	.00092	.00104	.00025	.00005	.00114	.00003	.00020	.00122
STANDARDIZED RATE (2)	.01002	.00024	.00021	.00096	.00328	.00096	.00067	.00043	.00005	.00067	.00004	.00023	.00227
GEOMETRIC MEAN	.00694												

LIFE TABLE FOR ALL CAUSES COMBINED

Age (x)	Midyear Population	Deaths During Year	$_nM_x$	$_nq_x$	l_x	$_nd_x$	$_nL_x$	$_nm_x$	$_na_x$	T_x	$_nr_x$	$\overset{\circ}{e}_x$	Age (x)
0	90249	7366	.081619	.076670	100000	7667	93933	.081622	.208752	6672186	.000000	66.722	0
1	346754	2319	.006688	.026307	92333	2429	363260	.006687	1.500000	6578253	.000000	71.245	1
5	414924	393	.000947	.004727	89904	425	448458	.000948	2.500000	6214993	.000000	69.129	5
10	413472	239	.000578	.002883	89479	258	446723	.000578	2.394218	5766536	.005703	64.446	10
15	379001	250	.000660	.003295	89221	294	445404	.000660	2.615505	5319813	.010728	59.625	15
20	366481	347	.000947	.004734	88927	421	443641	.000949	2.639549	4874409	.008298	54.814	20
25	346888	453	.001306	.006508	88506	576	441146	.001306	2.558018	4430768	.009102	50.062	25
30	330177	521	.001578	.007870	87930	692	437579	.001580	2.585802	3989621	.008484	45.373	30
35	304818	603	.001978	.009870	87238	861	434118	.001983	2.593157	3551642	.020625	40.712	35
40	258268	647	.002505	.012469	86377	1077	429331	.002509	2.628830	3117524	.016361	36.092	40
45	265686	959	.003610	.017902	85300	1527	422940	.003610	2.668768	2688193	-.000509	31.515	45
50	255770	1430	.005591	.027622	83773	2314	413421	.005597	2.647292	2265253	.007093	27.040	50
55	223382	1761	.007883	.038829	81459	3163	399938	.007909	2.674017	1851832	.018364	22.733	55
60	187607	2432	.012963	.063298	78296	4956	380172	.013036	2.718256	1451894	.024481	18.544	60
65	151629	3630	.023940	.113935	73340	8356	347413	.024052	2.691803	1071722	.019391	14.613	65
70	121955	5204	.042671	.194648	64984	12649	295148	.042857	2.646273	724310	.018270	11.146	70
75	80280	6269	.078089	.329359	52335	17237	219669	.078468	2.563006	429162	.018348	8.200	75
80	44841	6138	.136884	.508918	35098	17862	129764	.137650	2.440015	209493	.018348	5.969	80
85+	26956	5836	.216180	1.000000	17236	17236	79730	.216180	4.625771	79730	.000000	4.626	85+

NUMBER OF PERSONS DYING (OUT OF 100,000 AT BIRTH) ABOVE AGE X FROM SPECIFIED CAUSES

Age (x)	All Causes	Respiratory T.B.	Other Infec. and Paras.	Neoplasms	Cardio-vascular	Infl., Pneu., Bronch.	Diar-rheal	Certain Degenerative	Maternal	Cert. Dis. of Infancy	Motor Vehicle	Other Violence	Other and Unknown	Age (x)
0	100000	1825	1286	9416	38521	8263	3435	4166	336	3033	293	1926	27500	0
1	92333	1800	1030	9413	38520	6981	1382	4151	336	0	293	1894	26533	1
5	89904	1764	773	9387	38506	6366	648	4065	336	0	274	1690	26095	5
10	89479	1763	694	9366	38491	6292	627	4047	336	0	245	1619	25999	10
15	89221	1742	659	9340	38454	6260	620	4033	336	0	238	1596	25943	15
20	88927	1702	633	9313	38414	6244	617	4015	326	0	232	1544	25887	20
25	88506	1604	607	9270	38357	6228	615	3992	279	0	228	1509	25817	25
30	87930	1440	580	9220	38288	6214	608	3941	218	0	220	1468	25733	30
35	87238	1289	552	9124	38180	6178	605	3885	133	0	212	1430	25650	35
40	86377	1158	498	8940	38062	6131	598	3825	56	0	205	1383	25521	40
45	85300	1026	465	8624	37855	6094	591	3742	12	0	197	1324	25370	45
50	83773	885	431	8142	37483	6010	580	3603	1	0	185	1257	25196	50
55	81459	764	393	7411	36777	5919	564	3343	1	0	161	1168	24958	55
60	78256	649	351	6552	35582	5745	539	3005	1	0	131	1108	24633	60
65	73340	494	284	5411	33373	5430	492	2609	1	0	111	1016	24119	65
70	64984	313	215	4027	29037	4829	430	2004	1	0	83	876	23169	70
75	52335	163	157	2544	22255	3840	301	1325	1	0	37	681	21031	75
80	35058	67	86	1308	13153	2584	158	631	1	0	12	418	16680	80
85+	17236	12	32	434	5659	1217	65	219	0	0	3	230	9365	85+

NUMBER OF PERSONS SURVIVING TO AGE X IF SPECIFIED CAUSES WERE ELIMINATED

Age (x)	No Causes	Respiratory T.B. (1)	Other Infec. and Paras. (2)	Neoplasms (3)	Cardiovascular (4)	Infl., Pneu., Bronch. (5)	Diarrheal (6)	Certain Degenerative (7)	Maternal (8)	Cert. Dis. of Infancy (9)	Motor Vehicle (10)	Other Violence (11)	Other and Unknown (12)	(1)+(2)	(1)+(2)+(5)+(6)+(8)	(1)+(2)+(5)+(6)+(8)+part of(9)&(12)	(10)+(11)	Age (x)
0	100000	100000	100000	100000	100000	100000	100000	100000	100000	100000	100000	100000	100000	100000	100000	100000	100000	0
1	92333	92357	92336	92334	92347	94326	92347	92333	95293	92333	92364	93267	92603		95873	99889	92364	1
5	89904	89963	90398	89932	89919	91728	92588	90003	89904	92786	89923	90136	91251	90458	95048	99423	90154	5
10	89479	89539	90050	89528	89509	91370	92172	89595	89479	92348	89527	89780	90017	90110	94784	99203	89828	10
15	89221	89301	89826	89296	89288	91139	91913	89351	89221	92081	89275	89545	90711	89907	94611	99052	89599	15
20	88927	89047	89556	89029	89033	90855	91613	89075	88937	91778	88927	89302	90469	89677	94400	98855	89362	20
25	88506	88724	89158	88650	88669	90441	91182	88676	88563	91343	88570	88914	90112	89377	94153	98639	88978	25
30	87930	88310	88605	88123	88161	89867	90596	88150	88047	90749	88002	88376	89611	88988	93831	98353	88448	30
35	87238	87766	87936	87526	87575	89196	89886	87512	87439	90035	87317	87719	88990	88468	93415	97963	87798	35
40	86377	87031	87123	86828	86824	88364	89006	86708	86653	89146	86462	86900	88243	87782	92830	97412	86986	40
45	85300	86078	86069	86079	85953	87300	87903	85710	85616	88035	85392	85876	87296	86854	91943	96528	85968	45
50	83773	84678	84562	85022	84787	85822	86341	84314	84095	86459	83875	84405	85910	85476	90598	95156	84508	50
55	81459	82460	82264	83408	83153	83544	83972	82244	81772	84070	81582	82162	83778	83275	88379	92860	82286	55
60	78256	79372	79111	81036	81129	80475	80737	79385	78597	80806	78444	79031	80853	80199	85327	89699	79180	60
65	73340	74500	74169	77056	78244	75695	75673	74749	73622	75691	73498	74118	76251	75342	80544	84746	74278	65
70	64984	66184	65784	69653	73823	67657	67112	66814	65234	67067	65150	65807	68502	66999	72316	76219	65975	70
75	52335	53437	53032	57527	66768	55417	54168	54434	52536	54013	52510	53175	57238	54148	59573	63081	53352	75
80	35058	35915	35623	39685	55251	38261	36447	37091	35233	36223	35235	35878	42509	36453	41423	44410	36018	80
85+	17236	17676	17532	20179	36565	19840	17965	18516	17303	17789	17310	17751	27933	17979	21654	24245	17827	85+

ADDED YRS OF LIFE

	No Causes	(1)	(2)	(3)	(4)	(5)	(6)	(7)	(8)	(9)	(10)	(11)	(12)	(1)+(2)	big	part	(10)+(11)
TOTAL		.541	.585	1.555	5.046	2.039	2.061	.689	.144	2.133	.085	.498	4.366	1.132	5.544	9.393	.584
WORK	2.387	.309	.086	.505	.509	.105	.017	.194	.115	.000	.023	.131	.299	.395	.636	.741	.154

POPULATION, DEATHS, DEATH RATES FOR ALL CAUSES COMBINED, AND SPECIFIED CAUSES

Age Start of Interval	Midyear Population	Deaths During Year	All Causes	Respiratory T. B.	Other Infec. and Paras.	Neoplasms	Cardiovascular	Infl., Pneu., Bronch.	Diarrheal	Certain Degenerative	Maternal	Cert. Dis. of Infancy	Motor Vehicle	Other Violence	Other and Unknown	Age Start of Interval
0	100600	8310	.08260	.00008	.00291	.00006	.00018	.01383	.02236	.00031	.00000	.02999	.00000	.00024	.01265	0
1	369250	2471	.00669	.00003	.00074	.00011	.00003	.00175	.00217	.00022	.00000	.00000	.00013	.00045	.00106	1
5	449350	552	.00123	.00000	.00018	.00013	.00004	.00026	.00006	.00007	.00000	.00000	.00010	.00017	.00023	5
10	435100	335	.00077	.00000	.00008	.00008	.00007	.00008	.00002	.00005	.00000	.00000	.00007	.00020	.00011	10
15	356150	519	.00146	.00003	.00010	.00012	.00012	.00012	.00001	.00007	.00000	.00000	.00017	.00048	.00025	15
20	323850	460	.00142	.00011	.00006	.00010	.00012	.00005	.00000	.00009	.00000	.00000	.00022	.00045	.00022	20
25	323850	658	.00203	.00027	.00006	.00013	.00015	.00010	.00000	.00016	.00000	.00000	.00034	.00056	.00026	25
30	324850	705	.00217	.00045	.00007	.00016	.00021	.00009	.00001	.00024	.00000	.00000	.00025	.00044	.00026	30
35	292100	977	.00334	.00057	.00010	.00034	.00040	.00024	.00001	.00037	.00000	.00000	.00031	.00060	.00040	35
40	238950	1290	.00540	.00083	.00010	.00069	.00087	.00030	.00003	.00082	.00000	.00000	.00041	.00079	.00057	40
45	258200	1536	.00595	.00077	.00008	.00089	.00110	.00047	.00002	.00096	.00000	.00000	.00028	.00072	.00065	45
50	244950	2364	.00965	.00103	.00018	.00166	.00239	.00078	.00004	.00152	.00000	.00000	.00028	.00085	.00090	50
55	200600	3151	.01571	.00122	.00024	.00310	.00485	.00125	.00007	.00218	.00000	.00000	.00034	.00106	.00140	55
60	154700	3846	.02486	.00142	.00022	.00495	.00903	.00230	.00012	.00317	.00000	.00000	.00027	.00131	.00209	60
65	119500	4417	.03696	.00128	.00033	.00597	.01619	.00356	.00019	.00384	.00000	.00000	.00018	.00141	.00362	65
70	90500	5464	.06038	.00055	.00031	.00824	.02973	.00621	.00022	.00485	.00000	.00000	.00034	.00181	.00770	70
75	54011	5510	.10202	.00118	.00022	.01033	.04882	.01041	.00050	.00561	.00000	.00000	.00044	.00165	.02285	75
80	26162	4086	.15618	.00054	.00031	.01101	.06464	.01495	.00057	.00482	.00000	.00000	.00042	.00191	.05703	80
85+	12227	2789	.22810	.00041	.00008	.01006	.07361	.02364	.00082	.00523	.00000	.00000	.00025	.00311	.11090	85+
ALL	4374900	49440														

CRUDE DEATH RATE			.01130	.00043	.00024	.00115	.00313	.00129	.00074	.00082	.00000	.00069	.00022	.00061	.00197	
STANDARDIZED RATE (1)			.00909	.00032	.00029	.00072	.00174	.00119	.00108	.00055	.00000	.00106	.00020	.00052	.00142	
STANDARDIZED RATE (2)			.01332	.00046	.00024	.00137	.00411	.00147	.00069	.00094	.00000	.00062	.00023	.00065	.00253	
GEOMETRIC MEAN			.01026													

LIFE TABLE FOR ALL CAUSES COMBINED

Age (x)	Midyear Population	Deaths During Year	$_nM_x$	$_nq_x$	l_x	$_nd_x$	$_nL_x$	$_nm_x$	$_na_x$	T_x	$_nr_x$	$\overset{\circ}{e}_x$	Age (x)
0	100600	8310	.082604	.077550	100000	7755	93877	.082608	.210427	6216986	.000000	62.170	0
1	369250	2471	.006692	.026321	92245	2428	362910	.006690	1.500000	6123109	.000000	66.379	1
5	449350	552	.001228	.006124	89817	550	447710	.001228	2.500000	5760199	.000000	64.133	5
10	435100	335	.000770	.003842	89267	343	445498	.000770	2.559524	5312489	.015200	59.512	10
15	356150	519	.001457	.007287	88924	648	443059	.001463	2.590664	4866991	.028383	54.732	15
20	323850	460	.001420	.007080	88276	625	439867	.001421	2.579667	4423933	.014704	50.115	20
25	323850	658	.002032	.010120	87651	887	436102	.002034	2.573046	3984065	.000888	45.454	25
30	324850	705	.002170	.010788	86764	936	431593	.002169	2.621083	3547963	.002231	40.892	30
35	292100	977	.003345	.016673	85828	1431	425837	.003360	2.691737	3116370	.024004	36.309	35
40	238950	1290	.005399	.026655	84397	2253	416556	.005409	2.590250	2690533	.015047	31.879	40
45	258200	1536	.005949	.029302	82144	2407	405018	.005943	2.631215	2273977	-.007187	27.683	45
50	244950	2364	.009651	.047268	79737	3769	389966	.009665	2.686555	1868959	.007386	23.439	50
55	200600	3151	.015708	.076611	75968	5782	366324	.015784	2.662393	1478993	.024642	19.469	55
60	154700	3846	.024861	.117915	70186	8276	331231	.024986	2.619759	1112669	.028222	15.853	60
65	119500	4417	.036962	.170263	61910	10541	284300	.037077	2.604552	781438	.017642	12.622	65
70	90500	5464	.060376	.264089	51369	13566	223944	.060578	2.574712	497138	.015535	9.678	70
75	54011	5510	.102016	.407534	37803	15406	150262	.102527	2.484584	273195	.019657	7.227	75
80	26162	4086	.156181	.554806	22397	12426	79219	.156856	2.363123	122932	.019657	5.489	80
85+	12227	2789	.228102	1.000000	9971	9971	43713	.228102	4.384009	43713	.000000	4.384	85+

NUMBER OF PERSONS DYING (OUT OF 100,000 AT BIRTH) ABOVE AGE X FROM SPECIFIED CAUSES

Age (x)	All Causes	Respira-tory T. B.	Other Infec. and Paras.	Neo-plasms	Cardio-vascular	Infl., Pneu., Bronch.	Diar-rheal	Certain Degener-ative	Maternal	Cert. Dis. of Infancy	Motor Vehicle	Other Violence	Other and Unknown	Age (x)
0	100000	3438	1363	11018	34070	10508	3298	7388	0	2816	1539	4576	19986	0
1	92245	3430	1090	11012	34053	9209	1199	7360	0	0	1539	4554	18799	1
5	89817	3418	820	10973	34042	8575	412	7281	0	0	1491	4391	18414	5
10	89267	3418	742	10916	34026	8460	384	7249	0	0	1444	4316	18312	10
15	88924	3417	705	10879	33993	8424	377	7228	0	0	1411	4227	18263	15
20	88276	3406	663	10828	33941	8373	374	7195	0	0	1333	4012	18151	20
25	87651	3357	634	10784	33889	8352	373	7156	0	0	1238	3812	18056	25
30	86764	3237	610	10727	33823	8307	372	7087	0	0	1090	3568	17943	30
35	85828	3043	578	10656	33734	8270	368	6985	0	0	982	3378	17834	35
40	84397	2798	534	10512	33564	8166	362	6826	0	0	848	3124	17663	40
45	82144	2453	491	10225	33200	8040	351	6485	0	0	679	2796	17424	45
50	79737	2142	459	9864	32754	7851	342	6097	0	0	566	2504	17158	50
55	75968	1739	388	9215	31821	7545	326	5502	0	0	456	2171	16805	55
60	70186	1293	298	8074	30034	7084	300	4699	0	0	330	1781	16293	60
65	61910	822	225	6430	27022	6316	261	3647	0	0	242	1348	15597	65
70	51369	458	132	4731	22399	5187	207	2553	0	0	190	948	14564	70
75	37803	246	63	2881	15716	3792	157	1465	0	0	113	542	12828	75
80	22397	67	30	1325	8347	2221	81	621	0	0	46	294	9365	80
85+	9971	18	4	440	3218	1033	36	229	0	0	11	136	4846	85+

NUMBER OF PERSONS SURVIVING TO AGE X IF SPECIFIED CAUSES WERE ELIMINATED

Age (x)	No Causes	Respira-tory T. B.	Other Infec. and Paras.	Neo-plasms	Cardio-vascular	Infl., Pneu., Bronch.	Diar-rheal	Certain Degener-ative	Maternal	Cert. Dis. of Infancy	Motor Vehicle	Other Violence	Other and Unknown	(1) + (2)	(1) + (2) + (5) + (6) + (8)	(1)+(2)+ (5)+(6)+ (8)+part of(9)&(12)	(10) + (11)	Age (x)
		(1)	(2)	(3)	(4)	(5)	(6)	(7)	(8)	(9)	(10)	(11)	(12)					
0	100000	100000	100000	100000	100000	100000	100000	100000	100000	100000	100000	100000	100000	100000	100000	100000	100000	0
1	92245	92253	92508	92251	92261	93501	94283	92272	92245	94589	92245	92266	93392	92515	95846	99843	92266	1
5	89817	89836	90340	89861	89844	91676	92598	89921	89817	92489	89864	89999	91319	90360	95086	99401	90046	5
10	89267	89286	89865	89368	89310	91232	92060	89402	89267	91922	89361	89522	90863	89885	94737	99092	89617	10
15	88924	88944	89557	89061	88999	90918	91713	89080	88924	91569	89051	89268	90564	89577	94459	98816	89395	15
20	88276	88307	88947	88463	88403	90307	91048	88464	88276	90902	88480	88832	90018	88978	93884	98239	89037	20
25	87651	87731	88346	87881	87829	89689	90404	87876	87651	90258	87948	88404	89477	88426	93325	97675	88704	25
30	86764	86962	87476	87048	87006	88828	89491	87006	86764	89345	87206	87755	88686	87676	92582	96928	88220	30
35	85828	86218	86564	86180	86156	87907	88529	86219	85828	88381	86373	86999	87840	86958	91867	96219	87552	35
40	84397	85025	85165	84887	84889	86547	87059	84940	84397	86907	85067	85804	86550	85799	90760	95119	86485	40
45	82144	83099	82934	82906	82985	84364	84747	83012	82144	84587	82964	83843	84481	83898	88896	93235	84680	45
50	79737	80974	80536	80837	80999	82084	82272	80566	79737	82109	80645	81681	82276	81785	86870	91186	82611	50
55	75968	77546	76799	77661	78102	78512	78400	77731	75968	78228	76942	78153	78743	78395	83614	87861	79155	55
60	70186	72082	71041	72880	73947	72996	72458	72608	70186	72274	71208	72590	73261	72961	78338	82430	73648	60
65	61910	64037	62734	65907	68280	65144	63952	65075	61910	63752	62895	64451	65309	64888	70530	74353	65477	65
70	51369	53474	52138	56350	61498	53114	55047	55069	51369	52857	52234	53856	55193	54274	60242	63708	54763	70
75	37803	39538	38428	43229	52640	41879	39131	41510	37803	38927	38506	39995	42260	40191	46089	49024	40740	75
80	22397	23565	22792	26584	40031	26169	23244	25297	22397	23063	22865	23892	28220	23981	29079	31513	24391	80
85+	9971	10525	10164	12726	24890	12587	10378	11553	9971	10268	10203	10747	16863	10728	14097	16039	10996	85+

ADDED YRS OF LIFE

		(1)	(2)	(3)	(4)	(5)	(6)	(7)	(8)	(9)	(10)	(11)	(12)				
TOTAL		.751	.582	1.579	4.510	2.329	1.967	1.216	.000	1.843	.476	1.194	3.346	1.343	5.853	9.421	1.686
WORK	4.056	.443	.099	.478	.653	.250	.014	.455	.000	.000	.297	.639	.431	.543	.814	.922	.942

POPULATION, DEATHS, DEATH RATES FOR ALL CAUSES COMBINED, AND SPECIFIED CAUSES

Age Start of Interval	Midyear Population	Deaths During Year	All Causes	Respiratory T. B.	Other Infec. and Paras.	Neoplasms	Cardiovascular	Infl., Pneu., Bronch.	Diarrheal	Certain Degenerative	Maternal	Cert. Dis. of Infancy	Motor Vehicle	Other Violence	Other and Unknown	Age Start of Interval
0	93600	6675	.07131	.00007	.00237	.00011	.00009	.01269	.02066	.00021	.00000	.02410	.00001	.00031	.01068	0
1	350850	2195	.00626	.00002	.00063	.00008	.00004	.00178	.00202	.00020	.00000	.00000	.00010	.00041	.00100	1
5	430150	481	.00112	.00001	.00020	.00007	.00005	.00021	.00005	.00007	.00000	.00000	.00008	.00014	.00023	5
10	427350	242	.00057	.00002	.00007	.00004	.00007	.00007	.00002	.00003	.00000	.00000	.00004	.00007	.00014	10
15	374400	251	.00067	.00003	.00008	.00006	.00010	.00004	.00000	.00005	.00001	.00000	.00001	.00011	.00018	15
20	366300	286	.00078	.00010	.00005	.00008	.00009	.00004	.00002	.00007	.00009	.00000	.00003	.00008	.00013	20
25	352300	352	.00100	.00020	.00005	.00010	.00012	.00006	.00002	.00008	.00011	.00000	.00002	.00009	.00016	25
30	355050	450	.00127	.00022	.00008	.00020	.00020	.00005	.00001	.00012	.00010	.00000	.00003	.00010	.00015	30
35	313700	596	.00190	.00023	.00007	.00039	.00032	.00013	.00001	.00022	.00016	.00000	.00003	.00014	.00022	35
40	255700	726	.00284	.00023	.00009	.00088	.00052	.00011	.00001	.00038	.00007	.00000	.00006	.00013	.00036	40
45	275900	845	.00306	.00017	.00005	.00100	.00079	.00014	.00002	.00043	.00001	.00000	.00006	.00013	.00029	45
50	275950	1439	.00521	.00025	.00005	.00175	.00160	.00026	.00002	.00071	.00000	.00000	.00006	.00016	.00036	50
55	241450	1858	.00770	.00020	.00009	.00202	.00270	.00046	.00005	.00120	.00000	.00000	.00006	.00024	.00068	55
60	197750	2765	.01398	.00030	.00010	.00328	.00625	.00056	.00007	.00160	.00000	.00000	.00011	.00035	.00097	60
65	160050	3655	.02284	.00036	.00015	.00438	.01159	.00178	.00017	.00207	.00000	.00000	.00005	.00039	.00189	65
70	131850	5317	.04033	.00036	.00014	.00508	.02211	.00350	.00022	.00240	.00000	.00000	.00015	.00068	.00569	70
75	87633	6700	.07646	.00035	.00032	.00677	.04076	.00644	.00045	.00324	.00000	.00000	.00018	.00097	.01698	75
80	48948	6380	.13034	.00029	.00018	.00695	.05745	.01009	.00057	.00345	.00000	.00000	.00016	.00157	.04962	80
85+	29469	6225	.21124	.00031	.00010	.00682	.07449	.01476	.00064	.00302	.00000	.00000	.00017	.00258	.10835	85+
ALL	4768400	47438														

	All Causes	Respiratory T. B.	Other Infec. and Paras.	Neoplasms	Cardiovascular	Infl., Pneu., Bronch.	Diarrheal	Certain Degenerative	Maternal	Cert. Dis. of Infancy	Motor Vehicle	Other Violence	Other and Unknown
CRUDE DEATH RATE	.00995	.00015	.00018	.00105	.00343	.00099	.00060	.00053	.00004	.00047	.00005	.00023	.00222
STANDARDIZED RATE (1)	.00667	.00012	.00024	.00056	.00132	.00092	.00099	.00030	.00004	.00085	.00005	.00018	.00111
STANDARDIZED RATE (2)	.00951	.00015	.00018	.00101	.00323	.00098	.00063	.00051	.00004	.00050	.00005	.00022	.00200
GEOMETRIC MEAN	.00658												

LIFE TABLE FOR ALL CAUSES COMBINED

Age (x)	Midyear Population	Deaths During Year	$_nM_x$	$_nq_x$	l_x	$_nd_x$	$_nL_x$	$_nm_x$	$_na_x$	T_x	$_nr_x$	$\overset{\circ}{e}_x$	Age (x)
0	93600	6675	.071314	.067430	100000	6743	94546	.071319	.191234	6784658	.000000	67.847	0
1	350850	2195	.006256	.024631	93257	2297	367286	.006254	1.500000	6690111	.000000	71.738	1
5	430150	481	.001118	.005585	90960	508	453530	.001120	2.500000	6322826	.000000	69.512	5
10	427350	242	.000566	.002819	90452	255	451580	.000565	2.331699	5869296	.009418	64.889	10
15	374400	251	.000670	.003348	90197	302	450250	.000671	2.566225	5417716	.015051	60.065	15
20	366300	286	.000781	.003905	89895	351	448627	.000782	2.585470	4967466	.008245	55.259	20
25	352300	352	.000999	.004981	89544	446	446649	.000999	2.599496	4518839	.003100	50.465	25
30	355050	450	.001267	.006330	89098	564	444162	.001271	2.645907	4072189	.004302	45.705	30
35	313700	596	.001900	.009499	88534	841	440708	.001908	2.666964	3628027	.027305	40.979	35
40	255700	726	.002839	.014117	87693	1238	435468	.002843	2.579429	3187319	.018663	36.346	40
45	275900	845	.003063	.015187	86455	1313	429192	.003059	2.651688	2751851	-.006926	31.830	45
50	275950	1439	.005215	.025769	85142	2194	420607	.005216	2.674339	2322659	.001800	27.280	50
55	241450	1858	.007695	.037964	82948	3149	407543	.007727	2.714420	1902052	.018745	22.931	55
60	197750	2765	.013982	.068109	79799	5435	386438	.014064	2.689551	1494509	.026819	18.728	60
65	160050	3655	.022837	.108843	74364	8094	353006	.022929	2.675516	1108071	.018708	14.901	65
70	131850	5317	.040326	.184910	66270	12254	302672	.040486	2.659727	755066	.016430	11.394	70
75	87633	6700	.076455	.323774	54016	17489	227541	.076661	2.567662	452393	.019464	8.375	75
80	48948	6380	.130342	.490979	36527	17934	136834	.131064	2.446122	224853	.019464	6.156	80
85+	29469	6225	.211239	1.000000	18593	18593	88019	.211239	4.733976	88019	.000000	4.734	85+

NUMBER OF PERSONS DYING (OUT OF 100,000 AT BIRTH) ABOVE AGE X FROM SPECIFIED CAUSES

Age (x)	All Causes	Respiratory T. B.	Other Infec. and Paras.	Neoplasms	Cardiovascular	Infl., Pneu., Bronch.	Diarrheal	Certain Degenerative	Maternal	Cert. Dis. of Infancy	Motor Vehicle	Other Violence	Other and Unknown	Age (x)
0	100000	1232	1084	10314	39818	8758	3183	5083	245	2279	419	1933	25652	0
1	93257	1225	880	10304	39810	7557	1229	5063	245	0	418	1904	24642	1
5	90960	1218	630	10274	39796	6905	490	4991	245	0	382	1754	24275	5
10	90452	1214	537	10241	39773	6809	465	4961	245	0	344	1691	24172	10
15	90197	1205	505	10221	39743	6778	458	4949	245	0	325	1659	24109	15
20	89895	1192	469	10192	39700	6759	457	4928	239	0	323	1609	24027	20
25	89544	1145	446	10156	39660	6741	449	4895	198	0	308	1573	23973	25
30	89098	1055	423	10113	39608	6715	440	4859	150	0	299	1534	23902	30
35	88534	959	388	10023	39519	6692	437	4806	104	0	288	1487	23831	35
40	87693	859	359	9851	39376	6636	434	4707	32	0	277	1427	23735	40
45	86455	759	321	9467	39151	6586	429	4539	4	0	249	1373	23577	45
50	85142	687	301	9040	38814	6524	419	4353	1	0	234	1315	23454	50
55	82948	583	281	8302	38141	6416	410	4054	1	0	208	1248	23304	55
60	79799	501	244	7476	37036	6229	392	3565	1	0	184	1148	23023	60
65	74364	385	205	6203	34604	5855	366	2945	1	0	143	1011	22646	65
70	66270	257	152	4654	30493	5224	304	2214	1	0	126	872	21973	70
75	54016	149	108	3114	23774	4159	237	1488	1	0	80	667	20239	75
80	36527	69	35	1570	14457	2687	136	749	1	0	38	445	16340	80
85+	18593	27	9	600	6556	1299	57	266	0	0	15	227	9537	85+

NUMBER OF PERSONS SURVIVING TO AGE X IF SPECIFIED CAUSES WERE ELIMINATED

Age (x)	No Causes	Respiratory T. B. (1)	Other Infec. and Paras. (2)	Neoplasms (3)	Cardiovascular (4)	Infl., Pneu., Bronch. (5)	Diarrheal (6)	Certain Degenerative (7)	Maternal (8)	Cert. Dis. of Infancy (9)	Motor Vehicle (10)	Other Violence (11)	Other and Unknown (12)	(1)+(2)	(1)+(2)+(5)+(6)+(8)	(1)+(2)+(5)+(6)+(8)+part of(9)&(12)	(10)+(11)	Age (x)
0	100000	100000	100000	100000	100000	100000	100000	100000	100000	100000	100000	100000	100000	100000	100000	100000	100000	0
1	93257	93264	93474	93267	93265	94424	95163	93276	93257	95484	93258	93285	94237	93480	96584	99863	93286	1
5	90960	90974	91399	90999	90981	92752	93567	91050	90960	93132	90997	91136	92283	91413	95885	99474	91172	5
10	90452	90469	90982	90524	90456	92332	93070	90571	90452	92612	90526	90690	91872	90999	95579	99217	90764	10
15	90197	90223	90758	90289	90271	92103	92814	90328	90197	92350	90290	90466	91677	90784	95393	99052	90559	15
20	89895	89934	90490	90015	90012	91814	92505	90047	89901	92041	89990	90213	91453	90529	95153	98833	90308	20
25	89544	89630	90160	89700	89700	91474	92152	89728	89591	91682	89653	89897	91151	90246	94926	98625	90007	25
30	89098	89274	89734	89296	89305	91045	91702	89317	89193	91225	89216	89488	90769	89910	94661	98351	89607	30
35	88534	88804	89201	88821	88829	90492	91125	88805	88674	90648	88662	88969	90267	89473	94277	98024	89097	35
40	87693	88061	88383	88149	88128	89650	90262	88060	87903	89787	87831	88184	89507	88753	93657	97416	88322	40
45	86455	86917	87173	87289	87109	88474	88993	86985	86690	88519	86619	86993	88403	87639	92570	96321	87157	45
50	85142	85669	85869	86292	86124	87193	87652	85849	85377	87175	85318	85729	87186	86400	91341	95062	85907	50
55	82948	83565	83676	84908	84579	85056	85402	83935	83177	84928	83145	83587	85091	84298	89243	92898	83786	55
60	79799	80473	80536	82517	82482	82015	82178	81235	80019	81704	80012	80513	82143	81216	86198	89762	80728	60
65	74364	75105	75089	78177	79331	76801	76607	76313	74569	76139	74602	75162	76924	75837	80908	84299	75403	65
70	66270	67052	66966	71216	74962	69060	68329	68716	66453	67852	66498	67114	69215	67756	73004	76150	67345	70
75	54016	54751	54623	59548	68347	57299	55756	56688	54165	55306	54244	54891	58086	55367	60791	63638	55122	75
80	36527	37089	36598	41667	56688	40040	37789	38966	36628	37399	36715	37302	42506	37567	42720	45226	37494	80
85+	18593	18909	18851	21998	38990	21475	19293	20198	18645	19037	18705	19144	28216	19171	23040	25269	19259	85+

ADDED YRS OF LIFE

	No Causes	(1)	(2)	(3)	(4)	(5)	(6)	(7)	(8)	(9)	(10)	(11)	(12)	(1)+(2)	(1)+(2)+(5)+(6)+(8)	(1)+(2)+(5)+(6)+(8)+part of(9)&(12)	(10)+(11)
TOTAL		.330	.532	1.673	5.310	2.108	2.001	.871	.107	1.616	.131	.476	3.557	.866	5.222	8.398	.608
WORK	2.220	.185	.077	.496	.483	.113	.016	.255	.084	.000	.034	.134	.257	.263	.478	.556	.168

POPULATION, DEATHS, DEATH RATES FOR ALL CAUSES COMBINED, AND SPECIFIED CAUSES

Age Start of Interval	Midyear Population	Deaths During Year	All Causes	Respiratory T.B.	Other Infec. and Paras.	Neoplasms	Cardiovascular	Infl., Pneu., Bronch.	Diarrheal	Certain Degenerative	Maternal	Cert. Dis. of Infancy	Motor Vehicle	Other Violence	Other and Unknown	Age Start of Interval
0	38468	1875	.04874	.00003	.00135	.00008	.00016	.00454	.00832	.00010	.00000	.02256	.00000	.00055	.01066	0
1	142311	411	.00289	.00003	.00029	.00012	.00006	.00052	.00053	.00006	.00000	.00000	.00003	.00017	.00108	1
5	167002	160	.00096	.00001	.00013	.00006	.00008	.00011	.00002	.00005	.00000	.00000	.00006	.00020	.00023	5
10	163292	119	.00073	.00002	.00004	.00009	.00004	.00004	.00000	.00002	.00000	.00000	.00009	.00024	.00014	10
15	123394	165	.00134	.00006	.00002	.00012	.00008	.00005	.00002	.00005	.00000	.00000	.00019	.00045	.00029	15
20	80307	172	.00214	.00010	.00006	.00016	.00007	.00005	.00000	.00007	.00000	.00000	.00046	.00092	.00024	20
25	62371	121	.00194	.00022	.00000	.00003	.00011	.00008	.00002	.00010	.00000	.00000	.00042	.00074	.00022	25
30	59102	172	.00291	.00046	.00022	.00019	.00003	.00000	.00027	.00000	.00000	.00032	.00085	.00051		30
35	61990	216	.00348	.00035	.00008	.00031	.00050	.00003	.00000	.00034	.00000	.00000	.00021	.00102	.00061	35
40	53430	260	.00487	.00069	.00007	.00060	.00066	.00017	.00002	.00047	.00000	.00000	.00030	.00120	.00069	40
45	54128	320	.00591	.00063	.00015	.00085	.00122	.00015	.00004	.00070	.00000	.00000	.00022	.00120	.00076	45
50	40089	400	.00998	.00132	.00007	.00229	.00274	.00017	.00008	.00080	.00000	.00000	.00035	.00117	.00105	50
55	34626	418	.01207	.00101	.00017	.00280	.00390	.00026	.00006	.00110	.00000	.00000	.00043	.00081	.00153	55
60	29283	571	.01950	.00089	.00031	.00509	.00789	.00024	.00017	.00157	.00000	.00000	.00034	.00079	.00222	60
65	24683	692	.02804	.00126	.00053	.00725	.01045	.00061	.00016	.00280	.00000	.00000	.00041	.00113	.00344	65
70	16476	721	.04376	.00140	.00036	.01062	.01918	.00103	.00012	.00225	.00000	.00000	.00055	.00134	.00692	70
75	10341	552	.05338	.00114	.00058	.01083	.02582	.00155	.00048	.00251	.00000	.00000	.00029	.00116	.00841	75
80	4666	510	.10930	.00171	.00086	.01414	.05851	.00343	.00064	.00471	.00000	.00000	.00021	.00214	.02293	80
85+	4314	823	.19077	.00209	.00162	.01854	.09736	.01043	.00278	.00603	.00000	.00000	.00023	.00394	.04775	85+
ALL	1170273	8678														

	All Causes	Respiratory T.B.	Other Infec. and Paras.	Neoplasms	Cardiovascular	Infl., Pneu., Bronch.	Diarrheal	Certain Degenerative	Maternal	Cert. Dis. of Infancy	Motor Vehicle	Other Violence	Other and Unknown
CRUDE DEATH RATE	.00742	.00031	.00018	.00097	.00189	.00039	.00038	.00037	.00000	.00074	.00020	.00062	.00137
STANDARDIZED RATE (1)	.00647	.00030	.00016	.00079	.00134	.00036	.00038	.00033	.00000	.00079	.00022	.00063	.00117
STANDARDIZED RATE (2)	.00972	.00046	.00017	.00157	.00317	.00038	.00027	.00057	.00000	.00047	.00025	.00076	.00166
GEOMETRIC MEAN	.00858												

LIFE TABLE FOR ALL CAUSES COMBINED

Age (x)	Midyear Population	Deaths During Year	$_nM_x$	$_nq_x$	l_x	$_nd_x$	$_nL_x$	$_nm_x$	$_na_x$	T_x	$_nr_x$	$\overset{\circ}{e}_x$	Age (x)
0	38468	1875	.048742	.046810	100000	4681	96035	.048743	.152861	6739193	.000000	67.392	0
1	142311	411	.002888	.011467	95319	1093	378544	.002887	1.500000	6643158	.000000	69.694	1
5	167002	160	.000958	.004776	94226	450	470005	.000957	2.500000	6264615	.000000	66.485	5
10	163292	119	.000729	.003647	93776	342	468062	.000731	2.607822	5794610	.015540	61.792	10
15	123394	165	.001337	.006711	93434	627	465737	.001346	2.714979	5326548	.056601	57.009	15
20	80307	172	.002142	.010657	92807	989	461617	.002142	2.554769	4860811	.069444	52.375	20
25	62371	121	.001940	.009660	91818	887	456940	.001941	2.576569	4399194	.043571	47.912	25
30	59102	172	.002910	.014462	90931	1315	451506	.002912	2.605038	3942254	.006897	43.354	30
35	61990	216	.003484	.017296	89616	1550	444372	.003488	2.608065	3490748	.006496	38.952	35
40	53430	260	.004866	.024061	88066	2119	435233	.004869	2.594581	3046375	.006594	34.592	40
45	54128	320	.005912	.029227	85947	2512	423865	.005926	2.663134	2611142	.015587	30.381	45
50	40089	400	.009978	.048972	83435	4086	407410	.010029	2.610030	2187278	.033486	26.215	50
55	34626	418	.012072	.058854	79349	4670	385672	.012109	2.628881	1779868	.022812	22.431	55
60	29283	571	.019499	.093400	74679	6975	356844	.019546	2.627121	1394196	.014401	18.669	60
65	24683	692	.028035	.131839	67704	8926	317184	.028141	2.609658	1037352	.022735	15.322	65
70	16476	721	.043761	.198629	58778	11675	265174	.044028	2.540382	720168	.036567	12.252	70
75	10341	552	.053380	.231543	47103	11189	208382	.053695	2.575074	454994	.058798	9.660	75
80	4666	510	.109301	.437350	35914	15707	140650	.111642	2.524697	246611	.058798	6.867	80
85+	4314	823	.190774	1.000000	20207	20207	105921	.190774	5.241798	105921	.000000	5.242	85+

NUMBER OF PERSONS DYING (OUT OF 100,000 AT BIRTH) ABOVE AGE X FROM SPECIFIED CAUSES

Age (x)	All Causes	Respiratory T. B.	Other Infec. and Paras.	Neoplasms	Cardiovascular	Infl., Pneu., Bronch.	Diarrheal	Certain Degenerative	Maternal	Cert. Dis. of Infancy	Motor Vehicle	Other Violence	Other and Unknown	Age (x)
0	100000	4004	1412	16381	39360	3638	1707	5587	0	2167	1863	5929	17952	0
1	95319	4002	1282	16374	39345	3164	908	5577	0	0	1863	5876	16928	1
5	94226	3991	1173	16329	39321	2967	706	5553	0	0	1853	5812	16521	5
10	93776	3986	1111	16300	39284	2914	695	5530	0	0	1825	5717	16414	10
15	93434	3977	1091	16257	39264	2897	695	5522	0	0	1781	5602	16348	15
20	92807	3950	1080	16201	39227	2874	687	5499	0	0	1689	5387	16213	20
25	91818	3903	1051	16128	39196	2851	687	5465	0	0	1474	4958	16105	25
30	90931	3800	1051	16113	39145	2814	680	5420	0	0	1284	4622	16002	30
35	89616	3593	1021	16014	39060	2799	680	5258	0	0	1139	4240	15772	35
40	88066	3421	985	15877	38838	2785	680	5147	0	0	1046	3788	15499	40
45	85947	3119	952	15616	38552	2711	672	4943	0	0	915	3266	15201	45
50	83435	2852	889	15254	38033	2649	656	4645	0	0	821	2758	14878	50
55	79349	2312	859	14312	36906	2577	656	4319	0	0	679	2281	14448	55
60	74679	1923	792	13228	35395	2477	633	3894	0	0	511	1970	13856	60
65	67704	1606	682	11407	32572	2391	572	3332	0	0	390	1689	13063	65
70	58778	1207	514	9099	29243	2197	521	2444	0	0	261	1329	11963	70
75	47103	835	418	6270	24117	1922	488	1849	0	0	116	974	10114	75
80	35914	472	296	4017	18689	1596	386	1323	0	0	57	733	8345	80
85+	20207	221	172	1964	10312	1105	295	638	0	0	25	417	5058	85+

NUMBER OF PERSONS SURVIVING TO AGE X IF SPECIFIED CAUSES WERE ELIMINATED

Age (x)	No Causes	Respiratory T. B. (1)	Other Infec. and Paras. (2)	Neoplasms (3)	Cardiovascular (4)	Infl., Pneu., Bronch. (5)	Diarrheal (6)	Certain Degenerative (7)	Maternal (8)	Cert. Dis. of Infancy (9)	Motor Vehicle (10)	Other Violence (11)	Other and Unknown (12)	(1)+(2)	(1)+(2)+(5)+(6)+(8)	(1)+(2)+(5)+(6)+(8)+part of(9)&(12)	(10)+(11)	Age (x)
0	100000	100000	100000	100000	100000	100000	100000	100000	100000	100000	100000	100000	100000	100000	100000	100000	100000	0
1	95319	95321	95446	95326	95334	95783	96102	95329	95319	97458	95319	95971	96324	95448	96701	99727	95371	1
5	94226	94239	94460	94278	94264	94882	95203	94260	94226	96341	94236	94341	95629	94473	96117	99447	94351	5
10	93776	93794	94071	93856	93851	94482	94759	93832	93776	95880	93814	93985	95281	94089	95791	99153	94023	10
15	93434	93461	93748	93557	93529	94154	94414	93498	93434	95531	93516	93758	95000	93775	95489	98852	93840	15
20	92807	92860	93130	92985	92938	93545	93788	92894	92807	94890	92908	93344	94500	93184	94918	98281	93518	20
25	91818	91918	92166	92067	91979	92572	92789	91938	91818	93879	92204	92779	93602	92266	94007	97351	93169	25
30	90931	91132	91276	91192	91141	91715	91899	91094	90931	92972	91503	92221	92802	91478	93249	96586	92801	30
35	89616	90021	89986	89972	89908	90403	90570	89898	89616	91627	90324	91273	91694	90392	92157	95512	91995	35
40	88066	88635	88465	88553	88574	88654	88994	88494	88066	90042	88855	90152	90385	89037	90790	94145	90960	40
45	85947	86803	86370	86682	86727	86789	86870	86567	85947	87876	86848	88512	88513	87230	89031	92394	89440	45
50	83435	84532	83908	84509	84710	84314	84347	84333	83435	85307	84403	86441	86254	85011	86846	90191	87444	50
55	79349	80927	79828	81307	81686	80256	80217	80525	79349	81130	80410	82690	82465	81416	83247	86533	83796	55
60	74679	76549	75195	77667	78404	75631	75518	76205	74679	76355	75842	78138	78210	77078	78938	82143	79355	60
65	67704	69709	68278	72183	73959	68650	68524	69636	67704	69223	68875	71120	71700	70299	72145	75152	72350	65
70	58778	60901	59433	64999	67688	59783	59537	61309	58778	60097	59917	62096	63344	61580	63443	66207	63299	70
75	47103	49149	47714	54953	59753	48160	47742	49685	47103	48160	48147	50096	52577	49787	51594	53991	51207	75
80	35914	37803	36488	44232	52014	37012	36491	38367	35914	36720	36761	38418	41849	38407	40217	42261	39325	80
85+	20207	21466	20623	26830	35771	21202	20600	22136	20207	20660	20708	21868	26558	21908	23435	24856	22410	85+

ADDED YRS OF LIFE

	No Causes	(1)	(2)	(3)	(4)	(5)	(6)	(7)	(8)	(9)	(10)	(11)	(12)	(1)+(2)	(1)+(2)+(5)+(6)+(8)	(1)+(2)+(5)+(6)+(8)+part	(10)+(11)
TOTAL		.857	.393	2.451	6.408	.836	.771	.541	.000	1.509	.595	1.749	3.308	1.259	2.932	5.685	2.370
WORK	4.094	.401	.066	.495	.615	.088	.014	.303	.000	.000	.353	.950	.534	.468	.571	.667	1.314

POPULATION, DEATHS, DEATH RATES FOR ALL CAUSES COMBINED, AND SPECIFIED CAUSES

Age Start of Interval	Midyear Population	Deaths During Year	All Causes	Respiratory T. B.	Other Infec. and Paras.	Neoplasms	Cardiovascular	Infl., Pneu., Bronch.	Diarrheal	Certain Degenerative	Maternal	Cert. Dis. of Infancy	Motor Vehicle	Other Violence	Other and Unknown	Age Start of Interval
0	37898	1439	.03797	.00003	.00071	.00011	.00034	.00385	.00657	.00005	.00000	.01718	.00000	.00037	.00876	0
1	137990	445	.00322	.00001	.00045	.00008	.00004	.00069	.00063	.00005	.00000	.00001	.00002	.00017	.00107	1
5	162621	125	.00077	.00001	.00013	.00004	.00001	.00007	.00004	.00007	.00000	.00000	.00001	.00010	.00028	5
10	159968	74	.00046	.00002	.00003	.00007	.00005	.00002	.00001	.00005	.00000	.00000	.00000	.00012	.00011	10
15	125044	96	.00077	.00004	.00002	.00008	.00009	.00002	.00001	.00001	.00004	.00000	.00002	.00018	.00026	15
20	92454	107	.00116	.00013	.00002	.00008	.00011	.00002	.00002	.00004	.00006	.00000	.00002	.00036	.00029	20
25	74688	114	.00153	.00035	.00005	.00011	.00013	.00000	.00000	.00008	.00009	.00000	.00003	.00033	.00035	25
30	68436	118	.00172	.00034	.00003	.00019	.00028	.00006	.00003	.00010	.00007	.00000	.00007	.00034	.00022	30
35	69509	165	.00237	.00055	.00000	.00043	.00037	.00000	.00001	.00016	.00012	.00000	.00004	.00020	.00049	35
40	54609	171	.00313	.00048	.00004	.00062	.00070	.00011	.00002	.00027	.00004	.00000	.00002	.00020	.00064	40
45	52135	206	.00395	.00052	.00004	.00115	.00104	.00012	.00000	.00027	.00004	.00000	.00004	.00023	.00052	45
50	35600	264	.00742	.00073	.00014	.00228	.00177	.00014	.00006	.00070	.00000	.00000	.00008	.00020	.00132	50
55	31667	243	.00767	.00047	.00009	.00246	.00253	.00025	.00009	.00060	.00000	.00000	.00003	.00013	.00101	55
60	29158	390	.01338	.00089	.00017	.00408	.00425	.00045	.00003	.00123	.00000	.00000	.00000	.00017	.00199	60
65	23728	440	.01854	.00097	.00008	.00362	.00822	.00038	.00017	.00148	.00000	.00000	.00008	.00055	.00299	65
70	15230	506	.03322	.00105	.00046	.00762	.01530	.00131	.00026	.00289	.00000	.00000	.00000	.00053	.00381	70
75	11030	440	.03989	.00063	.00036	.00617	.02140	.00163	.00036	.00209	.00000	.00000	.00027	.00062	.00617	75
80	5523	510	.09234	.00109	.00000	.01050	.05269	.00326	.00036	.00561	.00000	.00000	.00000	.00018	.00127	.01738	80
85+	6997	1260	.18008	.00186	.00057	.01201	.09904	.01143	.00229	.00529	.00000	.00000	.00000	.00314	.04445	85+
ALL	1194285	7113															

	All Causes	Respiratory T. B.	Other Infec. and Paras.	Neoplasms	Cardiovascular	Infl., Pneu., Bronch.	Diarrheal	Certain Degenerative	Maternal	Cert. Dis. of Infancy	Motor Vehicle	Other Violence	Other and Unknown
CRUDE DEATH RATE	.00596	.00025	.00013	.00074	.00177	.00037	.00032	.00028	.00003	.00055	.00003	.00024	.00124
STANDARDIZED RATE (1)	.00483	.00024	.00013	.00063	.00106	.00032	.00033	.00023	.00003	.00061	.00003	.00023	.00099
STANDARDIZED RATE (2)	.00730	.00035	.00012	.00117	.00259	.00036	.00024	.00043	.00003	.00036	.00004	.00027	.00135
GEOMETRIC MEAN	.00616												

LIFE TABLE FOR ALL CAUSES COMBINED

Age (x)	Midyear Population	Deaths During Year	$_nM_x$	$_nq_x$	l_x	$_nd_x$	$_nL_x$	$_nm_x$	$_na_x$	T_x	$_nr_x$	$\overset{\circ}{e}_x$	Age (x)
0	37898	1439	.037970	.036760	100000	3676	96819	.037968	.134550	7202402	.000000	72.024	0
1	137990	445	.003225	.012801	96324	1233	382214	.003226	1.500000	7105584	.000000	73.768	1
5	162621	125	.000769	.003838	95091	365	474543	.000769	2.500000	6723370	.000000	70.705	5
10	159968	74	.000463	.002301	94726	218	473085	.000461	2.500000	6248828	.014639	65.967	10
15	125044	96	.000768	.003862	94508	365	471696	.000774	2.686644	5775743	.044997	61.114	15
20	92454	107	.001157	.005789	94143	545	469425	.001161	2.633410	5304047	.051911	56.340	20
25	74688	114	.001526	.007628	93598	714	466258	.001531	2.573821	4834622	.038660	51.653	25
30	68436	118	.001724	.008591	92884	798	462503	.001725	2.597901	4368364	.010559	47.030	30
35	69509	165	.002374	.011826	92086	1089	457837	.002379	2.618610	3905861	.017371	42.415	35
40	54609	171	.003131	.015583	90997	1418	451581	.003140	2.599171	3448024	.022002	37.892	40
45	52135	206	.003951	.019592	89579	1764	443860	.003974	2.712821	2996444	.032352	33.450	45
50	35600	264	.007416	.036668	87815	3220	431323	.007465	2.592650	2552583	.046387	29.068	50
55	31667	243	.007674	.037780	84595	3196	415416	.007693	2.634739	2121260	.019461	25.075	55
60	29158	390	.013375	.064952	81399	5287	394530	.013401	2.642330	1705844	.011652	20.957	60
65	23728	440	.018543	.089447	76112	6808	364675	.018669	2.666685	1311314	.036982	17.229	65
70	15230	506	.033224	.154863	69304	10734	320506	.033491	2.576470	946639	.042451	13.659	70
75	11030	440	.039891	.183507	58570	10748	267564	.040170	2.647392	626134	.050624	10.690	75
80	5523	510	.092341	.383464	47822	18338	194840	.094118	2.585865	358569	.050624	7.498	80
85+	6997	1260	.180077	1.000000	29484	29484	163730	.180077	5.553175	163730	.000000	5.553	85+

NUMBER OF PERSONS DYING (OUT OF 100,000 AT BIRTH) ABOVE AGE X FROM SPECIFIED CAUSES

Age (x)	All Causes	Respira-tory T. B.	Other Infec. and Paras.	Neo-plasms	Cardio-vascular	Infl., Pneu., Bronch.	Diar-rheal	Certain Degen-erative	Maternal	Cert. Dis. of Infancy	Motor Vehicle	Other Violence	Other and Unknown	Age (x)
0	100000	3372	947	14430	45218	4688	1711	5566	214	1666	358	2622	19208	0
1	96324	3370	878	14420	45185	4315	1075	5561	214	3	358	2587	18358	1
5	95091	3364	706	14389	45169	4052	834	5542	214	0	350	2520	17951	5
10	94726	3358	645	14369	45163	4020	813	5510	214	0	344	2473	17817	10
15	94508	3349	633	14336	45139	4011	811	5486	214	0	344	2417	17768	15
20	94143	3330	622	14258	45098	4003	807	5482	195	0	332	2329	17647	20
25	93598	3268	611	14263	45047	3993	797	5462	164	0	322	2161	17510	25
30	92884	3104	586	14213	44985	3993	797	5424	120	0	310	2005	17347	30
35	92086	2949	573	14125	44856	3966	783	5377	86	0	276	1849	17246	35
40	90997	2698	573	13926	44684	3966	777	5304	34	0	256	1757	17022	40
45	89579	2483	556	13644	44368	3916	768	5180	17	0	248	1666	16733	45
50	87815	2253	535	13128	43906	3865	768	5060	0	0	231	1564	16501	50
55	84595	1937	478	12140	43136	3804	744	4754	0	0	194	1480	15928	55
60	81399	1740	438	11114	42083	3699	704	4505	0	0	181	1427	15508	60
65	76112	1388	371	9502	40400	3523	691	4017	0	0	140	1359	14721	65
70	69304	1034	340	8176	37375	3383	628	3475	0	0	110	1158	13625	70
75	58570	698	191	5717	32426	2957	544	2544	0	0	110	989	12394	75
80	47822	530	95	4074	26644	2518	446	1986	0	0	36	770	10723	80
85+	29484	304	94	1966	16216	1872	374	866	0	0	0	515	7277	85+

NUMBER OF PERSONS SURVIVING TO AGE X IF SPECIFIED CAUSES WERE ELIMINATED

Age (x)	No Causes	Respira-tory T. B.	Other Infec. and Paras.	Neo-plasms	Cardio-vascular	Infl., Pneu., Bronch.	Diar-rheal	Certain Degen-erative	Maternal	Cert. Dis. of Infancy	Motor Vehicle	Other Violence	Other and Unknown	(1) + (2)	(1) + (2) + (5) + (6) + (8)	(1)+(2)+ (5)+(6)+ (8)+part of(9)&(12)	(10) + (11)	Age (x)
		(1)	(2)	(3)	(4)	(5)	(6)	(7)	(8)	(9)	(10)	(11)	(12)					
0	100000	100000	100000	100000	100000	100000	100000	100000	100000	100000	100000	100000	100000	100000	100000	100000	100000	0
1	96324	96326	96392	96334	96356	96691	96950	96329	96324	97970	96324	96358	97162	96394	97390	99733	96358	1
5	95091	95099	95329	95131	95139	95716	95950	95115	95091	96719	95099	95192	96327	95337	96831	99513	95199	5
10	94726	94740	95024	94786	94780	95380	95603	94782	94726	96348	94740	94873	96093	95038	96581	99329	94887	10
15	94508	94531	94818	94601	94586	95170	95385	94587	94508	96126	94522	94711	95921	94840	96391	99144	94725	15
20	94143	94185	94462	94274	94261	94811	95021	94226	94162	95755	94169	94433	95673	94504	96081	98857	94459	20
25	93598	93701	93926	93763	93766	94272	94481	93701	93648	95200	93634	94055	95258	94030	95651	98458	94090	25
30	92884	93150	93235	93098	93113	93553	93760	93024	92977	94474	92931	93493	94697	93502	95159	98024	93541	30
35	92086	92505	92447	92386	92442	92776	92969	92271	92212	93662	92167	92847	93986	92867	94590	97475	92928	35
40	90997	91662	91354	91492	91521	91679	91875	91253	91174	92555	91057	91841	93102	92021	93787	96732	91941	40
45	89579	90449	89947	90348	90410	90300	90453	89954	89770	91113	89685	90501	91945	90820	92641	95633	90608	45
50	87815	88898	88193	89086	89093	88573	88671	88303	88019	89318	87936	88821	90371	89280	91140	94134	88943	50
55	84595	85952	85019	86809	86597	85385	85444	85367	84791	86043	84748	85647	87638	86383	88269	91275	85802	55
60	81399	82901	81846	84568	84389	82264	82255	82389	81588	82793	81559	82464	84754	83357	85326	88293	82626	60
65	76112	77864	76595	80709	80615	77092	76926	77516	76289	77415	76301	77175	80046	78358	80402	83310	77366	65
70	69304	71244	69774	74842	76529	70333	70106	71111	69465	70490	69505	70466	73992	71728	73805	76593	70670	70
75	58570	60526	59105	65732	69900	59838	59326	60979	58706	59573	58740	59710	63751	61079	63353	65879	59883	75
80	47822	49574	48345	55345	63660	49263	48528	50313	47933	48641	48028	48954	53726	50116	52510	54755	49164	80
85+	29484	30747	29807	36073	51674	30894	29976	31950	29552	29989	29639	30385	36275	31084	33191	34811	30545	85+

ADDED YRS OF LIFE																	
TOTAL		.811	.344	2.378	7.719	.902	.754	.841	.097	1.231	.094	.704	3.448	1.161	2.982	5.497	.800
WORK	2.761	.368	.042	.534	.522	.057	.021	.177	.071	.000	.042	.302	.501	.411	.561	.701	.345

POPULATION, DEATHS, DEATH RATES FOR ALL CAUSES COMBINED, AND SPECIFIED CAUSES

Age Start of Interval	Midyear Population	Deaths During Year	All Causes	Respiratory T. B.	Other Infec. and Paras.	Neo-plasms	Cardio-vascular	Infl., Pneu., Bronch.	Diar-rheal	Certain Degen-erative	Maternal	Cert. Dis. of Infancy	Motor Vehicle	Other Violence	Other and Unknown	Age Start of Interval
0	39000	2375	.06090	.00000	.00138	.00013	.00028	.00523	.01077	.00010	.00000	.03151	.00003	.00072	.01074	0
1	142200	360	.00253	.00000	.00034	.00009	.00006	.00048	.00059	.00001	.00000	.00000	.00006	.00017	.00075	1
5	166700	134	.00080	.00000	.00010	.00006	.00004	.00004	.00006	.00002	.00000	.00000	.00011	.00018	.00020	5
10	161100	105	.00065	.00001	.00005	.00002	.00006	.00001	.00001	.00002	.00000	.00000	.00013	.00023	.00012	10
15	123200	179	.00145	.00002	.00002	.00010	.00006	.00005	.00000	.00005	.00000	.00000	.00030	.00054	.00032	15
20	103000	190	.00184	.00009	.00004	.00012	.00010	.00007	.00001	.00009	.00000	.00000	.00038	.00062	.00034	20
25	81200	170	.00209	.00005	.00002	.00009	.00020	.00000	.00000	.00020	.00000	.00000	.00038	.00090	.00026	25
30	68400	193	.00282	.00019	.00003	.00028	.00025	.00007	.00001	.00025	.00000	.00000	.00044	.00096	.00034	30
35	63400	227	.00358	.00032	.00003	.00021	.00044	.00011	.00000	.00039	.00000	.00000	.00028	.00104	.00076	35
40	63800	297	.00466	.00055	.00009	.00066	.00080	.00009	.00002	.00067	.00000	.00000	.00022	.00094	.00061	40
45	58400	370	.00634	.00051	.00009	.00094	.00128	.00014	.00005	.00075	.00000	.00000	.00031	.00134	.00092	45
50	51100	480	.00939	.00051	.00016	.00204	.00256	.00016	.00006	.00127	.00000	.00000	.00045	.00104	.00115	50
55	39000	519	.01331	.00079	.00013	.00300	.00436	.00028	.00000	.00156	.00000	.00000	.00036	.00118	.00164	55
60	31500	625	.01984	.00086	.00051	.00457	.00759	.00048	.00003	.00194	.00000	.00000	.00038	.00108	.00241	60
65	26500	820	.03094	.00109	.00030	.00660	.01340	.00075	.00030	.00264	.00000	.00000	.00045	.00117	.00423	65
70	20200	819	.04054	.00114	.00035	.00777	.01916	.00178	.00050	.00302	.00000	.00000	.00030	.00094	.00559	70
75	13274	773	.05823	.00158	.00045	.01032	.02938	.00279	.00015	.00331	.00000	.00000	.00068	.00151	.00806	75
80	5989	689	.11504	.00150	.00050	.01703	.05811	.00518	.00083	.00484	.00000	.00000	.00017	.00200	.02488	80
85+	5537	1121	.20246	.00144	.00054	.02149	.11089	.01318	.00108	.00578	.00000	.00000	.00036	.00235	.04533	85+
ALL	1263500	10446														

	All Causes	Respiratory T. B.	Other Infec. and Paras.	Neo-plasms	Cardio-vascular	Infl., Pneu., Bronch.	Diar-rheal	Certain Degen-erative	Maternal	Cert. Dis. of Infancy	Motor Vehicle	Other Violence	Other and Unknown
CRUDE DEATH RATE	.00827	.00023	.00016	.00099	.00227	.00044	.00044	.00047	.00000	.00097	.00025	.00065	.00140
STANDARDIZED RATE (1)	.00692	.00020	.00016	.00074	.00144	.00038	.00048	.00039	.00000	.00111	.00025	.00064	.00115
STANDARDIZED RATE (2)	.01018	.00032	.00016	.00148	.00340	.00046	.00032	.00068	.00000	.00065	.00028	.00077	.00166
GEOMETRIC MEAN	.00863												

LIFE TABLE FOR ALL CAUSES COMBINED

Age (x)	Midyear Population	Deaths During Year	$_nM_x$	$_nq_x$	l_x	$_nd_x$	$_nL_x$	$_nm_x$	$_na_x$	T_x	$_nr_x$	$\overset{\circ}{e}_x$	Age (x)
0	39000	2375	.060897	.057980	100000	5798	95208	.060898	.173526	6647402	.000000	66.474	0
1	142200	360	.002532	.010063	94202	948	374438	.002532	1.500000	6552194	.000000	69.555	1
5	166700	134	.000804	.004000	93254	373	465338	.000802	2.500000	6177756	.000000	66.247	5
10	161100	105	.000652	.003262	92881	303	463710	.000653	2.707646	5712419	.019875	61.503	10
15	123200	179	.001453	.007291	92578	675	461316	.001463	2.667593	5248708	.038655	56.695	15
20	103000	190	.001845	.009205	91903	846	457457	.001849	2.567967	4787393	.039281	52.092	20
25	81200	170	.002094	.010444	91057	951	452995	.002099	2.592227	4329935	.041092	47.552	25
30	68400	193	.002822	.014061	90106	1267	447493	.002831	2.603058	3876940	.029582	43.026	30
35	63400	227	.003580	.017762	88839	1578	440405	.003583	2.598094	3429447	.009781	38.603	35
40	63800	297	.004655	.023034	87261	2010	431506	.004658	2.612666	2989042	.003334	34.254	40
45	58400	370	.006336	.031261	85251	2665	419967	.006346	2.640557	2557536	.010322	30.000	45
50	51100	480	.009393	.046110	82586	3808	403919	.009428	2.633655	2137569	.024845	25.883	50
55	39000	519	.013308	.064840	78778	5108	381786	.013379	2.630473	1733650	.035104	22.007	55
60	31500	625	.019841	.095113	73670	7007	351771	.019919	2.634003	1351863	.022778	18.350	60
65	26500	820	.030943	.144233	66663	9615	310014	.031015	2.576595	1000092	.014917	15.002	65
70	20200	819	.040545	.184792	57048	10542	259375	.040644	2.546461	690078	.019153	12.096	70
75	13274	773	.058234	.257300	46506	11966	203679	.058749	2.588950	430703	.049361	9.261	75
80	5989	689	.115044	.453127	34540	15651	133724	.117039	2.509704	227024	.049361	6.573	80
85+	5537	1121	.202456	1.000000	18889	18889	93299	.202456	4.939340	93299	.000000	4.939	85+

NUMBER OF PERSONS DYING (OUT OF 100,000 AT BIRTH) ABOVE AGE X FROM SPECIFIED CAUSES

Age (x)	All Causes	Respiratory T. B.	Other Infec. and Paras.	Neoplasms	Cardiovascular	Infl., Pneu., Bronch.	Diarrheal	Certain Degenerative	Maternal	Cert. Dis. of Infancy	Motor Vehicle	Other Violence	Other and Unknown	Age (x)
0	100000	2865	1157	15223	40267	4481	1820	6360	0	3000	2036	5788	17003	0
1	94202	2865	1025	15211	40240	3983	794	6350	0	0	2033	5720	15981	1
5	93254	2865	899	15177	40219	3804	573	6348	0	0	2012	5656	15701	5
10	92881	2865	854	15149	40202	3784	545	6339	0	0	1962	5573	15608	10
15	92578	2862	832	15140	40176	3778	543	6330	0	0	1902	5466	15549	15
20	91903	2854	820	15095	40150	3756	543	6308	0	0	1762	5217	15398	20
25	91057	2814	803	15042	40105	3725	538	6267	0	0	1588	4932	15243	25
30	90106	2791	791	15002	40015	3725	538	6177	0	0	1415	4523	15129	30
35	88839	2706	778	14877	39904	3692	532	6066	0	0	1219	4091	14974	35
40	87261	2566	764	14787	39709	3643	532	5892	0	0	1094	3632	14642	40
45	85251	2330	724	14503	39364	3603	525	5601	0	0	1000	3226	14375	45
50	82586	2114	688	14106	38823	3545	503	5284	0	0	870	2665	13988	50
55	78778	1908	624	13279	37781	3481	480	4768	0	0	688	2247	13522	55
60	73670	1603	575	12127	36104	3373	480	4169	0	0	551	1796	12892	60
65	66663	1301	396	10513	33421	3205	468	3486	0	0	417	1417	12039	65
70	57048	962	302	8463	29256	2970	374	2666	0	0	277	1054	10724	70
75	46506	666	212	6443	24271	2505	246	1882	0	0	200	810	9271	75
80	34540	343	120	4328	18229	1932	216	1206	0	0	61	501	7604	80
85+	18889	135	51	2005	10346	1230	101	539	0	0	34	219	4229	85+

NUMBER OF PERSONS SURVIVING TO AGE X IF SPECIFIED CAUSES WERE ELIMINATED

Age (x)	No Causes	Respiratory T. B. (1)	Other Infec. and Paras. (2)	Neoplasms (3)	Cardiovascular (4)	Infl., Pneu., Bronch. (5)	Diarrheal (6)	Certain Degenerative (7)	Maternal (8)	Cert. Dis. of Infancy (9)	Motor Vehicle (10)	Other Violence (11)	Other and Unknown (12)	(1)+(2)	(1)+(2)+(5)+(6)+(8)	(1)+(2)+(5)+(6)+(8)+part of(9)&(12)	(10)+(11)	Age (x)
0	100000	100000	100000	100000	100000	100000	100000	100000	100000	100000	100000	100000	100000	100000	100000	100000	100000	0
1	94202	94202	94330	94214	94228	94687	95203	94212	94202	97159	94205	94268	95199	94330	95823	99597	94271	1
5	93254	93254	93507	93299	93301	93913	94467	93266	93254	96181	93278	93383	94523	93507	95392	99383	93407	5
10	92881	92881	93178	92954	92945	93557	94118	92902	92881	95796	92955	93093	94239	93178	95106	99118	93166	10
15	92578	92581	92896	92660	92667	93258	93813	92607	92578	95484	92711	92896	93991	92896	94829	98838	93030	15
20	91903	91914	92230	92029	92018	92600	93129	91954	91903	94788	92175	92468	93459	92241	94181	98175	92742	20
25	91057	91108	91398	91235	91216	91779	92277	91149	91057	93915	91501	91903	92756	91449	93409	97392	92350	25
30	90106	90179	90456	90322	90353	90820	91313	90286	90106	92934	90718	91354	91902	90529	92469	96417	91975	30
35	88839	88996	89197	89176	89193	89576	90035	89127	88839	91627	89638	90506	90767	89354	91308	95228	91320	35
40	87261	87554	87626	87682	87803	88034	88436	87717	87261	90000	88171	89363	89492	87921	89894	93810	90295	40
45	85251	85772	85648	85945	86124	86046	86406	85986	85251	87927	86234	87716	87701	86171	88152	92046	88727	45
50	82586	83304	83006	83654	83972	83414	83726	83614	82586	85178	83668	85543	85353	83728	85735	89582	86664	50
55	78778	79666	79241	80619	81142	79631	79889	80270	78778	81251	79990	82022	81885	80135	82144	85883	83284	55
60	73670	74799	74151	76540	77571	74573	74709	75657	73670	75982	74938	77158	77215	75288	77285	80872	78486	60
65	66663	67976	67270	70873	72935	67643	67615	69131	66663	68755	67940	70197	70726	68595	70596	73969	71541	65
70	57048	58491	57654	62696	66777	58108	57951	59949	57048	58839	58272	60425	61829	59113	61164	64212	61721	70
75	46506	47956	47082	53147	59566	47801	47359	49617	46506	47956	47574	49491	51843	48550	50817	53511	50628	75
80	34540	35902	35047	41594	51755	36010	35199	37470	34540	35624	35455	37039	40143	36429	38705	40925	38021	80
85+	18889	19792	19217	24879	38359	20234	19335	21025	18889	19482	19410	20477	25004	20136	22079	23617	21042	85+

ADDED YRS OF LIFE

	No Causes	(1)	(2)	(3)	(4)	(5)	(6)	(7)	(8)	(9)	(10)	(11)	(12)	(1)+(2)	(1)+(2)+(5)+(6)+(8)	part	(10)+(11)
TOTAL		.548	.364	2.183	6.627	.877	.939	1.085	.000	2.081	.657	1.719	3.095	.918	2.794	5.949	2.406
WORK	4.108	.241	.056	.487	.651	.086	.012	.392	.000	.000	.381	.948	.575	.298	.397	.470	1.340

POPULATION, DEATHS, DEATH RATES FOR ALL CAUSES COMBINED, AND SPECIFIED CAUSES

Age Start of Interval	Midyear Population	Deaths During Year	All Causes	Respiratory T.B.	Other Infec. and Paras.	Neoplasms	Cardiovascular	Infl., Pneu., Bronch.	Diarrheal	Certain Degenerative	Maternal	Cert. Dis. of Infancy	Motor Vehicle	Other Violence	Other and Unknown	Age Start of Interval
0	38000	1709	.04497	.00003	.00132	.00003	.00018	.00408	.00897	.00005	.00000	.02076	.00000	.00058	.00897	0
1	138100	387	.00280	.00002	.00035	.00007	.00004	.00059	.00064	.00001	.00000	.00001	.00004	.00014	.00089	1
5	163900	88	.00054	.00000	.00007	.00003	.00004	.00005	.00004	.00003	.00000	.00000	.00008	.00004	.00016	5
10	157100	65	.00041	.00000	.00003	.00004	.00006	.00001	.00000	.00005	.00000	.00000	.00003	.00008	.00012	10
15	129200	103	.00080	.00002	.00002	.00009	.00006	.00005	.00000	.00003	.00005	.00000	.00005	.00019	.00024	15
20	107700	91	.00084	.00006	.00003	.00008	.00011	.00005	.00000	.00003	.00008	.00000	.00005	.00021	.00015	20
25	94500	115	.00122	.00012	.00004	.00007	.00016	.00005	.00001	.00006	.00007	.00000	.00006	.00025	.00031	25
30	86600	117	.00135	.00018	.00005	.00022	.00020	.00005	.00002	.00012	.00008	.00000	.00007	.00012	.00025	30
35	76200	152	.00199	.00025	.00004	.00038	.00030	.00007	.00001	.00022	.00007	.00000	.00005	.00026	.00034	35
40	66200	161	.00243	.00030	.00005	.00053	.00050	.00006	.00000	.00017	.00008	.00000	.00006	.00015	.00054	40
45	59100	206	.00349	.00046	.00003	.00107	.00074	.00007	.00002	.00041	.00000	.00000	.00005	.00015	.00049	45
50	49600	279	.00562	.00030	.00008	.00169	.00161	.00014	.00002	.00054	.00002	.00000	.00004	.00014	.00103	50
55	37400	283	.00757	.00029	.00011	.00214	.00238	.00019	.00003	.00094	.00000	.00000	.00003	.00019	.00128	55
60	31800	439	.01381	.00057	.00016	.00362	.00506	.00019	.00006	.00167	.00000	.00000	.00006	.00019	.00223	60
65	26000	556	.02138	.00038	.00015	.00465	.01012	.00058	.00004	.00169	.00000	.00000	.00012	.00027	.00338	65
70	19800	558	.02818	.00056	.00020	.00500	.01490	.00076	.00005	.00192	.00000	.00000	.00015	.00030	.00434	70
75	12880	569	.04418	.00039	.00023	.00699	.02189	.00148	.00039	.00427	.00000	.00000	.00039	.00085	.00730	75
80	6449	676	.10482	.00124	.00047	.01209	.05830	.00481	.00105	.00574	.00000	.00000	.00031	.00171	.01907	80
85+	8171	1566	.19165	.00147	.00061	.01322	.10953	.01114	.00306	.00538	.00000	.00000	.00037	.00465	.04222	85+
ALL	1308700	8120														
CRUDE DEATH RATE			.00620	.00015	.00013	.00074	.00200	.00036	.00037	.00032	.00003	.00060	.00006	.00021	.00123	
STANDARDIZED RATE (1)			.00485	.00013	.00013	.00057	.00109	.00031	.00041	.00025	.00003	.00073	.00006	.00018	.00096	
STANDARDIZED RATE (2)			.00737	.00020	.00012	.00109	.00273	.00035	.00028	.00048	.00003	.00043	.00007	.00018	.00137	
GEOMETRIC MEAN			.00563													

LIFE TABLE FOR ALL CAUSES COMBINED

Age (x)	Midyear Population	Deaths During Year	$_nM_x$	$_nq_x$	l_x	$_nd_x$	$_nL_x$	$_nm_x$	$_na_x$	T_x	$_nr_x$	$\overset{\circ}{e}_x$	Age (x)
0	38000	1709	.044974	.043310	100000	4331	96303	.044972	.146455	7207656	.000000	72.077	0
1	138100	387	.002802	.011132	95669	1065	380014	.002803	1.500000	7111352	.000000	74.333	1
5	163900	88	.000537	.002674	94604	253	472388	.000536	2.500000	6731339	.000000	71.153	5
10	157100	65	.000414	.002077	94351	196	471291	.000416	2.630740	6258951	.015179	66.337	10
15	129200	103	.000797	.003993	94155	376	469877	.000800	2.610816	5787661	.032785	61.470	15
20	107700	91	.000845	.004223	93779	396	467945	.000846	2.601010	5317784	.032559	56.705	20
25	94500	115	.001217	.006082	93383	568	465543	.001220	2.584360	4849839	.023731	51.935	25
30	86600	117	.001351	.006745	92815	626	462583	.001353	2.616480	4384296	.019968	47.237	30
35	76200	152	.001995	.009958	92189	918	458750	.002001	2.608932	3921713	.024100	42.540	35
40	66200	161	.002432	.012118	91271	1106	453725	.002438	2.621873	3462963	.023369	37.942	40
45	59100	206	.003486	.017357	90165	1565	447197	.003500	2.681976	3009239	.022044	33.375	45
50	49600	279	.005625	.027741	88600	2473	437164	.005657	2.639928	2562041	.036252	28.917	50
55	37400	283	.007567	.037456	86127	3226	423216	.007623	2.700156	2124878	.038535	24.671	55
60	31800	439	.013805	.067225	82901	5573	401544	.013879	2.674390	1701662	.025786	20.526	60
65	26000	556	.021385	.102046	77328	7891	367669	.021462	2.595890	1300117	.024500	16.813	65
70	19800	558	.028182	.132566	69437	9205	325073	.028317	2.597796	932448	.033356	13.429	70
75	12880	569	.044177	.202749	60232	12212	272562	.044739	2.690949	607376	.054936	10.084	75
80	6449	676	.104822	.424781	48020	20398	190289	.107195	2.558043	334414	.054936	6.964	80
85+	8171	1566	.191653	1.000000	27622	27622	144125	.191653	5.217752	144125	.000000	5.218	85+

NUMBER OF PERSONS DYING (OUT OF 100,000 AT BIRTH) ABOVE AGE X FROM SPECIFIED CAUSES

Age (x)	All Causes	Respiratory T. B.	Other Infec. and Paras.	Neoplasms	Cardiovascular	Infl., Pneu., Bronch.	Diarrheal	Certain Degenerative	Maternal	Cert. Dis. of Infancy	Motor Vehicle	Other Violence	Other and Unknown	Age (x)
0	100000	2016	931	13827	46576	4452	1991	6156	207	2002	617	2440	18785	0
1	95669	2013	804	13824	46558	4059	1127	6151	207	3	617	2384	17922	1
5	94604	2005	669	13799	46542	3836	882	6145	207	0	603	2332	17584	5
10	94351	2005	638	13785	46524	3810	865	6131	207	0	566	2312	17508	10
15	94155	2005	626	13767	46497	3804	865	6107	207	0	551	2276	17450	15
20	93779	1994	619	13727	46468	3783	865	6092	184	0	525	2184	17338	20
25	93383	1967	605	13688	46416	3761	865	6079	145	0	503	2084	17270	25
30	92815	1913	586	13653	46342	3736	860	6049	111	0	474	1966	17125	30
35	92189	1827	564	13551	46251	3715	849	5996	73	0	442	1913	17008	35
40	91271	1713	546	13375	46112	3685	843	5893	43	0	418	1792	16851	40
45	90165	1575	526	13134	45884	3657	843	5818	9	0	390	1724	16605	45
50	88600	1371	511	12655	45549	3627	836	5635	9	0	368	1656	16383	50
55	86127	1239	475	11911	44839	3565	827	5396	0	0	350	1594	15931	55
60	82901	1114	430	11000	43822	3485	816	4996	0	0	339	1515	15384	60
65	77328	886	366	9542	41773	3409	790	4325	0	0	313	1439	14485	65
70	69437	745	310	7828	38035	3196	776	3702	0	0	271	1340	13234	70
75	60232	564	244	6199	33167	2948	759	3074	0	0	221	1240	11816	75
80	48020	458	180	4277	27110	2537	651	1896	0	0	114	1003	9794	80
85+	27622	212	88	1905	15787	1605	441	776	0	0	53	670	6085	85+

NUMBER OF PERSONS SURVIVING TO AGE X IF SPECIFIED CAUSES WERE ELIMINATED

Age (x)	No Causes	Respiratory T. B.	Other Infec. and Paras.	Neoplasms	Cardiovascular	Infl., Pneu., Bronch.	Diarrheal	Certain Degenerative	Maternal	Cert. Dis. of Infancy	Motor Vehicle	Other Violence	Other and Unknown	(1) + (2)	(1) + (2) + (5) + (6) + (8)	(1)+(2)+ (5)+(6)+ (8)+part of(9)&(12)	(10) + (11)	Age (x)
		(1)	(2)	(3)	(4)	(5)	(6)	(7)	(8)	(9)	(10)	(11)	(12)					
0	100000	100000	100000	100000	100000	100000	100000	100000	100000	100000	100000	100000	100000	100000	100000	100000	100000	0
1	95669	95672	95793	95672	95687	96054	96518	95674	95669	97644	95669	95724	96517	95796	97035	99753	95724	1
5	94604	94615	94861	94632	94637	95208	95689	94615	94604	96560	94618	94710	95782	94872	96573	99579	94724	5
10	94351	94362	94639	94393	94402	94979	95451	94376	94351	96302	94402	94477	95603	94650	96390	99424	94528	10
15	94155	94166	94454	94215	94233	94788	95252	94204	94155	96102	94221	94316	95463	94465	96209	99244	94382	15
20	93779	93801	94084	93878	93886	94431	94872	93842	93802	95718	93870	94032	95155	94106	95888	98941	94123	20
25	93383	93432	93701	93521	93541	94054	94471	93459	93445	95314	93496	93735	94862	93750	95587	98653	93848	25
30	92815	92917	93150	92957	93046	93507	93902	92921	92910	94734	92956	93283	94432	93252	95145	98247	93425	30
35	92189	92376	92544	92462	92510	92857	93280	92347	92322	94095	92361	92707	93914	92732	94686	97815	92880	35
40	91271	91570	91640	91717	91727	92002	92357	91530	91432	93158	91465	91905	93138	91940	93945	97094	92101	40
45	90165	90558	90549	90847	90844	90916	91238	90496	90358	92029	90385	90859	92259	90985	93032	96217	91081	45
50	88600	89229	88953	89749	89602	89368	89661	89107	88790	90432	88838	89350	90883	89625	91680	94863	89590	50
55	86127	86869	86544	87991	87813	86935	87167	86857	86320	87908	86376	86918	88805	87291	89374	92536	87169	55
60	82901	83739	83347	85612	85547	83758	83913	84001	83087	84615	83152	83740	86033	84190	86292	89401	83993	60
65	77328	78332	77806	81323	81867	78201	78258	79012	77502	78927	77587	78185	81156	78817	80888	83881	78447	65
70	69437	70474	69920	74749	77364	70426	70321	71553	69593	70873	69710	70301	74128	70964	73054	75840	70577	70
75	60232	61302	60712	66489	72350	61325	61015	62674	60367	61477	60515	61076	65726	61791	63873	66405	61364	75
80	48020	48969	48460	54922	64544	49267	48743	51066	48128	49013	48341	48908	54404	49417	51579	53761	49235	80
85+	27622	28356	27945	33691	50467	29065	28158	30280	27684	28193	27853	28388	34605	28688	30884	32478	28625	85+
ADDED YRS OF LIFE																		
TOTAL		.440	.336	2.121	7.750	.853	.904	.893	.095	1.488	.168	.557	3.208	.779	2.685	5.320	.728	
WORK	2.339	.196	.045	.472	.458	.071	.011	.196	.070	.000	.064	.227	.436	.242	.396	.496	.291	

POPULATION, DEATHS, DEATH RATES FOR ALL CAUSES COMBINED, AND SPECIFIED CAUSES

Age Start of Interval	Midyear Population	Deaths During Year	All Causes	Respiratory T. B.	Other Infec. and Paras.	Neo-plasms	Cardio-vascular	Infl., Pneu., Bronch.	Diar-rheal	Certain Degen-erative	Maternal	Cert. Dis. of Infancy	Motor Vehicle	Other Violence	Other and Unknown	Age Start of Interval
0	45087	1969	.04367	.00007	.00151	.00002	.00018	.00592	.00259	.00009	.00000	.02233	.00000	.00208	.00887	0
1	196235	358	.00182	.00008	.00032	.00009	.00003	.00025	.00006	.00002	.00000	.00000	.00021	.00026	.00050	1
5	202758	187	.00092	.00002	.00014	.00009	.00002	.00003	.00002	.00002	.00000	.00000	.00025	.00018	.00014	5
10	155940	101	.00052	.00004	.00004	.00006	.00004	.00001	.00000	.00001	.00000	.00000	.00011	.00012	.00010	10
15	173406	200	.00115	.00016	.00009	.00014	.00009	.00003	.00002	.00004	.00000	.00000	.00016	.00022	.00020	15
20	172638	244	.00141	.00036	.00005	.00012	.00021	.00001	.00002	.00005	.00000	.00000	.00016	.00025	.00018	20
25	187486	353	.00188	.00045	.00004	.00028	.00025	.00005	.00001	.00008	.00000	.00000	.00016	.00040	.00018	25
30	166302	375	.00225	.00049	.00010	.00030	.00041	.00012	.00000	.00013	.00000	.00000	.00015	.00018	.00025	30
35	177906	497	.00279	.00048	.00008	.00056	.00060	.00012	.00001	.00023	.00000	.00000	.00009	.00030	.00038	35
40	180256	793	.00440	.00054	.00009	.00083	.00133	.00026	.00002	.00032	.00000	.00000	.00006	.00026	.00051	40
45	168910	1309	.00775	.00071	.00014	.00172	.00258	.00059	.00001	.00046	.00000	.00000	.00006	.00044	.00096	45
50	141554	1922	.01358	.00078	.00013	.00306	.00548	.00119	.00004	.00075	.00000	.00000	.00015	.00055	.00145	50
55	115926	2443	.02107	.00107	.00019	.00454	.00926	.00204	.00009	.00083	.00000	.00000	.00013	.00080	.00211	55
60	98043	3227	.03291	.00118	.00032	.00640	.01596	.00375	.00008	.00121	.00000	.00000	.00019	.00075	.00306	60
65	83341	4014	.04816	.00108	.00046	.00929	.02504	.00457	.00018	.00173	.00000	.00000	.00028	.00100	.00455	65
70	65803	4778	.07261	.00064	.00040	.01184	.04219	.00663	.00015	.00196	.00000	.00000	.00033	.00111	.00737	70
75	41644	4982	.11963	.00062	.00053	.01635	.07218	.01085	.00026	.00276	.00000	.00000	.00038	.00195	.01374	75
80	17849	3412	.19116	.00022	.00050	.01821	.11928	.01961	.00050	.00437	.00000	.00000	.00038	.00195	.01374	80
85+	6381	1952	.30591	.00047	.00031	.01693	.19166	.02680	.00063	.00282	.00000	.00000	.00045	.00286	.02516	85+
ALL	2437465	33116														

CRUDE DEATH RATE			.01359	.00045	.00018	.00205	.00640	.00127	.00009	.00043	.00000	.00041	.00016	.00049	.00165	
STANDARDIZED RATE (1)			.00809	.00033	.00019	.00107	.00292	.00078	.00012	.00024	.00000	.00079	.00016	.00041	.00109	
STANDARDIZED RATE (2)			.01453	.00043	.00018	.00208	.00700	.00137	.00010	.00043	.00000	.00046	.00016	.00041	.00181	
GEOMETRIC MEAN			.00972													

LIFE TABLE FOR ALL CAUSES COMBINED

Age (x)	Midyear Population	Deaths During Year	$_nM_x$	$_nq_x$	l_x	$_nd_x$	$_nL_x$	$_nm_x$	$_na_x$	T_x	$_nr_x$	$\overset{\circ}{e}_x$	Age (x)
0	45087	1969	.043671	.042100	100000	4210	96397	.043673	.144241	6411283	.000000	64.113	0
1	196235	358	.001824	.007266	95790	696	381420	.001825	1.500000	6314886	.000000	65.924	1
5	202758	187	.000922	.004595	95094	437	474378	.000921	2.500000	5933466	.000000	62.396	5
10	155940	101	.000515	.002578	94657	244	472697	.000516	2.591359	5459088	.010995	57.672	10
15	173406	200	.001153	.005762	94413	544	470792	.001155	2.659697	4986391	.015654	52.815	15
20	172638	244	.001413	.007042	93869	661	467761	.001413	2.603694	4515599	-.005225	48.105	20
25	187486	353	.001883	.009369	93208	873	463936	.001883	2.589490	4047838	-.000669	43.428	25
30	166302	375	.002255	.011220	92335	1036	459167	.002256	2.578829	3583902	.005007	38.814	30
35	177906	497	.002794	.013856	91299	1265	453525	.002789	2.652009	3124736	-.008761	34.225	35
40	180256	793	.004399	.021758	90034	1959	445709	.004395	2.723009	2671211	-.004085	29.669	40
45	168910	1309	.007750	.038172	88075	3362	432728	.007769	2.725498	2225501	.009632	25.268	45
50	141554	1922	.013578	.066082	84713	5598	410529	.013636	2.671341	1792773	.021612	21.163	50
55	115926	2443	.021074	.100689	79115	7966	376756	.021144	2.637616	1382244	.018707	17.471	55
60	98043	3227	.032914	.152637	71149	10860	329640	.032945	2.596186	1005488	.005640	14.132	60
65	83341	4014	.048164	.215296	60289	12980	269762	.048117	2.559081	675848	-.006175	11.210	65
70	65803	4778	.072611	.307362	47309	14541	200621	.072480	2.529486	406086	-.009537	8.584	70
75	41644	4982	.119633	.458923	32768	15038	125554	.119774	2.454019	205465	-.004337	6.270	75
80	17849	3412	.191159	.632939	17730	11222	58637	.191380	2.325547	79912	.004337	4.507	80
85+	6381	1952	.305908	1.000000	6508	6508	21274	.305908	3.268955	21274	.000000	3.269	85+

NUMBER OF PERSONS DYING (OUT OF 100,000 AT BIRTH) ABOVE AGE X FROM SPECIFIED CAUSES

Age (x)	All Causes	Respiratory T. B.	Other Infec. and Paras.	Neoplasms	Cardiovascular	Infl., Pneu., Bronch.	Diarrheal	Certain Degenerative	Maternal	Cert. Dis. of Infancy	Motor Vehicle	Other Violence	Other and Unknown	Age (x)
0	100000	3149	1155	15310	48865	9356	552	3162	0	2153	1034	3350	11914	0
1	95790	3143	1009	15307	48847	8785	302	3153	0	0	1034	3149	11061	1
5	95054	3112	887	15274	48836	8690	281	3147	0	0	952	3048	10867	5
10	94657	3100	821	15230	48824	8676	271	3136	0	0	833	2964	10802	10
15	94413	3081	802	15203	48807	8674	271	3131	0	0	782	2906	10756	15
20	93869	3007	759	15138	48763	8657	263	3112	0	0	706	2800	10664	20
25	93208	2836	734	15081	48666	8652	255	3090	0	0	630	2683	10581	25
30	92335	2626	714	14953	48550	8627	250	3053	0	0	566	2498	10498	30
35	91299	2402	667	14814	48359	8572	250	2992	0	0	497	2360	10386	35
40	90034	2186	632	14563	48090	8519	245	2888	0	0	456	2243	10212	40
45	88075	1946	592	14192	47499	8405	235	2744	0	0	429	2045	9988	45
50	84713	1638	533	13445	46379	8148	232	2544	0	0	403	1819	9572	50
55	79115	1316	481	12184	44116	7655	218	2236	0	0	342	1593	8974	55
60	71149	912	409	10469	40611	6882	182	1923	0	0	293	1290	8178	60
65	60289	522	305	8360	35344	5643	155	1523	0	0	229	1041	7167	65
70	47309	231	182	5856	28597	4411	106	1057	0	0	155	773	5941	70
75	32768	102	103	3484	20150	3084	76	664	0	0	88	550	4467	75
80	17730	24	36	1429	11077	1719	43	317	0	0	40	306	2739	80
85+	6508	10	7	360	4078	570	13	60	0	0	13	137	1260	85+

NUMBER OF PERSONS SURVIVING TO AGE X IF SPECIFIED CAUSES WERE ELIMINATED

Age (x)	No Causes	Respiratory T. B.	Other Infec. and Paras.	Neoplasms	Cardiovascular	Infl., Pneu., Bronch.	Diarrheal	Certain Degenerative	Maternal	Cert. Dis. of Infancy	Motor Vehicle	Other Violence	Other and Unknown	(1) + (2)	(1) + (2) + (5) + (6) + (8)	(1)+(2)+ (5)+(6)+ (8)+part of(9)&(12)	(10) + (11)	Age (x)
		(1)	(2)	(3)	(4)	(5)	(6)	(7)	(8)	(9)	(10)	(11)	(12)					
0	100000	100000	100000	100000	100000	100000	100000	100000	100000	100000	100000	100000	100000	100000	100000	100000	100000	0
1	95790	95796	95933	95793	95808	96350	96035	95799	95790	97920	95790	95987	96628	95939	96747	99178	95987	1
5	95054	95131	95358	95130	95122	95744	95358	95109	95094	97209	95176	95390	96122	95395	96315	98843	95472	5
10	94657	94706	94986	94737	94697	95320	94930	94683	94657	96762	94857	95036	95745	95034	95976	98513	95237	10
15	94413	94480	94760	94519	94470	95076	94685	94444	94413	96513	94664	94849	95545	94827	95769	98310	95101	15
20	93869	94010	94257	94040	93970	94545	94148	93918	93869	95957	94154	94409	95087	94398	95361	97922	94736	20
25	93208	93519	93618	93434	93405	93885	93493	93279	93208	95281	93607	93862	94502	93930	94901	97481	94263	25
30	92335	92853	92761	92667	92646	93030	92622	92442	92335	94389	92794	93168	93700	93281	94276	96867	93632	30
35	91299	92035	91767	91786	91797	92042	91583	91466	91299	93329	91822	92261	92762	92507	93550	96163	92790	35
40	90034	90976	90531	90765	90794	90819	90319	90302	90034	92208	90591	91100	91603	91478	92568	91664	40	
45	88075	89237	88601	89161	89410	88957	88364	88480	88075	90034	88647	89316	89884	89770	90966	93612	89896	45
50	84713	86137	85277	86503	87120	85817	84994	85300	84713	86597	85288	86132	86870	86710	88131	90787	86717	50
55	79115	80761	79692	82040	83645	80630	79391	79963	79115	80875	79712	80662	81724	81350	83197	85815	81270	55
60	71149	73020	71737	75483	78821	73263	71431	72211	71149	72731	71732	72833	74278	73624	76112	78656	73430	60
65	60289	62242	60884	66051	72382	63264	60553	61563	60289	61630	60843	61950	63518	62856	66246	68649	62518	65
70	47309	49105	47885	54307	64441	50796	47560	48730	47309	48361	47809	48855	51319	49703	53648	55778	49372	70
75	32768	34120	33232	39924	55272	36380	32966	34086	32768	33497	33170	34029	36896	34603	38650	40363	34447	75
80	17730	18518	18030	23472	43356	20813	17861	18705	17730	18124	17982	18597	21429	18832	22270	23449	18861	80
85+	6508	6806	6635	9479	29734	8465	6574	7025	6508	6653	6616	6930	8977	6939	9117	9760	7045	85+
ADDED YRS OF LIFE TOTAL		.759	.378	2.101	7.791	1.376	.220	.465	.000	1.423	.349	.856	2.010	1.144	2.807	4.839	1.212	
WORK	4.344	.484	.092	.738	1.216	.258	.017	.208	.000	.000	.143	.370	.454	.578	.861	.978	.515	

POPULATION, DEATHS, DEATH RATES FOR ALL CAUSES COMBINED, AND SPECIFIED CAUSES

Age Start of Interval	Midyear Population	Deaths During Year	All Causes	Respiratory T.B.	Other Infec. and Paras.	Neoplasms	Cardiovascular	Infl., Pneu., Bronch.	Diarrheal	Certain Degenerative	Maternal	Cert. Dis. of Infancy	Motor Vehicle	Other Violence	Other and Unknown	Age Start of Interval
0	42657	1422	.03334	.00014	.00131	.00002	.00007	.00469	.00176	.00005	.00000	.01674	.00000	.00150	.00706	0
1	187412	306	.00163	.00005	.00045	.00011	.00000	.00029	.00005	.00002	.00000	.00012	.00000	.00015	.00037	1
5	195552	122	.00062	.00003	.00010	.00004	.00003	.00004	.00001	.00002	.00000	.00000	.00010	.00007	.00016	5
10	191067	99	.00052	.00003	.00007	.00004	.00008	.00003	.00002	.00006	.00000	.00000	.00003	.00002	.00014	10
15	188902	177	.00094	.00028	.00010	.00007	.00013	.00005	.00001	.00005	.00001	.00000	.00004	.00005	.00016	15
20	191934	274	.00143	.00072	.00006	.00010	.00015	.00005	.00001	.00007	.00005	.00000	.00003	.00004	.00015	20
25	194190	343	.00177	.00069	.00006	.00017	.00026	.00004	.00003	.00007	.00018	.00000	.00001	.00006	.00022	25
30	179036	361	.00202	.00051	.00005	.00035	.00037	.00008	.00004	.00009	.00015	.00000	.00002	.00010	.00026	30
35	191064	476	.00249	.00036	.00009	.00055	.00057	.00014	.00002	.00013	.00007	.00000	.00005	.00009	.00038	35
40	190364	660	.00347	.00037	.00007	.00110	.00097	.00014	.00001	.00014	.00005	.00000	.00000	.00015	.00047	40
45	181091	906	.00500	.00019	.00008	.00172	.00152	.00029	.00003	.00028	.00001	.00000	.00003	.00018	.00066	45
50	166805	1307	.00784	.00019	.00010	.00230	.00290	.00053	.00007	.00032	.00000	.00000	.00002	.00026	.00116	50
55	145074	1791	.01235	.00026	.00019	.00328	.00571	.00074	.00005	.00055	.00000	.00000	.00003	.00032	.00121	55
60	126946	2481	.01954	.00024	.00014	.00471	.00978	.00108	.00009	.00085	.00000	.00000	.00007	.00028	.00228	60
65	109063	3665	.03360	.00020	.00009	.00647	.01901	.00254	.00027	.00145	.00000	.00000	.00008	.00047	.00303	65
70	85722	4825	.05629	.00019	.00029	.00944	.03381	.00426	.00023	.00205	.00000	.00000	.00009	.00091	.00502	70
75	56230	5355	.09523	.00016	.00032	.01161	.06168	.00799	.00037	.00205	.00000	.00000	.00018	.00197	.00891	75
80	28059	4447	.15849	.00014	.00018	.01433	.10193	.01572	.00071	.00185	.00000	.00000	.00007	.00463	.01892	80
85+	13467	3645	.27066	.00015	.00045	.01448	.17183	.02770	.00126	.00230	.00000	.00000	.00022	.01025	.04203	85+
ALL	2664635	32662														

	All Causes	Resp. T.B.	Other Infec.	Neoplasms	Cardiovascular	Infl. Pneu. Bronch.	Diarrheal	Certain Degen.	Maternal	Cert. Dis. Infancy	Motor Vehicle	Other Violence	Other and Unknown
CRUDE DEATH RATE	.01226	.00029	.00015	.00188	.00635	.00099	.00009	.00036	.00004	.00027	.00005	.00033	.00145
STANDARDIZED RATE (1)	.00600	.00027	.00018	.00085	.00220	.00052	.00010	.00017	.00004	.00059	.00005	.00020	.00084
STANDARDIZED RATE (2)	.01091	.00029	.00015	.00162	.00549	.00090	.00010	.00031	.00004	.00035	.00005	.00030	.00132
GEOMETRIC MEAN	.00760												

LIFE TABLE FOR ALL CAUSES COMBINED

Age (x)	Midyear Population	Deaths During Year	$_nM_x$	$_nq_x$	l_x	$_nd_x$	$_nL_x$	$_nm_x$	$_na_x$	T_x	$_nr_x$	$\overset{\circ}{e}_x$	Age (x)
0	42657	1422	.033336	.032390	100000	3239	97171	.033333	.126671	6836085	.000000	68.361	0
1	187412	306	.001633	.006511	96761	630	385469	.001634	1.500000	6738914	.000000	69.645	1
5	195552	122	.000624	.003110	96131	299	479508	.000623	2.500000	6353445	.000000	66.092	5
10	191067	99	.000518	.002588	95832	248	478571	.000518	2.624328	5873537	.002704	61.290	10
15	188902	177	.000937	.004677	95584	447	476892	.000937	2.699478	5394966	.000500	56.442	15
20	191934	274	.001428	.007106	95137	676	474075	.001426	2.618343	4918075	-.004879	51.695	20
25	194190	343	.001766	.008797	94461	831	470282	.001767	2.566165	4444000	.003399	47.046	25
30	179036	361	.002016	.010040	93630	940	465866	.002018	2.569814	3973717	.002366	42.441	30
35	191064	476	.002491	.012364	92690	1146	460717	.002487	2.615256	3507851	-.007793	37.845	35
40	190364	660	.003467	.017194	91544	1574	454010	.003467	2.643080	3047134	-.001327	33.286	40
45	181091	906	.005003	.024753	89970	2227	444659	.005008	2.669230	2593124	.004784	28.822	45
50	166805	1307	.007835	.038556	87743	3383	430851	.007852	2.675387	2148465	.011571	24.486	50
55	145074	1791	.012345	.060159	84360	5075	409955	.012379	2.665928	1717614	.014906	20.361	55
60	126946	2481	.019544	.093649	79285	7425	379138	.019584	2.671829	1307659	.010088	16.493	60
65	109063	3665	.033604	.155845	71860	11199	332469	.033642	2.641810	928521	.005313	12.921	65
70	85722	4825	.056287	.248067	60661	15048	267017	.056356	2.588550	595630	.005778	9.819	70
75	56230	5355	.095234	.385745	45613	17595	184225	.095508	2.508407	328613	.011507	7.204	75
80	28059	4447	.158487	.562424	28018	15758	99091	.159025	2.398213	144387	.011507	5.153	80
85+	13467	3645	.270662	1.000000	12260	12260	45296	.270662	3.694650	45296	.000000	3.695	85+

NUMBER OF PERSONS DYING (OUT OF 100,000 AT BIRTH) ABOVE AGE X FROM SPECIFIED CAUSES

Age (x)	All Causes	Respiratory T. B.	Other Infec. and Paras.	Neo-plasms	Cardio-vascular	Infl., Pneu., Bronch.	Diar-rheal	Certain Degen-erative	Maternal	Cert. Dis. of Infancy	Motor Vehicle	Other Violence	Other and Unknown	Age (x)
0	100000	1987	1001	14980	53865	8177	699	2816	245	1626	343	2590	11671	0
1	96761	1973	873	14978	53858	7722	528	2811	245	0	343	2444	10986	1
5	96131	1938	658	14937	53858	7609	509	2803	245	0	306	2385	10843	5
10	95832	1923	652	14917	53844	7589	507	2796	245	0	240	2353	10766	10
15	95584	1911	617	14900	53806	7574	497	2766	245	0	225	2345	10698	15
20	95137	1777	571	14867	53745	7551	494	2740	240	0	205	2322	10625	20
25	94461	1434	541	14820	53674	7529	489	2708	215	0	193	2303	10555	25
30	93630	1109	512	14740	53553	7512	477	2677	130	0	190	2276	10454	30
35	92690	873	489	14576	53381	7476	459	2633	60	0	182	2229	10332	35
40	91544	706	448	14304	53119	7413	449	2572	26	0	161	2186	10160	40
45	89970	537	417	13806	52680	7349	447	2508	5	0	161	2117	9943	45
50	87743	451	380	13039	52001	7218	432	2385	0	0	148	2038	9651	50
55	84360	368	339	12046	50750	6990	404	2248	0	0	141	1927	9147	55
60	79285	261	260	10658	48399	6687	384	2021	0	0	129	1797	8649	60
65	71860	168	206	8909	44680	6277	348	1698	0	0	102	1689	7783	65
70	60661	101	175	6753	38344	5430	259	1215	0	0	75	1533	6776	70
75	45613	51	97	4231	29304	4292	157	667	0	0	50	1290	5434	75
80	28018	22	38	2088	17908	2816	128	290	0	0	17	925	3786	80
85+	12260	7	20	656	7783	1255	57	104	0	0	10	464	1904	85+

NUMBER OF PERSONS SURVIVING TO AGE X IF SPECIFIED CAUSES WERE ELIMINATED

Age (x)	No Causes	Respiratory T. B. (1)	Other Infec. and Paras. (2)	Neo-plasms (3)	Cardio-vascular (4)	Infl., Pneu., Bronch. (5)	Diar-rheal (6)	Certain Degener-ative (7)	Maternal (8)	Cert. Dis. of Infancy (9)	Motor Vehicle (10)	Other Violence (11)	Other and Unknown (12)	(1)+(2)	(1)+(2)+(5)+(6)+(8)	(1)+(2)+(5)+(6)+(8)+part of(9)&(12)	(10)+(11)	Age (x)
0	100000	100000	100000	100000	100000	100000	100000	100000	100000	100000	100000	100000	100000	100000	100000	100000	100000	0
1	96761	96775	96887	96763	96768	97210	96929	96766	96761	98374	96761	96905	97437	96901	97519	99434	96905	1
5	96131	96180	96431	96174	96138	96690	96317	96144	96131	97733	96168	96333	96546	96480	97229	99241	96370	5
10	95832	95895	96177	95895	95853	96409	96020	95852	95832	97429	95935	96065	96722	96241	97010	99047	96168	10
15	95584	95659	95963	95664	95643	96175	95781	95634	95584	97177	95701	95824	96541	96039	96832	98893	95942	15
20	95137	95346	95561	95249	95256	95748	95336	95212	95142	96723	95274	95399	96163	95770	96593	98692	95537	20
25	94461	95011	94912	94619	94650	95090	94664	94568	94491	96035	94609	94740	95550	95465	96337	98482	94889	25
30	93630	94502	94106	93667	93939	94270	93843	93767	93744	95190	93780	93934	94811	94982	95966	98170	94084	30
35	92690	93790	93184	93088	93167	93360	92919	92869	92873	94235	92846	93038	93982	94290	95394	97644	93195	35
40	91544	92798	92073	92209	92278	92269	91780	91782	91758	93070	91719	91930	92994	93334	94537	96826	92106	40
45	89970	91373	90521	91122	91131	90746	90204	90267	90202	91469	90142	90419	91614	91932	93206	95510	90591	45
50	87743	89197	88317	89637	89557	88631	87986	88155	87974	89205	87924	88259	89640	89780	91179	93477	88441	50
55	84360	85841	84952	87181	87366	85440	84621	84891	84582	85766	84540	84965	86690	86443	88051	90341	85147	55
60	79285	80782	79918	83297	84506	80598	79550	80006	79494	80606	79466	79981	81972	81427	83270	85493	80164	60
65	71860	73307	72486	77304	80463	73448	72135	72824	72049	73058	72050	72594	75152	73945	76067	78178	72786	65
70	60661	61944	61218	67414	74763	62802	60975	61925	60821	61672	60846	61426	64412	62513	65225	67139	61613	70
75	45613	46622	46100	53158	66733	48252	45902	47046	45733	46373	45774	46402	49680	47119	50294	51897	46565	75
80	28018	28660	28362	34625	56229	30879	28249	29195	28092	28485	28142	28794	31945	29012	32324	33512	28922	80
85+	12260	12551	12422	16333	41845	14665	12407	12900	12292	12464	12319	12908	15429	12717	15435	16193	12970	85+

ADDED YRS OF LIFE

		(1)	(2)	(3)	(4)	(5)	(6)	(7)	(8)	(9)	(10)	(11)	(12)				
TOTAL		.739	.403	2.200	8.840	1.142	.204	.427	.101	1.137	.124	.443	1.941	1.148	2.644	4.410	.569
WORK	3.272	.517	.088	.658	.860	.149	.025	.142	.080	.000	.028	.109	.401	.606	.866	.996	.137

POPULATION, DEATHS, DEATH RATES FOR ALL CAUSES COMBINED, AND SPECIFIED CAUSES

Age Start of Interval	Midyear Population	Deaths During Year	All Causes	Respiratory T. B.	Other Infec. and Paras.	Neoplasms	Cardiovascular	Infl., Pneu., Bronch.	Diarrheal	Certain Degenerative	Maternal	Cert. Dis. of Infancy	Motor Vehicle	Other Violence	Other and Unknown	Age Start of Interval
0	49134	1542	.03138	.00000	.00024	.00012	.00010	.00358	.00085	.00002	.00000	.01769	.00000	.00201	.00676	0
1	189261	223	.00118	.00000	.00005	.00013	.00002	.00022	.00005	.00003	.00000	.00000	.00016	.00017	.00035	1
5	214665	121	.00056	.00000	.00001	.00007	.00002	.00003	.00001	.00001	.00000	.00000	.00012	.00011	.00017	5
10	228414	105	.00046	.00000	.00000	.00007	.00004	.00000	.00000	.00000	.00000	.00000	.00008	.00015	.00011	10
15	192715	134	.00070	.00000	.00001	.00007	.00002	.00002	.00000	.00003	.00000	.00000	.00020	.00024	.00012	15
20	185154	188	.00102	.00002	.00000	.00011	.00009	.00004	.00001	.00005	.00000	.00000	.00025	.00033	.00013	20
25	176834	216	.00122	.00003	.00002	.00019	.00018	.00003	.00002	.00007	.00000	.00000	.00020	.00036	.00012	25
30	174655	273	.00156	.00010	.00002	.00020	.00036	.00005	.00002	.00005	.00000	.00000	.00018	.00038	.00017	30
35	178215	392	.00220	.00011	.00003	.00045	.00067	.00004	.00001	.00010	.00000	.00000	.00017	.00040	.00021	35
40	153403	562	.00366	.00011	.00005	.00074	.00152	.00015	.00005	.00015	.00000	.00000	.00018	.00044	.00029	40
45	172271	1069	.00621	.00011	.00005	.00154	.00280	.00030	.00001	.00024	.00000	.00000	.00017	.00050	.00049	45
50	164669	1957	.01188	.00025	.00006	.00304	.00560	.00077	.00005	.00052	.00000	.00000	.00017	.00065	.00078	50
55	146351	2933	.02004	.00037	.00012	.00521	.00991	.00149	.00006	.00049	.00000	.00000	.00017	.00077	.00134	55
60	109862	3508	.03193	.00044	.00010	.00844	.01572	.00319	.00007	.00083	.00000	.00000	.00028	.00080	.00208	60
65	83261	3982	.04783	.00053	.00026	.01093	.02561	.00462	.00012	.00141	.00000	.00000	.00017	.00072	.00346	65
70	59731	4348	.07279	.00055	.00013	.01373	.04182	.00732	.00020	.00204	.00000	.00000	.00039	.00116	.00546	70
75	40563	4274	.10537	.00057	.00005	.01738	.06508	.00895	.00015	.00253	.00000	.00000	.00047	.00153	.00826	75
80	21782	3620	.16619	.00046	.00018	.01956	.10770	.01377	.00055	.00381	.00000	.00000	.00051	.00298	.01667	80
85+	9615	2235	.23245	.00031	.00010	.01872	.16214	.01778	.00042	.00374	.00000	.00000	.00125	.00468	.02330	85+
ALL	2550555	31682														

	All Causes	Respiratory T. B.	Other Infec. and Paras.	Neoplasms	Cardiovascular	Infl., Pneu., Bronch.	Diarrheal	Certain Degenerative	Maternal	Cert. Dis. of Infancy	Motor Vehicle	Other Violence	Other and Unknown
CRUDE DEATH RATE	.01242	.00013	.00005	.00230	.00637	.00105	.00005	.00034	.00000	.00034	.00019	.00049	.00110
STANDARDIZED RATE (1)	.00688	.00008	.00004	.00116	.00283	.00060	.00006	.00017	.00000	.00062	.00017	.00040	.00075
STANDARDIZED RATE (2)	.01286	.00013	.00005	.00230	.00667	.00110	.00006	.00034	.00000	.00037	.00019	.00049	.00116
GEOMETRIC MEAN	.00770												

LIFE TABLE FOR ALL CAUSES COMBINED

Age (x)	Midyear Population	Deaths During Year	$_nM_x$	$_nq_x$	l_x	$_nd_x$	$_nL_x$	$_nm_x$	$_na_x$	T_x	$_nr_x$	$\overset{\circ}{e}_x$	Age (x)
0	49134	1542	.031384	.030540	100000	3054	97323	.031380	.123352	6647067	.000000	66.471	0
1	189261	223	.001178	.004704	96946	456	386644	.001179	1.500000	6549744	.000000	67.561	1
5	214665	121	.000564	.002809	96490	271	481773	.000563	2.500000	6163100	.000000	63.873	5
10	228414	105	.000460	.002297	96219	221	480556	.000460	2.560332	5681328	.005523	59.046	10
15	192715	134	.000695	.003490	95998	335	479207	.000699	2.664179	5200772	.019081	54.176	15
20	185154	188	.001015	.005070	95663	485	477154	.001016	2.605241	4721564	.010393	49.356	20
25	176834	216	.001221	.006094	95178	580	474492	.001222	2.590158	4244411	.007830	44.594	25
30	174655	273	.001563	.007780	94598	736	471244	.001562	2.627095	3769918	-.002620	39.852	30
35	178215	392	.002200	.010963	93862	1029	466936	.002204	2.692744	3298675	.008776	35.144	35
40	153403	562	.003664	.018183	92833	1688	460310	.003667	2.716109	2831739	.004798	30.504	40
45	172271	1069	.006205	.030501	91145	2780	449488	.006185	2.756370	2371429	-.012097	26.018	45
50	164669	1957	.011884	.057817	88365	5109	430138	.011878	2.712452	1921942	-.002309	21.750	50
55	146351	2933	.020041	.095969	83256	7990	397575	.020097	2.659001	1491804	.013558	17.918	55
60	109862	3508	.031931	.148899	75266	11207	349514	.032065	2.607169	1094228	.023222	14.538	60
65	83261	3982	.047826	.214724	64059	13755	286803	.047960	2.565128	744715	.016125	11.625	65
70	59731	4348	.072793	.308266	50304	15507	212893	.072839	2.509068	457911	.003534	9.103	70
75	40563	4274	.105367	.414691	34797	14430	137126	.105232	2.445657	245018	-.006951	7.041	75
80	21782	3620	.166192	.576570	20367	11743	70792	.165881	2.356457	107892	-.006951	5.297	80
85+	9615	2235	.232449	1.000000	8624	8624	37101	.232449	4.302013	37101	.000000	4.302	85+

NUMBER OF PERSONS DYING (OUT OF 100,000 AT BIRTH) ABOVE AGE X FROM SPECIFIED CAUSES

Age (x)	All Causes	Respiratory T. B.	Other Infec. and Paras.	Neo-plasms	Cardio-vascular	Infl., Pneu., Bronch.	Diar-rheal	Certain Degen-erative	Maternal	Cert. Dis. of Infancy	Motor Vehicle	Other Violence	Other and Unknown	Age (x)
0	100000	1019	363	18516	53298	8526	376	2714	0	1721	1352	3541	8574	0
1	96946	1019	339	18504	53288	8178	293	2712	0	0	1352	3345	7916	1
5	96490	1019	321	18455	53280	8092	274	2702	0	0	1289	3280	7778	5
10	96219	1019	314	18419	53271	8076	270	2697	0	0	1231	3226	7696	10
15	95998	1019	312	18383	53254	8074	268	2697	0	0	1191	3154	7646	15
20	95663	1019	309	18351	53247	8066	268	2685	0	0	1094	3039	7585	20
25	95178	1011	309	18299	53206	8048	265	2661	0	0	972	2882	7525	25
30	94598	998	301	18208	53122	8032	257	2629	0	0	876	2710	7465	30
35	93862	952	293	18114	52952	8008	249	2586	0	0	792	2530	7386	35
40	92833	899	278	17901	52640	7990	247	2539	0	0	711	2341	7287	40
45	91145	848	256	17562	51939	7920	225	2470	0	0	630	2140	7155	45
50	88365	799	236	16870	50686	7788	223	2361	0	0	554	1916	6932	50
55	83256	692	210	15565	48279	7459	202	2136	0	0	481	1636	6596	55
60	75266	545	163	13486	44229	6864	178	1940	0	0	370	1329	6062	60
65	64059	392	128	10526	38810	5745	152	1649	0	0	278	1049	5330	65
70	50304	240	52	7386	31442	4415	117	1245	0	0	229	842	4336	70
75	34797	123	24	4463	22532	2857	75	810	0	0	147	596	3170	75
80	20367	45	17	2081	13620	1631	54	408	0	0	83	387	2041	80
85+	8624	12	4	695	6016	660	15	139	0	0	46	174	863	85+

NUMBER OF PERSONS SURVIVING TO AGE X IF SPECIFIED CAUSES WERE ELIMINATED

Age (x)	No Causes	Respiratory T. B.	Other Infec. and Paras.	Neo-plasms	Cardio-vascular	Infl., Pneu., Bronch.	Diar-rheal	Certain Degener-ative	Maternal	Cert. Dis. of Infancy	Motor Vehicle	Other Violence	Other and Unknown	(1) + (2)	(1) + (2) + (5) + (6) + (8)	(1)+(2)+ (5)+(6)+ (8)+part of(9)&(12)	(10) + (11)	Age (x)
		(1)	(2)	(3)	(4)	(5)	(6)	(7)	(8)	(9)	(10)	(11)	(12)					
0	100000	100000	100000	100000	100000	100000	100000	100000	100000	100000	100000	100000	100000	100000	100000	100000	100000	0
1	96946	96946	96970	96958	96956	97289	97028	96948	96946	98655	96946	97139	97596	96970	97395	98994	97139	1
5	96490	96490	96531	96551	96508	96918	96590	96502	96490	98191	96553	96747	97276	96531	97060	98708	96810	5
10	96219	96219	96267	96315	96246	96662	96323	96236	96219	97916	96340	96530	97085	96267	96815	98471	96651	10
15	95998	95998	96048	96130	96042	96442	96104	96015	95998	97691	96158	96380	96912	96048	96598	98252	96541	15
20	95663	95663	95716	95827	95713	96113	95768	95692	95663	97350	95920	96155	96636	95716	96272	97923	96417	20
25	95178	95186	95231	95393	95269	95644	95286	95231	95178	96856	95556	95829	96206	95239	95813	97461	96209	25
30	94598	94619	94658	94903	94772	95077	94713	94682	94598	96266	95069	95418	95681	94679	95275	96918	95893	30
35	93862	93929	93930	94258	94205	94361	93984	93988	93862	95517	94414	94857	95016	93997	94620	96262	95414	35
40	92833	92952	92915	93438	93484	93345	92956	93005	92833	94470	93460	94007	94074	93034	93671	95306	94642	40
45	91145	91312	91247	92078	92487	91717	91288	91382	91145	92752	91841	92499	92496	91415	92133	93756	93206	45
50	88365	88575	88484	89560	90927	89051	88505	88703	88365	89923	89115	89902	89898	88695	89525	91120	90665	50
55	83256	83558	83393	86058	88108	84225	83408	83793	83256	84724	84034	84980	85032	83696	84825	86371	85775	55
60	75266	75679	75435	79869	83726	76717	75427	75939	75266	76593	76076	77122	77349	75849	77477	78947	77952	60
65	64059	64552	64235	70530	77151	66355	64220	64903	64059	65188	64833	65902	66566	64730	67218	68585	66699	65
70	50304	50826	50510	58849	68972	53339	50461	51330	50304	51191	50956	51939	53195	51034	54282	55507	52612	70
75	34797	35255	34961	43621	58987	38286	34940	35875	34797	35411	35317	36138	37831	35422	39134	40152	36678	75
80	20367	20694	20468	27872	48115	23445	20467	21313	20367	20726	20720	21317	23094	20797	24057	24787	21686	80
85+	8624	8784	8675	13062	35542	10659	8691	9204	8624	8776	8797	9168	10659	8836	11005	11437	9352	85+

ADDED YRS OF LIFE																		
TOTAL		.167	.086	2.550	10.535	1.156	.109	.358	.000	1.170	.413	.918	1.511	.254	1.541	2.804	1.341	
WORK	3.582	.081	.025	.714	1.263	.170	.017	.131	.000	.000	.224	.425	.282	.106	.294	.320	.652	

POPULATION, DEATHS, DEATH RATES FOR ALL CAUSES COMBINED, AND SPECIFIED CAUSES

Age Start of Interval	Midyear Population	Deaths During Year	All Causes	Respiratory T.B.	Other Infec. and Paras.	Neoplasms	Cardiovascular	Infl., Pneu., Bronch.	Diarrheal	Certain Degenerative	Maternal	Cert. Dis. of Infancy	Motor Vehicle	Other Violence	Other and Unknown	Age Start of Interval
0	46667	1131	.02424	.00000	.00030	.00009	.00006	.00238	.00054	.00011	.00000	.01271	.00004	.00105	.00696	0
1	181031	156	.00086	.00001	.00004	.00007	.00003	.00021	.00002	.00001	.00000	.00001	.00012	.00012	.00024	1
5	205152	97	.00047	.00000	.00003	.00005	.00001	.00003	.00000	.00002	.00000	.00000	.00011	.00012	.00024	5
10	218025	57	.00026	.00000	.00000	.00004	.00003	.00002	.00000	.00002	.00000	.00000	.00003	.00006	.00015	10
15	186595	75	.00040	.00000	.00002	.00004	.00005	.00002	.00001	.00004	.00001	.00000	.00008	.00005	.00010	15
20	179598	89	.00050	.00002	.00001	.00008	.00008	.00003	.00001	.00004	.00004	.00000	.00006	.00006	.00008	20
25	172446	130	.00075	.00007	.00002	.00022	.00010	.00003	.00001	.00003	.00003	.00000	.00002	.00007	.00014	25
30	174599	166	.00095	.00008	.00001	.00024	.00022	.00005	.00003	.00005	.00006	.00000	.00001	.00013	.00007	30
35	180595	332	.00184	.00012	.00002	.00058	.00047	.00009	.00002	.00005	.00003	.00000	.00001	.00016	.00030	35
40	162611	427	.00263	.00007	.00002	.00108	.00068	.00010	.00001	.00010	.00002	.00000	.00002	.00015	.00038	40
45	182988	746	.00408	.00006	.00003	.00173	.00126	.00014	.00004	.00015	.00002	.00000	.00004	.00020	.00043	45
50	175982	1144	.00650	.00005	.00006	.00261	.00241	.00023	.00002	.00023	.00000	.00000	.00009	.00024	.00057	50
55	165100	1651	.01000	.00005	.00009	.00321	.00445	.00037	.00006	.00047	.00000	.00000	.00005	.00024	.00100	55
60	142675	2345	.01644	.00007	.00008	.00465	.00861	.00067	.00006	.00065	.00000	.00000	.00008	.00032	.00125	60
65	118985	3370	.02832	.00008	.00010	.00604	.01667	.00125	.00011	.00104	.00000	.00000	.00011	.00062	.00229	65
70	92231	4338	.04703	.00013	.00010	.00838	.02959	.00242	.00030	.00163	.00000	.00000	.00021	.00083	.00345	70
75	65033	5021	.07721	.00011	.00017	.01012	.05231	.00447	.00042	.00188	.00000	.00000	.00018	.00191	.00564	75
80	35719	4755	.13312	.00014	.00011	.01259	.09460	.00750	.00073	.00283	.00000	.00000	.00017	.00384	.01022	80
85+	17136	4052	.23646	.00006	.00006	.01658	.17186	.01622	.00064	.00175	.00000	.00000	.00018	.00934	.01937	85+
ALL	2703168	30082														

			All Causes	Resp. T.B.	Other Infec.	Neoplasms	Cardio.	Infl. Pneu.	Diarrheal	Certain Degen.	Maternal	Cert. Dis. Infancy	Motor Vehicle	Other Violence	Other Unknown
CRUDE DEATH RATE			.01113	.00005	.00005	.00196	.00642	.00061	.00007	.00031	.00001	.00022	.00007	.00034	.00103
STANDARDIZED RATE (1)			.00456	.00003	.00004	.00081	.00189	.00028	.00004	.00013	.00001	.00045	.00006	.00018	.00062
STANDARDIZED RATE (2)			.00875	.00005	.00004	.00154	.00484	.00049	.00006	.00025	.00001	.00026	.00007	.00028	.00086
GEOMETRIC MEAN			.00508												

LIFE TABLE FOR ALL CAUSES COMBINED

Age (x)	Midyear Population	Deaths During Year	$_nM_x$	$_nq_x$	l_x	$_nd_x$	$_nL_x$	$_nm_x$	$_na_x$	T_x	$_nr_x$	$\overset{\circ}{e}_x$	Age (x)
0	46667	1131	.024236	.023720	100000	2372	97892	.024231	.111200	7189266	.000000	71.893	0
1	181031	156	.000862	.003442	97628	336	389672	.000862	1.500000	7091374	.000000	72.637	1
5	205152	97	.000473	.002364	97292	230	485885	.000473	2.500000	6701702	.000000	68.882	5
10	218025	57	.000261	.001308	97062	127	484985	.000262	2.442585	6215817	.004759	64.040	10
15	186595	75	.000402	.002012	96935	195	484211	.000403	2.620726	5730832	.017645	59.120	15
20	179598	89	.000496	.002481	96740	240	483135	.000497	2.645833	5246621	.010244	54.234	20
25	172446	130	.000754	.003762	96500	363	481637	.000754	2.623993	4763486	.005959	49.363	25
30	174599	166	.000951	.004733	96137	455	479655	.000949	2.735348	4281848	-.005236	44.539	30
35	180595	332	.001838	.009166	95682	877	476380	.001841	2.685766	3802194	-.004031	39.738	35
40	162611	427	.002626	.013048	94805	1237	471142	.002626	2.669766	3325813	-.000074	35.081	40
45	182988	746	.004077	.020146	93568	1885	463481	.004067	2.687666	2854671	-.011897	30.509	45
50	175982	1144	.006501	.032012	91683	2935	451590	.006499	2.674475	2391190	-.001050	26.081	50
55	165100	1651	.010000	.048936	88748	4343	433667	.010015	2.680655	1939600	-.006897	21.855	55
60	142675	2345	.016436	.079391	84405	6701	406524	.016484	2.686655	1505933	.013478	17.842	60
65	118985	3370	.028323	.133172	77704	10348	364220	.028461	2.652284	1099409	.014573	14.149	65
70	92231	4338	.047034	.211785	67356	14265	302560	.047148	2.601092	735184	.011863	10.915	70
75	65033	5021	.077207	.325291	53091	17270	223029	.077434	2.543368	432624	.013145	8.149	75
80	35719	4755	.133122	.498550	35821	17860	133637	.133645	2.454227	209595	.013145	5.851	80
85+	17136	4052	.236461	1.000000	17961	17961	75957	.236461	4.229023	75957	.000000	4.229	85+

NUMBER OF PERSONS DYING (OUT OF 100,000 AT BIRTH) ABOVE AGE X FROM SPECIFIED CAUSES

Age (x)	All Causes	Respiratory T.B.	Other Infec. and Paras.	Neo-plasms	Cardio-vascular	Infl., Pneu., Bronch.	Diar-rheal	Certain Degenerative	Maternal	Cert. Dis. of Infancy	Motor Vehicle	Other Violence	Other and Unknown	Age (x)
0	100000	390	343	16447	60429	5517	555	2635	96	1246	504	3046	8792	0
1	97628	390	314	16439	60423	5284	503	2624	96	2	500	2944	8109	1
5	97292	388	299	16413	60412	5202	497	2620	96	0	452	2896	8017	5
10	97062	388	282	16389	60405	5188	494	2608	96	0	398	2868	7946	10
15	96935	388	282	16369	60392	5179	492	2599	96	0	382	2859	7897	15
20	96740	388	272	16351	60368	5171	489	2581	90	0	346	2835	7849	20
25	96500	380	269	16313	60328	5158	489	2562	69	0	319	2806	7807	25
30	96137	346	258	16207	60278	5144	484	2548	52	0	308	2772	7740	30
35	95682	308	255	16092	60171	5122	467	2523	25	0	305	2709	7705	35
40	94805	250	247	15817	59946	5080	457	2500	12	0	300	2635	7561	40
45	93568	215	238	15310	55628	5033	451	2450	0	0	291	2566	7386	45
50	91683	187	223	14511	59047	4968	431	2380	0	0	274	2475	7187	50
55	88748	166	197	13334	57559	4863	420	2277	0	0	235	2364	6933	55
60	84405	143	158	11940	56025	4702	394	2072	0	0	214	2259	6498	60
65	77704	114	124	10048	52510	4430	371	1806	0	0	180	2131	5990	65
70	67356	87	87	7843	46415	3973	331	1426	0	0	140	1904	5150	70
75	53091	47	58	5304	37438	3239	239	933	0	0	77	1650	4106	75
80	35821	23	20	3044	25733	2238	146	514	0	0	36	1223	2844	80
85+	17961	4	4	1290	13054	1232	49	133	0	0	13	709	1473	85+

NUMBER OF PERSONS SURVIVING TO AGE X IF SPECIFIED CAUSES WERE ELIMINATED

Age (x)	No Causes	Respiratory T.B. (1)	Other Infec. and Paras. (2)	Neo-plasms (3)	Cardio-vascular (4)	Infl., Pneu., Bronch. (5)	Diar-rheal (6)	Certain Degenerative (7)	Maternal (8)	Cert. Dis. of Infancy (9)	Motor Vehicle (10)	Other Violence (11)	Other and Unknown (12)	(1)+(2)	(1)+(2)+(5)+(6)+(8)	(1)+(2)+(5)+(6)+(8)+part of(9)&(12)	(10)+(11)	Age (x)
0	100000	100000	100000	100000	100000	100000	100000	100000	100000	100000	100000	100000	100000	100000	100000	100000	100000	0
1	97628	97628	97657	97636	97634	97858	97679	97639	97628	98865	97632	97729	98305	97657	97939	99296	97733	1
5	97292	97294	97336	97326	97309	97604	97349	97307	97292	98527	97344	97440	98059	97338	97707	99102	97492	5
10	97062	97064	97122	97120	97086	97387	97122	97089	97062	98294	97168	97238	97899	97124	97510	98918	97344	10
15	96935	96937	96995	97013	96972	97269	96957	96971	96935	98165	97057	97120	97820	96997	97393	98807	97242	15
20	96740	96742	96810	96836	96801	97081	96805	96794	96746	97968	96897	96949	97672	96812	97225	98644	97106	20
25	96500	96510	96573	96633	96601	96853	96565	96573	96527	97725	96684	96737	97472	96583	97029	98455	96922	25
30	96137	96181	96221	96287	96262	96503	96206	96223	96181	97357	96331	96407	97173	96265	96745	98186	96602	30
35	95682	95764	95768	96035	95938	96068	95768	95793	95753	96896	95878	96014	96748	95850	96395	97840	96211	35
40	94805	94944	94899	95430	95284	95230	94900	94938	94888	96008	95005	95208	96007	95037	95642	97102	95408	40
45	93568	93740	93669	94653	94359	94034	93668	93749	93662	94755	93774	94034	94930	93841	94504	95955	94241	45
50	91683	91879	91757	93589	93040	92204	91801	91930	91775	92846	91902	92231	93218	91993	92728	94177	92451	50
55	88748	88958	88884	91782	91155	89357	88873	89088	88837	89874	88998	89388	90488	89095	89922	91342	89640	55
60	84405	84627	84572	88707	88654	85142	84549	84930	84490	85476	84663	85117	86493	84795	85768	87151	85377	60
65	77704	77937	77891	83591	85239	78646	77859	78444	77782	78690	77975	78483	80127	78124	79308	80616	78756	65
70	67356	67583	67552	74693	80382	68605	67528	68355	67423	68211	67628	68245	70266	67780	69282	70473	68520	70
75	53091	53305	53271	61410	73608	54743	53308	54321	53144	53765	53361	54020	56357	53486	55431	56451	54295	75
80	35821	35985	35974	43601	64871	37788	36043	36999	35857	36276	36036	36806	39133	36138	38397	39184	37027	80
85+	17961	18056	18049	23396	53098	19658	18140	18827	17979	18189	18085	18825	20689	18144	20118	20606	18955	85+

ADDED YRS OF LIFE

	No Causes	(1)	(2)	(3)	(4)	(5)	(6)	(7)	(8)	(9)	(10)	(11)	(12)	(1)+(2)	...	...	(10)+(11)
TOTAL		.103	.097	2.525	12.409	.738	.107	.366	.042	.911	.168	.491	1.603	.201	1.097	2.244	.661
WORK	2.221	.061	.024	.718	.666	.084	.020	.092	.032	.000	.046	.130	.260	.085	.222	.257	.177

POPULATION, DEATHS, DEATH RATES FOR ALL CAUSES COMBINED, AND SPECIFIED CAUSES

Age Start of Interval	Midyear Population	Deaths During Year	All Causes	Respiratory T.B.	Other Infec. and Paras.	Neoplasms	Cardiovascular	Infl., Pneu., Bronch.	Diarrheal	Certain Degenerative	Maternal	Cert. Dis. of Infancy	Motor Vehicle	Other Violence	Other and Unknown	Age Start of Interval
0	51000	1440	.02824	.00000	.00027	.00012	.00014	.00288	.00043	.00002	.00000	.01557	.00002	.00214	.00665	0
1	198000	179	.00090	.00000	.00006	.00010	.00001	.00012	.00002	.00001	.00000	.00000	.00014	.00021	.00027	1
5	226000	117	.00052	.00000	.00000	.00008	.00001	.00001	.00002	.00001	.00000	.00000	.00019	.00013	.00010	5
10	208000	91	.00044	.00000	.00001	.00008	.00001	.00004	.00000	.00000	.00000	.00000	.00011	.00008	.00010	10
15	211000	177	.00084	.00000	.00000	.00006	.00005	.00002	.00000	.00003	.00000	.00000	.00030	.00022	.00016	15
20	170000	177	.00104	.00000	.00001	.00001	.00005	.00002	.00001	.00007	.00000	.00000	.00035	.00031	.00009	20
25	156000	175	.00112	.00002	.00001	.00018	.00013	.00003	.00001	.00006	.00000	.00000	.00018	.00035	.00014	25
30	157000	208	.00132	.00003	.00001	.00024	.00029	.00005	.00000	.00005	.00000	.00000	.00022	.00035	.00012	30
35	159000	392	.00247	.00005	.00001	.00045	.00086	.00006	.00001	.00008	.00000	.00000	.00023	.00042	.00029	35
40	172000	682	.00397	.00004	.00001	.00087	.00177	.00020	.00001	.00015	.00000	.00000	.00019	.00042	.00030	40
45	140000	960	.00686	.00011	.00002	.00168	.00323	.00041	.00001	.00021	.00000	.00000	.00016	.00055	.00049	45
50	161000	1846	.01147	.00012	.00007	.00300	.00577	.00076	.00004	.00029	.00000	.00000	.00023	.00057	.00062	50
55	151000	2951	.01954	.00021	.00004	.00528	.01010	.00156	.00006	.00042	.00000	.00000	.00027	.00068	.00093	55
60	126000	4165	.03306	.00035	.00008	.00864	.01690	.00300	.00006	.00083	.00000	.00000	.00036	.00094	.00190	60
65	86000	4181	.04862	.00049	.00013	.01209	.02612	.00453	.00005	.00121	.00000	.00000	.00026	.00073	.00301	65
70	60000	4343	.07238	.00060	.00022	.01568	.04110	.00758	.00012	.00157	.00000	.00000	.00040	.00090	.00422	70
75	39000	4082	.10467	.00054	.00013	.01872	.06103	.01049	.00005	.00310	.00000	.00000	.00041	.00050	.00828	75
80	21000	3182	.15152	.00052	.00019	.02114	.09386	.01390	.00062	.00329	.00000	.00000	.00000	.00192	.01357	80
85+	10000	2415	.24150	.00020	.00000	.02230	.16120	.02480	.00050	.00420	.00000	.00000	.00000	.00095	.02170	85+
ALL	2502000	31763														

		All Causes	Respiratory T.B.	Other Infec. and Paras.	Neoplasms	Cardiovascular	Infl., Pneu., Bronch.	Diarrheal	Certain Degenerative	Maternal	Cert. Dis. of Infancy	Motor Vehicle	Other Violence	Other and Unknown
CRUDE DEATH RATE		.01270	.00010	.00004	.00254	.00649	.00113	.00003	.00030	.00000	.00032	.00023	.00050	.00100
STANDARDIZED RATE (1)		.00675	.00005	.00003	.00124	.00284	.00058	.00003	.00015	.00000	.00055	.00021	.00050	.00068
STANDARDIZED RATE (2)		.01271	.00009	.00004	.00247	.00655	.00114	.00003	.00030	.00000	.00055	.00021	.00040	.00068
GEOMETRIC MEAN		.00757									.00032	.00023	.00050	.00103

LIFE TABLE FOR ALL CAUSES COMBINED

Age (x)	Midyear Population	Deaths During Year	$_nM_x$	$_nq_x$	l_x	$_nd_x$	$_nL_x$	$_nm_x$	$_na_x$	T_x	$_nr_x$	$\overset{\circ}{e}_x$	Age (x)
0	51000	1440	.028235	.027550	100000	2755	97570	.028236	.118000	6668001	.000000	66.680	0
1	198000	179	.000904	.003609	97245	351	388103	.000904	1.500000	6570431	.000000	67.566	1
5	226000	117	.000518	.002580	96894	250	483845	.000517	2.500000	6182328	.000000	63.805	5
10	208000	91	.000437	.002183	96644	211	482725	.000437	2.653041	5698483	.000000	58.964	10
15	211000	177	.000839	.004200	96433	405	481212	.000842	2.648148	5215759	.003099	54.087	15
20	170000	177	.001041	.005196	96028	499	478920	.001042	2.554275	4734546	.012974	49.304	20
25	156000	175	.001122	.005600	95525	535	476334	.001123	2.550234	4255626	-.029104	44.548	25
30	157000	208	.001325	.006611	94994	628	473529	.001326	2.705016	3779292	.013285	39.785	30
35	159000	392	.002465	.012218	94366	1153	469199	.002457	2.717910	3305763	-.002886	35.031	35
40	172000	682	.003965	.019675	93213	1834	461883	.003971	2.719693	2836565	-.011965	30.431	40
45	140000	960	.006857	.033782	91379	3087	449819	.006863	2.707793	2374682	-.004291	25.987	45
50	161000	1846	.011466	.055645	88292	4913	430157	.011421	2.699301	1924863	-.004895	21.801	50
55	151000	2951	.019543	.093393	83379	7787	398823	.019525	2.679225	1494706	-.017337	17.927	55
60	126000	4165	.033056	.153614	75592	11612	350215	.033157	2.610626	1095883	-.004224	14.497	60
65	86000	4181	.048616	.218064	63980	13953	285799	.048821	2.555977	745668	.015972	11.655	65
70	60000	4343	.072383	.307054	50027	15361	211806	.072524	2.504788	459870	.025167	9.192	70
75	39000	4082	.104667	.412681	34666	14306	136661	.104683	2.436758	248064	.011131	7.156	75
80	21000	3182	.151524	.541306	20360	11021	72732	.151529	2.362497	111403	.000555	5.472	80
85+	10000	2415	.241500	1.000000	9339	9339	38671	.241500	4.140787	38671	.000000	4.141	85+

NUMBER OF PERSONS DYING (OUT OF 100,000 AT BIRTH) ABOVE AGE X FROM SPECIFIED CAUSES

Age (x)	All Causes	Respiratory T.B.	Other Infec. and Paras.	Neoplasms	Cardiovascular	Infl., Pneu., Bronch.	Diarrheal	Certain Degenerative	Maternal	Cert. Dis. of Infancy	Motor Vehicle	Other Violence	Other and Unknown	Age (x)
0	100000	762	278	19974	52997	9034	237	2394	0	1519	1612	3588	7605	0
1	97245	762	251	19963	52984	8753	195	2392	0	0	1610	3379	6956	1
5	96894	762	229	19926	52582	8707	189	2390	0	0	1557	3259	6853	5
10	96644	762	227	19887	52578	8703	189	2390	0	0	1467	3237	6804	10
15	96433	762	223	19848	52971	8682	189	2390	0	0	1416	3197	6755	15
20	96028	762	220	19818	52548	8671	189	2376	0	0	1272	3092	6680	20
25	95529	762	217	19753	52525	8660	186	2342	0	0	1103	2942	6639	25
30	94994	753	211	19667	52861	8644	183	2312	0	0	1018	2774	6571	30
35	94366	738	205	19555	52725	8620	183	2288	0	0	915	2624	6513	35
40	93213	714	199	19344	52322	8591	180	2249	0	0	806	2429	6379	40
45	91379	695	197	18940	51505	8497	172	2182	0	0	717	2233	6241	45
50	88292	647	187	18184	50051	8313	169	2089	0	0	644	1985	6023	50
55	83379	594	158	16899	47579	7989	153	1964	0	0	545	1742	5756	55
60	75592	509	142	14794	43555	7369	129	1798	0	0	437	1473	5386	60
65	63980	387	114	11758	37619	6315	110	1505	0	0	311	1145	4716	65
70	50027	247	77	8291	30119	5012	96	1158	0	0	238	936	3853	70
75	34666	120	31	4965	21395	3403	71	825	0	0	154	745	2957	75
80	20360	46	14	2407	13055	1970	64	401	0	0	97	482	1824	80
85+	9339	8	0	862	6234	959	19	162	0	0	27	228	840	85+

NUMBER OF PERSONS SURVIVING TO AGE X IF SPECIFIED CAUSES WERE ELIMINATED

Age (x)	No Causes	Respiratory T.B. (1)	Other Infec. and Paras. (2)	Neoplasms (3)	Cardiovascular (4)	Infl., Pneu., Bronch. (5)	Diarrheal (6)	Certain Degenerative (7)	Maternal (8)	Cert. Dis. of Infancy (9)	Motor Vehicle (10)	Other Violence (11)	Other and Unknown (12)	(1)+(2)	(1)+(2)+(5)+(6)+(8)	(1)+(2)+(5)+(6)+(8)+part of(9)&(12)	(10)+(11)	Age (x)
0	100000	100000	100000	100000	100000	100000	100000	100000	100000	100000	100000	100000	100000	100000	100000	100000	100000	0
1	97245	97245	97272	97256	97258	97522	97286	97247	97245	98754	97247	97451	97887	97272	97591	98878	97453	1
5	96894	96894	96943	96942	96909	97217	96941	96898	96894	98398	96949	97180	97637	96943	97313	98628	97235	5
10	96644	96644	96694	96731	96663	96970	96691	96648	96644	98144	96789	96991	97435	96694	97068	98381	97136	10
15	96433	96433	96487	96558	96459	96779	96480	96437	96433	97930	96628	96819	97271	96487	96881	98199	97016	15
20	96028	96028	96085	96183	96077	96384	96075	96046	96028	97519	96367	96518	96938	96085	96488	97804	96858	20
25	95529	95529	95589	95748	95600	95894	95579	95581	95529	97012	96035	96167	96476	95589	96004	97315	96677	25
30	94994	95003	95059	95298	95129	95373	95046	95075	94994	96469	95553	95797	96004	95508	95500	96810	96391	30
35	94366	94390	94437	94780	94636	94766	94418	94471	94366	95831	95054	95315	95428	94461	94914	96220	96010	35
40	93213	93260	93289	93833	93882	93637	93267	93355	93213	94660	94002	94346	94357	93336	93816	95115	95144	40
45	91379	91444	91456	92390	92853	91889	91440	91585	91379	92797	92241	92686	92678	91521	92093	93378	93561	45
50	88292	88402	88376	90024	91181	88666	88354	88583	88292	89663	89157	89802	89764	88486	89225	90485	90723	50
55	83379	83535	83486	86297	88624	84334	83453	83775	83379	84673	84331	85045	85033	83642	84676	85900	86016	55
60	75592	75814	75704	80239	84523	77058	75682	76110	75592	76765	76559	77364	77452	75927	77491	78649	78353	60
65	63980	64281	64101	71026	77907	66216	64074	64690	63980	64973	64915	65787	66189	64402	66750	67820	66749	65
70	50027	50386	50154	55930	69537	52980	50113	50892	50027	50804	50823	51628	52548	50514	53587	54541	52449	70
75	34666	35020	34792	44269	59360	38151	34746	35548	34666	35204	35288	35939	37202	35147	38770	39566	36584	75
80	20360	20623	20447	28571	47576	23630	20412	21211	20360	20676	20769	21318	22758	20711	24099	24716	21746	80
85+	9339	9485	9388	14619	35350	11642	9393	9895	9339	9484	9574	9956	11211	9535	11955	12355	10206	85+

ADDED YRS OF LIFE

	No Causes	(1)	(2)	(3)	(4)	(5)	(6)	(7)	(8)	(9)	(10)	(11)	(12)	(1)+(2)	(1)+(2)+(5)+(6)+(8)	combo	(10)+(11)
TOTAL		.106	.070	2.742	9.983	1.145	.055	.303	.000	1.033	.506	.905	1.365	.177	1.394	2.404	1.422
WORK	3.646	.040	.015	.744	1.349	.183	.009	.110	.000	.000	.278	.403	.264	.056	.249	.269	.684

POPULATION, DEATHS, DEATH RATES FOR ALL CAUSES COMBINED, AND SPECIFIED CAUSES

Age Start of Interval	Midyear Population	Deaths During Year	All Causes	Respiratory T. B.	Other Infec. and Paras.	Neoplasms	Cardiovascular	Infl., Pneu., Bronch.	Diarrheal	Certain Degenerative	Maternal	Cert. Dis. of Infancy	Motor Vehicle	Other Violence	Other and Unknown	Age Start of Interval
0	49000	1068	.02180	.00002	.00027	.00004	.00008	.00222	.00073	.00002	.00000	.01090	.00000	.00137	.00614	0
1	187000	168	.00090	.00000	.00004	.00009	.00002	.00013	.00005	.00001	.00000	.00000	.00010	.00016	.00030	1
5	216000	56	.00026	.00000	.00002	.00004	.00000	.00002	.00001	.00001	.00000	.00000	.00006	.00003	.00006	5
10	199000	68	.00034	.00000	.00000	.00004	.00004	.00003	.00001	.00002	.00000	.00000	.00006	.00005	.00010	10
15	208000	80	.00038	.00000	.00000	.00006	.00004	.00002	.00001	.00003	.00000	.00000	.00008	.00003	.00011	15
20	175000	86	.00049	.00000	.00002	.00005	.00007	.00002	.00001	.00001	.00002	.00000	.00009	.00011	.00009	20
25	163000	115	.00071	.00002	.00002	.00010	.00015	.00004	.00002	.00002	.00006	.00000	.00002	.00012	.00013	25
30	162000	153	.00094	.00004	.00002	.00022	.00023	.00006	.00001	.00004	.00004	.00000	.00003	.00010	.00015	30
35	166000	238	.00143	.00005	.00000	.00049	.00032	.00003	.00001	.00006	.00002	.00000	.00002	.00023	.00020	35
40	181000	466	.00257	.00007	.00002	.00102	.00077	.00012	.00003	.00003	.00001	.00000	.00003	.00017	.00030	40
45	155000	654	.00422	.00005	.00003	.00182	.00132	.00017	.00002	.00007	.00000	.00000	.00009	.00023	.00041	45
50	175000	1152	.00658	.00006	.00002	.00254	.00252	.00026	.00001	.00019	.00000	.00000	.00007	.00034	.00057	50
55	168000	1682	.01001	.00005	.00004	.00352	.00444	.00046	.00004	.00027	.00000	.00000	.00007	.00025	.00087	55
60	152000	2393	.01574	.00005	.00009	.00453	.00841	.00057	.00008	.00040	.00000	.00000	.00015	.00038	.00109	60
65	126000	3337	.02648	.00009	.00006	.00636	.01540	.00115	.00011	.00069	.00000	.00000	.00016	.00053	.00193	65
70	98000	4240	.04327	.00004	.00007	.00813	.02778	.00223	.00020	.00105	.00000	.00000	.00018	.00083	.00274	70
75	69000	4738	.06867	.00009	.00017	.00956	.04622	.00410	.00042	.00164	.00000	.00000	.00029	.00159	.00419	75
80	38000	4443	.11692	.00008	.00013	.01363	.08197	.00745	.00066	.00205	.00000	.00000	.00029	.00368	.00697	80
85+	20000	4139	.20695	.00005	.00025	.01655	.15040	.01425	.00065	.00170	.00000	.00000	.00000	.00025	.01445	85+
ALL	2707000	29276														

		All Causes	Respiratory T. B.	Other Infec. and Paras.	Neoplasms	Cardiovascular	Infl., Pneu., Bronch.	Diarrheal	Certain Degenerative	Maternal	Cert. Dis. of Infancy	Motor Vehicle	Other Violence	Other and Unknown
CRUDE DEATH RATE		.01081	.00003	.00004	.00204	.00626	.00061	.00007	.00022	.00001	.00020	.00008	.00037	.00088
STANDARDIZED RATE (1)		.00422	.00002	.00003	.00081	.00175	.00026	.00005	.00009	.00001	.00038	.00007	.00021	.00054
STANDARDIZED RATE (2)		.00803	.00003	.00003	.00154	.00442	.00046	.00006	.00017	.00001	.00023	.00008	.00030	.00072
GEOMETRIC MEAN		.00474												

LIFE TABLE FOR ALL CAUSES COMBINED

Age (x)	Midyear Population	Deaths During Year	$_nM_x$	$_nq_x$	l_x	$_nd_x$	$_nL_x$	$_nm_x$	$_na_x$	T_x	$_nr_x$	$\overset{\circ}{e}_x$	Age (x)
0	49000	1068	.021796	.021380	100000	2138	98091	.021796	.107053	7280300	.000000	72.803	0
1	187000	168	.000898	.003587	97862	351	390571	.000899	1.500000	7182210	.000000	73.391	1
5	216000	56	.000259	.001292	97511	126	487240	.000259	2.500000	6791639	.000000	69.650	5
10	199000	68	.000342	.001705	97385	166	486523	.000341	2.576556	6304399	.000000	64.737	10
15	208000	80	.000385	.001923	97219	187	485643	.000385	2.581328	5817876	.001642	59.843	15
20	175000	86	.000491	.002463	97032	239	484595	.000493	2.635112	5332234	.007240	54.953	20
25	163000	115	.000706	.003533	96793	342	483155	.000708	2.630970	4847639	.022723	50.083	25
30	162000	153	.000944	.004707	96451	454	481191	.000943	2.656938	4364484	.011853	45.251	30
35	166000	238	.001434	.007125	95997	684	478435	.001430	2.733309	3883293	.003152	40.452	35
40	181000	466	.002575	.012800	95313	1220	473782	.002575	2.719092	3404858	-.011992	35.723	40
45	155000	654	.004219	.020905	94093	1967	465914	.004222	2.686303	2931076	.000545	31.151	45
50	175000	1152	.006583	.032336	92126	2979	453681	.006566	2.667282	2465162	.002604	26.759	50
55	168000	1682	.010012	.048897	89147	4359	435560	.010008	2.665845	2011481	-.013719	22.564	55
60	152000	2393	.015743	.076060	84788	6449	408950	.015770	2.675576	1575921	-.001706	18.587	60
65	126000	3337	.026484	.125021	78339	9794	368672	.026566	2.649305	1166971	.008053	14.896	65
70	98000	4240	.043265	.196484	68545	13468	310400	.043389	2.599866	798299	.014897	11.646	70
75	69000	4738	.068667	.295041	55077	16250	235622	.068566	2.553077	487899	.014255	8.858	75
80	38000	4443	.116921	.453499	38827	17608	149744	.117587	2.478939	252276	.020713	6.497	80
85+	20000	4139	.206950	1.000000	21219	21219	102532	.206950	4.832085	102532	.020713	4.832	85+
											.000000		

NUMBER OF PERSONS DYING (OUT OF 100,000 AT BIRTH) ABOVE AGE X FROM SPECIFIED CAUSES

Age (x)	All Causes	Respiratory T.B.	Other Infec. and Paras.	Neoplasms	Cardiovascular	Infl., Pneu., Bronch.	Diarrheal	Certain Degenerative	Maternal	Cert. Dis. of Infancy	Motor Vehicle	Other Violence	Other and Unknown	Age (x)
0	100000	263	297	17377	60972	5740	582	1967	70	1069	643	3380	7640	0
1	97862	261	271	17373	60964	5521	510	1965	70	0	643	3246	7038	1
5	97511	261	257	17340	60957	5469	489	1963	70	0	604	3183	6918	5
10	97385	259	248	17320	60955	5460	483	1956	70	0	577	3168	6889	10
15	97219	259	248	17300	60938	5448	478	1947	70	0	547	3143	6841	15
20	97032	259	247	17270	60917	5436	471	1933	70	0	510	3129	6790	20
25	96793	259	239	17245	60881	5425	465	1927	61	0	466	3076	6749	25
30	96451	247	230	17197	60810	5404	456	1915	35	0	457	3017	6683	30
35	95997	229	221	17090	60697	5378	453	1897	14	0	442	2967	6609	35
40	95313	206	221	16858	60545	5363	448	1869	5	0	433	2854	6511	40
45	94093	172	211	16376	60181	5306	435	1853	0	0	418	2776	6365	45
50	92126	148	196	15528	59564	5228	426	1820	0	0	376	2667	6173	50
55	89147	122	185	14376	58425	5109	420	1734	0	0	344	2512	5920	55
60	84788	101	167	12842	56492	4909	402	1618	0	0	316	2403	5538	60
65	78339	82	132	10989	53046	4675	370	1453	0	0	254	2247	5091	65
70	68545	50	109	8641	47346	4249	329	1198	0	0	195	2050	4378	70
75	55077	38	87	6113	38697	3552	265	871	0	0	138	1793	3523	75
80	38827	17	46	3762	27756	2581	166	484	0	0	70	1415	2530	80
85+	21219	5	26	1697	15421	1461	67	174	0	0	26	861	1481	85+

NUMBER OF PERSONS SURVIVING TO AGE X IF SPECIFIED CAUSES WERE ELIMINATED

Age (x)	No Causes	Respiratory T.B. (1)	Other Infec. and Paras. (2)	Neoplasms (3)	Cardiovascular (4)	Infl., Pneu., Bronch. (5)	Diarrheal (6)	Certain Degenerative (7)	Maternal (8)	Cert. Dis. of Infancy (9)	Motor Vehicle (10)	Other Violence (11)	Other and Unknown (12)	(1)+(2)	(1)+(2)+(5)+(6)+(8)	(1)+(2)+(5)+(6)+(8)+part of(9)&(12)	(10)+(11)	Age (x)
0	100000	100000	100000	100000	100000	100000	100000	100000	100000	100000	100000	100000	100000	100000	100000	100000	100000	0
1	97862	97864	97888	97866	97870	98079	97933	97864	97862	98925	97862	97995	98459	97890	98178	99317	97995	1
5	97511	97513	97551	97548	97526	97779	97603	97515	97511	98570	97550	97706	98227	97553	97913	99095	97745	5
10	97385	97389	97434	97442	97402	97662	97483	97396	97385	98443	97451	97595	98129	97438	97813	99001	97661	10
15	97219	97223	97267	97296	97253	97507	97322	97239	97219	98275	97315	97454	98010	97271	97663	98857	97550	15
20	97032	97036	97081	97139	97087	97332	97141	97066	97032	98086	97165	97280	97873	97085	97495	98695	97413	20
25	96793	96797	96850	96924	96884	97103	96908	96833	96802	97845	96969	97094	97673	96854	97289	98493	97270	25
30	96451	96467	96517	96630	96612	96781	96575	96503	96486	97499	96636	96810	97395	96533	97023	98242	96995	30
35	95997	96031	96072	96282	96270	96352	96123	96066	96053	97040	96156	96404	97011	96106	96643	97873	96604	35
40	95313	95369	95387	95828	95737	95680	95443	95410	95377	96349	95519	95830	96418	95444	96007	97238	96038	40
45	94093	94183	94176	95084	94875	94512	94235	94204	94161	95115	94312	94682	95231	94266	94897	96130	94902	45
50	92126	92237	92222	93948	93510	92614	92274	92268	92193	93127	92382	92811	93531	92334	93039	94262	93068	50
55	89147	89280	89251	92073	91631	89737	89256	89369	89212	90116	89426	89963	90759	89385	90192	91392	90245	55
60	84788	84935	84905	89129	89111	85546	84947	85113	84850	85709	85081	85672	86701	85052	86035	87205	85967	60
65	78339	78493	78480	84240	85891		78517	78798	78356	79190	78669	79307	80547	78635	79804	80913	79641	65
70	68545	68710	68690	76101	81234	69761	68739	69187	68595	69290	68889	69578	71165	68855	70326	71343	69927	70
75	55077	55220	55213	63699	75129	56694	55290	55888	55117	55675	55405	56141	57980	55357	57244	58123	56475	75
80	38827	38945	38957	47218	67035	40812	39061	39727	38855	39249	39115	39902	41755	39076	41351	42052	40198	80
85+	21219	21293	21305	27700	55939	23177	21419	21543	21234	21450	21409	22225	23655	21379	23589	24055	22424	85+

ADDED YRS OF LIFE

	No Causes	(1)	(2)	(3)	(4)	(5)	(6)	(7)	(8)	(9)	(10)	(11)	(12)	(1)+(2)	sum	sum+part	(10)+(11)
TOTAL		.065	.079	2.707	13.731	.761	.136	.261	.031	.790	.188	.605	1.479	.144	1.083	2.064	.795
WORK	2.161	.033	.018	.690	.673	.090	.018	.058	.023	.000	.064	.162	.248	.051	.183	.213	.226

POPULATION, DEATHS, DEATH RATES FOR ALL CAUSES COMBINED, AND SPECIFIED CAUSES

Age Start of Interval	Midyear Population	Deaths During Year	All Causes	Respiratory T. B.	Other Infec. and Paras.	Neoplasms	Cardiovascular	Infl., Pneu., Bronch.	Diarrheal	Certain Degenerative	Maternal	Cert. Dis. of Infancy	Motor Vehicle	Other Violence	Other and Unknown	Age Start of Interval
0	17000	3350	.19706	.00124	.01876	.00000	.00000	.05918	.04594	.00094	.00000	.03059	.00000	.00129	.03912	0
1	59000	1944	.03295	.00207	.00610	.00000	.00002	.01180	.00834	.00085	.00000	.00000	.00010	.00058	.00310	1
5	63000	322	.00511	.00075	.00108	.00003	.00024	.00124	.00041	.00014	.00000	.00000	.00014	.00038	.00065	5
10	54105	178	.00329	.00068	.00055	.00000	.00024	.00057	.00009	.00009	.00000	.00000	.00007	.00037	.00061	10
15	45360	265	.00584	.00276	.00055	.00004	.00031	.00068	.00007	.00009	.00000	.00000	.00009	.00064	.00062	15
20	39110	341	.00872	.00447	.00066	.00003	.00041	.00102	.00003	.00015	.00000	.00000	.00033	.00087	.00074	20
25	34840	346	.00993	.00511	.00063	.00011	.00075	.00092	.00003	.00014	.00000	.00000	.00029	.00118	.00077	25
30	30090	311	.01034	.00479	.00120	.00013	.00063	.00090	.00013	.00043	.00000	.00000	.00027	.00080	.00106	30
35	24150	316	.01308	.00522	.00137	.00025	.00128	.00153	.00012	.00037	.00000	.00000	.00000	.00112	.00137	35
40	20010	362	.01809	.00675	.00170	.00100	.00265	.00185	.00020	.00065	.00000	.00000	.00050	.00135	.00145	40
45	17070	351	.02056	.00680	.00205	.00117	.00357	.00246	.00012	.00059	.00000	.00000	.00064	.00064	.00252	45
50	14850	346	.02330	.00626	.00155	.00202	.00519	.00330	.00000	.00108	.00000	.00000	.00054	.00101	.00236	50
55	11780	310	.02632	.00556	.00136	.00263	.00747	.00374	.00034	.00144	.00000	.00000	.00042	.00051	.00255	55
60	9490	403	.04247	.00769	.00179	.00369	.01338	.00695	.00074	.00179	.00000	.00000	.00074	.00095	.00474	60
65	6170	374	.06062	.00616	.00211	.00519	.02010	.01264	.00130	.00340	.00000	.00000	.00065	.00065	.00843	65
70	4320	326	.07546	.00463	.00208	.00926	.02431	.01134	.00231	.00278	.00000	.00000	.00046	.00139	.01690	70
75	2730	241	.08828	.00440	.00110	.00513	.03297	.01355	.00183	.00366	.00000	.00000	.00000	.00110	.02454	75
80	1160	202	.17414	.00517	.00345	.00690	.05172	.03276	.00345	.00345	.00000	.00000	.00000	.00172	.06552	80
85+	720	204	.28333	.00417	.00000	.00278	.07361	.04583	.00139	.00417	.00000	.00000	.00000	.00278	.14861	85+
ALL	454955	10492														

CRUDE DEATH RATE			.02306	.00339	.00236	.00055	.00214	.00539	.00299	.00053	.00000	.00114	.00025	.00075	.00358	
STANDARDIZED RATE (1)			.02278	.00352	.00228	.00061	.00228	.00520	.00281	.00054	.00000	.00108	.00026	.00076	.00345	
STANDARDIZED RATE (2)			.02593	.00413	.00195	.00114	.00456	.00507	.00193	.00077	.00000	.00063	.00031	.00082	.00462	
GEOMETRIC MEAN			.02693													

LIFE TABLE FOR ALL CAUSES COMBINED

Age (x)	Midyear Population	Deaths During Year	$_nM_x$	$_nq_x$	l_x	$_nd_x$	$_nL_x$	$_nm_x$	$_na_x$	T_x	$_nr_x$	$\overset{\circ}{e}_x$	Age (x)
0	17000	3350	.197059	.176380	100000	17638	89505	.197061	.405000	4037261	.000000	40.373	0
1	59000	1944	.032949	.121767	82362	10029	304376	.032949	1.500000	3947755	.000000	47.932	1
5	63000	322	.005111	.025231	72333	1825	357103	.005111	2.500000	3643380	.000000	50.370	5
10	54105	178	.003290	.016310	70508	1150	349704	.003288	2.533514	3286277	.021942	46.609	10
15	45360	265	.005842	.028980	69358	2010	342126	.005875	2.679415	2936574	.026937	42.339	15
20	39110	341	.008719	.042778	67348	2881	329770	.008736	2.580701	2594448	.020700	38.523	20
25	34840	346	.009931	.048490	64467	3126	314565	.009938	2.514262	2264678	.015893	35.129	25
30	30090	311	.010336	.050456	61341	3095	299088	.010348	2.539041	1950114	.022966	31.791	30
35	24150	316	.013085	.063627	58246	3706	282306	.013128	2.592080	1651025	.027695	28.346	35
40	20010	362	.018091	.086780	54540	4733	261111	.018126	2.551412	1368719	.021222	25.096	40
45	17070	351	.020562	.097858	49807	4874	236895	.020574	2.509275	1107608	.011084	22.238	45
50	14850	346	.023300	.110164	44933	4950	212306	.023315	2.503325	870713	.013190	19.378	50
55	11780	310	.026316	.123878	39983	4953	187911	.026358	2.576427	658406	.014100	16.467	55
60	9490	403	.042646	.193177	35030	6767	158754	.042626	2.577090	470495	.020288	13.431	60
65	6170	374	.060616	.263843	28263	7457	122633	.060807	2.494692	311741	.022097	11.030	65
70	4320	326	.075463	.316111	20806	6577	87104	.075507	2.426512	189108	.006009	9.089	70
75	2730	241	.088278	.361023	14229	5137	58079	.088449	2.456403	102004	.025372	7.169	75
80	1160	202	.174138	.605147	9092	5502	31255	.176036	2.418212	43926	.025372	4.831	80
85+	720	204	.283333	1.000000	3590	3590	12671	.283333	3.529412	12671	.000000	3.529	85+

NUMBER OF PERSONS DYING (OUT OF 100,000 AT BIRTH) ABOVE AGE X FROM SPECIFIED CAUSES

Age (x)	All Causes	Respiratory T.B.	Other Infec. and Paras.	Neo-plasms	Cardio-vascular	Infl., Pneu., Bronch.	Diar-rheal	Certain Degen-erative	Maternal	Cert. Dis. of Infancy	Motor Vehicle	Other Violence	Other and Unknown	Age (x)
0	100000	16878	7883	4229	16459	15621	7800	2917	0	2738	1262	3312	16901	0
1	82362	16768	6203	4229	16459	14324	3688	2833	0	0	1262	3196	13400	1
5	72333	16138	4346	4229	16454	10734	1150	2575	0	0	1231	3021	12455	5
10	70508	15855	3961	4218	16369	10291	1003	2524	0	0	1180	2884	12223	10
15	69358	15613	3768	4218	16285	10092	971	2492	0	0	1155	2755	12009	15
20	67348	14663	3579	4203	16179	9858	949	2461	0	0	1124	2535	11797	20
25	64467	13184	3360	4194	16044	9520	940	2411	0	0	1014	2248	11552	25
30	61341	11576	3160	4158	15809	9231	931	2365	0	0	924	1877	11310	30
35	58246	10145	2801	4118	15619	8562	891	2236	0	0	844	1639	10991	35
40	54540	8669	2415	4047	15254	8528	856	2130	0	0	715	1323	10603	40
45	49807	6905	1970	3784	14559	8044	804	1960	0	0	584	971	10226	45
50	44933	5296	1485	3506	13711	7460	776	1821	0	0	432	818	9628	50
55	39983	3966	1156	3077	12608	6759	776	1592	0	0	317	604	9128	55
60	35030	2866	901	2581	11201	6056	712	1320	0	0	238	508	8647	60
65	28263	1643	616	1994	9067	4946	594	1035	0	0	120	357	7891	65
70	20806	889	357	1355	6594	3390	434	616	0	0	41	278	6852	70
75	14229	486	176	548	4476	2402	232	374	0	0	1	157	5377	75
80	9092	231	112	253	2557	1613	126	161	0	0	1	93	3945	80
85+	3590	53	0	35	933	581	18	53	0	0	0	35	1882	85+

NUMBER OF PERSONS SURVIVING TO AGE X IF SPECIFIED CAUSES WERE ELIMINATED

Age (x)	No Causes	Respiratory T.B. (1)	Other Infec. and Paras. (2)	Neo-plasms (3)	Cardio-vascular (4)	Infl., Pneu., Bronch. (5)	Diar-rheal (6)	Certain Degener-ative (7)	Maternal (8)	Cert. Dis. of Infancy (9)	Motor Vehicle (10)	Other Violence (11)	Other and Unknown (12)	(1)+(2)	(1)+(2)+(5)+(6)+(8)	(1)+(2)+(5)+(6)+(8)+part of (9)&(12)	(10)+(11)	Age (x)
0	100000	100000	100000	100000	100000	100000	100000	100000	100000	100000	100000	100000	100000	100000	100000	100000	100000	0
1	82362	82462	83898	82362	82362	87304	86173	82438	82362	84881	82362	82467	85596	84000	93161	99660	82467	1
5	72333	73014	75475	72333	72338	80321	78208	72642	72333	74545	72362	72590	76099	76186	91471	98994	72619	5
10	70508	71454	73969	70519	70597	78782	76392	70860	70508	72664	70587	70894	74420	74961	90748	98464	70973	10
15	69358	70532	72983	69369	69529	77718	75181	69736	69358	71479	69460	69867	73431	74199	90122	97998	69969	15
20	67348	69447	71045	67373	67618	75724	73025	67746	67348	69408	67478	68060	71524	73260	89315	97354	68192	20
25	64467	67986	68232	64500	64859	72858	69911	64897	64467	66438	64699	65433	68719	71956	88189	96404	65669	25
30	61341	66364	65130	61408	61945	69644	66531	61795	61341	63217	61650	62629	65639	70464	86770	95120	62944	30
35	58246	64541	62217	58348	59007	66428	63216	58804	58246	60027	58618	59706	62661	68942	85336	93926	60087	35
40	54540	62037	58658	54705	55612	62683	59231	55166	54540	56208	55014	56221	59079	66722	83278	92105	56710	40
45	49807	58602	54027	50211	51469	57777	54145	50544	49807	51330	50306	51689	54344	63567	80160	89062	52270	45
50	44933	54693	49242	45565	47273	52771	48875	45732	44933	46307	45584	46781	49650	59937	76568	85754	47459	50
55	39983	50215	44157	40958	43176	47741	43491	40915	39983	41206	40672	41838	44704	55457	72026	81172	42559	55
60	35030	45302	38950	36363	39279	42620	38169	36107	35030	36101	35708	36749	39672	50372	66778	75718	37460	60
65	28263	37988	31711	29889	33913	35623	30911	29397	28263	29127	28518	29791	32788	42622	58756	67354	30482	65
70	20806	28833	23592	22590	27635	27955	22907	22016	20806	21442	21357	22002	25198	32694	48363	56460	22584	70
75	14229	20176	16302	16187	21362	20232	15850	15267	14229	14664	14638	15153	18783	23116	36612	44036	15589	75
80	9092	13178	10473	10603	16137	13851	10220	9937	9092	9370	9353	9736	13614	15181	25997	32593	10015	80
85+	3590	5362	4214	4343	8383	6510	4110	3996	3590	3700	3694	3882	7616	6295	13069	18940	3994	85+

ADDED YRS OF LIFE

	No Causes	(1)	(2)	(3)	(4)	(5)	(6)	(7)	(8)	(9)	(10)	(11)	(12)	(1)+(2)	(1)+(2)+(5)+(6)+(8)	(1)+(2)+(5)+(6)+(8)+part of (9)&(12)	(10)+(11)
TOTAL		4.825	2.867	.582	2.481	6.457	3.413	.594	.000	1.222	.316	.966	4.120	8.183	21.449	28.866	1.295
WORK	12.155	4.267	.840	.321	1.155	1.104	.073	.280	.000	.000	.267	.760	.939	5.266	6.737	7.567	1.035

POPULATION, DEATHS, DEATH RATES FOR ALL CAUSES COMBINED, AND SPECIFIED CAUSES

Age Start of Interval	Midyear Population	Deaths During Year	All Causes	Respiratory T.B.	Other Infec. and Paras.	Neoplasms	Cardiovascular	Infl., Pneu., Bronch.	Diarrheal	Certain Degenerative	Maternal	Cert. Dis. of Infancy	Motor Vehicle	Other Violence	Other and Unknown	Age Start of Interval
0	17100	2979	.17421	.00111	.01855	.00000	.00000	.05474	.04076	.00058	.00000	.02392	.00000	.00123	.03292	0
1	58700	1970	.03356	.00186	.00610	.00007	.00002	.01266	.00850	.00087	.00000	.00000	.00003	.00068	.00278	1
5	63000	339	.00538	.00110	.00108	.00003	.00017	.00170	.00029	.00010	.00000	.00000	.00014	.00030	.00048	5
10	54010	226	.00418	.00152	.00076	.00009	.00028	.00080	.00004	.00007	.00002	.00000	.00006	.00013	.00043	10
15	44805	364	.00812	.00442	.00060	.00002	.00045	.00103	.00004	.00004	.00047	.00000	.00002	.00016	.00087	15
20	38130	423	.01109	.00716	.00055	.00008	.00034	.00084	.00021	.00005	.00089	.00000	.00005	.00029	.00063	20
25	33580	405	.01206	.00640	.00074	.00012	.00074	.00110	.00009	.00024	.00137	.00000	.00006	.00012	.00107	25
30	28755	313	.01089	.00574	.00035	.00045	.00083	.00077	.00007	.00024	.00143	.00000	.00003	.00010	.00087	30
35	23000	261	.01135	.00417	.00052	.00048	.00170	.00078	.00022	.00052	.00135	.00000	.00013	.00022	.00126	35
40	18880	256	.01356	.00450	.00143	.00111	.00238	.00132	.00000	.00021	.00132	.00000	.00000	.00042	.00085	40
45	16075	244	.01518	.00379	.00062	.00212	.00442	.00106	.00019	.00087	.00050	.00000	.00000	.00025	.00137	45
50	13930	227	.01630	.00294	.00136	.00187	.00553	.00115	.00022	.00079	.00000	.00000	.00007	.00036	.00201	50
55	10820	218	.02015	.00305	.00083	.00268	.00712	.00203	.00028	.00139	.00000	.00000	.00018	.00009	.00250	55
60	8090	327	.04042	.00371	.00136	.00507	.01718	.00445	.00037	.00309	.00000	.00000	.00000	.00074	.00445	60
65	5580	308	.05520	.00502	.00179	.00430	.02384	.00771	.00125	.00269	.00000	.00000	.00108	.00036	.00717	65
70	4040	263	.06510	.00347	.00173	.00718	.02822	.00916	.00124	.00099	.00000	.00000	.00000	.00074	.01238	70
75	1710	211	.12339	.00351	.00175	.00702	.05556	.01988	.00117	.00409	.00000	.00000	.00117	.00000	.02924	75
80	1140	214	.18772	.00263	.00088	.00877	.06842	.02544	.00263	.00526	.00000	.00000	.00000	.00351	.07018	80
85+	810	236	.29136	.00370	.00123	.00247	.08025	.03333	.00247	.00617	.00000	.00000	.00000	.00247	.15926	85+
ALL	442155	9784														

	All Causes	Respiratory T.B.	Other Infec. and Paras.	Neoplasms	Cardiovascular	Infl., Pneu., Bronch.	Diarrheal	Certain Degenerative	Maternal	Cert. Dis. of Infancy	Motor Vehicle	Other Violence	Other and Unknown
CRUDE DEATH RATE	.02213	.00346	.00223	.00061	.00236	.00513	.00287	.00047	.00047	.00093	.00008	.00034	.00319
STANDARDIZED RATE (1)	.02187	.00357	.00210	.00072	.00273	.00485	.00261	.00050	.00049	.00084	.00008	.00034	.00305
STANDARDIZED RATE (2)	.02512	.00378	.00169	.00127	.00564	.00444	.00178	.00074	.00051	.00050	.00011	.00036	.00433
GEOMETRIC MEAN	.02663												

LIFE TABLE FOR ALL CAUSES COMBINED

Age (x)	Midyear Population	Deaths During Year	$_nM_x$	$_nq_x$	l_x	$_nd_x$	$_nL_x$	$_nm_x$	$_na_x$	T_x	$_nr_x$	$\overset{\circ}{e}_x$	Age (x)
0	17100	2979	.174211	.156890	100000	15689	90056	.174214	.366158	4135306	.000000	41.353	0
1	58700	1970	.033560	.123851	84311	10442	311139	.033561	1.500000	4045251	.000000	47.980	1
5	63000	339	.005381	.026493	73869	1957	364453	.005370	2.500000	3734112	.000000	50.550	5
10	54010	226	.004184	.020761	71912	1493	356007	.004194	2.620563	3369659	.022050	46.858	10
15	44805	364	.008124	.040060	70419	2821	345493	.008165	2.659813	3013652	.027290	42.796	15
20	38130	423	.011094	.054099	67598	3657	329039	.011114	2.552468	2668158	.020844	39.471	20
25	33580	405	.012061	.058523	63941	3742	310252	.012061	2.473777	2339119	.015989	36.582	25
30	28755	313	.010885	.052924	60199	3186	292907	.010877	2.461289	2028867	.023226	33.703	30
35	23000	261	.011348	.055251	57013	3150	277264	.011361	2.523347	1735960	.029824	30.449	35
40	18880	256	.013559	.065704	53863	3539	260579	.013561	2.531377	1458697	.025615	27.082	40
45	16075	244	.015179	.073186	50324	3683	242437	.015192	2.506618	1198118	.016686	23.808	45
50	13930	227	.016296	.078366	46641	3656	224164	.016310	2.527010	955681	.020125	20.490	50
55	10820	218	.020148	.096708	42985	4157	205271	.020251	2.677612	731518	.028239	17.018	55
60	8090	327	.040420	.185433	38828	7200	176873	.040707	2.601823	526247	.031106	13.553	60
65	5580	308	.055197	.242696	31628	7676	138852	.055282	2.487271	349374	.012423	11.046	65
70	4040	263	.065099	.281020	23952	6731	103026	.065333	2.513835	210521	.043686	8.789	70
75	1710	211	.123392	.471692	17221	8123	65579	.123866	2.473096	107496	.011658	6.242	75
80	1140	214	.187719	.624533	9098	5682	30192	.188192	2.307726	41917	.011658	4.607	80
85+	810	236	.291358	1.000000	3416	3416	11724	.291358	3.432203	11724	.000000	3.432	85+

NUMBER OF PERSONS DYING (OUT OF 100,000 AT BIRTH) ABOVE AGE X FROM SPECIFIED CAUSES

Age (x)	All Causes	Respiratory T.B.	Other Infec. and Paras.	Neoplasms	Cardiovascular	Infl., Pneu., Bronch.	Diarrheal	Certain Degenerative	Maternal	Cert. Dis. of Infancy	Motor Vehicle	Other Violence	Other and Unknown	Age (x)
0	100000	15797	6563	5176	21746	17744	7330	2964	2147	2154	453	1420	16106	0
1	84311	15697	5257	5176	21746	12814	3660	2912	2147	0	453	1309	13140	1
5	73869	15119	3359	5155	21740	8876	1015	2641	2147	0	442	1097	12278	5
10	71912	14721	2967	5143	21677	8258	911	2607	2147	0	390	987	12104	10
15	70419	14175	2697	5111	21578	7977	858	2580	2140	0	371	942	11950	15
20	67598	12637	2490	5103	21423	7622	882	2565	1976	0	363	887	11650	20
25	63941	10277	2308	5077	21311	7345	813	2548	1681	0	346	792	11443	25
30	60199	8292	2077	5040	21079	7004	786	2473	1255	0	327	756	11110	30
35	57013	6615	1976	4907	20833	6780	765	2402	838	0	317	725	10855	35
40	53863	5461	1830	4773	20361	6562	705	2257	464	0	281	664	10505	40
45	50324	4288	1456	4481	19736	6217	705	2202	120	0	281	554	10284	45
50	46641	3369	1306	3967	18662	5960	659	1990	1	0	281	493	9953	50
55	42985	2710	1000	3549	17421	5702	611	1812	1	0	265	413	9501	55
60	38828	2084	829	2996	15950	5282	554	1526	1	0	227	394	8985	60
65	31628	1425	588	2095	12886	4487	488	976	1	0	226	262	8194	65
70	23952	728	338	1497	9572	3415	313	603	1	0	77	212	7196	70
75	17221	375	160	755	6653	2467	186	503	1	0	77	136	5908	75
80	9098	144	45	294	2997	1158	109	233	1	0	1	135	3981	80
85+	3416	43	14	29	941	391	29	72	0	0	0	29	1868	85+

NUMBER OF PERSONS SURVIVING TO AGE X IF SPECIFIED CAUSES WERE ELIMINATED

Age (x)	No Causes	Respiratory T.B. (1)	Other Infec. and Paras. (2)	Neoplasms (3)	Cardiovascular (4)	Infl., Pneu., Bronch. (5)	Diarrheal (6)	Certain Degenerative (7)	Maternal (8)	Cert. Dis. of Infancy (9)	Motor Vehicle (10)	Other Violence (11)	Other and Unknown (12)	(1)+(2)	(1)+(2) +(5)+ (6)+(8)	(1)+(2)+ (5)+(6)+ (8)+part of(9)&(12)	(10)+(11)	Age (x)
0	100000	100000	100000	100000	100000	100000	100000	100000	100000	100000	100000	100000	100000	100000	100000	100000	100000	0
1	84311	84403	85890	84311	84311	88956	87745	84359	84311	86310	84311	84413	87075	85984	94415	99737	84413	1
5	73869	74493	77083	73889	73875	81523	79456	74165	73869	75620	73879	74157	77128	77734	92776	99023	74167	5
10	71912	72915	75446	71943	71980	80432	77500	72234	71912	73617	71973	72302	75264	76499	92212	98619	72363	10
15	70419	71952	74160	70481	70583	79074	75505	70761	70426	72088	70498	70845	73862	75775	91726	98277	70925	15
20	67598	70628	71403	67665	67908	76297	72881	67941	67766	69201	67682	68061	71211	74603	91010	97894	68145	20
25	63941	69248	67727	64030	64344	72474	69011	64282	64638	65457	64037	64472	67571	73348	90356	97473	64569	25
30	60199	67313	64001	60319	60806	68609	65000	60593	61038	61626	60307	60734	63959	71565	89295	96786	60844	30
35	57013	65601	60718	57257	57830	65226	61582	57456	58221	58365	57126	57550	60839	69864	88163	95906	57664	35
40	53863	63278	57515	54225	55103	61865	58243	54424	55376	55140	54004	54431	57841	67569	86277	94268	54574	40
45	50324	60466	54124	50948	52106	58185	54416	50902	52080	51517	50456	50962	54270	65032	84141	92197	51096	45
50	46641	57112	50318	47723	49377	54213	50482	47384	48386	47747	46763	47292	50644	61614	80414	88382	47416	50
55	42985	53414	46692	44394	46786	50253	46575	43844	44593	44004	43113	43662	47148	58020	76242	84132	43793	55
60	38828	48990	42352	40647	43812	45862	42129	39882	40280	39748	38980	39458	43129	53437	71045	78743	39613	60
65	31628	40945	34736	33568	38945	38216	34382	32998	32811	32378	31753	32262	35933	44654	60847	67860	32390	65
70	23952	31575	26544	26285	33255	30089	26204	25325	24848	24520	24177	24476	28219	34993	49891	56311	24706	70
75	17221	23091	19250	19597	27588	22664	18957	18295	17865	17629	17382	17663	21623	25811	38791	44610	17828	75
80	9098	12416	10259	10724	19412	13269	10074	9875	9438	9314	9239	9332	13312	14001	23457	28153	9476	80
85+	3416	4744	3873	4215	10389	5686	3835	3812	3544	3497	3469	3568	7195	5378	10429	13833	3624	85+

ADDED YRS OF LIFE																		
TOTAL		5.275	2.707	.782	3.282	6.227	3.268	.573	.699	.972	.098	.422	3.714	8.420	22.082	28.161	.521	
WORK	12.165	4.762	.581	.463	1.346	.871	.103	.253	.803	.000	.041	.180	.884	5.449	7.630	8.451	.221	

POPULATION, DEATHS, DEATH RATES FOR ALL CAUSES COMBINED, AND SPECIFIED CAUSES

Age Start of Interval	Midyear Population	Deaths During Year	All Causes	Respiratory T.B.	Other Infec. and Paras.	Neoplasms	Cardiovascular	Infl., Pneu., Bronch.	Diarrheal	Certain Degenerative	Maternal	Cert. Dis. of Infancy	Motor Vehicle	Other Violence	Other and Unknown	Age Start of Interval
0	27050	1599	.05911	.00004	.0C373	.00000	.00000	.01054	.01412	.00011	.00000	.01589	.00004	.00037	.01028	0
1	96353	509	.00528	.00002	.00132	.00003	.00004	.00092	.00093	.00010	.00000	.00000	.00004	.00039	.00147	1
5	107357	181	.00169	.00001	.00045	.00003	.00018	.00019	.00006	.00004	.00000	.00000	.00011	.00021	.00042	5
10	108827	142	.00130	.00001	.00027	.00004	.00020	.00008	.00004	.00004	.00000	.00000	.00006	.00027	.00031	10
15	101557	179	.00176	.00007	.00013	.00003	.00018	.00015	.00001	.00006	.00000	.00000	.00027	.00041	.00046	15
20	98263	218	.00222	.00021	.00018	.00007	.00009	.00012	.00000	.00009	.00000	.00000	.00044	.00068	.00033	20
25	96002	225	.00234	.00026	.00027	.00010	.00018	.00018	.00002	.00016	.00000	.00000	.00031	.00050	.00036	25
30	93317	248	.00266	.00032	.00020	.00011	.00044	.00026	.00001	.00013	.00000	.00000	.00023	.00058	.00039	30
35	75662	268	.00354	.00040	.00032	.00028	.00059	.00030	.00001	.00036	.00000	.00000	.00029	.00045	.00054	35
40	59413	367	.00618	.00052	.00034	.00057	.00148	.00059	.00003	.00049	.00000	.00000	.00022	.00081	.00113	40
45	56683	544	.00960	.00058	.00049	.00108	.00272	.00108	.00004	.00074	.00000	.00000	.00030	.00078	.00180	45
50	49055	735	.01498	.00088	.00063	.00228	.00475	.00116	.00008	.00112	.00000	.00000	.00035	.00080	.00294	50
55	42286	842	.01991	.00080	.00102	.00286	.00731	.00168	.00012	.00184	.00000	.00000	.00050	.00073	.00305	55
60	37431	1133	.03027	.00112	.00054	.00612	.01167	.00264	.00008	.00198	.00000	.00000	.00051	.00056	.00425	60
65	28111	1240	.04411	.00078	.00121	.00747	.01793	.00370	.00032	.00409	.00000	.00000	.00043	.00107	.00711	65
70	18098	1235	.06824	.00050	.00105	.01315	.02812	.00530	.00050	.00536	.00000	.00000	.00039	.00116	.01271	70
75	9964	985	.09866	.00070	.00141	.01616	.04035	.00943	.00100	.00572	.00000	.00000	.00050	.00130	.02228	75
80	4369	711	.16274	.00092	.00183	.01213	.06477	.02129	.00160	.00847	.00000	.00000	.00092	.00206	.04875	80
85+	1908	514	.26939	.00000	.00210	.01887	.C8386	.03512	.00524	.00629	.00000	.00000	.00105	.00734	.10954	85+
ALL	1111706	11875														

	All Causes	Respiratory T.B.	Other Infec. and Paras.	Neoplasms	Cardiovascular	Infl., Pneu., Bronch.	Diarrheal	Certain Degenerative	Maternal	Cert. Dis. of Infancy	Motor Vehicle	Other Violence	Other and Unknown
CRUDE DEATH RATE	.01068	.00031	.00058	.00118	.00293	.00114	.00049	.00062	.00000	.00048	.00025	.00057	.00213
STANDARDIZED RATE (1)	.00924	.00025	.00061	.00084	.00208	.00107	.00066	.00046	.00000	.00070	.00025	.00057	.00182
STANDARDIZED RATE (2)	.01454	.00035	.00061	.00174	.00454	.00153	.00048	.00087	.00000	.00041	.00027	.00062	.00311
GEOMETRIC MEAN	.01219												

LIFE TABLE FOR ALL CAUSES COMBINED

Age (x)	Midyear Population	Deaths During Year	$_nM_x$	$_nq_x$	l_x	$_nd_x$	$_nL_x$	$_nm_x$	$_na_x$	T_x	$_nr_x$	$\overset{\circ}{e}_x$	Age (x)
0	27050	1599	.059113	.056350	100000	5635	95326	.059113	.170492	6144531	.000000	61.445	0
1	96353	509	.005283	.020855	94365	1968	372540	.005283	1.500000	6049205	.000000	64.104	1
5	107357	181	.001686	.008399	92397	776	460045	.001687	2.500000	5676665	.000000	61.438	5
10	108827	142	.001305	.006494	91621	595	456622	.001303	2.508403	5216620	.002137	56.937	10
15	101557	179	.001763	.008789	91026	800	453214	.001765	2.604427	4759998	.007713	52.293	15
20	98263	218	.002219	.011039	90226	996	448690	.002202	2.549992	4306784	.005140	47.733	20
25	96002	225	.002344	.011644	89230	1039	443588	.002342	2.534087	3858094	.001043	43.238	25
30	93317	248	.002658	.013221	88191	1166	438144	.002661	2.589337	3414506	.012182	38.717	30
35	75662	268	.003542	.017685	87025	1539	431580	.003566	2.696556	2976362	.037224	34.201	35
40	59413	367	.006177	.030625	85486	2618	421376	.006213	2.687723	2544782	.028674	29.768	40
45	56683	544	.009597	.047039	82868	3898	405242	.009619	2.666004	2123406	.012361	25.624	45
50	49055	735	.014983	.072483	78970	5724	381180	.015017	2.611774	1718164	.015579	21.757	50
55	42286	842	.019912	.095145	73246	6969	349565	.019936	2.608726	1336984	.008125	18.253	55
60	37431	1133	.030269	.141241	66277	9361	308900	.030304	2.598058	987419	.007051	14.898	60
65	28111	1240	.044111	.159856	56916	11375	256915	.044265	2.573223	678518	.020975	11.921	65
70	18098	1235	.068240	.293340	45541	13359	194601	.068648	2.521973	421543	.031218	9.256	70
75	9964	985	.098856	.397241	32182	12784	128490	.099494	2.464001	226942	.036365	7.052	75
80	4369	711	.162737	.574802	19398	11150	67835	.164370	2.385183	98452	.036365	7.052	80
85+	1908	514	.269392	1.000000	8248	8248	30617	.269392	3.712062	30617	.000000	3.712	85+

NUMBER OF PERSONS DYING (OUT OF 100,000 AT BIRTH) ABOVE AGE X FROM SPECIFIED CAUSES

Age (x)	All Causes	Respiratory T.B.	Other Infec. and Paras.	Neoplasms	Cardiovascular	Infl., Pneu., Bronch.	Diarrheal	Certain Degenerative	Maternal	Cert. Dis. of Infancy	Motor Vehicle	Other Violence	Other and Unknown	Age (x)
0	100000	2449	3780	12745	32907	10200	2467	6242	0	1896	1800	4119	21395	0
1	94365	2446	3425	12745	32907	9195	1120	6231	0	0	1796	4084	20416	1
5	92397	2438	2934	12733	32891	8851	773	6193	0	0	1781	3937	19866	5
10	91621	2434	2728	12721	32810	8765	747	6175	0	0	1729	3839	19673	10
15	91026	2430	2606	12704	32717	8728	730	6159	0	0	1704	3717	19531	15
20	90226	2398	2548	12690	32637	8661	726	6132	0	0	1583	3529	19322	20
25	89230	2302	2466	12658	32596	8606	726	6091	0	0	1387	3223	19175	25
30	88191	2187	2346	12612	32517	8527	716	6021	0	0	1248	3001	19016	30
35	87025	2046	2257	12565	32324	8414	712	5965	0	0	1150	2748	18844	35
40	85486	1874	2119	12444	32065	8282	706	5809	0	0	1024	2554	18609	40
45	82868	1654	1977	12201	31436	8032	692	5603	0	0	932	2212	18129	45
50	78970	1417	1776	11763	30331	7596	677	5302	0	0	810	1898	17400	50
55	73246	1083	1535	10890	28515	7152	646	4873	0	0	678	1595	16279	55
60	66277	802	1179	9888	25957	6564	605	4228	0	0	504	1338	15212	60
65	56916	455	890	7996	22346	5746	580	3616	0	0	347	1041	13899	65
70	45541	255	579	6070	17721	4793	497	2561	0	0	238	767	12060	70
75	32182	158	375	3495	12215	3754	400	1514	0	0	163	540	9568	75
80	19398	68	194	1415	6999	2529	269	778	0	0	98	372	6676	80
85+	8248	0	64	578	2567	1075	160	193	0	0	32	225	3354	85+

NUMBER OF PERSONS SURVIVING TO AGE X IF SPECIFIED CAUSES WERE ELIMINATED

Age (x)	No Causes	Respiratory T.B. (1)	Other Infec. and Paras. (2)	Neoplasms (3)	Cardiovascular (4)	Infl., Pneu., Bronch. (5)	Diarrheal (6)	Certain Degenerative (7)	Maternal (8)	Cert. Dis. of Infancy (9)	Motor Vehicle (10)	Other Violence (11)	Other and Unknown (12)	(1)+(2)	(1)+(2)+(5)+(6)+(8)	(1)+(2)+(5)+(6)+(8)+part of(9)&(12)	(10)+(11)	Age (x)
0	100000	100000	100000	100000	100000	100000	100000	100000	100000	100000	100000	100000	100000	100000	100000	100000	100000	0
1	94365	94368	94710	94365	94365	95346	95682	94376	94365	96225	94369	94399	95321	94713	97034	99895	94403	1
5	92397	92408	93224	92409	92413	93702	94036	92445	92397	94218	92416	92576	93884	93235	96229	99557	92595	5
10	91621	91636	92648	91645	91717	93002	93272	91687	91621	93427	91691	91896	93291	92663	95756	99182	91967	10
15	91026	91045	92170	91067	91215	92436	92684	91107	91026	92820	91121	91422	92829	92189	95321	98793	91517	15
20	90226	90276	91418	90280	90493	91691	91873	90333	90226	92004	90441	90806	92226	91469	94652	98161	91022	20
25	89230	89375	90492	89315	89535	90734	90859	89377	89230	90988	89638	90111	91357	90639	93850	97373	90522	25
30	88191	88449	89559	88321	88571	89758	89811	88406	88191	89929	88733	89284	90456	89821	93097	96655	89833	30
35	87025	87420	88465	87200	87553	88686	88628	87293	87025	88740	87658	88359	89435	88867	92230	95822	89001	35
40	85486	86046	87039	85778	86303	87251	87067	85904	85486	87171	86233	86992	88093	87609	91071	94706	87752	40
45	82868	83629	84516	83352	84288	84830	84414	83478	82868	84501	83684	84671	85894	85292	88941	92645	85504	45
50	78970	79929	80741	79901	81428	81276	80458	79847	78970	80526	79680	81001	82585	81721	85693	89488	81922	50
55	73246	74461	75126	74965	77352	75826	74657	74479	73246	74689	74207	75429	77735	76372	80586	84437	76419	55
60	66277	67648	68326	68817	72611	69193	67593	68019	66277	67583	67314	68504	71422	69739	74254	78058	69576	60
65	56916	58421	58951	60944	66129	60216	58070	58996	56916	58038	57954	59112	62659	60509	65316	68932	60190	65
70	45541	46926	47456	50639	57936	49095	46541	48193	45541	46438	46047	47552	51981	48899	53865	57181	48521	70
75	32182	33243	33711	38260	47238	35639	32972	34989	32182	32816	32902	33800	39200	34822	39510	42304	34556	75
80	19358	20109	20465	25016	34998	22559	19978	21707	19358	19780	19883	20508	26520	21215	25410	27734	21021	80
85+	8248	8555	8789	11342	20506	10724	8566	9653	8248	8411	8497	8819	14549	9159	12367	14294	9085	85+

ADDED YRS OF LIFE

	No Causes	(1)	(2)	(3)	(4)	(5)	(6)	(7)	(8)	(9)	(10)	(11)	(12)	(1)+(2)	(1)+(2)+(5)+(6)+(8)	(1)+(2)+(5)+(6)+(8)+part of(9)&(12)	(10)+(11)
TOTAL		.544	1.233	1.604	4.632	2.008	1.174	.884	.000	1.208	.499	1.119	3.749	1.795	5.177	8.237	1.634
WORK	5.161	.347	.299	.440	1.064	.401	.021	.326	.000	.000	.328	.624	.821	.650	1.085	1.320	.959

POPULATION, DEATHS, DEATH RATES FOR ALL CAUSES COMBINED, AND SPECIFIED CAUSES

Age Start of Interval	Midyear Population	Deaths During Year	All Causes	Respiratory T.B.	Other Infec. and Paras.	Neoplasms	Cardiovascular	Infl., Pneu., Bronch.	Diarrheal	Certain Degenerative	Maternal	Cert. Dis. of Infancy	Motor Vehicle	Other Violence	Other and Unknown	Age Start of Interval
0	25783	1181	.04581	.00008	.00291	.00000	.00000	.00795	.01133	.00019	.00000	.01571	.00000	.00043	.00721	0
1	93651	463	.00494	.00006	.00135	.00005	.00004	.00109	.00072	.00007	.00000	.00000	.00004	.00036	.00115	1
5	103814	146	.00141	.00000	.00037	.00001	.00023	.00011	.00005	.00004	.00000	.00000	.00008	.00010	.00043	5
10	104812	102	.00097	.00003	.00021	.00004	.00024	.00006	.00000	.00003	.00000	.00000	.00005	.00009	.00024	10
15	98297	146	.00149	.00012	.00018	.00004	.00018	.00016	.00001	.00006	.00008	.00000	.00012	.00015	.00037	15
20	95257	181	.00190	.00041	.00014	.00008	.00029	.00012	.00002	.00007	.00023	.00000	.00008	.00005	.00040	20
25	95545	210	.00220	.00039	.00021	.00019	.00029	.00010	.00002	.00010	.00030	.00000	.00003	.00018	.00038	25
30	91646	252	.00275	.00037	.00020	.00029	.00044	.00023	.00000	.00017	.00036	.00000	.00009	.00010	.00050	30
35	73975	243	.00328	.00032	.00015	.00049	.00066	.00022	.00001	.00022	.00043	.00000	.00004	.00018	.00057	35
40	61774	290	.00469	.00032	.00019	.00110	.00117	.00024	.00006	.00044	.00018	.00000	.00008	.00011	.00079	40
45	57248	378	.00660	.00023	.00028	.00168	.00203	.00044	.00002	.00070	.00002	.00000	.00009	.00010	.00103	45
50	49408	484	.00980	.00020	.00026	.00233	.00350	.00059	.00004	.00077	.00000	.00000	.00016	.00032	.00162	50
55	40676	551	.01355	.00015	.00047	.00342	.00497	.00084	.00005	.00143	.00000	.00000	.00020	.00032	.00172	55
60	33780	689	.02040	.00024	.00068	.00385	.00805	.00145	.00033	.00240	.00000	.00000	.00021	.00027	.00293	60
65	25329	776	.03064	.00039	.00055	.00683	.01315	.00190	.00039	.00324	.00000	.00000	.00012	.00051	.00355	65
70	17444	872	.04999	.00017	.00066	.00900	.02264	.00424	.00069	.00504	.00000	.00000	.00011	.00080	.00642	70
75	10059	780	.07754	.00030	.00089	.01084	.03529	.00925	.00060	.00427	.00000	.00000	.00010	.00209	.01392	75
80	4709	592	.12572	.00021	.00106	.01444	.05628	.01253	.00234	.00680	.00000	.00000	.00021	.00297	.02888	80
85+	2369	522	.22035	.00000	.00338	.01393	.07556	.02702	.00549	.00802	.00000	.00000	.00042	.01055	.07598	85+
ALL	1085576	8858														

			All Causes	Respiratory T.B.	Other Infec. and Paras.	Neoplasms	Cardiovascular	Infl., Pneu., Bronch.	Diarrheal	Certain Degenerative	Maternal	Cert. Dis. of Infancy	Motor Vehicle	Other Violence	Other and Unknown
CRUDE DEATH RATE			.00816	.00021	.00044	.00110	.00237	.00082	.00041	.00054	.00013	.00037	.00008	.00024	.00145
STANDARDIZED RATE (1)			.00710	.00019	.00049	.00080	.00168	.00079	.00054	.00040	.00011	.00055	.00008	.00021	.00125
STANDARDIZED RATE (2)			.01098	.00021	.00046	.00155	.00368	.00108	.00041	.00075	.00011	.00033	.00009	.00031	.00200
GEOMETRIC MEAN			.00965												

LIFE TABLE FOR ALL CAUSES COMBINED

Age (x)	Midyear Population	Deaths During Year	$_nM_x$	$_nq_x$	l_x	$_nd_x$	$_nL_x$	$_nm_x$	$_na_x$	T_x	$_nr_x$	$\overset{\circ}{e}_x$	Age (x)
0	25783	1181	.045805	.044080	100000	4408	96244	.045800	.147869	6578801	.000000	65.788	0
1	93651	463	.004944	.019541	95592	1868	377698	.004946	1.500000	6482557	.000000	67.815	1
5	103814	146	.001406	.006999	93724	656	466980	.001405	2.500000	6104859	.000000	65.137	5
10	104812	102	.000973	.004857	93068	452	464216	.000974	2.513827	5637879	.002308	60.578	10
15	98297	146	.001485	.007407	92616	686	461452	.001487	2.626944	5173662	.007885	55.861	15
20	95257	181	.001900	.009464	91930	870	457539	.001901	2.573994	4712210	.003215	51.259	20
25	95545	210	.002198	.010927	91060	995	452888	.002197	2.575796	4254671	-.001150	46.724	25
30	91646	252	.002750	.013679	90065	1232	447340	.002754	2.577449	3801783	.014368	42.212	30
35	73975	243	.003285	.016357	88833	1453	440700	.003297	2.615135	3354443	.033356	37.761	35
40	61774	290	.004665	.023289	87380	2035	432089	.004710	2.636057	2913743	.025088	33.346	40
45	57248	378	.006603	.032597	85345	2782	420172	.006621	2.644530	2481654	.016109	29.078	45
50	49408	484	.009756	.048024	82563	3965	403401	.009829	2.625736	2061481	.022567	24.969	50
55	40676	551	.013546	.065841	78598	5175	380720	.013593	2.629026	1658080	.023385	21.096	55
60	33780	689	.020397	.097653	73423	7170	350093	.020460	2.625930	1277360	.024696	17.397	60
65	25329	776	.030637	.143526	66253	9509	308653	.030808	2.622012	927267	.030815	13.996	65
70	17444	872	.049989	.224500	56744	12739	252897	.050312	2.580454	618615	.037331	10.902	70
75	10059	780	.077542	.327826	44005	14426	184265	.078290	2.521113	365718	.047647	8.311	75
80	4709	592	.125717	.480104	29579	14201	111663	.127177	2.448625	181453	.047647	6.135	80
85+	2369	522	.220346	1.000000	15378	15378	69790	.220346	4.538314	69790	.000000	4.538	85+

NUMBER OF PERSONS DYING (OUT OF 100,000 AT BIRTH) ABOVE AGE X FROM SPECIFIED CAUSES

Age (x)	All Causes	Respiratory T. B.	Other Infec. and Paras.	Neoplasms	Cardiovascular	Infl., Pneu., Bronch.	Diarrheal	Certain Degenerative	Maternal	Cert. Dis. of Infancy	Motor Vehicle	Other Violence	Other and Unknown	Age (x)
0	100000	1477	3091	14349	36626	9673	2653	6957	718	1512	664	2824	19456	0
1	95592	1470	2811	14349	36626	8907	1563	6938	718	0	664	2783	18763	1
5	93724	1446	2303	14329	36610	8496	1293	6910	718	0	648	2646	18325	5
10	93068	1446	2132	14324	36502	8446	1270	6892	718	0	612	2601	18125	10
15	92616	1432	2035	14307	36391	8420	1270	6879	718	0	589	2561	18014	15
20	91930	1376	1950	14288	36307	8345	1266	6851	680	0	533	2491	17843	20
25	91060	1188	1888	14249	36172	8292	1256	6817	574	0	495	2467	17662	25
30	90065	1013	1793	14164	36039	8244	1247	6770	437	0	480	2386	17492	30
35	88833	847	1705	14032	35844	8142	1247	6691	276	0	441	2343	17265	35
40	87380	704	1640	13815	35550	8046	1241	6595	85	0	424	2265	17015	40
45	85345	564	1555	13337	35043	7941	1213	6406	10	0	388	2216	16672	45
50	82563	469	1438	12631	34189	7757	1205	6111	2	0	352	2172	16237	50
55	78598	388	1332	11689	32771	7520	1189	5800	2	0	286	2041	15580	55
60	73423	332	1153	10384	30872	7200	1170	5254	2	0	211	1919	14926	60
65	66253	248	914	9032	28039	6690	1055	4411	2	0	139	1826	13897	65
70	56744	126	744	6913	23955	6101	933	3408	2	0	102	1666	12794	70
75	44005	83	525	4627	18182	5015	758	2126	2	0	73	1461	11153	75
80	29579	28	360	2621	11617	3291	647	1340	2	0	55	1071	8547	80
85+	15378	0	236	972	5273	1885	383	560	0	0	29	736	5304	85+

NUMBER OF PERSONS SURVIVING TO AGE X IF SPECIFIED CAUSES WERE ELIMINATED

Age (x)	No Causes	Respiratory T. B. (1)	Other Infec. and Paras. (2)	Neoplasms (3)	Cardiovascular (4)	Infl., Pneu., Bronch. (5)	Diarrheal (6)	Certain Degenerative (7)	Maternal (8)	Cert. Dis. of Infancy (9)	Motor Vehicle (10)	Other Violence (11)	Other and Unknown (12)	(1)+(2)	(1)+(2)+(5)+(6)+(8)	(1)+(2)+(5)+(6)+(8)+part of(9)&(12)	(10)+(11)	Age (x)
0	100000	100000	100000	100000	100000	100000	100000	100000	100000	100000	100000	100000	100000	100000	100000	100000	100000	0
1	95592	95599	95866	95592	95592	96344	96664	95611	95592	97082	95592	95632	96272	95873	97710	99877	95632	1
5	93724	93754	94499	93744	93740	94872	95045	93770	93724	95185	93740	93899	94828	94529	97036	99579	93915	5
10	93068	93098	94009	93093	93191	94259	94403	93132	93068	94518	93120	93287	94267	93440	96609	99254	93339	10
15	92616	92660	93560	92657	92850	93827	93945	92692	92616	94059	92690	92874	94021	93695	96282	98965	92948	15
20	91930	92030	93042	91950	92246	93208	93253	92034	91568	93363	92060	92256	93497	93143	95837	98599	92386	20
25	91060	91346	92224	91158	91508	92379	92381	91197	91203	92479	91226	91407	92796	92514	95365	98232	91574	25
30	90065	90523	91312	90247	90641	91418	91380	90247	90343	91469	90244	90489	91954	91776	94808	97761	90669	30
35	88833	89590	90152	89144	89596	90271	90130	89091	89268	90217	89049	89294	90927	90778	94053	97109	89511	35
40	87380	88130	88743	87902	88426	88891	88662	87729	87998	88742	87609	87911	89654	89504	93042	96179	88142	40
45	85345	86217	86761	86332	86675	86926	86625	85874	86023	86675	85604	85912	87953	87648	91331	94507	86174	45
50	82563	83501	84050	84223	84903	84277	83810	83367	83227	83850	82850	83156	85529	85005	88788	91959	83444	50
55	78598	79571	80119	81121	82261	80466	79801	79671	79230	79823	78935	79291	82087	81111	84987	88117	79631	55
60	73423	74386	75020	77092	78790	75486	74565	74962	74013	74567	73811	74189	77345	76005	79994	83031	74581	60
65	66253	67203	67926	70924	74044	68614	67395	68464	66786	67285	66671	67033	70829	68900	73169	76120	67457	65
70	56744	57672	58338	62877	67783	59334	57837	59603	57200	57628	57136	57562	61762	59291	63699	66410	57960	70
75	44005	44762	45438	51026	58587	47027	45009	47413	44359	44691	44335	44824	49499	46220	50927	53336	45160	75
80	29579	30133	30680	36231	47500	33150	30346	32557	29817	30040	29815	30456	35765	31255	36226	38420	30699	80
85+	15378	15686	16042	20323	33077	18388	15970	17545	15503	15618	15519	16080	21590	16363	20485	22272	16228	85+

ADDED YRS OF LIFE

	No Causes	(1)	(2)	(3)	(4)	(5)	(6)	(7)	(8)	(9)	(10)	(11)	(12)				
TOTAL		.486	1.106	2.154	5.478	1.816	1.057	1.020	.292	1.023	.197	.522	3.369	1.603	4.955	7.562	.723
WORK	4.151	.327	.219	.642	.953	.255	.025	.289	.235	.000	.095	.154	.673	.548	1.074	1.324	.250

POPULATION, DEATHS, DEATH RATES FOR ALL CAUSES COMBINED, AND SPECIFIED CAUSES

Age Start of Interval	Midyear Population	Deaths During Year	All Causes	Respiratory T. B.	Other Infec. and Paras.	Neoplasms	Cardiovascular	Infl., Pneu., Bronch.	Diarrheal	Certain Degenerative	Maternal	Cert. Dis. of Infancy	Motor Vehicle	Other Violence	Other and Unknown	Age Start of Interval
0	20867	3510	.16821	.00278	.01481	.00005	.00029	.03676	.04716	.00029	.00000	.05166	.00010	.00101	.01332	0
1	72505	2014	.02778	.00272	.00444	.00011	.00006	.00789	.00839	.00066	.00000	.00000	.00014	.00052	.00285	1
5	75053	274	.00365	.00071	.00079	.00004	.00020	.00056	.00025	.00012	.00000	.00000	.00012	.00023	.00064	5
10	69916	161	.00230	.00060	.00036	.00000	.00026	.00027	.00006	.00010	.00000	.00000	.00009	.00033	.00064	10
15	56754	247	.00435	.00183	.00035	.00007	.00037	.00035	.00011	.00009	.00000	.00000	.00009	.00024	.00033	15
20	49206	376	.00764	.00390	.00037	.00006	.00049	.00051	.00002	.00008	.00000	.00000	.00023	.00060	.00035	20
25	40741	365	.00896	.00439	.00066	.00010	.00064	.00076	.00000	.00025	.00000	.00000	.00039	.00112	.00071	25
30	33943	327	.00963	.00424	.00068	.00027	.00109	.00047	.00009	.00029	.00000	.00000	.00039	.00108	.00069	30
35	29784	354	.01189	.00541	.00067	.00037	.00148	.00111	.00007	.00027	.00000	.00000	.00027	.00087	.00082	35
40	25887	388	.01499	.00576	.00104	.00058	.00263	.00155	.00012	.00050	.00000	.00000	.00058	.00089	.00135	40
45	21304	408	.01915	.00648	.00169	.00131	.00418	.00122	.00028	.00080	.00000	.00000	.00070	.00099	.00150	45
50	16496	408	.02473	.00643	.00152	.00230	.00740	.00230	.00018	.00115	.00000	.00000	.00024	.00079	.00242	50
55	10920	373	.03416	.00733	.00165	.00485	.01062	.00321	.00037	.00128	.00000	.00000	.00046	.00101	.00339	55
60	10111	442	.04371	.00821	.00099	.00603	.01731	.00504	.00020	.00099	.00000	.00000	.00020	.00059	.00415	60
65	8198	458	.05587	.00695	.00110	.00598	.02501	.00586	.00012	.00195	.00000	.00000	.00049	.00134	.00707	65
70	5172	423	.08179	.00560	.00213	.01025	.03094	.01411	.00193	.00290	.00000	.00000	.00000	.00116	.01257	70
75	3099	310	.10003	.00516	.00129	.01065	.04808	.01162	.00097	.00323	.00000	.00000	.00065	.00065	.01775	75
80	1598	232	.14518	.00438	.00313	.01001	.05820	.02628	.00250	.00250	.00000	.00000	.00063	.00188	.03567	80
85+	1251	253	.20224	.00480	.00000	.01119	.08553	.02958	.00320	.00639	.00000	.00000	.00000	.00160	.05995	85+
ALL	552805	11323														

	All Causes	Respiratory T. B.	Other Infec. and Paras.	Neoplasms	Cardiovascular	Infl., Pneu., Bronch.	Diarrheal	Certain Degenerative	Maternal	Cert. Dis. of Infancy	Motor Vehicle	Other Violence	Other and Unknown
CRUDE DEATH RATE	.02048	.00326	.00175	.00073	.00268	.00353	.00302	.00042	.00000	.00195	.00027	.00070	.00218
STANDARDIZED RATE (1)	.02043	.00343	.00169	.00083	.00289	.00340	.00279	.00044	.00000	.00182	.00027	.00070	.00218
STANDARDIZED RATE (2)	.02411	.00408	.00146	.00159	.00580	.00350	.00186	.00063	.00000	.00182	.00028	.00072	.00213
GEOMETRIC MEAN	.02421		.00146	.00159	.00580	.00350		.00063	.00000	.00107	.00032	.00079	.00300

LIFE TABLE FOR ALL CAUSES COMBINED

Age (x)	Midyear Population	Deaths During Year	$_nM_x$	$_nq_x$	l_x	$_nd_x$	$_nL_x$	$_nm_x$	$_na_x$	T_x	$_nr_x$	$\overset{\circ}{e}_x$	Age (x)
0	20867	3510	.168208	.151770	100000	15177	90225	.168212	.355954	4346419	.000000	43.464	0
1	72505	2014	.027777	.103887	84823	8812	317262	.027775	1.500000	4256194	.000000	50.177	1
5	75053	274	.003651	.018089	76011	1375	376618	.003651	2.500000	3938932	.000000	51.821	5
10	69916	161	.002303	.011456	74636	855	371090	.002304	2.555068	3562314	.017853	47.729	10
15	56754	247	.004352	.021699	73781	1601	365291	.004383	2.742427	3191225	.028600	43.253	15
20	49206	376	.007641	.037656	72180	2718	354406	.007669	2.610912	2825934	.025921	39.151	20
25	40741	365	.008959	.043880	69462	3048	339776	.008971	2.528092	2471528	.028675	35.581	25
30	33943	327	.009634	.047114	66414	3129	324375	.009646	2.540814	2131752	.024263	32.098	30
35	29784	354	.011886	.057849	63285	3661	307520	.011905	2.567661	1807377	.016749	28.559	35
40	25887	388	.014988	.072421	59624	4318	287619	.015013	2.567981	1499857	.017473	25.155	40
45	21304	408	.019151	.091672	55306	5070	264182	.019191	2.564431	1212238	.020343	21.919	45
50	16496	408	.024733	.117167	50236	5886	236869	.024849	2.568666	948057	.039796	18.872	50
55	10920	373	.034158	.158061	44350	7010	204531	.034274	2.543598	711187	.026739	16.036	55
60	10111	442	.043715	.196920	37340	7353	168390	.043667	2.509803	506657	-.009624	13.569	60
65	8198	458	.055867	.245306	29987	7356	131613	.055891	2.509261	338267	.002569	11.280	65
70	5172	423	.081787	.339358	22631	7680	93660	.081999	2.461534	206654	.015272	9.131	70
75	3099	310	.100032	.397164	14951	5938	59298	.100139	2.396886	112994	.012598	7.558	75
80	1598	232	.145181	.526018	9013	4741	32573	.145549	2.365139	53697	.012598	5.958	80
85+	1251	253	.202238	1.000000	4272	4272	21124	.202238	4.944664	21124	.000000	4.945	85+

NUMBER OF PERSONS DYING (OUT OF 100,000 AT BIRTH) ABOVE AGE X FROM SPECIFIED CAUSES

Age (x)	All Causes	Respiratory T. B.	Other Infec. and Paras.	Neo-plasms	Cardio-vascular	Infl., Pneu., Bronch.	Diar-rheal	Certain Degen-erative	Maternal	Cert. Dis. of Infancy	Motor Vehicle	Other Violence	Other and Unknown	Age (x)
0	100000	18000	6221	6354	23023	14286	7791	2639	0	4661	1401	3491	12133	0
1	84823	17749	4885	6350	22997	10969	3536	2613	0	0	1392	3400	10932	1
5	76011	16887	3476	6315	22580	8466	876	2403	0	0	1349	3233	10026	5
10	74636	16621	3180	6300	22504	8256	781	2358	0	0	1303	3148	9785	10
15	73781	16397	3048	6300	22809	8155	760	2320	0	0	1271	3057	9664	15
20	72180	15721	2920	6274	22673	8026	721	2288	0	0	1187	2837	9533	20
25	69462	14332	2789	6252	22500	7845	714	2259	0	0	1050	2439	9282	25
30	66414	12838	2563	6218	22282	7586	714	2175	0	0	916	2072	9050	30
35	63285	11461	2344	6132	21927	7433	685	2080	0	0	744	1700	8779	35
40	59624	9797	2137	6018	21471	7091	664	1997	0	0	662	1432	8355	40
45	55306	8141	1836	5850	20713	6647	631	1852	0	0	495	1176	7965	45
50	50236	6428	1389	5501	19604	6324	556	1640	0	0	309	916	7569	50
55	44350	4906	1030	4950	17839	5774	513	1366	0	0	252	730	6990	55
60	37340	3405	693	3952	15656	5115	438	1104	0	0	159	523	6295	60
65	29987	2023	526	2936	12746	4267	405	938	0	0	125	424	5597	65
70	22631	1108	382	2149	9454	3496	389	681	0	0	61	247	4664	70
75	14951	565	182	1187	6549	2170	207	409	0	0	61	138	3483	75
80	9013	259	106	556	3694	1481	150	217	0	0	23	100	2427	80
85+	4272	101	0	236	1807	625	68	135	0	0	0	34	1266	85+

NUMBER OF PERSONS SURVIVING TO AGE X IF SPECIFIED CAUSES WERE ELIMINATED

Age (x)	No Causes	Respiratory T. B. (1)	Other Infec. and Paras. (2)	Neo-plasms (3)	Cardio-vascular (4)	Infl., Pneu., Bronch. (5)	Diar-rheal (6)	Certain Degener-ative (7)	Maternal (8)	Cert. Dis. of Infancy (9)	Motor Vehicle (10)	Other Violence (11)	Other and Unknown (12)	(1)+(2)	(1)+(2)+(5)+(6)+(8)	(1)+(2)+(5)+(6)+(8)+part of(9)&(12)	(10)+(11)	Age (x)
0	100000	100000	100000	100000	100000	100000	100000	100000	100000	100000	100000	100000	100000	100000	100000	100000	100000	0
1	84823	85054	86061	84827	84847	87930	88829	84847	84823	89221	84831	84907	85935	86296	93682	99725	84915	1
5	76011	77040	78485	76047	76049	81289	82281	76231	76011	79952	76059	76244	77881	79548	92088	99074	76293	5
10	74636	75914	77369	74687	74748	80041	80854	74897	74636	78506	74729	74950	76717	78694	91469	98649	75043	10
15	73781	75272	76618	73831	73987	79232	79990	74077	73781	77607	73905	74182	75962	78166	91006	98253	74306	15
20	72180	74324	75087	72255	72516	77650	78256	72501	72180	75923	72384	72791	74447	77318	90225	97526	72997	20
25	69462	72942	72394	69555	69956	74917	75355	69800	69462	73064	69793	70445	71898	76021	88947	96381	70781	25
30	66414	71292	69448	66537	67102	71903	72049	66820	66414	69858	66863	67719	68979	74549	87558	95104	68176	30
35	63285	69391	66400	63486	64292	68678	68685	63765	63285	66566	63882	64899	66004	72806	85752	93385	65511	35
40	59624	67171	62770	59925	61024	65066	64734	60158	59624	62572	60412	61412	62617	70715	83783	91676	62073	40
45	55306	64127	58530	55148	57358	60822	60080	55942	55306	58174	56065	57218	58477	67866	81078	89089	58003	45
50	50236	60169	53617	50975	53210	55586	54650	51019	50236	52841	51105	52229	53517	64218	77301	85289	53132	50
55	44350	54854	47695	45533	48767	49649	48291	45303	44350	46650	45171	46291	47830	58991	71908	79793	47148	55
60	37340	47913	40488	38288	43323	42484	40733	38387	37340	39276	38118	39172	40962	51952	64480	72048	39988	60
65	29987	40090	32675	32520	37957	34993	32743	30981	29987	31542	30642	31551	33590	43685	55662	62670	32240	65
70	22631	31322	24796	25291	32490	27203	24728	23613	22631	23804	23182	23973	26276	34319	45074	51275	24557	70
75	14951	21297	16559	17600	25106	19311	16499	15830	14951	15726	15314	15929	18507	23588	33621	39104	16317	75
80	9013	13173	10046	11150	19333	12338	9953	9699	9013	9480	9263	9633	12218	14682	22284	26464	9900	80
85+	4272	6401	4842	5578	12334	6692	4758	4657	4272	4494	4406	4614	6953	7254	12763	16117	4759	85+

ADDED YRS OF LIFE																		
TOTAL		5.035	2.260	.881	3.971	4.409	3.671	.529	.000	2.235	.388	1.002	2.710	7.671	18.148	24.356	1.405	
WORK	11.332	3.877	.594	.405	1.466	.736	.074	.260	.000	.000	.331	.802	.827	4.576	5.567	6.194	1.143	

POPULATION, DEATHS, DEATH RATES FOR ALL CAUSES COMBINED, AND SPECIFIED CAUSES

Age Start of Interval	Midyear Population	Deaths During Year	All Causes	Respiratory T.B.	Other Infec. and Paras.	Neoplasms	Cardiovascular	Infl., Pneu., Bronch.	Diarrheal	Certain Degenerative	Maternal	Cert. Dis. of Infancy	Motor Vehicle	Other Violence	Other and Unknown	Age Start of Interval
0	21164	3107	.14681	.00217	.01181	.00009	.00024	.03572	.04366	.00028	.00000	.04049	.00000	.00128	.01106	0
1	72346	2098	.02900	.00272	.00470	.00012	.00006	.00817	.00922	.00059	.00000	.00000	.00010	.00054	.00278	1
5	74496	304	.00408	.00085	.00090	.00005	.00020	.00068	.00034	.00016	.00000	.00000	.00012	.00026	.00052	5
10	68727	211	.00307	.00105	.00045	.00003	.00055	.00016	.00006	.00007	.00000	.00000	.00003	.00020	.00047	10
15	59451	320	.00538	.00309	.00039	.00003	.00039	.00047	.00003	.00012	.00020	.00000	.00003	.00017	.00045	15
20	52540	436	.00830	.00497	.00036	.00011	.00042	.00053	.00017	.00015	.00059	.00000	.00006	.00023	.00070	20
25	40874	338	.00827	.00489	.00044	.00020	.00056	.00051	.00007	.00005	.00049	.00000	.00007	.00020	.00078	25
30	32968	294	.00892	.00400	.00027	.00045	.00109	.00067	.00015	.00039	.00067	.00000	.00018	.00033	.00070	30
35	29653	259	.00873	.00317	.00044	.00084	.00148	.00064	.00003	.00024	.00091	.00000	.00003	.00030	.00064	35
40	24840	269	.01083	.00246	.00068	.00121	.00290	.00072	.00004	.00056	.00056	.00000	.00000	.00040	.00129	40
45	19895	260	.01307	.00256	.00070	.00176	.00417	.00136	.00005	.00070	.00010	.00000	.00000	.00035	.00131	45
50	15736	290	.01843	.00337	.00089	.00248	.00693	.00140	.00013	.00070	.00013	.00000	.00019	.00038	.00184	50
55	10574	212	.02005	.00208	.00123	.00274	.00946	.00227	.00028	.00057	.00000	.00000	.00028	.00000	.00113	55
60	11317	335	.02960	.00274	.00080	.00415	.01476	.00283	.00053	.00088	.00000	.00000	.00009	.00027	.00256	60
65	8295	342	.04123	.00253	.00048	.00458	.02363	.00362	.00084	.00169	.00000	.00000	.00012	.00024	.00350	65
70	5443	312	.05732	.00312	.00092	.00533	.02976	.00606	.00092	.00257	.00000	.00000	.00018	.00092	.00753	70
75	3099	265	.08551	.00226	.00097	.00904	.04840	.00807	.00097	.00097	.00000	.00000	.00032	.00129	.01323	75
80	1762	224	.12713	.00114	.00284	.01249	.05675	.01873	.00114	.00357	.00000	.00000	.00000	.00284	.02724	80
85+	1626	265	.16298	.00000	.00123	.00800	.07196	.02645	.00123	.00185	.00000	.00000	.00000	.00246	.04982	85+
ALL	554806	10141														

	All Causes	Respiratory T.B.	Other Infec. and Paras.	Neoplasms	Cardiovascular	Infl., Pneu., Bronch.	Diarrheal	Certain Degenerative	Maternal	Cert. Dis. of Infancy	Motor Vehicle	Other Violence	Other and Unknown
CRUDE DEATH RATE	.01828	.00273	.00154	.00069	.00264	.00327	.00301	.00036	.00023	.00154	.00008	.00035	.00182
STANDARDIZED RATE (1)	.01776	.00276	.00147	.00076	.00277	.00307	.00278	.00037	.00024	.00143	.00008	.00034	.00170
STANDARDIZED RATE (2)	.01981	.00282	.00119	.00135	.00551	.00281	.00184	.00051	.00025	.00084	.00009	.00037	.00223
GEOMETRIC MEAN	.02073												

LIFE TABLE FOR ALL CAUSES COMBINED

Age (x)	Midyear Population	Deaths During Year	$_nM_x$	$_nq_x$	l_x	$_nd_x$	$_nL_x$	$_nm_x$	$_na_x$	T_x	$_nr_x$	$\overset{\circ}{e}_x$	Age (x)
0	21164	3107	.146806	.133470	100000	13347	90918	.146802	.319570	4672082	.000000	46.721	0
1	72346	2098	.029000	.108156	86653	9372	323182	.028999	1.500000	4581164	.000000	52.868	1
5	74496	304	.004081	.020186	77281	1560	382505	.004078	2.500000	4257982	.000000	55.097	5
10	68727	211	.003070	.015253	75721	1155	375807	.003073	2.577381	3875477	.014145	51.181	10
15	59451	320	.005383	.026674	74566	1989	368233	.005401	2.688956	3499670	.018671	46.934	15
20	52540	436	.008298	.040770	72577	2959	355661	.008320	2.558508	3131437	.025238	43.146	20
25	40874	338	.008269	.040507	69618	2820	341031	.008269	2.496749	2775776	.037475	39.872	25
30	32968	294	.008918	.043639	66798	2915	326684	.008923	2.493711	2434745	.027830	36.449	30
35	29653	259	.008734	.042766	63883	2732	312651	.008738	2.524250	2108061	.019232	32.999	35
40	24840	269	.010829	.052869	61151	3233	297870	.010854	2.561024	1795410	.027198	29.360	40
45	19895	260	.013069	.063521	57918	3679	280720	.013106	2.588962	1497540	.027265	25.856	45
50	15736	290	.018429	.088571	54239	4804	259405	.018519	2.545752	1216820	.046618	22.434	50
55	10574	212	.020049	.095762	49435	4734	235625	.020091	2.560115	957415	.023568	19.367	55
60	11317	335	.029601	.138028	44701	6170	208601	.029578	2.584414	721791	-.004812	16.147	60
65	8295	342	.041230	.187745	38531	7234	174929	.041354	2.549679	513190	.021181	13.319	65
70	5443	312	.057321	.252261	31297	7895	136963	.057643	2.527312	338261	.037474	10.808	70
75	3099	265	.085511	.353346	23402	8269	96204	.085953	2.483876	201297	.027486	8.602	75
80	1762	224	.127128	.475416	15133	7255	56755	.127830	2.393522	105093	.027486	6.945	80
85+	1626	265	.162977	1.000000	7878	7878	48338	.162977	6.135849	48338	.000000	6.136	85+

NUMBER OF PERSONS DYING (OUT OF 100,000 AT BIRTH) ABOVE AGE X FROM SPECIFIED CAUSES

Age (x)	All Causes	Respiratory T. B.	Other Infec. and Paras.	Neo-plasms	Cardio-vascular	Infl., Pneu., Bronch.	Diar-rheal	Certain Degen-erative	Maternal	Cert. Dis. of Infancy	Motor Vehicle	Other Violence	Other and Unknown	Age (x)
0	100000	13233	5370	7138	30427	13852	7987	2551	1185	3681	429	1827	12320	0
1	86653	13036	4296	7129	30405	10604	4017	2525	1185	0	429	1711	11316	1
5	77281	12156	2778	7089	30387	7964	1038	2333	1185	0	398	1537	10416	5
10	75721	11832	2434	7069	30310	7703	909	2271	1185	0	351	1439	10218	10
15	74566	11437	2265	7058	30102	7643	888	2244	1184	0	341	1363	10041	15
20	72577	10291	2123	7045	29960	7469	875	2200	1109	0	328	1301	9876	20
25	69618	8520	1994	7004	29811	7279	814	2146	899	0	308	1219	9624	25
30	66798	6854	1844	6937	29617	7104	789	2129	732	0	283	1153	9356	30
35	63883	5549	1755	6787	29259	6885	740	2000	513	0	223	1043	9129	35
40	61151	4560	1617	6522	28793	6685	730	1926	228	0	213	948	8929	40
45	57918	3830	1413	6161	27925	6468	718	1757	62	0	213	828	8543	45
50	54239	3109	1215	5665	26748	6086	703	1559	35	0	213	730	8176	50
55	49435	2234	983	5019	24936	5722	670	1378	2	0	162	631	7698	55
60	44701	1746	693	4372	22700	5185	602	1245	2	0	95	631	7430	60
65	38531	1174	527	3506	19625	4596	492	1061	2	0	77	576	6895	65
70	31297	731	443	2703	15478	3961	344	764	2	0	56	534	6281	70
75	23402	303	316	1970	11381	3125	218	411	2	0	30	407	5239	75
80	15133	87	223	1056	6702	2344	125	319	2	0	0	282	3953	80
85+	7878	0	59	386	3478	1278	59	89	0	0	0	119	2410	85+

NUMBER OF PERSONS SURVIVING TO AGE X IF SPECIFIED CAUSES WERE ELIMINATED

Age (x)	No Causes	Respiratory T. B. (1)	Other Infec. and Paras. (2)	Neo-plasms (3)	Cardio-vascular (4)	Infl., Pneu., Bronch. (5)	Diar-rheal (6)	Certain Degener-ative (7)	Maternal (8)	Cert. Dis. of Infancy (9)	Motor Vehicle (10)	Other Violence (11)	Other and Unknown (12)	(1) + (2)	(1) + (2) + (5) + (6) + (8)	(1)+(2)+ (5)+(6)+ (8)+part of(9)&(12)	(10) + (11)	Age (x)
0	100000	100000	100000	100000	100000	100000	100000	100000	100000	100000	100000	100000	100000	100000	100000	100000	100000	0
1	86653	86836	87658	86661	86673	89727	90425	86677	86653	90145	86653	86761	87592	87843	94919	99714	86761	1
5	77281	78281	79640	77326	77316	82645	83633	77484	77281	80395	77310	77542	78982	80671	93361	99103	77571	5
10	75721	77026	78384	75785	75832	81253	82084	75982	75721	78773	75796	76074	77588	79735	92751	98653	76150	10
15	74566	76252	77362	74640	74882	80078	80854	74849	74567	77571	74650	74989	76585	79111	92125	98140	75074	15
20	72577	75383	75444	72662	73025	78126	78711	72896	72652	75502	72672	73051	74709	78361	91577	97742	73146	20
25	69618	74134	72499	69740	70195	75142	75567	69977	69856	72424	69728	70153	71918	77200	90810	97224	70264	25
30	66798	72889	69716	66981	67544	72283	72533	67160	67229	69490	66929	67377	69276	76073	89965	96643	67508	30
35	63883	71114	66764	64205	64952	69361	69419	64356	64512	66458	64067	64545	66484	74321	88551	95355	64731	35
40	61151	69157	64051	61721	62640	66607	66461	61677	62035	63615	61336	61879	63845	72436	86990	93867	62066	40
45	57918	66307	60873	58814	60201	63317	62960	58582	58919	60252	58094	58725	60863	69690	84249	91185	58904	45
50	54239	62899	57207	55568	57514	59700	58977	55055	55202	56425	54404	55091	57371	66341	80809	87694	55258	50
55	49435	58303	52375	51282	54346	54756	53787	50354	50345	51427	49634	50307	52773	61770	75868	82602	50510	55
60	44701	53267	47652	47013	51537	50118	48707	45661	45524	46728	44945	45490	47992	56783	70647	77053	45738	60
65	38531	46550	41237	41377	47841	43917	42096	39534	39240	40084	38758	39263	41905	49819	63033	68975	39494	65
70	31297	38292	33515	34390	43780	36246	34338	32387	31873	32558	31500	31930	34646	41080	53160	58375	32138	70
75	23402	29084	25223	26417	38063	27951	25795	24532	23833	24345	23576	23988	26926	31348	42028	46546	24167	75
80	15133	19017	16391	17889	31493	18837	16761	15938	15412	15743	15270	15615	18642	20598	28920	32402	15756	80
85+	7878	9978	8660	9927	21913	10793	8778	8470	8024	8195	7949	8249	11150	10968	17054	19761	8324	85+

ADDED YRS OF LIFE

		(1)	(2)	(3)	(4)	(5)	(6)	(7)	(8)	(9)	(10)	(11)	(12)				
TOTAL		4.780	2.204	1.193	6.062	4.658	3.989	.568	.413	1.870	.127	.532	2.827	7.266	18.661	24.034	.662
WORK	9.949	3.581	.430	.569	1.586	.649	.086	.252	.426	.000	.065	.233	.747	4.066	5.415	5.988	.299

POPULATION, DEATHS, DEATH RATES FOR ALL CAUSES COMBINED, AND SPECIFIED CAUSES

Age Start of Interval	Midyear Population	Deaths During Year	All Causes	Respiratory T. B.	Other Infec. and Paras.	Neo-plasms	Cardio-vascular	Infl., Pneu., Bronch.	Diar-rheal	Certain Degen-erative	Maternal	Cert. Dis. of Infancy	Motor Vehicle	Other Violence	Other and Unknown	Age Start of Interval
0	32168	1244	.03867	.00006	.00180	.00006	.00016	.00435	.CC544	.00016	.00000	.02077	.00003	.00059	.00525	0
1	129525	351	.00271	.00001	.00076	.00015	.00001	.00049	.0C028	.00007	.00000	.00000	.00010	.00036	.00049	1
5	140250	160	.00114	.00000	.00030	.00014	.00008	.C0006	.CC000	.00004	.00000	.CC000	.00009	.00023	.00021	5
10	125564	79	.00063	.00000	.00007	.00006	.00014	.00001	.00001	.00001	.00000	.00000	.00010	.00014	.00009	10
15	108699	171	.00157	.00001	.00009	.00010	.00017	.C0006	.00001	.00006	.00000	.00000	.00029	.00061	.00017	15
20	104322	217	.00208	.00007	.00003	.00014	.00023	.00008	.00001	.00003	.00000	.C0000	.00052	.00073	.00025	20
25	98947	235	.00238	.00017	.00014	.00017	.00032	.00007	.00000	.00007	.00000	.C0000	.00034	.00081	.00027	25
30	97235	253	.00260	.00014	.00008	.00022	.00051	.00012	.0000C	.00020	.00000	.C0000	.00025	.00076	.00032	30
35	96619	335	.C0347	.00025	.00012	.00028	.00094	.00023	.00001	.00023	.00000	.C0000	.00036	.00073	.00031	35
40	92371	496	.00537	.00032	.0C014	.00061	.00202	.00038	.00002	.00042	.00000	.00000	.00018	.00070	.00056	40
45	73254	640	.00874	.00031	.00029	.00123	.00380	.00048	.C0003	.00055	.00000	.C0000	.00029	.00086	.00091	45
50	55027	721	.01310	.C0044	.00033	.00236	.00585	.00085	.00004	.00084	.00000	.C0000	.00013	.00087	.00140	50
55	49448	1051	.02125	.00051	.00034	.00384	.01044	.00150	.00004	.00105	.00000	.00000	.00036	.00097	.00220	55
60	39980	1244	.03112	.00103	.00043	.00605	.01481	.00208	.00010	.00183	.00000	.00000	.00038	.00100	.00343	60
65	31771	1409	.04435	.CC085	.00050	.00831	.02345	.00274	.00022	.00217	.00000	.00000	.00031	.00076	.00504	65
70	24581	1544	.06281	.00049	.00057	.01212	.03145	.00521	.C0012	.00350	.00000	.00000	.00053	.00077	.00806	70
75	15328	1339	.08736	.00052	.00072	.01409	.04443	.00835	.00059	.00489	.00000	.00000	.00065	.00124	.01187	75
80	7378	1065	.14435	.00027	.00054	.01748	.07238	.01654	.00108	.00610	.00000	.00000	.00000	.00244	.02684	80
85+	3237	804	.24838	.00031	.00185	.02286	.10133	.03769	.C0309	.01267	.00000	.00000	.00000	.00525	.06333	85+
ALL	1325704	13358														ALL

CRUDE DEATH RATE	.01008	.00020 .0CC29 .00138 .00393 .00C85 .C0020 .00049 .00000 .C0050 .00025 .00064 .00135
STANCARDIZED RATE (1)	.00775	.00015 .00031 .0C095 .00256 .00065 .00025 .00034 .C0000 .00073 .00024 .00058 .00100
STANCARDIZED RATE (2)	.01305	.C0C23 .CC030 .00188 .00550 .00113 .00019 .00065 .00000 .00043 .00027 .00068 .00180
GEOMETRIC MEAN	.01035	

LIFE TABLE FOR ALL CAUSES COMBINED

Age (x)	Midyear Population	Deaths During Year	$_nM_x$	$_nq_x$	l_x	$_nd_x$	$_nL_x$	$_nm_x$	$_na_x$	T_x	$_nr_x$	$\overset{\circ}{e}_x$	Age (x)
0	32168	1244	.038672	.037420	100000	3742	96766	.038671	.135742	6421864	.000000	64.219	0
1	129525	351	.002710	.010773	96258	1037	382440	.002712	1.500000	6325098	.000000	65.710	1
5	140250	160	.001141	.005682	95221	541	474753	.001140	2.500000	5942659	.000000	62.409	5
10	125564	79	.000629	.003137	94680	297	472700	.000628	2.641695	5467906	.019724	57.751	10
15	108699	171	.001573	.007872	94383	743	470158	.001580	2.688706	4995207	.019373	52.925	15
20	104322	217	.002080	.010359	93640	970	465848	.002082	2.575387	4525009	.010440	48.323	20
25	98947	235	.002375	.011805	92670	1094	460660	.002375	2.540753	4059161	.006860	43.802	25
30	97235	253	.002602	.012929	91576	1184	455016	.002602	2.581116	3598501	.001661	39.295	30
35	96619	335	.003467	.017203	90392	1555	448318	.003469	2.657690	3143485	-.001164	34.776	35
40	92371	496	.005370	.026577	88837	2361	438735	.005381	2.691656	2695167	.012377	30.338	40
45	73254	640	.008737	.043099	86476	3727	423672	.008797	2.663671	2256432	.038340	26.093	45
50	55027	721	.013103	.063916	82749	5289	401383	.013177	2.662641	1832760	.031221	22.148	50
55	49448	1051	.021255	.101420	77460	7856	368661	.021310	2.627957	1431377	.014498	18.479	55
60	39980	1244	.031116	.145006	69604	10093	323632	.031187	2.583701	1062716	.014662	15.268	60
65	31771	1409	.044349	.200148	59511	11911	268370	.044383	2.549726	739084	.005667	12.419	65
70	24581	1544	.062813	.271765	47600	12936	205772	.062866	2.508632	470714	.005240	9.889	70
75	15328	1339	.087356	.359076	34664	12447	141954	.087684	2.479999	264943	.023186	7.643	75
80	7378	1065	.144348	.528469	22217	11741	80811	.145289	2.421553	122989	.023186	5.536	80
85+	3237	804	.248378	1.000000	10476	10476	42178	.248378	4.026119	42178	.000000	4.026	85+

NUMBER OF PERSONS DYING (OUT OF 100,000 AT BIRTH) ABOVE AGE X FROM SPECIFIED CAUSES

Age (x)	All Causes	Respiratory T. B.	Other Infec. and Paras.	Neo-plasms	Cardio-vascular	Infl., Pneu., Bronch.	Diar-rheal	Certain Degen-erative	Maternal	Cert. Dis. of Infancy	Motor Vehicle	Other Violence	Other and Unknown	Age (x)
0	100000	1711	1913	14828	43907	8769	1120	5101	0	2009	1800	4715	14127	0
1	96258	1705	1738	14822	43892	8348	593	5066	0	0	1797	4658	13619	1
5	95221	1702	1449	14762	43889	8162	487	5060	0	C	1759	4522	13429	5
10	94680	1702	1307	14698	43852	8135	487	5040	0	0	1715	4413	13331	10
15	94383	1702	1273	14668	43788	8131	483	5036	0	0	1666	4345	13291	15
20	93640	1698	1230	14620	43710	8101	479	5005	0	0	1527	4058	13212	20
25	92670	1666	1217	14553	43602	8065	474	4992	0	C	1285	3719	13097	25
30	91576	1587	1152	14474	43453	8032	474	4959	0	C	1127	3346	12972	30
35	90392	1522	1114	14376	43219	7976	474	4870	0	0	1015	3000	12826	35
40	88837	1410	1059	14251	42797	7874	470	4768	0	0	853	2671	12684	40
45	86476	1268	997	13984	41906	7708	460	4583	0	0	772	2362	12436	45
50	82749	1134	874	13458	40285	7504	449	4350	0	0	650	1997	12048	50
55	77460	959	743	12503	37520	7159	434	4013	0	C	599	1646	11484	55
60	69604	772	616	11082	34063	6605	419	3625	0	0	465	1288	10669	60
65	59511	440	478	9119	29259	5932	386	3032	0	0	344	965	9556	65
70	47600	212	343	6887	22960	5197	327	2449	0	C	259	762	8204	70
75	34664	111	226	4391	16485	4124	302	1728	0	0	150	603	6544	75
80	22217	37	124	2387	10154	2932	218	1032	0	0	57	426	4850	80
85+	10476	13	78	964	4274	1590	130	534	0	0	0	222	2671	85+

NUMBER OF PERSONS SURVIVING TO AGE X IF SPECIFIED CAUSES WERE ELIMINATED

Age (x)	No Causes	Respiratory T. B.	Other Infec. and Paras.	Neo-plasms	Cardio-vascular	Infl., Pneu., Bronch.	Diar-rheal	Certain Degener-ative	Maternal	Cert. Dis. of Infancy	Motor Vehicle	Other Violence	Other and Unknown	(1) + (2) + (5) + (6) + (8)	(1) + (2) + (5) + (6) + (8)	(1)+(2)+ (5)+(6)+ (8)+part of(9)&(12)	(10) + (11)	Age (x)
		(1)	(2)	(3)	(4)	(5)	(6)	(7)	(8)	(9)	(10)	(11)	(12)					
0	100000	100000	100000	100000	100000	100000	100000	100000	100000	100000	100000	100000	100000	100000	100000	100000	100000	0
1	96258	96264	96430	96264	96273	96672	96776	96273	96258	98249	96261	96314	96758	96436	97372	99702	96317	1
5	95221	95230	95679	95287	95239	95816	95840	95261	95221	97191	95262	95412	95905	95688	96912	99367	95453	5
10	94680	94689	95278	95280	94734	95299	95295	94740	94680	96639	94764	94979	95459	95287	96533	99017	95063	10
15	94383	94392	95013	94542	94501	95004	95000	94447	94383	96335	94516	94749	95200	95022	96273	98757	94882	15
20	93640	93653	94309	93845	93835	94286	94257	93734	93640	95577	93911	94290	94530	94321	95598	98074	94563	20
25	92670	92714	93345	92940	92971	93368	92776	92670	94587	93180	93654	93666	93389	94695	97160	94169	25
30	91576	91698	92308	91922	92022	92277	92184	91714	91576	93470	92238	92924	92686	92431	93757	96222	93595	30
35	90392	90578	91152	90831	91066	91140	90992	90617	90392	92262	91157	92072	91635	91340	92707	95167	92851	35
40	88837	89131	89639	89393	89922	89674	89431	89159	88837	90675	89751	90820	90201	89936	91390	93844	91755	40
45	86476	86902	87319	87283	88427	87466	86973	86476	88265	87446	88719	88053	87749	89347	91793	89714	45
50	82749	83289	83677	84043	86253	83889	83322	83454	82749	84461	83798	85262	84645	84223	85975	88386	86343	50
55	77460	78136	78457	79615	83162	78866	78011	78449	77460	79062	78492	80162	79795	79141	81151	83510	81230	55
60	69604	70390	70621	72938	78756	71404	70114	70866	69604	71044	70660	72383	72502	71419	73803	76053	73481	60
65	59511	60494	60510	64291	72552	61691	59978	61150	59511	60742	60527	62196	63069	61509	64262	66372	63258	65
70	47600	48591	48521	53621	65308	50030	48026	49448	47600	48585	48489	49935	51743	49531	52526	54401	50868	70
75	34664	35471	35436	41508	55734	37409	34996	36653	34664	35381	35406	36506	39249	36261	39507	41114	37288	75
80	22217	22794	22794	28562	44791	25025	22498	24081	22217	22677	22768	23547	26734	23386	26674	27989	24131	80
85+	10476	10764	10780	14753	30776	12859	10669	11723	10476	10693	10775	11249	14493	11077	13846	14850	11570	85+

ADDED YRS OF LIFE																		
TOTAL		.344	.648	2.041	7.108	1.311	.462	.704	.000	1.326	.555	1.361	2.154	.998	2.845	4.839	1.936	
WORK	4.906	.185	.135	.547	1.491	.248	.012	.243	.000	.000	.350	.799	.477	.321	.585	.656	1.157	

POPULATION, DEATHS, DEATH RATES FOR ALL CAUSES COMBINED, AND SPECIFIED CAUSES

Age Start of Interval	Midyear Population	Deaths During Year	All Causes	Respiratory T. B.	Other Infec. and Paras.	Neo-plasms	Cardio-vascular	Infl., Pneu., Bronch.	Diar-rheal	Certain Degen-erative	Maternal	Cert. Dis. of Infancy	Motor Vehicle	Other Violence	Other and Unknown	Age Start of Interval
0	30881	977	.03164	.00003	.00149	.00019	.00006	.00499	.00473	.00003	.00000	.01541	.00006	.00042	.00421	0
1	124751	269	.00216	.00002	.00063	.00008	.00000	.00047	.00016	.00004	.00000	.00000	.00003	.00023	.00421	1
5	135775	120	.00088	.00001	.00029	.00010	.00010	.00004	.00001	.00001	.00000	.00000	.00006	.00050	.00050	5
10	121368	84	.00069	.00001	.00011	.00007	.00026	.00003	.00002	.00005	.00000	.00000	.00006	.00007	.00019	10
15	105391	92	.00087	.00004	.00004	.00009	.00012	.00006	.00002	.00005	.00007	.00000	.00004	.00002	.00009	15
20	103589	130	.00125	.00024	.00005	.00011	.00014	.00004	.00002	.00005	.00016	.00000	.00009	.00012	.00019	20
25	99499	131	.00132	.00023	.00006	.00013	.00024	.00011	.00001	.00010	.00011	.00000	.00005	.00015	.00027	25
30	96693	176	.00182	.00022	.00009	.00034	.00034	.00009	.00000	.00014	.00012	.00000	.00005	.00005	.00022	30
35	96633	242	.00250	.00011	.00006	.00055	.00075	.00007	.00002	.00016	.00020	.00000	.00004	.00017	.00026	35
40	91058	308	.00338	.00013	.00012	.00086	.00101	.00013	.00001	.00027	.00009	.00000	.00001	.00017	.00041	40
45	72133	359	.00498	.00019	.00014	.00110	.00187	.00024	.00006	.00043	.00000	.00000	.00008	.00019	.00049	45
50	58228	499	.00857	.00017	.00015	.00235	.00381	.00034	.00000	.00058	.00000	.00000	.00008	.00029	.00058	50
55	52654	641	.01217	.00019	.00011	.00306	.00606	.00036	.00008	.00076	.00000	.00000	.00007	.00029	.00079	55
60	44461	857	.01928	.00025	.00020	.00414	.00999	.00072	.00004	.00151	.00000	.00000	.00011	.00021	.00123	60
65	34647	956	.02759	.00012	.00026	.00603	.01495	.00193	.00029	.00147	.00000	.00000	.00000	.00034	.00198	65
70	25483	1127	.04423	.00020	.00063	.00797	.02460	.00259	.00059	.00314	.00000	.00000	.00016	.00043	.00211	70
75	16101	1166	.07242	.00019	.00062	.01155	.03900	.00596	.00081	.00385	.00000	.00000	.00016	.00067	.00369	75
80	8504	949	.11159	.00035	.00094	.01446	.05856	.01023	.00071	.00517	.00000	.00000	.00006	.00174	.00863	80
85+	4378	868	.19826	.00000	.00183	.01599	.10416	.02376	.00114	.00594	.00000	.00000	.00012	.00254	.01811	85+
ALL	1322227	9951														

	All Causes	Respiratory T. B.	Other Infec. and Paras.	Neo-plasms	Cardio-vascular	Infl., Pneu., Bronch.	Diar-rheal	Certain Degen-erative	Maternal	Cert. Dis. of Infancy	Motor Vehicle	Other Violence	Other and Unknown
CRUDE DEATH RATE	.00753	.00012	.00023	.00120	.00313	.00059	.00018	.00040	.00006	.00036	.00006	.00025	.00096
STANDARDIZED RATE (1)	.00544	.00011	.00024	.00078	.00181	.00047	.00022	.00026	.00005	.00054	.00006	.00019	.00071
STANDARDIZED RATE (2)	.00518	.00013	.00023	.00150	.00409	.00070	.00018	.00049	.00005	.00032	.00006	.00028	.00115
GEOMETRIC MEAN	.00719												

LIFE TABLE FOR ALL CAUSES COMBINED

Age (x)	Midyear Population	Deaths During Year	$_nM_x$	$_nq_x$	l_x	$_nd_x$	$_nL_x$	$_nm_x$	$_na_x$	T_x	$_nr_x$	$\overset{\circ}{e}_x$	Age (x)
0	30881	977	.031638	.030780	100000	3078	97303	.031633	.123784	6970223	.000000	69.702	0
1	124751	269	.002156	.008584	96922	832	385608	.002158	1.500000	6872920	.000000	70.912	1
5	135775	120	.000884	.004413	96090	424	479390	.000884	2.500000	6487312	.000000	67.513	5
10	121368	84	.000692	.003450	95666	330	477503	.000691	2.494949	6007922	.020080	62.801	10
15	105391	92	.000873	.004364	95336	416	475695	.000875	2.632212	5530418	.018060	58.010	15
20	103589	130	.001255	.006258	94920	594	473157	.001253	2.571549	5054723	.007401	53.252	20
25	99499	131	.001317	.006573	94326	620	470133	.001319	2.585685	4581566	.006637	48.572	25
30	96693	176	.001820	.009060	93706	849	466519	.001820	2.631527	4111433	.002729	43.876	30
35	96633	242	.002504	.012449	92857	1156	461539	.002505	2.624892	3644914	.000006	39.253	35
40	91058	308	.003382	.016816	91701	1542	454875	.003390	2.645644	3183374	.016764	34.715	40
45	72133	359	.004977	.024778	90159	2234	445662	.005013	2.702365	2728500	.036585	30.263	45
50	58228	499	.008570	.042218	87925	3712	430920	.008614	2.655015	2282838	.028026	25.963	50
55	52654	641	.012174	.059326	84213	4996	409327	.012205	2.650620	1851917	.015947	21.991	55
60	44461	857	.019275	.092455	79217	7324	378681	.019341	2.623652	1442590	.020421	18.211	60
65	34647	956	.027593	.129957	71893	9343	337200	.027708	2.616955	1063909	.024671	14.799	65
70	25483	1127	.044226	.200943	62550	12569	282601	.044476	2.601291	726709	.028215	11.618	70
75	16101	1166	.072418	.309197	49981	15454	211798	.072966	2.534161	444108	.034441	8.886	75
80	8504	949	.111595	.437426	34527	15103	134340	.112424	2.464411	232310	.034441	6.728	80
85+	4378	868	.198264	1.000000	19424	19424	97970	.198264	5.043779	97970	.000000	5.044	85+

NUMBER OF PERSONS DYING (OUT OF 100,000 AT BIRTH) ABOVE AGE X FROM SPECIFIED CAUSES

Age (x)	All Causes	Respiratory T. B.	Other Infec. and Paras.	Neo-plasms	Cardio-vascular	Infl., Pneu., Bronch.	Diar-rheal	Certain Degen-erative	Maternal	Cert. Dis. of Infancy	Motor Vehicle	Other Violence	Other and Unknown	Age (x)
0	100000	991	1729	15720	48659	7990	1279	5231	350	1500	443	3103	13005	0
1	96922	988	1584	15701	48652	7505	819	5228	350	0	437	3062	12596	1
5	96090	982	1343	15670	48652	7323	758	5213	350	0	425	2972	12402	5
10	95666	975	1205	15624	48603	7301	754	5205	350	0	396	2941	12312	10
15	95336	971	1155	15589	48481	7286	746	5182	350	0	377	2933	12266	15
20	94920	952	1137	15548	48422	7259	737	5159	318	0	336	2874	12178	20
25	94326	838	1114	15498	48358	7240	737	5136	241	0	313	2801	12050	25
30	93706	729	1085	15437	48245	7188	722	5089	189	0	290	2777	11945	30
35	92857	628	1042	15277	48085	7145	732	5021	131	0	270	2700	11826	35
40	91701	576	1013	15024	47741	7111	723	4950	40	0	266	2624	11633	40
45	90159	516	958	14634	47280	7051	718	4824	0	0	230	2538	11410	45
50	87925	429	896	14141	46438	6945	693	4632	0	0	193	2408	11150	50
55	84213	355	830	13122	44784	6797	693	4379	0	0	164	2283	10806	55
60	79217	277	783	11868	42296	6649	662	4067	0	0	117	2197	10301	60
65	71893	183	706	10296	38500	6374	645	3495	0	0	75	2069	9550	65
70	62550	145	618	8256	33436	5718	546	2997	0	0	75	1922	8837	70
75	49981	89	440	5996	26444	4981	379	2105	0	0	30	1732	7785	75
80	34527	49	308	3536	18124	3706	207	1286	0	0	17	1360	5934	80
85+	19424	0	179	1566	10204	2327	112	582	0	0	0	962	3492	85+

NUMBER OF PERSONS SURVIVING TO AGE X IF SPECIFIED CAUSES WERE ELIMINATED

Age (x)	No Causes	Respiratory T. B.	Other Infec. and Paras.	Neo-plasms	Cardio-vascular	Infl., Pneu., Bronch.	Diar-rheal	Certain Degener-ative	Maternal	Cert. Dis. of Infancy	Motor Vehicle	Other Violence	Other and Unknown	(1) + (2)	(1) + (2) + (5) + (6) + (8)	(1)+(2)+ (5)+(6)+ (8)+part of(9)&(12)	(10) + (11)	Age (x)
		(1)	(2)	(3)	(4)	(5)	(6)	(7)	(8)	(9)	(10)	(11)	(12)					
0	100000	100000	100000	100000	100000	100000	100000	100000	100000	100000	100000	100000	100000	100000	100000	100000	100000	0
1	96922	96925	97065	96941	96929	97401	97376	96925	96922	98410	96928	96962	97325	97068	98004	99797	96968	1
5	96090	96099	96472	96139	96057	96747	96601	96108	96090	97565	96108	96220	96684	96481	97657	99598	96238	5
10	95666	95682	96185	95761	95722	96342	96179	95692	95666	97135	95713	95826	96348	96201	97400	99383	95873	10
15	95336	95356	95903	95466	95513	96025	95855	95385	95336	96800	95401	95504	96062	95923	97142	99133	95569	15
20	94920	94959	95503	95090	95156	95633	95446	94991	94952	96377	95026	95146	95731	95542	96825	98839	95252	20
25	94326	94478	94928	94545	94624	95054	94849	94420	94435	95774	94454	94623	95261	95081	96457	98529	94752	25
30	93706	93966	94333	93985	94115	94481	94230	93846	93866	95145	93857	94025	94740	94595	96075	98191	94176	30
35	92857	93216	93522	93293	93423	93668	93376	93064	93073	94283	93026	93250	94002	93883	95454	97599	93420	35
40	91701	92107	92387	92385	92604	92536	92223	91976	92005	93109	91872	92165	92796	94486	96654	92337		40
45	90159	90618	90888	91221	91510	91040	90677	90555	90458	91543	90363	90701	91686	91351	93122	95298	90906	45
50	87925	88459	88698	89455	90091	88890	88455	88501	88255	89275	88160	88583	89676	89236	91100	93268	88820	50
55	84213	84797	85018	86699	87963	85284	84721	85015	84529	85506	84467	84966	86234	85608	87547	89660	85223	55
60	79217	79843	80020	82816	85304	80370	79725	80277	79515	80433	79502	80010	81621	80652	82660	84690	80297	60
65	71893	72551	72656	76740	81411	73207	72370	73409	72163	72997	72191	72736	74814	73361	75480	77388	73037	65
70	62550	63158	63332	68825	76384	64319	63059	64344	62785	63510	62809	63422	65786	63947	66540	68296	63685	70
75	49981	50517	50767	57252	69144	52076	50538	52239	50169	50748	50229	50851	53568	51311	54261	55797	51102	75
80	34527	34930	35180	41937	58277	37094	35054	36796	34657	35057	34708	35443	38694	35590	38967	40284	35630	80
85+	19424	19688	19889	25431	44328	21994	19792	21263	19497	19722	19539	20244	23890	20158	23345	24429	20364	85+

ADDED YRS OF LIFE																		
TOTAL		.304	.588	2.410	8.524	1.248	.460	.755	.152	1.068	.150	.539	2.065	.896	2.822	4.580	.691	
WORK	3.150	.187	.086	.609	.976	.128	.016	.205	.118	.000	.067	.177	.414	.274	.538	.644	.244	

POPULATION, DEATHS, DEATH RATES FOR ALL CAUSES COMBINED, AND SPECIFIED CAUSES

Age Start of Interval	Midyear Population	Deaths During Year	All Causes	Respiratory T.B.	Other Infec. and Paras.	Neoplasms	Cardiovascular	Infl., Pneu., Bronch.	Diarrheal	Certain Degenerative	Maternal	Cert. Dis. of Infancy	Motor Vehicle	Other Violence	Other and Unknown	Age Start of Interval
0	28652	4796	.16739	.00091	.00855	.00003	.00000	.03054	.06261	.00045	.00000	.04624	.00007	.00101	.01696	0
1	104713	2091	.01957	.00074	.00229	.00008	.00001	.00478	.00812	.00026	.00000	.00000	.00017	.00053	.00298	1
5	112360	215	.00191	.00008	.00029	.00011	.00007	.00029	.00012	.00006	.00000	.00000	.00020	.00037	.00031	5
10	90975	124	.00136	.00008	.00014	.00007	.00010	.00013	.00003	.00001	.00000	.00000	.00016	.00033	.00031	10
15	70525	154	.00218	.00031	.00010	.00006	.00020	.00013	.00003	.00007	.00000	.00000	.00024	.00069	.00035	15
20	64987	281	.00432	.00072	.00009	.00015	.00034	.00017	.00006	.00012	.00000	.00000	.00058	.00165	.00043	20
25	53594	260	.00485	.00007	.00017	.00017	.00034	.00022	.00006	.00007	.00000	.00000	.00069	.00183	.00054	25
30	45946	289	.00629	.00141	.00017	.00044	.00070	.00044	.00004	.00013	.00000	.00000	.00076	.00135	.00085	30
35	37974	303	.00798	.00169	.00026	.00071	.00166	.00050	.00008	.00026	.00000	.00000	.00092	.00113	.00076	35
40	31725	311	.00980	.00148	.00044	.00132	.00233	.00050	.00013	.00028	.00000	.00000	.00085	.00104	.00142	40
45	27509	353	.01283	.00207	.00062	.00182	.00338	.00091	.00015	.00051	.00000	.00000	.00051	.00120	.00167	45
50	22239	449	.02019	.00247	.00085	.00301	.00683	.00108	.00013	.00076	.00000	.00000	.00112	.00144	.00247	50
55	17265	451	.02612	.00278	.00122	.00458	.00875	.00290	.00035	.00098	.00000	.00000	.00058	.00122	.00237	55
60	11576	538	.04648	.00544	.00095	.00691	.01710	.00510	.00078	.00181	.00000	.00000	.00104	.00121	.00613	60
65	8847	504	.05697	.00486	.00136	.00938	.02362	.00543	.00057	.00170	.00000	.00000	.00090	.00079	.00836	65
70	6227	467	.07500	.00450	.00096	.00787	.03372	.01012	.00064	.00177	.00000	.00000	.00064	.00161	.01317	70
75	3942	397	.10071	.00583	.00127	.01040	.04338	.00964	.00101	.00330	.00000	.00000	.00127	.00254	.02207	75
80	1882	273	.14506	.00372	.00213	.01700	.05260	.02179	.00266	.00372	.00000	.00000	.00000	.00000	.04145	80
85+	1347	302	.22420	.00297	.00074	.01262	.08315	.02673	.01114	.00297	.00000	.00000	.00000	.00000	.08388	85+
ALL	742285	12558														
CRUDE DEATH RATE			.01692	.00099	.00092	.00087	.00220	.00255	.00368	.00028	.00000	.00179	.00044	.00092	.00228	
STANDARDIZED RATE (1)			.01699	.00111	.00087	.00104	.00261	.00244	.00329	.00028	.00000	.00163	.00044	.00092	.00227	
STANDARDIZED RATE (2)			.02079	.00156	.00078	.00192	.00539	.00259	.00217	.00050	.00000	.00096	.00056	.00106	.00330	
GEOMETRIC MEAN			.01823													

LIFE TABLE FOR ALL CAUSES COMBINED

Age (x)	Midyear Population	Deaths During Year	$_nM_x$	$_nq_x$	l_x	$_nd_x$	$_nL_x$	$_nm_x$	$_na_x$	T_x	$_nr_x$	$\overset{\circ}{e}_x$	Age (x)
0	28652	4796	.167388	.151070	100000	15107	90249	.167392	.354560	4862474	.000000	48.625	0
1	104713	2091	.019969	.076072	84893	6458	323427	.019967	1.500000	4772224	.000000	56.215	1
5	112360	215	.001913	.009537	78435	748	390305	.001916	2.500000	4448797	.000000	56.720	5
10	90975	124	.001363	.006784	77687	527	387138	.001361	2.538346	4058492	.036540	52.242	10
15	70525	154	.002184	.010851	77160	845	383919	.002201	2.774162	3671355	.034058	47.581	15
20	64987	281	.004324	.021477	76315	1639	377675	.004340	2.620627	3287455	.024782	43.077	20
25	53594	260	.004851	.024024	74676	1794	369025	.004861	2.572580	2909760	.028838	38.965	25
30	45946	289	.006290	.031064	72882	2264	358954	.006307	2.589996	2540735	.027872	34.861	30
35	37974	303	.007979	.039253	70618	2772	346367	.008003	2.574555	2181781	.029945	30.896	35
40	31725	311	.009803	.047991	67846	3256	331353	.009826	2.580748	1835415	.024206	27.053	40
45	27509	353	.012832	.062455	64590	4034	313406	.012871	2.634017	1504062	.021903	23.286	45
50	22239	449	.020190	.096621	60556	5851	288721	.020265	2.597134	1190656	.023864	19.662	50
55	17265	451	.026122	.123608	54705	6762	257496	.026261	2.629584	901935	.034865	16.487	55
60	11576	538	.046475	.209770	47943	10057	215131	.046748	2.555517	644439	.028999	13.442	60
65	8847	504	.056968	.249221	37886	9442	165597	.057018	2.475883	429308	.009111	11.332	65
70	6227	467	.074996	.315146	28444	8964	119468	.075033	2.461861	263711	.003741	9.271	70
75	3942	397	.100710	.400462	19480	7801	77310	.100906	2.424662	144243	.013607	7.405	75
80	1882	273	.145058	.525987	11679	6143	42241	.145428	2.370313	66933	.013607	5.731	80
85+	1347	302	.224202	1.000000	5536	5536	24692	.224202	4.460265	24692	.000000	4.460	85+

NUMBER OF PERSONS DYING (OUT OF 100,000 AT BIRTH) ABOVE AGE X FROM SPECIFIED CAUSES

Age (x)	All Causes	Respiratory T. B.	Other Infec. and Paras.	Neo-plasms	Cardio-vascular	Infl., Pneu., Bronch.	Diar-rheal	Certain Degen-erative	Maternal	Cert. Dis. of Infancy	Motor Vehicle	Other Violence	Other and Unknown	Age (x)
0	100000	7940	3628	9643	26597	12052	9457	2495	0	4174	2889	5314	15811	0
1	84893	7858	2856	9640	26597	9296	3806	2454	0	0	2883	5223	14280	1
5	78435	7617	2115	9615	26594	7748	1181	2370	0	0	2828	5050	13317	5
10	77687	7586	2000	9573	26566	7633	1132	2346	0	0	2751	4904	13196	10
15	77160	7556	1945	9548	26527	7583	1120	2342	0	0	2687	4776	13076	15
20	76315	7434	1907	9526	26450	7534	1109	2314	0	0	2594	4506	12941	20
25	74676	7160	1872	9468	26322	7470	1085	2268	0	0	2372	3881	12778	25
30	72882	6877	1810	9405	26198	7387	1065	2240	0	0	2117	3207	12576	30
35	70618	6367	1747	9248	25945	7230	1049	2193	0	0	1843	2724	12272	35
40	67846	5783	1656	9000	25367	7056	1021	2101	0	0	1523	2333	12006	40
45	64590	5291	1509	8559	24591	6889	980	2007	0	0	1242	1988	11534	45
50	60556	4641	1315	7987	23526	6603	934	1847	0	0	1082	1612	11009	50
55	54705	3925	1067	7113	21544	6289	895	1625	0	0	757	1196	10294	55
60	47943	3206	753	5824	19278	5536	804	1370	0	0	609	883	9680	60
65	37886	2029	549	4330	15573	4434	636	978	0	0	385	623	8349	65
70	28444	1225	324	2775	11656	3535	543	698	0	0	235	492	6961	70
75	19480	687	209	1835	7625	2325	466	486	0	0	159	300	5388	75
80	11679	236	111	1029	4267	1579	387	231	0	0	60	104	3675	80
85+	5536	73	18	312	2053	660	275	73	0	0	55	92	1925	85+

NUMBER OF PERSONS SURVIVING TO AGE X IF SPECIFIED CAUSES WERE ELIMINATED

Age (x)	No Causes	Respiratory T. B. (1)	Other Infec. and Paras. (2)	Neo-plasms (3)	Cardio-vascular (4)	Infl., Pneu., Bronch. (5)	Diar-rheal (6)	Certain Degener-ative (7)	Maternal (8)	Cert. Dis. of Infancy (9)	Motor Vehicle (10)	Other Violence (11)	Other and Unknown (12)	(1) + (2)	(1) + (2) + (5) + (6) + (8)	(1)+(2)+ (5)+(6)+ (8)+part of(9)&(12)	(10) + (11)	Age (x)
0	100000	100000	100000	100000	100000	100000	100000	100000	100000	100000	100000	100000	100000	100000	100000	100000	100000	0
1	84893	84969	85606	84896	84893	87468	90256	84931	84893	88823	84899	84977	86314	85683	93859	99755	84982	1
5	78435	78737	79816	78462	78438	82361	86116	78551	78435	82066	78493	78675	80654	80123	92372	99268	78737	5
10	77687	78017	79171	77755	77718	81656	85348	77825	77687	81283	77821	78075	80049	79507	91856	98788	78209	10
15	77160	77518	78690	77253	77229	81194	84782	77302	77160	80732	77357	77673	79629	79055	91406	98359	77872	15
20	76315	76791	77867	76429	76460	80356	83866	76483	76315	79848	76603	77093	78896	78352	90664	97614	77384	20
25	74676	75415	76230	74845	74945	78697	82051	74886	74676	78133	75178	76605	77368	76984	89185	96077	76577	25
30	72882	73886	74461	73109	73268	76893	80140	73115	72882	76256	73626	74919	75716	75487	87573	94413	75684	30
35	70618	72102	72211	70993	71243	74668	77668	70890	70618	73687	71612	73081	73676	73728	85740	92586	74110	35
40	67846	69858	69468	68452	69021	71917	74650	68198	67846	70987	69120	70609	71056	71528	83424	90207	71935	40
45	64590	67001	66281	65602	66484	68639	71111	65017	64590	67580	66082	67572	68130	68756	80443	87172	69133	45
50	60556	63472	62335	62070	63403	64647	66719	61113	60556	63359	62113	63733	64413	65337	76849	83512	65372	50
55	54705	58056	56555	56932	59284	58721	60313	55421	54705	57237	56429	57991	58916	60019	71030	77435	59819	55
60	47943	51598	49868	51165	54306	52226	52952	48813	47943	50162	49596	51133	52257	53670	64573	70654	52895	60
65	37886	41912	39594	41869	46809	42348	42009	38928	37886	39640	39397	40651	42605	43801	54288	59966	42273	65
70	28444	32237	29930	32950	39592	32675	31628	29474	28444	29761	29712	30641	33368	33921	43328	48369	32007	70
75	19480	22581	20596	23470	32152	23554	21731	20367	19480	20382	20413	21157	24432	23874	32202	36584	22170	75
80	11679	13941	12428	14836	24008	14825	13057	12418	11679	12220	12318	12847	16407	14835	21118	24614	13550	80
85+	5536	6741	5958	7673	14894	7858	6293	6000	5536	5792	5843	6099	9620	7254	11705	14520	6436	85+

ADDED YRS OF LIFE																	
TOTAL		1.705	1.277	1.440	4.243	3.497	4.852	.433	.000	2.235	.774	1.599	3.390	3.053	12.519	17.966	2.418
WORK	7.983	1.112	.250	.691	1.424	.430	.075	.207	.000	.000	.611	1.252	.824	1.374	1.917	2.194	1.889

POPULATION, DEATHS, DEATH RATES FOR ALL CAUSES COMBINED, AND SPECIFIED CAUSES

Age Start of Interval	Midyear Population	Deaths During Year	All Causes	Respiratory T.B.	Other Infec. and Paras.	Neo-plasms	Cardio-vascular	Infl., Pneu., Bronch.	Diar-rheal	Certain Degen-erative	Maternal	Cert. Dis. of Infancy	Motor Vehicle	Other Violence	Other and Unknown	Age Start of Interval
0	29023	4209	.14502	.00096	.00844	.00010	.00003	.03018	.05485	.00024	.00000	.03394	.00000	.00121	.01506	0
1	105201	1981	.01883	.00064	.00241	.00008	.00003	.00442	.00775	.00022	.00000	.00000	.00008	.00054	.00267	1
5	111658	194	.00174	.00004	.00046	.00004	.00008	.00024	.00013	.00004	.00000	.00000	.00013	.00022	.00037	5
10	91105	90	.00099	.00014	.00013	.00003	.00013	.00007	.00007	.00002	.00000	.00000	.00008	.00010	.00022	10
15	71752	130	.00181	.00028	.00013	.00011	.00028	.00021	.00004	.00004	.00013	.00000	.00000	.00020	.00035	15
20	67913	223	.00328	.00099	.00021	.00010	.00047	.00013	.00003	.00010	.00043	.00000	.00007	.00019	.00056	20
25	55883	203	.00363	.00120	.00016	.00025	.00030	.00016	.00011	.00009	.00045	.00000	.00005	.00032	.00054	25
30	45929	188	.00409	.00072	.00015	.00020	.00074	.00033	.00002	.00020	.00044	.00000	.00015	.00033	.00083	30
35	36727	218	.00594	.00101	.00025	.00076	.00123	.00041	.00011	.00025	.00068	.00000	.00038	.00019	.00068	35
40	30996	223	.00719	.00126	.00016	.00126	.00200	.00032	.00003	.00019	.00071	.00000	.00006	.00019	.00084	40
45	27083	283	.01045	.00107	.00022	.00144	.00443	.00059	.00015	.00055	.00022	.00000	.00022	.00011	.00144	45
50	21296	316	.01484	.00103	.00061	.00169	.00765	.00047	.00000	.00117	.00005	.00000	.00023	.00028	.00164	50
55	16206	279	.01722	.00123	.00062	.00259	.00889	.00086	.00019	.00074	.00005	.00000	.00019	.00019	.00173	55
60	13303	374	.02811	.00098	.00060	.00421	.01376	.00180	.00030	.00210	.00000	.00000	.00045	.00038	.00353	60
65	9610	415	.04318	.00177	.00062	.00489	.02456	.00343	.00083	.00250	.00000	.00000	.00000	.00052	.00406	65
70	7147	410	.05737	.00126	.00112	.00672	.03428	.00434	.00056	.00196	.00000	.00000	.00000	.00042	.00672	70
75	4227	371	.08777	.00308	.00000	.00875	.04826	.00686	.00118	.00260	.00000	.00000	.00024	.00118	.01561	75
80	2301	316	.13733	.00174	.00000	.00608	.07301	.01347	.00348	.00217	.00000	.00000	.00000	.00261	.03477	80
85+	1891	393	.20783	.00053	.00000	.01481	.09096	.02909	.00423	.00370	.00000	.00000	.00053	.00423	.05976	85+
ALL	749251	10816														

	All Causes	Respiratory T.B.	Other Infec. and Paras.	Neo-plasms	Cardio-vascular	Infl., Pneu., Bronch.	Diar-rheal	Certain Degen-erative	Maternal	Cert. Dis. of Infancy	Motor Vehicle	Other Violence	Other and Unknown
CRUDE DEATH RATE	.01443	.00067	.00089	.00063	.00250	.00226	.00332	.00029	.00018	.00131	.00011	.00033	.00194
STANDARDIZED RATE (1)	.01390	.00071	.00082	.00070	.00271	.00205	.00296	.00032	.00020	.00119	.00012	.00032	.00181
STANDARDIZED RATE (2)	.01666	.00085	.00064	.00127	.00572	.00189	.00154	.00052	.00021	.00070	.00014	.00035	.00243
GEOMETRIC MEAN	.01428												

LIFE TABLE FOR ALL CAUSES COMBINED

Age (x)	Midyear Population	Deaths During Year	$_nM_x$	$_nq_x$	l_x	$_nd_x$	$_nL_x$	$_nm_x$	$_na_x$	T_x	$_nr_x$	$\overset{\circ}{e}_x$	Age (x)
0	29023	4209	.145023	.131940	100000	13194	90982	.145017	.316539	5337541	.000000	53.375	0
1	105201	1981	.018831	.071942	86806	6245	331612	.018832	1.500000	5246559	.000000	60.440	1
5	111658	194	.001737	.008664	80561	698	401060	.001740	2.500000	4914947	.000000	61.009	5
10	91105	90	.000988	.004908	79863	392	398340	.000984	2.512755	4513887	.035334	56.520	10
15	71752	130	.001812	.009085	79471	722	395736	.001824	2.758253	4115547	.030782	51.787	15
20	67913	223	.003284	.016343	78749	1287	390668	.003294	2.609104	3719811	.021709	47.236	20
25	55883	203	.003633	.018022	77462	1396	383874	.003637	2.538801	3329143	.031840	42.978	25
30	45929	188	.004093	.020338	76066	1547	376628	.004108	2.606927	2945268	.036535	38.720	30
35	36727	218	.005936	.029388	74519	2190	367332	.005962	2.596842	2568641	.036207	34.470	35
40	30996	223	.007194	.035463	72329	2565	355520	.007215	2.612086	2201308	.025692	30.435	40
45	27083	283	.010449	.051173	69764	3570	340352	.010489	2.627976	1845788	.024490	26.458	45
50	21296	316	.014838	.071880	66194	4758	319393	.014897	2.566861	1505437	.035633	22.743	50
55	16206	279	.017216	.082964	61436	5097	295000	.017278	2.610359	1186043	.030401	19.305	55
60	13303	374	.028114	.132377	56339	7458	263583	.028252	2.625089	891043	.025914	15.816	60
65	9610	415	.043184	.195884	48881	9575	220975	.043331	2.553046	627061	.020533	12.828	65
70	7147	410	.057367	.251768	39306	9896	172007	.057532	2.521958	406085	.021213	10.331	70
75	4227	371	.087769	.361034	29410	10618	120433	.088165	2.493250	234078	.022439	7.959	75
80	2301	316	.137332	.508301	18792	9552	69184	.138066	2.406237	113645	.022439	6.047	80
85+	1891	393	.207827	1.000000	9240	9240	44460	.207827	4.811705	44460	.000000	4.812	85+

NUMBER OF PERSONS DYING (OUT OF 100,000 AT BIRTH) ABOVE AGE X FROM SPECIFIED CAUSES

Age (x)	All Causes	Respiratory T.B.	Other Infec. and Paras.	Neoplasms	Cardiovascular	Infl., Pneu., Bronch.	Diarrheal	Certain Degenerative	Maternal	Cert. Dis. of Infancy	Motor Vehicle	Other Violence	Other and Unknown	Age (x)
0	100000	4872	3147	8349	38523	10578	8805	3308	1149	3088	776	1998	15407	0
1	86806	4785	2379	8339	38520	7832	3814	3286	1149	0	776	1889	14037	1
5	80561	4573	1578	8314	38510	6366	1245	3213	1149	0	751	1709	13153	5
10	79863	4555	1395	8300	38478	6269	1194	3199	1149	0	701	1619	13004	10
15	79471	4498	1343	8286	38425	6243	1169	3190	1149	0	671	1580	12917	15
20	78749	4386	1294	8242	38314	6160	1152	3174	1098	0	648	1502	12779	20
25	77462	3999	1213	8202	38130	6108	1141	3133	931	0	620	1427	12558	25
30	76066	3539	1151	8105	38013	6046	1099	3059	759	0	599	1303	12353	30
35	74519	3269	1094	8030	37731	5922	1091	3024	594	0	541	1181	12042	35
40	72329	2898	1004	7747	37278	5772	1051	2934	343	0	400	1111	11791	40
45	69764	2450	946	7298	36561	5657	1040	2865	92	0	378	985	11492	45
50	66154	2086	870	6808	35044	5456	989	2675	18	0	302	947	10999	50
55	61436	1756	674	6265	32586	5305	989	2299	3	0	227	857	10475	55
60	56339	1392	492	5457	29956	5048	934	2080	3	0	173	802	9962	60
65	48881	1134	333	4382	26304	4569	854	1521	3	0	53	702	9026	65
70	39306	742	195	3298	20856	3807	670	969	3	0	53	587	8126	70
75	29410	525	2	2140	14943	3059	573	632	3	0	53	515	6965	75
80	18792	153	2	1084	9107	2228	430	318	3	0	25	371	5071	80
85+	9240	24	0	658	4044	1293	188	165	0	0	24	188	2656	85+

NUMBER OF PERSONS SURVIVING TO AGE X IF SPECIFIED CAUSES WERE ELIMINATED

Age (x)	No Causes	Respiratory T.B. (1)	Other Infec. and Paras. (2)	Neoplasms (3)	Cardiovascular (4)	Infl., Pneu., Bronch. (5)	Diarrheal (6)	Certain Degenerative (7)	Maternal (8)	Cert. Dis. of Infancy (9)	Motor Vehicle (10)	Other Violence (11)	Other and Unknown (12)	(1)+(2)	(1)+(2)+(5)+(6)+(8)	(1)+(2)+(5)+(6)+(8)+part of(9)&(12)	(10)+(11)	Age (x)
0	100000	100000	100000	100000	100000	100000	100000	100000	100000	100000	100000	100000	100000	100000	100000	100000	100000	0
1	86806	86887	87524	86815	86809	89400	91579	86826	86806	89729	86806	86908	88091	87606	95185	99767	86908	1
5	80561	80841	82009	80594	80573	84436	87641	80650	80561	83274	80585	80829	82622	82294	93832	99333	80853	5
10	79863	80158	81484	79909	79907	83805	86937	79966	79863	82552	79937	80219	82058	81785	93425	99019	80293	10
15	79471	79822	81137	79531	79568	83421	86538	79582	79471	82147	79574	79864	81745	81495	93153	98787	79968	15
20	78749	79209	80450	78852	78956	82750	85770	78875	78800	81401	78874	79216	81144	80920	92672	98368	79342	20
25	77462	78302	79217	77603	77848	81452	84380	77627	77678	80070	77613	77997	80044	80076	91975	97810	78149	25
30	76066	77352	77852	76301	76562	80049	82905	76261	76449	78627	76235	76715	78811	79169	91262	97225	76885	30
35	74519	76051	76327	74824	75287	78550	81227	74785	75059	77028	74742	75276	77528	77896	90149	96241	75502	35
40	72329	74190	74174	72906	73526	76397	78883	72676	73102	74764	72685	73134	75507	76083	88581	94717	73494	40
45	69764	72012	71602	70766	71319	73807	76597	70167	70759	72113	70129	70665	73137	73909	86508	92651	71035	45
50	66194	68693	68014	67630	69510	70238	72257	66763	67211	68423	66615	67087	69899	70582	83009	89065	67513	50
55	61436	64085	63320	63306	67049	65344	67064	62330	62394	63505	61899	62352	65409	66051	77882	83676	62822	55
60	56339	59132	58246	58817	64295	60185	61557	57372	57217	58236	56816	57233	60508	61134	72469	77987	57717	60
65	48881	51556	50688	52124	59805	52698	53490	50310	49643	50527	49407	49751	53441	53462	64055	69116	50286	65
70	39306	41828	40887	42959	54451	43117	43193	40964	39919	40629	39728	40110	43862	43511	53267	57677	40541	70
75	29410	31496	30765	33251	48448	32976	32410	30952	29869	30400	29726	30075	33964	32947	41345	44988	30398	75
80	18792	20443	19655	22203	39572	21825	20836	20038	19085	19425	19016	19336	23528	21381	27961	30809	19566	80
85+	9240	10148	9666	11268	28347	11503	10431	9965	9386	9551	9351	9637	13843	10616	15156	17259	9753	85+

ADDED YRS OF LIFE

	No Causes	(1)	(2)	(3)	(4)	(5)	(6)	(7)	(8)	(9)	(10)	(11)	(12)	(1)+(2)	(1)+(2)+(5)+(6)+(8)	+part of(9)&(12)	(10)+(11)
TOTAL		1.375	1.383	1.319	6.897	3.415	4.808	.574	.408	1.787	.232	.578	3.349	2.803	12.399	17.059	.814
WORK	6.104	.916	.214	.580	1.645	.307	.066	.237	.390	.000	.136	.251	.769	1.137	1.936	2.289	.388

POPULATION, DEATHS, DEATH RATES FOR ALL CAUSES COMBINED, AND SPECIFIED CAUSES

Age Start of Interval	Midyear Population	Deaths During Year	All Causes	Respiratory T. B.	Other Infec. and Paras.	Neoplasms	Cardiovascular	Infl., Pneu., Bronch.	Diarrheal	Certain Degenerative	Maternal	Cert. Dis. of Infancy	Motor Vehicle	Other Violence	Other and Unknown	Age Start of Interval
0	35982	1291	.03588	.00003	.00081	.00014	.00003	.00389	.00295	.00006	.00000	.02015	.00008	.00058	.00717	0
1	143259	253	.00177	.00001	.00026	.00008	.00000	.00029	.00017	.00002	.00000	.00000	.00009	.00033	.00052	1
5	166706	97	.00058	.00000	.00012	.00010	.00001	.00002	.00001	.00000	.00000	.00000	.00011	.00033	.00052	5
10	160225	94	.00059	.00000	.00002	.00006	.00005	.00004	.00001	.00000	.00000	.00000	.00011	.00007	.00014	10
15	137607	195	.00142	.00000	.00004	.00017	.00007	.00001	.00001	.00004	.00000	.00000	.00011	.00016	.00009	15
20	118128	307	.00260	.00002	.00003	.00009	.00010	.00004	.00001	.00002	.00000	.00000	.00049	.00049	.00010	20
25	104088	242	.00232	.00005	.00007	.00017	.00017	.00006	.00000	.00012	.00000	.00000	.00097	.00111	.00017	25
30	102784	298	.00290	.00001	.00007	.00029	.00049	.00005	.00003	.00006	.00000	.00000	.00073	.00074	.00022	30
35	97939	363	.00371	.00007	.00004	.00040	.00116	.00015	.00000	.00006	.00000	.00000	.00052	.00098	.00041	35
40	92527	515	.00557	.00009	.00005	.00073	.00224	.00017	.00001	.00014	.00000	.00000	.00044	.00088	.00042	40
45	92368	762	.00825	.00012	.00010	.00104	.00397	.00025	.00001	.00036	.00000	.00000	.00051	.00088	.00053	45
50	83623	1132	.01354	.00029	.00012	.00200	.00692	.00063	.00002	.00053	.00000	.00000	.00052	.00080	.00091	50
55	60124	1164	.01936	.00030	.00018	.00383	.00976	.00103	.00003	.00067	.00000	.00000	.00055	.00109	.00124	55
60	44253	1406	.03177	.00027	.00034	.00649	.01684	.00160	.00014	.00158	.00000	.00000	.00075	.00073	.00185	60
65	35233	1653	.04652	.00060	.00048	.01005	.02461	.00326	.00011	.00156	.00000	.00000	.00045	.00088	.00312	65
70	24556	1719	.07000	.00077	.00024	.01360	.03665	.00554	.00029	.00257	.00000	.00000	.00033	.00098	.00485	70
75	16760	1559	.09302	.00066	.00060	.01742	.04809	.00710	.00042	.00340	.00000	.00000	.00060	.00143	.00904	75
80	9339	1280	.13706	.00086	.00054	.02131	.06735	.01617	.00064	.00450	.00000	.00000	.00000	.00143	.01331	80
85+	4801	1059	.22058	.00021	.00062	.02479	.09852	.03124	.00125	.00583	.00000	.00000	.00000	.00257	.02217	85+
ALL	1530302	15389														

	All Causes	Respiratory T. B.	Other Infec. and Paras.	Neoplasms	Cardiovascular	Infl., Pneu., Bronch.	Diarrheal	Certain Degenerative	Maternal	Cert. Dis. of Infancy	Motor Vehicle	Other Violence	Other and Unknown
CRUDE DEATH RATE	.01006	.00010	.00014	.00151	.00417	.00073	.00012	.00037	.00000	.00047	.00043	.00068	.00134
STANDARDIZED RATE (1)	.00760	.00007	.00014	.00102	.00268	.00053	.00015	.00025	.00000	.00071	.00041	.00061	.00103
STANDARDIZED RATE (2)	.01006	.00013	.00015	.00209	.00577	.00098	.00012	.00048	.00000	.00042	.00046	.00073	.00174
GEOMETRIC MEAN	.00983												

LIFE TABLE FOR ALL CAUSES COMBINED

Age (x)	Midyear Population	Deaths During Year	nM_x	nq_x	l_x	nd_x	nL_x	nm_x	na_x	T_x	nr_x	$\overset{\circ}{e}_x$	Age (x)
0	35982	1291	.035879	.034790	100000	3479	96977	.035875	.130994	6455197	.000000	64.552	0
1	143259	253	.001766	.007035	96521	679	384387	.001766	1.500000	6358220	.000000	65.874	1
5	166706	97	.000582	.002901	95842	278	478515	.000581	2.500000	5973834	.000000	62.330	5
10	160225	94	.000587	.002940	95564	281	477201	.000589	2.795819	5495319	.012204	57.504	10
15	137607	195	.001417	.007105	95283	677	474919	.001426	2.790497	5018118	.025182	52.665	15
20	118128	307	.002599	.012948	94606	1225	470051	.002606	2.568537	4543199	.027689	48.022	20
25	104088	242	.002325	.011566	93381	1080	464227	.002326	2.520062	4073148	.016831	43.619	25
30	102784	298	.002899	.014399	92301	1329	458306	.002900	2.592958	3608921	.005538	39.099	30
35	97939	363	.003706	.018390	90972	1673	450912	.003710	2.640217	3150615	.007326	34.633	35
40	92527	515	.005566	.027492	89299	2455	440741	.005570	2.656144	2699703	.002661	30.232	40
45	92368	762	.008250	.040452	86844	3513	426068	.008245	2.679571	2258962	-.002619	26.012	45
50	83623	1132	.013537	.065798	83331	5483	403727	.013581	2.642182	1832894	.018853	21.995	50
55	60124	1164	.019360	.093194	77848	7255	372142	.019495	2.643263	1429167	.040858	18.358	55
60	44253	1406	.031772	.148343	70593	10472	327916	.031935	2.607986	1057025	.027534	14.974	60
65	35233	1653	.046916	.210958	60121	12683	269663	.047033	2.560333	729109	.015098	12.127	65
70	24556	1719	.070003	.298179	47438	14145	201791	.070057	2.497423	459446	.007974	9.685	70
75	16760	1559	.093019	.375695	33293	12508	134436	.093041	2.439289	257655	.001357	7.739	75
80	9339	1280	.137060	.505172	20785	10500	76592	.137090	2.356885	123220	.001357	5.928	80
85+	4801	1059	.220579	1.000000	10285	10285	46627	.220579	4.533522	46627	.000000	4.534	85+

NUMBER OF PERSONS DYING (OUT OF 100,000 AT BIRTH) ABOVE AGE X FROM SPECIFIED CAUSES

Age (x)	All Causes	Respiratory T.B.	Other Infec. and Paras.	Neo-plasms	Cardio-vascular	Infl., Pneu., Bronch.	Diar-rheal	Certain Degenerative	Maternal	Cert. Dis. of Infancy	Motor Vehicle	Other Violence	Other and Unknown	Age (x)
0	100000	960	981	16385	45909	7665	714	3741	0	1954	3119	5177	13395	0
1	96521	957	903	16371	45906	7288	428	3736	0	0	3111	5120	12701	1
5	95842	955	804	16339	45906	7178	361	3728	0	0	3076	4994	12501	5
10	95564	955	746	16293	45901	7169	358	3728	0	0	3021	4959	12434	10
15	95283	955	734	16263	45877	7151	352	3710	0	0	2970	4881	12390	15
20	94606	955	717	16180	45846	7144	346	3699	0	0	2733	4645	12341	20
25	93381	947	705	16137	45798	7124	342	3671	0	0	2275	4122	12260	25
30	92301	924	674	16056	45717	7097	342	3618	0	0	1936	3779	12158	30
35	90972	920	643	15922	45493	7075	328	3591	0	0	1700	3328	11972	35
40	89299	888	624	15742	44967	7006	328	3526	0	0	1502	2933	11783	40
45	86844	849	600	15418	43980	6930	323	3369	0	0	1278	2547	11550	45
50	83331	799	559	14976	42289	6824	319	3143	0	0	1057	2206	11159	50
55	77848	683	511	14165	39484	6567	309	2872	0	0	835	1766	10656	55
60	70593	571	442	12728	35824	6180	297	2536	0	0	556	1495	9964	60
65	60121	482	330	10590	30274	5650	252	2015	0	0	386	1206	8936	65
70	47438	321	200	7874	23622	4767	221	1593	0	0	264	953	7623	70
75	33293	164	151	5126	16217	3647	164	1075	0	0	198	756	5795	75
80	20785	76	70	2784	9750	2693	107	618	0	0	118	563	4006	80
85+	10285	10	29	1156	4594	1457	58	272	0	0	39	359	2311	85+

NUMBER OF PERSONS SURVIVING TO AGE X IF SPECIFIED CAUSES WERE ELIMINATED

Age (x)	No Causes	Respiratory T.B. (1)	Other Infec. and Paras. (2)	Neo-plasms (3)	Cardio-vascular (4)	Infl., Pneu., Bronch. (5)	Diar-rheal (6)	Certain Degener-ative (7)	Maternal (8)	Cert. Dis. of Infancy (9)	Motor Vehicle (10)	Other Violence (11)	Other and Unknown (12)	(1)+(2)	(1)+(2)+(5)+(6)+(8)	(1)+(2)+(5)+(6)+(8)+part of(9)&(12)	(10)+(11)	Age (x)
0	100000	100000	100000	100000	100000	100000	100000	100000	100000	100000	100000	100000	100000	100000	100000	100000	100000	0
1	96521	96524	96598	96535	96524	96852	96802	96526	96521	98460	96529	96577	97205	96601	97255	99630	96585	1
5	95842	95847	96017	95888	95845	96321	96188	95855	95842	97767	95885	96023	96722	96022	96850	99335	96066	5
10	95564	95569	95796	95655	95572	96050	95912	95577	95564	97484	95662	95780	96509	95801	96640	99143	95878	10
15	95283	95288	95527	95404	95315	95786	95636	95314	95283	97197	95411	95576	96270	95532	96392	98895	95725	15
20	94606	94611	94865	94609	94669	95112	94963	94647	94606	96506	94990	95133	95635	94870	95737	98226	95520	20
25	93381	93394	93649	93624	93490	93901	93737	93450	93381	95257	94218	94425	94478	93661	94542	97003	95272	25
30	92301	92336	92556	92622	92490	92842	92653	92422	92301	94155	93469	93679	93488	92632	93530	95973	94864	30
35	90972	91011	91294	91422	91382	91527	91333	91118	90972	92799	92360	92785	92329	91333	92255	94677	94202	35
40	89299	89369	89634	89920	90026	89913	89653	89507	89299	91093	90861	91479	90822	89704	90679	93075	93079	40
45	86844	86951	87194	87771	88735	87516	87194	87201	86844	88588	88588	89354	88559	87301	88330	90680	91149	45
50	83331	83482	83707	84659	86856	84081	83670	83896	83331	85005	85225	86084	85368	83859	84958	87244	88041	50
55	77848	78102	78246	79890	84016	78800	78175	78640	77848	79412	79837	80859	80250	78501	79794	81985	82925	55
60	70593	70930	71020	73863	80041	71830	70901	71635	70593	72011	72669	73590	73454	71358	72925	74990	75754	60
65	60121	60490	60588	65003	74223	61675	60425	61497	60121	61329	62049	62551	63551	60960	62852	64715	64970	65
70	47438	47873	47922	53958	66312	49476	47705	48906	47438	48391	49070	49905	51393	48362	50724	52364	51621	70
75	33293	33730	33673	40559	56014	35712	33529	34772	33293	33962	34494	35196	37764	34115	36853	38241	36466	75
80	20785	21127	21087	27649	44606	23115	20977	22084	20785	21203	21601	22134	25226	21434	24057	25151	23003	80
85+	10285	10500	10463	15258	31181	12425	10414	11184	10285	10492	10745	11104	13984	10682	13068	13909	11600	85+

ADDED YRS OF LIFE																		
TOTAL		.147	.282	2.213	7.778	1.066	.276	.531	.000	1.294	.982	1.453	2.187	.430	1.807	3.702	2.472	
WORK	4.987	.060	.062	.560	1.528	.147	.013	.197	.000	.000	.669	.858	.441	.123	.284	.315	1.586	

POPULATION, DEATHS, DEATH RATES FOR ALL CAUSES COMBINED, AND SPECIFIED CAUSES

Age Start of Interval	Midyear Population	Deaths During Year	All Causes	Respiratory T.B.	Other Infec. and Paras.	Neoplasms	Cardiovascular	Infl., Pneu., Bronch.	Diarrheal	Certain Degenerative	Maternal	Cert. Dis. of Infancy	Motor Vehicle	Other Violence	Other and Unknown	Age Start of Interval
0	34536	965	.02794	.00000	.00043	.00009	.00000	.00359	.00252	.00003	.00000	.01619	.00017	.00041	.00452	0
1	138027	210	.00152	.00000	.00025	.00013	.00001	.00033	.00013	.00004	.00000	.00000	.00009	.00023	.00030	1
5	160559	87	.00054	.00000	.00010	.00004	.00000	.00004	.00001	.00001	.00000	.00000	.00012	.00007	.00016	5
10	153988	63	.00041	.00000	.00005	.00003	.00003	.00003	.00000	.00004	.00000	.00000	.00006	.00010	.00008	10
15	133836	93	.00069	.00001	.00004	.00008	.00007	.00003	.00001	.00001	.00001	.00000	.00020	.00009	.00014	15
20	115622	81	.00070	.00002	.00003	.00006	.00010	.00003	.00001	.00003	.00003	.00000	.00009	.00014	.00017	20
25	102001	97	.00095	.00001	.00002	.00011	.00018	.00004	.00001	.00006	.00008	.00000	.00009	.00015	.00022	25
30	102132	144	.00141	.00002	.00007	.00030	.00031	.00003	.00000	.00009	.00012	.00000	.00011	.00017	.00020	30
35	98305	201	.00204	.00003	.00003	.00048	.00065	.00004	.00004	.00008	.00010	.00000	.00012	.00017	.00030	35
40	93328	291	.00312	.00004	.00003	.00094	.00096	.00010	.00004	.00011	.00009	.00000	.00014	.00017	.00049	40
45	92964	470	.00506	.00006	.00001	.00160	.00193	.00022	.00002	.00032	.00000	.00000	.00018	.00020	.00051	45
50	84679	608	.00718	.00004	.00015	.00203	.00321	.00027	.00000	.00043	.00001	.00000	.00015	.00026	.00063	50
55	62337	680	.01091	.00008	.00010	.00284	.00539	.00048	.00006	.00063	.00000	.00000	.00021	.00018	.00095	55
60	51245	834	.01627	.00004	.00014	.00355	.00861	.00088	.00016	.00058	.00000	.00000	.00016	.00012	.00166	60
65	43137	1108	.02569	.00014	.00023	.00471	.01440	.00160	.00019	.00155	.00000	.00000	.00016	.00037	.00234	65
70	32716	1328	.04059	.00000	.00018	.00862	.02265	.00217	.00021	.00180	.00000	.00000	.00034	.00095	.00367	70
75	21844	1451	.06643	.00009	.00046	.00966	.03653	.00568	.00050	.00311	.00000	.00000	.00005	.00151	.00884	75
80	12209	1346	.11025	.00016	.00016	.01499	.05733	.01155	.00131	.00467	.00000	.00000	.00066	.00319	.01622	80
85+	6837	1343	.19643	.00000	.00102	.01492	.09741	.02399	.00132	.00468	.00000	.00000	.00044	.00892	.04373	85+
ALL	1540302	11400														
CRUDE DEATH RATE			.00740	.00003	.00010	.00123	.00324	.00058	.00012	.00032	.00003	.00036	.00014	.00026	.00100	
STANDARDIZED RATE (1)			.00473	.00002	.00010	.00073	.00163	.00038	.00013	.00019	.00003	.00057	.00013	.00019	.00064	
STANDARDIZED RATE (2)			.00830	.00003	.00010	.00140	.00377	.00064	.00012	.00037	.00003	.00034	.00014	.00028	.00109	
GEOMETRIC MEAN			.00587													

LIFE TABLE FOR ALL CAUSES COMBINED

Age (x)	Midyear Population	Deaths During Year	$_nM_x$	$_nq_x$	l_x	$_nd_x$	$_nL_x$	$_nm_x$	$_na_x$	T_x	$_nr_x$	$\overset{\circ}{e}_x$	Age (x)
0	34536	965	.027942	.027270	100000	2727	97593	.027942	.117501	7156135	.000000	71.561	0
1	138027	210	.001521	.006065	97273	590	387617	.001522	1.500000	7058542	.000000	72.564	1
5	160559	87	.000542	.002700	96683	261	482763	.000541	2.500000	6670925	.000000	68.998	5
10	153988	63	.000409	.002043	96422	197	481633	.000409	2.578257	6188162	.011756	64.178	10
15	133836	93	.000695	.003481	96225	335	480316	.000697	2.586443	5706529	.024018	59.304	15
20	115622	81	.000701	.003504	95890	336	478635	.000702	2.573785	5226213	.028090	54.502	20
25	102001	97	.000951	.004751	95554	454	476704	.000952	2.652808	4747578	.017172	49.685	25
30	102132	144	.001410	.007035	95100	669	473933	.001412	2.658196	4270874	.004754	44.909	30
35	98305	201	.002045	.010187	94431	962	469912	.002047	2.668702	3796940	.007071	40.209	35
40	93328	291	.003118	.015492	93469	1448	464004	.003121	2.692363	3327028	.004056	35.595	40
45	92964	470	.005056	.024983	92021	2299	454718	.005056	2.656862	2863025	.000013	31.113	45
50	84679	608	.007180	.035432	89722	3179	441148	.007206	2.652826	2408306	.023032	26.842	50
55	62337	680	.010908	.053511	86543	4631	421818	.010979	2.646971	1967158	.038670	22.730	55
60	51245	834	.016275	.078694	81912	6446	394390	.016344	2.646603	1545340	.024653	18.866	60
65	43137	1108	.025686	.121472	75466	9167	355635	.025776	2.633404	1150950	.018638	15.251	65
70	32716	1328	.040592	.185764	66299	12316	302026	.040778	2.607279	795315	.023345	11.996	70
75	21844	1451	.066426	.287294	53983	15509	232056	.066833	2.558877	493288	.028187	9.138	75
80	12209	1346	.110247	.434033	38474	16699	150380	.111046	2.485453	261233	.028187	6.790	80
85+	6837	1343	.196431	1.000000	21775	21775	110853	.196431	5.090841	110853	.000000	5.091	85+

NUMBER OF PERSONS DYING (OUT OF 100,000 AT BIRTH) ABOVE AGE X FROM SPECIFIED CAUSES

Age (x)	All Causes	Respiratory T.B.	Other Infec. and Paras.	Neo-plasms	Cardio-vascular	Infl., Pneu., Bronch.	Diar-rheal	Certain Degenerative	Maternal	Cert. Dis. of Infancy	Motor Vehicle	Other Violence	Other and Unknown	Age (x)
0	100000	251	864	15731	49107	8367	1043	4265	206	1580	1119	3204	14263	0
1	97273	251	821	15723	49107	8016	797	4262	206	0	1102	3164	13824	1
5	96683	251	723	15672	49101	7887	746	4248	206	0	1065	3074	13710	5
10	96422	251	675	15654	49101	7869	743	4242	206	0	1005	3041	13635	10
15	96225	251	653	15641	49085	7857	743	4223	206	0	974	2994	13598	15
20	95890	247	635	15602	49049	7842	740	4216	203	0	877	2951	13528	20
25	95554	239	623	15573	49004	7830	736	4199	186	0	836	2885	13443	25
30	95100	234	613	15521	48919	7811	731	4171	148	0	794	2815	13343	30
35	94431	225	581	15377	48770	7797	731	4129	93	0	743	2736	13249	35
40	93469	210	567	15152	48464	7778	712	4091	45	0	685	2655	13110	40
45	92021	190	552	14714	48016	7733	692	4041	5	0	621	2575	12882	45
50	89722	161	547	13985	47141	7635	682	3895	5	0	538	2482	12651	50
55	86543	145	479	13087	45716	7515	682	3706	0	0	470	2368	12375	55
60	81912	111	438	11884	43425	7310	655	3441	0	0	382	2294	11972	60
65	75466	96	384	10479	40014	6962	593	3054	0	0	320	2247	11317	65
70	66299	47	302	8800	34876	6391	527	2501	0	0	263	2114	10478	70
75	53983	47	246	6187	28005	5731	462	1954	0	0	161	1826	9364	75
80	38474	25	139	3939	19478	4401	344	1227	0	0	150	1473	7298	80
85+	21775	0	113	1654	10798	2659	146	519	0	0	49	989	4848	85+

NUMBER OF PERSONS SURVIVING TO AGE X IF SPECIFIED CAUSES WERE ELIMINATED

Age (x)	No Causes	Respiratory T.B. (1)	Other Infec. and Paras. (2)	Neo-plasms (3)	Cardio-vascular (4)	Infl., Pneu., Bronch. (5)	Diar-rheal (6)	Certain Degenerative (7)	Maternal (8)	Cert. Dis. of Infancy (9)	Motor Vehicle (10)	Other Violence (11)	Other and Unknown (12)	(1)+(2)	(1)+(2)+(5)+(6)+(8)	(1)+(2)+(5)+(6)+(8)+part of (9)&(12)	(10)+(11)	Age (x)
0	100000	100000	100000	100000	100000	100000	100000	100000	100000	100000	100000	100000	100000	100000	100000	100000	100000	0
1	97273	97273	97315	97281	97273	97620	97516	97276	97273	98844	97290	97312	97707	97315	97906	99735	97329	1
5	96683	96683	96823	96742	96689	97157	96975	96700	96683	98244	96737	96812	97229	96823	97592	99483	96866	5
10	96422	96422	96610	96499	96428	96913	96717	96445	96422	97979	96535	96584	97041	96610	97398	99314	96697	10
15	96225	96225	96434	96314	96247	96727	96519	96267	96225	97779	96369	96433	96880	96434	97233	99154	96578	15
20	95890	95894	96117	96018	95948	96405	96186	95939	95893	97438	96131	96141	96613	96121	96938	98865	96382	20
25	95554	95566	95792	95711	95657	96075	95853	95619	95574	97097	95835	95870	96360	95804	96652	98591	96152	25
30	95100	95117	95347	95308	95287	95642	95403	95193	95158	96636	95422	95484	96003	95364	96270	98225	95807	30
35	94431	94457	94708	94781	94766	94983	94731	94565	94543	95956	94801	94892	95422	94734	95704	97665	95264	35
40	93469	93509	93757	94041	94106	94034	93785	93640	93628	94978	93893	94006	94590	93798	94845	96809	94433	40
45	92021	92081	92319	93022	93097	92623	92352	92239	92217	93507	92503	92630	93354	92379	93517	95480	93114	45
50	89722	89805	90018	91429	91650	90406	90055	90079	89913	91171	90274	90408	91253	90105	91323	93256	90964	50
55	86543	86642	86895	89092	89844	87322	86864	87074	86732	87941	87143	87317	88296	86995	88297	90186	87922	55
60	81912	82039	82286	85537	87383	82851	82242	82674	82091	83235	82566	82717	83972	82413	83877	85702	83377	60
65	75466	75598	75862	80225	84076	76670	75830	76544	75631	76685	76128	76254	78011	75995	77749	79495	76922	65
70	66299	66460	66724	72172	79425	67902	66681	67773	66444	67370	66934	67118	69352	66887	69049	70677	67761	70
75	53983	54114	54380	61377	72524	55903	54353	55688	54101	54855	54593	54913	57532	54512	56962	58381	55533	75
80	38474	38586	38847	45929	62253	41024	38839	40323	38558	39095	38917	39440	42904	38960	42028	43306	39895	80
85+	21775	21857	22006	28100	47364	24638	22130	23379	21823	22127	22102	22693	26397	22089	25457	26539	23034	85+

ADDED YRS OF LIFE

	No Causes	(1)	(2)	(3)	(4)	(5)	(6)	(7)	(8)	(9)	(10)	(11)	(12)	(1)+(2)	(1)+(2)+(5)+(6)+(8)	part	(10)+(11)
TOTAL		.057	.262	2.415	8.231	1.130	.301	.584	.085	1.154	.358	.570	2.090	.319	1.867	3.534	.933
WORK	2.657	.028	.048	.612	.877	.092	.019	.131	.062	.000	.154	.174	.340	.075	.249	.296	.329

POPULATION, DEATHS, DEATH RATES FOR ALL CAUSES COMBINED, AND SPECIFIED CAUSES

Age Start of Interval	Midyear Population	Deaths During Year	All Causes	Respiratory T. B.	Other Infec. and Paras.	Neo-plasms	Cardio-vascular	Infl., Pneu., Bronch.	Diar-rheal	Certain Degen-erative	Maternal	Cert. Dis. of Infancy	Motor Vehicle	Other Violence	Other and Unknown	Age Start of Interval
0	256457	42529	.16583	.00035	.00547	.00001	.00089	.02357	.06671	.00065	.00000	.02834	.00000	.00035	.03910	0
1	1059130	26260	.02479	.00027	.00324	.00002	.00024	.00315	.00559	.00048	.00000	.00000	.00000	.00032	.01149	1
5	1305652	5164	.00396	.00012	.00076	.00001	.00015	.00031	.00000	.00013	.00000	.00000	.00000	.00032	.01149	5
10	1146568	2714	.00237	.00014	.00038	.00000	.00018	.00014	.00000	.00008	.00000	.00000	.00000	.00024	.00223	10
15	1073960	4679	.00436	.00104	.00054	.00002	.00028	.00025	.00000	.00011	.00000	.00000	.00000	.00025	.00119	15
20	1029320	5644	.00548	.00180	.00050	.00003	.00033	.00033	.00000	.00013	.00000	.00000	.00000	.00049	.00163	20
25	925301	5405	.00584	.00185	.00043	.00005	.00040	.00032	.00000	.00018	.00000	.00000	.00000	.00058	.00178	25
30	796397	4733	.00594	.00165	.00037	.00012	.00051	.00041	.00000	.00022	.00000	.00000	.00000	.00064	.00197	30
35	681373	4944	.00726	.00174	.00036	.00021	.00068	.00054	.00000	.00035	.00000	.00000	.00000	.00054	.00211	35
40	651923	5885	.00903	.00171	.00031	.00049	.00111	.00072	.00000	.00053	.00000	.00000	.00000	.00055	.00282	40
45	555055	6634	.01195	.00185	.00036	.00086	.00168	.00104	.00000	.00079	.00000	.00000	.00000	.00062	.00353	45
50	527699	8245	.01562	.00171	.00032	.00150	.00279	.00133	.00000	.00120	.00000	.00000	.00000	.00070	.00467	50
55	422079	9852	.02334	.00173	.00042	.00249	.00510	.00222	.00000	.00189	.00000	.00000	.00000	.00071	.00606	55
60	383519	14127	.03684	.00117	.00043	.00289	.01031	.00327	.00001	.00266	.00000	.00000	.00000	.00078	.00871	60
65	280280	14642	.05224	.00123	.00047	.00430	.01641	.00445	.00001	.00401	.00000	.00000	.00000	.00081	.01529	65
70	191431	15033	.07853	.00123	.00045	.00593	.02629	.00673	.00001	.00613	.00000	.00000	.00000	.00062	.02075	70
75	102718	12123	.11802	.00114	.00053	.00717	.04112	.01064	.00002	.00919	.00000	.00000	.00000	.00105	.03071	75
80	46715	8872	.18992	.00101	.00062	.00822	.06231	.01742	.00004	.01319	.00000	.00000	.00000	.00132	.04689	80
85+	18734	6289	.33570	.00069	.00085	.00859	.09384	.03160	.00011	.01820	.00000	.00000	.00000	.00197	.08513	85+
ALL	11454311	203774														

			All Causes	Respiratory T. B.	Other Infec. and Paras.	Neo-plasms	Cardio-vascular	Infl., Pneu., Bronch.	Diar-rheal	Certain Degen-erative	Maternal	Cert. Dis. of Infancy	Motor Vehicle	Other Violence	Other and Unknown
CRUDE DEATH RATE			.01779	.00112	.00083	.00068	.00267	.00180	.00201	.00080	.00000	.00063	.00000	.00053	.00672
STANDARDIZED RATE (1)			.01797	.00103	.00098	.00049	.00192	.00196	.00301	.00063	.00000	.00100	.00000	.00049	.00646
STANDARDIZED RATE (2)			.02200	.00118	.00078	.00057	.00421	.00216	.00183	.00115	.00000	.00059	.00000	.00057	.00857
GEOMETRIC MEAN			.02076												

LIFE TABLE FOR ALL CAUSES COMBINED

Age (x)	Midyear Population	Deaths During Year	$_nM_x$	$_nq_x$	l_x	$_nd_x$	$_nL_x$	$_nm_x$	$_na_x$	T_x	$_nr_x$	$\overset{\circ}{e}_x$	Age (x)
0	256457	42529	.165833	.149740	100000	14974	90296	.165833	.351916	4720755	.000000	47.208	0
1	1059130	26260	.024794	.093383	85026	7940	320254	.024793	1.500000	4630459	.000000	54.459	1
5	1305652	5164	.003955	.019589	77086	1510	381655	.003956	2.500000	4310205	.000000	55.914	5
10	1146568	2714	.002367	.011763	75576	889	375679	.002366	2.523903	3928550	.014274	51.981	10
15	1073960	4679	.004357	.021583	74687	1612	369632	.004361	2.640741	3552871	.008305	47.570	15
20	1029320	5644	.005483	.027068	73075	1978	360521	.005487	2.545816	3183239	.007715	43.561	20
25	925301	5405	.005841	.028792	71097	2047	350377	.005842	2.504783	2822719	.015760	39.702	25
30	796397	4733	.005943	.029327	69050	2025	340259	.005951	2.535494	2472341	.024450	35.805	30
35	681373	4944	.007256	.035668	67025	2392	329319	.007263	2.572638	2132082	.015583	31.810	35
40	651923	5885	.009027	.044234	64633	2859	316267	.009040	2.587443	1802763	.012745	27.892	40
45	555055	6634	.011952	.058147	61774	3592	300209	.011965	2.588681	1486496	.009538	24.063	45
50	527699	8245	.015624	.075419	58182	4388	280433	.015647	2.612380	1186287	.011069	20.389	50
55	422079	9852	.023342	.110774	53794	5959	254845	.023383	2.629566	905854	.009357	16.839	55
60	383519	14127	.036835	.169207	47835	8094	219618	.036855	2.583807	651009	.003466	13.609	60
65	280280	14642	.052241	.231876	39741	9215	176075	.052236	2.544199	431391	.011728	10.855	65
70	191431	15033	.078530	.329195	30526	10049	127525	.078800	2.501783	255316	.018425	8.364	70
75	102718	12123	.118022	.454217	20477	9301	78512	.118466	2.433273	127791	.017977	6.241	75
80	46715	8872	.189918	.632606	11176	7070	37048	.190834	2.336339	49279	.017977	4.409	80
85+	18734	6289	.335700	1.000000	4106	4106	12231	.335700	2.978852	12231	.000000	2.979	85+

NUMBER OF PERSONS DYING (OUT OF 100,000 AT BIRTH) ABOVE AGE X FROM SPECIFIED CAUSES

Age (x)	All Causes	Respiratory T.B.	Other Infec. and Paras.	Neoplasms	Cardiovascular	Infl., Pneu., Bronch.	Diarrheal	Certain Degenerative	Maternal	Cert. Dis. of Infancy	Motor Vehicle	Other Violence	Other and Unknown	Age (x)
0	100000	5822	3453	4759	19218	9706	7825	5374	0	2559	0	2744	38540	0
1	85026	5790	2959	4758	19138	7541	1802	5315	0	0	0	2713	35010	1
5	77086	5704	1922	4752	19062	6532	12	5160	0	0	0	2612	31330	5
10	75576	5658	1633	4748	19003	6413	12	5112	0	0	0	2519	30478	10
15	74687	5606	1489	4746	18934	6360	12	5081	0	0	0	2427	30032	15
20	73075	5220	1291	4740	18831	6267	12	5040	0	0	0	2245	29429	20
25	71097	4570	1111	4728	18712	6147	12	4994	0	0	0	2037	28786	25
30	69050	3921	959	4711	18572	6035	12	4932	0	0	0	1813	28095	30
35	67025	3358	832	4669	18397	5896	10	4857	0	0	0	1628	27378	35
40	64633	2785	712	4601	18171	5719	10	4741	0	0	0	1447	26447	40
45	61774	2245	615	4445	17820	5490	9	4572	0	0	0	1249	25329	45
50	58182	1690	506	4186	17315	5177	9	4336	0	0	0	1038	23925	50
55	53794	1210	417	3764	16532	4804	9	3998	0	0	0	838	22222	55
60	47835	770	310	3128	15228	4239	8	3515	0	0	0	640	19997	60
65	39741	514	217	2493	12962	3519	7	2929	0	0	0	462	16638	65
70	30526	298	135	1735	10067	2734	6	2221	0	0	0	353	12977	70
75	20477	141	77	976	6702	1873	4	1437	0	0	0	219	9048	75
80	11176	52	35	412	3461	1034	3	713	0	0	0	114	5352	80
85+	4106	8	10	105	1148	387	1	223	0	0	0	39	2185	85+

NUMBER OF PERSONS SURVIVING TO AGE X IF SPECIFIED CAUSES WERE ELIMINATED

Age (x)	No Causes	Respiratory T.B. (1)	Other Infec. and Paras. (2)	Neoplasms (3)	Cardiovascular (4)	Infl., Pneu., Bronch. (5)	Diarrheal (6)	Certain Degenerative (7)	Maternal (8)	Cert. Dis. of Infancy (9)	Motor Vehicle (10)	Other Violence (11)	Other and Unknown (12)	(1)+(2)	(1)+(2)+(5)+(6)+(8)	(1)+(2)+(5)+(6)+(8)+part of (9)&(12)	(10)+(11)	Age (x)
0	100000	100000	100000	100000	100000	100000	100000	100000	100000	100000	100000	100000	100000	100000	100000	100000	100000	0
1	85026	85055	85482	85027	85100	87044	90759	85080	85026	87416	85026	85055	88340	85512	93443	99688	85055	1
5	77086	77195	78498	77093	77225	79905	84122	77283	77086	79253	77086	77208	83814	78609	88921	98916	77208	5
10	75576	75728	77253	75586	75771	78462	82474	75817	75576	77700	75576	75788	83095	77408	87699	98311	75788	10
15	74687	74889	76490	74699	74949	77593	81504	74956	74687	76786	74687	74988	82606	76697	86955	97803	74988	15
20	73075	73657	75040	73093	73433	76014	79745	73379	73075	75129	73075	73551	81485	75638	85862	97103	73551	20
25	71097	72312	73191	71126	71564	74080	77586	71438	71097	73095	71097	71767	79990	74443	84646	96338	71767	25
30	69050	70884	71238	69095	69642	72062	75353	69443	69050	70991	69050	69924	78457	73130	83287	95423	69924	30
35	67025	69377	69278	67110	67774	70092	73145	67481	67025	68909	67025	68058	76963	71709	81838	94392	68058	35
40	64633	67485	66928	64782	65580	67713	70535	65187	64633	66450	64633	65809	75274	69881	79967	93014	65809	40
45	61774	65053	64065	62070	63029	65010	67416	62471	61774	63510	61774	63096	73228	67466	77484	90924	63096	45
50	58182	61840	60450	58714	59866	61550	63496	59070	58182	59817	58182	59636	70604	64250	74177	87957	59636	50
55	53794	57667	55980	54697	56132	57289	58707	54946	53794	55306	53794	55335	67296	60010	69745	83588	55335	55
60	47835	51723	49883	49251	51216	51513	52205	49327	47835	49180	47835	49397	62524	53938	63391	76970	49397	60
65	39741	43221	41531	41516	44822	43508	43372	41534	39741	40858	39741	41205	56099	45168	53967	66673	41205	65
70	30526	33404	31975	32588	37409	34178	33316	32557	30526	31384	30526	31749	47848	34989	42756	53911	31749	70
75	20477	22546	21498	22526	28688	23725	22350	22530	20477	21053	20477	21411	37517	23670	29933	38791	21411	75
80	11176	12375	11765	12749	19337	13676	12199	12888	11176	11490	11176	11765	26061	13027	17401	23512	11765	80
85+	4106	4575	4338	4892	9858	5507	4483	5075	4106	4221	4106	4369	14994	4833	7077	10385	4369	85+

ADDED YRS OF LIFE

	No Causes	(1)	(2)	(3)	(4)	(5)	(6)	(7)	(8)	(9)	(10)	(11)	(12)	(1)+(2)	(1)+(2)+(5)+(6)+(8)	part combo	(10)+(11)
TOTAL		1.710	1.491	.598	2.483	2.677	4.235	.795	.000	1.317	.000	.766	10.566	3.271	10.995	20.665	.766
WORK	8.206	1.585	.415	.284	.808	.513	.001	.336	.000	.000	.000	.567	2.738	2.022	2.576	4.158	.567

POPULATION, DEATHS, DEATH RATES FOR ALL CAUSES COMBINED, AND SPECIFIED CAUSES

Age Start of Interval	Midyear Popula- tion	Deaths During Year	All Causes	Respira- tory T. B.	Other Infec. and Paras.	Neo- plasms	Cardio- vascular	Infl., Pneu., Bronch.	Diar- rheal	Certain Degen- erative	Maternal	Cert. Dis. of Infancy	Motor Vehicle	Other Violence	Other and Unknown	Age Start of Interval
0	245312	34925	.14237	.00031	.00536	.00001	.00079	.02051	.05873	.00049	.00000	.02342	.00000	.00021	.03253	0
1	1030676	24570	.02384	.00024	.00316	.00001	.00019	.00302	.00542	.00042	.00000	.00000	.00000	.00023	.01117	1
5	1264574	4782	.00378	.00013	.00077	.00001	.00015	.00030	.00000	.00011	.00000	.00000	.00000	.00011	.00221	5
10	1131799	2731	.00241	.00035	.00044	.00001	.00019	.00014	.00000	.00007	.00000	.00000	.00000	.00005	.00114	10
15	1101828	4440	.00403	.00136	.00059	.00002	.00025	.00020	.00000	.00010	.00005	.00000	.00000	.00010	.00136	15
20	1090958	5610	.00514	.00191	.00051	.00003	.00036	.00023	.00000	.00013	.00038	.00000	.00000	.00010	.00148	20
25	982519	5568	.00567	.00162	.00047	.00006	.00047	.00028	.00000	.00021	.00066	.00000	.00000	.00009	.00182	25
30	845974	4818	.00570	.00132	.00037	.00018	.00059	.00029	.00000	.00025	.00061	.00000	.00000	.00009	.00200	30
35	740942	4578	.00618	.00110	.00034	.00035	.00077	.00034	.00000	.00035	.00059	.00000	.00000	.00009	.00224	35
40	693648	4761	.00686	.00059	.00030	.00073	.00106	.00036	.00000	.00043	.00038	.00000	.00000	.00014	.00248	40
45	558650	4800	.00802	.00087	.00029	.00107	.00160	.00046	.00000	.00058	.00008	.00000	.00000	.00017	.00289	45
50	580029	5990	.01033	.00074	.00032	.00169	.00251	.00054	.00000	.00084	.00000	.00000	.00000	.00013	.00354	50
55	477033	7257	.01521	.00070	.00030	.00228	.00405	.00097	.00000	.00118	.00000	.00000	.00000	.00020	.00553	55
60	443172	13042	.02943	.00054	.00040	.00242	.00929	.00219	.00000	.00158	.00000	.00000	.00000	.00029	.01272	60
65	320263	13522	.04222	.00057	.00044	.00360	.01477	.00297	.00000	.00238	.00000	.00000	.00000	.00022	.01726	65
70	233484	14873	.06370	.00057	.00043	.00497	.02368	.00449	.00000	.00363	.00000	.00000	.00000	.00037	.02555	70
75	129814	12476	.09611	.00053	.00050	.00602	.03702	.00711	.00001	.00546	.00000	.00000	.00000	.00046	.03899	75
80	73150	11341	.15504	.00046	.00060	.00689	.05612	.01162	.00003	.00783	.00000	.00000	.00000	.00068	.07080	80
85+	38722	10630	.27452	.00031	.00083	.00723	.08453	.02107	.00005	.01082	.00000	.00000	.00000	.00114	.14855	85+
ALL	12022547	150714														

	All Causes	Respira- tory T. B.	Other Infec. and Paras.	Neo- plasms	Cardio- vascular	Infl., Pneu., Bronch.	Diar- rheal	Certain Degen- erative	Maternal	Cert. Dis. of Infancy	Motor Vehicle	Other Violence	Other and Unknown
CRUDE DEATH RATE	.01586	.00088	.00079	.00073	.00288	.00140	.00166	.00062	.00020	.00048	.00000	.00015	.00608
STANDARDIZED RATE (1)	.01540	.00064	.00097	.00048	.00175	.00156	.00271	.00045	.00019	.00082	.00000	.00014	.00549
STANDARDIZED RATE (2)	.01824	.00087	.00077	.00090	.00381	.00157	.00165	.00076	.00019	.00048	.00000	.00016	.00708
GEOMETRIC MEAN	.01739												

LIFE TABLE FOR ALL CAUSES COMBINED

Age (x)	Midyear Popula- tion	Deaths During Year	$_nM_x$	$_nq_x$	l_x	$_nd_x$	$_nL_x$	$_nm_x$	$_na_x$	T_x	$_nr_x$	$\overset{\circ}{e}_x$	Age (x)
0	245312	34925	.142370	.129670	100000	12967	91079	.142371	.312029	5078024	.000000	50.780	0
1	1030676	24570	.023839	.089989	87033	7832	328552	.023838	1.500000	4986945	.000000	57.299	1
5	1264574	4782	.003782	.018737	79201	1484	392295	.003783	2.500000	4658393	.000000	58.817	5
10	1131799	2731	.002413	.011992	77717	932	386265	.002413	2.510730	4266098	.010274	54.893	10
15	1101828	4440	.004030	.019952	76785	1532	380299	.004028	2.633268	3879833	.001595	50.529	15
20	1090958	5610	.005142	.025408	75253	1912	371593	.005145	2.556442	3499533	.003081	46.504	20
25	982519	5568	.005667	.027952	73341	2050	361599	.005669	2.509146	3127940	.015113	42.649	25
30	845974	4818	.005695	.028082	71291	2002	351462	.005696	2.596140	2766342	.022369	38.804	30
35	740942	4578	.006179	.030438	69289	2109	341228	.006181	2.526474	2414879	.015319	34.852	35
40	693648	4761	.006864	.033790	67180	2270	330318	.006872	2.540841	2073651	.015560	30.867	40
45	598650	4800	.008018	.039347	64910	2554	318348	.008023	2.571620	1743333	.010548	26.858	45
50	580029	5990	.010327	.050484	62356	3148	304287	.010346	2.619653	1424985	.012053	22.852	50
55	477033	7257	.015213	.073672	59208	4362	286054	.015249	2.710626	1120699	.010414	18.928	55
60	443172	13042	.029429	.137804	54846	7558	256317	.029487	2.629912	834645	.009595	15.218	60
65	320263	13522	.042222	.191909	47288	9075	214378	.042332	2.568893	578328	.016606	12.230	65
70	233484	14873	.063700	.276320	38213	10559	165011	.063990	2.532555	363950	.024720	9.524	70
75	129814	12476	.096107	.387828	27654	10725	111212	.096437	2.477137	198939	.017362	7.194	75
80	73150	11341	.155038	.554197	16929	9382	60235	.155756	2.398254	87727	.017362	5.182	80
85+	38722	10630	.274521	1.000000	7547	7547	27492	.274521	3.642709	27492	.000000	3.643	85+

NUMBER OF PERSONS DYING (OUT OF 100,000 AT BIRTH) ABOVE AGE X FROM SPECIFIED CAUSES

Age (x)	All Causes	Respiratory T.B.	Other Infec. and Paras.	Neoplasms	Cardiovascular	Infl., Pneu., Bronch.	Diarrheal	Certain Degenerative	Maternal	Cert. Dis. of Infancy	Motor Vehicle	Other Violence	Other and Unknown	Age (x)
0	100000	4429	3590	5491	23259	8243	7138	4441	968	2133	0	836	39472	0
1	87033	4400	3102	5490	23187	6374	1788	4356	968	0	0	817	36511	1
5	79201	4322	2064	5488	23124	5382	9	4260	968	0	0	743	32841	5
10	77717	4271	1764	5486	23064	5265	9	4217	968	0	0	701	31972	10
15	76785	4133	1594	5482	22989	5209	9	4190	968	0	0	680	31531	15
20	75253	3617	1370	5474	22895	5132	9	4153	948	0	0	641	31014	20
25	73341	2907	1179	5463	22763	5046	8	4103	807	0	0	603	30462	25
30	71291	2322	1010	5441	22594	4945	8	4028	569	0	0	569	29805	30
35	69289	1860	879	5375	22386	4844	8	3940	356	0	0	537	29104	35
40	67180	1486	762	5255	22124	4727	8	3821	155	0	0	505	28337	40
45	64910	1159	664	5014	21774	4608	8	3681	28	0	0	458	27516	45
50	62356	881	570	4674	21262	4461	8	3495	3	0	0	405	26597	50
55	59208	655	473	4158	20495	4297	6	3238	2	0	0	365	25519	55
60	54846	454	387	3506	19332	4020	6	2902	2	0	0	307	23930	60
65	47288	317	283	2886	16946	3458	5	2495	1	0	0	233	20664	65
70	38213	196	188	2111	13769	2820	5	1983	1	0	0	186	16954	70
75	27654	102	117	1288	9843	2075	4	1381	1	0	0	125	12718	75
80	16929	42	61	618	5712	1282	3	771	1	0	0	73	8366	80
85+	7547	9	23	199	2324	579	1	297	0	0	0	31	4084	85+

NUMBER OF PERSONS SURVIVING TO AGE X IF SPECIFIED CAUSES WERE ELIMINATED

Age (x)	No Causes	Respiratory T.B. (1)	Other Infec. and Paras. (2)	Neoplasms (3)	Cardiovascular (4)	Infl., Pneu., Bronch. (5)	Diarrheal (6)	Certain Degenerative (7)	Maternal (8)	Cert. Dis. of Infancy (9)	Motor Vehicle (10)	Other Violence (11)	Other and Unknown (12)	(1)+(2)	(1)+(2)+(5)+(6)+(8)	(1)+(2)+(5)+(6)+(8)+part of(9)&(12)	(10)+(11)	Age (x)
0	100000	100000	100000	100000	100000	100000	100000	100000	100000	100000	100000	100000	100000	100000	100000	100000	100000	0
1	87033	87060	87489	87034	87100	88793	92166	87075	87033	89044	87033	87051	89837	87516	94551	99759	87051	1
5	79201	79300	80617	79204	79322	81773	85688	79369	79201	81031	79201	79288	85446	80718	90165	99139	79288	5
10	77717	77865	79410	77722	77896	80361	84082	77925	77717	79513	77717	77844	84779	79561	89005	98692	77844	10
15	76785	77069	78630	76794	77036	79455	83074	77017	76785	78559	76785	76931	84242	78921	88353	98384	76931	15
20	75253	76046	77289	75269	75593	77548	81416	75517	75273	76992	75253	75435	83125	78103	87549	98037	75435	20
25	73341	74825	75519	73368	73803	76056	79349	73648	73500	75036	73341	73556	81617	77047	86631	97610	73556	25
30	71291	73324	73580	71339	71908	74033	77131	71664	71681	72938	71291	71534	80060	75678	85492	97015	71534	30
35	69289	71735	71647	69401	70096	72058	74965	69739	69880	70890	69289	69556	78592	74176	84170	96181	69556	35
40	67180	69933	69585	67407	68224	69984	72683	67734	67952	68732	67180	67471	77061	72437	82581	95007	67471	40
45	64910	67905	67334	65368	66269	67742	70227	65584	65782	66410	64910	65237	75388	70441	80605	93268	65237	45
50	62356	65519	64780	63132	64177	65227	67464	63188	63219	63797	62356	62723	73476	68066	78097	90801	62723	50
55	59208	62442	61608	60456	61711	62101	64060	60252	60028	60576	59208	59595	71015	64973	74754	87280	59595	55
60	54846	58046	57155	56645	58344	57807	59341	56143	55606	56113	54846	55261	67645	60489	69935	82117	55261	60
65	47288	50180	49379	49435	52718	50393	51164	48794	47944	48381	47288	47715	62183	52399	61255	72794	47715	65
70	38213	40665	39991	40681	45904	41336	41345	39907	38743	39096	38213	38600	54819	42557	50500	60849	38600	70
75	27654	29512	29003	30189	37468	30605	29922	29417	28038	28293	27654	27986	45165	30952	37578	46131	27986	75
80	16929	18115	17800	19050	27707	19428	18318	18517	17164	17320	16929	17173	33751	19047	23981	30289	17173	80
85+	7547	8099	7961	8805	16536	9201	8168	8599	7652	7721	7547	7684	21755	8543	11430	15272	7684	85+

ADDED YRS OF LIFE																		
TOTAL		1.589	1.632	.790	3.181	2.416	4.091	.730	.359	1.166	.000	.233	10.753	3.284	10.916	20.011	.233
WORK	7.003	1.382	.442	.370	.841	.328	.001	.302	.364	.000	.000	.112	2.210	1.843	2.580	3.950	.112

POPULATION, DEATHS, DEATH RATES FOR ALL CAUSES COMBINED, AND SPECIFIED CAUSES

Age Start of Interval	Midyear Population	Deaths During Year	All Causes	Respiratory T. B.	Other Infec. and Paras.	Neoplasms	Cardiovascular	Infl., Pneu., Bronch.	Diarrheal	Certain Degenerative	Maternal	Cert. Dis. of Infancy	Motor Vehicle	Other Violence	Other and Unknown	Age Start of Interval
0	223424	37402	.16740	.00055	.01018	.00005	.00340	.03760	.05484	.00066	.00000	.04015	.00000	.00060	.01937	0
1	911314	15788	.01732	.00028	.00329	.00002	.00084	.00473	.00393	.00043	.00000	.00000	.00000	.00038	.00343	1
5	1386444	5475	.00395	.00014	.00090	.00002	.00040	.00065	.00027	.00017	.00000	.00000	.00000	.00030	.00110	5
10	1373083	3401	.00248	.00015	.00053	.00002	.00032	.00027	.00010	.00008	.00000	.00000	.00000	.00033	.00067	10
15	1245122	5802	.00466	.00078	.00073	.00002	.00051	.00039	.00008	.00009	.00000	.00000	.00000	.00117	.00090	15
20	1012516	9980	.00986	.00201	.00071	.00004	.00082	.00046	.00008	.00014	.00000	.00000	.00000	.00434	.00127	20
25	950025	10608	.01117	.00187	.00057	.00005	.00089	.00047	.00009	.00018	.00000	.00000	.00000	.00561	.00143	25
30	926371	9868	.01065	.00152	.00051	.00012	.00056	.00054	.00010	.00020	.00000	.00000	.00000	.00518	.00152	30
35	823724	9179	.01114	.00143	.00061	.00026	.00118	.00082	.00014	.00027	.00000	.00000	.00000	.00454	.00188	35
40	731792	8921	.01219	.00155	.00067	.00050	.00174	.00116	.00017	.00042	.00000	.00000	.00000	.00373	.00225	40
45	626114	9938	.01587	.00181	.00085	.00089	.00304	.00176	.00026	.00058	.00000	.00000	.00000	.00358	.00310	45
50	570628	10874	.01906	.00171	.00088	.00155	.00446	.00243	.00038	.00088	.00000	.00000	.00000	.00290	.00387	50
55	464434	12236	.02635	.00182	.00098	.00238	.00760	.00351	.00060	.00147	.00000	.00000	.00000	.00275	.00523	55
60	421531	15554	.03690	.00155	.00109	.00333	.01259	.00502	.00100	.00263	.00000	.00000	.00000	.00257	.00711	60
65	308541	16559	.05367	.00131	.00135	.00482	.02048	.00763	.00157	.00370	.00000	.00000	.00000	.00214	.01067	65
70	207506	17321	.08347	.00099	.00148	.00561	.03457	.01019	.00176	.00602	.00000	.00000	.00000	.00175	.02110	70
75	123325	15580	.12633	.00092	.00172	.00680	.05408	.01613	.00320	.00908	.00000	.00000	.00000	.00221	.03219	75
80	56086	11312	.20169	.00082	.00205	.00779	.08195	.02641	.00793	.01302	.00000	.00000	.00000	.00326	.05846	80
85+	22492	7715	.34301	.00053	.00280	.00818	.12347	.04784	.01418	.01756	.00000	.00000	.00000	.00538	.12267	85+
ALL	12384472	233513														

	All Causes	Respiratory T. B.	Other Infec. and Paras.	Neoplasms	Cardiovascular	Infl., Pneu., Bronch.	Diarrheal	Certain Degenerative	Maternal	Cert. Dis. of Infancy	Motor Vehicle	Other Violence	Other and Unknown
CRUDE DEATH RATE	.01886	.00110	.00112	.00072	.00394	.00264	.00162	.00075	.00000	.00072	.00000	.00256	.00368
STANDARDIZED RATE (1)	.01920	.00101	.00138	.00051	.00288	.00308	.00265	.00058	.00000	.00141	.00000	.00233	.00338
STANDARDIZED RATE (2)	.02401	.00115	.00121	.00100	.00583	.00338	.00193	.00107	.00000	.00083	.00000	.00263	.00499
GEOMETRIC MEAN	.02450												

LIFE TABLE FOR ALL CAUSES COMBINED

Age (x)	Midyear Population	Deaths During Year	$_nM_x$	$_nq_x$	l_x	$_nd_x$	$_nL_x$	$_nm_x$	$_na_x$	T_x	$_nr_x$	$\overset{\circ}{e}_x$	Age (x)
0	223424	37402	.167404	.151080	100000	15108	90249	.167403	.354586	4529615	.000000	45.296	0
1	911314	15788	.017324	.066426	84892	5639	325471	.017326	1.500000	4439366	.000000	52.294	1
5	1386444	5475	.003949	.019545	79253	1549	392393	.003948	2.500000	4113896	.000000	51.908	5
10	1373083	3401	.002477	.012316	77704	957	386176	.002478	2.550505	3721503	.002477	47.893	10
15	1245122	5802	.004660	.023206	76747	1781	379838	.004689	2.811740	3335327	.020319	43.459	15
20	1012516	9980	.009857	.048135	74966	3622	366211	.009890	2.620445	2955490	.022287	39.424	20
25	950025	10608	.011166	.054314	71344	3875	347007	.011167	2.493441	2589278	.003028	36.293	25
30	926371	9868	.010652	.051876	67469	3500	328510	.010654	2.475774	2242271	.001829	33.234	30
35	823724	9179	.011143	.054214	63969	3468	311193	.011144	2.505106	1913761	.009268	29.917	35
40	731792	8921	.012191	.059255	60501	3585	293727	.012205	2.551371	1602568	.014499	26.488	40
45	626114	9938	.015873	.076464	56916	4352	273951	.015886	2.557780	1308842	.010090	22.996	45
50	570628	10874	.019056	.091165	52564	4792	251167	.019079	2.568169	1034890	.011032	19.688	50
55	464434	12236	.026346	.123922	47772	5920	224538	.026365	2.580764	783724	.005835	16.406	55
60	421531	15554	.036899	.169335	41852	7087	192030	.036906	2.569847	559185	.001265	13.361	60
65	308541	16559	.053669	.237653	34765	8262	153603	.053788	2.552399	367155	.013017	10.561	65
70	207506	17321	.083472	.345810	26503	9165	109602	.083621	2.499955	213552	.009092	8.058	70
75	123325	15580	.126333	.476410	17338	8260	65368	.126362	2.418609	103950	.001180	5.996	75
80	56086	11312	.201690	.654109	9078	5938	29428	.201780	2.311911	38582	.001180	4.250	80
85+	22492	7715	.343011	1.000000	3140	3140	9154	.343011	2.915360	9154	.000000	2.915	85+

NUMBER OF PERSONS DYING (OUT OF 100,000 AT BIRTH) ABOVE AGE X FROM SPECIFIED CAUSES

Age (x)	All Causes	Respiratory T. B.	Other Infec. and Paras.	Neo-plasms	Cardio-vascular	Infl., Pneu., Bronch.	Diar-rheal	Certain Degen-erative	Maternal	Cert. Dis. of Infancy	Motor Vehicle	Other Violence	Other and Unknown	Age (x)
0	100000	5370	5284	4248	22575	13956	8089	4311	0	3624	0	12257	19886	0
1	84892	5321	4365	4243	22669	10563	3140	4252	0	0	0	12203	18136	1
5	79253	5230	3256	4235	22395	9024	1862	4112	0	0	0	12078	17021	5
10	77704	5176	2944	4229	22237	8767	1757	4044	0	0	0	11961	16589	10
15	76747	5116	2741	4222	22112	8663	1720	4012	0	0	0	11833	16328	15
20	74966	4817	2464	4215	21919	8515	1689	3977	0	0	0	11383	15987	20
25	71344	4077	2206	4202	21618	8348	1659	3926	0	0	0	9786	15522	25
30	67469	3428	2010	4183	21308	8185	1627	3865	0	0	0	7839	15024	30
35	63969	2930	1843	4142	20591	8008	1594	3799	0	0	0	6137	14525	35
40	60501	2484	1653	4060	20622	7753	1550	3714	0	0	0	4727	13938	40
45	56916	2029	1457	3914	20110	7410	1500	3589	0	0	0	3631	13276	45
50	52564	1533	1223	3669	19275	6929	1429	3430	0	0	0	2649	12427	50
55	47772	1105	1003	3280	18152	6317	1334	3208	0	0	0	1922	11451	55
60	41852	657	782	2745	16443	5528	1199	2876	0	0	0	1306	10276	60
65	34765	400	572	2105	14024	4563	1007	2372	0	0	0	812	8910	65
70	26503	199	364	1364	10870	3388	766	1802	0	0	0	483	7267	70
75	17338	91	202	748	7073	2270	573	1141	0	0	0	292	4948	75
80	9078	31	89	304	3537	1215	364	547	0	0	0	148	2843	80
85+	3140	5	26	75	1130	438	130	164	0	0	0	49	1123	85+

NUMBER OF PERSONS SURVIVING TO AGE X IF SPECIFIED CAUSES WERE ELIMINATED

Age (x)	No Causes	Respiratory T. B. (1)	Other Infec. and Paras. (2)	Neo-plasms (3)	Cardio-vascular (4)	Infl., Pneu., Bronch. (5)	Diar-rheal (6)	Certain Degener-ative (7)	Maternal (8)	Cert. Dis. of Infancy (9)	Motor Vehicle (10)	Other Violence (11)	Other and Unknown (12)	(1)+(2)	(1)+(2) +(5)+ (6)+(8)	(1)+(2)+ (5)+(6)+ (8)+part of(9)&(12)	(10) +(11)	Age (x)
0	100000	100000	100000	100000	100000	100000	100000	100000	100000	100000	100000	100000	100000	100000	100000	100000	100000	0
1	84892	84937	85742	84897	85174	88073	89571	84946	84892	88294	84892	84942	86518	85788	93908	99289	84942	1
5	79253	79383	81056	79265	79782	83780	84934	79439	79253	82429	79253	79420	81876	81230	92024	98467	79420	5
10	77704	77885	79869	77722	78381	82412	83386	77954	77704	80818	77704	77984	80719	80055	91113	97862	77984	10
15	76747	76686	79093	76771	77541	81506	82398	77026	76747	79822	76747	77152	79995	79339	90463	97354	77152	15
20	74966	75496	77540	74997	75934	79770	80519	75273	74966	77970	74966	75810	78490	78088	89247	96272	75810	20
25	71344	72579	74054	71386	72563	76609	76660	71686	71344	74203	71344	73741	75174	75336	86333	93353	73741	25
30	67469	69282	70229	67527	68929	72126	72530	67852	67469	70173	67469	71721	71603	72116	82876	89813	71721	30
35	63969	66187	66756	64064	65670	68569	68802	64397	63969	66532	63969	69784	68407	69070	79630	86487	69784	35
40	60501	63049	63330	60671	62480	65118	65118	60989	60501	62925	60501	67512	65312	65997	76454	83292	67512	40
45	56916	59774	59776	57219	59253	61619	61311	57498	56916	59197	56916	64707	62139	62778	73215	80086	64707	45
50	52564	55706	55442	53081	55603	57411	56697	53256	52564	54670	52564	60839	58285	58756	69220	76147	60839	50
55	47772	51061	50609	48619	51681	52818	51626	48616	47772	49686	47772	56098	54013	54093	64632	71593	56098	55
60	41852	45141	44556	43106	47042	47096	45365	42909	41852	43529	41852	49824	48578	48058	58620	65493	49824	60
65	34765	37788	37215	36412	41636	40122	37874	36117	34765	36158	34765	41922	41821	40451	50858	57415	41922	65
70	26503	28996	28564	28440	35212	31789	29102	28054	26503	27565	26503	32302	33655	31251	41159	47161	32302	70
75	17338	19061	18825	19138	27470	21897	19208	18923	17338	18033	17338	21316	24522	20697	28958	34015	21316	75
80	9078	10026	9943	10371	18979	12454	10225	10379	9078	9442	9078	11286	15145	10982	16970	20720	11286	80
85+	3140	3484	3478	3737	10055	4950	3688	3844	3140	3266	3140	3974	7125	3859	7146	9453	3974	85+

ADDED YRS OF LIFE

	No Causes	(1)	(2)	(3)	(4)	(5)	(6)	(7)	(8)	(9)	(10)	(11)	(12)	(1)+(2)	(1)+(2)+(5)+(6)+(8)	part of(9)&(12)	(10)+(11)
TOTAL		1.505	1.948	.540	3.542	3.989	3.488	.630	.000	1.801	.000	3.687	4.430	3.542	12.130	17.634	3.687
WORK	11.325	1.348	.584	.256	1.251	.706	.120	.244	.000	.000	.000	3.464	1.543	1.961	2.864	3.471	3.464

POPULATION, DEATHS, DEATH RATES FOR ALL CAUSES COMBINED, AND SPECIFIED CAUSES

Age Start of Interval	Midyear Population	Deaths During Year	All Causes	Respiratory T. B.	Other Infec. and Paras.	Neoplasms	Cardiovascular	Infl., Pneu., Bronch.	Diarrheal	Certain Degenerative	Maternal	Cert. Dis. of Infancy	Motor Vehicle	Other Violence	Other and Unknown	Age Start of Interval
0	218651	31093	.14220	.00048	.00913	.00003	.00291	.03080	.04862	.00057	.00000	.03296	.00000	.00073	.01597	0
1	888905	15200	.01710	.00028	.00322	.00001	.00081	.00476	.00411	.00033	.00000	.00000	.00000	.00030	.00328	1
5	1365769	5146	.00377	.00015	.00096	.00002	.00039	.00066	.00026	.00016	.00000	.00000	.00000	.00017	.00101	5
10	1361227	3208	.00236	.00023	.00057	.00001	.00036	.00030	.00010	.00009	.00000	.00000	.00000	.00008	.00062	10
15	1293431	4409	.00341	.00092	.00070	.00002	.00046	.00032	.00007	.00010	.00004	.00000	.00000	.00012	.00066	15
20	1163890	4944	.00425	.00139	.00060	.00003	.00056	.00032	.00006	.00012	.00025	.00000	.00000	.00019	.00073	20
25	1104198	5284	.00479	.00130	.00056	.00006	.00077	.00040	.00008	.00014	.00042	.00000	.00000	.00017	.00090	25
30	990751	4969	.00502	.00104	.00054	.00015	.00095	.00049	.00007	.00019	.00046	.00000	.00000	.00020	.00092	30
35	905547	5013	.00554	.00089	.00049	.00035	.00116	.00054	.00008	.00024	.00041	.00000	.00000	.00021	.00115	35
40	805513	5047	.00627	.00081	.00052	.00063	.00146	.00068	.00013	.00031	.00024	.00000	.00000	.00025	.00125	40
45	699810	5302	.00758	.00070	.00049	.00104	.00200	.00084	.00014	.00050	.00005	.00000	.00000	.00030	.00151	45
50	620134	6372	.01028	.00067	.00051	.00148	.00324	.00115	.00026	.00069	.00001	.00000	.00000	.00030	.00196	50
55	528287	7731	.01463	.00073	.00059	.00212	.00504	.00169	.00036	.00100	.00000	.00000	.00000	.00043	.00267	55
60	511869	11533	.02253	.00064	.00071	.00268	.00879	.00297	.00074	.00165	.00000	.00000	.00000	.00038	.00397	60
65	390574	13915	.03563	.00068	.00085	.00362	.01532	.00478	.00125	.00240	.00000	.00000	.00000	.00043	.00629	65
70	267770	17418	.06505	.00084	.00110	.00436	.02816	.00757	.00153	.00362	.00000	.00000	.00000	.00051	.01755	70
75	166313	16437	.09883	.00060	.00129	.00527	.04403	.01200	.00279	.00542	.00000	.00000	.00000	.00064	.02679	75
80	93717	14878	.15875	.00053	.00153	.00604	.06672	.01963	.00691	.00779	.00000	.00000	.00000	.00095	.04865	80
85+	49609	13476	.27164	.00034	.00212	.00633	.10053	.03558	.01236	.01074	.00000	.00000	.00000	.00157	.10208	85+
ALL	13425965	191375														

	All Causes	Respiratory T. B.	Other Infec. and Paras.	Neoplasms	Cardiovascular	Infl., Pneu., Bronch.	Diarrheal	Certain Degenerative	Maternal	Cert. Dis. of Infancy	Motor Vehicle	Other Violence	Other and Unknown
CRUDE DEATH RATE	.01425	.00073	.00097	.00072	.00375	.00210	.00139	.00060	.00014	.00054	.00000	.00025	.00307
STANDARDIZED RATE (1)	.01400	.00068	.00126	.00045	.00228	.00247	.00240	.00042	.00013	.00116	.00000	.00024	.00251
STANDARDIZED RATE (2)	.01693	.00072	.00105	.00085	.00460	.00253	.00172	.00071	.00013	.00068	.00000	.00027	.00368
GEOMETRIC MEAN	.01591												

LIFE TABLE FOR ALL CAUSES COMBINED

Age (x)	Midyear Population	Deaths During Year	$_nM_x$	$_nq_x$	l_x	$_nd_x$	$_nL_x$	$_nm_x$	$_na_x$	T_x	$_nr_x$	$\overset{\circ}{e}_x$	Age (x)
0	218651	31093	.142204	.129530	100000	12953	91085	.142208	.311746	5318991	.000000	53.190	0
1	888905	15200	.017100	.065597	87047	5710	333913	.017100	1.500000	5227906	.000000	60.058	1
5	1365769	5146	.003768	.018663	81337	1518	402890	.003768	2.500000	4893993	.000000	60.169	5
10	1361227	3208	.002357	.011714	79819	935	396719	.002357	2.459225	4491103	.000130	56.266	10
15	1293431	4409	.003409	.016924	78884	1335	391227	.003412	2.608614	4094383	.009565	51.904	15
20	1163890	4944	.004248	.021030	77549	1631	383764	.004250	2.558885	3703156	.011333	47.752	20
25	1104198	5284	.004785	.023657	75918	1796	375143	.004788	2.523896	3319392	.010740	43.723	25
30	990751	4969	.005015	.024783	74122	1837	366055	.005018	2.520300	2944249	.013944	39.722	30
35	905547	5013	.005536	.027322	72285	1975	356557	.005539	2.535338	2578185	.014028	35.667	35
40	805513	5047	.006266	.030892	70310	2172	346237	.006273	2.554098	2221637	.018452	31.598	40
45	699810	5302	.007576	.037263	68138	2539	334577	.007589	2.592474	1875400	.017945	27.524	45
50	620134	6372	.010275	.050290	65599	3299	320137	.010305	2.618218	1540822	.020038	23.489	50
55	528287	7731	.014634	.070803	62300	4411	301076	.014651	2.636826	1220685	.007944	19.594	55
60	511869	11533	.022531	.107032	57889	6196	274813	.022546	2.638530	919609	.003689	15.886	60
65	390574	13915	.035627	.165032	51693	8531	238384	.035787	2.646085	644796	.021255	12.474	65
70	267770	17418	.065048	.282146	43162	12178	186142	.065423	2.563828	406412	.023761	9.416	70
75	166313	16437	.098832	.395753	30984	12262	123919	.098952	2.471779	220270	.005782	7.109	75
80	93717	14878	.158755	.561746	18722	10517	66146	.158998	2.388573	96351	.005782	5.146	80
85+	49609	13476	.271644	1.000000	8205	8205	30205	.271644	3.681285	30205	.000000	3.681	85+

NUMBER OF PERSONS DYING (OUT OF 100,000 AT BIRTH) ABOVE AGE X FROM SPECIFIED CAUSES

Age (x)	All Causes	Respiratory T.B.	Other Infec. and Paras.	Neo-plasms	Cardio-vascular	Infl., Pneu., Bronch.	Diar-rheal	Certain Degen-erative	Maternal	Cert. Dis. of Infancy	Motor Vehicle	Other Violence	Other and Unknown	Age (x)
0	100000	3902	5227	5582	30292	14192	8328	4570	690	3002	0	1508	22707	0
1	87047	3858	4395	5579	30027	11387	3899	4518	690	0	0	1442	21252	1
5	81337	3765	3320	5576	29757	9796	2526	4408	690	0	0	1340	20159	5
10	79819	3705	2933	5570	29600	9531	2423	4344	690	0	0	1273	19750	10
15	78884	3613	2709	5565	29459	9412	2385	4307	690	0	0	1240	19504	15
20	77549	3252	2434	5558	29278	9285	2358	4269	675	0	0	1193	19247	20
25	75918	2718	2202	5547	29064	9161	2336	4224	578	0	0	1118	18970	25
30	74122	2230	1991	5526	28776	9013	2306	4173	419	0	0	1056	18632	30
35	72285	1851	1792	5471	28426	8834	2278	4103	251	0	0	984	18295	35
40	70310	1533	1616	5345	28012	8640	2250	4016	105	0	0	908	17885	40
45	68138	1254	1435	5127	27506	8404	2205	3910	23	0	0	821	17453	45
50	65599	1020	1272	4780	26833	8121	2159	3742	5	0	0	720	16947	50
55	62300	805	1110	4304	25792	7751	2076	3520	1	0	0	622	16319	55
60	57889	584	931	3664	24273	7242	1968	3218	1	0	0	493	15515	60
65	51693	407	736	2927	21856	6425	1764	2764	1	0	0	389	14424	65
70	43162	244	533	2063	18185	5282	1464	2190	1	0	0	287	12913	70
75	30984	124	328	1248	12913	3864	1178	1514	1	0	0	191	9623	75
80	18722	50	168	555	7450	2376	832	841	1	0	0	111	6298	80
85+	8205	10	64	191	3036	1075	373	325	0	0	0	47	3084	85+

NUMBER OF PERSONS SURVIVING TO AGE X IF SPECIFIED CAUSES WERE ELIMINATED

Age (x)	No Causes	Respiratory T.B. (1)	Other Infec. and Paras. (2)	Neo-plasms (3)	Cardio-vascular (4)	Infl., Pneu., Bronch. (5)	Diar-rheal (6)	Certain Degener-ative (7)	Maternal (8)	Cert. Dis. of Infancy (9)	Motor Vehicle (10)	Other Violence (11)	Other and Unknown (12)	(1)+(2)	(1)+(2)+(5)+(6)+(8)	(1)+(2)+(5)+(6)+(8)+part of(9)&(12)	(10)+(11)	Age (x)
0	100000	100000	100000	100000	100000	100000	100000	100000	100000	100000	100000	100000	100000	100000	100000	100000	100000	0
1	87047	87088	87826	87050	87294	89702	91275	87095	87047	89891	87047	87109	88414	87867	94946	99372	87109	1
5	81337	81465	83120	81343	81830	85417	86651	81489	81337	83995	81337	81493	83694	83251	93182	98666	81493	5
10	79819	80004	81961	79830	80460	84099	85182	80031	79819	82427	79819	80039	82550	82152	92372	98174	80039	10
15	78884	79159	81230	78900	79659	83239	84224	79131	78884	81461	78884	79134	81837	81513	91836	97812	79134	15
20	77549	78180	80137	77572	78492	81963	82827	77829	77564	80083	77549	77842	80716	80788	91216	97391	77842	20
25	75918	77070	78689	75551	77056	80369	81109	76237	76029	78398	75918	76275	79304	75883	90480	96865	76279	25
30	74122	75737	77044	74175	75522	78623	79222	74484	74388	76544	74122	74536	77778	78723	89567	96195	74536	30
35	72285	74244	75339	72391	74004	76862	77288	72708	72711	74647	72285	72760	76200	77380	88492	95319	72760	35
40	70310	72538	73461	70538	72401	74965	75206	70808	70869	72607	70310	70848	74546	75789	87121	94139	70848	40
45	68138	70581	71378	68555	70679	72858	72930	68726	68761	70364	68138	68746	72695	73937	85439	92595	68746	45
50	65599	68189	68886	66363	68734	70479	70261	66331	66216	67742	65599	66284	70518	71605	83175	90391	66284	50
55	62300	64977	65588	63497	66350	67323	66814	63215	62890	64336	62300	63047	67633	68406	80029	87239	63047	55
60	57889	60599	61125	59633	63232	63089	62195	59035	58437	59780	57889	58709	63691	63987	75632	82757	58709	60
65	51693	54287	54777	53571	59016	57184	55746	53155	52183	53382	51693	52524	58019	57526	69277	76216	52524	65
70	43162	45483	45933	45691	53255	48913	46841	44923	43571	44572	43162	43950	50024	48403	60093	66660	43950	70
75	30984	32756	33156	33675	44128	36491	33887	32845	31278	31996	30984	31632	39285	35052	45578	51606	31632	75
80	18722	19851	20165	20896	33371	23440	20772	20402	18899	19334	18722	19176	27216	21382	29984	35043	19176	80
85+	8205	8727	8910	9453	20676	11376	9437	9310	8293	8473	8205	8446	15347	9477	15258	19045	8446	85+

ADDED YRS OF LIFE

	No Causes	(1)	(2)	(3)	(4)	(5)	(6)	(7)	(8)	(9)	(10)	(11)	(12)	(1)+(2)	(1)+(2)+(5)+(6)+(8)	+part of(9)&(12)	(10)+(11)
TOTAL		1.357	2.231	.815	4.730	4.160	3.814	.719	.261	1.728	.000	.434	4.682	3.660	13.001	18.692	.434
WORK	6.270	1.078	.601	.352	1.221	.557	.104	.249	.254	.000	.000	.208	1.085	1.699	2.674	3.327	.208

POPULATION, DEATHS, DEATH RATES FOR ALL CAUSES COMBINED, AND SPECIFIED CAUSES

Age Start of Interval	Midyear Population	Deaths During Year	All Causes	Respiratory T.B.	Other Infec. and Paras.	Neo plasms	Cardio vascular	Infl., Pneu., Bronch.	Diarrheal	Certain Degen erative	Maternal	Cert. Dis. of Infancy	Motor Vehicle	Other Violence	Other and Unknown	Age Start of Interval
0	326850	16592	.05076	.00019	.00211	.00018	.00094	.00900	.00356	.00013	.00000	.01729	.00000	.00020	.01715	0
1	1204789	2594	.00215	.00003	.00035	.00009	.00009	.00049	.00020	.00003	.00000	.00000	.00002	.00009	.00076	1
5	1394426	1007	.00072	.00001	.00008	.00007	.00006	.00007	.00002	.00002	.00000	.00000	.00003	.00012	.00024	5
10	1328533	779	.00059	.00001	.00005	.00007	.00009	.00005	.00001	.00002	.00000	.00000	.00004	.00011	.00015	10
15	1174648	1172	.00100	.00003	.00006	.00008	.00015	.00005	.00000	.00005	.00000	.00000	.00010	.00030	.00018	15
20	1127892	1336	.00118	.00006	.00005	.00008	.00016	.00003	.00000	.00006	.00000	.00000	.00020	.00038	.00016	20
25	1184513	1880	.00159	.00018	.00006	.00011	.00020	.00004	.00001	.00008	.00000	.00000	.00023	.00047	.00021	25
30	1168829	2184	.00187	.00026	.00006	.00015	.00028	.00004	.00001	.00011	.00000	.00000	.00022	.00044	.00029	30
35	1070777	2635	.00246	.00036	.00009	.00027	.00042	.00006	.00001	.00018	.00000	.00000	.00020	.00047	.00039	35
40	843698	2909	.00345	.00038	.00011	.00053	.00068	.00009	.00002	.00030	.00000	.00000	.00021	.00053	.00058	40
45	816375	4369	.00535	.00055	.00013	.00104	.00116	.00021	.00003	.00051	.00000	.00000	.00019	.00058	.00094	45
50	777311	6716	.00864	.00070	.00017	.00193	.00227	.00039	.00005	.00078	.00000	.00000	.00015	.00059	.00162	50
55	687547	9473	.01378	.00084	.00022	.00318	.00407	.00074	.00006	.00118	.00000	.00000	.00016	.00070	.00263	55
60	569865	11943	.02096	.00099	.00030	.00466	.00700	.00140	.00011	.00168	.00000	.00000	.00017	.00069	.00396	60
65	409569	14572	.03558	.00097	.00048	.00724	.01322	.00268	.00022	.00282	.00000	.00000	.00017	.00078	.00701	65
70	311615	17353	.05569	.00099	.00052	.00916	.02286	.00478	.00039	.00381	.00000	.00000	.00013	.00101	.01203	70
75	188150	16688	.08870	.00096	.00058	.01201	.03819	.00885	.00088	.00531	.00000	.00000	.00013	.00111	.02067	75
80	87967	13056	.14942	.00061	.00085	.01479	.06367	.01564	.00183	.00804	.00000	.00000	.00014	.00149	.04136	80
85+	38753	9274	.23931	.00036	.00067	.01486	.09024	.02748	.00335	.00968	.00000	.00000	.00010	.00199	.09057	85+
ALL	14712107	136532														

CRUDE DEATH RATE	.00928	.00031	.00020	.00127	.00278	.00085	.00016	.00055	.00000	.00038	.00014	.00042	.00222
STANDARDIZED RATE (1)	.00670	.00022	.00021	.00076	.00154	.00070	.00018	.00033	.00000	.00061	.00012	.00034	.00168
STANDARDIZED RATE (2)	.01117	.00032	.00020	.00152	.00360	.00103	.00017	.00067	.00000	.00036	.00014	.00043	.00272
GEOMETRIC MEAN	.00792												

LIFE TABLE FOR ALL CAUSES COMBINED

Age (x)	Midyear Population	Deaths During Year	$_nM_x$	$_nq_x$	l_x	$_nd_x$	$_nL_x$	$_nm_x$	$_na_x$	T_x	$_nr_x$	$\overset{\circ}{e}_x$	Age (x)
0	326850	16592	.050763	.048680	100000	4868	95893	.050765	.156298	6694083	.000000	66.941	0
1	1204789	2594	.002153	.008567	95132	815	378451	.002153	1.500000	6598191	.000000	69.358	1
5	1394426	1007	.000722	.003594	94317	339	470738	.000720	2.500000	6219700	.000000	65.945	5
10	1328533	779	.000586	.002937	93978	276	469227	.000588	2.596618	5748963	.012080	61.173	10
15	1174648	1172	.000998	.004984	93702	467	467400	.000999	2.622680	5279736	.017585	56.346	15
20	1127892	1336	.001185	.005910	93235	551	464853	.001185	2.600197	4812336	.003426	51.615	20
25	1184513	1880	.001587	.007898	92684	732	461654	.001586	2.586806	4347483	-.004559	46.907	25
30	1168829	2184	.001869	.009309	91952	856	457700	.001870	2.593945	3885830	.001194	42.259	30
35	1070777	2635	.002461	.012273	91096	1118	452829	.002469	2.628391	3428129	.023601	37.632	35
40	843698	2909	.003448	.017171	89978	1545	446282	.003462	2.664914	2975301	.027451	33.067	40
45	816375	4369	.005352	.026472	88433	2341	436751	.005360	2.687420	2529019	.007618	28.598	45
50	777311	6716	.008640	.042408	86092	3651	421993	.008652	2.681001	2092267	.007059	24.303	50
55	687547	9473	.013778	.066672	82441	5513	399271	.013808	2.653841	1670274	.012338	20.260	55
60	569865	11943	.020958	.100380	76928	7722	366562	.021066	2.658961	1271003	.026187	16.522	60
65	409569	14572	.035579	.164798	69206	11405	318871	.035767	2.618661	904441	.025770	13.069	65
70	311615	17353	.055687	.245982	57801	14218	254401	.055888	2.566157	585570	.018844	10.131	70
75	188150	16688	.088695	.365280	43583	15920	178262	.089307	2.509239	331169	.030748	7.599	75
80	87967	13056	.148419	.539493	27663	14924	99675	.149726	2.410856	152907	.030748	5.528	80
85+	38753	9274	.239311	1.000000	12739	12739	53232	.239311	4.178672	53232	.000000	4.179	85+

NUMBER OF PERSONS DYING (OUT OF 100,000 AT BIRTH) ABOVE AGE X FROM SPECIFIED CAUSES

Age (x)	All Causes	Respiratory T. B.	Other Infec. and Paras.	Neo-plasms	Cardio-vascular	Infl., Pneu., Bronch.	Diar-rheal	Certain Degen-erative	Maternal	Cert. Dis. of Infancy	Motor Vehicle	Other Violence	Other and Unknown	Age (x)
0	100000	2677	1435	14028	34865	9020	1244	6194	0	1658	973	3347	24559	0
1	95132	2659	1232	14011	34774	8158	902	6181	0	0	973	3328	22914	1
5	94317	2646	1099	13978	34742	7971	826	6171	0	0	964	3295	22625	5
10	93978	2639	1063	13944	34714	7936	816	6163	0	0	951	3240	22512	10
15	93702	2634	1041	13913	34673	7913	813	6152	0	0	932	3188	22443	15
20	93235	2622	1014	13876	34602	7891	811	6130	0	0	884	3049	22356	20
25	92684	2592	989	13839	34527	7878	809	6102	0	0	793	2872	22283	25
30	91952	2507	960	13787	34437	7861	805	6064	0	0	689	2656	22186	30
35	91096	2389	930	13717	34307	7842	802	6012	0	0	590	2453	22054	35
40	89978	2225	888	13592	34114	7816	797	5930	0	0	499	2240	21877	40
45	88433	2056	838	13352	33807	7775	788	5797	0	0	403	2002	21615	45
50	86092	1816	782	12896	33301	7682	775	5573	0	0	318	1748	21201	50
55	82441	1519	711	12081	32341	7515	756	5243	0	0	255	1501	20519	55
60	76928	1185	621	10809	30710	7218	730	4773	0	0	192	1219	19471	60
65	69206	821	510	9096	28128	6703	691	4153	0	0	131	965	18008	65
70	57801	511	358	6777	23887	5844	620	3249	0	0	78	717	15760	70
75	43583	258	227	4441	18048	4621	521	2278	0	0	44	460	12685	75
80	27663	88	123	2291	11191	3030	362	1327	0	0	21	261	8969	80
85+	12739	19	36	791	4804	1463	179	515	0	0	5	106	4821	85+

NUMBER OF PERSONS SURVIVING TO AGE X IF SPECIFIED CAUSES WERE ELIMINATED

Age (x)	No Causes	Respiratory T. B. (1)	Other Infec. and Paras. (2)	Neo-plasms (3)	Cardio-vascular (4)	Infl., Pneu., Bronch. (5)	Diar-rheal (6)	Certain Degen-erative (7)	Maternal (8)	Cert. Dis. of Infancy (9)	Motor Vehicle (10)	Other Violence (11)	Other and Unknown (12)	(1) + (2)	(1) + (2) + (5) + (6) + (8)	(1)+(2)+ (5)+(6)+ (8)+part of(9)&(12)	(10) + (11)	Age (x)
0	100000	100000	100000	100000	100000	100000	100000	100000	100000	100000	100000	100000	100000	100000	100000	100000	100000	0
1	95132	95150	95330	95149	95221	95976	95466	95145	95132	96763	95132	95151	96750	95348	96532	99555	95151	1
5	94317	94347	94646	94366	94437	95342	94724	94340	94317	95934	94326	94368	96214	94677	96119	99364	94377	5
10	93978	94015	94342	94061	94125	95035	94394	94008	93978	95589	94000	94084	95983	94380	95863	99146	94106	10
15	93702	93744	94087	93816	93890	94779	94120	93743	93702	95308	93743	93860	95772	94129	95636	98929	93901	15
20	93235	93289	93645	93385	93493	94329	93653	93298	93235	94833	93324	93531	95383	93699	95223	98518	93620	20
25	92684	92768	93117	92870	93016	93784	93101	92775	92684	94273	92863	93155	94894	93201	94732	98021	93335	25
30	91952	92120	92410	92189	92371	93061	92370	92080	91952	93528	92233	92636	94244	92579	94121	97411	92920	30
35	91096	91380	91580	91400	91641	92214	91513	91274	91096	92658	91474	91977	93501	91866	93418	96716	92359	35
40	89978	90422	90498	90403	90710	91108	90395	90236	89978	91520	90442	91063	92534	90945	92514	95827	91532	40
45	88433	89038	88994	89091	89460	89585	88852	88819	88433	89949	88984	89738	91213	89603	91200	94524	90298	45
50	86092	86919	86694	87187	87598	87306	86512	86690	86092	87568	86713	87617	89221	87527	89195	92538	88249	50
55	82441	83527	83087	84301	84845	83770	82862	83339	82441	83854	83098	84147	86132	84182	85976	89333	84818	55
60	76928	78268	77619	79930	80810	78460	77346	78226	76928	78247	77602	78798	81436	78971	80982	84329	79488	60
65	69206	70763	69934	73613	75318	71085	69620	70974	69206	70392	69871	71134	74745	71506	73887	77194	71817	65
70	57801	59389	58549	63769	67268	60182	58212	60129	57801	58792	58404	59644	64684	60157	63080	66261	60266	70
75	43583	45004	44261	50354	56965	46497	43979	46217	43583	44330	44067	45201	51848	45703	49203	52170	45703	75
80	27663	28701	28176	33967	43978	30887	28043	30138	27663	28137	27989	28852	36604	29233	33088	35709	29191	80
85+	12739	13264	13034	16910	28223	15430	13037	14477	12739	12957	12900	13394	20910	13571	16823	18862	13563	85+

ADDED YRS OF LIFE		(1)	(2)	(3)	(4)	(5)	(6)	(7)	(8)	(9)	(10)	(11)	(12)				
TOTAL		.569	.455	1.920	4.629	1.508	.367	.807	.000	1.145	.314	.887	4.203	1.030	2.983	5.891	1.208
WORK	3.306	.282	.094	.479	.653	.114	.015	.233	.000	.000	.206	.501	.527	.377	.508	.613	.711

POPULATION, DEATHS, DEATH RATES FOR ALL CAUSES COMBINED, AND SPECIFIED CAUSES

Age Start of Interval	Midyear Population	Deaths During Year	All Causes	Respiratory T. B.	Other Infec. and Paras.	Neoplasms	Cardiovascular	Infl., Pneu., Bronch.	Diarrheal	Certain Degenerative	Maternal	Cert. Dis. of Infancy	Motor Vehicle	Other Violence	Other and Unknown	Age Start of Interval
0	310462	12327	.03971	.00014	.00166	.00015	.00059	.00758	.00318	.00010	.00000	.01316	.00000	.00016	.01298	0
1	1161892	2177	.00187	.00002	.00030	.00008	.00007	.00052	.00017	.00002	.00000	.00000	.00001	.00007	.00061	1
5	1288642	726	.00056	.00001	.00007	.00006	.00005	.00007	.00002	.00002	.00000	.00000	.00002	.00006	.00020	5
10	1296637	576	.00044	.00001	.00004	.00006	.00009	.00005	.00000	.00002	.00000	.00000	.00002	.00004	.00011	10
15	1222403	633	.00052	.00003	.00004	.00006	.00010	.00002	.00000	.00004	.00000	.00000	.00003	.00006	.00013	15
20	1096343	810	.00074	.00008	.00005	.00007	.00015	.00003	.00000	.00005	.00005	.00000	.00005	.00007	.00015	20
25	1245207	1344	.00108	.00014	.00005	.00011	.00022	.00003	.00001	.00007	.00011	.00000	.00005	.00009	.00021	25
30	1176895	1467	.00125	.00015	.00005	.00016	.00027	.00004	.00000	.00008	.00010	.00000	.00005	.00009	.00026	30
35	1151722	1962	.00170	.00015	.00007	.00035	.00040	.00004	.00000	.00010	.00010	.00000	.00005	.00012	.00032	35
40	958930	2318	.00242	.00012	.00008	.00067	.00065	.00006	.00001	.00016	.00006	.00000	.00004	.00014	.00042	40
45	923589	3242	.00351	.00017	.00011	.00109	.00099	.00009	.00001	.00023	.00002	.00000	.00004	.00015	.00060	45
50	874429	4471	.00511	.00016	.00011	.00165	.00151	.00017	.00002	.00034	.00000	.00000	.00004	.00017	.00094	50
55	766729	6145	.00801	.00021	.00012	.00227	.00268	.00031	.00004	.00066	.00000	.00000	.00004	.00023	.00145	55
60	680450	8599	.01264	.00025	.00016	.00297	.00499	.00067	.00007	.00106	.00000	.00000	.00003	.00023	.00221	60
65	533561	12174	.02282	.00034	.00025	.00431	.00987	.00136	.00016	.00175	.00000	.00000	.00005	.00032	.00441	65
70	427047	16782	.03930	.00041	.00035	.00566	.01843	.00297	.00033	.00257	.00000	.00000	.00004	.00041	.00814	70
75	277830	18844	.06783	.00044	.00046	.00762	.03273	.00615	.00071	.00356	.00000	.00000	.00003	.00059	.01554	75
80	147519	18592	.12603	.00077	.00066	.00980	.05919	.01226	.00158	.00559	.00000	.00000	.00005	.00080	.03533	80
85+	80868	18131	.22420	.00070	.00085	.01244	.09357	.02442	.00279	.00648	.00000	.00000	.00002	.00130	.08161	85+
ALL	15621155	131320														

CRUDE DEATH RATE			.00841	.00014	.00015	.00111	.00311	.00075	.00014	.00043	.00003	.00026	.00004	.00014	.00210	
STANDARDIZED RATE (1)			.00483	.00010	.00016	.00056	.00125	.00054	.00016	.00021	.00003	.00046	.00003	.00010	.00124	
STANDARDIZED RATE (2)			.00819	.00013	.00015	.00107	.00302	.00074	.00015	.00042	.00003	.00027	.00003	.00014	.00203	
GEOMETRIC MEAN			.00553													

LIFE TABLE FOR ALL CAUSES COMBINED

Age (x)	Midyear Population	Deaths During Year	$_nM_x$	$_nq_x$	l_x	$_nd_x$	$_nL_x$	$_nm_x$	$_na_x$	T_x	$_nr_x$	$\overset{\circ}{e}_x$	Age (x)
0	310462	12327	.039705	.038390	100000	3839	96689	.039705	.137499	7166944	.000000	71.669	0
1	1161892	2177	.001874	.007456	96161	717	382852	.001873	1.500000	7070256	.000000	73.525	1
5	1288642	726	.000563	.002818	95444	269	476548	.000564	2.500000	6687404	.000000	70.066	5
10	1296637	576	.000444	.002217	95175	211	475343	.000444	2.477291	6210857	.000901	65.257	10
15	1222403	633	.000518	.002590	94964	246	474234	.000519	2.617717	5735514	.015667	60.397	15
20	1096343	810	.000739	.003695	94718	350	472769	.000740	2.655357	5261280	.003185	55.547	20
25	1245207	1344	.001079	.005373	94368	507	470621	.001077	2.595743	4788511	-.007619	50.743	25
30	1176895	1467	.001247	.006211	93861	583	467907	.001246	2.602201	4317890	.001159	46.003	30
35	1151722	1962	.001704	.008501	93278	793	464518	.001707	2.639765	3849982	.013820	41.274	35
40	958930	2318	.002417	.012056	92485	1115	459804	.002425	2.649477	3385464	.021041	36.606	40
45	923589	3242	.003510	.017435	91370	1593	453109	.003516	2.651444	2925660	.007957	32.020	45
50	874429	4471	.005113	.025318	89777	2273	443590	.005124	2.670256	2472551	.011631	27.541	50
55	766729	6145	.008015	.039438	87504	3451	429459	.008035	2.675734	2028962	.014610	23.187	55
60	680450	8599	.012637	.061675	84053	5184	408375	.012694	2.706445	1599463	.020684	19.029	60
65	533561	12174	.022817	.108889	78869	8588	374439	.022936	2.682134	1191087	.022473	15.102	65
70	427047	16782	.039298	.180589	70281	12692	321405	.039489	2.636306	816648	.021930	11.620	70
75	277830	18844	.067826	.293320	57589	16892	247158	.068345	2.585432	495243	.031320	8.600	75
80	147519	18592	.126031	.482075	40697	19619	154073	.127336	2.481417	248085	.031320	6.096	80
85+	80868	18131	.224205	1.000000	21078	21078	94012	.224205	4.460206	94012	.000000	4.460	85+

NUMBER OF PERSONS DYING (OUT OF 100,000 AT BIRTH) ABOVE AGE X FROM SPECIFIED CAUSES

Age (x)	All Causes	Respiratory T.B.	Other Infec. and Paras.	Neoplasms	Cardiovascular	Infl., Pneu., Bronch.	Diarrheal	Certain Degenerative	Maternal	Cert. Dis. of Infancy	Motor Vehicle	Other Violence	Other and Unknown	Age (x)
0	100000	1240	1210	12225	41139	8821	1315	5092	204	1273	259	1336	25886	0
1	96161	1227	1049	12211	41081	8088	1008	5083	204	0	259	1320	24631	1
5	95444	1217	933	12181	41055	7890	944	5074	204	0	253	1295	24398	5
10	95175	1212	900	12154	41030	7857	936	5066	204	0	246	1268	24302	10
15	94964	1206	881	12127	40985	7834	933	5056	204	0	239	1248	24251	15
20	94718	1190	862	12097	40937	7826	931	5038	202	0	225	1221	24189	20
25	94368	1152	839	12066	40868	7814	929	5016	180	0	200	1189	24115	25
30	93861	1085	815	12016	40766	7800	927	4985	128	0	177	1148	24014	30
35	93278	1017	793	11939	40640	7782	925	4948	80	0	153	1106	23895	35
40	92485	948	761	11775	40452	7761	923	4902	36	0	129	1050	23748	40
45	91370	892	725	11466	40154	7733	917	4828	8	0	107	985	23555	45
50	89777	815	674	10969	39704	7691	910	4725	0	0	91	915	23283	50
55	87504	746	626	10237	39031	7617	900	4573	0	0	75	838	22861	55
60	84053	657	573	9258	37875	7481	882	4288	0	0	59	738	22242	60
65	78869	557	506	8043	35827	7206	853	3853	0	0	46	646	21332	65
70	70281	427	413	6425	32110	6653	793	3196	0	0	28	526	19670	70
75	57589	296	300	4603	26154	5732	686	2368	0	0	16	395	17039	75
80	40697	188	185	2713	18001	4198	508	1484	0	0	10	248	13162	80
85+	21078	66	80	1170	8797	2296	263	609	0	0	2	122	7673	85+

NUMBER OF PERSONS SURVIVING TO AGE X IF SPECIFIED CAUSES WERE ELIMINATED

Age (x)	No Causes	Respiratory T.B. (1)	Other Infec. and Paras. (2)	Neoplasms (3)	Cardiovascular (4)	Infl., Pneu., Bronch. (5)	Diarrheal (6)	Certain Degenerative (7)	Maternal (8)	Cert. Dis. of Infancy (9)	Motor Vehicle (10)	Other Violence (11)	Other and Unknown (12)	(1)+(2)	(1)+(2)+(5)+(6)+(8)	(1)+(2)+(5)+(6)+(8)+part of(9)&(12)	(10)+(11)	Age (x)
0	100000	100000	100000	100000	100000	100000	100000	100000	100000	100000	100000	100000	100000	100000	100000	100000	100000	0
1	96161	96174	96319	96175	96218	96882	96463	96170	96161	97417	96161	96177	97400	96332	97359	99711	96177	1
5	95444	95467	95717	95488	95526	96359	95462	95444	95444	96691	95450	95484	96909	95739	97025	99563	95490	5
10	95175	95203	95480	95245	95282	96121	95545	95201	95175	96419	95188	95242	96733	95508	96832	99410	95255	10
15	94964	94997	95287	95061	95116	95931	95336	95000	94964	96205	94984	95051	96570	95321	96669	99260	95071	15
20	94718	94767	95060	94845	94918	95690	95091	94771	94752	95956	94752	94832	96383	95109	96446	99069	94866	20
25	94368	94455	94731	94636	94742	95539	94742	94443	94392	95601	94427	94514	96102	94819	96209	98831	94572	25
30	93861	94015	94246	94068	94229	94851	94235	93967	93937	95087	93942	94047	95688	94401	95853	98508	94128	30
35	93278	93499	93683	93560	93770	94280	93652	93420	93401	94497	93383	93505	95215	93905	95419	98104	93610	35
40	92485	92773	92919	92929	93162	93499	92858	92672	92651	93693	92613	92765	94955	93207	94779	97486	92894	40
45	91370	91710	91834	92118	92337	92467	91744	91628	91562	92564	91518	91712	93612	92176	93793	96506	91861	45
50	89777	90188	90284	91010	91179	90831	90152	90133	89973	90950	89938	90183	92256	90697	92346	95057	90345	50
55	87504	87973	88046	89441	89548	88606	87879	88002	87695	88647	87677	87976	90349	88517	90213	92909	88150	55
60	84053	84591	84626	86899	87185	85246	84431	84813	84237	85151	84235	84605	87415	85167	86955	89621	84866	60
65	78869	79471	79472	82764	83892	80260	79252	80008	79042	79899	79052	79476	82946	80078	82065	84685	79661	65
70	70281	70941	70906	75367	78585	72015	70679	71927	70435	71199	70461	70936	75582	71572	73915	76471	71118	70
75	57589	58248	58204	63540	70705	59909	58013	59706	57715	58341	57748	58245	64546	58871	61828	64313	58405	75
80	40697	41254	41228	46666	59073	43694	41147	42962	40786	41229	40814	41284	49408	41792	45466	47860	41403	80
85+	21078	21454	21428	25453	41658	24121	21487	22913	21124	21353	21144	21473	30761	21811	25499	27685	21540	85+

ADDED YRS OF LIFE

	No Causes	(1)	(2)	(3)	(4)	(5)	(6)	(7)	(8)	(9)	(10)	(11)	(12)	(1)+(2)	(1)+(2)+(5)+(6)+(8)	(1)+(2)+(5)+(6)+(8)+part of(9)&(12)	(10)+(11)
TOTAL		.287	.398	1.839	5.544	1.359	.355	.648	.088	.935	.092	.306	4.003	.687	2.585	5.035	.399
WORK	2.146	.134	.073	.471	.551	.065	.010	.139	.065	.000	.052	.117	.391	.207	.348	.433	.169

POPULATION, DEATHS, DEATH RATES FOR ALL CAUSES COMBINED, AND SPECIFIED CAUSES

Age Start of Interval	Midyear Population	Deaths During Year	All Causes	Respiratory T. B.	Other Infec. and Paras.	Neoplasms	Cardiovascular	Infl., Pneu., Bronch.	Diarrheal	Certain Degenerative	Maternal	Cert. Dis. of Infancy	Motor Vehicle	Other Violence	Other and Unknown	Age Start of Interval
0	65366	5453	.08342	.00073	.00877	.00003	.00005	.01210	.01222	.00011	.00000	.03286	.00000	.00063	.01593	0
1	253328	2416	.00954	.00037	.00381	.00007	.00010	.00176	.00061	.00011	.00000	.00000	.00000	.00054	.00217	1
5	297406	1009	.00339	.00018	.00148	.00003	.00018	.00019	.00012	.00010	.00000	.00000	.00000	.00048	.00064	5
10	281460	752	.00267	.00031	.00093	.00002	.00018	.00011	.00004	.00014	.00000	.00000	.00000	.00049	.00047	10
15	262245	1186	.00452	.00157	.00085	.00004	.00026	.00017	.00005	.00022	.00000	.00000	.00000	.00075	.00061	15
20	228933	1327	.00580	.00245	.00079	.00008	.00031	.00025	.00004	.00021	.00000	.00000	.00000	.00106	.00060	20
25	199735	1343	.00672	.00294	.00069	.00014	.00040	.00034	.00004	.00027	.00000	.00000	.00000	.00126	.00065	25
30	181261	1088	.00600	.00227	.00050	.00017	.00044	.00038	.00005	.00035	.00000	.00000	.00000	.00119	.00066	30
35	156778	1005	.00641	.00200	.00040	.00036	.00064	.00050	.00006	.00044	.00000	.00000	.00000	.00121	.00079	35
40	132390	980	.00740	.00180	.00045	.00068	.00097	.00067	.00008	.00051	.00000	.00000	.00000	.00122	.00102	40
45	134660	1240	.00921	.00168	.00047	.00120	.00151	.00092	.00010	.00070	.00000	.00000	.00000	.00129	.00134	45
50	122535	1494	.01219	.00177	.00058	.00207	.00224	.00122	.00011	.00109	.00000	.00000	.00000	.00149	.00162	50
55	104645	1805	.01725	.00179	.00060	.00326	.00370	.00189	.00016	.00145	.00000	.00000	.00000	.00161	.00278	55
60	89693	2216	.02471	.00178	.00048	.00458	.00574	.00309	.00022	.00158	.00000	.00000	.00000	.00186	.00536	60
65	76730	2610	.03402	.00188	.00053	.00683	.00912	.00420	.00036	.00240	.00000	.00000	.00000	.00142	.00727	65
70	57776	3317	.05741	.00156	.00048	.00633	.01307	.00440	.00024	.00152	.00000	.00000	.00000	.00142	.02839	70
75	41667	3541	.08498	.00144	.00055	.00768	.02045	.00696	.00046	.00230	.00000	.00000	.00000	.00180	.04334	75
80	21379	2968	.13883	.00126	.00065	.00879	.03096	.01137	.00112	.00332	.00000	.00000	.00000	.00267	.07868	80
85+	9647	2453	.25428	.00083	.00093	.00923	.04675	.02052	.00197	.00456	.00000	.00000	.00000	.00435	.16513	85+
ALL	2717634	38203														

	All Causes	Respiratory T. B.	Other Infec. and Paras.	Neoplasms	Cardiovascular	Infl., Pneu., Bronch.	Diarrheal	Certain Degenerative	Maternal	Cert. Dis. of Infancy	Motor Vehicle	Other Violence	Other and Unknown
CRUDE DEATH RATE	.01406	.00144	.00123	.00107	.00201	.00139	.00045	.00054	.00000	.00079	.00000	.00102	.00410
STANDARDIZED RATE (1)	.01158	.00136	.00143	.00068	.00118	.00124	.00058	.00041	.00000	.00116	.00000	.00093	.00262
STANDARDIZED RATE (2)	.01528	.00151	.00113	.00129	.00239	.00149	.00041	.00061	.00000	.00068	.00000	.00108	.00468
GEOMETRIC MEAN	.01626												

LIFE TABLE FOR ALL CAUSES COMBINED

Age (x)	Midyear Population	Deaths During Year	$_nM_x$	$_nq_x$	l_x	$_nd_x$	$_nL_x$	$_nm_x$	$_na_x$	T_x	$_nr_x$	$\overset{\circ}{e}_x$	Age (x)
0	65366	5453	.083423	.078280	100000	7828	93830	.083427	.211818	5659001	.000000	56.590	0
1	253328	2416	.009537	.037256	92172	3434	360103	.009536	1.500000	5565171	.000000	60.378	1
5	297406	1009	.003393	.016814	88738	1492	439960	.003391	2.500000	5205068	.000000	58.657	5
10	281460	752	.002672	.013273	87246	1158	433426	.002672	2.578800	4765108	.006147	54.617	10
15	262245	1186	.004522	.022419	86088	1930	425876	.004532	2.635039	4331682	.012842	50.317	15
20	228933	1327	.005796	.028625	84158	2409	414929	.005806	2.566936	3905806	.020198	46.410	20
25	199735	1343	.006724	.033077	81749	2704	401970	.006727	2.494376	3490877	.017976	42.702	25
30	181261	1088	.006002	.029553	79045	2336	389326	.006000	2.474939	3088908	.016126	39.078	30
35	156778	1005	.006410	.031587	76709	2423	377564	.006417	2.531555	2699581	.025444	35.192	35
40	132390	980	.007402	.036386	74286	2703	364839	.007409	2.561737	2322017	.014037	31.258	40
45	134660	1240	.009208	.045039	71583	3224	350136	.009208	2.587301	1957178	-.000453	27.341	45
50	122535	1494	.012192	.059305	68359	4054	332100	.012207	2.608586	1607041	.009126	23.509	50
55	104645	1805	.017249	.082995	64305	5337	308771	.017285	2.610354	1274941	.013907	19.826	55
60	89693	2216	.024706	.116690	58968	6881	278234	.024731	2.586742	966170	.007586	16.385	60
65	76730	2610	.034015	.157467	52087	8202	240800	.034061	2.606057	687935	.008177	13.207	65
70	57776	3317	.057411	.251977	43885	11058	192471	.057453	2.562474	447135	.003410	10.189	70
75	41667	3541	.084983	.350870	32827	11518	135312	.085122	2.497594	254664	.008679	7.758	75
80	21379	2968	.138828	.512694	21309	10925	78514	.139146	2.434268	119352	.008679	5.601	80
85+	9647	2453	.254276	1.000000	10384	10384	40838	.254276	3.932735	40838	.000000	3.933	85+

NUMBER OF PERSONS DYING (OUT OF 100,000 AT BIRTH) ABOVE AGE X FROM SPECIFIED CAUSES

Age (x)	All Causes	Respiratory T.B.	Other Infec. and Paras.	Neoplasms	Cardiovascular	Infl., Pneu., Bronch.	Diarrheal	Certain Degenerative	Maternal	Cert. Dis. of Infancy	Motor Vehicle	Other Violence	Other and Unknown	Age (x)
0	100000	8889	5792	8974	17223	9497	2107	4063	0	3084	0	6523	33848	0
1	92172	8820	4969	8972	17218	8361	960	4053	0	0	0	6464	32355	1
5	88738	8688	3598	8947	17181	7728	741	4011	0	0	0	6270	31574	5
10	87246	8607	2947	8936	17101	7645	689	3967	0	0	0	6060	31294	10
15	86088	8472	2544	8926	17023	7599	674	3908	0	0	0	5849	31093	15
20	84158	7800	2180	8910	16912	7527	653	3814	0	0	0	5530	30832	20
25	81749	6783	1852	8875	16782	7423	637	3725	0	0	0	5088	30584	25
30	79045	5601	1575	8821	16620	7288	620	3616	0	0	0	4581	30323	30
35	76709	4720	1380	8754	16450	7140	601	3481	0	0	0	4119	30064	35
40	74286	3965	1229	8618	16206	6951	577	3314	0	0	0	3662	29764	40
45	71583	3309	1066	8369	15850	6706	549	3127	0	0	0	3215	29392	45
50	68359	2722	902	7948	15322	6383	516	2882	0	0	0	2763	28921	50
55	64305	2134	710	7259	14575	5979	478	2521	0	0	0	2267	28382	55
60	58968	1582	524	6250	13430	5393	427	2072	0	0	0	1768	27522	60
65	52087	1085	390	4974	11830	4533	365	1631	0	0	0	1250	26029	65
70	43885	634	262	3328	9631	3522	277	1054	0	0	0	908	24269	70
75	32827	334	168	2109	7114	2675	231	761	0	0	0	634	18801	75
80	21309	139	94	1069	4343	1732	169	449	0	0	0	391	12923	80
85+	10384	34	38	377	1909	838	80	186	0	0	0	178	6744	85+

NUMBER OF PERSONS SURVIVING TO AGE X IF SPECIFIED CAUSES WERE ELIMINATED

Age (x)	No Causes	Respiratory T.B.	Other Infec. and Paras.	Neoplasms	Cardiovascular	Infl., Pneu., Bronch.	Diarrheal	Certain Degenerative	Maternal	Cert. Dis. of Infancy	Motor Vehicle	Other Violence	Other and Unknown	(1) + (2)	(1) + (2) + (5) + (6) + (8)	(1)+(2)+ (5)+(6)+ (8)+part of(9)&(12)	(10) + (11)	Age (x)
		(1)	(2)	(3)	(4)	(5)	(6)	(7)	(8)	(9)	(10)	(11)	(12)					
0	100000	100000	100000	100000	100000	100000	100000	100000	100000	100000	100000	100000	100000	100000	100000	100000	100000	0
1	92172	92238	92965	92174	92177	93269	93279	92182	92172	95180	92172	92229	93616	93032	95270	99810	92229	1
5	88738	88931	90869	88764	88779	90425	90022	88788	88738	91634	88738	88983	90910	91067	94140	99385	88983	5
10	87246	87516	90005	87283	87366	88988	88561	87339	87246	90093	87246	87696	89666	90284	93474	98906	87696	10
15	86088	86490	89224	86134	86284	87854	87400	86239	86088	88898	86088	86743	88682	89640	92873	98413	86743	15
20	84158	85221	87997	84219	84459	85957	85462	84398	84158	86905	84158	85117	86960	88704	92003	97694	85117	20
25	81749	83803	85426	81843	82170	83601	83032	82071	81749	84417	81749	83122	84723	87573	90962	96784	83122	25
30	79045	82231	82886	79189	79613	80972	80302	79464	79045	81625	79045	80881	82187	86227	89734	95682	80881	30
35	76709	80709	80638	76915	77429	78728	77948	77249	76709	79212	76709	78958	80024	84842	88482	94535	78958	35
40	74286	78945	78247	74620	75226	76433	75510	74975	74286	76710	74286	76928	77805	83154	86967	93111	76928	40
45	71583	76755	75568	72151	72844	73900	72790	72242	71583	73919	71583	74585	75358	81033	85066	91294	74585	45
50	68359	73919	72334	69318	70091	70898	69545	69413	68359	70590	68359	71687	72450	78217	82530	88812	71687	50
55	64305	70154	68242	65889	66681	67101	65458	65653	64305	66404	64305	67941	68710	74448	79078	85338	67941	55
60	58968	64909	62767	61418	62295	62121	60075	60644	58968	60892	58968	62808	63895	69090	74150	80364	62808	60
65	52087	57849	55576	55514	56639	55730	53124	53595	52087	53787	52087	55998	57980	61724	67355	73565	55998	65
70	43885	49198	46949	48403	49962	47953	44841	46041	43885	45317	43885	47515	50701	52633	58764	64808	47515	70
75	32827	37088	35205	37372	39921	36672	33582	34701	32827	33898	32827	35797	43818	39775	45455	51822	35797	75
80	21309	24249	22915	25216	28751	24662	21850	22791	21309	22004	21309	23449	35475	26077	30947	37087	23449	80
85+	10384	11898	11208	12860	16444	12746	10710	11300	10384	10723	10384	11588	25960	12843	16260	21492	11588	85+

ADDED YRS OF LIFE																		
TOTAL		2.939	2.733	1.332	2.411	2.261	.959	.813	.000	1.840	.000	1.935	6.860	5.851	9.572	15.056	1.935	
WORK	7.674	2.152	.637	.445	.710	.471	.059	.399	.000	.000	.000	1.132	.856	2.832	3.418	3.918	1.132	

POPULATION, DEATHS, DEATH RATES FOR ALL CAUSES COMBINED, AND SPECIFIED CAUSES

Age Start of Interval	Midyear Population	Deaths During Year	All Causes	Respiratory T.B.	Other Infec. and Paras.	Neo-plasms	Cardio-vascular	Infl., Pneu., Bronch.	Diar-rheal	Certain Degen-erative	Maternal	Cert. Dis. of Infancy	Motor Vehicle	Other Violence	Other and Unknown	Age Start of Interval
0	61981	4124	.06654	.00048	.CC887	.00005	.C0008	.C0915	.CC907	.00011	.00000	.02554	.00000	.00073	.01246	0
1	242852	2122	.00874	.00034	.0C364	.00003	.00012	.00161	.00061	.00008	.C0000	.C0000	.00000	.00035	.00196	1
5	287932	988	.00343	.CCC37	.0C161	.00001	.00021	.00022	.CC011	.00013	.C00C0	.C0000	.00000	.00012	.00066	5
10	272161	760	.00279	.00074	.00087	.00003	.00024	.00012	.C0005	.00017	.00000	.C0000	.00000	.00008	.00050	10
15	253503	1088	.00429	.00215	.CC065	.00005	.00035	.00016	.00002	.00020	.00003	.C0000	.00000	.00015	.00053	15
20	231557	1124	.00485	.00273	.0CC49	.00007	.00035	.00015	.CC0C5	.00019	.00023	.C0000	.00000	.00015	.00044	20
25	206447	1148	.00556	.C0317	.00035	.00015	.00045	.00018	.C0007	.00023	.00036	.C0000	.00000	.00016	.00046	25
30	189292	1078	.00569	.00268	.00032	.00026	.00060	.00024	.00011	.00033	.00048	.C0000	.00000	.00013	.00055	30
35	166336	1038	.00624	.00246	.00031	.00051	.00078	.00034	.C0013	.00041	.00047	.C0000	.00000	.00013	.00070	35
40	146893	1011	.00688	.00221	.CC040	.0C092	.00092	.00051	.00010	.00048	.00023	.C0000	.00000	.00016	.00095	40
45	152591	1225	.008C3	.00155	.00043	.00142	.00131	.C0069	.C0010	.00062	.00010	.C0000	.00000	.00018	.00122	45
50	141315	1321	.0C935	.00163	.C0036	.00215	.00191	.00078	.00012	.00086	.00000	.C0000	.00000	.00022	.00132	50
55	120053	1582	.01318	.00146	.00036	.003C6	.00322	.00131	.00017	.00108	.00000	.C0000	.00000	.00025	.00227	55
60	105610	2087	.01976	.00153	.00045	.00384	.00516	.00253	.00027	.00108	.00000	.C0000	.00000	.00034	.00455	60
65	92806	2558	.02799	.0C161	.CC050	.00572	.00822	.00343	.00044	.00163	.00000	.C0000	.00000	.00027	.00618	65
70	72091	3726	.05168	.00115	.00047	.00547	.01194	.00444	.00026	.00089	.00000	.00000	.00000	.00051	.02655	70
75	53066	4084	.07696	.00107	.CC055	.00660	.01869	.00703	.00047	.00134	.C00C0	.00000	.00000	.00066	.04055	75
80	28974	3670	.12667	.0CC97	.00066	.00756	.02834	.01149	.00117	.00193	.00000	.00000	.00000	.00097	.07358	80
85+	14916	3485	.23364	.00060	.00094	.00791	.04264	.02085	.C0208	.00261	.00000	.C0000	.00000	.00161	.15440	85+
ALL	2840376	38259														

CRUDE DEATH RATE			.01347	.00165	.001C6	.00115	.00221	.00128	.00038	.00046	.00012	.00056	.00000	.00022	.00439	
STANDARDIZED RATE (1)			.01002	.00158	.00132	.00065	.00113	.00101	.00048	.C0034	.00013	.00090	.00000	.00020	.00230	
STANDARDIZED RATE (2)			.01332	.00168	.00101	.00119	.00222	.00126	.00037	.00047	.0C013	.00053	.00000	.00022	.00423	
GEOMETRIC MEAN			.01441													

LIFE TABLE FOR ALL CAUSES COMBINED

Age (x)	Midyear Population	Deaths During Year	$_nM_x$	$_nq_x$	l_x	$_nd_x$	$_nL_x$	$_nm_x$	$_na_x$	T_x	$_nr_x$	$\overset{\circ}{e}_x$	Age (x)
0	61981	4124	.066537	.063110	1C0000	6311	94845	.066540	.183112	5949010	.000000	59.490	0
1	242852	2122	.008738	.034198	93689	3204	366746	.008736	1.500000	5854166	.000000	62.485	1
5	287932	988	.003431	.017CC8	90485	1539	448578	.003431	2.500000	5487420	.000000	60.645	5
10	272161	760	.002792	.013814	88946	1234	441713	.002794	2.555038	5038842	.006910	56.651	10
15	253503	1088	.004292	.021263	87712	1865	434070	.004297	2.592270	4597129	.010238	52.412	15
20	231557	1124	.004854	.023996	85847	2060	424175	.004856	2.543892	4163060	.014503	48.494	20
25	206447	1148	.005561	.027439	83787	2299	413235	.005563	2.520752	3738884	.014759	44.624	25
30	189292	1078	.005699	.028090	81488	2289	401746	.005698	2.512469	3325649	.014349	40.812	30
35	166336	1038	.006240	.030758	79199	2436	389969	.006247	2.526427	2923903	.020715	36.918	35
40	146893	1011	.006883	.033844	76763	2598	377421	.006884	2.538732	2533934	.007858	33.010	40
45	152591	1225	.008028	.039358	74165	2919	363665	.008027	2.547248	2156513	-.004455	29.077	45
50	141315	1321	.009348	.045757	71246	3260	348379	.009358	2.591705	1792848	.009166	25.164	50
55	120053	1582	.013178	.064043	67986	4354	329618	.013209	2.631632	1444469	.015777	21.247	55
60	105610	2087	.019761	.094465	63632	6011	303804	.019786	2.611740	1114850	.007849	17.520	60
65	92806	2558	.027994	.131515	57621	7578	270305	.028035	2.651150	811046	.007899	14.076	65
70	72091	3726	.051685	.229982	50043	11509	222461	.051735	2.588481	540741	.004405	10.806	70
75	53066	4084	.076961	.323507	38534	12466	161714	.077087	2.516762	318280	.008839	8.260	75
80	28974	3670	.126665	.479975	26068	12512	98546	.126967	2.458889	156566	.008839	6.006	80
85+	14916	3485	.233642	1.C00000	13556	13556	58020	.233642	4.280057	58020	.000000	4.280	85+

NUMBER OF PERSONS DYING (OUT OF 100,000 AT BIRTH) ABOVE AGE X FROM SPECIFIED CAUSES

Age (x)	All Causes	Respira- tory T. B.	Other Infec. and Paras.	Neo- plasms	Cardio- vascular	Infl., Pneu., Bronch.	Diar- rheal	Certain Degener- ative	Maternal	Cert. Dis. of Infancy	Motor Vehicle	Other Violence	Other and Unknown	Age (x)
0	100000	10157	5298	9283	18594	9364	2053	3317	761	2422	0	1456	37295	0
1	93689	10111	4456	9278	18586	8497	1193	3306	761	0	0	1387	36114	1
5	90485	9987	3120	9266	18544	7905	971	3277	761	0	0	1258	35396	5
10	88946	9822	2399	9260	18450	7807	922	3221	761	0	0	1204	35100	10
15	87712	9495	2017	9248	18345	7753	901	3145	761	0	0	1170	34877	15
20	85847	8561	1736	9228	18192	7683	890	3058	747	0	0	1103	34649	20
25	83787	7400	1530	9197	18042	7621	868	2979	650	0	0	1041	34459	25
30	81488	6091	1384	9134	17858	7546	840	2885	501	0	0	977	34272	30
35	79199	5014	1254	9030	17615	7449	798	2753	310	0	0	926	34050	35
40	76763	4056	1135	8832	17310	7315	748	2591	125	0	0	874	33777	40
45	74165	3224	983	8484	16963	7122	712	2408	38	0	0	812	33419	45
50	71246	2513	828	7968	16486	6872	674	2184	0	0	0	746	32975	50
55	67986	1947	702	7217	15820	6600	632	1883	0	0	0	669	32516	55
60	63632	1466	584	6208	14754	6167	575	1526	0	0	0	587	31765	60
65	57621	1000	449	5039	13183	5398	491	1198	0	0	0	483	30380	65
70	50043	567	315	3491	10999	4471	372	758	0	0	0	410	28700	70
75	38534	311	210	2275	8299	3483	313	561	0	0	0	296	22786	75
80	26068	137	122	1208	5271	2344	237	344	0	0	0	189	16216	80
85+	13556	35	54	459	2474	1210	121	152	0	0	0	93	8958	85+

NUMBER OF PERSONS SURVIVING TO AGE X IF SPECIFIED CAUSES WERE ELIMINATED

Age (x)	No Causes	Respira- tory T. B.	Other Infec. and Paras.	Neo- plasms	Cardio- vascular	Infl., Pneu., Bronch.	Diar- rheal	Certain Degener- ative	Maternal	Cert. Dis. of Infancy	Motor Vehicle	Other Violence	Other and Unknown	(1) + (2)	(1) + (2) + (5) + (6) + (8)	(1)+(2)+ (5)+(6)+ (8)+part of(9)&(12)	(10) + (11)	Age (x)
		(1)	(2)	(3)	(4)	(5)	(6)	(7)	(8)	(9)	(10)	(11)	(12)					
0	100000	100000	100000	100000	100000	100000	100000	100000	100000	100000	100000	100000	100000	100000	100000	100000	100000	0
1	93689	93734	94507	93694	93697	94532	94525	93700	93689	96012	93689	93756	94839	94552	96254	99776	93756	1
5	90485	90650	92609	90501	90534	91888	91513	90524	90485	92777	90485	90676	92313	92778	95287	99481	90676	5
10	88946	89272	91769	88568	89087	90424	90005	89040	88946	91199	88946	89188	91043	92105	94751	99193	89188	10
15	87712	88360	90888	87746	87956	89224	88778	87880	87712	89934	87712	87984	90006	91560	94269	98882	87984	15
20	85847	87418	89244	85900	86237	87397	86501	86098	85861	88022	85847	86180	88234	90876	93669	98459	86180	20
25	83787	86496	87314	83869	84317	85362	84838	84110	83897	85910	83787	84174	86358	90137	93105	98048	84174	25
30	81488	85466	85068	81630	82186	83055	82538	81895	81742	83552	81488	81927	84218	89221	92440	97526	81927	30
35	79199	84186	82812	79440	80120	80859	80262	79726	79635	81205	79199	79677	82079	88026	91578	96815	79677	35
40	76763	82604	80388	77193	77960	78507	77843	77434	77369	78708	76763	77277	79833	86505	90422	95817	77277	40
45	74165	80693	77824	74925	75669	76044	75244	74995	74836	76044	74165	74723	77498	84674	88879	94442	74723	45
50	71246	78278	74920	72490	73170	73303	72320	72266	71928	73051	71246	71848	74904	82315	86792	92495	71848	50
55	67986	75305	71621	69923	70493	70223	69053	69258	68637	69708	67986	68636	71950	79332	84025	89759	68636	55
60	63632	70998	67155	66456	67057	66160	64687	65175	64241	65244	63632	64320	68116	74929	79955	85707	64320	60
65	57621	64787	60946	61351	62319	60676	58657	59338	58173	59081	57621	58344	63109	68526	74160	80068	58344	65
70	50043	56718	53063	54833	56407	53610	51055	51956	50522	51311	50043	50740	56569	60141	66361	72268	50740	70
75	38534	43925	40556	43393	46133	42215	39365	40183	38903	39510	38534	39172	49851	46685	52748	59425	39172	75
80	26068	29875	27782	30345	34314	29596	26695	27369	26318	26728	26068	26588	41449	31839	37372	44337	26588	80
85+	13556	15619	14499	16410	20653	16330	13966	14376	13686	13899	13556	13896	31497	16705	20931	27513	13896	85+

ADDED YRS OF LIFE																		
TOTAL		3.727	2.633	1.500	2.719	2.037	.866	.752	.293	1.503	.000	.427	7.614	6.560	10.307	15.618	.427	
WORK	6.835	2.587	.446	.526	.759	.338	.080	.360	.246	.000	.000	.159	.735	3.068	3.807	4.319	.159	

POPULATION, DEATHS, DEATH RATES FOR ALL CAUSES COMBINED, AND SPECIFIED CAUSES

Age Start of Interval	Midyear Population	Deaths During Year	All Causes	Respiratory T. B.	Other Infec. and Paras.	Neo-plasms	Cardio-vascular	Infl., Pneu., Bronch.	Diar-rheal	Certain Degen-erative	Maternal	Cert. Dis. of Infancy	Motor Vehicle	Other Violence	Other and Unknown	Age Start of Interval
0	62364	5055	.08106	.00055	.00895	.00003	.00006	.01371	.00770	.00006	.00000	.03547	.00000	.00075	.01377	0
1	225024	1822	.00810	.00029	.00313	.00006	.00010	.00159	.00026	.00013	.00000	.00000	.00000	.00064	.00190	1
5	291257	973	.00334	.00016	.00160	.00002	.00021	.00034	.00004	.00010	.00000	.00000	.00000	.00039	.00047	5
10	301015	773	.00257	.00023	.00087	.00005	.00017	.00023	.00002	.00017	.00000	.00000	.00000	.00038	.00045	10
15	282358	1201	.00425	.00125	.00069	.00005	.00025	.00072	.00003	.00018	.00000	.00000	.00000	.00055	.00054	15
20	255987	1591	.00622	.00228	.00065	.00005	.00023	.00131	.00004	.00024	.00000	.00000	.00000	.00086	.00055	20
25	222425	1600	.00719	.00273	.00056	.00009	.00029	.00158	.00005	.00028	.00000	.00000	.00000	.00102	.00059	25
30	199773	1199	.00600	.00191	.00047	.00016	.00038	.00122	.00006	.00026	.00000	.00000	.00000	.00093	.00062	30
35	179938	1087	.00604	.00158	.00044	.00032	.00052	.00111	.00005	.00034	.00000	.00000	.00000	.00096	.00072	35
40	165855	1096	.00661	.00136	.00055	.00053	.00060	.00106	.00004	.00055	.00000	.00000	.00000	.00101	.00092	40
45	143657	1187	.00826	.00125	.00058	.00109	.00111	.00109	.00004	.00079	.00000	.00000	.00000	.00108	.00123	45
50	119951	1324	.01104	.00145	.00052	.00203	.00196	.00118	.00007	.00110	.00000	.00000	.00000	.00120	.00153	50
55	118480	1828	.01543	.00151	.00051	.00323	.00356	.00154	.00010	.00140	.00000	.00000	.00000	.00126	.00230	55
60	102998	2338	.02270	.00146	.00055	.00490	.00637	.00237	.00016	.00154	.00000	.00000	.00000	.00136	.00399	60
65	81723	2601	.03183	.00154	.00060	.00731	.01013	.00322	.00026	.00231	.00000	.00000	.00000	.00105	.00541	65
70	61975	3589	.05791	.00106	.00050	.00686	.01778	.00379	.00013	.00158	.00000	.00000	.00000	.00113	.02507	70
75	42230	3632	.08601	.00097	.00059	.00829	.02782	.00604	.00021	.00237	.00000	.00000	.00000	.00142	.03829	75
80	22129	3069	.13869	.00086	.00068	.00949	.04216	.00585	.00054	.00343	.00000	.00000	.00000	.00212	.06955	80
85+	11062	2742	.24788	.00054	.00099	.00994	.06346	.01781	.00099	.00470	.00000	.00000	.00000	.00353	.14590	85+
ALL	2890201	38707														

	All Causes	Respiratory T. B.	Other Infec. and Paras.	Neo-plasms	Cardio-vascular	Infl., Pneu., Bronch.	Diar-rheal	Certain Degen-erative	Maternal	Cert. Dis. of Infancy	Motor Vehicle	Other Violence	Other and Unknown
CRUDE DEATH RATE	.01339	.00124	.00108	.00112	.00236	.00165	.00025	.00055	.00000	.00077	.00000	.00084	.00353
STANDARDIZED RATE (1)	.01109	.00115	.00134	.00069	.00127	.00160	.00035	.00040	.00000	.00125	.00000	.00077	.00227
STANDARDIZED RATE (2)	.01473	.00126	.00106	.00133	.00280	.00174	.00025	.00061	.00000	.00073	.00000	.00088	.00406
GEOMETRIC MEAN	.01558												

LIFE TABLE FOR ALL CAUSES COMBINED

Age (x)	Midyear Population	Deaths During Year	$_nM_x$	$_nq_x$	l_x	$_nd_x$	$_nL_x$	$_nm_x$	$_na_x$	T_x	$_nr_x$	$\overset{\circ}{e}_x$	Age (x)
0	62364	5055	.081056	.076170	100000	7617	93966	.081061	.207796	5751483	.000000	57.515	0
1	225024	1822	.008097	.031737	92383	2932	362202	.008095	1.500000	5657517	.000000	61.240	1
5	291257	973	.003341	.016568	89451	1482	443550	.003341	2.500000	5295315	.000000	59.198	5
10	301015	773	.002568	.012754	87969	1122	437113	.002567	2.564988	4851765	-.001912	55.153	10
15	282358	1201	.004253	.021095	86847	1832	429964	.004261	2.668873	4414652	.007662	50.833	15
20	255987	1591	.006215	.030665	85015	2607	418782	.006225	2.586226	3984688	.015308	46.870	20
25	222425	1600	.007193	.035324	82408	2911	404709	.007193	2.481464	3565906	.017868	43.271	25
30	199773	1199	.006002	.025536	79497	2348	391487	.005998	2.445432	3161197	.016031	39.765	30
35	179938	1087	.006041	.029761	77149	2296	380023	.006042	2.507985	2769710	.013220	35.901	35
40	165855	1096	.006608	.032544	74853	2436	368309	.006614	2.555162	2389687	.013131	31.925	40
45	143657	1187	.008263	.040612	72417	2941	355005	.008284	2.592514	2021378	.023799	27.913	45
50	119951	1324	.011038	.053860	69476	3742	338431	.011057	2.608621	1666373	.013782	23.985	50
55	118480	1828	.015429	.074421	65734	4892	317027	.015431	2.619924	1327941	.000096	20.202	55
60	102998	2338	.022699	.107787	60842	6558	288474	.022733	2.600482	1010915	.010507	16.615	60
65	81723	2601	.031827	.148386	54284	8055	252366	.031918	2.634518	722441	.015828	13.309	65
70	61975	3589	.057910	.254364	46229	11759	202615	.058036	2.573738	470075	.009405	10.168	70
75	42230	3632	.086005	.354424	34470	12217	141733	.086197	2.493895	267460	.012061	7.759	75
80	22129	3069	.138687	.512335	22253	11401	81947	.139126	2.428497	125727	.012061	5.650	80
85+	11062	2742	.247876	1.000000	10852	10852	43780	.247876	4.034282	43780	.000000	4.034	85+

NUMBER OF PERSONS DYING (OUT OF 100,000 AT BIRTH) ABOVE AGE X FROM SPECIFIED CAUSES

Age (x)	All Causes	Respiratory T. B.	Other Infec. and Paras.	Neoplasms	Cardiovascular	Infl., Pneu., Bronch.	Diarrheal	Certain Degenerative	Maternal	Cert. Dis. of Infancy	Motor Vehicle	Other Violence	Other and Unknown	Age (x)
0	100000	7454	5555	9673	21500	10895	1272	4173	0	3333	0	5357	30788	0
1	92383	7403	4714	9670	21494	9607	549	4167	0	0	0	5287	29492	1
5	89451	7297	3581	9647	21459	9032	454	4121	0	0	0	5055	28805	5
10	87969	7224	2871	9638	21366	8880	435	4076	0	0	0	4880	28599	10
15	86847	7122	2492	9616	21290	8778	428	4002	0	0	0	4714	28405	15
20	85015	6585	2194	9593	21183	8468	416	3926	0	0	0	4478	28172	20
25	82408	5627	1923	9570	21085	7919	398	3825	0	0	0	4119	27942	25
30	79497	4523	1695	9532	20967	7280	378	3712	0	0	0	3707	27703	30
35	77149	3776	1511	9469	20818	6805	356	3610	0	0	0	3343	27461	35
40	74853	3177	1344	9346	20621	6383	337	3479	0	0	0	2980	27186	40
45	72417	2675	1142	9150	20401	5994	324	3276	0	0	0	2609	26846	45
50	69476	2233	937	8759	20003	5608	309	2993	0	0	0	2225	26409	50
55	65734	1742	762	8072	19338	5207	287	2620	0	0	0	1819	25887	55
60	60842	1263	599	7047	18208	4718	254	2176	0	0	0	1420	25157	60
65	54284	843	439	5630	16367	4033	210	1730	0	0	0	1028	24004	65
70	46229	454	288	3785	13802	3220	145	1146	0	0	0	763	22626	70
75	34470	238	187	2395	10192	2451	119	826	0	0	0	534	17528	75
80	22253	101	103	1219	6239	1593	88	490	0	0	0	332	12088	80
85+	10852	24	44	435	2778	780	44	206	0	0	0	154	6387	85+

NUMBER OF PERSONS SURVIVING TO AGE X IF SPECIFIED CAUSES WERE ELIMINATED

Age (x)	No Causes	Respiratory T. B.	Other Infec. and Paras.	Neoplasms	Cardiovascular	Infl., Pneu., Bronch.	Diarrheal	Certain Degenerative	Maternal	Cert. Dis. of Infancy	Motor Vehicle	Other Violence	Other and Unknown	(1) + (2)	(1) + (2) + (5) + (6) + (8)	(1)+(2)+(5)+(6)+(8)+part of(9)&(12)	(10) + (11)	Age (x)
		(1)	(2)	(3)	(4)	(5)	(6)	(7)	(8)	(9)	(10)	(11)	(12)					
0	100000	100000	100000	100000	100000	100000	100000	100000	100000	100000	100000	100000	100000	100000	100000	100000	100000	0
1	92383	92432	93195	92386	92389	93629	93080	92389	92383	95642	92383	92450	93637	93244	95215	99775	92450	1
5	89451	89603	91369	89476	89491	91233	90220	89502	89451	92606	89451	89745	91353	91524	94150	99294	89745	5
10	87969	88191	90577	88003	88101	89875	88745	88064	87969	91072	87969	88432	90048	90805	93591	98877	88432	10
15	86847	87168	89810	86902	87053	88832	87620	87014	86847	89911	86847	87470	89057	90142	93023	98415	87470	15
20	85015	85864	88221	85092	85322	87273	85784	85254	85015	88014	85015	85861	87454	89102	92295	97837	85861	20
25	82408	84190	85793	82505	82803	85153	83171	82739	82408	85315	82408	83586	85006	87647	91406	97095	83586	25
30	79497	82331	82995	79628	79995	82756	80253	79928	79497	82301	79497	81044	82245	85954	90372	96209	81044	30
35	77149	80664	80733	77339	77780	80840	77904	77669	77149	75870	77149	79017	80063	84412	89316	95285	79017	35
40	74853	78883	78503	75159	75661	78871	75605	75487	74853	77493	74853	77033	77962	82729	88045	94131	77033	40
45	72417	76837	76157	72907	73418	76708	73157	73232	72417	74572	72417	74902	75774	80805	86468	92671	74902	45
50	69476	74177	73275	70333	70833	73994	70201	70539	69476	71927	69476	72250	73146	78233	84190	90462	72250	50
55	65734	70693	69508	67225	67681	71425	66442	67109	65734	68053	65734	68770	69743	74752	80948	87206	68770	55
60	60842	65928	64501	63239	63775	65690	61529	62552	60842	62988	60842	64054	65303	69893	76314	82479	64054	60
65	54284	59252	57708	57831	58755	59311	54939	56244	54284	56199	54284	57539	59445	62990	69654	75647	57539	65
70	46229	50850	49292	51088	52663	51333	46847	48456	46229	47860	46229	49259	52053	54219	61010	66651	49259	70
75	34470	38116	36846	39423	42969	39014	34953	36616	34470	35686	34470	36938	44112	40743	46761	52185	36938	75
80	22253	24726	23858	26536	31958	25973	22590	23793	22253	23038	22253	24018	34616	26509	31409	36192	24018	80
85+	10852	12117	11678	13596	19381	13332	11047	11813	10852	11235	10852	11845	24174	13039	16306	20001	11845	85+

ADDED YRS OF LIFE																		
TOTAL		2.519	2.593	1.401	2.817	3.162	.585	.831	.000	2.022	.000	1.629	5.750	5.256	9.506	14.590	1.629	
WORK	7.486	1.844	.576	.418	.593	1.181	.046	.388	.000	.000	.000	.902	.777	2.453	3.780	4.279	.902	

POPULATION, DEATHS, DEATH RATES FOR ALL CAUSES COMBINED, AND SPECIFIED CAUSES

Age Start of Interval	Midyear Population	Deaths During Year	All Causes	Respiratory T. B.	Other Infec. and Paras.	Neoplasms	Cardiovascular	Infl., Pneu., Bronch.	Diarrheal	Certain Degenerative	Maternal	Cert. Dis. of Infancy	Motor Vehicle	Other Violence	Other and Unknown	Age Start of Interval
0	59315	3726	.06282	.00029	.00831	.00007	.00002	.01125	.00551	.00005	.00000	.02630	.00000	.00069	.01033	0
1	216138	1661	.00768	.00023	.00334	.00004	.00009	.00167	.00031	.00011	.00000	.00000	.00000	.00031	.00159	1
5	280778	940	.00335	.00026	.00170	.00000	.00022	.00038	.00007	.00013	.00000	.00000	.00000	.00010	.00050	5
10	288980	753	.00261	.00061	.00076	.00002	.00024	.00028	.00004	.00016	.00000	.00000	.00000	.00007	.00043	10
15	273557	1162	.00425	.00196	.00074	.00007	.00027	.00043	.00004	.00016	.00007	.00000	.00000	.00010	.00041	15
20	250979	1215	.00484	.00224	.00057	.00010	.00022	.00069	.00006	.00016	.00025	.00000	.00000	.00014	.00043	20
25	229051	1270	.00554	.00254	.00047	.00018	.00027	.00086	.00007	.00019	.00035	.00000	.00000	.00016	.00045	25
30	212402	1185	.00558	.00215	.00043	.00026	.00044	.00093	.00007	.00027	.00039	.00000	.00000	.00016	.00049	30
35	190891	1148	.00601	.00195	.00038	.00054	.00063	.00095	.00008	.00035	.00035	.00000	.00000	.00016	.00060	35
40	175232	1107	.00632	.00167	.00033	.00112	.00080	.00074	.00007	.00045	.00021	.00000	.00000	.00016	.00076	40
45	153359	1161	.00757	.00144	.00031	.00177	.00129	.00076	.00009	.00058	.00010	.00000	.00000	.00018	.00104	45
50	134183	1262	.00941	.00130	.00039	.00247	.00190	.00056	.00012	.00074	.00000	.00000	.00000	.00022	.00130	50
55	136770	1775	.01298	.00121	.00040	.00335	.00336	.00135	.00014	.00094	.00000	.00000	.00000	.00027	.00196	55
60	121916	2350	.01928	.00124	.00036	.00422	.00617	.00220	.00014	.00115	.00000	.00000	.00000	.00038	.00342	60
65	97438	2696	.02767	.00131	.00040	.00628	.00981	.00299	.00023	.00172	.00000	.00000	.00000	.00029	.00464	65
70	76257	4018	.05269	.00105	.00037	.00640	.01570	.00368	.00014	.00105	.00000	.00000	.00000	.00066	.02364	70
75	54568	4269	.07823	.00095	.00044	.00773	.02454	.00585	.00026	.00156	.00000	.00000	.00000	.00081	.03610	75
80	30725	3890	.12661	.00085	.00052	.00885	.03717	.00957	.00065	.00225	.00000	.00000	.00000	.00120	.06555	80
85+	16844	3833	.22756	.00053	.00071	.00926	.05598	.01734	.00119	.00309	.00000	.00000	.00000	.00196	.13750	85+
ALL	2995383	39421														

	All Causes	Respiratory T. B.	Other Infec. and Paras.	Neoplasms	Cardiovascular	Infl., Pneu., Bronch.	Diarrheal	Certain Degenerative	Maternal	Cert. Dis. of Infancy	Motor Vehicle	Other Violence	Other and Unknown
CRUDE DEATH RATE	.01314	.00137	.00097	.00133	.00265	.00146	.00022	.00045	.00012	.00052	.00000	.00023	.00382
STANDARDIZED RATE (1)	.00966	.00127	.00128	.00075	.00123	.00132	.00030	.00032	.00012	.00093	.00000	.00020	.00196
STANDARDIZED RATE (2)	.01304	.00136	.00099	.00136	.00261	.00147	.00023	.00046	.00012	.00054	.00000	.00023	.00367
GEOMETRIC MEAN	.01401												

LIFE TABLE FOR ALL CAUSES COMBINED

Age (x)	Midyear Population	Deaths During Year	$_nM_x$	$_nq_x$	l_x	$_nd_x$	$_nL_x$	$_nm_x$	$_na_x$	T_x	$_nr_x$	$\overset{\circ}{e}_x$	Age (x)
0	59315	3726	.062817	.059730	100000	5973	95083	.062819	.176789	6021088	.000000	60.211	0
1	216138	1661	.007685	.030162	94027	2836	369018	.007685	1.500000	5926005	.000000	63.025	1
5	280778	940	.003348	.016603	91191	1514	452170	.003348	2.500000	5556987	.000000	60.938	5
10	288980	753	.002606	.012935	89677	1160	445558	.002603	2.562680	5104817	-.002206	56.924	10
15	273557	1162	.004248	.021047	88517	1863	438118	.004252	2.602210	4659259	-.006662	52.637	15
20	250979	1215	.004841	.023934	86654	2074	428179	.004844	2.545303	4221141	-.011732	48.713	20
25	229051	1270	.005545	.027359	84580	2314	417154	.005547	2.517016	3792962	-.011198	44.845	25
30	212402	1185	.005579	.027508	82266	2263	405684	.005578	2.505247	3375808	-.012126	41.035	30
35	190891	1148	.006014	.029636	80003	2371	394120	.006016	2.513532	2970124	-.012938	37.125	35
40	175232	1107	.006317	.031134	77632	2417	382207	.006324	2.536978	2576004	-.013536	33.182	40
45	153359	1161	.007570	.037227	75215	2800	369266	.007583	2.568155	2193797	-.020441	29.167	45
50	134183	1262	.009405	.046026	72415	3333	354065	.009414	2.596635	1824531	-.007827	25.195	50
55	136770	1775	.012978	.062911	69082	4346	335095	.012969	2.626553	1470467	-.004257	21.286	55
60	121916	2350	.019276	.092267	64736	5973	309438	.019303	2.615551	1135372	-.009457	17.538	60
65	97438	2696	.027669	.130337	58763	7659	275916	.027758	2.663016	825934	-.016277	14.055	65
70	76257	4018	.052690	.234150	51104	11966	226682	.052788	2.590029	550018	-.007809	10.763	70
75	54568	4269	.078233	.327814	39138	12830	163750	.078351	2.510506	323336	-.008455	8.261	75
80	30725	3890	.126607	.479436	26308	12613	99404	.126887	2.452133	159586	-.008455	6.066	80
85+	16844	3833	.227559	1.000000	13695	13695	60182	.227559	4.394469	60182	.000000	4.394	85+

NUMBER OF PERSONS DYING (OUT OF 100,000 AT BIRTH) ABOVE AGE X FROM SPECIFIED CAUSES

Age (x)	All Causes	Respiratory T.B.	Other Infec. and Paras.	Neoplasms	Cardio-vascular	Infl., Pneu., Bronch.	Diarrheal	Certain Degenerative	Maternal	Cert. Dis. of Infancy	Motor Vehicle	Other Violence	Other and Unknown	Age (x)
0	100000	8308	5208	10785	22864	10231	1289	3341	706	2501	0	1566	33201	0
1	94027	8281	4417	10778	22862	9162	765	3336	706	0	0	1500	32220	1
5	91191	8197	3185	10763	22830	8545	649	3297	706	0	0	1386	31633	5
10	89677	8081	2418	10763	22730	8373	616	3237	706	0	0	1342	31411	10
15	88517	7812	2079	10755	22622	8250	598	3165	706	0	0	1311	31219	15
20	86654	6952	1755	10726	22503	8062	579	3094	676	0	0	1266	31041	20
25	84580	5995	1511	10682	22410	7766	555	3026	570	0	0	1208	30857	25
30	82266	4936	1315	10605	22297	7409	527	2946	422	0	0	1141	30668	30
35	80003	4064	1139	10500	22119	7033	499	2837	266	0	0	1078	30468	35
40	77632	3297	989	10284	21870	6659	468	2698	119	0	0	1014	30234	40
45	75215	2660	862	9855	21562	6376	439	2528	39	0	0	953	29941	45
50	72415	2129	747	9201	21084	6094	406	2313	1	0	0	885	29555	50
55	69082	1667	609	8326	20410	5753	363	2052	1	0	0	806	29095	55
60	64736	1263	475	7205	19286	5300	317	1736	1	0	0	716	28437	60
65	58763	880	363	5896	17374	4619	274	1380	1	0	0	599	27377	65
70	51104	517	252	4161	14659	3794	211	904	1	0	0	519	26086	70
75	39138	280	169	2710	11095	2958	179	667	1	0	0	370	20709	75
80	26308	124	97	1442	7071	1999	136	411	1	0	0	238	14789	80
85+	13695	32	43	557	3369	1043	71	186	0	0	0	118	8276	85+

NUMBER OF PERSONS SURVIVING TO AGE X IF SPECIFIED CAUSES WERE ELIMINATED

Age (x)	No Causes	Respiratory T.B. (1)	Other Infec. and Paras. (2)	Neoplasms (3)	Cardio-vascular (4)	Infl., Pneu., Bronch. (5)	Diarrheal (6)	Certain Degenerative (7)	Maternal (8)	Cert. Dis. of Infancy (9)	Motor Vehicle (10)	Other Violence (11)	Other and Unknown (12)	(1)+(2)+(5)+(6)+(8)	(1)+(2)+(5)+(6)+(8)+part of(9)&(12)	(10)+(11)	Age (x)
0	100000	100000	100000	100000	100000	100000	100000	100000	100000	100000	100000	100000	100000	100000	100000	100000	0
1	94027	94053	94797	94034	94029	95069	94536	94032	94027	96483	94027	94091	94983	94823	96394	99802	1
5	91191	91299	93169	91212	91224	92818	91800	91234	91191	93573	91191	91365	92704	93280	95578	99531	5
10	89677	89898	92403	89658	89809	91451	90309	89779	89677	92020	89677	89892	91389	92631	95129	99268	10
15	88517	89004	91555	88546	88755	90393	89159	88689	88517	90829	88517	88760	90401	92059	94691	98976	15
20	86654	87991	89960	86711	87005	88680	87301	86893	86684	88918	86654	86937	88679	91348	94215	98647	20
25	84580	86850	88057	84679	85015	86858	85235	84881	84714	86790	84580	84914	86742	90421	93724	98315	25
30	82266	85553	85850	82438	82801	84844	82931	82638	82543	84415	82266	82657	84561	89280	93135	97883	30
35	80003	84098	83669	80275	80700	82893	80678	80473	80427	82093	80003	80446	82437	87953	92385	97282	35
40	77632	82404	81344	78110	78557	80819	78318	78226	78189	79660	77632	78125	80232	86344	91333	96371	40
45	75215	80506	78943	76104	76419	78593	75908	75959	75833	77180	75215	75753	78033	84496	89837	94991	45
50	72415	78068	76122	73924	74052	75557	73115	73345	73048	74307	72415	73000	75522	82065	87671	92901	50
55	69082	74962	72761	71399	71321	72811	69792	70227	69686	70887	69082	69718	72516	78954	84806	90065	55
60	64736	70671	68320	68038	67568	68694	65449	66121	65302	66427	64736	65420	66627	74583	80711	85954	60
65	58763	64549	62128	63084	63641	63048	59449	60367	59277	60298	58763	59496	63374	68245	74724	79918	65
70	51104	56506	54139	56618	58152	55659	51760	52954	51551	52439	51104	51817	56445	59862	66612	71604	70
75	39138	43501	41539	44773	48213	43425	39668	40766	39480	40160	39138	39816	48763	46169	52374	57534	75
80	26308	29380	27984	31291	36706	30070	26700	27620	26538	26995	26308	26873	35383	31251	36569	41507	80
85+	13695	15367	14608	17093	23143	16447	13946	14546	13815	14053	13695	14076	28720	16392	20223	24484	85+

ADDED YRS OF LIFE

	No Causes	(1)	(2)	(3)	(4)	(5)	(6)	(7)	(8)	(9)	(10)	(11)	(12)	(1)+(2)+(5)+(6)+(8)	(1)+(2)+(5)+(6)+(8)+part of(9)&(12)	(10)+(11)
TOTAL		3.023	2.622	1.755	3.160	2.769	.548	.715	.277	1.569	.000	.420	6.145	5.805	9.926	14.392	.420
WORK	6.694	2.107	.512	.617	.654	.796	.070	.314	.232	.000	.000	.156	.644	2.651	3.851	4.303	.156

POPULATION, DEATHS, DEATH RATES FOR ALL CAUSES COMBINED, AND SPECIFIED CAUSES

Age Start of Interval	Midyear Population	Deaths During Year	All Causes	Respiratory T. B.	Other Infec. and Paras.	Neoplasms	Cardiovascular	Infl., Pneu., Bronch.	Diarrheal	Certain Degenerative	Maternal	Cert. Dis. of Infancy	Motor Vehicle	Other Violence	Other and Unknown	Age Start of Interval
0	45922	2975	.06478	.00024	.00473	.00002	.00009	.01067	.00514	.00007	.00000	.03262	.00000	.00052	.01069	0
1	185025	746	.00403	.00011	.00105	.00005	.00008	.00075	.00021	.00005	.00000	.00000	.00000	.00053	.00121	1
5	266882	513	.00192	.00005	.00054	.00005	.00015	.00014	.00001	.00006	.00000	.00000	.00000	.00042	.00045	5
10	277916	434	.00156	.00017	.00041	.00004	.00015	.00010	.00001	.00008	.00000	.00000	.00000	.00034	.00025	10
15	284603	857	.00301	.00103	.00048	.00009	.00020	.00016	.00003	.00009	.00000	.00000	.00000	.00056	.00036	15
20	280662	1106	.00394	.00192	.00051	.00007	.00021	.00022	.00002	.00011	.00000	.00000	.00000	.00085	.00044	20
25	250761	1023	.00408	.00168	.00048	.00009	.00021	.00016	.00003	.00019	.00000	.00000	.00000	.00083	.00041	25
30	227759	969	.00425	.00144	.00048	.00017	.00033	.00022	.00003	.00027	.00000	.00000	.00000	.00086	.00046	30
35	204042	938	.00460	.00120	.00039	.00034	.00052	.00033	.00002	.00027	.00000	.00000	.00000	.00087	.00065	35
40	186615	1091	.00585	.00116	.00051	.00070	.00079	.00043	.00004	.00053	.00000	.00000	.00000	.00088	.00079	40
45	168558	1235	.00733	.00102	.00052	.00105	.00125	.00054	.00005	.00081	.00000	.00000	.00000	.00104	.00105	45
50	153428	1543	.01006	.00093	.00068	.00185	.00214	.00071	.00008	.00095	.00000	.00000	.00000	.00122	.00151	50
55	130101	1816	.01396	.00105	.00071	.00291	.00370	.00108	.00011	.00115	.00000	.00000	.00000	.00119	.00206	55
60	103538	2662	.02571	.00132	.00085	.00559	.00894	.00176	.00009	.00171	.00000	.00000	.00000	.00143	.00402	60
65	95175	2795	.02937	.00110	.00074	.00660	.01128	.00189	.00011	.00204	.00000	.00000	.00000	.00128	.00433	65
70	73434	4189	.05704	.00076	.00059	.00869	.02229	.00276	.00012	.00147	.00000	.00000	.00000	.00140	.01896	70
75	47224	3981	.08430	.00070	.00070	.01050	.03486	.00438	.00021	.00222	.00000	.00000	.00000	.00178	.02895	75
80	25016	3312	.13240	.00064	.00084	.01203	.05281	.00716	.00052	.00320	.00000	.00000	.00000	.00264	.05257	80
85+	11865	2689	.22663	.00042	.00110	.01264	.07956	.01298	.00093	.00438	.00000	.00000	.00000	.00430	.11032	85+
ALL	3018526	34874														

	All Causes	Respiratory T. B.	Other Infec. and Paras.	Neoplasms	Cardiovascular	Infl., Pneu., Bronch.	Diarrheal	Certain Degenerative	Maternal	Cert. Dis. of Infancy	Motor Vehicle	Other Violence	Other and Unknown
CRUDE DEATH RATE	.01155	.00094	.00063	.00132	.00304	.00082	.00014	.00050	.00000	.00050	.00000	.00085	.00282
STANDARDIZED RATE (1)	.00879	.00081	.00073	.00074	.00149	.00083	.00024	.00033	.00000	.00115	.00000	.00073	.00176
STANDARDIZED RATE (2)	.01274	.00090	.00067	.00145	.00338	.00094	.00017	.00053	.00000	.00068	.00000	.00086	.00316
GEOMETRIC MEAN	.01228												

LIFE TABLE FOR ALL CAUSES COMBINED

Age (x)	Midyear Population	Deaths During Year	$_nM_x$	$_nq_x$	l_x	$_nd_x$	$_nL_x$	$_nm_x$	$_na_x$	T_x	$_nr_x$	$\overset{\circ}{e}_x$	Age (x)
0	45922	2975	.064784	.061520	100000	6152	94956	.064788	.180132	6213870	.000000	62.139	0
1	185025	746	.004032	.015962	93848	1498	371647	.004031	1.500000	6118914	.000000	65.200	1
5	266882	513	.001922	.009572	92350	884	459540	.001924	2.500000	5747267	.000000	62.234	5
10	277916	434	.001562	.007773	91466	711	455651	.001560	2.638010	5287727	-.006766	57.811	10
15	284603	857	.003011	.014930	90755	1355	450603	.003007	2.658979	4832076	-.006509	53.243	15
20	280662	1106	.003941	.019519	89400	1745	442724	.003942	2.549666	4381473	.003828	49.010	20
25	250761	1023	.004080	.020204	87655	1771	433861	.004082	2.507411	3938749	.013801	44.935	25
30	227759	969	.004254	.021052	85884	1808	424930	.004255	2.516362	3504888	.015902	40.810	30
35	204042	938	.004557	.022753	84076	1913	415715	.004602	2.561422	3079959	.015597	36.633	35
40	186615	1091	.005846	.028869	82163	2372	405086	.005856	2.584581	2664244	.014068	32.426	40
45	168558	1235	.007327	.036044	79791	2876	392059	.007336	2.602283	2259158	.012287	28.313	45
50	153428	1543	.010057	.049197	76915	3784	375550	.010076	2.615068	1867099	.012991	24.275	50
55	130101	1816	.013958	.067906	73131	4966	354174	.014021	2.688071	1491548	.023562	20.396	55
60	103538	2662	.025710	.121279	68165	8267	320836	.025767	2.582028	1137374	.013351	16.686	60
65	95175	2795	.029367	.137250	59898	8221	279920	.029369	2.619486	816539	.000659	13.632	65
70	73434	4189	.057044	.251214	51677	12982	227030	.057182	2.584717	536619	.009986	10.384	70
75	47224	3981	.084300	.348882	38695	13500	159621	.084575	2.492284	309589	.017833	8.001	75
80	25016	3312	.132395	.495416	25195	12482	93873	.132966	2.428163	149968	.017833	5.952	80
85+	11865	2689	.226633	1.000000	12713	12713	56095	.226633	4.412421	56095	.000000	4.412	85+

NUMBER OF PERSONS DYING (OUT OF 100,000 AT BIRTH) ABOVE AGE X FROM SPECIFIED CAUSES

Age (x)	All Causes	Respiratory T. B.	Other Infec. and Paras.	Neoplasms	Cardiovascular	Infl., Pneu., Bronch.	Diarrheal	Certain Degenerative	Maternal	Cert. Dis. of Infancy	Motor Vehicle	Other Violence	Other and Unknown	Age (x)
0	100000	5855	4077	11967	29878	6729	959	4149	0	3058	0	5871	27417	0
1	93848	5832	3628	11965	29870	5716	471	4143	0	0	0	5821	26402	1
5	92350	5792	3239	11945	29839	5439	393	4124	0	0	0	5624	25955	5
10	91466	5751	2989	11921	29770	5375	386	4095	0	0	0	5433	25746	10
15	90755	5674	2800	11901	29700	5331	379	4061	0	0	0	5277	25632	15
20	89400	5210	2583	11861	29608	5258	367	4018	0	0	0	5026	25469	20
25	87655	4534	2359	11831	29517	5162	357	3969	0	0	0	4650	25276	25
30	85884	3804	2152	11793	29427	5093	345	3886	0	0	0	4290	25094	30
35	84076	3195	1947	11720	29284	5001	332	3770	0	0	0	3927	24900	35
40	82163	2696	1786	11577	29066	4864	324	3656	0	0	0	3564	24630	40
45	79791	2228	1577	11292	28744	4690	306	3440	0	0	0	3206	24308	45
50	76915	1828	1375	10879	28252	4478	288	3123	0	0	0	2796	23896	50
55	73131	1480	1117	10182	27446	4211	258	2768	0	0	0	2338	23331	55
60	68165	1109	867	9145	26124	3828	220	2359	0	0	0	1916	22597	60
65	59898	685	594	7346	23247	3263	192	1809	0	0	0	1457	21305	65
70	51677	376	388	5499	20087	2734	163	1239	0	0	0	1098	20093	70
75	38695	203	255	3524	15014	2105	135	905	0	0	0	779	15775	75
80	25195	91	143	1845	9431	1403	101	549	0	0	0	495	11137	80
85+	12713	24	61	709	4463	728	52	246	0	0	0	241	6189	85+

NUMBER OF PERSONS SURVIVING TO AGE X IF SPECIFIED CAUSES WERE ELIMINATED

Age (x)	No Causes	Respiratory T. B.	Other Infec. and Paras.	Neoplasms	Cardiovascular	Infl., Pneu., Bronch.	Diarrheal	Certain Degenerative	Maternal	Cert. Dis. of Infancy	Motor Vehicle	Other Violence	Other and Unknown	(1) + (2)	(1) + (2) + (5) + (6) + (8)	(1)+(2)+(5)+(6)+(8)+part of(9)&(12)	(10) + (11)	Age (x)
		(1)	(2)	(3)	(4)	(5)	(6)	(7)	(8)	(9)	(10)	(11)	(12)					
0	100000	100000	100000	100000	100000	100000	100000	100000	100000	100000	100000	100000	100000	100000	100000	100000	100000	0
1	93848	93870	94284	93850	93856	94834	94322	93854	93848	96897	93848	93896	94836	94306	95779	99795	93896	1
5	92350	92412	93167	92372	92388	93599	92894	92375	92350	95351	92350	92593	93772	93230	95047	99388	92593	5
10	91466	91568	92527	91511	91573	92767	92012	91519	91466	94438	91466	91898	93086	92630	94508	98945	91898	10
15	90755	90933	91998	90820	90931	92091	91304	90842	90755	93704	90755	91340	92478	92179	94101	98584	91340	15
20	89400	90038	90843	89504	89665	90789	89952	89528	89400	92305	89400	90227	91262	91492	93487	98055	90227	20
25	87655	88957	89296	87786	88005	89114	88207	87829	87655	90503	87655	88843	89676	90622	92710	97378	88843	25
30	85884	87896	87701	86051	86316	87383	86436	86137	85884	88674	85884	87409	88048	89755	91909	96666	87409	30
35	84076	86665	86062	84312	84642	85636	84630	84439	84076	86808	84076	85936	86392	88711	90952	95784	85936	35
40	82163	85202	84266	82535	82933	83825	82712	82631	82163	84833	82163	84438	84701	87384	89748	94666	84438	40
45	79791	83222	82045	80435	80860	81581	80342	80460	79791	82383	79791	82276	82583	85573	88097	93081	82276	45
50	76915	80632	79292	77946	78437	78853	77464	77874	76915	79414	76915	79726	80027	83124	85827	90844	79726	50
55	73131	77022	75651	74804	75384	75241	73683	74394	73131	75507	73131	76267	76665	79675	82593	87605	76267	55
60	68165	72169	70763	70156	71596	70513	68716	69745	68165	70380	68165	71513	72206	74919	78127	83080	71513	60
65	59898	63837	62446	63949	65812	62511	60408	61815	59898	61844	59898	63292	64743	66553	70048	74768	63292	65
70	51677	55379	54074	57028	60096	54445	52144	53877	51677	53356	51677	54956	57099	57948	61603	65974	54956	70
75	38695	41624	40608	44610	50387	41341	39069	40639	38695	39952	38695	41441	47095	43682	47121	51008	41441	75
80	25195	27197	26534	30625	39180	27526	25466	26762	25195	26014	25195	27227	35545	28643	31630	34792	27227	80
85+	12713	13774	13449	16445	25955	14413	12885	13730	12713	13126	12713	13931	23522	14571	16742	19003	13931	85+

ADDED YRS OF LIFE																		
TOTAL		1.956	1.570	1.704	4.116	1.684	.437	.768	.000	2.013	.000	1.706	4.689	3.597	5.907	9.894	1.706	
WORK	5.754	1.382	.525	.458	.657	.320	.035	.334	.000	.000	.000	.887	.669	1.930	2.309	2.644	.887	

POPULATION, DEATHS, DEATH RATES FOR ALL CAUSES COMBINED, AND SPECIFIED CAUSES

Age Start of Interval	Midyear Population	Deaths During Year	All Causes	Respiratory T.B.	Other Infec. and Paras.	Neoplasms	Cardiovascular	Infl., Pneu., Bronch.	Diarrheal	Certain Degenerative	Maternal	Cert. Dis. of Infancy	Motor Vehicle	Other Violence	Other and Unknown	Age Start of Interval
0	44254	2152	.04863	.00020	.00434	.00005	.00002	.00766	.00314	.00005	.00000	.02633	.00000	.00059	.00626	0
1	178437	699	.00392	.00011	.00115	.00003	.00006	.00077	.00020	.00011	.00000	.00000	.00000	.00033	.00115	1
5	256881	428	.00167	.00007	.00062	.00002	.00014	.00014	.00010	.00007	.00000	.00000	.00000	.00015	.00035	5
10	267213	410	.00153	.00032	.00037	.00003	.00012	.00010	.00005	.00005	.00000	.00000	.00000	.00012	.00033	10
15	273510	874	.00320	.00163	.00049	.00006	.00019	.00016	.00003	.00011	.00008	.00000	.00000	.00012	.00033	15
20	274833	1058	.00385	.00211	.00051	.00008	.00019	.00013	.00002	.00011	.00019	.00000	.00000	.00016	.00034	20
25	255245	1000	.00392	.00205	.00041	.00012	.00025	.00016	.00004	.00012	.00026	.00000	.00000	.00015	.00036	25
30	235130	953	.00405	.00161	.00038	.00026	.00039	.00018	.00006	.00023	.00039	.00000	.00000	.00015	.00036	30
35	216425	966	.00446	.00139	.00037	.00055	.00061	.00024	.00004	.00025	.00028	.00000	.00000	.00010	.00046	35
40	201226	1014	.00504	.00108	.00046	.00091	.00087	.00029	.00003	.00031	.00016	.00000	.00000	.00013	.00061	40
45	179765	1173	.00653	.00095	.00046	.00170	.00116	.00045	.00007	.00047	.00002	.00000	.00000	.00022	.00103	45
50	162971	1530	.00939	.00098	.00045	.00281	.00215	.00049	.00004	.00076	.00001	.00000	.00000	.00020	.00150	50
55	139616	1680	.01203	.00084	.00057	.00317	.00352	.00074	.00012	.00096	.00000	.00000	.00000	.00027	.00186	55
60	118038	2339	.01982	.00120	.00053	.00448	.00714	.00141	.00014	.00132	.00000	.00000	.00000	.00030	.00328	60
65	112803	3251	.02882	.00126	.00059	.00667	.01137	.00192	.00024	.00199	.00000	.00000	.00000	.00035	.00444	65
70	89621	4821	.05379	.00086	.00051	.00722	.02129	.00285	.00008	.00133	.00000	.00000	.00000	.00114	.01852	70
75	58657	4680	.07979	.00078	.00060	.00875	.03331	.00450	.00015	.00199	.00000	.00000	.00000	.00143	.02827	75
80	32612	4105	.12587	.00071	.00071	.01000	.05044	.00736	.00037	.00285	.00000	.00000	.00000	.00212	.02827	80
85+	17412	3783	.21726	.00046	.00098	.01051	.07598	.01338	.00069	.00396	.00000	.00000	.00000	.00356	.10774	85+
ALL	3114649	36916														
CRUDE DEATH RATE			.01185	.00111	.00057	.00148	.00342	.00079	.00012	.00046	.00011	.00037	.00000	.00028	.00314	
STANDARDIZED RATE (1)			.00777	.00097	.00069	.00077	.00141	.00068	.00019	.00028	.00010	.00093	.00000	.00022	.00153	
STANDARDIZED RATE (2)			.01159	.00105	.00061	.00143	.00321	.00082	.00015	.00045	.00010	.00054	.00000	.00027	.00296	
GEOMETRIC MEAN			.01133													

LIFE TABLE FOR ALL CAUSES COMBINED

Age (x)	Midyear Population	Deaths During Year	$_nM_x$	$_nq_x$	l_x	$_nd_x$	$_nL_x$	$_nm_x$	$_na_x$	T_x	$_nr_x$	$\overset{\circ}{e}_x$	Age (x)
0	44254	2152	.048628	.046700	100000	4670	96043	.048624	.152668	6418081	.000000	64.181	0
1	178437	699	.003917	.015525	95330	1480	377620	.003919	1.500000	6322038	.000000	66.317	1
5	256881	428	.001666	.008300	93850	779	467303	.001667	2.500000	5944418	.000000	63.340	5
10	267213	410	.001534	.007639	93071	711	463720	.001533	2.700422	5477115	-.006409	58.849	10
15	273510	874	.003195	.015840	92360	1463	458355	.003192	2.645534	5013395	-.007187	54.281	15
20	274833	1058	.003850	.019066	90897	1733	450208	.003852	2.532098	4555040	-.000754	50.112	20
25	255245	1000	.003918	.019402	89164	1730	441499	.003918	2.502529	4104832	.008546	46.037	25
30	235130	953	.004053	.020061	87434	1754	432819	.004053	2.519361	3663332	.011812	41.898	30
35	216425	966	.004463	.022094	85680	1893	423737	.004467	2.536648	3230513	.010896	37.704	35
40	201226	1014	.005039	.024908	83787	2087	413871	.005034	2.573571	2806776	.012627	33.499	40
45	179765	1173	.006525	.032191	81700	2630	402248	.006538	2.622703	2392905	.013868	29.289	45
50	162971	1530	.009388	.045985	79070	3636	386634	.009404	2.602963	1990658	.014357	25.176	50
55	139616	1680	.012033	.058687	75434	4427	366747	.012071	2.645556	1604023	.020771	21.264	55
60	118038	2339	.019816	.094765	71007	6729	339096	.019844	2.631335	1237276	.007772	17.425	60
65	112803	3251	.028820	.134867	64278	8669	301077	.028793	2.656881	898180	-.004350	13.973	65
70	89621	4821	.053793	.238397	55609	13257	246039	.053882	2.585709	597103	-.007282	10.738	70
75	58657	4680	.079786	.333467	42352	14123	176499	.080018	2.503260	351064	.015777	8.289	75
80	32612	4105	.125874	.477452	28229	13478	106671	.126351	2.442205	174565	.015777	6.184	80
85+	17412	3783	.217264	1.000000	14751	14751	67894	.217264	4.602656	67894	.000000	4.603	85+

NUMBER OF PERSONS DYING (OUT OF 100,000 AT BIRTH) ABOVE AGE X FROM SPECIFIED CAUSES

Age (x)	All Causes	Respiratory T.B.	Other Infec. and Paras.	Neoplasms	Cardiovascular	Infl., Pneu., Bronch.	Diarrheal	Certain Degenerative	Maternal	Cert. Dis. of Infancy	Motor Vehicle	Other Violence	Other and Unknown	Age (x)
0	100000	6879	3761	12456	31367	6539	887	3746	598	2528	0	2142	29097	0
1	95330	6659	3344	12452	31365	5804	585	3741	598	0	0	2086	28496	1
5	93850	6819	2908	12439	31342	5514	509	3699	598	0	0	1961	28061	5
10	93071	6786	2617	12430	31274	5450	461	3665	598	0	0	1892	27898	10
15	92360	6640	2443	12416	31217	5403	437	3625	598	0	0	1835	27746	15
20	90897	5895	2217	12388	31132	5328	425	3576	563	0	0	1778	27595	20
25	89164	4945	1986	12353	31047	5269	417	3525	476	0	0	1704	27442	25
30	87434	4043	1806	12301	30936	5199	398	3472	360	0	0	1638	27281	30
35	85680	3348	1642	12187	30766	5120	374	3372	192	0	0	1594	27085	35
40	83787	2761	1487	11953	30505	5018	358	3264	75	0	0	1537	26829	40
45	81700	2315	1296	11576	30143	4897	344	3137	10	0	0	1475	26507	45
50	79070	1935	1110	10889	29674	4717	315	2948	3	0	0	1386	26093	50
55	75434	1558	937	9800	28841	4527	298	2653	1	0	0	1308	25511	55
60	71007	1250	729	8637	27544	4253	253	2301	1	0	0	1210	24829	60
65	64278	842	551	7116	25118	3772	205	1852	1	0	0	1107	23714	65
70	55609	463	375	5109	21697	3194	132	1254	1	0	0	1003	22381	70
75	42352	252	249	3332	16449	2492	113	927	1	0	0	722	17815	75
80	28229	113	143	1786	10552	1696	86	574	1	0	0	469	12809	80
85+	14751	31	66	714	5159	909	47	269	0	0	0	242	7314	85+

NUMBER OF PERSONS SURVIVING TO AGE X IF SPECIFIED CAUSES WERE ELIMINATED

Age (x)	No Causes	Respiratory T.B.	Other Infec. and Paras.	Neoplasms	Cardiovascular	Infl., Pneu., Bronch.	Diarrheal	Certain Degenerative	Maternal	Cert. Dis. of Infancy	Motor Vehicle	Other Violence	Other and Unknown	(1)+(2)	(1)+(2)+(5)+(6)+(8)	(1)+(2)+(5)+(6)+(8)+part of(9)&(12)	(10)+(11)	Age (x)
		(1)	(2)	(3)	(4)	(5)	(6)	(7)	(8)	(9)	(10)	(11)	(12)					
0	100000	100000	100000	100000	100000	100000	100000	100000	100000	100000	100000	100000	100000	100000	100000	100000	100000	0
1	95330	95350	95334	95738	95232	96050	95625	95335	95330	97830	95330	95385	95919	95758	96780	99792	95385	1
5	93850	93909	94687	93867	93875	94849	94216	93896	93850	96311	93850	94028	94865	94747	96129	99489	94028	5
10	93071	93162	94194	93097	93163	94127	93482	93151	93071	95512	93071	93316	94242	94286	95777	99247	93316	10
15	92360	92596	93650	92399	92508	93455	92792	92479	92360	94782	92360	92660	93675	93890	95447	99019	92660	15
20	90897	91874	92394	90963	91128	92050	91334	91063	90932	93281	90897	91249	92343	93387	95063	98755	91249	20
25	89164	91078	90865	89264	89475	90354	89601	89377	89284	91503	89164	89583	90737	92816	94643	98461	89583	25
30	87434	90228	89284	87584	87849	88671	87881	87696	87667	89727	87434	87911	89139	92137	94169	98115	87911	30
35	85680	89130	87659	85940	86256	86972	86142	86036	86075	87927	85680	86191	87548	91189	93493	97570	86191	35
40	83787	87767	85879	84274	84611	85153	84255	84243	84290	85585	83787	84344	85673	89958	92487	96694	84344	40
45	81700	86043	83934	82550	82865	83153	82170	82270	82255	83843	81700	82304	84061	88395	91100	95420	82304	45
50	79070	83667	81420	80579	80667	80657	79554	79810	79614	81144	79070	79743	81775	86153	89028	93420	79743	50
55	75434	80210	77850	77965	77793	77137	75912	76431	75955	77412	75434	76153	78605	82778	85772	90172	76153	55
60	71007	75820	73489	74564	74538	74239	71501	72292	71497	72869	71007	71780	74684	78471	81664	86031	71780	60
65	64278	69050	66700	69033	69943	66447	64771	65877	64722	65964	64278	65076	68731	71651	75153	79432	65076	65
70	55609	60114	57873	61753	64071	58042	56104	57562	55993	57067	55609	56398	60814	62562	66335	70370	56398	70
75	42352	45978	44189	48765	54352	44846	42745	44131	42644	43463	42352	43202	50892	47973	51623	55393	43202	75
80	28229	30767	29543	33967	42915	30583	28513	29714	28424	28969	28229	29004	39178	32199	35478	38717	29004	80
85+	14751	16141	15495	18690	29075	16598	14928	15757	14854	15138	14751	15323	26674	16955	19441	21920	15323	85+

ADDED YRS OF LIFE

	No Causes	(1)	(2)	(3)	(4)	(5)	(6)	(7)	(8)	(9)	(10)	(11)	(12)	(1)+(2)	(1)+(2)+(5)+(6)+(8)	+part	(10)+(11)
TOTAL		2.480	1.554	1.968	4.376	1.477	.375	.694	.243	1.680	.000	.507	4.758	4.115	6.425	9.925	.507
WORK	5.444	1.733	.480	.620	.670	.252	.043	.260	.196	.000	.000	.160	.625	2.237	2.765	3.136	.160

POPULATION, DEATHS, DEATH RATES FOR ALL CAUSES COMBINED, AND SPECIFIED CAUSES

Age Start of Interval	Midyear Population	Deaths During Year	All Causes	Respiratory T. B.	Other Infec. and Paras.	Neoplasms	Cardiovascular	Infl., Pneu., Bronch.	Diarrheal	Certain Degenerative	Maternal	Cert. Dis. of Infancy	Motor Vehicle	Other Violence	Other and Unknown	Age Start of Interval
0	47274	2174	.04599	.00023	.00332	.00013	.00004	.00965	.00137	.00006	.00000	.02340	.00000	.00076	.00702	0
1	179597	446	.00248	.00008	.00062	.00009	.00004	.00051	.00011	.00004	.00000	.00000	.00000	.00053	.00046	1
5	208550	240	.00115	.00003	.00029	.00009	.00005	.00009	.00002	.00003	.00000	.00000	.00000	.00037	.00019	5
10	226705	189	.00083	.00004	.00013	.00006	.00009	.00001	.00001	.00003	.00000	.00000	.00000	.00024	.00022	10
15	264118	529	.00200	.00053	.00028	.00009	.00014	.00008	.00002	.00008	.00000	.00000	.00000	.00048	.00031	15
20	273081	800	.00293	.00084	.00031	.00010	.00016	.00010	.00000	.00009	.00000	.00000	.00000	.00106	.00025	20
25	276117	789	.00286	.00085	.00029	.00008	.00018	.00011	.00001	.00010	.00000	.00000	.00000	.00092	.00026	25
30	274412	733	.00267	.00077	.00022	.00017	.00023	.00012	.00001	.00012	.00000	.00000	.00000	.00075	.00029	30
35	247262	819	.00331	.00071	.00027	.00022	.00049	.00013	.00000	.00025	.00000	.00000	.00000	.00093	.00032	35
40	222761	983	.00441	.00080	.00027	.00053	.00088	.00017	.00003	.00031	.00000	.00000	.00000	.00096	.00046	40
45	196971	1258	.00639	.00077	.00026	.00107	.00162	.00025	.00003	.00052	.00000	.00000	.00000	.00122	.00063	45
50	176334	1674	.00949	.00074	.00035	.00182	.00305	.00044	.00002	.00073	.00000	.00000	.00000	.00124	.00111	50
55	154474	2150	.01392	.00074	.00046	.00330	.00478	.00056	.00003	.00098	.00000	.00000	.00000	.00133	.00174	55
60	134011	2988	.02230	.00090	.00058	.00481	.00969	.00108	.00004	.00127	.00000	.00000	.00000	.00113	.00280	60
65	105331	3442	.03268	.00095	.00064	.00716	.01543	.00147	.00007	.00191	.00000	.00000	.00000	.00127	.00379	65
70	73400	4656	.06343	.00084	.00049	.00974	.02920	.00354	.00005	.00147	.00000	.00000	.00000	.00155	.01654	70
75	53866	5062	.09397	.00078	.00056	.01179	.04567	.00563	.00009	.00221	.00000	.00000	.00000	.00199	.02527	75
80	28853	4194	.14536	.00069	.00066	.01348	.06918	.00918	.00021	.00315	.00000	.00000	.00000	.00295	.04585	80
85+	12733	3085	.24228	.00047	.00094	.01414	.10422	.01665	.00039	.00440	.00000	.00000	.00000	.00487	.09621	85+
ALL	3155850	36211														

CRUDE DEATH RATE			.01147	.00062	.00038	.00150	.00412	.00073	.00005	.00044	.00000	.00035	.00000	.00092	.00237	
STANDARDIZED RATE (1)			.00733	.00048	.00043	.00077	.00181	.00066	.00008	.00025	.00000	.00082	.00000	.00075	.00127	
STANDARDIZED RATE (2)			.01199	.00057	.00041	.00152	.00429	.00081	.00006	.00043	.00000	.00048	.00000	.00089	.00253	
GEOMETRIC MEAN			.00997													

LIFE TABLE FOR ALL CAUSES COMBINED

Age (x)	Midyear Population	Deaths During Year	$_nM_x$	$_nq_x$	l_x	$_nd_x$	$_nL_x$	$_nm_x$	$_na_x$	T_x	$_nr_x$	$\overset{\circ}{e}_x$	Age (x)
0	47274	2174	.045987	.044250	100000	4425	96231	.045983	.148178	6529242	.000000	65.292	0
1	179597	446	.002483	.009877	95575	944	379940	.002485	1.500000	6433012	.000000	67.309	1
5	208550	240	.001151	.005759	94631	545	471793	.001155	2.500000	6053072	.000000	63.965	5
10	226705	189	.000834	.004135	94086	389	469538	.000828	2.706191	5581279	-.019095	59.321	10
15	264118	529	.002003	.009926	93697	930	466360	.001994	2.714830	5111742	-.022571	54.556	15
20	273081	800	.002930	.014531	92767	1348	460541	.002927	2.556720	4645382	-.011136	50.076	20
25	276117	789	.002857	.014187	91419	1297	453821	.002858	2.475585	4184840	-.006866	45.776	25
30	274412	733	.002671	.013271	90122	1196	447655	.002672	2.528916	3731019	.003028	41.400	30
35	247262	819	.003312	.016452	88926	1463	441122	.003313	2.602387	3283365	.013934	36.922	35
40	222761	983	.004413	.021895	87463	1915	432785	.004425	2.634356	2842243	.017364	32.497	40
45	196971	1258	.006387	.031538	85548	2698	421399	.006402	2.649880	2409458	.017230	28.165	45
50	176334	1674	.009493	.046542	82850	3856	405160	.009517	2.642527	1988058	.015584	23.996	50
55	154474	2150	.013918	.067549	78994	5336	382455	.013952	2.654610	1582899	.013323	20.038	55
60	134011	2988	.022297	.106112	73658	7816	349730	.022349	2.625331	1200444	.013344	16.298	60
65	105331	3442	.032678	.152456	65842	10038	305689	.032837	2.656800	850714	.024054	12.921	65
70	73400	4656	.063433	.275446	55804	15371	241699	.063596	2.571956	545025	.010558	9.767	70
75	53866	5062	.093974	.379566	40433	15347	163351	.093951	2.470896	303327	-.001503	7.502	75
80	28853	4194	.145358	.527266	25086	13227	91029	.145305	2.399156	139976	-.001503	5.580	80
85+	12733	3085	.242284	1.000000	11859	11859	48947	.242284	4.127391	48947	.000000	4.127	85+

NUMBER OF PERSONS DYING (OUT OF 100,000 AT BIRTH) ABOVE AGE X FROM SPECIFIED CAUSES

Age (x)	All Causes	Respiratory T.B.	Other Infec. and Paras.	Neoplasms	Cardio-vascular	Infl., Pneu., Bronch.	Diarrheal	Certain Degenerative	Maternal	Cert. Dis. of Infancy	Motor Vehicle	Other Violence	Other and Unknown	Age (x)
0	100000	4049	2634	13218	38833	6243	349	3615	0	2251	0	6374	22434	0
1	95575	4026	2314	13205	38829	5315	217	3609	0	0	0	6300	21760	1
5	94631	3994	2077	13171	38814	5123	175	3594	0	0	0	6099	21584	5
10	94086	3979	1943	13128	38791	5082	166	3578	0	0	0	5924	21495	10
15	93697	3959	1881	13101	38748	5078	162	3564	0	0	0	5811	21393	15
20	92767	3715	1751	13059	38681	5041	153	3527	0	0	0	5590	21250	20
25	91419	3328	1608	13014	38605	4994	151	3484	0	0	0	5102	21133	25
30	90122	2941	1476	12953	38525	4943	148	3440	0	0	0	4682	21014	30
35	88926	2599	1380	12874	38423	4889	143	3386	0	0	0	4348	20884	35
40	87463	2285	1260	12778	38207	4833	141	3277	0	0	0	3939	20743	40
45	85548	1939	1144	12547	37824	4759	127	3141	0	0	0	3523	20544	45
50	82850	1614	1032	12094	37137	4652	117	2920	0	0	0	3009	20275	50
55	78994	1313	892	11354	35896	4472	110	2625	0	0	0	2506	19826	55
60	73658	1028	716	10088	34060	4259	100	2251	0	0	0	1998	19158	60
65	65842	715	512	8401	30660	3880	87	1806	0	0	0	1604	18177	65
70	55804	424	318	6206	25920	3427	67	1222	0	0	0	1215	17005	70
75	40433	220	199	3848	18844	2568	53	866	0	0	0	839	12996	75
80	25086	93	108	1923	11386	1650	38	506	0	0	0	514	8868	80
85+	11859	23	46	692	5101	815	19	215	0	0	0	238	4710	85+

NUMBER OF PERSONS SURVIVING TO AGE X IF SPECIFIED CAUSES WERE ELIMINATED

Age (x)	No Causes	Respiratory T.B. (1)	Other Infec. and Paras. (2)	Neoplasms (3)	Cardio-vascular (4)	Infl., Pneu., Bronch. (5)	Diarrheal (6)	Certain Degenerative (7)	Maternal (8)	Cert. Dis. of Infancy (9)	Motor Vehicle (10)	Other Violence (11)	Other and Unknown (12)	(1)+(2)	(1)+(2)+(5)+(6)+(8)	(1)+(2)+(5)+(6)+(8)+part of(9)&(12)	(10)+(11)	Age (x)
0	100000	100000	100000	100000	100000	100000	100000	100000	100000	100000	100000	100000	100000	100000	100000	100000	100000	0
1	95575	95597	95888	95588	95579	96486	95704	95581	95575	97801	95575	95647	96236	95911	96956	99708	95647	1
5	94631	94685	95178	94677	94650	95727	94801	94652	94631	96835	94631	94903	95462	95233	96508	99367	94903	5
10	94086	94155	94764	94175	94128	95217	94264	94123	94086	96277	94086	94532	95002	94834	96155	99044	94532	10
15	93697	93785	94435	93813	93781	94627	93878	93747	93697	95879	93697	94254	94712	94524	95849	98763	94254	15
20	92767	93098	93628	92923	92917	93923	92955	92854	92767	94928	92767	93540	93916	93962	95326	98304	93540	20
25	91419	92132	92411	91618	91643	92605	91606	91547	91419	93548	91419	92671	92669	93131	94533	97545	92671	25
30	90122	91212	91232	90379	90422	91343	90310	90292	90122	92221	90122	91780	91474	92336	93782	96832	91780	30
35	88926	90346	90118	89258	89324	90185	89116	89148	88926	90997	88926	90900	90391	91558	93053	96144	90900	35
40	87463	89177	88756	87885	88070	88758	87652	87789	87463	89500	87463	89820	89046	90496	92034	95147	89820	40
45	85548	87574	86929	86191	86524	86889	85747	86002	85548	87540	85548	88277	87297	88988	90593	93727	88277	45
50	82850	85140	84300	83923	84482	84255	83052	83509	82850	84780	82850	86016	84815	86629	88314	91436	86016	50
55	78994	81479	80516	80753	81796	80513	79194	79913	78994	80834	78994	82523	81317	83048	84859	87549	82523	55
60	73658	76259	75250	76558	78131	75284	73854	74881	73658	75374	73658	77462	76491	77907	79839	82852	77462	60
65	65842	68473	67462	70111	73337	67663	66030	67364	65842	67375	65842	69633	69344	70157	72303	75172	69633	65
70	55804	58311	57358	61604	67205	57777	55981	57643	55804	57104	55804	59394	59930	59935	62252	64858	59394	70
75	40433	42427	41661	46881	56479	42625	40573	42073	40433	41375	40433	43372	47250	43716	46246	48612	43372	75
80	25086	26426	25921	30865	44199	27213	25185	26397	25086	25670	25086	27182	33341	27305	29736	31673	27182	80
85+	11859	12542	12297	15645	29829	13487	11919	12686	11859	12135	11859	13052	19947	13005	14865	16244	13052	85+

ADDED YRS OF LIFE

	No Causes	(1)	(2)	(3)	(4)	(5)	(6)	(7)	(8)	(9)	(10)	(11)	(12)	(1)+(2)	+(5)+(6)+(8)	part(9)&(12)	(10)+(11)
TOTAL		1.217	.970	1.818	5.451	1.349	.152	.598	.000	1.517	.000	1.844	3.171	2.214	3.796	6.305	1.844
WORK	4.523	.812	.311	.467	.762	.168	.015	.240	.000	.000	.000	.975	.457	1.131	1.321	1.486	.975

POPULATION, DEATHS, DEATH RATES FOR ALL CAUSES COMBINED, AND SPECIFIED CAUSES

Age Start of Interval	Midyear Population	Deaths During Year	All Causes	Respiratory T.B.	Other Infec. and Paras.	Neoplasms	Cardiovascular	Infl., Pneu., Bronch.	Diarrheal	Certain Degenerative	Maternal	Cert. Dis. of Infancy	Motor Vehicle	Other Violence	Other and Unknown	Age Start of Interval
0	45108	1584	.03512	.00011	.00224	.00002	.00002	.00743	.00086	.00002	.00000	.01869	.00000	.00047	.00525	0
1	172677	327	.00189	.00005	.00049	.00008	.00005	.00048	.00003	.00003	.00000	.00000	.00000	.00030	.00039	1
5	200183	203	.00101	.00005	.00029	.00005	.00007	.00010	.00002	.00008	.00000	.00000	.00000	.00014	.00019	5
10	219547	188	.00086	.00014	.00024	.00007	.00007	.00005	.00001	.00004	.00000	.00000	.00000	.00008	.00016	10
15	255213	402	.00158	.00062	.00029	.00005	.00011	.00004	.00001	.00007	.00005	.00000	.00000	.00010	.00023	15
20	264610	510	.00193	.00090	.00023	.00008	.00012	.00005	.00001	.00007	.00013	.00000	.00000	.00011	.00022	20
25	268300	582	.00217	.00055	.00023	.00015	.00016	.00006	.00003	.00014	.00016	.00000	.00000	.00010	.00020	25
30	269416	669	.00248	.00091	.00018	.00029	.00032	.00008	.00001	.00011	.00018	.00000	.00000	.00013	.00028	30
35	250350	720	.00288	.00072	.00018	.00052	.00054	.00012	.00000	.00016	.00018	.00000	.00000	.00016	.00030	35
40	229275	828	.00361	.00058	.00023	.00055	.00076	.00013	.00013	.00024	.00009	.00000	.00000	.00014	.00048	40
45	208272	1091	.00524	.00053	.00022	.00163	.00122	.00019	.00002	.00036	.00001	.00000	.00000	.00025	.00081	45
50	190057	1454	.00765	.00051	.00018	.00238	.00265	.00037	.00003	.00042	.00000	.00000	.00000	.00018	.00092	50
55	165985	1837	.01107	.00048	.00033	.00319	.00422	.00063	.00002	.00052	.00000	.00000	.00000	.00026	.00142	55
60	144700	2708	.01871	.00062	.00043	.00431	.00832	.00122	.00003	.00097	.00000	.00000	.00000	.00041	.00241	60
65	115937	3211	.02770	.00066	.00047	.00643	.01325	.00165	.00004	.00146	.00000	.00000	.00000	.00047	.00327	65
70	86459	5131	.05935	.00066	.00049	.00785	.02821	.00401	.00005	.00138	.00000	.00000	.00000	.00160	.01511	70
75	66958	5918	.08838	.00063	.00055	.00951	.04413	.00635	.00007	.00208	.00000	.00000	.00000	.00200	.02306	75
80	37086	5096	.13741	.00057	.00067	.01089	.06684	.01041	.00019	.00299	.00000	.00000	.00000	.00297	.04188	80
85+	17777	4078	.22940	.00039	.00090	.01142	.10069	.01884	.00034	.00411	.00000	.00000	.00000	.00489	.08781	85+
ALL	3207910	36537														

	All Causes	Respiratory T.B.	Other Infec. and Paras.	Neoplasms	Cardiovascular	Infl., Pneu., Bronch.	Diarrheal	Certain Degenerative	Maternal	Cert. Dis. of Infancy	Motor Vehicle	Other Violence	Other and Unknown
CRUDE DEATH RATE	.01139	.00057	.00032	.00161	.00449	.00082	.00004	.00038	.00006	.00026	.00000	.00032	.00252
STANDARDIZED RATE (1)	.00613	.00047	.00036	.00077	.00166	.00059	.00005	.00020	.00006	.00066	.00000	.00021	.00110
STANDARDIZED RATE (2)	.01050	.00052	.00034	.00145	.00399	.00081	.00004	.00034	.00006	.00039	.00000	.00030	.00226
GEOMETRIC MEAN	.00842												

LIFE TABLE FOR ALL CAUSES COMBINED

Age (x)	Midyear Population	Deaths During Year	$_nM_x$	$_nq_x$	l_x	$_nd_x$	$_nL_x$	$_nm_x$	$_na_x$	T_x	$_nr_x$	$\overset{\circ}{e}_x$	Age (x)
0	45108	1584	.035116	.034070	100000	3407	97035	.035111	.129697	6799216	.000000	67.992	0
1	172677	327	.001894	.007547	96593	729	384550	.001896	1.500000	6702181	.000000	69.386	1
5	200183	203	.001014	.005070	95864	486	478105	.001017	2.500000	6317631	.000000	65.902	5
10	219547	188	.000856	.004257	95378	406	475929	.000853	2.631876	5839526	-.019697	61.225	10
15	255213	402	.001575	.007823	94972	743	473106	.001570	2.639356	5363598	-.022391	56.476	15
20	264610	510	.001927	.009583	94229	903	468942	.001926	2.560908	4890492	-.010855	51.900	20
25	268300	582	.002169	.010790	93326	1007	464162	.002170	2.548825	4421549	-.006777	47.377	25
30	269416	669	.002483	.012338	92319	1139	458809	.002483	2.554141	3957388	.000289	42.866	30
35	250350	720	.002876	.014290	91180	1303	452741	.002878	2.575627	3498578	.009855	38.370	35
40	229275	828	.003611	.017936	89877	1612	445560	.003618	2.627300	3045837	.013792	33.889	40
45	208272	1091	.005238	.025922	88265	2288	435944	.005248	2.648055	2600277	.013232	29.460	45
50	190057	1454	.007650	.037661	85977	3238	422246	.007669	2.640776	2164333	.014466	25.173	50
55	165985	1837	.011067	.054098	82739	4476	403296	.011099	2.676683	1742088	.015092	21.055	55
60	144700	2708	.018715	.089876	78263	7034	374739	.018770	2.643381	1338792	.015607	17.106	60
65	115937	3211	.027696	.130803	71229	9317	334739	.027834	2.702453	964053	.022023	13.535	65
70	86459	5131	.059346	.259853	61912	16088	270848	.059399	2.593716	629315	.003513	10.165	70
75	66958	5918	.088384	.361252	45824	16554	187472	.088301	2.484118	358467	-.005294	7.823	75
80	37086	5096	.137410	.506525	29270	14826	108030	.137240	2.415337	170995	-.005294	5.842	80
85+	17777	4078	.229398	1.000000	14444	14444	62965	.229398	4.359245	62965	.000000	4.359	85+

NUMBER OF PERSONS DYING (OUT OF 100,000 AT BIRTH) ABOVE AGE X FROM SPECIFIED CAUSES

Age (x)	All Causes	Respiratory T. B.	Other Infec. and Paras.	Neoplasms	Cardiovascular	Infl., Pneu., Bronch.	Diarrheal	Certain Degenerative	Maternal	Cert. Dis. of Infancy	Motor Vehicle	Other Violence	Other and Unknown	Age (x)
0	100000	3754	2269	13610	41411	7293	268	3172	368	1813	0	2647	23395	0
1	96593	3744	2052	13607	41409	6573	184	3170	368	0	0	2602	22884	1
5	95864	3723	1863	13578	41391	6388	173	3159	368	0	0	2486	22735	5
10	95378	3699	1721	13552	41358	6337	161	3118	368	0	0	2419	22645	10
15	94972	3636	1609	13517	41325	6311	154	3101	368	0	0	2382	22569	15
20	94229	3344	1471	13491	41275	6291	151	3066	345	0	0	2334	22461	20
25	93326	2921	1363	13453	41217	6268	147	3034	284	0	0	2282	22357	25
30	92319	2480	1254	13385	41144	6242	135	2970	210	0	0	2237	22262	30
35	91180	2065	1171	13254	40998	6204	130	2920	127	0	0	2178	22133	35
40	89877	1738	1089	13018	40753	6152	130	2850	44	0	0	2105	21998	40
45	88265	1477	986	12595	40412	6093	124	2743	5	0	0	2045	21785	45
50	85977	1247	892	11882	39879	6012	114	2588	1	0	0	1934	21428	50
55	82739	1032	817	10876	38755	5853	100	2410	1	0	0	1856	21039	55
60	78263	837	685	9588	37045	5597	93	2198	1	0	0	1751	20468	60
65	71229	607	524	7968	33916	5140	83	1834	1	0	0	1596	19560	65
70	61912	387	366	5813	29458	4585	68	1345	1	0	0	1436	18453	70
75	45824	209	234	3685	21810	3497	56	972	1	0	0	1003	14357	75
80	29270	91	130	1902	13545	2309	42	584	1	0	0	628	10038	80
85+	14444	25	57	719	6340	1187	21	259	0	0	0	308	5528	85+

NUMBER OF PERSONS SURVIVING TO AGE X IF SPECIFIED CAUSES WERE ELIMINATED

Age (x)	No Causes	Respiratory T. B. (1)	Other Infec. and Paras. (2)	Neoplasms (3)	Cardiovascular (4)	Infl., Pneu., Bronch. (5)	Diarrheal (6)	Certain Degenerative (7)	Maternal (8)	Cert. Dis. of Infancy (9)	Motor Vehicle (10)	Other Violence (11)	Other and Unknown (12)	(1) + (2)	(1) + (2) + (5) + (6) + (8)	(1)+(2)+(5)+(6)+(8)+part of(9)&(12)	(10) + (11)	Age (x)
0	100000	100000	100000	100000	100000	100000	100000	100000	100000	100000	100000	100000	100000	100000	100000	100000	100000	0
1	96593	96603	96806	96596	96595	97303	96676	96595	96593	98391	96593	96637	97097	96816	97612	99834	96637	1
5	95864	95895	96265	95884	95884	95957	95877	95864	95864	97649	95864	96024	96513	96296	97284	99607	96024	5
10	95378	95432	95919	95436	95431	95816	95482	95432	95378	97154	95378	95604	96114	95974	97023	99394	95604	10
15	94972	95089	95623	95064	95057	95932	95083	95043	94972	96740	94972	95234	95781	95741	96822	99237	95234	15
20	94229	94637	95014	94347	94364	95201	94342	94334	94252	95983	94229	94537	95141	95425	96549	99042	94537	20
25	93326	94154	94212	93480	93517	94312	93442	93462	93409	95063	93326	93683	94333	95047	96257	98828	93683	25
30	92319	93581	93304	92539	92561	93321	92446	92517	92475	94038	92319	92717	93411	94580	95900	98534	92717	30
35	91180	92846	92237	91528	91584	92207	91310	91425	91417	92878	91180	91632	92389	93922	95363	98067	91632	35
40	89877	91850	91001	90456	90520	90942	90005	90189	90193	91550	89877	90395	91204	92999	94566	97316	90395	40
45	88265	90467	89472	89257	89238	89370	88357	88678	88614	89908	88265	88834	89713	91704	93359	96151	88834	45
50	85977	88355	87247	87658	87459	87134	86115	86533	86321	87578	85977	86641	87815	89660	91377	94193	86641	50
55	82739	85244	84036	85368	85294	84011	82886	83449	83070	84279	82739	83455	84898	86580	88420	91213	83455	55
60	78263	80828	79620	82052	82414	79720	78640	79143	78576	75720	78263	79044	80877	82229	84251	87006	79044	60
65	71229	73789	72620	76313	78218	73000	71371	72382	71514	72555	71229	72089	74508	75231	77564	80236	72089	65
70	61912	64349	63270	68508	72704	63984	62050	63376	62160	63065	61912	62811	65860	65761	68385	70878	62811	70
75	45824	47784	46944	52747	62087	48331	45936	47233	46007	46677	45824	46867	52643	48952	51964	54348	46867	75
80	29270	30618	30069	35344	49611	31882	29353	30488	29387	29815	29270	30240	37806	31454	34495	36573	30240	80
85+	14444	15157	14890	18453	34507	16597	14499	15280	14503	14713	14444	15152	23128	15625	18095	19705	15152	85+

ADDED YRS OF LIFE

	No Causes	(1)	(2)	(3)	(4)	(5)	(6)	(7)	(8)	(9)	(10)	(11)	(12)	(1)+(2)	(1)+(2)+(5)+(6)+(8)	(1)+(2)+(5)+(6)+(8)+part of(9)&(12)	(10)+(11)
TOTAL		1.268	.852	2.099	5.866	1.325	.105	.519	.154	1.264	.000	.525	3.176	2.142	3.812	6.100	.525
WORK	3.675	.844	.260	.638	.698	.130	.015	.184	.121	.000	.000	.152	.427	1.110	1.386	1.578	.152

POPULATION, DEATHS, DEATH RATES FOR ALL CAUSES COMBINED, AND SPECIFIED CAUSES

Age Start of Interval	Midyear Population	Deaths During Year	All Causes	Respiratory T.B.	Other Infec. and Paras.	Neoplasms	Cardiovascular	Infl., Pneu., Bronch.	Diarrheal	Certain Degenerative	Maternal	Cert. Dis. of Infancy	Motor Vehicle	Other Violence	Other and Unknown	Age Start of Interval
0	56916	1385	.02433	.00002	.00033	.00012	.00009	.00227	.00044	.00000	.00000	.01560	.00000	.00040	.00506	0
1	250544	337	.00135	.00000	.00007	.00016	.00004	.00016	.00002	.00001	.00000	.00000	.00009	.00032	.00048	1
5	310606	235	.00076	.00000	.00004	.00012	.00002	.00004	.00000	.00001	.00000	.00000	.00012	.00027	.00014	5
10	232591	120	.00052	.00000	.00001	.00008	.00003	.00003	.00001	.00002	.00000	.00000	.00006	.00015	.00013	10
15	210882	219	.00104	.00004	.00001	.00008	.00003	.00003	.00000	.00004	.00000	.00000	.00027	.00037	.00011	15
20	228733	322	.00141	.00017	.00006	.00015	.00007	.00002	.00001	.00001	.00000	.00000	.00024	.00055	.00011	20
25	264463	358	.00135	.00021	.00004	.00012	.00007	.00002	.00000	.00016	.00000	.00000	.00014	.00045	.00014	25
30	277336	452	.00163	.00022	.00005	.00018	.00021	.00001	.00001	.00010	.00000	.00000	.00017	.00050	.00017	30
35	274236	524	.00191	.00020	.00007	.00031	.00022	.00003	.00001	.00018	.00000	.00000	.00013	.00053	.00023	35
40	273335	792	.00290	.00029	.00008	.00055	.00062	.00007	.00001	.00023	.00000	.00000	.00016	.00056	.00033	40
45	244005	1147	.00470	.00032	.00009	.00097	.00144	.00011	.00001	.00039	.00000	.00000	.00009	.00076	.00052	45
50	216076	1555	.00720	.00046	.00012	.00167	.00249	.00014	.00005	.00056	.00000	.00000	.00013	.00084	.00074	50
55	185128	2167	.01171	.00041	.00012	.00291	.00496	.00024	.00001	.00080	.00000	.00000	.00014	.00082	.00130	55
60	157530	2998	.01903	.00044	.00022	.00468	.00891	.00050	.00003	.00105	.00000	.00000	.00025	.00095	.00199	60
65	129395	3873	.02993	.00057	.00022	.00668	.01566	.00093	.00005	.00133	.00000	.00000	.00024	.00107	.00318	65
70	98908	4899	.04953	.00068	.00025	.00990	.02717	.00212	.00009	.00165	.00000	.00000	.00032	.00136	.00599	70
75	63605	5287	.08312	.00063	.00016	.01305	.04655	.00483	.00009	.00193	.00000	.00000	.00053	.00154	.01380	75
80	30810	4384	.14229	.00071	.00019	.01587	.07939	.00915	.00023	.00295	.00000	.00000	.00049	.00282	.03048	80
85+	15990	4285	.26798	.00069	.00019	.01620	.12752	.01945	.00025	.00244	.00000	.00000	.00025	.00613	.09487	85+
ALL	3521089	35339														

	All Causes	Respiratory T.B.	Other Infec. and Paras.	Neoplasms	Cardiovascular	Infl., Pneu., Bronch.	Diarrheal	Certain Degenerative	Maternal	Cert. Dis. of Infancy	Motor Vehicle	Other Violence	Other and Unknown
CRUDE DEATH RATE	.01004	.00024	.00009	.00164	.00447	.00047	.00003	.00038	.00000	.00025	.00017	.00062	.00169
STANDARDIZED RATE (1)	.00523	.00015	.00007	.00078	.00175	.00026	.00003	.00019	.00000	.00055	.00015	.00047	.00083
STANDARDIZED RATE (2)	.00978	.00022	.00008	.00155	.00433	.00047	.00003	.00035	.00000	.00032	.00017	.00060	.00166
GEOMETRIC MEAN	.00689												

LIFE TABLE FOR ALL CAUSES COMBINED

Age (x)	Midyear Population	Deaths During Year	$_nM_x$	$_nq_x$	l_x	$_nd_x$	$_nL_x$	$_nm_x$	$_na_x$	T_x	$_nr_x$	$\overset{\circ}{e}_x$	Age (x)
0	56916	1385	.024334	.023820	100000	2382	97883	.024335	.111368	7003328	.000000	70.033	0
1	250544	337	.001345	.005358	97618	523	389165	.001344	1.500000	6905445	.000000	70.739	1
5	310606	235	.000757	.003780	97095	367	484558	.000757	2.500000	6516280	.000000	67.112	5
10	232591	120	.000516	.002574	96728	249	483045	.000515	2.612115	6031723	.034792	62.358	10
15	210882	219	.001038	.005193	96479	501	481231	.001041	2.676314	5548677	.013053	57.512	15
20	228733	322	.001408	.007012	95978	673	478237	.001407	2.543648	5067446	-.015156	52.798	20
25	264463	358	.001354	.006736	95305	642	474940	.001352	2.530828	4589209	-.022051	48.153	25
30	277336	452	.001630	.008113	94663	768	471447	.001629	2.568088	4114270	-.009791	43.462	30
35	274236	524	.001911	.009511	93895	893	467561	.001911	2.633212	3642822	-.004017	38.797	35
40	273335	792	.002898	.014398	93002	1339	461922	.002899	2.693552	3175461	.003915	34.144	40
45	244005	1147	.004701	.023314	91663	2137	453356	.004714	2.679477	2713539	.015019	29.603	45
50	216076	1555	.007197	.035520	89526	3180	440264	.007223	2.683569	2260183	.018890	25.246	50
55	185128	2167	.011705	.057200	86346	4939	420270	.011752	2.679650	1819919	.019796	21.077	55
60	157530	2998	.019031	.091380	81407	7439	389568	.019096	2.651986	1399650	.017329	17.193	60
65	129395	3873	.029932	.140142	73968	10366	345317	.030019	2.634313	1010082	.015302	13.656	65
70	98908	4899	.049531	.222037	63602	14122	284120	.049704	2.600213	664764	.016467	10.452	70
75	63605	5287	.083122	.346717	49480	17159	205093	.083665	2.534396	380644	.027090	7.693	75
80	30810	4384	.142291	.524582	32321	16955	118211	.143430	2.440652	175551	.027090	5.431	80
85+	15990	4285	.267980	1.000000	15366	15366	57340	.267980	3.731622	57340	.000000	3.732	85+

NUMBER OF PERSONS DYING (OUT OF 100,000 AT BIRTH) ABOVE AGE X FROM SPECIFIED CAUSES

Age (x)	All Causes	Respiratory T. B.	Other Infec. and Paras.	Neo-plasms	Cardio-vascular	Infl., Pneu., Bronch.	Diar-rheal	Certain Degenerative	Maternal	Cert. Dis. of Infancy	Motor Vehicle	Other Violence	Other and Unknown	Age (x)
0	100000	1981	674	15706	47527	4941	221	3351	0	1529	1268	4951	17951	0
1	97618	1879	642	15654	47518	4719	178	3351	0	2	1268	4912	17455	1
5	97095	1879	615	15632	47503	4657	172	3348	0	0	1234	4787	17268	5
10	96728	1879	597	15574	47492	4637	172	3343	0	0	1178	4658	17198	10
15	96479	1877	593	15527	47477	4624	168	3334	0	0	1146	4587	17136	15
20	95978	1856	586	15498	47438	4611	166	3314	0	0	1016	4411	17082	20
25	95305	1773	556	15425	47405	4600	161	3308	0	0	899	4150	17028	25
30	94663	1674	537	15367	47371	4589	161	3233	0	0	832	3938	16961	30
35	93895	1570	511	15284	47274	4583	156	3185	0	0	752	3700	16880	35
40	93002	1475	479	15140	47171	4567	153	3103	0	0	691	3454	16769	40
45	91663	1340	443	14886	46885	4537	146	2995	0	0	618	3197	16616	45
50	89526	1193	404	14444	46230	4486	142	2818	0	0	575	2853	16381	50
55	86346	991	353	13705	45126	4425	120	2571	0	0	516	2484	16055	55
60	81407	821	303	12479	43029	4325	115	2232	0	0	457	2139	15507	60
65	73968	647	216	10651	39543	4128	103	1823	0	0	358	1768	14731	65
70	63602	450	139	8337	34117	3807	87	1363	0	0	275	1399	13628	70
75	49480	257	67	5519	26370	3200	61	894	0	0	183	1011	11918	75
80	32321	128	35	2832	16759	2202	42	496	0	0	73	694	9060	80
85+	15366	39	11	929	7312	1115	14	140	0	0	14	351	5441	85+

NUMBER OF PERSONS SURVIVING TO AGE X IF SPECIFIED CAUSES WERE ELIMINATED

Age (x)	No Causes	Respiratory T. B. (1)	Other Infec. and Paras. (2)	Neo-plasms (3)	Cardio-vascular (4)	Infl., Pneu., Bronch. (5)	Diar-rheal (6)	Certain Degener-ative (7)	Maternal (8)	Cert. Dis. of Infancy (9)	Motor Vehicle (10)	Other Violence (11)	Other and Unknown (12)	(1) + (2)	(1) + (2) + (5) + (6) + (8)	(1)+(2)+ (5)+(6)+ (8)+part of(9)&(12)	(10) + (11)	Age (x)
0	100000	100000	100000	100000	100000	100000	100000	100000	100000	100000	100000	100000	100000	100000	100000	100000	100000	0
1	97618	97620	97660	97630	97627	97838	97660	97618	97618	99138	97618	98109	98109	97618	97914	99598	97657	1
5	97095	97097	97153	97169	97119	97375	97143	97098	97095	98609	97129	97258	97771	97155	97484	99216	97292	5
10	96728	96730	96804	96859	96763	97027	96776	96736	96728	98237	96818	97020	97472	96806	97154	98889	97110	10
15	96479	96483	96559	96647	96529	96791	96531	96496	96479	97984	96600	96841	97284	96563	96927	98665	96963	15
20	95978	96003	96065	96184	96066	96301	96022	96015	95978	97475	96229	96514	96833	96089	96467	98202	96767	20
25	95305	95413	95421	95583	95426	95637	95363	95348	95305	96791	95671	96100	96208	95528	95920	97657	96469	25
30	94663	94869	94797	94997	94817	95003	94721	94780	94663	96139	95054	95665	95627	95003	95403	97146	96101	30
35	93895	94203	94054	94309	94144	94239	93957	94059	93895	95359	94402	95129	94933	94362	94771	96519	95643	35
40	93002	93402	93191	93556	93352	93358	93067	93246	93002	94452	93565	94473	94142	93552	94016	95772	95045	40
45	91663	92192	91885	92463	92293	92044	91734	92011	91663	93093	92291	93372	92940	92415	92871	94633	94012	45
50	89526	90188	89782	90749	90796	89949	89559	90042	89526	90922	90182	91542	91009	90446	90948	92704	92213	50
55	86346	87185	86643	88265	88678	86814	86438	87088	86346	87653	87037	88661	88103	87485	88053	89792	89371	55
60	81407	82364	81736	84442	85724	81946	81499	82439	81407	82116	83934	83608	82697	83338	85025	84665	60	60
65	73968	75005	74350	78553	81471	74647	74063	75300	73968	75122	74708	76628	76731	75392	76182	77779	77394	65
70	63602	64679	64002	69856	75820	64488	63698	65181	63602	64594	64315	66243	67047	65085	66092	67549	66986	70
75	49480	50489	49854	57126	67658	50716	49578	51131	49480	50252	50117	51889	53778	50871	52245	53515	52557	75
80	32321	33084	32590	39864	56130	33963	32400	33728	32321	32825	32826	34160	37728	33360	35140	36207	34693	80
85+	15366	15790	15510	20602	40383	16935	15423	16287	15366	15606	15646	16486	21022	15939	17630	18433	16787	85+

ACCED YRS OF LIFE																		
TOTAL		.426	.182	2.151	6.548	.598	.062	.528	.000	1.091	.401	1.288	2.296	.610	1.287	2.731	1.701
WORK	2.958	.234	.065	.488	.647	.055	.011	.194	.000	.000	.212	.605	.257	.300	.366	.410	.821

POPULATION, DEATHS, DEATH RATES FOR ALL CAUSES COMBINED, AND SPECIFIED CAUSES

Age Start of Interval	Midyear Population	Deaths During Year	All Causes	Respiratory T.B.	Other Infec. and Paras.	Neoplasms	Cardiovascular	Infl., Pneu., Bronch.	Diarrheal	Certain Degenerative	Maternal	Cert. Dis. of Infancy	Motor Vehicle	Other Violence	Other and Unknown	Age Start of Interval
0	53562	993	.01854	.00000	.00021	.00009	.00009	.00202	.00026	.00002	.00000	.01163	.00000	.00032	.00390	0
1	238170	263	.00110	.00000	.00008	.00016	.00005	.00019	.00002	.00003	.00000	.00000	.00010	.00017	.00031	1
5	295758	128	.00043	.00001	.00003	.00008	.00002	.00002	.00000	.00002	.00000	.00000	.00007	.00006	.00012	5
10	224208	90	.00040	.00002	.00001	.00005	.00006	.00005	.00000	.00001	.00000	.00000	.00005	.00001	.00012	10
15	205548	125	.00061	.00004	.00006	.00006	.00006	.00004	.00000	.00004	.00002	.00000	.00006	.00009	.00014	15
20	228010	184	.00081	.00015	.00005	.00013	.00007	.00002	.00000	.00007	.00000	.00000	.00004	.00008	.00010	20
25	259920	229	.00088	.00020	.00003	.00013	.00008	.00004	.00000	.00005	.00008	.00000	.00002	.00010	.00013	25
30	271212	329	.00121	.00020	.00004	.00029	.00015	.00003	.00000	.00010	.00006	.00000	.00001	.00014	.00020	30
35	268231	429	.00160	.00019	.00004	.00047	.00034	.00001	.00000	.00008	.00009	.00000	.00001	.00012	.00024	35
40	269163	589	.00219	.00020	.00004	.00081	.00039	.00006	.00001	.00014	.00003	.00000	.00002	.00014	.00033	40
45	248172	948	.00382	.00018	.00007	.00146	.00103	.00011	.00001	.00020	.00001	.00000	.00002	.00020	.00054	45
50	224142	1274	.00568	.00020	.00008	.00209	.00191	.00015	.00002	.00033	.00000	.00000	.00005	.00016	.00070	50
55	198519	1778	.00896	.00024	.00009	.00327	.00348	.00021	.00002	.00042	.00000	.00000	.00000	.00021	.00100	55
60	174606	2481	.01421	.00036	.00007	.00388	.00675	.00041	.00002	.00074	.00000	.00000	.00003	.00026	.00169	60
65	144306	3509	.02432	.00030	.00012	.00547	.01308	.00087	.00006	.00102	.00000	.00000	.00004	.00038	.00299	65
70	111639	4849	.04343	.00047	.00022	.00744	.02530	.00234	.00010	.00172	.00000	.00000	.00004	.00081	.00500	70
75	73238	5682	.07758	.00044	.00022	.01015	.04696	.00457	.00011	.00214	.00000	.00000	.00012	.00164	.01084	75
80	38356	5068	.13213	.00055	.00013	.01288	.07702	.00944	.00021	.00224	.00000	.00000	.00016	.00342	.02610	80
85+	22436	5512	.24568	.00013	.00022	.01270	.12395	.01738	.00049	.00165	.00000	.00000	.00004	.00798	.08112	85+
ALL	3549156	34460														
CRUDE DEATH RATE			.00971	.00017	.00007	.00166	.00472	.00053	.00002	.00031	.00003	.00018	.00004	.00028	.00170	
STANDARDIZED RATE (1)			.00422	.00011	.00006	.00075	.00154	.00025	.00002	.00015	.00003	.00041	.00005	.00015	.00070	
STANDARDIZED RATE (2)			.00829	.00015	.00006	.00140	.00395	.00047	.00002	.00027	.00003	.00024	.00004	.00024	.00141	
GEOMETRIC MEAN			.00526													

LIFE TABLE FOR ALL CAUSES COMBINED

Age (x)	Midyear Population	Deaths During Year	$_nM_x$	$_nq_x$	l_x	$_nd_x$	$_nL_x$	$_nm_x$	$_na_x$	T_x	$_nr_x$	$\overset{\circ}{e}_x$	Age (x)
0	53562	993	.018539	.018240	100000	1824	98361	.018544	.101517	7270866	.000000	72.709	0
1	238170	263	.001104	.004400	98176	432	391624	.001103	1.500000	7172505	.000000	73.058	1
5	295758	128	.000433	.002159	97744	211	488193	.000432	2.500000	6780881	.000000	69.374	5
10	224208	90	.000401	.002010	97533	196	487193	.000402	2.590349	6292689	.033414	64.519	10
15	205548	125	.000608	.003041	97337	296	485985	.000609	2.636543	5805496	.010128	59.643	15
20	228010	184	.000807	.004019	97041	390	484257	.000805	2.568376	5319511	-.016609	54.817	20
25	259920	229	.000881	.004387	96651	424	482235	.000879	2.593848	4835254	-.020305	50.028	25
30	271212	329	.001213	.006038	96227	581	479753	.001211	2.621199	4353019	-.008613	45.237	30
35	268231	429	.001599	.007967	95646	762	476419	.001599	2.623578	3873266	-.003456	40.496	35
40	269163	589	.002188	.010887	94884	1033	472050	.002188	2.705510	3396847	.001750	35.800	40
45	248172	948	.003820	.018977	93851	1781	465127	.003803	2.682014	2924797	.011126	31.164	45
50	224142	1274	.005684	.028120	92070	2589	454327	.005699	2.673490	2459671	.015312	26.715	50
55	198519	1778	.008956	.043958	89481	3937	438253	.008983	2.675366	2005344	.015485	22.411	55
60	174606	2481	.014209	.069005	85544	5903	414059	.014256	2.685817	1567091	.016262	18.319	60
65	144306	3509	.024316	.115544	79641	9202	376873	.024417	2.681822	1153032	.017925	14.478	65
70	111639	4849	.043435	.197817	70439	13934	319302	.043639	2.639392	776158	.020170	11.019	70
75	73238	5682	.077583	.327847	56505	18525	237243	.078085	2.555623	456856	.025115	8.085	75
80	38356	5068	.132131	.497104	37980	18880	141869	.133081	2.455972	219613	.025115	5.782	80
85+	22436	5512	.245677	1.000000	19100	19100	77744	.245677	4.070392	77744	.000000	4.070	85+

NUMBER OF PERSONS DYING (OUT OF 100,000 AT BIRTH) ABOVE AGE X FROM SPECIFIED CAUSES

Age (x)	All Causes	Respiratory T.B.	Other Infec. and Paras.	Neo-plasms	Cardio-vascular	Infl., Pneu., Bronch.	Diar-rheal	Certain Degen-erative	Maternal	Cert. Dis. of Infancy	Motor Vehicle	Other Violence	Other and Unknown	Age (x)
0	100000	1371	540	15429	51183	5750	225	2904	179	1144	312	2716	18247	0
1	98176	1371	519	15419	51174	5552	199	2902	179	0	312	2685	17864	1
5	97744	1371	488	15359	51154	5476	191	2893	179	0	275	2618	17740	5
10	97533	1368	475	15321	51143	5465	189	2883	179	0	240	2590	17680	10
15	97337	1359	469	15295	51114	5439	187	2876	179	0	216	2583	17620	15
20	97041	1337	438	15266	51086	5420	187	2857	167	0	188	2540	17555	20
25	96651	1263	414	15203	51054	5409	185	2815	131	0	169	2502	17506	25
30	96227	1165	398	15142	51013	5391	183	2789	92	0	158	2454	17442	30
35	95646	1070	380	15001	50943	5376	181	2743	64	0	154	2389	17345	35
40	94884	977	362	14775	50781	5373	179	2704	19	0	147	2334	17233	40
45	93851	881	341	14391	50599	5347	174	2637	4	0	138	2265	17074	45
50	92070	758	309	13711	50119	5296	169	2543	0	0	131	2171	16823	50
55	89481	709	271	12758	49248	5229	160	2393	0	0	108	2100	16505	55
60	85544	603	233	11323	47716	5136	154	2207	0	0	99	2010	16063	60
65	79641	456	205	9712	44910	4964	147	1898	0	0	85	1903	15361	65
70	70439	343	160	7647	39959	4635	126	1513	0	0	70	1759	14227	70
75	56505	194	88	5264	31840	3884	94	962	0	0	55	1500	12624	75
80	37980	91	37	2848	20628	2696	68	452	0	0	26	1108	10026	80
85+	19100	10	17	988	9637	1351	38	128	0	0	3	620	6308	85+

NUMBER OF PERSONS SURVIVING TO AGE X IF SPECIFIED CAUSES WERE ELIMINATED

Age (x)	No Causes	Respiratory T.B. (1)	Other Infec. and Paras. (2)	Neo-plasms (3)	Cardio-vascular (4)	Infl., Pneu., Bronch. (5)	Diar-rheal (6)	Certain Degener-ative (7)	Maternal (8)	Cert. Dis. of Infancy (9)	Motor Vehicle (10)	Other Violence (11)	Other and Unknown (12)	(1) + (2)	(1) + (2) + (5) + (6) + (8)	(1)+(2)+(5)+(6)+(8)+part of(9)&(12)	(10) + (11)	Age (x)
0	100000	100000	100000	100000	100000	100000	100000	100000	100000	100000	100000	100000	100000	100000	100000	100000	100000	0
1	98176	98176	98197	98186	98185	98372	98202	98178	98176	99316	98176	98207	98556	98197	98419	99678	98207	1
5	97744	97744	97796	97814	97773	98016	97778	97755	97744	98879	97781	97841	98247	97796	98101	99403	97878	5
10	97533	97536	97598	97641	97573	97815	97569	97554	97533	98666	97605	97658	98095	97601	97918	99230	97730	10
15	97337	97339	97407	97410	97406	97644	97374	97365	97337	98467	97433	97469	97958	97419	97765	99093	97565	15
20	97041	97075	97142	97203	97137	97367	97078	97088	97053	98168	97164	97216	97726	97176	97552	98901	97339	20
25	96651	96759	96776	96875	96779	96986	96690	96740	96699	97773	96793	96863	97382	96884	97307	98675	97005	25
30	96227	96432	96367	96511	96395	96575	96268	96341	96314	97344	96379	96486	97019	96573	97054	98450	96639	30
35	95646	95945	95803	95883	95611	95689	95805	95760	95717	96757	95801	95968	96531	96103	96627	98049	96124	35
40	94884	95273	95058	95531	95281	95249	94928	95081	95042	95986	95045	95259	95875	95448	96020	97461	95421	40
45	93851	94332	94044	94876	94426	94238	93900	94113	94022	94941	94019	94291	94991	94526	95138	96597	94460	45
50	92070	92625	92291	93759	93114	92500	92123	92420	92242	93139	92242	92595	93440	92847	93509	94972	92768	50
55	89481	90108	85733	92084	91369	89565	89541	89970	89648	90520	89671	90061	91131	90362	91083	93253	90253	55
60	85544	86248	85823	89487	88893	86099	85608	86194	85704	86537	85734	86187	87563	86529	87317	88742	86379	60
65	79641	80439	79927	84551	85622	80325	79707	80547	79790	80566	79832	80344	82217	80728	81641	83021	80536	65
70	70439	71252	70735	77229	80906	71358	70517	71607	70571	71257	70622	71197	73825	71551	72700	73999	71382	70
75	56505	57291	56807	64320	73802	57928	56596	57943	56610	57161	56665	57348	60744	57597	59253	60438	57511	75
80	37980	38592	38224	45511	63083	39943	38062	39369	38051	38421	38111	38873	43183	38840	41012	42034	39007	80
85+	19100	19465	19237	24491	47334	21095	19162	20034	19136	19322	19182	19900	24865	19604	21764	22602	19985	85+

ADDED YRS OF LIFE

	No Causes	(1)	(2)	(3)	(4)	(5)	(6)	(7)	(8)	(9)	(10)	(11)	(12)	(1)+(2)	(1)+(2)+(5)+(6)+(8)	part of(9)&(12)	(10)+(11)
TOTAL		.347	.159	2.363	7.218	.678	.049	.436	.080	.843	.122	.437	2.269	.507	1.330	2.542	.560
WORK	2.203	.189	.059	.633	.511	.058	.006	.130	.060	.000	.035	.138	.300	.249	.374	.442	.173

POPULATION, DEATHS, DEATH RATES FOR ALL CAUSES COMBINED, AND SPECIFIED CAUSES

Age Start of Interval	Midyear Population	Deaths During Year	All Causes	Respiratory T.B.	Other Infec. and Paras.	Neoplasms	Cardiovascular	Infl., Pneu., Bronch.	Diarrheal	Certain Degenerative	Maternal	Cert. Dis. of Infancy	Motor Vehicle	Other Violence	Other and Unknown	Age Start of Interval
0	44031	993	.02255	.00000	.00007	.00016	.00005	.00077	.00025	.00000	.00000	.01588	.00000	.00025	.00513	0
1	215609	205	.00095	.00000	.00003	.00012	.00000	.00011	.00004	.00001	.00000	.00000	.00011	.00026	.00027	1
5	273881	140	.00051	.00000	.00000	.00008	.00001	.00000	.00001	.00001	.00000	.00000	.00013	.00015	.00011	5
10	312176	121	.00039	.00000	.00001	.00008	.00002	.00002	.00000	.00001	.00000	.00000	.00009	.00007	.00008	10
15	302911	258	.00085	.00001	.00002	.00010	.00003	.00005	.00000	.00002	.00000	.00000	.00031	.00024	.00007	15
20	235516	250	.00106	.00000	.00002	.00013	.00004	.00003	.00000	.00003	.00000	.00000	.00026	.00042	.00012	20
25	219574	251	.00114	.00000	.00000	.00013	.00008	.00003	.00001	.00010	.00000	.00000	.00019	.00048	.00011	25
30	236021	322	.00136	.00004	.00003	.00019	.00016	.00003	.00002	.00011	.00000	.00000	.00013	.00056	.00011	30
35	268512	471	.00175	.00007	.00001	.00029	.00027	.00004	.00001	.00013	.00000	.00000	.00017	.00062	.00015	35
40	270198	683	.00253	.00006	.00002	.00054	.00050	.00007	.00002	.00021	.00000	.00000	.00020	.00062	.00030	40
45	268628	1067	.00397	.00008	.00004	.00092	.00121	.00007	.00002	.00024	.00000	.00000	.00015	.00087	.00037	45
50	260845	1612	.00618	.00011	.00006	.00152	.00237	.00015	.00001	.00042	.00000	.00000	.00020	.00080	.00056	50
55	225928	2561	.01134	.00010	.00005	.00277	.00536	.00039	.00001	.00063	.00000	.00000	.00027	.00089	.00089	55
60	190708	3513	.01842	.00022	.00008	.00444	.00967	.00047	.00004	.00089	.00000	.00000	.00031	.00095	.00136	60
65	152288	4563	.02996	.00033	.00011	.00749	.01594	.00099	.00007	.00132	.00000	.00000	.00044	.00093	.00235	65
70	115728	5868	.05071	.00045	.00015	.01120	.02846	.00243	.00014	.00166	.00000	.00000	.00048	.00133	.00442	70
75	78085	6284	.08048	.00061	.00024	.01429	.04797	.00525	.00019	.00224	.00000	.00000	.00058	.00183	.00726	75
80	43496	5765	.13254	.00060	.00016	.01950	.08141	.00984	.00055	.00285	.00000	.00000	.00055	.00301	.01407	80
85+	20229	4584	.22661	.00054	.00035	.01765	.13985	.02304	.00069	.00287	.00000	.00000	.00040	.00692	.03431	85+
ALL	3734364	39511														

	All Causes	Resp. T.B.	Other Infec.	Neoplasms	Cardiovascular	Infl. Pneu. Bronch.	Diarrheal	Certain Degen.	Maternal	Cert. Dis. Infancy	Motor Vehicle	Other Violence	Other Unknown
CRUDE DEATH RATE	.01058	.00010	.00004	.00196	.00539	.00056	.00004	.00037	.00000	.00019	.00022	.00065	.00107
STANDARDIZED RATE (1)	.00482	.00004	.00003	.00080	.00178	.00021	.00003	.00017	.00000	.00056	.00018	.00044	.00058
STANDARDIZED RATE (2)	.00915	.00008	.00004	.00164	.00448	.00048	.00004	.00031	.00000	.00033	.00021	.00058	.00096
GEOMETRIC MEAN	.00594												

LIFE TABLE FOR ALL CAUSES COMBINED

Age (x)	Midyear Population	Deaths During Year	$_nM_x$	$_nq_x$	l_x	$_nd_x$	$_nL_x$	$_nm_x$	$_na_x$	T_x	$_nr_x$	$\overset{\circ}{e}_x$	Age (x)
0	44031	993	.022552	.022110	100000	2211	98029	.022555	.108339	7114221	.000000	71.142	0
1	215609	205	.000951	.003794	97789	371	390229	.000951	1.500000	7016192	.000000	71.748	1
5	273881	140	.000511	.002556	97418	249	486468	.000512	2.500000	6625964	.000000	68.016	5
10	312176	121	.000388	.001935	97169	188	485409	.000387	2.681738	6139496	-.014506	63.184	10
15	302911	258	.000852	.004259	96981	413	483940	.000853	2.663438	5654087	.015740	58.301	15
20	235516	250	.001061	.005302	96568	512	481588	.001063	2.554932	5170147	.032498	53.539	20
25	219574	251	.001143	.005705	96056	548	478938	.001144	2.551703	4688559	.010288	48.811	25
30	236021	322	.001364	.006785	95508	648	475978	.001361	2.589699	4209621	-.014562	44.076	30
35	268512	471	.001754	.008718	94860	827	472343	.001751	2.634019	3733642	-.017450	39.360	35
40	270198	683	.002528	.012549	94033	1180	467423	.002524	2.676377	3261299	-.006205	34.682	40
45	268628	1067	.003972	.019665	92853	1826	460033	.003969	2.682206	2793876	-.003501	30.089	45
50	260845	1612	.006180	.030507	91027	2777	448831	.006187	2.730014	2333843	.005669	25.639	50
55	225928	2561	.011335	.055433	88250	4892	429981	.011337	2.696367	1885012	.016310	21.360	55
60	190708	3513	.018421	.088630	83358	7388	399524	.018492	2.662933	1455031	.019572	17.455	60
65	152288	4563	.029963	.140450	75970	10670	354718	.030080	2.644642	1055508	.019197	13.894	65
70	115728	5868	.050705	.226565	65300	14796	290826	.050876	2.588932	700789	.015976	10.732	70
75	78085	6284	.080476	.336330	50504	16986	210438	.080717	2.522531	409963	.014147	8.117	75
80	43496	5765	.132541	.496241	33518	16633	125013	.133050	2.440204	199526	.014147	5.953	80
85+	20229	4584	.226605	1.000000	16885	16885	74513	.226605	4.412958	74513	.000000	4.413	85+

NUMBER OF PERSONS DYING (OUT OF 100,000 AT BIRTH) ABOVE AGE X FROM SPECIFIED CAUSES

Age (x)	All Causes	Respiratory T.B.	Other Infec. and Paras.	Neo-plasms	Cardio-vascular	Infl., Pneu., Bronch.	Diar-rheal	Certain Degen-erative	Maternal	Cert. Dis. of Infancy	Motor Vehicle	Other Violence	Other and Unknown	Age (x)
0	100000	8C7	349	17578	53C84	5817	336	3220	0	1556	1657	5156	10440	0
1	97789	8C7	342	17563	53080	5741	312	3220	0	0	1657	5132	9935	1
5	97418	8C7	330	17518	53078	5700	297	3217	0	0	1616	5028	9827	5
10	97169	805	328	17479	53073	5698	290	3213	0	0	1553	4956	9774	10
15	96981	805	323	17440	53062	5687	290	3209	0	0	1509	4920	9736	15
20	96568	799	314	17390	53C48	5665	290	3197	0	0	1360	4801	9704	20
25	96056	797	303	17329	53027	5652	288	3183	0	0	1235	4596	9646	25
30	95508	795	301	17268	52988	5639	282	3135	0	0	1146	4364	9590	30
35	94860	777	289	17179	52913	5625	273	3080	0	0	1086	4098	9540	35
40	94033	743	286	17042	52787	5606	270	3019	0	0	1005	3807	9468	40
45	92853	716	277	16789	52554	5575	261	2922	0	0	913	3518	9328	45
50	91027	678	258	16368	51997	5542	251	2813	0	0	845	3117	9158	50
55	88250	628	232	15685	50933	5477	246	2625	0	0	757	2759	8908	55
60	83358	584	211	14492	48620	5311	242	2354	0	0	641	2378	8525	60
65	75970	496	178	12712	44740	5121	227	1999	0	0	517	1999	7981	65
70	65300	377	140	10048	39063	4767	202	1530	0	0	360	1670	7143	70
75	50504	246	98	6783	30754	4057	161	1046	0	0	222	1282	5855	75
80	33518	116	46	3770	20626	2948	121	574	0	0	101	896	4320	80
85+	16885	41	26	1315	10421	1716	52	214	0	0	29	516	2555	85+

NUMBER OF PERSONS SURVIVING TO AGE X IF SPECIFIED CAUSES WERE ELIMINATED

Age (x)	No Causes	Respiratory T.B. (1)	Other Infec. and Paras. (2)	Neo-plasms (3)	Cardio-vascular (4)	Infl., Pneu., Bronch. (5)	Diar-rheal (6)	Certain Degener-ative (7)	Maternal (8)	Cert. Dis. of Infancy (9)	Motor Vehicle (10)	Other Violence (11)	Other and Unknown (12)	(1)+(2)	(1)+(2)+(5)+(6)+(8)	(1)+(2)+(5)+(6)+(8)+part of(9)&(12)	(10)+(11)	Age (x)
0	100000	100000	100000	1C0000	100000	100000	1C0C00	100000	100000	100000	100000	100000	100000	100000	100000	100000	100000	0
1	97789	97789	97796	97804	97793	97864	97813	97789	97789	99340	97789	97813	98290	97796	97895	99361	97813	1
5	97418	97418	97437	97478	97424	97534	97457	97421	97418	98963	97459	97546	98025	97437	97591	99081	97587	5
10	97169	97171	97190	97268	97180	97287	97215	97176	97169	98710	97273	97368	97828	97192	97355	98845	97472	10
15	96981	96983	97007	97118	97003	97109	97026	96992	96981	98519	97129	97216	97677	97009	97183	98674	97364	15
20	96568	96576	96603	96755	96604	96718	96613	96591	96568	98099	96864	96921	97293	96611	96806	98295	97218	20
25	96056	96066	96101	96303	96113	96218	96103	96093	96056	97579	96476	96613	96835	96111	96321	97806	97035	25
30	95508	95520	95555	95814	95603	95682	95561	95592	95508	97023	96014	96294	96339	95567	95794	97274	96805	30
35	94860	94890	94919	95253	95029	95047	94921	94999	94860	96364	95423	95909	95736	94949	95197	96672	96478	35
40	94033	94096	94094	94560	94327	94237	94097	94231	94033	95524	94672	95366	94974	94158	94426	95895	96014	40
45	92853	92942	92922	93627	93376	93C85	92925	93146	92853	94326	93576	94461	93923	93012	93317	94779	95197	45
50	91027	91152	91114	92207	92096	91288	91107	91422	91027	92471	91804	93008	92246	91239	91581	93026	93801	50
55	88250	88421	88360	90077	90353	88567	88333	88819	88250	89650	89091	90531	89681	88531	88932	90350	91393	55
60	83358	83562	83482	86276	87679	83819	83440	84161	83358	84680	84266	85892	85089	83687	84233	85595	86827	60
65	75970	76240	76115	80407	83900	76573	76059	77044	75970	77175	76917	78652	78079	76385	77082	78355	79632	65
70	65300	65643	65460	71773	78166	66151	65400	66664	65300	66336	66261	67920	67916	65803	66763	67909	68919	70
75	50504	50884	50664	58736	69848	51801	50617	51992	50504	51305	51369	52884	53716	51046	52474	53457	53790	75
80	33518	33876	33666	41900	59209	35316	33626	34898	33518	34050	34191	35425	36598	34025	35966	36757	36136	80
85+	16885	17118	16974	23356	45427	18717	16988	17843	16885	17153	17275	18127	20044	17208	19191	19748	18546	85+

ADDED YRS OF LIFE

	No Causes	(1)	(2)	(3)	(4)	(5)	(6)	(7)	(8)	(9)	(10)	(11)	(12)	(1)+(2)	(1)+(2)+(5)+(6)+(8)	+part	(10)+(11)
TOTAL		.122	.074	2.362	8.991	.580	.067	.473	.000	1.127	.500	1.248	1.546	.196	.854	2.041	1.764
WORK	2.583	.042	.025	.474	.623	.066	.012	.152	.000	.000	.248	.602	.224	.067	.145	.159	.855

POPULATION, DEATHS, DEATH RATES FOR ALL CAUSES COMBINED, AND SPECIFIED CAUSES

Age Start of Interval	Midyear Population	Deaths During Year	All Causes	Respiratory T.B.	Other Infec. and Paras.	Neoplasms	Cardiovascular	Infl., Pneu., Bronch.	Diarrheal	Certain Degenerative	Maternal	Cert. Dis. of Infancy	Motor Vehicle	Other Violence	Other and Unknown	Age Start of Interval
0	42001	706	.01681	.00000	.00012	.00012	.00000	.00057	.00010	.00000	.00000	.01083	.00000	.00029	.00479	0
1	202976	158	.00078	.00000	.00004	.00015	.00001	.00011	.00001	.00000	.00000	.00000	.00004	.00010	.00031	1
5	258953	85	.00033	.00000	.00002	.00007	.00000	.00003	.00000	.00000	.00000	.00000	.00008	.00005	.00007	5
10	297267	75	.00025	.00000	.00001	.00007	.00002	.00001	.00000	.00003	.00000	.00000	.00004	.00002	.00006	10
15	290613	115	.00040	.00000	.00001	.00007	.00003	.00002	.00000	.00002	.00001	.00000	.00004	.00002	.00006	15
20	230139	103	.00045	.00001	.00000	.00008	.00003	.00000	.00001	.00006	.00002	.00000	.00007	.00010	.00007	20
25	215310	143	.00066	.00002	.00001	.00015	.00007	.00001	.00001	.00007	.00003	.00000	.00004	.00013	.00013	25
30	233548	189	.00081	.00002	.00000	.00027	.00005	.00001	.00001	.00009	.00003	.00000	.00004	.00012	.00013	30
35	264349	320	.00121	.00003	.00002	.00049	.00017	.00003	.00001	.00009	.00004	.00000	.00004	.00011	.00013	35
40	265137	460	.00173	.00006	.00003	.00082	.00026	.00005	.00000	.00012	.00004	.00000	.00003	.00011	.00017	40
45	264468	830	.00314	.00007	.00003	.00145	.00071	.00007	.00000	.00015	.00000	.00000	.00007	.00020	.00038	45
50	260408	1184	.00455	.00004	.00003	.00210	.00121	.00007	.00001	.00024	.00000	.00000	.00004	.00026	.00052	50
55	234920	1633	.00695	.00004	.00007	.00291	.00226	.00023	.00002	.00032	.00000	.00000	.00004	.00027	.00075	55
60	205269	2384	.01161	.00003	.00005	.00408	.00495	.00038	.00002	.00058	.00000	.00000	.00012	.00027	.00114	60
65	173107	3483	.02012	.00014	.00011	.00513	.01036	.00090	.00007	.00099	.00000	.00000	.00012	.00048	.00183	65
70	137634	5292	.03845	.00024	.00010	.00766	.02259	.00225	.00015	.00160	.00000	.00000	.00015	.00081	.00296	70
75	94276	6390	.06778	.00024	.00018	.01058	.04274	.00455	.00027	.00223	.00000	.00000	.00013	.00189	.00499	75
80	53860	6210	.11530	.00028	.00011	.01285	.07558	.00882	.00059	.00256	.00000	.00000	.00017	.00434	.00999	80
85+	27421	5822	.21232	.00022	.00033	.01291	.13694	.02028	.00088	.00306	.00000	.00000	.00026	.00977	.02768	85+
ALL	3751656	35582														
CRUDE DEATH RATE			.00948	.00005	.00004	.00186	.00506	.00058	.00004	.00033	.00001	.00012	.00007	.00035	.00097	
STANDARDIZED RATE (1)			.00351	.00002	.00003	.00074	.00129	.00017	.00002	.00013	.00001	.00038	.00006	.00016	.00050	
STANDARDIZED RATE (2)			.00701	.00004	.00003	.00139	.00352	.00041	.00003	.00025	.00001	.00022	.00007	.00027	.00076	
GEOMETRIC MEAN			.00404													

LIFE TABLE FOR ALL CAUSES COMBINED

Age (x)	Midyear Population	Deaths During Year	$_nM_x$	$_nq_x$	l_x	$_nd_x$	$_nL_x$	$_nm_x$	$_na_x$	T_x	$_nr_x$	$\overset{\circ}{e}_x$	Age (x)
0	42001	706	.016809	.016560	100000	1656	98507	.016811	.098576	7488639	.000000	74.886	0
1	202976	158	.000778	.003101	98344	305	392614	.000777	1.500000	7390131	.000000	75.146	1
5	258953	85	.000328	.001642	98039	161	489793	.000329	2.500000	6997518	.000000	71.375	5
10	297267	75	.000252	.001267	97878	124	489087	.000254	2.553763	6507725	-.015272	66.488	10
15	290613	115	.000396	.001974	97754	193	488307	.000395	2.602547	6018639	.013822	61.569	15
20	230139	103	.000448	.002259	97561	219	487285	.000449	2.623668	5530331	.030646	56.686	20
25	215310	143	.000664	.003318	97342	323	485938	.000665	2.610939	5043047	.009216	51.808	25
30	233548	189	.000809	.004030	97019	391	484171	.000808	2.638001	4557109	-.014974	46.971	30
35	264349	320	.001211	.006023	96628	582	481776	.001208	2.656429	4072937	-.016353	42.151	35
40	265137	460	.001735	.008621	96046	828	478348	.001731	2.726701	3591161	-.005228	37.350	40
45	264468	830	.003138	.015575	95218	1483	472649	.003138	2.679956	3112813	-.003375	32.691	45
50	260408	1184	.004547	.022500	93735	2109	463748	.004548	2.663980	2640164	-.003079	28.166	50
55	234920	1633	.006951	.034302	91626	3143	450880	.006971	2.693154	2176416	.012975	23.753	55
60	205269	2384	.011614	.056768	88483	5023	430882	.011657	2.703937	1725536	.017201	19.501	60
65	173107	3483	.020121	.096573	83460	8060	398886	.020206	2.715390	1294654	.017536	15.512	65
70	137634	5292	.038450	.177135	75400	13356	345710	.038634	2.657248	895768	.019404	11.880	70
75	94276	6390	.067780	.252389	62044	18141	266192	.068150	2.573027	550058	.022508	8.866	75
80	53860	6210	.115299	.449058	43903	19715	169943	.116010	2.485555	283866	.022508	6.466	80
85+	27421	5822	.212319	1.000000	24188	24188	113923	.212319	4.709894	113923	.000000	4.710	85+

NUMBER OF PERSONS DYING (OUT OF 100,000 AT BIRTH) ABOVE AGE X FROM SPECIFIED CAUSES

Age (x)	All Causes	Respiratory T.B.	Other Infec. and Paras.	Neoplasms	Cardiovascular	Infl., Pneu., Bronch.	Diarrheal	Certain Degenerative	Maternal	Cert. Dis. of Infancy	Motor Vehicle	Other Violence	Other and Unknown	Age (x)
0	100000	427	345	16590	56347	6686	410	3147	74	1067	571	3701	10235	0
1	98344	427	333	16578	56347	6629	400	3147	74	0	571	3672	9766	1
5	98039	427	318	16920	56343	6585	396	3145	74	0	554	3634	9643	5
10	97878	427	306	16884	56341	6572	396	3144	74	0	514	3611	9609	10
15	97754	427	303	16850	56331	6567	396	3130	74	0	494	3601	9581	15
20	97561	427	296	16818	56318	6558	396	3120	67	0	447	3571	9543	20
25	97342	421	294	16779	56305	6556	392	3090	59	0	413	3524	9509	25
30	97019	412	290	16707	56273	6550	388	3054	43	0	395	3463	9444	30
35	96628	401	290	16579	56232	6543	381	3011	31	0	377	3403	9380	35
40	96046	387	281	16343	56148	6529	376	2969	12	0	357	3352	9292	40
45	95218	358	266	15952	56024	6507	374	2911	0	0	331	3280	9215	45
50	93735	326	250	15266	55687	6475	372	2842	0	0	299	3185	9033	50
55	91626	296	236	14293	55124	6445	369	2729	0	0	280	3064	8790	55
60	88483	277	205	12980	54100	6341	361	2587	0	0	239	2941	8452	60
65	83460	264	184	11218	51954	6174	350	2336	0	0	189	2834	7957	65
70	75400	206	140	9167	47799	5814	323	1938	0	0	143	2642	7228	70
75	62044	138	105	6512	39947	5034	272	1384	0	0	92	2361	6199	75
80	43903	73	57	3688	28504	3814	201	789	0	0	59	1855	4863	80
85+	24188	25	37	1471	15600	2310	100	349	0	0	29	1113	3154	85+

NUMBER OF PERSONS SURVIVING TO AGE X IF SPECIFIED CAUSES WERE ELIMINATED

Age (x)	No Causes	Respiratory T.B. (1)	Other Infec. and Paras. (2)	Neoplasms (3)	Cardiovascular (4)	Infl., Pneu., Bronch. (5)	Diarrheal (6)	Certain Degenerative (7)	Maternal (8)	Cert. Dis. of Infancy (9)	Motor Vehicle (10)	Other Violence (11)	Other and Unknown (12)	(1)+(2)	(1)+(2)+(5)+(6)+(8)	(1)+(2)+(5)+(6)+(8)+part of(9)&(12)	(10)+(11)	Age (x)
0	100000	100000	100000	100000	100000	100000	100000	100000	100000	100000	100000	100000	100000	100000	100000	100000	100000	0
1	98344	98344	98356	98356	98344	98401	98344	98344	98344	99408	98344	98373	98810	98356	98422	99431	98373	1
5	98039	98039	98066	98109	98043	98139	98053	98041	98039	99100	98056	98106	98627	98066	98180	99229	98123	5
10	97878	97878	97917	97984	97884	97991	97892	97881	97878	98937	97935	97968	98499	97917	98044	99098	98025	10
15	97754	97754	97796	97894	97770	97872	97768	97771	97754	98811	97831	97853	98403	97796	97928	98983	97930	15
20	97561	97561	97610	97732	97590	97688	97575	97588	97561	98616	97685	97690	98247	97610	97757	98817	97814	20
25	97342	97348	97393	97552	97384	97471	97360	97399	97357	98395	97499	97518	98060	97399	97560	98621	97676	25
30	97019	97034	97073	97300	97093	97153	97041	97112	97050	98068	97194	97255	97800	97088	97275	98344	97431	30
35	96628	96654	96682	97036	96742	96769	96657	96763	96671	97673	96820	96923	97471	96708	96920	97792	97116	35
40	96046	96086	96109	96689	96244	96200	96079	96222	96107	97085	96257	96391	96972	96149	96398	97474	96602	40
45	95218	95286	95295	96248	95538	95392	95253	95451	95291	96248	95453	95632	96214	95363	95646	96723	95868	45
50	93735	93834	93827	95439	94386	93938	93772	94033	93807	94749	93998	94237	94858	93926	94238	95311	94502	50
55	91626	91752	91730	94276	92825	91855	91665	92029	91656	92617	91902	92237	93006	91856	92195	93254	92515	55
60	88483	88624	88614	92379	90667	88806	88528	89013	88551	89440	88790	89195	90153	88754	89193	90237	89504	60
65	83460	83605	83604	88937	87684	83928	83513	84205	83524	84363	83798	84236	85527	83749	84337	85348	84577	65
70	75400	75587	75571	82446	83480	76168	75474	76455	75458	76216	75749	76285	77979	75758	76664	77630	76639	70
75	62044	62259	62217	70512	77046	63396	62151	63421	62091	62715	62378	63031	65135	62432	63951	64831	63370	75
80	43903	44109	44065	52634	67824	45917	44039	45385	43937	44378	44166	45036	47280	44272	46481	47222	45306	80
85+	24188	24337	24292	31009	55200	26475	24337	25340	24207	24450	24355	25375	27430	24442	26937	27498	25551	85+

ADDED YRS OF LIFE

	No Causes	(1)	(2)	(3)	(4)	(5)	(6)	(7)	(8)	(9)	(10)	(11)	(12)	(1)+(2)	(1)+(2)+(5)+(6)+(8)	(1)+(2)+(5)+(6)+(8)+part of(9)&(12)	(10)+(11)
TOTAL		.076	.081	2.657	9.822	.631	.050	.435	.034	.809	.183	.520	1.555	.158	.883	1.795	.705
WORK	1.675	.030	.018	.629	.334	.038	.009	.110	.024	.000	.072	.148	.214	.049	.120	.140	.220

POPULATION, DEATHS, DEATH RATES FOR ALL CAUSES COMBINED, AND SPECIFIED CAUSES

Age Start of Interval	Midyear Population	Deaths During Year	All Causes	Respiratory T. B.	Other Infec. and Paras.	Neoplasms	Cardiovascular	Infl., Pneu., Bronch.	Diarrheal	Certain Degenerative	Maternal	Cert. Dis. of Infancy	Motor Vehicle	Other Violence	Other and Unknown	Age Start of Interval
0	60000	1001	.01668	.00000	.00012	.00015	.00003	.00065	.00015	.00000	.00000	.01062	.00002	.00033	.00462	0
1	215000	150	.00070	.00000	.00001	.00013	.00001	.00004	.00001	.00000	.00000	.00000	.00007	.00022	.00022	1
5	271000	131	.00048	.00000	.00001	.00007	.00001	.00002	.00001	.00000	.00000	.00000	.00011	.00018	.00008	5
10	282000	121	.00043	.00000	.00001	.00009	.00001	.00002	.00001	.00001	.00000	.00000	.00012	.00010	.00006	10
15	326000	335	.00103	.00000	.00002	.00010	.00005	.00003	.00001	.00001	.00000	.00000	.00043	.00031	.00007	15
20	283000	331	.00117	.00000	.00000	.00013	.00004	.00002	.00001	.00005	.00000	.00000	.00032	.00049	.00011	20
25	234000	262	.00112	.00000	.00001	.00015	.00006	.00001	.00000	.00008	.00000	.00000	.00021	.00051	.00009	25
30	225000	285	.00127	.00000	.00001	.00018	.00012	.00000	.00002	.00015	.00000	.00000	.00018	.00045	.00015	30
35	244000	454	.00186	.00002	.00001	.00028	.00029	.00003	.00000	.00014	.00000	.00000	.00018	.00074	.00017	35
40	279000	699	.00251	.00004	.00004	.00051	.00058	.00003	.00000	.00020	.00000	.00000	.00020	.00068	.00022	40
45	258000	1036	.00402	.00006	.00002	.00081	.00133	.00007	.00001	.00029	.00000	.00000	.00017	.00086	.00041	45
50	266000	1701	.00639	.00007	.00004	.00164	.00240	.00012	.00002	.00043	.00000	.00000	.00020	.00052	.00057	50
55	243000	2711	.01116	.00009	.00009	.00267	.00527	.00023	.00003	.00061	.00000	.00000	.00034	.00101	.00081	55
60	205000	3656	.01783	.00016	.00007	.00429	.00918	.00046	.00007	.00076	.00000	.00000	.00039	.00096	.00149	60
65	164000	4962	.03026	.00022	.00011	.00763	.01654	.00089	.00012	.00110	.00000	.00000	.00045	.00084	.00235	65
70	121000	5878	.04858	.00026	.00017	.01097	.02774	.00179	.00019	.00189	.00000	.00000	.00052	.00110	.00394	70
75	83000	6646	.08007	.00035	.00014	.01604	.04712	.00514	.00020	.00239	.00000	.00000	.00058	.00145	.00666	75
80	44000	5775	.13125	.00039	.00023	.02057	.08064	.01027	.00043	.00330	.00000	.00000	.00080	.00280	.01184	80
85+	22000	4985	.22659	.00059	.00050	.02318	.14705	.02232	.00068	.00436	.00000	.00000	.00050	.00473	.02268	85+
ALL	3825000	41119														

	All Causes	Respiratory T. B.	Other Infec. and Paras.	Neoplasms	Cardiovascular	Infl., Pneu., Bronch.	Diarrheal	Certain Degenerative	Maternal	Cert. Dis. of Infancy	Motor Vehicle	Other Violence	Other and Unknown
CRUDE DEATH RATE	.01075	.00006	.00004	.00207	.00555	.00053	.00004	.00039	.00000	.00017	.00026	.00065	.00099
STANDARDIZED RATE (1)	.00457	.00002	.00003	.00081	.00178	.00018	.00002	.00017	.00000	.00037	.00021	.00046	.00053
STANDARDIZED RATE (2)	.00895	.00005	.00004	.00169	.00448	.00044	.00003	.00032	.00000	.00022	.00024	.00059	.00085
GEOMETRIC MEAN	.00583												

LIFE TABLE FOR ALL CAUSES COMBINED

Age (x)	Midyear Population	Deaths During Year	$_nM_x$	$_nq_x$	l_x	$_nd_x$	$_nL_x$	$_nm_x$	$_na_x$	T_x	$_nr_x$	$\overset{\circ}{e}_x$	Age (x)
0	60000	1001	.016683	.016440	100000	1644	98518	.016687	.098362	7164153	.000000	71.642	0
1	215000	150	.000698	.002786	98356	274	392739	.000698	1.500000	7065636	.000000	71.837	1
5	271000	131	.000483	.002416	98082	237	489818	.000484	2.500000	6672897	.000000	68.034	5
10	282000	121	.000429	.002136	97845	209	488757	.000428	2.762161	6183079	-.016288	63.193	10
15	326000	335	.001028	.005121	97636	500	487004	.001027	2.648750	5694322	-.011020	58.322	15
20	283000	331	.001170	.005827	97136	566	484273	.001169	2.514723	5207317	.022828	53.609	20
25	234000	262	.001120	.005592	96570	540	481508	.001121	2.515432	4723044	.026023	48.908	25
30	225000	285	.001267	.006311	96030	606	478706	.001266	2.617574	4241536	.005620	44.169	30
35	244000	454	.001861	.009243	95424	882	475034	.001857	2.634401	3762829	-.018798	39.433	35
40	279000	699	.002505	.012428	94542	1175	469975	.002500	2.672695	3287796	-.012568	34.776	40
45	258000	1036	.004016	.019879	93367	1856	462551	.004013	2.691608	2817821	-.001617	30.180	45
50	266000	1701	.006395	.031493	91511	2882	450969	.006391	2.714912	2355270	-.003582	25.738	50
55	243000	2711	.011156	.054486	88629	4829	431972	.011179	2.686245	1904301	.009438	21.486	55
60	205000	3656	.017834	.085907	83800	7199	402259	.017896	2.674532	1472329	.017513	17.570	60
65	164000	4962	.030256	.141774	76601	10860	357343	.030391	2.637028	1070070	.021431	13.969	65
70	121000	5878	.048579	.218159	65741	14342	294179	.048753	2.592677	712727	.018052	10.841	70
75	83000	6646	.080072	.335415	51399	17240	214416	.080405	2.530211	418547	.018088	8.143	75
80	44000	5775	.131250	.493047	34159	16842	127707	.131879	2.441664	204132	.018088	5.976	80
85+	22000	4985	.226591	1.000000	17317	17317	76424	.226591	4.413240	76424	.000000	4.413	85+

NUMBER OF PERSONS DYING (OUT OF 100,000 AT BIRTH) ABOVE AGE X FROM SPECIFIED CAUSES

Age (x)	All Causes	Respiratory T.B.	Other Infec. and Paras.	Neo-plasms	Cardio-vascular	Infl., Pneu., Bronch.	Diar-rheal	Certain Degenerative	Maternal	Cert. Dis. of Infancy	Motor Vehicle	Other Violence	Other and Unknown	Age (x)
0	100000	514	348	18621	54095	5517	355	3430	0	1046	1917	5068	9089	0
1	98356	514	336	18606	54092	5453	349	3430	0	0	1916	5035	8634	1
5	98082	514	332	18555	54088	5438	335	3428	0	0	1890	4953	8549	5
10	97845	514	325	18523	54085	5428	331	3426	0	0	1838	4866	8509	10
15	97636	514	322	18481	54080	5417	328	3421	0	0	1779	4816	8478	15
20	97136	514	313	18433	54057	5401	325	3415	0	0	1570	4665	8443	20
25	96570	512	311	18372	54037	5390	320	3393	0	0	1417	4426	8392	25
30	96030	512	307	18297	54008	5386	318	3355	0	0	1319	4181	8347	30
35	95424	512	303	18212	53950	5384	309	3283	0	0	1231	3964	8276	35
40	94542	504	299	18081	53813	5371	307	3217	0	0	1144	3612	8194	40
45	93367	484	282	17840	53543	5356	305	3123	0	0	1049	3294	8091	45
50	91511	457	273	17468	52926	5325	302	2990	0	0	972	2894	7904	50
55	88629	427	256	16731	51844	5269	293	2797	0	0	884	2481	7647	55
60	83800	387	219	15575	49563	5168	279	2532	0	0	736	2045	7296	60
65	76601	324	189	13841	45857	4980	251	2225	0	0	579	1659	6696	65
70	65741	246	150	11102	39917	4660	208	1829	0	0	420	1358	5851	70
75	51399	170	99	7867	31724	4129	152	1271	0	0	267	1034	4686	75
80	34159	95	68	4419	21576	3019	108	758	0	0	142	723	3251	80
85+	17317	45	38	1772	11238	1706	52	333	0	0	38	361	1734	85+

NUMBER OF PERSONS SURVIVING TO AGE X IF SPECIFIED CAUSES WERE ELIMINATED

Age (x)	No Causes	Respiratory T.B. (1)	Other Infec. and Paras. (2)	Neo-plasms (3)	Cardio-vascular (4)	Infl., Pneu., Bronch. (5)	Diar-rheal (6)	Certain Degenerative (7)	Maternal (8)	Cert. Dis. of Infancy (9)	Motor Vehicle (10)	Other Violence (11)	Other and Unknown (12)	(1)+(2)	(1)+(2)+(5)+(6)+(8)	(1)+(2)+(5)+(6)+(8)+part of(9)&(12)	(10)+(11)	Age (x)
0	100000	100000	100000	100000	100000	100000	100000	100000	100000	100000	100000	100000	100000	100000	100000	100000	100000	0
1	98356	98356	98368	98371	98359	98419	98371	98356	98356	99399	98357	98389	98808	98368	98446	99399	98390	1
5	98082	98082	98098	98149	98089	98160	98102	98084	98082	99122	98109	98198	98618	98098	98196	99157	98224	5
10	97845	97845	97868	97943	97855	97933	97869	97849	97845	98882	97924	98046	98420	97868	97980	98943	98125	10
15	97636	97636	97662	97775	97651	97735	97663	97645	97636	98671	97774	97887	98241	97662	97787	98752	98025	15
20	97136	97136	97171	97323	97174	97250	97166	97151	97136	98166	97482	97537	97773	97171	97315	98277	97884	20
25	96570	96572	96606	96617	96628	96695	96604	96607	96570	97594	97067	97208	97255	96606	96768	97726	97709	25
30	96030	96032	96070	96350	96116	96158	96066	96105	96030	97048	96623	96911	96756	96072	96236	97191	97509	30
35	95424	95426	95468	95827	95568	95553	95469	95570	95424	96436	96101	96518	96217	95470	95644	96595	97203	35
40	94542	94552	94590	95073	94821	94683	94589	94752	94542	95544	95300	95981	95410	94599	94787	95732	96750	40
45	93367	93397	93431	94132	93912	93521	93415	93667	93367	94357	95109		94327	93461	93663	94602	95969	45
50	91511	91567	91582	92633	92662	91693	91561	91939	91511	92481	92415	93622	92639	91638	91871	92799	94547	50
55	88629	88713	88715	90453	90829	88860	88666	89234	88629	89569	89592	91090	89578	88799	89088	89999	92080	55
60	83800	83918	83917	86679	88185	84117	83868	84632	83800	84689	84856	86563	85423	84035	84422	85300	87654	60
65	76601	76769	76737	80566	84426	77072	76690	77658	76601	77413	77718	79507	78671	76905	77468	78301	80666	65
70	65741	65957	65894	72217	78779	66444	65857	67020	65741	66438	66848	68523	68325	66111	66936	67695	69677	70
75	51399	51635	51563	59676	70895	52429	51539	52902	51399	51944	52401	53871	54498	51800	52982	53641	54922	75
80	34159	34376	34293	43017	59937	35779	34288	35585	34159	34521	34927	36066	37472	34511	36284	36836	36877	80
85+	17317	17462	17406	24265	46107	19125	17421	18352	17317	17501	17781	18553	20195	17552	19502	19913	19050	85+

ADDED YRS OF LIFE

	No Causes	(1)	(2)	(3)	(4)	(5)	(6)	(7)	(8)	(9)	(10)	(11)	(12)	(1)+(2)	(1)+(2)+(5)+(6)+(8)	(1)+(2)+(5)+(6)+(8)+part of(9)&(12)	(10)+(11)
TOTAL		.070	.068	2.450	9.565	.504	.058	.487	.000	.759	.579	1.316	1.395	.138	.709	1.483	1.914
WORK	2.638	.020	.019	.463	.630	.044	.011	.158	.000	.000	.305	.651	.221	.039	.094	.103	.962

POPULATION, DEATHS, DEATH RATES FOR ALL CAUSES COMBINED, AND SPECIFIED CAUSES

Age Start of Interval	Midyear Population	Deaths During Year	All Causes	Respiratory T. B.	Other Infec. and Paras.	Neoplasms	Cardiovascular	Infl., Pneu., Bronch.	Diarrheal	Certain Degenerative	Maternal	Cert. Dis. of Infancy	Motor Vehicle	Other Violence	Other and Unknown	Age Start of Interval
0	57000	743	.01304	.00000	.00014	.00004	.00007	.00035	.00012	.00000	.00000	.00846	.00007	.00028	.00351	0
1	204000	119	.00058	.00000	.00003	.00013	.00001	.00004	.00001	.00000	.00000	.00000	.00005	.00013	.00017	1
5	256000	77	.00030	.00000	.00001	.00008	.00002	.00000	.00000	.00000	.00000	.00000	.00008	.00005	.00006	5
10	267000	63	.00024	.00000	.00001	.00007	.00003	.00001	.00000	.00001	.00000	.00000	.00004	.00001	.00005	10
15	312000	127	.00041	.00000	.00001	.00005	.00002	.00001	.00001	.00002	.00000	.00000	.00014	.00006	.00008	15
20	271000	126	.00046	.00000	.00000	.00006	.00004	.00003	.00000	.00005	.00001	.00000	.00007	.00010	.00010	20
25	224000	141	.00063	.00000	.00000	.00015	.00006	.00000	.00003	.00004	.00003	.00000	.00005	.00017	.00010	25
30	221000	168	.00076	.00001	.00001	.00018	.00010	.00004	.00000	.00007	.00001	.00000	.00003	.00018	.00012	30
35	241000	287	.00119	.00001	.00002	.00046	.00017	.00002	.00000	.00009	.00003	.00000	.00006	.00019	.00014	35
40	275000	458	.00167	.00001	.00001	.00076	.00022	.00004	.00001	.00009	.00001	.00000	.00008	.00020	.00023	40
45	255000	696	.00273	.00003	.00003	.00134	.00054	.00002	.00001	.00010	.00001	.00000	.00005	.00025	.00035	45
50	263000	1141	.00434	.00003	.00004	.00215	.00101	.00005	.00002	.00017	.00000	.00000	.00008	.00030	.00048	50
55	249000	1594	.00640	.00004	.00004	.00292	.00207	.00009	.00002	.00029	.00000	.00000	.00010	.00028	.00055	55
60	220000	2444	.01111	.00004	.00009	.00385	.00467	.00032	.00005	.00059	.00000	.00000	.00012	.00034	.00104	60
65	185000	3472	.01877	.00006	.00005	.00525	.00944	.00058	.00004	.00102	.00000	.00000	.00017	.00040	.00174	65
70	146000	4998	.03423	.00010	.00013	.00751	.01965	.00158	.00012	.00155	.00000	.00000	.00018	.00059	.00283	70
75	104000	6489	.06239	.00022	.00023	.01014	.03873	.00385	.00043	.00251	.00000	.00000	.00023	.00115	.00489	75
80	57000	6184	.10849	.00033	.00025	.01328	.07168	.00763	.00070	.00314	.00000	.00000	.00019	.00225	.00904	80
85+	31000	6215	.20048	.00023	.00048	.01555	.13555	.01703	.00084	.00377	.00000	.00000	.00016	.00574	.02113	85+
ALL	3838000	35542														

	All Causes	Respiratory T. B.	Other Infec. and Paras.	Neoplasms	Cardiovascular	Infl., Pneu., Bronch.	Diarrheal	Certain Degenerative	Maternal	Cert. Dis. of Infancy	Motor Vehicle	Other Violence	Other and Unknown
CRUDE DEATH RATE	.00926	.00003	.00004	.00191	.00496	.00049	.00005	.00035	.00001	.00013	.00009	.00030	.00090
STANDARDIZED RATE (1)	.00315	.00001	.00003	.00072	.00119	.00013	.00002	.00012	.00001	.00030	.00008	.00016	.00041
STANDARDIZED RATE (2)	.00645	.00002	.00003	.00137	.00325	.00032	.00004	.00025	.00001	.00018	.00008	.00024	.00066
GEOMETRIC MEAN	.00373												

LIFE TABLE FOR ALL CAUSES COMBINED

Age (x)	Midyear Population	Deaths During Year	$_nM_x$	$_nq_x$	l_x	$_nd_x$	$_nL_x$	$_nm_x$	$_na_x$	T_x	$_nr_x$	$\overset{\circ}{e}_x$	Age (x)
0	57000	743	.013035	.012880	100000	1288	98831	.013032	.092160	7593264	.000000	75.933	0
1	204000	119	.000583	.002330	98712	230	354273	.000583	1.500000	7494433	.000000	75.922	1
5	256000	77	.000301	.001503	98482	148	492040	.000301	2.500000	7100160	.000000	72.096	5
10	267000	63	.000236	.001180	98334	116	491391	.000236	2.593391	6608120	-.017066	67.201	10
15	312000	127	.000407	.002036	98218	200	490613	.000408	2.616667	6116729	-.011971	62.277	15
20	271000	126	.000465	.002326	98018	228	489542	.000466	2.598684	5626116	.023487	57.399	20
25	224000	141	.000629	.003150	97790	308	488210	.000631	2.596050	5136573	.024878	52.527	25
30	221000	168	.000760	.003796	97482	370	486541	.000760	2.650338	4648364	.002867	47.684	30
35	241000	287	.001191	.005921	97112	575	484212	.001187	2.655435	4161823	-.019274	42.856	35
40	275000	458	.001665	.008277	96537	799	480838	.001662	2.688517	3677611	-.012151	38.055	40
45	255000	696	.002729	.013558	95738	1298	475701	.002729	2.697058	3196773	-.000487	33.391	45
50	263000	1141	.004338	.021463	94440	2027	467470	.004336	2.666502	2721072	-.003691	28.813	50
55	249000	1594	.006402	.031576	92413	2918	455361	.006408	2.702479	2253602	.006364	24.386	55
60	220000	2444	.011109	.054338	89495	4863	436303	.011146	2.702593	1798241	.014886	20.093	60
65	185000	3472	.018768	.090356	84632	7647	405583	.018854	2.701441	1361939	.019741	16.092	65
70	146000	4998	.034233	.159213	76985	12257	356369	.034394	2.670209	956356	.019477	12.423	70
75	104000	6489	.062394	.272849	64728	17661	281144	.062818	2.593792	599987	.027129	9.269	75
80	57000	6184	.108491	.429345	47067	20208	184872	.109308	2.502825	318843	.027129	6.774	80
85+	31000	6215	.200484	1.000000	26859	26859	133971	.200484	4.987932	133971	.000000	4.988	85+

NUMBER OF PERSONS DYING (OUT OF 100,000 AT BIRTH) ABOVE AGE X FROM SPECIFIED CAUSES

Age (x)	All Causes	Respiratory T. B.	Other Infec. and Paras.	Neo-plasms	Cardio-vascular	Infl., Pneu., Bronch.	Diar-rheal	Certain Degen-erative	Maternal	Cert. Dis. of Infancy	Motor Vehicle	Other Violence	Other and Unknown	Age (x)
0	100000	293	400	17850	57399	5936	521	3469	48	836	727	2960	9561	0
1	98712	293	386	17846	57392	5902	509	3469	48	0	720	2932	9215	1
5	98482	293	375	17794	57388	5884	503	3469	48	0	699	2880	9149	5
10	98334	293	371	17756	57379	5882	503	3469	48	0	659	2857	9117	10
15	98218	293	365	17721	57364	5879	501	3464	48	0	639	2853	9091	15
20	98018	293	359	17696	57356	5876	498	3454	46	0	568	2822	9050	20
25	97790	293	357	17665	57338	5861	496	3431	41	0	534	2774	9000	25
30	97482	293	355	17590	57309	5859	483	3411	28	0	510	2691	8953	30
35	97112	286	348	17502	57263	5839	481	3376	21	0	495	2605	8896	35
40	96537	282	340	17278	57181	5827	479	3334	7	0	465	2515	8829	40
45	95738	279	333	16916	57077	5810	472	3288	4	0	424	2419	8716	45
50	94440	264	318	16278	56821	5802	466	3242	0	0	398	2302	8549	50
55	92413	248	299	15274	56349	5777	456	3164	0	0	359	2161	8326	55
60	89495	231	282	13945	55403	5735	445	3030	0	0	312	2035	8077	60
65	84632	214	245	12262	53355	5594	425	2771	0	0	258	1888	7620	65
70	76985	189	223	10126	49502	5355	407	2355	0	0	190	1725	6913	70
75	64728	155	176	7441	42461	4789	365	1802	0	0	124	1515	5900	75
80	47067	92	111	4578	31490	3699	243	1093	0	0	59	1188	4514	80
85+	26859	30	65	2083	18160	2282	112	506	0	0	22	769	2830	85+

NUMBER OF PERSONS SURVIVING TO AGE X IF SPECIFIED CAUSES WERE ELIMINATED

Age (x)	No Causes	Respiratory T. B. (1)	Other Infec. and Paras. (2)	Neo-plasms (3)	Cardio-vascular (4)	Infl., Pneu., Bronch. (5)	Diar-rheal (6)	Certain Degener-ative (7)	Maternal (8)	Cert. Dis. of Infancy (9)	Motor Vehicle (10)	Other Violence (11)	Other and Unknown (12)	(1) + (2)	(1) + (2) + (5) + (6) + (8)	(1)+(2)+ (5)+(6)+ (8)+part of(9)&(12)	(10) + (11)	Age (x)
0	100000	100000	100000	100000	100000	100000	100000	100000	100000	100000	100000	100000	100000	100000	100000	100000	100000	0
1	98712	98712	98726	98716	98719	98746	98724	98712	98712	99546	98719	98740	99056	98726	98772	99439	98747	1
5	98482	98482	98507	98538	98493	98534	98500	98482	98482	99314	98510	98562	98892	98507	98576	99257	98590	5
10	98334	98334	98363	98428	98388	98352	98334	98334	98334	99165	98402	98437	98775	98363	98434	99115	98505	10
15	98218	98218	98253	98347	98253	98275	98238	98223	98218	99048	98306	98324	98665	98253	98329	99013	98412	15
20	98018	98018	98059	98171	98061	98077	98041	98033	98020	98846	98177	98155	98525	98059	98143	98829	98314	20
25	97790	97790	97833	97974	97851	97864	97815	97828	97797	98616	97982	97975	98346	97833	97939	98630	98168	25
30	97482	97482	97526	97741	97571	97520	97540	97540	97508	98306	97698	97749	98084	97526	97660	98355	97966	30
35	97112	97119	97163	97458	97247	97208	97152	97205	97139	97933	97342	97465	97768	97170	97333	98033	97695	35
40	96537	96548	96596	97105	96753	96644	96578	96671	96578	97353	96795	96978	97257	96607	96796	97498	97237	40
45	95738	95752	95803	96665	96056	95861	95786	95917	95781	96547	96035	96271	96585	95817	96032	96734	96570	45
50	94440	94469	94519	95996	95010	94569	94493	94662	94487	95238	94759	95083	95424	94548	94778	95478	95404	50
55	92413	92457	92510	94951	93441	92564	92475	92708	92459	93194	92764	93182	93599	92553	92813	93507	93536	55
60	89495	89554	89605	93305	91438	89683	89566	89913	89539	90251	89881	90365	90892	89664	89969	90650	90755	60
65	84632	84704	84772	89956	88530	84948	84718	85281	84674	85347	85050	85599	86405	84845	85290	85958	86022	65
70	76985	77075	77134	84017	84472	77502	77081	77975	77023	77636	77430	78021	79289	77223	77877	78517	78473	70
75	64728	64835	64896	73364	78472	65689	64847	66074	64760	65275	65163	65794	67626	65003	66122	66724	66236	75
80	47067	47198	47244	56153	69566	48717	47258	48661	47090	47465	47438	48126	50418	47376	49260	49811	48505	80
85+	26859	26980	26995	34342	57475	28916	27066	28225	26872	27086	27099	27785	30148	27116	29433	29887	28032	85+

ADDED YRS OF LIFE																		
TOTAL		.039	.080	2.760	10.942	.524	.069	.435	.022	.641	.233	.544	1.395	.119	.744	1.356	.781	
WORK	1.589	.010	.017	.594	.295	.032	.013	.087	.015	.000	.092	.188	.203	.027	.088	.103	.281	

POPULATION, DEATHS, DEATH RATES FOR ALL CAUSES COMBINED, AND SPECIFIED CAUSES

Age Start of Interval	Midyear Population	Deaths During Year	All Causes	Respiratory T. B.	Other Infec. and Paras.	Neoplasms	Cardiovascular	Infl., Pneu., Bronch.	Diarrheal	Certain Degenerative	Maternal	Cert. Dis. of Infancy	Motor Vehicle	Other Violence	Other and Unknown	Age Start of Interval
0	31481	2034	.06461	.00022	.00378	.00013	.00064	.00547	.00746	.00029	.00000	.02884	.00006	.00105	.01267	0
1	132839	640	.00482	.00015	.00121	.00009	.00013	.00104	.00017	.00009	.00000	.00000	.00012	.00076	.00106	1
5	175219	322	.00184	.00002	.00058	.00009	.00009	.00014	.00002	.00004	.00000	.00000	.00009	.00024	.00053	5
10	163979	250	.00152	.00009	.00033	.00007	.00013	.00004	.00001	.00007	.00000	.00000	.00010	.00027	.00040	10
15	180047	470	.00261	.00052	.00034	.00005	.00014	.00007	.00001	.00009	.00000	.00000	.00016	.00069	.00054	15
20	181649	695	.00383	.00100	.00048	.00005	.00015	.00015	.00002	.00013	.00000	.00000	.00032	.00095	.00053	20
25	169327	697	.00412	.00116	.00043	.00013	.00019	.00017	.00001	.00017	.00000	.00000	.00025	.00104	.00057	25
30	151600	647	.00427	.00118	.00037	.00014	.00028	.00030	.00001	.00020	.00000	.00000	.00024	.00091	.00063	30
35	133493	713	.00534	.00127	.00038	.00034	.00053	.00042	.00001	.00034	.00000	.00000	.00022	.00100	.00082	35
40	121681	885	.00727	.00131	.00054	.00066	.00087	.00052	.00002	.00060	.00000	.00000	.00000	.00135	.00117	40
45	117670	1222	.01038	.00144	.00066	.00142	.00174	.00072	.00003	.00091	.00000	.00000	.00024	.00159	.00163	45
50	110187	1644	.01492	.00170	.00084	.00286	.00301	.00097	.00006	.00131	.00000	.00000	.00021	.00174	.00221	50
55	93068	2104	.02261	.00185	.00096	.00474	.00596	.00164	.00009	.00178	.00000	.00000	.00021	.00202	.00336	55
60	71839	2314	.03221	.00189	.00092	.00715	.01006	.00260	.00004	.00232	.00000	.00000	.00021	.00242	.00458	60
65	54781	2733	.04989	.00184	.00099	.01015	.01833	.00451	.00011	.00287	.00000	.00000	.00020	.00274	.00816	65
70	35206	2403	.06826	.00159	.00108	.01335	.02920	.00591	.00023	.00324	.00000	.00000	.00011	.00270	.01085	70
75	18359	2188	.11918	.00142	.00125	.01623	.05017	.01367	.00049	.00359	.00000	.00000	.00022	.00338	.02876	75
80	8002	1313	.16408	.00150	.00125	.01500	.06598	.02299	.00075	.00300	.00000	.00000	.00050	.00387	.04924	80
85+	3074	849	.27619	.00098	.00195	.01561	.09922	.04196	.00130	.00423	.00000	.00000	.00000	.00683	.10345	85+
ALL	1953501	24123														

	All Causes	Respiratory T. B.	Other Infec. and Paras.	Neoplasms	Cardiovascular	Infl., Pneu., Bronch.	Diarrheal	Certain Degenerative	Maternal	Cert. Dis. of Infancy	Motor Vehicle	Other Violence	Other and Unknown
CRUDE DEATH RATE	.01235	.00097	.00066	.00162	.00306	.00115	.00017	.00062	.00000	.00046	.00020	.00114	.00229
STANDARDIZED RATE (1)	.01043	.00076	.00072	.00104	.00197	.00107	.00031	.00043	.00000	.00102	.00018	.00096	.00197
STANDARDIZED RATE (2)	.01612	.00056	.00071	.00207	.00452	.00164	.00022	.00072	.00000	.00060	.00020	.00121	.00329
GEOMETRIC MEAN	.01457												

LIFE TABLE FOR ALL CAUSES COMBINED

Age (x)	Midyear Population	Deaths During Year	$_nM_x$	$_nq_x$	l_x	$_nd_x$	$_nL_x$	$_nm_x$	$_na_x$	T_x	$_nr_x$	$\overset{o}{e}_x$	Age (x)
0	31481	2034	.064610	.061360	100000	6136	94967	.064612	.179838	5911887	.000000	59.119	0
1	132839	640	.004818	.019038	93864	1787	370989	.004817	1.500000	5816920	.000000	61.972	1
5	175219	322	.001838	.009145	92077	842	458280	.001837	2.500000	5445931	.000000	59.145	5
10	163979	250	.001525	.007596	91235	693	454511	.001525	2.599206	4987651	-.001411	54.668	10
15	180047	470	.002610	.012944	90542	1172	449989	.002605	2.677937	4533140	-.012493	50.067	15
20	181649	695	.003826	.018955	89370	1694	442743	.003826	2.575512	4083152	-.002874	45.688	20
25	169327	697	.004116	.020370	87676	1786	433940	.004116	2.514231	3640409	.009060	41.521	25
30	151600	647	.004268	.021143	85890	1816	425001	.004273	2.549904	3206468	.017040	37.332	30
35	133493	713	.005341	.026417	84074	2221	415050	.005351	2.604495	2781468	.018361	33.084	35
40	121681	885	.007273	.035796	81853	2930	402311	.007283	2.626493	2366418	.009507	28.911	40
45	117670	1222	.010385	.050682	78923	4000	385130	.010386	2.628750	1964107	.000662	24.886	45
50	110187	1644	.014920	.072101	74923	5402	361834	.014930	2.633978	1578977	-.004095	21.075	50
55	93068	2104	.022607	.107507	69521	7474	329732	.022667	2.608654	1217144	-.016413	17.508	55
60	71839	2314	.032211	.149886	62047	9300	287877	.032305	2.595968	887412	-.018660	14.302	60
65	54781	2733	.049890	.222913	52747	11758	234906	.050054	2.548176	599534	-.018733	11.366	65
70	35206	2403	.068255	.293225	40989	12019	175226	.068591	2.527335	364628	-.031910	8.896	70
75	18359	2188	.119179	.460304	28970	13335	110867	.120279	2.451631	189402	-.031450	6.538	75
80	8002	1313	.164084	.570707	15635	8923	54232	.164535	2.316672	78534	-.031450	5.023	80
85+	3074	849	.276187	1.000000	6712	6712	24302	.276187	3.620730	24302	.000000	3.621	85+

NUMBER OF PERSONS DYING (OUT OF 100,000 AT BIRTH) ABOVE AGE X FROM SPECIFIED CAUSES

Age (x)	All Causes	Respiratory T.B.	Other Infec. and Paras.	Neo-plasms	Cardio-vascular	Infl., Pneu., Bronch.	Diar-rheal	Certain Degenerative	Maternal	Cert. Dis. of Infancy	Motor Vehicle	Other Violence	Other and Unknown	Age (x)
0	100000	6169	4133	13671	28826	5876	1083	4749	0	2739	1186	7630	19938	0
1	93864	6148	3774	13659	28766	8978	374	4722	0	0	1180	7531	18732	1
5	92077	6093	3325	13625	28718	8592	313	4688	0	0	1135	7249	18339	5
10	91235	6085	3058	13586	28677	8529	303	4670	0	0	1094	7139	18094	10
15	90542	6043	2908	13553	28616	8510	300	4640	0	0	1047	7014	17911	15
20	89370	5812	2754	13530	28553	8478	297	4600	0	0	974	6703	17669	20
25	87676	5368	2539	13491	28487	8412	290	4541	0	0	831	6281	17436	25
30	85890	4866	2355	13435	28403	8340	285	4467	0	0	720	5830	17189	30
35	84074	4364	2198	13376	28285	8211	279	4380	0	0	620	5443	16918	35
40	81853	3838	2039	13232	28063	8036	273	4239	0	0	526	5029	16578	40
45	78923	3309	1821	12967	27711	7828	266	3997	0	0	430	4486	16108	45
50	74923	2753	1565	12420	27040	7549	257	3647	0	0	339	3874	15479	50
55	69521	2139	1260	11385	25549	7198	234	3174	0	0	263	3244	14675	55
60	62047	1529	944	9817	23975	6654	205	2585	0	0	196	2577	13565	60
65	52747	984	680	7752	21065	5902	193	1914	0	0	136	1879	12242	65
70	40989	551	448	5361	16141	4839	167	1240	0	0	89	1235	10318	70
75	28970	273	259	3015	11594	3797	127	672	0	0	69	762	8402	75
80	15635	116	119	1207	5983	2263	72	272	0	0	44	385	5174	80
85+	6712	24	47	379	2411	1020	32	103	0	0	16	166	2514	85+

NUMBER OF PERSONS SURVIVING TO AGE X IF SPECIFIED CAUSES WERE ELIMINATED

Age (x)	No Causes	Respiratory T.B. (1)	Other Infec. and Paras. (2)	Neo-plasms (3)	Cardio-vascular (4)	Infl., Pneu., Bronch. (5)	Diar-rheal (6)	Certain Degenerative (7)	Maternal (8)	Cert. Dis. of Infancy (9)	Motor Vehicle (10)	Other Violence (11)	Other and Unknown (12)	(1)+(2)	(1)+(2)+(5)+(6)+(8)	(1)+(2)+(5)+(6)+(8)+part of(9)&(12)	(10)+(11)	Age (x)
0	100000	100000	100000	100000	100000	100000	100000	100000	100000	100000	100000	100000	100000	100000	100000	100000	100000	0
1	93864	93884	94212	93876	93922	94738	94553	93890	93864	96555	93870	93960	95040	94233	95809	99412	93966	1
5	92077	92151	92866	92122	92182	93321	92814	92136	92077	94717	92127	92451	93625	92941	94951	98807	92502	5
10	91235	91317	92285	91319	91380	92531	91975	91312	91235	93851	91326	91716	93017	92368	94441	98429	91807	10
15	90542	90665	91736	90658	90746	91847	91280	90648	90542	93138	90679	91144	92497	91860	93944	97994	91282	15
20	89370	89722	90703	89507	89634	90691	90101	89514	89370	91932	89578	90276	91545	91060	93162	97297	90486	20
25	87676	88464	89200	87649	88001	89038	88440	87876	87676	90190	88022	88988	90047	90002	92155	96372	89339	25
30	85890	87164	87569	86115	86292	87297	86605	86160	85890	88352	86339	87630	88464	88868	91075	95377	88088	30
35	84074	85827	85876	84353	84585	85581	84779	84424	84074	86484	84613	86168	86870	87666	89986	94391	86721	35
40	81853	84091	83768	82268	82571	83496	82546	82334	81853	84200	82471	84312	84923	86058	88528	93037	84948	40
45	78923	81616	80988	79585	79965	80716	79598	79626	78923	81186	79614	81844	82363	83751	86386	90994	82561	45
50	74923	78041	77140	76092	76578	76903	75573	75935	74923	77071	75668	78316	78831	80350	83189	87860	79096	50
55	69521	73031	71881	71626	72141	71707	70146	70923	69521	71514	70286	73306	73966	75510	78584	83257	74113	55
60	62047	65786	64461	65470	66352	64530	62632	63868	62047	63826	62794	66091	67138	68346	71752	76320	66886	60
65	52747	56458	55051	57700	59354	55584	53256	54934	52747	54259	53438	56871	58410	58924	62692	66988	57616	65
70	40989	44278	42992	47194	50618	44190	41408	43307	40989	42164	41567	44805	47303	46442	50580	54444	45437	70
75	28970	31543	30550	35680	41518	32189	29300	31110	28970	29801	29395	32098	35345	33263	37380	40582	32569	75
80	15635	17144	16593	20906	29035	18660	15854	17097	15635	16083	15883	17624	22187	18195	22018	24592	17903	80
85+	6712	7424	7172	9708	17486	9012	6832	7458	6712	6904	6837	7724	12255	7933	10842	12835	7868	85+

ADDED YRS OF LIFE

	No Causes	(1)	(2)	(3)	(4)	(5)	(6)	(7)	(8)	(9)	(10)	(11)	(12)	(1)+(2)	(1)+(2)+(5)+(6)+(8)	(1)+(2)+(5)+(6)+(8)+part	(10)+(11)
TOTAL		1.590	1.400	1.815	3.769	1.817	.515	.790	.000	1.650	.375	1.934	3.651	3.049	5.609	9.208	2.331
WORK	6.555	1.122	.475	.552	.730	.347	.018	.364	.000	.000	.240	1.087	.900	1.616	2.006	2.387	1.335

POPULATION, DEATHS, DEATH RATES FOR ALL CAUSES COMBINED, AND SPECIFIED CAUSES

Age Start of Interval	Midyear Population	Deaths During Year	All Causes	Respiratory T. B.	Other Infec. and Paras.	Neoplasms	Cardio-vascular	Infl., Pneu., Bronch.	Diarrheal	Certain Degenerative	Maternal	Cert. Dis. of Infancy	Motor Vehicle	Other Violence	Other and Unknown	Age Start of Interval
0	30226	1518	.05022	.00030	.00351	.00013	.00043	.00738	.00549	.00007	.00000	.02150	.00000	.00073	.01069	0
1	129812	521	.00401	.00007	.00116	.00010	.00008	.00076	.00021	.00005	.00000	.00000	.00007	.00059	.00092	1
5	171615	282	.00164	.00003	.00052	.00006	.00010	.00020	.00003	.00006	.00000	.00000	.00005	.00016	.00044	5
10	160874	211	.00131	.00024	.00039	.00006	.00012	.00002	.00001	.00007	.00000	.00000	.00004	.00006	.00031	10
15	182222	478	.00262	.00113	.00043	.00009	.00013	.00008	.00001	.00009	.00003	.00000	.00003	.00018	.00043	15
20	193392	594	.00307	.00135	.00040	.00008	.00014	.00013	.00001	.00007	.00026	.00000	.00002	.00017	.00044	20
25	184439	644	.00349	.00160	.00036	.00011	.00019	.00015	.00001	.00009	.00036	.00000	.00002	.00019	.00048	25
30	169826	620	.00365	.00111	.00034	.00024	.00031	.00022	.00001	.00015	.00045	.00000	.00003	.00023	.00057	30
35	150112	635	.00423	.00091	.00033	.00052	.00055	.00027	.00001	.00024	.00044	.00000	.00003	.00026	.00069	35
40	135316	660	.00488	.00075	.00035	.00099	.00082	.00030	.00002	.00037	.00018	.00000	.00001	.00029	.00079	40
45	126896	849	.00669	.00072	.00039	.00162	.00155	.00039	.00002	.00058	.00006	.00000	.00000	.00032	.00105	45
50	121100	1153	.00952	.00094	.00050	.00248	.00255	.00041	.00001	.00091	.00001	.00000	.00002	.00033	.00137	50
55	103294	1582	.01532	.00114	.00059	.00370	.00508	.00089	.00003	.00129	.00000	.00000	.00004	.00042	.00214	55
60	84512	1937	.02292	.00140	.00064	.00528	.00852	.00166	.00006	.00172	.00000	.00000	.00006	.00057	.00303	60
65	68574	2622	.03824	.00159	.00083	.00722	.01613	.00362	.00013	.00226	.00000	.00000	.00009	.00082	.00556	65
70	47459	2708	.05706	.00173	.00124	.00944	.02750	.00611	.00023	.00291	.00000	.00000	.00015	.00082	.00693	70
75	26008	2692	.10351	.00158	.00146	.01165	.04756	.01334	.00050	.00338	.00000	.00000	.00012	.00223	.02169	75
80	12515	1835	.14662	.00096	.00104	.01159	.06312	.02078	.00072	.00280	.00000	.00000	.00000	.00439	.04123	80
85+	5173	1275	.24647	.00058	.00155	.01218	.09511	.03750	.00116	.00387	.00000	.00000	.00000	.00812	.08641	85+
ALL	2103365	22816														

CRUDE DEATH RATE			.01085	.00092	.00056	.00149	.00336	.00105	.00013	.00052	.00014	.00031	.00003	.00037	.00197	
STANDARDIZED RATE (1)			.00820	.00075	.00064	.00087	.00179	.00084	.00024	.00032	.00012	.00076	.00003	.00037	.00152	
STANDARDIZED RATE (2)			.01288	.00088	.00061	.00164	.00416	.00136	.00017	.00055	.00012	.00045	.00004	.00032	.00249	
GEOMETRIC MEAN			.01162													

LIFE TABLE FOR ALL CAUSES COMBINED

Age (x)	Midyear Population	Deaths During Year	$_nM_x$	$_nq_x$	l_x	$_nd_x$	$_nL_x$	$_nm_x$	$_na_x$	T_x	$_nr_x$	$\overset{\circ}{e}_x$	Age (x)
0	30226	1518	.050222	.048180	100000	4818	95931	.050224	.155377	6337170	.000000	63.372	0
1	129812	521	.004013	.015896	95182	1513	376946	.004014	1.500000	6241239	.000000	65.572	1
5	171615	282	.001643	.008178	93669	766	466430	.001642	2.500000	5864294	.000000	62.607	5
10	160874	211	.001312	.006534	92903	607	463088	.001311	2.648957	5397864	-.002898	58.102	10
15	182222	478	.002623	.013002	92296	1200	458643	.002616	2.635590	4934776	-.019033	53.467	15
20	193392	594	.003071	.015237	91096	1388	452084	.003070	2.552984	4476133	-.010015	49.136	20
25	184439	644	.003492	.017312	89708	1553	444701	.003492	2.527903	4024050	.003761	44.857	25
30	169826	620	.003651	.018104	88155	1596	436839	.003654	2.534070	3579349	.013296	40.603	30
35	150112	635	.004230	.020957	86559	1814	428354	.004235	2.551567	3142509	.018159	36.305	35
40	135316	660	.004877	.024131	84745	2045	418802	.004883	2.592910	2714156	.014687	32.027	40
45	126896	849	.006691	.032963	82700	2726	407036	.006697	2.628699	2295353	.006042	27.755	45
50	121100	1153	.009521	.046628	79974	3729	391157	.009533	2.663527	1888318	.007536	23.612	50
55	103294	1582	.015316	.074143	76245	5653	367920	.015365	2.646309	1497160	.018124	19.636	55
60	84512	1937	.022920	.109063	70592	7699	334836	.022993	2.645906	1129241	-.017080	15.997	60
65	68574	2622	.038236	.175616	62893	11045	287970	.038355	2.601215	794405	-.015967	12.631	65
70	47459	2708	.057060	.251987	51848	13065	227619	.057399	2.579714	506434	.031041	9.768	70
75	26008	2692	.103507	.413686	38783	16044	153596	.104566	2.486963	278815	.031494	7.189	75
80	12515	1835	.146624	.530410	22739	12061	81896	.147272	2.363506	125220	.031494	5.507	80
85+	5173	1275	.246472	1.000000	10678	10678	43323	.246472	4.057255	43323	.000000	4.057	85+

NUMBER OF PERSONS DYING (OUT OF 100,000 AT BIRTH) ABOVE AGE X FROM SPECIFIED CAUSES

Age (x)	All Causes	Respiratory T. B.	Other Infec. and Paras.	Neo-plasms	Cardio-vascular	Infl., Pneu., Bronch.	Diar-rheal	Certain Degen-erative	Maternal	Cert. Dis. of Infancy	Motor Vehicle	Other Violence	Other and Unknown	Age (x)
0	100000	5967	3853	13284	35109	10641	965	4407	757	2063	242	3047	19665	0
1	95182	5938	3517	13271	35068	9934	438	4401	757	0	242	2977	18639	1
5	93669	5912	3078	13233	35039	9646	360	4380	757	0	216	2757	18291	5
10	92903	5898	2836	13203	34990	9554	346	4353	757	0	194	2683	18089	10
15	92296	5786	2658	13174	34932	9545	343	4322	757	0	177	2657	17945	15
20	91056	5272	2461	13132	34872	9510	341	4281	742	0	161	2577	17747	20
25	89708	4660	2281	13097	34806	9452	338	4249	623	0	152	2502	17548	25
30	88155	3947	2122	13046	34722	9386	336	4209	491	0	145	2418	17334	30
35	86559	3461	1976	12940	34588	9291	333	4143	292	0	132	2317	17086	35
40	84745	3074	1833	12716	34353	9177	331	4040	104	0	121	2206	16790	40
45	82700	2759	1687	12300	34008	9050	321	3885	27	0	118	2085	16460	45
50	79974	2467	1530	11639	33375	8893	312	3647	5	0	118	1957	16031	50
55	76245	2098	1336	10668	32375	8731	308	3292	2	0	111	1828	15496	55
60	70592	1677	1115	9304	30497	8401	298	2817	2	0	97	1674	14706	60
65	62893	1209	905	7533	27633	7844	278	2241	2	0	77	1484	13687	65
70	51848	751	665	5450	22970	6798	240	1589	2	0	52	1248	12083	70
75	38783	358	381	3295	16670	5396	187	925	2	0	18	1060	10491	75
80	22739	115	155	1497	9303	3325	109	404	2	0	0	713	7116	80
85+	10678	25	67	528	4120	1625	50	167	0	0	0	352	3744	85+

NUMBER OF PERSONS SURVIVING TO AGE X IF SPECIFIED CAUSES WERE ELIMINATED

Age (x)	No Causes	Respiratory T. B.	Other Infec. and Paras.	Neo-plasms	Cardio-vascular	Infl., Pneu., Bronch.	Diar-rheal	Certain Degener-ative	Maternal	Cert. Dis. of Infancy	Motor Vehicle	Other Violence	Other and Unknown	(1) + (2)	(1) + (2) + (5) + (6) + (8)	(1)+(2)+ (5)+(6)+ (8)+part of(9)&(12)	(10) + (11)	Age (x)
		(1)	(2)	(3)	(4)	(5)	(6)	(7)	(8)	(9)	(10)	(11)	(12)					
0	100000	100000	100000	100000	100000	100000	100000	100000	100000	100000	100000	100000	100000	100000	100000	100000	100000	0
1	95182	95210	95510	95195	95222	95874	95697	95188	95182	97216	95182	95250	96188	95539	96755	99629	95250	1
5	93669	93723	94430	93719	93737	94638	94254	93696	93669	95671	93695	93955	95009	94484	96058	99173	93981	5
10	92903	92970	93901	92983	93019	93957	93497	92956	92903	94888	92951	93260	94436	93969	95643	98882	93308	10
15	92296	92475	93467	92404	92470	93352	92889	92380	92296	94268	92360	92677	93965	93648	95329	98656	92742	15
20	91056	91785	92450	91244	91327	92174	91684	91220	91111	93043	91175	91552	92944	93150	94876	98349	91632	20
25	89708	91001	91223	89889	90001	90828	90290	89861	89841	91625	89795	90232	91729	92538	94440	98074	90319	25
30	88155	90145	89804	88384	88527	89221	88729	88347	88417	90039	88247	88754	90358	91832	93930	97733	88847	30
35	86559	89007	88326	86889	87058	87800	87125	86812	87014	88409	86663	87248	88975	90823	93216	97179	87352	35
40	84745	87536	86619	85291	85467	86674	85201	85095	85378	86556	84857	85530	87412	89472	92155	96255	85643	40
45	82700	85745	84677	83648	83750	84125	83253	83195	83394	84467	82813	83587	85639	87794	90658	94839	83701	45
50	79974	83217	82044	81551	81622	81509	80518	80689	80667	81683	80083	80959	83254	85370	88359	92569	81069	50
55	76245	79712	78412	78721	78820	77870	76767	77277	76908	77874	76356	77311	79918	81978	85032	89223	77423	55
60	70592	74226	72813	74251	74870	72422	71085	72012	71206	72100	70708	71729	74793	76562	79783	83897	71847	60
65	62893	66595	65080	67931	69636	65066	63351	64713	63440	64237	63015	64089	67663	68911	72436	76391	64213	65
70	51848	55339	53876	58073	62292	54632	52261	53958	52299	52956	51571	53051	57365	57504	61605	65313	53177	70
75	38783	41754	40554	45557	53600	42162	39138	40957	39120	39612	38905	39849	44464	43660	48315	51564	39974	75
80	22739	24674	23954	28333	40132	26450	23007	24426	22937	23225	22823	23638	29208	25992	30902	33766	23726	80
85+	10678	11652	11311	14138	26079	13838	10844	11642	10772	10906	10718	11354	16943	12342	16386	18770	11396	85+

ADDED YRS OF LIFE																		
TOTAL		1.820	1.392	1.967	4.785	1.709	.438	.709	.291	1.351	.078	.690	3.433	3.269	5.954	9.269	.769	
WORK	5.140	1.242	.417	.627	.720	.238	.010	.266	.241	.000	.024	.243	.716	1.674	2.191	2.598	.267	

POPULATION, DEATHS, DEATH RATES FOR ALL CAUSES COMBINED, AND SPECIFIED CAUSES

Age Start of Interval	Midyear Population	Deaths During Year	All Causes	Respiratory T.B.	Other Infec. and Paras.	Neoplasms	Cardiovascular	Infl., Pneu., Bronch.	Diarrheal	Certain Degenerative	Maternal	Cert. Dis. of Infancy	Motor Vehicle	Other Violence	Other and Unknown	Age Start of Interval
0	32319	1662	.05142	.00028	.00179	.00006	.00046	.00569	.00368	.00025	.00000	.02642	.00000	.00065	.01213	0
1	122519	398	.00325	.00002	.00064	.00015	.00004	.00041	.00006	.00002	.00000	.00000	.00007	.00075	.00110	1
5	159172	208	.00131	.00004	.00035	.00005	.00006	.00006	.00001	.00004	.00000	.00000	.00006	.00021	.00044	5
10	163909	204	.00124	.00005	.00025	.00007	.00006	.00007	.00001	.00007	.00000	.00000	.00003	.00024	.00040	10
15	171133	371	.00217	.00026	.00033	.00013	.00011	.00009	.00000	.00005	.00000	.00000	.00006	.00070	.00044	15
20	162800	453	.00278	.00062	.00027	.00008	.00008	.00006	.00000	.00007	.00000	.00000	.00004	.00106	.00050	20
25	165218	534	.00323	.00077	.00027	.00011	.00012	.00005	.00000	.00011	.00000	.00000	.00005	.00122	.00053	25
30	174224	513	.00294	.00062	.00030	.00016	.00018	.00007	.00000	.00016	.00000	.00000	.00005	.00092	.00048	30
35	165513	605	.00366	.00064	.00033	.00037	.00041	.00010	.00001	.00026	.00000	.00000	.00005	.00089	.00059	35
40	149459	774	.00518	.00078	.00036	.00076	.00077	.00011	.00001	.00041	.00000	.00000	.00005	.00103	.00059	40
45	128712	1023	.00795	.00091	.00042	.00148	.00167	.00023	.00001	.00072	.00000	.00000	.00006	.00121	.00123	45
50	111979	1299	.01160	.00105	.00054	.00246	.00279	.00045	.00002	.00125	.00000	.00000	.00007	.00150	.00147	50
55	102637	1883	.01835	.00118	.00064	.00428	.00558	.00079	.00002	.00174	.00000	.00000	.00008	.00181	.00222	55
60	89139	2476	.02778	.00126	.00077	.00738	.00958	.00108	.00000	.00225	.00000	.00000	.00008	.00220	.00319	60
65	70070	3160	.04510	.00140	.00091	.01069	.01840	.00237	.00003	.00280	.00000	.00000	.00007	.00254	.00589	65
70	44802	2934	.06549	.00163	.00109	.01413	.03058	.00388	.00007	.00326	.00000	.00000	.00004	.00246	.00835	70
75	26787	2950	.11013	.00153	.00116	.01699	.05372	.00944	.00019	.00351	.00000	.00000	.00004	.00332	.02023	75
80	11154	1763	.15806	.00081	.00090	.01587	.07899	.01748	.00036	.00260	.00000	.00000	.00009	.00457	.03640	80
85+	3603	930	.25812	.00056	.00139	.01665	.11879	.03164	.00083	.00361	.00000	.00000	.00000	.00833	.07633	85+
ALL	2055149	24140														
CRUDE DEATH RATE			.01175	.00064	.00046	.00191	.00373	.00073	.00007	.00063	.00000	.00042	.00005	.00112	.00198	
STANDARDIZED RATE (1)			.00855	.00047	.00046	.00106	.00196	.00058	.00014	.00038	.00000	.00093	.00005	.00090	.00161	
STANDARDIZED RATE (2)			.01392	.00061	.00048	.00212	.00473	.00098	.00010	.00065	.00000	.00055	.00005	.00114	.00251	
GEOMETRIC MEAN			.01168													

LIFE TABLE FOR ALL CAUSES COMBINED

Age (x)	Midyear Population	Deaths During Year	$_nM_x$	$_nq_x$	l_x	$_nd_x$	$_nL_x$	$_nm_x$	$_na_x$	T_x	$_nr_x$	$\overset{\circ}{e}_x$	Age (x)
0	32319	1662	.051425	.049290	100000	4929	95847	.051426	.157422	6278359	.000000	62.784	0
1	122519	398	.003248	.012885	95071	1225	377222	.003247	1.500000	6182512	.000000	65.030	1
5	159172	208	.001307	.006521	93846	612	467700	.001309	2.500000	5805291	.000000	61.860	5
10	163909	204	.001245	.006199	93234	578	464806	.001244	2.639490	5337591	-.007758	57.249	10
15	171133	371	.002169	.010782	92656	999	460926	.002167	2.643477	4872785	-.003784	52.590	15
20	162800	453	.002783	.013812	91657	1266	455214	.002781	2.574052	4411859	.001733	48.134	20
25	165218	534	.003232	.016030	90391	1449	448340	.003232	2.504888	3956645	-.007727	43.773	25
30	174224	513	.002944	.014616	88942	1300	441489	.002945	2.522436	3508306	-.006732	39.445	30
35	165513	605	.003655	.018131	87642	1589	434426	.003658	2.618917	3066817	-.005915	34.993	35
40	149459	774	.005179	.025647	86053	2207	425100	.005192	2.659908	2632390	.015967	30.590	40
45	128712	1023	.007948	.039155	83846	3283	411513	.007978	2.649317	2207290	.021260	26.326	45
50	111979	1299	.011600	.056602	80563	4560	392125	.011629	2.655610	1795777	.014152	22.290	50
55	102637	1883	.018346	.088010	76003	6689	364226	.018365	2.639564	1403653	-.006154	18.468	55
60	89139	2476	.027777	.130435	69314	9041	325135	.027807	2.629111	1039427	.005776	14.996	60
65	70070	3160	.045098	.203939	60273	12292	271581	.045261	2.576947	714292	-.019188	11.851	65
70	44802	2934	.065488	.283050	47981	13581	206494	.065769	2.535869	442711	-.024032	9.227	70
75	26787	2950	.110128	.432878	34400	14891	134212	.110951	2.462379	236217	-.028365	6.867	75
80	11154	1763	.158060	.558306	19509	10892	68621	.158727	2.344458	102005	-.028365	5.229	80
85+	3603	930	.258118	1.000000	8617	8617	33384	.258118	3.874194	33384	.000000	3.874	85+

NUMBER OF PERSONS DYING (OUT OF 100,000 AT BIRTH) ABOVE AGE X FROM SPECIFIED CAUSES

Age (x)	All Causes	Respiratory T.B.	Other Infec. and Paras.	Neoplasms	Cardiovascular	Infl., Pneu., Bronch.	Diarrheal	Certain Degenerative	Maternal	Cert. Dis. of Infancy	Motor Vehicle	Other Violence	Other and Unknown	Age (x)
0	100000	4336	3127	16156	35806	6873	502	4927	0	2533	344	7846	17550	0
1	95071	4309	2955	16150	35761	6327	150	4903	0	0	344	7784	16388	1
5	93846	4303	2715	16094	35746	6173	128	4894	0	0	320	7500	15973	5
10	93234	4282	2553	16071	35719	6147	125	4873	0	0	293	7403	15768	10
15	92656	4260	2437	16037	35691	6116	122	4839	0	0	279	7293	15582	15
20	91657	4141	2283	15975	35643	6075	122	4815	0	0	252	6973	15378	20
25	90391	3859	2160	15939	35606	6047	122	4782	0	0	232	6492	15152	25
30	88942	3511	2041	15890	35552	6023	122	4733	0	0	211	5946	14913	30
35	87642	3238	1909	15819	35474	5990	122	4662	0	0	190	5538	14700	35
40	86053	2959	1765	15656	35295	5948	120	4549	0	0	167	5150	14444	40
45	83846	2629	1611	15333	34966	5899	117	4372	0	0	144	4711	14064	45
50	80563	2255	1438	14719	34275	5803	114	4073	0	0	118	4212	13556	50
55	76003	1841	1228	13750	33178	5627	107	3582	0	0	90	3623	12977	55
60	69314	1412	993	12190	31142	5339	99	2946	0	0	62	2962	12169	60
65	60273	1003	742	9787	28022	4989	99	2213	0	0	40	2247	11131	65
70	47981	623	493	6876	23003	4342	92	1451	0	0	21	1556	9524	70
75	34400	286	267	3951	16656	3534	78	778	0	0	12	1049	7789	75
80	19509	80	111	1664	9390	2254	52	306	0	0	7	601	5044	80
85+	8617	19	46	556	3966	1056	28	120	0	0	0	278	2548	85+

NUMBER OF PERSONS SURVIVING TO AGE X IF SPECIFIED CAUSES WERE ELIMINATED

Age (x)	No Causes	Respiratory T.B. (1)	Other Infec. and Paras. (2)	Neoplasms (3)	Cardiovascular (4)	Infl., Pneu., Bronch. (5)	Diarrheal (6)	Certain Degenerative (7)	Maternal (8)	Cert. Dis. of Infancy (9)	Motor Vehicle (10)	Other Violence (11)	Other and Unknown (12)	(1)+(2)	(1)+(2)+(6)+(8)	(1)+(2)+(5)+(6)+(8)+part of(9)&(12)	(10)+(11)	Age (x)
0	100000	100000	100000	100000	100000	100000	100000	100000	100000	100000	100000	100000	100000	100000	100000	100000	100000	0
1	95071	95097	95239	95077	95115	95605	95415	95094	95071	97573	95071	95131	96211	95265	96147	99440	95131	1
5	93846	93878	94251	93907	93904	94527	94207	93878	93846	96316	93870	94188	95389	94283	95333	99825	94212	5
10	93234	93287	93799	93318	93319	93937	93556	93287	93234	95688	93285	93671	94575	93852	94926	98515	93722	10
15	92656	92730	93333	92773	92768	93385	93019	92742	92656	95094	92720	93201	94575	93408	94512	98172	93265	15
20	91657	91849	92481	91835	91816	92420	92016	91766	91657	94069	91747	92517	93763	92675	93812	97530	92608	20
25	90391	90862	91327	90602	90584	91171	90745	90532	90391	92770	90500	91722	92658	91803	92958	96742	91833	25
30	88942	89753	89983	89199	89186	89734	89290	89129	88942	91283	89070	90803	91455	90803	91970	95817	90934	30
35	87642	88715	88800	87566	87560	88455	87985	87897	87642	89948	87789	89890	90336	89887	91076	94578	90041	35
40	86053	87386	87335	86533	86544	86893	86392	86416	86053	88318	86220	88656	88850	88688	89907	93856	88828	40
45	83846	85476	85529	84635	84652	84714	84179	84375	83846	86052	84032	86829	87067	86907	88155	92148	87022	45
50	80563	82504	82084	81931	82024	81492	80886	81367	80563	82683	80767	83937	84176	84061	85372	89367	84150	50
55	76003	78246	77646	78257	78475	77053	76315	77245	76003	78003	76223	79784	80001	79937	81373	85309	80014	55
60	69314	71782	71041	72921	73606	70550	69606	71065	69314	71138	69541	73426	73776	73570	75198	78978	73667	60
65	60273	62813	62014	65809	67174	61682	60527	62498	60273	61855	60491	64556	65192	64628	66416	69896	64789	65
70	47981	50355	49595	55289	58707	49697	48189	50458	47981	49244	48171	52049	53468	52048	54144	57185	52256	70
75	34400	36398	35753	42568	49187	36347	34561	36772	34400	35305	34544	37779	40008	37830	40158	42627	37937	75
80	19509	20800	20394	26304	36802	21653	19620	21225	19509	20022	19554	21791	25215	21745	24272	26142	21886	80
85+	8617	9230	9052	12625	24419	10464	8682	9507	8617	8844	8659	9861	13431	9696	11862	13166	9909	85+

ADDED YRS OF LIFE

	No Causes	(1)	(2)	(3)	(4)	(5)	(6)	(7)	(8)	(9)	(10)	(11)	(12)	(1)+(2)	(1)+(2)+(6)+(8)	(1)+(2)+(5)+(6)+(8)+part of(9)&(12)	(10)+(11)
TOTAL		1.069	.975	2.181	4.873	1.062	.255	.783	.000	1.648	.116	2.023	3.303	2.072	3.478	6.516	2.145
WORK	5.119	.691	.358	.598	.683	.138	.003	.309	.000	.000	.056	1.110	.739	1.057	1.204	1.447	1.169

POPULATION, DEATHS, DEATH RATES FOR ALL CAUSES COMBINED, AND SPECIFIED CAUSES

Age Start of Interval	Midyear Population	Deaths During Year	All Causes	Respiratory T.B.	Other Infec. and Paras.	Neoplasms	Cardiovascular	Infl., Pneu., Bronch.	Diarrheal	Certain Degenerative	Maternal	Cert. Dis. of Infancy	Motor Vehicle	Other Violence	Other and Unknown	Age Start of Interval
0	31365	1297	.04135	.00019	.00172	.00016	.00048	.00532	.00239	.00003	.00000	.02120	.00000	.00045	.00941	0
1	118639	323	.00272	.00001	.00054	.00013	.00004	.00052	.00007	.00007	.00000	.00000	.00003	.00044	.00087	1
5	153931	194	.00126	.00005	.00034	.00004	.00004	.00007	.00001	.00004	.00000	.00000	.00003	.00016	.00048	5
10	159650	168	.00105	.00008	.00033	.00009	.00006	.00005	.00001	.00004	.00000	.00000	.00002	.00007	.00032	10
15	168425	245	.00145	.00035	.00034	.00010	.00007	.00004	.00001	.00004	.00002	.00000	.00000	.00017	.00033	15
20	162361	339	.00209	.00071	.00031	.00008	.00004	.00004	.00001	.00004	.00015	.00000	.00001	.00022	.00041	20
25	168903	414	.00245	.00086	.00028	.00012	.00013	.00005	.00001	.00005	.00020	.00000	.00002	.00025	.00047	25
30	184237	448	.00243	.00070	.00023	.00022	.00017	.00008	.00000	.00008	.00019	.00000	.00001	.00021	.00054	30
35	178746	510	.00285	.00062	.00021	.00045	.00031	.00010	.00000	.00015	.00017	.00000	.00001	.00021	.00062	35
40	167994	585	.00348	.00051	.00021	.00087	.00045	.00010	.00001	.00030	.00010	.00000	.00001	.00026	.00067	40
45	147096	761	.00517	.00045	.00023	.00146	.00111	.00015	.00001	.00052	.00005	.00000	.00001	.00031	.00090	45
50	128700	986	.00766	.00048	.00030	.00221	.00204	.00021	.00001	.00078	.00000	.00000	.00000	.00033	.00131	50
55	117014	1466	.01253	.00056	.00038	.00335	.00443	.00044	.00001	.00114	.00000	.00000	.00001	.00038	.00184	55
60	105568	1977	.01873	.00073	.00051	.00496	.00766	.00064	.00003	.00159	.00000	.00000	.00002	.00041	.00217	60
65	86122	2827	.03283	.00099	.00069	.00709	.01576	.00171	.00003	.00206	.00000	.00000	.00001	.00062	.00388	65
70	58645	3025	.05158	.00148	.00087	.00977	.02764	.00312	.00005	.00244	.00000	.00000	.00000	.00084	.00537	70
75	38563	3543	.09188	.00156	.00117	.01258	.05000	.00757	.00010	.00280	.00000	.00000	.00003	.00197	.01411	75
80	17703	2539	.14342	.00085	.00147	.01423	.07818	.01423	.00023	.00260	.00000	.00000	.00000	.00006	.00390	.02768	80
85+	6726	1549	.23030	.00059	.00208	.01487	.11775	.02587	.00030	.00357	.00000	.00000	.00000	.00015	.00390	.02768	85+
ALL	2200388	23196														

	All Causes	Respiratory T.B.	Other Infec. and Paras.	Neoplasms	Cardiovascular	Infl., Pneu., Bronch.	Diarrheal	Certain Degenerative	Maternal	Cert. Dis. of Infancy	Motor Vehicle	Other Violence	Other and Unknown
CRUDE DEATH RATE	.01054	.00054	.00039	.00173	.00413	.00070	.00005	.00050	.00007	.00030	.00001	.00036	.00176
STANDARDIZED RATE (1)	.00660	.00041	.00040	.00085	.00171	.00050	.00010	.00026	.00006	.00075	.00002	.00028	.00126
STANDARDIZED RATE (2)	.01091	.00050	.00041	.00164	.00425	.00079	.00007	.00047	.00006	.00044	.00001	.00038	.00189
GEOMETRIC MEAN	.00899												

LIFE TABLE FOR ALL CAUSES COMBINED

Age (x)	Midyear Population	Deaths During Year	$_nM_x$	$_nq_x$	l_x	$_nd_x$	$_nL_x$	$_nm_x$	$_na_x$	T_x	$_nr_x$	$\overset{\circ}{e}_x$	Age (x)
0	31365	1297	.041352	.039930	100000	3993	96567	.041349	.140298	6698793	.000000	66.988	0
1	118639	323	.002723	.010822	96007	1039	381431	.002724	1.500000	6602226	.000000	68.768	1
5	153931	194	.001260	.006276	94968	596	473350	.001259	2.500000	6220795	.000000	65.504	5
10	159650	168	.001052	.005245	94372	495	470640	.001052	2.535354	5747445	-.008865	60.902	10
15	168425	245	.001455	.007244	93877	680	467784	.001454	2.644914	5276805	-.005265	56.210	15
20	162361	339	.002088	.010387	93197	968	463657	.002088	2.595558	4809022	-.000559	51.601	20
25	168903	414	.002451	.012187	92229	1124	458362	.002452	2.524466	4345364	-.012274	47.115	25
30	184237	448	.002432	.012074	91105	1100	452806	.002429	2.528598	3887002	-.011450	42.665	30
35	178746	510	.002853	.014166	90005	1275	446928	.002853	2.571078	3434195	-.000741	38.156	35
40	167994	585	.003482	.017300	88730	1535	440013	.003489	2.630429	2987267	.011082	33.667	40
45	147096	761	.005173	.025644	87195	2236	430733	.005191	2.655784	2547254	.019841	29.213	45
50	128700	986	.007661	.037748	84959	3207	417350	.007684	2.678516	2116521	.017278	24.912	50
55	117014	1466	.012528	.060965	81752	4984	397069	.012552	2.654285	1699171	.009587	20.784	55
60	105568	1977	.018727	.089855	76768	6898	367783	.018756	2.672182	1302102	.007514	16.962	60
65	86122	2827	.032826	.152927	69870	10685	324042	.032974	2.631454	934319	-.021550	13.372	65
70	58645	3025	.051582	.230464	59185	13640	263168	.051830	2.558470	610277	.023698	10.311	70
75	38563	3543	.091876	.376155	45545	17132	185158	.092526	2.515371	347109	.026238	7.621	75
80	17703	2539	.143422	.524549	28413	14904	103292	.144289	2.398517	161951	.026238	5.700	80
85+	6726	1549	.230300	1.000000	13509	13509	58658	.230300	4.342156	58658	.000000	4.342	85+

NUMBER OF PERSONS DYING (OUT OF 100,000 AT BIRTH) ABOVE AGE X FROM SPECIFIED CAUSES

Age (x)	All Causes	Respiratory T.B.	Other Infec. and Paras.	Neoplasms	Cardiovascular	Infl., Pneu., Bronch.	Diarrheal	Certain Degenerative	Maternal	Cert. Dis. of Infancy	Motor Vehicle	Other Violence	Other and Unknown	Age (x)
0	100000	3805	2919	15260	43369	7306	382	4267	395	2047	92	3105	17053	0
1	96007	3787	2752	15245	43322	6792	151	4264	395	0	92	3062	16145	1
5	94968	3784	2547	15193	43306	6592	125	4238	395	0	79	2895	15814	5
10	94372	3759	2387	15175	43288	6558	122	4220	395	0	64	2818	15586	10
15	93877	3724	2233	15134	43258	6535	119	4202	395	0	55	2785	15437	15
20	93197	3560	2075	15086	43225	6518	116	4186	387	0	55	2705	15284	20
25	92229	3229	1930	15049	43182	6498	111	4166	318	0	49	2602	15095	25
30	91105	2833	1799	14992	43123	6476	108	4141	226	0	41	2488	14878	30
35	90005	2516	1693	14892	43044	6440	108	4107	140	0	39	2395	14631	35
40	88730	2238	1601	14689	42907	6395	108	4039	63	0	36	2300	14354	40
45	87195	2016	1507	14306	42707	6353	105	3905	21	0	34	2184	14057	45
50	84959	1822	1407	13674	42227	6288	102	3682	0	0	34	2052	13671	50
55	81752	1621	1283	12751	41373	6200	99	3354	0	0	34	1916	13121	55
60	76768	1397	1134	11418	39610	6027	96	2902	0	0	30	1763	12391	60
65	69870	1129	946	9591	36786	5789	85	2316	0	0	23	1613	11592	65
70	59185	808	723	7285	31652	5232	74	1649	0	0	19	1413	10330	70
75	45545	416	494	4706	24338	4405	60	1006	0	0	19	1192	8909	75
80	28413	128	277	2368	15015	2990	41	486	0	0	15	824	6269	80
85+	13509	35	122	872	6907	1517	17	209	0	0	9	419	3402	85+

NUMBER OF PERSONS SURVIVING TO AGE X IF SPECIFIED CAUSES WERE ELIMINATED

Age (x)	No Causes	Respiratory T.B. (1)	Other Infec. and Paras. (2)	Neoplasms (3)	Cardiovascular (4)	Infl., Pneu., Bronch. (5)	Diarrheal (6)	Certain Degenerative (7)	Maternal (8)	Cert. Dis. of Infancy (9)	Motor Vehicle (10)	Other Violence (11)	Other and Unknown (12)	(1)+(2)	(1)+(2)+(5)+(6)+(8)	(1)+(2)+(5)+(6)+(8)+part of(9)&(12)	(10)+(11)	Age (x)
0	100000	100000	100000	100000	100000	100000	100000	100000	100000	100000	100000	100000	100000	100000	100000	100000	100000	0
1	96007	96025	96171	96022	96053	96512	96234	96010	96007	98034	96007	96049	96501	96188	96923	99577	96049	1
5	94968	94988	95334	95034	95029	95668	95218	94997	94968	96973	94981	95176	96185	95355	96310	99158	95189	5
10	94372	94417	94896	94456	94451	95101	94623	94419	94372	96364	94400	94656	95812	94942	95931	98911	94684	10
15	93877	93957	94553	94001	93986	94626	94130	93941	93877	95859	93914	94192	95460	94634	95646	98714	94229	15
20	93197	93440	94027	93368	93338	93957	93451	93277	93205	95164	93233	93590	94924	94272	95309	98474	93626	20
25	92229	92800	93196	92435	92411	93001	92486	92328	92306	94176	92271	92721	94130	93773	94901	98198	92763	25
30	91105	92066	92192	91366	91344	91890	91362	91228	91272	93028	91154	91705	93203	93164	94405	97850	91754	30
35	90005	91273	91185	90362	90320	90817	90258	90160	90256	91905	90056	90691	92329	92470	93828	97421	90742	35
40	88730	90261	89986	89285	89177	89575	88980	88950	89054	90603	88783	89501	91304	91539	93009	96719	89554	40
45	87195	88923	88524	88123	87834	88068	87444	87545	87555	89036	87249	88069	90028	90279	91820	95587	88123	45
50	84959	86838	86354	86496	86060	85874	85204	85521	85331	86752	85012	85942	88113	88264	89864	93367	85995	50
55	81752	83762	83218	84158	83665	82720	81991	82617	82110	83478	81803	82833	85348	85264	86904	90647	82884	55
60	76768	78878	78292	80368	80334	77847	76995	78024	77104	78389	76820	77533	80886	80443	82173	85814	77985	60
65	69870	72053	71440	74991	75993	71083	70087	71583	70176	71345	69924	71075	74425	73671	75512	78957	71130	65
70	59185	61338	60724	65834	69724	60737	59379	61265	59444	60434	59234	60393	64290	62933	65079	68205	60443	70
75	45545	47557	46934	53221	61754	47491	45707	47727	45744	46506	45583	46672	50847	49007	51507	54159	46711	75
80	28413	29899	29453	35384	45801	30811	28529	30197	28537	29013	28440	29415	34131	30994	33895	35992	29442	80
85+	13509	14282	14112	18127	35481	15766	13580	14557	13568	13794	13526	14271	18723	14920	17581	19060	14288	85+

ADDED YRS OF LIFE

	No Causes	(1)	(2)	(3)	(4)	(5)	(6)	(7)	(8)	(9)	(10)	(11)	(12)	(1)+(2)	(1)+(2)+(5)+(6)+(8)	+part of(9)&(12)	(10)+(11)
TOTAL		1.072	.961	2.221	6.317	1.114	.155	.666	.161	1.411	.036	.695	3.128	2.056	3.619	6.462	.732
WORK	3.743	.676	.313	.605	.551	.098	.007	.211	.128	.000	.008	.260	.666	.995	1.235	1.552	.267

POPULATION, DEATHS, DEATH RATES FOR ALL CAUSES COMBINED, AND SPECIFIED CAUSES

Age Start of Interval	Midyear Population	Deaths During Year	All Causes	Respiratory T. B.	Other Infec. and Paras.	Neo-plasms	Cardio-vascular	Infl., Pneu., Bronch.	Diar-rheal	Certain Degen-erative	Maternal	Cert. Dis. of Infancy	Motor Vehicle	Other Violence	Other and Unknown	Age Start of Interval
0	41657	1428	.03428	.00012	.00079	.00014	.00029	.00206	.00161	.00002	.00000	.02062	.00000	.00101	.00761	0
1	170652	384	.00225	.00005	.00026	.00016	.00003	.00018	.00012	.00005	.00000	.00004	.00015	.00067	.00055	1
5	202616	170	.00084	.00001	.00014	.00010	.00004	.00003	.00002	.00002	.00000	.00000	.00015	.00016	.00015	5
10	155174	116	.00075	.00000	.00008	.00008	.00003	.00005	.00000	.00001	.00000	.00000	.00009	.00024	.00016	10
15	160855	209	.00130	.00006	.00009	.00007	.00005	.00006	.00000	.00004	.00000	.00000	.00021	.00055	.00019	15
20	169484	304	.00179	.00014	.00012	.00015	.00010	.00002	.00000	.00005	.00000	.00000	.00032	.00076	.00013	20
25	180693	334	.00185	.00020	.00008	.00015	.00013	.00003	.00002	.00009	.00000	.00000	.00028	.00066	.00020	25
30	170175	388	.00228	.00036	.00013	.00015	.00025	.00003	.00001	.00013	.00000	.00000	.00025	.00071	.00023	30
35	174705	470	.00269	.00037	.00011	.00038	.00038	.00003	.00001	.00010	.00000	.00000	.00023	.00073	.00035	35
40	178396	655	.00367	.00038	.00015	.00070	.00071	.00006	.00001	.00028	.00000	.00000	.00018	.00081	.00040	40
45	163966	1006	.00614	.00052	.00014	.00137	.00171	.00010	.00000	.00045	.00000	.00000	.00019	.00104	.00062	45
50	141734	1408	.00993	.00063	.00028	.00248	.00305	.00023	.00003	.00085	.00000	.00000	.00031	.00113	.00096	50
55	116430	1827	.01569	.00077	.00030	.00434	.00524	.00048	.00008	.00120	.00000	.00000	.00028	.00141	.00159	55
60	95142	2336	.02455	.00080	.00044	.00675	.00968	.00079	.00011	.00180	.00000	.00000	.00036	.00170	.00213	60
65	79189	3128	.03950	.00102	.00047	.01035	.01739	.00157	.00014	.00208	.00000	.00000	.00045	.00205	.00398	65
70	58588	3770	.06435	.00111	.00061	.01461	.03182	.00348	.00029	.00311	.00000	.00000	.00041	.00229	.00662	70
75	35202	3605	.10241	.00148	.00054	.01724	.05664	.00716	.00026	.00330	.00000	.00000	.00054	.00293	.01233	75
80	15159	2427	.16010	.00145	.00046	.02137	.08919	.01366	.00059	.00330	.00000	.00000	.00026	.00409	.02573	80
85+	5665	1596	.28173	.00124	.00053	.02383	.15269	.02860	.00035	.00459	.00000	.00000	.00053	.00936	.06002	85+
ALL	2315482	25561														

	All Causes	Respiratory T.B.	Other Infec. and Paras.	Neo-plasms	Cardio-vascular	Infl., Pneu., Bronch.	Diar-rheal	Certain Degen-erative	Maternal	Cert. Dis. of Infancy	Motor Vehicle	Other Violence	Other and Unknown
CRUDE DEATH RATE	.01104	.00036	.00021	.00208	.00432	.00056	.00007	.00051	.00000	.00037	.00024	.00092	.00139
STANDARDIZED RATE (1)	.00685	.00024	.00019	.00108	.00202	.00033	.00009	.00028	.00000	.00073	.00021	.00072	.00096
STANDARDIZED RATE (2)	.01226	.00035	.00021	.00219	.00502	.00068	.00008	.00052	.00000	.00043	.00024	.00092	.00162
GEOMETRIC MEAN	.00859												

LIFE TABLE FOR ALL CAUSES COMBINED

Age (x)	Midyear Population	Deaths During Year	$_nM_x$	$_nq_x$	l_x	$_nd_x$	$_nL_x$	$_nm_x$	$_na_x$	T_x	$_nr_x$	$\overset{\circ}{e}_x$	Age (x)
0	41657	1428	.034280	.033290	100000	3329	97098	.034285	.128276	6639115	.000000	66.391	0
1	170652	384	.002250	.008948	96671	865	384522	.002250	1.500000	6542017	.000000	67.673	1
5	202616	170	.000835	.004175	95806	400	478030	.000837	2.500000	6157495	.000000	64.270	5
10	155174	116	.000748	.003742	95406	357	476182	.000750	2.625467	5679465	.022555	59.529	10
15	160855	209	.001299	.006470	95049	615	473809	.001298	2.664634	5203283	-.001447	54.743	15
20	169484	304	.001794	.008927	94434	843	470114	.001793	2.560795	4729474	-.012247	50.082	20
25	180693	334	.001848	.009200	93591	861	465846	.001848	2.550329	4259360	-.005750	45.510	25
30	170175	388	.002280	.011334	92730	1051	461098	.002279	2.572154	3793514	-.001342	40.909	30
35	174705	470	.002690	.013362	91679	1225	455456	.002690	2.601020	3332416	-.006661	36.349	35
40	178396	655	.003672	.018166	90454	1645	448463	.003668	2.685917	2876960	-.002007	31.806	40
45	163966	1006	.006135	.030324	88809	2693	437844	.006151	2.697425	2428496	.011061	27.345	45
50	141734	1408	.009934	.048737	86116	4197	420824	.009973	2.675373	1990652	.020668	23.116	50
55	116430	1827	.015692	.076002	81919	6226	394991	.015762	2.654359	1569829	.024599	19.163	55
60	95142	2336	.024553	.116391	75693	8810	357661	.024632	2.638645	1174838	.016763	15.521	60
65	79189	3128	.039500	.180748	66883	12089	305537	.039566	2.611206	817176	.008777	12.218	65
70	58588	3770	.064348	.278552	54794	15263	236660	.064493	2.555540	511639	.010646	9.338	70
75	35202	3605	.102409	.408743	39531	16158	156837	.103024	2.473852	274979	.026305	6.956	75
80	15159	2427	.160103	.566252	23373	13235	82157	.161094	2.377550	118142	.026305	5.055	80
85+	5665	1596	.281730	1.000000	10138	10138	35985	.281730	3.549499	35985	.000000	3.549	85+

NUMBER OF PERSONS DYING (OUT OF 100,000 AT BIRTH) ABOVE AGE X FROM SPECIFIED CAUSES

Age (x)	All Causes	Respiratory T.B.	Other Infec. and Paras.	Neoplasms	Cardiovascular	Infl., Pneu., Bronch.	Diarrheal	Certain Degenerative	Maternal	Cert. Dis. of Infancy	Motor Vehicle	Other Violence	Other and Unknown	Age (x)
0	100000	2785	1483	18682	43081	5618	528	4359	0	2016	1674	6895	12879	0
1	96671	2773	1406	18668	43053	5417	372	4357	0	14	1674	6797	12140	1
5	95806	2753	1307	18605	43042	5350	327	4339	0	0	1615	6540	11928	5
10	95406	2746	1239	18558	43023	5336	317	4327	0	0	1542	6462	11856	10
15	95049	2746	1199	18518	43008	5314	317	4321	0	0	1499	6348	11779	15
20	94434	2719	1158	18482	42984	5288	317	4303	0	0	1402	6089	11692	20
25	93591	2656	1100	18413	42937	5277	317	4281	0	0	1250	5731	11629	25
30	92730	2560	1063	18341	42875	5261	309	4240	0	0	1118	5424	11539	30
35	91679	2395	1004	18254	42759	5248	304	4180	0	0	1004	5099	11432	35
40	90454	2228	954	18082	42584	5232	299	4136	0	0	897	4768	11274	40
45	88809	2060	886	17771	42265	5204	294	4010	0	0	817	4406	11096	45
50	86116	1833	825	17171	41513	5161	294	3812	0	0	734	3952	10821	50
55	81919	1568	709	16121	40224	5066	282	3454	0	0	603	3476	10416	55
60	75693	1262	590	14399	38142	4875	251	2978	0	0	491	2919	9786	60
65	66883	976	432	11979	34666	4592	213	2334	0	0	363	2309	9019	65
70	54794	664	289	8810	29342	4112	171	1696	0	0	224	1684	7802	70
75	39531	401	143	5348	21792	3285	102	960	0	0	127	1142	6231	75
80	23373	168	59	2635	12848	2153	62	443	0	0	42	681	4282	80
85+	10138	44	19	858	5495	1029	13	165	0	0	19	337	2159	85+

NUMBER OF PERSONS SURVIVING TO AGE X IF SPECIFIED CAUSES WERE ELIMINATED

Age (x)	No Causes	Respiratory T.B. (1)	Other Infec. and Paras. (2)	Neoplasms (3)	Cardiovascular (4)	Infl., Pneu., Bronch. (5)	Diarrheal (6)	Certain Degenerative (7)	Maternal (8)	Cert. Dis. of Infancy (9)	Motor Vehicle (10)	Other Violence (11)	Other and Unknown (12)	(1)+(2)	(1)+(2)+(5)+(6)+(8)	(1)+(2)+(5)+(6)+(8)+part of(9)&(12)	(10)+(11)	Age (x)
0	100000	100000	100000	100000	100000	100000	100000	100000	100000	100000	100000	100000	100000	100000	100000	100000	100000	0
1	96671	96683	96747	96685	96699	96869	96824	96673	96671	98659	96671	96767	97400	96759	97110	99186	96767	1
5	95806	95838	95980	95882	95844	96069	96003	95826	95806	97791	95865	96158	96742	96011	96473	98618	96217	5
10	95406	95444	95647	95529	95463	95682	95612	95438	95406	97383	95537	95835	96410	95686	96170	98330	95967	10
15	95049	95087	95329	95212	95121	95346	95254	95087	95049	97018	95223	95590	96127	95368	95872	98044	95765	15
20	94434	94499	94753	94631	94529	94755	94638	94489	94434	96390	94704	95232	95593	94819	95346	97522	95504	20
25	93591	93718	93965	93856	93732	93920	93793	93668	93591	95530	94010	94742	94803	94093	94628	96798	95166	25
30	92730	92952	93138	93064	92932	93072	92938	92847	92730	94651	93277	94180	94022	93361	93916	96089	94736	30
35	91679	92063	92141	92096	91994	92030	91890	91854	91679	93578	92334	93441	93064	92527	93095	95277	94109	35
40	90454	90999	90960	91037	90940	90816	90667	90671	90454	92328	91208	92528	91980	91509	92092	94287	93299	40
45	88809	89512	89374	89693	89604	89193	89023	89147	88809	90649	89629	91213	90487	90081	90688	92884	92055	45
50	86116	87023	86724	87572	87638	86531	86324	86640	86116	87900	86993	88907	88019	87638	88272	90448	89813	50
55	81919	83043	82611	84352	84656	82407	82128	82769	81919	83616	82883	85054	84134	83745	84459	86594	86055	55
60	75693	77030	76448	79664	80320	76329	75916	76942	75693	77261	76692	79147	78364	77798	78683	80747	80191	60
65	66883	68337	67700	72825	74527	67714	67116	68603	66883	68269	67887	70535	69993	69172	70275	72192	71594	65
70	54794	56273	55593	62856	66669	55917	55023	56795	54794	55929	55744	58381	58505	57094	58508	60213	59393	70
75	39531	40825	40232	48813	56551	41065	39755	41621	39531	40350	40299	42606	43653	41549	43406	44815	43433	75
80	23373	24320	23851	31490	44762	25197	23535	25019	23373	23857	23892	25569	27510	24817	26940	28001	26136	80
85+	10138	10632	10371	15280	30881	11733	10240	11044	10138	10348	10378	11334	13643	10876	12714	13430	11602	85+

ADDED YRS OF LIFE																	
TOTAL		.569	.427	2.494	6.050	.641	.178	.622	.000	1.373	.512	1.736	2.027	1.002	1.857	3.576	2.271
WORK	3.854	.305	.139	.626	.726	.075	.011	.216	.000	.000	.278	.844	.372	.446	.534	.598	1.129

POPULATION, DEATHS, DEATH RATES FOR ALL CAUSES COMBINED, AND SPECIFIED CAUSES

Age Start of Interval	Midyear Population	Deaths During Year	All Causes	Respiratory T. B.	Other Infec. and Paras.	Neo-plasms	Cardio-vascular	Infl., Pneu., Bronch.	Diar-rheal	Certain Degen-erative	Maternal	Cert. Dis. of Infancy	Motor Vehicle	Other Violence	Other and Unknown	Age Start of Interval
0	39496	1039	.02631	.00000	.00035	.00020	.00023	.00215	.00071	.00005	.00000	.01501	.00005	.00061	.00694	0
1	163120	277	.00170	.00001	.00022	.00013	.00002	.00024	.00009	.00001	.00000	.00001	.00001	.00008	.00048	1
5	194805	124	.00064	.00001	.00012	.00009	.00003	.00002	.00001	.00003	.00000	.00000	.00007	.00009	.00018	5
10	150590	58	.00039	.00002	.00003	.00004	.00002	.00003	.00000	.00003	.00000	.00000	.00001	.00005	.00015	10
15	159071	83	.00052	.00004	.00006	.00006	.00004	.00004	.00001	.00002	.00001	.00000	.00003	.00008	.00012	15
20	172072	156	.00091	.00015	.00013	.00005	.00005	.00003	.00001	.00005	.00007	.00000	.00003	.00020	.00015	20
25	182165	247	.00136	.00024	.00008	.00015	.00015	.00003	.00001	.00008	.00015	.00000	.00001	.00021	.00024	25
30	167337	254	.00152	.00025	.00012	.00022	.00010	.00004	.00000	.00005	.00017	.00000	.00004	.00020	.00033	30
35	174334	329	.00189	.00016	.00010	.00052	.00021	.00009	.00001	.00008	.00016	.00000	.00003	.00022	.00032	35
40	184539	494	.00268	.00017	.00012	.00083	.00049	.00009	.00002	.00021	.00010	.00000	.00003	.00020	.00041	40
45	175567	755	.00430	.00019	.00015	.00151	.00099	.00014	.00002	.00033	.00002	.00000	.00005	.00029	.00060	45
50	160292	977	.00610	.00020	.00015	.00210	.00173	.00019	.00002	.00057	.00001	.00000	.00007	.00030	.00076	50
55	136629	1346	.00985	.00023	.00020	.00305	.00364	.00024	.00002	.00084	.00000	.00000	.00009	.00042	.00113	55
60	114923	1901	.01654	.00033	.00025	.00466	.00716	.00058	.00003	.00141	.00000	.00000	.00009	.00050	.00153	60
65	97502	2664	.02732	.00056	.00028	.00676	.01352	.00108	.00006	.00184	.00000	.00000	.00003	.00044	.00276	65
70	77183	3748	.04856	.00069	.00039	.00882	.02769	.00281	.00010	.00244	.00000	.00000	.00016	.00096	.00451	70
75	49571	4080	.08231	.00119	.00046	.01317	.04866	.00589	.00038	.00317	.00000	.00000	.00016	.00176	.00746	75
80	23458	3260	.13897	.00102	.00060	.01607	.08517	.01202	.00043	.00315	.00000	.00000	.00004	.00401	.01645	80
85+	10512	2599	.24724	.00095	.00067	.01931	.14003	.03006	.00086	.00304	.00000	.00000	.00029	.01065	.04138	85+
ALL	2433166	24391														

	All Causes	Respiratory T. B.	Other Infec. and Paras.	Neo-plasms	Cardio-vascular	Infl., Pneu., Bronch.	Diar-rheal	Certain Degen-erative	Maternal	Cert. Dis. of Infancy	Motor Vehicle	Other Violence	Other and Unknown
CRUDE DEATH RATE	.01002	.00021	.00016	.00185	.00465	.00064	.00005	.00048	.00005	.00024	.00005	.00038	.00126
STANDARDIZED RATE (1)	.00455	.00013	.00014	.00082	.00162	.00031	.00005	.00022	.00005	.00053	.00005	.00026	.00079
STANDARDIZED RATE (2)	.00921	.00019	.00016	.00162	.00421	.00060	.00005	.00041	.00005	.00031	.00005	.00036	.00119
GEOMETRIC MEAN	.00612												

LIFE TABLE FOR ALL CAUSES COMBINED

Age (x)	Midyear Population	Deaths During Year	$_nM_x$	$_nq_x$	l_x	$_nd_x$	$_nL_x$	$_nm_x$	$_na_x$	T_x	$_nr_x$	$\overset{\circ}{e}_x$	Age (x)
0	39496	1039	.026306	.025710	100000	2571	97724	.026309	.114721	7088982	.000000	70.890	0
1	163120	277	.001698	.006764	97429	659	388069	.001698	1.500000	6991259	.000000	71.757	1
5	194805	124	.000637	.003183	96770	308	483070	.000638	2.500000	6603190	.000000	68.236	5
10	150590	58	.000385	.001918	96462	185	481835	.000384	2.434685	6120110	.021032	63.446	10
15	159071	83	.000522	.002597	96277	250	480812	.000520	2.707500	5638275	-.004944	58.563	15
20	172072	156	.000907	.004520	96027	434	479132	.000906	2.689612	5157463	-.014887	53.708	20
25	182165	247	.001356	.006747	95593	645	476412	.001354	2.592054	4678330	-.003301	48.940	25
30	167337	254	.001518	.007573	94948	719	472992	.001520	2.569251	4201919	-.004252	44.255	30
35	174334	329	.001887	.009381	94229	884	469044	.001885	2.622785	3728926	-.008949	39.573	35
40	184539	494	.002677	.013284	93345	1240	463850	.002673	2.681116	3259883	-.006907	34.923	40
45	175567	755	.004300	.021302	92105	1962	455927	.004304	2.656728	2796033	.004517	30.357	45
50	160292	977	.006095	.030130	90143	2716	444397	.006112	2.673892	2340106	.014372	25.960	50
55	136629	1346	.009851	.048372	87427	4229	427382	.009895	2.693850	1895708	.021801	21.683	55
60	114923	1901	.016542	.079942	83198	6651	400535	.016605	2.676227	1468326	.018944	17.649	60
65	97502	2664	.027323	.128744	76547	9855	359744	.027395	2.667026	1067792	.012018	13.949	65
70	77183	3748	.048560	.218197	66692	14552	298765	.048707	2.615820	708048	.013100	10.617	70
75	49571	4080	.082306	.344170	52140	17945	216479	.082895	2.535723	409283	-.029434	7.850	75
80	23458	3260	.138972	.515543	34195	17629	125801	.140134	2.437456	192804	-.029434	5.638	80
85+	10512	2599	.247241	1.000000	16566	16566	67003	.247241	4.044633	67003	.000000	4.045	85+

NUMBER OF PERSONS DYING (OUT OF 100,000 AT BIRTH) ABOVE AGE X FROM SPECIFIED CAUSES

Age (x)	All Causes	Respiratory T. B.	Other Infec. and Paras.	Neoplasms	Cardiovascular	Infl., Pneu., Bronch.	Diarrheal	Certain Degenerative	Maternal	Cert. Dis. of Infancy	Motor Vehicle	Other Violence	Other and Unknown	Age (x)
0	100000	1764	1245	17085	50175	7012	413	4285	331	1472	398	3499	12321	0
1	97429	1764	1210	17065	50153	6802	344	4281	331	5	393	3440	11641	1
5	96770	1759	1125	17015	50144	6709	311	4276	331	0	362	3285	11453	5
10	96462	1754	1068	16973	50131	6659	308	4261	331	0	329	3243	11365	10
15	96277	1744	1052	16954	50122	6686	308	4245	331	0	326	3217	11292	15
20	96027	1726	1022	16923	50100	6665	305	4236	325	0	311	3178	11236	20
25	95593	1657	958	16901	50076	6651	303	4214	292	0	297	3083	11161	25
30	94948	1544	918	16831	50002	6638	297	4177	218	0	292	2981	11050	30
35	94229	1426	862	16726	49957	6621	297	4152	136	0	275	2888	10889	35
40	93345	1350	816	16484	49658	6581	295	4114	61	0	262	2786	10738	40
45	92105	1270	761	16058	49632	6538	287	4019	13	0	244	2696	10547	45
50	90143	1182	691	15409	49180	6476	279	3868	3	0	221	2563	10271	50
55	87427	1093	624	14473	48409	6392	268	3615	0	0	190	2430	9933	55
60	83198	996	539	13164	46844	6289	259	3254	0	0	152	2251	9450	60
65	76547	863	438	11290	43561	6054	248	2688	0	0	118	2052	8835	65
70	66692	660	339	8855	39082	5665	226	2026	0	0	107	1893	7839	70
75	52140	454	222	6214	30782	4821	195	1297	0	0	60	1606	6489	75
80	34195	195	121	3348	20169	3534	111	609	0	0	25	1222	4861	80
85+	16566	64	45	1294	9383	2014	57	204	0	0	19	714	2772	85+

NUMBER OF PERSONS SURVIVING TO AGE X IF SPECIFIED CAUSES WERE ELIMINATED

Age (x)	No Causes	Respiratory T. B.	Other Infec. and Paras.	Neoplasms	Cardiovascular	Infl., Pneu., Bronch.	Diarrheal	Certain Degenerative	Maternal	Cert. Dis. of Infancy	Motor Vehicle	Other Violence	Other and Unknown	(1) + (2)	(1) + (2) + (5) + (6) + (8)	(1)+(2)+ (5)+(6)+ (8)+part of(9)&(12)	(10) + (11)	Age (x)
		(1)	(2)	(3)	(4)	(5)	(6)	(7)	(8)	(9)	(10)	(11)	(12)					
0	100000	100000	100000	100000	100000	100000	100000	100000	100000	100000	100000	100000	100000	100000	100000	100000	100000	0
1	97429	97429	97464	97449	97451	97636	97497	97433	97429	98888	97434	97487	98102	97464	97739	99327	97492	1
5	96770	96775	96889	96839	97069	96871	96779	96770	98224	96806	96983	97628	96894	97295	98966	97018	5
10	96462	96472	96638	96573	96505	96770	96565	96486	96462	97911	96531	96716	97406	96648	97060	98758	96785	10
15	96277	96297	96468	96407	96329	96598	96380	96317	96277	97724	96349	96556	97293	96488	96913	98634	96628	15
20	96027	96065	96248	96188	96101	96368	96133	96076	96033	97470	96113	96345	97096	96286	96740	98481	96431	20
25	95593	95700	95877	95775	95691	95946	95700	95663	95632	97029	95693	96005	96733	95984	96486	98261	96105	25
30	94948	95167	95270	95199	95119	95312	95061	95055	95060	96375	95052	95459	96193	95489	96083	97903	95564	30
35	94229	94564	94605	94583	94444	94607	94341	94360	94422	95645	94349	94829	95627	94941	95631	97524	94950	35
40	93345	93753	93763	93538	93656	93760	93458	93513	93611	94748	93477	94042	94882	94172	94975	96506	94175	40
45	92105	92587	92572	93076	92638	92557	92224	92365	92416	93489	92253	92883	93815	93057	93950	95904	93032	45
50	90143	90702	90670	91785	91116	90647	90268	90547	90457	91497	90311	91037	92095	91233	92189	94147	91206	50
55	87427	88058	88004	89563	89142	87999	87559	88070	87734	88741	87621	88426	89661	88639	89668	91609	88622	55
60	83198	83893	83831	86402	85640	83494	83332	83491	83419	84325	83508	84532	85625	84286	85625	87517	84550	60
65	76547	77315	77227	81883	82421	77369	76681	77987	76816	77697	76783	77777	79559	78002	79255	81056	78017	65
70	66692	67553	67377	73805	76889	67777	66829	68577	66926	67694	66908	67914	70288	68246	69744	71409	68134	70
75	52140	52996	52779	60325	69184	53753	52275	54275	52323	52923	52350	53354	56218	53646	55644	57091	53570	75
80	34195	34967	34696	42301	58240	36340	34351	36169	34315	34709	34361	35310	38311	35479	38011	39159	35481	80
85+	16566	17032	16861	22299	43959	18740	16679	17817	16624	16815	16650	17467	20224	17335	19814	20614	17556	85+

ADDED YRS OF LIFE																		
TOTAL		.373	.364	2.444	7.400	.788	.108	.610	.137	1.063	.121	.688	2.056	.741	1.809	3.340	.811	
WORK	2.528	.191	.127	.611	.492	.079	.010	.162	.103	.000	.039	.230	.372	.318	.513	.623	.269	

POPULATION, DEATHS, DEATH RATES FOR ALL CAUSES COMBINED, AND SPECIFIED CAUSES

Age Start of Interval	Midyear Population	Deaths During Year	All Causes	Respiratory T.B.	Other Infec. and Paras.	Neoplasms	Cardiovascular	Infl., Pneu., Bronch.	Diarrheal	Certain Degenerative	Maternal	Cert. Dis. of Infancy	Motor Vehicle	Other Violence	Other and Unknown	Age Start of Interval
0	46900	1161	.02475	.00002	.00047	.00013	.00011	.00109	.00038	.00004	.00000	.01591	.00000	.00070	.00591	0
1	179011	271	.00151	.00000	.00006	.00011	.00002	.00014	.00006	.00001	.00000	.00002	.00023	.00041	.00045	1
5	205703	125	.00061	.00000	.00004	.00009	.00000	.00001	.00000	.00000	.00000	.00002	.00014	.00017	.00015	5
10	218942	105	.00048	.00000	.00004	.00007	.00001	.00000	.00000	.00000	.00000	.00000	.00013	.00011	.00011	10
15	207916	212	.00102	.00000	.00001	.00009	.00002	.00002	.00000	.00002	.00000	.00000	.00029	.00044	.00012	15
20	172189	338	.00196	.00001	.00002	.00011	.00009	.00003	.00001	.00002	.00000	.00000	.00064	.00088	.00015	20
25	177287	276	.00156	.00002	.00002	.00016	.00012	.00002	.00000	.00005	.00000	.00000	.00043	.00060	.00015	25
30	178271	321	.00180	.00006	.00002	.00025	.00030	.00002	.00001	.00007	.00000	.00000	.00033	.00061	.00012	30
35	186199	353	.00190	.00009	.00003	.00025	.00038	.00005	.00001	.00005	.00000	.00000	.00031	.00055	.00019	35
40	167528	503	.00300	.00006	.00007	.00054	.00071	.00008	.00003	.00015	.00000	.00000	.00032	.00064	.00040	40
45	179632	880	.00490	.00013	.00008	.00102	.00145	.00015	.00003	.00023	.00000	.00000	.00043	.00082	.00055	45
50	174128	1425	.00818	.00029	.00012	.00218	.00271	.00026	.00003	.00049	.00000	.00000	.00045	.00090	.00075	50
55	151595	2042	.01347	.00031	.00017	.00372	.00499	.00051	.00006	.00078	.00000	.00000	.00045	.00109	.00140	55
60	121238	2775	.02289	.00049	.00028	.00635	.00913	.00069	.00007	.00153	.00000	.00000	.00057	.00129	.00247	60
65	89765	3233	.03602	.00047	.00032	.00967	.01561	.00140	.00014	.00213	.00000	.00000	.00051	.00159	.00417	65
70	64200	3628	.05651	.00067	.00036	.01380	.02748	.00324	.00009	.00266	.00000	.00000	.00083	.00160	.00578	70
75	42825	4020	.09387	.00061	.00068	.01721	.05168	.00658	.00026	.00346	.00000	.00000	.00098	.00290	.00953	75
80	21762	3225	.14819	.00087	.00046	.02206	.08639	.01158	.00046	.00363	.00000	.00000	.00115	.00437	.01723	80
85+	8684	2139	.24632	.00069	.00035	.02522	.14590	.02614	.00081	.00415	.00000	.00000	.00069	.00668	.03570	85+
ALL	2593775	27032														
CRUDE DEATH RATE			.01042	.00014	.00010	.00208	.00440	.00056	.00004	.00043	.00000	.00029	.00038	.00077	.00123	
STANDARDIZED RATE (1)			.00575	.00007	.00008	.00099	.00184	.00027	.00004	.00021	.00000	.00056	.00032	.00059	.00078	
STANDARDIZED RATE (2)			.01072	.00013	.00010	.00206	.00462	.00060	.00005	.00042	.00000	.00033	.00037	.00076	.00128	
GEOMETRIC MEAN			.00738													

LIFE TABLE FOR ALL CAUSES COMBINED

Age (x)	Midyear Population	Deaths During Year	$_nM_x$	$_nq_x$	l_x	$_nd_x$	$_nL_x$	$_nm_x$	$_na_x$	T_x	$_nr_x$	$\overset{\circ}{e}_x$	Age (x)
0	46900	1161	.024755	.024220	100000	2422	97849	.024752	.112083	6879085	.000000	68.791	0
1	179011	271	.001514	.006036	97578	589	388840	.001515	1.500000	6781236	.000000	69.496	1
5	205703	125	.000608	.003031	96989	294	484210	.000607	2.500000	6392396	.000000	65.908	5
10	218942	105	.000480	.002399	96695	232	482936	.000480	2.678700	5908186	-.005876	61.101	10
15	207916	212	.001020	.005111	96463	493	481230	.001024	2.798766	5425250	.016920	56.242	15
20	172189	338	.001963	.009784	95970	939	477553	.001966	2.553914	4944020	.018210	51.516	20
25	177287	276	.001557	.007745	95031	736	473392	.001555	2.473392	4466467	.001009	47.000	25
30	178271	321	.001801	.008961	94295	845	469393	.001800	2.535956	3993172	-.006803	42.348	30
35	186199	353	.001896	.009438	93450	882	465157	.001896	2.626606	3523779	.001635	37.708	35
40	167528	503	.003002	.014919	92568	1381	459663	.003004	2.699584	3058622	.003068	33.042	40
45	179632	880	.004899	.024181	91187	2205	450880	.004890	2.707294	2598959	-.008795	28.501	45
50	174128	1425	.008184	.040177	88982	3575	436679	.008187	2.697727	2148079	-.002303	24.141	50
55	151595	2042	.013470	.065545	85407	5598	414110	.013518	2.691102	1711400	.016194	20.038	55
60	121238	2775	.022889	.109136	79809	8710	378571	.023008	2.649421	1297290	.026059	16.255	60
65	89765	3233	.036016	.166599	71099	11845	327145	.036207	2.606567	918719	.028213	12.922	65
70	64200	3628	.056511	.249249	59254	14769	260412	.056714	2.572054	591574	.018065	9.984	70
75	42825	4020	.093870	.381099	44485	16953	180040	.094162	2.499865	331162	.013171	7.444	75
80	21762	3225	.148194	.536031	27532	14758	99262	.148678	2.398134	151122	.013171	5.489	80
85+	8684	2139	.246315	1.000000	12774	12774	51860	.246315	4.055841	51860	.000000	4.060	85+

NUMBER OF PERSONS DYING (OUT OF 100,000 AT BIRTH) ABOVE AGE X FROM SPECIFIED CAUSES

Age (x)	All Causes	Respira-tory T. B.	Other Infec. and Paras.	Neo-plasms	Cardio-vascular	Infl., Pneu., Bronch.	Diar-rheal	Certain Degen-erative	Maternal	Cert. Dis. of Infancy	Motor Vehicle	Other Violence	Other and Unknown	Age (x)
0	100000	1179	838	19558	45983	5940	372	3995	0	1563	2823	6079	11670	0
1	97578	1177	792	19545	45972	5833	334	3991	0	7	2823	6010	11094	1
5	96989	1177	768	19502	45964	5779	312	3989	0	0	2732	5849	10917	5
10	96695	1177	749	19457	45964	5772	310	3986	0	0	2666	5767	10847	10
15	96463	1177	731	19424	45957	5770	310	3984	0	0	2602	5714	10794	15
20	95970	1177	727	19380	45945	5760	310	3975	0	0	2460	5500	10736	20
25	95031	1171	716	19327	45901	5744	307	3966	0	0	2154	5078	10667	25
30	94295	1163	708	19252	45842	5736	307	3945	0	0	1952	4792	10598	30
35	93450	1134	697	19134	45703	5725	305	3911	0	0	1796	4505	10540	35
40	92568	1094	685	19019	45528	5700	300	3888	0	0	1654	4250	10450	40
45	91187	1067	652	18772	45201	5662	286	3820	0	0	1505	3957	10265	45
50	88982	1007	617	18314	44548	5594	271	3717	0	0	1312	3585	10017	50
55	85407	879	564	17363	43363	5481	256	3504	0	0	1114	3192	9691	55
60	79809	750	493	15817	41290	5270	231	3180	0	0	928	2740	9110	60
65	71099	562	386	13400	37812	5006	206	2596	0	0	713	2249	8169	65
70	59254	409	280	10222	32673	4543	158	1898	0	0	545	1727	6799	70
75	44485	234	187	6620	25486	3695	134	1203	0	0	329	1309	5288	75
80	27532	125	65	3516	16149	2504	88	580	0	0	152	786	3567	80
85+	12774	36	18	1308	7566	1356	42	215	0	0	36	346	1851	85+

NUMBER OF PERSONS SURVIVING TO AGE X IF SPECIFIED CAUSES WERE ELIMINATED

Age (x)	No Causes	Respira-tory T. B.	Other Infec. and Paras.	Neo-plasms	Cardio-vascular	Infl., Pneu., Bronch.	Diar-rheal	Certain Degener-ative	Maternal	Cert. Dis. of Infancy	Motor Vehicle	Other Violence	Other and Unknown	(1) + (2)	(1) + (2) + (5) + (6) + (8)	(1)+(2)+ (5)+(6)+ (8)+part of(9)&(12)	(10) + (11)	Age (x)
		(1)	(2)	(3)	(4)	(5)	(6)	(7)	(8)	(9)	(10)	(11)	(12)					
0	100000	100000	100000	100000	100000	100000	100000	100000	100000	100000	100000	100000	100000	100000	100000	100000	100000	0
1	97578	97580	97623	97591	97589	97684	97616	97582	97578	99127	97578	97646	98149	97625	97769	99183	97646	1
5	96989	96991	97058	97045	97008	97148	97048	96995	96989	98536	97080	97218	97005	97734	97060	97279	98732	97309	5
10	96695	96697	96783	96795	96714	96861	96756	96704	96695	98237	96851	97005	97508	96785	97012	98470	97162	10
15	96463	96465	96569	96596	96489	96630	96524	96474	96463	98002	96683	96825	97327	96571	96799	98260	97046	15
20	95970	95972	96079	96146	96008	96146	96031	95990	95970	97501	96331	96545	96888	96081	96318	97774	96908	20
25	95031	95039	95150	95259	95112	95222	95094	95060	95031	96547	95565	96024	96010	95158	95412	96857	96694	25
30	94295	94311	94421	94596	94434	94492	94358	94344	94295	95799	95156	95568	95336	94437	94697	96134	96441	30
35	93450	93495	93586	93866	93727	93656	93514	93533	93450	94940	94460	95002	94540	93631	93901	95330	96029	35
40	92568	92652	92715	93095	93017	92797	92636	92673	92568	94044	93712	94364	93738	92799	93097	94523	95530	40
45	91187	91297	91364	91953	91956	91451	91268	91358	91187	92641	92464	93253	92526	91474	91820	93244	94558	45
50	88982	89148	89190	90187	90386	89307	89076	89251	88982	90401	90421	91374	90537	89356	89777	91192	92852	50
55	85407	85692	85658	87514	87942	85830	85512	85875	85407	86769	86985	88099	87225	85944	86476	87870	89726	55
60	79809	80201	80113	83323	84268	80409	79931	80562	79809	81082	81467	82775	82084	80506	81235	82596	84494	60
65	71099	71626	71471	76648	78619	71885	71232	72327	71099	72233	72782	74222	74045	72000	72932	74223	75979	65
70	59254	59833	59660	67075	70920	60340	59408	60927	59254	60199	60813	62353	63022	60243	61507	62693	63994	70
75	44485	45072	44871	53987	61235	46056	44621	46359	44485	45195	45847	47191	48719	45462	47212	48244	48635	75
80	27532	27980	27866	36449	49401	29485	27653	29196	27532	27971	28515	29642	31658	28319	30461	31273	30701	80
85+	12774	13042	12961	18970	35825	14522	12861	13806	12774	12978	13310	14072	16060	13233	15146	15692	14662	85+

ADDED YRS OF LIFE																	
TOTAL		.183	.182	2.580	7.076	.617	.081	.501	.000	1.095	.841	1.520	1.834	.366	1.082	2.246	2.393
WORK	3.282	.070	.043	.552	.654	.078	.013	.126	.000	.000	.460	.757	.306	.113	.204	.227	1.228

POPULATION, DEATHS, DEATH RATES FOR ALL CAUSES COMBINED, AND SPECIFIED CAUSES

Age Start of Interval	Midyear Population	Deaths During Year	All Causes	Respiratory T. B.	Other Infec. and Paras.	Neo-plasms	Cardio-vascular	Infl., Pneu., Bronch.	Diar-rheal	Certain Degen-erative	Maternal	Cert. Dis. of Infancy	Motor Vehicle	Other Violence	Other and Unknown	Age Start of Interval
0	44980	832	.01850	.00000	.00022	.00009	.00007	.00062	.00044	.00000	.00000	.01074	.00000	.00082	.00549	0
1	170707	186	.00109	.00000	.00007	.00009	.00002	.00014	.00005	.00001	.00000	.00002	.00013	.00028	.00029	1
5	196854	68	.00035	.00000	.00002	.00006	.00001	.00005	.00000	.00001	.00000	.00000	.00006	.00003	.00011	5
10	203707	58	.00028	.00000	.00000	.00008	.00001	.00001	.00000	.00000	.00000	.00000	.00004	.00003	.00011	10
15	198850	75	.00038	.00000	.00003	.00008	.00001	.00002	.00000	.00002	.00000	.00000	.00007	.00005	.00008	15
20	195867	117	.00060	.00001	.00002	.00006	.00004	.00003	.00000	.00003	.00006	.00000	.00006	.00011	.00007	20
25	214831	136	.00063	.00002	.00002	.00014	.00003	.00001	.00000	.00002	.00005	.00000	.00006	.00016	.00014	25
30	205882	146	.00071	.00003	.00002	.00016	.00012	.00002	.00000	.00002	.00005	.00000	.00005	.00013	.00011	30
35	189241	238	.00126	.00001	.00005	.00047	.00013	.00002	.00001	.00005	.00008	.00000	.00005	.00018	.00021	35
40	157716	316	.00200	.00004	.00004	.00087	.00030	.00006	.00002	.00008	.00003	.00000	.00005	.00018	.00030	40
45	175280	525	.00300	.00008	.00004	.00128	.00062	.00007	.00001	.00017	.00001	.00000	.00006	.00025	.00042	45
50	178264	847	.00475	.00006	.00010	.00191	.00125	.00007	.00003	.00029	.00001	.00000	.00010	.00030	.00064	50
55	165051	1243	.00753	.00008	.00011	.00272	.00249	.00026	.00001	.00048	.00000	.00000	.00007	.00041	.00090	55
60	143456	1866	.01301	.00010	.00018	.00415	.00522	.00045	.00007	.00080	.00000	.00000	.00007	.00041	.00156	60
65	115334	2524	.02188	.00010	.00021	.00590	.01042	.00079	.00011	.00132	.00000	.00000	.00015	.00055	.00233	65
70	88358	3431	.03883	.00032	.00037	.00792	.02106	.00197	.00026	.00206	.00000	.00000	.00026	.00103	.00358	70
75	61923	4397	.07101	.00069	.00032	.01145	.04320	.00413	.00027	.00283	.00000	.00000	.00032	.00182	.00596	75
80	35021	4370	.12478	.00063	.00031	.01542	.08167	.00877	.00066	.00348	.00000	.00000	.00000	.00057	.00934	80
85+	15763	3687	.23390	.00051	.00063	.01916	.15149	.02297	.00070	.00349	.00000	.00000	.00000	.00057	.00934	85+
ALL	2757085	25062														

CRUDE DEATH RATE			.00909	.00007	.00008	.00178	.00457	.00051	.00005	.00036	.00002	.00018	.00009	.00039	.00099	
STANDARDIZED RATE (1)			.00377	.00003	.00005	.00074	.00132	.00018	.00003	.00014	.00002	.00038	.00007	.00023	.00057	
STANDARDIZED RATE (2)			.00749	.00006	.00007	.00146	.00363	.00041	.00005	.00030	.00002	.00022	.00009	.00034	.00086	
GEOMETRIC MEAN			.00434													

LIFE TABLE FOR ALL CAUSES COMBINED

Age (x)	Midyear Population	Deaths During Year	$_nM_x$	$_nq_x$	l_x	$_nd_x$	$_nL_x$	$_nm_x$	$_na_x$	T_x	$_nr_x$	$\overset{\circ}{e}_x$	Age (x)
0	44980	832	.018497	.018190	100000	1819	98366	.018492	.101445	7407902	.000000	74.079	0
1	170707	186	.001090	.004349	98181	427	391657	.001090	1.500000	7309536	.000000	74.450	1
5	196854	68	.000345	.001729	97754	169	488348	.000346	2.500000	6917880	.000000	70.768	5
10	203707	58	.000285	.001424	97585	139	487580	.000285	2.520983	6429532	.000000	70.768	10
15	198850	75	.000377	.001878	97446	183	486804	.000376	2.671903	5941952	-.002394	65.886	15
20	195867	117	.000597	.002982	97263	290	485616	.000597	2.589080	5455148	-.004214	60.977	20
25	214831	136	.000633	.003163	96973	307	484108	.000634	2.535288	4969532	-.005228	56.087	25
30	205882	146	.000709	.003538	96666	342	482537	.000709	2.682749	4485424	-.007953	51.247	30
35	189241	238	.001258	.006302	96324	607	480231	.001264	2.711079	4002886	-.004227	46.401	35
40	157716	316	.002004	.009958	95717	957	476359	.002009	2.673938	3522656	.022911	41.556	40
45	175280	525	.002995	.014837	94760	1406	470542	.002988	2.682995	3046297	.014015	36.803	45
50	178264	847	.004751	.023481	93354	2192	461701	.004748	2.687709	2575755	-.010987	32.147	50
55	165051	1243	.007531	.037088	91162	3381	448060	.007546	2.707779	2114053	-.003672	27.591	55
60	143456	1866	.013007	.063385	87781	5564	426084	.013058	2.695678	1665993	.018401	23.190	60
65	115334	2524	.021884	.104686	82217	8607	391150	.022004	2.683886	1239909	.024308	18.979	65
70	88358	3431	.038821	.178794	73610	13161	337185	.039032	2.654829	848759	.021996	15.081	70
75	61923	4397	.071008	.304190	60449	18388	257709	.071352	2.578006	511574	.018988	11.530	75
80	35021	4370	.124782	.476594	42061	20046	159744	.125488	2.477749	253865	.018988	8.463	80
85+	15763	3687	.233902	1.000000	22015	22015	94121	.233902	4.275292	94121	.000000	6.036	85+
												4.275	

NUMBER OF PERSONS DYING (OUT OF 100,000 AT BIRTH) ABOVE AGE X FROM SPECIFIED CAUSES

Age (x)	All Causes	Respira-tory T. B.	Other Infec. and Paras.	Neo-plasms	Cardio-vascular	Infl., Pneu., Bronch.	Diar-rheal	Certain Degen-erative	Maternal	Cert. Dis. of Infancy	Motor Vehicle	Other Violence	Other and Unknown	Age (x)
0	100000	668	737	17693	54348	6209	502	3718	134	1063	752	3904	10272	0
1	98181	668	716	17684	54342	6148	458	3718	134	7	752	3823	9731	1
5	97754	668	688	17647	54335	6093	440	3716	134	0	701	3715	9617	5
10	97585	668	678	17617	54332	6070	440	3711	134	0	672	3700	9563	10
15	97446	666	676	17579	54325	6066	440	3709	134	0	652	3676	9523	15
20	97263	666	663	17542	54220	6058	440	3701	134	0	621	3625	9493	20
25	96973	663	653	17515	54300	6043	440	3689	107	0	591	3545	9427	25
30	96666	654	644	17448	54285	6039	440	3678	82	0	564	3466	9366	30
35	96324	640	635	17372	54226	6030	437	3668	59	0	540	3403	9314	35
40	95717	635	610	17145	54162	6022	435	3643	21	0	517	3314	9213	40
45	94760	617	592	16730	54020	5995	426	3606	6	0	469	3230	9069	45
50	93354	579	573	16130	53728	5962	423	3529	3	0	440	3112	8875	50
55	91162	553	529	15247	53154	5929	407	3394	0	0	393	2974	8582	55
60	87781	518	480	14027	52035	5812	405	3179	0	0	360	2790	8175	60
65	82217	474	402	12254	49798	5618	375	2836	0	0	328	2623	7509	65
70	73610	436	321	9938	45694	5307	330	2319	0	0	270	2405	6590	70
75	60449	328	195	7258	38547	4638	242	1622	0	0	182	2056	5381	75
80	42061	149	111	4298	27353	3566	171	891	0	0	98	1583	3841	80
85+	22015	48	60	1803	14259	2161	66	328	0	0	6	949	2335	85+

NUMBER OF PERSONS SURVIVING TO AGE X IF SPECIFIED CAUSES WERE ELIMINATED

Age (x)	No Causes	Respira-tory T. B. (1)	Other Infec. and Paras. (2)	Neo-plasms (3)	Cardio-vascular (4)	Infl., Pneu., Bronch. (5)	Diar-rheal (6)	Certain Degener-ative (7)	Maternal (8)	Cert. Dis. of Infancy (9)	Motor Vehicle (10)	Other Violence (11)	Other and Unknown (12)	(1) + (2)	(1) + (2) + (5) + (6) + (8)	(1)+(2)+ (5)+(6)+ (8)+part of(9)&(12)	(10) + (11)	Age (x)
0	100000	100000	100000	100000	100000	100000	100000	100000	100000	100000	100000	100000	100000	100000	100000	100000	100000	0
1	98181	98181	98202	98187	98241	98225	98181	98181	99233	98181	98261	98719	98202	98306	99209	98261	1
5	97754	97754	97803	97800	97767	97869	97815	97756	97754	98808	97805	97942	98404	97803	97979	98920	97993	5
10	97585	97585	97644	97661	97601	97723	97646	97592	97585	98638	97665	97788	98288	97644	97843	98798	97868	10
15	97446	97448	97506	97560	97469	97588	97507	97455	97446	98497	97546	97672	98188	97508	97712	98669	97772	15
20	97263	97265	97336	97413	97291	97412	97324	97280	97263	98312	97394	97540	98034	97338	97549	98509	97671	20
25	96973	96978	97056	97150	97021	97137	97034	97002	97000	98019	97133	97329	97808	97061	97313	98287	97490	25
30	96666	96680	96758	96909	96729	96834	96727	96706	96718	97709	96853	97100	97560	96772	97052	98035	97288	30
35	96324	96352	96425	96643	96445	96500	96387	96374	96399	97363	96534	96820	97267	96452	96767	97758	97031	35
40	95717	95750	95842	96261	95901	95900	95782	95791	95829	96749	95949	96299	96756	95875	96236	97236	96532	40
45	94760	94810	94902	95715	95084	94968	94833	94870	94886	95782	95037	95420	95933	94952	95360	96368	95699	45
50	93354	93441	93512	94898	93965	93592	93429	93539	93481	94361	93656	94123	94705	93600	94041	95050	94427	50
55	91162	91273	91360	93561	92332	91427	91251	91477	91289	92145	91503	92050	92776	91471	91955	92960	92395	55
60	87781	87922	88020	91327	90027	88151	87869	88296	87903	88728	88142	88818	89742	88162	88746	89744	89184	60
65	82217	82392	82516	87341	86572	82753	82329	83034	82332	83104	82586	83352	84715	82692	83459	84445	83726	65
70	73610	73803	73955	80553	81712	74387	73753	74836	73713	74404	73996	74835	76746	74148	75181	76124	75228	70
75	60449	60706	60846	68846	74692	61703	60646	62098	60533	61101	60846	61777	64172	61105	62662	63544	62182	75
80	42061	42388	42406	50762	64839	43853	42257	43830	42120	42515	42407	43388	46023	42736	44827	45572	43745	80
85+	22015	22259	22232	28759	51800	24019	22192	23362	22046	22252	22262	23179	25289	22478	24756	25278	23439	85+

ADDED YRS OF LIFE		(1)	(2)	(3)	(4)	(5)	(6)	(7)	(8)	(9)	(10)	(11)	(12)				
TOTAL		.091	.157	2.553	8.861	.588	.050	.451	.059	.798	.214	.685	1.672	.248	.999	1.845	.903
WORK	1.747	.028	.041	.577	.334	.045	.007	.084	.042	.000	.076	.204	.254	.069	.163	.195	.280

POPULATION, DEATHS, DEATH RATES FOR ALL CAUSES COMBINED, AND SPECIFIED CAUSES

Age Start of Interval	Midyear Population	Deaths During Year	All Causes	Respiratory T. B.	Other Infec. and Paras.	Neo-plasms	Cardio-vascular	Infl., Pneu., Bronch.	Diar-rheal	Certain Degen-erative	Maternal	Cert. Dis. of Infancy	Motor Vehicle	Other Violence	Other and Unknown	Age Start of Interval
0	56860	1248	.02195	.00002	.00037	.00007	.00018	.00084	.00053	.00002	.00000	.01335	.00000	.00065	.00593	0
1	180540	232	.00129	.00000	.00007	.00010	.00003	.00007	.00008	.00001	.00000	.00001	.00018	.00034	.00042	1
5	219650	142	.00065	.00000	.00002	.00007	.00000	.00002	.00000	.00000	.00000	.00000	.00019	.00015	.00019	5
10	211700	100	.00047	.00000	.00002	.00008	.00003	.00000	.00001	.00001	.00000	.00000	.00010	.00014	.00009	10
15	240500	259	.00108	.00000	.00001	.00010	.00004	.00001	.00000	.00001	.00000	.00000	.00032	.00049	.00010	15
20	260900	359	.00138	.00000	.00001	.00013	.00004	.00002	.00000	.00002	.00000	.00000	.00041	.00062	.00012	20
25	226200	308	.00136	.00000	.00001	.00018	.00011	.00000	.00000	.00002	.00000	.00000	.00035	.00057	.00011	25
30	206400	308	.00149	.00001	.00002	.00023	.00020	.00000	.00001	.00006	.00000	.00000	.00019	.00062	.00014	30
35	188900	379	.00201	.00004	.00003	.00034	.00033	.00003	.00002	.00007	.00000	.00000	.00028	.00064	.00021	35
40	177300	611	.00345	.00006	.00004	.00063	.00093	.00005	.00001	.00014	.00000	.00000	.00037	.00074	.00049	40
45	163050	762	.00467	.00018	.00006	.00109	.00136	.00008	.00001	.00039	.00000	.00000	.00038	.00062	.00052	45
50	171200	1437	.00839	.00012	.00006	.00210	.00278	.00019	.00005	.00071	.00000	.00000	.00053	.00075	.00110	50
55	156400	2165	.01384	.00024	.00015	.00418	.00464	.00029	.00003	.00113	.00000	.00000	.00055	.00104	.00159	55
60	130250	3003	.02306	.00029	.00018	.00706	.00856	.00053	.00005	.00177	.00000	.00000	.00064	.00121	.00277	60
65	99000	3573	.03609	.00051	.00033	.00925	.01608	.00086	.00006	.00275	.00000	.00000	.00070	.00155	.00401	65
70	70300	3827	.05444	.00057	.00027	.01304	.02656	.00111	.00026	.00344	.00000	.00000	.00088	.00199	.00632	70
75	45350	3802	.08384	.00082	.00031	.01689	.04536	.00287	.00024	.00406	.00000	.00000	.00101	.00232	.00997	75
80	24720	3286	.13293	.00085	.00032	.02149	.07832	.00566	.00020	.00457	.00000	.00000	.00121	.00396	.01634	80
85+	10130	2508	.24758	.00109	.00010	.02784	.15271	.01382	.00099	.00592	.00000	.00000	.00197	.00800	.03514	85+
ALL	2839350	28309														

CRUDE DEATH RATE			.00997	.00011	.00007	.00208	.00418	.00029	.00004	.00054	.00000	.00027	.00038	.00073	.00128	
STANDARDIZED RATE (1)			.00546	.00005	.00006	.00101	.00176	.00015	.00004	.00026	.00000	.00047	.00030	.00055	.00080	
STANDARDIZED RATE (2)			.01024	.00011	.00007	.00208	.00440	.00031	.00005	.00053	.00000	.00028	.00037	.00072	.00133	
GEOMETRIC MEAN			.00703													

LIFE TABLE FOR ALL CAUSES COMBINED

Age (x)	Midyear Population	Deaths During Year	nM_x	nq_x	l_x	nd_x	nL_x	nm_x	na_x	T_x	nr_x	$\overset{\circ}{e}_x$	Age (x)
0	56860	1248	.021949	.021530	100000	2153	98078	.021952	.107313	6939032	.000000	69.390	0
1	180540	232	.001285	.005120	97847	501	390136	.001284	1.500000	6840954	.000000	69.915	1
5	219650	142	.000646	.003226	97346	314	485945	.000646	2.500000	6450818	.000000	66.267	5
10	211700	100	.000472	.002360	97032	229	484630	.000473	2.685590	5964873	-.004232	61.473	10
15	240500	259	.001077	.005351	96803	518	482810	.001073	2.673343	5480243	-.021760	56.612	15
20	260900	359	.001376	.006855	96285	660	479802	.001073	2.541351	4997433	-.004779	51.903	20
25	226200	308	.001362	.006787	95625	649	476512	.001362	2.515087	4517631	.016590	47.243	25
30	206400	308	.001492	.007444	94976	707	473174	.001494	2.586928	4041119	.017159	42.549	30
35	188900	379	.002006	.010014	94269	944	469171	.002012	2.696857	3567945	.013778	37.849	35
40	177300	611	.003446	.017134	93325	1599	462873	.003455	2.653481	3098774	.014010	33.204	40
45	163050	762	.004673	.023134	91726	2122	453760	.004676	2.704759	2635901	.003157	28.737	45
50	171200	1437	.008394	.041125	89604	3685	439567	.008383	2.706242	2182142	-.005418	24.353	50
55	156400	2165	.013843	.067156	85919	5770	416234	.013862	2.684431	1742574	.007045	20.282	55
60	130250	3003	.023056	.109708	80149	8793	380039	.023137	2.645144	1326340	.018058	16.548	60
65	99000	3573	.036091	.166713	71356	11896	328195	.036247	2.597056	946301	.023568	13.262	65
70	70300	3827	.054438	.241086	59460	14335	262253	.054661	2.555153	618107	.022914	10.395	70
75	45350	3802	.083837	.347723	45125	15691	186462	.084151	2.504089	355853	.018650	7.886	75
80	24720	3286	.132929	.497486	29434	14643	109650	.133543	2.437669	169392	.018650	5.755	80
85+	10130	2508	.247581	1.000000	14791	14791	59742	.247581	4.039075	59742	.000000	4.039	85+

NUMBER OF PERSONS DYING (OUT OF 100,000 AT BIRTH) ABOVE AGE X FROM SPECIFIED CAUSES

Age (x)	All Causes	Respiratory T. B.	Other Infec. and Paras.	Neo-plasms	Cardio-vascular	Infl., Pneu., Bronch.	Diar-rheal	Certain Degen-erative	Maternal	Cert. Dis. of Infancy	Motor Vehicle	Other Violence	Other and Unknown	Age (x)
0	100000	1024	606	20403	46392	3173	377	5215	0	1312	2914	5970	12614	0
1	97847	1022	570	20396	46374	3090	326	5213	0	2	2914	5907	12033	1
5	97346	1022	544	20357	46364	3064	295	5211	0	0	2842	5775	11872	5
10	97032	1022	535	20324	46364	3053	295	5211	0	0	2749	5700	11779	10
15	96803	1022	523	20287	46348	3053	291	5207	0	0	2701	5633	11738	15
20	96285	1022	517	20241	46330	3049	291	5203	0	0	2545	5398	11689	20
25	95625	1022	514	20180	46309	3040	291	5193	0	0	2347	5098	11631	25
30	94976	1020	507	20096	46254	3040	289	5185	0	0	2179	4828	11578	30
35	94269	1015	498	19986	46158	3037	284	5157	0	0	2087	4532	11515	35
40	93325	995	483	19824	46000	3022	277	5122	0	0	1955	4232	11415	40
45	91726	969	465	19530	45568	3001	274	5059	0	0	1783	3887	11190	45
50	89604	888	440	19034	44953	2965	268	4884	0	0	1610	3606	10956	50
55	85919	837	412	18112	43732	2883	248	4571	0	0	1377	3278	10469	55
60	80149	739	348	16368	41797	2763	235	4102	0	0	1148	2844	9805	60
65	71356	627	280	13676	38528	2561	214	3429	0	0	905	2385	8751	65
70	59460	461	171	10630	33222	2278	194	2524	0	0	676	1876	7428	70
75	45125	311	100	7199	26222	1985	126	1619	0	0	444	1353	5766	75
80	29434	159	42	4042	17727	1448	81	861	0	0	255	920	3899	80
85+	14791	65	6	1663	9123	826	59	354	0	0	118	478	2099	85+

NUMBER OF PERSONS SURVIVING TO AGE X IF SPECIFIED CAUSES WERE ELIMINATED

Age (x)	No Causes	Respiratory T. B.	Other Infec. and Paras.	Neo-plasms	Cardio-vascular	Infl., Pneu., Bronch.	Diar-rheal	Certain Degen-erative	Maternal	Cert. Dis. of Infancy	Motor Vehicle	Other Violence	Other and Unknown	(1) + (2)	(1) + (2) + (5) + (6) + (8)	(1)+(2)+ (5)+(6)+ (8)+part of(9)&(12)	(10) + (11)	Age (x)
		(1)	(2)	(3)	(4)	(5)	(6)	(7)	(8)	(9)	(10)	(11)	(12)					
0	100000	100000	100000	100000	100000	100000	100000	100000	100000	100000	100000	100000	100000	100000	100000	100000	100000	0
1	97847	97849	97883	97854	97865	97929	97857	97849	97847	99151	97847	97909	98423	97885	98017	99255	97909	1
5	97346	97348	97407	97392	97374	97454	97427	97350	97346	98646	97418	97540	98081	97409	97598	98871	97612	5
10	97032	97034	97102	97111	97060	97150	97113	97036	97032	98328	97197	97300	97858	97104	97304	98581	97465	10
15	96803	96805	96885	96918	96847	96921	96888	96811	96803	98096	97015	97138	97669	96887	97090	98368	97351	15
20	96285	96287	96373	96446	96346	96406	96389	96297	96285	97571	96652	96853	97195	96374	96580	97853	97223	20
25	95625	95627	95715	95846	95707	95755	95709	95647	95625	96902	96188	96491	96587	95717	95930	97196	97059	25
30	94976	94980	95072	95279	95112	95105	95061	95006	94976	96244	95704	96108	95985	95076	95290	96548	96844	30
35	94269	94278	94374	94680	94500	94400	94358	94326	94269	95528	95084	95691	95334	94382	94603	95854	96518	35
40	93325	93354	93443	93854	93711	93469	93421	93417	93325	94571	94264	95036	94480	93472	93713	94959	95993	40
45	91726	91780	91860	92579	92537	91889	91823	91879	91726	92951	92821	93757	93088	91914	92175	93412	94876	45
50	89604	89737	89760	90933	91012	89799	89705	89927	89604	90800	90847	91872	91169	89893	90189	91418	93146	50
55	85919	86096	86096	88115	88492	86186	86035	86536	85919	87066	87342	88423	87906	86274	86659	87867	89888	55
60	80149	80405	80376	83944	84497	80515	80270	81182	80149	81219	81701	82917	82661	80637	81127	82296	84522	60
65	71356	71694	71622	77438	78553	71873	71483	72921	71356	72309	72971	74268	74624	71961	72612	73712	75949	65
70	59460	59893	59782	67607	71014	60151	59585	61612	59460	60254	61019	62370	63457	60217	61045	62038	64005	70
75	45125	45585	45430	54800	61681	45909	45279	47575	45125	45728	46514	47810	49724	45893	46849	47682	49282	75
80	29434	29856	29679	38931	50739	30390	29570	31673	29434	29827	30495	31553	34125	30105	31227	31875	32691	80
85+	14791	15070	14940	21878	38202	15725	14875	16300	14791	14988	15423	16189	18662	15221	16273	16696	16881	85+

ADDED YRS OF LIFE																		
TOTAL		.138	.139	2.770	7.401	.350	.092	.658	.000	.925	.789	1.454	1.978	.278	.729	1.724	2.274	
WORK	3.163	.042	.031	.602	.669	.043	.010	.155	.000	.000	.395	.708	.329	.073	.126	.143	1.112	

POPULATION, DEATHS, DEATH RATES FOR ALL CAUSES COMBINED, AND SPECIFIED CAUSES

Age Start of Interval	Midyear Population	Deaths During Year	All Causes	Respiratory T.B.	Other Infec. and Paras.	Neoplasms	Cardiovascular	Infl., Pneu., Bronch.	Diarrheal	Certain Degenerative	Maternal	Cert. Dis. of Infancy	Motor Vehicle	Other Violence	Other and Unknown	Age Start of Interval
0	54020	854	.01655	.00002	.00030	.00013	.00013	.00061	.00033	.00000	.00000	.00940	.00004	.00044	.00515	0
1	174080	177	.00102	.00001	.00005	.00010	.00001	.00007	.00003	.00001	.00000	.00001	.00018	.00023	.00033	1
5	209950	73	.00035	.00000	.00001	.00008	.00001	.00001	.00000	.00000	.00000	.00000	.00008	.00004	.00011	5
10	203500	50	.00025	.00000	.00000	.00006	.00001	.00001	.00000	.00000	.00000	.00000	.00004	.00005	.00007	10
15	233850	84	.00036	.00000	.00001	.00006	.00003	.00001	.00001	.00000	.00000	.00000	.00007	.00007	.00009	15
20	242800	112	.00046	.00000	.00001	.00007	.00005	.00001	.00000	.00001	.00005	.00000	.00007	.00013	.00007	20
25	204750	131	.00064	.00000	.00002	.00009	.00006	.00001	.00000	.00004	.00006	.00000	.00007	.00013	.00007	25
30	198650	161	.00081	.00002	.00001	.00020	.00009	.00001	.00001	.00002	.00007	.00000	.00007	.00014	.00020	30
35	192650	226	.00117	.00004	.00002	.00045	.00012	.00002	.00000	.00006	.00005	.00000	.00005	.00017	.00020	35
40	182300	334	.00183	.00002	.00002	.00071	.00026	.00002	.00001	.00006	.00007	.00000	.00009	.00022	.00035	40
45	162300	461	.00284	.00003	.00004	.00124	.00052	.00004	.00001	.00014	.00000	.00000	.00009	.00022	.00035	45
50	180000	740	.00411	.00004	.00006	.00182	.00096	.00001	.00001	.00028	.00000	.00000	.00008	.00021	.00062	50
55	175450	1266	.00722	.00007	.00009	.00286	.00209	.00009	.00002	.00050	.00000	.00000	.00009	.00032	.00109	55
60	158450	1813	.01144	.00006	.00009	.00393	.00444	.00017	.00006	.00082	.00000	.00000	.00015	.00038	.00133	60
65	131600	2635	.02002	.00016	.00018	.00559	.00919	.00042	.00012	.00131	.00000	.00000	.00020	.00064	.00223	65
70	99900	3520	.03524	.00018	.00018	.00744	.01939	.00077	.00013	.00220	.00000	.00000	.00022	.00064	.00223	70
75	68850	4329	.06288	.00041	.00031	.01072	.03842	.00183	.00026	.00305	.00000	.00000	.00033	.00195	.00561	75
80	40200	4342	.10801	.00035	.00025	.01418	.07107	.00363	.00052	.00358	.00000	.00000	.00045	.00473	.00886	80
85+	18850	3952	.20966	.00080	.00074	.01798	.14249	.01082	.00090	.00483	.00000	.00000	.00027	.01013	.02069	85+
ALL	2932150	25300														

	All Causes	Respiratory T.B.	Other Infec. and Paras.	Neoplasms	Cardiovascular	Infl., Pneu., Bronch.	Diarrheal	Certain Degenerative	Maternal	Cert. Dis. of Infancy	Motor Vehicle	Other Violence	Other and Unknown
CRUDE DEATH RATE	.00863	.00005	.00006	.00175	.00436	.00025	.00005	.00040	.00002	.00017	.00010	.00040	.00101
STANDARDIZED RATE (1)	.00341	.00002	.00004	.00071	.00117	.00009	.00003	.00014	.00002	.00033	.00009	.00021	.00056
STANDARDIZED RATE (2)	.00672	.00004	.00005	.00138	.00324	.00019	.00004	.00031	.00002	.00020	.00010	.00033	.00083
GEOMETRIC MEAN	.00399												

LIFE TABLE FOR ALL CAUSES COMBINED

Age (x)	Midyear Population	Deaths During Year	$_nM_x$	$_nq_x$	l_x	$_nd_x$	$_nL_x$	$_nm_x$	$_na_x$	T_x	$_nr_x$	$\overset{\circ}{e}_x$	Age (x)
0	54020	854	.016549	.016310	100000	1631	98529	.016553	.098134	7523051	.000000	75.231	0
1	174080	177	.001017	.004056	98369	399	392479	.001017	1.500000	7424522	.000000	75.476	1
5	209950	73	.000348	.001735	97970	170	489425	.000347	2.500000	7032044	.000000	71.778	5
10	203500	50	.000246	.001227	97800	120	488701	.000246	2.508701	6542019	-.005960	66.898	10
15	233850	84	.000359	.001792	97680	175	487984	.000359	2.625000	6053918	-.020297	61.977	15
20	242800	112	.000461	.002308	97505	225	486991	.000462	2.625926	5565933	-.003195	57.084	20
25	204750	131	.000640	.003197	97280	311	485657	.000640	2.612540	5078943	.018155	52.210	25
30	198650	161	.000810	.004053	96969	393	483515	.000812	2.634648	4593285	.008347	47.369	30
35	192650	226	.001173	.005850	96576	565	481569	.001173	2.678835	4109370	.005619	42.551	35
40	182300	334	.001832	.009145	96011	878	478022	.001837	2.684842	3627801	.015402	37.785	40
45	162300	461	.002840	.014128	95133	1344	472519	.002844	2.659195	3149779	-.004990	33.109	45
50	180000	740	.004111	.020312	93789	1905	464582	.004100	2.709646	2677260	-.010980	28.546	50
55	175450	1266	.007216	.035490	91884	3261	451502	.007216	2.694662	2212678	-.000114	24.081	55
60	158450	1813	.011442	.055877	88623	4952	431731	.011470	2.701223	1760776	-.011272	19.868	60
65	131600	2635	.020023	.096138	83671	8044	399792	.020120	2.692302	1329044	.021349	15.884	65
70	99900	3520	.035235	.163658	75627	12377	349133	.035451	2.656793	929252	.026365	12.287	70
75	68850	4329	.062876	.274451	63250	17359	274364	.063270	2.587055	580119	.025697	9.172	75
80	40200	4342	.108010	.427840	45891	19634	180516	.108766	2.507428	305755	.025697	6.663	80
85+	18850	3952	.209655	1.000000	26257	26257	125239	.209655	4.769737	125239	.000000	4.770	85+

NUMBER OF PERSONS DYING (OUT OF 100,000 AT BIRTH) ABOVE AGE X FROM SPECIFIED CAUSES

Age (x)	All Causes	Respiratory T. B.	Other Infec. and Paras.	Neo-plasms	Cardio-vascular	Infl., Pneu., Bronch.	Diar-rheal	Certain Degen-erative	Maternal	Cert. Dis. of Infancy	Motor Vehicle	Other Violence	Other and Unknown	Age (x)
0	100000	535	580	17950	55743	3232	483	4340	143	929	873	4447	10745	0
1	98369	533	551	17937	55730	3172	450	4340	143	2	870	4403	10238	1
5	97970	531	533	17896	55726	3143	439	4337	143	0	800	4313	10109	5
10	97800	531	528	17857	55721	3138	437	4337	143	0	762	4292	10054	10
15	97680	531	528	17826	55716	3133	437	4337	142	0	741	4268	10020	15
20	97505	531	524	17794	55702	3129	432	4335	143	0	707	4233	9975	20
25	97280	531	520	17762	55680	3125	430	4331	117	0	675	4169	9940	25
30	96969	528	510	17717	55651	3118	428	4310	89	0	633	4088	9897	30
35	96576	521	508	17622	55610	3115	426	4300	57	0	599	4020	9798	35
40	96011	501	500	17404	55552	3105	426	4273	34	0	574	3940	9702	40
45	95133	493	490	17064	55428	3095	420	4244	0	0	532	3832	9535	45
50	93789	479	470	16479	55183	3074	417	4177	0	0	494	3733	9283	50
55	91884	458	441	15636	54741	3072	412	4048	0	0	471	3607	8998	55
60	88623	427	400	14346	53796	3033	402	3824	0	0	429	3462	8504	60
65	83671	403	359	12646	51871	2959	375	3469	0	0	364	3299	7926	65
70	75627	339	286	10407	48174	2791	326	2944	0	0	285	3042	7033	70
75	63250	275	223	7801	41353	2520	280	2172	0	0	208	2666	5752	75
80	45891	163	139	4849	30738	2014	208	1332	0	0	116	2128	4204	80
85+	26257	100	93	2252	17846	1355	113	605	0	0	33	1269	2591	85+

NUMBER OF PERSONS SURVIVING TO AGE X IF SPECIFIED CAUSES WERE ELIMINATED

Age (x)	No Causes	Respiratory T. B. (1)	Other Infec. and Paras. (2)	Neo-plasms (3)	Cardio-vascular (4)	Infl., Pneu., Bronch. (5)	Diar-rheal (6)	Certain Degener-ative (7)	Maternal (8)	Cert. Dis. of Infancy (9)	Motor Vehicle (10)	Other Violence (11)	Other and Unknown (12)	(1) + (2)	(1) + (2) + (5) + (6) + (8)	(1)+(2)+ (5)+(6)+ (8)+part of(9)&(12)	(10) + (11)	Age (x)
0	100000	100000	100000	100000	100000	100000	100000	100000	100000	100000	100000	100000	100000	100000	100000	100000	100000	0
1	98369	98371	98398	98382	98382	98429	98402	98369	98369	99293	98372	98413	98873	98400	98492	99392	98416	1
5	97970	97974	98017	98024	97567	98058	98014	97973	97970	98892	98043	98103	98602	98021	98153	99079	98176	5
10	97800	97804	97852	97893	97822	97893	97846	97803	97800	98720	97911	97954	98486	97856	97994	98925	98065	10
15	97680	97684	97731	97804	97707	97778	97725	97683	97680	98599	97812	97858	98399	97735	97879	98811	97990	15
20	97505	97509	97560	97660	97546	97607	97555	97510	97505	98423	97670	97718	98268	97564	97717	98652	97883	20
25	97280	97284	97339	97467	97343	97386	97332	97289	97306	98195	97477	97556	98077	97343	97527	98467	97754	25
30	96969	96976	97038	97200	97060	97081	97023	96999	97023	97882	97207	97326	97806	97045	97265	98211	97565	30
35	96576	96590	96647	96902	96708	96691	96632	96616	96662	97485	96847	96999	97510	96661	96917	97875	97272	35
40	96011	96045	96089	96553	96200	96135	96077	96119	96119	96028	96306	96512	97036	96123	96411	97377	96808	40
45	95133	95174	95221	96011	95444	95266	95194	95228	95274	96028	95467	95737	96317	95262	95598	96571	96074	45
50	93789	93844	93895	95243	94340	93941	93852	93949	93928	94672	94156	94484	95210	93950	94305	95279	94854	50
55	91884	91958	92017	94159	92865	92035	91951	92169	92020	92749	92267	92690	93563	92091	92446	93411	93076	55
60	88623	88725	88791	92125	90513	88807	88657	89119	88754	89457	89033	89544	90737	88894	89285	90238	89959	60
65	83671	83791	83870	88709	87389	83517	83767	84486	83795	84458	84122	84701	86243	83990	84459	85382	85157	65
70	75627	75796	75876	82463	82750	76010	75761	76869	75739	76339	76110	76805	78831	76046	76679	77561	77296	70
75	63250	63450	63516	71602	76384	63820	63404	65008	63344	63845	63724	64585	67158	63717	64543	65333	65069	75
80	45891	46131	46155	54846	67455	46741	46064	47899	45959	46323	46313	47330	50135	46396	47504	48153	47765	80
85+	26257	26442	26443	33786	55686	27249	26427	27978	26296	26504	26561	27750	30032	26629	27855	28298	28071	85+

ADDED YRS OF LIFE

	No Causes	(1)	(2)	(3)	(4)	(5)	(6)	(7)	(8)	(9)	(10)	(11)	(12)	(1)+(2)	(1)+(2)+(5)+(6)+(8)	(1)+(2)+(5)+(6)+(8)+part of(9)&(12)	(10)+(11)
TOTAL		.073	.117	2.669	10.324	.322	.080	.512	.064	.707	.265	.693	1.790	.190	.664	1.464	.963
WORK	1.629	.018	.023	.552	.289	.020	.008	.079	.045	.000	.086	.188	.274	.041	.115	.141	.274

POPULATION, DEATHS, DEATH RATES FOR ALL CAUSES COMBINED, AND SPECIFIED CAUSES

Age Start of Interval	Midyear Population	Deaths During Year	All Causes	Respiratory T. B.	Other Infec. and Paras.	Neoplasms	Cardiovascular	Infl., Pneu., Bronch.	Diarrheal	Certain Degenerative	Maternal	Cert. Dis. of Infancy	Motor Vehicle	Other Violence	Other and Unknown	Age Start of Interval
0	49197	14271	.29008	.00035	.05828	.00028	.00106	.07466	.01051	.00073	.00000	.05311	.00000	.00081	.09029	0
1	215353	10277	.04772	.00022	.00756	.00007	.00038	.02050	.00408	.00081	.00000	.00000	.00000	.00072	.01338	1
5	252764	3154	.01248	.00009	.00230	.00000	.00017	.00529	.00081	.00042	.00000	.00000	.00000	.00053	.00287	5
10	224817	1478	.00657	.00011	.00120	.00001	.00010	.00257	.00028	.00028	.00000	.00000	.00000	.00053	.00287	10
15	196023	2117	.01080	.00045	.00185	.00001	.00023	.00463	.00032	.00033	.00000	.00000	.00000	.00057	.00146	15
20	177762	2868	.01613	.00130	.00252	.00005	.00028	.00687	.00051	.00043	.00000	.00000	.00000	.00070	.00229	20
25	151594	3237	.02135	.00192	.00316	.00007	.00032	.00933	.00079	.00046	.00000	.00000	.00000	.00114	.00304	25
30	142186	3717	.02614	.00298	.00360	.00006	.00047	.01077	.00056	.00072	.00000	.00000	.00000	.00115	.00415	30
35	136240	4101	.03010	.00422	.00374	.00017	.00058	.01118	.00128	.00103	.00000	.00000	.00000	.00132	.00527	35
40	108679	3808	.03504	.00500	.00403	.00033	.00081	.01296	.00141	.00128	.00000	.00000	.00000	.00109	.00680	40
45	85521	3395	.03970	.00658	.00412	.00046	.00092	.01278	.00173	.00191	.00000	.00000	.00000	.00100	.00822	45
50	57737	2706	.04687	.00774	.00433	.00066	.00165	.01344	.00216	.00220	.00000	.00000	.00000	.00089	.01031	50
55	37586	2240	.05960	.00862	.00415	.00125	.00245	.01634	.00237	.00282	.00000	.00000	.00000	.00114	.01354	55
60	27490	2117	.07701	.00993	.00473	.00142	.00258	.01935	.00378	.00349	.00000	.00000	.00000	.00109	.02051	60
65	16623	1744	.10491	.01047	.00626	.00205	.00415	.02238	.00421	.00596	.00000	.00000	.00000	.00095	.03077	65
70	8617	982	.11396	.00928	.00650	.00128	.00534	.02147	.00255	.00545	.00000	.00000	.00000	.00132	.04813	70
75	3676	617	.16785	.00871	.00762	.00163	.00843	.03400	.00462	.00816	.00000	.00000	.00000	.00174	.06035	75
80	1197	336	.28070	.00752	.00919	.00167	.01253	.05557	.01170	.01170	.00000	.00000	.00000	.00218	.09249	80
85+	479	255	.53236	.00418	.01253	.00209	.01879	.10021	.01879	.01879	.00000	.00000	.00000	.00334	.16708	85+
ALL	1893541	63420														

CRUDE DEATH RATE	.03349	.00220	.00485	.00018	.00057	.01152	.00158	.00088	.00000	.00138	.00000	.00089	.00944
STANDARDIZED RATE (1)	.03950	.00242	.00549	.00023	.00074	.01277	.00181	.00105	.00000	.00187	.00000	.00090	.01221
STANDARDIZED RATE (2)	.04637	.00353	.00455	.00039	.00126	.01364	.00196	.00162	.00000	.00110	.00000	.00102	.01690
GEOMETRIC MEAN	.05124												

LIFE TABLE FOR ALL CAUSES COMBINED

Age (x)	Midyear Population	Deaths During Year	$_nM_x$	$_nq_x$	l_x	$_nd_x$	$_nL_x$	$_nm_x$	$_na_x$	T_x	$_nr_x$	$\overset{\circ}{e}_x$	Age (x)
0	49197	14271	.290079	.257450	100000	25745	88753	.290075	.563134	2668498	.000000	26.685	0
1	215353	10277	.047722	.170547	74255	12664	265360	.047724	1.500000	2579745	.000000	34.742	1
5	252764	3154	.012478	.060561	61591	3730	298630	.012490	2.500000	2314385	.000000	37.577	5
10	224817	1478	.006574	.032267	57861	1867	284476	.006563	2.413631	2015755	.013213	34.838	10
15	196023	2117	.010800	.052791	55994	2956	273051	.010826	2.659210	1731278	.013207	30.919	15
20	177762	2868	.016134	.077793	53038	4126	255294	.016162	2.601491	1458228	.011217	27.494	20
25	151594	3237	.021353	.101529	48912	4966	232408	.021368	2.552985	1202934	.006683	24.594	25
30	142186	3717	.026142	.122628	43946	5389	206347	.026116	2.516585	970526	-.011756	22.085	30
35	136240	4101	.030101	.139923	38557	5395	179287	.030091	2.498146	764179	-.007735	19.819	35
40	108679	3808	.035039	.161058	33162	5341	152380	.035050	2.485529	584892	.005773	17.637	40
45	85521	3395	.039658	.180583	27821	5024	126430	.039737	2.477110	432511	.016535	15.546	45
50	57737	2706	.046868	.210072	22797	4789	101940	.046979	2.484774	306081	.033370	13.426	50
55	37586	2240	.059557	.259551	18008	4674	78252	.059730	2.477981	204142	.020600	11.336	55
60	27490	2117	.077010	.322109	13334	4295	55735	.077061	2.454065	125890	.004926	9.441	60
65	16623	1744	.104915	.412324	9039	3727	35465	.105088	2.389433	70154	-.010582	7.761	65
70	8617	982	.113961	.436182	5312	2317	20354	.113834	2.321608	34689	.025217	6.530	70
75	3676	617	.167845	.581970	2995	1743	10340	.168565	2.340911	14335	.022577	4.786	75
80	1197	336	.280702	.787540	1252	986	3495	.282117	2.195740	3995	.022577	3.191	80
85+	479	255	.532359	1.000000	266	266	500	.532359	1.878431	500	.000000	1.878	85+

NUMBER OF PERSONS DYING (OUT OF 100,000 AT BIRTH) ABOVE AGE X FROM SPECIFIED CAUSES

Age (x)	All Causes	Respiratory T. B.	Other Infec. and Paras.	Neo-plasms	Cardio-vascular	Infl., Pneu., Bronch.	Diar-rheal	Certain Degen-erative	Maternal	Cert. Dis. of Infancy	Motor Vehicle	Other Violence	Other and Unknown	Age (x)
0	100000	6718	14145	593	1825	32954	4514	2657	0	4714	0	2444	29436	0
1	74255	6687	8972	568	1731	26328	3581	2592	0	0	0	2372	21424	1
5	61591	6628	6965	551	1630	20887	2500	2376	0	0	0	2181	17873	5
10	57861	6600	6278	551	1580	19307	2258	2251	0	0	0	2021	17015	10
15	55994	6568	5937	548	1552	18577	2179	2172	0	0	0	1859	16602	15
20	53038	6445	5432	545	1488	17311	2093	2083	0	0	0	1668	15973	20
25	48912	6112	4788	534	1416	15553	1963	1974	0	0	0	1378	15194	25
30	43946	5665	4053	517	1343	13382	1779	1868	0	0	0	1109	14230	30
35	38557	5051	3310	505	1245	11161	1582	1720	0	0	0	836	13147	35
40	33162	4295	2639	475	1142	9158	1352	1535	0	0	0	640	11926	40
45	27821	3533	2025	425	1018	7182	1137	1340	0	0	0	487	10674	45
50	22797	2700	1504	367	901	5566	918	1099	0	0	0	375	9367	50
55	18008	1909	1063	299	732	4194	657	874	0	0	0	258	7982	55
60	13334	1234	738	201	540	2914	511	653	0	0	0	173	6370	60
65	9039	680	474	122	396	1835	300	458	0	0	0	120	4654	65
70	5312	309	252	49	249	1040	151	246	0	0	0	73	2943	70
75	2955	121	120	24	140	604	99	136	0	0	0	38	1713	75
80	1252	31	41	7	52	251	51	51	0	0	0	15	753	80
85+	266	2	6	1	9	50	9	9	0	0	0	3	177	85+

NUMBER OF PERSONS SURVIVING TO AGE X IF SPECIFIED CAUSES WERE ELIMINATED

Age (x)	No Causes	Respiratory T. B. (1)	Other Infec. and Paras. (2)	Neo-plasms (3)	Cardio-vascular (4)	Infl., Pneu., Bronch. (5)	Diar-rheal (6)	Certain Degener-ative (7)	Maternal (8)	Cert. Dis. of Infancy (9)	Motor Vehicle (10)	Other Violence (11)	Other and Unknown (12)	(1)+(2)	(1)+(2)+(5)+(6)+(8)	(1)+(2)+(5)+(6)+(8)+part of(9)&(12)	(10)+(11)	Age (x)
0	100000	100000	100000	100000	100000	100000	100000	100000	100000	100000	100000	100000	100000	100000	100000	100000	100000	0
1	74255	74282	78832	74276	74336	80167	75060	74311	74255	78414	74255	74317	81462	78860	86062	99416	74317	1
5	61591	61667	67354	61624	61750	72058	62261	61834	61591	65041	61591	61816	71206	67437	81036	98351	61816	5
10	57861	57959	64007	57892	58059	69509	59671	58211	57861	61102	57861	58228	67862	64116	79433	97637	58228	10
15	55994	56121	62314	56027	56213	68134	57826	56411	55994	59131	55994	56510	66151	62455	78482	97040	56510	15
20	53038	53279	59574	53072	53308	66054	54860	53520	53038	56009	53038	53715	63386	59844	77090	96259	53715	20
25	48912	49457	55638	48954	49231	63054	50721	49462	48912	51652	48912	49819	59355	56257	75206	95143	49819	25
30	43946	44866	50787	44000	44302	59367	45753	44542	43946	46408	43946	45021	54449	51850	72924	93968	45021	30
35	38557	39557	45369	38616	38962	54570	40335	39221	38557	40717	38557	39762	49046	47016	70121	92464	39762	35
40	33162	35101	39759	33241	33607	49997	34915	33908	33162	35020	33162	34386	43648	42083	66801	90763	34386	40
45	27821	30195	34035	27933	28310	44758	29499	28631	27821	29379	27821	28992	38159	36939	63012	88749	28992	45
50	22797	25574	28469	22942	23306	39096	24383	23686	22797	24074	22797	23862	32934	31938	58584	86268	23862	50
55	18008	21003	22981	18183	18564	33038	19472	18919	18008	19017	18008	18958	27857	26803	53171	82866	18958	55
60	13334	16239	17373	13549	13917	26558	14591	14209	13334	14081	13334	14114	22888	21159	46116	78154	14114	60
65	9039	11572	12061	9251	9557	19843	10082	9804	9039	9545	9039	9613	18136	15441	37809	72791	9613	65
70	5312	7166	7316	5493	5737	13052	6051	5939	5312	5610	5312	5688	13627	9869	27623	64109	5688	70
75	2955	4230	4261	3116	3324	8193	3454	3440	2955	3163	2955	3235	10443	6018	18987	55341	3235	75
80	1252	1846	1852	1313	1452	4092	1480	1501	1252	1322	1252	1368	7087	2731	10553	43820	1368	80
85+	266	411	416	282	330	1192	336	341	266	281	266	296	3722	642	3632	29694	296	85+
ACCED YRS OF LIFE																		
TOTAL		1.139	4.074	.081	.304	10.077	1.156	.486	.000	1.463	.000	.577	8.074	5.527	21.591	45.577	.577	
WORK	20.334	1.490	1.740	.075	.268	5.654	.479	.413	.000	.000	.000	.581	3.143	3.408	11.225	16.195	.581	

POPULATION, DEATHS, DEATH RATES FOR ALL CAUSES COMBINED, AND SPECIFIED CAUSES

Age Start of Interval	Midyear Population	Deaths During Year	All Causes	Respiratory T. B.	Other Infec. and Paras.	Neoplasms	Cardiovascular	Infl., Pneu., Bronch.	Diarrheal	Certain Degenerative	Maternal	Cert. Dis. of Infancy	Motor Vehicle	Other Violence	Other and Unknown	Age Start of Interval
0	48216	11367	.23575	.00033	.04430	.00010	.00071	.06048	.01010	.00062	.00000	.04107	.00000	.00058	.07746	0
1	207157	11319	.05464	.00026	.00913	.00010	.00057	.02156	.00469	.00142	.00000	.00000	.00000	.00080	.01612	1
5	236856	3550	.01499	.00008	.00296	.00002	.00019	.00672	.00076	.00062	.00000	.00000	.00000	.00037	.00328	5
10	205132	1619	.00789	.00013	.00146	.00002	.00010	.00364	.00026	.00032	.00000	.00000	.00000	.00037	.00160	10
15	174702	2087	.01195	.00052	.00161	.00000	.00018	.00521	.00028	.00045	.00082	.00000	.00000	.00069	.00219	15
20	150226	2586	.01721	.00109	.00226	.00005	.00028	.00742	.00048	.00056	.00140	.00000	.00000	.00070	.00299	20
25	124759	2566	.02057	.00128	.00275	.00005	.00034	.00931	.00074	.00069	.00142	.00000	.00000	.00052	.00348	25
30	114590	2693	.02350	.00198	.00271	.00016	.00045	.00982	.00068	.00089	.00140	.00000	.00000	.00054	.00487	30
35	115357	2716	.02354	.00235	.00288	.00029	.00043	.00898	.00104	.00094	.00146	.00000	.00000	.00043	.00475	35
40	97721	2291	.02344	.00258	.00284	.00040	.00065	.00866	.00098	.00116	.00092	.00000	.00000	.00029	.00496	40
45	82422	2058	.02497	.00308	.00271	.00062	.00072	.00888	.00116	.00121	.00021	.00000	.00000	.00033	.00605	45
50	61552	1844	.02956	.00370	.00349	.00063	.00110	.00973	.00128	.00169	.00002	.00000	.00000	.00041	.00790	50
55	44461	1665	.03745	.00400	.00367	.00088	.00110	.01005	.00160	.00232	.00000	.00000	.00000	.00034	.01349	55
60	39333	1903	.04838	.00486	.00455	.00092	.00198	.01182	.00254	.00272	.00008	.00000	.00000	.00051	.01841	60
65	27735	1848	.06663	.00559	.00523	.00144	.00267	.01233	.00278	.00397	.00000	.00000	.00000	.00061	.03202	65
70	16993	1415	.08327	.00583	.00468	.00129	.00441	.01130	.00241	.00388	.00000	.00000	.00000	.00077	.04849	70
75	9279	1140	.12286	.00539	.00571	.00151	.00701	.01800	.00442	.00582	.00000	.00000	.00000	.00097	.07404	75
80	3769	787	.20881	.00478	.00650	.00166	.01061	.02945	.01114	.00849	.00000	.00000	.00000	.00133	.13425	80
85+	1507	603	.40013	.00398	.00929	.00199	.01593	.05309	.01991	.01128	.00000	.00000	.00000	.00265	.28202	85+
ALL	1761767	56057														

	All Causes	Respiratory T. B.	Other Infec. and Paras.	Neoplasms	Cardiovascular	Infl., Pneu., Bronch.	Diarrheal	Certain Degenerative	Maternal	Cert. Dis. of Infancy	Motor Vehicle	Other Violence	Other and Unknown
CRUDE DEATH RATE	.03182	.00139	.00455	.00022	.00058	.01081	.00158	.00102	.00055	.00112	.00000	.00052	.00946
STANDARDIZED RATE (1)	.03389	.00139	.00489	.00022	.00061	.01128	.00166	.00104	.00055	.00145	.00000	.00053	.01028
STANDARDIZED RATE (2)	.03687	.00157	.00431	.00036	.00098	.01091	.00171	.00139	.00055	.00085	.00000	.00053	.01331
GEOMETRIC MEAN	.04189												

LIFE TABLE FOR ALL CAUSES COMBINED

Age (x)	Midyear Population	Deaths During Year	$_nM_x$	$_nq_x$	l_x	$_nd_x$	$_nL_x$	$_nm_x$	$_na_x$	T_x	$_nr_x$	$\overset{\circ}{e}_x$	Age (x)
0	48216	11367	.235752	.209600	100000	20960	88908	.235751	.470778	2918417	.000000	29.184	0
1	207157	11319	.054640	.192995	79040	15199	278163	.054641	1.500000	2829509	.000000	35.798	1
5	236856	3550	.014988	.072352	63841	4619	307658	.015013	2.500000	2551347	.000000	39.964	5
10	205132	1619	.007892	.038567	59222	2284	290129	.007872	2.381239	2243689	.015331	37.886	10
15	174702	2087	.011946	.058256	56938	3317	276846	.011981	2.635351	1953561	.018532	34.310	15
20	150226	2586	.017214	.082785	53621	4439	257320	.017251	2.570399	1676714	.018185	31.270	20
25	124759	2566	.020568	.097942	49182	4817	233968	.020588	2.520803	1419394	.013188	28.860	25
30	114590	2693	.023501	.110898	44365	4920	209434	.023492	2.481538	1185426	-.009200	26.720	30
35	115357	2716	.023544	.111066	39445	4381	186056	.023547	2.450496	975992	-.010837	24.743	35
40	97721	2291	.023444	.110626	35064	3879	165474	.023442	2.461652	789937	.003800	22.528	40
45	82422	2058	.024969	.117589	31185	3667	146751	.024988	2.498125	624463	-.014020	20.024	45
50	61552	1844	.025958	.139763	27518	3846	128057	.030033	2.521343	477712	-.031207	17.360	50
55	44461	1665	.037449	.171553	23672	4061	108288	.037502	2.519905	349655	.014744	14.771	55
60	39333	1903	.048382	.215899	19611	4234	87539	.048367	2.516336	241367	-.002058	12.308	60
65	27735	1848	.066631	.285686	15377	4393	65807	.066756	2.478327	153828	.012815	10.004	65
70	16993	1415	.083270	.343864	10984	3777	45265	.083442	2.443754	88020	.020127	8.014	70
75	9279	1140	.122858	.468156	7207	3374	27351	.123361	2.426089	42755	.020631	5.932	75
80	3769	787	.208809	.673102	3833	2580	12273	.210215	2.328731	15405	.020631	4.019	80
85+	1507	603	.400133	1.000000	1253	1253	3131	.400133	2.499171	3131	.000000	2.499	85+

NUMBER OF PERSONS DYING (OUT OF 100,000 AT BIRTH) ABOVE AGE X FROM SPECIFIED CAUSES

Age (x)	All Causes	Respiratory T.B.	Other Infec. and Paras.	Neoplasms	Cardiovascular	Infl., Pneu., Bronch.	Diarrheal	Certain Degenerative	Maternal	Cert. Dis. of Infancy	Motor Vehicle	Other Violence	Other and Unknown	Age (x)
0	100000	4805	13540	796	2082	32222	4729	3339	1678	3651	0	1536	31622	0
1	79040	4776	9602	786	2019	26845	3831	3284	1678	0	0	1484	24735	1
5	63841	4705	7062	759	1861	20848	2525	2888	1678	0	0	1263	20252	5
10	59222	4681	6150	753	1803	18778	2293	2697	1677	0	0	1148	19242	10
15	56938	4643	5729	747	1774	17725	2218	2604	1676	0	0	1042	18780	15
20	53621	4498	5281	747	1724	16279	2140	2480	1447	0	0	852	18173	20
25	49182	4217	4658	735	1652	14367	2016	2336	1086	0	0	672	17403	25
30	44365	3917	4054	724	1573	12188	1844	2174	754	0	0	550	16587	30
35	39445	3502	3466	691	1478	10131	1701	1988	462	0	0	437	15569	35
40	35064	3066	2951	638	1398	8460	1508	1814	191	0	0	356	14682	40
45	31185	2639	2480	572	1289	7028	1345	1622	38	0	0	309	13863	45
50	27518	2186	2083	481	1184	5724	1174	1444	9	0	0	260	12973	50
55	23672	1711	1634	400	1042	4477	1010	1227	7	0	0	208	11956	55
60	19611	1277	1237	305	923	3387	836	976	7	0	0	172	10491	60
65	15377	852	839	224	749	2353	614	737	0	0	0	127	8882	65
70	10984	484	494	129	573	1541	431	476	0	0	0	87	6769	70
75	7207	220	273	71	373	1029	322	300	0	0	0	52	4567	75
80	3833	73	117	30	180	535	200	140	0	0	0	26	2532	80
85+	1253	12	29	6	50	166	62	35	0	0	0	8	885	85+

NUMBER OF PERSONS SURVIVING TO AGE X IF SPECIFIED CAUSES WERE ELIMINATED

Age (x)	No Causes	Respiratory T.B. (1)	Other Infec. and Paras. (2)	Neoplasms (3)	Cardiovascular (4)	Infl., Pneu., Bronch. (5)	Diarrheal (6)	Certain Degenerative (7)	Maternal (8)	Cert. Dis. of Infancy (9)	Motor Vehicle (10)	Other Violence (11)	Other and Unknown (12)	(1)+(2)	(1)+(2)+(5)+(6)+(8)	(1)+(2)+(5)+(6)+(8)+part of(9)&(12)	(10)+(11)	Age (x)
0	100000	100000	100000	100000	100000	100000	100000	100000	100000	100000	100000	100000	100000	100000	100000	100000	100000	0
1	79040	79066	82611	79049	79096	83956	79841	79089	79040	82346	79040	79086	85391	82638	88667	99595	79086	1
5	63841	63926	69150	63872	64028	73714	65662	64237	63841	66511	63841	64077	73455	69242	82322	98015	64077	5
10	59222	59323	65106	59257	59452	70779	61160	59775	59223	61699	59222	59552	65269	65217	80495	97264	59552	10
15	56938	57073	63050	56577	57187	69294	58877	57561	56940	59319	56938	57360	67129	63199	79536	96774	57360	15
20	53621	53890	59860	53658	53905	66987	55526	54330	53846	55864	53621	54204	63916	60160	78151	95597	54204	20
25	49182	49700	55531	49228	49511	63772	51052	49972	49737	51239	49182	49891	59510	56115	76380	95080	49891	25
30	44365	45121	50787	44417	44738	60271	46222	45234	45185	46220	44365	45122	54628	51652	74459	94168	45122	30
35	39445	40518	45771	39522	39867	56284	41237	40397	40455	41095	39445	40226	45767	47016	71930	92964	40226	35
40	35064	36443	41277	35183	35515	52329	36848	36079	36224	36530	35064	35836	45306	42900	69507	91755	35836	40
45	31185	32833	37237	31354	31691	48558	32933	32275	32365	32489	31185	31917	41305	39204	66962	90309	31917	45
50	27518	29423	33306	27753	28065	44833	29231	28653	28587	28669	27518	28211	37573	35612	64025	88602	28211	50
55	23672	25786	29159	23950	24277	40493	25307	24859	24593	24662	23672	24318	33638	31762	60346	86309	24318	55
60	19611	21795	24604	19929	20224	35280	21136	20835	20374	20431	19611	20179	29830	27345	55081	83226	20179	60
65	15377	17511	19737	15699	16017	29350	16785	16563	15982	16020	15377	15864	25662	22477	48672	79161	15864	65
70	10984	12864	14474	11296	11597	22300	12158	12069	11416	11443	10984	11366	21570	16952	39591	72725	11366	70
75	7207	8691	9731	7459	7782	15485	8074	8075	7490	7508	7207	7487	18117	11735	29357	64116	7487	75
80	3833	4747	5327	3997	4291	9025	4394	4425	3984	3993	3833	4001	14117	6597	18531	52612	4001	80
85+	1253	1593	1809	1320	1484	3466	1525	1514	1302	1305	1253	1318	9422	2301	8050	37750	1318	85+

ADDED YRS OF LIFE

	No Causes	(1)	(2)	(3)	(4)	(5)	(6)	(7)	(8)	(9)	(10)	(11)	(12)				
TOTAL		.949	4.258	.128	.369	11.129	1.311	.730	.462	1.201	.000	.432	9.313	5.441	23.343	46.819	.432
WORK	18.391	1.064	1.629	.111	.262	5.808	.446	.517	.704	.000	.000	.353	2.802	2.793	11.233	15.241	.353

POPULATION, DEATHS, DEATH RATES FOR ALL CAUSES COMBINED, AND SPECIFIED CAUSES

Age Start of Interval	Midyear Population	Deaths During Year	All Causes	Respiratory T. B.	Other Infec. and Paras.	Neoplasms	Cardiovascular	Infl., Pneu., Bronch.	Diarrheal	Certain Degenerative	Maternal	Cert. Dis. of Infancy	Motor Vehicle	Other Violence	Other and Unknown	Age Start of Interval
0	69934	16961	.24253	.00031	.05464	.00014	.00107	.06735	.04940	.00001	.00000	.03819	.00000	.00067	.03073	0
1	324805	7525	.02317	.00015	.00217	.00001	.00014	.00822	.00837	.00001	.00000	.00000	.00000	.00060	.00348	1
5	300249	1257	.00419	.00007	.00074	.00000	.00012	.00105	.00077	.00002	.00000	.00000	.00000	.00047	.00095	5
10	252738	701	.00277	.00008	.00057	.00003	.00008	.00051	.00038	.00001	.00000	.00000	.00000	.00036	.00076	10
15	251808	1186	.00471	.00047	.00097	.00003	.00017	.00097	.00044	.00002	.00000	.00000	.00000	.00060	.00103	15
20	225812	1472	.00652	.00093	.00103	.00003	.00021	.00136	.00058	.00003	.00000	.00000	.00000	.00088	.00146	20
25	190266	1595	.00838	.00162	.00121	.00002	.00036	.00181	.00074	.00008	.00000	.00000	.00000	.00096	.00159	25
30	161515	1544	.00956	.00202	.00126	.00009	.00037	.00201	.00091	.00011	.00000	.00000	.00000	.00089	.00190	30
35	133249	1572	.01180	.00254	.00142	.00009	.00062	.00233	.00116	.00015	.00000	.00000	.00000	.00080	.00268	35
40	120262	1948	.01620	.00339	.00158	.00028	.00086	.00315	.00206	.00028	.00000	.00000	.00000	.00096	.00362	40
45	108470	2405	.02217	.00479	.00183	.00079	.00153	.00479	.00261	.00041	.00000	.00000	.00000	.00077	.00465	45
50	81316	2220	.02730	.00598	.00171	.00079	.00223	.00529	.00380	.00034	.00000	.00000	.00000	.00097	.00620	50
55	59183	2166	.03660	.00716	.00223	.00159	.00296	.00725	.00488	.00041	.00000	.00000	.00000	.00081	.00931	55
60	35345	1775	.05022	.00767	.00243	.00184	.00532	.00965	.00685	.00062	.00000	.00000	.00000	.00113	.01471	60
65	19437	1384	.07120	.00839	.00252	.00211	.00885	.01405	.01024	.00072	.00000	.00000	.00000	.00144	.02289	65
70	11658	999	.08569	.00798	.00232	.00214	.01064	.01527	.01004	.00034	.00000	.00000	.00000	.00172	.03525	70
75	4973	640	.12869	.00744	.00282	.00261	.01669	.02413	.01830	.00060	.00000	.00000	.00000	.00221	.05389	75
80	1620	363	.22407	.00679	.00309	.00309	.02531	.03951	.04506	.00062	.00000	.00000	.00000	.00309	.09753	80
85+	648	268	.41358	.00309	.00463	.00309	.03858	.07253	.08025	.00154	.00000	.00000	.00000	.00463	.20525	85+
ALL	2353288	47981														

CRUDE DEATH RATE			.02039	.00163	.00291	.00021	.00074	.00516	.00386	.00011	.00000	.00114	.00000	.00072	.00393	
STANDARDIZED RATE (1)			.02385	.00183	.00322	.00027	.00106	.00584	.00437	.00012	.00000	.00134	.00000	.00074	.00505	
STANDARDIZED RATE (2)			.02882	.00271	.00259	.00050	.00208	.00628	.00477	.00019	.00000	.00079	.00000	.00086	.00805	
GEOMETRIC MEAN			.02775													

LIFE TABLE FOR ALL CAUSES COMBINED

Age (x)	Midyear Population	Deaths During Year	$_nM_x$	$_nq_x$	l_x	$_nd_x$	$_nL_x$	$_nm_x$	$_na_x$	T_x	$_nr_x$	$\overset{\circ}{e}_x$	Age (x)
0	69934	16961	.242529	.215470	100000	21547	88845	.242523	.482299	4000573	.000000	40.006	0
1	324805	7525	.023168	.087607	78453	6873	296630	.023170	1.500000	3911728	.000000	49.961	1
5	300249	1257	.004187	.020704	71580	1482	354195	.004184	2.500000	3615098	.000000	50.504	5
10	252738	701	.002774	.013781	70098	966	348102	.002779	2.528037	3260903	.012543	46.519	10
15	251808	1186	.004710	.023318	69132	1612	341881	.004715	2.655733	2912801	.005536	42.134	15
20	225812	1472	.006519	.032153	67520	2171	332397	.006531	2.603351	2570920	.017282	38.076	20
25	190266	1595	.008383	.041148	65349	2689	320181	.008398	2.558959	2238523	.023302	34.255	25
30	161515	1544	.009559	.046792	62660	2932	306125	.009578	2.552865	1918342	.026155	30.615	30
35	133249	1572	.011797	.057477	59728	3433	290362	.011823	2.588601	1612217	.021899	26.993	35
40	120262	1948	.016198	.078018	56295	4392	270919	.016212	2.596435	1321856	.006168	23.481	40
45	108470	2405	.022172	.105312	51903	5466	246176	.022204	2.559611	1050937	.012297	20.248	45
50	81316	2220	.027301	.128266	46437	5956	217579	.027374	2.547676	804761	.026277	17.330	50
55	59183	2166	.036598	.168696	40481	6829	185669	.036781	2.549208	587182	.038723	14.505	55
60	35345	1775	.050219	.224920	33652	7569	149563	.050607	2.529809	401514	.058285	11.931	60
65	19437	1384	.071204	.303339	26083	7912	110390	.071673	2.469034	251951	.044915	9.660	65
70	11658	999	.085692	.351824	18171	6393	74419	.085905	2.429122	141561	.042255	7.790	70
75	4973	640	.128695	.487095	11778	5737	44103	.130081	2.422579	67141	.057708	5.701	75
80	1620	363	.224074	.705347	6041	4261	18734	.227445	2.307548	23038	.057708	3.814	80
85+	648	268	.413580	1.000000	1780	1780	4304	.413580	2.417910	4304	.000000	2.418	85+

NUMBER OF PERSONS DYING (OUT OF 100,000 AT BIRTH) ABOVE AGE X FROM SPECIFIED CAUSES

Age (x)	All Causes	Respiratory T. B.	Other Infec. and Paras.	Neoplasms	Cardio-vascular	Infl., Pneu., Bronch.	Diarrheal	Certain Degenerative	Maternal	Cert. Dis. of Infancy	Motor Vehicle	Other Violence	Other and Unknown	Age (x)
0	100000	10378	10517	1706	6363	22469	16352	705	0	3393	0	3293	24824	0
1	78453	10350	5663	1693	6268	16486	11963	704	0	0	0	3233	22093	1
5	71580	10305	5019	1690	6225	14046	9479	701	0	0	0	3055	21060	5
10	70098	10281	4757	1689	6184	13674	9208	695	0	0	0	2889	20721	10
15	69132	10254	4557	1679	6158	13498	9074	692	0	0	0	2762	20458	15
20	67520	10092	4225	1669	6099	13166	8924	684	0	0	0	2555	20106	20
25	65349	9780	3882	1660	6028	12712	8730	673	0	0	0	2263	19621	25
30	62660	9259	3494	1653	5912	12132	8494	648	0	0	0	1957	19111	30
35	59728	8637	3108	1626	5800	11515	8215	616	0	0	0	1684	18527	35
40	56295	7897	2695	1600	5618	10836	7878	572	0	0	0	1451	17748	40
45	51903	6977	2267	1523	5384	9981	7319	495	0	0	0	1190	16767	45
50	46437	5795	1815	1328	5006	8800	6676	395	0	0	0	1002	15620	50
55	40481	4492	1443	1156	4520	7647	5846	320	0	0	0	790	14267	55
60	33652	3159	1028	859	3967	6294	4935	245	0	0	0	640	12525	60
65	26083	2011	663	583	3161	4841	3902	151	0	0	0	469	10302	65
70	18171	1083	385	349	2176	3280	2765	71	0	0	0	309	7753	70
75	11778	492	213	190	1383	2143	2018	46	0	0	0	181	5112	75
80	6041	165	88	74	639	1066	1197	19	0	0	0	83	2710	80
85+	1780	13	20	13	166	312	345	7	0	0	0	20	884	85+

NUMBER OF PERSONS SURVIVING TO AGE X IF SPECIFIED CAUSES WERE ELIMINATED

Age (x)	No Causes	Respiratory T. B.	Other Infec. and Paras.	Neoplasms	Cardio-vascular	Infl., Pneu., Bronch.	Diarrheal	Certain Degenerative	Maternal	Cert. Dis. of Infancy	Motor Vehicle	Other Violence	Other and Unknown	(1) + (2)	(1) + (2) + (5) + (6) + (8)	(1)+(2)+ (5)+(6)+ (8)+part of(9)&(12)	(10) + (11)	Age (x)
		(1)	(2)	(3)	(4)	(5)	(6)	(7)	(8)	(9)	(10)	(11)	(12)					
0	100000	100000	100000	100000	100000	100000	100000	100000	100000	100000	100000	100000	100000	100000	100000	100000	100000	0
1	78453	78478	82861	78464	78537	83922	82428	78454	78453	81509	78453	78506	80904	82887	93158	99734	78506	1
5	71580	71646	76254	71593	71698	79103	77741	71584	71580	74368	71580	71799	74840	76324	91605	99380	71799	5
10	70098	70186	74952	70112	70254	77873	76423	70108	70098	72829	70098	70477	73642	75046	90893	98991	70477	10
15	69132	69246	74132	69156	69312	76994	75515	69144	69132	71825	69132	69633	72902	74254	90334	98667	69633	15
20	67520	67792	72756	67553	67754	75565	73916	67540	67520	70150	67520	68215	71570	73049	89497	98144	68215	20
25	65349	65921	70781	65390	65646	73637	71749	65379	65349	67895	65349	66313	69776	71401	88336	97418	66313	25
30	62660	63726	68281	62706	63059	71250	69051	62713	62660	65101	62660	63889	67440	69568	87015	96569	63889	30
35	59728	61365	65498	59798	60218	68604	66121	59810	59728	62055	59728	61171	64901	67292	85565	95569	61171	35
40	56295	58580	62174	56387	56936	65422	62684	56415	56295	58488	56295	57887	61998	64698	83720	94669	57887	40
45	51903	54937	57778	52062	52721	61280	58394	52088	51903	53925	51903	53629	58208	61156	81234	93216	53629	45
50	46437	50349	52171	46765	47534	56160	52933	46637	46437	42058	46437	53308	56565	77980	91170	48165	50	50
55	40481	45228	45870	40929	41905	50275	47036	40778	40481	42058	40481	42192	47945	51249	73954	88636	42192	55
60	33652	38975	38562	34299	35362	43352	40076	33968	33652	34963	33652	35216	41784	44661	68519	85236	35216	60
65	26083	31393	30256	26832	28165	35285	32162	26411	26083	27099	26083	27453	34908	36415	60744	79922	27453	65
70	18171	22810	21345	18892	20527	26517	23599	18466	18171	18879	18171	19265	27336	26795	50555	72425	19265	70
75	11778	15382	13996	12377	14040	18478	16089	11989	11778	12237	11778	12596	21219	18279	39116	63731	12596	75
80	6041	8187	7282	6434	7852	10744	9089	6169	6041	6276	6041	6534	14396	9869	26417	52391	6534	80
85+	1780	2520	2189	1929	2650	3930	3419	1824	1780	1849	1780	1960	7161	3097	13141	38595	1960	85+

ADDED YRS OF LIFE																	
TOTAL		1.983	3.872	.228	.859	6.922	4.971	.120	.000	1.540	.000	.888	5.467	6.144	22.533	37.934	.888
WORK	11.511	1.785	1.081	.149	.493	1.922	.998	.104	.000	.000	.000	.701	2.068	2.957	6.458	8.667	.701

POPULATION, DEATHS, DEATH RATES FOR ALL CAUSES COMBINED, AND SPECIFIED CAUSES

Age Start of Interval	Midyear Population	Deaths During Year	All Causes	Respiratory T. B.	Other Infec. and Paras.	Neoplasms	Cardiovascular	Infl., Pneu., Bronch.	Diarrheal	Certain Degenerative	Maternal	Cert. Dis. of Infancy	Motor Vehicle	Other Violence	Other and Unknown	Age Start of Interval
0	68551	13703	.19989	.00036	.04101	.00009	.00069	.05635	.04579	.00000	.00000	.03056	.00000	.00064	.02441	0
1	314777	8422	.02676	.00022	.00234	.00003	.00012	.00903	.01049	.00000	.00000	.00000	.00000	.00054	.00398	1
5	289705	1117	.00386	.00004	.00070	.00001	.00010	.00104	.00087	.00002	.00000	.00000	.00000	.00016	.00092	5
10	239096	563	.00235	.00009	.00048	.00001	.00009	.00062	.00041	.00000	.00000	.00000	.00000	.00019	.00046	10
15	236222	1104	.00467	.00047	.00067	.00001	.00016	.00091	.00047	.00001	.00054	.00000	.00000	.00055	.00088	15
20	200092	1252	.00626	.00082	.00071	.00002	.00021	.00101	.00063	.00005	.00058	.00000	.00000	.00063	.00118	20
25	167853	1224	.00729	.00116	.00083	.00005	.00041	.00108	.00092	.00008	.00086	.00000	.00000	.00043	.00148	25
30	139524	1159	.00831	.00123	.00092	.00014	.00047	.00133	.00105	.00006	.00102	.00000	.00006	.00032	.00175	30
35	111899	1077	.00962	.00150	.00107	.00036	.00042	.00139	.00122	.00007	.00114	.00000	.00006	.00032	.00216	35
40	102344	1166	.01139	.00196	.00109	.00064	.00063	.00185	.00141	.00011	.00084	.00000	.00000	.00035	.00251	40
45	100333	1255	.01251	.00235	.00109	.00084	.00091	.00207	.00181	.00012	.00011	.00000	.00000	.00041	.00280	45
50	83450	1323	.01585	.00259	.00103	.00097	.00156	.00288	.00229	.00020	.00001	.00000	.00000	.00042	.00391	50
55	67672	1493	.02206	.00364	.00136	.00132	.00205	.00383	.00334	.00034	.00004	.00000	.00000	.00037	.00578	55
60	46252	1427	.03085	.00426	.00141	.00149	.00370	.00515	.00510	.00032	.00000	.00000	.00000	.00048	.00895	60
65	29875	1386	.04639	.00402	.00191	.00151	.00653	.00733	.00730	.00044	.00000	.00000	.00000	.00050	.01687	65
70	22409	1407	.06279	.00442	.00196	.00147	.00928	.00915	.00625	.00040	.00000	.00000	.00000	.00049	.02936	70
75	12237	1159	.09471	.00409	.00229	.00180	.01455	.01455	.01144	.00057	.00000	.00000	.00000	.00065	.04478	75
80	4970	823	.16559	.00362	.00262	.00221	.02213	.02374	.02817	.00080	.00000	.00000	.00000	.00101	.08129	80
85+	1988	612	.30785	.00252	.00402	.00201	.03320	.04326	.05030	.00101	.00000	.00000	.00000	.00101	.17052	85+
ALL	2239249	41672														

	All Causes	Respiratory T.B.	Other Infec.	Neoplasms	Cardiovascular	Infl. Pneu.	Diarrheal	Certain Degen.	Maternal	Cert. Dis. Infancy	Motor Vehicle	Other Violence	Other Unknown
CRUDE DEATH RATE	.01861	.00104	.00231	.00027	.00078	.00448	.00410	.00007	.00038	.00094	.00000	.00041	.00384
STANDARDIZED RATE (1)	.01936	.00107	.00247	.00028	.00083	.00461	.00414	.00008	.00039	.00108	.00000	.00040	.00403
STANDARDIZED RATE (2)	.02184	.00151	.00195	.00046	.00167	.00439	.00359	.00012	.00039	.00063	.00000	.00041	.00632
GEOMETRIC MEAN	.02140												

LIFE TABLE FOR ALL CAUSES COMBINED

Age (x)	Midyear Population	Deaths During Year	$_nM_x$	$_nq_x$	l_x	$_nd_x$	$_nL_x$	$_nm_x$	$_na_x$	T_x	$_nr_x$	$\overset{\circ}{e}_x$	Age (x)
0	68551	13703	.199895	.178800	100000	17880	89448	.199894	.409821	4485128	.000000	44.851	0
1	314777	8422	.026755	.100317	82120	8238	307885	.026757	1.500000	4395681	.000000	53.528	1
5	289705	1117	.003856	.019084	73882	1410	365885	.003854	2.500000	4087796	.000000	55.329	5
10	239096	563	.002355	.011715	72472	849	360289	.002356	2.561101	3721911	.014449	51.357	10
15	236222	1104	.004674	.023163	71623	1659	354241	.004683	2.664632	3361621	.011007	46.935	15
20	200092	1252	.006257	.030873	69964	2160	344581	.006268	2.574653	3007381	.024128	42.985	20
25	167853	1224	.007292	.035883	67804	2433	333043	.007305	2.543242	2662799	.026853	39.272	25
30	139524	1159	.008307	.040767	65371	2665	320301	.008320	2.540650	2329757	.031964	35.639	30
35	111899	1077	.009625	.047093	62706	2953	306282	.009641	2.545646	2009456	.027757	32.046	35
40	102344	1166	.011393	.055428	59753	3312	290584	.011398	2.529753	1703174	.005366	28.504	40
45	100333	1255	.012508	.060701	56441	3426	273795	.012513	2.545181	1412590	.004599	25.028	45
50	83450	1323	.015854	.076488	53015	4055	255296	.015884	2.588471	1138795	.017092	21.481	50
55	67672	1493	.022062	.105147	48960	5148	232405	.022151	2.592188	883499	.029037	18.045	55
60	46252	1427	.030853	.144549	43812	6333	203789	.031016	2.588623	651094	.048727	14.861	60
65	29875	1386	.046393	.209237	37479	7842	168151	.046637	2.546093	447306	.032727	11.935	65
70	22409	1407	.062787	.272227	29637	8068	128113	.062976	2.512162	279154	.021089	9.419	70
75	12237	1159	.094713	.385414	21569	8313	86997	.095555	2.492081	151041	.044362	7.003	75
80	4970	823	.165594	.584792	13256	7752	46165	.167918	2.405240	64044	.044362	4.831	80
85+	1988	612	.307847	1.000000	5504	5504	17879	.307847	3.248366	17879	.000000	3.248	85+

NUMBER OF PERSONS DYING (OUT OF 100,000 AT BIRTH) ABOVE AGE X FROM SPECIFIED CAUSES

Age (x)	All Causes	Respiratory T. B.	Other Infec. and Paras.	Neo-plasms	Cardio-vascular	Infl., Pneu., Bronch.	Diar-rheal	Certain Degen-erative	Maternal	Cert. Dis. of Infancy	Motor Vehicle	Other Violence	Other and Unknown	Age (x)
0	100000	7261	8660	2227	7981	19676	17776	591	1785	2734	0	1871	29438	0
1	82120	7229	4992	2219	7920	14635	13680	591	1785	0	0	1814	27255	1
5	73882	7160	4272	2211	7882	11855	10449	590	1785	0	0	1648	26030	5
10	72472	7145	4014	2208	7846	11476	10130	583	1785	0	0	1590	25695	10
15	71623	7113	3841	2205	7815	11252	9981	582	1783	0	0	1522	25529	15
20	69964	6946	3604	2202	7758	10929	9813	579	1591	0	0	1325	25217	20
25	67804	6662	3357	2193	7685	10579	9596	561	1253	0	0	1108	24810	25
30	65371	6274	3081	2175	7549	10219	9287	536	967	0	0	966	24317	30
35	62706	5879	2785	2128	7398	9792	8951	515	639	0	0	865	23754	35
40	59753	5418	2456	2018	7269	9367	8576	493	288	0	0	778	23090	40
45	56441	4847	2138	1830	7087	8830	8167	462	45	0	0	676	22359	45
50	53015	4203	1840	1601	6839	8262	7670	429	15	0	0	564	21592	50
55	48960	3541	1577	1353	6440	7526	7084	377	12	0	0	457	20593	55
60	43812	2694	1260	1046	5960	6633	6304	297	1	0	0	371	19246	60
65	37479	1824	973	742	5198	5578	5257	231	1	0	0	273	17402	65
70	29637	1149	652	489	4093	4340	4026	158	1	0	0	189	14540	70
75	21569	583	400	300	2900	3165	3225	107	1	0	0	126	10762	75
80	13256	228	200	143	1624	1888	2216	56	1	0	0	69	6831	80
85+	5504	45	72	36	594	773	899	18	0	0	0	18	3049	85+

NUMBER OF PERSONS SURVIVING TO AGE X IF SPECIFIED CAUSES WERE ELIMINATED

Age (x)	No Causes	Respiratory T. B. (1)	Other Infec. and Paras. (2)	Neo-plasms (3)	Cardio-vascular (4)	Infl., Pneu., Bronch. (5)	Diar-rheal (6)	Certain Degener-ative (7)	Maternal (8)	Cert. Dis. of Infancy (9)	Motor Vehicle (10)	Other Violence (11)	Other and Unknown (12)	(1) + (2)	(1) + (2) + (5) + (6) + (8)	(1)+(2)+ (5)+(6)+ (8)+part of(9)&(12)	(10) + (11)	Age (x)
0	100000	100000	100000	100000	100000	100000	100000	100000	100000	100000	100000	100000	100000	100000	100000	100000	100000	0
1	82120	82149	85507	82127	82175	86810	85911	82120	82120	84631	82120	82172	84119	85537	94596	99809	82172	1
5	73882	73974	77643	73896	73968	80564	80564	73883	73882	76141	73882	74086	76880	77739	92866	99489	74086	5
10	72472	72577	76430	72489	72592	79805	79372	72480	72472	74688	72472	72730	75758	76540	92311	99304	72730	10
15	71623	71758	75716	71643	71772	79116	78605	71632	71625	73813	71623	71946	75044	75859	91966	99127	71946	15
20	69964	70262	74210	69986	70166	77637	76966	69976	70156	72103	69964	70475	73629	74526	91226	98687	70475	20
25	67804	68374	72178	67834	68072	75623	74826	67833	68325	69877	67804	68515	71779	72785	90273	98122	68515	25
30	65371	66306	69877	65418	65764	73305	72476	65423	66156	67370	65371	66197	69718	70876	89176	97530	66197	30
35	62706	63996	67339	62797	63232	70787	69887	62777	63785	64624	62706	63598	67466	68724	87954	96915	63598	35
40	59753	61444	64513	59948	60381	67923	67005	59842	61131	61580	59753	60689	64990	66339	86512	96206	60689	40
45	56441	58612	61272	56809	57213	64755	63739	56555	57984	58167	56441	57426	62165	63628	84692	95142	57426	45
50	53015	55706	57866	53584	53985	61459	60416	53154	54493	54636	53015	54051	59217	60803	82568	93757	54051	50
55	48960	52117	53717	49727	50248	57584	56441	49139	50328	50457	48960	50021	55770	57181	79694	91810	50021	55
60	43812	47497	48398	44794	45433	52531	51364	44048	45047	45152	43812	44845	51379	52468	75833	89287	44845	60
65	37479	41509	41655	38606	39605	46121	45088	37742	38535	38625	37479	38455	46002	46178	70290	85542	38455	65
70	29637	33489	33288	30759	32373	37846	36987	29910	30472	30543	29637	30485	39645	37615	61635	79633	30485	70
75	21569	24917	24466	22551	24694	28846	27776	21811	22177	22229	21569	22241	33498	28264	50050	71263	22241	75
80	13256	15629	15212	13986	16352	19104	18118	13445	13630	13661	13256	13714	25916	17934	36324	60067	13714	80
85+	5504	6625	6408	5878	7630	9001	8734	5606	5660	5672	5504	5727	16523	7714	20587	45788	5727	85+

ADDED YRS OF LIFE																		
TOTAL		1.593	3.434	.379	1.065	6.642	5.926	.102	.632	1.359	.000	.602	6.425	5.200	22.283	36.990	.602	
WORK	9.310	1.217	.821	.243	.456	1.321	1.004	.069	.706	.000	.000	.419	1.755	2.079	5.501	7.237	.419	

POPULATION, DEATHS, DEATH RATES FOR ALL CAUSES COMBINED, AND SPECIFIED CAUSES

Age Start of Interval	Midyear Population	Deaths During Year	All Causes	Respiratory T.B.	Other Infec. and Paras.	Neo-plasms	Cardio-vascular	Infl., Pneu., Bronch.	Diar-rheal	Certain Degen-erative	Maternal	Cert. Dis. of Infancy	Motor Vehicle	Other Violence	Other and Unknown	Age Start of Interval
0	99977	18625	.18629	.00108	.04680	.00027	.00082	.05638	.03158	.00006	.00000	.01104	.00000	.00072	.03754	0
1	356928	10435	.02924	.00045	.00579	.00007	.00036	.01004	.00689	.00003	.00000	.00000	.00000	.00068	.00494	1
5	371762	1684	.00453	.00010	.00101	.00004	.00011	.00136	.00037	.00003	.00000	.00000	.00000	.00068	.00494	5
10	296096	831	.00281	.00012	.00068	.00003	.00012	.00066	.00014	.00002	.00000	.00000	.00000	.00034	.00116	10
15	252537	1148	.00455	.00053	.00096	.00002	.00019	.00095	.00015	.00005	.00000	.00000	.00000	.00031	.00073	15
20	234501	1556	.00706	.00137	.00128	.00004	.00020	.00145	.00019	.00012	.00000	.00000	.00000	.00050	.00118	20
25	217213	1771	.00815	.00181	.00128	.00006	.00023	.00175	.00023	.00023	.00000	.00000	.00000	.00092	.00149	25
30	180722	1804	.00998	.00217	.00146	.00011	.00034	.00234	.00037	.00024	.00000	.00000	.00000	.00088	.00168	30
35	151020	1783	.01181	.00239	.00134	.00026	.00062	.00279	.00048	.00033	.00000	.00000	.00000	.00075	.00223	35
40	120548	2030	.01684	.00323	.00183	.00045	.00100	.00399	.00075	.00051	.00000	.00000	.00000	.00083	.00425	40
45	103381	2266	.02192	.00444	.00186	.00081	.00161	.00511	.00083	.00092	.00000	.00000	.00000	.00095	.00546	45
50	91541	2640	.02884	.00553	.00189	.00145	.00236	.00664	.00126	.00110	.00000	.00000	.00000	.00094	.00767	50
55	69332	2632	.03796	.00678	.00251	.00212	.00417	.00754	.00199	.00149	.00000	.00000	.00000	.00102	.01034	55
60	49506	2435	.04919	.00780	.00252	.00277	.00675	.00982	.00232	.00149	.00000	.00000	.00000	.00105	.01466	60
65	26956	1922	.07130	.01028	.00260	.00282	.01106	.01354	.00378	.00185	.00000	.00000	.00000	.00126	.02411	65
70	13598	1254	.09222	.00765	.00368	.00316	.01375	.01434	.00463	.00132	.00000	.00000	.00000	.00132	.04236	70
75	5801	789	.13601	.00690	.00431	.00379	.02138	.02293	.00845	.00190	.00000	.00000	.00000	.00172	.06464	75
80	1889	433	.22922	.00635	.00529	.00424	.03229	.03706	.02065	.00265	.00000	.00000	.00000	.00265	.11805	80
85+	756	319	.42196	.00397	.00661	.00397	.04894	.06746	.03704	.00397	.00000	.00000	.00000	.00397	.24603	85+
ALL	2644064	56457														

CRUDE DEATH RATE			.02135	.00174	.00365	.00033	.00091	.00574	.00261	.00028	.00000	.00042	.00000	.00068	.00500	
STANDARDIZED RATE (1)			.02291	.00194	.00351	.00041	.00128	.00586	.00257	.00033	.00000	.00039	.00000	.00068	.00500	
STANDARDIZED RATE (2)			.02874	.00279	.00292	.00072	.00258	.00634	.00246	.00052	.00000	.00000	.00000	.00070	.00594	
GEOMETRIC MEAN			.02832													

LIFE TABLE FOR ALL CAUSES COMBINED

Age (x)	Midyear Population	Deaths During Year	$_nM_x$	$_nq_x$	l_x	$_nd_x$	$_nL_x$	$_nm_x$	$_na_x$	T_x	$_nr_x$	$\overset{\circ}{e}_x$	Age (x)
0	99977	18625	.186293	.167190	100000	16719	89746	.186292	.386658	4120264	.000000	41.203	0
1	356928	10435	.029236	.108980	83281	9076	310434	.029236	1.500000	4030518	.000000	48.397	1
5	371762	1684	.004530	.022424	74205	1664	366865	.004536	2.500000	3720084	.000000	50.133	5
10	296096	831	.002807	.013909	72541	1009	360172	.002801	2.490089	3353219	.029327	46.225	10
15	252537	1148	.004546	.022591	71532	1616	353916	.004566	2.683194	2993046	.023304	41.842	15
20	234501	1656	.007062	.034756	69916	2430	343731	.007069	2.592936	2639130	.010475	37.747	20
25	217213	1771	.008153	.040008	67486	2700	330832	.008161	2.556481	2295400	.014575	34.013	25
30	180722	1804	.009982	.048807	64786	3162	316201	.010000	2.555806	1964567	.023288	30.324	30
35	151020	1783	.011806	.057559	61624	3547	299576	.011840	2.591157	1648366	.027466	26.749	35
40	120548	2030	.016840	.081168	58077	4714	279019	.016895	2.588875	1348790	.025567	23.224	40
45	103381	2266	.021919	.104155	53363	5558	253281	.021944	2.564884	1069771	.009303	20.047	45
50	91541	2640	.028840	.134819	47805	6445	223253	.028869	2.552786	816490	.008870	17.080	50
55	69332	2632	.037962	.173864	41360	7191	189046	.038038	2.531115	593237	.017117	14.343	55
60	49506	2435	.049186	.220053	34169	7519	152240	.049389	2.525602	404191	.034765	11.829	60
65	26956	1922	.071301	.304503	26650	8115	112841	.071915	2.485059	251951	.053527	9.454	65
70	13598	1254	.092219	.374265	18535	6937	74864	.092662	2.432428	139110	.056885	7.505	70
75	5801	789	.136011	.505651	11598	5865	42732	.137250	2.398515	64246	.054549	5.539	75
80	1889	433	.229222	.711669	5733	4080	17596	.231865	2.287122	21514	.054549	3.753	80
85+	756	319	.421958	1.000000	1653	1653	3917	.421958	2.369906	3917	.000000	2.370	85+

NUMBER OF PERSONS DYING (OUT OF 100,000 AT BIRTH) ABOVE AGE X FROM SPECIFIED CAUSES

Age (x)	All Causes	Respiratory T.B.	Other Infec. and Paras.	Neo-plasms	Cardio-vascular	Infl., Pneu., Bronch.	Diar-rheal	Certain Degen-erative	Maternal	Cert. Dis. of Infancy	Motor Vehicle	Other Violence	Other and Unknown	Age (x)
0	100000	10898	11828	2517	7791	23267	8706	1933	0	951	0	3173	28896	0
1	83281	10801	7628	2493	7717	18206	5872	1928	0	0	0	3108	25528	1
5	74205	10661	5831	2472	7606	15090	3733	1920	0	0	0	2898	23994	5
10	72541	10623	5459	2458	7565	14589	3597	1908	0	0	0	2773	23569	10
15	71532	10578	5217	2446	7521	14353	3548	1902	0	0	0	2660	23307	15
20	69916	10387	4875	2438	7454	14014	3494	1884	0	0	0	2481	22889	20
25	67486	9916	4437	2423	7383	13517	3430	1841	0	0	0	2164	22375	25
30	64786	9316	4011	2405	7307	12937	3352	1763	0	0	0	1873	21822	30
35	61624	8628	3549	2371	7200	12197	3234	1688	0	0	0	1642	21115	35
40	58077	7910	3148	2293	7014	11358	3091	1588	0	0	0	1404	20271	40
45	53363	7007	2636	2168	6735	10241	2880	1444	0	0	0	1172	19080	45
50	47805	5881	2165	1961	6328	8946	2669	1211	0	0	0	947	17697	50
55	41360	4646	1743	1636	5800	7462	2388	964	0	0	0	737	15984	55
60	34169	3363	1268	1235	5009	6034	2011	683	0	0	0	543	14023	60
65	26650	2173	884	812	3975	4533	1656	455	0	0	0	383	11779	65
70	18535	1008	590	454	2715	2996	1224	245	0	0	0	240	9023	70
75	11598	444	313	257	1681	1921	876	148	0	0	0	141	5817	75
80	5733	150	129	95	759	931	509	66	0	0	0	67	3027	80
85+	1653	16	26	16	192	264	145	16	0	0	0	16	962	85+

NUMBER OF PERSONS SURVIVING TO AGE X IF SPECIFIED CAUSES WERE ELIMINATED

Age (x)	No Causes	Respiratory T.B. (1)	Other Infec. and Paras. (2)	Neo-plasms (3)	Cardio-vascular (4)	Infl., Pneu., Bronch. (5)	Diar-rheal (6)	Certain Degener-ative (7)	Maternal (8)	Cert. Dis. of Infancy (9)	Motor Vehicle (10)	Other Violence (11)	Other and Unknown (12)	(1)+(2)	(1)+(2)+(5)+(6)+(8)	(1)+(2)+(5)+(6)+(8)+part of(9)&(12)	(10)+(11)	Age (x)
0	100000	100000	100000	100000	100000	100000	100000	100000	100000	100000	100000	100000	100000	100000	100000	100000	100000	0
1	83281	83369	87198	83303	83348	88023	85904	83286	83281	84189	83281	83340	86408	87290	95167	99752	83340	1
5	74205	74416	75490	74244	74370	81600	78652	74217	74205	75014	74205	74456	78507	79717	92915	99219	74456	5
10	72541	72785	78103	72593	72743	80317	77031	72564	72541	73332	72541	72911	77192	78366	92137	98871	72911	10
15	71532	71818	77276	71595	71775	79459	76011	71561	71532	72312	71532	72010	76396	77584	91579	98547	72010	15
20	69916	70385	75896	69986	70220	78037	74351	69962	69916	70678	69916	70561	75113	76405	90690	98037	70561	20
25	67486	68407	73727	67568	67849	75872	71834	67573	67486	68222	67486	68424	73047	74732	89432	97233	68424	25
30	64786	66268	71234	64883	65210	73478	69041	64946	64786	65492	64786	65976	70713	72864	88068	96381	65976	30
35	61624	63724	68254	61749	62132	70716	65794	61849	61624	62296	61624	62585	68019	70580	86474	95507	62985	35
40	58077	60781	64758	58271	58739	67586	62156	58387	58077	58710	58077	59596	65015	67773	84409	94254	59596	40
45	53363	56760	60051	53662	54242	63359	57327	53787	53363	53945	53363	54967	61029	63874	81473	92502	54987	45
50	47805	51994	54299	48271	48596	58233	51571	48408	47805	48326	47805	49479	56190	59057	77607	89924	49479	50
55	41360	46249	47425	42070	42889	52088	44902	42114	41360	41811	41360	43011	50523	53031	72507	86385	43011	55
60	34169	39531	39676	35128	36187	44654	37468	35052	34169	34542	34169	35716	43972	45902	65838	81274	35716	60
65	26650	32065	31338	27782	29209	36630	29568	27545	26650	26941	26650	28003	36943	37706	57503	74499	28003	65
70	18535	23487	22083	19597	21494	27285	20966	19337	18535	18737	18535	19600	29087	27982	46596	65349	19600	70
75	11598	15253	14079	12459	14422	18353	13432	12177	11598	11724	11598	12346	22645	18516	33933	54326	12346	75
80	5733	7802	7113	6278	7965	10222	6943	6079	5733	5796	5733	6157	15667	9680	20904	40921	6157	80
85+	1653	2343	2116	1854	2730	3612	2237	1780	1653	1671	1653	1803	8477	3000	8871	25806	1803	85+

ADDED YRS OF LIFE

	No Causes	(1)	(2)	(3)	(4)	(5)	(6)	(7)	(8)	(9)	(10)	(11)	(12)	(1)+(2)	(1)+(2)+(5)+(6)+(8)	(1)+(2)+(5)+(6)+(8)+part of(9)&(12)	(10)+(11)
TOTAL		2.158	4.381	.350	1.020	7.150	2.975	.316	.000	.445	.000	.852	6.734	6.881	20.350	31.943	.852
WORK	11.680	1.824	1.167	.217	.514	2.125	.346	.261	.000	.000	.000	.655	2.312	3.089	6.001	8.290	.655

POPULATION, DEATHS, DEATH RATES FOR ALL CAUSES COMBINED, AND SPECIFIED CAUSES

Age Start of Interval	Midyear Population	Deaths During Year	All Causes	Respiratory T. B.	Other Infec. and Paras.	Neo-plasms	Cardio-vascular	Infl., Pneu., Bronch.	Diar-rheal	Certain Degen-erative	Maternal	Cert. Dis. of Infancy	Motor Vehicle	Other Violence	Other and Unknown	Age Start of Interval
0	109728	14494	.13209	.00067	.03153	.00023	.00061	.03988	.02457	.00004	.00000	.00730	.00000	.00051	.02676	0
1	346325	11250	.03248	.00049	.00653	.00007	.00044	.01063	.00819	.00003	.00000	.00000	.00000	.00058	.00552	1
5	358366	1563	.00436	.00012	.00108	.00002	.00013	.00123	.00036	.00003	.00000	.00000	.00000	.00015	.00125	5
10	287318	783	.00273	.00014	.00063	.00002	.00013	.00069	.00015	.00001	.00000	.00000	.00000	.00018	.00077	10
15	243622	1055	.00433	.00051	.00070	.00002	.00017	.00083	.00011	.00004	.00048	.00000	.00000	.00039	.00106	15
20	223652	1346	.00602	.00088	.00071	.00004	.00021	.00106	.00015	.00007	.00104	.00000	.00000	.00055	.00131	20
25	202315	1328	.00656	.00128	.00084	.00011	.00026	.00104	.00014	.00011	.00087	.00000	.00000	.00033	.00159	25
30	163094	1339	.00821	.00131	.00107	.00026	.00039	.00125	.00033	.00018	.00100	.00000	.00000	.00025	.00217	30
35	135119	1300	.00962	.00139	.00115	.00050	.00069	.00152	.00040	.00022	.00115	.00000	.00000	.00027	.00232	35
40	104838	1118	.01066	.00162	.00097	.00083	.00072	.00165	.00052	.00029	.00076	.00000	.00000	.00036	.00294	40
45	92075	1216	.01321	.00218	.00110	.00126	.00133	.00230	.00060	.00041	.00017	.00000	.00000	.00042	.00343	45
50	88696	1528	.01723	.00277	.00108	.00149	.00214	.00311	.00077	.00059	.00000	.00000	.00000	.00044	.00484	50
55	76443	1795	.02348	.00315	.00153	.00182	.00306	.00442	.00122	.00056	.00001	.00000	.00000	.00029	.00742	55
60	61411	1955	.03183	.00388	.00151	.00204	.00466	.00541	.00179	.00068	.00000	.00000	.00000	.00041	.01146	60
65	39896	1915	.04800	.00446	.00213	.00221	.00757	.00759	.00311	.00065	.00000	.00000	.00000	.00060	.01968	65
70	24322	1677	.06895	.00502	.00271	.00234	.01139	.00970	.00333	.00078	.00000	.00000	.00000	.00078	.03289	70
75	13282	1360	.10239	.00467	.00316	.00286	.01784	.01543	.00610	.00120	.00000	.00000	.00000	.00098	.05014	75
80	5394	931	.17260	.00408	.00371	.00334	.02707	.02521	.01502	.00167	.00000	.00000	.00000	.00148	.09103	80
85+	2158	694	.32159	.00324	.00510	.00324	.04078	.04588	.02734	.00232	.00000	.00000	.00000	.00232	.19138	85+
ALL	2578054	48647														

CRUDE DEATH RATE			.01887	.00109	.00305	.00039	.00099	.00468	.00260	.00016	.00037	.00031	.00000	.00037	.00486
STANDARDIZED RATE (1)			.01792	.00112	.00274	.00041	.00105	.00430	.00232	.00017	.00038	.00026	.00000	.00037	.00479
STANDARDIZED RATE (2)			.02152	.00156	.00222	.00068	.00208	.00431	.00209	.00027	.00039	.00015	.00000	.00040	.00738
GEOMETRIC MEAN			.02170												

LIFE TABLE FOR ALL CAUSES COMBINED

Age (x)	Midyear Population	Deaths During Year	$_nM_x$	$_nq_x$	l_x	$_nd_x$	$_nL_x$	$_nm_x$	$_na_x$	T_x	$_nr_x$	$\overset{\circ}{e}_x$	Age (x)
0	109728	14494	.132090	.120830	100000	12083	91476	.132089	.294553	4669480	.000000	46.695	0
1	346325	11250	.032484	.120182	87917	10566	325253	.032485	1.500000	4578004	.000000	52.072	1
5	358366	1563	.004361	.021590	77351	1670	382580	.004365	2.500000	4252751	.000000	54.980	5
10	287318	783	.002725	.013517	75681	1023	375834	.002722	2.486966	3870171	.029070	51.138	10
15	243622	1055	.004330	.021511	74658	1606	369514	.004346	2.648661	3494337	.024537	46.805	15
20	223652	1346	.006018	.029691	73052	2169	359981	.006025	2.565987	3124823	.013689	42.775	20
25	202315	1328	.006564	.032349	70883	2293	348807	.006574	2.554241	2764843	.020984	39.006	25
30	163094	1339	.008210	.040327	68590	2766	336203	.008227	2.560707	2416036	.029134	35.224	30
35	135119	1300	.009621	.047080	65824	3099	321476	.009640	2.533546	2079833	.033734	31.597	35
40	104838	1118	.010664	.052053	62725	3265	305610	.010684	2.545304	1758357	.032943	28.033	40
45	92075	1216	.013207	.064060	59460	3809	288056	.013223	2.573182	1452746	.010883	24.432	45
50	88696	1528	.017227	.082712	55651	4603	267136	.017231	2.584501	1164690	.001786	20.928	50
55	76443	1795	.023482	.111189	51048	5676	241492	.023504	2.577960	897553	.007656	17.583	55
60	61411	1955	.031835	.148263	45372	6727	210600	.031942	2.582906	656061	.023509	14.460	60
65	39896	1915	.048000	.216147	38645	8353	172808	.048337	2.555694	445461	.040537	11.527	65
70	24322	1677	.068950	.295788	30292	8960	129138	.069583	2.508673	272653	.038720	9.001	70
75	13282	1360	.102394	.409057	21332	8726	84552	.103202	2.466479	143515	.041604	6.728	75
80	5394	931	.172599	.599397	12606	7556	43260	.174666	2.383509	58963	.041604	4.677	80
85+	2158	694	.321594	1.000000	5050	5050	15703	.321594	3.109510	15703	.000000	3.110	85+

NUMBER OF PERSONS DYING (OUT OF 100,000 AT BIRTH) ABOVE AGE X FROM SPECIFIED CAUSES

Age (x)	All Causes	Respiratory T.B.	Other Infec. and Paras.	Neoplasms	Cardiovascular	Infl., Pneu., Bronch.	Diarrheal	Certain Degenerative	Maternal	Cert. Dis. of Infancy	Motor Vehicle	Other Violence	Other and Unknown	Age (x)
0	100000	7672	10026	3379	9919	19734	9280	1312	1855	668	0	1888	34267	0
1	87917	7611	7141	3358	9863	16086	7032	1309	1855	0	0	1841	31821	1
5	77351	7450	5017	3337	9720	12630	4367	1301	1855	0	0	1651	30023	5
10	75681	7403	4604	3330	9671	12161	4229	1289	1855	0	0	1593	29546	10
15	74658	7349	4368	3321	9624	11902	4173	1285	1854	0	0	1526	29256	15
20	73052	7158	4108	3314	9560	11593	4132	1270	1673	0	0	1380	28864	20
25	70883	6840	3852	3301	9482	11211	4079	1244	1297	0	0	1182	28395	25
30	68590	6393	3560	3262	9393	10847	4031	1204	992	0	0	1069	27839	30
35	65824	5951	3199	3175	9262	10426	3919	1142	656	0	0	986	27108	35
40	62725	5503	2830	3012	9040	9935	3790	1070	287	0	0	898	26360	40
45	59460	5006	2533	2757	8820	9429	3629	983	56	0	0	787	25460	45
50	55651	4377	2217	2394	8438	8765	3457	863	7	0	0	665	24468	50
55	51048	3636	1928	1996	7865	7934	3252	707	7	0	0	548	23175	55
60	45372	2874	1558	1557	7125	6865	2958	571	3	0	0	478	21383	60
65	38645	2057	1239	1128	6140	5723	2579	427	3	0	0	392	18957	65
70	30292	1284	869	746	4821	4404	2038	314	3	0	0	287	15526	70
75	21332	635	517	443	3340	3144	1606	213	3	0	0	186	11245	75
80	12606	241	249	200	1819	1828	1084	110	3	0	0	103	6969	80
85+	5050	51	80	51	640	720	429	36	0	0	0	36	3007	85+

NUMBER OF PERSONS SURVIVING TO AGE X IF SPECIFIED CAUSES WERE ELIMINATED

Age (x)	No Causes	Respiratory T.B. (1)	Other Infec. and Paras. (2)	Neoplasms (3)	Cardiovascular (4)	Infl., Pneu., Bronch. (5)	Diarrheal (6)	Certain Degenerative (7)	Maternal (8)	Cert. Dis. of Infancy (9)	Motor Vehicle (10)	Other Violence (11)	Other and Unknown (12)	(1)+(2)	(1)+(2)+(5)+(6)+(8)	(1)+(2)+(5)+(6)+(8)+part of(9)&(12)	(10)+(11)	Age (x)
0	100000	100000	100000	100000	100000	100000	100000	100000	100000	100000	100000	100000	100000	100000	100000	100000	100000	0
1	87917	87974	90662	87937	87969	91402	90049	87920	87917	88545	87917	87961	90239	90721	96605	99818	87961	1
5	77351	77552	81846	77388	77531	83857	81827	77361	77351	77904	77351	77568	81143	82059	94109	99292	77568	5
10	75681	75925	80512	75724	75906	82551	80205	75703	75681	76222	75681	75951	79887	80772	93370	99063	75951	10
15	74658	74952	79674	74709	74927	81716	79180	74683	74659	75191	74658	74991	79112	79988	92854	98830	74991	15
20	73052	73530	78235	73109	73379	80254	77519	73092	73232	73574	73052	73523	77822	78747	92073	98420	73523	20
25	70883	71663	76182	70951	71277	78324	75273	70947	71430	71389	70883	71537	76005	77021	91075	97872	71537	25
30	68590	69791	74027	68695	69060	76187	72888	68691	69422	69080	68590	69335	74136	75323	89988	97352	69335	30
35	65824	67418	71425	66010	66404	73574	70066	65982	66957	66294	65824	66621	71924	73154	88535	96640	66621	35
40	62725	64693	68454	63062	63497	70648	69901	62946	64172	63173	62725	63571	69340	70602	86770	95564	63571	40
45	59460	61827	65206	60030	60409	67528	63586	59755	61061	59885	59460	60372	66707	67802	84563	94120	60372	45
50	55651	58503	61365	56540	56917	63936	59651	56044	57157	56049	55651	56624	63520	64510	81703	91961	56624	50
55	51048	54414	56595	52252	52773	59569	54965	51559	52466	51413	51048	52055	59667	60327	77905	89025	52055	55
60	45372	49134	50690	46667	47633	54134	49153	45955	46637	45656	45372	46334	55074	54893	72929	85360	46334	60
65	38645	42671	43503	40327	41536	47379	42246	39276	39722	38921	38645	39545	49708	48035	66174	80278	39545	65
70	30292	34206	34469	31563	33836	38552	33640	30888	31136	30508	30292	31092	43074	38923	56604	72998	31092	70
75	21332	24703	24609	22775	25251	28548	24093	21837	21927	21484	21332	21982	35680	28497	44274	62685	21982	75
80	12606	14541	14776	13655	16353	18264	14697	12985	12957	12656	12606	13055	27448	17513	30408	49939	13055	80
85+	5050	6125	6042	5570	7556	8367	6374	5249	5193	5086	5050	5272	17764	7327	15756	34360	5272	85+

ADDED YRS OF LIFE	No Causes	(1)	(2)	(3)	(4)	(5)	(6)	(7)	(8)	(9)	(10)	(11)	(12)	(1)+(2)	combo	combo	(10)+(11)
TOTAL		1.706	4.045	.578	1.360	6.416	3.282	.240	.651	.332	.000	.565	7.976	5.957	19.007	30.104	.565
WORK	9.162	1.209	.854	.358	.539	1.338	.289	.167	.705	.000	.000	.352	2.079	2.104	4.700	6.534	.352

POPULATION, DEATHS, DEATH RATES FOR ALL CAUSES COMBINED, AND SPECIFIED CAUSES

Age Start of Interval	Midyear Population	Deaths During Year	All Causes	Respiratory T.B.	Other Infec. and Paras.	Neoplasms	Cardiovascular	Infl., Pneu., Bronch.	Diarrheal	Certain Degenerative	Maternal	Cert. Dis. of Infancy	Motor Vehicle	Other Violence	Other and Unknown	Age Start of Interval
0	202952	7834	.03860	.0000S	.00458	.00000	.00072	.00845	.00696	.00014	.00000	.01436	.00001	.00049	.00280	0
1	782294	4839	.00619	.00008	.00102	.00003	.00011	.00154	.00187	.00012	.00000	.00000	.00003	.00062	.00076	1
5	882946	1055	.00119	.00003	.00017	.00002	.00006	.00018	.00012	.00006	.00000	.00000	.00001	.00030	.00025	5
10	591090	527	.00089	.00002	.00009	.00002	.00008	.00008	.00004	.00005	.00000	.00000	.00000	.00032	.00019	10
15	494218	760	.00154	.00006	.00008	.00004	.00014	.00008	.00002	.00011	.00000	.00000	.00002	.00077	.00023	15
20	322212	876	.00272	.00018	.00011	.00009	.00022	.00009	.00003	.00014	.00000	.00000	.00002	.00137	.00046	20
25	396921	970	.00244	.00030	.00009	.00015	.00024	.00008	.00004	.00014	.00000	.00000	.00004	.00094	.00043	25
30	384010	1160	.00302	.00046	.00009	.00022	.00034	.00010	.00007	.00027	.00000	.00000	.00004	.00087	.00056	30
35	236856	1268	.00376	.00060	.00009	.00043	.00048	.00012	.00007	.00042	.00000	.00000	.00003	.00079	.00073	35
40	273655	1541	.00563	.00096	.00016	.00073	.00090	.00020	.00011	.00063	.00000	.00000	.00005	.00087	.00104	40
45	251651	2061	.00819	.00121	.00020	.00119	.00188	.00030	.00019	.00095	.00000	.00000	.00002	.00085	.00141	45
50	184926	2413	.01305	.00173	.00034	.00180	.00360	.00056	.00029	.00151	.00000	.00000	.00005	.00101	.00218	50
55	130966	2710	.02069	.00260	.00034	.00263	.00596	.00118	.00055	.00250	.00000	.00000	.00004	.00100	.00389	55
60	87107	2684	.03081	.00351	.00063	.00344	.00988	.00180	.00067	.00344	.00000	.00000	.00007	.00101	.00635	60
65	53077	2679	.05047	.00416	.00036	.00509	.01681	.00403	.00143	.00454	.00000	.00000	.00004	.00124	.01277	65
70	32001	2413	.07540	.00494	.00056	.00522	.02269	.00650	.00228	.00634	.00000	.00000	.00009	.00125	.02553	70
75	16845	1946	.11552	.00427	.00071	.00576	.03259	.01027	.00421	.00701	.00000	.00000	.00006	.00202	.04862	75
80	5793	1008	.17400	.00363	.00052	.00380	.03867	.01502	.00414	.00811	.00000	.00000	.00000	.00207	.09805	80
85+	1289	433	.33592	.00465	.00233	.01009	.07215	.03103	.01086	.00465	.00000	.00000	.00000	.00310	.19705	85+
ALL	5430809	39177														

	All Causes	Respiratory T.B.	Other Infec. and Paras.	Neoplasms	Cardiovascular	Infl., Pneu., Bronch.	Diarrheal	Certain Degenerative	Maternal	Cert. Dis. of Infancy	Motor Vehicle	Other Violence	Other and Unknown
CRUDE DEATH RATE	.00721	.00050	.00045	.00045	.00117	.00084	.00067	.00047	.00000	.00054	.00003	.00071	.00141
STANDARDIZED RATE (1)	.00883	.00060	.00042	.00057	.00169	.00093	.00065	.00060	.00000	.00051	.00003	.00076	.00208
STANDARDIZED RATE (2)	.01510	.00101	.00037	.00103	.00361	.00132	.00068	.00108	.00000	.00030	.00003	.00085	.00483
GEOMETRIC MEAN	.01200												

LIFE TABLE FOR ALL CAUSES COMBINED

Age (x)	Midyear Population	Deaths During Year	$_nM_x$	$_nq_x$	l_x	$_nd_x$	$_nL_x$	$_nm_x$	$_na_x$	T_x	$_nr_x$	$\overset{\circ}{e}_x$	Age (x)
0	202952	7834	.038600	.037350	100000	3735	96772	.038596	.135620	6229684	.000000	62.297	0
1	782294	4839	.006186	.024370	96265	2346	379195	.006187	1.500000	6132912	.000000	63.709	1
5	882946	1055	.001195	.005963	93919	560	468195	.001196	2.500000	5753717	.000000	61.263	5
10	591090	527	.000892	.004445	93359	415	465750	.000891	2.579317	5285522	.042255	56.615	10
15	494218	760	.001538	.007725	92944	718	463099	.001550	2.742282	4819732	.060249	51.856	15
20	322212	876	.002719	.013554	92226	1250	458086	.002729	2.564500	4356633	.037242	47.239	20
25	396921	970	.002444	.012146	90976	1105	452138	.002444	2.518477	3898547	-.012092	42.852	25
30	384010	1160	.003021	.014999	89871	1348	446100	.003022	2.585312	3446409	.004151	38.348	30
35	236856	1268	.003764	.018718	88523	1657	438696	.003777	2.635033	3000309	.025148	33.893	35
40	273655	1541	.005631	.027882	86866	2422	428640	.005650	2.650616	2561613	.023424	29.489	40
45	251651	2061	.008190	.040358	84444	3408	414273	.008226	2.668232	2132973	.025267	25.259	45
50	184926	2413	.013048	.063848	81036	5174	393107	.013162	2.666659	1718700	.045505	21.209	50
55	130966	2710	.020692	.099483	75862	7547	361426	.020881	2.630322	1325593	.051502	17.474	55
60	87107	2684	.030813	.144844	68315	9895	318028	.031114	2.620284	964166	.057249	14.114	60
65	53077	2679	.050474	.226977	58420	13260	259892	.051021	2.571016	646139	.053566	11.060	65
70	32001	2413	.075404	.319198	45160	14415	189877	.075918	2.507920	386247	.037615	8.553	70
75	16845	1946	.115524	.449114	30745	13808	118312	.116709	2.435303	196370	.049918	6.387	75
80	5793	1008	.174003	.597922	16937	10127	57786	.175250	2.343837	78059	.049918	4.609	80
85+	1289	433	.335919	1.000000	6810	6810	20273	.335919	2.976905	20273	.000000	2.977	85+

NUMBER OF PERSONS DYING (OUT OF 100,000 AT BIRTH) ABOVE AGE X FROM SPECIFIED CAUSES

Age (x)	All Causes	Respiratory T.B.	Other Infec. and Paras.	Neo-plasms	Cardio-vascular	Infl., Pneu., Bronch.	Diar-rheal	Certain Degen-erative	Maternal	Cert. Dis. of Infancy	Motor Vehicle	Other Violence	Other and Unknown	Age (x)
0	100000	7305	2136	7479	25116	8200	3995	7685	0	1390	203	5530	30957	0
1	96265	7296	1693	7479	25047	7383	3322	7675	0	0	202	5482	30686	1
5	93919	7267	1305	7467	25004	6799	2611	7631	0	0	191	5246	30398	5
10	93359	7255	1226	7459	24976	6716	2555	7604	0	0	186	5104	30278	10
15	92944	7243	1185	7451	24939	6680	2538	7578	0	0	184	4955	30191	15
20	92226	7216	1146	7433	24877	6644	2528	7529	0	0	175	4593	30085	20
25	90976	7131	1097	7391	24774	6604	2512	7464	0	0	168	3963	29872	25
30	89871	6996	1058	7224	24665	6567	2494	7399	0	0	152	3539	29677	30
35	88523	6792	1016	7224	24514	6524	2465	7277	0	0	135	3150	29426	35
40	86866	6528	977	7034	24302	6473	2432	7091	0	0	121	2803	29105	40
45	84444	6115	908	6719	23915	6388	2387	6821	0	0	100	2432	28659	45
50	81036	5613	825	6225	23133	6264	2306	6427	0	0	90	2079	28074	50
55	75862	4930	690	5512	21704	6042	2192	5829	0	0	71	1683	27209	55
60	68315	3985	568	4556	19526	5609	1991	4915	0	0	57	1322	25786	60
65	58420	2861	366	3453	16345	5028	1777	3813	0	0	35	1000	23742	65
70	45160	1774	274	2121	11932	3965	1400	2624	0	0	26	676	20368	70
75	30745	835	167	1130	7601	2721	963	1414	0	0	8	438	15468	75
80	16937	331	82	448	3714	1493	459	583	0	0	1	197	9629	80
85+	6810	94	47	204	1463	629	220	94	0	0	0	63	3996	85+

NUMBER OF PERSONS SURVIVING TO AGE X IF SPECIFIED CAUSES WERE ELIMINATED

Age (x)	No Causes	Respiratory T.B. (1)	Other Infec. and Paras. (2)	Neo-plasms (3)	Cardio-vascular (4)	Infl., Pneu., Bronch. (5)	Diar-rheal (6)	Certain Degener-ative (7)	Maternal (8)	Cert. Dis. of Infancy (9)	Motor Vehicle (10)	Other Violence (11)	Other and Unknown (12)	(1)+(2)	(1)+(2)+(5)+(6)+(8)	(1)+(2)+(5)+(6)+(8)+part of(9)&(12)	(10)+(11)	Age (x)
0	100000	100000	100000	100000	100000	100000	100000	100000	100000	100000	100000	100000	100000	100000	100000	100000	100000	0
1	96265	96274	96701	96265	96333	97070	96928	96279	96265	97638	96266	96312	96531	96709	98189	99758	96313	1
5	93919	93956	94730	93931	94028	95288	95215	93976	93919	95259	93931	94198	94464	94767	97537	99345	94210	5
10	93359	93408	94244	93379	93495	94804	94764	93442	93359	94691	93376	93779	94022	94294	97194	99062	93796	10
15	92944	93005	93867	92972	93116	94419	94360	93053	92944	94270	92963	93511	93691	93928	96872	98764	93530	15
20	92226	92313	93181	92271	92459	93726	93641	92383	92226	93542	92253	93153	93074	93269	96240	98140	93180	20
25	90976	91147	91967	91063	91308	92496	92388	91196	90976	92274	91010	92524	92026	92140	95132	97052	92559	25
30	89871	90174	90889	90023	90308	91410	91284	90153	89871	91153	89921	91830	91105	91196	94215	96169	91880	30
35	88523	89025	89568	88772	89104	90082	89944	88922	88523	89786	88589	90848	89991	90076	93134	95142	90915	35
40	86866	87622	87931	87300	87648	88447	88294	87443	86866	88105	86944	89500	88630	88696	91795	93874	89581	40
45	84444	85591	85548	85178	85550	86067	85877	85273	84444	85649	84541	87382	86609	86709	89875	92059	87743	45
50	81036	82636	82178	82230	82917	82717	82492	82223	81036	82192	81139	84214	83703	83800	87075	89368	84321	50
55	75862	78036	77063	77683	79051	77656	77337	77562	75862	76944	75977	79235	79228	79272	82724	85153	79355	55
60	68315	71200	69514	70889	73374	70352	69838	70738	68315	69290	68431	71710	72771	72450	76274	78946	71832	60
65	58420	61976	59635	61686	65985	60719	59925	61553	58420	59253	58540	61635	64280	63265	67449	70425	61761	65
70	45160	48925	46180	48528	55556	47918	46664	48689	45160	45804	45260	47944	53070	50030	54855	58284	48050	70
75	30745	34144	31529	34192	42447	33724	32143	34229	30745	31184	30828	32846	41213	35015	40155	44307	32935	75
80	16937	19211	17432	19398	27633	19550	18097	19535	16937	17179	16988	18284	29298	19773	24436	29041	18338	80
85+	6810	7891	7031	7969	13605	8513	7434	8208	6810	6907	6831	7441	19554	8147	11119	15431	7464	85+

ADDED YRS OF LIFE

	No Causes	(1)	(2)	(3)	(4)	(5)	(6)	(7)	(8)	(9)	(10)	(11)	(12)	(1)+(2)	(1)+(2)+(5)+(6)+(8)	(1)+(2)+(5)+(6)+(8)+part of(9)&(12)	(10)+(11)
TOTAL		1.206	.818	1.090	3.229	1.634	1.196	1.124	.000	.887	.056	1.691	4.436	2.049	5.122	7.607	1.749
WORK	5.096	.583	.134	.465	.845	.183	.091	.450	.000	.000	.032	1.022	.826	.721	1.006	1.232	1.055

POPULATION, DEATHS, DEATH RATES FOR ALL CAUSES COMBINED, AND SPECIFIED CAUSES

Age Start of Interval	Midyear Popula-tion	Deaths During Year	All Causes	Respiratory T. B.	Other Infec. and Paras.	Neo-plasms	Cardio-vascular	Infl., Pneu., Bronch.	Diar-rheal	Certain Degen-erative	Maternal	Cert. Dis. of Infancy	Motor Vehicle	Other Violence	Other and Unknown	Age Start of Interval
0	191596	6852	.03576	.00014	.00363	.00001	.00059	.00856	.00721	.00012	.00000	.01273	.00000	.00043	.00235	0
1	743583	5096	.00685	.00007	.00103	.00002	.00013	.00190	.00220	.00017	.00000	.00000	.00001	.00052	.00081	1
5	838260	786	.00094	.00002	.00018	.00001	.00005	.00017	.00011	.00005	.00000	.00000	.00001	.00052	.00081	5
10	556763	386	.00069	.00003	.00006	.00001	.00009	.00007	.00003	.00004	.00000	.00000	.00001	.00013	.00017	10
15	464521	596	.00128	.00006	.00005	.00003	.00012	.00008	.00002	.00005	.00003	.00000	.00001	.00053	.00026	15
20	441742	769	.00174	.00011	.00009	.00006	.00019	.00006	.00007	.00020	.00000	.00000	.00001	.00063	.00027	20
25	388821	722	.00186	.00022	.00012	.00009	.00025	.00010	.00004	.00015	.00021	.00000	.00000	.00033	.00036	25
30	340099	836	.00246	.00027	.00009	.00025	.00033	.00013	.00006	.00021	.00036	.00000	.00000	.00030	.00046	30
35	280909	898	.00320	.00042	.00010	.00046	.00058	.00014	.00005	.00033	.00028	.00000	.00000	.00026	.00056	35
40	219586	922	.00420	.00040	.00010	.00075	.00087	.00020	.00007	.00040	.00021	.00000	.00000	.00038	.00082	40
45	196890	1125	.00571	.00060	.00014	.00124	.00145	.00024	.00010	.00055	.00004	.00000	.00001	.00037	.00098	45
50	157468	1290	.00819	.00088	.00015	.00156	.00233	.00041	.00022	.00084	.00000	.00000	.00001	.00030	.00152	50
55	119035	1497	.01258	.00120	.00022	.00215	.00370	.00067	.00035	.00136	.00000	.00000	.00000	.00047	.00244	55
60	88659	1818	.02051	.00192	.00025	.00254	.00673	.00106	.00058	.00211	.00000	.00000	.00000	.00052	.00480	60
65	61546	1962	.03188	.00200	.00026	.00270	.01066	.00219	.00112	.00325	.00000	.00000	.00000	.00055	.00915	65
70	44862	2421	.05397	.00261	.00040	.00325	.01741	.00352	.00169	.00381	.00002	.00000	.00000	.00089	.02035	70
75	29472	2609	.08852	.00238	.00058	.00305	.02541	.00665	.00353	.00526	.00000	.00000	.00003	.00092	.04072	75
80	12989	1721	.13250	.00146	.00031	.00339	.02949	.00901	.00370	.00577	.00000	.00000	.00015	.00108	.07814	80
85+	4162	1002	.24075	.00120	.00072	.00360	.04613	.01586	.00601	.00865	.00000	.00000	.00000	.00288	.15569	85+
ALL	5180963	33308														

CRUDE DEATH RATE			.00643	.00028	.00038	.00037	.00105	.00085	.00071	.00035	.00009	.00047	.00001	.00037	.00149
STANDARDIZED RATE (1)			.00682	.00033	.00035	.00044	.00124	.00082	.00066	.00040	.00009	.00045	.00001	.00038	.00165
STANDARDIZED RATE (2)			.01107	.00052	.00029	.00075	.00261	.00095	.00062	.00073	.00009	.00026	.00001	.00042	.00381
GEOMETRIC MEAN			.00901												

LIFE TABLE FOR ALL CAUSES COMBINED

Age (x)	Midyear Popula-tion	Deaths During Year	$_nM_x$	$_nq_x$	l_x	$_nd_x$	$_nL_x$	$_nm_x$	$_na_x$	T_x	$_nr_x$	$\overset{\circ}{e}_x$	Age (x)
0	191596	6852	.035763	.034680	100000	3468	96986	.035758	.130797	6638338	.000000	66.383	0
1	743583	5096	.006853	.026955	96532	2602	379623	.006854	1.500000	6541352	.000000	67.764	1
5	838260	786	.000938	.004695	93930	441	468548	.000941	2.500000	6161729	.000000	65.599	5
10	556763	386	.000693	.003444	93489	322	466673	.000690	2.602226	5693182	.050785	60.897	10
15	464521	596	.001283	.006429	93167	599	464438	.001290	2.667293	5226509	.029869	56.098	15
20	441742	769	.001741	.008675	92568	803	460885	.001742	2.565120	4762071	.017995	51.444	20
25	388821	722	.001857	.009243	91765	850	456765	.001861	2.576225	4301186	.022207	46.872	25
30	340099	836	.002458	.012253	90915	1114	451911	.002465	2.608468	3844422	.026068	42.286	30
35	280909	898	.003197	.015924	89801	1430	445582	.003209	2.606352	3392511	.038535	37.778	35
40	219586	922	.004199	.020867	88371	1844	437457	.004215	2.615013	2946929	.034180	33.347	40
45	196890	1125	.005714	.028292	86527	2448	426839	.005735	2.632336	2509472	.026473	29.002	45
50	157468	1290	.008192	.040426	84079	3399	412422	.008242	2.654396	2082633	.037957	24.770	50
55	119035	1497	.012576	.061564	80680	4967	391830	.012676	2.670584	1670210	.042448	20.702	55
60	88659	1818	.020506	.098609	75713	7466	360988	.020682	2.645688	1278381	.045474	16.885	60
65	61546	1962	.031875	.149281	68247	10188	317109	.032128	2.631875	917393	.040331	13.442	65
70	44862	2421	.053965	.239670	58059	13915	256738	.054199	2.588424	600284	.019818	10.339	70
75	29472	2609	.088525	.364560	44144	16094	180484	.089171	2.499948	343546	.031644	7.782	75
80	12989	1721	.132497	.495936	28050	13911	104333	.133333	2.418095	163062	.031644	5.813	80
85+	4162	1002	.240750	1.000000	14139	14139	58729	.240750	4.153693	58729	.000000	4.154	85+

NUMBER OF PERSONS DYING (OUT OF 100,000 AT BIRTH) ABOVE AGE X FROM SPECIFIED CAUSES

Age (x)	All Causes	Respiratory T.B.	Other Infec. and Paras.	Neo-plasms	Cardio-vascular	Infl., Pneu., Bronch.	Diar-rheal	Certain Degen-erative	Maternal	Cert. Dis. of Infancy	Motor Vehicle	Other Violence	Other and Unknown	Age (x)
0	100000	4485	1766	6525	25046	7599	4384	6657	609	1234	53	3009	38633	0
1	96532	4472	1414	6524	24989	6769	3685	6645	609	0	53	2968	38404	1
5	93930	4443	1023	6515	24941	6047	2850	6582	609	0	49	2772	38099	5
10	93489	4433	940	6510	24917	5969	2798	6559	609	0	46	2712	37996	10
15	93167	4421	912	6504	24877	5936	2783	6541	608	0	42	2627	37916	15
20	92568	4395	889	6490	24819	5899	2774	6500	593	0	37	2378	37794	20
25	91765	4343	847	6461	24729	5871	2757	6467	499	0	33	2088	37670	25
30	90915	4244	792	6418	24616	5826	2741	6400	403	0	33	1936	37506	30
35	89801	4123	753	6306	24465	5768	2715	6305	238	0	32	1799	37297	35
40	88371	3934	711	6100	24204	5704	2691	6156	113	0	31	1683	37044	40
45	86527	3760	665	5771	23819	5618	2659	5980	23	0	31	1515	36686	45
50	84079	3503	604	5240	23196	5516	2616	5745	8	0	28	1357	36266	50
55	80680	3140	543	4595	22228	5347	2526	5396	8	0	26	1234	35637	55
60	75713	2666	457	3749	20766	5081	2386	4859	8	0	22	1049	34670	60
65	68247	1970	368	2831	18211	4694	2177	4091	8	0	22	861	32914	65
70	58059	1335	285	1974	14906	3992	1918	3056	8	0	22	686	29977	70
75	44144	664	182	1138	10420	3083	1381	2075	2	0	22	456	24721	75
80	28050	236	77	566	5808	1874	739	1121	2	0	16	290	17301	80
85+	14139	71	42	212	2709	931	353	508	0	0	0	169	9144	85+

NUMBER OF PERSONS SURVIVING TO AGE X IF SPECIFIED CAUSES WERE ELIMINATED

Age (x)	No Causes	Respiratory T.B. (1)	Other Infec. and Paras. (2)	Neo-plasms (3)	Cardio-vascular (4)	Infl., Pneu., Bronch. (5)	Diar-rheal (6)	Certain Degener-ative (7)	Maternal (8)	Cert. Dis. of Infancy (9)	Motor Vehicle (10)	Other Violence (11)	Other and Unknown (12)	(1) + (2)	(1) + (2) + (5) + (6) + (8)	(1)+(2)+ (5)+(6)+ (8)+part of(9)&(12)	(10) + (11)	Age (x)
0	100000	100000	100000	100000	100000	100000	100000	100000	100000	100000	100000	100000	100000	100000	100000	100000	100000	0
1	96532	96545	96878	96533	96588	97351	97221	96544	96532	97752	96532	96572	96757	96891	98411	99805	96572	1
5	93930	93971	94655	93940	94032	95448	95434	94004	93930	95117	93934	94163	94451	94696	97767	99426	94167	5
10	93489	93540	94294	93504	93614	95079	95038	93585	93489	94671	93496	93781	94111	94345	97540	99267	93788	10
15	93167	93230	93997	93188	93332	94785	94726	93281	93168	94344	93178	93543	93867	94061	97297	99050	93554	15
20	92568	92656	93416	92603	92790	94213	94126	92722	92584	93738	92584	93191	93387	93505	96786	98560	93207	20
25	91765	91904	92648	91828	92075	93424	93327	91951	91875	92925	91785	92674	92701	92789	96189	97598	92694	25
30	90915	91152	91845	91020	91335	92604	92479	91166	91119	92064	90934	91968	92007	92084	95623	97500	91988	30
35	89801	90156	90759	90017	90367	91528	91372	90144	90167	90936	89821	90979	91091	91117	94880	96844	90999	35
40	88371	88908	89356	88788	89189	90136	89941	88857	89856	89488	88392	89647	89895	89899	93835	95880	89668	40
45	86527	87226	87537	87264	87713	88342	88057	87118	87091	87621	86547	87945	88380	88245	92328	94451	87966	45
50	84079	85014	85122	85324	85656	85945	85647	84945	84642	85142	84102	85615	86304	86069	90220	92402	85638	50
55	80680	81938	81741	82518	83360	82640	82275	81857	81220	81700	80704	82277	83450	83015	87293	89573	82301	55
60	75713	77361	76793	78280	79705	77817	77348	77347	76220	76670	75739	77394	79288	78464	82938	85358	77421	60
65	68247	70439	69306	71464	74341	70522	69924	70468	68704	69110	68271	69944	73239	71502	76208	78898	69969	65
70	58059	60502	59037	61624	66753	60667	60667	60939	58448	58793	58079	59668	65289	61522	66685	69835	59689	70
75	44144	46609	44979	47626	55432	46960	45881	47231	44445	44702	44159	45572	55079	47490	52865	56796	45588	75
80	28050	29967	28664	30728	40080	30874	29685	30823	28241	28405	28065	29091	43198	30623	35914	40884	29107	80
85+	14139	15229	14473	15777	23534	16302	15250	16013	14237	14318	14158	14752	32539	15589	19521	24729	14771	85+

ADDED YRS OF LIFE																		
TOTAL		.832	.766	1.135	3.408	1.792	1.391	1.005	.242	.837	.016	.949	6.552	1.612	5.252	7.871	.965	
WORK	3.748	.343	.110	.462	.717	.168	.073	.311	.192	.000	.006	.473	.655	.454	.898	1.106	.479	

POPULATION, DEATHS, DEATH RATES FOR ALL CAUSES COMBINED, AND SPECIFIED CAUSES

Age Start of Interval	Midyear Population	Deaths During Year	All Causes	Respiratory T. B.	Other Infec. and Paras.	Neo-plasms	Cardio-vascular	Infl., Pneu., Bronch.	Diar-rheal	Certain Degen-erative	Maternal	Cert. Dis. of Infancy	Motor Vehicle	Other Violence	Other and Unknown	Age Start of Interval
0	200794	5864	.02920	.00004	.00234	.00012	.00037	.00825	.00324	.00008	.00000	.01056	.00001	.00055	.00364	0
1	821207	3290	.00401	.00004	.00071	.00008	.00005	.00103	.00061	.00009	.00000	.00000	.00005	.00063	.00069	1
5	964956	804	.00083	.00001	.00010	.00005	.00003	.00012	.00005	.00005	.00000	.00000	.00003	.00021	.00018	5
10	841146	596	.00071	.00002	.00005	.00006	.00005	.00005	.00001	.00004	.00000	.00000	.00002	.00026	.00015	10
15	531428	668	.00126	.00004	.00004	.00006	.00010	.00006	.00001	.00006	.00000	.00000	.00006	.00065	.00019	15
20	318826	932	.00292	.00017	.00004	.00019	.00018	.00008	.00001	.00014	.00000	.00000	.00013	.00161	.00037	20
25	445106	925	.00208	.00020	.00004	.00015	.00015	.00006	.00001	.00011	.00000	.00000	.00012	.00054	.00030	25
30	423287	1108	.00262	.00036	.00004	.00026	.00022	.00007	.00002	.00026	.00000	.00000	.00012	.00051	.00037	30
35	400660	1410	.00352	.00053	.00005	.00043	.00040	.00007	.00004	.00042	.00000	.00000	.00012	.00054	.00052	35
40	336099	1679	.00500	.00083	.00008	.00082	.00079	.00016	.00005	.00057	.00000	.00000	.00009	.00090	.00071	40
45	270331	2017	.00746	.00111	.00011	.00126	.00145	.00026	.00006	.00099	.00000	.00000	.00014	.00105	.00102	45
50	236988	2810	.01186	.00189	.00014	.00157	.00300	.00048	.00013	.00151	.00000	.00000	.00011	.00104	.00159	50
55	163501	2946	.01802	.00196	.00019	.00295	.00557	.00106	.00017	.00221	.00000	.00000	.00014	.00108	.00268	55
60	108910	3214	.02951	.00308	.00032	.00373	.01027	.00200	.00049	.00373	.00000	.00000	.00013	.00124	.00454	60
65	67351	3098	.04600	.00414	.00028	.00566	.01624	.00445	.00065	.00517	.00000	.00000	.00030	.00141	.00769	65
70	36587	2586	.07068	.00503	.00044	.00541	.02575	.00784	.00153	.00700	.00000	.00000	.00016	.00164	.01588	70
75	19571	2043	.10439	.00439	.00041	.00690	.03377	.01405	.00347	.00991	.00000	.00000	.00026	.00199	.02923	75
80	7973	1185	.14863	.00464	.00050	.00564	.04616	.02320	.00615	.01066	.00000	.00000	.00025	.00226	.04917	80
85+	1564	553	.35358	.00448	.00256	.01023	.09974	.06074	.01471	.02302	.00000	.00000	.00128	.00128	.13555	85+
ALL	6196285	37728														

			All Causes	Respiratory T. B.	Other Infec. and Paras.	Neo-plasms	Cardio-vascular	Infl., Pneu., Bronch.	Diar-rheal	Certain Degen-erative	Maternal	Cert. Dis. of Infancy	Motor Vehicle	Other Violence	Other and Unknown
CRUDE DEATH RATE			.00609	.00046	.00024	.00055	.00117	.00074	.00026	.00050	.00000	.00034	.00008	.00072	.00103
STANDARDIZED RATE (1)			.00763	.00054	.00024	.00065	.00167	.00093	.00030	.00063	.00000	.00037	.00009	.00079	.00142
STANDARDIZED RATE (2)			.01361	.00054	.00022	.00117	.00378	.00157	.00042	.00125	.00000	.00022	.00011	.00090	.00304
GEOMETRIC MEAN			.01041												

LIFE TABLE FOR ALL CAUSES COMBINED

Age (x)	Midyear Population	Deaths During Year	$_nM_x$	$_nq_x$	l_x	$_nd_x$	$_nL_x$	$_nm_x$	$_na_x$	T_x	$_nr_x$	$\overset{\circ}{e}_x$	Age (x)
0	200794	5864	.029204	.028470	100000	2847	97494	.029202	.119647	6454811	.000000	64.548	0
1	821207	3290	.004006	.015872	97153	1542	384757	.004008	1.500000	6357318	.000000	65.436	1
5	964956	804	.000833	.004152	95611	397	477063	.000832	2.500000	5572561	.000000	62.467	5
10	841146	596	.000709	.003539	95214	337	475265	.000709	2.610658	5495498	-.036214	57.717	10
15	531428	668	.001257	.006071	94877	576	473161	.001217	2.875756	5020233	.093884	52.913	15
20	318826	932	.002923	.014592	94301	1376	468145	.002939	2.558291	4547072	.043078	48.219	20
25	445106	925	.002078	.010342	92925	961	462185	.002079	2.460978	4078927	-.020181	43.895	25
30	423287	1108	.002618	.013005	91964	1196	456960	.002617	2.608870	3616742	-.000167	39.328	30
35	400660	1410	.003519	.017473	90768	1586	450087	.003524	2.633459	3159781	.011895	34.812	35
40	336099	1679	.004996	.024803	89182	2212	440717	.005019	2.652388	2709695	.030535	30.384	40
45	270331	2017	.007461	.036840	86970	3204	427392	.007497	2.672181	2268978	.026800	26.089	45
50	236988	2810	.011857	.058019	83766	4860	407446	.011928	2.657707	1841586	.031928	21.985	50
55	163501	2946	.018018	.087230	78906	6883	378400	.018190	2.656575	1434140	.052562	18.175	55
60	108910	3214	.029511	.135303	72023	10033	336298	.029830	2.626146	1055739	.056329	14.658	60
65	67351	3098	.045998	.209034	61990	12958	278562	.046517	2.577751	719441	.062066	11.606	65
70	36587	2586	.070681	.303251	49032	14869	208239	.071404	2.516912	440879	.054662	8.992	70
75	19571	2043	.104389	.414630	34163	14165	134546	.105280	2.439508	232640	.047998	6.810	75
80	7973	1185	.148627	.537854	19998	10756	71956	.149481	2.393625	98094	.047998	4.905	80
85+	1564	553	.353581	1.000000	9242	9242	26138	.353581	2.828210	26138	.000000	2.828	85+

NUMBER OF PERSONS DYING (OUT OF 100,000 AT BIRTH) ABOVE AGE X FROM SPECIFIED CAUSES

Age (x)	All Causes	Respiratory T.B.	Other Infec. and Paras.	Neo-plasms	Cardio-vascular	Infl., Pneu., Bronch.	Diar-rheal	Certain Degenerative	Maternal	Cert. Dis. of Infancy	Motor Vehicle	Other Violence	Other and Unknown	Age (x)
0	100000	7317	1322	9049	28521	10976	2756	9568	0	1030	750	6170	22121	0
1	97153	7313	1094	9037	28885	10172	2440	9580	0	0	750	6116	21766	1
5	95611	7296	819	9004	28864	9775	2204	9543	0	0	730	5873	21503	5
10	95214	7291	772	8979	28850	9719	2179	9522	0	0	715	5772	21415	10
15	94977	7281	747	8953	28825	9695	2173	9504	0	0	704	5648	21347	15
20	94301	7264	731	8925	28788	9671	2170	9479	0	0	675	5334	21264	20
25	92925	7184	712	8833	28704	9635	2167	9411	0	0	613	4578	21088	25
30	91964	7091	694	8764	28634	9608	2163	9362	0	0	557	4144	20947	30
35	90768	6927	676	8647	28531	9576	2155	9245	0	0	501	3729	20781	35
40	89182	6688	653	8452	28351	9545	2138	9056	0	0	447	3305	20547	40
45	86670	6322	617	8089	27599	9475	2117	8806	0	0	407	2906	20232	45
50	83766	5847	567	7548	27373	9363	2092	8380	0	0	346	2455	19795	50
55	78906	5072	512	6738	26140	9167	2038	7761	0	0	301	2032	19145	55
60	72023	4327	440	5615	24007	8758	1972	6915	0	0	248	1622	18119	60
65	61990	3283	331	4353	20511	8074	1806	5649	0	0	204	1204	16575	65
70	49032	2121	252	2765	15933	6812	1622	4198	0	0	121	810	14398	70
75	34163	1070	161	1638	10519	5156	1297	2729	0	0	87	467	11039	75
80	19998	481	106	706	5945	3243	823	1386	0	0	52	198	7058	80
85+	9242	117	67	267	2607	1588	384	602	0	0	33	33	3544	85+

NUMBER OF PERSONS SURVIVING TO AGE X IF SPECIFIED CAUSES WERE ELIMINATED

Age (x)	No Causes	Respiratory T.B. (1)	Other Infec. and Paras. (2)	Neo-plasms (3)	Cardio-vascular (4)	Infl., Pneu., Bronch. (5)	Diar-rheal (6)	Certain Degenerative (7)	Maternal (8)	Cert. Dis. of Infancy (9)	Motor Vehicle (10)	Other Violence (11)	Other and Unknown (12)	(1)+(2)+(5)+(6)+(8)	(1)+(2)+(5)+(6)+(8)+part of(9)&(12)	(10)+(11)	Age (x)
0	100000	100000	100000	100000	100000	100000	100000	100000	100000	100000	100000	100000	100000	100000	100000	100000	0
1	97153	97157	97378	97165	97188	97949	97465	97161	97153	98174	97153	97206	97504	97382	98495	99783	97206	1
5	95611	95632	96106	95665	95667	96792	96153	95655	95611	96615	95631	95905	96218	96127	97866	99342	95925	5
10	95214	95240	95754	95283	95284	96447	95779	95279	95214	96214	95249	95608	95907	95780	97596	99107	95643	10
15	94877	94913	95441	94972	94971	96130	95446	94960	94877	95874	94923	95394	95636	95476	97317	98841	95440	15
20	94301	94353	94877	94423	94432	95570	94870	94408	94301	95292	94375	95130	95139	94930	96787	98314	95205	20
25	92925	93056	93512	93137	93137	94212	93488	93098	92925	93901	93060	94502	93927	93644	95516	97043	94639	25
30	91964	92186	92563	92243	92244	93265	92525	92185	91964	92930	92153	93565	93058	92787	94673	96212	94158	30
35	90768	91151	91377	91160	91147	92084	91330	91102	90768	91721	91010	93165	92054	91763	93670	95229	93414	35
40	89182	89797	89803	89761	89734	90506	89751	89699	89182	90119	89474	91956	90681	90422	92351	93945	92270	40
45	86670	87934	87612	87857	87332	88332	87723	86670	87884	87294	90095	88749	88583	90566	92214	90431		45
50	83766	85167	84433	85197	85245	85189	84346	84914	83766	84646	84138	87235	85918	85846	87908	89618	87623	50
55	78906	80993	79588	81057	81528	80441	79505	80598	78906	79735	79301	82601	81583	81694	83915	85723	83014	55
60	72023	74661	72715	75095	76553	73824	72633	74397	72023	72780	72434	75806	75487	75434	77918	79836	76238	60
65	61990	65270	62688	65863	69427	64195	62671	65256	61990	62641	62385	66653	66490	66005	69103	71192	66071	65
70	49032	52719	49654	53608	59658	51953	49736	52985	49032	49547	49418	52299	54712	53389	57382	59703	52711	70
75	34163	37674	34673	38377	47404	37690	34931	38255	34163	34522	34460	36742	41384	38236	43133	45892	37061	75
80	19998	22539	20338	23263	32962	23728	20822	23555	19998	20208	20198	21726	28192	22922	28318	31527	21943	80
85+	9242	10692	9425	11095	19357	12349	9931	11516	9242	9339	9347	10160	16765	10904	15656	19013	10276	85+

ADDED YRS OF LIFE

	No Causes	(1)	(2)	(3)	(4)	(5)	(6)	(7)	(8)	(9)	(10)	(11)	(12)				
TOTAL		1.166	.490	1.380	3.560	1.658	.550	1.271	.000	.677	.198	1.860	2.856	1.671	4.143	6.038	2.068
WORK	4.670	.516	.063	.538	.723	.153	.034	.431	.000	.000	.118	1.106	.601	.580	.774	.904	1.228

POPULATION, DEATHS, DEATH RATES FOR ALL CAUSES COMBINED, AND SPECIFIED CAUSES

Age Start of Interval	Midyear Population	Deaths During Year	All Causes	Respiratory T.B.	Other Infec. and Paras.	Neoplasms	Cardiovascular	Infl., Pneu., Bronch.	Diarrheal	Certain Degenerative	Maternal	Cert. Dis. of Infancy	Motor Vehicle	Other Violence	Other and Unknown	Age Start of Interval
0	189037	4969	.02625	.00006	.00229	.00013	.00022	.00787	.00318	.00009	.00000	.00910	.00002	.00047	.00286	0
1	776517	3430	.00442	.00006	.00078	.00006	.00005	.00132	.00074	.00010	.00000	.00000	.00005	.00051	.00073	1
5	916269	602	.00066	.00002	.00009	.00003	.00004	.00012	.00004	.00003	.00000	.00000	.00002	.00011	.00016	5
10	799199	427	.00053	.00002	.00003	.00004	.00006	.00005	.00001	.00004	.00000	.00000	.00002	.00014	.00012	10
15	503091	491	.00098	.00004	.00005	.00007	.00009	.00006	.00002	.00005	.00003	.00000	.00003	.00041	.00013	15
20	470153	647	.00138	.00008	.00004	.00008	.00011	.00005	.00002	.00010	.00013	.00000	.00002	.00054	.00020	20
25	429185	699	.00163	.00021	.00006	.00017	.00021	.00006	.00001	.00010	.00016	.00000	.00001	.00035	.00028	25
30	377645	738	.00195	.00022	.00005	.00023	.00029	.00009	.00003	.00019	.00019	.00000	.00001	.00029	.00036	30
35	325684	848	.00260	.00033	.00007	.00048	.00043	.00008	.00020	.00021	.00021	.00000	.00002	.00032	.00045	35
40	265734	924	.00348	.00042	.00008	.00076	.00075	.00020	.00005	.00035	.00014	.00000	.00003	.00027	.00044	40
45	209086	1065	.00509	.00056	.00007	.00125	.00128	.00024	.00009	.00051	.00002	.00000	.00003	.00038	.00064	45
50	186234	1360	.00730	.00068	.00010	.00171	.00224	.00031	.00005	.00078	.00000	.00000	.00003	.00038	.00104	50
55	143373	1578	.01101	.00068	.00015	.00207	.00368	.00068	.00019	.00133	.00000	.00000	.00001	.00041	.00157	55
60	105412	2002	.01899	.00162	.00015	.00294	.00703	.00114	.00028	.00186	.00000	.00000	.00005	.00066	.00326	60
65	74716	2231	.02986	.00214	.00017	.00353	.01142	.00257	.00048	.00316	.00000	.00000	.00003	.00076	.00559	65
70	48300	2345	.04855	.00246	.00027	.00387	.01874	.00505	.00114	.00484	.00000	.00000	.00006	.00099	.01112	70
75	31898	2561	.08029	.00245	.00031	.00480	.02972	.00919	.00238	.00627	.00000	.00000	.00000	.00132	.02386	75
80	17449	2084	.11943	.00235	.00034	.00395	.03639	.01524	.00533	.00768	.00000	.00000	.00000	.00149	.04665	80
85+	4836	1339	.27688	.00310	.00083	.00517	.07506	.03825	.00951	.01179	.00000	.00000	.00041	.00331	.12945	85+
ALL	5873818	30340														

	All Causes	Respiratory T.B.	Other Infec. and Paras.	Neoplasms	Cardiovascular	Infl., Pneu., Bronch.	Diarrheal	Certain Degenerative	Maternal	Cert. Dis. of Infancy	Motor Vehicle	Other Violence	Other and Unknown
CRUDE DEATH RATE	.00517	.00026	.00024	.00044	.00110	.00074	.00028	.00034	.00006	.00029	.00003	.00035	.00104
STANDARDIZED RATE (1)	.00567	.00029	.00024	.00051	.00128	.00078	.00029	.00039	.00006	.00032	.00003	.00037	.00112
STANDARDIZED RATE (2)	.00988	.00049	.00019	.00088	.00289	.00113	.00035	.00077	.00006	.00019	.00003	.00042	.00248
GEOMETRIC MEAN	.00757												

LIFE TABLE FOR ALL CAUSES COMBINED

Age (x)	Midyear Population	Deaths During Year	$_nM_x$	$_nq_x$	l_x	$_nd_x$	$_nL_x$	$_nm_x$	$_na_x$	T_x	$_n r_x$	$\overset{\circ}{e}_x$	Age (x)
0	189037	4969	.026286	.025690	100000	2569	97726	.026288	.114686	6895158	.000000	68.952	0
1	776517	3430	.004417	.017469	97431	1702	385469	.004415	1.500000	6797432	.000000	69.767	1
5	916269	602	.000657	.003291	95729	315	477558	.000659	2.500000	6411963	.000000	66.980	5
10	799199	427	.000534	.002662	95414	254	476466	.000533	2.623852	5934106	.045280	62.193	10
15	503091	491	.000976	.004857	95160	466	474718	.000982	2.677486	5457639	.057394	57.352	15
20	470153	647	.001376	.006875	94694	651	471904	.001380	2.595046	4982922	.023564	52.621	20
25	429185	699	.001629	.008113	94043	763	468361	.001631	2.570719	4511017	.020311	47.968	25
30	377645	738	.001954	.009756	93280	910	464216	.001960	2.599817	4042656	.023548	43.339	30
35	325684	848	.002604	.012980	92370	1199	458992	.002612	2.616416	3578440	.028605	38.740	35
40	265734	924	.003477	.017330	91171	1580	452127	.003495	2.640691	3119448	.039617	34.215	40
45	209086	1065	.005094	.025293	89591	2266	442617	.005120	2.644252	2667321	.033167	29.772	45
50	186234	1360	.007303	.036061	87325	3149	429229	.007336	2.651238	2224704	.028258	25.476	50
55	143373	1578	.011006	.054077	84176	4552	410365	.011093	2.690118	1795475	.041250	21.330	55
60	105412	2002	.018992	.091719	79624	7303	381033	.019166	2.660237	1385110	.044226	17.396	60
65	74716	2231	.029860	.140609	72321	10169	337496	.030131	2.629192	1004077	.047855	13.884	65
70	48300	2345	.048551	.218563	62152	13609	278019	.048950	2.594178	666581	.039714	10.725	70
75	31898	2561	.080287	.336217	48543	16321	202167	.080730	2.515624	388562	.024577	8.004	75
80	17449	2084	.119434	.460338	32222	14833	123591	.120017	2.470575	186394	.024577	5.785	80
85+	4836	1339	.276882	1.000000	17389	17389	62803	.276882	3.611650	62803	.000000	3.612	85+

NUMBER OF PERSONS DYING (OUT OF 100,000 AT BIRTH) ABOVE AGE X FROM SPECIFIED CAUSES

Age (x)	All Causes	Respiratory T. B.	Other Infec. and Paras.	Neo-plasms	Cardio-vascular	Infl., Pneu., Bronch.	Diar-rheal	Certain Degen-erative	Maternal	Cert. Dis. of Infancy	Motor Vehicle	Other Violence	Other and Unknown	Age (x)
0	100000	4599	1226	8256	31129	11022	3158	7778	417	889	199	3343	27984	0
1	97431	4593	1002	8244	31107	10253	2847	7769	417	0	198	3297	27704	1
5	95729	4570	703	8219	31087	9744	2561	7729	417	0	177	3099	27423	5
10	95414	4561	662	8206	31069	9686	2542	7714	417	0	168	3045	27344	10
15	95160	4553	646	8186	31041	9662	2537	7693	417	0	161	2976	27288	15
20	94694	4534	623	8152	30997	9635	2530	7671	400	0	148	2779	27225	20
25	94043	4496	602	8113	30943	9610	2523	7622	340	0	137	2524	27133	25
30	93280	4396	574	8032	30846	9583	2517	7573	264	0	132	2361	27002	30
35	92370	4295	551	7924	30712	9541	2502	7484	174	0	126	2226	26835	35
40	91171	4142	520	7703	30512	9506	2493	7392	75	0	117	2081	26630	40
45	89591	3950	488	7358	30171	9415	2472	7231	11	0	105	1958	26434	45
50	87325	3700	454	6801	29601	9306	2432	7003	1	0	91	1788	26148	50
55	84176	3409	412	6066	28634	9172	2411	6667	1	0	77	1627	25700	55
60	79624	3028	352	5212	27111	8891	2333	6117	1	0	71	1457	25051	60
65	72321	2405	294	4086	24406	8452	2227	5403	1	0	53	1203	23791	65
70	62152	1679	235	2890	20516	7572	2062	4327	1	0	44	944	21882	70
75	48543	993	160	1811	15265	6153	1741	2972	1	0	27	667	18753	75
80	32222	498	96	839	9229	4284	1255	1700	1	0	27	400	13893	80
85+	17389	195	52	325	4714	2403	557	740	0	0	26	208	8129	85+

NUMBER OF PERSONS SURVIVING TO AGE X IF SPECIFIED CAUSES WERE ELIMINATED

Age (x)	No Causes	Respiratory T. B. (1)	Other Infec. and Paras. (2)	Neo-plasms (3)	Cardio-vascular (4)	Infl., Pneu., Bronch. (5)	Diar-rheal (6)	Certain Degener-ative (7)	Maternal (8)	Cert. Dis. of Infancy (9)	Motor Vehicle (10)	Other Violence (11)	Other and Unknown (12)	(1) + (2)	(1) + (2) + (5) + (6) + (8)	(1)+(2)+ (5)+(6)+ (8)+part of(9)&(12)	(10) + (11)	Age (x)
0	100000	100000	100000	100000	100000	100000	100000	100000	100000	100000	100000	100000	100000	100000	100000	100000	100000	0
1	97431	97437	97652	97443	97453	98193	97738	97440	97431	98312	97432	97476	97708	97658	98733	99833	97477	1
5	95729	95758	96244	95765	95770	96988	96316	95777	95729	96595	95751	95970	96281	96273	98136	99457	95992	5
10	95414	95452	95968	95463	95473	96727	96018	95477	95414	96277	95445	95708	96043	96006	97944	99306	95739	10
15	95160	95205	95729	95229	95247	96494	95767	95244	95160	96021	95198	95523	95844	95775	97737	99112	95561	15
20	94694	94758	95283	94797	94824	96049	95306	94800	94711	95551	94744	95253	95438	95348	97354	98739	95303	20
25	94043	94145	94649	94184	94226	95414	94657	94197	94120	94894	94104	94854	94874	94752	96839	98243	94915	25
30	93280	93481	93910	93501	93559	94855	93881	93432	93432	94124	93936	94249	94236	94111	96297	97744	94314	30
35	92370	92669	93016	92696	92780	93786	92994	92658	92610	93206	92441	93464	93485	93318	95636	97137	93536	35
40	91171	91619	91840	91714	91775	92604	91796	91547	91507	91996	91250	92397	92478	92291	94732	96289	92477	40
45	89591	90223	90282	90469	90526	91090	90226	90121	89984	90402	89680	90919	91072	90919	93505	95102	91010	45
50	87325	88190	88031	88738	88807	88886	87964	88068	87718	88115	87426	88790	89056	88902	91595	93227	88893	50
55	84176	85298	84899	86274	86576	85824	84832	85226	84555	84938	84287	85749	86295	86030	88796	90463	85862	55
60	79624	81062	80366	82463	83432	81463	80321	81160	79983	80344	79735	81280	82278	81817	84819	86552	81393	60
65	72321	74233	73050	76017	78530	74421	73056	74413	72647	72975	72439	74072	75584	74982	78294	80163	74193	65
70	62152	64487	62834	66498	71516	64803	62939	64983	62432	62714	62262	63902	67187	65194	69146	71246	64015	70
75	48543	50993	49142	52958	61440	51937	49446	52014	48762	48982	48643	50161	55557	51622	56513	59029	50264	75
80	32222	34265	32672	36011	47433	36134	33228	35638	32367	32514	32288	33518	41699	34743	40359	43500	33587	80
85+	17389	18726	17664	19854	30884	21087	18429	20016	17468	17546	17426	18233	28599	19022	24559	28569	18272	85+

ADDED YRS OF LIFE																		
TOTAL		.795	.530	1.421	3.979	1.850	.645	1.050	.171	.623	.065	.963	3.621	1.334	4.186	6.199	1.029	
WORK	3.199	.299	.069	.511	.648	.141	.038	.275	.132	.000	.024	.437	.449	.369	.685	.809	.462	

POPULATION, DEATHS, DEATH RATES FOR ALL CAUSES COMBINED, AND SPECIFIED CAUSES

Age Start of Interval	Midyear Population	Deaths During Year	All Causes	Respiratory T. B.	Other Infec. and Paras.	Neoplasms	Cardiovascular	Infl., Pneu., Bronch.	Diarrheal	Certain Degenerative	Maternal	Cert. Dis. of Infancy	Motor Vehicle	Other Violence	Other and Unknown	Age Start of Interval
0	16900	789	.04669	.00006	.00136	.00012	.00030	.00609	.00521	.00059	.00000	.02704	.00000	.00065	.00527	0
1	61550	178	.00289	.00000	.00010	.00013	.00011	.00091	.00047	.00026	.00000	.00000	.00003	.00023	.00065	1
5	66750	46	.00069	.00000	.00007	.00003	.00003	.00012	.00000	.00000	.00000	.00000	.00007	.00016	.00019	5
10	54350	48	.00088	.00002	.00005	.00009	.00015	.00004	.00000	.00000	.00000	.00000	.00007	.00024	.00018	10
15	47050	50	.00106	.00000	.00004	.00000	.00019	.00004	.00000	.00000	.00000	.00000	.00006	.00057	.00015	15
20	36250	58	.00160	.00000	.00000	.00011	.00017	.00011	.00003	.00003	.00000	.00000	.00019	.00074	.00022	20
25	30300	54	.00178	.00000	.00013	.00010	.00013	.00000	.00007	.00003	.00000	.00000	.00007	.00092	.00033	25
30	25550	54	.00211	.00000	.00004	.00008	.00043	.00000	.00000	.00027	.00000	.00000	.00023	.00063	.00043	30
35	23200	82	.00353	.00009	.00004	.00017	.00103	.00013	.00004	.00043	.00000	.00000	.00013	.00082	.00065	35
40	23500	117	.00498	.00000	.00030	.00021	.00170	.00021	.00004	.00030	.00000	.00000	.00034	.00111	.00077	40
45	19850	145	.00730	.00005	.00035	.00065	.00297	.00020	.00005	.00071	.00000	.00000	.00035	.00086	.00111	45
50	17300	195	.01127	.00012	.00052	.00145	.00561	.00035	.00006	.00110	.00000	.00000	.00017	.00081	.00110	50
55	12650	265	.02095	.00032	.00079	.00292	.01083	.00040	.00016	.00237	.00000	.00000	.00040	.00103	.00174	55
60	10050	310	.03085	.00109	.00050	.00308	.01672	.00169	.00000	.00229	.00000	.00000	.00050	.00109	.00358	60
65	5850	363	.06205	.00103	.00051	.00684	.03641	.00444	.00051	.00325	.00000	.00000	.00034	.00154	.00718	65
70	4350	301	.06920	.00138	.00138	.00575	.03425	.00506	.00069	.00460	.00000	.00000	.00023	.00046	.01540	70
75	2200	252	.11455	.00136	.00273	.01182	.05364	.00545	.00182	.00545	.00000	.00000	.00000	.00273	.02955	75
80	1150	166	.14435	.00261	.00067	.01217	.07043	.01130	.00522	.00656	.00000	.00000	.00087	.00087	.03304	80
85+	750	186	.24800	.00267	.00133	.00800	.12133	.02133	.00267	.00800	.00000	.00000	.00000	.00400	.07867	85+
ALL	459550	3659														

CRUDE DEATH RATE	.00796	.00009	.00022	.00055	.00267	.00066	.00032	.00044	.00000	.00099	.00014	.00058	.00129	
STANDARDIZED RATE (1)	.00823	.00010	.00022	.00060	.00287	.00065	.00031	.00046	.00000	.00095	.00014	.00061	.00131	
STANDARDIZED RATE (2)	.01409	.00021	.00031	.00120	.00624	.00095	.00032	.00084	.00000	.00056	.00018	.00073	.00256	
GEOMETRIC MEAN	.00556													

LIFE TABLE FOR ALL CAUSES COMBINED

Age (x)	Midyear Population	Deaths During Year	$_nM_x$	$_nq_x$	l_x	$_nd_x$	$_nL_x$	$_nm_x$	$_na_x$	T_x	$_nr_x$	$\overset{\circ}{e}_x$	Age (x)
0	16900	789	.046686	.044900	100000	4490	96181	.046683	.149367	6365567	.000000	63.656	0
1	61550	178	.002892	.011486	95510	1097	379298	.002892	1.500000	6269386	.000000	65.641	1
5	66750	46	.000689	.003432	94413	324	471255	.000688	2.500000	5890089	.000000	62.386	5
10	54350	48	.000883	.004402	94089	416	469441	.000886	2.587139	5418834	.025429	57.593	10
15	47050	50	.001063	.005316	93673	498	467189	.001066	2.637634	4949393	.035257	52.837	15
20	36250	58	.001600	.007956	93175	745	464080	.001605	2.590604	4482204	.042310	48.105	20
25	30300	54	.001782	.008893	92430	822	460141	.001786	2.556265	4018124	.035995	43.472	25
30	25550	54	.002114	.010556	91608	967	455783	.002122	2.665891	3557983	.030657	38.839	30
35	23200	82	.003534	.017564	90641	1592	449481	.003542	2.660568	3102200	.010291	34.225	35
40	23500	117	.004979	.024638	89049	2194	440080	.004985	2.645852	2652719	.008578	29.789	40
45	19850	145	.007305	.036014	86855	3128	426962	.007326	2.662244	2212639	.017965	25.475	45
50	17300	195	.011272	.055099	83727	4630	408063	.011346	2.716703	1785677	.029530	21.327	50
55	12650	265	.020949	.100434	79097	7944	376810	.021082	2.649222	1377613	.030850	17.417	55
60	10050	310	.030846	.145040	71153	10320	331744	.031108	2.672380	1000803	.041528	14.066	60
65	5850	363	.062051	.270955	60833	16483	263529	.062547	2.534670	669059	.031994	10.998	65
70	4350	301	.069195	.294543	44350	13063	188559	.069278	2.459124	405530	.022119	9.144	70
75	2200	252	.114545	.444913	31287	13920	120799	.115233	2.439940	216971	.022926	6.935	75
80	1150	166	.144348	.521103	17367	9050	62636	.144485	2.326105	96173	.022926	5.538	80
85+	750	186	.248000	1.000000	8317	8317	33536	.248000	4.032258	33536	.000000	4.032	85+

NUMBER OF PERSONS DYING (OUT OF 100,000 AT BIRTH) ABOVE AGE X FROM SPECIFIED CAUSES

Age (x)	All Causes	Respiratory T. B.	Other Infec. and Paras.	Neoplasms	Cardiovascular	Infl., Pneu., Bronch.	Diarrheal	Certain Degenerative	Maternal	Cert. Dis. of Infancy	Motor Vehicle	Other Violence	Other and Unknown	Age (x)
0	100000	1560	2154	8806	46213	6395	1903	6150	0	2601	1242	4995	17981	0
1	95510	1554	2023	8795	46184	5809	1403	6094	0	0	1242	4932	17474	1
5	94413	1554	1986	8746	46141	5464	1224	5995	0	0	1230	4846	17227	5
10	94089	1554	1951	8732	46127	5407	1224	5995	0	0	1194	4769	17136	10
15	93673	1546	1908	8688	46058	5390	1224	5995	0	0	1160	4656	17048	15
20	93175	1546	1888	8688	45968	5370	1224	5995	0	0	1130	4385	16981	20
25	92430	1546	1888	8637	45892	5319	1211	5982	0	0	1040	4038	16877	25
30	91608	1546	1827	8591	45831	5319	1180	5966	0	0	1010	3613	16725	30
35	90641	1545	1809	8556	45632	5319	1180	5840	0	0	902	3329	16529	35
40	89049	1507	1790	8478	45166	5261	1161	5646	0	0	844	2960	16236	40
45	86855	1507	1658	8384	44415	5167	1142	5515	0	0	694	2473	15900	45
50	83727	1485	1508	8103	43140	5081	1121	5213	0	0	544	2108	15424	50
55	79097	1437	1294	7508	40834	4939	1097	4761	0	0	473	1777	14977	55
60	71153	1316	996	6400	36725	4788	1037	3863	0	0	323	1389	14316	60
65	60833	950	832	5371	31126	4217	903	3103	0	0	192	1026	13113	65
70	44350	679	656	3555	21456	3034	768	2241	0	0	102	619	11200	70
75	31287	419	434	2472	15000	2081	637	1373	0	0	59	533	8279	75
80	17367	253	103	1035	8483	1419	415	712	0	0	59	201	4687	80
85+	8317	89	45	268	4069	715	89	268	0	0	0	134	2640	85+

NUMBER OF PERSONS SURVIVING TO AGE X IF SPECIFIED CAUSES WERE ELIMINATED

Age (x)	No Causes	Respiratory T. B.	Other Infec. and Paras.	Neoplasms	Cardiovascular	Infl., Pneu., Bronch.	Diarrheal	Certain Degenerative	Maternal	Cert. Dis. of Infancy	Motor Vehicle	Other Violence	Other and Unknown	(1) + (2)	(1) + (2) + (5) + (6) + (8)	(1)+(2)+ (5)+(6)+ (8)+part of(9)&(12)	(10) + (11)	Age (x)
		(1)	(2)	(3)	(4)	(5)	(6)	(7)	(8)	(9)	(10)	(11)	(12)					
0	100000	100000	100000	100000	100000	100000	100000	100000	100000	100000	100000	100000	100000	100000	100000	100000	100000	0
1	95510	95516	95538	95521	95538	96084	96000	95565	95510	98086	95510	95572	96007	95644	96713	99473	95572	1
5	94413	94419	94576	94472	94484	95326	95076	94566	94413	96959	94425	94559	95151	94582	96168	99083	94571	5
10	94089	94095	94287	94162	94174	95057	94750	94241	94089	96627	94137	94312	94916	94293	95932	98877	94360	10
15	93673	93687	93913	93790	93826	94654	94331	93824	93673	96199	93755	94008	94585	93927	95577	98530	94090	15
20	93175	93189	93434	93291	93417	94171	93830	93326	93175	95688	93286	93780	94150	93447	95109	98055	93892	20
25	92430	92444	92687	92596	92746	93469	93092	92592	92430	94923	92630	93379	93502	92700	94414	97349	93581	25
30	91608	91621	91923	91819	91982	92638	92256	91785	91608	94079	91836	92977	92824	91937	93668	96602	93208	30
35	90641	90655	90971	90884	91211	91660	91321	90942	90641	93086	90974	92282	92041	90985	92699	95607	92622	35
40	89049	89101	89392	89365	90075	90108	89736	89538	89049	91451	89434	91034	90720	89444	91207	94100	91428	40
45	86855	86905	87321	87257	88609	87982	87544	87462	86855	89157	87380	89284	88824	87371	89208	92084	89824	45
50	83727	83797	84324	84393	86705	84899	84412	84611	83727	85985	84381	86437	86104	84395	86277	89110	87112	50
55	79097	79210	79871	80311	84266	80344	79768	80378	79097	81230	79784	81989	81789	79985	81935	84674	82701	55
60	71153	71371	72134	73318	80070	72422	71814	73174	71153	73072	71914	74136	74227	72354	74329	76872	74929	60
65	60833	61358	61823	63670	74536	62460	61523	63283	60833	62474	61605	63732	64632	62357	64751	67133	64541	65
70	44350	44964	45190	48059	65358	46582	44969	46903	44350	45546	44989	46823	48894	45816	48793	50811	47499	70
75	31287	31941	32107	34894	54772	33705	31836	33865	31287	32131	31774	33106	37327	32778	35931	37888	33621	75
80	17367	17853	18072	20586	40041	19236	17842	19325	17367	17835	17637	18639	24125	18578	21140	22749	18929	80
85+	8317	8665	8656	10494	27460	9755	8774	9595	8317	8541	8487	8975	13647	9059	11210	12427	9158	85+

ADDED YRS OF LIFE

		(1)	(2)	(3)	(4)	(5)	(6)	(7)	(8)	(9)	(10)	(11)	(12)				
TOTAL		.171	.445	1.120	7.489	1.197	.566	.905	.000	1.713	.322	1.390	2.635	.621	2.453	4.762	1.724
WORK	4.306	.037	.146	.312	1.406	.119	.039	.318	.000	.000	.191	.859	.550	.183	.344	.400	1.055

POPULATION, DEATHS, DEATH RATES FOR ALL CAUSES COMBINED, AND SPECIFIED CAUSES

Age Start of Interval	Midyear Population	Deaths During Year	All Causes	Respiratory T. B.	Other Infec. and Paras.	Neoplasms	Cardiovascular	Infl., Pneu., Bronch.	Diarrheal	Certain Degenerative	Maternal	Cert. Dis. of Infancy	Motor Vehicle	Other Violence	Other and Unknown	Age Start of Interval
0	16250	581	.03575	.00000	.00049	.00012	.00025	.00455	.00542	.00031	.00000	.02018	.00000	.00049	.00394	0
1	59600	149	.00250	.00002	.00017	.00008	.00005	.00081	.00050	.00017	.00000	.00000	.00000	.00012	.00059	1
5	65750	29	.00044	.00002	.00005	.00000	.00005	.00006	.00003	.00002	.00000	.00000	.00006	.00009	.00008	5
10	54050	18	.00033	.00000	.00000	.00000	.00007	.00002	.00002	.00000	.00000	.00000	.00004	.00007	.00011	10
15	47850	35	.00073	.00000	.00000	.00004	.00019	.00002	.00000	.00006	.00002	.00000	.00000	.00010	.00029	15
20	38100	42	.00110	.00000	.00003	.00003	.00034	.00005	.00000	.00003	.00024	.00000	.00000	.00016	.00024	20
25	31050	48	.00155	.00000	.00010	.00016	.00032	.00006	.00000	.00016	.00026	.00000	.00000	.00016	.00032	25
30	27100	60	.00221	.00000	.00011	.00011	.00052	.00007	.00000	.00022	.00041	.00000	.00000	.00022	.00055	30
35	23750	71	.00299	.00017	.00021	.00051	.00080	.00008	.00000	.00034	.00029	.00000	.00000	.00004	.00055	35
40	23550	101	.00429	.00017	.00013	.00106	.00132	.00008	.00008	.00059	.00013	.00000	.00000	.00025	.00047	40
45	18400	107	.00582	.00016	.00005	.00163	.00223	.00005	.00005	.00060	.00000	.00000	.00000	.00022	.00082	45
50	16300	158	.00969	.00006	.00012	.00209	.00417	.00037	.00006	.00129	.00000	.00000	.00000	.00037	.00117	50
55	11400	187	.01640	.00026	.00035	.00307	.00816	.00035	.00018	.00140	.00000	.00000	.00009	.00044	.00211	55
60	10050	215	.02139	.00040	.00010	.00378	.01124	.00119	.00050	.00199	.00000	.00000	.00020	.00050	.00149	60
65	6850	258	.03766	.00015	.00015	.00672	.01766	.00146	.00058	.00423	.00000	.00000	.00029	.00088	.00555	65
70	6050	255	.04215	.00033	.00033	.00628	.02331	.00198	.00066	.00215	.00000	.00000	.00000	.00050	.00661	70
75	3000	228	.07600	.00000	.00133	.00900	.04567	.00433	.00100	.00333	.00000	.00000	.00000	.00100	.01033	75
80	1800	202	.11222	.00056	.00111	.00889	.05389	.00944	.00278	.00167	.00000	.00000	.00000	.00000	.03389	80
85+	1550	263	.16968	.00000	.00129	.00710	.07935	.01290	.00387	.00581	.00000	.00000	.00000	.00258	.05677	85+
ALL	462450	3007														

CRUDE DEATH RATE			.00650	.00005	.00012	.00071	.00226	.00050	.00023	.00040	.00008	.00071	.00002	.00019	.00111	
STANDARDIZED RATE (1)			.00600	.00005	.00012	.00070	.00202	.00045	.00031	.00040	.00009	.00071	.00002	.00019	.00093	
STANDARDIZED RATE (2)			.00956	.00008	.00015	.00131	.00436	.00061	.00030	.00066	.00009	.00042	.00003	.00024	.00171	
GEOMETRIC MEAN			.00726													

LIFE TABLE FOR ALL CAUSES COMBINED

Age (x)	Midyear Population	Deaths During Year	nM_x	nq_x	l_x	nd_x	nL_x	nm_x	na_x	T_x	nr_x	$\overset{\circ}{e}_x$	Age (x)
0	16250	581	.035754	.034680	100000	3468	96986	.035758	.130782	6833501	.000000	68.335	0
1	59600	149	.002500	.009935	96532	959	383731	.002499	1.500000	6736515	.000000	69.785	1
5	65750	29	.000441	.002197	95573	210	477340	.000440	2.500000	6352785	.000000	66.470	5
10	54050	18	.000333	.001667	95363	159	476447	.000334	2.683438	5875445	.023902	61.611	10
15	47850	35	.000731	.003676	95204	350	475221	.000736	2.717262	5398998	.030123	56.710	15
20	38100	42	.001102	.005524	94854	524	473039	.001108	2.651081	4923777	.040906	51.909	20
25	31050	48	.001546	.007739	94330	730	469931	.001553	2.645833	4450738	.035171	47.183	25
30	27100	60	.002214	.011058	93600	1035	465547	.002223	2.630032	3980806	.029806	42.530	30
35	23750	71	.002989	.014865	92565	1376	459574	.002994	2.637173	3515259	.013791	37.976	35
40	23550	101	.004289	.021265	91189	1941	451342	.004301	2.628370	3055686	.018186	33.509	40
45	18400	107	.005815	.028819	89248	2572	440268	.005842	2.678120	2604344	.026249	29.181	45
50	16300	158	.009693	.047764	86676	4140	423859	.009767	2.700181	2164076	.035845	24.967	50
55	11400	187	.016404	.079359	82536	6550	397062	.016496	2.615585	1740217	.033675	21.084	55
60	10050	215	.021393	.102308	75986	7774	361587	.021500	2.640479	1343155	.031055	17.676	60
65	6850	258	.037664	.172873	68212	11792	312212	.037769	2.553585	981568	.016849	14.390	65
70	6050	255	.042149	.191546	56420	10807	255696	.042265	2.556792	669356	.028219	11.864	70
75	3000	228	.076000	.323110	45613	14738	191787	.076846	2.538463	413660	.042646	9.069	75
80	1800	202	.112222	.438154	30875	13528	119637	.113075	2.432178	221873	.042646	7.186	80
85+	1550	263	.169677	1.000000	17347	17347	102235	.169677	5.893536	102235	.000000	5.894	85+

NUMBER OF PERSONS DYING (OUT OF 100,000 AT BIRTH) ABOVE AGE X FROM SPECIFIED CAUSES

Age (x)	All Causes	Respiratory T.B.	Other Infec. and Paras.	Neoplasms	Cardiovascular	Infl., Pneu., Bronch.	Diarrheal	Certain Degenerative	Maternal	Cert. Dis. of Infancy	Motor Vehicle	Other Violence	Other and Unknown	Age (x)
0	100000	713	1306	12385	46792	5984	2358	6163	627	1958	245	2079	19390	0
1	96532	713	1258	12373	46768	5543	1833	6133	627	0	245	2031	19008	1
5	95573	707	1194	12341	46748	5234	1640	6069	627	0	245	1986	18782	5
10	95363	700	1172	12341	46727	5205	1625	6062	627	0	216	1943	18745	10
15	95204	700	1172	12340	46691	5196	1616	6062	627	0	199	1908	18693	15
20	94854	700	1172	12321	46601	5186	1616	6032	616	0	199	1858	18553	20
25	94330	700	1159	12308	46439	5161	1616	6019	504	0	199	1783	18442	25
30	93600	700	1113	12232	46287	5131	1616	5943	382	0	199	1707	18290	30
35	92565	699	1062	12180	46046	5096	1616	5839	193	0	199	1604	18031	35
40	91189	622	965	11946	45677	5057	1616	5684	58	0	199	1585	17780	40
45	89248	545	908	11465	45080	5019	1578	5415	1	0	199	1469	17569	45
50	86676	474	884	10745	44093	4995	1554	5151	1	0	199	1374	17206	50
55	82536	448	831	9856	42308	4837	1528	4601	1	0	199	1217	16710	55
60	75986	342	691	8632	39047	4696	1457	4042	1	0	163	1042	15873	60
65	68212	198	656	7259	34963	4262	1276	3318	1	0	91	862	15326	65
70	56420	153	610	5157	29431	3805	1093	1994	1	0	0	588	13588	70
75	45613	68	524	3551	23445	3295	924	1448	1	0	0	461	11896	75
80	30875	68	265	1813	14594	2451	730	805	1	0	0	268	9880	80
85+	17347	0	132	726	8113	1319	396	594	0	0	0	264	5803	85+

NUMBER OF PERSONS SURVIVING TO AGE X IF SPECIFIED CAUSES WERE ELIMINATED

Age (x)	No Causes	Respiratory T.B. (1)	Other Infec. and Paras. (2)	Neoplasms (3)	Cardiovascular (4)	Infl., Pneu., Bronch. (5)	Diarrheal (6)	Certain Degenerative (7)	Maternal (8)	Cert. Dis. of Infancy (9)	Motor Vehicle (10)	Other Violence (11)	Other and Unknown (12)	(1)+(2)	(1)+(2)+(5)+(6)+(8)	(1)+(2)+(5)+(6)+(8)+part of(9)&(12)	(10)+(11)	Age (x)
0	100000	100000	100000	100000	100000	100000	100000	100000	100000	100000	100000	100000	100000	100000	100000	100000	100000	0
1	96532	96532	96579	96544	96556	96966	97049	96561	96532	98475	96532	96579	96908	96579	97533	99644	96579	1
5	95573	95579	95683	95617	95616	96232	96278	95666	95573	97497	95573	95665	96171	95689	97141	99426	95665	5
10	95363	95376	95495	95406	95427	96130	96082	95463	95363	97282	95392	95497	95957	95508	97002	99299	95526	10
15	95204	95217	95336	95248	95304	95679	95931	95304	95204	97120	95250	95373	95889	95349	96858	99162	95419	15
20	94854	94867	94985	94917	95044	95636	95578	94983	94865	96763	94900	95073	95678	94998	96524	98833	95118	20
25	94330	94343	94474	94406	94681	95123	95050	94471	94453	96229	94375	94622	95261	94487	96143	98485	94668	25
30	93600	93613	93789	93751	94100	94427	94314	93816	93844	95484	93645	93966	94677	93801	95600	97984	94011	30
35	92565	92579	92802	92766	93301	93418	93272	92883	92994	94428	92610	93030	93891	92816	94824	97284	93075	35
40	91189	91279	91519	91620	92284	92068	91885	91656	91747	93024	91233	91666	92748	91610	93768	96283	91710	40
45	89248	89412	89628	90150	90919	90146	89967	89973	89850	91044	89251	89830	90986	89793	92044	94546	89873	45
50	86676	86905	87069	88271	89296	87572	87398	87643	87261	88421	86718	87336	88730	87299	89537	91996	87378	50
55	82536	82780	82962	84542	86845	83545	83249	84001	83393	84157	82576	83318	84988	83207	85526	87512	83359	55
60	75986	76313	76513	79418	83315	77053	76712	77882	76499	77515	76057	76876	79073	76842	79196	81474	76948	60
65	68212	68642	68718	72665	79152	65558	69037	70621	68672	69585	68344	69183	71527	69151	71881	74010	69318	65
70	56420	56816	56881	62169	71568	57982	57270	59667	56801	57556	56612	57475	60845	57280	60157	62065	57671	70
75	45613	46010	46065	51867	65110	47351	46454	48752	45921	46531	45767	46581	50854	46465	49457	51185	46739	75
80	30875	31143	31396	36748	55651	32780	31607	33560	31083	31496	30979	31690	36332	31668	34652	36065	31798	80
85+	17347	17548	17740	21626	41243	19328	18013	19026	17465	17696	17406	17808	24286	17946	20903	22433	17868	85+

ADDED YRS OF LIFE

	No Causes	(1)	(2)	(3)	(4)	(5)	(6)	(7)	(8)	(9)	(10)	(11)	(12)	(1)+(2)	...(8)	...part	(10)+(11)
TOTAL		.149	.297	2.014	6.671	1.119	.687	1.092	.259	1.373	.059	.505	3.058	.447	2.582	4.654	.565
WORK	3.600	.063	.097	.577	1.210	.098	.024	.346	.203	.000	.004	.196	.555	.161	.489	.603	.200

POPULATION, DEATHS, DEATH RATES FOR ALL CAUSES COMBINED, AND SPECIFIED CAUSES

Age Start of Interval	Midyear Population	Deaths During Year	All Causes	Respiratory T. B.	Other Infec. and Paras.	Neoplasms	Cardiovascular	Infl., Pneu., Bronch.	Diarrheal	Certain Degenerative	Maternal	Cert. Dis. of Infancy	Motor Vehicle	Other Violence	Other and Unknown	Age Start of Interval
0	221096	39712	.17961	.00137	.01252	.00006	.00372	.02729	.04452	.00080	.00000	.04084	.00000	.00142	.04708	0
1	822636	16962	.02062	.00044	.00617	.00004	.00046	.00486	.00311	.00023	.00000	.00000	.00000	.00088	.00443	1
5	997052	4711	.00472	.00014	.00195	.00002	.00031	.00054	.00014	.00016	.00000	.00000	.00000	.00052	.00096	5
10	911482	2663	.00292	.00016	.00073	.00002	.00032	.00022	.00005	.00013	.00000	.00000	.00000	.00063	.00067	10
15	881181	4311	.00489	.00109	.00090	.00003	.00041	.00049	.00007	.00019	.00000	.00000	.00000	.00091	.00082	15
20	919860	6449	.00701	.00224	.00108	.00004	.00043	.00071	.00009	.00028	.00000	.00000	.00000	.00128	.00086	20
25	915609	7211	.00788	.00261	.00098	.00006	.00055	.00084	.00009	.00042	.00000	.00000	.00000	.00132	.00099	25
30	834777	7297	.00874	.00268	.00094	.00012	.00080	.00098	.00012	.00059	.00000	.00000	.00000	.00139	.00111	30
35	765239	7713	.01008	.00266	.00095	.00020	.00111	.00117	.00015	.00083	.00000	.00000	.00000	.00162	.00138	35
40	653940	7523	.01150	.00234	.00099	.00037	.00161	.00140	.00016	.00122	.00000	.00000	.00000	.00172	.00165	40
45	519631	7265	.01398	.00241	.00105	.00064	.00246	.00179	.00027	.00167	.00000	.00000	.00000	.00168	.00200	45
50	446314	7972	.01786	.00238	.00112	.00108	.00382	.00225	.00038	.00243	.00000	.00000	.00000	.00180	.00261	50
55	343124	8511	.02480	.00246	.00136	.00170	.00643	.00311	.00064	.00355	.00000	.00000	.00000	.00187	.00368	55
60	276478	9374	.03391	.00249	.00150	.00233	.01011	.00431	.00099	.00506	.00000	.00000	.00000	.00210	.00501	60
65	202049	10167	.05032	.00267	.00199	.00330	.01666	.00643	.00155	.00674	.00000	.00000	.00000	.00231	.00868	65
70	141114	10262	.07272	.00243	.00264	.00441	.02485	.00946	.00220	.00856	.00000	.00000	.00000	.00255	.01523	70
75	86212	9386	.10887	.00258	.00341	.00494	.03647	.01457	.00351	.01163	.00000	.00000	.00000	.00309	.02867	75
80	39614	6819	.17214	.00225	.00457	.00520	.05066	.02380	.00591	.01348	.00000	.00000	.00000	.00442	.06144	80
85+	17446	4708	.26986	.00218	.00573	.00562	.05973	.03525	.00791	.01393	.00000	.00000	.00000	.00613	.13338	85+
ALL	9994854	179016														

CRUDE DEATH RATE	.01791	.00173	.00166	.00048	.00267	.00249	.00153	.00124	.00000	.00090	.00000	.00131	.00371
STANDARDIZED RATE (1)	.01882	.00149	.00219	.00038	.00219	.00274	.00217	.00101	.00000	.00144	.00000	.00120	.00401
STANDARDIZED RATE (2)	.02227	.00176	.00193	.00072	.00420	.00306	.00161	.00176	.00000	.00085	.00000	.00141	.00496
GEOMETRIC MEAN	.02265												

LIFE TABLE FOR ALL CAUSES COMBINED

Age (x)	Midyear Population	Deaths During Year	$_nM_x$	$_nq_x$	l_x	$_nd_x$	$_nL_x$	$_nm_x$	$_na_x$	T_x	$_nr_x$	$\overset{\circ}{e}_x$	Age (x)
0	221096	39712	.179614	.161500	100000	16150	89912	.179620	.375344	4564642	.000000	45.646	0
1	822636	16962	.020619	.078426	83850	6576	318960	.020617	1.500000	4474730	.000000	53.366	1
5	997052	4711	.004725	.023358	77274	1805	381858	.004727	2.500000	4155770	.000000	53.780	5
10	911482	2663	.002922	.014496	75469	1094	374609	.002920	2.498667	3773913	.008822	50.006	10
15	881181	4311	.004892	.024175	74375	1798	367673	.004890	2.662912	3399304	-.001020	45.705	15
20	919860	6449	.007011	.034446	72577	2500	356824	.007006	2.575667	3031631	-.010268	41.771	20
25	915609	7211	.007876	.038615	70077	2706	343700	.007873	2.529564	2674807	-.002247	38.170	25
30	834777	7297	.008741	.042808	67371	2884	329742	.008746	2.533663	2331107	.006059	34.601	30
35	765239	7713	.010079	.049188	64487	3172	314620	.010082	2.536255	2001365	.010057	31.035	35
40	653940	7523	.011504	.056038	61315	3436	298141	.011525	2.545414	1686745	.023578	27.509	40
45	519631	7265	.013981	.067745	57879	3921	279841	.014012	2.563494	1388604	.024102	23.991	45
50	446314	7972	.017862	.085826	53958	4631	258602	.017908	2.584035	1108762	.023155	20.549	50
55	343124	8511	.024804	.117360	49327	5789	232622	.024886	2.579389	850161	.023793	17.235	55
60	276478	9374	.033905	.157035	43538	6837	201109	.033997	2.574746	617539	.019092	14.184	60
65	202049	10167	.050319	.224572	36701	8242	163303	.050471	2.548911	416430	.017945	11.347	65
70	141114	10262	.072721	.308233	28459	8772	120399	.072858	2.503871	253127	.011230	8.894	70
75	86212	9386	.108871	.426931	19687	8405	76988	.109173	2.448319	132728	.013395	6.742	75
80	39614	6819	.172136	.592714	11282	6687	38713	.172734	2.353478	55740	.013395	4.941	80
85+	17446	4708	.269861	1.000000	4595	4595	17027	.269861	3.705607	17027	.000000	3.706	85+

NUMBER OF PERSONS DYING (OUT OF 100,000 AT BIRTH) ABOVE AGE X FROM SPECIFIED CAUSES

Age (x)	All Causes	Respiratory T. B.	Other Infec. and Paras.	Neo-plasms	Cardio-vascular	Infl., Pneu., Bronch.	Diar-rheal	Certain Degen-erative	Maternal	Cert. Dis. of Infancy	Motor Vehicle	Other Violence	Other and Unknown	Age (x)
0	100000	8317	8471	3373	19056	13643	6974	8182	0	3672	0	6568	21744	0
1	83850	8194	7345	3367	18722	11189	2971	8110	0	0	0	6441	17511	1
5	77274	8054	5377	3356	18576	9639	1980	8037	0	0	0	6159	16096	5
10	75469	8002	4633	3349	18456	9434	1928	7978	0	0	0	5960	15729	10
15	74375	7943	4362	3341	18335	9353	1909	7928	0	0	0	5725	15479	15
20	72577	7543	4033	3331	18185	9172	1985	7859	0	0	0	5391	15178	20
25	70077	6744	3648	3317	18032	8921	1854	7758	0	0	0	4935	14868	25
30	67371	5846	3310	3296	17841	8632	1822	7615	0	0	0	4480	14529	30
35	64487	4962	3000	3255	17576	8309	1783	7419	0	0	0	4023	14160	35
40	61315	4124	2700	3191	17227	7940	1736	7157	0	0	0	3512	13728	40
45	57879	3426	2404	3080	16744	7521	1678	6792	0	0	0	2998	13236	45
50	53958	2753	2109	2899	16052	7019	1602	6322	0	0	0	2528	12674	50
55	49327	2138	1820	2618	15061	6437	1503	5690	0	0	0	2061	11999	55
60	43538	1564	1502	2220	13558	5712	1354	4862	0	0	0	1627	11139	60
65	36701	1063	1200	1750	11517	4844	1154	3841	0	0	0	1204	10128	65
70	28459	627	874	1210	8787	3790	900	2738	0	0	0	827	8706	70
75	19687	334	557	678	5790	2649	635	1658	0	0	0	520	6866	75
80	11282	136	293	297	2976	1524	363	761	0	0	0	282	4650	80
85+	4595	37	98	96	1017	600	135	237	0	0	0	104	2271	85+

NUMBER OF PERSONS SURVIVING TO AGE X IF SPECIFIED CAUSES WERE ELIMINATED

Age (x)	No Causes	Respiratory T. B.	Other Infec. and Paras.	Neo-plasms	Cardio-vascular	Infl., Pneu., Bronch.	Diar-rheal	Certain Degener-ative	Maternal	Cert. Dis. of Infancy	Motor Vehicle	Other Violence	Other and Unknown	(1) + (2)	(1) + (2) + (5) + (6) + (8)	(1)+(2)+ (5)+(6)+ (8)+part of(9)&(12)	(10) + (11)	Age (x)
		(1)	(2)	(3)	(4)	(5)	(6)	(7)	(8)	(9)	(10)	(11)	(12)					
0	100000	100000	100000	100000	100000	100000	100000	100000	100000	100000	100000	100000	100000	100000	100000	100000	100000	0
1	83850	83963	84886	83855	84156	86125	87552	83916	83850	87276	83850	83966	87812	85000	91202	98855	83966	1
5	77274	77512	80164	77290	77697	80913	81722	77405	77274	80432	77274	77653	82360	80412	89045	98057	77653	5
10	75469	75753	79059	75491	76001	79235	79868	75565	75469	78553	75469	76037	80824	79356	88173	97439	76037	10
15	74375	75753	78195	74405	75021	78171	78730	74608	74375	77414	74375	75170	79918	78551	87395	96743	75170	15
20	72577	74714	76647	72616	73356	76470	76852	72873	72577	75543	72577	73687	78306	77417	86373	95657	73687	20
25	70077	73306	74407	70128	70982	74096	74237	70463	70077	72940	70077	71605	75538	76002	85130	94753	71605	25
30	67371	71579	71886	67441	68431	71535	71403	67883	67371	70124	67371	69297	73367	74393	83718	93484	69297	30
35	64487	69720	69133	64594	65766	68809	68387	65171	64487	67122	64487	66792	70620	72509	82048	91937	66792	35
40	61315	67636	66047	61480	62879	65810	65072	62224	61315	63820	61315	64025	67610	70201	79963	89951	64025	40
45	57879	65171	62656	58143	59839	62560	61465	59098	57879	60244	57879	60960	64350	67380	77368	87391	60960	45
50	53958	62243	58720	54380	56481	58848	57398	55560	53958	56163	53958	57310	60597	63912	74148	84142	57310	50
55	49327	58729	53981	49985	52636	54408	52573	51418	49327	51343	49327	52866	56126	59457	69896	79734	52866	55
60	43538	54330	47973	44499	47992	48779	46552	46202	43538	45317	43538	47100	50466	53496	64085	73591	47100	60
65	36701	48550	40745	37954	42575	42021	39439	39952	36701	38201	36701	40124	43631	46005	56603	65529	40124	65
70	28459	41439	31914	29524	35919	33661	30823	32050	28459	29622	28459	31475	35355	36518	46781	54886	31475	70
75	19687	32565	22372	21166	28181	24429	21561	23197	19687	20491	19687	22054	26434	25912	35214	42260	22054	75
80	11282	22803	13045	12435	19449	15083	12581	14100	11282	11743	11282	12837	17570	15306	22819	28636	12837	80
85+	4595	13237	5454	5203	10306	6955	5283	6161	4595	4783	4595	5355	9851	6485	11286	15767	5355	85+

ADDED YRS OF LIFE																		
TOTAL		2.338	3.244	.452	2.959	3.795	2.876	1.321	.000	1.850	.000	1.819	5.767	5.812	13.945	21.933	1.819	
WORK	9.894	2.049	.913	.210	1.053	.953	.131	.684	.000	.000	.000	1.257	1.166	3.030	4.255	4.997	1.257	

POPULATION, DEATHS, DEATH RATES FOR ALL CAUSES COMBINED, AND SPECIFIED CAUSES

Age Start of Interval	Midyear Population	Deaths During Year	All Causes	Respiratory T.B.	Other Infec. and Paras.	Neoplasms	Cardiovascular	Infl., Pneu., Bronch.	Diarrheal	Certain Degenerative	Maternal	Cert. Dis. of Infancy	Motor Vehicle	Other Violence	Other and Unknown	Age Start of Interval
0	216688	31583	.14575	.00115	.01109	.00006	.00285	.02184	.03845	.00060	.00000	.03092	.00000	.00119	.03762	0
1	811216	15550	.01917	.00038	.00595	.00003	.00040	.00465	.00288	.00021	.00000	.00000	.00000	.00061	.00408	1
5	985781	4566	.00463	.00020	.00207	.00001	.00033	.00059	.00013	.00017	.00000	.00000	.00000	.00061	.00408	5
10	906239	2785	.00307	.00044	.00087	.00002	.00043	.00030	.00006	.00015	.00000	.00000	.00000	.00027	.00086	10
15	922762	4473	.00485	.00160	.00090	.00003	.00042	.00039	.00008	.00020	.00020	.00000	.00000	.00013	.00066	15
20	992196	6619	.00667	.00247	.00085	.00007	.00047	.00048	.00010	.00038	.00054	.00000	.00000	.00021	.00082	20
25	928802	7382	.00795	.00286	.00077	.00016	.00062	.00062	.00016	.00050	.00068	.00000	.00000	.00031	.00101	25
30	800241	6752	.00844	.00256	.00078	.00034	.00082	.00074	.00017	.00063	.00065	.00000	.00000	.00027	.00129	30
35	721132	6678	.00926	.00225	.00073	.00068	.00117	.00093	.00020	.00086	.00055	.00000	.00000	.00028	.00146	35
40	603076	6272	.01040	.00199	.00070	.00125	.00169	.00108	.00024	.00120	.00033	.00000	.00000	.00029	.00159	40
45	497499	6202	.01247	.00165	.00069	.00187	.00264	.00141	.00032	.00143	.00004	.00000	.00000	.00029	.00168	45
50	429200	6970	.01624	.00152	.00084	.00248	.00393	.00207	.00047	.00211	.00001	.00000	.00000	.00035	.00207	50
55	344247	7646	.02221	.00159	.00097	.00327	.00612	.00314	.00071	.00276	.00001	.00000	.00000	.00042	.00239	55
60	287788	8678	.03015	.00165	.00122	.00377	.00893	.00490	.00097	.00363	.00000	.00000	.00000	.00050	.00314	60
65	213705	9469	.04431	.00158	.00162	.00443	.01403	.00769	.00174	.00463	.00000	.00000	.00000	.00055	.00454	65
70	147904	9962	.06735	.00211	.00224	.00506	.02187	.01191	.00278	.00556	.00001	.00000	.00000	.00085	.00734	70
75	92991	9155	.09845	.00241	.00320	.00583	.03122	.01787	.00397	.00670	.00001	.00000	.00000	.00123	.01419	75
80	45012	7286	.16187	.00199	.00453	.00638	.04419	.02917	.00644	.00740	.00000	.00000	.00000	.00201	.02523	80
85+	24113	6173	.25600	.00145	.00506	.00635	.05300	.04118	.00912	.00730	.00000	.00000	.00000	.00420	.05758	85+
ALL	9970592	164201														
CRUDE DEATH RATE			.01647	.00162	.00168	.00087	.00258	.00242	.00142	.00101	.00025	.00067	.00000	.00041	.00354	
STANDARDIZED RATE (1)			.01677	.00144	.00202	.00068	.00203	.00253	.00156	.00083	.00021	.00109	.00000	.00040	.00359	
STANDARDIZED RATE (2)			.02015	.00160	.00173	.00119	.00381	.00310	.00153	.00132	.00021	.00064	.00000	.00049	.00359	
GEOMETRIC MEAN			.02106													

LIFE TABLE FOR ALL CAUSES COMBINED

Age (x)	Midyear Population	Deaths During Year	$_nM_x$	$_nq_x$	l_x	$_nd_x$	$_nL_x$	$_nm_x$	$_na_x$	T_x	$_nr_x$	$\overset{\circ}{e}_x$	Age (x)
0	216688	31583	.145753	.132570	100000	13257	90956	.145752	.317781	4835375	.000000	48.354	0
1	811216	15550	.019169	.073170	86743	6347	331105	.019169	1.500000	4744419	.000000	54.695	1
5	985781	4566	.004632	.022899	80396	1841	397378	.004633	2.500000	4413314	.000000	54.895	5
10	906239	2785	.003073	.015238	78555	1197	389785	.003071	2.501740	4015937	.000000	51.123	10
15	922762	4473	.004847	.023928	77358	1851	382429	.004940	2.643954	3626152	-.009700	46.875	15
20	992196	6619	.006671	.032792	75507	2476	371553	.006664	2.583889	3243723	-.011440	42.959	20
25	928802	7382	.007948	.038997	73031	2848	358124	.007953	2.531089	2872171	.007266	39.328	25
30	800241	6752	.008437	.041335	70183	2901	343704	.008402	2.514363	2514047	.014542	35.821	30
35	721132	6678	.009260	.045302	67282	3048	328865	.009268	2.524606	2170343	.016399	32.257	35
40	603076	6272	.010400	.050768	64234	3261	313152	.010413	2.541398	1841478	.025138	28.668	40
45	497499	6202	.012466	.060617	60973	3696	295880	.012492	2.569050	1528325	.022242	25.066	45
50	429200	6970	.016240	.078321	57277	4486	275562	.016279	2.587355	1232445	.021056	21.517	50
55	344247	7646	.022211	.105643	52791	5577	250463	.022267	2.580763	956883	.018730	18.126	55
60	287788	8678	.030154	.140806	47214	6648	219984	.030220	2.580287	706420	.015949	14.962	60
65	213705	9469	.044309	.200636	40566	8139	183052	.044463	2.569982	486437	.020694	11.991	65
70	147904	9962	.067355	.289327	32427	9382	138880	.067555	2.521340	303385	.016092	9.356	70
75	92991	9155	.098450	.394880	23045	9100	92177	.098723	2.467285	164504	.015189	7.138	75
80	45012	7286	.161868	.570312	13945	7953	48921	.162568	2.384137	72327	.015189	5.187	80
85+	24113	6173	.256003	1.000000	5992	5992	23406	.256003	3.906204	23406	.000000	3.906	85+

NUMBER OF PERSONS DYING (OUT OF 100,000 AT BIRTH) ABOVE AGE X FROM SPECIFIED CAUSES

Age (x)	All Causes	Respiratory T.B.	Other Infec. and Paras.	Neoplasms	Cardiovascular	Infl., Pneu., Bronch.	Diarrheal	Certain Degenerative	Maternal	Cert. Dis. of Infancy	Motor Vehicle	Other Violence	Other and Unknown	Age (x)
0	100000	7957	8000	6265	19740	15304	7066	6857	1045	2812	0	2406	22548	0
1	86743	7852	6992	6260	19481	13317	3569	6802	1045	0	0	2297	19128	1
5	80396	7727	5021	6251	19349	11779	2616	6734	1045	0	0	2097	17777	5
10	78555	7648	4197	6246	19218	11543	2564	6667	1045	0	0	1990	17437	10
15	77358	7475	3859	6237	19048	11426	2540	6608	1044	0	0	1940	17181	15
20	75507	6864	3516	6227	18888	11276	2510	6532	969	0	0	1858	16867	20
25	73031	5946	3199	6200	18713	11099	2474	6391	769	0	0	1745	16495	25
30	70183	4921	2922	6142	18490	10876	2418	6210	525	0	0	1648	16031	30
35	67282	4040	2654	6026	18208	10621	2359	5993	303	0	0	1550	15528	35
40	64234	3301	2415	5800	17821	10316	2292	5708	122	0	0	1454	15005	40
45	60973	2690	2196	5408	17290	9978	2218	5333	20	0	0	1364	14476	45
50	57277	2202	1991	4852	16507	9560	2124	4910	9	0	0	1259	13863	50
55	52791	1784	1759	4168	15421	8987	1994	4326	7	0	0	1142	13203	55
60	47214	1384	1515	3348	13883	8198	1816	3634	6	0	0	1017	12413	60
65	40566	1021	1247	2518	11913	7117	1603	2834	6	0	0	895	11412	65
70	32427	658	950	1706	9234	5704	1283	1985	5	0	0	740	10062	70
75	23045	365	639	1002	6289	4045	856	1155	4	0	0	568	8082	75
80	13945	143	343	464	3404	2393	529	537	3	0	0	382	5747	80
85+	5992	34	118	149	1241	964	214	171	0	0	0	176	2925	85+

NUMBER OF PERSONS SURVIVING TO AGE X IF SPECIFIED CAUSES WERE ELIMINATED

Age (x)	No Causes	Respiratory T.B. (1)	Other Infec. and Paras. (2)	Neoplasms (3)	Cardiovascular (4)	Infl., Pneu., Bronch. (5)	Diarrheal (6)	Certain Degenerative (7)	Maternal (8)	Cert. Dis. of Infancy (9)	Motor Vehicle (10)	Other Violence (11)	Other and Unknown (12)	(1)+(2)	(1)+(2)+(5)+(6)+(8)	(1)+(2)+(5)+(6)+(8)+part of (9)&(12)	(10)+(11)	Age (x)
0	100000	100000	100000	100000	100000	100000	100000	100000	100000	100000	100000	100000	100000	100000	100000	100000	100000	0
1	86743	86841	87686	86748	86584	88612	90059	86794	86743	89400	86743	86844	85985	87785	93104	99137	86844	1
5	80396	80607	83211	80409	80747	83654	84427	80509	80396	82858	80396	80683	84760	83429	91163	98522	80683	5
10	78555	78839	82153	78573	79028	81982	82548	78732	78555	80961	78555	78942	83175	82450	90421	98052	78942	10
15	77358	77811	81252	77384	77994	80854	81315	77591	77359	79727	77358	77789	82177	81728	89792	97593	77789	15
20	75507	76559	79665	75543	76287	79074	79401	75810	75582	77820	75507	76009	80540	80774	89041	97090	76009	20
25	73031	74969	77382	73092	73560	76664	76834	73463	73301	75268	73031	73628	78290	79435	88054	96390	73628	25
30	70183	73084	74652	70299	71257	73904	73896	70777	70683	72332	70183	70853	75727	77738	86804	95495	70853	30
35	67282	70967	71846	67507	68632	71113	70902	68066	67980	69343	67282	68021	73130	75781	85281	94303	68021	35
40	64234	68517	68841	64671	65910	68207	67759	65265	65079	66060	64234	65034	70374	73431	83334	92596	65034	40
45	60973	65676	65575	61774	63097	65095	64395	62324	61876	62840	60973	61822	67369	70632	80819	90175	61822	45
50	57277	62205	61814	58578	60064	61583	60588	58967	58136	59031	57277	58177	63945	67132	77457	86822	58177	50
55	52791	57770	57213	54666	56464	57355	55975	54929	53584	54408	52791	53735	59647	62609	73208	82366	53735	55
60	47214	52081	51419	49699	52080	52113	50240	49811	47924	48660	47214	48179	54197	56720	67621	76486	48179	60
65	40566	45119	44450	43516	46806	45895	43377	43585	41176	41808	40566	41510	47643	49439	60709	69206	41510	65
70	32427	36427	35822	35567	40168	38142	34981	35661	32916	33420	32427	33323	39530	40241	51831	59868	33323	70
75	23045	26163	25747	25928	31892	28794	25213	26117	23393	23751	23045	23831	30203	29230	40563	48085	23831	75
80	13945	16024	15836	16157	22619	19087	15568	16345	14157	14372	13945	14570	20815	18197	28230	35144	14570	80
85+	5992	6966	6969	7179	12229	9546	6917	7302	6085	6176	5992	6399	12070	8101	15130	21271	6399	85+

ADDED YRS OF LIFE

	No Causes	(1)	(2)	(3)	(4)	(5)	(6)	(7)	(8)	(9)	(10)	(11)	(12)	(1)+(2)	(1)+(2)+(5)+(6)+(8)	(1)+(2)+(5)+(6)+(8)+part of (9)&(12)	(10)+(11)
TOTAL		2.473	3.199	1.017	3.162	3.788	2.777	1.257	.372	1.471	.000	.604	5.763	5.887	14.406	22.106	.604
WORK	9.413	2.071	.754	.555	1.120	.781	.171	.685	.386	.000	.000	.268	1.313	2.878	4.379	5.307	.268

POPULATION, DEATHS, DEATH RATES FOR ALL CAUSES COMBINED, AND SPECIFIED CAUSES

Age Start of Interval	Midyear Population	Deaths During Year	All Causes	Respiratory T.B.	Other Infec. and Paras.	Neoplasms	Cardiovascular	Infl., Pneu., Bronch.	Diarrheal	Certain Degenerative	Maternal	Cert. Dis. of Infancy	Motor Vehicle	Other Violence	Other and Unknown	Age Start of Interval
0	521945	76290	.14616	.00079	.01063	.00008	.00202	.02277	.04187	.00075	.00000	.03797	.00000	.00152	.02778	0
1	1964987	28946	.01473	.00024	.00460	.00006	.00022	.00337	.00256	.00021	.00000	.00000	.00001	.00091	.00215	1
5	2260512	8163	.00361	.00008	.00146	.00003	.00026	.00038	.00010	.00013	.00000	.00000	.00005	.00052	.00062	5
10	2157475	5239	.00243	.00013	.00059	.00003	.00032	.00019	.00003	.00012	.00000	.00000	.00003	.00052	.00048	10
15	2222736	8844	.00398	.00065	.00072	.00004	.00035	.00034	.00002	.00017	.00000	.00000	.00001	.00092	.00056	15
20	2397351	13731	.00573	.00164	.00081	.00006	.00034	.00044	.00002	.00023	.00000	.00000	.00002	.00162	.00056	20
25	2324456	14966	.00644	.00151	.00077	.00008	.00044	.00050	.00002	.00036	.00000	.00000	.00002	.00172	.00062	25
30	2045875	15509	.00758	.00216	.00079	.00013	.00071	.00068	.00003	.00055	.00000	.00000	.00002	.00171	.00080	30
35	1887488	17328	.00918	.00229	.00086	.00023	.00105	.00094	.00004	.00085	.00000	.00000	.00003	.00190	.00099	35
40	1616494	17617	.01090	.00231	.00090	.00045	.00162	.00115	.00005	.00129	.00000	.00000	.00002	.00189	.00121	40
45	1372795	18589	.01354	.00221	.00100	.00081	.00249	.00145	.00007	.00193	.00000	.00000	.00004	.00207	.00149	45
50	1171527	20272	.01730	.00212	.00108	.00132	.00395	.00187	.00011	.00279	.00000	.00000	.00003	.00205	.00198	50
55	831385	20182	.02428	.00228	.00127	.00215	.00685	.00253	.00015	.00422	.00000	.00000	.00003	.00226	.00254	55
60	658306	22641	.03439	.00217	.00121	.00325	.01150	.00360	.00029	.00616	.00000	.00000	.00005	.00245	.00372	60
65	491796	24268	.04935	.00216	.00154	.00435	.01918	.00504	.00045	.00835	.00000	.00000	.00007	.00259	.00558	65
70	327264	23838	.07284	.00191	.00174	.00561	.03069	.00775	.00085	.01150	.00000	.00000	.00006	.00302	.00970	70
75	193905	21151	.10908	.00181	.00240	.00649	.04788	.01222	.00163	.01508	.00000	.00000	.00008	.00379	.01770	75
80	89263	14924	.16719	.00162	.00325	.00744	.06917	.01996	.00307	.01898	.00000	.00000	.00010	.00547	.03813	80
85+	42411	10851	.25585	.00118	.00434	.00776	.09297	.03270	.00535	.02318	.00000	.00000	.00009	.00943	.07885	85+
ALL	24577971	383349														

	All Causes	Respiratory T.B.	Other Infec. and Paras.	Neoplasms	Cardiovascular	Infl., Pneu., Bronch.	Diarrheal	Certain Degenerative	Maternal	Cert. Dis. of Infancy	Motor Vehicle	Other Violence	Other and Unknown
CRUDE DEATH RATE	.01560	.00143	.00146	.00061	.00291	.00191	.00123	.00142	.00000	.00081	.00003	.00153	.00227
STANDARDIZED RATE (1)	.01619	.00120	.00174	.00049	.00236	.00214	.00151	.00116	.00000	.00134	.00003	.00137	.00245
STANDARDIZED RATE (2)	.02031	.00144	.00153	.00054	.00497	.00245	.00127	.00214	.00000	.00079	.00003	.00164	.00311
GEOMETRIC MEAN	.02032												

LIFE TABLE FOR ALL CAUSES COMBINED

Age (x)	Midyear Population	Deaths During Year	$_nM_x$	$_nq_x$	l_x	$_nd_x$	$_nL_x$	$_nm_x$	$_na_x$	T_x	$_nr_x$	$\overset{\circ}{e}_x$	Age (x)
0	521945	76290	.146165	.132920	100000	13292	90941	.146160	.318480	4949255	.000000	49.493	0
1	1964987	28946	.014731	.056834	86708	4928	334512	.014732	1.500000	4858314	.000000	56.031	1
5	2260512	8163	.003611	.017889	81780	1463	405243	.003610	2.500000	4523802	.000000	55.317	5
10	2157475	5239	.002428	.012077	80317	970	399180	.002430	2.521048	4118560	.001347	51.279	10
15	2222736	8844	.003979	.019673	79347	1561	393087	.003971	2.663357	3719379	-.010812	46.875	15
20	2397351	13731	.005728	.028206	77786	2194	383619	.005719	2.575288	3326292	-.013478	42.762	20
25	2324456	14966	.006438	.031696	75592	2396	372081	.006439	2.546345	2942673	.003235	38.928	25
30	2045875	15509	.007581	.037256	73196	2727	359323	.007589	2.558825	2570592	.010939	35.119	30
35	1887488	17328	.009180	.044928	70469	3166	344607	.009187	2.555999	2211269	.012229	31.379	35
40	1616494	17617	.010858	.053163	67303	3578	327782	.010916	2.559216	1866661	.015721	27.735	40
45	1372795	18589	.013541	.065641	63725	4183	308456	.013561	2.568880	1538880	.016514	24.149	45
50	1171527	20272	.017304	.083319	59542	4961	285746	.017362	2.588398	1230424	.027912	20.665	50
55	831385	20182	.024275	.115205	54581	6288	257753	.024395	2.590284	944678	.034544	17.308	55
60	658306	22641	.034393	.159154	48293	7686	222807	.034496	2.572507	686925	.020867	14.224	60
65	491796	24268	.049346	.220725	40607	8963	181064	.049502	2.548719	464118	.019629	11.430	65
70	327264	23838	.072840	.309127	31644	9782	133846	.073084	2.508242	283054	.018657	8.945	70
75	193905	21151	.109079	.427683	21862	9350	85411	.109471	2.443962	149208	.017654	6.825	75
80	89263	14924	.167191	.580802	12512	7267	43297	.167840	2.349262	63797	.017654	5.099	80
85+	42411	10851	.255853	1.000000	5245	5245	20500	.255853	3.908488	20500	.000000	3.908	85+

NUMBER OF PERSONS DYING (OUT OF 100,000 AT BIRTH) ABOVE AGE X FROM SPECIFIED CAUSES

Age (x)	All Causes	Respiratory T.B.	Other Infec. and Paras.	Neoplasms	Cardiovascular	Infl., Pneu., Bronch.	Diarrheal	Certain Degenerative	Maternal	Cert. Dis. of Infancy	Motor Vehicle	Other Violence	Other and Unknown	Age (x)
0	100000	7502	7250	4884	24940	11844	5643	10965	0	3453	151	8362	15006	0
1	86708	7430	6284	4877	24757	9773	1836	10898	0	0	151	8224	12478	1
5	81780	7342	4746	4857	24682	8645	847	10828	0	0	149	7921	11763	5
10	80317	7310	4156	4846	24579	8493	808	10774	0	0	131	7709	11511	10
15	79347	7259	3922	4834	24451	8419	797	10727	0	0	120	7500	11318	15
20	77786	6926	3640	4819	24314	8285	790	10659	0	0	115	7140	11098	20
25	75592	6299	3330	4798	24182	8118	784	10573	0	0	107	6519	10882	25
30	73196	5588	3045	4768	24018	7931	775	10439	0	0	99	5880	10653	30
35	70469	4811	2761	4719	23762	7688	765	10242	0	0	91	5266	10364	35
40	67303	4023	2465	4641	23399	7365	751	9947	0	0	80	4611	10021	40
45	63725	3266	2170	4491	22867	6986	734	9525	0	0	73	3990	9623	45
50	59542	2584	1861	4242	22096	6535	712	8928	0	0	62	3353	9165	50
55	54581	1979	1551	3863	20961	6002	681	8127	0	0	53	2767	8597	55
60	48293	1392	1222	3306	19181	5346	642	7035	0	0	45	2185	7939	60
65	40607	909	952	2580	16607	4541	577	5658	0	0	35	1639	7109	65
70	31644	518	673	1790	13121	3626	496	4134	0	0	22	1170	6094	70
75	21862	263	439	1038	8997	2585	382	2591	0	0	13	765	4789	75
80	12512	108	234	482	4893	1537	242	1300	0	0	6	441	3269	80
85+	5245	24	89	159	1906	670	110	475	0	0	2	193	1617	85+

NUMBER OF PERSONS SURVIVING TO AGE X IF SPECIFIED CAUSES WERE ELIMINATED

Age (x)	No Causes	Respiratory T.B. (1)	Other Infec. and Paras. (2)	Neoplasms (3)	Cardiovascular (4)	Infl., Pneu., Bronch. (5)	Diarrheal (6)	Certain Degenerative (7)	Maternal (8)	Cert. Dis. of Infancy (9)	Motor Vehicle (10)	Other Violence (11)	Other and Unknown (12)	(1)+(2)	(1)+(2)+(5)+(6)+(8)	(1)+(2)+(5)+(6)+(8)+part of(9)&(12)	(10)+(11)	Age (x)
0	100000	100000	100000	100000	100000	100000	100000	100000	100000	100000	100000	100000	100000	100000	100000	100000	100000	0
1	86708	86775	87611	86715	86878	88656	90323	86770	86708	89981	86708	86836	89092	87679	93387	99232	86836	1
5	81780	81929	84155	81806	82014	84745	86196	81907	81780	84617	81782	82196	84745	84308	92083	98587	82198	5
10	80317	80495	83253	80353	80649	83385	84695	80495	80317	83349	80337	80937	83488	83438	91347	98004	80957	10
15	79347	79574	82489	79395	79803	82455	83684	79570	79347	82342	79377	80169	82680	82725	90663	97382	80200	15
20	77786	78340	81157	77847	78369	80970	82045	78072	77786	80722	77781	78953	81280	81735	89739	96541	78989	20
25	75592	76755	79187	75672	76290	78858	79737	75592	75592	78445	75634	77350	79210	80406	88479	95337	77393	25
30	73196	75036	76972	73303	74035	76551	77219	73680	73196	75955	73244	75545	76936	78907	87059	93965	75594	30
35	70469	73026	74397	70621	71532	73949	74352	71130	70469	73129	70523	73354	74365	77097	85362	92334	73411	35
40	67303	70547	71361	67524	68675	70959	71026	68226	67303	69943	67366	70728	71382	74401	83226	90250	70794	40
45	63725	67573	67872	64082	65559	67268	65017	63725	63725	66130	63791	67605	67999	71970	80562	87603	67675	45
50	59542	63839	63735	60118	62028	63600	62875	61342	59542	61789	59614	63823	64010	68335	77077	84058	63901	50
55	54581	59143	58743	55477	58005	58853	57667	57027	54581	56641	54656	59109	59264	63652	72515	79348	59190	55
60	48293	52928	52309	49621	53135	52742	51063	51541	48293	50116	48367	53112	53112	57329	66201	72704	52974	60
65	40607	44989	44251	42413	47355	45160	42959	44705	40607	42140	40678	45024	45503	49027	57735	63688	45103	65
70	31644	35439	34751	33784	40669	36099	33584	36344	31644	32838	31711	35544	36477	38920	47121	52288	35620	70
75	21862	24718	24221	24010	32845	25942	23303	26612	21862	22687	21916	24933	26481	27385	34637	38806	24994	75
80	12512	14275	14032	14199	24018	15807	13449	16442	12512	12984	12548	14546	16609	16009	21740	24804	14588	80
85+	5245	6045	5985	6187	14393	7350	5728	7607	5245	5443	5263	6281	8484	6897	10556	12575	6302	85+

ADDED YRS OF LIFE

	No Causes	(1)	(2)	(3)	(4)	(5)	(6)	(7)	(8)	(9)	(10)	(11)	(12)	(1)+(2)	(1)+(2)+(5)+(6)+(8)	(1)+(2)+(5)+(6)+(8)+part of(9)&(12)	(10)+(11)
TOTAL		2.060	2.792	.655	3.758	3.182	2.747	1.666	.000	1.856	.042	2.292	3.667	5.016	11.942	17.289	2.337
WORK	8.974	1.709	.783	.270	1.055	.722	.034	.740	.000	.000	.021	1.547	.838	2.541	3.378	3.822	1.569

POPULATION, DEATHS, DEATH RATES FOR ALL CAUSES COMBINED, AND SPECIFIED CAUSES

Age Start of Interval	Midyear Population	Deaths During Year	All Causes	Respiratory T. B.	Other Infec. and Paras.	Neo-plasms	Cardio-vascular	Infl., Pneu., Bronch.	Diar-rheal	Certain Degen-erative	Maternal	Cert. Dis. of Infancy	Motor Vehicle	Other Violence	Other and Unknown	Age Start of Interval
0	508284	60136	.11831	.00065	.00971	.00006	.00152	.01803	.03485	.00053	.00000	.02918	.00001	.00122	.02255	0
1	1923032	25966	.01350	.00023	.00450	.00004	.00022	.00312	.00263	.00019	.00000	.00000	.00001	.00072	.00184	1
5	2225082	7522	.00338	.00011	.00150	.00003	.00029	.00038	.00009	.00012	.00000	.00000	.00002	.00027	.00058	5
10	2128134	4956	.00233	.00002	.00067	.00002	.00035	.00015	.00003	.00015	.00000	.00000	.00002	.00027	.00045	10
15	2222983	7894	.00355	.00111	.00065	.00004	.00036	.00022	.00002	.00020	.00023	.00000	.00000	.00012	.00050	15
20	2300242	11513	.00501	.00178	.00063	.00006	.00038	.00029	.00003	.00025	.00065	.00000	.00001	.00028	.00064	20
25	2099471	12332	.00587	.00199	.00057	.00016	.00048	.00038	.00004	.00039	.00081	.00000	.00000	.00026	.00078	25
30	1834289	11921	.00650	.00188	.00051	.00038	.00070	.00046	.00004	.00054	.00081	.00000	.00000	.00026	.00078	30
35	1701742	12601	.00740	.00165	.00055	.00069	.00102	.00057	.00005	.00075	.00072	.00000	.00000	.00027	.00090	35
40	1435557	12312	.00858	.00144	.00053	.00129	.00155	.00068	.00008	.00109	.00039	.00000	.00001	.00031	.00121	40
45	1224877	12855	.01049	.00120	.00055	.00202	.00241	.00088	.00010	.00152	.00005	.00000	.00000	.00034	.00143	45
50	1041743	14589	.01400	.00115	.00058	.00270	.00376	.00126	.00013	.00225	.00000	.00000	.00001	.00042	.00175	50
55	760955	15043	.01977	.00118	.00067	.00363	.00605	.00201	.00024	.00333	.00000	.00000	.00001	.00048	.00217	55
60	632102	17959	.02841	.00121	.00075	.00445	.00998	.00337	.00032	.00456	.00000	.00000	.00002	.00061	.00312	60
65	485778	21043	.04332	.00138	.00113	.00576	.01635	.00557	.00067	.00643	.00000	.00000	.00001	.00103	.00499	65
70	335415	21954	.06545	.00160	.00155	.00683	.02640	.00925	.00121	.00876	.00000	.00000	.00002	.00169	.00815	70
75	207661	20536	.09889	.00161	.00188	.00825	.04084	.01483	.00206	.01128	.00000	.00000	.00002	.00310	.01503	75
80	102132	15836	.15505	.00132	.00307	.00878	.06258	.02473	.00361	.01395	.00000	.00000	.00000	.00570	.03130	80
85+	54056	13291	.24587	.00081	.00388	.00869	.08328	.03946	.00618	.01670	.00000	.00000	.00002	.01214	.07470	85+
ALL	23223535	320259														

	All Causes	Respiratory T. B.	Other Infec. and Paras.	Neo-plasms	Cardio-vascular	Infl., Pneu., Bronch.	Diar-rheal	Certain Degen-erative	Maternal	Cert. Dis. of Infancy	Motor Vehicle	Other Violence	Other and Unknown
CRUDE DEATH RATE	.01379	.00115	.00126	.00101	.00278	.00176	.00112	.00117	.00030	.00064	.00001	.00046	.00213
STANDARDIZED RATE (1)	.01380	.00101	.00154	.00080	.00213	.00185	.00165	.00054	.00026	.00103	.00001	.00043	.00215
STANDARDIZED RATE (2)	.01760	.00114	.00129	.00143	.00441	.00232	.00115	.00168	.00026	.00060	.00001	.00057	.00274
GEOMETRIC MEAN	.01766												

LIFE TABLE FOR ALL CAUSES COMBINED

Age (x)	Midyear Population	Deaths During Year	$_nM_x$	$_nq_x$	l_x	$_nd_x$	$_nL_x$	$_nm_x$	$_na_x$	T_x	$_nr_x$	$\overset{\circ}{e}_x$	Age (x)
0	508284	60136	.118312	.108920	100000	10892	92061	.118313	.271130	5313351	.000000	53.134	0
1	1923032	25966	.013503	.052251	89108	4656	344792	.013504	1.500000	5221290	.000000	58.595	1
5	2225082	7522	.003381	.016755	84452	1415	418723	.003379	2.500000	4876498	.000000	57.743	5
10	2128134	4956	.002329	.011573	83037	961	412788	.002328	2.506070	4457775	-.000195	53.684	10
15	2222983	7894	.003551	.017581	82076	1443	406987	.003546	2.648995	4044987	-.010202	49.283	15
20	2300242	11513	.005005	.024717	80633	1993	398356	.005003	2.587285	3638000	-.004740	45.118	20
25	2099471	12332	.005874	.028967	78640	2278	387599	.005877	2.541246	3239643	-.012208	41.196	25
30	1834289	11921	.006499	.032005	76362	2444	375766	.006504	2.535120	2852044	-.013803	37.349	30
35	1701742	12601	.007405	.036392	73918	2690	362980	.007411	2.542828	2476258	-.014817	33.500	35
40	1435557	12312	.008576	.042076	71228	2997	348816	.008592	2.556167	2113278	-.023015	29.669	40
45	1224877	12855	.010495	.051267	68231	3498	332703	.010514	2.583738	1764682	-.019584	25.860	45
50	1041743	14589	.014004	.068018	64733	4403	313120	.014062	2.605089	1431759	-.030091	22.118	50
55	760955	15043	.019769	.094795	60330	5719	287952	.019861	2.604913	1118639	-.032498	18.542	55
60	632102	17959	.028412	.133361	54611	7283	255955	.028944	2.602579	830687	-.018600	15.211	60
65	485778	21043	.043318	.166607	47328	9305	214098	.043461	2.577467	575092	-.018987	12.151	65
70	335415	21954	.065453	.282540	38023	10743	163572	.065677	2.529321	360994	-.018248	9.494	70
75	207661	20536	.098892	.396518	27280	10817	109016	.099224	2.468414	197421	-.016739	7.237	75
80	102132	15836	.155054	.552937	16463	9103	58471	.155683	2.380694	88405	-.016739	5.370	80
85+	54056	13291	.245875	1.000000	7360	7360	29934	.245875	4.067113	29934	.000000	4.067	85+

NUMBER OF PERSONS DYING (OUT OF 100,000 AT BIRTH) ABOVE AGE X FROM SPECIFIED CAUSES

Age (x)	All Causes	Respiratory T. B.	Other Infec. and Paras.	Neoplasms	Cardiovascular	Infl., Pneu., Bronch.	Diarrheal	Certain Degenerative	Maternal	Cert. Dis. of Infancy	Motor Vehicle	Other Violence	Other and Unknown	Age (x)
0	100000	6300	6415	8729	26932	13049	5458	10132	1392	2687	42	3225	15639	0
1	89108	6240	5521	8724	26792	11390	2249	10083	1392	0	42	3112	13563	1
5	84452	6162	3570	8709	26715	10313	1341	10017	1392	0	40	2864	12929	5
10	83037	6116	3344	8699	26592	10156	1302	9966	1392	0	32	2753	12685	10
15	82076	5993	3067	8691	26431	10076	1290	9904	1390	0	30	2702	12502	15
20	80633	5541	2802	8676	26286	9986	1282	9824	1295	0	28	2612	12301	20
25	78640	4831	2550	8652	26135	9872	1270	9724	1035	0	26	2500	12045	25
30	76362	4060	2329	8590	25948	9723	1253	9571	722	0	25	2399	11742	30
35	73918	3355	2135	8448	25685	9550	1237	9368	416	0	23	2298	11403	35
40	71228	2756	1937	8197	25316	9344	1218	9094	156	0	20	2183	11007	40
45	68231	2254	1753	7745	24773	9105	1190	8713	20	0	18	2078	10582	45
50	64733	1857	1570	7072	23967	8810	1158	8207	4	0	17	1965	10106	50
55	60330	1498	1386	6224	22782	8415	1116	7501	4	0	15	1833	9556	55
60	54611	1158	1194	5175	21028	7832	1048	6538	4	0	12	1653	8929	60
65	47328	847	1001	4035	18467	6967	965	5369	4	0	7	1536	8130	65
70	38023	550	759	2800	14953	5769	820	3989	4	0	6	1315	7058	70
75	27280	289	505	1682	10619	4251	621	2553	4	0	3	1038	5715	75
80	16463	113	299	781	6152	2628	396	1321	4	0	1	698	4070	80
85+	7360	24	116	260	2493	1181	185	500	0	0	1	363	2237	85+

NUMBER OF PERSONS SURVIVING TO AGE X IF SPECIFIED CAUSES WERE ELIMINATED

Age (x)	No Causes	Respiratory T. B. (1)	Other Infec. and Paras. (2)	Neoplasms (3)	Cardiovascular (4)	Infl., Pneu., Bronch. (5)	Diarrheal (6)	Certain Degenerative (7)	Maternal (8)	Cert. Dis. of Infancy (9)	Motor Vehicle (10)	Other Violence (11)	Other and Unknown (12)	(1) + (2)	(1) + (2) + (5) + (6) + (8)	(1)+(2)+ (5)+(6)+ (8)+part of(9)&(12)	(10) + (11)	Age (x)
0	100000	100000	100000	100000	100000	100000	100000	100000	100000	100000	100000	100000	100000	100000	100000	100000	100000	0
1	89108	89165	89955	89113	89240	90687	92188	89154	89108	91679	89108	89215	91088	90013	94774	99424	89215	1
5	84452	84582	86793	84471	84652	87022	88290	84560	84452	86889	84454	84795	86562	86926	93642	98884	84797	5
10	83037	83210	85979	83066	83356	85725	86851	83194	83037	85433	82047	83485	85754	86158	93032	98453	83495	10
15	82076	82370	85270	82112	82552	84815	85858	82293	82078	84445	82088	82570	84950	85575	92508	98035	82582	15
20	80633	81373	84044	80684	81246	83416	84357	80926	80729	82960	80646	81208	83663	84815	91904	97572	81221	20
25	78640	80072	82226	78713	79388	81470	82284	79025	78992	80909	78655	79312	81858	83724	91162	97026	79327	25
30	76362	78530	80072	76494	77275	79263	75918	76887	77014	78566	76378	77115	79798	82345	90218	96301	77131	30
35	73918	76733	77710	74186	75064	76903	77377	74628	74853	76051	73935	74747	77593	80669	88965	95248	74765	35
40	71228	74553	75086	71735	72701	74315	74581	72184	72388	73283	71247	72141	75179	78591	87254	93702	72161	40
45	68231	71931	72117	69164	70187	71433	71471	69526	69477	70200	68252	69210	72456	76028	84897	91406	69231	45
50	64733	68652	68608	66286	67402	68072	67840	66466	65930	66601	64754	65774	69235	72761	81670	88123	65794	50
55	60330	64350	64130	62621	64021	63844	63268	62649	61446	62071	60351	61429	65096	68403	77317	83613	61451	55
60	54611	58595	58245	57729	59151	58383	57338	57669	55621	56187	54633	55742	59572	62494	71444	77457	55764	60
65	47328	51091	50669	51161	54459	51465	49773	51139	48203	48694	47352	48457	52444	54697	63708	69314	48481	65
70	38023	41332	40939	42310	47526	42530	40124	42438	38726	39120	38043	39133	43210	44502	53500	58544	39154	70
75	27280	29892	29603	31416	38590	31981	28966	31824	27785	28067	27297	28319	32220	32437	41125	45450	28336	75
80	16463	18186	18036	19765	28986	20821	17665	20333	16768	16938	16475	17365	21074	19924	27540	31016	17377	80
85+	7360	8194	8195	9253	17910	10579	8046	9775	7499	7572	7365	7997	11079	9124	14609	17178	8002	85+

ADDED YRS OF LIFE		(1)	(2)	(3)	(4)	(5)	(6)	(7)	(8)	(9)	(10)	(11)	(12)				
TOTAL		1.966	2.693	1.374	4.107	3.044	2.556	1.617	.517	1.526	.013	.736	3.688	4.788	11.909	16.840	.750
WORK	7.723	1.560	.578	.640	1.087	.511	.053	.693	.500	.000	.005	.281	.910	2.167	3.322	3.874	.286

POPULATION, DEATHS, DEATH RATES FOR ALL CAUSES COMBINED, AND SPECIFIED CAUSES

Age Start of Interval	Midyear Population	Deaths During Year	All Causes	Respiratory T. B.	Other Infec. and Paras.	Neoplasms	Cardiovascular	Infl., Pneu., Bronch.	Diarrheal	Certain Degenerative	Maternal	Cert. Dis. of Infancy	Motor Vehicle	Other Violence	Other and Unknown	Age Start of Interval
0	940656	97176	.10331	.00039	.00861	.00007	.00102	.01893	.01807	.00040	.00000	.03638	.00002	.00127	.01816	0
1	3708708	38056	.01026	.00013	.00305	.00006	.00016	.00311	.00151	.00012	.00000	.00000	.00011	.00075	.00125	1
5	4555314	14218	.00312	.00007	.00059	.00003	.00018	.00053	.00007	.00005	.00000	.00000	.00024	.00040	.00053	5
10	4182062	10226	.00245	.00010	.00046	.00002	.00026	.00039	.00002	.00010	.00000	.00000	.00015	.00049	.00046	10
15	3750618	15506	.00413	.00061	.00048	.00004	.00030	.00097	.00001	.00014	.00000	.00000	.00011	.00088	.00059	15
20	3640777	19706	.00541	.00133	.00048	.00006	.00029	.00115	.00002	.00018	.00000	.00000	.00013	.00118	.00060	20
25	3807819	22397	.00588	.00143	.00043	.00008	.00034	.00149	.00002	.00024	.00000	.00000	.00013	.00113	.00058	25
30	3438191	24028	.00699	.00148	.00051	.00015	.00050	.00198	.00003	.00033	.00000	.00000	.00013	.00118	.00058	30
35	3425282	26584	.00776	.00149	.00067	.00024	.00076	.00190	.00005	.00048	.00000	.00000	.00012	.00125	.00080	35
40	2847896	24798	.00871	.00147	.00078	.00044	.00124	.00167	.00005	.00076	.00000	.00000	.00012	.00121	.00097	40
45	2527203	27704	.01096	.00150	.00084	.00083	.00207	.00173	.00007	.00124	.00000	.00000	.00013	.00131	.00125	45
50	2159009	31255	.01448	.00152	.00092	.00143	.00353	.00199	.00008	.00192	.00000	.00000	.00016	.00137	.00157	50
55	1603370	33267	.02075	.00156	.00101	.00246	.00624	.00245	.00010	.00312	.00000	.00000	.00017	.00150	.00213	55
60	1339456	39025	.02913	.00155	.00105	.00353	.01035	.00317	.00014	.00457	.00000	.00000	.00023	.00159	.00295	60
65	901619	40434	.04485	.00171	.00128	.00501	.01775	.00479	.00022	.00746	.00000	.00000	.00029	.00195	.00438	65
70	594506	40952	.06888	.00163	.00134	.00703	.02987	.00723	.00043	.01131	.00000	.00000	.00032	.00235	.00738	70
75	352920	36867	.10446	.00156	.00165	.00854	.04889	.01083	.00076	.01656	.00000	.00000	.00041	.00292	.01195	75
80	156658	25177	.16071	.00132	.00207	.00935	.07603	.01729	.00160	.02426	.00000	.00000	.00045	.00515	.02319	80
85+	74330	18760	.25239	.00121	.00309	.00996	.11172	.02887	.00221	.03421	.00000	.00000	.00048	.00927	.05137	85+
ALL	44006394	586136														

CRUDE DEATH RATE			.01332	.00099	.00108	.00072	.00279	.00225	.00058	.00120	.00000	.00078	.00015	.00109	.00169	
STANDARDIZED RATE (1)			.01322	.00065	.00125	.00056	.00217	.00236	.00087	.00094	.00000	.00128	.00015	.00101	.00177	
STANDARDIZED RATE (2)			.01762	.00103	.00111	.00110	.00484	.00265	.00059	.00193	.00000	.00075	.00016	.00120	.00224	
GEOMETRIC MEAN			.01793													

LIFE TABLE FOR ALL CAUSES COMBINED

Age (x)	Midyear Population	Deaths During Year	$_nM_x$	$_nq_x$	l_x	$_nd_x$	$_nL_x$	$_nm_x$	$_na_x$	T_x	$_nr_x$	$\overset{\circ}{e}_x$	Age (x)
0	940656	97176	.103307	.095840	100000	9584	92770	.103309	.245621	5400968	.000000	54.010	0
1	3708708	38056	.010261	.040015	90416	3618	352619	.010260	1.500000	5308198	.000000	58.709	1
5	4555314	14218	.003121	.015473	86798	1343	430633	.003119	2.500000	4955579	.000000	57.093	5
10	4182062	10226	.002445	.012170	85455	1040	424756	.002448	2.577724	4524946	.013039	52.951	10
15	3750618	15506	.004134	.020506	84415	1731	417991	.004141	2.640574	4100190	.013825	48.572	15
20	3640777	19706	.005413	.026704	82684	2208	408025	.005411	2.556801	3682200	-.002967	44.533	20
25	3807819	22397	.005882	.028990	80476	2333	396647	.005882	2.542595	3274174	-.001469	40.685	25
30	3438191	24028	.006989	.034360	78143	2685	384115	.006990	2.541977	2877527	.001667	36.824	30
35	3425282	26584	.007761	.038067	75458	2874	370191	.007764	2.529938	2493412	.006663	33.044	35
40	2847896	24798	.008707	.042682	72584	3098	355350	.008718	2.556623	2123221	.019494	29.252	40
45	2527203	27704	.010962	.053478	69486	3716	338456	.010979	2.585161	1767871	.014618	25.442	45
50	2159009	31255	.014477	.070199	65770	4617	317797	.014528	2.606039	1429414	.027449	21.734	50
55	1603370	33267	.020748	.099194	61153	6066	291206	.020831	2.599577	1111617	.027249	18.178	55
60	1339456	39025	.029135	.136657	55087	7528	257367	.029250	2.599877	820411	.025271	14.893	60
65	901619	40434	.044846	.203432	47559	9675	214371	.045132	2.578941	563044	.035019	11.839	65
70	594506	40952	.068884	.295481	37884	11194	161723	.069217	2.525758	348673	.025292	9.204	70
75	352920	36867	.104463	.414350	26690	11059	105316	.105008	2.455994	186949	.025581	7.004	75
80	156658	25177	.160713	.566694	15631	8858	54798	.161649	2.363142	81633	.025581	5.223	80
85+	74330	18760	.252388	1.000000	6773	6773	26836	.252388	3.962154	26836	.000000	3.962	85+

NUMBER OF PERSONS DYING (OUT OF 100,000 AT BIRTH) ABOVE AGE X FROM SPECIFIED CAUSES

Age (x)	All Causes	Respiratory T.B.	Other Infec. and Paras.	Neoplasms	Cardiovascular	Infl., Pneu., Bronch.	Diarrheal	Certain Degenerative	Maternal	Cert. Dis. of Infancy	Motor Vehicle	Other Violence	Other and Unknown	Age (x)
0	100000	5916	5793	6704	29009	14609	2772	11588	C	3375	891	6789	12554	0
1	90416	5880	4994	6658	28915	12853	1095	11551	0	0	890	6672	10868	1
5	86798	5833	3919	6677	28857	11756	563	11507	0	0	849	6408	10429	5
10	85455	5804	3494	6664	28780	11527	535	11468	0	0	747	6234	10202	10
15	84415	5762	3301	6653	28671	11361	528	11424	0	0	682	6027	10006	15
20	82684	5504	3102	6636	28546	10956	522	11365	0	0	634	5658	9761	20
25	80476	4963	2907	6612	28426	10488	515	11290	0	0	582	5176	9517	25
30	78143	4395	2736	6580	28291	9896	506	11197	0	0	531	4727	9284	30
35	75458	3828	2539	6523	28058	9136	494	11069	0	0	482	4272	9017	35
40	72584	3278	2290	6433	27815	8433	477	10892	C	0	438	3808	8720	40
45	69486	2756	2012	6276	27373	7839	460	10621	0	0	396	3376	8377	45
50	65770	2247	1727	5995	26669	7255	437	10201	0	0	353	2933	7953	50
55	61153	1765	1435	5538	25542	6622	411	9587	0	0	303	2496	7454	55
60	55087	1310	1141	4817	23714	5905	382	8675	0	0	254	2059	6830	60
65	47559	910	869	3906	21035	5086	344	7495	0	0	196	1650	6068	65
70	37884	543	594	2827	17200	4053	297	5884	0	0	133	1230	5123	70
75	26690	280	377	1686	12342	2879	227	4046	0	0	82	849	3922	75
80	15631	115	203	785	7163	1732	147	2252	0	0	39	540	2655	80
85+	6773	32	83	267	2998	775	59	918	0	0	13	249	1379	85+

NUMBER OF PERSONS SURVIVING TO AGE X IF SPECIFIED CAUSES WERE ELIMINATED

Age (x)	No Causes	Respiratory T.B. (1)	Other Infec. and Paras. (2)	Neoplasms (3)	Cardiovascular (4)	Infl., Pneu., Bronch. (5)	Diarrheal (6)	Certain Degenerative (7)	Maternal (8)	Cert. Dis. of Infancy (9)	Motor Vehicle (10)	Other Violence (11)	Other and Unknown (12)	(1)+(2)	(1)+(2)+(5)+(6)+(8)	(1)+(2)+(5)+(6)+(3)+part of(9)&(12)	(10)+(11)	Age (x)
0	100000	100000	100000	100000	100000	100000	100000	100000	100000	100000	100000	100000	100000	100000	100000	100000	100000	0
1	90416	90450	91179	90422	90505	92101	92024	90451	90416	93681	90417	90527	92033	91213	94565	99434	90528	1
5	86798	86877	88599	86824	86941	89517	88874	86875	86798	89933	86839	87164	88789	88679	93644	98888	87205	5
10	85455	85561	87659	85494	85672	88366	87527	85569	85455	88541	85597	85989	87646	87769	92959	98330	86132	10
15	84415	84562	86789	84464	84738	87462	86465	84572	84415	87464	84620	85150	86779	86941	92270	97710	85356	15
20	82684	83084	85212	82749	83125	86084	84702	82896	82684	86570	82932	83773	85249	85625	91322	96872	84024	20
25	80476	81404	83135	80563	81024	84268	82447	80757	80476	83382	80769	82019	83221	84094	90213	95872	82318	25
30	78143	79612	80899	78259	78809	82438	80066	78508	78143	80965	78478	80093	81046	82420	89091	94857	80437	30
35	75458	77446	78320	75626	76293	80397	77327	75937	75458	78830	75705	77801	78534	80384	87767	93655	78184	35
40	72584	75052	75591	72834	73665	78073	74399	73220	72584	75205	72985	75308	75847	78162	86174	92173	75724	40
45	69486	72378	72649	69880	70965	75368	71241	70363	69486	71996	69911	72533	72961	75673	84151	90231	72977	45
50	65770	69025	69054	66419	67874	71956	67454	67015	65770	68145	66215	69105	69494	72471	81317	87475	69572	50
55	61153	64668	64502	62204	64242	67575	62744	62917	61153	63362	61615	64698	65125	68209	77333	83370	65196	55
60	55087	58710	58338	56734	59723	61627	56549	57574	55087	57076	55550	58719	59299	62239	71476	77282	59213	60
65	47559	51083	50685	49859	54334	54062	48857	50865	47559	49277	48013	51100	51962	54440	63574	68969	51587	65
70	37884	41041	40635	40735	47371	44122	38961	42081	37884	39252	38302	41107	42322	44021	52727	57453	41560	70
75	26690	29150	28921	29737	38863	32247	27509	31400	26690	27654	27027	29305	30960	31477	39198	42989	29676	75
80	15631	17206	17021	18183	29257	19962	16174	20054	15631	16196	15861	17420	19282	18735	24757	27419	17677	80
85+	6773	7514	7459	8274	18784	9468	7067	9856	6773	7018	6890	7758	9425	8275	12069	13634	7892	85+

ADDED YRS OF LIFE

	No Causes	(1)	(2)	(3)	(4)	(5)	(6)	(7)	(8)	(9)	(10)	(11)	(12)	(1)+(2)	...	...	(10)+(11)
TOTAL		1.633	2.204	.881	4.281	4.183	1.360	1.537	.000	1.942	.272	1.883	2.975	3.932	10.170	14.701	2.171
WORK	8.098	1.252	.565	.304	.916	1.459	.033	.514	.000	.000	.122	1.129	.779	1.843	3.480	3.940	1.256

POPULATION, DEATHS, DEATH RATES FOR ALL CAUSES COMBINED, AND SPECIFIED CAUSES

Age Start of Interval	Midyear Population	Deaths During Year	All Causes	Respiratory T. B.	Other Infec. and Paras.	Neoplasms	Cardiovascular	Infl., Pneu., Bronch.	Diarrheal	Certain Degenerative	Maternal	Cert. Dis. of Infancy	Motor Vehicle	Other Violence	Other and Unknown	Age Start of Interval
0	918373	73882	.08045	.00031	.00776	.00005	.00071	.01463	.01430	.00027	.00000	.02764	.00002	.00100	.01376	0
1	3618500	34149	.00944	.00012	.00256	.00004	.00015	.00286	.00131	.00011	.00000	.00000	.00007	.00069	.00112	1
5	4463524	12364	.00277	.00008	.00058	.00002	.00021	.00052	.00006	.00009	.00000	.00000	.00009	.00026	.00047	5
10	4133259	8855	.00214	.00024	.00046	.00002	.00030	.00039	.00002	.00012	.00001	.00000	.00003	.00014	.00041	10
15	3798468	14824	.00390	.00106	.00050	.00004	.00030	.00071	.00001	.00015	.00039	.00000	.00004	.00020	.00050	15
20	3804677	22757	.00598	.00174	.00051	.00007	.00034	.00125	.00002	.00020	.00090	.00000	.00003	.00025	.00066	20
25	3842467	25913	.00674	.00160	.00043	.00015	.00046	.00181	.00003	.00025	.00102	.00000	.00003	.00024	.00072	25
30	3292654	24655	.00749	.00142	.00042	.00038	.00064	.00199	.00003	.00038	.00105	.00000	.00003	.00025	.00089	30
35	3087147	23937	.00775	.00127	.00043	.00072	.00092	.00164	.00004	.00054	.00086	.00000	.00003	.00025	.00103	35
40	2625338	21503	.00819	.00106	.00043	.00130	.00135	.00131	.00004	.00080	.00042	.00000	.00003	.00027	.00118	40
45	2233808	22813	.01021	.00094	.00046	.00192	.00229	.00139	.00007	.00125	.00008	.00000	.00005	.00031	.00147	45
50	1909617	25417	.01331	.00089	.00048	.00266	.00358	.00165	.00008	.00189	.00001	.00000	.00006	.00035	.00167	50
55	1460417	27358	.01873	.00092	.00054	.00363	.00577	.00222	.00011	.00290	.00000	.00000	.00008	.00042	.00213	55
60	1220070	32537	.02667	.00097	.00060	.00466	.00974	.00295	.00016	.00422	.00000	.00000	.00011	.00056	.00268	60
65	853045	35015	.04105	.00122	.00072	.00589	.01671	.00476	.00026	.00667	.00000	.00000	.00013	.00087	.00381	65
70	593601	37667	.06346	.00126	.00098	.00753	.02790	.00804	.00049	.00957	.00000	.00000	.00014	.00158	.00596	70
75	372325	36356	.09765	.00134	.00146	.00893	.04615	.01256	.00090	.01343	.00000	.00000	.00015	.00317	.00955	75
80	184302	27857	.15115	.00112	.00173	.01053	.07177	.02041	.00156	.01818	.00000	.00000	.00018	.00632	.01935	80
85+	98848	24075	.24356	.00109	.00228	.01058	.10952	.03220	.00284	.02338	.00000	.00000	.00008	.01271	.04887	85+
ALL	42510440	531934														
CRUDE DEATH RATE			.01251	.00092	.00092	.00105	.00283	.00213	.00049	.00110	.00038	.00060	.00005	.00042	.00161	
STANDARDIZED RATE (1)			.01195	.00083	.00111	.00082	.00212	.00215	.00071	.00086	.00034	.00097	.00005	.00040	.00158	
STANDARDIZED RATE (2)			.01628	.00093	.00093	.00150	.00465	.00256	.00050	.00167	.00034	.00057	.00006	.00054	.00203	
GEOMETRIC MEAN			.01693													

LIFE TABLE FOR ALL CAUSES COMBINED

Age (x)	Midyear Population	Deaths During Year	$_nM_x$	$_nq_x$	l_x	$_nd_x$	$_nL_x$	$_nm_x$	$_na_x$	T_x	$_nr_x$	$\overset{\circ}{e}_x$	Age (x)
0	918373	73882	.080449	.075620	100000	7562	94002	.080445	.206763	5592026	.000000	55.920	0
1	3618500	34149	.009437	.036879	92438	3409	361230	.009437	1.500000	5498025	.000000	59.478	1
5	4463524	12364	.002770	.013748	89029	1224	442085	.002769	2.500000	5136795	.000000	57.698	5
10	4133259	8855	.002142	.010660	87805	936	436781	.002143	2.602163	4694710	.011352	53.467	10
15	3798468	14824	.003903	.019374	86869	1683	430465	.003910	2.694841	4257929	.008542	49.016	15
20	3804677	22757	.005981	.029465	85186	2510	419876	.005979	2.587981	3827464	-.005545	44.931	20
25	3842467	25913	.006744	.033178	82676	2743	406612	.006746	2.532583	3407588	.003271	41.216	25
30	3292654	24655	.007488	.036768	79933	2939	392356	.007491	2.513185	3000976	.012225	37.544	30
35	3087147	23937	.007754	.038042	76994	2929	377655	.007756	2.502632	2608620	.012485	33.881	35
40	2625338	21503	.008191	.040181	74065	2976	363014	.008198	2.543473	2230965	.021971	30.122	40
45	2233808	22813	.010213	.049937	71089	3550	346860	.010235	2.581808	1867950	.020182	26.276	45
50	1909617	25417	.013310	.064703	67539	4370	327214	.013355	2.601688	1521090	.027293	22.522	50
55	1460417	27358	.018733	.089965	63169	5683	302234	.018803	2.604918	1193876	.026272	18.900	55
60	1220070	32537	.026668	.125805	57486	7232	270131	.026772	2.608027	891642	.024912	15.511	60
65	853045	35015	.041047	.187706	50254	9433	228523	.041278	2.588541	621511	.030666	12.367	65
70	593601	37667	.063455	.275373	40821	11241	176457	.063704	2.540477	392988	.020701	9.627	70
75	372325	36356	.097646	.392732	29580	11617	118549	.097994	2.473405	216530	.017165	7.320	75
80	184302	27857	.151149	.543228	17963	9758	64294	.151773	2.384561	97982	.017165	5.455	80
85+	98848	24075	.243556	1.000000	8205	8205	33688	.243556	4.105836	33688	.000000	4.106	85+

NUMBER OF PERSONS DYING (OUT OF 100,000 AT BIRTH) ABOVE AGE X FROM SPECIFIED CAUSES

Age (x)	All Causes	Respira-tory T. B.	Other Infec. and Paras.	Neo-plasms	Cardio-vascular	Infl., Pneu., Bronch.	Diar-rheal	Certain Degen-erative	Maternal	Cert. Dis. of Infancy	Motor Vehicle	Other Violence	Other and Unknown	Age (x)
0	100000	5413	4866	9739	30858	15166	2495	10912	1891	2598	335	3295	12432	0
1	92438	5393	4137	9734	30791	13791	1152	10887	1891	0	333	3201	11138	1
5	89029	5340	3067	9718	30736	12757	679	10846	1891	0	309	2952	10734	5
10	87805	5303	2635	9709	30644	12526	653	10808	1891	0	268	2839	10529	10
15	86869	5195	2437	9698	30512	12357	645	10755	1886	0	257	2779	10348	15
20	85186	4740	2222	9680	30382	12050	639	10691	1715	0	240	2694	10133	20
25	82676	4008	2007	9649	30238	11526	631	10608	1338	0	227	2589	9855	25
30	79933	3358	1832	9588	30049	10789	617	10508	923	0	216	2492	9561	30
35	76994	2801	1668	9437	29797	10007	604	10358	510	0	204	2395	9213	35
40	74065	2322	1505	9164	29450	9389	588	10155	185	0	191	2293	8823	40
45	71089	1937	1347	8689	28959	8913	575	9864	33	0	181	2195	8396	45
50	67539	1611	1187	8021	28162	8433	551	9431	5	0	163	2088	7887	50
55	63169	1321	1029	7147	26986	7892	525	8810	3	0	141	1974	7341	55
60	57486	1042	867	6047	25232	7218	492	7928	3	0	117	1846	6694	60
65	50254	779	703	4786	22585	6418	448	6783	3	0	87	1695	5967	65
70	40821	499	538	3436	18740	5324	389	5250	3	0	56	1494	5092	70
75	29580	276	365	2103	13794	3899	303	3557	3	0	32	1214	4034	75
80	17963	117	191	1043	8301	2404	156	1960	3	0	15	835	2898	80
85+	8205	37	77	356	3690	1085	96	788	0	0	3	428	1645	85+

NUMBER OF PERSONS SURVIVING TO AGE X IF SPECIFIED CAUSES WERE ELIMINATED

Age (x)	No Causes	Respira-tory T. B. (1)	Other Infec. and Paras. (2)	Neo-plasms (3)	Cardio-vascular (4)	Infl., Pneu., Bronch. (5)	Diar-rheal (6)	Certain Degener-ative (7)	Maternal (8)	Cert. Dis. of Infancy (9)	Motor Vehicle (10)	Other Violence (11)	Other and Unknown (12)	(1) + (2)	(1) + (2) + (5) + (6) + (8)	(1)+(2)+ (5)+(6)+ (8)+part of(9)&(12)	(10) + (11)	Age (x)
0	100000	100000	100000	100000	100000	100000	100000	100000	100000	100000	100000	100000	100000	100000	100000	100000	100000	0
1	92438	92467	93141	92443	92502	93769	93738	92462	92438	94969	92440	92528	93690	93170	95841	99587	92530	1
5	89029	89095	90771	89049	89145	91346	90753	89092	89029	91467	89054	89361	90638	90842	95011	99109	89386	5
10	87805	87911	89961	87834	88011	90326	89532	87905	87805	90209	87871	88245	89599	90070	94478	98715	88311	10
15	86869	87081	89204	86909	87205	89536	88585	87021	86874	89248	86945	87364	88828	89422	93994	98342	87441	15
20	85186	85847	87695	85243	85644	88116	86875	85399	85361	87519	85277	85757	87325	88375	93418	97931	85849	20
25	82676	84047	85329	82762	83263	86055	84323	82964	83219	84940	82778	83334	85033	86744	92693	97439	83436	25
30	79933	81911	82676	80076	80668	83958	81540	80311	80669	82122	80042	80665	82510	84721	91839	96826	80775	30
35	76994	79461	79802	77281	77972	81681	78555	77506	78307	79102	77111	77795	79829	82359	90664	95903	77913	35
40	74065	76924	76932	74610	75352	79219	75582	74758	75652	76093	74190	74937	77190	79902	89082	94537	75064	40
45	71089	74226	74002	72083	72815	76535	72558	72043	72764	73036	71219	72023	74526	77267	86907	92481	72155	45
50	67539	70851	70469	69147	69580	73219	68959	68875	69158	69388	67680	68532	71326	73925	83788	89381	68675	50
55	63169	66561	66069	65544	66642	69050	64523	65034	64685	64899	63322	64210	67271	69617	79595	85096	64365	55
60	57486	60853	60286	60745	62440	63544	58750	60056	58866	59060	57648	58557	61879	63818	73825	79121	58723	60
65	50254	53458	52863	54361	57342	56382	51401	53630	51460	51630	50424	51334	54829	56232	66079	71006	51508	65
70	40821	43691	43096	45486	50703	46618	41807	45059	41801	41939	40987	41884	45404	46125	55599	59959	42054	70
75	29580	31860	31383	34236	42344	35416	30370	34270	30290	30390	29720	30596	33914	33803	42549	46148	30741	75
80	17963	19478	19200	21748	32565	22933	18528	22281	18394	18455	18061	18887	21628	20820	28074	30725	18990	80
85+	8205	8954	8851	10497	21541	11645	8531	11182	8404	8430	8258	8914	10925	9659	14600	16287	8971	85+

ADDED YRS OF LIFE																		
TOTAL		1.695	2.030	1.512	4.721	4.031	1.166	1.543	.718	1.526	.098	.723	2.894	3.805	10.494	14.506	.822	
WORK	8.139	1.293	.453	.635	.996	1.414	.034	.531	.652	.000	.036	.247	.875	1.765	4.023	4.617	.283	

POPULATION, DEATHS, DEATH RATES FOR ALL CAUSES COMBINED, AND SPECIFIED CAUSES

Age Start of Interval	Midyear Population	Deaths During Year	All Causes	Respiratory T. B.	Other Infec. and Paras.	Neoplasms	Cardiovascular	Infl., Pneu., Bronch.	Diarrheal	Certain Degenerative	Maternal	Cert. Dis. of Infancy	Motor Vehicle	Other Violence	Other and Unknown	Age Start of Interval
0	866145	84772	.09787	.00033	.00789	.00007	.00105	.01741	.01765	.00037	.00000	.03546	.00002	.00113	.01649	0
1	3391976	33329	.00983	.00010	.00302	.00006	.00016	.00292	.00144	.00012	.00000	.00000	.00012	.00072	.00115	1
5	4136465	12673	.00306	.00004	.00098	.00003	.00019	.00050	.00007	.00009	.00000	.00000	.00025	.00040	.00051	5
10	3787986	8813	.00233	.00006	.00042	.00003	.00026	.00035	.00001	.00010	.00000	.00000	.00016	.00047	.00045	10
15	3395561	12753	.00376	.00045	.00041	.00004	.00030	.00090	.00001	.00014	.00000	.00000	.00012	.00082	.00045	15
20	3302706	15636	.00473	.00104	.00039	.00006	.00027	.00104	.00002	.00017	.00000	.00000	.00013	.00105	.00057	20
25	3486586	18820	.00540	.00124	.00036	.00008	.00030	.00143	.00002	.00023	.00000	.00000	.00013	.00106	.00055	25
30	3184204	20696	.00650	.00133	.00044	.00015	.00043	.00191	.00003	.00031	.00000	.00000	.00013	.00111	.00055	30
35	3134758	22487	.00717	.00134	.00059	.00025	.00065	.00180	.00004	.00044	.00000	.00000	.00013	.00111	.00065	35
40	2610122	21359	.00818	.00137	.00071	.00045	.00111	.00156	.00004	.00072	.00000	.00000	.00012	.00119	.00075	40
45	2313747	23927	.01034	.00139	.00077	.00086	.00190	.00160	.00007	.00115	.00000	.00000	.00014	.00129	.00118	45
50	1993487	27506	.01380	.00143	.00083	.00147	.00328	.00188	.00008	.00181	.00000	.00000	.00016	.00137	.00149	50
55	1501302	30493	.02031	.00150	.00096	.00253	.00608	.00241	.00010	.00300	.00000	.00000	.00017	.00206	.00149	55
60	1259612	36173	.02872	.00149	.00098	.00364	.01024	.00310	.00014	.00447	.00000	.00000	.00023	.00160	.00284	60
65	847361	37695	.04449	.00162	.00119	.00520	.01777	.00475	.00022	.00729	.00000	.00000	.00030	.00197	.00417	65
70	560651	38416	.06852	.00154	.00125	.00733	.02997	.00723	.00041	.01109	.00000	.00000	.00033	.00235	.00701	70
75	333970	34966	.10470	.00154	.00155	.00884	.04952	.01090	.00076	.01688	.00000	.00000	.00043	.00296	.01132	75
80	147197	23791	.16163	.00121	.00186	.00980	.07760	.01748	.00161	.02421	.00000	.00000	.00045	.00525	.01132	80
85+	67740	17135	.25295	.00105	.00282	.01056	.11568	.02948	.00224	.03415	.00000	.00000	.00050	.00957	.04691	85+
ALL	40321576	521440														

CRUDE DEATH RATE			.01293	.00088	.00101	.00076	.00281	.00216	.00056	.00115	.00000	.00076	.00016	.00106	.00160
STANDARDIZED RATE (1)			.01265	.00074	.00117	.00058	.00214	.00223	.00084	.00092	.00000	.00125	.00016	.00097	.00165
STANDARDIZED RATE (2)			.01712	.00092	.00104	.00114	.00483	.00255	.00057	.00189	.00000	.00073	.00017	.00117	.00210
GEOMETRIC MEAN			.01715												

LIFE TABLE FOR ALL CAUSES COMBINED

Age (x)	Midyear Population	Deaths During Year	$_nM_x$	$_nq_x$	l_x	$_nd_x$	$_nL_x$	$_nm_x$	$_na_x$	T_x	$_nr_x$	$\overset{\circ}{e}_x$	Age (x)
0	866145	84772	.097873	.091070	100000	9107	93046	.097877	.236384	5501985	.000000	55.020	0
1	3391976	33329	.009826	.038353	90893	3486	354857	.009824	1.500000	5408939	.000000	59.509	1
5	4136465	12673	.003064	.015205	87407	1329	433713	.003064	2.500000	5054082	.000000	57.822	5
10	3787986	8813	.002327	.011571	86078	996	427954	.002327	2.553757	4620369	.013408	53.677	10
15	3395561	12753	.003756	.018641	85082	1586	421645	.003761	2.625841	4192416	.014181	49.275	15
20	3302706	15636	.004734	.023402	83456	1954	412717	.004734	2.562479	3770771	-.003060	45.161	20
25	3486586	18820	.005398	.026637	81542	2172	402402	.005398	2.556112	3358054	-.002991	41.182	25
30	3184204	20696	.006500	.031989	79370	2539	390614	.006500	2.544063	2955652	.001507	37.239	30
35	3134758	22487	.007173	.035259	76831	2709	377474	.007177	2.533684	2565038	.008026	33.385	35
40	2610122	21359	.008183	.040164	74122	2977	363352	.008193	2.562003	2187564	.020269	29.513	40
45	2313747	23927	.010341	.050531	71145	3595	347061	.010358	2.589882	1824212	.014962	25.641	45
50	1993487	27506	.013798	.067032	67550	4528	326957	.013849	2.616451	1477151	.026269	21.868	50
55	1501302	30493	.020311	.097204	63022	6126	300450	.020389	2.606921	1150194	.025716	18.251	55
60	1259612	36173	.028718	.134693	56896	7672	266055	.028832	2.603651	849744	.024910	14.935	60
65	847361	37695	.044485	.201995	49224	9943	222072	.044774	2.581381	583649	.035125	11.857	65
70	560651	38416	.068520	.294188	39281	11556	167842	.068851	2.528268	361577	.024870	9.205	70
75	333970	34966	.104698	.415185	27725	11511	109362	.105256	2.457794	193736	.025621	6.988	75
80	147197	23791	.161627	.568891	16214	9224	56740	.162565	2.362338	84374	.025621	5.204	80
85+	67740	17135	.252952	1.000000	6990	6990	27634	.252952	3.953312	27634	.000000	3.953	85+

NUMBER OF PERSONS DYING (OUT OF 100,000 AT BIRTH) ABOVE AGE X FROM SPECIFIED CAUSES

Age (x)	All Causes	Respiratory T.B.	Other Infec. and Paras.	Neoplasms	Cardiovascular	Infl., Pneu., Bronch.	Diarrheal	Certain Degenerative	Maternal	Cert. Dis. of Infancy	Motor Vehicle	Other Violence	Other and Unknown	Age (x)
0	100000	5451	5470	7179	29934	14421	2724	11700	0	3300	945	6767	12109	0
1	90893	5420	4736	7173	29837	12801	1082	11666	0	0	944	6662	10572	1
5	87407	5383	3663	7152	29779	11764	570	11623	0	0	900	6407	10166	5
10	86078	5365	3238	7137	29698	11546	541	11585	0	0	791	6233	9944	10
15	85082	5338	3058	7126	29586	11395	535	11540	0	0	722	6031	9751	15
20	83496	5146	2884	7108	29461	11015	530	11482	0	0	673	5686	9511	20
25	81542	4718	2723	7083	29348	10586	522	11412	0	0	618	5248	9284	25
30	79370	4219	2577	7050	29227	10010	513	11322	0	0	565	4824	9063	30
35	76831	3698	2403	6993	29058	9263	503	11201	0	0	514	4389	8809	35
40	74122	3192	2182	6899	28812	8585	486	11034	0	0	468	3939	8525	40
45	71145	2696	1923	6736	28407	8017	470	10773	0	0	423	3504	8196	45
50	67550	2212	1655	6438	27743	7463	447	10373	0	0	376	3056	7787	50
55	63022	1743	1383	5955	26662	6848	422	9779	0	0	323	2608	7299	55
60	56896	1291	1095	5192	24824	6122	393	8873	0	0	272	2157	6677	60
65	49224	995	834	4219	22084	5296	355	7679	0	0	210	1731	5921	65
70	39281	535	569	3058	18106	4235	307	6048	0	0	143	1292	4988	70
75	27725	276	359	1823	13047	3015	237	4177	0	0	88	897	3806	75
80	16214	108	189	854	7599	1817	154	2322	0	0	40	572	2559	80
85+	6990	29	78	292	3197	815	62	944	0	0	14	264	1295	85+

NUMBER OF PERSONS SURVIVING TO AGE X IF SPECIFIED CAUSES WERE ELIMINATED

Age (x)	No Causes	Respiratory T.B. (1)	Other Infec. and Paras. (2)	Neoplasms (3)	Cardiovascular (4)	Infl., Pneu., Bronch. (5)	Diarrheal (6)	Certain Degenerative (7)	Maternal (8)	Cert. Dis. of Infancy (9)	Motor Vehicle (10)	Other Violence (11)	Other and Unknown (12)	(1)+(2)	(1)+(2)+(5)+(6)+(8)	(1)+(2)+(5)+(6)+(8)+part of(9)&(12)	(10)+(11)	Age (x)
0	100000	100000	100000	100000	100000	100000	100000	100000	100000	100000	100000	100000	100000	100000	100000	100000	100000	0
1	90893	90923	91555	90899	90985	92450	92471	90925	90893	94093	90894	90993	92370	91625	94813	99458	90994	1
5	87407	87472	89149	87433	87553	89945	89437	87480	87407	90484	87451	87754	89233	89215	93937	98528	87798	5
10	86078	86160	88225	86119	86302	88800	88107	86188	86078	89108	86230	86593	88101	88308	93248	98359	86746	10
15	85082	85190	87387	85133	85415	87927	87093	85236	85082	88077	85301	85794	87278	87498	92562	97735	86014	15
20	83496	83792	85936	83564	83947	86678	85475	83704	83496	86436	83759	84540	85895	86241	91650	96925	84806	20
25	81542	82257	84088	81633	82095	85091	83483	81815	81542	84413	81654	83001	84116	84826	90625	95598	83318	25
30	79370	80564	81997	79491	80029	83420	81268	79725	79370	82164	79726	81216	82101	83231	89570	95045	81581	30
35	76831	78509	79551	77005	77637	81527	78678	77294	76831	79057	77226	79057	79733	81289	88332	93925	79464	35
40	74122	76250	76971	74382	75144	79362	75921	74734	74122	76732	74548	76726	77212	79181	86838	92540	77167	40
45	71145	73689	74144	71555	72530	76772	72888	71991	71145	73650	71599	74087	74448	76795	84900	90683	74559	45
50	67550	70455	70670	68233	69528	73477	69228	68749	67550	69928	68027	70799	71104	73709	82169	87982	71298	50
55	63022	66206	66208	64132	65953	69201	64612	64728	63022	65241	63518	66507	66835	69552	78298	84051	67031	55
60	56896	60221	60059	58641	61400	63235	58360	59327	56896	58899	57393	60495	60968	63570	72470	78015	61023	60
65	49224	52499	52217	51674	55946	55567	50527	52498	49224	50957	49712	52759	53505	55681	64521	69675	53282	65
70	39281	42229	41919	42335	48870	45423	40365	43473	39281	40664	39730	42522	43611	45065	53549	58062	43008	70
75	27725	30036	29773	31009	40188	33260	28550	32463	27725	28701	28088	30369	31899	31289	39846	43466	30767	75
80	16214	17701	17549	18962	30313	20567	16762	20696	16214	16785	16463	18030	19776	19158	25123	27658	18307	80
85+	6990	7686	7643	8605	19525	9715	7287	10117	6990	7236	7114	7995	9567	8404	12177	13657	8137	85+

ADDED YRS OF LIFE

	No Causes	(1)	(2)	(3)	(4)	(5)	(6)	(7)	(8)	(9)	(10)	(11)	(12)	(1)+(2)	...	...	(10)+(11)
TOTAL		1.462	2.108	.941	4.386	4.035	1.347	1.531	.000	1.929	.291	1.847	2.836	3.650	9.656	13.967	2.154
WORK	7.585	1.102	.502	.319	.866	1.437	.032	.495	.000	.000	.128	1.083	.748	1.624	3.182	3.610	1.215

POPULATION, DEATHS, DEATH RATES FOR ALL CAUSES COMBINED, AND SPECIFIED CAUSES

Age Start of Interval	Midyear Population	Deaths During Year	All Causes	Respiratory T. B.	Other Infec. and Paras.	Neo-plasms	Cardio-vascular	Infl., Pneu., Bronch.	Diar-rheal	Certain Degen-erative	Maternal	Cert. Dis. of Infancy	Motor Vehicle	Other Violence	Other and Unknown	Age Start of Interval
0	841788	63927	.07594	.00024	.00711	.00005	.00072	.01340	.01350	.00025	.00000	.02696	.00002	.00088	.01242	0
1	3300350	29659	.00899	.00009	.00292	.00004	.00015	.00269	.00125	.00011	.00000	.00000	.00007	.00064	.00103	1
5	4044869	10743	.00266	.00005	.00096	.00002	.00021	.00049	.00006	.00009	.00000	.00000	.00010	.00022	.00046	5
10	3733835	7281	.00195	.00016	.00042	.00002	.00031	.00035	.00002	.00012	.00000	.00000	.00003	.00013	.00039	10
15	3415822	11431	.00335	.00084	.00042	.00004	.00030	.00063	.00001	.00014	.00030	.00000	.00004	.00018	.00044	15
20	3420390	17954	.00525	.00143	.00041	.00007	.00031	.00117	.00002	.00018	.00084	.00000	.00003	.00023	.00056	20
25	3484529	21477	.00616	.00138	.00036	.00013	.00040	.00175	.00003	.00023	.00100	.00000	.00003	.00022	.00064	25
30	3026399	20822	.00688	.00125	.00035	.00025	.00058	.00193	.00003	.00035	.00102	.00000	.00003	.00023	.00077	30
35	2816312	19789	.00703	.00112	.00036	.00067	.00079	.00156	.00003	.00046	.00083	.00000	.00004	.00026	.00091	35
40	2410301	18009	.00747	.00095	.00038	.00125	.00115	.00122	.00003	.00072	.00040	.00000	.00003	.00027	.00106	40
45	2075851	19466	.00938	.00084	.00041	.00188	.00202	.00128	.00006	.00114	.00007	.00000	.00005	.00031	.00133	45
50	1786223	22318	.01249	.00079	.00043	.00265	.00328	.00154	.00007	.00175	.00001	.00000	.00007	.00034	.00157	50
55	1382762	24914	.01802	.00087	.00048	.00364	.00545	.00213	.00010	.00280	.00000	.00000	.00008	.00042	.00205	55
60	1157630	30035	.02595	.00092	.00056	.00469	.00946	.00282	.00015	.00414	.00000	.00000	.00012	.00056	.00253	60
65	809756	32690	.04037	.00118	.00067	.00597	.01644	.00468	.00025	.00658	.00000	.00000	.00014	.00087	.00360	65
70	562209	35535	.06321	.00122	.00069	.00769	.02792	.00806	.00047	.00960	.00000	.00000	.00014	.00159	.00561	70
75	354724	34721	.09788	.00131	.00138	.00913	.04649	.01273	.00089	.01345	.00000	.00000	.00015	.00323	.00911	75
80	173753	26515	.15260	.00106	.00165	.01089	.07333	.02082	.00162	.01835	.00000	.00000	.00018	.00650	.01819	80
85+	89973	22133	.24600	.00108	.00211	.01109	.11380	.03349	.00288	.02364	.00000	.00000	.00009	.01343	.04439	85+
ALL	38887476	469419														

CRUDE DEATH RATE	.01207	.00079	.00085	.00107	.00284	.00205	.00047	.00109	.00036	.00058	.00005	.00041	.00149		
STANDARDIZED RATE (1)	.01131	.00071	.00103	.00081	.00206	.00203	.00069	.00083	.00032	.00095	.00005	.00038	.00145		
STANDARDIZED RATE (2)	.01570	.00081	.00086	.00150	.00460	.00247	.00049	.00163	.00032	.00056	.00006	.00053	.00188		
GEOMETRIC MEAN	.01598														

LIFE TABLE FOR ALL CAUSES COMBINED

Age (x)	Midyear Population	Deaths During Year	$_nM_x$	$_nq_x$	l_x	$_nd_x$	$_nL_x$	$_nm_x$	$_na_x$	T_x	$_nr_x$	$\overset{\circ}{e}_x$	Age (x)
0	841788	63927	.075942	.071590	100000	7159	94266	.075944	.199101	5713374	.000000	57.134	0
1	3300350	29659	.008587	.035157	92841	3264	363204	.008587	1.500000	5619108	.000000	60.524	1
5	4044869	10743	.002656	.013184	89577	1181	444933	.002654	2.500000	5255904	.000000	58.675	5
10	3733835	7281	.001950	.009706	88396	858	439892	.001950	2.566774	4810971	.012105	54.425	10
15	3415822	11431	.003346	.016633	87538	1456	434336	.003352	2.696314	4371079	.009624	49.934	15
20	3420390	17954	.005249	.025930	86082	2230	425062	.005246	2.601831	3936743	-.005115	45.732	20
25	3484529	21477	.006164	.030363	83852	2546	413004	.006165	2.542632	3511681	.001910	41.880	25
30	3026399	20822	.006880	.033835	81306	2751	399687	.006883	2.512647	3098678	.011709	38.111	30
35	2816312	19789	.007027	.034536	78555	2713	386000	.007029	2.502611	2658990	.013328	34.358	35
40	2410301	18009	.007472	.036721	75842	2785	372382	.007479	2.548175	2312991	.021314	30.497	40
45	2075851	19466	.009377	.045950	73057	3357	357196	.009398	2.590483	1940609	.019220	26.563	45
50	1786223	22318	.012495	.060815	69700	4243	338375	.012539	2.613766	1583413	.026219	22.718	50
55	1382762	24914	.018018	.086683	65457	5674	313744	.018085	2.613419	1245038	.025318	19.021	55
60	1157630	30035	.025945	.122644	59783	7332	281424	.026053	2.614424	931294	.024954	15.578	60
65	809756	32690	.040370	.184954	52451	9701	238920	.040604	2.594578	649870	.031442	12.390	65
70	562209	35535	.063206	.274526	42750	11736	184932	.063461	2.544466	410950	.020754	9.613	70
75	354724	34721	.097882	.393596	31014	12207	124250	.098245	2.475253	226018	.017254	7.288	75
80	173753	26515	.152602	.546924	18807	10286	67129	.153227	2.384207	101768	.017254	5.411	80
85+	89973	22133	.245996	1.000000	8521	8521	34639	.245996	4.065106	34639	.000000	4.065	85+

NUMBER OF PERSONS DYING (OUT OF 100,000 AT BIRTH) ABOVE AGE X FROM SPECIFIED CAUSES

Age (x)	All Causes	Respiratory T.B.	Other Infec. and Paras.	Neoplasms	Cardiovascular	Infl., Pneu., Bronch.	Diarrheal	Certain Degenerative	Maternal	Cert. Dis. of Infancy	Motor Vehicle	Other Violence	Other and Unknown	Age (x)
0	100000	4856	4554	10171	31790	15149	2438	11126	1809	2542	359	3357	11849	0
1	92841	4833	3884	10167	31723	13887	1128	11103	1809	0	357	3273	10677	1
5	89577	4802	2823	10150	31668	12910	675	11063	1809	0	332	3040	10305	5
10	88396	4780	2395	10141	31574	12693	650	11024	1809	0	289	2941	10100	10
15	87538	4710	2211	10130	31438	12540	644	10971	1808	0	276	2883	9927	15
20	86082	4343	2028	10112	31309	12268	639	10911	1675	0	257	2806	9734	20
25	83852	3737	1853	10084	31177	11772	632	10832	1318	0	244	2709	9494	25
30	81306	3168	1704	10028	31012	11049	620	10738	906	0	233	2618	9230	30
35	78555	2671	1564	9887	30779	10280	609	10600	499	0	220	2526	8920	35
40	75842	2239	1426	9628	30472	9679	597	10421	179	0	206	2426	8569	40
45	73057	1885	1285	9159	30040	9225	586	10151	30	0	195	2326	8175	45
50	69700	1586	1140	8487	29316	8768	565	9743	5	0	176	2216	7698	50
55	65457	1319	993	7587	28201	8245	542	9146	3	0	153	2102	7166	55
60	59783	1045	843	6441	26482	7573	510	8265	3	0	127	1969	6525	60
65	52451	787	687	5117	23806	6777	467	7094	3	0	94	1811	5808	65
70	42750	504	526	3687	19851	5651	408	5513	3	0	61	1601	4945	70
75	31014	279	358	2263	14662	4154	320	3732	3	0	35	1306	3902	75
80	18807	116	187	1126	8863	2565	209	2055	3	0	16	903	2764	80
85+	8521	37	73	384	3942	1160	100	819	0	0	3	465	1538	85+

NUMBER OF PERSONS SURVIVING TO AGE X IF SPECIFIED CAUSES WERE ELIMINATED

Age (x)	No Causes	Respiratory T.B. (1)	Other Infec. and Paras. (2)	Neoplasms (3)	Cardiovascular (4)	Infl., Pneu., Bronch. (5)	Diarrheal (6)	Certain Degenerative (7)	Maternal (8)	Cert. Dis. of Infancy (9)	Motor Vehicle (10)	Other Violence (11)	Other and Unknown (12)	(1) + (2)	(1) + (2) + (5) + (6) + (8)	(1)+(2)+(5)+(6)+(8)+part of(9)&(12)	(10) + (11)	Age (x)
0	100000	100000	100000	100000	100000	100000	100000	100000	100000	100000	100000	100000	100000	100000	100000	100000	100000	0
1	92841	92863	93489	92845	92906	94065	94112	92863	92841	95322	92922		93977	93511	96040	99613	92924	1
5	89577	89629	91257	89597	89693	91735	91255	89638	89577	91971	89603	89884	91044	91310	95262	99158	89911	5
10	88396	88469	90489	88425	88604	90747	90077	88495	88396	90759	88465	88758	90050	90563	94740	98775	88867	10
15	87538	87680	89798	87578	87880	90022	89209	87689	87539	89878	87619	87994	89352	89944	94263	98395	88076	15
20	86082	86587	88490	86139	86547	88803	87730	86290	86121	88383	86181	86607	88061	89010	93726	98000	86707	20
25	83852	84948	86376	83935	84436	87009	85465	84132	84335	86093	83961	84460	86023	87504	93079	97550	84570	25
30	81306	82938	83904	81442	82036	85109	82882	81671	82184	83479	81422	81986	83678	85588	92314	97002	82103	30
35	78555	80631	81207	78826	79492	83024	80088	79044	79808	80655	78680	79303	81161	83354	91249	96161	79430	35
40	75842	78283	78543	76360	77053	80783	77334	76491	77372	77869	75977	76664	78715	81071	89828	94938	76800	40
45	73057	75768	75802	74021	74656	78292	74506	73951	74679	75010	73198	73948	76227	78615	87827	93051	74090	45
50	69700	72589	72466	71288	71992	75174	71103	70957	71272	71563	69853	70659	73212	75470	84909	90157	70813	50
55	65457	68440	68203	67846	68698	71147	66797	67230	66936	67206	65623	66469	69298	71311	80883	86057	66637	55
60	59783	62781	62440	63109	64492	65681	61038	62273	61133	61381	59959	60836	63942	65571	75214	80209	61016	60
65	52451	55335	54934	56691	59355	58450	53594	55789	53636	53853	52637	53526	56822	57955	67480	72136	53715	65
70	42750	45369	44926	47615	52589	48785	43736	47011	43716	43893	42931	43820	47162	47678	56920	61051	44005	70
75	31014	33115	32742	35907	43978	36872	31806	35803	31715	31843	31167	32049	35204	34960	43588	46999	32207	75
80	18807	20213	19994	22801	33835	23864	19376	23247	19232	19310	18914	19761	22371	21489	28726	31242	19873	80
85+	8521	9214	9139	10938	22389	12047	8853	11584	8716	8749	8578	9260	11139	9882	14846	16436	9322	85+

ADDED YRS OF LIFE

	No Causes	(1)	(2)	(3)	(4)	(5)	(6)	(7)	(8)	(9)	(10)	(11)	(12)	(1)+(2)	(1)+(2)+(5)+(6)+(8)	part	(10)+(11)
TOTAL		1.481	1.933	1.559	4.786	3.915	1.148	1.539	.693	1.522	.105	.704	2.714	3.478	9.920	13.704	.812
WORK	7.490	1.122	.389	.632	.924	1.362	.029	.502	.623	.000	.038	.238	.803	1.525	3.671	4.198	.276

UNITED STATES: NONWHITE (REGISTRATION STATES) 1920 MALES

POPULATION, DEATHS, DEATH RATES FOR ALL CAUSES COMBINED, AND SPECIFIED CAUSES

Age Start of Interval	Midyear Population	Deaths During Year	All Causes	Respiratory T.B.	Other Infec. and Paras.	Neoplasms	Cardiovascular	Infl., Pneu., Bronch.	Diarrheal	Certain Degenerative	Maternal	Cert. Dis. of Infancy	Motor Vehicle	Other Violence	Other and Unknown	Age Start of Interval
0	74511	12413	.16659	.00106	.01704	.00005	.00068	.03653	.02258	.00070	.00000	.04704	.00003	.00280	.03767	0
1	316732	4723	.01491	.00046	.00332	.00003	.00016	.00513	.00222	.00017	.00000	.00000	.00004	.00109	.00229	1
5	418849	1544	.00369	.00030	.00106	.00001	.00011	.00084	.00006	.00011	.00000	.00000	.00011	.00041	.00068	5
10	394076	1413	.00359	.00043	.00078	.00001	.00020	.00074	.00003	.00011	.00000	.00000	.00008	.00064	.00056	10
15	355057	2755	.00776	.00218	.00108	.00003	.00033	.00164	.00003	.00016	.00000	.00000	.00007	.00150	.00074	15
20	338071	4080	.01207	.00416	.00134	.00005	.00049	.00219	.00002	.00033	.00000	.00000	.00009	.00235	.00105	20
25	321233	3578	.01114	.00349	.00116	.00005	.00079	.00218	.00003	.00036	.00000	.00000	.00008	.00200	.00099	25
30	253987	3333	.01312	.00325	.00138	.00019	.00140	.00276	.00007	.00064	.00000	.00000	.00010	.00207	.00126	30
35	290524	4101	.01412	.00305	.00159	.00019	.00196	.00302	.00007	.00086	.00000	.00000	.00009	.00192	.00138	35
40	237774	3441	.01447	.00263	.00157	.00037	.00266	.00285	.00008	.00122	.00000	.00000	.00005	.00143	.00160	40
45	213456	3777	.01769	.00268	.00161	.00050	.00390	.00315	.00009	.00222	.00000	.00000	.00006	.00153	.00198	45
50	165522	3753	.02267	.00250	.00194	.00058	.00646	.00331	.00014	.00330	.00000	.00000	.00007	.00138	.00260	50
55	102068	2773	.02717	.00244	.00178	.00150	.00852	.00313	.00016	.00482	.00000	.00000	.00015	.00149	.00318	55
60	79844	2851	.03571	.00257	.00224	.00174	.01216	.00440	.00020	.00612	.00000	.00000	.00016	.00149	.00471	60
65	54258	2737	.05044	.00310	.00267	.00155	.01738	.00544	.00026	.01014	.00000	.00000	.00011	.00170	.00770	65
70	33855	2529	.07470	.00307	.00292	.00192	.02791	.00709	.00068	.01498	.00000	.00000	.00015	.00242	.01356	70
75	18950	1893	.09989	.00201	.00327	.00322	.03778	.00950	.00079	.01821	.00000	.00000	.00000	.00206	.02306	75
80	9461	1380	.14586	.00307	.00539	.00243	.05137	.01416	.00137	.02494	.00000	.00000	.00000	.00042	.03921	80
85+	6590	1622	.24613	.00288	.00592	.00379	.07086	.02261	.00182	.03475	.00000	.00000	.00030	.00607	.09712	85+
ALL	3684818	64696														
CRUDE DEATH RATE			.01756	.00216	.00187	.00030	.00261	.00330	.00073	.00137	.00000	.00095	.00008	.00149	.00270	
STANDARDIZED RATE (1)			.01959	.00199	.00215	.00028	.00248	.00383	.00114	.00132	.00000	.00166	.00008	.00145	.00321	
STANDARDIZED RATE (2)			.02329	.00224	.00203	.00050	.00484	.00379	.00077	.00252	.00000	.00097	.00009	.00155	.00398	
GEOMETRIC MEAN			.02542													

LIFE TABLE FOR ALL CAUSES COMBINED

Age (x)	Midyear Population	Deaths During Year	$_nM_x$	$_nq_x$	l_x	$_nd_x$	$_nL_x$	$_nm_x$	$_na_x$	T_x	$_nr_x$	$\overset{\circ}{e}_x$	Age (x)
0	74511	12413	.166593	.150390	100000	15039	90273	.166595	.353208	4422509	.000000	44.225	0
1	316732	4723	.014912	.057497	84961	4885	327632	.014910	1.500000	4332236	.000000	50.991	1
5	418849	1544	.003686	.018220	80076	1459	396733	.003678	2.500000	4004605	.000000	50.010	5
10	394076	1413	.003586	.017821	78617	1401	389893	.003593	2.721717	3607872	.009466	45.892	10
15	355057	2755	.007759	.038205	77216	2950	379320	.007777	2.708333	3217979	.010416	41.675	15
20	338071	4080	.012068	.058587	74266	4351	360627	.012065	2.540125	2838660	-.002133	38.223	20
25	321233	3578	.011138	.054180	69915	3788	340074	.011139	2.491860	2478033	.015357	35.444	25
30	253987	3333	.013123	.063560	66127	4203	320218	.013125	2.521463	2137959	.003241	32.331	30
35	290524	4101	.014116	.068164	61924	4221	299032	.014116	2.491560	1817741	-.009240	29.354	35
40	237774	3441	.014472	.069875	57703	4032	278505	.014477	2.517309	1518709	-.010879	26.319	40
45	213456	3777	.017695	.084868	53671	4556	257228	.017712	2.557708	1240204	.010689	23.108	45
50	165522	3753	.022674	.107788	49115	5294	232557	.022764	2.541045	982976	.042378	20.014	50
55	102068	2773	.027168	.127770	43821	5599	205316	.027270	2.537321	750419	-.047882	17.125	55
60	79844	2851	.035707	.164748	38222	6297	175700	.035839	2.552869	545102	.029954	14.261	60
65	54258	2737	.050444	.225435	31925	7197	141949	.050701	2.543913	369402	.033109	11.571	65
70	33855	2529	.074701	.315998	24728	7814	104009	.075128	2.487736	227454	.032490	9.198	70
75	18950	1893	.099894	.398309	16914	6737	67222	.100220	2.425010	123444	.025428	7.298	75
80	9461	1380	.145862	.529527	10177	5389	36769	.146564	2.380582	56222	.025428	5.524	80
85+	6590	1622	.246131	1.000000	4788	4788	19453	.246131	4.062885	19453	.000000	4.063	85+

NUMBER OF PERSONS DYING (OUT OF 100,000 AT BIRTH) ABOVE AGE X FROM SPECIFIED CAUSES

Age (x)	All Causes	Respiratory T.B.	Other Infec. and Paras.	Neoplasms	Cardiovascular	Infl., Pneu., Bronch.	Diarrheal	Certain Degenerative	Maternal	Cert. Dis. of Infancy	Motor Vehicle	Other Violence	Other and Unknown	Age (x)
0	100000	10035	8845	2126	20217	16455	3302	10560	0	4246	391	6907	16916	0
1	84961	9939	7306	2121	20156	13157	1228	10497	0	0	388	6654	13515	1
5	80076	9787	6217	2110	20104	11478	501	10441	0	0	376	6297	12765	5
10	78617	9668	5799	2105	20061	11147	477	10398	0	0	333	6134	12495	10
15	77216	9501	5494	2100	19983	10858	466	10356	0	0	302	5882	12274	15
20	74266	8670	5083	2091	19857	10236	455	10295	0	0	275	5313	11991	20
25	69915	7169	4601	2073	19681	9446	447	10176	0	0	243	4467	11613	25
30	66127	5981	4206	2054	19412	8706	435	10052	0	0	217	3786	11278	30
35	61924	4940	3765	1993	18964	7821	413	9848	0	0	184	3124	10872	35
40	57703	4027	3290	1937	18378	6918	394	9592	0	0	157	2550	10460	40
45	53671	3295	2852	1835	17636	6124	370	9252	0	0	142	2152	10013	45
50	49115	2607	2439	1706	16631	5314	348	8680	0	0	127	1759	9504	50
55	43821	2027	1987	1475	15119	4544	315	7908	0	0	112	1438	8896	55
60	38222	1527	1621	1165	13358	3902	283	6912	0	0	81	1132	8241	60
65	31925	1075	1226	859	11212	3126	247	5832	0	0	53	886	7409	65
70	24728	635	846	581	8731	2352	210	4384	0	0	37	644	6308	70
75	16914	316	541	381	5810	1611	139	2818	0	0	22	391	4885	75
80	10177	181	321	164	3262	971	86	1591	0	0	22	253	3326	80
85+	4788	56	115	74	1379	440	35	676	0	0	6	118	1889	85+

NUMBER OF PERSONS SURVIVING TO AGE X IF SPECIFIED CAUSES WERE ELIMINATED

Age (x)	No Causes	Respiratory T.B. (1)	Other Infec. and Paras. (2)	Neoplasms (3)	Cardiovascular (4)	Infl., Pneu., Bronch. (5)	Diarrheal (6)	Certain Degenerative (7)	Maternal (8)	Cert. Dis. of Infancy (9)	Motor Vehicle (10)	Other Violence (11)	Other and Unknown (12)	(1) + (2)	(1) + (2) + (5) + (6) + (8)	(1)+(2)+(5)+(6)+(8)+part of (9)&(12)	(10) + (11)	Age (x)
0	100000	100000	100000	100000	100000	100000	100000	100000	100000	100000	100000	100000	100000	100000	100000	100000	100000	0
1	84961	85049	86390	84966	85017	88052	86892	85019	84961	88962	84964	85194	88151	86480	91684	99155	85197	1
5	80076	80307	82505	80091	80179	84656	82621	80185	80076	83847	80090	80644	83841	82743	90258	98464	80658	5
10	78617	78962	81430	78637	78761	83501	81140	78767	78617	82319	78674	79337	82594	81787	89655	98013	79395	10
15	77216	77722	80292	77240	77435	82217	79706	77405	77216	80852	77302	78176	81353	80818	88935	97406	78264	15
20	74266	75578	77644	74298	74601	79825	76672	74508	74266	77763	74376	75757	78537	79016	87681	96285	75868	20
25	69915	72649	73586	69963	70402	75577	72188	70258	69915	73207	70049	72160	74021	76643	85793	94558	72299	25
30	66127	69921	70004	66191	66852	72647	68289	66573	66127	69241	66279	68937	70645	74021	83977	92866	69096	30
35	61924	66550	66008	62043	63044	68577	63570	62541	61924	64840	62099	65226	66576	70939	81629	90630	65410	35
40	57703	62967	61999	57868	59326	65253	59629	58529	57703	60420	57892	61366	62467	67655	79060	88146	61566	40
45	53671	59341	58122	53924	55922	61565	55486	54773	53671	56158	53861	57487	58571	64263	76208	85344	57690	45
50	49115	55035	53617	49470	52188	57233	50758	50686	49115	51428	49303	53010	54133	60080	72410	81475	53213	50
55	43821	49719	48306	44359	48107	51917	45355	45982	43821	45884	44003	47624	48935	54807	67205	76007	47822	55
60	38222	43898	42511	38985	43805	45998	39591	41095	38222	40022	38410	41850	43371	48824	60860	69175	42056	60
65	31925	37141	35910	32848	38905	39281	33102	35402	31925	33428	32108	35201	37100	41777	53299	61020	35402	65
70	24728	29219	28191	25694	32911	31271	25614	28869	24728	25892	24883	27500	29885	33310	43734	50596	27673	70
75	16914	20293	19568	17745	25550	22172	17622	21306	16914	17710	17033	19042	21913	23478	32064	37676	19175	75
80	10177	12332	11970	10853	18919	14000	10645	14057	10177	10656	10248	11575	14844	14505	20872	25120	11656	80
85+	4788	5904	5796	5171	11584	7095	5044	7517	4788	5013	4832	5550	8539	7147	11159	14067	5601	85+

ADDED YRS OF LIFE

	No Causes	(1)	(2)	(3)	(4)	(5)	(6)	(7)	(8)	(9)	(10)	(11)	(12)	(1)+(2)	(1)+(2)+(5)+(6)+(8)	+part of(9)&(12)	(10)+(11)
TOTAL		2.944	2.970	.320	3.301	5.367	1.464	1.565	.000	2.066	.113	2.088	4.286	6.213	14.621	21.531	2.210
WORK	13.109	2.581	1.116	.170	1.380	2.022	.043	.683	.000	.000	.065	1.519	1.041	3.811	6.206	6.967	1.588

UNITED STATES: NONWHITE (REGISTRATION STATES) 1920 FEMALES

POPULATION, DEATHS, DEATH RATES FOR ALL CAUSES COMBINED, AND SPECIFIED CAUSES

Age Start of Interval	Midyear Popula-tion	Deaths During Year	All Causes	Respira-tory T. B.	Other Infec. and Paras.	Neo-plasms	Cardio-vascular	Infl., Pneu., Bronch.	Diar-rheal	Certain Degen-erative	Maternal	Cert. Dis. of Infancy	Motor Vehicle	Other Violence	Other and Unknown	Age Start of Interval
0	76585	9958	.13003	.00116	.01494	.00007	.00068	.02823	.01865	.00047	.00000	.03503	.00000	.00230	.02850	0
1	318150	4487	.01410	.00049	.00337	.00004	.00014	.00470	.00195	.00015	.00000	.00000	.00004	.00115	.00209	1
5	418655	1619	.00387	.00040	.00112	.00002	.00016	.00083	.00010	.00007	.00000	.00000	.00004	.00057	.00055	5
10	399424	1574	.00394	.00106	.00081	.00003	.00024	.00076	.00003	.00012	.00009	.00000	.00000	.00020	.00061	10
15	382646	3399	.00888	.00297	.00118	.00004	.00036	.00148	.00004	.00024	.00122	.00000	.00001	.00037	.00099	15
20	384287	4808	.01251	.00458	.00139	.00013	.00065	.00197	.00006	.00031	.00140	.00000	.00002	.00046	.00155	20
25	357938	4442	.01241	.00373	.00113	.00031	.00111	.00242	.00009	.00044	.00126	.00000	.00002	.00041	.00149	25
30	266255	3836	.01441	.00342	.00118	.00075	.00133	.00277	.00009	.00079	.00144	.00000	.00002	.00044	.00218	30
35	270835	4155	.01534	.00283	.00121	.00128	.00220	.00247	.00013	.00129	.00121	.00000	.00002	.00040	.00229	35
40	215037	3498	.01627	.00231	.00106	.00187	.00352	.00232	.00012	.00165	.00061	.00000	.00002	.00030	.00250	40
45	157957	3353	.02123	.00229	.00120	.00246	.00582	.00280	.00022	.00265	.00021	.00000	.00003	.00032	.00324	45
50	123394	3104	.02516	.00227	.00120	.00283	.00789	.00317	.00022	.00387	.00002	.00000	.00002	.00047	.00320	50
55	77655	2443	.03146	.00184	.00161	.00341	.01159	.00380	.00026	.00482	.00000	.00000	.00044	.00367		55
60	62440	2498	.04001	.00202	.00149	.00404	.01505	.00538	.00037	.00564	.00000	.00000	.00008	.00050	.00545	60
65	43289	2316	.05350	.00199	.00162	.00444	.02183	.00621	.00044	.00841	.00000	.00000	.00005	.00090	.00762	65
70	31392	2127	.06776	.00207	.00229	.00478	.02749	.00768	.00067	.00858	.00000	.00000	.00003	.00143	.01233	70
75	17601	1624	.09227	.00187	.00312	.00483	.03898	.00858	.00114	.01284	.00000	.00000	.00205	.01846		75
80	10549	1334	.12646	.00218	.00313	.00446	.04579	.01346	.00047	.01526	.00000	.00000	.00009	.00322	.03839	80
85+	8875	1940	.21859	.00124	.00394	.00541	.06603	.01904	.00248	.02073	.00000	.00000	.00000	.00530	.09442	85+
ALL	3622564	62515														

	All Causes	Respira-tory T. B.	Other Infec. and Paras.	Neo-plasms	Cardio-vascular	Infl., Pneu., Bronch.	Diar-rheal	Certain Degen-erative	Maternal	Cert. Dis. of Infancy	Motor Vehicle	Other Violence	Other and Unknown
CRUDE DEATH RATE	.01726	.00231	.00168	.00081	.00277	.00299	.00068	.00118	.00065	.00074	.00002	.00055	.00287
STANDARDIZED RATE (1)	.01906	.00211	.00154	.00083	.00292	.00344	.00100	.00124	.00056	.00123	.00002	.00060	.00317
STANDARDIZED RATE (2)	.02318	.00223	.00175	.00133	.00547	.00356	.00071	.00215	.00054	.00073	.00002	.00062	.00406
GEOMETRIC MEAN	.02519												

LIFE TABLE FOR ALL CAUSES COMBINED

Age (x)	Midyear Popula-tion	Deaths During Year	$_nM_x$	$_nq_x$	l_x	$_nd_x$	$_nL_x$	$_nm_x$	$_na_x$	T_x	$_nr_x$	$\overset{\circ}{e}_x$	Age (x)
0	76585	9958	.130025	.119050	100000	11905	91560	.130024	.291043	4471998	.000000	44.720	0
1	318150	4487	.014103	.054498	88095	4801	340378	.014105	1.500000	4380438	.000000	49.724	1
5	418655	1619	.003867	.019101	83294	1591	412493	.003857	2.500000	4040061	.000000	48.504	5
10	399424	1574	.003941	.019559	81703	1598	404915	.003947	2.746923	3627568	-.004324	44.399	10
15	382646	3399	.008883	.043505	80105	3485	392448	.008880	2.682269	3222653	-.001256	40.230	15
20	384287	4808	.012511	.060650	76620	4647	371659	.012503	2.538017	2830206	-.009575	36.938	20
25	357938	4442	.012410	.060203	71973	4333	349045	.012414	2.502933	2458547	.017145	34.159	25
30	266255	3836	.014407	.069604	67640	4708	326496	.014420	2.513983	2109501	.017221	31.187	30
35	270835	4155	.015341	.073873	62932	4649	303008	.015343	2.493592	1783006	.002991	28.332	35
40	215037	3498	.016267	.078325	58283	4565	280166	.016294	2.535871	1479998	.029875	25.393	40
45	157957	3353	.021227	.101177	53718	5435	255246	.021293	2.544810	1199832	.031531	22.336	45
50	123394	3104	.025155	.118758	48283	5734	227246	.025233	2.528957	944586	.043099	19.564	50
55	77655	2443	.031460	.146466	42549	6232	197351	.031578	2.529819	717339	.040993	16.859	55
60	62440	2498	.040006	.182449	36317	6626	165184	.040113	2.524682	519989	.023383	14.318	60
65	43289	2316	.053501	.236334	29691	7017	130901	.053606	2.498308	354805	.016132	11.950	65
70	31392	2127	.067756	.289715	22674	6569	96740	.067904	2.468412	223904	.020210	9.875	70
75	17601	1624	.092267	.373859	16105	6021	65106	.092480	2.439067	127164	.016455	7.896	75
80	10549	1334	.126457	.476795	10084	4808	37922	.126785	2.400686	62059	.016455	6.154	80
85+	8875	1940	.218592	1.000000	5276	5276	24136	.218592	4.574742	24136	.000000	4.575	85+

NUMBER OF PERSONS DYING (OUT OF 100,000 AT BIRTH) ABOVE AGE X FROM SPECIFIED CAUSES

Age (x)	All Causes	Respiratory T. B.	Other Infec. and Paras.	Neoplasms	Cardiovascular	Infl., Pneu., Bronch.	Diarrheal	Certain Degenerative	Maternal	Cert. Dis. of Infancy	Motor Vehicle	Other Violence	Other and Unknown	Age (x)
0	100000	10157	7724	5643	22612	15497	3091	8986	2538	3208	106	2724	17714	0
1	88095	10050	6356	5637	22550	12912	1384	8943	2538	0	106	2514	15105	1
5	83294	9884	5210	5624	22504	11312	720	8892	2538	0	93	2122	14395	5
10	81703	9720	4751	5616	22436	10969	678	8862	2538	0	79	1886	14168	10
15	80105	9292	4424	5604	22340	10661	667	8812	2502	0	78	1806	13919	15
20	76620	8126	3961	5590	22199	10079	650	8720	2025	0	76	1662	13532	20
25	71973	6424	3443	5543	21960	9348	628	8605	1506	0	68	1491	12957	25
30	67640	5123	3049	5435	21573	8503	595	8453	1067	0	60	1347	12435	30
35	62932	4008	2664	5188	21138	7599	566	8193	597	0	54	1204	11721	35
40	58283	3150	2296	4801	20469	6849	525	7801	232	0	48	1083	11029	40
45	53718	2504	2001	4275	19479	6200	491	7338	62	0	43	999	10326	45
50	48283	1921	1693	3647	17984	5484	436	6657	10	0	37	918	9496	50
55	42549	1406	1420	3002	16182	4763	386	5774	5	0	31	810	8770	55
60	36317	1044	1102	2327	13882	4010	335	4820	5	0	26	724	8042	60
65	29691	710	856	1659	11387	3119	274	3887	5	0	13	642	7139	65
70	22674	450	644	1078	8523	2304	217	2784	5	0	7	523	6139	70
75	16105	250	421	616	5858	1560	152	1914	5	0	4	384	4941	75
80	10084	128	217	301	3315	975	78	1076	5	0	4	251	3734	80
85+	5276	30	95	131	1594	460	60	500	0	0	0	128	2278	85+

NUMBER OF PERSONS SURVIVING TO AGE X IF SPECIFIED CAUSES WERE ELIMINATED

Age (x)	No Causes	Respiratory T. B.	Other Infec. and Paras.	Neoplasms	Cardiovascular	Infl., Pneu., Bronch.	Diarrheal	Certain Degenerative	Maternal	Cert. Dis. of Infancy	Motor Vehicle	Other Violence	Other and Unknown	(1) + (2)	(1) + (2) + (5) + (6) + (8)	(1)+(2)+(5)+(6)+(8)+part of(9)&(12)	(10) + (11)	Age (x)
		(1)	(2)	(3)	(4)	(5)	(6)	(7)	(8)	(9)	(10)	(11)	(12)					
0	100000	100000	100000	100000	100000	100000	100000	100000	100000	100000	100000	100000	100000	100000	100000	100000	100000	0
1	88095	88195	89388	88101	88153	90553	89711	88135	88095	91156	88095	88292	90576	89489	93674	99334	88292	1
5	83294	83551	85654	83312	83394	87232	85482	83382	83294	86188	83307	83863	86353	85918	92344	98636	83876	5
10	81703	82117	84487	81729	81868	85523	83892	81819	81703	84542	81729	82497	84937	84916	91693	98140	82521	10
15	80105	80939	83170	80142	80362	84563	82262	80268	80141	82888	80132	80964	83532	84036	91142	97798	80991	15
20	76620	78579	80023	76669	77005	81487	78700	76866	77122	79282	76648	77584	80294	82068	90239	97247	77612	20
25	71973	75523	77655	72065	72568	78074	73949	72316	72953	74474	72007	73046	76010	79429	88846	96383	73080	25
30	67640	72311	71540	67832	68579	73534	69530	68111	68993	69990	67679	68790	71971	76480	87178	95135	68830	30
35	62932	68435	66955	63350	64233	69370	64719	63624	64655	65119	62974	64142	67698	72810	84796	93274	64186	35
40	58283	64282	62386	59047	60150	65045	59979	59307	60239	60308	58328	59523	63418	68808	81677	90463	59569	40
45	53718	59934	57803	54937	56431	60649	55314	55117	55689	55584	53764	54943	55189	64492	77727	88876	54990	45
50	48283	54489	52269	49991	52234	55284	49772	50208	50105	49961	48330	49462	54074	58987	72249	80977	49511	50
55	42549	48564	46340	44685	47899	49458	43909	45116	44159	44027	42556	43692	48420	52891	65900	74229	43741	55
60	36317	41833	39873	38799	43347	43065	37527	39452	37691	37579	36362	37374	42100	45929	58407	66117	37420	60
65	29691	34548	32842	32370	38233	38173	30737	33182	30814	30723	29740	30632	35378	38215	50023	57045	30682	65
70	22674	26647	25285	25276	32597	28502	23524	26437	23532	23462	22716	23500	28079	29715	40220	46261	23544	70
75	16105	19123	18170	18387	26601	21043	16766	19646	16714	16665	16137	16813	21234	21575	30457	35539	16847	75
80	10084	12087	11558	11795	20295	13787	10558	13129	10466	10434	10104	10637	14615	13853	20582	24485	10659	80
85+	5276	6408	6147	6314	13390	7732	5537	7423	5479	5459	5289	5659	9304	7466	11926	14831	5673	85+

ADDED YRS OF LIFE

	No Causes	(1)	(2)	(3)	(4)	(5)	(6)	(7)	(8)	(9)	(10)	(11)	(12)	(1)+(2)	(1)+(2)+(5)+(6)+(8)	combo+part	(10)+(11)
TOTAL		3.139	2.704	1.005	4.054	4.795	1.290	1.496	.830	1.544	.030	.814	4.441	6.112	14.772	20.963	.845
WORK	14.199	2.634	.950	.633	1.654	1.805	.076	.775	.852	.000	.014	.309	1.491	3.681	6.896	8.097	.323

POPULATION, DEATHS, DEATH RATES FOR ALL CAUSES COMBINED, AND SPECIFIED CAUSES

Age Start of Interval	Midyear Population	Deaths During Year	All Causes	Respiratory T.B.	Other Infec. and Paras.	Neo-plasms	Cardio-vascular	Infl., Pneu., Bronch.	Diar-rheal	Certain Degen-erative	Maternal	Cert. Dis. of Infancy	Motor Vehicle	Other Violence	Other and Unknown	Age Start of Interval
0	1049309	81251	.07743	.00022	.00520	.00008	.00054	.01267	.00543	.00016	.00000	.03181	.00008	.00113	.01611	0
1	4445634	26675	.00600	.00009	.00153	.00009	.00011	.00133	.00104	.00008	.00000	.00000	.00017	.00052	.00105	1
5	6053720	12666	.00209	.00004	.00052	.00006	.00014	.00024	.00005	.00006	.00000	.00000	.00024	.00028	.00046	5
10	5796286	9804	.00169	.00006	.00028	.00005	.00017	.00015	.00001	.00007	.00000	.00000	.00016	.00035	.00039	10
15	5485717	15955	.00292	.00023	.00034	.00007	.00022	.00029	.00001	.00009	.00000	.00000	.00036	.00069	.00051	15
20	5297331	20955	.00396	.00073	.00037	.00008	.00026	.00036	.00001	.00015	.00000	.00000	.00049	.00099	.00052	20
25	4659862	21141	.00454	.00091	.00034	.00012	.00036	.00042	.00001	.00021	.00000	.00000	.00042	.00115	.00060	25
30	4376310	22905	.00523	.00098	.00041	.00019	.00057	.00051	.00001	.00032	.00000	.00000	.00036	.00118	.00071	30
35	4492770	28931	.00644	.00098	.00047	.00030	.00092	.00065	.00002	.00050	.00000	.00000	.00035	.00131	.00089	35
40	4007891	34346	.00857	.00106	.00058	.00056	.00166	.00090	.00002	.00086	.00000	.00000	.00040	.00145	.00109	40
45	3546361	40758	.01149	.00112	.00073	.00093	.00288	.00109	.00003	.00128	.00000	.00000	.00044	.00159	.00140	45
50	3039697	48560	.01598	.00113	.00084	.00165	.00490	.00135	.00004	.00204	.00000	.00000	.00051	.00171	.00180	50
55	2367000	52263	.02208	.00114	.00092	.00267	.00781	.00166	.00006	.00316	.00000	.00000	.00060	.00178	.00227	55
60	1888535	60425	.03200	.00113	.00098	.00404	.01279	.00223	.00008	.00481	.00000	.00000	.00067	.00206	.00321	60
65	1384709	64383	.04650	.00119	.00107	.00602	.02035	.00302	.00013	.00725	.00000	.00000	.00085	.00224	.00436	65
70	964822	66569	.06900	.00120	.00104	.00831	.03263	.00457	.00020	.01105	.00000	.00000	.00101	.00253	.00646	70
75	536413	54681	.10194	.00111	.00122	.01005	.05103	.00724	.00037	.01661	.00000	.00000	.00111	.00335	.00986	75
80	246358	37543	.15239	.00099	.00145	.01152	.07733	.01185	.00091	.02385	.00000	.00000	.00143	.00518	.01790	80
85+	113833	26829	.23569	.00065	.00200	.01208	.11650	.02148	.00163	.03291	.00000	.00000	.00148	.00941	.03756	85+
ALL	59752558	726680														

	All Causes	Resp. T.B.	Other Infec.	Neo-plasms	Cardio-vascular	Infl. Pneu.	Diar-rheal	Certain Degen.	Maternal	Cert. Dis. Infancy	Motor Vehicle	Other Violence	Other and Unknown
CRUDE DEATH RATE	.01216	.00067	.00070	.00092	.00347	.00117	.00028	.00129	.00000	.00056	.00039	.00112	.00158
STANDARDIZED RATE (1)	.01118	.00056	.00079	.00067	.00243	.00125	.00049	.00092	.00000	.00112	.00035	.00098	.00163
STANDARDIZED RATE (2)	.01619	.00069	.00075	.00131	.00537	.00148	.00033	.00190	.00000	.00066	.00043	.00123	.00204
GEOMETRIC MEAN	.01546												

LIFE TABLE FOR ALL CAUSES COMBINED

Age (x)	Midyear Population	Deaths During Year	$_nM_x$	$_nq_x$	l_x	$_nd_x$	$_nL_x$	$_nm_x$	$_na_x$	T_x	$_nr_x$	$\overset{\circ}{e}_x$	Age (x)
0	1049309	81251	.077433	.072920	100000	7292	94178	.077428	.201636	5757645	.000000	57.576	0
1	4445634	26675	.006000	.023655	92708	2193	365350	.006002	1.500000	5663467	.000000	61.089	1
5	6053720	12666	.002092	.010396	90515	941	450223	.002090	2.500000	5298117	.000000	58.533	5
10	5796286	9804	.001691	.008429	89574	755	446055	.001693	2.595475	4847895	.006471	54.122	10
15	5485717	15955	.002916	.014490	88819	1287	441078	.002918	2.655724	4401840	.005345	49.560	15
20	5297331	20955	.003956	.019616	87532	1717	433501	.003961	2.577655	3960762	.009736	45.249	20
25	4659862	21141	.004537	.022455	85815	1927	424351	.004541	2.548759	3527262	.016354	41.103	25
30	4376310	22905	.005234	.025844	83888	2168	414158	.005235	2.563807	3102910	-.002398	36.989	30
35	4492770	28931	.006439	.031706	81720	2591	402364	.006439	2.593111	2688752	-.000089	32.902	35
40	4007891	34346	.008570	.042033	79129	3326	387675	.008579	2.603728	2286388	.011618	28.894	40
45	3546361	40758	.011493	.056027	75803	4247	368655	.011514	2.607625	1898713	.013473	25.048	45
50	3039697	48560	.015975	.077142	71556	5520	344542	.016021	2.601864	1529858	.021493	21.380	50
55	2367000	52263	.022080	.105185	66036	6946	313499	.022156	2.598468	1185316	.024675	17.950	55
60	1888535	60425	.031996	.148976	59090	8803	274189	.032106	2.584796	871817	.022147	14.754	60
65	1384709	64383	.046496	.209378	50287	10529	225726	.046645	2.558252	597628	.019402	11.884	65
70	964822	66569	.068996	.295463	39758	11747	169600	.069263	2.515146	371902	.021807	9.354	70
75	536413	54681	.101938	.406376	28011	11383	111042	.102511	2.451188	202302	.029958	7.222	75
80	246358	37543	.152392	.546067	16628	9080	59235	.153289	2.367245	91260	.029958	5.488	80
85+	113833	26829	.235687	1.000000	7548	7548	32025	.235687	4.242909	32025	.000000	4.243	85+

NUMBER OF PERSONS DYING (OUT OF 100,000 AT BIRTH) ABOVE AGE X FROM SPECIFIED CAUSES

Age (x)	All Causes	Respiratory T.B.	Other Infec. and Paras.	Neoplasms	Cardiovascular	Infl., Pneu., Bronch.	Diarrheal	Certain Degenerative	Maternal	Cert. Dis. of Infancy	Motor Vehicle	Other Violence	Other and Unknown	Age (x)
0	100000	4313	4273	8461	34776	8818	1608	12319	0	2995	2578	7606	12253	0
1	92708	4292	3783	8453	34725	7625	720	12303	0	0	2570	7500	10737	1
5	90515	4259	3223	8421	34686	7140	340	12275	0	0	2506	7311	10354	5
10	89574	4240	2988	8395	34624	7032	317	12250	0	0	2397	7185	10146	10
15	88819	4212	2862	8373	34547	6965	312	12220	0	0	2326	7029	9973	15
20	87532	4064	2711	8342	34449	6837	308	12179	0	0	2167	6725	9750	20
25	85815	3746	2552	8308	34238	6682	303	12113	0	0	1954	6297	9522	25
30	83888	3359	2407	8256	34185	6506	298	12022	0	0	1776	5810	9269	30
35	81720	2955	2238	8178	33950	6294	293	11888	0	0	1628	5321	8975	35
40	79129	2558	2049	8057	33578	6016	286	11687	0	0	1486	4794	8618	40
45	75803	2148	1826	7840	32931	5668	277	11354	0	0	1332	4231	8196	45
50	71556	1737	1557	7496	31867	5266	266	10879	0	0	1169	3644	7675	50
55	66036	1348	1266	6926	30170	4799	252	10172	0	0	994	3053	7056	55
60	59090	990	977	6084	27709	4278	232	9176	0	0	807	2494	6343	60
65	50287	680	710	4971	24188	3667	210	7851	0	0	624	1927	5459	65
70	39758	412	467	3608	19577	2982	181	6208	0	0	431	1421	4471	70
75	28011	209	290	2194	14018	2204	147	4326	0	0	259	991	3373	75
80	16628	86	155	1075	8317	1395	106	2471	0	0	136	617	2270	80
85+	7548	21	64	387	3731	688	52	1054	0	0	48	301	1202	85+

NUMBER OF PERSONS SURVIVING TO AGE X IF SPECIFIED CAUSES WERE ELIMINATED

Age (x)	No Causes	Respiratory T.B. (1)	Other Infec. and Paras. (2)	Neoplasms (3)	Cardiovascular (4)	Infl., Pneu., Bronch. (5)	Diarrheal (6)	Certain Degenerative (7)	Maternal (8)	Cert. Dis. of Infancy (9)	Motor Vehicle (10)	Other Violence (11)	Other and Unknown (12)	(1) + (2)	(1)+(2)+(5)+(6)+(8)	(1)+(2)+(5)+(6)+(8)+part of (9)&(12)	(10)+(11)	Age (x)
0	100000	100000	100000	100000	100000	100000	100000	100000	100000	100000	100000	100000	100000	100000	100000	100000	100000	0
1	92708	92728	93181	92716	92757	93864	93567	92723	92708	95636	92716	92810	94179	93201	95237	99487	92818	1
5	90515	90567	91535	90554	90602	92130	91733	90558	90515	93374	90586	90802	92336	91587	94476	99025	90873	5
10	89574	89645	90820	89639	89721	91281	90803	89641	89574	92403	89753	89984	91588	90891	93894	98535	90163	10
15	88819	88917	90181	88905	89042	90580	90042	88915	88819	91625	89067	89381	90992	90281	93339	98026	89631	15
20	87532	87776	89027	87648	87849	89397	88742	87668	87532	90297	87935	88391	89901	89275	92437	97178	88797	20
25	85815	86371	87441	85962	86236	87800	87006	86014	85815	88526	86422	87086	88369	88007	91293	96083	87702	25
30	83888	84817	85624	84083	84452	86007	85057	84172	83888	86538	84659	85620	86643	86572	89996	94838	86407	30
35	81720	83029	83581	81987	82504	83999	82864	82130	81720	84301	82618	83901	84704	84920	88510	93413	84823	35
40	79129	80794	81122	79508	80259	81618	80244	79725	79129	81628	80140	81775	82383	82829	86637	91594	82820	40
45	75803	77809	77936	76380	77531	78539	76880	76703	75803	78197	76924	79351	79998	79905	84063	89037	80076	45
50	71556	73860	73838	72438	74253	74544	72583	72875	71556	73816	72775	75083	75437	76215	80538	85481	76362	50
55	66036	68548	68431	67407	70239	69262	66958	67949	66036	68122	67332	69888	70247	71034	75589	80399	71260	55
60	59090	61689	61516	61136	65378	62499	59970	61779	59090	60956	60430	63097	63579	64222	68934	73479	64528	60
65	50287	52756	52607	53100	59351	53783	51056	53868	50287	51875	51600	54256	54990	55233	59976	64089	55673	65
70	39758	41991	41817	43278	52017	43176	40392	44180	39758	41014	40971	43381	44445	44166	48728	52217	44704	70
75	28011	29762	29616	31799	43266	31134	28487	32923	28011	28896	29013	30955	32355	31467	35569	38255	32063	75
80	16628	17765	17689	19860	33365	19181	16943	21276	16628	17153	17319	18692	20205	18898	22213	24021	19469	80
85+	7548	8110	8093	9571	22570	9259	7727	10925	7548	7786	7922	8722	10064	8696	10920	11935	9154	85+

ADDED YRS OF LIFE

	No Causes	(1)	(2)	(3)	(4)	(5)	(6)	(7)	(8)	(9)	(10)	(11)	(12)	(1)+(2)	(1)+(2)+(5)+(6)+(8)	+part of (9)&(12)	(10)+(11)
TOTAL		1.140	1.484	1.142	5.582	2.226	.817	1.624	.000	1.812	.699	1.554	2.961	2.670	5.957	9.620	2.696
WORK	7.169	.822	.451	.373	1.158	.587	.017	.528	.000	.000	.412	1.156	.817	1.287	1.922	2.228	1.584

POPULATION, DEATHS, DEATH RATES FOR ALL CAUSES COMBINED, AND SPECIFIED CAUSES

Age Start of Interval	Midyear Population	Deaths During Year	All Causes	Respiratory T. B.	Other Infec. and Paras.	Neoplasms	Cardiovascular	Infl., Pneu., Bronch.	Diarrheal	Certain Degenerative	Maternal	Cert. Dis. of Infancy	Motor Vehicle	Other Violence	Other and Unknown	Age Start of Interval
0	1016519	62081	.06107	.00019	.00476	.00007	.00041	.01013	.00736	.00013	.00000	.02440	.00005	.00095	.01260	0
1	4284665	22494	.00525	.00009	.00142	.00008	.00010	.00120	.00087	.00006	.00000	.00000	.00012	.00043	.00088	1
5	5906876	10028	.00170	.00005	.00046	.00004	.00014	.00022	.00004	.00005	.00000	.00000	.00012	.00016	.00041	5
10	5675704	7678	.00135	.00013	.00025	.00004	.00020	.00015	.00001	.00008	.00001	.00000	.00006	.00010	.00032	10
15	5514459	14565	.00264	.00064	.00030	.00006	.00024	.00021	.00001	.00012	.00033	.00000	.00012	.00018	.00042	15
20	5284359	19869	.00376	.00108	.00033	.00009	.00032	.00026	.00001	.00015	.00058	.00000	.00011	.00025	.00058	20
25	4772410	20115	.00421	.00106	.00031	.00021	.00040	.00030	.00002	.00021	.00066	.00000	.00009	.00026	.00070	25
30	4380810	20271	.00463	.00086	.00029	.00042	.00057	.00035	.00002	.00031	.00067	.00000	.00009	.00024	.00081	30
35	4356843	23835	.00547	.00072	.00032	.00075	.00082	.00041	.00002	.00048	.00060	.00000	.00009	.00026	.00099	35
40	3741237	25776	.00689	.00062	.00036	.00135	.00141	.00049	.00002	.00081	.00030	.00000	.00010	.00028	.00115	40
45	3265041	29539	.00905	.00058	.00039	.00157	.00237	.00065	.00003	.00119	.00005	.00000	.00014	.00030	.00139	45
50	2771344	34332	.01239	.00056	.00042	.00267	.00376	.00081	.00004	.00185	.00000	.00000	.00018	.00036	.00173	50
55	2175578	37909	.01742	.00055	.00043	.00389	.00591	.00116	.00006	.00283	.00000	.00000	.00023	.00044	.00210	55
60	1769643	45362	.02563	.00063	.00045	.00474	.00995	.00179	.00009	.00436	.00000	.00000	.00023	.00063	.00273	60
65	1328302	50595	.03809	.00079	.00053	.00609	.01638	.00271	.00012	.00665	.00000	.00000	.00038	.00092	.00351	65
70	939819	55088	.05862	.00086	.00067	.00815	.02766	.00439	.00025	.00972	.00000	.00000	.00041	.00163	.00486	70
75	551253	49296	.08943	.00100	.00092	.00955	.04511	.00742	.00047	.01375	.00000	.00000	.00049	.00357	.00715	75
80	279826	38318	.13694	.00092	.00126	.01123	.07037	.01258	.00096	.01874	.00000	.00000	.00050	.00695	.01343	80
85+	152364	33409	.21927	.00063	.00176	.01224	.10994	.02058	.00179	.02495	.00000	.00000	.00033	.01471	.03193	85+
ALL	58167052	600560														

CRUDE DEATH RATE			.01032	.00058	.00053	.00119	.00304	.00055	.00024	.00116	.00026	.00043	.00013	.00041	.00141	
STANDARDIZED RATE (1)			.00929	.00052	.00064	.00087	.00206	.00100	.00039	.00082	.00023	.00086	.00012	.00036	.00141	
STANDARDIZED RATE (2)			.01365	.00058	.00057	.00158	.00459	.00124	.00028	.00166	.00023	.00051	.00015	.00053	.00174	
GEOMETRIC MEAN			.01309													

LIFE TABLE FOR ALL CAUSES COMBINED

Age (x)	Midyear Population	Deaths During Year	$_nM_x$	$_nq_x$	l_x	$_nd_x$	$_nL_x$	$_nm_x$	$_na_x$	T_x	$_nr_x$	$\overset{\circ}{e}_x$	Age (x)
0	1016519	62081	.061072	.058140	100000	5814	95197	.061074	.173823	6100989	.000000	61.010	0
1	4284665	22494	.005250	.020725	94186	1952	371864	.005249	1.500000	6005792	.000000	63.765	1
5	5906876	10028	.001698	.008446	92234	779	459223	.001696	2.500000	5633928	.000000	61.083	5
10	5675704	7678	.001353	.006746	91455	617	455819	.001354	2.639789	5174706	.004259	56.582	10
15	5514459	14565	.002641	.013133	90838	1193	451427	.002643	2.684234	4718887	.003628	51.948	15
20	5284359	19869	.003760	.018651	89645	1672	444179	.003764	2.580119	4267460	.008025	47.604	20
25	4772410	20115	.004215	.020870	87973	1836	435337	.004217	2.533928	3823281	.014956	43.460	25
30	4380810	20271	.004627	.022882	86137	1971	425849	.004628	2.546191	3387944	.006336	39.332	30
35	4356843	23835	.005471	.027006	84166	2273	415316	.005473	2.574241	2962095	.007121	35.193	35
40	3741237	25776	.006890	.033959	81893	2781	402770	.006905	2.592742	2546779	.018902	31.099	40
45	3265041	29539	.009047	.044380	79112	3511	387154	.009069	2.605739	2144008	.019054	27.101	45
50	2771344	34332	.012388	.060356	75601	4563	367109	.012430	2.612088	1756855	.025924	23.239	50
55	2175578	37909	.017425	.083583	71038	5966	340967	.017497	2.616040	1389746	.027339	19.563	55
60	1769643	45362	.025633	.121189	65072	7886	306488	.025730	2.606861	1048778	.024011	16.117	60
65	1328302	50555	.038090	.175060	57186	10011	261378	.038241	2.588569	742291	.023232	12.980	65
70	939819	55088	.058616	.257382	47175	12142	206111	.058910	2.548695	480501	.026468	10.186	70
75	551253	49296	.089425	.366768	35033	12849	142659	.089942	2.485683	274390	.028628	7.832	75
80	279826	38318	.136935	.507528	22184	11259	81707	.137796	2.405409	131532	.028628	5.929	80
85+	152364	33409	.219271	1.000000	10925	10925	49824	.219271	4.560568	49824	.000000	4.561	85+

NUMBER OF PERSONS DYING (OUT OF 100,000 AT BIRTH) ABOVE AGE X FROM SPECIFIED CAUSES

Age (x)	All Causes	Respiratory T. B.	Other Infec. and Paras.	Neoplasms	Cardio-vascular	Infl., Pneu., Bronch.	Diarrheal	Certain Degenerative	Maternal	Cert. Dis. of Infancy	Motor Vehicle	Other Violence	Other and Unknown	Age (x)
0	100000	3748	3321	11935	36979	8705	1490	12937	1373	2323	978	3952	12219	0
1	94186	3729	2867	11929	36940	7740	789	12925	1373	0	973	3901	11020	1
5	92234	3696	2338	11900	36901	7294	467	12901	1373	0	931	3740	10693	5
10	91455	3675	2126	11882	36838	7195	446	12877	1373	0	876	3664	10503	10
15	90838	3614	2014	11865	36748	7125	441	12841	1368	0	849	3618	10355	15
20	89645	3325	1876	11837	36639	7029	436	12789	1217	0	795	3537	10165	20
25	87973	2843	1732	11797	36496	6915	430	12724	955	0	744	3426	9907	25
30	86137	2382	1595	11708	36322	6783	423	12631	673	0	706	3314	9600	30
35	84166	2016	1471	11527	36079	6634	416	12500	389	0	666	3210	9258	35
40	81893	1715	1336	11213	35737	6465	406	12299	141	0	630	3102	8849	40
45	79112	1464	1191	10666	35166	6268	396	11973	21	0	590	2991	8386	45
50	75601	1242	1041	9902	34244	6016	384	11511	3	0	537	2876	7845	50
55	71038	1035	888	8917	32859	5719	368	10829	2	0	471	2742	7208	55
60	65072	835	740	7654	30834	5320	349	9860	2	0	394	2592	6492	60
65	57186	642	603	6197	27768	4768	320	8517	2	0	315	2399	5655	65
70	47175	435	464	4599	23459	4057	287	6769	2	0	214	2156	4733	70
75	35033	257	326	2913	17724	3146	235	4758	2	0	129	1817	3726	75
80	22184	113	194	1544	11240	2078	168	2784	2	0	59	1302	2700	80
85+	10925	31	88	610	5478	1045	89	1243	0	0	17	733	1591	85+

NUMBER OF PERSONS SURVIVING TO AGE X IF SPECIFIED CAUSES WERE ELIMINATED

Age (x)	No Causes	Respiratory T. B.	Other Infec. and Paras.	Neoplasms	Cardio-vascular	Infl., Pneu., Bronch.	Diarrheal	Certain Degenerative	Maternal	Cert. Dis. of Infancy	Motor Vehicle	Other Violence	Other and Unknown	(1) + (2)	(1) + (2) + (5) + (6) + (8)	(1)+(2)+ (5)+(6)+ (8)+part of(9)&(12)	(10) + (11)	Age (x)
		(1)	(2)	(3)	(4)	(5)	(6)	(7)	(8)	(9)	(10)	(11)	(12)					
0	100000	100000	100000	100000	100000	100000	100000	100000	100000	100000	100000	100000	100000	100000	100000	100000	100000	0
1	94186	94204	94628	94192	94224	95127	94869	94198	94186	96467	94191	94274	95357	94646	96285	99601	94279	1
5	92234	92285	93194	92268	92310	93602	93224	92269	92234	94468	92280	92480	93709	93245	95644	99223	92527	5
10	91455	91526	92620	91507	91593	92912	92458	91514	91455	93670	91556	91775	93110	92692	95202	98886	91876	10
15	90838	90970	92109	90907	91065	92356	91839	90932	90843	93038	90965	91202	92632	92242	94822	98579	91329	15
20	89645	90063	91038	89741	89977	91240	90638	89790	89800	91816	89824	90085	91608	91462	94284	98159	90265	20
25	87973	88864	89465	88107	88442	89653	88953	88180	88382	90104	88089	88515	90161	90391	93577	97624	88713	25
30	86137	87471	87755	86356	86769	87915	87104	86432	86822	88223	86356	86779	88591	89115	92707	96945	87041	30
35	84166	85838	85872	84560	85026	86054	85118	84584	85119	86205	84459	84897	86912	87578	91580	95986	85193	35
40	81893	83823	83689	82588	83072	83901	82829	82499	83067	83877	82214	82712	84983	85661	90037	94585	83036	40
45	79112	81229	80993	80328	80822	81259	80026	80021	80366	81028	79461	80013	82570	83160	87764	92361	80367	45
50	75601	77847	77548	77525	78162	77858	76487	76928	76817	77432	75987	76576	79459	79852	84580	89148	76967	50
55	71038	73355	73020	73831	74847	73493	71886	72961	72181	72759	71465	72086	75315	75401	80209	84666	72519	55
60	65072	67392	67033	68898	70635	67717	65867	67793	66119	66648	65537	66178	69719	69422	74304	78554	66651	60
65	57186	59411	59041	62008	65276	60051	57912	60903	58106	58571	57669	62114	61339	66280	70195	58835		65
70	47175	49206	48835	52745	58506	50221	47804	51957	47934	48318	47666	48354	52155	50937	55834	59257	48857	70
75	35033	36699	36388	40814	50015	38138	35546	40530	35597	35882	35471	36210	39697	38119	42783	45535	36662	75
80	22184	23357	23150	27121	39897	25087	22563	27524	22541	22721	22517	23356	26072	24374	28486	30451	23707	80
85+	10925	11562	11477	14165	28233	13184	11167	14935	11102	11190	11118	11922	13768	12147	15226	16423	12132	85+

ADDED YRS OF LIFE																		
TOTAL		1.179	1.308	1.906	6.042	1.989	.714	1.787	.545	1.474	.262	.756	2.948	2.521	6.025	9.321	1.024	
WORK	6.223	.841	.340	.719	1.046	.359	.020	.525	.466	.000	.115	.262	.882	1.189	2.116	2.541	.379	

POPULATION, DEATHS, DEATH RATES FOR ALL CAUSES COMBINED, AND SPECIFIED CAUSES

Age Start of Interval	Midyear Population	Deaths During Year	All Causes	Respiratory T. B.	Other Infec. and Paras.	Neoplasms	Cardiovascular	Infl., Pneu., Bronch.	Diarrheal	Certain Degenerative	Maternal	Cert. Dis. of Infancy	Motor Vehicle	Other Violence	Other and Unknown	Age Start of Interval
0	1028386	63612	.06186	.00010	.00313	.00013	.00036	.00994	.00452	.00013	.00000	.02923	.00006	.00137	.01289	0
1	4334694	13502	.00311	.00005	.00053	.00012	.00006	.00072	.00033	.00005	.00000	.00000	.00015	.00042	.00069	1
5	5427194	6650	.00123	.00002	.00017	.00008	.00009	.00011	.00001	.00004	.00000	.00000	.00018	.00023	.00030	5
10	5961524	6770	.00114	.00003	.00010	.00005	.00013	.00008	.00001	.00005	.00000	.00000	.00014	.00028	.00026	10
15	6189700	11758	.00190	.00017	.00012	.00008	.00016	.00012	.00001	.00007	.00000	.00000	.00036	.00048	.00033	15
20	5701186	15473	.00271	.00038	.00014	.00010	.00019	.00012	.00001	.00012	.00000	.00000	.00055	.00075	.00034	20
25	5459082	16760	.00307	.00049	.00017	.00013	.00030	.00016	.00001	.00016	.00000	.00000	.00044	.00084	.00037	25
30	5078145	18909	.00372	.00056	.00025	.00019	.00052	.00021	.00001	.00026	.00000	.00000	.00038	.00088	.00046	30
35	4752990	23138	.00487	.00064	.00034	.00031	.00094	.00030	.00001	.00042	.00000	.00000	.00036	.00098	.00059	35
40	4425962	30847	.00697	.00079	.00044	.00061	.00188	.00041	.00002	.00069	.00000	.00000	.00035	.00102	.00076	40
45	4215772	42752	.01014	.00086	.00054	.00109	.00338	.00057	.00001	.00110	.00000	.00000	.00043	.00114	.00102	45
50	3758547	56821	.01512	.00097	.00069	.00188	.00585	.00079	.00002	.00177	.00000	.00000	.00048	.00129	.00137	50
55	3016016	66500	.02205	.00105	.00082	.00301	.00943	.00108	.00003	.00272	.00000	.00000	.00059	.00147	.00185	55
60	2401520	75619	.03149	.00105	.00089	.00458	.01457	.00148	.00004	.00406	.00000	.00000	.00068	.00159	.00255	60
65	1899017	85319	.04493	.00100	.00092	.00642	.02221	.00209	.00005	.00605	.00000	.00000	.00077	.00175	.00366	65
70	1272930	86537	.06798	.00102	.00095	.00918	.03503	.00342	.00008	.00941	.00000	.00000	.00097	.00227	.00565	70
75	724798	75157	.10369	.00091	.00092	.01242	.05533	.00604	.00016	.01461	.00000	.00000	.00119	.00317	.00896	75
80	359566	56300	.15658	.00078	.00080	.01426	.08585	.01064	.00029	.02218	.00000	.00000	.00120	.00580	.01477	80
85+	156616	38579	.24633	.00068	.00114	.01484	.13233	.02177	.00068	.03226	.00000	.00000	.00125	.01027	.03111	85+
ALL	66163645	791003														

CRUDE DEATH RATE			.01196	.00050	.00042	.00121	.00452	.00080	.00011	.00129	.00000	.00045	.00040	.00093	.00130	
STANDARDIZED RATE (1)			.00942	.00038	.00043	.00076	.00266	.00082	.00021	.00078	.00000	.00103	.00034	.00077	.00124	
STANDARDIZED RATE (2)			.01481	.00050	.00046	.00150	.00593	.00102	.00014	.00165	.00000	.00061	.00041	.00100	.00160	
GEOMETRIC MEAN			.01252													

LIFE TABLE FOR ALL CAUSES COMBINED

Age (x)	Midyear Population	Deaths During Year	$_nM_x$	$_nq_x$	l_x	$_nd_x$	$_nL_x$	$_nm_x$	$_na_x$	T_x	$_nr_x$	$\overset{\circ}{e}_x$	Age (x)
0	1028386	63612	.061856	.058850	100000	5885	95146	.061852	.175155	6102361	.000000	61.024	0
1	4334694	13502	.003115	.012368	94115	1164	373550	.003116	1.500000	6007215	.000000	63.828	1
5	5427194	6650	.001225	.006122	92951	569	463333	.001228	2.500000	5633665	.000000	60.609	5
10	5961524	6770	.001136	.005650	92382	522	460667	.001133	2.619333	5170333	-.013783	55.967	10
15	6189700	11758	.001900	.009449	91860	868	457277	.001898	2.669211	4709665	-.002717	51.270	15
20	5701186	15473	.002714	.013485	90992	1227	451997	.002715	2.585065	4252388	.007314	46.734	20
25	5459082	16760	.003070	.015251	89765	1369	445487	.003073	2.561785	3800392	.007865	42.337	25
30	5078145	18909	.003724	.018474	88396	1633	438048	.003728	2.591983	3354904	.009630	37.953	30
35	4752990	23138	.004868	.024089	86763	2090	428855	.004873	2.626894	2916857	.009553	33.619	35
40	4425962	30847	.006970	.034320	84673	2906	416509	.006977	2.640586	2488002	.006218	29.384	40
45	4215772	42752	.010141	.049543	81767	4051	399286	.010146	2.642866	2071493	.004050	25.334	45
50	3758547	56821	.015118	.073138	77716	5684	375102	.015153	2.628834	1672207	-.013714	21.517	50
55	3016016	66500	.022049	.105037	72032	7566	342030	.022121	2.603726	1297104	.021809	18.007	55
60	2401520	75619	.031488	.146604	64466	9451	299492	.031561	2.579269	955075	.015832	14.815	60
65	1899017	85319	.044924	.202890	55015	11162	247870	.045032	2.562713	655623	.014765	11.917	65
70	1272930	86537	.067983	.292135	43853	12811	187575	.068258	2.526312	407753	.024842	9.298	70
75	724798	75157	.103694	.411700	31042	12780	122706	.104151	2.456671	220178	.021025	7.093	75
80	359566	56300	.156578	.555963	18262	10153	64553	.157282	2.364593	97472	.021025	5.337	80
85+	156616	38579	.246329	1.000000	8109	8109	32919	.246329	4.059618	32919	.000000	4.060	85+

NUMBER OF PERSONS DYING (OUT OF 100,000 AT BIRTH) ABOVE AGE X FROM SPECIFIED CAUSES

Age (x)	All Causes	Respiratory T. B.	Other Infec. and Paras.	Neoplasms	Cardiovascular	Infl., Pneu., Bronch.	Diarrheal	Certain Degenerative	Maternal	Cert. Dis. of Infancy	Motor Vehicle	Other Violence	Other and Unknown	Age (x)
0	100000	3383	2888	10541	41889	6532	712	11639	0	2781	2676	6588	10371	0
1	94115	3373	2589	10529	41855	5597	282	11627	0	0	2671	6458	9144	1
5	92951	3354	2391	10485	41831	5319	159	11608	0	0	2616	6301	8887	5
10	92382	3344	2312	10450	41788	5267	153	11591	0	0	2535	6195	8747	10
15	91860	3329	2264	10426	41729	5230	151	11569	0	0	2470	6065	8627	15
20	90992	3250	2212	10390	41655	5173	147	11536	0	0	2305	5845	8479	20
25	89765	3078	2148	10343	41568	5117	144	11483	0	0	2054	5505	8325	25
30	88396	2859	2073	10287	41435	5045	140	11410	0	0	1859	5130	8158	30
35	86763	2611	1963	10205	41206	4952	136	11297	0	0	1694	4743	7956	35
40	84673	2339	1819	10073	40803	4824	130	11119	0	0	1542	4324	7700	40
45	81767	2010	1635	9818	40020	4653	124	10832	0	0	1395	3897	7393	45
50	77716	1667	1418	9384	38670	4425	118	10393	0	0	1224	3440	6977	50
55	72032	1303	1158	8678	36469	4130	109	9728	0	0	1045	2954	6458	55
60	64466	945	878	7643	33230	3758	99	8795	0	0	844	2449	5825	60
65	55015	629	612	6269	28855	3313	88	7576	0	0	640	1971	5062	65
70	43853	381	384	4673	23334	2794	76	6072	0	0	450	1537	4152	70
75	31042	190	205	2944	16729	2150	60	4298	0	0	268	1110	3088	75
80	18262	78	93	1415	9909	1405	41	2498	0	0	122	719	1982	80
85+	8109	22	37	488	4356	717	22	1062	0	0	41	338	1026	85+

NUMBER OF PERSONS SURVIVING TO AGE X IF SPECIFIED CAUSES WERE ELIMINATED

Age (x)	No Causes	Respiratory T. B. (1)	Other Infec. and Paras. (2)	Neoplasms (3)	Cardiovascular (4)	Infl., Pneu., Bronch. (5)	Diarrheal (6)	Certain Degenerative (7)	Maternal (8)	Cert. Dis. of Infancy (9)	Motor Vehicle (10)	Other Violence (11)	Other and Unknown (12)	(1)+(2)	(1)+(2)+(5)+(6)+(8)	(1)+(2)+(5)+(6)+(8)+part of(9)&(12)	(10)+(11)	Age (x)
0	100000	100000	100000	100000	100000	100000	100000	100000	100000	100000	100000	100000	100000	100000	100000	100000	100000	0
1	94115	94125	94405	94127	94148	95036	94533	94127	94115	96852	94120	94241	95213	94415	95763	99378	94246	1
5	92951	92979	93435	93006	93007	94130	93467	92981	92951	95654	93010	93232	94393	93464	95195	98971	93292	5
10	92382	92420	92943	92472	92481	93606	92920	92429	92382	95068	92522	92767	93957	92981	94763	98573	92908	10
15	91860	91913	92466	91973	92017	93115	92397	91929	91860	94531	92064	92373	93548	92519	94332	98157	92579	15
20	90992	91123	91644	91140	91222	92292	91528	91093	90992	93638	91359	91721	92814	91776	93637	97476	92091	20
25	89765	90066	90472	89958	90078	91104	90297	89917	89765	92375	90378	90825	91719	90775	92676	96521	91445	25
30	88396	88911	89168	88642	88837	89787	88924	88619	88396	90566	89194	89817	90489	89687	91643	95500	90628	30
35	86763	87515	87630	87086	87424	88222	87285	87094	86763	89286	87711	88548	89023	88390	90418	94293	89516	35
40	84673	85679	85663	85119	85721	86226	85189	85173	84673	87135	85750	86683	87138	86681	88808	92697	87544	40
45	81767	83066	82906	82450	83562	83438	82271	82534	81767	84145	82954	84289	84469	84223	86474	90352	85513	45
50	77716	79290	79013	78793	80779	79521	78201	78878	77716	79976	79013	80573	80653	80614	83012	86831	81918	50
55	72032	73849	73489	73723	77108	74005	72490	73762	72032	74126	73409	75166	75312	75343	77899	81584	76603	55
60	64466	66439	66040	66989	72369	66554	64885	66924	64466	66340	65892	67770	68030	68061	70766	74215	69269	60
65	55015	56999	56609	58502	66466	57257	55383	58293	55015	56615	56424	58298	58804	58651	61449	64542	59792	65
70	43853	45662	45332	48167	59275	46124	44157	47908	43853	45128	45150	46880	47748	47202	49991	52602	48266	70
75	31042	32487	32243	35719	50147	33223	31271	35574	31042	31945	32116	33568	34783	33744	36381	38377	34729	75
80	18262	19199	19055	22381	39171	20162	18411	22552	18262	18793	19008	20071	21425	20033	22298	23613	20890	80
85+	8109	8563	8499	10702	27116	9459	8188	11232	8109	8345	8495	9188	10265	8975	10571	11271	9625	85+

ADDED YRS OF LIFE

	No Causes	(1)	(2)	(3)	(4)	(5)	(6)	(7)	(8)	(9)	(10)	(11)	(12)	(1)+(2)	...	...	(10)+(11)
TOTAL		.816	.845	1.416	6.958	1.498	.374	1.470	.000	1.769	.730	1.635	2.358	1.681	3.646	6.518	2.401
WORK	5.867	.540	.282	.438	1.339	.285	.012	.458	.000	.000	.441	.886	.585	.828	1.135	1.288	1.340

POPULATION, DEATHS, DEATH RATES FOR ALL CAUSES COMBINED, AND SPECIFIED CAUSES

Age Start of Interval	Midyear Population	Deaths During Year	All Causes	Respiratory T. B.	Other Infec. and Paras.	Neo-plasms	Cardio-vascular	Infl., Pneu., Bronch.	Diar-rheal	Certain Degen-erative	Maternal	Cert. Dis. of Infancy	Motor Vehicle	Other Violence	Other and Unknown	Age Start of Interval
0	995364	47464	.04769	.00011	.00265	.00011	.00029	.00796	.00360	.00010	.00000	.02164	.00006	.00113	.01002	0
1	4201741	11209	.00267	.00005	.00052	.00010	.00006	.00061	.00027	.00004	.00000	.00000	.00010	.00032	.00058	1
5	5276346	4938	.00094	.00002	.00014	.00005	.00010	.00010	.00001	.00004	.00000	.00000	.00009	.00013	.00025	5
10	5805210	4930	.00085	.00007	.00009	.00006	.00015	.00008	.00000	.00005	.00001	.00000	.00006	.00008	.00022	10
15	6165694	9442	.00153	.00032	.00011	.00006	.00016	.00011	.00008	.00018	.00000	.00000	.00012	.00012	.00026	15
20	5907251	12403	.00210	.00054	.00014	.00009	.00020	.00012	.00001	.00010	.00030	.00000	.00012	.00018	.00030	20
25	5657284	13981	.00247	.00056	.00015	.00019	.00026	.00015	.00001	.00014	.00035	.00000	.00010	.00020	.00037	25
30	5182435	15722	.00303	.00049	.00018	.00041	.00043	.00019	.00001	.00021	.00035	.00000	.00009	.00022	.00046	30
35	4809331	18592	.00387	.00044	.00019	.00074	.00069	.00022	.00002	.00034	.00031	.00000	.00009	.00022	.00060	35
40	4377458	22915	.00523	.00038	.00022	.00125	.00126	.00026	.00002	.00063	.00013	.00000	.00009	.00024	.00076	40
45	4054059	28936	.00714	.00032	.00024	.00191	.00213	.00034	.00002	.00090	.00002	.00000	.00011	.00027	.00089	45
50	3511114	36113	.01029	.00032	.00028	.00263	.00351	.00046	.00002	.00144	.00000	.00000	.00014	.00030	.00118	50
55	2838174	42107	.01484	.00036	.00029	.00352	.00562	.00065	.00003	.00233	.00000	.00000	.00018	.00037	.00149	55
60	2335192	51415	.02202	.00040	.00031	.00468	.00924	.00097	.00004	.00367	.00000	.00000	.00020	.00054	.00198	60
65	1914396	63894	.03338	.00048	.00034	.00594	.01575	.00157	.00006	.00554	.00000	.00000	.00026	.00090	.00254	65
70	1301166	70625	.05428	.00057	.00041	.00811	.02769	.00286	.00011	.00880	.00000	.00000	.00032	.00172	.00371	70
75	781865	67561	.08641	.00065	.00046	.01025	.04710	.00523	.00019	.01282	.00000	.00000	.00038	.00369	.00563	75
80	416212	56541	.13565	.00061	.00051	.01179	.07676	.01007	.00037	.01832	.00000	.00000	.00035	.00734	.00972	80
85+	208795	47478	.22739	.00056	.00084	.01310	.12553	.02089	.00077	.02605	.00000	.00000	.00027	.01530	.02410	85+
ALL	65739087	626266														

CRUDE DEATH RATE			.00953	.00034	.00025	.00137	.00359	.00066	.00009	.00117	.00014	.00033	.00012	.00042	.00105	
STANDARDIZED RATE (1)			.00724	.00028	.00030	.00086	.00198	.00065	.00017	.00069	.00012	.00076	.00011	.00032	.00099	
STANDARDIZED RATE (2)			.01159	.00033	.00028	.00157	.00460	.00083	.00012	.00144	.00012	.00045	.00013	.00050	.00123	
GEOMETRIC MEAN			.00973													

LIFE TABLE FOR ALL CAUSES COMBINED

Age (x)	Midyear Population	Deaths During Year	$_nM_x$	$_nq_x$	l_x	$_nd_x$	$_nL_x$	$_nm_x$	$_na_x$	T_x	$_nr_x$	$\overset{\circ}{e}_x$	Age (x)
0	995364	47464	.047685	.045830	100000	4583	96109	.047685	.151065	6543023	.000000	65.430	0
1	4201741	11209	.002668	.010596	95417	1011	379141	.002667	1.500000	6446914	.000000	67.566	1
5	5276346	4938	.000936	.004682	94406	442	470925	.000935	2.500000	6067773	.000000	64.273	5
10	5805210	4930	.000849	.004225	93964	397	468884	.000847	2.642212	5596848	-.014693	59.564	10
15	6165694	9442	.001531	.007620	93567	713	466172	.001529	2.667426	5127964	-.007579	54.805	15
20	5907251	12403	.002100	.010447	92854	970	461932	.002100	2.589562	4661792	.002599	50.206	20
25	5657284	13981	.002471	.012298	91884	1130	456678	.002474	2.573378	4199860	.008248	45.708	25
30	5182435	15722	.003034	.015074	90754	1368	450472	.003037	2.588938	3743182	.012003	41.245	30
35	4809331	18592	.003866	.019175	89386	1714	442833	.003871	2.609636	3292711	.012937	36.837	35
40	4377458	22915	.005235	.025852	87672	2270	432953	.005243	2.618209	2849878	.011931	32.506	40
45	4054059	28936	.007138	.035151	85402	3002	419857	.007149	2.630469	2416925	.012297	28.301	45
50	3511114	36113	.010285	.050364	82400	4150	402172	.010319	2.631928	1997028	.021722	24.236	50
55	2838174	42107	.014836	.071949	78250	5630	377898	.014898	2.628367	1594855	.026349	20.382	55
60	2335192	51415	.022017	.104910	72620	7619	344980	.022085	2.621735	1216958	.018194	16.758	60
65	1914396	63894	.033376	.155105	65001	10082	300973	.033498	2.616317	871978	.020152	13.415	65
70	1301166	70625	.054278	.241228	54919	13248	242415	.054637	2.575452	571005	.032043	10.397	70
75	781865	67561	.086410	.357083	41671	14880	171215	.086908	2.504018	328530	.026258	7.884	75
80	416212	56541	.135847	.505207	26791	13535	99019	.136690	2.418868	157316	.026258	5.872	80
85+	208795	47478	.227391	1.000000	13256	13256	58296	.227391	4.397721	58296	.000000	4.398	85+

NUMBER OF PERSONS DYING (OUT OF 100,000 AT BIRTH) ABOVE AGE X FROM SPECIFIED CAUSES

Age (x)	All Causes	Respiratory T.B.	Other Infec. and Paras.	Neoplasms	Cardiovascular	Infl., Pneu., Bronch.	Diarrheal	Certain Degenerative	Maternal	Cert. Dis. of Infancy	Motor Vehicle	Other Violence	Other and Unknown	Age (x)
0	100000	2336	1817	13609	43730	6751	689	13218	747	2079	899	4368	9757	0
1	95417	2325	1562	13598	43702	5986	343	13208	747	0	893	4259	8794	1
5	94406	2305	1365	13561	43677	5754	240	13192	747	0	855	4136	8574	5
10	93964	2294	1298	13535	43632	5705	234	13173	747	0	812	4076	8458	10
15	93567	2264	1256	13509	43563	5668	232	13148	744	0	786	4041	8356	15
20	92854	2114	1206	13482	43490	5617	229	13112	658	0	729	3984	8233	20
25	91884	1864	1140	13440	43398	5564	226	13067	519	0	674	3900	8092	25
30	90754	1607	1072	13354	43278	5497	220	13005	360	0	629	3810	7922	30
35	89386	1385	992	13170	43082	5413	215	12909	204	0	591	3711	7714	35
40	87672	1189	906	12839	42778	5318	208	12758	66	0	551	3612	7447	40
45	85402	1026	812	12295	42231	5205	200	12486	9	0	512	3509	7117	45
50	82400	892	713	11491	41335	5063	193	12109	2	0	465	3395	6742	50
55	78250	763	599	10430	39918	4877	185	11527	1	0	409	3273	6268	55
60	72620	628	490	9095	37783	4630	172	10641	1	0	341	3135	5704	60
65	65001	492	382	7478	34583	4294	158	9372	1	0	273	2949	5019	65
70	54919	349	281	5687	29821	3819	140	7697	1	0	195	2677	4252	70
75	41671	209	182	3714	23057	3120	115	5551	1	0	117	2257	3348	75
80	26791	98	102	1953	14942	2219	81	3345	1	0	52	1621	2377	80
85+	13256	32	49	764	7318	1218	45	1519	0	0	16	892	1403	85+

NUMBER OF PERSONS SURVIVING TO AGE X IF SPECIFIED CAUSES WERE ELIMINATED

Age (x)	No Causes	Respiratory T.B. (1)	Other Infec. and Paras. (2)	Neoplasms (3)	Cardiovascular (4)	Infl., Pneu., Bronch. (5)	Diarrheal (6)	Certain Degenerative (7)	Maternal (8)	Cert. Dis. of Infancy (9)	Motor Vehicle (10)	Other Violence (11)	Other and Unknown (12)	(1)+(2)	(1)+(2)+(5)+(6)+(8)	(1)+(2)+(5)+(6)+(8)+part of(9)&(12)	(10)+(11)	Age (x)
0	100000	100000	100000	100000	100000	100000	100000	100000	100000	100000	100000	100000	100000	100000	100000	100000	100000	0
1	95417	95428	95666	95428	95444	96167	95756	95427	95417	97469	95423	95524	96362	95677	96771	99502	95529	1
5	94406	94437	94849	94453	94458	95381	94844	94432	94406	96437	94450	94634	95562	94880	96305	99182	94678	5
10	93964	94005	94473	94037	94061	94994	94406	94008	93964	95985	94050	94251	95232	94514	95989	98907	94338	10
15	93567	93638	94116	93666	93732	94620	94009	93636	93570	95580	93679	93888	94933	94187	95700	98650	94000	15
20	92854	93074	93448	92979	93091	93950	93296	92959	92943	94851	93022	93229	94334	93670	95318	98331	93398	20
25	91884	92352	92538	92050	92210	93022	92324	92032	92110	93860	92105	92339	93491	93009	94845	97936	92561	25
30	90754	91473	91468	91003	91196	91946	91155	90962	91136	92706	91017	91294	92514	92193	94252	97428	91558	30
35	89386	90316	90170	89815	90017	90644	89825	89687	89918	91309	89663	90016	91330	91108	93396	96649	90315	35
40	87672	88781	88527	88423	88595	89001	88109	88117	88331	89558	88003	88389	89849	89646	92147	95460	88723	40
45	85402	86645	86328	86677	86848	86810	85836	86106	86101	87239	85763	86203	87657	87584	90213	93536	86567	45
50	82400	83733	83392	84435	84696	83901	82826	83453	83081	84172	82795	83286	85148	84740	87446	90728	83685	50
55	78250	79643	79304	81249	81863	79860	78662	79827	78898	79933	78680	79211	81338	80716	83496	86690	79646	55
60	72620	74045	73705	76749	78156	74357	73015	74960	73221	74182	73085	73647	76052	75151	78008	81052	74118	60
65	65001	66408	66075	70330	73293	66882	65368	68346	66539	66399	65481	66099	66756	67505	70429	73240	66587	65
70	54919	56241	55921	61222	67063	56959	55246	59384	55373	56100	55357	56101	58838	57267	60242	62710	56590	70
75	41671	42798	42518	48394	58597	43854	41941	47116	42016	42567	42102	42944	45492	43668	46636	48618	43388	75
80	26791	27605	27400	32768	47953	28962	26992	32334	27013	27367	27119	28139	30102	28233	31004	32397	28484	80
85+	13256	13706	13595	17247	35266	15096	13380	17591	13366	13541	13444	14461	15668	14056	16291	17103	14666	85+

ADDED YRS OF LIFE

	No Causes	(1)	(2)	(3)	(4)	(5)	(6)	(7)	(8)	(9)	(10)	(11)	(12)	(1)+(2)	+(5)+(6)+(8)	+(9)&(12)	(10)+(11)
TOTAL		.717	.667	2.170	7.193	1.397	.337	1.703	.312	1.404	.259	.741	2.243	1.395	3.526	5.969	1.006
WORK	4.514	.478	.185	.741	.955	.219	.013	.420	.255	.000	.118	.223	.569	.666	1.165	1.371	.341

POPULATION, DEATHS, DEATH RATES FOR ALL CAUSES COMBINED, AND SPECIFIED CAUSES

Age Start of Interval	Midyear Population	Deaths During Year	All Causes	Respiratory T.B.	Other Infec. and Paras.	Neoplasms	Cardiovascular	Infl., Pneu., Bronch.	Diarrheal	Certain Degenerative	Maternal	Cert. Dis. of Infancy	Motor Vehicle	Other Violence	Other and Unknown	Age Start of Interval
0	1612971	59759	.03705	.00004	.00089	.00014	.00013	.00313	.00131	.00008	.00000	.02219	.00009	.00123	.00782	0
1	6678824	10075	.00151	.00002	.00020	.00014	.00003	.00023	.00005	.00003	.00000	.00000	.00013	.00030	.00038	1
5	6759887	4770	.00071	.00000	.00008	.00005	.00003	.00004	.00001	.00002	.00000	.00000	.00012	.00018	.00013	5
10	5698708	4010	.00070	.00001	.00006	.00007	.00005	.00003	.00000	.00003	.00000	.00000	.00011	.00024	.00011	10
15	5347185	7483	.00140	.00005	.00006	.00010	.00009	.00003	.00000	.00005	.00000	.00000	.00046	.00042	.00014	15
20	5644000	10879	.00193	.00010	.00006	.00011	.00012	.00004	.00001	.00007	.00000	.00000	.00066	.00061	.00015	20
25	6012199	11792	.00196	.00015	.00006	.00016	.00021	.00004	.00001	.00010	.00000	.00000	.00046	.00063	.00016	25
30	5662416	13356	.00236	.00020	.00006	.00022	.00042	.00005	.00001	.00014	.00000	.00000	.00035	.00068	.00023	30
35	5554582	18511	.00333	.00027	.00008	.00035	.00092	.00008	.00001	.00024	.00000	.00000	.00033	.00074	.00033	35
40	5104261	26946	.00528	.00037	.00011	.00061	.00202	.00015	.00001	.00041	.00000	.00000	.00032	.00081	.00046	40
45	4556718	38112	.00836	.00046	.00018	.00117	.00385	.00022	.00002	.00059	.00000	.00000	.00033	.00088	.00068	45
50	4156256	54339	.01307	.00060	.00024	.00206	.00678	.00031	.00003	.00083	.00000	.00000	.00034	.00096	.00091	50
55	3654211	72229	.01977	.00076	.00031	.00340	.01087	.00045	.00003	.00115	.00000	.00000	.00041	.00110	.00134	55
60	3058004	88345	.02889	.00076	.00038	.00515	.01668	.00066	.00006	.00160	.00000	.00000	.00046	.00119	.00195	60
65	2440735	99809	.04089	.00085	.00045	.00681	.02483	.00100	.00007	.00214	.00000	.00000	.00055	.00137	.00282	65
70	1639650	98807	.06026	.00085	.00050	.00953	.03799	.00167	.00011	.00297	.00000	.00000	.00064	.00170	.00430	70
75	1008435	89831	.08908	.00088	.00051	.01229	.05870	.00277	.00015	.00447	.00000	.00000	.00080	.00244	.00668	75
80	508318	67407	.13261	.00078	.00047	.01549	.09017	.00483	.00026	.00555	.00000	.00000	.00095	.00398	.01012	80
85+	238406	51289	.21513	.00065	.00048	.01674	.14849	.01093	.00047	.00746	.00000	.00000	.00078	.00802	.02112	85+
ALL	75335766	827749														

	All Causes	Respiratory T.B.	Other Infec. and Paras.	Neoplasms	Cardiovascular	Infl., Pneu., Bronch.	Diarrheal	Certain Degenerative	Maternal	Cert. Dis. of Infancy	Motor Vehicle	Other Violence	Other and Unknown
CRUDE DEATH RATE	.01099	.00028	.00017	.00145	.00559	.00037	.00005	.00053	.00000	.00048	.00035	.00075	.00097
STANDARDIZED RATE (1)	.00717	.00019	.00015	.00082	.00287	.00029	.00007	.00031	.00000	.00078	.00032	.00060	.00077
STANDARDIZED RATE (2)	.01221	.00028	.00017	.00161	.00645	.00041	.00005	.00058	.00000	.00046	.00036	.00077	.00106
GEOMETRIC MEAN	.00929												

LIFE TABLE FOR ALL CAUSES COMBINED

Age (x)	Midyear Population	Deaths During Year	$_nM_x$	$_nq_x$	l_x	$_nd_x$	$_nL_x$	$_nm_x$	$_na_x$	T_x	$_nr_x$	$\overset{\circ}{e}_x$	Age (x)
0	1612971	59759	.037049	.035900	100000	3590	96887	.037053	.132983	6545816	.000000	65.458	0
1	6678824	10075	.001508	.006006	96410	579	384193	.001507	1.500000	6448929	.000000	66.891	1
5	6759887	4770	.000706	.003506	95831	336	478315	.000702	2.500000	6064736	.000000	63.286	5
10	5698708	4010	.000704	.003529	95495	337	476701	.000707	2.703388	5586421	.020764	58.500	10
15	5347185	7483	.001399	.006988	95158	665	474246	.001402	2.678258	5109720	.007329	53.697	15
20	5644000	10879	.001928	.009588	94493	906	470252	.001927	2.557027	4635474	-.010299	49.056	20
25	6012199	11792	.001961	.009756	93587	913	465690	.001961	2.541302	4165223	-.005667	44.506	25
30	5662416	13356	.002359	.011729	92674	1087	460778	.002359	2.615379	3699532	.002915	39.920	30
35	5554582	18511	.003333	.016542	91587	1515	454412	.003334	2.674367	3238754	.004545	35.363	35
40	5104261	26946	.005279	.026146	90072	2355	444908	.005293	2.684979	2784343	.012326	30.912	40
45	4556718	38112	.008364	.041109	87717	3606	430192	.008382	2.672629	2339435	.012667	26.670	45
50	4156256	54339	.013074	.063523	84111	5343	407998	.013096	2.649768	1909242	.009217	22.699	50
55	3654211	72229	.019766	.094543	78768	7447	376119	.019800	2.620323	1501244	.010425	19.059	55
60	3058004	88345	.028890	.135220	71321	9644	333338	.028932	2.587446	1125126	.009565	15.776	60
65	2440735	99809	.040893	.186374	61677	11495	280390	.040996	2.564630	791788	.016583	12.838	65
70	1639650	98807	.060261	.263242	50182	13210	218302	.060513	2.531558	511397	.024537	10.191	70
75	1008435	89831	.089080	.365033	36972	13496	150790	.089502	2.475564	293095	.025541	7.927	75
80	508318	67407	.132608	.495272	23476	11627	87227	.133295	2.406683	142305	.025541	6.062	80
85+	238406	51289	.215133	1.000000	11849	11849	55078	.215133	4.648287	55078	.000000	4.648	85+

NUMBER OF PERSONS DYING (OUT OF 100,000 AT BIRTH) ABOVE AGE X FROM SPECIFIED CAUSES

Age (x)	All Causes	Respiratory T. B.	Other Infec. and Paras.	Neo-plasms	Cardio-vascular	Infl., Pneu., Bronch.	Diar-rheal	Certain Degen-erative	Maternal	Cert. Dis. of Infancy	Motor Vehicle	Other Violence	Other and Unknown	Age (x)
0	100000	2161	1220	13336	56156	3305	340	4825	0	2151	2494	5728	8284	0
1	96410	2157	1133	13322	56143	3001	213	4818	0	1	2485	5608	7529	1
5	95831	2149	1059	13270	56132	2914	192	4806	0	0	2436	5494	7379	5
10	95495	2147	1019	13228	56116	2895	189	4794	0	0	2377	5409	7321	10
15	95158	2143	991	13192	56092	2879	189	4782	0	0	2323	5296	7271	15
20	94493	2121	964	13145	56048	2864	187	4761	0	0	2104	5057	7202	20
25	93587	2072	938	13054	55991	2846	184	4730	0	0	1792	4811	7129	25
30	92674	2003	911	13020	55895	2829	180	4686	0	0	1580	4517	7053	30
35	91587	1913	882	12920	55703	2806	177	4621	0	0	1418	4202	6945	35
40	90072	1791	847	12760	55296	2769	173	4514	0	0	1269	3868	6795	40
45	87717	1627	797	12487	54382	2703	168	4329	0	0	1127	3506	6591	45
50	84111	1427	720	11984	52723	2610	159	4074	0	0	986	3127	6301	50
55	78768	1182	623	11142	49950	2482	147	3735	0	0	847	2734	5926	55
60	71321	919	506	9862	45852	2312	135	3302	0	0	694	2319	5420	60
65	61677	666	379	8143	40281	2092	115	2768	0	0	541	1923	4769	65
70	50182	426	253	6230	33299	1811	95	2165	0	0	388	1537	3978	70
75	36972	240	145	4143	24567	1445	71	1516	0	0	248	1165	3032	75
80	23476	107	68	2285	16071	1025	48	899	0	0	127	795	2051	80
85+	11849	36	26	922	8179	602	26	411	0	0	43	442	1162	85+

NUMBER OF PERSONS SURVIVING TO AGE X IF SPECIFIED CAUSES WERE ELIMINATED

Age (x)	No Causes	Respiratory T. B. (1)	Other Infec. and Paras. (2)	Neo-plasms (3)	Cardio-vascular (4)	Infl., Pneu., Bronch. (5)	Diar-rheal (6)	Certain Degener-ative (7)	Maternal (8)	Cert. Dis. of Infancy (9)	Motor Vehicle (10)	Other Violence (11)	Other and Unknown (12)	(1) + (2)	(1) + (2) + (5) + (6) + (8)	(1)+(2)+(5)+(6)+(8)+part of(9)&(12)	(10) + (11)	Age (x)
0	100000	100000	100000	100000	100000	100000	100000	100000	100000	100000	100000	100000	100000	100000	100000	100000	100000	0
1	96410	96414	96495	96423	96423	96709	96535	96417	96410	98544	96419	96528	97154	96499	96924	99134	96537	1
5	95831	95843	95990	95897	95855	96215	95976	95850	95831	97953	95889	96062	96721	96002	96532	98802	96120	5
10	95495	95509	95693	95602	95535	95897	95642	95526	95495	97610	95611	95810	96441	95707	96258	98536	95927	10
15	95158	95176	95384	95301	95221	95575	95305	95201	95158	97266	95328	95585	96151	95401	95967	98246	95756	15
20	94493	94533	94744	94682	94600	94922	94641	94556	94493	96586	94881	95117	95548	94784	95363	97635	95507	20
25	93587	93675	93862	93825	93750	94029	93737	93681	93587	95660	94283	94492	94706	93950	94545	96806	95195	25
30	92674	92830	92973	92983	92931	93129	92826	92810	92674	94726	93576	93866	93858	93129	93740	95993	94780	30
35	91587	91831	91911	91993	92033	92060	91740	91787	91587	93615	92641	93083	92866	92156	92787	95033	94154	35
40	90072	90433	90426	90630	90927	90574	90227	90375	90072	92067	91258	91880	91481	90788	91451	93688	93090	40
45	87717	88231	88111	88532	89455	88271	87873	88195	87717	89660	89014	89842	89294	88627	89346	91559	91171	45
50	84111	84801	84565	85392	87451	84734	84269	84821	84111	85974	85499	86529	85913	85258	86051	88217	87953	50
55	78768	79653	79287	80799	84735	79476	78928	79764	78768	80513	80201	81424	80826	80178	81063	83140	82905	55
60	71321	72375	71903	74420	81035	72126	71477	72641	71321	72901	72766	74134	73680	72966	73951	75887	75637	60
65	61677	62827	62299	66045	76216	62580	61830	63325	61677	63043	63072	64492	64345	63461	64550	66285	65951	65
70	50182	51337	50802	55610	70294	51174	50325	52083	50182	51293	51457	52836	53101	51972	53151	54628	54179	70
75	36972	37985	37522	42992	62806	38024	37098	38952	36972	37791	38034	39263	39988	38550	39782	40937	40390	75
80	23476	24226	23886	29050	53823	24489	23574	25250	23476	23996	24248	25243	26244	24649	25820	26616	26073	80
85+	11849	12279	12086	15886	43210	12672	11914	13116	11849	12111	12299	13008	13957	12524	13467	13920	13502	85+

ADDED YRS OF LIFE

	No Causes	(1)	(2)	(3)	(4)	(5)	(6)	(7)	(8)	(9)	(10)	(11)	(12)				
TOTAL		.441	.333	1.895	12.464	.608	.126	.701	.000	1.447	.768	1.440	1.648	.779	1.534	3.209	2.238
WORK	4.624	.234	.056	.514	1.517	.058	.011	.249	.000	.000	.474	.722	.346	.331	.441	.482	1.206

POPULATION, DEATHS, DEATH RATES FOR ALL CAUSES COMBINED, AND SPECIFIED CAUSES

Age Start of Interval	Midyear Population	Deaths During Year	All Causes	Respiratory T. B.	Other Infec. and Paras.	Neoplasms	Cardiovascular	Infl., Pneu., Bronch.	Diarrheal	Certain Degenerative	Maternal	Cert. Dis. of Infancy	Motor Vehicle	Other Violence	Other and Unknown	Age Start of Interval
0	1556354	44121	.02835	.00003	.00080	.00012	.00008	.00256	.00105	.00004	.00000	.01618	.00008	.00095	.00646	0
1	6430130	8092	.00126	.00002	.00018	.00012	.00003	.00020	.00005	.00003	.00000	.00000	.00010	.00021	.00032	1
5	6533451	3387	.00052	.00001	.00007	.00007	.00004	.00004	.00000	.00002	.00000	.00000	.00007	.00009	.00011	5
10	5499609	2453	.00045	.00002	.00005	.00006	.00006	.00002	.00000	.00003	.00000	.00000	.00005	.00007	.00009	10
15	5344792	4061	.00076	.00008	.00004	.00007	.00009	.00003	.00000	.00004	.00005	.00000	.00013	.00010	.00012	15
20	5919257	5916	.00100	.00016	.00004	.00009	.00013	.00003	.00001	.00005	.00009	.00000	.00012	.00013	.00014	20
25	6316739	7738	.00122	.00017	.00005	.00017	.00019	.00004	.00001	.00007	.00010	.00000	.00010	.00015	.00018	25
30	5935962	9632	.00162	.00019	.00005	.00032	.00031	.00005	.00001	.00012	.00011	.00000	.00008	.00016	.00022	30
35	5771361	13432	.00233	.00019	.00006	.00062	.00058	.00007	.00001	.00017	.00010	.00000	.00008	.00019	.00027	35
40	5171718	18126	.00350	.00017	.00007	.00110	.00111	.00008	.00001	.00026	.00005	.00000	.00009	.00021	.00037	40
45	4577742	23826	.00520	.00015	.00008	.00167	.00198	.00011	.00002	.00039	.00001	.00000	.00010	.00023	.00049	45
50	4174116	31947	.00765	.00014	.00009	.00237	.00331	.00017	.00002	.00056	.00000	.00000	.00012	.00024	.00063	50
55	3631564	40908	.01126	.00015	.00011	.00330	.00539	.00022	.00003	.00085	.00000	.00000	.00013	.00027	.00082	55
60	3043800	52891	.01738	.00019	.00012	.00433	.00936	.00033	.00004	.00131	.00000	.00000	.00017	.00036	.00117	60
65	2597380	66848	.02574	.00022	.00016	.00531	.01525	.00056	.00007	.00187	.00000	.00000	.00020	.00050	.00160	65
70	1796194	77131	.04294	.00030	.00019	.00727	.02752	.00111	.00011	.00265	.00000	.00000	.00021	.00100	.00254	70
75	1159031	80111	.06912	.00038	.00024	.00932	.04704	.00208	.00019	.00361	.00000	.00000	.00025	.00214	.00385	75
80	624927	68758	.11003	.00035	.00028	.01152	.07794	.00413	.00027	.00466	.00000	.00000	.00025	.00444	.00614	80
85+	342575	65327	.19069	.00030	.00038	.01317	.13623	.00947	.00050	.00610	.00000	.00000	.00022	.01058	.01374	85+
ALL	76426702	624705														

	All Causes	Resp. T.B.	Other Infec.	Neoplasms	Cardiovascular	Infl. Pneu. Bronch.	Diarrheal	Certain Degen.	Maternal	Cert. Dis. Infancy	Motor Vehicle	Other Violence	Other Unknown
CRUDE DEATH RATE	.00817	.00013	.00010	.00140	.00424	.00029	.00005	.00045	.00004	.00033	.00011	.00033	.00070
STANDARDIZED RATE (1)	.00491	.00010	.00011	.00079	.00189	.00022	.00005	.00024	.00004	.00057	.00010	.00023	.00057
STANDARDIZED RATE (2)	.00657	.00013	.00010	.00144	.00454	.00030	.00005	.00047	.00004	.00033	.00011	.00034	.00072
GEOMETRIC MEAN	.00625												

LIFE TABLE FOR ALL CAUSES COMBINED

Age (x)	Midyear Population	Deaths During Year	$_nM_x$	$_nq_x$	l_x	$_nd_x$	$_nL_x$	$_nm_x$	$_na_x$	T_x	$_nr_x$	$\overset{\circ}{e}_x$	Age (x)
0	1556354	44121	.028349	.027660	100000	2766	97561	.028352	.118193	7102863	.000000	71.029	0
1	6430130	8092	.001258	.005019	97234	488	387716	.001259	1.500000	7005302	.000000	72.046	1
5	6533451	3387	.000518	.002584	96746	250	483105	.000517	2.500000	6617586	.000000	68.402	5
10	5499609	2453	.000446	.002228	96496	215	481966	.000446	2.611434	6134481	.019371	63.572	10
15	5344792	4061	.000760	.003791	96281	365	480547	.000760	2.650114	5652515	.000712	58.709	15
20	5919257	5916	.000999	.004984	95916	478	478430	.000999	2.594578	5171968	-.015903	53.922	20
25	6316739	7738	.001225	.006098	95438	582	475795	.001223	2.603451	4693538	-.006468	49.179	25
30	5935962	9632	.001623	.008086	94856	767	472469	.001623	2.638255	4217742	.003747	44.465	30
35	5771361	13432	.002327	.011595	94089	1091	467855	.002332	2.663077	3745274	.007994	39.806	35
40	5171718	18126	.003505	.017430	92998	1621	461201	.003515	2.662451	3277378	.017409	35.241	40
45	4577742	23826	.005205	.025772	91377	2355	451359	.005218	2.653309	2816178	.016786	30.819	45
50	4174116	31947	.007654	.037676	89022	3354	437217	.007671	2.646653	2364819	.014622	26.564	50
55	3631564	40908	.011265	.055050	85668	4716	417262	.011302	2.651037	1927602	.019640	22.501	55
60	3043800	52891	.017377	.083602	80952	6773	388726	.017424	2.632727	1510340	.015511	18.657	60
65	2597380	66848	.025737	.121746	74179	9031	349566	.025835	2.638228	1121121	.021121	15.120	65
70	1796194	77131	.042941	.195938	65148	12765	295190	.043243	2.606721	772048	.033329	11.851	70
75	1159031	80111	.069119	.297234	52383	15570	223652	.069617	2.542536	476858	.034010	9.103	75
80	624927	68758	.110026	.433108	36813	15944	143768	.110901	2.472612	253205	.034010	6.878	80
85+	342575	65327	.190694	1.000000	20869	20869	109437	.190694	5.244003	109437	.000000	5.244	85+

NUMBER OF PERSONS DYING (OUT OF 100,000 AT BIRTH) ABOVE AGE X FROM SPECIFIED CAUSES

Age (x)	All Causes	Respiratory T. B.	Other Infec. and Paras.	Neo-plasms	Cardio-vascular	Infl., Pneu., Bronch.	Diar-rheal	Certain Degen-erative	Maternal	Cert. Dis. of Infancy	Motor Vehicle	Other Violence	Other and Unknown	Age (x)
0	100000	1089	767	15332	59778	3468	385	5265	240	1579	851	3913	7333	0
1	97234	1086	689	15321	59770	3219	283	5261	240	0	844	3820	6701	1
5	96746	1078	618	15275	59760	3142	263	5251	240	0	806	3737	6576	5
10	96456	1075	585	15239	59741	3123	261	5241	240	0	774	3692	6525	10
15	96281	1067	563	15211	59710	3112	259	5228	239	0	751	3658	6483	15
20	95916	1028	542	15176	59667	3098	257	5206	213	0	689	3611	6429	20
25	95438	952	521	15131	59605	3082	254	5182	170	0	631	3551	6359	25
30	94856	869	498	15050	59515	3064	251	5147	121	0	583	3481	6277	30
35	94089	779	475	14897	59368	3041	247	5092	70	0	544	3405	6171	35
40	92998	692	448	14606	59095	3011	242	5012	24	0	507	3318	6043	40
45	91377	616	417	14098	58582	2973	238	4891	3	0	466	3220	5873	45
50	89022	546	381	13342	57686	2923	231	4719	1	0	421	3118	5654	50
55	85668	483	340	12304	56234	2849	223	4476	1	0	369	3011	5378	55
60	80952	419	296	10923	53976	2758	212	4120	0	0	314	2897	5037	60
65	74179	345	248	9238	50326	2629	195	3609	0	0	248	2758	4583	65
70	65148	266	193	7379	44969	2433	171	2954	0	0	180	2583	4020	70
75	52383	177	138	5223	36782	2103	137	2158	0	0	117	2284	3264	75
80	36813	91	83	3129	26178	1632	95	1346	0	0	61	1800	2398	80
85+	20869	33	41	1441	14909	1036	55	667	0	0	24	1158	1505	85+

NUMBER OF PERSONS SURVIVING TO AGE X IF SPECIFIED CAUSES WERE ELIMINATED

Age (x)	No Causes	Respiratory T. B. (1)	Other Infec. and Paras. (2)	Neo-plasms (3)	Cardio-vascular (4)	Infl., Pneu., Bronch. (5)	Diar-rheal (6)	Certain Degener-ative (7)	Maternal (8)	Cert. Dis. of Infancy (9)	Motor Vehicle (10)	Other Violence (11)	Other and Unknown (12)	(1) + (2)	(1) + (2) + (5) + (6) + (8)	(1)+(2)+ (5)+(6)+ (8)+part of(9)&(12)	(10) + (11)	Age (x)
0	100000	100000	100000	100000	100000	100000	100000	100000	100000	100000	100000	100000	100000	100000	100000	100000	100000	0
1	97234	97237	97311	97245	97242	97480	97335	97238	97234	98803	97241	97326	97859	97314	97661	99380	97333	1
5	96746	96757	96893	96803	96764	97068	96866	96760	96746	98308	96791	96920	97494	96904	97347	99123	96965	5
10	96456	96510	96676	96589	96533	96836	96618	96520	96456	98054	96513	96715	97293	96690	97153	98940	96792	10
15	96281	96303	96483	96401	96349	96631	96405	96318	96282	97835	96380	96533	97119	96505	96981	98776	96633	15
20	95916	95977	96138	96071	96026	96279	96041	95975	95943	97464	96077	96214	96805	96199	96716	98524	96376	20
25	95438	95574	95680	95637	95610	95815	95565	95520	95508	96979	95656	95795	96393	95816	96394	98224	96014	25
30	94856	95074	95119	95135	95117	95249	94986	94973	94974	96387	95121	95281	95888	95338	95983	97835	95547	30
35	94089	94395	94373	94519	94494	94502	94222	94260	94257	95608	94391	94586	95219	94681	95400	97272	94890	35
40	92998	93388	93306	93714	93672	93436	93134	93246	93210	94499	93333	93577	94244	93697	94490	96372	93914	40
45	91377	91836	91710	92589	92553	91845	91515	91741	91606	92852	91747	92043	92772	92170	93015	94887	92416	45
50	89022	89538	89382	90962	91068	89528	89168	89548	89247	90459	89427	89773	90601	89901	90783	92628	90181	50
55	85668	86227	86055	88581	89107	86227	85812	86414	85885	87051	86109	86496	87463	86616	87549	89345	86941	55
60	80952	81543	81361	85104	86517	81570	81098	82007	81158	82259	81422	81846	82987	81954	82939	84657	82322	60
65	74179	74791	74600	79695	83103	74870	74329	75642	74367	75376	74673	75133	76490	75215	76263	77862	75634	65
70	65148	65760	65569	71883	78834	65940	65303	67061	65314	66200	65646	66152	67723	66185	67320	68755	66658	70
75	52383	52955	52771	59959	72913	53321	52538	54657	52516	53229	52840	53464	55161	53348	54601	55795	53930	75
80	36813	37287	37132	44170	65173	37875	36957	39120	36907	37407	37181	37989	39532	37610	38945	39832	38369	80
85+	20869	21182	21081	26591	55182	21932	20980	22720	20922	21206	21105	22034	23134	21397	22664	23216	22283	85+

ADDED YRS OF LIFE																		
TOTAL		.305	.266	2.536	14.240	.583	.124	.758	.107	1.145	.271	.672	1.533	.572	1.401	2.842	.947	
WORK	2.941	.174	.063	.704	.901	.070	.010	.194	.081	.000	.121	.182	.255	.238	.400	.458	.304	

POPULATION, DEATHS, DEATH RATES FOR ALL CAUSES COMBINED, AND SPECIFIED CAUSES

Age Start of Interval	Midyear Population	Deaths During Year	All Causes	Respiratory T. B.	Other Infec. and Paras.	Neoplasms	Cardiovascular	Infl., Pneu., Bronch.	Diarrheal	Certain Degenerative	Maternal	Cert. Dis. of Infancy	Motor Vehicle	Other Violence	Other and Unknown	Age Start of Interval
0	1404121	47617	.03391	.00002	.00071	.00014	.00012	.00252	.00107	.00007	.00000	.02087	.00009	.00107	.00723	0
1	5863256	7930	.00135	.00001	.00017	.00014	.00003	.00018	.00004	.00003	.00000	.00000	.00013	.00027	.00035	1
5	5934046	3985	.00067	.00000	.00009	.00009	.00003	.00003	.00000	.00002	.00000	.00000	.00012	.00017	.00012	5
10	4560347	3322	.00067	.00001	.00006	.00008	.00005	.00003	.00000	.00002	.00000	.00000	.00011	.00021	.00012	10
15	4700810	6125	.00130	.00002	.00005	.00010	.00008	.00003	.00000	.00004	.00000	.00000	.00048	.00037	.00013	15
20	5018780	8665	.00173	.00005	.00004	.00011	.00010	.00003	.00001	.00006	.00000	.00000	.00068	.00050	.00013	20
25	5366815	9115	.00170	.00009	.00004	.00016	.00018	.00003	.00001	.00009	.00000	.00000	.00044	.00052	.00014	25
30	5056857	10233	.00201	.00012	.00005	.00022	.00035	.00004	.00001	.00013	.00000	.00000	.00034	.00056	.00020	30
35	4971790	14557	.00293	.00020	.00005	.00034	.00081	.00006	.00001	.00022	.00000	.00000	.00031	.00064	.00028	35
40	4588155	21774	.00475	.00029	.00007	.00060	.00185	.00012	.00001	.00038	.00000	.00000	.00031	.00072	.00040	40
45	4093222	31594	.00772	.00037	.00011	.00114	.00362	.00018	.00002	.00056	.00000	.00000	.00031	.00082	.00060	45
50	3768137	45622	.01211	.00051	.00016	.00158	.00634	.00025	.00003	.00078	.00000	.00000	.00032	.00093	.00081	50
55	3361604	63098	.01877	.00062	.00024	.00334	.01039	.00039	.00003	.00109	.00000	.00000	.00039	.00108	.00121	55
60	2838447	79435	.02799	.00071	.00032	.00512	.01620	.00058	.00006	.00154	.00000	.00000	.00045	.00118	.00183	60
65	2230123	90482	.04057	.00080	.00040	.00692	.02475	.00093	.00007	.00209	.00000	.00000	.00055	.00140	.00267	65
70	1518147	91430	.06022	.00081	.00045	.00973	.03815	.00159	.00011	.00288	.00000	.00000	.00065	.00172	.00412	70
75	936315	84140	.08986	.00085	.00047	.01262	.05948	.00274	.00014	.00398	.00000	.00000	.00081	.00251	.00625	75
80	474035	63956	.13492	.00077	.00043	.01602	.09224	.00487	.00026	.00549	.00000	.00000	.00097	.00412	.00974	80
85+	218858	48286	.22063	.00064	.00046	.01744	.15358	.01105	.00047	.00739	.00000	.00000	.00079	.00839	.02042	85+
ALL	67343865	731366														
CRUDE DEATH RATE			.01086	.00023	.00014	.00150	.00568	.00034	.00005	.00052	.00000	.00044	.00035	.00070	.00091	
STANDARDIZED RATE (1)			.00681	.00015	.00012	.00082	.00281	.00025	.00005	.00030	.00000	.00074	.00032	.00055	.00071	
STANDARDIZED RATE (2)			.01188	.00023	.00014	.00162	.00641	.00038	.00005	.00056	.00000	.00043	.00036	.00072	.00099	
GEOMETRIC MEAN			.00871													

LIFE TABLE FOR ALL CAUSES COMBINED

Age (x)	Midyear Population	Deaths During Year	$_nM_x$	$_nq_x$	l_x	$_nd_x$	$_nL_x$	$_nm_x$	$_na_x$	T_x	$_nr_x$	$\overset{\circ}{e}_x$	Age (x)
0	1404121	47617	.033912	.032940	100000	3294	97126	.033915	.127651	6627230	.000000	66.272	0
1	5863256	7930	.001352	.005387	96706	521	385522	.001351	1.500000	6530104	.000000	67.525	1
5	5934046	3985	.000672	.003337	96185	321	480123	.000669	2.500000	6144582	.000000	63.883	5
10	4960347	3322	.000670	.003359	95864	322	478577	.000673	2.694099	5664460	.021061	59.088	10
15	4700810	6125	.001303	.006500	95542	621	476260	.001304	2.665727	5185882	-.005731	54.279	15
20	5018780	8665	.001727	.008597	94921	816	472601	.001727	2.544424	4709622	-.011726	49.616	20
25	5366815	9115	.001698	.008448	94105	795	468562	.001697	2.530660	4237021	-.006891	45.024	25
30	5056857	10233	.002008	.009999	93310	933	464332	.002009	2.622588	3768459	.002575	40.386	30
35	4971790	14557	.002928	.014549	92377	1344	458777	.002930	2.687562	3304127	.004960	35.768	35
40	4588155	21774	.004746	.023541	91033	2143	450231	.004760	2.697737	2845350	.012560	31.256	40
45	4093222	31594	.007719	.038002	88890	3378	436609	.007737	2.678730	2395119	.012809	26.945	45
50	3768137	45622	.012107	.058961	85512	5041	415762	.012125	2.659649	1958510	.008216	22.903	50
55	3361604	63098	.018770	.089983	80471	7241	385206	.018798	2.631658	1542748	.008624	19.171	55
60	2838447	79435	.027985	.131326	73230	9617	343052	.028034	2.598263	1157542	.010346	15.807	60
65	2230123	90482	.040573	.185135	63613	11777	289460	.040686	2.571149	814489	.017667	12.804	65
70	1518147	91430	.060225	.263118	51836	13639	225555	.060469	2.534613	525029	.023464	10.129	70
75	936315	84140	.089863	.367647	38197	14043	155560	.090274	2.477376	299474	.024043	7.840	75
80	474035	63956	.134918	.501532	24154	12114	89343	.135550	2.405705	143914	.024043	5.958	80
85+	218858	48286	.220627	1.000000	12040	12040	54572	.220627	4.532535	54572	.000000	4.533	85+

NUMBER OF PERSONS DYING (OUT OF 100,000 AT BIRTH) ABOVE AGE X FROM SPECIFIED CAUSES

Age (x)	All Causes	Respiratory T. B.	Other Infec. and Paras.	Neo-plasms	Cardio-vascular	Infl., Pneu., Bronch.	Diar-rheal	Certain Degen-erative	Maternal	Cert. Dis. of Infancy	Motor Vehicle	Other Violence	Other and Unknown	Age (x)
0	100000	1874	1018	13798	57185	3114	308	4762	0	2025	2506	5509	7897	0
1	96706	1872	949	13784	57173	2870	204	4756	0	1	2497	5405	7195	1
5	96185	1867	883	13730	57163	2801	188	4745	0	0	2446	5302	7060	5
10	95864	1866	846	13686	57149	2784	186	4734	0	0	2387	5223	7003	10
15	95542	1863	818	13649	57127	2770	185	4722	0	0	2331	5120	6957	15
20	94921	1854	794	13601	57088	2757	184	4701	0	0	2101	4945	6896	20
25	94105	1830	773	13548	57040	2742	180	4672	0	0	1782	4707	6831	25
30	93310	1788	752	13474	56955	2729	176	4631	0	0	1575	4463	6767	30
35	92377	1731	730	13372	56790	2712	174	4572	0	0	1419	4201	6676	35
40	91033	1639	706	13214	56418	2683	169	4470	0	0	1277	3908	6549	40
45	88890	1509	674	12945	55582	2631	165	4297	0	0	1138	3581	6368	45
50	85512	1347	627	12447	53997	2554	158	4050	0	0	1002	3224	6106	50
55	80471	1136	559	11620	51357	2449	146	3726	0	0	869	2839	5770	55
60	73230	898	468	10333	47347	2299	135	3305	0	0	719	2424	5302	60
65	63613	656	358	8573	41778	2099	115	2777	0	0	564	2020	4673	65
70	51836	422	241	6566	34592	1829	96	2172	0	0	405	1615	3898	70
75	38197	239	138	4364	25948	1469	71	1520	0	0	258	1225	2965	75
80	24154	107	65	2395	16649	1039	49	898	0	0	131	832	1989	80
85+	12040	35	25	952	8381	603	26	403	0	0	43	458	1114	85+

NUMBER OF PERSONS SURVIVING TO AGE X IF SPECIFIED CAUSES WERE ELIMINATED

Age (x)	No Causes	Respiratory T. B.	Other Infec. and Paras.	Neo-plasms	Cardio-vascular	Infl., Pneu., Bronch.	Diar-rheal	Certain Degen-erative	Maternal	Cert. Dis. of Infancy	Motor Vehicle	Other Violence	Other and Unknown	(1) + (2)	(1) + (2) + (5) + (6) + (8)	(1)+(2)+ (5)+(6)+ (8)+part of(9)&(12)	(10) + (11)	Age (x)
		(1)	(2)	(3)	(4)	(5)	(6)	(7)	(8)	(9)	(10)	(11)	(12)					
0	100000	100000	100000	100000	100000	100000	100000	100000	100000	100000	100000	100000	100000	100000	100000	100000	100000	0
1	96706	96708	96774	96720	96712	96946	96808	96712	96706	98721	96715	96808	97399	96776	97119	99143	96817	1
5	96185	96192	96318	96253	96207	96493	96303	96202	96185	98190	96245	96390	97010	96325	96752	98825	96449	5
10	95864	95872	96034	95975	95900	96188	95983	95892	95864	97862	95982	96147	96743	96042	96486	98566	96266	10
15	95542	95553	95739	95690	95599	95879	95662	95582	95542	97534	95716	95927	96465	95750	96209	98290	96102	15
20	94921	94941	95141	95116	95017	95269	95041	94981	94921	96900	95324	95479	95899	95161	95630	97704	95884	20
25	94105	94149	94344	94351	94248	94465	94228	94194	94105	96067	94824	94897	95140	94388	94873	96936	95622	25
30	93310	93395	93568	93628	93537	93680	93436	93439	93310	95255	94231	94341	94401	93653	94151	96206	95271	30
35	92377	92518	92654	92794	92766	92760	92504	92563	92377	94303	93945	93661	93549	92796	93308	95536	94744	35
40	91033	91263	91330	91601	91788	91439	91163	91318	91033	92931	92228	92594	92315	91561	92101	94138	93810	40
45	88890	89244	89212	89713	90465	89338	89021	89340	88890	90743	90156	90743	90324	89567	90151	92166	92077	45
50	85512	86012	85868	86698	88624	86015	85645	86189	85512	87295	86904	87652	87153	86370	87017	88987	89079	50
55	80471	81147	80872	82500	86097	81051	80608	81425	80471	82149	81912	82868	82348	81552	82279	84170	84352	55
60	73230	74074	73682	76346	82551	73902	73345	74505	73230	74757	74687	75819	75356	74532	75354	77120	77327	60
65	63613	64574	64109	68050	77805	64385	63749	65223	63613	64935	65025	66252	66100	65078	66008	67594	67723	65
70	51836	52833	52346	57418	71842	52712	51964	53709	51836	52917	53133	54366	54593	53353	54388	55739	55727	70
75	38197	39090	38661	44442	64253	39158	38313	40158	38197	38993	39281	40412	41078	39565	40683	41739	41559	75
80	24154	24824	24505	29557	55063	25113	24244	25913	24154	24658	24942	25884	26617	25185	26282	27008	26729	80
85+	12040	12425	12243	16224	44143	12836	12101	13289	12040	12291	12456	13183	14057	12635	13538	13947	13682	85+

ADDED YRS OF LIFE																		
TOTAL		.352	.275	1.940	12.536	.525	.107	.682	.000	1.375	.778	1.320	1.534	.631	1.279	2.806	2.125	
WORK	4.246	.171	.071	.514	1.433	.080	.010	.238	.000	.000	.476	.636	.307	.243	.334	.364	1.122	

UNITED STATES (WHITE) 1950 FEMALES

POPULATION, DEATHS, DEATH RATES FOR ALL CAUSES COMBINED, AND SPECIFIED CAUSES

Age Start of Interval	Midyear Population	Deaths During Year	All Causes	Respiratory T. B.	Other Infec. and Paras.	Neoplasms	Cardiovascular	Infl., Pneu., Bronch.	Diarrheal	Certain Degenerative	Maternal	Cert. Dis. of Infancy	Motor Vehicle	Other Violence	Other and Unknown	Age Start of Interval
0	1345821	34432	.02558	.00002	.00064	.00012	.00007	.00202	.00086	.00004	.00000	.01492	.00008	.00079	.00603	0
1	5618947	6286	.00112	.00002	.00016	.00012	.00002	.00016	.00004	.00003	.00000	.00000	.00008	.00017	.00029	1
5	5701478	2741	.00048	.00000	.00006	.00008	.00003	.00004	.00000	.00002	.00000	.00000	.00006	.00008	.00010	5
10	4766745	1963	.00041	.00001	.00004	.00006	.00006	.00002	.00000	.00003	.00000	.00000	.00006	.00008	.00010	10
15	4661075	2897	.00062	.00003	.00003	.00007	.00007	.00002	.00000	.00004	.00003	.00000	.00005	.00007	.00008	15
20	5194660	4132	.00080	.00008	.00004	.00009	.00010	.00003	.00001	.00005	.00007	.00000	.00013	.00008	.00010	20
25	5594758	5435	.00097	.00010	.00004	.00016	.00015	.00003	.00001	.00006	.00007	.00000	.00012	.00010	.00011	25
30	5294326	6806	.00129	.00012	.00003	.00030	.00023	.00003	.00001	.00009	.00008	.00000	.00010	.00011	.00014	30
35	5120526	9589	.00187	.00013	.00004	.00057	.00042	.00004	.00001	.00009	.00008	.00000	.00008	.00013	.00018	35
40	4633042	13342	.00288	.00012	.00004	.00103	.00081	.00006	.00001	.00013	.00007	.00000	.00008	.00017	.00022	40
45	4103601	18146	.00442	.00011	.00005	.00160	.00151	.00007	.00001	.00032	.00000	.00000	.00010	.00019	.00030	45
50	3792642	24974	.00656	.00010	.00006	.00227	.00265	.00011	.00002	.00045	.00000	.00000	.00012	.00023	.00041	50
55	3356640	34059	.01015	.00012	.00008	.00321	.00464	.00017	.00002	.00076	.00000	.00000	.00012	.00023	.00054	55
60	2833163	45792	.01616	.00016	.00010	.00427	.00849	.00026	.00004	.00124	.00000	.00000	.00017	.00027	.00075	60
65	2370904	59606	.02514	.00020	.00014	.00541	.01477	.00051	.00007	.00182	.00000	.00000	.00020	.00050	.00109	65
70	1674150	71189	.04252	.00029	.00016	.00740	.02724	.00103	.00012	.00262	.00000	.00000	.00022	.00100	.00152	70
75	1087352	75749	.06966	.00038	.00023	.00958	.04749	.00206	.00019	.00357	.00000	.00000	.00022	.00100	.00244	75
80	587088	65857	.11218	.00040	.00027	.01189	.07969	.00413	.00027	.00466	.00000	.00000	.00025	.00220	.00373	80
85+	315063	61824	.19623	.00029	.00038	.01372	.14101	.00567	.00052	.00611	.00000	.00000	.00022	.00600	.01314	85+
ALL	68051981	544719														
CRUDE DEATH RATE			.00800	.00010	.00008	.00143	.00424	.00026	.00004	.00044	.00003	.00030	.00011	.00032	.00066	
STANDARDIZED RATE (1)			.00453	.00007	.00009	.00077	.00177	.00018	.00005	.00022	.00003	.00053	.00010	.00021	.00052	
STANDARDIZED RATE (2)			.00818	.00009	.00008	.00143	.00439	.00027	.00004	.00044	.00003	.00031	.00011	.00032	.00067	
GEOMETRIC MEAN			.00558	.00009	.00008	.00143	.00439	.00027	.00004	.00044	.00003	.00031	.00011	.00032	.00067	

LIFE TABLE FOR ALL CAUSES COMBINED

Age (x)	Midyear Population	Deaths During Year	$_nM_x$	$_nq_x$	l_x	$_nd_x$	$_nL_x$	$_nm_x$	$_na_x$	T_x	$_nr_x$	$\overset{\circ}{e}_x$	Age (x)
0	1345821	34432	.025584	.025020	100000	2502	97782	.025588	.113493	7205723	.000000	72.057	0
1	5618947	6286	.001119	.004462	97498	435	388905	.001119	1.500000	7107941	.000000	72.903	1
5	5701478	2741	.000481	.002401	97063	233	484733	.000481	2.500000	6719037	.000000	69.223	5
10	4766745	1963	.000412	.002055	96830	199	483666	.000411	2.570142	6234304	.019682	64.384	10
15	4661075	2897	.000622	.003105	96631	300	482443	.000622	2.627083	5750638	-.000038	59.511	15
20	5194660	4132	.000795	.003953	96331	382	480734	.000795	2.589442	5268194	-.017040	54.688	20
25	5594758	5435	.000971	.004836	95949	464	478633	.000969	2.603269	4787460	-.008055	49.896	25
30	5294326	6806	.001286	.006409	95485	612	475583	.001286	2.643655	4308827	-.003507	45.126	30
35	5120526	9589	.001873	.009339	94873	886	472303	.001876	2.673062	3832844	.008039	40.400	35
40	4633042	13342	.002880	.014342	93987	1348	468804	.002888	2.677269	3360541	.017076	35.755	40
45	4103601	18146	.004422	.021945	92639	2033	458443	.004435	2.662424	2893737	.016505	31.237	45
50	3792642	24974	.006558	.032371	90606	2933	446182	.006574	2.665289	2435294	.013015	26.878	50
55	3356640	34059	.010147	.049730	87673	4360	428209	.010182	2.670728	1989112	.017622	22.688	55
60	2833163	45792	.016163	.078091	83313	6506	401299	.016212	2.653544	1560903	.016997	18.735	60
65	2370904	59606	.025141	.119155	76807	9155	362529	.025253	2.650919	1159604	.022480	15.098	65
70	1674150	71189	.042522	.194200	67652	13138	306907	.042808	2.613554	797075	.031519	11.782	70
75	1087352	75749	.069664	.299299	54514	16316	232541	.070164	2.546669	490168	.032524	8.992	75
80	587088	65857	.112176	.439630	38198	16793	148544	.113051	2.472384	257626	.032524	6.744	80
85+	315063	61824	.196227	1.000000	21405	21405	109083	.196227	5.096128	109083	.000000	5.096	85+

NUMBER OF PERSONS DYING (OUT OF 100,000 AT BIRTH) ABOVE AGE X FROM SPECIFIED CAUSES

Age (x)	All Causes	Respiratory T.B.	Other Infec. and Paras.	Neoplasms	Cardiovascular	Infl., Pneu., Bronch.	Diarrheal	Certain Degenerative	Maternal	Cert. Dis. of Infancy	Motor Vehicle	Other Violence	Other and Unknown	Age (x)
0	100000	850	641	15802	60421	2304	364	5158	173	1460	869	3961	6997	0
1	97458	848	578	15750	60414	3106	280	5154	173	0	862	3884	6409	1
5	97063	842	517	15742	60405	3044	263	5144	173	0	823	3816	6294	5
10	96830	840	487	15705	60390	3027	261	5135	173	0	792	3779	6241	10
15	96631	837	466	15675	60362	3018	260	5122	172	0	769	3746	6204	15
20	96331	820	449	15640	60327	3007	258	5103	158	0	704	3707	6158	20
25	95949	780	432	15556	60277	2994	255	5082	126	0	647	3660	6100	25
30	95485	731	414	15519	60207	2981	252	5051	91	0	600	3605	6034	30
35	94873	672	397	15378	60097	2966	248	5007	54	0	561	3544	5949	35
40	93987	610	381	15107	59901	2946	243	4944	20	0	526	3466	5843	40
45	92639	556	360	14626	59523	2919	240	4849	3	0	485	3375	5703	45
50	90606	504	337	13893	58826	2885	234	4702	1	0	440	3274	5510	50
55	87673	459	309	12877	57640	2835	227	4498	1	0	387	3170	5270	55
60	83313	408	275	11458	55643	2763	216	4171	0	0	332	3056	4951	60
65	76807	344	237	9782	52221	2657	200	3674	0	0	262	2916	4514	65
70	67652	270	186	7815	46837	2472	177	3011	0	0	188	2734	3962	70
75	54514	181	136	5534	38412	2154	141	2202	0	0	122	2424	3208	75
80	38198	92	82	3298	27284	1671	97	1368	0	0	63	1908	2335	80
85+	21405	32	41	1497	15381	1055	56	666	0	0	24	1218	1435	85+

NUMBER OF PERSONS SURVIVING TO AGE X IF SPECIFIED CAUSES WERE ELIMINATED

Age (x)	No Causes	Respiratory T.B. (1)	Other Infec. and Paras. (2)	Neoplasms (3)	Cardiovascular (4)	Infl., Pneu., Bronch. (5)	Diarrheal (6)	Certain Degenerative (7)	Maternal (8)	Cert. Dis. of Infancy (9)	Motor Vehicle (10)	Other Violence (11)	Other and Unknown (12)	(1)+(2)	(1)+(2)+(5)+(6)+(8)	(1)+(2)+(5)+(6)+(8)+part of(9)&(12)	(10)+(11)	Age (x)
0	100000	100000	100000	100000	100000	100000	100000	100000	100000	100000	100000	100000	100000	100000	100000	100000	100000	0
1	97458	97500	97560	97510	97505	97594	97581	97502	97458	98950	97505	97574	98080	97562	97841	99405	97581	1
5	97063	97071	97186	97123	97079	97320	97163	97077	97063	98509	97109	97207	97758	97194	97551	99163	97253	5
10	96830	96840	96983	96927	96861	97103	96931	96853	96830	98272	96907	97010	97577	96993	97368	98993	97087	10
15	96631	96644	96804	96757	96690	96913	96733	96667	96632	98070	96731	96844	97414	96817	97203	98833	96944	15
20	96331	96361	96521	96492	96425	96623	96435	96386	96346	97766	96455	96582	97157	96551	96963	98600	96747	20
25	95949	96019	96155	96153	96092	96253	96055	96024	95996	97378	96170	96246	96831	96225	96684	98335	96468	25
30	95485	95603	95708	95765	95697	95800	95594	95591	95567	96907	95751	95836	96429	95827	96335	98001	96103	30
35	94873	95049	95112	95293	95194	95201	94985	95022	94991	96286	95177	95283	95896	95288	95850	97529	95588	35
40	93987	94224	94239	94674	94501	94332	94103	94198	94138	95387	94323	94471	95107	94476	95093	96778	94800	40
45	92639	92926	92909	93799	93524	93006	92756	92941	92804	94019	93011	93207	93884	93196	93852	95529	93581	45
50	90606	90938	90892	92477	92170	90999	90727	91048	90770	91956	91014	91262	92017	91226	91909	93564	91673	50
55	87673	88039	87978	90509	90382	88102	87797	88302	87831	88979	88121	88411	89279	88345	89064	90679	88862	55
60	83313	83710	83636	87406	87919	83792	83441	84233	83465	84554	83792	84126	85156	84035	84802	86354	84610	60
65	76807	77235	77141	82325	84597	77351	76941	78138	76947	77951	77316	77692	78936	77571	78399	79850	78207	65
70	67652	68099	67994	74512	80294	68306	67791	69459	67775	68660	68170	68605	70060	68443	69374	70678	69130	70
75	54514	54954	54835	62326	74221	55330	54659	56717	54613	55326	54991	55565	57158	55277	56356	57445	56051	75
80	38198	38581	38468	45838	66393	39182	38336	40467	38267	38767	38581	39377	40818	38853	40071	40878	39772	80
85+	21405	21664	21587	27332	56089	22428	21513	23232	21444	21724	21649	22597	23594	21848	23049	23548	22855	85+

ADDED YRS OF LIFE

	No Causes	(1)	(2)	(3)	(4)	(5)	(6)	(7)	(8)	(9)	(10)	(11)	(12)	(1)+(2)	(1)+(2)+(5)+(6)+(8)	combo	(10)+(11)
TOTAL		.209	.219	2.564	13.982	.498	.108	.711	.077	1.072	.276	.624	1.420	.429	1.123	2.424	.905
WORK	2.489	.109	.047	.683	.728	.051	.010	.165	.058	.000	.122	.160	.251	.156	.274	.315	.282

POPULATION, DEATHS, DEATH RATES FOR ALL CAUSES COMBINED, AND SPECIFIED CAUSES

Age Start of Interval	Midyear Population	Deaths During Year	All Causes	Respiratory T.B.	Other Infec. and Paras.	Neoplasms	Cardiovascular	Infl., Pneu., Bronch.	Diarrheal	Certain Degenerative	Maternal	Cert. Dis. of Infancy	Motor Vehicle	Other Violence	Other and Unknown	Age Start of Interval
0	203582	12149	.05968	.00013	.00213	.00014	.00018	.00748	.00304	.00017	.00000	.03183	.00009	.00242	.01207	
1	793755	2144	.00270	.00009	.00039	.00010	.00006	.00059	.00013	.00005	.00000	.00000	.00012	.00054	.00064	0
5	803764	787	.00098	.00002	.00011	.00007	.00006	.00008	.00001	.00002	.00000	.00000	.00012	.00027	.00064	1
10	719749	687	.00095	.00002	.00006	.00005	.00008	.00006	.00001	.00003	.00000	.00000	.00012	.00039	.00020	5
15	628912	1359	.00216	.00025	.00010	.00008	.00019	.00007	.00000	.00006	.00000	.00000	.00009	.00082	.00015	10
20	606787	2212	.00365	.00055	.00015	.00009	.00027	.00008	.00000	.00010	.00000	.00000	.00031	.00148	.00028	15
25	625749	2680	.00428	.00066	.00017	.00016	.00043	.00012	.00001	.00017	.00000	.00000	.00058	.00148	.00034	20
30	547066	3122	.00571	.00086	.00023	.00022	.00101	.00018	.00002	.00025	.00000	.00000	.00059	.00161	.00035	25
35	564651	3954	.00700	.00088	.00029	.00042	.00188	.00025	.00001	.00038	.00000	.00000	.00052	.00180	.00061	30
40	499436	5175	.01036	.00112	.00050	.00075	.00368	.00043	.00003	.00072	.00000	.00000	.00048	.00161	.00079	35
45	448614	6522	.01454	.00133	.00081	.00148	.00606	.00059	.00004	.00087	.00000	.00000	.00045	.00166	.00101	40
50	374545	8719	.02328	.00155	.00101	.00289	.01152	.00094	.00005	.00138	.00000	.00000	.00047	.00144	.00144	45
55	280673	9134	.03254	.00171	.00123	.00424	.01710	.00124	.00007	.00188	.00000	.00000	.00058	.00137	.00199	50
60	209570	8913	.04253	.00153	.00120	.00581	.02397	.00176	.00012	.00253	.00000	.00000	.00061	.00149	.00298	55
65	202641	9326	.04602	.00140	.00093	.00586	.02676	.00179	.00011	.00286	.00000	.00000	.00061	.00136	.00365	60
70	116148	7371	.06346	.00146	.00106	.00731	.03764	.00276	.00009	.00424	.00000	.00000	.00054	.00116	.00462	65
75	68827	5686	.08261	.00135	.00105	.00837	.05075	.00321	.00009	.00548	.00000	.00000	.00051	.00152	.00687	70
80	32623	3446	.10563	.00098	.00095	.00858	.06462	.00457	.00018	.00668	.00000	.00000	.00064	.00158	.00989	75
85+	18769	2997	.15968	.00075	.00069	.00927	.09521	.00991	.00048	.00858	.00000	.00000	.00071	.00212	.01625	80
ALL	7745861	96383														85+
CRUDE DEATH RATE			.01244	.00066	.00045	.00108	.00494	.00068	.00012	.00062	.00000	.00084	.00038	.00118	.00150	
STANDARDIZED RATE (1)			.01050	.00055	.00040	.00081	.00357	.00065	.00014	.00047	.00000	.00112	.00038	.00118	.00150	
STANDARDIZED RATE (2)			.01562	.00073	.00048	.00147	.00708	.00078	.00011	.00085	.00000	.00112	.00035	.00110	.00134	
GEOMETRIC MEAN			.01373							.00066	.00000	.00066	.00040	.00121	.00184	

LIFE TABLE FOR ALL CAUSES COMBINED

Age (x)	Midyear Population	Deaths During Year	$_nM_x$	$_nq_x$	l_x	$_nd_x$	$_nL_x$	$_nm_x$	$_na_x$	T_x	$_nr_x$	$\overset{\circ}{e}_x$	Age (x)
0	203582	12149	.059676	.056860	100000	5686	95289	.059671	.171450	5864840	.000000	58.648	
1	793755	2144	.002701	.010741	94314	1013	374724	.002703	1.500000	5769551	.000000	61.174	0
5	803764	787	.000979	.004855	93301	453	465373	.000973	2.500000	5394828	.000000	57.822	1
10	719749	687	.000954	.004782	92848	444	463244	.000958	2.756194	4929455	.018547	53.092	5
15	628912	1359	.002161	.010811	92404	999	459774	.002173	2.751919	4466211	.019291	48.334	10
20	606787	2212	.003645	.018073	91405	1652	453083	.003646	2.614003	4006437	.000674	43.832	15
25	625749	2680	.004283	.021203	89753	1903	444179	.004284	2.589989	3553354	.004658	39.590	20
30	547066	3122	.005707	.028162	87850	2474	433281	.005710	2.587325	3109175	.005651	35.392	25
35	564651	3954	.007003	.034436	85376	2940	419884	.007002	2.620536	2675894	.000613	31.342	30
40	499436	5175	.010362	.050645	82436	4175	402278	.010378	2.628293	2256010	.009995	27.367	35
45	448614	6522	.014538	.070418	78261	5511	378334	.014567	2.646298	1853732	.011128	23.687	40
50	374545	8719	.023279	.110584	72750	8045	344529	.023351	2.610757	1475398	.019066	20.280	45
55	280673	9134	.032543	.151271	64705	9788	299577	.032673	2.553318	1130869	.030220	17.477	50
60	209570	8913	.042530	.192108	54917	10550	248077	.042527	2.487382	831292	-.001539	15.137	55
65	202641	9326	.046022	.206212	44367	9149	198781	.046025	2.480212	583216	.001379	13.145	60
70	116148	7371	.063462	.274888	35218	9681	151802	.063774	2.491134	384434	.035133	10.916	65
75	68827	5686	.082613	.342131	25537	8737	105281	.082988	2.435714	232632	.042126	9.110	70
80	32623	3446	.105631	.415774	16800	6985	65884	.106019	2.406466	127352	.042126	7.580	75
85+	18769	2997	.159678	1.000000	9815	9815	61467	.159678	6.262596	61467	.000000	6.263	80
										61467	.000000	6.263	85+

NUMBER OF PERSONS DYING (OUT OF 100,000 AT BIRTH) ABOVE AGE X FROM SPECIFIED CAUSES

Age (x)	All Causes	Respiratory T. B.	Other Infec. and Paras.	Neo-plasms	Cardio-vascular	Infl., Pneu., Bronch.	Diar-rheal	Certain Degen-erative	Maternal	Cert. Dis. of Infancy	Motor Vehicle	Other Violence	Other and Unknown	Age (x)
0	100000	4605	2932	9417	47140	4861	572	5527	0	3033	2477	7466	11970	0
1	94314	4592	2729	9404	47123	4149	283	5511	0	0	2468	7235	10820	1
5	93301	4558	2583	9367	47102	3927	234	5492	0	0	2425	7033	10580	5
10	92848	4549	2530	9334	47072	3888	229	5481	0	0	2369	6907	10489	10
15	92404	4537	2501	9309	47035	3861	227	5468	0	0	2326	6724	10416	15
20	91405	4422	2457	9270	46949	3828	224	5441	0	0	2183	6345	10286	20
25	89753	4174	2386	9230	46825	3794	223	5395	0	0	1919	5673	10134	25
30	87850	3881	2309	9157	46634	3741	217	5320	0	0	1658	4956	9977	30
35	85376	3506	2210	9059	46195	3661	210	5210	0	0	1435	4176	9714	35
40	82436	3136	2089	8882	45404	3557	204	5050	0	0	1232	3498	9384	40
45	78261	2686	1886	8578	43918	3382	193	4761	0	0	1051	2830	8976	45
50	72750	2183	1579	8017	41619	3160	176	4432	0	0	874	2278	8432	50
55	64705	1648	1229	7017	37636	2836	159	3957	0	0	673	1806	7744	55
60	54917	1135	862	5740	32489	2464	138	3392	0	0	491	1358	6848	60
65	44367	757	564	4299	26543	2028	108	2765	0	0	341	1021	5941	65
70	35218	479	379	3135	21224	1672	87	2196	0	0	233	790	5023	70
75	25537	258	218	2022	15479	1251	72	1548	0	0	156	560	3973	75
80	16800	116	108	1139	10110	911	41	969	0	0	88	392	2926	80
85+	9815	46	43	570	5852	609	29	527	0	0	39	246	1854	85+

NUMBER OF PERSONS SURVIVING TO AGE X IF SPECIFIED CAUSES WERE ELIMINATED

Age (x)	No Causes	Respiratory T. B. (1)	Other Infec. and Paras. (2)	Neo-plasms (3)	Cardio-vascular (4)	Infl., Pneu., Bronch. (5)	Diar-rheal (6)	Certain Degener-ative (7)	Maternal (8)	Cert. Dis. of Infancy (9)	Motor Vehicle (10)	Other Violence (11)	Other and Unknown (12)	(1) + (2)	(1) + (2) + (5) + (6) + (8)	(1)+(2)+ (5)+(6)+ (8)+part of(9)&(12)	(10) + (11)	Age (x)
0	100000	100000	100000	100000	100000	100000	100000	100000	100000	100000	100000	100000	100000	100000	100000	100000	100000	0
1	94314	94327	94511	94327	94331	95008	94595	94330	94314	97306	94323	94539	95437	94524	95503	98892	94547	1
5	93301	93347	93642	93350	93338	94210	93628	93335	93301	96260	93352	93725	94654	93688	94933	98448	93776	5
10	92848	92903	93240	92930	92915	93792	93178	92893	92848	95793	92955	93396	94287	93296	94579	98110	93504	10
15	92404	92471	92823	92511	92508	93371	92462	92462	92404	95335	92554	93133	93910	92891	94198	97729	93284	15
20	91405	91586	91864	91549	91593	92394	91735	91489	91405	94304	91696	92507	93026	92045	93378	96909	92801	20
25	89753	90177	90274	89934	90061	90759	90078	89881	89753	92600	90301	91512	91498	90701	92049	95568	92070	25
30	87850	88557	88437	88100	88341	88887	88174	88050	87850	90637	88646	90297	89717	89148	90534	94035	91116	30
35	85376	86436	86045	85716	86290	86444	85698	85679	85376	88372	86372	88084	87455	87113	88556	92052	89581	35
40	82436	83828	83202	82939	84109	83590	82753	82887	82436	85051	83599	86192	84776	84607	86121	89602	87408	40
45	78261	80030	79188	79038	81341	79530	78573	78972	78261	80743	79544	82508	80893	80977	82618	86054	83861	45
50	72750	74891	73911	74021	77955	74147	73056	73732	72750	75058	74116	77260	76086	77874	81236	78710		50
55	64705	67129	66073	66802	73480	64953	66034	66578	64705	66757	66113	69188	68043	68548	70508	73675	70694	55
60	54917	57464	56423	57524	67987	56588	55181	56578	54917	56659	56283	59163	58623	59040	61130	64013	60634	60
65	44367	46779	45858	48180	61949	46122	44607	46292	44367	45774	45608	48122	48238	48351	50536	53035	49468	65
70	35218	37393	36571	39383	56245	36942	35428	37278	35218	36335	36301	38421	39191	38830	40972	43100	39603	70
75	25537	27312	26659	29629	49361	27164	25702	27619	25537	26347	26439	29073	29428	28513	30525	32216	29010	75
80	16800	18089	17630	20330	42013	18163	16934	18681	16800	17333	17417	18617	20361	18983	20687	21922	19301	80
85+	9815	10625	10352	12409	34061	10861	9902	11291	9815	10126	10214	10999	12918	11206	12511	13341	11447	85+

ADDED YRS OF LIFE		(1)	(2)	(3)	(4)	(5)	(6)	(7)	(8)	(9)	(10)	(11)	(12)				
TOTAL		1.100	.752	1.504	11.411	1.179	.243	.871	.000	1.855	.705	2.268	2.551	1.883	3.399	6.000	3.021
WORK	7.978	.721	.291	.518	2.235	.236	.016	.343	.000	.000	.469	1.391	.657	1.022	1.287	1.432	1.882

POPULATION, DEATHS, DEATH RATES FOR ALL CAUSES COMBINED, AND SPECIFIED CAUSES

Age Start of Interval	Midyear Population	Deaths During Year	All Causes	Respiratory T.B.	Other Infec. and Paras.	Neoplasms	Cardiovascular	Infl., Pneu., Bronch.	Diarrheal	Certain Degenerative	Maternal	Cert. Dis. of Infancy	Motor Vehicle	Other Violence	Other and Unknown	Age Start of Interval
0	204851	9692	.04731	.00011	.00189	.00010	.00018	.00615	.00235	.00009	.00000	.02488	.00007	.00208	.00942	0
1	787706	1808	.00230	.00005	.00037	.00008	.00005	.00048	.00011	.00003	.00000	.00000	.00009	.00050	.00053	1
5	808119	644	.00080	.00003	.00010	.00005	.00008	.00008	.00000	.00003	.00000	.00000	.00008	.00020	.00015	5
10	712784	490	.00069	.00009	.00006	.00004	.00011	.00005	.00000	.00004	.00002	.00000	.00004	.00010	.00015	10
15	664203	1167	.00176	.00040	.00011	.00009	.00020	.00008	.00000	.00004	.00022	.00000	.00004	.00010	.00013	15
20	702985	1779	.00253	.00074	.00011	.00011	.00032	.00006	.00001	.00009	.00027	.00000	.00015	.00022	.00025	20
25	698918	2304	.00330	.00074	.00013	.00024	.00055	.00014	.00001	.00016	.00034	.00000	.00012	.00032	.00034	25
30	619963	2824	.00456	.00076	.00018	.00057	.00101	.00019	.00001	.00032	.00034	.00000	.00012	.00042	.00045	30
35	629763	3848	.00611	.00065	.00023	.00104	.00198	.00024	.00002	.00049	.00030	.00000	.00011	.00044	.00059	35
40	519793	4786	.00921	.00061	.00028	.00178	.00382	.00032	.00003	.00078	.00012	.00000	.00012	.00038	.00098	40
45	457427	5682	.01242	.00052	.00033	.00239	.00621	.00044	.00004	.00093	.00001	.00000	.00010	.00029	.00114	45
50	366234	7080	.01933	.00062	.00044	.00349	.01031	.00074	.00004	.00162	.00001	.00000	.00010	.00037	.00157	50
55	261665	6851	.02618	.00057	.00045	.00460	.01524	.00090	.00005	.00203	.00000	.00000	.00016	.00037	.00181	55
60	199524	7100	.03558	.00066	.00050	.00541	.02217	.00127	.00005	.00249	.00000	.00000	.00014	.00048	.00238	60
65	216993	7245	.03339	.00047	.00037	.00441	.02120	.00118	.00011	.00241	.00000	.00000	.00012	.00053	.00258	65
70	115486	5939	.05143	.00047	.00051	.00581	.03304	.00233	.00009	.00377	.00000	.00000	.00012	.00112	.00414	70
75	67447	4357	.06460	.00047	.00044	.00583	.04282	.00262	.00027	.00449	.00000	.00000	.00019	.00133	.00612	75
80	35557	2893	.08136	.00034	.00062	.00602	.05400	.00436	.00028	.00484	.00000	.00000	.00028	.00180	.00883	80
85+	26261	3497	.13316	.00042	.00038	.00720	.08530	.00743	.00038	.00625	.00000	.00000	.00019	.00404	.02159	85+
ALL	8095679	79586	.00983	.00045	.00027	.00117	.00436	.00054	.00009	.00060	.00013	.00063	.00011	.00042	.00111	

	All Causes	Respiratory T.B.	Other Infec. and Paras.	Neoplasms	Cardiovascular	Infl., Pneu., Bronch.	Diarrheal	Certain Degenerative	Maternal	Cert. Dis. of Infancy	Motor Vehicle	Other Violence	Other and Unknown
CRUDE DEATH RATE	.00989	.00045	.00027	.00117	.00436	.00054	.00009	.00060	.00013	.00063	.00011	.00042	.00111
STANDARDIZED RATE (1)	.00846	.00039	.00027	.00091	.00324	.00053	.00009	.00060	.00013	.00063	.00011	.00042	.00111
STANDARDIZED RATE (2)	.01255	.00045	.00028	.00151	.00630	.00053	.00011	.00047	.00012	.00088	.00010	.00040	.00102
GEOMETRIC MEAN	.01101	.00045	.00028	.00151	.00630	.00063	.00009	.00081	.00012	.00051	.00011	.00044	.00130

LIFE TABLE FOR ALL CAUSES COMBINED

Age (x)	Midyear Population	Deaths During Year	$_nM_x$	$_nq_x$	l_x	$_nd_x$	$_nL_x$	$_nm_x$	$_n\bar{a}_x$	T_x	$_nr_x$	$\overset{\circ}{e}_x$	Age (x)
0	204851	9692	.047312	.045480	100000	4548	96136	.047308	.150431	6267764	.000000	62.678	0
1	787706	1808	.002295	.009135	95452	872	379628	.002297	1.500000	6171628	.000000	64.657	1
5	808119	644	.000797	.003954	94580	374	471965	.000792	2.500000	5792000	.000000	61.239	5
10	712784	490	.000687	.003450	94206	325	470311	.000691	2.787821	5320035	.017201	56.472	10
15	664203	1167	.001757	.008766	93881	823	467523	.001760	2.713649	4849724	.005891	51.658	15
20	702985	1779	.002531	.012562	93058	1169	462509	.002528	2.621364	4382201	-.007625	47.091	20
25	698918	2304	.003297	.016368	91889	1504	455866	.003299	2.620373	3919691	-.005917	42.657	25
30	619963	2824	.004555	.022548	90385	2038	447072	.004559	2.618580	3463825	-.005420	38.323	30
35	629763	3848	.006110	.030154	88347	2664	435457	.006118	2.643346	3016754	.007618	34.147	35
40	519793	4786	.009208	.045178	85683	3871	419214	.009234	2.623030	2581297	.020000	30.126	40
45	457427	5682	.012422	.060505	81812	4950	397365	.012457	2.637374	2162083	.019161	26.427	45
50	366234	7080	.019332	.092829	76862	7135	367238	.019429	2.607276	1764718	.031097	22.960	50
55	261665	6851	.026182	.123682	69727	8624	327607	.026319	2.568607	1397480	.042410	20.042	55
60	199524	7100	.035585	.163249	61103	9975	280422	.035571	2.484440	1069813	-.004612	17.508	60
65	216993	7245	.033388	.154103	51128	7879	235937	.033394	2.499339	789391	-.002728	15.440	65
70	115486	5939	.051426	.230063	43249	9950	191660	.051915	2.529188	553454	.055153	12.797	70
75	67447	4357	.064599	.278477	33299	9273	142934	.064876	2.459201	361793	.052858	10.865	75
80	35557	2893	.081362	.338550	24026	8134	99517	.081735	2.465833	218859	.052858	9.109	80
85+	26261	3497	.133163	1.000000	15892	15892	119342	.133163	7.505580	119342	.000000	7.510	85+

NUMBER OF PERSONS DYING (OUT OF 100,000 AT BIRTH) ABOVE AGE X FROM SPECIFIED CAUSES

Age (x)	All Causes	Respiratory T. B.	Other Infec. and Paras.	Neo-plasms	Cardio-vascular	Infl., Pneu., Bronch.	Diar-rheal	Certain Degen-erative	Maternal	Cert. Dis. of Infancy	Motor Vehicle	Other Violence	Other and Unknown	Age (x)
0	100000	2993	1802	11472	54173	4819	528	6359	754	2391	729	3191	10749	0
1	95452	2982	1620	11462	54156	4228	302	6390	754	0	723	2991	9844	1
5	94580	2963	1479	11433	54137	4046	261	6378	754	0	687	2800	9642	5
10	94206	2951	1432	11409	54100	4009	259	6364	754	0	649	2707	9572	10
15	93881	2908	1404	11389	54047	3987	257	6345	745	0	628	2660	9511	15
20	93058	2723	1350	11349	53952	3948	255	6308	644	0	583	2557	9389	20
25	91889	2379	1299	11297	53803	3918	252	6266	519	0	516	2407	9233	25
30	90385	2040	1240	11187	53554	3856	249	6193	362	0	462	2217	9025	30
35	88347	1701	1160	10932	53102	3771	245	6052	190	0	413	2020	8761	35
40	85683	1419	1059	10480	52240	3664	238	5839	58	0	366	1860	8460	40
45	81812	1163	944	9733	50630	3532	227	5509	8	0	315	1702	8049	45
50	76862	956	811	8781	48152	3355	209	5137	3	0	275	1589	7594	50
55	69727	730	648	7493	44343	3082	196	4538	1	0	230	1453	7013	55
60	61103	543	499	5980	39317	2786	180	3370	1	0	177	1330	6420	60
65	51129	358	360	4462	33104	2429	155	3173	1	0	138	1197	5751	65
70	43249	247	271	3423	28101	2150	129	2603	1	0	109	1072	5143	70
75	33299	157	173	2303	21705	1698	112	1875	1	0	79	855	4341	75
80	24026	89	110	1471	15555	1321	73	1231	1	0	52	663	3460	80
85+	15892	50	45	859	10180	886	45	745	0	0	23	482	2577	85+

NUMBER OF PERSONS SURVIVING TO AGE X IF SPECIFIED CAUSES WERE ELIMINATED

Age (x)	No Causes	Respiratory T. B. (1)	Other Infec. and Paras. (2)	Neo-plasms (3)	Cardio-vascular (4)	Infl., Pneu., Bronch. (5)	Diar-rheal (6)	Certain Degener-ative (7)	Maternal (8)	Cert. Dis. of Infancy (9)	Motor Vehicle (10)	Other Violence (11)	Other and Unknown (12)	(1) + (2)	(1) + (2) + (5) + (6) + (8)	(1)+(2)+ (5)+(6)+ (8)+part of(9)&(12)	(10) + (11)	Age (x)
0	100000	100000	100000	100000	100000	100000	100000	100000	100000	100000	100000	100000	100000	100000	100000	100000	100000	0
1	95452	95463	95630	95462	95469	96031	95673	95461	95452	97817	95458	95648	96340	95641	96444	99104	95653	1
5	94580	94610	94897	94619	94615	95336	94840	94601	94580	96923	94622	94965	95663	94927	95949	98715	95006	5
10	94206	94247	94569	94268	94278	94996	94467	94241	94206	96540	94295	94692	95356	94610	95669	98451	94762	10
15	93881	93965	94271	93963	94006	94691	94143	93934	93890	96207	93981	94403	95088	94355	95444	98245	94503	15
20	93058	93326	93498	93179	93277	93900	93320	93148	93168	95363	93202	93678	94378	93768	94994	97851	93823	20
25	91889	92497	92375	92061	92253	92750	92150	92019	92122	94165	92058	92652	93350	92986	94363	97291	92862	25
30	90385	91322	90922	90663	90992	90645	90586	90770	92624	90644	91325	92032	91864	93452	96457	91587	30
35	88347	89602	88951	88872	89391	89321	88605	88683	88894	90536	88649	89463	90222	90215	92042	95109	89769	35
40	85683	87182	86369	86642	87560	86734	85940	86220	86344	87806	86022	86925	87805	87880	89914	92995	87269	40
45	81812	83498	82580	83469	85228	82946	82069	82650	82492	83839	82654	84282	84251	84282	86431	89464	83534	45
50	76862	78650	77714	79365	82614	78102	77120	77506	77254	78766	77252	78234	79608	79522	81756	84683	78631	50
55	69727	71569	70657	73275	78949	71116	69974	71353	70313	71454	70124	71104	72793	72523	74854	77598	71508	55
60	61103	62897	62059	65715	74722	62603	61334	63170	61617	62617	61501	62426	64371	63880	66249	68727	62833	60
65	51128	52803	52056	56496	69869	52719	51345	53520	51558	52395	51496	52360	54510	53761	56137	58290	52737	65
70	43249	44770	44117	48854	65730	44860	43456	45824	43612	44320	43587	44409	46710	45669	47998	49883	44757	70
75	33299	34551	34055	38733	59873	34952	33474	35962	33579	34124	33586	34388	36731	35336	37598	39134	34685	75
80	24026	24989	24626	28773	53648	25556	24185	26541	24228	24621	24256	24980	27340	25613	27655	28844	25219	80
85+	15892	16562	16342	19633	46630	17282	16020	17995	16026	16286	16068	16676	18914	17031	18828	19706	16860	85+

ADDED YRS OF LIFE																		
TOTAL		.936	.578	2.255	16.079	1.166	.213	1.145	.296	1.549	.233	.921	2.457	1.528	3.287	5.528	1.159
WORK	6.750	.630	.188	.870	2.346	.216	.014	.411	.240	.000	.116	.343	.620	.823	1.309	1.496	.460

POPULATION, DEATHS, DEATH RATES FOR ALL CAUSES COMBINED, AND SPECIFIED CAUSES

Age Start of Interval	Midyear Population	Deaths During Year	All Causes	Respiratory T. B.	Other Infec. and Paras.	Neo-plasms	Cardio-vascular	Infl., Pneu., Bronch.	Diar-rheal	Certain Degen-erative	Maternal	Cert. Dis. of Infancy	Motor Vehicle	Other Violence	Other and Unknown	Age Start of Interval
0	2096966	63957	.03050	.00001	.00041	.00011	.00014	.00286	.00069	.00006	.00000	.01864	.00009	.00059	.00651	0
1	8267645	9851	.00119	.00000	.00008	.00013	.00003	.00019	.00004	.00001	.00000	.00000	.00011	.00025	.00035	1
5	9536463	5354	.00056	.00000	.00002	.00009	.00002	.00004	.00000	.00001	.00000	.00000	.00011	.00014	.00012	5
10	8553074	4693	.00055	.00000	.00001	.00007	.00003	.00002	.00000	.00001	.00000	.00000	.00011	.00014	.00012	10
15	6656062	8636	.00130	.00000	.00002	.00010	.00005	.00003	.00000	.00003	.00000	.00000	.00010	.00020	.00010	15
20	5290144	9484	.00179	.00001	.00002	.00011	.00009	.00004	.00000	.00005	.00000	.00000	.00052	.00041	.00014	20
25	5351084	9286	.00174	.00002	.00002	.00017	.00016	.00004	.00001	.00008	.00000	.00000	.00073	.00059	.00015	25
30	5865966	11739	.00200	.00003	.00002	.00022	.00035	.00006	.00001	.00013	.00000	.00000	.00046	.00062	.00017	30
35	6100042	17605	.00289	.00004	.00003	.00037	.00087	.00010	.00001	.00022	.00000	.00000	.00034	.00061	.00023	35
40	5695048	26250	.00461	.00007	.00004	.00066	.00187	.00015	.00001	.00036	.00000	.00000	.00030	.00067	.00028	40
45	5376018	40847	.00760	.00011	.00006	.00123	.00359	.00022	.00002	.00057	.00000	.00000	.00030	.00072	.00043	45
50	4750818	59344	.01249	.00017	.00008	.00232	.00642	.00037	.00003	.00085	.00000	.00000	.00031	.00082	.00066	50
55	4141182	76541	.01848	.00022	.00014	.00371	.01009	.00051	.00004	.00106	.00000	.00000	.00032	.00093	.00101	55
60	3420832	97590	.02853	.00029	.00018	.00578	.01627	.00087	.00007	.00143	.00000	.00000	.00034	.00095	.00143	60
65	2940986	121385	.04127	.00033	.00025	.00793	.02461	.00135	.00010	.00190	.00000	.00000	.00038	.00100	.00226	65
70	2192595	130157	.05936	.00043	.00029	.01035	.03708	.00221	.00015	.00245	.00000	.00000	.00042	.00108	.00330	70
75	1364015	117185	.08591	.00048	.00029	.01284	.05675	.00352	.00021	.00308	.00000	.00000	.00051	.00132	.00458	75
80	667339	88960	.13331	.00055	.00033	.01626	.09224	.00639	.00033	.00416	.00000	.00000	.00062	.00186	.00626	80
85+	363499	76784	.21124	.00062	.00040	.01753	.15283	.01308	.00054	.00497	.00000	.00000	.00074	.00307	.00922	85+
ALL	88629778	975648														

	All Causes	Respiratory T. B.	Other Infec. and Paras.	Neo-plasms	Cardio-vascular	Infl., Pneu., Bronch.	Diar-rheal	Certain Degen-erative	Maternal	Cert. Dis. of Infancy	Motor Vehicle	Other Violence	Other and Unknown
CRUDE DEATH RATE	.01101	.00008	.00008	.00164	.00582	.00046	.00005	.00047	.00000	.00044	.00032	.00064	.00100
STANDARDIZED RATE (1)	.00662	.00005	.00006	.00089	.00277	.00031	.00004	.00027	.00000	.00044	.00032	.00064	.00100
STANDARDIZED RATE (2)	.01166	.00009	.00008	.00175	.00631	.00048	.00005	.00049	.00000	.00066	.00031	.00053	.00073
GEOMETRIC MEAN	.00840									.00039	.00034	.00067	.00103

LIFE TABLE FOR ALL CAUSES COMBINED

Age (x)	Midyear Population	Deaths During Year	$_nM_x$	$_nq_x$	l_x	$_nd_x$	$_nL_x$	$_nm_x$	$_na_x$	T_x	$_nr_x$	$\overset{\circ}{e}_x$	Age (x)
0	2096966	63957	.030500	.029700	100000	2970	97392	.030495	.121850	6665119	.000000	66.651	0
1	8267645	9851	.001192	.004751	97030	461	386968	.001191	1.500000	6567727	.000000	67.688	1
5	9536463	5354	.000561	.002756	96569	270	482170	.000560	2.500000	6180759	.000000	64.004	5
10	8553074	4693	.000549	.002752	96299	265	480907	.000560	2.780660	5698589	.024202	59.176	10
15	6656062	8636	.001297	.006529	96034	627	478725	.001310	2.695375	5217683	.045056	54.332	15
20	5290144	9484	.001793	.008941	95407	853	474942	.001796	2.546405	4738958	.031391	49.671	20
25	5351084	9286	.001735	.008641	94554	817	470744	.001736	2.519890	4264015	-.000832	45.096	25
30	5865966	11739	.002001	.009932	93737	931	466464	.001996	2.614572	3793272	-.014220	40.467	30
35	6100042	17605	.002886	.014320	92806	1329	460949	.002883	2.681527	3326808	-.004768	35.847	35
40	5695048	26250	.004609	.022836	91477	2089	452582	.004616	2.700854	2865859	.004551	31.329	40
45	5376018	40847	.007598	.037399	89388	3343	439237	.007611	2.695869	2413277	.008348	26.998	45
50	4750818	59344	.012491	.060805	86045	5232	417943	.012518	2.652467	1974039	.011988	22.942	50
55	4141182	76541	.018483	.088748	80813	7172	387096	.018528	2.633970	1556097	.014459	19.256	55
60	3420832	97590	.028528	.133676	73641	9844	344594	.028567	2.601437	1169001	.008383	15.874	60
65	2940986	121385	.041274	.187548	63797	11965	289820	.041284	2.562509	824407	.001822	12.922	65
70	2192595	130157	.059362	.259184	51832	13434	225918	.059464	2.525557	534587	.010500	10.314	70
75	1364015	117185	.085912	.354524	38398	13613	157730	.086306	2.483273	308669	.025993	8.039	75
80	667339	88960	.133306	.497922	24785	12341	92028	.134100	2.415390	150939	.025993	6.090	80
85+	363499	76784	.211236	1.000000	12444	12444	58910	.211236	4.734046	58910	.000000	4.734	85+

NUMBER OF PERSONS DYING (OUT OF 100,000 AT BIRTH) ABOVE AGE X FROM SPECIFIED CAUSES

Age (x)	All Causes	Respiratory T.B.	Other Infec. and Paras.	Neo-plasms	Cardio-vascular	Infl., Pneu., Bronch.	Diar-rheal	Certain Degen-erative	Maternal	Cert. Dis. of Infancy	Motor Vehicle	Other Violence	Other and Unknown	Age (x)
0	100000	738	570	15052	57457	4131	328	4211	0	1816	2370	5044	8283	0
1	97030	738	530	15041	57443	3852	260	4205	0	1	2362	4948	7650	1
5	96569	737	500	14991	57434	3778	245	4200	0	0	2317	4851	7516	5
10	96299	737	489	14946	57424	3760	244	4194	0	0	2265	4782	7458	10
15	96034	736	483	14912	57412	3750	243	4187	0	0	2217	4683	7411	15
20	95407	735	476	14862	57396	3735	241	4175	0	0	1967	4486	7344	20
25	94554	733	467	14808	57345	3717	239	4149	0	0	1620	4204	7272	25
30	93737	725	460	14729	57269	3697	236	4110	0	0	1403	3914	7194	30
35	92806	713	450	14626	57108	3669	232	4049	0	0	1243	3629	7087	35
40	91477	693	437	14457	56709	3625	228	3947	0	0	1105	3320	6956	40
45	89388	661	420	14159	55861	3558	222	3782	0	0	970	2995	6760	45
50	86045	613	392	13619	54279	3460	212	3531	0	0	834	2633	6472	50
55	80813	544	358	12646	51591	3307	199	3176	0	0	700	2246	6046	55
60	73641	458	305	11206	47676	3109	184	2764	0	0	569	1879	5491	60
65	63797	357	242	9212	42059	2811	158	2273	0	0	439	1534	4712	65
70	51832	261	168	6914	34924	2420	128	1722	0	0	318	1221	3756	70
75	38398	164	101	4573	26531	1920	95	1168	0	0	203	923	2720	75
80	24785	88	55	2542	17533	1361	62	680	0	0	106	627	1731	80
85+	12444	36	24	1033	9003	771	32	293	0	0	37	341	874	85+

NUMBER OF PERSONS SURVIVING TO AGE X IF SPECIFIED CAUSES WERE ELIMINATED

Age (x)	No Causes	Respiratory T.B. (1)	Other Infec. and Paras. (2)	Neo-plasms (3)	Cardio-vascular (4)	Infl., Pneu., Bronch. (5)	Diar-rheal (6)	Certain Degener-ative (7)	Maternal (8)	Cert. Dis. of Infancy (9)	Motor Vehicle (10)	Other Violence (11)	Other and Unknown (12)	(1) + (2)	(1) + (2) + (5) + (6) + (8)	(1)+(2)+ (5)+(6)+ (8)+part of(9)&(12)	(10) + (11)	Age (x)
0	100000	100000	100000	100000	100000	100000	100000	100000	100000	100000	100000	100000	100000	100000	100000	100000	100000	0
1	97030	97030	97069	97041	97044	97305	97057	97036	97030	98834	97038	97125	97656	97069	97412	99223	97132	1
5	96569	96570	96638	96630	96592	96917	96651	96580	96569	98366	96622	96760	97326	96639	97099	98925	96813	5
10	96299	96300	96379	96404	96332	96664	96381	96316	96299	98091	96404	96559	97112	96380	96828	98698	96663	10
15	96034	96036	96120	96173	96079	96408	96117	96058	96034	97821	96186	96392	96893	96122	96580	98438	96545	15
20	95407	95410	95499	95595	95477	95794	95492	95443	95407	97182	95608	95960	96327	95502	95974	97824	96364	20
25	94554	94559	94654	94794	94664	94955	94640	94615	94554	96313	95299	95385	95539	94659	95147	96984	96137	25
30	93737	93750	93843	94054	93922	94155	93825	93837	93737	95481	94694	94852	94792	93856	94363	96189	95820	30
35	92806	92831	92921	93223	93150	93248	92857	92965	92806	94533	93914	94198	93958	92946	93480	95296	95322	35
40	91477	91521	91604	92057	92215	91956	91571	91736	91477	93179	92708	93160	92744	91648	92222	94023	94414	40
45	89388	89463	89529	90252	90958	89923	89466	89804	89388	91051	90726	91361	90823	89603	90238	92013	92728	45
50	86045	86164	86208	87413	88561	86657	86149	86693	86045	87646	87468	88307	87714	86327	87046	88775	89768	50
55	80813	80992	80999	83062	86473	81537	80923	81769	80813	82317	82281	83323	82802	81178	82017	83670	84837	55
60	73641	73886	73861	77116	82901	74491	73756	74911	73641	75011	75106	76289	75598	74107	75080	76623	77807	60
65	63797	64104	64046	68777	77950	64815	63921	65362	63797	64984	65189	66423	66591	64354	65508	66895	67872	65
70	51832	52168	52101	58149	71687	53018	51959	53613	51832	52796	53074	54258	55007	52439	53771	55458	55558	70
75	38398	38730	38655	45382	64069	39719	38521	40210	38398	39112	39419	40463	41702	38989	40459	41407	41539	75
80	24785	25060	24987	31257	55263	26104	24891	26363	24785	25246	25523	26368	27785	25264	26722	27397	27152	80
85+	12444	12619	12567	17073	44672	13545	12518	13525	12444	12676	12864	13452	14634	12744	13954	14348	13906	85+

ADDED YRS OF LIFE																		
TOTAL		.113	.135	2.160	13.499	.671	.089	.632	.000	1.238	.776	1.321	1.609	.248	1.019	2.377	2.122	
WORK	4.253	.044	.033	.565	1.421	.109	.011	.232	.000	.000	.496	.685	.349	.077	.198	.217	1.191	

POPULATION, DEATHS, DEATH RATES FOR ALL CAUSES COMBINED, AND SPECIFIED CAUSES

Age Start of Interval	Midyear Population	Deaths During Year	All Causes	Respiratory T.B.	Other Infec. and Paras.	Neoplasms	Cardiovascular	Infl., Pneu., Bronch.	Diarrheal	Certain Degenerative	Maternal	Cert. Dis. of Infancy	Motor Vehicle	Other Violence	Other and Unknown	Age Start of Interval
0	2029428	46950	.02313	.00000	.00028	.00010	.00009	.00221	.00058	.00003	.00000	.01379	.00007	.00080	.00517	0
1	7998248	7841	.00098	.00000	.00007	.00010	.00002	.00017	.00003	.00001	.00000	.00000	.00008	.00019	.00030	1
5	9220979	3814	.00041	.00000	.00002	.00007	.00002	.00003	.00000	.00001	.00000	.00000	.00006	.00008	.00011	5
10	8279343	2686	.00032	.00000	.00001	.00006	.00003	.00002	.00000	.00002	.00000	.00000	.00004	.00005	.00009	10
15	6609643	3562	.00054	.00000	.00001	.00006	.00004	.00003	.00000	.00003	.00002	.00000	.00016	.00008	.00010	15
20	5548620	3871	.00070	.00001	.00002	.00008	.00009	.00003	.00001	.00003	.00003	.00000	.00016	.00008	.00010	20
25	5556276	4936	.00089	.00002	.00002	.00014	.00015	.00004	.00001	.00006	.00005	.00000	.00010	.00012	.00015	25
30	6125260	7472	.00122	.00003	.00002	.00028	.00023	.00005	.00001	.00009	.00006	.00000	.00009	.00017	.00019	30
35	6424986	11571	.00180	.00004	.00002	.00053	.00041	.00006	.00001	.00015	.00005	.00000	.00009	.00019	.00026	35
40	5946007	16713	.00281	.00004	.00003	.00094	.00079	.00009	.00001	.00022	.00002	.00000	.00010	.00021	.00036	40
45	5541734	23468	.00423	.00004	.00004	.00154	.00137	.00012	.00002	.00034	.00000	.00000	.00011	.00023	.00044	45
50	4888922	31289	.00640	.00004	.00005	.00224	.00241	.00015	.00003	.00049	.00000	.00000	.00012	.00025	.00060	50
55	4318340	40260	.00932	.00004	.00007	.00295	.00420	.00023	.00003	.00062	.00000	.00000	.00015	.00026	.00077	55
60	3746773	55914	.01492	.00005	.00008	.00398	.00788	.00036	.00005	.00097	.00000	.00000	.00016	.00031	.00108	60
65	3338977	75305	.02255	.00007	.00010	.00505	.01323	.00057	.00008	.00140	.00000	.00000	.00018	.00038	.00148	65
70	2563046	93638	.03653	.00005	.00012	.00644	.02366	.00106	.00014	.00195	.00000	.00000	.00021	.00068	.00219	70
75	1700325	102881	.06051	.00014	.00016	.00843	.04215	.00206	.00020	.00251	.00000	.00000	.00023	.00127	.00335	75
80	918176	96343	.10493	.00020	.00021	.01056	.07715	.00432	.00036	.00327	.00000	.00000	.00023	.00290	.00532	80
85+	569048	107820	.18947	.00022	.00033	.01283	.14436	.01059	.00056	.00385	.00000	.00000	.00022	.00636	.01016	85+
ALL	91324131	736334														
CRUDE DEATH RATE			.00806	.00003	.00005	.00139	.00446	.00033	.00004	.00037	.00002	.00031	.00011	.00029	.00067	
STANDARDIZED RATE (1)			.00412	.00002	.00004	.00071	.00162	.00020	.00004	.00018	.00002	.00049	.00010	.00020	.00050	
STANDARDIZED RATE (2)			.00745	.00003	.00005	.00132	.00406	.00030	.00004	.00035	.00002	.00029	.00011	.00027	.00063	
GEOMETRIC MEAN			.00507													

LIFE TABLE FOR ALL CAUSES COMBINED

Age (x)	Midyear Population	Deaths During Year	$_nM_x$	$_nq_x$	l_x	$_nd_x$	$_nL_x$	$_nm_x$	$_na_x$	T_x	$_nr_x$	$\overset{\circ}{e}_x$	Age (x)
0	2029428	46950	.023135	.022670	100000	2267	97981	.023137	.109329	7325912	.000000	73.259	0
1	7998248	7841	.000980	.003909	97733	382	389977	.000980	1.500000	7227931	.000000	73.956	1
5	9220979	3814	.000414	.002065	97351	201	486253	.000413	2.500000	6837954	.000000	70.240	5
10	8279343	2686	.000324	.001626	97150	158	485368	.000326	2.580432	6351701	.023367	65.380	10
15	6609643	3562	.000539	.002701	96992	262	484342	.000541	2.643130	5866334	.038774	60.483	15
20	5548620	3871	.000698	.003494	96730	338	482839	.000700	2.601701	5381991	.026331	55.639	20
25	5556276	4936	.000888	.004430	96392	427	480943	.000888	2.619048	4899152	-.000572	50.825	25
30	6125260	7472	.001220	.006065	95965	582	478459	.001216	2.653207	4418208	-.014796	46.040	30
35	6424986	11571	.001801	.008964	95383	855	474931	.001800	2.680068	3939749	-.004512	41.305	35
40	5946007	16713	.002811	.013975	94528	1321	469567	.002813	2.674111	3464818	.007599	36.654	40
45	5541734	23468	.004235	.021018	93207	1959	461463	.004245	2.666220	2995250	.012846	32.135	45
50	4888922	31289	.006400	.031606	91248	2884	449464	.006417	2.650615	2533787	.017176	27.768	50
55	4318340	40260	.009323	.045765	88364	4044	432378	.009353	2.665214	2084323	.018014	23.588	55
60	3746773	55914	.014923	.072237	84320	6091	407279	.014955	2.648751	1651945	.012122	19.591	60
65	3338977	75305	.022553	.107288	78229	8393	371350	.022601	2.641462	1244666	.011548	15.911	65
70	2563046	93638	.036534	.168824	69836	11790	321170	.036709	2.624293	873316	.023549	12.505	70
75	1700325	102881	.060507	.265772	58046	15427	252927	.060994	2.581972	552146	.035904	9.512	75
80	918176	96343	.104929	.419062	42619	17860	168547	.105965	2.505704	299219	.035904	7.021	80
85+	569048	107820	.189474	1.000000	24759	24759	130672	.189474	5.277759	130672	.000000	5.278	85+

NUMBER OF PERSONS DYING (OUT OF 100,000 AT BIRTH) ABOVE AGE X FROM SPECIFIED CAUSES

Age (x)	All Causes	Respiratory T.B.	Other Infec. and Paras.	Neoplasms	Cardiovascular	Infl., Pneu., Bronch.	Diarrheal	Certain Degenerative	Maternal	Cert. Dis. of Infancy	Motor Vehicle	Other Violence	Other and Unknown	Age (x)
0	100000	296	437	15356	62913	4018	404	4188	127	1352	902	3124	6883	0
1	97733	296	409	15346	62904	3802	348	4185	127	0	895	3045	6376	1
5	97351	295	383	15307	62897	3734	337	4180	127	0	862	2970	6259	5
10	97150	295	372	15273	62889	3718	336	4175	127	0	831	2929	6205	10
15	96992	295	366	15243	62877	3708	335	4166	126	0	810	2905	6161	15
20	96730	293	359	15212	62855	3695	333	4153	117	0	732	2867	6114	20
25	96392	289	350	15172	62811	3680	331	4137	91	0	665	2811	6055	25
30	95965	281	338	15103	62741	3661	328	4108	63	0	619	2740	5983	30
35	95383	269	326	14970	62630	3636	325	4065	36	0	577	2658	5891	35
40	94528	252	315	14718	62437	3606	321	3995	11	0	536	2569	5768	40
45	93207	233	302	14275	62063	3566	314	3891	1	0	491	2471	5600	45
50	91248	215	285	13564	61430	3512	307	3735	0	0	442	2364	5394	50
55	88364	195	263	12553	60341	3443	295	3515	0	0	386	2250	5123	55
60	84320	177	231	11277	58515	3344	282	3244	0	0	322	2138	4790	60
65	78229	157	198	9655	55295	3198	261	2849	0	0	258	2010	4348	65
70	69836	129	159	7777	50368	2986	230	2328	0	0	193	1869	3797	70
75	58046	99	121	5703	42728	2644	186	1701	0	0	127	1648	3089	75
80	42619	62	79	3560	31971	2118	134	1064	0	0	68	1324	2239	80
85+	24759	28	43	1677	18864	1384	73	503	0	0	29	831	1327	85+

NUMBER OF PERSONS SURVIVING TO AGE X IF SPECIFIED CAUSES WERE ELIMINATED

Age (x)	No Causes	Respiratory T.B. (1)	Other Infec. and Paras. (2)	Neoplasms (3)	Cardiovascular (4)	Infl., Pneu., Bronch. (5)	Diarrheal (6)	Certain Degenerative (7)	Maternal (8)	Cert. Dis. of Infancy (9)	Motor Vehicle (10)	Other Violence (11)	Other and Unknown (12)	(1)+(2)	(1)+(2)+(5)+(6)+(8)	(1)+(2)+(5)+(6)+(8)+part of(9)&(12)	(10)+(11)	Age (x)
0	100000	100000	100000	100000	100000	100000	100000	100000	100000	100000	100000	100000	100000	100000	100000	100000	100000	0
1	97733	97733	97761	97743	97742	97947	97788	97736	97733	99079	97740	97811	98235	97761	98030	99395	97818	1
5	97351	97352	97405	97400	97367	97632	97417	97359	97351	98691	97391	97504	97969	97406	97753	99162	97544	5
10	97150	97151	97214	97233	97174	97446	97217	97163	97150	98488	97221	97343	97821	97215	97579	98996	97414	10
15	96992	96993	97062	97105	97028	97298	97060	97014	96993	98328	97084	97209	97706	97063	97439	98860	97301	15
20	96730	96733	96873	96788	96748	97048	96800	96765	96740	98062	96899	96985	97490	96810	97209	98634	97154	20
25	96392	96399	96478	96575	96493	96724	96463	96443	96428	97719	96628	96702	97208	96485	96925	98359	96938	25
30	95965	95980	96062	96216	96136	96315	96039	96044	96029	97286	96246	96345	96850	96077	96566	98009	96626	30
35	95383	95410	95492	95765	95664	95756	95460	95505	95413	96656	95842	96355		95519	96060	97510	96165	35
40	94528	94571	94647	95159	94999	94608	94719	94642		95830	94887	95072	95615	94690	95286	96739	95433	40
45	93207	93269	93337	94273	94046	93640	93293	93458	93330	94490	93606	93842	94448	93399	94043	95491	94243	45
50	91248	91326	91392	93006	92703	91726	91335	91668	91369	92504	91687	91976	92670	91471	92164	93594	92419	50
55	88364	88459	88525	91086	90869	88895	88464	89008	88481	89581	88845	89182	90012	88621	89373	90773	89667	55
60	84320	84429	84505	88211	88566	84924	84428	85202	84432	85481	84842	85211	86224	84614	85443	86796	85738	60
65	78229	78349	78433	83488	85493	78931	78349	79432	78333	79306	78775	79180	80432	78553	79486	80761	79732	65
70	69836	69970	70055	76443	81584	70665	69973	71411	69929	70798	70385	70820	72339	70189	71256	72421	71376	70
75	58046	58184	58262	65631	76453	59052	58200	59940	58123	58562	60797	60157		58401	59650	60652	59594	75
80	42619	42752	42814	50287	59647	43818	42776	44570	42676	43206	43048	43653	45403	42947	44377	45158	44093	80
85+	24759	24862	24899	30935	60274	26030	24897	26338	24792	25100	25038	25743	27118	25003	26468	26971	26033	85+

ACCID YRS OF LIFE	No Causes	(1)	(2)	(3)	(4)	(5)	(6)	(7)	(8)	(9)	(10)	(11)	(12)	(1)+(2)	(1)+(2)+(5)+(6)+(8)	+part of(9)&(12)	(10)+(11)
TOTAL		.058	.121	2.536	16.745	.611	.093	.626	.059	1.007	.297	.607	1.432	.179	.949	2.095	.908
WORK	2.351	.025	.030	.645	.676	.072	.010	.160	.043	.000	.137	.182	.275	.055	.180	.210	.319

POPULATION, DEATHS, DEATH RATES FOR ALL CAUSES COMBINED, AND SPECIFIED CAUSES

Age Start of Interval	Midyear Popula-tion	Deaths During Year	All Causes	Respira-tory T. B.	Other Infec. and Paras.	Neo-plasms	Cardio-vascular	Infl., Pneu., Bronch.	Diar-rheal	Certain Degen-erative	Maternal	Cert. Dis. of Infancy	Motor Vehicle	Other Violence	Other and Unknown	Age Start of Interval
0	2C61000	57365	.02783	.0C0C0	.00037	.00009	.00015	.00244	.C0054	.00005	.00000	.01713	.00009	.00089	.00608	0
1	8470000	8883	.001C5	.000C0	.00007	.00011	.00003	.00015	.C0003	.00001	.00000	.00000	.00012	.00025	.00029	1
5	10304000	5315	.00052	.00000	.00002	.00008	.00001	.00003	.00003	.00000	.00000	.00000	.00012	.00013	.00011	5
10	9351000	4927	.00053	.00000	.00001	.00007	.00002	.00002	.0000C	.00001	.0C000	.00000	.00011	.00018	.00010	10
15	8133000	10794	.00133	.000C0	.00002	.00010	.00005	.00002	.0000C	.00002	.00000	.C0000	.00011	.00042	.00015	15
20	6303000	11619	.00184	.000C0	.00001	.00011	.00008	.00003	.00001	.00004	.00000	.C0000	.00080	.00058	.00017	20
25	5441000	9802	.00180	.00001	.00002	.00016	.00016	.00003	.00001	.00007	.00000	.C0000	.00053	.00064	.00018	25
30	5441000	11757	.00216	.00002	.00002	.00023	.00036	.00005	.00001	.00014	.00000	.00000	.00042	.00067	.00025	30
35	5930000	17807	.00300	.000C3	.00002	.00038	.00086	.00007	.00001	.00025	.00000	.00000	.00037	.00070	.00032	35
40	6012000	28028	.00466	.000C4	.00003	.00070	.00186	.00011	.C0002	.00036	.00000	.00000	.00034	.00074	.00046	40
45	5526000	41098	.00744	.00007	.000C4	.00126	.00347	.00C18	.00002	.00056	.00000	.00000	.00035	.00081	.00067	45
50	5093000	61329	.01204	.00011	.000C7	.00234	.00610	.00028	.00003	.00081	.00000	.00000	.00037	.00090	.00103	50
55	4366000	81833	.01874	.00016	.00011	.00388	.01013	.00042	.C0006	.00110	.00000	.00000	.00039	.00095	.00155	55
60	3654000	102082	.02794	.00021	.00016	.00594	.01564	.00069	.C0006	.00145	.00000	.00000	.00040	.00101	.00239	60
65	2855000	121222	.04246	.00027	.00022	.00862	.02489	.00125	.C0012	.00187	.00000	.00000	.00049	.00105	.00368	65
70	2294000	135639	.05913	.00032	.00029	.01085	.03647	.00190	.00016	.00226	.00000	.00000	.00056	.00126	.00505	70
75	1518000	126796	.08353	.00041	.00032	.01325	.05413	.00320	.00021	.00294	.00000	.00000	.00065	.00177	.00666	75
80	786000	97704	.12431	.00043	.00035	.01541	.08529	.00561	.00034	.00380	.00000	.C0000	.00078	.00283	.00946	80
85+	395000	83778	.21210	.00051	.00051	.01824	.15313	.01252	.00055	.00493	.00000	.00000	.00062	.00544	.01565	85+
ALL	95933000	1017778														

	All Causes	Respira-tory T.B.	Other Infec. and Paras.	Neo-plasms	Cardio-vascular	Infl., Pneu., Bronch.	Diar-rheal	Certain Degen-erative	Maternal	Cert. Dis. of Infancy	Motor Vehicle	Other Violence	Other and Unknown
CRUDE DEATH RATE	.01084	.00006	.0C0C7	.00170	.00572	.00040	.00004	.00046	.C0000	.00038	.00036	.00064	.00103
STANDARDIZED RATE (1)	.00648	.00003	.000C5	.00092	.00270	.00026	.00004	.00026	.00000	.00038	.00036	.00064	.00103
STANDARDIZED RATE (2)	.01148	.C00C6	.00007	.CC180	.00613	.00042	.00004	.00048	.C0000	.00060	.00035	.00053	.00073
GEOMETRIC MEAN	.00828									.00035	.00038	.00066	.00107

LIFE TABLE FOR ALL CAUSES COMBINED

Age (x)	Midyear Popula-tion	Deaths During Year	$_nM_x$	$_nq_x$	l_x	$_nd_x$	$_nL_x$	$_nm_x$	$_na_x$	T_x	$_nr_x$	$\overset{\circ}{e}_x$	Age (x)
0	2C61000	57365	.027834	.027170	100000	2717	97602	.027838	.117317	6690530	.000000	66.905	0
1	8470000	8883	.001049	.004184	97283	407	388115	.001049	1.500000	6592928	.000000	67.771	1
5	10304000	5315	.000516	.002560	96876	248	483760	.000513	2.500000	6204813	.000000	64.049	5
10	9351000	4927	.000527	.002639	96628	255	482585	.000528	2.821895	5721053	.015086	59.207	10
15	8133000	10794	.001327	.006662	96373	642	480390	.001336	2.703141	5238469	.031965	54.356	15
20	6303000	11619	.001843	.009203	95731	881	476496	.001849	2.549423	4758078	.040596	49.703	20
25	5441000	9802	.001802	.008972	94850	851	472149	.001802	2.531580	4281582	.023239	45.141	25
30	5441000	11757	.002161	.010745	93999	1010	467581	.002160	2.609736	3809433	-.001845	40.526	30
35	5930000	17807	.003003	.014873	92989	1383	461717	.002995	2.666004	3341852	-.012956	35.938	35
40	6012000	28028	.004662	.023055	91606	2112	453144	.004661	2.686622	2880135	-.002490	31.440	40
45	5526000	41098	.007437	.036595	89494	3275	439896	.007445	2.687405	2426991	.005866	27.119	45
50	5093000	61329	.012042	.058665	86219	5058	419288	.012063	2.665744	1987095	.009474	23.047	50
55	4366000	81833	.018743	.089932	81161	7299	388523	.018787	2.632296	1567806	.012767	19.317	55
60	3654000	102082	.027937	.131231	73862	9693	346131	.028004	2.608734	1179283	.014840	15.966	60
65	2855000	121222	.042460	.192585	64169	12358	290713	.042509	2.561751	833152	.007347	12.984	65
70	2294000	135639	.059128	.257783	51811	13356	225860	.059134	2.514631	542439	.000487	10.470	70
75	1518000	126796	.083528	.345755	38455	13296	158727	.083166	2.476873	316578	.017100	8.232	75
80	786000	97704	.124305	.472157	25159	11880	95242	.124735	2.428223	157851	.017100	6.274	80
85+	395000	83778	.212096	1.000000	13279	13279	62608	.212096	4.714842	62608	.000000	4.715	85+

NUMBER OF PERSONS DYING (OUT OF 100,000 AT BIRTH) ABOVE AGE X FROM SPECIFIED CAUSES

Age (x)	All Causes	Respira-tory T.B.	Other Infec. and Paras.	Neo-plasms	Cardio-vascular	Infl., Pneu., Bronch.	Diar-rheal	Certain Degen-erative	Maternal	Cert. Dis. of Infancy	Motor Vehicle	Other Violence	Other and Unknown	Age (x)
0	100000	546	528	15699	56879	3684	328	4141	0	1673	2665	5027	8830	0
1	97283	546	492	15691	56865	3446	275	4136	0	1	2656	4940	8235	1
5	96876	546	466	15648	56855	3390	265	4132	0	0	2610	4842	8122	5
10	96628	546	455	15607	56849	3377	263	4128	0	0	2553	4779	8071	10
15	96373	545	450	15571	56840	3369	262	4123	0	0	2500	4690	8023	15
20	95731	545	442	15525	56817	3358	260	4111	0	0	2234	4486	7953	20
25	94850	543	435	15471	56779	3345	257	4090	0	0	1852	4207	7871	25
30	93999	539	427	15395	56703	3329	255	4055	0	0	1603	3906	7787	30
35	92989	531	419	15286	56536	3307	250	3990	0	0	1408	3591	7671	35
40	91606	516	407	15113	56142	3273	246	3876	0	0	1239	3270	7524	40
45	89494	497	393	14796	55300	3222	238	3714	0	0	1083	2937	7314	45
50	86219	467	374	14242	53770	3142	229	3465	0	0	929	2580	7021	50
55	81161	423	344	13257	51208	3023	215	3123	0	0	774	2205	6589	55
60	73862	361	300	11746	47260	2861	192	2697	0	0	624	1835	5986	60
65	64169	290	245	9684	41833	2622	171	2195	0	0	485	1486	5158	65
70	51811	210	182	7175	34587	2259	137	1651	0	0	344	1180	4086	70
75	38455	137	117	4723	26350	1829	100	1142	0	0	218	894	2945	75
80	25159	73	66	2617	17732	1320	67	674	0	0	114	612	1884	80
85+	13279	32	32	1142	9587	784	35	309	0	0	39	341	978	85+

NUMBER OF PERSONS SURVIVING TO AGE X IF SPECIFIED CAUSES WERE ELIMINATED

Age (x)	No Causes	Respira-tory T.B. (1)	Other Infec. and Paras. (2)	Neo-plasms (3)	Cardio-vascular (4)	Infl., Pneu., Bronch. (5)	Diar-rheal (6)	Certain Degener-ative (7)	Maternal (8)	Cert. Dis. of Infancy (9)	Motor Vehicle (10)	Other Violence (11)	Other and Unknown (12)	(1)+(2)	(1)+(2)+(5)+(6)+(8)	(1)+(2)+(5)+(6)+(8)+part of(9)&(12)	(10)+(11)	Age (x)
0	100000	100000	100000	100000	100000	100000	100000	100000	100000	100000	100000	100000	100000	100000	100000	100000	100000	0
1	97283	97283	97319	97291	97297	97518	97335	97288	97283	98946	97292	97369	97872	97319	97606	99250	97378	1
5	96876	96876	96937	96927	96900	97166	96938	96885	96876	98533	96931	97059	97576	96937	97290	98965	97114	5
10	96628	96628	96700	96720	96658	96930	96652	96641	96628	98281	96740	96874	97377	96700	97067	98745	96986	10
15	96373	96374	96450	96500	96412	96683	96438	96391	96373	98022	96537	96708	97169	96451	96826	98503	96872	15
20	95731	95732	95815	95903	95752	96050	95757	95761	95731	97369	96160	96268	96592	95816	96202	97871	96699	20
25	94850	94853	94941	95075	94949	95179	94919	94900	94850	96473	95658	95661	95785	94944	95341	96998	96476	25
30	93999	94006	94097	94258	94172	94341	94069	94084	93999	95607	95050	95106	95010	94104	94516	96162	96169	30
35	92989	93004	93094	93293	93327	93349	93063	93138	92989	94580	94225	94401	94106	93109	93544	95178	95656	35
40	91606	91635	91721	92177	92333	91994	91683	91866	91606	93173	92993	93321	92854	91751	92217	93837	94735	40
45	89494	89542	89620	90368	91047	89524	89577	89909	89494	91025	91006	91505	90924	89668	90183	91777	93051	45
50	86219	86294	86359	87612	89257	86712	86308	86864	86219	87654	87829	88515	87889	86435	87019	88571	90168	50
55	81161	81275	81322	83449	86634	81741	81258	82103	81161	82549	82830	83696	83161	81436	82117	83601	85417	55
60	73862	74025	74051	77441	82967	74546	73973	75131	73862	75126	75526	76533	76274	74214	75013	76394	78257	60
65	64169	64376	64384	69321	77589	64989	64285	65748	64169	65267	65747	66826	67066	64592	65536	66777	68469	65
70	51811	52050	52041	58452	71391	52804	51935	53587	51811	52697	53214	54241	55164	52282	53412	54472	55710	70
75	38455	38695	38682	45817	63656	39571	38579	40226	38455	39113	39607	40516	41998	38924	40183	41032	41730	75
80	25159	25368	25348	32046	54893	26315	25267	26712	25159	25589	25998	26747	28421	25559	26847	27465	27639	80
85+	13279	13419	13403	18310	44902	14295	13359	14378	13279	13506	13778	14324	15750	13544	14669	15049	14862	85+

ADDED YRS OF LIFE

	No Causes	(1)	(2)	(3)	(4)	(5)	(6)	(7)	(8)	(9)	(10)	(11)	(12)	(1)+(2)	...	...	(10)+(11)
TOTAL		.080	.121	2.265	13.299	.570	.079	.627	.000	1.143	.874	1.329	1.658	.201	.858	2.083	2.231
WORK	4.289	.028	.029	.578	1.385	.085	.012	.231	.000	.000	.557	.701	.372	.057	.155	.171	1.270

POPULATION, DEATHS, DEATH RATES FOR ALL CAUSES COMBINED, AND SPECIFIED CAUSES

Age Start of Interval	Midyear Population	Deaths During Year	All Causes	Respiratory T. B.	Other Infec. and Paras.	Neoplasms	Cardiovascular	Infl., Pneu., Bronch.	Diarrheal	Certain Degenerative	Maternal	Cert. Dis. of Infancy	Motor Vehicle	Other Violence	Other and Unknown	Age Start of Interval
0	1977000	42446	.02147	.00000	.00029	.00008	.00012	.00192	.00046	.00004	.00000	.01264	.00009	.00072	.00512	0
1	8149000	7100	.00087	.00000	.00006	.00008	.00002	.00013	.00003	.00001	.00000	.00000	.00009	.00026	.00026	1
5	9973000	3722	.00037	.00000	.00002	.00007	.00001	.00003	.00000	.00001	.00000	.00000	.00007	.00007	.00010	5
10	9043000	2793	.00031	.00000	.00001	.00006	.00002	.00002	.00000	.00001	.00000	.00000	.00005	.00005	.00008	10
15	8030000	4396	.00055	.00000	.00001	.00007	.00004	.00002	.00000	.00002	.00001	.00000	.00018	.00008	.00010	15
20	6550000	4692	.00072	.00000	.00001	.00009	.00009	.00002	.00000	.00003	.00004	.00000	.00019	.00012	.00010	20
25	5633000	4936	.00088	.00001	.00002	.00014	.00013	.00003	.00001	.00006	.00005	.00000	.00012	.00017	.00015	25
30	5654000	7160	.00127	.00001	.00002	.00028	.00023	.00004	.00001	.00010	.00005	.00000	.00012	.00020	.00021	30
35	6206000	11562	.00186	.00002	.00003	.00052	.00042	.00005	.00001	.00016	.00005	.00000	.00012	.00022	.00027	35
40	6352000	17516	.00276	.00002	.00002	.00091	.00074	.00007	.00001	.00024	.00002	.00000	.00013	.00023	.00036	40
45	5802000	24204	.00417	.00003	.00004	.00149	.00128	.00010	.00002	.00035	.00000	.00000	.00013	.00025	.00049	45
50	5344000	34073	.00638	.00003	.00005	.00225	.00236	.00012	.00002	.00048	.00000	.00000	.00014	.00027	.00064	50
55	4647000	42642	.00918	.00003	.00006	.00297	.00394	.00018	.00003	.00067	.00000	.00000	.00017	.00028	.00084	55
60	4025000	56582	.01406	.00004	.00008	.00384	.00722	.00028	.00006	.00092	.00000	.00000	.00018	.00031	.00113	60
65	3391000	75562	.02228	.00005	.00010	.00516	.01288	.00045	.00009	.00131	.00000	.00000	.00022	.00041	.00161	65
70	2868000	98612	.03438	.00007	.00011	.00629	.02197	.00085	.00015	.00180	.00000	.00000	.00023	.00062	.00229	70
75	1988000	111268	.05597	.00010	.00017	.00789	.03873	.00167	.00025	.00241	.00000	.00000	.00027	.00109	.00340	75
80	1123000	107501	.09573	.00014	.00025	.01013	.07032	.00363	.00038	.00301	.00000	.00000	.00028	.00233	.00525	80
85+	642000	123506	.19238	.00022	.00031	.01281	.14830	.00954	.00075	.00397	.00000	.00000	.00025	.00588	.01035	85+
ALL	97397000	780273														

	All Causes	Respiratory T. B.	Other Infec. and Paras.	Neoplasms	Cardiovascular	Infl., Pneu., Bronch.	Diarrheal	Certain Degenerative	Maternal	Cert. Dis. of Infancy	Motor Vehicle	Other Violence	Other and Unknown
CRUDE DEATH RATE	.00801	.00002	.00005	.00139	.00448	.00028	.00004	.00037	.00001	.00026	.00013	.00028	.00069
STANDARDIZED RATE (1)	.00354	.00001	.00004	.00070	.00153	.00017	.00003	.00018	.00002	.00045	.00012	.00020	.00050
STANDARDIZED RATE (2)	.00713	.00002	.00004	.00129	.00383	.00024	.00004	.00034	.00002	.00026	.00014	.00026	.00064
GEOMETRIC MEAN	.00491												

LIFE TABLE FOR ALL CAUSES COMBINED

Age (x)	Midyear Population	Deaths During Year	$_nM_x$	$_nq_x$	l_x	$_nd_x$	$_nL_x$	$_nm_x$	$_na_x$	T_x	$_nr_x$	$\overset{\circ}{e}_x$	Age (x)
0	1977000	42446	.021470	.021070	100000	2107	98117	.021474	.106499	7377687	.000000	73.777	0
1	8149000	7100	.000871	.003473	97893	340	390722	.000870	1.500000	7279569	.000000	74.363	1
5	9973000	3722	.000373	.001866	97553	182	487310	.000373	2.500000	6888847	.000000	70.616	5
10	9043000	2793	.000309	.001540	97371	150	486458	.000308	2.618056	6401537	.014717	65.744	10
15	8030000	4396	.000547	.002746	97221	267	485479	.000550	2.654494	5915040	.026613	60.841	15
20	6550000	4692	.000716	.003569	96954	348	483932	.000719	2.593391	5429561	.035620	56.001	20
25	5633000	4936	.000876	.004379	96606	423	482026	.000878	2.627561	4945628	.023027	51.194	25
30	5654000	7160	.001266	.006311	96183	607	479454	.001266	2.658567	4463602	-.001880	46.407	30
35	6206000	11562	.001863	.009260	95576	885	475811	.001860	2.662194	3984108	-.013572	41.685	35
40	6352000	17516	.002758	.013687	94691	1296	470433	.002755	2.668467	3508297	-.001789	37.050	40
45	5802000	24204	.004172	.020697	93395	1933	462472	.004180	2.670611	3037864	.009138	32.527	45
50	5344000	34073	.006376	.031478	91462	2879	450541	.006390	2.648851	2575392	.013649	28.158	50
55	4647000	42642	.009176	.045043	88583	3990	433543	.009203	2.651211	2124851	.017691	23.987	55
60	4025000	56582	.014058	.068268	84593	5775	409438	.014105	2.657612	1691307	.018186	19.993	60
65	3391000	75562	.022283	.106054	78818	8359	374327	.022331	2.635757	1281869	.012279	16.264	65
70	2868000	98612	.034384	.159270	70459	11222	325559	.034470	2.617533	907542	.013036	12.880	70
75	1988000	111268	.055970	.247987	59237	14690	260740	.056340	2.587106	581983	.030716	9.825	75
80	1123000	107501	.095727	.385791	44547	17364	179943	.096497	2.535586	321244	.030716	7.211	80
85+	642000	123506	.192377	1.000000	27183	27183	141301	.192377	5.198128	141301	.000000	5.198	85+

NUMBER OF PERSONS DYING (OUT OF 100,000 AT BIRTH) ABOVE AGE X FROM SPECIFIED CAUSES

Age (x)	All Causes	Respira-tory T. B.	Other Infec. and Paras.	Neo-plasms	Cardio-vascular	Infl., Pneu., Bronch.	Diar-rheal	Certain Degen-erative	Maternal	Cert. Dis. of Infancy	Motor Vehicle	Other Violence	Other and Unknown	Age (x)
0	100000	219	420	15336	63041	3552	457	4180	105	1241	1105	3076	7268	0
1	97853	218	392	15329	63029	3364	412	4176	105	1	1096	3006	6765	1
5	97553	218	370	15296	63020	3313	401	4172	105	1	1061	2922	6664	5
10	97371	218	360	15263	63013	3301	400	4168	105	0	1029	2897	6617	10
15	97221	218	354	15235	63002	3293	399	4161	105	0	1004	2871	6579	15
20	96954	216	349	15202	62983	3283	397	4150	98	0	914	2831	6531	20
25	96606	215	343	15160	62941	3274	395	4134	79	0	824	2771	6470	25
30	96183	211	335	15093	62876	3260	392	4107	55	0	765	2690	6399	30
35	95576	204	325	14958	62766	3241	389	4058	32	0	708	2595	6300	35
40	94691	194	313	14713	62566	3216	385	3983	9	0	651	2489	6172	40
45	93395	183	302	14287	62216	3183	379	3869	1	0	592	2382	6001	45
50	91462	170	285	13597	61621	3139	371	3707	0	0	530	2267	5775	50
55	88583	156	264	12580	60554	3084	360	3489	0	0	467	2145	5484	55
60	84593	142	239	11289	58838	3005	345	3198	0	0	391	2024	5122	60
65	78818	127	208	9712	55871	2890	321	2818	0	0	316	1895	4660	65
70	70459	108	170	7777	51037	2722	287	2329	0	0	232	1742	4055	70
75	59237	84	134	5727	43862	2445	239	1740	0	0	156	1540	3310	75
80	44547	57	90	3664	33689	2005	174	1110	0	0	87	1254	2417	80
85+	27183	31	44	1810	20955	1348	106	560	0	0	35	831	1463	85+

NUMBER OF PERSONS SURVIVING TO AGE X IF SPECIFIED CAUSES WERE ELIMINATED

Age (x)	No Causes	Respira-tory T. B.	Other Infec. and Paras.	Neo-plasms	Cardio-vascular	Infl., Pneu., Bronch.	Diar-rheal	Certain Degener-ative	Maternal	Cert. Dis. of Infancy	Motor Vehicle	Other Violence	Other and Unknown	(1) + (2)	(1) + (2) + (5) + (6) + (8)	(1)+(2)+ (5)+(6)+ (8)+part of(9)&(12)	(10) + (11)	Age (x)
		(1)	(2)	(3)	(4)	(5)	(6)	(7)	(8)	(9)	(10)	(11)	(12)					
0	100000	100000	100000	100000	100000	100000	100000	100000	100000	100000	100000	100000	100000	100000	100000	100000	100000	0
1	97853	97894	97921	97900	97905	58079	97938	97897	97893	99128	97902	97962	98392	97922	98153	99405	97971	1
5	97553	97554	97603	97553	97574	57790	97608	97561	97553	98783	97597	97696	98152	97604	97896	99181	97740	5
10	97371	97372	97430	97444	97399	57619	97427	97383	97371	98600	97447	97549	98016	97431	97736	99028	97625	10
15	97221	97222	97286	97322	97260	57477	97278	97240	97221	98448	97322	97425	97903	97287	97601	98896	97525	15
20	96954	96957	97024	97087	97012	57219	97013	96984	96961	98178	97144	97197	97682	97027	97359	98656	97388	20
25	96606	96610	96682	96781	96705	56879	96667	96652	96632	97825	96886	96908	97393	96686	97046	98348	97189	25
30	96183	96191	96267	96424	96347	56469	96247	96255	96233	97397	96521	96565	97038	96275	96675	97982	96904	30
35	95576	95591	95669	95951	95849	55879	95642	95697	95648	96782	95968	96051	96525	95684	96127	97439	96445	35
40	94691	94716	94795	95207	95161	55060	94760	94886	94786	95886	95137	95267	95760	94820	95311	96624	95716	40
45	93395	93430	93509	94430	94209	53749	93470	93700	93496	94574	93894	94070	94622	93544	94075	95382	94573	45
50	91462	91509	91590	93168	92855	51852	91543	91922	91562	92616	92012	92238	92890	91638	92211	93503	92793	50
55	88583	88643	88728	91261	91005	89015	88672	89244	88680	89701	89178	89456	90257	88788	89408	90672	90056	55
60	84593	84664	84756	88459	88693	84693	85511	84686	85661	85236	85546	86553	84827	85512	86735	86196	60
65	78818	78898	79000	84025	85653	79387	78934	80045	78904	79813	79490	79831	81101	79080	79855	81013	80512	65
70	70459	70549	70657	77085	81703	71128	70595	72026	70536	71348	71139	71511	73090	70747	71635	72693	72202	70
75	59237	59334	59437	66886	76759	60056	59395	61107	59302	59985	59879	60310	62160	59534	60586	61507	60963	75
80	44547	44644	44735	52340	70337	45552	44722	46515	44596	45109	45090	45607	47560	44832	46074	46809	46162	80
85+	27183	27262	27334	33668	61657	28321	27343	28832	27213	27526	27555	28167	29820	27413	28760	29257	28552	85+

ADDED YRS OF LIFE																		
TOTAL		.040	.111	2.558	17.068	.518	.090	.637	.048	.930	.366	.625	1.483	.151	.814	1.859	.997	
WORK	2.344	.015	.024	.637	.643	.056	.010	.166	.035	.000	.173	.201	.288	.040	.141	.165	.375	

POPULATION, DEATHS, DEATH RATES FOR ALL CAUSES COMBINED, AND SPECIFIED CAUSES

Age Start of Interval	Midyear Population	Deaths During Year	All Causes	Respiratory T. B.	Other Infec. and Paras.	Neoplasms	Cardiovascular	Infl., Pneu., Bronch.	Diarrheal	Certain Degenerative	Maternal	Cert. Dis. of Infancy	Motor Vehicle	Other Violence	Other and Unknown	Age Start of Interval
0	118523	5869	.08327	.00008	.00364	.00012	.00014	.00835	.01385	.00013	.00000	.02589	.00002	.00053	.03049	0
1	430610	3049	.00708	.00004	.00081	.00009	.00002	.00082	.00115	.00007	.00000	.00000	.00010	.00036	.00359	1
5	444237	842	.00190	.00002	.00029	.00006	.00003	.00012	.00011	.00004	.00000	.00000	.00015	.00026	.00081	5
10	374405	423	.00113	.00001	.00015	.00007	.00005	.00002	.00005	.00002	.00000	.00000	.00013	.00024	.00041	10
15	309883	541	.00175	.00006	.00007	.00009	.00011	.00005	.00001	.00004	.00000	.00000	.00026	.00062	.00045	15
20	305375	748	.00245	.00009	.00009	.00006	.00009	.00004	.00000	.00007	.00000	.00000	.00044	.00104	.00052	20
25	261993	789	.00301	.00011	.00011	.00011	.00021	.00008	.00002	.00008	.00000	.00000	.00059	.00102	.00067	25
30	219613	792	.00361	.00025	.00012	.00017	.00033	.00004	.00003	.00015	.00000	.00000	.00046	.00115	.00090	30
35	200878	817	.00407	.00019	.00021	.00028	.00070	.00004	.00002	.00021	.00000	.00000	.00046	.00090	.00103	35
40	160101	929	.00580	.00029	.00032	.00047	.00118	.00010	.00002	.00034	.00000	.00000	.00049	.00097	.00162	40
45	124635	1208	.00969	.00067	.00065	.00101	.00246	.00008	.00006	.00051	.00000	.00000	.00062	.00058	.00266	45
50	104096	1304	.01253	.00077	.00064	.00171	.00340	.00012	.00007	.00088	.00000	.00000	.00043	.00104	.00347	50
55	66024	1347	.02040	.00101	.00094	.00323	.00591	.00035	.00018	.00158	.00000	.00000	.00047	.00106	.00568	55
60	51597	1712	.03318	.00149	.00089	.00516	.01000	.00066	.00023	.00205	.00000	.00000	.00047	.00112	.01111	60
65	27652	1159	.04191	.00130	.00105	.00611	.01378	.00119	.00029	.00264	.00000	.00000	.00054	.00098	.01403	65
70	19236	1114	.05791	.00158	.00140	.00738	.01923	.00109	.00057	.00400	.00000	.00000	.00057	.00135	.02033	70
75	9818	845	.08607	.00154	.00153	.01161	.02933	.00214	.00051	.00346	.00000	.00000	.00051	.00143	.03361	75
80	7214	747	.10355	.00125	.00222	.00929	.03410	.00194	.00069	.00610	.00000	.00000	.00042	.00291	.04464	80
85+	5110	962	.18826	.00156	.00274	.01311	.05108	.00783	.00157	.00626	.00000	.00000	.00078	.00352	.09941	85+
ALL	3241000	29157														

	All Causes	Respiratory T.B.	Other Infec.	Neoplasms	Cardiovascular	Infl., Pneu.	Diarrheal	Certain Degen.	Maternal	Cert. Dis. Infancy	Motor Vehicle	Other Violence	Other/Unknown
CRUDE DEATH RATE	.00901	.00021	.00047	.00052	.00114	.00052	.00072	.00027	.00000	.00095	.00031	.00069	.00321
STANDARDIZED RATE (1)	.00959	.00025	.00049	.00070	.00154	.00052	.00069	.00035	.00000	.00091	.00032	.00065	.00321
STANDARDIZED RATE (2)	.01382	.00041	.00053	.00137	.00325	.00049	.00048	.00065	.00000	.00091	.00032	.00071	.00350
GEOMETRIC MEAN	.01228												

LIFE TABLE FOR ALL CAUSES COMBINED

Age (x)	Midyear Population	Deaths During Year	$_nM_x$	$_nq_x$	l_x	$_nd_x$	$_nL_x$	$_nm_x$	$_na_x$	T_x	$_nr_x$	$\overset{\circ}{e}_x$	Age (x)
0	118523	5869	.083267	.078140	100000	7814	93839	.083270	.211553	6002159	.000000	60.022	0
1	430610	3049	.007081	.027824	92186	2565	362332	.007079	1.500000	5908320	.000000	64.091	1
5	444237	842	.001895	.009451	89621	847	445988	.001899	2.500000	5545989	.000000	61.883	5
10	374405	423	.001130	.005621	88774	499	442606	.001127	2.467852	5100001	.028996	57.449	10
15	309883	541	.001746	.008723	88275	770	439568	.001752	2.653680	4657395	.022525	52.760	15
20	305375	748	.002449	.012194	87505	1067	434967	.002453	2.602507	4217826	.013202	48.201	20
25	261993	789	.003012	.014982	86438	1295	429048	.003018	2.573520	3782859	.027310	43.764	25
30	219613	792	.003606	.017899	85143	1524	421987	.003611	2.553724	3353812	.023924	39.390	30
35	200878	817	.004067	.020187	83619	1688	414049	.004077	2.603303	2931825	.023541	35.062	35
40	160101	929	.005803	.028817	81931	2361	404190	.005841	2.685303	2517775	.039431	30.730	40
45	124635	1208	.009692	.047606	79570	3788	388855	.009741	2.625341	2113585	.032055	26.563	45
50	104096	1304	.012527	.061228	75782	4640	367977	.012609	2.643678	1724731	.046334	22.759	50
55	66024	1347	.020402	.098226	71142	6988	339342	.020593	2.657770	1356754	.047389	19.071	55
60	51597	1712	.033180	.154815	64154	9932	296639	.033482	2.570416	1017411	.052948	15.859	60
65	27652	1159	.041914	.190790	54222	10345	245508	.042137	2.525153	720772	.055592	13.293	65
70	19236	1114	.057912	.254826	43877	11181	191689	.058329	2.522974	475264	.051244	10.832	70
75	9818	845	.086066	.354111	32696	11578	134004	.086400	2.454170	283575	.021612	8.673	75
80	7214	747	.103549	.408846	21118	8634	83257	.103702	2.413424	149571	.021612	7.083	80
85+	5110	962	.188258	1.000000	12484	12484	66313	.188258	5.311850	66313	.000000	5.312	85+

NUMBER OF PERSONS DYING (OUT OF 100,000 AT BIRTH) ABOVE AGE X FROM SPECIFIED CAUSES

Age (x)	All Causes	Respiratory T.B.	Other Infec. and Paras.	Neoplasms	Cardiovascular	Infl., Pneu., Bronch.	Diarrheal	Certain Degenerative	Maternal	Cert. Dis. of Infancy	Motor Vehicle	Other Violence	Other and Unknown	Age (x)
0	100000	2598	3401	10406	25669	3156	2443	4930	0	2431	2405	5458	36703	0
1	92186	2990	3059	10395	25656	2372	1143	4917	0	1	2403	5409	33841	1
5	89621	2977	2765	10364	25648	2077	713	4893	0	0	2367	5279	32538	5
10	88774	2967	2635	10339	25616	2023	663	4875	0	0	2301	5162	32173	10
15	88275	2964	2571	10309	25616	2012	641	4864	0	0	2245	5058	31995	15
20	87505	2939	2539	10271	25569	1993	635	4846	0	0	2130	4785	31798	20
25	86438	2897	2500	10246	25528	1974	634	4817	0	0	1940	4331	31571	25
30	85143	2840	2454	10200	25439	1941	625	4781	0	0	1686	3894	31283	30
35	83619	2736	2402	10127	25297	1924	612	4717	0	0	1492	3408	30904	35
40	81931	2655	2312	10009	25005	1905	602	4630	0	0	1300	3035	30478	40
45	79570	2535	2183	9815	24523	1865	594	4493	0	0	1103	2641	29818	45
50	75782	2275	1929	9418	23562	1834	569	4295	0	0	863	2261	28776	50
55	71142	1991	1691	8782	22300	1790	544	3966	0	0	705	1879	27494	55
60	64154	1645	1371	7676	20275	1670	481	3428	0	0	545	1519	25544	60
65	54222	1200	1107	6134	17278	1472	412	2814	0	0	407	1185	22213	65
70	43877	880	848	4629	13873	1177	340	2162	0	0	274	946	18748	70
75	32656	499	578	3206	10158	967	230	1391	0	0	164	685	14818	75
80	21118	240	373	1645	6211	679	162	926	0	0	96	494	10292	80
85+	12484	130	182	869	3387	519	104	415	0	0	52	234	6592	85+

NUMBER OF PERSONS SURVIVING TO AGE X IF SPECIFIED CAUSES WERE ELIMINATED

Age (x)	No Causes	Respiratory T.B. (1)	Other Infec. and Paras. (2)	Neoplasms (3)	Cardiovascular (4)	Infl., Pneu., Bronch. (5)	Diarrheal (6)	Certain Degenerative (7)	Maternal (8)	Cert. Dis. of Infancy (9)	Motor Vehicle (10)	Other Violence (11)	Other and Unknown (12)	(1)+(2)	(1)+(2)+(5)+(6)+(8)	(1)+(2)+(5)+(6)+(8)+part of(9)&(12)	(10)+(11)	Age (x)
0	100000	100000	100000	100000	100000	100000	100000	100000	100000	100000	100000	100000	100000	100000	100000	100000	100000	0
1	92186	92194	92515	92198	92942	93442	92198	92186	94548	92188	92233	94974	92523	94552	99717	92235		1
5	89621	89641	90232	89662	89641	90649	91273	89657	89621	91919	89658	89795	93665	90253	92971	99207	89833	5
10	88774	88804	89510	88839	88806	89847	90461	88827	88774	91050	88877	89063	93160	89540	92345	98743	89166	10
15	88275	88308	89071	88370	88327	89353	89975	88339	88275	90538	88433	88667	92823	89104	91929	98360	88825	15
20	87505	87562	88326	87637	87603		89156	87586	87505	89748	87777	88167	92220	88384	91212	97625	88440	20
25	86438	86537	87288	86593	86576	87532	88110	86547	86438	88654	86896	87547	91333	87388	90205	96577	88011	25
30	85143	85297	86027	85342	85367	86253	86799	85286	85143	87326	85848	86676	90268	86182	89004	95337	87394	30
35	83619	83873	84539	83887	83980	84727	85258	83823	83619	85763	84505	85616	89051	84796	87604	93905	86524	35
40	81931	82261	82922	82311	82576	83035	83547	82218	81931	84031	82991	84267	87704	83256	86043	92308	85357	40
45	79570	80009	80662	80131	80677	80682	81148	79984	79570	81610	80797	82238	85875	81107	83871	90107	83506	45
50	75782	76456	77073	76708	77793	76872	77310	76371	75782	77725	77188	78707	82892	77759	80467	86690	80167	50
55	71142	72052	72589	72638	74296	72209	72601	72017	71142	72956	72618	74272	79187	73518	76150	82292	75813	55
60	64154	65308	65769	66584	69037	65232	65531	65462	64154	65799	65639	67333	73501	66951	69537	75512	68892	60
65	54222	55614	55835	57764	61389	55319	55450	55905	54222	55612	55607	57230	65730	57268	59749	65426	58692	65
70	43877	45298	45422	48203	53264	45036	44937	45847	43877	45002	45120	46537	57099	46893	49294	54506	47855	70
75	32656	34094	34088	37287	43767	33745	33583	34861	32656	33534	33719	34917	47191	35545	37680	42245	36009	75
80	21118	22234	22187	25542	32811	22034	21746	22911	21118	21659	21834	22715	36180	23359	25097	28702	23485	80
85+	12484	13232	13269	15830	23035	13153	12901	13972	12484	12804	12942	13643	26792	14064	15313	17932	14143	85+

ADDED YRS OF LIFE	No Causes	(1)	(2)	(3)	(4)	(5)	(6)	(7)	(8)	(9)	(10)	(11)	(12)	(1)+(2)	(1)+(2)+(5)+(6)+(8)	(1)+(2)+(5)+(6)+(8)+part of(9)&(12)	(10)+(11)
TOTAL		.542	.966	1.516	3.909	.965	1.221	.735	.000	1.534	.722	1.603	9.012	1.527	3.815	8.979	2.359
WORK	5.405	.254	.226	.421	.882	.074	.029	.243	.000	.000	.472	1.003	1.296	.482	.588	.803	1.490

POPULATION, DEATHS, DEATH RATES FOR ALL CAUSES COMBINED, AND SPECIFIED CAUSES

Age Start of Interval	Midyear Population	Deaths During Year	All Causes	Respiratory T. B.	Other Infec. and Paras.	Neoplasms	Cardiovascular	Infl., Pneu., Bronch.	Diarrheal	Certain Degenerative	Maternal	Cert. Dis. of Infancy	Motor Vehicle	Other Violence	Other and Unknown	Age Start of Interval
0	110559	8039	.07271	.00013	.00335	.00011	.00004	.00756	.01300	.00010	.00000	.01968	.00003	.00052	.02780	0
1	401778	3172	.00789	.00005	.00080	.00009	.00002	.00100	.00132	.00005	.00000	.00001	.00008	.00025	.00422	1
5	410488	747	.00182	.00003	.00024	.00006	.00002	.00013	.00011	.00003	.00000	.00000	.00010	.00019	.00091	5
10	338587	308	.00091	.00002	.00009	.00007	.00004	.00004	.00001	.00004	.00001	.00000	.00002	.00017	.00038	10
15	312049	399	.00128	.00008	.00008	.00006	.00007	.00002	.00001	.00005	.00012	.00000	.00002	.00017	.00051	15
20	296126	512	.00173	.00016	.00009	.00009	.00012	.00003	.00002	.00007	.00021	.00000	.00005	.00022	.00066	20
25	246855	531	.00215	.00022	.00009	.00018	.00017	.00007	.00002	.00006	.00030	.00000	.00004	.00019	.00080	25
30	195081	621	.00318	.00025	.00013	.00033	.00033	.00005	.00005	.00011	.00040	.00000	.00004	.00018	.00130	30
35	179859	642	.00357	.00020	.00016	.00053	.00051	.00007	.00003	.00015	.00038	.00000	.00007	.00016	.00131	35
40	141103	733	.00519	.00035	.00025	.00120	.00090	.00007	.00005	.00023	.00016	.00000	.00005	.00014	.00181	40
45	107354	818	.00762	.00044	.00021	.00156	.00154	.00012	.00007	.00034	.00005	.00000	.00012	.00016	.00262	45
50	100645	892	.00886	.00040	.00028	.00207	.00218	.00010	.00007	.00049	.00002	.00000	.00011	.00019	.00297	50
55	61388	991	.01614	.00067	.00047	.00394	.00424	.00026	.00008	.00085	.00000	.00000	.00000	.00026	.00520	55
60	62189	1465	.02356	.00074	.00042	.00455	.00712	.00063	.00016	.00174	.00000	.00000	.00008	.00026	.00786	60
65	32146	979	.03045	.00078	.00050	.00603	.01023	.00065	.00022	.00190	.00000	.00000	.00016	.00037	.00921	65
70	27840	1151	.04134	.00119	.00075	.00772	.01354	.00119	.00065	.00169	.00000	.00000	.00018	.00050	.01394	70
75	13620	937	.06880	.00110	.00073	.01028	.02606	.00272	.00066	.00367	.00000	.00000	.00015	.00059	.02283	75
80	12919	1129	.08739	.00132	.00139	.00960	.02910	.00418	.00077	.00410	.00000	.00000	.00000	.00023	.00124	.03545	80
85+	9414	1756	.18653	.00191	.00191	.01317	.06044	.01073	.00127	.00478	.00000	.00000	.00011	.00308	.08912	85+
ALL	3060000	25822														ALL

CRUDE DEATH RATE			.00844	.00020	.00039	.00074	.00115	.00057	.00070	.00023	.00012	.00071	.00007	.00023	.00335
STANDARDIZED RATE (1)			.00834	.00021	.00038	.00082	.00117	.00053	.00070	.00024	.00011	.00069	.00007	.00023	.00321
STANDARDIZED RATE (2)			.01117	.00030	.00037	.00151	.00255	.00052	.00067	.00045	.00012	.00041	.00008	.00025	.00415
GEOMETRIC MEAN			.01001												

LIFE TABLE FOR ALL CAUSES COMBINED

Age (x)	Midyear Population	Deaths During Year	$_nM_x$	$_nq_x$	l_x	$_nd_x$	$_nL_x$	$_nm_x$	$_na_x$	T_x	$_nr_x$	$\overset{\circ}{e}_x$	Age (x)
0	110559	8039	.072712	.068690	100000	6869	94461	.072718	.193611	6355745	.000000	63.557	0
1	401778	3172	.007895	.030967	93131	2884	365314	.007895	1.500000	6261285	.000000	67.231	1
5	410488	747	.001820	.009075	90247	819	449188	.001823	2.500000	5895971	.000000	65.331	5
10	338587	308	.000910	.004518	89428	404	446078	.000906	2.370565	5446783	.022797	60.907	10
15	312049	399	.001279	.006380	89024	568	443775	.001280	2.631675	5000705	.013727	56.173	15
20	296126	512	.001729	.008626	88456	763	440451	.001732	2.602392	4556531	.016328	51.516	20
25	246855	531	.002151	.010753	87693	943	436235	.002162	2.634986	4116480	.035795	46.942	25
30	195081	621	.003183	.015839	86750	1374	430434	.003192	2.586730	3680245	.031262	42.424	30
35	179859	642	.003569	.017745	85376	1515	423257	.003579	2.608911	3249811	.025053	38.065	35
40	141103	733	.005195	.025828	83861	2166	414213	.005229	2.645181	2826553	.045800	33.705	40
45	107354	818	.007620	.037530	81695	3066	401074	.007644	2.586160	2412340	.026916	29.529	45
50	100645	892	.008863	.043673	78629	3434	385147	.008916	2.671083	2011266	.044132	25.579	50
55	61388	991	.016143	.078276	75195	5886	362161	.016252	2.653153	1626119	.033609	21.625	55
60	62189	1465	.023557	.111977	69309	7761	327742	.023680	2.577256	1263907	.038135	18.237	60
65	32146	979	.030455	.142393	61548	8764	286293	.030612	2.552820	936215	.046893	15.211	65
70	27840	1151	.041343	.189129	52784	9983	239764	.041637	2.580303	649922	.048031	12.313	70
75	13620	937	.068756	.294666	42801	12612	182654	.065049	2.514173	410158	.017875	9.583	75
80	12919	1129	.087391	.359104	30189	10841	123779	.087584	2.494120	227504	.017875	7.536	80
85+	9414	1756	.186531	1.000000	19348	19348	103726	.186531	5.361048	103726	.000000	5.361	85+

NUMBER OF PERSONS DYING (OUT OF 100,000 AT BIRTH) ABOVE AGE X FROM SPECIFIED CAUSES

Age (x)	All Causes	Respiratory T.B.	Other Infec. and Paras.	Neo-plasms	Cardio-vascular	Infl., Pneu., Bronch.	Diar-rheal	Certain Degenerative	Maternal	Cert. Dis. of Infancy	Motor Vehicle	Other Violence	Other and Unknown	Age (x)
0	100000	2488	2550	13664	27159	4321	2558	4181	708	1863	547	1927	38014	0
1	93131	2476	2234	13674	27155	3569	1330	4171	708	4	545	1877	35388	1
5	90247	2456	1942	13642	27149	3203	846	4152	708	0	515	1787	33847	5
10	89428	2443	1835	13614	27139	3143	795	4140	708	0	472	1703	33436	10
15	89024	2433	1795	13581	27122	3123	788	4120	703	0	462	1626	33271	15
20	88456	2398	1761	13555	27092	3116	784	4099	647	0	446	1514	33044	20
25	87693	2330	1720	13515	27036	3104	774	4068	556	0	422	1416	32752	25
30	86750	2227	1679	13437	26962	3072	765	4043	426	0	405	1334	32400	30
35	85376	2121	1624	13292	26817	3050	743	3994	252	0	387	1255	31841	35
40	83861	2036	1555	13065	26600	3022	728	3930	92	0	359	1187	31287	40
45	81655	1891	1452	12563	26223	2993	708	3836	29	0	338	1128	30534	45
50	78629	1715	1366	11776	25604	2944	678	3701	11	0	289	1065	29480	50
55	75195	1562	1258	10975	24758	2905	651	3512	3	0	247	992	28332	55
60	69309	1319	1086	9540	23212	2810	621	3202	3	0	182	897	26437	60
65	61548	1076	949	8044	20861	2603	568	2629	3	0	156	813	23846	65
70	52784	853	689	6307	17912	2415	505	2086	3	0	111	705	21198	70
75	42801	567	509	4447	14639	2127	348	1680	3	0	68	584	17829	75
80	30189	366	374	2566	9861	1628	227	1007	3	0	41	476	13640	80
85+	19348	198	198	1366	6269	1113	132	456	0	0	11	320	9245	85+

NUMBER OF PERSONS SURVIVING TO AGE X IF SPECIFIED CAUSES WERE ELIMINATED

Age (x)	No Causes	Respiratory T.B. (1)	Other Infec. and Paras. (2)	Neo-plasms (3)	Cardio-vascular (4)	Infl., Pneu., Bronch. (5)	Diar-rheal (6)	Certain Degenerative (7)	Maternal (8)	Cert. Dis. of Infancy (9)	Motor Vehicle (10)	Other Violence (11)	Other and Unknown (12)	(1)+(2)	(1)+(2)+(5)+(6)+(8)	(1)+(2)+(5)+(6)+(8)+part of(9)&(12)	(10)+(11)	Age (x)
0	100000	100000	100000	100000	100000	100000	100000	100000	100000	100000	100000	100000	100000	100000	100000	100000	100000	0
1	93131	93143	93436	93141	93135	93859	94323	93141	93131	94942	93133	93179	95659	93181	95385	99773	93181	1
5	90247	90278	90832	90288	90257	91317	91886	90275	90247	92006	90278	90382	94308	90863	93610	99359	90414	5
10	89428	89472	90115	89496	89448	90548	91104	89468	89428	91171	89502	89646	93880	90159	92999	98967	89720	10
15	89024	89077	89748	89125	89060	90160	90700	89084	89029	90759	89108	89318	93625	89802	92664	98673	89402	15
20	88456	88544	89209	88582	88522	89551	90125	88536	88517	90180	87815	88192	93270	89298	92214	98294	88960	20
25	87693	87848	88481	87814	87831	88831	89358	87803	87844	89402	87815	88192	92773	88637	91649	97845	88315	25
30	86750	87006	87571	86991	86944	87908	88406	86884	87029	88441	86888	87325	92146	87829	90992	97352	87464	30
35	85376	85733	86239	85758	85711	86537	87028	85557	85824	87040	85529	86021	91278	86600	89946	96524	86176	35
40	83861	84297	84778	84462	84406	85030	85459	84102	84460	85495	84039	84563	90247	85218	88723	95444	84743	40
45	81695	82263	82691	82782	82602	82863	83311	82023	82341	83287	81890	82437	88719	83266	86808	93600	82634	45
50	78629	79350	79673	80461	80118	79802	80214	79078	79269	80162	78865	79406	86520	80403	83925	90704	79644	50
55	75195	76036	76300	77753	77467	76355	76738	75810	75815	76661	75461	76010	83986	77153	80610	87312	76279	55
60	69309	70320	70495	73104	72950	70471	70760	70177	69880	70660	69617	70152	79470	71523	74857	81369	70464	60
65	61548	62678	62733	66419	67157	62779	62888	62868	62055	62748	61846	62377	73424	63884	67129	73327	62679	65
70	52784	53963	54046	58722	60650	54017	53993	54430	53219	53813	53081	53596	65961	55253	58316	64057	53898	70
75	42801	44020	43989	49507	52683	44068	43926	44513	43154	43635	43081	43570	57409	45241	48199	53462	43855	75
80	30189	31220	31142	36774	42414	31517	31086	31987	30438	30777	30409	30823	45479	32206	34907	39232	31048	80
85+	19348	20147	20104	24758	31500	20631	20000	20935	19510	19725	19513	19881	34909	20934	23268	26861	20051	85+

ADDED YRS OF LIFE

	No Causes	(1)	(2)	(3)	(4)	(5)	(6)	(7)	(8)	(9)	(10)	(11)	(12)				
TOTAL		.533	.833	2.296	4.056	1.129	1.250	.639	.291	1.235	.163	.548	9.511	1.378	4.216	9.672	.713
WORK	4.344	.254	.157	.688	.667	.069	.038	.175	.238	.000	.063	.218	1.470	.413	.763	1.223	.281

POPULATION, DEATHS, DEATH RATES FOR ALL CAUSES COMBINED, AND SPECIFIED CAUSES

Age Start of Interval	Midyear Population	Deaths During Year	All Causes	Respiratory T. B.	Other Infec. and Paras.	Neoplasms	Cardiovascular	Infl., Pneu., Bronch.	Diarrheal	Certain Degenerative	Maternal	Cert. Dis. of Infancy	Motor Vehicle	Other Violence	Other and Unknown	Age Start of Interval
0	176168	10149	.05761	.00007	.00299	.00007	.00008	.00513	.00781	.00014	.00000	.02121	.00000	.00056	.01954	0
1	601572	3533	.00587	.00003	.00078	.00008	.00003	.00068	.00090	.00004	.00000	.00000	.00013	.00026	.00292	1
5	633844	1010	.00159	.00001	.00035	.00006	.00003	.00009	.00008	.00003	.00000	.00000	.00015	.00017	.00063	5
10	537230	611	.00114	.00001	.00012	.00006	.00003	.00004	.00002	.00002	.00000	.00000	.00017	.00032	.00035	10
15	414904	699	.00168	.00002	.00010	.00006	.00006	.00006	.00001	.00004	.00000	.00000	.00028	.00061	.00042	15
20	330312	817	.00247	.00005	.00006	.00011	.00010	.00002	.00002	.00006	.00000	.00000	.00054	.00107	.00042	20
25	300465	833	.00277	.00009	.00009	.00010	.00013	.00001	.00001	.00009	.00000	.00000	.00064	.00107	.00055	25
30	275823	857	.00311	.00016	.00012	.00012	.00022	.00004	.00001	.00015	.00000	.00000	.00058	.00103	.00069	30
35	244489	906	.00371	.00015	.00018	.00029	.00045	.00006	.00004	.00023	.00000	.00000	.00051	.00095	.00086	35
40	194886	1068	.00548	.00022	.00030	.00051	.00115	.00008	.00003	.00035	.00000	.00000	.00047	.00102	.00135	40
45	163310	1119	.00685	.00036	.00034	.00076	.00160	.00009	.00002	.00055	.00000	.00000	.00047	.00088	.00179	45
50	133297	1538	.01154	.00044	.00055	.00172	.00299	.00017	.00006	.00098	.00000	.00000	.00035	.00111	.00317	50
55	96269	1507	.01565	.00066	.00078	.00272	.00443	.00034	.00012	.00113	.00000	.00000	.00042	.00087	.00418	55
60	73586	2095	.02847	.00077	.00137	.00458	.00897	.00057	.00008	.00158	.00000	.00000	.00046	.00111	.00856	60
65	48752	1337	.02742	.00078	.00086	.00453	.00919	.00059	.00027	.00170	.00000	.00000	.00037	.00074	.00839	65
70	26703	1448	.05423	.00105	.00101	.00723	.01865	.00154	.00037	.00397	.00000	.00000	.00067	.00124	.01850	70
75	14387	1011	.07027	.00125	.00181	.00938	.02634	.00229	.00056	.00389	.00000	.00000	.00056	.00174	.02245	75
80	9352	981	.10490	.00139	.00150	.01037	.03796	.00438	.00086	.00406	.00000	.00000	.00086	.00160	.04192	80
85+	5381	1065	.19792	.00223	.00260	.01152	.06188	.01134	.00204	.00539	.00000	.00000	.00112	.00335	.09645	85+
ALL	4280730	32584														
CRUDE DEATH RATE			.00761	.00013	.00045	.00049	.00101	.00042	.00049	.00026	.00000	.00087	.00032	.00065	.00253	
STANDARDIZED RATE (1)			.00805	.00016	.00044	.00062	.00131	.00039	.00043	.00032	.00000	.00075	.00034	.00069	.00261	
STANDARDIZED RATE (2)			.01162	.00026	.00048	.00121	.00289	.00044	.00031	.00058	.00000	.00044	.00039	.00080	.00383	
GEOMETRIC MEAN			.01071													

LIFE TABLE FOR ALL CAUSES COMBINED

Age (x)	Midyear Population	Deaths During Year	$_nM_x$	$_nq_x$	l_x	$_nd_x$	$_nL_x$	$_nm_x$	$_na_x$	T_x	$_nr_x$	$\overset{\circ}{e}_x$	Age (x)
0	176168	10149	.057610	.054970	100000	5497	95426	.057605	.167937	6374165	.000000	63.742	0
1	601572	3533	.005873	.023153	94503	2188	372542	.005873	1.500000	6278739	.000000	66.440	1
5	633844	1010	.001593	.007940	92315	733	459743	.001594	2.500000	5906197	.000000	63.979	5
10	537230	611	.001137	.005667	91582	519	456620	.001137	2.514451	5446454	.029882	59.471	10
15	414904	699	.001685	.008445	91063	769	453516	.001696	2.661194	4989834	.045427	54.795	15
20	330312	817	.002473	.012337	90294	1114	448781	.002482	2.586026	4536318	.036047	50.239	20
25	300465	833	.002772	.013781	89180	1229	442878	.002775	2.541192	4087537	.020140	45.835	25
30	275823	857	.003107	.015429	87951	1357	436439	.003109	2.556344	3644659	.015964	41.440	30
35	244489	906	.003706	.018431	86594	1596	429178	.003719	2.624138	3208220	.026317	37.049	35
40	194886	1068	.005480	.027154	84998	2308	419471	.005502	2.608770	2779042	.034286	32.695	40
45	163310	1119	.006852	.033874	82690	2801	406907	.006884	2.664227	2359571	.029386	28.535	45
50	133297	1538	.011538	.056528	79889	4516	388766	.011616	2.635214	1952663	.038641	24.442	50
55	96269	1507	.015654	.076048	75373	5732	363536	.015767	2.674641	1563898	.041791	20.749	55
60	73586	2095	.028470	.133944	69641	9321	325327	.028651	2.545574	1200362	.038757	17.236	60
65	48752	1337	.027425	.128830	60320	7771	282899	.027469	2.593483	875034	.059382	14.507	65
70	26703	1448	.054226	.243734	52549	12808	231586	.055306	2.567227	592135	.075675	11.268	70
75	14387	1011	.070272	.299540	39741	11904	168697	.070564	2.479156	360549	.038874	9.072	75
80	9352	981	.104897	.417322	27837	11617	109900	.105706	2.479090	191852	.038874	6.892	80
85+	5381	1065	.197919	1.000000	16220	16220	81953	.197919	5.052582	81953	.000000	5.053	85+

NUMBER OF PERSONS DYING (OUT OF 100,000 AT BIRTH) ABOVE AGE X FROM SPECIFIED CAUSES

Age (x)	All Causes	Respiratory T.B.	Other Infec. and Paras.	Neo-plasms	Cardio-vascular	Infl., Pneu., Bronch.	Diar-rheal	Certain Degenerative	Maternal	Cert. Dis. of Infancy	Motor Vehicle	Other Violence	Other and Unknown	Age (x)
0	100000	2162	3412	10750	28088	3666	1813	5087	0	2025	2691	5629	34677	0
1	94503	2155	3127	10743	28081	3176	1068	5073	0	1	2691	5576	32812	1
5	92315	2142	2834	10714	28070	2923	733	5056	0	0	2641	5478	31724	5
10	91582	2137	2673	10687	28059	2882	694	5045	0	0	2574	5358	31433	10
15	91063	2130	2619	10662	28044	2866	683	5035	0	0	2495	5252	31277	15
20	90294	2119	2574	10637	28005	2839	677	5019	0	0	2366	4972	31086	20
25	89180	2096	2547	10589	27960	2830	666	4993	0	0	2124	4489	30886	25
30	87951	2055	2509	10545	27904	2824	660	4954	0	0	1841	4016	30643	30
35	86594	1986	2458	10494	27807	2807	655	4889	0	0	1590	3565	30343	35
40	84998	1923	2381	10368	27613	2782	639	4789	0	0	1372	3158	29973	40
45	82690	1832	2255	10152	27125	2750	627	4641	0	0	1174	2729	29405	45
50	79889	1687	2118	9840	26471	2715	616	4416	0	0	985	2371	28670	50
55	75373	1514	1903	9166	25298	2647	593	4034	0	0	851	1939	27428	55
60	69641	1271	1618	8169	23674	2521	547	3621	0	0	700	1622	25898	60
65	60320	1019	1170	6670	20735	2334	521	2972	0	0	550	1259	23090	65
70	52549	758	930	5388	18127	2165	444	2489	0	0	446	1052	20710	70
75	39741	553	693	3687	13716	1800	356	1551	0	0	287	761	16337	75
80	27837	341	386	2100	9251	1410	262	895	0	0	193	467	12532	80
85+	16220	183	213	944	5072	929	168	442	0	0	91	274	7904	85+

NUMBER OF PERSONS SURVIVING TO AGE X IF SPECIFIED CAUSES WERE ELIMINATED

Age (x)	No Causes	Respiratory T.B. (1)	Other Infec. and Paras. (2)	Neo-plasms (3)	Cardio-vascular (4)	Infl., Pneu., Bronch. (5)	Diar-rheal (6)	Certain Degenerative (7)	Maternal (8)	Cert. Dis. of Infancy (9)	Motor Vehicle (10)	Other Violence (11)	Other and Unknown (12)	(1)+(2)	(1)+(2)+(5)+(6)+(8)	(1)+(2)+(5)+(6)+(8)+part of(9)&(12)	(10)+(11)	Age (x)
0	100000	100000	100000	100000	100000	100000	100000	100000	100000	100000	100000	100000	100000	100000	100000	100000	100000	0
1	94503	94510	94780	94510	94510	94580	95230	94517	94503	96491	94503	94555	96333	94787	95999	99716	94555	1
5	92315	92334	92877	92350	92333	93033	93359	92345	92315	94258	92364	92462	95205	92897	94678	99281	92512	5
10	91582	91606	92301	91644	91610	92336	92657	91623	91582	93509	91658	91808	94749	92325	94178	98931	91924	10
15	91063	91094	91832	91150	91106	91828	92143	91114	91063	92980	91257	91434	94373	91864	93735	98505	91629	15
20	90294	90336	91102	90405	90376	91260	91371	90360	90294	92194	90615	90942	93773	91144	93034	97801	91266	20
25	89180	89244	90005	89337	89305	89965	90255	89271	89180	91057	89739	90305	92823	90070	91958	96686	90871	25
30	87951	88055	88803	88150	88130	88732	89017	88080	87951	89802	88786	89537	91795	88908	90784	95476	90387	30
35	86594	86765	87484	86840	86867	87379	87649	86785	86594	88417	87667	88612	90690	87656	89529	94200	89711	35
40	84998	85228	85548	85365	85459	85754	86049	85285	84998	86787	86270	87393	89404	86181	88065	92718	88701	40
45	82690	83004	83740	83262	83624	83496	83725	83116	82690	84430	84126	85455	87567	84059	85940	90574	86939	45
50	79889	80336	81040	80751	81445	80703	80900	80523	79889	81570	81465	82925	85370	81493	83365	87985	84561	50
55	75373	75964	76671	76851	78011	76208	76349	76346	75373	76959	76993	78673	81843	77272	79140	83722	80364	55
60	69641	70422	71120	71590	73714	70535	70588	70943	69641	71107	71286	73008	77233	71917	73830	78380	74732	60
65	60320	61233	62027	63812	66809	61270	61165	62065	60320	61590	61887	63590	69857	62966	64854	69269	65242	65
70	52549	53554	54265	56868	60960	53538	53358	54535	52549	53655	54013	55600	63485	55302	57210	61444	57150	70
75	39741	40717	41251	44629	50761	40813	40430	42094	39741	40577	40990	42316	52816	42264	44157	47929	43646	75
80	27837	28701	29161	32776	40641	28925	28400	30064	27837	28423	28792	29902	41461	30066	31873	35089	30927	80
85+	16220	16847	17129	20152	28759	17235	16620	17890	16220	16561	16856	17580	29958	17791	19371	21928	18270	85+

ADDED YRS OF LIFE	No Causes	(1)	(2)	(3)	(4)	(5)	(6)	(7)	(8)	(9)	(10)	(11)	(12)	(1)+(2)	(1)+(2)+(5)+(6)+(8)	(1)+(2)+(5)+(6)+(8)+part	(10)+(11)
TOTAL		.388	.970	1.579	4.095	.825	.827	.783	.000	1.338	.852	1.721	7.575	1.372	3.098	7.112	2.612
WORK	4.814	.161	.195	.399	.715	.066	.027	.248	.000	.000	.519	1.025	1.074	.357	.452	.602	1.561

POPULATION, DEATHS, DEATH RATES FOR ALL CAUSES COMBINED, AND SPECIFIED CAUSES

Age Start of Interval	Midyear Population	Deaths During Year	All Causes	Respiratory T. B.	Other Infec. and Paras.	Neo-plasms	Cardio-vascular	Infl., Pneu., Bronch.	Diar-rheal	Certain Degen-erative	Maternal	Cert. Dis. of Infancy	Motor Vehicle	Other Violence	Other and Unknown	Age Start of Interval
0	170890	8175	.04784	.00003	.00277	.00008	.00008	.00470	.00723	.00006	.00000	.01550	.00003	.00039	.01699	0
1	579627	3581	.00618	.00004	.00088	.00007	.00002	.00082	.00090	.00003	.00000	.00000	.00007	.00019	.00316	1
5	606509	804	.00133	.00001	.00025	.00005	.00001	.00006	.00009	.00004	.00000	.00000	.00007	.00007	.00068	5
10	511574	350	.00068	.00001	.00010	.00004	.00002	.00003	.00001	.00003	.00001	.00000	.00004	.00011	.00028	10
15	408505	430	.00105	.00006	.00006	.00008	.00007	.00002	.00001	.00004	.00007	.00000	.00005	.00022	.00036	15
20	335297	490	.00146	.00009	.00007	.00010	.00013	.00003	.00001	.00008	.00023	.00000	.00006	.00020	.00048	20
25	287564	533	.00185	.00018	.00013	.00013	.00018	.00005	.00001	.00008	.00023	.00000	.00007	.00014	.00065	25
30	256755	594	.00231	.00014	.00011	.00039	.00027	.00003	.00002	.00010	.00027	.00000	.00005	.00019	.00074	30
35	224228	764	.00341	.00021	.00014	.00062	.00039	.00004	.00003	.00015	.00034	.00000	.00005	.00021	.00122	35
40	176949	754	.00426	.00029	.00021	.00111	.00059	.00005	.00003	.00019	.00016	.00000	.00010	.00012	.00140	40
45	147818	846	.00572	.00028	.00020	.00160	.00114	.00009	.00003	.00030	.00007	.00000	.00006	.00013	.00185	45
50	127962	1106	.00864	.00038	.00040	.00219	.00184	.00012	.00005	.00066	.00000	.00000	.00007	.00020	.00275	50
55	94708	1094	.01155	.00034	.00040	.00273	.00299	.00024	.00011	.00068	.00000	.00000	.00014	.00020	.00373	55
60	74417	1908	.02564	.00075	.00063	.00477	.00786	.00074	.00023	.00165	.00000	.00000	.00027	.00039	.00834	60
65	57839	1210	.02092	.00052	.00040	.00394	.00698	.00067	.00016	.00116	.00000	.00000	.00012	.00021	.00676	65
70	34674	1481	.04271	.00075	.00089	.00730	.01419	.00138	.00023	.00277	.00000	.00000	.00012	.00052	.01456	70
75	20566	1146	.05572	.00088	.00068	.00836	.02076	.00248	.00039	.00263	.00000	.00000	.00019	.00112	.01823	75
80	15215	1338	.08794	.00112	.00145	.01032	.03174	.00427	.00085	.00335	.00000	.00000	.00013	.00177	.03293	80
85+	14972	2093	.13979	.00080	.00174	.00822	.04865	.00902	.00087	.00381	.00000	.00000	.00020	.00334	.06312	85+
ALL	4146069	28697														

CRUDE DEATH RATE			.00692	.00014	.00040	.00065	.00102	.00044	.00047	.00021	.00009	.00064	.00007	.00020	.00261	
STANDARDIZED RATE (1)			.00656	.00015	.00037	.00073	.00101	.00038	.00040	.00023	.00009	.00055	.00007	.00021	.00240	
STANDARDIZED RATE (2)			.00932	.00022	.00036	.00132	.00225	.00042	.00029	.00041	.00010	.00032	.00008	.00023	.00332	
GEOMETRIC MEAN			.00823													

LIFE TABLE FOR ALL CAUSES COMBINED

Age (x)	Midyear Population	Deaths During Year	$_nM_x$	$_nq_x$	l_x	$_nd_x$	$_nL_x$	$_nm_x$	$_na_x$	T_x	$_nr_x$	$\overset{\circ}{e}_x$	Age (x)
0	170890	8175	.047838	.045970	100000	4597	96099	.047836	.151324	6770618	.000000	67.706	0
1	579627	3581	.006178	.024339	95403	2322	375807	.006179	1.500000	6674519	.000000	69.961	1
5	606509	804	.001326	.006618	93081	616	463865	.001328	2.500000	6298712	.000000	67.669	5
10	511574	350	.000684	.003407	92465	315	461510	.000683	2.414021	5834847	.028916	63.103	10
15	408505	430	.001053	.005274	92150	486	459609	.001057	2.652178	5373337	.039410	58.311	15
20	335297	490	.001461	.007309	91664	670	456719	.001467	2.610697	4913728	.036344	53.606	20
25	287564	533	.001854	.009253	90994	842	452942	.001859	2.591548	4457009	.028324	48.981	25
30	256755	594	.002313	.011536	90152	1040	448299	.002320	2.634014	4004066	.022016	44.415	30
35	224228	764	.003407	.016956	89112	1511	441952	.003419	2.612370	3555767	.030036	39.902	35
40	176949	754	.004261	.021176	87601	1855	433559	.004279	2.603324	3113815	.037877	35.545	40
45	147818	846	.005723	.028351	85746	2431	423004	.005747	2.644745	2680256	.027645	31.258	45
50	127962	1106	.008643	.042537	83315	3544	408153	.008683	2.623507	2257251	.032787	27.093	50
55	94708	1094	.011551	.056813	79771	4532	388686	.011660	2.756056	1849099	.041198	23.180	55
60	74417	1908	.025639	.121147	75239	9115	353835	.025761	2.546946	1460413	.028292	19.410	60
65	57839	1210	.020920	.099601	66124	6586	314694	.020928	2.581897	1106577	.040679	16.735	65
70	34674	1481	.042712	.196580	59538	11704	269506	.043428	2.591938	791883	.065746	13.300	70
75	20566	1146	.055723	.245662	47834	11751	210079	.055936	2.524395	522377	.030567	10.921	75
80	15215	1338	.087940	.362498	36083	13080	147749	.088529	2.502596	312298	.030567	8.655	80
85+	14972	2093	.139794	1.000000	23003	23003	164549	.139794	7.153368	164549	.000000	7.153	85+

NUMBER OF PERSONS DYING (OUT OF 100,000 AT BIRTH) ABOVE AGE X FROM SPECIFIED CAUSES

Age (x)	All Causes	Respiratory T.B.	Other Infec. and Paras.	Neoplasms	Cardiovascular	Infl., Pneu., Bronch.	Diarrheal	Certain Degenerative	Maternal	Cert. Dis. of Infancy	Motor Vehicle	Other Violence	Other and Unknown	Age (x)
0	100000	1985	2724	13387	29152	4575	1745	4391	618	1489	619	2290	37025	0
1	95403	1983	2457	13379	29146	4124	1050	4385	618	0	616	2253	35392	1
5	93081	1968	2127	13353	29139	3817	713	4372	618	0	590	2180	34204	5
10	92465	1964	2010	13329	29136	3789	672	4353	618	0	557	2146	33891	10
15	92150	1959	1965	13310	29125	3775	667	4338	614	0	540	2097	33760	15
20	91664	1930	1936	13273	29095	3764	664	4317	581	0	517	1995	33592	20
25	90994	1890	1906	13230	29036	3752	661	4281	474	0	492	1904	33368	25
30	90152	1806	1849	13169	28955	3729	655	4246	370	0	460	1840	33073	30
35	89112	1741	1800	12993	28834	3717	644	4202	249	0	436	1752	32744	35
40	87601	1648	1737	12718	28660	3699	632	4135	98	0	412	1662	32200	40
45	85746	1523	1644	12232	28400	3677	618	4053	30	0	368	1611	31590	45
50	83315	1406	1560	11554	27917	3640	606	3927	2	0	342	1556	30805	50
55	79771	1252	1397	10657	27162	3592	587	3654	2	0	313	1476	29679	55
60	75239	1120	1241	9588	25985	3496	545	3389	2	0	259	1398	28216	60
65	66124	853	1017	7894	23188	3233	464	2802	2	0	164	1260	25247	65
70	59538	691	892	6654	20986	3020	415	2437	2	0	126	1195	23120	70
75	47834	486	647	4659	17095	2639	352	1679	2	0	95	1051	19129	75
80	36083	302	504	2899	12713	2115	270	1128	2	0	54	815	15281	80
85+	23003	132	286	1352	8012	1484	143	626	0	0	33	550	10385	85+

NUMBER OF PERSONS SURVIVING TO AGE X IF SPECIFIED CAUSES WERE ELIMINATED

Age (x)	No Causes	Respiratory T.B. (1)	Other Infec. and Paras. (2)	Neoplasms (3)	Cardiovascular (4)	Infl., Pneu., Bronch. (5)	Diarrheal (6)	Certain Degenerative (7)	Maternal (8)	Cert. Dis. of Infancy (9)	Motor Vehicle (10)	Other Violence (11)	Other and Unknown (12)	(1)+(2)	(1)+(2)+(5)+(6)+(8)	(1)+(2)+(5)+(6)+(8)+part of (9)&(12)	(10)+(11)	Age (x)
0	100000	100000	100000	100000	100000	100000	100000	100000	100000	100000	100000	100000	100000	100000	100000	100000	100000	0
1	95403	95405	95664	95411	95409	95844	96084	95409	95403	96868	95406	95439	97011	95666	96795	99809	95442	1
5	93081	93098	93663	93114	93094	93817	94081	93100	93081	94511	93110	93188	95851	93680	95435	99495	93217	5
10	92465	92486	93161	92522	92481	93224	93500	92502	92465	93885	92526	92606	95538	93182	94998	99249	92667	10
15	92150	92176	92889	92226	92176	92921	93187	92202	92154	93565	92228	92335	95348	92914	94750	99045	92417	15
20	91664	91718	92428	91776	91720	92442	92698	91737	91701	93072	91765	91954	95019	92483	94358	98694	92055	20
25	90994	91088	91782	91148	91109	91778	92024	91102	91137	92392	91119	91373	94556	91877	93865	98283	91498	25
30	90152	90329	90990	90366	90346	90952	91178	90294	90358	91537	90308	90591	93587	91169	93278	97828	90748	30
35	89112	89351	89990	89499	89425	89915	90137	89296	89476	90481	89290	89634	93244	90232	92468	97107	89813	35
40	87601	87929	88527	88256	88082	88408	88621	87849	88109	88947	87799	88204	92229	88858	91247	96031	88404	40
45	85746	86191	86746	86873	86476	86558	86758	86070	86311	87063	85984	86387	90914	87196	89647	94519	86627	45
50	83315	83863	84370	85090	84506	84141	84311	83755	83891	84595	83572	83593	89160	84925	87392	92286	84252	50
55	79771	80448	80943	82371	81664	80609	80743	80461	80323	80996	80045	80499	86555	81629	84070	88973	80776	55
60	75239	76007	76498	78769	78205	76124	76197	76150	75159	75550	75559	76002	83193	77278	79731	84602	76316	60
65	66124	67052	67443	70907	71511	67152	67043	67483	66581	67140	66487	66925	76256	68390	70905	75668	67292	65
70	59538	60529	60847	65117	66688	60669	60412	61116	59950	60452	59901	60321	71027	61859	64403	69016	60689	70
75	47834	48816	49109	54301	57625	49092	48994	49801	48165	48569	48153	48595	61485	50118	52614	56873	48919	75
80	36083	36986	37172	42720	48292	37502	36729	38063	36333	36637	36359	36866	50870	38102	40588	44356	37148	80
85+	23003	23717	23875	28724	36193	24433	23517	24688	23164	23356	23196	23718	38382	24617	26918	30120	23916	85+

ACCUM YRS OF LIFE

	No Causes	(1)	(2)	(3)	(4)	(5)	(6)	(7)	(8)	(9)	(10)	(11)	(12)	(1)+(2)	(1)+(2)+(5)+(6)+(8)	(1)+(2)+(5)+(6)+(8)+part	(10)+(11)
TOTAL		.441	.899	2.405	4.817	.995	.845	.723	.264	1.038	.188	.544	9.042	1.351	3.555	7.787	.735
WORK	3.658	.193	.154	.661	.555	.058	.024	.180	.201	.000	.072	.205	1.163	.349	.637	.965	.278

POPULATION, DEATHS, DEATH RATES FOR ALL CAUSES COMBINED, AND SPECIFIED CAUSES

Age Start of Interval	Midyear Popula-tion	Deaths During Year	All Causes	Respira-tory T. B.	Other Infec. and Paras.	Neo-plasms	Cardio-vascular	Infl., Pneu., Bronch.	Diar-rheal	Certain Degen-erative	Maternal	Cert. Dis. of Infancy	Motor Vehicle	Other Violence	Other and Unknown	Age Start of Interval
0	210557	18557	.08812	.00021	.00504	.00005	.00015	.01658	.00555	.00003	.00000	.03062	.00000	.00039	.02550	0
1	784033	3326	.00424	.00006	.00088	.00010	.00003	.00092	.00049	.00002	.00000	.00000	.00000	.00042	.02550	0
5	1027854	755	.00077	.00001	.00011	.00008	.00002	.00006	.00000	.00001	.00000	.00000	.00000	.00042	.00133	1
10	940026	574	.00061	.00001	.00006	.00006	.00003	.00002	.00001	.00002	.00000	.00000	.00000	.00025	.00023	5
15	697711	772	.00111	.00004	.00004	.00010	.00005	.00003	.00000	.00003	.00000	.00000	.00000	.00024	.00017	10
20	800831	1153	.00144	.00014	.00005	.00010	.00010	.00001	.00000	.00003	.00000	.00000	.00000	.00055	.00022	15
25	828549	1464	.00177	.00033	.00005	.00012	.00013	.00002	.00001	.00007	.00000	.00000	.00000	.00078	.00021	20
30	770232	1600	.00208	.00048	.00004	.00018	.00020	.00002	.00000	.00011	.00000	.00000	.00000	.00079	.00024	25
35	565698	1413	.00250	.00051	.00006	.00027	.00030	.00003	.00000	.00011	.00000	.00000	.00000	.00079	.00026	30
40	344357	1300	.00378	.00063	.00012	.00049	.00059	.00008	.00002	.00031	.00000	.00000	.00000	.00079	.00041	35
45	424909	2279	.00536	.00081	.00013	.00100	.00103	.00015	.00001	.00033	.00000	.00000	.00000	.00094	.00060	40
50	485529	4263	.00878	.00118	.00016	.00164	.00203	.00035	.00002	.00064	.00000	.00000	.00000	.00099	.00090	45
55	411131	6029	.01466	.00184	.00024	.00293	.00385	.00071	.00005	.00096	.00000	.00000	.00000	.00111	.00164	50
60	312408	7494	.02399	.00222	.00031	.00441	.00789	.00130	.00008	.00133	.00000	.00000	.00000	.00122	.00287	55
65	185025	7283	.03936	.00261	.00037	.00673	.01426	.00226	.00011	.00199	.00000	.00000	.00000	.00132	.00513	60
70	136968	8012	.05850	.00195	.00035	.00749	.02395	.00361	.00015	.00210	.00000	.00000	.00000	.00153	.00952	65
75	86616	7745	.08942	.00192	.00037	.00843	.03677	.00588	.00044	.00195	.00000	.00000	.00000	.00158	.01730	70
80	41846	5730	.13693	.00122	.00019	.00746	.04968	.01013	.00033	.00165	.00000	.00000	.00000	.00178	.03189	75
85+	22194	4324	.19483	.00077	.00045	.00581	.06231	.01194	.00063	.00131	.00000	.00000	.00000	.00251	.06376	80
ALL	9076514	84113													.10926	85+

	All Causes	Respira-tory T. B.	Other Infec. and Paras.	Neo-plasms	Cardio-vascular	Infl., Pneu., Bronch.	Diar-rheal	Certain Degen-erative	Maternal	Cert. Dis. of Infancy	Motor Vehicle	Other Violence	Other and Unknown
CRUDE DEATH RATE	.00927	.00052	.00029	.00090	.00208	.00082	.00029	.00029	.00000	.00071	.00000	.00073	.00263
STANDARDIZED RATE (1)	.00848	.00041	.00036	.00066	.00142	.00093	.00041	.00022	.00000	.00108	.00000	.00066	.00233
STANDARDIZED RATE (2)	.01229	.00063	.00029	.00124	.00332	.00098	.00027	.00038	.00000	.00063	.00000	.00080	.00374
GEOMETRIC MEAN	.00882												

LIFE TABLE FOR ALL CAUSES COMBINED

Age (x)	Midyear Popula-tion	Deaths During Year	$_nM_x$	$_nq_x$	l_x	$_nd_x$	$_nL_x$	$_nm_x$	$_na_x$	T_x	$_nr_x$	$\overset{\circ}{e}_x$	Age (x)
0	210557	18557	.088116	.082450	100000	8245	93567	.088118	.219797	6357543	.000000	63.575	0
1	784033	3326	.004242	.016784	91755	1540	363170	.004240	1.500000	6263975	.000000	68.268	1
5	1027854	755	.000773	.003857	90215	348	450205	.000773	2.500000	5900805	.000000	65.408	5
10	940026	574	.000611	.003060	89867	275	448678	.000613	2.612121	5450600	.031666	60.652	10
15	697711	772	.001106	.005536	89592	496	446796	.001110	2.652470	5001922	.025552	55.830	15
20	800831	1153	.001440	.007161	89096	638	443944	.001437	2.592085	4555126	-.011051	51.126	20
25	828549	1464	.001767	.008795	88458	778	440401	.001767	2.572301	4111183	-.005024	46.466	25
30	770232	1600	.002077	.010356	87680	908	436192	.002082	2.568833	3670781	-.017720	41.866	30
35	565698	1413	.002498	.012423	86772	1078	431312	.002499	2.636441	3234589	.070465	37.277	35
40	344357	1300	.003775	.018834	85694	1614	424672	.003801	2.646892	2803277	-.048067	32.713	40
45	424909	2279	.005364	.026356	84080	2216	415255	.005336	2.678343	2378605	-.024428	28.290	45
50	485529	4263	.008780	.042888	81864	3511	401242	.008750	2.699136	1963349	-.015415	23.983	50
55	411131	6029	.014664	.071114	78353	5572	378840	.014708	2.680441	1562108	-.013788	19.937	55
60	312408	7494	.023988	.114549	72781	8337	344336	.024212	2.652783	1183267	.046438	16.258	60
65	185025	7283	.039362	.181336	64444	11686	294087	.039737	2.592614	838931	.048616	13.018	65
70	136968	8012	.058495	.256492	52758	13532	230521	.058702	2.541476	544844	.020717	10.327	70
75	86616	7745	.089418	.366594	39226	14380	159984	.089884	2.486353	314323	.025479	8.013	75
80	41846	5730	.136931	.506721	24846	12590	91432	.137698	2.394907	154339	.025479	6.212	80
85+	22194	4324	.194827	1.000000	12256	12256	62907	.194827	5.132747	62907	.000000	5.133	85+

NUMBER OF PERSONS DYING (OUT OF 100,000 AT BIRTH) ABOVE AGE X FROM SPECIFIED CAUSES

Age (x)	All Causes	Respiratory T. B.	Other Infec. and Paras.	Neo-plasms	Cardio-vascular	Infl., Pneu., Bronch.	Diar-rheal	Certain Degen-erative	Maternal	Cert. Dis. of Infancy	Motor Vehicle	Other Violence	Other and Unknown	Age (x)
0	100000	4949	1635	10500	30274	7059	1359	3173	0	2865	0	5701	32481	0
1	91755	4929	1167	10495	30260	5507	465	3170	0	0	0	5664	30098	1
5	90215	4908	849	10459	30250	5173	287	3164	0	0	0	5512	29613	5
10	89867	4902	802	10425	30242	5146	286	3160	0	0	0	5398	29506	10
15	89592	4896	776	10400	30227	5139	284	3151	0	0	0	5290	29429	15
20	89096	4877	757	10353	30188	5127	283	3136	0	0	0	5043	29332	20
25	88458	4813	734	10309	30144	5120	282	3117	0	0	0	4699	29240	25
30	87680	4667	712	10257	30087	5111	280	3084	0	0	0	4350	29132	30
35	86772	4457	694	10178	30000	5103	278	3036	0	0	0	4005	29021	35
40	85694	4236	666	10061	29873	5091	278	2981	0	0	0	3663	28845	40
45	84080	3969	615	9848	29618	5059	271	2847	0	0	0	3261	28592	45
50	81864	3635	560	9436	29194	4997	265	2709	0	0	0	2849	28219	50
55	78353	3164	496	8780	28382	4855	256	2452	0	0	0	2403	27565	55
60	72781	2465	404	7668	26518	4585	236	2087	0	0	0	1942	26476	60
65	64444	1658	296	6138	24168	4134	209	1625	0	0	0	1486	24690	65
70	52758	931	187	4146	19927	3463	177	1037	0	0	0	1035	21855	70
75	39226	483	106	2417	14382	2626	141	552	0	0	0	672	17847	75
80	24846	176	47	1067	8471	1680	70	240	0	0	0	386	12709	80
85+	12256	48	28	366	3920	751	40	82	0	0	0	147	6874	85+

NUMBER OF PERSONS SURVIVING TO AGE X IF SPECIFIED CAUSES WERE ELIMINATED

Age (x)	No Causes	Respiratory T. B. (1)	Other Infec. and Paras. (2)	Neo-plasms (3)	Cardio-vascular (4)	Infl., Pneu., Bronch. (5)	Diar-rheal (6)	Certain Degen-erative (7)	Maternal (8)	Cert. Dis. of Infancy (9)	Motor Vehicle (10)	Other Violence (11)	Other and Unknown (12)	(1)+(2)	(1)+(2)+(5)+(6)+(8)	(1)+(2)+(5)+(6)+(8)+part of (9)&(12)	(10)+(11)	Age (x)
0	100000	100000	100000	100000	100000	100000	100000	100000	100000	100000	100000	100000	100000	100000	100000	100000	100000	0
1	91755	91774	92208	91760	91768	93253	92615	91758	91755	94540	91755	91790	94066	92227	94612	99831	91790	1
5	90215	90255	90978	90255	90238	92025	91239	90224	90215	92953	90215	90401	92981	91018	93898	99505	90401	5
10	89867	89912	90674	89941	89898	91658	90888	89880	89867	92595	89867	90166	92733	90720	93620	99250	90166	10
15	89592	89643	90423	89691	89638	91424	90612	89614	89592	92311	89592	89998	92528	90475	93376	99009	89998	15
20	89096	89166	89942	89241	89181	90930	90111	89133	89096	91800	89096	89748	92116	90012	92912	98530	89748	20
25	88458	88591	89321	88646	88566	90286	89467	88513	88458	91143	88458	89451	91551	89455	92346	97947	89451	25
30	87680	87958	88557	87918	87864	89501	88682	87768	87680	90341	87680	89017	90857	88838	91720	97315	89017	30
35	86772	87257	87658	87087	87040	88583	87766	86907	86772	89406	86772	88444	90031	88148	91018	96607	88444	35
40	85694	86394	86597	86122	86086	87494	86675	85882	85694	88295	85694	87692	89094	87305	90160	95753	87692	40
45	84080	85034	85017	84712	84719	85879	85050	84397	84080	86632	84080	86449	87677	85982	88835	95419	86449	45
50	81864	83127	82831	82890	82909	83678	82814	82310	81864	84349	81864	84589	85751	84109	86971	92541	84589	50
55	78353	80030	79342	79988	80162	80232	79272	79033	78353	80731	78353	81412	82746	81041	83957	89510	81412	55
60	72781	75029	73790	75401	75921	74793	73768	73760	72781	74990	72781	76085	77978	76069	79109	84635	76085	60
65	64444	67180	65440	68270	69980	66663	65242	65759	64444	66400	64444	67817	70871	68218	71442	76844	67817	65
70	52758	55720	53673	57824	61612	55206	53441	54377	52758	54359	52758	55948	60913	56686	60084	65189	55948	70
75	39226	41830	39976	44639	51731	41806	39765	40858	39226	40417	39226	41927	49462	42630	46059	50624	41927	75
80	24846	26750	25368	29497	39519	27289	25245	26132	24846	25600	24846	26797	36925	27312	30479	34335	26797	80
85+	12256	13291	12527	15134	25167	14182	12474	13005	12256	12628	12256	13397	25273	13584	15998	19014	13397	85+

ADDED YRS OF LIFE

	No Causes	(1)	(2)	(3)	(4)	(5)	(6)	(7)	(8)	(9)	(10)	(11)	(12)	(1)+(2)	(1)+(2)+(5)+(6)+(8)	part combo	(10)+(11)
TOTAL		.994	.727	1.574	4.094	1.822	.749	.506	.000	1.923	.000	1.612	6.658	1.737	4.439	9.223	1.612
WORK	3.534	.485	.081	.456	.548	.086	.008	.188	.000	.000	.000	.902	.557	.568	.666	.801	.902

POPULATION, DEATHS, DEATH RATES FOR ALL CAUSES COMBINED, AND SPECIFIED CAUSES

Age Start of Interval	Midyear Population	Deaths During Year	All Causes	Respiratory T. B.	Other Infec. and Paras.	Neoplasms	Cardiovascular	Infl., Pneu., Bronch.	Diarrheal	Certain Degenerative	Maternal	Cert. Dis. of Infancy	Motor Vehicle	Other Violence	Other and Unknown	Age Start of Interval
0	203066	16096	.07926	.00016	.00444	.00007	.00016	.01612	.00857	.00000	.00000	.02644	.00000	.00035	.02295	0
1	747628	3390	.00453	.00007	.00097	.00006	.00003	.00115	.00058	.00002	.00000	.00000	.00000	.00030	.00136	1
5	581995	638	.00065	.00001	.00013	.00005	.00002	.00007	.00000	.00001	.00000	.00000	.00000	.00011	.00023	5
10	900983	407	.00045	.00005	.00005	.00006	.00003	.00003	.00000	.00002	.00000	.00000	.00000	.00009	.00015	10
15	686456	565	.00082	.00012	.00005	.00006	.00007	.00001	.00000	.00003	.00004	.00000	.00000	.00022	.00021	15
20	787678	932	.00118	.00027	.00007	.00007	.00009	.00003	.00001	.00004	.00014	.00000	.00000	.00021	.00025	20
25	826211	1272	.00154	.00044	.00007	.00014	.00016	.00004	.00000	.00008	.00018	.00000	.00000	.00014	.00030	25
30	795003	1344	.00169	.00038	.00007	.00022	.00025	.00004	.00001	.00010	.00015	.00000	.00000	.00016	.00031	30
35	685233	1390	.00203	.00034	.00007	.00042	.00030	.00003	.00001	.00014	.00017	.00000	.00000	.00018	.00037	35
40	415918	1203	.00289	.00038	.00010	.00073	.00055	.00008	.00001	.00019	.00011	.00000	.00000	.00019	.00057	40
45	493745	1871	.00379	.00037	.00010	.00107	.00099	.00012	.00001	.00022	.00002	.00000	.00000	.00023	.00067	45
50	516740	3165	.00612	.00046	.00012	.00162	.00181	.00019	.00001	.00039	.00001	.00000	.00000	.00033	.00118	50
55	443620	4113	.00927	.00057	.00015	.00212	.00319	.00030	.00002	.00055	.00001	.00000	.00000	.00034	.00203	55
60	374087	6007	.01606	.00072	.00014	.00258	.00630	.00071	.00006	.00076	.00000	.00000	.00000	.00040	.00398	60
65	247258	7173	.02901	.00086	.00023	.00409	.01291	.00153	.00007	.00110	.00001	.00000	.00000	.00053	.00769	65
70	202699	9693	.04782	.00077	.00023	.00473	.02198	.00283	.00014	.00124	.00000	.00000	.00000	.00068	.01523	70
75	125828	9810	.07796	.00068	.00031	.00521	.03578	.00436	.00019	.00129	.00000	.00000	.00000	.00108	.02906	75
80	66217	7889	.11914	.00059	.00027	.00595	.05017	.00655	.00027	.00109	.00000	.00000	.00000	.00133	.05252	80
85+	36203	6376	.17612	.00044	.00022	.00439	.06251	.01055	.00050	.00102	.00000	.00000	.00000	.00193	.09455	85+
ALL	9536568	83334														
CRUDE DEATH RATE			.00874	.00031	.00026	.00081	.00251	.00076	.00025	.00021	.00006	.00056	.00000	.00025	.00275	
STANDARDIZED RATE (1)			.00709	.00024	.00035	.00052	.00131	.00088	.00038	.00014	.00006	.00093	.00000	.00022	.00206	
STANDARDIZED RATE (2)			.01003	.00032	.00026	.00093	.00310	.00083	.00024	.00024	.00006	.00055	.00000	.00027	.00323	
GEOMETRIC MEAN			.00704													

LIFE TABLE FOR ALL CAUSES COMBINED

Age (x)	Midyear Population	Deaths During Year	$_nM_x$	$_nq_x$	l_x	$_nd_x$	$_nL_x$	$_nm_x$	$_na_x$	T_x	$_nr_x$	$\overset{\circ}{e}_x$	Age (x)
0	203066	16096	.079265	.074560	100000	7456	94071	.079260	.204750	6687077	.000000	66.871	0
1	747628	3390	.004534	.017937	92544	1660	366026	.004535	1.500000	6593007	.000000	71.242	1
5	581995	638	.000650	.003246	90884	295	453683	.000650	2.500000	6226981	.000000	68.516	5
10	900983	407	.000452	.002252	90589	204	452451	.000451	2.579657	5773298	.029521	63.731	10
15	686456	565	.000823	.004127	90385	373	451060	.000827	2.682082	5320847	.023054	58.869	15
20	787678	932	.001183	.005888	90012	530	448800	.001181	2.623035	4869787	-.012450	54.102	20
25	826211	1272	.001540	.007666	89482	686	445740	.001539	2.566205	4420986	-.006222	49.406	25
30	795003	1344	.001691	.008424	88796	748	442153	.001692	2.557375	3975246	.002704	44.768	30
35	685233	1390	.002029	.010131	88048	892	438116	.002036	2.619114	3533093	.052031	40.127	35
40	415918	1203	.002892	.014434	87156	1258	432784	.002907	2.618740	3094977	-.046123	35.511	40
45	493745	1871	.003789	.018732	85898	1609	425735	.003779	2.666511	2662192	-.013934	30.992	45
50	516740	3165	.006125	.030182	84289	2544	415525	.006122	2.672956	2236457	-.002214	26.533	50
55	443620	4113	.009271	.045520	81745	3721	400161	.009299	2.698591	1820932	.013068	22.276	55
60	374087	6007	.016058	.078066	78024	6091	376167	.016192	2.709325	1420770	.035899	18.209	60
65	247258	7173	.029010	.136808	71933	9841	336577	.029238	2.653927	1044603	.035346	14.522	65
70	202699	9693	.047820	.215197	62092	13362	278340	.048006	2.596153	708026	.019138	11.403	70
75	125828	9810	.077964	.328504	48730	16008	203970	.078482	2.521226	429686	.029863	8.818	75
80	66217	7889	.119139	.458193	32722	14993	125051	.119895	2.428175	225716	.029863	6.898	80
85+	36203	6376	.176118	1.000000	17729	17729	100665	.176118	5.678011	100665	.000000	5.678	85+

NUMBER OF PERSONS DYING (OUT OF 100,000 AT BIRTH) ABOVE AGE X FROM SPECIFIED CAUSES

Age (x)	All Causes	Respiratory T. B.	Other Infec. and Paras.	Neo-plasms	Cardio-vascular	Infl., Pneu., Bronch.	Diar-rheal	Certain Degen-erative	Maternal	Cert. Dis. of Infancy	Motor Vehicle	Other Violence	Other and Unknown	Age (x)
0	100000	2532	1515	8880	35989	6745	1256	2257	360	2487	0	2205	35774	0
1	92544	2516	1097	8873	35974	5229	450	2257	360	0	0	2173	33615	1
5	90884	2490	743	8852	35965	4809	238	2250	360	0	0	2061	33116	5
10	90589	2485	684	8827	35954	4777	237	2244	360	0	0	2010	33011	10
15	90385	2473	662	8802	35939	4762	237	2235	359	0	0	1970	32946	15
20	90012	2419	638	8775	35906	4756	237	2222	341	0	0	1870	32848	20
25	89482	2298	606	8746	35864	4740	235	2204	280	0	0	1774	32735	25
30	88796	2100	574	8684	35795	4724	233	2170	201	0	0	1712	32603	30
35	88048	1933	541	8585	35686	4706	231	2127	134	0	0	1640	32465	35
40	87156	1786	510	8398	35552	4692	228	2067	60	0	0	1559	32304	40
45	85859	1621	466	8079	35314	4658	225	1987	15	0	0	1477	32056	45
50	84289	1465	425	7624	34893	4609	222	1893	7	0	0	1379	31772	50
55	81745	1272	375	6949	34140	4531	218	1731	4	0	0	1244	31281	55
60	78024	1044	314	6098	32861	4409	210	1510	4	0	0	1107	30467	60
65	71933	771	261	4972	30466	4140	188	1223	4	0	0	955	28953	65
70	62092	480	184	3590	26283	3620	163	853	1	0	0	775	26343	70
75	48730	265	121	2273	19941	2830	123	508	1	0	0	586	22082	75
80	32722	126	58	1207	12598	1934	84	245	1	0	0	364	16105	80
85+	17729	44	22	442	6292	1062	50	103	0	0	0	195	9519	85+

NUMBER OF PERSONS SURVIVING TO AGE X IF SPECIFIED CAUSES WERE ELIMINATED

Age (x)	No Causes	Respiratory T. B. (1)	Other Infec. and Paras. (2)	Neo-plasms (3)	Cardio-vascular (4)	Infl., Pneu., Bronch. (5)	Diar-rheal (6)	Certain Degener-ative (7)	Maternal (8)	Cert. Dis. of Infancy (9)	Motor Vehicle (10)	Other Violence (11)	Other and Unknown (12)	(1) + (2)	(1) + (2) + (5) + (6) + (8)	(1)+(2)+ (5)+(6)+ (8)+part of(9)&(12)	(10) + (11)	Age (x)
0	100000	100000	100000	100000	100000	100000	100000	100000	100000	100000	100000	100000	100000	100000	100000	100000	100000	0
1	92544	92559	92947	92551	92558	94014	93322	92544	92544	94967	92544	92575	94644	92962	95233	99851	92575	1
5	90884	90925	91633	90911	90907	92751	91861	90884	90884	93264	90884	91025	93453	91674	94562	99620	91025	5
10	90589	90635	91395	90641	90623	92483	91563	90602	90589	92961	90589	90781	93258	91441	94356	99461	90781	10
15	90385	90443	91211	90462	90434	92290	91357	90407	90386	92752	90385	90616	93115	91269	94196	99318	90616	15
20	90012	90123	90859	90116	90094	91915	90980	90047	90031	92369	90012	90343	92831	90971	93913	99060	90343	20
25	89482	89714	90356	89614	89605	91390	90447	89535	89562	91825	89482	89907	92401	90590	93602	98800	89907	25
30	88796	89224	89695	88989	88987	90706	89755	88882	88954	91121	88796	89280	91828	90128	93226	98489	89280	30
35	88048	88639	88973	88338	88346	89960	89001	88176	88271	90353	88048	88600	91197	89571	92741	98049	88600	35
40	87156	87889	88103	87630	87585	89063	88102	87343	87451	89438	87156	87783	90439	88844	92084	97420	87783	40
45	85859	86785	86875	86664	86559	87812	86834	86162	86233	88147	85859	86598	89390	88773	91060	96417	86598	45
50	84289	85316	85289	85517	85359	86216	85210	84641	84626	86496	84289	85074	88009	86328	89625	94958	85074	50
55	81745	82933	82765	83613	83537	83693	82642	82247	82075	83885	81745	82640	85859	83968	87264	92544	82640	55
60	78024	79384	79058	80661	81023	80005	78889	78720	78339	80067	78024	79014	82790	80436	83729	88926	79014	60
65	71933	73454	72937	75488	77126	74025	72751	72853	72223	73816	71933	72993	77886	74479	77831	82887	72993	65
70	62092	63679	63031	66516	71085	64397	62822	63234	62345	63718	62092	63176	69910	64643	68108	72892	63176	70
75	48730	50169	49523	53454	62360	51268	49339	49935	48929	50006	48730	49751	59286	50985	54533	58916	49751	75
80	32722	33803	33306	36848	50254	35201	33163	33748	32856	33579	32722	33592	46220	34406	37665	41387	33592	80
85+	17729	18376	18072	20599	35234	19764	17993	18391	17802	18193	17729	18326	32779	18732	21280	24163	18326	85+

ADDED YRS OF LIFE

	No Causes	(1)	(2)	(3)	(4)	(5)	(6)	(7)	(8)	(9)	(10)	(11)	(12)	(1)+(2)	(1)+(2)+(5)+(6)+(8)	+part	(10)+(11)
TOTAL		.675	.751	1.509	5.229	1.897	.740	.394	.155	1.746	.000	.583	7.327	1.435	4.335	8.862	.583
WORK	2.689	.376	.089	.482	.528	.069	.006	.141	.123	.000	.000	.234	.520	.466	.668	.838	.234

POPULATION, DEATHS, DEATH RATES FOR ALL CAUSES COMBINED, AND SPECIFIED CAUSES

Age Start of Interval	Midyear Population	Deaths During Year	All Causes	Respiratory T.B.	Other Infec. and Paras.	Neoplasms	Cardiovascular	Infl., Pneu., Bronch.	Diarrheal	Certain Degenerative	Maternal	Cert. Dis. of Infancy	Motor Vehicle	Other Violence	Other and Unknown	Age Start of Interval
0	190000	16260	.08558	.00008	.00383	.00008	.00023	.01419	.00699	.00003	.00000	.04174	.00000	.00040	.01801	0
1	759000	3337	.00440	.00002	.00107	.00009	.00004	.00097	.00034	.00002	.00000	.00000	.00000	.00039	.00146	1
5	983000	695	.00071	.00001	.00009	.00008	.00002	.00005	.00000	.00002	.00000	.00000	.00000	.00022	.00020	5
10	1005000	592	.00059	.00001	.00004	.00006	.00002	.00002	.00000	.00001	.00000	.00000	.00000	.00023	.00018	10
15	805000	739	.00092	.00002	.00003	.00008	.00008	.00002	.00000	.00002	.00000	.00000	.00000	.00049	.00018	15
20	754000	907	.00120	.00005	.00002	.00011	.00011	.00002	.00000	.00003	.00000	.00000	.00000	.00070	.00017	20
25	833000	1246	.00150	.00017	.00003	.00012	.00013	.00003	.00000	.00006	.00000	.00000	.00000	.00076	.00020	25
30	850000	1622	.00191	.00030	.00004	.00017	.00022	.00002	.00000	.00010	.00000	.00000	.00000	.00075	.00030	30
35	688000	1781	.00259	.00036	.00006	.00030	.00039	.00004	.00000	.00017	.00000	.00000	.00000	.00079	.00048	35
40	517000	2002	.00387	.00050	.00008	.00050	.00068	.00009	.00001	.00025	.00000	.00000	.00000	.00099	.00077	40
45	289000	1609	.00557	.00065	.00010	.00094	.00106	.00015	.00000	.00041	.00000	.00000	.00000	.00104	.00123	45
50	462000	4272	.00925	.00092	.00013	.00175	.00223	.00035	.00002	.00069	.00000	.00000	.00000	.00119	.00196	50
55	434000	6804	.01568	.00130	.00019	.00304	.00454	.00063	.00002	.00100	.00000	.00000	.00000	.00138	.00356	55
60	351000	9322	.02656	.00170	.00022	.00480	.00916	.00150	.00002	.00138	.00000	.00000	.00000	.00139	.00639	60
65	226000	9348	.04136	.00192	.00035	.00680	.01542	.00260	.00003	.00152	.00000	.00000	.00000	.00141	.01133	65
70	136000	9137	.06718	.00178	.00030	.00779	.02785	.00470	.00008	.00200	.00000	.00000	.00000	.00155	.02112	70
75	94000	9647	.10263	.00159	.00034	.00820	.04136	.00843	.00005	.00189	.00000	.00000	.00000	.00206	.03870	75
80	50000	7233	.14466	.00090	.00028	.00814	.05512	.01138	.00022	.00160	.00000	.00000	.00000	.00210	.06492	80
85+	30000	4844	.16147	.00053	.00023	.00397	.05487	.01343	.00007	.00097	.00000	.00000	.00000	.00180	.08560	85+
ALL	9456000	91397														

CRUDE DEATH RATE	.00967	.00039	.00024	.00096	.00246	.00081	.00018	.00029	.00000	.00084	.00000	.00073	.00278	
STANDARDIZED RATE (1)	.00866	.00029	.00033	.00068	.00159	.00050	.00029	.00021	.00000	.00147	.00000	.00064	.00226	
STANDARDIZED RATE (2)	.01286	.00046	.00025	.00127	.00369	.00105	.00018	.00037	.00000	.00086	.00000	.00079	.00393	
GEOMETRIC MEAN	.00871													

LIFE TABLE FOR ALL CAUSES COMBINED

Age (x)	Midyear Population	Deaths During Year	$_nM_x$	$_nq_x$	l_x	$_nd_x$	$_nL_x$	$_nm_x$	$_na_x$	T_x	$_nr_x$	$\overset{\circ}{e}_x$	Age (x)
0	190000	16260	.085579	.080190	100000	8019	93709	.085573	.215484	6331435	.000000	63.314	0
1	759000	3337	.004397	.017395	91981	1600	363924	.004397	1.500000	6237726	.000000	67.815	1
5	983000	695	.000707	.003530	90381	319	451108	.000707	2.500000	5873802	.000000	64.989	5
10	1005000	592	.000589	.002942	90062	265	449667	.000589	2.573899	5422695	.012048	60.211	10
15	805000	739	.000918	.004599	89797	413	448009	.000922	2.637207	4973028	.029329	55.381	15
20	754000	907	.001203	.006008	89384	537	445629	.001205	2.596214	4525018	.006050	50.624	20
25	833000	1246	.001496	.007440	88847	661	442645	.001493	2.554869	4079389	-.013629	45.915	25
30	850000	1622	.001908	.009503	88186	838	438932	.001909	2.616348	3636744	.006585	41.239	30
35	688000	1781	.002589	.012925	87348	1129	434089	.002601	2.651498	3197812	.029015	36.610	35
40	517000	2002	.003872	.019242	86219	1659	427200	.003883	2.651949	2763723	-.081332	32.055	40
45	289000	1609	.005567	.027661	84560	2339	417375	.005604	2.680633	2336523	.035174	27.632	45
50	462000	4272	.009247	.044843	82221	3687	402636	.009157	2.703135	1919148	-.040386	23.341	50
55	434000	6804	.015677	.075560	78534	5934	378966	.015658	2.650568	1516512	-.005210	19.310	55
60	351000	9322	.026558	.125551	72600	9115	341486	.026692	2.639719	1137546	-.024847	15.669	60
65	226000	9348	.041363	.189761	63485	12047	288514	.041755	2.600181	796060	.050157	12.539	65
70	136000	9137	.067184	.289825	51438	14908	220507	.067608	2.539352	507546	.029975	9.867	70
75	94000	9647	.102628	.406871	36530	14863	144744	.102685	2.449651	287039	.002715	7.858	75
80	50000	7233	.144660	.522269	21667	11316	78189	.144727	2.335962	142295	.002715	6.567	80
85+	30000	4844	.161467	1.000000	10351	10351	64106	.161467	6.193229	64106	.000000	6.193	85+

NUMBER OF PERSONS DYING (OUT OF 100,000 AT BIRTH) ABOVE AGE X FROM SPECIFIED CAUSES

Age (x)	All Causes	Respiratory T. B.	Other Infec. and Paras.	Neo-plasms	Cardio-vascular	Infl., Pneu., Bronch.	Diar-rheal	Certain Degen-erative	Maternal	Cert. Dis. of Infancy	Motor Vehicle	Other Violence	Other and Unknown	Age (x)
0	100000	3639	1412	10344	31444	7533	861	2952	0	3911	0	5558	32306	0
1	91981	3631	1054	10336	31422	6203	206	2949	0	0	0	5561	30619	1
5	90381	3623	666	10304	31407	5850	83	2942	0	0	0	5418	30088	5
10	90062	3619	624	10267	31397	5825	81	2934	0	0	0	5317	29998	10
15	89797	3616	606	10237	31386	5816	81	2928	0	0	0	5212	29915	15
20	89384	3606	594	10201	31349	5807	81	2917	0	0	0	4993	29836	20
25	88847	3585	586	10150	31302	5800	80	2904	0	0	0	4681	29759	25
30	88186	3509	571	10096	31243	5792	80	2879	0	0	0	4346	29670	30
35	87348	3377	555	10023	31144	5781	79	2833	0	0	0	4015	29541	35
40	86219	3219	531	9893	30975	5764	79	2759	0	0	0	3671	29328	40
45	84560	3004	496	9676	30684	5727	77	2650	0	0	0	3247	28999	45
50	82221	2731	456	9281	30240	5665	77	2477	0	0	0	2813	28481	50
55	78534	2361	403	8584	29357	5525	69	2200	0	0	0	2334	27701	55
60	72600	1867	330	7432	27639	5285	63	1821	0	0	0	1809	26354	60
65	63485	1287	254	5787	24492	4770	55	1347	0	0	0	1335	24158	65
70	51438	734	153	3815	19992	4012	47	908	0	0	0	928	20849	70
75	36530	341	87	2093	13809	2968	29	465	0	0	0	585	16153	75
80	21667	112	38	905	7819	1748	21	191	0	0	0	286	10547	80
85+	10351	34	15	254	3517	861	4	62	0	0	0	115	5489	85+

NUMBER OF PERSONS SURVIVING TO AGE X IF SPECIFIED CAUSES WERE ELIMINATED

Age (x)	No Causes	Respiratory T. B.	Other Infec. and Paras.	Neo-plasms	Cardio-vascular	Infl., Pneu., Bronch.	Diar-rheal	Certain Degener-ative	Maternal	Cert. Dis. of Infancy	Motor Vehicle	Other Violence	Other and Unknown	(1)+(2)	(1)+(2)+(5)+(6)+(8)	(1)+(2)+(5)+(6)+(8)+part of(9)&(12)	(10)+(11)	Age (x)
		(1)	(2)	(3)	(4)	(5)	(6)	(7)	(8)	(9)	(10)	(11)	(12)					
0	100000	100000	100000	100000	100000	100000	100000	100000	100000	100000	100000	100000	100000	100000	100000	100000	100000	0
1	91981	91989	92325	91989	92002	93265	92611	91984	91981	95808	91981	92016	93613	92333	94263	99759	92016	1
5	90381	90396	91106	90420	90417	91998	91123	90391	90381	94142	90381	90558	92522	91121	93513	99437	90558	5
10	90062	90081	90826	90138	90107	91699	90803	90080	90062	93809	90062	90339	92287	90846	93259	99197	90339	10
15	89797	89819	90577	89903	89853	91438	90536	89821	89797	93533	89797	90179	92101	90600	93015	98953	90179	15
20	89384	89416	90173	89525	89477	91027	90120	89419	89384	93103	89384	89984	91758	90205	92620	98541	89984	20
25	88847	88900	89639	89038	88986	90487	89579	88894	88847	92544	88847	89757	91285	89693	92101	97996	89757	25
30	88186	88314	88987	88430	88383	89822	88913	88258	88186	91855	88186	89427	90657	89117	91518	97393	89427	30
35	87348	87607	88158	87663	87642	88980	87965	87348	87348	90983	87348	88912	89968	88419	90814	96675	88912	35
40	86219	86632	87042	86659	86678	87847	86931	86408	86219	89807	86219	88111	89023	87459	89846	95696	88111	40
45	84560	85179	85403	85208	85300	86194	85260	84854	84560	88079	84560	86845	87647	86028	88416	94252	86845	45
50	82221	83095	83080	83245	83384	83872	82902	82678	82221	85642	82221	84883	85754	83963	86358	92175	84883	50
55	78534	79734	79407	80205	80526	80251	79192	79243	78534	81802	78534	81561	82707	80621	83073	88839	81561	55
60	72600	74193	73478	75283	76156	74424	73214	73624	72600	75621	72600	75923	77834	75090	77627	83277	75923	60
65	63485	65432	64324	67443	69755	65576	64030	64829	63485	66127	63485	66853	70300	66297	69068	74504	66853	65
70	51438	53527	52210	56553	61146	53841	51886	52930	51438	53578	51438	54550	60356	54330	57364	62463	54550	70
75	36530	38353	37133	41766	50051	39166	36864	37970	36530	38050	36530	39044	47761	38986	42182	46678	39044	75
80	21667	22927	22062	25813	36631	24251	21871	22735	21667	22569	21667	23401	34544	23346	26376	30146	23401	80
85+	10351	11009	10556	12867	23174	12276	10460	10953	10351	10782	10351	11305	22959	11227	13455	16215	11305	85+

ADDED YRS OF LIFE

		(1)	(2)	(3)	(4)	(5)	(6)	(7)	(8)	(9)	(10)	(11)	(12)				
TOTAL		.680	.645	1.550	4.550	1.752	.526	.476	.000	2.626	.000	1.549	6.535	1.334	3.708	8.688	1.549
WORK	3.484	.330	.056	.462	.613	.086	.003	.189	.000	.000	.000	.879	.638	.387	.478	.598	.879

POPULATION, DEATHS, DEATH RATES FOR ALL CAUSES COMBINED, AND SPECIFIED CAUSES

Age Start of Interval	Midyear Population	Deaths During Year	All Causes	Respiratory T. B.	Other Infec. and Paras.	Neoplasms	Cardiovascular	Infl., Pneu., Bronch.	Diarrheal	Certain Degenerative	Maternal	Cert. Dis. of Infancy	Motor Vehicl	Other Violence	Other and Unknown	Age Start of Interval
0	180000	14161	.07867	.00011	.00357	.00009	.00018	.01433	.00654	.00002	.00000	.03632	.00000	.00042	.01671	0
1	719000	3563	.00496	.00003	.00121	.00008	.00004	.00108	.00041	.00003	.00000	.00000	.00000	.00026	.00181	1
5	927000	545	.00059	.00000	.00012	.00005	.00003	.00006	.00001	.00001	.00000	.00000	.00000	.00010	.00021	5
10	958000	403	.00042	.00001	.00004	.00007	.00004	.00001	.00000	.00002	.00000	.00000	.00000	.00010	.00014	10
15	770000	496	.00064	.00004	.00004	.00007	.00008	.00001	.00000	.00003	.00003	.00000	.00000	.00020	.00015	15
20	725000	720	.00099	.00011	.00010	.00009	.00011	.00003	.00000	.00005	.00011	.00000	.00000	.00019	.00020	20
25	809000	972	.00120	.00019	.00009	.00012	.00016	.00002	.00000	.00007	.00014	.00000	.00000	.00016	.00025	25
30	827000	1298	.00157	.00024	.00010	.00022	.00023	.00003	.00000	.00010	.00014	.00000	.00000	.00017	.00034	30
35	759000	1449	.00191	.00029	.00007	.00036	.00033	.00003	.00000	.00013	.00014	.00000	.00000	.00018	.00039	35
40	629000	1688	.00268	.00025	.00005	.00075	.00055	.00005	.00000	.00015	.00008	.00000	.00000	.00022	.00058	40
45	358000	1388	.00388	.00027	.00008	.00109	.00096	.00008	.00001	.00025	.00002	.00000	.00000	.00026	.00086	45
50	528000	3273	.00620	.00035	.00008	.00157	.00185	.00019	.00001	.00038	.00001	.00000	.00000	.00034	.00142	50
55	461000	4634	.01005	.00038	.00010	.00216	.00369	.00033	.00002	.00065	.00000	.00000	.00000	.00033	.00239	55
60	400000	6777	.01694	.00052	.00012	.00282	.00725	.00067	.00002	.00082	.00000	.00000	.00000	.00045	.00426	60
65	293000	8598	.02934	.00072	.00015	.00364	.01304	.00147	.00005	.00104	.00000	.00000	.00000	.00055	.00868	65
70	200000	10137	.05068	.00066	.00019	.00475	.02326	.00351	.00007	.00125	.00000	.00000	.00000	.00067	.01631	70
75	148000	12425	.08395	.00056	.00014	.00541	.03716	.00557	.00009	.00123	.00000	.00000	.00000	.00111	.03228	75
80	80000	9970	.12462	.00046	.00016	.00489	.05225	.00924	.00011	.00097	.00000	.00000	.00000	.00115	.05539	80
85+	52000	7361	.14156	.00033	.00015	.00333	.05194	.00992	.00019	.00054	.00000	.00000	.00000	.00112	.07404	85+
ALL	9823000	85858														

	All Causes	Respiratory T.B.	Other Infec. and Paras.	Neoplasms	Cardiovascular	Infl., Pneu., Bronch.	Diarrheal	Certain Degenerative	Maternal	Cert. Dis. of Infancy	Motor Vehicl	Other Violence	Other and Unknown
CRUDE DEATH RATE	.00915	.00021	.00023	.00082	.00285	.00075	.00017	.00022	.00005	.00067	.00000	.00026	.00293
STANDARDIZED RATE (1)	.00714	.00015	.00034	.00051	.00137	.00082	.00030	.00014	.00005	.00128	.00000	.00022	.00195
STANDARDIZED RATE (2)	.01016	.00021	.00025	.00089	.00322	.00084	.00019	.00024	.00005	.00075	.00000	.00027	.00325
GEOMETRIC MEAN	.00674												

LIFE TABLE FOR ALL CAUSES COMBINED

Age (x)	Midyear Population	Deaths During Year	$_nM_x$	$_nq_x$	l_x	$_nd_x$	$_nL_x$	$_nm_x$	$_na_x$	T_x	$_nr_x$	$\overset{\circ}{e}_x$	Age (x)
0	180000	14161	.078672	.074030	100000	7403	94105	.078667	.203743	6693703	.000000	66.937	0
1	719000	3563	.004955	.019579	92597	1813	365856	.004956	1.500000	6599597	.000000	71.272	1
5	927000	545	.000588	.002941	90784	267	453253	.000589	2.500000	6233742	.000000	68.666	5
10	958000	403	.000420	.002099	90517	190	452115	.000420	2.527412	5780489	.010935	63.861	10
15	770000	496	.000644	.003233	90327	292	450958	.000648	2.682648	5328374	.028797	58.990	15
20	725000	720	.000993	.004954	90035	446	449111	.000993	2.613976	4877416	.004501	54.172	20
25	809000	972	.001201	.005983	89589	536	446657	.001200	2.597170	4428305	-.013088	49.429	25
30	827000	1298	.001570	.007816	89053	696	443589	.001569	2.591295	3981648	-.000737	44.711	30
35	759000	1449	.001909	.009518	88357	841	439782	.001912	2.617915	3538059	-.009170	40.043	35
40	629000	1688	.002684	.013392	87516	1172	434822	.002695	2.647184	3098278	.065926	35.402	40
45	358000	1388	.003877	.019330	86344	1669	427840	.003901	2.675005	2663455	.035597	30.847	45
50	528000	3273	.006199	.030399	84675	2574	417434	.006166	2.691822	2235616	-.024498	26.402	50
55	461000	4634	.010052	.049196	82101	4039	401202	.010067	2.656831	1818182	-.006187	22.146	55
60	400000	6777	.016942	.081858	78062	6390	375560	.017015	2.691673	1416979	.019798	18.152	60
65	293000	8598	.029345	.138380	71672	9918	335153	.029592	2.660147	1041420	.037799	14.530	65
70	200000	10137	.050685	.226933	61754	14014	275127	.050936	2.599365	706266	.022206	11.437	70
75	148000	12425	.083953	.347759	47740	16602	197329	.084134	2.508069	431139	.009600	9.031	75
80	80000	9970	.124625	.470711	31138	14657	117384	.124864	2.386488	233810	.009600	7.509	80
85+	52000	7361	.141558	1.000000	16481	16481	116426	.141558	7.064258	116426	.000000	7.064	85+

NUMBER OF PERSONS DYING (OUT OF 100,000 AT BIRTH) ABOVE AGE X FROM SPECIFIED CAUSES

Age (x)	All Causes	Respiratory T. B.	Other Infec. and Paras.	Neo-plasms	Cardio-vascular	Infl., Pneu., Bronch.	Diar-rheal	Certain Degenerative	Maternal	Cert. Dis. of Infancy	Motor Vehicle	Other Violence	Other and Unknown	Age (x)
0	100000	1761	1382	8429	36484	7235	923	2214	292	3417	u	2142	35721	0
1	92597	1751	1046	8420	36467	5886	270	2211	292	0	0	2103	34151	1
5	90784	1738	603	8391	36454	5450	121	2202	292	0	0	2006	33487	5
10	90517	1736	547	8369	36442	5464	118	2198	292	0	0	1959	33392	10
15	90327	1734	531	8340	36424	5458	118	2188	292	0	0	1912	33330	15
20	90035	1717	511	8306	36389	5454	118	2175	280	0	0	1823	33262	20
25	89589	1670	466	8266	36338	5441	117	2153	230	0	0	1737	33171	25
30	89053	1585	425	8215	36266	5431	116	2122	168	0	0	1663	33062	30
35	88357	1477	381	8116	36164	5420	115	2079	105	0	0	1588	32912	35
40	87516	1348	351	7958	36021	5407	113	2024	43	0	0	1510	32741	40
45	86344	1240	329	7629	35779	5385	111	1956	10	0	0	1414	32491	45
50	84675	1125	293	7158	35363	5353	109	1848	4	0	0	1303	32119	50
55	82101	979	259	6505	34597	5273	106	1690	1	0	0	1160	31531	55
60	78062	827	217	5637	33115	5142	98	1429	1	0	0	1027	30569	60
65	71672	632	170	4576	30378	4888	89	1120	1	0	0	857	28961	65
70	61754	390	118	3350	25967	4389	72	770	1	0	0	674	26023	70
75	47740	207	66	2041	19536	3418	53	424	1	0	0	487	21507	75
80	31138	97	38	972	12190	2238	36	182	1	0	0	267	15117	80
85+	16481	38	18	387	6047	1155	22	63	0	0	0	130	8621	85+

NUMBER OF PERSONS SURVIVING TO AGE X IF SPECIFIED CAUSES WERE ELIMINATED

Age (x)	No Causes	Respiratory T. B. (1)	Other Infec. and Paras. (2)	Neo-plasms (3)	Cardio-vascular (4)	Infl., Pneu., Bronch. (5)	Diar-rheal (6)	Certain Degenerative (7)	Maternal (8)	Cert. Dis. of Infancy (9)	Motor Vehicle (10)	Other Violence (11)	Other and Unknown (12)	(1)+(2)	(1)+(2)+(5)+(6)+(8)	(1)+(2)+(5)+(6)+(8)+part of(9)&(12)	(10)+(11)	Age (x)
0	100000	100000	100000	100000	100000	100000	100000	100000	100000	100000	100000	100000	100000	100000	100000	100000	100000	0
1	92597	92607	92921	92606	92613	93904	93227	92600	92597	95943	92597	92635	94120	92930	94884	99784	92635	1
5	90784	90806	91543	90821	90813	92464	91551	90796	90784	94065	90784	90917	92948	91565	94047	99530	90917	5
10	90517	90541	91330	90576	90558	92218	91284	90523	90517	93788	90517	90697	92771	91354	93860	99385	90697	10
15	90327	90353	91154	90415	90386	92031	91093	90353	90327	93591	90327	90553	92640	91181	93688	99216	90553	15
20	90035	90078	90880	90157	90129	91737	90798	90074	90047	93289	90035	90350	92410	90923	93440	98971	90350	20
25	89589	89679	90475	89750	89733	91296	90350	89649	89651	92827	89589	89988	92046	90566	93139	98696	89988	25
30	89053	89227	89975	89264	89268	90740	89810	89144	89176	92271	89053	89524	91607	90151	92788	98380	89524	30
35	88357	88638	89316	88665	88672	90062	89109	88490	88542	91550	88357	88899	91045	89600	92299	97930	88899	35
40	87516	87923	88496	87979	87971	89218	88263	87703	87761	90679	87516	88131	90354	88907	91666	97325	88131	40
45	86344	86853	87333	87130	87035	88045	87083	86596	86619	89464	86344	87047	89400	87848	90633	96284	87047	45
50	84675	85289	85681	85918	85769	86376	85402	85029	84950	87735	84675	85475	88055	86302	89080	94695	85475	50
55	82101	82841	83110	83961	83930	83831	82809	82601	82371	85068	82101	83019	85982	83859	86648	92197	83019	55
60	78062	78915	79063	80700	81293	79837	78743	78794	78319	80883	78062	79066	82741	79927	82728	88141	79066	60
65	71672	72644	72637	75150	77421	73552	72306	72642	71908	74262	71672	72759	77620	73622	76471	81659	72759	65
70	61754	62818	62634	65949	71277	63852	62316	62919	61957	63986	61754	62862	69899	63713	66695	71587	62862	70
75	47740	48724	48466	52216	62006	50252	48191	48948	47897	49465	47740	48763	58721	49465	52732	57210	48763	75
80	31138	31868	31634	34995	48845	33787	31446	32122	31240	32263	31138	31985	45180	32375	35593	39460	31985	80
85+	16481	16911	16758	18999	33753	18744	16654	17090	16536	17077	16481	17030	31703	17195	19827	22893	17030	85+

ADDED YRS OF LIFE

	No Causes	(1)	(2)	(3)	(4)	(5)	(6)	(7)	(8)	(9)	(10)	(11)	(12)	(1)+(2)	(1)+(2)+(5)+(6)+(8)	part	(10)+(11)
TOTAL		.422	.739	1.481	5.849	1.836	.578	.401	.126	2.412	.000	.584	7.673	1.168	3.789	8.649	.584
WORK	2.540	.219	.090	.480	.562	.056	.004	.143	.101	.000	.000	.236	.537	.310	.473	.603	.236